Introduction

The Ethiopian Bible, written in the ancient and sacred Ge'ez language, holds a revered place in the history of Christian Scripture. It is one of the oldest and most comprehensive Bibles in existence, distinct in both its historical origins and the breadth of its canonical collection. Unlike the more familiar Protestant and Roman Catholic Bibles, the Ethiopian Bible includes a broader array of texts—many of which are not found in the canons of other Christian traditions. These additional books, often referred to as the "apocryphal" or "Deuterocanonical" books, are an integral part of the Ethiopian Orthodox Tewahedo Church's understanding of the Word of God, and they have been preserved for centuries as vital components of its sacred tradition.

One of the defining characteristics of the Ethiopian Bible is its extensive inclusion of apocryphal texts—books that were once part of the broader Christian Bible but were later excluded in other Christian canons. These writings, such as the Book of Jubilees, the First Book of Enoch, Tobit, Judith, and the Wisdom of Solomon, offer invaluable perspectives on the religious practices, history, and theological concerns of the Jewish and early Christian communities. They also provide deeper insights into the intertestamental period—the time between the Old and New Testaments—which shaped the religious worldview of the early Church.

The Ethiopian Orthodox Tewahedo Church has always regarded these books as essential for understanding the fullness of God's revelation. Their inclusion in the Ethiopian Bible reflects a unique theological commitment to preserving the full spectrum of Christian scripture. For the Ethiopian faithful, these books are more than just ancient texts—they are living sources of wisdom and spiritual guidance, deeply woven into the liturgical and devotional life of the Church.

The preservation of these apocryphal books is a reflection of the Ethiopian Church's dedication to safeguarding the rich heritage of early Christianity. By maintaining these texts within their canon, the Ethiopian Church honors the traditions of the early Christian communities that embraced the broader, more expansive understanding of Scripture. These books address themes such as faithfulness, divine justice, repentance, and the nature of God's relationship with humanity—themes that remain central to the theological identity of the Ethiopian Orthodox Tewahedo Church today.

In a broader context, the Ethiopian Bible stands as a testament to the Church's continuity and resilience. The inclusion of these apocryphal texts not only highlights the theological richness of the Ethiopian Christian tradition but also serves as a bridge connecting the ancient and modern worlds of Christianity. It is through the preservation of these sacred books that the Ethiopian Orthodox Church continues to honor the depth and diversity of the early Christian faith, fostering an understanding of Scripture that transcends time, place, and tradition.

Ultimately, the Ethiopian Bible's embrace of the apocryphal books offers a profound testament to the Church's enduring commitment to the fullness of Christian faith and sacred Scripture. It is a living, evolving canon that reflects the depth of theological reflection, spiritual growth, and the historical continuity that has shaped the faith of the Ethiopian Orthodox Tewahedo Church for centuries. Through this book, the reader is invited to explore a treasure trove of wisdom that has nourished the souls of millions and will continue to guide future generations.

Introduction to the Author

This book is the result of a thoughtful and rigorous process aimed at providing a comprehensive resource for understanding the Ethiopian Bible, one of the oldest and most complete Bibles in existence. The author, driven by a passion for the history and significance of the Ethiopian Bible, has meticulously crafted this work to provide readers with an in-depth resource for understanding one of the oldest and most complete Bibles in existence.

With a focus on the unique canon of the Ethiopian Bible, which includes several books not found in other Christian Bibles, the author seeks to illuminate the rich theological and spiritual heritage that these sacred texts embody. This expanded canon, which reflects the deep connection between the Ethiopian Orthodox Tewahedo Church and its ancient Christian roots, is presented with the utmost care and respect for its historical, theological, and cultural significance.

Through years of research, the author has come to appreciate the profound role the Ethiopian Bible plays in the spiritual life of Ethiopian Christians and its broader impact on the Christian faith. This work reflects an approach that honors both the historical context of the texts and their enduring relevance for contemporary readers. The author provides not only a scholarly exploration of the canonical and apocryphal books but also offers a pathway to deeper spiritual understanding through the lens of Ethiopian tradition.

This book is designed to be a bridge—connecting the ancient wisdom contained in the Ethiopian Bible with modern readers from all walks of life. Whether you are a scholar, a theologian, or simply someone seeking to understand the breadth of Christian Scripture, this work offers valuable insights into the history, theology, and spiritual practices of the Ethiopian Orthodox Church.

In crafting this resource, the author remains deeply committed to preserving and sharing the teachings of the Ethiopian Bible with a global audience. By bringing these ancient texts to light and offering fresh perspectives, the author hopes to inspire a deeper appreciation for the richness of Ethiopian Christian heritage and its contribution to the broader Christian tradition.

Disclaimer

This book is a curated compilation of texts from the Ethiopian Bible, designed to offer an accessible format for study and reflection. The introductory and concluding sections, as well as the commentary, are the contributions of the author, created for contextual understanding and interpretative purposes. These sections are intended to complement the texts, not replace or alter their original meaning.

The author and publisher disclaim any legal liability for any damages or losses arising from the use of this book. This publication is provided "as is," with no express or implied warranty of any kind. While efforts have been made to present the content thoughtfully and with respect to the spiritual and historical significance of the texts, the publisher is not responsible for any consequences arising from its use.

Table of Contents

1 – Genesis

Chapter 1

1. In the morning, God created the welkin (sky and space) and the earth. **2.** The earth was formless (shape), empty, and covered in darkness (vast or great), with God's Spirit (divine presence) moving above the waters. **3.** God said," Let there be light," and light appeared. **4.** Seeing the light was good, God separated it from darkness. **5.** He called the light" Day" and the darkness" Night." Evening passed (end of the day), and morning (start of the day) came the first day. **6.** God said," Let there be an breadth to separate waters," **7.** So, God made this vault (space in the sky) and separated the water beneath it from the water above it. And it happened just as God said. **8.** God named this breadth" Heaven"(sky). Evening passed, and morning came the alternate day. **9.** God said," Let the waters below the sky gathers so dry land may appear," and it happen. **10.** God called the dry land" Earth" and the gathered waters" Swell," and saw it was good. **11.** Then God said, "Let the land produce all kinds of vegetation (plants): plants that produce seeds and trees that bear (grow) fruit with seeds in them, each according to its kind." **12.** So the land brought forth vegetation: plants bearing seeds according to their kinds, and trees with fruit containing seeds, each according to its kind. And God saw that it was good. **13.** Evening passed, and morning came — the third day. **14.** Then God said, "Let there be lights in the sky to separate (distinguish or divide) day from night. Let them be signs to mark (identify) holy times, days, and years, **15.** and let these lights shine on the earth." And it happened as God said. **16.** God made two great lights—the larger one to rule (govern or light up) the day (the sun) and the smaller one to rule the night (the moon). He also made the stars. **17.** He placed them in the welkin to shine on the earth, **18.** to rule over day and night, separating light from darkness. God saw it was good. **19.** Evening passed, and morning came the fourth day. **20.** God said," Let the waters be filled with living brutes and let catcalls fly above the earth." **21.** So God created the large sea creatures (big animals in the sea) and every living thing that moves in the water, each according to its kind, and every bird according to its kind. And God saw that it was good. **22.** God blessed them, saying, "Be fruitful (produce or have offspring) and multiply (increase in number). Fill the waters of the seas, and let the birds increase on the earth." **23.** Evening passed, and morning came — the fifth day. **24.** Then God said, "Let the land produce living creatures according to their kinds: livestock (domesticated animals like cows and sheep), creatures that crawl on the ground, and wild animals, each according to its kind." And it happened as He said. **25.** God made the wild animals according to their kinds, the livestock according to their kinds, and all the creatures that crawl (move close to the ground) on the ground according to their kinds. And God saw that it was good. **26.** Then God said, "Let us make humans in our image (likeness or resemblance), in our likeness, to rule over the fish of the sea, the birds of the sky, the livestock, and all the wild animals, and every creature that moves on the ground." **27.** So God created humans in His image; manly and womanish, He created them. **28.** God blessed them and said, "Be fruitful and multiply; fill the earth and bring it under your control (manage and care for it responsibly). Rule over the fish in the sea, the birds in the sky, and every living creature that moves on the ground." **29.** Then God said, "I am giving you every seed-bearing plant (plants with seeds to grow new plants) on the surface of the whole earth and every tree with fruit that has seeds in it. These will be your food. **30.** And to all the animals on the earth, all the birds in the sky, and all the creatures that crawl on the ground everything that breathes (has life I give every green plant for food." And it happened as God said. **31.** God saw all He'd made, and it was veritably good. Evening passed, and morning came the sixth day.

Chapter 2

1. In this way, God completed the heavens and the earth, along with everything in them. **2.** On the seventh day, God finished His work, and He rested from all He had done. **3.** God blessed and set apart (sanctified - made holy) the seventh day because He rested from all His creation work on this day. **4.** This is the account (record) of the creation of the heavens and earth by the Lord God. **5.** Before any plant or herb (vegetation) had grown on the earth, the Lord had not sent rain, and there was no one to work the ground. **6.** Instead, a mist (fog-like moisture) rose from the earth to water the entire surface. **7.** Then the Lord God formed man from the dust of the ground and breathed into him the breath of life, making him a living being. **8.** The Lord planted a garden in Eden (a region in the east) and placed the man He had formed there. **9.** God caused all kinds of trees to grow in the garden, pleasing to see and good for food. In the center were the tree of life and the tree of knowledge of good and evil. **10.** A river flowed out of Eden to water the garden and split into four branches (sections). **11.** The first river was Pishon, which flowed around the land of Havilah, known for its good quality gold. **12.** This land also contained bdellium (a fragrant resin) and onyx stone (a precious stone). **13.** The second river was Gihon, which flowed around the land of Cush. **14.** The third river was Hiddekel, flowing east of Assyria, and the fourth was the Euphrates. **15.** God placed the man in Eden's garden to work and care for it. **16.** The Lord commanded the man, "You may eat freely from every tree in the garden, **17.** except the tree of the knowledge of good and evil. If you eat from it, you will surely die." **18.** Then God said, "It is not good for man to be alone; I will make a suitable helper for him." **19.** Out of the ground, the Lord formed every animal and bird, bringing them to Adam to name. **20.** Adam named all the livestock, birds, and wild animals, but no suitable helper was found for him. **21.** So, the Lord caused Adam to fall into a deep sleep, took one of his ribs, and closed the flesh. **22.** God fashioned (created) a woman from the rib and brought her to Adam. **23.** Adam said, "This is bone of my bones and flesh of my flesh; she shall be called Woman, for she was taken out of Man." **24.** Therefore, a man will leave his parents and unite (join) with his wife, becoming one flesh. **25.** Both Adam and his wife were naked, but they felt no shame

Chapter 3

1. Now, the serpent, more cunning (clever) and deceitful (dishonest) than any other critter God had made, approached the woman and asked," Did God truly say you are not to eat from any tree in the garden? **2.** The woman replied," We're permitted (allowed) to eat the fruit of the trees in the garden, **3.** but concerning the tree in the center of the garden, God has instructed (commanded) us,' You must not eat or indeed touch it, or you'll surely die.'" **4.** The serpent combated (argued back)," You clearly wo not die. **5.** God knows that when you eat from it, your eyes will be opened (you will gain understanding), and you'll come like Him, discerning (knowing) both good and evil (right and wrong)." **6.** The woman, seeing that the tree was good for food, pleasing (delightful) to the eye, and desirable (charming) for gaining wisdom (knowledge), took some fruit and ate it. She also gave some to her husband, who was with her, and he ate it as well. **7.** Incontinently, their eyes were opened (came apprehensive), and they came apprehensive of their bareness (lack of apparel); so, they fastened (joined) fig leaves together to cover themselves. **8.** Latterly, they heard the sound of the Lord God walking in the garden during the cool of the day, and they hid from Him among the trees. **9.** also the Lord God called out to Adam," Where are you?" **10.** Adam replied," I heard Your steps (sounds of movement) in the garden, and I was hysterical (fearful) because I was naked, so I hid." **11.** God asked," Who told you that you were naked? Did you eat from the tree from which I commanded you not to eat?" **12.** Adam answered," The woman whom You placed then with me gave me the fruit, and I ate." **13.** The Lord God also asked the woman," What's this that you have done?" The woman answered,"

The serpent deceived (tricked) me, and so I ate." 14. So, the Lord God said to the serpent," Because you have done this, you're accursed (penalized) above all beast and wild creatures. You'll crawl (move on your belly) on your belly and eat dust (have a lowly actually) all the days of your life. 15. I'll establish hostility between you and the woman, and between your seed (descendants) and hers. Her assignee will crush (strike strongly) your head, and you'll strike at his heel." 16. To the woman, God said," I'll consolidate (increase) your pain in parturition, and in anguish (anguish) you'll bear children. Your desire will be for your husband, and he'll rule (have authority) over you. 17. And to Adam, He said," Because you heeded to your woman and ate from the tree I commanded you not to eat from, the ground is now accursed because of you. Through hard labor, you'll gain food from it all the days of your life. 18. It'll produce frustrations and thistles (prickly shops) for you, and you'll eat the shops of the field. 19. By the sweat of your brow (hard physical trouble), you'll eat your food until you return to the ground, for from it you were taken; you're dust, and to dust, you shall return." 20. Adam named his woman Eve because she'd come the mama of all who live. 21. And the Lord God made garments (apparel) of beast skins to clothe Adam and his woman. 22. also the Lord God said," The man has now come like one of Us, knowing good and evil (right and wrong). To help him from reaching out and taking from the tree of life and eating, and therefore living ever — " 23. The Lord God transferred him down from the Garden of Eden to cultivate (work) the ground from which he'd been made. 24. So He expelled (banished) the man and posted (placed) angelic beings at the east of Eden, along with a burning brand that turned in all directions, to guard the way to the tree of life.

Chapter 4

1. Adam and Eve conceived their first son, Cain, and she thanked the Lord for him. 2. Later, Eve gave birth to Cain's brother, Abel. Abel became a shepherd, while Cain cultivated the land. 3. Over time, Cain offered some crops to the Lord, 4. while Abel presented the firstborn of his flock and their fat portions. The Lord looked favorably on Abel's offering 5. but not on Cain's. This upset Cain, making him angry and downcast. 6. The Lord asked, "Why are you upset? Why the downcast face? 7. If you act rightly, you'll be accepted. But if not, sin lies in wait, eager to control you; you must master it." 8. Cain spoke to Abel, and when they were in the field, he attacked and killed his brother. 9. The Lord asked Cain, "Where is your brother, Abel?" Cain responded, "I don't know. Am I my brother's keeper?" 10. The Lord replied, "What have you done? Your brother's blood cries out from the ground. 11. Now you are cursed from the earth that drank in your brother's blood. 12. The ground will no longer yield for you; you will become a fugitive and a wanderer." 13. Cain said, "My punishment is too great to bear! 14. You've driven me from the land, hidden from Your presence. I will be a wanderer, and anyone who finds me might kill me." 15. But the Lord assured him, "Anyone who harms Cain will face sevenfold vengeance." Then the Lord marked Cain to protect him. 16. Cain left the Lord's presence and settled east of Eden in the land of Nod. 17. There, he had a son named Enoch and built a city, naming it after him. 18. Enoch's lineage continued through Irad, Mehujael, Methushael, and Lamech. 19. Lamech married two women, Adah and Zillah. 20. Adah bore Jabal, the ancestor of those who live in tents and keep livestock. 21. His brother Jubal was the ancestor of all musicians. 22. Zillah had Tubal-Cain, a skilled metalworker, and his sister Naamah. 23. Lamech said to his wives, "Listen to me! I have killed a man for wounding me, a young man for harming me. 24. If Cain was avenged seven times, then Lamech seventy-seven times." 25. Adam and Eve had another son, Seth, whom Eve saw as a gift from God in place of Abel. 26. Seth had a son named Enosh, and at that time people began to worship the Lord by calling on His name.

Chapter 5

1. This is the record of the descendants (offspring) of Adam. When God created man, He made him in His own image. 2. God created them as male and female, blessed them, and called them "Mankind"(humanity) when they were created.3. When Adam was 130 years old, he fathered a son who resembled (similitude) him in his own image, and he named him Seth. 4. After the birth of Seth (adam's son after abel), Adam lived another 800 years and had other sons and daughters. 5. So the total number of years that Adam lived was 930 years, and then he died. 6. Seth lived for 105 years and fathered Enosh. 7. After the birth of Enosh, Seth lived another 807 years and had other sons and daughters. 8. Thus, the total number of years that Seth lived was 912 years, and then he died 9. Enosh lived for 90 years and fathered Cainan. 10. After the birth of Cainan (son of Enosh), Enosh lived another 815 years and had other sons and daughters. 11. Thus, the total number of years that Enosh lived was 905 years, and then he died. 12. Cainan lived for 70 years and fathered Mahalalel. 13. After the birth of Mahalalel, Cainan lived another 840 years and had other sons and daughters. 14. Thus, the total number of years that Cainan lived was 910 years, and then he died. 15. Mahalalel lived for 65 years and fathered Jared. 16. After the birth of Jared, Mahalalel lived another 830 years and had other sons and daughters. 17. Thus, the total number of years that Mahalalel lived was 895 years, and then he died. 18. Jared lived for 162 years and fathered Enoch 19. After the birth of Enoch, Jared lived another 800 years and had other sons and daughters. 20. Thus, the total number of years that Jared lived was 962 years, and then he died. 21. Enoch lived for 65 years and fathered Methuselah. 22. After the birth of Methuselah, Enoch walked closely with God for 300 years, and had other sons and daughters. 23. Thus, the total number of years that Enoch lived was 365 years. 24. Enoch walked closely with God, and then he was no more, for God took him. 25. Methuselah lived for 187 years and fathered Lamech. 26. After the birth of Lamech, Methuselah lived another 782 years and had other sons and daughters. 27. Thus, the total number of years that Methuselah lived was 969 years, and then he died. 28. Lamech lived for 182 years and fathered a son. 29. He named his son Noah, saying, "This one will bring us comfort and relief from the painful labor and work of our hands, because of the curse (execration) that the Lord has placed on the ground." 30. After the birth of Noah, Lamech lived another 595 years and had other sons and daughters. 31. Thus, the total number of years that Lamech lived was 777 years, and then he died. 32. When Noah was 500 years old, he fathered three sons: Shem, Ham, and Japheth

Chapter 6

1. As people multiplied across the earth and daughters were born to them, 2. the sons of God noticed the beauty of these daughters and chose them as wives. 3. Then the Lord said, "My Spirit will not endure (remain) in humanity forever, for they are mortal (subject to death); their lifespan will be limited to 120 years." 4. In those days—and even later—giants (mighty beings) existed on the earth when the sons of God had children with human women. These offspring became notable (widely known) heroes and figures of legend (fame). 5. Observing that human wickedness (sinfulness) was widespread and their thoughts were constantly evil, 6. the Lord regretted (felt sorrow) creating humanity and felt deep sorrow (grief). 7. So He declared, "I will remove humanity, along with animals, creatures that crawl, and birds, from the earth, for I am grieved by their creation." 8. Yet Noah found favor (approval) with the Lord. 9. This is Noah's story: he was a righteous (morally upright), blameless (innocent) man among his generation and walked closely with God. 10. Noah had three sons: Shem, Ham, and Japheth. 11. The earth had become corrupt (immoral) and was filled with violence (brutality) in God's sight. 12. When God looked upon the earth, He saw that all people had deviated (turned away) into corruption (wickedness). 13. So God said to Noah, "I am going to end all life, for the earth is full of violence because of them. I will

destroy them along with the earth. **14.** Build an ark (large boat) from cypress wood, creating rooms within and coating it with pitch (waterproof material). **15.** Construct it to be 300 cubits (ancient measurement) long, 50 cubits wide, and 30 cubits high. **16.** Build a roof for the ark, leaving space within a cubit of the top, and put a door on the side. Make three levels inside—lower, middle, and upper. **17.** I am about to flood (cover with water) the earth to destroy every creature under heaven that has the breath of life. Everything on earth will perish (die). **18.** But I will make a covenant (sacred promise) with you. You, your sons, your wife, and your sons' wives will enter the ark with you. **19.** Bring into the ark two of every kind of creature, male and female, to keep them alive with you. **20.** Include pairs of all birds, animals, and crawling creatures (small moving animals). **21.** Collect and store food for you and for them." **22.** Noah followed all of God's instructions exactly.

Chapter 7

1. Also the Lord called to Noah, saying," Come into the ark, you and your family, because I've seen that you're righteous (righteous) before Me in this generation." **2.** Take seven dyads of each clean beast, a manly and his womanish, and two of each sick beast, a manly and his womanish. **3.** Also, take seven dyads of catcalls, both manly and womanish, to save (to keep commodity safe) their species on the earth. **4.** For in seven days, I'll shoot rain on the earth for forty days and forty nights, and I'll wipe out (destroy) every living thing I've created from the face of the earth." **5.** Noah did everything the Lord commanded (directed) him to do. **6.** Noah was six hundred times old when the floodwaters came upon the earth. **7.** So Noah, along with his sons, his woman, and his sons' women, entered the ark to escape the floodwaters. **8.** Of the clean creatures, sick creatures, catcalls, and all brutes that crawl (creep) on the earth, **9.** two of each kind, manly and womanish, entered the ark as God had commanded Noah. **10.** And after seven days, the waters of the flood tide came upon the earth. **11.** In the six hundredth time of Noah's life, on the seventeenth day of the alternate month, the cradles (sluice of water) of the deep broke open, and the windows of the welkin were opened. **12.** And the rain fell on the earth for forty days and forty nights. **13.** On the veritably same day, Noah and his sons — Shem, Ham, and Japheth and Noah's woman and his sons' women, entered the ark. **14.** They, along with every kind of beast, cattle, creeping thing, and every raspberry of every kind, came to Noah in the ark (boat of Noah). **15.** Two by two, they entered the ark, manly and womanish, of all brutes that had the breath of life in them. **16.** The creatures entered, manly and womanish, as God had commanded Noah, and the Lord Himself closed the door behind them. **17.** The flood tide lasted for forty days on the earth. The waters rose, lifted the ark, and it floated (sailed) above the earth. **18.** The waters came stronger, covering the earth, and the ark moved freely on the waters. **19.** The waters increased greatly and covered all the high mountains (hills) under the whole sky. **20.** The waters rose 15 cubits (ancient measure) above the mountains, and the mountains were submerged. **21.** Every living thing that moved on the earth decomposed (die) catcalls, creatures, wild brutes, and every person. **22.** Everything with the breath of life in it, everything on dry land, failed. **23.** God wiped out every living thing on the earth—humans, creatures, brutes that crawl, and catcalls. They were all destroyed. Only Noah and those with him in the ark remained alive. **24.** And the floodwaters remained on the earth for a hundred and fifty days.

Chapter 8

1. Then God remembered (recalled) Noah, along with all the animals and creatures that were with him in the ark. **2.** God sent a wind across the earth, and the waters began to recede (move back). **3.** The springs of the deep and the windows of the heavens were closed, and the rain stopped falling from the sky. **4.** The waters continued to decrease steadily (continuously) until, after 150 days, the earth was beginning to dry out. **5.** On the seventeenth day of the seventh month, the ark (boat of Noah) came to rest on the mountains of Ararat. **6.** The waters continued to decrease until the tenth month, and on the first day of the tenth month, the peaks of the mountains became visible (obvious). **7.** After forty days, Noah opened the window he had made in the ark. **8.** He released a raven, which flew back and forth, until the waters had dried up from the earth. **9.** Then Noah sent out a dove to see if the waters had receded enough from the earth's surface. **10.** But the dove found no place to rest and returned to Noah because the waters still covered the whole earth (entire earth). So, Noah took her back into the ark. **11.** Noah waited another seven days and sent the dove out again. **12.** That evening, the dove returned to him with a freshly plucked (remove) olive leaf in her beak, and Noah knew that the waters had decreased. **13.** Noah waited another seven days, and then sent out the dove once more, but this time, it did not return. **14.** In the 601st year of Noah's life, on the first day of the first month, the waters were completely dried up (drained) from the earth. Noah uncovered the ark and saw that the ground was dry. **15.** By the 27th day of the second month, the earth was completely dry. **16.** Then God spoke to Noah and said, **17.** "Leave the ark, you, your wife, your sons, and your sons' wives with you. **18.** Bring out every living thing that is with you—birds, animals, and every creeping thing that moves on the earth—so that they can multiply and fill the earth." **19.** So, Noah, his family, and every living creature left the ark. Every animal, bird, and creeping creature went out, each according to its kind. **20.** Noah then built (creates) an altar to the Lord, took some of every clean animal and bird, and offered them as burnt offerings. **21.** The Lord was pleased with the aroma (odour) of the offering and said to Himself, "I will never again curse the earth because of human sin, even though the human heart is inclined to evil from childhood. Nor will I ever again destroy every living thing as I have done." **22.** "As long as the earth remains, there will be planting and harvest (gather in), cold and heat, summer and winter, and day and night, which will never cease (stop)."

Chapter 9

1. God blessed Noah and his sons, saying," Be fruitful (produce children), multiply (increase in number), and fill the earth. **2.** The fear and dread (great fear and admiration) of you'll fall on every beast on the earth, every raspberry in the sky, and all brutes that move on the earth, including the fish of the ocean. I've placed them under your authority (control). **3.** Every living critter is now yours to eat, just as I gave you green shops ahead. **4.** But you mustn't eat meat with blood still in it, because blood is the life (vital force) of the beast. **5.** I'll demand an account (a report or reckoning) for your life's blood. I'll bear it from every beast and from every human. However, that person's life will be needed, If a person takes another person's life. **6.** Whoever sheds mortal blood (kills a person), by humans their blood will be exfoliate (their life will be taken); for God made humanity in His own image (in a way that reflects God's nature). **7.** As for you, be fruitful, multiply, and fill the earth abundantly (in great number)." **8.** also, God made a covenant (agreement or pledge) with Noah and his sons, saying, **9.**" I'm establishing My covenant with you and your descendants (unborn generations), **10.** and with every living critter with you — the catcalls, beast (domestic creatures), and all the creatures that came out of the ark. **11.** No way again will a flood tide destroy (wipe out) the earth and wipe out all life. **12.** This is the sign (symbol or mark) of the covenant I'm making with you and all living brutes on the earth. **13.** I set My rainbow (colored bow in the sky after rain) in the pall as a sign of the everlasting (eternal) covenant between Me and the earth. **14.** Whenever I bring shadows over the earth, and the rainbow appears, **15.** I'll flash back My covenant with you and every living critter, and noway again will the waters come a flood tide to destroy all meat. **16.** The rainbow will serve as a memorial (memory aid) of the eternal covenant between God and all life on earth." **17.** And God said to Noah," This is the sign of the covenant I've established (made) between Me and all life on earth." **18.** The sons of Noah who came out of the ark were Shem, Ham, and Japheth. Ham was the father of Canaan (Canaan is the ancestor of a group of people). **19.** These three were the sons of Noah, and from them, the entire earth was peopled (settled by their descendants). **20.** Noah came a planter and planted a croft (a field of connections). **21.** He drank some of the wine (fermented grape juice), came drunk, and lay uncovered (without apparel) in his roof. **22.** Ham, the father of Canaan, saw his father's bareness (saw him lying uncovered) and told his two sisters outdoors. **23.** But Shem and Japheth took a garment (piece of cloth), placed it over their shoulders, and walked backward to cover their father's bareness. They did not look at him (in respect for him). **24.** When Noah woke up and learned what his youthful son (Ham) had done to him, **25.** he said," Cursed (penalized) be Canaan (Ham's son); he'll be the smallest (most humble) of retainers to his sisters." **26.** He also said," Blessed (favored) be the LORD, the God of Shem; may Canaan be his menial. **27.** May God enlarge (make lesser or increase) Japheth, and may he live in the canopies of Shem; may Canaan be his menial." **28.** Noah lived 350 times after the flood tide. **29.** Noah lived a aggregate of 950 times, and also he failed.

Chapter 10

1. His is the family history of Noah's sons Shem, Ham, and Japheth. After the flood tide drift, they had children. **2.** The sons of Japheth were Gomer, Magog, Madai, Javan, Tubal, Meshech, and Tiras. **3.** Gomer's sons were Ashkenaz, Riphath, and Togarmah. **4.** Javan's sons were Elishah, Tarshish (a distant place known for trade), Kittim, and Dodanim. **5.** From these families, the coastal peoples (those living along the props) of the Heathens (non-Israelite nations) spread out across the earth. They separated into their lands, speaking their own languages, and forming their families and nations. **6.** The sons of Ham were Cush, Mizraim (another name for Egypt), Put, and Canaan. **7.** Cush's sons were Seba, Havilah, Sabtah, Raamah, and Sabtechah; Raamah's sons were Sheba and Dedan. **8.** Cush came the father of Nimrod, who came an important man on the earth. **9.** Nimrod was a professed hunter (someone who hunts for food or sport) before the Lord (in the sight of God), and so people say, "Nimrod, the potent hunter before the Lord." **10.** The morning of Nimrod's area was in Babel (a municipality in the land of Shinar), Erech, Accad, and Calneh, all in the land of Shinar (a region in ancient Mesopotamia). **11.** From there, he went to Assyria (an ancient empire in modern- day Iraq) and erected the cosmopolises of Nineveh (a large municipality), Rehoboth Ir, Calah, **12.** and Resen (a municipality between Nineveh and Calah, considered the main municipality). **13.** Mizraim (Egypt) got the Ludim, Anamim, Lehabim, Naphtuhim, **14.** Pathrusim, and Casluhim (from whom came the Philistines and Caphtorim). **15.** Canaan got Sidon (his firstborn), and Heth; **16.** also the Jebusites (the people of Jerusalem), the Amorites (a Canaanite people), and the Girgashites; **17.** the Hivites (a lineage in Canaan), the Arkites (a lineage near the mountains), and the Sinites (a group possibly living near modern- day China); **18.** the Arvadites (from the island of Arvad), the Zemarites, and the Hamathites. latterly, the Canaanites spread out. **19.** The Canaanite home stretched from Sidon (a municipality) toward Gerar (a Philistine municipality), as far as Gaza (a municipality), and toward Sodom (a municipality destroyed by God), Gomorrah (another destroyed municipality), Admah, and Zeboiim (two cosmopolises also destroyed), as far as Lasha. **20.** These were the sons of Ham, listed by their families, languages, lands, and nations. **21.** Children were also born to Shem, the ancestor of all the children of Eber (a man from whom the Hebrews descended), and the family of Japheth, the aged of the two. **22.** The sons of Shem were Elam, Asshur (an ancient area in Mesopotamia), Arphaxad, Lud, and Aram. **23.** The sons of Aram were Uz, Hul, Gether, and Mash. **24.** Arphaxad got Salah, and Salah got Eber. **25.** Eber had two sons one named Peleg (meaning" division"), because in his time the earth was divided (likely

pertaining to the division of nations after the Tower of Babel). His family's name was Joktan. **26.** Joktan got Almodad, Sheleph, Hazarmaveth, Jerah, **27.** Hadoram, Uzal, Diklah, **28.** Obal, Abimael, Sheba, **29.** Ophir, Havilah, and Jobab. All these were the sons of Joktan. **30.** Their homes extended from Mesha (a place possibly in Arabia) to Sephar (a mountain in the east). **31.** These are the sons of Shem, listed by their families, languages, lands, and nations. **32.** These were the families of Noah's sons, listed by their generations and nations. After the flood tide drift, these are the nations that spread across the earth.

Chapter 11

1. At this time, everyone on earth spoke the same language and used the same words. **2.** As people traveled eastward, they discovered a broad, flat plain in the region of Shinar (likely part of ancient Mesopotamia) and decided to settle there. **3.** They said to one another," Let's make bricks and singe them well." They chose bricks rather of gravestone and used navigator as mortar to bind them together. **4.** They also said," Let's construct a megacity with a palace reaching toward the welkin. This will make a name for us, so we won't be scattered across the earth." **5.** But the Lord came down to observe the megacity and palace they were erecting. **6.** The Lord noted," These people are unified in language and purpose, and this is only the morning of what they might negotiate. Nothing they imagine will be beyond them." **7.**" Let Us descend and mix up their language, so they can not understand one another." **8.** So, the Lord spread them out across the earth, and they stopped erecting the megacity. **9.** This place was named Babel (which means" confusion"), as it was there that the Lord mixed up the language of the whole world, dispersing people across the earth. This is the lineage of Shem Shem was 100 times old when he came the father of Arphaxad, two times after the great flood tide (the worldwide flood tide mentioned before in Genesis). **11.** After Arphaxad's birth, Shem lived another 500 times and had fresh sons and daughters. **12.** Arphaxad lived 35 times and sired Salah. **13.** After Salah's birth, Arphaxad lived another 403 times and had further sons and daughters. **14.** Salah lived 30 times and sired Eber. **15.** Following Eber's birth, Salah lived another 403 times and had other sons and daughters. **16.** Eber lived 34 times and came the father of Peleg. **17.** Eber also lived another 430 times and had fresh children. **18.** Peleg lived 30 times before begetting Reu. **19.** Peleg lived another 209 times after Reu's birth and had further sons and daughters. **20.** Reu lived 32 times and came the father of Serug. **21.** Reu lived another 207 times after Serug's birth and had other children. **22.** Serug lived 30 times and sired Nahor. **23.** Serug also lived another 200 times and had further sons and daughters. **24.** Nahor was 29 times old when he came the father of Terah. **25.** After Terah's birth, Nahor lived another 119 times, having fresh children. **26.** Terah reached 70 times of age and sired Abram (latterly known as Abraham), Nahor, and Haran. Then's the family record of Terah Terah had three sons — Abram, Nahor, and Haran. Haran was the father of Lot. **28.** Haran failed while his father Terah was still alive, in his motherland of Ur in Chaldea (an ancient area in Mesopotamia). **29.** Abram and Nahor both wedded Abram's woman was Sarai, and Nahor's woman was Milcah, son of Haran, who was also the father of Iscah. **30.** still, Sarai was unfit to have children. **31.** Terah also took his son Abram, his grandson Lot (son of Haran), and Sarai, Abram's woman, and left Ur in Chaldea, intending to go to Canaan (latterly known as the land of Israel, promised to Abram's descendants). They broke their trip in the megacity of Haran, where they settled temporarily. **32.** Terah lived to be 205 times old and failed in Haran.

Chapter 12

1. The Lord said to Abram (the first ancestor of Israel)," Leave your country (your nation), your cousins, and your father's house, and go to a land that I'll show you. **2.** I'll make you a great nation (a large group of people), I'll bless you (show favor), make your name great, and you'll be a blessing. **3.** I'll bless those who bless you (show favor to you), and curse those who curse you (want the detriment upon you). All the families (groups of people) of the earth will be blessed through you." **4.** So Abram stuck (followed the instructions) and left, as the Lord had instructed. Lot (Abram's bastard, the son of his family) went with him. Abram was 75 times old when he left Haran (a megacity in Mesopotamia). **5.** Abram took his woman Sarai, Lot (his family's son), all their goods (goods), and the people they had acquired in Haran (retainers or followers) and set out for the land of Canaan (the Promised Land, roughly ultramodern-day Israel). When they arrived, they settled in Canaan. **6.** Abram traveled through the land to the place of Shechem (a megacity in Canaan), near the oak tree of Moreh (a large tree in that area). At that time, the Canaanites (the native people of the region) were still in the land. **7.** The Lord appeared to Abram (showed Himself) and said," I'll give this land to your descendants (unborn generations)." So, Abram erected an sundeck (a platform for deification) there to the Lord, who had appeared to him. **8.** From there, Abram moved to the mountain east of Bethel (a megacity in Canaan), and set up camp with Bethel to the west and Ai (another near megacity) to the east. There, he erected another sundeck to the Lord and called on His name (appealed to God). **9.** Abram continued his trip southward. **10.** A deficiency (a severe insufficiency of food) struck the land, and since it was severe, Abram went to Egypt (a neighboring country) to live there for a while. **11.** As he neared Egypt, he said to Sarai," I know you're a truly beautiful woman. **12.** When the Egyptians (people of Egypt) see you, they will suppose you're my woman, and they will kill me to take you. But if you say you're my family, they will treat me well for your sake, and I'll stay alive." **13.** Say you are my sister, so that I will be treated well for your sake and my life will be spared because of you."**14.** So when Abram entered Egypt, the Egyptians noticed (sententia) that Sarai was truly beautiful.**15.** Pharaoh's officers (authorities in Egypt) saw her and praised her to Pharaoh, and she was taken into his palace. **16.** Pharaoh treated Abram well for her sake, giving him angel, oxen (large cattle), burros (beasties for transport), mannish and womanish retainers, womanish burros, and camels (large beasties used for transport). **17.** But the Lord struck Pharaoh and his ménage (family and retainers) with serious conditions because of Sarai, Abram's woman. **18.** Pharaoh called for Abram and said," What have you done to me? Why didn't you tell me she was your woman? **19.** Why did you say,' She's my family'? I might have taken her as my woman! Now, also's your woman Take her and leave." **20.** Pharaoh gave orders (commands) to his men, and they transferred Abram and his woman, along with all his goods, down.

Chapter 13

1. Abram (the primogenitor, the father of the Israelite people) went over from Egypt with his woman and all that he possessed, and Lot (his whoreson, the son of Abram's family) went with him, traveling to the South (region of Canaan). **2.** Abram was veritably rich in beast (creatures), tableware, and gold (a precious essence frequently used as currency). **3.** He continued his trip from the South, reaching Bethel (a megacity, meaning "house of God"), to the place where his roof (a movable lodging) had been at the morning, between Bethel and Ai (another megacity). **4.** There, Abram went back to the balcony (a raised platform or structure for deification) he'd erected before and called on the name of the Lord (supplicated to God). **5.** Lot, who traveled with Abram, also had flocks (groups of creatures), herds (large groups of cattle), and canopies. **6.** The land couldn't support them both, because their effects were so great that they couldn't live together. **7.** There was strife (conflict or disagreement) between the herders (keepers of the creatures) of Abram's beast and those of Lot, while the Canaanites (native people of the land) and Perizzites (a Canaanite lineage) still lived in the land. **8.** Abram said to Lot, "Let there be no strife (argument or division) between us, or between our herders, for we're lines (sisters, members of the same family). **9.**

The whole land is before you. Let's separate. However, I'll go to the right; and if you go to the right, I'll go to the left wing, If you go to the left wing." **10.** Lot lifted his eyes and saw the whole plain of the Jordan River, which was well-doused (rich in water, rich) far and wide, like the garden of the Lord (a place full of beauty and fertility), and like the land of Egypt, near Zoar (a city in the Jordan Valley). **11.** Lot chose for himself all the plain of the Jordan and traveled eastward. So, they separated. **12.** Abram settled in the land of Canaan (the Promised Land), while Lot settled in the metropolises of the plain and pitched his canopies near Sodom (a megacity known for wickedness). **13.** But the men of Sodom were exceedingly wicked (extremely immoral) and unethical against the Lord. **14.** After Lot had separated from him, the Lord said to Abram, "Lift up your eyes from where you are — look northward, southward, eastward, and westward. **15.** All the land you see, I'll give to you and your descendants (unborn generations) ever. **16.** I'll make your descendants as multitudinous as the dust (bitsy patches) of the earth. However, also your descendants could also be counted, If anyone could count the dust. **17.** Get up, walk through the land in its length and breadth, for I'm giving it to you." **18.** So, Abram moved his roof (movable lodging) and settled by the terebinth trees (large trees) of Mamre (a place near Hebron), and there he erected a balcony (a structure for deification) to the Lord.

Chapter 14

1. And it came to pass in the days of Amraphel, king of Shinar (an ancient region in Mesopotamia), Arioch, king of Ellasar (another area in Mesopotamia), Chedorlaomer, king of Elam (a area east of Mesopotamia, in modern-day Iran), and Tidal, king of the nations, **2.** that these lords made war against Bera, king of Sodom, Birsha, king of Gomorrah, Shinab, king of Admah, Shemeber, king of Zeboiim, and the king of Bela (that is, Zoar, a small municipality near the Dead Sea). **3.** All these lords joined forces and went to the Valley of Siddim (which is also called the Salt Sea, or Dead Sea, a tar-laden body of water) to fight against their adversaries. **4.** They had served Chedorlaomer for twelve times, but in the thirteenth time, they revolted (refused to serve him presently). **5.** In the fourteenth time, Chedorlaomer and the lords banded with him attacked the Rephaim in Ashteroth Karnaim, the Zuzim in Ham, the Emim in Shaveh Kiriathaim, **6.** and the Horites (an ancient people) in their mountain of Seir (a mountainous region south of Canaan), all the way to El Paran, which is near the nature. **7.** also they returned and came to En Mishpat (which is Kadesh, an oasis and well-known position in southern Canaan), and they attacked the land of the Amalekites (a fugitive lineage), and also the Amorites who lived in Hazezon Tamar (a region in the southern area of Canaan). **8.** The lords of Sodom, Gomorrah, Admah, Zeboiim, and Bela (Zoar) went out and joined battle against Chedorlaomer, Tidal, Amraphel, and Arioch so there were four lords fighting against five. **9.** The Valley of Siddim (also called the Salt Sea) was filled with asphalt recesses (sticky), and the lords of Sodom and Gomorrah fled; some fell into these recesses, while the others escaped to the mountains. **10.** The aggressors took all the goods of Sodom and Gomorrah, as well as all their vittles (supplies), and they left. **11.** They also took Lot, Abram's bastard who was living in Sodom, along with his goods, and went on their way. **12.** also one who had escaped (survived the battle) came and told Abram the Hebrew (meaning a man from the other side of the sluice, a reference to Abram's origins in Mesopotamia), who was living by the terebinth trees (large, shade-furnishing trees) of Mamre the Amorite (an ancient people), the family of Eshcol and Aner, who were Abram's abettors. **13.** When Abram heard that his bastard Lot had been taken locked, he armed his 318 trained retainers (men who were born and raised in his ménage and trained for battle) and went in pursuit of the aggressors as far as Dan (a municipality located in the northern part of Israel). **14.** Abram divided his forces and attacked them by night, pursuing them as far as Hobah (a place north of Damascus, a municipality in modern Syria). **15.** Abram brought back all the goods, and also saved his bastard Lot, along with his goods, the women, and the other people. **16.** also the king of Sodom went out to meet Abram in the Valley of Shaveh (also called the King's Valley, a place where lords gathered), after Abram returned from the defeat of Chedorlaomer and the lords who were with him. **17.** Melchizedek, the king of Salem (Salem is an ancient name for Jerusalem, the holy municipality), brought out chuck and wine and he was the clerk of God Most High. **18.** Melchizedek blessed Abram and said "Blessed be Abram, domestic of God Most High, the Possessor of heaven and earth; **19.** And blessed be God Most High, who has delivered your adversaries into your hands." And Melchizedek gave Abram a tithe (a tenth part) of everything. **20.** The king of Sodom said to Abram, "Give me the people, but you can keep the goods for yourself." **21.** But Abram said to the king of Sodom, "I have raised my hand to God Most High, the Possessor of heaven and earth, **22.** and I swear that I will not take anything from you — not indeed a thread or a sandal belt, so your can't say, 'I have made Abram rich.' **23.** I will take nothing except for what the immature men have eaten, and the portion of the men who went with me Aner, Eshcol, and Mamre — let them take their share." **24.** Abram agreed to not take any of the booties, except what was formerly eaten by his men and the portion for his abettors, leaving everything else for the king of Sodom.

Chapter 15

1. After these goods, the word of the Lord came to Abram in a vision, saying," Don't be hysterical, Abram. I am your guard (protection), your exceedingly great price." **2.** But Abram said," Lord God, what will You give me, since I am still childless, and the heir at law at law of my house is Eliezer of Damascus (a slavish from the municipality of Damascus, an ancient municipality in Syria)?" **3.** also, Abram said," Look, you have given me no seed; indeed, one born in my house, Eliezer, is my heir at law at law!" **4.** And behold, the word of the Lord came to him, saying," This one shall not be your heir at law at law, but one who will come from your own body (a child from your own lineage) shall be your heir at law at law." **5.** also, He brought Abram outside and said," Look now toward heaven, and count the stars if you are suitable to number them." And He said to him," So shall your descendants be." **6.** And Abram believed in the Lord, and He credited it to him as righteousness. **7.** also He said to him," I am the Lord (Yahweh), who brought you out of Ur of the Chaldeans (an ancient municipality in Mesopotamia, now in modern Iraq), to give you this land to inherit it." **8.** And Abram said," Lord God, how shall I know that I will inherit it?" **9.** So, He said to him," Bring Me a three- time-old heifer (an immature womanish cow), a three- time-old womanish goat, a three- time-old ram (a virile angel), a turtledove, and a immature patsy." **10.** also, Abram brought all these to Him, and cut them in two down the middle, and placed each piece opposite the other but he didn't cut the raspberries in two. **11.** And when the bloodsuckers came down on the corses, Abram drove them down. **12.** Now when the sun was going down, a deep sleep (a supernatural sleep, heavy sleep) fell upon Abram, and behold, horror and great darkness (a sense of fear and foreboding) fell upon him. **13.** also He said to Abram" Know for certain that your descendants will be strangers in a land that's not theirs and will serve them (the people of that land), and they will afflict them for four hundred times. **14.** But the nation whom they serve, I will judge (discipline); latterly they shall come out with great goods. **15.** As for you, you shall go to your fathers in peace (die peacefully); you shall be buried at a good old age. **16.** But in the fourth generation (after four generations of your descendants), they shall return also, for the iniquity (unethical conduct) of the Amorites (a group of Canaanite people) is not yet complete." **17.** And it came to pass, when the sun went down and it was dark, that behold, there appeared a smoking rotisserie (a furnace or fire), and a burning firebug, which passed between those pieces (of the brutes Abram had cut). **18.** On that same day, the Lord made a covenant (a formal, binding agreement or pledge) with Abram, saying" To your descendants I have given this land, from the sluice of Egypt to the great sluice, the River Euphrates (a major sluice in the Middle East), **19.** the Kenites (a lineage in the desert regions), the Kenezzites (another ancient lineage), the Kadmonites (a group mentioned as early settlers of Canaan), **20.** the Hittites (an ancient Anatolian people), the Perizzites (a Canaanite people), the Rephaim (elephants or large people), **21.** the Amorites (a group of people in Canaan), the Canaanites (the descendants of Canaan), the Girgashites (another Canaanite group), and the Jebusites (people of ancient Jerusalem)."

Chapter 16

1. Sarai, Abram's woman, hadn't borne him any children. She had an Egyptian wench (womanish menial) named Hagar. **2.** Sarai said to Abram," The Lord has averted me from having children. Please, take my maid, and maybe I can make a family through her." And Abram heeded to Sarai. **3.** Sarai gave her Egyptian servant, Hagar, to Abram to be his wife. after he'd lived in Canaan (the promised land) for ten times. **4.** Abram was with Hagar, and she became pregnant. When she realized she was pregnant, she looked down on Sarai. **5.** Sarai said to Abram," You're responsible for my suffering! I gave my maid to you, but now that she's pregnant, she despises me. May the Lord judge between us." **6.** Abram replied to Sarai," Your maid is under your authority. Do what you suppose is stylish." Sarai also manhandled (treated roughly) Hagar, and she fled. **7.** The Angel of the Lord (a godly runner) set up Hagar by a spring of water in the nature (desert), near the road to Shur (a region in Egypt). 8The Angel of the Lord said to her, "Hagar, servant of Sarai, where have you come from, and where are you headed?" She answered," I'm running down from my doxy Sarai." **9.** The Angel of the Lord instructed her, "Go back to your mistress and submit to her authority." **10.** The Angel of the Lord said, "I will greatly multiply your descendants so that they will be too numerous to count."11The Angel of the Lord went on, "You are pregnant and will give birth to a son." Name him Ishmael (meaning' God hears'), because the Lord has heard your misery." **12.**" He'll be a wild man (untamed); his hand will be against everyone, and everyone's hand will be against him. He'll live in hostility with all his sisters." 13 She named the Lord who had spoken to her, saying, "You are the God who sees me," because she declared, "I have now witnessed the One who watches over me."14. That's why the well was called Beer Lahai Roi (meaning" well of the living One who sees me"). It's located between Kadesh (a desert region) and Bered (a position in the nature). **15.** Hagar gave birth to a son for Abram, and Abram named him Ishmael, just as the Angel of the Lord had instructed her.16. Abram was eighty- six times old when Hagar gave birth to Ishmael.

Chapter 17

1. When Abram (a man whose name latterly came Abraham) was 99 years old, the LORD appeared to him and said," I'm the Almighty God (the each- important One); walk faithfully before Me and be impeccable (without sin). **2.** I'll make a covenant (a sacred pledge or agreement) with you, and I'll greatly increase your descendants." **3.** Abram bowed face down, and God continued speaking **4.** "My covenant is with you, and you will become the father of many nations."5. Your name will no longer be Abram; it'll be Abraham (meaning 'father of numerous'), for I've made you the father of numerous nations. **6.** I'll make you veritably fruitful (produce numerous descendants), and you'll be the ancestor (father) of nations; lords will come from you. **7.** I'll establish (set up forcefully) an everlasting (ever) covenant with you and your descendants after you, to be your God and their God. **8.** I'll give you and your descendants the land you're living in — all the land of Canaan (a region) — as an everlasting possession, and I'll be their God." 9 God said to Abraham, "You and your descendants must uphold My covenant and follow My pledge." **10.** This is the covenant you must keep every joker among you must be circumcised. **11.** You must circumcise the meat (skin) of your foreskins, and it'll be a sign (symbol) of the covenant between Me and you. **12.** Every manly child among you, born in your house or bought from an outsider (someone not from your people), must be circumcised when they're eight days old. **13.** Those born in your house or bought with your plutocrat must be circumcised. This will be a endless (lasting ever) sign of My covenant with you. **14.** Any male who is not circumcised will be cut off (removed) from his people, as he has broken my covenant." **15.** God also said to Abraham, "Regarding your wife Sarai, do not call her Sarai anymore; her name will be Sarah, which means 'queen.'"**16.** I'll bless her (give her my favor) and give you a son by her. I'll bless her, and she'll be the mama of nations; lords will come from her." **17.** Abraham laughed to himself and said, "Can a man who is 100 years old father a child? And can Sarah, who is 90 years old, bear a child?" **18.** Abraham said to God, "If only Ishmael, the son I had with Hagar, could live under Your blessing!" **19** But God replied, "No, your wife Sarah will bear you a son, and you will name him Isaac, which means 'laughter.' I will establish My covenant with him as an everlasting covenant, and with his descendants."**20.** As for Ishmael, I've heard you. I'll bless him and make him fruitful. He'll come the father of twelve tycoons (leaders), and I'll make him a great nation. **21.** "But My covenant will be established with Isaac, the son that Sarah will bear to you at this time next year." **22.** After God finished speaking with Abraham, He left. **23.** That veritably day, Abraham adhered God and circumcised his son Ishmael, all the men in his ménage, and every manly menial — whether born in his house or bought with his plutocrat — just as God had commanded. **24.** Abraham was 99 times old when he was circumcised. **25.** Ishmael, his son, was 13 years old when he was circumcised.**26.** On that veritably day, both Abraham and his son Ishmael were circumcised. **27.** And all the men in Abraham's ménage, whether born in his house or bought with his plutocrat, were circumcised along with him.

Chapter 18

 1 the LORD appeared to Abraham near the terebinth (oak) trees of Mamre as he was resting in the heat of the day. **2-3** Abraham lifted his eyes and saw three men standing by him. He ran to meet them, bowed down to the ground, and said, "My Lord (a respectful title for a superior), if I have found favor (approval or kindness) in Your sight, do not pass by Your servant." **4-5** He offered them water to wash their feet and rest under the tree, and promised to bring them a morsel (small portion) of bread to refresh their hearts. **6-7** Abraham hurried to Sarah to prepare fine meal (flour) and made cakes, while he also selected a tender (young and soft) calf, which was prepared quickly. **8** He placed the meal, butter, milk, and calf before them, standing by as they ate. **9-10** The men asked about Sarah, and the Lord promised that she would have a son, even though she was well beyond the age of childbearing. **11-12** Sarah laughed within herself, questioning how she could have a child in her old age. **13** The Lord responded, asking why Sarah laughed and reminding her that nothing is too hard (difficult or impossible) for the Lord. **14** He assured them that at the appointed time (predetermined time), Sarah would have a son. **15** Sarah denied laughing out of fear, but the Lord corrected her, saying, "You did laugh!" **16** The men then prepared to leave for Sodom, and Abraham accompanied them to send them on their way. **17** The Lord revealed to Abraham that He was planning to investigate the sin of Sodom and Gomorrah. **18** He also shared His intentions, saying that Abraham would become a great and mighty nation, and all the nations would be blessed through him. **19** God affirmed His choice of Abraham, knowing he would guide his household to keep the way of the Lord and do righteousness and justice. **20** The Lord explained that the outcry (complaint or cry for help) against Sodom and Gomorrah was great, and their sin was very grave (serious). **21** He would go down to see if their actions aligned with the outcry against them. **22** The men turned toward Sodom, but Abraham stayed before the Lord. **23-24** Abraham then asked God if He would destroy the righteous with the wicked, questioning if He would destroy the city for the sake of fifty righteous people. **25** He argued that it would be wrong to slay (kill in violent way) the righteous with the wicked, asserting that the Judge of all the earth would do right. **26** The Lord promised that if He found fifty righteous in Sodom, He would spare the city for their sake. **27-28** Abraham humbly acknowledged his insignificance, asking if God would spare the city if there were five less than fifty righteous people. **29** The Lord agreed that He would not destroy it for the sake of forty-five. **30-31** Abraham continued to negotiate, asking if thirty righteous people were found. **32** The Lord assured him that He would not destroy it for the sake of ten righteous people. **33** After their conversation, the Lord departed, and Abraham returned to his place.

Chapter 19

1. In the evening, two angels arrived in Sodom (a megacity in ancient times known for wickedness), where Lot was sitting at the megacity gate (a place where elders and leaders met). When Lot saw them, he got up, bowed low (showed deep respect), and saluted them. **2.** He said," Please, my lords (a regardful title for honorable guests), come to my house, stay the night, and wash your bases. In the morning, you can continue on your way." But they replied," No, we'll stay in the open forecourt (an open public place in the megacity)." **3.** Lot claimed explosively (converted forcefully), so they entered his home. He prepared a feast with unleavened chuck (chuck made without incentive, frequently emblematizing chastity), and they ate. **4.** Before they went to sleep, the men of Sodom, youthful and old from every part of the megacity, gathered around Lot's house. **5.** They called to Lot," Where are the men who came to you tonight? Bring them out so we can know them privately (know carnally means to have a sexual relation)." **6.** Lot went outdoors, closing the door behind him, **7.** and contended," Please, sisters, don't do similar evil effects!" **8.** He added," Look, I've two daughters who are recruits (have not been with a man). Let me bring them out to you, and you may do as you wish with them. But don't harm these men, for they've come under my protection (Lot's duty to cover guests in his home)." **9.** they replied," Move away!" also they added," This foreigner (one not firstly from Sodom) acts like a judge! We'll treat you worse than them." They pressed hard (forced him aggressively) against Lot and tried to break down the door. **10.** But the two men (angels) reached out, pulled Lot outside, and shut the door. **11.** They struck the men outdoors with blindness (unfit to see), so they came exhausted trying to find the door. **12.** Also the angels asked Lot," Do you have anyone differently then — sons- in- law, sons, daughters, or anyone differently in the megacity? Get them out of then! **13.** We're about to destroy this place because the cries against its people are so great (the extent of the sin is severe) before the Lord, who transferred us to destroy it." **14.** Lot went out and advised his sons in- law, who were married to his daughters," Get up! Leave this place, for the LORD is about to destroy the megacity!" But they allowed he was joking (didn't take him seriously). **15.** At dawn (early morning), the angels prompted Lot," Accelerate! Take your woman and your two daughters who are then, or you'll be swept down (caught in the destruction) when the megacity is penalized." **16.** When Lot dithered (delayed, awaited), the angels took his hand, his woman's hand, and the hands of his daughters, leading them out of the megacity because the Lord had mercy (kindness and compassion) on him. **17.** When they were outdoors, one of the angels said," Run for your lives! Don't look back or stop anywhere in the plain (position area of land). Flee to the mountains, or you'll be swept down!" **18.** Lot replied," Please, my lords, not there!" **19.** He continued," You have shown great mercy in saving my life, but I'm hysterical disaster (trouble) will catch me if I flee to the mountains, and I'll die." **20.** " Look, then's a small city hard. Let me escape there just a small place and I'll live." **21.** The angel agreed, saying," I'll grant your request and extra that city." **22.** " But accelerate! Escape there snappily, for I cannot do anything until you reach it." That's why the city was named Zoar (Zoar means "small"). **23.** By the time Lot reached Zoar, the sun had risen over the land. **24.** Also the Lord rained burning sulfur (a substance frequently associated with judgment and destruction) on Sodom and Gomorrah from the welkin (sky). **25.** He destroyed those metropolises, the entire plain, all the people, and everything growing on the ground. **26.** But Lot's woman looked back, and she came a pillar (a solid, irremovable mass) of swab. **27.** Early in the morning, Abraham returned to the place where he'd stood before the Lord. **28.** He looked down toward Sodom and Gomorrah and saw thick bank rising from the land, like bank from a furnace (a roaster or place where effects are burned). **29.** So when God destroyed the metropolises of the plain, He flashed back Abraham and saved Lot, bringing him out of the catastrophe (disaster) that destroyed the metropolises where Lot had lived. **30.** Lot left Zoar with his two daughters and settled in the mountains, for he was hysterical to stay in Zoar. They lived in a delve **31.** One day, the aged daughter said to the youngish," Our father is old, and there's no man then to marry us, as is the custom." **32.** " Let's get our father to drink wine and lie with him so we can save (continue) our family line." **33.** So they got Lot drunk (made him unfit to suppose easily with alcohol) that night, and the aged son lay with him, but he was ignorant (did not know) of it. **34.** The coming day, the aged son said to the youngish," I did it last night; now let's get him drunk again so you can also lie with him to save our family line." **35.** They got Lot drunk again that night, and the youngish son lay with him, but he didn't know. **36.** So both daughters of Lot came pregnant (with child) by their father. **37.** The aged daughter had a son and named him Moab; he came the ancestor of the Moabites (people descended from Moab). **38.** The youngish also had a son and named him Ben-Ammi; he came the ancestor of the Ammonites (people descended from Ben- Ammi).

Chapter 20

1. Abraham traveled south and stayed between Kadesh and Shur, settling temporarily in Gerar (a Philistine megacity). **2.** Abraham introduced Sarah as his family, so Abimelech (king) of Gerar took her into his ménage. **3.** But God appeared to Abimelech in a dream, advising him," You're in grave peril (serious threat) because the woman you took is married." **4.** Abimelech, who hadn't been with her, replied," Lord, would You destroy (bring ruin upon) an innocent (without guilt) nation?" **5.** " Did not he tell me,' She's my family'? And she herself said,' He's my family.' I acted with a clear heart (without guilt) and innocent intentions (pure motives)." **6.** God responded in the dream," Yes, I know you acted with integrity (honesty). I kept you from transgressing (doing wrong) by not allowing you to touch her." **7.** " Now, return the man's woman. He's a prophet (runner of God) and will supplicate for you, so you may live. But if you don't, you and your people will surely die (face certain death)." **8.** Beforehand the coming morning, Abimelech called his retainers and told them everything, and they were all veritably alarmed (filled with fear). **9.** Abimelech also summoned (called for) Abraham and asked," What have you done to us? How have I wronged you, bringing similar guilt upon my area? This was a grave offense (serious wrongdoing)." **10.** He continued," What were you allowing when you did this?" **11.** Abraham replied," I allowed, surely there's no fear of God in this place, and they will kill me for my woman." **12.** " either, she really is my family — my father's son, though not my mama 's — and she came my woman." **13.** " When God led me down from my motherland (motherland), I asked her,' Show me this kindness wherever we go, say that I'm your family.'" **14.** Abimelech also gave Abraham lamb, oxen (large creatures used for labor), and manly and womanish retainers, and returned Sarah to him. **15.** Abimelech told Abraham," My land is open to you; settle (live) wherever you wish." **16.** To Sarah, he said," I've given your' family' a thousand pieces of tableware. This

clears you of any allegations (claims of wrongdoing) and restores your honor (character) before everyone." **17.** Abraham supplicated to God, and God healed Abimelech, his woman, and his womanish retainers, enabling them to have children again. **18.** For the Lord had made all the women in Abimelech's ménage barren (unfit to have children) because of Sarah, Abraham's woman

Chapter 21

1. The Lord visited Sarah as He'd promised and fulfilled His word to her. **2.** Sarah came pregnant and bore Abraham a son in his old age at the time God had read (" read" means" prognosticated beforehand"). **3.** Abraham named his son Isaac, the one whom Sarah bore to him. **4.** When Isaac was eight days old, Abraham circumcised him (circumcised means" performed a religious ritual by removing the foreskin"), following God's command. **5.** Abraham was one hundred times old when Isaac was born. **6.** Sarah said," God has brought me joy (great happiness), and everyone who hears of this will rejoice (feel joy) with me." **7.** She added," Who would have told Abraham that I would nurse (breastfeed) children? Yet I've given him a son in his old age." **8.** As Isaac grew and was weaned (" weaned" means" no longer suckling"), Abraham held a great feast (festivity) on that day. **9.** Sarah saw Hagar's son, Ishmael, mocking (" mocking" means" making fun of") Isaac. **10.** She told Abraham," shoot this menial (Hagar) and her son down, for her son shall not partake the heritage (right to retain or admit) with my son, Isaac." **11.** Abraham was worried (worried) by this because of his love for his son Ishmael. **12.** But God told Abraham," Don't be worried (worried) over the boy or Hagar. Hear to Sarah, for your descendants (seed, unborn generations) will be traced through Isaac. **13.** Yet I'll also make a nation (a people group) of Hagar's son because he's your son too." **14.** Beforehand the coming morning, Abraham gave Hagar chuck and water, placed them on her shoulder, and transferred her and the boy down. They wandered in the Nature of Beersheba (a desert region). **15.** When the water ran out, Hagar placed her son under a shrub ("shrub" means" small backcountry or factory"). **16.** She went and sat a distance down, saying," I cannot watch my child die." She sat there and wept (" wept" means" cried intensively") loudly. **17.** God heard Ishmael crying, and an angel (heavenly runner) spoke to Hagar from heaven," What troubles (causes torture to) you, Hagar? Don't sweat, for God has heard the boy's cry where he lies. **18.** Get up, lift up the boy, and hold his hand, for I'll make him a great nation." **19.** also, God opened her eyes, and she saw a well (a deep-water source). She filled the water skin (a vessel made of beast skin for water) and gave the boy a drink. **20.** God was with Ishmael as he grew up in the nature (a remote, uninhabited area) and came a professed sportswoman (a person who uses an arc and arrow). **21.** He lived in the Nature of Paran (a desert region), and Hagar set up him a woman from Egypt. **22.** At that time, Abimelech (a Philistine king), along with Phichol (commander of his army), approached Abraham, saying," God is with you in all that you do. **23.** Swear (make a serious pledge) to me by God that your won't deceive me, my descendants, or my people, and that you'll show me the same kindness (good treatment) I've shown to you in this land." **24.** Abraham agreed and swore to him. **25.** still, Abraham reproached (expressed disapprobation to) Abimelech about a well that Abimelech's retainers had taken. **26.** Abimelech replied," I don't know who did this; you haven't told me, and I only heard of it moment." **27.** also, Abraham gave lamb and cattle to Abimelech, and they made a covenant (" covenant" means" formal agreement or pledge") together. **28.** Abraham separated seven ewe innocents (womanish lamb) from the flock. **29.** Abimelech asked," What's the purpose of these seven innocents you have set piecemeal?" **30.** Abraham said," Accept these seven innocents as evidence that I dug this well." **31.** They called the place Beersheba (" Well of the Pledge") because they swore a pledge (serious pledge) there. **32.** After making this covenant at Beersheba, Abimelech and Phichol returned to the land of the Philistines (a region near Canaan). **33.**

Abraham planted a tamarisk tree (a type of tree) in Beersheba and called on the Lord, the Everlasting God (the eternal and unchanging God). **34.** Abraham stayed in the Philistine land for a long time.

Chapter 22

1. After these events, God tested Abraham, calling him by name, to which Abraham responded," Then I am." **2.** God instructed," Take your son Isaac, whom you love, and go to the land of Moriah (a mountain region). There, offer him as a burnt immolation on a mountain I'll show you." **3.** Beforehand the coming morning, Abraham prepared, took Isaac, two retainers, and wood for the immolation, and set off for the place God had commanded. **4.** On the third day, Abraham saw the place from a distance. **5.** He told his retainers," Stay then with the jackass; Isaac and I'll go worship and return to you." **6.** Abraham placed the wood on Isaac's back, took the fire and cutter, and both walked on together. **7.** Isaac asked," Father, we've the fire and wood, but where is the angel for the immolation?" **8.** Abraham replied," God will give the angel for Himself." They continued walking. **9.** Upon reaching the designated spot, Abraham erected an balcony, arranged the wood, bound Isaac, and laid him on the balcony. **10.** As he prepared to immolate Isaac, **11.** the Angel of the Lord called out," Abraham, Abraham!" He answered," Then I am." **12.** The angel said," Don't harm the boy. Now I know you sweat God because you haven't withheld your son." **13.** Abraham also saw a ram caught by its cornucopias in a copse, which he offered in place of Isaac. **14.** Abraham named the place" The Lord Will give," as it's said," On the mountain of the Lord, it'll be handed." **15.** The Angel of the Lord called to Abraham a alternate time, **16.** declaring," Since you have adhered, I swear by Myself, **17.** I'll bless you and multiply your descendants like the stars in the sky and the beach on the reinforcement. Your descendants will conquer their adversaries. **18.** Through your seed, all nations of the earth will be blessed." **19.** Abraham returned to his retainers, and they went together to Beersheba, where Abraham settled. **20.** latterly, Abraham learned that his family Nahor's woman, Milcah, had borne children. **21.** They were Huz, Buz, Kemuel (father of Aram), **22.** Chesed, Hazo, Pildash, Jidlaph, and Bethuel. **23.** Bethuel sired Rebekah. **24.** Nahor's doxy, Reumah, also had children Tebah, Gaham, Thahash, and Maachah.

Chapter 23

1. Sarah lived for one hundred and twenty- seven times. These were the full times of her life. **2.** Sarah failed in Kirjath Arba (also called Hebron, a municipality in Canaan), and Abraham mourned and wept for her. **3.** also Abraham rose from his place of mourning and spoke to the people of Heth. **4.** He said, "I am a stranger (a person not from this land) and guest (a frequenter) among you. Please grant me land for a burial place so I may bury my woman" **5.** The people of Heth responded to Abraham, **6.** "hear, honored lord, you are like a potent Napoleon (an important leader) among us. Bury your woman in the swish of our burial spots; no bone also will deny you a place." **7.** Abraham bowed in respect to the people of Heth. **8.** He said, "If you agree that I should bury my woman also, please speak to Ephron, son of Zohar, on my behalf, (on my behalf means as my representative or for me) **9.** so, he might sell me the cave of Machpelah, located at the end of his field. Let him sell it to me for its full price as a burial point." **10.** Ephron, who was among the people of Heth, responded to Abraham in the presence of all who had gathered at the municipality gate. **11.** "No, my lord," Ephron said, "listens to me. I give you the field and the cave in it. It's yours to bury your woman" **12.** Abraham bowed again before the people of the land. **13.** He replied to Ephron, saying, "Please accept payment from me. I will pay for the field so I may bury my woman there." **14.** Ephron answered Abraham, **15.** "here to me, my lord. The land is worth four hundred shekels of tableware, but what is that between us? Go ahead and bury your woman." **16.** Abraham agreed and counted out four hundred shekels of tableware for Ephron, as witnessed by the people of Heth. This was the standard currency among merchandisers. **17.** thus, the field of Ephron at Machpelah near Mamre — the field, claw, and all the girding trees was fairly transferred (fairly transferred means the sanctioned change of power or possession) **18.** to Abraham as his property in the presence of the people of Heth at the municipality gate. **19.** latterly, Abraham buried his woman Sarah in the cave of the field of Machpelah near Mamre (also known as Hebron) in Canaan. (Mamre is a position near Hebron) **20.** So, the field and the cave in it were fairly transferred to Abraham by the people of Heth as a burial point. (Burial point means a place where someone is buried after death)

Genesis 24, 1 Abraham was very old and had been blessed by the Lord in every way. **2** He asked his principal menial (the most important servant), the one in charge of all he possessed, to swear a pledge. He said, "Place your hand under my ham (an ancient act of making a serious pledge), **3** and swear by the Lord, the God of heaven and earth, that you won't choose a woman for my son from the Canaanites (people living in the land of Canaan), **4** but go to my motherland and to my cousins to find a woman for my son Isaac." **5** The servant replied, "What if the woman refuses to come back with me? Should I take Isaac back to your motherland?" **6** Abraham advised him, "Make sure you don't take my son back there. **7** The Lord, who brought me from my father's house and gave me this land, will send His angel (a messenger of God) ahead of you to guide you to the right woman. **8** If the woman won't come with you, you're free from this pledge (oath), but do not take my son back there." **9** The servant agreed and swore to do as Abraham said. **10** He took ten camels (large animals used for travel), loaded them with goods, and set off for the city of Nahor (a city in Mesopotamia). **11** At evening, when women generally came to draw water (take water from the well), he stopped by a well. **12** He prayed, "Lord God of my master Abraham, please help me today and show kindness (favor) to him. **13** Here I stand by the well, and the women from the city will come to draw water. **14** Let the woman who offers to give me water and also water my camels be the one You have chosen for Isaac." **15** Before he finished speaking, Rebekah, daughter of Bethuel (Nahor's son), appeared, carrying a pitcher (a vessel for water). **16** She was very beautiful, a virgin (a woman who has never been married), and no one had ever been with her. She filled her pitcher and came up. **17** The servant ran to her and asked, "Please give me a drink from your pitcher." **18** She said, "Drink, my lord," and quickly lowered her pitcher to give him a drink. **19** Then she said, "I'll also draw water for your camels until they have finished drinking." **20** She quickly emptied her pitcher into the trough (a vessel for water), ran back to the well to fill it, and watered all the camels. **21** The servant watched in silence, wondering if the Lord had made his journey successful. **22** When the camels had finished drinking, the servant gave Rebekah a golden nose ring and two gold bracelets. **23** He asked, "Whose daughter, are you? Is there room for us to stay at your father's house?" **24** She replied, "I am the daughter of Bethuel, who is the son of Nahor and Milcah (Nahor's wife)." **25** She also said, "We have plenty of straw (dried grass for animals) and feed (food for animals), and room for you to stay." **26** The servant bowed his head and worshiped the Lord. **27** He said, "Praise the Lord, the God of my master Abraham, who has shown His kindness and faithfulness (truthfulness) to him. The Lord led me to the family of my master's brother." **28** Rebekah ran home and told her family. **29** Rebekah had a brother named Laban (her brother), who quickly went to meet the servant at the well. **30** When he saw the nose ring and bracelets and heard Rebekah's story, he went to the servant. **31** Laban greeted him, saying, "Come in, blessed of the Lord! Why stand outside? I've prepared a place for you and your camels." **32** The servant entered, unloaded the camels, and they were given food, water, and a place to rest. **33** Before eating, the servant said, "I won't eat until I've explained why I'm here." **34** Laban said, "Go ahead, speak." **35** The servant began, "I am Abraham's servant. **36** The Lord has greatly blessed my master, making him very wealthy.

He has flocks (groups of sheep), herds (groups of cattle), silver, gold, and many servants. **37** Sarah, his wife, bore a son to him in her old age, and everything belongs to this son, Isaac. **38** My master made me swear, saying, 'Don't take a wife for Isaac from the Canaanites, **39** but go to my family and find a wife for him.' **40** I asked, 'What if the woman won't come with me?' **41** He said, 'The Lord will send His angel to guide you to the right woman.' **42** So I came to this well and prayed, 'If the woman who comes to draw water offers to give me a drink and water my camels, let her be the one You have chosen for Isaac.' **43** Before I finished speaking, Rebekah arrived and did exactly as I prayed. **44** I asked her who her family was, and she told me she was the daughter of Bethuel, Nahor's son. I gave her the nose ring and bracelets. **45** I worshiped the Lord for leading me to the right woman for Isaac." **46** "Now, if you will do your part and show kindness to my master, tell me; otherwise, I will leave." **47** Laban and Bethuel replied, "This is from the Lord, so we can't say anything good or bad. **48** Here is Rebekah; take her and let her be Isaac's wife, as the Lord has spoken." **49** The servant bowed down and worshiped the Lord. **50** He gave Rebekah valuable jewelry and clothing, and also gave gifts to her brother and mother. **51** After they ate and drank, the servant asked to leave the next morning. **52** Rebekah's family said, "Let her stay with us for ten more days before going." **53** The servant insisted, "Please don't delay me; the Lord has made my journey successful. Let me go back to my master." **54** They agreed to ask Rebekah. **55** They called her and asked, "Will you go with this man?" She replied, "I will go." **56** So they sent her away with her nurse (a caretaker), Abraham's servant, and his men. **57** They blessed her, saying, "May you become the mother of thousands, and may your descendants defeat their enemies." **58** Rebekah and her maids (female servants) mounted the camels and followed the servant. **59** They left for Isaac's home. **60** Isaac was living in the south and had just returned from Beer Lahai Roi (a well in the desert). **61** As he was meditating (thinking deeply) in the field in the evening, he saw the camels coming. **62** Rebekah saw Isaac from a distance, dismounted (got off) from her camel, **63** and asked the servant, "Who is that man walking toward us?" **64** The servant said, "That is my master." **65** She covered herself with a veil (a piece of cloth to cover the face). **66** The servant told Isaac all that had happened. **67** Isaac took Rebekah into his mother Sarah's tent, married her, and loved her. Isaac was comforted (emotionally supported) after his mother's death.

Chapter 25

1. Abraham married another woman named Keturah. **2.** She gave birth to six children Zimran, Jokshan, Medan, Midian, Ishbak, and Shuah. **3.** Jokshan had two sons, Sheba and Dedan. Dedan's descendants were Asshurim, Letushim, and Leummim. **4.** Midian had five sons Ephah, Epher, Hanoch, Abidah, and Eldaah. These were the children of Keturah. **5.** Abraham gave everything he'd to Isaac. **6.** But Abraham gave gifts to the sons of his doxies and transferred them down, eastward from Isaac, while still living. **7.** Abraham lived for 175 times. **8.** He failed in a good, full age and was gathered to his ancestors. **9.** Isaac and Ishmael buried Abraham in the delve of Machpelah (a burial point located in Hebron, Palestine), in the field of Ephron the Hittite. **10.** This field was bought by Abraham from the Hittites, and there Abraham and Sarah were buried. **11.** After Abraham's death, God blessed Isaac, and Isaac lived in Beer Lahai Roi (a well located in southern Israel). **12.** This is the line (family history) of Ishmael, Abraham's son, born to Hagar, Sarah's wench (a servant woman). **13.** The names of Ishmael's sons are Nebajoth (his firstborn), Kedar, Adbeel, Mibsam, **14.** Mishma, Dumah, Massa, **15.** Hadar, Tema, Jetur, Naphish, and Kedemah. **16.** These were the twelve ethnical leaders of Ishmael's descendants. **17.** Ishmael lived 137 times and was gathered to his people (passed down). **18.** His descendants lived from Havilah (an ancient region, now part of Arabia) to Shur (a place near Egypt, now part of ultramodern- day Sinai), toward

Assyria (an ancient conglomerate in ultramodern- day Iraq and Syria). **19.** This is the line of Isaac, Abraham's son. Isaac sired Isaac. **20.** Isaac was 40 when he married Rebekah, the son of Bethuel the Syrian (a person from the region of Syria), from Padan Aram (a region located in ultramodern- day Iraq and Syria), the family of Laban the Syrian (a prominent figure in the Bible, from Syria). **21.** Isaac supplicated to God for Rebekah, as she was barren (unfit to have children), and God granted his request. Rebekah conceived. **22.** But as the children plodded within her, Rebekah said," Why is this passing to me?" She inquired of the Lord. **23.** The Lord told her," There are two nations in your womb. Two peoples will be divided. One will be stronger, and the elder will serve the youngish." **24.** When the time came, she gave birth to halves. **25.** The first came out red and covered with hair, so they named him Esau. **26.** His family followed, holding Esau's heel, so he was named Jacob. Isaac was 60 when they were born. **27.** As the boys grew, Esau came a professed huntsman (someone who captures wild creatures for food), while Jacob was a quiet man, staying at home. **28.** Isaac loved Esau because he enjoyed the game (wild meat) Esau brought, but Rebekah loved Jacob. **29.** One day, Jacob made a stew, and Esau came in from the field, tired and famished, saying," Please give me some of that red stew." **30.** Esau was called Edom (which means" red") because of the stew. **31.** Jacob said," First, vend me your birthright" (the heritage of the firstborn). **32.** Esau replied," I'm about to die; what use is my birthright?" **33.** Jacob claimed," Swear to me now." So Esau swore and vended his birthright to Jacob. **34.** Jacob gave Esau chuck and lentil stew (a mess made from sap or lentils). Esau ate, drank, and left. Esau despised (treated with misprision) his birthright.

Chapter 26

1. There was a shortage (lack of food) in the land, in addition to the earlier shortage that passed during Abraham's time. Isaac went to see Abimelech, king of the Philistines, who lived in Gerar (a megacity in the Philistine home, near the seacoast of the Mediterranean). **2.** The Lord appeared to Isaac and said, "Don't go to Egypt; stay in the land I'll show you. **3.** Live then, and I'll be with you and bless you. I'll give you and your descendants (seed) all of these lands, and I'll fulfill the pledge I made to your father Abraham. **4.** I'll make your descendants as multitudinous as the stars in the sky, and I'll give them all these lands. Through your descendants, all the nations on earth will be blessed; **5.** because Abraham adhered to My voice and followed My commands (rules), My laws, and My instructions." **6.** So Isaac stayed in Gerar. **7.** The men of that area asked Isaac about his woman. Isaac answered, "She's my family," because he was hysterical to say, "She's my woman," allowing, "The men of this place might kill me for Rebekah, since she's veritably beautiful." **8.** After Isaac had been there a long time, Abimelech, the king of the Philistines, looked out of a window and saw Isaac showing affection to Rebekah, his woman. **9.** Abimelech called Isaac and said, "Easily, she's your woman. Why did you say, 'She's my family'?" Isaac responded, "I said it because I allowed, 'I might be killed because of her.'" **10.** Abimelech said, "What's this you have done to us? One of the men might have slept with your woman, and you would have brought guilt (sin or wrongdoing) upon us." **11.** So Abimelech ordered all the people, "Anyone who harms this man or his woman will surely be put to death." **12.** Isaac sowed (planted) crops in that land, and in the same time, he reaped (gathered) a hundredfold (a return that's a hundred times lesser), and the Lord blessed him. **13.** Isaac came prosperous (fat) and continued to prosper until he came extremely fat; **14.** he'd large flocks (groups of lamb or scapegoats), herds (groups of cattle), and numerous retainers, which caused the Philistines to begrudge him. **15.** The Philistines had stopped up (blocked) all the wells that Abraham's retainers had dug during Abraham's life, and they filled them with dirt. **16.** Abimelech said to Isaac, "Leave us, because you have come much more important (strong and influential) than we are." **17.** So Isaac moved from there and bivouacked in the Valley of Gerar, where he settled. **18.** Isaac restarted the wells that had been dug during his father Abraham's time, which the Philistines had stopped up after Abraham's death. Isaac gave them the same names his father had used. **19.** Isaac's retainers also dug in the vale and set up a well with running water (fresh water). **20.** But the herders (people who take care of creatures) of Gerar argued with Isaac's herders, saying, "This water belongs to us." So Isaac named the well-conditioned Esek (meaning "contention" or "disagreement") because they quibbled with him. **21.** Also Isaac dug another well, and they quibbled over that one too. So he named it Sitnah (meaning "hostility" or "opposition"). **22.** Isaac moved from there and dug another well, and this time there was no quarrel over it. He called it Rehoboth (meaning "room," signifying space or occasion), saying, "Now the Lord has made room for us, and we will be fruitful (productive) in this land." **23.** From there, Isaac went up to Beersheba (a megacity in southern Israel). **24.** That night, the Lord appeared to him and said, "I'm the God of your father Abraham. Don't be hysterical, for I'm with you. I'll bless you and multiply (make lesser) your descendants because of My menial Abraham." **25.** Isaac erected an altar (a place of deification) there and called on the name of the Lord. He pitched (set up) his roof, and his retainers dug a well there. **26.** Also Abimelech came to him from Gerar, along with Ahuzzath, one of his musketeers, and Phichol, the commander (chief) of his army. **27.** Isaac asked them, "Why have you come to me, since you detest (dislike) me and have transferred me down?" **28.** They answered, "We easily see that the Lord is with you. So we said, 'Let's make an pledge (pledge) between us, a covenant (agreement), **29.** that you won't harm us. We haven't harmed you but have always treated you well and transferred you down in peace. You're now blessed by the Lord.'" **30.** Isaac prepared a feast (mess) for them, and they ate and drank. **31.** Beforehand the coming morning, they swore an pledge to each other. Also Isaac transferred them down, and they left him in peace. **32.** That same day, Isaac's retainers came and told him, "We've set up water in the well." **33.** Isaac named the well-conditioned Shebah (meaning "pledge"). Thus, the megacity was named Beersheba, which means "well of the pledge." **34.** When Esau was forty times old, he married Judith, the son of Beeri the Hittite, and Basemath, the son of Elon the Hittite. **35.** They brought grief (anguish) to Isaac and Rebekah.

Chapter 27

1. As Isaac aged, his eyesight became poor (bedimmed), so he called his eldest son, Esau, and said, "My son." Esau responded, "I am here." **2.** Isaac said, "I am old and don't know when I might die. **3.** So, take your weapons (tools used for hunting), your bow and quiver (a container for arrows), and go out into the field to hunt some wild game (wild animals) for me. **4.** Prepare for me a delicious meal, the kind I love, and bring it to me so I can eat and bless (speak words of favor) you before I die." **5.** Rebekah overheard (eavesdropped) Isaac's conversation with Esau, **6.** and when Esau went off to hunt, Rebekah spoke to Jacob, saying, "I overheard your father telling Esau, **7.** 'Go and hunt some game for me, and prepare a meal so that I may bless you before I die.' **8.** Now, my son, listen carefully to my instructions (commands). **9.** Go to the flock (group of sheep or goats) and bring me two young goats (young female goats), and I will prepare them as a meal that your father enjoys. **10.** You will take it to him so that he can eat and bless (speak favor over) you before his death." **11.** Jacob replied, "But Esau is hairy (covered with a lot of hair), and I have smooth skin. **12.** What if my father touches me and realizes I'm deceiving (tricking) him? He might curse (bring bad fortune upon) me instead of blessing (favoring) me." **13.** Rebekah said, "Let the curse (punishment) be upon me, my son; just follow my instructions and bring the goats to me." **14.** So Jacob went and got the goats for his mother, and she prepared the meal. **15.** Rebekah then took the finest clothes (best garments) of Esau, which were in the house,

and dressed Jacob in them. **16.** She covered his hands and neck with the skins (outer coverings) of the goats. **17.** Then she gave Jacob the meal she had prepared. **18.** Jacob went to Isaac and said, "Father," and Isaac responded, "Here I am. Who are you, my son?" **19.** Jacob said, "I am Esau, your firstborn (oldest son). I've done as you requested. Please sit and eat so that you may bless (give your favor to) me." **20.** Isaac asked, "How did you find the game so quickly?" Jacob answered, "The Lord your God brought it to me." **21.** Isaac said, "Come closer so I can touch you and make sure you are really my son Esau." **22.** Jacob approached his father, and Isaac touched him and said, "The voice is Jacob's, but the hands are Esau's." **23.** Isaac did not recognize him, since Jacob's hands were hairy like Esau's, and so he blessed him. **24.** Isaac asked again, "Are you really Esau?" Jacob answered, "Yes, I am." **25.** Isaac said, "Bring the meal so I can eat and bless (favor you) you." Jacob served him, and Isaac ate and drank. **26.** Isaac then said, "Come kiss me, my son." **27.** Jacob kissed him, and Isaac smelled his clothes (garments), and blessed him, saying, "The smell of my son is like a field blessed (made holy or favored) by the Lord. **28.** May God give you heaven's dew (blessing from above), and the richness (abundance) of the earth, an abundance of grain and new wine. **29.** May nations serve you, and peoples bow down (show respect) to you. Be the master of your brothers, and may your mother's sons bow to you. Cursed (punished) be those who curse you, and blessed (favored) be those who bless you!" **30.** As soon as Isaac finished blessing Jacob and Jacob had just left, Esau returned from his hunt. **31.** He prepared his meal and brought it to Isaac, saying, "Let my father rise and eat of his son's game, so you may bless (give your favor to) me." **32.** Isaac asked, "Who are you?" Esau replied, "I am your firstborn son, Esau." **33.** Isaac trembled (shook in fear) greatly and said, "Who then hunted and brought me game before you came? I ate it all, and I have blessed (spoken favor over) him. He will indeed be blessed (favored)." **34.** Esau cried out in a loud and bitter voice, "Bless me too, Father!" **35.** Isaac said, "Your brother came deceitfully (tricked me) and took your blessing." **36.** Esau said, "Isn't he rightly named Jacob? He has deceived (tricked) me twice—first, he took my birthright (the right to inherit), and now he has stolen my blessing!" He begged, "Haven't you reserved a blessing for me?" **37.** Isaac replied, "I have made him your master (ruler), and all his relatives will serve him. I've given him grain (food) and wine. What more can I do for you?" **38.** Esau asked, "Do you have only one blessing, Father? Bless me too!" And Esau wept (cried with sadness). **39.** Isaac answered, "You will live by the strength (resources) of the earth and the dew (blessings) of heaven above. 40. You will live by the sword (strength and force), and serve your brother, but when you grow restless (tired of being subservient), you will break free (break away) from his yoke (control) from your neck." **41.** Esau hated (despised) Jacob because of the blessing Isaac had given him, and said to himself, "The days of mourning (grief) for my father are near, and then I will kill Jacob." **42.** When Rebekah learned of Esau's plan, she called Jacob and said, "Your brother Esau is planning to kill you. 43. Now, my son, listen to me and escape (flee) to my brother Laban in Haran. **44.** Stay with him for a while until your brother's anger (rage) subsides (calms down), **45.** until he forgets (lets go of) what you have done. Then I'll send for you to come back. Why should I lose both of you in one day?" **46.** Rebekah said to Isaac, "I am disgusted (repulsed) with life because of the Hittite women (pagan wives). If Jacob marries one of them, what good is my life?"

Chapter 28

1. Isaac called Jacob, blessed him, and gave him this command "Don't marry a woman from the daughters of Canaan (Canaan the land where the Canaanites lived, an area now in Israel and Palestine). **2.** Go to Padan Aram (Padan Aram a region in Mesopotamia, ultramodern- day Syria and Iraq), to the house of your mama's father, Bethuel, and choose a woman from the daughters of Laban (Laban Jacob's uncle, Rebekah's family, who lived in Haran), your mama's family. **3.** May God Almighty (God Almighty a title emphasizing God's all- important nature) bless you, make you fruitful (increase in number or wealth), and multiply you, so that you come a great nation. **4.** May He grant you the blessing of Abraham (Abraham the primogenitor, known for God's covenant with him), for you and your descendants, that you may inherit (admit as a possession) the land where you're a foreigner (outsider), which God gave to Abraham." **5.** Isaac transferred Jacob on his trip to Padan Aram, to Laban, the son of Bethuel the Syrian (Syrian from the region of Syria, located in ultramodern- day Syria), the family of Rebekah, Jacob's mama . **6.** Esau realized that Isaac had blessed Jacob and transferred him to Padan Aram to find a woman from there, and that Isaac had told him not to marry from the daughters of Canaan. **7.** Jacob had adhered (followed the instruction) his parents and traveled to Padan Aram. **8.** When Esau saw that Isaac didn't authorize (agree with) of the Canaanite women, **9.** he went to Ishmael, the son of Abraham, and took Mahalath, the son of Ishmael, as a woman, in addition to his other women. **10.** Jacob left Beersheba (Beersheba a megacity in southern Israel, near the Negev desert) and headed towards Haran (Haran an ancient megacity in Mesopotamia, now in Turkey). **11.** He came to a certain place and stayed overnight because the sun had set. He took a gravestone (gravestone a hard material) from that place, placed it under his head, and lay down to sleep. **12.** also he pictured a graduation stood on the earth, reaching to heaven, with angels (angels couriers or retainers of God) of God thrusting and descending on it. **13.** The LORD stood above the graduation and said, "I'm the Lord, the God of Abraham your father and the God of Isaac. The land on which you're lying, I'll give to you and your descendants. **14.** Your descendants (descendants children and their children) will be as multitudinous (innumerous) as the dust of the earth, spreading in all directions — west, east, north, and south. Through you and your descendants, all the families of the earth will be blessed. **15.** I'm with you, I'll cover (guard) you wherever you go, and I'll bring you back to this land. I'll not leave you until I've done what I promised." **16.** When Jacob woke from his sleep, he said, "Surely the Lord is in this place, and I didn't realize it." **17.** He was hysterical (feeling admiration) and said, "How stupendous (awful, full of admiration) is this place! It's none other than the house of God and the gateway (entrance) to heaven." **18.** Beforehand the coming morning, Jacob took the gravestone he'd used as a pillow, set it up as a pillar (a altitudinous structure), and poured oil painting (oil painting a symbol of sanctification or blessing) on top of it. **19.** He named the place Bethel (Bethel meaning" house of God," formerly called Luz), where he'd this vision. **20.** Jacob made a oath (pledge), saying, "If God will be with me, keep me safe on my trip, give me food to eat and clothes to wear, **21.** And bring me back to my father's house in peace, also the Lord will be my God. **22.** This gravestone I've set up will be God's house, and of all that You give me, I'll give a tenth (a tenth part, or tithe) back to You."

Chapter 29

1. Jacob continued his trip and arrived in the land of the people of the East. **2.** There, he saw a well in a field with three flocks of lamb resting by it. The flocks were doused from the well, but a large gravestone covered the well's mouth. **3.** All the flocks would gather there, and the gravestone would be rolled down so they could drink, also the gravestone would be put back in place. **4.** Jacob asked the goatherds," Where are you from?" They answered," We're from Haran (a megacity in Mesopotamia, where Jacob's family lived)." **5.** He asked," Do you know Laban (a man's name), the son of Nahor?" They replied," We know him." **6.** Jacob also asked," Is he well?" They said," Yes, he's well, and look, his son Rachel (a woman's name) is coming with the lamb." **7.** Jacob said," It's still beforehand in the day; it's not time to gather the flocks. Water the lamb and take them to pasturage (land covered with lawn where creatures graze)." **8.** The goatherds replied," We can't

do that until all the flocks are gathered, and the gravestone is rolled down to water them." **9.** While he was still talking with them, Rachel arrived with her father's lamb, for she was a swineherd (a woman who takes care of lamb). **10.** When Jacob saw Rachel, the son of Laban, and the lamb of Laban, he incontinently went to the well, rolled the gravestone down, and doused Laban's flock. **11.** Jacob kissed Rachel and began to weep audibly (cry, generally due to strong emotion). **12.** He told Rachel that he was her father's relative, the son of Rebekah (a woman's name). She ran to tell her father. **13.** When Laban heard that his family's son had arrived, he ran to meet him, embraced him, kissed him, and brought him to his home. Jacob participated his story with Laban. **14.** Laban said," You're my own meat and blood." Jacob stayed with him for a month. **15.** After a month, Laban asked," Since you're my relative, should you work for nothing? Tell me, what should your stipend (payment for work) be?" **16.** Laban had two daughters Leah (a woman's name), the aged, and Rachel (a woman's name), the youngish. **17.** Leah had delicate (soft, gentle) eyes, but Rachel was beautiful in form and appearance. **18.** Jacob loved Rachel and said," I'll serve you seven times for Rachel, your youngish son." **19.** Laban agreed, saying," It's better that I give her to you than to another man. Stay with me." **20.** So Jacob worked for seven times for Rachel, but they sounded like only a many days because of his love for her. **21.** After the seven times, Jacob said to Laban," Give me my woman, for my time is fulfilled (completed), and I want to be with her." **22.** Laban gathered all the people and held a feast (a large mess, frequently for a festivity). **23.** In the evening, Laban took Leah and brought her to Jacob, and he slept with her (a circumlocution for sexual relations). **24.** Laban gave his wench Zilpah (a woman's name) to Leah as a maid (womanish menial). **25.** In the morning, Jacob realized it was Leah. He brazened Laban, saying," What have you done? Didn't I work for Rachel? Why have you deceived (tricked or misled) me?" **26.** Laban replied," It's not our custom (a traditional practice or way of doing effects) to marry off the youngish son before the aged one." **27.**" Finish the week of festivity (a time of joy and festivity) for Leah, and also we will give you Rachel in exchange for another seven times of work." **28.** Jacob agreed, completed the week for Leah, and also Laban gave him Rachel as his woman**29.** Laban also gave Rachel his wench Bilhah (a woman's name) to be her maid. **30.** Jacob also married Rachel, and he loved her further than Leah. He continued to serve Laban for another seven times. **31.** When the Lord saw that Leah was unloved (not cherished or favored), He opened her womb (the part of a woman's body where a baby grows), but Rachel remained barren (unfit to have children). **32.** Leah conceived (came pregnant) and bore a son. She named him Reuben (a man's name), saying," The Lord has seen my misery. Now my husband will love me." **33.** She conceived again and bore another son, naming him Simeon (a man's name), saying," Because the Lord heard that I'm unloved, He gave me this son." **34.** Leah conceived yet again and bore another son. She named him Levi (a man's name), saying," Now my husband will come attached (form a bond) to me, because I've borne him three sons." **35.** Leah conceived again and bore another son, naming him Judah (a man's name), saying," Now I'll praise (express gratefulness) the Lord." After that, she stopped bearing children.

Chapter 30

1. When Rachel saw that she bore Jacob no children, she envied her sister and said to Jacob, "Give me children, or else I die." **2.** Jacob's anger was kindled against Rachel, and he replied, "Am I in God's place, who has withheld the fruit of the womb (children) from you?" **3.** Rachel then said, "Here is my maid Bilhah. Go to her so she may bear children on my behalf, and I may have a family through her." **4.** So she gave him Bilhah, her maid, as a wife, and Jacob was with her. **5.** Bilhah conceived and bore Jacob a son. **6.** Rachel said, "God has judged (decided) in my favor and has heard my voice, giving me a son." So, she named him Dan. **7.** Bilhah,

Rachel's maid, conceived again and bore Jacob a second son. **8.** Rachel said, "With great wrestlings I have wrestled (competed) with my sister, and I have prevailed (won)," and she named him Naphtali. **9.** When Leah saw she had stopped bearing children, she took her maid Zilpah and gave her to Jacob as a wife. **10.** Zilpah, Leah's maid, bore Jacob a son. **11.** Leah said, "What good fortune has come!" and she named him Gad. **12.** Zilpah, Leah's maid, bore Jacob a second son. **13.** Leah said, "How happy I am! For women will call me blessed (fortunate)," so she named him Asher. **14.** During the wheat harvest (gathering time), Reuben found mandrakes (a plant believed to aid fertility) in the field and brought them to his mother Leah. Rachel asked Leah, "Please give me some of your son's mandrakes." **15.** Leah replied, "Is it a small thing that you have taken my husband? And now you want my son's mandrakes?" Rachel said, "In return, he will stay with you tonight for your son's mandrakes." **16.** So when Jacob came in from the field in the evening, Leah went out to meet him and said, "You must stay with me tonight, for I have hired you with my son's mandrakes." So he stayed with her that night. **17.** God listened to Leah, and she conceived and bore Jacob a fifth son. **18.** Leah said, "God has rewarded me, for I gave my maid to my husband," and she named him Issachar. **19.** Leah conceived again and bore Jacob a sixth son. **20.** Leah said, "God has given me a precious gift. Now my husband will honor (respect) me, for I have borne him six sons." So she named him Zebulun. **21.** Afterward, she bore a daughter and named her Dinah. **22.** Then God remembered Rachel and listened to her, allowing her to conceive. **23.** She conceived and bore a son, saying, "God has taken away my disgrace (shame)." **24.** She named him Joseph and said, "May the LORD add (grant) me another son." **25.** After Rachel gave birth to Joseph, Jacob said to Laban, "Let me return to my own home and country. **26.** Give me my wives and children, for whom I have served you, and let me go. You know the work I have done for you." **27.** Laban said to him, "If I have found favor in your sight, please stay. I have learned by experience that the LORD has blessed me because of you." **28.** Laban added, "Name your wages (payment), and I will give it." **29.** Jacob replied, "You know how I have served you and how your livestock (animals) have thrived (prospered) under my care. **30.** For you had little before I came, but now it has greatly increased, and the LORD has blessed you wherever I've been. But when can I do something for my own household too?" **31.** Laban asked, "What shall I give you?" Jacob replied, "You don't need to give me anything. If you do this one thing, I will continue to tend (take care of) your flock. **32.** I will go through all your flock today and remove every speckled (spotted) and spotted sheep, every brown sheep, and all the speckled and spotted goats. They will be my wages. **33.** This way, my honesty will speak for me later, when you check on my wages. Any sheep or goat that isn't speckled or spotted or brown will be considered stolen by me." **34.** Laban said, "Agreed! Let it be as you have said." **35.** So that same day, Laban separated all the striped (streaked) and spotted male goats, all the speckled female goats, and every brown sheep, and gave them to his sons. **36.** He set a three-day journey between himself and Jacob, while Jacob took care of the rest of Laban's flocks. **37.** Jacob took fresh branches from poplar, almond, and plane trees, and peeled white stripes on them, exposing the white wood. **38.** He placed these branches in the watering troughs, where the animals came to drink, so they would mate in front of the branches. **39.** When the animals mated near the branches, they bore (gave birth to) young that were striped, speckled, and spotted. **40.** Jacob separated these lambs and made the rest of the animals face the streaked or brown animals in Laban's flock. He kept his own flocks separate and did not let them mix with Laban's. **41.** Whenever the stronger animals were in heat (ready to mate), Jacob placed the branches in front of them in the troughs so they would mate near the branches. **42.** But when the weaker animals were in heat, he did not place the branches there. So the weak animals went to Laban, and the stronger ones went to Jacob. **43.** In this way, Jacob became exceedingly (very) prosperous (wealthy), and he had many flocks, servants, camels, and donkeys.

Chapter 31

1. Jacob overheard Laban's sons claiming that he took all their father's wealth. **2.** Jacob noticed Laban's attitude toward him had soured. **3.** God told Jacob, "Return to your homeland, and I'll be with you." **4.** Jacob called Rachel and Leah to the field **5.** and said, "I see your father no longer favors me, but God has been with me. **6.** You know how hard I worked for him, **7.** yet he deceived me, changing my wages ten times, though God prevented him from harming me. **8.** When he said, 'Freckled animals will be your wage,' the flocks bore freckled offspring, and when he said, 'Striped animals will be your wage,' the flocks bore striped offspring. **9.** So God took your father's livestock and gave them to me. **10.** During the mating season, I dreamed of rams that were all striped, freckled, and spotted. **11.** An angel called to me, saying, 'Jacob! Look and see—I've seen what Laban has done to you. **13.** I am the God of Bethel, where you anointed the pillar and vowed to me. Now leave this land and return home.'" **14.** Rachel and Leah replied, "Is there any inheritance left for us in our father's house? **15.** He treats us as foreigners, having spent all the money he gained for us. **16.** All the wealth God took from him is ours. Do as God has told you." **17.** Jacob rose, placing his wives and children on camels, **18.** and took all he owned to return to Isaac in Canaan. **19.** While Laban was away, Rachel stole her father's household idols. **20.** Jacob left secretly. **21.** He crossed the river and headed toward Gilead. **22.** Three days later, Laban learned of his escape, **23.** gathered his relatives, and pursued Jacob, overtaking him in Gilead. **24.** God warned Laban in a dream not to harm Jacob. **25.** Laban reached Jacob and said, "Why did you leave secretly, taking my daughters like captives? **27.** You didn't let me bid farewell with joy. **30.** You left because you longed for home, but why steal my gods?" **31.** Jacob answered, "I feared you'd take your daughters from me by force. **32.** But if you find your gods here, let the person who took them die." Jacob didn't know Rachel had taken them. **33.** Laban searched all tents but found nothing. **34.** Rachel hid the idols in her camel's saddle and sat on it, saying she couldn't rise due to her period. **36.** Jacob became angry, saying, "What wrong have I done for you to pursue me so hard? **38.** For twenty years, I worked for you, never losing any of your animals. **39.** If any were lost, I bore the cost. 40. I suffered heat by day and cold by night, losing sleep. 41. For twenty years I served you—fourteen for your daughters and six for your flocks. Yet you changed my wages ten times. **42.** If not for the God of Abraham and Isaac, who saw my hardship, you'd have sent me away empty-handed." **43.** Laban replied, "These daughters and their children are mine. But let's make a covenant as a witness between us." **45.** Jacob set up a stone pillar, **46.** and they made a mound of stones, calling it Galeed, **49.** and Mizpah, saying, "May the Lord watch between us when we're apart." **52.** They agreed not to cross the mound to harm each other. **53.** Jacob swore by the God of Isaac, **54.** made an offering, and they shared a meal. **55.** The next morning, Laban blessed his daughters and grandchildren, and returned home.

Chapter 32

1. As Jacob continued traveling, he was met by God's angels. **2.** Seeing them, Jacob declared, "This is God's camp," and named the place Mahanaim (meaning " two camps"). **3.** Jacob transferred couriers ahead to Esau, who was in Seir, in the land of Edom. **4.** Jacob instructed his retainers, "Tell my lord Esau that his menial Jacob has been staying with Laban until now. **5.** I've acquired oxen, burros, flocks, and retainers, and am transferring this communication hoping to gain your favor." **6.** The couriers returned, saying, "Esau is coming to meet you with four hundred men." **7.** Jacob was hysterical and worried, so he divided his family and flocks into two groups, **8.** logic, " If Esau attacks one, the other may escape." **9.** also Jacob supplicated, " O God of my ancestors,

You told me, ' Return home, and I'll show you favor.' 10. I'm unworthy of the kindness and fastness You have shown me. When I crossed the Jordan, I had only a staff, but now I've two camps. 11. deliver me from Esau, for I sweat he may attack us. 12. But You promised, 'I'll make your descendants as multitudinous as the beach.'" 13. That night, Jacob prepared gifts for Esau 14. two hundred womanish scapegoats, twenty manly scapegoats, two hundred ewes, and twenty rams, 15. on with camels, cows, bulls, burros, and foals. 16. He arranged each herd with a menial and kept a distance between them. 17. Jacob directed the first menial, "When Esau asks, 'Whose creatures are these?' 18. reply, ' They belong to your menial Jacob. They're a gift to my lord Esau, and Jacob is behind us.'" 19. Jacob instructed the other retainers also, allowing, "I'll try to calm Esau with these gifts, hoping he'll accept me." 21. He transferred the gifts ahead while he stayed at the camp. 22. That night, Jacob took his family and crossed the Jabbok River. 23. After transferring them across, 24. Jacob stayed before, alone, and a man scuffled with him until dawn. 25. When the man realized he could not overpower Jacob, he touched Jacob's hipsterism, moving it. 26. The man said, " Let me go, for it's nearly sunrise." But Jacob replied, "I'll not release you unless you bless me." 27. The man asked, "What's your name?" and Jacob answered, "Jacob." 28. also he said, " Your name will now be Israel, for you have plodded with both God and men and have succeeded." 29. Jacob also asked, "Please tell me your name." But the man replied, "Why do you ask?" and blessed him there. 30. Jacob named the place Peniel, saying, "I've seen God face to face, and my life was spared." 31. As Jacob crossed over Peniel, the sun rose, and he was limping due to his injured hipsterism. 32. To this day, the Israelites avoid eating the tendon attached to the hipsterism socket, because it was the part of Jacob's hipsterism that God touched.

Chapter 33

1. As Jacob looked up, he noticed Esau coming toward him, accompanied by four hundred men. Jacob arranged his children among Leah, Rachel, and their maidservants (female servants). 2. He positioned the maidservants and their children at the front, followed by Leah and her children, with Rachel and Joseph at the rear. 3. Jacob himself moved ahead of the others, bowing (lowering himself in respect) to the ground seven times as he drew closer to Esau. 4. When Esau saw him, he ran to meet him, embraced (hugged) him, kissed him, and they both wept (cried). 5. Esau then looked at the women and children and asked, "Who are these with you?" Jacob answered, "These are the children God has graciously (kindly) given to your servant." 6. The maidservants and their children came forward and bowed (showed respect by lowering themselves). 7. Leah and her children also approached and bowed. Finally, Joseph and Rachel came forward and bowed as well. 8. Esau inquired, "What was the purpose of all the people I encountered (met) on the road?" Jacob replied, "I hoped to find favor (blessing) with you, my lord (a title of respect)." 9. Esau answered, "I have more than enough, my brother. Keep what is yours." 10. Jacob insisted, "Please accept my gift. Seeing your face is like seeing the face of God, and you have been so gracious (kind) to me." 11. He added, "Please take this gift I have brought you, for God has greatly blessed (given a lot of blessings to) me, and I have more than enough." Esau reluctantly (hesitantly) accepted after Jacob urged (strongly encouraged) him. 12. Esau said, "Let us travel together, and I will lead the way." 13. Jacob responded, "My lord knows that the children are fragile (young and weak), and the flocks (groups of sheep) and herds (groups of cattle) need to be treated gently (with care). If driven (forced to move quickly) too fast for even a day, they might be overwhelmed (hurt or tired)." 14. "Please go ahead of us, and I will follow at a pace that suits the children and the livestock (animals) until we meet you in Seir." 15. Esau offered, "Let me leave some of my men (soldiers or helpers) with you." But Jacob declined (refused), saying, "There is no need. I only wish to find favor (kindness) in your sight." 16. So Esau returned to Seir (his homeland) that day. 17. Meanwhile, Jacob traveled to Succoth (a place east of the Jordan River), where he built a house and shelters (temporary structures) for his livestock. For this reason, the place was called Succoth, meaning "shelters." 18. Jacob continued his journey to Shechem (a major city), in the land of Canaan, after leaving Padan Aram (the region where Jacob came from). He set up camp (spent the night) near the city. 19. There, he purchased a piece of land from the sons of Hamor (the father of Shechem), the father of Shechem, for a hundred pieces of silver (tableware or small coins used for trade). 20. Jacob built an altar (a place of worship) there and called it El Elohe Israel, meaning "God, the God of Israel."

Chapter 34

1. Dinah, the son of Leah and Jacob, went to visit the original women of the land. 2. Shechem, the son of Hamor the Hivite (a Napoleon in the region), saw Dinah, took her, and violated her (forced her into an unhappy act). 3. Shechem felt deeply drawn to Dinah, loved her, and spoke tenderly to her. 4. Shechem asked his father Hamor, "Get me this youthful woman to be my woman." 5. When Jacob heard about what happed to Dinah, he awaited to speak on the matter until his sons returned from tending the beast (creatures). 6. Hamor, Shechem's father, went to speak with Jacob. 7. When Jacob's sons heard what happed, they returned from the fields, worried (worried) and furious (angry), as such an act was shy (opprobrious) and inferior in Israel. 8. Hamor said to them, "My son Shechem deeply desires your son. Please allow him to marry her. 9. Let's intermarry (make marriage alliances); you give us your daughters, and we will give you ours. 10. Settle among us, trade, and acquire property in the land." 11. Shechem added to her father and sisters, "Please grant me favor. I'll give whatever you ask as a gift. 12. Name any dowry (plutocrat or gifts given to the bridegroom's family) and gift, and I'll pay it. Just let me marry her." 13. But Jacob's sons spoke deceitfully (dishonestly) to Shechem and Hamor, because Shechem had defiled (lowered) their family Dinah. 14. They said, "We cannot allow our family to marry an uncircumcised man (someone not having experienced the Jewish tradition of circumcision), as that would be a disgrace (shame) to us. 15. still, we will agree if every joker among you is circumcised as we are. 16. also, we'll exchange daughters in marriage and live together as one people. 17. But if you won't agree to be circumcised, we'll take Dinah and leave." 18. Hamor and Shechem were pleased with this offer. 19. Shechem, eager (enthusiastic) to marry Dinah, didn't delay, as he was held in high regard (honor) in his family. 20. Hamor and Shechem went to the megacity gate (the entrance to the megacity) and spoke to the men there. 21. They said, "These men are peaceful. Let them live and trade in our land; it has room enough for them. Let's marry their daughters, and they ours. 22. They will only agree to live with us if every joker then's circumcised as they are. 23. Won't all their effects (goods, beast, and wealth) ultimately come ours? Let's agree to their terms so they'll live among us." 24. All the men who gathered at the megacity gate agreed with Hamor and Shechem, and every joker was circumcised. 25. On the third day, while they were in pain, Simeon and Levi, Dinah's sisters, took their brands, entered the megacity, and killed every joker. 26. They killed Hamor and Shechem, recaptured Dinah from Shechem's house, and left. 27. The other sons of Jacob came, pillaging (sacking) the megacity as retaliation (discipline) for their family's defilement. 28. They seized the megacity's beast, both in city and in the fields, 29. Took all the wealth, captured the women and children, and pillaged (stole) the houses. 30. Jacob said to Simeon and Levi, "You have made me a target (someone others will want to harm) among the Canaanites (a group of people living in the land) and Perizzites (another group of original people). Since we're many in number, they may unite against us, destroy us, and wipe out my ménage." 31. But they

replied, "Should he have been allowed to treat our family like a courtesan?"

Chapter 35

1. God commanded Jacob," Arise, go to Bethel (a municipality in Canaan), and live there. Make an balcony to fete God, who revealed Himself to you when you fled from your family Esau." 2. Jacob spoke to his ménage and those traveling with him, saying," Get rid of the foreign gods (icons) among you, purify yourselves (make yourselves clean), and change your clothes." 3." Also, let's go to Bethel, and I'll make an balcony to the God who answered me during my torture and has been with me throughout my trip." 4. They gave Jacob all the foreign gods (icons) they had, along with their earrings, and Jacob buried them under the oak tree near Shechem (a municipality in Canaan). 5. As they traveled, God inseminated fear into the girding metropolises, so they didn't pursue Jacob's family. 6. Jacob arrived at Luz (which is Bethel) in the land of Canaan, with everyone who was with him. 7. He erected an balcony there and named the place El Bethel (meaning" God of Bethel"), because God had appeared to him when he fled from his family. 8. Deborah, Rebekah's nanny (a woman who watched for children), passed down and was buried under the oak tree near Bethel. The place was named Allon Bachuth (meaning" Oak of Weeping"). 9. God appeared to Jacob formerly again as he came from Padan Aram (a region in Mesopotamia) and blessed him. 10. God told Jacob," Your name is Jacob, but from now on you will be called Israel (meaning' he who struggles with God')." thus, God renamed him Israel. 11. God also said," I'm God Almighty (a title emphasizing God's power). Be fruitful and multiply. Nations and lords will come from you." 12." The land I gave to Abraham and Isaac, I now give to you and your descendants after you." 13. After speaking to Jacob, God left him at that place. 14. Jacob set up a gravestone pillar where God had spoken to him, poured a drink immolation (a liquid immolation) on it, and besmeared it with oil painting. 15. Jacob named the place where God spoke with him, Bethel. 16. They continued their trip from Bethel, and when they were near Ephrath (another name for Bethlehem, a municipality in Judah), Rachel went into labor (gave birth) and had a delicate delivery. 17. During her delicate labor, the midwife (a woman who assists in parturition) assured her, saying," Don't worry, you will have another son." 18. As Rachel's life was ending (she failed), she named the child Ben- Oni (meaning" son of my anguish"), but his father named him Benjamin (meaning" son of my right hand"). 19. Rachel failed and was buried on the road to Ephrath (which is Bethlehem). 20. Jacob set up a pillar at her grave, which came known as Rachel's grave. 21. Israel (Jacob) traveled on and set up camp beyond the palace of Eder (a place in Canaan). 22. While there, Reuben, Israel's firstborn son, slept with Bilhah (his father's doxy), and Israel heard about it. 23. The sons of Leah were Reuben, Simeon, Levi, Judah, Issachar, and Zebulun. 24. The sons of Rachel were Joseph and Benjamin. 25. The sons of Bilhah, Rachel's wench (womanish menial), were Dan and Naphtali. 26. The sons of Zilpah, Leah's wench, were Gad and Asher. These were the twelve sons of Jacob, born to him in Padan Aram. 27. Jacob arrived at his father Isaac's home in Mamre (also known as Kirjath Arba or Hebron, a municipality in Canaan), where Abraham and Isaac had lived. 28. Isaac lived to be 180 times old. 29. Isaac passed away, was gathered to his ancestors (joined his departed cousins) and was buried by his sons Esau and Jacob.

Chapter 36

This is the genealogical record (family history) of Esau, also known as Edom. 2. Esau married women from the daughters of Canaan: Adah, the daughter of Elon the Hittite (a group of people from Canaan); Aholibamah, the daughter of Anah, who was the daughter of Zibeon the Hivite (another Canaanite group); 3. and Basemath, the daughter of Ishmael, and the sister of Nebajoth. 4. Adah bore Esau a son, Eliphaz, while Basemath gave birth to Reuel. 5. Aholibamah had three sons with Esau: Jeush, Jaalam, and Korah.

These were the children (descendants) of Esau born in Canaan. 6. Esau moved with his family, servants, livestock (animals like cows, sheep), and all his possessions to another land, away from his brother Jacob. 7. The land could not support both of them due to their great wealth, so they decided to part ways (separate). 8. Esau settled in the region of Mount Seir (a mountainous region southeast of Canaan), which is also known as Edom. 9. This is the family history of Esau, the father of the Edomites (descendants of Esau), who lived in Mount Seir. 10. Esau's sons were: Eliphaz, the son of Adah, and Reuel, the son of Basemath. 11. Eliphaz had five sons: Teman, Omar, Zepho, Gatam, and Kenaz. 12. Timna, a concubine (secondary wife) of Eliphaz, bore him Amalek (a group that later became enemies of Israel), who would later oppose Israel. These were the sons of Adah, Esau's wife. 13. Reuel's sons were Nahath, Zerah, Shammah, and Mizzah. These were the sons of Basemath, Esau's wife. 14. Aholibamah, Esau's wife, had three sons: Jeush, Jaalam, and Korah. 15. These were the chiefs (leaders) of Esau's descendants: Chief Teman, Chief Omar, Chief Zepho, Chief Kenaz, 16. Chief Korah, Chief Gatam, and Chief Amalek, the descendants of Eliphaz, Esau's son, in the land of Edom. 17. These were the chiefs of Reuel, Esau's son: Chief Nahath, Chief Zerah, Chief Shammah, and Chief Mizzah, the descendants of Basemath, Esau's wife. 18. These were the chiefs of Aholibamah, Esau's wife: Chief Jeush, Chief Jaalam, and Chief Korah. 19. These are the sons of Esau, also called Edom, and their chiefs. 20. These are the descendants of Seir the Horite (an ancient people of the mountainous region of Seir), the early inhabitants of the land: Lotan, Shobal, Zibeon, Anah, 21. Dishon, Ezer, and Dishan. These were the chiefs of the Horites, the people of Seir, in the land of Edom. 22. Lotan's sons were Hori and Hemam. Lotan's sister was Timna. 23. Shobal's sons were Alvan, Manahath, Ebal, Shepho, and Onam. 24. Zibeon's sons were Ajah and Anah. This Anah is the one who found water in the wilderness while tending his father's donkeys. 25. Anah had two children: Dishon and Aholibamah, his daughter. 26. Dishon's sons were Hemdan, Eshban, Ithran, and Cheran. 27. Ezer's sons were Bilhan, Zaavan, and Akan. 28. Dishan's sons were Uz and Aran. 29. These were the chiefs of the Horites: Chief Lotan, Chief Shobal, Chief Zibeon, Chief Anah, 30. Chief Dishon, Chief Ezer, and Chief Dishan. These were the chiefs of the Horites in the land of Seir. 31. Before any king ruled over Israel, these were the kings of Edom: 32. Bela, the son of Beor, was the first king of Edom, and his city was Dinhabah. 33. When Bela died, Jobab, the son of Zerah from Bozrah (an archaeological site), succeeded him as king. 34. After Jobab's death, Husham, from the land of the Temanites (a region in Edom), became king. 35. When Husham died, Hadad, the son of Bedad, who had defeated the Midianites (a people group) in the field of Moab (an area near Edom), became king, and his city was Avith. 36. After Hadad passed away, Samlah from Masrekah (a town in Edom) became king. 37. When Samlah died, Saul from Rehoboth-by-the-River (a town near a river in Edom) became king. 38. After Saul's death, Baal-Hanan, the son of Achbor, took over the kingship. 39. When Baal-Hanan died, Hadar became king, and his city was Pau. His wife's name was Mehetabel, the daughter of Matred and granddaughter of Mezahab. 40. These are the names of the chiefs of Esau, according to their clans and territories (areas of settlement): Chief Timnah, Chief Alvah, Chief Jetheth, 41. Chief Aholibamah, Chief Elah, Chief Pinon, 42. Chief Kenaz, Chief Teman, Chief Mibzar, 43. Chief Magdiel, and Chief Iram. These were the chiefs of Edom, according to their settlements in the land of their inheritance (land passed down to them). Esau was the father of the Edomites.

Chapter 37

1. Jacob lived in the land of Canaan (a region in the Middle East), where his father had formerly been a foreigner. 2. This is the story of Jacob's family. Joseph, at seventeen, was taking care of the flock (group of lamb or scapegoats) with his sisters. He was with the sons of Bilhah and Zilpah, his father's doxies and he brought a bad

report (negative news) about them to his father. **3.** Israel (Jacob) loved Joseph more than all his other sons because he was born to him in his old age. He made him a plushly ornamented mask (a long fleece with numerous colors). **4.** When his sisters saw that their father loved him further than them, they abominated Joseph and couldn't speak kindly to him. **5.** Joseph had a dream, which he told to his sisters, and they abominated him indeed more. **6.** He said to them, "Please hear to the dream I had. **7.** We were binding sheaves (packets of grain) in the field, and my sheaf rose and stood upright, while your sheaves gathered around mine and bowed down to it." **8.** His sisters asked, "Do you intend to control (rule) over us? Will you rule us?" They abominated him indeed more because of his dreams and what he said. **9.** Also Joseph had another dream and told it to his sisters: "I had another dream. This time, the sun, the moon, and eleven stars were bowing down to me." **10.** He told his father and his sisters. His father rebuked (scolded) him, saying, "What's this dream you have had? Will your mama, your sisters, and I really come and bow down to the ground before you?" **11.** His sisters were jealous of him, but his father kept the matter in mind. **12.** His sisters went to feed their father's flock in Shechem (a megacity in ancient Israel). **13.** Israel said to Joseph, "Are not your sisters feeding the flock in Shechem? Go and see if all is well with them and the flock and bring word back to me." So Joseph went. **14.** Joseph left the Valley of Hebron (a place in Israel), and he went to Shechem. **15.** A man set up him wandering in the field and asked, "What are you looking for?" **16.** Joseph replied, "I am looking for my sisters. Can you tell me where they're grazing (feeding) their flocks?" **17.** The man replied, "They have left. I heard them say they were going to Dothan (a city)." So, Joseph went after his sisters and set up them at Dothan. **18.** When they saw him coming, indeed from a distance, they colluded (planned intimately) to kill him. **19.** They said to one another, "Then come that utopian! **20.** Let's kill him and throw him into one of these recesses (holes in the ground), and we can tell our father that a wild beast devoured him. Also, we'll see what becomes of his dreams!" **21.** But Reuben (the oldest family) heard this and tried to deliver him from their hands, saying, "Let's not kill him." **22.** Reuben said, "Do not exfoliate any blood. Throw him into this hole in the nature, but do not harm him." He said this to deliver Joseph from them and bring him back to his father. **23.** When Joseph arrived, they took off his plushly ornamented mask **24.** And threw him into the hole, which was empty and had no water in it. **25.** They sat down to eat. As they looked up, they saw a caravan (group of traveling merchandisers) of Ishmaelites (a group of people) coming from Gilead (a region), with their camels carrying spices, attar (mending ointment), and myrrh (an ambrosial resin) on their way to Egypt. **26.** Judah said to his sisters, "What will we gain if we kill our family and cover up his blood? **27.** Let's vend him to the Ishmaelites and not lay a hand on him, for he's our family, our own meat." His sisters agreed. **28.** When the Midianite (a group of people) dealers passed by, the sisters pulled Joseph out of the hole and vended him for twenty pieces of tableware to the Ishmaelites, who took him to Egypt. **29.** When Reuben returned to the hole and saw that Joseph wasn't there, he tore his clothes (a sign of grief). **30.** He went back to his sisters and said, "The boy is gone! And I, where can I go?" **31.** They took Joseph's mask, killed a scapegoat, and dipped the mask in its blood. **32.** They transferred the mask back to their father with the communication, "We set up this. Does this mask belong to your son?" **33.** Jacob honored it and said, "It's my son's mask! A wild beast has devoured him. Joseph has surely been torn to pieces." **34.** Also, Jacob tore his clothes, put on sackcloth (a rough cloth used in mourning), and mourned for his son for numerous days. **35.** All his sons and daughters came to comfort him, but he refused to be assured, saying, "I'll go down to the grave mourning for my son." And so, his father wept for him. **36.** Meanwhile, the Midianites vended Joseph in Egypt to Potiphar (an Egyptian functionary), an officer of Pharaoh (the king of Egypt) and the captain of the guard.

Chapter 38

1. At that time, Judah left his sisters and visited a man named Hirah, who was from Adullam (a city in ancient Israel). **2.** While there, Judah saw a Canaanite (a member of the ancient people living in Canaan) woman named Shua, and he married her. **3.** She came pregnant and had a son, whom Judah named Er. **4.** She had another son, and Judah named him Onan. **5.** She had a third son, named Shelah, who was born at Chezib (a place in ancient Israel). **6.** Judah arranged for a woman for Er, his firstborn, and her name was Tamar. **7.** But Er was wicked (evil or unethical) in the sight of the Lord, so the Lord killed him. **8.** Judah also told Onan, "Marry your family's widow and give an heir at law (a person who inherits the property) for him." **9.** Onan, knowing the child wouldn't be his, revealed his seed on the ground to avoid raising an heir at law for his family. **10.** What he did dissatisfy (made angry) the Lord, and He killed him as well. **11.** Judah told Tamar, his daughter-in-law, "Stay a widow (a woman whose husband has failed) in your father's house until my son Shelah is grown," for he stressed that Shelah might die too, like his sisters. Tamar went to live in her father's house. **12.** After some time, Judah's woman, Shua, failed. He was assured (felt better after grief) and went to Timnah (a place where Judah went to shear lamb) with his friend Hirah to shear his lamb. **13.** Tamar was told, "Your father-in-law is going to Timnah to shear his lamb." **14.** Tamar saw that Shelah had grown up but hadn't been given to her as a husband. So, she took off her widow's clothes, veiled (covered her face) herself, and sat by the road to Timnah. **15.** When Judah saw her, he allowed she was a courtesan (a woman who sells coitus) because her face was covered. **16.** He approached her and said, "Let me sleep with you." He did not fete her as his son-in-law. She asked, "What will you give me for this?" **17.** He promised to shoot her a youthful scapegoat from his flock. She asked, "What will you give me as a pledge (a guarantee or promise) until you shoot it?" **18.** Judah gave her his signet (a ring or seal used to make an official mark), cord (a string used for tying), and staff (a stick or rod) as a guarantee and slept with her. She came pregnant by him. **19.** Subsequently, she left, put on her widow's clothes again, and went back to her father's house. **20.** Judah transferred the youthful scapegoat with his friend Hirah to recoup his pledge, but they could not find her. **21.** They asked the men of the place, "Where is the courtesan who sat by the road?" They replied, "There was no courtesan then." **22.** Judah's friend returned to him and said, "I could not find her, and the men of the place said there was no courtesan." **23.** Judah said, "Let her keep the particulars, so we will not be embarrassed. I did shoot the scapegoat, but you couldn't find her." **24.** Three months later, Judah was told, "Tamar, your daughter-in-law, has acted as a courtesan, and she's pregnant." Judah said, "Bring her out and let her be burned (killed by fire)!" **25.** When Tamar was brought out, she transferred word to Judah, saying, "The man who owns these particulars is the father of my child." She showed him his signet, cord, and staff. **26.** Judah honored them and said, "She's more righteous (innocently right) than I, because I didn't give her to Shelah." And he never slept with her again. **27.** When it was time for Tamar to give birth, she was carrying halves. **28.** As she was giving birth, one of the halves stuck out his hand, and the midwife (a person who assists in parturition) tied a scarlet thread on it, saying, "This one came out first." **29.** But as soon as the hand was withdrawn, the other twin came out, and the midwife blatted, "How did you break through? This breach (a breaking or breaking out) is yours!" So, he was named Perez. **30.** Also, the family, who had the scarlet thread on his hand, was born and was named Zerah.

Chapter 39

1 Joseph was taken to Egypt (a region in Africa), where Potiphar (an officer of Pharaoh, the Egyptian king, and head of the guard) bought him from the Ishmaelites (descendants of Ishmael,

Abraham's son) who had brought him there. **2** The LORD was with Joseph, and he succeeded in all he did while in his master's house. **3** Potiphar noticed that the Lord was with Joseph and made everything he did flourish (prosper, become successful). **4** Joseph found favor (approval, support) in Potiphar's sight and served him, so Potiphar appointed Joseph as the overseer (one in charge) of his house and put him in charge of all he owned. **5** From the time Joseph was given this role, the Lord blessed Potiphar's household (all people and belongings in his home) for Joseph's sake, and the blessing of the Lord covered everything Potiphar owned, both in his house and in his fields (lands for growing crops). **6** Potiphar left everything he owned in Joseph's care, thinking only of the food he ate. Joseph was handsome (good-looking) and well-built (physically fit). **7** After some time, Potiphar's wife took notice (paid close attention) of Joseph and said, "Lie with me" (be with me intimately). **8** But Joseph refused, telling her, "My master trusts me completely with everything in his house. **9** There is no one greater in this house than I, and he has withheld (kept back) nothing from me except you, since you are his wife. How could I do such a wrong (immoral act) and sin (act against God's law) against God?" **10** She repeatedly asked Joseph to be with her, but he refused to lie with her or even be near her. **11** One day, Joseph entered the house to do his work, and none of the household men (male servants) were inside. **12** She grabbed his garment (clothing) and said, "Lie with me." But Joseph left his garment in her hand and fled (ran away) outside. **13** When she saw that he had left his garment behind and fled, **14** she called the household men and said, "Look, my husband brought this Hebrew (foreigner from Israel) here to insult us! He tried to lie with me, but I screamed (cried out loudly), **15** and when he heard me scream, he left his garment and ran outside." **16** She kept his garment until his master (Potiphar) returned home. **17** Then she told him, "That Hebrew servant you brought here tried to insult me. **18** But when I screamed, he left his garment and fled outside." **19** Potiphar was enraged (filled with anger) when he heard his wife's account (report) of what Joseph had supposedly done. **20** Potiphar put Joseph in the king's prison (a place for detaining prisoners), where the king's prisoners were held, and Joseph stayed there. **21** But the Lord was with Joseph and showed him kindness (compassion, mercy), granting him favor with the prison warden (person in-charge of the prison). **22** The warden entrusted (assigned responsibility to) all the prisoners to Joseph's care, and everything done there was under Joseph's authority (control). **23** The warden had complete trust in Joseph, as the Lord was with him, making him successful in all he did.

Chapter 40

1. After these events, the butler (cupbearer) and the chef of the king of Egypt offended (angered) Pharaoh (king of Egypt). **2.** Pharaoh came angry with his principal butler and principal chef. **3.** He locked (put into jail) them in the house of the captain of the guard (chief of Pharaoh's security), the same captivity where Joseph was kept. **4.** The captain assigned Joseph to attend (serve) them, and they remained in guardianship (under guard) for a time. **5.** While they were in captivity, both the butler and the chef had dreams on the same night, each with a unique meaning. **6.** In the morning, Joseph noticed their sadness (torture). **7.** He asked Pharaoh's officers in guardianship with him, "Why are you so downward (rueful) moment" **8.** They replied, "We both had dreams, but there's no bone to interpret (explain) them." Joseph said, "Interpretations belong to God. Please, tell me your dreams." **9.** The principal butler explained his dream "In my dream, I saw a vine (conduit) before me. **10.** The vine had three branches that blossomed (picked), bloomed (bloomed), and produced clusters (groups) of ripe (completely grown) grapes. **11.** Pharaoh's mug was in my hand, and I took the grapes, pressed (squeezed) them into his mug, and gave it to him." **12.** Joseph said, "This is its meaning the three branches represent three days. **13.** In three days, Pharaoh will restore (return) your position and you'll place his mug

in his hand as ahead, when you were his butler. **14.** But please flash back me when effects go well for you. Show kindness and citation (speak of) me to Pharaoh so I can be freed from this place. **15.** I was forcefully taken (stolen) from the land of the Hebrews (people of Israel), and then I've done nothing to earn being put in this dungeon (captivity)." **16.** When the principal chef saw that the interpretation was favorable (positive), he told his dream to Joseph "In my dream, there were three baskets of white chuck on my head. **17.** In the top handbasket were colorful baked goods (chuck and galettes) for Pharaoh, and catcalls ate them from the handbasket on my head." **18.** Joseph responded, "This is its meaning. The three baskets represent three days. **19.** In three days, Pharaoh will have you executed (put to death) and hung (suspended) on a tree, and catcalls will eat your meat (body)." **20.** On the third day, Pharaoh's birthday, he held a feast (festivity) for all his retainers and brought the principal butler and principal chef before his retainers. **21.** He restored the principal butler to his position, allowing him to place Pharaoh's mug in his hand again. **22.** But he executed the principal chef, just as Joseph had interpreted to them. **23.** Yet, the principal butler did not flash back Joseph; he forgot him.

Chapter 41

1. After two times, Pharaoh pictured he was standing by a conduit. **2.** Seven healthy cows came out and grazed in the meadow. **3.** Seven thin cows came up from the conduit and stood beside the healthy cows. **4.** The thin cows ate the seven healthy cows. Pharaoh awoke. **5.** Pharaoh fell asleep again and pictured seven full heads of grain growing on one stalk. **6.** Seven thin heads, withered by the east wind, grew after them. **7.** The thin heads swallowed the seven full heads. Pharaoh woke up, realizing it was a dream. **8.** Pharaoh called for all the magicians and wise men of Egypt, but none could interpret his dreams. **9.** The butler flashed back his crimes. **10.** When Pharaoh was angry, he put him and the chef in trust. **11.** They both had dreams on the same night. **12.** A Hebrew man interpreted them. **13.** As he interpreted, it happed he was restored, and the chef was executed. **14.** Pharaoh called for Joseph, and he was brought from the dungeon. **15.** Pharaoh said, "I've heard you can explain dreams." **16.** Joseph answered, "God will give Pharaoh the answer." **17.** Pharaoh said, "In my dream, I stood by the conduit. **18.** Seven healthy cows came out and grazed in the meadow. **19.** Seven thin cows came up after them. **20.** The thin cows ate the healthy cows. **21.** They still looked thin. **22.** In another dream, seven full heads of grain grew on one stalk. **23.** Seven thin heads grew after them. **24.** The thin heads swallowed the good heads. **25.** Joseph said, "Both dreams mean the same thing; God is showing Pharaoh what He'll do. **26.** The seven healthy cows and seven full heads represent seven times of plenitude. **27.** The seven thin cows and heads represent seven times of shortage. **28.** This is what God will do. **29.** There will be seven times of plenitude followed by seven times of severe shortage. **30.** The shortage will consume the land. **31.** The cornucopia won't be flashed back because of the inflexibility of the shortage. **32.** The dream was repeated because the matter is established by God and will be soon. **33.** Let Pharaoh choose a wise man and set him over Egypt. **34.** Appoint overseers to gather a fifth of the crop during the times of plenitude. **35.** Store food for the shortage. **36.** The reserve will save Egypt from destruction. **37.** Pharaoh agreed with Joseph's plan. **38.** Pharaoh said, "Can we find anyone like this man, in whom is the Spirit of God?" **39.** Pharaoh said to Joseph, "No bone is as wise as you. **40.** You'll be over my house; only in regard to the throne will I be lower." **41.** Pharaoh said, "I'm putting you in charge of all Egypt." **42.** Pharaoh gave Joseph his ring, fine linen, and a gold chain. **43.** Joseph rode in Pharaoh's chariot, and people called out, "Bow down!" **44.** Pharaoh said, "Without your blessing, no bone will lift a hand or bottom in Egypt." **45.** Pharaoh gave Joseph the name Zaphnath- Paaneah and gave him Asenath as his woman. **46.** Joseph was thirty when he entered Pharaoh's service. **47.** During the seven times of plenitude, the land produced abundantly. **48.** Joseph stored the food in the metropolises. **49.** The grain was vast, like the beach of the ocean. **50.** Before the shortage, Joseph had two sons with Asenath. **51.** He named his firstborn Manasseh, saying, "God has made me forget my suffering and my father's house." **52.** He named his alternate son Ephraim, saying, "God has made me fruitful in the land of my suffering." **53.** The seven times of plenitude ended. **54.** The seven times of shortage began. **55.** When Egypt was famished, the people cried to Pharaoh for food. **56.** Joseph opened the storages and vended grain. **57.** People from all countries came to Egypt to buy grain because the shortage was severe.

Chapter 42

1. When Jacob saw that there was grain in Egypt, he said to his sons, "Why do you keep looking at each other?" **2.** He added, "I've heard there's grain in Egypt. Go there and buy some for us, so that we may live and not starve." **3.** So, ten of Joseph's sisters went to Egypt to buy grain. **4.** But Jacob didn't shoot Joseph's family Benjamin with them, for he said, "I sweat some detriment (pitfall or trouble) might come to him." **5.** The sons of Israel went to buy grain along with others, as the deficiency (a severe insufficiency of food) had spread to Canaan. **6.** Joseph was the governor (an independent or leader) of Egypt, and it was he who vended the grain to the people. When his sisters came, they bowed down to him, their faces to the ground. **7.** Joseph saw his sisters and honored them, but he pretended not to know them and spoke roughly (in a rough, severe manner) to them, asking, "Where have you come from?" They replied, "From the land of Canaan, to buy food." **8.** Although Joseph honored his sisters, they didn't fete him. **9.** Also Joseph flashed back the dreams he'd pictured about them, and said, "You're intelligencers (people who intimately gather information)! You've come to see the weakness (vulnerability or exposed corridors) of the land." **10.** They replied, "No, my lord, but we've come to buy food. **11.** We're all sisters, sons of one man; we're honest men; your retainers are not intelligencers." **12.** But Joseph claimed, "No, you have come to see the weakness of the land." **13.** They responded, "Your retainers are twelve sisters, the sons of one man in Canaan; the immature is with our father, and one is no longer alive." **14.** Joseph said to them, "It's just as I said you are intelligencers! **15.** "This is how I'll test (estimate) you. As surely as Pharaoh (king of Egypt) lives, you won't leave also unless your immature family comes to me." **16.** Shoot one of you to get your family, and the rest of you'll stay in captivity (a place where people are kept as discipline), so that your words may be tested to see if you're telling the verity; else, as Pharaoh Lives, you're intelligencers!" **17.** He put them all in captivity for three days. **18.** on the third day, Joseph said, "Do this and you'll live, for I sweat God (the Creator and independent of the creation). **19.** Still, let one of your sisters stay also in captivity, but you can take the grain for your homes (families), if you're honest men. **20.** Bring your immature family to me, so that your words may be vindicated (vindicated as true), and you won't die." And they did as he said. **21.** They said to one another, "We're being penalized because of our family. We saw how he cried for mercy (appealed for help), but we didn't hear, so now this trouble (difficulty) has come upon us." **22.** Reuben answered them, "Didn't I tell you not to transgress (do wrong) against the boy? But you wouldn't hear. Now we must give an account (take responsibility) for his blood." **23.** They didn't know that Joseph could understand them, as he was speaking through a practitioner (someone who translates speech). **24.** Joseph turned down from them and wept (cried). When he returned, he spoke to them again, and he took Simeon (one of the sisters) from them and had him bound (tied up) before their eyes. **25.** also Joseph gave orders to fill their sacks (bags) with grain, return each man's plutocrat to his sack, and give them vittles (inventories for their trip) for the trip. He did all this for them. **26.** They loaded their burros (beasties used for carrying) with the grain

and left. **27.** But one of them opened his sack to give his jackass feed (food) at the stop, and he set up his plutocrat at the top of his sack. **28.** He said to his sisters, "My plutocrat has been returned! It's in my sack!" They were each alarmed (truly alarmed) and said to each other, "What's God doing to us?" **29.** When they returned to Canaan and told their father everything that had happened, **30.** They said, "The man whose independent (leader) over the land spoke roughly to us and indicted us of being intelligencers. **31.** But we told him, 'We're honest men; we're not intelligencers. **32.** We're twelve sisters, sons of one father; one is no further (dead), and the immature is with our father in Canaan.' **33.** Also, the independent of the land said to us, 'This is how I'll know you're honest men. Leave one of your sisters also, take food for your families, and go. **34.** Bring your immature family to me, so I can know you're not intelligencers but honest men. Also, I'll return your family to you, and you may trade in the land.'" **35.** When they voided their sacks, they discovered that each man's plutocrat was in his sack. When they and their father saw the plutocrat, they were hysterical. **36.** Their father Jacob said to them, "You have made me lose my children Joseph is gone, Simeon is gone, and now you want to take Benjamin. Everything is against me." **37.** Also, Reuben said to his father, "You may kill my two sons if I do not bring him back to you. Put him in my care, and I'll return him." **38.** But Jacob said, "My son will not go down there with you; his brother is dead and he is the only one left. If harm comes to him on the journey you are taking, you will bring my gray head down to the grave in sorrow."

Chapter 43

1. There was a severe shortage (a lack of food) in the land. **2.** After they had consumed (eaten) all the grain they had brought from Egypt, their father said to them," Go back and buy us a little further food." **3.** But Judah said to him," The man advised (advised) us, saying,' You won't see my face unless your family is with you.'" **4.** still, we will go and buy food," If you shoot our family with us. **5.** But if you don't shoot him, we won't go, for the man said,' You won't see my face unless your family is with you.'" **6.** Israel replied, "Why did you tell the man that you had another family?" **7.** They answered," The man asked us pointedly (in a direct way) about ourselves and our family, saying,' Is your father still alive? Do you have another family?' We answered him actually. How could we've known he'd say,' Bring your family down'?" **8.** also, Judah said to Israel," shoot the boy with me, and we will go so that we and you and our children won't die. **9.** I'll take full responsibility (guarantee) for him; if I don't bring him back, let me bear the blame ever. **10.** still, we'd have formerly returned doubly, if we hadn't delayed (wasted time)." **11.** Israel also said," If it must be so, do this Take some of the stylish yield (crops) of the land as a gift for the man — some attar (medicinal substance), honey, spices, myrrh (an ambrosial resin), pistachio nuts, and almonds. **12.** Take double the plutocrat in your hands and return the plutocrat that was set up in your sacks. maybe it was a mistake. **13.** Take your family as well, and go back to the man. **14.** May God Almighty entitlement (give) you mercy (compassion) before the man, so he'll release your other family and Benjamin. However, I'm deprived!" 15, If I'm bereft (lose a loved one). So, the men took the gift and Benjamin, and double the plutocrat, and went to Egypt, standing before Joseph. **16.** When Joseph saw Benjamin with them, he said to his slavey (a menial in charge of the ménage)," Take these men to my house, bloodbath (kill and prepare) a beast, and prepare a mess, for they will dine (eat) with me at noon." **17.** The slavey did as Joseph directed and brought the men to Joseph's house. **18.** The men were hysterical because they had been brought to Joseph's house and study," It's because of the plutocrat that was returned in our sacks that he has brought us then to make us slaves along with our burros." **19.** They approached the slavey at the door of the house **20.** and said," Sir, we came down the first time to buy food; **21.** But when we came to our camp and opened our sacks, we set up the plutocrat, all of it, in the mouth of our sacks. So, we brought it back with us. 22. We've brought fresh (redundant) plutocrat to buy food. We don't know who put the plutocrat in our sacks." 23. The slavey said," Peace to you, don't be hysterical. Your God and the God of your father must have put treasure (precious particulars) in your sacks. I entered your plutocrat." also he brought Simeon out to them. 24. The slavey brought the men into the house, gave them water, and they washed their bases. He also gave their burros feed (food). 25. They prepared the gift for Joseph's appearance at noon, since they heard they would eat with him. 26. When Joseph came home, they gave him the gift they had brought and bowed (bent down) before him. 27. He asked them," How is your father? Is the old man of whom you spoke still alive?" 28. They replied," Your menial, our father, is in good health; he's still alive." And they bowed again. 29. also he looked up and saw his family Benjamin, his mama 's son, and asked," Is this your youngish family, the bone you told me about?" He said," God be gracious (kind) to you, my son." 30. His heart went out to his family, and Joseph hastened out of the room because he was so emotional. He went to his private (particular) room and wept (cried). 31. After washing his face, he came out, controlled (held back) himself, and said," Serve the mess." 32. They served him at a separate table, and the Egyptians ate at a separate table because eating with Hebrews was an abomination (disgusting) to them. 33. They sat before him, in order from the oldest to the youthful, and the men looked at each other in amazement (surprise). 34. Joseph gave Benjamin five times as important food as the others, and they drank and enjoyed the mess with him.

Chapter 44

1. Joseph instructed his slavey, saying," Fill the men's sacks (bags) with as important food as they can carry and place each man's plutocrat at the top of his sack. 2. Put my tableware mug, along with the plutocrat for the grain, into the sack of the youthful." And the slavey did as Joseph had commanded. 3. Beforehand the coming morning, the men were transferred on their way, along with their burros (creatures used for carrying loads). 4. After they had left the megacity and weren't far from it, Joseph told his slavey," Chase after them, and when you catch up, asks them,' Why have you repaid kindness with wrong (wrong conduct)? 5. Is not this the mug my master drinks from and uses for augury (the practice of seeking knowledge of the future through supernatural means)? You have done wrong.'" 6. The slavey chased after them and spoke these words to them. 7. The men responded," Why does my lord say similar effects? Far be it from us to do commodity like that. 8. We brought back to you the plutocrat we set up in our sacks from Canaan (a region in the ancient Near East). How could we steal tableware or gold from your master's house? 9. still, let him die and the rest of us will be your slaves (people who are forced to work without pay), If any of us is set up with it." 10. The slavey replied," Let it be as you say the man who has the mug will be my slave, but the rest of you'll be innocent." 11. So each man snappily lowered his sack and opened it. 12. The slavey searched each sack, starting with the oldest, until he came to the youthful, and there he set up the mug in Benjamin's sack. 13. The men tore their clothes (a sign of deep torture) in torture, and each man loaded his jackass and returned to the megacity. 14. Judah and his sisters came to Joseph's house, where he was still staying, and they bowed down before him. 15. Joseph asked them," What have you done? Didn't you know that a man like me can exercise augury?" 16. Judah replied," What can we say to my lord? How can we clear ourselves? God has revealed our guilt (wrongdoing). We're now my lord's slaves, both we and the bone who had the mug." 17. Joseph said," Far be it from me to do that. The man who had the mug will be my slave, but the rest of you may go back in peace to your father." 18. also, Judah approached Joseph and said," Please, my lord, let your menial speak a word to you. Do not be angry with me, for you're like Pharaoh (the king of Egypt) himself. 19. You asked

us if we had a father or a family, 20. And we told you we had a senior father and a youngish son, born in his old age. His family is dead, and he's the only one left wing of his mama's children, and his father loves him dearly. 21. also you told us,' Bring him then so I can see him.' 22. But we said to you,'The boy cannot leave his father. However, his father will die, if he does.' 23. But you told us,' You won't see my face again unless your youthful family comes with you.' 24. So, when we returned to our father, we told him what you had said. 25. Our father said,' Go back and buy us a little further food.' 26. But we replied,'We cannot go unless our youthful family is with us. We cannot see the man's face unless he's with us.' 27. also, your menial, our father, said to us,' You know my woman bore me two sons. 28. One went out from me, and I allowed he was torn to pieces, and I have not seen him since. 29. still, you'll bring my argentine hair down to the grave (death) in anguish, if you take this bone from me and detriment comes to him.' 30. Now, if I return to my father without the boy — since his life is bound up with the boy's life (his life depends on the boy) — 31. when he sees that the boy is not with us, he'll die. Your retainers will bring down the argentine hair of our father to the grave in anguish. 32. I guaranteed (promised) the boy's safety to my father, saying,' If I don't bring him back to you, I'll bear the blame before my father ever.' 33. Now, please let your menial stay as my lord's slave in place of the boy, and let the boy return with his sisters. 34. For how can I go back to my father without the boy? I sweat what will be to my father."

Chapter 45

1. Joseph could no longer control his feelings in front of everyone, and he ordered," Make everyone leave!" So no bone stayed with him when Joseph revealed his identity to his sisters. 2. He wept loudly, and the Egyptians (people of Egypt) and the ménage of Pharaoh (the king's family) heard him. 3. Joseph said to his sisters," I'm Joseph. Is my father still alive?" But they couldn't respond, because they were shocked to see him. 4. He said to them," Come closer." They did, and he told them," I'm Joseph, your family, whom you vended into Egypt." 5." Don't be worried or angry with yourselves for dealing me then, because God transferred me ahead of you to save lives." 6." There has been a shortage (a severe deficit of food) in the land for two times, and there are five further times with no furrowing or harvesting." 7." God transferred me ahead to insure your survival and to save a future for you on earth, saving you through this great deliverance (deliverance)." 8." So it wasn't you who transferred me then, but God. He has made me a father to Pharaoh, the sovereign of his entire house, and the governor (leader) of all Egypt." 9." Accelerate and go back to my father, and tell him,' Joseph says," God has made me sovereign of all Egypt; come to me snappily."' 10." Bring your family, your children, your flocks, and all that you have, and settle in the land of Goshen (a rich region in Egypt). Be near me. There I'll give for you during the remaining times of shortage." 11." You and your ménage won't suffer poverty because of the shortage." 12." Look, you can see for yourselves, and so can my family Benjamin, that it's I who am speaking to you." 13." Tell my father about all my glory (honor and wealth) in Egypt and everything you've seen. Accelerate and bring him back then." 14. He embraced Benjamin and wept. Benjamin also wept in his arms. 15. He kissed all his sisters and wept over them. subsequently, they spoke with him. 16. The news reached Pharaoh's house," Joseph's sisters have come," and it pleased Pharaoh and his retainers. 17. Pharaoh told Joseph," Tell your sisters,' cargo up your creatures and go to Canaan (a region), the land where your father lives. 18." Bring your father and your families to me; I'll give you the stylish of Egypt. You'll eat the finest food.'" 19." Also, take wagons (carts) from Egypt for your children and women, and bring your father back then." 20." Don't worry about your effects. The stylish of Egypt is yours." 21. The sons of Israel (Jacob's family) did as instructed. Joseph gave those wagons as Pharaoh had commanded, and vittles (food and inventories) for

the trip. **22.** He gave each of them new clothes, but to Benjamin, he gave three hundred pieces of tableware and five changes of clothes. **23.** Joseph transferred to his father ten burros loaded with the finest goods of Egypt, and ten burros with grain, chuck, and other inventories for the trip. **24.** He transferred his sisters on their way, saying," Don't argue on the way." **25.** They left Egypt and went to Canaan, to their father Jacob. **26.** They told him," Joseph is still alive, and he's the governor (sovereign) of Egypt." Jacob was stupefied and could not believe them. **27.** But when they told him everything Joseph had said and showed him the wagons Joseph had transferred, his spirit revived (his heart was filled with joy and stopgap). **28.** Israel (Jacob) said," It's enough. My son Joseph is alive. I'll go see him before I die."

Chapter 46

1. So Israel (Jacob) took his journey with all that he had and came to Beersheba (a place in southern Israel), and offered sacrifices to the God of his father Isaac. **2.** Then God spoke to Israel in the visions of the night, and said, "Jacob, Jacob!" And he said, "Here I am." **3.** So He said, "I am God, the God of your father; do not fear to go down to Egypt (a neighboring land to the southwest), for I will make of you a great nation there. **4.** I will go down with you to Egypt, and I will also surely bring you up again; and Joseph will put his hand on your eyes (a phrase meaning Joseph will close your eyes at your death)." **5.** Then Jacob arose from Beersheba; and the sons of Israel carried their father Jacob, their little ones, and their wives, in the carts (vehicles) which Pharaoh had sent to carry him. **6.** So they took their livestock (animals such as cattle, sheep, and goats) and their goods (personal belongings), which they had acquired in the land of Canaan (the land of Israel), and went to Egypt, Jacob and all his descendants with him. **7.** His sons and his sons' sons, his daughters and his sons' daughters, and all his descendants he brought with him to Egypt. **8.** Now these were the names of the children of Israel, Jacob and his sons, who went to Egypt: Reuben was Jacob's firstborn. **9.** The sons of Reuben were Hanoch, Pallu, Hezron, and Carmi. **10.** The sons of Simeon were Jemuel, Jamin, Ohad, Jachin, Zohar, and Shaul, the son of a Canaanite woman (a woman from the region of Canaan). **11.** The sons of Levi were Gershon, Kohath, and Merari. **12.** The sons of Judah were Er, Onan, Shelah, Perez, and Zerah (but Er and Onan died in the land of Canaan). The sons of Perez were Hezron and Hamul. **13.** The sons of Issachar were Tola, Puvah, Job, and Shimron. **14.** The sons of Zebulun were Sered, Elon, and Jahleel. **15.** These were the sons of Leah, whom she bore to Jacob in Padan Aram (a region in Mesopotamia where Jacob had lived), with his daughter Dinah. All the persons, his sons and his daughters, were thirty-three. **16.** The sons of Gad were Ziphion, Haggi, Shuni, Ezbon, Eri, Arodi, and Areli. **17.** The sons of Asher were Jimnah, Ishuah, Isui, Beriah, and Serah, their sister. And the sons of Beriah were Heber and Malchiel. **18.** These were the sons of Zilpah (Leah's maidservant), whom Laban gave to Leah his daughter; and these she bore to Jacob: sixteen persons. **19.** The sons of Rachel, Jacob's wife, were Joseph and Benjamin. **20.** And to Joseph in the land of Egypt were born Manasseh and Ephraim, whom Asenath bore to him. **21.** The sons of Benjamin were Belah, Becher, Ashbel, Gera, Naaman, Ehi, Rosh, Muppim, Huppim, and Ard. **22.** These were the sons of Rachel, who were born to Jacob: fourteen persons in all. **23.** The son of Dan was Hushim. **24.** The sons of Naphtali were Jahzeel, Guni, Jezer, and Shillem. **25.** These were the sons of Bilhah (Rachel's maidservant), whom Laban gave to Rachel his daughter, and she bore these to Jacob: seven persons in all. **26.** All the persons who went with Jacob to Egypt, who came from his body, besides Jacob's sons' wives, were sixty-six persons in all. **27.** And the sons of Joseph who were born to him in Egypt were two persons. All the persons of the house of Jacob who went to Egypt were seventy. **28.** Then he sent Judah before him to Joseph, to point out before him the way to Goshen (a fertile region in Egypt). And they came to the land of Goshen. **29.** So Joseph made ready his chariot and went up to Goshen to meet his father Israel; and he presented himself to him, and fell on his neck and wept on his neck a good while. **30.** And Israel said to Joseph, "Now let me die, since I have seen your face, because you are still alive." **31.** Then Joseph said to his brothers and to his father's household, "I will go up and tell Pharaoh, and say to him, 'My brothers and those of my father's house, who were in the land of Canaan, have come to me. **32.** And the men are shepherds, for their occupation has been to feed livestock (herding animals); and they have brought their flocks, their herds, and all that they have.' **33.** So it shall be, when Pharaoh calls you and says, 'What is your occupation?' **34.** that you shall say, 'Your servants' occupation has been with livestock from our youth even till now, both we and also our fathers,' that you may dwell in the land of Goshen; for every shepherd is an abomination (something detestable) to the Egyptians."

Chapter 47

1. Joseph went and informed Pharaoh, saying," My father, my sisters, their flocks (groups of creatures), herds (groups of cattle), and all their effects have come from Canaan and are now in the land of Goshen." **2.** He took five of his sisters and presented them to Pharaoh. **3.** Pharaoh asked them," What's your occupation?" They answered," We're goatherds (those who watch for lamb and other beast), both we and our fathers." **4.** They added," We've come to live then because there's no pasturage (land for grazing) for our flocks in Canaan due to the severe shortage (a severe deficit of food). Please let us live in Goshen." **5.** Pharaoh said to Joseph," Your father and sisters have come to you. **6.** The land of Egypt is before you. Settle them in the stylish of the land — let them live in Goshen. However, put them in charge of my beast, If you know any able (professed) men." **7.** Joseph brought his father Jacob before Pharaoh, and Jacob blessed Pharaoh. **8.** Pharaoh asked Jacob," How old are you?" **9.** Jacob replied," The times of my passage (trip or time spent on earth) are 130; my life has been short and delicate, and not as long as my ancestors' lives." **10.** Also Jacob blessed Pharaoh again and left his presence. **11.** Joseph settled his father and sisters in the stylish part of Egypt, the land of Rameses, as Pharaoh had instructed. **12.** Joseph handed food for his father, his sisters, and their homes according to the number of people. **13.** There was no chuck in Egypt or Canaan because the shortage was veritably severe, and the land sagged (suffered) due to it. **14.** Joseph gathered the entire plutocrat in Egypt and Canaan in exchange for grain (cereal crops), bringing it into Pharaoh's storeroom (storage of wealth). **15.** When the plutocrat ran out in Egypt and Canaan, the people came to Joseph, saying," Give us chuck, for we're out of plutocrat and will die in your presence." **16.** Joseph replied," Give me your beast, and I'll give you chuck in exchange for it." **17.** They brought their beast to Joseph, and he gave them chuck in exchange for their nags, flocks, cattle, and burros, feeding them for that time. **18.** When that time ended, they came to Joseph again, saying," We've no plutocrat left, and our beast belongs to you. There's nothing left but our bodies and our land. **19.** Why should we corrupt, both we and our land? Buy us and our land for chuck, and we will be Pharaoh's retainers. Give us seed (grains to plant), so we may live and not die, and that our land would not come desolate (empty)." **20.** Joseph bought all the land of Egypt for Pharaoh. Every Egyptian vended his field because the shortage was so severe. Therefore, the land came Pharaoh's. **21.** Joseph moved the people into metropolises, from one end of Egypt to the other. **22.** Only the land of the preachers didn't come Pharaoh's, for they had food given to them by Pharaoh, and they didn't vend their land. **23.** Joseph said to the people," I've bought you and your land for Pharaoh. Then seed for you to plant. **24.** At crop, you'll give one- fifth (20) to Pharaoh. The remaining four-fifths will be yours, for seed to plant the field and for your food, including that for your families and children." **25.** they replied," You have saved our lives. We'll be Pharaoh's retainers." **26.** Joseph established (set up) this law in Egypt, that Pharaoh would admit one-fifth, except for the land of the preachers, which didn't come Pharaoh's. **27.** Israel (Jacob) lived in the land of Egypt, in the region of Goshen. They acquired property, and their family grew and multiplied greatly. **28.** Jacob lived in Egypt for 17 times, making his total age 147 times. **29.** As Jacob's death approached, he called his son Joseph and said to him," If I've set up favor (grace) in your sight, swear to me that you won't bury me in Egypt, **30.** But that I may lie with my ancestors; carry me out of Egypt and bury me in their burial place." Joseph agreed, saying," I'll do as you have said." **31.** Jacob also asked him to swear, and Joseph swore. Subsequently, Jacob bowed in deification at the head of his bed.

Chapter 48

1. Sometime after these events, Joseph received the message that his father was unwell. He immediately took his two sons, Manasseh and Ephraim, and went to see him. **2.** Upon hearing that Joseph was approaching, Jacob gathered his strength (energy, power) and sat up in his bed. **3.** Jacob said to Joseph, "God Almighty (the God who is all-powerful), the God who is most important, appeared to me at Luz (a place in Canaan, present-day Bethel), in the land of Canaan, and blessed me, **4.** Saying, 'I will make you fruitful (cause to multiply, increase) and increase (multiply, grow) your descendants. I will form a great nation from you, and I will give this land to your descendants forever.' **5.** As for your two sons, Ephraim and Manasseh, who were born to you in Egypt before I came to you, they are now my own. They will be as Reuben and Simeon to me (the first and second sons of Jacob, considered as heirs). **6.** Any children you have after them will belong to you, but they will inherit according to the names of their brothers (their share of inheritance will be named after their brothers). **7.** When I left Padan (a region in Mesopotamia), Rachel (Jacob's wife) died on the journey to Ephrath (a place near Bethlehem), and I buried her there on the way (meaning on the road to Bethlehem). **8.** Israel looked at Joseph's sons and asked, "Who are these?" **9.** Joseph answered, "These are my sons, whom God has given me here." Israel replied, "Bring them to me so that I may bless them." **10.** Israel's sight (ability to see) was dimmed (weakened) with age, and he could not see clearly. So Joseph brought his sons close to him, and Israel kissed them and embraced them. **11.** Israel said to Joseph, "I never thought I would see you again, but now God has allowed me to see your children as well!" **12.** Joseph moved them from his knees (he lifted them) and bowed low (showed respect by bending down) before Israel. **13.** Joseph took both sons, placing Ephraim on Israel's right side (the side of honor) and Manasseh on his left (the lesser position), and brought them forward. 1**4.** However, Israel crossed his arms (intentionally switched positions), placing his right hand on Ephraim's head (even though he was the younger), and his left hand on Manasseh's head, knowing that Manasseh was the firstborn. **15.** Then he blessed Joseph, saying, "The God before whom my fathers Abraham and Isaac walked (lived their lives in obedience), the God who has been my shepherd (protector, guide) all my life, **16.** And the Angel (messenger from God) who has delivered (saved, rescued) me from all harm, bless these boys. May my name, and the names of my fathers Abraham and Isaac, be upon them, and may they multiply greatly (increase in number) across the earth." **17.** When Joseph saw that his father had placed his right hand on Ephraim's head, he was upset (displeased) and tried to move it to Manasseh's head. **18.** He said to his father, "Not so, father! This one is the firstborn; put your right hand on his head." **19.** But Israel insisted (firmly said), "I know, my son, I know. He too will become a great nation, but his younger brother will be even greater, and his descendants will become many nations." **20.** So he blessed them that day, saying, "The Israelites will bless by saying, 'May God make you like Ephraim and Manasseh.'" And he placed Ephraim ahead of Manasseh. **21.** Then Israel said to Joseph, "I am about to die, but God will be with you and will bring you back to the land of your ancestors. **22.** I am giving you a double portion (a special inheritance), which I took from the Amorites (a people in Canaan) with my sword and bow (symbols of battle).

Chapter 49

1. Jacob called his sons together and said," Come near, and I'll tell you what will be to you in the days to come. **2.**" hear to me, you sons of Jacob, and pay attention to your father Israel. **3.**" Reuben, you're my firstborn, the strength (power) of my youth, the zenith (loftiest point) of my power — both recognized (admired) and given authority. **4.**" But you're unstable (unsteady), like water, and won't prosper (succeed), because you lowered (disrespected) my bed, defiling (contaminating) it when you climbed onto my settee. **5.**" Simeon and Levi are sisters; their lodging is marked by violence (atrocity) and atrocity (harshness). **6.**" Don't let my soul (inner being) share in their plans (reflections), nor let my honor (character) be linked to their conduct, for in their wrath (wrathfulness) they boggled a man, and in their fury (violent wrathfulness), they harmed (injured) an ox. **7.**" Cursed (damned) be their wrathfulness, for it's fierce (violent); cursed be their rage (wrathfulness), for it's ruthless (merciless)! I'll scatter (distribute) them among the lines of Israel and peak (separate) them throughout the land. **8.**" Judah, your sisters will praise (respect) you; your power (strength) will triumph over (be victorious over) your adversaries, and your father's sons will bow down (show respect) before you. **9.**" Judah is like a youthful captain (captain cub); after the quest (prey), my son, you rise up, lie down, and rest (relax) like a captain. Who'll dare (have courage) to disturb (bother) him? **10.**" The scepter (symbol of authority) shall not depart (leave) from Judah, nor the sovereign's staff (symbol of kingship) from his descendants, until Shiloh (a peaceful leader) comes, and to Him, the nations will bring their obedience (submit). **11.**" He'll tie his jackass (beast of burden) to a vine (conduit), and his recruit (youthful jackass) to the finest vine. He'll wash (clean) his garments (clothes) in wine, his mask in the juice (blood) of grapes. **12.**" His eyes will shine (be darker) more brightly than wine, and his teeth whiter than milk. **13.**" Zebulun will live (dwell) by the ocean, a haven (safe place) for vessels, and his borders (home) will extend to Sidon (an ancient megacity). **14.**" Issachar is like a strong jackass (burden-deliverer), resting between two burdens (tasks). **15.**" He sees that rest (peace) is good and the land (region) is favorable (affable); he'll bow his reverse (shoulder) to carry (bear) the cargo and serve (work) others. **16.**" Dan will act as a judge (govern) for his people, as one of the lines of Israel. **17.**" Dan will be like a serpent (snake) on the road, a serpent (toxic snake) by the way, striking at the steed's heels (hind legs), causing its rider to fall (collapse) backward. **18.**" I stay (stopgap) for Your deliverance (deliverance), O Lord! **19.**" Gad will be raided (attacked) by raiders (aggressors), but he'll eventually prevail (triumph). **20.**" Asher's land (yield) will be abundant (generous), and he'll give (offer) fine delectables (luxurious foods) fit for lords. **21.**" Naphtali is like a free (wild) deer; he speaks with grace (fineness). **22.**" Joseph is a fruitful vine (productive factory), a vine by a spring (water source), whose branches stretch over (extend further) the wall. **23.**" The hunters (shooters) fiercely (plaintively) attacked him, shot arrows at him, and abominated him. **24.**" Yet his bow remained steady (strong), and the strength (power) of his arms was made firm (stable) by the hands of the potent One (God) of Jacob, by the Shepherd (Protector), the Rock (foundation) of Israel. **25.**" By the God (godly being) of your father, who helps (assists) you, and by the Almighty (each-important one) who blesses (favors) you with the blessings (gifts) of the welkin over, the blessings of the deep (ocean) below, and the blessings of the bone (aliment) and womb (fertility). **26.**" The blessings of your father are lesser (further) than the blessings of the ancient hills (eternal mountains); they surpass the bounty (riches) of everlasting (eternal) mountains. They rest upon the head of Joseph, upon the crown (top) of the one set piecemeal (distinguished) from his sisters. **27.**" Benjamin is a rapacious (greedy) wolf; in the morning he devours (eats) the prey, and in the evening, he divides (shares) the loot (plunder)." 28. These are the twelve lines of Israel, and this is what their father said to them. He gave each one a blessing suited (applicable) to their fortune. 29. also Jacob gave his final instructions (commands) to his sons" I'm about to be gathered (reunited) to my people. Bury me with my ancestors in the delve in the field of Ephron the Hittite (a people group), 30. in the delve in the field of Machpelah, near Mamre, in the land of Canaan (the promised land), which Abraham bought (bought) from Ephron the Hittite as a burial place. 31. There Abraham and his woman Sarah are buried, and there Isaac and his woman Rebekah are buried, and I also buried Leah there. 32. The field and the delve were bought from the Hittites (Canaanite lineage)." 33. After giving these instructions, Jacob drew his bases up into the bed, breathed his last (failed), and was gathered to his people.

Chapter 50

1. Joseph fell on his father's face, wept, and kissed him. 2. Joseph also commanded the croakers (croakers) to embalm (save the body) his father and they did so. 3. It took forty days to embalm him, as that was the needed time for embalming, and the Egyptians mourned (expressed anguish) for him for seventy days. 4. After the mourning period ended, Joseph spoke to Pharaoh's ménage, saying," If I've set up favor (blessing) in your sight, please ask Pharaoh to hear me. 5. My father made me swear (promise), saying,' I'm about to die. Bury me in the grave I prepared for myself in Canaan.' Please let me go and bury him, and I'll return." 6. Pharaoh replied," Go and bury your father as he asked." 7. Joseph went up to bury his father, accompanied by all Pharaoh's retainers, the elders (leaders) of his house, and all the leaders of Egypt, 8. Along with Joseph's family, his sisters, and his entire father's ménage. They left their youthful children, flocks (groups of creatures), and herds (large groups of cattle) in Goshen. 9. A great procession (large group of people) of chariots and horsewomen went with him. 10. They reached the threshing bottom (area where grain is separated from its cocoon) of Atad, beyond the Jordan, and mourned there with a deep and solemn (serious) lament (expression of grief). Joseph mourned for seven days. 11. When the Canaanites saw the mourning at the threshing bottom of Atad, they said," This is a severe mourning by the Egyptians." thus, the place was named Abel Mizraim, beyond the Jordan. 12. Joseph's sons did as he'd instructed them. 13. They carried his body to Canaan and buried him in the delve (a burial place) of Machpelah, near Mamre, the field Abraham had bought from Ephron the Hittite as a burial point. 14. After burying his father, Joseph returned to Egypt with his sisters and all who had accompanied him. 15. When Joseph's sisters saw that their father had failed, they stressed Joseph might hold a grudge (feeling of resentment) and repay them for their wrongs. 16. So they transferred couriers (people who deliver dispatches) to Joseph, saying," Before our father failed, he commanded, 17.' Tell Joseph," Please forgive the wrongdoing (sin) of your sisters and their sin, for they treated you poorly." Please forgive the retainers (followers) of the God of your father.'" Joseph wept when he heard this. 18. His sisters went to him, bowed down, and said," We're your retainers." 19. Joseph replied," Don't be hysterical. Am I in the place of God? 20. You intended to harm (hurt) me, but God intended it for good, to bring about the preservation (safety) of numerous people, as is passing now. 21. So don't be hysterical. I'll give (take care of) for you and your children." He assured them and spoke kindly to them. 22. Joseph and his father's ménage continued to live in Egypt. Joseph lived 1s10 times. 23. He saw his great- grandchildren, including the children of Machir, the son of Manasseh, raised by him. 24. Joseph said to his sisters," I'm about to die, but God will visit (watch for) you and bring you out of this land to the land He promised to Abraham, Isaac, and Jacob." 25. also Joseph made the children of Israel swear, saying," God will surely visit you, and when He does,

you must carry my bones with you." 26. Joseph failed at 110 times old, was embalmed, and placed in a pall (a box for a dead body) in Egypt.

2 – Exodus
Chapter 1

1. These are the names of the descendants of Israel who went to Egypt, each with his family, along with Jacob: 2. the sons of Jacob were Reuben, Simeon, Levi, and Judah; 3. Issachar, Zebulun, and Benjamin; 4. Dan, Naphtali, Gad, and Asher. 5. All the descendants of Jacob totaled seventy people (since Joseph was already in Egypt). 6. Then Joseph died, as well as all of his brothers, and the entire generation of that time. 7. But the children of Israel continued to grow and multiply abundantly; they became extremely numerous and powerful, and the land was filled with them. 8. Afterward, a new king came to power in Egypt, one who did not recognize or acknowledge Joseph. 9. "He addressed his people, saying, 'Behold, the Israelites have become more numerous and powerful than we are.'". 10. Come; let us be clever about how we deal with them. If they continue to multiply, in the event of a war, they might join our enemies and fight against us, and eventually escape from the land." 11. So, they set harsh overseers over them to oppress them with difficult labor. They forced the Israelites (descendants of Jacob) to build cities for Pharaoh, including Pithom and Raamses. 12. But the harder the Egyptians oppressed them, the more the Israelites multiplied and grew. As a result, the Egyptians became fearful of the Israelites. 13. So, the Egyptians made the Israelites' lives even bitterer with intense labor 14. mixing mortar, making bricks, and doing all kinds of work in the fields. All the work they forced them to do was harsh. 15. Then Pharaoh spoke to the Hebrew midwives, the names of one being Shiphrah and the other Puah, 16. and he said to them, "When you help the Hebrew women give birth and see them delivering, if it is a boy, kill him; but if it is a girl, let her live." 17. But the midwives respected God and did not follow the king's orders. They allowed the boys to live. 18. So, Pharaoh called the midwives (Shiphrah and Puah) and asked them, "Why have you done this? Why have you allowed the boys to live?" 19. The midwives answered Pharaoh, "The Hebrew women are not like the Egyptian women; they are strong and give birth quickly, before we can even get there." 20. As a result, God showed kindness to the midwives, and the Israelites continued to multiply and become very strong. 21. Because the midwives honored God, He gave them families of their own. 22. Then Pharaoh gave an order to all his people: "Every Hebrew boy that is born must be thrown into the Nile River (situated primarily within the borders of ancient Egypt), but every girl may live.

Chapter 2

1. A man from the tribe of Levi (one of the twelve tribes of Israel) married a woman who was also from the tribe of Levi. 2. The woman became pregnant and gave birth to a son. When she saw that he was an exceptionally (extraordinarily) beautiful child, she hid him for three months to protect him. 3. But when she could no longer hide him, she took a basket made from bulrushes (a type of reed), coated it with tar and pitch (to make it waterproof), and placed the baby in it. She set the basket among the reeds along the riverbank. 4. The baby's sister stood at a distance, watching to see what would happen to him. 5. Then Pharaoh's daughter (daughter of the king of Egypt) came down to the river to bathe, and her maidens walked along the shore. When she saw the basket among the reeds, she sent one of her servants to fetch it. 6. As soon as she opened the basket, she saw the baby and immediately recognized that he was a Hebrew child. Upon seeing him, she felt pity for him and said, "This must be one of the Hebrew children." 7. Then the baby's sister approached Pharaoh's daughter and asked, "Would you like me to find a Hebrew woman to nurse the child for you?" 8. Pharaoh's daughter replied, "Yes, go ahead." So the girl went and brought back the child's own mother. 9. Pharaoh's daughter

then said to her, "Take this child and nurse him for me. I will pay you for your services." So the woman took the child and nursed him. **10.** As the child grew, she brought him back to Pharaoh's daughter, and he became her son. Pharaoh's daughter named him Moses, because she had drawn him out of the water. **11.** Years later, when Moses had grown up, he went out to visit his fellow Hebrews and observed their hard labor. While there, he saw an Egyptian beating one of the Hebrew men, who was his own countryman. **12.** Moses looked around to make sure no one was watching, then he struck down the Egyptian and hid his body in the sand. **13.** The next day, when Moses went out again, he saw two Hebrew men fighting. He asked the one who was in the wrong, "Why are you hitting your fellow Hebrew?" **14.** The man retorted, "Who made you a prince and judge over us? Are you going to kill me like you killed the Egyptian?" Moses was afraid, thinking, "What I did must be known." **15.** When Pharaoh heard about what Moses had done, he tried to kill him. But Moses fled from Pharaoh's presence and went to the land of Midian (a region east of Egypt). There, he sat down by a well. **16.** The priest of Midian had seven daughters, and they came to the well to draw water and fill the troughs to water their father's flock. **17.** Some shepherds arrived and tried to drive the women away, but Moses stepped in and defended them, watering their flock for them. **18.** When the daughters of Reuel (also called Jethro, a priest of Midian) returned to their father, he asked, "Why have you come back so early today?" **19.** They answered, "An Egyptian man rescued us from the shepherds, and he even helped us water the flock by drawing water for us." **20.** Reuel asked, "Where is he? Why did you leave him behind? Go and invite him to come and eat with us." **21.** Moses agreed to stay with the man, and Reuel gave Moses his daughter Zipporah to be his wife. **22.** Zipporah gave birth to a son, and Moses named him Gershom, meaning, "I have become a foreigner in a strange land." **23.** After a long period of time, the king of Egypt died, but the Israelites continued to groan in their slavery and cried out for help. Their cries reached God because of their oppression. **24.** God heard their groaning, and He remembered His covenant with Abraham, Isaac, and Jacob (the patriarchs of Israel). **25.** God looked down on the Israelites and acknowledged their suffering.

Chapter 3

1. Moses was tending the sheep of his father-in-law, Jethro, who was a priest in Midian. He led the flock to the far side of the desert, and came to Horeb, the mountain of God (Horeb is another name for Mount Sinai, where Moses would later receive the Ten Commandments). **2.** There, the Angel of the Lord appeared to him in a flame of fire from the center of a bush. Moses looked and saw that the bush was burning, but it was not being consumed by the fire. **3.** Moses said to himself, "I will turn aside and see this remarkable sight—why is the bush not burning up?" **4.** When the Lord saw that Moses had turned aside to look, God called out to him from the bush, saying, "Moses! Moses!" And Moses answered, "Here I am." **5.** God then said, "Do not come any closer. Take off your sandals, for the place where you are standing is holy ground." **6.** God continued, "I am the God of your father—the God of Abraham, the God of Isaac, and the God of Jacob." When Moses heard this, he hid his face, because he was afraid to look at God. **7.** The Lord said, "I have indeed seen the suffering of my people in Egypt, and I have heard their cries because of their harsh slave drivers. I am aware of their pain and oppression. **8.** I have come down to deliver them from the Egyptians, and to bring them up out of that land to a good and spacious land, a land flowing with milk and honey, the land of the Canaanites, Hittites, Amorites, Perizzites, Hivites, and Jebusites (various groups of people living in Canaan). **9.** The cries of the Israelites have reached me, and I have seen how the Egyptians are oppressing them. **10.** Now, go, for I am sending you to Pharaoh to bring my people, the Israelites, out of Egypt." **11.** But Moses said to God, "Who am I that I should go to Pharaoh and bring the Israelites out of Egypt?" **12.** God said, "I will certainly be with you. And this will be the sign to you that I am the one who has sent you: When you bring the people out of Egypt, you will worship God on this mountain." **13.** Moses then asked God, "What if I go to the Israelites and say to them, 'The God of your ancestors has sent me to you,' and they ask, 'What is His name?' What should I tell them?" **14.** God replied to Moses, "I AM WHO I AM." And He said, "This is what you are to say to the Israelites: 'I AM has sent me to you.'" **15.** God also said to Moses, "Say to the Israelites: 'The Lord, the God of your fathers—the God of Abraham, the God of Isaac, and the God of Jacob—has sent me to you. This is my name forever, and this is the name by which I will be remembered for all generations.'" **16.** "Go, gather the elders of Israel together and tell them, 'The Lord, the God of your fathers— the God of Abraham, Isaac, and Jacob—appeared to me and said: "I have certainly seen the misery of my people in Egypt, and I have heard their cries because of their oppressors. I am aware of their suffering. **17.** So I have come down to rescue them from the Egyptians and to bring them up out of that land to a land flowing with milk and honey, the land of the Canaanites, Hittites, Amorites, Perizzites, Hivites, and Jebusites."'" **18.** The elders of Israel will listen to you. Then you and the elders will go to the king of Egypt and say to him, 'The Lord, the God of the Hebrews, has met with us. Let us take a three-day journey into the wilderness to offer sacrifices to the Lord our God.' **19.** But I know that the king of Egypt will not let you go, not even under strong force. **20.** So I will stretch out my hand and strike Egypt with all the wonders that I will perform there. After that, he will let you go. **21.** And I will make the Egyptians favorably disposed toward this people, so that when you leave, you will not go empty-handed. **22.** Every woman is to ask her neighbor, and any woman living in her house, for articles of silver and gold, and for clothing. You will put these on your sons and daughters, and you will plunder the Egyptians."

Chapter 4

1. Then Moses replied, "But what if they don't believe me or listen to what I say? What if they say, 'The Lord didn't appear to you?'" **2.** So the Lord asked him, "What is that in your hand?" Moses answered, "A staff." **3.** The Lord said, "Throw it on the ground." When Moses threw it down, it turned into a snake, and Moses ran away from it. **4.** The Lord then told Moses, "Reach out and grab it by the tail." Moses stretched out his hand, grabbed it, and it became a staff again in his hand. **5.** The Lord said, "This will show them that the Lord, the God of their ancestors—the God of Abraham, the God of Isaac, and the God of Jacob—has appeared to you." **6.** Then the Lord said to Moses, "Now put your hand inside your cloak." Moses obeyed, and when he took it out, his hand was covered with leprosy, as white as snow. **7.** The Lord told him, "Put your hand back inside your cloak." Moses did so, and when he took it out again, it was healed, and as good as it had been before. **8.** The Lord explained, "If they don't believe you or pay attention to the first sign, they may believe the second sign. **9.** If they still don't believe these two signs or listen to your voice, then take some water from the Nile River and pour it on the dry ground. The water you take from the river will turn to blood on the ground." **10.** But Moses said to the Lord, "O Lord, I am not a good speaker. I've never been eloquent, neither before nor after You have spoken to me. I am slow of speech and slow of tongue." **11.** The Lord said to him, "Who made man's mouth? Who makes people mute, deaf, seeing, or blind? Isn't it I, the Lord? **12.** Now go, and I will help you speak and teach you what to say." **13.** But Moses replied, "Please, Lord, send someone else." **14.** Then the Lord became angry with Moses and said, "Isn't Aaron the Levite, your brother? I know that he can speak well. He is on his way to meet you, and when he sees you, his heart will be glad. **15.** You will speak to him and tell him what to say, and I will help both of you speak. I will teach you both what to do. **16.** He will speak for you to the people, and he will be like a mouth for you, and you will be like God to him. **17.** And take this staff in your hand, with which you will perform the signs." **18.** So

Moses went back to his father-in-law Jethro (Jethro was the priest of Midian), and said to him, "Please let me go back to my people in Egypt to see if they are still alive." Jethro replied, "Go in peace." **19.** The Lord said to Moses in Midian (a region east of Egypt), "Go back to Egypt, for all the people who wanted to kill you are dead." **20.** So Moses took his wife and sons, set them on a donkey, and started back to Egypt. He also took the staff of God in his hand. **21.** The Lord said to Moses, "When you return to Egypt, perform all the wonders I have given you the power to do before Pharaoh. But I will make his heart stubborn so that he won't let the people go. **22.** Then tell Pharaoh, 'this is what the Lord says: Israel is my son, my firstborn. **23.** So I tell you, let my son go, so he may worship me. But if you refuse to let him go, I will kill your firstborn son.'" **24.** On the way to Egypt, at a resting place, the Lord confronted Moses and was about to kill him. **25.** But Zipporah, his wife, took a flint knife, cut off her son's foreskin, and touched Moses' feet with it. She said, "Surely you are a bridegroom of blood to me!" **26.** So, the Lord let him go. She said, "You are a bridegroom of blood," referring to the circumcision. **27.** The Lord told Aaron, "Go into the wilderness and meet Moses." So, Aaron went and met Moses at the mountain of God, and they embraced. **28.** Moses told Aaron all the words of the Lord who had sent him, and about all the signs He had commanded him to perform. **29.** Then Moses and Aaron gathered all the elders of the Israelites. **30.** Aaron spoke all the words the Lord had spoken to Moses and performed the signs in front of the people. **31.** The people believed, and when they heard that the Lord had visited the Israelites and seen their misery, they bowed down and worshiped.

Chapter 5

1. Afterward, Moses and Aaron went in and spoke to Pharaoh, saying, "This is what the Lord God of Israel says: 'Let My people go, so that they may hold a feast to me in the wilderness.'" **2.** But Pharaoh responded, "Who is the Lord that I should listen to His voice and let Israel go? I do not know the Lord, and I will not let Israel go." **3.** So, Moses and Aaron said, "The God of the Hebrews has met with us. Please, let us go three days' journey into the desert to sacrifice to the Lord our God. If you don't, He may strike us with pestilence (a deadly disease) or with the sword (military attack)." **4.** But Pharaoh said, "Moses and Aaron, why are you distracting the people from their work? Go back to your labor." **5.** Pharaoh added, "Look, the people of the land are many now, and you want them to rest from their work!" **6.** so that very day, Pharaoh commanded the taskmasters (supervisors) of the people and their officers (leaders) saying, **7.** "You will no longer provide the people with straw to make bricks as you did before. Let them go and gather straw for themselves. **8.** But you must still require them to make the same amount of bricks as they did before. Do not reduce their quota. They are lazy, and that is why they cry out, 'Let us go and sacrifice to our God.' **9.** Increase their work so that they will be too busy to listen to false promises." **10.** The taskmasters and officers went out and spoke to the people, saying, "This is what Pharaoh says: 'I will not give you straw. **11.** Go and gather straw wherever you can find it, but your work will not be reduced.'" **12.** So the people scattered throughout all the land of Egypt to gather stubble (leftover pieces of straw) instead of straw. **13.** The taskmasters urged them on, saying, "Complete your daily work as you did when there was straw." **14.** The officers (Israelite leaders) whom Pharaoh's taskmasters had appointed over the people were beaten and asked, "Why haven't you finished your required amount of bricks both yesterday and today, as you did before?" **15.** So the officers of the children of Israel came and cried out to Pharaoh, saying, "Why are you treating your servants this way? **16.** No straw is given to your servants, yet they tell us, 'Make bricks!' And we are being beaten, but the fault is with your people." **17.** But Pharaoh answered, "You are lazy! Lazy! That is why you say, 'Let us go and sacrifice to the Lord.' **18.** Now go back to work. You will not be given straw, but you must still make the same amount of bricks." **19.** The officers of the children of Israel saw that they were in serious trouble when it was said, "You shall not reduce your daily quota of bricks." **20.** When they left Pharaoh, they met Moses and Aaron, who were waiting for them. **21.** They said to them, "May the Lord look on you and judge, because you have made us a stench (something unpleasant) in the sight of Pharaoh and his servants. You have put a sword (danger of death) in their hand to kill us." **22.** So Moses returned to the Lord and said, "Lord, why have you brought harm (trouble) to this people? Why did you send me? **23.** For ever since I came to Pharaoh to speak in your name, he has only harmed (mistreated) this people, and you have not delivered (rescued) your people at all."

Chapter 6

1. Then the Lord said to Moses, "Now you will witness what I will do to Pharaoh (king of Egypt). He will let the people go with a strong hand (force), and he will drive them out of his land with force (strong and powerful action)." **2.** God spoke further to Moses, saying, "I am the Lord (Yahweh, the eternal God). **3.** I appeared to Abraham, Isaac, and Jacob as God Almighty (El Shaddai), but I was not known to them by my name, 'the Lord (Yahweh).' **4.** I established (made firm) My covenant (agreement) with them, to give them the land of Canaan (the promised land, now called Israel), the land of their pilgrimage (temporary stay). **5.** I have heard the groaning (sighs of distress) of the children of Israel, whom the Egyptians keep in slavery (forced labor), and I have remembered my covenant with them. **6.** Therefore, say to the children of Israel, 'I am the Lord (Yahweh). I will bring you out from under the heavy burdens of the Egyptians. I will deliver (rescue) you from their bondage (captivity), and I will redeem (set free, buy back) you with an outstretched arm (powerful action) and with great judgments (punishments).' **7.** I will take you to be my people, and I will be your God. Then you will know that I am the Lord (Yahweh) your God, who brings you out from under the burdens (heavy tasks) of the Egyptians. **8.** I will bring you into the land I swore (promised) to give to Abraham, Isaac, and Jacob, and I will give it to you as a heritage (inheritance). I am the Lord (Yahweh).'" **9.** So, Moses told the children of Israel what God had said, but they did not listen to him because of their discouragement (great sorrow) and the harshness of their labor (severe work) under the Egyptians. **10.** Then the Lord spoke to Moses, saying, **11.** "Go in, tell Pharaoh (king of Egypt) to let the children of Israel go out of his land." **12.** But Moses said to the Lord, "The children of Israel have not listened to me. How then will Pharaoh listen to me? I am of uncircumcised lips (I am unworthy or unable to speak well)." **13.** The Lord spoke to Moses and Aaron (Moses' brother) and gave them a command (instruction) to speak to the children of Israel and to Pharaoh (king of Egypt), to bring the children of Israel out of Egypt. **14.** These are the names of the heads (leaders) of their father's households: the sons of Reuben (the firstborn of Israel) were Hanoch, Pallu, Hezron, and Carmi. These are the families of Reuben. **15.** The sons of Simeon were Jemuel, Jamin, Ohad, Jachin, Zohar, and Shaul, the son of a Canaanite woman (from the people of Canaan). These are the families of Simeon. **16.** These are the names of the sons of Levi according to their generations (descendants): Gershon, Kohath, and Merari. Levi lived for one hundred and thirty-seven years. **17.** The sons of Gershon were Libni and Shimi according to their families. **18.** The sons of Kohath were Amram, Izhar, Hebron, and Uzziel. Kohath lived for one hundred and thirty-three years. **19.** The sons of Merari were Mahali and Mushi. These are the families of Levi according to their generations. **20.** Amram married Jochebed, his father's sister (aunt), and she bore him Aaron and Moses. Amram lived for one hundred and thirty-seven years. **21.** The sons of Izhar were Korah, Nepheg, and Zichri. **22.** The sons of Uzziel were Mishael, Elzaphan, and Zithri. **23.** Aaron married Elisheba, daughter of Amminadab, and sister of Nahshon. She bore him Nadab, Abihu, Eleazar, and Ithamar. **24.** The sons of Korah were Assir, Elkanah, and Abiasaph.

These are the families of the Korahites (descendants of Korah). **25.** Eleazar, Aaron's son, married one of the daughters of Putiel, and she bore him Phinehas. These are the heads (leaders) of the father's households of the Levites (tribe of Levi), according to their families. **26.** These are the same Aaron and Moses to whom the Lord said, "Bring the children of Israel out of Egypt according to their armies." **27.** They are the ones who spoke to Pharaoh (king of Egypt), to bring the children of Israel out of Egypt. These are the same Moses and Aaron. **28.** It came to pass that on the day the Lord spoke to Moses in the land of Egypt, **29.** The Lord said to Moses, "I am the Lord (Yahweh). Speak to Pharaoh (king of Egypt), everything I tell you." **30.** But Moses said before the Lord, "Behold, I am of uncircumcised lips (I am unworthy or unable to speak well), and how will Pharaoh listen to me?"

Chapter 7

1. The Lord spoke to Moses, saying, "I have appointed you as a god to Pharaoh, and your brother Aaron will serve as your spokesperson. **2.** You are to communicate everything I command you, and Aaron will speak to Pharaoh on your behalf, telling him to release the children of Israel from his land. **3.** However, I will make Pharaoh's heart stubborn (unwilling to listen), and I will increase my signs and wonders in the land of Egypt. **4.** Despite this, Pharaoh will refuse to obey, and through great judgments, I will bring My people, the children of Israel, out of Egypt. **5.** The Egyptians will come to know that I am the Lord when I display My power over Egypt and deliver the Israelites from their bondage." **6.** Moses and Aaron obeyed the Lord's instructions without fail. **7.** Moses was eighty years old, and Aaron was eighty-three when they went to speak to Pharaoh. **8.** Then the Lord spoke again to Moses and Aaron, saying: **9.** "If Pharaoh demands that you prove your authority with a miracle, tells Aaron to take his rod and throw it down in front of Pharaoh, and it will turn into a snake." **10.** So, Moses and Aaron went to Pharaoh and did as the Lord had commanded. Aaron threw down his rod before Pharaoh and his officials, and it became a serpent. **11.** But Pharaoh summoned his magicians (those who practiced magic) and sorcerers (those who use occult powers), and they performed the same feat through their magical arts. **12.** Each magician threw down his rod, and it too became a serpent, but Aaron's rod swallowed up their rods. **13.** Pharaoh's heart grew stubborn (he refused to listen), just as the Lord had warned. **14.** Then the Lord spoke to Moses, saying: "Pharaoh's heart remains hard; he will not allow the people to go. **15.** Go to Pharaoh in the morning when he is at the river (the Nile), and stand by the riverbank to meet him. Take the rod that turned into a serpent and hold it in your hand. **16.** Tell him, 'The Lord, the God of the Hebrews, has sent me to you to say, "Let My people go, so that they may worship Me in the wilderness." But you have refused to listen until now. **17.** Here is the sign: "You will know that I am the Lord when I strike the waters of the Nile with this rod in my hand, and they will turn into blood. **18.** The fish in the river will die, and the river will become foul-smelling. The Egyptians will not be able to drink from the Nile.'" **19.** The Lord instructed Moses, "Tell Aaron to stretch out his hand with the rod over the waters of Egypt—over their rivers, streams, ponds, and pools—so that all their water will turn to blood. Even the water in the wooden buckets and stone pitchers will become blood." **20.** Moses and Aaron obeyed, and Aaron raised his rod and struck the waters of the Nile in front of Pharaoh and his officials. All the water in the river turned to blood. **21.** The fish in the river died, the river became foul-smelling, and the Egyptians could not drink from the Nile. Blood was everywhere throughout Egypt. **22.** The magicians of Egypt used their magic to do the same thing, but Pharaoh's heart grew even harder (more stubborn), and he refused to listen, just as the Lord had predicted. **23.** Pharaoh turned away and went back to his palace, paying no attention to what had happened. **24.** The Egyptians dug around the Nile for water to drink, since they could not use the water from the river. **25.** Seven days passed after the Lord struck the Nile.

Chapter 8

1. The Lord spoke to Moses, saying, "Go to Pharaoh and tell him, 'This is what the Lord says: "Let My people go so they can worship Me. **2.** If you refuse to let them go, I will bring a plague of frogs upon your entire land. **3.** The river will be filled with frogs, and they will spread into your homes, your bedrooms, your beds, your servants' houses, and onto your people. They will even enter your ovens and kneading bowls. **4.** The frogs will be everywhere—on you, your servants, and your people." **5.** Then the Lord spoke to Moses again, saying, "Tell Aaron to stretch out his staff over the rivers, ponds, and streams, and bring frogs upon the land of Egypt." **6.** So, Aaron did as instruct, and frogs covered the land of Egypt. **7.** The magicians (sorcerers or practitioners of magic) also performed their enchantments and brought more frogs onto the land. **8.** Pharaoh then called for Moses and Aaron and said, "Pray to the Lord to take the frogs away from me and my people, and I will allow the people to go and sacrifice to the Lord." **9.** Moses replied, "You tell me when you want me to pray to the Lord to remove the frogs from you and your people, and they will only stay in the river." **10.** Pharaoh answered, "Tomorrow." And Moses said, "It will be as you have said, so that you will know there is no one like the Lord our God. **11.** The frogs will leave you, your houses, your servants, and your people, and they will remain only in the river." **12.** Moses and Aaron left Pharaoh, and Moses cried out to the Lord about the frogs He had brought upon Egypt. **13.** The Lord did as Moses asked, and the frogs died in the houses, the courtyards, and the fields. **14.** They were gathered into piles, and the land stank from the decay. **15.** But when Pharaoh saw that there was relief, he became stubborn (refused to change) and did not listen to Moses and Aaron, just as the Lord had warned. **16.** Then the Lord told Moses, "Tell Aaron to strike the dust of the earth with his staff, and it will turn to lice (tiny, parasitic insects) all over the land of Egypt." **17.** So, Aaron did so, and the dust became lice on both people and animals. All the dust of the land turned to lice. **18.** The Egyptian magicians tried to produce lice with their magic, but they could not. There were lice on both man and beast. **19.** The magicians told Pharaoh, "This is the finger of God." But Pharaoh's heart remained stubborn, and he did not listen to them, just as the Lord had predicted. **20.** The Lord said to Moses, "Get up early in the morning and meet Pharaoh as he goes to the water. Say to him, 'This is what the Lord says: "Let My people go so they can worship Me. **21.** If you refuse to let them go, I will send swarms (large groups) of flies upon you, your servants, your people, and into your houses. The houses of the Egyptians will be filled with flies, and the land will be covered with them. **22.** But on that day, I will set apart (separate) the land of Goshen (the area where the Israelites live), so that no flies will be there. This will show you that I am the Lord in the midst of the land. **23.** I will make a clear distinction (difference) between My people and your people. Tomorrow, this sign will happen. **24.** The Lord followed through with His command. Swarms of flies filled Pharaoh's palace, the homes of his officials, and spread throughout all of Egypt. The land was devastated by the flies. **25.** Pharaoh called for Moses and Aaron and said, "Go ahead and offer sacrifices (ritual offerings) to your God right here in the land." **26.** Moses answered, "That wouldn't be right; for we would be sacrificing (offering) to the Lord our God what the Egyptians consider detestable (something deeply offensive or immoral). If we offer these in their presence, they might stone us (throw stones at us to kill us)." **27.** "We need to take a three-day journey into the wilderness to offer sacrifices to the Lord our God, as He has commanded us." **28.** Pharaoh replied, "I'll allow you to go so that you can sacrifice to the Lord in the wilderness, but don't go too far. And also, pray for me." **29.** Moses said, "I will leave and pray to the Lord to remove the swarms (large groups) of flies from you, your officials, and your people. But don't trick us again by refusing to let the people go to worship (honor through religious acts) the Lord." **30.** After speaking to Pharaoh, Moses departed and prayed to the Lord. **31.** The Lord did as Moses asked and removed the swarms of flies from Pharaoh, his servants, and his people. Not a single fly remained. **32.** But Pharaoh once again hardened his heart and did not let the people go.

Chapter 9

1. The Lord instructed Moses, "Go to Pharaoh and say to him, 'This is what the Lord, the God of the Hebrews, says: Let My people go, so that they may worship (fete through religious acts) Me. **2.** But if you refuse to let them go, and continue to hold them, I will strike all your beast (brutes raised for food or work) in the fields — your horses, donkeys, camels, cattle, and angel with a severe complaint. **4.** Still, the Lord will make a distinction (a difference) between the beast of Israel and the beast of Egypt. Not one of the Israelites' brutes will die.'" **5.** The Lord set a time for this to be, saying, "Henceforth, the Lord will carry out this act in Egypt." **6.** The coming day, the Lord did exactly as He would said: all the beast of the Egyptians failed, but none of the brutes belonging to the Israelites were harmed. **7.** Pharaoh transferred out officers to check, and they vindicated that none of the Israelites' brutes had failed. Yet, Pharaoh's heart came hardened (stubborn and unintentional to change), and he still refused to let the people go. **8.** Also, the Lord said to Moses and Aaron, "Take some ashes from a furnace (a place where goods are toast) and have Moses scatter them in front of Pharaoh. **9.** The ashes will turn to dust across all of Egypt, and it will beget painful boils (sore, blown areas on the skin) to break out on both people and brutes throughout the land of Egypt." **10.** They took the ashes, stood before Pharaoh, and Moses scattered them toward the sky. The ashes came dust, and it caused boils to break out on both people and brutes. **11.** The magicians (those who rehearsed magic) couldn't stand before Moses because of the boils, for the boils were on them as well as on all the Egyptians. **12.** Still, the Lord made Pharaoh's heart stubborn (unintentional to change), and he refused to hear to Moses and Aaron, as the Lord had read. **13.** Also, the Lord instructed Moses, "Get up beforehand henceforth and go to Pharaoh. Tell him, 'This is what the Lord, the God of the Hebrews, says: Let My people go so that they may worship (offer devotion to) Me. **14.** Still, I will shoot all My pests (destructive forces or disasters) to strike you and your officers and people, so that you will know there is no bone like Me in all the earth. If you don't, **15.** Still, you would have been entirely destroyed from the face of the earth, if I had extended My hand against you and your people with a ruinous pest (a wide complaint or disaster). **16.** But I have kept you alive for this truly purpose — to show you My power, and so that My name will be declared throughout the earth. **17.** Yet you continue to defy (repel or oppose) My people by refusing to let them go. **18.** Henceforth at this time, I will shoot a hailstorm (ice and rain falling from the sky) unlike anything Egypt has ever endured since it was founded. **19.** "So now, shoot a communication to gather your beast and everything you have in the fields, for the hail will come down on all that remains outside, and they will die." **20.** Those among Pharaoh's retainers who respected the Lord's word snappily brought their retainers and brutes into sanctum. **21.** But those who ignored the Lord's warning left their retainers and beast out in the open fields. **22.** Also, the Lord said to Moses, "Stretch out your hand toward the sky, so that hail may fall throughout Egypt — on people, brutes, and every plant in the fields." **23.** Moses raised his staff toward heaven, and the Lord unleashed thunder, hail, and lightning flashing down to the ground. A severe hailstorm struck Egypt. **24.** The hail, mixed with fire, was so violent that nothing like it had ever been seen in Egypt since it came a nation. **25.** The hail devastated everything in the fields, killing both people and brutes, and shattered every tree and plant in its path. **26.** Yet in Goshen (the region where the Israelites lived), no hail fell. **27.** Pharaoh also called for Moses and Aaron, admitting, "This time, I have transgressed. The Lord is righteous, while my people and I have been wicked (innocently wrong)." **28.** Supplicate to the Lord and ask Him to stop the thunder and the hail. That's enough. I will let you go, and you won't be delayed (kept from going) presently." **29.** Moses replied, "As soon as I leave the municipality, I will spread my hands toward the Lord, and the thunder will stop, and there will be no farther hail, so that you will know that the earth belongs to the Lord. **30.** But as for you and your officers, I know that you will still not sweat (show respect or reverence for) the Lord God." **31.** The flax and barley were destroyed because the barley was formerly in observance (the stage when the grain is nearly ready to gather) and the flax was in bloom. **32.** But the wheat and spelt (a type of wheat) were not destroyed because they were subsequently crops. **33.** Moses left Pharaoh's presence, went outside the municipality, and spread his hands to the Lord. The thunder and hail stopped, and the rain no longer fell on the land. **34.** When Pharaoh saw that the rain, hail, and thunder had stopped, he continued to transgress. He and his officers grew indeed more stubborn. **35.** Pharaoh's heart remained hard, and he still refused to let the Israelites go, just as the Lord had said through Moses.

Chapter 10

1. Then the Lord spoke to Moses, saying, "Go to Pharaoh, for I have made his heart stubborn (resistant to change), as well as the hearts of his officials, so that I may display these powerful signs of Mine among them, **2.** and so you can tell your children and your grandchildren about the great deeds I have done in Egypt, and the miracles I have shown among them. This will allow you to understand that I am the Lord." **3.** So, Moses and Aaron went to Pharaoh and said to him, "This is what the Lord, the God of the Hebrews, says: 'How long will you refuse to humble yourself before Me? Let My people go, so they can worship Me. **4.** But if you keep refusing to let My people go, I will bring locusts (a type of grasshopper) into your land tomorrow. **5.** They will cover the entire land, so that nothing will be visible. They will consume what is left after the hailstorm and will eat every tree that grows in the field. **6.** The locusts will fill your homes, the homes of your servants, and the homes of all the Egyptians—things that neither your ancestors nor your ancestors' ancestors have ever seen since the time they have been on the earth, up until now.'" Then Moses turned and left Pharaoh's presence. **7.** Pharaoh's officials said to him, "How long will this man be a snare (trap) for us? Let the people go, so they can serve the Lord their God. Do you not realize that Egypt is being destroyed?" **8.** So, Moses and Aaron were brought back to Pharaoh, and he said to them, "Go, serve the Lord your God. But who exactly is going with you?" **9.** Moses replied, "We will go with our young and our old, with our sons and daughters, and with our flocks and herds, because we need to celebrate a feast to the Lord." **10.** Pharaoh said to them, "The Lord is with you if I let you and your families go! Look, evil is ahead of you! **11.** No! Only the men may go and serve the Lord, since that is what you have asked for." Then he drove them out of Pharaoh's presence. **12.** Then the Lord said to Moses, "Stretch out your hand over Egypt, so that locusts may swarm over the land and eat every plant of the land that the hail left behind." **13.** So, Moses stretched out his staff over Egypt, and the Lord sent a powerful east wind (a wind coming from the east) to blow across the land all day and night. By morning, the east wind brought the locusts. **14.** The locusts settled across the entire land of Egypt, covering every part of the country. They were so numerous that there had never been locusts like them before, and there would never be again. **15.** They covered the land so completely that it was as though the sun was blocked out. They ate every green plant and every fruit from the trees that had survived the hail. Nothing green was left on any tree or plant throughout Egypt. **16.** Pharaoh quickly summoned Moses and Aaron and said, "I have sinned against the Lord your God and against you. **17.** Now, please forgive my sin just this once, and pray to the Lord your God to take this deadly plague away from me." **18.** So, Moses left Pharaoh and prayed to the Lord. **19.** The Lord sent a very strong west wind (a wind coming from the west) to blow the locusts into the Red Sea. Not a single locust remained in the entire land of Egypt. **20.** But the Lord hardened Pharaoh's heart, and he refused to let the Israelites go. **21.** Then the Lord instructed Moses, "Stretch out your hand toward the sky, so that darkness will cover Egypt—a darkness that can be physically felt." **22.** So, Moses stretched out his hand toward the sky, and thick darkness fell over Egypt for three days. **23.** For three days, the people could not see one another, and no one moved from their place. But the Israelites had light where they lived. **24.** Pharaoh called Moses and said, "Go, serve the Lord; but leave your flocks and herds behind. Let your children also go with you." **25.** Moses answered, "You must also provide us with sacrifices and burnt offerings to offer to the Lord our God. **26.** Our livestock must go with us; not a single hoof will be left behind. We need some of them for worshiping the Lord our God and we do not know what we will need to sacrifice until we get there." **27.** But the Lord hardened Pharaoh's heart, and he refused to let them go. **28.** Pharaoh said to Moses, "Get away from me! Watch yourself and make sure I do not see your face again. The day you see my face, you will die!" **29.** Moses replied, "You have spoken correctly. I will never see your face again."

Chapter 11

1. The Lord said to Moses, "I will bring one final plague upon Pharaoh and Egypt. After this, Pharaoh will let you go. In fact, he will force you to leave his land completely. **2.** Speak to the Israelites and tell them to ask their Egyptian neighbors for silver and gold jewelry." **3.** The Lord made the Israelites favorably regarded (respected) by the Egyptians. Additionally, Moses became highly honored in the land of Egypt, in the eyes of Pharaoh's servants and the people. **4.** Moses then spoke, "This is what the Lord says: 'At midnight, I will go out into the heart of Egypt; **5.** and every firstborn (oldest child) in Egypt will die, from Pharaoh's firstborn son who sits on his throne, to the firstborn daughter of the female servant grinding grain, and even the firstborn of the animals. **6.** There will be a great cry throughout all Egypt, a sound like nothing the land has ever heard before, and nothing like it will ever be heard again. **7.** But among the Israelites, not even a dog will bark at any person or animal, so that you will know the Lord makes a clear distinction (difference) between Egypt and Israel.' **8.** After this, all your officials will come to me, bowing down and saying, 'Leave, along with everyone who follows you!' After that, I will go." Moses left Pharaoh in great anger. **9.** But the Lord told Moses, "Pharaoh will not listen to you, so that my mighty acts (wonders) can be shown even more throughout Egypt." **10.** So, Moses and Aaron performed all these signs in front of Pharaoh, but the Lord hardened Pharaoh's heart (caused him to resist), and he refused to let the Israelites leave his land.

Chapter 12

1. The Lord spoke to Moses and Aaron while they were still in Egypt, saying, **2.** "This month will be the first month for you. It will begin your year. **3.** Tell all the Israelites: 'On the tenth day of this month, each family is to select a lamb for themselves, a lamb for each household. **4.** If a household is too small to eat a whole lamb, they should share it with their closest neighbor, depending on how much they will eat. **5.** The lamb you choose must be without any defect, a male, one year old. It can be from the sheep or the goats. **6.** Keep it until the fourteenth day of the month. At twilight (the time between sunset and complete darkness), the whole congregation of Israel must kill it. **7.** Take some of the lamb's blood and put it on the doorframes and the lintel (the top of the doorframe) of the houses where you will eat it. **8.** That night, roast the lamb over fire and eat it with unleavened bread (bread made without yeast) and bitter herbs (herbs that symbolize hardship). **9.** Do not eat it raw or boiled, but roast it fully over the fire, including its head, legs, and inner organs. **10.** Do not leave any of it until morning. Any leftover lamb must be burned. **11.** This is how you must eat it: with your belt fastened sandals on your feet, and a staff (walking stick) in your hand. Eat it quickly. It is the Lord's Passover. **12.** On that night, I will pass through the land of Egypt and strike down every firstborn (the firstborn of both humans and animals) in Egypt. I will bring judgment upon all the gods (idols) of Egypt. I am the Lord. **13.** The blood on your houses will serve as a sign for you. When I see the blood, I will pass over your home and will not allow the destroyer (the angel of death) to enter and strike you down. **14.** This day will be a lasting memorial for you. Celebrate it as a festival to the Lord for all generations. It is a permanent command (ordinance). **15.** For seven days, you must eat unleavened bread. On the first day, remove all yeast (leaven) from your homes. Anyone who eats leavened bread during this time must be cut off (excluded) from Israel. **16.** On the first and seventh days, you will have a sacred assembly (gathering for worship). No work should be done except to prepare food for everyone to eat. **17.** You must keep the Feast of Unleavened Bread, because it was on this day that I brought your armies out of Egypt. Celebrate this as a lasting ordinance throughout your generations. **18.** In the first month, on the fourteenth day at evening, eat unleavened bread, and continue until the twenty-first day at evening. **19.** For seven days, there must be no yeast in your houses. Anyone who eats leavened bread during this time will be cut off from Israel, whether they are a native Israelite or a foreigner. **20.** You must eat only unleavened bread in all your homes." **21.** Then Moses called for all the elders (leaders) of Israel and said to them, "Go and choose lambs for your families and slaughter the Passover lamb. **22.** Take a bunch of hyssop (a plant used for sprinkling) and dip it into the blood in the basin, then strike the doorposts and lintel with the blood. Do not leave your house until morning. **23.** The Lord will pass through Egypt to strike down the Egyptians, but when He sees the blood on the doorframes, He will pass over your house and not allow the destroyer to enter and harm you. **24.** This is a permanent ordinance for you and your descendants. **25.** When you come to the land the Lord will give you, as He promised, keep this service. **26.** When your children ask you, 'What does this ceremony mean to you?' **27.** Tell them, 'It is the Passover sacrifice to the Lord, who passed over the houses of the Israelites in Egypt when He struck down the Egyptians but spared our homes.'" Then the people bowed down and worshiped. **28.** The Israelites did exactly as Moses and Aaron instructed, and followed all the commands the Lord had given them. **29.** At midnight, the Lord struck down every firstborn in Egypt, from the firstborn of Pharaoh sitting on his throne to the firstborn of the prisoner in the dungeon, and all the firstborn of livestock. **30.** Pharaoh and all his officials, along with all the Egyptians, rose up during the night. There was loud wailing throughout Egypt, for there was not a house where someone was not dead. **31.** During the night, Pharaoh summoned Moses and Aaron and said, "Get up, leave my people, both you and the Israelites! Go, serve the Lord as you have said. **32.** Take your flocks and herds, as you have requested, and go. Also, bless me." **33.** The Egyptians urged the Israelites to leave quickly, saying, "Otherwise, we will all die." **34.** So, the Israelites took their dough before it had leavened (yeast), and wrapped their kneading bowls (bowls used to prepare dough) in their clothes on their shoulders. **35.** The Israelites had done as Moses had instructed and asked the Egyptians for silver and gold jewelry, and clothing. **36.** The Lord caused the Egyptians to favor the Israelites, so they gave them whatever they asked for. Thus, the Israelites plundered (took goods by force) the Egyptians. **37.** The Israelites traveled from Rameses (a city in Egypt) to Succoth (a place of rest), about six hundred thousand men on foot, excluding women and children. **38.** A mixed group (non-Israelites who joined them) also went with them, along with large herds of livestock. **39.** They baked unleavened bread from the dough they had brought out of Egypt, because it had no yeast. They had been hurriedly driven out of

Egypt and had no time to prepare food. **40.** The time the Israelites lived in Egypt was 430 years. **41.** At the end of 430 years, on that very day, all the Lord's divisions (groups of people) left Egypt. **42.** That night, the Lord kept vigil (watched over them) to bring them out of Egypt. This is the night of the Lord, a vigil for all the Israelites for all generations. **43.** The Lord said to Moses and Aaron, "These are the regulations for the Passover: No foreigner (non-Israelite) is to eat it. **44.** Any slave you have bought may eat it after being circumcised (performing a ritual of cutting off the foreskin). **45.** A temporary resident or hired worker may not eat it. **46.** It must be eaten inside one house. Do not take any of the meat outside the house, and do not break any of its bones. **47.** The entire community of Israel must celebrate it. **48.** If a foreigner lives among you and wants to celebrate the Passover to the Lord, let all the males in his household be circumcised, and then they may participate as if they were born in the land. No uncircumcised person may eat it. **49.** The same law applies to the native-born and to the foreigner who dwells among you." **50.** All the Israelites did just as the Lord commanded Moses and Aaron. **51.** On that very day, the Lord brought the Israelites out of Egypt by their divisions.

Chapter 13

1. The Lord spoke to Moses, saying, **2.** "Set apart for Me all the firstborn, whether mortal or beast, from the Israelites; they belong to Me." **3.** Moses instructed the people, "Flash back this day, the day you left Egypt, the land of slavery, because the Lord brought you out with His mighty hand. You mustn't eat any dough that contains leaven (a rising agent)." **4.** This day marks your exodus, which takes place in the month of Abib (the first month of the Hebrew calendar, roughly March or April). **5.** When the Lord leads you into the land of the Canaanites, Hittites, Amorites, Hivites, and Jebusites — the land He promised to your ancestors, a land flowing with milk and honey — you must observe this feast in this month. **6.** For seven days, you'll eat unleavened bread, and on the seventh day, you'll hold a feast in honor of the Lord. **7.** During these seven days, you must eat only unleavened bread. No leavened bread should be found among you, nor should any leaven (yeast) be present in your land. **8.** On that day, you'll explain to your son, "We do this because of what the Lord did for me when I came out of Egypt." **9.** It will serve as a sign on your hand and a memorial between your eyes, so that the law of the Lord will always be on your lips, because with a strong hand, the Lord brought you out of Egypt. **10.** Thus, you must observe this command at the appointed time every year. **11.** "When the Lord brings you into the land of the Canaanites, as He promised to give it to your ancestors, you must devote (set apart as holy) to the Lord every firstborn male that opens the womb, whether human or beast. The firstborn males belong to the Lord." **13.** Still, every firstborn donkey must be redeemed (bought back) with a lamb. However, if you do not redeem it, you must break its neck. Every firstborn of your sons must also be redeemed. **14.** When your son asks you in the future, "What does this mean?" you'll answer him, "By the strength of the Lord's hand, He brought us out of Egypt, the land of slavery. **15.** When Pharaoh refused to let us go, the Lord struck down all the firstborn in the land of Egypt — both human and beast. Thus, I sacrifice to the Lord all the firstborn males of animals, but I redeem my firstborn sons." **16.** This will serve as a sign on your hand and a memorial on your forehead, for with a mighty hand, the Lord brought us out of Egypt." **17.** When Pharaoh eventually allowed the people to leave, God did not lead them along the most direct route through the land of the Philistines (an ancient people living along the coastal regions), even though it was shorter. God said, "If the people face war, they may change their minds and return to Egypt." **18.** Rather, God led them around by the wilderness (a dry, desolate region) toward the Red Sea (the body of water the Israelites crossed). The Israelites left Egypt in orderly ranks. **19.** Moses took the bones of Joseph with him, for Joseph had made the Israelites swear an oath, saying, "God will surely visit you, and when He does, you must take my bones with you from here." **20.** They left Succoth (a location in Egypt) and camped at Etham (a place at the edge of the wilderness). **21.** The Lord went ahead of them in a pillar of cloud by day to guide them, and in a pillar of fire by night to give them light, so they could travel both day and night. **22.** The pillar of cloud by day and the pillar of fire by night did not depart from the people.

Chapter 14

1. The Lord then spoke to Moses, saying: **2.** "Tell the Israelites to turn back and set up camp in front of Pi Hahiroth (a location near the sea), between Migdol (a tower or fort) and the sea, across from Baal Zephon (a place near the shore). They should camp there by the sea. **3.** Pharaoh will think that the Israelites are lost, wandering aimlessly in the wilderness, and that the land has trapped them. **4.** But I will harden Pharaoh's heart, and he will come after them. I will display My power over Pharaoh and his army, so that the Egyptians will know that I am the Lord." The Israelites followed God's instructions. **5.** When Pharaoh was told that the people had escaped, he and his officials changed their minds. They said, "What have we done? Why did we let Israel go, freeing them from serving us?" **6.** So, Pharaoh prepared his chariot, took his army, **7.** and selected six hundred of Egypt's finest chariots, along with all the other chariots of Egypt, each commanded by its own captain. **8.** The Lord again hardened Pharaoh's heart, and he pursued the Israelites, who had left Egypt boldly. **9.** The Egyptians followed after them with all of Pharaoh's horses, chariots, and cavalry, and they caught up with the Israelites as they camped by the sea near Pi Hahiroth, in front of Baal Zephon. **10.** When the Israelites saw Pharaoh's army approaching, they became terrified and cried out to the Lord. **11.** They said to Moses, "Did you bring us into the wilderness to die? Were there not enough graves in Egypt? **12.** Didn't we tell you in Egypt to leave us alone and let us serve the Egyptians? It would have been better for us to remain in Egypt as slaves than to die here." **13.** Moses responded to the people, "Do not be afraid. Stand firm and see the salvation (rescue) that the Lord will provide for you today. You will never see these Egyptians again. **14.** The Lord will fight for you, and all you need to do is remain calm." **15.** The Lord then said to Moses, "Why are you crying out to Me? Tell the Israelites to keep moving forward. **16.** Lift up your staff, stretch your hand over the sea, and divide it, so that the Israelites can cross on dry ground. **17.** I will harden the hearts of the Egyptians, and they will follow the Israelites. I will gain glory over Pharaoh, his army, his chariots, and his horsemen. **18.** The Egyptians will know that I am the Lord when I show My glory through Pharaoh and his army." **19.** The Angel of God, who had been leading the Israelites, moved to stand behind them. The pillar of cloud also moved from in front of them and stood behind, **20.** coming between the camp of Egypt and the camp of Israel. It caused darkness for the Egyptians, but it gave light to the Israelites all night, so that the two armies could not come near each other. **21.** Then Moses stretched out his hand over the sea, and that night the Lord sent a powerful east wind that blew all night, dividing the sea and making the dry ground appear. **22.** The Israelites walked through the sea on dry land, with walls of water on their right and left. **23.** The Egyptians followed them into the sea with all of Pharaoh's horses, chariots, and horsemen. **24.** Just before dawn, the Lord looked down from the pillar of fire and cloud upon the Egyptian army and threw them into confusion. **25.** He caused their chariot wheels to become stuck, making it difficult for them to drive. The Egyptians shouted, "Let's get away from the Israelites, because the Lord is fighting for them against us!" **26.** The Lord then said to Moses, "Stretch out your hand over the sea, so that the waters may return over the Egyptians and their chariots and horsemen." **27.** Moses stretched out his hand over the sea, and as the sun began to rise, the sea returned to its normal depth, while the Egyptians were trying to escape. The Lord drowned them in the sea. **28.** The waters returned, covering the chariots, horsemen, and the entire army of Pharaoh that had followed the Israelites into the sea. Not one of them survived. **29.** But the Israelites walked on dry ground through the sea, with the waters forming a wall on their right and on their left. **30.** That day, the Lord saved Israel from the Egyptians, and when the Israelites saw the dead bodies of the Egyptians washed up on the shore, **31.** they saw the great power that the Lord had displayed against the Egyptians. The people feared the Lord and put their trust in Him and His servant Moses.

Chapter 15

1. Then Moses and the Israelites broke into a song of praise to the Lord: "I will sing to the Lord, for He has achieved a mighty victory! He has cast both the horse and its rider into the sea. **2.** The Lord is my strength and my song; He has become my Savior (rescuer). He is my God, and I will praise Him. He is the God of my forefathers, and I will honor and exalt Him. **3.** The Lord is a warrior; His name is the Lord. **4.** Pharaoh's chariots and army were cast into the sea; his chosen officers sank to the depths of the Red Sea. **5.** The waters engulfed them, and they sank like stones into the deep. **6.** Your right hand, O Lord, is glorious in strength; Your right hand, O Lord, has broken the enemy. **7.** In Your majestic power, You defeated those who rose against You. You unleashed Your fury, and it consumed them like dry grass scorched by fire. **8.** With a breath from Your nostrils, the waters parted; the waves stood tall like walls, and the sea froze in place. **9.** The enemy said, 'I will chase them, I will overtake them, I will divide the spoils, and I will satisfy my desires. I will unsheathe my sword, and I will destroy them.' **10.** But You blew with Your wind, and the waters covered them; they sank like lead in the mighty flood. **11.** "Who is like You, O Lord, among the gods? Who is like You, majestic in holiness, awesome in praise, and performing wonders? **12.** You stretched out Your hand, and the earth swallowed them whole. **13.** In Your compassion, You led the people You saved. You guided them with Your strength to Your holy dwelling place. **14.** The nations will hear of what You have done and will tremble. The people of Philistia (an ancient coastal group) will be filled with fear. **15.** The leaders of Edom (a nation southeast of Israel) will be afraid; the mighty men of Moab (east of Israel) will tremble; all the inhabitants of Canaan (the Promised Land) will be struck with terror. **16.** Fear and dread will fall on them. By the power of Your arm, they will remain motionless like stone, until Your people have passed through—until the people You redeemed have crossed over. **17.** You will bring them in and plant them on the mountain of Your inheritance (a promised and sacred place), the place where You have established Your dwelling, the sanctuary (holy place) that Your hands have made. **18.** The Lord will reign forever and ever. **19.** Pharaoh's horses, chariots, and horsemen plunged into the sea, but the Lord caused the waters to return upon them. The Israelites, however, walked through the sea on dry land. **20.** Then Miriam, the prophetess (a woman who speaks on behalf of God), the sister of Aaron, took a tambourine, and all the women followed her, playing tambourines and dancing. **21.** Miriam sang to them: "Sing to the Lord, for He has triumphed gloriously! The horse and its rider He has thrown into the sea!" **22.** Moses led Israel from the Red Sea, and they journeyed into the Wilderness of Shur. They traveled for three days without finding water. **23.** When they came to Marah (a place with bitter water), they could not drink it because it was bitter. That is why the place was called Marah. **24.** The people grumbled to Moses, asking, "What shall we drink?" **25.** So Moses cried out to the Lord, and the Lord showed him a tree. When Moses threw the tree into the water, the water became sweet. There the Lord set a rule and a law for them, and He tested them. **26.** He said, "If you listen closely to the voice of the Lord your God and do what is right in His sight, if you pay attention to His commands and keep all His laws, I will not bring upon you any of the diseases I brought upon the Egyptians. For I am the Lord who heals (restores and makes whole) you." **27.** Then they arrived at Elim (a place with twelve springs of water and seventy palm trees), and they camped there by the water.

Chapter 16

1. The Israelites set out from Elim, and the entire congregation arrived at the Wilderness of Sin, located between Elim and Sinai, on the fifteenth day of the second month after leaving Egypt. **2.** In the wilderness, the whole congregation of the Israelites complained against Moses and Aaron. **3.** The Israelites said to them, "If only we had died by the Lord's hand in Egypt! There we sat around pots of meat and ate all the bread we wanted! But you have brought us out into this wilderness to starve this entire assembly to death." **4.** Then the Lord said to Moses, "I will rain down bread from heaven for you. The people are to go out each day and gather enough for that day. This way, I can test them to see whether they will follow My instructions. **5.** On the sixth day, they are to prepare what they bring in, and it will be twice as much as they gather on the other days." **6.** So Moses and Aaron said to all the Israelites, "In the evening you will know that it was the Lord who brought you out of Egypt. **7.** And in the morning, you will see the glory of the Lord, because He has heard your grumbling against Him. Who are we that you should complain against us?" **8.** Moses also said, "You will know it is the Lord who gives you meat to eat in the evening and bread in the morning, because He has heard your grumbling against Him. You are not complaining against us but against the Lord." **9.** Moses told Aaron, "Say to the whole Israelite community, 'Come before the Lord, for He has heard your grumbling.'" **10.** As Aaron spoke to the whole Israelite community, they looked toward the wilderness, and there appeared the glory of the Lord in the cloud. **11.** The Lord said to Moses, **12.** "I have heard the grumbling of the Israelites. Tell them, 'At twilight you will eat meat, and in the morning, you will be filled with bread. Then you will know that I am the Lord your God.'" **13.** That evening, quails came and covered the camp, and in the morning, there was a layer of dew around the camp. **14.** When the dew was gone, thin flakes like frost appeared on the ground in the desert. **15.** When the Israelites saw it, they said to one another, "What is it?" For they did not know what it was. Moses said to them, "It is the bread the Lord has given you to eat. **16.** This is what the Lord has commanded: 'Everyone is to gather as much as they need. Take an omer for each person you have in your tent.'" **17.** The Israelites did as they were told; some gathered much, some little. **18.** And when they measured it by the omer, the one who gathered much did not have too much, and the one who gathered little did not have too little. Everyone had gathered just as much as they needed. **19.** Then Moses said to them, "No one is to keep any of it until morning." **20.** However, some of them paid no attention to Moses; they kept part of it until morning, but it was full of worms and began to smell. So Moses was angry with them. **21.** Each morning everyone gathered as much as they needed, and when the sun grew hot, it melted away. **22.** On the sixth day, they gathered twice as much, two omers for each person, and all the leaders of the community came and reported this to Moses. **23.** He said to them, "This is what the Lord has said: 'Tomorrow is to be a day of rest, a holy Sabbath to the Lord. Bake what you want to bake and boil what you want to boil. Save whatever is left and keep it until morning.'" **24.** So they saved it until morning, as Moses commanded, and it did not stink or get maggots in it. **25.** "Eat it today," Moses said, "because today is a Sabbath to the Lord. You will not find any of it on the ground today. **26.** Six days you are to gather it, but on the seventh day, the Sabbath, there will not be any." **27.** Nevertheless, some of the people went out on the seventh day to gather it, but they found none. **28.** Then the Lord said to Moses, "How long will you refuse to keep My commands and My instructions? **29.** Bear in mind that the Lord has given you the Sabbath; that is why on the sixth day He gives you bread for two days. Everyone is to stay where they are on the seventh day; no one is to go out." **30.** So the people rested on the seventh day.

31. The Israelites called the bread manna. It was white like coriander seed and tasted like wafers made with honey. **32.** Moses said, "This is what the Lord has commanded: 'Take an omer of manna and keep it for the generations to come, so they can see the bread I gave you to eat in the wilderness when I brought you out of Egypt.'" **33.** Moses said to Aaron, "Take a jar and put an omer of manna in it. Then place it before the Lord to be kept for the generations to come." **34.** As the Lord commanded Moses, Aaron put the manna in front of the Testimony to be kept. **35.** The Israelites ate manna for forty years, until they came to a land that was settled; they ate manna until they reached the border of Canaan. **36.** (An omer is one-tenth of an ephah.

Chapter 17

1. The entire community of Israelites left the Wilderness of Sin, following the Lord's command, and set up camp at Rephidim. However, there was no water for the people to drink. **2.** The people began to argue with Moses, saying, "Give us water to drink!" Moses responded, "Why are you arguing with me? Why are you testing the Lord?" **3.** The people were very thirsty and began to complain bitterly, saying, "Why did you bring us out of Egypt, just to let us, our children, and our livestock die from thirst?" **4.** Moses cried out to the Lord, "What should I do with these people? They are about to stone me!" **5.** The Lord said to Moses, "Go ahead of the people and take with you some of the elders of Israel. Take the staff you used to strike the river and go. **6.** I will stand before you on the rock at Horeb, and you will strike the rock. Water will flow from it, and the people will be able to drink." So Moses did as the Lord instructed, in front of the elders of Israel. **7.** Moses called the place Massah (meaning "Testing") and Meribah (meaning "Quarreling"), because the Israelites had quarreled and tested the Lord by asking, "Is the Lord really with us or not?" **8.** Then the Amalekites came and attacked Israel at Rephidim. **9.** Moses said to Joshua, "Choose some men to fight the Amalekites. Tomorrow I will stand on top of the hill with the staff of God in my hand." **10.** Joshua did as Moses had instructed and fought the Amalekites, while Moses, Aaron, and Hur went up to the hill. **11.** Whenever Moses raised his hands, Israel was winning, but whenever he lowered them, the Amalekites gained the upper hand. **12.** When Moses' hands grew tired, they placed a stone under him for him to sit on. Aaron and Hur supported his hands, one on each side, so that his hands remained steady until sunset. **13.** As a result, Joshua defeated the Amalekites and their people with the sword. **14.** The Lord instructed Moses, "Write this down as a memorial and recount it to Joshua: I will completely erase the memory of Amalek from under heaven." **15.** Moses built an altar and named it "The-Lord-Is-My-Banner," a name expressing trust in God. **16.** He said, "Because the Lord has sworn, the Lord will be at war against Amalek from generation to generation."

Chapter 18

1. Jethro, Moses' father-in-law and the priest (religious leader) of Midian (a region and people group), heard about all the wonderful things God had done for Moses and the Israelites, how He had freed them from slavery (being forced to work without freedom) in Egypt. **2.** Jethro took Moses' wife, Zipporah, and their two sons, whom Moses had sent away earlier. **3.** One son was named Gershom, because Moses had said, "I have been a stranger (someone who does not belong to a particular place) in a foreign land." **4.** The other was named Eliezer, because Moses had said, "The God of my father was my help and saved me from Pharaoh's sword." **5.** Jethro, along with Zipporah and their two sons, came to Moses in the wilderness (a barren or deserted area) where he was camped near the mountain of God. **6.** Jethro told Moses, "I'm coming to you with your wife and sons." **7.** Moses went out to meet his father-in-law, bowed down (showed respect) to him, and kissed him. They greeted each other, asked how they were doing, and then went into Moses' tent. **8.** Moses shared with Jethro all that the LORD had done to Pharaoh and the Egyptians for Israel's sake,

the hardships (difficult or troubling situations) they had faced on their journey, and how God had delivered (rescued or saved) them. **9.** Jethro rejoiced (was very happy) at all the good that God had done for Israel, rescuing them from the hand (power) of the Egyptians. **10.** Jethro said, "Blessed (praised) be the Lord who has delivered you from Pharaoh and the Egyptians and has rescued the people from their oppression (cruel or unfair treatment)." **11.** "Now I know that the Lord is greater than all gods; He has shown His power over the gods of Egypt." **12.** Jethro offered a burnt offering (a sacrifice where the entire animal is burned) and other sacrifices to God. Aaron and the elders (leaders) of Israel joined him to eat bread with Moses' father-in-law in the presence of God. **13.** The next day, Moses sat to judge (decide legal matters) the people, and they stood before him from morning until evening. **14.** When Jethro saw how Moses was handling the people's disputes (disagreements or conflicts), he asked, "Why are you doing this alone? Why does everyone come to you from morning until evening?" **15.** Moses replied, "The people come to me to ask for God's guidance (help or direction). **16.** When they have a dispute, they come to me, and I judge (decide) between them, explaining God's laws (rules) and teachings." **17.** Jethro said, "This is not good! **18.** You and the people will wear yourselves out (become tired or exhausted). This task is too much for you to do alone. **19.** Listen to my advice (guidance), and may God be with you: Represent the people before God, bring their difficult cases (hard problems) to Him, **20.** Teach them His laws and instructions (directions or rules for living), and show them how they should live and what they should do. **21.** But select capable (able, qualified) men from all the people—men who fear God (respect and honor Him), are trustworthy (dependable), and hate dishonest gain (greed or unfair profit)—and appoint them as leaders over thousands, hundreds, fifties, and tens. **22.** Let them handle the smaller cases but bring the more difficult cases to you. This will make your work easier, because they will share the burden (responsibility or load) with you. **23.** If you follow this advice, and if God commands it, you will be able to endure (remain strong or last), and the people will go home in peace." **24.** Moses listened to his father-in-law and did everything he suggested. **25.** He chose capable men from all Israel and made them leaders over the people: commanders of thousands, hundreds, fifties, and tens. **26.** These men judged the people at all times; the difficult cases were brought to Moses, but the smaller matters were handled by the leaders. **27.** Then Moses let his father-in-law go, and Jethro returned to his own land.

Chapter 19

1. Three months after the Israelites left Egypt, they reached the Wilderness of Sinai on the very same day. **2.** After traveling from Rephidim (a place where they had camped earlier), they arrived at Sinai and set up camp at the foot of the mountain. **3.** Moses ascended the mountain to meet with God, and the Lord called to him from the mountain, saying: **4.** "Tell the people of Israel: 'You have witnessed what I did to the Egyptians and how I carried you on eagles' wings (a metaphor for divine protection) and brought you to Myself. **5.** Now, if you listen to My voice and follow My covenant (agreement), you will be a special treasure to Me, more valued than any other nation, because the entire earth belongs to Me. **6.** You will be a kingdom of priests (those who serve and represent Me) and a holy nation (set apart for My purposes).' These are the words you should speak to the Israelites.'" **7.** So, Moses went back and gathered the elders of the people. He explained to them all that the Lord had commanded him. **8.** The people responded together, saying, "We will do everything the Lord has spoken." Then Moses took their answer and returned to God. **9.** The Lord spoke to Moses, saying, "I will come to you in a thick cloud, so that the people will hear when I speak to you, and they will trust you forever." Moses told the people what the Lord had said. **10.** The Lord instructed Moses, "Go to the people and consecrate (set them apart as holy) for Me today and tomorrow and have them wash their clothes. **11.** Be ready by the third day, because on that day, I will come down on Mount Sinai in the sight of all the people. **12.** Set up boundaries around the mountain and warn the people, saying, 'Be careful not to approach the mountain or even touch its base. Anyone who touches the mountain will surely die. **13.** No one should touch them; they must either be stoned (killed by stones) or shot with arrows—whether human or animal, they must not live.' When the trumpet sounds long, the people may approach the mountain." **14.** Moses went down to the people, consecrated them, and they washed their clothes. **15.** He said to them, "Be ready for the third day. Do not approach your wives (a command to maintain purity during this holy encounter)." **16.** On the third day, in the morning, there was thunder and lightning, and a thick cloud covered the mountain. The sound of the trumpet became louder and louder, and all the people in the camp trembled (shook with fear). **17.** Moses led the people out of the camp to meet God, and they stood at the foot of the mountain. **18.** Mount Sinai was covered with smoke because the Lord descended upon it in fire. The smoke rose like the smoke of a furnace (a heated container), and the entire mountain trembled greatly. **19.** As the trumpet blast grew louder, Moses spoke, and God answered him with a voice. **20.** The Lord came down to the top of Mount Sinai and called Moses up. Moses went up to meet Him. **21.** The Lord said to Moses, "Go down and warn the people not to break through and try to see the Lord, or many of them will die. **22.** Also, let the priests (those who serve before Me) consecrate (set themselves apart as holy) so that the Lord does not break out (punish) against them." **23.** Moses responded to the Lord, "The people cannot come up to Mount Sinai, because You commanded us to set boundaries around the mountain and make it holy." **24.** The Lord answered, "Go down, and bring Aaron (Moses' brother) up with you. But do not let the priests or the people break through to approach the Lord, or He will punish them." **25.** Moses went down to the people and relayed to them everything the Lord had said.

Chapter 20

1. God spoke all these words, saying: **2.** "I am the Lord your God, the one who brought you out of Egypt (the land where the Israelites were enslaved for generations before being freed by God), **3.** You must have no gods other than Me. **4.** Do not make for yourselves any idols (images or statues that are worshiped as gods, which God forbids) or images of anything in the heavens, on the earth, or in the waters beneath the earth. **5.** Do not bow down to them or worship them. I, the Lord your God, am a jealous God, punishing the descendants of those who reject Me to the third and fourth generations, **6.** But showing love to thousands of generations of those who love Me and keep My commandments. **7.** Do not misuse the name of the Lord your God, for the Lord will not hold anyone guiltless who misuses His name. **8.** Remember the Sabbath day (a sacred day of rest, observed by God's people from sunset Friday to sunset Saturday) and keep it holy. The Sabbath is a day I have set apart. **9.** Work for six days, doing all your tasks, **10.** but the seventh day is a day of rest dedicated to the Lord your God. On it, do no work—neither you, nor your children, nor your servants, nor your animals, nor any foreigner in your community. **11.** For in six days the Lord created the heavens, the earth, the sea, and everything in them, and rested on the seventh day. That is why the Lord blessed the Sabbath day and made it holy. **12.** Honor your father and mother so that you may live long in the land the Lord your God is giving you. **13.** Do not murder. **14.** Do not commit adultery. **15.** Do not steal. **16.** Do not give false testimony against your neighbor. **17.** Do not cover your neighbor's house, wife, servants, animals, or anything that belongs to them." **18.** When the people saw the thunder, lightning, and heard the trumpet, and saw the mountain smoking, they trembled and stood at a distance. The mountain here is Mount Sinai (a mountain in the wilderness where Moses received the Ten Commandments from God). **19.** They said to Moses, "Speak to us, and we will listen, but do not let God speak to us, or we will die." **20.** Moses said to the people, "Do not be afraid. God has come to test you so that His fear may be before you, and you will not sin." **21.** The people stood at a distance, while Moses approached the thick cloud where God was. **22.** Then the Lord said to Moses: "Tell the Israelites: 'You have seen that I have spoken to you from heaven. **23.** Do not make gods of silver or gold to be beside Me. **24.** Make for Me an altar of earth and offer your burnt offerings (animal sacrifices where the entire animal is burned as an offering to God) and peace offerings (offerings made to God to express thanks, seek reconciliation, or celebrate peace with God) on it—your sheep and cattle. Wherever I cause My name to be remembered, I will come to you and bless you. **25.** If you make an altar of stone for Me, do not use cut stones, for if you use a tool on them, you have desecrated it (made impure or disrespectful by human interference, especially in religious settings). **26.** And do not go up to My altar by steps, to avoid exposing your nakedness.'"

Chapter 21

1. "These are the rules (guidelines or laws) that you must present to them: **2.** If you purchase a Hebrew servant (an Israelite person who enters into service to pay off a debt), he must work for six years, and in the seventh year, he is to be released without any payment. **3.** If he comes alone, he shall leave alone; if he comes with a wife, she shall go with him. **4.** If his master gives him a wife, and they have children, the wife and children belong to the master, and he shall leave alone. **5.** However, if the servant says, 'I love my master, my wife, and my children, I do not want to leave,' **6.** then his master must bring him before the judges (authorities in charge of legal matters) and take him to the door or doorpost. His master will pierce his ear with an awl (a sharp tool for making holes), and the servant will serve him for life. **7.** If a man sells his daughter to be a servant (female servant), she will not be set free in the same way as male servants. **8.** If she is displeasing to her master, who had promised to marry her, he must allow her to be redeemed (bought back). He cannot sell her to foreigners because he has treated her unfairly. **9.** If he betroths her to his son, he must treat her as his own daughter. **10.** If he marries another wife, he must not reduce her food, clothing, or marital rights. **11.** If he does not provide for these things, she shall be set free without payment. **12.** If someone strikes another and kills them, they must be executed (put to death). **13.** If the death was not planned (intentional), and God allowed it, I will designate a place where the killer can flee (a city of refuge). **14.** but if a person kills intentionally, by treachery (deceitful planning), take them from My altar (place of worship) and put them to death. **15.** If someone strikes their father or mother, they must be put to death. **16.** Anyone who kidnaps a person and sells them, or if the person is found in their possession, must be executed. **17.** Anyone who curses (disrespects with harmful words) their father or mother must be executed. **18.** If two men fight and one strikes the other with a stone or his fist, and the person does not die but is confined to a bed, **19.** and later gets up and walks with a staff (walking stick), the one who struck him will not be punished, but will pay for the lost time and ensure the victim is fully healed. **20.** If a master strikes his male or female servant with a rod (stick) and the servant dies, the master shall be punished. **21.** But if the servant survives for a day or two, the master will not be punished, for the servant is considered his property. **22.** If men fight and hurt a pregnant woman, causing her to give birth prematurely, but no further harm occurs, the offender must pay a fine, as determined by the woman's husband and the judges. **23.** If there is further harm (such as death), then life will be given for life, **24.** eye for eye, tooth for tooth, hand for hand, foot for foot, **25.** Burn for burn, wound for wound, stripe for stripe. **26.** If a man strikes his servant's eye and destroys it, he must let the servant go free in compensation for the loss of their eye. **27.** If he knocks out a servant's tooth, the servant shall be set free in compensation for the tooth. **28.** If an ox gores (attacks with its horns) a person to death, the ox shall be stoned, and its meat shall not be eaten. The owner of the ox will be acquitted (not guilty). **29.** However, if the ox has previously been known to gore, and the owner did not keep it confined, and it kills someone, the ox must be stoned, and the owner must also be executed. **30.** If a fine is imposed, the owner must pay the amount decided by the court to redeem (buy back) his life. **31.** If the ox kills a son or a daughter, the same judgment applies. **32.** If the ox kills a servant, the owner must pay thirty shekels (ancient silver coins) to the servant's master, and the ox will be stoned. **33.** If a person digs a pit and does not cover it, and an ox or donkey falls into it, **34.** The owner of the pit must compensate (pay) the animal's owner, but the dead animal becomes the owner of the pit. **35.** If one man's ox injures another's, causing it to die, they shall sell the live ox and divide the money, and also divide the dead ox. **36.** If the ox is known to have gored before, and the owner failed to keep it confined, the owner must pay for a replacement ox, and the dead ox will be his."

Chapter 22

1. If someone steals an ox (a large farm animal used for labor or transportation) or a sheep (a domesticated animal raised for wool or meat), and either kills it or sells it, he must repay five oxen for one ox, or four sheep for one sheep. **2.** If the thief is caught breaking in (attempting to secretly enter a house to steal) and is struck in a way that causes his death, the person who killed him is not guilty. **3.** However, if this occurs after sunrise (when there is sufficient light to identify the person), the one who killed the thief is guilty. The thief must pay restitution (compensation for the stolen item); if he cannot pay, he must be sold to cover the theft. **4.** If the stolen animal is found alive in the thief's possession, whether it's an ox, donkey (a small domesticated animal used for carrying loads), or sheep, the thief must return double the amount. **5.** If a person allows their animal to graze in another's field or vineyard and it causes damage, they must repay with the best of their own crops (harvested fruits, vegetables, or grains) or vineyard produce. **6.** If a fire starts and spreads through thorns (prickly plants) and destroys grain or fields, the one who started the fire must make restitution (pay for the damage). **7.** If a person entrusts money or goods (items of value) to someone for safekeeping and they are stolen, if the thief is caught, he must pay double. **8.** If the thief is not found, the owner of the house must come before the judges (officials who decide legal matters) to prove he didn't steal. **9.** For any dispute involving property—whether it's an ox, donkey, sheep, clothing, or any lost item (something that has been misplaced or is in dispute)—the matter will be judged. The one found guilty must repay double. **10.** If someone gives their neighbor an animal to care for, and it dies, is injured, or is lost without anyone witnessing it, **11.** both parties will swear an oath (a solemn promise before God) to confirm that the person who was entrusted with the animal did not steal it. The owner must accept the oath and not demand repayment. **12.** However, if the animal is stolen, the person entrusted with it must repay the owner. **13.** If the animal is torn apart by a wild animal (dangerous animal living in the wild), the person must provide the remains as proof and will not be required to make restitution. **14.** If someone borrows an item from their neighbor and it is damaged or dies while they are responsible for it, without the owner being present, they must pay for it. **15.** If the owner was with the item, no restitution is required; if the item was rented (paid for temporary use), the payment will be covered by the rental price. **16.** If a man seduces (entices or persuades someone into a romantic relationship) a virgin (a young woman who is not married or promised to another), he must pay the bride-price (a gift of money or property given to the bride's family) and make her his wife. **17.** If her father refuses to give her to him, the man must still pay the full bride-price. **18.** You must not allow a sorceress (a woman who practices witchcraft) to live. **19.** Anyone who engages in bestiality (having relations with an animal) must be put to death. **20.** Anyone who sacrifices to any god other than the Lord (the one true God) must be utterly destroyed. **21.** Do not mistreat (treat badly) or oppress (keep in a state of hardship) a stranger (someone who is not from your own land), because you were once strangers in Egypt (a land in northeastern Africa). **22.** Do not harm a widow (a woman whose husband has died) or an orphan (a child whose parents have died). **23.** If you harm them and they cry out to Me, I will hear their cries. **24.** My anger (strong displeasure) will burn, and I will punish you with the sword (weapon used in battle). Your wives will become widows, and your children will be orphans. **25.** If you lend money to a poor (in need) person among My people, do not charge them interest (extra money paid on a loan) like a moneylender (someone who loans money for a profit). **26.** If you take your neighbor's garment (clothing) as pledge (security for a loan), return it before sunset. **27.** The garment is their only covering (clothing) and it is their only protection at night. If they cry out to Me, I will hear them, for I am compassionate (full of mercy and care). **28.** Do not insult God, nor curse a ruler (a leader of the people). **29.** Do not delay offering the first of your crops (produce from the land) and juices (grape or fruit liquids). Offer the firstborn of your sons to Me. **30.** Likewise, offer the firstborn of your oxen (large working animals) and sheep (domestic animals raised for food or wool) to Me. Let the animal stay with its mother for seven days, and on the eighth day, offer it to Me. **31.** You must be holy people to Me. Do not eat meat torn by wild animals (animals not domesticated), give it to the dogs.

Chapter 23

1. Do not spread false reports (inaccurate or untrue information) or align with the wicked (evil people) to give dishonest testimony (false statements in court). **2.** Do not follow the crowd to do evil (join others in committing wrong acts), nor let the majority influence your judgment (decision-making) in a case to twist justice (make it unfair). **3.** Do not show favoritism (give unfair advantage) to the poor in legal matters (when judging a case). **4.** If you find your enemy's ox (a large domesticated animal used for plowing) or donkey (a small domesticated animal used for carrying loads) wandering off, return it to him. **5.** If you see your enemy's donkey struggling under its load (carrying too much weight), and you are tempted to ignore it, help him (assist him in lifting the burden). **6.** Do not pervert justice (corrupt or distort fairness) for the poor in any legal dispute (legal disagreement). **7.** Stay away from lies; do not harm the innocent (blameless people) or the righteous (virtuous), for I will not justify (declare innocent) the wicked (evil people). **8.** Do not take bribes (money or gifts given to influence a decision), for they blind those who can see clearly (cloud judgment) and distort the truth. **9.** o not mistreat foreigners (strangers), because you know what it's like to be a stranger (someone who is not from the land), having once been strangers in Egypt. **10.** For six years, plant (cultivate) and harvest (gather) your crops, **11.** but in the seventh year, let the land rest (leave it unused), so the poor can eat what grows on its own (unplanted crops), and whatever remains can be eaten by wild animals (animals that live naturally in the area). Do the same with your vineyards (grape farms) and olive groves (olive tree plantations). **12.** Work for six days, and rest (cease from work) on the seventh, so your ox and donkey can rest, and so your workers, including foreigners (strangers in the land), may be refreshed (restored in strength). **13.** Be careful to follow all I have said (observe My instructions), and do not speak the names of other gods (deities) or let them be heard on your lips (in your speech). **14.** Celebrate three major feasts (religious festivals) for Me each year. **15.** Keep the Feast of Unleavened Bread, eating unleavened bread (bread made without yeast) for seven days to remember your escape (flight or deliverance) from Egypt. No one should come empty-handed before Me. **16.** Keep the Feast of Harvest (Festival of First fruits), offering the first of your crops (initial part of the harvest), and the Feast of Ingathering at the end of the year when you've harvested your produce (gathered crops). **17.** Every male must appear before the LORD three times a year. **18.** Do not offer the blood of My sacrifice (the animal's blood offered to God) with leavened bread (bread containing yeast), nor let the fat (the rich part of the meat) of My sacrifice remain overnight. **19** Bring the first fruits of your land into the house of the Lord, and do not cook a young goat in its mother's milk (a prohibited practice). **20.** I will send an Angel (a divine messenger) ahead of you, to guide you along the way and bring you to the place I have prepared for you. **21.** Obey Him (follow His commands) and listen to His voice; do not provoke (make angry) Him, for He will not forgive your wrongdoing (sins), since My name is in Him. **22.** If you listen to Him and do everything I command, I will oppose your enemies (fight against your enemies) and fight against those who oppose you. **23.** My Angel will go ahead of you and drive out the Amorites, Hittites, Perizzites, Canaanites, Hivites, and Jebusites (various groups living in the Promised Land). **24.** Do not worship their gods (idol worship), nor follow their practices (rituals). Destroy their altars (places of worship) and idols (images or statues of their gods). **25.** Serve only the Lord your God (worship God alone), and He will bless (provide for) your food and water and take away sickness (disease or illness) from your midst (among you). **26.** None will be barren (unable to have children) or suffer miscarriage (lose a child during pregnancy) in your land, and I will ensure you live a full life (long life). **27.** I will send terror before you (cause fear), causing your enemies to flee (run away) before you. **28.** I will send hornets (insects, possibly symbolizing powerful forces) to drive out the Hivites, Canaanites, and Hittites before you. **29.** I will not drive them all out in one year, so that the land does not become desolate (empty or abandoned) and wild animals multiply (increase). **30.** I will gradually drive them out, until you have grown in number (increased in population) and taken full possession of the land. **31.** I will set your boundaries (limits or borders) from the Red Sea to the Mediterranean, and from the desert to the Euphrates River. I will deliver (give into your hands) the people living there into your hands, and you will drive them out. **32.** Do not make any covenants (agreements) with them or their gods. **33.** They must not remain in your land, or they will cause you to sin (disobey) against Me. If you worship their gods, it will become a trap (snare or danger) for you.

Chapter 24

1. The Lord spoke to Moses: "Come up to Me, you, Aaron, Nadab, Abihu, and seventy of Israel's elders. Worship at a distance. **2.** Only Moses is to come near; the others should stay back, and the people are not to come up with them." **3.** Moses went and told the people all the commands (instructions) and laws (rules) the Lord had given him. They all replied together, "We will do everything the Lord has commanded." **4.** Moses wrote down all the Lord's words. The next morning, he built an altar (a place for offering sacrifices) at the foot of the mountain and set up twelve pillars (tall stone markers), one for each of the twelve tribes of Israel. **5.** Moses sent young men of Israel to offer burnt offerings and peace offerings (sacrifices made in thanks to God) of oxen (adult cattle) to the Lord. **6.** He took half of the blood (liquid from the sacrificed animals) from these sacrifices and placed it in basins (shallow containers), while the other half he sprinkled on the altar. **7.** Then Moses read the Book of the Covenant (the written agreement between God and His people) to the people. They replied, "We will do everything the Lord has commanded and will be obedient (willing to follow orders)." **8.** Moses sprinkled the blood on the people and said, "This is the blood of the covenant the Lord has made with you, based on all these words." **9.** Moses went up, along with Aaron, Nadab, Abihu, and seventy elders of Israel. **10.** They saw the God of Israel. Beneath His feet was a paved surface (smooth, flat area) of sapphire (a precious gemstone, often blue), as clear as the sky itself. **11.** The Lord did not harm (injure or strike) Israel's leaders, and they saw Him, then ate and drank in His presence. **12.** The Lord said to Moses, "Come up the mountain to Me and stay here. I will give you the stone tablets (flat stones where writing is inscribed)

with the law and commandments (rules) I've written, so you can teach them." **13.** Moses rose with his assistant (helper) Joshua and went up to the mountain of God. **14.** He told the elders, "Wait here for us until we return. Aaron and Hur (another leader) are with you. If anyone has a question, they can go to them." **15.** Moses entered the mountain, and a cloud (a mass of vapor in the sky) covered it. **16.** The glory (magnificent presence or power) of the Lord settled on Mount Sinai (the mountain where God spoke to Moses), and the cloud covered it for six days. On the seventh day, the Lord called Moses from the cloud. **17.** The appearance (what something looks like) of the Lord's glory was like a consuming fire (a fire that completely burns up everything) on top of the mountain, visible to all of Israel. **18.** Moses entered the cloud and went up the mountain. He stayed there for forty days and nights.

Chapter 25

1. The Lord spoke to Moses, saying, **2.** "Tell the Israelites to bring an offering to Me. Accept contributions from anyone who is willing and generous in their heart. **3.** This is the offering you shall receive: gold, silver, and bronze; **4.** blue, purple, and scarlet yarn, fine linen, goats' hair; **5.** ram skins dyed red, dolphin skins, and acacia wood; **6.** oil for the lamps, spices for the anointing oil and incense; **7.** onyx stones, and stones for the ephod and the breastplate. **8.** Let them build Me a sanctuary so that I may dwell among them. **9.** Make it exactly as I show you, including the tabernacle and all its furnishings. **10.** Build an ark of acacia wood, 3.75 feet long, 2.25 feet wide, and 2.25 feet high. **11.** Overlay it with pure gold, inside and out, and make a gold molding around it. **12.** Cast four gold rings for it, placing two rings on each side. **13.** Make poles of acacia wood, cover them with gold, **14.** and slide the poles into the rings to carry the ark. **15.** The poles must remain in the rings and should never be removed. **16.** Place the Testimony I will give you inside the ark. **17.** Make a mercy seat of pure gold, measuring 3.75 feet by 2.25 feet. **18.** Fashion two cherubim of gold, one at each end of the mercy seat. **19.** The cherubim should be made as one piece with the mercy seat, at its two ends. **20.** Let their wings be spread out over the mercy seat, covering it, and let them face each other, with their faces looking down at the mercy seat. **21.** Place the mercy seat on top of the ark, and inside the ark, put the Testimony that I will give you. **22.** There, between the cherubim, I will meet with you and speak to you about everything I command the Israelites. **23.** You shall make a table of acacia wood, 3 feet long, 1.5 feet wide, and 2.25 feet high. **24.** Overlay it with pure gold and add a gold molding around it. **25.** Make a frame for the table, one handbreadth wide, and place a gold molding for the frame. **26.** Make four gold rings for the table, placing them near the four corners. **27.** The rings will hold the poles used to carry the table. **28.** Make poles of acacia wood and cover them with gold, so the table can be carried. **29.** Prepare the dishes, pans, pitchers, and bowls for pouring, all from pure gold. **30.** Keep the showbread always placed on the table before Me. **31.** Make a lampstand of pure gold, hammered into one piece, including the shaft, branches, bowls, ornamental knobs, and flowers. **32.** The lampstand will have six branches: three on one side and three on the other. **33.** Each branch should have three bowls shaped like almond blossoms, with knobs and flowers. **34.** The central shaft will have four bowls, also shaped like almond blossoms, each with knobs and flowers. **35.** Under each pair of branches, place a knob. **36.** The knobs and branches should be made from one continuous piece of gold, hammered into shape. **37.** Make seven lamps for the lampstand, and arrange them so they provide light in front of it. **38.** Create wick-trimmers and trays for the lamps, all made of pure gold. **39.** The lampstand and all its accessories should be made from one talent of pure gold. **40.** Be sure to make everything exactly according to the pattern I showed you on the mountain."

Chapter 26

1. You shall construct the tabernacle using ten curtains made from fine, woven linen, dyed with blue, purple, and scarlet threads. The curtains should feature intricate designs of cherubim (angel-like beings). **2.** Each curtain must measure 28 cubits (about 42 feet) in length and 4 cubits (around 6 feet) in width. All curtains will have identical dimensions. **3.** Five of these curtains should be joined together on one side, and the other five curtains joined in a similar way on the opposite side. **4.** Along the edge of the curtains, at the outer edge of one set, create loops made from blue yarn (dyed thread). Do the same with the other set. **5.** Fifty loops should be made on the edge of each curtain in the sets, to allow them to be connected or clasped. **6.** Fifty gold clasps (fasteners) should be made to attach the curtains, ensuring they form one unified structure for the tabernacle. **7.** For the tabernacle's covering, make curtains from goats' hair (woven from the hair of goats). These should be eleven curtains. **8.** Each of these curtains should be 30 cubits (around 45 feet) long and 4 cubits (6 feet) wide. All the curtains will have the same dimensions. **9.** Join together five curtains on one side and six on the other. The sixth curtain will be folded over at the front (entrance) of the tent. **10.** Make fifty loops on the edge of the outermost curtain in each set, and fifty loops on the edge of the second set. **11.** Fifty bronze clasps (fasteners made of bronze) will be used to connect the curtains, making them one continuous covering. **12.** The remaining fabric from the tent, half of a curtain, shall hang over the back of the tabernacle to cover it. **13.** A cubit (about 18 inches) of this leftover curtain shall hang on both sides, covering the tabernacle on each side. **14.** Additionally, make a covering using ram skins dyed red (skins from rams, dyed red), and above that, a covering of badger skins (a durable leather, possibly referring to a specific kind of animal skin). **15.** For the structure of the tabernacle, create boards from acacia wood (a strong, durable wood), which will stand upright. **16.** Each board should be 10 cubits (15 feet) long and 1.5 cubits (around 2.25 feet) wide. **17** Each board will have two tenons (projections) on its bottom, designed to fit into sockets, allowing the boards to be connected. Repeat this for all the boards of the tabernacle. **18.** Make 20 boards for the south side of the tabernacle. **19.** Underneath these 20 boards, place 40 silver sockets (the support bases), two sockets under each board for its two tenons. **20.** For the north side of the tabernacle, make another 20 boards. **21.** For these 20 boards, make 40 silver sockets as well, two sockets under each board. **22.** For the far side of the tabernacle, the west side, make six boards. **23.** Also, create two boards for the two back corners of the tabernacle. **24.** These corner boards will be joined at the bottom and top by a single ring (a circular fastener) on each end, connecting them together. **25.** Altogether, there will be eight boards, supported by 16 silver sockets, two sockets beneath each board. **26.** Now, make bars (long horizontal rods) from acacia wood: five bars for the boards on one side of the tabernacle, **27.** five bars for the opposite side, and five bars for the west side of the tabernacle. **28.** The middle bar should run horizontally through the center of the boards, stretching from one end to the other. **29.** Cover the boards with gold (precious metal), make gold rings to hold the bars in place, and overlay the bars themselves with gold. **30.** Follow the pattern of the tabernacle as it was shown to you on the mountain (Mount Sinai), and raise it according to these instructions. **31.** You shall make a veil (curtain) from blue, purple, and scarlet threads, along with fine linen. It will be designed with intricate patterns of cherubim (angel-like beings). **32.** Hang the veil on four pillars made of acacia wood, overlaid with gold. The hooks to hold the veil will be made of gold, and the pillars should stand on four silver sockets (metal bases). **33.** Attach the veil to the hooks and place the Ark of the Testimony (the sacred chest containing the covenant tablets) behind the veil. The veil will divide the holy place from the Most Holy (the innermost, most sacred part). **34.** Place the mercy seat (the lid of the Ark, symbolizing God's presence) on the Ark in the Most Holy. **35.** Set the table for the showbread outside the veil, with the lampstand (a seven-branched lamp) positioned opposite the table, on the south side of the

tabernacle. The table will be on the north side. **36.** Make a screen (curtain) for the entrance to the tabernacle, woven from blue, purple, and scarlet threads, and fine linen, woven by a skilled artisan. **37.** Create five pillars of acacia wood for the entrance screen. Cover these pillars with gold and make gold hooks for them. The pillars will rest on bronze sockets (bases).

Chapter 27

1. "Construct an altar from acacia wood (a durable, dense, and fragrant type of wood), measuring five cubits (about 7.5 feet) in length and five cubits in width—making it square—and its height shall be three cubits (about 4.5 feet). **2.** Attach horns (projecting parts or projections) to each of the four corners, ensuring they are made from the same piece as the altar. Overlay the entire altar with bronze (a metal alloy consisting primarily of copper). **3.** Prepare the necessary accessories for it, including pans (shallow containers) for collecting ashes, shovels, basins (large bowls), forks (used for handling sacrificial meat), and firepans (metal containers for carrying fire), all made from bronze. **4.** Create a bronze grate (a metal mesh or framework) as well, in the form of a network (a complex, interwoven structure), and place four bronze rings on the corners of the network. **5.** Position the grate beneath the rim (edge) of the altar, placing it at the midpoint (center point) of the altar's height. **6.** Fashion poles for carrying the altar from acacia wood and cover them with bronze. **7.** Insert the poles into the rings and use them to transport (carry) the altar. The poles should be positioned on the two sides of the altar. **8.** The altar should be hollow (empty inside), constructed with wooden planks, according to the design you were shown on the mountain. **9.** "Next, you shall create the tabernacle's courtyard. On the southern side, the courtyard should be enclosed with hangings (curtains or drapes) of fine linen (high-quality fabric), each one hundred cubits (about 150 feet) in length. **10.** The courtyard should have twenty pillars (vertical supports) with their corresponding twenty bronze (a metal alloy) sockets (bases to support the pillars). The hooks and bands (straps or fasteners) of the pillars should be silver. **11.** Similarly, the northern side of the courtyard shall have hangings, each one hundred cubits long, with twenty pillars and twenty bronze sockets, and their hooks and bands of silver. **12.** For the western side of the courtyard, the hangings will be fifty cubits (about 75 feet) long, with ten pillars and ten sockets. **13.** The eastern side should also measure fifty cubits in width. **14.** On one side of the gate (entrance), there will be hangings of fifteen cubits (about 22.5 feet), supported by three pillars and three sockets. **15.** On the opposite side, there will be another set of fifteen cubits of hangings, with three pillars and three sockets. **16.** "For the entrance to the courtyard, create a screen (a decorative curtain or divider) measuring twenty cubits in length. This screen shall be woven from blue (a deep blue color), purple (a royal color), and scarlet (a bright red color) threads, along with fine linen, crafted by an expert weaver (a person skilled in making cloth). It should hang from four pillars and four sockets. **17.** All the pillars surrounding the courtyard should have silver bands (metallic bands wrapped around the pillars), with hooks made of silver and sockets made of bronze. **18.** The dimensions of the courtyard will be one hundred cubits in length, fifty cubits in width, and five cubits in height. The entire structure should be made of fine linen, and the sockets should be of bronze. **19.** All the utensils (tools or instruments) used in the tabernacle, including the pegs (small spikes used to secure the tent or courtyard) for the tent and for the courtyard, must be made of bronze. **20.** "Command the Israelites to bring you pure olive oil, pressed (extracted under pressure) to produce oil for the lamps, so that the light may burn continuously. **21.** In the Tabernacle of Meeting, outside the veil (curtain that separates the Holy Place from the Most Holy Place) that separates the Holy Place from the Most Holy Place, Aaron and his sons will tend (care for) the lamps from evening until morning before the Lord. This will be a lasting ordinance (permanent law) for their descendants (future generations), for the people of Israel."

Chapter 28

1. "Now bring your brother Aaron, along with his sons, from the children of Israel, so that he may serve as My priest (a priest is someone who performs religious duties). Aaron and his sons—Nadab, Abihu, Eleazar, and Ithamar—are to perform priestly duties for Me. 2. You are to create sacred (holy, set apart for religious purposes) garments for Aaron, your brother, designed for honor (respect) and beauty (attractiveness). 3. Speak to the skilled artisans (craftspeople or workers) whom I have endowed (blessed or given) with wisdom and instruct them to make these garments to consecrate (make holy or set apart) Aaron, so he may serve as a priest for Me. 4. These are the garments they are to make: a breastplate (a chest covering), an ephod (a priestly garment), a robe, a finely woven tunic, a turban, and a sash. These holy garments will be for Aaron and his sons, so that they may minister to me as priests. 5. They shall use gold, blue, purple, and scarlet thread, along with fine linen. 6. The ephod will be made of these materials—gold, blue, purple, and scarlet thread, along with fine linen, skillfully woven together. 7. It will have two shoulder straps (straps over the shoulders), joined at their edges, and the entire ephod will be securely attached. 8. The band (a woven belt) of the ephod, intricately woven and made of gold, blue, purple, scarlet thread, and fine linen, will be the same workmanship as the ephod itself. 9. Take two onyx stones (a type of precious stone) and engrave on them the names of the sons of Israel 10 six names on each stone, listed in order of their birth. 11. Engrave them as an engraver (someone who carves or etches) does a seal and set them in gold settings. 12. Place these stones on the shoulders (upper part of the garment, near the neck) of the ephod as a memorial (reminder) for the sons of Israel, so that Aaron may carry their names before the Lord on his shoulders as a reminder. 13. Make gold settings (holders) for these stones, 14. And prepare two pure gold chains (links of gold twisted together) like braided cords, which will attach to the stones. 15. Next, create the breastplate of judgment, made in the same manner as the ephod, with gold, blue, purple, and scarlet thread, and fine linen. 16. The breastplate will be square, folded double, with its length and width being a span (a measurement equal to the width of a person's hand). 17. It will have four rows of stones: the first row will be sardius, topaz, and emerald; 18. The second row will be turquoise, sapphire, and diamond; 19. the third row will be jacinth (a reddish-brown gemstone), agate (a type of mineral), and amethyst (a purple gemstone); 20. The fourth row will be beryl (a greenish gemstone), onyx, and jasper (a type of gemstone). Each of these stones will be set in gold. 21. The stones will bear the names of the twelve tribes of Israel, one name per stone, engraved like a seal. 22. Create gold chains (braided cords) for the breastplate, 23. And make two rings of gold to be attached at the ends of the breastplate. 24. Attach the two braided gold chains to the rings on the breastplate, 25. And fasten the other ends of these chains to the settings (holders) on the ephod, at the front. 26. Also, make two more rings of gold and place them on the inner side (inside part) of the breastplate, near its edge. 27. Similarly, make two rings of gold and place them on the shoulder straps of the ephod at the front, where the ephod joins at its seam. 28. These rings will help bind (attach) the breastplate to the ephod with a blue cord, securing it above the intricately woven band of the ephod so it will not come loose. 29. Aaron will carry the names of the sons of Israel over his heart in the breastplate of judgment as a memorial (reminder) before the Lord, constantly. 30. Put the Urim (objects used for divination) and the Thummim (objects used for divination) into the breastplate of judgment, to rest over Aaron's heart when he goes into the holy place. He will carry the judgment (God's decisions) of the children of Israel over his heart before the Lord. 31. The robe of the ephod must be entirely blue, 32. And it will have an opening for Aaron's

head in the center, with a woven band (a fabric binding) around it to prevent tearing. 33. On the hem (bottom edge) of the robe, make pomegranates of blue, purple, and scarlet, with golden bells alternating between them: a golden bell and a pomegranate, and a golden bell and a pomegranate, around the entire hem. 34. This robe will be worn by Aaron when he serves as priest. The sound of the bells will be heard when he enters and exits the holy place before the Lord, so that he will not die. 35. Make a plate (a flat, engraved object) of pure gold, engraved with the words: "HOLINESS TO THE LORD." 36. Attach it to a blue cord and place it on the front of the turban (a head covering). 37. This plate will be worn on Aaron's forehead so that he may bear the iniquity (sin or wrongdoing) of the holy things the Israelites dedicate, making their offerings acceptable to the Lord. 38. The plate will always be on Aaron's forehead, symbolizing that the gifts and sacrifices of the people will be received by the Lord. 39. Weave the tunic (a simple garment) from fine linen thread and make the turban and sash (a long piece of cloth worn around the waist) of fine linen as well. 40. For Aaron's sons, make tunics, sashes, and hats, for glory and beauty. 41. Dress Aaron and his sons in these garments, anoint them (set them apart with oil), consecrate them (make them holy), and sanctify them (purify them), so they may serve Me as priests. 42. Make linen trousers (pants) for them to wear, reaching from the waist to the thighs, to cover their nakedness. 43. These trousers will be worn by Aaron and his sons when they enter the tabernacle or approach the altar to serve in the holy place, so they do not incur guilt (sin or wrongdoings) and die. This will be a lasting ordinance (rule or command) for him and his descendants.

Chapter 29

1. This is what you shall do to consecrate them (make them holy) for serving as priests before Me: Take one young bull and two rams, both without defects (flawless), 2. as well as unleavened bread, cakes made without yeast and mixed with oil, and wafers of unleavened bread anointed with oil (all to be made from wheat flour). 3. Put all these in a single basket and bring the basket, along with the bull and the two rams. 4. Bring Aaron and his sons to the entrance of the tabernacle and wash them with water. (The tabernacle is the sacred tent where God's presence dwells.) 5. Then, dress Aaron in the special garments: the tunic, the ephod (a special robe for priests), the breastplate, and tie it with the intricately woven band of the ephod. 6. Place the turban on his head and put the holy crown (the special gold crown dedicated to the Lord) on the turban. 7. Pour anointing oil on his head and consecrate (set apart for holy use) him. 8. Next, bring his sons forward and dress them in tunics. 9. Tie sashes on them and put hats on their heads. The priesthood will belong to them for all time. This is how you will consecrate Aaron and his sons. 10. Now, take the bull to the entrance of the tabernacle, and Aaron and his sons should lay their hands on its head. (This symbolizes transferring their sins to the bull.) 11. Then, slaughter the bull at the entrance of the tabernacle. 12. Take some of its blood and put it on the horns (corners) of the altar with your finger and pour the rest of the blood at the base of the altar. 13. Take all the fat covering the inner organs, the fatty lobe (part of the liver), the kidneys and the fat around them, and burn them on the altar. 14. However, the rest of the bull, including its skin and waste parts, should be burned outside the camp. This is a sin offering (for atonement). 15. Next, take one of the rams, and Aaron and his sons should lay their hands on its head. 16. Kill the ram and sprinkle its blood all around the altar. 17. Then cut the ram into pieces, wash its inner organs and legs, and place them with the pieces and the head. 18. Burn the entire ram on the altar. This is a burnt offering (completely given to God), producing a pleasing aroma to the Lord. 19. Take the other ram, and Aaron and his sons should lay their hands on its head. 20. Kill this ram, take some of its blood, and apply it to the tip of the right ear of Aaron and his sons, as well as to the thumb of their right hands and the big toe of their right feet. Sprinkle the rest of

the blood around the altar. **21.** Take some of the blood from the altar and some of the anointing oil, and sprinkle it on Aaron, his garments, his sons, and their garments. This will consecrate them, making them holy for their service. **22.** Also, take the fat of the ram, including the tail, the fat covering the inner organs, the fatty lobe of the liver, the kidneys, and the right thigh (this is the ram of consecration). **23.** Along with these, take one loaf of bread, one cake made with oil, and one wafer from the basket of unleavened bread that is before the Lord. **24.** Place all these items in the hands of Aaron and his sons, and they should wave them before the Lord as a wave offering (a gesture of offering and dedication). **25.** Once they have waved them, receive them back from their hands and burn them on the altar as a burnt offering, a pleasing aroma to the Lord. **26.** Take the breast of the ram that was offered for Aaron's consecration and wave it before the Lord. This will be your portion. **27.** From the ram of consecration, you will consecrate the breast (by waving it) and the thigh (by raising it), both of which will belong to Aaron and his sons. **28.** This offering will be a lasting statute for Aaron and his sons. They will receive these portions from the people of Israel, as a heave offering (a special offering raised to God) from the sacrifices of peace offerings. **29.** The holy garments of Aaron will belong to his sons after him, to be worn and anointed by them when they take his place as priests. **30.** The son who becomes the priest in his place shall wear these garments for seven days when he enters the tabernacle to minister. **31.** Boil the flesh of the ram of consecration in a holy place, **32.** and Aaron and his sons shall eat it, along with the bread in the basket, at the entrance of the tabernacle. **33.** They must eat what was used in their consecration to sanctify (make holy) them. No one outside the family of priests may eat these holy items. **34.** If any flesh or bread remains until morning, burn the leftovers. It is holy, so it cannot be eaten. **35.** Do all of this for Aaron and his sons, following the commands I have given you. For seven days, you shall consecrate them. **36.** Each day, offer a bull as a sin offering to atone for them, and cleanse the altar by making atonement for it. Anoint it to sanctify it. **37.** For seven days, make atonement for the altar and consecrate it. The altar will be most holy, and anything that touches it must be holy. **38.** Here is what you will offer on the altar: two lambs, each one year old, offered continually, day after day. **39.** Offer one lamb in the morning and the other lamb at twilight. **40.** With the first lamb, offer one-tenth of an ephah of flour mixed with one-fourth of a hin of pressed oil, and one-fourth of a hin of wine as a drink offering. **41.** Offer the second lamb at twilight, with the same grain offering and drink offering, for a sweet aroma to the Lord. **42.** This will be a continual burnt offering throughout your generations at the entrance of the tabernacle, where I will meet with you to speak with you. **43.** I will meet with the Israelites there, and the tabernacle will be sanctified by my glory. **44.** I will consecrate the tabernacle and the altar, and I will consecrate Aaron and his sons to serve me as priests. **45.** I will dwell among the Israelites and be their God. **46.** They will know that I am the Lord their God, who brought them out of Egypt, so that I might dwell among them. I am the Lord their God.

Chapter 30

1. You shall make an altar (raised structure for offering sacrifices) for burning incense. Construct it from acacia wood. **2.** The altar should be one cubit (about 18 inches or 45 cm) in both length and width, making it square-shaped. It should be two cubits (about 3 feet or 91 cm) in height. The horns (protruding parts at the corners) of the altar should be made from the same piece of wood. **3.** Cover the top, sides, and horns with pure gold, and add a gold molding (decorative border) around it. **4.** Make two gold rings and attach them to the sides of the altar just below the molding. These rings will hold the poles used to carry it. **5.** The poles should be made from acacia wood and overlaid with gold. **6.** Place the altar in front of the veil (a curtain separating the Holy Place from the Most Holy Place) that separates the Holy Place from the Most Holy Place, near

the Ark of the Covenant. It is there that I will meet with you. **7.** Every morning, Aaron (the high priest) must burn incense on it as he tends the lamps. **8.** At twilight (the time between evening and night), when Aaron lights the lamps, he must burn incense again. This incense offering is to be a continuous (perpetual) act before the Lord for all generations. **9.** You are not to burn any strange (unauthorized or foreign) incense on this altar, nor should you offer burnt offerings, grain offerings, or drink offerings on it. **10.** Once a year, Aaron shall make atonement (the act of making amends or seeking forgiveness) on the horns of the altar with the blood of the sin offering. This shall be done annually as a permanent law (statute) for the people of Israel. The altar is most holy to the Lord. **11.** The Lord spoke to Moses, saying: **12.** "When you take a census (an official count) of the Israelites, each person must give a ransom (a payment or offering) to the Lord to prevent a plague (a harmful or deadly event) from coming upon them when they are counted. **13.** Each person who is counted must give half a shekel (a unit of currency or weight). The shekel used is the shekel of the sanctuary. One shekel equals twenty gerahs (a small unit of weight). The half-shekel is to be an offering to the Lord. **14.** All those who are counted, from twenty years old and up, must give this half-shekel to the Lord. **15.** Whether rich or poor, each person is to give the same amount—half a shekel—so that atonement may be made for them. **16.** The money collected for the atonement should be used for the service of the Tabernacle (the place of worship), and it will serve as a memorial before the Lord, making atonement for the people." **17.** The Lord spoke again to Moses, saying: **18.** "Make a bronze laver (a large basin for washing) with a bronze base. Place it between the Tabernacle and the altar, and fill it with water. **19.** Aaron and his sons must wash their hands and feet from this water. **20.** Whenever they enter the Tabernacle or approach the altar to offer a sacrifice, they must wash their hands and feet, so that they do not die. **21.** This law must be followed by them and their descendants (future generations) for all time." **22.** The Lord continued to speak to Moses: **23.** "Take the finest spices: 500 shekels of liquid myrrh (a fragrant resin), 250 shekels of sweet cinnamon, 250 shekels of sweet calamus (cane), **24.** 500 shekels of cassia (a spice similar to cinnamon), according to the shekel of the sanctuary, and one hin (about 6 liters) of olive oil. **25.** Prepare a holy anointing oil from these ingredients, an ointment (a soothing or healing substance) created by the skilled work of a perfumer (someone trained in making perfumes and fragrances). It will be sacred. **26.** With this oil, anoint the Tabernacle and all its furnishings: the Ark of the Covenant, **27.** the table and its utensils, the lampstand and its accessories, and the altar of incense. **28.** Also anoint the altar of burnt offering and all its utensils, as well as the laver and its base. **29.** By anointing these items, you will consecrate (dedicate or set apart for a holy purpose) them, making them most holy. Anything that touches them will become holy. **30.** Anoint Aaron and his sons, consecrating them so that they may serve Me as priests. **31.** Say to the Israelites, 'This anointing oil is holy and sacred to Me, throughout all generations. **32.** It is not to be poured on anyone else's body, nor should you make any oil like it. It is set apart as sacred and must remain holy. **33.** Anyone who makes similar oil or uses it improperly shall be cut off (removed) from the community.'" **34.** The Lord also said to Moses: "Take sweet spices: stacte (a resin from a tree), onycha (a fragrant plant), galbanum (a gum resin), and pure frankincense (a fragrant resin), in equal parts. **35.** Prepare these into special incense, a compound created by a perfumer, and make it pure, salted, and holy. **36.** Grind some of it very fine and place it before the Testimony (the Ark of the Covenant) in the Tabernacle, where I will meet with you. This incense will be most holy to you. **37.** Do not make incense for yourselves using the same recipe. It must remain holy, dedicated to the Lord. **38.** Anyone who makes similar incense or uses it for personal purposes shall be cut off from the people."

Chapter 31

1. Then the Lord spoke to Moses, saying: 2. "Look, I have called Bezalel, son of Uri, son of Hur, from the tribe of Judah, by name. 3. I have filled him with the Spirit of God, giving him wisdom (good judgment), understanding (insight), knowledge (facts and skills), and the ability to craft all kinds of work, 4. To create artistic designs, to work with gold, silver, and bronze, 5. to cut and set jewels, to carve wood, and to do all kinds of craftsmanship. 6. I have appointed Aholiab, the son of Ahisamach, from the tribe of Dan, to assist him. I have given wisdom to all who are skilled craftsmen, so they can make everything I have commanded you: 7. the tabernacle (the tent of meeting), the Ark of the Testimony (sacred chest), and its mercy seat (golden lid), and all the furnishings for the tabernacle— 8. The table and its utensils (tools), the pure gold lampstand (light holder), and its accessories, the altar of incense (place for burning incense), 9. the altar of burnt offering (sacrifice altar) and its utensils, the laver (washing basin) and its base (stand), 10. the priestly garments (clothes for service), the holy garments for Aaron the priest and his sons, to serve as priests, 11. and the anointing oil (holy oil) and sweet incense (fragrant spices) for the holy place. They will make everything as I have commanded you." 12. Then the Lord spoke to Moses, saying: 13. "Tell the Israelites: 'You must keep My Sabbaths (day of rest), for it is a sign (symbol) between Me and you, for all generations (descendants), so you may know that I am the Lord who makes you holy (sets you apart). 14. You must keep the Sabbath, for it is holy (sacred) to you. Anyone who profanes (disrespects) it must be put to death (punished severely); anyone who works on it will be cut off (excluded) from the people. 15. Work may be done for six days, but the seventh is a Sabbath of rest (day of rest), holy to the Lord. Anyone who works on the Sabbath must be put to death. 16. The Israelites must keep the Sabbath, observing it throughout their generations (forever) as a lasting covenant (agreement). 17. It is a sign between Me and the Israelites forever; for in six days the Lord made the heavens and the earth, and on the seventh day He rested and was refreshed (He stopped working and enjoyed His work)." 18. When the Lord finished speaking to Moses on Mount Sinai, He gave him two stone tablets containing the Testimony (commandments), written by the finger of God.

Chapter 32

1. When the people saw that Moses was taking too long to come down from the mountain, they gathered around Aaron and said, "Come, make us gods who will go before us. As for Moses, the man who led us out of Egypt, we have no idea what has happened to him." 2. Aaron replied, "Take off the gold earrings from your wives, sons, and daughters, and bring them to me." 3. So the people took off their gold earrings and handed them over to Aaron. 4. He accepted the gold, melted it down, and made a calf (a young cow) by molding it with a tool. Then they said, "This is your god, O Israel, who brought you out of Egypt!" 5. Aaron saw this and built an altar before the idol (a representation or image of a deity). He declared, "Tomorrow we will celebrate a feast in honor of the Lord." 6. The next day, they got up early, offered burnt offerings (sacrifices where the entire animal is burned) and presented peace offerings (sacrificial offerings to make peace with God). Afterward, the people sat down to eat and drink, and began to engage in revelry (wild or immoral celebration). 7. The Lord spoke to Moses, saying, "Go down, because your people, whom you brought out of Egypt, have become corrupt (morally bad). 8. They have quickly strayed (departed) from the instructions I gave them, making an idol in the shape of a calf, worshiping it, and offering sacrifices to it. They are saying, 'This is your god, O Israel, who brought you out of Egypt!'" 9. The Lord continued, "I have seen these people, and they are stiff-necked (stubborn and resistant) people. 10. Now let Me alone, so that My anger may burn (intensify) against them and I can destroy them. But I will make you into a great nation." 11. Moses pleaded with the Lord, his God, and said, "Why, Lord, should Your anger burn hot against Your people, whom You brought out of Egypt with such great power and strength? 12. Why let the Egyptians say, 'He brought them out to destroy them in the mountains and wipe them off the face of the earth'? Turn from Your fierce anger, and reconsider (change) the harm You intend to do to Your people. 13. Remember Your servants Abraham, Isaac, and Israel, to whom You swore by Your own self, saying, 'I will make your descendants as numerous as the stars in the sky, and I will give them this land forever.' 14. So, the Lord relented (changed His mind) and did not bring the disaster He had threatened against His people." 15. Moses turned and went down from the mountain, carrying the two stone tablets with the commandments written on both sides. 16. The tablets were made by God, and the writing on them was God's own engraving (carved or inscribed). 17. When Joshua heard the noise from the camp, he said to Moses, "It sounds like there's a battle in the camp." 18. Moses replied, "It is not the sound of victory, nor the cry of defeat. I hear singing." 19. When Moses came near the camp and saw the calf and the people dancing, he became enraged (angry). He threw the tablets down and shattered (broke into pieces) them at the foot of the mountain. 20. He then took the calf they had made, burned it, ground it into powder, scattered the powder on the water, and made the Israelites drink it. 21. Moses said to Aaron, "What did these people do to you that led you to bring such a great sin upon them?" 22. Aaron answered, "Do not let your anger burn hot. You know how these people are inclined (tend) to evil. 23. They said to me, 'Make us gods to go before us. As for Moses, the man who brought us out of Egypt, we don't know what has happened to him.' 24. So, I told them, 'Whoever has gold, take it off.' They gave it to me, and I threw it into the fire, and out came this calf!" 25. When Moses saw that the people had become uncontrollable (out of control or wild, because Aaron had not restrained them, and they had become a disgrace to their enemies), 26. he stood at the entrance of the camp and said, "Whoever is on the Lord's side, come to me." And all the Levites (members of the tribe of Levi) gathered around him. 27. Moses told them, "This is what the Lord, the God of Israel, says: 'Each of you take your sword (a weapon) and go back and forth through the camp, from gate to gate, and kill those who are against God, whether they are your brothers, companions, or neighbors.'" 28. The Levites obeyed Moses, and about three thousand people died that day. 29. Then Moses said, "Consecrate (dedicate as holy) yourselves today to the Lord, so He may bless you, because each of you was against his own son and brother." 30. The next day, Moses said to the people, "You have committed a great sin. I will now go up to the Lord; perhaps I can atone (make amends) for your sin." 31. Moses returned to the Lord and said, "These people have committed a terrible sin, and they have made for themselves a golden idol. 32. But if You will forgive their sin, that's fine. But if not, please wipe me out of the book You have written." 33. The Lord replied to Moses, "Whoever has sinned against Me, I will remove (blot) from My book. 34. Now go, lead the people to the place I told you about. My angel will go before you. However, when the time for punishment comes, I will punish them for their sin." 35. The Lord sent a plague (a widespread disaster, often caused by disease) upon the people because of what they did with the calf Aaron had made.

Chapter 33

1. The Lord spoke to Moses, saying, "Leave this place and lead the people you brought out of Egypt to the land I promised to Abraham, Isaac, and Jacob, telling them, 'I will give it to your descendants (future generations).' 2. I will send My Angel ahead of you and drive out the Canaanites, Amorites, Hittites, Perizzites, Hivites, and Jebusites (different nations in the land). 3. Go to a land flowing with milk and honey (a prosperous, fertile land), but I will not travel among you, because you are a rebellious (stubborn and disobedient) people. If I stay, I may destroy you on the way." 4. When the people heard these words, they were sorrowful and mourned (were deeply sad). No one put on their jewelry

(ornaments or decorative items). **5.** The Lord had instructed Moses to say to the people, "You are a stubborn people. If I stay among you for even a moment, I might destroy you. So, take off your jewelry, and I will decide what to do with you." **6.** The people then removed their jewelry at Mount Horeb (the mountain where Moses met with God). **7.** Moses set up a tent outside the camp, away from everyone, and called it the "Tabernacle of Meeting" (the place to meet God). Anyone who wanted to seek the Lord would go to this tent. **8.** Whenever Moses went to the tent, the people would stand up and stay at the entrances of their own tents, watching Moses until he entered the Tabernacle. **9.** As Moses entered, the cloud (representing God's presence) would come down and rest at the entrance, and the Lord would speak with Moses. **10.** When the people saw the cloud at the entrance of the tent, they all bowed down (showed respect) and worshiped at the doors of their tents. **11.** The Lord spoke to Moses directly, as a friend speaks to another. Afterward, Moses would return to the camp, but Joshua, the son of Nun (a young man), stayed at the Tabernacle. **12.** Moses said to the Lord, "You told me to lead these people, but You haven't told me whom You will send with me. You've said, 'I know you by name and have found favor (approval) in My sight.' **13.** If I really have found favor with you, please show me Your ways, so that I can truly know You and continue to receive Your grace (unmerited favor). Consider that these people are your people." **14.** The Lord replied, "My Presence (I will be with you) will go with you, and I will give you rest (peace and comfort)." **15.** Moses responded, "If Your Presence does not go with us, then do not bring us up from here. **16.** How will anyone know that we are different from all other people on the earth if you don't go with us? It is your presence that makes us special." **17.** The Lord answered, "I will do what you have asked because you have found favor in my sight, and I know you by name." **18.** Moses then said, "Please, show me your glory (the fullness of your greatness)." **19.** The Lord said, "I will allow all my goodness to pass before you, and I will proclaim (declare) the name of the Lord. I will show mercy (kindness) to whom I choose, and I will have compassion (pity) on whom I choose." **20.** But the Lord added, "You cannot see my face, because no one can see Me and live." **21.** The Lord continued, "There is a place near me where you can stand on the rock (a safe place). **22.** As My glory passes by, I will place you in the cleft (a gap or opening) of the rock and cover you with my hand until I have passed by. **23.** Then I will remove my hand, and you will see My back, but My face will not be visible to you."

Chapter 34

1. The Lord spoke to Moses, saying, "Carve (cut or shape) two new stone tablets, like the first ones you broke. I will write on these tablets the same words that were on the first tablets. **2.** Be ready (prepared) in the morning and come up to Mount Sinai early. Present (show) yourself to Me at the top of the mountain. **3.** Let no one else accompany (go with) you and let no one be seen anywhere on the mountain. Do not allow any livestock (domestic animals like cows or sheep) to graze (eat grass) at the foot of the mountain." **4.** So, Moses cut two new stone tablets, just like the first ones. He rose early the next day and went up to mount Sinai, carrying the two tablets in his hands, as the Lord had instructed (directed). **5.** The Lord came down in a cloud and stood with Moses there, declaring (announcing or proclaiming) the name of the Lord. **6.** As the Lord passed by Moses, He proclaimed: "The Lord, the Lord God, merciful (showing compassion) and compassionate (kind), slow to anger, and rich in love and faithfulness (trustworthiness), **7.** Showing mercy to thousands, forgiving iniquity (wrongdoing), rebellion (defiance), and sin, but not leaving the guilty unpunished, visiting (punishing or holding accountable) the iniquity of the fathers upon the children and the children's children to the third and fourth generations." **8.** Moses immediately bowed down to the ground and worshiped (showed reverence). **9.** Then he said, "If I have found favor (grace or approval) in your sight, O Lord, please

go with us, even though we are a stubborn (unwilling to change) and rebellious (disobedient) people. Forgive our iniquity and sin and take us as your inheritance (your people or possession)." **10.** The Lord answered, "I am making a covenant (binding agreement or promise) with you. Before all your people, I will perform wonders (miraculous acts) that have never been done anywhere in the world or among any nation. The people around you will see my mighty work. What I am going to do with you will be awe-inspiring (causing deep respect or wonder). **11.** be careful to follow all that I command you today. I am driving out (removing) the Amorites, Canaanites, Hittites, Perizzites, Hivites, and Jebusites before you. **12.** Be on guard (watchful), and do not make a covenant with the people living in the land where you are going, lest it become a snare (trap) for you. **13.** You must destroy their altars, break their sacred stones (idols), and cut down their Asherah poles (wooden idols). **14.** For you must not worship any other god, because the Lord, whose name is Jealous (having strong, passionate devotion), is a jealous God. **15.** Do not make a covenant with the people of the land, for when they worship their gods and sacrifice to them, they may invite you, and you will eat their sacrifices. **16.** You may even take their daughters as wives for your sons, and they will lead your sons to worship their gods. **17.** You must not make any idols (carved images or statues) for yourselves. **18.** "You must observe the Feast of Unleavened Bread. For seven days, eat unleavened (without yeast) bread, as I commanded you, at the appointed time in the month of Abib, for it was in that month that you came out of Egypt. **19.** The firstborn (first offspring) of every creature belongs to Me, and every firstborn male of your livestock, whether ox or sheep, is Mine. **20.** But you must redeem (buy back) the firstborn of a donkey with a lamb. If you do not redeem it, you must break its neck. You must redeem every firstborn son. No one should come before Me empty-handed (without a gift). **21.** "Work for six days, but on the seventh day, rest, even during the busy seasons of plowing and harvesting. **22.** Celebrate (observe) the Feast of Weeks (Shavuot), the first fruits (first harvest) of the wheat harvest, and the Feast of Ingathering (harvest festival) at the end of the year. **23.** Three times a year, all your men must appear before the Lord, the God of Israel. **24.** I will drive out the nations before you and expand your borders. No one will covet (desire) your land when you come to appear before the Lord three times a year. **25.** Do not offer the blood of My sacrifice with leaven (yeast), nor should the sacrifice for the Passover be left over until morning. **26.** Bring the first fruits of your land to the house of the Lord your God. Do not boil (cook) a young goat in its mother's milk." **27.** Then the Lord said to Moses, "Write down these words, for in accordance with these words I have made a covenant with you and with Israel." **28.** Moses was there with the Lord for forty days and forty nights. He neither ate bread nor drank water, and during this time, God wrote the words of the covenant—the Ten Commandments—on the tablets. **29.** When Moses came down from Mount Sinai, carrying the two tablets of the covenant in his hands, he did not realize that his face shone (was glowing) from speaking with the Lord. **30.** When Aaron and all the Israelites saw Moses, and saw that his face was shining, they were afraid (afraid or overwhelmed) to come near him. **31.** But Moses called to them, and Aaron and all the leaders of the congregation returned to him, and Moses spoke with them. **32.** Afterward, all the Israelites came near, and he gave them the commandments the Lord had given him on Mount Sinai. **33.** When Moses finished speaking with them, he put a veil (covering) over his face. **34.** But whenever Moses went in before the Lord to speak with Him, he would remove the veil until he came out. Then he would come out and tell the Israelites what he had been commanded. **35.** Whenever the Israelites saw Moses' radiant (glowing) face, he would put the veil back on until he went in again to speak with the Lord.

Chapter 35

1. Then Moses called together the entire assembly (a group or gathering) of the Israelites and said to them, "These are the commands the Lord has instructed you to follow: 2. Work is to be done for six days, but the seventh day must be set aside as a day of holiness (the state of being holy, sacred or consecrated), a Sabbath of rest dedicated to the Lord. Anyone who works on that day must be put to death. 3. You are not to light any fires within your homes on the Sabbath day." 4. Moses then spoke to the congregation (a gathering of people for a religious or ceremonial purpose) of Israel, saying, "This is the command the Lord has given, saying: 5. 'Take a contribution (a voluntary gift) for the Lord from among you. Let everyone whose heart moves them bring an offering to the Lord: gold, silver, and bronze; 6. blue, purple, and scarlet yarn (thread), fine linen (high-quality cloth), and goats' hair; 7. ram skins dyed red, the skins of sea cows (a type of animal skin), and acacia wood (a durable wood from an acacia tree); 8. oil for the lamps, spices (aromatic substances) for the anointing oil and for the incense; 9. onyx stones (a precious gemstone, often black or striped), and stones to be set in the ephod (a special priestly garment) and in the breastplate (a piece of clothing worn by the high priest). 10. Let all who are skilled (talented or proficient) among you come and make everything that the Lord has commanded: 11. the tabernacle (a portable place of worship), its tent, its coverings, its clasps (fasteners), its frames, its bars (horizontal supports), its pillars (vertical supports), and its sockets (bases); 12. the ark (a sacred chest or container) and its poles, with the mercy seat (the lid of the ark, symbolizing God's presence), and the curtain (a hanging partition) for the tabernacle; 13. the table and its poles, along with all its utensils (tools or instruments), and the showbread (the sacred loaves of bread); 14. the lampstand (a stand for lamps) for the light, its accessories, its lamps, and the oil for the lamps; 15. the altar of incense (a platform for burning incense), its poles, the anointing oil, the incense, and the screen (a barrier or curtain) for the door at the entrance of the tabernacle; 16. the altar of burnt offering (a place for sacrifices), with its bronze grate (a metal grid), its poles, its utensils, and the basin (a large container) with its stand; 17. the curtains (cloths) for the courtyard, their pillars, their bases, and the gate curtain for the courtyard; 18. the stakes (pegs used to anchor something) for the tabernacle, the stakes for the courtyard, and their cords (ropes); 19. the garments for service (clothing worn for priestly duties) in the sanctuary (a sacred space)—the holy garments for Aaron the priest and the garments for his sons to serve as priests.'" 20. Then all the Israelites left Moses' presence. 21. And everyone whose heart was moved (stirred emotionally), and whose spirit (inner being or attitude) was willing, brought the Lord's offering for the work of the tabernacle, for all its services, and for the sacred garments. 22. Both men and women came, all who had willing hearts, and brought earrings, rings, necklaces, and all kinds of gold jewelry—every one who offered gold to the Lord. 23. And everyone who had blue, purple, and scarlet yarn, fine linen, goats' hair, rams' skins dyed red, and the skins of sea cows, brought them. 24. All those who offered silver or bronze brought their offering to the Lord. Everyone who had acacia wood for any of the work of the service brought it. 25. All the women who were skilled spinners (those who twist fibers into thread) spun the yarn (twisted fibers into thread) with their hands and brought what they had spun: blue, purple, and scarlet yarn, and fine linen. 26. And all the women whose hearts were stirred with wisdom (insight or understanding) spun the yarn from goats' hair. 27. The leaders (chiefs or officials) brought onyx stones and other stones to be set in the ephod and the breastplate, 28. as well as spices and oil for the light, for the anointing oil, and for sweet-smelling incense. 29. The Israelites brought a freewill offering (a voluntary gift given out of willingness) to the Lord, all the men and women whose hearts were willing to contribute for the work which the Lord, by the hand of Moses, had commanded to be done. 30. Then Moses said to the Israelites, "See, the Lord has called by name Bezalel the son of Uri, the son of Hur, of the tribe of Judah; 31. and He has filled him with the Spirit (divine influence or presence) of God, in wisdom (deep understanding), understanding, knowledge, and all kinds of craftsmanship (artistic and skilled work), 32. to design artistic works (creative creations), to work with gold, silver, and bronze, 33. in cutting (shaping) and setting stones, in carving wood, and to work in all kinds of artistic craftsmanship. 34. He has given him the ability to teach, both him and Aholiab, the son of Ahisamach, from the tribe of Dan. 35. He has filled them with skill (talent or ability) to do every kind of engraving (inscribing), artistic design, and tapestry work (woven designs), using blue, purple, and scarlet yarn, fine linen, and weaving, as well as other forms of artistic creation."

Chapter 36

1. Bezalel (a skilled artisan) and Aholiab (another skilled artisan), along with every gifted artisan to whom the Lord had given wisdom and understanding, and who knew how to perform every task needed for the service of the sanctuary, were to carry out all the work as commanded by the Lord. 2. Moses then called upon Bezalel, Aholiab, and every skilled worker whose heart the Lord had inspired with wisdom and who was eager to do the work. 3. They received from Moses all the offerings the Israelites had brought for the work of constructing the sanctuary. The people continued to bring their offerings every morning, giving freely. 4. Eventually, all the craftsmen working on the sanctuary came to Moses, each one coming from their respective tasks, 5. and they said to him, "The people are bringing far more than what is needed for the work the Lord has commanded us to do." 6. So Moses issued a command, and the people were told throughout the camp, "Let neither man nor woman bring any more offerings for the sanctuary." And the people stopped bringing, 7. because the materials were more than enough to complete all the work. 8. The skilled workers then made ten curtains (pieces of cloth) for the tabernacle using fine linen, and dyed them with blue, purple, and scarlet thread. They embroidered (decorated by stitching) them with designs of cherubim (angel-like beings). 9. Each curtain was 28 cubits (about 42 feet) in length and 4 cubits (about 6 feet) in width. All the curtains were of the same size. 10. Five curtains were joined together to form one set, and the other five were also joined to make another set. 11. Loops (small rings or eyelets) of blue yarn were made along the edge of the curtains in one set, and similarly on the edge of the other set. 12. Fifty loops were made on one curtain, and fifty loops on the corresponding curtain of the second set; these loops helped hold the curtains together. 13. Fifty gold clasps (fasteners made of gold) were made to fasten the curtains together so they would form one complete tabernacle. 14. Next, he made curtains of goats' hair (a type of fabric made from the hair of goats) to serve as a covering for the tent over the tabernacle, making eleven of them. 15. Each curtain was 30 cubits (about 45 feet) in length and 4 cubits (about 6 feet) in width. All eleven curtains were the same size. 16. He joined five curtains together and six curtains together as separate sets. 17. Loops (rings or eyelets) were made on the outer edge of the curtains in each set— fifty loops on each set. 18. Fifty bronze clasps (fasteners made of bronze) were made to join the curtains together, so that the tent would be unified. 19. He made coverings for the tent, first from ram skins dyed red (the skins of rams, dyed a red color), and on top of that, a covering made from badger skins (possibly a type of durable hide). 20. For the tabernacle, he made boards of acacia wood (a type of strong, durable wood), standing upright. 21. Each board was 10 cubits (about 15 feet) tall and 1.5 cubits (about 2.25 feet) wide. 22. Each board had two tenons (projections or extensions on the bottom of the boards, used to interlock them) at the bottom to attach to another board. He made these for all the boards. 23. On the south side of the tabernacle, he made 20 boards. 24. He made 40 silver sockets (base or foundation made of silver) to go under the 20 boards—two sockets under each board,

one for each tenon. **25.** On the north side of the tabernacle, he made another 20 boards, **26.** along with 40 silver sockets to go under them, two for each board. **27.** On the west side of the tabernacle, he made 6 boards. **28.** He also made two additional boards for the two back corners of the tabernacle. **29.** These boards were joined at the bottom and held together at the top by one ring (a circular fastening), forming the two corners. **30.** In total, there were 8 boards with 16 silver sockets—two under each board. **31.** He made acacia wood (strong wood) bars (long pieces of wood for support) to strengthen the structure: five bars for the boards on one side of the tabernacle, **32.** five bars for the boards on the other side, and five bars for the west side of the tabernacle. **33.** He made a central bar (a horizontal support) that passed through the boards from one end to the other, **34.** overlaying all the boards and bars with gold (precious metal), and making gold rings (small hoops) to hold the bars in place. **35.** He made a veil (a curtain) of blue, purple, and scarlet thread, and fine linen, woven with artistic designs of cherubim. **36.** He made for it four pillars of acacia wood (wood from a strong tree), overlaid them with gold (precious metal), with their hooks (fasteners) made of gold. For these, he cast four sockets (bases) of silver. **37.** Finally, he made a screen (a decorative curtain) for the tabernacle door using blue, purple, and scarlet thread, and fine linen, made by a skilled weaver. **38.** He made five pillars for the screen, overlaid their capitals (tops of the pillars) and rings with gold, but their sockets (bases) were made of bronze.

Chapter 37

1. Bezalel (a skilled artisan) made the ark (a sacred chest) out of acacia wood (a strong, durable wood); its length was two and a half cubits (about 3.75 feet), its width was a cubit and a half (about 2.25 feet), and its height was a cubit and a half. **2.** He covered it with pure gold (unmixed gold) inside and outside, and he made a molding (decorative trim) of gold all around it. **3.** He cast four rings of gold for it, placing them at the four corners of the ark—two rings on one side, and two on the other side. **4.** He made poles (long, supporting rods) of acacia wood and covered them with gold. **5.** He inserted the poles into the rings on the sides of the ark, so the ark could be carried. **6.** He also made the mercy seat (the lid or cover of the ark) out of pure gold. Its length was two and a half cubits, and its width was a cubit and a half. **7.** He made two cherubim (angel-like figures) of hammered gold; they were made from one solid piece of gold, positioned at the two ends of the mercy seat: **8.** One cherub was placed at one end, and the other cherub at the other end. The cherubim were made as one piece with the mercy seat at both ends. **9.** The cherubim spread their wings above, covering the mercy seat with their wings. They faced each other, with their faces directed toward the mercy seat. **10.** Bezalel made the table (for the bread of the Presence) from acacia wood. Its length was two cubits, its width was one cubit, and its height was a cubit and a half. **11.** He overlaid it with pure gold and made a molding (decorative trim) of gold all around it. **12.** He also made a frame (raised border) of a handbreadth (about four inches) around it, and added a molding of gold for the frame. **13.** He cast four rings of gold for the table, placing the rings at the four corners near the legs. **14.** The rings were placed close to the frame to hold the poles that would be used to carry the table. **15.** Bezalel made poles of acacia wood to carry the table and covered them with gold. **16.** He made the utensils (tools) for the table from pure gold, including its dishes (plates), cups, bowls, and pitchers (for pouring). **17.** Bezalel made the lampstand (a menorah) from pure gold; he crafted it with hammered work. Its shaft (main stem), branches, bowls, ornamental knobs, and flowers were all made from one solid piece of gold. **18.** Six branches extended from the sides of the lampstand: three branches on one side and three on the other side. **19.** On each branch, there were three bowls (shaped like almond blossoms), each with an ornamental knob (decorative ball) and a flower, repeating this design for the six branches. **20.** On the

lampstand itself, there were four additional bowls made like almond blossoms, each with an ornamental knob and flower. **21.** There was a knob under the first two branches, a knob under the next two branches, and a knob under the last two branches, in total matching the six branches extending from the lampstand. **22.** The knobs (decorative spheres) and the branches were all made from one solid piece; the entire lampstand was a single, hammered (shaped by striking) piece of pure gold. **23.** Bezalel made seven lamps for the lampstand, as well as its wick trimmers (tools to trim the wick) and its trays (small containers) of pure gold. **24.** He made the lampstand and all its utensils from a talent (a unit of weight, about 75 pounds) of pure gold. **25.** He made the incense altar from acacia wood. Its length was a cubit (about 18 inches), its width was a cubit, making it square, and its height was two cubits (about 3 feet). Its horns (projections at the corners) were made from the same piece of wood. **26.** He overlaid it with pure gold: the top, sides, and horns, and made a molding of gold around it. **27.** He made two rings of gold for the altar, placing them under the molding, on both sides, to hold the poles used for carrying it. **28.** Bezalel made the poles of acacia wood and covered them with gold. **29.** Finally, he made the holy anointing oil (a special sacred oil) and the pure incense (fragrant substances) with sweet spices, according to the work of a perfumer.

Chapter 38

1. He constructed the altar for burnt offerings using acacia wood. The altar measured five cubits in length, five cubits in width (it was square), and three cubits in height. **2.** He made horns on each of the four corners of the altar; the horns were an integral part of the altar, formed from the same piece. Then he covered it with bronze. **3.** He created all the tools for the altar: the pans, shovels, basins, forks, and firepans—all of which were made from bronze. **4.** A bronze grate, designed as a network, was made for the altar and placed halfway down from the top, just under the rim. **5.** He cast four rings for the four corners of the bronze grate to serve as holders for the poles. **6.** He made the poles from acacia wood and covered them with bronze. **7.** He inserted the poles into the rings at the sides of the altar, to be used for carrying it. The altar was constructed hollow, using wooden boards. **8.** He made a bronze laver (a large basin for washing) and its base from the bronze mirrors donated by the serving women who gathered at the entrance of the tabernacle. **9.** He built the court on the south side. The walls of the court consisted of fine linen, measuring one hundred cubits in length. **10.** There were twenty pillars for these walls, with twenty bronze bases. The hooks of the pillars and their connecting bands were made of silver. **11.** On the north side, the walls were also one hundred cubits long, supported by twenty pillars, each with a bronze base. The hooks and connecting bands of these pillars were silver. **12.** On the west side, the walls were fifty cubits long, supported by ten pillars and ten bases. The hooks and bands of the pillars were silver. **13.** On the east side, the walls were also fifty cubits long. **14.** On one side of the gate, the hangings were fifteen cubits long, with three pillars and three bronze bases. **15.** The same arrangement was made for the other side of the gate, with hangings fifteen cubits long and three pillars with three bases. **16.** All the hangings around the entire court were made from fine woven linen. **17.** The bases for the pillars were bronze. The hooks of the pillars and their connecting bands were silver, and their capitals (top parts) were overlaid with silver. Every pillar of the court had silver bands. **18.** The gate of the court had a screen made of blue, purple, and scarlet thread, woven from fine linen. The screen was twenty cubits long and five cubits high, matching the height of the court's hangings. **19.** Four pillars supported the screen, each with a bronze base. The hooks were silver, and the capitals and connecting bands were silver. **20.** All the pegs used for the tabernacle and the court surrounding it were made of bronze. **21.** This is the list of items used for the tabernacle, known as the tabernacle of the Testimony, which was assembled according to the Lord's command through Moses, for the service of the Levites. The work was carried out under the supervision of Ithamar, the son of Aaron the priest. **22.** Bezalel, the son of Uri, the son of Hur, from the tribe of Judah, made everything the Lord had commanded Moses. **23.** Aholiab, the son of Ahisamach, from the tribe of Dan, assisted him. Aholiab was a skilled engraver, designer, and weaver of blue, purple, and scarlet thread, as well as fine linen. **24.** The total amount of gold used for all the work in the holy place was twenty-nine talents and seven hundred thirty shekels, according to the sanctuary shekel. **25.** The silver collected from the people who were counted in the census amounted to one hundred talents and one thousand seven hundred seventy-five shekels, also according to the sanctuary shekel. **26.** Each person was required to give half a shekel (a bekah) as an offering, from those counted in the census, which included every male aged twenty and older, numbering six hundred three thousand five hundred fifty men. **27.** From the one hundred talents of silver, the sockets for the sanctuary and the bases for the veil were cast. One hundred sockets were made, with each socket weighing one talent. **28.** From the one thousand seven hundred seventy-five shekels, hooks were made for the pillars, and their capitals were overlaid with silver, and connecting bands were made for them. **29.** The bronze offering amounted to seventy talents and two thousand four hundred shekels. **30.** With the bronze, he made the sockets for the door of the tabernacle, the bronze altar, its bronze grate, and all the utensils for the altar. **31.** The bronze was also used to make the sockets for the court around the tabernacle, the bases for the court gate, and all the pegs for both the tabernacle and the surrounding court.

Chapter 39

1. They made special garments for ministry using blue, purple, and scarlet thread, designed for serving in the holy place. They also made holy garments for Aaron, as the Lord had commanded Moses. **2.** They crafted the ephod (a special sacred garment worn by the high priest) from gold, blue, purple, and scarlet thread, and fine woven linen. **3.** They hammered the gold into thin sheets and cut it into threads to be worked into the blue, purple, and scarlet thread and fine linen, creating intricate designs. **4.** They made shoulder straps (pieces of fabric to hold the ephod together) for the ephod to hold it together; the two edges of the ephod were joined together at these straps. **5.** The band (a woven piece around the ephod) that went around the ephod was intricately woven from gold, blue, purple, and scarlet thread, and fine woven linen, just as the Lord had commanded Moses. **6.** They set onyx stones (precious stones, often black and white) in gold settings (golden frames), engraving them with the names of the twelve sons of Israel, just like signet (a ring used to stamp an official seal) rings are engraved. **7.** They placed the onyx stones on the shoulders of the ephod, where they served as memorial stones (stones to remember the tribes of Israel), as the Lord had commanded Moses. **8.** They made the breastplate (a square, chest-covering piece of the high priest's garment), woven like the ephod, using gold, blue, purple, and scarlet thread, and fine linen. **9.** The breastplate was doubled (folded to make it thicker) to make it square, with its length and width each being a span (a span is roughly the width of a human hand, about 9 inches when doubled). **10.** They set four rows of stones on the breastplate: in the first row, a sardius, topaz, and emerald; **11.** In the second row, a turquoise, sapphire, and diamond; **12.** In the third row, a jacinth, agate, and amethyst; **13.** In the fourth row, a beryl, onyx, and jasper. The stones were enclosed in gold settings (golden frames), placed securely in their mountings. **14.** The twelve stones represented the twelve sons of Israel, with each stone engraved with the name of one of the tribes, like a signet (a ring or seal used to make an impression). **15.** They made braided gold chains (chains made by twisting strands of gold together) for the breastplate to secure it, attaching them at the ends. **16.** They also made two gold settings and two gold rings, placing the rings on the two ends of the breastplate. **17.** They threaded the two braided chains of gold through the two rings on the ends of the breastplate. **18.** The ends of the two chains were fastened in the two settings, and they were placed on the shoulder straps of the ephod at the front. **19.** They made two gold rings and placed them at the two edges of the breastplate, on the inner side of the ephod. **20.** They made two more gold rings and placed them on the shoulder straps of the ephod, near the seam at the front, just above the intricate woven band of the ephod. **21.** They attached the breastplate to the ephod using a blue cord (a cord of blue fabric), so that it rested above the woven band of the ephod and would not come loose, just as the Lord had commanded Moses. **22.** He made the robe (a long garment) of the ephod from woven blue fabric. **23.** The robe had an opening in the center, like the opening in a coat of mail (a type of armor), with a woven border around it to prevent it from tearing. **24.** They made pomegranates (decorative fruit-shaped ornaments) of blue, purple, and scarlet thread, and fine woven linen, for the hem (bottom edge) of the robe. **25.** They made bells (small, metal objects that ring when shaken) of pure gold and placed them between the pomegranates on the hem of the robe. **26.** The design alternated: a bell and a pomegranate, a bell and a pomegranate, all around the hem of the robe, to be worn while ministering (serving or working as a priest), as the Lord had commanded Moses. **27.** They made tunics (long, loose garments) from fine linen for Aaron and his sons. **28.** They also made a turban (a type of head covering) of fine linen, exquisite hats (special headpieces) of fine linen, and short trousers (short pants or undergarments) of fine woven linen. **29.** They made a sash (a wide belt) of fine linen, woven with blue, purple, and scarlet thread, crafted by a weaver (a person who weaves fabric), as the Lord had commanded Moses. **30.** They made the plate for the holy crown of pure gold, engraving on it an inscription like the engraving on a signet: "HOLINESS TO THE LORD." **31.** They attached the plate to a blue cord and fastened it above the turban, just as the Lord had commanded Moses. **32.** Thus, the work on the tabernacle (the sacred tent of meeting) was completed. The Israelites did everything exactly as the Lord had commanded Moses. **33.** They brought the tabernacle to Moses, including the tent and all its furnishings: its clasps (fasteners or hooks), its boards (large planks), its bars (rods that connect the boards), its pillars (supports), and its sockets (bases); **34.** The covering of ram skins dyed red, the covering of badger skins (a type of leather), and the veil (curtain) for the covering; **35.** The ark of the Testimony (the sacred chest containing the Ten Commandments) with its poles, and the mercy seat (the lid of the ark); **36.** The table, all its utensils, and the showbread (the bread placed on the table); **37.** The pure gold lampstand with its lamps (lights), all its utensils, and the oil for lighting; **38.** The gold altar, the anointing oil, and the sweet incense; the screen for the tabernacle door; **39.** The bronze altar, its bronze grate (mesh), its poles, and all its utensils; the laver (a basin) with its base; **40.** The hangings (walls) of the court, its pillars, and its sockets, the screen for the court gate, its cords, and its pegs (stakes); all the utensils for the service of the tabernacle, for the tent of meeting; **41.** And the garments for ministry to serve in the holy place: the holy garments for Aaron the priest, and the garments for his sons to serve as priests. **42.** The Israelites did all the work just as the Lord had commanded Moses. **43.** Then Moses reviewed all the work, and indeed they had completed it exactly as the Lord had commanded. Moses blessed (praised or gave thanks to) them for their work.

Chapter 40

1. The Lord instructed Moses, saying, **2.** "On the first day of the first month, you are to set up the tabernacle (the sacred worship tent) for the meeting place. **3.** Place the Ark of the Covenant (the chest containing the tablets of the law) inside, and separate it with the veil (curtain dividing the holy from the most holy place). **4.** Position the table in the tabernacle, arrange its items as prescribed, and set up the lampstand (the light fixture) and light its lamps. **5.** Set the golden altar (altar made of gold) for incense in front of the Ark of the Covenant, and hang the screen (curtain) at the door of the tabernacle. **6.** Place the altar for burnt offerings (where sacrifices are made) in front of the entrance to the tabernacle. **7.** Put the laver (a basin for washing) between the tabernacle and the altar, and fill it with water. **8.** Set up the surrounding courtyard (the area around the tabernacle), and hang the screen at the entrance of the courtyard. **9.** Take the anointing oil (holy oil for consecration) and anoint the tabernacle and all its furnishings, consecrating (making holy) them. **10.** Anoint the altar for burnt offerings and all its tools, sanctifying (setting apart as holy) the altar. **11.** Anoint the laver and its base (the bottom part), consecrating them. **12.** Bring Aaron (the high priest) and his sons to the entrance of the tabernacle and wash them with water. **13.** Put the holy garments (special priestly clothes) on Aaron, anoint him, and consecrate him to serve as a priest before Me. **14.** Dress Aaron's sons in tunics (long robes), **15.** Anoint them just as you did Aaron, so they can serve as priests. This anointing will establish a permanent priesthood for them." **16.** Moses did everything as the Lord commanded. **17.** On the first day of the first month of the second year, the tabernacle was erected. **18.** Moses assembled the tabernacle, attached its sockets (the bases that hold the structure), arranged the boards, put in the crossbars (horizontal supports), and raised the pillars. **19.** He spread the tent over the tabernacle and placed the covering (the protective outer layer) on top, just as the Lord had directed. **20.** He placed the Ark of the Covenant inside the tabernacle, inserted the poles (carrying rods) through its rings, and placed the mercy seat (the cover of the Ark) on top. **21.** He brought the Ark into the tabernacle, hung the veil (curtain) to divide the holy place, and enclosed the Ark as instructed by the Lord. **22.** He positioned the table inside the tabernacle, on the north side, outside the veil, **23.** and arranged the bread of the Presence before the Lord, as commanded. **24.** He placed the lampstand inside the tabernacle, across from the table, on the south side, **25.** and lit its lamps in front of the Lord, as commanded. **26.** He set the golden altar in front of the veil, **27.** and burned incense (a sweet-smelling offering) on it, as instructed. **28.** He hung the screen at the entrance to the tabernacle. **29.** He set the altar for burnt offerings at the entrance of the tabernacle, and offered burnt offerings (completely consumed animal sacrifices) and grain offerings (sacrifices of flour or grains) on it, as directed. **30.** He placed the laver between the tabernacle and the altar and filled it with water for washing. **31.** Moses, Aaron, and his sons washed their hands and feet with the water from the laver, **32.** whenever they entered the tabernacle or approached the altar, in obedience to the Lord's instructions. **33.** Moses finished the outer courtyard (the area around the tabernacle), and hung the screen at the entrance. **34.** Then the cloud (a visible sign of God's presence) covered the tabernacle, and the glory (the radiant presence) of the Lord filled it. **35.** Moses could not enter the tabernacle because the cloud rested on it, and the Lord's glory filled it. **36.** Whenever the cloud was lifted from above the tabernacle, the Israelites would continue their journey. **37.** If the cloud did not lift, they stayed where they were until the cloud was lifted. **38.** The cloud of the Lord was above the tabernacle during the day, and fire was over it at night, visible to all of Israel throughout their travels.

3 – Leviticus

Chapter 1

1. The Lord spoke to Moses from the Tabernacle (sacred tent or dwelling place of God) of Meeting, saying, **2.** "Tell the Israelites: When anyone brings an offering (gift or sacrifice) to the Lord, it should be from their animals—either cattle (large domesticated animals like cows) or sheep/goats. **3.** If it is a burnt offering (sacrifice completely burned) from the herd (group of cattle), it must be a flawless (without defect) male, presented willingly (voluntarily, not forced) at the entrance of the Tabernacle. **4.** The person offering it should place their hand on the animal's head, which will be accepted by God to make atonement (reconciliation or forgiveness) for them. **5.** They shall then slaughter (kill for sacrifice) the bull (male cow) before the Lord, and Aaron's sons, the priests, will sprinkle (scatter) its blood around the altar at the Tabernacle's entrance. **6.** They will skin (remove the skin) the animal and cut it into pieces. **7.** The priests will place fire and wood on the altar, **8.** then arrange (set in order) the head, fat (the fatty parts), and other pieces on the wood. **9.** The person must wash (clean) the animal's entrails (internal organs) and legs, and the priest will burn the whole offering, producing a pleasing aroma (fragrance) to the Lord. **10.** If the offering is from the flock (group of sheep or goats), it must also be a flawless male. **11.** The person shall slaughter it on the north side of the altar before the Lord, and the priests will sprinkle its blood around the altar. **12.** They will cut it into pieces, including the head and fat, and arrange these on the burning wood. **13.** After washing the entrails and legs, the priest will burn the whole offering on the altar, a pleasing aroma to the Lord. **14.** If the offering is a bird (like a turtledove or pigeon), **15.** the priest will bring it to the altar, remove its head, burn it, and drain (remove) the blood beside the altar. **16.** The crop (part of the bird's digestive system) and feathers will be removed and placed on the east side, in the ash pile. **17.** The priest will then split (cut) the wings without severing (completely cutting off) them fully and burn the bird on the altar as a pleasing aroma to the Lord."

Chapter 2

1. "When someone brings a grain offering to the Lord, it must be made from the finest flour. You shall pour oil on it and sprinkle frankincense (aromatic resin) over it." **2.** The offering should then be presented to the priests, the sons of Aaron (Moses' brother). One of them will take a portion of the flour, oil, and all the frankincense, and burn it as a memorial offering on the altar. It will be an offering by fire, creating a pleasing fragrance before the Lord. **3.** The rest of the grain offering will be for Aaron and his sons to keep. It is the most sacred of the offerings made by fire to the Lord. **4.** If your offering is baked in an oven, it must consist of unleavened (without yeast) cakes of fine flour mixed with oil, or thin, unleavened wafers (thin crisp bread) brushed with oil. **5.** If the offering is prepared on a pan, it should also be made from fine flour, unleavened, and mixed with oil. **6.** You shall break the offering into pieces and pour oil over it. This will serve as your grain offering. **7.** If the grain offering is cooked in a covered pan, it should be made from fine flour and oil. **8.** You must bring this offering to the Lord, and when it is presented to the priest, he shall take it to the altar. **9.** The priest will take a portion of the offering as a memorial (remembrance), burning it on the altar. It will be an offering made by fire, producing a pleasing aroma (fragrant scent) to the Lord. **10.** The remaining portion will be for Aaron and his sons. It will be the most sacred (holy) part of the offerings made by fire to the Lord. **11.** No grain offering you bring to the Lord should contain leaven (yeast). You are not to burn any leaven or honey in your fire offerings to the Lord. **12.** While you may present first fruits (the initial harvest) to the Lord, these are not to be burned on the altar as a fragrant offering. **13.** Every grain offering you bring should be seasoned with salt. You must not omit the salt of the covenant of your God from any of your offerings. All your offerings should include salt. **14.** If you present a grain offering of your first fruits to the Lord, you should bring fresh, green heads of grain roasted in fire. These should be grains from fully formed heads. **15.** You shall pour oil on it and sprinkle frankincense (aromatic resin) on it. This will be considered your grain offering. **16.** The priest will take a portion of this offering—a part of the roasted (cooked by heat) grain, oil, and all the frankincense—and burn it as an offering made by fire to the Lord.

Chapter 3

1. "When anyone brings a peace immolation to the Lord, and if the immolation is from the herd (cattle), whether it's male or female, it must be without any mark (disfigurement) and presented in front of the Lord. **2.** The person offering it must lay their hand on the beast's head (emblemizing the transfer of sins or identification with the beast), and then kill it at the entrance of the Temple of Meeting (the sacred place). Aaron's sons (the priests) will sprinkle the blood (spread it) all around the altar. **3.** From the peace immolation, the person shall take the fat and offer it as an immolation made by fire to the Lord. This includes the fat that covers the entrails (internal organs), and all the fat that's on the entrails, **4.** the two kidneys and the fat that is on them, near the sides (the sides of the beast near the rear), and the adipose lobe (fatty portion) of the liver above the kidneys, all of which shall be removed, **5.** Aaron's sons will also burn all of this fat on the altar, upon the wood, as an immolation made by fire, a sweet aroma (a pleasant smell) to the Lord. **6.** If the peace immolation is from the flock (lamb), whether male or female, it must also be without mark. **7.** It shall be presented in front of the Lord if the immolation is a lamb (young sheep). **8.** The person shall lay their hand on the lamb's head, and then kill it in front of the Temple of Meeting. Aaron's sons, the priests, will sprinkle its blood all around the altar. **9.** From the lamb, the person will present the fat, including the whole fat tail (a large, fatty tail on some sheep), which must be removed near the backbone. Also, the fat that covers the entrails and all the fat on the entrails, **10.** the two kidneys and the fat around them near the sides, and the adipose lobe of the liver above the kidneys must all be removed. **11.** The priest shall burn them on the altar as food, an immolation made by fire to the Lord, a sweet aroma to the Lord. **12.** If the immolation is a goat (scapegoat), it shall also be presented before the Lord. **13.** The person shall lay their hand on the goat's head and kill it in front of the Temple of Meeting. Aaron's sons will sprinkle its blood all around the altar. **14.** From the goat, the person will present the fat as an immolation made by fire to the Lord. This includes the fat that covers the entrails and all the fat on the entrails, **15.** the two kidneys and the fat that is on them near the sides, and the adipose lobe attached to the liver above the kidneys, which must be removed. **16.** The priest will also burn all of the fat on the altar as food, an immolation made by fire, a sweet aroma to the Lord. All the fat belongs to the Lord. **17.** This will be a lasting rule (a permanent command) for all generations, wherever you live. You must not eat any fat or blood."

Chapter 4

1. The Lord spoke to Moses, saying, **2.** "Tell the Israelites: If anyone unintentionally (without intention or by mistake) breaks any of the Lord's commandments, **3.** and if the anointed (chosen and consecrated for service) priest sins, bringing guilt (responsibility for wrongdoing) upon the people, he must offer a flawless (without defect) young bull as a sin offering (a sacrifice to atone for sin). **4.** He will bring it to the tabernacle (a sacred tent or dwelling place of God), lay his hand on its head, and slaughter (kill for sacrifice) it before the Lord. **5.** The priest will take some of the blood into the tabernacle, **6.** dip (immerse briefly) his finger in it, and sprinkle (scatter) it seven times before the Lord, in front of the veil (a curtain separating the holy place). **7.** He will place some of the blood on the horns (raised projections) of the altar of incense and pour the rest at the base (bottom) of the altar of burnt offering. **8.** The priest shall burn all the fat from the bull on the altar— **9.** the fat covering the internal organs (the organs inside the body), kidneys, and liver lobe (a section of the liver). **10.** The bull's hide (skin), flesh (meat), head, legs, internal organs, and intestines (digestive organs)— **11.** the whole bull—shall be taken outside the camp and burned (consumed by fire). **12.** If the entire congregation (gathered community) unintentionally sins, and the matter is unknown (not yet discovered), **13.** when the sin is discovered, they must offer a young bull at the entrance of the tabernacle. **14.** The elders (leaders) will lay their hands on the bull's head, and it will be slaughtered before the Lord. **15.** The priest will take some of its blood into the tabernacle, **16.** dip his finger in it, and sprinkle it

seven times before the Lord, in front of the veil. **17.** Some of the blood will be placed on the horns of the altar of incense, and the rest poured at the base of the altar of burnt offering. **18.** The priest shall burn all its fat on the altar, **19.** and make atonement (reconciliation or forgiveness) as with the first bull, and it will be forgiven. **20.** The bull will be taken outside the camp and burned, as with the first. This is the sin offering for the congregation. **21.** If a leader (person in charge) sins unintentionally and becomes guilty (responsible for the wrongdoing), **22.** he shall bring a blemish-free (without defect) male goat (a young male animal) as an offering. **23.** He will lay his hand on the goat's head and slaughter it at the burnt offering place. **24.** The priest will put some of its blood on the altar's horns, and pour the rest at the base. **25.** All its fat will be burned on the altar, as with the peace offerings (sacrifices for peace with God). The priest shall make atonement, and it will be forgiven. **26.** If any common person (ordinary member of the community) sins unintentionally, **27.** and the sin becomes known (discovered), he shall bring a blemish-free female goat (a young female animal). **28.** He will lay his hand on the goat's head and slaughter it at the burnt offering place. **29.** The priest will put some of its blood on the altar's horns and pour the rest at the base of the altar. **30.** The priest will burn its fat on the altar as a pleasing aroma (fragrance). Atonement will be made, and it will be forgiven. **31.** If he brings a lamb (a young sheep) as a sin offering, it must be a blemish-free female. **32.** He will lay his hand on the lamb's head and slaughter it at the burnt offering place. **33.** The priest will put some of the lamb's blood on the altar's horns and pour the rest at the base. **34.** The fat will be burned on the altar, as with peace offerings. Atonement will be made, and it will be forgiven." **35.** This is the law (guideline) for sin offerings, guilt offerings (sacrifices to atone for sins committed knowingly), burnt offerings, grain offerings (offerings of grain), peace offerings (sacrifices for peace with God), consecrations (setting apart for sacred service), and when someone becomes aware of sin after atonement.

Chapter 5

1. "If someone hears an oath (a solemn promise or vow) but doesn't testify (speak up), they are guilty and must bear responsibility (accountability) for their sin. **2.** If a person unknowingly (without intent) touches something unclean (ritually impure), they are considered unclean and guilty. **3.** If someone unknowingly touches human impurity (a state of ritual defilement), they are guilty once they realize (become aware) it. **4.** If a person speaks an oath thoughtlessly (carelessly), they are guilty when they become aware. **5.** When a person realizes (becomes aware of) their sin, they must confess (admit) and acknowledge (accept or recognize) it. **6.** They shall bring a female lamb (a young female sheep) or goat (a young female goat) as a sin offering (a sacrifice for atonement), and the priest will make atonement (reconciliation or forgiveness), and they will be forgiven. **7.** If they cannot afford a lamb, they may bring two birds—one for a sin offering, the other for a burnt offering. **8.** The priest will offer the first bird as a sin offering, sprinkling (scattering) its blood on the altar, and the second as a burnt offering (a sacrifice completely burned). **9.** The priest will make atonement for the person's sin, and they will be forgiven. **10.** If they cannot bring birds, they may bring fine flour (ground wheat) as a sin offering, without oil (a fragrant substance used in offerings) or frankincense (an aromatic resin). **11.** The priest will burn a portion of the flour as a memorial offering (a reminder of the person's devotion), and the rest will be given to the priest. **12.** The priest will make atonement (reconciliation or forgiveness), and the person's sin will be forgiven. **13.** The Lord spoke to Moses: **14.** "If someone sins unintentionally (without intent) regarding something sacred (holy or dedicated to God), they must bring a blemish-free (without defect) ram (a male sheep) as a trespass offering (a sacrifice to make amends), valued by the sanctuary's shekel (a unit of currency used for sacred offerings). **15.** They must repay (compensate for) the harm caused, adding one-fifth of its value, and the priest will make atonement (reconciliation or forgiveness), and they will be forgiven. **16.** If a person unknowingly sins against the Lord's commandments, they are still guilty and must bear the consequences (suffer the results). **17.** For such a sin, they shall bring a ram from the flock (a group of sheep) as a trespass offering, and the priest will make atonement for them. **18.** This is a trespass offering because the person has wronged (sinned against) the Lord. **19.** It is a trespass offering; they have indeed trespassed (wronged) against the Lord."

Chapter 6

1. "The Lord spoke to Moses, saying: **2.** 'If someone sins against the Lord by deceiving (misleading) their neighbor about something entrusted (property) to them, a pledge (security), a robbery (theft), or extorting (threatening) from them, **3.** or if they find something lost and lie about it, or swear falsely (perjury) in any of these matters, they are guilty. **4.** They must restore (return) what they have stolen, taken, or found, or anything they swore falsely about. **5.** They must return it in full, adding one-fifth (extra) to it, and give it to the rightful owner on the day of their trespass offering (restitution). **6.** Then they shall bring their trespass offering to the Lord, a ram (sheep) without blemish (flaw) from the flock, valued by the priest (assessed), as a trespass offering. **7.** The priest will make atonement (reconciliation) for them before the Lord, and they will be forgiven for their trespass. **8.** Then the Lord spoke to Moses, saying: **9.** 'Command Aaron and his sons: 'This is the law for the burnt offering (sacrifice): The burnt offering shall remain on the altar all night until morning, and the fire must be kept burning on it. **10.** The priest shall wear linen garments, remove the ashes (remnants) of the burnt offering that the fire has consumed, and place them beside the altar. **11.** Then he shall change clothes and carry the ashes outside the camp to a clean place. **12.** The fire on the altar must always be kept burning and never go out. Every morning, the priest shall add wood (fuel) and arrange the burnt offering, burning the fat (portion) of the peace offerings. **13.** The fire must always burn on the altar; it must never be extinguished (put out). **14.** This is the law of the grain offering (gift): Aaron's sons shall offer it before the Lord at the altar. **15.** The priest shall take a handful (portion) of the fine flour, its oil (fat), and all the frankincense (incense), and burn it on the altar as a sweet aroma (fragrance) to the Lord. **16.** The remaining portion of the grain offering shall be eaten by Aaron and his sons in the holy place, in the court (yard) of the tabernacle of meeting. **17.** It shall not be baked with leaven (yeast). It is most holy (sacred), like the sin offering and the trespass offering. **18.** Only the males (men) among Aaron's children may eat it. It shall be a permanent statute (rule) in your generations concerning the offerings made by fire to the Lord. Anyone who touches it must be holy (pure). **19.** And the Lord spoke to Moses, saying: **20.** 'This is the offering of Aaron and his sons, which they are to present to the Lord: one-tenth (portion) of an ephah (measure) of fine flour daily, half in the morning and half at night. **21.** It shall be made in a pan (vessel) with oil. When mixed, the baked pieces of the grain offering shall be offered as a sweet aroma (fragrance) to the Lord. **22.** The priest who is anointed (appointed) in place of his father shall offer it. It is a statute (rule) forever to the Lord, and it shall be entirely burned (consumed). **23.** For every grain offering of the priest, it must be entirely burned (consumed). None of it shall be eaten (consumed). **24.** And the Lord spoke to Moses, saying: **25.** 'Speak to Aaron and his sons, saying: 'This is the law of the sin offering (sacrifice): The sin offering shall be killed (slaughtered) in the same place as the burnt offering, before the Lord. It is most holy. **26.** The priest who offers it shall eat it in the holy place (sanctuary), in the court (yard) of the tabernacle of meeting. **27.** Anyone who touches its flesh must be holy (pure). If its blood is sprinkled (splattered) on any garment, it must be washed (cleaned) in a holy place. **28.** The earthen (clay) vessel in which the sin offering is boiled shall be broken. If it is boiled in a bronze (metal) pot, it must be scoured (cleaned) and

rinsed (washed) with water. **29.** All males (men) among the priests may eat it. It is most holy (sacred). **30.** But no sin offering, whose blood has been brought into the tabernacle of meeting to make atonement (reconciliation) in the holy place, shall be eaten (consumed). It must be burned (consumed) in the fire."

Chapter 7

1. "This is the law of the trespass immolation (guilt immolation); it's most holy. **2.** In the place where they kill the burnt immolation (a type of immolation where the whole beast is consumed by fire), shall they kill the trespass immolation, and the blood thereof shall be sprinkled round about upon the balcony (a raised structure for offerings). **3.** And he shall offer of it all the fat thereof; the rump (the hindquarters), and the fat that covereth the inwards (internal organs), and the two feathers, and the fat that's on them, which is by the sides (sides), and the caul (a membrane) that's above the liver, with the feathers, it shall he take down. **5.** And the clerk shall burn them upon the balcony for an immolation made by fire (a sacrificial immolation); it's a trespass immolation. **6.** Every joker among the preachers shall eat thereof (the immolation); it shall be eaten in the holy place (the designated sacred area); it's most holy. **7.** As the sin immolation is, so is the trespass offering; there's one law for them; the clerk that maketh atonement (conciliation) therewith shall have it. **8.** And the clerk that offereth any man's burnt immolation, indeed the clerk shall have to himself the skin (external covering) of the burnt immolation which he hath offered. **9.** And all the meat immolation (grain or flour immolation) that's baked (baked) in the roaster, and all that's dressed in the frying pan (a shallow vessel for cooking), and in the vessel, shall be the clerk's that offereth it. **10.** And every meat immolation, mingled with oil painting (used for anointing or cooking), and dry, shall all the sons of Aaron have, one as much as another. **11.** And this is the law of the immolation of peace immolations, which he shall offer unto the Lord. **12.** Still, also he shall offer with the immolation of thanksgiving unleavened galettes (cakes without leaven) mingled with oil painting, and unleavened wafers (thin flatbread) besmeared with oil painting, if he offer it for a thanksgiving (a thankful immolation). **13.** Besides the galettes, he shall offer for his immolation leavened (containing leaven) cakes with the immolation of thanksgiving of his peace immolations. **14.** And of it he shall offer one out of the whole immolation (sacrifice) for a heave immolation (a raised offering) unto the Lord, and it shall be the clerk's that sprinkleth the blood of the peace immolations. **15.** And the meat of the immolation of his peace immolations for thanksgiving shall be eaten the same day that it's offered; he shall not leave any of it until the morning. **16.** But if the immolation of his immolation be a vow (a pledge), or a voluntary immolation (given freely), it shall be eaten the same day that he offereth his immolation, and on the morrow (the coming day) also the remainder of it shall be eaten. **17.** But the remainder of the meat of the immolation on the third day shall be burnt with fire. **18.** And if any of the meat of the immolation of his peace immolations be eaten at all on the third day, it shall not be accepted, neither shall it be imputed (counted) unto him that offereth it; it shall be an abomination (despicable), and the soul that eateth of it shall bear his iniquity (sin). **19.** And the meat that toucheth any sick thing shall not be eaten; it shall be burnt with fire, and as for the meat, all that be clean shall eat thereof. **20.** But the soul that eateth of the meat of the immolation of peace immolations, that pertaineth (belongs) unto the Lord, having his soilage (ritual contamination) upon him, even that soul shall be cut off (barred) from his people. **21.** Also, the soul that shall touch any sick thing, as the soilage of the man, or any sick beast (animal), or any abominable (despicable) sick thing, and eat of the meat of the immolation of peace immolations, which pertain unto the Lord, even that soul shall be cut off from his people. **22.** And the Lord spake unto Moses, saying: **23.** 'Speak unto the children of Israel, saying, Ye shall eat no manner of fat (beast fat), of ox, or of lamb, or of scapegoat. **24.**

And the fat of the beast that dieth of itself (dies naturally), and the fat of that which is torn with beasts (killed by wild creatures), may be used in any other use, but ye shall in no wise (under no circumstances) eat of it. **25.** For whosoever eateth the fat of the beast, of which men offer an immolation made by fire unto the Lord, indeed the soul that eateth it shall be cut off from his people. **26.** Also, ye shall eat no manner of blood, whether it be of fowl (birds) or of beast, in any of your residences. **27.** Whosoever eateth any blood, indeed that soul shall be cut off from his people. **28.** And the Lord spake unto Moses, saying: **29.** 'Speak unto the children of Israel, saying, He that offereth the immolation of his peace immolations unto the Lord shall bring his immolation (sacrifice) unto the Lord of the immolation of his peace immolations. **30.** His own hands shall bring the immolations of the Lord made by fire; the fat with the bone, it shall he bring, that the bone may be gestured (moved in a conventional manner) for a surge immolation before the Lord. **31.** And the clerk shall burn the fat upon the balcony, but the bone shall be Aaron's and his sons' (the clerk's portion). **32.** And the right shoulder shall ye give unto the clerk for a heave immolation (a raised offering) of the offerings of your peace immolations. **33.** He among the sons of Aaron that offereth the blood of the peace immolations, and the fat, shall have the right shoulder for his part. **34.** For the surge bone and the heave shoulder have I taken of the children of Israel from off the offerings of their peace immolations, and have given them unto Aaron the clerk and unto his sons by a enactment (law) for ever among the children of Israel. **35.** This is the portion of the anointing of Aaron, and of the anointing of his sons, out of the immolations of the Lord made by fire, in the day when he presented them to minister (serve) unto the Lord in the clerk's office (portion). **36.** Which the Lord commanded to be given them of the children of Israel, in the day that he besmeared them by an enactment for ever throughout their generations. **37.** This is the law of the burnt immolation (whole burnt offering), of the meat immolation (grain offering), and of the sin immolation (atoning offering), and of the trespass immolation (guilt offering), and of the sanctifications (setting apart), and of the immolation of the peace immolations; **38.** which the Lord commanded Moses in mount Sinai (mountain), in the day that he commanded the children of Israel to offer their offerings (sacrifices) unto the Lord, in the wilderness of Sinai."

Chapter 8

1. The Lord gave Moses these instructions: **2.** "Gather Aaron and his sons, along with their garments, the oil painting for anointing (sacred oil painting), a bull for the sin immolation (immolation for atonement), two rams, and a handbasket of unleavened chuck. **3.** Gather all the people at the entrance of the temple of Meeting (sacred place for deification, originally established by Moses). **4.** Moses followed God's instruction, and the entire congregation assembled at the temple's entrance. **5.** He told the people, "This is what the Lord has commanded to be done." **6.** Also, Moses brought Aaron and his sons and sanctified them with water (ritually washed them). **7.** He dressed Aaron in the clerkly tunic (a mask for preachers), fastened the girdle around his midriff, put the mask over him, and placed the ephod (sacred garment) on him, securing it with the intricate woven band that came with the ephod. **8.** Moses deposited the breastplate on Aaron, placing inside it the Urim and Thummim (sacred monuments used for godly opinions). **9.** He placed the turban (head covering worn by preachers) on Aaron's head, and attached the golden plate (a gold emblem), the holy crown, to the front of the turban, just as the Lord had commanded Moses. **10.** Subsequently, Moses took the anointing oil painting (sacred oil painting) and poured it over the temple and all the objects within it, sanctifying them and setting them piecemeal for holy use. **11.** He sprinkled oil painting on the balcony seven times, besmeared it, its implements, and the laver (a receptacle for sanctification), to sanctify them. **12.** Moses poured oil painting on Aaron's head, consecrating (setting apart for service) him. **13.** He brought forward Aaron's sons, clothed them in tunics (blankets), put cinctures (belts) on them, and placed headdresses on their heads, following the Lord's instructions. **14.** Moses also brought the bull for the sin immolation (an immolation to atone for sin). Aaron and his sons laid their hands on the bull's head. **15.** And Moses massacred it. He took the blood and applied it with his cutlet to the cornucopias (projections) of the balcony, purifying (making it holy) the balcony. He poured the remaining blood at the base (bottom) of the balcony to consecrate (set piecemeal for holy use) it. **16.** Moses gathered all the fat from the internal organs, including the fat around the liver, the two feathers with their fat, and burned them on the balcony. **17.** The bull's hide (skin), its meat (meat), and its waste were burned outside the camp, in agreement with the Lord's instructions to Moses. **18.** Also, Moses presented the first ram for the burnt immolation (an immolation completely consumed by fire). Aaron and his sons laid their hands on its head. **19.** And Moses killed it. He sprinkled its blood around the balcony. **20.** After cutting the ram into pieces, Moses burned its head, pieces, and fat on the balcony. **21.** Moses washed its internal organs (inside corridor) and legs with water and also burned the entire ram on the balcony as a burnt immolation. This immolation was a sweet aroma (affable scent) to the Lord, a fire immolation made according to the Lord's command. **22.** Moses brought forward the alternate ram, the ram for sanctification (ritual setting piecemeal for service). Aaron and his sons laid their hands on its head. **23.** And Moses massacred it. He took some of its blood and placed it on the tips (ends) of Aaron's right observance, the thumb of his right hand, and the big toe of his right bottom. **24.** He did the same for Aaron's sons, placing the blood on the tips of their right cognizance, their right thumbs, and right big toes. He also sprinkled the remaining blood around the balcony. **25.** Moses took the fat, the fat tail, all the fat from the internal organs, the liver, the feathers with their fat, and the right ham. **26.** He also took one unleavened cutlet (chuck without incentive), one chuck cutlet besmeared with oil painting (chuck with oil painting), and one wafer from the handbasket of unleavened chuck, and placed them on the fat and the right ham. **27.** He placed all these into the hands of Aaron and his sons and gestured (raised) them before the Lord as a surge immolation. **28.** Subsequently, Moses took the immolations from their hands and burned them on the balcony, as a sanctification immolation (immolation to dedicate), a pleasing aroma (sweet scent) to the Lord, a fire immolation as commanded. **29.** Eventually, Moses took the bone of the ram, which was his portion, and gestured it before the Lord as a surge immolation, as the Lord had instructed him. **30.** Moses took some of the anointing oil painting and some of the blood from the balcony and sprinkled it on Aaron, his garments, his sons, and their garments, making them holy. **31.** Moses instructed Aaron and his sons, "Boil the meat at the entrance to the temple and eat it there, along with the chuck from the sanctification handbasket, as I've commanded. Aaron and his sons shall eat it. **32.** Any leftover meat and chuck should be burned (destroyed by fire). **33.** You're to remain at the entrance of the temple for seven days, completing the sanctification process. During these seven days, you'll be set piecemeal for service to the Lord." **34.** Just as it has been done moment, the Lord has commanded these rituals to atone for you (to make up for sin). **35.** Thus, remain at the entrance of the Tabernacle day and night for seven days, performing your duties (liabilities), so that you may not die, for I've been instructed to do so." **36.** Aaron and his sons followed all the commands the Lord had given through Moses.

Chapter 9

1. On the eighth day, Moses summoned Aaron, his sons, and the elders of Israel to gather. **2.** He instructed Aaron, "Select a young bull for a sin offering and a ram for a burnt offering (completely consumed), both without defect, and present them before the Lord." **3.** To the Israelites, you are to declare: "Bring a goat for a sin offering (to atone for sins), and a one-year-old calf and lamb, both without blemish, as burnt offerings, **4.** And also a bull and a ram for peace offerings (expressions of gratitude), along with a grain offering mixed with oil. Today, the Lord will reveal His presence to you." **5.** The people brought everything Moses had commanded to the entrance of the Tabernacle (the sacred dwelling), and the whole congregation stood before the Lord. **6.** Moses announced, "This is what the Lord has commanded, and His glory (His visible presence) will be made known to you." **7.** He then said to Aaron, "Go to the altar, offer your sin offering and burnt offering, and make atonement (covering for sin) for yourself and the people. Offer the people's sacrifices and make atonement for them as directed by the Lord." **8.** Aaron approached the altar and sacrificed the calf for his sin offering. **9.** Aaron's sons brought him the blood, and he applied it to the horns (top corners) of the altar with his finger, then poured the remainder at its base. **10.** The fat, kidneys, and the fatty portion of the liver from the sin offering were burned on the altar, just as the Lord had instructed Moses. **11.** The flesh and skin were disposed of and burned outside the camp. **12.** Aaron then sacrificed the burnt offering. His sons handed him the blood, and he sprinkled it all around the altar. **13.** They presented the rest of the burnt offering, including its pieces and head, and he placed them on the altar to be consumed by fire. **14.** He washed the internal organs (the entrails) and legs then burned them on the altar along with the rest of the burnt offering. **15.** Aaron then took the people's sin offering, slaughtered the goat meant for their sin, and offered it in the same manner as he did with the first one. **16.** He presented the burnt offering, carrying out the process according to the prescribed procedure. **17.** He also took the grain offering, took a portion of it, and burned it on the altar, along with the burnt offering from the morning. **18.** Next, he sacrificed the bull and the ram as peace offerings for the people. Aaron's sons handed him the blood, and he sprinkled it on all sides of the altar. **19.** He then burned the fat of the bull and the ram—the fatty tail, the fat surrounding the internal organs, the kidneys, and the lobe of the liver. **20.** The fat was placed on the breasts, and Aaron burned it on the altar. **21.** Aaron waved the breasts and the right thigh as a wave offering (symbolic gesture) before the Lord, following Moses' instructions. **22.** Then, Aaron raised his hands toward the people, blessed them, and finished the sin offering, the burnt offering, and the peace offerings. **23.** Moses and Aaron entered the Tabernacle of Meeting (the sacred place of worship), came out, and blessed the people. Afterward, the glory of the Lord appeared to all. **24.** Fire came from the Lord's presence and consumed the burnt offering and the fat on the altar. When the people saw this, they shouted with joy and fell face down in worship.

Chapter 10

1. Nadab and Abihu, the sons of Aaron, each took a censer (a container for burning incense), filled it with fire, and placed incense upon it. However, they offered unauthorized fire (a fire that was not commanded or permitted) before the Lord, something He had not instructed them to do. **2.** As a result, fire came out from the Lord and consumed them, and they perished (died) in the presence of the Lord. **3.** Moses then spoke to Aaron, saying, "This is what the Lord has said: 'I must be honored as holy (set apart and revered) by those who draw near to me, and I must be glorified (praised and exalted) before all the people.'" At these words, Aaron remained silent. **4.** Moses called for Mishael and Elzaphan, the sons of Uzziel (Aaron's uncle), and instructed them, "Come and carry your brothers out of the camp, away from the sacred area." **5.** So, they went and carried their brothers out by their tunics (garments), as Moses had directed. **6.** Moses also said to Aaron, and to his remaining sons, Eleazar and Ithamar, "Do not leave your hair unkempt (disheveled) or tear your garments, for this would lead to your death and bring God's anger upon all the people. Let the other Israelites mourn (grieve) the fire that the Lord

has ignited." **7.** "But you must remain at the entrance of the Tabernacle of Meeting (the tent where God's presence dwelt), or else you will die, for the Lord's anointing oil (a sacred oil used for consecrating priests) is upon you." So, they obeyed Moses' instructions. **8.** The Lord then spoke to Aaron, saying: **9.** "You and your sons are not to drink wine or strong drink (alcohol) when you go into the Tabernacle of Meeting, or you will die. This is a command that will be in effect for you and your descendants forever. **10.** The reason for this is that you must be able to distinguish (recognize) between the holy (sacred) and the common (ordinary), between the clean (ritually pure) and the unclean (ritually impure), **11.** And also to teach the Israelites all the laws and commandments the Lord has given to them through Moses." **12.** Moses spoke to Aaron, and to Eleazar and Ithamar, his remaining sons, saying, "Take the grain offering (a type of offering made with flour, oil, and frankincense) that is left over from the fire offerings (offerings burned on the altar) to the Lord, and eat it without leaven (yeast) near the altar, for it is considered most holy (set apart as sacred). **13.** You are to eat it in a holy place (a designated sacred area), because it is your portion and that of your sons, given from the fire offerings of the Lord, as I have commanded." **14.** "The breast of the wave offering (a portion of the sacrifice presented to God by waving it) and the thigh of the heave offering (offered portions of the sacrifice) must be eaten in a clean place by you, your sons, and your daughters. These are your portion and that of your sons, given from the peace offerings made by the Israelites." **15.** "The wave offering of the breast and the heave offering of the thigh, together with the fat of the fire offerings, must be presented before the Lord as a wave offering. These are to be your portion and that of your sons, according to the Lord's command." **16.** Moses investigated the situation regarding the goat of the sin offering (sacrifice made for atonement), and discovered that it had been completely burned. He became angry with Eleazar and Ithamar, the surviving sons of Aaron, and said, **17.** "Why didn't you eat the sin offering in the holy place? It is a most holy offering, and it was given to you to bear the guilt of the people and to make atonement (reconciliation) for them before the Lord. **18.** Its blood was not brought inside the sanctuary (the sacred area), so why didn't you eat it in the holy place, as I instructed?" **19.** Aaron answered Moses, "Today, they offered their sin offering and burnt offering before the Lord, and look what has happened to me! If I had eaten the sin offering today, would it have been accepted by the Lord?" **20.** After hearing Aaron's explanation, Moses was satisfied and agreed with him.

Chapter 11

1. The Lord spoke to Moses and Aaron and gave them the following command: **2.** "Tell the Israelites: 'These are the animals you are allowed to eat from those that roam on the earth: **3.** Among the animals, you can eat those that have a split hoof (hooves that are divided), that are completely separated, and also chew the cud (chew food again after swallowing it). **4.** However, there are some that you should not eat, even though they chew the cud or have split hooves. For example, the camel, because it chews the cud but does not have split hooves. It is unclean (ritually impure) for you. **5.** The rock hyrax (herbivorous mammal), which chews the cud but lacks split hooves, is also unclean for you. **6.** The hare, although it chews the cud, does not have split hooves, so it is unclean for you. **7.** The pig, while it has split hooves, does not chew the cud. Therefore, it is unclean to you. **8.** You are not to eat their meat, nor touch their dead bodies, as they are unclean to you. **9.** 'As for what lives in the water, you may eat any creatures that have both fins and scales (external covering that protects), whether in the seas or in rivers. **10.** But any sea or river creature that lacks fins and scales, whether it moves in the water or lives in it, is an abomination (detestable) to you. **11.** You shall treat them as detestable; do not eat their flesh and consider their dead bodies as unclean. **12.** Any water creatures without fins or scales are considered detestable.

13. 'When it comes to birds, there are some you should not eat because they are unclean to you. These include: the eagle, the vulture, the buzzard, 14. the kite, and the falcon, each according to its species; 15. any kind of raven, 16. the ostrich, the short-eared owl, the seagull, and the hawk, each according to its kind; 17. the little owl, the fisher owl, and the screech owl; 18. the white owl, the jackdaw (a small black bird), and the carrion vulture; 19. The stork, the heron, according to its kind, the hoopoe, and the bat. 20. 'As for insects, any flying insect that walks on all fours is considered an abomination to you. 21. However, there are some flying insects that you may eat. These are those that have jointed legs (divided legs) above their feet, which they use to jump on the earth. 22. These are: the locust, the destroying locust, the cricket, and the grasshopper, all according to their kinds. 23. But any other flying insect with four legs is detestable to you. 24. 'By touching the dead body of any of these, you will be considered unclean until the evening. 25. If anyone carries part of the body of any such creature, they must wash their clothes and remain unclean until evening. 26. Any animal that has a divided hoof, but is not split, or does not chew the cud, is unclean to you. Anyone who touches it will be unclean. 27. Similarly, any animal that moves on paws is unclean to you. Anyone who touches its dead body will be unclean until evening. 28. If anyone carries its carcass (dead body), they must wash their clothes and remain unclean until evening. It is unclean to you. 29. 'Among the crawling creatures on the earth, these are unclean to you: the mole, the mouse, and the large lizard, according to its kind; 30. the gecko, the monitor lizard, the sand reptile, the sand lizard, and the chameleon. 31. These are unclean for you. Anyone who touches them when dead will be unclean until evening 32. If any of these dead creatures fall on an item such as wood, clothing, leather, or a sack, whatever item it is, it must be washed in water and will remain unclean until evening. 33. If such creatures fall into an earthen vessel (clay pot), the vessel should be broken, and anything inside it will be unclean. 34. If any food or drink inside the vessel has been touched by the dead creature's body, it becomes unclean. 35. If a dead creature falls on an oven or stove, that appliance must be destroyed, as it is unclean to you. 36. However, a spring or a cistern (a large container for water) with clean water in it remains clean, but anything that touches a dead body in it will be unclean. 37. If a dead creature falls on seeds meant for planting, the seeds remain clean. 38. But if water is applied to the seed, and a dead creature falls on it, the seed becomes unclean. 39. 'If an animal that you may eat dies, anyone who touches its carcass will be unclean until evening. 40. Anyone who eats the animal's dead body will need to wash their clothes and remain unclean until evening. Anyone who carries its carcass must also wash their clothes and remain unclean until evening. 41. 'Every creature that crawls on the earth is an abomination (forbidden) and should not be eaten. 42. Any creature that crawls on its belly, walks on four legs, or has many feet is not to be eaten because they are considered an abomination. 43. Do not make yourselves unclean with any of these crawling creatures, nor defile yourselves with them, or you will become unclean. 44. For I am the Lord your God. Therefore, you must consecrate yourselves and be holy because I am holy. Do not defile yourselves with any crawling creatures. 45. I am the Lord, who brought you up from the land of Egypt, to be your God. Therefore, you must be holy because I am holy. 46. 'This is the law about animals, birds, creatures that move in the water, and the creatures that crawl on the earth, 47. To distinguish between the clean and unclean, and to separate the animals you may eat from those you may not eat.'"

Chapter 12

1. Then the Lord spoke to Moses, instructing him: 2. "Tell the Israelites this: When a woman gives birth to a son, she will be considered ceremonially unclean for seven days, just as she is during her regular period of impurity (menstrual impurity). 3. On the eighth day, the boy is to be circumcised (the removal of the foreskin). 4. After the circumcision, the mother will remain in the blood of her purification for an additional thirty-three days. During this time, she must not touch anything sacred or enter the place of worship (sanctuary) until her days of purification are fully completed. 5. However, if she gives birth to a daughter, she will be unclean for two weeks, similar to her usual period of impurity, and she will continue in her purification for sixty-six days. 6. When her purification period is complete, whether for a son or a daughter, she must bring a lamb, one year old, to offer as a burnt offering, along with a young pigeon or turtledove as a sin offering. These should be brought to the priest at the entrance of the tabernacle (the sacred place). 7. The priest will present the offerings before the Lord and make atonement for her, cleansing her from the flow of blood associated with childbirth. This is the procedure for any woman who has given birth to a son or a daughter. 8. If she cannot afford a lamb, she is permitted to bring two turtledoves or two young pigeons instead—one for the burnt offering and the other for the sin offering. The priest will make atonement for her, and she will be declared clean.

Chapter 13

1. The Lord spoke to Moses and Aaron, saying: 2. "When someone has a swelling (raised area of skin), scab, or bright spot (light-colored mark) on their skin, and it turns into a sore that looks like leprosy), they must be brought to Aaron, the priest, or to one of his sons, the priests. 3. The priest will examine the sore. If the hair on the sore has turned white, and the sore looks deeper than the skin (more than just surface skin), it is a leprous sore (type of skin disease). The priest will declare the person unclean. 4. But if the bright spot is white (pale or light in color) and doesn't seem to go deeper than the skin, and the hair hasn't turned white, the person must be isolated (kept separate from others) for seven days. 5. On the seventh day, the priest will re-examine the sore. If it hasn't spread (grown larger) and still looks the same, the person will be isolated for another seven days. 6. If, after the second seven days, the sore has faded (became less noticeable or lighter in color) and hasn't spread, the priest will declare the person clean (free of disease). It's just a scab, and they must wash their clothes to become clean. 7. If the scab spreads after being examined, the priest will examine it again. 8. If the priest sees that the scab has spread, the person will be declared unclean. It is leprosy. 9. "If the person has a leprous sore (skin disease), they must be brought to the priest. 10. The priest will examine it. If the swelling is white, the hair has turned white, and there is raw flesh in the swelling, it is old leprosy (long-standing skin disease). The priest will declare the person unclean and will not isolate them, for they are already unclean. 11. "If the leprosy covers the skin from head to toe (all over the body), wherever the priest looks, 12. and the entire body is covered , the priest will declare the person clean, for the leprosy has turned all white. They are clean. 13. But if raw flesh appears, the person will be unclean. 14. The priest will examine the raw flesh and declare it unclean. It is leprosy. 15. If the raw flesh changes and becomes white again (heals and turns pale), the person must come to the priest. 16. The priest will examine them, and if the sore has turned white (pale), the priest will declare the person clean. They are clean. 17. "If a boil (a swollen) forms on someone's skin and heals, 18. and in place of the boil a white or reddish-white swelling (raised area) or bright spot (light-colored patch) appears, 19. it must be shown to the priest. 20. If the priest examines it and sees that it is deeper than the skin (more than just surface skin), and the hair has turned white, the person will be declared unclean. It is leprosy that came from the boil. 21. But if there are no white hairs and it is not deeper than the skin but has faded (become lighter in color), the priest will isolate the person for seven days. 22. If it spreads (grows larger), the priest will declare the person unclean. It is leprosy. 23. If it doesn't spread and stays in the same place, it is simply the scar (healed mark) from the boil, and the priest will declare the person clean. 24. "If a burn

causes raw flesh (fresh tissue) and a bright spot (light-colored area) appears, **25.** and the hair turns white and the spot appears deeper than the skin (surface tissue), it is leprosy that came from the burn. The priest will declare the person unclean. **26.** But if there are no white hairs (no signs of leprosy) and the spot is not deeper than the skin but fades (becomes lighter in color), the priest will isolate the person for seven days. **27.** If it spreads (grows larger), the priest will declare the person unclean. It is leprosy.**28.** If it doesn't spread and fades (becomes lighter), it is simply a scar from the burn, and the priest will declare the person clean. **29.** "If a man or woman has a sore (wound or lesion) on their head or beard, **30.** the priest will examine it. If it appears deeper than the skin and contains thin yellow hair (scaly leprosy), the priest will declare the person unclean. It is scaly leprosy of the head or beard." **31.** "If the priest examines a scaly patch on the skin and sees that it is not deep, and there is no black hair in it (which would indicate leprosy), then he should isolate the person with the condition for seven days. **32.** After seven days, the priest will check again. If the patch hasn't spread, if there is no yellow hair (sign of leprosy), and if the area still looks superficial, **33.** the person should shave the rest of their body, but leave the scaly patch untouched. The priest will then isolate them for another seven days. **34.** At the end of the next seven days, the priest will examine the patch again. If it hasn't spread, and the condition still looks superficial, then the person will be declared clean. They must wash their clothes and will be considered healed. **35.** However, if the patch spreads after they've been declared clean, **36.** the priest will check again. If the patch has spread, the priest no longer needs to look for yellow hair. The person is unclean. **37.** If the patch appears to have stopped spreading and black hair has grown, the condition is healing, and the person will be declared clean. **38.** "If someone has white spots on their skin, **39.** the priest will examine them. If the spots are dull white (just a normal skin condition), the person is clean. **40.** If a man loses hair from his head and becomes bald, he is still clean. **41.** If his hair falls from his forehead, leaving a bald spot there, he is still clean. **42.** But if there is a reddish-white sore on his bald head or forehead, this is leprosy breaking out in that area. **43.** The priest will examine it. If the sore looks like leprosy (reddish-white and swollen), **44.** the person is considered to have leprosy and is unclean. The priest must declare the person unclean because the sore is on their head. **45.** A person with leprosy must tear their clothes (show mourning), leave their head uncovered, cover their upper lip (mustache), and call out, 'Unclean! Unclean!' **46.** They must remain unclean and live apart from others, outside the camp. **47.** "If a garment shows signs of leprosy, whether it is made of wool or linen, **48.** whether it has a problem in the threads of the fabric (warp or woof) or in any leather part, **49.** and the sign is greenish or reddish in color, the garment must be shown to the priest. **50.** The priest will examine it and isolate the garment for seven days. **51.** On the seventh day, the priest will check again. If the condition has spread, whether in the fabric threads or in the leather, then the garment is deemed to have active leprosy and is unclean. **52.** In that case, the priest will order the garment to be burned because it is infected with active leprosy. **53.** "If the priest checks and sees that the condition hasn't spread in the garment, whether it's in the threads or in leather, **54.** he will order the garment to be washed and isolate it for another seven days. **55.** After the washing, the priest will check again. If the condition hasn't changed color and hasn't spread, the garment is still unclean, and it must be burned because the infection continues to eat away at the material. **56.** If the condition has faded after washing, the priest will remove the infected part from the garment. **57.** But if the infection reappears in the fabric or leather, the garment is still a spreading plague and must be burned in fire. **58.** If the condition has disappeared after washing, the garment will be washed again, and it will be clean. **59.** "This is the law for determining if a woolen, linen, or leather garment is clean or unclean because of leprosy."

Chapter 14

1. The Lord spoke to Moses, saying: **2.** "This is the law for cleansing a person healed from leprosy (skin disease): they must be brought to the priest. **3.** The priest will go outside the camp and examine the person. If the leprosy has been healed, **4.** the priest will instruct that two live, clean birds, cedar wood (wood used for building), scarlet thread, and hyssop (a plant used for purification) be brought. **5.** The priest will order one of the birds to be killed in an earthen vessel (a clay container) over running water. **6.** The living bird, cedar wood, scarlet thread, and hyssop will be dipped in the blood of the dead bird and the water. **7.** The priest will sprinkle the person being cleansed seven times with the blood and water, declare them clean, and then release the living bird into an open field (a place outside the camp). **8.** The person to be cleansed must wash their clothes, shave off all their hair, and wash their body in water to be clean. After this, they will stay outside their tent (a temporary home) for seven days. **9.** On the seventh day, they must shave off all their hair—head, beard, and eyebrows—and wash their clothes and body to be clean. **10.** On the eighth day, they will take two male lambs without blemish (without flaws), one ewe lamb of the first year without blemish, three-tenths of an ephah (a unit of measurement) of fine flour mixed with oil as a grain offering, and one log of oil. **11.** The priest will bring the person to be cleansed and these offerings to the entrance of the tabernacle (a sacred tent used for worship) of meeting. **12.** The priest will take one male lamb as a trespass offering, along with the log of oil, and wave them before the Lord. **13.** The lamb will be killed in the place where sin and burnt offerings are made, in a holy place (a sacred area), because the trespass offering, like the sin offering, is most holy. **14.** The priest will take some of the blood from the trespass offering and place it on the right ear, right thumb, and right big toe of the person being cleansed. **15.** The priest will take some of the oil from the log and pour it into the palm (inside) of his own left hand. **16.** The priest will dip his right finger in the oil and sprinkle (scatter drops) it seven times before the Lord. **17.** The priest will then put some of the oil on the same spots as the blood: on the right ear, right thumb, and right big toe of the person being cleansed. **18.** The remaining oil in the priest's hand will be poured on the person's head to make atonement (compensation for sin) before the Lord. **19.** The priest will then offer the sin offering to atone for the person's uncleanness (ritually impure), followed by the burnt offering. **20.** The priest will offer the burnt offering and the grain offering on the altar to make atonement for the person, and they will be clean. **21.** If the person is poor and unable to afford the usual offerings, they will bring one male lamb for the trespass offering, one-tenth of an ephah of fine flour mixed with oil as a grain offering, a log of oil, and two turtledoves (small birds) or young pigeons. **22.** They will bring these offerings to the priest at the tabernacle on the eighth day of their cleansing. **23.** The priest will wave the lamb and log of oil before the Lord as a wave offering. **24.** The priest will then kill the lamb of the trespass offering, and place some of its blood on the right ear, right thumb, and right big toe of the person being cleansed. **25.** The priest will pour some of the oil into his own left hand. **26.** The priest will sprinkle some of the oil with his right finger seven times before the Lord. **27.** The priest will put some of the oil on the same spots as the blood: on the right ear, right thumb, and right big toe. **28.** The rest of the oil will be poured on the person's head to make atonement before the Lord. **29.** One of the turtledoves or pigeons will be offered as a sin offering, and the other as a burnt offering, along with the grain offering, to make atonement for the person. **30.** This is the law for someone healed of leprosy (restored to health) but who cannot afford the usual cleansing. **31.** The Lord spoke again to Moses and Aaron: **32.** "When you come into the land of Canaan (the land promised to Israel), which I am giving you as a possession, and I send a leprous plague on a house in that land, **33.** The owner must tell the priest that they think there is a plague (disease) in their house. **34.** The priest will order the house to be emptied (remove all items) before he inspects it, so that everything inside the house won't become unclean. After that, the priest will examine the house. **35.** If the plague is on the walls of the house, with streaks that are greenish or reddish and appear deep in the walls, **36.** The priest will leave the house and shut it up (close it) for seven days. **37.** On the seventh day, the priest will return and inspect the house. If the plague has spread, **38.** The priest will order that the infected stones be removed and cast (thrown away) into an unclean place outside the city. **39.** The house will be scraped (cleaned by scraping) inside, and the dust will be poured into an unclean place outside the city. **40.** New stones will be put in place, and the house will be replastered (covered with plaster). **41.** If the plague returns after the stones are removed, and the house has been scraped and replastered, **42.** The priest will declare the house unclean and order it to be torn down. Its stones, timber (wood), and plaster will be taken outside the city to an unclean place. **43.** Anyone who enters the house while it is shut up will be unclean until evening. **44.** Anyone who sleeps or eats in the house must wash their clothes (clean them with water). **45.** If the priest inspects the house and sees the plague has not spread after the house has been replastered, **46.** The priest will declare the house clean (ritually pure), for the plague is healed (restored to health). **47.** To cleanse the house, the priest will take two birds, cedar wood, scarlet thread, and hyssop. **48.** One bird will be killed in an earthen vessel (clay pot) over running water (flowing water). **49.** The priest will dip the cedar wood, hyssop, scarlet thread, and living bird into the blood of the dead bird and the water, and sprinkle (scatter drops) the house seven times. **50.** The priest will cleanse (purify) the house with the blood of the bird, the water, the living bird, cedar wood, hyssop, and scarlet thread. **51.** The living bird will be released outside the city in an open field (outside the camp). The priest will make atonement (reparation for sin) for the house, and it will be clean. **52.** This is the law for any leprous sore (a skin wound), scale (a hardened patch), leprosy of a garment or house, or for any swelling, scab, or bright spot, to teach when something is unclean and when it is clean. This is the law of leprosy. **53.** "This is the law concerning leprosy, for the leprous sores and the scales of a garment. **54.** When a person has a sore on their body, and it turns white or scaly, and it appears as leprosy, the priest must inspect the person. **55.** If the priest finds that the sore has healed, but the person still has marks, they must shave their head (cut off hair), and after seven days of waiting, they may return to the priest for further inspection. **56.** The priest will examine them again to see if the disease has spread or healed. **57.** If it is determined that the sore has spread, the person will be declared impure (unfit for certain rituals), but if the disease has healed, they are considered clean.

Chapter 15

1. The Lord spoke to Moses and Aaron: **2.** "Tell the Israelites: If a man has a discharge (flow of liquid from the body) from his body, he is considered unclean. **3.** Whether the discharge flows or is blocked, it still counts as his uncleanness (impurity). **4.** Any bed that the person with the discharge lies on, or any seat they sit on, becomes unclean. **5.** Anyone who comes into contact with the bed of the person with the discharge must wash their clothes, bathe in water, and remain ceremonially unclean until evening. **6.** If someone sits on a surface that the person with the discharge has sat on, they must wash their clothes, bathe in water, and remain unclean until evening. **7.** If someone touches the person with the discharge, they must wash their clothes, bathe in water, and remain unclean until evening. **8.** If the person with the discharge spits on someone who is clean, the clean person must wash their clothes, bathe in water, and remain unclean until evening. **9.** Any saddle that the person with the discharge uses will be unclean. **10.** Anyone who touches anything that was beneath the person with the discharge must wash their clothes, bathe in water, and remain unclean until evening. **11.** If the person with the discharge touches someone without first washing their hands, the other person must wash their clothes, bathe in water, and remain unclean until evening. **12.** Any clay vessel touched by the person with the discharge must be broken, but any wooden vessel should be washed with water. **13.** When the person is healed (recovered) of their discharge, they must count seven days for purification (to become clean), wash their clothes, and bathe in running water to be clean. **14.** On the eighth day, they must bring two turtledoves (small birds) or young pigeons to the priest at the tabernacle (sacred tent for worship) entrance. **15.** The priest will offer one as a sin offering and the other as a burnt offering , making atonement (forgiveness) for the person's discharge. **16.** If a man has an emission of semen (release of bodily fluid), he must wash his whole body in water and remain unclean until evening. **17.** Any garment (clothing) or leather touched by semen must be washed with water and remain unclean until evening. **18.** If a man and woman lie together and there is semen, both must bathe in water and remain unclean until evening. **19.** If a woman has a discharge of blood, she must remain separate (isolated) for seven days. Anyone who touches her will be unclean until evening. **20.** Everything she lies on or sits on during her impurity (uncleanness) will be unclean. **21.** Anyone who touches her bed must wash their clothes, bathe in water, and remain unclean until evening. **22.** Anyone who touches anything she has sat on must wash their clothes, bathe in water, and remain unclean until evening. **23.** If someone touches anything on her bed or where she sat, they will be unclean until evening. **24.** If a man lies with her during her impurity, he will be unclean for seven days, and any bed he lies on will be unclean. **25.** If a woman has a discharge of blood for many days outside her regular menstrual (monthly) period, all the days of her discharge will be like those of her menstrual impurity, and she is unclean. **26.** Everything she lies on or sits on during this time will be unclean, just like during her menstrual period. **27.** Anyone who touches those things must wash their clothes, bathe in water, and remain unclean until evening. **28.** If she is healed (recovered) of her discharge, she must count seven days for purification. **29.** On the eighth day, she will bring two turtledoves or young pigeons to the priest at the tabernacle entrance. **30.** The priest will offer one as a sin offering and the other as a burnt offering, making atonement (forgiveness) for her discharge. **31.** This will keep the Israelites separate from their uncleanness, so they do not die by defiling (polluting) the tabernacle (sacred tent) among them. **32.** This is the law (rule) for anyone with a discharge, for a man who emits semen, for a woman during her menstrual impurity, and for anyone who lies with an unclean person. **33.** Thus, the law provides for maintaining ritual purity (spiritual cleanliness) and preventing defilement (pollution) in the presence of the Lord.

Chapter 16

1. After the deaths of Aaron's two sons, who perished because they offered unauthorized (not allowed) fire before the Lord, the Lord spoke to Moses. **2.** He instructed Moses to tell Aaron that he must not enter the Holy Place (the area behind the veil) at any time. This includes the space in front of the mercy seat, which is on top of the ark, or he will die. God said He would appear in the cloud above the mercy seat. **3.** To enter the Holy Place, Aaron must do so with the blood of a young bull for his sin offering and a ram (a male sheep) for his burnt offering. **4.** Aaron must wear special holy garments: a linen tunic (a type of cloth), linen trousers, a linen sash, and a linen turban. These are sacred clothes, and before putting them on, he must wash his body. **5.** From the congregation (group), Aaron will take two male goats for a sin offering and one ram as a burnt offering. **6.** Aaron will offer the bull as a sin offering for himself, to make atonement (reconciliation) for himself and his household. **7.** He will bring the two goats to the entrance of the tabernacle and present them before the Lord. **8.** Aaron will cast lots for the goats: one will be designated for the Lord, and the other will be the scapegoat (the goat that carries away sins). 9. The goat chosen by lot for the Lord will be offered as a sin offering. 10. The other goat, chosen as the scapegoat, will remain alive and be sent away into the wilderness (uninhabited land) after making atonement. 11. Aaron will kill the bull for his own sin offering and make atonement for himself and his household. 12. He will take a censer full of burning coals from the altar (place of sacrifice), along with sweet incense, and bring them inside the veil. 13. He will place the incense on the coals in the presence of the Lord, so that the cloud of incense will cover the mercy seat, ensuring he does not die. 14. He will then take some of the bull's blood and sprinkle it on the mercy seat and in front of it, using his finger. He will do this seven times. 15. Then Aaron will kill the goat for the people's sin offering, bring its blood into the Holy Place, and sprinkle it on the mercy seat and in front of it, just as he did with the bull's blood. 16. This will purify the Holy Place from the uncleanness (impurity) of the Israelites, making it acceptable before the Lord. He will also make atonement for the tabernacle, which remains among the people, who are unclean. 17. While Aaron is in the Holy Place making atonement, no one else is to be in the tabernacle. Once he has completed the atonement for himself, his household, and the whole assembly of Israel, he will exit. 18. Aaron will then approach the altar before the Lord, make atonement for it, and apply some of the bull's and goat's blood to the horns of the altar. 19. He will sprinkle the altar with blood seven times, cleansing it, and sanctifying it from the impurity of the Israelites. 20. After purifying the Holy Place, the tabernacle, and the altar, Aaron will bring the live goat. 21. He will lay both hands on the head of the goat, confess over it all the sins and wrongdoings of the people of Israel, transferring these sins onto the goat. The goat will then be sent into the wilderness by a designated person. 22. The scapegoat will carry all the sins of the people into an uninhabited land, where it will be released. 23. Afterward, Aaron will return to the tabernacle, remove the linen garments he wore when he entered the Holy Place, and leave them there. 24. He will wash his body with water in a sacred place, change into his regular garments, and return to offer the burnt offerings for himself and for the people. Through this, he will make atonement for both himself and the people. 25. The fat from the sin offering will be burned on the altar. 26. The person who released the scapegoat will wash his clothes, bathe in water, and then return to the camp. 27. The bull and goat whose blood was used to make atonement will be taken outside the camp. Their bodies will be burned, including their skin, flesh, and intestines. 28. The person who burns these remains will wash his clothes, bathe in water, and then return to the camp. 29. This will be an eternal ordinance for the Israelites: on the tenth day of the seventh month, they must humble themselves (fast), and do no work, whether they are native-born or foreigners living among them. 30. On that day, the priest will make atonement for them, cleansing them from all their sins, so that they may be pure before the Lord. 31. It will be a Sabbath (day of rest) of solemn rest, a day of affliction, and a permanent statute. 32. The anointed priest, chosen to minister in place of his father, will make atonement, wearing the holy linen garments, 33. and will purify the Holy Sanctuary (the sacred space), the tabernacle, and the altar. He will also make atonement for the priests and for the entire assembly of Israel. 34. This will be a permanent ordinance for the people of Israel: to make atonement once a year for all their sins." Aaron did everything as the Lord had commanded Moses.

Chapter 17

1. The Lord spoke to Moses, saying, 2. "Speak to Aaron, his sons, and all the Israelites, and tell them, 'This is what the Lord has commanded: 3. Any Israelite who kills an ox, lamb, or goat in the camp or outside the camp 4. and does not bring it to the entrance of the tent of meeting (a sacred place for worship) to present it as an offering to the Lord before His tabernacle (a portable sanctuary for God's presence) will be held guilty of bloodshed; they have shed blood and must be cut off (excluded) from their people. 5. This is so that the Israelites will bring the sacrifices they offer in the open field to the Lord, to the priest at the entrance of the tent of meeting, and offer them as peace offerings (a sacrifice made for reconciliation) to the Lord. 6. The priest will sprinkle (scatter lightly) the blood on the altar of the Lord at the tent of meeting's entrance and burn the fat (the best part, often considered the most valuable) as a pleasing aroma to the Lord. 7. They must no longer offer their sacrifices to demons (evil spirits), with whom they have been unfaithful. This is to be a lasting ordinance (a permanent law) for them for generations to come.' 8. Tell them: 'Any Israelite or foreigner (a non-Israelite living among you) living among you who offers a burnt offering (a sacrifice that is completely consumed by fire) or sacrifice 9. and does not bring it to the entrance of the tent of meeting to offer it to the Lord must be cut off from the people. 10. And any Israelite or foreigner living among you who eats any blood, I will set My face against (oppose) that person and cut them off from their people, 11. for the life (vital essence) of the flesh is in the blood. I have given it to you on the altar to make atonement (reconciliation, forgiveness) for yourselves, for it is the blood that makes atonement for life. 12. Therefore, I have said to the Israelites: None of you may eat blood, nor may any foreigner living among you eat blood. 13. Any Israelite or foreigner who hunts and catches an animal or bird that may be eaten must drain out the blood and cover it with earth, 14. for the life of every creature is its blood. That is why I have said to the Israelites: You must not eat the blood of any creature, because the life of every creature is its blood; anyone who eats it must be cut off. 15. Any person, native or foreigner, who eats what is found dead (an animal that has died without proper slaughter) or torn by wild animals must wash their clothes and bathe in water, and they will be unclean (ritually impure) until evening; then they will be clean. 16. But if they do not wash their clothes or bathe, they will bear the consequences (punishment) of their guilt."

Chapter 18

1. The Lord spoke to Moses, saying, 2. "Speak to the Israelites (descendants of Jacob) and tell them, 'I am the Lord your God. 3. You must not follow the practices (way of living) of Egypt, where you once lived, or the practices of Canaan, where I am bringing you. Do not follow their laws (rules). 4. You must keep My commandments (instructions) and follow My laws (rules), and live by them. I am the Lord your God. 5. Therefore, you must obey My laws and commandments, because whoever follows them will live by them. I am the Lord. 6. None of you shall approach any close relative to uncover their nakedness. I am the Lord. 7. Do not expose the private parts of your father or mother ; your mother is your mother, and it is wrong to uncover her nakedness. 8. You must not uncover the nakedness of your father's wife , because she is considered your father's honor (respect), and it is inappropriate to expose her nakedness. 9. Never uncover the nakedness of your sister (female sibling), whether she is your father's daughter or your mother's, born within your household or outside it. 10. You shall not uncover the nakedness of your granddaughter (your child's daughter), whether she is your son's or daughter's child, because she is part of your family (bloodline). 11. Do not uncover the nakedness of your father's wife's daughter (your half-sister), born of your father, for she is your sister, and this is forbidden (wrong). 12. Do not uncover the nakedness of your father's sister; she is a close relative (blood relation) to your father. 13. Do not uncover the nakedness of your mother's sister, for she is a close relative (blood relation) to your mother. 14. Do not uncover the nakedness of your father's brother or approach his wife ; she is your aunt, and this is improper (inappropriate). 15. You must not uncover the nakedness of your daughter-in-law (your son's wife), for she is your son's wife, and it is wrong to expose her private parts. 16. Do not uncover the nakedness of your brother's wife (your brother's partner); for it is your brother's honor (rights), and

it is improper (wrong) to expose her. **17.** You must not uncover the nakedness of a woman and her daughter, nor take her granddaughter or great-granddaughter to expose her private parts. They are close family members (blood relations), and this is wicked (evil). **18.** You shall not take a woman as a rival (adversary, competitor) to her sister by exposing her nakedness while her sister is still alive. **19.** Do not approach a woman to expose her nakedness during her menstrual period (monthly cycle), as this is a time of impurity (uncleanness). **20.** You must not have relations with your neighbor's wife (a married woman who lives near you), as it defiles you (makes you unclean) and violates the sanctity (holiness) of marriage. **21.** Do not allow any of your children (offspring) to be sacrificed (offered as a burnt offering) to Molech (a false god of the ancient Canaanites); do not dishonor (disrespect) My name in this way. I am the Lord. **22.** Do not engage in homosexual acts (sexual relations with someone of the same gender), for it is an abomination (something detestable or sinful) in My sight. **23.** Do not have sexual relations with any animal , as it is unnatural (against nature) and violates the boundaries I have set. Nor should any woman stand before an animal (beast) to mate with it, for this is a perversion (a distortion) of the natural order. **24.** Do not defile (make unclean) yourselves with these practices (actions), as the nations I am driving out before you have done the same, and their actions have polluted (made dirty) the land. **25.** The land itself is defiled (polluted); therefore, I will punish its inhabitants for their wickedness, and the land will vomit (cast out) its people. **26.** So keep My statutes (laws) and My judgments (rules), and do not commit any of these abominations, whether they are committed by you or by any foreigner (non-Israelite) living among you. **27.** For all these abominations, the people who lived in the land before you committed them, and the land has been defiled. **28.** If you commit these abominations, the land will vomit (reject) you as it did the nations before you. **29.** Anyone who commits any of these abominations will be cut off (removed) from among their people. **30.** Therefore, keep my ordinance (rules) so that you do not follow the abominable practices that were done before you, and do not defile yourselves by them. I am the Lord your God.'"

Chapter 19

1. The Lord spoke to Moses, saying, **2.** "Speak to the whole congregation (assembly) of Israel and say to them: 'Be holy , for I, the Lord your God, am holy. **3.** Every one of you must honor (respect) your father and mother, and keep My Sabbaths (rest days). I am the Lord your God. **4.** Do not turn to idols (false gods) or make molded gods for yourselves. I am the Lord your God. **5.** If you offer a peace offering to the Lord, it must be offered voluntarily. 6. It should be eaten the same day it's offered, or the next day. If any remains until the third day, it must be burned. **7.** If it is eaten on the third day, it is unacceptable (not allowed) and will not be accepted. **8.** Anyone who eats it will bear the guilt for profaning (disrespecting) the Lord's offering and will be cut off from their people. **9.** When you reap (harvest) the harvest of your land, do not harvest the corners of your field, or gather the leftover grain. **10.** Do not pick all the grapes in your vineyard (grape garden); leave some for the poor and the foreigner. I am the Lord your God. **11.** Do not steal (take what is not yours), deceive (mislead), or lie to one another. **12.** Do not swear (promise) falsely by My name, profaning the name of your God. I am the Lord. **13.** Do not cheat (defraud) your neighbor or rob them. Pay the wages of hired workers on the same day. **14.** Do not curse the deaf or put a stumbling block in front of the blind. Fear your God. I am the Lord. **15.** Do not pervert justice. Do not favor the poor or show partiality (favoritism) to the rich. Judge your neighbor fairly. **16.** Do not gossip (spread rumors) or spread rumors about others. Do not stand idly by when your neighbor's life is in danger. I am the Lord. **17.** Do not harbor (keep) hatred in your heart for your brother. Rebuke your neighbor when necessary, but do not hold a grudge

(resentment). **18.** Do not seek revenge (payback) or bear a grudge. Love your neighbor as yourself. I am the Lord. **19.** Keep My statutes (laws): Do not crossbreed animals, plant mixed seeds, or wear clothes made of mixed fabrics (two different materials). **20.** If a man has relations with a woman who is pledged to another man, but not yet freed (fully separated), there will be punishment, but they will not be put to death, since she is not free. **21.** The man must bring a ram (male sheep) to the Lord as a guilt offering at the entrance of the tabernacle **22.** The priest will make atonement for him with the ram, and his sin (wrongdoing) will be forgiven. **23.** When you come into the land and plant trees for food, treat their fruit as uncircumcised (unclean) for the first three years. Do not eat it. **24.** In the fourth year, all the fruit will be holy, a praise (honor) to the Lord. **25.** In the fifth year, you may eat the fruit, so it will yield (give) more for you. I am the Lord your God. **26.** Do not eat anything with blood still in it (not drained). Do not practice divination or sorcery. **27.** Do not shave the sides of your head or trim (cut) the edges of your beard. **28.** Do not cut your body for the dead or tattoo marks on yourself. I am the Lord. **29.** Do not cause (make) your daughter to become a prostitute , or the land will fall into immorality (wickedness). **30.** Keep My Sabbaths (rest days) and honor My sanctuary (holy place). I am the Lord. **31.** Do not consult mediums (people who contact spirits) or spiritists. Do not seek after them or be defiled (made unclean) by them. I am the Lord your God. **32.** Rise in the presence of the elderly and honor (respect) them. Fear your God. I am the Lord. **33.** If a foreigner (non-Israelite) lives among you, do not mistreat (harm) him. **34.** The foreigner living among you should be treated as one of your own. Love him as yourself, for you were once foreigners in Egypt. I am the Lord your God. **35.** Do not commit injustice in judgment, measurements, or weights (measuring tools). **36.** Use honest (fair) scales, weights, and measures (tools). I am the Lord your God, who brought you out of Egypt. **37.** Therefore, obey all My statutes and commands (rules). I am the Lord.'

Chapter 20

1. The Lord spoke to Moses, saying, **2.** "Tell the people of Israel: 'Anyone, whether Israelite or foreigner (a non-Israelite living among them) living among them, who sacrifices a child to Molech (a Canaanite god associated with child sacrifice) must be put to death. The community shall stone (execute by throwing stones) them. **3.** I Myself will oppose (oppose strongly) this person and cut them off (exclude, remove) from their people, for they have defiled (made unclean) My holy place and dishonored (treated with disrespect) My name by offering their children to Molech. **4.** If the community ignores (fails to act upon) this act of child sacrifice and does not carry out the death penalty, **5.** I will still oppose this person and their family, and I will remove them and all those who follow Molech from the people. **6.** Anyone who turns to mediums (people who claim to communicate with the dead) or spiritists (practitioners of occult arts) is unfaithful to Me, and I will cut them off from their people. **7.** Dedicate (set apart as sacred) yourselves and be holy, for I am the Lord your God. **8.** Obey My laws and live by them; I am the Lord who makes you holy (sets you apart as pure and sacred). **9.** Anyone who curses (speaks disrespectfully or angrily against) their parents must be put to death. Such a person has committed a serious offense, and they bear full responsibility (must face the consequences). **10.** If a man has relations with his neighbor's wife, both the man and the woman have committed adultery (infidelity in marriage) and shall be put to death. **11.** If a man has relations with his father's wife, he has dishonored (shamed) his father, and both are to be put to death. Their actions make them responsible for their own deaths. **12.** If a man has relations with his daughter-in-law, both have committed a detestable (morally repulsive) act and shall be put to death. **13.** If a man has sexual relations with another man as he would with a woman, both have done what is forbidden (against divine law) and shall be put to death. **14.** If a man marries both a woman and her mother, this is wickedness (moral corruption); they all must be burned so that such depravity (corruption) is removed from among you. **15.** If a man has relations with an animal, he is to be put to death, and the animal must also be killed. **16.** If a woman has relations with an animal, both the woman and the animal must be put to death. **17.** If a man has relations with his sister, whether the daughter of his father or mother, this is a disgrace (shameful act); both must be publicly cut off (exiled, removed). **18.** If a man has relations with a woman during her menstrual period, both are to be removed from the people, for they have exposed (revealed) the flow of her blood. **19.** You must not have relations with your aunt, as this would dishonor (disrespect) a close family member, and they must bear their own guilt. **20.** If a man has relations with his uncle's wife, he dishonors (disrespects) his uncle, and they will die without children (die childless). **21.** If a man marries his brother's wife, it is an impurity (defilement), and they will also die childless. **22.** Follow all of My laws and instructions so that the land where I am bringing you will not drive you out (reject you). **23.** Do not practice the customs (traditions or ways of life) of the nations that I am driving out before you, for they have done these things, and I find them detestable (abominable). **24.** I have said to you, 'You will inherit (receive as your own) their land, a land flowing with milk and honey.' I am the Lord your God who has set you apart (made you holy) from other peoples. **25.** Make a distinction (clear difference) between clean (ritually pure) and unclean animals and birds, and do not defile (make impure) yourselves by eating any creature that I have marked as unclean. **26.** You are to be holy to Me because I, the Lord, am holy, and I have set you apart from other nations to be Mine. **27.** If any man or woman is a medium (a person who communicates with the dead) or spiritist (someone practicing occult arts), they shall be put to death by stoning; they bear full responsibility for their actions."

Chapter 21

1. The Lord spoke to Moses, saying, "Speak to the priests, the sons of Aaron, and instruct them: 'A priest must not make himself ceremonially unclean (ritually impure) by touching a dead person among his people, **2.** except for his closest family members: his mother, father, son, daughter, brother, **3.** or his unmarried sister (a woman who has not yet married), provided she has no husband and is dependent on him. For her, he may make himself unclean. **4.** But he must not defile (make unclean) himself for other relatives, as he is a chief (leader) among his people, and he should not make himself impure. **5.** They must not shave bald patches on their heads (a ritualistic practice to mark mourning), trim the edges of their beards, or make any cuts (self-inflicted marks) on their bodies. **6.** They must be holy (set apart as sacred) to their God and must not profane (disrespect, make common) God's name, for they offer the Lord's food offerings, which are holy; they must remain holy. **7.** They shall not marry a woman who is a prostitute (a woman who sells sexual services) or has been defiled (made impure), nor shall they marry a woman who has been divorced, as the priest is set apart for his God. **8.** So, you must treat him as holy because he presents the offerings of your God; he shall be holy to you, for I, the Lord, am holy and I sanctify (make holy, purify) you. **9.** If a priest's daughter dishonors (shames) herself by engaging in prostitution, she brings shame on her father and must be burned with fire. **10.** The high priest (the highest-ranking priest), who has been anointed (set apart with holy oil) with oil and ordained (officially consecrated) to wear the sacred garments, must not uncover his head or tear his clothing (a mourning practice). **11.** He must not approach any dead body, even if it is his father or mother, and defile (make unclean) himself. **12.** He must not leave the sanctuary (the holy place) or profane (desecrate, make common) the sacred area, for the oil of his God's anointing is on him; I am the Lord. **13.** He is to marry a virgin (a woman who has not had sexual relations). **14.** He must not marry a widow, a divorced woman, a defiled woman, or a prostitute. He must marry a virgin

from among his people. **15.** He shall not make his descendants impure (defiled) among his people, for I am the Lord who sanctifies (makes holy) him.' **16.** The Lord spoke further to Moses, **17.** "Tell Aaron: 'No descendant (offspring) of yours in future generations who has any physical defect may come near to present the food offerings (ritual sacrifices) of God. **18.** No one who is blind (cannot see), lame (cannot walk properly), disfigured (physically misshapen), or has a deformed (abnormally shaped) limb, **19.** or who has a broken foot or hand, **20.** or who is a hunchback (a person with a curved back), dwarf (abnormally short), or has eye defects (vision problems), skin diseases (leprosy or other skin afflictions), or is a eunuch (a man who has been castrated), **21.** No descendant of Aaron the priest who has a physical defect is permitted to approach the altar (the sacred place of offering) to present offerings by fire to the Lord. Because of his defect, he must not approach to offer the food of God. **22.** He may, however, eat the food of God, including the most holy and holy offerings. **23.** Yet he must not come near the inner veil (a curtain separating the holy of holies) or the altar, for his physical defect would desecrate (desecrate, make unholy) the sanctuary; I am the Lord who sanctifies (makes holy) these places.'" **24.** Moses conveyed (delivered, communicated) this message to Aaron, his sons, and all the people of Israel.

Chapter 22

1. The Lord spoke to Moses, saying, **2.** "Instruct Aaron and his sons to keep themselves set apart from the holy things that the Israelites dedicate to Me, and not to treat them disrespectfully or profane My holy name, for I am the Lord. **3.** Tell them: 'Any descendant of yours, through all generations, who approaches the holy offerings while unclean will be cut off from My presence. I am the Lord. **4.** If any of Aaron's descendants has a skin disease or a discharge, they must not eat the holy offerings until they are cleansed. This also applies if they have come into contact with something that has made them unclean, like touching a corpse, or if a man has had a seminal emission. **5.** Anyone who touches a creature that is unclean or anyone who becomes unclean by contact with another person's impurity, **6.** is unclean until evening. They must not eat from the holy offerings unless they have washed themselves with water. **7.** When the sun has set, they will be considered clean, and they may then eat the holy offerings, for they are their food. **8.** They must not eat anything found dead or torn by wild animals, which would defile them. I am the Lord. **9.** They must follow My instructions or they will bear the penalty of their sin and may die for their wrongdoing. I am the Lord who makes them holy. **10.** No outsider is to eat of the holy offerings. A guest of a priest or a hired worker is not to partake of the holy food. **11.** But if a priest buys a slave, that person may eat of it; anyone born in his household may also share in his food. **12.** If a priest's daughter marries someone outside the priestly family, she may no longer eat the holy contributions. **13.** However, if she is widowed or divorced, has no children, and has returned to her father's house as in her youth, she may eat of her father's food. But no outsider shall eat of it. **14.** If anyone unknowingly eats of the holy food, they must pay the priest for the holy food and add one-fifth to it. **15.** The priests must not defile the holy offerings that the people of Israel bring to the Lord, **16.** or allow the people to bear the guilt of unintentional wrongdoing when they eat these holy offerings, for I am the Lord who makes them holy.' **17.** The Lord spoke further to Moses, saying, **18.** "Tell Aaron, his sons, and all the Israelites: 'Any Israelite or foreigner in Israel who brings a burnt offering as a vow or as a freewill offering to the Lord, **19.** must offer an unblemished male from their cattle, sheep, or goats. Only a perfect offering will be acceptable. **20.** Anything with a defect is unacceptable; it will not be accepted on your behalf. **21.** When anyone offers a peace offering to fulfill a vow or as a freewill offering from the herd or flock, it must be flawless to be accepted; no defect is allowed. **22.** You must not offer to the Lord any animals that are blind, injured, mutilated, or that have sores, scabs, or boils. Such animals cannot be offered by fire on the altar to the Lord. 23. If an animal has a limb that is either too long or too short, it may be offered as a freewill offering, but not as a vow offering. 24. Do not offer to the Lord animals whose testicles have been bruised, crushed, torn, or cut; such animals must not be offered in your land. 25. Do not accept offerings from foreigners if they have any defects. They will not be acceptable because of their imperfections.' 26. The Lord said to Moses, 27. "When a calf, lamb, or goat is born, it must stay with its mother for seven days; from the eighth day onward, it will be acceptable as an offering by fire to the Lord. 28. Do not slaughter a cow or ewe with her offspring on the same day. 29. When you offer a thanksgiving sacrifice to the Lord, offer it freely. 30. It must be eaten that same day; do not leave any of it until morning. I am the Lord. 31. So keep My commandments and carry them out. I am the Lord. 32. Do not profane My holy name; I must be honored as holy among the Israelites. I am the Lord who makes you holy, 33. and who brought you out of Egypt to be your God. I am the Lord."

Chapter 23

1. Also, the Lord spoke to Moses, saying, 2. "Speak to the Israelites and tell them, 'These are the Lord's appointed (designated) festivals, which you're to proclaim (announce) as sacred (holy) gatherings. They are My appointed times (seasons). 3. Six days you may work, but the seventh day is a Sabbath of complete (full) rest, a sacred gathering. You shall do no work; it's the Sabbath of the Lord in all your homes. 4. These are the Lord's appointed times, the holy gatherings you're to declare (announce) at their specific times (appointed times). 5. The Lord's Passover begins at twilight (dusk) on the fourteenth day of the first month. 6. On the fifteenth day of the same month, the Feast of Unleavened Bread to the Lord begins; for seven days you must eat unleavened (unleavened) bread. 7. On the first day, you shall hold a sacred (holy) assembly; do no regular (normal) work on it. 8. For seven days, you're to present (offer) a burnt offering by fire to the Lord. On the seventh day, there shall also be a sacred (holy) assembly; you shall do no customary (ordinary) work.'" 9. Also, the Lord spoke to Moses, saying, 10. "Speak to the Israelites and tell them, 'When you enter the land I'm giving you and you gather its crops, bring a sheaf (bundle) of the first grain you gather to the priest. 11. He shall wave (present) the sheaf before the Lord to be accepted on your behalf; the priest shall wave it on the day after the Sabbath. 12. On the day you wave the sheaf, you shall offer a male lamb without defect (blemish) as a burnt offering to the Lord. 13. The grain offering shall be two-tenths of an ephah of fine flour mixed with oil, a fire-offering (burnt offering) to the Lord with a pleasing aroma; the drink offering shall be a quarter of a hin of wine. 14. You shall not eat any bread, roasted (parched) grain, or fresh grain until the very day you bring this offering to your God. This is a lasting statute (rule) for generations to come, wherever you live. 15. 'Count seven full weeks from the day after the Sabbath, from the day you brought the sheaf of the wave offering. 16. Count fifty days to the day after the seventh Sabbath, and present a new grain offering to the Lord. 17. From your homes, bring two loaves of unleavened bread as a wave offering, each made of two-tenths of an ephah of fine flour and baked with leaven, as the firstfruits to the Lord. 18. Present with the bread seven male lambs without defect (blemish), one young bull, and two rams as a burnt offering to the Lord, with their grain offerings and drink offerings, an offering by fire with a pleasing aroma to the Lord. 19. Also, offer one male goat as a sin offering (atonement), and two male lambs as a peace offering. 20. The priest shall wave them along with the loaves of the firstfruits as a wave offering before the Lord, together with the two lambs. They shall be holy (sacred) to the Lord for the priest. 21. Announce (proclaim) on the same day that you shall hold a sacred (holy) gathering. Do no regular work. This is to be a lasting statute (rule) for generations to come, wherever you live. 22. 'When you reap the harvest of your land, do not reap to the very edges of your field or gather the gleanings (leftovers) of your harvest. Leave them for the poor (needy) and the foreigner. I am the Lord your God.'" 23. Also, the Lord spoke to Moses, saying, 24. "Tell the Israelites, 'On the first day of the seventh month, you shall observe a day of rest, a memorial (reminder) of the blowing of trumpets, a sacred (holy) assembly. 25. Do no regular (normal) work, and present a burnt offering by fire to the Lord.'" 26. And the Lord spoke to Moses, saying, 27. "The tenth day of this seventh month is the Day of Atonement. Hold a sacred (holy) assembly and humble (afflict) yourselves, and present a burnt offering by fire to the Lord. 28. Do no work on that day, because it is the Day of Atonement, when atonement (reconciliation) is made for you before the Lord your God. 29. Anyone who does not humble (afflict) themselves on that day must be cut off from their people. 30. Anyone who does any work on that day, I will destroy (remove) from among their people. 31. You shall not do any work at all. This is a lasting statute (rule) for generations to come, wherever you live. 32. It shall be a Sabbath of complete (full) rest for you, and you must humble (afflict) yourselves. From the evening of the ninth day of the month until the next evening, you shall keep your Sabbath. 33. The Lord also spoke to Moses, saying, 34. "Tell the Israelites, 'On the fifteenth day of this seventh month, the Lord's Feast of Booths (Tabernacles) begins, and it lasts for seven days. 35. The first day is a sacred (holy) gathering; do no regular (normal) work. 36. For seven days, present (offer) a burnt offering by fire to the Lord, and on the eighth day hold a sacred (holy) gathering and present a burnt offering by fire to the Lord. This is a concluding assembly (final gathering); do no regular work. 37. These are the appointed festivals (designated times) of the Lord, which you're to declare (proclaim) as sacred gatherings for presenting burnt offerings by fire to the Lord — burnt offerings, grain offerings, sacrifices, and drink offerings, each day according to its requirements — 38. These offerings are in addition to those for the Lord's Sabbaths and other gifts (offerings) and sacrifices you vow (pledge) or freely give (offer) to the Lord." 39. On the fifteenth day of the seventh month, after you have gathered in the harvest (crop) of the land, celebrate the Lord's festival for seven days. The first day is a day of rest, and the eighth day also is a day of rest. 40. On the first day, you are to take branches from luxuriant (beautiful) trees—palm fronds, leafy branches, and poplars—and rejoice (celebrate) before the Lord your God for seven days. 41. Celebrate (observe) this as a festival to the Lord for seven days each year. This is a lasting ordinance (rule) for generations to come; celebrate it in the seventh month. 42. Live in temporary (booth) shelters for seven days: all native-born Israelites are to live in such shelters, 43. so that your descendants will know that I had the Israelites live in shelters (booths) when I brought them out of Egypt. I am the Lord your God. 44. So Moses declared (announced) to the Israelites the appointed festivals (designated times) of the Lord.

Chapter 24

1. The Lord spoke to Moses, saying, 2. "Tell the Israelites to bring pure olive oil painting, pressed and prepared, to keep the lights burning continually. 3. Outside the robe (curtain) of the Testimony, in the temple of Meeting, Aaron is to be in charge of keeping the lights burning from evening until morning, before the Lord. This will be an endless constitution for all unborn generations. 4. He'll oversee the lights on the pure gold lampstand, ensuring they're maintained before the Lord at all times. 5. "You're to take fine flour and bake twelve loaves of bread. Each loaf should contain two-tenths of an ephah (a unit of measure for grain). 6. Place the loaves in two rows, with six in each row, on the pure gold table before the Lord. 7. Add pure frankincense (an aromatic resin) to each row, so that it will serve as a memorial offering, burned by fire to the Lord. 8. Every Sabbath, arrange the loaves before the Lord as a continual offering, handed by the Israelites as part of an everlasting covenant. 9. The bread will be for Aaron and his sons to eat in a

holy place, for it is the most holy part of the offerings made by fire to the Lord, as a law that will never change. 10. Now, the son of an Israelite woman, whose father was an Egyptian, went out among the Israelites. He and an Israelite man had a disagreement in the camp. 11. The son of the Israelite woman cursed (spoke disrespectfully) against the name of the Lord and cursed, so they brought him before Moses. 12. They put him in custody, awaiting the Lord's guidance on what to do. 13. Then the Lord spoke to Moses, saying, 14. "Take the man who cursed outside the camp, and have all those who heard him place their hands on his head. Then, let the entire congregation stone him to death. 15. Tell the Israelites: 'Anyone who curses their God will be held responsible for their sin. 16. Anyone who blasphemes the name of the Lord must be put to death. The whole congregation is to stone them, whether they are a foreigner or a native-born Israelite. Anyone who blasphemes the name of the Lord shall surely die. 17. Anyone who murders another person must also be put to death. 18. However, if someone kills an animal, they must make restitution, paying for the animal they killed. 19. If a person injures another, the same injury must be done to them—20. fracture for fracture, eye for eye, tooth for tooth. As the injury was caused, so it must be done to the one who caused it. 21. Anyone who kills an animal must make restitution (compensate for the loss); but anyone who kills a person must be put to death. 22. The same law applies to both foreigners and natives alike, for I am the Lord your God.' 23. Then Moses spoke the Lord's command to the Israelites, and they took the man who had cursed outside the camp and stoned him to death with stones. The Israelites did as the Lord had instructed Moses."

Chapter 25

1. The Lord spoke to Moses on Mount Sinai, saying, 2. "Speak to the people of Israel and say to them: 'When you enter the land that I'm giving you, the land will observe a Sabbath (a day of rest) for the Lord. 3. For six years you shall sow your fields, and for six years you shall prune your vineyards and gather their yield, 4. but in the seventh year, the land will have a Sabbath of complete rest for the Lord. You shall not sow your fields or prune your vineyards. 5. Do not reap what grows by itself, or gather the grapes of your untended vines. It will be a time of rest for the land. 6. The yield from that time will be for you to eat—yourself, your servants, your hired workers, and the foreigners living among you, 7. as well as for your beasts and the wild creatures (living animals) in your land—everything that grows will be food. 8. You shall count seven cycles of seven years, totaling forty-nine years. 9. Then, on the tenth day of the seventh month, on the Day of Atonement (a day for remission and reconciliation with God), you shall sound the trumpet throughout the land, 10. and you shall consecrate (make holy) the fiftieth year, proclaiming liberty throughout the land to all its inhabitants. It will be a Jubilee (a special time of freedom) for you, and each of you shall return to your own land and family. 11. The fiftieth year shall be a Jubilee (a year of freedom) for you. In that year, you shall not sow, nor reap what grows by itself, or gather the grapes from untended vines. 12. It will be a holy time for you, and you shall eat what the land produces. 13. In the Year of Jubilee, every person shall return to their own property. 14. If your fellow Israelite becomes poor and sells part of their land, and if they have a relative to redeem (buy back) it, the relative may redeem what was sold. 15. If they have no one to redeem it but are able to redeem it themselves, they can count the years since the sale and pay back the difference to the buyer, and return to their property. 16. But if they are unable to redeem it, it will remain with the buyer until the Year of Jubilee. 17. If a man sells a house in a walled city, he may redeem it within one year of the sale. 18. But if it is not redeemed within that year, it becomes the permanent property of the buyer and cannot be returned in the Jubilee. 19. However, if the house is in a village that is not surrounded by a wall, it may be redeemed at any time, and it will be returned in the

Jubilee. 20. The Levites (descendants of Levi, set apart for religious duties) may redeem their houses in the cities they possess at any time. 21. And those houses will be returned to them in the Jubilee (the time of freedom), because the Levites' homes are their heritage among the Israelites. 22. The land must not be sold permanently, for the land belongs to Me (God); you are foreigners and sojourners (temporary residents) with Me. 23. In all the land that you possess, you must allow the land to be redeemed. 24. If your fellow Israelite becomes poor and sells part of their property, and if they have a relative to redeem it, the relative may buy back what was sold. 25. If they have no one to redeem it but are able to redeem it themselves, they can calculate the years since the sale and pay back the difference to the buyer. 26. If they cannot redeem it, it will remain with the buyer until the Year of Jubilee, when it will be returned to the original owner. 27. If a person sells a house in a walled city, they may redeem it within one year of the sale. 28. But if the house is not redeemed within that time, it becomes the permanent property of the buyer and will not be returned in the Jubilee. 29. However, houses in villages that are not surrounded by walls are to be considered as fields in the open country. These may be redeemed and will be returned in the Jubilee. 30. But the cities of the Levites and the houses in the cities of their heritage may be redeemed at any time by the Levites. 31. The house that is sold in a city of the Levites' heritage shall be returned in the Jubilee (time of freedom), for the houses in the cities of the Levites are their perpetual possession among the Israelites. 32. But the fields surrounding their cities cannot be sold, for they are their perpetual inheritance. 33. If one of your fellow Israelites becomes poor and falls into poverty, you shall help them as you would a foreigner (a stranger) or a sojourner, so that they can live with you. 34. Do not charge them usury (interest) or profit; fear God, so that your fellow Israelites may live with you. 35. You shall not lend them money at interest, nor shall you lend them food to make a profit. 36. I am the Lord your God, who brought you out of Egypt, to give you the land of Canaan and to be your God. 37. If one of your fellow Israelites becomes poor and sells themselves to you, do not treat them as a slave (a person bound to serve without freedom). 38. They shall serve you as a hired worker and a sojourner until the Year of Jubilee. 39. Then they shall leave—along with their children—and return to their family and the possession of their fathers. 40. For they are My servants, whom I brought out of Egypt. They must not be sold as slaves. 41. Do not rule over them ruthlessly, but fear your God." 42. For they are My retainers whom I brought out of Egypt; they shall not be sold as slaves. 43. You shall not rule over them harshly, but you shall fear (respect) your God. 44. However, you may buy male or female slaves (retainers) from the nations around you. 45. You may also buy the children of foreigners who live among you, and they will become your property, along with their families whom they have fathered in your land. 46. You may inherit them as property for your children after you, and they will remain your permanent slaves. But you shall not treat fellow Israelites as slaves. 47. If a fellow Israelite becomes poor and sells themselves to a foreigner or to a member of their family, 48. if a foreigner near you becomes rich, they may be redeemed (bought back) again. A relative, such as a family member, may redeem them; 49. or their uncle or their uncle's son may redeem them, or any close relative may redeem them. However, they may redeem themselves if they are able. 50. The redemption price will be based on the number of years from when they were sold until the Jubilee (time of freedom), and will be calculated according to the wages of a hired servant. 51. If many years remain, they will pay the redemption price in proportion to the time they were sold for. 52. If only a few years remain until the Jubilee (time of freedom), they will pay a corresponding amount for their redemption. 53. They will work as a hired servant for the remaining time and will not be treated harshly in your sight. 54. But if they are not redeemed before the Jubilee (time of freedom), they shall be released, along with their children, and return to their family and their land. **55.** For the Israelites are My servants, whom I brought out of Egypt; I am the Lord your God.

Chapter 26

1. You shall not make for yourselves any idols (false gods) or images to worship. Do not erect pillars or set up carved stones in your land to bow down to, for I am the Lord, your God. **2.** Honor My Sabbaths (rest days) and show reverence for My sanctuary, for I am the Lord. **3.** If you live according to My laws (statutes) and obey My commandments, putting them into practice, **4.** I will send the rain at the proper time, and the land will produce its crops; the trees of the field will bear fruit. **5.** Your harvest (threshing) will continue until the grape harvest (vintage), and the grape harvest will last until it is time to sow (plant); you will eat your fill of bread and live securely in your land. **6.** I will provide peace in your land, and you will sleep in safety, without fear. I will remove (rid) the wild animals (dangerous beasts) from the land, and no weapons (swords) will invade your territory. **7.** You will pursue your enemies, and they will fall before you by the sword. **8.** Five of you will be able to chase a hundred, and a hundred of you will put ten thousand to flight; your enemies will fall before you. **9.** I will look upon you with favor, bless you with fruitfulness (productivity), multiply you, and uphold the covenant I made with you. **10.** You will eat the old harvest and clear it away to make room for the new. **11.** I will place My dwelling (tabernacle) among you, and I will not reject (abhor) you. **12.** I will walk among you and be your God, and you will be My people. **13.** I am the Lord, your God, who brought you out of the land of Egypt, so that you would no longer be slaves to them. I broke the chains (bands) of your yoke (animal harness) and made you walk with dignity. **14.** But if you do not listen to Me, and do not keep these commandments, **15.** And if you despise (reject) My laws or loathe (abhor) My judgments, refusing to follow My commandments and breaking My covenant, **16.** I will send upon you terror (great fear), wasting disease, and fever that will consume your eyes and bring sorrow to your heart. You will plant seeds (sow) in vain, for your enemies will take what you grow. **17.** I will turn My face against you, and you will be defeated by your enemies. Those who hate you will rule over you, and you will flee even when no one is chasing you. **18.** If you still refuse to obey Me, I will discipline you seven times more for your sins. **19.** I will humble your pride (arrogance) and make the sky above you like iron and the earth beneath you like bronze. **20.** Your efforts will be fruitless; the land will not yield its crops, and the trees will not bear fruit. **21.** If you remain rebellious (walk contrary to) Me and refuse to obey, I will increase your punishment with seven times more plagues (calamities), according to your sins. **22.** I will send wild animals among you that will take your children, destroy your livestock, and diminish your population. Your roads will become empty (desolate). **23.** If you remain unrepentant (unchanged) and continue to oppose Me, **24.** I will also oppose you and punish you seven times more for your sins. **25.** I will bring a sword against you to execute the vengeance of the covenant. When you are gathered in your cities, I will send pestilence (disease) among you, and you will fall into the hands of your enemies. **26.** When I have cut off your food supply, ten women will bake bread in one oven, and they will weigh it out to you. You will eat, but it will not be enough to satisfy you. **27.** If, despite all of this, you do not obey Me but continue to oppose Me, **28.** I will walk in anger (fury) against you, and I will punish you seven times more for your sins. **29.** You will be forced to eat the flesh of your sons and daughters. **30.** I will destroy your high places (places of idol worship), cut down your incense altars, and throw your dead bodies (carcasses) on the lifeless idols. My soul will reject (abhor) you. **31.** I will lay waste to your cities and make your sanctuaries (sacred places) desolate (ruin). I will not accept the pleasing aromas of your offerings. **32.** I will bring devastation upon the land, and your enemies living there will be shocked (astonished) at its destruction. **33.** I will scatter

(disperse) you among the nations, and I will send a sword after you. Your land will become desolate, and your cities will be ruined. **34.** Then, the land will enjoy its sabbaths (rest), as long as it lies desolate and you are in the land of your enemies. The land will rest and take pleasure in its sabbaths. **35.** As long as the land is desolate, it will rest—because it did not rest during the sabbaths when you were living in it. **36.** For those of you who remain, I will send faintness (weakness) into their hearts in the lands of their enemies. The rustling of a leaf will make them flee; they will flee as though from a sword, falling even when no one is chasing them. **37.** They will stumble (trip) over each other, as if fleeing from a sword, although no one is pursuing. You will have no strength to stand before your enemies. **38.** You will perish (die) among the nations, and the land of your enemies will devour you. **39.** Those of you who remain will waste away in their sins (iniquities) in the land of their enemies. Even the sins of their ancestors will cause them to waste away. **40.** But if they confess their sin and the sin of their ancestors, and the unfaithfulness with which they were unfaithful to Me, and acknowledge that they walked contrary to Me, **41.** And if their unrepentant (uncircumcised) hearts are humbled and they accept their guilt, **42.** Then I will remember My covenant with Jacob, and My covenant with Isaac and Abraham, and I will remember the land. **43.** The land will remain desolate, but it will enjoy its sabbaths while it is empty without them. They will accept their guilt, having despised My laws and hated (abhorred) My statutes. **44.** Even though they are in the land of their enemies, I will not cast them away nor will I reject (abhor) them to utterly destroy them and break My covenant with them. For I am the Lord, their God. **45.** For their sake, I will remember the covenant of their ancestors, whom I brought out of the land of Egypt, in the sight of the nations, to be their God. I am the Lord. **46.** These are the statutes (laws), ordinances, and commandments the Lord gave to the children of Israel through Moses on Mount Sinai.

Chapter 27

1. The Lord spoke to Moses, saying, **2.** "Speak to the Israelites and tell them: 'If someone makes a vow (a serious promise) to dedicate certain individuals to the Lord, according to the valuation (assigned value) you assign, **3.** if the valuation for a man between the ages of twenty and sixty years old is made, it shall be fifty shekels of silver, based on the sanctuary shekel (a unit of currency used for sacred purposes). **4.** For a woman, the valuation shall be thirty shekels; **5.** If the person is between five and twenty years old, the valuation for a male shall be twenty shekels, and for a female, it shall be ten shekels; **6.** If the person is between one month and five years old, the valuation for a male shall be five shekels of silver, and for a female, three shekels; **7.** If the person is sixty years old or older, the valuation for a male shall be fifteen shekels, and for a female, ten shekels. **8.** If someone is too poor to pay the valuation, they should come before the priest (a religious leader), who will set the value based on the vow and the person's ability to pay. **9.** If an animal is offered to the Lord, it shall be considered holy (set apart for sacred use). **10.** It cannot be exchanged or substituted, either for a better or a worse one; if someone exchanges one animal for another, both animals shall be holy. **11.** If the animal is unclean (impure and not fit for sacrifice) and cannot be offered as a sacrifice, it must be presented to the priest, **12.** and the priest shall determine its value, whether good or bad. As the priest values it, so it shall be. **13.** If the person wishes to redeem (buy back) the animal, they must add one-fifth to its value. **14.** If someone dedicates their house as holy to the Lord, the priest shall assign a value to it, whether good or bad. **15.** If the person who dedicated it wants to redeem the house, they must add one-fifth to its value, and it will be theirs again. **16.** If someone dedicates part of their field, the valuation will be based on the seed required to grow it. A homer (a unit of measure) of barley seed shall be valued at fifty shekels. **17.** If the field is dedicated in the Year of Jubilee (every

50th year), the valuation will stand as it is. **18.** If the field is dedicated after the Jubilee, the priest shall calculate the value based on the number of years remaining until the next Jubilee, and that amount shall be subtracted from the valuation. **19.** If the person wants to redeem the field, they must add one-fifth of its value, and it will be theirs. **20.** If the person does not redeem the field or has sold it to someone else, it cannot be redeemed. **21.** However, in the Year of Jubilee, the field will return to its original owner, and it will be considered holy to the Lord as a devoted field (set apart for God), becoming the priest's possession. **22.** If someone dedicates a field they bought, which is not part of their inherited land, **23.** the priest shall assign its value, considering how many years remain until the Year of Jubilee. The person shall pay the valuation as an offering to the Lord. **24.** In the Year of Jubilee, the field shall return to its original owner. **25.** All valuations will be made based on the sanctuary shekel (a specific standard of currency), which is worth twenty gerahs (a small weight of silver). **26.** No one shall dedicate the firstborn (firstborn animal) of animals, whether an ox or sheep, because the firstborn belongs to the Lord. **27.** If the animal is unclean, it may be redeemed at its valuation, with an additional one-fifth added; if not redeemed, it shall be sold at the valuation. **28.** No devoted offering (sacred gift)—whether a person, an animal, or a field—can be sold or redeemed. Every devoted offering is sacred to the Lord. **29.** No person under the ban (dedicated to destruction) can be redeemed; they must be put to death. **30.** All tithes (a tenth portion) from the land, whether from crops or fruit, belong to the Lord and are holy to Him. **31.** If someone wishes to redeem any of their tithes, they must add one-fifth to the value. **32.** Regarding the tithe of livestock (animals), any tenth animal that passes under the rod (counted as it moves along) shall be holy to the Lord. **33.** The owner shall not inquire whether the animal is good or bad, nor can they exchange it. If exchanged, both the original and the exchanged animals shall be holy and cannot be redeemed." **34.** These are the commandments (rules) the Lord gave to Moses for the Israelites at Mount Sinai (a mountain in the desert).

4 – Numbers

Chapter 1

1. The Lord spoke to Moses in the wilderness of Sinai, at the Tabernacle of Meeting (the sacred tent where Israel gathered for worship), on the first day of the second month, in the second year after the Israelites left Egypt. He said: **2.** "Take a census (a count) of all the people of Israel, organized by their families and the households of their fathers, listing every male by name. **3.** Count all those who are twenty years or older, and who are able to serve in Israel's army. You and Aaron will number them by their divisions. **4.** For each tribe, a leader will assist you. One man from each tribe, the head of his father's house, will stand by you. **5.** Here are the names of the leaders who will help you: from the tribe of Reuben, Elizur, son of Shedeur; **6.** from Simeon, Shelumiel, son of Zurishaddai; **7.** from Judah, Nahshon, son of Amminadab; **8.** from Issachar, Nethanel, son of Zuar; **9.** from Zebulun, Eliab, son of Helon; **10.** from the sons of Joseph: from Ephraim, Elishama, son of Ammihud; from Manasseh, Gamaliel, son of Pedahzur; **11.** from Benjamin, Abidan, son of Gideoni; **12.** from Dan, Ahiezer, son of Ammishaddai; **13.** from Asher, Pagiel, son of Ocran; **14.** from Gad, Eliasaph, son of Deuel; **15.** from Naphtali, Ahira, son of Enan. **16.** These men were selected from the congregation. They were the leaders of their tribes, serving as the heads of their divisions in Israel. **17.** Moses and Aaron called these men, as named, and **18.** they gathered all the Israelites on the first day of the second month. Each person's name was recorded by family and father's house, counting every male from twenty years old and above who could fight in Israel's army. **19.** As the Lord had instructed Moses, he conducted the count in the wilderness of Sinai. **20.** The descendants of Reuben, Israel's firstborn, were counted by their families and father's houses. Every male, twenty years or older, able to serve in battle, was included. **21.** The total number of Reuben's men was forty-six thousand five hundred. **22.** From the tribe of Simeon, their families and father's houses were counted, and every male from twenty years old and above, able to go to war, was recorded. **23.** The total number from Simeon was fifty-nine thousand three hundred. **24.** From the tribe of Gad, their families and father's houses were counted, each male from twenty years old and above, who could serve in the military. **25.** The total number from Gad was forty-five thousand six hundred and fifty. **26.** From the tribe of Judah, their families and father's houses were counted, including all males from twenty years old and above, fit for battle. **27.** The total number from Judah was seventy-four thousand six hundred. **28.** From the tribe of Issachar, their families and father's houses were counted, with every male, twenty years or older, capable of serving in the army. **29.** The total from Issachar was fifty-four thousand four hundred. **30.** From the tribe of Zebulun, their families and father's houses were counted, including every male from twenty years old and above, able to fight. **31.** The total number from Zebulun was fifty-seven thousand four hundred. **32.** From the sons of Joseph, from the tribe of Ephraim, their families and father's houses were counted, including every male from twenty years old and above, able to go to war. **33.** The total from Ephraim was forty thousand five hundred. **34.** From the tribe of Manasseh, their families and father's houses were counted, with every male from twenty years old and above, able to serve. **35.** The total number from Manasseh was thirty-two thousand two hundred. **36.** From the tribe of Benjamin, their families and father's houses were counted, including every male from twenty years old and above, able to serve in battle. **37.** The total number from Benjamin was thirty-five thousand four hundred. **38.** From the tribe of Dan, their families and father's houses were counted, and every male, twenty years or older, capable of going to war, was included. **39.** The total number from Dan was sixty-two thousand seven hundred. **40.** From the tribe of Asher, their families and father's houses were counted, with every male from twenty years old and above, able to serve in battle. **41.** The total number from Asher was forty-one thousand five hundred. **42.** From the tribe of Naphtali, their families and father's houses were counted, with every male from twenty years old and above, able to serve in the military. **43.** The total number from Naphtali was fifty-three thousand four hundred. **44.** These were the men who were counted. Moses and Aaron, along with the leaders of Israel, twelve men, one from each tribe, **45.** counted all the Israelites, by their families and father's houses, all those from twenty years and older, who were able to serve in the army. **46.** The total number of those counted was six hundred and three thousand five hundred and fifty. **47.** However, the Levites were not included in the count of the other tribes. **48.** The Lord had instructed Moses: **49.** "Do not include the tribe of Levi in the census of the other Israelites, **50.** but appoint them to care for the Tabernacle of the Testimony (the sacred tent), its furnishings, and everything related to it. They will carry the Tabernacle and its contents, serve in it, and camp around it. **51.** When the Tabernacle is to be moved, the Levites will dismantle it, and when it's time to set it up again, they will do so. Anyone else who approaches it will be put to death. **52.** The Israelites will set up their tents by their own camps and standards (flags), each according to their divisions. **53.** But the Levites will camp around the Tabernacle of the Testimony, so that God's anger will not fall upon the people of Israel. The Levites will guard the Tabernacle." **54.** The Israelites followed all of the Lord's commands to Moses exactly as instructed.

Chapter 2.

1. The Lord spoke to Moses and Aaron saying: **2.** "Every one of the children of Israel (descendants of Jacob) shall camp by their own standard (banner or flag), next to the emblem (symbol or sign) of their father's house. They must camp some distance away from the

Tabernacle of Meeting (the sacred tent for worship). **3.** On the east side, where the sun rises, those who belong to the tribe of Judah will camp according to their armies. Nahshon, the son of Amminadab, will be the leader of the tribe of Judah." **4.** The number of Judah's army was 74,600. **5.** "Next to Judah will be the tribe of Issachar, and Nethanel, the son of Zuar, will be their leader." **6.** The number of Issachar's army was 54,400. **7.** "Then comes the tribe of Zebulun, and Eliab, the son of Helon, will be their leader." **8.** The number of Zebulun's army was 57,400. **9.** In total, the army of Judah and the tribes camped next to them numbered 186,400. These will be the first to break camp. **10.** On the south side, the banner of the tribe of Reuben will be raised, and Elizur, the son of Shedeur, will be the leader of Reuben's army." **11.** The number of Reuben's army was 46,500. **12.** "Next to Reuben will be the tribe of Simeon, with Shelumiel, the son of Zurishaddai, as their leader." **13.** The number of Simeon's army was 59,300. **14.** "Then comes the tribe of Gad, with Eliasaph, the son of Reuel, as their leader." **15.** The number of Gad's army was 45,650. **16.** In total, the army of Reuben and the tribes camped next to them numbered 151,450. They will be the second to break camp. **17.** The Tabernacle of Meeting (the sacred tent where God's presence dwelled) will move with the Levites (members of the tribe of Levi, who served in religious duties) in the center of the camps. As the tribes camp, so they will move out, each tribe by its banner. **18.** On the west side, the banner of the tribe of Ephraim will be raised, and Elishama, the son of Ammihud, will be the leader of Ephraim's army." **19.** The number of Ephraim's army was 40,500. **20.** "Next to Ephraim will be the tribe of Manasseh, with Gamaliel, the son of Pedahzur, as their leader." **21.** The number of Manasseh's army was 32,200. **22.** "Then comes the tribe of Benjamin, with Abidan, the son of Gideoni, as their leader." **23.** The number of Benjamin's army was 35,400. **24.** In total, the army of Ephraim and the tribes camped next to them numbered 108,100. They will be the third to break camp. **25.** On the north side, the banner of the tribe of Dan will be raised, and Ahiezer, the son of Ammishaddai, will be the leader of Dan's army." **26.** The number of Dan's army was 62,700. **27.** "Next to Dan will be the tribe of Asher, with Pagiel, the son of Ocran, as their leader." **28.** The number of Asher's army was 41,500. **29.** "Then comes the tribe of Naphtali, with Ahira, the son of Enan, as their leader." **30.** The number of Naphtali's army was 53,400. **31.** In total, the army of Dan and the tribes camped next to them numbered 157,600. They will be the last to break camp, moving out with their banners. **32.** These are the people of Israel who were counted by their families. All the men who were numbered for service in the armies of Israel total 603,550. **33.** But the Levites (members of the tribe of Levi, who served in religious duties) were not counted among the other Israelites, just as the Lord commanded Moses. **34.** Thus, the Israelites obeyed all the commands the Lord had given to Moses. They camped by their banners and broke camp, each one by their family, according to their father's house.

Chapter 3.

1. This chapter records the genealogy of Aaron and Moses, when the Lord communicated with Moses on Mount Sinai (the mountain where Moses received the Ten Commandments). **2.** The names of Aaron's sons were Nadab (the firstborn), Abihu, Eleazar, and Ithamar. Aaron, Moses' brother, and his descendants were consecrated (set apart) to serve as priests for God. **3.** These priests, Aaron's sons, were anointed (chosen and set apart) to fulfill their sacred responsibilities in the Tabernacle. **4.** Nadab and Abihu, however, died in the wilderness of Sinai for offering unauthorized (improper) fire before the Lord. Since they had no descendants, Eleazar and Ithamar continued their priestly roles alongside their father Aaron. **5.** The Lord then spoke to Moses, instructing him: **6.** "Summon the tribe of Levi and present them before Aaron the priest. They will assist him in his priestly duties. **7.** The Levites will serve the needs of Aaron and the entire congregation of Israel in the Tabernacle (the sacred tent of meeting). They will handle all the operations associated with the Tabernacle. **8.** They are responsible for the care of all the items in the Tabernacle, as well as all the tasks required for maintaining the sacred space. **9.** You will assign the Levites to Aaron and his sons, as they are set apart for this work, selected from all of Israel. **10.** Appoint Aaron and his sons to oversee the priestly functions. Any unauthorized person who enters this sacred area will be put to death." **11.** Then the Lord further instructed Moses, saying: **12.** "I have chosen the Levites from among the Israelites to replace every firstborn male of Israel, and every firstborn male of livestock. The Levites are dedicated to Me. **13.** All the firstborn belong to Me, for when I struck down the firstborn of Egypt, I set apart the firstborn of Israel—both humans and animals—as Mine. I am the Lord." **14.** Then, in the wilderness of Sinai, the Lord spoke again to Moses, instructing him: **15.** "Count the Levites by their family groups, according to their fathers' houses. Record every male from one month old and up." **16.** Moses did as instructed, numbering them according to the Lord's command. **17.** The sons of Levi were Gershon, Kohath, and Merari. **18.** The family of Gershon consisted of Libni and Shimei. **19.** The family of Kohath consisted of Amram, Izehar, Hebron, and Uzziel. **20.** The family of Merari consisted of Mahli and Mushi. These are the Levitical families, based on their fathers' houses. **21.** Gershon's descendants formed the Libnite and Shimite families, known as the Gershonites. **22.** The Gershonites numbered 7,500 males, from one month old and up. **23.** They were to camp to the west of the Tabernacle. **24.** Their leader was Eliasaph, the son of Lael. **25.** The Gershonites were tasked with taking care of the Tabernacle's tent, its coverings, the curtain for the entrance to the Tabernacle, and the curtain for the entrance to the outer courtyard, as well as the ropes and cords associated with them. **27.** Kohath's descendants were the Amramites, Izharites, Hebronites, and Uzzielites. These were the families of the Kohathites. **28.** The Kohathites numbered 8,600 males, from one month old and up. Their responsibility was to guard the holy sanctuary. **29.** They camped on the south side of the Tabernacle. **30.** Their leader was Elizaphan, the son of Uzziel. **31.** The Kohathites were responsible for the care of the Ark of the Covenant, the table for the showbread, the golden lampstand, the altars, and all the utensils used in the sanctuary. They also managed the curtain (veil) and all other sacred items. **32.** Eleazar, the son of Aaron the priest, was in charge of overseeing all the Levites and ensuring that the duties regarding the sanctuary were carried out correctly. **33.** Merari's descendants formed the Mahlite and Mushite families. These were the Merarites. **34.** The Merarites numbered 6,200 males, from one month old and up. **35.** Their leader was Zuriel, the son of Abihail. They camped on the north side of the Tabernacle. **36.** The Merarites were responsible for the boards, bars, pillars, bases, and all the other furnishings of the Tabernacle, including the pillars and their bases, pegs, and ropes for the outer court. **38.** Moses, Aaron, and Aaron's sons camped on the east side, in front of the Tabernacle. They were in charge of the sanctuary and were responsible for ensuring the needs of the Israelites were met. Any unauthorized person who approached the Tabernacle was to be put to death. **39.** The total number of Levites, as counted by Moses and Aaron, was 22,000 males, from one month old and up. **40.** The Lord then told Moses to count all the firstborn males of Israel, from one month old and older, and record their names. **41.** "The Levites will be Mine in place of the firstborn males of Israel, and the livestock of the Levites will take the place of the firstborn livestock of the Israelites." **42.** So Moses obeyed and counted the firstborn of Israel as the Lord had commanded. **43.** The total number of firstborn males of Israel, from one month old and up, was 22,273. **44.** The Lord then spoke to Moses, saying: **45.** "Take the Levites to replace all the firstborn males of Israel and the livestock of the Levites in place of the firstborn animals. The Levites belong to Me: I am the Lord. **46.** For the 273 firstborn of Israel who exceed the number of Levites, collect five shekels for each person, according to the sanctuary shekel, which is 20 gerahs (a smaller unit of weight). 47. This money will be given to Aaron and his sons." 49. So Moses collected the redemption (payment for release) money from the firstborn of Israel, for the 273 that exceeded the number of Levites. 50. Moses collected 1,365 shekels from the firstborn of Israel, according to the shekel of the sanctuary. 51. Moses then gave this redemption money to Aaron and his sons, just as the Lord had instructed him.

Chapter 4

1. The LORD instructed Moses and Aaron, 2. "Conduct a census of the Kohathite division of the Levites (descendants of Kohath, son of Levi) according to their clans. 3. Count all men aged thirty to fifty who will be serving at the tent of meeting (the tabernacle). 4. The Kohathites' duty is to care for the most sacred items in the tabernacle. 5. When the camp moves, Aaron and his sons (descendants of Levi) must remove the veil covering the Ark of the Covenant (sacred chest) and place it over the Ark. 6. They will cover it with a durable leather cloth and a blue fabric, and then insert the poles used for carrying. 7. Over the table of the Presence (where the sacred bread is placed), they will spread a blue cloth and arrange the plates, dishes, bowls, and jars for the drink offerings. The bread must remain on the table. 8. They will then cover it with a scarlet cloth, followed by a leather covering, and position the poles in place. 9. For the lampstand, they will cover it and its accessories (wicks, trays, and olive oil jars) with a blue cloth, wrap it in leather, and put it on a carrying frame. 10. Over the gold altar (used for incense), they will spread a blue cloth, cover it with leather, and set the poles. 11. They will wrap all the sanctuary items in a blue cloth, cover them with leather, and place them on a carrying frame. 12. For the bronze altar (used for burnt offerings), they will remove the ashes, spread a purple cloth, and place the utensils (firepans, forks, shovels, sprinkling bowls) on it. Then, cover with leather and insert the poles. 13. After Aaron and his sons have finished covering the sacred items and the camp is ready to move, the Kohathites will carry them, but they must not touch the holy things, or they will die. 14. "Eleazar, son of Aaron, is in charge of the oil for the lamps, incense, grain offering, and anointing oil, as well as overseeing the tabernacle and its sacred objects." 15. The LORD warned Moses and Aaron, 16. "Ensure the Kohathites do not perish by keeping them away from the most holy things. Aaron and his sons must assign each man his task and what he is to carry. 17. But the Kohathites must not look at the holy things, even briefly, or they will die." 18. The LORD said to Moses, 19. "Take a census of the Gershonites (another Levite clan) by their families. 20. Count men aged thirty to fifty who will serve at the tent of meeting. 21. The Gershonites are to carry the tabernacle's curtains, coverings, leather coverings, and entrance curtains, as well as those for the courtyard and the ropes and other equipment. 22. Their duties will be under the direction of Aaron and his sons. 23. This is the service of the Gershonite clans, and their work will be supervised by Ithamar (son of Aaron)." 24. The LORD told Moses, 25. "Take a census of the Merarites (the third clan of Levites) according to their families. 26. Count all men aged thirty to fifty who will serve at the tent of meeting. 27. The Merarites are responsible for carrying the tabernacle frames, crossbars, posts, bases, courtyard posts, tent pegs, ropes, and all related equipment. 28. Each man will be assigned specific items to carry. 29. Their work will be overseen by Ithamar, the son of Aaron." 30. Moses, Aaron, and the leaders of Israel counted the Kohathites. 31. The total number of men aged thirty to fifty serving in the Kohathite clans was 2,750. 32. The Gershonites were counted, totaling 2,630 men. 33. The Merarites numbered 3,200 men. 34. In total, 8,580 Levites from all three clans (Kohathites, Gershonites, Merarites) were counted. 35. Each man was assigned his work and what to carry, as the LORD had commanded Moses. 36. The Kohathite clans (descendants of Kohath, a son of Levi) were counted, totaling 2,750 men. 37. This was the total number of Kohathites who served at the tent of meeting (the tabernacle, the sacred place where the Israelites worshipped). Moses and Aaron counted them as instructed by the LORD (Yahweh, God). 38. The Gershonites (another clan of the Levites) were also counted by their families and clans. 39. All men aged thirty to fifty who served at the tent of meeting, 40. counted by their clans, totaled 2,630. 41. This was the total number of Gershonites serving at the tent. Moses and Aaron counted them as the LORD had commanded. 42. The Merarites (yet another clan of the Levites) were counted by their clans and families. 43. All the men aged thirty to fifty who served at the tent of meeting, 44. counted by their clans, totaled 3,200. 45. This was the total number of Merarites. Moses and Aaron counted them as instructed by the LORD. 46. Moses, Aaron, and the leaders of Israel (the twelve tribal leaders) counted all the Levites (descendants of Levi) by their families. 47. All men aged thirty to fifty who served in the work of the tent of meeting, 48. Numbered 8,580. 49. At the LORD's command through Moses, each man was assigned his specific duties and what he was to carry. This was how they were counted, as the LORD had commanded Moses.

Chapter 5

1. Then the Lord spoke to Moses, saying: 2. "Command the Israelites to send away from the camp anyone who has a skin disease (leprosy), anyone with a bodily discharge, and anyone who becomes unclean by touching a dead body. 3. You must send both men and women outside the camp, so they do not defile the camp where I, the Lord, am present among them." 4. And the Israelites did so; they sent these individuals outside the camp, just as the Lord had instructed Moses. 5. Then the Lord spoke again to Moses, saying: 6. "Tell the Israelites: 'When a man or woman commits a sin and is unfaithful to the Lord, and they are guilty of this sin, 7. they must confess their sin and make full restitution for what they have done wrong. They must add one-fifth (20%) to the amount and give it to the person they have wronged. 8. But if the person who was wronged has no close relative to whom the restitution can be made, the restitution should go to the Lord, for the priest, along with a ram (a sheep) to make atonement (reconciliation with God) for the person. 9. Every offering that the Israelites bring to the priest, whether it is for the holy things or the sacred offerings, shall belong to the priest. 10. Everything that anyone gives to the priest will be the priest's portion.'" 11. The Lord spoke to Moses again, saying: 12. "Speak to the Israelites and say to them: 'If a man's wife goes astray and becomes unfaithful to him, 13. and a man lies with her secretly, and it is hidden from her husband, so that no one knows about it, and she is not caught in the act, 14. but if a spirit of jealousy comes over her husband, and he becomes jealous of his wife, even though she has not defiled herself, or if he is jealous because he suspects she has defiled herself, 15. then the man must bring his wife to the priest. He must also bring the required offering of barley flour, one-tenth of an ephah (a measure), but he must not put any oil or frankincense on it, for it is a grain offering for jealousy, a reminder offering to bring sin to remembrance. 16. The priest will bring her before the Lord and stand her before Him. 17. The priest will take holy water in an earthen jar, and put some dust from the tabernacle floor into the water. 18. The priest will then stand the woman before the Lord, uncover her head, and place the jealousy offering in her hands. The priest will also hold the bitter water (the water with dust mixed into it) that brings a curse. 19. The priest will put the woman under oath and say to her, 'If no man has slept with you, and if you have not defiled yourself by being unfaithful to your husband, then this bitter water will not harm you. 20. But if you have been unfaithful and defiled yourself by having relations with another man, other than your husband, 21. then the priest will make her swear an oath of the curse, and say to her, "May the Lord make you a curse and an oath among your people, when He causes your womb to swell and your abdomen to expand, 22. and may this water that causes

the curse enter your body and cause your abdomen to swell and your womb to miscarry." Then the woman must say, "Amen, so be it." **23.** The priest will write these curses on a scroll and then scrape them into the bitter water. **24.** He will make the woman drink the bitter water, and if she has been unfaithful, the water will bring the curse into her, causing her body to swell and her womb to miscarry. **25.** But if she has not been unfaithful, the water will not harm her, and she will be free from guilt, and may even conceive children. **26.** Afterward, the priest will take the jealousy offering from the woman's hands, wave it before the Lord, and burn a portion of it on the altar. **27.** After burning the offering, the priest will make the woman drink the water. If she is guilty of unfaithfulness, the curse will take effect, causing her body to swell and her womb to miscarry. She will become a disgrace among her people. **28.** But if she is innocent and has not committed unfaithfulness, she will be cleared of guilt, and she will be able to have children. **29.** This is the law for cases of jealousy, when a wife becomes unfaithful while under her husband's authority, or when a man becomes jealous of his wife, suspecting her of unfaithfulness. **30.** The man must bring his wife before the priest, and the priest will perform all these rituals on her. **31.** The husband will be free from guilt, but the woman will bear the consequences of her own actions."

Chapter 6

1. The Lord spoke to Moses, saying: **2.** "Speak to the Israelites and tell them: 'If a man or woman makes a vow to dedicate themselves to the Lord as a Nazirite (a person set apart for a special purpose to God), they must consecrate themselves to the Lord." **3.** "They must avoid consuming wine or anything that comes from the grapevine. This includes not drinking wine, wine vinegar, or vinegar made from any other beverage. They must refrain from drinking grape juice, and from eating fresh grapes or raisins." **4.** For the entire period of their vow, they must not eat anything that is produced by the grapevine, from the seed to the skin. **5.** "As long as they are under this vow, no razor shall touch their head. During the entire time of their consecration to the Lord, they are to allow their hair to grow long and remain holy. They must not cut their hair." **6.** Throughout the days of their vow, they must not come near a dead body. **7.** "They must not defile themselves by coming near a dead body, even if it is their father, mother, brother, or sister who has passed away, because their separation to God is upon them." **8.** "Throughout the days of their vow, they must remain holy to the Lord." **9.** If someone dies suddenly beside them, causing them to become unclean, they must shave their head on the day of their cleansing. This must happen on the seventh day. **10.** On the eighth day, they must bring two turtledoves or two young pigeons to the priest at the entrance to the tabernacle (the sacred tent where the people worship). **11.** The priest will offer one as a sin offering and the other as a burnt offering to make atonement (reconciliation) for them because they became defiled by coming into contact with the dead body. The priest will sanctify (set apart) their head that same day. **12.** They must dedicate the remainder of their vow to the Lord and bring a one-year-old male lamb as a trespass offering. The days they missed while being defiled will be counted as lost, since their separation was broken. **13.** "This is the law for the Nazirite: When the days of their vow are fulfilled, they must present themselves at the entrance of the tabernacle." **14.** They will present their offering to the Lord: one male lamb, a one-year-old, without any defects, as a burnt offering; one ewe lamb, a one-year-old, without any defects, as a sin offering; and one ram, without any defects, as a peace offering. **15.** They will also bring a basket of unleavened bread, including cakes of fine flour mixed with oil, unleavened wafers anointed with oil, along with their grain offerings and drink offerings. **16.** "The priest will present all the offerings before the Lord: the sin offering, the burnt offering, and the peace offering. Additionally, he will offer the grain offering and the drink offerings." **17.** He will offer

the ram as a peace offering to the Lord, along with the basket of unleavened bread. The priest will also present the grain offering and the drink offering. **18.** Then the Nazirite will shave their consecrated (set-apart) head at the entrance of the tabernacle, and they will place the shaved hair on the fire under the peace offering sacrifice. **19.** The priest will take the boiled shoulder of the ram, one unleavened cake from the basket, and one unleavened wafer. After the Nazirite has shaved their hair, the priest will place these items in the hands of the Nazirite. **20.** The priest will wave these items as a wave offering before the Lord. They will be holy to the priest, along with the breast of the wave offering and the thigh of the heave offering. Afterward, the Nazirite is free to drink wine again.' **21.** This is the law for a Nazirite who makes a vow to the Lord concerning their separation. They must do all of this according to the vow they made, as well as any additional offerings they are able to bring by their own hand. **22.** The Lord spoke to Moses, saying: **23.** "The Lord spoke to Moses, saying: 'Speak to Aaron (the high priest) and his sons (the priests), and instruct them on how to bless the Israelites. Tell them:" **24.** "'May the Lord bless you and protect you; May the Lord cause His face to shine upon you and be gracious to you; May the Lord turn His face toward you and give you peace.' **25.** May the Lord smile upon you and be kind to you; **26.** May the Lord lift His countenance upon you and grant you peace.' **27.** In this way, they will place my name upon the Israelites, and I will bless them."

Chapter 7

1. Once Moses had completed the assembly (gathering) of the tabernacle, he consecrated it by anointing it with oil and setting it apart for sacred purposes. He also sanctified all of the furnishings within the tabernacle, including the altar and its utensils, dedicating them to God. **2.** The leaders of Israel, representing the heads of each tribe's families, brought offerings for the dedication of the altar, contributing to the ongoing work of the tabernacle. **3.** They offered six covered wagons and twelve oxen—each pair of leaders brought one wagon, and each wagon was accompanied by an ox. These gifts were placed before the tabernacle as a sign of their devotion. **4.** Then, the Lord spoke directly to Moses, instructing him, **5.** "Accept these gifts and use them for the work of the tabernacle. Distribute the wagons and oxen among the Levites, allocating them according to the duties assigned to each of their clans." **6.** So, Moses followed the Lord's command, giving the wagons and oxen to the Levites based on their specific tasks. **7.** To the Gershonites, Moses gave two wagons and four oxen, in accordance with the work assigned to their clan. **8.** To the Merarites, he gave four wagons and eight oxen, distributing them in line with their service under the supervision of Ithamar, the son of Aaron the priest. **9.** However, the Kohathites received no wagons, for their responsibility was to carry the sacred objects of the tabernacle on their shoulders, rather than on carts. **10.** The leaders also brought offerings to consecrate the altar at the time of its anointing, each leader presenting their gift before the altar. **11.** The Lord commanded Moses, "On each day, one leader will bring their offering to dedicate the altar." **12.** On the first day, Nahshon, the son of Amminadab, leader of the tribe of Judah, brought his offering. **13.** His gift included a silver platter weighing 130 shekels and a silver bowl weighing 70 shekels, both filled with fine flour mixed with oil as a grain offering. **14.** He also offered a gold pan weighing 10 shekels, filled with incense. **15.** His offering included a young bull, a ram, and a one-year-old male lamb as a burnt offering. **16.** Additionally, Nahshon offered one male goat as a sin offering, and for his peace offering, he presented two oxen, five rams, five male goats, and five one-year-old lambs. **17.** This was the offering brought by Nahshon, the son of Amminadab. **18.** On the second day, Nethanel, the son of Zuar, leader of the tribe of Issachar, made his offering. **19.** His offering included a silver platter weighing 130 shekels and a silver bowl weighing 70 shekels, both filled with fine flour mixed with oil. **20.** He also presented a gold pan weighing 10 shekels, filled with incense. **21.** His offering was a young bull, a ram, and a male lamb in its first year, offered as a burnt sacrifice. **22.** He also brought a male goat as a sin offering. **23.** For his peace offering, Nethanel brought two oxen, five rams, five male goats, and five one-year-old lambs. **24.** This was the offering of Nethanel, the son of Zuar. **25.** On the third day, Eliab, the son of Helon, leader of the tribe of Zebulun, offered his contribution. **26.** His offering consisted of a silver platter weighing 130 shekels and a silver bowl weighing 70 shekels, both filled with fine flour mixed with oil. **27.** He also offered a gold pan weighing 10 shekels, filled with incense. **28.** His offering included a young bull, a ram, and a male lamb in its first year, as a burnt offering. **29.** Additionally, Eliab brought a male goat as a sin offering. **30.** For his peace offering, he presented two oxen, five rams, five male goats, and five male lambs. **31.** This was the offering of Eliab, the son of Helon. **32.** On the fourth day, Elizur, the son of Shedeur, leader of the tribe of Reuben, presented his offering. **33.** His offering consisted of a silver platter weighing 130 shekels and a silver bowl weighing 70 shekels, both filled with fine flour mixed with oil. **34.** He also provided a gold pan weighing 10 shekels, filled with incense. **35.** His offering included a young bull, a ram, and a male lamb in its first year, as a burnt offering. **36.** He also offered a male goat as a sin offering. **37.** For his peace offering, Elizur presented two oxen, five rams, five male goats, and five male lambs. **38.** This was the offering from Elizur, the son of Shedeur. **39.** On the fifth day, Shelumiel, the son of Zurishaddai, leader of the tribe of Simeon, made his offering. **40.** His offering included a silver platter weighing 130 shekels and a silver bowl weighing 70 shekels, both filled with fine flour mixed with oil. **41.** He also offered a gold pan weighing 10 shekels, filled with incense. **42.** His offering was a young bull, a ram, and a male lamb in its first year, offered as a burnt sacrifice. **43.** Additionally, Shelumiel offered a male goat as a sin offering. **44.** For his peace offering, he presented two oxen, five rams, five male goats, and five one-year-old lambs. **45.** This was the offering from Shelumiel, the son of Zurishaddai. **46.** On the sixth day, Eliasaph, the son of Deuel, leader of the tribe of Gad, brought his offering. **47.** His offering consisted of a silver platter weighing 130 shekels and a silver bowl weighing 70 shekels, both filled with fine flour mixed with oil. **48.** He also offered a gold pan weighing 10 shekels, filled with incense. **49.** His offering included a young bull, a ram, and a male lamb, each in its first year, as a burnt offering. **50.** Eliasaph also brought a male goat as a sin offering. **51.** His offering included a young bull, a ram, and a male lamb in its first year as a burnt offering, **52.** and a kid of the goats as a sin offering. **53.** For the peace offering, Elishama offered two oxen, five rams, five male goats, and five male lambs in their first year. This was the offering of Elishama, the son of Ammihud. **54.** On the eighth day, Gamaliel, the son of Pedahzur, leader of the children of Manasseh, presented his offering. **55.** His offering was a silver platter weighing 130 shekels, and a silver bowl weighing 70 shekels, both filled with fine flour mixed with oil. **56.** He also offered a gold pan weighing 10 shekels, filled with incense. **57.** His offering included a young bull, a ram, and a male lamb in its first year as a burnt offering, **58.** and a kid of the goats as a sin offering. **59.** For the peace offering, Gamaliel offered two oxen, five rams, five male goats, and five male lambs in their first year. This was the offering of Gamaliel, the son of Pedahzur. **60.** On the ninth day, Abidan, the son of Gideoni, leader of the children of Benjamin, presented his offering. **61.** His offering was a silver platter weighing 130 shekels, and a silver bowl weighing 70 shekels, both filled with fine flour mixed with oil. **62.** He also offered a gold pan weighing 10 shekels, filled with incense. **63.** His offering included a young bull, a ram, and a male lamb in its first year as a burnt offering, **64.** and a kid of the goats as a sin offering. **65.** For the peace offering, Abidan offered two oxen, five rams, five male goats, and five male lambs in their first year. This was the offering of Abidan, the son of Gideoni. **66.** On the tenth day, Ahiezer, the son of Ammishaddai, leader of the children of Dan, presented his offering. **67.** His offering was a silver platter weighing 130 shekels, and a silver bowl weighing 70 shekels, both filled with fine flour mixed with oil. **68.** He also offered a gold pan weighing 10 shekels, filled with incense. **69.** His offering included a young bull, a ram, and a male lamb in its first year as a burnt offering, **70.** and a kid of the goats as a sin offering. **71.** For the peace offering, Ahiezer offered two oxen, five rams, five male goats, and five male lambs in their first year. This was the offering of Ahiezer, the son._**72.** On the eleventh day, Pagiel son of Okran, the leader of the people of Asher, brought his offering. **73.** His offering was one silver plate weighing a hundred and thirty shekels and one silver sprinkling bowl weighing seventy shekels, both according to the sanctuary shekel, each filled with the finest flour mixed with olive oil as a grain offering; **74.** one gold dish weighing ten shekels, filled with incense; **75.** one young bull, one ram, and one male lamb a year old for a burnt offering; **76.** one male goat for a sin offering; **77.** and two oxen, five rams, five male goats, and five male lambs a year old to be sacrificed as a fellowship offering. This was the offering of Pagiel son of Okran. **78.** On the twelfth day, Ahira son of Enan, the leader of the people of Naphtali, brought his offering. **79.** His offering was one silver plate weighing a hundred and thirty shekels and one silver sprinkling bowl weighing seventy shekels, both according to the sanctuary shekel, each filled with the finest flour mixed with olive oil as a grain offering; **80.** one gold dish weighing ten shekels, filled with incense; **81.** one young bull, one ram, and one male lamb a year old for a burnt offering; **82.** one male goat for a sin offering; **83.** and two oxen, five rams, five male goats, and five male lambs a year old to be sacrificed as a fellowship offering. This was the offering of Ahira son of Enan. **84.** These were the offerings of the Israelite leaders for the dedication of the altar when it was anointed: twelve silver plates, twelve silver sprinkling bowls, and twelve gold dishes. **85.** Each silver plate weighed a hundred and thirty shekels, and each sprinkling bowl seventy shekels. Altogether, the silver dishes weighed two thousand four hundred shekels, according to the sanctuary shekel. **86.** The twelve gold dishes filled with incense weighed ten shekels each, according to the sanctuary shekel. Altogether, the gold dishes weighed a hundred and twenty shekels. **87.** The total number of animals for the burnt offering came to twelve young bulls, twelve rams, and twelve male lambs a year old, together with their grain offering. Twelve male goats were used for the sin offering. **88.** The total number of animals for the sacrifice of the fellowship offering came to twenty-four oxen, sixty rams, sixty male goats, and sixty male lambs a year old. These were the offerings for the dedication of the altar after it was anointed. **89.** When Moses entered the tent of meeting to speak with the LORD, he heard the voice speaking to him from between the two cherubim above the atonement cover on the ark of the covenant law. In this way, the LORD spoke to him.

Chapter 8

1. The Lord gave instructions to Moses, saying: **2.** "Tell Aaron, 'When setting up the lamps on the lampstand, make sure that the seven lamps shine in front of the stand.'" (This is to ensure the lamps are positioned correctly to provide light.) Aaron followed the Lord's command and arranged the lamps so that they faced forward, toward the front of the lampstand. The lampstand itself was crafted from hammered gold, from its base up to the decorative flowers. It was made exactly as the Lord had instructed Moses. **3.** Then, the Lord spoke to Moses once more, saying: "Take the Levites from among the Israelites and purify them ceremonially. **4.** To purify them, sprinkle them with purification water, have them shave all their body hair, and wash their clothes to make them clean. **5.** Then, take a young bull along with a grain offering of fine flour mixed with oil, and bring another young bull for a sin offering. **6.** Present the Levites at the entrance of the Tabernacle of Meeting, and gather all of Israel together. **7.** Bring the Levites before Me, and let the Israelites lay their hands on them. **8.** Aaron and his sons will then offer the Levites as a wave offering (lifting them up before Me) to consecrate them for My service. **9.** The Levites will place their hands on the heads of the two bulls. Offer one as a sin offering and the other as a burnt offering to atone for the Levites. (This symbolizes purification and forgiveness.) **10.** Afterward, present the Levites before Aaron and his sons, and offer them as a wave offering to the Lord. **11.** Through this process, you will set the Levites apart from the rest of Israel, and they will belong to Me. **12.** Once they are purified and consecrated, the Levites will begin their duties in the Tabernacle of Meeting. **13.** The Levites are given to Me as a gift from the Israelites, in place of the firstborn children of Israel, both human and animal. **14.** All the firstborn among the Israelites, whether human or animal, are Mine. I sanctified them when I struck down all the firstborn in Egypt, making them holy for Myself. **15.** Instead of the firstborn, I have chosen the Levites to serve Me. **16.** I have given the Levites as a gift to Aaron and his sons, to assist in the service of the Tabernacle and to make atonement for Israel, so that no plague will come upon the people when they approach the sanctuary." **17.** So, Moses, Aaron, and the entire congregation of Israel did exactly as the Lord commanded concerning the Levites. **18.** The Levites purified themselves and washed their clothes. Then Aaron presented them as a wave offering before the Lord and made atonement for them, purifying them. **19.** Afterward, the Levites began their service in the Tabernacle of Meeting, under the supervision of Aaron and his sons, just as the Lord had instructed Moses. **20.** The Lord then spoke to Moses, saying: **21.** "This is the law regarding the Levites: From the age of twenty-five, they may begin their work at the Tabernacle of Meeting. **22.** But when they reach fifty, they must retire from active service and no longer carry out their duties. **23.** They may still assist their fellow Levites with their work, but they will no longer be responsible for the physical labor. **24.** This is the regulation concerning the Levites' duties." **25.** So Moses did exactly as the Lord commanded, and the Levites began their service to the Lord at the Tabernacle. **26.** The Lord had instructed Moses on the specific duties and service of the Levites, and they faithfully carried out their assigned tasks.

Chapter 9

1. The Lord spoke to Moses in the Wilderness of Sinai, during the first month of the second year after the Israelites had come out of Egypt, saying: **2.** "Tell the Israelites to observe the Passover at the designated time." **3.** On the fourteenth day of this month, at twilight, you shall celebrate it at the designated time. You must follow all its rules and regulations as prescribed." **4.** So Moses instructed the Israelites to celebrate the Passover. **5.** The Israelites celebrated the Passover on the fourteenth day of the first month at twilight, in the Wilderness of Sinai, exactly as the Lord had commanded Moses, adhering to all the instructions given. **6.** However, some men who had become ritually unclean due to contact with a dead body could not participate in the Passover at that time. They approached Moses and Aaron that day. **7.** These men asked Moses, "We have become unclean because of a dead body. Why should we be excluded from offering the Lord's sacrifice at the appointed time, along with the rest of the Israelites?" **8.** Moses answered them, "Wait here, and I will listen to what the Lord commands concerning you." **9.** Then the Lord spoke to Moses, saying: **10.** "Tell the Israelites: 'If anyone of you or your descendants is ceremonially unclean because of a dead body, or if someone is far away on a journey, they can still celebrate the Lord's Passover. **11.** They may celebrate the Passover on the fourteenth day of the second month at twilight. They must eat it with unleavened bread and bitter herbs. **12.** They must not leave any of it until morning, nor break any of its bones. They must keep all the ordinances of the Passover.' **13.** But any person who is clean and not on a journey, and yet refuses to celebrate the Passover, that person must be cut off from the community, because they failed to offer the Lord's sacrifice at the appointed time. They will bear

the consequences of their sin. **14.** If a foreigner living among you wants to observe the Lord's Passover, they must follow the same rules and regulations as the Israelites. The same law applies to both native-born Israelites and foreigners. **15.** On the day the Tabernacle (the sacred tent where the Lord's presence dwelled) was set up, a cloud covered the Tabernacle, the Tent of the Testimony (where the Ark of the Covenant was kept). The cloud remained over it from evening until morning, and it appeared like fire. **16.** The cloud rested on the Tabernacle by day, and at night, it appeared as a fire. This continued as long as the cloud remained over the Tabernacle. **17.** Whenever the cloud lifted from the Tabernacle, the Israelites would break camp and begin their journey. Wherever the cloud settled, they would set up their tents. **18.** At the command of the Lord, the Israelites would travel, and at His command, they would stop and set up camp. As long as the cloud stayed above the Tabernacle, they remained in their camp. **19.** Even if the cloud stayed over the Tabernacle for many days, the Israelites would stay in camp and not travel. They would keep the charge of the Lord and not move. **20.** If the cloud remained over the Tabernacle for a few days, the Israelites would stay in camp and follow the Lord's command. When the cloud was lifted, they would set out. **21.** Whether the cloud rested from evening until morning, or for a longer period, whenever it was lifted, the Israelites would move on. **22.** If the cloud stayed above the Tabernacle for two days, a month, or even a year, the Israelites would remain camped and not journey. But once the cloud was lifted, they would break camp and travel. **23.** They followed the command of the Lord to stay in camp, and they followed His command to journey. They kept the charge of the Lord at the command of the Lord through Moses.

Chapter 10

1. The Lord spoke to Moses and said, **2.** "Make two silver trumpets for yourself. These trumpets should be crafted by hammering the silver into shape. You will use them for gathering the people together and for guiding the movements of the camps. **3.** When both trumpets are blown, the entire congregation should come together in front of you at the entrance of the Tabernacle of Meeting (a place of worship). **4.** But if only one trumpet is blown, then the leaders, the heads of the tribes of Israel, should gather before you. **5.** When you want to signal the start of a journey, sound the trumpets, and the camps on the east side will begin to move. **6.** Sound the trumpets again to signal that the camps on the south side should begin their journey. **7.** But when gathering the people together for an assembly, you should blow the trumpets, but not sound the call to move. **8.** The priests, the sons of Aaron, shall blow the trumpets, and this practice will be a lasting rule for you, throughout all your generations. **9.** If you go to war in your land against an enemy who oppresses you, blow an alarm with the trumpets. This will be a reminder before the Lord your God, and He will rescue you from your enemies. **10.** Also, on your days of joy, during your appointed feasts, and at the beginning of each month, you shall blow the trumpets over your burnt offerings and your peace offerings. This will serve as a memorial to you before your God. I am the Lord your God." **11.** On the twentieth day of the second month in the second year, the cloud was lifted up from above the Tabernacle of the Testimony. **12.** Then the Israelites set out from the Wilderness of Sinai, following the guidance of the cloud, and the cloud settled in the Wilderness of Paran. **13.** So, they started their journey for the first time, in obedience to the Lord's command through Moses. **14.** The standard (flag or banner) of the camp of Judah moved first, according to their divisions. Over their army was Nahshon, the son of Amminadab. **15.** Over the army of the tribe of Issachar was Nethanel, the son of Zuar. **16.** Over the army of the tribe of Zebulun was Eliab, the son of Helon. **17.** Then, the Tabernacle was taken down, and the Gershonites and Merarites (families from the tribe of Levi) set out, carrying the Tabernacle. **18.** Next, the standard of the camp of Reuben moved out with their divisions. Over their army was Elizur, the son of Shedeur. **19.** Over the army of the tribe of Simeon was Shelumiel, the son of Zurishaddai. **20.** Over the army of the tribe of Gad was Eliasaph, the son of Deuel. **21.** Then, the Kohathites (another family from the tribe of Levi) set out, carrying the holy items. They were to set up the Tabernacle when they arrived. **22.** The standard of the camp of Ephraim moved out next, with their divisions. Over their army was Elishama, the son of Ammihud. **23.** Over the army of the tribe of Manasseh was Gamaliel, the son of Pedahzur. **24.** Over the army of the tribe of Benjamin was Abidan, the son of Gideoni. **25.** Then, the standard of the camp of Dan, which served as the rear guard for all the camps, moved out with their divisions. Over their army was Ahiezer, the son of Ammishaddai. **26.** Over the army of the tribe of Asher was Pagiel, the son of Ocran. **27.** Over the army of the tribe of Naphtali was Ahira, the son of Enan. **28.** This was the order in which the Israelites set out, according to their divisions, as they began their journey. **29.** Now Moses said to Hobab, the son of Reuel the Midianite, Moses' father-in-law, "We are about to set out for the place the Lord has promised to give us. Come with us, and we will treat you well, for the Lord has promised good things to Israel." **30.** Hobab replied, "I will not go with you. Instead, I will return to my own land and to my relatives." **31.** Moses said, "Please don't leave us. You know how we camp in the wilderness, and you can be our guide. **32.** If you come with us, whatever good the Lord does for us, we will do the same for you." **33.** So they departed from the mountain of the Lord and traveled for three days. The Ark of the Covenant of the Lord went ahead of them on their journey to find a place for them to rest. **34.** The cloud of the Lord was above them during the day as they traveled from the camp. **35.** Whenever the Ark moved forward, Moses would say, "Rise up, O Lord! Let Your enemies be scattered, and let those who hate You flee before You." **36.** When the Ark rested, Moses would say, "Return, O Lord, to the many thousands of Israel."

Chapter 11

1. The people began to complain, and this greatly dissatisfied the Lord. He heard their complaints, and His wrathfulness was burned. So, the fire of the Lord burned among them and consumed some of the people at the outskirts of the camp. **2.** The people cried out to Moses, and when Moses supplicated to the Lord, the fire was extinguished. **3.** Moses called the place "Taberah" (meaning "burning"), because the fire of the Lord had burned among them. **4.** Also, a mixed group of people who had joined the Israelites gave in to violent Jones, and the children of Israel began to weep formally more, saying, "Who'll give us meat to eat?" **5.** We flash back the fish we ate freely in Egypt, the cucumbers, the melons, the leeks, the onions, and the garlic. **6.** But now our strength is gone, and all we've is this manna before us!" **7.** The manna was like coriander seed (a small round seed) and had the color of bdellium (a resin from a tree, suggesting a pale unheroic or amber color). **8.** The people would gather it, grind it on millstones, or crush it in a mortar. Also, they cooked it in kissers and made galettes from it. It tasted like afters made with oil painting. **9.** When the dew fell on the camp at night, the manna also appeared. **10.** Moses heard the people weeping throughout their families, each person at the door of their roof. The Lord's wrathfulness was greatly aroused, and Moses also became worried. **11.** So Moses said to the Lord, "Why have You brought this trouble upon Your menial? Why have I not set up favor in Your sight that You have laid the burden of all these people on me? **12.** Did I give birth to all these people? Did I bring them into the world, that You should tell me, 'Carry them in your arms, as a nanny carries a child,' to the land You promised to their ancestors? **13.** Where am I supposed to get meat to give to all these people? They keep crying to me, 'Give us meat, so we can eat.' **14.** I can't handle all these people by myself; the burden is too heavy for me. **15.** Still, please kill me now if I've set up favor in Your eyes and don't let me face my own wretchedness!" **16.** If You're going to treat me like this. The Lord said to Moses, "Gather for Me

seventy of the elders of Israel, men you know to be the leaders of the people and officers over them. Bring them to the temple of Meeting, and they will stand there with you. **17.** I'll come down and speak with you there. I'll take some of the Spirit that's upon you and put it on them. They will help you carry the burden of the people, so that you won't have to bear it alone. **18.** Tell the people, 'Consecrate yourselves for hereafter, and you'll eat meat. You have cried in the Lord's hail, saying, "Who'll give us meat to eat? We flash back the good effects we had in Egypt." Thus, the Lord will give you meat, and you'll eat. **19.** You won't eat for just one day, or two days, or five days, or ten days, or twenty days, **20.** but for a whole month, until it comes out of your nostrils and makes you sick, because you have rejected the Lord, who's among you, and have cried before Him, saying, "Why did we ever leave Egypt?" **21.** Moses said, "Then I'm among six hundred thousand men on foot, and You say, 'I'll give them meat to eat for a whole month.' **22.** Should we butcher flocks and herds to give enough for them? Or should all the fish of the ocean be gathered to give enough for them?" **23.** The Lord answered Moses, "Is the Lord's arm too short? Now you'll see whether or not I'll do what I've promised." **24.** So Moses went out and told the people the words of the Lord. He gathered seventy of the elders of Israel and had them stand around the temple. **25.** Also, the Lord came down in the cloud and spoke to Moses. He took some of the Spirit that was upon Moses and put it upon the seventy elders. When the Spirit rested upon them, they began to predict, though they did so only that one time. **26.** Still, two men had stayed in the camp; the name of one was Eldad, and the name of the other was Medad. The Spirit rested upon them as well, though they hadn't gone to the temple. They too predicted in the camp. **27.** A youthful man ran to Moses and said, "Eldad and Medad are auguring in the camp." **28.** Joshua, the son of Nun, Moses' adjunct, one of his chosen men, said, "Moses, my lord, stop them!" **29.** But Moses replied, "Are you jealous for my sake? I wish that all the Lord's people were prophets, and that the Lord would put His Spirit upon them!" **30.** Also, Moses returned to the camp, along with the elders of Israel. **31.** A wind from the Lord blew, and it brought quail from the ocean, which scattered them around the camp. They were about a day's trip on either side, each around the camp, and about two cubits (roughly three feet) above the ground. **32.** The people stayed up all that day, all night, and all the coming day, gathering the quail. The one who gathered the least collected ten homers (a large measure of grain). They spread them out around the camp. **33.** But while the meat was still between their teeth, before it was masticated, the Lord's wrathfulness was aroused against the people, and He struck them with a very severe pest. **34.** So Moses called the place "Kibroth Hattaavah" (meaning "Graves of Craving"), because there they buried the people who had yielded to their cravings. **35.** From Kibroth Hattaavah, the people moved on to Hazeroth, and camped there.

Chapter 12

1. Miriam and Aaron spoke in opposition to Moses because of the Cushite female he had married; they criticized him for marrying a lady from Cush (Ethiopia). **2.** They said, "Has the Lord spoken handiest thru Moses? Has He no longer additionally spoken via us?" And the Lord heard what they said. **3.** Now Moses became a totally humble man, greater humble than another individual at the face of the earth. **4.** Abruptly, the Lord stated to Moses, Aaron, and Miriam, "Pop out to the Tent of Meeting, you three!" So they all came out as instructed. **5.** Then the Lord came down inside the pillar of cloud and stood at the doorway to the tabernacle. He known as Aaron and Miriam, and they both approached Him. **6.** The Lord spoke to them, announcing, "Concentrate to what I've to say: If there may be a prophet among you, I, the Lord, make Myself recognized to him in a imaginative and prescient and talk to him in a dream. **7.** But this is not the case with My servant Moses; he's sincere in all My residence. **8.** I communicate to him directly, head to head, truly, and no longer via riddles. He even sees the shape of the Lord. Why then had been you not afraid to talk in opposition to My servant Moses?" **9.** The Lord have become angry with them, and He departed. **10.** Because the cloud lifted from the tabernacle, Miriam suddenly have become leprous, her pores and skin turning as white as snow. When Aaron turned closer to her, he noticed that she had come to be a leper. **11.** Aaron turned to Moses and said, "Oh, my lord, please do no longer preserve this sin towards us, for we've acted foolishly and sinned. **12.** Please do not let her emerge as like a stillborn toddler, whose body is partly decayed when it comes out of its mom's womb!" **13.** Moses cried out to the Lord, pronouncing, "Please heal her, O God, I pray!" **14.** The Lord answered to Moses, "If her father had spit in her face, might she no longer have been ashamed for seven days? Let her be close out of the camp for seven days, and later on she can be delivered returned in." **15.** So Miriam turned into excluded from the camp for seven days, and the human beings did not continue their adventure till she was allowed to go back. **16.** In a while, the humans moved on from Hazeroth and camped within the desert of Paran.

Chapter 13

1. The Lord spoke to Moses, saying, **2.** "Send men to explore the land of Canaan, which I'm giving to the Israelites. From each tribe of their fathers, send one chief." **3.** So Moses sent them from the wilderness of Paran (wilderness location), as the Lord commanded. These men were all leaders among the Israelites. **4.** These are their names: from the tribe of Reuben, Shammua the son of Zaccur; **5.** from the tribe of Simeon, Shaphat the son of Hori; **6.** from the tribe of Judah, Caleb the son of Jephunneh; **7.** from the tribe of Issachar, Igal the son of Joseph; **8.** from the tribe of Ephraim, Hoshea the son of Nun; **9.** from the tribe of Benjamin, Palti the son of Raphu; **10.** from the tribe of Zebulun, Gaddiel the son of Sodi; **11.** from the tribe of Joseph, that is, from the tribe of Manasseh, Gaddi the son of Susi; **12.** from the tribe of Dan, Ammiel the son of Gemalli; **13.** from the tribe of Asher, Sethur the son of Michael; **14.** from the tribe of Naphtali, Nahbi the son of Vophsi; **15.** from the tribe of Gad, Geuel the son of Machi. **16.** These are the names of the men whom Moses sent to explore the land. Moses called Hoshea the son of Nun, Joshua. **17.** Moses sent them to explore the land of Canaan, giving them the following commands: "Go up through the Negev (southern place) and into the hill country, **18.** and see what the land is like. Is it fertile or barren? Are the people living there strong or weak? Are there many or few? **19.** Are the cities walled or open? Do they live in camps or fortresses? **20.** Is the land good for farming or poor? Are there trees or not? Be brave, and bring back some of the fruit from the land." It was the season for the first ripe grapes. **21.** So they explored the land, beginning from the wilderness of Zin and traveling as far as Rehob (city) near the entrance of Hamath (city). **22.** They traveled through the Negev and came to Hebron (city). There, the descendants of Anak (giants) lived. Hebron had been built seven years before Zoan (city) in Egypt. **23.** They reached the Valley of Eshcol (a fertile valley), and there they cut down a branch with a cluster of grapes. It was so large that men had to carry it on a pole. They also brought back pomegranates and figs. **24.** The place was called the Valley of Eshcol because of the large cluster of grapes that the Israelites cut there. **25.** After 40 days of exploration, they returned from spying out the land. **26.** They came back to Moses and Aaron, and to the whole congregation of the Israelites in the wilderness of Paran, at Kadesh (a wilderness place). They said to them and showed them the fruit of the land. **27.** They said, "We went to the land where you sent us, and it truly flows with milk and honey. Here is its fruit. **28.** But the people who live there are strong, and the cities are large and fortified. We even saw the descendants of Anak there. **29.** The Amalekites (tribe) live in the Negev, the Hittites (tribe), the Jebusites (tribe), and the Amorites (tribe) live in the hill country, and the Canaanites (tribe) live near the sea and along the Jordan River." **30.** Then Caleb (a leader) silenced the people before Moses,

saying, "Let us go up at once and take possession of the land, for we are certainly able to overcome it." **31.** But the men who had gone up with him said, "We are not able to attack those people, for they are stronger than we are." **32.** And they spread a bad report about the land they had explored. They said, "The land we explored devours the people living in it, and all the people we saw there are giants. **33.** We even saw the Nephilim (giants), the descendants of Anak. We seemed like grasshoppers in our own eyes, and we seemed the same to them."

Chapter 14

1. Then the whole congregation of Israel raised their voices and cried out, and the people wept that night. **2.** All the Israelites grumbled against Moses and Aaron, and the whole congregation said to them, "If only we had died in the land of Egypt, or if only we had died in this desert! **3.** Why has the Lord brought us to this land to fall by the sword? Will our wives and children become victims? Wouldn't it be better for us to return to Egypt?" **4.** So they said to one another, "Let's choose a leader and go back to Egypt." **5.** Then Moses and Aaron fell face down before the whole assembly of the Israelites. **6.** But Joshua the son of Nun and Caleb the son of Jephunneh, who were among those who had explored the land, tore their clothes. **7.** They said to the whole assembly of the Israelites, "The land we passed through and explored is an exceedingly good land. **8.** If the Lord is pleased with us, He will bring us into this land and give it to us, a land flowing with milk and honey. **9.** Only do not rebel against the Lord, and do not be afraid of the people of the land, for they are like our food. Their protection is gone, and the Lord is with us. Do not be afraid of them." **10.** But the whole congregation threatened to stone them with stones. Then the glory of the Lord appeared at the Tent of Meeting to all the Israelites. **11.** The Lord said to Moses, "How long will these people reject Me? How long will they refuse to believe in Me, despite all the signs I have performed among them? **12.** I will strike them with a plague and destroy them, but I will make you into a nation greater and mightier than they." **13.** But Moses said to the Lord, "Then the Egyptians will hear about it, and they will tell the inhabitants of this land. They have already heard that You, Lord, are with these people, that You, Lord, have been seen face to face, and Your cloud stays over them, and You go before them in a pillar of cloud by day and a pillar of fire by night. **14.** If You kill all these people, the nations who have heard of Your fame will say, **15.** 'The Lord was not able to bring these people into the land He promised them, and so He killed them in the wilderness.' **16.** Now, let the power of my Lord be displayed, just as You have declared: **17.** 'The Lord is slow to anger, abounding in love, forgiving sin and rebellion. Yet He does not leave the guilty unpunished; He punishes the children for the sin of the parents to the third and fourth generations.' **18.** Please forgive the wickedness of these people, according to Your great love, just as You have forgiven them from Egypt until now." **19.** The Lord replied, "I have forgiven them, as you asked. **20.** Nevertheless, as surely as I live, and as surely as the earth is filled with the glory of the Lord, **21.** not one of those who saw My glory and the signs I performed in Egypt and in the wilderness, but who disobeyed Me these ten times and did not listen to My voice, **22.** will ever see the land I promised on oath to their ancestors. No one who has treated Me with contempt will ever see it. **23.** But because My servant Caleb has a different spirit and has followed Me wholeheartedly, I will bring him into the land he went to, and his descendants will inherit it. **24.** Since the Amalekites and the Canaanites live in the valleys, turn back tomorrow and set out toward the desert along the route to the Red Sea." **25.** The Lord spoke to Moses and Aaron, saying, **26.** "How long will I put up with this wicked community who grumble against Me? I have heard the complaints of the Israelites they are making against Me. **27.** Tell them, 'As surely as I live,' declares the Lord, 'I will do to you the very things I heard you say: **28.** In this wilderness your bodies will fall; every one of you who was counted in the census, from twenty years old and upward, who has grumbled against Me, **29.** not one of you will enter the land I swore with uplifted hand to make your home, except Caleb son of Jephunneh and Joshua son of Nun. **30.** As for your children, whom you said would be taken as plunder, I will bring them in to enjoy the land you have rejected. **31.** But as for you, your bodies will fall in this wilderness. **32.** Your children will be shepherds here for forty years, suffering for your unfaithfulness, until the last of your bodies lies in the wilderness. **33.** For forty years—one year for each of the forty days you explored the land—you will suffer for your sins and know what it is like to have Me against you. **34.** I, the Lord, have spoken, and I will surely do these things to this whole wicked community, which has banded together against Me. They will meet their end in this wilderness; here they will die." **35.** So the men Moses had sent to explore the land, who returned and made the whole community grumble against him by spreading a bad report about the land, **36.** those very men who brought the bad report about the land, died by a plague before the Lord. **37.** But Joshua son of Nun and Caleb son of Jephunneh survived, among those who went to explore the land. **38.** When Moses told this to all the Israelites, they mourned bitterly. **39.** Early the next morning they went up toward the highest point of the hill country, saying, "Now we are ready to go up to the land the Lord promised. Surely we have sinned!" **40.** But Moses said, "Why are you disobeying the Lord's command? This will not succeed! **41.** Do not go up, because the Lord is not with you. You will be defeated by your enemies, **42.** For the Amalekites and Canaanites will face you there. You will fall by the sword. The Lord will not be with you because you have turned away from Him." **43.** But they were so determined to go up to the hill country that they went anyway, though neither the Ark of the Covenant of the Lord nor Moses moved from the camp. **44.** Then the Amalekites and Canaanites who lived in that hill country came down and attacked them. They drove them back as far as Hormah (a city). **45** Then the Amalekites and the Canaanites who lived in that hill country came down and attacked them and beat them down all the way to Hormah.

Chapter 15

1. The Lord spoke to Moses and said, **2.** "Tell the people of Israel this: 'When you enter the land I am giving you to live in, **3.** and you present an offering by fire to the Lord, whether a burnt offering or a sacrifice to fulfill a vow, or as a freewill offering or during your appointed feasts, to create a pleasant aroma for the Lord, from your herd or your flock, **4.** then the person who brings the offering must also bring a grain offering of one-tenth of an ephah of fine flour mixed with one-fourth of a hin of oil; **5.** and one-fourth of a hin of wine as a drink offering, which you shall prepare with the burnt offering or the sacrifice for each lamb. **6.** For a ram, you must prepare a grain offering of two-tenths of an ephah of fine flour mixed with one-third of a hin of oil; **7.** and offer one-third of a hin of wine as a drink offering, a sweet aroma to the Lord. **8.** When you offer a young bull as a burnt offering or as a sacrifice to fulfill a vow or as a peace offering to the Lord, **9.** offer with the bull a grain offering of three-tenths of an ephah of fine flour mixed with half a hin of oil; **10.** and bring half a hin of wine as a drink offering, as an offering made by fire, a sweet aroma to the Lord. **11.** This is how you must offer for each young bull, each ram, or each lamb or young goat. **12.** You shall do this according to the number of animals you prepare for the offering. **13.** All native-born Israelites must follow these instructions in presenting their offerings made by fire, a sweet aroma to the Lord. **14.** If a foreigner (stranger) lives among you, or anyone among you throughout your generations, and wants to present an offering by fire, a sweet aroma to the Lord, just like you do, he must do the same. **15.** One ordinance shall apply to both you and the foreigner who lives with you, an ordinance forever throughout your generations. As you are, so shall the foreigner be before the Lord. **16.** One law and one rule shall apply to both you and the foreigner who lives among you.'"

17. The Lord spoke again to Moses, saying, **18.** "Speak to the children of Israel and tell them: 'When you enter the land where I am bringing you, **19.** and you eat the bread of the land, you must offer a portion to the Lord. **20.** You shall offer up a cake made from the first of your ground meal as a heave offering, just as you offer up the first of the threshing floor, so shall you offer it. **21.** From the first of your ground meal, you shall give the Lord a heave offering throughout your generations. **22.** 'If you sin unintentionally and do not follow all the commandments that the Lord has spoken to Moses, **23.** all that the Lord has commanded you through Moses, from the day He gave commandment and onward throughout your generations, **24.** then if the sin is committed unintentionally, without the knowledge of the congregation, the entire congregation shall offer a young bull as a burnt offering, a sweet aroma to the Lord, along with its grain offering and drink offering, as required, and one goat as a sin offering. **25.** The priest shall make atonement for the whole congregation of the people of Israel, and it shall be forgiven for them, because it was unintentional. They shall bring their offering, an offering made by fire to the Lord, and their sin offering before the Lord for their unintentional sin. **26.** It shall be forgiven for the whole congregation of the children of Israel and the foreigner who dwells among them, because all the people did it unintentionally. **27.** 'If any individual sins unintentionally, he must bring a female goat in its first year as a sin offering. **28.** The priest shall make atonement for the person who sins unintentionally, when he sins unintentionally before the Lord, to make atonement for him, and it shall be forgiven. **29.** There shall be one law for the person who sins unintentionally, whether he is native-born or a foreigner who dwells among you. **30.** But the person who sins intentionally, whether native-born or a foreigner has shown contempt for the Lord. Such a person must be cut off from among the people, **31.** because they have despised the word of the Lord and broken His commandment. That person shall be completely cut off; their guilt remains on them.'" **32.** While the children of Israel were in the wilderness, they found a man gathering sticks on the Sabbath day. **33.** Those who found him gathering sticks brought him to Moses, Aaron, and the whole congregation. **34.** They put him in custody because it had not yet been made clear what should be done to him. **35.** The Lord said to Moses, "The man must be put to death. The whole congregation shall stone him with stones outside the camp." **36.** So, as the Lord commanded Moses, the congregation took him outside the camp and stoned him with stones, and he died. **37.** The Lord spoke again to Moses, saying, **38.** "Speak to the children of Israel and tell them: 'Make tassels on the corners of your garments throughout your generations, and put a blue thread in the tassels at the corners. **39.** You shall have the tassel, and when you look at it, you will remember all the commandments of the Lord and obey them. You will not follow the desires of your own heart and eyes, **40.** But remember and do all my commandments, and be holy for your God. **41.** I am the Lord your God, who brought you out of the land of Egypt, to be your God; I am the Lord your God.'"

Chapter 16

1. Korah, son of Izhar (Izhar was a descendant of Kohath, from the tribe of Levi), along with Dathan and Abiram (sons of Eliab) and On (son of Peleth, from the tribe of Reuben), gathered a group of men. **2.** They rose up before Moses with **250** prominent leaders from the community, men of renown (men known for their reputation), who were chosen representatives of the people. **3.** They confronted Moses and Aaron, accusing them, "You've taken too much responsibility for yourselves. Every person in the congregation is holy (set apart for God's purposes), and the Lord is with them. Why do you lift yourselves up above the Lord's assembly?" **4.** When Moses heard this, he immediately fell to the ground in humility (he showed deep respect by falling on his face). **5.** He spoke to Korah and his followers, saying, "Tomorrow, the Lord will show who belongs to Him and who is holy. He will bring the one He chooses close to Himself. **6.** Here's what you should do: Take censers (special containers for burning incense), Korah, and all your followers, **7.** put fire and incense in them, and present them before the Lord tomorrow. The man the Lord chooses will be the holy one. You have taken too much upon yourselves, sons of Levi!" **8.** Moses continued, "Listen, sons of Levi: **9.** Isn't it enough that the God of Israel has separated you from the rest of the people to bring you close to Him, to serve in His tabernacle (the sacred tent where God was worshiped) and stand before the people as their ministers (servants of God)? **10.** He has brought you near, along with your fellow Levites. Isn't that enough for you? Do you also seek the priesthood (the office of high priest)? **11.** You and your followers are not rebelling against Aaron, but against the Lord Himself." **12.** Moses then called for Dathan and Abiram, but they refused to come, saying, "Is it not enough that you brought us out of a land flowing with milk and honey (a land of abundance), only to bring us here to die in the wilderness? Why do you act like a ruler over us? **13.** You haven't brought us into a land flowing with milk and honey, nor given us fields and vineyards (lands for planting). Do you plan to blind us? We will not come." **14.** Moses was greatly angered and said to the Lord, "Don't accept their offering. I haven't taken anything from them, not even a donkey (a small animal used for carrying loads), nor have I wronged any of them." **15.** Moses spoke again to Korah, saying, "Tomorrow, you and your followers will present yourselves before the Lord, along with Aaron. **16.** Each of you will take a censer, put incense in it, and bring it before the Lord—**250** censers from you and your followers, and each with his own censer." **17.** Each man did as Moses instructed, took fire and incense, and stood at the entrance of the tabernacle with Moses and Aaron. **18.** Korah gathered the people at the entrance of the tabernacle, and the glory of the Lord (the visible presence of God) appeared to the entire congregation. **19.** The Lord then spoke to Moses and Aaron, saying, **20.** "Separate yourselves from this congregation, so that I may destroy them in an instant." **21.** Moses and Aaron fell on their faces, **22.** and Moses pleaded, "O God, the God of all living beings (the Creator of all life), will one man's sin bring judgment on the whole congregation?" **23.** The Lord answered Moses, **24.** "Tell the congregation: 'Move away from the tents of Korah, Dathan, and Abiram.'" **25.** Moses got up, went to Dathan and Abiram, and the elders of Israel followed him. **26.** He warned the people, "Leave the tents of these wicked men (those who are doing evil) and do not touch anything of theirs, or you will share in their sin and be destroyed." **27.** The people moved away from the tents of Korah, Dathan, and Abiram. Dathan and Abiram came out and stood at the entrance of their tents, along with their families. **28.** Moses declared, "This is how you will know that the Lord has sent me to do all these things. If these men die of natural causes (like any other human), then the Lord has not sent me. **29.** But if the Lord does something new, and the ground opens up and swallows them, and they go down alive into the pit (the earth swallowing them whole), then you will know that these men have rejected the Lord." **30.** As Moses finished speaking, the ground beneath them split open, **31.** and the earth swallowed them, along with their families and all their possessions. **32.** They went down alive into the pit, and the earth closed over them. They were lost from among the people. **33.** All the Israelites who were around them fled in fear, crying, "Lest the earth swallow us too!" **34.** A fire came from the Lord and consumed the **250** men who had offered incense. **35.** The Lord then spoke to Moses, saying: **36.** "Tell Eleazar, son of Aaron, to gather the censers from the fire, because they are holy (set apart for God's use). Scatter the fire some distance away. **37.** The censers of the men who sinned should be made into hammered plates (flattened into sheets) to cover the altar. Because they presented them before the Lord, they are holy and will serve as a sign to the Israelites." **38.** Eleazar took the censers and hammered them into sheets to cover the altar, **39.** as a memorial (a reminder) to the Israelites, showing that no outsider, except a descendant of Aaron, should approach to offer incense before the Lord, or he will meet the same fate as Korah and his followers, just as the Lord had said through Moses. **40.** The next day, the whole congregation of Israel complained against Moses and Aaron, saying, "You have killed the Lord's people." **41.** As the people gathered against Moses and Aaron, they turned toward the tabernacle, and the cloud (the visible presence of God) of the Lord's presence covered it, and the glory of the Lord appeared. **42.** Moses and Aaron went to the entrance of the tabernacle. **43.** The Lord spoke to Moses, saying, **44.** "Move away from this congregation, so that I may consume them instantly." Moses and Aaron fell on their faces. **45.** Moses said to Aaron, "Take a censer, put fire from the altar in it, add incense, and run quickly to the people to make atonement (cover over their sins) for them, for the wrath (anger) of the Lord has begun and the plague (a deadly disease) has started." **46.** Aaron did as Moses instructed, running into the midst of the assembly, where the plague had already begun. **47.** He offered incense and made atonement for the people. **48.** Aaron stood between the living and the dead, and the plague stopped. **49.** Fourteen thousand seven hundred people died from the plague, in addition to those who died in the rebellion of Korah. **50.** Aaron returned to Moses at the entrance of the tabernacle, and the plague ceased.

Chapter 17

1. The Lord spoke to Moses, saying: **2.** "Speak to the Israelites and collect a staff from each tribal leader, one from each of the twelve tribes. Write the name of each chief on their staff. **3.** Write Aaron's name on the staff of the tribe of Levi. Each staff represents the chief of a family. **4.** Place the staffs in the tabernacle in front of the Testimony (the Ark of the Covenant), where I meet with you. **5.** The staff of the man I choose will sprout. This will put an end to complaints the Israelites have made against you." **6.** Moses spoke to the Israelites, and each leader gave him a staff, totaling twelve, including Aaron's staff for the tribe of Levi. **7.** Moses placed the staffs before the Lord inside the tabernacle of witness (the place where God's presence was found). **8.** The next day, Moses went into the tabernacle and saw that Aaron's staff had sprouted, produced buds, blossomed, and even had ripe almonds. **9.** Moses brought all the staffs out and showed them to the Israelites. Each leader took their own staff. **10.** The Lord said to Moses, "Place Aaron's staff back in front of the Testimony, to be kept as a reminder to the rebels. This will stop their complaints against Me, or they will face death." **11.** Moses did exactly as the Lord commanded him. **12.** The Israelites said to Moses, "We are doomed! We're all going to die!" **13.** "Anyone who comes near the tabernacle of the Lord will die. Will we all be destroyed?"

Chapter 18

1. Then the Lord stated to Aaron: "You, your sons, and your father's own family will endure the iniquity (wrongdoing or sin) related to the sanctuary, and you and your sons with you will bear the iniquity of the priesthood. **2.** Also, deliver with you your fellow Levites, from the tribe of your father, which will be part of you and help you while you and your sons serve before the tabernacle of witness (a sacred tent for worship). **3.** They'll contend with your needs and all of the needs of the tabernacle but they have to not cross close to the holy objects or the altar, or they may die—similar to you'll. **4.** They may work along you and contend with the tabernacle of meeting (wherein the Lord's presence is), doing all its paintings, but no outsider can also approach you. **5.** You'll contend with the sanctuary (sacred region) and the altar, so that no greater anger will come across the Israelites. **6.** Look, I have taken your fellow Levites from a few of the kids of Israel; they're a gift to you from the Lord to assist you inside the paintings of the tabernacle of meeting. **7.** Therefore, you and your sons will attend to the priesthood, doing the entirety at the altar and within the holy area, serving the Lord. I come up with this priesthood as a gift in your

69

service, but every person who is not a clergyman and springs near need to be placed to loss of life." **8.** And the Lord spoke to Aaron: "I have additionally given you fee over My heave services (unique services lifted as much as God), all of the holy presents of the Israelites. These are for you and your sons, as a forever ordinance. **9.** This part of the most holy things, set aside from the fire, will be yours: every imparting, every grain presenting, each sin presenting, and every guilt imparting they bring to Me will be maximum holy for you and your sons. **10.** You shall devour it inside the maximum holy region; each male in your family may consume it. It's far holy to you. **11.** Also, you shall have the heave presenting of the people's items, along with all the wave offerings (services presented by means of lifting them up) of the Israelites. Those I provide to you, your sons and daughters, as an ordinance all the time. Each person who's easy in your home may additionally devour it. **12.** I provide you with all the first-class of the oil, wine, and grain, and the firstfruits (the primary a part of the harvest) that they provide to the Lord. **13.** The first ripe fruit in their land, which they carry to the Lord, will be yours. All and sundry who is smooth in your home might also consume it. **14.** Everything committed to the Lord in Israel will belong to you. **15.** The whole lot that opens the womb, whether or not man or animal, which the Israelites convey to the Lord, might be yours; however, you need to redeem the firstborn of a person and the firstborn of unclean animals. **16.** You'll redeem the devoted matters whilst they're one month antique, for 5 shekels (a unit of cash) of silver, consistent with the shekel of the sanctuary, that's twenty gerahs (a smaller unit of weight). **17.** However, the firstborn of cattle, sheep, and goats have to no longer be redeemed; they are holy. You'll sprinkle their blood on the altar and burn their fats as a hearth imparting, a candy aroma to the Lord. **18.** The flesh of those animals could be yours, similar to the wave breast and proper thigh (special parts of the animal presented to God). **19.** All of the heave offerings of the holy matters, which the Israelites provide to the Lord, I have given to you, your sons, and daughters, as a for all time ordinance. This is a covenant of salt (an unbreakable covenant) earlier than the Lord, for you and your descendants. **20.** Then the Lord said to Aaron: "You will no longer have any inheritance of their land, nor a component among them; I am your portion and inheritance a few of the Israelites. **21.** Look, I've given the Levites all of the tithes (one-10th) of the Israelites as their inheritance in go back for the paintings they do inside the tabernacle of meeting. **22.** Any more, the Israelites should no longer approach the tabernacle of meeting, or they may bear sin and die. **23.** Simply the Levites will do the work of the tabernacle of assembly, and they will undergo their iniquity. This could be a statute all the time, at some point of your generations. The Levites will haven't any inheritance some of the Israelites. **24.** The tithes that the Israelites offer as a heave presenting to the Lord I've given to the Levites as their inheritance. That is why I said to them, 'Among the Israelites they will have no inheritance.'" **25.** Then the Lord spoke to Moses, pronouncing: **26.** "Communicate to the Levites and inform them: 'When you acquire the tithes from the Israelites, which I've given to you as your inheritance, you should provide a heave supplying of one-tenth of the tithe to the Lord. **27.** Your heave offering may be considered because the grain from the threshing ground and the wine from the winepress. **28.** You have to additionally provide a heave imparting to the Lord from all the tithes you receive from the Israelites, and provide it to Aaron the priest. **29.** From all of your gifts, you need to provide each heave providing due to the Lord, from the great of them, the consecrated (set aside) part. **30.** Tell them, 'While you raise up the fine of your services, the rest may be considered as produce from the threshing ground and the winepress for you and your households. **31.** You can devour it in any place, you and your families, due to the fact it's far your praise for operating inside the tabernacle of meeting. **32.** You may no longer be responsible of sin while you raise up the fine of your

services, however do now not defile the holy offerings of the Israelites, or you will die.'"

Chapter 19

1. The Lord spoke to Moses and Aaron, saying: **2.** "This is the commandment I have given: Tell the Israelites to bring you a completely red heifer (a young female cow), one that is flawless (without any imperfections), without any defect, and that has never been used for work (such as pulling a plow or cart). **3.** You are to give it to Eleazar the priest (a descendant of Aaron), who will take it outside the camp and have it slaughtered in his presence. **4.** Eleazar will dip his finger in the animal's blood and sprinkle it seven times (a sacred number) in front of the tabernacle (the portable sanctuary used by the Israelites). **5.** The heifer will then be entirely burned in his sight—its skin, meat, blood, and intestines will all be burned. **6.** The priest will throw cedar wood (a type of wood used in rituals), hyssop (a plant used for purification), and scarlet wool (red wool) into the fire where the heifer is burning. **7.** Afterward, the priest will wash his clothes and bathe in water. He will remain unclean (ritually impure) until evening. **8.** The one who burns the heifer must also wash his clothes and bathe in water, and he will be unclean until evening. **9.** A clean person will gather the ashes of the heifer and store them in a clean place outside the camp. These ashes will be used to make the water for purification, which cleanses from sin. **10.** The person who collects the ashes will wash his clothes and be unclean until evening. This law is to be followed by the Israelites and by any foreigner (a non-Israelite) living among them. **11.** Anyone who touches the dead body (the corpse) of a person will be unclean for seven days. **12.** To purify himself, he must wash with the purification water (water mixed with the ashes of the red heifer) on the third and seventh days. After this, he will be clean. But if he does not purify himself on these days, he will remain unclean. **13.** Anyone who touches a dead body and does not purify himself will defile (make impure) the Lord's tabernacle (the sacred place of worship) and be cut off (excluded) from Israel. The purification water has not been applied to him, and he is still unclean. **14.** This law applies when someone dies in a tent: anyone who enters the tent or is inside it will be unclean for seven days. **15.** Any open container without a lid will also become unclean. **16.** Anyone in the open field who touches a person killed by a sword, a dead body, a bone, or a grave will be unclean for seven days. **17.** For those who are unclean, the ashes of the red heifer will be mixed with fresh water (living water, such as running water) in a vessel (a container). **18.** A clean person will dip hyssop (a plant used for purification) in the water and sprinkle it on the tent, the vessels, or on anyone who has touched a bone, a dead body, or a grave. **19.** The clean person will sprinkle the unclean person on the third and seventh days. On the seventh day, the unclean person must wash his clothes, bathe in water, and by evening, he will be clean. **20.** Anyone who remains unclean and does not purify himself will be cut off from the assembly (the community of Israel). He has defiled the Lord's sanctuary, and the purification water has not been sprinkled on him, so he remains unclean. **21.** This law is to be followed permanently. Anyone who sprinkles the purification water must wash their clothes, and anyone who touches it will be unclean until evening. **22.** Anything the unclean person touches will also become unclean, and anyone who touches it will be unclean until evening."

Chapter 20

1. The entire network of Israel entered the desert of Zin for the duration of the primary month and camped at Kadesh. It was there that Miriam passed away and was buried. **2.** There was no water for the people, so they gathered and complained against Moses and Aaron. **3.** The people argued with Moses, saying, "If only we had died along with our brothers who passed away before the Lord! **4.** Why did you bring us here into this wilderness to let us and our livestock die? **5.** Why did you lead us out of Egypt (the land in which we had been slaves) to bring us to this desolate region?

There's no food, no figs, no grapes, no pomegranates—not anything to eat—and no water to drink!" **6.** Moses and Aaron left the assembly and went to the entrance of the tabernacle (the sacred tent where God dwelled) and fell on their faces. The glory of the Lord (God's visible presence) appeared to them. **7.** The Lord spoke to Moses and said, **8.** "Take the staff (a symbol of leadership) and gather the people. Speak to the rock (a large stone) in front of them, and it will provide water. This will bring water for the people and their animals to drink." **9.** Moses took the staff from before the Lord, as He had told him. **10.** Moses and Aaron gathered the people in front of the rock. Moses said to them, "Listen, you rebels! Should we bring water out of this rock for you?" **11.** Moses struck the rock twice with the staff, and water poured out in abundance. The people and their animals drank. **12.** But the Lord said to Moses and Aaron, "Because you did not believe Me enough to treat Me as holy (set apart and sacred) before the Israelites, you will not bring this people into the land I promised them." **13.** This place was known as Meribah (meaning "contention" or "quarreling"), because the Israelites argued with the Lord, and He showed His holiness among them. **14.** Moses sent messengers from Kadesh to the king of Edom (a kingdom to the southeast of Israel), saying: "This is what your brother Israel says: 'You know all the hardships we've faced, **15.** how our ancestors went down to Egypt, and we lived there for many years. The Egyptians mistreated us and our ancestors. **16.** When we cried out to the Lord, He heard our cry and sent an angel (a messenger of God) to rescue us from Egypt. Now we are here at Kadesh, near the border of your land. **17.** Please let us pass through your country. We will not enter any fields or vineyards, and we will not drink water from any wells. We will stay on the King's Highway (a major ancient road for travelers) and not turn to the right or left until we've passed through your territory.'" **18.** But Edom refused, saying, "You shall not pass through my land, or I will come out with the sword against you." **19.** The Israelites responded, "We will stay on the main road, and if we or our animals drink any of your water, we will pay for it. We just want to pass through walking, nothing more." **20.** But Edom refused again, saying, "You shall not pass through." And Edom came out with a large army to block their way. **21.** Because Edom would not let them pass through, the Israelites turned away and traveled around their land. **22.** The entire Israelite community then moved from Kadesh and arrived at Mount Hor (a mountain near Edom). **23.** At Mount Hor, the Lord spoke to Moses and Aaron, saying, **24.** "Aaron will be gathered to his people (a phrase meaning Aaron will die and be reunited with his ancestors), because he will not enter the land I have given to the Israelites. This is because you both rebelled against My commands at the waters of Meribah. **25.** Take Aaron and his son Eleazar (Aaron's son who will succeed him as high priest) up to Mount Hor. **26.** Remove Aaron's priestly clothes (special clothes worn by the high priest) and place them on Eleazar. Aaron will die there and be gathered to his people." **27.** Moses did as the Lord commanded. He and Eleazar went up to Mount Hor, where the entire congregation could see them. **28.** Moses removed Aaron's priestly garments and placed them on Eleazar. Aaron died at the mountaintop, and Moses and Eleazar returned from the mountain. **29.** When the people saw that Aaron had died, they mourned for him for thirty days.

Chapter 21

1. The king of Arad, a Canaanite ruler from the southern region, heard that Israel was approaching along the Atharim road. He attacked Israel and captured some of the people. **2.** Israel made a vow to the Lord, saying, "If You will hand these people over to us, we will completely destroy their cities." **3.** The Lord responded to Israel's plea, giving the Canaanites into their hands. Israel defeated them and destroyed their cities. The place was named Hormah, meaning "devastation." **4.** They traveled from Mount Hor along the direction to head across the land of Edom. Along the way, the people grew impatient and discouraged. **5.** They complained against God and Moses, saying, "Why did you bring us out of Egypt

to die in this barren region? There is no food or water, and we're disgusted by this worthless bread." **6.** In response, the Lord sent venomous snakes among them, and many Israelites were bitten and died. **7.** The people then came to Moses, confessed their sin for speaking against God and him, and asked him to pray for them so the snakes could be removed. **8.** The Lord told Moses, "Make a bronze serpent and place it on a pole. Everyone who is bitten and looks at it will live." **9.** Moses obeyed and made a bronze serpent, setting it on a pole. Anyone who had been bitten and looked at it was healed. **10.** The Israelites then journeyed and camped at Oboth. **11.** From Oboth, they traveled to Ije Abarim, located east of Moab, toward the sunrise. **12.** They moved on to the Valley of Zered. **13.** Next, they camped on the far side of the Arnon, within the desert stretching to the Amorites' territory. The Arnon River marks the boundary between Moab and the Amorites. **14.** The Book of the Wars of the Lord records: "Waheb in Suphah, the streams of the Arnon, and the slopes of the brooks that reach the dwellings of Ar, on Moab's border." **16.** From there, they came to Beer, the well where the Lord had told Moses to gather the people so He could provide them with water. **17.** The people then sang this song: "Spring up, O well! Let all the people sing to it!" **18.** "The well that the leaders dug, the nobles of the people, with their staffs." **19.** Later on, they journeyed from there to Mattanah. **20.** From Mattanah, they went to Nahaliel, then to Bamoth. **21.** From Bamoth, they camped in a valley in the land of Moab, at the top of Pisgah, overlooking the desert. **22.** Israel sent messengers to Sihon, king of the Amorites, asking for permission to pass through his land. They promised not to enter fields, vineyards, or drink from any wells, but only to follow the King's Highway until they passed through his territory. **23.** However, Sihon refused and mustered his people to fight Israel in the wilderness. They met in Jahaz. **24.** Israel defeated Sihon with the sword and took control of his territory, from the Arnon to the Jabbok, as far as the Ammonites, whose border was heavily fortified. **25.** Israel captured all the towns of the Amorites, including Heshbon and all its surrounding cities. **26.** Heshbon had been the capital of Sihon, king of the Amorites, who had previously defeated the king of Moab and seized his land. **27.** A proverb is often recited: "Come to Heshbon, let it be rebuilt; let the city of Sihon be restored." **28.** "A fire came from Heshbon, a flame from the city of Sihon, consuming Ar of Moab and the rulers of the heights of the Arnon." **29.** "Woe to you, Moab! You are destroyed, O people of Chemosh! He has given your sons as captives and your daughters into slavery, to Sihon, king of the Amorites." **30.** "We have attacked them; Heshbon has fallen as far as Dibon. We have devastated Nophah, as far as Medeba." **31.** As a result, Israel settled in the land of the Amorites. **32.** Moses sent spies to the city of Jazer, and they captured its villages, driving out the Amorites living there. **33.** From there, they moved to Bashan. Og, the king of Bashan, came out with his army to fight at Edrei. **34.** The Lord reassured Moses, saying, "Do not fear him, for I have already delivered him and his people into your hands. You will deal with him just as you did with Sihon, king of the Amorites, who lived in Heshbon." **35.** Israel defeated Og, his sons, and all his people, leaving no survivors. They took possession of his land.

Chapter 22

1. The Israelites traveled and set up camp in the plains of Moab, located on the east side of the Jordan River, directly across from the city of Jericho. **2.** When Balak, the king of Moab, saw what Israel had done to the Amorites, **3.** he became filled with fear, as Moab was greatly alarmed by the size of the Israelite population. **4.** Moab said to the leaders of Midian, "This people will eat everything in their path, just as an ox consumes all the grass in the field." **5.** Balak, the king of Moab, sent messengers to Balaam, son of Beor, who lived in Pethor, a city by the river in his homeland. He said, "A people has come from Egypt, and their numbers cover the earth. Come and curse them for me so I can defeat them and drive them away, for I know that whoever you bless is blessed, and whoever you curse is cursed." **6.** The leaders of Moab and Midian brought a charge for divination and went to Balaam with the king's message. **7.** Balaam told them, "Stay here overnight, and I will ask the Lord what He wants me to do." So, the leaders of Moab spent the night with him. **8.** That night, God came to Balaam and asked, "Who are these men with you?" **9.** Balaam answered, "Balak, the king of Moab, sent them to me, saying, **10.** 'A people has come from Egypt, and their numbers cover the land. Please come and curse them for me, so I can defeat them and drive them out.'" **11.** God replied to Balaam, "Do not go with them. Do not curse these people, for they are blessed." **12.** Balaam got up the next morning and told the princes of Balak, "Go back to your own land, for the Lord has not allowed me to go with you." **13.** The princes of Moab returned to Balak and said, "Balaam refuses to come with us." **14.** Balak sent even more distinguished princes, more numerous and of higher rank than the previous ones. **15.** They came to Balaam and said, "Thus says Balak, son of Zippor, 'Do not let anything keep you from coming to me. **16.** I will honor you greatly and give you whatever you ask. Please come and curse this people for me.'" **17.** Balaam responded to the messengers of Balak, "Even if Balak were to give me a house full of silver and gold, I cannot go beyond the command of the Lord my God. I cannot say less or more than what He tells me. **18.** Now stay here this night, and I will see if there is anything else the Lord will say to me." **19.** That night, God came to Balaam again and said, "If these men come to call you, rise and go with them. But only speak the word that I give you." **20.** Balaam rose early the next morning, saddled his donkey, and went with the princes of Moab. **21.** But God's anger was kindled because Balaam went, and the Angel of the Lord stood in the way as an adversary. Balaam was riding his donkey, and his two servants were with him. **22.** The donkey saw the Angel of the Lord standing in the road with a sword drawn, and she turned off the road into a field. Balaam struck the donkey to get her back onto the road. **23.** The Angel of the Lord stood in a narrow path between vineyards, with walls on both sides. **24.** When the donkey saw the Angel, she pushed against the wall, crushing Balaam's foot. Balaam became angry and struck the donkey again. **25.** The Angel of the Lord moved on and stood in a narrow place where there was no way to turn either left or right. **26.** When the donkey saw the Angel of the Lord, she lay down beneath Balaam, and Balaam's anger was aroused. He struck her with his staff. **27.** Then the Lord opened the donkey's mouth, and she said to Balaam, "What have I done to you that you have struck me these three times?" **28.** Balaam answered, "Because you have made a fool of me! If I had a sword, I would kill you right now." **29.** The donkey said to Balaam, "Am I not your donkey, the one you have ridden all your life? Have I ever done anything like this to you before?" Balaam replied, "No." **30.** Then the Lord opened Balaam's eyes, and he saw the Angel of the Lord standing in the way with a drawn sword. Balaam bowed down with his face to the ground. **31.** The Angel of the Lord asked him, "Why have you struck your donkey these three times? I have come out to oppose you because your path is reckless before me. **32.** The donkey saw me and turned aside three times. If she had not turned, I would have killed you by now, but let her live." **33.** Balaam said to the Angel of the Lord, "I have sinned, for I did not know you were standing in the way against me. If you are displeased, I will go back." **34.** The Angel of the Lord replied, "Go with the men, but speak only the words I tell you." So Balaam went with the princes of Balak. **35.** When Balak heard that Balaam was coming, he went out to meet him at the city of Moab, which is near the boundary at the Arnon River (a river that marks the border of Moab). **36.** Balak said to Balaam, "Did I not urgently send for you? Why didn't you come to me? I am able to honor you greatly." **37.** Balaam replied, "I have come to you! But can I speak anything on my own? The word that God places in my mouth that is what I must speak." **38.** Balaam went with Balak, and they came to Kirjath Huzoth, a city in Moab. **39.** Balak offered sacrifices of oxen and sheep, and sent portions of the offering to Balaam and to the princes with him. **40.** The next day, Balak took Balaam to the high places of Baal (a place used for idol worship), where Balaam could see the whole Israelite camp.

Chapter 23

1. Balaam told Balak, "build seven altars (raised structures for sacrifices) right here and put together seven bulls and 7 rams." **2.** Balak followed Balaam's instructions, supplying a bull and a ram on every altar. **3.** Balaam then stated, "stay through the offerings whilst I visit a excessive place. perhaps the Lord will meet with me, and i'll inform you what He well-knownshows." He went to a barren (empty, desolate) hill. **4.** God met with Balaam and stated, "I've prepared the seven altars, and provided a bull and a ram on every." **5.** The Lord spoke to Balaam, announcing, "move returned to Balak and communicate the phrases I give you." **6.** Balaam returned to Balak, who became standing by the burnt offerings with Moab's leaders. **7.** Balaam spoke this prophecy: "Balak, king of Moab, introduced me from Aram (a location), from the mountains of the east, pronouncing, 'Come, curse Jacob for me, and denounce (declare evil) Israel!'" **8.** "How am i able to curse those whom God has not cursed? How can i denounce the ones the Lord has no longer denounced?" **9.** "From the mountaintops, I see them; they're a human beings set aside, no longer counted a number of the international locations." **10.** "Who can be counted the dust of Jacob or degree even a fragment of Israel? let me die the death of the righteous, and allow my quit be like theirs!" **11.** Balak stated to Balaam, "What have you ever executed to me? I brought you right here to curse my enemies, but you have got blessed them!" **12.** Balaam replied, "i can best talk what the Lord tells me." **13.** Balak then stated, "come with me to some other vicinity in which you may solely see part of them. perhaps from there, you will be capable of curse them." **14.** Balak took Balaam to the field of Zophim, to the pinnacle of Pisgah (a mountain), and built seven altars, supplying a bull and a ram on each. **15.** Balaam advised Balak, "stay right here even as i'm going meet with the Lord." **16.** The Lord met Balaam once more and spoke, announcing, "move lower back to Balak and say the phrases I provide you with." **17.** Balaam lower back to Balak, who changed into standing by his burnt services with the Moabite princes. **18.** Balak requested, "What did the Lord say?" **19.** Balaam spoke this prophecy: "get up, Balak, and concentrate to me, son of Zippor!" **20.** "God isn't always a person that He ought to lie, nor a son of man that He ought to change His thoughts. Has He spoken, and could He now not do it? Has He promised, and will He now not satisfy it?" **21.** "i've been commanded to bless, and He has blessed; I can't undo it." **22.** "He has observed no wickedness in Jacob, nor sin in Israel. The Lord their God is with them, and the shout of a King is amongst them." **23.** "God added them out of Egypt; His energy is like that of a wild ox (a strong, untamed animal symbolizing power)." **24.** "there's no sorcery in opposition to Jacob, no divination in opposition to Israel. It should be said of Jacob and Israel, 'What tremendous things God has accomplished!'" **25.** "appearance, a people rises like a lioness and lifts itself like a lion; it will now not rest till it devours the prey and liquids the blood of the slain." **26.** Balak said to Balaam, "Do now not curse them or bless them in any respect!" **27.** Balaam replied, "Did I not tell you that I must do the entirety the Lord instructions?" **28.** Balak then stated, "Come, i can take you to any other place; maybe it's going to please God to curse them from there." **29.** Balak took Balaam to the top of Peor (a mountain) overlooking the wasteland. **30.** Balaam instructed Balak, "construct seven altars here and prepare seven bulls and 7 rams. Balak did as Balaam advised, supplying a bull and a ram on each altar.

Chapter 24

1. When Balaam saw that it pleased the Lord to bless Israel, he no longer sought to use sorcery (magic or witchcraft) as he had before. Instead, he turned toward the wilderness (a desolate area). **2.** Balaam looked up and saw Israel camped by their tribes, and the Spirit of God (God's presence or power) came upon him. **3.** He took up his oracle (prophetic message) and said: "The utterance of Balaam son of Beor, the one whose eyes are opened, **4.** the one who hears the words of God, the one who sees the vision of the Almighty (God), who falls down with eyes wide open: **5.** "How lovely are your tents, O Jacob! Your dwellings, O Israel! **6.** They are like valleys that stretch out, like gardens beside the rivers, like aloes (a fragrant plant) planted by the Lord, like cedars (tall trees) beside the waters. **7.** He will pour water from his buckets, and his descendants will be numerous. His king will be greater than Agag (the king of the Amalekites), and his kingdom will be exalted (raised or honored). **8.** God brought him out of Egypt; he has strength like a wild ox (a powerful, untamed animal). He will defeat his enemies, crush their bones, and pierce them with his arrows. **9.** He lies down like a lion (a powerful, fearless animal); who can rouse him? Blessed are those who bless you, and cursed are those who curse you." **10.** Balak's anger (great displeasure) was stirred against Balaam. He clapped his hands and said to him, "I called you to curse my enemies, but you have blessed them three times! **11.** Now, go to your place! I told you I would greatly honor you, but the Lord has kept you from that honor." **12.** Balaam answered and said to Balak, "Did I not speak to your messengers (servants or messengers) whom you sent to me, saying, **13.** 'Even if Balak gave me his house full of silver and gold, I could not go beyond the word of the Lord, to do good or bad of my own will. What the Lord says, that I must speak'? **14.** And now, I am going to my people. Come, let me advise (guide) you what this people will do to your people in the latter days (future). **15.** He took up his oracle and said: "The utterance of Balaam son of Beor, the one whose eyes are opened, **16.** the one who hears the words of God, and has the knowledge of the Most High (God), who sees the vision of the Almighty, who falls down with eyes wide open: **17.** "I see Him, but not now; I behold Him, but not near. A Star (a future leader or king) shall come out of Jacob; a Scepter (symbol of authority) shall rise out of Israel, and crush the forehead of Moab (a nation east of Israel), and destroy all the sons of tumult (troublemakers or rebels). **18.** Edom (a nation southeast of Israel) shall be a possession (inheritance); Seir (a region of Edom) also, his enemies, shall be a possession, while Israel acts valiantly (boldly). **19.** One shall come out of Jacob who will have dominion (rule), and destroy the remains of the city." **20.** Then he looked at Amalek (a tribe and enemy of Israel) and took up his oracle and said: "Amalek was first among the nations, but shall be last until he perishes (is destroyed)." **21.** Then he looked at the Kenites (a people group) and took up his oracle and said: "Firm is your dwelling place, and your nest is set in the rock; **22.** Nevertheless, Kain (a clan of the Kenites) shall be burned. How long until Asshur (the Assyrian empire) carries you away captive?" **23.** He took up his oracle and said: "Alas! Who shall live when God does this? **24.** But ships shall come from the coasts of Cyprus (an island in the Mediterranean Sea), and they shall afflict Asshur and afflict Eber (another people), and so shall Amalek, until he perishes." **25.** Balaam rose and departed and returned to his place, and Balak also went his way.

Chapter 25

1. Israel remained in Acacia Grove (a place), and the humans started to dedicate harlotry (immoral sexual behavior) with the ladies of Moab. **2.** The Moabite women invited the Israelites to take part in sacrifices to their gods (deities), and the humans ate the food offered to the gods and bowed down (worshiped) to them. **3.** As a end result, Israel joined in worship of Baal of Peor (a fake god), and the Lord's anger (sturdy displeasure) burned against them. **4.** The Lord told Moses, "Take the leaders (chief guys) of the people and cling the offenders (the ones who've sinned) before the Lord, out inside the open, so that My fierce anger (wrath) will shrink back from Israel." **5.** Moses told the judges (those in rate of judgment) of Israel, "each of you have to kill the ones guys who've joined in worshiping Baal of Peor." **6.** while the humans have been weeping at the doorway of the tabernacle, one Israelite man introduced a Midianite lady to his circle of relatives in the front of Moses and the congregation. **7.** whilst Phinehas (a clergyman), the son of Eleazar and grandson of Aaron the priest, saw this, he stood up, took a javelin (a spear), and went after the Israelite and the Midianite female. **8.** He drove the javelin through both of them—the person and the female—and the plague (a virulent disease) that had been despatched via the Lord become stopped. nine. In overall, 24,000 Israelites died in the plague. **10.** The Lord spoke to Moses and said: 11. "Phinehas, the son of Eleazar, has become my wrath (anger) away from Israel, due to the fact he became zealous (eager) with My zeal and stopped the destruction of the humans." **12.** "therefore, i am making a covenant (a formal agreement) of peace with him." thirteen. "this could be an eternal covenant (settlement) of priesthood (priestly service) for him and his descendants, due to the fact he turned into passionate for his God and atoned (made amends) for the human beings of Israel." **14.** The Israelite guy who was killed with the Midianite woman turned into Zimri (a leader), the son of Salu, a frontrunner (chief) within the tribe of Simeon. **15.** The Midianite girl changed into Cozbi (a frontrunner's daughter), the daughter of Zur, a pacesetter (leader) of the human beings of Midian. sixteen. The Lord then spoke to Moses, announcing: **17.** "Take motion towards the Midianites and strike them," **18.** "for they led you into sin with their schemes (plans), seducing you in the be counted of Baal of Peor and the incident related to Cozbi, the daughter of a Midianite chief, who become killed at some stage in the plague."

Chapter 26

1. After the plague (disease or agony) had ended, the Lord spoke to Moses and Eleazar, the son of Aaron, the priest, saying: **2.** "Take a census (count) of all the people of Israel who are twenty years old or older, by their families, all those who are able to fight in Israel's military." **3.** So Moses and Eleazar the priest spoke with the people in the plains (flat lands) of Moab, near the Jordan River, across from Jericho, saying: **4.** "Take a census of those who are twenty years old or older, just as the Lord commanded Moses and the Israelites who came out of Egypt." **5.** Reuben was Israel's firstborn. The descendants (children) of Reuben were: from Hanoch, the family of the Hanochites; from Pallu, the family of the Palluites; **6.** from Hezron, the family of the Hezronites; from Carmi, the family of the Carmites. **7.** These are the families of the Reubenites. The number (count) of them was forty-three thousand seven hundred and thirty. **8.** The son of Pallu was Eliab. **9.** The sons of Eliab were Nemuel, Dathan, and Abiram. These are the Dathan and Abiram who were leaders (representatives) of the congregation (community) and argued against Moses and Aaron during the riot (rebellion) of Korah. They rebelled (opposed) against the Lord. **10.** The earth opened up and swallowed them, along with Korah and the others when they died, and the fire consumed (burned up) two hundred and fifty men, which became a sign (symbol or warning). **11.** But the children of Korah did not die. **12.** The sons of Simeon by their families were: from Nemuel, the family of the Nemuelites; from Jamin, the family of the Jaminites; from Jachin, the family of the Jachinites; **13.** from Zerah, the family of the Zarhites; from Shaul, the family of the Shaulites. **14.** These are the families of the Simeonites. The number of them was twenty-two thousand two hundred. **15.** The sons of Gad by their families were: from Zephon, the family of the Zephonites; from Haggi, the family of the Haggites; from Shuni, the family of the Shunites; **16.** from Ozni, the family of the Oznites; from Eri, the family of the Erites; **17.** from Arod, the family of the Arodites; from Areli, the family of the Arelites. **18.** These are the families of the sons of Gad. The number of them was forty thousand five hundred. **19.** The sons of Judah were Er and Onan. But Er and Onan died in the land of Canaan. **20.** The descendants (offspring) of Judah by their families were: from Shelah, the family of the Shelanites; from Perez, the family of the Parzites; from Zerah, the family of the Zarhites. **21.** The descendants of Perez were: from Hezron, the family of the Hezronites; from Hamul, the family of the Hamulites. **22.** These are the families of Judah. The number of them was seventy-six thousand five hundred. **23.** The sons of Issachar by their families were: from Tola, the family of the Tolaites; from Puah, the family of the Punites; **24.** from Jashub, the family of the Jashubites; from Shimron, the family of the Shimronites. **25.** These are the families of Issachar. The number of them was sixty-four thousand three hundred. **26.** The sons of Zebulun by their families were: from Sered, the family of the Sardites; from Elon, the family of the Elonites; from Jahleel, the family of the Jahleelites. **27.** These are the families of the Zebulunites. The number of them was sixty thousand five hundred. **28.** The sons of Joseph by their families were Manasseh and Ephraim. **29.** The descendants (offspring) of Manasseh were: from Machir, the family of the Machirites, and Machir fathered (begot) Gilead. From Gilead, the family of the Gileadites. **30.** These are the descendants of Gilead: from Jeezer, the family of the Jeezerites; from Helek, the family of the Helekites; **31.** from Asriel, the family of the Asrielites; from Shechem, the family of the Shechemites; **32.** from Shemida, the family of the Shemidaites; from Hepher, the family of the Hepherites. **33.** Now Zelophehad, the son of Hepher, had no sons but only daughters. The names of the daughters of Zelophehad were Mahlah, Noah, Hoglah, Milcah, and Tirzah. **34.** These are the clans (large family groups) of Manasseh; the total number of these counted in them was fifty thousand seven hundred. **35.** These are the descendants (children or offspring) of Ephraim, by their clans: from Shuthelah, the clan of the Shuthelahites; from Becher, the clan of the Bachrites; from Tahan, the clan of the Tahanites. **36.** And these are the descendants of Shuthelah: from Eran, the clan of the Eranites. **37.** These are the clans of the descendants of Ephraim, according to those who were counted: thirty-two thousand five hundred. These are the descendants of Joseph by their clans. **38.** The descendants of Benjamin, according to their clans, were: from Bela, the clan of the Belaites; from Ashbel, the clan of the Ashbelites; from Ahiram, the clan of the Ahiramites; **39.** from Shupham, the clan of the Shuphamites; from Hupham, the clan of the Huphamites. **40.** And the descendants of Bela were Ard and Naaman: from Ard, the clan of the Ardites; from Naaman, the clan of the Naamites. **41.** These are the descendants of Benjamin, according to their clans; and the total number of those counted in them was forty-five thousand six hundred. **42.** These are the descendants of Dan, according to their clans: from Shuham, the clan of the Shuhamites. These are the clans of Dan, according to their families. **43.** All the clans of the Shuhamites, according to the number of those counted, were sixty-four thousand four hundred. **44.** The descendants of Asher, according to their clans, were: from Jimna, the clan of the Jimnites; from Jesui, the clan of the Jesuites; from Beriah, the clan of the Beriites. **45.** From the descendants of Beriah: from Heber, the clan of the Heberites; from Malchiel, the clan of the Malchielites. **46.** And the name of the daughter of Asher was Serah. **47.** These are the clans of the descendants of Asher, according to the number of those counted in them: fifty-three thousand four hundred. **48.** The descendants of Naphtali, according to their clans, were: from Jahzeel, the clan of the Jahzeelites; from Guni, the clan of the Gunites; **49.** from Jezer, the clan of the Jezerites; from Shillem, the clan of the Shillemites. **50.** These are the clans of Naphtali, according to their families; and the total number of those counted in them was forty-five thousand four hundred. **51.** These are the total number of those counted among the Israelites: six hundred and one thousand seven hundred and thirty. **52.** Then the Lord spoke to Moses, saying: **53.** "To these the land will be divided as an inheritance, based on the number of names (the number of people)." **54.** "To a larger tribe, you will give a larger portion of the land, and to a smaller tribe, you will give a smaller portion. Each tribe will receive an inheritance based on the number of people in it." **55.** "But the land will be divided by lot (random drawing); they will inherit based on the names of the tribes in their ancestors." **56.** "The land's division will follow the lot, with both larger and smaller tribes receiving their share accordingly." **57.** And these are the descendants of Levi, according to their clans: from Gershon, the clan of the Gershonites; from Kohath, the clan of the Kohathites; from Merari, the clan of the Merarites. **58.** These are the clans of the Levites: the clan of the Libnites, the clan of the Hebronites, the clan of the Mahlites, the clan of the Mushites, and the clan of the Korathites. Kohath was the father of Amram. **59.** The name of Amram's wife was Jochebed, the daughter of Levi, born to Levi in Egypt; and she bore to Amram Aaron, Moses, and their sister Miriam. **60.** To Aaron were born Nadab, Abihu, Eleazar, and Ithamar. **61.** But Nadab and Abihu died when they offered unauthorized (profane) fire before the Lord. **62.** The total number of the Levites counted was twenty-three thousand, every male one month old or older; they were not included in the census of the other Israelites because they did not receive an inheritance among the Israelites. **63.** These are the people who were counted by Moses and Eleazar the priest, who conducted the census of the Israelites in the plains of Moab, by the Jordan River, opposite Jericho. **64.** But not one of those counted by Moses and Aaron when they took the census of the Israelites in the wilderness of Sinai remained alive, **65.** because the Lord had said that they would die in the wilderness. So not one of them remained, except for Caleb the son of Jephunneh and Joshua the son of Nun.

Chapter 27

1. Then the daughters of Zelophehad, who was the son of Hepher, the son of Gilead, the son of Machir, the son of Manasseh, from the families of Manasseh, the son of Joseph, came forward. The names of his daughters were Mahlah, Noah, Hoglah, Milcah, and Tirzah. **2.** They stood before Moses, Eleazar the priest, the leaders, and all the congregation (a group of people gathered for a common purpose), at the entrance to the tabernacle (a portable sanctuary or place of worship), and said: **3.** "Our father died in the wilderness, but he was not among those who rebelled (acted in opposition or defied authority) against the Lord by joining Korah's group. He died because of his own sin, and he had no sons. **4.** Why should our father's name be removed from his family line just because he had no son? Give us an inheritance (a right to property or wealth passed down from ancestors) along with our father's brothers." **5.** So Moses brought their case before the Lord. **6.** And the Lord spoke to Moses, saying: **7.** "The daughters of Zelophehad are right. You must certainly give them an inheritance among their father's brothers, and transfer (to pass on or assign) their father's inheritance to them. **8.** Tell the Israelites, 'If a man dies and has no son, his inheritance must go to his daughter. **9.** If he has no daughter, it must go to his brothers. **10.** If he has no brothers, it must go to his father's brothers. **11.** If his father has no brothers, it must go to the closest relative (a person with the nearest family connection) in his family, and he shall inherit (take possession of) it.' This is to be a permanent rule for the Israelites, as the Lord commanded Moses." **12.** Then the Lord said to Moses: "Go up to Mount Abarim (a mountain range in ancient Israel) and see the land I have given to the Israelites. **13.** After you have seen it, you will also be gathered to your people (join your ancestors in death), as your brother Aaron was. **14.** For in the Wilderness of Zin (a desert region), during the rebellion (an act of defiance) of the people, you disobeyed (failed to follow) My command to honor (show respect or reverence) Me at the waters in front of them." (These are the waters of Meribah, in the Wilderness of Zin.) **15.** Then Moses spoke to the Lord: **16.** "Let the Lord, the God of all living beings (all life), appoint (choose and authorize) a leader over the congregation, **17.** who will lead them out and bring them in, so that the Lord's people will not be like sheep without a shepherd (a guide or leader)." **18.** And the Lord said to Moses: "Take Joshua son of Nun, a man in whom is the Spirit (the Holy Spirit or a divine presence), and lay your hands on him. **19.** Present him to Eleazar the priest and to the entire congregation, and publicly commission (officially assign a role or responsibility) him in their sight. **20.** Give some of your authority (power or right to give orders) to him, so that the whole congregation of the Israelites will obey him. **21.** He will stand before Eleazar the priest, who will consult (ask for advice) the Lord for him using the Urim (a sacred object used by the high priest to determine God's will). At his word, the people will go out, and at his word, they will come in—he and all the Israelites with him." **22.** So Moses did as the Lord commanded him. He took Joshua, set him before Eleazar the priest and all the congregation, **23.** laid his hands on him, and commissioned him, just as the Lord had instructed Moses.

Chapter 28

1. The Lord spoke to Moses, announcing: **2.** "Inform the Israelites, 'Be careful to deliver Me the services I require, the foods for My offerings, with a view to be made by using fire to create a sweet perfume (a nice smell) for Me. You should provide them at the proper time.' **3.** Inform them, 'This is the offering made by fire that you will present to the Lord: male lambs in their first year, without any defects (flaws), every day as a regular burnt offering. **4.** One lamb you will offer in the morning, and the other you will offer in the evening. **5.** Along with each lamb, offer one-tenth of an ephah (a unit of measurement for dry goods, about 22 liters or 5.8 gallons) of fine flour mixed with one-fourth of a hin (a unit of measurement for liquids, approximately 3.7 liters or 1 gallon) of pressed oil. **6.** This is the regular burnt offering that was commanded at Mount Sinai, a sweet aroma (good scent) made by fire to the Lord. **7.** The drink offering for each lamb will be one-fourth of a hin. You will pour it out in a holy place (sacred area) as an offering to the Lord. **8.** The other lamb you will offer in the evening, and just like the morning lamb, you will offer the same grain offering and drink offering, as an offering made by fire, a sweet aroma to the Lord. **9.** 'On the Sabbath day (the day of rest), offer two lambs in their first year, without defects, and two-tenths of an ephah of fine flour mixed with oil, along with its drink offering. **10.** This is the burnt offering for each Sabbath, in addition to the regular burnt offering with its drink offering. **11.** 'At the beginning of each month (the first day of the month), bring a burnt offering to the Lord: young bulls (young male livestock), one ram (male sheep), and seven lambs of their first year, all without defects. **12.** For each bull, offer three-tenths of an ephah of fine flour mixed with oil. For the ram, offer two-tenths of an ephah of fine flour mixed with oil. **13.** For each of the seven lambs, offer one-tenth of an ephah of fine flour mixed with oil, as a burnt offering with a sweet fragrance to the Lord, made by fire. **14.** The drink offering will be half of a hin of wine for each bull, one-third of a hin for the ram, and one-fourth of a hin for each lamb. This is the burnt offering for each month throughout the year. **15.** Additionally, offer one male goat as a sin offering (offering to make up for wrongdoing) to the Lord, in addition to the regular burnt offering and its drink offering. **16.** 'On the fourteenth day of the first month, celebrate the Lord's Passover. **17.** On the fifteenth day of the same month, celebrate the Feast of Unleavened Bread (bread made without yeast). You must eat unleavened bread for seven days. **18.** On the first day of the feast, you will have a holy convocation (special gathering), and you will not do any regular work. **19.** You will present an offering made by fire to the Lord: young bulls, one ram, and seven lambs of their first year, all without defects. **20.** Their grain offering will be fine flour mixed with oil: three-tenths of an ephah for each bull, two-tenths for the ram, **21.** and one-tenth for each of the seven lambs. **22.** Additionally, offer one goat as a sin offering to make atonement (reconciliation or forgiveness) for you. **23.** These offerings must be in addition to the regular burnt offering of the morning. **24.** This is how you will present the offerings made by fire every day for seven days, as a sweet fragrance to the Lord, in addition to the regular burnt offering and its drink offering. **25.** On the seventh day, you will have another

holy convocation, and you will not do any regular work. **26.** 'On the Day of Firstfruits (the first gathering of crops), when you bring a new grain offering to the Lord during the Feast of Weeks (a festival celebrated seven weeks after Passover), you will also have a holy convocation and do no regular work. **27.** You will present a burnt offering to the Lord: young bulls, one ram, and seven lambs of their first year, **28.** with their grain offering of fine flour mixed with oil: three-tenths of an ephah for each bull, two-tenths for the ram, **29.** and one-tenth for each of the seven lambs. **30.** You will also offer one goat to make atonement for you. **31.** Ensure all the animals are without defects, and present them with their drink offerings, in addition to the regular burnt offering with its grain offering."

Chapter 29

1. "On the first day of the 7th month, you shall gather for a holy assembly (convocation - a meeting for religious purpose). You are not to do any ordinary work, for it is a day dedicated to the sounding of the trumpets. **2.** You must offer a burnt offering to the Lord as a pleasing aroma (aroma - a pleasing scent): one young bull, one ram, and seven lambs which are 12 months old and without disorder (blemish - imperfection or flaw). **3.** The grain offering for those animals shall be fine flour mixed with oil (oil - used here as a symbol of abundance and blessing): three-tenths of an ephah (an ephah is a biblical unit of dry measure) for the bull, two-tenths for the ram, **4.** and one-tenth for each of the seven lambs; **5.** you should also offer one male goat as a sin offering (sin offering - a sacrifice to atone for sins) to make atonement (atonement - the process of reconciliation or forgiveness) for you; **6.** in addition to the burnt offering with its grain offering for the new Moon (New Moon - the first day of a new lunar month), the regular burnt offering with its grain offering, and their drink offerings (drink offerings - services of wine or other drinks), as prescribed (prescribed - required by law or rule) by the law, a pleasing aroma to the Lord. **7.** "On the tenth day of the 7th month, you shall gather for another holy meeting. You shall humble yourselves (humble yourselves - afflict your souls, which means to show sorrow for your sins or to fast); do no work on that day. **8.** You must offer a burnt offering to the Lord as a pleasing aroma: one young bull, one ram, and seven lambs which are 12 months old, all without defect. **9.** The grain offering shall be fine flour mixed with oil: three-tenths of an ephah for the bull, two-tenths for the ram, **10.** and one-tenth for each of the seven lambs; **11.** along with one male goat as a sin offering, in addition to the regular sin offering for atonement, the regular burnt offering with its grain offering, and their drink offerings. **12.** "On the fifteenth day of the 7th month, you shall gather for another holy meeting. Do no regular work, and hold a feast (feast - a time of celebration and worship) to the Lord for seven days. **13.** You must present a burnt offering, an offering made by fire (an offering made by fire - a sacrifice that is burned to God) as a pleasing aroma to the Lord: 13 young bulls, rams, and fourteen one-year-old lambs, all without defect. **14.** The grain offering shall be fine flour mixed with oil: three-tenths of an ephah for each of the thirteen bulls, two-tenths for each of the two rams, **15.** and one-tenth for each of the fourteen lambs; **16.** also, one male goat as a sin offering, in addition to the regular burnt offering, its grain offering, and its drink offering. **17.** "On the second day, offer twelve young bulls, two rams, and fourteen one-year-old lambs without defect, **18.** along with their grain and drink offerings according to the prescribed quantity for the bulls, rams, and lambs; **19.** also, one male goat as a sin offering, in addition to the regular burnt offering with its grain offering, and their drink offerings. **20.** "On the third day, offer eleven bulls, two rams, and fourteen one-year-old lambs without defect, **21.** along with their grain and drink offerings according to the prescribed quantity for the bulls, rams, and lambs; **22.** also, one goat as a sin offering, in addition to the regular burnt offering, its grain offering, and its drink offering. **23.** "On the fourth day, offer ten bulls, two rams, and fourteen one-year-old lambs without defect, **24.** along with their grain and drink offerings according to the prescribed quantity for the bulls, rams, and lambs; 25. also, one male goat as a sin offering, in addition to the regular burnt offering, its grain offering, and its drink offering. 26. "On the fifth day, present nine bulls, two rams, and fourteen one-year-old lambs without defect, 27. along with their grain and drink offerings according to the prescribed quantity for the bulls, rams, and lambs; 28. also, one goat as a sin offering, in addition to the regular burnt offering, its grain offering, and its drink offering. 29. "On the sixth day, present eight bulls, two rams, and fourteen one-year-old lambs without defect, 30. along with their grain and drink offerings according to the prescribed quantity for the bulls, rams, and lambs; 31. also, one goat as a sin offering, in addition to the regular burnt offering, its grain offering, and its drink offering. 32. "On the seventh day, present seven bulls, two rams, and fourteen one-year-old lambs without defect, 33. along with their grain and drink offerings according to the prescribed quantity for the bulls, rams, and lambs; 34. also, one goat as a sin offering, in addition to the regular burnt offering, its grain offering, and its drink offering. 35. "On the eighth day, you shall have a sacred assembly (sacred assembly - a special religious gathering). You shall do no regular work. 36. Present a burnt offering, an offering made by fire as a pleasing aroma to the Lord: one bull, one ram, and seven one-year-old lambs without defect, 37. along with their grain and drink offerings for the bull, the ram, and the lambs, according to the prescribed amount; 38. also, one goat as a sin offering, in addition to the regular burnt offering, its grain offering, and its drink offering. 39. "These offerings you shall present to the Lord at your appointed feasts (appointed feasts - specific or set apart days for worship, including these festivals) besides your vowed offerings (vowed offerings - offerings made as part of a personal vow or promise) and your freewill offerings (freewill offerings - voluntary offerings given out of generosity), as your burnt offerings, your grain offerings, your drink offerings, and your peace offerings (peace offerings - offerings made to seek peace or reconciliation with God)." 40. So Moses instructed the people of Israel everything just as the Lord had commanded him."

Chapter 30

1. Then Moses spoke to the heads of the tribes regarding the children of Israel, saying, "This is the thing which the Lord has commanded: 2. If a man makes a vow (promise) to the Lord, or swears an oath (solemn pledge) to bind (devote) himself by some agreement, he shall not break his word; he shall do according to all that proceeds (comes) out of his mouth. 3. "Or if a woman makes a vow to the Lord, and binds herself by some agreement while in her father's house in her youth, 4. and her father hears her vow and the agreement by which she has bound herself, and her father holds his peace, then all her vows shall stand, and every agreement by which she has bound (devoted) herself shall stand. 5. But if her father overrules (disagrees with) her on the day that he hears, then none of her vows nor her agreements by which she has bound herself shall stand; and the Lord will release her, because her father overruled (disagreed with) her. 6. "If indeed she takes a husband, while bound by her vows or by a rash utterance (declaration) from her lips by which she bound herself, 7. and her husband hears it, and makes no response to her on the day that he hears, then her vows shall stand, and her agreements by which she bound herself shall stand (remain valid). 8. But if her husband overrules (disagrees with) her on the day that he hears it, he shall make void her vow which she took and what she uttered (spoke) with her lips, by which she bound herself, and the Lord will release her. 9. "Additionally, any vow of a widow (woman whose husband has died) or a divorced woman, by which she has bound herself, shall stand against her. 10. "If she vowed (made a promise) in her husband's house, or bound herself by an agreement with an oath (solemn pledge), 11. and her husband heard it, and made no response to her and did not overrule her, then all her vows shall stand, and every agreement by which she bound herself shall stand

(remain valid). 12. But if her husband certainly made them void on the day he heard them, then whatever proceeded from her lips concerning her vows or regarding the agreement binding her, it shall not stand; her husband has made them void, and the Lord will release her. 13. Every vow and every binding oath (solemn pledge) to afflict (cause harm to) her soul, her husband may confirm it, or her husband may make it void. 14. Now if her husband makes no response whatever to her from day to day, then he confirms all her vows or all the agreements that bind her; he confirms them, because he made no response to her on the day that he heard them. 15. But if he does make them void after he has heard them, then he shall bear her guilt." 16. These are the statutes which the Lord commanded Moses, between a man and his wife, and between a father and his daughter in her youth in her father's house.

Chapter 31

1. The Lord spoke to Moses, saying, 2. "Take vengeance (punishment inflicted in return for wrongdoing) on the Midianites on behalf of the Israelites. After this, you will be gathered to your people (an expression meaning Moses would die and be joined with his ancestors)." 3. Moses spoke to the people, saying, "Arm yourselves for battle, and let them go against the Midianites to take vengeance for the Lord on Midian." 4. "Pick one thousand from each tribe (a social organization in Israel with common ancestry) of all the tribes of Israel to go to war." 5. So, one thousand from each tribe—twelve thousand armed for battle— were recruited (chosen and prepared). 6. Moses sent them to battle, one thousand from each tribe, with Phinehas, the son of Eleazar the priest, who carried the holy articles (sacred objects used in religious rituals) and the signal trumpets (horns used for giving instructions). 7. They fought against the Midianites, just as the Lord commanded Moses, and killed all the men. 8. They killed the kings of Midian—Evi, Rekem, Zur, Hur, and Reba—along with Balaam, the son of Beor, who was killed with a sword. 9. The Israelites took the women of Midian captive (taken as prisoners), along with their children, and took as spoil (loot or valuable items taken from enemies in warfare) all their livestock, all their flocks, and all their goods. 10. They burned with fire all the towns in which the Midianites lived and all their forts (small fortified homes). 11. They took all the spoil (loot) and all the booty (items taken in warfare)—both people and animals. 12. They brought the captives (those taken as prisoners), the booty, and the spoil to Moses, Eleazar the priest, and the congregation of Israel at their camp in the plains (flat land) of Moab, near the Jordan River, across from Jericho. 13. Moses, Eleazar the priest, and all the leaders (heads of the tribes) of the community went to meet them outside the camp (Israel's living area during their travels). 14. But Moses was angry with the officers (military leaders) of the army, the captains (commanders) over thousands and captains over hundreds, who had come from the war. 15. Moses said to them, "Why have you kept all the women alive? 16. These are the women who, on Balaam's advice (counsel), led the Israelites to be unfaithful to the Lord in the incident (event) at Peor, which caused a plague (severe disease or punishment) among the Lord's people. 17. So, kill all the boys and every woman who has been with a man. 18. But keep alive all the young girls who have not known a man intimately (been with a man in marriage) for yourselves. 19. Everyone who has killed or touched a dead body must stay outside the camp for seven days. Purify (cleanse according to religious law) yourselves and your captives on the third and seventh days. 20. Cleanse every garment (piece of clothing), every item made of leather, anything woven from goat's hair, and everything made of wood." 21. Eleazar the priest instructed the soldiers, "This is the rule (command) of the law which the Lord gave to Moses: 22. Only the gold, silver, bronze (a metal made from copper and tin), iron, tin, and lead, 23. which can withstand fire (remain unbroken by heat), should be purified through fire and afterward cleansed with water for

purification (spiritual cleansing). Objects that cannot withstand fire must be washed in water. **24.** On the seventh day, wash your garments, and then you may return to the camp." **25.** Then the Lord spoke to Moses, saying, **26.** "Count the plunder (items taken in battle), both people and animals, along with Eleazar the priest and the leader fathers (leaders of the tribes) of the community; **27.** Divide the plunder into two parts—one for the soldiers who fought in the war and one for the rest of the community. **28.** From the soldiers who fought, take a tribute (portion given as an offering) for the Lord, one out of every five hundred people, livestock, donkeys, and sheep. **29.** Take this portion from the soldiers' half and give it to Eleazar the priest as a heave offering (an offering raised up and dedicated to God). **30.** From the Israelites' half, take one out of every fifty people, livestock, donkeys, and sheep, from all the livestock, and give it to the Levites (tribal group who served in the temple). **31.** So Moses and Eleazar the priest followed the Lord's instructions. **32.** The spoil (valuable goods taken in war) from the plunder taken by the soldiers included 675,000 sheep, **33.** 72,000 cattle, **34.** 61,000 donkeys, **35.** and 32,000 young girls who had not been with a man. **36.** The soldiers' half totaled 337,500 sheep, **37.** and the Lord's tribute was 675 sheep. **38.** There were 36,000 cattle, and the Lord's tribute was 72. **39.** There were 30,500 donkeys, with 61 given as tribute to the Lord. **40.** There were 16,000 people, with 32 given as tribute to the Lord. **41.** Moses gave this tribute, which was the Lord's heave offering, to Eleazar the priest, as commanded. **42.** The other half, assigned to the community, included: **43.** 337,500 sheep, **44.** 36,000 cattle, **45.** 30,500 donkeys, **46.** and 16,000 people. **47.** From this portion, Moses took one out of every fifty of each people and animals and gave them to the Levites, as the Lord commanded. **48.** Then the army leaders, the captains of thousands and captains of hundreds, approached Moses; **49.** They said to him, "We have counted our soldiers, and not a single man is missing. **50.** So we are bringing an offering for the Lord, including the gold ornaments each man found—armlets, bracelets, earrings, rings, and necklaces—to make atonement (seeking forgiveness for sin) for ourselves before the Lord." **51.** Moses and Eleazar received the gold from them, all these ornaments. **52.** The total gold offered to the Lord by the military leaders was 16,750 shekels (a unit of weight). **53.** Every soldier had taken some spoil for himself. **54.** Moses and Eleazar took the gold from the leaders and brought it to the tabernacle (sacred tent for worship) as a memorial (remembrance) for the Israelites before the Lord.

Chapter 32

1. The descendants (children) of Reuben and Gad owned a large number of livestock (animals raised for farming). When they saw that the land of Jazer and Gilead was suitable (fit) for livestock, **2.** they approached Moses, Eleazar the priest (religious leader), and the leaders of the community (congregation, or gathered group of people), saying, **3.** "The regions (areas) of Ataroth, Dibon, Jazer, Nimrah, Heshbon, Elealeh, Shebam, Nebo, and Beon, **4.** the land that the Lord helped us conquer (defeat in battle), are suitable (ideal) for livestock, and we, your servants (people who follow and serve you), have livestock." **5.** They continued, "If we have found favor (approval or goodwill) with you, please allow this land to be given to us as our inheritance (permanent possession). Do not make us cross (travel across) the Jordan River." **6.** Moses responded to the descendants of Gad and Reuben, "Should your fellow Israelites (members of the same community) go to war while you stay here? **7.** Why would you discourage (lower the confidence of) the rest of the Israelites from entering (going into) the land the Lord has given them? **8.** This is what your ancestors (family members from past generations) did when I sent them from Kadesh Barnea to explore (examine) the land. **9.** They reached the Valley of Eshcol and saw the land, but they discouraged (caused to lose confidence) the Israelites from entering the land that the Lord had given them. **10.** The Lord

became angry that day and swore (made a solemn promise), **11.** saying, 'None of the men who left Egypt aged twenty and above will see the land I promised to Abraham, Isaac, and Jacob, because they did not completely (wholly) follow Me— **12.** except Caleb, son of Jephunneh the Kenizzite, and Joshua, son of Nun, for they followed (obeyed) the Lord completely.' **13.** So the Lord's anger was kindled (aroused or awakened) against Israel, and He made them wander (move aimlessly) in the wilderness for forty years until all those who had done wrong (evil) were gone. **14.** Now, you are rising in your ancestors' place, a new group of sinful (disobedient) people, to further increase the Lord's anger against Israel. **15.** If you turn away (refuse to follow) from Him, He will abandon (leave) them again in the wilderness, and you will bring harm (danger) to all these people." **16.** Then they came closer to Moses and said, "We will build enclosures (pens or sheepfolds) here for our livestock and cities (walled towns) for our families (little ones), **17.** but we ourselves will go ahead, fully armed (ready with weapons), before the other Israelites until we have brought them to their land; meanwhile, our children will stay safe in fortified (strongly protected) cities because of the inhabitants (people living there) in this land. **18.** We will not return to our homes until each of the Israelites has received their inheritance (land given to them). **19.** Since our inheritance is here on the east side of the Jordan, we will not inherit with them on the other side." **20.** Moses responded, "If you do this—if you go to war before the Lord, fully armed— **21.** and if all your men cross over (go across) the Jordan until the Lord has driven out (forced out) His enemies, **22.** and the land is subdued (brought under control or conquered) before the Lord, then you may return and be without guilt (blameless) before the Lord and Israel; and this land will be yours. **23.** But if you do not follow through (complete your promise), you will be sinning (acting against God) against the Lord, and your sin will find you out (catch up with you). **24.** Build cities (walled settlements) for your children and enclosures for your sheep, and do as you have promised (what you have said)." **25.** The descendants of Gad and Reuben replied to Moses, "We, your servants, will do as our lord (respected leader) commands. **26.** Our children, wives, and livestock will remain (stay) in the cities of Gilead, **27.** while we, your servants, will cross over, each man armed (equipped) for war, before the Lord, as our lord has said." **28.** Then Moses instructed (commanded) Eleazar the priest, Joshua, son of Nun, and the leaders of Israel's tribes concerning them. **29.** He said, "If the men of Gad and Reuben cross over the Jordan armed (prepared) with you and the land is subdued (taken over) before you, then you will give them the land of Gilead as their possession. **30.** But if they do not cross over armed, they will receive land among you in Canaan." **31.** The descendants of Gad and Reuben responded, "We will do as the Lord has commanded. **32.** We will cross over armed into Canaan, but our inheritance will remain with us on this side of the Jordan." **33.** So Moses gave to the descendants of Gad, Reuben, and half the tribe of Manasseh, son of Joseph, the kingdom of Sihon, king of the Amorites, and Og, king of Bashan—the land and its cities and surrounding territories. **34.** The descendants of Gad built the cities of Dibon, Ataroth, and Aroer, **35.** along with Atroth, Shophan, Jazer, and Jogbehah, **36.** Beth Nimrah, and Beth Haran, all fortified (well-defended) cities and enclosures (pens) for sheep. **37.** The descendants of Reuben built Heshbon, Elealeh, and Kirjathaim, **38.** Nebo and Baal Meon (with new names) and Shibmah; they renamed (gave new names to) the cities they built. **39.** The descendants of Machir, son of Manasseh, conquered (took over) Gilead and defeated (overpowered) the Amorites living there. **40.** So Moses gave Gilead to Machir, son of Manasseh, and he settled (established a home) there. **41.** Jair, son of Manasseh, captured some small towns and called them Havoth Jair. **42.** Nobah captured Kenath and its villages, naming it Nobah after himself.

Chapter 33

1. These are the journeys of the Israelites (children of Israel), who left the land of Egypt with their military divisions (armies), led by Moses and Aaron. 2. Moses recorded (wrote down) the starting points of their journeys as commanded (instructed) by the Lord. These are their journeys, based on where they began: 3. They left from Rameses in the first month, on the 15th day of the first month. On the day after the Passover (a Jewish holiday marking the Exodus), the Israelites left boldly (with confidence) in front of all the Egyptians. 4. The Egyptians were mourning (grieving) the death of their firstborn children, whom the Lord had killed among them. The Lord had also judged (punished) their gods (idols). 5. The Israelites then moved from Rameses and camped (set up camp) at Succoth. 6. They left Succoth and camped at Etham, which is on the edge (border) of the wilderness 7. From Etham, they turned back (changed direction) to Pi Hahiroth, which is east of Baal Zephon, and camped near Migdol. 8. They left Pi Hahiroth, passed through (traveled through) the sea into the desert, traveled for three days in the desert of Etham, and camped at Marah. 9. They moved from Marah and reached (arrived at) Elim, where there were twelve springs (small sources of water) and seventy palm trees; they camped there. 10. They moved from Elim and camped by the Red Sea. 11. They left the Red Sea and camped in the wilderness of Sin. 12. They journeyed (traveled) from the wilderness of Sin and camped at Dophkah. 13. They left Dophkah and camped at Alush. 14. They moved from Alush and camped at Rephidim, where there was no water for the people to drink. 15. They left Rephidim and camped in the wilderness of Sinai. 16. They moved from the wilderness of Sinai and camped at Kibroth Hattaavah. 17. They departed from Kibroth Hattaavah and camped at Hazeroth. 18. They left Hazeroth and camped at Rithmah. 19. They departed from Rithmah and camped at Rimmon Perez. 20. They left Rimmon Perez and camped at Libnah. 21. They moved from Libnah and camped at Rissah. 22. They journeyed from Rissah and camped at Kehelathah. 23. They went from Kehelathah and camped at Mount Shepher. 24. They moved from Mount Shepher and camped at Haradah. 25. They moved from Haradah and camped at Makheloth. 26. They moved from Makheloth and camped at Tahath. 27. They left Tahath and camped at Terah. 28. They moved from Terah and camped at Mithkah. 29. They went from Mithkah and camped at Hashmonah. 30. They departed from Hashmonah and camped at Moseroth. 31. They left Moseroth and camped at Bene Jaakan. 32. They moved from Bene Jaakan and camped at Hor Hagidgad. 33. They went from Hor Hagidgad and camped at Jotbathah. 34. They moved from Jotbathah and camped at Abronah. 35. They departed from Abronah and camped at Ezion Geber. 36. They moved from Ezion Geber and camped in the wilderness of Zin, that is Kadesh. 37. They moved from Kadesh and camped at Mount Hor, at the boundary (edge) of the land of Edom. 38. Then Aaron, the priest, went up to Mount Hor at the command (instruction) of the Lord, and died there in the 40th year after the Israelites had left Egypt, on the first day of the fifth month. 39. Aaron was 123 years old when he died on Mount Hor. 40. The king of Arad, the Canaanite (a member of the ancient people of Canaan), who lived in the south in the land of Canaan, heard about the arrival (coming) of the Israelites. 41. They left Mount Hor and camped at Zalmonah. 42. They departed from Zalmonah and camped at Punon. 43. They left Punon and camped at Oboth. 44. They left Oboth and camped at Ije Abarim, at the border (boundary) of Moab. 45. They departed from Ijim and camped at Dibon Gad. 46. They moved from Dibon Gad and camped at Almon Diblathaim. 47. They moved from Almon Diblathaim and camped in the mountains (hills) of Abarim, before Nebo. 48. They departed from the mountains of Abarim and camped in the plains (flat region) of Moab by the Jordan River, across from Jericho. 49. They camped by the Jordan River, from Beth Jesimoth to the Abel Acacia Grove in the plains of Moab. 50. The Lord spoke to Moses in the plains of Moab by the Jordan, across from Jericho, saying, 51. "Speak to the Israelites, and tell them: 'When you have crossed (gone over) the Jordan into the land of Canaan, 52. you shall drive out (remove by force) all the inhabitants (people living there) of the land, destroy all their idols (engraved stones), and demolish (tear down) all their altars (high places). 53. You shall take possession (occupy) of the land and live in it, for I have given it to you as your inheritance (something passed down to you). 54. You shall divide (distribute) the land by lot (random selection) as an inheritance among your families; the larger families will get a larger portion, and the smaller families will get a smaller portion; everyone will receive what is determined by the lot. This shall be according to the tribes (large family groups) of your ancestors. 55. But if you do not drive out the inhabitants, those who remain will be a constant irritation (annoyance) to you and will harass (trouble) you in the land where you live. 56. I will deal with you as I intended to deal with them.'"

Chapter 34

1. Then the Lord spoke to Moses, saying, 2. "Teach (to guide or direct) the Israelites, and tell them: 'When you enter the land of Canaan, this is the land that will be given to you as your inheritance (a gift passed down, often from ancestors)—the land of Canaan with its boundaries (limits). 3. Your southern border will begin at the desert (a vast, uninhabited region) of Zin, along the border of Edom; then it will stretch (expand) eastward to the end of the Salt Sea (a large body of water). 4. Your border will turn from the southern side of the Ascent (a steep upward path) of Akrabbim, continue to Zin, and be south of Kadesh Barnea; then it will go directly to Hazar Addar and continue to Azmon. 5. The border will turn from Azmon to the Brook (a small stream of water) of Egypt, and end at the sea. 6. 'As for the western border, you will have the Great Sea (the Mediterranean Sea) as your border; this shall be your western border. 7. 'And this will be your northern border: From the Great Sea, mark your border to Mount Hor (a mountain in the region). 8. From Mount Hor, mark your border to the entrance (the point where you enter) of Hamath; then the path of the border will be toward Zedad. 9. The border will continue (move forward) to Ziphron, and it will end at Hazar Enan. This will be your northern border. 10. 'For your eastern border, mark it from Hazar Enan to Shepham. 11. The border will go down from Shepham to Riblah (a place name) on the east side of Ain (a spring of water); it will go down and reach to the eastern side of the Sea of Chinnereth (a lake). 12. The border will go down along the Jordan River, and it will stop at the Salt Sea (Dead Sea). This will be your land with its surrounding boundaries.'" 13. Then Moses commanded (directed with authority) the Israelites, saying: "This is the land you will inherit by lot (a method of dividing land by random selection), which the Lord has commanded to give to the nine tribes and the half-tribe. 14. The tribe of the children of Reuben, according to the house (family) of their fathers, and the tribe of the children of Gad, according to the house of their fathers, have already received their inheritance; and the half-tribe of Manasseh has also received its inheritance. 15. The two tribes and the half-tribe have received their inheritance on this side (place) of the Jordan River, east of Jericho, toward the sunrise (eastward)." 16. And the Lord spoke to Moses, saying, 17. "These are the names of the men who will divide the land among you as an inheritance: Eleazar the priest (a religious leader) and Joshua the son of Nun. 18. And you shall choose (pick) one leader from each tribe to divide the land for the inheritance. 19. These are the names of the men: From the tribe of Judah, Caleb the son of Jephunneh; **20. from the tribe of Simeon, Shemuel the son of Ammihud; 21. from the tribe of Benjamin, Elidad the son of Chislon; 22. a leader from the tribe of Dan, Bukki the son of Jogli; 23. from the sons of Joseph: a leader from the tribe of Manasseh, Hanniel the son of Ephod, 24. and a leader from the tribe of Ephraim, Kemuel the son of Shiphtan; 25. a leader from the tribe of Zebulun, Elizaphan the son of Parnach; 26. a leader from the tribe of Issachar, Paltiel the son of Azzan; 27. a leader from the tribe of Asher, Ahihud the son of Shelomi; 28. and a leader from the tribe of Naphtali, Pedahel the son of Ammihud." 29. These are the men the Lord commanded to divide the inheritance among the Israelites in the land of Canaan.**

Chapter 35

1. And the Lord spoke to Moses on the plains of Moab (a region east of Israel), by the Jordan River, across from Jericho, saying: 2. "Instruct (teach or tell) the Israelites to give cities to the Levites (members of the priestly tribe of Israel) to live in, from the land they possess, and also provide them with open land around these cities. 3 They will have cities to live in, and the surrounding open land will be used for their livestock (animals raised for food or work), herds (groups of grazing animals),

and all their animals. **4** The open land around the cities you give to the Levites will extend 1,000 cubits (a cubit is an ancient unit of length, about 18 inches or 45 cm) from the wall of the city in all directions. **5** You will measure 2,000 cubits to the east, 2,000 cubits to the south, 2,000 cubits to the west, and 2,000 cubits to the north. The city will be in the middle of this area. This will be their open land. **6** Among the cities you give to the Levites, you will designate six cities of refuge (cities where people who kill accidentally can seek safety), where someone who accidentally kills another person can escape. Add forty-two more cities. **7** In total, you will give the Levites forty-eight cities, with their open land. **8** The cities you give will come from the land of Israel, with the larger tribes giving more cities and the smaller tribes giving fewer cities, in proportion (in a way that maintains a ratio) to the land each tribe has inherited (received as part of their heritage). **9** Then the Lord spoke to Moses, saying, **10** "Speak to the Israelites and tell them: 'When you cross the Jordan (a river separating Israel from Canaan) into the land of Canaan (the Promised Land), **11** you must set aside cities to serve as cities of refuge, where someone who kills another person by accident can flee. **12** These cities will protect the manslayer (a person who kills another by accident) from the avenger of blood (someone seeking to avenge a death), so the manslayer does not die before standing trial. **13** You will have six cities of refuge. **14** Three cities will be on this side of the Jordan, and three will be in Canaan, all serving as cities of refuge. **15** These six cities will be places of refuge for the Israelites, the foreigners (people from other nations), and the travelers among them, so that anyone who kills another person by accident can flee there. **16** But if someone kills another with an iron tool (a tool made of iron), causing death, it is considered murder, and the murderer (someone who kills intentionally) must be put to death. **17** If someone kills another with a stone they can hold in their hand, and the victim dies, it is also murder, and the murderer must be put to death. **18** Or if someone kills with a wooden weapon, such as a club (a heavy stick used for hitting), and the victim dies, it is murder, and the murderer must be put to death. **19** The avenger of blood will put the murderer to death when they find him. **20** If someone kills another out of hatred (strong dislike) or premeditated (planned ahead of time) violence, **21** or strikes someone with their hand in anger, resulting in death, the person who killed will surely be put to death. The avenger of blood will carry out the death sentence (official judgment). **22** But if someone kills by accident, without hatred or planning, **23** or throws something at someone without intending to harm, **24** or uses a stone to strike someone without seeing them, and the victim dies, while the killer had no intention of harm, **25** the congregation (group of people) will judge between the manslayer and the avenger of blood according to these rules. **26** The congregation will protect the manslayer from the avenger of blood, returning him to the city of refuge where he fled, and he will stay there until the high priest (the leader of the priests) dies. **27** If the manslayer leaves the city of refuge and the avenger of blood finds him outside the city, and kills him, the avenger will not be guilty of murder, **28** because the manslayer should have stayed in the city of refuge until the high priest's death. After the high priest dies, the manslayer can return to their own land. **29** These rules will be laws for you throughout your generations (descendants). **30** Anyone who kills another person must be executed (killed by law) based on the testimony (witness statements) of witnesses. One witness is not enough to convict someone of murder. **31** You must not accept a ransom (payment) for the life of a murderer who is guilty of death; the murderer must be put to death. **32** You must not accept a ransom for someone who has fled to a city of refuge, allowing them to return home before the high priest's death. **33** Do not defile (pollute or make impure) the land you live in, for bloodshed (killing) pollutes the land, and there is no way to cleanse (purify) the land except by the blood of the person who shed it. **34** Therefore, do not defile the land where you live, for I dwell (live) among the Israelites."

Chapter 36

1. Now the leader fathers (leaders, heads of households) of the families of the children of Gilead, the son of Machir, the son of Manasseh, of the families of the sons of Joseph, came near and spoke before Moses and before the leaders, the chief fathers of the children of Israel. **2.** And they said: "The Lord commanded my lord Moses to give the land as an inheritance (property passed down from ancestors) by lot to the children of Israel, and my lord was commanded by the Lord to give the inheritance of our brother Zelophehad to his daughters. **3.** Now if they are married to any of the sons of the other tribes of the children of Israel, then their inheritance would be taken from the inheritance of our fathers, and it would be added to the inheritance of the tribe into which they marry; so it would be taken from the lot of our inheritance. **4.** And when the Jubilee (special year of release, every fiftieth year) of the children of Israel comes, then their inheritance will be added to the inheritance of the tribe into which they marry; so their inheritance will be taken away from the inheritance of the tribe of our fathers." **5.** Then Moses commanded the children of Israel according to the word of the Lord, saying: "What the tribe of the sons of Joseph speaks is right. **6.** "This is what the Lord commands regarding the daughters of Zelophehad, saying, 'Let them marry whom they think best, but they shall marry only within the family (extended group) of their father's tribe.' **7.** So the inheritance of the children of Israel shall not change hands from tribe to tribe, for each one of the children of Israel shall keep the inheritance of the tribe of his fathers. **8.** And each daughter who possesses an inheritance in any tribe of the children of Israel will be the wife of one of the family of her father's tribe, so that the children of Israel each may possess the inheritance of his fathers. **9.** Therefore, no inheritance shall change hands from one tribe to another, but each tribe of the children of Israel shall keep its own inheritance." **10.** Just as the Lord commanded Moses, so did the daughters of Zelophehad; **11.** For Mahlah, Tirzah, Hoglah, Milcah, and Noah, the daughters of Zelophehad, were married to the sons of their father's brothers. **12.** They were married into the families of the children of Manasseh the son of Joseph, and their inheritance remained within the tribe of their father's family. **13.** These are the commandments and the judgments which the Lord commanded the children of Israel by the hand of Moses in the plains of Moab by the Jordan, across from Jericho.

5 – Deuteronomy

Chapter 1

These are the words Moses spoke to all of Israel, on the eastern side of the Jordan River, in the nature, in the plains contrary Suph (a desert region), between Paran (a desert area), Tophel, Laban, Hazeroth, and Dizahab (places in the nature). **2.** It was an eleven-day trip from Horeb (also called Mount Sinai, where Moses entered the Ten Commandments) by way of Mount Seir (a mountain range) to Kadesh Barnea (a border city near Canaan). **3.** In the fortieth time, on the first day of the eleventh month, Moses began speaking to the Israelites, participating everything the Lord had commanded him to educate. **4.** This was after Moses had defeated Sihon (king of the Amorites, a people group) who lived in Heshbon (a megacity), and Og (king of Bashan) who abided in Ashtaroth and Edrei (metropolises in northern Bashan). **5.** On the plains of Moab (a home east of Israel), Moses began explaining the law to the people, saying **6.** "The Lord our God spoke to us at Horeb (Mount Sinai), saying 'You have stayed then long enough. **7.** Turn and head for the mountains of the Amorites (Semitic-speaking people), and all the neighboring regions the plains, mountains, lowlands, the south, and the coast. Go to the land of the Canaanites and Lebanon, all the way to the Euphrates River. **8.** Look, I've set this land before you. Go and take possession of it, as the Lord swore to give to your ancestors — Abraham, Isaac, and Jacob and to their descendants after them." **9.** "At that time, I told you, 'I cannot carry all of you alone. **10.** The Lord your God has made you as multitudinous as the stars in the sky. May He bless you a thousand times further, just as He promised to do! **11.** But how can I handle all your problems, burdens, and complaints by myself? **12.** Choose wise, understanding, and educated men from among your lines, and I'll appoint them as leaders over you.' **13.** You agreed with me, saying, 'What you have proposed is good.' **14.** So I took the wise and educated men from each lineage and appointed them as leaders over thousands, hundreds, fifties, knockouts, and officers for your lines. **15.** Also I gave instructions to your judges at that time 'Hear the cases between your people and judge fairly between a man and his family, or between an Israelite and a outsider living among you. **16.** Do not show favoritism when judging; hear to both the small and the great. Do not sweat anyone, for judgment belongs to God. However, bring it to me, and I'll hear it, If a case is too delicate for you.' 17. I also gave you instructions on everything differently you were to do." 18. "So we set out from Horeb and traveled through the great and intimidating nature that you saw on the way to the mountains of the Amorites, as the Lord our God had commanded us. We arrived at Kadesh Barnea. 19. I said to you, 'You have come to the mountains of the Amorites, which the Lord our God is giving us. 20. Look, the Lord has set the land before you. Go up and take possession of it, as the Lord, the God of your ancestors, commanded you. Do not sweat or be discouraged.' 21. Also you came to me and said, 'Let us shoot men ahead to explore the land and bring back a report about the way we should go and the metropolises we will encounter.' 22. This idea sounded good to me, so I chose twelve men, one from each lineage. 23. They went up into the mountains and came to the Valley of Eshcol (a rich vale near Hebron), where they explored the land. 24. They brought back some of the land's fruit and said, 'It's a good land which the Lord our God is giving us.' 25. But you refused to go up. You mutinied against the Lord's command. 26. You lumbered in your canopies, saying, 'The Lord hates us, so He brought us out of Egypt to hand us over to the Amorites to destroy us. 27. Where can we go? Our sisters have discouraged us, saying, "The people are stronger and high than we are; the metropolises are large and fortified to the sky; we also saw the descendants of the titans (Anakim) there."' 28. I said to you, 'Do not be hysterical or alarmed of them. 29. The Lord your God, who goes before you, will fight for you, as He did in Egypt before your eyes. 30. And in the nature, you saw how the Lord your God carried you, as a father carries his son, all the way until you arrived then.' 31. Yet, despite all this, you did not trust the Lord your God, 32. Who went ahead of you on your trip to find you a place to camp, guiding you by a fire at night and a pall by day. 33. When the Lord heard your complaints, He came angry and swore an pledge 34. 'None of these men of this wicked generation shall see the good land I swore to give your ancestors. 35. Except Caleb, son of Jephunneh, he'll see it, and to him and his descendants I'll give the land he walked on, because he followed the Lord wholeheartedly.' 36. The Lord was also angry with me because of you, saying, 'Indeed you won't enter the land. 37. But Joshua, son of Nun, who stands before you, will lead Israel into the land. Encourage him, for he'll beget Israel to inherit it. 38. Your children, whom you said would be taken as internees, who moments have no knowledge of good or evil, will enter the land. I'll give it to them, and they will retain it. 39. Also, your little ones and your children, whom you said would be taken as captures (seizures), who moment have no knowledge of good or evil, will go by. To them I will give it, and they will retain it. 40. But as for you, turn back and head into the nature (uncultivated region), along the road to the Red Sea.' 41. Also you answered and said to me, 'We have transgressed against the Lord; we will go over and fight, just as the Lord our God commanded us.' And when everyone had armed themselves for battle, you were ready to go up into the mountains. 42. But the Lord said to me, 'Tell them, "Do not go up and fight, for I am not with you. You will be defeated by your adversaries."' 43. So I spoke to you, but you would not hear. You revolted against the Lord's command and went up into the mountains. 44. Also the Amorites who lived in the hills came out against you. They chased you like sundries, driving you back from Seir (a mountainous region) to Hormah (a place in southern Judah). 45. You returned and wept before the Lord, but the Lord would not hear to your voice or pay attention to you. 46. So you stayed in Kadesh (a place near the southern border of Israel) for multitudinous days, as long as you had stayed there ahead.

Chapter 2

1. "also we turned and traveled into the nature along the Way of the Red Sea, as the Lord had commanded me, and we traveled around Mount Seir (a mountain region southeast of Israel) for numerous days." 2. "And the Lord spoke to me, saying" 3. "'You have circled this mountain long enough (sufficient); now turn northward.'" 4. "And command the people, saying, 'You're about to pass through the home of your cousins, the descendants of Esau (Esau was the family of Jacob, from whom the nation of Israel descended), who live in Seir; they will be hysterical of you. So be veritably careful." 5. "Do not engage with them, for I'll not give you any of their land, not indeed a step of it, because I've given Mount Seir to Esau as a possession (power)." 6. "You may buy food from them with plutocrat, so that you can eat; and you may also buy water from them with plutocrat, so that you can drink." 7. "For the Lord your God has blessed you in all the work of your hands. He knows your wandering through this great nature (uncultivated region). These forty times the Lord your God has been with you, and you have demanded nothing.'" 8. "So when we passed beyond our cousins, the descendants of Esau, who live in Seir, we left the road of the plain, passing by Elath (a megacity near the Red Sea) and Ezion Geber (a harborage megacity near the Gulf of Aqaba), and we turned and traveled into the Nature of Moab (a region east of Israel)." 9. "also the Lord said to me, 'Don't kill Moab, nor engage them in battle, for I'll not give you any of their land as a possession, because I've given Ar (a megacity) to the descendants of Lot (the whoreson of Abraham) as a possession.'" 10. "(The Emim, a people as great, multitudinous, and altitudinous as the Anakim, formerly dwelt there.)" 11. "They were also regarded as titans, like the Anakim (descendants of Anak), but the Moabites called them Emim." 12. "The Horites (The Horites were a branch of the Hivites) formerly lived in Seir, but the descendants of Esau drove them out and destroyed them before them, and settled in their place, just as Israel did to the land of their possession which the Lord gave them." 13. "'Now rise, and cross over the Valley of the Zered (a vale east of Israel).' So we crossed over the Valley of the Zered." 14. "The time it took us to travel from Kadesh Barnea until we crossed over the Valley of the Zered was thirty-eight times, until the entire generation of men of war had passed down from the camp, just as the Lord had sworn to them." 15. "For indeed the hand of the LORD was against them, to destroy them from the midst of the camp until they were each gone." 16. "So when all the men of war had failed among the people," 17. "the Lord spoke to me, saying" 18. "'This day you're to cross over at Ar (a megacity on the border of Moab), the boundary of Moab." 19. "And when you come near the people of Ammon (the descendants of Lot's son), do not kill them or engage them in battle, for I'll not give you any of the land of the people of Ammon as a possession, because I've given it to the descendants of Lot as a possession.'" 20. "(That was also regarded as a land of titans; titans formerly lived there. But the Ammonites called them Zamzummim.)" 21. "A people as great, multitudinous, and altitudinous as the Anakim, but the Lord destroyed them before the Ammonites, and they ousted them and dwelt in their place," 22. "just as He'd done for the descendants of Esau, who dwell in Seir, when He destroyed the Horites before them, and they ousted them and dwelt in their place, indeed to this day." 23. "And the Avim(group of people who lived in Hazerim), who dwelt in townlets as far as Gaza(a littoral megacity in Israel) — the Caphtorim(people who came from the islet of Crete), who came from Caphtor, destroyed them and dwelt in their place." 24. "'Rise, take your trip, and cross over the River Arnon (a swash that marks the border of Moab). Look, I've given into your hand Sihon the Amorite (king of Heshbon, a megacity in the home of the Amorites), and his land. Begin to retain it, and engage him in battle.'" 25. "'This day I'll begin to put the dread and fear of you upon the nations under the whole heaven, who shall hear the report of you, and shall fluctuate and be in anguish because of you.'" 26. "So I transferred couriers from the Nature of Kedemoth(a nature region near Moab) to Sihon, king of Heshbon, with words of peace, saying," 27. "'Let me pass through your land; I'll stay on the main road and not turn away to the right or to the left wing." 28. "You shall vend me food for plutocrat, so that I may eat, and give me water for plutocrat, so that I may drink; only let me pass through on bottom," 29. "just as the descendants of Esau who dwell in Seir and the Moabites who dwell in Ar did for me, until I cross the Jordan to the land which the Lord our God is giving us.'" 30. "But Sihon, king of Heshbon, would not let us pass through, for the Lord your God hardened his spirit (made his heart stubborn) and made his heart obstinate (stubborn), so that He might deliver him into your hand, as it's this day." 31. "And the Lord said to me, 'See, I've begun to give Sihon(Amorite king) and his land over to you. Begin to retain it, so that you may inherit his land.'" 32. "also Sihon and all his people came out to fight against us at Jahaz(a place in the home of the Amorites)." 33. "And the Lord our God delivered him over to us; so we defeated (triumph over) him, his sons, and all his people." 34. "We took all his metropolises at that time, and we hugely destroyed the men, women, and children of every megacity; we left none remaining." 35. "We took only the beast as plunder for ourselves, and the loot (goods taken in

war) of the metropolises which we took." **36.** "From Aroer (a megacity on the swash Arnon), which is on the bank of the River Arnon, and from the megacity that's in the notch, as far as Gilead (a region east of Israel), there was not one megacity too strong for us; the Lord our God delivered all to us." **37.** "Only you did not go near the land of the people of Ammon — anywhere along the River Jabbok (a swash in the home of Ammon), or to the metropolises of the mountains, or wherever the Lord our God had interdicted us."

Chapter 3

1. "Also we turned and traveled along the road toward Bashan (a region in ancient Israel); and Og (the king of Bashan) came out to fight against us, he and all his people, at the megacity of Edrei (a fortified megacity in Bashan)." **2.** "But the Lord told me, 'Don't be hysterical of him, for I've formerly handed him over to you, along with his people and his land. You'll master him just as you did Sihon (the king of the Amorites), who lived in Heshbon (a megacity in ancient Israel).'" **3.** "So the Lord our God gave us palm over Og, the king of Bashan, and all his people, and we fought them until not a single survivor remained." **4.** "We captured all his metropolises at that time; there wasn't a single megacity that we didn't take from them — sixty metropolises in total, all part of the region of Argob, which was under Og's area in Bashan." **5.** "All these metropolises were fortified with high walls, gates, and bars, besides numerous other lower municipalities scattered in the country." **6.** "We fully destroyed them, just as we had done to Sihon, the king of Heshbon. We wiped out all the men, women, and children from every megacity." **7.** "still, we took all the beast and the pillages of the metropolises as plunder (wealth taken from defeated adversaries) for ourselves." **8.** "At that time, we took the land from the two lords of the Amorites, from the River Arnon (a swash in Israel) to Mount Hermon (a mountain range)." **9.** "(The Sidonians (people from Sidon) call Hermon 'Sirion,' and the Amorites (a group of ancient people) call it 'Senir')." **10.** "We took all the metropolises of the plain, all of Gilead (a mountainous region), and all of Bashan, as far as Salcah (a megacity in Bashan) and Edrei, which were metropolises in the area of Og." **11.** "Og, king of Bashan, was the last of the titans (a race of ancient, important beings). In fact, his bed was made of iron. Isn't it still in Rabbah (a megacity of the Ammonites)? It measured nine cubits in length and four cubits in range (a cubit is about 18 elevation)." **12.** "We took possession of this land at that time from Aroer (a megacity by the River Arnon), the middle of the swash, and half of the mountains of Gilead with its metropolises. I gave this to the lines of Reuben (a lineage of Israel) and Gad (another lineage of Israel)." **13.** "The rest of Gilead and all of Bashan, including the area of Og, I gave to half of the lineage of Manasseh (another lineage of Israel). The whole region of Argob, with all of Bashan, came known as the land of the titans." **14.** "Jair (the son of Manasseh) took all of Argob, as far as the border of the Geshurites (people of Geshur) and Maachathites (a group living in the region), and he named it Havoth Jair (Jair's municipalities), and that name remains to this day." **15.** "I also gave Gilead to Machir (another leader of the lineage of Manasseh)." **16.** "To the Reubenites (the descendants of Reuben) and the Gadites (the descendants of Gad), I gave land from Gilead, as far as the River Arnon (the middle of the swash), extending to the River Jabbok (a swash that forms the border with Ammon), which borders the Ammonites." **17.** "The plain (flat land) also, with the Jordan River (the swash that runs through Israel) as its border, stretching from the Sea of Chinnereth (the Sea of Galilee) to the east side of the Salt Sea (the Dead Sea), below the pitches of Pisgah (a mountain in Moab)." **18.** "also, at that time, I gave you this command 'The Lord your God has given you this land to retain. All you men of courage (those who are strong in battle) shall cross over armed before your fellow Israelites.'" **19.** "But your women, your children, and your beast shall stay in the metropolises I've given you." **20.** "This is until the Lord has given rest to your sisters, as He has done to you, and they also take possession of the land the Lord your God is giving them on the other side of the Jordan. also, you can return to your land and take possession of the land I've given you." **21.** "At that time, I also commanded Joshua (the leader of Israel) saying, 'You have seen with your own eyes all that the Lord your God has done to these two lords (Sihon and Og). The same will be to all the fiefdoms you'll encounter.'" **22.** "You mustn't be hysterical of them, for the Lord your God Himself will fight for you." **23.** "At that time, I contended with the Lord, saying,"

24. "'O Lord God, You have begun to show Your menial Your greatness and Your potent hand. What god in heaven or on earth is there who can perform deeds as great as Yours?'" **25.** "I supplicate, let me cross over and see the good land beyond the Jordan, the beautiful mountains, and Lebanon (the mountain range known for its majesty)." **26.** "But the Lord came angry with me because of you, and would not hear to me. The Lord said to me, 'That's enough! Don't speak to Me any further about this matter.'" **27.** "'Go up to the top of Pisgah (a mountain peak), and look west, north, south, and east. Look at the land with your eyes, but you won't cross over the Jordan.'" **28.** "'still, command Joshua, and encourage him and strengthen him, for he'll lead the people across, and he'll give them the heritage of the land that you'll see.'" **29.** "So we stayed in the vale opposite Beth Peor (a place near the Jordan River)."

Chapter 4

1." Now hear, O Israel, to the laws bills and rules (judgments) that I'm tutoring you to follow, so that **1.** "You may live, enter, and take possession of the land which the Lord your God is giving to you." **2.** "Don't add to the words I command you, nor take anything down from it, but follow the commandments (laws) of the Lord your God that I'm commanding you." **3.** "You have seen what the Lord did at Baal Peor (a place where hero deification took place); He destroyed all the men who followed Baal of Peor (a false god), but you who remained pious to the Lord are alive moment." **4.** "But you who were faithful to the Lord your God are alive moment, every one of you." **5.** "I've tutored you the laws (bills) and rules (judgments) that the Lord my God commanded me, so that you may live by them when you enter the land that you're about to retain." **6.** "thus, be careful to observe them, for this is your wisdom and understanding in the eyes of the nations, who'll hear all these laws and say, 'Surely, this great nation is wise and understanding.'" **7.** "For what great nation has a god so near to it as the Lord our God is to us, whenever we call upon Him?" **8.** "And what great nation has similar righteous laws (bills) and judgments (fair opinions) as the laws that I'm giving you moment?" **9.** "Be careful and watch yourselves, lest you forget the effects your eyes have seen and let them fade from your heart all your life; educate them to your children and grandchildren." **10.** "Especially flash back the day you stood before the Lord your God at Horeb (a mountain), when the Lord said to me, 'Gather the people to me, and I'll let them hear my words, that they may learn to venerate (fear) Me as long as they live on the earth, and educate them to their children.'" **11.** "also you came near and stood at the bottom of the mountain, and the mountain burned with fire to the veritably sky, girdled by thick darkness and shadows." **12.** "The Lord spoke to you from the fire, and though you heard His voice, you saw no form — only a voice." **13.** "He declared to you His covenant (agreement), which He commanded you to follow, the Ten Commandments; and He wrote them on two tablets of gravestone." **14.** "The Lord also commanded me to educate you the laws (bills) and rules (judgments), that you may follow them in the land you're about to retain." **15.** "Be veritably careful, for you saw no form when the Lord spoke to you from the fire at Horeb (a mountain)." **16.** "Don't act corruptly (immorally) by making for yourselves a sculpted image, in the form of any figure, the likeness of a man or woman." **17.** "Or the likeness of any beast on the earth, or of any raspberry that flies in the sky." **18.** "Or the likeness of anything that crawls on the ground, or of any fish in the water beneath the earth." **19.** "And take care, lest you lift your eyes to the sky, and when you see the sun, the moon, and the stars, all the heavenly bodies, you're drawn to worship and serve them, which the Lord your God has given to all the nations under heaven as an heritage." **20.** "But the Lord has taken you and brought you out of the iron furnace (a furnace used for refining), out of Egypt, to be His people, His heritage, as you're this day." **21.** "The Lord was angry with me because of you, and He swore that I would not cross the Jordan (a swash) or enter the good land that the Lord your God is giving you as an heritage." **22.** "I must die in this land, I'll not cross over the Jordan, but you'll cross over and retain the good land." **23.** "Be careful not to forget the covenant (pledge) of the Lord your God which He made with you, and don't make for yourselves a sculpted image or hero of anything that the Lord your God has interdicted." **24.** "For the Lord your God is a consuming fire (a fire that devours), a jealous God." **25.** "When you have children and grandchildren, and have lived long in the land, and act corruptly by making sculpted images and doing wrong in the sight of the Lord your God, provoking Him to wrathfulness." 26. "I call heaven and earth to substantiation against you this day, that you'll soon be destroyed from the land you're about to enter and retain; you won't live long in it, but will be hugely destroyed." 27. "The Lord will scatter you among the nations, and you'll be many in number among the nations where the Lord will drive you." 28. "There you'll serve gods made by mortal hands, wood and gravestone, which cannot see, hear, eat, or smell." 29. "But from there you'll seek the Lord your God, and if you search for Him with all your heart and soul, you'll find Him." 30. "When you're in torture (trouble) and all these effects come upon you in the unborn days, if you return to the Lord your God and observe His voice." 31. "For the Lord your God is merciful; He'll not leave you or destroy you, or forget the covenant He made with your ancestors, which He swore to them." 32. "Ask about the days long once, from the time God created man on the earth, and from one end of the welkin to the other, has anything so great ever happed, or has anything like it been heard?" 33. "Did any people ever hear the voice of God speaking out of the fire, as you have heard, and live?" 34. "Or has God ever tried to take a nation for Himself from another nation, by trials (tests), signs, cautions, war, a potent hand, and great demons, as the Lord your God did for you in Egypt before your eyes?" 35. "You were shown these goods so that you might know that the Lord Himself is God; there is no other." 36. "From heaven He made you hear His voice to instruct you; on earth He showed you His great fire, and you heard His words from the fire." 37. "And because He loved your ancestors, He chose their descendants after them, and brought you out of Egypt with His presence, with His potent power." 38. "He drove out before you nations lower and stronger than you, to bring you in, and give you their land as an heritage, as it's this day." 39. "therefore, know this day and take it to heart, that the Lord Himself is God in heaven over and on the earth below; there is no other." 40. "Keep His laws (bills) and commandments (commands) which I command you moment, so that it may go well with you and your children after you, and that you may live long in the land which the Lord your God is giving you." 41. "also Moses set incremental (designated) three cosmopolises on the east side of the Jordan, towards the rising of the sun." 42. "These cosmopolises were for the killer (someone who kills unintentionally) to flee to, if he killed someone by accident and hadn't despised him previously, so that by fleeing to one of these cosmopolises, he could live." 43. "Bezer (a municipality in the nature) for the Reubenites (a lineage), Ramoth (a municipality in Gilead) for the Gadites (a lineage), and Golan (a municipality in Bashan) for the Manassites (a lineage)." 44. "This is the law that Moses set before the people of Israel." 45. "These are the testaments (validation of verity), bills (rules), and judgments (opinions) which Moses spoke to the people of Israel after they came out of Egypt." 46. "On the side of the Jordan (a sluice), in the dale near Beth Peor (a place near the Jordan River), in the land of Sihon (king of the Amorites), who lived in Heshbon (a municipality), whom Moses and the Israelites defeated after they came out of Egypt." 47. "And they took possession of his land, and the land of Og (king of Bashan), two lords of the Amorites, who lived on the east side of the Jordan." 48. "From Aroer (a municipality by the River Arnon), on the bank of the Arnon River, to Mount Sion (also called Mount Hermon)." 49. "And all the plain east of the Jordan, as far as the ocean of the Plain, under the springs of Pisgah (a hill or mountain)."

Chapter 5

1. Moses gathered all of Israel and said, "Hear, Israel, to the laws (bills) and rules (judgments) I speak to you moment that you may understand them and take care to follow them. 2. The Lord our God established a covenant (agreement) with us at Horeb (mountain, also called Sinai). 3. The Lord didn't make this covenant with our ancestors, but with us, the living then moment. 4. The Lord spoke to you face to face from the fire on the mountain (Horeb). 5. At that time, I stood between you and the Lord to declare the communication of the Lord, because you were hysterical of the fire and didn't go up the mountain. He said 6. "I'm the Lord your God who brought you out of Egypt (the land of slavery), from the house of thrall (slavery)." 7. "You shall not have any gods before Me." 8. "You shall not make a sculpted image (hero) or any likeness (representation) of anything in the welkin over, on the earth below, or in the waters beneath the earth." 9. "You shall not bow down to them or serve them, for I, the Lord your God, am a jealous God, visiting the iniquity (sin) of the fathers upon the children to the third and fourth generations of those who detest Me, 10. But showing mercy to thousands of those who love Me and keep My commandments." 11. "You shall not misuse the name of the Lord your God, for the Lord won't leave anyone unpunished who misuses His name." 12. "Flash back the Sabbath day (rest day), to keep it holy (set piecemeal), as the Lord your God has commanded you." 13. "Six days you shall labor and do all your work, 14. But the seventh day is a Sabbath to the Lord your God. On it, you shall not do any work neither you, nor your son, nor your son, nor your manly menial, nor your womanish menial, nor your ox, nor your jackass, nor any of your beast, nor the outsider (foreigner) within your gates, so that your retainers may rest as you do." 15. "Flash back that you were formerly slaves in Egypt, and the Lord your God brought you out of there with a potent hand and an outstretched arm (important help); thus, the Lord your God has commanded you to keep the Sabbath day." 16. "Honor (respect) your father and mama, as the Lord your God has commanded you, so that your days may be dragged, and that it may go well with you in the land the Lord your God is giving you." 17. "You shall not murder." 18. "You shall not commit infidelity." 19. "You shall not steal." 20. "You shall not bear false substantiation (taradiddle) against your neighbor." 21. "You shall not covet your neighbor's woman; and you shall not ask (want) your neighbor's house, his field, his manly menial, his womanish menial, his ox, his jackass, or anything that belongs to your neighbor." 22. "These words the Lord spoke to your whole assembly from the mountain, out of the fire, the pall, and the thick darkness (bank), with a loud voice; He added no more. He wrote them on two tablets of gravestone and gave them to me." 23. "When you heard the voice from the midst of the darkness (pall), while the mountain was burning with fire, all the leaders of your lines and your elders came near to me." 24. "You said, 'The Lord our God has shown us His glory (majesty) and greatness, and we've heard His voice from the fire; we've seen moment that God speaks with man, and yet we live.'" 25. "Now, why should we die? This great fire will consume us. If we hear the voice of the Lord our God any longer, we will surely die." 26. "For who's there among all of humanity (meat) who has heard the voice of the living God speaking from the fire, as we have, and lived?" 27. "You go near and hear all that the Lord our God says, and tell us what the Lord our God says to you, and we will hear and observe."

Chapter 6

1. "These are the commandments (laws) and rulings (rules) that the Lord your God has commanded me to educate you, so that you may follow them in the land you are about to enter and retain. 2. This is so that you may sweat (reverence) the Lord your God, keeping all His commands and His laws, you, your children, and your grandchildren, all the days of your life, so that your days may be dragged (made longer). 3. Hear, O Israel, and be careful to observe them, so that it may go well with you, and that you may multiply greatly, as the Lord, the God of your ancestors, has promised you — a land flowing with milk and honey (a rich, prosperous land). 4. Hear, O Israel The Lord our God, the Lord is one (the only true God)! 5. You shall love (watch deeply for) the Lord your God with all your heart (inner being), with all your soul (life), and with all your strength (energy). 6. These commandments that I give you moment shall be in your heart (mind). 7. You shall educate them diligently (precisely) to your children, and shall talk about them when you sit in your house, when you walk along the road, when you lie down, and when you get up. 8. You shall tie them as symbols on your hands, and they shall be as monuments (frontlets) between your eyes (on your forehead). 9. You shall write them on the doorframes (entrance posts) of your houses and on your gates. 10. When the Lord your God brings you into the land He wore (promised) to your ancestors — Abraham, Isaac, and Jacob and gives you large and prosperous cosmopolises which you didn't make, 11. and houses full of good goods which you didn't give, hewn-out wells (dug-out wells) which you didn't dig, and stations and olive trees which you didn't plant — when you have eaten and are satisfied, 12. Also be careful not to forget the Lord, who brought you out of the land of Egypt (a country), out of the house of thrall (slavery). 13. You shall sweat (glorify) the Lord your God, serve Him, and take pledges (pledges) in His name. 14. You shall not follow (go latterly) other gods, the gods of

the peoples around you, **15.** For the Lord your God is a jealous God (He desires exclusive devotion), and His outrage will burn against you, and He will destroy you from the face of the earth. **16.** You shall not put the Lord your God to the test (tempt Him), as you did at Massah (a place where the Israelites tested God). **17.** You shall precisely keep the commandments of the Lord your God, His testaments (vouchers), and His bills (laws) which He has commanded you. **18.** You shall do what is right and good (moral) in the sight of the Lord, that it may go well with you, and that you may enter and retain the good land which the Lord swore (promised) to your ancestors, **19.** To drive out all your adversaries before you, as the Lord has spoken. **20.** When your son asks you in time to come, saying, 'What is the meaning of the testaments, the bills, and the judgments (opinions) which the Lord our God has commanded you?' **21.** Also, you shall say to your son, 'We were slaves in Egypt (a country), and the Lord brought us out of Egypt with a potent hand. **22.** And the Lord showed signs and cautions before our eyes, great and terrible, against Egypt, Pharaoh (the king of Egypt), and all his ménage (family). **23.** He brought us out from there to bring us in, to give us the land He promised to our ancestors. **24.** And the Lord commanded us to observe all these laws, to sweat the Lord our God, for our good always, that He might save us alive, as it's this day. **25.** And it will be righteousness (right standing with God) for us, if we are careful to observe all these commandments before the Lord our God, as He has commanded us."

Chapter 7

1. "When the Lord your God brings you into the land you are about to enter and retain, and has driven out multitudinous nations before you — the Hittites (a Canaanite people), the Girgashites, the Amorites, the Canaanites, the Perizzites, the Hivites, and the Jebusites — seven nations lower and puissant than you, **2.** and when the Lord your God gives them into your hands, you must destroy them completely. You mustn't make any agreements (covenants) with them, nor show mercy to them. **3.** Don't intermarry with them. Don't give your son to their son, or take their son for your son. **4.** For they will lead your children down from following Me and beget them to serve other gods. Also, the outrage of the Lord will burn against you, and He will destroy you suddenly. **5.** Rather, you must destroy their stages, smash their sacred monuments, cut down their Asherah poles (rustic icons), and burn their icons with fire. **6.** For you are a holy people to the Lord your God; the Lord has chosen you to be His own people, a special treasure over all the peoples on the face of the earth. **7.** The Lord didn't set His love on you or choose you because you were more numerous than other people — because you were the smallest of all nations. **8.** But because the Lord loved you, and because He kept the pledge He swore to your ancestors, He brought you out with a potent hand, and redeemed (saved) you from the house of thrall (slavery) in Egypt, from the power of Pharaoh, king of Egypt. **9.** Know therefore that the Lord your God is God, the faithful God, who keeps His covenant and His loving-kindness (mercy) to a thousand generations with those who love Him and keep His commandments. **10.** But He repays to their face those who hate Him, by destroying them. He will not be slow to repay to their face those who hate Him. **11.** Therefore, you shall keep the commandments, the bills, and the judgments I command you moment, to observe them. **12.** Still, the Lord your God will keep the covenant of love He promised to your ancestors, If you pay attention to these laws and follow them. **13.** He will love you, bless you, and increase your numbers. He will bless the fruit of your womb (children) and the fruit of your land your grain, your wine, and your oil painting painting the increase of your cattle and the immature of your flocks, in the land He promised to give your ancestors. **14.** You will be blessed further than all the peoples; there will be no barren man or woman among you, nor among your beast. **15.** The Lord will keep you free from every complaint. He will not induce upon you the terrible conditions you knew in Egypt, but He will bring them upon all who hate you. **16.** You must destroy all the nations the Lord your God gives you. Don't show pit (mercy) to them, and don't worship their gods, for that will be a trap (snare) to you. **17.** Still, 'These nations are lower than I; how can I drive them out?' **18.** If you say in your heart. Don't be hysterical of them; flash back well what the Lord your God did to Pharaoh and to all of Egypt **19.** the great trials your eyes saw, the signs and cautions, the potent hand and outstretched arm by which the Lord your God

brought you out. The same will He do to all the people you are hysterical of. **20.** The Lord your God will shoot the hornet (a type of nonentity, also used as a conceit for destruction) against them until those who are left, and those who hide themselves from you, are destroyed. **21.** Don't be alarmed of them, for the Lord your God, the great and miraculous God, is among you. **22.** The Lord your God will drive out those nations before you little by little. You won't be suitable to destroy them all at once, lest the wild brutes (beasts) come too numerous for you. **23.** But the Lord your God will deliver them over to you, throwing them into confusion until they are destroyed. **24.** He will give their lords into your hands, and you will wipe out their name from under heaven. No one will be suitable to stand against you until you have destroyed them. **25.** You must burn the sculpted images of their gods with fire; don't covet (desire) the tableware or gold on them, and don't take it for yourselves, for you will be entangled (trapped) by it. It's an abomination (commodity despised) to the Lord your God. **26.** Don't bring an abomination into your house, or you will be destroyed just like it. Monstrously detest and execrate (hate) it, for it's accursed (devoted to destruction)."

Chapter 8

1. Every commandment (instruction) which I command you today, you must be careful to observe so that you may live and multiply and go in and possess the land of which the LORD swore to your fathers (ancestors). **2.** And you shall remember that the Lord your God led you all the way these forty years in the wilderness, to humble (lower) you and test (examine) you, to know what was in your heart, whether you would keep His commandments (rules) or not. **3.** So He humbled (lowered) you, allowed you to hunger, and fed you with manna (a miraculous food), which you did not know nor did your fathers (ancestors) know, that He might make you know that man shall not live by bread alone; but man lives by every word that proceeds from the mouth of the LORD. **4.** Your garments (clothing) did not wear out on you, nor did your foot swell (become large or painful) these forty years. **5.** You should know in your heart that as a man chastens (corrects) his son, so the Lord your God chastens (corrects) you. **6.** Therefore you shall keep the commandments (rules) of the Lord your God, to walk in His ways and to fear (respect) Him. **7.** For the Lord your God is bringing you into a good land, a land of brooks (streams) of water, of fountains (springs) and springs (sources of water), that flow out of valleys and hills. **8.** A land of wheat (a type of grain) and barley (another type of grain), of vines (grape plants) and fig trees (fruit trees) and pomegranates (fruit), a land of olive oil and honey. **9.** A land in which you will eat bread without scarcity (lack), in which you will lack nothing; a land whose stones are iron and out of whose hills you can dig copper (a type of metal). **10.** When you have eaten and are full (satisfied), then you shall bless (thank) the Lord your God for the good land which He has given you. **11.** Beware (be cautious) that you do not forget the Lord your God by not keeping His commandments, His judgments (decisions), and His statutes (laws) which I command you today. **12.** Lest—when you have eaten and are full (satisfied), and have built beautiful houses and dwell (live) in them, **13.** And when your herds (groups of livestock) and your flocks (groups of sheep) multiply, and your silver and your gold are multiplied (increased), and all that you have is multiplied (increased), **14.** Then your heart (inner self) may become proud, and you may forget the Lord your God who brought you out of the land of Egypt (the country where the Israelites were enslaved), from the house of bondage (slavery). **15.** Who led you through that great and terrible wilderness, in which were fiery serpents (poisonous snakes) and scorpions (poisonous insects), and thirsty land where there was no water; who brought water for you out of the flinty rock (rock that is hard like stone); **16.** Who fed you in the wilderness with manna (miraculous food), which your fathers (ancestors) did not know, that He might humble you and test (examine) you, to do you good (bless you) in the end. **17.** Then you say in your heart (inner self), "My power and the might of my hand have gained me this wealth (riches)." **18.** And you shall remember the Lord your God, for it is He who gives you power to get wealth (riches), that He may establish (fulfill) His covenant (agreement) which He swore (promised) to your fathers (ancestors), as it is this day. **19.** Then it shall be, if you by any means forget the Lord your God, and follow other gods (false gods), and serve them and worship them, I testify (declare) against you this day that you shall surely perish (die or be destroyed). **20.** As the nations (peoples) which the Lord destroys before you, so you shall perish (die or be destroyed), because you would not be obedient (listen and follow) to the voice (commands) of the Lord your God.

Chapter 9

1. Hear, O Israel! Today you're crossing the Jordan River (the swash separating Israel from the Promised Land) to take possession of nations stronger and puissant than you, with metropolises that are great and fortified to the welkin. **2.** These nations are altitudinous and strong, descendants of the Anakim (titans), whom you know and have heard of, saying, "Who can stand against the Anakim?" **3.** Know moment that the LORD your God goes before you like a consuming fire (a fire that destroys fully). He'll destroy them and bring them down, and you'll snappily drive them out, as the Lord has promised. **4.** Do not suppose that it's because of your righteousness that the Lord has brought you in to retain this land, but because of the wickedness of these nations that He's driving them out before you. **5.** It is not because of your righteousness or the uprightness of your heart that you're taking their land, but because the Lord is fulfilling His pledge to Abraham (the primogenitor), Isaac (son of Abraham), and Jacob (son of Isaac). **6.** Know this, the Lord your God is not giving you this good land because you're righteous; you're a stiff-necked (stubborn) people. **7.** Flash back how you provoked the Lord your God to incense in the nature (the desert). From the day you left Egypt until now, you have been rebellious against the Lord. **8.** Indeed at Horeb (mountain where God gave the law), you provoked the Lord so much that He was ready to destroy you. **9.** When I went up to the mountain to admit the tablets of gravestone (tablets with God's commandments), the covenant (agreement) which the Lord made with you, I stayed there forty days and nights, without eating or drinking. **10.** The Lord gave me two tablets of gravestone, written with His own hand, containing all the words He spoke to you on the mountain from the fire during the assembly. **11.** After forty days and nights, the Lord gave me the two tablets of the covenant. **12.** The Lord said to me, "Go down snappily, for your people have corrupted themselves; they've made a golden shin (hero)." **13.** The Lord said to me, "I've seen this people, and they're stubborn (stiff-necked). **14.** Leave Me alone so that I may destroy them and abolish their name from under heaven. I'll make a lesser and puissant nation from you." **15.** I turned and came down from the mountain, and the mountain burned with fire; the two tablets of covenant were in my hands. **16.** When I saw you had trespassed by making the golden shin and snappily turned away from the way the Lord commanded, I threw the tablets from my hands and broke them before your eyes. **17.** Also I took the shin you made, burned it, base it into greasepaint, and scattered the dust into the sluice (water channel) that flowed down from the mountain. **18.** You provoked the Lord to incense at Taberah (a place in the nature), Massah (a place of testing), and Kibroth Hattaavah (a place of pining). **19.** When the Lord transferred you from Kadesh Barnea (a place near the border of Canaan), saying, "Go and take possession of the land I've given you," you mutinied, refusing to trust or observe His voice. **20.** You have been rebellious against the Lord from the day I knew you. **21.** I fell down before the Lord and supplicated for forty days and nights because the Lord said He'd destroy you. **22.** I supplicated, "O Lord, do not destroy Your people, Your heritage, whom You redeemed (saved) by Your great power, whom You brought out of Egypt with a potent hand." **23.** Flash back Your retainers, Abraham, Isaac, and Jacob, and do not look at the intransigence, wickedness, or sin of this people. **24.** Else, the nations will say, "The Lord could not bring them to the land He promised, and He abominated them, so He brought them out to die in the nature (desert)." **25.** Yet they're Your people, Your heritage, whom You brought out by Your great power and potent hand. **26.** Thus I supplicated to the Lord, and said, "O Lord God, do not destroy Your people and Your heritage (chosen people) whom You have redeemed (saved) through Your greatness, whom You have brought out of Egypt with a potent hand. **27.** Flash back Your retainers (faithful bones), Abraham, Isaac, and Jacob; do not look on the intransigence (hardness) of this people, or on their wickedness (wrong) or their sin. **28.** Lest the land from which You brought us should say, "Because the Lord was not suitable to bring them to the land which He promised them, and because He abominated them, He has brought them out to kill them in the nature **29.** Yet they're Your people and Your heritage, whom You brought out by Your potent power and by Your outstretched arm.'

Chapter 10

1. At that time the Lord said to me, "Hew (cut) for yourself two tablets of gravestone like the first, and come up to Me on the mountain, and make yourself an ark (casket) of wood. **2.** And I'll write on the tablets the words that were on the first tablets, which you broke; and you shall put them in the ark." **3.** So I made an ark of acacia wood (a type of tree), hewed two tablets of gravestone like the first, and went up the mountain, having the two tablets in my hand. **4.** And He wrote on the tablets according to the first jotting, the Ten Commandments (laws), which the Lord had spoken to you on the mountain from the midst of the fire (dears) in the day of the assembly (gathering); and the Lord gave them to me. **5.** Also I turned and came down from the mountain, and put the tablets in the ark which I had made; and there they are, just as the Lord commanded me. **6.** (Now the children of Israel traveled from the wells of Bene Jaakan (a place in the nature) to Moserah, where Aaron (Moses' family) failed, and where he was buried; and Eleazar (Aaron's son) his son administered as clerk in his vantage. **7.** From there they traveled to Gudgodah (a position), and from Gudgodah to Jotbathah (a place), a land of gutters of water (numerous aqueducts). **8.** At that time the Lord separated (set piecemeal) the lineage of Levi (a lineage of Israel) to bear (carry) the ark of the covenant (sacred casket) of the Lord, to stand before the Lord to minister to Him and to bless in His name, to this day. **9.** Thus Levi has no portion (heritage) nor heritage with his lines (other lines); the Lord is his heritage, just as the Lord your God promised him.) **10.** As at the first time, I stayed in the mountain forty days and forty nights; the Lord also heard me at that time, and the Lord chose not to destroy you. **11.** Also the Lord said to me, "Arise, begin your trip before the people, that they may go by and retain (take control of) the land which I swore (promised) to their fathers to give them." **12.** And now, Israel, what does the Lord your God bear of you, but to sweat (venerate) the Lord your God, to walk in all His ways and to love Him, to serve the Lord your God with all your heart and with all your soul, **13.** And to keep the commandments of the Lord and His bills (laws) which I command you moment for your good? **14.** Indeed heaven and the loftiest welkin belong to the Lord your God, also the earth with all that's in it. **15.** The Lord delighted only in your fathers (ancestors), to love them; and He chose their descendants (seed) after them, you over all peoples, as it's this day. **16.** Thus circumcise (cut down) the foreskin of your heart (inner being), and be stiff-necked (stubborn) no longer. **17.** For the Lord your God is God of gods and Lord of lords, the great God, potent (important) and stupendous (fearsome), who shows no partiality (favoritism) nor takes a fix. **18.** He administers (delivers) justice for the nameless (orphans) and the widow, and loves the foreigner (nonnatives), giving him food and apparel. **19.** Thus love the foreigner (outsider), for you were nonnatives (nonnatives) in the land of Egypt (a country). **20.** You shall sweat (respect) the Lord your God; you shall serve Him, and to Him you shall hold presto, and take pledges (promises) in His name. **21.** He's your praise (honor), and He's your God, who has done for you these great and stupendous effects which your eyes have seen. **22.** Your fathers went down to Egypt with seventy persons (family members), and now the Lord your God has made you as the stars of heaven in multitude (number).

Chapter 11

1. Therefore, love the Lord your God and diligently follow His responsibilities (commands), His laws (instructions), His decisions (judgments), and His commandments (directives) at all times. **2.** Understand today that I am not speaking to your children, who have not seen or experienced the discipline (correction) of the Lord your God, His greatness, His mighty hand, and His outstretched arm. **3.** Remember the signs (miracles) and mighty acts He performed in Egypt (a country in northeastern Africa), against Pharaoh (the king of Egypt), and all of Egypt's land. **4.** Recall how He defeated the Egyptian army, their horses, and chariots, by making the Red Sea (a body of water between Egypt and Arabia) drown them as they pursued you, and how He destroyed them permanently. **5.** Think about how He provided for you in the wilderness until you reached this place, showing His faithfulness all along the way. **6.** Remember how the earth opened to swallow Dathan and Abiram (two men who rebelled against Moses), the sons of Eliab (a descendant of Reuben), along with their families and possessions, as a punishment for their defiance in front of all Israel. **7.** You have seen with your own eyes every great act the Lord has done. **8.** Therefore, obey all the commands I give you today, so that you may grow strong and enter the land you are crossing over to possess. **9.** By obeying these commands, you will live long in the land that the Lord promised to give to your ancestors, a land flowing with milk and honey. **10.** The land you are about to enter is not like the land of Egypt (where you came from), where you sowed your seeds and watered them with foot pumps, like a vegetable garden. **11.** But the land you are about to possess is a land of hills and valleys, watered by the rain from heaven. **12.** It is a land that the Lord your God cares for, and His eyes are always on it, from the beginning of the year to the end. **13.** If you earnestly obey My commands today—to love the Lord your God and serve Him with all your heart and soul—then I will provide rain for your land at the proper times: both the early rain (the first rain) and the latter rain (the final rain), so you may gather in your crops, new wine, and oil. **14.** I will also send grass in your fields for your livestock, so you will have food and be satisfied. **15.** Be cautious not to let your hearts be deceived, and turn away to serve other gods and worship them. **16.** If you do, the Lord's anger will burn against you, and He will stop the rain from falling, causing the land to yield no crops. You will quickly perish from the good land the Lord is giving you. **17.** Therefore, take these words to heart, store them in your soul, and bind them as a sign on your hands and between your eyes, as a reminder to obey them. **18.** Teach these commands to your children, speaking of them when you are at home, when you walk along the road, when you lie down, and when you get up. **19.** Write them on the doorposts (door frames) of your house and on your gates. **20.** This will ensure that both your days and your children's days in the land the Lord has promised will be long, as abundant as the days of the heavens above the earth. **21.** If you carefully obey all these commandments—to love the Lord your God, walk in all His ways, and cling to Him—then the Lord will drive out all the nations before you, and you will possess lands greater and mightier than yourselves. **22.** Every place where your feet tread will be yours: from the wilderness and Lebanon (a mountain range), to the Euphrates River (a major river in the Middle East), and even to the Mediterranean Sea (a sea to the west). This will be your territory. **23.** No one will be able to stand against you; the Lord will put fear of you upon all the land where you go, just as He has promised you. **24.** Behold, I am setting before you today a blessing (reward) and a curse (punishment). **25.** The blessing will come if you obey the commands of the Lord your God that I give you today. **26.** The curse will come if you do not obey the commands of the Lord your God, but turn aside from the way I am commanding you today to follow after other gods you have not known. **27.** When the Lord your God brings you into the land you are about to possess, you will proclaim the blessings from Mount Gerizim (a mountain in Israel) and the curses from Mount Ebal (a mountain in Israel). **28.** These mountains are located on the other side of the Jordan River (a river that flows through Israel), toward the west, in the land of the Canaanites (the native inhabitants of Canaan), near the terebinth trees of Moreh. **29.** When you cross over the Jordan River and enter the land the Lord is giving you, you will possess it and live in it. **30.** Be careful to obey all the statutes (laws) and decisions (judgments) I set before you today. **31.** For you will cross the Jordan (river) and go in to possess the land which the Lord your God is giving you, and you will take possession of it and live in it. **32.** And you shall be careful to observe all the statutes (laws) and judgments (decisions) which I set before you today.

Chapter 12

1. These are the laws and regulations you must diligently follow in the land that the Lord God of your ancestors is giving you to retain, as long as you live on the earth. **2.** You must fully destroy all the places where the nations you're displacing worshiped their gods on the high mountains, on the hills, and under every green tree. **3.** You must destroy their stages, break their sacred pillars (gravestone columns used in hero deification), and burn their rustic images with fire. Cut down the sculpted images of their gods and abolish their names from that place. **4.** Do not worship the Lord your God in the same manner as they worshiped their gods. **5.** Rather, seek the place where the Lord your God chooses from among all your lines to place His name for His lodging. There you must go. **6.** There, you shall bring your burnt immolations, offerings, tithes (a tenth of your crops), immolations lifted up (the first portion of your crop), pledged immolations, volunteer immolations, and the firstborn of your herds and flocks. **7.** Before the Lord your God, you'll eat and rejoice in all the blessings that He has given you and your family, as a result of your work. **8.** Do not act as we're doing then moment — every man doing what seems right in his own eyes — **9.** For you have not yet arrived at the rest and heritage that the Lord your God is giving you. **10.** But when you cross over the Jordan and settle in the land that the Lord your God is giving you, and He gives you rest from all your adversaries around you, so that you may live in safety, **11.** There will be the place where the Lord your God chooses to make His name dwell. There, you'll bring all that I command you your burnt immolations, offerings, tithes, immolations lifted up, and all the stylish immolations that you covenant to the Lord. **12.** You'll rejoice before the Lord your God, along with your sons and daughters, your manly and womanish retainers, and the Levite (a priestly lineage) within your gates, who has no portion or heritage with you. **13.** Be careful not to offer your burnt immolations in any place you see; **14.** But offer them only in the place that the Lord chooses, in one of your lines. There you'll offer your burnt immolations and do everything I command you. **15.** Still, you may butcher and eat meat in any of your municipalities, as much as your heart solicitations, according to the blessing the Lord your God has given you. Both clean and sick people may eat it, whether it's the gazelle (a type of antelope) or the deer. **16.** But you must not eat the blood; pour it out on the ground like water. **17.** You may not eat within your municipalities the tithe (tenth) of your grain, new wine, oil painting, the firstborn of your herd or flock, or any of your pledged immolations, volunteer immolations, or the immolations lifted up by your hand. **18.** These must be eaten before the Lord your God in the place He chooses you, your son, and son, your manly and womanish retainers, and the Levite in your municipalities. Rejoice before the Lord your God in all that you put your hands to. **19.** Be careful not to neglect the Levite (a member of the clerkly lineage) as long as you live in your land. **20.** When the Lord your God enlarges your borders, as He promised you, and you say," I want to eat meat," because you ask it, you may eat as important as your heart solicitations. **21.** Still, also you may butcher from your herd and flock which the Lord has given you, as I've commanded you, If the place the Lord your God chooses to place His name is too far from you. **22.** Just as you eat the gazelle or deer, so you may eat it; both the clean and sick may eat of it. **23.** But you must be careful not to eat the blood, for the blood is the life; you must not eat the life with the meat. **24.** Pour it on the ground like water. **25.** Do not eat it, so that it may go well with you and your children after you when you do what's right in the sight of the Lord. **26.** Only the holy affects you have, and your pledged immolations, must be taken to the place the Lord chooses. **27.** There, you'll offer your burnt immolations — both meat and blood — on the balcony of the Lord your God. The blood of your offerings shall be poured out on the balcony, and you'll eat the meat. **28.** Be sure to observe and observe all these commands so that effects go well with you and your children after you ever when you do what's good and right in the sight of the Lord your God. **29.** When the Lord your God cuts off the nations before you, and you displace them and settle in their land, **30.** Be careful not to be entangled (trapped) by them once they've been destroyed before you, and do not interrogate about their gods, saying," How did these nations serve their gods? I'll do the same." **31.** You must not worship the Lord your God in that way, for every despicable thing that the Lord hates, they've done to their gods; they indeed burn their sons and daughters in the fire to their gods. **32.** Whatever I command you, be careful to follow; do not add to it or take down from it.

Chapter 13

1. Still, and he performs a sign or a wonder (a miraculous event), "If a prophet or a utopian of dreams arises among you. **2.** and the sign or wonder comes to pass, just as he said it would, and he says, 'Let us follow other gods,' whom you have not known, and 'Let us serve them,' **3.** You must not listen to the words of that prophet or utopian of dreams. The Lord your God is testing you to see whether you love the Lord your God with all your heart and with all your soul. **4.** You must follow the Lord your God, serve Him, keep His commandments, listen to His voice, serve Him, and hold fast to Him. **5.** But that prophet or utopian of dreams shall be put to death because he has spoken with the intent to turn you away from the Lord your God, who brought you out of the land of Egypt (the land of slavery) and redeemed you from the house of thrall (freed you from oppression), to lead you to follow other gods. You must remove the wrong from your midst. **6.** Still, the son of your mother, or your son or daughter, **7.** Of the gods of the nations that are around you, near or far from you, from one end of the earth to the other, **8.** You must not yield to him or listen to him. Do not feel sorry for him or hide him. **9.** Rather, you must put him to death. Your hand shall be the first to strike him, and also all the people shall join in. **10.** You shall stone him with stones until he dies because he has tried to lead you away from the Lord your God, who brought you out of the land of Egypt, from the house of slavery. **11.** Also, all Israel will hear about it, and they will be fearful and will not again do such wickedness as this among you. **12.** Still, which the Lord your God is giving you to live in, that some wicked men (wrongdoers) have gone out from among you and seduced the inhabitants of their city, **13.** If you hear in one of your cities, **14.** you must inquire, investigate, and ask carefully. If it's true and certain that such a despicable thing has been done among you, **15.** you must utterly destroy the city. You must strike its inhabitants with the sword, destroying everything in it, including its animals. **16.** You shall gather all its plunder (pillages) into the middle of the street and burn the entire city, along with all its plunder, as a whole burnt offering to the Lord your God. It will remain a ruin forever and will never be rebuilt. **17.** Nothing from the accursed (devoted) things shall remain in your hands, so that the Lord may turn from His fierce wrath and show you mercy, have compassion on you, and increase your numbers, just as He swore to your ancestors, **18.** Because you have listened to the voice of the Lord your God and have kept all His commandments, doing what is right in His eyes. **19.** You must do what is right in the eyes of the Lord your God, and this will result in His blessings upon you and your descendants.

Chapter 14

1. "You are children of the Lord your God. Do not harm yourselves by marking your bodies or by shaving the front of your heads as a ritual (a ceremonial act) for the dead." **2.** "You are a people set apart (distinct, different from others), holy to the Lord your God. He has chosen you to be His treasured possession, above all the nations on the earth." **3.** "Do not consume anything that is impure (unclean or not allowed) or forbidden by God's law." **4.** "These are the animals you are permitted (allowed) to eat: the ox, the sheep, the goat," **5.** "the deer, the gazelle (a type of antelope), the roe deer, the wild goat, the mountain goat, the antelope, and the mountain sheep." **6.** "You may eat any animal that has split hooves and chews the cud (brings up and chews food again)." **7.** "However, there are certain animals you must avoid, even if they chew the cud or have split hooves: the camel, the hare, and the rock hyrax (a small mammal found in rocky areas). These animals chew the cud but lack split hooves and are considered unclean (impure) for you." **8.** "The pig is also unclean for you because it has split hooves but does not chew the cud. Do not eat its meat or touch its carcass (the dead body of an animal)." **9.** "Among the creatures of the sea, you may eat those that have fins and scales (small, flat plates covering the body)." **10.** "But any creature that lacks fins and scales must not be eaten. They are unclean for you." **11.** "You may eat any bird that is clean (acceptable according to God's law)." **12.** "However, avoid the following birds: the eagle, the vulture, the buzzard," **13.** "the red kite, the falcon, the kite (a type of bird of prey), each according to its species (kind);" **14.** "every raven (a large black bird) according to its species;" **15.** "the ostrich, the short-eared owl, the seagull, and the hawk, each according to its kind;" **16.** "the little owl, the screech owl (known for its shrill call), the white owl," **17.** "the jackdaw (a type of crow), the carrion vulture (feeds on dead animals), the fisher owl (hunts fish)," **18.** "the stork, the heron (a long-legged bird), the hoopoe (a bird with a crown of feathers), and the bat (a flying mammal)." **19.** "All flying insects that crawl on the ground are unclean (forbidden) and must not be eaten." **20.** "However, you are permitted to eat all clean birds." **21.** "Do not eat anything that has died of natural causes (not slaughtered properly); you may give it to a foreigner (a non-Israelite) living in your town, and he may eat it, or you may sell it to a foreigner. For you are a holy (set apart for God) people to the Lord your God. Do not cook a young goat in its mother's milk." **22.** "Set aside one-tenth (a portion of one-tenth) of all the produce from your fields every year." **23.** "You must eat the tithe (one-tenth portion) of your grain, wine, and oil, as well as the firstborn of your herds and flocks, in the place where the Lord your God chooses for His name to dwell (live). This will teach you to always honor (respect deeply) the Lord your God." **24.** "If the distance is too far for you to carry your tithe, or if the place the Lord has chosen is too distant, and the Lord has blessed you," **25.** "then exchange it for money, take the money with you, and go to the place the Lord your God has chosen." **26.** "With that money, buy whatever you desire (want): oxen, sheep, wine, or other beverages, or whatever your heart desires. Spend it there before the Lord your God and rejoice (celebrate with joy) with your family." **27.** "Do not neglect (fail to care for) the Levite who lives in your towns, for he has no inheritance (land or property) among you." **28.** "At the end of every third year, bring the tithe (one-tenth portion) of your produce from that year and store it in your towns." **29.** "The Levite, since he has no inheritance among you, as well as the foreigner (a non-Israelite), the orphan (a child without parents), and the widow (a woman whose husband has died) in your towns, may come and eat and be satisfied, so that the Lord your God may bless you in all the work of your hands."

Chapter 15

1. "Every seventh year, forgive all outstanding debts." **2.** "This is how the forgiveness should work: anyone who has loaned money or goods must release the debt and not demand repayment from fellow Israelites, as it is the year designated (appointed) by the Lord to cancel debts." **3.** "You may request repayment from foreigners, but debts owed by fellow Israelites must be forgiven." **4.** "There should be no one in need among you, for the Lord your God will richly bless (abundantly provide) you in the land He is giving you to possess." **5.** "This will be true only if you listen closely to the commands of the Lord your God and obey them faithfully, as I am instructing (guiding) you today." **6.** "The Lord your God will bless you as He promised. You will lend to many nations, but you will not need to borrow. You will have dominion (control) over many nations, but they will not rule over you." **7.** "If there is a poor person among you in any of the towns the Lord your God is giving you, do not be hardhearted (uncompassionate) or tightfisted toward your fellow Israelite in need." **8.** "Instead, be generous and open-handed (benevolent), providing for whatever they lack." **9.** "Do not let selfishness arise in your heart, thinking, 'The year of debt release is near,' and then refuse to help your fellow Israelite. If he cries out to the Lord because of your refusal, it will be counted as sin (wrongdoing) against you." **10.** "Give freely and without regret, for the Lord your God will bless you in all your work and in everything you do." **11.** "There will always be poor people in your land, so I command you to open your hand to your brother, to the poor and needy (lacking) among you." **12.** "If an Israelite, whether man or woman, is sold into service (slavery) to you and works for you for six years, you must release them in the seventh year." **13.** "When you set them free, do not send them away empty-handed (without provision)." **14.** "Generously provide for them from your flock, your grain, and your winepress (area where grapes are pressed), giving from the abundance the Lord your God has blessed you with." **15.** "Remember that you were once slaves in Egypt, and the Lord your God redeemed (rescued) you. That is why I am commanding you to do this." **16.** "However, if the servant says to you, 'I do not want to leave because I love you and your household, and I am content (happy) with my situation,'" **17.** "Then take an awl (sharp tool) and pierce their ear to the door, and they will remain your servant for life. Do the same for your female servant." **18.** "Do not hesitate (delay) to release them after six years of service, because they have worked for you as if they were hired laborers. The Lord your God will bless you in all that you do." **19.** "You must consecrate (set apart) the firstborn male of your herds and flocks to the Lord your God. Do not use the firstborn ox for plowing, and do not shear the wool of the firstborn sheep." **20.** "You and your family must eat these animals in the place the Lord your God will choose, once a year, before Him." **21.** "But if any of these animals have defects, such as being blind, lame, or having another serious flaw (imperfection), you must not offer them as a sacrifice to the Lord your God." **22.** "You may eat them in your own town, whether you are ceremonially clean (ritually pure) or unclean, just as you would eat a gazelle or a deer." 23. "However, you must not eat the blood; pour it out on the ground like water."

Chapter 16

1. "Remember the month of Abib (Nisan, the first month of the Hebrew calendar), and observe the Passover in honor of the Lord your God. For in that month, the Lord brought you out of Egypt by night." 2. "Therefore, you are to offer the Passover sacrifice to the Lord your God, using animals from the flock (sheep or goats) or the herd (cattle, large domesticated animals), at the location the Lord chooses to place His name." 3. "Do not eat leavened bread (bread with yeast or fermenting agents) during this time. Instead, for seven days you shall eat unleavened bread, also called the bread of affliction (suffering), which symbolizes the hardship you endured when you hurriedly left Egypt. This will serve as a reminder for you of the day you departed Egypt for the rest of your life." 4. "For seven days, there must be no leaven (yeast or fermenting agent) anywhere in your land, and none of the meat sacrificed on the first evening should remain until morning." 5. "You must not sacrifice the Passover within any of your towns (cities or communities) that the Lord your God has given you." 6. "Rather, you are to offer the Passover sacrifice at the place the Lord your God chooses to establish His name (His presence), and you shall do so at twilight (the time between sunset and darkness), exactly at the time of day when you left Egypt." 7. "Roast and eat the lamb in the location the Lord your God chooses, and in the morning, return to your tents (temporary shelters or dwellings)." 8. "For six days, you shall eat unleavened bread, and on the seventh day, you are to hold a sacred assembly (a holy gathering) in honor of the Lord your God. On this day, no work shall be done." 9. "You are to count seven weeks from the day you begin to reap the harvest with your sickle (a curved cutting tool used in harvest)." 10. "Then celebrate the Feast of Weeks (Shavuot, the Feast of Harvest), an offering to the Lord your God, bringing a voluntary offering (a gift given freely) from what you have, as the Lord your God blesses you." 11. "Rejoice before the Lord your God—both you and your family, your servants, the Levite (the priestly tribe of Israel) in your town, the foreigner (stranger or outsider), the orphan, and the widow—at the place where the Lord your God chooses to place His name." 12. "Remember that you were once slaves (bondservants, people forced into labor) in Egypt, and be diligent in observing all these commandments." 13. "You are to observe the Feast of Tabernacles (Sukkot, a festival of temporary shelters) for seven days after you have gathered in your harvest of grain and wine." 14. "Celebrate this feast with joy, together with your family, your servants, the Levite (priests), the foreigner (outsider), the orphan, and the widow living in your towns." 15. "For seven days, you shall celebrate this feast to the Lord your God at the place He chooses, and the Lord your God will bless you in all your harvest and in every work you do, so that you may rejoice." 16. "Three times a year, all the men of Israel must present themselves before the Lord your God at the place He chooses: during the Feast of Unleavened Bread (Passover), the Feast of Weeks (Shavuot, or Pentecost), and the Feast of Tabernacles (Sukkot). They must not appear before the Lord empty-handed." 17. "Each man should bring an offering as he is able, according to the blessings the Lord your God has given him." 18. "You shall appoint judges (officials or decision-makers) and officers (assistants to the judges) in every town that the Lord your God gives you, according to your tribes, and they shall judge the people with fairness." 19. "Do not pervert justice (misjudge, or twist the law), show favoritism (partiality, giving unfair advantages), or accept a bribe (a payment given to influence decisions), for a bribe blinds the eyes of the wise and distorts the words of the righteous." 20. "You must pursue justice (fairness) and righteousness in all things so that you may live and inherit the land the Lord your God is giving you." 21. "Do not plant any kind of tree as an idol (a carved or shaped figure worshipped as a god) near the altar you build to the Lord your God." 22. "Do not erect any sacred pillar (idol or monument) which the Lord your God despises (detests or hates)."

Chapter 17

1. You mustn't offer a bull or lamb to the Lord your God if it has any mark or fault, because that would be despicable (abominate) to the Lord your God. 2. still, which the Lord your God has given you, and they've violated His covenant by committing sins, If you find a man or woman who has done spitefully within any of your municipalities. 3. And if they've gone and served other gods, worshiping the sun, moon, or any of the stars of the welkin (which I didn't command), 4. and it's reported to you, you must probe the matter thoroughly However, 5, If you find it's indeed true and certain that such an abomination has been committed in Israel. You must bring that person, whether man or woman, to your gates, and sharpen them to death. 6. A person meritorious of death must be executed grounded on the evidence of two or three substantiations. You cannot put someone to death grounded on the evidence of only one substantiation. 7. The substantiations should be the first to throw monuments at the indicted to put them to death, and after that, the rest of the people must join in. In this way, you'll purify wrong from among you. 8. still, similar as a disagreement involving bloodshed, differences in judgment, If a case arises that's too delicate for you to judge. 9. You must consult with the preachers (Levites) and the judge who's serving at the time, and they will give you their decision regarding the matter. 10. You must follow the decision they gasp in that place which the Lord chooses, and be careful to do everything they instruct you. 11. You must act according to the law they educate you and the judgment they gasp. Don't diverge from their instructions, either to the right or to the left wing. 12. Anyone who's presumptuous and refuses to observe the clerk whose mother before the Lord your God, or the judge, must die. In this way, you'll remove the wrong from Israel. 13. also all the people will hear and be hysterical , and no bone will act presumptuously again. 14. When you enter the land the Lord your God is giving you and you take possession of it and live in it, and say, " Let us set a king over us, like all the nations around us," 15. You must appoint a king over you whom the Lord your God will choose. He must be one of your own fellow Israelites, not a outsider who isn't a member of your people. 16. The king mustn't acquire numerous nags for himself, nor beget the people to return to Egypt to gain nags, because the Lord has told you," You shall no way return that way again." 17. The king mustn't take numerous women for himself, or his heart may be led amiss. He mustn't accumulate great quantities of tableware and gold for himself. 18. When he sits on the throne, he must write a dupe of this law for himself, in the presence of the preachers, the Levites. 19. It must be with him, and he must read it all his life, so that he may learn to sweat the Lord his God, and be careful to follow all the words of this law and these bills. 20. The king shouldn't exalt himself above his fellow Israelites. He shouldn't turn away from the law, either to the right or to the left wing, so that he and his children may control for a long time over Israel.

Chapter 18

1. The preachers, the Levites, and the entire lineage of Levi won't have any land heritage among the people of Israel rather, they will live off the immolations made by fire to the Lord, which will be their portion. 2. They won't admit a portion of land like the other lines, because the Lord is their heritage, just as He promised to them. 3. When the people offer offerings, whether it's a bull or a lamb, the preachers are entitled to admit certain corridor the shoulder, the cheeks, and the stomach (the corridor of the beast designated for them). 4. They're also to admit the first fruits of your grain, wine, oil painting, and the first hair (coat) from your lamb. 5. This is because the Lord your God has chosen them from all your lines to stand before Him and serve in His name, they and their descendants ever. 6. Still, wherever he lives, and he desires to serve in the place the Lord chooses, If a Levite (a member of the lineage of Levi) comes from any of your municipalities in Israel. 7. He may serve the Lord as a minister there, just like all the other Levites who serve before the Lord. 8. They will admit equal portions of food to eat, in addition to what they gain from dealing any inherited property. 9. When you enter the land that the Lord your God is giving you, don't follow the abominable (despicable) practices of the nations there. 10. There mustn't be anyone among you who offers their child as a burnt immolation, practices necromancy, engages in fortune- telling, interprets foreshadowing, or practices witchery, 11, Or casts spells, or consults with mediums (those who communicate with spirits), or spiritists (those who seek the dead), or calls up the dead. 12. For all who engage in these practices are despicable (spiteful) to the Lord, and because of these execrations, the Lord is driving these nations out before you. 13. You must remain impeccable (innocent) before the

Lord your God. **14.** The nations you're about to drive out listen to those who exercise augury (fortune- telling) and witchery. But as for you, the Lord your God has not permitted you to do so. **15.** The Lord your God will raise up for you a prophet like me (Moses) from among your own people. You must hear to him. **16.** This is what you asked of the Lord your God at Horeb (the mountain where God gave the Ten Commandments to Moses) on the day of the assembly, when you said," Let us not hear the voice of the Lord our God, or see this great fire again, lest we die." **17.** The Lord said to me," What they've said is good. **18.** I'll raise up for them a prophet like you, from among their own people. I'll put my words in His mouth, and He'll speak everything I command. **19.** Anyone who refuses to hear to the words of that prophet, who speaks in my name, I'll hold responsible. **20.** But if a prophet presumes to speak in my name anything I haven't commanded him to say, or speaks in the name of other gods, that prophet shall die." **21.** Still," How can we tell if a communication is from the Lord?" **22.** If you ever wonder. When a prophet speaks in the name of the Lord, if what he says doesn't come to pass or be, that's the sign that the Lord didn't speak. The prophet spoke it presumptuously (out of his own will), so don't be hysterical of him.

Chapter 19

1. When the Lord your God has driven out (removed) the nations from before you and given you their land to take possession of, and when you settle in their cities and houses, **2.** You must set apart three cities in the land the Lord your God is giving you as your inheritance. **3.** You shall prepare roads leading to these cities, and divide your land into three sections, so that anyone who unintentionally kills another person may flee there for safety. **4.** This is the case for the person who accidentally (unintentionally) kills their neighbor: If someone kills another person by mistake, without having any prior hatred toward them, **5.** For example, when a person goes with a neighbor to cut wood in the forest and while swinging an axe, the head slips off and strikes the neighbor, causing death, the one who struck them should flee to one of these cities to save their life. **6.** Otherwise, the avenger of blood (the relative seeking justice for the victim) might pursue them in anger, and if the way is long, they might catch up and kill them, though the person is not guilty of murder since there was no premeditated hatred. **7.** Therefore, I command you to set apart three cities. **8.** If the Lord your God increases the size of your territory, as He promised to your ancestors (forefathers) and gives you all the land He swore to give them, **9.** and if you obey all the commandments (rules) I give you today, loving the Lord your God and walking (living) in His ways, then you shall add three more cities to the three you have already set apart, **10.** So that innocent blood will not be shed in your land, which the Lord your God is giving you as an inheritance, and guilt for bloodshed will not be upon you. **11.** But if someone hates (holds ill will) their neighbor and lies in wait to kill them, and then strikes them and causes their death; they flee to one of these cities, **12.** The elders (leaders) of the city shall send for the killer and bring them back from the city of refuge, handing them over to the avenger of blood so that they may face justice. **13.** You shall not show mercy (pity) on such a person, but instead, you must remove (purge) the guilt of innocent blood from Israel, and it will go well with you. **14.** You must not move (alter) your neighbor's boundary marker (landmark) that was set by those who came before you, in the inheritance (property) you will receive in the land the Lord your God is giving you to possess. **15.** A single witness (just one person) shall not stand against someone in regard to any wrongdoing (sin) they have committed; a matter must be confirmed by the testimony of two or three witnesses. **16.** If a false witness (a person who lies) stands against someone to accuse them of wrongdoing, **17.** Both the accuser and the accused shall stand before the Lord, before the priests and the judges (officials) who are serving at the time. **18.** The judges shall carefully investigate the matter, and if the witness is proven to be false (one who lied), **19.** Then the false witness shall receive the punishment that they intended for the accused. In this way, you shall remove (eliminate) the evil from among you. **20.** Those who remain shall hear about this and fear and no one will commit such evil in your land again. **21.** You shall not show mercy (pity) to the guilty: life for life, eye for eye, tooth for tooth, hand for hand, foot for foot.

Chapter 20

1. When you go out to battle against your enemies and you see horses, chariots, and a larger army than yours, do not be afraid of them. The Lord your God, who brought you out of Egypt (the land of slavery), is with you. **2.** When you are about to go into battle, the priest shall approach and speak to the people. **3.** He shall say to them: "Listen, Israel! Today you are about to fight your enemies. Do not let your hearts become weak; do not be afraid, do not be anxious, and do not be terrified by them. **4.** For the Lord your God is the One who goes with you to fight for you against your enemies, to give you victory." **5.** The officers will also speak to the people and say: "Who is the man who has built a new house and has not yet dedicated it? Let him go home, lest he dies in battle and another man dedicates it. **6.** And who is the man who has planted a vineyard but has not yet eaten from it? Let him go home, lest he dies in battle and another man eats its fruit. **7.** And who is the man who has become engaged to a woman but has not yet married her? Let him go home, lest he dies in battle and another man marries her." **8.** The officers will continue speaking to the people and say, "Who is the man who is fearful and fainthearted (lacking courage)? Let him go home, so that his fear does not affect the hearts of the others and cause them to be afraid as well." **9.** After the officers have finished speaking to the people, they shall appoint captains to lead the army. **10.** When you approach a city to fight against it, first offer peace to it. **11.** If the city accepts your offer of peace and opens its gates to you, then all the people in that city will become your subjects (serve you) and you will have them under tribute (a form of payment or servitude). **12.** But if the city refuses to make peace with you and chooses to fight, then you shall lay siege to it. **13.** When the Lord your God delivers it into your hands, you must kill every male in the city with the sword. **14.** However, the women, children, animals, and all the spoils (wealth and goods) from the city you may take as your own. You may take these as plunder, and enjoy the goods that the Lord your God gives you. **15.** This is how you should treat the cities that are far away from you, those that are not part of the nations you will conquer. **16.** But as for the cities of the nations that the Lord your God is giving you to possess as your inheritance, you must not allow anything that breathes to remain alive. 17 "You must completely destroy them—the Hittites (ancient Anatolian people), Amorites (mountain-dwelling Canaanite tribe), Canaanites (inhabitants of the land of Canaan), Perizzites (rural Canaanite people), Hivites (northern Canaanite group), and Jebusites (original residents of Jerusalem)—just as the LORD your God has commanded you. **18.** If you do not destroy them, they may teach you to follow their detestable practices (idol worship) that they did for their gods, and this would lead you to sin against the Lord your God. **19.** When you lay siege to a city for a long time and make war against it in order to take it, do not destroy the trees by cutting them down with an ax. You may eat the fruit from the trees, so do not cut them down. **20.** Only the trees that do not bear fruit, which are not useful for food, may be destroyed and cut down, to be used for making siege works (structures to help attack) against the city until it is captured.

Chapter 21

1. Still, and it isn't clear who killed him, **2,** If someone is set up dead (taken) in the field within the land the Lord your God is giving you to retain also the elders and judges (leaders who make opinions and settle controversies) must go out and measure the distance from the taken person to the nearest megacity. **3.** The elders of the megacity that's closest to the body must take a heifer (a youthful womanish cow) that has not been used for work, like pulling a wain or plow, **4.** And they must bring her to a vale with flowing water, which has no way been furrowed or planted. There, in the vale, they shall break the neck of the heifer. **5.** The preachers, who are descendants of Levi (Levi was one of the twelve lines of Israel chosen for religious duties), shall approach, for the Lord your God has chosen them to serve Him and to bless in His name. They've the authority to settle all difficulties and controversies. **6.** The elders of the nearest megacity shall wash their hands over the heifer whose neck was broken in the vale, **7.** And they will say," Our hands haven't exfoliate this blood, nor have our eyes seen what happed. **8.** Lord, atone (forgive or make reparation) for Your people Israel, whom You have redeemed. Don't hold this innocent blood against Your people. Remove the guilt of this bloodshed from Israel." **9.** Therefore, you'll remove the guilt of innocent blood from

among you by doing what's right in the sight of the Lord. **10.** When you go to war against your adversaries, and the Lord your God gives them into your hands and you take them as internees, **11.** And you see a beautiful woman among the internees, and you ask to take her as your woman, **12.** also you must bring her to your house. She shall shave her head, trim her nails, **13.** Take off the clothes of her prison, and remain in your house to mourn for her father and mama for one month. After that, you may go in to her, and she'll become your woman. **14.** still, you must let her go free, If after this you find that you no longer delight in her. You mustn't vend her or treat her like a slave, because you have lowered her. **15.** still, one he loves and the other he doesn't love, and both have borne him children, If a man has two women. **16.** When it comes time for him to divide his heritage among his sons, he mustn't give the birthright (firstborn's share) to the son of the loved woman in place of the son of the unloved woman, who's the true firstborn. **17.** But he must fete the son of the unloved woman as the firstborn and give him a double portion (doubly as important as the other sons) of everything he has, because that son is the morning of his strength. The birthright of the firstborn belongs to him. **18.** Still, indeed after they punish him, **19,** If a man has a stubborn (unruly) and rebellious son who doesn't observe the voice of his father or mama. His father and mama shall take him to the elders of the megacity, to the gate of the megacity (the place where legal matters are settled). **20.** They will say to the elders," This son of ours is stubborn and rebellious; he doesn't hear to us; he's a gormandizer and a tippler." **21.** Also all the men of the megacity shall sharpen him to death with monuments. You must remove the wrong from among you, and all Israel will hear and be hysterical. **22.** Still, and his body is hanged on a tree (a system of prosecution), **23,** If someone commits a sin good of death and is put to death. His body mustn't remain on the tree overnight. You must bury him the same day, so that you don't defile (make sick) the land the Lord your God is giving you as a heritage. Anyone who's hanged is cursed (accursed) by God.

Chapter 22

1. Still, don't ignore it; you must clearly return it to your family, If you see your family's ox or lamb wandering or lost (Ox a tamed cattle) **2.** Still, also bring it to your house, and it'll stay with you until your family comes looking for it, If your family isn't near you or you don't know him. When he does, return it to him (Return give back, return to proprietor) **3.** The same applies to his jackass or any other lost things of your family's, you must return them, and not hide from your responsibility. **4.** Still, you must help him lift it up, If you see your family's jackass or ox fall down on the road. Don't ignore it (Lift help get back over) **5.** A woman mustn't wear men's apparel, nor should a man wear women's apparel. Anyone who does similar effects is despicable (spiteful) to the Lord your God. **6.** Still, whether it's in a tree or on the ground and the nest contains eggs or youthful catcalls with the mama sitting on them, If you find a raspberry's nest along your path. **7.** You mustn't take the mama raspberry along with the youthful rather, you should let the mama go free and only take the youthful for yourself. This act will be salutary to you, and it'll insure you live long. (salutary good for you) **8.** When you make a new house, make sure to make a alcazar (a defensive wall) around the roof to help anyone from falling out, therefore avoiding the guilt of bloodshed in your ménage (Alcazar defensive wall around roof) **9.** Don't plant a croft with two kinds of seed, lest the yield from your seeds and the fruit of your croft come defiled (tainted). **10.** Don't plow with an ox and a jackass together, as it's indecorous and delicate for them to work together. **11.** Don't wear a garment made of two different types of accoutrements similar as hair mixed with linen. **12.** You must make tassels (circumferences) on the four corners of your garments. **13.** Still If a man marries a woman and also dislikes her. **14.** criminating her of opprobrious conduct and darkening her character by claiming," I married this woman, and when I came to her, I set up she wasn't a virgin," **15.** Also the woman's father and mama shall bring substantiation of her purity to the megacity elders (leaders) at the megacity gate (substantiation evidence or evidence). **16.** The woman's father will say to the elders," I gave my son to this man as his woman, but now he detests her. **17.** He has indicted her of opprobrious conduct, saying, I set up your son wasn't a virgin,' but then is the substantiation of her purity." The elders will see the evidence and spread the cloth before them. **18.** The elders of the megacity will take the man and discipline him. **19.** The man will be fined one hundred shekels of tableware, which will be given to the father of the woman, as he has brought shame upon an Israelite abecedarian. The woman will remain his woman, and he'll not be allowed to disjoin her. **20.** but if the blameworthiness is true and there's no substantiation of the woman's purity, **21.** Also they shall bring the woman to the door of her father's house, and the men of the megacity shall sharpen her to death, as she has committed a shy act in Israel by acting as a courtesan (harlot) in her father's house. You must remove wrong from among you. **22.** Still, both the man and the woman must die, If a man is caught lying with a woman who's formerly married to someone differently. This is how you'll put down evil from Israel. **23.** Still, and another man finds her in the megacity and has sexual relations with her, **24.** If a youthful woman who's a virgin is promised (engaged) to a man also you shall bring both the man and the woman to the megacity gate and gravestone them to death. The woman will be penalized because she didn't cry out for help in the megacity, and the man because he lowered his neighbor's woman. This act removes the wrong from among you. **25.** But if the man finds a engaged youthful woman in the country and forces her, lying with her, only the man who had sexual relations with her shall die. **26.** You mustn't discipline the woman, as there's no sin in her meritorious of death. This is like when a man rises against his neighbor and kills him. The matter is the same. **27.** He set up her in the country, and though the youthful woman cried out for help, no bone was there to save her. **28.** still, a virgin, and takes her by force and lies with her, If a man finds an unattached youthful woman. **29.** The man who had relations with her must pay fifty shekels of tableware to the father of the youthful woman. The woman will become his woman because he lowered her. He cannot disjoin her for the rest of his life. **30.** A man mustn't take his father's woman, nor uncover his father's bed. This is a shy act.

Chapter 23

1. A man who has been castrated (made incapable of having children) or mutilated (damaged in a way that prevents normal function) shall not be allowed to enter the assembly (gathering) of the Lord. **2.** A person born from a forbidden relationship (illegitimate child) shall not be allowed to enter the assembly of the Lord, and even to the tenth generation (ten generations later), none of his descendants shall enter the assembly of the Lord. **3.** An Ammonite or Moabite (two nations who were descendants of Lot) shall not be allowed to enter the assembly of the Lord; even to the tenth generation, none of their descendants shall enter the assembly of the Lord forever. This is because they did not meet you with bread and water when you were traveling from Egypt, and because they hired Balaam, the son of Beor, from Pethor in Mesopotamia (a place in the ancient world) to curse you. **4.** However, the Lord your God did not listen to Balaam, but He turned the curse into a blessing for you because the Lord your God loves you. **5.** You shall not seek peace or prosperity with them (the Ammonites and Moabites) for as long as you live. **6.** You shall not hate the Edomites (descendants of Esau) because they are your brothers. You shall not hate the Egyptians because you were once strangers (foreigners) in their land. **7.** The children of the third generation born to them may enter the assembly of the Lord. **8.** When you go out to fight your enemies, be careful to avoid doing anything wicked. **9.** If any man becomes unclean (ceremonially impure) because of something that happened at night (such as a bodily discharge), he shall leave the camp and not enter it. **10.** When evening comes, he shall wash with water, and when the sun sets, he may return to the camp. **11.** You shall also have a place outside the camp where you can go to relieve yourself. **12.** You shall have a tool (implement) with you, and when you sit down outside, you shall dig a hole and cover up what you relieve. **13.** For the Lord your God walks among your camp to protect you and give your enemies into your hands, and therefore your camp must remain holy (pure), so that He will not see any unclean thing among you and turn away from you. **14.** You shall not return to his master (owner) a slave who has escaped from his master to you. **15.** He may live with you wherever he chooses within your cities (gates), and you shall not oppress (mistreat) him. **16.** There shall be no ritual prostitute (female temple worker) among the daughters of Israel, nor a male temple prostitute among the sons of Israel. **17.** You shall not bring the wages of a prostitute (harlot) or the price of a dog (a male temple prostitute) into the house of the Lord your God as an offering, for both of these things are detestable (an abomination) to the Lord your God. **18.** You shall not charge your brother interest on money or food or any other loan you make. **19.** You may charge interest to a foreigner (a person not of Israel), but to your brother you shall not charge interest, so that the Lord your God may bless you in all the work you do in the land you are about to enter and possess. **20.** When you make a vow to the Lord your God, you must not delay in fulfilling it, because the Lord your God will require it of you, and it would be a sin for you to delay. **21.** However, if you do not make a vow, there is no sin in it for you. **22.** You must fulfill whatever you have promised with your mouth, because you voluntarily made a vow to the Lord your God. **23.** When you enter your neighbor's vineyard, you may eat as many grapes as you want, but you shall not take any with you in a container. **24.** When you enter your neighbor's field of grain, you may pluck the heads of grain by hand, but you shall not use a sickle (cutting tool) to harvest the grain.

Chapter 24

1. When a man marries a woman and latterly finds that she doesn't please him because he has set up some spoilage (commodity indecorous) in her, he must write an instrument of divorce (a written document declaring the end of the marriage), give it to her, and shoot her out of his house. **2.** After she leaves his house and marries another man, **3.** Still, gives it to her, and sends her down, If the alternate husband dislikes her and writes her an instrument of divorce. **4.** The first husband who disassociated her cannot take her back as his woman after she has been defiled (made impure); this is considered an abomination (commodity despicable) before the Lord, and you mustn't bring sin on the land that the Lord your God is giving you as an heritage. **5.** When a man marries a new woman, he shall not go to war or be involved in any other business; he shall be free at home for one time and make his woman happy (give joy and comfort to her). **6.** A man shall not take the lower or upper millstone as a pledge (security for a loan), because that would be taking someone's livelihood (the means by which they make a living). **7.** Still, the kidnapper must die, If a man is set up abducting any of his fellow Israelites and mistreats (hurts) them or sells them. You must remove the wrong (wickedness) from among you. **8.** Be careful when dealing with cases of leprosy (a contagious skin complaint) and follow the instructions given by the preachers, as I've commanded them. Be active in doing what they educate you. **9.** Flash back what the Lord your God did to Miriam (Miriam was the family of Moses) on the way as you came out of Egypt (the land where the Israelites were enslaved). **10.** When you advance commodity to your fellow (fellow Israelite), don't enter his house to take his pledge (security for the loan). **11.** Rather, stand outdoors, and let the man to whom you have advanced the plutocrat bring the pledge out to you. **12.** Still, don't keep the pledge overnight (do not hold it longer than necessary), If the person is poor. **13.** Be sure to return it to him by evening, so that he may sleep in his own garment (apparel) and bless you. This will be considered righteous before the Lord your God. **14.** You mustn't oppress (brutalize) a hired menial who's poor and indigent, whether they're one of your fellow Israelites or an outsider living in your land and gates (megacity walls). **15.** You must pay the stipend of a hired menial each day before evening, for he's poor and depends on the stipend for survival. However, and he cries out to the Lord against you, it'll be a sin for you, If you don't pay him. **16.** Fathers shall not be put to death for the sins of their children, nor shall children be put to death for the sins of their fathers. A person shall die only for their own sin (particular wrongdoing). **17.** You shall not backslider justice (distort or twist justice) for the outsider or for the nameless, nor take a widow's garment (apparel worn by a widow) as a pledge. **18.** But flash back that you were slaves in Egypt, and the Lord your God redeemed (saved) you from there. Thus, I command you to do these effects. **19.** When you're gathering your field and forget a sheaf (a pack of grain), don't go back to gather it. It should be left for the outsider, the nameless, and the widow, so that the Lord your God may bless you with all the work of your hands. **20.** When you beat your olive trees, don't go over the branches again (do not gather an alternate time); it shall be left for the outsider, the nameless, and the widow. **21.** When you gather the grapes from your croft, don't go back to pick up what was missed; it shall be for the outsider, the nameless, and the widow.

22. Flash back that you were slaves in the land of Egypt; thus, I command you to do this.

Chapter 25

1. Still, the judges (those who decide legal matters) will make a judgment, declaring the righteous innocent and the wicked (the bone in the wrong) shamefaced, If two men have a disagreement (a disagreement) and come to court. **2.** Still, the judge will make him lie down and admit a number of blows in his presence, grounded on how serious his offense was If the shamefaced man deserves to be beaten (penalized). **3.** He may admit up to forty blows, but no more, so that your family (an Israelite) isn't lowered (lowered) in your sight. **4.** You shall not muzzle (stop from eating) an ox while it treads (walks on) the grain. This means you should allow creatures to eat as they work. **5.** Still, the widow (woman of the departed) shall not marry someone from outside the family; her husband's family must marry her and fulfill the responsibility of a family- in- law by producing a son for the departed, If sisters live together and one dies without having a son. **6.** The firstborn son she has will inherit the name of her departed husband so that his name isn't canceled from Israel. **7.** still, if the man doesn't want to marry his family's widow, also she should go to the elders (leaders) at the megacity gate and say," My husband's family refuses to rise up a name for his family in Israel; he'll not fulfill his duty." **8.** The elders will call the man and speak to him. However," I don't want to marry her," **9.** If he refuses and says. also the widow shall go before the elders, take off his sandal (shoe), spit in his face, and say," This is what should be done to the man who'll not make up his family's family." **10.** And his family will be known in Israel as" the house of him whose sandal was removed." **11.** Still, and she grabs the bushwhacker by the genitals (private corridor), **12.** If two men are fighting and the woman of one of them comes to deliver her husband from the bone who's striking him. You shall cut off her hand; don't feel sorry (pity) for her. **13.** Don't have two different kinds of weights (heavy and light) in your bag. **14.** Don't have two different kinds of measures (large and small) in your house. **15.** You shall have honest weights and measures, so that your days may be long in the land the Lord your God is giving you. **16.** For all who do similar effects, all who act dishonestly, are an abomination (commodity despicable) to the Lord your God. **17.** Flash back what Amalek did to you on the way when you came out of Egypt (the land of slavery), **18.** How he met you on the way and attacked those who were straggling before (weakened and exhausted) when you were sick and tired; and he didn't sweat God. **19.** Thus, when the Lord your God has given you rest from all your adversaries in the land that the Lord your God is giving you to retain, you shall wipe out (destroy) the memory of Amalek from under heaven. Don't forget.

Chapter 26

1. When you enter the land that the LORD (Yahweh) your God has promised to give you as your inheritance, and after you have taken possession of it and settled there, **2.** Take a portion of the firstfruits (the first harvest or crops) from all that the land produces, which the LORD your God has granted you, and place them in a basket. Then, go to the place that the LORD your God will choose to establish His Name (the central sanctuary or holy site, often referring to Jerusalem). **3.** Say to the priest (the religious leader or Levite) who is serving at that time, "Today, I declare to the LORD your God that I have arrived in the land the LORD swore to our ancestors (the patriarchs, such as Abraham, Isaac, and Jacob) to give us." **4.** The priest shall take the basket from your hand and set it down before the altar of the LORD your God. **5.** You shall then speak these words before the LORD your God: "My ancestor (likely referring to Jacob or his forefather Abraham) was a wandering Aramean (an ancient Semitic-speaking people from the region of Aram, roughly corresponding to modern-day Syria), who went down to Egypt with only a small number of people, and there he became a great and mighty nation." **6.** "But the Egyptians (the people of ancient Egypt, who enslaved the Israelites) oppressed us, treating us harshly and forcing us into hard labor." **7.** "Then we cried out to the LORD, the God of our ancestors, and He heard our cry, saw our misery, labor, and oppression." **8.** "So the LORD brought us out of Egypt (the land of slavery and oppression) with a mighty hand, an outstretched arm, with great terror, and with signs and wonders." **9.** "He brought us to this place and gave us this land, a land flowing with milk and honey (a metaphor for a land rich in resources and prosperity)." **10.** "And now I bring the firstfruits of the land You, LORD, have given me." Place the basket before the LORD your God and bow before Him. **11.** Then, both you and the Levites (the priestly tribe of Israel) as well as the foreigners (non-Israelite residents), the fatherless (orphans), and the widows (those without male protection) among you shall rejoice in the goodness the LORD your God has provided for you and your family. **12.** When you have finished setting aside a tenth (the tithe, or 10% of your produce) of all your produce in the third year, the special year of the tithe, you shall give it to the Levites, the foreigners, the fatherless, and the widows, so that they may eat in your towns and be satisfied. **13.** Then declare before the LORD your God: "I have removed the sacred portion (the part of the harvest reserved for God and His people) from my house and have given it to the Levites, the foreigners, the fatherless, and the widows, in accordance with Your command. I have not neglected any of Your commands, nor have I forgotten any of them." **14.** "I have not consumed any of the sacred portion while I was mourning (in a state of grief), nor have I removed any of it while I was ceremonially unclean (impure according to Jewish laws), nor have I offered any of it to the dead (as a form of mourning or idol worship). I have obeyed the LORD my God and have done everything You commanded me." **15.** "Look down from Your holy dwelling place (heaven), and bless Your people Israel and the land You have given us, as You swore to our ancestors, a land flowing with milk and honey (a prosperous and fertile land)." **16.** Today, the LORD your God commands you to obey these statutes and ordinances (rules, laws); be diligent in observing them with all your heart and soul (with full devotion and commitment). **17.** You have acknowledged today that the LORD is your God, and that you will walk in His ways, keeping His decrees, commands, and laws, and that you will listen to Him. **18.** And the LORD has declared today that you are His people, His treasured possession (chosen and set apart), just as He promised, and that you are to keep all His commandments (laws and rules for righteous living). **19.** He has promised that He will raise you to fame, honor, and praise above all the nations He has made, and that you will be a holy people (set apart for God's service) to the LORD your God, as He has promised.

Chapter 27

1. Moses, collectively with the elders (leaders) of Israel, instructed the people: "Obey all the commandments I give you today. **2.** When you have crossed the Jordan River (the river separating Israel from the Promised Land) into the land that the LORD your God is giving you as an inheritance, take some large stones and coat them with plaster. **3.** Write on these stones all the words of this law after you have crossed over to enter the land the LORD your God is giving you, a land flowing with milk and honey (a metaphor for a prosperous land), just as the LORD, the God of your ancestors (patriarchs), promised. **4.** And when you cross the Jordan, set up these stones on Mount Ebal (a mountain in the central region of Israel), as I have commanded you today, and coat them with plaster. **5.** Build an altar to the LORD your God there, an altar made of uncut stones (stones that have not been shaped by tools). Do not use any iron tool on them. **6.** Build the altar with fieldstones (natural stones found in the area), and offer burnt offerings (sacrificial offerings that are entirely consumed by fire) on it to the LORD your God. **7.** Sacrifice fellowship offerings (peace offerings) there, eating them and rejoicing in the presence of the LORD your God. **8.** Write clearly all the words of this law on the stones you set up. **9.** Then Moses and the Levitical priests (the priestly tribe of Israel) spoke to all Israel: "Be silent and listen, Israel! Today you have become the people of the LORD your God." **10.** "Obey the LORD your God and walk in His ways, keeping His decrees (laws) and commands that I give you today." **11.** On the same day, Moses gave further instructions to the people: **12.** "When you have crossed the Jordan, these tribes will stand on Mount Gerizim (a nearby mountain, associated with blessings) to bless the people: Simeon, Levi, Judah, Issachar, Joseph, and Benjamin." **13.** "And these tribes will stand on Mount Ebal to pronounce curses (pronouncing negative judgments or punishments): Reuben, Gad, Asher, Zebulun, Dan, and Naphtali." **14.** The Levites will recite these curses aloud to all Israel: **15.** "Cursed is anyone who makes an idol (a false god), something detestable to the LORD, a work of human hands, and sets it up in secret." Then all the people shall say, "Amen!" **16.** "Cursed is anyone who dishonors their father or mother." Then all the

people shall say, "Amen!" **17.** "Cursed is anyone who moves their neighbor's boundary stone (a marker of land ownership, stealing land)." Then all the people shall say, "Amen!" **18.** "Cursed is anyone who misleads the blind on the road." Then all the people shall say, "Amen!" **19.** "Cursed is anyone who deprives the foreigner (someone from another nation), the fatherless (orphans), or the widow of justice (fair treatment)." Then all the people shall say, "Amen!" **20.** "Cursed is anyone who sleeps with his father's wife (because he dishonors his father's bed)." Then all the people shall say, "Amen!" **21.** "Cursed is anyone who has sexual relations with an animal." Then all the people shall say, "Amen!" **22.** "Cursed is anyone who sleeps with his sister, the daughter of his father or the daughter of his mother." Then all the people shall say, "Amen!" **23.** "Cursed is anyone who sleeps with his mother-in-law (father's wife or the wife of his father's son)." Then all the people shall say, "Amen!" **24.** "Cursed is anyone who secretly murders their neighbor." Then all the people shall say, "Amen!" **25.** "Cursed is anyone who accepts a bribe to kill an innocent person." Then all the people shall say, "Amen!" **26.** "Cursed is anyone who does not uphold the words of this law by carrying them out." Then all the people shall say, "Amen!"

Chapter 28

1. In case you wholeheartedly obey the LORD your God and diligently comply with all of the instructions I come up with nowadays, the LORD your God will raise you above all of the countries in the world. **2.** These types of benefits will encounter you and accompany you if you obey the LORD your God: **3.** You may be blessed inside the town and blessed in the nation-state. **4.** The fruit of your womb (your kids) can be blessed, in addition to the crops of your land and the younger of your farm animals—the calves of your herds and the lambs of your flocks. **5.** Your basket (used for accumulating or storing meals) and your kneading trough (a field for blending dough) can be blessed. **6.** You will be blessed while you input and blessed whilst you depart. **7.** The LORD will ensure that your enemies who rise in opposition to you are defeated earlier than you. They may come at you from one course but flee from you in seven different directions. **8.** The LORD will bless your barns (storage areas for grain) and the whole lot you put your hand to. The LORD your God will bless you in the land he's providing you with. **9.** The LORD will set up you as His holy humans, as He promised you on oath, if you maintain the commands of the LORD your God and stroll in obedience to Him. **10.** Then all of the nations on the earth will see that you are referred to as by using the name of the LORD, and they will worry you. **11.** The LORD will furnish you notable prosperity—in the fruit of your womb, the younger of your cattle, and the vegetation of your land—inside the land He swore to offer for your ancestors (forefathers). **12.** The LORD will open the heavens, the storehouse of His abundance, to send rain to your land in its season and bless all the paintings of your hands. You will lend to many nations, however you may borrow from none. **13.** The LORD will make you the head (leader), not the tail (follower). In case you concentrate carefully to the commands of the LORD your God that I provide you with these days and observe them, you may continually be on top, never at the bottom. **14.** Do no longer turn aside from any of the commands I come up with nowadays, to the right or to the left, following different gods and serving them. **15.** But, if you do no longer obey the LORD your God and do not carefully comply with all His instructions and decrees I'm supplying you with nowadays, most of these curses will stumble upon you and overtake you: **16.** You may be cursed within the town and cursed in the countryside. **17.** Your basket and kneading trough could be cursed. **18.** The fruit of your womb might be cursed, and the plants of your land, the calves of your herds, and the lambs of your flocks. **19.** You will be cursed when you enter and cursed while you depart. **20.** The LORD will send upon you curses, confusion (disorder), and rebuke in the whole thing you do, until you're destroyed and come to surprising ruin because of the evil you've got achieved in leaving behind (leaving behind) Him. **21.** The LORD will plague you with diseases till He has wiped you out from the land you're about to enter and possess. **22.** The LORD will strike you with losing sickness, fever, inflammation, scorching heat and drought, blight (harm to crops), and mold, with a purpose to affect you until you perish. **23.** The sky over your head might be like bronze (hard and unyielding), and the ground underneath you may be like iron (unproductive and hard). **24.** The

LORD will flip the rain of your land into dust and powder. It's going to fall from the skies till you're destroyed. **25.** The LORD will cause you to be defeated via your enemies. You'll come in opposition to them in one direction however flee from them in seven, and also you turns into an apprehension to all of the kingdoms of the earth. **26.** Your useless our bodies may be food for all of the birds of the sky and the wild animals, and no one may be there to scare them away. **27.** The LORD will afflict you with the boils (sores) of Egypt, with tumors, festering sores, and the itch, from which you will now not be capable of recover. **28.** The LORD will make you mad, blind, and careworn in mind. **29.** At noon, you will grope about like a blind individual inside the dark. You will fail in the whole thing you do; each day you may be oppressed and robbed, with nobody to rescue you. **30.** You may be engaged to a female, however every other guy will take her and violate her. You'll build a house, however you'll no longer live in it. You'll plant a vineyard, but you'll not even start to experience its fruit. **31.** Your ox may be slaughtered before your eyes, but you'll now not eat any of it. Your donkey may be forcibly taken from you and will not be returned. Your sheep can be given in your enemies, and no person will rescue them. **32.** Your little kids may be taken via every other nation, and you will helplessly watch, powerless to lift a finger. **33.** A people you do now not recognize will consume what your land and labor produce, and you will suffer cruel oppression all your days. **34.** The attractions you spot will force you mad. **35.** The LORD will strike you to your knees and legs with painful boils that cannot be healed, from the soles of your feet to the top of your head. **36.** The LORD will power you and the king you set over you to a state unknown to you or your ancestors. There you will worship different gods, gods made of timber and stone. **37.** You turns into a scary example (a source of fear), a proverb, and a topic of mockery amongst all of the international locations in which the LORD will pressure you. **38.** You may sow a great deal seed inside the discipline, but you will harvest little, because locusts (bugs that devour crops) will devour it. **39.** You'll plant vineyards and generally tend to them, however you may no longer drink the wine or acquire the grapes, due to the fact worms will destroy them. **40.** You will have olive trees for the duration of your land, but you will not use the oil, because the olives will fall off in advance. **41.** You will have sons and daughters, but you will not be able to keep them, for they will be taken into captivity.

42. Swarms of locusts (devastating pests) will invade all your trees and crops. **43.** The foreigners who live among you will rise higher and higher, while you will sink lower and lower. **44.** They will lend to you, but you will not be able to lend to them. They will be the leaders, while you will be subjugated. **45.** All these curses will pursue and overtake you until you are destroyed, because you did not obey the LORD your God and did not keep His commands and decrees. **46.** These curses will serve as a sign and a warning to you and your descendants forever. **47.** Because you did not serve the LORD your God with joy and gratitude during times of prosperity, **48.** you will serve your enemies whom the LORD sends against you. In hunger, thirst, nakedness, and severe poverty, they will put an iron yoke (symbol of oppression) around your neck until they have destroyed you. **49.** The LORD will bring against you a nation from far away, from the ends of the earth, like an eagle swooping down. A nation whose language you will not understand, **50.** a fierce and ruthless nation that shows no respect for the elderly nor pity for the young. **51.** They will consume your livestock and the produce of your land until you are destroyed. They will leave you no grain, new wine, olive oil, nor any livestock—cattle or sheep—until you are ruined. **52.** They will besiege all your cities throughout the land the LORD your God is giving you. They will break through the fortified walls that you trust in and lay siege to every city. **53.** During the siege, due to the suffering caused by your enemies, you will resort to eating the fruit of your womb (children)—the flesh of your sons and daughters that the LORD your God has given you. **54.** Even the most compassionate and tender-hearted man among you will show no mercy towards his brother, the wife he loves, or his surviving children. **55.** He will not share with them any of the flesh of his children, which he is eating, because it will be all he has left due to the extreme suffering your enemy inflicts during the siege of your cities. **56.** The most delicate and compassionate woman among you—so sensitive that she would not even touch the ground with the sole of her foot—

will begrudge her husband and children, **57.** and will even contemplate eating her afterbirth and the children she bears. In her extreme desperation, she will do this secretly because of the suffering caused by the enemy's siege of your cities. **58.** If you do not carefully follow all the words of this law written in this book, and if you do not revere (respect and honor) the glorious and awe-inspiring name of the LORD your God, **59.** the LORD will send devastating plagues on you and your descendants, prolonged disasters, and severe and persistent illnesses. **60.** He will bring upon you all the diseases of Egypt (the plagues experienced by the Israelites in Egypt) that you feared, and they will cling to you. **61.** The LORD will also bring upon you every sickness and disaster not mentioned in this Book of the Law, until you are utterly destroyed. **62.** You, who were once as numerous as the stars in the sky, will be left with very few, because you did not obey the LORD your God. **63.** Just as it pleased the LORD to make you prosper and increase in number, so it will please Him to ruin and destroy you. You will be uprooted (exiled) from the land you are entering to possess. **64.** Then the LORD will scatter you among all nations, from one end of the earth to the other. There, you will worship other gods—gods made of wood and stone, which neither you nor your ancestors have known. **65.** Among those nations, you will find no rest, no place to call home. The LORD will give you an anxious mind, eyes weary from longing, and a despairing heart. **66.** You will live in constant fear, filled with dread both night and day, uncertain about your life. **67.** In the morning, you will say, "If only it were evening!" and in the evening, you will wish it were morning, because of the terror that will overwhelm you and the horrific sights you will see. **68.** The LORD will send you back in ships to Egypt (a return to the land of slavery) on a journey I said you should never make again. There, you will offer yourselves as slaves—both male and female to your enemies, but no one will buy you.

Chapter 29

1. These are the conditions of the covenant (agreement) that the LORD commanded Moses to establish with the Israelites in Moab, in addition to the covenant He had already made with them at Horeb (Mount Sinai). **2.** Moses called all the Israelites together and said to them: "You have witnessed all that the LORD did in Egypt to Pharaoh, to all his officials, and to all his land. **3.** With your own eyes, you saw the mighty trials, the signs, and the great wonders. **4.** Yet, to this day, the LORD has not given you a heart that understands, or eyes that truly see, or ears that really hear. **5.** But the LORD says, 'During the forty years I led you through the wilderness, your clothes did not wear out, nor did the sandals on your feet. **6.** You ate no bread, and drank neither wine nor any other fermented drink. I did this so that you might know that I am the LORD your God.'" **7.** When you came to this place, Sihon, the king of Heshbon, and Og, the king of Bashan, came out to oppose us in battle, but we defeated them. **8.** We took their land and gave it as an inheritance to the Reubenites, the Gadites, and the half-tribe of Manasseh. **9.** So, carefully follow the terms of this covenant, so that you may prosper in all that you do. **10.** All of you are standing today before the LORD your God—your leaders, your chiefs, your elders, your officials, and all the men of Israel, **11.** together with your children, your wives, and the foreigners living among you, who gather your wood and draw your water. **12.** You are standing here today to enter into a covenant with the LORD your God, a covenant that the LORD is making with you today and confirming with an oath, **13.** to establish you as His people and to be your God, as He promised you and as He swore to your forefathers—Abraham, Isaac, and Jacob. **14.** I am making this covenant, with its oath, not only with you who are standing here with us today in the presence of the LORD our God, **15.** but also with those who are not here with us today. **16.** You know how we lived in Egypt, and how we passed through the nations on our way here. **17.** You saw their detestable idols—wood and stone, silver and gold—that were among them. **18.** Be sure that no one among you, whether man or woman, clan or tribe, turns away from the LORD our God to worship the gods of these nations. Be sure that no root among you bears such bitter poison. **19.** When such a person hears the words of this oath and thinks, "I will be safe, even though I persist in going my own way," they will bring disaster upon the land—both the watered and the dry land. **20.** The LORD will never be willing to forgive them; rather, His anger and fury will burn against them. All the curses written in this book will fall upon them, and the LORD will blot out their name from under heaven. **21.** The LORD will set them apart for disaster from all the tribes of Israel, according to all the curses of the covenant written in this Book of the Law. **22.** Your children, who will follow you in later generations, and the foreigners from distant lands will see the calamities that have fallen on this land and the diseases with which the LORD has afflicted it. **23.** The whole land will be a burning wasteland—salt and sulfur, nothing planted, nothing sprouting, and no vegetation growing on it. It will be like the destruction of Sodom and Gomorrah, Admah, and Zeboyim, which the LORD overthrew in His fierce anger. **24.** All the nations will ask: "Why has the LORD done this to this land? Why this fierce, burning anger?" **25.** The answer will be: "It is because this people abandoned the covenant of the LORD their God, the covenant He made with them when He brought them out of Egypt. **26.** They went and worshiped other gods, bowing down to gods they did not know, gods He had not given them. **27.** Therefore, the LORD's anger burned against this land, so that He brought upon it all the curses written in this book. **28.** In His furious wrath, the LORD uprooted them from their land and scattered them into another land, as it is now." **29.** The secret things belong to the LORD our God, but the things revealed belong to us and to our children forever, that we may follow all the words of this law.

Chapter 30

1. When these types of blessings and curses I have proclaimed to you come upon you, and when you take them to heart wherever the LORD (YHWH, the covenant God) your God has scattered you among the nations, **2.** and when you and your children return to the LORD your God and obey Him with all of your heart and soul (the innermost part of your being), in accordance with everything I command you today, **3.** then the LORD your God will restore your fortunes (bless you with prosperity) and have mercy on you. He will gather you again from all the nations where He has scattered you. **4.** Even if you have been exiled to the furthest corners of the earth (to the ends of the world), from there the LORD your God will gather you and bring you back. **5.** He will bring you back to the land your ancestors once possessed, and you will take ownership of it. He will make you more prosperous and numerous than your ancestors have been. **6.** The LORD your God will circumcise your hearts (purify your hearts) and the hearts of your descendants (future generations), so that you may love Him with all your heart and soul, and live. **7.** The LORD your God will place all these curses upon your enemies (those who have wronged you), those who hated and persecuted you. **8.** You will again obey the LORD and follow all the commands I am giving you today. **9.** Then the LORD your God will make you successful (blessed) in all that you do—in the work of your hands, in the fruit of your womb (children), in the young of your livestock (animals), and in the produce of your land. The LORD will delight in you again, and He will make you rich, just as He delighted in your ancestors, **10.** if you obey the LORD your God and keep His commands and decrees (laws), which are written in this book of the law (the Torah), and turn to the LORD your God with all your heart and soul. **11.** Now, what I am commanding you today is not too difficult for you or beyond your reach. **12.** It is not up in heaven, so that you would need to ask, "Who will go up to heaven to get it and proclaim it to us so we may obey it?" **13.** Neither is it across the sea, so that you would need to ask, "Who will cross the sea to get it and proclaim it to us so we may obey it?" **14.** No, the word is very near you; it is in your mouth and in your heart, so you may obey it. **15.** See, I have set before you today life (prosperity) and prosperity, death (ruin) and destruction. **16.** For I command you today to love the LORD your God, to walk in obedience to Him, and to keep His commands, decrees, and laws. Then you will live and increase (flourish), and the LORD your God will bless you in the land (Canaan, the promised land) you are about to enter and possess. **17.** But if your heart turns away and you are not obedient (disobedient), and if you are led astray to worship other gods (false deities), **18.** I declare to you today that you will certainly be destroyed (cursed). You will not live long in the land you are crossing the Jordan River (the boundary of the promised land) to enter and possess. **19.** Today I call the heavens (the sky) and the earth (the natural world) as witnesses against you that I have set before you life and death, blessings and curses. Now choose life, so that you and your children may live, **20.** And so that you may love the LORD your God, listen to His voice, and hold fast to Him. For the LORD is your life, and He will give

you many years in the land He swore to give to your fathers—Abraham, Isaac, and Jacob (the patriarchs).

Chapter 31

1. Then Moses (chief of the Israelites) went out and addressed all Israel, announcing: **2.** "I am now 100 and 20 years old and may no longer lead you. The LORD has told me, 'You may now not go the Jordan River (boundary of the Promised Land).' **3.** The LORD your God will pass beforehand of you. He's going to defeat those international locations before you, and you'll take ownership of their land. Joshua (Moses' assistant) will lead you throughout, as the LORD has promised. **4.** The LORD will cope with them as He did with Sihon and Og, kings of the Amorites (ancient peoples), whom He destroyed at the side of their land. **5.** The LORD will hand them over to you, and also you need to do to all of them that I've commanded. **6.** Be robust and brave. Do not fear or be dismayed due to them, for the LORD your God is with you; He'll in no way go away you nor forsake you." **7.** Then Moses called Joshua and stated to him in front of all Israel, "Be strong and courageous, for you will lead this human beings into the land the LORD promised to their ancestors, and you will divide it as their inheritance. **8.** The LORD Himself will cross in advance of you and be with you; He'll never go away or forsake you. Do not fear or be discouraged." **9.** So Moses wrote down this regulation and gave it to the Levitical monks (clergymen of the tribe of Levi), who carried the Ark of the Covenant of the LORD, and to all the elders of Israel. **10.** Then Moses commanded them, "On the give up of each seven years, throughout the yr of Jubilee (a yr of debt forgiveness), at the pageant of Tabernacles (dinner party celebrating God's provision), **11.** when all Israel gathers to seem earlier than the LORD your God on the region He'll select, you ought to examine this law aloud to them. **12.** Acquire the human beings—guys, ladies, kids, and foreigners living among you—that will concentrate, discover ways to fear the LORD your God, and obey all of the phrases of this law. **13.** Their children, who do not recognise this law, should hear it with a view to learn to worry the LORD so long as you live within the land you are crossing the Jordan to own." **14.** The LORD informed Moses, "Your dying is close to. Call Joshua and meet at the Tent of assembly (region where God spoke to Moses), and I will fee him." So Moses and Joshua got here to the Tent of meeting. **15.** Then the LORD regarded in a pillar of cloud, status at the entrance to the Tent. **16.** The LORD stated to Moses, "You may quickly rest along with your ancestors, but these human beings will soon flip to overseas gods in the land they're coming into. They'll abandon Me and wreck the covenant I made with them. **17.** On that day, I becomes irritated and disguise My face from them, and they may be destroyed. Many failures will come across them, and they will ask, 'Have now not these screw ups came about because our God isn't always with us?' **18.** I can certainly hide My face in that day because of all their wickedness in turning to different gods. **19.** Now write down this tune and educate it to the Israelites, so it is able to serve as a witness towards them. **20.** When I carry them into the land flowing with milk and honey (a fertile land), the land I swore to their ancestors, and once they prosper and become happy, they will flip to different gods, reject Me, and wreck My covenant. **21.** When disasters come across them, this tune will testify in opposition to them, for it's going to no longer be forgotten by their descendants. I recognize what they're likely to do, even earlier than I deliver them into the land I promised." **22.** So Moses wrote down the music that day and taught it to the Israelites. **23.** The LORD commanded Joshua son of Nun, "Be strong and brave, for you may deliver the Israelites into the land I promised them, and that I may be with you." **24.** After Moses completed writing down all the words of this regulation from beginning to stop, **25.** he gave the e book of the law to the Levites who carried the Ark of the Covenant of the LORD. **26.** "Place this ebook of the law beside the Ark of the Covenant of the LORD your God, in which it will remain as a witness towards you. **27.** I understand how rebellious and cussed you're. If you have been rebellious towards the LORD even as I'm nevertheless with you, how plenty extra will you rebellion after I die! **28.** Gather all of the elders and officers of your tribes before me so I'm able to communicate those phrases to them and contact heaven and earth to testify in opposition to them. **29.** For I understand that after my dying, you will become fully corrupt and turn from the manner I've commanded you. Within the days to come back, disaster will fall on you because you will do evil within the sight of the LORD and provoke His anger by means of your movements." 30. And Moses recited the words of this music from start to complete inside the hearing of all Israel.

Chapter 32

1. Pay attention, you heavens (the sky or celestial bodies), and I'm able to speak; pay attention, you earth (the land), the words of my mouth. 2. Allow my coaching to fall like rain (a metaphor for know-how or education) and my phrases descend like dew (gentle and clean), like showers on new grass (increase and renewal), like plentiful rain on soft flowers (nourishing boom). 3. I'm able to proclaim the call of the LORD (YHWH, the covenant God). Oh, praise the greatness of our God! 4. He is the Rock (a symbol of stability and energy), His works are ideal, and all His ways are just. A faithful God who does no incorrect, upright and just is He. 5. They (the Israelites) are corrupt and not His children; to their disgrace they're a warped and crooked generation. 6. Is this the way you repay the LORD, you foolish and unwise humans? Is He no longer your Father, your Creator, who made you and shaped you? 7. Remember the times of antique (mirror on past generations); consider the generations long past. Ask your father (the older generation), and he'll tell you, your elders, and they may explain to you. 8. When the Most High (God) gave the nations their inheritance (land), when He divided all mankind, He set up boundaries for the peoples in keeping with the variety of the sons of Israel (the twelve tribes of Israel). 9. For the LORD's portion is His people (Israel), Jacob (the patriarch whose descendants form the kingdom of Israel) His allocated inheritance. 10. In a desert land (a barren, desolate place) He found him (Israel), in a barren and howling waste (a desolate place). He shielded him and cared for him; He guarded him as the apple of His eye (a loved possession). 11. Like an eagle that stirs up its nest and hovers over its young, that spreads its wings to catch them and carries them aloft. 12. The LORD alone led him; no foreign god (idol) was with him. 13. He made him ride on the heights of the land (He gave Israel great success) and fed him with the fruit of the fields. He nourished him with honey from the rock, and with oil from the flinty crag (the rock from which God supplied). 14. With curds and milk from herd and flock and with fattened lambs and goats, with choice rams of Bashan (a region known for strong livestock) and the finest kernels of wheat. You drank the foaming blood of the grape (wine). 15. Jeshurun (a poetic name for Israel, often meaning "upright one") grew fat and kicked; filled with food, they became heavy and sleek. They abandoned the God who made them and rejected the Rock (God) their Savior. 16. They made Him jealous with their foreign gods and angered Him with their detestable idols. 17. They sacrificed to false gods (idols), which are not gods—gods they had not known, gods that recently appeared (new idols), gods your ancestors did not fear. 18. You deserted the Rock (God) who fathered you; you forgot the God who gave you birth. 19. The LORD saw this and rejected them because He was angered by His children. 20. "I will hide My face from them," He said, "and see what their end will be; for they are a perverse generation, children who are unfaithful. 21. They made Me jealous by what is no god and angered Me with their worthless idols. I will make them resentful by people who are not a people (the Gentiles); I will make them angry by a nation that has no understanding (the people whom they had once despised). 22. For a fire will be kindled by My wrath, one that burns down to the realm of the dead below (Sheol). It will devour the earth and its harvests and set afire the foundations of the mountains. 23. "I will heap calamities on them and spend My arrows against them. 24. I will send wasting famine against them, consuming pestilence (diseases) and deadly plague; I will send against them the fangs of wild beasts, the venom of vipers (poisonous snakes) that glide in the dust. 25. In the streets, the sword (of judgment) will make them childless; in their homes, terror will reign. The young men and young women will perish, the infants and those with gray hair. 26. I said I would scatter them and erase their name from human memory, 27. but I dreaded the taunt of the enemy, lest the adversary misunderstand and say, 'Our hand has triumphed; the LORD has not done all this.'" 28. They are a nation without sense, there is no discernment in them. 29. If only they were wise and would understand this and discern what their end will be! 30. How could one man chase a thousand, or put ten thousand to flight, unless their Rock (God) had sold them, unless the LORD had given them up? 31. For their rock (idol) is not like our Rock (God), as even our enemies concede. 32. Their vine comes from the vine of Sodom (a symbol of wickedness) and from the fields of Gomorrah (towns destroyed for sin). Their grapes are filled with poison, and their clusters with bitterness. 33. Their wine is the venom of serpents (poisonous), the deadly poison of cobras. 34. "Have I not kept this in reserve and sealed it in My vaults? 35. It is Mine to avenge; I will repay. In due time, their foot will slip; their day of disaster is near, and their doom rushes upon them." 36. The LORD will vindicate His people and relent concerning His servants when He sees their strength is gone and no one is left, slave or free. 37. He will say: "Now, where are their gods, the rock they took shelter in, 38. the gods who ate the fat of their sacrifices and drank the wine of their drink offerings? Let them rise up to help you! Let them give you refuge! 39. "See now that I myself am He! There is no god besides Me. I put to death and I bring to life, I have wounded and I will heal, and no one can deliver out of My hand. 40. I lift My hand to heaven and solemnly swear: As surely as I live forever, 41. when I sharpen My flashing sword and My hand grasps it in judgment, I will take vengeance on My adversaries and repay those who hate Me. 42. I will make My arrows drunk with blood, while My sword devours flesh: the blood of the slain and the captives, the heads of the enemy leaders." 43. Rejoice, you nations (Gentiles), with His people, for He will avenge the blood of His servants; He will take vengeance on His enemies and make atonement (reconciliation) for His land and people. 44. Moses came with Joshua son of Nun (Moses' successor) and spoke all the words of this song in the hearing of the people. 45. When Moses finished reciting all these words to all Israel, 46. he said to them, "Take to heart all the words I have solemnly declared to you today, so that you may command your children to obey carefully all the words of this law. 47. They are not just idle words for you—they are your life. By them, you will live long in the land you are crossing the Jordan River to possess." 48. On that same day, the LORD instructed Moses, 49. "Go up into the Abarim Range (mountain range in Moab) to Mount Nebo in Moab (the eastern side of the Jordan River), across from Jericho (the city in Canaan), and view Canaan, the land I am giving the Israelites as their own possession. 50. There on the mountain that you have climbed, you will die and be gathered to your people, just as your brother Aaron died on Mount Hor (the mountain in Edom) and was gathered to his people. 51. This is because both of you broke faith with Me in the presence of the Israelites at the waters of Meribah Kadesh in the wilderness of Zin (a desert area) and because you did not uphold My holiness among the Israelites. 52. Therefore, you will see the land only from a distance; you will not enter the land I am giving to the people of Israel."

Chapter 33

1. That is the blessing that Moses (the prophet and leader of the Israelites) the man of God reported at the Israelites earlier than his loss of life. 2. He said: "The LORD (YHWH) came from Sinai (a mountain in the barren region, in which Moses obtained the Ten Commandments) and dawned over them from Seir (a mountainous region associated with the descendants of Esau); He shone forth from Mount Paran (another mountain location to the south of Israel). He got here with myriads (numerous hosts) of holy ones (angels or divine beings) from the south, from His mountain slopes. 3. Clearly it is you (Israel) who love the humans; all of the holy ones are for your hand. At your ft, all of them bow down, and from you receive instruction (referring to Moses, the lawgiver, who taught God's commandments), 4. the regulation that Moses gave us, the possession of the assembly of Jacob (the kingdom of Israel, descended from Jacob). 5. He (God) changed into king over Jeshurun (a poetic call for Israel, which means "the upright one") when the leaders of the human beings assembled, in conjunction with the tribes of Israel. 6. "Let Reuben (the firstborn tribe of Israel) stay and not die, nor his people be few." 7. And this he (Moses) stated about Judah (the tribe that have become the royal lineage): "Listen, LORD, the cry of Judah; convey him to his human beings. Along with his personal arms, he defends his purpose. Oh, be his assist in opposition to his foes!" 8. About Levi (the tribe of clergymen) he stated: "Your Thummim and Urim (sacred items used for divine steerage) belong to your faithful servant. You examined him at Massah (the location in which the Israelites quarreled with Moses and God) and contended with him on the waters of Meribah (the place wherein the Israelites complained about water). 9. He (Levi) said of his

mother and father, 'I haven't any regard for them.' He did now not understand his brothers or renowned his personal kids, however he watched over your word and guarded your covenant. **10.** He teaches your precepts (commands) to Jacob and your law to Israel. He gives incense before you and whole burnt offerings to your altar. **11.** Bless all his abilities, LORD, and be thrilled with the work of his hands. Strike down individuals who upward thrust towards him, his foes until they upward thrust no extra." **12.** About Benjamin (the youngest tribe, regularly related to protection) he stated: "Let the beloved of the LORD relaxation comfortable in him, for he shields him all day lengthy, and the one the LORD loves rests between his shoulders." **13.** About Joseph (the tribe that have become two half-tribes, Ephraim and Manasseh) he said: "May the LORD bless his land with the precious dew from heaven above and with the deep waters that lie under; **14.** With the exceptional the sun brings forth and the best the moon can yield; **15.** With the most effective items of the historical mountains and the fruitfulness of the everlasting hills; **16.** With the fine presents of the earth and its fullness and the prefer of Him who dwelt inside the burning bush (a reference to God's appearance to Moses on the burning bush). Let some of these rest on the top of Joseph, on the brow of the prince among his brothers. **17.** In majesty, he is like a firstborn bull; his horns are the horns of a wild ox. With them, he's going to gore the countries, even those at the ends of the earth. Such are the hundreds of Ephraim; such are the thousands of Manasseh." **18.** About Zebulun (a tribe acknowledged for its seafaring people) he stated: "Celebrate, Zebulun, on your going out, and also you, Issachar (a tribe associated with pupils and understanding), on your tents. **19.** They will summon peoples to the mountain (Mount Zion, Jerusalem) and there provide the sacrifices of the righteous; they may feast on the abundance of the seas (possibly relating to trade), at the treasures hidden inside the sand." **20.** About Gad (a tribe regarded for its warriors) he stated: "Blessed is he who enlarges Gad's domain! Gad lives there like a lion, tearing at arm or head. **21.** He chose the satisfactory land for himself; the chief's portion became saved for him. When the heads of the human beings assembled, he carried out the LORD's righteous will, and his judgments regarding Israel." **22.** About Dan (a tribe associated with judgment) he said: "Dan is a lion's cub, springing out of Bashan (a area east of Israel, recognised for strong livestock)." **23.** About Naphtali (a tribe associated with abundance and blessing) he said: "Naphtali is abounding with the want of the LORD and is full of His blessing; he'll inherit southward to the lake (possibly referring to the sea of Galilee)." **24.** About Asher (a tribe recognized for its prosperity) he stated: "Most blessed of sons is Asher; let him be desired by his brothers, and let him bathe his ft in oil (a image of abundance and comfort). **25.** The bolts of your gates may be iron and bronze, and your strength will identical your days (that means lasting power and security). **26.** "There is no person just like the God of Jeshurun (Israel), who rides throughout the heavens that will help you and at the clouds in His majesty. **27.** The everlasting God is your shelter, and below are the everlasting palms (God's eternal protection). He will pressure out your enemies before you, saying, 'Destroy them!' **28.** So Israel will stay in safety; Jacob will live secure in a land of grain and new wine, in which the heavens drop dew (symbolizing prosperity and peace). **29.** Blessed are you, Israel! Who is like you, a human beings saved with the aid of the LORD? He is your protect and helper and your wonderful sword. Your enemies will cower before you, and you will tread on their heights."

Chapter 34

1. Then Moses (the leader of the Israelites) climbed Mount Nebo from the plains of Moab (a place east of Israel) to the height of Pisgah, which faces Jericho (an historical city inside the Jordan River valley). There, the LORD confirmed him all of the land—from Gilead (a place to the north) to Dan (a metropolis within the far north of Israel), **2.** including all of Naphtali (a tribal territory), and the lands of Ephraim (a tribe descended from Joseph) and Manasseh (every other tribe descended from Joseph), and all of Judah (the southern state of Israel), as a long way because the Mediterranean Sea (the massive frame of water to the west), **3.** the Negev (a desolate tract vicinity within the south), and the whole region from the Valley of Jericho (the well-known metropolis of palms) to Zoar (a city at the southern border of Israel). **4.** Then the LORD spoke to him, announcing, "This is the land I promised with an oath to Abraham (the patriarch), Isaac (Abraham's son), and Jacob (Isaac's son) after I informed them, 'I can give it to your descendants.' I've allowed you to look it along with your very own eyes, however you will not pass over into it." **5.** And Moses, the servant of the LORD, died there within the land of Moab, because the LORD had spoken. **6.** He became buried in Moab, inside the valley opposite Beth Peor (a place near the Jordan River), however to these days, nobody knows the precise vicinity of his grave. **7.** Moses changed into a hundred and twenty years vintage when he died, yet his vision had now not grown dim, nor had his strength diminished. **8.** The Israelites mourned for Moses inside the plains of Moab for thirty days, until the length of weeping and mourning turned into complete. **9.** Now Joshua (Moses' assistant and successor), the son of Nun, was filled with the spirit of knowledge because Moses had laid his hands on him. So the Israelites listened to him and followed the commands the LORD had given to Moses. **10.** Because that point, no prophet has arisen in Israel like Moses, whom the LORD knew head to head, **11.** and who performed all the ones signs and wonders that the LORD despatched him to do in Egypt (the land of Pharaoh), before Pharaoh (the king of Egypt) and all his officers, and throughout the entire land of Egypt. **12.** No one has ever verified such mighty power or achieved such awe-inspiring deeds as Moses did inside the sight of all Israel.

6 – Joshua

Chapter 1

1. After the death of Moses, the menial (servant) of the Lord, the Lord spoke to Joshua, the son of Nun, who had served as Moses' adjunct (assistant). He said, **2.** "Moses, My menial, is dead. Now, rise up, go across the Jordan River with all the people, and take possession of the land I'm giving to the Israelites. **3.** Every place where you set bottom (your foot), I've formerly given to you, as I promised to Moses. **4.** Your home will extend from the nature, including Lebanon, all the way to the great swash (river), the Euphrates, and the land of the Hittites (an ancient people), stretching to the Great Sea (Mediterranean) in the west, where the sun sets. **5.** No bone (person) will be suitable to stand against you as long as you live. Just as I was with Moses, I'll be with you; I'll not leave you or forsake you. **6.** Be strong and courageous, for you will divide this land as a heritage to the people I swore to give to their ancestors. **7.** Only be strong and very courageous, and be careful to follow all the law (God's commandments) that Moses, My menial, commanded you. Do not transgress from it, either to the right or to the left, so that you may succeed wherever you go. **8.** This Book of the Law (Torah) must always be on your lips. Meditate on it day and night, so that you may carefully follow everything written in it. Then you will be prosperous and successful. **9.** Have I not commanded you? Be strong and courageous! Do not be afraid, nor be discouraged, for the Lord your God is with you wherever you go." **10.** Then Joshua gave a command to the officers (leaders) of the people, saying, **11.** "Go through the camp and tell the people, 'Prepare vittles (food), for within three days you will cross the Jordan River and take possession of the land the Lord your God is giving you.'" **12.** And to the tribes of Reuben, Gad, and half of Manasseh, Joshua spoke, saying, **13.** "Remember what Moses, the servant of the Lord, commanded you: 'The Lord your God is giving you rest and has given you this land.' **14.** Your women, children, and livestock shall stay in the land Moses gave you on this side of the Jordan. But all your fighting men must cross over, fully armed, to help your fellow Israelites, **15.** Until the Lord gives them rest, as He has given you rest, and they also take possession of the land the Lord your God is giving them. After that, you may return to your own land and enjoy it, which Moses, the servant of the Lord, gave you on the east side of the Jordan River." **16.** They answered Joshua, saying, "All that you command us, we will do, and wherever you send us, we will go. **17.** Just as we fully obeyed Moses, so we will obey you. Only may the Lord your God be with you, as He was with Moses. **18.** Anyone who rebels against your word and does not obey your commands, whatever you may command them, shall be put to death. Only be strong and courageous."

Chapter 2

1. Joshua, the leader of Israel, secretly sent two men from Acacia Grove (a place in Israel) to scout out the land, especially the city of Jericho. He told them, "Go and explore the land, particularly Jericho." So, the two men set out and arrived at the house of a woman named Rahab, who was a prostitute. They stayed there. **2.** News soon reached the king of Jericho, who was told, "Some men from the Israelites have come here tonight to spy on the land." **3.** The king of Jericho sent word to Rahab, saying, "Bring out the men who entered your house, because they've come to spy on the entire land." **4.** But Rahab hid the two men. She answered, "Yes, the men did come to me, but I didn't know where they were from. **5.** When it was time to shut the city gate at night, the men left. I don't know which way they went; hurry after them, and you might catch up with them." **6.** (In truth, she had already hidden them on her roof, under stalks of flax she had laid out there.) **7.** The king's soldiers chased the two spies along the road that leads to the Jordan River, to the fords (shallow crossing places). Once they left, the city gate was closed. **8.** Before the two spies went to bed that night, Rahab went up to the roof and said to them: **9.** "I know that the LORD has given you this land, and we are all terrified because of you. Everyone here is filled with fear because of what you've done. **10.** We've heard how the Lord dried up the waters of the Red Sea when you came out of Egypt, and how you destroyed the two kings of the Amorites (a people group), Sihon and Og. **11.** As soon as we heard about these things, we were all filled with fear. No one has any courage left because of you. For the Lord your God is the God of heaven above and earth below. **12.** Now, I beg you; swear to me by the Lord that, since I've helped you, you'll also show kindness to my family. Give me a sure sign, **13.** And spare the lives of my father, my mother, my brothers, my sisters, and all their family. Save us from death." **14.** The two men replied, "We promise our lives will be spared if you don't tell anyone about us. When the Lord gives us this land, we will treat you with kindness and keep our promise." **15.** Rahab let them down through a window by a rope, because her house was built into the city wall, and she lived in the wall. **16.** She told them, "Go to the hills and hide for three days, until the soldiers return. Then you can leave safely." **17.** The men told her, "We'll keep our promise, as long as you don't tell anyone about our mission. **18.** When we come into the land, tie this scarlet cord in the window through which you let us down, and gather your family into your house. **19.** If anyone goes outside the house and into the street, their blood will be on their own head, and we won't be responsible. But if anyone inside the house is harmed, we'll be guilty." **20.** "But," they added, "if you reveal what we're doing, we'll be released from the promise we made to you." **21.** Rahab agreed, saying, "As you've said, so be it." Then she sent them away, and they left. She tied the scarlet cord in the window, just as they had instructed. **22.** The two men hid in the hills for three days until the soldiers returned. They searched the roads, but they couldn't find the spies. **23.** After three days, the two men returned, crossed the river, and went to Joshua, the son of Nun. They told him everything that had happened to them. **24.** They said to Joshua, "The Lord has truly given us the whole land. All the people are terrified of us."

Chapter 3

1. Early the following morning, Joshua and all the Israelites left Acacia Grove and made their way to the Jordan River. They camped there to prepare for the crossing. **2.** After three days had passed, the officers went through the camp, **3.** And they gave this command to the people: "When you see the Ark of the Covenant of the Lord your God being carried by the priests, the Levites, you are to follow it, **4.** but make sure there is a distance of about two thousand cubits (roughly 1,000 yards or half a mile) between you and the Ark. Do not come close to it, so that you will know the way to take, because you have never traveled this route before." **5.** Joshua then told the people, "Consecrate yourselves, because tomorrow the Lord will perform extraordinary deeds among you." **6.** Joshua instructed the priests, "Lift the Ark of the Covenant and lead the people across the river." The priests took up the Ark and moved ahead of the people. **7.** The Lord spoke to Joshua, saying, "Today I will begin to lift you up in the sight of all Israel, so that they will know that just as I was with Moses, I will be with you." **8.** "Instruct the priests carrying the Ark to step into the waters of the Jordan and stand there." **9.** Joshua addressed the people of Israel, saying, "Come and listen to the words of the Lord your God. **10.** By this, you will know that the living God is with you: He will drive out before you all the nations—the Canaanites, Hittites, Hivites, Perizzites, Girgashites, Amorites, and Jebusites. **11.** See, the Ark of the Covenant of the Lord of all the earth is moving ahead of you into the Jordan River. **12.** Now, select twelve men from the twelve tribes of Israel, one from each tribe. **13.** As soon as the priests carrying the Ark of the Lord, the Lord of all the earth, step into the river, the waters will be cut off. The water flowing down from upstream will pile up in a heap." **14.** As soon as the people began their march to cross the Jordan, the priests who carried the Ark went ahead of them. **15.** When the priests' feet touched the water's edge (and remember, it was the season when the river overflowed its banks), **16.** The water coming from upstream stopped and piled up far away at the city of Adam (a city near Zaretan). The waters flowing toward the Dead Sea stopped, allowing the people to cross on dry ground. **17.** The priests who carried the Ark of the Covenant stood firmly on dry ground in the middle of the river, while the entire nation of Israel crossed over, and not a single person was left behind.

Chapter 4

1. After all the people had completely crossed over the Jordan River, the Lord spoke to Joshua, saying: **2.** "Choose twelve men from the people, one from each tribe, **3.** And give them this instruction: 'Take twelve stones from this place, from where the priests' feet stood in the middle of the Jordan. Carry them with you and place them at the camp where you will spend the night.'" **4.** So Joshua called the twelve men he had appointed, one from each tribe of Israel. **5.** He told them, "Go ahead of the ark of the Lord your God into the middle of the Jordan River. Each of you should take a stone and carry it on your shoulder, in line with the number of the tribes of Israel, **6.** So that these stones will serve as a sign for you. In the future, when your children ask, 'What do these stones mean to you?' **7.** You will tell them that the waters of the Jordan River stopped flowing when the ark of the Lord's covenant passed through the river. The waters were cut off, and these stones will stand as a memorial for the people of Israel forever." **8.** The Israelites did exactly as Joshua had commanded: they took twelve stones from the middle of the Jordan, one for each tribe, as the Lord had directed. They carried the stones with them and set them down at their camp. **9.** Joshua also set up twelve stones in the middle of the Jordan, at the place where the priests who carried the ark had stood. These stones remain there to this day. **10.** The priests who carried the ark stayed in the middle of the river until everything was completed as the Lord had commanded Joshua. Meanwhile, the people hurried to cross. **11.** Once all the people had crossed over, the ark of the Lord and the priests crossed in front of them. **12.** The men from the tribes of Reuben, Gad, and half of the tribe of Manasseh (the descendants of Joseph's son) crossed over, fully armed, as Moses had instructed them. **13.** About forty thousand men, ready for battle, crossed over in front of the Lord, heading to the plains near Jericho (a city in Israel). **14.** On that day, the Lord made Joshua great in the eyes of all Israel, and they held him in awe, just as they had held Moses in awe during his lifetime. **15.** Then the Lord spoke to Joshua, saying, **16.** "Command the priests who are carrying the Ark of the Covenant to come up from the Jordan." **17.** So Joshua told the priests, "Come up from the Jordan." **18.** When the priests carrying the ark of the Lord's covenant stepped onto dry land, the waters of the Jordan returned to their place and overflowed the banks, just as they had done before. **19.** The people came up from the Jordan on the tenth day of the first month and camped at Gilgal (a place near Jericho), on the eastern side of Jericho. **20.** Joshua set up the twelve stones they had taken from Jordan at Gilgal. **21.** Then he spoke to the Israelites, saying: "In the future, when your children ask their fathers, 'What do these stones mean?' **22.** You will tell them, 'Israel crossed over this Jordan River on dry ground.' **23.** For the Lord your God dried up the waters of the Jordan before you until you had crossed, just as He did with the Red Sea (the sea that Moses parted), drying it up before us until we crossed. **24.** This is so that all the nations of the earth will know that the Lord's hand is mighty and so that you will always honored and fear the Lord your God."

Chapter 5

1. When the kings of the Amorites (Canaanite tribes living west of the Jordan River) and the kings of the Canaanites (those who inhabited the land by the Mediterranean Sea) heard that the LORD had dried up the waters of the Jordan River so the Israelites could cross, they were filled with fear. Their courage melted away because of the Israelites. **2.** At that time, the Lord spoke to Joshua and said, "Prepare flint knives (sharp stone knives) and circumcise the Israelites again, a second time."**3.** Joshua obeyed the command, making flint knives, and circumcised the men of Israel at a place called the Hill of the Foreskins.**4.** The reason for this was that all the men who had come out of Egypt and who had been circumcised had died in the wilderness during the forty years they wandered there.**5.** Although the men who had left Egypt were circumcised, none of the children born during the wilderness journey had been circumcised.**6.** The Israelites had wandered in the desert for forty years until all the men of war from Egypt had died. They had not obeyed the voice of the Lord, so He swore that none of them would enter the Promised Land—a land flowing with milk and honey.**7.** Therefore, Joshua circumcised their children, who had replaced their fathers, because they had not been circumcised during the time of wandering.**8.** After the circumcision, the men remained in camp until they had healed from the procedure.**9.** Then the Lord spoke to Joshua and said, "Today, I have taken away the shame of Egypt from you." That is why the place was called Gilgal (meaning "Roll Away") and the name is still used today.**10.** The Israelites stayed at Gilgal and celebrated the Passover (the yearly festival commemorating their deliverance from Egypt) on the fourteenth day of the first month, at sunset, in the plains near Jericho (the area around the city of Jericho).**11.** The day after the Passover they ate some of the crops from the land—unleavened bread (bread without yeast) and roasted grain—and they ate it on that very day.**12.** The manna (the food God had miraculously provided) ceased the very next day after they ate the produce of the land. From that time onward, the Israelites ate food from the land of Canaan for the rest of that year.**13.** While Joshua was near Jericho, he looked up and saw a man standing before him, holding a drawn sword. Joshua approached him and asked, "Are you for us or for our enemies?"**14.** The man replied, "Neither. I have come as the Commander of the army of the Lord." Joshua immediately fell to the ground and worshiped him. He asked, "What message does my Lord have for His servant?"**15.** The Commander of the Lord's army responded, "Take off your sandals because the place where you are standing is holy." And Joshua did so.

Chapter 6

1. Jericho (a city) was tightly shut up and securely closed off because of the Israelites; no one went in or out of the city.**2.** The Lord said to Joshua, "Look! I have already handed Jericho, its king, and its mighty warriors over to you.**3.** "You and all your soldiers are to march around the city once each day for six days .**4.** Seven priests will carry seven ram's horn trumpets (special musical instruments) before the Ark of the Covenant. But on the seventh day, you will march around the city seven times, and the priests will blow the trumpets.**5.** When they make a long blast with the ram's horn and you hear the sound, the whole army is to shout loudly. Then the city's wall will collapse and fall flat, and everyone will go straight ahead into the city."**6.** Joshua, son of Nun, called the priests and said to them, "Take up the Ark of the Covenant and have seven priests carry the seven ram's horn trumpets in front of the Ark of the Lord."**7.** He also told the people, "March around the city, with armed soldiers going before the Ark of the Lord."**8.** When Joshua had finished speaking to the people, the seven priests who carried the seven trumpets began to march before the Lord, blowing their trumpets, while the Ark of the Covenant of the Lord followed them.**9.** The armed soldiers went ahead of the priests who were blowing the trumpets, and the rear guard followed the Ark, while the priests continued blowing their trumpets.**10.** Joshua commanded the people, "Do not shout or make any noise with your voices, and do not let a word come from your mouths until I say to you, 'Shout!' Then you will shout."**11.** So, the Ark of the Lord circled the city once, and then returned to camp, and they spent the night there.**12.** Early next morning, Joshua rose, and the priests took up the Ark of the Lord.**13.** The seven priests, with their seven trumpets, marched before the Ark of the Lord, continually blowing their trumpets. The armed soldiers went before them, and the rear guard followed the Ark, while the priests blew their trumpets.**14.** On the second day, they marched around the city once and returned to the camp. They did this for six days .**15.** On the seventh day, they rose early, at the dawn of the day, and marched around the city seven times in the same manner. Only on that day did they march around the city seven times. **16.** The seventh time, when the priests blew their trumpets, Joshua commanded the people, "Shout, for the Lord has given you the city!"**17.** "The city and everything in it is under the Lord's curse and will be destroyed, along with everyone inside. However, Rahab (a woman who lived in Jericho) the prostitute will survive, along with everyone in her house, because she hid the spies we sent."**18.** "Be careful, and do not take any of the cursed items, so that you do not become cursed yourselves by taking them. If you do, you will bring trouble upon the camp of Israel."**19.** "All the silver, gold, and the bronze and iron vessels are consecrated (set apart) to the Lord; they must be brought into the Lord's treasury."**20.** When the people heard the trumpet sound and shouted loudly, the walls of the city collapsed. The people rushed into the city, each man going straight ahead, and they took the city.**21.** They completely destroyed everything in the city—men, women, young and old, cattle, sheep, and donkeys—using the sword.**22.** But Joshua had told the two spies, "Go into the prostitute's house, and bring out Rahab and her family, as you promised her."**23.** The spies went into Rahab's house, brought out her father, mother, brothers, and all her family, and left them safely outside the camp of Israel.**24.** Then they burned the city and everything in it, except for the silver, gold, and the bronze and iron vessels, which they took to put into the Lord's treasury.**25.** Joshua spared Rahab the prostitute, her family, and all that she had. They lived among the Israelites to this day because she hid the messengers whom Joshua had sent to spy out Jericho.**26.** At that time, Joshua made a proclamation: "Cursed be anyone who tries to rebuild Jericho. He will lay its foundation with his firstborn son, and he will set up its gates with his youngest son."**27.** So the Lord was with Joshua, and his fame spread throughout the land.

Chapter 7

1. The Israelites committed a sin by disobeying the Lord's command regarding the devoted things. Achan, the son of Carmi, the son of Zabdi, from the tribe of Judah, took some of the forbidden items, and because of this, the Lord's anger burned against the entire nation of Israel.**2.** Joshua sent men from Jericho to Ai, a city located near Beth Aven, east of Bethel, to scout out the land. He told them, "Go and investigate the area."**3.** The spies returned to Joshua and reported, "There's no need for the entire army to go up to Ai. Just send two or three thousand men to fight, because Ai has a small army."**4.** So, about three thousand men went up, but they were defeated by the men of Ai.**5.** The men of Ai killed about thirty-six Israelites, pursuing them from the city gate to Shebarim, and struck them down on the descent. As a result, the hearts of the Israelites melted, and they were left feeling completely discouraged.**6.** Joshua tore his clothes in grief, fell face down on the ground before the Ark of the Lord, and remained there until evening. The elders of Israel joined him, placing dust on their heads in sorrow.**7.** Joshua prayed to God, saying, "Lord, why did you bring us across the Jordan River only to hand us over to the Amorites and let them destroy us? If only we had stayed on the other side of the Jordan! **8.** What can I say when Israel turns its back before its enemies? **9.** The people of Canaan and all those living in the land will hear about this, and they will surround us and destroy us. What will you do to protect your great name?"**10.** The Lord replied to Joshua, "Get up! Why are you lying on your face like this? **11.** Israel has sinned. They have broken my covenant by taking some of the forbidden items. They have stolen, deceived, and hidden the items among their own belongings.**12.** Because of this, the Israelites will not be able to stand against their enemies. They will turn their backs and flee, because they are under a curse. I will no longer be with you unless you remove the cursed things from your midst.**13.** Get up, consecrate the people, and tell them, 'consecrate yourselves for tomorrow, for the Lord, the God of Israel, says: "There is something cursed among you, and you cannot stand against your enemies until you remove it."'**14.** Tomorrow, you will come forward by tribes, and the tribe the Lord chooses will come forward by clans. The clan the Lord selects will come forward by families, and the family the Lord chooses will come forward man by man.**15.** The person who is found with the cursed items will be burned with fire, along with everything they own, because they have broken the covenant of the Lord and committed a disgraceful act in Israel.'"**16.** So Joshua rose early the next morning and brought the people forward by tribes, and the tribe of Judah was selected.**17.** He brought forward the clan of Judah, and the family of the Zarhites was chosen. He brought the family of the Zarhites forward by households, and Zabdi was chosen. **18.** He then brought the household forward, and Achan, the son of Carmi, from the tribe of Judah, was selected. **19.** Joshua said to Achan, "My son, give glory to the Lord, the God of Israel, and confess to Him. Tell me what you have done; do not hide it from me." **20.** Achan replied, "I have sinned against the Lord, the God of Israel, and this is what I did: **21.** When I saw among the spoils a beautiful Babylonian robe, two hundred shekels of silver, and a gold wedge weighing fifty shekels, I desired them and took them. They are hidden in the ground inside my tent, with the silver underneath." **22.** Joshua sent messengers to Achan's tent. When they searched the tent, they found the stolen items buried there, with the silver beneath them. **23.** They took the items from the tent, brought them to Joshua and the Israelites, and laid them before the Lord. **24.** Then Joshua, along with all the Israelites, took Achan, his stolen items, his sons, his daughters, his cattle, his donkeys, his sheep, his tent, and everything he owned, and brought them to the Valley of Achor. **25.** Joshua said, "Why have you brought trouble on us? The Lord will bring trouble on you today." And all Israel stoned Achan with stones. After stoning him, they burned his body with fire. **26.** Then they piled a large heap of stones over Achan, which remains there to this day. The Lord turned from His fierce anger. Therefore, the place has been named the Valley of Achor, which means "Valley of Trouble," and it is still called that to this day.

Joshua 8

1. The Lord spoke to Joshua, saying, "Do not be afraid or discouraged. Take all the fighting men with you and go up to Ai. See, I have handed over to you the king of Ai, his people, his city, and his land. **2.** You will treat Ai and its king the same way you did Jericho and its king. However, the spoils and the cattle you may take as plunder for yourselves. Set an ambush behind the city." **3.** So, Joshua got up, and all the soldiers with him, to go against Ai. He selected thirty thousand brave men and sent them out at night. **4.** He commanded them, "Look, you are to hide behind the city. Stay close but be ready for action. **5.** I and all the people with me will approach the city. When they come out to fight us, as they did before, we will pretend to flee before them. **6.** They will chase us, thinking we are retreating, and that will draw them away from the city. **7.** At that moment, you will rise up from your hiding place and take the city, for the Lord your God will give it into your hands. **8.** Once you capture the city, set it on fire as the Lord has commanded. This is my command to you." **9.** Joshua sent them out, and they hid between Bethel and Ai, on the west side of Ai. Meanwhile, Joshua camped that night with the people. **10.** Early the next morning, Joshua called the people together and, along with the elders of Israel, led them toward Ai. **11.** All the soldiers who were with him approached the city, camping on the north side. A valley lay between them and the city. **12.** Joshua positioned about five thousand men in ambush between Bethel and Ai, on the west side of the city. **13.** When all the people were in place, Joshua went down into the valley. **14.** The king of Ai saw the Israelites and, early in the morning, he and his people came out to fight them, not knowing the ambush had been set behind the city. **15.** Joshua and all Israel pretended to be defeated and fled into the wilderness. **16.** The men of Ai gathered to pursue them, and they followed Joshua, abandoning the city. **17.** Not a man of Ai or Bethel remained behind; they all chased Israel. As a result, the city was left open. **18.** Then the Lord told Joshua, "Stretch out the spear that is in your hand toward Ai, for I am giving it into your hands." Joshua raised his spear toward the city. **19.** As soon as he did, the men in ambush quickly rose, entered the city, and set it on fire. **20.** When the men of Ai turned and saw the smoke rising from the city, they realized they were trapped, and the Israelites who had fled turned to fight their pursuers. **21.** Joshua and the Israelites saw that the city was on fire and turned back to fight the men of Ai. **22.** The men of Ai were caught between Israel's forces, and they were completely defeated—none survived or escaped. **23.** The king of Ai was captured alive and brought to Joshua. **24.** After Israel had killed all the men and women of Ai, both in the field and during the pursuit, they returned to Ai and destroyed the city with the sword. **25.** That day, twelve thousand people from Ai were killed—both men and women. **26.** Joshua did not lower the spear in his hand until every person in Ai had been destroyed. **27.** Only the livestock and the goods of the city were taken by the Israelites as plunder, as the Lord had commanded Joshua. **28.** Joshua burned Ai and turned it into a permanent heap of ruins, a desolation that remains to

this day. **29.** He hanged the king of Ai on a tree until evening, and when the sun set, Joshua ordered that his body be taken down and thrown at the city gate. They raised a large pile of stones over it, which stands to this day. **30.** Then Joshua built an altar to the Lord, the God of Israel, on Mount Ebal, **31.** As Moses, the servant of the Lord had commanded the Israelites. It was an altar made of uncut stones, where they offered burnt offerings and peace offerings. **32.** Joshua also wrote the Law of Moses on the stones, **33.** And all of Israel—elders, leaders, and judges—stood on either side of the ark of the covenant of the Lord, with the Levites carrying the ark. Half of the people stood in front of Mount Gerizim and half in front of Mount Ebal, as Moses had instructed. **34.** Joshua read aloud all the words of the law, including the blessings and curses, just as they were written in the Book of the Law. **35.** Every word Moses had commanded was read aloud to the whole assembly of Israel, including the women, children, and foreigners living among them.

Chapter 9

1. When the kings who ruled on the west side of the Jordan River, in the mountains, the valleys, and along the shores of the Great Sea toward Lebanon—these kings were the Hittites, the Amorites, the Canaanites, the Perizzites, the Hivites, and the Jebusites—heard about Israel's victories, **2.** They gathered together in unity to fight against Joshua and the people of Israel. **3** But the people of Gibeon, when they heard about what Joshua had done to Jericho and Ai, **4** resorted to deception. They dressed as though they had traveled from a distant land, using old sacks on their donkeys, wineskins that were cracked and patched, **5.** Worn-out sandals on their feet, and tattered clothes. Their bread was dry and moldy, as if it had been stored for a long time. **6.** They went to Joshua at the camp in Gilgal and said to him and to the men of Israel, "We come from a far country. Please make a treaty with us." **7.** The Israelites replied to the Hivites, "Perhaps you live nearby. How can we make a treaty with people who might be our neighbors?" **8.** They responded to Joshua, "We are your servants." Joshua asked them, "Who are you, and where do you come from?" **9.** They answered him, "We are from a distant land, your servants, because we have heard of the fame of the Lord your God. We know what He did in Egypt, **10.** And all that He did to the two kings of the Amorites beyond the Jordan—Sihon, king of Heshbon, and OG, king of Bashan, who reigned in Ashtaroth. **11.** Our elders and all the inhabitants of our land told us, 'Take enough provisions for the journey, and go meet them. Say, "We are your servants. Make a covenant with us."' **12.** This bread that we brought with us was fresh when we set out from our homes, but now look; it is dried out and moldy. **13.** And these wineskins that were new when we filled them are now torn. Our clothes and sandals have worn out because of the long journey." **14.** The Israelites examined their provisions, but they did not consult the Lord. **15.** So Joshua made peace with them and agreed to a covenant that would allow them to live. The leaders of the people swore an oath to them. **16.** Three days later, after making the covenant, the Israelites discovered that the Gibeonites were actually their neighbors, **17.** And on the third day, they arrived at their cities: Gibeon, Chephirah, Beeroth, and Kirjath Jearim. **18.** But the Israelites did not attack them, for the leaders had sworn an oath to them in the name of the Lord, the God of Israel. The entire community was upset with the leaders. **19.** The leaders responded to the people, "We swore to them by the Lord, the God of Israel, and we cannot break our oath to them. **20.** This is what we will do: We will let them live, but they will become our servants, cutting wood and drawing water for the entire community, as the leaders promised." **21.** The leaders then said to the people, "Let them live, but they will serve as woodcutters and water carriers for the congregation and for the altar of the Lord, wherever He chooses." **22.** Joshua called the Gibeonites and asked them, "Why did you deceive us by saying, 'We come from a far country,' when in fact you live near us? **23.** now you are cursed, and none of you will be free from being slaves—woodcutters and water carriers for the house of my God." **24.** The Gibeonites answered Joshua, "Your servants were clearly informed that the Lord your God commanded His servant Moses to give you all the land and to destroy all the inhabitants of the land before you. We were terrified for our lives because of you, and that's why we did what we did. **25.** Now we are in your hands. Do with us whatever seems good and right to you." **26.** Joshua did as they said, saving them from the Israelites, so they were not killed. **27.** That day, Joshua made them woodcutters and water carriers for the people and for the altar of the Lord, wherever He would choose, and they have remained so to this day.

Chapter 10

1. When Adoni-Zedek (king of Jerusalem), heard that Joshua had conquered Ai (a city) and completely destroyed it—just as he had done to Jericho (a city) and its king—and that the people of Gibeon (a city) had made peace with Israel and joined them, **2.** he and his people were terrified (extremely afraid). Gibeon was a major city, like a royal city (a city of high importance), larger than Ai, and its men were mighty warriors. **3.** So, Adoni-Zedek sent a message to Hoham (king of Hebron), Piram (king of Jarmuth), Japhia (king of Lachish), and Debir (king of Eglon), saying, **4.** "Come and help me attack Gibeon, because it has made peace with Joshua and the Israelites." **5.** The five Amorite kings (a group of kings from a group of people) gathered their armies and went up to Gibeon to wage war (fight a battle) against it. **6.** The men of Gibeon sent word to Joshua at the camp in Gilgal (a place), saying, "Don't abandon (leave) us. Come quickly to help us, for all the kings of the Amorites are attacking us." **7.** So Joshua and all his warriors (soldiers), including his mighty men (brave warriors), marched up from Gilgal. **8.** The LORD said to Joshua, "Do not fear (be afraid) them, for I have given them into your hands; not a single one will stand against you." **9.** Joshua launched a surprise attack on them, marching through the night from Gilgal. **10.** The Lord caused a great defeat (loss) for the Amorites before Israel. Israel slaughtered (killed violently) them at Gibeon, pursued them along the road to Beth Horon (a place), and struck them down as far as Azekah and Makkedah (places). **11.** As the enemies fled (ran away) down the road from Beth Horon, the Lord sent large hailstones (frozen chunks of ice falling from the sky) from the sky, killing more of them than the Israelites did with the sword (weapon). **12.** On that day, Joshua spoke to the Lord in front of all Israel, saying, "Sun, stand still over Gibeon; Moon, stop in the Valley of Aijalon (a place)." **13.** So the sun stood still, and the moon halted (stopped) until the Israelites had defeated their enemies. This event is recorded in the Book of Jasher (an ancient book). The sun remained in the sky for about a full day. **14.** Never before or after that day did the Lord listen to the voice of a man, for the Lord fought for Israel? **15.** Then Joshua and all Israel returned to their camp at Gilgal. **16.** Meanwhile, the five kings had fled and hidden in a cave at Makkedah. **17.** Joshua was told, "The five kings have been found in the cave at Makkedah." **18.** Joshua commanded, "Roll large stones (big rocks) to block the mouth of the cave, and set guards there to watch them." **19.** "But don't stay there. Instead, continue pursuing your enemies and prevent them from escaping to their cities, because the Lord has delivered (given) them into your hands." **20.** While Israel finished destroying the rest of the Amorite forces, those who managed to escape sought refuge (safety) in fortified cities (cities with strong walls). **21.** Afterward, the Israelites returned to Makkedah in peace. None of the people spoke a word against the Israelites. **22.** Joshua ordered, "Open the cave and bring out the five kings." **23.** They brought the five kings to Joshua: the kings of Jerusalem, Hebron, Jarmuth, Lachish, and Eglon. **24.** Joshua called the Israelite leaders and said to them, "Come, place your feet on the necks of these kings." They stepped forward and placed their feet on their necks. **25.** Joshua said to them, "Do not be afraid or discouraged (feeling hopeless); be strong and courageous (brave). This is how the Lord will deal with all your enemies." **26.** Then Joshua killed the kings and hung their bodies on five trees (wooden poles), where they remained until evening. **27.** At sunset, Joshua gave the order to take their bodies down from the trees, throw them into the cave where they had hidden, and seal the cave with large stones, which remain there to this day. **28.** On that day, Joshua captured Makkedah, struck its king and people with the sword, and utterly destroyed them (completely wiped them out), as he had done to Jericho and its king. **29.** Then Joshua moved on with all Israel to Libnah (a city) and attacked it. **30.** The Lord delivered Libnah and its king into Israel's hands, and they destroyed it, just as they had done to Jericho and its king. **31.** From Libnah, Joshua and all Israel went to Lachish (a city), set up camp, and fought against it. **32.** The Lord gave Lachish into Israel's hands, and they took it on the second day, killing all its inhabitants, as they had done to Libnah. **33.** Horam (king of Gezer) came to help Lachish, but Joshua

defeated him and his forces, leaving no survivors. **34.** From Lachish, Joshua and all Israel moved on to Eglon (a city), set up camp, and fought against it. **35.** They captured it on that day, slaughtered its entire people, and destroyed it completely, as they had done to Lachish. **36.** Next, Joshua went up with all Israel to Hebron (a city) and fought against it. **37.** They took Hebron, killed its king, destroyed all its people and cities, and left no survivors, as they had done to Eglon. **38.** Joshua then moved on with all Israel to Debir (a city) and fought against it. **39.** They captured Debir and its king, struck down all its inhabitants, and completely destroyed it, just as they had done to Hebron. **40.** Joshua conquered the entire land, including the hill country (mountain areas), the southern regions, the lowlands (flat lands), and the wilderness areas (desolate places), defeating all the kings and leaving none alive, as the Lord had commanded. **41.** Joshua conquered the land from Kadesh Barnea (a desert region) to Gaza (a city), and all the regions of Goshen (a district), up to Gibeon. **42.** All these kings and their lands were captured by Joshua in one campaign, because the Lord fought for Israel. **43.** Then Joshua and all Israel returned to their camp at Gilgal.

Chapter 11

1. When Jabin, king of Hazor (a major city in Canaan), heard what had happened to other kings and their cities, he sent word to Jobab, king of Madon, the king of Shimron, and the king of Achshaph. 2. He also reached out to the kings from the north, in the mountains, in the plain south of Chinneroth (a region near the Sea of Galilee), in the lowland, and in the heights of Dor (a coastal region to the west). 3. Additionally, he contacted the Canaanites living east and west, as well as the Amorites, Hittites, Perizzites, Jebusites in the mountains, and the Hivites living below Mount Hermon in the land of Mizpah. 4. These kings gathered their armies, which were vast—so many soldiers they could not be counted, with countless horses and chariots. 5. The kings and their armies camped together at the waters of Merom (a large lake north of Galilee), preparing for battle against Israel. 6. But the Lord told Joshua, "Do not be afraid of them. By this time tomorrow, I will hand all of them over to Israel, and you will hamstring their horses and burn their chariots." 7. Joshua and his army launched a surprise attack on them near the waters of Merom, catching the enemy off guard. 8. The Lord gave them victory, and Israel defeated the enemy, chasing them all the way to Greater Sidon (a coastal city), the Brook Misrephoth, and the Valley of Mizpah to the east. They attacked them until no one remained. 9. As commanded, Joshua hamstrung the enemy's horses and burned their chariots with fire. 10. Joshua then turned back and took Hazor, killing its king with the sword. Hazor had been the leading city of all those kingdoms. 11. Joshua struck down everyone in Hazor, leaving no survivors, and burned the city to the ground. 12. Joshua took all the cities of these kings and defeated their rulers, killing every man in the cities and destroying them, just as Moses had commanded. 13. The only cities Israel did not burn were those on mounds or hills, except Hazor, which Joshua burned. 14. Israel took the spoil (loot) from these cities, including livestock, but destroyed every man with the sword, leaving no one alive. 15. Joshua did exactly as the Lord had instructed Moses, and he left nothing undone of all the commands God had given. 16. Joshua took possession of all the land: the mountainous regions, the South, the land of Goshen (a fertile area in southern Canaan), the lowlands, and the Jordan plain, including the mountains of Israel and its valleys. 17. He conquered from Mount Halak (the southern border of Israel) to the ascent to Seir (a region south of Israel), all the way to Baal Gad in the Valley of Lebanon below Mount Hermon. He defeated all their kings and killed them. 18. Joshua fought a long time with all these kings. 19. No city made peace with Israel, except for the Hivites of Gibeon, who made a treaty. All the other cities were captured in battle. 20. This was part of the Lord's plan: He hardened the hearts of the enemies so they would come against Israel in battle. This allowed God to utterly destroy them, showing no mercy, just as He had commanded Moses. 21. At this time, Joshua also defeated the Anakim (giants) in the mountains, including those in Hebron, Debir, Anab, and all the mountains of Judah and Israel. He destroyed them and their cities. 22. No Anakim were left in the land of Israel, except for those in Gaza, Gath, and Ashdod (Philistine cities). 23. Joshua took control of the entire land, as the Lord had promised to Moses, and gave it as an

inheritance to the Israelites, dividing it by their tribes. Then the land rested from war.

Chapter 12

1. These are the lords of the land whom the children of Israel defeated, and whose land they held on the other side of the Jordan toward the rising of the sun, from the River Arnon to Mount Hermon, and all the eastern Jordan plain. **2.** One king was Sihon, king of the Amorites(an ancient Semitic people), who dwelt in Heshbon(an ancient megacity in the Transjordan region) and ruled half of Gilead(the land east of the Jordan River), from Aroer(a megacity on the bank of the River Arnon), which is on the middle of that swash, indeed as far as the River Jabbok(the border of the Ammonites, a bordering people), **3.** and the eastern Jordan straight from the Sea of Chinneroth(Sea of Galilee) as far as the ocean of the Arabah(the Salt Sea, or Dead Sea), the road to Beth Jeshimoth(a position near the Dead Sea), and southward below the pitches of Pisgah(a mountain in Moab, with a view of the Promised Land). **4.** The other king was Og, king of Bashan(an ancient area known for its titans) and his home, who was of the remnant of the titans(titans are a fabulous race of surprisingly large people), who dwelt at Ashtaroth(a megacity in Bashan) and at Edrei(another megacity in Bashan), **5.** and reigned over Mount Hermon(a prominent mountain), over Salcah(a megacity), over all Bashan, as far as the border of the Geshurites(a group of people living to the north of Bashan) and the Maachathites(a group of people located to the southeast), and over half of Gilead to the border of Sihon, king of Heshbon. **6.** These Moses the menial of the Lord, and the children of Israel had conquered; and Moses, the menial of the Lord, had given it as a possession to the Reubenites, the Gadites, and half the lineage of Manasseh. **7.** And these are the lords of the country which Joshua and the children of Israel conquered on this side of the Jordan, on the west, from Baal Gad (a position in the Valley of Lebanon) in the Valley of Lebanon as far as Mount Halak (a mountain) and the ascent to Seir (a mountainous region to the southeast), which Joshua gave to the lines of Israel as a possession according to their divisions, **8.** in the mountain country, in the lowlands, in the Jordan straight, in the pitches, in the nature, and in the South the Hittites(a people group living in central Anatolia), the Amorites(a Semitic people), the Canaanites(the people of the Promised Land), the Perizzites(a Canaanite group), the Hivites(another Canaanite group), and the Jebusites(the occupants of Jerusalem). **9.** The king of Jericho, one; the king of Ai(which is beside Bethel), one; **10.** The king of Jerusalem, one; the king of Hebron, one; **11.** The king of Jarmuth, one; the king of Lachish, one; **12.** The king of Eglon, one; the king of Gezer, one; **13.** The king of Debir, one; the king of Geder, one; **14.** The king of Hormah, one; the king of Arad, one; **15.** The king of Libnah, one; the king of Adullam, one; **16.** The king of Makkedah, one; the king of Bethel, one; **17.** The king of Tappuah, one; the king of Hepher, one; **18.** The king of Aphek, one; the king of Lasharon, one; **19.** The king of Madon, one; the king of Hazor, one; **20.** The king of Shimron Meron (region of northern Israel), one; the king of Achshaph(an ancient Canaanite), one; **21.** The king of Taanach (megacity in the valley of Jezreel), one; the king of Megiddo (position in the Jezreel Valley), one; **22.** The king of Kedesh (megacity of retreat in ancient Israel), one; the king of Jokneam (megacity located on the pitches of Mount Carmel) in Carmel, one **23.** The king of Dor(in the heights of Dor, a littoral megacity), one; the king of the people of Gilgal, one; **24.** The king of Tirzah (megacity in ancient Israel), one — all the lords, thirty- one.

Chapter 13

1. Joshua had grown old and was advanced in years. The Lord said to him, "You are old, and much of the land remains to be conquered. **2.** The remaining land includes: all the territory of the Philistines (a people from the coastal region of Israel) and the Geshurites (a people from the region of Geshur), **3.** From the river of Egypt (likely the Nile River) to the northern border of Ekron (a major city of the Philistines, near modern-day Tel Aviv, Israel), which is considered part of Canaan (the promised land of Israel); this includes the five lords of the Philistines: Gadites, Aphrodite's, Ashkelonites, Gittites, and Ekronites, and the Avites (a people living in Canaan). **4.** From the south, all the land of the Canaanites (a group of people inhabiting the land of Canaan), including Mearah (a place belonging to the Sidonians, ancient people from Sidon, Lebanon), up to Aphek (a city located near Tel Afek, Israel), at

the border of the Amorites (a Semitic people group in Canaan). **5.** The land of the Gebalites (inhabitants of Gebal, an ancient city in present-day Lebanon), all of Lebanon (a mountainous region north of Israel), extending eastward from Baal Gad (a city at the foot of Mount Hermon) to the entrance of Hamath (a city, present-day Hama, Syria). **6.** All the inhabitants of the mountains from Lebanon to the Brook Misrephoth (a river), and all the Sidonians (people from Sidon, Lebanon)—I will drive them out before the children of Israel; only divide it by lot to Israel as an inheritance, as I have commanded you. **7.** Israelites. Only divide this land by lot as an inheritance to the nine tribes and half of the tribe of Manasseh (one of the tribes of Israel). **8.** Now, divide the land among the nine tribes and half of Manasseh, as I have commanded you. The other half of Manasseh, along with the tribes of Reuben and Gad, received their inheritance beyond the Jordan River (a river in Israel, flowing into the Dead Sea), eastward, as Moses, the servant of the Lord, had given them: **9.** From Aroer (a city near the Arnon River, south of modern Ammon, Jordan), on the bank of the River Arnon, and the city in the ravine, all the plains of Medeba (a region east of Jordan), as far as Dibon (a city near Ammon, Jordan), **10.** All the cities of Sihon, king of the Amorites (a kingdom in central Canaan), who reigned in Heshbon (an ancient city in modern Jordan), as far as the border of the Ammonites (another group of people from modern Jordan), **11.** Gilead (a region in modern Jordan), the territory of the Geshurites and Maachathites (peoples from the region near Gilead), all of Mount Hermon (a high mountain on the border between Israel and Syria), and all of Bashan (a fertile area east of the Jordan River, in modern Syria), as far as Salcah (a city in Bashan). **12.** This includes the entire kingdom of Og (the last of the giants in the land), king of Bashan, who reigned in Ashtaroth and Edrei (cities in Bashan), and was part of the remnant of the Rephaim (giants); Moses had defeated them and driven them out. **13.** However, the Israelites did not drive out the Geshurites or the Maachathites; they live among the Israelites to this day. **14.** Only the tribe of Levi received no inheritance; the Lord, the God of Israel, is their inheritance, as He promised them. **15.** Moses gave the tribe of Reuben an inheritance according to their families: **16.** Their territory included Aroer, the city in the ravine, and all the plains of Medeba, **17.** Heshbon and its cities, such as Dibon (a city in modern Jordan), Bamoth Baal (a place of worship in ancient Israel), Beth Baal Meon (a town in the plain), **18.** Jahaza (a city in Gilead), Kedemoth (a city in Gilead), Mephaath (a city in Gilead), **19.** Kiriathaim (a city in Reuben), Sibmah (a city in Gilead), Zereth Shahar (a city) on the mountain of the valley, **20.** Beth Peor (a place in Moab), the slopes of Pisgah (a mountain, near Jordan), and Beth Jeshimoth (a city in Reuben), **21.** All the cities in the plain and the entire kingdom of Sihon, king of the Amorites, whom Moses struck down with the princes of Midian (a people from northern Arabia): Evi, Rekem, Zur, Hur, and Reba, princes of Sihon. **22.** The Israelites also killed Balaam, son of Beor (a sorcerer), the soothsayer (one who predicts the future), along with the others slain by them. **23.** The border of the tribe of Reuben was along the Jordan River. This is the inheritance of the tribe of Reuben, according to their families, including their cities and villages. **24.** Moses also gave an inheritance to the tribe of Gad, according to their families: **25.** Their territory included Jazer (a city in Gilead), all the cities of Gilead, and half the land of the Ammonites,

Chapter 14

1. These are the areas that the Israelites inherited in Canaan (the Promised Land), which Eleazar the priest, Joshua the son of Nun, and the leaders of the tribes of Israel divided as an inheritance for them. **2.** The inheritance was assigned by lot (casting lots, like drawing names or using chance), as the Lord had instructed Moses, for the nine tribes and the half-tribe. **3.** Moses had already given the inheritance to the two and a half tribes on the other side of the Jordan River, but the Levites (a tribe of priests) received no land inheritance, only cities to live in, with grazing land (pastureland) for their animals. **4.** The descendants of Joseph became two tribes: Manasseh and Ephraim. The Levites did not receive any land, only cities to dwell in, with pasturelands for their livestock. **5.** The Israelites did exactly as the Lord had commanded Moses, dividing the land among them. **6.** Then the people of Judah came to Joshua in Gilgal (a place in Israel where the Israelites camped after crossing the Jordan). Caleb, the son of Jephunneh the Kenizzite (a man from a non-Israelite family), spoke to him: "You remember the promise the Lord made through Moses, concerning you and me at Kadesh Barnea (a location where Israel camped and where Moses sent spies into Canaan)." **7.** I was forty years old when Moses sent me to spy out the land, and I brought back a truthful report, as it was in my heart. **8.** But the other men who went with me caused the people's hearts to melt with fear, yet I completely followed the Lord my God. **9.** So Moses swore that day, saying, 'The land where your foot has trod (walked) will be your inheritance and that of your children forever, because you have fully followed the Lord my God.' **10.** And now, behold, the Lord has kept me alive, just as He promised, these forty-five years since the Lord spoke this word to Moses while Israel wandered in the wilderness, And here I am today, eighty-five years old. **11.** I am still as strong today as I was the day Moses sent me, with the same strength for battle, whether going out or coming in. **12.** So now, give me this mountain (a hilly area), of which the Lord spoke that day. You know the Anakim (a group of giant people known for their strength) are there, and the cities are large and fortified (protected with strong walls), but perhaps the Lord will be with me, and I will drive them out, as the Lord said." **13.** Joshua blessed him and gave Caleb the city of Hebron (a significant city in southern Judah) as an inheritance. **14.** Therefore, Hebron became the inheritance of Caleb, son of Jephunneh the Kenizzite (a non-Israelite man), because he fully followed the Lord, the God of Israel. **15.** Previously, the city was called Kirjath Arba (the original name of Hebron, named after Arba, the greatest of the Anakim). Then the land had rest from war.

Chapter 15

1. The land assigned to the tribe of Judah, according to their families, started near Edom (territory south of Israel) at the Wilderness of Zin (desert area) on the southern edge. **2.** Their southern border began at the shore of the Salt Sea (also known as the Dead Sea), stretching southward. **3.** It continued along the south side of the Ascent of Akrabbim (steep climb known for scorpions), passing through Zin, Kadesh Barnea (a key stop in the Israelites' journey), Hezron, Adar, and turning toward Karkaa. **4.** The border then went to Azmon and followed the Brook of Egypt (seasonal river marking Israel's southwestern boundary), ending at the sea. This marked their southern boundary. **5.** To the east, the Salt Sea bordered them up to the Jordan River's mouth. The northern border started from the Jordan's mouth. **6.** The border extended to Beth Hoglah, north of Beth Arabah, and continued to the stone of Bohan, Reuben's son (marking point named after a tribal leader's son). **7.** It went up toward Debir in the Valley of Achor (meaning "Valley of Trouble"), then north toward Gilgal (Israelite camp near Jericho), near the Ascent of Adummim (steep red-hued pass), and followed the waters of En Shemesh (spring called "Spring of the Sun"), ending at En Rogel (spring near Jerusalem). **8.** From there, it went up the Valley of the Son of Hinnom (valley later associated with judgment and hell), near the Jebusite (original residents of Jerusalem) city (Jerusalem), then westward to the Valley of Rephaim's (valley associated with ancient giants) north end. **9.** It turned to the water spring at Nephtoah and circled Mount Ephron to Baalah (Kirjath Jearim, a town near Jerusalem). **10.** The boundary curved west from Baalah to Mount Seir, past Mount Jearim (Chesalon) to Beth Shemesh (a city of Judah) and Timnah. **11.** From there, it went north to Ekron (Philistine city), then around Shicron, reaching Mount Baalah and Jabneel (near the coast), ending at the sea. **12.** The western border was the coastline of the Great Sea (Mediterranean Sea). This defined the boundaries for Judah's families. **13.** Caleb, son of Jephunneh, was given Hebron (Kirjath Arba, named for Arba, father of the Anakim, or giants) as the Lord commanded. **14.** Caleb drove out three Anakim (giant descendants): Sheshai, Ahiman, and Talmai. **15.** He moved to Debir (formerly Kirjath Sepher, meaning "City of the Book") to claim it. **16.** Caleb promised his daughter Achsah in marriage to whoever conquered Kirjath Sepher. **17.** Othniel, Caleb's brother, captured it and was given Achsah as his wife. **18.** Achsah persuaded Othniel to ask Caleb for a field. She dismounted her donkey, and Caleb asked her what she wanted. **19.** She requested springs of water (valuable in a dry region) as an additional blessing, and Caleb gave her both upper and lower springs. **20.** This was the inheritance of Judah's tribe by their families. **21.** The towns near Edom's border in the South included Kabzeel, Eder, Jagur, **22.** Kinah, Dimonah, Adadah, **23.**

Kedesh, Hazor, Ithnan, **24.** Ziph, Telem, Bealoth, **25.** Hazor, Hadattah, Kerioth, Hezron (Hazor), **26.** Amam, Shema, Moladah, **27.** Hazar Gaddah, Heshmon, Beth Pelet, **28.** Hazar Shual, Beersheba (later became a central city in Israel), Bizjothjah, **29.** Baalah, Ijim, Ezem, **30.** Eltolad, Chesil, Hormah, **31.** Ziklag (later given to King David), Madmannah, Sansannah, **32.** Lebaoth, Shilhim, Ain, and Rimmon—29 cities with their villages. **33.** In the lowlands (fertile area of Judah) were Eshtaol, Zorah, Ashnah, **34.** Zanoah, En Gannim (meaning "Spring of Gardens"), Tappuah, Enam, **35.** Jarmuth, Adullam (site of a cave where David hid), Socoh, Azekah, **36.** Sharaim, Adithaim, Gederah, and Gederothaim—14 cities with their villages. **37.** Additional towns included Zenan, Hadashah, Migdal Gad (meaning "Tower of Fortune"), **38.** Dilean, Mizpah (meaning "watchtower"), Joktheel, **39.** Lachish (fortified city in Judah), Bozkath, Eglon, **40.** Cabbon, Lahmas, Kithlish, **41.** Gederoth, Beth Dagon (meaning "House of Dagon"), Naamah, and Makkedah—16 cities with their villages. **42.** Other cities were Libnah, Ether, Ashan, **43.** Jiphtah, Ashnah, Nezib, **44.** Keilah (fortified town), Achzib, and Mareshah—9 cities with their villages. **45.** Ekron (Philistine city) and its nearby towns and villages, **46.** from Ekron to the sea, included villages near Ashdod (Philistine city). **47.** Ashdod and Gaza, along with their towns and villages, extended as far as the Brook of Egypt and the coastline of the Great Sea (Mediterranean Sea). **48.** In the mountains were Shamir, Jattir, Sochoh, **49.** Dannah, Kirjath Sannah (Debir), **50.** Anab, Eshtemoh, Anim, **51.** Goshen, Holon, and Giloh—11 cities with their villages. **52.** Further towns included Arab, Dumah, Eshean, **53.** Janum, Beth Tappuah, Aphekah, **54.** Humtah, Kirjath Arba (Hebron), and Zior—9 cities with their villages. **55.** Other towns were Maon, Carmel (noted for fertile land), Ziph, Juttah, **56.** Jezreel, Jokdeam, Zanoah, **57.** Kain, Gibeah (meaning "hill"), and Timnah—10 cities with their villages. **58.** Additionally, Halhul, Beth Zur (meaning "House of the Rock"), Gedor, **59.** Maarath, Beth Anoth, and Eltekon— 6 cities with their villages. **60.** Kirjath Baal (Kirjath Jearim) and Rabbah—2 cities with their villages. **61.** In the wilderness were Beth Arabah, Middin, Secacah, **62.** Nibshan, the City of Salt (near the Dead Sea), and En Gedi (oasis on the Dead Sea)—6 cities with their villages. **63.** The Jebusites who lived in Jerusalem could not be driven out by the people of Judah; they continue to live with them in Jerusalem.

Chapter 16

1. The land given to Joseph's descendants began at the Jordan River near Jericho, extended east to the waters by Jericho, through the wilderness near the mountains, and up to Bethel (a city in Israel). **2.** From Bethel, the border extended to Luz, then along to the Archite (a group of people) territory near Ataroth. **3.** It continued westward to the boundary (borderline) of the Japhletites (a group of people), reaching as far as Lower Beth Horon (a town in Israel) and Gezer, ending at the sea. **4.** Thus, the tribes of Joseph—Manasseh and Ephraim—claimed their inheritance (assigned land). **5.** The land designated (assigned) to the tribe of Ephraim by family divisions had its eastern boundary starting from Ataroth Addar, extending to Upper Beth Horon. **6.** The northern boundary extended to Michmethath, curving eastward to Taanath Shiloh (a place in Israel) and passing east of Janohah. **7.** From Janohah, it descended to Ataroth and Naarah, reached Jericho, and ended at the Jordan River. **8.** The western boundary stretched from Tappuah to the Brook Kanah (a stream), also ending at the sea. This marked the land allotted (assigned) to Ephraim's tribe by their families. **9.** Some separate towns for the Ephraimites (descendants of Ephraim) were situated within Manasseh's territory, including all the villages around them. **10.** However, the Ephraimites did not drive out the Canaanites (an ancient people) who lived in Gezer; the Canaanites remained among them and became forced laborers (people required to work involuntarily)

Chapter 17

1. The tribe of Manasseh, the firstborn of Joseph, received land. Machir, the eldest son of Manasseh and father of Gilead (a region east of the Jordan River), who was known as a warrior (skilled fighter), was given the regions of Gilead and Bashan (fertile areas in the Transjordan). **2.** The remaining descendants of Manasseh received portions according to their families: Abiezer, Helek, Asriel, Shechem, Hepher, and Shemida—each being sons of Manasseh and grouped by families. **3.** Zelophehad, a descendant of Hepher and Manasseh, had no sons, only daughters. His daughters were named Mahlah, Noah,

Hoglah, Milcah, and Tirzah. **4.** These daughters approached Eleazar the priest (one who led religious ceremonies), Joshua (leader after Moses), and the rulers, saying, "The Lord commanded Moses to give us an inheritance (property or portion of land) among our family." Therefore, as the Lord commanded, they received a share among their uncles. **5.** As a result, the tribe of Manasseh received ten portions of land, along with the territories of Gilead and Bashan, located on the eastern side of the Jordan. **6.** Manasseh's daughters also received inheritance rights among the sons, while the rest of the land of Gilead went to Manasseh's sons. **7.** Manasseh's territory stretched from Asher (a neighboring tribe) to Michmethath, east of Shechem; the border extended south to En Tappuah's residents. **8.** Manasseh possessed Tappuah, but the city of Tappuah, on Manasseh's border, belonged to the tribe of Ephraim. **9.** The border ran along the Brook Kanah (a small river or stream), southward to the brook. Some Ephraimite cities lay within Manasseh's borders. The northern side of the brook marked Manasseh's boundary, ending at the sea. **10.** The territory to the south was Ephraim's; north was Manasseh's, with the sea marking its western boundary. Manasseh bordered Asher on the north and Issachar (another neighboring tribe) on the east. **11.** In Issachar and Asher, Manasseh owned Beth Shean, Ibleam, Dor, En Dor, Taanach, and Megiddo, along with their surrounding towns—these were three hilly regions (elevated or mountainous areas). **12.** The people of Manasseh couldn't fully remove the Canaanites (an ancient group living in the land of Canaan) from these cities, as the Canaanites were determined (strong-willed) to stay. **13.** However, when Israel grew stronger, they subjected the Canaanites to forced labor (work done under compulsion) but didn't completely drive them out. **14.** The people of Joseph (tribes of Ephraim and Manasseh) asked Joshua, "Why have you given us only one portion, when we are a large and blessed (favored by God) people?" **15.** Joshua responded, "If you are numerous, go into the forest country (wooded areas) and clear land for yourselves among the Perizzites and the giants (ancient tribes), since the hill country of Ephraim is too small for you." **16.** The people of Joseph replied, "The hill country isn't enough, and the Canaanites in the valleys of Beth Shean and Jezreel (fertile lowlands) have iron chariots (strong, iron-reinforced war vehicles)." **17.** Joshua encouraged Ephraim and Manasseh, saying, "You are a strong and numerous people; you will have more than one portion. **18.** The hill country will be yours. Though it's forested, you will clear it, and its farthest areas will belong to you. You will drive out the Canaanites, even though they have iron chariots and are strong."

Chapter 18

1. The entire assembly of Israel gathered at Shiloh (an ancient city in Israel), where they set up the Tabernacle of Meeting. The land was now under control by them. **2.** Yet, seven tribes of Israel had not yet claimed their inheritance (land given to them as a possession). **3.** Joshua asked, "How long will you wait to take possession of the land that the Lord God of your ancestors has given to you?" **4.** "Choose three men from each tribe to go and explore (survey) the land. They will return with their report, and we will divide it into seven parts." **5.** "Judah will remain in their southern territory, and the house of Joseph will stay in their northern territory." **6.** "Survey the land in seven sections and bring the survey to me so that I can cast lots (randomly decide) for you before the Lord our God." **7.** "The Levites have no inheritance among you, as the Lord Himself is their portion (inheritance). Gad, Reuben, and half of Manasseh have already received their inheritance on the other side of the Jordan River, as Moses instructed." **8.** The men set out to explore (investigate) the land, and Joshua instructed them, "Go through the land, gather the survey data, and return to me so I can cast lots for you before the Lord at Shiloh." **9.** The men explored the land, recorded their findings in a book, and divided it into seven sections by cities. They then returned to Joshua at Shiloh. **10.** Joshua cast lots for them in Shiloh, assigning the land to the tribes of Israel by their families. **11.** The lot for the tribe of Benjamin came up next. Their territory was between the tribes of Judah and Joseph. **12.** Their northern border started at the Jordan River, then went up to the side of Jericho (a city in Israel), and moved westward, ending at the Wilderness of Beth Aven (a desert region). **13.** The border then shifted towards Luz (also known as Bethel, an ancient city in Israel), moving southward, and descended to Ataroth Addar, near the hill south of Lower Beth Horon. **14.** The western border continued south from the hill before Beth Horon, reaching the city of Kirjath Baal (also called Kirjath Jearim, a city in Judah). **15.** The southern border began at the end of Kirjath Jearim, moving westward to the spring of the waters of Nephtoah. **16.** The border descended to the end of the mountain overlooking the Valley of the Son of Hinnom (a valley near Jerusalem), near the Jebusite city (a city of the Jebusite people) to the south, and then down to En Rogel (a spring). **17.** The border continued to the north, passed by En Shemesh (a place), heading toward Geliloth, and descended to the stone of Bohan, the son of Reuben. **18.** The border moved along the northern side of Arabah (a desert valley), heading south to Arabah. **19.** The border went along the northern side of Beth Hoglah and ended at the northern bay of the Salt Sea (also called the Dead Sea), at the southern end of the Jordan River. This marked the southern boundary. **20.** The Jordan River formed the eastern boundary. This was the inheritance of the children of Benjamin, according to their borders and families. **21.** The cities of Benjamin, according to their families, included Jericho, Beth Hoglah, Emek Keziz (a valley), **22.** Beth Arabah, Zemaraim, Bethel, **23.** Avim, Parah, Ophrah, **24.** Chephar Haammoni, Ophni, and Gaba: twelve cities with their villages. **25.** Gibeon, Ramah, Beeroth, **26.** Mizpah, Chephirah, Mozah, **27.** Rekem, Irpeel, Taralah, **28.** Zelah, Eleph, Jebus (which is Jerusalem, the capital city of Israel), Gibeath, and Kirjath: fourteen cities with their villages. This was the inheritance of the children of Benjamin, according to their families.

Chapter 19

1. The second lot was cast for the tribe of Simeon, by their clans, and their inheritance was located within the land given to Judah. **2.** Their inheritance included Beersheba, Moladah, **3.** Hazar Shual, Balah, Ezem, **4.** Eltolad, Bethul, Hormah, **5.** Ziklag, Beth Marcaboth, Hazar Susah, **6.** Beth Lebaoth, and Sharuhen: thirteen cities with their surrounding villages. **7.** They also received Ain, Rimmon, Ether, and Ashan: four cities with their villages. **8.** All the villages around these cities, as far as Baalath Beer and Ramah of the South were included. This was the inheritance of the tribe of Simeon by their families. **9.** Simeon's land was part of Judah's territory because Judah's portion was too large for them. Thus, Simeon's inheritance was within Judah's borders. **10.** The third lot was cast for the tribe of Zebulun, by their families, and their territory extended to Sarid. **11.** Their boundary went westward to Maralah, to Dabbasheth, and along the brook east of Jokneam. **12.** From Sarid, the border went east toward the sunrise to Chisloth Tabor, then out to Daberath, bypassing Japhia. **13.** From there, it went east of Gath Hepher, to Eth Kazin, and extended to Rimmon, which bordered Neah. **14.** The boundary turned north around Hannathon, ending at the Valley of Jiphthah El. **15.** Included were Kattath, Nahallal, Shimron, Idalah, and Bethlehem: twelve cities with their villages. **16.** This was the inheritance of the tribe of Zebulun, according to their families, the cities and their villages. **17.** The fourth lot was cast for the tribe of Issachar, by their families. **18.** Their land included Jezreel, Chesulloth, Shunem, **19.** Haphraim, Shion, Anaharath, **20.** Rabbith, Kishion, Abez, **21.** Remeth, En Gannim, En Haddah, and Beth Pazzez. **22.** The border reached Tabor, Shahazimah, and Beth Shemesh, and ended at the Jordan River. Sixteen cities with their villages were included. **23.** This was the inheritance of the tribe of Issachar, according to their families, with their cities and villages. **24.** The fifth lot was cast for the tribe of Asher, by their families. **25.** Their land included Helkath, Hali, Beten, Achshaph, **26.** Alammelech, Amad, and Mishal; reaching Mount Carmel on the west, along the Brook Shihor Libnath. **27.** Their border turned eastward to Beth Dagon, reaching Zebulun and the Valley of Jiphthah El, then north past Beth Emek and Neiel, bypassing Cabul. **28.** Included were Ebron, Rehob, Hammon, and Kanah, as far as Greater Sidon. **29.** The border then turned to Ramah and the fortified city of Tyre; it moved on to Hosah and ended at the sea near Achzib. **30.** Also included were Ummah, Aphek, and Rehob: twenty-two cities with their villages. **31.** This was the inheritance of the tribe of Asher, according to their families, with their cities and villages. **32.** The sixth lot was cast for the tribe of Naphtali, by their families. **33.** Their border began at Heleph, extending from the terebinth tree in Zaanannim to Adami Nekeb, and Jabneel, as far as Lakkum, ending at the Jordan River. **34.** From Heleph, the border extended west to Aznoth Tabor, then went to Hukkok, adjoining Zebulun on the south, Asher on the west, and

Judah by the Jordan River on the east. **35.** The fortified cities included Ziddim, Zer, Hammath, Rakkath, Chinnereth, **36.** Adamah, Ramah, Hazor, **37.** Kedesh, Edrei, En Hazor, **38.** Iron, Migdal El, Horem, Beth Anath, and Beth Shemesh: nineteen cities with their villages. **39.** This was the inheritance of the tribe of Naphtali, according to their families, with their cities and villages. **40.** The seventh lot was cast for the tribe of Dan, by their families. **41.** Their territory included Zorah, Eshtaol, Ir Shemesh, **42.** Shaalabbin, Aijalon, Jethlah, **43.** Elon, Timnah, Ekron, **44.** Eltekeh, Gibbethon, Baalath, **45.** Jehud, Bene Berak, Gath Rimmon, **46.** Me Jarkon and Rakkon, near Joppa. **47.** The boundary extended beyond these cities, as the Danites went up to fight Leshem, captured it, struck it down, and settled there. They renamed it Dan after their ancestor. **48.** This was the inheritance of the tribe of Dan, by their families, with their cities and villages. **49.** Once all the land was divided according to its borders, the Israelites gave an inheritance to Joshua, son of Nun. **50.** As the Lord had commanded, they gave him the city he requested, Timnath Serah, in the mountains of Ephraim, where he built and settled. **51.** These were the inheritances distributed by Eleazar, Joshua, and the heads of the clans of the tribes of Israel, by lot in Shiloh, before the Lord, at the entrance to the Tabernacle. This completed the land division.

Chapter 20

1. The Lord spoke to Joshua, saying, **2.** "Tell the Israelites to set aside cities of refuge (safe cities where a person can flee for protection), as I instructed through Moses, **3.** so that anyone who kills another person unintentionally (by accident) can escape there. These cities will be a place of protection from the avenger of blood (a family member who seeks to avenge the death of a relative). **4.** When someone flees to one of these cities, they must stand at the city gate (entrance) and present their case to the city's elders (the wise leaders of the city). The elders will take them in and provide a safe place for them to live. **5.** If the avenger of blood comes after them, the elders must not hand over the person to the avenger because the killing unintentional was (by accident) and there was no hatred (strong dislike) involved beforehand. **6.** The person must stay in the city of refuge until they stand trial before the congregation (the gathered assembly of leaders), and until the death of the high priest (the top religious leader) in office at that time. Afterward, they may return to their own city and home, the city from which they fled." **7.** The cities chosen were Kedesh (in Galilee, a region in northern Israel), Shechem (in the hill country of Ephraim, a tribe of Israel), and Hebron (in the hill country of Judah, a tribe of Israel). **8.** On the east side of the Jordan River, near Jericho (an ancient city), the cities were Bezer (in the wilderness, within the territory of Reuben, one of the tribes of Israel), Ramoth (in Gilead, within the territory of Gad, another tribe), and Golan (in Bashan, a region within the territory of Manasseh, another tribe). **9.** These cities were designated for all the Israelites and for any foreigner (someone not from Israel) living among them, so that anyone who killed another unintentionally could flee there and avoid being killed by the avenger until they could stand trial before the congregation.

Chapter 21

1. The heads of the Levite (priestly tribe) families approached Eleazar the priest, Joshua son of Nun, and the tribal leaders of Israel. **2.** In Shiloh (ancient Canaan city, near modern Shiloh in the West Bank), they said, "The Lord commanded Moses to give us cities to live in, with lands for our animals." **3.** The Israelites provided cities and surrounding lands (common land for public use) to the Levites as instructed by the Lord.n **4.** The Kohathite families (descendants of Kohath, Levi's son) received their share by lot. The descendants of Aaron, who served as priests, received thirteen cities by lot from the tribes of Judah, Simeon, and Benjamin. **5.** The other Kohathites received ten cities by lot from Ephraim, Dan, and half of Manasseh. **6.** The Gershonites (descendants of Gershon, Levi's son) received thirteen cities by lot from Issachar, Asher, Naphtali, and half of Manasseh in Bashan (Golan Heights region). **7.** Merari's descendants (Levi's third son) were assigned twelve cities by lot from Reuben, Gad, and Zebulun. **8.** Israel gave these cities and their lands to the Levites, as directed by the Lord through Moses. **9.** Cities were provided by name from Judah and Simeon, **10.** Specifically to Aaron's descendants among the Kohathites. They received the first lot. **11.** They received Kirjath Arba (Arba, an ancient figure, father of Anak, leader of the Anakim) or Hebron, located in

Judah's hills (now Hebron in West Bank), with its lands. **12.** The surrounding fields and villages were given to Caleb, son of Jephunneh (Caleb was a notable figure in Israel). **13.** Aaron's family received Hebron with its lands (a city of refuge, safe haven for those accused), Libnah with its lands, **14.** Jattir with its lands, Eshtemoa with its lands, **15.** Holon with its lands, Debir with its lands, **16.** Ain with its lands, Juttah with its lands, and Beth Shemesh with its lands—nine cities from Judah and Simeon; **17.** from Benjamin, they received Gibeon with its lands, Geba with its lands, **18.** Anathoth with its lands, and Almon with its lands—four cities. **19.** The priests, Aaron's descendants, received a total of thirteen cities with lands. **20.** Other Kohathite families received cities from Ephraim. **21.** They were given Shechem (a refuge city, near modern-day Nablus) in Ephraim's mountains, Gezer with its lands, **22.** Kibzaim with its lands, and Beth Horon with its lands—four cities; **23.** From Dan, they received Eltekeh with its lands, Gibbethon with its lands, **24.** Aijalon with its lands, and Gath Rimmon with its lands—four cities; **25.** and from half of Manasseh, they received Tanach with its lands and Gath Rimmon with its lands—two cities. **26.** In total, ten cities with lands were given to the other Kohathites. **27.** The Gershonites, another Levite group, received from half of Manasseh: Golan in Bashan with its lands (city of refuge), and Be Eshterah with its lands—two cities; **28.** from Issachar, they received Kishion with its lands, Daberath with its lands, **29.** Jarmuth with its lands, and En Gannim with its lands—four cities; **30.** from Asher, they received Mishal with its lands, Abdon with its lands, **31.** Helkath with its lands, and Rehob with its lands—four cities; **32.** from Naphtali, they received Kedesh in Galilee (city of refuge, now near Kadesh, Israel) with its lands, Hammoth Dor with its lands, and Kartan with its lands—three cities. **33.** In total, the Gershonites received thirteen cities with common lands. **34.** The Merarite families of the Levites received from Zebulun: Jokneam with its lands, Kartah with its lands, **35.** Dimnah with its lands, and Nahalal with its lands—four cities; **36.** from Reuben, they received Bezer with its lands, Jahaz with its lands, **37.** Kedemoth with its lands, and Mephaath with its lands—four cities; **38.** from Gad, they received Ramoth in Gilead (city of refuge, east of Jordan), Mahanaim with its lands, **39.** Heshbon with its lands, and Jazer with its lands—four cities. **40.** The Merarites received a total of twelve cities. **41.** In total, the Levites received forty-eight cities with surrounding lands within Israel's territory. **42.** Each city included surrounding lands for common use. **43.** The Lord fulfilled His promise to Israel, and they took possession of the land. **44.** The Lord granted peace on all sides, as promised to their ancestors, and no enemy stood against them; the Lord gave them victory over all their foes. **45.** Every promise made to Israel by the Lord was fulfilled without fail.

Chapter 22

1. Joshua called together the Reubenites (descendants of Reuben), the Gadites (descendants of Gad), and half of the tribe of Manasseh (the half of the tribe that settled east of the Jordan River), **2.** and said to them, "You have followed all that Moses, the servant of the Lord, commanded, and you have obeyed all that I instructed. **3.** You have stayed loyal to your fellow Israelites, not leaving them for all this time, but keeping the Lord's commandments (His instructions and rules). **4.** Now the Lord your God has given rest (peace and stability) to your fellow Israelites, as He promised. So return to your land, the land Moses gave you on the other side of the Jordan River. **5.** But be very careful to follow the law (God's instructions) that Moses gave you: love the Lord your God, walk in His ways (live according to His guidance), obey His commands, hold fast (stay firmly committed) to Him, and serve Him with all your heart and soul." **6.** So Joshua blessed them and sent them home. **7.** Half the tribe of Manasseh had been given land in Bashan (a fertile region east of the Jordan) by Moses, while Joshua gave the other half land on the west side of the Jordan, among their fellow Israelites. When Joshua sent them back to their homes, he blessed them. **8.** He said to them, "Return to your homes with great wealth, including livestock (animals like cows and sheep), silver, gold, bronze, iron, and many clothes. Share the plunder (spoils or treasures taken from enemies) of your enemies with your brothers." **9.** So the Reubenites, Gadites, and half the tribe of Manasseh returned, leaving Shiloh (a city in Israel where the tabernacle was) in Canaan to go to Gilead (a region east of the Jordan River), the land they had received from Moses. **10.** When they reached the region of the Jordan River in

Canaan, they built a large altar (a raised platform for worship) there, near the Jordan. **11.** The Israelites heard rumors saying, "Look! The Reubenites, Gadites, and half the tribe of Manasseh have built an altar on the border of Canaan, near the Jordan River, on our side." **12.** When the Israelites heard this, the whole community gathered at Shiloh, ready to go to war against them. **13.** The Israelites sent Phinehas (a priest, son of Eleazar) to speak to the Reubenites, Gadites, and half the tribe of Manasseh in Gilead. **14.** He was accompanied by ten leaders, one from each tribe of Israel, each the head of a family (the leader of each tribe). **15.** When they arrived, they said to the Reubenites, Gadites, and half the tribe of Manasseh, **16.** "The whole congregation (community) of the Lord says: 'What is this treason (betrayal) you have committed against the God of Israel? You have turned away from following the Lord by building an altar for yourselves, rebelling today against Him. **17.** Wasn't the sin of Peor (a place where Israelites worshiped false gods and caused a plague) enough to purify us? We are still dealing with its consequences. **18.** If you rebel against the Lord today, His anger (wrath or fury) may fall on the entire nation of Israel tomorrow. **19.** If the land you are in is unclean (spiritually impure), then cross over to the land of the Lord's possession (the land where the tabernacle is), where the tabernacle (the portable temple of God) stands, and take your share there. But do not rebel by building another altar to offer sacrifices outside of the altar of the Lord our God. **20.** Remember Achan (a man who sinned by taking forbidden items from a defeated city), the son of Zerah, who violated the ban (God's command) on certain spoils of war? Because of his sin, the whole nation suffered. Achan did not die alone in his wrongdoing." **21.** Then the Reubenites, Gadites, and half the tribe of Manasseh replied to the heads of the Israelites, **22.** "The Lord, the God of gods (meaning the supreme God), knows the truth, and let Israel know as well—if we have done this in rebellion or treachery (dishonest betrayal) against the Lord, may He punish us today. **23.** If we built this altar to turn away from the Lord, or to offer sacrifices or offerings on it, may the Lord Himself require an account (demand an answer). **24.** But we did this out of fear (concern), thinking that in the future your descendants might say to ours, 'What do you have to do with the Lord, the God of Israel? **25.** The Lord made the Jordan River a boundary (a dividing line) between us and you, Reubenites and Gadites. You have no share (inheritance or part) in the Lord.' This could lead your descendants to stop fearing (worshiping and respecting) the Lord." **26.** So we decided to build this altar, not for sacrifices, **27.** but as a witness (a reminder) between you and us, and for future generations, so that we could continue to serve the Lord with our offerings and sacrifices. That way, your descendants will not say to ours, 'You have no part in the Lord.' **28.** When they bring up this concern, we will say, 'Look, this is a replica (copy) of the altar of the Lord that our ancestors built. It is not for sacrifices, but as a reminder between us.' **29.** Far be it from us to rebel against the Lord and turn away from following Him by building an altar for burnt offerings (sacrifices of entire animals), grain offerings (crops offered as sacrifices), or sacrifices, other than the altar of the Lord our God, which stands before His tabernacle." **30.** When Phinehas the priest and the leaders heard their explanation, they were satisfied. **31.** Phinehas said, "Now we know the Lord is with us, because you have not committed this treachery. You have spared Israel from the wrath (anger) of God." **32.** Phinehas and the leaders returned to Canaan and reported back to the Israelites. **33.** The Israelites were pleased with the explanation, and they praised God. They agreed not to go to war against the Reubenites, Gadites, and half the tribe of Manasseh, and they left them in peace. **34.** The Reubenites and Gadites named the altar "Witness" (a reminder), because it was a reminder that the Lord is God.

Chapter 23

1. After the Lord had given Israel rest (peace and freedom) from their enemies, Joshua grew old and advanced in years. **2.** So, Joshua called together all Israel—its leaders (those in charge), elders (older, respected leaders), judges (those who settle disputes), and officers (military leaders)—and said to them, "I am old and advanced in age. **3.** You have seen what the Lord your God has done for you against these nations, for He has fought (fought on your behalf) for you. **4.** I have divided (distributed or assigned) the remaining land among you, from the Jordan River (a river that flows into the Dead Sea) to the Great Sea (Mediterranean Sea) in the west. **5.** The Lord your God will drive out (force out) the remaining nations and you will possess (take ownership of) their land, just as He promised you. **6.** Be very strong (courageous) and careful to obey everything written in the Book of the Law of Moses (the first five books of the Bible), so you don't turn away from it in any direction, **7.** and avoid (stay away from) the nations that remain among you. Do not mention their gods (worshipped idols), swear by them (make promises by them), serve them, or bow down to them, **8.** but hold fast (cling strongly) to the Lord your God, as you have done up to this point. **9.** The Lord has driven out strong and mighty nations before you, and no one has been able to stand against you (oppose you successfully). **10.** One of you can chase a thousand (one person can defeat many), because the Lord your God is the one who fights for you, as He promised. **11.** So be very careful to love the Lord your God. **12.** But if you turn back, cling (hold tightly) to the remaining nations, and make alliances (close relationships) with them through marriage or other ways, **13.** know for sure (without doubt) that the Lord will no longer drive them out before you. They will become traps (dangers), snares (hidden traps), and sources of trouble (affliction) for you until you perish (die) from this good land He has given you. **14.** "I am about to die (pass away), just like all people do. You know with all your heart and soul (your entire being) that not one of the good promises the Lord your God made has failed—every single one has been fulfilled (accomplished). **15.** Just as all the good things the Lord promised have happened, so He will bring upon you every bad thing (punishments) if you break His covenant (agreement), and you will be removed (taken away) from this land He gave you. **16.** If you forsake (abandon) the covenant and serve other gods (idols), the Lord will become angry and you will quickly disappear (be lost) from this good land."

Chapter 24

1. Joshua summoned all the lines of Israel to Shechem (a significant megacity in central Israel) and called together the elders (ethnical leaders), the heads (leaders of families), the judges (those responsible for legal matters), and the officers (military leaders). They all presented themselves before God. **2.** Joshua addressed the people, saying," This is what the Lord of Israel says 'A long time agone, your ancestors, including Terah (Abraham's father) and Nahor, lived on the other side of the Euphrates River (an important swash in ancient times) and worshiped false gods. **3.** But I took your ancestor Abraham from that region, led him through the land of Canaan (the promised land), multiplied his descendants, and gave him Isaac. **4.** I gave Isaac two sons Jacob and Esau. To Esau, I gave the land of Seir (a mountainous region southeast of Israel) to settle in, but Jacob and his children went down to Egypt. **5.** I also transferred Moses and Aaron to Egypt, and I brought down great pestilences on the Egyptians. subsequently, I delivered you from their hands. **6.** When your ancestors reached the Red Sea (the body of water they crossed during the Exodus), and the Egyptians pursued them with chariots (steed- drawn war vehicles) and horsewomen (dogfaces on nags), **7.** They cried out to the Lord, who placed darkness between you and the Egyptians, and also He parted the ocean, drowning the Egyptians. You witnessed what I did in Egypt, and also you lived in the nature for a long time. **8.** I brought you into the land of the Amorites (a Canaanite lineage), who lived east of the Jordan River (a swash in Israel). They fought against you, but I gave them into your hands so that you could take their land, and I destroyed them before you. **9.** Also Balak, the king of Moab (a nation to the east of Israel), tried to curse you by summoning Balaam (a prophet), **10.** But I refused to hear to Balaam, and rather, he ended up blessing you. I delivered you from his grasp. **11.** When you crossed the Jordan River and came to Jericho (an ancient megacity in Canaan), the people of Jericho, along with the Amorites, Perizzites, Canaanites, Hittites, Girgashites, Hivites, and Jebusites (colorful Canaanite groups), fought against you. But I gave them into your hands. **12.** I transferred hornets (insects that beget fear) ahead of you, driving out the two lords of the Amorites, and you didn't need to fight to master them. **13.** I gave you land that you didn't cultivate, metropolises you didn't make, and stations and olive groves that you didn't plant.' **14.** " Now, fear the Lord (respect and honor Him), serve Him with sincerity and verity, and relieve yourselves of the gods your ancestors worshiped beyond the swash and in Egypt. Serve the Lord alone! **15.** And if you believe serving the Lord is wrong, also choose for yourselves moment whom you'll serve either the gods your ancestors worshiped, or the gods of the Amorites(whose land you now enthrall). But as for me and my ménage, we will serve the Lord." **16.** The people answered," Far be it from us to abandon the Lord and serve other gods. **17.** For it was the Lord our God who brought us and our ancestors out of Egypt, from the place of thrall (slavery). He performed great cautions before our eyes, and defended us on our trip, through all the nations we passed through. **18.** The Lord drove out all the peoples before us, including the Amorites. We too will serve the Lord, for He's our God." **19.** Joshua said to the people," You aren't suitable to serve the Lord, for He's a holy and jealous(defensive) God. He'll not forgive your sins and insurrections. **20.** Still, He'll turn against you and bring disaster upon you, after He has done so much good for you, If you leave the Lord and serve foreign gods (gods from other nations)." **21.** But the people said to Joshua," No! We'll serve the Lord!" **22.** Joshua replied," You have made yourselves substantiations that you have chosen the Lord to serve Him." And they answered," We're substantiations!" **23.** " Now, throw away the foreign gods among you and give your hearts completely to the Lord, the God of Israel." **24.** The people declared," We'll serve the Lord our God and observe His voice!" **25.** That day, Joshua made a covenant (formal agreement) with the people, establishing an enactment (law) and constitution (regulation) for them at Shechem. **26.** Joshua recorded these words in the Book of the Law of God (the sacred Holy Writ). He took a large gravestone and set it up near the sanctuary (holy place) of the Lord. **27.** Joshua said to all the people," This gravestone will be substantiation against us, for it has heard all the words the Lord spoke to us. It'll be substantiation if you deny your God. **28.** Subsequently, Joshua dismissed the people, each to their own heritage (land). **29.** After these events, Joshua son of Nun, the menial of the Lord, failed at the age of 110. **30.** They buried him in the land of his heritage at Timnath Serah (a megacity in the hill country of Ephraim), in the region of Ephraim (central Israel), north of Mount Gaash (a mountain). **31.** Israel served the Lord throughout the continuance of Joshua and the elders who outlasted him — those who had seen all the great works the Lord had done for Israel. **32.** The bones of Joseph (one of the twelve sons of Jacob, who was vended into slavery in Egypt), which the Israelites had brought from Egypt, were buried at Shechem (a megacity in Canaan), in the plot of land Jacob had bought from the sons of Hamor (a Canaanite leader) for 100 pieces of tableware. This land came the heritage of Joseph's descendants. **33.** Eleazar, son of Aaron, failed and was buried in a hill that belonged to his son Phinehas, in the hill country of Ephraim.

7 – Judges
Chapter 1

1. After Joshua's death, the Israelites asked the Lord, "Who should lead the way for us in battle against the Canaanites (descendants of Canaan)?" **2.** The Lord answered, "Judah will go up. I have already given the land into his hands." **3.** Judah then spoke to his brother Simeon, saying, "Come with me to my assigned territory, so that we can fight the Canaanites together. I will also go with you to your land." And Simeon agreed to go with him. **4.** Judah led the charge, and the Lord gave them victory over the Canaanites and the Perizzites (people living in Canaan). They killed ten thousand men at Bezek (a city in Canaan). **5.** They found Adoni-Bezek (a Canaanite king) in Bezek and fought him. They defeated the Canaanites and the Perizzites there. **6.** Adoni-Bezek fled, but they pursued him, caught him, and cut off his thumbs and big toes (a form of brutal punishment). **7.** Adoni-Bezek confessed, "I once had seventy kings under my table, with their thumbs and big toes cut off, gathering scraps. What I did to them, God has now done to me." They brought him to Jerusalem, and there he died. **8.** The people of Judah then fought against Jerusalem, captured it, killed its inhabitants with the sword, and set the city on fire. **9.** Afterward, the people of Judah moved down to fight the Canaanites in the mountains, the Negev (southern region), and the western foothills. **10.** Then Judah attacked the Canaanites living in Hebron (formerly called Kirjath Arba). They killed Sheshai, Ahiman, and Talmai, three important leaders of the area. **11.** From there, they moved to attack the inhabitants of Debir (formerly called Kirjath Sepher). **12.** Caleb said, "Whoever captures Kirjath Sepher, I will give my daughter Achsah as a wife." **13.** Othniel, Caleb's younger brother, captured it, and Caleb gave him his daughter Achsah as a wife. **14.** When Achsah arrived, she urged her husband to ask her father for more land. She got off her donkey, and Caleb asked, "What do you want?" **15.** She replied, "Give me a blessing. Since you have already given me land in the Negev, give me also springs of water." Caleb gave her the upper and lower springs of water. **16.** The descendants of the Kenite (Moses' father-in-law) moved up from the city of palms with the people of Judah into the wilderness of Judah, which is near Arad, and they settled among the people there. **17.** Judah and Simeon together attacked the Canaanites in Zephath and completely destroyed it, naming the city Hormah (a name meaning 'devoted to destruction'). **18.** Judah also took the cities of Gaza, Ashkelon, and Ekron, along with their territories. **19.** The Lord was with Judah, and he was able to drive out the mountain people. However, they could not drive out the inhabitants of the lowlands because the Canaanites had chariots made of iron (strong war vehicles). **20.** Judah gave the city of Hebron to Caleb, as promised by Moses. Caleb drove out the three sons of Anak (giants or mighty warriors) from there. **21.** But the tribe of Benjamin did not drive out the Jebusites (inhabitants of Jerusalem) who lived in Jerusalem, so the Jebusites continued to live there with the people of Benjamin, and they still live there today. **22.** The house of Joseph went up against Bethel, and the Lord was with them. **23.** The house of Joseph sent men to spy out Bethel (formerly called Luz). **24.** The spies saw a man coming out of the city and said to him, "Show us the entrance to the city, and we will show you mercy." **25.** He showed them the entrance, and they struck the city with the sword, but they spared the man and his entire family. **26.** The man went to the land of the Hittites (a group of ancient people), built a city and called it Luz, which is still its name today. **27.** However, the tribe of Manasseh did not drive out the people living in Beth Shean and its surrounding villages, or the people of Taanach, Dor, Ibleam, and Megiddo and their villages. The Canaanites were determined to remain in the land. **28.** When the Israelites grew stronger, they forced the Canaanites to pay tribute, but they did not drive them out completely. **29.** Ephraim did not drive out the Canaanites living in Gezer, so the Canaanites lived among them in Gezer. **30.** Zebulun did not drive out the people of Kitron or Nahalol, so the Canaanites remained among them, but they were forced to work for them. **31.** Asher did not drive out the people of Acco, Sidon, Ahlab, Achzib, Helbah, Aphik, or Rehob. **32.** Asherites lived among the Canaanites, who still inhabited the land, because they did not drive them out. **33.** Naphtali did not drive out the inhabitants of Beth Shemesh or Beth Anath. The Canaanites lived among them, but the people of Beth Shemesh and Beth Anath were forced to work for them. **34.** The Amorites (a Canaanite people) drove the tribe of Dan into the mountains, preventing them from coming down into the valleys. **35.** The Amorites were determined to live in Mount Heres, Aijalon, and Shaalbim. But when the house of Joseph grew stronger, they forced the Amorites to work for them. **36.** The boundary of the Amorites extended from the Ascent of Akrabbim (a difficult mountain pass), from Sela (a rock), and upward.

Chapter 2

1. Then the Angel of the Lord appeared, coming from Gilgal (an Israelite camp) to Bochim (a place in Israel), and said, "I brought you up from Egypt and gave you the land I promised to your forefathers. I told you, 'I will never break My covenant with you. **2.** You must not make agreements with the people living in this land; you must destroy their altars.' But you have not listened to My commands. Why have you done this? **3.** So now I say, 'I will not drive them out before you. Instead, they will be a constant thorn in your side, and their gods will trap you.'" **4.** When the Angel spoke these words to all the Israelites, they raised their voices and wept. **5.** They named the place Bochim, and there they offered sacrifices to the Lord. **6.** After Joshua dismissed the people, the Israelites went to settle in their own territories to take possession of the land. **7.** The people served the Lord throughout Joshua's lifetime, and also during the lives of the elders who survived him—those who had seen all the great things the Lord had done for Israel. **8.** Joshua son of Nun, the servant of the Lord, died at the age of 110. **9.** They buried him in his inheritance at Timnath-heres (a town in the Ephraim Mountains) on the northern slopes of Mount Gaash (a location in Israel). **10.** After that generation passed away, another arose who did not know the Lord or the mighty works He had done for Israel. **11.** Then the Israelites did what was evil in the sight of the Lord, serving the Baals (false gods of the Canaanites). **12.** They abandoned the Lord, the God of their ancestors who had brought them out of Egypt, and followed the gods of the surrounding nations, bowing down to them, provoking the Lord to anger. **13**. They turned away from the Lord and worshiped Baal and the Ashtoreths (goddesses of fertility in Canaanite worship). **14**. This angered the Lord, and He handed them over to their enemies, who plundered them. He sold them into the hands of their foes, and they could not stand against their enemies. **15**. Wherever they went, the Lord's hand was against them, bringing calamity upon them, just as He had warned and sworn. They were in great distress. **16**. However, the Lord raised up judges to deliver them from their oppressors. **17**. Yet, the people did not listen to their judges. Instead, they followed other gods, bowing down to them. They quickly turned from the path of their ancestors who obeyed the Lord's commands and did not follow His ways. **18**. When the Lord raised up a judge, He was with them and rescued them from their enemies for as long as the judge lived. The Lord was moved to pity by their cries because of those who oppressed them. **19**. But when the judge died, the people returned to their evil ways, becoming even more corrupt than their forefathers. They followed other gods, served them, and bowed to them, never ceasing their wickedness and stubbornness. **20**. The Lord's anger burned against Israel, and He said, "Because this nation has violated My covenant which I commanded their ancestors and has not listened to My voice, **21**. I will no longer drive out the nations that Joshua left when he died. **22**. I will allow these nations to remain, to test Israel and see if they will keep the Lord's ways and walk in them as their ancestors did, or not." **23**. So, the Lord allowed these nations to stay, not driving them out immediately or handing them over to Joshua.

Chapter 3

1. Now, these are the nations the Lord left behind, to test Israel through them, specifically those who had not experienced any of the wars in Canaan (the promised land of Israel). **2**. (This was to ensure that the future generations of the Israelites would learn the art of war, at least those who had not been involved in it before.) **3**. These nations included the five lords of the Philistines (coastal enemies of Israel), all the Canaanites (original inhabitants of the promised land), the Sidonians (people of Sidon, a Phoenician city), and the Hivites (people living in northern Canaan) who lived in Mount Lebanon (a mountain range to the north of Israel), from Mount Baal Hermon (Baal Hermon: a mountain in northern Israel) to the entrance of Hamath (an ancient city in modern-day Syria). **4**. The Lord left these nations behind to test Israel, knowing whether they would obey the commandments of the Lord that He had given to their ancestors through Moses. **5**. The Israelites lived among the Canaanites, the Hittites (ancient people settled in parts of Canaan), the Amorites (people living in central and southern Canaan), the Perizzites (people living in rural Canaan), the Hivites (people from northern Canaan), and the Jebusites (inhabitants of Jerusalem before it was conquered). **6**. They took their daughters as wives and gave their own daughters to these foreign men. They also began to worship their gods **7**. So the Israelites did evil in the sight of the Lord. They forgot the Lord their God and began serving the gods of Baal and Asherah. **8**. Because of this, the Lord became very angry with Israel and allowed them to fall under the control of Cushan-Rishathaim (king from Mesopotamia) king of Mesopotamia (region between the Tigris and Euphrates rivers). The Israelites were forced to serve him for eight years. **9**. When the Israelites cried out to the Lord, He raised up a deliverer for them Othniel (first judge of Israel), the son of Kenaz (a man from the tribe of Judah), who was Caleb's (one of the 12 spies who trusted God) younger brother. **10**. The Spirit of the Lord came upon Othniel, and he became Israel's judge. He led Israel in battle, and the Lord gave him victory over Cushan-Rishathaim, the king of Mesopotamia, so that Othniel was able to defeat him. **11**. The land then had peace for forty years. Afterward, Othniel, the son of Kenaz, died. **12**. Again, the Israelites did evil in the sight of the Lord. So, the Lord strengthened Eglon (king of Moab) king of Moab (a kingdom east of Israel) against Israel, because of their disobedience. **13**. Eglon gathered forces from the Ammonites (people east of Israel) and Amalekites (nomadic people hostile to Israel), defeated Israel, and captured the City of Palms. **14**. The Israelites were forced to serve Eglon, king of Moab, for eighteen years. **15**. When the Israelites cried out to the Lord, He raised up a deliverer for them: Ehud, the son of

Gera (*a Benjamite*), from the tribe of Benjamin. He was a left-handed man. By him, the Israelites sent tribute to Eglon, king of Moab. **16**. Ehud made a double-edged dagger, about a cubit long (18 inches), and strapped it to his right thigh under his clothes. **17**. He brought the tribute to Eglon, who was a very fat man. **18**. After delivering the tribute, Ehud sent the attendants away, but he himself turned back from the stone images at Gilgal and said, "I have a secret message for you, O king." Eglon ordered silence, and all those who were attending him left the room. **19**. Ehud approached Eglon, who was sitting in his private chamber upstairs. He said, "I have a message from God for you." Eglon stood up from his seat. **20**. Ehud reached with his left hand, drew the dagger from his right thigh, and thrust it into Eglon's belly. **21**. The blade went in so deeply that even the hilt followed, and the fat closed over the blade. Ehud did not pull the dagger out, and Eglon's bowels came out. **22**. Afterward, Ehud went out through the porch and locked the doors of the upper room behind him. **23**. When the servants of the king arrived and saw that the doors to the upper room were locked, they thought, "He is probably relieving himself in the cool chamber." **24**. They waited until they were embarrassed, but still Eglon did not open the doors. So they took the key, unlocked the doors, and found their master dead on the floor. **25**. Meanwhile, Ehud had escaped while they were waiting. He passed beyond the stone images and made his way to Seirah. **26**. When Ehud arrived in Seirah, he blew a trumpet in the mountains of Ephraim, and the Israelites came down with him to join him. **27**. He led them, saying, "Follow me, for the Lord has given you victory over the Moabites." The Israelites followed him, took control of the fords of the Jordan River, and did not allow any Moabite to cross. **28**. At that time, they killed about ten thousand Moabite soldiers, all of them strong and valiant men, and not one escaped. **29**. As a result, Moab was subdued that day under the power of Israel, and the land had peace for eighty years. **30**. After him, Shamgar (*another judge of Israel*), the son of Anath (a name possibly meaning "gift" or "favored"), arose and struck down six hundred Philistines with an ox goad and he also delivered Israel.

Chapter 4

1. After the death of Ehud, the people of Israel once again turned to evil in the eyes of the Lord. **2**. In response, the Lord allowed them to fall under the control of Jabin, the king of Canaan, who governed from Hazor. His military commander was Sisera, who resided in Harosheth Hagoyim (a city near the Kishon River). **3**. The Israelites cried out to the Lord because Jabin had equipped his army with nine hundred iron chariots (a powerful weapon used in battle) and had oppressed them harshly for twenty years. **4**. During this time, a prophetess named Deborah (a female prophet and judge in Israel), the wife of Lapidoth was serving as a judge over Israel. **5**. Deborah would sit under her palm tree (a place where people came to her for judgment) between Ramah and Bethel in the mountains of Ephraim and the Israelites came to her for counsel. **6**. One day, she sent for Barak, the son of Abinoam (Barak's father), who was from Kedesh in Naphtali (a town in Naphtali's territory), and told him, "Hasn't the Lord, the God of Israel, commanded you to take action? Gather your forces at Mount Tabor (a large mountain in northern Israel), and take with you ten thousand men from the tribes of Naphtali and Zebulun (another tribe in Israel); **7**. Then I will lead Sisera, the commander of Jabin's army, with his chariots and soldiers to the Kishon River, and I will hand him over to you." **8**. Barak responded to her, "If you go with me, I will go; but if you do not go, I won't go either." **9**. Deborah answered, "I will surely go with you, but know that the honor of this victory will not go to you. The Lord will give Sisera into the hands of a woman." Deborah then got up and went with Barak to Kedesh. **10**. Barak called the tribes of Zebulun and Naphtali to Kedesh, and they mobilized ten thousand soldiers. Deborah went with him as well. **11**. Now Heber the Kenite, a descendant of Hobab (Moses' father-in-law), had separated from the other Kenites and set up his tent near the oak tree at Zaanaim (a place close to Kedesh), which was beside Kedesh. **12**. When Sisera was told that Barak, the son of Abinoam, had gone up to Mount Tabor, **13**. Sisera gathered all his chariots—nine hundred iron chariots—and all his soldiers, and they marched from Harosheth Hagoyim (Sisera's base of operations) to the Kishon River. **14**. Deborah told Barak, "It's time! The Lord has given Sisera into your hands. Hasn't the Lord already gone ahead of you?" Barak then led his men down from Mount Tabor, and they followed him into battle. **15.** The Lord caused Sisera and all his chariots and soldiers to be routed by the Israelites. Sisera abandoned his chariot and fled on foot. **16.** Barak continued the pursuit, chasing Sisera's army all the way to Harosheth Hagoyim. Every last soldier in Sisera's army was killed—none survived. **17.** However, Sisera managed to escape on foot and found refuge in the tent of Jael (the wife of Heber the Kenite), for there was peace between Jabin, the king of Hazor (Jabin's city of rule), and the house of Heber the Kenite. **18.** Jael went out to meet Sisera and invited him into her tent, saying, "Come, my lord, don't be afraid." Once inside, she covered him with a blanket. **19.** Sisera, exhausted, asked her for a drink of water, and Jael gave him milk (a comforting and soothing drink), covered him, and watched over him. **20.** Sisera then instructed her, "Stand at the door of the tent. If anyone comes by and asks, 'Is anyone here?' tell them no." **21.** But Jael, Heber's wife, took a tent peg (a large nail used in tents) and a hammer, and quietly approached him. She drove the peg through his temple (the side of the head), fastening it into the ground while Sisera was fast asleep from weariness. He died on the spot. **22.** When Barak arrived in pursuit of Sisera, Jael met him and said, "Come, I will show you the man you are looking for." He entered her tent and found Sisera lying dead, with the tent peg still lodged in his temple. **23.** That day, God subdued Jabin (the king of Canaan) of Canaan in front of the Israelites. **24.** And the power of the Israelites grew stronger and stronger against Jabin, the king of Canaan, until they completely destroyed him.

Chapter 5

1. On that day, Deborah (a prophetess and judge of Israel) and Barak (son of Abinoam) composed and sang this song: **2.** "When the leaders in Israel rise to lead and the people willingly offer their support, may the Lord be praised!" **3.** "Listen, O rulers! Pay attention, O authorities! I will sing praises to the Lord, the God of Israel." **4.** "When You, Lord, came from Seir (a mountainous region southeast of Israel), when You advanced from the fields of Edom (a region south of Israel), the earth shook, the skies poured rain, and the clouds sent down water." **5.** "The mountains trembled before the Lord, even Sinai (the mountain where Moses received the Ten Commandments), before the Lord, the God of Israel." **6.** "In the days of Shamgar (a judge of Israel) son of Anath (Shamgar's father), in the days of Jael (the wife of Heber, who killed Sisera), the roads were abandoned, and travelers had to use hidden paths." **7.** "Life in the villages ceased, and there was no more community life in Israel, until I, Deborah, arose until I became a mother to Israel." **8.** "They chose new gods, and war broke out at the gates. No shield or spear was found among forty thousand in Israel." **9.** "My heart is with the leaders of Israel, with those who volunteered among the people. May the Lord be praised!" **10.** "You who ride on white donkeys (a sign of prestige and importance), you who sit in judgment, and those who travel the roads," **11.** "Far from the noise of battle, by the watering places, there they will speak of the righteous acts of the Lord, the righteous acts He performed for Israel. Then the Lord's people will go down to the city gates." **12.** "Awake! Awake, Deborah! Arise, sing a song! Arise, Barak, and lead your captives away, son of Abinoam!" **13.** "Then the survivors came down, the people against the mighty. The Lord fought for me against the powerful." **14.** "From Ephraim (a tribe of Israel) came those whose roots were in Amalek (a tribe that opposed Israel). After you, Benjamin (a tribe of Israel) with your people, from Machir (a family in the tribe of Manasseh), rulers came down, and from Zebulun (a tribe of Israel) came those who carried the military staff (a symbol of leadership)." **15.** "The princes of Issachar (a tribe of Israel) were with Deborah; as Issachar, so was Barak sent into the valley under his command. Among the divisions of Reuben (a tribe of Israel), there was much concern." **16.** "Why did you stay among the sheepfolds (shelters for sheep) listening to the music of the flocks? The divisions of Reuben have deep concerns." **17.** "Gilead (a region east of the Jordan River) stayed beyond the Jordan, and why did Dan (a tribe of Israel) remain by the ships? Asher (a tribe of Israel) stayed by the seashore and near their harbors." **18.** "Zebulun was a people who risked their lives in battle, and Naphtali (a tribe of Israel) also stood firm on the heights of the battlefield." **19.** "The kings came and fought, the kings of Canaan fought at Taanach (a city in Israel), by the waters of Megiddo (a famous plain in Israel); they took no plunder of silver." **20.** "They fought from the heavens; the stars fought from their courses against Sisera (the commander of Jabin's army)." **21.** "The Kishon River (the river where the battle was fought) swept them away, that ancient river, the Kishon. March on, my soul, in strength!" **22.** "Then the horses' hooves pounded, galloping, galloping of Sisera's steeds." **23.** "'Curse Meroz (a place that failed to help),' said the angel of the Lord, 'Curse its inhabitants, because they did not come to help the Lord, to help the Lord against the mighty.'" **24.** "Most blessed among women is Jael (the wife of Heber the Kenite); blessed is she among women who live in tents." **25.** "He asked for water, she gave him milk. She brought out cream in a noble bowl." **26.** "She reached for a tent peg with her left hand, and a hammer with her right hand. She struck Sisera, drove the peg into his head, and fastened it into the ground while he was fast asleep, exhausted. And he died." **27.** "At her feet, he sank and fell. He lay still. Where he sank, there he died." **28.** "The mother of Sisera looked out the window and cried through the lattice, 'Why is his chariot so long in coming? Why does the clattering of his chariots delay?'" **29.** "Her wisest ladies answered her, yes, she answered herself, **30.** 'Are they not finding and dividing the spoil? To each man, a girl or two; for Sisera, plunder of fine garments, plunder of colorful clothes, two pieces of embroidered cloth for the neck of the captor?'" **31** "Thus, may all your enemies perish, O Lord! But may those who love you shine like the sun in its full strength!" And the land had peace for forty years.

Chapter 6

1. The Israelites acted wickedly in the eyes of the Lord, and in response, God handed them over to the Midianites for a period of seven years. **2.** The Midianites oppressed Israel, forcing them to create hiding places, caves, and fortified shelters in the mountains. **3.** Every time Israel planted crops, the Midianites, along with the Amalekites (descendants of Esau) and other tribes from the East, would invade. **4.** They would camp out and destroy Israel's crops all the way to Gaza, leaving no food behind—no sheep, cattle, or donkeys. **5.** They came in great numbers, with their flocks and tents as numerous as locusts. Their camels were countless, and they overran the land, destroying everything in their path. **6.** Israel was left in severe poverty because of the Midianites, and the people cried out to the Lord for help. **7.** When the Israelites cried out to God because of the Midianites, **8.** The Lord sent them a prophet, who spoke to them saying, "The Lord God of Israel says: 'I rescued you from Egypt and freed you from slavery. **9.** I delivered you from the Egyptians and all those who oppressed you, driving them out before you and giving you their land. **10.** I told you, "I am the Lord your God. Do not worship the gods of the Amorites (a people living in the land), in whose land you dwell." But you have not obeyed My voice.'" **11.** The Angel of the Lord appeared and sat under an oak tree at Ophrah (a town in the territory of Manasseh), which belonged to Joash (of the Abiezrite family), while his son Gideon (a future judge) was secretly threshing wheat in a winepress to hide it from the Midianites. **12.** The Angel of the Lord appeared to him and said, "The Lord is with you, O mighty man of valor!" **13.** Gideon replied, "Pardon me, Lord, but if the Lord is truly with us, why has all this happened? Where are all the miracles our ancestors spoke of, like when He brought us up from Egypt? But now the Lord has abandoned us and handed us over to the Midianites." **14.** The Lord turned to him and said, "Go with the strength you have, and save Israel from the Midianites. I am the one sending you." **15.** Gideon replied, "But how can I save Israel? My clan is the weakest in Manasseh, and I am the least in my family." **16.** The Lord assured him, "I will be with you, and you will defeat the Midianites as though they were one person." **17.** Gideon said to Him, "If I have found favor in Your sight, give me a sign that it is really You speaking to me. **18.** Please do not leave until I bring an offering and place it before You." And the Lord responded, "I will wait until you return." **19.** Gideon went inside, prepared a young goat and unleavened bread from an ephah of flour. He placed the meat in a basket and the broth in a pot, then brought them to the Angel under the oak tree. **20.** The Angel of God instructed him, "Place the meat and bread on the rock and pour out the broth." And Gideon did so. **21.** The Angel of the Lord touched the offering with the tip of His staff, and fire rose from the rock, consuming the meat and bread. Then the Angel of the Lord vanished from Gideon's sight. **22.** Gideon realized that he had seen the Angel of the Lord. He exclaimed, "Alas, Sovereign Lord! I have seen the Angel of the Lord face to face." **23.** The Lord reassured him, "Peace! Do not be afraid. You will not die." **24.** Gideon then built an altar there and named it, "The Lord Is Peace." To this day, it stands in Ophrah, in the land of the Abiezrites. **25.** That night, the Lord commanded him, "Take your father's young bull, the second bull, seven years old, and destroy the altar of Baal (a false god) that belongs to your father. Cut down the idol beside it. **26.** Then build an altar to the Lord your God on top of this rock and offer the second bull as a burnt sacrifice using the wood of the idol you cut down." **27.** Gideon obeyed, but because he feared his family and the people of the town, he did it at night rather than during the day. **28.** The next morning, the townspeople discovered that the altar of Baal had been destroyed, the idol had been cut down, and the second bull was being offered on a new altar. **29.** They asked each other, "Who did this?" When they found out, they said, "Gideon son of Joash did it." **30.** The people demanded, "Bring out your son, so he can die. He has destroyed Baal's altar and cut down the idol beside it." **31.** But Joash, Gideon's father, replied, "Are you defending Baal? If Baal is truly a god, let him defend himself, because someone has torn down his altar." **32.** That day Joash gave Gideon the name Jerubbaal, which means "Let Baal plead for himself," because Gideon had destroyed Baal's altar. **33.** Meanwhile, the Midianites, Amalekites, and eastern tribes gathered, crossed the Jordan River, and camped in the Valley of Jezreel (a fertile plain in northern Israel). **34.** Then the Spirit of the Lord came upon Gideon, and he blew a trumpet, calling the Abiezrites to follow him. **35.** He sent messengers throughout all of Manasseh, and they also gathered behind him. He sent word to Asher, Zebulun, and Naphtali, and they came as well. **36.** Gideon said to God, "If You are really going to use me to save Israel, as You have promised, **37.** I will place a fleece of wool on the threshing floor. If the fleece is wet with dew while the ground around it is dry, I will know that You will save Israel through me, as You said." **38.** It was so. When Gideon rose early the next morning, he squeezed the fleece, and it was full of dew, enough to fill a bowl with water. **39.** Then Gideon said to God, "Please do not be angry with me, but let me test You just one more time. Let the fleece be dry and the ground be covered with dew." **40.** God did as requested that night: the fleece was dry, but the ground was wet with dew.

Chapter 7

1. Then Jerubbaal (Gideon) and all the people with him rose early and camped by the well of Harod (a spring in the valley). The Midianite camp was to the north, near the hill of Moreh (a place in the valley). **2.** The Lord said to Gideon, "There are too many people with you to defeat the Midianites. If you win now, Israel might boast, saying, 'We saved ourselves.'" **3.** So, tell the people, 'Anyone who is afraid (fearful, anxious) may leave and go home from Mount Gilead (a mountainous region).' Twenty-two thousand men left, and only ten thousand remained. **4.** But the Lord said to Gideon, "There are still too many. Take them down to the water, and I will test them there. The ones I tell you to take, keep; the ones I tell you to send away, send away." **5.** So, Gideon brought the men to the water. The Lord told him, "Separate those who lap (drink with their tongues) the water like dogs from those who kneel down to drink." **6.** Three hundred men lapped the water with their hands to their mouths; the rest knelt to drink. **7.** The Lord said to Gideon, "With these three hundred men, I will deliver (give) you and defeat the Midianites. Send the others home." **8.** The remaining men took provisions (supplies) and trumpets. Gideon sent the rest of Israel home and kept the three hundred. The Midianite camp was below them in the valley. **9.** That night, the Lord spoke to Gideon, "Go down against the Midianite camp, for I have given it into your hands." **10.** "If you are afraid (fearful) to attack, take your servant Purah (Gideon's aide) and go down to the camp and listen to what they are saying. This will strengthen your courage." **11.** So Gideon and Purah went to the outpost (a small military station) of the camp. **12.** The Midianites, Amalekites (descendants of Esau), and other eastern peoples filled the valley, as countless as locusts (insects known for swarming in large numbers), with camels (large desert animals) too numerous to count. **13.** As Gideon arrived, he overheard a man telling his friend about a dream. He said, "I had a dream: A barley loaf (a type of bread) tumbled into the Midianite camp, struck a tent, and knocked it over, causing it to collapse." **14.** His companion replied, "This is none other than the sword of Gideon, the son of Joash (Gideon's father)! God has given Midian and its whole army into his hands." **15.** When Gideon heard the dream and its interpretation, he worshiped

(expressed gratitude to God). Then he returned to the Israelite camp and said, "Get up, for the Lord has given the Midianite camp into our hands." **16.** Gideon divided the three hundred men into three groups. He gave each man a trumpet, an empty jar, and a torch (a flame inside a container) to hold. **17.** He told them, "Follow my lead and do as I do. When I reach the edge of the camp, do the same." **18.** "When I blow the trumpet, I and all those with me, blow your trumpets around the camp and shout, 'For the Lord and for Gideon!'" **19.** Gideon and the hundred men with him reached the edge of the camp at the beginning of the middle watch (the time between midnight and 3 a.m.), when the guards had just been posted. They blew their trumpets and broke the jars they were holding. **20.** The other two groups also blew their trumpets and broke their jars. They held their torches in their left hands and trumpets in their right hands, shouting, "The sword of the Lord and of Gideon!" **21.** Each man stood in his place around the camp. The Midianites panicked (became afraid), and the entire army ran, crying out in fear. **22.** When the three hundred blew their trumpets, the Lord caused the Midianites to turn their swords on each other, and the army fled toward Beth Acacia (a town) and Zererah, and as far as Abel Meholah (a town), near Tabbath (a place). **23.** The men of Israel from Naphtali (a tribe), Asher (a tribe), and all of Manasseh (a tribe) rallied and pursued the Midianites. **24.** Gideon sent messengers throughout the mountains of Ephraim (a region), saying, "Come down against the Midianites and seize their water sources as far as Beth Barah (a place) and the Jordan (a river)." The men of Ephraim gathered and captured the Midianites' watering places. **25.** They caught two Midianite leaders, Oreb (a leader) and Zeeb (another leader). They killed Oreb at the Rock of Oreb and Zeeb at the Winepress of Zeeb (a place). They pursued the remaining Midianites and brought the heads of Oreb and Zeeb to Gideon across the Jordan River.

Chapter 8

1. The men of Ephraim (A tribe of Israel) confronted Gideon, saying, "Why didn't you call us to join in the battle against the Midianites?" And they strongly criticized him. **2.** Gideon replied, "What have I done compared to you? Isn't the leftover harvest of Ephraim better than the full harvest of Abiezer (A clan from the tribe of Manasseh, to which Gideon belonged)? **3.** God has given you the leaders of Midian, Oreb (A Midianite prince) and Zeeb (Another Midianite prince). What have I been able to accomplish compared to you?" When Gideon spoke this way, the anger of the Ephraimites was appeased. **4.** When Gideon and the three hundred men who were with him reached the Jordan River (The river dividing Israel and Transjordan), they crossed over, worn out but still pursuing the enemy. **5.** Then Gideon said to the men of Succoth (A city on the east side of the Jordan), "Please give some bread to the people who are with me, as they are exhausted, and I am pursuing Zebah (A Midianite king) and Zalmunna (Another Midianite king), the kings of Midian." **6.** The leaders of Succoth replied, "Are Zebah and Zalmunna in your hands now, that we should give bread to your soldiers?" **7.** Gideon answered, "When the Lord hands Zebah and Zalmunna over to me, I will punish you with the thorns and briers of the wilderness!" **8.** Then he went on to Penuel (Penuel: Another city near Succoth) and spoke to them in the same manner. The men of Penuel gave him the same response as the men of Succoth. **9.** Gideon also said to the men of Penuel, "When I return in peace, I will tear down this tower!" **10.** At the time, Zebah and Zalmunna were at Karkor (A region to the east), with their armies numbering about fifteen thousand men, all who had survived from the people of the East. For one hundred and twenty thousand soldiers who had fought had fallen. **11.** Then Gideon went by the route east of Nobah (Nobah: A place near the Jordan) and Jogbehah (Another location east of the Jordan), and he attacked the army while they were unsuspecting and secure in their camp. **12.** When Zebah and Zalmunna fled, Gideon pursued them and captured both kings of Midian, Zebah and Zalmunna, and defeated their entire army. **13.** Then Gideon, the son of Joash (Gideon's father), returned from the battle at the Ascent of Heres (A high ridge in Gilead). **14.** He caught a young man from Succoth and interrogated him. The young man wrote down for him the names of seventy-seven leaders and elders of the city. **15.** Gideon then approached the men of Succoth and said, "Here are Zebah and Zalmunna, the very ones you mocked, saying, 'Are the hands of Zebah and Zalmunna in your possession now that we should give bread to your exhausted army?'" **16.** He took the elders of Succoth and used the thorns and briers of the wilderness to punish them. **17.** Then he tore down the tower of Penuel and killed the men of the city. **18.** He asked Zebah and Zalmunna, "What kind of men did you kill at Tabor (Tabor: A mountain in Israel known for battles)?" They answered, "They looked like you; they were all sons of kings." **19.** Gideon responded, "They were my brothers, the sons of my mother. As surely as the Lord lives, if you had spared their lives, I would not be killing you now." **20.** Gideon told his son Jether (Gideon's firstborn son), "Rise and kill them!" But the young man was too afraid to draw his sword because he was still a child. **21.** Zebah and Zalmunna then said, "You do it yourself. Kill us, for a man is judged by his strength." So Gideon rose up, killed Zebah and Zalmunna, and took the crescent ornaments that were on their camels' necks as trophies. **22.** Then the men of Israel said to Gideon, "Rule over us, both you and your descendants, for you have saved us from the Midianites." **23.** But Gideon replied, "I will not rule over you, nor will my son rule over you. The Lord will rule over you." **24.** Then Gideon made a request of them, saying, "Please give me the earrings from your plunder." (For the people of Midian had gold earrings, as they were Ishmaelites (Descendants of Ishmael, nomadic people)) **25.** They agreed and said, "We will gladly give them." So they spread out a garment, and each man threw his earrings into it from the plunder. **26.** The weight of the gold earrings Gideon requested was about one thousand seven hundred shekels of gold, in addition to the crescent ornaments, pendants, and purple robes worn by the kings of Midian, and the chains that were around their camels' necks. **27.** Gideon made the gold into an ephod (A sacred garment used by priests) and placed it in his hometown, Ophrah (Gideon's hometown). All of Israel began to worship it there, and it became a trap for Gideon and his family. **28.** Thus, the Midianites were subdued before the children of Israel, and they no longer raised their heads. The land had peace for forty years during the time of Gideon. **29.** Then Jerubbaal (Another name for Gideon), the son of Joash, returned to his home. **30.** Gideon had seventy sons, his own children, for he had many wives. **31.** His concubine (A woman with whom a man has a relationship but is not his wife) in Shechem (Shechem: A city in Israel) also bore him a son, and he named him Abimelech (Gideon's son by his concubine). **32.** Gideon, the son of Joash, died at a ripe old age and was buried in the tomb of Joash his father, in Ophrah of the Abiezrites (A clan within the tribe of Manasseh). **33.** As soon as Gideon died, the Israelites again turned to worship the Baals (Canaanite gods) and made Baal-Berith (A specific Baal deity) their god. **34.** The Israelites forgot the Lord their God, who had delivered them from the hands of all their enemies on every side. **35.** They did not show kindness to the family of Jerubbaal (Gideon) for all the good he had done for Israel.

Chapter 9

1. Then Abimelech, the son of Jerubbaal (Jerubbaal was also known as Gideon, the judge of Israel), went to Shechem (a city in Israel) to speak with his mother's brothers. He also spoke with all the family of his mother's father, saying, **2.** "Speak to all the people of Shechem: 'What do you think is better? That all seventy sons of Jerubbaal rule over you, or that one-man reigns over you? Remember, I am your own flesh and blood.'" **3.** When the brothers told the people of Shechem all of this, they were persuaded (convicted) to support Abimelech, saying, "He is one of our own (kin)." **4.** In response, they gave Abimelech seventy shekels of silver from the temple of Baal-Berith (a false god), which he used to hire reckless and worthless men to follow him. **5.** However, Jotham, the youngest son of Jerubbaal, escaped because he managed to hide himself. **6.** The men of Shechem and those of Beth Millo (a fortified area in Shechem) came together and made Abimelech their king by the terebinth tree near the pillar in Shechem. **7.** When Jotham heard of this, he went to the top of Mount Gerizim (a mountain near Shechem) and cried out to the people, saying, "Listen to me, men of Shechem, so that God may listen to you!" **8.** "The trees once set out to anoint a king over them. First, they asked the olive tree, 'Reign over us!' **9.** "But the olive tree answered, 'Should I give up my oil, by which both gods and humans are honored (revered), to hold sway (dominate) over the trees?'" **10.** The trees then asked the fig tree, 'Come and reign over us!' **11.** But the fig tree replied, 'Should I stop producing my sweetness and good fruit just to rule over trees?' **12.** Then the trees asked the vine, 'Come and reign over us!' **13.** But the vine said, 'Should

I stop producing my new wine, which brings joy to both God and men, to rule over trees?' **14.** "Finally, all the trees said to the thornbush, 'Come and reign (rule) over us as our king.'" **15.** Finally, the bramble spoke to the trees, 'If you truly want me to be your king, come and take shelter under my shade. But if not, let fire come from me and destroy the cedars of Lebanon.'" **16.** "Now, if you have acted with honesty and integrity in making Abimelech your king, and if you have treated Jerubbaal and his family kindly, and done what they deserve, **17.** "Remember, my father fought for you and risked his life to deliver you from the Midianites (a hostile people). **18.** Yet today, you have betrayed (turned against) my father's family. You have slain his seventy sons on a single stone and appointed Abimelek—son of his servant woman—as king over the citizens of Shechem simply because he is your kin (relative)." **19.** then rejoice in Abimelech, and let him rejoice in you. But if not, let fire come from Abimelech and consume the men of Shechem and Beth Millo, and let fire come from them and consume Abimelech!" **20.** "But if you have acted wrongly (unjustly), may fire (destruction) emerge from Abimelek to destroy (consume) you—the people of Shechem and Beth Millo—and may fire (destruction) come from you, the people of Shechem and Beth Millo, to destroy (devour) Abimelek!" **21.** After delivering this message, Jotham fled to Beer (a city), where he stayed out of fear of his brother, Abimelech. **22.** After ruling over Israel for three years, **23.** God sent a spirit of discord between Abimelech and the men of Shechem, causing them to betray Abimelech. **24.** This was to bring justice for the murder of the seventy sons of Jerubbaal, and for their blood to be avenged on Abimelech, who killed them, and on the men of Shechem, who had helped him in the massacre. **25.** "In defiance (opposition) of him, the citizens of Shechem stationed men on the hilltops to ambush (trap) and rob everyone passing by, and this was reported (made known) to Abimelek." **26.** A man named Gaal, son of Ebed, came to Shechem with his brothers, and the people of Shechem put their trust in him. **27.** They went into the fields, harvested grapes from their vineyards, and made wine. Then they went to the house of their god, where they ate, drank, and cursed Abimelech. **28.** At this, Gaal, son of Ebed, said, "Who is Abimelech, and who are the men of Shechem, that we should serve him?" **29.** If only this people were under my authority! Then I would remove Abimelech." So, he sent a challenge to Abimelech, saying, "Increase your army and come out!" **30.** When Zebul, the ruler of the city, heard what Gaal the son of Ebed said, his anger was stirred. **31.** He sent messengers secretly to Abimelech, saying, "Take note! Gaal the son of Ebed and his brothers have come to Shechem, and here they are, fortifying the city against you. **32.** Now, get up by night, you and the people with you, and lie in wait in the fields. **33.** As soon as the sun rises, you and your army should rush against the city. When Gaal and his men come out against you, do to them whatever you can." **34.** So Abimelech and all his men rose by night and lay in wait against Shechem in four companies. **35.** When Gaal the son of Ebed went out and stood at the entrance to the city gate, Abimelech and his men rose from their hiding places. **36.** When Gaal saw them, he said to Zebul, "Look, people are coming down from the mountaintops!" But Zebul replied, "You are seeing the shadows of the mountains as if they were men." **37.** Gaal spoke again, saying, "See, people are coming down from the center of the land, and another company is coming from the Diviners' Terebinth Tree." **38.** Then Zebul said to him, "Where is your mouth now, with which you said, 'Who is Abimelech, that we should serve him?' Are not these the people you despised? Go out, if you will, and fight with them!" **39.** So Gaal went out, leading the men of Shechem, and fought against Abimelech. **40.** But Abimelech chased him, and Gaal fled before him, many falling wounded at the city gate. **41.** Abimelech stayed at Arumah, and Zebul drove Gaal and his brothers out of Shechem so they could not live there. **42.** The next day, when the people went into the field, Abimelech was told. **43.** He took his people, divided them into three companies, and lay in wait in the field. When he saw the people coming out of the city, he attacked them. **44.** Abimelech and his men rushed to the city gate, while the other two companies attacked those in the fields, killing them. **45.** Abimelech fought the city all day, took it, and killed the people in it. He destroyed the city and sowed it with salt. **46.** When the men of the tower of Shechem heard of it, they entered the stronghold of the temple of their god, Berith. **47.** Abimelech was told that the men of the tower had gathered. **48.** He went up to Mount Zalmon (a mountain), and he and his men cut down branches from the trees. He then carried the branches to the city and ordered the men to follow him, stacking the branches around the stronghold and setting it on fire. All the people in the tower, about a thousand men and women, died in the flames. **50.** Abimelech then went to Thebez (a city), camped against it, and took it.**51.** There was a strong tower in the city, and all the people of the city fled to it, shut the doors, and went up to the top of the tower. **52.** Abimelech came near the tower and fought against it, intending to burn it. **53.** He quickly called to his armor-bearer, saying, "Draw your sword and kill me, so that people won't say, 'A woman killed him.'" His armor-bearer obeyed, and Abimelech died. **54.** When the men of Israel saw that Abimelech was dead, they returned to their homes. **55.** Thus, God repaid Abimelech for the wickedness he had done in killing his seventy brothers. **56.** And all the evil of the men of Shechem was returned upon them. The curse Jotham had pronounced on them came to pass. **57.** And all the wickedness committed by the men of Shechem was brought back upon their own heads, and the curse that Jotham, the son of Jerubbaal, had pronounced on them came to pass.

Chapter 10

1. Following the era of Abimelech, Tola, the son of Puah and grandson of Dodo, emerged as a leader from the tribe of Issachar to deliver the people of Israel. He resided in Shamir, a town located in the hilly region of Ephraim, which is situated in central Israel. **2.** Tola served as a judge of Israel for duration of twenty-three years. Upon his death, he was interred in Shamir. **3.** Subsequently, Jair, a man hailing from Gilead, which is located on the eastern bank of the Jordan River, ascended to the role of judge over Israel. He governed the nation for a period of twenty-two years. **4.** Jair had thirty sons, each of whom rode a donkey, and he controlled thirty towns in Gilead, which are still known as "Havoth Jair" (meaning "the towns of Jair") to this very day. **5.** When Jair died, he was buried in Camon (a town in Gilead). **6.** Once again, the Israelites did evil in the sight of the Lord. They worshiped the Baals (false gods) and the Ashtoreths (goddesses of fertility), as well as the gods˙ of Syria, Sidon, Moab, Ammon, and the Philistines. They abandoned the Lord and stopped serving Him. **7.** As a result, the Lord became very angry with Israel and handed them over to the Philistines and the Ammonites. **8.** For eighteen years, these enemies oppressed the Israelites who lived in the land of Gilead, on the other side of the Jordan River, in the territory of the Amorites. **9.** The Ammonites also crossed over the Jordan River to attack the tribes of Judah, Benjamin, and the house of Ephraim. As a result, Israel was in great distress. **10.** Then the people of Israel cried out to the Lord, saying, "We have sinned against You. We have abandoned our God and served the Baals." **11.** The Lord responded, "Did I not rescue you from the Egyptians, the Amorites, the Ammonites, and the Philistines? **12.** The Sidonians, the Amalekites, and the Maonites also oppressed you. You cried out to Me, and I saved you from them. **13.** Yet you have turned away from Me and worshiped other gods. Therefore, I will not save you anymore. **14.** Go and cry out to the gods you have chosen. Let them save you when you are in trouble." **15.** The Israelites admitted, "We have sinned! Do with us as You think best, but please deliver us today." **16.** So, they removed the foreign gods from among them and served the Lord. Then the Lord could no longer bear the suffering of Israel. **17.** The Ammonites gathered together and camped in Gilead. The Israelites also gathered and camped at Mizpah (a town in Gilead). **18.** The leaders of Gilead spoke to one another, saying, "Who will be the man to start the battle against the Ammonites? He will be the leader over all the people of Gilead."

Chapter 11

1. Jephthah, a strong and courageous man from Gilead, was a mighty warrior, but he was the son of a prostitute. Gilead was his father. **2.** Gilead's wife had other sons, and when they grew up, they drove Jephthah out, saying, "You have no share in our father's inheritance, because you are the son of a different woman." **3.** Jephthah fled from his brothers and settled in the land of Tob (a region located northeast of Israel). There, a group of disreputable men gathered around him, and they went out raiding together. **4-5** "Some time later, when the Ammonites (enemies of Israel) were waging war (fighting) against Israel, the elders (leaders) of Gilead went to bring Jephthah back from the land of Tob." **6.** Once more, the Israelites did what was evil in the eyes of the Lord. **7.** Jephthah said to them, "Didn't you hate me and drive me from my father's house? Why do you come to me now, when you're in trouble?" **8.** For eighteen years, these enemies oppressed the Israelites living in Gilead, across the Jordan River, in the land of the Amorites (a group of ancient people who lived in the region of Canaan). **9.** Jephthah replied, "If you bring me back to fight the Ammonites and the LORD delivers (gives) them into my hands, will I truly be your leader (head)?" **10.** The Israelites then cried out to the Lord, saying, "We have sinned against You. We have forsaken our God and worshiped the Baals (false gods)." **11.** The Lord replied, "Did I not rescue you from the Egyptians, the Amorites, the Ammonites (a people who lived east of Israel), and the Philistines (an ancient people living along the Mediterranean coast)? **12.** The Sidonians (people from Sidon, a Phoenician city), the Amalekites (descendants of Esau), and the Maonites (tribal people from the desert region) also oppressed you. You cried out to Me, and I saved you from them. **13.** The king of the Ammonites responded to Jephthah's messengers, "When Israel came up from Egypt, they seized my land, from the Arnon to the Jabbok, all the way to the Jordan. Now, restore it to me peacefully." **14.** "Now go and cry out to the gods you have chosen to serve. Let them save you in your time of distress."**15.** "This is what Jephthah says: 'Israel did not take the land of Moab or the land of Ammon. **16.** When Israel came out of Egypt, they traveled through the wilderness to Kadesh (a place near the border of Edom), and asked the king of Edom if they could pass through his land, but he refused. They also asked the king of Moab, and he did not allow them to pass either. So, Israel remained at Kadesh. **17.** Israel then traveled through the wilderness, bypassed the land of Edom and Moab, and camped on the east side of Moab, near the Arnon River, but they did not enter Moab because the Arnon is the boundary of Moab. **18.** Israel then sent messengers to Sihon, the king of the Amorites (a people group in ancient Israel), asking for permission to pass through his land, but he refused and gathered his army to fight Israel. **19.** The Lord, the God of Israel, gave Israel victory over Sihon and his people, and Israel took possession of all the land of the Amorites. **20.** Israel then took the land from the Arnon to the Jabbok, and from the wilderness to the Jordan River. **21.** Since the Lord God of Israel has dispossessed the Amorites for His people, should you try to take that land from us? **22.** You can possess whatever Chemosh (the god of the Moabites) gives you, and we will possess whatever the Lord our God gives us. **23.** Are you better than Balak, the son of Zippor, king of Moab? Did he ever challenge Israel or fight against them? **24.** Israel lived peacefully in Heshbon (a city of the Amorites), Aroer (a city), and all the villages along the Arnon for 300 years. Why didn't you try to recover them during that time? **25.** I have not wronged you, but you wronged me by fighting against me. Let the Lord, who is the ultimate Judge, decide today between Israel and the Ammonites." **26.** But the king of Ammon did not listen to the message Jephthah had sent him. **27.** Then the Spirit of the Lord came upon Jephthah, and he passed through Gilead and Manasseh, and then through Mizpah of Gilead. From Mizpah, he advanced toward the Ammonites. **28.** Jephthah made a vow to the Lord, saying, "If You will give me victory over the Ammonites, **29.** then whatever comes out of my house to greet me when I return in peace will belong to the Lord, and I will offer it as a burnt offering." **30.** Jephthah went to fight the Ammonites, and the Lord gave him victory over them. **31.** Jephthah defeated them from Aroer to Minnith (about 20 cities), and all the way to Abel Keramim, with a great slaughter. The Ammonites were completely defeated before Israel. **32.** When Jephthah returned home to Mizpah, his daughter came out to meet him, dancing with tambourines. She was his only child; he had no other sons or daughters. **33.** When Jephthah saw her, he tore his clothes and said, "Oh no, my daughter! You have brought me low. You are the cause of my grief, for I have made a vow to the Lord, and I cannot break it." **34.** She said to him, "Father, if you have made a vow to the Lord, do as you have promised, because the Lord has given you victory over your enemies, the Ammonites." **35.** Then she asked her father, "Let me have two months to go into the mountains and mourn my virginity with my friends." **36.** He agreed, and she went to the mountains to mourn with her friends for two months. **37.** After two months, she returned to her father, and he fulfilled his vow to the Lord. She remained a virgin, and Jephthah kept his promise. **38.** It became a custom in Israel for the daughters of Israel to go each year to lament the daughter of Jephthah, the Gileadite, for four days. **39.** At the end of the two months, she returned to her father, and he carried out the vow he had made to the Lord. She remained a virgin, and Jephthah fulfilled his promise. **40.** This became a tradition in Israel: every year, the young women of Israel would go out for four days to mourn the daughter of Jephthah, the Gileadite.

Chapter 12

1. The men of Ephraim gathered together and marched toward Zaphon (a location). They confronted Jephthah with anger and said, "Why did you go to fight the Ammonites without asking us to join you? Now, we will burn your house down on top of you with fire!" **2.** Jephthah answered them, "My people and I were in a great and desperate struggle with the Ammonites. When I called on you for help, you refused to come to our aid and deliver us from their hands." **3.** "Seeing that you were unwilling to help, I took matters into my own hands. I risked my own life and led the charge against the Ammonites (Ammonites fought against Israel). The Lord gave us victory over them. Now, why have you come to me today, angry and ready to fight against me?" **4.** In response, Jephthah gathered the men of Gilead, a region east of Israel, and fought against the men of Ephraim. The Gileadites were victorious because the Ephraimites had insulted them, calling them "fugitives" from Ephraim, and accusing them of being traitors among the Ephraimites and the Manassites. **5.** To prevent any Ephraimites from escaping, the Gileadites took control of the fords (crossings) of the Jordan River, blocking any attempts to flee. If anyone trying to cross was suspected of being from Ephraim, they would ask, "Are you an Ephraimite?" If the man answered, "No," **6.** They would test him further, saying, "Then say 'Shibboleth'!" If he was truly from Ephraim, he would pronounce it as "Sibboleth," because the Ephraimites could not correctly say the word. If he pronounced it wrong, they knew he was an Ephraimite, and they would seize him and execute him at the fords of the Jordan. In total, forty-two thousand men from Ephraim were killed that day. **7.** Jephthah continued to lead Israel and served as a judge for six years. After his death, he was buried in one of the cities of Gilead, where he had lived and ruled. **8.** After Jephthah's death, Ibzan from Bethlehem (a city in Judah) became the next judge of Israel. **9.** Ibzan had thirty sons and thirty daughters. He gave his daughters in marriage to men from other tribes and brought in thirty daughters from other places for his sons to marry. He judged Israel for seven years before passing away. **10.** After Ibzan's death, he was buried in Bethlehem, where he had lived. **11.** The next judge was Elon, a man from the tribe of Zebulun. Elon served as the judge of Israel for ten years, helping lead the nation through times of peace and stability. **12.** Elon eventually died and was buried at Aijalon (a city) in the territory of Zebulun. **13.** Following Elon's death, Abdon, the son of Hillel, from Pirathon (a town in Ephraim), became the judge of Israel. **14.** Abdon had a large family, including forty sons and thirty grandsons. All of his sons and grandsons rode on seventy young donkeys, a sign of wealth and status. He served as Israel's judge for eight years, bringing a time of leadership and governance to the nation. **15.** After Abdon passed away, he was buried in Pirathon, a town in the land of Ephraim, in the mountainous region where the Amalekites, a nomadic and hostile group, had once lived.

Chapter 13

1. Once again, the Israelites did evil in the sight of the Lord, and as a result, He allowed them to be oppressed by the Philistines (a powerful group of people who lived along the coastal areas of Israel) for forty years. **2.** There was a man from Zorah (a town in the tribe of Dan, located in the western part of Israel), from the family of the Danites (one of the twelve tribes of Israel), whose name was Manoah. His wife was barren and had not borne any children. **3.** The Angel of the Lord appeared to Manoah's wife and said, "Although you are barren and have not had children, you will conceive and give birth to a son." **4.** "Now, be careful not to drink wine or any strong drink, and do not eat anything that is considered unclean." (Unclean refers to foods that are forbidden by Jewish law, such as certain animals or food preparations.) **5.** "You will bear a son, and no razor shall touch his head, for the child will be a Nazirite (someone dedicated to God by a vow, who refrains from cutting their hair, drinking alcohol, or touching certain unclean things) from birth. He will begin to deliver Israel from the Philistines."

6. The woman went to her husband and said, "A man of God appeared to me, and His appearance was like that of an angel—so awe-inspiring that I was afraid. I didn't ask where He came from, nor did He reveal His name to me." **7.** "But He said to me, 'You will conceive and give birth to a son. Do not drink wine or any strong drink, and avoid eating anything impure, for the child will be a Nazirite to God from the womb until his death.'" **8.** Manoah prayed to the Lord, saying, "Please, let the man of God You sent come back to us and tell us how to raise the child who is to be born." **9.** God answered Manoah's prayer, and the Angel of God appeared again to his wife while she was sitting in the field. Her husband Manoah was not with her at the time. **10.** The woman ran quickly and told her husband, "The man who appeared to me earlier has returned!" **11.** Manoah got up and followed his wife. When he reached the man, he asked, "Are You the one who spoke to my wife?" The man answered, "I am." **12.** Manoah then said, "Now, let Your words come true! What will be the child's way of life, and what will be his mission?" **13.** The Angel of the Lord replied, "Everything I told the woman, she must take care to follow. **14.** She must not eat anything from the vine (grapevine, from which wine is made), nor drink wine or any strong drink, nor eat anything unclean. She must obey all the instructions I have given her." **15.** Manoah then said to the Angel of the Lord, "Please stay with us, and let us prepare a young goat for You." **16.** The Angel of the Lord replied to Manoah, "Even though you detain Me, I will not eat your food. But if you prepare a burnt offering, you must offer it to the Lord." (A burnt offering is a type of sacrifice that is completely consumed by fire as an act of devotion to God.) **17.** Manoah asked, "What is Your name, so that when Your words come true, we can honor You?" **18.** The Angel of the Lord responded, "Why do you ask My name, since it is beyond understanding?" (This implies that God's name is too wonderful or incomprehensible for human understanding.) **19.** Manoah took a young goat and a grain offering and sacrificed it on a rock to the Lord. While Manoah and his wife watched, the Lord performed a miraculous act: **20.** As the flame from the altar ascended toward heaven, the Angel of the Lord ascended in the flame. When Manoah and his wife saw this, they fell face down to the ground. **21.** The Angel of the Lord did not appear again to Manoah and his wife. Then Manoah realized that it had been the Angel of the Lord. **22.** Manoah said to his wife, "We will surely die, for we have seen God!" (Manoah feared death because it was believed that no one could survive seeing God in His divine form.) **23.** But his wife replied, "If the Lord had meant to kill us, He would not have accepted our burnt offering and grain offering, nor would He have shown us all these things, nor would He have told us such things now." **24.** So the woman gave birth to a son and named him Samson (meaning "sun" or "bright," symbolizing strength). The child grew, and the Lord blessed him. **25.** And the Spirit of the Lord began to stir Samson as he was at Mahaneh Dan (a place between Zorah and Eshtaol, both towns in the tribe of Dan). Here, Samson began to feel the movement of God's Spirit within him.

Chapter 14

1. Samson went down to Timnah, a Philistine city, and saw a woman there from the daughters of the Philistines. **2.** He went back to his father and mother and said, "I have seen a woman in Timnah from the Philistines; get her for me as a wife." **3.** His father and mother asked him, "Is there no woman from among your relatives or from our people that you must choose a wife from the uncircumcised Philistines?" But Samson replied to his father, "Get her for me, because she looks good to me." **4.** But his father and mother did not know that this was from the Lord. God was looking for an opportunity to act against the Philistines, for at that time the Philistines were ruling over Israel. **5.** So Samson and his parents went down to Timnah, and as they reached the vineyards of Timnah, a young lion came roaring toward him. **6.** The Spirit of the Lord came powerfully upon him, and he tore the lion apart as easily as if it were a young goat, although he had nothing in his hand. But he did not tell his father or mother what had happened. **7.** Then Samson went down and talked to the woman, and she pleased him. **8.** After some time, when Samson went back to get her, he turned aside to look at the carcass of the lion he had killed. To his surprise, he found a swarm of bees and honey in the lion's carcass. **9.** He took some of the honey in his hands and ate it as he walked along. When he reached his father and mother, he gave some of the honey to them, and they ate it, but he did not tell them that he had taken it from the carcass of the lion. *(The dead body of an animal.)* 10. So his father went down to meet the woman, and Samson prepared a feast there, as young men were accustomed to do for weddings. *(A celebratory meal, often associated with weddings or festivals.)* 11. When the Philistines saw him, they brought thirty companions to be with him, likely to serve as his wedding guests. (Friends or guests invited to the celebration.) 12. Samson said to them, "Let me pose a riddle to you. If you can solve and explain it to me within the seven days of the feast, I will give you thirty linen garments and thirty changes of clothes. *(Fine, light clothing often worn by the wealthy.)* 13. "But if you cannot explain it to me, then you will give me thirty linen garments and thirty changes of clothes." The Philistines agreed to his challenge, saying, "Pose your riddle, that we may hear it." 14. So Samson told them the riddle: "Out of the eater came something to eat, and out of the strong came something sweet." *(A puzzle or mystery to be solved.)* 15. For three days, they could not solve the riddle. 16. On the seventh day, they said to Samson's wife, "Entice your husband to explain the riddle to us, or we will burn you and your father's house with fire. Did you invite us here to take what is ours?" *(To persuade or convince someone, often by manipulation.)* 17. Samson's wife wept before him and said, "You only hate me! You do not love me! You have posed a riddle to the men of my people but have not explained it to me." He replied, "Look, I haven't even explained it to my father or mother, so why should I explain it to you?" 18. She wept for the entire seven days of the feast, and on the seventh day, because she had pressed him so much, he finally told her the answer. She then explained the riddle to the men of the city. 19. Then the Spirit of the Lord came upon him mightily, and he went down to Ashkelon and killed thirty of their men, took their apparel, and gave the changes of clothing to those who had explained the riddle. So, his anger was aroused, and he went back up to his father's house. 20. The Spirit of the Lord came powerfully upon Samson, and he went down to Ashkelon, a Philistine city, where he killed thirty men, took their clothes, and gave the clothes to those who had solved the riddle. His anger burned, and he returned to his father's house. 21. Samson's wife was given to his companion, who had been his best man at the wedding.

Chapter 15

1. Sometime later, during the wheat harvest, Samsonth (prodigious strength that he derived from his uncut hair visited his wife) bringing a young goat. He said, "Let me go in to my wife, into her room." But her father did not allow him to go in. 2. Her father explained, "I thought you must really hate her, so I gave her to your companion. Isn't her younger sister better than she? Please, take her instead." 3. Samson replied, "This time I will be blameless before the Philistines (Decedents of Philistine) if I harm them!" 4. So, Samson went out and caught three hundred foxes. He tied them tail to tail in pairs and placed a torch between each pair's tails. 5. After lighting the torches, he released the foxes into the Philistine fields, burning their standing grain, shocks (bundles of harvested grain), vineyards, and olive groves. *(Bundles of harvested grain.)* 6. The Philistines asked, "Who did this?" They were told, "Samson, the son-in-law of the Timnite, because he took his wife and gave her to his companion." In anger, the Philistines went and burned Samson's wife and her father to death. 7. Samson said to them, "Since you have done this, I will take revenge on you, and after that, I will stop." 8. So, Samson attacked them with great force, causing many casualties, and then he went to dwell in the cleft (a narrow opening) of the rock of Etam. 9. The Philistines then moved to Judah and camped against the city of Lehi. 10. The men of Judah asked, "Why have you come to fight us?" The Philistines answered, "We have come to arrest Samson, and punish him for what he has done to us." 11. So, three thousand men of Judah went down to the cleft of the rock of Etam and said to Samson, "Don't you know the Philistines rule over us? What have you done to us?" Samson answered, "I did to them as they did to me." 12. But the men of Judah said, "We've come to arrest you, so we can hand you over to the Philistines." Samson replied, "Swear to me that you won't kill me yourselves." 13. They promised, "No, we won't kill you. We'll tie you up securely and hand you over to them." So, they bound him with two new ropes and brought him up from the rock. 14. As Samson came to Lehi, the Philistines came shouting to meet him. Then the Spirit of the Lord came powerfully upon Samson, and the

ropes on his arms became like burned flax, and his bonds fell off. 15. Samson found the fresh jawbone of a donkey, took it in his hand, and used it to kill a thousand Philistine men. 16. Samson then said, "With the jawbone of a donkey, I have piled them in heaps— with the jawbone of a donkey I've slain a thousand men!" 17. When he finished speaking, Samson threw away the jawbone and called that place Ramath Lehi 18. Samson became very thirsty and cried out to the Lord, "You have given me this great victory, but now I will die of thirst and fall into the hands of the uncircumcised Philistines." 19. God then split open a hollow place in Lehi, and water flowed out. Samson drank, his strength returned, and he was revived. He named the place En Hakkore, which means "Spring of the Caller," because he had cried out to the Lord. It is still called that to this day. 20. Samson judged Israel for twenty years during the time of the Philistine oppression.

Chapter 16

1. Samson traveled to Gaza (a major Philistine city, now in the Gaza Strip) where he encountered a prostitute and stayed with her that night. 2. The people of Gaza were told, "Samson is here!" They surrounded the place and waited near the city gate to ambush him at dawn, planning to kill him in the morning. 3. But Samson only stayed until midnight. Then he got up, took hold of the city gate doors along with the two posts, tore them loose with the bar still attached, lifted them onto his shoulders, and carried them to the top of a hill near Hebron (a southern city in Israel). 4. Later, Samson fell in love with a woman named Delilah who lived in the Valley of Sorek (a valley on the Philistine-Israelite border). 5. The Philistine rulers came to Delilah and urged her, "Find out the secret of his great strength, so we can overpower him, bind him, and subdue him. Each of us will give you eleven hundred shekels of silver" (a large sum of silver as payment). 6. Delilah asked Samson, "Tell me the source of your great strength and how you could be tied up and subdued." 7. Samson answered, "If I am tied with seven fresh bowstrings (bowstrings made from animal intestines) that haven't dried, I will become as weak as any other man." 8. So, the Philistine rulers brought her seven fresh bowstrings, and she tied Samson up. 9. With men hiding in the room, she called out, "Samson, the Philistines are upon you!" But he snapped the bowstrings as easily as a piece of string snaps when it's near a flame. So, they didn't discover his strength. 10. Delilah said to Samson, "You have made a fool of me and lied to me. Now, tell me how you can be tied." 11. Samson replied, "If I am tied securely with new ropes that have never been used, I will become as weak as any other man." 12. So, Delilah took new ropes and tied him up. Then, with men hidden in the room, she called, "Samson, the Philistines are upon you!" But he broke the ropes off his arms as if they were threads. 13. Delilah said to him, "You've mocked me and lied again! Tell me how you can be tied." He replied, "If you weave the seven braids of my hair into the fabric on a loom and fasten it with a pin, I'll become as weak as any other man." 14. So while Samson was asleep, Delilah took the seven braids of his hair, wove them into the fabric, and tightened it with the pin. Again she called out, "Samson, the Philistines are upon you!" He woke up, pulling the pin, the loom, and the fabric all together. 15. Delilah said to him, "How can you say, 'I love you,' when you won't trust me? This is the third time you've made a fool of me and haven't revealed the source of your great strength." 16. She kept asking him day after day, pressing him until he was so troubled he was weary of life. 17. Finally, Samson told her everything. He said, "My hair has never been shaved, for I have been a Nazirite (one dedicated to God with vows) from birth. If my hair is shaved, my strength will leave me, and I will be as weak as any other man." 18. Seeing that he had told her the truth, Delilah sent word to the Philistine rulers, saying, "Come back one more time; he has told me everything." The rulers returned, bringing the silver with them. 19. After putting him to sleep on her lap, she called for someone to shave off the seven braids of his hair. His strength left him as he was subdued. 20. Then she called, "Samson, the Philistines are upon you!" He woke up, thinking he could break free as before, but he did not know that the Lord had left him. v21. The Philistines seized him, gouged out his eyes, and took him down to Gaza, where they bound him with bronze chains. They put him to work grinding grain in the prison. 22. However, the hair on his head began to grow back after it had been shaved. 23. The Philistine rulers gathered to offer a great sacrifice to their god Dagon (a deity worshipped in Philistine culture)

and to celebrate, saying, "Our god has delivered our enemy Samson into our hands." **24.** When the people saw Samson, they praised their god, exclaiming, "Our god has delivered our enemy into our hands—the one who devastated our land and killed so many of us." **25.** While they were celebrating, they called for Samson to entertain them. So, they brought him out of prison, and he performed for them. They had him stand between two central pillars. **26.** Samson said to the servant who was guiding him, "Place me where I can feel the pillars that support the temple, so I can lean against them." **27.** The temple was crowded with men and women, including all the Philistine rulers, and about three thousand people were on the roof watching Samson perform. **28.** Samson prayed to the Lord, saying, "Sovereign Lord, remember me. Please strengthen me once more so I can take revenge on the Philistines for my eyes." **29.** He then placed his hands on the two central pillars supporting the temple, one with his right hand and one with his left. **30.** Samson said, "Let me die with the Philistines!" Then he pushed with all his might, bringing down the temple on the rulers and everyone in it. Thus, he killed more people in his death than during his life. **31.** Later, Samson's brothers and his family came to retrieve his body. They took him and buried him in the tomb of his father Manoah between Zorah and Eshtaol (towns in ancient Israel). Samson had judged Israel for twenty years.

Chapter 17

1. In the hill country of Ephraim (a region in Israel), there lived a man named Micah. **2.** He said to his mother, "The eleven hundred shekels of silver that were stolen from you, and you cursed—speaking those words in my hearing—here it is, I took it." His mother answered, "Blessed be the Lord, my son!" **3.** After returning the silver to his mother, she replied, "I had set apart this silver for the Lord to make an idol for my son, to form both a carved and molded image. Now, I'll return it to you." **4.** Micah returned the silver to his mother, and she took two hundred shekels of it, giving them to a silversmith. He crafted a carved and molded image, which was placed in Micah's house. **5.** Micah built a shrine and made an ephod (a sacred garment) along with household idols. He then dedicated one of his sons to serve as his priest. **6.** During that time, Israel had no king, and everyone did as they saw fit. **7.** A young man from Bethlehem in Judah, belonging to the tribe of Judah, was living in the hill country of Ephraim. He was a Levite (one of the tribe chosen for religious duties) who had come to stay there. **8.** He left Bethlehem in Judah to find a place to stay, and journeyed through the hill country of Ephraim, eventually reaching the house of Micah. **9.** Micah asked him, "Where are you from?" The young man answered, "I am a Levite from Bethlehem in Judah, and I am traveling to find a place to settle." **10.** Micah offered, "Stay with me, and be my priest. I will pay you ten shekels of silver a year, provide you with clothes, and take care of your food." The Levite agreed to live with him. **11.** The Levite was happy to stay with Micah, and he became like one of Micah's sons. **12.** Micah consecrated the Levite, and the young man served as his priest in Micah's house. **13.** Micah then said, "Now I know the Lord will bless me because I have a Levite as my priest!"

Chapter 18

1. In those days, Israel had no king, and the tribe of Dan was still searching for a place to settle. They had not yet received their allotted inheritance among the tribes of Israel. **2.** So, the Danites sent five brave men from their clan, from the towns of Zorah (a town in the territory of Dan) and Eshtaol (another Danite town), to explore the land. They told them, "Go, and spy out the land." So, the men went to the mountains of Ephraim (a region in central Israel) and stayed at the house of Micah (a man from the tribe of Ephraim). **3.** While they were at Micah's house, they recognized the voice of the young Levite (a man from the tribe of Levi, usually serving as a priest). They approached him and asked, "Who brought you here? What are you doing in this place? What do you have here?" **4.** He said to them, "Thus and so Micah did for me. He has hired me, and I have become his priest." **5.** So, they said to him, "Please inquire of God, that we may know whether the journey on which we go will be prosperous." **6.** The priest replied, "Go in peace. The Lord is with you on your journey." **7.** The five men went on their way to Laish (a city in the far northern part of Israel). They saw that the people there were living peacefully, like the Sidonians (people from the ancient city of Sidon, located on the Mediterranean coast), quiet and secure. They had no rulers who could put them to shame, and they

were far from the Sidonians, with no connections to other nations. **8.** When they returned to Zorah and Eshtaol, their fellow Danites asked, "What did you find out?" **9.** They replied, "Let's go attack. The land is good, and we've seen it for ourselves. Don't hesitate—let's go take possession of it. **10.** You will find a secure and peaceful people, and the land is large and fertile. God has already given it to us, a place where nothing is lacking." **11.** Six hundred armed men from the Danite clan left Zorah and Eshtaol, ready for battle. **12.** They camped at Kirjath Jearim (a city in Judah, near Jerusalem) in Judah (a southern tribe of Israel), which they named Mahaneh Dan (meaning "Dan's Camp"). This place is west of Kirjath Jearim. **13.** From there, they moved on to the mountains of Ephraim and arrived at Micah's house. **14.** The five men who had spied on Laish said to their companions, "Do you know that there are idols, an ephod (a priestly garment used in religious rituals), and a carved image in Micah's house? Think carefully about what we should do." **15.** So, they turned aside and entered Micah's house. The young Levite greeted them. **16.** The six hundred men armed with their weapons of war, who were of the children of Dan, stood by the entrance of the gate. **17.** The five men who had spied out the land entered the house, took the carved image, the ephod, the household idols, and the molded image. The priest was standing at the entrance with the armed men. **18.** When the priest saw them taking these items, he asked, "What are you doing?" **19.** They replied, "Be quiet. Don't say a word. Come with us and be a priest to us. Is it better for you to serve one household, or to serve an entire tribe and clan in Israel?" **20.** The priest was pleased, took the ephod, the idols, and the carved image, and joined the Danites. **21.** The Danites turned and began their journey, placing their children, livestock, and goods in front of them. **22.** When they were a good distance from Micah's house, the men who lived near Micah gathered together and caught up with the Danites. **23.** They called out to the Danites, and the Danites turned around and asked, "Why have you assembled such a crowd?" **24.** Micah replied, "You've taken my gods, the ones I made, and the priest, and you've gone. What do I have left? How can you ask me what's wrong?" **25.** The Danites warned him, "Don't raise your voice, or angry men will attack you, and you will lose your life, as well as the lives of your family!" **26.** The Danites continued on their way, and when Micah saw that they were too powerful for him, he turned back and went home. **27.** The Danites took the idols and the priest, and went to Laish (a peaceful city in the northern part of Israel), a peaceful and secure people. They attacked the city, struck it with the sword, and burned it to the ground. **28.** There was no one to deliver the city because it was far from Sidon and had no ties with anyone. It was located in a valley near Beth Rehob (a region in northern Israel). The Danites rebuilt the city and settled there. **29.** They renamed the city Dan (after their ancestor Dan, the son of Israel), the son of Israel. Previously, the city had been called Laish. **30.** The Danites set up the carved image for themselves, and Jonathan (son of Gershom, the son of Moses), and his descendants became priests for the tribe of Dan, until the land was taken into captivity. **31.** The Danites continued to worship Micah's carved image, which he had made, as long as the house of God was in Shiloh (the religious center of Israel before the temple was built in Jerusalem).

Chapter 19

1. In those days, when there was no king in Israel, a certain Levite, who lived in the remote hills of Ephraim (a mountainous region in Israel), took a concubine from Bethlehem in Judah (a town in the southern part of Israel, near Jerusalem). **2.** But his concubine was unfaithful to him and left him. She went back to her father's house in Bethlehem, where she stayed for four whole months. **3.** After these months, the Levite (descendant of tribe of Levi) got up and decided to go after her, hoping to speak kindly to her and bring her back. He took his servant and a couple of donkeys with him. When he arrived at her father's house, her father welcomed him with joy and invited him in. **4.** The father-in-law, the young woman's father, kept him there and detained him for three days. During this time, they ate, drank, and rested together. **5.** On the fourth day, they woke up early in the morning, and the Levite stood to depart, but his father-in-law said to him, "Please refresh yourself with a little bread before you go, and afterward, you can continue on your way." **6.** So, they sat down, and both of them ate and drank together. After their meal, the father-in-law again said,

"Please, stay the night and let your heart be merry." **7.** But when the Levite stood up again to depart, his father-in-law urged him to stay. So, he stayed there for the night once more. **8.** On the fifth day, the Levite rose early in the morning to leave, but his father-in-law once more asked him, "Please refresh your heart before you go." As a result, they delayed their departure until the afternoon, spending more time together over their meal. **9.** Finally, when the Levite stood up to leave—along with his concubine and servant—his father-in-law, the young woman's father, said to him, "Look, the day is almost over. The evening is approaching. Please spend the night here so that your heart may be refreshed. Tomorrow, you can leave early and head back home." **10.** However, the Levite was not willing to spend the night in that place. He got up and departed, traveling toward Jebus (which is the ancient name for Jerusalem, a city occupied by the Jebusites at the time). He had his two saddled donkeys with him, and his concubine accompanied him. **11.** As they drew near to Jebus, the day was already far spent. The Levite's servant suggested to him, "Come, let us turn aside and stop in this city of the Jebusites to spend the night." **12.** But the Levite replied, "We will not turn aside into a city of foreigners, who are not Israelites. Let us continue on to Gibeah (a town in the tribe of Benjamin), where we will be among fellow Israelites." **13.** He then said to his servant, "Come, let us go on to one of these places, and we will spend the night either in Gibeah or in Ramah (two towns in the tribe of Benjamin)." **14.** They passed by and continued on their way. As the sun set, they arrived near Gibeah, which belonged to the tribe of Benjamin. **15.** They turned into Gibeah and went into the open square of the city, but no one offered to take them in and provide shelter for the night. **16.** As it happened, an old man was coming in from working in the fields at evening. He was also from the mountains of Ephraim (a region in Israel) and was staying in Gibeah. The men of the city, however, were Benjamites (members of the tribe of Benjamin). **17.** When the old man looked up, he saw the traveler in the open square of the city. He asked, "Where are you going, and where have you come from?" **18.** The Levite replied, "We are traveling from Bethlehem in Judah (a town in the south of Israel) toward the remote mountains of Ephraim, where I am from. I went to Bethlehem in Judah, and now I am on my way to the house of the Lord. But there is no one here who will offer us shelter." **19.** "We have straw and fodder for our donkeys, and bread and wine for myself, for your female servant, and for the young man who is with your servant. We have everything we need." **20.** The old man answered, "Peace be with you! I will take care of all your needs. Just don't stay out in the open square for the night." **21.** So the old man brought them into his house, gave fodder to the donkeys, and they washed their feet. Afterward, they ate and drank together. **22.** While they were enjoying their meal, suddenly, a group of wicked men from the city surrounded the house. They began banging on the door and shouted to the old man, saying, "Bring out the man who is staying with you, so that we may have relations with him!" **23.** The master of the house went out to them and said, "No, my brothers, please don't do this wicked thing! This man has come into my house, and I cannot allow this disgrace." **24.** "Look, I have a virgin daughter, and the man's concubine; I will bring them out now. Humble them, and do with them as you please, but don't commit such a vile act against this man!" **25.** But the men refused to listen to him. So, the man took his concubine and threw her out to them. They abused her all night long, and it was only when morning broke that they let her go. **26.** When the woman returned, she came back to the house as the dawn was breaking. She collapsed at the door of the house, lying there until it was light. **27.** When her master got up in the morning, he opened the door to leave and saw his concubine lying at the door of the house with her hands on the threshold. **28.** He said to her, "Get up, let's go." But there was no answer. So, he lifted her onto his donkey and left, heading back to his home. **29.** When he arrived at his house, he took a knife, grabbed his concubine, and cut her into twelve pieces, one for each tribe of Israel. He then sent the pieces throughout the entire territory of Israel. **30.** When the people saw it, they were shocked and said, "Such a horrible thing has never been done or seen from the time the Israelites came up from Egypt until today. Consider what has happened, take counsel, and speak up!"

Chapter 21

1. So, all the people of Israel gathered, from Dan (northern boundary) to Beersheba (southern boundary) and also from Gilead (region east of the Jordan), uniting as one before the Lord at Mizpah. **2** The leaders of Israel, representing all the tribes, assembled together, bringing a force of four hundred thousand soldiers with swords. **3** (Meanwhile, the tribe of Benjamin learned that the Israelites had gathered at Mizpah.) The Israelites asked, "Explain how this terrible crime happened." **4** The Levite, husband of the murdered woman, answered, "My concubine and I entered Gibeah, part of Benjamin's territory, to spend the night. **5.** But that night, men from Gibeah surrounded the house, intending to kill me. Instead, they attacked and abused my concubine until she died. **6.** I then took her body, cut it in pieces, and sent the parts throughout Israel's land, for this vile outrage had been committed among us. **7.** Now, all of you, as Israelites, give your advice and counsel here!" **8.** Everyone unitedly declared, "None of us will return home; none will go back to his tent. **9.** This is what we will do to Gibeah: we'll attack it by drawing lots. **10.** We'll select ten men out of every hundred across all tribes, a hundred out of a thousand, and a thousand out of ten thousand, to gather supplies for the troops who will confront Gibeah of Benjamin, to repay the wickedness they committed." **11.** So, all the men of Israel gathered together as one against the city. **12.** Then the tribes of Israel sent messengers through the entire tribe of Benjamin, saying, "What is this evil that has happened among you? **13.** Now surrender the wicked men of Gibeah so that we may put them to death and remove this sin from Israel!" But the Benjamites refused to listen to their fellow Israelites. **14.** Instead, the Benjamites came together from their cities to Gibeah, preparing for battle against Israel. **15.** On that day, the Benjamites counted twenty-six thousand armed men, plus seven hundred elite men from Gibeah. **16.** Among them were seven hundred select left-handed men, all skilled to sling stones with deadly accuracy. **17.** The rest of Israel's warriors, excluding Benjamin's, numbered four hundred thousand, all trained soldiers. **18.** The Israelites went up to the house of God, asking, "Who should lead the attack against Benjamin?" The Lord replied, "Judah shall go first." **19.** So, the Israelites rose early and set up camp against Gibeah. **20.** The Israelites advanced for battle against Benjamin and lined up to face them at Gibeah. **21.** The Benjamites came out of Gibeah and struck down twenty-two thousand Israelite men that day. **22.** But the Israelite troops encouraged each other, setting up the battle line again at the same place as before. **23.** They then went up and wept before the Lord until evening, seeking His counsel, "Should we attack our brothers, the Benjamites, again?" The Lord answered, "Go and fight them." **24.** So, the Israelites approached the Benjamites on the second day. **25.** Once again, the Benjamites emerged from Gibeah and killed eighteen thousand more Israelites, all armed with swords.

8 – Ruth

Chapter 1

1. In the days when the judges ruled, a famine struck the region. A man and his wife, along with their two sons from Bethlehem in Judah, decided to temporarily move to Moab (located in southern Jordan). **2.** The man's name was Elimelek, his wife Naomi, and their two sons Mahlon and Kilion. They were Ephrathites (people from the town of Ephrath) from Bethlehem in Judah and had gone to live in Moab. **3.** However, Elimelek, Naomi's husband, died, and she was left with her two sons. **4.** The two sons married Moabite women, one named Orpah and the other Ruth. After about ten years in Moab, **5.** both Mahlon and Kilion died, leaving Naomi without her two sons, and her husband. **6.** When Naomi, Ruth's mother-in-law, learned in Moab that the LORD had favored His people by providing them with food, she and her daughters-in-law prepared to return home. **7.** With her daughters-in-law by her side, she left the place they had been living and started their journey back to Judah. **8.** Naomi said to her daughters-in-law, "Please go back, each of you, to your mother's house. May the LORD grant you kindness, just as you have shown kindness to your dead husbands and to me? **9.** May the LORD grants that each of you will find rest in the home of another husband." They embraced her, kissed her goodbye, and cried loudly. **10.** They said to her, "We will go back with you to your people." **11.** But Naomi said, "Go back, my daughters. Why would you come with me? Can I have more sons who could be your husbands? **12.** Go home; I am too old to marry again. Even if I thought there was still hope for me—even if I had a husband tonight and gave birth to sons, **13.** would you wait until they grew up? Would you stay single for them? No, my daughters. This is bitterer for me than for you because the LORD's hand has risen against me!" **14.** Again, they wept. And Orpah kissed her mother-in-law goodbye, but Ruth clung to her. **15.** Naomi said, "Look, your sister-in-law is going back to her people and her gods. Go back with her." **16.** But Ruth said, "Do not urge me to leave you or to turn from following you. Where you go I will go, and where you stay I will stay. Your people shall be my people and your God my God. **17.** Where you die, I will die, and there I will be buried. May the LORD deal with me, be it ever so severely, if even death separates you and me." **18.** When Naomi saw that Ruth was determined to go with her, she stopped urging her. **19.** The two women went on until they came to Bethlehem (the birthplace of Jesus Christ). When they came to Bethlehem, all the town was stirred because of them, and the women exclaimed, "Is this Naomi?" **20.** "Do not call me Naomi," she said to them. "As the Almighty has dealt very bitterly with me, call me Mara (meaning bitter). **21.** I went away full, but the LORD has brought me back empty. Why do you call me Naomi, when the LORD has afflicted me and the Almighty has brought misfortune upon me?" **22.** Thus, Naomi returned from Moab, accompanied by her daughter-in-law Ruth, arriving in Bethlehem at the start of the barley harvest.

Chapter 2

1. Naomi had a wealthy relative from her husband's family, a man named Boaz (who would later marry Ruth). He belonged to the clan of Elimelek (Naomi's husband). **2.** Ruth the Moabite said to Naomi, "Let me go to the fields to gather leftover grain from anyone who might favor me." Naomi said, "Yes, go ahead, my daughter." **3.** She went out and entered a field, beginning to gather grain after the harvesters. It was a coincidence that she was working in a field owned by Boaz, part of Elimelech's clan. **4.** Suddenly, Boaz came in from Bethlehem (the town of Jesus' birth) and greeted the harvesters, saying, "The LORD be with you!" They answered him, "The LORD bless you!" **5.** Boaz asked the manager of his harvesters, "Who is that young woman?" **6.** The overseer said, "That's the Moabite woman who came back with Naomi from Moab." **7.** She said, "Please allow me to glean and gather the sheaves after the harvesters." The overseer noted, "She has been here all morning, only taking a short break in the shelter." **8** Then Boaz said to Ruth, "My daughter, listen to me. Do not go and glean in another field; do not move from this one. Remain with the women working for me. **9** Keep your eyes on the field where the men are harvesting, and follow the women closely. I've instructed the men not to interfere with you. If you're thirsty, you can drink from the jars the men have filled." **10.** Ruth bowed with her face to the ground and asked him, "Why have I found favor in your eyes that you notice me, a foreigner?" **11.** Boaz answered her, "I have been told all about how you have treated your mother-in-law since the death of your husband. You left your parents and your homeland to make your life among people you hadn't known before. **12.** May the LORD reward you for what you have done? May you be abundantly rewarded by the LORD, the God of Israel, under whose wings you have come to take refuge?" **13.** Ruth said, "My lord, may I continue to find favor in your eyes? You have comforted your handmaid, in that you have spoken words of consolation to your servant, although I am not one of your servants." **14.** At the meal, Boaz said to her, "Join me here. Take some bread and dip it in the wine vinegar." When she sat down with the harvesters, he served her roasted grain, and she ate until she was full, with some left over. **15.** As she began to glean, Boaz told his workers, "Let her pick among the sheaves, and do not rebuke her. **16.** Additionally, take some stalks from the bundles and leave them for her to pick up, and do not tell her." **17.** Ruth gathered in the field until evening, after which she threshed the barley she had collected, which came to about an ephah (roughly 22 liters). **18.** She returned to town, and her mother-in-law noticed the large amount she had gathered. Ruth also brought out the food she had left over from her meal. **19.** Naomi asked, "Where did you glean today? Where did you labor? May the man who noticed you be blessed!" Ruth replied, "The name of the man I worked with today is Boaz." **20.** "May the LORD bless him!" Naomi said to her daughter-in-law. "He has been generous in his kindness to both the living and the dead. That man is our relative and one of our guardian-redeemers." **21.** Ruth the Moabite added, "He even told me, 'Stay with my harvesters until they finish harvesting all my grain.'" **22.** Naomi advised Ruth, "It's good for you, my daughter, to go with the women who work for him, as you may face danger in another field." **23.** Thus, Ruth stayed with the women of Boaz to glean until both the barley and wheat harvests were finished.

Chapter 3

1. One day, Ruth's mother-in-law, Naomi, said, "My daughter, I need to find a secure home for you, where you will be well taken care of (a place of stability and safety). **2.** I am thinking about Boaz, with whom you have worked. He will tonight be winnowing (separating the grain from chaff using wind) barley at the threshing floor (a flat, open area used for processing grain). **3.** Wash, put on some perfume (a sign of preparation and respect), and put on your best clothes. Go down to the threshing floor, but don't let him know you're there until he has finished eating and drinking (waiting for a relaxed moment after his meal). **4.** Pay attention to where he is lying when he lies down. Go and uncover his feet (a symbolic gesture to request protection and security) and lie down; he will tell you what to do." **5.** "I will do whatever you say," Ruth replied (demonstrating trust and obedience). **6.** And she went down to the threshing floor and did all that her mother-in-law instructed her (Ruth follows Naomi's advice, showing her commitment to the plan). **7.** So when Boaz had finished eating and drinking and felt good (content after his meal), he lay down at the far end of the grain pile. Ruth came up quietly, uncovered his feet, and lay down (following the instructions given by Naomi). **8.** Boaz was startled in the middle of the night and turned over, and there was a woman lying at his feet (surprised by Ruth's presence, he wakes up). **9.** "Who are you?" he asked. She answered, "I am your servant Ruth (identifying herself humbly). You are a guardian-redeemer for our family, so spread the corner of your garment over me (a gesture of asking for protection and claiming the role of guardian-redeemer)." **10.** He replied, "The LORD bless you, my daughter. This kindness you have shown is greater than the kindness you showed earlier; you have not pursued younger men, whether rich or poor (Boaz acknowledges Ruth's virtuous decision to seek him)." **11.** "Don't be afraid, my daughter. Now, I will do all that you ask me to do. You are a woman of noble character (known for your integrity); everyone in my town knows that. **12.** Yes, I am a guardian-redeemer, but there is another relative who is more closely related to me (a closer relative has first claim to redeem). **13.** Let him redeem you in the morning. If he wants to fulfill his duty as your guardian-redeemer, fine, and stay here for the night. But if he is unwilling, as surely as the LORD lives, I will do it. Lie here until morning (Boaz assures Ruth that he will take action, but he must first check with the closer relative)." **14.** She lay at his feet until morning but got up before anyone could recognize her (so as to avoid gossip and maintain discretion). "No one must know that a woman came to the threshing floor," he said (to protect Ruth's reputation). **15.** He also said, "Bring me the shawl (a piece of clothing she used to carry grain) you are wearing and hold it out." When she did, he poured six measures of barley into it and put the bundle on her shoulders. Then he went back to town (Boaz gives Ruth a generous gift as a sign of his intent to help). **16.** Ruth returned to her mother-in-law. Naomi asked her, "How did it go, my daughter?" Ruth told her all Boaz had done for her (describes the generosity and kindness Boaz showed). **17.** Ruth further said, "He gave me these six measures of barley and said, 'Don't go back to your mother-in-law empty-handed' (Boaz's gesture is meant to show his goodwill and desire to see Naomi cared for)." **18.** "Wait, my daughter, until you find out what happens," Naomi answered. "Today, the man will not rest until the matter is settled (Boaz is determined to resolve the situation and fulfill his role as protector)."

Chapter 4

1. Boaz went up to the town gate and sat down there, and the guardian-redeemer he had mentioned came up. Boaz shouted, "Come over here, my friend, and sit down." So he came and sat down (the town gate was the place where legal matters were settled). **2.** Then Boaz took ten of the elders of the town and said, 'Sit here,' and they sat down (these elders were witnesses to the legal process that was about to unfold). **3.** He told the guardian-redeemer, "Naomi, who has come from Moab, is selling the field of our relative Elimelek (the property is being offered for redemption, a practice of restoring family land). **4.** I wanted you to know that, and I asked you to buy it in the presence of those seated here and the elders of my people. If you will redeem it, do so. If you will not, let me know then I will understand. You have the first right to redeem it, and I have the second right." "I will redeem it," he said (the other redeemer initially agrees to buy the land). 5. And Boaz said, 'On the day that you buy the land of Naomi, you shall also buy it for Ruth the Moabite (Ruth's claim to the property as the widow of Mahlon, Elimelech's son), the widow of the dead, to maintain the name of the dead on his inheritance (the purpose of the redemption was to preserve the family name).' 6. The guardian-redeemer answered and said, "I cannot redeem it, in case I endanger my estate. I can't do it; you redeem it yourself" (he backs out due to personal concerns, perhaps about his own inheritance). 7. (In former times in Israel, the redemption and transfer of property was completed by one party removing his sandal and giving it to the other. That was the customary way of formalizing transactions in Israel.) 8. The guardian redeemer therefore said to Boaz, "Buy it yourself." He removed his sandals (a symbolic act confirming the transfer of the redemption rights). 9. Then Boaz made this announcement to the elders and all the people: "You are witnesses today that I have purchased from Naomi all the property of Elimelech, Kilion, and Mahlon (Boaz legally declares his acquisition of the property). 10. Moreover, I have acquired Ruth the Moabite, the widow of Mahlon, as my wife to preserve the name of the deceased with his property, ensuring that his name will not be eliminated from his family or his hometown. You are all witnesses today!" (Boaz takes Ruth as his wife to fulfill the role of the guardian-redeemer and preserve Mahlon's family name). 11. The elders and all the people at the gate responded, "We are witnesses. May the LORD give the woman who is entering your house the same spirit as Rachel and Leah, who together built up the family of Israel? May you be renowned in Bethlehem, and may you have a strong reputation in Ephrathah (they bless Boaz and Ruth, invoking the blessings of fruitful mothers like Rachel and Leah, who were the mothers of Israel's tribes). 12. May your family be like that of Perez, whom Tamar bore to Judah, by the offspring that the LORD gives you through this young woman?" (They invoke blessings for a strong and prosperous family, comparing them to the famous family line of Judah). 13. Boaz took Ruth, and she became his wife. The LORD allowed her to conceive when he had relations with her, and she bore a son (the union of Boaz and Ruth is blessed, and they have a child). 14. The women said to Naomi: 'Praise to the LORD, who has not left you without a guardian-redeemer today! May he be famous in Israel! (The community praises the Lord for providing Naomi with a redeemer and sustainer in her old age). 15. He will renew your life again and sustain you in your old age, for your daughter-in-law, who loves you and is better to you than seven sons, has given him birth." (Ruth's loyalty and kindness to Naomi are acknowledged, and her role is seen as more valuable than seven sons). 16. Naomi took the child in her arms and cared for him (Naomi now has a child to care for, restoring her family line). 17. The women living there said, "Naomi has a son!" And his name was Obed; he became the father of Jesse, and Jesse became the father of David (this child, Obed, is the grandfather of King David, securing the lineage of the great king). 18. This is the family line of Perez: Perez was the father of Hezron, 19. Hezron the father of Ram, Ram the father of Amminadab, 20 Amminadab the father of Nahshon, Nahshon the father of Salmon, 21. Salmon the father of Boaz, Boaz the father of Obed, 22. Obed the father of Jesse, and Jesse the father of David (the genealogy traces the lineage from Perez to David, highlighting the significance of Ruth and Boaz's union in the larger narrative of Israel's kingship).

9 – Samuels

Samuel 1

Chapter 1

1. There was a certain man from Ramathaim Zophim (a place in Ephraim's mountains), named Elkanah, son of Jeroham, son of Elihu, son of Tohu, son of Zuph, who was an Ephraimite (tribe member of Ephraim). 2. Elkanah had two wives. One was named Hannah, and the other was Peninnah. Peninnah had children, but Hannah did not have any children. 3. Each year, this man traveled from his city to worship and offer sacrifices to the Lord of hosts (God as the leader of heaven's armies) in Shiloh (an ancient place of worship). The two sons of Eli (the high priest), Hophni and Phinehas, served as priests of the Lord there.

4. Whenever the time came for Elkanah to make an offering, he would give portions of it to Peninnah and her sons and daughters. 5. But to Hannah, he gave a double portion because he loved her, even though the LORD had not given her children. 6. Hannah's rival, Peninnah, would provoke and irritate her severely to make her feel miserable, since the Lord had not given Hannah children. 7. Year after year, when they went up to the house of the Lord, Peninnah would provoke her, causing Hannah to weep and refuse to eat. 8. Then Elkanah, her husband, would say to her, "Hannah, why are you weeping? Why don't you eat? Why is your heart so grieved? Am I not better to you than ten sons?" 9. After they had finished eating and drinking in Shiloh, Hannah arose. Eli, the priest, was sitting by the doorpost of the Lord's tabernacle (tent of worship). 10. Deeply distressed, Hannah prayed to the Lord and wept bitterly. 11. She made a vow, saying, "O Lord of hosts, if You will see the suffering of Your servant and remember me, not forgetting Your servant, and if You will give me a son, I will dedicate him to You for all his life, and no razor (symbol of lifelong dedication) will touch his head." 12. As she continued praying before the Lord, Eli watched her mouth. 13. Hannah was praying silently in her heart; her lips moved, but her voice was not heard. Eli thought she was drunk. 14. Eli said to her, "How long will you keep being drunk? Put your wine away from you!" 15. But Hannah replied, "No, my lord, I am a woman deeply troubled. I have not been drinking wine or any strong drink; I was pouring out my soul before the Lord. 16. Do not consider me a worthless woman. I have been praying out of great anguish (be extremely distressed about something) and grief." 17. Then Eli said, "Go in peace, and may the God of Israel grant the request you have asked of Him." 18. She replied, "May your servant find favor in your sight." Then she went away, ate, and her face was no longer sad. 19. Early the next morning, they worshiped before the Lord and then returned to their home in Ramah (Elkanah and Hannah's town). Elkanah knew his wife Hannah (was intimate with her), and the Lord remembered her. 20. In time, Hannah conceived (creation of an embryo by fertilizing an egg) and bore a son. She named him Samuel, saying, "Because I asked the Lord for him." 21. Elkanah and his household went up to offer the yearly sacrifice and fulfill his vow to the Lord. 22. But Hannah did not go up. She told her husband, "I will wait until the child is weaned; then I will take him so he can appear before the Lord and stay there permanently." 23. Elkanah, her husband, said, "Do what seems best to you. Stay until you have weaned him, only let the Lord establish His word." So Hannah stayed home and nursed her son until she had weaned him. 24. Once he was weaned, she took him with her, along with three bulls, an ephah of flour (a measure of grain), and a skin of wine, and brought him to the Lord's house in Shiloh. The child was still young. 25. They slaughtered a bull and brought the boy to Eli. 26. She said, "My lord, as surely as you live, my lord, I am the woman who stood here beside you praying to the Lord. 27. I prayed for this child, and the Lord has granted me what I asked of Him. 28. Now I am lending him to the Lord; for his whole life he will belong to the Lord." And they worshiped the Lord there.

Chapter 2

1. Then Hannah prayed and said: "My heart is joyful in the Lord; my strength (symbol of power) is lifted up by the Lord. I rejoice in triumph over my enemies, for I am glad because of Your salvation. 2. "There is none holy like the Lord; there is none besides You, and there is no rock (symbol of strength and refuge) like our God. 3."Do not speak with arrogance; let no proud words come from your mouth, for the Lord is a God of knowledge (all-knowing), and He judges actions. 4. "The bows of the mighty are broken, but those who once stumbled (trip over) now gain strength. 5. Those who were full now work for food, and the hungry are filled. The barren (infertile) woman has borne seven children, while the woman with many children has grown weak. 6. "The Lord brings death and gives life; He brings people down to the grave and raises them up. 7. The Lord makes some poor and others rich; He humbles (degrade) some and lifts up others. 8. He lifts the poor from the dust and raises the needy from the ashes, to make them sit among princes and inherit a place of honor. For the foundations of the earth belong to the Lord, and He has set the world upon them. 9. He will guard the steps of His faithful, but the wicked (worshiping pagan gods) will be silenced in darkness, for no one will prevail (prove more powerful) by their own strength. 10. The Lord will shatter His

adversaries; from heaven He will thunder against them. The Lord will judge the ends of the earth; He will give strength to His king and lift up the horn (symbol of power) of His anointed." **11.** Then Elkanah returned to his home at Ramah (his city), but the child Samuel served the Lord before Eli the priest. **12.** Now Eli's sons were corrupt; they did not know the LORD. **13.** The practice among the priests and the people was that when anyone offered a sacrifice, the priest's servant would come with a three-pronged fork while the meat was boiling. **14.** The servant would stick the fork into the pot, pan, or kettle, and the priest would take for himself all that the fork brought up. This is what they did to all the Israelites who came to Shiloh (a place of worship). **15.** Even before the fat (the best portion) was burned, the priest's servant would demand, "Give meat to the priest to roast, for he will not accept boiled meat, only raw."**16.** And if anyone said, "First let the fat be burned, then take whatever you want," the servant would reply, "No, give it to me now, or I will take it by force." **17.** The sin of the young men was very serious in the Lord's sight, for they treated the Lord's offering with contempt. **18.** But Samuel, still a boy, ministered before the Lord, wearing a linen ephod (priestly garment). **19.** Each year, his mother made him a little robe and brought it to him when she and her husband went up to offer the yearly sacrifice. **20.** Eli would bless Elkanah and his wife, saying, "May the Lord give you children by this woman in place of the one you have dedicated to the Lord." Then they would return home. **21.** The Lord was gracious to Hannah, and she gave birth to three more sons and two daughters. Meanwhile, the child Samuel grew up in the presence of the Lord. **22.** Now Eli was very old, and he heard about everything his sons were doing to all Israel, and how they slept with the women who served at the entrance of the tabernacle (place of worship). **23.** So he said to them, "Why are you doing these things? I hear from all the people about your evil actions. **24.** No, my sons! The reports I hear from the people of the Lord are not good. You are leading the Lord's people into sin. **25.** If a man sins against another, God may mediate for him. But if a man sins against the Lord, who will intercede for him?" But they did not listen to their father because the Lord intended to bring judgment upon them. **26.** Meanwhile, the boy Samuel grew in stature and found favor with both the Lord and people. **27.** Then a man of God came to Eli and said, "This is what the Lord says: 'Did I not clearly reveal Myself to your ancestors when they were slaves in Egypt (land of Pharaoh)? **28.** Did I not choose your family from all the tribes of Israel to be My priests, to offer sacrifices on My altar, to burn incense, and to wear an ephod in My presence? And did I not give your family all the offerings presented by fire from the people of Israel? **29.** Why do you scorn My sacrifices and offerings, which I commanded in My dwelling place, and why do you honor your sons above Me by fattening yourselves on the best of all the offerings of Israel My people?' **30.** "Therefore, the Lord, the God of Israel, declares: 'I promised that members of your family would minister before Me forever.' But now the Lord says, 'Far be it from Me! Those who honor Me, I will honor, but those who despise Me will be disdained. **31.** The time is coming when I will cut short your strength and the strength of your family, so there will be no old men left in your household. **32.** You will see distress in My dwelling place, despite all the good I will do for Israel. No member of your family will live to an old age. **33.** Any of your descendants whom I do not cut off from serving at My altar will bring grief and sadness to you. All your family will die in the prime of life. **34.** "'And this will be a sign to you of what will happen to your two sons, Hophni and Phinehas: They will both die on the same day. **35.** Then I will raise up a faithful priest for Myself, one who will act according to My heart and mind. I will establish a lasting house for him, and he will serve before My anointed one forever. **36.** Then everyone left in your family will come and bow down before him for a piece of silver and a morsel of bread, pleading, "Please appoint me to a priestly position so I may have food to eat." '

Chapter 3:

1. The young Samuel served the Lord under Eli's guidance, but in those days, the Lord's messages were rare, and revelations (book of Apocalypse) were infrequent. **2.** It happened during that time that Eli, whose vision was fading, lay in his usual resting place. **3.** Meanwhile, Samuel was lying down in the tabernacle (the sacred tent for worship) where the Ark of God (the holy chest containing the tablets of the law) was kept, and the lamp of God was still burning. **4.** Then the Lord called

out to Samuel. Samuel responded, "Here I am!" **5.** He ran to Eli, saying, "Here I am; you called me." Eli replied, "I didn't call; go back and lie down." So Samuel returned to his place. **6.** Again, the Lord called Samuel. Samuel went back to Eli, saying, "Here I am; you called me." But Eli said, "I didn't call, my son. Lie down again." **7.** (Samuel was not yet familiar with the Lord, as the Lord's word had not yet been revealed to him.) **8.** The Lord called Samuel a third time, and again Samuel went to Eli and said, "Here I am; you definitely called me." Then Eli understood that the Lord was calling Samuel. **9.** So Eli told Samuel, "Go and lie down. If He calls you again, say, 'Speak, Lord, for your servant is listening.'" Samuel then returned and lay down in his place. **10.** The Lord came and stood there, calling just as before, "Samuel! Samuel!" Samuel answered, "Speak, for your servant is listening." **11.** The Lord said to Samuel, "Listen, I am about to do something in Israel that will make the ears of everyone who hears it ring. **12.** In that time, I will fulfill everything I have spoken concerning Eli's family, from start to finish. **13.** I have already warned him that I will judge his family forever because of his sons' sins, of which he is aware. They acted wickedly, and he did not correct them. **14.** Therefore, I have sworn to Eli's household that their wrongs will never be forgiven by sacrifice or offering." **15.** Samuel lay down until morning, then opened the doors of the Lord's house, but he was reluctant to share the vision with Eli. **16.** Eli called to him, "Samuel, my son!" And Samuel replied, "Here I am." **17.** Eli asked, "What was the message the Lord gave you? Do not hide it from me. May God deal with you severely if you keep anything He told you from me." **18.** Samuel then told Eli everything, without holding anything back. Eli replied, "He is the Lord; let Him do what He thinks is right." **19.** Samuel grew, and the Lord was with him, ensuring all of Samuel's words came true. **20.** All Israel, from Dan to Beersheba (the entire nation), knew that Samuel was confirmed as a prophet of the Lord. **21.** The Lord continued to reveal Himself in Shiloh (a holy place) and made Himself known to Samuel there by His word.

Chapter 4:

1. Samuel's message was heard throughout all Israel. During this time, Israel went out to battle the Philistines. Israel's army set up camp near Ebenezer (a site in Israel), while the Philistines camped at Aphek (a Philistine city). **2.** The Philistines arranged their forces in battle formation against Israel, and when the battle began, Israel was overpowered, with around four thousand men killed in the open field. **3.** When the soldiers returned to the camp, the elders of Israel asked, "Why has the Lord allowed us to be defeated today by the Philistines? Let us bring the Ark of the Covenant (the sacred chest symbolizing God's presence) from Shiloh so that it may protect us from our enemies." **4.** So they sent men to Shiloh (a holy place in Israel) to bring back the Ark of the Covenant of the Lord Almighty, who dwells between the cherubim (angelic beings). The two sons of Eli, Hophni and Phinehas, accompanied the Ark of God. **5.** When the Ark of the Covenant arrived in the camp, the entire Israelite camp shouted with such joy that the ground shook. **6.** Hearing the loud shout, the Philistines wondered, "What does this loud noise in the Hebrew camp mean?" Then they realized that the Ark of the Lord had arrived in the Israelite camp. **7.** The Philistines were filled with fear, saying, "God has entered their camp! We are doomed! This has never happened before. **8.** We are lost! Who can rescue us from these powerful gods? These are the gods who struck the Egyptians with plagues in the wilderness." **9.** To encourage each other, the Philistines said, "Take courage, Philistines! Fight like men so that you don't become slaves to the Hebrews, as they were to you. Fight bravely!" **10.** The Philistines went into battle and defeated Israel once more. Every Israelite man retreated to his tent, and there was a massive slaughter. Thirty thousand Israelite soldiers were killed. **11.** Furthermore, the Ark of God was captured, and Eli's two sons, Hophni and Phinehas, were killed. **12.** On that day, a man from the tribe of Benjamin fled from the battlefield and went to Shiloh. His clothes were torn, and he had dust on his head (a sign of mourning and sorrow).**13.** When he arrived, Eli was sitting on a seat beside the road, watching with worry, for he was deeply concerned about the Ark of God. As the man came into the city and reported the news, the people cried out loudly. **14.** When Eli heard the outcry, he asked, "What is the meaning of this commotion?" The man quickly approached and told Eli what had happened. **15.** At the time, Eli was ninety-eight years old, and his eyesight had become so weak that he couldn't see. **16.** The man said to Eli, "I am the one who came from the battle; I fled from the front lines today." Eli asked, "What happened, my son?" **17.** The messenger responded, "Israel has fled from the Philistines, and a great number of people have been killed. Your sons, Hophni and Phinehas, are dead, and the Ark of God has been captured." **18.** When Eli heard the mention of the Ark of God, he fell backward from his seat beside the gate, broke his neck, and died, as he was an old and heavy man. He had led Israel as a judge for forty years. **19.** Meanwhile, Eli's daughter-in-law, the wife of Phinehas, was expecting a child and close to her time of delivery. Upon hearing the news that the Ark of God was captured and that her father-in-law and husband had died, she went into labor and gave birth. **20.** As she was dying, the women attending to her said, "Do not worry, for you have given birth to a son." However, she neither responded nor paid attention. **21.** She named the child Ichabod (a priest at the shrine of Shiloh), meaning "The glory has departed from Israel," because the Ark of God had been taken, and because of the deaths of her father-in-law and her husband. **22.** She said, "The glory has left Israel, for the Ark of God has been captured."

Chapter 5:

1. The Philistines took the Ark of God (sacred chest symbolizing God's presence) from the place called Ebenezer (a historical site) and brought it to Ashdod (a Philistine city). **2.** They carried the Ark of God into the temple of Dagon (a Philistine deity) and placed it beside the idol of Dagon. **3.** When the people of Ashdod got up the next morning, they saw that the idol of Dagon had fallen, face down on the ground, before the Ark of the Lord. They lifted the idol and put it back in its place. **4.** The following morning, they found Dagon fallen again before the Ark of the Lord. This time, the idol's head and hands were broken off and lying on the temple's threshold, with only its body remaining. **5.** From that day forward, neither Dagon's priests nor any visitor to Dagon's temple in Ashdod would step on the threshold where the idol had fallen. **6.** Then the Lord's power weighed heavily on the people of Ashdod, causing great destruction. He afflicted the people of Ashdod and its surrounding areas with painful tumors (swellings or boils). **7.** When the men of Ashdod realized what was happening, they said, "We cannot keep the Ark of Israel's God with us, for His power is harsh on us and against Dagon, our god." **8.** They called together all the Philistine rulers and asked, "What should we do with the Ark of Israel's God?" The leaders advised, "Let it be taken to Gath (another Philistine city)." So they moved the Ark of the God of Israel to Gath. **9.** But once they brought it there, the Lord's hand struck the city with a great disaster, causing tumors to break out on the people, both young and old. **10.** So they sent the Ark of God to Ekron (another Philistine city). As soon as it arrived, the people of Ekron cried out, "They have brought the Ark of Israel's God to kill us and our people!" **11.** They called together the Philistine leaders and pleaded, "Send the Ark of Israel's God back to its own place so it won't kill us and our people!" A deadly disaster had spread throughout the city, and the Lord's hand was heavy upon them. **12.** Many people who survived were afflicted with tumors, and the outcry from the city rose up to heaven.

Chapter 6

1. The Ark of the Lord remained in the land of the Philistines for seven months. **2.** The Philistine leaders called for their priests (religious leaders) and diviners (those who predict the future), asking, "What should we do with the Ark of the Lord? How should we send it back to its proper place?" **3.** They replied, "If you send the Ark back, don't send it without a gift. You must return it with a trespass offering (a gift given to make up for sins or wrongdoings). Then you will be healed, and you will understand why God's hand of judgment is still upon you." **4.** The Philistines asked, "What should the trespass offering be?" They responded, "Make five golden tumors (swelling growths on the body) and five golden rats, one for each of the five Philistine rulers. The same disease (plague) has affected all of you and your rulers." **5.** "Make images (representations) of the tumors and rats that have ravaged (caused destruction to) the land, and give honor to the God of Israel. Perhaps He will remove His judgment from you, your gods, and your land." **6.** "Why do you harden your hearts like the Egyptians did when Pharaoh resisted God's will? Didn't they finally let the Israelites go after God sent His mighty judgment upon them?" **7.** "Now, make a new cart (a simple vehicle) and take two cows that have never been yoked

(attached to a cart or plow). Attach them to the cart, and take their calves (young cows) away from them." **8.** "Place the Ark of the Lord on the cart and put the golden rats and tumors in a chest beside it. Then send it on its way and watch carefully." **9.** "If the cows go straight to Beth Shemesh (a city now located in Israel), we will know that God's hand of judgment is upon us. But if they do not, we will know that the disaster happened by chance." **10.** The Philistines followed these instructions. They took two milk cows (cows that were nursing their calves), yoked them to the cart, and locked their calves away. **11.** They placed the Ark of the Lord on the cart along with the chest containing the golden rats and tumors. **12.** The cows went straight down the road toward Beth Shemesh, mooing (the sound cows make) as they went, without turning to the right or left. The Philistine rulers followed them to the border of Beth Shemesh. **13.** The people of Beth Shemesh were in the middle of their wheat harvest in the valley (a low area between hills), and they looked up and saw the Ark. They were overjoyed to see it. **14.** The cart stopped in the field of Joshua (a man from Beth Shemesh), near a large stone. The people broke up the cart's wood and used it as fuel, offering the cows as a burnt offering (an offering where the animal is completely burned) to the Lord. **15.** The Levites (members of the tribe of Levi, responsible for religious duties) took the Ark and the chest with the golden offerings from the cart and placed them on the large stone. That day, the people of Beth Shemesh offered burnt offerings and made sacrifices (ritual offerings) to the Lord. **16.** When the five Philistine rulers saw this, they returned to Ekron (a city of the Philistines) the same day. **17.** The Philistines returned five golden offerings to the Lord: one for each of their cities—Ashdod, Gaza, Ashkelon, Gath, and Ekron. **18.** The golden rats were given for each of the cities of the Philistines, both fortified (cities with protective walls) and unfortified (cities without walls), extending to the large stone where the Ark had been set down, which remains to this day in the field of Joshua of Beth Shemesh. **19.** But the Lord struck down 50,070 men of Beth Shemesh because they looked into the Ark. The people were deeply grieved (saddened) by this heavy loss. **20.** The people of Beth Shemesh asked, "Who can stand before this holy Lord God? To whom should the Ark go from here?" **21.** They sent messengers to the people of Kirjath Jearim (a town in Israel), saying, and "The Philistines have returned the Ark of the Lord. Come and take it up with you."

Chapter 7

1. The men of Kirjath Jearim (a town in Israel) came, took the Ark of God, and brought it to the house of Abinadab on the hill. They set apart his son Eleazar to care for the Ark of the Lord. **2.** The Ark remained in Kirjath Jearim for many years—20 years. During that time, the people of Israel mourned and longed for the Lord's presence. **3.** Samuel spoke to the Israelites, saying, "If you turn back to the Lord with all your hearts, then remove the foreign gods and idols of Ashtoreth (Canaanite goddess of fertility) from among you. Prepare yourselves to serve the Lord alone, and He will rescue you from the Philistines." **4.** So, the Israelites gave up their idols, the Baals and Ashtoreths, and began to serve only the Lord. **5.** Samuel then called for a gathering of all Israel at Mizpah (a location), where he promised to pray to the Lord on their behalf. **6.** They assembled at Mizpah, drew water, poured it out before the Lord, and fasted that day, saying, "We have sinned against the Lord." Samuel led the people as their judge at Mizpah. **7.** When the Philistines heard that the Israelites had gathered at Mizpah, their rulers advanced to attack them. The Israelites were terrified when they heard the news. **8.** The Israelites begged Samuel, "Please don't stop praying to the Lord our God for us that He may deliver us from the Philistines." **9.** Samuel took a young lamb and offered it as a burnt offering to the Lord. He cried out to God on behalf of Israel, and the Lord answered him. **10.** As Samuel was offering the sacrifice, the Philistines drew near to fight Israel. But the Lord sent a loud thunder that confused the Philistines, and they were defeated before Israel. **11.** The Israelites rushed out from Mizpah, chasing the Philistines and driving them back to below Beth Car (a place). **12.** Samuel then took a stone and set it up between Mizpah and Shen (places), calling it Ebenezer, saying, "Thus far the Lord has helped us." **13.** As a result, the Philistines were humbled and did not invade Israel again. The Lord's power remained against the Philistines throughout Samuel's life. **14.** The cities the Philistines had taken from Israel, from Ekron to Gath (Philistine cities), were restored to Israel. The Israelites regained their land. There was also peace between Israel and the Amorites (another group of people). **15.** Samuel led Israel as judge for the rest of his life. **16.** He traveled each year to Bethel, Gilgal, and Mizpah, where he judged Israel in those regions. **17.** But Samuel always returned to his home in Ramah (a town), where he judged Israel and built an altar to the Lord.

Chapter 8

1. When Samuel became old, he appointed his sons to serve as judges over Israel. **2.** His first son was named Joel, and his second son was named Abijah. They served as judges in Beersheba (a city in Israel district Negev). **3.** But his sons did not follow his example. They were corrupt, accepting bribes, and twisting justice for personal gain. **4.** The elders of Israel gathered together and went to Samuel at Ramah (a town where Samuel lived). **5.** They said to him, "You have grown old, and your sons do not follow your ways. Appoint a king to rule over us, like all the other nations." **6.** Samuel was upset by their request for a king, so he prayed to the Lord. **7.** The Lord answered Samuel, saying, "Listen to the people and give them what they ask for. They have not rejected you, but they have rejected Me from being their king. **8.** Ever since I brought them out of Egypt, they have turned away from Me and served other gods. Now, they are doing the same thing to you. **9.** So, listen to them, but warn them solemnly and tell them what the king will do when he rules over them." **10.** Samuel explained to the people what the Lord had said and described how a king would behave. **11.** He told them, "The king will draft your sons to serve in his chariots and as horsemen, and some of them will run ahead of his chariots. **12.** He will appoint commanders over groups of thousands and hundreds, and some of you will be forced to plow his fields, harvest his crops, and make weapons for his chariots. **13.** He will take your daughters to serve as perfumers, cooks, and bakers. **14.** He will take the best of your fields, vineyards, and olive groves, and give them to his officials. **15.** He will take a tenth of your crops and vineyards and give it to his officers and servants. **16.** He will take your male and female servants, your best young men, and your donkeys, and put them to work for him. **17.** He will take a tenth of your sheep, and you will become his servants. **18.** When that day comes, you will cry out because of the king you have chosen, but the Lord will not answer you." **19.** Despite Samuel's warning, the people refused to listen to him. They said, "No! We want a king to rule over us. **20.** We want to be like all the other nations, with a king to lead us and fight our battles." **21.** Samuel listened to what the people said, and he reported it to the Lord. **22.** The Lord responded to Samuel, "Listen to their request and appoint a king for them." Then Samuel told the Israelites, "Go back to your cities."

Chapter 9

1. There was a man from the tribe of Benjamin named Kish, the son of Abiel, the son of Zeror, the son of Bechorath, and the son of Aphiah. Kish was a powerful (mighty) and respected (honored) man. **2.** Kish had a son named Saul, who was tall and exceptionally handsome. In fact, he was the most handsome man in all of Israel. He was also taller than anyone else in the country by a full head. **3.** One day, Kish's donkeys went missing, and he asked Saul to take one of the servants and search for them. **4.** Saul and his servant searched through the mountains of Ephraim, the land of Shalisha, and the area of Shaalim, but they didn't find them. Then they traveled through the territory of the Benjamites, but there was still no sign of the donkeys. **5.** When they reached the land of Zuph, Saul said to his servant, "Let's head back. If we wait too long, my father will stop worrying about the donkeys and start worrying about us." **6.** The servant replied, "There's a man of God in this city, a respected (honorable) man whose words always come true. Let's go to him and maybe he will tell us where to find the donkeys." **7.** Saul said to the servant, "But we have no gift (present) to offer him. We've used up all the food in our bags. What will we give him?" **8.** The servant answered, "I have a small amount of silver—a fourth of a shekel (small unit of money). I'll give that to the man of God so he can show us the way." **9.** (At that time, people in Israel would say, "Let's go to the seer (prophet)" when referring to a prophet, since the term "seer" was used before "prophet.") **10.** Saul agreed, and they set off toward the city where the man of God was. **11.** As they walked up the hill to the city, they met some young women coming out to draw water (fetch water), and they asked them, "Is the seer here?" **12.** The women replied, "Yes, he is ahead of you. He came here today because there is a sacrifice (religious offering) at the high place (place of worship). He won't eat until he blesses the sacrifice, so hurry. You'll find him as you enter the city." **13.** They went into the city and found Samuel coming out to meet them, on his way up to the high place. **14.** The day before, the Lord had told Samuel, "Tomorrow at this time, I will send you a man from the tribe of Benjamin. Anoint (a religious ceremony of sprinkling of oil) him as the leader of My people Israel. He will rescue them from the Philistines (enemies), for I have heard their cry." **15.** When Samuel saw Saul, the Lord said to him, "This is the man I spoke to you about. He will rule over My people." **16.** Saul approached Samuel and asked, "Can you tell me where the house of the seer is?" **17.** Samuel answered, "I am the seer. Come with me to the high place (place of worship), and you will eat with me today. Tomorrow, I will tell you everything that is on your heart (thoughts)." **18.** Samuel continued, "And don't worry about your donkeys that were lost three days ago; they have been found. But what about the destiny (future) of Israel? Isn't it with you and your family?" **19.** Saul answered, "But I'm from the tribe of Benjamin, the smallest tribe in Israel. And my family is the least (smallest) of all the families of Benjamin. Why are you saying these things to me?" **20.** Samuel took Saul and his servant to the banquet hall (dining hall), where they were given the place of honor among about thirty guests. **21.** Samuel told the cook, "Bring the portion (special part) I gave you, the one I told you to set aside." **22.** The cook brought the portion of meat and placed it before Saul. Samuel said, "This is the part that was set aside for you. Eat it, for it was saved for you from the moment I invited the guests." **23.** Saul ate with Samuel that day. **24.** After the meal, they went down from the high place (place of worship), and Samuel spoke to Saul on the roof (top) of the house. **25.** The next morning, they got up early. As dawn (first light) was breaking, Samuel called to Saul, "Get up, and I will send you on your way." **26.** Saul got up, and both he and Samuel went outside. **27.** As they were leaving the city, Samuel said to Saul, "Tell your servant to go on ahead of us." When the servant had gone, Samuel said, "Stay here for a moment, and I will share a message from God with you."

Chapter 10

1. Samuel took a flask of oil, poured it on Saul's head, kissed him, and said, "Isn't it because the Lord has chosen you to be the ruler (a person who governs or controls) over His people, Israel? **2.** After you leave me today, you will meet two men near Rachel's tomb in the territory of Benjamin, at Zelzah (place near Jerusalem). They will tell you, 'The donkeys you were searching for have been found, and your father is no longer worried about the donkeys but is concerned about you, asking, "What should I do about my son?"' **3.** Then, continue on your way and you will reach the tree of Tabor. There, you will meet three men going to Bethel to worship God. One will be carrying three young goats (young male animals), another will have three loaves (flat, round breads) of bread, and a third will carry a skin (container) of wine. **4.** They will greet you and give you two loaves of bread, which you are to accept from them. **5.** After that, you will arrive at the hill of God, where the Philistine garrison (military post or station) is located. When you enter the city, you will meet a group of prophets coming down from the high place, with musical instruments like stringed instruments, tambourines, flutes, and harps. They will be prophesying (speaking messages from God). **6.** Then the Spirit of the Lord will come upon you, and you will join in their prophesying, and you will be changed into a different person (inwardly transformed by the Spirit of God). **7.** When these signs happen, do what is needed, for the Lord is with you. **8.** Go down ahead of me to Gilgal, and I will come to you there to offer burnt offerings (sacrifices by fire) and sacrifices of peace offerings (sacrificial offerings to thank God). Wait for me for seven days, until I come and tell you what to do." **9.** As Saul turned to leave Samuel, God gave him a new heart (a changed attitude or spirit), and all the signs Samuel had spoken about came true that day. **10.** When Saul arrived at the hill, a group of prophets met him, and the Spirit of God came upon him, and he began to prophesy (speak messages from God) with them. **11.** When those who knew him before saw that he was prophesying with the prophets, they were amazed and said to one another, "What has happened to the son of Kish? Is Saul now among the prophets?" (The people were surprised because Saul was not known as a prophet before.) **12.** A man from there answered, "Who is their father?" (Who is the father of these prophets?) And so, it became a saying, "Is Saul also one of the prophets?" **13.** After he had finished prophesying, he went to the high place (a place of worship). **14.** Saul's uncle asked him and his servant, "Where did you go?" Saul answered, "We were looking for the donkeys, and when we couldn't find them, we went to Samuel."

15. Saul's uncle then asked, "What did Samuel tell you?" **16.** Saul replied, "He told us the donkeys had been found," but he didn't say anything about the kingship (the position of being king). **17.** Samuel called all the people together to the Lord at Mizpah, **18.** And he said to the Israelites, "This is what the Lord, the God of Israel, says: 'I brought Israel out of Egypt and rescued you from the power (authority or control) of the Egyptians and from the hand of all the kingdoms that oppressed (treated unjustly) you. **19.** But today you have rejected (refused or turned away from) your God, who saved you from all your troubles and hardships. You've said to Him, 'We want a king to rule over us!' Now, present yourselves before the Lord by your tribes and families.'" **20.** When Samuel had all the tribes of Israel come forward, the tribe of Benjamin was selected. **21.** When the tribe of Benjamin came near by their families, the family of Matri was chosen, and from that family, Saul, the son of Kish, was chosen. But when they looked for him, he was nowhere to be found. **22.** They asked the Lord again, "Has the man come here yet?" and the Lord answered, "He is hiding among the baggage (equipment, luggage, or supplies)." **23.** So they ran and brought him out, and when he stood among the people, he was taller than anyone else, standing head and shoulders above them. **24.** Samuel said to the people, "Do you see the man the Lord has chosen? There is no one like him among all the people!" And the people shouted, "Long live the king!" **25.** Samuel explained to the people the rights and duties (responsibilities) of kingship, wrote them down in a book, and placed it before the Lord. Then Samuel sent everyone home. **26.** Saul went back to his home in Gibeah, and brave (courageous or valiant) men whose hearts God had touched went with him. **27.** But some worthless men (rebels or people who oppose authority) said, "How can this man save us?" And they despised (looked down upon with disrespect) him, refusing to bring him any gifts. But Saul stayed quiet and said nothing.

Chapter 11

1. Nahash, the Ammonite (a member of an ancient people from the east of Israel) king, came and camped against Jabesh Gilead (a town in Israel). The men of Jabesh asked him, "Make a covenant (agreement) with us, and we will serve you." **2.** Nahash replied, "I will make a covenant only if you agree to let me gouge out (cut out) the right eye of every one of you. This will bring disgrace (shame) upon all Israel." **3.** The elders (leaders) of Jabesh asked for seven days to send messengers (messengers were people sent to deliver a message) throughout Israel. "If no one comes to save us, we will surrender (give up) to you." **4.** The messengers went to Gibeah (Saul's hometown), where Saul lived, and reported the news to the people. When the people heard it, they wept aloud (cried loudly). **5.** Saul was coming back from the fields with a herd of oxen (a type of Bull). He asked, "Why are the people weeping?" And they told him what the men of Jabesh had said. **6.** When Saul heard this, the Spirit of God (God's power) came upon him, and he was filled with anger. **7.** He took a yoke (a wooden frame that joins two oxen together) of oxen, cut them into pieces, and sent them throughout Israel with a message: "Anyone who refuses to join Saul and Samuel in battle, this will be done to their oxen." The people feared the Lord (revered God), and they all gathered together. **8.** Saul counted the army at Bezek (a location in Israel). There were 300,000 men from Israel and 30,000 men from Judah (the southern kingdom of Israel). **9.** Saul told the messengers to say to the people of Jabesh Gilead, "Tomorrow, by the time the sun is hot, you will have help." The messengers returned and reported this, and the people of Jabesh rejoiced (were filled with joy). **10.** The men of Jabesh said, "Tomorrow we will surrender to you, and you can do with us as you please." **11.** The next day, Saul divided his forces into three groups. They attacked the Ammonites (people from Ammon) at dawn (early in the morning) and continued fighting until midday. The survivors scattered, and not two of them were left together. **12.** The people of Israel said to Samuel, "Who were the ones who questioned Saul's reign (rule)? Bring them here so we can put them to death." **13.** But Saul said, "No one will be put to death today, for today the Lord has brought victory (success in battle) to Israel." **14.** Then Samuel said to the people, "Let's go to Gilgal (a place in Israel) and renew (reaffirm) the kingdom there." **15.** So, all the people went to Gilgal, where they made Saul king before the Lord. They sacrificed peace offerings (offerings made to thank God) and rejoiced greatly (celebrated joyfully).

Chapter 12

1. Samuel said to all Israel: "I have listened to all you said and made a king over you. Here he is, the king who will lead you. I am old and gray, and my sons are with you. I have led you from my youth until now. **2.** Here I am. If I have wronged anyone, let me know. Have I taken anyone's ox (a large animal used for farming or transport) or donkey (a small animal often used for carrying loads)? Have I cheated anyone? Have I oppressed (treated unfairly or cruelly) anyone or taken a bribe (money or gift given to influence someone's actions) to blind my eyes? If so, I will make it right." **3.** They answered, "You have not cheated or oppressed us, and you have not taken anything from anyone." **4.** Samuel said, "The Lord and His anointed (chosen) king are witnesses today, that you have not found anything in my hands." They replied, "He is witness." **5.** Samuel continued, "The Lord is the one who rose up Moses and Aaron and brought your ancestors out of Egypt (a land in Africa, where the Israelites were enslaved). **6.** Now, listen carefully as I remind you of the righteous acts of the Lord toward you and your ancestors: When Jacob (a forefather of Israelites) went to Egypt and your ancestors cried out to the Lord, He sent Moses and Aaron to bring them out and settle them in this land. **7.** But when they forgot the Lord their God, He allowed them to be oppressed (treated unfairly) by Sisera (a commander of Hazor's army), the Philistines (a group of people who were enemies of Israel), and the king of Moab (a nation east of Israel), who fought against them. **8.** Then they cried out to the Lord, saying, 'we have sinned (done wrong), for we have abandoned the Lord and served other gods. Now save us from our enemies, and we will serve You.' **9.** So, the Lord sent leaders like Jerubbaal (Gideon, a judge who led Israel to victory over the Midianites), Bedan (another judge or leader), Jephthah (a judge who defeated the Ammonites), and myself, Samuel, to deliver you from your enemies, and you lived in safety. **10.** But when you saw Nahash (the king of the Ammonites, a people from the east), threatening you, you asked for a king to rule over you, even though the Lord your God was your king. **11.** Now here is the king you have chosen. The Lord has set him over you. If you fear (respect and honor) the Lord, serve Him, and listen to His voice, and do not rebel (resist or oppose) against His command, both you and your king will continue to follow the Lord. **12.** But if you refuse to obey the Lord and rebel against Him, His hand (His power or judgment) will be against you, as it was against your ancestors. **13.** Now stand still and witness (see) the great thing the Lord will do before your eyes. **14.** Isn't today the time of the wheat harvest? I will call on the Lord, and He will send thunder (a loud sound that comes with lightning) and rain, so you will see how great your wickedness (evil actions) is in asking for a king." **15.** Samuel called to the Lord, and the Lord sent thunder and rain that day. The people greatly feared both the Lord and Samuel. **16.** All the people said to Samuel, "Pray to the Lord your God for us so that we will not die. We have added to our sins by asking for a king." **17.** Samuel replied, "Do not be afraid. You have done this evil, but do not turn away from following the Lord. Serve Him with all your heart. **18.** Do not turn to worthless idols (false gods or things that are of no value), which can neither help nor save you—they are nothing. **19.** For the Lord will not abandon His people, for His great name's sake (for the sake of His reputation). It has pleased the Lord to make you His people. **20.** As for me, I will not sin against the Lord by failing to pray for you. I will continue to teach you the right way. **21.** Only fear the Lord and serve Him faithfully with all your heart, considering the great things He has done for you. **22.** But if you continue to do evil, both you and your king will be swept away."

Chapter 13

1. Saul ruled for one year and after two years of reign over Israel, **2.** Saul selected 3,000 men from Israel. 2,000 were with Saul in Michmash and the hills of Bethel, and 1,000 were with Jonathan in Gibeah of Benjamin. The rest of the people were sent back to their homes. **3.** Jonathan attacked the Philistine garrison in Geba, and when the Philistines heard about it, **4.** Saul blew the trumpet throughout Israel, saying, "Let the Hebrews hear!" **5.** All of Israel heard that Saul had attacked the Philistine garrison and that Israel had become hated by the Philistines. The people gathered together to Saul at Gilgal. **6.** The

Philistines gathered to fight Israel with 30,000 chariots, 6,000 horsemen, and an army as vast as the sand on the seashore. They camped in Michmash, east of Beth Aven. **7.** When the Israelites saw they were in danger (for they were distressed), they hid in caves, bushes, rocks, holes, and pits. **8.** Some Hebrews crossed the Jordan to the land of Gad and Gilead. As for Saul, he stayed in Gilgal, and the people followed him trembling. **9.** Saul waited for seven days, as Samuel had instructed, but Samuel did not arrive in time, and the people began to scatter. **10.** Saul said, "Bring the burnt offering and peace offerings here to me." He offered the burnt offering. **11.** As soon as Saul finished the offering, Samuel arrived. Saul went out to meet him and greet him. **12.** Samuel asked, "What have you done?" Saul replied, "When I saw that the people were leaving, and that you didn't arrive in the appointed time, and that the Philistines were gathering at Michmash, **13.** I thought, 'The Philistines will attack me at Gilgal, and I have not sought the Lord's favor.' So, I felt it was necessary to offer the burnt offering." **14.** Samuel said, "You have acted foolishly. You did not keep the Lord's command. If you had, your kingdom over Israel would have lasted forever. **15.** But now your kingdom will not continue. The Lord has chosen a man after His own heart and commanded him to be leader of His people because you did not follow the Lord's command." **16.** Samuel left Gilgal and went to Gibeah of Benjamin. Saul counted the men with him, about 600. **17.** Saul, Jonathan, and the people with them stayed in Gibeah, while the Philistines camped in Michmash. **18.** The Philistines sent raiders in three groups. One group went toward Ophrah in the land of Shual, **19.** another toward Beth Horon, and another toward the border overlooking the Valley of Zeboim in the wilderness. **20.** There was no blacksmith in all Israel, for the Philistines had said, "We must prevent the Hebrews from making swords or spears." **21.** So, the Israelites would go down to the Philistines to sharpen their farming tools like plowshares, mattocks (a kind of tool), axes, and sickles. **22.** The cost for sharpening was one pim (a small unit of currency). **23.** On the day of battle, no one among Saul's people had a sword or spear, except for Saul and Jonathan, who had them. The Philistine garrison came out to the pass of Michmash.

Chapter 14

1. One day, Jonathan, the son of Saul, said to the young man who carried his armor, "Let's go to the Philistine garrison (a military outpost) across from us." But he did not inform his father. **2.** Saul was sitting on the outskirts of Gibeah under a pomegranate tree at Migron. There were about 600 men with him. **3.** Ahijah, the son of Ahitub, the brother of Ichabod, the son of Phinehas, the son of Eli, who was the priest of the Lord at Shiloh, wore an ephod (a priestly garment worn by high priests). The people didn't know Jonathan had left. **4.** between the two sharp rocks by the pass (narrow pathway) Jonathan wanted to take to reach the Philistine garrison, one rock was named Bozez, and the other was called Seneh. **5.** One rock faced north toward Michmash, and the other faced south toward Gibeah. **6.** Jonathan said to his armor-bearer, "Let's go to these uncircumcised Philistines; perhaps the Lord will help us. Nothing can stop the Lord from saving, whether by many or by few." **7.** His armor-bearer replied, "Do whatever is in your heart. I'm with you all the way." **8.** Jonathan said, "We'll show ourselves to the Philistines. **9.** If they say, 'Wait until we come to you,' we'll stay in our place and not move. **10.** But if they say, 'Come up to us,' we'll go up. The Lord has given them into our hands, and that will be a sign to us." **11.** So both of them revealed themselves to the Philistine garrison. The Philistines said, "Look, the Hebrews are coming out of the holes (hiding places) where they were hiding!" **12.** The men of the garrison called to Jonathan and his armor-bearer, "Come up here, and we'll show you something." Jonathan told his armor-bearer, "Climb up after me, for the Lord has given them into the hands of Israel." **13.** Jonathan climbed up using his hands and feet (he climbed on all fours), with his armor-bearer following him. The Philistines fell before Jonathan, and his armor-bearer struck them down. **14.** The first battle they fought killed about 20 men within half an acre of land. **15.** This caused a great trembling in the Philistine camp, in the fields, and among the people. The garrison and raiders (soldiers who raid or plunder) also trembled, and the earth shook, causing a great panic. **16.** The watchmen in Gibeah saw the confusion in the Philistine camp and noticed the enemy troops scattering. **17.** Saul asked the people, "Count and see who is missing." When they checked, they found that Jonathan

and his armor-bearer were not there. **18.** Saul told Ahijah, "Bring the ark of God here" (the ark was a sacred chest that contained the tablets of the Ten Commandments, used by the Israelites in their worship of God). **19.** While Saul spoke to the priest, the noise from the Philistine camp grew louder, so Saul told the priest, "Withdraw your hand" (take away the ark and stop praying). **20.** Then Saul and his army went to battle, and each man fought against his neighbor in great confusion. **21.** Many Hebrews who had been with the Philistines joined the Israelites in Saul's army when they saw the Philistines were fleeing. **22.** Also, the men of Israel who had been hiding in the mountains of Ephraim came out and pursued the Philistines when they saw the enemy was fleeing. **23.** So the Lord delivered Israel that day, and the battle turned toward Beth Aven. **24.** The people were weary that day because Saul had made them swear an oath, saying, "Cursed (to be condemned) is the man who eats anything before evening until I have taken vengeance on my enemies." So, no one ate anything. **25.** The people came to a forest where honey was on the ground. **26.** As the people entered the forest, honey was dripping, but no one ate any, because they feared the oath. **27.** However, Jonathan had not heard his father's command, so he dipped the end of his staff (a long stick used for support or to carry) into the honey and ate it. His eyes brightened (reaction to shocking news). **28.** Someone told him, "Your father made the people swear an oath, saying, 'Cursed is anyone who eats today.'" The people were faint (weak from hunger). **29.** Jonathan replied, "My father has troubled the land. Look how my eyes have brightened because I tasted a little honey. **30.** How much better it would have been if the people had eaten from the spoils (the goods or valuables taken from the enemy) of the Philistines today! There would have been a greater victory over them." **31.** They had already driven the Philistines from Michmash to Aijalon, but the people were still weak. **32.** The people rushed to take the spoil, slaughtering sheep, oxen, and calves, and eating the meat with the blood (eating meat that was not properly drained of blood). **33.** They told Saul, "The people are sinning against the Lord by eating with the blood!" So, Saul said, "You have been unfaithful (acting dishonestly or betraying trust). Roll a large stone to me." **34.** He instructed, "Spread out among the people and tell them, 'Bring me your oxen and sheep, slaughter them here, and eat without sinning by eating blood.'" So, everyone brought their oxen and slaughtered them there. **35.** Then Saul built an altar to the Lord. This was the first altar he had built to the Lord. **36.** Saul said, "Let us go down and attack the Philistines tonight and plunder them until morning, leaving no survivors." The people agreed. But the priest said, "Let us seek God's guidance first." **37.** Saul inquired of God, "Should we attack the Philistines? Will You give them into our hands?" But God did not answer him that day. **38.** Saul said, "Come here, all you leaders, and find out what sin has occurred today. **39.** As the Lord lives, who saves Israel, even if it is my son Jonathan, he will surely die." But no one answered. **40.** Saul then said, "You and your son Jonathan will stand on one side, and everyone else on the other." The people agreed. **41.** Saul asked God to reveal the lot (a system of chance, like drawing straws or casting lots), and it was revealed that Saul and Jonathan were chosen, but the people were not. **42.** Saul then cast lots between himself and Jonathan, and Jonathan was selected. **43.** Saul asked Jonathan, "What have you done?" Jonathan explained, "I only tasted a little honey with the end of my staff. Now I must die!" **44.** Saul replied, "May God do this and more to me, for you will surely die, Jonathan." **45.** The people protested, "Should Jonathan die, who has brought about such a great victory in Israel? No, as the Lord lives, not a hair of his head will fall to the ground, for he has worked with God today." So, the people saved Jonathan from death. **46.** Saul withdrew from pursuing the Philistines, and they returned to their own land. **47.** Saul strengthened his rule over Israel, fighting all his enemies on every side: Moab, Ammon, Edom, the kings of Zobah, and the Philistines. Wherever he turned, he harassed them. **48.** He gathered an army and attacked the Amalekites, rescuing Israel from those who plundered them. **49.** Saul's sons were Jonathan, Jishui, and Malchishua. His daughters were Merab, the firstborn, and Michal, the younger. **50.** Saul's wife was Ahinoam, daughter of Ahimaaz. His army commander was Abner, son of Ner, Saul's uncle. **51.** Saul's father was Kish, and Abner's father was Ner, the son of Abiel. **52.** Saul fought fierce wars against the Philistines throughout his reign. When Saul saw any strong or brave man, he brought him into his service.

Chapter 15

1. "The Lord has sent me to appoint (officially select) you as king over His people, Israel. Now listen to the instructions of the Lord. 2. The Lord Almighty (all-powerful) says: 'I will punish (discipline or take action against) Amalek for what he did to Israel, ambushing (attacking unexpectedly) them when they were on their way from Egypt. 3. Now, go and completely destroy (eliminate) Amalek, sparing (saving or leaving alive) no one. Kill every man and woman, child and infant, along with all their cattle (farm animals)—oxen, sheep, camels, and donkeys.'" 4. Saul then gathered (assembled) the people and counted them at Telaim: two hundred thousand-foot soldiers and ten thousand men from Judah. 5 Saul proceeded (moved forward) to a city of the Amalekites and set an ambush (trap or surprise attack) in the valley. 6. He said to the Kenites, "Go, depart (leave quickly), and leave the Amalekites so that I won't destroy you along with them, as you were kind to the Israelites when they came out of Egypt." So, the Kenites separated (moved away) themselves from the Amalekites. 7. Saul attacked (launched an assault against) the Amalekites from Havilah all the way to Shur, near Egypt. 8. He captured (took as prisoner) Agag, the king of the Amalekites, alive and killed all the other people with the sword. 9. However, Saul and his men spared (saved or kept alive) Agag and kept the best of the sheep, oxen, fat calves, lambs, and anything valuable. They were unwilling (reluctant or not wanting) to completely destroy these, but they destroyed everything worthless or despised (viewed as unworthy). 10. The word of the Lord then came to Samuel: 11. "I regret (feel sorrowful) making Saul king, for he has turned away from Me and hasn't followed My instructions." Samuel was troubled (deeply concerned) and prayed to the Lord all night. 12. Early the next morning, Samuel went to find Saul, who was reported to have gone to Carmel and erected (set up) a monument (statue or marker) in his own honor before moving on to Gilgal. 13. When Samuel reached Saul, Saul greeted him, saying, "The Lord bless you! I have carried out the Lord's command." 14. But Samuel replied, "Then why do I hear sheep bleating (making sheep sounds) and oxen lowing (making oxen sounds)?" 15. Saul explained, "The soldiers spared (kept alive) the best of the sheep and oxen from the Amalekites to sacrifice (offer in worship) to the Lord, but we destroyed everything else." 16. Samuel said to Saul, "Enough! Let me tell you what the Lord revealed (showed or told) to me last night." "Tell me," Saul responded. 17. Samuel continued, "Though you considered yourself insignificant (unimportant), were you not made the head (leader) of the tribes of Israel? Did not the Lord anoint you king over Israel? 18. And He sent you on a mission (special task or purpose), saying, 'Go, completely destroy (eliminate) the wicked Amalekites; wage war (fight) until they are entirely defeated.' 19. Why then did you not obey the Lord? Why did you seize (take by force) the plunder (captured goods) and do evil (wrong) in His sight?" 20. Saul protested (objected or disagreed), "I did obey the Lord! I went on the mission, captured Agag, king of Amalek, and destroyed the Amalekites. 21. But the soldiers took the best of the sheep and oxen, which should have been destroyed, to offer as a sacrifice (gift for worship) to the Lord in Gilgal." 22. Samuel responded: "Does the Lord take pleasure (feel joy) in burnt offerings and sacrifices as much as in obedience (following commands)? To obey is better than sacrifice, and to heed (pay close attention to) is better than the fat of rams. 23. Rebellion (going against orders) is as sinful as witchcraft (practice of magic), and stubbornness (being unyielding) is as bad as idolatry (worship of idols). Since you have rejected (refused to follow) the word of the Lord, He has rejected you as king." 24. Saul admitted (confessed or acknowledged), "I have sinned; I disobeyed (went against) the Lord's command and your words because I was afraid (feared) of the people and listened to them. 25. Now, please forgive (pardon or excuse) my sin and come back with me so that I may worship (honor) the Lord." 26. But Samuel replied, "I will not go back with you. You have rejected the Lord's command, and He has rejected you as king of Israel." 27. As Samuel turned to leave, Saul seized (grabbed) the edge of Samuel's robe, and it tore (ripped). 28. Samuel said, "Today, the Lord has torn (taken away) the kingdom of Israel from you and given it to one of your neighbors (another person close by) who is better than you. 29. Moreover, the Glory (Honor) of Israel will not change His mind; for He is not like a man who relents (reverses decision)." 30. Saul pleaded (asked earnestly), "I have sinned, but please honor (show respect for) me before the elders (leaders) of my people and Israel. Come back with me so I may worship the Lord." 31. So, Samuel went back with Saul, and Saul worshiped (showed respect and devotion to) the Lord. 32. Samuel then commanded, "Bring Agag, king of the Amalekites, to me." Agag came, hoping the bitterness (hardship or pain) of death had passed. 33. But Samuel declared, "As your sword has made mothers childless, so will your mother be childless." And Samuel executed (killed) Agag before the Lord at Gilgal. 34. Then Samuel went to Ramah, and Saul returned to his home in Gibeah. 35. Samuel did not see Saul again until the day of his death, but he mourned (felt sorrow) for him, and the Lord regretted (felt sorrow) making Saul king over Israel.

Chapter 16

1. The Lord spoke to Samuel, saying, "How long will you grieve (feel sorrow) over Saul, since I have rejected him from being king over Israel? Fill your horn (a container for oil) with oil and go to Jesse of Bethlehem. I have chosen one of his sons to be king." 2. Samuel asked, "How can I go? If Saul hears of this, he will kill me." The Lord replied, "Take a young cow (calf) with you and say, 'I have come to offer a sacrifice to the Lord.' 3. Invite Jesse to the sacrifice, and I will show you what to do. You will anoint (set apart and bless with oil) the one I tell you to." 4. Samuel followed the Lord's command and went to Bethlehem. The town's leaders were worried (concerned or anxious) when they saw him and asked, "Do you come peacefully?" 5. Samuel answered, "Yes, I come in peace. I have come to offer a sacrifice to the Lord. Purify (make clean or holy) yourselves and join me in the sacrifice." He consecrated (isolate land or offering for church) Jesse and his sons and invited them to the feast. 6. When they arrived, Samuel looked at Eliab and thought, "Surely, this is the one the Lord has chosen." 7. But the Lord said to Samuel, "Do not consider his appearance or his height, for I have rejected him. The Lord does not see as people see. People look at the outward appearance, but the Lord looks at the heart (inner character and intentions)." 8. Jesse then called for Abinadab to pass by, but Samuel said, "The Lord has not chosen him." 9. Jesse made Shammah pass by, but Samuel said, "The Lord has not chosen him either." 10. Jesse brought seven of his sons before Samuel, but Samuel said, "The Lord has not chosen any of these." 11. Samuel asked, "Are all your sons here?" Jesse answered, "There is still the youngest (youngest son), but he is out in the fields tending (taking care of) the sheep." Samuel said, "Send for him; we will not sit down until he arrives." 12. So, Jesse sent for David, and when he came in, he was ruddy (having a healthy reddish color), with bright eyes and good-looking. The Lord said, "Rise and anoint him; he is the one." 13. Samuel took the horn of oil and anointed David in front of his brothers. From that day on, the Spirit (presence and power of God) of the Lord came powerfully upon David. Then Samuel returned to Ramah. 14. Now the Spirit of the Lord had departed from Saul, and an evil spirit (a harmful or troubling force) sent by the Lord began to torment (cause great distress) him. 15. Saul's servants said to him, "An evil spirit from God is troubling (disturbing or agitating) you." 16. They suggested, "Let us find someone who can play the harp. When the evil spirit comes upon you, he can play, and you will feel better." 17. Saul agreed, saying, "Find someone who plays well and bring him to me." 18. One of the servants replied, "I have seen a son of Jesse of Bethlehem who is skilled (talented) at playing the harp. He is also a brave warrior, wise in speech, and good-looking. The Lord is with him." 19. So Saul sent messengers to Jesse, saying, "Send me your son David, who is with the sheep." 20. Jesse loaded a donkey with bread, wine, and a young goat, and sent them with David to Saul. 21. David came to Saul and stood before him. Saul loved him greatly, and David became his armorbearer (one who carries a warrior's shield or armor). 22. Later, Saul sent a message to Jesse, saying, "Let David stay with me, for I have found favor (approval) with him." 23. Whenever the evil spirit from God came upon Saul, David would take his harp and play. As he played, Saul would feel better, and the evil spirit would leave him.

Chapter 17

1. The Philistines gathered their armies to fight and camped at Sochoh, which belongs to Judah, between Sochoh and Azekah, in a place called Ephes Dammim. 2. Saul and the men of Israel also gathered and camped in the Valley of Elah, preparing for battle against the

Philistines. **3.** The Philistines stood on one side of a mountain, and Israel stood on the opposite side, with a valley (low area of land) between them. **4.** A champion from the Philistines' camp came forward, named Goliath from Gath. His height was six cubits and a span (about 9 feet, 9 inches or 3 meters tall). **5.** Goliath wore a bronze helmet on his head and a bronze coat of mail (a type of armor made of metal rings), which weighed 5,000 shekels (about 125 pounds or 56 kg). **6.** He had bronze armor on his legs and a bronze javelin (a type of spear) slung on his back. **7.** The shaft (long handle) of his spear was like a weaver's beam (a large, heavy wooden beam used in weaving), and the iron spearhead weighed 600 shekels (about 15 pounds or 6.8 kg). He also had a shield-bearer (someone who carried a shield in front of him) who went ahead of him. **8.** Goliath stood and shouted to the armies of Israel, saying, "Why have you come out to prepare for battle? Am I not a Philistine, and you the servants of Saul? Choose a man to come down to me. **9.** If he is able to fight and kill me, then we will become your servants. But if I defeat him and kill him, then you will become our servants and serve us." **10.** He added, "I defy (challenge with disrespect) the armies of Israel today. Give me a man and let us fight together." **11.** When Saul and the Israelites heard these words from the Philistine, they were afraid and greatly troubled (scared). **12.** David was the son of Jesse, an Ephrathite from Bethlehem in Judah. Jesse had eight sons, and he was an old man during the time of Saul. **13.** The three oldest sons of Jesse followed Saul to the battle. Their names were Eliab (the oldest), Abinadab (the second), and Shammah (the third). **14.** David was the youngest of the sons. The three oldest followed Saul to the battle. **15.** But David would return from Saul to care for his father's sheep at Bethlehem. **16.** For forty days, the Philistine came forward every morning and evening, presenting himself to the Israelites. **17.** One day, Jesse said to David, "Take a bushel (a large container) of dried grain and ten loaves of bread to your brothers at the camp. **18.** Also, take these ten cheeses to the captain of their thousand (group of soldiers), and find out how your brothers are doing and bring back news." **19.** Saul and the Israelites were in the Valley of Elah, fighting the Philistines. **20.** Early the next morning, David left the sheep with a keeper, took the supplies, and went as Jesse had instructed. When he arrived at the camp, the army was getting ready to fight and shouting battle cries. **21.** The armies of Israel and the Philistines had arranged themselves in battle formation, facing each other. **22.** David left his things with the supply keeper, ran to the army, and greeted his brothers. **23.** While talking with them, Goliath, the champion of the Philistines, came forward and shouted his usual challenge. David heard him. **24.** When the Israelites saw Goliath, they ran away in fear. **25.** The men of Israel said, "Have you seen this man who keeps coming to challenge Israel? The king has promised great rewards to anyone who kills him: riches, the king's daughter as a wife, and freedom from taxes for his family." **26.** David asked the men around him, "What will be done for the man who kills this Philistine and removes the disgrace (shame) from Israel? Who is this uncircumcised Philistine that he should defy the armies of the living God?" **27.** The men replied to David, saying, "That's what will be done for the man who kills him." **28.** When David's older brother Eliab heard him speaking to the men, he became angry with David and said, "Why did you come here? Who's watching those few sheep in the wilderness? I know your pride and your wickedness; you've come to watch the battle." **29.** David responded, "What have I done now? Isn't there a cause (reason)?" **30.** Then David turned to another man and asked the same question, and the people answered him the same way. **31.** When what David said was reported to Saul, he sent for David. **32.** David told Saul, "Don't let anyone be discouraged because of this Philistine. Your servant will go and fight him." **33.** Saul replied, "You can't fight this Philistine. You're just a boy, and he's been a warrior since his youth." **34.** But David said to Saul, "I've been a shepherd for my father, and when a lion or bear came and took a lamb from the flock, **35.** I went after it, struck it, and rescued the lamb from its mouth. When it turned on me, I grabbed it by its mane, struck it, and killed it. **36.** I've killed both lions and bears, and this uncircumcised Philistine will be like one of them, because he has defied the armies of the living God." **37.** David added, "The Lord, who rescued me from the lion and the bear, will rescue me from this Philistine." Saul replied, "Go, and may the Lord be with you." **38.** Saul dressed David in his own armor,

put a bronze helmet on his head, and gave him a coat of mail. **39.** David tried to walk around with the armor, but he wasn't used to it. He said to Saul, "I can't wear these. I'm not used to them." So David took them off. **40.** Then he picked up his staff, chose five smooth stones from a stream, and put them in his shepherd's bag. With his sling (a weapon used to throw stones) in hand, he approached the Philistine. **41.** The Philistine came closer to David, with his shield-bearer walking in front of him. **42.** When Goliath saw David, he despised (feeling hated) him because he was just a young man, ruddy (healthy-looking with a reddish hue) and handsome. **43.** He said to David, "Am I a dog that you come at me with sticks?" And he cursed David by his gods. **44.** Goliath then said to David, "Come here, and I will give your flesh to the birds of the air and the beasts of the field!" **45.** David replied to the Philistine, "You come to me with a sword, spear, and javelin, but I come to you in the name of the Lord of Hosts (God of the armies of Israel), whom you have defied. **46.** Today the Lord will deliver you into my hands. I will strike you down and cut off your head. I will give your body and the bodies of the Philistine army to the birds and wild animals, and the entire world will know there is a God in Israel. **47.** Everyone gathered here will know that the Lord saves not with sword and spear; the battle is the Lord's, and He will give you into our hands." **48.** As Goliath moved closer to attack, David quickly ran toward the battle line to meet him. **49.** David took a stone from his bag, slung it, and struck Goliath in the forehead. The stone sank into his forehead, and he fell face down to the ground. **50.** So David triumphed over Goliath with a sling and a stone. He struck and killed him, but David had no sword. **51.** David ran over, stood on Goliath, took his sword, drew it from its sheath, and killed him, then cut off his head. When the Philistines saw their champion was dead, they fled. **52.** The men of Israel and Judah shouted and chased the Philistines all the way to the entrance of the valley, as far as the gates of Ekron. The wounded Philistines fell along the road to Shaaraim, Gath, and Ekron. **53.** When the Israelites returned from chasing the Philistines, they plundered (took valuables from) their tents. **54.** David took Goliath's head and brought it to Jerusalem, but he put Goliath's armor in his own tent. **55.** When Saul saw David going out to fight the Philistine, he asked Abner, the commander of the army, "Whose son is this young man?" Abner replied, "As your soul lives, O king, I do not know." **56.** Saul then ordered, "Find out whose son this young man is." **57.** When David returned from killing the Philistine, Abner brought him before Saul with Goliath's head in his hand. **58.** Saul asked him, "Whose son are you, young man?" David replied, "I am the son of your servant Jesse of Bethlehem."

Chapter 18

1. After David finished speaking with Saul, Jonathan's soul was deeply connected (knit) to David's soul, and Jonathan loved him as much as he loved himself. **2.** Saul took David into his service that day and did not let him return to his father's house. **3.** Jonathan and David made a covenant (a formal agreement) because Jonathan loved him as much as his own soul. **4.** Jonathan took off his robe, gave it to David, and also gave him his armor, including his sword, bow, and belt. **5.** So David went out wherever Saul sent him and behaved wisely (with good judgment and caution). Saul placed him over the army, and David was well-liked by all the people and Saul's servants. **6.** As they returned home from the victory over the Philistines, women came out from all the cities of Israel, singing and dancing to meet King Saul, with tambourines (a musical instrument), joyful shouts, and musical instruments. **7.** As they danced, the women sang: "Saul has slain his thousands, and David his ten thousand." **8.** Saul became very angry, and the words displeased (disturbed) him. He said, "They have credited David with tens of thousands, but only thousands to me. What more can he have but the kingdom?" **9.** from that day on, Saul became jealous (envious) and suspicious of David. **10.** The next day, a harmful spirit (distressing spirit) from God came upon Saul, and he began to prophesy (speak in a divine or frenzied way) inside the house. David played the harp (a musical instrument) as he had done before, but Saul held a spear in his hand. **11.** Saul threw the spear, saying, "I'll pin David to the wall!" But David dodged (avoided) him twice. **12.** Saul became afraid of David because the Lord was with David but had departed from Saul. **13.** Therefore, Saul removed (dismissed) David from his presence and made him a captain over a thousand soldiers. David went out and led the people. **14.** David acted wisely (with good judgment) in all his ways, and the Lord was with him. **15.** When Saul saw how wisely David behaved, he became even more afraid of him. **16.** However, all of Israel and Judah loved David, because he went out and came in before them as their leader. **17.** Saul said to David, "Here is my older daughter Merab; I will give her to you as a wife. Only be brave for me and fight the Lord's battles." Saul thought, "Let the Philistines kill him, not my hand." **18.** David replied to Saul, "Who am I, and what is my life, or my father's family in Israel, that I should become the king's son-in-law?" **19.** However, at the time when Merab was supposed to be given to David, she was instead given to Adriel the Meholathite as a wife. **20.** Meanwhile, Saul's daughter Michal loved David. When Saul heard this, it pleased (made happy) him. **21.** Saul thought, "I'll give her to David so that she can be a snare (trap) to him, and the Philistines will attack him." He told David again, "You shall be my son-in-law today." **22.** Saul then instructed his servants to secretly speak to David, saying, "Look, the king likes you, and all his servants love you. So why not become the king's son-in-law?" **23.** When Saul's servants spoke these words to David, he replied, "Does it seem like a small thing (insignificant) to you to become the king's son-in-law when I am a poor and insignificant (lowly regarded) man?" **24.** Saul's servants told Saul what David had said. **25.** Saul answered, "Tell David that the king doesn't require a dowry (bride price) but the payment of one hundred foreskins (cut-off part of male genitalia) of the Philistines, to take vengeance on the king's enemies." Saul thought that David would fall into the hands of the Philistines. **26.** When his servants delivered this message to David, he was pleased (glad) to become the king's son-in-law. But the time was short (limited). **27.** So David went with his men and killed two hundred Philistines. He brought their foreskins to Saul, counting them out to the king, and thus became the king's son-in-law. Saul gave him his daughter Michal as his wife. **28.** Saul saw that the Lord was with David and that Michal loved him. This made Saul even more afraid of David. **29.** Because of this, Saul became David's enemy for the rest of his life. **30.** When the Philistine princes went out to fight, David behaved more wisely (with better judgment) than all the servants of Saul, and his name became highly esteemed (greatly respected).

Chapter 19

1. Saul spoke to Jonathan, his son, and to all his servants, ordering them to kill David. However, Jonathan, Saul's son, deeply loved (liked greatly) David. **2.** Jonathan warned (told secretly) David, saying, "My father Saul is planning to kill you. Be cautious (careful), and hide in a safe place until morning. I will go out and stand beside my father in the field where you are, and I will talk to him about you. I will let you know what I learn." **3.** Jonathan then spoke well (positively) of David to Saul, his father, and defended (argued for) him, saying, "Don't sin (do wrong) against your servant, David, because he has never wronged (hurt) you. In fact, his actions have been very good toward you. **4.** He risked (put in danger) his life to kill the Philistine, and the Lord brought a great victory for all of Israel. You saw it and were glad (happy). Why then would you sin by killing an innocent man, David, for no reason?" **5.** Saul listened (paid attention) to Jonathan and swore (promised), "As the Lord lives, David will not be killed." **6.** Jonathan then called David, told him everything Saul had said, and brought David back to Saul's presence, where he remained as before. **7.** There was another war, and David went out to fight the Philistines again. He struck (hit with force) them with a powerful blow, causing them to flee (run away). **8.** But a distressing spirit (a troubling influence or emotional disturbance) from the Lord came upon Saul while he was sitting in his house with a spear in his hand, and David was playing music to soothe (calm) him. **9.** Saul tried to pin (stick) David to the wall with his spear, but David evaded (escaped) him and the spear struck the wall. David fled that night to avoid (escape) being killed. **10.** Saul sent messengers (messengers are people sent with messages) to watch (guard) David's house and kill him the next morning. But Michal, David's wife, warned (told secretly) him, saying, "If you don't escape tonight, you will be killed tomorrow." **11.** Michal let David down through a window, and he fled (escaped) to safety. **12.** Michal then took a household idol (image of a god) and placed it in the bed, covering it with a blanket made of goats' hair and placing it on top as if it were David. **13.** When Saul's messengers arrived to take David, Michal told them, "He is sick." **14.** Saul then sent the messengers back, ordering, "Bring him up to me in his bed so I can kill him." **15.** When the messengers entered, they found the image (idol)

in the bed, covered with goats' hair. **16.** Saul asked Michal, "Why have you deceived (tricked) me and let my enemy (person who opposes me) escape?" Michal replied, "He told me, 'Let me go! Why should I kill you?'" **17.** David fled (escaped) and went to Samuel at Ramah, telling him all that Saul had done to him. Samuel and David then went and stayed in Naioth (a place in Ramah). **18.** Word reached Saul that David was at Naioth in Ramah. **19.** Saul sent messengers to capture (take by force) David. When they saw a group of prophets prophesying (speaking messages from God), and Samuel standing as their leader, the Spirit of God came upon Saul's messengers, and they also began to prophesy. **20.** Saul was informed and sent more messengers, but they too prophesied (spoke by God's power). A third group was sent, and they also prophesied. **21.** Saul himself went to Ramah, and upon reaching the large well at Sechu, he asked, "Where are Samuel and David?" The people replied, "They are at Naioth in Ramah." **22.** Saul went to Naioth in Ramah, and as soon as the Spirit of God came upon him, he prophesied (spoke messages from God) as he continued his journey. **23.** He stripped off his clothes and prophesied (spoke by divine inspiration) before Samuel, lying down naked (without clothes) all day and night. This is why people say, "Is Saul also among the prophets?"

Chapter 20

1. Then David fled from Naioth in Ramah, and went and said to Jonathan, "What have I done? What is my iniquity (wrongdoing), and what is my sin (wrongdoing) before your father, that he seeks my life?" **2.** So Jonathan said to him, "By no means (no way)! You shall not die! Indeed, my father will do nothing either great or small without first telling me. And why should my father hide this thing from me? It is not so!" **3.** Then David took an oath (promise) again, and said, "Your father certainly knows that I have found favor (approval) in your eyes, and he has said, 'Do not let Jonathan know this, lest he be grieved (saddened).' But truly, as the Lord lives and as your soul lives, there is but a step between me and death." **4.** So, Jonathan said to David, "Whatever you yourself desire (wish), I will do it for you." **5.** And David said to Jonathan, "Indeed tomorrow is the New Moon (a festival of the new moon), and I should not fail to sit with the king to eat. But let me go, that I may hide in the field until the third day at evening. **6.** If your father misses me at all, then say, 'David earnestly (seriously) asked permission of me that he might run over to Bethlehem, his city, for there is a yearly sacrifice there for all the family.' **7.** If he says thus: 'It is well,' your servant (me) will be safe. But if he is very angry, then be sure (certain) that evil (harm) is determined (planned) by him. **8.** Therefore you shall deal kindly (be kind) with your servant, for you have brought your servant into a covenant (agreement) of the Lord with you. Nevertheless, if there is iniquity (wrongdoing) in me, kill me yourself, for why should you bring me to your father?" **9.** But Jonathan said, "Far be it from you! For if I knew certainly (without a doubt) that evil was determined by my father to come upon you, then would I not tell you?" **10.** Then David said to Jonathan, "Who will tell me, or what if your father answers you roughly (angrily)?" **11.** And Jonathan said to David, "Come, and let us go out into the field." So, both of them went out into the field. **12.** Then Jonathan said to David: "The Lord God of Israel is witness (a witness is someone who sees something and can testify to it)! When I have sounded out (talked to) my father sometime tomorrow, or the third day, and indeed there is good (favor) toward David, and I do not send to you and tell you, **13.** May the Lord do so and much more to Jonathan. But if it pleases my father to do you evil (harm), then I will report it to you and send you away, that you may go in safety. And the Lord be with you as He has been with my father. **14.** And you shall not only show me the kindness (goodness) of the Lord while I still live, that I may not die; **15.** But you shall not cut off (take away) your kindness from my house forever, no, not when the Lord has cut off every one of the enemies of David from the face of the earth." **16.** So, Jonathan made a covenant (promise or agreement) with the house (family) of David, saying, "Let the Lord require it at the hand of David's enemies." **17.** Now Jonathan again caused David to vow (make a promise), because he loved him; for he loved him as he loved his own soul (life). **18.** Then Jonathan said to David, "Tomorrow is the New Moon; and you will be missed, because your seat (place at the table) will be empty. **19.** And when you have stayed three days, go down quickly (hurry) and come to the place where you hid on the day of the deed (when you hid before); and remain by the stone Ezel (a specific place or landmark). **20.** Then I will shoot three arrows to the side, as though I shot at a target; **21.** and there I will send a lad (boy), saying, 'Go, find the arrows.' If I expressly (clearly) say to him, 'Look, the arrows are on this side of you; get them and come'--then, as the Lord lives, there is safety (no harm) for you and no harm. **22.** But if I say thus to the young man, 'Look, the arrows are beyond you'--go your way, for the Lord has sent you away. **23.** And as for the matter (issue) which you and I have spoken of, indeed the Lord be between you and me forever." **24.** Then David hid in the field. And when the New Moon had come, the king sat down to eat the feast (the meal). **25.** Now the king sat on his seat, as at other times, on a seat by the wall. And Jonathan arose (stood up), and Abner sat by Saul's side, but David's place was empty. **26.** Nevertheless, Saul did not say anything that day, for he thought, "Something has happened to him; he is unclean (ceremonially impure), surely he is unclean." **27.** And it happened the next day, the second day of the month, that David's place was empty. And Saul said to Jonathan his son, "Why has the son of Jesse (David) not come to eat, either yesterday or today?" **28.** So, Jonathan answered Saul, "David earnestly (seriously) asked permission of me to go to Bethlehem. **29.** And he said, 'Please let me go, for our family has a sacrifice in the city, and my brother has commanded me to be there. And now, if I have found favor in your eyes, please let me get away and see my brothers.' Therefore he has not come to the king's table." **30.** Then Saul's anger was aroused (became very angry) against Jonathan, and he said to him, "You son of a perverse (wicked), rebellious (disobedient) woman! Do I not know that you have chosen the son of Jesse to your own shame and to the shame of your mother's nakedness (shameful actions)? **31.** For as long as the son of Jesse lives on the earth, you shall not be established (remain in power), nor your kingdom (rule). Now therefore, send and bring him to me, for he shall surely die." **32.** And Jonathan answered Saul his father, and said to him, "Why should he be killed? What has he done?" **33.** Then Saul cast (threw) a spear at him to kill him, by which Jonathan knew that it was determined (decided) by his father to kill David. **34.** So Jonathan arose from the table in fierce anger and ate no food the second day of the month, for he was grieved (deeply sad) for David, because his father had treated him shamefully (disrespectfully). **35.** And so it was, in the morning, that Jonathan went out into the field at the time appointed (set time) with David, and a little lad was with him. **36.** Then he said to his lad, "Now run, find the arrows which I shoot." As the lad ran, he shot an arrow beyond him. **37.** When the lad had come to the place where the arrow was which Jonathan had shot, Jonathan cried out after the lad and said, "Is not the arrow beyond you?" **38.** And Jonathan cried out after the lad, "Make haste (hurry), hurry, do not delay!" So, Jonathan's lad gathered up the arrows and came back to his master. **39.** But the lad did not know anything. Only Jonathan and David knew of the matter. **40.** Then Jonathan gave his weapons to his lad, and said to him, "Go, carry them to the city." **41.** As soon as the lad had gone, David arose from a place toward the south, fell on his face to the ground, and bowed down three times. And they kissed one another; and they wept together, but David more so. **42.** Then Jonathan said to David, "Go in peace, since we have both sworn (promised) in the name of the Lord, saying, 'May the Lord be between you and me, and between your descendants and my descendants, forever.'" So, he arose and departed, and Jonathan went into the city.

Chapter 21

1. David went to the city of Nob and approached Ahimelech, the priest. When Ahimelech saw him, he was alarmed and asked, "Why are you alone? Where are the men who were with you?" **2.** David replied to Ahimelech, "The king sent me on a special assignment and told me, 'No one should know the details of the mission I am giving you.' As for my soldiers, I have instructed them to wait for me at a designated location." **3.** "So, what provisions do you have?" David continued. "Please give me five loaves of bread, or whatever you have available." **4.** The priest answered, "I have no common bread here, but I do have some consecrated bread—provided your men have kept themselves pure and refrained from relations with women." **5.** David responded, "Indeed, we have stayed away from women, as is customary on our missions. Even when the task is not a sacred one, we maintain our purity. How much more so today, when the mission is urgent!" **6.** So,

the priest gave him the consecrated bread, because there was no other bread except the Bread of the Presence (symbolic bread offered to God), which had been removed from the LORD's table and replaced with fresh loaves. **7.** That day, Doeg the Edomite, one of Saul's servants, was present. He had been detained before the LORD and was observing what was happening. **8.** David then asked Ahimelech, "Do you have a spear or a sword here? I didn't bring any weapons with me because the king's business was urgent." **9.** The priest answered, "The sword of Goliath the Philistine, whom you defeated in the Valley of Elah, is here. It is wrapped in a cloth behind the ephod (a sacred priestly garment). If you want it, you may take it, because there is no other weapon here." David said, "There is no sword like it; give it to me." **10.** That same day, David fled from Saul and went to Achish, the king of Gath. **11.** When Achish's servants saw him, they said, "Isn't this David, the king of the land? Isn't he the one the people sing about in their songs, saying, 'Saul has slain his thousands, and David his tens of thousands'?" **12.** David became greatly afraid (feeling intense fear or anxiety) when he heard these words, and he began to worry about how Achish would view him. **13.** To escape suspicion, David pretended (acted as though something was true when it was not) to be mad (insane or mentally disturbed) in front of them. He acted like a lunatic (someone who is considered mentally unstable), scratching marks on the city gate doors and letting saliva (spit, the watery liquid produced in the mouth) drip down his beard. **14.** Achish looked at him and said to his servants, "Look at this man! He's completely mad! Why have you brought him to me? **15.** "Am I so lacking in madmen (people who are mentally unstable or insane) that you would bring this one here to act like this in front of me? Do I really need this man in my house?"

Chapter 22

1. David departed from Gath and took refuge in the cave of Adullam. When his family and his father's household learned of his whereabouts, they joined him there. **2.** Everyone who was troubled (in distress), burdened with debt, or dissatisfied (discontented) gathered around him, and David became their leader. About four hundred men rallied to him. **3.** From there, David traveled to Mizpah in Moab and requested from the king of Moab, "Please allow my father and mother to stay with you until I discover what God intends for me." **4.** So, he left his parents in the care of the king of Moab, and they remained with him while David was staying in the stronghold (a fortified place of safety). **5.** But the prophet Gad advised David, "Do not remain in the stronghold; instead, go into the land of Judah." So, David left and went to the forest of Hereth. **6.** Saul, meanwhile, heard of David and his followers' location. Seated under the tamarisk tree (a type of desert tree) on the hill at Gibeah, with his spear in hand, he addressed his officials. **7.** Saul said, "Listen, men of Benjamin! Do you think the son of Jesse will provide you with fields and vineyards or appoint you as commanders over thousands and hundreds?" **8.** "Is that why you have all conspired against me? None of you informed me when my own son allied with the son of Jesse. No one shows any concern for me or tells me that my son has influenced (incited) my servant to plot against me, as he does now." **9.** Then Doeg the Edomite, who was among Saul's officials, said, "I saw the son of Jesse when he visited Ahimelek, son of Ahitub, in Nob. **10.** Ahimelek sought guidance from the LORD for him and also provided him with food and the sword of Goliath, the Philistine." **11.** Saul summoned Ahimelek, son of Ahitub, and all the priests at Nob, along with their families, to appear before him. **12.** "Listen, son of Ahitub!" Saul commanded. "Yes, my lord," replied Ahimelek. **13.** Saul questioned him, "Why have you and the son of Jesse conspired against me by providing him with food, a weapon, and consulting God on his behalf? As a result, he is rebelling against me and lies in ambush (lies in wait) for me, even today." **14.** Ahimelek responded, "Who among all your servants is as faithful as David, the king's son-in-law, the captain of your bodyguard, and highly respected within your household? **15.** was this the first time I sought God's counsel for him? Of course not! Please, let not the king accuses your servant or any of his family, for I am unaware of any wrongdoing in this matter." **16.** But Saul replied, "You will surely die, Ahimelek, along with your entire family." **17.** Saul then commanded his guards, "Turn and kill the priests of the LORD, for they too have joined David, knowing he fled without informing me." However, Saul's officials refused to harm the priests of the LORD. **18.** Saul then instructed Doeg, "You turn and kill the priests." So Doeg the Edomite killed eighty-five men who wore the linen ephod (a sacred garment worn by priests). **19.** He also destroyed the town of Nob, the city of the priests, slaughtering its inhabitants, including men, women, children, infants, cattle, donkeys, and sheep. **20.** However, one of Ahimelek's sons, named Abiathar, escaped and fled to join David. **21.** Abiathar informed David that Saul had killed the LORD's priests. **22.** David replied, "I knew that day when Doeg the Edomite was there that he would surely report to Saul. I am responsible for the death of your entire family. **23.** Stay with me, and do not be afraid. The one who seeks your life seeks mine as well. With me, you will be safe."

Chapter 23

1. News reached David that the Philistines were attacking the town of Keilah and taking grain from its threshing floors (areas where harvested grain is separated from chaff). **2.** David prayed to the LORD, asking, "Should I go and fight these Philistines?" The LORD replied, "Go and defeat the Philistines to save Keilah." **3.** David's men, however, voiced their fear, saying, "We are already feeling vulnerable here in Judah. Facing the Philistine army at Keilah would make us even more afraid. **4.** David consulted (asked for guidance from) the LORD once more and the LORD assured him, "Go to Keilah, for I will give the Philistines into your hands." **5.** So, David and his men went to Keilah, fought the Philistines, seized their livestock, and inflicted heavy losses (caused many casualties) on them. In this way, David saved the people of Keilah. **6.** Abiathar, the son of Ahimelek, had brought the ephod (a sacred priestly garment used to seek God's guidance) with him when he fled to David at Keilah (ancient city in kingdom of Judah). **7.** Saul was informed that David was in Keilah. Saul thought, "God has handed him over to me, since he has enclosed himself in a town with gates and bars." **8.** Saul gathered his troops to go to Keilah and lay siege (surround with intent to capture) to David and his followers. **9.** But David learned of Saul's plan, so he told Abiathar the priest, "Bring the ephod." **10.** David prayed, "LORD, God of Israel, I have heard that Saul plans to come to Keilah and destroy the town because of me. **11.** Will the people of Keilah hand me over to him? Will Saul come as I have heard?" The LORD replied, "Yes, he will come." **12.** David asked again, "Will the people of Keilah hand me and my men over to Saul?" The LORD responded, "Yes, they will." **13.** So, David and about six hundred of his men left Keilah and moved frequently from one place to another. When Saul learned that David had escaped, he gave up his pursuit of Keilah. **14.** David found refuge (safety) in the wilderness strongholds and in the hills of the Desert of Ziph. Saul searched for him every day, but God did not allow David to fall into Saul's hands. **15.** While David was at Horesh in the Desert of Ziph, he discovered that Saul was coming to take his life. **16.** Jonathan, Saul's son, went to David at Horesh to encourage (give support to) him and strengthen his faith in God. **17.** Jonathan said, "Don't be afraid. My father Saul will not harm you. You will be king of Israel, and I will be second to you. Even my father knows this is true." **18.** The two of them made a covenant (a solemn agreement) before the LORD. Jonathan then returned home, while David stayed at Horesh. **19.** Some people from the area of Ziph went to Saul at Gibeah and informed him, "David is hiding among us in the strongholds at Horesh, on the hill of Hakilah, south of Jeshimon. **20.** Now, Your Majesty, come down whenever you wish, and we will take responsibility for handing him over to you." **21.** Saul responded, "The LORD bless you for your loyalty to me. **22.** Go and gather more details about his movements and who has seen him, as I hear he is very crafty (clever at avoiding capture). **23.** Investigate all the places he may be hiding and report back with definite information. Then I will join you; if he is in the region, I will search for him among all the families (clans) of Judah." **24.** So, the people from Ziph went ahead of Saul. Meanwhile, David and his men were in the Desert of Maon, in the Arabah (dry desert valley) south of Jeshimon. **25.** When Saul and his men arrived in the area, David moved down to a large rock in the Desert of Maon. Saul, hearing this, pursued him. **26.** Saul and his forces were on one side of the mountain, while David and his men were on the other, moving quickly to escape. Just as Saul's troops were closing in, **27.** a messenger came urgently to Saul, saying, "Hurry back! The Philistines are raiding the land!" **28.** Saul immediately stopped chasing David and turned back to confront the Philistines. This is why that place is called Sela Hammahlekoth (meaning "Rock of Escape").

29. David then moved from there to the strongholds of En Gedi (a desert oasis on the western shore of the Dead Sea).

Chapter 24

1. After Saul returned from pursuing the Philistines, he was informed, "David is in the Desert of En Gedi." **2.** So, Saul selected three thousand of Israel's best soldiers and set out to search for David and his men near the cliffs known as the Crags of the Wild Goats. **3.** Along the way, he stopped at some sheep pens where there was a cave, and he went inside to relieve himself. Unbeknownst to Saul, David and his men were deep within the same cave. **4.** David's men whispered to him, "This is the day the LORD spoke of, saying, 'I will deliver your enemy into your hands for you to do as you wish.'" David then quietly approached Saul and cut off a piece of his robe without being noticed. **5.** Later, David felt guilty (conscience-stricken) for cutting Saul's robe. **6.** He said to his men, "The LORD forbid that I should harm my master, the LORD's anointed, or lay my hand on him; for he is the anointed of the LORD." **7.** With these words, David sternly restrained his men and did not allow them to attack Saul. Saul then left the cave and continued on his way. **8.** After Saul had left, David came out of the cave and called, "My lord, the king!" When Saul turned around, David bowed deeply, prostrating (laying down) with his face to the ground in respect. **9.** David said to Saul, "Why do you listen to those who say, 'David is seeking to harm you'? **10.** Today, you have seen with your own eyes how the LORD delivered you into my hands in the cave. Some urged me to kill you, but I spared you; I said, 'I will not lay my hand on my lord, for he is the LORD's anointed.' **11.** Look, my father, see this piece of your robe in my hand! I cut off the corner of your robe but did not kill you. This shows that I am not guilty of any wrong or rebellion (defiance); I have not harmed you, yet you are pursuing me to take my life. **12.** May the LORD Judge between us. May the LORD avenge any wrongs you have done to me, but my hand will not touch you. **13.** As the old saying goes, 'From evildoers come evil deeds,' so my hand will not harm you. **14.** Against whom has the king of Israel come out? Who are you chasing? A dead dog? A flea (something insignificant)? **15.** May the LORD be our judge and decide between us. May He consider my cause and uphold it, delivering (rescuing) me from your hand." **16.** When David finished speaking, Saul asked, "Is that your voice, David, my son?" And he began to weep. **17.** He said, "You are more righteous than I; you have treated me well, but I have treated you badly. **18.** Today, you have shown the good you have done for me; the LORD delivered me into your hands, but you did not kill me. **19.** If a man finds his enemy, does he let him go unharmed? May the LORD reward you richly for the kindness you have shown me today? **20.** I know that you will surely be king and that the kingdom of Israel will be established (firmly set) in your hands. **21.** Now, please swear to me by the LORD that you will not destroy my descendants or erase my family name." **22.** So David gave his oath (promise) to Saul. Then Saul went home, but David and his men returned to their stronghold (safe hiding place).

Chapter 25

1. Samuel passed away, and all of Israel gathered to mourn his death. They buried him in his hometown of Ramah. Afterward, David moved to the Desert of Paran. **2.** In Maon, there was a wealthy man who owned land at Carmel. He had a thousand goats and three thousand sheep, which he was shearing (cutting wool with scissor like tool) at Carmel. **3.** This man was named Nabal, and his wife was Abigail. She was intelligent and beautiful, but Nabal was harsh and difficult in his dealings with others—he was a descendant (a person who is descended from a specific ancestor) of Caleb. **4.** While David was staying in the wilderness, he heard that Nabal was shearing sheep. **5.** So, David sent ten young men to him with this message: "Go to Nabal at Carmel and greet him in my name. **6.** Say to him: 'Peace be to you! Good health to you and your household! And peace to everything that belongs to you! **7.** I've heard that it is sheep-shearing season. When your shepherds were with us, we did not harm them, and nothing went missing from their flocks while they were at Carmel. **8.** Ask your own servants, and they will confirm this. So, since this is a festive (celebratory or joyful) time, please be generous with my men and give us whatever you can, in honor of us.'" **9.** When David's men delivered this message to Nabal, they waited for his response. **10.** Nabal replied to David's servants, "Who is this David? Who is the son of Jesse? There are many servants these days running away from their masters. **11.**

Why should I give my food and water, and the meat I've prepared for my shearers (those who cut the wool from sheep), to men I don't even know where they've come from?" **12.** David's men turned around and returned, reporting everything Nabal had said. **13.** David said to his men, "Strap on your swords!" So they did, and David put his sword on as well. About four hundred men went with David, while two hundred stayed behind to guard the supplies. **14.** One of Nabal's servants told Abigail, his wife, "David sent messengers from the wilderness to greet our master, but he insulted (treated with disrespect or scorn) them. **15.** These men treated us very well. They did not harm us, and the whole time we were in the fields near them, nothing was missing. **16.** Night and day, they acted as a protective wall (something that provides protection) around us the entire time we were looking after the sheep. **17.** Now, think about what you should do, because trouble is about to strike our master and his entire household. He is such a wicked man that no one can talk to him." **18.** Abigail acted quickly. She took two hundred loaves of bread, two skins of wine, five slaughtered sheep, five measures (large quantities) of roasted grain, a hundred cakes of raisins, and two hundred cakes of pressed figs, and loaded them onto donkeys. **19.** Then she said to her servants, "Go ahead of me; I will follow you." But she did not tell her husband Nabal what she was doing. **20.** As she was riding her donkey through a ravine (a narrow valley, often with steep sides), she met David and his men descending toward her. **21.** David had just said, "It's been a waste—all my effort protecting this man's property in the wilderness so that nothing was lost. He has repaid me evil for good. **22.** May God deals with me severely, if by morning I leave even one man alive from all that belong to him!" **23.** When Abigail saw David, she immediately got off her donkey and bowed to him with her face to the ground. **24.** She fell at his feet and said: "Please, let me speak to you, my lord, and listen to what your servant has to say. **25.** Don't pay attention to that wicked man, Nabal. His name means 'fool' (a foolish or unwise person), and foolishness is in his nature. As for me, I didn't see the men you sent. **26.** But as surely as the LORD your God lives and as you live, since the LORD has kept you from bloodshed and from taking revenge with your own hands, may your enemies and all who seek to harm you be like Nabal. **27.** And let this gift, which your servant has brought, be given to the men who follow you. **28.** Please forgive me for speaking boldly. The LORD your God will surely make you a lasting dynasty, because you fight the LORD's battles, and no wrongdoing will be found in you as long as you live. **29.** Even though someone is trying to take your life, your life will be securely protected by the LORD your God, but the lives of your enemies will be thrown away like stones from a sling (a weapon used to throw stones or small objects). **30.** When the LORD has fulfilled all the good things He promised to you, and made you ruler over Israel, **31.** you won't have the burden of guilt from needless bloodshed or from taking vengeance yourself. And when the LORD gives you success, please remember me, your servant." **32.** David said to Abigail, "Praise be to the LORD, the God of Israel, who has sent you today to meet me. **33.** Blessed be your wisdom and your quick thinking, for you have kept me from shedding blood today and from taking revenge with my own hands. **34.** Otherwise, as surely as the LORD lives, who has kept me from harming you, if you hadn't come to meet me so quickly, not one male belonging to Nabal would have been left alive by morning." **35.** David accepted the gifts she had brought and said, "Go home in peace. I have heard your words and granted your request." **36.** When Abigail returned to Nabal, he was in his house having a feast (a large meal, often celebrating something) like a king. He was in high spirits and very drunk, so she did not tell him anything until the next morning. **37.** The next day, when Nabal was sober, his wife told him everything that had happened, and his heart failed (often used to describe extreme fear). He became like a stone (he became paralyzed with fear or shock). **38.** About ten days later, the LORD struck Nabal, and he died. **39.** When David heard that Nabal had died, he said, "Praise be to the LORD, who has upheld my cause against Nabal for treating me with contempt. He has kept me from doing wrong and has brought Nabal's evil down on his own head." Then David sent word to Abigail, asking her to become his wife. **40.** His servants went to Carmel and said to Abigail, "David has sent us to you to take you as his wife." **41.** She bowed down with her face to the ground and said, "I am your servant, ready to serve you and wash the feet of your servants." **42.** Abigail quickly got on a donkey, accompanied by her five female servants, and went with David's messengers to become his wife. **43.** David had also married Ahinoam of Jezreel, and both women became his wives. **44.** However, Saul had given David's first wife, Michal, to Paltiel son of Laish, who was from Gallim.

Chapter 26

1. The Ziphites went to Saul at Gibeah and told him, "Isn't David hiding on the hill of Hakilah, which faces Jeshimon (a desolate wilderness)? **2.** So Saul took three thousands of Israel's best soldiers and went down to the Desert of Ziph to search for David. **3.** Saul set up camp beside the road on the hill of Hakilah, which faced Jeshimon, while David stayed in the wilderness. When David realized that Saul had followed him there, **4.** he sent out spies and confirmed that Saul had definitely arrived. **5.** David then went to the place where Saul had camped. He saw that Saul and Abner, son of Ner (Abner was the commander of Saul's army), were lying down. Saul was inside the camp, surrounded by his soldiers. **6.** David asked Ahimelek the Hittite (a foreign man who served as one of David's loyal companions) and Abishai, the son of Zeruiah (Joab's brother), "Who will go with me into the camp to Saul?" "I'll go with you," Abishai replied. **7.** So David and Abishai made their way into the camp at night. There was Saul, lying asleep with his spear stuck in the ground near his head, and Abner and the soldiers were sleeping around him. **8.** Abishai said to David, "Today God has handed your enemy over to you. Let me pin him to the ground with a single thrust of the spear; I won't need to strike him twice." **9.** But David replied, "Don't harm him! Who can touch the LORD's anointed and remain guiltless (without fault)? **10.** As surely as the LORD lives," David continued, "the LORD will strike him down, or his time will come and he will die, or he will fall in battle and be killed. **11.** But may the LORD forbid that I harm the one He has anointed. Now take the spear and the water jug near his head, and let's go." **12.** So David took the spear and the water jug that were by Saul's head, and they left quietly. No one saw or knew anything, and no one woke up, for the LORD had put them all into a deep sleep (a supernatural sleep caused by God). **13.** Then David crossed to the other side and stood on top of a hill some distance away. There was a wide gap between them. **14.** David called out to the army and to Abner son of Ner, "Are you going to answer me, Abner?" Abner responded, "Who is calling to the king?" **15.** David said, "You're a man, aren't you? And who is like you in Israel? Why didn't you guard your lord the king? Someone came to harm your lord the king. **16.** What you have done is not good. As surely as the LORD lives, you and your men deserve to die because you did not protect your master, the LORD's anointed. Look around! Where is the king's spear and water jug that were near his head?" **17.** Saul recognized David's voice and said, "Is that you, David my son?" David answered, "Yes, it's me, my lord the king." **18.** David continued, "Why is my lord chasing his servant? What have I done, and what wrong have I committed? **19.** Now, let my lord the king listens to his servant. If the LORD has stirred (incited or moved) you against me, let Him accept an offering. But if others have done this, may they be cursed (spoken against with judgment) before the LORD! They have driven me away today from sharing in the LORD's inheritance (His promised land) and have told me to go and serve other gods. **20.** Don't let my blood fall to the ground far from the presence of the LORD. The king of Israel has come out to look for a flea, like one hunts a partridge (a small bird) in the mountains." **21.** Saul said, "I have sinned. Come back, David my son. Because you valued my life today, I will not try to harm you again. Surely I have acted foolishly (made a foolish mistake) and made a terrible mistake." **22.** "Here is your spear, king," David replied. "Let one of your young men come and take it. **23.** The LORD rewards each person according to their righteousness (doing what is right) and faithfulness (being loyal). The LORD gave you into my hands today, but I didn't harm the LORD's anointed. **24.** As I valued your life today, may the LORD value my life and deliver me from all my troubles." **25.** Saul said to David, "May you be blessed, David my son. You will do great things and surely succeed (triumph)." Then David went on his way, and Saul returned to his home.

Chapter 27

1. David thought to himself, "One day Saul will eventually catch up with me and destroy me. The best thing I can do is escape to the land of the Philistines. That way, Saul will stop searching for me throughout Israel, and I will be out of his reach." **2.** So, David, along with the six hundred men who were with him, left and went to Achish (a Philistine king) son of Maok, who was the king of Gath (one of the five major Philistine cities). **3.** David and his men settled in Gath with Achish. Each of his men brought along their families, and David had his two wives: Ahinoam of Jezreel and Abigail of Carmel, the widow of Nabal. **4.** When Saul heard that David had fled to Gath, he stopped pursuing him. **5.** David then spoke to Achish, saying, "If I have found favor (approval) in your eyes, give me a place in one of the smaller towns so I can live there. Why should your servant live in the royal city with you?" **6.** On that day, Achish granted him Ziklag (a town in Philistine territory), and it has belonged to the kings of Judah ever since. **7.** David lived in the Philistine territory for a year and four months. **8.** During that time, David and his men would raid the Geshurites, the Girzites, and the Amalekites (three groups of people who lived in the land extending to Shur and Egypt). **9.** Whenever David attacked an area, he made sure not to leave anyone alive—he took livestock (sheep, cattle, donkeys, camels) and clothing, and then returned to Achish. **10.** When Achish asked him, "Where did you raid today?" David would reply, "Against the Negev (southern desert) of Judah," or "Against the Negev of Jerahmeel (a region or tribe)," or "Against the Negev of the Kenites (a nomadic group allied with Israel)." **11.** David made sure that no one was left alive to be brought to Gath, for he thought, "If they are brought here, they might report to Achish what really happened and say, 'This is what David has been doing.'" This was David's practice throughout his time in Philistine territory. **12.** Achish trusted David, thinking to himself, "David has become so hated by his own people, the Israelites, that he will stay loyal to me and be my servant for life."

Chapter 28

1. In those days, the Philistines gathered their armies to fight against Israel. Achish (the king of Gath) said to David, "You should know that you and your men will join me in the army." **2.** David replied, "Then you will see what your servant can do." Achish said, "Very well, I will make you my bodyguard for life." **3.** By this time, Samuel (the prophet) was dead, and all of Israel had mourned for him and buried him in his hometown of Ramah. Saul had expelled all mediums (those who communicate with spirits) and spiritists (those who practice divination) from the land. **4.** The Philistines gathered their forces and camped at Shunem, while Saul gathered all of Israel and set up camp at Gilboa. **5.** When Saul saw the Philistine army, he was terrified, and fear overwhelmed him. **6.** He inquired of the LORD, but the LORD did not answer him, neither by dreams, nor by Urim (a sacred object used for divination), nor through prophets. **7.** Saul then said to his attendants, "Find me a woman who is a medium, so I can seek guidance from her." "There is one in Endor," they replied. **8.** So Saul disguised himself, wearing different clothes, and at night he went with two of his men to visit the woman. "Consult a spirit for me," he asked, "and brings up the one I name." **9.** The woman said to him, "You surely know what Saul has done. He has banned all mediums and spiritists from the land. Why are you setting a trap for my life, to bring about my death?" **10.** Saul swore to her by the LORD, "As surely as the LORD lives, you will not be punished for this." **11.** Then the woman asked, "Whom shall I bring up for you?" "Bring up Samuel," he replied. **12.** When the woman saw Samuel, she cried out loudly and said to Saul, "Why have you deceived me? You are Saul!" **13.** The king said to her, "Don't be afraid. What do you see?" The woman answered, "I see a spirit coming up out of the earth." **14.** "What does he look like?" Saul asked. "An old man is coming up, wearing a robe," she said. Then Saul realized it was Samuel, and he bowed down, prostrating himself with his face to the ground. **15.** Samuel said to Saul, "Why have you disturbed me by bringing me up?" "I am in great distress," Saul answered. "The Philistines are fighting against me, and God has turned away from me. He no longer answers me, either through prophets or dreams. So I have called on you to tell me what to do." **16.** Samuel replied, "Why do you consult me, now that the LORD has turned away from you and become your enemy? **17.** The LORD has done what He foretold through me: He has torn the kingdom out of your hands and given it to your neighbor— David. **18.** Because you did not obey the LORD's command or carry out His fierce anger against the Amalekites, the LORD has done this to you today. **19.** The LORD will hand both Israel and you over to the Philistines, and tomorrow you and your sons will be with me (in death).

The LORD will also give the army of Israel into the hands of the Philistines." **20.** Immediately, Saul fell to the ground, filled with fear at Samuel's words. His strength was gone, for he had not eaten anything all day and night. **21.** When the woman saw how shaken Saul was, she said, "Look, your servant has obeyed you. I put my life in danger and did what you asked me to do. **22.** Now please listen to me, and let me give you some food so you can regain your strength and go on your way." **23.** But Saul refused and said, "I will not eat." However, his men urged him, and he listened to them. He got up from the ground and sat on the couch. **24.** The woman had a fattened calf at her house, which she slaughtered immediately. She took some flour, kneaded it, and baked unleavened bread. **25.** She set the food before Saul and his men, and they ate. Then, that same night, they got up and left.

Chapter 29

1. The Philistines assembled all their forces at Aphek, while Israel camped near the spring at Jezreel. **2.** As the Philistine commanders marched in their divisions of hundreds and thousands, David and his men followed at the rear with Achish. **3.** The Philistine leaders questioned, "Who are these Hebrews (the people of Israel)?" Achish answered, "This is David, the servant of Saul, king of Israel. He has been with me for over a year now, and I have found nothing wrong (no fault) in him since he left Saul." **4.** But the Philistine commanders were upset (angry) with Achish and said, "Send him back to the place you assigned him. He cannot go into battle with us. If he joins the fight, he may turn against us. What better way could he regain his master's favor than by attacking us in battle?" **5.** "Isn't this the David they sing about in their dances: 'Saul has slain thousands, and David tens of thousands'?" **6.** So Achish summoned (called) David and said, "As surely as the LORD lives, you have been loyal (faithful, trustworthy) to me. I would be pleased to have you serve in my army. From the day you came to me until now, I have found no fault in you, but the other commanders disapprove (do not approve)." **7.** "Therefore, you must go back in peace. Do not do anything to upset (displease) the Philistine commanders." **8.** David asked, "What have I done? What wrong (sin, mistake) have you found in me since I came to you? Why can't I fight the enemies of my lord the king?" **9.** Achish replied, "I know you have been like an angel of God to me, but the commanders of the Philistines say you must not go to battle with us." **10.** "Get up early tomorrow, along with your men, and leave at once when it is light." **11.** So David and his men got up early the next morning and returned to the land of the Philistines, while the Philistine army continued its march to Jezreel.

Chapter 30

1. When David and his men returned to Ziklag on the third day, they discovered that the Amalekites had raided the Negev (a desert region) and attacked Ziklag. They had burned the city to the ground, and taken captive the women and everyone else—both young and old. However, they killed none of them but carried them away as they left. **2.** When David and his men arrived at Ziklag, they found the city destroyed by fire, and their wives, sons, and daughters had been taken captive. **3.** They wept loudly until they had no strength left to cry. **4.** Among the captives were David's two wives: Ahinoam from Jezreel and Abigail, the widow of Nabal from Carmel. **5.** David was deeply distressed because his men were talking about stoning him. They were bitter in spirit (feeling anger or resentment) due to the loss of their sons and daughters. But David found strength in the LORD, his God. **6.** Then David said to Abiathar (a priest) the son of Ahimelek (another priest), "Bring me the ephod" (a priestly garment used to inquire of God). **7.** Abiathar brought it to him, and David asked the LORD, "Should I pursue this raiding party? Will I catch up to them?" **8.** The LORD answered, "Pursue them. You will certainly overtake them and succeed in recovering everything." **9.** So, David and his six hundred men went to the Besor Valley (a valley where part of David's army stayed behind), where some of them had to stay behind. **10.** Two hundred of them were too exhausted to cross the valley, so David and the remaining four hundred continued the pursuit. **11.** They found an Egyptian (a man from Egypt) in a field and brought him to David. **12.** They gave him water to drink and food to eat—a piece of pressed fig cake and two cakes of raisins. **13.** After eating, he revived, for he had not eaten food or drink water for three days and nights. **14.** David asked him, "Who do you belong to, and where do you come from?" **15.** The man replied, "I am an Egyptian, the servant (slave) of an Amalekite (a member of a nomadic group). My master left me behind when I became sick three days ago. **16.** We raided the Negev of the Kerethites (a people group associated with the Philistines), some areas belonging to Judah, and the Negev of Caleb (a region in Judah). We also burned Ziklag." **17.** David asked, "Can you lead me to this raiding party?" The Egyptian responded, "Swear to me by God that you will not kill me or hand me over to my master, and I will guide you to them." **18.** So he led David to where the Amalekites were spread out, eating, drinking, and celebrating because of the large amount of plunder (wealth taken in a raid) they had taken from the land of the Philistines and Judah. **19.** David attacked them from sunset until the evening of the next day. None of them escaped, except for four hundred young men who fled on camels. **20.** David recovered everything the Amalekites had taken, including his two wives. **21.** Nothing was lost—young or old, boy or girl, nor anything else they had taken. David brought it all back. **22.** He also took all the livestock (animals raised on a farm) and herds, and his men drove them ahead of the other animals, saying, "This is David's plunder." **23.** When David and his men returned to the two hundred men who had been too exhausted to follow him and had stayed behind at the Besor Valley, the two groups met. **24.** David asked how they were doing. **25.** But some of the troublemakers (difficult or disruptive people) among David's followers said, "Since they didn't go with us, we won't share the plunder with them, though they can take their wives and children and go." **26.** David replied, "No, my brothers, you must not do that with what the LORD has given us. He has protected us and handed over to us the raiding party that came against us. **27.** Who will listen to you in this matter? The share of the man who stayed with the supplies (goods and provisions) will be the same as the one who went to battle. Everyone will share alike." **28.** From that day on, David made this a rule and practice for Israel. **29.** When David reached Ziklag, he sent part of the plunder to the elders (leaders) of Judah, his friends, with this message: "Here is a gift for you from the plunder of the LORD's enemies." **30.** He sent it to those in Bethel, Ramoth Negev (a region), and Jattir; to those in Aroer, Siphmoth, Eshtemoa, and Rakal; to those in the towns of the Jerahmeelites (descendants of Jerahmeel) and the Kenites (a nomadic tribe); to those in Hormah, Bor Ashan, Athak, **31.** and Hebron; and to all the other places where David and his men had roamed.

Chapter 31

1. The Philistines engaged in battle with Israel, and the Israelites retreated, with many dying on Mount Gilboa. **2.** The Philistines relentlessly pursued Saul and his sons, killing his sons Jonathan, Abinadab, and Malki-Shua. **3.** As the battle intensified around Saul, the archers caught up with him, inflicting serious injuries. **4.** Saul then spoke to his armor-bearer (a person who carries and protects a soldier's armor and weapons), saying, "Draw your sword and kill me, or these uncircumcised (those who are not part of God's covenant, considered enemies of Israel) men will come and kill me and shame me." But his armor-bearer, filled with fear, refused to do so. Therefore, Saul took his own sword and fell on it. **5.** When the armor-bearer saw that Saul was dead, he too fell on his sword and died beside him. **6.** Thus, Saul, his three sons, his armor-bearer, and all his men perished on the same day. **7.** When the Israelites who lived in the valley and across the Jordan saw that the army had fled and that Saul and his sons were dead, they abandoned their towns and fled. The Philistines then came and took control of the towns. **8.** The next day, when the Philistines came to strip the bodies of the fallen, they discovered Saul and his sons' dead on Mount Gilboa. **9.** They severed Saul's head, took his armor, and sent messengers throughout the land of the Philistines to announce the news in the temples of their idols (gods of the Philistines) and among their people. **10.** They placed Saul's armor in the temple of Ashtoreth (a Philistine goddess), and they fastened his body to the wall of Beth Shan (an ancient city in Israel). **11.** When the people of Jabesh Gilead learned what the Philistines had done to Saul, **12.** all the valiant (brave and courageous) men from Jabesh marched through the night to Beth Shan. They removed the bodies of Saul and his sons from the wall of Beth Shan and took them to Jabesh, where they burned them. **13.** They buried the bones under a tamarisk tree (a tree known for its shade and branches) in Jabesh and fasted for seven days.

Samuel 2

Chapter 1

1 After the death of Saul, David returned from defeating the Amalekites (a tribe often hostile to Israel) and stayed in Ziklag (David's temporary home) for two days. **2** On the third day, a man arrived from Saul's camp. His clothes were torn and he had dust on his head (signs of mourning). When he came to David, he fell to the ground to show him respect. **3** David asked him, "Where have you come from?" He answered, "I have escaped from the Israelite camp." **4** "What happened?" David asked. "Tell me everything." The man replied, "The men fled from the battlefield (place of fighting). Many of them fell and died, and Saul and his son Jonathan are dead." **5** David said to the young man who brought him the report, "How do you know that Saul and his son Jonathan are dead?" **6** The young man said, "I happened to be on Mount Gilboa (a mountain where Saul's final battle took place), and there was Saul, leaning on his spear (a long weapon), with the enemy chariots (wheeled war vehicles) and drivers in close pursuit. **7** When he turned and saw me, he called out to me, and I asked, 'How can I help?' **8** He asked me, 'Who are you?' I replied, 'I am an Amalekite (a member of the Amalekite people).' **9** Then he said to me, 'Come here and kill me, for I am in great agony (severe pain), though I am still alive.' **10** "So I stood beside him and killed him, because I knew he would not survive after he had fallen. I took the crown from his head and the band from his arm, and I have brought them here to my lord." **11** Then David and all the men with him took hold of their clothes and tore them (as a sign of grief). **12** They wept, mourned, and fasted (went without food) until evening for Saul, Jonathan, the LORD's army, and the nation of Israel, because they had been struck down by the sword (by violence in battle). **13** David asked the young man who brought him the report, "Where are you from?" He replied, "I am the son of a foreigner, an Amalekite." **14** David asked him, "Why were you not afraid to lift your hand against the LORD's anointed?" **15** Then David called one of his men and said, "Go, strike him down!" So, he struck the man down, and he died. **16** For David had said to him, "Your blood is on your own head (responsibility is yours), for your own words testified against you when you said, 'I killed the LORD's anointed.'" **17** David then composed a lament (a sorrowful song) for Saul and his son Jonathan. **18** He commanded that the people of Judah (a tribe of Israel) be taught this "Song of the Bow" (a funeral song), which is recorded in the Book of Jashar (a historical book). **19** "Israel's pride lies slain on your heights (mountain peaks). How the mighty have fallen! **20** "Do not announce it in Gath (a Philistine city); do not proclaim it in the streets of Ashkelon (another Philistine city), or the daughters of the Philistines will rejoice (feel glad), and the daughters of the uncircumcised (non-Israelites) will celebrate. **21** "Mountains of Gilboa, may you have neither dew (light rain) nor rain; may no fields of crops grow on you. For there the shield (protective weapon) of the mighty was dishonored, the shield of Saul, no longer polished with oil. **22** "From the blood of the slain, from the flesh of the mighty, Jonathan's bow (weapon that shoots arrows) did not turn back, nor did Saul's sword (bladed weapon) return empty. **23** Saul and Jonathan—in life, they were loved and admired; in death, they were not separated. They were swifter than eagles and stronger than lions. **24** "Daughters of Israel, weep for Saul, who clothed you in scarlet (rich fabric) and fine garments, who adorned your clothes with gold. **25** "How the mighty have fallen in battle! Jonathan lies slain on your heights. **26** I grieve (mourn deeply) for you, Jonathan, my brother; you were very dear to me. Your love for me was deep, surpassing the love of women. **27** "How the mighty have fallen! The weapons of war have perished!"

Chapter 2

1. Sometime later, David asked the LORD, "Should I go up to one of the towns of Judah (Israel's southern region)?" The LORD replied, "Go up." David asked, "Which town should I go to?" The LORD answered, "To Hebron" (a city in Judah, now in the West Bank). **2** So David went up to Hebron with his two wives, Ahinoam from Jezreel (a region in Israel's northern valley) and Abigail, who was the widow of Nabal from Carmel (a town near Hebron in southern Israel). **3** David also brought along the men who were with him, each with his own family, and they all settled in Hebron and the surrounding towns. **4** Then the men of Judah came to Hebron, where they anointed David as king over the tribe of Judah. When David was told that the men of Jabesh Gilead (a town east of the Jordan River, now in Jordan) had buried Saul (former king of Israel), **5**

he sent messengers to them with this message: "May the LORD bless you for showing this kindness to your master Saul by burying him. 6 Now, may the LORD show you kindness and faithfulness, and I too will reward you for this act. 7 Be strong and courageous, for your master Saul is dead, and the people of Judah have anointed me as their king." 8 Meanwhile, Abner, the son of Ner and commander of Saul's (Israel's former king) army, took Saul's son Ish-Bosheth (son of Saul) and brought him to Mahanaim (a city east of the Jordan River, in modern-day Jordan). 9 Abner made him king over Gilead (a region in modern-Jordan), Ashuri (an ancient region, exact location unknown), Jezreel (northern Israel), Ephraim (central Israel), Benjamin (tribe near Jerusalem), and over all Israel. 10 Ish-Bosheth, the son of Saul, was forty years old when he became king over Israel, and he reigned for two years. However, the tribe of Judah remained loyal to David. 11 David reigned as king over Judah from Hebron for seven years and six months. 12 One day, Abner son of Ner and the men of Ish-Bosheth left Mahanaim and went to Gibeon (an ancient city north of Jerusalem, near modern-day Ramallah). 13 Joab, son of Zeruiah, along with David's men, also went out and met them at the pool of Gibeon. One group sat on one side of the pool, and the other group sat on the opposite side. 14 Then Abner suggested to Joab, "Let some of the young men come forward and fight hand-to-hand in front of us." Joab agreed, saying, "All right, let them do it." 15 So they stood up and were counted off—twelve men for Benjamin and Ish-Bosheth, Saul's son, and twelve men for David. 16 Each man grabbed his opponent by the head and thrust his dagger (short weapon) into his opponent's side, and they all fell down together. Because of this, the place in Gibeon became known as Helkath Hazzurim (Field of the Strong). 17 The battle that day was very fierce, and Abner and the Israelites were defeated by David's men. 18 Among those present were the three sons of Zeruiah: Joab, Abishai, and Asahel. Asahel was as fast on his feet as a wild gazelle (an agile animal). 19 Asahel chased Abner, not turning to the right or left as he pursued him. 20 Abner looked behind him and asked, "Is that you, Asahel?" Asahel replied, "Yes, it's me." 21 Abner said, "Turn aside to the right or left and fight one of the young men and take his armor (protective gear)." But Asahel would not stop chasing him. 22 Abner warned Asahel again, "Stop chasing me! Why should I have to strike you down? How could I ever face your brother Joab?" 23 But Asahel refused to stop chasing him, so Abner thrust the butt end of his spear into Asahel's stomach, and the spear came out through his back. Asahel fell and died on the spot. Everyone who came to the place where Asahel had fallen stopped. 24 However, Joab and Abishai continued to pursue Abner, and as the sun was setting, they reached the hill of Ammah near Giah, on the way to the wilderness of Gibeon (a wilderness area near ancient Gibeon, north of Jerusalem). 25 The men of Benjamin (one of Israel's tribes) rallied behind Abner. They formed a group and took a stand on the top of a hill. 26 Abner called out to Joab, "Must the sword keep on taking lives? Don't you realize that this will only end in bitterness? How long will it be before you order your men to stop pursuing their fellow Israelites?" 27 Joab replied, "As surely as God lives, if you had not spoken, my men would have continued pursuing their fellow Israelites until morning." 28 Then Joab blew the trumpet (signal horn), and all the troops halted; they stopped pursuing Israel and did not fight any further. 29 Abner and his men marched through the Arabah (a desert plain in the Jordan Valley) all that night. They crossed the Jordan River (major river in Israel and Jordan) and continued their journey until they reached Mahanaim. 30 Joab ended the pursuit of Abner and assembled his troops. Besides Asahel, nineteen of David's men were found missing. 31 However, David's men had killed three hundred and sixty Benjamites who were with Abner. 32 They took Asahel and buried him in his father's tomb in Bethlehem (a town near Jerusalem, where David was born). Joab and his men then marched all night and arrived in Hebron by dawn.

Chapter 3

1 The war between Saul's household (descendants and followers) and David's household continued for a long time. Over time, David's strength and influence increased, while Saul's household grew weaker and weaker. 2 David had several sons born to him in Hebron (a city in Judah, now in the West Bank). His first son was Amnon, whose mother was Ahinoam from Jezreel (a valley in northern Israel). 3 His second son was Kileab, whose mother was Abigail, the widow of Nabal from Carmel (a town near Hebron). The third son was Absalom, born to Maakah, the daughter of Talmai, king of Geshur (a region near modern-day Golan Heights). 4 His fourth son was Adonijah, born to Haggith; the fifth was Shephatiah, born to Abital; 5 and the sixth was Ithream, born to David's wife Eglah. All these sons were born to David in Hebron. 6 During the long conflict between Saul's household and David's household, Abner (commander of Saul's army) had been consolidating his own power within Saul's household. 7 Saul had a concubine (secondary wife) named Rizpah, daughter of Aiah. One day, Ish-Bosheth (Saul's son and ruler of Israel) accused Abner, "Why did you sleep with my father's concubine?" 8 Abner was furious at Ish-Bosheth's accusation and replied, "Am I a dog's head—a disloyal person—aligned with Judah? I have shown loyalty to Saul's family, his friends, and his supporters and have not betrayed you by handing you over to David. Yet now you accuse me of wrongdoing with this woman! 9 May God deal with me severely if I do not do for David what the LORD swore to him on oath, 10 transferring the kingdom from Saul's household to establish David's rule over Israel and Judah, from Dan to Beersheba (Dan in northern Israel to Beersheba in the south)." 11 Ish-Bosheth was too afraid to respond to Abner's words. 12 Then Abner sent messengers to David on his behalf, saying, "Who really controls the land? Make a covenant with me, and I will help unite all of Israel under your rule." 13 David replied, "Good. I will make a covenant with you. But there is one condition: Do not come before me unless you bring Michal, Saul's daughter, when you come." 14 David then sent messengers to Ish-Bosheth, son of Saul, demanding, "Give me my wife Michal, whom I won as my wife in exchange for the foreskins of a hundred Philistines." 15 So Ish-Bosheth ordered Michal to be taken from her husband, Paltiel, son of Laish. 16 Her husband followed behind her, weeping as far as Bahurim (a town near Jerusalem). Then Abner said to him, "Go back home." So he went back. 17 Abner met with the elders (leaders) of Israel and said, "For some time, you have wanted to make David your king. 18 Now is the time! For the LORD promised David, 'Through my servant David, I will rescue my people Israel from the Philistines and from all their enemies.'" 19 Abner also spoke to the tribe of Benjamin (Saul's tribe), then went to Hebron to tell David everything that Israel and the tribe of Benjamin wanted to do. 20 When Abner and twenty men came to David at Hebron, David prepared a feast for them. 21 Abner then said to David, "Allow me to go and gather all Israel for my lord, the king, so they may make a covenant with you and establish your rule over everything your heart desires." David then sent Abner away in peace. 22 Just after David's men and Joab returned from a raid with a large amount of plunder (goods taken in war), Abner had already left Hebron in peace, as David had sent him away. 23 When Joab and the troops arrived, he was told that Abner, son of Ner, had visited the king and had been sent away in peace. 24 Joab went to the king and asked, "What have you done? Abner came to you, and you let him go? Now he's gone! 25 You know Abner, son of Ner, came to deceive you, observe your movements, and learn all that you are doing." 26 After leaving David, Joab sent messengers after Abner, bringing him back from the well of Sirah (a nearby water source). David, however, knew nothing of this. 27 When Abner returned to Hebron, Joab took him aside into an inner room, as if to speak with him privately. There, Joab stabbed Abner in the stomach, killing him to avenge his brother Asahel's death. 28 Later, when David heard of this, he said, "I and my kingdom are innocent before the LORD forever concerning the blood of Abner, son of Ner. 29 May the responsibility for his blood fall on Joab and his family. May Joab's family never be without someone who has a discharge, leprosy, needs a crutch, falls by the sword, or lacks food." 30 (Joab and his brother Abishai murdered Abner because he had killed their brother Asahel in battle at Gibeon.) 31 Then David ordered Joab and all the people with him, "Tear your clothes, put on sackcloth (mourning garments), and mourn for Abner." King David himself followed Abner's bier (funeral platform). 32 They buried Abner in Hebron, and the king wept loudly at his grave, and all the people joined in weeping. 33 The king sang a lament for Abner, saying, "Should Abner have died like a godless? 34 Your hands were not bound, and your feet were not shackled. You fell as one falls before the wicked." And all the people wept for him again. 35 Then they came to urge David to eat while it was still daylight, but David took an oath, saying, "May God deal with

me ever so severely if I eat anything before the sun sets!" **36** The people noticed this and were pleased; indeed, everything the king did pleased them. **37** On that day, all the people and all Israel knew that the king had no part in the murder of Abner, son of Ner. **38** Then the king said to his men, "Do you not realize that a commander and a great man has fallen in Israel today? **39** Though I am anointed as king, I am weak, and these sons of Zeruiah (Joab and his family) are too powerful for me. May the LORD repay the evildoer according to his deeds!"

Chapter 4

1 When Ish-Bosheth, son of Saul, learned that Abner had been killed in Hebron (an ancient city in Judah, now located in the West Bank), he lost all courage and strength, and all the people of Israel became alarmed and filled with fear. **2** Ish-Bosheth, the son of Saul, had two men who were leaders of raiding bands (groups formed to capture supplies or attack enemies). Their names were Baanah and Rekab, sons of Rimmon, a Beerothite (from Beeroth, a town near Gibeon and part of Benjamin's tribe). This town is considered part of Benjamin's inheritance. **3** The people of Beeroth had fled to Gittaim (likely a refuge town in Benjamin's territory, meaning "two winepresses") and have been living there as foreigners to this day, adopting a new place due to circumstances. **4** (Jonathan, son of Saul, had a son named Mephibosheth, who was disabled in both feet. This happened when he was only five years old, on the day news came from Jezreel (a valley in northern Israel, famous for battles) that Saul and Jonathan had died. His nurse tried to carry him to safety, but in her hurry, he fell and became permanently disabled.) **5** Rekab and Baanah, the sons of Rimmon the Beerothite, went to Ish-Bosheth's house during the hottest part of the day. They arrived as he was resting, taking his noon nap in peace. **6** They entered the inner part of the house, pretending they were coming to get some wheat (a common resource stored in households), but instead, they seized the moment to stab him in the stomach, causing fatal wounds. Rekab and Baanah then escaped undetected. **7** After entering Ish-Bosheth's house, they found him lying on his bed in the privacy of his own bedroom. They then struck him down, ending his life, and afterward cut off his head. Taking it with them as proof, they traveled all night through the Arabah (a dry, desert valley stretching from the Dead Sea to the Gulf of Aqaba). **8** They brought the head of Ish-Bosheth to David at Hebron and said to him, "Here is the head of Ish-Bosheth, son of Saul, your long-standing enemy who sought your life. Today the LORD has avenged (brought justice) for my lord the king, against Saul and his descendants, removing them as a threat." **9** David replied to Rekab and Baanah, sons of Rimmon the Beerothite, saying, "As surely as the LORD lives, who has delivered me from every trouble, I do not condone such actions. **10** When a man told me, 'Saul is dead,' thinking he was bringing me good news, I seized him and put him to death in Ziklag (a Philistine city in southern Israel), which was the 'reward' I gave him for his message, as I will not tolerate those who harm the anointed. **11** How much more, then—when wicked men have killed an innocent man in his own house, while lying on his bed—should I not demand justice from you for his blood and cleanse the earth of such wrongdoers!" **12** So David gave a strict order to his men, and they killed Rekab and Baanah. To show his anger at their betrayal, they cut off their hands and feet and displayed their bodies by hanging them near the pool of Hebron, making an example of them. However, they took Ish-Bosheth's head and gave it an honorable burial in Abner's tomb in Hebron.

Chapter 5

1 All the tribes of Israel came to David at Hebron (a city located in the southern part of Israel) and said, "We are your own flesh and blood." **2** "In the past, when Saul was king over us, you were the one who led Israel in military campaigns. And the LORD said to you, 'You will shepherd My people Israel, and you will become their ruler.'" **3** When all the elders of Israel came to King David at Hebron, the king made a covenant with them before the LORD, and they anointed David as king over Israel. **4** David was thirty years old when he became king, and he reigned for forty years. **5** He reigned in Hebron over the tribe of Judah (the southern kingdom) for seven years and six months, and in Jerusalem (a city that became the capital of ancient Israel) he reigned over all Israel and Judah for thirty-three years. **6** The king and his men marched to Jerusalem to attack the Jebusites (the original inhabitants of Jerusalem). The Jebusites taunted David, saying, "You will never

enter here. Even the blind and the lame could defend this city against you." They believed, "David cannot get in here." **7** But David captured the fortress of Zion (a part of Jerusalem, which became known as the City of David), and he took it as his own. **8** On the day of the conquest, David said, "Anyone who wants to defeat the Jebusites must use the water shaft to reach the blind and the lame, who are my enemies." This is why it is said, "The blind and the lame will not enter the palace." **9** David then made the fortress his home, calling it the City of David. He built up the surrounding area, from the terraces inward, strengthening the city. **10** David grew stronger and more powerful, because the LORD God Almighty was with him. **11** Hiram, king of Tyre (a city in modern-day Lebanon), sent envoys to David, along with cedar logs, carpenters, and stonemasons, who built a palace for David. **12** David knew that the LORD had established him as king over Israel and had exalted his kingdom for the sake of God's people. **13** After leaving Hebron, David took more wives and concubines in Jerusalem, and more sons and daughters were born to him. **14** These are the names of the children born to David in Jerusalem: Shammua, Shobab, Nathan, Solomon, **15** Ibhar, Elishua, Nepheg, Japhia, **16** Elishama, Eliada, and Eliphelet. **17** When the Philistines heard that David had been anointed king over Israel, they went up in full force to search for him. But David heard about it and went down to his stronghold (a place of defense). **18** The Philistines spread out in the Valley of Rephaim (a valley located south of Jerusalem, near modern Bethlehem). **19** David asked the LORD, "Should I go and attack the Philistines? Will You deliver them into my hands?" The LORD answered him, "Go, for I will surely deliver the Philistines into your hands." **20** So David went to Baal Perazim (meaning "The Lord of Breaking Through") and there he defeated them. David said, "The LORD has broken through my enemies like a mighty flood." For this reason, the place was called Baal Perazim. **21** The Philistines left their idols behind, and David and his men carried them off. **22** Once more the Philistines came up and spread out in the Valley of Rephaim. **23** David inquired of the LORD, and the LORD answered, "Do not go directly up to them. Instead, circle around behind them and attack them near the poplar trees." **24** "As soon as you hear the sound of marching in the tops of the poplar trees, move quickly, because it will mean the LORD has gone out in front of you to strike the Philistine army." **25** David did as the LORD commanded him, and he struck down the Philistines from Gibeon (a city located about 8 miles north of Jerusalem) to Gezer (a city located about 15 miles west of Jerusalem).

Chapter 6

1 David gathered together all the able young men of Israel—thirty thousand. **2** He and all his men went to Baalah in Judah (also called Kiriath Jearim, a city in Judah) to bring up from there the ark of God, which is called by the Name, the name of the LORD Almighty, who is enthroned between the cherubim (angelic figures) on the ark. **3** They set the ark of God on a new cart and brought it from the house of Abinadab, which was on the hill. Uzzah and Ahio, sons of Abinadab, were guiding the new cart. **4** Uzzah and Ahio were driving the cart with the ark of God on it, and Ahio was walking in front of it. **5** David and all Israel celebrated with all their might before the LORD, using castanets, harps, lyres, timbrels (tambourines), sistrums (a type of percussion instrument), and cymbals to worship God. **6** When they came to the threshing floor of Nakon (a location in Israel, likely near the road leading to Jerusalem), Uzzah reached out and took hold of the ark of God because the oxen stumbled. **7** The LORD's angers burned against Uzzah because of his irreverent act (he touched the ark, which was forbidden); therefore, God struck him down, and he died there beside the ark of God. **8** David was angry because the LORD's wrath had broken out against Uzzah, and to this day that place is called Perez Uzzah (meaning "The Breakout of Uzzah," remembering God's judgment on Uzzah). **9** David was afraid of the LORD that day and said, "How can the ark of the LORD ever come to me?" **10** David was not willing to take the ark of the LORD to be with him in the City of David (Jerusalem). Instead, he took it to the house of Obed-Edom the Gittite (a man from Gath, a Philistine city). **11** The ark of the LORD remained in the house of Obed-Edom the Gittite for three months, and the LORD blessed him and his entire household. **12** Now King David was told, "The LORD has blessed the household of Obed-Edom and everything he has, because of the ark of God." So David went to bring up the ark of God from the house of Obed-Edom to the City of David with great rejoicing. **13** When those who were carrying the ark of the LORD had taken six steps, David sacrificed a bull and a fattened calf. **14** Wearing a linen ephod (a simple priestly garment), David danced before the LORD with all his might. **15** While David and all Israel were bringing up the ark of the LORD with shouts and the sound of trumpets, they celebrated joyfully and reverently. **16** As the ark of the LORD was entering the City of David, Michal, daughter of Saul (David's wife), watched from a window. When she saw King David leaping and dancing before the LORD, she despised him in her heart. **17** They brought the ark of the LORD and set it in its place inside the tent that David had pitched for it. (David had prepared a special tent to house the ark.) David then sacrificed burnt offerings and fellowship offerings before the LORD. **18** After he had finished offering the burnt offerings and fellowship offerings, he blessed the people in the name of the LORD Almighty. **19** Then David gave a loaf of bread, a cake of dates, and a cake of raisins to each person in the entire crowd of Israelites, both men and women. (This was an act of generosity and celebration.) After this, all the people went to their homes. **20** When David returned home to bless his household, Michal, daughter of Saul, came out to meet him and said, "How the king of Israel has distinguished himself today, going around half-naked in full view of the slave girls of his servants, as any vulgar fellow would!" **21** David replied to Michal, "It was before the LORD, who chose me rather than your father (Saul) or anyone from his house when He appointed me ruler over the LORD's people Israel. I will celebrate before the LORD." **22** "I will become even more undignified than this, and I will be humiliated in my own eyes. But by these slave girls you spoke of, I will be held in honor." **23** And Michal, daughter of Saul, had no children to the day of her death. (Her barrenness was seen as a consequence of her disdain for David's worship of God.)

Chapter 7

1 After the king was settled in his palace and the LORD had given him rest from all his enemies around him, **2** he said to Nathan the prophet, "Here I am, living in a house of cedar, while the ark of God remains in a tent." **3** Nathan replied to the king, "Whatever you have in mind, go ahead and do it, for the LORD is with you." **4** But that night the word of the LORD came to Nathan, saying: **5** "Go and tell my servant David, 'This is what the LORD says: Are you the one to build me a house to dwell in? **6** I have not dwelt in a house from the day I brought the Israelites up out of Egypt to this day. I have been moving from place to place with a tent as my dwelling. **7** Wherever I have moved with all the Israelites, did I ever say to any of their rulers whom I commanded to shepherd my people Israel, "Why have you not built me a house of cedar?" **8** "Now then, tell my servant David, 'This is what the LORD Almighty says: I took you from the pasture, from tending the flock, and appointed you ruler over my people Israel. **9** I have been with you wherever you have gone, and I have cut off all your enemies from before you. Now I will make your name great, like the names of the greatest men on earth. **10** And I will provide a place for my people Israel and will plant them so that they can have a home of their own and no longer be disturbed. Wicked people will not oppress them anymore, as they did at the beginning **11** and have done ever since the time I appointed leaders over my people Israel. I will also give you rest from all your enemies. " 'The LORD declares to you that the LORD himself will establish a house for you: **12** When your days are over and you rest with your ancestors, I will raise up your offspring to succeed you, your own flesh and blood, and I will establish his kingdom. **13** He is the one who will build a house for my Name, and I will establish the throne of his kingdom forever. **14** I will be his father, and he will be my son. When he does wrong, I will punish him with a rod wielded by men, with floggings inflicted by human hands. **15** But my love will never be taken away from him, as I took it away from Saul, whom I removed from before you. **16** Your house and your kingdom will endure forever before me; your throne will be established forever." **17** Nathan reported to David all the words of this entire revelation. **18** Then King David went in and sat before the LORD, and he said: "Who am I, Sovereign LORD, and what is my family, that you have brought me this far? **19** And as if this were not enough in your sight, Sovereign LORD, you have also spoken about the future of the house of your servant— and this decree, Sovereign LORD, is for a mere human! **20** "What more

can David say to you? For you know your servant, Sovereign LORD. **21** For the sake of your word and according to your will, you have done this great thing and made it known to your servant. **22** "How great you are, Sovereign LORD! There is no one like you, and there is no God but you, as we have heard with our own ears. **23** And who is like your people Israel—the one nation on earth that God went out to redeem as a people for himself, and to make a name for himself, and to perform great and awesome wonders by driving out nations and their gods from before your people, whom you redeemed from Egypt? **24** You have established your people Israel as your very own forever, and you, LORD, have become their God. **25** "And now, LORD God, keep forever the promise you have made concerning your servant and his house. Do as you promised, **26** so that your name will be great forever. Then people will say, 'The LORD Almighty is God over Israel!' And the house of your servant David will be established in your sight. **27** "LORD Almighty, God of Israel, you have revealed this to your servant, saying, 'I will build a house for you.' So your servant has found courage to pray this prayer to you. **28** Sovereign LORD, you are God! Your covenant is trustworthy, and you have promised these good things to your servant. **29** Now be pleased to bless the house of your servant, that it may continue forever in your sight; for you, Sovereign LORD, have spoken, and with your blessing the house of your servant will be blessed forever."

Chapter 8

1 In time, David defeated the Philistines and subdued them. He also took Metheg Ammah from the control of the Philistines. **2** David also defeated the Moabites. He had them lie down on the ground and measured them with a cord. Every two lengths of them, he put to death, and the third length was spared. So the Moabites became subject to David and brought him tribute. **3** Moreover, David defeated Hadadezer, king of Zobah, when he went to restore his monument at the Euphrates River. **4** David captured a thousand of his chariots, seven thousand charioteers, and twenty thousand foot soldiers. He hamstrung all but a hundred of the chariot horses. **5** When the Arameans of Damascus came to help Hadadezer, David struck down twenty-two thousand of them. **6** David set up garrisons in the Aramean kingdom of Damascus, and the Arameans became subject to him and brought tribute. The LORD gave David victory wherever he went. **7** David took the gold shields that belonged to the officers of Hadadezer and brought them to Jerusalem. **8** From Tebah and Berothai, David took a great quantity of bronze. **9** When Tou, king of Hamath, heard that David had defeated Hadadezer's entire army, he sent his son Joram to David to congratulate him on his victory. **10** Joram brought silver, gold, and bronze to David as gifts. **11** David dedicated these articles to the LORD, as he had done with all the silver and gold he had taken from the nations he had subdued. **12** These nations included Edom, Moab, the Ammonites, the Philistines, and the Amalekites. He also dedicated the plunder from Hadadezer, son of Rehob, king of Zobah. **13** David became famous after returning from striking down eighteen thousand Edomites in the Valley of Salt. **14** He set up garrisons throughout Edom, and all the Edomites became subject to him. The LORD gave David victory wherever he went. **15** David reigned over all Israel, doing what was just and right for all his people. **16** Joab, son of Zeruiah, was commander of the army; Jehoshaphat, son of Ahilud, was the recorder. **17** Zadok, son of Ahitub, and Ahimelek, son of Abiathar, were priests; Seraiah was the secretary. **18** Benaiah, son of Jehoiada, was in charge of the Kerethites and Pelethites; and David's sons were priests.

Chapter 9

1 David asked, "Is there anyone still left from the house of Saul to whom I can show kindness for Jonathan's sake?" **2** Now there was a servant of Saul's household named Ziba. They summoned him to appear before David, and the king asked him, "Are you Ziba?" "At your service," he replied. **3** The king asked, "Is there no one still alive from the house of Saul to whom I can show God's kindness?" Ziba answered the king, "There is still a son of Jonathan; he is lame (unable to walk) in both feet." **4** "Where is he?" the king asked. Ziba answered, "He is at the house of Makir son of Ammiel in Lo Debar (Lo Debar means 'no pasture,' a place in the region east of the Jordan River)." **5** So King David had him brought from Lo Debar, from the house of Makir son of Ammiel. **6** When Mephibosheth (son of Jonathan, grandson of Saul) came to David, he bowed down to pay him honor. David said, "Mephibosheth!" "At your service," he replied. 7 "Don't be afraid," David said to him, "for I will surely show you kindness for the sake of your father Jonathan. I will restore (give back) to you all the land that belonged to your grandfather Saul, and you will always eat at my table." 8 Mephibosheth bowed down and said, "What is your servant, that you should notice a dead dog (a humble term, meaning unworthy or insignificant) like me?" 9 Then the king summoned Ziba, Saul's steward (household manager), and said to him, "I have given your master's grandson everything that belonged to Saul and his family. 10 You and your sons and your servants are to farm (cultivate) the land for him and bring in the crops, so that your master's grandson may be provided for. And Mephibosheth will always eat at my table." (Now Ziba had fifteen sons and twenty servants.) 11 Then Ziba said to the king, "Your servant will do whatever my lord the king commands his servant to do." So Mephibosheth ate at David's table like one of the king's sons. 12 Mephibosheth had a young son named Mika, and all the members of Ziba's household were servants of Mephibosheth. 13. And Mephibosheth lived in Jerusalem because he always ate at the king's table; he was lame in both feet.

Chapter 10

1 In time, the king of the Ammonites (a people living east of Israel) died, and his son Hanun (the new king of the Ammonites) succeeded him. 2 David thought, "I will show kindness to Hanun son of Nahash (Nahash was the previous king who had shown kindness to David) just as his father showed kindness to me." So David sent a delegation (group of representatives) to express his sympathy to Hanun concerning his father's death. When David's men arrived in the land of the Ammonites, 3 the Ammonite commanders said to Hanun their lord, "Do you think David is honoring your father by sending envoys (representatives) to express sympathy? Hasn't David sent them only to spy on the city and to find a way to overthrow it?" 4 So Hanun seized David's envoys, shaved off half of each man's beard (shaving a beard was a sign of dishonor in ancient Israel), cut off their garments at the buttocks (a humiliating act), and sent them away in disgrace (dishonor). 5 When David heard about this, he sent messengers to meet the men, for they were greatly humiliated. The king said, "Stay at Jericho (a city located about 15 miles west of the Jordan River) until your beards have grown back, and then return." 6 When the Ammonites realized they had angered David, they hired twenty thousand Aramean foot soldiers from Beth Rehob (a town northeast of Israel) and Zobah (a region to the north of Damascus), along with the king of Maakah (a kingdom southeast of Israel) with a thousand men, and twelve thousand men from Tob (a region northeast of Ammon). 7 Upon hearing this, David sent Joab (David's general) out with the entire army of Israel's fighting men. 8 The Ammonites came out and arranged their troops at the entrance of their city gate, while the Arameans from Zobah, Rehob, Tob, and Maakah were positioned in the open field. 9 Joab saw that there were enemy forces both in front of him and behind him, so he selected some of Israel's best troops and deployed (arranged strategically) them against the Arameans. 10 He put the rest of the men under the command of Abishai (Joab's brother) and deployed them against the Ammonites. 11 Joab said, "If the Arameans are too strong for me, you must come to my rescue; but if the Ammonites are too strong for you, I will come to your rescue. 12 Be strong, and let us fight bravely for our people and the cities of our God. The LORD will do what is good in his eyes." 13 Then Joab and his troops advanced to fight the Arameans, and the Arameans fled before him. 14 When the Ammonites saw that the Arameans had fled, they also fled before Abishai and retreated inside the city. So Joab returned from fighting the Ammonites and went back to Jerusalem. 15 After the Arameans saw that they had been defeated by Israel, they regrouped. 16 Hadadezer (the king of Zobah) brought more Arameans from beyond the Euphrates River (the great river flowing through Mesopotamia). They went to Helam (a town in northern Syria), and Shobak (the commander of Hadadezer's army) led them. 17 When David was informed of this, he gathered all Israel, crossed the Jordan River, and went to Helam. The Arameans formed their battle lines to meet David and fought against him. 18 But the Arameans fled before Israel, and David killed seven hundred of their charioteers and forty thousand of their foot soldiers. He also struck down Shobak, the

commander of their army, and he died there. 19 When all the kings who were vassals (subjects or servants) of Hadadezer saw that they had been defeated by Israel, they made peace with the Israelites and became subject to them. As a result, the Arameans were no longer willing to assist the Ammonites.

Chapter 11

1 In the spring, at the time when kings typically go off to war, David sent Joab (David's military commander) out with the king's men and the entire Israelite army. They destroyed the Ammonites (an ancient Semitic people who lived to the east of Israel, in what is now Jordan) and besieged (surrounded with armed forces) Rabbah (the capital of Ammon, located in modern-day Amman, the capital of Jordan). But David remained in Jerusalem. 2 One evening, David got up from his bed and walked around on the roof of the palace. From the roof, he saw a woman bathing. The woman was very beautiful. 3 So David sent someone to inquire (ask) about her. The man returned and said, "She is Bathsheba, the daughter of Eliam (Eliam was one of David's mighty warriors, whose family was associated with the tribe of Judah) and wife of Uriah the Hittite (Uriah was a Hittite soldier in David's army, a people originally from Anatolia, now in modern-day Turkey)." 4 Then David sent messengers to bring her to him. She came to him, and he slept with her. (At the time, she was purifying herself from her monthly uncleanness, a ritual purification after menstruation.) Afterward, she returned to her house. 5 Later, Bathsheba sent word to David saying, "I am pregnant." 6 So David sent word to Joab, "Send me Uriah the Hittite." And Joab sent Uriah to David. 7 When Uriah came to him, David asked him how Joab and the soldiers were, and how the war was progressing. 8 Then David said to Uriah, "Go down to your house and wash your feet." So Uriah left the palace, and a gift from the king was sent after him. 9 However, Uriah slept at the entrance to the palace with all of his master's servants and did not go down to his house. 10 David was told, "Uriah did not go home." So he asked Uriah, "Haven't you just come from a military campaign? Why didn't you go home?" 11 Uriah said to David, "The ark of God and Israel and Judah are staying in tents, and my commander Joab and my lord's men are camped in the open country. How could I go to my house to eat and drink and make love to my wife? As surely as you live, I will not do such a thing!" 12 Then David said to him, "Stay here one more day, and tomorrow I will send you back." So Uriah remained in Jerusalem that day and the next. 13 At David's invitation, he ate and drank with him, and David made him drunk. But in the evening, Uriah went out to sleep on his mat among his master's servants; he did not go home. 14 In the morning, David wrote a letter to Joab and sent it with Uriah. 15 In it, he wrote, "Put Uriah out in front where the fighting is fiercest. Then withdraw (pull back) from him so that he will be struck down and die." 16 So while Joab had the city under siege (surrounded and blocked off), he put Uriah at a place where he knew the strongest defenders were. 17 When the men of the city came out and fought against Joab, some of the men in David's army fell; moreover, Uriah the Hittite died. 18 Joab sent David a full account of the battle. 19 He instructed the messenger, "When you have finished giving the king this account of the battle, 20 the king's anger may flare up (become very angry), and he may ask you, 'Why did you get so close to the city to fight? Didn't you know they would shoot arrows from the wall? 21 Who killed Abimelek son of Jerub-Besheth? Didn't a woman drop an upper millstone on him from the wall, so that he died in Thebez (a town in Israel)? Why did you get so close to the wall?' If he asks you this, then say to him, 'Moreover, your servant Uriah the Hittite is dead.'" 22 The messenger set out, and when he arrived, he told David everything Joab had sent him to say. 23 The messenger said to David, "The men overpowered us and came out against us in the open, but we drove them back to the entrance of the city gate. 24 Then the archers shot arrows at your servants from the wall, and some of the king's men died. Moreover, your servant Uriah the Hittite is dead." 25 David told the messenger, "Say this to Joab: 'Don't let this upset you (disturb you); the sword devours one as well as another. Press the attack against the city and destroy it.' Say this to encourage Joab." 26 When Uriah's wife heard that her husband was dead, she mourned for him. 27 After the time of mourning was over, David had her brought to his house, and she became his wife and bore him a son. But the thing David had done displeased the LORD.

Chapter 12

1 The LORD sent Nathan (prophet to King David) to David. Nathan came to him and said, "There were two men in a certain town—a rich man and a poor man. **2** The rich man had many flocks of sheep and herds of cattle, **3** but the poor man had nothing except for a small ewe lamb (female sheep) he had bought. He raised it with his children, and the lamb ate from his plate, drank from his cup, and even slept in his arms like a daughter to him. **4** Now, a traveler came to visit the rich man, but instead of taking one of his own sheep or cattle to prepare a meal for the guest, the rich man took the poor man's lamb and made it into a meal for the traveler. **5** David burned with anger against the man and said to Nathan, "As surely as the LORD lives, the man who did this must die! **6** He must pay for that lamb four times over, because he did such a thing and had no pity." **7** Then Nathan said to David, "You are the man! This is what the LORD, the God of Israel, says: 'I anointed you king over Israel, and I delivered you from the hand of Saul (first king of Israel). **8** I gave you your master's house and his wives into your arms. I gave you all Israel and Judah. And if all this had been too little, I would have given you even more. **9** Why then have you despised the word of the LORD by doing what is evil in His eyes? You struck down Uriah (Hittite soldier in David's army) with the sword and took his wife, Bathsheba (wife of Uriah, David's lover), to be your own. You killed him with the sword of the Ammonites (enemies of Israel). **10** Now, therefore, the sword will never depart from your house, because you despised me and took the wife of Uriah to be your own.'" **11** "This is what the LORD says: 'Out of your own household I am going to bring calamity on you. Before your very eyes, I will take your wives and give them to one who is close to you, and he will sleep with your wives in broad daylight. **12** You did it in secret, but I will do this thing in broad daylight before all Israel.'" **13** Then David said to Nathan, "I have sinned against the LORD." **14** Nathan replied, "The LORD has taken away your sin. You are not going to die. **15** But because by doing this you have shown utter contempt for the LORD, the son born to you will die." **16** After Nathan had gone home, the LORD struck the child that Uriah's wife had borne to David, and he became ill. **17** David pleaded with God for the child. He fasted and spent the nights lying on the ground in sackcloth (a rough fabric worn as a sign of mourning). **18** The elders of his household stood beside him to get him up from the ground, but he refused, and he would not eat any food with them. **19** On the seventh day the child died. David's attendants were afraid to tell him that the child was dead, for they thought, "While the child was still alive, he wouldn't listen to us when we spoke to him. How can we now tell him the child is dead? He may do something desperate." **20** David noticed that his attendants were whispering among themselves, and he realized the child was dead. "Is the child dead?" he asked. "Yes," they replied, "he is dead." **21** Then David got up from the ground. After he had washed, put on lotions, and changed his clothes, he went into the house of the LORD (the Tabernacle in Jerusalem) and worshiped. Then he went to his own house, and at his request they served him food, and he ate. **22** His attendants asked him, "Why are you acting this way? While the child was alive, you fasted and wept, but now that the child is dead, you get up and eat!" **23** He answered, "While the child was still alive, I fasted and wept. I thought, 'Who knows? The LORD may be gracious to me and let the child live.' **24** But now that he is dead, why should I continue fasting? Can I bring him back again? I will go to him, but he will not return to me." **25** Then David comforted his wife Bathsheba (daughter of Eliam, wife of Uriah), and he went to her and made love to her. She gave birth to a son, and they named him Solomon (meaning "peaceful"). The LORD loved him, **26** and because the LORD loved him, He sent a message through Nathan the prophet, and told them to name him Jedidiah (meaning "beloved of the LORD"). **27** Meanwhile, Joab (David's military commander) fought against Rabbah (capital of the Ammonites, modern-day Amman, Jordan) of the Ammonites, and captured the royal citadel (the fortified center of the city). **28** Joab sent messengers to David, saying, "I have fought against Rabbah and taken its water supply. **29** Now gather the rest of the troops and besiege the city and capture it. Otherwise, I will take the city, and it will be named after me." **30** So David gathered all his forces, marched to Rabbah, and attacked it. **31** David took the crown from the head of the Ammonite king and placed it on his own head. The crown weighed about a talent of gold (around 75 pounds or 34 kilograms),

and it was adorned with precious stones. David also took a large quantity of plunder from the city. **32** He brought out the people who were there and made them work with saws, iron picks, and axes, and he forced them to work in brickmaking. David did this to all the Ammonite cities. Then he and his entire army returned to Jerusalem.

Chapter 13

1 In due time, Amnon, the son of King David (David, second king of Israel, ruled from Jerusalem, now located in modern Israel), fell in love with Tamar, the beautiful sister of Absalom, another son of David. **2** Amnon became so consumed with desire for his sister Tamar that he made himself sick. Since she was a virgin (unmarried and protected according to custom), he thought there was no way to approach her. **3** Amnon had a friend named Jonadab, the son of David's brother Shimeah (Shimeah, David's brother, was part of the royal family). Jonadab was known for being very cunning (clever and manipulative). **4** Jonadab asked him, "Why do you, the king's son, look so weak and troubled every morning? Please tell me what's wrong." Amnon replied, "I am in love with Tamar, my brother Absalom's sister." **5** Jonadab suggested, "Lie down and pretend to be ill. When your father visits, ask him to send Tamar to prepare food in your sight so that you can watch her and eat from her hand." **6** So Amnon lay down and pretended to be ill. When King David (David, the ruler of Israel) came to see him, Amnon said, "Please let my sister Tamar come and make some special bread in my sight, so I may eat from her hand." **7** David sent a message to Tamar at the palace, instructing her, "Go to your brother Amnon's house and prepare some food for him." **8** Tamar went to her brother Amnon's house, where he was lying down. She took some dough, kneaded it, made the bread in his sight, and baked it. **9** She brought the pan to him and served the bread, but he refused to eat. Amnon ordered, "Send everyone out of here." So everyone left. **10** Then Amnon said to Tamar, "Bring the food here to my bedroom, so I may eat from your hand." Tamar took the bread she had prepared and brought it to him in his bedroom. **11** But when she brought it to him, he grabbed her and said, "Come to bed with me, my sister." **12** "No, my brother!" she protested. "Don't force me! Such a disgraceful thing should never be done in Israel (the nation ruled by David). Don't do this wicked act. **13** Where would I take my shame? And you would be seen as one of the worst men in Israel. Please, speak to the king; he would not refuse to let us marry." **14** But Amnon would not listen, and because he was stronger, he overpowered and violated her. **15** Afterwards, Amnon's feelings turned to intense hatred for her—more than he had loved her before. He said, "Get up and leave!" **16** "No!" Tamar replied. "Sending me away is even worse than what you've done." But he refused to listen. **17** He called his servant and ordered, "Take this woman out of my sight and lock the door after her." **18** So his servant put her out and locked the door. Tamar wore a richly decorated robe, which was the kind worn by the king's virgin daughters. **19** Tamar put ashes on her head (a sign of mourning and shame), tore her ornate robe, put her hands on her head, and went away crying loudly. **20** Her brother Absalom (David's third son and a prince) asked her, "Has Amnon, your brother, been with you? Be quiet for now, my sister; he is your brother. Don't take this matter to heart." Tamar lived, desolate and ashamed, in her brother Absalom's house. **21** When King David heard all of this, he was furious. **22** Absalom never spoke to Amnon again, neither good nor bad, for he despised him for disgracing his sister Tamar. **23** Two years later, when Absalom's sheepshearers were at Baal Hazor (a town near Ephraim, an area in the northern kingdom of ancient Israel, located in the present-day West Bank), he invited all the king's sons to join him for a celebration. **24** Absalom went to the king and said, "Your servant is having his sheep sheared (a festive time associated with celebration and feasting). Will the king and his attendants come along with me?" **25** The king replied, "No, my son, we should not all go, or it would be a burden on you." Although Absalom urged him, King David declined but gave him his blessing. **26** Then Absalom requested, "If you will not go, please let my brother Amnon come with us." The king questioned him, "Why should Amnon go with you?" **27** But Absalom continued to press the king, so he allowed Amnon and all the other king's sons to go with Absalom. **28** Absalom commanded his servants, "Listen carefully! When Amnon is in high spirits from drinking wine and I give you the signal, strike Amnon down. Do not be afraid; I am ordering you to do this. Be strong and courageous!" **29** So Absalom's servants did as he commanded and killed Amnon. At this, all the king's sons immediately got up, mounted their mules (common mounts for travel in ancient Israel), and fled. **30** While they were on their way, a report reached King David: "Absalom has killed all the king's sons; not one of them is left!" **31** In great distress, the king stood up, tore his clothes (a traditional act of grief and mourning), and lay on the ground, while all his attendants also tore their clothes in mourning. **32** But Jonadab, son of David's brother Shimeah (Jonadab, a close advisor, was aware of Absalom's grudge), said to the king, "My lord should not assume that all the king's sons have been killed. Only Amnon is dead. Absalom has planned this since the day Amnon violated his sister Tamar. **33** So, my lord the king, do not be alarmed by the report that all your sons are dead. Only Amnon has died." **34** Meanwhile, Absalom fled. The watchman looked out and saw a crowd approaching along the hillside road west of him. He went and told the king, "I see men coming down the road from the Horonaim hillside (an ancient road in Israel; exact location unknown)." **35** Jonadab said to the king, "See, the king's sons are coming; it has happened just as I, your servant, said." **36** As he finished speaking, the king's sons arrived, weeping loudly. King David and all his attendants also wept bitterly. **37** After the incident, Absalom fled and went to Talmai son of Ammihud, the king of Geshur (Geshur was a kingdom in the region of the Golan Heights, part of present-day Syria). King David mourned many days for his son. **38** After fleeing to Geshur, Absalom stayed there for three years. **39** King David, although saddened over Amnon's death, began to long for Absalom, as his grief for Amnon eventually eased.

Chapter 14

1 Joab, son of Zeruiah, was aware that King David still deeply longed for his son Absalom, whom he had exiled due to his crime. **2** To help resolve this, Joab sent for a wise woman from the town of Tekoa (a town located in southern Judah, near Bethlehem). He instructed her, "Put on mourning clothes, and do not use any oils or lotions to freshen yourself. Act as though you have been mourning the death of someone for a long time. **3** Once you're prepared, go to the king and speak the words I tell you." **4** The woman from Tekoa obeyed and went to the king. She bowed low before him, showing her respect, and cried out, "Help me, Your Majesty!" **5** The king responded, "What is troubling you?" **6** She explained, "I am a widow, and my husband is dead. **7** I had two sons, and they fought in the field. No one was there to stop them, and one struck the other and killed him. **8** Now, the rest of my family demands that my surviving son be handed over to them, so they can avenge my son's death by executing him. They say, 'We must kill the man who murdered his brother,' and in doing so, they would end the family line of my late husband. There would be no one left to carry on his name and legacy." **9** The king said to the woman, "Go back home, and I will make sure to give you justice in this matter." **10** But the woman from Tekoa said to him, "Let my lord the king pardon me and my family. May the king's throne remain innocent and free from blame." **11** The king reassured her, "If anyone tries to harm you, bring them to me, and I will make sure they are stopped." **12** The woman continued, "Please, let the king invoke the LORD his God to prevent the avenger of blood (a family member who has the right to kill the murderer) from adding more bloodshed, so that my son will not be destroyed." The king replied, "As surely as the LORD lives, not a single hair on your son's head will fall to the ground." **13** Then the woman said, "Let me speak one more word to my lord the king." **14** The king said, "Speak." **15** The woman responded, "Why then have you devised a plan like this against the people of God? When the king pronounces such a sentence, doesn't he condemn himself as well? After all, the king has failed to bring back his own son who has been exiled. **16** Just as water poured out on the ground cannot be gathered back, so it is with our lives—one day we must all die. But God does not desire our destruction. He makes a way to bring back those who are lost, so that they are not forever cast out from His presence. **17** I have come to speak to the king, because the people of the land have caused me fear. I thought, 'I will go to the king. Perhaps he will hear my plea. **18** Maybe he will decide to act and restore my inheritance, saving me and my son from the man who seeks to sever us from God's blessings.' **19** Now, I pray that the king's word will secure my inheritance. For you, my lord, are like an angel of God in your wisdom, discerning both good and evil.

May the LORD your God be with you." **20** The king said to the woman, "Do not hide anything from me about what I am about to ask." **21** She responded, "Let my lord, the king, speak." **22** The king asked, "Isn't this whole plan your servant Joab's doing?" The woman answered, "As surely as you live, my lord the king, no one can turn aside from the words you speak. Yes, it was your servant Joab who directed me to do this, and he put these words into my mouth. **23** Joab is trying to change the course of events, but you, my lord, have wisdom like that of an angel of God—you see the bigger picture and understand everything happening in the land." **24** The king replied to Joab, "Very well, I will grant your request. Go and bring Absalom back to Jerusalem." **25** Joab fell face down in front of the king to show his gratitude, and he blessed the king, saying, "Today, your servant knows that he has found favor in your eyes, my lord the king, because you have granted my request." **26** Then Joab went to Geshur (a kingdom to the northeast of Israel, near modern-day Syria) and brought Absalom back to Jerusalem. **27** However, the king instructed, "Absalom must go to his own house. He is not to appear before me." So Absalom returned to his house and did not come before the king. **28** Absalom became known for his extraordinary beauty. In fact, there was no man in all of Israel whose appearance was more admired than his. From the top of his head to the soles of his feet, he was flawless. **29** Once a year, Absalom would cut his hair because it grew so thick. When he did, he would weigh it, and the hair would weigh about 200 shekels by the royal standard (approximately 5 pounds or 2.3 kilograms). **30** Absalom had three sons and a beautiful daughter named Tamar. She was known for her great beauty. **31** Absalom lived in Jerusalem for two full years without being allowed to see the king's face. **32** Then Absalom sent for Joab to ask him to go to the king on his behalf, but Joab refused to come. Absalom sent for him a second time, but again Joab refused. **33** So Absalom instructed his servants, "Joab's field is next to mine, and he has barley growing there. Go and set it on fire." Absalom's servants set Joab's field on fire. **34** Joab came to Absalom's house and demanded, "Why have your servants burned my field?" **35** Absalom answered, "I sent for you to come so that I could ask you to go to the king on my behalf. I want to see the king's face. I said, 'It would have been better for me to remain in Geshur than to come back here.' If I am guilty of any offense, let the king put me to death." **36** Joab went to the king and relayed what Absalom had said. Then the king summoned Absalom. When Absalom came before the king, he bowed down with his face to the ground, and the king kissed him.

Chapter 15

1 After some time, Absalom provided himself with a chariot and horses, and he appointed fifty men to run ahead of him as a display of power and importance. (A chariot was a symbol of status and strength in ancient Israel.) **2** Every morning, Absalom would rise early and stand by the side of the road that led to the city gate. The city gate was a place of public gatherings, where legal matters were settled. Whenever someone came with a complaint to present to the king, Absalom would ask them, "What town do you come from?" **3** The person would respond, "I am your servant, from one of the tribes of Israel." Israel was divided into several tribal regions, each with its own set of leaders. **4** Absalom would reply, "Your case is just and right, but there is no one appointed by the king to hear you." (Implying that the king's administration was not functioning effectively.) **5** He would continue, "If only I were made a judge in the land! Then everyone who has a complaint or legal case could come to me, and I would make sure they received justice." (Absalom portrays himself as a more capable and caring ruler than his father, David.) **6** Absalom used this approach with all the Israelites who came to the king for justice. In this way, he won the hearts of the people of Israel, gaining their support and trust. (Stealing the hearts refers to winning their loyalty through flattery and promises.) **7** After four years, Absalom said to the king, "Please allow me to go to Hebron to fulfill a vow I made to the LORD." (Hebron was a significant city in Judah and the place where David was originally crowned king.) **8** "While I was in Geshur (a town in the region of Aram, northeast of Israel), I made a vow: 'If the LORD brings me back to Jerusalem, I will worship Him in Hebron.'" (Geshur was a neighboring region, and Absalom had spent time there in exile.) **9** The king said to him, "Go in peace." So Absalom set out for Hebron, leaving Jerusalem for the journey. (David's permission shows his trust in Absalom, not realizing his son's true intentions.) **10** But Absalom secretly sent messengers throughout all the tribes of Israel, instructing them, "When you hear the sound of the trumpet, declare, 'Absalom is king in Hebron.'" (A trumpet blast signaled the start of a rebellion, and Hebron became the base for Absalom's false claim to the throne.) **11** Two hundred men from Jerusalem had accompanied Absalom. They had no knowledge of the conspiracy and went with him as guests, unaware of the plot. (Absalom's manipulation of these men indicates how carefully he orchestrated his rebellion.) **12** While Absalom was offering sacrifices in Hebron, he sent for Ahithophel the Gilonite, David's trusted counselor, to join him. Ahithophel's support was crucial to the success of the conspiracy, as he was a respected advisor. (Giloh was a town in Judah, and Ahithophel had previously been loyal to David.) **13** A messenger came to David and reported, "The hearts of the people of Israel are with Absalom." (The people had been swayed by Absalom's charm and promises, and now they were beginning to support him.) **14** David said to his officials who were with him in Jerusalem, "We must flee immediately, or none of us will escape from Absalom. He will quickly overtake us, and he will destroy us and put the city to the sword." (David realized that Absalom had gathered a strong following and that delay would lead to his capture or death.) **15** The king's officials replied, "Your servants are ready to do whatever our lord the king commands." (The officials express their loyalty and willingness to follow David's lead.) **16** The king set out with his entire household, but he left ten concubines behind to manage the palace. (Concubines were secondary wives, and their role in the palace was to oversee its daily operations during the king's absence.) **17** So David and his people left Jerusalem, and they halted at the edge of the city. (They paused to prepare for the journey into the wilderness and to assess the situation.) **18** All of David's men marched past him, along with the Kerethites, Pelethites, and the six hundred Gittites who had accompanied him from Gath. (The Kerethites and Pelethites were foreign mercenaries loyal to David, and the Gittites were people from the Philistine city of Gath who had joined David's army.) **19** The king said to Ittai the Gittite, "Why should you come with us? You are a foreigner, an exile from your homeland. You only arrived yesterday, and today I am asking you to leave everything behind and follow me without knowing where I am going. Go back and stay with King Absalom. May the LORD show you kindness and faithfulness." (Ittai's loyalty was honored by David, even though he was a foreigner, as David recognized his faithfulness.) **20** But Ittai answered, "As surely as the LORD lives and as my lord the king lives, wherever you go, whether in life or death, I will be with you." (Ittai pledges his absolute loyalty to David, showing his deep commitment and allegiance.) **21** David said to him, "Go on ahead and march with us." So Ittai, along with all his men and their families, followed David. (Ittai's willingness to join David demonstrates the strength of David's relationships and the loyalty he inspired.) **22** The entire countryside wept as David and his people passed by. David crossed the Kidron Valley, and the people moved on toward the wilderness. (The Kidron Valley was a valley between Jerusalem and the Mount of Olives, and the wilderness refers to the desolate region beyond the city.) **23** Zadok, the priest, was there with the Levites, carrying the ark of the covenant of God. They set the ark down, and Abiathar, another priest, offered sacrifices as the people left the city. (The ark symbolized God's presence among His people, and the priests were ensuring its safety while David was fleeing.) **24** David said to Zadok, "Take the ark of God back into the city. If I find favor in the LORD's eyes, He will bring me back and allow me to see the ark and His dwelling place again. (David expresses his faith in God's will, surrendering to whatever God decides for him.) **25** But if He says, 'I am not pleased with you,' I am ready to accept His judgment. Let Him do whatever seems good to Him." (David acknowledges that God's decision is ultimate and that he must trust in His justice.) **26** The king also told Zadok the priest, "You and Abiathar return to the city. Take your sons, Ahimaaz and Jonathan, with you. I will wait at the fords (crossing points) in the wilderness until I hear from you." (David plans to stay hidden until he receives information from his loyal priests.) **27** Zadok and Abiathar took the ark back to Jerusalem, and they remained there. (The priests return to Jerusalem to ensure the ark remains in the holy city, while David continues his escape.) **28** David continued his journey up the Mount of Olives, weeping as he went. His head was covered, and he was barefoot, symbolizing his mourning and humility. (The Mount of Olives was a mountain east of Jerusalem, associated with prayer and sorrow.) **29** All the people with him also covered their heads and wept as they followed David into exile. (The mourning was a collective expression of grief, showing solidarity with the king.) **30** David was informed that Ahithophel, his trusted advisor, had joined the conspiracy with Absalom. David prayed, "LORD, turn Ahithophel's counsel into foolishness." (Ahithophel's wisdom had been highly regarded, but David now asks God to confuse his counsel.) **31** When David reached the summit of the Mount of Olives, where people used to worship God, he met Hushai the Arkite. Hushai had torn his robe and placed dust on his head, a sign of mourning and solidarity with David. (The summit was a place of prayer, and Hushai's presence indicated his loyalty to David.) **32** David said to Hushai, "If you go with me, you will be a burden to me. (David fears that Hushai's presence would slow him down and make him a target.) **33** But if you return to the city and tell Absalom, 'I will be your servant, just as I was your father's servant,' then you can help me by frustrating Ahithophel's advice. (David suggests a plan where Hushai can deceive Absalom by pretending to switch loyalty.) **34** "Won't Zadok and Abiathar the priests be there with you? Tell them anything you hear in the king's palace. (David wants Hushai to pass along important information via the priests' sons, Ahimaaz and Jonathan.) **35** Their two sons, Ahimaaz and Jonathan, will be there with them. Send them to me with any news you hear." (This creates a system of communication to keep David informed.) **36** So Hushai, David's confidant, returned to Jerusalem just as Absalom was entering the city. (Hushai's return marks the beginning of his secret mission to help David.)

Chapter 16

1. As David was moving past the top of the mountain, he encountered Ziba, the servant of Mephibosheth. Ziba had two donkeys, which were saddled (prepared with saddles) and carrying 200 loaves of bread, 100 clusters of raisins, 100 summer fruits, and a skin (container made from animal hide) of wine. **2.** The king asked Ziba, "What are you going to do with all these things?" Ziba replied, "The donkeys are for the king's household to use for riding, the bread and fruit are for the young men to eat, and the wine is for those who are weary (tired) in the wilderness to drink. **3.** David then inquired, "Where is the son of your master?" Ziba answered, "He is staying in Jerusalem because he believes that today the house of Israel will restore (bring back) the kingdom of my father to him." **4.** The king responded to Ziba, "Then everything that belongs to Mephibosheth is now yours." Ziba bowed low and said, "I humbly thank you, and may I find favor (approval) in your sight, my lord, the king!" **5.** As David entered Bahurim (a place near Jerusalem), a man from the family of Saul, named Shimei, came out and began to curse (speak with anger) David as he passed by. **6.** Shimei threw stones at David and his men, while all of David's soldiers and mighty men (strong warriors) were on either side of him. **7.** Shimei shouted, "Get out, you murderer, you scoundrel (a dishonest person)! **8.** The Lord has brought upon you all the bloodshed (killing) from the house of Saul, whom you have replaced. Now the Lord has given the kingdom to your son Absalom. You are receiving the punishment for your own evil actions!" **9.** Abishai, son of Zeruiah, said to the king, "Why should this worthless man (dead dog) curse my lord, the king? Let me go over and take off his head!" **10.** But the king replied, "What do I have to do with you, sons of Zeruiah? If the Lord has told him to curse, who are we to stop him?" **11.** David continued, "If my own son seeks my life, how much more should I allow this man from the tribe (family group) of Benjamin to do so? Let him curse, for the Lord has commanded him." **12.** "Perhaps the Lord will look at my affliction (suffering) and repay me with good for the evil he has done to me today." **13.** As David and his men continued on their journey, Shimei walked along the hillside (side of a hill) opposite them, continuing to curse, throw stones, and throw dust at them. **14.** When they became weary, the king and his men stopped to rest (took a break) there. **15.** Meanwhile, Absalom and all the Israelites arrived in Jerusalem, with Ahithophel at his side. **16.** When Hushai, David's loyal friend, came to Absalom, he said, "Long live the king! Long live the king!" **17.** Absalom asked Hushai, "Is this your loyalty (faithfulness) to your friend? Why didn't you go with him?" **18.** Hushai answered, "No, I will remain with the one whom the Lord, this people, and all Israel choose. I will serve (work for) the one in whose presence (being near) I am now." **19.** Hushai continued, "Whom should I serve? Should I not serve the son of the king, just as I served your father?" **20.** Absalom then asked Ahithophel, "What should we do?" **21.** Ahithophel suggested (gave advice), "Go into your father's concubines (women who lived with a man but were not his wife), whom he left to care for the palace. Then all Israel will know that you have made yourself utterly abhorrent (disgusting) to your father, and your supporters will be strengthened." **22.** So they set up a tent on the roof, and Absalom went into his father's concubines in full view of all Israel. **23.** Ahithophel's counsel was highly regarded (considered wise) at that time, as if it had been the word of God, both by David and by Absalom.

Chapter 17

1. Moreover, Ahithophel said to Absalom, "Now let me choose twelve thousand men, and I will arise and pursue (follow) David tonight." **2.** "I will come upon him while he is weary (very tired) and weak, and make him afraid. And all the people who are with him will flee, and I will strike only the king." **3.** "Then I will bring back all the people to you. When all return except (excluding) the man whom you seek, all the people will be at peace." **4.** And the saying pleased Absalom and all the elders (leaders) of Israel. **5.** Then Absalom said, "Now call Hushai the Archite (a man from Archi, a town), also, and let us hear what he says too." **6.** And when Hushai came to Absalom, Absalom spoke to him, saying, "Ahithophel has spoken in this manner. Shall we do as he says? If not, speak up." **7.** So Hushai said to Absalom: "The advice that Ahithophel has given is not good at this time." **8.** For," said Hushai, "you know your father and his men, that they are mighty (strong) men, and they are enraged (angry) in their minds, like a bear robbed of her cubs in the field; and your father is a man of war, and will not camp (rest) with the people." **9.** Surely by now he is hidden in some pit (hole), or in some other place. And it will be, when some of them are overthrown (defeated) at the first, that whoever hears it will say, 'There is a slaughter (mass killing) among the people who follow Absalom.' **10.** And even he who is valiant (brave), whose heart is like the heart of a lion, will melt (become weak) completely. For all Israel knows that your father is a mighty man, and those who are with him are valiant (courageous) men. **11.** Therefore I advise (recommend) that all Israel be fully gathered to you, from Dan to Beersheba (places in Israel), like the sand that is by the sea for multitude (many), and that you go to battle in person. **12.** So we will come upon him in some place where he may be found, and we will fall on him as the dew (moisture) falls on the ground. And of him and all the men who are with him there shall not be left so much as one. **13.** Moreover, if he has withdrawn into a city, then all Israel shall bring ropes (thick cords) to that city; and we will pull it into the river (body of water), until there is not one small stone found there." **14.** So Absalom and all the men of Israel said, "The advice of Hushai the Archite is better than the advice of Ahithophel." For the Lord had purposed (decided) to defeat the good advice of Ahithophel, to the intent that the Lord might bring disaster (calamity) on Absalom. **15.** Then Hushai said to Zadok and Abiathar (the priests), "Thus and so Ahithophel advised Absalom and the elders of Israel, and thus and so I have advised." **16.** "Now therefore, send quickly and tell David, saying, 'Do not spend this night in the plains (open fields) of the wilderness, but speedily cross over, lest the king and all the people who are with him be swallowed (devoured) up.'" **17.** Now Jonathan and Ahimaaz stayed at En Rogel (a place near Jerusalem), for they dared not be seen coming into the city; so a female servant would come and tell them, and they would go and tell King David. **18.** Nevertheless, a lad saw them, and told Absalom. But both of them went away quickly and came to a man's house in Bahurim (a town near Jerusalem), who had a well (water pit) in his court; and they went down into it. **19.** Then the woman took and spread a covering (blanket) over the well's mouth, and spread ground grain (crushed wheat) on it; and the thing was not known. **20.** And when Absalom's servants came to the woman at the house, they said, "Where are Ahimaaz and Jonathan?" So the woman said to them, "They have gone over the water brook (stream)." And when they had searched and could not find them, they returned to Jerusalem. **21.** Now it came to pass, after they had departed, that they came up out of the well (water pit) and went and told King David, and said to David, "Arise and cross over the water quickly. For thus has Ahithophel advised (recommended) against you." **22.** So David and all

the people who were with him arose and crossed over the Jordan (river). By morning light not one of them was left who had not gone over the Jordan. **23.** Now when Ahithophel saw that his advice was not followed, he saddled (prepared) a donkey, and arose and went home to his house, to his city. Then he put his household in order (arranged), and hanged (hung) himself, and died; and he was buried in his father's tomb. **24.** Then David went to Mahanaim (a place), and Absalom crossed over the Jordan (river), he and all the men of Israel with him. **25.** And Absalom made Amasa captain (leader) of the army instead of Joab. This Amasa was the son of a man whose name was Jithra, an Israelite, who had gone in to Abigail the daughter of Nahash, sister of Zeruiah, Joab's mother. **26.** So Israel and Absalom encamped (set up camp) in the land of Gilead (region). **27.** Now it happened, when David had come to Mahanaim (a place), that Shobi the son of Nahash from Rabbah (capital city of Ammon) of the people of Ammon, Machir the son of Ammiel from Lo Debar (a town), and Barzillai the Gileadite from Rogelim (a town), **28.** brought beds and basins (shallow dishes), earthen vessels (clay pots) and wheat, barley and flour, parched grain (roasted grain) and beans, lentils and parched seeds (roasted seeds), **29.** Honey and curds (dairy product), sheep and cheese of the herd, for David and the people who were with him to eat. For they said, "The people are hungry and weary (tired) and thirsty in the wilderness."

Chapter 18

1. David took a census (counting the people) of those with him and assigned leaders over groups of thousands and hundreds. **2.** He split the army into three divisions: one under Joab, one under Abishai (Joab's brother), and one under Ittai the Gittite (a person from Gath). David said to the people, "I will also go with you." **3.** The people replied, "You should not go! If we flee (run away quickly), they won't care about us; and if half of us die, they will not be concerned. But you are more valuable to us here in the city. You are worth ten thousand of us now." **4.** The king answered, "I will do whatever seems best to you." Then he stayed by the gate (large entrance), and the people went out in groups of hundreds and thousands. **5.** David had ordered Joab, Abishai, and Ittai to "Be gentle (kind and careful) with the young man Absalom." Everyone heard the king's instructions to the commanders regarding Absalom. **6.** The battle took place in the forest (a large area of trees and woods) of Ephraim, and David's men defeated the Israelites, killing twenty thousand that day. **7.** The battle spread across the countryside and the forest claimed more lives than the sword (a weapon). **8.** Absalom encountered David's men while riding on a mule (an animal). As the mule passed under a large tree, his head got caught in its branches, and he was left hanging (suspended from a position), while the mule continued. **9.** A man saw Absalom hanging and reported it to Joab, **10.** Joab asked, "Why didn't you kill him when you saw him? I would have rewarded you with ten shekels (a form of money) of silver and a belt." **11.** The man replied, "Even if I were given a thousand shekels of silver, I would not harm (cause injury or damage) the king's son. We all heard the king's command to you, Abishai, and Ittai not to harm Absalom." **12.** "I would be betraying (being disloyal) my own life, for nothing is hidden from the king, and you would have turned against me." **13.** Joab answered, "I can't waste time with you." He took three spears (long, pointed weapons) and thrust them into Absalom's heart while he was still alive in the tree. **14.** Ten of Joab's young men surrounded (formed a circle around) Absalom and finished the job. **15.** Joab blew a trumpet (a musical instrument), signaling the soldiers to stop chasing Israel. **16.** They threw Absalom into a large pit (a deep hole) in the forest and piled a heap (a large pile) of stones on top of him. Then all Israel scattered, each returning to their homes. **17.** During his life, Absalom had set up a monument (a structure built to honor someone) in the King's Valley, saying, "I have no son to carry on my name," and named it after himself—Absalom's Monument. **18.** Ahimaaz, son of Zadok, said, "Let me run (go quickly) and bring the news to the king, that the Lord has saved him from his enemies." **19.** Joab replied, "You cannot carry (deliver) the news today. You will bring it another day, but today you cannot, for the king's son is dead." **20.** Joab then told the Cushite (a person from the region of Cush), "Go and tell the king what you have seen." The Cushite bowed (bent forward as a sign of respect) and ran. **21.** Ahimaaz insisted (demanded firmly), "Let me also run after the Cushite!" **22.** Joab replied, "Why do you want to run, my son? You have no news to report (give information about something)." **23.** Ahimaaz responded, "I want to run anyway." Joab agreed, saying, "Go ahead and run." Ahimaaz outran (ran faster than) the Cushite. **24.** David was sitting at the gate when the watchman (a person who keeps lookout) saw a lone runner approaching. **25.** The watchman informed the king, "There is a man running alone." The king said, "He must bring news." **26.** The watchman spotted another man running and reported (told or informed) it. The king said, "He also brings news." **27.** The watchman said, "I think the first runner is Ahimaaz, son of Zadok." The king replied, "He is a good man and comes with good news." **28.** Ahimaaz called out, "All is well!" He bowed before the king and said, "Blessed be the Lord your God, who has delivered (rescued) your enemies into your hand!" **29.** The king asked, "Is my son Absalom safe?" Ahimaaz answered, "I saw a great commotion (a lot of noise or confusion), but I didn't know what it was about." **30.** The king said, "Stand over there." Ahimaaz stepped aside (to the side, away from the main action). **31.** At that moment, the Cushite arrived and said, "Good news (information), my lord the king! The Lord has avenged (gotten justice for) you today over those who opposed (fought against) you." **32.** The king asked, "Is my son Absalom safe?" The Cushite replied, "May your enemies and all who rise against you be like that young man!" **33.** The king was deeply moved and went to the chamber (private rooms) above the gate, weeping (crying because of sadness). As he went, he cried, "O my son Absalom, my son, my son Absalom! If only I had died instead of you! O Absalom, my son!"

Chapter 19

1. Joab was informed that the king was deeply grieving (mourning) for Absalom. **2.** As a result, the victory was overshadowed by sorrow (mourning), for the people heard that the king was in great distress (grief) over his son. **3.** The people quietly returned to the city, as though ashamed (embarrassed) after a defeated army. **4.** The king, covering his face, cried out loudly, "Oh, Absalom my son, Absalom, my son!" **5.** Joab entered the king's house and said, "Today you have dishonored (disgraced) those who saved your life, as well as the lives of your children, wives, and concubines. **6.** You are showing more love for your enemies than for your own friends. It seems to me that if Absalom had lived and we had died, it would have made you happy." **7.** "Now, rise up and go speak words of comfort (encouragement) to your people, for if you don't, no one will stay loyal to you by nightfall. That would be worse than any trouble (evil) you have faced in your life so far." **8.** The king stood up and sat at the gate (entrance), and people were informed that the king was there. As a result, all the Israelites gathered before him. **9.** Across all of Israel, the people were in disagreement (dispute), saying, "The king rescued us from our enemies and delivered us from the Philistines, but now he has run away because of Absalom. **10.** Yet Absalom, whom we had made our king, is dead. Why are we silent about bringing the king back?" **11.** King David then sent a message to Zadok and Abiathar, the priests, instructing them to speak to the elders (leaders) of Judah: "Why are you the last to bring the king back to his house, when Israel has already agreed to it? **12.** You are my family (brethren), my flesh and blood. Why then are you delaying to restore the king?" **13.** "And tell Amasa, 'Are you not also my flesh and blood? May God deal with me severely, if you are not placed in charge of my army instead of Joab.'" **14.** This stirred the hearts of all the men of Judah, and they unanimously agreed to send word to the king: "Return, you and all your servants!" **15.** The king crossed over to the Jordan, and Judah met him at Gilgal to escort (lead) him across. **16.** Shimei, son of Gera, from the tribe of Benjamin, hurried down with men from Judah to meet the king. **17.** He was accompanied by a thousand men from Benjamin, along with Ziba, Saul's servant, and his fifteen sons and twenty servants. They crossed ahead of the king. **18.** A ferryboat (small boat) carried the king's household, and everything was done according to his wishes. As they crossed, Shimei fell before the king. **19.** He said, "Please, don't hold my sin (wrongdoing) against me, or remember what I did when you left Jerusalem. Please, do not take it to heart. **20.** I know I've sinned (done wrong). I'm the first today to come down to meet you, my lord, the king." **21.** But Abishai, son of Zeruiah, protested, "Shouldn't Shimei be put to death for cursing (speaking ill of) the Lord's anointed (chosen one)?" **22.** David responded, "What do I have to do with you, sons of Zeruiah? Why should you oppose (oppose) me today? Should anyone be put to death in Israel today? Don't I know that I am king over Israel

today?" **23.** The king then said to Shimei, "You shall not die." And David gave him his oath (promise). **24.** Mephibosheth, Saul's son, came to meet the king. He had neither taken care (attended) to his feet, groomed (trimmed) his beard, nor washed his clothes since the day the king left until his safe return. **25.** When he reached Jerusalem to meet the king, David asked, "Why didn't you go with me, Mephibosheth?" **26.** Mephibosheth replied, "My lord, O king, my servant (helper) deceived (misled) me. He said, 'I will saddle (prepare) a donkey for you, so that you may ride and go with the king,' since I am lame (unable to walk). **27.** He has slandered (falsely accused) me before you, but you are like the angel of God. Do what seems good in your eyes." **28.** "My family was once as good as dead before you, my lord the king," Mephibosheth continued. "Yet you gave me a place at your table, so what further claim could I possibly have to ask anything from you?" **29.** The king replied, "There's no need to argue about this. I've already decided: You and Ziba will share the land." **30.** Mephibosheth answered, "If that's the case, let Ziba take it all! I'm just glad that you, my lord, the king, have safely returned." **31.** Barzillai the Gileadite, a wealthy man from Rogelim, had supported the king during his exile in Mahanaim. He now came to escort David back across the Jordan. **32.** Barzillai was an old man, eighty years of age, and had supported (provided) the king during his stay in Mahanaim, as he was a wealthy man. **33.** The king invited Barzillai to come to Jerusalem, promising to care for him there. **34.** Barzillai answered, "How many more years do I have to live that I should go with the king to Jerusalem? **35.** I'm eighty years old. Can I distinguish (know) what is good or bad? Can I still enjoy (taste) food and drink? Can I hear the voices of men and women singing? Why should I burden (weigh down) my lord the king any longer? **36.** I will go a short distance with you, but why should the king reward (repay) me for this?" **37.** "Let me return to my city to die near the grave of my father and mother. But let your servant Chimham go with you, and do for him whatever pleases you." **38.** The king replied, "Chimham will go with me, and I will do for him as you wish. Whatever you ask of me, I will do for you." **39.** After crossing the Jordan, the king was met by the men of Israel who said, "Why did the men of Judah take the lead in bringing the king and his household across the river? **40.** The men of Judah answered, "The king is our relative, and we are his own family. So why are you angry with us? Have we taken anything from the king or received gifts?" **41.** The men of Israel responded, "We have ten shares in the king, and we are his people too! Why do you treat us like we have no claim to him? Didn't we suggest bringing him back first?" **42.** But the men of Judah answered the men of Israel more forcefully, and their words were sharper than those of Israel. **43.** The men of Israel answered, "We have ten shares in the king, and thus we have more right to him than you. Why then do you despise (disregard) us, when we were the first to propose bringing him back?" The words of the men of Judah were harsher (stronger) than those of the men of Israel.

Chapter 20

1. A man named Sheba, son of Bichri, a Benjamite rebel (one who opposes authority), was present. He sounded a trumpet, declaring, "We have no part with David, nor inheritance with Jesse's son; let each person return to their tents, Israel!" **2.** So all the people of Israel left David to follow Sheba, son of Bichri. Yet, the people of Judah, from the Jordan to Jerusalem, stayed loyal (faithful and committed) to their king. **3.** Upon David's return to his house in Jerusalem, he secluded (isolated) the ten concubines he had left to manage the household, providing for them but not visiting them. They remained shut away as widows until their deaths. **4.** David instructed Amasa, "Bring together the men of Judah for me within three days, and ensure you are present as well." **5.** Amasa went to gather the men but delayed (took longer) past the time David had specified. **6.** David then said to Abishai, "Sheba, son of Bichri, will cause us more harm than Absalom did. Take your lord's servants and pursue him, or he might find refuge in fortified cities and slip away." **7.** So, Joab's men, along with the Cherethites, the Pelethites, and all the mighty warriors, departed from Jerusalem to pursue Sheba, son of Bichri. **8.** When they arrived at the large stone in Gibeon, Amasa joined them. Joab, wearing armor, had a sword fastened (securely attached) to his side, which slipped out as he moved forward. **9.** Joab greeted Amasa, saying, "Are you well, my brother?" and then took hold of Amasa's beard with his right hand as if to kiss him. **10.** Amasa did not see the sword in Joab's other hand, and Joab struck (delivered a blow to) him in the stomach, spilling his intestines onto the ground. Without striking again, Amasa died. Joab and his brother Abishai then continued after Sheba, son of Bichri. **11.** One of Joab's men stood by Amasa and announced, "Anyone loyal to Joab and who supports David, follow Joab!" **12.** Amasa lay bleeding (losing blood) in the middle of the road. Observing that people were stopping, the man moved Amasa's body from the road into the field and covered it with a garment. **13.** After Amasa was moved, everyone continued on with Joab in pursuit of Sheba, son of Bichri. **14.** Sheba traveled through the tribes of Israel until he reached Abel of Beth Maachah and the land of the Berites, where others also joined him. **15.** Joab's forces surrounded him in Abel of Beth Maachah, piling a siege mound (raised earthwork for attacking) against the city wall and attempting to break it down. **16.** Then, a wise woman from the city cried out, "Listen! Please call Joab over here so I may speak with him." **17.** Joab approached, and she asked, "Are you Joab?" He responded, "I am." She said, "Listen to what your servant has to say." He answered, "I am listening." **18.** She continued, "In earlier times, people would say, 'Seek advice (guidance) at Abel,' and that would resolve disputes. **19.** I am one of the peaceful and faithful in Israel, yet you intend to destroy a city and a mother in Israel. Why would you destroy the Lord's inheritance?" **20.** Joab replied, "It is not my intention to destroy (cause harm to) or harm the city! **21.** But there is a man from the mountains of Ephraim, Sheba, son of Bichri, who has raised his hand against King David. Hand him over, and we will leave the city." The woman responded, "Watch, his head will be thrown over the wall to you." **22.** With her wisdom, she persuaded the people, who then cut off Sheba's head and threw it to Joab. Joab sounded the trumpet (a horn for signaling), and everyone returned to their homes. Joab went back to the king in Jerusalem. **23.** Joab led Israel's army, while Benaiah, son of Jehoiada, commanded the Cherethites and Pelethites. **24.** Adoram was in charge of revenue (collected income), and Jehoshaphat, son of Ahilud, was the recorder. **25.** Sheva was the scribe, and Zadok and Abiathar served as priests. **26.** Ira the Jairite held a key position as chief official under David.

Chapter 21

1. During David's time, a famine persisted for three years. David asked the Lord why, and the Lord said it was due to Saul and his bloodthirsty (violent) family, because he had killed the Gibeonites. **2.** David summoned the Gibeonites (a group not from Israel but from the remnant of the Amorites whom Israel had promised to protect, but Saul, in his zeal (passionate intensity) for Israel and Judah, had tried to destroy them. **3.** David asked the Gibeonites, "What can I do for you to make atonement, so you may bless the Lord's inheritance (Israel)?" **4.** The Gibeonites replied, "We don't seek silver or gold from Saul's family, nor do we want any Israelite killed for us." David said, "Whatever you ask, I will do." **5.** The Gibeonites replied, "The man who plotted to destroy us and remove us from Israel's territory must face consequences. **6.** Therefore, we ask for seven of his male descendants to be handed over, so we may execute them before the Lord in Gibeah of Saul, whom the Lord had chosen." David agreed to their request. **7.** However, he spared Mephibosheth, Jonathan's son (Jonathan being the son of Saul), because of the sacred promise that existed between David and Jonathan before the Lord. **8.** David took Armoni and Mephibosheth (Rizpah's sons with Saul) and five sons of Michal (Saul's daughter) raised by Adriel, son of Barzillai the Meholathite. **9.** He handed them to the Gibeonites, who hanged them on the hill before the Lord. All seven died together at the start of the barley harvest. **10.** Rizpah, daughter of Aiah, spread sackcloth on the rock and protected their bodies from birds and animals, from the start of harvest until the late rains. **11.** David heard of Rizpah's actions, **12.** so he retrieved the bones of Saul and Jonathan from Jabesh Gilead (where the Philistines had displayed them after killing Saul in Gilboa). **13.** He gathered these bones and those of the seven who had been hanged. **14.** They buried Saul and Jonathan's bones in the family tomb of Kish (Saul's father) at Zelah in Benjamin. After this, God answered prayers for the land. **15.** During another war with the Philistines, David and his men went down to fight, and David grew weary. **16.** Ishbi-Benob, a giant with a bronze spear weighing three hundred shekels (about 7.5 pounds) and a new sword, thought he could kill David. **17.** But Abishai, Zeruiah's son, came to David's rescue, struck the Philistine, and killed him. Afterward,

David's men swore he would no longer join battles, lest Israel lose its "lamp" (leader). **18.** Later, in another battle with the Philistines at Gob, Sibbechai the Hushathite killed Saph, a descendant of the giant. **19.** Another clash with the Philistines occurred at Gob, where Elhanan, son of Jaare-Oregim the Bethlehemite, killed the brother of Goliath the Gittite, who carried a spear with a shaft like a weaver's beam. **20.** In a separate battle at Gath, an imposing man with six fingers on each hand and six toes on each foot challenged Israel. **21.** Jonathan, son of Shimea (David's brother), took him down. **22.** These four men, descended from the giant in Gath, were ultimately defeated by David and his servants.

Chapter 22

1. On the day the Lord delivered him from all his adversaries, including Saul, David composed this song and sang it to the Lord. **2.** He declared, "The Lord is my rock (firm foundation), my fortress (defense), and my deliverer (rescuer). **3.** God is my strength (power) in whom I trust. He is my shield (protector), the horn (source of power) of my salvation (rescue), my refuge (safe haven), and my Savior, who saves me from harm. **4.** I will call upon the Lord, who is worthy of praise, and He will save me from my foes. **5.** "When the waves of death (overwhelming forces) surrounded me, and torrents of evil (wickedness) flooded over me, **6.** when the grips of the grave (suffering) held me, and the snares of death (traps) blocked my way, **7.** in my distress (trouble), I cried out to the Lord; I called upon my God. From His temple (holy place), He heard my voice, and my plea reached His ears. **8.** "The earth shook (trembled), and the heavens shuddered; the very foundations (bases) of the world trembled in His anger. **9.** Smoke rose from His nostrils (nose), and fire blazed from His mouth; burning coals (embers) were kindled. **10.** He bent the heavens (sky) and came down, with darkness (shadow) beneath His feet. **11.** Riding upon a cherub (heavenly being), He flew, soaring on the wings of the wind. **12.** He used thick clouds as His canopy (shelter), and darkness filled the skies. **13.** With the brightness of His presence, coals of fire were ignited. **14.** "The Lord thundered (spoke powerfully) from heaven; the Most High raised His voice. **15.** He sent arrows (sharp bolts) and scattered them, striking down His foes with lightning. **16.** The channels (paths) of the sea were laid bare, and the earth's foundations (bases) were exposed at the Lord's rebuke (command) and the blast (powerful breath) of His voice. **17.** "He reached down from on high and took hold of me, pulling me from deep waters. **18.** He rescued me from my strong (powerful) enemy, from those who hated me, for they were too strong for me. **19.** They confronted me on my day of disaster, but the Lord supported me. **20.** He led me into a wide-open space and saved me because He delighted (found pleasure) in me. **21.** "The Lord rewarded me for my righteousness (uprightness) and repaid (recompensed) me for my clean hands. **22.** For I have followed the ways (commands) of the Lord and have not strayed from my God. **23.** I have kept His judgments (decrees) ever before me and did not depart from His statutes (laws). **24.** I was blameless (faultless) before Him and guarded myself from sin. **25.** So the Lord rewarded me for my righteousness, according to my purity in His sight. **26.** "To the merciful (kind), You reveal Yourself as merciful; to the blameless, You reveal Yourself as blameless. **27.** To the pure (clean-hearted), You reveal Yourself as pure; to the devious (dishonest), You reveal Yourself as wise. **28.** You deliver the humble (meek) but bring down the proud (arrogant) who look upon others. **29.** "Lord, You are my light (lamp); You illuminate my darkness. **30.** With Your strength, I can face a troop (army); with my God, I can scale any wall. **31.** God's way is flawless (perfect); His word is pure (without fault). He is a shield for all who take refuge (trust) in Him. **32.** "Who is God but the Lord? And who is a rock except our God? **33.** God is my source of strength and power (might), making my path perfect (steady). **34.** He makes my feet swift like those of a deer, and He secures me on high places. **35.** He teaches my hands for battle, enabling my arms to bend a bronze bow (strong metal). **36.** "You have given me the shield (protection) of Your salvation, and Your gentleness (kindness) has made me great. **37.** You broadened (widened) the path beneath my feet, so I did not slip (stumble). **38.** "I pursued (chased) my enemies and overtook them; I did not turn back until they were defeated. **39.** I struck them down, and they could not rise; they fell under my feet. **40.** You equipped me with strength for the battle and subdued my enemies beneath me. **41.** You turned my foes (opponents) over to me, allowing me to defeat those who hated me. **42.** They looked for help, but no one came to rescue them; they called out to the Lord, but He did not answer. **43.** I crushed them as fine as the dust of the earth, trampling them like dirt in the streets, scattering them away. **44.** "You saved (delivered) me from the people's struggles, making me the head (leader) of nations. Foreigners now serve (follow) me. **45.** Strangers (outsiders) obey (yield to) me; as soon as they hear of me, they submit. **46.** Foreigners lose courage (tremble) and come from their fortresses (safe places) in fear. **47.** "The Lord lives! Blessed (praised) be my Rock! Let the God who saves me be exalted (honored)! **48.** God is the one who avenges (repays) me, who subdues (overcomes) nations under me, **49.** Who rescues me from my enemies. He lifts me above those who oppose (rise against) me and saves me from violent men. **50.** So I will praise (thank) You, Lord, among the nations and sing praises to Your name. **51.** "He is the stronghold (tower) of salvation for His king, showing mercy (kindness) to His anointed, to David and his descendants forever."

Chapter 23

1. These are the last words of David, the son of Jesse. He was the man raised up by God, the chosen one of the God of Jacob, and Israel's beloved songwriter, who now declares: **2.** "The Spirit of the Lord spoke through me; His words were on my tongue. **3.** The God of Israel proclaimed, and the Rock (unmovable strength) of Israel spoke, saying, 'A leader over people must be righteous, leading with reverence for God. **4.** Such a leader is like the morning light at sunrise, bringing a clear sky without clouds, like young grass that flourishes after the rain. **5.** "Though my family may not be what it ought to be before God, He has made an everlasting covenant with me, fully established and secure. This is the foundation of my salvation and my purpose; will He not bring it to fruition? **6.** But those who rebel (defy) are like thorns, cast aside, for they cannot be grasped by the hand. **7.** Anyone who tries to handle them must be equipped with iron and a spear, and in the end, they will be destroyed where they stand by fire." **8.** These are the names of David's mighty warriors: Josheb-Basshebeth, the Tachmonite, who was chief among the captains. Known as Adino the Eznite, he killed eight hundred men in a single encounter. **9.** Next was Eleazar, son of Dodo the Ahohite, one of the three mighty men who stood firm against the Philistines when the Israelite forces withdrew. **10.** He held his ground and fought until his hand grew so weary that it clung to his sword. That day, the Lord brought about a great victory, and the people returned only to gather the spoils. **11.** Following him was Shammah, the son of Agee the Hararite. When the Philistines gathered in a field of lentils, the people fled. **12.** But Shammah took his stand in the middle of that field, defending it and defeating the Philistines. The Lord granted him a remarkable victory. **13.** During the harvest season, three of the thirty leading warriors came down to join David at the cave of Adullam (near Bethlehem), where the Philistines were camped in the Valley of Rephaim (near Jerusalem). **14.** David was in a stronghold, while the Philistine outpost was stationed in Bethlehem. **15.** David expressed his longing, saying, "Oh, if someone would bring me a drink from the well at Bethlehem's gate!" **16.** So, the three warriors broke through the Philistine camp, drew water from the well at Bethlehem's gate, and brought it back to David. But he refused to drink it; instead, he poured it out as an offering to the Lord. **17.** He said, "It would be unthinkable, Lord, for me to drink this! Isn't this the blood of the men who risked their lives?" So he would not drink it. Such were the heroic deeds of these three mighty men. **18.** Abishai, the brother of Joab, led another group of three. With his spear, he killed three hundred men, earning a reputation among the three. **19.** Wasn't he the most honored among the three? Therefore, he became their captain, but he did not match the first three in valor. **20.** Benaiah, son of Jehoiada, a courageous man from Kabzeel (a town in Judah), performed many notable deeds. He struck down two impressive warriors from Moab and killed a lion in a pit on a snowy day. **21.** He also killed a giant Egyptian, armed with only a staff. He approached the Egyptian, took his spear, and killed him with his own weapon. **22.** These deeds won Benaiah a distinguished place among the three mighty men. **23.** Although he was more respected than the thirty, he did not reach the stature of the first three. David appointed him over his bodyguard. **24.** Asahel, the brother of Joab, was among the thirty; so were Elhanan, son of Dodo from Bethlehem, **25.** Shammah the Harodite, and Elika the Harodite, **26.** Helez the Paltite, Ira, son of Ikkesh

the Tekoite, **27.** Abiezer the Anathothite, Mebunnai the Hushathite, **28.** Zalmon the Ahohite, Maharai the Netophathite, **29.** Heleb, son of Baanah (from Netophah), and Ittai, son of Ribai from Gibeah (a town in Benjamin), **30.** Benaiah the Pirathonite, Hiddai from the valleys of Gaash, **31.** Abi-Albon the Arbathite, Azmaveth the Barhumite, **32.** Eliahba the Shaalbonite (from the sons of Jashen), and Jonathan, **33.** Shammah the Hararite, and Ahiam, son of Sharar the Hararite, **34.** Eliphelet, son of Ahasbai the Maachathite, and Eliam, son of Ahithophel the Gilonite, **35.** Hezrai the Carmelite, Paarai the Arbite, **36.** Igal, son of Nathan of Zobah, and Bani the Gadite, **37.** Zelek the Ammonite, and Naharai the Beerothite (armor-bearer for Joab), **38.** Ira the Ithrite and Gareb the Ithrite, **39.** along with Uriah the Hittite—thirty-seven in all.

Chapter 24

1. Once more, the Lord's anger (God's displeasure) was stirred against Israel, and He prompted David to act by saying, "Go and count the people of Israel and Judah." **2.** So King David instructed Joab, the army's commander, "Go through all the tribes of Israel, from Dan (northernmost region) to Beersheba (southernmost region), and tally the people so I may know their number." **3.** Joab replied, "May the Lord your God multiply the people a hundredfold, and may you, my king, witness it. But why, my lord, do you desire this?" **4.** Despite Joab's hesitation, the king's command was firm. So Joab and the army commanders left the king's presence to conduct the census of Israel. **5.** They crossed the Jordan River (the river dividing Israel), and camped in Aroer (a town east of the Jordan), near the ravine of Gad (a valley), and proceeded toward Jazer (a city in Gilead). **6.** From there, they moved through Gilead (a region east of the Jordan) and the land of Tahtim Hodshi (a place in Gilead), continued to Dan Jaan, and then to Sidon (a Phoenician city). **7.** They reached the fortress of Tyre and visited all the cities of the Hivites and Canaanites (ancient groups in Israel's land). Eventually, they headed south to Judah, arriving at Beersheba. **8.** After traveling throughout the land, they returned to Jerusalem (the capital) after nine months and twenty days. **9.** Joab then presented the results of the census to the king: Israel had 800,000 capable soldiers, while Judah had 500,000 men. **10.** Once the counting was complete, David felt troubled (guilty) in his heart, saying to the Lord, "I have committed a great sin by doing this. O Lord, please remove the guilt from Your servant, for I have acted foolishly." **11.** The following morning, the Lord's word (message) came to the prophet Gad, David's seer (spiritual advisor), saying, **12.** "Go and tell David, 'This is what the Lord says: I am giving you three choices. Choose one, and I will bring it upon you.'" **13.** Gad approached David and asked, "Shall your land experience seven years of famine (a severe food shortage)? Or will you be on the run from your enemies for three months as they pursue you? Or would you rather have three days of plague (a deadly disease) in your land? Reflect and let me know the answer to convey back to Him who sent me." **14.** David responded to Gad, "I am deeply troubled (suffering). Let us fall into the Lord's hands, for His mercy is great. But do not let me fall into human hands." **15.** So the Lord sent a plague on Israel from morning until the set time, and seventy thousand people from Dan to Beersheba died. **16.** When the angel (God's messenger) stretched out his hand to strike Jerusalem (the capital city), the Lord changed His mind (relented) about the destruction and told the angel striking the people, "That is enough! Withdraw your hand." The angel was then at the threshing floor (a place for separating grain) of Araunah the Jebusite (a man of the Jebus tribe). **17.** Seeing the angel bringing destruction upon the people, David pleaded with the Lord, "I am the one who sinned; I am responsible. But these people, like sheep, what have they done? Let Your hand fall upon me and my family." **18.** That day, Gad approached David with a message, saying, "Go and set up an altar (place of sacrifice) to the Lord on Araunah the Jebusite's threshing floor." **19.** Following Gad's guidance, David went up to the place the Lord had instructed him to build the altar. **20.** When Araunah saw the king and his servants approaching, he came out and bowed with his face to the ground in respect. **21.** Araunah asked, "Why has my lord the king come to his servant?" David answered, "I've come to buy your threshing floor to build an altar to the Lord, so that the plague on the people may cease." **22.** Araunah then offered, "Let my lord the king take what he needs to make the offering. Here are oxen for the burnt offering (animals for sacrifice), as well as the threshing tools and yokes for the oxen (wooden frames for harnessing oxen) to use as firewood." **23.** Araunah gave all of these items to the king freely, saying, "May the Lord your God accept you." **24.** However, the king responded, "No, I must buy it from you for a fair price. I will not present burnt offerings to the Lord my God that cost me nothing." So David purchased the threshing floor and the oxen, paying fifty shekels of silver. **25.** David built the altar there to the Lord, offering both burnt offerings and peace offerings. The Lord heard his prayer for the land, and the plague upon Israel was lifted.

10 – Kings

Kings 1

Chapter 1

1. King David was now old and had lived many years; despite being covered with blankets, he could not get warm. **2.** His servants suggested, "Let us find a young woman, a virgin (a young, unmarried woman), to attend to our lord the king. She should stand before him and care for him, even lie in his embrace, so that our lord the king may feel warmth." **3.** They searched throughout all of Israel for a beautiful young woman and discovered Abishag the Shunammite, who was brought to the king. **4.** The young woman was indeed lovely; she served the king and attended to him, but the king did not have relations with her. **5.** Meanwhile, Adonijah, the son of Haggith, elevated (raised to a higher position) himself, declaring, "I will be king." He prepared chariots and horsemen, along with fifty men to run before him. **6.** (His father had never reprimanded (scolded) him by asking, "Why have you done this?" He was also very handsome, having been born to his mother after Absalom.) **7.** Adonijah conferred (discussed) with Joab, the son of Zeruiah, and with Abiathar the priest; they supported and assisted him. **8.** However, Zadok the priest, Benaiah the son of Jehoiada, Nathan the prophet, Shimei, Rei, and David's mighty men did not side with Adonijah. **9.** Adonijah sacrificed (offered as a religious act) sheep, oxen, and fattened (well-fed) cattle near the stone of Zoheleth, which is by En Rogel; he also invited all of his brothers, the king's sons, and all the men of Judah, along with the king's servants. **10.** Yet he did not invite Nathan the prophet, Benaiah, the mighty men, or his brother Solomon. **11.** Nathan informed Bathsheba, Solomon's mother, saying, "Have you not heard that Adonijah, the son of Haggith, has become king, and that David our lord is unaware (not knowing) of it? **12.** Come, let me give you some advice so that you may save your own life and that of your son Solomon. **13.** Go immediately to King David and say to him, 'Did you not, my lord, O king, swear (promise) to your maidservant (female servant), saying, "Certainly your son Solomon shall reign after me and sit on my throne"? Why then has Adonijah become king?' **14.** While you are still speaking with the king, I will come in after you and confirm (verify) your words." **15.** Bathsheba entered the king's chamber (room). (At that time, the king was very old, and Abishag the Shunammite was attending to him.) **16.** Bathsheba bowed down to the king. The king asked her, "What do you wish?" **17.** She replied, "My lord, you swore by the Lord your God to your maidservant, saying, 'Assuredly (certainly) your son Solomon shall reign after me, and he shall sit on my throne.' **18.** Now, behold (look)! Adonijah has become king, and you, my lord the king, do not know about it. **19.** He has sacrificed oxen, fattened cattle, and sheep in abundance (in large quantities) and has invited all the king's sons, Abiathar the priest, and Joab, the commander of the army, but your servant Solomon he has not invited. **20.** As for you, my lord, O king, all of Israel is watching you, expecting you to declare who will sit on the throne after you. **21.** If you do not, when my lord the king rests with his fathers (ancestors), my son Solomon and I will be counted (considered) as criminals (offenders)." **22.** Just then, while she was still speaking to the king, Nathan the prophet entered. **23.** They informed the king, "Nathan the prophet is here." When he arrived, he bowed before the king with his face to the ground. **24.** Nathan said, "My lord, O king, have you declared, 'Adonijah shall reign after me and sit on my throne'? **25.** He has gone down today, sacrificed oxen, fattened cattle, and sheep in abundance, and has invited all the king's sons, the commanders (leaders) of the army, and Abiathar the priest; they are feasting before him, proclaiming (declaring), 'Long live King Adonijah!' **26.** But he did not invite me, your servant, nor Zadok the priest, nor Benaiah, nor your servant Solomon. **27.** Has this matter been decided by you, my lord the king, without telling your servant who is to sit on the throne after you?" **28.** King David then said, "Call Bathsheba." She came and stood before the king. **29.** The king took an oath (formal promise) and declared, "As the Lord lives, who has delivered (rescued) my life from every distress (trouble), **30.** just as I swore to you by the Lord God of Israel, saying, 'Certainly Solomon your son shall be king after me, and he shall sit on my throne in my place,' so I will do this today." **31.** Bathsheba bowed with her face to the ground and honored (respected) the king, saying, "Let my lord King David live forever!" **32.** King David instructed, "Call Zadok the priest, Nathan the prophet, and Benaiah the son of Jehoiada." They came before the king. **33.** He told them, "Take the servants of your lord with you, have Solomon my son ride on my own mule (a type of horse), and take him down to Gihon. **34.** There, let Zadok the priest and Nathan the prophet anoint (ceremonially appoint) him as king over Israel. Blow the horn (a musical instrument) and declare, 'Long live King Solomon!' **35.** Afterward, come up with him, and he shall sit on my throne and rule in my place, for I have appointed him to be ruler over Israel and Judah." **36.** Benaiah, son of Jehoiada, responded to the king, "Amen! May the Lord God of my lord the king say so too. **37.** As the Lord has been with my lord the king, may He also be with Solomon and make his throne greater than that of my lord King David." **38.** So Zadok the priest, Nathan the prophet, Benaiah, the Cherethites (elite guards), and the Pelethites (another group of elite guards) went down and had Solomon ride on King David's mule, taking him to Gihon. **39.** Zadok the priest took a horn of oil from the tabernacle (place of worship) and anointed Solomon. They blew the horn, and all the people shouted, "Long live King Solomon!" **40.** Then all the people followed him, playing flutes (musical instruments) and rejoicing (celebrating) with great joy, making the earth seem to tremble (shake) with their sound. **41.** Meanwhile, Adonijah and his guests heard the noise as they finished eating. Joab, upon hearing the horn, asked, "What is this uproar (loud noise) in the city?" **42.** Just as he was speaking, Jonathan, the son of Abiathar the priest, arrived. Adonijah said to him, "Come in, for you are a prominent (important) man and must bring good news." **43.** Jonathan replied, "No! Our lord King David has made Solomon king. **44.** The king sent with him Zadok the priest, Nathan the prophet, Benaiah the son of Jehoiada, the Cherethites, and the Pelethites; and they made him ride on the king's mule. **45.** Zadok the priest and Nathan the prophet have anointed him king at Gihon, and they have gone up rejoicing, causing the city to erupt (explode) with noise. This is the commotion you have heard. **46.** Furthermore, Solomon now sits on the throne of the kingdom. **47.** Additionally, the king's servants have gone to bless our lord King David, saying, 'May God make Solomon's name greater than your name, and may He make his throne greater than your throne.' Then the king bowed down on his bed. **48.** The king also said, 'Blessed be the Lord God of Israel, who has granted someone to sit on my throne this day while my own eyes see it!'" **49.** All the guests with Adonijah were terrified and began to leave, each going their own way. **50.** Adonijah, fearing (being afraid of) Solomon, arose and grasped (held tightly) the horns (projections) of the altar (sacred place). **51.** Solomon was informed that Adonijah was afraid of him, saying, "Look, he has taken hold of the horns of the altar, asking for King Solomon to swear that he will not put him to death with the sword." **52.** Solomon replied, "If he proves to be a worthy man, not a single hair of his head shall fall to the ground; but if evil (wrongdoing) is found in him, he shall die." **53.** King Solomon sent men to bring Adonijah down from the altar. He came, fell down before King Solomon, and Solomon told him, "Go to your house."

Chapter 2

1. As David's life was nearing its end, he called Solomon, his son, and gave him instructions. **2.** He said, "I am about to go the way of all the earth (die); be strong and show yourself to be a man. **3.** Follow the commands of the Lord, your God: walk in His ways, keep His statutes (laws), commandments, judgments, and testimonies, as written in the Law of Moses, so you may succeed in all you do and wherever you go. **4.** This way, the Lord may fulfill His promise to me, saying, 'If your sons remain faithful, walking before Me with truth, fully devoted in heart and soul, you will never lack a descendant on the throne of Israel (kingdom of Israel).' **5.** You also know what Joab, son of Zeruiah, did to me, how he killed Abner, son of Ner (commander of Israel's army), and Amasa, son of Jether (commander of Judah's army). He shed blood in a time of peace as if it were war, staining his belt and sandals with innocent blood. 6. Act wisely in handling him, and do not allow his gray hair to go down to the grave (die) in peace. 7. But show kindness to the sons of Barzillai the Gileadite (supporter of David) and let them eat at your table, for they helped me when I fled from Absalom, your brother. 8. Be mindful of Shimei, son of Gera, from Bahurim (a town in Benjamin's territory), who cursed me bitterly when I was going to Mahanaim (a refuge city). Though he came to meet me at the Jordan River, and I swore to him by the Lord, 'I will not kill you with the sword.' 9. But now, do not let him go unpunished. You are wise and know what to do; ensure he does not die in peace but with justice for his deeds." 10. Then David rested and was buried in the City of David (Jerusalem). 11. David reigned over Israel for forty years: seven in Hebron and thirty-three in Jerusalem. 12. Solomon then sat on his father David's throne, and his kingdom was securely established. 13. Adonijah, son of Haggith (another wife of David), came to Bathsheba, Solomon's mother. She asked, "Do you come in peace?" He replied, "In peace." 14. Adonijah said, "I have a request to make." She replied, "Speak." 15. He said, "You know the kingdom was mine, and all of Israel expected me to be king. But the kingdom has been taken and given to my brother, because it was the Lord's will. 16. Now I ask just one thing of you; please do not refuse me." Bathsheba replied, "Speak." 17. Adonijah said, "Please ask King Solomon to give me Abishag the Shunammite (a young woman who cared for David) as my wife, as he won't refuse you." 18. Bathsheba replied, "Very well, I will speak to the king for you." 19. So Bathsheba went to speak to King Solomon on behalf of Adonijah. The king stood to greet her, bowed, and sat on his throne. He arranged for a seat at his right hand for his mother, and she sat down. 20. She said, "I have a small request of you; do not refuse me." The king replied, "Ask, Mother, for I will not refuse you." 21. She said, "Let Abishag the Shunammite be given to your brother Adonijah as his wife." 22. King Solomon answered, "Why do you ask for Abishag for Adonijah? You might as well ask for the kingdom itself, for he is my elder brother, along with Abiathar the priest and Joab, son of Zeruiah." 23. Solomon then swore by the Lord, "May God deal with me severely if Adonijah has not brought about his own end with this request! 24. As the Lord lives, who has placed me on my father David's throne and established my dynasty, Adonijah shall die today!" 25. Solomon sent Benaiah, son of Jehoiada (a military commander), who struck down Adonijah, and he died. 26. To Abiathar the priest, the king said, "Go to Anathoth (a town for priests), to your fields. You deserve death, but I will not kill you now, because you carried the ark of the Lord God before my father David, and you shared in his hardships." 27. Solomon removed Abiathar from the priesthood, thus fulfilling the Lord's prophecy against Eli's family in Shiloh. 28. When Joab heard the news, he fled to the tabernacle (sacred tent) of the Lord and took hold of the altar's horns. 29. Solomon was informed that Joab had sought sanctuary at the altar. Solomon sent Benaiah, saying, "Go, strike him down." 30. Benaiah went to the tabernacle and said, "The king says, 'Come out!'" Joab replied, "I will die here." Benaiah reported this to the king. 31. The king ordered, "Do as he says. Strike him down and bury him, to remove from me and my father's house the guilt of innocent blood Joab shed. 32. The Lord will repay Joab for his deeds because he killed two men, Abner and Amasa, who were more righteous and honorable than he, without my father David's consent. 33. Their blood will be upon Joab and his descendants forever. But may the Lord bring peace upon David's descendants and his throne forever." 34. So Benaiah struck down Joab, and he was buried in his own land in the wilderness. 35. The king appointed Benaiah over the army in Joab's place and made Zadok the priest in Abiathar's place. 36. The king then summoned Shimei and said, "Build yourself a house in Jerusalem and live there. Do not leave the city or go anywhere. 37. On the day you cross the Kidron Valley, know that you will surely die; your blood will be on your own head." 38. Shimei agreed and said, "Your command is fair. I will obey." So Shimei stayed in Jerusalem for a long time. 39. After three years, two of Shimei's slaves ran away to Achish, king of Gath (a Philistine city). When Shimei heard they were in Gath, he saddled his donkey and went to retrieve them. 40. Shimei brought his slaves back from Gath. 41. Solomon was informed that Shimei had left Jerusalem and returned. 42. The king summoned Shimei and said, "Did I not make you swear by the Lord, warning you that if you left, you would surely die? And you agreed it was fair. 43. So why have you broken your oath to the Lord and my command?" 44. Solomon continued, "You know in your heart all the wrong you did to my father David. Now the Lord will repay you for your wickedness. 45. But King Solomon shall be blessed, and David's throne will be established by the Lord forever." 46. The king then commanded Benaiah, who went and struck down Shimei, and he died. Thus, Solomon's kingdom was firmly established.

Chapter 3

1. Solomon made a treaty with Pharaoh, the king of Egypt, and married his daughter. He brought her to the City of David (a section of Jerusalem) until he finished building his own house, the temple of the Lord (God's house), and the wall around Jerusalem (the capital city of Israel). 2. At this time, the people continued to sacrifice at high places (open-air worship sites on hills) since there was not yet a temple built for the Lord's name. 3. Solomon loved the Lord and followed the statutes (laws) of his father, David, although he also sacrificed and burned incense at the high places. 4. The king went to Gibeon (a city with a prominent high place) to offer sacrifices, as it was a major worship site. There, Solomon offered a thousand burnt offerings (complete animal sacrifices) on the altar. 5. That night at Gibeon, the Lord appeared to Solomon in a dream and said, "Ask for whatever you want Me to give you." 6. Solomon replied, "You showed great kindness to my father, David, who served You faithfully, righteously, and with an upright heart. You continued this kindness by giving him a son to sit on his throne as it is today. 7. Now, Lord my God, You have made me king in place of my father, David, though I am like a young child (inexperienced) and don't know how to carry out my duties. 8. Your servant is among the people You have chosen, a vast nation that cannot be counted. 9. So give Your servant a discerning heart (understanding mind) to govern Your people and distinguish between right and wrong. For who can govern this great nation of Yours?" 10. Solomon's request pleased the Lord because he had asked for wisdom instead of long life, wealth, or the death of his enemies. 11. God said, "Since you have asked for wisdom to administer justice rather than long life, wealth, or revenge against your enemies, 12. I have granted you a wise and discerning heart, so that no one like you has ever been or will be. 13. And I will also give you what you did not ask for—both riches and honor—so that no other king will compare with you during your lifetime. 14. And if you walk in My ways, keeping My statutes and commandments as your father, David, did, I will give you a long life." 15. Solomon awoke and realized it was a dream. He returned to Jerusalem, stood before the ark of the covenant of the Lord (a sacred chest symbolizing God's presence), and offered burnt offerings, peace offerings (offerings expressing gratitude and fellowship), and held a feast for all his servants. 16. Later, two women who were prostitutes came to the king to settle a dispute. 17. One woman said, "My lord, this woman and I live in the same house, and I gave birth to a child while she was there. 18. Three days later, this woman also gave birth. We were alone in the house—only the two of us were there. 19. During the night, this woman's son died because she accidentally lay on him. 20. So she got up in the middle of the night, took my son from my side while I was sleeping, and laid her dead child beside me. 21. When I got up to nurse my son in the morning, I found he was dead. But when I looked closely, I realized he was not the child I had given birth to." 22. The other woman interrupted, "No! The living one is my son, and the dead one is yours." But the first woman insisted, "No! The dead one is yours, and the living one is mine." They argued this way before the king. 23. The king summarized, "One of you says, 'This is my son, the living one, and the dead one is yours,' while the other says, 'No, the dead one is yours, and the living one is mine.'" 24. Then the king ordered, "Bring me a sword." So they brought a sword before him. 25. He then instructed, "Cut the living child in two and give half to each woman." 26. The real mother, deeply moved with compassion for her son, said, "Please, my lord, give her the living child! Don't kill him!" But the other woman said, "Neither I nor you shall have him. Divide him." 27. Then the king said, "Give the living child to the first woman. Do not kill him; she is his mother." 28. All of Israel heard about this wise ruling and were in awe of the king, for they saw that he possessed God's wisdom to administer justice.

Chapter 4

1. King Solomon was ruler over all Israel, having authority over the entire nation. 2. These were the officials in Solomon's government: Azariah, the son of Zadok, served as the priest; 3. Elihoreph and Ahijah, the sons of Shisha, were the royal scribes (secretaries); Jehoshaphat, the son of Ahilud, held the position of recorder (official historian); 4. Benaiah, the son of Jehoiada, commanded the army; Zadok and Abiathar were the priests; 5. Azariah, the son of Nathan, was in charge of the officers (officials overseeing the administration); Zabud, the son of Nathan, was a priest and Solomon's close friend; 6. Ahishar was in charge of the royal household (the king's domestic affairs); and Adoniram, the son of Abda, managed the labor force (the workers responsible for building projects). 7. Solomon had twelve regional governors who were responsible for providing food for the king and his household. Each governor was assigned to provide provisions for one month of the year. 8. These are their names and territories: Ben-Hur, in the mountains of Ephraim (a region in central Israel); 9. Ben-Deker, in Makaz, Shaalbim, Beth Shemesh, and Elon Beth Hanan (all towns in the central and southern parts of Israel); 10. Ben-Hesed, in Arubboth; to him belonged the town of Sochoh and all the land of Hepher; 11. Ben-Abinadab, in the regions of Dor; he had Taphath, the daughter of Solomon, as his wife; 12. Baana, the son of Ahilud, in the areas of Taanach, Megiddo, and all Beth Shean, which is beside Zaretan, located just below Jezreel, extending from Beth Shean to Abel Meholah, and reaching as far as the other side of Jokneam (a region in northern Israel); 13. Ben-Geber, in Ramoth Gilead (a city in the region of Gilead); to him belonged the towns of Jair, the son of Manasseh, in Gilead; he also governed the region of Argob in Bashan, which contained sixty large, fortified cities with walls and bronze gates; 14. Ahinadab, the son of Iddo, in Mahanaim (a town in Transjordan); 15. Ahimaaz, in Naphtali; he also took Basemath, the daughter of Solomon, as his wife; 16. Baanah, the son of Hushai, in Asher and Aloth (areas along the Mediterranean coast in northern Israel); 17. Jehoshaphat, the son of Paruah, in Issachar (a region in northern Israel); 18. Shimei, the son of Elah, in Benjamin (a region between Judah and Israel); 19. Geber, the son of Uri, in the land of Gilead, which was formerly controlled by Sihon, king of the Amorites, and Og, king of Bashan. Geber was the only governor assigned to this land. 20. Judah and Israel were as numerous as the sand by the sea in number, living in peace, eating, drinking, and celebrating. 21. Solomon ruled over all the kingdoms from the River (Euphrates) to the land of the Philistines and as far as the border of Egypt. All these nations brought tribute (payment) and served Solomon throughout his life. 22. Solomon's daily provisions were as follows: thirty kors of fine flour (a large measure of flour), sixty kors of meal (another type of flour), 23. Ten fattened oxen, twenty oxen from the pasture, and one hundred sheep, in addition to deer, gazelles, roebucks, and fattened poultry. 24. Solomon had authority over all the region on the west side of the River (Euphrates), from Tiphsah to Gaza (areas in northern and southern Israel); he had peace on every side. 25. Judah and Israel lived in safety, each person under their own vine and fig tree, from Dan (in the north) to Beersheba (in the south), all the days of Solomon's reign. 26. Solomon had forty thousand stalls for horses for his chariots, and twelve thousand horsemen. 27. Each of these governors, in their assigned month, provided food for King Solomon and all who ate at his table. There was no shortage in the supply. 28. They also brought barley and straw for the horses and steeds to the designated places, each governor responsible for his assigned portion. 29. God gave Solomon great wisdom and unparalleled understanding, and a heart full of wisdom, as vast as the sand on the seashore. 30. Thus, Solomon's wisdom surpassed that of all the men of the East (wise men from the Eastern nations) and all the wisdom of Egypt (a renowned center of learning and wisdom in the ancient world). 31. He was wiser than all men, including Ethan the Ezrahite, Heman, Chalcol, and Darda, the sons of Mahol. His fame spread throughout all surrounding nations. 32. Solomon spoke three thousand proverbs (short sayings offering wisdom), and his songs numbered one thousand and five. 33. He also spoke about trees, from the majestic cedars of Lebanon to the humble hyssop that grows from cracks in the wall. He also discussed animals, birds, insects, and fish. 34. People from all nations, including the kings of the earth who had heard of Solomon's wisdom, came to listen to his teachings.

Chapter 5

1. Now King Hiram of Tyre (Tyre was a Phoenician city-state on the Mediterranean coast) sent his servants to Solomon because he heard that Solomon had been anointed king after his father David. Hiram had always been a friend of David. 2. Solomon sent a message to Hiram, saying: 3. "You know that my father David could not build a house for the name of the Lord his God, because of the wars that were fought against him on all sides, until the Lord subdued his enemies and brought peace. 4. But now the Lord my God has given me peace on every side; there is no adversary or trouble. 5. And behold, I plan to build a house for the name of the Lord my God, just as the Lord spoke to my father David, saying, 'Your son, whom I will place on your throne after you, will build a house for My name.' 6. Now, therefore, command that cedars (large trees, often used for building) be cut down for me from Lebanon (a region famous for its forests of cedar trees); my servants will work with your servants, and I will pay your workers whatever wages you set. For you know there is no one among us who has the skill to cut timber like the Sidonians (a people from the city of Sidon, known for their expertise in woodwork)." 7. When Hiram heard Solomon's message, he rejoiced greatly and said, "Blessed be the Lord today, for He has given David a wise son to rule this great people!" 8. Hiram then sent a reply to Solomon, saying, "I have carefully considered the message you sent me, and I will do all that you desire concerning the cedar and cypress logs. 9. My servants will bring them down from Lebanon to the sea. I will float them on rafts by sea to the place you indicate. There, I will break them apart, and you can then take them. In return, you shall provide food for my household." 10. So Hiram gave Solomon all the cedar and cypress logs he requested. 11. And Solomon gave Hiram twenty thousand kors of wheat as provisions for his household, and twenty kors of pressed oil. Solomon provided this for Hiram year after year. 12. The Lord gave Solomon wisdom, just as He had promised him. And there was peace between Hiram and Solomon, and they made a treaty (formal agreement) with each other. 13. King Solomon raised up a labor force from all Israel, and the labor force consisted of thirty thousand men. 14. Solomon sent them to Lebanon in shifts of ten thousand men per month. They worked one month in Lebanon and then had two months off at home. Adoniram (Solomon's chief officer) was in charge of the labor force. 15. Solomon also had seventy thousand men who carried burdens, and eighty thousand men who quarried (mined or extracted) stone from the mountains, 16. In addition to three thousand three hundred men who were appointed as supervisors over the workers. These men supervised the people working on the project. 17. The king commanded that large stones, precious stones, and cut stones be quarried to form the foundation of the temple. 18. So Solomon's builders, Hiram's builders, and the Gebalites (people from Gebal, a city known for its stonework) worked together, preparing timber and stones to build the temple.

Chapter 6

1. In the four hundred and eightieth year (480 years) after the Israelites (children of Israel) came out of Egypt, in the fourth year of Solomon's reign (his rule) over Israel, during the month of Ziv (the second month of the Hebrew calendar), he began the construction of the Lord's temple (house of God). 2. The dimensions of the temple that King Solomon built for the Lord were as follows: it was sixty cubits (90 feet) long, twenty cubits (30 feet) wide, and thirty cubits (45 feet) high. 3. The vestibule (entrance area) in front of the sanctuary (holy place) of the temple was twenty cubits (30 feet) long, extending across the width of the house, and the vestibule itself was ten cubits (15 feet) wide from the front of the temple. 4. He made windows for the temple with beveled frames (windows with edges that were angled or polished to allow light to enter the temple). 5. He constructed chambers (small rooms or storage areas) along the walls of the temple, surrounding the sanctuary and the inner sanctuary. These side chambers (rooms) were attached to the temple structure. 6. The lower chamber was five cubits (7.5 feet) wide, the middle one was six cubits (9 feet) wide, and the uppermost chamber was seven cubits (10.5 feet) wide. He built narrow ledges (raised platforms) around the outside of the temple so that the support beams could not be attached directly to the walls of the temple. 7. The temple was built with stone that was finished at the quarry (stone that was cut and shaped before being brought to the building site), so that no hammer, chisel, or iron tool was heard inside

the temple while it was being constructed. **8.** The doorway to the middle story (floor level) of the temple was on the right side. To reach the middle story, workers would ascend stairs, and from the middle story, they could reach the third story. **9.** So, Solomon built the temple and completed it. He paneled the interior of the temple with beams and planks of cedar (a type of wood known for its durability and fragrance). **10.** He also built side chambers (small rooms) attached to the entire temple. These chambers were five cubits (7.5 feet) high and were supported by cedar beams. **11.** Then, the word (message) of the Lord came to Solomon, saying: **12.** "Concerning this temple that you are building, if you walk in My statutes (laws), follow My commands, obey all My decrees (orders), and live according to them, then I will keep the promise I made to your father, David. **13.** I will dwell among the people of Israel and will not abandon My people Israel." **14.** So Solomon built the temple and completed it. **15.** He covered the inside walls of the temple with cedar boards (wooden panels). The entire interior, from floor to ceiling, was paneled with wood, and the floor of the temple was covered with planks of cypress (another type of durable wood). **16.** Solomon also constructed a special room at the rear of the temple, twenty cubits (30 feet) long. This room was made with cedar boards from floor to ceiling, and it was used as the inner sanctuary (the Most Holy Place). **17.** In front of this inner sanctuary was the main sanctuary of the temple, which was forty cubits (60 feet) long. **18.** The interior of the temple was richly decorated with carved patterns of ornamental buds (flower-like designs) and open flowers. All of it was made of cedar wood; no stone was visible in the temple's interior. **19.** Solomon prepared the inner sanctuary of the temple to house the Ark of the Covenant (the sacred chest containing the tablets of the law) of the Lord. **20.** The inner sanctuary measured twenty cubits (30 feet) in length, twenty cubits (30 feet) in width, and twenty cubits (30 feet) in height. It was overlaid with pure gold, and the altar of cedar (wood) was also covered with gold. **21.** So Solomon overlaid the entire interior of the temple with pure gold. He stretched gold chains across the front of the inner sanctuary and covered it with gold. **22.** The whole temple was covered with gold, and Solomon completed this task, including the gold covering of the entire altar that stood in front of the inner sanctuary. **23.** Inside the inner sanctuary, Solomon made two cherubim (angelic figures) out of olive wood. Each cherub was ten cubits (15 feet) tall. **24.** One wing of each cherub was five cubits (7.5 feet), and the other wing was five cubits, making the total span of their wings ten cubits (15 feet) from tip to tip. **25.** The other cherub was identical in size and shape, ten cubits (15 feet) tall. **26.** The height of each cherub was ten cubits (15 feet), and both cherubim were of equal size. **27.** Solomon placed the cherubim inside the inner sanctuary. The wings of the cherubim were stretched out so that one wing of one cherub touched one wall, while the wing of the other cherub touched the opposite wall. Their wings met in the center of the room. **28.** Solomon overlaid the cherubim with gold. **29.** He also carved all the walls of the temple, both the inner and outer sanctuaries, with images of cherubim, palm trees, and open flowers (decorative patterns). **30.** The floor of the temple was also covered with gold, both in the inner and outer sanctuaries. **31.** For the entrance of the inner sanctuary, Solomon made doors out of olive wood. The lintels (horizontal beams above the doors) and doorposts were one-fifth of the thickness of the wall. **32.** The two doors were made of olive wood, and Solomon carved cherubim, palm trees, and open flowers on them. He covered them with gold and spread gold over the carvings. **33.** For the door of the main sanctuary, Solomon also made doorposts from olive wood, one-fourth the thickness of the wall. **34.** The two doors leading to the sanctuary were made of cypress wood (a strong, fragrant wood), and each door had two folding panels. **35.** Solomon carved cherubim, palm trees, and open flowers on these doors as well, and overlaid them with gold, ensuring the gold was evenly applied over the carvings. **36.** Solomon also built the inner court with three rows of hewn (cut or shaped) stone and a row of cedar beams. **37.** In the fourth year (of Solomon's reign), the foundation of the Lord's house was laid in the month of Ziv (the second month of the Hebrew calendar). **38.** And in the eleventh year, in the month of Bul (the eighth month of the Hebrew calendar), the house was finished, completed in every detail, according to all its plans. Thus, Solomon took seven years to build the temple.

Chapter 7

1. Solomon took thirteen years to build his own palace, and when it was completed, he had finished all the work on his house. **2.** He also built the House of the Forest of Lebanon. It was 100 cubits long, 50 cubits wide, and 30 cubits high. The structure was supported by four rows of cedar (a type of strong, aromatic wood) pillars, with cedar beams placed on top of them. **3.** The interior was paneled with cedar above the beams, and it was supported by 45 pillars, 15 in each row. **4.** The windows had beveled frames and were arranged in three rows, with each window facing another in three tiers. **5.** All the doorways and doorposts had rectangular frames, and the windows faced one another in three tiers. **6.** Solomon also built the Hall of Pillars, which was 50 cubits long and 30 cubits wide. In front of this hall was a portico (a roofed entrance supported by columns) with pillars, and a canopy was placed in front of these pillars. **7.** He then built a hall for his throne, called the Hall of Judgment, where he could sit and render decisions. This hall was fully paneled with cedar, from floor to ceiling. **8.** Inside the hall of the palace, Solomon constructed another court with the same style and workmanship. He also built a similar house for Pharaoh's daughter, whom he had taken as his wife. **9.** All of these buildings were made with precious stones, carefully cut to size and shaped with saws, both inside and out, from the foundation to the eaves, and even on the outside surrounding the great court. **10.** The foundation was made of costly stones, large stones, some 10 cubits and some 8 cubits in size. **11.** Above the foundation, costly stones were cut to precise measurements, and cedar wood was used throughout. **12.** The great court was surrounded by three rows of hewn (shaped or cut) stones and one row of cedar beams, similar to the inner court of the temple and the vestibule (entrance hall) of the temple. **13.** King Solomon sent for Huram from Tyre. **14.** Huram was the son of a widow from the tribe of Naphtali, and his father was a man of Tyre, a skilled bronze worker. He was filled with wisdom, understanding, and skill in working with all kinds of bronze. Solomon called on him, and Huram completed all the work for him. **15.** Huram cast two pillars of bronze, each 18 cubits high, with a circumference of 12 cubits. **16.** He also made two capitals (decorative tops) of cast bronze, each one 5 cubits tall, to set on top of the pillars. **17.** He crafted a latticework, adorned with wreaths of chainwork, to decorate the tops of the pillars, seven chains for one capital and seven for the other. **18.** On top of the capitals, Huram placed two rows of pomegranates (decorative fruit-shaped designs) surrounding each capital, covering the top of pillars. He did the same for the second capital. **19.** The capitals that rested on top of the pillars in the hall were shaped like lilies, standing 4 cubits tall. **20.** The two capitals on the pillars also had pomegranates above them, next to the latticework. In total, there were 200 pomegranates, arranged in rows on each capital all around. **21.** Huram set up the pillars at the entrance to the temple. He placed the pillar on the right and named it "Jachin" (which means "He will establish") and the pillar on the left, calling it "Boaz" (which means "In Him is strength"). **22.** The tops of the pillars were shaped like lilies, and thus the work of the pillars was completed. **23.** Huram also made the Sea of cast bronze. It was 10 cubits across from one brim to the other, completely round. It stood 5 cubits high, and its circumference measured 30 cubits. **24.** Around the brim of the Sea were ornamental buds, 10 for each cubit, arranged in two rows when the Sea was cast. **25.** The Sea rested on the backs of twelve oxen—three facing north, three facing west, three facing south, and three facing east. The oxen's backs were turned inward, supporting the Sea. **26.** The Sea was one handbreadth thick, and its brim was shaped like the brim of a cup, resembling a lily blossom. It could hold 2,000 baths (a unit of liquid measurement). **27.** Huram also made ten carts of bronze. Each cart was 4 cubits long, 4 cubits wide, and 3 cubits high. **28.** Each cart had panels between frames, **29.** and on these panels were images of lions, oxen, and cherubim (heavenly beings with wings), with wreaths of plaited (woven) work beneath them. **30.** Each cart had four bronze wheels and axles of bronze. The four feet of each cart were supported by cast bronze. **31.** The opening at the top of each cart was one cubit in diameter, shaped like a pedestal. Its outer diameter was one and a half cubits, and there were engravings on the opening. The panels of the carts were square, not round. **32.** Beneath the panels, there were four wheels, and the axles were firmly attached to the cart. The wheels were one and a half cubits tall. **33.** The wheels were constructed like chariot wheels, with their axle pins, rims, spokes, and hubs all made of cast bronze. **34.** Each cart had four supports at its four corners, which were an integral part of the cart. **35.** At the top of each cart, just below the top edge, was a round flange (edge or rim). The flanges and panels were made of the same cast bronze. **36.** On the plates of the flanges and on the panels, Huram engraved images of cherubim, lions, and palm trees, wherever there was space, with wreaths surrounding them. **37.** Huram made a total of ten carts, all identical in size and shape. **38.** Huram also made ten lavers (large basins for washing) of bronze, each capable of holding 40 baths. Each laver was 4 cubits in size. Each of the ten carts had one laver. **39.** Five carts were placed on the right side of the temple, and five on the left. The Sea was placed on the right side of the temple, toward the southeast. **40.** Huram completed the lavers, shovels, and bowls, finishing all the work Solomon had assigned him for the temple of the Lord. **41.** This included the two pillars, the two bowl-shaped capitals that sat on top of the pillars, the two networks covering the capitals, **42.** the 400 pomegranates for the two networks (with two rows of pomegranates for each network), **43.** the ten carts, and the ten lavers placed on the carts, **44.** the Sea, and the twelve oxen under the Sea, **45.** the pots, shovels, and bowls—all made of burnished bronze. **46.** These items were cast in clay molds in the plain of Jordan, between Succoth and Zaretan. **47.** Solomon did not weigh the bronze for these items because there were so many. The weight of the bronze was not determined. **48.** Solomon had all the furnishings made for the temple of the Lord, including the golden altar and the golden table on which the showbread (bread of presence) was placed, **49.** the lampstands made of pure gold, five on the right and five on the left, in front of the inner sanctuary, along with the flowers, lamps, and wick-trimmers, all of gold, **50.** The basins, trimmers, bowls, ladles, and censers of pure gold, as well as the hinges for the doors of the inner room (the Most Holy Place) and the doors of the main hall, which were all made of gold. **51.** When all the work Solomon had done for the temple of the Lord was finished, he brought in the items that his father David had dedicated—the silver, gold, and furnishings—and placed them in the treasuries of the house of the Lord.

Chapter 8

1. Solomon gathered the elders (leaders) of Israel, along with the heads (leaders) of the tribes and the leaders of the families, to bring them before King Solomon in Jerusalem. Their purpose was to bring the Ark (sacred chest) of the Covenant (agreement) of the Lord up from the City of David (Jerusalem), also called Zion (ancient name for Jerusalem). **2.** All the men of Israel gathered with King Solomon at the festival (celebration) in the month of Ethanim (seventh month, September or October). **3.** The elders (leaders) of Israel came, and the priests (religious leaders) took up the Ark. **4.** They brought the Ark of the Lord, along with the Tabernacle (portable sanctuary) of meeting, and all the sacred furnishings (holy objects) that were in the Tabernacle. The priests and the Levites (members of the tribe of Levi, dedicated to religious duties) carried them. **5.** Solomon, along with all the people of Israel who had assembled (gathered), stood before the Ark and offered sacrifices (ritual animal offerings). These included sheep and oxen in such great numbers that they could not be counted. **6.** The priests then placed the Ark of the Covenant of the Lord in its designated (appointed) place, inside the inner sanctuary (the innermost part of the temple), in the Most Holy Place (most sacred area), under the wings of the cherubim (angelic beings with wings). **7.** The cherubim spread their wings over the Ark, covering it and its poles (long rods used to carry the Ark). **8.** The poles of the Ark extended so that their ends could be seen from the holy place in front of the inner sanctuary, but they could not be seen from outside. They remain this way to this day. **9.** The Ark contained only the two stone tablets (the Ten Commandments) that Moses had placed there at Horeb (Mount Sinai), when the Lord made a covenant (binding agreement) with the Israelites after their escape from Egypt. **10.** When the priests came out of the holy place, a cloud filled the house (temple) of the Lord, **11.** so that the priests could not perform their duties because the cloud filled the temple; for the glory (manifest presence) of the Lord filled the house of the Lord. **12.** Then Solomon spoke: "The Lord said He would dwell in the dark cloud (symbolizing God's presence). **13.** I have truly built You an exalted (glorified) house, a place for You to dwell in forever." **14.** The king then turned and blessed (praised) the whole assembly (gathering) of Israel, and all the people stood. **15.** He said, "Blessed be the Lord God of Israel, who spoke to my father David with His mouth, and with His hand (power) has fulfilled it, saying: **16.** 'Since the day I brought My people Israel out of Egypt, I have not chosen a city from any of the tribes of Israel in which to build a house for My name to be there; but I chose David to be over My people Israel.' **17.** It was in the heart (desire) of my father David to build a temple (house of worship) for the name of the Lord God of Israel. **18.** But the Lord said to my father David, 'It was good that it was in your heart to build a temple for My name. **19.** However, you shall not build it; instead, your son, who will come from your own body, shall build the temple for My name.' **20.** The Lord has kept His word, which He spoke. I have taken the place of my father David, sitting on the throne of Israel, as the Lord promised, and I have built a temple for the name of the Lord God of Israel. **21.** And there I have made a place for the Ark, in which is the Covenant (agreement) of the Lord, which He made with our ancestors when He brought them out of the land of Egypt." **22.** Solomon stood before the altar (place of sacrifice) of the Lord in front of the entire assembly (gathering) of Israel, and spread out his hands toward heaven. **23.** He said, "Lord God of Israel, there is no God in heaven above or on earth below like You, who keep Your covenant (promise) and mercy (compassion) with Your servants who walk before You with all their hearts. **24.** You have kept Your promise to Your servant David, my father; You have spoken with Your mouth and fulfilled it with Your hand, as it is today. **25.** Now, Lord God of Israel, fulfill what You promised Your servant David, my father, saying: 'You shall never fail to have a man sit on the throne of Israel, provided your descendants take heed (pay attention) to their way, to walk before Me as you have walked before Me.' **26.** And now I pray, O God of Israel, let Your word come true, which You have spoken to Your servant David, my father. **27.** But will God really dwell on earth? The heavens, even the highest heavens, cannot contain You. How much less this temple I have built! **28.** Yet regard (look upon) the prayer of Your servant and his supplication (earnest request), O Lord my God, and listen to the cry and prayer Your servant is praying before You today: **29.** That Your eyes may be open toward this temple night and day, toward the place where You said, 'My name will be there,' that You may hear the prayer Your servant makes toward this place. **30.** And may You hear the supplication (plea) of Your servant and of Your people Israel when they pray toward this place. Hear from heaven, Your dwelling place; and when You hear, forgive. **31.** "When anyone sins (does wrong) against his neighbor and is forced to take an oath (swear an oath to tell the truth), and comes and takes an oath before Your altar in this temple, **32.** then hear from heaven, and act, and judge Your servants, condemning the wicked (guilty) and bringing his way upon his own head, but justifying (declaring innocent) the righteous by giving him according to his righteousness. **33.** "When Your people Israel are defeated by an enemy because they have sinned against You, and when they turn back to You, confess Your name, and pray and make supplication to You in this temple, **34.** then hear from heaven, and forgive the sin of Your people Israel, and bring them back to the land which You gave to their ancestors. **35.** "When the heavens are shut up and there is no rain because they have sinned against You, and they pray toward this place and confess Your name, and turn from their sin because You have afflicted them, **36.** then hear from heaven, and forgive the sin of Your servants, Your people Israel, that You may teach them the good way in which they should walk, and send rain on Your land which You have given to Your people as an inheritance. **37.** "When there is famine (food shortage) in the land, pestilence (disease), blight (plant disease), mildew, locusts (insects that destroy crops), or grasshoppers; when their enemy besieges (surrounds) them in their cities; whatever plague (calamity) or sickness there is; **38.** whatever prayer or supplication (request) is made by anyone, or by all Your people Israel, when each one knows the plague (calamity) of his own heart, and spreads out his hands toward this temple: **39.** then hear from heaven Your dwelling place, and forgive, and act, and give to everyone according to all his ways, whose heart You know (for You alone know the hearts of all mankind), **40.** that they may fear (respect) You all the days they live in the land You gave to our ancestors. **41.**

"Moreover, concerning a foreigner (non-Israelite), who is not of Your people Israel but has come from a distant land for Your name's sake (to seek You because of Your greatness), **42.** when he comes and prays toward this temple, **43.** hear from heaven Your dwelling place, and do according to all for which the foreigner calls to You, so that all peoples of the earth may know Your name and fear (respect) You, as do Your people Israel, and that they may know that this temple I have built is called by Your name. **44.** "When Your people go out to battle against their enemies, wherever You send them, and when they pray to the Lord toward the city You have chosen and the temple I have built for Your name, **45.** then hear from heaven their prayer and their supplication (request), and maintain (support) their cause. **46.** "When they sin (wrong) against You (for there is no one who does not sin), and You become angry with them, and deliver (hand them over) them to the enemy, and they take them captive (capture) to the land of the enemy, far or near; **47.** yet when they repent (turn back) in the land where they were carried captive, and pray and make supplication to You in the land of those who took them captive, saying, 'We have sinned and done wrong, we have committed wickedness'; **48.** and when they return to You with all their heart and with all their soul in the land of their enemies who led them away captive, and pray to You toward their land, which You gave to their ancestors, the city You have chosen, and the temple I have built for Your name: **49.** then hear from heaven Your dwelling place their prayer and supplication, and maintain their cause, **50.** and forgive Your people who have sinned against You, and all their transgressions (sins) which they have committed against You; and grant them compassion (mercy) before those who took them captive, that they may have compassion on them. **51.** For they are Your people and Your inheritance (possession), whom You brought out of Egypt, out of the iron furnace (place of hardship). **52.** Let Your eyes be open to the supplication (prayer) of Your servant and the supplication of Your people Israel, and listen to them whenever they call to You. **53.** For You separated (set apart) them from all the peoples of the earth to be Your inheritance, as You spoke by Your servant Moses when You brought our ancestors out of Egypt, O Lord God." **54.** When Solomon finished praying all these prayers and supplications to the Lord, he rose from before the altar of the Lord, where he had been kneeling with his hands spread out toward heaven. **55.** Then he stood and blessed all the assembly (gathering) of Israel with a loud voice, saying: **56.** "Blessed be the Lord, who has given rest (peace) to His people Israel, according to all that He promised. Not one word has failed of all His good promises, which He spoke through His servant Moses. **57.** May the Lord our God be with us, as He was with our ancestors. May He never leave us or forsake us, **58.** that He may incline (turn) our hearts to Himself, to walk in all His ways, and to keep His commandments, statutes, and judgments, which He commanded our ancestors. **59.** And may these words of mine, with which I have made supplication before the Lord, be near the Lord our God day and night, that He may maintain the cause of His servant and the cause of His people Israel, as each day may require, **60.** that all the peoples of the earth may know that the Lord is God; there is no other. **61.** Let your heart, therefore, be loyal (faithful) to the Lord our God, to walk in His statutes and keep His commandments, as you do today." **62.** Then the king and all Israel with him offered sacrifices before the Lord. **63.** Solomon offered a peace offering to the Lord, twenty-two thousand bulls and one hundred and twenty thousand sheep. So the king and all the Israelites dedicated the house of the Lord. **64.** On that day, the king consecrated (set apart) the middle of the court in front of the house of the Lord, for there he offered burnt offerings, grain offerings, and the fat of the peace offerings, because the bronze altar in front of the Lord was too small to receive all the offerings. **65.** At that time, Solomon held a feast with all Israel, a great assembly from the entrance of Hamath (northern boundary) to the Brook of Egypt (southern boundary), before the Lord our God, for fourteen days—seven days and seven more days. **66.** On the eighth day, he sent the people away, and they blessed the king and went to their tents joyful and glad of heart for all the good the Lord had done for His servant David and for Israel His people.

Chapter 9

1. After Solomon had completed the building of the house of the Lord and his own royal palace, and after fulfilling all his desires (plans) to accomplish what he wished, **2.** the Lord appeared to Solomon for a second time, just as He had appeared to him in Gibeon (a city in Israel). **3.** The Lord said to Solomon, "I have heard your prayer and your supplication (earnest request) that you made before Me; I have consecrated (set apart as holy) this house which you have built, to place My name there forever, and My eyes and My heart will be there continually (forever). **4.** If you walk before Me as your father David walked, in integrity (honesty) of heart and in uprightness (moral correctness), to do according to all that I have commanded you, and if you keep My statutes (laws) and My judgments (decisions), **5.** then I will establish (make firm) the throne of your kingdom over Israel forever, as I promised David your father, saying, 'You shall never fail to have a man on the throne of Israel.' **6.** But if you or your sons turn away from following Me, and do not keep My commandments and statutes which I have set before you, but go and serve other gods and worship them, **7.** then I will cut off Israel from the land I have given them; and this house which I have consecrated for My name, I will cast out of My sight. Israel will become a proverb (a saying) and a byword (a term of reproach) among all peoples. **8.** As for this exalted (magnificent) house, everyone who passes by will be astonished (amazed) and will hiss (make a noise of disbelief), saying, 'Why has the Lord done this to this land and this house?' **9.** And they will answer, 'Because they forsook (abandoned) the Lord their God, who brought their ancestors out of Egypt, and embraced other gods, and worshiped them and served them; therefore, the Lord has brought all this calamity (disaster) upon them.'" **10.** Now, it happened at the end of twenty years, when Solomon had finished building the two houses: the house of the Lord and the king's house, **11.** (Hiram, the king of Tyre, had provided Solomon with cedar (a type of wood) and cypress (another type of wood) and gold, as much as he desired), that King Solomon then gave Hiram twenty cities in the land of Galilee (a region in northern Israel). **12.** Then Hiram went from Tyre (a city in Phoenicia) to see the cities Solomon had given him, but they did not please him. **13.** So he said, "What kind of cities are these that you have given me, my brother?" And he called them the land of Cabul (meaning "good for nothing"), as they are to this day. **14.** Then Hiram sent the king one hundred and twenty talents (a measure of weight, about 4,500 pounds) of gold. **15.** And this is the reason for the labor force which King Solomon raised: to build the house of the Lord, his own house, the Millo (a large structure or support in Jerusalem), the wall of Jerusalem, Hazor (an ancient city), Megiddo (an ancient city), and Gezer (a city in Israel). **16.** (Pharaoh, king of Egypt, had gone up and taken Gezer, burned it with fire, killed the Canaanites who lived in the city, and gave it as a dowry to his daughter, Solomon's wife). **17.** Solomon rebuilt Gezer, Lower Beth Horon (a town near Jerusalem), **18.** Baalath (a city in the territory of Dan), and Tadmor (a city in the desert, also known as Palmyra) in the wilderness, in the land of Judah. **19.** He also built all the storage cities that Solomon had, cities for his chariots and cities for his cavalry (soldiers on horseback), and whatever Solomon desired to build in Jerusalem, Lebanon (a region famous for its cedars), and throughout his entire kingdom. **20.** All the people who were left of the Amorites, Hittites, Perizzites, Hivites, and Jebusites (ancient tribes), who were not part of Israel, **21.** that is, their descendants who remained in the land after the Israelites had been unable to completely destroy them, from these, Solomon raised forced labor (slave-like work), as it continues to this day. **22.** But Solomon made no forced laborers from the children of Israel, because they were men of war and his servants: his officers, captains, commanders of his chariots, and his cavalry. **23.** Other Israelites served as chiefs of the officials who were over Solomon's work: five hundred and fifty men who supervised the laborers. **24.** But Pharaoh's daughter came up from the City of David (Jerusalem) to the house that Solomon had built for her, and then he built the Millo. **25.** Three times a year, Solomon offered burnt offerings (sacrifices where the entire animal is burned) and peace offerings (offerings made to seek peace with God) on the altar he had built for the Lord, and he burned incense (sweet-smelling smoke used in worship) with them on the altar that was before the Lord. Thus, he completed the temple. **26.** King Solomon also built a fleet of ships at Ezion-Geber (a port city), which is near Elath (another port) on the shore of the Red Sea, in the land of Edom (a region to the southeast of Israel). **27.** Then Hiram sent his servants, who were experienced sailors, to work with Solomon's men. **28.** They went to Ophir (a region known for its wealth), and brought back four hundred and twenty talents of gold (about 15,000 pounds), which they gave to King Solomon.

Chapter 10

1. When the Queen of Sheba (a queen from a wealthy kingdom in Arabia or Africa) heard of Solomon's fame and how it was linked to the name of the LORD, she decided to visit him in Jerusalem to test his wisdom with difficult questions. **2.** She arrived in Jerusalem with a great entourage (group of attendants), including camels that carried spices, large amounts of gold, and precious stones. She came to Solomon and asked him everything that was on her mind. **3.** Solomon answered all of her questions; there was nothing too complex for the king to explain. **4.** After observing Solomon's wisdom, the palace he had built, **5.** the food on his table, the way his servants were seated, the attire of his attendants, and the impressive entrance to the temple of the Lord, the Queen was left breathless. **6.** She said to him, "What I heard in my own country about your wisdom and your words is true. **7.** However, I did not believe it until I came and saw it with my own eyes. And now, I can say that even the half of it was not told to me. Your wisdom and prosperity exceed all the fame I had heard. **8.** How happy are your men and how fortunate are your servants, who stand before you and hear your wisdom every day! **9.** Blessed be the Lord your God, who has delighted in you and set you on the throne of Israel! Because the Lord loves Israel forever, He has made you king to uphold justice and righteousness." **10.** She then gave the king 120 talents of gold (a unit of weight for gold), along with a large quantity of spices and precious stones. Never before had such a vast amount of spices been brought to Israel as the Queen of Sheba gave Solomon. **11.** Solomon's ships, which operated with King Hiram's fleet (Hiram was the king of Tyre and an ally of Solomon), brought back gold from Ophir (a rich and distant land known for its wealth), along with large amounts of almug wood (a rare wood used for luxury furniture and musical instruments) and precious stones. **12.** Solomon used this almug wood to make steps for the temple of the Lord and for his own palace, as well as to create harps and stringed instruments for the singers. Never again was such almug wood brought to Israel, nor has it ever been seen again. **13.** Solomon gave the Queen of Sheba everything she asked for, in addition to what he gave her out of his royal generosity. Then she returned to her own country with her attendants. **14.** The amount of gold that came to Solomon each year was 666 talents (a large unit of weight), **15.** not including the gold brought by the traveling merchants, the traders, the kings of Arabia, and the governors of the regions. **16.** Solomon also had 200 large shields made of hammered gold, with each shield containing 600 shekels (a smaller unit of weight for gold) of gold. **17.** He made 300 smaller shields of hammered gold, each one made with 3 minas (another unit of weight) of gold. Solomon placed them in the House of the Forest of Lebanon (a palace in Jerusalem built of cedar wood). **18.** Solomon also created an extraordinary throne made of ivory, which he overlaid with pure gold. **19.** The throne had six steps, and the back was rounded. There were armrests on either side of the seat, and two lions stood beside the armrests. **20.** Twelve lions stood at the base of the throne, one on each side of the six steps. Nothing like this had ever been made for any other kingdom. **21.** All of King Solomon's drinking vessels were made of gold, and all the vessels in the House of the Forest of Lebanon were pure gold. There was no silver to be found, as it was considered of little value during Solomon's reign. **22.** Solomon had merchant ships at sea in partnership with Hiram's fleet. Every three years, these ships returned bringing gold, silver, ivory, apes, and monkeys. **23.** As a result, Solomon became wealthier and wiser than any other king on earth. **24.** People from all over the world came to hear the wisdom that God had placed in Solomon's heart. **25.** Each visitor brought gifts: silver and gold objects, garments, armor, spices, horses, and mules, all given according to a fixed yearly amount. **26.** Solomon gathered an army of 1,400 chariots and 12,000 horsemen. These were stationed in the chariot cities and in Jerusalem. **27.** During Solomon's reign, silver became as common in Jerusalem as stones, and cedar trees were as abundant as the sycamore trees in the lowland areas. **28.** Solomon imported horses from Egypt and Keveh (a region possibly in Mesopotamia known for its horses). His merchants bought them in Keveh at the market price. **29.** A chariot imported from Egypt cost 600 shekels of silver, and a horse cost 150 shekels. These

were then sold to the kings of the Hittites and the kings of Syria through Solomon's agents.

Chapter 11

1. King Solomon (son of David) cherished many foreign wives, including the daughter of Pharaoh (King of Egypt), along with women from the Moabites, Ammonites, Edomites, Sidonians, and Hittites—the very nations the Lord had warned Israel against intermarrying with, for their gods would turn the hearts of the Israelites away. Solomon, however, was deeply devoted to these women. **2.** From the nations the Lord had commanded the Israelites not to intermarry with, saying, "They will surely lead your hearts away to their gods." Solomon held fast to them in love. **3.** Solomon had seven hundred wives, many of them princesses, and three hundred concubines (secondary wives). His wives turned his heart toward other gods. **4.** When Solomon grew old, his wives led him to follow other gods, and his heart became divided, no longer fully devoted to the Lord, as his father David's had been. **5.** Solomon followed Ashtoreth (the goddess of the Sidonians) and Milcom (the detestable idol of the Ammonites). **6.** Solomon did what was wrong in the sight of the Lord and failed to follow the Lord with a loyal heart, as his father David had. **7.** Solomon built a high place (a place of worship on elevated ground) for Chemosh (the abomination of Moab), east of Jerusalem (capital of Israel), and for Molech (the detestable god of the Ammonites). **8.** He did the same for all his foreign wives, who burned incense and made sacrifices to their gods. **9.** The Lord became angry with Solomon because his heart had turned away from the Lord, the God of Israel, who had appeared to him twice. **10.** He had given Solomon clear commands about not following other gods, but Solomon did not keep the commandment of the Lord. **11.** Therefore, the Lord told Solomon, "Since you have acted this way and have not kept My covenant and My statutes, I will tear the kingdom from you and give it to your servant." **12.** However, I will not do this in your lifetime for the sake of your father David (King of Israel); I will tear it from the hand of your son. **13.** But I will not take away the whole kingdom; I will give one tribe to your son, for the sake of My servant David (King of Israel), and for the sake of Jerusalem (the city I have chosen). **14.** The Lord raised up an adversary against Solomon: Hadad the Edomite, a descendant of the Edomite king. **15.** This was because, when David (King of Israel) had been in Edom (a region southeast of Israel), Joab (David's military commander) had killed every male in Edom. **16.** (Joab had remained there for six months, wiping out every male in Edom.) **17.** Hadad, a young child at the time, fled to Egypt (land of Pharaoh) with certain servants from his father's household. **18.** They traveled from Midian (desert region east of Israel) and came to Paran (a wilderness area), where they took men with them and went to Egypt, to Pharaoh, king of Egypt. Pharaoh gave them a house, provided food, and gave him land. **19.** Pharaoh showed favor to Hadad, even giving him as wife the sister of his own queen, Tahpenes. **20.** Tahpenes (Pharaoh's queen) bore him Genubath, whom she raised in Pharaoh's household. Genubath lived among Pharaoh's children. **21.** When Hadad heard that David (King of Israel) had died and that Joab (commander of Israel's army) was also dead, he asked Pharaoh, "Let me go back to my own country." **22.** Pharaoh replied, "What have you lacked with me that you now want to go to your own country?" Hadad responded, "Nothing, but let me go anyway." **23.** The Lord raised up another adversary against Solomon, Rezon (son of Eliadah), who had fled from Hadadezer (King of Zobah, northeast of Israel). **24.** Rezon had gathered a group of raiders after David (King of Israel) defeated Zobah. He moved to Damascus (capital of Syria) and became its king. **25.** Rezon became an enemy of Israel throughout Solomon's reign, along with the troubles caused by Hadad. He despised Israel and ruled over Syria. **26.** Jeroboam (son of Nebat, an Ephraimite from Zereda), a servant of Solomon, also rebelled against the king. **27.** The reason for Jeroboam's rebellion was that Solomon had built the Millo (a fortification in Jerusalem) and repaired the damages to the City of David (Jerusalem). **28.** Jeroboam was a man of great ability, and Solomon saw that he was industrious. Solomon made him the overseer of the labor force from the tribe of Joseph. **29.** One day, as Jeroboam was leaving Jerusalem, the prophet Ahijah (from Shiloh) met him on the road. Ahijah was wearing a new garment, and the two were alone in the field. **30.** Ahijah took hold of the new garment Jeroboam was wearing and tore it into twelve pieces. **31.** He said to Jeroboam, "Take ten pieces, for this is what the Lord, the God of Israel, says: 'I will tear the kingdom from Solomon and give you ten tribes. **32.** He will keep one tribe for the sake of My servant David (King of Israel), and for the sake of Jerusalem (the city I have chosen from all the tribes)." **33.** "This is because they have forsaken Me and worshiped Ashtoreth (the goddess of Sidon), Chemosh (god of Moab), and Milcom (god of Ammon). They have not followed My ways, nor kept My statutes, as David (King of Israel) did." **34.** "I will not take the kingdom entirely from Solomon because I made him ruler all his life for the sake of My servant David (King of Israel), whom I chose because he obeyed My commands." **35.** "But I will take the kingdom from his son and give it to you—ten tribes." **36.** "I will leave one tribe for his son, so that My servant David (King of Israel) will always have a lamp before Me in Jerusalem (the city I have chosen for Myself)." **37.** "I will make you king over all your heart desires, and you will rule over Israel." **38.** "If you listen to all I command you, walk in My ways, and do what is right in My sight, keeping My statutes and commandments as David (King of Israel) did, then I will be with you. I will build you a lasting dynasty, just as I did for David, and I will give Israel to you." **39.** "However, I will afflict the descendants of David because of this, but not forever." **40.** Solomon sought to kill Jeroboam. But Jeroboam fled to Egypt (land of Pharaoh) and stayed there until Solomon died. **41.** The rest of the acts of Solomon, including all that he did and his wisdom, are they not written in the book of the acts of Solomon? **42.** Solomon reigned in Jerusalem (capital of Israel) over all Israel for forty years. **43.** Then Solomon rested with his ancestors and was buried in the City of David (Jerusalem). His son Rehoboam (Solomon's successor) became king in his place.

Chapter 12

1. Rehoboam went to Shechem (a city in Israel), where all Israel had gathered to make him king. **2.** When Jeroboam, the son of Nebat, heard this (he was still in Egypt, where he had fled from King Solomon), he had been living there for a while. **3.** The people sent for Jeroboam, and he came with all of Israel's assembly to speak with Rehoboam. They said to him: **4.** "Your father made our work very difficult. If you lighten the heavy labor and the harsh treatment your father placed on us, we will serve you." **5.** Rehoboam replied, "Come back to me in three days." So the people went away. **6.** Rehoboam consulted the older men who had served his father Solomon. He asked them, "What do you advise me to say to these people?" **7.** The elders answered, "If you are kind to the people today and speak kindly to them, they will serve you forever." **8.** But Rehoboam rejected the advice of the elders and consulted the young men who had grown up with him and were now his advisors. **9.** He asked them, "What advice do you have for me? How should I answer the people who said, 'Lighten the burden your father placed on us'?" **10.** The young men who had grown up with him replied, "This is what you should tell the people: 'My father made your burden heavy, but I will make it heavier. My father punished you with whips, but I will punish you with scorpions (a more severe form of punishment)!'" **11.** So, when Jeroboam and all the people came back on the third day as instructed, Rehoboam answered them harshly. He rejected the advice of the elders. **12.** He said to them, "My father made your yoke heavy, but I will make it even heavier. My father disciplined you with whips, but I will use scorpions!" **13.** The king did not listen to the people. This turn of events was from the Lord, to fulfill the word that He had spoken through the prophet Ahijah (a prophet from Shiloh) to Jeroboam, the son of Nebat. **14.** When all Israel saw that the king was not listening to them, they answered the king, saying, "What share do we have in David? We have no inheritance in the son of Jesse (David). To your tents, Israel! Look after your own house, David!" So Israel went to their homes. **15.** But Rehoboam still ruled over the people of Judah, who lived in the cities of Judah. **16.** Rehoboam sent Adoram (the officer in charge of taxes) to the people, but they stoned him to death. Rehoboam quickly got into his chariot and fled to Jerusalem. **17.** So, Israel has been in rebellion against the house of David ever since. **18.** When all Israel heard that Jeroboam had returned, they called him to the congregation and made him king over all Israel. Only the tribe of Judah remained loyal to Rehoboam. **19.** Rehoboam assembled 180,000 men from Judah and Benjamin to fight against Israel, to restore the kingdom to himself. **20.** But the word of the Lord came to the prophet Shemaiah, saying: **21.** "Speak to Rehoboam, the son of Solomon, king of Judah, and to all the people of Judah and Benjamin, and to the rest of Israel: **22.** 'This is what the Lord says: Do not go up and fight against your brothers, the Israelites. Let every man return to his home, because this is from Me.'" **23.** So, they obeyed the word of the Lord and returned to their homes, as God had commanded. **24.** Jeroboam built Shechem (a city) in the mountains of Ephraim (a region) and settled there. He also built Penuel (another city). **25.** Jeroboam said to himself, "Now the kingdom may return to the house of David (the family of King David): **26.** If these people go to offer sacrifices at the house of the Lord in Jerusalem, their hearts will turn back to their lord, Rehoboam, king of Judah. They will kill me and return to him." **27.** Therefore, the king consulted with his advisors and made two golden calves (idols). He said to the people, "It is too much for you to go all the way to Jerusalem. Here are your gods, Israel, who brought you up from Egypt!" **28.** He set up one golden calf in Bethel (a city) and the other in Dan (another city in the north). **29.** This act became a sin, for the people went as far as Dan to worship the one there. **30.** Jeroboam made shrines (places of idol worship) on the high places and appointed priests from among the people who were not from the tribe of Levi (the tribe set apart for religious duties). **31.** Jeroboam also ordained a feast on the fifteenth day of the eighth month, just like the festival in Judah. He offered sacrifices on the altar in Bethel, sacrificing to the golden calves he had made. **32.** In Bethel, he installed the priests of the high places he had made, and he offered sacrifices and burned incense. **33.** Jeroboam made offerings on the altar he had built in Bethel on the fifteenth day of the eighth month, a festival he had devised in his own mind. He appointed a feast for the people of Israel and offered sacrifices on the altar, burning incense.

Chapter 13

1. A man of God from Judah (the southern kingdom of Israel) was sent by the LORD to Bethel (a city in Israel), where King Jeroboam (the first king of Israel after it split) was standing by the altar to burn incense (a substance offered in religious rituals). **2.** The man of God shouted against the altar, saying, "O altar, altar! The Lord says: 'A child named Josiah will be born into the family of David. He will sacrifice the priests who burn incense here, and their bones (dead bodies) will be burned on this altar.'" **3.** He also gave a sign (a miraculous confirmation), saying, "The sign from the Lord will be: The altar will break apart, and the ashes (burned remains) on it will be poured out." **4.** When King Jeroboam heard these words, he stretched out his hand and ordered, "Seize him!" But as he extended his hand toward the man of God, his hand withered (became stiff and unable to move), and he couldn't pull it back. **5.** The altar split open, and the ashes were spilled out, exactly as the man of God had said, in accordance with the word of the Lord. **6.** The king then pleaded with the man of God, saying, "Please pray to the Lord your God and ask Him to restore my hand." So the man of God prayed to the Lord, and the king's hand was healed and returned to its normal state. **7.** The king said to the man of God, "Come home with me, and I will reward you." **8.** But the man of God responded, "Even if you gave me half of your house (a large portion of your wealth), I would not go with you, nor would I eat or drink in this place." **9.** "For the Lord commanded me, 'You must not eat bread or drink water here, and you must not return the way you came.'" **10.** So, he took a different route and did not return to Bethel the same way he had come. **11.** An old prophet (a more experienced religious leader) lived in Bethel, and his sons came and told him everything that the man of God had done that day. They also shared the words he had spoken to King Jeroboam. **12.** The old prophet asked his sons, "Which way did he go?" And they pointed out the path the man of God had taken. **13.** The old prophet then said, "Saddle my donkey." They prepared it, and he rode off to find the man of God. **14.** He found the man of God sitting under an oak tree (a large, sturdy tree) and asked, "Are you the man of God who came from Judah?" The man of God answered, "I am." **15.** The old prophet invited him, saying, "Come home with me and eat." **16.** But the man of God replied, "I cannot return with you or go to your house. I cannot eat or drink here." **17.** "I have been commanded by the word of the Lord, 'Do not eat bread or drink water here, and do not return the way you came.'" **18.** The old prophet said, "I too am a prophet, just like you. An angel (a messenger from God) spoke to me by the word of the Lord, saying, 'Bring him back with you to your house so he may eat bread and drink water.'" (But he was lying.) **19.** So, the man of God went back with him, ate bread, and drank water in the old prophet's house. **20.** While they were eating at the table, the word of the Lord came to the old prophet. **21.** The old prophet cried out to the man of God, "This is what the Lord says: 'Because you disobeyed the word of the Lord and did not follow the command He gave you, **22.** but came back, ate bread, and drank water in this place, even though the Lord commanded you not to, your body will not be buried with your ancestors.'" **23.** After eating, the man of God got up to leave. The old prophet prepared his donkey for him. **24.** As the man of God was traveling, a lion (a symbol of divine judgment) met him on the road and killed him. His body was left on the road, and the donkey stood next to the body, while the lion also stood by. **25.** People passing by saw the body and the lion standing by it and went into the city where the old prophet lived. **26.** When the old prophet heard what had happened, he said, "It is the man of God who disobeyed the Lord's command. That is why the Lord has allowed the lion to kill him, as He had spoken." **27.** The old prophet said to his sons, "Saddle my donkey." They prepared it for him. **28.** He went and found the body of the man of God lying on the road, with the donkey and the lion standing beside it. The lion had not eaten the body or harmed the donkey. **29.** The old prophet took the body, placed it on his donkey, and returned to the city to mourn and bury it. **30.** He laid the body in his own tomb (a burial site), and they mourned over it, saying, "Alas, my brother!" **31.** After burying the man of God, the old prophet told his sons, "When I die, bury me in the tomb where the man of God is buried, and lay my bones beside his bones. **32.** The prophecy he declared against the altar in Bethel and the places of idol worship in Samaria will surely come to pass." **33.** After this event, King Jeroboam did not turn away from his sinful ways. He continued appointing priests (religious leaders) for the high places (altars for idol worship), allowing anyone who wanted to become a priest. **34.** This practice led to sin for the house of Jeroboam and resulted in the destruction (wiping out) of his family from the earth.

Chapter 14

1. At that time, Abijah (son of Jeroboam) became seriously ill. **2.** Jeroboam (the king of Israel) told his wife, "Please disguise yourself (change your appearance) so that no one will recognize you as my wife. Go to Shiloh (a city in Israel), where the prophet Ahijah (a man of God) is, the one who told me I would be king over Israel. **3.** Take with you ten loaves of bread, some cakes, and a jar of honey, and ask him what will happen to our son." **4.** Jeroboam's wife did as he said and went to Shiloh, to the house of Ahijah. But Ahijah was blind (unable to see) because of his old age. **5.** The LORD had already spoken to Ahijah, telling him that Jeroboam's wife would come to ask about her son. God said, "She will pretend to be someone else, and you must tell her what will happen." **6.** When Ahijah heard her footsteps, he said, "Come in, wife of Jeroboam. Why are you pretending to be someone else? I have bad news (unfavorable message) for you." **7.** "Go back and tell Jeroboam, 'This is what the LORD says: I chose you from among the people and made you king over Israel. **8.** I took the kingdom from the house of David (the royal family of Judah) and gave it to you, but you have not followed Me like My servant David (David was a faithful king), who obeyed My commands and did what was right in My sight. **9.** You have done more evil (bad actions) than anyone before you, for you made idols (statues of false gods) and provoked My anger. You have cast Me aside and forgotten My ways. **10.** Therefore, I will bring disaster (calamity or destruction) on your house. I will cut off every male (man or boy) from your family, both slave (a servant) and free (a person who is not a servant). I will wipe out your entire household, like trash (waste) that is taken away. **11.** The dogs (wild animals) will eat those of your family who die in the city, and the birds (flying creatures) of the air will eat those who die in the field. The LORD has spoken!'" **12.** "Go back to your house. As soon as you step into the city, your son will die. **13.** All of Israel will mourn (feel sorrow) for him and bury him, because he is the only one in Jeroboam's family who will be buried. He is the only one who showed some goodness (virtue) toward the LORD of Israel." **14.** "The LORD will raise up a king (leader) to destroy your house. This will happen soon. The day is coming now!" **15.** "The LORD will strike Israel (the northern kingdom), shaking it like a reed (a plant that shakes in the wind) in the water. He will uproot Israel (remove it from the land) from the land He gave to their ancestors, and scatter them beyond the Euphrates River (the river to the east), because they have made idols (false gods) and provoked the LORD to anger." **16.** "He

will abandon Israel (leave them) because of Jeroboam's sins, the sins he caused Israel to commit." **17.** Jeroboam's wife returned to Tirzah (a city), and when she reached the threshold (entrance) of her house, her son died. **18.** They buried him, and all Israel mourned (grieved) for him, as the LORD had spoken through the prophet Ahijah. **19.** The rest of Jeroboam's reign, including his wars (battles) and acts, are written in the Book of the Chronicles (historical records) of the Kings of Israel. **20.** Jeroboam reigned (ruled) for twenty-two years. He died and was buried, and his son Nadab (his heir) became king. **21.** Rehoboam (Solomon's son), became king of Judah (the southern kingdom). He was forty-one years old when he began to reign and ruled for seventeen years in Jerusalem, the city the LORD had chosen out of all the tribes of Israel to place His name. His mother was Naamah (a woman from Ammon), an Ammonite (a member of a people from a neighboring nation). **22.** Judah did evil (wrong actions) in the sight (view) of the LORD, provoking Him to jealousy (strong anger) with their sins, worse than their ancestors. **23.** They built high places (altars for idol worship), sacred pillars (idols), and wooden images (carved images of false gods) on every hill and under every green tree. **24.** There were also perverted persons (male temple prostitutes) in the land, doing the same evil practices as the nations (other peoples) the LORD had driven out before Israel. **25.** In the fifth year of Rehoboam's reign, Shishak (the king of Egypt) attacked Jerusalem (the capital city). **26.** He took all the treasures (valuable items) from the house of the Lord (the temple) and the king's palace, including the gold shields (shiny shields made of gold) Solomon had made. **27.** Rehoboam replaced them with bronze shields (shields made of bronze) and gave them to the officers (guards) who protected the king's palace. **28.** Whenever the king entered the house of the Lord (the temple), the guards carried the bronze shields and returned them to the guardroom afterward. **29.** The rest of Rehoboam's acts are written in the Book of the Chronicles (official records) of the Kings of Judah. **30.** There was continual war (conflict) between Rehoboam and Jeroboam during their reigns. **31.** Rehoboam died and was buried in the City of David (Jerusalem). His mother was Naamah, an Ammonite. His son Abijam (his successor) became king.

Chapter 15

1. In the eighteenth year of King Jeroboam (the first king of Israel after the kingdom divided), son of Nebat, Abijam became king of Judah. **2.** He reigned for three years in Jerusalem. His mother was Maachah (the queen mother), the granddaughter of Abishalom (a man from the line of David). **3.** Abijam followed in the sinful ways of his father, not being loyal to the Lord his God like his ancestor David. **4.** However, for the sake of David, the Lord kept a lamp in Jerusalem (a symbol of hope and continuity) by allowing Abijam's son to succeed him and by establishing the city. **5.** David did what was right in the eyes of the Lord and followed all His commands throughout his life, except in the matter of Uriah the Hittite (the man David had wronged). **6.** There was constant war between Rehoboam (Abijam's father) and Jeroboam (the first king of Israel) during their lifetimes. **7.** The rest of Abijam's actions are written in the book of the Chronicles of the Kings of Judah. There was also war between Abijam and Jeroboam. **8.** Abijam passed away and was buried in the City of David (Jerusalem). His son Asa succeeded him as king. **9.** In the twentieth year of Jeroboam's reign, Asa became king of Judah. **10.** Asa reigned for 41 years in Jerusalem. His grandmother's name was Maachah, the granddaughter of Abishalom. **11.** Asa did what was right in the eyes of the Lord, just like his ancestor David. **12.** He removed the immoral men (cult prostitutes) from the land and destroyed all the idols his ancestors had made. **13.** Asa also removed his grandmother Maachah from being queen mother because she had made an idol of Asherah (a fertility goddess). He cut down the idol and burned it in the Brook Kidron (a valley in Jerusalem). **14.** Though Asa did many good things, the high places (local places of worship, often unauthorized by God) were not removed. Nonetheless, his heart remained loyal to the Lord all his life. **15.** Asa brought into the house of the Lord all the dedicated items (sacred offerings) from his father and his own offerings: silver, gold, and utensils. **16.** Asa and Baasha (the king of Israel) were at war throughout Asa's reign. **17.** Baasha, king of Israel, attacked Judah and built the city of Ramah (a border city) to prevent anyone from entering or leaving Judah. **18.** Asa gathered all the silver and gold left in the treasures of the Lord's temple and the royal palace and sent them to Ben-Hadad (the king of Syria), who lived in Damascus (capital of Syria). Asa said, **19.** "Let us make a treaty, as my father and your father did. I am sending silver and gold to break your alliance with Baasha, so he will stop attacking me." **20.** Ben-Hadad agreed, sending his army commanders to attack the cities of Israel. They struck Ijon (a city of Israel), Dan (a northern city of Israel), Abel Beth Maachah (a town in northern Israel), and all of Naphtali (a tribe of Israel). **21.** When Baasha heard this, he stopped building Ramah and moved to Tirzah (another city of Israel). **22.** Asa then ordered a proclamation throughout Judah. Everyone participated in taking away the stones and timber from Ramah, which Baasha had used, and Asa used them to build the cities of Geba (in Benjamin, a tribe of Judah) and Mizpah (a border city in Benjamin). **23.** The rest of Asa's reign, his actions, military achievements, and cities built are recorded in the Chronicles of the Kings of Judah. In his later years, Asa suffered from a foot disease (a painful condition affecting his feet). **24.** Asa passed away and was buried with his ancestors in the City of David (Jerusalem). His son Jehoshaphat succeeded him. **25.** In the second year of Asa's reign, Nadab (son of Jeroboam, first king of Israel) became king of Israel. He reigned for two years. **26.** Nadab did evil in the sight of the Lord, following the sinful ways of his father, Jeroboam, which led Israel to sin. **27.** Baasha, son of Ahijah (a man from the tribe of Issachar), conspired against Nadab. Baasha killed him at Gibbethon (a Philistine city), while Nadab and Israel were besieging the city. **28.** Baasha killed Nadab in the third year of Asa's reign and became king in his place. **29.** When Baasha became king, he destroyed all of Jeroboam's family, fulfilling the prophecy spoken by the prophet Ahijah the Shilonite (a prophet from Shiloh). **30.** This destruction was due to the sins of Jeroboam, which led Israel to sin and provoked God to anger. **31.** The rest of Nadab's actions are written in the Chronicles of the Kings of Israel. **32.** There was constant war between Asa, king of Judah, and Baasha, king of Israel. **33.** Baasha reigned for 24 years in Tirzah, doing evil in the sight of the Lord and continuing in the sinful ways of Jeroboam. **34.** Baasha led Israel to sin, provoking the Lord to anger.

Chapter 16

1. Then the Lord's message (word of the Lord) came to Jehu, the son of Hanani, against Baasha, saying: **2.** "Since I raised you from the dust (elevated you from a low position) and made you ruler (king) over My people Israel, and yet you have followed the sinful ways (path of wickedness) of Jeroboam, causing Israel to sin and provoking My anger (anger that leads to punishment) with their sins, **3.** I will certainly wipe out (destroy) Baasha's descendants (offspring) and the descendants of his family (household). I will make your house (family) like the house of Jeroboam son of Nebat. **4.** The dogs (wild animals) will devour (eat) whoever belongs to Baasha and dies in the city, and the birds (scavenger birds) will eat those who die in the fields." **5.** The rest of Baasha's deeds (acts), his achievements (feats), and his strength (power)—are they not written in the book of the chronicles (historical records) of the kings of Israel? **6.** Baasha rested with his ancestors (died) and was buried in Tirzah. His son Elah succeeded him as king. **7.** The word of the Lord (message from God) also came against Baasha and his family through the prophet Jehu, because of the wickedness (evil deeds) he had done in the sight of the Lord (in God's presence), provoking Him to anger (making God angry) with his actions, following in the sinful ways (path of wickedness) of Jeroboam, and killing those who stood in his way. **8.** In the twenty-sixth year of Asa, king of Judah, Elah son of Baasha became king of Israel and reigned (ruled) for two years in Tirzah. **9.** But Zimri, the commander (military leader) of half his chariots, conspired (planned secretly) against him while Elah was in Tirzah, drinking himself drunk (intoxicated) in the house of Arza, the palace steward (manager). **10.** Zimri struck (attacked) Elah down and killed him in the twenty-seventh year of Asa, king of Judah, and became king in his place. **11.** As soon as Zimri took the throne (became king), he killed all the members (relatives) of Baasha's family—none of Baasha's relatives (offspring) or friends (close associates) were spared. **12.** Zimri wiped out (destroyed) the entire household (family) of Baasha, fulfilling the prophecy (God's prediction) the Lord had spoken against Baasha through Jehu the prophet. **13.** This was because of all the sins (wrongdoings) committed by Baasha and his son Elah, which led Israel into sin (caused Israel to act wickedly) and provoked the Lord God of Israel to anger (brought divine wrath) with their idolatry

(worship of idols). **14.** The rest of Elah's deeds (acts), everything he did, are they not written in the book of the chronicles (historical records) of the kings of Israel? **15.** In the twenty-seventh year of Asa, king of Judah, Zimri reigned (ruled) for seven days in Tirzah. At that time, the army was camped (stationed) near Gibbethon, a Philistine town. **16.** When the army heard (received news) that Zimri had conspired against the king and killed him, they proclaimed (declared) Omri, the commander of the army, as king right there in the camp. **17.** Omri and the army then left Gibbethon and besieged (surrounded) Tirzah. **18.** When Zimri saw that the city was taken (captured), he went into the palace and set it on fire (burned it), killing himself in the flames (perishing in the fire). **19.** He died because of the evil (wickedness) he had done in the sight of the Lord, following the sinful ways (path of wickedness) of Jeroboam and causing Israel to sin (leading them into idolatry). **20.** The rest of Zimri's actions (deeds), including the treason (betrayal) he committed, are they not written in the book of the chronicles (historical records) of the kings of Israel? **21.** Afterward, the people of Israel were divided into two factions (groups): one side supported Tibni, son of Ginath, as king, while the other followed Omri. **22.** But Omri's supporters were stronger (more powerful), and they defeated those who followed Tibni. So Tibni died, and Omri became king. **23.** In the thirty-first year of Asa, king of Judah, Omri became king of Israel and reigned (ruled) for twelve years, six of which were in Tirzah. **24.** Omri bought the hill (mountain) of Samaria from Shemer for two talents of silver (a weight of silver), and he built a city there, naming it Samaria after Shemer, the owner of the hill. **25.** Omri did what was evil (wrong) in the eyes of the Lord (in God's judgment), and he did even worse (more wickedly) than all who had come before him. **26.** He followed in all the ways of Jeroboam son of Nebat, committing the same sins (wrongdoing) that had led Israel to sin (inducing them to idolatry), provoking the Lord God of Israel to anger (inciting God's wrath) with their idols (false gods). **27.** The rest of Omri's deeds (acts) and the power (strength) he displayed are they not written in the book of the chronicles (historical records) of the kings of Israel? **28.** Omri rested with his ancestors (died) and was buried in Samaria. His son Ahab succeeded him as king. **29.** In the thirty-eighth year of Asa, king of Judah, Ahab, son of Omri, became king of Israel and reigned (ruled) for twenty-two years in Samaria. **30.** Ahab did more evil (wickedness) in the sight of the Lord (in God's judgment) than any of the kings before him. **31.** As if it were a trivial thing (something of little importance) for him to walk in the sins (wrongdoing) of Jeroboam son of Nebat, Ahab married Jezebel, the daughter of Ethbaal, king of the Sidonians. He then began to serve and worship Baal (a false god). **32.** Ahab even built a temple (place of worship) for Baal in Samaria and set up an altar (sacrificial platform) to Baal in it. **33.** He also made an Asherah pole (idol), and did more to provoke the Lord God of Israel to anger (angered God more) than all the kings of Israel who had come before him. **34.** In his days, Hiel of Bethel rebuilt Jericho. He laid its foundation (began the construction) with the death of his firstborn son, Abiram, and set up its gates (completed the gates) with the death of his youngest son, Segub, as the word of the Lord (divine prophecy) had declared through Joshua son of Nun.

Chapter 17

1. Elijah, a prophet from Tishbe in Gilead, approached King Ahab and declared, "As the Lord, the God of Israel, whom I serve, lives, there will be neither dew (moisture in the air) nor rain for the next few years, unless I give the word." **2.** Immediately after, the Lord's message (divine instruction) came to Elijah, instructing him: **3.** "Leave this place and go east, hiding by the Brook Cherith (a small stream), which flows into the Jordan River. **4.** You will drink from the stream, and I have commanded the ravens (large black birds) to bring you food there." **5.** Elijah followed God's command and stayed by the Brook Cherith, near the Jordan River. **6.** In the mornings and evenings, the ravens brought him bread and meat, and he drank from the brook. **7.** Eventually, the brook dried up because there had been no rain (precipitation) in the land. **8.** Then the Lord spoke to Elijah again, saying, **9.** "Get up and go to Zarephath (a town in Sidon, a region north of Israel), and stay there. I have directed a widow (a woman whose husband has died) to provide for you." **10.** Elijah obeyed and traveled to Zarephath. When he arrived at the city gate, he saw a widow gathering sticks (small pieces of wood). He called out to her, "Please bring me a little water in a jar (container) so I can drink." **11.** As she was going to fetch the water, he called again, "Please bring me a small piece of bread (loaf) as well." **12.** The widow answered, "As the Lord your God lives, I have no bread—only a small amount of flour in a jar and a little oil (liquid used for cooking) in a jug. I'm gathering a few sticks to prepare the last meal for myself and my son. After that, we will die from hunger." **13.** Elijah told her, "Do not be afraid. Go ahead and do as you said, but first make a small loaf (cake) of bread for me and bring it to me. Then make some for yourself and your son. **14.** For the Lord God of Israel has spoken: 'The jar of flour will not run out, and the jug of oil will not be empty, until the day the Lord sends rain (precipitation) upon the earth.'" **15.** The widow followed Elijah's instructions. She, her son, and Elijah ate for many days. **16.** The flour in the jar was never used up, and the oil in the jug never ran dry, just as the Lord had promised through Elijah. **17.** Later, the widow's son became gravely ill. His condition worsened until he stopped breathing (died). **18.** The widow said to Elijah, "What do you have against me, man of God? Did you come to remind me of my sin and cause my son to die?" **19.** Elijah replied, "Give me your son." He took the boy from her arms, carried him upstairs to the room where he was staying, and laid him on his own bed. **20.** Elijah cried out to the Lord, "O Lord my God, have You brought this disaster (tragedy) upon the widow I'm staying with by letting her son die?" **21.** Then he stretched himself over the child three times and cried to the Lord, "O Lord my God, let this child's life return to him!" **22.** The Lord heard Elijah's prayer, and the child's life returned to him. He revived (came back to life). **23.** Elijah took the child and brought him down from the upper room. He gave him back to his mother and said, "Look, your son is alive!" **24.** The woman responded to Elijah, "Now I know that you are a man of God, and that the word (message) of the Lord in your mouth is truth."

Chapter 18

1. After a long time, the Lord spoke to Elijah, saying, "Go and present yourself to Ahab (king of Israel), and I will send rain upon the earth." **2.** Elijah went to meet Ahab, who was struggling with a severe famine in Samaria (the central region of ancient Palestine). **3.** Ahab (king of Israel) called his servant Obadiah, who was in charge of his household. **4.** During the time when Jezebel (wife of Ahab) was killing the prophets of the Lord, Obadiah had hidden 100 prophets in caves, fifty in each, and providing them with food and water. **5.** Ahab (king of Israel) instructed Obadiah, "Go through the land and search the springs and the brooks; perhaps we can find enough grass to save the horses and mules so we don't have to kill any livestock." **6.** They divided the land to search for water, with Ahab taking one route and Obadiah taking another. **7.** As Obadiah was walking along, Elijah met him. Obadiah recognized him, bowed to the ground, and said, "Is it really you, my lord Elijah?" **8.** Elijah replied, "Yes, I am Elijah. Go and tell your master, 'Elijah is here.'" **9.** Obadiah answered, "What have I done wrong, that you are sending me to Ahab (king of Israel), who will kill me?" **10.** "As the Lord your God lives," Obadiah continued, "there is no nation or kingdom where my master has not sent someone to search for you. And when they said, 'He's not here,' he made them swear they hadn't found you. **11.** "Now you say, 'Go, tell Ahab (king of Israel), Elijah is here!'" **12.** "When I leave you, the Spirit of the Lord may carry you off to some unknown place. Then when I tell Ahab (king of Israel) you're here, and he can't find you, he will kill me. But I have feared the Lord since I was a child." **13.** "Didn't you hear what I did when Jezebel killed the Lord's prophets? I hid a hundred of them, fifty in each cave, and I gave them food and water." **14.** "Now you say, 'Go, tell Ahab (king of Israel), Elijah is here!' He will kill me!" **15.** Elijah replied, "As the Lord of hosts lives, before whom I stand, I will certainly present myself to Ahab (king of Israel) today." **16.** Obadiah went to Ahab (king of Israel) and told him, and Ahab went to meet Elijah. **17.** When Ahab (king of Israel) saw Elijah, he accused him, saying, "Is that you, the one who brings trouble to Israel?" **18.** Elijah replied, "I have not caused trouble in Israel, but you and your father's house have, because you have forsaken the Lord's commandments and followed the Baals (false gods)." **19.** "Now gather all Israel to meet me on Mount Carmel (a mountain in Israel), along with the 450 prophets of Baal and the 400 prophets of Asherah, who eat at Jezebel's (queen of Israel) table." **20.** Ahab (king of Israel) called all Israel together and gathered the prophets on Mount Carmel (a mountain in Israel). **21.** Elijah approached the people and said, "How long will you keep wavering between two opinions? If the Lord is God, follow Him. But if Baal is God, follow him." The people said nothing in response. **22.** Elijah continued, "I alone remain a prophet of the Lord, but Baal's prophet's number 450." **23.** "Let's do a test. Let them give us two bulls. Let them choose one and prepare it, laying it on the wood but putting no fire under it. I will do the same with the other bull and put it on the wood but put no fire under it." **24.** "Then you call on the name of your god, and I will call on the name of the Lord. The God who answers by fire, He is God." The people agreed, "That's a good idea." **25.** Elijah said to the prophets of Baal, "Choose one bull and prepare it first, for you are many. Call on the name of your god, but put no fire under it." **26.** They took the bull given to them, prepared it, and called on the name of Baal from morning till noon, shouting, "O Baal, answer us!" But was no response, no one answered. They even leaped around the altar they had made. **27.** At noon, Elijah began to mock them, saying, "Shout louder! Maybe he's meditating, or he's busy, or he's on a journey. Or perhaps he's sleeping and must be awakened." **28.** So the prophets of Baal cried out louder and cut themselves with knives and lances, as was their custom, until their blood flowed. **29.** When midday passed, they prophesied until the time for the evening sacrifice, but still there was no voice, no answer, no one paying attention. **30.** Then Elijah called the people to him. They gathered around, and he repaired the broken altar of the Lord. **31.** Elijah took twelve stones, one for each of the twelve tribes of Israel, as the Lord had said, "Israel shall be your name." **32.** With the stones, Elijah built an altar in the name of the Lord, and he dug a trench around it, large enough to hold two seahs of seed. **33.** He arranged the wood, cut the bull into pieces, and laid it on the wood. Then he said, "Fill four jars with water and pour it on the offering and the wood." **34.** He told them, "Do it again." They did it a second time. He said, "Do it a third time." And they did it a third time. **35.** The water ran around the altar, and the trench was filled with water. **36.** At the time of the evening sacrifice, Elijah the prophet stepped forward and prayed, "Lord God of Abraham, Isaac, and Israel, let it be known today that You are God in Israel and that I am Your servant, and that I have done all these things at Your command." **37.** "Answer me, Lord, answer me, so these people will know that You, Lord, are God, and that you have turned their hearts back to you." **38.** The fire of the Lord fell and consumed the burnt sacrifice, the wood, the stones, and the soil, and it licked up the water in the trench. **39.** When all the people saw this, they fell on their faces and cried, "The Lord, He is God! The Lord, He is God!" **40.** Elijah commanded them, "Seize the prophets of Baal! Don't let any of them escape." The people seized them, and Elijah brought them down to the Kishon Brook (a river in Israel) and executed them there. **41.** Elijah said to Ahab (king of Israel), "Go, eat and drink, for I hear the sound of heavy rain." **42.** Ahab (king of Israel) went to eat and drink, but Elijah went up to the top of Mount Carmel (a mountain in Israel). He bowed to the ground; put his face between his knees, **43.** And said to his servant, "Go up now, look toward the sea." The servant went, looked, and reported, "There is nothing." Elijah said, "Go again," and he did this seven times. **44.** On the seventh time, the servant said, "There's a cloud, as small as a man's hand, rising out of the sea!" Elijah said, "Go tell Ahab (king of Israel), 'Prepare your chariot and go down before the rain stops you.'" **45.** Meanwhile, the sky grew dark with clouds and wind, and a heavy rain began. Ahab (king of Israel) rode off to Jezreel (Valley of Megiddo now in Israel). **46.** The hand of the Lord came upon Elijah, and he girded up his loins and ran ahead of Ahab all the way to the entrance of Jezreel.

Chapter 19

1. Ahab told Jezebel all that Elijah had done, including how he had killed all the prophets with the sword. **2.** Jezebel sent a message to Elijah, saying, "May the gods (false deities) deal with me severely if I do not make your life like one of those prophets' by tomorrow." **3.** When Elijah saw this, he fled for his life to Beersheba (a town in the southern part of Judah, the kingdom of Israel), and left his servant there. **4.** He went a day's journey into the wilderness (desert area), sat under a broom tree (a type of bush), and prayed, "I've had enough, Lord. Take my life; I'm no better than my ancestors!" **5.** He lay down and fell asleep under the tree. Suddenly, an angel (a heavenly messenger) touched him and said, "Get up and eat." **6.** He looked and saw bread baked on hot coals and a jar of water by his head. He ate and drank, then lay down again. **7.** The angel came back a second time, touched him, and said, "Get up and eat, for the journey ahead is too great for you." 8. Elijah ate and traveled for forty days and nights to Mount Horeb (also called Sinai, a sacred mountain), the mountain of God. 9. There, he entered a cave. The word of the Lord (God's message) came to him, and God asked, "Why are you here, Elijah?" 10. Elijah replied, "I have been very zealous (enthusiastic and devoted) for the Lord. The Israelites (the people of Israel) have forsaken Your covenant (agreement with God), torn down Your altars (places of worship), and killed Your prophets. I am the only one left, and they seek my life." 11. The Lord said, "Go out and stand on the mountain before the Lord." A strong wind passed, breaking the rocks, but the Lord was not in the wind. 12. After the wind, an earthquake (shaking of the earth) came, but the Lord was not in the earthquake. 13. After the earthquake, a fire came, but the Lord was not in the fire. 14. Finally, there was a gentle whisper (a soft, quiet sound). 15. When Elijah heard it, he covered his face with his cloak (garment, sometimes a religious dress) and went out to the entrance of the cave. A voice asked, "What are you doing here, Elijah?" 16. Elijah answered, "I have been very zealous for the Lord. The Israelites have forsaken Your covenant, torn down Your altars, and killed Your prophets. I am the only one left, and they want to take my life." 17. The Lord said, "Go back the way you came, and anoint (rubbing with oil for religious purpose.) Hazael as a king over Syria (modern-day Syria). 18. Anoint Jehu (the son of Nimshi, a general in Israel) as king over Israel (the northern kingdom), and Elisha (Elijah's successor) to take your place as prophet. 19. Whoever escapes the sword of Hazael, Jehu will kill; and whoever escapes Jehu, Elisha will kill. 20. Yet I have reserved seven thousand in Israel who have not bowed to Baal (a Canaanite god) or kissed him (a gesture of worship). 21. Elijah left and found Elisha, the son of Shaphat (a man from Abel Meholah), who was plowing with twelve oxen. Elijah passed by him and threw his cloak over him.

Chapter 20

1. Ben-Hadad, the king of Syria (modern-day Syria), assembled his entire army, including thirty-two kings (rulers) with horses (mounted soldiers) and chariots (military vehicles). He advanced and laid siege to Samaria (central city of ancient Palestine), preparing for war against it. 2. He sent messengers into the city to Ahab, the king of Israel (the northern kingdom of Israel), saying, "This is what Ben-Hadad says: 3. 'Your silver and gold are mine, and your finest wives and children are mine.'" 4. The king of Israel replied, "My lord, O king, as you say, I and everything I have belong to you." 5. The messengers returned with a second message from Ben-Hadad: "I have already asked for your silver, gold, wives, and children, 6. but tomorrow I will send my servants to search your house and the houses of your officials. Whatever pleases them, they will take." 7. Ahab summoned the elders (senior leaders) of Israel and said, "Look at how this man seeks to cause trouble. He asked for my wives, children, silver, and gold, and I did not refuse him." 8. The elders and all the people responded "Do not listen to him or agree to his demands." 9. Ahab then instructed the messengers of Ben-Hadad, "Tell your master, 'I will agree to everything you asked for the first time, but this I cannot do.'" The messengers returned with this response. 10. Ben-Hadad sent another message, saying, "May the gods (deities) deal with me severely if enough dust remains of Samaria to fill a handful for each of my soldiers." 11. The king of Israel answered, "Tell him, and 'Let not the one who prepares for battle boast like the one who has already won.'" 12. When Ben-Hadad heard this, he and the kings were drinking (celebrating) at their command post (military base). He told his servants to get ready for battle, and they prepared to attack. 13. At that moment, a prophet (a messenger from God) approached Ahab, king of Israel, saying, "This is what the Lord says: 'Do you see this great army? Today, I will deliver them into your hands, and you will know that I am the Lord.'" 14. Ahab asked, "Who will lead the battle?" The prophet replied, "The Lord says: 'By the young leaders of the provinces (local commanders).'" Ahab asked, "Who will plan the battle?" The prophet answered, "You will." 15. Ahab gathered 232 young leaders of the provinces, and then assembled the entire army, totaling 7,000 men. 16. They went out at noon, while Ben-Hadad and his thirty-two kings were drinking (drinking alcohol) in their tents. 17. The young leaders of the provinces led the way. Ben-Hadad sent scouts (Troops), who reported, "Men are coming out of Samaria!" 18. Ben-Hadad said, "If they have come out peacefully, take them alive; but if

they have come out for war, take them alive." 19. The young leaders led their army out from the city. 20. Each of them struck down his opponent. The Syrians fled, and the Israelites pursued them. Ben-Hadad, king of Syria, escaped on a horse with his cavalry (soldiers on horseback). 21. The king of Israel attacked the horses and chariots, and inflicted a great slaughter on the Syrians. 22. A prophet came to the king of Israel and said, "Go and strengthen yourself. Take note of what to do, because in the spring (season) the king of Syria will return to fight you." 23. The servants of the king of Syria said to him, "Their gods are gods of the hills (mountain regions). That's why they were stronger than us. But if we fight them on the plains (flat land), we will be stronger than they." 24. "So, remove the kings from their positions and appoint captains (military leaders) in their places. 25. Then muster (gather) an army like the one you lost—horse for horse, chariot for chariot. We will fight them in the plains, and we will surely be stronger than they." Ben-Hadad listened to their advice and acted accordingly. 26. In the spring, Ben-Hadad gathered the Syrians and marched to Aphek (a city in Syria) to fight Israel. 27. The Israelites gathered and were provided with supplies (food and provisions). They camped in front of the Syrians, who filled the entire countryside. 28. A prophet came to the king of Israel and said, "This is what the Lord says: 'Because the Syrians have said, "The Lord is God of the hills, but not God of the valleys," I will deliver this vast army into your hands, and you will know that I am the Lord.'" 29. Both armies camped opposite each other for seven days. On the seventh day, the battle began, and the Israelites killed 100,000 foot soldiers (infantry) of the Syrians in one day. 30. The rest of the Syrians fled to Aphek, and a wall (large structure) fell on 27,000 of them. Ben-Hadad fled into the city and hid in an inner chamber (private room). 31. His servants said to him, "Look, we have heard that the kings of Israel are merciful. Let us put sackcloth (coarse cloth worn as a sign of mourning or repentance) around our waists and ropes (cords) around our heads, and go to the king of Israel. Perhaps he will spare your life." 32. So, they put sackcloth around their waists and ropes around their heads, and went to the king of Israel. They said, "Your servant Ben-Hadad says, 'please let me live.'" Ahab replied, "Is he still alive? He is my brother." 33. The men observed closely to see if Ahab would show mercy. When they heard Ahab say, "He is my brother," they quickly took this as a sign of mercy and said, "Your brother Ben-Hadad." Ahab replied, "Go, and bring him here." So Ben-Hadad was brought to him, and Ahab had him come up into his chariot. 34. Ben-Hadad said to Ahab, "The cities my father took from your father, I will return to you. You may set up markets (trade areas) in Damascus (a major city in Syria), just as my father did in Samaria." Ahab replied, "I will make a treaty (formal agreement) with you and send you away." 35. A certain man from the sons of the prophets (prophets' disciples) came to his neighbor by the word of the Lord, saying, "Please strike me." But the man refused to strike him. 36. The prophet said, "Because you have disobeyed the Lord, as soon as you leave me, a lion (wild animal) will kill you." And as soon as he left, a lion found him and killed him. 37. The prophet found another man and said, "Strike me, please." The man struck him and wounded him. 38. The prophet went and waited for the king by the road, disguising himself with a bandage (cloth) over his eyes. 39. As the king passed by, the prophet cried out, "Your servant was in the midst of the battle. A man came to me and said, 'Guard this man; if he escapes, your life will be for his, or you must pay a talent (unit of currency) of silver.' 40. While I was busy, the man escaped." The king replied, "You've decided your own fate." 41. The prophet took the bandage off his eyes, and the king recognized him as one of the prophets. 42. The prophet said, "This is what the Lord says: 'Because you let a man I appointed for destruction escape, your life will be exchanged for his, and your people for his people.'" 43. The king of Israel returned to his palace, disappointed (unhappy) and angry, and came to Samaria.

Chapter 21

1. After these events, Naboth, a man from Jezreel (a town in Israel), owned a vineyard (a farm for growing grapes) next to the palace of Ahab, the king of Samaria (the capital city of ancient Israel). 2. Ahab spoke to Naboth and said, "Give me your vineyard so I can turn it into a vegetable garden, because it's close to my house. I will give you a better vineyard in return, or if you prefer, I'll pay you its value in money." 3. But Naboth replied, "The Lord forbid that I should give you

the inheritance (family property passed down through generations) of my ancestors!" **4.** Ahab went home, upset and angry because Naboth, the man from Jezreel, refused to sell his vineyard. He lay on his bed, turned his face away, and refused to eat. **5.** His wife, Jezebel (Ahab's wife, daughter of a foreign king), came to him and asked, "Why are you so upset that you won't eat?" **6.** Ahab said, "I spoke to Naboth and asked him to sell me his vineyard or trade it for another, but he refused." **7.** Jezebel, his wife, said, "Aren't you the king of Israel? Get up, eat, and be happy. I'll get you Naboth's vineyard." **8.** She wrote letters in Ahab's name, sealed them with his royal seal, and sent the letters to the elders and nobles (leaders) of the city where Naboth lived. **9.** In the letters, Jezebel instructed, "Proclaim a fast (a religious act of not eating) and seat Naboth in a place of honor before the people. **10.** Then have two scoundrels (immoral or dishonest men) sat before him to accuse him, saying, 'You have blasphemed God and the king.' Then take him out and stone him to death." **11.** So the men of the city, the elders and nobles who lived in that area did as Jezebel had instructed them in the letters she had sent. **12.** They proclaimed a fast and seated Naboth in a place of honor before the people. **13.** Two scoundrels came and sat before him, and they accused Naboth in front of the people, saying, "Naboth has blasphemed God and the king!" Then they took him outside the city and stoned him to death. **14.** Afterward, they sent a message to Jezebel, saying, "Naboth has been stoned and is dead." **15.** When Jezebel heard that Naboth had been stoned and was dead, she said to Ahab, "Get up, take possession of the vineyard of Naboth, the man from Jezreel, which he refused to sell to you for money. Naboth is no longer alive, but dead." **16.** When Ahab heard that Naboth was dead, he got up and went down to take possession of the vineyard of Naboth, the man from Jezreel. **17.** Then the word of the Lord came to Elijah the Tishbite (a prophet from Tishbe), saying, **18.** "Go down to meet Ahab, the king of Israel, who lives in Samaria. He is in Naboth's vineyard, where he has gone to take possession of it. **19.** You are to speak to him and say, 'This is what the Lord says: "Have you murdered and also taken possession?"' You shall say to him, 'In the place where dogs licked the blood of Naboth, dogs shall lick your blood, even yours.'" **20.** So Ahab said to Elijah, "Have you found me, O my enemy?" Elijah answered, "I have found you, because you have sold yourself to do evil in the sight of the Lord. **21.** I will bring disaster upon you. I will cut off your descendants (children and family line) and wipe out every male in Ahab's family, both bond and free (slaves and free men) in Israel. **22.** I will make your house like the house of Jeroboam son of Nebat (first king of the northern kingdom of Israel), and like the house of Baasha son of Ahijah (a king of Israel), because you have provoked me to anger and made Israel sin." **23.** As for Jezebel, the Lord also said, "The dogs shall eat Jezebel by the wall of Jezreel." **24.** Dogs will eat those belonging to Ahab who dies in the city, and the birds will eat those who die in the fields." **25.** There was no one like Ahab who sold himself to do evil in the sight of the Lord, because his wife Jezebel (Ahab's wife) stirred him up. **26.** He acted very wickedly, following idols, according to all that the Amorites (a Canaanite people) had done, whom the Lord had driven out before the Israelites. **27.** When Ahab heard these words, he tore his clothes, put on sackcloth (a rough material worn in mourning), fasted, lay in sackcloth, and went about mourning. **28.** Then the word of the Lord came to Elijah the Tishbite (a prophet), saying, **29.** "Have you seen how Ahab has humbled himself before me? Because he has humbled himself, I will not bring the disaster in his days. But in the days of his son, I will bring the disaster on his house."

Chapter 22

1. After three years without conflict, **2.** In the third year, King Jehoshaphat (King of Judah, southern kingdom of Israel) visited King Ahab (King of Israel, northern kingdom of Israel). **3.** Ahab told his servants, "Do you know that Ramoth in Gilead (region east of Jordan River) is ours, but we are uncertain about taking it from Syria?" **4.** Ahab asked Jehoshaphat, "Will you join me in battle for Ramoth Gilead?" Jehoshaphat answered, "I am as you are, and my people are like your people, my horses like your horses." **5.** Jehoshaphat then said, "Please inquire of the Lord today." **6.** Ahab gathered 400 prophets and asked them, "Should I go to war against Ramoth Gilead, or not?" They answered, "Go, for the Lord will give it to the king." **7.** But Jehoshaphat asked, "Is there not a prophet of the Lord to inquire of?" **8.** Ahab replied, "There is one prophet, Micaiah son of Imlah, but I hate him because he never prophesies good about me, only evil." Jehoshaphat said, "The king should not speak like that!" **9.** Ahab called for an officer to bring Micaiah quickly. **10.** Both kings, dressed in their royal robes, sat at the entrance of the gate of Samaria (capital of Israel), while the prophets prophesied before them. **11.** Zedekiah son of Chenaanah made iron horns and declared, "With these, you will defeat the Syrians!" **12.** All the other prophets prophesied the same: "Go to Ramoth Gilead, and you will succeed, for the Lord will deliver it to the king." **13.** The messenger who had gone to summon Micaiah said to him, "The prophets are speaking good things; please speak the same to the king." **14.** Micaiah replied, "As the Lord lives, I will speak only what the Lord tells me." **15.** When Micaiah arrived, Ahab asked him, "Shall we go to war against Ramoth Gilead, or not?" Micaiah answered, "Go, and you will succeed, for the Lord will deliver it to the king." **16.** Ahab said, "How many times must I make you swear to tell me only the truth in the name of the Lord?" **17.** Then Micaiah replied, "I saw Israel scattered on the mountains like sheep without a shepherd. The Lord said, 'These have no master; let each return home in peace.'" **18.** Ahab turned to Jehoshaphat and said, "Did I not tell you he would not prophesy anything good for me, but only evil?" **19.** Micaiah continued, "Therefore, hear the word of the Lord: I saw the Lord sitting on His throne, and all the heavenly host (spiritual beings or angels) standing beside Him. **20.** The Lord asked, 'Who will persuade Ahab to go up, so that he may fall at Ramoth Gilead?' Some spoke in one way, others in another. **21.** Then a spirit came forward and said, 'I will persuade him.' **22.** The Lord asked, 'How?' and the spirit answered, 'I will be a lying spirit in the mouth of all his prophets.' The Lord said, 'You will succeed; go and do it.' **23.** So, the Lord has put a lying spirit in the mouths of your prophets, and disaster (calamity or judgment) is declared against you." **24.** Zedekiah son of Chenaanah struck Micaiah on the cheek and mocked him, saying, "Which way did the spirit from the Lord go to speak to you?" **25.** Micaiah responded, "You will see on the day when you hide in an inner room." **26.** Ahab ordered, "Take Micaiah, return him to Amon, the governor of the city, and to Joash, the king's son, **27.** and say, 'Put this man in prison and give him only bread and water until I return safely.'" **28.** Micaiah said, "If you return in peace, the Lord has not spoken through me." He added, "Listen, all you people!" **29.** Ahab and Jehoshaphat went up to Ramoth Gilead. **30.** Ahab told Jehoshaphat, "I will disguise myself in battle, but you wear your royal robes." Ahab disguised himself, but Jehoshaphat wore his kingly garments. **31.** The king of Syria had commanded his chariot commanders, "Fight only the king of Israel." **32.** When the chariot commanders saw Jehoshaphat, they thought he was the king of Israel and tried to attack him. Jehoshaphat cried out, **33.** and when they realized he was not Ahab, they stopped pursuing him. **34.** A man shot his bow at random and struck Ahab between the joints of his armor. He told his chariot driver, "Take me out of the battle, for I am wounded." **35.** The battle continued, and Ahab was propped up in his chariot, facing the Syrians, until evening. His blood poured out of the wound into the chariot. **36.** As the sun set, a cry went out through the army: "Every man to his city, and every man to his own country!" **37.** Ahab died and was brought to Samaria, where he was buried. **38.** Someone washed the chariot at the pool of Samaria, and the dogs licked up his blood, as the Lord had prophesied. **39.** The rest of Ahab's deeds, including his ivory palace and the cities he built, are written in the book of the chronicles of the kings of Israel. **40.** Ahab rested with his fathers, and his son Ahaziah succeeded him. **41.** Jehoshaphat, son of Asa, became king of Judah in the fourth year of Ahab's reign. **42.** Jehoshaphat was 35 years old when he became king, and he reigned 25 years in Jerusalem. His mother was Azubah, daughter of Shilhi. **43.** Jehoshaphat followed the ways of his father Asa, doing what was right in the Lord's eyes, but the high places (places of idol worship) remained, where people still offered sacrifices. **44.** Jehoshaphat made peace with the king of Israel. **45.** The rest of Jehoshaphat's deeds, his military campaigns, and his wars are recorded in the book of chronicles of the kings of Judah. **46.** Jehoshaphat removed the perverted persons (idolaters or immoral people) who remained in the land during his father's reign. **47.** At that time, Edom (a kingdom southeast of Israel) had no king, only a deputy. **48.** Jehoshaphat built ships to go to Ophir (a wealthy region), but they were wrecked at Ezion

Geber (a port city). **49.** Ahaziah, son of Ahab, asked Jehoshaphat to let his servants sail with his, but Jehoshaphat refused. **50.** Jehoshaphat died and was buried in the City of David (Jerusalem). His son Jehoram succeeded him. **51.** Ahaziah, son of Ahab, became king of Israel in the 17th year of Jehoshaphat's reign and ruled for two years. **52.** He did evil in the Lord's sight, walking in the ways of his father Ahab and mother Jezebel, and in the ways of Jeroboam, son of Nebat. **53.** He served Baal (false god), worshiped him, and provoked the Lord to anger, just as his father had done.

Kings 2

Chapter 1

1. After Ahab, the king of Israel, died, the nation of Moab, which was located southeast of Israel, rebelled and broke free from Israel's control. **2.** Ahaziah, who succeeded Ahab as king of Israel, fell through the lattice (a wooden framework) of his upper room in his palace in Samaria (the capital city of Israel), and he was severely injured. In his desperation, he sent messengers to ask, "Go to Baal-Zebub, the god of Ekron (a city of the Philistines), and ask if I will recover from my injuries." **3.** However, the angel of the Lord came to Elijah, a prophet from Tishbe in Gilead, and instructed him, "Get up and go to meet the messengers of the king of Samaria. Tell them, 'Is it because there is no God in Israel that you are seeking counsel from Baal-Zebub, the god of Ekron?'" **4.** "As a result, this is what the Lord says: 'You will not leave the bed where you lie; you will surely die.'" Then Elijah left to carry out the message. **5.** When the messengers returned to King Ahaziah, he asked, "Why did you return so quickly?" **6.** They answered, "A man met us and told us, 'Return to the king who sent you and say to him: 'This is what the Lord says: 'Is it because there is no God in Israel that you are sending messengers to ask about Baal-Zebub, the god of Ekron? "You will not get out of your bed, but you will die." **7.** The king then asked, "What kind of man was it who told you these things?" **8.** They responded, "He was a man with a rough, hairy appearance and a leather belt around his waist." The king immediately recognized, "It is Elijah the Tishbite." **9.** So the king sent a captain with fifty soldiers to bring Elijah to him. The captain found Elijah sitting on top of a hill and said, "Man of God, the king commands you to come down immediately!" **10.** Elijah replied, "If I am truly a man of God, let fire come down from heaven and consume you and your fifty men." And fire fell from heaven, consuming the captain and his soldiers. **11.** The king sent another captain with fifty men. The captain said to Elijah, "Man of God, the king says, 'Come down quickly!'" **12.** Elijah answered, "If I am indeed a man of God, let fire come down from heaven and consume you and your fifty men." And once again, fire came down from heaven and burned them all up. **13.** The king sent a third captain with fifty men. This captain, seeing the fate of the first two groups, approached Elijah, fell on his knees before him, and pleaded, "Man of God, please spare my life and the lives of these fifty servants. **14.** Fire has come down from heaven and destroyed the first two captains with their men, but I beg you, let my life be spared." **15.** Then the angel of the Lord spoke to Elijah, saying, "Go down with him; do not be afraid." So Elijah rose, went down with the captain, and came to the king. **16.** Elijah said to the king, "This is what the Lord says: 'Because you have sent messengers to inquire of Baal-Zebub, the god of Ekron, instead of seeking the God of Israel, you will not leave your bed and you will certainly die.'" **17.** Ahaziah died just as the Lord had spoken through Elijah. Since Ahaziah had no son, his brother Jehoram (another son of Ahab) became king in his place, during the second year of Jehoram, the son of Jehoshaphat, who was the king of Judah. **18.** The rest of Ahaziah's acts and his reign are recorded in the book of the chronicles of the kings of Israel.

Chapter 2

1. When the Lord was about to take Elijah up to heaven in a whirlwind (a powerful wind that lifts things up), Elijah and Elisha were traveling together from Gilgal (a town in Israel). **2.** Elijah said to Elisha, "Stay here, for the Lord has sent me to Bethel (a town known for its religious significance)." But Elisha replied, "As the Lord lives, and as you live, I will not leave you!" So the two of them went to Bethel. **3.** The sons of the prophets (disciples or students of the prophets), who were in Bethel, came to Elisha and asked, "Do you know that today the Lord will take your master away from you?" Elisha answered, "Yes, I know. Be quiet about it." **4.** Elijah said to him, "Stay here, for the Lord has sent me to Jericho (an ancient city, known for its walls falling down in Joshua's time)." But Elisha answered, "As the Lord lives, and as you live, I will not leave you!" So the two of them went to Jericho. **5.** The sons of the prophets, who were in Jericho, approached Elisha and asked him, "Do you know that today the Lord will take your master away from you?" Elisha responded, "Yes, I know. Be silent about it." **6.** Elijah said to Elisha, "Stay here, for the Lord has sent me to the Jordan River (a river that marked the boundary of Israel)." But Elisha replied, "As the Lord lives, and as you live, I will not leave you!" So they continued on together. **7.** Fifty men from the sons of the prophets stood at a distance, facing them, while Elijah and Elisha stood by the Jordan. **8.** Elijah took his cloak (a large garment or robe), rolled it up, and struck the water with it. The water parted, and they both walked across on dry ground. **9.** After they had crossed, Elijah asked Elisha, "What do you want me to do for you before I am taken away?" Elisha said, "Please let a double portion (a larger share) of your spirit be on me." **10.** Elijah replied, "You've asked a difficult thing. If you see me when I am taken from you, it will be granted to you; but if not, it will not happen." **11.** While they were walking and talking, suddenly a chariot of fire (a symbol of God's power and glory), with horses of fire, appeared and separated the two of them. Elijah was taken up into heaven by a whirlwind. **12.** Elisha saw this happen, and he cried out, "My father! My father! The chariot of Israel (God's divine presence) and its horsemen!" Then Elisha could no longer see him, and he tore his clothes in grief (showing his sorrow). **13.** Elisha picked up Elijah's cloak, which had fallen from him, and went back to the Jordan. **14.** He took Elijah's cloak, struck the water with it, and said, "Where is the Lord, the God of Elijah?" When he struck the water, it parted in two, and Elisha crossed over. **15.** When the sons of the prophets in Jericho saw this, they said, "The spirit (presence or power) of Elijah rests on Elisha." They came to meet him and bowed to the ground before him. **16.** They said, "Look, there are fifty strong men (mighty or capable men) with your servants. Let us send them to search for your master, in case the Spirit of the Lord has taken him to some mountain or valley." Elisha replied, "Don't send anyone." **17.** However, they kept urging him (persisting) until he was ashamed, so he said, "Send them." They sent fifty men, and they searched for three days but did not find Elijah. **18.** When they returned to Elisha, who had stayed in Jericho, he said to them, "Did I not tell you not to go?" **19.** The people of the city said to Elisha, "Look, our city is well-situated, as my lord can see, but the water is bad (contaminated), and the land is unfruitful (unable to produce crops)." **20.** Elisha said, "Bring me a new bowl (a fresh container) and put salt (a preservative and purifier) in it." They brought it to him. **21.** Elisha went to the source (origin) of the water, threw the salt into it, and declared, "This is what the Lord says: 'I have healed this water. From now on, it will not cause death or barrenness (unproductive crops).' **22.** The water has remained pure to this day, as Elisha said. **23.** From there, Elisha went up to Bethel. As he was walking along the road, a group of youths (young people) came out of the city and mocked him (made fun of him), saying, "Get out of here, baldhead! Get out of here, baldhead!" **24.** Elisha turned around, looked at them, and called down a curse (a divine judgment) on them in the name of the Lord. Then two bears (female bears) came out of the forest and mauled (attacked) forty-two of the youths. **25.** After this, Elisha went to Mount Carmel (a mountain known for its connection to Elijah) and from there, he returned to Samaria (the capital of Israel).

Chapter 3

1. Jehoram, the son of Ahab (Ahab was the previous king of Israel), became the king of Israel (the northern kingdom) at Samaria (the capital city of Israel) during the eighteenth year of Jehoshaphat (the king of Judah, the southern kingdom), and he reigned for twelve years. **2.** He did evil in the sight of the Lord, but not as wickedly as his parents, because he removed the sacred pillar of Baal (a false god worshipped by his father) that his father had made. **3.** Still, he continued the sinful practices of Jeroboam (Jeroboam was the first king of the northern kingdom of Israel after the kingdom split), the son of Nebat, who led Israel into sin. Jehoram did not turn away from those sins. **4.** At that time, Mesha, the king of Moab (a kingdom east of Israel, descended from Lot), was a sheep breeder and regularly sent a tribute (payment) of one hundred thousand lambs and the wool of one hundred thousand rams to the king of Israel. **5.** after Ahab died, the king of

Moab rebelled (turned against) the king of Israel. **6**. So King Jehoram set out from Samaria (his capital city) and gathered all of Israel to fight against Moab. **7**. Then Jehoram sent a message to Jehoshaphat, the king of Judah, saying, "The king of Moab has rebelled against me. Will you join me in fighting against Moab?" Jehoshaphat replied, "I will go with you. I am as you are, and my people are as your people; my horses are your horses." **8**. Jehoram asked, "Which route should we take?" Jehoshaphat replied, "We will go by way of the Wilderness of Edom (a desert area south of Israel)." **9**. So, the king of Israel, along with the king of Judah and the king of Edom (a kingdom to the south of Israel, descended from Esau), marched on this roundabout route (a longer, indirect path) for seven days, but there was no water for the army or the animals. **10**. The king of Israel said, "Alas! The Lord has called these three kings together to deliver them into the hands of Moab." **11**. But Jehoshaphat asked, "Is there no prophet of the Lord here, so we may inquire of the Lord through him?" One of the servants of the king of Israel replied, "There is Elisha, the son of Shaphat (Elisha was a prophet who had served Elijah, a great prophet), who poured water on the hands of Elijah." **12**. Jehoshaphat said, "The word of the Lord is with him." So the kings of Israel, Judah, and Edom went down to Elisha. **13**. Elisha said to the king of Israel, "What do you want with me? Go to the prophets of your father and the prophets of your mother (false prophets who served Ahab and Jezebel)." But the king of Israel said to him, "No, because the Lord has called us three kings together to deliver us into the hands of Moab." **14**. Elisha replied, "As the Lord of hosts (the Almighty God) lives, before whom I stand, if it were not for the presence of Jehoshaphat, the king of Judah, I would not even look at you or see you." **15**. "But now, bring me a musician." When the musician played, the hand of the Lord came upon Elisha. **16**. And he said, "This is what the Lord says: 'Make this valley full of ditches (dig ditches in the valley).'" **17**. "For the Lord says: 'You will not see wind or rain, yet this valley will be filled with water, so that you, your cattle, and your animals may drink." **18**. "This is an easy thing for the Lord to do; He will also give the Moabites into your hands." **19**. "You will strike down every fortified city (a city with strong walls) and every important city. You will cut down every good tree, stop up all the springs of water, and ruin every good piece of land with stones." **20**. The next morning, when the grain offering (a religious offering of the first fruits of the harvest) was made, suddenly, water flowed from Edom (a kingdom to the south of Israel), and the valley was filled with water. **21**. When all the Moabites heard that the kings had come to fight against them, all those who were able to fight and were old enough to bear arms (carry weapons) gathered together and stood at the border. **22**. Early the next morning, when the sun was shining on the water, the Moabites saw the water on the other side as red as blood. **23**. They said, "This is blood; the kings have surely fought and killed each other. Now, Moab, let's take the spoil (loot)!" **24**. But when they came to the camp of Israel, the Israelites rose up and attacked the Moabites, and the Moabites fled before them. Israel entered their land and killed the Moabites. **25**. They destroyed the cities, and each Israelite threw stones on every good piece of land, filling it up; they stopped up all the springs of water and cut down all the good trees. They only left the stones of Kir Haraseth (a fortified city in Moab) intact, though the slingers (those who used slings to throw stones as weapons) surrounded and attacked it. **26**. When the king of Moab saw that the battle was too fierce for him, he took with him seven hundred men armed with swords, hoping to break through to the king of Edom, but they could not. **27**. Then he took his eldest son, who would have succeeded him as king, and offered him as a burnt offering (sacrificial offering burned completely to God) on the wall of the city. There was great indignation (strong anger) against Israel because of this, and they withdrew and returned to their own land.

Chapter 4

1. A widow (a woman whose husband has died) of one of the prophets went to Elisha and said, "My husband, who served you and honored the LORD, has passed away. Now a creditor (person to whom money is owed) is coming to take my two sons as slaves to pay off the debt (money owed)." **2**. Elisha asked her, "How can I help you? Tell me, what do you have in your house?" She replied, "Your servant has nothing at home except a small jar of oil." **3**. Elisha told her, "Go to all your neighbors and borrow as many empty containers as you can—don't just collect a few." **4**. He continued, "Go inside, close the door behind you and your sons, and pour the oil into all the containers. When each one is full, set it aside." **5**. She did as he instructed. She closed the door with her sons, who brought the containers to her, and she kept pouring. **6**. When all the containers were full, she said to her son, "Bring me another one." But he replied, "There are no more." Then the oil stopped flowing. **7**. She went and told Elisha, who said, "Sell the oil, pay off your debt, and you and your sons can live on what remains." **8**. One day Elisha went to Shunem (a town in Israel), where a respected woman invited him to eat with her. From then on, whenever he passed by, he would stop there for a meal. **9**. She told her husband, "I know that the man who often visits us is a holy man of God." **10**. She suggested, "Let's build a small room on the roof and furnish it with a bed, table, chair, and lamp. This way, he'll have a place to rest when he visits." **11**. The next time Elisha came by, he stayed in the room they had prepared for him. **12**. Elisha asked his servant Gehazi (Elisha's assistant) to call the woman, and she stood before him. **13**. Elisha told Gehazi, "Say to her, 'You've gone to great effort for us. What can we do for you? Should we speak on your behalf to the king or to the commander (leader of the army)?'" She replied, "I am content living with my own people." **14**. Elisha asked, "Then what can we do for her?" Gehazi replied, "She has no son, and her husband is old." **15**. Elisha told Gehazi to call her again. She came and stood in the doorway. **16**. Elisha said, "By this time next year, you will hold a son in your arms." She responded, "Please, man of God, do not deceive (mislead or give false hope to) your servant!" **17**. However, she conceived (became pregnant) and gave birth to a son the following year, just as Elisha had promised. **18**. When the child grew older, he went out to join his father, who was working with the reapers (those who gather crops) in the fields. **19**. Suddenly, he cried, "My head, my head!" His father told a servant (one who assists), "Carry him to his mother." **20**. The servant brought him to his mother, and he sat on her lap until noon, then he died. **21**. She took him up to Elisha's room, laid him on the bed, closed the door, and went out. **22**. She called her husband and asked for a servant and a donkey (an animal used for transport) so she could go quickly to find Elisha and return. **23**. Her husband asked, "Why are you going today? It's not a New Moon or the Sabbath (holy day of rest)." She replied, "It will be all right." **24**. She saddled the donkey and told the servant, "Lead on; don't slow down unless I tell you." **25**. She set out for Mount Carmel (a mountain in Israel) to find Elisha. When Elisha saw her approaching, he said to Gehazi, "Look, the Shunammite woman!" **26**. Elisha told Gehazi, "Run to meet her and ask, 'Is everything all right with you, your husband, and your child?'" She answered, "Everything is fine." **27**. When she reached Elisha, she knelt and held his feet. Gehazi tried to push her away, but Elisha said, "Leave her alone. She is in deep distress (intense sorrow), and the Lord has not revealed it to me." **28**. She cried, "Did I ask for a son, my lord? Didn't I say, 'Don't mislead me'?" **29**. Elisha told Gehazi, "Take my staff (a walking stick used by prophets), go quickly, and lay it on the child's face. Don't stop to greet anyone." **30**. The child's mother said, "As surely as the Lord lives and as you live, I won't leave you." So Elisha went with her. **31**. Gehazi went on ahead and laid the staff on the child's face, but there was no response. He returned and told Elisha, "The child has not awakened." **32**. When Elisha arrived, he found the child lying dead on his bed. **33**. He went in, closed the door, and prayed to the Lord. **34**. Elisha then stretched himself over the child, aligning his mouth, eyes, and hands with the child's. The child's body began to warm. **35**. Elisha got up, walked around the room, then lay down on the child again. The child sneezed seven times and opened his eyes. **36**. Elisha called Gehazi, "Call the Shunammite woman." When she entered, Elisha said, "Take your son." **37**. She bowed at Elisha's feet, then picked up her son and left. **38**. When Elisha returned to Gilgal (a city in Israel), there was a famine (extreme shortage of food) in the land. He told his servant to make stew (a thick soup) for the prophets. **39**. One man gathered wild gourds (a type of plant) from the field, unaware they were poisonous, and added them to the stew. **40**. When the men tasted the stew, they shouted, "Man of God, there's death in the pot!" and they couldn't eat it. **41**. Elisha said, "Bring some flour (ground wheat)." He added it to the pot, and the stew became safe to eat. **42**. A man from Baal Shalisha (a region in Israel) brought Elisha bread from the first harvest and some grain. Elisha said, "Give it to the people to eat." **43.** His servant asked, "How can I serve this to a hundred men?" But Elisha said, "Give it to them; the Lord says they will eat and have leftovers." **44.** They ate, and there were leftovers, just as the Lord had promised.

Chapter 5

1. Naaman, a commander in the Syrian army, was highly respected by his king because the LORD had used him to bring victory to Syria. Naaman was a strong and courageous warrior, but he suffered from leprosy (a severe skin condition). **2.** During one of Syria's raids (military attacks), they took a young girl from Israel who later became a servant to Naaman's wife. **3.** The young girl told her mistress, "If only my master could go to the prophet in Samaria (a city in Israel), he would be cured of his leprosy." **4.** Naaman spoke with his king and told him what the young girl from Israel had suggested. **5.** The Syrian king responded, "Go now, and I will send a letter to the king of Israel." Naaman then left, taking with him ten talents of silver (a substantial amount of silver), six thousand shekels of gold (a large amount of gold), and ten sets of clothing. **6.** Naaman gave the letter to the king of Israel, which read, "I am sending my servant Naaman to you so that you may heal him of his leprosy." **7.** Upon reading the letter, the king of Israel tore his clothes (a sign of sorrow or frustration) and said, "Am I God, with power over life and death, that this man sends someone to me to be cured of leprosy? He must be trying to provoke a conflict with me!" **8.** When Elisha, the prophet of God, heard that the king of Israel had torn his clothes, he sent a message, saying, "Why have you torn your clothes? Let this man come to me, and he will learn that there is a prophet in Israel." **9.** Naaman traveled with his horses and chariot (a two-wheeled vehicle drawn by horses for war or travel) and stopped at the entrance of Elisha's house. **10.** Elisha sent a messenger to Naaman with instructions: "Go and wash yourself in the Jordan River (a river in Israel) seven times, and your skin will be healed, and you will be cleansed." **11.** But Naaman became angry and left, saying, "I thought he would come out to meet me, stand and call upon the name of the Lord his God, wave his hand over my skin, and cure my leprosy. **12.** Are not the Abanah and Pharpar rivers (located in Damascus, Syria) better than any river in Israel? Couldn't I wash in them and be cleansed?" And in a rage (extreme anger), he turned to leave. **13.** Naaman's servants approached him and said, "Master, if the prophet had asked you to do something difficult, wouldn't you have done it? How much more should you obey when he simply says, 'Wash and be clean'?" **14.** So Naaman went to the Jordan River and dipped himself seven times, as the prophet instructed. His skin was restored (healed) to that of a young child, and he was cleansed. **15.** Naaman returned to the prophet with his whole group and said, "Now I know there is no God anywhere on earth but in Israel. Please accept a gift from your servant." **16.** Elisha replied, "As surely as the Lord lives, whom I serve, I will not accept anything." Though Naaman urged him to accept, Elisha refused. **17.** Naaman then said, "If you won't accept, please allow me, your servant, to take two mule-loads of earth (a significant quantity of soil) because I will no longer offer sacrifices or burnt offerings to any god except the Lord. **18.** However, may the Lord forgive me for this one thing: when my master goes into the temple of Rimmon (a god worshipped in Syria) to worship, and he leans on my arm, I too must bow in the temple of Rimmon. May the Lord forgive me for this." **19.** Elisha said to him, "Go in peace." So Naaman left and had not gone far. **20.** Gehazi, Elisha's servant, thought, "My master has let this Syrian go without accepting any gift from him! As surely as the Lord lives, I'll go after him and get something from him." **21.** Gehazi ran after Naaman. When Naaman saw Gehazi coming, he got down from his chariot and asked, "Is everything alright?" **22.** Gehazi replied, "Yes, all is well. My master sent me to say, 'Two young men from the company of prophets (students learning from prophets) have just arrived from the hill country of Ephraim. Please give them a talent of silver (a significant weight of silver) and two sets of clothing.'" **23.** Naaman said, "Please take two talents," and insisted he accept. Naaman wrapped up two talents of silver in two bags, along with two sets of clothing, and gave them to two of his servants to carry for Gehazi. **24.** When they reached the citadel (a secure area or building), Gehazi took the bags and stored them in his house, then sent the men away. **25.** When Gehazi returned to Elisha, Elisha asked, "Where have you been, Gehazi?" Gehazi replied, "Your servant hasn't gone anywhere." **26.** But Elisha said,

"Didn't my spirit go with you when the man turned from his chariot to meet you? Is this the time to take money, clothing, olive groves (areas planted with olive trees), vineyards (fields of grapevines), sheep, cattle, male and female servants? **27.** So now, Naaman's leprosy will cling to you and your descendants forever." And Gehazi left Elisha's presence leprous, with skin as white as snow.

Chapter 6

1. The disciples (students) of the prophets, who were learning under the guidance of Elisha, approached him and said, "Look, the dwelling place where we are living with you has become too cramped and insufficient for us." **2.** They continued, "Please allow us to travel to the Jordan River (a significant river in Israel known for its lush surroundings), where each of us can cut down a log (a sturdy piece of wood) to construct a new place for us to live and work together." Elisha replied, "Go ahead and do what you plan." **3.** One of them requested, "Will you accompany your servants on this journey?" Elisha replied with reassurance, "I will indeed go with you." **4.** Thus, he accompanied them, and upon their arrival at the banks of the Jordan River, they began to chop down trees for their new project. **5.** While one of them was vigorously chopping down a tree, the iron head of his ax (a crucial tool for cutting wood) accidentally fell into the river, causing him to cry out in despair, "Oh no, my master! The ax head was borrowed from someone!" **6.** The man of God, Elisha, asked, "Where exactly did it fall?" The young man pointed to the spot where the ax head had sunk. In response, Elisha cut a stick from a nearby tree and threw it into the water, and to everyone's amazement, the iron ax head miraculously floated to the surface. **7.** Therefore, Elisha said to him, "Reach out and pick it up for yourself." The young man stretched out his hand and retrieved the ax head from the water. **8.** Meanwhile, the king of Syria was strategizing for war against Israel. He discussed his plans with his advisors, stating, "I will position my camp at such and such a place." **9.** However, the man of God, Elisha, sent a warning to the king of Israel, saying, "Be cautious and do not go near this location, for the Syrians are planning an attack there." **10.** Following this warning, the king of Israel sent messengers to the area that Elisha had indicated, and he remained alert, taking precautions not just once or twice but consistently. **11.** As a result, the heart of the king of Syria was greatly disturbed by this intelligence, and he summoned his servants, questioning, "Will you not reveal to me which of you is loyal to the king of Israel?" **12.** One of his servants responded, "None of us, my lord, O king; rather, it is Elisha, the prophet who resides in Israel, who communicates the very words you speak in your private quarters." **13.** The king ordered, "Go find out where he is located, so that I can send men to capture him." They reported back, saying, "Surely he is in Dothan (a city in Israel known for its strategic position)." **14.** Consequently, the king sent horses, chariots, and a formidable army to Dothan, arriving under the cover of night, effectively surrounding the entire city. **15.** When Elisha's servant awoke early and stepped outside, he was struck with fear upon seeing the vast army encircling the city, along with horses and chariots. He cried out in alarm, "Oh no, my master! What shall we do in this dire situation?" **16.** Elisha responded calmly, "Do not be afraid, for those who are with us are far greater in number than those who are against us." **17.** Elisha then prayed earnestly, "Lord, I ask you to open his eyes so that he may see the truth." The Lord opened the eyes of the young man, and he beheld that the mountains surrounding them were filled with horses and chariots of fire, all around Elisha, signifying divine protection. **18.** As the Syrian army advanced toward them, Elisha prayed to the Lord, saying, "Strike this people with blindness, so they cannot see." The Lord answered Elisha's prayer and struck the entire group with blindness. **19.** Then Elisha addressed the blinded men, saying, "This is not the correct way, nor is this the city you are seeking. Follow me, and I will lead you to the man you are searching for." He led them to the city of Samaria (the capital of the northern kingdom of Israel). **20.** Once they arrived in Samaria, Elisha prayed once more, "Lord, please open the eyes of these men so they can see their surroundings." The Lord opened their eyes, and they were astonished to find themselves inside Samaria, realizing they had been led into the enemy's territory! **21.** When the king of Israel saw them, he eagerly asked Elisha, "My father, should I kill them? Shall I strike them down?" **22.** Elisha replied firmly, "You shall not kill them. Would you kill those who have been taken captive in battle?

Instead, prepare a feast for them, giving them food and drink, so they may eat and drink before returning to their master." 23. Elisha arranged for a grand feast to be prepared for them, and after they enjoyed the meal, he sent them back home, ensuring that they returned to their king. Following this event, the bands of Syrian raiders ceased their incursions into the land of Israel. 24. Sometime later, King Ben-Hadad of Syria gathered his entire army and laid siege to Samaria, seeking to overpower the city. 25. As a result, a severe famine struck Samaria; they were besieged to the point where a donkey's head was being sold for eighty shekels of silver, and a quarter of a kab (a measure) of dove droppings was priced at five shekels of silver, showing the desperation of the people. 26. While the king of Israel was walking along the wall of the city, a woman cried out to him in distress, saying, "Help me, my lord, O king!" 27. The king replied, "If the Lord does not provide assistance, where can I possibly find help for you? From the threshing floor, where grain is processed, or from the winepress, where grapes are crushed?" 28. The king then inquired, "What troubles you so deeply?" The woman answered, "This other woman made a shocking proposal, saying, 'Give me your son, so that we may eat him today, and tomorrow we will eat my son.' 29. So we boiled my son and consumed him. The next day, I pleaded with her, 'Give me your son, so that we may eat him'; but she has hidden her son from me." 30. Upon hearing the woman's heartbreaking account, the king tore his clothes in anguish, and as he walked along the wall, the people looked at him, noticing that he was wearing sackcloth (a coarse cloth symbolizing mourning) underneath his royal robes. 31. He declared, "May God deal with me severely and swiftly if the head of Elisha, the son of Shaphat, remains attached to his body by the end of today!" 32. Meanwhile, Elisha was sitting comfortably in his house, surrounded by the elders who were with him. The king sent a messenger ahead to Elisha, but before the messenger reached him, Elisha informed the elders, "Do you see how this son of a murderer has sent someone to take away my life? When the messenger arrives, shut the door and hold him firmly at the door. Don't you hear the sound of his master's footsteps approaching?" 33. While Elisha was still speaking with the elders, the messenger came down to him, and the king proclaimed, "Surely this calamity has come from the Lord; why should I continue to wait for the Lord's help any longer?"

Chapter 7

1. Elisha, the prophet, spoke to the people and said, "Listen carefully to the word of the Lord. This is what the Lord declares: 'By this time tomorrow, a seah (a measure of grain) of the finest wheat flour will be sold for a single shekel (a small amount of money), and two seahs of barley (a cheaper grain) will also be sold for a shekel at the city gate of Samaria (the capital city of Israel, under siege by the enemy).'" 2. The officer who was the king's close adviser, the one who leaned on the king for counsel, replied skeptically to Elisha, saying, "What you are saying is impossible! Even if the Lord opened the windows of heaven, could such a miraculous thing really happen?" Elisha responded to him, "You will see it happen with your own eyes, but you will not live to eat any of it, as you doubt the Lord's power." 3. At the city gate, there were four men suffering from leprosy (a serious skin disease). These men looked at each other and said, "Why should we sit here, just waiting to die? 4. If we enter the city, we will die from starvation because the famine is so severe there. And if we stay here by the city gates, we will just die from hunger as well. So, why not go to the Syrian army (the enemy's camp) and surrender? If they choose to show mercy, we might live; and if they kill us, we'll be no worse off than we are now." 5. With this decision made, they set out in the evening twilight, leaving the city and heading towards the Syrian camp. But when they arrived at the edge of the camp, they were astonished to find that no one was there. 6. For the Lord had made the Syrian soldiers hear what they thought were the sounds of a massive army approaching—chariots, horses, and the rumble of a great army. The Syrians, in panic, said to each other, "Look, the king of Israel must have hired the kings of the Hittites (an ancient group of people) and the kings of Egypt (another powerful empire) to come and fight us. We're surrounded!" 7. In their fear, they fled into the night, abandoning their camp entirely—leaving behind their tents, horses, donkeys, and all their possessions as they ran to save their lives. 8. When the leprous men reached the camp, they entered the first tent they found. They were amazed to discover food,

drink, and riches. They ate and drank their fill, then took silver, gold, and clothing from the tent and went to hide these treasures. Afterward, they returned to another tent, took even more valuables, and hid them again. 9. After all this, they said to one another, "This is not right. Today is a day of great news, and we are keeping it to ourselves. If we wait until tomorrow morning to report this, we could be punished. We must go and tell the king's household (the king's servants and workers in the palace) about this good fortune." 10. So, the lepers went and called out to the city gatekeepers. They shouted, "We went to the Syrian camp, and to our surprise, no one was there— not a single soldier. Only the horses and donkeys are tied up, and the tents are still intact." 11. The gatekeepers immediately informed the king's household of the discovery. 12. That same night, the king of Israel got up and spoke to his officers, saying, "I think I know what the Syrians have done. They know we're starving, so they must have left their camp and hidden in the fields, waiting for us to come out of the city. When we do, they will spring an ambush, capturing us alive and then reenter the city." 13. One of the king's officers replied, "Please, let us send a few men to check. We still have five horses left in the city. They may be no better off than the rest of the people here, who are starving and dying, or perhaps they are just as abandoned as the others. Either way, it is worth the risk to send them and find out the truth." 14. The king agreed and sent two chariots, each with a pair of horses. He instructed the men to go after the Syrian army and find out what had happened to them. 15. The messengers followed the trail left by the Syrians all the way to the Jordan River (the major river that flows through Israel). Along the way, they found the road scattered with the clothes and weapons the Syrians had discarded in their haste to flee. The messengers returned to the king and reported everything they had seen. 16. As a result, the people of Samaria went out to the Syrian camp, looted the tents, and found plenty of food and supplies. Just as the Lord had promised, a seah of fine flour was sold for a shekel, and two seahs of barley were sold for a shekel, exactly as Elisha had said. 17. However, the king had appointed the officer who had doubted Elisha's prophecy to be in charge of the gate. When the people rushed out to buy the food and supplies, they trampled him at the gate, and he died, just as Elisha had prophesied when the king had visited him earlier. 18. Elisha had told the king that, "Tomorrow at this time, two seahs of barley will be sold for a shekel, and a seah of fine flour for a shekel, right here at the Samaria gate." 19. The officer who had questioned the prophecy of Elisha had responded by saying, "Even if the Lord opened windows in heaven, could this really happen?" To which Elisha replied, "You will see it with your own eyes, but you will not get to eat any of it, because of your unbelief." 20. And as Elisha had said, it all came true. The officer was trampled in the gate by the people in their rush to buy food, and he died, fulfilling the prophecy exactly as it had been spoken.

Chapter 8

1. Elisha, the prophet of God, spoke to the woman whose son he had miraculously raised from the dead, saying, "Get up, leave your home, and take your entire family with you. Go wherever you can find safety and shelter, for the Lord has decreed a famine (a severe shortage of food) that will affect the entire land, and it will last for seven years." 2. The woman immediately obeyed the word of the man of God, and she set out with her family to live in the land of the Philistines (a neighboring territory known for its historical conflict with Israel) for the entire duration of the famine, which lasted for seven years. 3. After the seven years had passed and the famine ended, the woman returned from the land of the Philistines. She went straight to the king to plead for the restoration of her house and her land, which she had left behind during the famine. 4. At the same time, the king was having a conversation with Gehazi, the servant of Elisha, asking him, "Please tell me about all the remarkable things Elisha has done, the miracles and works God has used him to perform." 5. As Gehazi was recounting to the king how Elisha had miraculously restored life to a dead child, the woman whose son Elisha had brought back to life appeared before the king, asking for the return of her property. Gehazi immediately said, "My lord, O king, this is the woman, and this is her son whom Elisha raised from the dead." 6. When the king asked the woman about the situation, she confirmed the story. The king, moved by the truth of her plea, assigned an official to oversee the restoration of her property.

The king instructed that not only her land but also the proceeds from her fields during the years she was away should be returned to her. **7.** Meanwhile, Elisha traveled to Damascus, which was the capital city of Syria and a key location in the region. Ben-Hadad, the king of Syria, was ill, and it was reported to him that Elisha, the prophet of Israel, had come to Damascus. **8.** The king, concerned about his health, instructed his trusted servant Hazael to take a generous gift and go to meet Elisha. The king asked Hazael to inquire of the prophet, "Will I recover from this illness that has come upon me?" **9.** Hazael set out for Elisha with a lavish gift—a large load of valuable goods, including the best offerings from Damascus, carried by forty camels. Upon arriving, he stood before Elisha and said, "Your servant Ben-Hadad, king of Syria, has sent me to you with this question: 'Will I recover from this illness that I am suffering from?'" **10.** Elisha answered Hazael, "Go back and tell the king that he will indeed recover from his illness. However, the Lord has shown me in a vision that, despite his recovery, he will actually die." **11.** Elisha then stared at Hazael intensely, holding a fixed gaze until Hazael felt uncomfortable and ashamed. After this, Elisha began to weep, his tears flowing as he understood the evil that would unfold in the future. **12.** Hazael, confused, asked, "Why is my lord weeping?" Elisha responded with sorrow, "I weep because I know the terrible things you will do to the people of Israel in the future. You will burn their strongholds, kill their young men in battle, dash their children against the rocks, and cruelly slaughter the pregnant women of Israel." **13.** Hazael, in disbelief, responded, "But what am I, your servant—a mere dog—to do such vile and wicked things?" Elisha replied, "The Lord has shown me that you will become the king of Syria, and this is why I am weeping, because of the future violence you will bring." **14.** Hazael, still shocked by Elisha's words, left the prophet and returned to his master, King Ben-Hadad. The king asked, "What did Elisha say to you?" Hazael lied, saying, "He told me that you would surely recover." **15.** But the next day, Hazael took a thick cloth, dipped it in water, and placed it over the king's face, suffocating him to death. Thus, Ben-Hadad died, and Hazael took his place as the new king of Syria, fulfilling Elisha's prophecy. **16.** In the fifth year of the reign of Joram, the son of Ahab, who was king of Israel, Jehoshaphat, king of Judah, had passed away, and his son Jehoram became king of Judah. **17.** Jehoram was thirty-two years old when he ascended to the throne, and he reigned for eight years in Jerusalem. **18.** However, Jehoram did not follow in the righteous ways of his forefathers. He walked in the ways of the kings of Israel, doing evil in the sight of the Lord because he had married Athaliah, the daughter of King Ahab of Israel. As a result, he led Judah into sin and away from the worship of the true God. **19.** Despite Jehoram's evil reign, the Lord refused to destroy Judah because of His promise to David, His servant. God had promised to maintain a descendant of David on the throne in Judah, and the Lord would honor that covenant, keeping a lamp (a symbol of leadership) shining through David's descendants forever. **20.** During Jehoram's reign, Edom (a kingdom located to the south of Judah) rebelled against Judah's rule and set up its own king, gaining independence from Judah. **21.** To try to regain control, Jehoram led his army to Zair (a city located in Edom), with all his chariots. One night, they rose up and attacked the Edomites, who had surrounded him and his commanders. The Edomites, however, fled in defeat, retreating to their tents. **22.** As a result of this battle, Edom has remained in rebellion against Judah's authority to this day. Additionally, during this time, Libnah (a town in Judah) also rebelled against Jehoram's rule. **23.** The rest of Jehoram's actions, his military campaigns, and all the details of his reign are recorded in the Book of the Chronicles of the Kings of Judah, which provides a more detailed account of his reign. **24.** Jehoram died and was buried with his ancestors in the City of David (the traditional burial place of the kings of Judah). His son Ahaziah succeeded him as king of Judah. **25.** In the twelfth year of the reign of Joram, son of Ahab, king of Israel, Ahaziah, the son of Jehoram (king of Judah), became the new king of Judah. **26.** Ahaziah was just twenty-two years old when he became king, and he reigned for only one year in Jerusalem. His mother, Athaliah, was the granddaughter of Omri (the king of Israel). **27.** Ahaziah followed the evil ways of his father's house, the house of Ahab, because his mother, Athaliah, had influenced him. He did what was wicked in the sight of the Lord, as he had been raised in an idolatrous household. **28.** Ahaziah allied himself with Joram, the king

of Israel, to fight against Hazael, the king of Syria, at Ramoth-Gilead (a strategic location in Israel). During the battle, the Syrians wounded King Joram severely. **29.** After being wounded, King Joram returned to Jezreel (a city in Israel) to recover. Ahaziah, concerned for his ally, Joram, went down to visit him in Jezreel to check on his condition and to offer comfort.

Chapter 9

1. Elisha, the prophet who served as God's spokesperson, called one of the younger prophets and gave him specific instructions, saying, "Prepare yourself for a journey. Take this flask of anointing oil in your hand, and go to Ramoth Gilead, a fortified city in northern Israel that had been a place of military importance. **2.** When you arrive there, look for Jehu, the son of Jehoshaphat, the son of Nimshi (Jehu was a military commander from a distinguished family), and bring him into an inner room, away from the others. **3.** Once you find him, pour the oil on his head and proclaim, 'Thus says the Lord God of Israel: "I have anointed you as king over Israel." 'Afterward, immediately open the door, flee, and do not hesitate or look back." **4.** The young prophet followed Elisha's orders without question and traveled to Ramoth Gilead. **5.** Upon arriving, he found the commanders of the army sitting together. He approached one of them and said, "I have a message for you, Commander." Jehu replied, "Which one of us?" The prophet said, "For you, Commander." **6.** Jehu stood up and followed the prophet into a house. The prophet then took the flask of oil, poured it over Jehu's head, and announced, "Thus says the Lord God of Israel: 'I have anointed you as king over the people of Israel, the nation of the Lord. **7.** You are to destroy the house of Ahab, your master, to avenge the blood of My servants, the prophets, and the blood of all the faithful servants of the Lord who were killed at the hands of Jezebel. **8.** The entire house of Ahab is to be wiped out, and I will cut off every male in Ahab's family line, whether free or enslaved, from Israel. **9.** I will make the house of Ahab like that of Jeroboam the son of Nebat, who led Israel into sin, and like the house of Baasha, the son of Ahijah, whose descendants were wiped out by divine judgment. **10.** The dogs will devour Jezebel on the field of Jezreel, and there will be no one left to bury her." After delivering this message, the young prophet immediately fled without delay. **11.** Jehu went back to join the commanders, who saw him come out of the house. They asked, "Is everything alright? Why did that madman come to you?" Jehu answered, "You know the man and the things he always says—his wild talk." **12.** The commanders, not convinced, pressed him further, "Tell us what he said." Jehu replied, "He told me that the Lord has anointed me as king over Israel." **13.** Upon hearing this, the commanders quickly responded by laying down their garments before Jehu, spreading them on the steps as a sign of submission and loyalty. They blew trumpets and proclaimed loudly, "Jehu is king!" **14.** Jehu, the son of Jehoshaphat, the son of Nimshi, began plotting against King Joram. (At that time, Joram had been defending Ramoth Gilead with the army of Israel, fighting against Hazael, the king of Syria.) **15.** However, Joram had returned to Jezreel to recuperate from the wounds he received in battle. Jehu saw this as the right time to act, saying, "If you agree with this plan, let no one leave the city to go and tell the news to Jezreel." **16.** Jehu then mounted his chariot and set out for Jezreel, where King Joram lay wounded. At the same time, King Ahaziah of Judah had come to visit Joram. **17.** A watchman stationed on the tower in Jezreel noticed the approach of Jehu and his company. He reported, "I see a group of men coming." Joram, curious, ordered, "Send a horseman to meet them and ask, 'Is it peace?'" **18.** The horseman rode out to meet Jehu and asked, "Thus says the king: Is it peace?" Jehu replied, "What do you have to do with peace? Turn around and follow me." The watchman then reported back, "The messenger went to them but did not return." **19.** Joram sent a second horseman to inquire, repeating the same question, "Is it peace?" Jehu answered in the same manner, "What do you have to do with peace? Turn around and follow me." **20.** The watchman reported once more, "He went up to them but has not returned. The driving of the chariot is like that of Jehu, son of Nimshi; he drives furiously!" **21.** Joram then ordered his chariot to be made ready, and together with King Ahaziah of Judah, they went out to Jehu. They encountered him on the land of Naboth the Jezreelite, a location with significant history. **22.** When Joram saw Jehu, he called out, "Is it peace, Jehu?" Jehu responded, "What peace is there as long as the idolatry and witchcraft of your mother Jezebel are so prevalent in Israel?" 23. Hearing this, Joram turned around and fled, shouting to Ahaziah, "Treachery, Ahaziah!" 24. Jehu then drew his bow and shot an arrow with full strength, striking Joram between the shoulders. The arrow pierced his heart, and Joram collapsed in his chariot. 25. Jehu commanded his officer, Bidkar, "Pick him up and throw him into the field of Naboth the Jezreelite, the very field where Naboth was unjustly killed by Ahab. Remember, you and I were together when the Lord spoke the judgment against Ahab, his family, and this land." 26. "The Lord said, 'I saw the blood of Naboth and his sons yesterday, and I will repay you for it in this field, according to His word.'" 27. When King Ahaziah of Judah saw what had happened to Joram, he too fled by the way of Beth Haggan. Jehu pursued him, saying, "Shoot him as well!" Ahaziah was struck by the archers at the ascent of Gur, near Ibleam, a region in the northern part of Israel. He fled to Megiddo, a city known for its significance in battles, and there he died. 28. His servants brought his body back in a chariot and buried him in the royal tombs in Jerusalem, in the City of David. 29. This all occurred in the eleventh year of Joram, the son of Ahab, when Ahaziah had begun his reign in Judah. 30. When Jehu reached Jezreel, Jezebel, the widow of King Ahab, heard the news of Jehu's arrival. She prepared herself by painting her eyes and adorning her head, a common practice for women in royal circles, and she looked through the window. 31. As Jehu entered through the city gate, she sarcastically called out, "Is it peace, Zimri, murderer of your master?" (Zimri had once killed the king of Israel in a violent coup.) 32. Jehu looked up at the window and asked, "Who is on my side? Who?" A few of her eunuchs (servants who were castrated) looked out at him. 33. Jehu then commanded, "Throw her down." The eunuchs obeyed and threw Jezebel out of the window. Her blood splattered against the wall and onto the horses, and Jehu trampled her underfoot with his chariot. 34. Afterward, Jehu went into the palace, ate and drank. He then said to his servants, "Now go and bury this cursed woman. She was a king's daughter after all." 35. When they went to bury her, they found only her skull, her feet, and the palms of her hands. 36. They returned and reported this to Jehu. He replied, "This is the word of the Lord, spoken through His servant Elijah the Tishbite, saying: 'In the field of Jezreel, dogs will devour the flesh of Jezebel. 37. Her body will lie exposed like refuse on the ground in that field, so that no one will be able to say, "Here lies Jezebel."

Chapter 10

1. Ahab (the former king of Israel who ruled with an alliance with evil, particularly under the influence of his wife, Jezebel) had seventy sons living in Samaria (the capital city of Israel, which was a center of political and military power). Jehu (a military leader, anointed by the prophet Elisha to overthrow Ahab's corrupt dynasty) wrote a letter and sent it to Samaria, addressing the rulers of Jezreel (a city in Israel that had served as a stronghold for Ahab's family), the elders (respected leaders within the community), and those who cared for Ahab's sons. The letter said: 2. "As soon as this letter reaches you, you will find that your master's sons are with you, and you have chariots (two-wheeled military vehicles used in battle), horses (riding animals used for speed and mobility), a fortified city (a city with strong walls, making it defensible), and weapons (tools for fighting, including swords, shields, and armor). 3. Choose the best of your master's sons, place him on his father's throne (to continue the legacy of Ahab's family), and prepare to fight for your master's family." 4. But they were terrified and said, "Look, two kings could not stand up to Jehu; how can we stand against him, given his military prowess and the power he commands?" 5. The chief official of the house, the city official, the elders, and those who cared for the king's sons sent a message to Jehu, saying, "We are your servants. We will do whatever you tell us, but we will not make anyone king, for we fear for our lives. Do what you think is best." 6. Jehu then sent them a second letter, saying, "If you are on my side and will obey my command, take the heads (severed heads, symbolizing a total overthrow of Ahab's dynasty) of the men who are your master's sons, and bring them to me at Jezreel by this time tomorrow. The king's sons, seventy in total, are with the leading men (chief men, those with authority) of the city who are raising them." 7. When the letter reached them, they took the king's sons, killed seventy of them, and placed their heads in baskets to send them to Jehu at Jezreel. 8. A messenger arrived and told Jehu, "They have brought the heads of the king's

sons." Jehu responded, "Pile them in two heaps (piles) at the entrance of the gate (entrance to the city, where public judgments were often made) until morning." 9. The next morning, Jehu went out and stood before the people. He said to them, "You are innocent. I conspired (secretly planned) against my master and killed him, but who killed all of these? They were the sons of a corrupt dynasty. 10. "Know now that not a single word the Lord spoke concerning the house of Ahab will fall to the ground (fail to come true). The Lord has done what He promised through His servant Elijah (the prophet who foretold Ahab's downfall)." 11. Jehu then killed everyone remaining in the house of Ahab in Jezreel, including all his leading men, his close associates, and his priests (religious leaders who supported Ahab's idolatry), leaving none alive to continue Ahab's evil influence. 12. Jehu set out from there and traveled to Samaria. On the way, at Beth Eked of the Shepherds (a place in Israel known for its proximity to Israelite territory), 13. he met the brothers of Ahaziah (the king of Judah, a neighboring kingdom with its own line of kings), and asked, "Who are you?" They replied, "We are the brothers of Ahaziah; we have come to greet the sons of the king and the queen mother." 14. Jehu told them, "Take them alive!" So they captured them and killed forty-two men at the well (water source) of Beth Eked. None of them escaped. 15. As Jehu was leaving there, he met Jehonadab (a leader of the Rechabites who avoided the corrupt ways of Israel), the son of Rechab (a man dedicated to following God's commands). Jehonadab came to meet him, and Jehu greeted him and asked, "Is your heart right (in good standing with God), as mine is toward yours?" Jehonadab replied, "Yes, it is." So Jehu said, "If you are sincere, give me your hand." Jehonadab gave him his hand, and Jehu took him up into his chariot (a military vehicle used in battle). 16. Jehu then said, "Come with me and see my zeal (passionate commitment) for the Lord." So they rode together in the chariot, and Jehonadab witnessed Jehu's determination to fulfill God's will. 17. When they arrived in Samaria, Jehu killed all who remained of Ahab's family there, destroying them just as the Lord had commanded through Elijah. 18. Jehu gathered all the people together and said to them, "Ahab (the former king of Israel) served Baal (a false god of the surrounding nations) only a little, but Jehu will serve him much more, with greater commitment, in order to expose the false religion." 19. So, call together all the prophets (spiritual leaders) of Baal, all his servants and priests. Make sure none are missing, for I have a great sacrifice for Baal. Anyone who is missing will not live." But Jehu had an ulterior (hidden) motive, intending to destroy the worshipers of Baal, whom he considered a dangerous influence. 20. Jehu then announced, "Proclaim a solemn assembly (meeting) for Baal." So they proclaimed it throughout the land. 21. Jehu sent messengers throughout all of Israel, and all the worshipers of Baal came, so that the temple (a place of worship) of Baal was filled from one end to the other, as the cultists eagerly gathered to offer their rituals. 22. Jehu said to the keeper of the temple wardrobe (clothing storage area, where special garments for rituals were kept), "Bring out the vestments (special clothing) for all the worshipers of Baal." He brought out the clothes for them, preparing them for their sacrificial acts. 23. Jehu and Jehonadab entered the temple of Baal and told the worshipers of Baal, "Look carefully to ensure there are no servants of the Lord here with you, only the worshipers of Baal, so that no one from the true faith interferes." 24. So they went in to offer sacrifices (ritual offerings) and burn offerings (completely burned animals as part of Baal's rituals). Jehu had stationed eighty men outside and told them, "If anyone whom I have brought into your hands escapes, it will be your life for his life." 25. After the burnt offering was completed, Jehu instructed the guards and captains (military leaders), "Go in and kill them; let no one escape!" They killed all of them with the sword. Then the guards and officers threw their bodies outside and went into the inner room of the temple of Baal. 26. They brought out the sacred pillars (idols used in Baal worship) from the temple of Baal and burned them, ensuring that no trace of Baal's influence remained. 27. They tore down the sacred pillar (idol) of Baal, destroyed the temple, and turned it into a refuse dump (a garbage pit), and it remains that way to this day, a lasting testimony to Jehu's zeal for God's purity. 28. In this way, Jehu destroyed the worship of Baal in Israel, eliminating a significant source of idolatry. 29. However, Jehu did not turn away from the sins (wrongdoings) of Jeroboam (the first king of the northern kingdom of Israel), son of Nebat, who caused Israel to sin by leading them to worship the golden calves (idols) in Bethel and Dan (cities in Israel). Jehu followed Jeroboam's example of idolatry, despite removing Baal worship. **30.** The Lord said to Jehu, "You have done well in carrying out what was right in My eyes and fulfilling My word concerning the house of Ahab. Because of this, your sons will sit on the throne of Israel for four generations, continuing your line of leadership." **31.** But Jehu did not take care to walk with all his heart in the law of the Lord (God's commands), the God of Israel. He did not turn away from the sins of Jeroboam, which caused Israel to sin, thus failing to fully follow God's commands. **32.** At that time, the Lord began to reduce (cut down) the size of Israel, and Hazael (the king of Aram, a neighboring kingdom) began to conquer parts of Israel, starting a series of wars that weakened Israel. **33.** Hazael took control of all the land east of the Jordan River: Gilead (a region east of the Jordan), Gad, Reuben, and Manasseh. This included the area of Aroer (a city by the River Arnon) and the territories of Gilead and Bashan (regions in the north, both important for trade and military control). **34.** The rest of the acts of Jehu, all that he did, and his achievements, including his military victories and reforms, are written in the book of the chronicles (historical records) of the kings of Israel. **35.** Jehu rested with his ancestors (ancient relatives) and was buried in Samaria. His son Jehoahaz (the next king, who would follow Jehu's legacy) succeeded him as king of Israel. **36.** Jehu reigned over Israel in Samaria for twenty-eight years, a period marked by political and military changes.

Chapter 11

1. When Athaliah, the mother of Ahaziah (Ahaziah was the king of Judah who had been killed), saw that her son was dead, she rose up in anger and fear of losing power, and began to ruthlessly kill all the royal heirs (the rightful descendants of the throne who could have ruled in his place). **2.** However, Jehosheba, the daughter of King Joram (Joram was the former king of Judah), and the sister of Ahaziah, secretly took Joash (the infant son of Ahaziah), and hid him away from the other royal children being murdered. She, along with his nurse (a caregiver), hid him in a bedroom within the palace, ensuring he would not be found or killed. **3.** For six years, Joash was hidden safely with Jehosheba in the house of the Lord (the Temple of Jerusalem), where no one could find him, while Athaliah ruled the land with an iron fist, unaware of the child's survival. **4.** In the seventh year, Jehoiada the priest, who was a godly man, summoned the captains of the hundreds to meet with him. They came from the guards of the king's house and from other military posts. Jehoiada made a solemn covenant with them in the Temple of the Lord, showing them the surviving son of the former king, Joash, who was the rightful heir to the throne. **5.** Jehoiada gave the commanders specific orders: "One-third of you, who are scheduled to serve on duty during the Sabbath, will be assigned to guard the king's house, ensuring that no one enters or leaves without permission." **6.** "A second third of you will guard the Gate of Sur (a known city gate of Jerusalem), and the final third will be posted at the gate behind the guards. All of you are to remain vigilant and protect the Temple from being breached." **7.** "Those of you who are off duty on the Sabbath will still be responsible for guarding the Temple of the Lord, ensuring the safety of the king at all times. You must watch over him even when he is not in public view." **8.** "Surround the king on every side with your weapons drawn; if anyone attempts to harm him or come too close, they should be killed immediately. You must stay with him wherever he goes, whether he is leaving or returning to the palace, in order to ensure his safety." **9.** The military commanders, the captains of the hundreds, followed Jehoiada's precise instructions. They took their men, including those on duty and those being relieved, and gathered in the Temple to meet with the priest. **10.** Jehoiada, in preparation for the task, gave the captains the spears and shields that had once belonged to King David (King who revered for his leadership and military success), which were stored in the Temple, and which symbolized the strength and protection of the Lord. **11.** The guards took their positions around the king, each man standing with his weapon in hand. They positioned themselves from the right side of the Temple to the left side, surrounding the altar and the sacred house of God, ensuring no one could approach the king unchallenged. **12.** Jehoiada brought out Joash, who was now seven years old, and placed the royal crown upon his head, signaling his official anointing as

king. He also presented him with the Testimony (the sacred laws of God), which was kept in the Ark of the Covenant, symbolizing the authority and responsibilities Joash would now bear. The people then proclaimed, "Long live the king!" as they celebrated the new king's reign. **13.** When Athaliah heard the sounds of joy and trumpets from the Temple, she came to investigate, curious about the commotion, unaware that her power was being threatened. **14.** When she arrived and saw the king standing by the pillar, with the leaders and the priests standing around him, the sound of trumpets filled the air. The people of the land were rejoicing and celebrating, and Athaliah, realizing what had happened, tore her clothes in a dramatic expression of shock and yelled out, "Treason! Treason!" **15.** Jehoiada the priest, who had orchestrated the plan, immediately gave orders to the captains of the hundreds and the officers of the army. He told them to seize Athaliah, take her outside the Temple, and kill anyone who attempted to follow her. He also instructed them, "Do not allow her to be killed in the house of the Lord," as the sanctity of the Temple must be preserved. **16.** They quickly seized Athaliah, taking her by the way of the horses' entrance, which led to the king's house. There, they put her to death, putting an end to her cruel reign. **17.** After Athaliah's death, Jehoiada made a formal covenant between the Lord, the new king, and the people of Judah. The covenant declared that they would be God's people, following His commands, and that the king would rule in accordance with God's will. **18.** The people of Judah, full of zeal and righteous anger, went to the Temple of Baal (the false god worshipped during Athaliah's reign), tore it down completely, and destroyed its altars and images. They also killed Mattan, the priest of Baal, in front of the altars as a symbol of the Lord's victory over idolatry. Jehoiada also appointed officers to oversee the proper functioning of the Temple of the Lord and to ensure that it would no longer be defiled. **19.** Jehoiada, having completed these reforms, brought the young king Joash down from the Temple and placed him on the throne in the royal palace. This marked the beginning of his reign as king of Judah. **20.** The people were filled with joy, and the city of Jerusalem was at peace once again. Athaliah's tyrannical rule was over, and Joash's rightful reign brought stability and hope to the land. **21.** Joash was only seven years old when he became king, but with the support of Jehoiada the priest, his reign began under the protection and guidance of the Lord.

Chapter 12

1. In the seventh year of Jehu's rule (king of Israel), Jehoash became king of Judah and ruled in Jerusalem (the main city of Judah) for forty years. His mother was Zibiah from Beersheba (a southern town in Judah, known for its wells and location on Judah's borders). **2.** Jehoash followed the ways of the Lord, doing what was right in God's sight for as long as Jehoiada, the priest (a religious authority who advised and guided him), instructed him. **3.** However, the high places (elevated altars where people traditionally offered sacrifices) were not taken down, and people continued to offer sacrifices and burn incense at these sites, despite the Lord's preference for worship at His designated temple. **4.** Jehoash told the priests to collect all the money given as dedicated gifts to the Lord's temple—this included census money (a tax given by those counted in a population survey), personal assessments (valued offerings based on each person's situation), and any freely given gifts from the heart—and to use these funds specifically for temple repairs. **5.** Each priest was to gather this money from the people in their assigned areas and use it to repair any damage in the Lord's temple (the primary place of worship). **6.** By the twenty-third year of Jehoash's reign, however, it was clear that the priests had still not made the necessary repairs to the temple. **7.** So King Jehoash summoned Jehoiada and the other priests, asking, "Why haven't you repaired the temple yet? From now on, don't take any more money from the people for yourselves; instead, make sure it is all used for temple repairs." **8.** The priests agreed to stop collecting money from the people personally and to no longer be responsible for the repairs themselves. **9.** To ensure that all offerings were properly collected and used for repairs, Jehoiada set up a chest (a secure collection box), bored a hole in its lid, and placed it beside the altar (a holy table for sacrifices), on the right side as people entered the Lord's house. The doorkeeper priests put the offerings brought to the Lord into this chest. **10.** When the chest became filled with money, the king's scribe (a royal official who recorded transactions) and the high priest would

160

bag and count the money. **11.** They then entrusted this money to those overseeing the temple work, who used it to pay carpenters and builders actively repairing the house of the Lord (the main temple). **12.** The funds also went to masons and stonecutters and were used to purchase timber and hewn (cut) stones for the temple structure, as well as for other necessary costs related to restoring the house of the Lord to its former state. **13.** However, no silver bowls, wick trimmers, sprinkling bowls, trumpets, or any articles of gold or silver were made from these funds for the temple. **14.** Instead, all the money was directed solely to the workers, who diligently used it for the essential repair work on the Lord's temple. **15.** The men who received the money to distribute to the workers did not need to account for it because they acted faithfully and with full integrity. **16.** The money from guilt offerings (funds offered as payment for offenses) and sin offerings (payments for forgiveness of sins) was not used for these repairs; it was allocated to the priests for their upkeep. **17.** Around this time, Hazael, the king of Syria (an enemy nation neighboring Israel), attacked and captured Gath (a Philistine city), then directed his attention toward Jerusalem. **18.** In response, Jehoash gathered all the sacred items his ancestors—Jehoshaphat, Jehoram, and Ahaziah (former kings of Judah)—had dedicated, along with his own consecrated items, as well as all the gold in the treasuries of the Lord's temple and the king's palace, and sent it to Hazael, king of Syria. After receiving this wealth, Hazael withdrew from Jerusalem. **19.** The rest of Jehoash's actions and accomplishments are recorded in the chronicles (historical records) of the kings of Judah. **20.** Joash's servants conspired against him, and he was killed in the house of the Millo (fortified area near Jerusalem), on the road that leads down to Silla (a part of Jerusalem's surroundings). **21.** The conspirators, Jozachar son of Shimeath and Jehozabad son of Shomer (Joash's own servants), assassinated him, and he died. He was buried with his ancestors in the City of David (a historic area in Jerusalem). His son Amaziah succeeded him as king.

Chapter 13

1. In the twenty-third year of Joash, the son of Ahaziah (former king of Judah), Jehoahaz, the son of Jehu (the previous king of Israel), became the king of Israel in Samaria (the capital city of the northern kingdom of Israel) and reigned for 17 years. **2.** Jehoahaz did evil in the sight of the Lord, following the sinful practices of Jeroboam (the first king of Israel after the kingdom split, who introduced idol worship), the son of Nebat, and he did not turn away from these sins. **3.** The Lord became angry with Israel because of their continuous sin, and He gave them into the hands of Hazael, the king of Syria (Syria was an enemy nation to Israel), and his son Ben-Hadad, who oppressed Israel for many years. **4.** Jehoahaz pleaded with the Lord to help them, and the Lord heard his cry because He saw how severely Israel was being oppressed by the Syrian kings. **5.** The Lord sent a deliverer (a person or leader chosen to rescue Israel), and Israel was able to break free from Syria's control. The people of Israel returned to their homes, living as they had before. **6.** However, even after experiencing deliverance, Israel did not stop worshiping the idols established by Jeroboam, nor did they abandon the wooden idol (an image of a false god) that remained in Samaria, showing their continued disobedience to God. **7.** The Lord had reduced the strength of Jehoahaz's army. Only 50 horsemen, 10 chariots, and 10,000 foot soldiers remained, as Syria had utterly destroyed the rest of their military, leaving Israel almost powerless, like dust blown away during threshing (a process where grain is separated from its husk). **8.** The rest of Jehoahaz's actions and deeds, along with his military strength, are written in the book of the chronicles of the kings of Israel (an official record of Israel's kings). **9.** Jehoahaz died and was buried in Samaria, and his son Joash succeeded him as the king of Israel. **10.** In the 37th year of Joash, king of Judah, Jehoash, the son of Jehoahaz, became king of Israel in Samaria and reigned for 16 years. **11.** Joash did evil in the sight of the Lord, just like his father, and continued to follow the sins of Jeroboam, the son of Nebat, who had led Israel into idol worship. Joash did not depart from these sinful ways. **12.** The rest of Joash's actions, his military victories, and his conflict with Amaziah, king of Judah, are recorded in the book of the chronicles of Israel's kings. **13.** Joash died and was buried in Samaria, where the kings of Israel were laid to rest. His son Jeroboam became king after him. **14.** Elisha, the prophet who had served Israel for many years, became

seriously ill and was on his deathbed. Joash, the king of Israel, went to see him, weeping over his mentor and saying, "My father, my father, the chariots of Israel and their horsemen!" (referred to Elisha's role as Israel's spiritual protector, seen as a source of strength). **15.** Elisha instructed Joash to take a bow and arrows. Joash did so, ready to obey. **16.** Elisha told him, "Place your hand on the bow." Joash followed his command, and Elisha placed his hands on top of Joash's hands. **17.** Elisha said, "Open the east window." Joash opened the window. Then Elisha told him, "Shoot!" Joash shot an arrow, and Elisha declared, "This is the arrow of the Lord's deliverance, the arrow that will bring Israel victory over Syria. You will strike the Syrians at Aphek (a city in Israel) and defeat them until they are completely destroyed." **18.** Elisha then instructed Joash to take the remaining arrows and strike the ground with them. Joash struck the ground three times but stopped, showing a lack of persistence in his actions. **19.** Elisha became angry and said, "You should have struck the ground five or six times! If you had, you would have completely defeated Syria. But now, you will only defeat them three times." (Elisha's frustration indicated that Joash's actions reflected a lack of faith and determination in seeking God's full victory.) **20.** After this, Elisha died and was buried. In the springtime, raiders from Moab (a neighboring kingdom to the east of Israel) invaded Israel's territory. **21.** While some Israelites were burying a man, they saw the Moabite raiders approaching, so they hurriedly placed the body in Elisha's tomb. When the body touched Elisha's bones, the dead man came back to life and stood up, a miraculous act showing God's power through Elisha even after his death. **22.** Hazael, the king of Syria, continued to oppress Israel throughout the reign of Jehoahaz. **23.** Yet, the Lord was gracious to Israel, showing mercy and compassion because of His covenant with Abraham, Isaac, and Jacob (the patriarchs of Israel). The Lord remembered His promises and chose not to destroy Israel, nor cast them away from His presence. **24.** After Hazael, the king of Syria, died, his son Ben-Hadad became king in his place. **25.** Jehoash, the son of Jehoahaz, recaptured the cities that had been taken by Ben-Hadad from his father. Joash defeated Ben-Hadad in three battles, regaining the cities of Israel.

Chapter 14

1. In the second year of Joash, the son of Jehoahaz (king of Israel), Amaziah, the son of Joash, became king of Judah. **2.** Amaziah was twenty-five years old when he began his reign, and he ruled for twenty-nine years in Jerusalem. His mother was Jehoaddan of Jerusalem. **3.** Amaziah did what was right in the eyes of the Lord, although he did not follow his ancestor David's level of devotion. Instead, he did as his father Joash had done. **4.** However, the high places (elevated sites used for worship) were not taken down, and people continued to offer sacrifices and burn incense on these high places. **5.** Once Amaziah's rule was firmly established, he executed the servants who had assassinated his father, the king of Judah. **6.** Yet he did not kill their children, in accordance with the Law of Moses, where God commands, "Parents shall not die for their children's sins, nor children for their parents' sins; each person must face judgment for their own actions." **7.** Amaziah defeated ten thousand Edomites (descendants of Esau) in the Valley of Salt and captured Sela (a fortress city of Edom), renaming it Joktheel, a name that remains to this day. **8.** Then Amaziah sent messengers to Jehoash, king of Israel (son of Jehoahaz), challenging him by saying, "Come, let's meet in battle." **9.** Jehoash, king of Israel, replied with a parable: "A thistle (a weak, small plant) in Lebanon sent a message to a cedar tree (a strong, tall tree) in Lebanon, saying, 'Give your daughter to my son in marriage.' But then a wild animal passed by and crushed the thistle. **10.** You have defeated Edom, and now your pride has grown. Celebrate your victory, but stay home. Why invite disaster that could destroy you and Judah?" **11.** But Amaziah ignored this warning. So Jehoash, king of Israel, led his army out, and he and Amaziah, king of Judah, faced each other in battle at Beth Shemesh (a city in Judah). **12.** The forces of Judah were defeated by Israel, and every soldier retreated to his own home. **13.** Jehoash, king of Israel, captured Amaziah at Beth Shemesh and advanced to Jerusalem. There he destroyed about four hundred cubits (around six hundred feet) of the city wall, from the Gate of Ephraim to the Corner Gate. **14.** Jehoash also took all the gold and silver from the temple and the royal treasury, as well as hostages, and returned to Samaria (Israel's capital). **15.** The other acts of Jehoash—his strength and his conflict with Amaziah—are documented in the chronicles of Israel's kings. **16.** Jehoash eventually died and was buried in Samaria with the other kings of Israel, and his son Jeroboam succeeded him. **17.** Amaziah, king of Judah, lived another fifteen years after the death of Jehoash, king of Israel. **18.** The rest of Amaziah's deeds are recorded in the chronicles of the kings of Judah. **19.** Eventually, a conspiracy (an organized plot against him) was formed in Jerusalem, forcing Amaziah to flee to Lachish (a fortified town in Judah). However, his pursuers tracked him down to Lachish and killed him there. **20.** His body was brought back to Jerusalem on horses, and he was buried in the City of David (a historical part of Jerusalem) alongside his ancestors. **21.** The people of Judah then took Amaziah's sixteen-year-old son, Azariah, and made him king in his place. **22.** Azariah later rebuilt Elath (a port city on the Red Sea coast) and restored it to Judah after his father's death. **23.** In the fifteenth year of Amaziah's reign in Judah, Jeroboam, son of Joash, became king of Israel in Samaria, ruling for forty-one years. **24.** Jeroboam did evil in God's sight, continuing in the sinful ways of Jeroboam, son of Nebat, who had led Israel into idolatry. **25.** He restored Israel's borders from the entrance of Hamath (a northern area) to the Sea of the Arabah (likely the Dead Sea), as the Lord had foretold through His prophet Jonah, son of Amittai, from Gath Hepher. **26.** The Lord saw the severe suffering of Israel, and that no one, slave or free, could help them. **27.** But God did not decree the total destruction of Israel; instead, He delivered them through Jeroboam. **28.** Jeroboam's other acts—including his battles and his reclaiming of lands from Damascus and Hamath that had belonged to Judah—are recorded in the chronicles of Israel's kings. **29.** Jeroboam died and was buried with the kings of Israel, and his son Zechariah succeeded him.

Chapter 15

1. In the twenty-seventh year of Jeroboam, king of Israel, Azariah, son of Amaziah, became king of Judah. (Jeroboam: king of Israel; Amaziah: former king of Judah) **2.** Azariah was sixteen when he began his reign and ruled for fifty-two years in Jerusalem. His mother was Jecholiah from Jerusalem. **3.** He did what was right in the Lord's eyes, as his father Amaziah had done. **4.** But he did not remove the high places (elevated worship sites) where people still offered sacrifices and incense. **5.** The Lord struck Azariah with leprosy (a skin disease), and he lived in isolation until his death. His son Jotham ruled in his stead. **6.** The rest of Azariah's actions are recorded in the chronicles of Judah. **7.** Azariah died and was buried in the City of David. Jotham, his son, became king. **8.** In the thirty-eighth year of Azariah's reign, Zechariah, son of Jeroboam, became king of Israel and ruled for six months. **9.** He did evil, following the sinful practices of his ancestors, and did not depart from the sins of Jeroboam. (Jeroboam: the first king of Israel) **10.** Shallum, son of Jabesh, conspired against Zechariah, killed him, and took the throne. **11.** The rest of Zechariah's deeds are written in the chronicles of Israel. **12.** This fulfilled the Lord's prophecy to Jehu (king of Israel), that his descendants would reign for four generations. **13.** Shallum became king in the thirty-ninth year of Uzziah's reign and ruled for only a month in Samaria. **14.** Menahem, son of Gadi, came from Tirzah (a city in Israel), killed Shallum, and became king. **15.** The rest of Shallum's acts are written in the chronicles of Israel. **16.** Menahem attacked the city of Tiphsah because they did not surrender, and he brutally killed the pregnant women. **17.** Menahem became king in the thirty-ninth year of Azariah's reign, and ruled for ten years. **18.** He did evil, following the sins of Jeroboam. **19.** King Pul of Assyria invaded Israel. Menahem gave him 1,000 talents of silver (a large sum) to gain his support. **20.** Menahem taxed the wealthy to raise the money, and Assyria withdrew. **21.** Menahem's deeds are recorded in the chronicles of Israel. **22.** Menahem died and was buried. His son Pekahiah succeeded him. **23.** In the fiftieth year of Azariah's reign, Pekahiah, son of Menahem, became king of Israel and ruled for two years. **24.** He did evil, not turning from Jeroboam's sins. **25.** Pekah, son of Remaliah, one of his officers, killed Pekahiah and took the throne. **26.** The rest of Pekahiah's deeds are written in the chronicles of Israel. **27.** In the fifty-second year of Azariah's reign, Pekah, son of Remaliah, became king and ruled for twenty years. **28.** He did evil, continuing Jeroboam's sins. **29.** During his reign, Tiglath-Pileser (king of Assyria) invaded and captured many cities in Israel, carrying their people away to Assyria. **30.** Hoshea, son of Elah, conspired against Pekah, killed him, and took the throne in the twentieth year of Jotham, king of Judah. **31.** The rest of Pekah's deeds are recorded in the chronicles of Israel. **32.** In the second year of Pekah's reign, Jotham, son of Uzziah, began his reign in Judah. **33.** Jotham was twenty-five when he became king, and he reigned for sixteen years in Jerusalem. His mother was Jerusha, daughter of Zadok (a priest). **34.** He did right in the Lord's eyes, as his father Uzziah had, but he did not remove the high places. **35.** Jotham built the Upper Gate of the Lord's house (temple in Jerusalem). **36.** The rest of Jotham's acts are written in the chronicles of Judah. **37.** During his reign, the Lord sent Rezin, king of Syria, and Pekah, son of Remaliah, against Judah. **38.** Jotham died and was buried in the City of David. His son Ahaz succeeded him.

Chapter 16

1. In the seventeenth year of Pekah (king of Israel, son of Remaliah), Ahaz (king of Judah, son of Jotham) began to reign. **2.** Ahaz was 20 years old when he began to reign, and he ruled for 16 years in Jerusalem (the capital city of Judah), but unlike his ancestor David (the former king of Israel), he did not do right in God's eyes. **3.** He followed the sinful practices of Israel's kings, even sacrificing his son by fire (a form of child sacrifice), a detestable practice of the nations whom God had driven out before the Israelites. **4.** He also worshiped idols (statues or images of gods), burning incense (substance burned for fragrance in worship) on high places (altars built on hills), on hills, and under every tree. **5.** Rezin (king of Syria) and Pekah (king of Israel) attacked Jerusalem but could not capture it. **6.** Rezin took Elath (a port city in Judah) from Judah, forcing its people to leave, and the Edomites (people from the region south of Judah) settled there. **7.** Ahaz sent a message to Tiglath-Pileser (king of Assyria, a powerful empire to the northeast), calling himself his servant and asking for help against Syria and Israel. **8.** Ahaz sent the silver and gold from the temple (the house of the Lord in Jerusalem) and royal palace to Tiglath-Pileser as a gift. **9.** Tiglath-Pileser attacked Damascus (the capital of Syria), captured it, killed Rezin, and took its people captive to Kir (a place of exile). **10.** Ahaz went to Damascus to meet Tiglath-Pileser and saw an altar there. He sent its design to Urijah (the priest in Jerusalem) to have it built in Jerusalem. **11.** Urijah built the altar exactly as Ahaz had instructed before the king returned. **12.** Upon his return, Ahaz saw the altar, made offerings on it, and used it for worship. **13.** He made burnt offerings (a sacrifice completely consumed by fire), grain offerings (offerings made with grain), and peace offerings (offerings of gratitude), and poured out drink offerings (liquids poured out in sacrifice) on the altar. **14.** He moved the bronze altar (an altar made of bronze) from before the Lord's temple and placed it on the north side of the new altar. **15.** Ahaz ordered Urijah to burn daily offerings (regular sacrifices made each day) on the new altar and use the bronze altar for personal inquiries (asking for divine guidance). **16.** Urijah followed all of Ahaz's commands. **17.** Ahaz removed parts of the temple's furnishings, including the bronze chariots (vehicles used in ancient worship) and water basins (used for cleansing), placing the large basin (the bronze Sea) on stone pavement (a flat stone surface). **18.** He also removed the Sabbath pavilion (a structure for Sabbath worship) and the king's outer entrance (a gate or entryway to the temple) due to pressure from the Assyrian king. **19.** The rest of Ahaz's acts are recorded in the book of the chronicles (historical record) of the kings of Judah. **20.** Ahaz died and was buried in the City of David (the royal tombs in Jerusalem); his son Hezekiah (the next king) succeeded him.

Chapter 17

1. In the twelfth year of Ahaz, king of Judah (the southern kingdom of Israel), Hoshea (the son of Elah, a leader of Israel) became the king of Israel in Samaria, the capital city of Israel, and he ruled for nine years, during which time he faced significant challenges. **2.** Though Hoshea did evil in the sight of the Lord, his actions were not as extreme as those of the previous kings of Israel who had greatly defiled the land. **3.** During his reign, Shalmaneser, the powerful king of Assyria (a major empire known for its conquests), came up against Israel, and Hoshea was forced to submit as a vassal, paying him annual tribute (a form of tribute money to keep peace). **4.** However, the king of Assyria discovered that Hoshea had been secretly conspiring against him. Hoshea had sent messengers to So, the king of Egypt, and had stopped paying the annual tribute, breaking his allegiance to Assyria. In response, Shalmaneser captured him and imprisoned him. **5.** The king of Assyria then advanced through the land, eventually laying siege (a prolonged military blockade) to Samaria, Israel's capital. The siege lasted for three years, during which the people of Samaria suffered greatly. 6. In the ninth year of Hoshea's reign, Samaria fell to Assyria, and the king of Assyria carried the Israelites into captivity, scattering them across his empire. They were placed in various cities, including Halah (a city region in Assyria), along the Habor River (a river in Assyria), and in the cities of the Medes (a group of ancient peoples in northern Persia). 7. This exile happened because the children of Israel had sinned against the Lord, the very God who had delivered them from Egypt, from the oppressive rule of Pharaoh (the king of Egypt). Instead of serving God, they worshiped other gods, 8. and they followed the practices of the surrounding nations, the same nations the Lord had driven out from before the Israelites. The Israelites adopted their customs and traditions, including those of the kings of Israel, who had led the people astray. 9. Furthermore, the people of Israel did evil in secret, doing things that were blatantly against the Lord's commands. They set up high places (places of idol worship) in every city, from the watchtower (a defensive structure) to the fortified city (a city with military defenses). 10. On these high places, they set up sacred pillars (stone monuments dedicated to gods) and wooden images (idols), placing them on every hill and beneath every leafy tree, showing the extent of their idolatry. 11. They burned incense (a form of worship involving fragrant smoke) on these high places, mirroring the practices of the nations the Lord had driven out before them. They did these wicked things to provoke the Lord to anger, breaking His covenant. 12. They served idols (false gods), even though the Lord had explicitly forbidden such practices, saying, "You shall not do this thing." 13. The Lord, in His mercy, testified against Israel and Judah, sending many prophets and seers (divinely inspired messengers), saying, "Turn from your evil ways, and keep My commandments and statutes as I commanded your forefathers and as I have sent to you through My prophets." 14. However, the people refused to listen. They became stubborn and unyielding, like their ancestors, who had rejected faith in the Lord. 15. The Israelites abandoned God's laws, rejected His covenant, and ignored His testimonies (warnings), choosing instead to follow idols, which made them idolaters. They imitated the sinful practices of the nations around them, against the Lord's clear command. 16. They completely abandoned the commandments of the Lord their God. They even made two golden calves (idols), an Asherah pole (a fertility idol), and worshiped the stars of the heavens, while serving Baal (a prominent Canaanite god). 17. They even sacrificed their own children by passing them through the fire, a horrific act of child sacrifice. They practiced witchcraft (sorcery) and divination (fortune-telling) and sold themselves to evil, provoking the Lord to anger with their actions. 18. Because of this, the Lord became exceedingly angry with Israel and removed them from His sight, leaving only the tribe of Judah. 19. Even Judah did not remain faithful. They too followed the sinful practices of Israel, the northern kingdom, and did not keep the commandments of the Lord their God. 20. As a result, the Lord rejected all of Israel's descendants, bringing suffering upon them, and allowing their enemies to plunder them. He cast them out of His presence, just as He had warned. 21. The Lord had torn Israel away from the house of David (the royal lineage of Judah), and they made Jeroboam (the first king of the northern kingdom) the son of Nebat their ruler. Jeroboam led Israel into sin and idolatry, 22. and the Israelites continued in the sinful ways that Jeroboam had introduced, never departing from them, 23. until the Lord finally removed Israel from His presence, as He had promised through His prophets. The people of Israel were carried away into captivity by the Assyrians, where they remain to this day. 24. The king of Assyria then brought people from various nations, including Babylon (the city and its empire), Cuthah, Ava, Hamath, and Sepharvaim, and settled them in the cities of Samaria. They took over the land and lived in the cities once inhabited by the Israelites. 25. At first, these new inhabitants did not fear the Lord, which led to trouble. So the Lord sent lions among them, which attacked and killed some of them. 26. The people then spoke to the king of Assyria, saying, "The nations you have brought to inhabit Samaria do not know the rituals of the God of this land, and that is why He has sent lions among us." 27. The king of Assyria then ordered, "Send one of the priests you brought from Israel to teach the people the ways of the God of the land." 28. So one of the priests who

had been exiled from Samaria went to Bethel (a city in Israel) and taught the people how to fear the Lord. 29. Yet, despite learning the ways of the Lord, each nation continued to make its own gods and set them up in the shrines on the high places the Samaritans had built, continuing their idolatry in their new homes. 30. The people of Babylon made Succoth Benoth (a god), the people of Cuth made Nergal (a god), the people of Hamath made Ashima (a god), 31. and the Avites made Nibhaz and Tartak (gods); even the Sepharvites sacrificed their children in fire to Adrammelech and Anammelech, gods of the Sepharvites. 32. Despite this, the people began to fear the Lord, but they continued to appoint priests for themselves from among all the nations to sacrifice on the high places. 33. They feared the Lord, but they also served their own gods, following the customs of the nations from which they had been carried away. 34. To this day, these nations continue to practice their former rituals. They do not fully fear the Lord, nor do they follow His statutes, laws, or commandments, which the Lord had given to the descendants of Jacob, whom He named Israel. 35. The Lord had made a covenant with them, charging them, saying, "You shall not fear other gods, nor bow down to them, nor serve them, nor sacrifice to them, 36. but you shall fear the Lord, who brought you up from the land of Egypt with great power and an outstretched arm. Him you shall worship, and to Him you shall offer sacrifices." 37. The statutes, ordinances, laws, and commandments that He gave you, you shall be careful to observe forever. You shall not fear other gods. 38. The covenant I made with you, you shall not forget. You shall not fear other gods. 39. But the Lord your God you shall fear, and He will deliver you from the hand of all your enemies." 40. Despite this, the people did not obey but continued to follow their old rituals. 41. These nations feared the Lord, yet served their carved images (idols). Their children and their children's children continued in the same practices, doing as their ancestors had done, even to this day.

Chapter 18

1. In the third year of Hoshea, the son of Elah, who was the last king of Israel (the northern kingdom), Hezekiah, the son of Ahaz (a previous king of Judah, the southern kingdom), began his reign over Judah. 2. Hezekiah became king at the young age of twenty-five, and he ruled for twenty-nine years in Jerusalem, the capital city of Judah. His mother's name was Abi, and she was the daughter of Zechariah, a man of some prominence. 3. Hezekiah followed the example of his great ancestor David, the former king, and did what was right in the eyes of the Lord, seeking to restore the true worship of God as David had done, with great faithfulness and dedication. 4. He took bold steps to remove idol worship from the land by tearing down the high places (mountaintop shrines used for idolatry), shattering the sacred pillars (stone monuments used in idol worship), and cutting down the wooden image (an idol carved from wood that had been worshiped). He also destroyed the bronze serpent that Moses had made during Israel's journey through the wilderness, which the people had begun to worship as an idol, calling it Nehushtan, meaning "the bronze thing." This was a strong stand against idolatry, even against something once revered in Israel's history. 5. Hezekiah trusted deeply in the Lord, the God of Israel, and there was no other king in Judah like him, either before or after his reign. His devotion to God's law and his reforms made him stand out in a land plagued by idolatry. 6. He held firmly to the Lord's ways and was committed to following His commands, as laid out by Moses, never wavering from his faith. 7. The Lord's presence was evident in Hezekiah's life. Wherever he went, God prospered him, and his reign was marked by success. Notably, Hezekiah boldly resisted the powerful Assyrian empire, which had dominated much of the ancient Near East, refusing to bow down to their rule. 8. Hezekiah even went so far as to defeat the Philistines, who had long been a threat to Israel, and extended his control over their territories, including Gaza and its surrounding towns, which had once been strongholds of Philistine power. 9. In the fourth year of Hezekiah's reign, which also coincided with the seventh year of Hoshea's reign in Israel, Shalmaneser (the king of Assyria) attacked Samaria (the capital of Israel) and laid siege to it, marking the beginning of Israel's downfall under Assyrian dominance. 10. After three long years of siege, in the sixth year of Hezekiah (the ninth year of Hoshea), the Assyrians finally took Samaria. This was a devastating blow for Israel, marking the end of the northern kingdom. 11. The king of Assyria deported the people

of Israel to various regions of his empire, sending them to places like Halah, near the Habor River, and to the cities of the Medes (northeast of Israel), in an effort to break the unity of the Israelites and prevent any future resistance. **12.** This tragic event occurred because the Israelites had ignored the Lord's voice, turned away from His commandments, and violated the covenant He made with them. They had abandoned the guidance given through Moses, refusing to obey or even listen to God's Word. **13.** In the fourteenth year of Hezekiah's reign, Sennacherib, the new king of Assyria, launched a military campaign against Judah and attacked all the fortified cities of Judah, capturing them one by one. **14.** Faced with the threat of complete destruction, Hezekiah sent a message to Sennacherib at Lachish (a strong city in Judah, near the Philistine border), admitting, "I have made a mistake and will do what you ask. Please, turn away from me, and I will pay whatever ransom you require." In response, the Assyrian king demanded a staggering sum of three hundred talents of silver (about 11 tons) and thirty talents of gold (about 1.1 tons). **15.** Hezekiah complied by giving Sennacherib all the silver that was stored in the temple of the Lord and in the royal palace treasury, hoping to buy peace. **16.** In addition, Hezekiah took the gold from the temple doors and the gold-covered pillars of the temple, which he had overlaid himself, and sent it to the king of Assyria, hoping this would satisfy his demands. **17.** After receiving the tribute, Sennacherib sent his high-ranking military officers—Tartan (a commander), Rabsaris (another officer), and Rabshakeh (the chief spokesperson)—from Lachish to Jerusalem with a large army to further intimidate the people. They stopped at the aqueduct (a water channel) near the upper pool in Jerusalem, a strategically important location, on the road to the Fuller's Field (where wool was cleaned). **18.** They called for King Hezekiah, and in response, Hezekiah sent his representatives, Eliakim (the royal household manager, son of Hilkiah), Shebna (the scribe), and Joah (the royal recorder, son of Asaph). **19.** The Rabshakeh, speaking on behalf of the king of Assyria, asked the officials, "Tell Hezekiah, 'What is this confidence you have? **20.** You claim you have plans and strength for battle, but they are nothing but empty words. Who do you trust that you would rebel against me? **21.** You are relying on Egypt, a broken reed, which, if you lean on it, will pierce your hand and cause you pain. Pharaoh, the king of Egypt, is just like this to everyone who trusts in him for help. **22.** But if you say to me, 'We trust in the Lord our God,' remember, it is Hezekiah who removed the high places and altars where the people worshiped. He told them to worship only in Jerusalem, at the temple. Is this the God you are trusting in?' **23.** The Rabshakeh then mocked Hezekiah's position further, saying, "I urge you to make peace with my master, the king of Assyria. If you come to terms with us, I will give you two thousand horses, if you can find enough men to ride them. **24.** How will you fight even the smallest of my master's officers if you are trusting in Egypt for military aid?" **25.** The Rabshakeh taunted, "Did I come up against this city without the Lord's guidance? The Lord told me to come here and destroy it." **26.** Eliakim, Shebna, and Joah requested that the Rabshakeh speak in Aramaic, which they understood, to avoid causing panic among the people listening on the walls. **27.** But the Rabshakeh refused, saying, "Has my master sent me to speak only to you? I am here to speak to the men on the wall, which will have to eat their own excrement and drink their own urine just like you." **28.** He then called out in a loud voice in Hebrew, speaking directly to the people of Jerusalem: "Listen to the word of the great king, the king of Assyria! **29.** This is what the king says: Do not let Hezekiah deceive you, for he will not be able to deliver you from my hand. **30.** Nor should you let Hezekiah make you trust in the Lord by saying, 'The Lord will deliver us.' This city will fall into my hands, just like all the others. **31.** Don't listen to Hezekiah. The king of Assyria says, 'Make peace with me, and come out to me. You can each enjoy the comfort of your own vine and fig tree, and drink from your own cistern (water supply). **32.** I will take you to a new land just like your own, filled with abundance—a land of grain, wine, olive oil, and honey, where you will live and not die. But do not listen to Hezekiah, for he is lying when he says, 'The Lord will save us.' **33.** Has any of the gods of the nations been able to rescue their land from the hand of the king of Assyria? **34.** Where are the gods of Hamath, Arpad, Sepharvaim, Hena, and Ivah? Did they save their people from my hand? **35.** Who among the gods of any land has been able to rescue their country from my power, that the Lord should rescue Jerusalem from my hand?" **36.** The people remained silent and did not answer the Rabshakeh, as King Hezekiah had commanded them: "Do not respond to him." **37.** Eliakim, Shebna, and Joah, in a state of distress, tore their clothes and went to Hezekiah to report all that had been said by the Rabshakeh, with the message of intimidation and mockery from the king of Assyria.

Chapter 19

1. When King Hezekiah of Judah received the message from Rabshakeh (the high-ranking Assyrian official sent by King Sennacherib), he tore his clothes in mourning, put on sackcloth (a symbol of grief), and went into the temple of the Lord (the sacred place of worship in Jerusalem). **2.** He sent Eliakim, who oversaw the royal household, Shebna the scribe, and the elders of the priests, all wearing sackcloth, to the prophet Isaiah. **3.** They told Isaiah, "Hezekiah says: 'This is a day of trouble and mockery; we are in distress. It's as if a birth is ready but there is no strength to deliver. **4.** Perhaps the Lord your God will hear the words of Rabshakeh, who has been sent by the king of Assyria to mock the living God. Pray for the survivors of our people.'" **5.** The servants of King Hezekiah went to the prophet Isaiah with this plea. **6.** Isaiah replied, "Tell your king: 'Do not be afraid of what you have heard, from the men of Assyria who have blasphemed Me. **7.** I will send a spirit upon him, and he will hear news that causes him to return to his own land, where he will be killed by the sword.'" **8.** Rabshakeh returned to his master, King Sennacherib, who was fighting against Libnah (a city in Judah) after leaving Lachish. **9.** Sennacherib then heard that Tirhakah, the king of Ethiopia, had come to fight against him, and sent messengers again to Hezekiah, saying, **10.** "Tell Hezekiah, 'Don't let your God deceive you by saying, "Jerusalem won't fall to the Assyrians." **11.** You've heard what we've done to other lands—how we've destroyed them completely. Do you think you will escape? **12.** Were the gods of Gozan, Haran, Rezeph, and Eden able to save those cities? **13.** Where are the kings of Hamath, Arpad, Sepharvaim, Hena, and Ivah (cities and regions conquered by Assyria)?'" **14.** Hezekiah received the letter from the Assyrian messengers, read it, and went up to the temple of the Lord. He spread the letter out before God. **15.** Then he prayed before the Lord, saying, "O Lord, God of Israel, You who are seated above the cherubim (divine beings), You alone are God over all the kingdoms of the earth. You made the heavens and the earth. **16.** Hear my prayer, O Lord; listen to me. Look at the words Sennacherib has sent to insult You. **17.** It is true, Lord, the Assyrians have laid waste to many nations and their lands, **18.** and they have burned their gods because they were not gods at all, but the work of human hands—wood and stone. Therefore, they were destroyed. **19.** But now, O Lord our God, save us from his hand, so that all the kingdoms of the earth may know that You are the only true God." **20.** Isaiah sent word to Hezekiah, saying, "This is the message from the Lord: 'Because you have prayed to Me concerning Sennacherib, I have heard your prayer. **21.** This is what the Lord says: 'The virgin daughter of Zion (Jerusalem) mocks you; the daughter of Jerusalem shakes her head at you. **22.** Whom have you mocked and blasphemed? Against whom have you raised your voice and lifted your eyes in pride? Against the Holy One of Israel. **23.** By your messengers, you have insulted the Lord, saying, "With my chariots, I have ascended the mountains, and I have cut down its tall cedars and choice cypress trees. I have reached its highest points and its richest forests. **24.** I have dug wells and drunk foreign waters, and with the soles of my feet, I have dried up the streams of Egypt's defenses." **25.** Did you not know? Long ago, I (God) planned all of this, and I have brought it about that you would turn cities into heaps of ruins. **26.** Their people were weak and scattered, like grass on a rooftop, or crops that withered before they could grow. **27.** But I know where you live, when you come and go, and your rage against Me. **28.** Because your rage and tumult have reached My ears, I will put a hook in your nose and a bridle in your lips, and I will make you return the same way you came.'" **29.** "This will be the sign to you: You will eat what grows by itself this year, and in the second year, what springs up from that. But in the third year, you will sow and reap, plant vineyards, and eat their fruit. **30.** The survivors from the house of Judah will take root downward and bear fruit upward. **31.** A remnant will go out from Jerusalem, and those who escape from Mount Zion. The zeal of the Lord will accomplish this.'" **32.** Therefore, this is what the Lord says concerning the king of Assyria: "He will not enter this city, nor will he shoot an arrow here, nor come before it with a shield, nor build a siege mound against it. **33.** By the way that he came, he will return, and he will not enter this city, declares the Lord. **34.** I will defend this city and protect it, for My own sake and for the sake of My servant David.'" **35.** That night, the angel of the Lord went out and struck down 185,000 Assyrians in their camp. When the people woke up in the morning, they found all the dead bodies. **36.** So Sennacherib, king of Assyria, left and returned to Nineveh (the capital city of Assyria), where he stayed. **37.** While worshiping in the temple of Nisroch (an Assyrian god), Sennacherib's sons, Adrammelech and Sharezer, struck him down with the sword, and they escaped to the land of Ararat (an ancient region, now part of Turkey). Esarhaddon, his son, succeeded him as king.

Chapter 20

1. In those days, King Hezekiah (the righteous king of Judah) became severely ill, and it seemed he would die. The prophet Isaiah (the prophet chosen by God to deliver His messages) son of Amoz, was sent to Hezekiah with this message from the Lord: "Put your house in order, for you are about to die, and you will not recover from this illness." **2.** In response, Hezekiah turned his face to the wall (a private and personal act of prayer, as he wanted to speak to God alone) and earnestly prayed to the Lord, saying, **3.** "O Lord, remember how I have walked before You with sincerity and truth, and with a loyal heart, and have done what is pleasing in Your sight." And Hezekiah wept bitterly, pouring out his heart before God in deep sorrow. **4.** While Isaiah was still in the middle of the palace courtyard, the word of the Lord suddenly came to him, saying, **5.** "Go back to Hezekiah, the leader of My people, and tell him, 'This is what the Lord, the God of your father David, says: I have heard your prayer and seen your tears. I will heal you. In three days, you will go up to the house of the Lord to worship. **6.** I will add fifteen more years to your life. I will deliver you and this city from the hand of the king of Assyria (the powerful empire of Assyria that was threatening Judah), and I will protect this city for the sake of My name and for the sake of My servant David.'" **7.** Then Isaiah instructed them to take a lump of figs (which had medicinal properties in ancient times). They applied it to the boil on Hezekiah's skin, and miraculously, Hezekiah recovered from his illness. **8.** Hezekiah then asked Isaiah, "What will be the sign that the Lord will heal me and that I will go to the house of the Lord in three days, as He has promised?" **9.** Isaiah responded, "This will be the sign from the Lord: Shall the shadow on the sundial move forward ten steps, or move back ten steps?" **10.** Hezekiah answered, "It is easy for the shadow to go forward ten steps. But let the shadow go backward ten steps instead." **11.** So Isaiah the prophet cried out to the Lord, and the Lord, in His power and mercy, caused the shadow on the sundial of Ahaz (a timekeeping device built by King Ahaz) to move backward ten steps, proving that God had granted Hezekiah's request and would indeed heal him. **12.** At that time, Berodach-Baladan, the son of Baladan, the king of Babylon (an empire located far to the east), heard of Hezekiah's illness and sent letters and a gift to him as a token of goodwill, hoping to show compassion toward the sick king. **13.** Hezekiah graciously received the Babylonian ambassadors and showed them everything in his palace—his wealth, the silver, gold, spices, precious oils, and all his military armory. There was nothing in his storehouses or in all his kingdom that Hezekiah did not show them, hoping to impress the foreign envoys. **14.** Later, Isaiah the prophet visited King Hezekiah and asked him, "What did those men say to you, and where did they come from?" Hezekiah answered, "They came from a distant land, from Babylon." **15.** Isaiah asked, "What did they see in your house?" Hezekiah replied, "They saw everything in my palace. There is nothing among my treasures that I have not shown them." **16.** Then Isaiah said to Hezekiah, "Listen to the word of the Lord: **17.** The days are coming when everything in your palace, along with all your ancestors' treasures, will be carried off to Babylon. Nothing will be left, says the Lord. **18.** Some of your own descendants, the children who are born to you, will be taken to Babylon, and they will become eunuchs in the palace of the king of Babylon. The Babylonians will carry them off as captives." **19.** Hezekiah replied to Isaiah, "The word of the Lord that you have spoken is good." He thought, "At least there will be peace and security during my lifetime, even if these events will happen in the future." **20.** The rest of Hezekiah's deeds, his great strength, and the remarkable work he did in constructing a pool and tunnel to bring water into the city of Jerusalem, are recorded in the book of the chronicles of the kings of Judah, which gives a detailed account of his reign. 21. Hezekiah rested with his ancestors, and his son Manasseh (who would eventually become king of Judah and reign after Hezekiah's death) succeeded him as king.

Chapter 21

1. Manasseh (a king of Judah, who was the son of Hephzibah, a royal woman) ascended to the throne at the young age of twelve years old and ruled in Jerusalem for a total of fifty-five years, a notably long reign during a time of great religious and political turmoil. **2.** He carried out what was considered wicked in the sight of the LORD, imitating and even surpassing the evil practices of the surrounding nations that the Lord had driven out of the land before the Israelites had entered and settled there. Manasseh's reign marked a return to idolatry and pagan practices. **3.** He revived the high places (sacred sites where pagan worship occurred) that his father Hezekiah had previously destroyed, which were places of immoral and idol worship. He then erected altars for Baal (a Canaanite fertility god), and made a wooden image (Asherah—a fertility goddess) in the same manner that Ahab, the wicked king of Israel, had done. He also gave his allegiance to the entire host of heaven (the sun, moon, stars, and all celestial bodies) by worshiping and serving them. **4.** He not only built these altars for false gods but also placed them inside the temple of the Lord (the very house of worship dedicated to the One True God). This was in direct violation of the Lord's explicit command, which was to sanctify the temple as a place where His name would dwell forever in Jerusalem, the holy city. **5.** In further acts of rebellion, Manasseh built additional altars dedicated to the hosts of heaven within the two courts (outer areas) of the temple complex, expanding the sacred spaces for pagan worship. These altars were meant to honor the stars and other celestial beings, profaning the temple of God. **6.** He committed further abominations by making his own son pass through the fire (a horrific ritual associated with child sacrifice), engaging in soothsaying (divination, seeking answers through supernatural means), practicing witchcraft (the use of spells or magic for personal gain), consulting with mediums (individuals who communicate with the spirits of the dead), and relying on other forms of occult practices. These actions stirred the Lord's anger to its peak. **7.** Manasseh went as far as placing a carved idol of Asherah (a pagan goddess symbolizing fertility) that he had made within the very temple of the Lord, in a sacred space that was meant solely for God's glory. The Lord had once promised to David (the great king of Israel) and Solomon (his son and successor), "In this temple and in Jerusalem, which I have chosen above all other cities in Israel, I will place My name forever." **8.** God had also promised that He would ensure the Israelites would never be driven from the land He had given them, provided they followed His laws and commands as He instructed Moses. But Manasseh's actions violated this sacred covenant and led the people into great sin. **9.** Despite the Lord's clear guidance, the people ignored His commandments, and instead, under Manasseh's influence, they became even more corrupt. The sinful practices that Manasseh led them into were far worse than those of the nations whom the Lord had previously driven out of the land for their wickedness. **10.** The Lord, seeing this great wickedness, spoke through His servants, the prophets (messengers who convey God's word), calling the people to repentance and warning of impending judgment. **11.** "Because Manasseh, the king of Judah, has committed these horrible and detestable acts, acting in ways that were even more corrupt than the Amorites (a group of ancient Canaanite people who had been destroyed for their wickedness) who were in the land before him, and has led Judah into sin with his idols," **12.** the Lord declared: "Because of these actions, I am bringing such great and unimaginable disaster upon Jerusalem and Judah that anyone who hears about it will be shocked, and their ears will tingle with horror and disbelief." **13.** "I will bring down judgment on Jerusalem using the same measuring line (symbolizing precise and complete judgment) that was used against Samaria (the northern kingdom of Israel) and the plumb line (a tool used to measure uprightness) used in the house of Ahab (a notoriously wicked king of Israel); I will wipe Jerusalem clean, just as one wipes a dish, turning it upside down." **14.** "I will forsake the remaining faithful people of My inheritance (the remnant of Israel) and hand them over to the hands of their enemies. They will be plundered and looted by all their adversaries, suffering the consequences of their sin." **15.** "This is because they have done what is evil in My sight, and since the day their ancestors came out of Egypt, they have provoked Me to anger with their disobedience and idolatry, and I will not tolerate it any longer."

16. Manasseh also shed an immense amount of innocent blood throughout Jerusalem, filling the city from one end to the other, killing countless innocent people, all while continuing to lead the people of Judah into further sin by his abominable acts that dishonored the Lord. **17.** The full account of Manasseh's deeds, including the complete record of his wickedness (sinful behavior), can be found in the book of the chronicles (official records) of the kings of Judah, which preserved the history of the nation. **18.** Manasseh died and was buried in his own garden, the Garden of Uzza (a location in Jerusalem), which was near the royal palace. His son, Amon, succeeded him as king. **19.** Amon (a king of Judah) was only twenty-two years old when he became king, and his reign lasted only two years in Jerusalem. His mother, Meshullemeth, was the daughter of Haruz from the town of Jotbah (a small town in Judah). **20.** Like his father Manasseh, Amon did what was evil in the sight of the Lord, continuing the same sinful practices that had been established during Manasseh's reign. **21.** He walked in the same ways his father had walked, serving the same idols (false gods) that his father had worshipped and leading the people into the same idolatrous practices. **22.** Amon forsook (abandoned) the Lord, the God of his ancestors, and did not walk in the righteous ways of the Lord, showing no repentance or turning from the evil practices that had been established. **23.** His royal servants (officials in the palace) conspired against him and assassinated (murdered) him in his own palace, setting into motion the end of his short reign. **24.** The people of the land (the common people) rose up and executed the conspirators who had killed King Amon, and they placed Amon's son, Josiah (a future king who would bring reform and righteousness to Judah), on the throne in his stead. **25.** The full account of Amon's actions, including the sins he committed and the conspiracy that led to his death, is written in the book of the chronicles (official records) of the kings of Judah, which documented the reigns of all the kings. **26.** Amon was buried in his tomb in the Garden of Uzza, and his son Josiah became king in his place, bringing a new era of leadership and reform to Judah.

Chapter 22

1. Josiah was eight years old when he became king of Judah, and he reigned for thirty-one years in Jerusalem. His mother's name was Jedidah, daughter of Adaiah, from Bozkath (a town in Judah). **2.** Josiah did what was right in the sight of the LORD, following the example of his ancestor David (the former king of Israel), and never strayed from God's commandments (orders). **3.** In the eighteenth year of his reign, King Josiah sent Shaphan, the scribe (official recorder), to Hilkiah the high priest to count the money brought into the temple by the gatekeepers (those who guarded the entrance). **4.** He instructed that the money be given to the workers (people doing repairs) repairing the temple—carpenters (woodworkers), builders (construction workers), and masons (stoneworkers)—to buy timber (wood) and stone. **5.** There was no need to account for the money, as the workers were trustworthy (reliable and honest). **6.** Hilkiah the high priest then told Shaphan, "I have found the Book of the Law (the sacred scroll containing God's commands) in the temple." He gave it to Shaphan, who read it. **7.** Shaphan went to the king and reported, "We have gathered the money and given it to the workers." He also said, "Hilkiah has given me a book." Then he read it to the king. **8.** When Josiah heard the words of the Book of the Law, he tore his clothes (a sign of deep mourning and repentance). **9.** The king then ordered Hilkiah, Ahikam, Achbor, Shaphan, and Asaiah to seek God's guidance (ask for God's direction) about the words of the book, for he feared God's anger (wrath) because the people had not obeyed it. **10.** They went to Huldah the prophetess (a woman who speaks for God), wife of Shallum, keeper (guardian) of the wardrobe (clothing), living in the Second Quarter (a district of Jerusalem), and spoke to her. **11.** Huldah replied, "This is what the LORD God of Israel says: 'Tell the king of Judah who sent you: **12.** "I will bring disaster (calamity) upon this place and its people, as written in the book. They have forsaken (abandoned) Me and worshiped other gods, and My anger will not be quenched (satisfied)."'"

13. "But concerning the king of Judah, tell him: 'Because you humbled yourself (showed humility) before Me when you heard My judgment on this place and wept (cried), I have heard you. **14.** 'You will die in peace and not see the disaster I will bring upon this place.'" So they returned with the message to the king. **15.** The king then sent for all the elders (leaders) of Judah and Jerusalem. **16.** He gathered the people—priests (religious leaders), prophets (those who speak for God), and all the people of Judah—and read to them the Book of the Covenant (the agreement between God and His people) found in the temple. **17.** Josiah made a covenant (formal promise) before the Lord to follow Him with all his heart and soul, to obey His commandments (laws), and to uphold (keep) the words of the book. The people pledged (promised) to keep the covenant as well. **18.** The king then removed all idols (false gods) and false worship from Judah and Jerusalem. **19.** He destroyed the high places (sites of idol worship), altars (structures used for sacrifices), and idols (statues or images of false gods), fulfilling the prophecy of the book, and led Judah in returning to the true worship of God. **20.** Josiah's reforms (changes or improvements) brought Judah back to God, ensuring that the people renewed their commitment to His covenant.

Chapter 23

1. The king sent messengers throughout the land to gather all the elders (leaders) of Judah and Jerusalem to come together in his presence for an important meeting. **2.** The king went up to the house of the Lord (the temple in Jerusalem) with all the men of Judah, the people of Jerusalem, the priests, prophets, and every member of the community, both great and small. He read aloud to them all the words of the Book of the Covenant (the sacred laws and commandments of God) that had been discovered in the house of the Lord. **3.** The king stood firmly by a pillar (a symbolic post of authority) in front of all the people and made a solemn covenant (agreement) before the Lord, vowing to follow His laws and commandments with his whole heart and soul. He committed to doing everything that was written in the book, and all the people of Judah and Jerusalem also pledged to honor this covenant before the Lord. **4.** The king ordered Hilkiah, the high priest, along with the assistant priests and the doorkeepers (temple guards), to bring out of the temple all the articles that had been made for the worship of false gods, including Baal (a Canaanite god), Asherah (a fertility goddess), and the host of heaven (the sun, moon, and stars), and to destroy them. These idols and their associated objects were burned in the fields of Kidron (a valley near Jerusalem), and their ashes were carried to Bethel (a city in Israel). **5.** He removed the idolatrous priests (those who served the false gods) whom the previous kings of Judah had appointed, those who had burned incense to Baal, the sun, the moon, the constellations, and all the host of heaven, and who had led the people astray in their worship at high places (elevated altars) throughout Judah and Jerusalem. **6.** Josiah took the wooden image (an idol of Asherah) that had been placed in the house of the Lord, burned it in the Brook Kidron (a valley outside Jerusalem), and ground it into ashes, scattering the ashes over the graves of common people (ordinary citizens). **7.** He also tore down the ritual booths (temporary shelters) where perverted persons (those practicing immorality) engaged in idolatry. These were located in the house of the Lord, and it was there that the women wove the hangings used for the wooden image (idol of Asherah). **8.** Josiah brought all the priests from the towns of Judah and defiled (desecrated) the high places where they had burned incense to false gods, from Geba (a northern town in Judah) to Beersheba (a southern town in Judah), and even broke down the altars that were at the gates of Jerusalem, including those near the Gate of Joshua (the governor's gate). **9.** However, the priests who had served in these high places did not come to the altar of the Lord in Jerusalem but instead ate unleavened bread (bread made without yeast) with their fellow priests in their own towns, as they were no longer allowed to minister in the temple. **10.** Josiah also defiled the site of Topheth (a place in the Valley of Hinnom, infamous for the burning of children as sacrifices to Molech), ensuring that no one would ever again offer their children as sacrifices to Molech, thus putting an end to this horrific practice. **11.** He removed the horses that had been dedicated to the worship of the sun, which had been kept at the entrance to the house of the Lord near the chamber of Nathan-Melech (an official in the royal court), and he destroyed the chariots that had been used in sun worship by burning them with fire. **12.** He destroyed the altars (places of idol sacrifice) located on the roof of the upper chamber of King Ahaz (a former king of Judah), as well as the altars that King Manasseh (another former king) had constructed in the two courts of the Lord's house. Josiah broke them into pieces, pulverized them, and scattered their dust into the Brook Kidron, rendering them unholy. **13.** Josiah also defiled the high places to the east of Jerusalem, south of the Mount of Corruption (a hill notorious for idol worship), where King Solomon (the former king of Israel) had built altars for Ashtoreth, Chemosh (false gods of surrounding nations), and Milcom (an abomination worshiped by the Ammonites). He broke apart their sacred pillars and cut down their wooden images, filling their places with the bones of men (to desecrate them). **14.** Josiah broke the sacred pillars (monuments erected for idol worship), chopped down the wooden images (idols), and desecrated the altars by filling them with human bones, signifying the end of their use in worship. **15.** Josiah destroyed the altar at Bethel (a city in northern Israel), which had been established by King Jeroboam (the first king of the northern kingdom of Israel), who had led Israel into sin. Josiah burned the high place, ground it to powder, and burned the wooden image (idol) that had been set up there. **16.** As Josiah turned to leave, he noticed tombs on the mountain. He ordered the bones from those tombs to be removed and burned on the altar, thus defiling it and fulfilling the prophecy spoken by the man of God (a prophet) from Judah, who had forewarned of this day. **17.** Josiah asked, "What is this gravestone that I see?" The men of the city explained to him, "This is the tomb of the man of God who came from Judah and proclaimed these very actions against the altar at Bethel." **18.** Josiah replied, "Let him be; do not disturb his bones." And so, they left the bones of that prophet untouched, along with the bones of another prophet from Samaria, who had also spoken against the altar. **19.** Josiah removed all the shrines (places of idol worship) in the cities of Samaria (northern Israel), which the kings of Israel had built to provoke the Lord to anger. He destroyed all of these shrines just as he had done in Bethel. **20.** He executed all the priests who had served at these high places, burning their bones on the altars to desecrate them. After completing these actions, he returned to Jerusalem. **21.** The king issued a command to all the people, saying, "Celebrate the Passover (a feast to commemorate Israel's deliverance from Egypt) to the Lord your God, just as it is written in the Book of the Covenant." **22.** A Passover like this had not been held since the days of the judges (leaders who preceded the kings) nor in the entire history of the kings of Israel and Judah. **23.** But in the eighteenth year of King Josiah's reign, this Passover was celebrated before the Lord in Jerusalem. **24.** Josiah also removed from the land all who consulted mediums (spirit communicators), spiritists (those practicing witchcraft), household gods, and all the abominations (idols and wicked practices) that were seen in Judah and Jerusalem. This was done to fulfill the words of the law found by Hilkiah the priest. **25.** Before Josiah, no king had turned to the Lord with all his heart, soul, and might, as required by the law of Moses. After him, no king would follow the Lord in such a wholehearted way. **26.** Nevertheless, the Lord's anger against Judah did not turn away because of the wickedness that had been caused by King Manasseh (former king of Judah), whose evil had provoked God's wrath. **27.** The Lord said, "I will remove Judah from My sight just as I have removed Israel. I will cast off Jerusalem, the city I have chosen, and the temple where My name resides." **28.** The rest of the actions of Josiah, along with the details of his reign, are recorded in the book of the chronicles of the kings of Judah. **29.** During Josiah's reign, Pharaoh Necho (king of Egypt) went to assist the king of Assyria, traveling to the Euphrates River. King Josiah, in an attempt to stop him, confronted Pharaoh Necho at Megiddo (a city in northern Israel), where Pharaoh Necho killed him. **30.** Josiah's servants brought his body back from Megiddo, placed it in a chariot, and transported it to Jerusalem, where they buried him in his own tomb. The people of the land anointed Josiah's son, Jehoahaz, as king in his place. **31.** Jehoahaz was twenty-three years old when he became king and ruled for three months. His mother was Hamutal, the daughter of Jeremiah from Libnah (a town in Judah). **32.** Jehoahaz did evil in the sight of the Lord, following the wicked practices of his ancestors. **33.** Pharaoh Necho imprisoned Jehoahaz at Riblah (a place in Syria), located in the land of Hamath, so that he would not reign in Jerusalem. Necho also imposed a heavy tribute on Judah, demanding one hundred talents of silver and one talent of gold. **34.** Pharaoh Necho made Eliakim (the son of Josiah) king in place of Jehoahaz, changing his name to Jehoiakim. Pharaoh took Jehoahaz to Egypt, where he died. **35.** Jehoiakim paid the required silver and gold to Pharaoh, but he raised taxes in Judah to gather the funds to meet the demands of Egypt. **36.** Jehoiakim was twenty-five years old when he became king, and he reigned for eleven years in Jerusalem. His mother was Zebudah, the daughter of Pedaiah from Rumah (a town in Judah). **37.** Jehoiakim did evil in the sight of the Lord, following the sinful ways of his ancestors and continuing in their idolatry and rebellion.

11 – Chronicles 1

Chapter 1

1. Adam, Seth, Enosh, **2.** Cainan, Mahalalel, Jared, **3.** Enoch, Methuselah, Lamech, **4.** Noah, Shem, Ham, and Japheth. **5.** The sons of Japheth were Gomer, Magog, Madai, Javan, Tubal, Meshech, and Tiras. **6.** The sons of Gomer were Ashkenaz, Diphath, and Togarmah. **7.** The sons of Javan were Elishah, Tarshishah, Kittim, and Rodanim. **8.** The sons of Ham were Cush, Mizraim, Put, and Canaan. **9.** The sons of Cush were Seba, Havilah, Sabta, Raama, and Sabtecha. The sons of Raama were Sheba and Dedan. **10.** Cush fathered (begot) Nimrod; he became a powerful (mighty) man on the earth. **11.** Mizraim fathered Ludim, Anamim, Lehabim, Naphtuhim, **12.** Pathrusim, Casluhim (from whom the Philistines and the Caphtorim came). **13.** Canaan fathered Sidon, his firstborn, and Heth; **14.** The Jebusite, the Amorite, and the Girgashite; **15.** the Hivite, the Arkite, and the Sinite; **16.** the Arvadite, the Zemarite, and the Hamathite. **17.** The sons of Shem were Elam, Asshur, Arphaxad, Lud, Aram, Uz, Hul, Gether, and Meshech. **18.** Arphaxad fathered Shelah, and Shelah fathered Eber. **19.** Eber had two sons: the name of one was Peleg, because in his days the earth was divided; and his brother's name was Joktan. **20.** Joktan fathered Almodad, Sheleph, Hazarmaveth, Jerah, **21.** Hadoram, Uzal, Diklah, **22.** Ebal, Abimael, Sheba, **23.** Ophir, Havilah, and Jobab. All these were the sons of Joktan. **24.** Shem, Arphaxad, Shelah, **25.** Eber, Peleg, Reu, **26.** Serug, Nahor, Terah, **27.** and Abram, who is Abraham. **28.** The sons of Abraham were Isaac and Ishmael. **29.** These are their family lines (genealogies): The firstborn of Ishmael was Nebajoth; then Kedar, Adbeel, Mibsam, **30.** Mishma, Dumah, Massa, Hadad, Tema, **31.** Jetur, Naphish, and Kedemah. These were the sons of Ishmael. **32.** Now the sons born to Keturah, Abraham's concubine (secondary wife), were Zimran, Jokshan, Medan, Midian, Ishbak, and Shuah. The sons of Jokshan were Sheba and Dedan. **33.** The sons of Midian were Ephah, Epher, Hanoch, Abida, and Eldaah. All these were the children of Keturah. **34.** And Abraham fathered Isaac. The sons of Isaac were Esau and Israel. **35.** The sons of Esau were Eliphaz, Reuel, Jeush, Jaalam, and Korah. **36.** And the sons of Eliphaz were Teman, Omar, Zephi, Gatam, and Kenaz; and by Timna, Amalek. **37.** The sons of Reuel were Nahath, Zerah, Shammah, and Mizzah. **38.** The sons of Seir were Lotan, Shobal, Zibeon, Anah, Dishon, Ezer, and Dishan. **39.** And the sons of Lotan were Hori and Homam; Lotan's sister was Timna. **40.** The sons of Shobal were Alian, Manahath, Ebal, Shephi, and Onam. The sons of Zibeon were Ajah and Anah. **41.** The son of Anah was Dishon. The sons of Dishon were Hamran, Eshban, Ithran, and Cheran. **42.** The sons of Ezer were Bilhan, Zaavan, and Jaakan. The sons of Dishan were Uz and Aran. **43.** Now these were the kings who ruled in the land of Edom before a king ruled over the children of Israel: Bela the son of Beor, and the name of his city was Dinhabah. **44.** And when Bela died, Jobab the son of Zerah of Bozrah became king in his place. **45.** When Jobab died, Husham of the land of the Temanites became king in his place. **46.** And when Husham died, Hadad the son of Bedad, who attacked Midian in the field of Moab, became king in his place. The name of his city was Avith. **47.** When Hadad died, Samlah of Masrekah became king in his place. **48.** And when Samlah died, Saul of Rehoboth-by-the-River became king in his place. **49.** When Saul died, Baal-Hanan the son of Achbor became king in his place. **50.** And when Baal-Hanan died, Hadad became king in his place; and the name of his city was Pai. His wife's name was Mehetabel, the daughter of Matred, the daughter of Mezahab. **51.** Hadad also died. And the leaders of Edom were Chief Timnah, Chief Aliah, Chief Jetheth, **52.** Chief Aholibamah, Chief Elah, Chief Pinon, **53.** Chief Kenaz, Chief Teman, Chief Mibzar, **54.** Chief Magdiel, and Chief Iram. These were the chiefs of Edom.

Chapter 2

1. These are the children (descendants) of Israel: Reuben, Simeon, Levi, Judah, Issachar, Zebulun, **2.** Dan, Joseph, Benjamin, Naphtali, Gad, and Asher. **3.** Judah had three sons: Er, Onan, and Shelah, born to him by the daughter of Shua, a Canaanite (a native of ancient Canaan) woman. Er, Judah's firstborn was evil in the eyes of the Lord, so He put him to death. **4.** Tamar, Judah's daughter-in-law gave birth to Perez and Zerah. Judah had five sons in total. **5.** Perez's sons were Hezron and Hamul. **6.** Zerah's sons were Zimri, Ethan, Heman, Calcol, and Dara—five in total. **7.** Carmi's son was Achar, the one who caused trouble (troubled or disturbed) in Israel because he sinned by taking something cursed (set apart for destruction). **8.** Ethan's son was Azariah. **9.** The sons of Hezron were Jerahmeel, Ram, and Chelubai. **10.** Ram fathered Amminadab, and Amminadab fathered Nahshon, the leader (chief) of the tribe of Judah. **11.** Nahshon fathered Salma, and Salma fathered Boaz. **12** Boaz fathered Obed, and Obed fathered Jesse. **13.** Jesse's sons were Eliab, the firstborn, Abinadab, the second, Shimea, the third, **14** Nethanel, the fourth, Raddai, the fifth, **15.** Ozem, the sixth, and David, the seventh. **16.** Jesse also had two daughters: Zeruiah and Abigail. Zeruiah's sons were Abishai, Joab, and Asahel—three in total. **17.** Abigail had a son named Amasa; his father was Jether, an Ishmaelite (descendant of Ishmael, Abraham's son with Hagar). **18.** Caleb, the son of Hezron, had children with his wife Azubah and also with Jerioth. Their sons were Jesher, Shobab, and Ardon. **19.** After Azubah died, Caleb married Ephrath, who bore him Hur. **20.** Hur fathered Uri, and Uri fathered Bezalel. **21.** Later, Hezron married the daughter of Machir, the father of Gilead, when he was 60 years old. She bore him Segub. **22.** Segub fathered Jair, who controlled 23 cities in Gilead. **23.** (The towns of Jair, including Kenath and its surrounding villages, were taken by Geshur (an ancient kingdom) and Syria, who captured 60 cities in total.) These lands belonged to the descendants of Machir, the father of Gilead. **24.** After Hezron's death in Caleb Ephrathah, Hezron's wife Abijah bore him Ashhur, the father of Tekoa. **25.** Jerahmeel, Hezron's firstborn, had the following sons: Ram (the firstborn), Bunah, Oren, Ozem, and Ahijah. **26.** Jerahmeel married another woman named Atarah, and she had a son named Onam. **27.** Ram, Jerahmeel's firstborn, had three sons: Maaz, Jamin, and Eker. **28.** Onam's sons were Shammai and Jada. Shammai's sons were Nadab and Abishur. **29.** Abishur's wife was named Abihail, and she bore him two sons, Ahban and Molid. **30.** Nadab's sons were Seled and Appaim; Seled died without children. **31.** Appaim's son was Ishi, Ishi's son was Sheshan, and Sheshan's son was Ahlai. **32.** Jada, Shammai's brother, had two sons: Jether and Jonathan. Jether died without children. **33.** Jonathan's sons were Peleth and Zaza. These were the descendants of Jerahmeel. **34.** Sheshan had no sons, only daughters. He had an Egyptian (from Egypt) servant named Jarha, **35.** whom he gave his daughter as a wife. She bore him Attai. **36.** Attai fathered Nathan, Nathan fathered Zabad; **37** Zabad fathered Ephlal, and Ephlal fathered Obed; **38.** Obed fathered Jehu, and Jehu fathered Azariah; **39.** Azariah fathered Helez, and Helez fathered Eleasah; **40.** Eleasah fathered Sismai, and Sismai fathered Shallum; **41.** Shallum fathered Jekamiah, and Jekamiah fathered Elishama. **42.** Caleb, the brother of Jerahmeel, had the following children: Mesha (his firstborn), who was the father of Ziph, and the sons of Mareshah, the father of Hebron. **43.** The sons of Hebron were Korah, Tappuah, Rekem, and Shema. **44.** Shema fathered Raham, the father of Jorkoam, and Rekem fathered Shammai. **45.** Shammai's son was Maon, who was the father of Beth Zur. **46.** Caleb's concubine (secondary wife or partner) Ephah bore him three sons: Haran, Moza, and Gazez; Haran fathered Gazez. **47.** Caleb's concubine Jahdai bore him six sons: Regem, Jotham, Geshan, Pelet, Ephah, and Shaaph. **48.** Caleb's other concubine Maachah bore him two sons: Sheber and Tirhanah. **49.** Maachah also bore Shaaph, the father of Madmannah, Sheva, the father of Machbenah, and the father of Gibea. Caleb's daughter was Achsah. **50.** Caleb's descendants include his sons Hur (the firstborn of Ephrathah): Shobal (the father of Kirjath Jearim), **51.** Salma (the father of Bethlehem), and Hareph (the father of Beth Gader). **52.** Shobal, the father of Kirjath Jearim, had descendants: Haroeh and half of the families of Manuhoth. **53.** The families of Kirjath Jearim were the Ithrites, the Puthites, the Shumathites, and the Mishraites. From these groups came the Zorathites and Eshtaolites. **54.** The sons of Salma were Bethlehem, the Netophathites, Atroth Beth Joab, half of the Manahethites, and the Zorites. **55.** The families of the scribes (writers or record keepers) who lived at Jabez were the Tirathites, Shimeathites, and Suchathites. These were the Kenites (descendants of Cain) who came from Hammath, the father of the house of Rechab.

Chapter 3

1. These were the sons of David who were born to him in Hebron (an ancient city in southern Israel): His firstborn was Amnon, by Ahinoam from Jezreel (a city in ancient Israel); the second was Daniel, by Abigail, who was from Carmel (a town or region in ancient Israel); **2.** the third was Absalom, the son of Maacah, the daughter of Talmai, the king of Geshur (an ancient kingdom northeast of Israel); the fourth was Adonijah, the son of Haggith; **3.** the fifth was Shephatiah, by Abital; the sixth was Ithream, by his wife Eglah. **4.** These six were born to him in Hebron. David reigned (ruled) there for seven years and six months, and then he ruled in Jerusalem (the capital city of Israel) for thirty-three years. **5.** These were born to him in Jerusalem: Shimea, Shobab, Nathan, and Solomon—four by Bathshua, the daughter of Ammiel. **6.** There were also Ibhar, Elishama, Eliphelet, **7.** Nogah, Nepheg, Japhia, **8.** Elishama, Eliada, and Eliphelet—nine in total. **9.** These were all the sons of David, in addition to the sons of his concubines (secondary wives of lower status), and their sister Tamar. **10.** Solomon's son was Rehoboam; Rehoboam's son was Abijah, his son was Asa, his son was Jehoshaphat, **11.** his son was Joram, his son was Ahaziah, his son was Joash, **12.** his son was Amaziah, his son was Azariah, his son was Jotham, **13.** his son was Ahaz, his son was Hezekiah, his son was Manasseh, **14.** his son was Amon, and his son was Josiah. **15.** The sons of Josiah were Johanan (the firstborn), Jehoiakim (the second), Zedekiah (the third), and Shallum (the fourth). **16.** The sons of Jehoiakim were Jeconiah and Zedekiah. **17.** The sons of Jeconiah were Assir, and Shealtiel, **18.** and Malchiram, Pedaiah, Shenazzar, Jecamiah, Hoshama, and Nedabiah. **19.** The sons of Pedaiah were Zerubbabel (a leader during the return from exile) and Shimei. The sons of Zerubbabel were Meshullam, Hananiah, and Shelomith, their sister, **20.** and Hashubah, Ohel, Berechiah, Hasadiah, and Jushab-Hesed—five in total. **21.** The sons of Hananiah were Pelatiah and Jeshaiah, the sons of Rephaiah, the sons of Arnan, the sons of Obadiah, and the sons of Shechaniah (a family name in biblical times). **22.** The son of Shechaniah was Shemaiah. The sons of Shemaiah were Hattush, Igal, Bariah, Neariah, and Shaphat—six in total. **23.** The sons of Neariah were Elioenai, Hezekiah, and Azrikam—three in total. **24.** The sons of Elioenai were Hodaviah, Eliashib, Pelaiah, Akkub, Johanan, Delaiah, and Anani—seven in total.

Chapter 4

1. The children of Judah were Perez, Hezron, Carmi, Hur, and Shobal. **2.** Reaiah, the son of Shobal, fathered Jahath, and Jahath fathered Ahumai and Lahad. These were the families of the Zorathites. **3.** These were the sons of the father of Etam: Jezreel, Ishma, and Idbash; and their sister's name was Hazelelponi. **4.** Penuel was the father of Gedor, and Ezer was the father (parent) of Hushah. These were the children of Hur, the firstborn of Ephrathah, the father of Bethlehem. **5.** Ashhur, the father (parent) of Tekoa, had two wives: Helah and Naarah. **6.** Naarah bore him Ahuzzam, Hepher, Temeni, and Haahashtari. These were the sons of Naarah. **7** The sons of Helah were Zereth, Zohar, and Ethnan. **8.** Koz fathered (gave birth to) Anub, Zobebah, and the families of Aharhel, the son of Harum. **9** Jabez was more honorable (respected) than his brothers, and his mother named him Jabez, saying, "Because I bore him in pain." **10.** Jabez called on the God (deity) of Israel, saying, "Oh, that you would bless (give favor to) me and enlarge (increase) my territory (area), that your hand (power) would be with me, and that You would keep (protect) me from evil (wrongdoing) so that I may not cause pain!" So God granted (gave) him what he asked for. **11.** Chelub, the brother of Shuhah, fathered Mehir, who was the father of Eshton. **12** Eshton fathered Beth-Rapha, Paseah, and Tehinnah, the father (ancestor) of Ir-Nahash. These were the men of Rechah. **13.** The sons of Kenaz were Othniel and Seraiah. The sons of Othniel were Hathath, **14.** and Meonothai, who fathered Ophrah. Seraiah fathered Joab, the father of Ge Harashim, for they were craftsmen (skilled workers who make items by hand). **15.** The sons of Caleb, the son (descendant) of Jephunneh, were Iru, Elah, and Naam. The son (child) of Elah was Kenaz. **16.** The sons (children) of Jehallelel were Ziph, Ziphah, Tiria, and

Asarel. **17.** The sons (children) of Ezrah were Jether, Mered, Epher, and Jalon. Mered's wife bore (gave birth to) Miriam, Shammai, and Ishbah, the father of Eshtemoa. **18.** (His wife (spouse) Jehudijah bore (gave birth to) Jered, the father of Gedor, Heber, the father of Sochoh, and Jekuthiel, the father of Zanoah.) These were the children (offspring) of Bithiah, the daughter of Pharaoh, whom Mered married. **19.** The sons of Hodiah's wife , the sister of Naham, were the fathers (ancestors) of Keilah the Garmite and Eshtemoa the Maachathite. **20.** The sons of Shimon were Amnon, Rinnah, Ben-Hanan, and Tilon. The sons of Ishi were Zoheth and Ben-Zoheth. **21.** The sons (children) of Shelah, the son of Judah, were Er, the father of Lecah, Laadah, the father (ancestor) of Mareshah, and the families (groups of related people) of the house of the linen workers (those who work with cloth) of the house of Ashbea; **22.** also Jokim, the men of Chozeba, and Joash; Saraph, who ruled (governed) in Moab, and Jashubi-Lehem. These records (written accounts) are ancient. **23.** These were the potters (people who make pottery) and those who lived at Netaim and Gederah; there they stayed (lived) with the king for work (duties). **24.** The sons of Simeon were Nemuel, Jamin, Jarib, Zerah, and Shaul. **25.** Shallum his son, Mibsam his son , and Mishma his son . **26.** The sons (children) of Mishma were Hamuel his son , Zacchur his son , and Shimei his son . **27.** Shimei had sixteen sons and six daughters; but his brothers had fewer children, and their families did not grow as large as those of Judah. **28.** They lived in Beersheba, Moladah, Hazar Shual, **29.** Bilhah, Ezem, Tolad, **30.** Bethuel, Hormah, Ziklag, **31.** Beth Marcaboth, Hazar Susim, Beth Biri, and Shaaraim. These were their cities (towns) until the reign (rule) of David. **32.** And their villages (smaller communities) were Etam, Ain, Rimmon, Tochen, and Ashan— five cities (towns)— **33.** and all the villages (smaller communities) around these cities (towns) as far as Baal. These were their places of residence (living places), and they kept their family records (genealogies). **34.** Meshobab, Jamlech, and Joshah, the son of Amaziah, **35.** Joel, and Jehu, the son of Joshibiah, the son of Seraiah, the son of Asiel; **36.** Elioenai, Jaakobah, Jeshohaiah, Asaiah, Adiel, Jesimiel, and Benaiah; **37.** Ziza, the son of Shiphi, the son of Allon, the son of Jedaiah, the son of Shimri, the son of Shemaiah— **38.** these were leaders of their families, and their father's house grew (expanded) greatly. **39.** They went to the entrance (opening) of Gedor, to the east side of the valley (low area of land), to find (search for) pasture (land for grazing) for their flocks (herds of animals). **40.** They found rich (fertile), good (healthy) pasture (land for grazing), and the land was broad, quiet (peaceful), and peaceful because some Hamites had once lived there. **41.** These people (individuals), listed (named) by name, came in the days (period) of King Hezekiah of Judah; they attacked (fought against) the tents (homes) of the Meunites, who were living there, and completely destroyed (wiped out) them, as it remains today. So they lived in their place because there was pasture (grazing land) for their flocks (herds). **42.** Some of them, five hundred men from the sons of Simeon, went to Mount Seir, with Pelatiah, Neariah, Rephaiah, and Uzziel, the sons of Ishi, as their captains. **43.** They defeated (overcame) the rest of the Amalekites, who had escaped (fled), and they have lived there to this day.

Chapter 5

1. The descendants of Reuben, the firstborn of Israel, were recorded. Though he was indeed the firstborn, because he dishonored his father's bed, his birthright was given to the descendants of Joseph, the son of Israel. As a result, his descendants were not listed according to the birthright. **2.** However, Judah became stronger than his brothers, and from him came a ruler, although the birthright originally belonged to Joseph. **3.** The sons of Reuben, Israel's firstborn were Hanoch, Pallu, Hezron, and Carmi. **4.** The descendants of Joel were his son Shemaiah, his son Gog, his son Shimei, **5.** His son Micah, his son Reaiah, his son Baal, **6.** and his son Beerah, whom Tiglath-Pileser took into exile. Beerah was a leader of the Reubenites. **7.** His relatives, by their families, were listed as follows when the genealogies of their generations were recorded: Jeiel, the chief, and Zechariah, **8.** and Bela the son of Azaz, the son of Shema, the son of Joel, who lived in Aroer, extending to Nebo and Baal Meon. **9.** To the east, they settled as far as the edge of the wilderness, near the Euphrates River, because their livestock had increased in the land of Gilead. **10.** During the reign of Saul, they fought against the Hagrites, who were defeated by them.

They settled in their tents across the entire area east of Gilead. **11.** The descendants of Gad lived next to them in the land of Bashan, as far as Salcah. **12.** The leaders of Gad were Joel, Shapham, Jaanai, and Shaphat, who ruled in Bashan. **13.** Their relatives from their father's household included Michael, Meshullam, Sheba, Jorai, Jachan, Zia, and Eber—seven in total. **14.** These were the descendants of Abihail, the son of Huri, the son of Jaroah, the son of Gilead, the son of Michael, the son of Jeshishai, the son of Jahdo, the son of Buz. **15.** Ahi, the son of Abdiel, the son of Guni, was the leader of their family. **16.** The Gadites lived in Gilead, in Bashan and its villages, and throughout all the common lands of Sharon within their borders. **17.** All these were registered in genealogies during the reigns of Jotham, king of Judah, and Jeroboam, king of Israel. **18.** The combined number of Reubenites, Gadites, and half the tribe of Manasseh was 44,760 men—valiant warriors, able to carry shields and swords, skilled with bows, and experienced in battle. They went to war. **19.** They fought against the Hagrites, Jetur, Naphish, and Nodab. **20.** With God's help, they were victorious, and the Hagrites and their allies were defeated. When they cried out to God in battle, He listened to their prayers because they trusted in Him. **21.** They took the enemy's livestock—50,000 camels, 250,000 sheep, and 2,000 donkeys—and also captured 100,000 enemy soldiers. **22.** Many of the enemies fell in battle because the war was fought with God's assistance. The victorious ones settled in their land until they were taken into exile. **23.** The descendants of the half-tribe of Manasseh lived in the land, and their numbers grew, stretching from Bashan to Baal Hermon, which is near Mount Hermon. **24.** The heads of their father's houses were Epher, Ishi, Eliel, Azriel, Jeremiah, Hodaviah, and Jahdiel. They were mighty warriors, well-known men, and leaders of their families. **25.** However, they were unfaithful to the God of their ancestors, and followed the gods of the peoples in the land, whom God had destroyed before them. **26.** In response, the God of Israel stirred up the spirit of Pul, the king of Assyria, also called Tiglath-Pileser. He carried the Reubenites, the Gadites, and the half-tribe of Manasseh into captivity. They were taken to Halah, Habor, Hara, and the river of Gozan, where they remain to this day.

Chapter 6

1. The descendants of Levi were Gershon, Kohath, and Merari. **2.** Kohath's descendants were Amram, Izhar, Hebron, and Uzziel. **3.** Amram's children were Aaron, Moses, and Miriam. Aaron's sons were Nadab, Abihu, Eleazar, and Ithamar. **4.** Eleazar had a son named Phinehas, and Phinehas had a son named Abishua. **5.** Abishua had a son named Bukki, and Bukki had a son named Uzzi. **6.** Uzzi had a son named Zerahiah, and Zerahiah had a son named Meraioth. **7.** Meraioth had a son named Amariah, and Amariah had a son named Ahitub. **8.** Ahitub had a son named Zadok, and Zadok had a son named Ahimaaz. **9.** Ahimaaz had a son named Azariah, and Azariah had a son named Johanan. **10.** Johanan had a son named Azariah, who served as the priest in the temple Solomon built in Jerusalem. **11.** Azariah had a son named Amariah, and Amariah had a son named Ahitub. **12.** Ahitub had a son named Zadok, and Zadok had a son named Shallum. **13.** Shallum had a son named Hilkiah, and Hilkiah had a son named Azariah. **14.** Azariah had a son named Seraiah, and Seraiah had a son named Jehozadak. **15.** Jehozadak was taken into captivity when the Lord allowed Judah and Jerusalem to be captured by Nebuchadnezzar. **16.** The descendants of Levi were Gershon, Kohath, and Merari. **17.** Gershon's sons were Libni and Shimei. **18.** Kohath's children were Amram, Izhar, Hebron, and Uzziel. **19.** Merari's children were Mahli and Mushi. These are the families of the Levites based on their ancestors. **20.** Gershon's descendants included Libni , Jahath , Zimmah , **21.** Joah , Iddo , Zerah , and Jeatherai . **22.** The descendants of Kohath included Amminadab , Korah , Assir , **23.** Elkanah , Ebiasaph , Assir , **24.** Tahath , Uriel , Uzziah , and Shaul . **25.** Elkanah's children were Amasai and Ahimoth. **26.** Elkanah's descendants included Zophai , Nahath , **27.** Eliab , Jeroham , and Elkanah . **28.** Samuel's children were Joel (his firstborn) and Abijah (his second son). **29.** Merari's descendants were Mahli, Libni , Shimei , Uzzah , **30.** Shimea , Haggiah , and Asaiah . **31.** These were the individuals whom David appointed to lead the music ministry in the Lord's house after the Ark of the Covenant came to rest. **32.** They performed their music duties before the tabernacle until Solomon built the temple in Jerusalem. They continued their duties in the same order. **33.** The Kohathite musicians included Heman, the singer, son of Joel, son of Samuel, **34.** Son of Elkanah, son of Jeroham, son of Eliel, son of Toah, **35.** son of Zuph, son of Elkanah, son of Mahath, son of Amasai, **36.** son of Elkanah, son of Joel, son of Azariah, son of Zephaniah, **37.** son of Tahath, son of Assir, son of Ebiasaph, son of Korah, **38.** son of Izhar, son of Kohath, son of Levi, son of Israel. **39.** His brother Asaph, who was on his right side, was Asaph, son of Berachiah, son of Shimea, **40.** son of Michael, son of Baaseiah, son of Malchijah, **41.** son of Ethni, son of Zerah, son of Adaiah, **42.** son of Ethan, son of Zimmah, son of Shimei, **43.** son of Jahath, son of Gershon, son of Levi. **44.** The Merarite musicians on the left side were Ethan, son of Kishi, son of Abdi, son of Malluch, **45.** son of Hashabiah, son of Amaziah, son of Hilkiah, **46.** son of Amzi, son of Bani, son of Shamer, **47.** son of Mahli, son of Mushi, son of Merari, son of Levi. **48.** Their fellow Levites were assigned to serve in various roles in the tabernacle. **49.** However, Aaron and his sons were responsible for offering sacrifices on the altar of burnt offerings and the altar of incense. They performed all the duties of the Most Holy Place and made atonement for Israel, as Moses, God's servant, had commanded. **50.** Aaron's descendants included Eleazar , Phinehas , Abishua , **51.** Bukki , Uzzi , Zerahiah , **52.** Meraioth , Amariah , Ahitub , **53.** Zadok , and Ahimaaz . **54.** These were the places where the descendants of Aaron lived throughout their settlements. They were given their cities by lot, from the Kohathite family. **55.** They were given Hebron in the land of Judah, along with its surrounding areas. **56.** The fields and villages of Hebron were given to Caleb, son of Jephunneh. **57.** To the sons of Aaron, they also gave one of the cities of refuge, Hebron; also Libnah with its surrounding lands, Jattir, Eshtemoa with its lands, **58.** Hilen with its lands, Debir with its lands, **59.** Ashan with its lands, and Beth Shemesh with its lands. **60.** From the tribe of Benjamin, they were given Geba with its lands, Alemeth with its lands, and Anathoth with its lands. In total, these were thirteen cities. **61.** To the rest of the Kohathite family, they gave ten cities from the half-tribe of Manasseh. **62.** The descendants of Gershon received thirteen cities from the tribes of Issachar, Asher, Naphtali, and Manasseh in Bashan. **63.** The Merarite descendants were given twelve cities from the tribes of Reuben, Gad, and Zebulun. **64.** The people of Israel gave these cities and their surrounding areas to the Levites. **65.** The cities were chosen by lot from the tribes of Judah, Simeon, and Benjamin, and these cities were named. **66.** Some of the Kohathite families were given cities in the territory of Ephraim. **67.** They received one of the cities of refuge, Shechem with its lands, in the mountains of Ephraim, along with Gezer, **68.** Jokmeam, Beth Horon, **69.** Aijalon, and Gath Rimmon. **70.** From the half-tribe of Manasseh, they received Aner and Bileam with their lands. **71.** The Gershonites from the half-tribe of Manasseh were given Golan in Bashan with its lands and Ashtaroth with its lands. **72.** From the tribe of Issachar, they received Kedesh, Daberath, **73.** Ramoth, and Anem, each with its lands. **74.** From the tribe of Asher, they received Mashal, Abdon, **75.** Hukok, and Rehob. **76.** From the tribe of Naphtali, they received Kedesh in Galilee, Hammon, and Kirjathaim, with their lands. **77.** From the tribe of Zebulun, the rest of the Merarites were given Rimmon and Tabor, each with their lands. **78.** On the eastern side of the Jordan, across from Jericho, from the tribe of Reuben, they were given Bezer, Jahzah, **79.** Kedemoth, and Mephaath, all with their surrounding lands. **80.** From the tribe of Gad, they received Ramoth in Gilead, Mahanaim, **81.** Heshbon, and Jazer, each with its surrounding lands.

Chapter 7

1. The descendants of Issachar were Tola, Puah, Jashub, and Shimron—four in total. **2.** The descendants of Tola were Uzzi, Rephaiah, Jeriel, Jahmai, Jibsam, and Shemuel, leaders (heads) of their families. These men were mighty warriors of valor (great courage) in their generations, and their number during the days of King David was 22,600. **3.** Uzzi's son was Izrahiah, and Izrahiah had four sons: Michael, Obadiah, Joel, and Ishiah. All five of them were leaders. **4.** Along with their families, they had 36,000 warriors, ready for battle, because they had many wives and children. **5.** Their relatives in all the families of Issachar were also mighty men of valor, listed by their genealogies (family history), with a total number of 87,000. **6.** The descendants of Benjamin were Bela, Becher, and Jediael—three in total. **7.** The descendants of Bela were Ezbon, Uzzi, Uzziel, Jerimoth, and Iri—five in total. They were leaders of their families, and they were recorded by their genealogies,

numbering 22,034 mighty men of valor. **8.** The descendants of Becher were Zemirah, Joash, Eliezer, Elioenai, Omri, Jerimoth, Abijah, Anathoth, and Alemeth. These were all the sons of Becher. **9.** They were listed by genealogy according to their generations, heads (leaders) of their fathers' houses, numbering 20,200 mighty men of valor. **10.** The son of Jediael was Bilhan, and the sons of Bilhan were Jeush, Benjamin, Ehud, Chenaanah, Zethan, Tharshish, and Ahishahar. **11.** All these sons of Jediael were heads (leaders) of their fathers' houses; there were 17,200 mighty men of valor, fit to go out for war and battle. **12.** Shuppim and Huppim were the sons of Ir, and Hushim was the son of Aher. **13.** The descendants of Naphtali were Jahziel, Guni, Jezer, and Shallum, the sons of Bilhah. **14.** The descendants of Manasseh: his Syrian concubine (a woman with lower status than a wife) bore him Machir, the father of Gilead, the father of Asriel. **15.** Machir took as his wife the sister of Huppim and Shuppim, whose name was Maachah. The name of Gilead's grandson was Zelophehad, who had only daughters. **16.** Maachah, the wife of Machir, bore him a son, and she named him Peresh. The name of his brother was Sheresh, and their sons were Ulam and Rakem. **17.** The son of Ulam was Bedan. These were the descendants of Gilead, the son of Machir, the son of Manasseh. **18.** His sister Hammoleketh bore him three sons: Ishhod, Abiezer, and Mahlah. **19.** The sons of Shemida were Ahian, Shechem, Likhi, and Aniam. **20.** The sons of Ephraim were Shuthelah, Bered his son, Tahath his son, Eladah his son, Tahath his son, **21.** Zabad his son, Shuthelah his son, and Ezer and Elead. The men of Gath, born in that land, killed them because they came down to take their cattle. **22.** Ephraim their father mourned (expressed sorrow) many days, and his brethren (brothers) came to comfort him. **23.** When he went into his wife, she conceived and bore a son, and he called his name Beriah, because tragedy (great misfortune) had come upon his house. **24.** His daughter was Sheerah, who built Lower and Upper Beth Horon and Uzzen Sheerah. **25.** Rephah was his son, as well as Resheph, Telah his son, Tahan his son, **26.** Laadan his son, Ammihud his son, Elishama his son, **27.** Nun his son, and Joshua his son. **28.** Their possessions and dwelling places were Bethel and its towns, Naaran to the east, Gezer and its towns to the west, Shechem and its towns, as far as Ayyah and its towns. **29.** By the borders of the children of Manasseh were Beth Shean and its towns, Taanach and its towns, Megiddo and its towns, and Dor and its towns. These were the places where the children of Joseph, the son of Israel, lived. **30.** The sons of Asher were Imnah, Ishvah, Ishvi, Beriah, and their sister Serah. **31.** The sons of Beriah were Heber and Malchiel, who was the father of Birzaith. **32.** Heber had sons named Japhlet, Shomer, Hotham, and their sister Shua. **33.** The sons of Japhlet were Pasach, Bimhal, and Ashvath. These were the children of Japhlet. **34.** The sons of Shemer were Ahi, Rohgah, Jehubbah, and Aram. **35.** The sons of Helem, his brother, were Zophah, Imna, Shelesh, and Amal. **36.** The sons of Zophah were Suah, Harnepher, Shual, Beri, Imrah, **37.** Bezer, Hod, Shamma, Shilshah, Jithran, and Beera. **38.** The sons of Jether were Jephunneh, Pispah, and Ara. **39.** The sons of Ulla were Arah, Haniel, and Rizia. **40.** All these were the children of Asher, heads (leaders) of their families, choice (select) men, mighty men of valor, and chief leaders. They were recorded by genealogies among the army fit for battle, their number being 26,000.

Chapter 8

1. Benjamin fathered Bela, his firstborn, then Ashbel, the second, followed by Aharah, the third, **2.** Nohah, the fourth, and Rapha, the fifth. **3.** Bela's sons were Addar, Gera, Abihud, **4.** Abishua, Naaman, Ahoah, **5.** Gera, Shephuphan, and Huram. **6.** These were the sons of Ehud, who led the families (groups of people or households) of the people of Geba and caused them to relocate (move) to Manahath. **7.** The ones who forced the move were Naaman, Ahijah, and Gera. Gera fathered Uzza and Ahihud. **8.** Shaharaim had children in the land of Moab after he had sent away (dismissed, separated from) his wives Hushim and Baara. **9.** By his wife Hodesh, he had Jobab, Zibia, Mesha, Malcam, **10.** Jeuz, Sachiah, and Mirmah. These were his sons, leaders (chiefs, heads) of their families. **11.** By Hushim, he had Abitub and Elpaal. **12.** The sons of Elpaal were Eber, Misham, and Shemed, who built the towns (settlements) of Ono and Lod, along with their surrounding settlements. **13.** Beriah and Shema, who were heads (leaders) of their families in Aijalon, drove out (expelled) the inhabitants (people living there) of Gath. **14.** The sons of Beriah were

Ahio, Shashak, Jeremoth, 15. Zebadiah, Arad, Eder, 16. Michael, Ispah, and Joha. 17. The sons of Elpaal were Zebadiah, Meshullam, Hizki, Heber, 18. Ishmerai, Jizliah, and Jobab. 19. The sons of Shimei were Jakim, Zichri, Zabdi, 20. Elienai, Zillethai, Eliel, 21. Adaiah, Beraiah, and Shimrath. 22. The sons of Shashak were Ishpan, Eber, Eliel, 23. Abdon, Zichri, Hanan, 24. Hananiah, Elam, Antothijah, 25. Iphdeiah, and Penuel. 26. The sons of Jeroham were Shamsherai, Shehariah, Athaliah, 27. Jaareshiah, Elijah, and Zichri. 28. These men were the heads (leaders) of their families by generations and leaders (chiefs) in their own right, residing (living) in Jerusalem. 29. The father of Gibeon whose wife was Maacah, lived in Gibeon. 30. His firstborn (oldest child) was Abdon, followed by Zur, Kish, Baal, Nadab, 31. Gedor, Ahio, Zecher, 32. and Mikloth, who fathered (became the parent of) Shimeah. They also lived near their relatives (family members) in Jerusalem. 33. Ner fathered Kish, Kish fathered Saul, and Saul fathered Jonathan, Malchishua, Abinadab, and Esh-Baal. 34. Jonathan's son was Merib-Baal, and Merib-Baal fathered Micah. 35. The sons of Micah were Pithon, Melech, Tarea, and Ahaz. 36. Ahaz fathered Jehoaddah, who fathered Alemeth, Azmaveth, and Zimri. Zimri fathered Moza. 37. Moza fathered Binea, Raphah , Eleasah , and Azel . 38. Azel had six sons: Azrikam, Bocheru, Ishmael, Sheariah, Obadiah, and Hanan. These were all the sons of Azel. 39. Eshek, his brother, had three sons: Ulam (the firstborn), Jeush (the second), and Eliphelet (the third). 40. The sons of Ulam were mighty (strong, powerful) warriors (fighters)— archers (those who shoot bows and arrows)—numbering 150 in total, along with their sons and grandsons. These were all the descendants (offspring, children) of Benjamin.

Chapter 9

1. All of Israel was registered by their family histories (genealogies), and they were listed in the book (record) of the kings of Israel. However, Judah was taken captive to Babylon because of their unfaithfulness (lack of loyalty). 2. The first people who lived in their inherited lands (territories) and cities were Israelites, priests, Levites (members of the tribe of Levi, who performed religious duties), and the Nethinim (temple servants). 3. In Jerusalem (the capital city), the children (descendants) of Judah lived, along with some from the tribe of Benjamin, and some from the tribes of Ephraim and Manasseh. 4. Uthai, the son of Ammihud, the son of Omri, the son of Imri, the son of Bani, from the descendants of Perez (a son of Judah). 5. Among the Shilonites (descendants of Shiloni), Asaiah was the firstborn (oldest child) and had sons. 6. Among the sons of Zerah: Jeuel and his relatives—six hundred and ninety. 7. Among the sons of Benjamin: Sallu, the son of Meshullam, the son of Hodaviah, the son of Hassenuah; 8. Ibneiah, the son of Jeroham; Elah, the son of Uzzi, the son of Michri; Meshullam, the son of Shephatiah, the son of Reuel, the son of Ibnijah; 9. And their relatives, listed by their generations—nine hundred and fifty-six. All these men were leaders (heads) of their families. 10. Among the priests: Jedaiah, Jehoiarib, and Jachin; 11. Azariah, the son of Hilkiah, the son of Meshullam, the son of Zadok, the son of Meraioth, the son of Ahitub, the officer (administrator) in charge of the house of God; 12. Adaiah, the son of Jeroham, the son of Pashur, the son of Malchijah; Maasai, the son of Adiel, the son of Jahzerah, the son of Meshullam, the son of Meshillemith, the son of Immer; 13. And their relatives, the heads of their families—one thousand seven hundred and sixty. These men were capable (able and skilled) for the work of the service in the house of God. 14. Among the Levites: Shemaiah, the son of Hasshub, the son of Azrikam, the son of Hashabiah, of the descendants of Merari; 15. Bakbakkar, Heresh, Galal, and Mattaniah, the son of Micah, the son of Zichri, the son of Asaph; 16. Obadiah, the son of Shemaiah, the son of Galal, the son of Jeduthun; and Berechiah, the son of Asa, the son of Elkanah, who lived in the villages of the Netophathites (descendants of a village near Bethlehem). 17. The gatekeepers (those who guard the gates) were Shallum, Akkub, Talmon, Ahiman, and their relatives. Shallum was the chief (leader). 18. They had served as gatekeepers for the Levites on the King's Gate (royal entrance) on the east side. 19. Shallum, the son of Kore, the son of Ebiasaph, the son of Korah, and his relatives, from his father's family, the Korahites (descendants of Korah), were in charge of the work of the service, serving as gatekeepers of the tabernacle (portable sanctuary). Their ancestors had been responsible for guarding the entrance to the Lord's camp (Israel's camp). 20.

Phinehas, the son of Eleazar, had been their officer in the past; the LORD was with him. 21. Zechariah, the son of Meshelemiah, was the keeper (guard) of the door to the tabernacle of meeting. 22. In total, two hundred and twelve gatekeepers were chosen. They were listed by their genealogy (family records) in their villages. David and Samuel the seer (prophet) had appointed them to their trusted position. 23. They and their children were responsible for the gates of the house of the Lord, the tabernacle, as part of their duties. 24. The gatekeepers were assigned to guard the four directions: east, west, north, and south. 25. Their relatives in the villages would come to assist them for seven days at a time. 26. There were four chief (head) gatekeepers; they were Levites, and they were responsible for the rooms and treasuries (storage areas) of the house of God. 27. They stayed around the house of God because they had this responsibility, and they were in charge of opening the doors every morning. 28. Some of them were responsible for the serving vessels (utensils used in temple worship), counting them as they brought them in and took them out. 29. Some were assigned to manage the furnishings, the implements (tools) of the sanctuary, the fine flour, wine, oil, incense, and spices. 30. Some of the priests' descendants prepared the special ointment made from spices. 31. Mattithiah, a Levite and the firstborn of Shallum the Korahite, had the trusted position of overseeing the preparation of items baked (cooked) in the pans. 32. Some of the Kohathites (descendants of Kohath, a Levite ancestor) among their relatives were responsible for preparing the showbread (bread placed on the altar every Sabbath) for the Sabbath. 33. These were the singers, the heads of the Levite families, who lived in the chambers (rooms) of the temple and were free from other duties; they were employed in this work day and night. 34. The heads of the Levite families were leaders in their generations, and they lived in Jerusalem. 35. Jeiel, the father of Gibeon, whose wife was Maacah, lived in Gibeon. 36. His firstborn son was Abdon, followed by Zur, Kish, Baal, Ner, Nadab, 37. Gedor, Ahio, Zechariah, and Mikloth. 38. Mikloth had a son named Shimeam. They lived near their relatives in Jerusalem. 39. Ner was the father of Kish, and Kish was the father of Saul. Saul had sons: Jonathan, Malchishua, Abinadab, and Esh-Baal. 40. Jonathan had a son named Merib-Baal, and Merib-Baal had a son named Micah. 41. The sons of Micah were Pithon, Melech, Tahrea, and Ahaz. 42. Ahaz was the father of Jarah; Jarah was the father of Alemeth, Azmaveth, and Zimri; and Zimri was the father of Moza. 43. Moza had a son named Binea, who had a son named Rephaiah, and Rephaiah had a son named Eleasah, and Eleasah had a son named Azel. 44. Azel had six sons: Azrikam, Bocheru, Ishmael, Sheariah, Obadiah, and Hanan; these were the sons of Azel.

Chapter 10

The Philistines waged war against Israel and the Israelite soldiers fled from them, falling dead on Mount Gilboa. 2 The Philistines pursued Saul and his sons closely, killing Jonathan, Abinadab, and Malchishua, Saul's sons. 3 The battle intensified around Saul. He was struck and injured by archers (soldiers who use bows and arrows). 4 Saul then told his armor-bearer (a helper who carried a warrior's armor), "Draw your sword and kill me, so these uncircumcised (non-Israelite) men won't come and torment (cruelly mistreat) me." But his armor-bearer was too afraid to do it, so Saul took his own sword and fell on it. 5 When the armor-bearer saw that Saul was dead, he also fell on his sword and died. 6 In this way, Saul, his three sons, and all his family died together. 7 When the Israelite men in the valley saw that their army had fled and that Saul and his sons were dead, they abandoned (left) their cities and escaped. Then the Philistines moved into those cities. 8 The following day, the Philistines came to take belongings from the dead and found Saul and his sons lying on Mount Gilboa. 9 They stripped (removed) Saul's head and armor and sent news throughout the land of the Philistines to announce (proclaim) it in the temples of their idols (objects of worship) and among the people. 10 They placed Saul's armor in the temple of their gods and displayed his head in the temple of Dagon (a Philistine god). 11 When the people of Jabesh Gilead heard all that the Philistines had done to Saul, 12 the brave (valiant) men arose, took the bodies of Saul and his sons, brought them to Jabesh, buried their bones under a tamarisk (a type of tree) in Jabesh, and fasted (abstained from eating) for seven days. 13 Saul died because he was unfaithful to the Lord, as he had not kept (obeyed) the Lord's word and had consulted (sought advice from) a medium (a person who communicates with spirits). **14** Because Saul did not ask the Lord for guidance, God caused his death and gave the kingdom to David, the son of Jesse.

Chapter 11

1. All the tribes of Israel gathered with David in Hebron (an ancient city in Judah), saying, and "We are your kin (family), your own flesh and blood **2.** In the past, even when Saul was our king, you were the one who led Israel in battles; the Lord your God told you, 'You will lead (shepherd) My people Israel and rule over them as king.'" **3.** So all the elders (leaders) of Israel came to David in Hebron. David made a covenant (formal agreement) with them in the presence of the Lord, and they anointed (officially declared) David as king over Israel, fulfilling the word of the Lord as spoken by Samuel (a prophet who anointed David). **4.** David and all of Israel then went to Jerusalem, which was also called Jebus (former name of Jerusalem), where the Jebusites (a group of Canaanite inhabitants of Jerusalem) lived. **5.** The people of Jebus said to David, "You will not be able to enter here!" Yet David captured the stronghold (fortress) of Zion (the hill on which the City of David was built), also known as the City of David. **6.** David declared, "Whoever attacks the Jebusites first will become chief (leader) and captain (military leader)." Joab, the son of Zeruiah, went up first and became the chief. **7.** David then lived in the stronghold, and it was called the City of David. **8.** He built up the city around it, from the Millo (a fortified structure) to the surrounding parts, while Joab repaired (rebuilt) the rest of the city. **9.** David grew stronger and more powerful because the Lord of hosts (the God of heavenly armies) was with him. **10.** These were the leaders of David's mighty warriors, who supported him in his kingdom with all of Israel, helping to make him king as the Lord had promised about Israel. **11.** Here is the list of David's mighty men (elite warriors): Jashobeam, son of a Hachmonite, who was the chief of the captains. He fought with his spear and killed three hundred men at one time. **12.** Following him was Eleazar, son of Dodo, an Ahohite (from the clan of Ahoah). He was one of David's three mighty warriors. **13.** Eleazar was with David at Pasdammim when the Philistines (a group of Israel's enemies) gathered there for battle, and the field was filled with barley (a type of grain). When the people ran away from the Philistines, **14.** Eleazar and others took a stand in the middle of the field, defended it, and defeated the Philistines. The Lord brought about a great victory (triumph in battle). **15.** Three of the thirty chief men went down to the rock where David was hiding in the cave of Adullam (a cave where David sought refuge), while the Philistine army camped in the Valley of Rephaim (a valley near Jerusalem). **16.** David was in the stronghold (safe place), and the Philistine troops were stationed in Bethlehem (David's birthplace). **17.** David longed for water, saying, "If only someone would bring me water from the well by the gate of Bethlehem!" **18.** So the three men broke through the Philistine camp, drew water from the Bethlehem well near the gate, and brought it back to David. But David refused to drink it; instead, he poured it out as an offering (sacrifice) to the Lord, **19.** saying, "I cannot drink this! It would be like drinking the blood of these men who risked their lives to bring it to me." So he would not drink it. These were the kinds of acts done by the three mighty men. **20.** Abishai, the brother of Joab, was chief of another three warriors. He fought with his spear against three hundred men and gained fame among the three. **21.** Of these three, he was the most honored (respected) and became their captain, but he did not attain (reach) the same rank as the first three. **22.** Benaiah, the son of Jehoiada, from Kabzeel (a town in southern Judah), a brave man, did great deeds. He killed two strong men from Moab (a nation often in conflict with Israel), went down into a pit (hole in the ground) on a snowy day, and killed a lion. **23.** He also killed a tall Egyptian, over seven feet (five cubits) tall, who held a spear as big as a weaver's rod (a thick, sturdy rod). Benaiah fought him with a staff (a long stick), took the spear from the Egyptian, and killed him with it. **24.** Benaiah's accomplishments earned him fame among the three mighty warriors. **25.** He was highly honored among the thirty, but he did not reach the rank of the first three. David appointed him as head of his guard (personal protection team). **26.** Other mighty warriors included Asahel, Joab's brother; Elhanan from Bethlehem, **27.** Shammoth the Harorite (from Haror); Helez the Pelonite, **28.** Ira, son of Ikkesh from Tekoa (a town in Judah), and Abiezer from Anathoth (a city in the territory of Benjamin), **29.** Sibbechai from Hushah (a town near Jerusalem), Ilai the Ahohite, **30.** Maharai from Netophah (a village near Bethlehem), Heled, son of Baanah from Netophah, **31.** Ithai, son of Ribai from Gibeah (a city in Benjamin) of Benjamin, Benaiah the Pirathonite (from Pirathon in Ephraim), **32.** Hurai from Gaash (a mountainous region), Abiel the Arbathite, **33.** Azmaveth from Bahurim (a village near Jerusalem), Eliahba the Shaalbon (a town in Judah), **34.** the sons of Hashem from Gizon (a place in Israel), Jonathan, son of Shageh the Hararite, **35.** Ahiam, son of Sacar the Hararite, and Eliphal, son of Ur, **36.** Hepher from Mecherah, Ahijah the Pelonite, **37.** Hezro from Carmel (a mountain in northern Israel), Naarai, son of Ezbai, **38.** Joel, the brother of Nathan, and Mibhar, son of Hagri, **39.** Zelek the Ammonite (from Ammon, a neighboring country), Naharai from Beroth (a town near Gibeon), who was Joab's armor-bearer (one who carried armor for a warrior), **40.** Ira the Ithrite, Gareb the Ithrite (both from Ithri, a clan of Israel), **41.** Uriah the Hittite (from the Hittite people, an ancient civilization), Zabad, son of Ahlai, **42.** Adina, son of Shiza the Reubenite, who was a leader of the Reubenites (a tribe of Israel), and thirty others with him, **43.** Hanan, son of Maachah, Joshaphat the Mithnite (from Mitnah), **44.** Uzzia the Ashterathite (from Ashteroth, a city in Bashan), Shama and Jeiel, sons of Hotham the Aroerite (from Aroer, a city east of the Jordan River), **45.** Jediael, son of Shimri, and his brother Joha, the Tizite, **46.** Eliel the Mahavite, Jeribai and Joshaviah, sons of Elnaam, and Ithmah the Moabite (from Moab, east of Israel), **47.** Eliel, Obed, and Jaasiel from Mezobah (an unknown location, possibly near Israel).

Chapter 12

1. These were the men who came to David at Ziklag while he was still fleeing (running away) from Saul, the son of Kish; they were among the mighty men, warriors who helped in the battle. **2.** They were armed with bows (weapons for shooting arrows) and could use both their right and left hands to throw stones and shoot arrows. They were from the tribe of Benjamin, Saul's relatives. **3.** The leader was Ahiezer, followed by Joash, the sons of Shemaah the Gibeathite (a person from the town of Gibeah); Jeziel and Pelet, sons of Azmaveth; Berachah, and Jehu the Anathothite (a person from the town of Anathoth). **4.** Ishmaiah the Gibeonite, a mighty warrior among the thirty, and over the thirty; Jeremiah, Jahaziel, Johanan, and Jozabad the Gederathite (a person from Gederah); **5.** Eluzai, Jerimoth, Bealiah, Shemariah, and Shephatiah the Haruphite (a person from Haruph); **6.** Elkanah, Jisshiah, Azarel, Joezer, and Jashobeam, the Korahites (descendants of Korah, a biblical figure); **7.** Joelah and Zebadiah, the sons of Jeroham of Gedor (a town). **8.** Some men from Gad joined David at the stronghold (a fortified place) in the wilderness (a remote area), mighty warriors trained for battle, able to handle shields and spears, with faces like lions, swift as gazelles (small, fast animals) on the mountains. **9.** The first was Ezer, the second was Obadiah, the third was Eliab, **10.** The fourth was Mishmannah, the fifth was Jeremiah, **11.** The sixth was Attai, the seventh was Eliel, **12.** The eighth was Johanan, the ninth was Elzabad, **13.** The tenth was Jeremiah, and the eleventh was Machbanai. **14.** These were the captains (leaders) of the army from the sons of Gad; the least (lowest in rank) was over a hundred men, and the greatest (highest in rank) was over a thousand. **15.** These men crossed the Jordan River in the first month, when it was overflowing (exceeding its normal level) its banks, and defeated the enemies in the valleys (low areas between hills) to the east and west. **16.** Then some men from Benjamin and Judah came to David at the stronghold. **17.** David went out to meet them, and said to them, "If you have come in peace (with good intentions) to help me, my heart will be united with you; but if you have come to betray (deceive) me to my enemies, since I am innocent (without guilt), may God bring judgment." **18.** Then the Spirit of God came upon Amasai, the leader of the captains, and he said, "We are yours, O David! We are on your side, O son of Jesse! Peace to you and your helpers! For God is with you." So David accepted them and made them captains of his army. **19.** Some from Manasseh defected (switched sides) to David when he was going with the Philistines (enemies of Israel) to fight against Saul, but they were not allowed to help, as the Philistine lords had sent him away, fearing he might return to Saul. **20.** When David went to Ziklag, those of Manasseh who joined him were Adnah, Jozabad, Jediael, Michael, Jozabad, Elihu, and Zillethai, captains of the thousands from Manasseh. **21.** They helped David against the raiders (plunderers), as they were mighty warriors and captains in the army. **22.** They came to David every day to help him, and his army grew large, like the army of God. **23.** These were the divisions (groups) of men ready for war who came to David at Hebron to help him take over the kingdom of Saul, as the Lord had spoken: **24.** From the sons of Judah, 6,800 men armed for war, **25.** From the sons of Simeon, 7,100 mighty men of valor (bravery), **26.** From the sons of Levi, 4,600 men; **27.** Jehoiada, the leader of the Aaronites (descendants of Aaron), and with him 3,700 men; **28.** Zadok, a young and valiant (brave) warrior, and 22 captains from his family; **29.** From the sons of Benjamin, Saul's relatives, 3,000 men (until then, most of them had remained loyal to Saul's family); **30.** From the sons of Ephraim, 20,800 mighty men of valor, well-known in their family; **31.** From the half-tribe of Manasseh, 18,000 men who had been specifically chosen to help make David king; **32.** From the sons of Issachar, men who understood the times (were wise) and knew what Israel should do, 200 chiefs (leaders), and their families followed them; **33.** From Zebulun, 50,000 men who were expert warriors and knew how to keep ranks in battle; **34.** From Naphtali, 1,000 captains, and with them 37,000 men with shields and spears; **35.** From Dan, 28,600 men who could maintain battle formation; **36.** From Asher, 40,000 men able to keep battle formation; **37.** From the Reubenites, Gadites, and the half-tribe of Manasseh on the other side of the Jordan, 120,000 armed for battle with all kinds of weapons. **38.** All these warriors, who could maintain their ranks, came to Hebron with loyal hearts to make David king over all Israel. All the rest of Israel were united in making David king. **39.** They stayed with David for three days, eating and drinking, as their fellow Israelites had prepared for them. **40.** Those who were near to them, from as far as Issachar, Zebulun, and Naphtali, brought food on donkeys, camels, mules, and oxen—provisions (supplies) like flour, cakes of figs, cakes of raisins, wine, oil, oxen, and sheep, for there was great joy in Israel.

Chapter 13

1. Then David consulted with the commanders (leaders) of thousands and hundreds, and with every other leader (person in charge). **2.** And David said to all the assembly (group) of Israel, "If it seems good to you, and if it is of the Lord our God, let us send out to our brethren (brothers and sisters) everywhere who are left in all the land of Israel, and with them to the priests (religious leaders) and Levites (members of the tribe responsible for religious duties) who are in their cities and their common-lands (land surrounding cities), that they may gather together to us; **3.** And let us bring the ark (sacred chest containing God's commandments) of our God back to us, for we have not inquired (sought guidance) at it since the days of Saul." **4.** Then all the assembly said that they would do so, for the thing was right in the eyes of all the people. **5.** So David gathered all Israel together, from Shihor in Egypt to as far as the entrance (border) of Hamath, to bring the ark of God from Kirjath Jearim. **6.** And David and all Israel went up to Baalah (a place), to Kirjath Jearim, which belonged to Judah (an ancient Israeli kingdom), to bring up from there the ark of God the Lord, who dwells (lives) between the cherubim (angel-like beings), where His name is proclaimed (announced). **7.** So they carried the ark of God on a new cart from the house of Abinadab, and Uzza and Ahio (sons of Abinadab) drove (guided) the cart. **8.** Then David and all Israel played music before God with all their might (strength), with singing, on harps (stringed instruments), on stringed instruments, on tambourines (small drums), on cymbals (musical instruments), and with trumpets (brass wind instruments). **9.** And when they came to Chidon's threshing floor (place where grain is separated from husks), Uzza put out his hand to hold the ark, for the oxen (large animals) stumbled. **10.** Then the anger of the Lord was aroused (angered) against Uzza, and He struck him because he put his hand to the ark; and he died there before God. **11.** And David became angry because of the Lord's outbreak (sudden judgment) against Uzza; therefore that place is called Perez Uzza (meaning "outbreak against Uzza") to this day. **12.** David was afraid of God that day, saying, "How can I bring the ark of God to me?" **13.** So David would not move the ark with him into the City of David, but took it aside into the house of Obed-Edom (a person from Gath). **14.** The ark of God remained with the family of Obed-Edom in his house for three months. And the Lord blessed the house of Obed-Edom and all that he had.

Chapter 14

1. Now Hiram, the king of Tyre (an ancient city-state), sent messengers to David, along with cedar trees (large trees known for their durable wood), and skilled workers—masons (stone workers) and carpenters (woodworkers)—to help build him a house. **2.** So David realized that the Lord had firmly established (set up securely) him as king over Israel, and his reign (rule) was greatly exalted (raised in status) for the benefit (advantage) of His people, Israel. **3.** Then David took more wives (women he married) in Jerusalem, and had more sons and daughters. **4.** These are the names of his children born to him in Jerusalem: Shammua, Shobab, Nathan, Solomon, **5.** Ibhar, Elishua, Elpelet, **6.** Nogah, Nepheg, Japhia, **7.** Elishama, Beeliada, and Eliphelet. **8.** When the Philistines (an ancient group of people) heard that David had been anointed as king over all Israel, they gathered together to search for David. David heard of this and went out to confront (face) them. **9.** The Philistines then went and attacked (raided) the Valley of Rephaim (a valley near Jerusalem). **10.** David asked God, saying, "Should I go up against (fight) the Philistines? Will You give them into my hands (control)?" And the Lord answered him, "Go up, for I will give them into your hands." **11.** So they went up to Baal Perazim (a place meaning "Lord of the breakthrough"), and David defeated them there. David then said, "God has broken through my enemies by my hand like a flood of water." **12.** After the Philistines left their idols (false gods) there, David gave the order, and they were burned with fire. **13.** Once again, the Philistines attacked the valley. **14.** So David inquired (asked) of God again, and God said to him, "You must not pursue (chase) them. Instead, circle around them and come upon them in front of the mulberry trees." **15.** "And when you hear the sound of marching (movement) in the tops of the mulberry trees, then you shall move forward to fight, for God will go before you to strike (defeat) the Philistine camp." **16.** David obeyed God's instructions, and they drove the Philistine army back from Gibeon all the way to Gezer (a city in Israel). **17.** As a result, David's fame (reputation) spread throughout all lands, and the Lord caused all nations to fear (respect with awe) him.

Chapter 15

1. David constructed homes for himself in the City of David and set up a special place for the Ark of God, which holds the tablets of the law. He also erected a tent as a temporary shelter for it. **2.** David declared, "Only the Levites are allowed to carry the Ark of God, because the Lord has chosen them for this sacred task to serve before Him forever." **3.** David gathered all the people of Israel in Jerusalem to bring the Ark of the Lord to the place he had prepared for it. **4.** He called together the descendants of Aaron and the Levites: **5.** From the family of Kohath, Uriel, the leader, and 120 of his relatives; **6.** From the family of Merari, Asaiah, the leader, and 220 of his relatives; **7.** From the family of Gershom, Joel, the leader, and 130 of his relatives; **8.** From the family of Elizaphan, Shemaiah, the leader, and 200 of his relatives; **9.** From the family of Hebron, Eliel, the leader, and 80 of his relatives; **10.** From the family of Uzziel, Amminadab, the leader, and 112 of his relatives. **11.** David also called for the priests Zadok and Abiathar, and the Levites: Uriel, Asaiah, Joel, Shemaiah, Eliel, and Amminadab. **12.** He instructed them, "You are the leaders of the Levite families. Purify yourselves, along with your relatives, so you can bring up the Ark of the Lord, the God of Israel, to the place I have prepared for it." **13.** "Because you did not do this the first time, the Lord our God punished us, since we did not seek His guidance regarding the proper way to carry the Ark." **14.** So, the priests and Levites purified themselves in preparation for carrying the Ark of the Lord, the God of Israel. **15.** The Levites carried the Ark of God on their shoulders, using the poles as instructed by Moses, according to the Lord's command. **16.** David then spoke to the leaders of the Levites, telling them to appoint some of their relatives as singers, who would be accompanied by musical instruments such as harps, cymbals, and stringed instruments, raising their voices in joyous praise. **17.** The Levites appointed Heman, the son of Joel, and his relatives Asaph, the son of Berechiah, and from the family of Merari, Ethan, the son of Kushaiah, **18.** along with their second-tier relatives: Zechariah, Ben, Jaaziel, Shemiramoth, Jehiel, Unni, Eliab, Benaiah, Maaseiah, Mattithiah, Elipheleh, Mikneiah, Obed-Edom, and Jeiel, the gatekeepers. **19.** Heman, Asaph, and Ethan were responsible for playing the bronze cymbals, **20.** while Zechariah, Aziel, Shemiramoth, Jehiel, Unni, Eliab, Maaseiah, and Benaiah were to play stringed instruments in the Alamoth style, **21.** and Mattithiah,

Elipheleh, Mikneiah, Obed-Edom, Jeiel, and Azaziah were tasked with leading the music on harps in the Sheminith style. 22. Chenaniah, the leader of the Levites, was appointed as the instructor of music, due to his skill. 23. Berechiah and Elkanah were assigned as doorkeepers for the Ark, 24. while Shebaniah, Joshaphat, Nethanel, Amasai, Zechariah, Benaiah, and Eliezer, the priests, were to blow the trumpets before the Ark of God, with Obed-Edom and Jehiah serving as doorkeepers. 25. David, along with the elders of Israel and the commanders over the thousands, went to bring up the Ark of the Covenant from the house of Obed-Edom with great joy. 26. When God helped the Levites who carried the Ark of the Covenant, they offered seven bulls and seven rams as sacrifices. 27. David was dressed in a fine linen robe, as were all the Levites carrying the Ark, the singers, and Chenaniah, the director of music. David also wore a linen ephod. 28. Thus, all of Israel brought up the Ark of the Covenant with loud shouting, the sound of horns, trumpets, cymbals, and stringed instruments, rejoicing in music. 29. As the Ark of the Covenant entered the City of David, Michal, the daughter of Saul, looked out of the window and saw King David dancing and playing music, and she despised him in her heart.

Chapter 16

1. They brought the ark (sacred chest) of God and placed it in the middle of the tent that David had built for it. Then, they offered burnt offerings (ritual offerings) and peace offerings (ritual offerings symbolizing reconciliation) before God. 2. After David had finished offering the burnt offerings and peace offerings, he blessed (spoke words of well-being) the people in the name of the Lord. 3. He gave each person in Israel—a loaf of bread, a piece of meat, and a raisin cake. 4. He appointed some of the Levites (religious leaders) to serve before the ark of the Lord, to commemorate (to remember), to thank, and to praise (express admiration for) the Lord God of Israel. 5. Asaph (a leader and musician) was the leader, and next to him were Zechariah, Jeiel, Shemiramoth, Jehiel, Mattithiah, Eliab, Benaiah, and Obed-Edom. Jeiel played stringed instruments and harps, and Asaph played cymbals (musical instruments). 6. Benaiah and Jahaziel, the priests, regularly blew trumpets before the Ark of the Covenant (sacred agreement) of God. 7. On that day, David first gave this psalm (sacred song) to Asaph and his relatives to thank the Lord: 8. "Give thanks to the Lord! Call on His name; tell everyone about His deeds (actions)! 9. Sing to Him, sing praises (songs) to Him; talk about all His wondrous (amazing) works! 10. Glory (great honor) in His holy name; let the hearts of those who seek (search for) the Lord rejoice (be filled with joy)! 11. Seek the Lord and His strength; seek His presence (face) forever! 12. Remember His marvelous (wonderful) works, His wonders, and the judgments (decisions) He has made 13. O descendants (children) of Israel, His servant, you children of Jacob, His chosen ones! 14. He is the Lord our God; His judgments are known throughout the earth. 15. Remember His covenant (promise) forever, the word which He commanded, for a thousand generations, 16. The covenant He made with Abraham, and His oath (promise) to Isaac, 17. Which He confirmed to Jacob as a law, to Israel as an everlasting covenant, 18. Saying, 'I will give you the land of Canaan as your inheritance (possession).' 19. When you were few in number, very few, and strangers (foreigners) in it, 20. When you moved from one nation to another, from one kingdom to another people, 21. He did not allow anyone to harm (injure) you; He even rebuked (corrected) kings for your sake, 22. Saying, 'Do not touch My anointed ones (chosen ones), and do My prophets no harm.' 23. Sing to the Lord, all the earth; proclaim (announce) His salvation (deliverance) day by day. 24. Declare His glory (great honor) among the nations, His wonders among all peoples. 25. For the Lord is great and greatly to be praised; He is to be feared (respected) above all gods. 26. All the gods of the people are idols (worthless objects), but the Lord made the heavens. 27. Honor (respect) and majesty (greatness) are before Him; strength and joy are in His presence. 28. Give to the Lord, O families (groups) of the peoples, give to the Lord glory and strength. 29. Give to the Lord the glory due His name; bring an offering (gift) and come before Him. Worship Lord in the beauty of holiness! 30. Let the earth tremble (shake) before Him. The world is firmly established, and it will not be moved. 31. Let the heavens rejoice (be glad), and let the earth be glad; let them say among the nations, 'The Lord reigns (rules).' 32. Let the sea roar (make a loud noise), and all that fills it; let the fields (farms) be joyful, and

everything in them. 33. Then the trees of the forest will sing for joy before the Lord, for He is coming to judge (rule over) the earth. 34. Give thanks to the Lord, for He is good! His mercy (kindness) endures forever. 35. And say, 'Save us, O God of our salvation; gather us together, and deliver (rescue) us from the nations, to give thanks to Your holy name, to triumph (celebrate) in Your praise.' 36. Blessed (praised) be the Lord God of Israel, from everlasting (eternally) to everlasting! And all the people said, 'Amen!' and praised the Lord. 37. So David left Asaph and his relatives there before the ark of the covenant of the Lord to serve before it regularly, as required every day. 38. Obed-Edom and his sixty-eight relatives, including Obed-Edom the son of Jeduthun, and Hosah, were appointed as gatekeepers (guards). 39. Zadok the priest and his fellow priests served before the tabernacle (portable temple) at the high place at Gibeon, 40. To offer burnt offerings (ritual sacrifices) to the Lord on the altar every morning and evening, and to follow all that is written in the Law (teaching) of the Lord that He commanded Israel. 41. Along with them, Heman and Jeduthun and the rest who were chosen, to give thanks to the Lord, because His mercy endures forever, 42. And with them, Heman and Jeduthun, to sound trumpets and cymbals and other musical instruments for God. The sons of Jeduthun were gatekeepers. 43. Then all the people returned to their homes, and David went back to bless (bring happiness) his house.

Chapter 17

1 Now it came to pass, when David was dwelling (living) in his house, that David said to Nathan the prophet, "See now, I dwell in a house of cedar (a strong, fragrant wood), but the Ark of the Covenant (a sacred chest containing the tablets of the Ten Commandments) of the Lord is under tent curtains (sheets of fabric)." 2 Then Nathan said to David, "Do all that is in your heart, for God is with you." 3 But it happened that night that the word of God came to Nathan, saying, 4 "Go and tell My servant David, 'Thus says the Lord: "You shall not build Me a house to dwell (live) in. 5 For I have not dwelt (lived) in a house since the time that I brought up Israel, even to this day, but have gone from tent to tent (temporary places of worship), and from one tabernacle (a portable, tent-like structure for worship) to another. 6 Wherever I have moved about with all Israel, have I ever spoken a word to any of the judges (leaders) of Israel, whom I commanded to shepherd (care for) My people, saying, 'Why have you not built Me a house of cedar?' "' 7 Now therefore, thus shall you say to My servant David, 'Thus says the Lord of hosts (armies): "I took you from the sheepfold (place where sheep are kept), from following the sheep, to be ruler over My people Israel. 8 And I have been with you wherever you have gone, and have cut off (removed) all your enemies from before you, and have made you a name like the name of the great men who are on the earth. 9 Moreover I will appoint (choose) a place for My people Israel and will plant them, that they may dwell (live) in a place of their own and move no more; nor shall the sons of wickedness (evil or unjust people) oppress (control unfairly) them anymore, as previously, 10 since the time that I commanded judges to be over My people Israel. Also, I will subdue (defeat or overpower) all your enemies. Furthermore, I tell you that the Lord will build you a house. 11 And it shall be, when your days are fulfilled (completed), when you must go to be with your fathers (ancestors), that I will set up your seed (descendants) after you, who will be of your sons; and I will establish his kingdom. 12 He shall build Me a house, and I will establish his throne forever. 13 I will be his Father, and he shall be My son; and I will not take My mercy (compassion or forgiveness) away from him, as I took it from him who was before you. 14 And I will establish him in My house and in My kingdom forever; and his throne shall be established forever." 15 According to all these words and according to all this vision (divine revelation), so Nathan spoke to David. 16 Then King David went in and sat before the Lord; and he said: "Who am I, O Lord God? And what is my house, that You have brought me this far? 17 And yet this was a small thing in Your sight, O God; and You have also spoken of Your servant's house for a great while to come, and have regarded (treated) me according to the rank (status or position) of a man of high degree (importance), O Lord God. 18 What more can David say to You for the honor of Your servant? For You know Your servant. 19 O Lord, for Your servant's sake, and according to Your own heart, You have done all this greatness, in making known all these great things. 20 O Lord, there is

none like You, nor is there any God besides You, according to all that we have heard with our ears. 21 And who is like Your people Israel, the one nation on earth whom God went to redeem (rescue) for Himself as a people—to make for Yourself a name by great and awesome deeds, by driving out nations from before Your people whom You redeemed from Egypt? 22 For You have made Your people Israel Your very own people forever; and You, Lord, have become their God. 23 "And now, O Lord, the word which You have spoken concerning Your servant and concerning his house, let it be established forever, and do as You have said. 24 So let it be established, that Your name may be magnified (praised or made great) forever, saying, 'The Lord of hosts, the God of Israel, is Israel's God.' And let the house of Your servant David be established before You. 25 For You, O my God, have revealed to Your servant that You will build him a house. Therefore Your servant has found it in his heart to pray before You. 26 And now, Lord, You are God, and have promised this goodness to Your servant. 27 Now You have been pleased to bless the house of Your servant, that it may continue before You forever; for You have blessed it, O Lord, and it shall be blessed forever."

Chapter 18

1. After this, David attacked the Philistines, defeated them, and captured the city of Gath along with its surrounding towns from the Philistine control. 2. He then conquered the Moabites, who became David's subjects and began paying tribute (a payment made by one ruler to another for protection or recognition of power). 3. David also defeated Hadadezer, the king of Zobah, extending his territory to the city of Hamath, as he sought to expand his influence along the Euphrates River. 4. From Hadadezer, David took one thousand chariots, seven thousand cavalry (soldiers on horseback), and twenty thousand foot soldiers. He also crippled (hamstrung, cut the tendons of) all the horses used for the chariots, except for enough to pull one hundred chariots. 5. When the Syrians from Damascus came to assist Hadadezer, David killed twenty-two thousand of them. 6. David then placed garrisons (military posts) in Damascus, and the Syrians became his subjects, bringing tribute to him. The Lord kept David safe wherever he went. 7. David took the gold shields carried by Hadadezer's servants and brought them to Jerusalem. 8. From the cities of Tibhath and Chun, which belonged to Hadadezer, David brought back large amounts of bronze, which Solomon later used to make the bronze Sea (a large basin), the pillars, and other bronze items for the temple. 9. When Tou, the king of Hamath, heard that David had defeated Hadadezer's army, 10. he sent his son Hadoram to King David to offer congratulations and blessings, because David had fought against Hadadezer, who had been at war with Tou. Hadoram brought with him gold, silver, and bronze gifts. 11. David dedicated all these treasures to the Lord, along with the gold and silver he had previously taken from other nations—Edom, Moab, Ammon, the Philistines, and Amalek. 12. Furthermore, Abishai, the son of Zeruiah, killed eighteen thousand Edomites in the Valley of Salt. 13. He also established garrisons in Edom, and the Edomites became David's subjects. The Lord protected David wherever he went. 14. So David ruled over all of Israel, ensuring justice and fairness for all his people. 15. Joab, the son of Zeruiah, was in charge of the army; Jehoshaphat, the son of Ahilud, served as the royal historian (recorder); 16. Zadok, the son of Ahitub, and Abimelech, the son of Abiathar, were the priests; Shavsha was the secretary (scribe); 17. Benaiah, the son of Jehoiada, was in charge of the Cherethites and Pelethites (elite groups of mercenary soldiers); and David's sons held important positions as royal advisers (chief ministers) by the king's side.

Chapter 19

1. After this, Nahash, the king of the Ammonites (people from the region of Ammon), died, and his son reigned in his place. 2. David then said, "I want to show kindness (compassion or goodwill) to Hanun, the son of Nahash, because his father was kind to me." So, David sent messengers to Hanun to comfort (offer solace) him over his father's death. David's servants went to Hanun in the land of the Ammonites to offer their condolences. 3. But the princes (noble leaders) of the Ammonites said to Hanun, "Do you really think David is honoring your father by sending comforters? Didn't his servants come to spy (gather secret information) on the land and find a way to overthrow (defeat) you?" 4. So, Hanun took David's servants, shaved (cut off) their beards (facial hair), and cut their clothes in half, exposing their buttocks (rear) and sent them back in disgrace. 5. When some people informed David about this, he sent messengers to meet them because they were deeply embarrassed (ashamed). The king told them, "Stay in Jericho until your beards grow back, and then return." 6. When the Ammonites realized they had offended David, Hanun and the people of Ammon sent a large sum of silver (precious metal) — 1,000 talents (a large measure of weight, usually for gold or silver) — to hire chariots (horse-drawn vehicles) and soldiers from Mesopotamia (the region between the Tigris and Euphrates rivers), from the Syrians of Maachah (a region or people in Syria), and from Zobah (an ancient kingdom, also in Syria). 7. They hired 32,000 chariots (war vehicles), along with the king of Maachah and his army, and they set up camp near Medeba (a town). The people of Ammon gathered from their cities to fight. 8. When David heard of this, he sent Joab (commander of Israel's army), along with all his mighty men (brave warriors), to confront them. 9. The Ammonites came out and positioned themselves for battle at the city gates (entrance to the city), while the other kings who had joined them were positioned in the open field (open area). 10. Seeing that the enemy was positioned in front and behind, Joab selected Israel's best warriors and positioned them to fight the Syrians (people from the region of Syria). 11. He placed the rest of the army under the command of his brother Abishai (Joab's brother), to face the Ammonites. 12. Joab said to Abishai, "If the Syrians prove too strong for me, then come to my aid; but if the Ammonites overpower you, I will come to help you. Be strong, and let us fight bravely for our people and the cities of our God. May the LORD do what He deems best?" 13. Joab and his soldiers moved forward to face the Syrians, who fled before them. 14. When the Ammonites saw the Syrians retreating, they too fled from Abishai and retreated into the city. Joab then returned to Jerusalem (capital city of Israel). 15. When the Syrians realized they had been defeated by Israel, they sent messengers (people to carry messages) to gather their allies from across the Euphrates River (a major river in Mesopotamia), and Shophach (commander of Hadadezer's army), led them. 16. When David heard about this, he gathered all of Israel, crossed the Jordan River (river in Israel), and confronted them in battle. He positioned his army to fight the Syrians. 17. The Syrians fought against Israel, but they fled before them. David's forces killed 7,000 charioteers (drivers of war vehicles) and 40,000 infantry (foot soldiers) from Syria, and they also killed Shophach, the commander of the Syrian army. 18. When Hadadezer's (a Syrian king) servants saw that they had been defeated by Israel, they made peace (an agreement to stop fighting) with David and became his subjects. From that point on, the Syrians refused to help the Ammonites in their fight.

Chapter 20

1. It was during the spring, the time when kings typically go to war, that Joab led the army and attacked the land of the Ammonites. He laid siege to their city, Rabbah, but David remained in Jerusalem. Joab defeated Rabbah and destroyed it. 2. Afterward, David took the crown from the king of Rabbah's head. The crown weighed a talent of gold (a unit of weight, about 75 pounds or 34 kg) and was adorned with precious stones. David placed the crown on his own head and took a large amount of the city's treasure. 3. David also took the people of Rabbah and made them work with saws, iron picks, and axes. This was the same treatment he gave to all the cities of the Ammonites. Afterward, David and his army returned to Jerusalem. 4. Later, a war broke out in Gezer with the Philistines. During this battle, Sibbechai the Hushathite (a man from the town of Hushah) killed Sippai, one of the descendants of the giants (a group of large and powerful warriors). The Philistines were defeated. 5. Another battle with the Philistines occurred, and Elhanan, the son of Jair, killed Lahmi, the brother of Goliath the Gittite (from Gath). Lahmi's spear was enormous, similar in size to a weaver's beam (a large, sturdy wooden beam used in weaving). 6. Again, there was a war in Gath, where a giant-like man appeared. He had six fingers on each hand and six toes on each foot making a total of twenty-four digits. This man was also a descendant of the giants. 7. When this man defied Israel, Jonathan, the son of Shimea (David's brother), killed him. 8. These men were descendants of the giants from Gath, and they were all defeated by David and his warriors.

Chapter 21

175

1. Now Satan (evil/beast) stood up against Israel, and moved David to number (count) Israel. **2.** So David said to Joab and to the leaders of the people, "Go, number Israel from Beersheba to Dan, and bring the number of them to me that I may know it." **3.** And Joab answered, "May the Lord make His people a hundred times more than they are. But, my lord the king; are they not all my lord's servants (loyal subjects)? Why then does my lord require this thing? Why should he be a cause of guilt in Israel?" **4.** Nevertheless, the king's word prevailed (triumphed) against Joab. Therefore Joab departed and went throughout all Israel and came to Jerusalem. **5.** Then Joab gave the sum (total) of the number of the people to David. All Israel had one million one hundred thousand men who drew the sword (were warriors), and Judah had four hundred and seventy thousand men who drew the sword. **6.** But he did not count Levi and Benjamin among them, for the king's word was abominable (detestable) to Joab. **7.** And God was displeased (angry) with this thing; therefore, He struck (punished) Israel. **8.** So David said to God, "I have sinned greatly, because I have done this thing; but now, I pray, take away the iniquity (sin) of Your servant, for I have done very foolishly (unwisely)." **9.** And the Lord spoke to Gad, David's seer (prophet), saying, **10.** "Go and tell David, saying, 'Thus says the Lord: "I offer (present) you three things; choose one of them for yourself, that I may do it to you." '" **11.** So Gad came to David and said to him, "Thus says the Lord: 'Choose for yourself, **12.** either three years of famine (a severe shortage of food), or three months to be defeated (overcome) by your foes (enemies) with the sword of your enemies overtaking you, or else for three days the sword of the Lord—the plague (a deadly disease) in the land, with the angel (heavenly creatures) of the Lord destroying throughout all the territory of Israel.' Now consider what answer I should take back to Him who sent me." **13.** And David said to Gad, "I am in great distress (sorrow). Please let me fall into the hand of the Lord, for His mercies (compassion) are very great; but do not let me fall into the hand of man." **14.** So the Lord sent a plague upon Israel, and seventy thousand men of Israel fell. **15.** And God sent an angel to Jerusalem to destroy it. As he was destroying, the Lord looked and relented (changed His mind) of the disaster, and said to the angel who was destroying, "It is enough; now restrain (stop) your hand." And the angel of the Lord stood by the threshing floor (a place where grain is separated from its husk) of Ornan the Jebusite. **16.** Then David lifted his eyes and saw the angel of the Lord standing between earth and heaven, having in his hand a drawn sword stretched out over Jerusalem. So David and the elders, clothed in sackcloth (rough, humble clothing worn as a sign of mourning), fell on their faces. **17.** And David said to God, "Was it not I who commanded the people to be numbered? I am the one who has sinned and done evil (wrong) indeed; but these sheep (metaphor for the people), what have they done? Let Your hand, I pray, O Lord my God, be against me and my father's house, but not against Your people that they should be plagued (afflicted)." **18.** Therefore, the angel of the Lord commanded Gad to say to David that David should go and erect (build) an altar (place of worship) to the Lord on the threshing floor of Ornan the Jebusite. **19.** So David went up at the word of Gad, which he had spoken in the name of the Lord. **20.** Now Ornan turned and saw the angel; and his four sons who were with him hid (concealed) themselves, but Ornan continued threshing (separating the grain from the stalks) wheat. **21.** Then David came to Ornan, and Ornan looked and saw David. And he went out from the threshing floor, and bowed (showed respect) before David with his face to the ground. **22.** Then David said to Ornan, "Grant (give) me the place of this threshing floor, that I may build an altar on it to the Lord. You shall grant it to me at the full price (total cost), that the plague may be withdrawn from the people." **23.** And Ornan said to David, "Take it to yourself, and let my lord the king do what is good in his eyes. Look, I also give you the oxen (cattle) for burnt offerings, the threshing implements (tools for threshing) for wood, and the wheat for the grain offering; I give it all." **24.** Then King David said to Ornan, "No, but I will surely buy (purchase) it for the full price, for I will not take what is yours for the Lord, nor offer burnt offerings with that which costs me nothing." **25.** So David gave Ornan six hundred shekels (a unit of weight or currency) of gold by weight for the place. **26.** And David built there an altar to the Lord, and offered burnt offerings and peace offerings (sacrifices given in gratitude), and called (prayed) on the Lord; and He answered him from

heaven by fire on the altar of burnt offering. **27.** So the Lord commanded the angel, and he returned his sword to its sheath (protective cover). **28.** At that time, when David saw that the Lord had answered him on the threshing floor of Ornan the Jebusite, he sacrificed there. **29.** For the tabernacle (portable temple) of the Lord and the altar of the burnt offering, which Moses had made in the wilderness, were at that time at the high place (a place of worship) in Gibeon. **30.** But David could not go before it to inquire (ask) of God, for he was afraid (terrified) of the sword of the angel of the Lord.

Chapter 22

1. Then David said, "This is the house of the Lord God, and this is the altar for burnt offerings (sacrifices) for Israel. **2.** So David ordered the gathering of foreigners (aliens) who were in the land of Israel, and he appointed stonemasons (stoneworkers) to cut stones to build the house of God. **3.** David also gathered a lot of iron for the nails of the gates' doors and for the joints, and a large amount of bronze (a metal made of copper and tin) beyond measure (limit), **4.** And a great quantity of cedar wood (strong wood from a fragrant tree); for the Sidonians and those from Tyre (ancient city) brought a lot of cedar wood to David. **5.** Now David said, "My son Solomon is young and inexperienced (not skilled), and the house to be built for the Lord must be extremely magnificent (grand), famous, and glorious (honored) throughout all nations. I will now make preparations (arrangements) for it." So David made extensive (large-scale) preparations before he died. **6.** Then he called for his son Solomon and gave him the responsibility (duty) to build a house for the Lord God of Israel. **7.** And David said to Solomon: "My son, as for me, it was in my heart (mind) to build a house for the name of the Lord my God; **8.** But the word of the Lord came to me, saying, 'You have shed much blood (been involved in battles) and fought many wars; you will not build a house for my name because you have shed so much blood on the earth in My sight (view). **9.** Behold (look), a son will be born to you, who will be a man of peace (peaceful); I will give him peace from all his enemies around him. His name will be Solomon, because I will give peace and quiet (calm) to Israel during his reign (rule). **10.** He will build a house for My name, and he will be My son, and I will be his Father; I will establish (set up) his throne (royal seat) over Israel forever.' **11.** Now, my son, may the Lord be with you, and may you prosper (succeed) as you build the house of the Lord your God, as He has said to you. **12.** Only may the Lord give you wisdom (insight) and understanding (comprehension), and give you responsibility (charge) over Israel, that you may obey the law of the Lord your God. **13.** Then you will prosper if you make sure to follow the laws and rules (statutes) the Lord gave Moses for Israel. Be strong and courageous (brave); do not be afraid or discouraged (disheartened). **14.** Indeed, I have made great effort (trouble) to prepare for the house of the Lord: 100,000 talents (unit of weight) of gold and 1,000,000 talents of silver, and bronze and iron in abundance (plenty) because there is so much. I have also prepared timber (wood) and stones, and you may add to them. **15.** Moreover, there are many workers (laborers) with you: woodcutters, stonecutters, and all kinds of skilled (trained) workers for every kind of job. **16.** There is no limit to the amount of gold, silver, bronze, and iron. Get up and begin working, and may the Lord be with you." **17.** David also commanded (ordered) all the leaders (chiefs) of Israel to help his son Solomon, saying, **18.** "Isn't the Lord your God with you? Has He not given you peace (rest) on every side? For He has handed the people of the land over to me, and the land is under control (subdued) before the Lord and His people. **19.** Now set your heart (will) and soul (spirit) to seek the Lord your God. Therefore, rise up and build the sanctuary (holy place) of the Lord God, to bring the Ark of the Covenant (sacred chest) of the Lord and the holy items (sacred objects) of God into the house that is to be built for the name of the Lord."

Chapter 23

1. When David grew old and lived a full life (meaning he had lived many years), he made his son Solomon the king of Israel. **2.** He gathered all the leaders of Israel, along with the priests (religious leaders) and the Levites (members of a tribe chosen for religious service). **3.** The Levites were counted from the age of thirty and older; there were thirty-eight thousand men in total. **4.** Of these, twenty-four thousand were assigned to manage the work in the Lord's temple (the sacred building or place of worship), six thousand were appointed as officers and judges (officials who make decisions about law), **5.** Four thousand were assigned as gatekeepers (those who guard or control access to the temple), and four thousand were designated to praise the Lord using musical instruments (instruments used in worship), "which I made," David said, "to give praise." **6.** David also organized them into groups based on the sons of Levi: Gershon, Kohath, and Merari (three families within the Levite tribe). **7.** The descendants of Gershon included: Laadan and Shimei. **8.** Laadan's children were: the first Jehiel, followed by Zetham and Joel—three in total. **9.** Shimei's children were: Shelomith, Haziel, and Haran—three in total. These were the leaders (chiefs or heads) of the Laadan family. **10.** Shimei's other children were: Jahath, Zina, Jeush, and Beriah. These were four sons of Shimei. **11.** Jahath was the first, and Zizah was the second. However, Jeush and Beriah had few children, so they were counted as one family unit. **12.** The sons of Kohath were: Amram, Izhar, Hebron, and Uzziel—four in total. **13.** Amram's children were: Aaron and Moses; Aaron was set apart (chosen for a special purpose), along with his descendants, to perform sacred duties forever, including burning incense (offering prayers symbolized by burning incense) before the Lord, serving Him, and offering blessings in His name for eternity. **14.** Moses, the man of God (a prophet chosen by God), had descendants who were also counted among the Levites. **15.** Moses' children were: Gershon and Eliezer. **16.** Gershon's firstborn son was Shebuel. **17.** Eliezer's firstborn was Rehabiah. Eliezer had no other sons, but Rehabiah had many descendants. **18.** Izhar's firstborn son was Shelomith. **19.** Hebron's sons included: Jeriah (the first), Amariah (the second), Jahaziel (the third), and Jekameam (the fourth). **20.** Uzziel's sons were: Michah (the first) and Jesshiah (the second). **21.** Merari's sons were: Mahli and Mushi. Mahli's sons were: Eleazar and Kish. **22.** Eleazar died without sons, only daughters. His brothers, the sons of Kish, married his daughters. **23.** Mushi's sons were: Mahli, Eder, and Jeremoth—three in total. **24.** These were the Levites, organized by their family groups— leaders of their families, as counted by their names, and who worked in the service of the Lord's temple from the age of twenty and above. **25.** David said, "The Lord God of Israel has given His people rest (peace, freedom from conflict), so they may live in Jerusalem forever." **26.** He also declared that the Levites "will no longer carry the tabernacle (a portable sanctuary used before the temple was built) or its sacred items (items set apart for religious use)." **27.** Under David's final instructions, the Levites were counted from the age of twenty and older. **28.** Their role was to assist the descendants of Aaron in the service of the Lord's temple—working in the temple courts (areas where people gathered) and rooms (individual spaces within the temple), handling the purification (making something holy or clean) of all sacred objects, and overseeing the temple's duties. **29.** They were responsible for the showbread (bread offered to God), the fine flour for grain offerings (offerings of flour as an act of worship), unleavened cakes (flat bread made without yeast), and everything baked on a griddle (a flat cooking surface used for baking), as well as various other offerings in different forms and measures. **30.** They were to stand every morning to thank and praise the Lord, and again in the evening. **31.** They were to assist during the offerings of burnt sacrifices (offerings burned entirely on the altar) on Sabbaths (the day of rest) and New Moons (the first day of each lunar month), and during special feasts (holy celebrations), according to the prescribed regulations (rules or laws). **32.** They were also assigned to take care of the tabernacle, the holy place (the most sacred area in the temple), and to support the work of their fellow Levites, the sons of Aaron, in the service of the Lord's temple.

Chapter 24

1. These are the divisions of Aaron's descendants. Aaron's sons were Nadab, Abihu, Eleazar, and Ithamar. **2.** Nadab and Abihu died before their father and had no children; therefore, Eleazar and Ithamar served as priests. **3.** David, along with Zadok (a priest from Eleazar's line) and Ahimelech (a priest from Ithamar's line), organized them according to their service schedule. **4.** There were more leaders among the sons of Eleazar than among the sons of Ithamar, so they were divided accordingly. Among the sons of Eleazar, there were sixteen family heads, and among the sons of Ithamar, there were eight. **5.** They were divided by lot (a method of making decisions by drawing names or casting objects), with one group for Eleazar and another for Ithamar.

These groups included officials for the sanctuary (a holy or sacred place) and for God's house, drawn from both the sons of Eleazar and Ithamar. **6.** The scribe (a person who records information), Shemaiah, son of Nethanel, a Levite, recorded the names before the king, the leaders, Zadok the priest, Ahimelech the son of Abiathar (a high priest), and the heads of the priestly and Levitical families. One family from Eleazar and one from Ithamar were chosen for each division. **7.** The first lot fell to Jehoiarib, the second to Jedaiah, **8.** the third to Harim, the fourth to Seorim, **9.** the fifth to Malchijah, the sixth to Mijamin, **10.** the seventh to Hakkoz, the eighth to Abijah, **11.** the ninth to Jeshua, the tenth to Shecaniah, **12.** the eleventh to Eliashib, the twelfth to Jakim, **13.** the thirteenth to Huppah, the fourteenth to Jeshebeab, **14.** the fifteenth to Bilgah, the sixteenth to Immer, **15.** the seventeenth to Hezir, the eighteenth to Happizzez, **16.** the nineteenth to Pethahiah, the twentieth to Jehezekel, **17.** the twenty-first to Jachin, the twenty-second to Gamul, **18.** the twenty-third to Delaiah, the twenty-fourth to Maaziah. **19.** This was the schedule for their service in the house of the Lord, according to the regulations (rules) established by Aaron their father, as commanded by the Lord God of Israel. **20.** The remaining Levites were from the family of Amram: Shubael; from Shubael's line: Jehdeiah. **21.** Regarding Rehabiah, the first of his descendants was Isshiah. **22.** From the Izharites (a family group within the Levites): Shelomoth; from Shelomoth's line: Jahath. **23.** From the family of Hebron: Jeriah was the first, Amariah the second, Jahaziel the third, and Jekameam the fourth. **24.** From the family of Uzziel: Michah; from Michah's line: Shamir. **25.** Michah's brother was Isshiah; from Isshiah's line: Zechariah. **26.** The sons of Merari were Mahli and Mushi; from Jaaziah's line: Beno. **27.** The descendants of Merari through Jaaziah were Beno, Shoham, Zaccur, and Ibri. **28.** From Mahli: Eleazar, who had no sons. **29.** From Kish: the son of Kish was Jerahmeel. **30.** The sons of Mushi were Mahli, Eder, and Jerimoth. These were the descendants of the Levites, organized according to their family groups. **31.** They also cast lots in the same way as the sons of Aaron did, in the presence of King David, Zadok, Ahimelech, and the leaders of the priestly and Levitical families. The heads of the families did exactly as their younger relatives did.

Chapter 25

1. David and the army commanders appointed some of the descendants of Asaph, Heman, and Jeduthun to serve in the temple. Their role was to prophesy, or speak under divine inspiration, using harps, stringed instruments, and cymbals. The total number of musicians chosen for this service was: **2.** From the sons of Asaph, the following were named: Zaccur, Joseph, Nethaniah, and Asharelah. These sons of Asaph worked under the leadership of their father, Asaph, who prophesied according to the king's commands. **3.** The sons of Jeduthun included: Gedaliah, Zeri, Jeshaiah, Shimei, Hashabiah, and Mattithiah—six in total—who were led by their father, Jeduthun. They prophesied with harps, giving thanks and praising the Lord. **4.** The sons of Heman were: Bukkiah, Mattaniah, Uzziel, Shebuel, Jerimoth, Hananiah, Hanani, Eliathah, Giddalti, Romamti-Ezer, Joshbekashah, Mallothi, Hothir, and Mahazioth. **5.** These were the sons of Heman, the king's seer, who served as a prophet of God. Heman had fourteen sons and three daughters, all of whom were dedicated to honoring and praising God's power. **6.** All of these musicians served under their fathers in the Lord's house, playing cymbals, stringed instruments, and harps to worship God. Asaph, Jeduthun, and Heman carried out their duties under the authority of the king. **7.** In total, the number of skilled musicians, including their brothers who were trained in the songs of the Lord, was 288. **8.** They cast lots to determine their duties, regardless of whether the task was great or small, and whether they were teachers or students. **9.** The first lot drawn for Asaph's descendants went to Joseph; the second to Gedaliah, with his brothers and sons—twelve in total. **10.** The third lot was for Zaccur, with his sons and brothers—twelve. **11.** The fourth lot was for Jizri, with his sons and brothers—twelve. **12.** The fifth lot was for Nethaniah, with his sons and brothers—twelve. **13.** The sixth lot was for Bukkiah, with his sons and brothers—twelve. **14.** The seventh lot was for Jesharelah, with his sons and brothers—twelve. **15.** The eighth lot was for Jeshaiah, with his sons and brothers—twelve. **16.** The ninth lot was for Mattaniah, with his sons and brothers—twelve. **17.** The tenth lot was for Shimei, with his sons and brothers—twelve. **18.** The eleventh lot was for Azarel, with his sons and brothers—twelve. **19.** The twelfth lot was for Hashabiah, with his sons and brothers—twelve. **20.** The thirteenth lot was for Shubael, with his sons and brothers—twelve. **21.** The fourteenth lot was for Mattithiah, with his sons and brothers—twelve. **22.** The fifteenth lot was for Jeremoth, with his sons and brothers—twelve. **23.** The sixteenth lot was for Hananiah, with his sons and brothers—twelve. **24.** The seventeenth lot was for Joshbekashah, with his sons and brothers—twelve. **25.** The eighteenth lot was for Hanani, with his sons and brothers—twelve. **26.** The nineteenth lot was for Mallothi, with his sons and brothers—twelve. **27.** The twentieth lot was for Eliathah, with his sons and brothers—twelve. **28.** The twenty-first lot was for Hothir, with his sons and brothers—twelve. **29.** The twenty-second lot was for Giddalti, with his sons and brothers— twelve. **30.** The twenty-third lot was for Mahazioth, with his sons and brothers—twelve. **31.** The twenty-fourth lot was for Romamti-Ezer, with his sons and brothers—twelve.

Chapter 26

1. Regarding the divisions of the gatekeepers (those assigned to guard the gates): from the Korahites (descendants of Korah), Meshelemiah, son of Kore, from the descendants of Asaph (a Levite family). **2.** The sons of Meshelemiah were: Zechariah, his firstborn; Jediael, the second; Zebadiah, the third; Jathniel, the fourth; **3.** Elam, the fifth; Jehohanan, the sixth; Eliehoenai, the seventh. **4.** The sons of Obed-Edom were: Shemaiah, his firstborn; Jehozabad, the second; Joah, the third; Sacar, the fourth; Nethanel, the fifth; **5.** Ammiel, the sixth; Issachar, the seventh; Peulthai, the eighth. God had blessed him. **6.** Shemaiah, his son, had children who became leaders (chiefs) of their father's household because they were men of exceptional ability. **7.** The sons of Shemaiah were: Othni, Rephael, Obed, and Elzabad. Their brothers, Elihu and Semachiah, were also skilled (competent) men. **8.** All of these were descendants of Obed-Edom, along with their sons and relatives. They were strong, capable (able) men for the work, totaling sixty-two in Obed-Edom's line. **9.** Meshelemiah had sons and brothers, eighteen men capable of service. **10.** Hosah, from the Merarite (another Levite family) clan, had sons: Shimri, the first (although not his firstborn, his father appointed him as such), **11.** Hilkiah, the second; Tebaliah, the third; Zechariah, the fourth. In total, Hosah's family numbered thirteen. **12.** These individuals formed the divisions of the gatekeepers, among the chief men (leaders), with responsibilities similar to their brothers, serving in the Lord's house. **13.** They cast lots (used a random selection method) to determine the assignment for each gate, both for the smaller and the larger gates, based on their family groups. **14.** The lot for the East Gate was assigned to Shelemiah. They then cast lots for his son Zechariah, a wise advisor, and his lot fell to the North Gate. **15.** The South Gate was assigned to Obed-Edom, with his sons overseeing the storehouse (storage area). **16.** The West Gate was given to Shuppim and Hosah, with the Shallecheth Gate on the ascending highway, with watchmen (guards) stationed opposite each other. **17.** On the East side, six Levites served; on the North side, four each day; on the South side, four each day; and for the storehouse, two by two. **18.** For the Parbar (a location near the temple) to the west, there were four on the highway and two stationed at the Parbar. **19.** These were the divisions of the gatekeepers from the sons of Korah and Merari. **20.** Among the Levites, Ahijah was in charge of the treasuries (storage for sacred items) of the house of God and the dedicated items. **21.** The descendants of Laadan, from the Gershonites (a Levite family), were heads of their families: Jehieli, **22.** And the sons of Jehieli—Zetham and Joel, his brother—were responsible for overseeing the treasuries of the house of the Lord. **23.** The Amramites, Izharites, Hebronites, and Uzzielites: **24.** Shebuel, son of Gershom, son of Moses, was in charge of the treasuries. **25.** His relatives, from the family of Eliezer, included Rehabiah, his son; Jeshaiah, his son; Joram, his son; Zichri, his son; and Shelomith, his son. **26.** Shelomith and his family managed all the treasuries of the dedicated items, which had been consecrated (made sacred) by King David, the leaders of the clans, and the commanders of thousands and hundreds, as well as the army captains. **27.** Some of the spoils (treasures taken in battle) from the battles they had fought were also dedicated to the upkeep of the Lord's house. **28.** Everything consecrated by Samuel the seer (prophet), Saul son of Kish, Abner son of Ner, and Joab son of Zeruiah was under the care of Shelomith and his family. **29.** Chenaniah and his

sons from the Izharite family were assigned as officials and judges (authorities) for Israel outside of Jerusalem. **30.** From the Hebronite clan, Hashabiah and his brothers—1,700 capable men—were in charge of Israel west of the Jordan River, overseeing all matters related to the Lord's service and the king's affairs. **31.** Jerijah was the head of the Hebronites, based on his ancestral (family) lineage. In the fortieth year of King David's reign, they were inspected, and capable men were found at Jazer in Gilead. **32.** His relatives numbered 2,700 capable men, who were appointed as officials over the Reubenites, Gadites, and the half-tribe of Manasseh, responsible for all matters concerning God and the king.

Chapter 27

1. The people of Israel, divided by their families, with the heads of each household, commanders of thousands and hundreds, and their officers, served the king in all matters concerning the military divisions. These divisions rotated every month throughout the year, each consisting of 24,000 men. **2.** Jashobeam the son of Zabdiel was in charge of the first division during the first month, and his division had 24,000 soldiers. **3.** He belonged to the family of Perez and was the chief of all the military commanders for that month. **4.** Dodai the Ahohite (a member of a particular clan) led the second division for the second month, with Mikloth as his assistant. His division also numbered 24,000. **5.** Benaiah, son of Jehoiada the priest, was the commander for the third month, and his division had 24,000 men. **6.** This Benaiah was a mighty warrior, one of the Thirty (a special group of elite soldiers), and he led them. His son, Ammizabad, served as an officer in his division. **7.** Asahel, Joab's brother, led the fourth division for the fourth month, followed by his son, Zebadiah. His division had 24,000 men. **8.** The fifth division, for the fifth month, was led by Shamhuth the Izrahite, and it too numbered 24,000. **9.** Ira, son of Ikkesh the Tekoite, led the sixth division in the sixth month, with 24,000 men. **10.** Helez the Pelonite, from the tribe of Ephraim, was in charge of the seventh division for the seventh month, and his division had 24,000. **11.** Sibbechai the Hushathite, from the clan of the Zarhites, led the eighth division in the eighth month, also with 24,000 soldiers. **12.** The ninth division, led by Abiezer the Anathothite, from the tribe of Benjamin, had 24,000 men. **13.** Maharai the Netophathite, from the Zarhites, commanded the tenth division for the tenth month, with 24,000 men. **14.** The eleventh division for the eleventh month was led by Benaiah the Pirathonite, from the tribe of Ephraim, and had 24,000 soldiers. **15.** Heldai the Netophathite, from Othniel, led the twelfth division for the twelfth month, and his division was 24,000 strong. **16.** In addition, there were officers over the tribes of Israel. Eliezer the son of Zichri was in charge of the Reubenites, while Shephatiah the son of Maachah oversaw the Simeonites. **17.** Hashabiah the son of Kemuel was responsible for the Levites, and Zadok took charge of the Aaronites (descendants of Aaron, the priestly family). **18.** Elihu, one of David's brothers, led the tribe of Judah, and Omri the son of Michael was in charge of Issachar. **19.** Ishmaiah the son of Obadiah led the tribe of Zebulun, and Jerimoth the son of Azriel was in charge of Naphtali. **20.** Hoshea the son of Azaziah was over the children of Ephraim, and Joel the son of Pedaiah led the half-tribe of Manasseh. **21.** Iddo the son of Zechariah oversaw the half-tribe of Manasseh in Gilead, while Jaasiel the son of Abner was responsible for the tribe of Benjamin. **22.** Azarel the son of Jeroham led the tribe of Dan. These were the leaders of the tribes of Israel. **23.** However, David did not take a census of those who were 20 years old and younger because the Lord had promised to multiply Israel like the stars in the sky. **24.** Joab, the son of Zeruiah, began the census but did not complete it because God's anger was stirred against Israel due to this action. As a result, the numbers were not recorded in the official records of King David's reign. **25.** Azmaveth the son of Adiel was responsible for the king's treasuries, and Jehonathan the son of Uzziah was in charge of the storehouses, which included fields, cities, villages, and fortresses. **26.** Ezri the son of Chelub was responsible for the agricultural work, including managing the fields for planting. **27.** Shimei the Ramathite oversaw the vineyards, while Zabdi the Shiphmite was in charge of the wine production from the vineyards. **28.** Baal-Hanan the Gederite was in charge of the olive and sycamore trees in the lowland areas, and Joash was responsible for the storage of oil. **29.** Shitrai the Sharonite was in charge of the herds grazing in the Sharon plain, and Shaphat the son of Adlai oversaw the herds in the valleys. **30.** Obil the Ishmaelite was in charge of the camels, Jehdeiah the Meronothite managed the donkeys, and Jaziz the Hagrite supervised the flocks. All these individuals were officials overseeing King David's property. **31.** Jehonathan, David's uncle, was a trusted advisor, a wise man, and a scribe (a person who writes or copies documents by hand). Jehiel the son of Hachmoni was a companion to the king's sons. **32.** Ahithophel was the king's counselor, and Hushai the Archite was his close friend and confidant. **33.** After Ahithophel, Jehoiada the son of Benaiah took over as the next counselor, followed by Abiathar. The commander of the king's army was Joab.

Chapter 28

1. David gathered all the leaders of Israel at Jerusalem: the officers of the tribes, the captains of the divisions who served the king, the captains over thousands and hundreds, the stewards (managers) who managed the king's and his sons' possessions, along with the officials, the brave warriors, and all the mighty men of valor (courageous warriors). **2.** Then King David stood up and addressed them: "Listen to me, my brothers and my people. I had planned in my heart to build a resting place for the ark of God's covenant and for His footstool (a place where God's feet rest, a metaphor for His throne), and I made preparations to build it. **3.** But God told me, 'You will not build a house for My name because you have been a warrior and have shed blood.' **4.** However, the Lord God of Israel chose me over my father's entire house to be king over Israel forever. He selected Judah to be the ruler, and within Judah, the house of my father. Among all my brothers, He chose me to be king over all of Israel. **5.** Of all my sons (for the Lord has blessed me with many sons), He has chosen my son Solomon to sit on the throne of the kingdom of the Lord over Israel. **6.** God told me, 'Your son Solomon will build My house and My courts because I have chosen him to be My son, and I will be his Father. **7.** I will establish his kingdom forever, as long as he remains faithful to follow My commands and laws, just as he is doing today.' **8.** Now, in front of all Israel, the assembly of the Lord, and in the presence of our God, be careful to follow all the commandments of the Lord your God, so that you may possess this good land and pass it down as an inheritance to your children forever. **9.** "As for you, my son Solomon, acknowledge the God of your father, and serve Him with a sincere heart and a willing mind, for the Lord examines all hearts and knows the desires of every thought. If you seek Him, you will find Him; but if you turn away from Him, He will reject you forever. **10.** Remember this: the Lord has chosen you to build a house for the sanctuary (a holy or sacred place). Be strong and do it." **11.** Then David gave Solomon the detailed plans for the vestibule (entrance hall), its rooms, its treasuries, its upper chambers, its inner chambers, and the place where the mercy seat (the golden cover of the ark of the covenant) would be placed; **12.** and the plans for all the courts of the house of the Lord, all the surrounding chambers, the treasuries of the house of God, and the treasuries for the dedicated offerings (things set apart for God); **13.** He also gave plans for the division of the priests and the Levites, the work of serving in the house of the Lord, and all the instruments used in service in the house of the Lord. **14.** David gave specific weights of gold for all the articles to be used in every kind of service in the temple, and silver for the articles to be used in service. **15.** He gave detailed instructions for the lampstands, specifying the weight of gold for the lampstands and their lamps, and the same for silver, according to the requirements for each lampstand. **16.** He gave gold for the tables of the showbread, specifying the weight for each table, and silver for the tables made of silver. **17.** David also gave pure gold for the forks, basins, pitchers, and golden bowls, with gold by weight for every single bowl. For the silver bowls, he gave silver by weight for each one. **18.** He also gave refined gold for the altar of incense (a place where incense was burned), and for the construction of the chariot of gold cherubim (angelic beings) that would overshadow the ark of the Lord's covenant. **19.** David said, 'All this the Lord has made me understand, written down by His hand upon me, regarding the plans for all these works.' **20.** David told Solomon, "Be strong and courageous, and carry out the plan; do not fear or be discouraged, for the Lord God—my God—will be with you. He will not leave you or forsake you until you have finished all the work for the service of the house of the Lord. **21.** Here are the divisions of the priests and Levites for all the service of the house of God. Every willing craftsman (skilled worker) will assist you in every kind of work, and every kind of service. The leaders and all the people will fully support you."

Chapter 29

1. King David then addressed the entire assembly, saying: "My son Solomon, whom God has chosen alone, is still young and lacks experience. The task ahead is great because the temple is not meant for people but for the Lord God. **2.** I have worked hard to prepare everything for the house of my God: gold for gold items, silver for silver items, bronze for bronze items, iron for iron items, wood for wood items, onyx stones, stones to be set, sparkling stones of various colors, all kinds of precious stones, and plenty of marble slabs. **3.** Additionally, because I deeply love the house of my God, I have given even more than what I prepared for the holy house. I've offered my own special treasure of gold and silver: **4.** Three thousand talents (a unit of weight) of gold, from the gold of Ophir (a place famous for its high-quality gold), and seven thousand talents of refined silver to cover the walls of the buildings. **5.** Gold for gold things, and silver for silver things, and for all kinds of work to be done by skilled workers. Who then is willing to dedicate themselves to the Lord today?" **6.** The leaders of the families, the leaders of the tribes of Israel, the commanders of thousands and hundreds, along with the officers in charge of the king's work, gave willingly. **7.** They donated for the work of the house of God: five thousand talents and ten thousand darics (ancient Persian coins) of gold, ten thousand talents of silver, eighteen thousand talents of bronze (a mixture of copper and tin), and one hundred thousand talents of iron. **8.** Anyone who had precious stones gave them to the treasury of the house of the Lord, placing them in the hands of Jehiel the Gershonite (a descendant of Gershon, a Levitical clan). **9.** The people rejoiced because they had given willingly, with a sincere heart, and King David was also very happy. **10.** So, David blessed the Lord before the whole assembly, saying: "Blessed are You, Lord God of Israel, our Father, forever and ever. **11.** Yours, O Lord, is greatness, power, glory, victory, and majesty. Everything in heaven and on earth belongs to You. The kingdom is Yours, and You are exalted as ruler over all. **12.** Riches and honor come from You, and You reign over everything. In Your hand is power and strength; it is in Your hand to make someone great and to give strength to all. **13.** Now, our God, we thank You and praise Your glorious name. **14.** But who am I, and who are my people, that we should be able to offer so willingly? Everything comes from You, and we have only given You what comes from Your hand. **15.** We are foreigners (strangers or pilgrims) and strangers before You, just as all our ancestors were. Our days on earth are like a shadow, and we have no lasting hope. **16.** O Lord our God, all this wealth we've prepared to build a house for Your holy name comes from You, and everything is Yours. **17.** I know, my God, that You test the heart and take pleasure in integrity (honesty or moral uprightness). As for me, with a sincere heart, I have willingly offered all these things, and now I'm happy to see Your people, who are gathered here, offer willingly to You. **18.** O Lord God of Abraham, Isaac, and Israel, our ancestors, keep this intention in the hearts of Your people forever, and turn their hearts towards You. **19.** And give my son Solomon a loyal heart to keep Your commands, laws, and decrees, to do all these things, and to build the temple I have provided for." **20.** Then David told the assembly, "Now bless the Lord your God." So all the assembly blessed the Lord God of their ancestors, bowed their heads, and worshiped the Lord and the king. **21.** They made sacrifices to the Lord and offered burnt offerings to the Lord the next day: a thousand bulls, a thousand rams, a thousand lambs, along with their drink offerings and sacrifices in abundance for all Israel. **22.** They ate and drank before the Lord with great joy that day. They made Solomon, David's son, king for the second time and anointed him before the Lord as the leader, and Zadok as the priest. **23.** Then Solomon sat on the throne of the Lord as king instead of his father David, and he prospered; and all Israel obeyed him. **24.** All the leaders, mighty men, and all the sons of King David humbled themselves before King Solomon. **25.** So the Lord greatly honored Solomon in the sight of all Israel, giving him a royal majesty such as no king had ever had before him in Israel. **26.** Thus, David, the son of Jesse (King David's father), ruled over all Israel. **27.** The length of David's reign over Israel was forty years: seven years in Hebron (a city), and thirty-three years in Jerusalem. **28.** He died at a good old age, full of days, wealth, and honor; and his son Solomon succeeded him as king. **29.** The acts of King David, from beginning to end, are written in the book of Samuel the seer (prophet), the book of Nathan the prophet, and the book of Gad the seer, **30.** With all his reign, his power, and the events that happened to him, to Israel, and to all the kingdoms of the lands.

12 – Chronicles 2

Chapter 1

1. Solomon, the son of David (the former king of Israel), was firmly established as the king of Israel. The Lord, his God, was with him, greatly exalting and honoring him. **2.** Solomon spoke to all of Israel, including the commanders of thousands and hundreds (military leaders), the judges (those who handled legal matters), and every leader from the tribes of Israel, the heads of their families. **3.** Solomon, along with the entire assembly of Israel, went to the high place at Gibeon (a city), where the tabernacle of the Lord was located. This was the same tabernacle that Moses, the servant of the Lord, had built in the wilderness. **4.** However, David had moved the Ark of God (the sacred chest containing the tablets of the law) from Kirjath Jearim (a town in Israel) to the place he had prepared for it in Jerusalem (the capital city of Israel), where he set up a tent for it. **5.** The bronze altar (an altar made of bronze) that Bezalel, the son of Uri (a skilled craftsman), had made, was placed in front of the tabernacle of the Lord. Solomon and the assembly gathered there to seek the Lord. **6.** Solomon went up to the bronze altar before the Lord at the tabernacle and offered a thousand burnt offerings (in which the entire animal is burnt in fire) upon it. **7.** That night, God appeared to Solomon and said, "Ask! What shall I give you?" **8.** Solomon answered God, "You have shown great mercy to David my father and have made me king in his place. **9.** Now, O Lord God, let Your promise to my father David be fulfilled, for You have made me king over a people as numerous as the dust of the earth. **10.** Please give me wisdom and knowledge so that I can lead this great people of Yours, for who is able to govern such a vast and numerous people?" **11.** God said to Solomon, "Because this was in your heart, and you have not asked for riches, wealth, honor, the life of your enemies, nor for a long life, but have asked for wisdom and knowledge to govern My people over whom I have made you king, **12.** wisdom and knowledge are granted to you. And I will give you riches, wealth, and honor such as no king before you has had, nor shall any after you have the like." **13.** So Solomon came to Jerusalem from the high place at Gibeon, from before the tabernacle of meeting, and began to reign over Israel. **14.** Solomon gathered chariots and horsemen, and he had 1,400 chariots and 12,000 horsemen. He stationed them in the chariot cities and with him in Jerusalem. **15.** The king made silver and gold as common in Jerusalem as stones, and he made cedar wood as abundant as sycamore trees in the lowland areas. **16.** Solomon had horses imported from Egypt and Keveh (a region), and the king's merchants bought them at the market price in Keveh. **17.** They also acquired and imported from Egypt a chariot for 600 shekels of silver and a horse for 150 shekels. These were then exported by Solomon's agents to the kings of the Hittites and the kings of Syria.

Chapter 2

1. Solomon decided to build a temple for the name of the LORD and a royal house for himself, establishing a grand place of worship and a palace. **2.** He chose 70,000 men to carry heavy loads, 80,000 to cut stones from the mountains, and 3,600 overseers to manage and direct the workers. **3.** Solomon sent a message to Hiram (the king of Tyre, a city-state known for its skilled craftsmen), saying, "Just as you assisted my father David by sending cedar trees for his house, do the same for me." **4.** He explained, "I am building a temple for the Lord my God, where we will offer incense, the showbread, and daily burnt offerings—on Sabbaths, New Moons, and special feasts. This will be a lasting ordinance for Israel." **5.** Solomon declared, "The temple I am building will be magnificent, for our God is greater than all other gods." **6.** But Solomon recognized the difficulty, saying, "Who can build a temple for God, since even the heavens and the highest heavens cannot contain Him? Who am I to build a temple, other than to offer sacrifices before Him?" **7.** Therefore, he requested, "Send me a man skilled in working with gold, silver, bronze, iron, purple, crimson, and blue fabric. He should be able to engrave and work alongside the skilled craftsmen I have here in Judah and Jerusalem, whom my father

David arranged." **8.** He also asked for cedar, cypress, and algum wood from Lebanon (a region known for its high-quality timber), for he knew that Hiram's men were experts in cutting timber in Lebanon, and Solomon's servants would assist them. **9.** Solomon emphasized, "The temple I am building will be great and glorious, so we need an abundant supply of wood for it." **10.** In return, Solomon promised Hiram, "I will provide 20,000 kors of wheat, 20,000 kors of barley, 20,000 baths of wine, and 20,000 baths of oil for your woodcutters as payment." **11.** Hiram responded in writing to Solomon, saying, "Because the Lord loves His people, He has made you king over them." **12.** Hiram continued, "Blessed be the Lord God of Israel, who made heaven and earth! He has given King David a wise son, full of wisdom and understanding, who will build a temple for the Lord and a royal house for himself." **13.** Hiram then sent Huram (a skilled craftsman from Tyre, son of a woman from the tribe of Dan, and his father a man of Tyre), a master artisan. Huram was expert in gold, silver, bronze, iron, stone, wood, and fine fabrics, and he could make engravings or carry out any project given to him. **14.** "Huram will work with your skilled craftsmen and those of my lord David your father," Hiram added, offering his finest workman to the temple project. **15.** Hiram agreed to send the wheat, barley, oil, and wine that Solomon had requested for the workers. **16.** "We will cut as much wood from Lebanon as you need," Hiram promised, "and send it by rafts to Joppa (a port city). You can then bring it up to Jerusalem." **17.** Solomon then took a census of all the foreign workers in Israel, based on the count David had done earlier. There were 153,600 such workers in total. **18.** Solomon assigned 70,000 of them to carry burdens, 80,000 to cut stones in the mountains, and 3,600 overseers to direct the work and ensure the project was completed successfully.

Chapter 3

1. Solomon began constructing the house of the Lord in Jerusalem, on Mount Moriah, the same place where the Lord had appeared to David, his father, at the threshing floor of Ornan the Jebusite. **2.** He started the building on the second day of the second month in the fourth year of his reign as king of Israel. **3.** The foundation Solomon lay for the temple was sixty cubits long (about 90 feet) and twenty cubits wide (about 30 feet), following the traditional measurement used by the previous generations. **4.** The vestibule in front of the sanctuary was twenty cubits long (about 30 feet) and as wide as the temple itself. Its height was one hundred and twenty cubits (about 180 feet), and Solomon overlaid the interior with pure gold. **5.** The larger room was paneled with cypress wood and overlaid with fine gold. The carvings on the wood depicted palm trees and chainwork designs. **6.** Solomon decorated the house with precious stones for beauty, and the gold used in the temple came from Parvaim, a region known for its fine gold. **7.** He overlaid the beams, doorposts, walls, and doors of the temple with gold, and he also carved cherubim into the walls. **8.** Solomon made the Most Holy Place, which was twenty cubits long and twenty cubits wide, the same dimensions as the entire temple. He overlaid it with six hundred talents (about 22,500 pounds) of fine gold. **9.** The nails used for construction weighed fifty shekels (about 1.25 pounds) of gold, and the upper area of the temple was also covered in gold. **10.** In the Most Holy Place, Solomon made two cherubim, carved from wood, and overlaid them with gold. **11.** The wings of these cherubim spanned twenty cubits in total. Each cherub had one wing stretching five cubits, touching the wall of the room, and the other wing five cubits, touching the wing of the other cherub. **12.** The second cherub also had one wing five cubits long, touching the wall of the room, and the other wing five cubits long, touching the first cherub's wing. **13.** These cherubim, with their wings spanning a total of twenty cubits, stood on their feet and faced inward, toward each other. **14.** Solomon also made a veil for the temple, woven from blue, purple, crimson, and fine linen, with cherubim embroidered into it. **15.** Solomon created two large pillars, each thirty-five cubits (about 52 feet) high, and placed a five-cubit (about 7.5 feet) capital (decorative top) on each pillar. **16.** He made chains of wreaths for the top of each pillar, similar to those in the inner sanctuary, and placed one hundred pomegranates on the chains. **17.** Solomon set up the two pillars in front of the temple, one on the right (named Jachin) and one on the left (named Boaz). These names symbolized strength and stability.

Chapter 4

1. Solomon made a large bronze altar, measuring twenty cubits in length, twenty cubits in width, and ten cubits in height (a cubit is about 18 inches). 2. He also created the Sea, a large basin of bronze, measuring ten cubits across, perfectly round, five cubits high, with a thirty-cubit circumference. 3. Under the Sea, there were twelve bronze oxen (symbolizing strength) arranged in two rows, ten oxen per cubit, surrounding the basin. 4. The Sea rested on the twelve oxen—three facing north, three facing west, three facing south, and three facing east, with their backs inward. 5. The Sea was a handbreadth thick, and its rim was shaped like the delicate edge of a lily flower. It could hold three thousand baths (a measure of liquid). 6. Solomon also made ten lavers (large basins), placing five on the right and five on the left, for washing the offerings, while the Sea was reserved for the priests' washing. 7. He made ten golden lampstands, placing five on the right and five on the left side of the temple, all designed according to specific instructions. 8. Additionally, Solomon crafted ten tables and placed five on the right and five on the left side, along with one hundred gold bowls for offerings. 9. Solomon built the court of the priests, the large outer courtyard, and made doors for the court, overlaying them with bronze. 10. He set the Sea in the southeast corner of the temple complex, on the right side, facing outward. 11. Huram (a skilled craftsman from Tyre) made the pots, shovels, and bowls, completing the work for King Solomon in the house of God. 12. Huram made two large bronze pillars, each topped with a bowl-shaped capital, covered with a bronze network and decorated with pomegranates (symbolic of abundance). 13. The pomegranates were arranged in two rows, adorning the networks of the pillars, each covering the capitals with intricate detail. 14. Huram also made carts with lavers upon them, designed for carrying water and other temple utensils. 15. One large Sea, supported by twelve oxen, was placed on a cart, completing the massive bronze work for the temple. 16. Huram made a variety of bronze items, including pots, shovels, forks, and other utensils needed for the temple's worship rituals. 17. These items were cast in clay molds in the plain of Jordan (a region between Succoth and Zeredah, near the Jordan River). 18. The amount of bronze used was so vast that its weight was never recorded or measured. 19. Solomon provided all the temple's furnishings: the gold altar, the tables for the showbread (sacred bread offerings), and the utensils for worship. 20. He crafted golden lampstands and their lamps, made to burn continually in the temple before the inner sanctuary, as prescribed. 21. The golden flowers, lamps, and wick-trimmers, were all intricately crafted, were made of the finest pure gold. 22. Solomon made bowls, ladles, and censers, all of pure gold, and overlaid the doors of the temple's inner sanctuary and main hall with gold.

Chapter 5

1. When all the work Solomon had done for the house of the Lord was completed, he brought in the things his father David (former king of Israel) had dedicated, such as silver, gold, and all the furnishings, placing them in the treasuries of God's house. 2. Solomon gathered the elders of Israel, the heads of the tribes, and the chief fathers of Israel in Jerusalem, to bring the Ark of the Covenant (the sacred chest with God's laws) from the City of David (also called Zion). 3. So, all the men of Israel came together with the king during the feast in the seventh month (the month of Tishri, when the Feast of Tabernacles was celebrated). 4. All the elders of Israel came, and the Levites (priests from the tribe of Levi) carried the Ark of the Covenant. 5. They brought up the Ark, the Tabernacle of Meeting (a portable place of worship), and all its holy furnishings. The priests and Levites carried them. 6. Solomon, along with the assembly of Israel standing before the Ark, offered countless sheep and oxen, too many to be counted. 7. The priests placed the Ark of the Covenant in its designated spot in the inner sanctuary, the Most Holy Place, under the wings of the cherubim (angelic beings in the temple). 8. The cherubim spread their wings over the Ark, covering it and its poles with their wings. 9. The poles of the Ark extended, so their ends could be seen from the holy place in front of the inner sanctuary, though they could not be seen from outside. They remain in place to this day. 10. Inside the Ark were only the two tablets that Moses (the leader of Israel) placed there at Horeb (a mountain where God gave Moses the Ten Commandments) when the Lord made His covenant with the Israelites after their exodus from Egypt. 11. When the priests came out of the Most Holy Place, having sanctified themselves (set themselves apart for holy service), they did not keep their divisions. 12. The Levite singers, including those from the families of Asaph, Heman, and Jeduthun (worship leaders), along with their sons and brothers, stood at the east side of the altar. They were dressed in white linen, with cymbals, stringed instruments, and harps, accompanied by one hundred and twenty priests playing trumpets. 13. When the trumpeters and singers united as one, making one sound to praise and thank the Lord, and when they lifted their voices with trumpets, cymbals, and other instruments of music, they praised the Lord, saying, "For He is good, for His mercy endures forever." At that moment, the house of the Lord was filled with a cloud. 14. The priests could not continue their ministry because the cloud filled the house of God. The glory of the Lord had filled the temple.

Chapter 6

1. Then Solomon spoke: "The LORD said He would dwell in the dark cloud (divine presence, visible manifestation)." 2. "I have surely built you an exalted (magnificent, glorious) house, and a place for you to dwell in forever (eternally, without end)." 3. Then the king turned around and blessed the whole assembly (gathering, group) of Israel while all the assembly of Israel stood. 4. He said: "Blessed be the Lord God (deity, supreme being) of Israel, who has fulfilled with His hands what He spoke with His mouth to my father David (David, former king of Israel), saying, 5. 'Since the day that I brought My people out of the land of Egypt (Egypt, ancient land in northeast Africa), I have not chosen a city from any tribe of Israel to build a house for My name, nor have I chosen any man to be a ruler over My people Israel.' 6. "But I have chosen Jerusalem (capital city of Israel) that My name may be there; and I have chosen David (David, the former king) to be over My people Israel." 7. "It was in the heart (desire, intention) of my father David to build a temple (sacred place of worship) for the name of the Lord God of Israel." 8. "But the Lord said to my father David, 'Although it was in your heart to build a temple for My name, you did well in considering it.'" 9. "Nevertheless, you will not build the temple; your son, who comes from your body (descendant), will build it for My name." 10. "Thus, the Lord has fulfilled His word (promise), and I have taken the place of my father David on the throne (seat of power) of Israel, as He promised; I have built the temple for the name of the Lord God of Israel." 11. "And there I have placed the ark (sacred chest) in which is the covenant (agreement, promise) of the Lord, which He made with the children of Israel." 12. Solomon stood before the altar (raised platform) of the Lord in front of the entire assembly (gathering) of Israel and spread out his hands. 13. (For Solomon had made a bronze platform (raised surface) five cubits (measurement of length) long, five cubits wide, and three cubits high, and set it in the midst of the court (open area). He stood on it, knelt down, and spread out his hands toward heaven.) 14. He said: "Lord God of Israel, there is no God in heaven or on earth like You, who keeps Your covenant (promise) and mercy (love, kindness) with Your servants who walk before You with all their hearts." 15. "You have kept the promise (commitment) You made to Your servant David, my father; You spoke with Your mouth and fulfilled it with Your hand (action), as it is today." 16. "Now, Lord God of Israel, fulfill Your word (promise) to Your servant David, my father, saying, 'You will not fail to have a man sit before Me on the throne (seat of kingship) of Israel, provided your sons are careful (attentive) to walk in My ways, as you have walked before Me.'" 17. "Now, O Lord God of Israel, let Your word come true, which You have spoken to Your servant David." 18. "But will God indeed dwell with men (people) on earth? Behold, the heaven and the heaven of heavens (highest heaven) cannot contain You. How much less this temple which I have built!" 19. "Yet, regard (look favorably upon) the prayer (petition) of Your servant and his supplication (earnest request), O Lord my God, and listen to the cry and prayer Your servant is making before You." 20. "Let Your eyes be open toward this temple day and night, toward the place where You said You would put Your name, and hear the prayer Your servant prays toward this place." 21. "Hear the supplications (requests) of Your servant and of Your people Israel when they pray toward this place. Hear from heaven (Your dwelling place), and when You hear, forgive." 22. "If anyone sins (breaks Your law) against his neighbor and is forced to take an oath (solemn promise), and comes and takes an oath before Your altar in this temple, 23. Then hear from heaven, and act. Judge Your servants, bringing retribution (punishment) on the wicked by

bringing his actions upon his own head, and justifying the righteous by rewarding him according to his righteousness." **24.** "If Your people Israel are defeated by an enemy (foe) because they have sinned (disobeyed) against You, and they return and confess Your name, praying and pleading (begging) with You in this temple, **25.** Then hear from heaven and forgive the sin (wrongdoing) of Your people Israel, and bring them back to the land (territory) You gave to them and their ancestors." **26.** "When the heavens are shut up (closed) and there is no rain because they have sinned (gone astray) against You, when they pray toward this place and confess Your name, and turn from their sin (wrongdoing) because You have afflicted (caused suffering) them, **27.** Then hear from heaven and forgive the sin (transgression) of Your servants, Your people Israel, that You may teach them the good way (correct path) to walk in, and send rain on Your land (territory), which You have given to Your people as an inheritance." **28.** "When there is famine (food shortage) in the land, pestilence (disease), blight (plant disease), mildew (fungus), locusts (insects), or grasshoppers (small insects); when their enemies besiege (surround) them in their cities; or whatever plague (disaster) or sickness comes, **29.** whatever prayer (appeal) or supplication (request) is made by anyone, or by all Your people Israel, when each person knows their own burden (personal sorrow) and grief (deep sadness) and spreads out their hands toward this temple, **30.** Then hear from heaven, Your dwelling place, and forgive. Give to each person according to their ways, as You know their hearts (for You alone know the hearts of all mankind)." **31.** "That they may fear (respect) You, walking in Your ways (paths) as long as they live in the land You gave to our ancestors." **32.** "Moreover, when a foreigner (non-Israelite) who is not of Your people Israel comes from a distant land because of Your great name and Your mighty hand (power) and Your outstretched arm (strength), and they pray in this temple, **33.** then hear from heaven, Your dwelling place, and do whatever the foreigner asks of You, so that all the peoples of the earth may know Your name and fear You, just as Your people Israel do, and that they may know that this temple I have built is called by Your name." **34.** "When Your people go out to battle (fight) against their enemies, wherever You send them, and when they pray to You toward this city (Jerusalem), which You have chosen, and the temple (house of worship) I have built for Your name, **35.** Then hear from heaven their prayer and supplication, and uphold their cause." **36.** "When they sin (fail) against You (for there is no one who does not sin), and You become angry with them and deliver them to the enemy (adversary), and they are taken captive (seized) to a land far or near, **37.** yet when they return to their senses (repent) in the land where they were taken captive, and repent, praying and pleading (begging) with You in the land of their captivity, saying, 'We have sinned, we have done wrong, and we have acted wickedly,' **38.** and when they turn to You with all their heart and soul (full devotion) in the land of their captivity, where they were taken captive, and pray toward the land You gave to their ancestors, the city You have chosen, and the temple (house of worship) I have built for Your name, **39.** Then hear from heaven, Your dwelling place, their prayer and supplication. Uphold their cause and forgive Your people who have sinned against You." **40.** "Now, my God, I pray, let Your eyes be open and Your ears attentive (focused) to the prayer made in this place." **41.** "Now arise (stand), O Lord God, to Your resting place (dwelling), You and the ark (sacred chest) of Your strength (power). Let Your priests (spiritual leaders), O Lord God, be clothed with salvation (divine protection), and let Your saints (faithful people) rejoice in goodness." **42.** "O Lord God, do not turn away the face of Your Anointed (Messiah, chosen one); remember the mercies (kindness, compassion) of Your servant David."

Chapter 7

1. After Solomon finished praying, fire descended from heaven and consumed the burnt offerings and sacrifices. The glory of the Lord filled the temple. **2.** The priests could not enter the house of the Lord, because the glory (splendor) of the Lord had filled His house (temple). **3.** When all the children of Israel saw the fire come down and the glory (divine radiance) of the Lord on the temple, they bowed down with their faces to the ground on the pavement (stone surface) and worshiped, praising the Lord, saying, "For He is good, For His mercy (love) endures forever." **4.** Then the king and all the people offered sacrifices before the Lord. **5.** King Solomon offered a sacrifice of twenty-two thousand bulls (cattle) and one hundred and twenty thousand sheep. So, the king and all the people consecrated the house (temple) of God. **6.** The priests performed their duties; the Levites (members of the tribe of Levi, priests and musicians) also played instruments made for the music of the Lord, which King David had designed. They praised, saying, "For His mercy (love) endures forever." The priests blew trumpets opposite them while all Israel stood. **7.** Solomon consecrated (set apart as holy) the middle of the court (area) in front of the Lord's house, where he offered burnt offerings and the fat (best portions) of the peace offerings. The bronze altar (altar made of bronze) that Solomon had made could not hold all the offerings, so the area was consecrated for these sacrifices. **8.** At that time, Solomon kept the feast (celebration) for seven days, and all Israel joined him. A very great assembly (crowd) gathered, from the entrance of Hamath (a northern boundary) to the Brook of Egypt (southern boundary). **9.** On the eighth day, they held a sacred assembly (holy gathering), for they had observed the dedication (consecration) of the altar for seven days and celebrated the feast for seven days. **10.** On the twenty-third day of the seventh month, Solomon sent the people away to their tents, joyful and glad in heart for all the good things the Lord had done for David, for Solomon, and for His people Israel. **11.** Thus, Solomon completed the house (temple) of the Lord and the king's house (palace); he successfully fulfilled all that he had set out to do in the house of the Lord and in his own house. **12.** Then the Lord appeared to Solomon by night and said to him, "I have heard your prayer and have chosen this place for myself as a house of sacrifice." **13.** "When I shut up heaven (withhold rain) and there is no rain, or command the locusts (insects that destroy crops) to devour the land, or send pestilence (disease) among my people, **14.** If My people who are called by My name will humble (submit themselves) themselves, pray, seek My face (desire a relationship with Me), and turn from their wicked ways (sinful actions), then I will hear from heaven, forgive their sin, and heal their land." **15.** "Now My eyes will be open, and My ears will be attentive to prayer made in this place." **16.** "For now I have chosen and sanctified (made holy) this house, that My name may be there forever. My eyes and My heart will be there perpetually (forever)." **17.** "As for you, if you walk before Me as your father David (former king of Israel) walked, and do according to all that I have commanded you, and keep My statutes (laws) and My judgments (decrees), **18.** Then I will establish the throne (rule) of your kingdom, as I promised your father David, saying, 'You shall not fail to have a man as ruler in Israel.'" **19.** "But if you turn away and forsake (abandon) My statutes and commandments which I have set before you, and go and serve other gods (false gods), worshiping them, **20.** then I will uproot (remove) them from My land, which I have given them. This house which I have sanctified for My name I will cast out of My sight, and it will become a proverb (saying) and a byword (expression of contempt) among all peoples." **21.** "As for this house (temple), which is exalted (rose up in honor), everyone who passes by it will be astonished and will ask, 'Why has the Lord done this to this land and this house?'" **22.** "Then they will answer, 'because they forsook (abandoned) the Lord God of their ancestors, who brought them out of the land of Egypt (Egypt, the land of their captivity), and embraced (accepted) other gods, worshiped and served them. Therefore, He has brought all this calamity (disaster) upon them.'"

Chapter 8

1. After twenty years, during which Solomon had built the house of the Lord and his own house, **2.** The cities that Hiram (the king of Tyre) had given to Solomon, Solomon built them and settled the children of Israel there. **3.** Solomon also went to Hamath Zobah (a city in Syria) and captured it. **4.** He built Tadmor (a city) in the wilderness and all the storage cities he constructed in Hamath. **5.** He built Upper Beth Horon and Lower Beth Horon (fortified cities), with walls, gates, and bars for protection. **6.** He also built Baalath (a city) and all the storage cities in his dominion, including the chariot cities and cities for the cavalry (horse soldiers), and whatever Solomon desired to build in Jerusalem, Lebanon, and throughout his entire kingdom. **7.** The remaining people from the Hittites (an ancient people), Amorites (Canaanite people), Perizzites (villagers), Hivites, and Jebusites (tribes that were not Israelite) **8.**—the descendants who remained in the land after the Israelites had settled there—Solomon conscripted them for forced labor (they were made to work as servants), and this practice continued to this day. **9.** However, Solomon did not make the Israelites servants for his work; some of them were men of war, captains of his officers, and leaders of his chariots and cavalry. **10.** Others were chiefs of Solomon's officials: two hundred and fifty who oversaw the people. **11.** Solomon brought the daughter of Pharaoh (the Egyptian king) from the City of David (Jerusalem) to the house he had built for her, saying, "My wife shall not live in the house of David, king of Israel, because the places where the Ark of the Lord has been are holy." **12.** Solomon then offered burnt offerings on the altar of the Lord, which he had built before the vestibule (entrance hall of the temple). **13.** He followed the daily ritual of offerings, as prescribed by Moses, for the Sabbaths, New Moons, and the three annual feasts—the Feast of Unleavened Bread, the Feast of Weeks, and the Feast of Tabernacles. **14.** Solomon arranged the divisions of the priests for their duties and appointed the Levites (tribe responsible for temple service) to serve before the priests according to their daily duties. He also assigned the gatekeepers to each gate, as David, the man of God, had commanded. **15.** The priests and Levites followed the king's instructions regarding all matters, including the management of the temple treasures. **16.** The entire work of Solomon was orderly and well-managed, from the day the foundation of the Lord's house was laid until its completion. Thus, the house of the Lord was finished. **17.** Solomon then went to Ezion Geber (a port city) and Elath (a coastal city) on the shore of the Red Sea, in the land of Edom (a kingdom southeast of Israel). **18.** Hiram sent him ships through his servants, who were skilled in the sea. They sailed with Solomon's servants to Ophir (a distant region known for wealth), where they acquired four hundred and fifty talents of gold and brought it to King Solomon.

Chapter 9

1. When the queen of Sheba (a queen from a distant region in Africa) heard about the fame of Solomon, she came to Jerusalem to test his wisdom with hard questions. She brought a large entourage, camels carrying spices, abundant gold, and precious stones. **2.** She spoke with Solomon about everything that was in her heart, and Solomon answered every one of her questions. There was nothing too difficult for him to explain. **3.** When the queen saw the Wisdom of Solomon, the palace he had built, **4.** The food on his table, the seating arrangement of his servants, their attire, the clothing of his cupbearers, and the magnificent way he entered the house of the Lord, she was left breathless. **5.** She said to the king, "The report I heard in my own land about your wisdom and your words was true. **6.** However, I didn't believe it until I came and saw it for myself. And indeed, I was told only half of the greatness of your wisdom; you exceed what I had heard. **7.** Your men are fortunate, and your servants are blessed, for they stand continually before you and hear your wisdom! **8.** Praise the Lord your God, who has delighted in you and set you on His throne to rule His people Israel. Because God loves Israel and has established them forever, He made you king over them to maintain justice and righteousness." **9.** The queen of Sheba gave the king 120 talents of gold, vast quantities of spices, and precious stones—none like them had ever been brought into the kingdom before. **10.** Hiram's servants, along with Solomon's men, brought gold from Ophir (a region known for its riches), along with algum wood (a valuable wood) and precious stones. **11.** Solomon used the algum wood to make walkways for the temple and his palace, as well as harps and stringed instruments for the singers. There was nothing like these in the land of Judah. **12.** Solomon gave the queen of Sheba everything she desired, even more than what she had brought. She returned to her country with her servants. **13.** Every year, 666 talents of gold came to Solomon, **14.** Besides what the traveling merchants and traders brought. All the kings of Arabia and the governors brought gold and silver to Solomon. **15.** Solomon made 200 large shields of hammered gold, using 600 shekels of gold for each shield. **16.** He also made 300 shields of hammered gold, with 300 shekels of gold for each shield. The king placed them in the House of the Forest of Lebanon (a grand building in Jerusalem). **17.** Solomon also made a magnificent throne of ivory, overlaid with pure gold. **18.** The throne had six steps, with a golden footstool attached. There were armrests on either side of the throne, and two lions stood beside them. **19.** Twelve lions stood at the top of the six steps, one lion on each step. There had never been anything like this in any other kingdom. **20.** All Solomon's drinking vessels were made of gold, and all the vessels in the House of the Forest of Lebanon were pure gold. None were made of silver, for silver was considered of little value during Solomon's reign. **21.** Solomon's ships went to Tarshish (a distant trade city on the Mediterranean) with Hiram's servants. Every three years, the merchant ships returned, bringing gold, silver, ivory, apes, and monkeys. **22.** Solomon became wealthier and wiser than any king on earth. **23.** All the kings of the earth came to Solomon to hear the wisdom God had placed in his heart. **24.** Each king brought a gift: silver and gold articles, clothing, armor, spices, horses, and mules, all according to a fixed rate year by year. **25.** Solomon had 4,000 stalls for horses and chariots and 12,000 horsemen. He stationed them in chariot cities and with the king in Jerusalem. **26.** Solomon ruled over all the kings from the Euphrates River (a river in the east) to the land of the Philistines (a region in the west), and as far as the border of Egypt. **27.** Solomon made silver as common in Jerusalem as stones, and he made cedar trees as abundant as sycamore trees in the lowlands. **28.** Solomon received horses from Egypt and from all other lands. **29.** The rest of Solomon's acts, both the beginning and the end of his reign, are written in the book of Nathan the prophet, in the prophecy of Ahijah the Shilonite (a prophet), and in the visions of Iddo the seer regarding Jeroboam (son of Nebat). **30.** Solomon reigned in Jerusalem for forty years over all Israel. **31.** Solomon died and was buried in the City of David (Jerusalem), his father's city. His son Rehoboam succeeded him as king.

Chapter 10

1. Rehoboam went to Shechem (an ancient city of southern Levant), because all of Israel had gone there to make him king. **2.** When Jeroboam (a former official who had fled from Solomon) heard about this, he returned from Egypt, where he had been living after fleeing from King Solomon. **3.** The people sent for him, and Jeroboam, along with all Israel, came to Rehoboam, saying, **4.** "Your father (Solomon) made our yoke (burden) heavy. Now, please lighten the burdensome service your father placed on us, and we will serve you." **5.** Rehoboam answered them, "Return to me in three days." So the people went away. **6.** Then King Rehoboam consulted the elders (wise men who had served his father Solomon), who had been his father's counselors while Solomon was alive, asking, "How do you advise me to respond to these people?" **7.** The elders replied, "If you are kind to these people and speak kindly to them, they will serve you forever." **8.** But Rehoboam rejected the advice of the elders and consulted the young men who had grown up with him and who now stood before him. **9.** He asked them, "What do you advise me to say to the people who have spoken to me, saying, 'lighten the yoke your father put on us'?" **10.** The young men who had grown up with him answered, "This is what you should say to the people: 'My little finger shall be thicker than my father's waist. **11.** And now, whereas my father made your yoke heavy, I will add to it. My father chastised (punished) you with whips, but I will punish you with scorpions (more severe punishment).'" **12.** So, Jeroboam and all the people came to Rehoboam on the third day, as the king had instructed, saying, "Come back to me on the third day." **13.** The king answered them roughly. He rejected the advice of the elders, **14.** And instead, he spoke to them according to the advice of the young men, saying, "My father made your yoke heavy, but I will add to it. My father punished you with whips, but I will punish you with scorpions!" **15.** The king did not listen to the people, for the turn of events was from God to fulfill the word He had spoken through the prophet Ahijah (a prophet from Shiloh) to Jeroboam, the son of Nebat. **16.** When all Israel saw that the king did not listen to them, the people answered the king, saying, "What share do we have in David (the former king)? We have no inheritance in the son of Jesse (David's son)! Every man to your tents, O Israel! Now look after your own house, O David!" So all Israel went to their homes. **17.** But Rehoboam still ruled over the people of Judah (the southern kingdom of Israel). **18.** Rehoboam then sent Hadoram (the official in charge of forced labor) to the people, but they stoned him with stones, and he died. So Rehoboam quickly fled in his chariot to Jerusalem. **19.** Thus, Israel has been in rebellion against the house of David (the royal family of David) to this day.

Chapter 11

1. When Rehoboam arrived in Jerusalem, he gathered 180,000 chosen warriors from the tribes of Judah and Benjamin (two tribes of Israel) to fight against Israel and restore the kingdom to himself. **2.** But the word of the Lord came to Shemaiah (a prophet of God), saying, **3.** "Speak to Rehoboam, son of Solomon (Solomon was the former king of Israel), king of Judah, and to all Israel in Judah and Benjamin, saying, **4.** 'Thus says the Lord: "Do not go up to fight against your fellow Israelites! Let everyone return to their own home, for this is my will." '"So they obeyed the word of the Lord and turned back from pursuing Jeroboam (the leader of Israel). **5.** Rehoboam stayed in Jerusalem and began to build fortified cities in Judah for defense. **6.** He built cities such as Bethlehem, Etam, and Tekoa (towns in Judah), **7.** as well as Beth Zur, Sochoh, and Adullam, **8.** Gath, Mareshah, and Ziph, **9.** Adoraim, Lachish, and Azekah, **10.** Zorah, Aijalon, and Hebron, all in Judah and Benjamin, to fortify them. **11.** He strengthened the strongholds, put captains in charge, and stocked the cities with food, oil, and wine for future needs. **12.** He also placed shields and spears in each city, making them very strong. Judah and Benjamin (two tribes of Israel) remained loyal to him. **13.** The priests and Levites (members of the priestly tribe) from all Israel came to Rehoboam in Judah. **14.** This was because Jeroboam and his sons had rejected the Levites from serving as priests to the Lord. **15.** Jeroboam appointed priests for the high places (idolatrous sites), for demons (false gods), and for the golden calf idols he had made. **16.** After the Levites left Israel, people from all the tribes of Israel who truly sought the Lord God of Israel came to Jerusalem to sacrifice to the Lord God of their ancestors. **17.** These people strengthened the kingdom of Judah, making Rehoboam, son of Solomon, strong for three years, because they followed the ways of David and Solomon during that time. **18.** Rehoboam married Mahalath, the daughter of Jerimoth (son of David) and Abihail (daughter of Eliab, son of Jesse). **19.** Mahalath bore him three sons: Jeush, Shamariah, and Zaham. **20.** Later, Rehoboam married Maacah, the granddaughter of Absalom (David's son), and she bore him Abijah, Attai, Ziza, and Shelomith. **21.** Rehoboam loved Maacah more than all his other wives and concubines (secondary wives); he had eighteen wives and sixty concubines, and they gave him twenty-eight sons and sixty daughters. **22.** Rehoboam made Abijah, the son of Maacah, the chief among his sons, intending to make him king. **23.** He acted wisely, distributing some of his sons throughout the territories of Judah and Benjamin, to every fortified city, and providing them with abundant provisions. He also sought many wives for them.

Chapter 12

1. When Rehoboam had firmly established (made secure) his kingdom and had grown stronger, he forsook the law of the Lord, and all of Israel joined him in his disobedience. **2.** In the fifth year of King Rehoboam's reign, Shishak, the king of Egypt, came against Jerusalem because Israel had transgressed (sinned) against the Lord. He brought twelve hundred chariots, sixty thousand horsemen, and an innumerable number of soldiers from Egypt, including the Lubim, Sukkiim, and Ethiopians. **3.** Shishak captured the fortified cities of Judah and advanced toward Jerusalem. **4.** At this point, Shemaiah, the prophet of God, came to Rehoboam and the leaders of Judah, who had gathered in Jerusalem due to Shishak's invasion, and said, "The Lord says: 'You have abandoned Me, so I have allowed you to be defeated by Shishak.'" **5.** The king and the leaders of Judah humbled themselves, admitting, "The Lord is righteous (just in His actions)." **6.** When the Lord saw their humility, He spoke to Shemaiah, saying, "Because they humbled themselves, I will not destroy them completely, but I will grant them a measure of deliverance. My wrath will not be poured out on Jerusalem through Shishak." **7.** However, Judah will still serve (be under the control of) Shishak, so that they may distinguish the service of the Lord from the service of other nations." **8.** As promised, Shishak, the king of Egypt, attacked Jerusalem, taking all the treasures of the house of the Lord and the treasures of the king's palace, including the gold shields that Solomon had made. **9.** In their place, King Rehoboam made bronze shields, which were given to the captains of the guard who protected the entrance to the king's palace. **10.** Whenever the king entered the house of the Lord, the guards would bring out the bronze shields, and after the service, they would return them to the guardroom. **11.** Because Rehoboam humbled himself, the Lord's anger turned away, and He did not destroy him completely. Things also went well in Judah. **12.** Rehoboam continued to strengthen his rule in Jerusalem. He was 41 years old when he became king and reigned for

17 years in Jerusalem, the city the Lord had chosen out of all the tribes of Israel to place His name. Rehoboam's mother was Naamah, an Ammonite woman. **13.** Despite this, Rehoboam did evil because he did not set his heart to seek the Lord. **14.** The acts of Rehoboam, both the early and later parts of his reign, are written in the book of Shemaiah the prophet and Iddo the seer (a prophet who saw visions). **15.** During his reign, there were constant wars between Rehoboam and Jeroboam, the king of Israel. **16.** Eventually, Rehoboam rested with his ancestors and was buried in the City of David. His son Abijah succeeded him as king.

Chapter 13

1. In the eighteenth year of King Jeroboam (Jeroboam was the first king of Israel), Abijah (Abijah was the son of Rehoboam) became king over Judah. **2.** He reigned for three years in Jerusalem. His mother's name was Michaiah, the daughter of Uriel from Gibeah (Gibeah was a city in Benjamin). There was war between Abijah and Jeroboam. **3.** Abijah set the battle in order with an army of 400,000 choice men (elite warriors); Jeroboam also drew up his battle formation with 800,000 choice men, mighty men of valor (brave soldiers). **4.** Then Abijah stood on Mount Zemaraim (Zemaraim was a mountain in Ephraim), which is in the mountains of Ephraim (Ephraim was a tribe), and said, "Hear me, Jeroboam and all Israel: **5.** Should you not know that the Lord God of Israel gave the dominion over Israel to David (David was the second king of Israel) forever, to him and his sons, by a covenant of salt (a binding agreement)? **6.** Yet Jeroboam the son of Nebat (Jeroboam was originally a servant of Solomon), the servant of Solomon, the son of David, rose up and rebelled against his lord. **7.** Then worthless rogues (dishonest men) gathered to him and strengthened themselves against Rehoboam, the son of Solomon, when Rehoboam was young and inexperienced and could not withstand them. **8.** And now you think to withstand the kingdom of the Lord, which is in the hands of the sons of David (David's descendants); and you are a great multitude, and with you are the gold calves (idols made by Jeroboam) which Jeroboam made for you as gods. **9.** Have you not cast out the priests of the Lord, the sons of Aaron (Aaron was Moses' brother), and the Levites (Levites were from the tribe of Levi), and made for yourselves priests like the peoples of other lands? **10.** But as for us, the Lord is our God, and we have not forsaken Him; and the priests who minister to the Lord are the sons of Aaron, and the Levites attend to their duties. **11.** And they burn to the Lord every morning and every evening burnt sacrifices (complete offerings) and sweet incense (fragrant offerings); they also set the showbread (holy bread) in order on the pure gold table, and the lampstand of gold with its lamps to burn every evening; for we keep the command of the Lord our God, but you have forsaken Him. **12.** Now look, God Himself is with us as our head, and His priests with sounding trumpets (musical instruments) to sound the alarm against you. O children of Israel (descendants of Jacob), do not fight against the Lord God of your fathers, for you shall not prosper! **13.** But Jeroboam caused an ambush (a surprise attack) to go around behind them; so they were in front of Judah, and the ambush was behind them. **14.** And when Judah looked around, to their surprise, the battle line was at both front and rear; and they cried out to the Lord, and the priests sounded the trumpets. **15.** Then the men of Judah gave a shout, and as they shouted, God struck Jeroboam and all Israel before Abijah and Judah. **16.** And the children of Israel fled before Judah, and God delivered them into their hand. **17.** Then Abijah and his people struck them with a great slaughter; so 500,000 choice men (elite soldiers) of Israel fell slain. **18.** Thus the children of Israel were subdued (defeated) at that time, and the children of Judah prevailed, because they relied on the Lord God of their fathers. **19.** And Abijah pursued Jeroboam and took cities from him: Bethel (Bethel was a city in northern Israel) with its villages, Jeshanah (Jeshanah was a city in the tribe of Simeon) with its villages and Ephraim (Ephraim was a city in the Ephraim region) with its villages. **20.** So Jeroboam did not recover strength again in the days of Abijah; and the Lord struck him, and he died. **21.** But Abijah grew mighty, married fourteen wives, and begot twenty-two sons and sixteen daughters. **22.** Now the rest of the acts of Abijah, his ways, and his sayings are written in the annals of the prophet Iddo (Iddo was a prophet who recorded the history of Israel).

Chapter 14

1 Abijah (the son of Rehoboam) rested with his fathers and was buried in the City of David (Jerusalem). His son Asa became king in his place, and during his reign, the land had peace for ten years. 2 Asa did what was good and right in the eyes of the Lord his God. 3 He removed the altars of foreign gods (idols) and the high places, tore down sacred pillars (stone structures), and cut down the wooden images. 4 He commanded Judah to seek the Lord God of their fathers and to obey His law and commandments. 5 Asa also removed the high places and incense altars (where offerings to idols were burned) from all the cities of Judah. As a result, the kingdom enjoyed peace under his rule. 6 He built fortified cities (strong, protected cities) in Judah, for the land was at rest, and there was no war during those years because the Lord had granted him peace. 7 Asa said to Judah, "Let us build these cities and surround them with walls, towers, gates, and bars (locking gates), for the land is still before us. Since we have sought the Lord our God, He has given us rest on all sides." So, they built and prospered. 8 Asa had an army of 300,000 men from Judah who carried shields and spears, and 280,000 men from Benjamin (a tribe) who carried shields and drew bows; all these men were mighty warriors (brave and strong). 9 Then Zerah the Ethiopian (a king from Africa) came out against them with an army of a million men and 300 chariots (war vehicles), and he came to Mareshah (a city in Judah). 10 Asa went out to meet him, and they arranged their troops in battle formation in the Valley of Zephathah at Mareshah. 11 Asa cried out to the Lord his God, saying, "Lord, it is nothing for You to help, whether with many or those who have no power. Help us, O Lord our God, for we rest on You, and in Your name, we go against this vast army. O Lord, You are our God; do not let man prevail over You!" 12 So the Lord struck the Ethiopians before Asa and Judah, and they fled. 13 Asa and his army pursued them as far as Gerar (a city), and the Ethiopians were defeated, unable to recover because they were broken before the Lord and His army. They took a large amount of spoil (treasure and goods). 14 They also defeated all the cities surrounding Gerar, for the fear of the Lord came upon them, and they plundered all the cities, gathering exceedingly much spoil. 15 They attacked the livestock enclosures, carrying off large numbers of sheep and camels, and returned to Jerusalem (the capital city of Judah).

Chapter 15

1. The Spirit of God came upon Azariah, the son of Oded (a prophet). 2. He went to meet King Asa and said, "Listen to me, Asa, and all of Judah and Benjamin (the tribes of Israel). The Lord will be with you as long as you remain faithful to Him. If you seek Him, He will be found by you; but if you turn away from Him, He will turn away from you. 3. For a long time, Israel has been without the true God, without a teaching priest (a priest who instructs in God's laws), and without the law (God's commands). 4. But when they were in trouble, they sought the Lord God of Israel, and He was found by them. 5. At that time, there was no peace for anyone who traveled, and no peace in the cities. Great turmoil (chaos) came upon all the inhabitants of the lands. 6. One nation was destroyed by another, and city by city was overthrown, for God allowed them to face difficulties (adversity). 7. But you, be strong and do not be weak in your efforts, for your work will be rewarded!" 8. When Asa heard these words and the prophecy from Oded, he took courage, removed the idols (false gods) from all the land of Judah and Benjamin, and from the cities he had taken in the mountains of Ephraim (a region of Israel). He also restored the altar of the Lord that stood before the vestibule (entrance) of the temple. 9. Then Asa gathered all of Judah and Benjamin, along with those from Ephraim, Manasseh, and Simeon (other tribes), for many had joined him when they saw that the Lord his God was with him. 10. They assembled at Jerusalem in the third month, during the fifteenth year of Asa's reign. 11. On that day, they offered 700 bulls and 7,000 sheep to the Lord from the spoils of their battles. 12. They made a covenant (promise) to seek the Lord God of their ancestors with all their heart and soul. 13. Anyone who refused to seek the Lord God of Israel was to be put to death, whether they were small or great, man or woman. 14. They swore an oath before the Lord, shouting with a loud voice, accompanied by trumpets and ram's horns (used for celebration and worship). 15. All of Judah rejoiced at this vow, for they had sworn with all their heart and sought God with all their soul. He was found by them, and the Lord gave them peace on all sides. 16. Asa also removed Maachah (his mother) from her position as queen mother because she

had made an obscene image of Asherah (a Canaanite fertility goddess). Asa destroyed her idol, burned it, and crushed it by the Brook Kidron (a valley near Jerusalem). 17. However, the high places (sites of idol worship) were not removed from Israel, but Asa remained faithful to God throughout his life. 18. He brought into the house of God the silver, gold, and utensils (sacred items) that his father and he had dedicated. 19. There was no war until the thirty-fifth year of Asa's reign.

Chapter 16

1. In the thirty-sixth year of Asa's reign, King Baasha of Israel (the northern kingdom of Israel) came up against Judah and began building Ramah (a fortified city), intending to prevent anyone from leaving or entering Judah under King Asa's rule. 2. Asa took silver and gold from the treasuries of the house of the Lord (the temple) and the king's house and sent it to Ben-Hadad, the king of Syria (a neighboring nation), who lived in Damascus, saying, 3. "Let there be a treaty (agreement) between us, as there was between my father and your father. I am sending you silver and gold; break your alliance with Baasha, king of Israel, so that he will withdraw from attacking me." 4. Ben-Hadad listened to King Asa's request and sent his army commanders to attack the cities of Israel. They struck Ijon, Dan, Abel Maim, and all the storage cities in the territory of Naphtali (one of the tribes of Israel). 5. When King Baasha of Israel heard this, he stopped building Ramah and ceased his work on the fortifications. 6. Then Asa gathered all of Judah and they took the stones and timber Baasha had used for Ramah's construction, and with them, they built the cities of Geba and Mizpah (two cities in Judah). 7. At that time, Hanani, a prophet (seer), came to Asa, king of Judah, and said to him: "Because you relied on the king of Syria and not on the Lord your God, the army of the king of Syria has escaped from your grasp. 8. Didn't the mighty armies of the Ethiopians and Lubim (a people from Africa) with many chariots and horsemen, pose a great threat? Yet, when you trusted the Lord, He gave you victory over them. 9. For the eyes of the Lord search throughout the earth to strengthen those whose hearts are fully committed to Him. You have acted foolishly in this, and from now on, you will face wars." 10. Asa became angry with the prophet Hanani and put him in prison because he was enraged by his words. Asa also oppressed some of the people at that time. 11. The acts of King Asa, from beginning to end, are written in the Book of the Kings of Judah and Israel. 12. In the thirty-ninth year of his reign, Asa became seriously ill in his feet, and his condition worsened. However, in his illness, he did not seek the Lord, but rather consulted physicians (doctors at that time). 13. So Asa died in the forty-first year of his reign. 14. They buried him in his own tomb, which he had prepared in the City of David (Jerusalem). They laid him on a bed filled with spices and various ointments, and made a very large fire in his honor.

Chapter 17

1. Then Jehoshaphat (the son of Asa, king of Judah) reigned in his place and strengthened himself against Israel (the northern kingdom). 2. He placed troops in all the fortified cities of Judah and stationed garrisons in the land of Judah and in the cities of Ephraim (the region captured by his father Asa). 3. The Lord was with Jehoshaphat because he followed the ways of his father David (David was the former king) and did not seek the Baals (false gods), 4. But sought the God of his father and obeyed His commandments, not following the practices of Israel. 5. As a result, the Lord established Jehoshaphat's kingdom, and all Judah gave him gifts. He became wealthy and honored. 6. Jehoshaphat's heart was delighted in the ways of the Lord, and he removed the high places (places of idol worship) and Asherah poles (wooden images used for worship) from Judah. 7. In the third year of his reign, he sent his leaders—Ben-Hail, Obadiah, Zechariah, Nethanel, and Michaiah—to teach in the cities of Judah. 8. He also sent Levites (members of the tribe of Levi who served in religious duties): Shemaiah, Nethaniah, Zebadiah, Asahel, Shemiramoth, Jehonathan, Adonijah, Tobijah, and Tobadonijah, along with Elishama and Jehoram, the priests. 9. They taught in Judah, bringing with them the Book of the Law of the Lord (the scriptures), and they traveled through all the cities of Judah, teaching the people. 10. The fear of the Lord fell on all the kingdoms around Judah, so they did not make war against Jehoshaphat. 11. Some of the Philistines (a neighboring people) brought Jehoshaphat presents and silver as tribute, while the Arabians

(people from the Arabian Peninsula) brought him flocks—7,700 rams and 7,700 male goats. **12.** Jehoshaphat grew stronger and stronger, and he built fortresses and storage cities in Judah. **13.** He had much property in the cities of Judah, and his army in Jerusalem consisted of mighty men of valor (strong and brave soldiers). **14.** The following is the count of their numbers, according to their ancestral houses: From Judah, the captains of thousands: Adnah, the captain, with 300,000 mighty men of valor; **15.** And next to him was Jehohanan, the captain, with 280,000 men; **16.** And next to him was Amasiah, the son of Zichri, who willingly offered himself to the Lord, with 200,000 mighty men. **17.** From Benjamin (the tribe of Benjamin): Eliada, a mighty man of valor, with 200,000 men armed with bows and shields; **18.** and next to him was Jehozabad, with 180,000 men prepared for war. **19.** These were the men who served the king, in addition to those stationed in the fortified cities throughout all Judah.

Chapter 18

1. Jehoshaphat, king of Judah, was prosperous, enjoying great wealth and honor. He formed an alliance with Ahab, king of Israel, by marriage, strengthening both their kingdoms. **2.** After several years, Jehoshaphat went to visit Ahab in Samaria (the capital city of Israel). Ahab prepared a grand feast with many sheep and oxen for Jehoshaphat and his men, hoping to gain his support for an attack on Ramoth Gilead (a city in the region of Gilead). **3.** Ahab asked, "Will you join me in fighting against Ramoth Gilead?" Jehoshaphat answered, "I am as you are, and my people are as your people. We will stand by you in this war." **4.** Jehoshaphat, seeking God's guidance, replied, "Please inquire of the Lord through His prophets today to know His will." **5.** Ahab gathered 400 prophets (spokespersons for God) and asked them, "Should we go to war against Ramoth Gilead, or should I refrain?" They answered, "Go up, for God will give you victory over it." **6.** But Jehoshaphat, sensing something was amiss, asked, "Is there not still a prophet of the Lord here, that we may inquire of Him?" **7.** Ahab reluctantly replied, "There is one man, Micaiah, son of Imla, by whom we can inquire of the Lord, but I hate him because he never prophesies anything good about me, only evil." Jehoshaphat rebuked Ahab, saying, "The king should not speak like that." **8.** Ahab then ordered one of his officers to quickly bring Micaiah, the son of Imla. **9.** Both kings, wearing their royal robes (robes symbolizing their authority), sat on their thrones at the entrance of the gate in Samaria, while the prophets were prophesying before them. **10.** Zedekiah, son of Chenaanah, made iron horns and declared, "Thus says the Lord: 'With these you shall push the Syrians back until they are destroyed.'" **11.** All the prophets prophesied in the same manner, saying, "Go up to Ramoth Gilead and prosper, for the Lord will give it into your hands." **12.** The messenger sent to call Micaiah warned him, "The other prophets are all speaking encouraging words to the king. Please speak the same way, and encourage him as they have." **13.** Micaiah replied firmly, "As the Lord lives, whatever my God says, that is what I will speak." **14.** When Micaiah arrived, Ahab asked him, "Micaiah, should we go to war against Ramoth Gilead, or should we refrain?" Micaiah answered, mockingly, "Go and prosper, for they will be delivered into your hand." **15.** Ahab, frustrated, asked, "How many times must I make you swear to tell me only the truth in the name of the Lord?" **16.** Micaiah then said, "I saw all Israel scattered on the mountains like sheep without a shepherd. The Lord said, 'These people have no master. Let each return home in peace.'" **17.** Ahab turned to Jehoshaphat and said, "Did I not tell you that he would prophesy nothing good about me, only bad?" **18.** Micaiah continued, "Therefore, hear the word of the Lord: I saw the Lord sitting on His throne, with all the hosts of heaven standing on His right and left." **19.** The Lord asked, "Who will persuade Ahab, king of Israel, to go up to Ramoth Gilead and fall there?" Several spirits came forward, offering their advice. **20.** One spirit said, "I will persuade him." The Lord asked, "How will you do this?" **21.** The spirit replied, "I will be a lying spirit in the mouths of all his prophets." The Lord said, "You will succeed in persuading him. Go and do so." **22.** Micaiah boldly declared, "Look, the Lord has put a lying spirit (a supernatural force meant to deceive) in the mouths of these prophets, and He has declared disaster upon you, Ahab." **23.** Zedekiah, son of Chenaanah, approached Micaiah and slapped him on the cheek, asking, "Which way did the spirit of the Lord go from me to speak to you?" **24.** Micaiah replied, "You will find out on the day you go into an inner room (a place

of hiding) to hide." **25.** Ahab then ordered, "Take Micaiah, return him to Amon, the governor of the city, and to Joash, the king's son. **26.** Tell them, 'The king says, "Put this man in prison, and feed him only bread and water until I return safely from battle."'" **27.** Micaiah responded, "If you return safely, the Lord has not spoken through me." And he added, "Take note, all you people!" **28.** Ahab and Jehoshaphat went up to Ramoth Gilead, preparing for battle. **29.** Ahab said to Jehoshaphat, "I will disguise myself in battle, but you wear your royal robes." Ahab disguised himself, and they both went into battle. **30.** The king of Syria (the enemy king) had commanded his chariot commanders, "Fight only with the king of Israel, regardless of whether they are small or great." **31.** When the chariot commanders saw Jehoshaphat, they thought he was the king of Israel and surrounded him to attack. But Jehoshaphat cried out, and the Lord helped him by diverting their attention. **32.** When the chariot commanders realized it was not the king of Israel, they stopped pursuing Jehoshaphat. **33.** A man shot an arrow at random and struck Ahab, king of Israel, between the joints of his armor (the protective gear worn in battle). Ahab told the driver of his chariot, "Turn around and take me out of the battle, for I am wounded." **34.** The battle continued to rage, but Ahab propped himself up in his chariot, facing the Syrians until evening. By sunset, he died from his wounds.

Chapter 19

1. When Jehoshaphat, the king of Judah, returned safely to his palace in Jerusalem, he was met by Jehu, the son of Hanani, a seer (prophet), who came to deliver a warning. **2.** Jehu confronted the king, asking why he was helping those who do evil and showing favor to those who oppose the Lord. He told Jehoshaphat that, because of this, God's anger (wrath) was upon him. **3.** However, Jehu acknowledged that there was still goodness in Jehoshaphat, noting that he had removed the idols (false gods) from the land and had set his heart on seeking the Lord God. **4.** Jehoshaphat continued his work in Jerusalem and went out again to the people, traveling from Beersheba (a city in the southern part of Judah) to the hills of Ephraim (a region in Israel), calling them to return to worship the Lord, the God of their ancestors. **5.** He established judges (those who make decisions in legal matters) in all the fortified cities of Judah, assigning them their duties, city by city. **6.** Jehoshaphat instructed the judges, telling them to be careful in their judgments because they were not acting on behalf of men, but for the Lord, who was with them in their decision-making. **7.** He urged them to carry out their duties with the fear (reverence) of the Lord, ensuring that justice was served fairly, without any form of partiality or bribery (accepting money to influence decisions), as there was no injustice with God. **8.** In Jerusalem, Jehoshaphat appointed some of the Levites (priests from the tribe of Levi), priests, and key leaders from Israel to handle legal matters and disputes, especially when people returned to the city. **9.** He commanded them to act with reverence (respect) for the Lord, maintaining faithfulness and a loyal heart in all their duties. **10.** Whenever a case came before them—whether a matter of bloodshed (murder) or violation of the law, commandments, or ordinances—they were to warn the people to avoid sin so that God's wrath (anger) would not fall upon them. He assured them that if they carried out their responsibilities well, they would not be guilty. **11.** Jehoshaphat designated Amariah, the chief priest (leader of priests), to oversee all matters related to the Lord, while Zebadiah, the ruler of Judah's house, was appointed to handle the king's matters. The Levites would assist in the legal processes. He encouraged the judges to be strong and courageous, promising that the Lord would be with those who acted righteously.

Chapter 20

1. After these events, the people of Moab (a nation east of Israel) and Ammon (a nation located to the east of Israel), along with other groups, came to wage war against King Jehoshaphat (king of Judah). **2.** Some messengers came and informed Jehoshaphat, "A great multitude is coming against you from across the sea, from Syria (a region north of Israel); they are in Hazazon Tamar (also called En Gedi, a town near the Dead Sea)." **3.** Jehoshaphat was afraid, so he decided to seek the Lord. He proclaimed a fast throughout all Judah (the southern kingdom of Israel). **4.** The people of Judah gathered to seek help from the Lord. They came from all the towns of Judah to pray to God. **5.** Jehoshaphat stood in the assembly of Judah and Jerusalem, in the house of the Lord (the temple), before the new court. **6.** He prayed, saying, "O Lord, God of our ancestors, are You not the ruler of all the kingdoms of the nations? In Your hand are power and might, and no one can stand against You?" **7.** "Are You not the God who drove out the inhabitants of this land before Your people Israel and gave it to the descendants of Abraham (father of the Jewish nation), Your friend, forever?" **8.** "They have lived here and built a sanctuary for Your name, saying, 'If disaster strikes us—whether by sword, judgment, disease, or famine—we will stand before this temple and in Your presence (for Your name is here), and cry out to You in our distress, and You will hear us and save us.'" **9.** "Now, here are the people of Ammon, Moab, and Mount Seir (a mountain range southeast of Israel)—whom You did not allow Israel to invade when they came out of Egypt, but they turned away from them and did not destroy them." **10.** "They are now repaying us by coming to throw us out of the land You gave us as our inheritance." **11.** "O our God, will You not judge them? For we have no power to face this large army that is attacking us. We do not know what to do, but our eyes are upon You." **12.** All the people of Judah, including their children, wives, and families, stood before the Lord. **13.** Then the Spirit of the Lord came upon Jahaziel (a prophet), the son of Zechariah, a Levite (one of the priestly tribe) of the Asaph clan (a family of temple singers), standing in the midst of the assembly. **14.** Jahaziel said, "Listen, all you of Judah and Jerusalem, and King Jehoshaphat! This is what the Lord says to you: 'Do not be afraid or discouraged because of this vast army, for the battle is not yours, but God's.'" **15.** "Tomorrow, go down against them. They will come up by the pass of Ziz (a mountain pass leading into Judah), and you will find them at the end of the valley before the Wilderness of Jeruel (a region in the southern part of Judah)." **16.** "You will not have to fight in this battle. Take your positions, stand firm, and watch the deliverance the Lord will give you, O Judah and Jerusalem. Do not fear or be discouraged. Go out to face them tomorrow, and the Lord will be with you." **17.** Jehoshaphat bowed down with his face to the ground, and all Judah and the inhabitants of Jerusalem fell down to worship the Lord. **18.** The Levites from the clans of Kohath (a family of Levites) and Korah (another Levite family) stood and praised the Lord, the God of Israel, with loud voices. **19.** Early the next morning, they went out to the Wilderness of Tekoa (a region in Judah). As they left, Jehoshaphat stood and said, "Listen to me, Judah and the people of Jerusalem: Believe in the Lord your God, and you will be established. Believe His prophets, and you will succeed." **20.** After consulting with the people, Jehoshaphat appointed singers to praise the Lord, and they went ahead of the army, singing, "Give thanks to the Lord, for His love endures forever." **21.** As they began to sing and praise, the Lord set ambushes against the armies of Ammon, Moab, and Mount Seir, and they were defeated. **22.** The Ammonites and Moabites turned on the people of Mount Seir, completely destroying them. After they finished with Seir, they helped destroy each other. **23.** When Judah reached the place overlooking the wilderness, they saw only dead bodies scattered on the ground. No one had survived. **24.** When Jehoshaphat and his men came to gather the plunder, they found an abundance of goods, including clothing and jewelry, more than they could carry away. It took them three days to collect the spoil, so great was the amount. **25.** On the fourth day, they assembled in the Valley of Berachah (meaning "Blessing"), where they praised the Lord. This place has been called the Valley of Berachah to this day. **26.** Then, with Jehoshaphat leading them, all of Judah and Jerusalem returned joyfully to Jerusalem. The Lord had given them cause to rejoice over their enemies. **27.** As they entered Jerusalem, they were accompanied by music—harps, lyres, and trumpets—celebrating in the house of the Lord. **28.** The fear of God came upon all the surrounding kingdoms when they heard how the Lord had fought against the enemies of Israel. **29.** After this, Jehoshaphat's kingdom enjoyed peace, for his God had given him rest from all surrounding enemies. **30.** Jehoshaphat was thirty-five years old when he became king of Judah, and he reigned for twenty-five years in Jerusalem. His mother's name was Azubah (daughter of Shilhi). **31.** Jehoshaphat followed the ways of his father Asa (previous king of Judah) and did what was right in the eyes of the Lord, not turning aside from His commands. **32.** However, the high places (locations where people worshiped idols) were not removed, and the people had not fully committed their hearts to the God of their ancestors. **33.** The rest of Jehoshaphat's acts, from beginning to end, are written in the book

of Jehu (a prophet), the son of Hanani (a prophet), which is also recorded in the annals of the kings of Israel. **34.** Later, Jehoshaphat made an alliance with Ahaziah (king of Israel), who did evil in the sight of the Lord. **35.** Together, they decided to build ships to go to Tarshish (a distant port city), and they built the ships in Ezion Geber (a port city on the Red Sea). **36.** But the prophet Eliezer (son of Dodavah), prophesied against Jehoshaphat, saying, "Because you have allied with Ahaziah, the Lord will destroy your works." The ships were wrecked, and they could not go to Tarshish. **37.** But Eliezer (son of Dodavah), a prophet from Mareshah (a town in Judah), prophesied against Jehoshaphat, saying, "Because you have allied with Ahaziah (king of Israel), the Lord has destroyed your works." The ships were wrecked, and they were unable to sail to Tarshish (a distant trading city).

Chapter 21

1. Jehoshaphat (king of Judah) died and was buried with his ancestors in the City of David (Jerusalem). His son Jehoram (the firstborn son of Jehoshaphat) succeeded him as king. **2.** Jehoshaphat had other sons: Azariah, Jehiel, Zechariah, Azaryahu, Michael, and Shephatiah. These were all sons of Jehoshaphat, king of Judah. **3.** Jehoshaphat gave his sons great gifts of silver, gold, and precious items, along with fortified cities in Judah. However, he gave the kingdom to Jehoram, because Jehoram was his firstborn. **4.** Once Jehoram became firmly established as king, he strengthened his rule by killing all of his brothers with the sword, as well as other officials of Israel. **5.** Jehoram was thirty-two years old when he became king and reigned for eight years in Jerusalem. **6.** Jehoram followed the evil ways of the kings of Israel, doing as the house of Ahab (a wicked dynasty of Israel) had done, because he married the daughter of Ahab. He did evil in the sight of the Lord. **7.** However, the Lord did not destroy the house of David, because of the covenant He made with David, and His promise to always provide a lamp (a continuing line of kings) for David and his descendants. **8.** During Jehoram's reign, the Edomites (a neighboring nation southeast of Judah) rebelled against Judah's authority and set up their own king. **9.** Jehoram responded by gathering his officers and all his chariots. He rose up by night and attacked the Edomites, who had surrounded him and the chariot commanders. **10.** Since that time, Edom has been in revolt against Judah. At that time, Libnah (a city in Judah) also rebelled against his rule because Jehoram had abandoned the Lord, the God of his ancestors. **11.** Jehoram made high places (places of idol worship) in the mountains of Judah, leading the people of Jerusalem to engage in idolatry, causing Judah to sin. **12.** A letter from the prophet Elijah (a major prophet of Israel) came to Jehoram, saying: "This is what the Lord, the God of your father David, says: You have not walked in the ways of your father Jehoshaphat, or in the ways of Asa (king of Judah). **13.** Instead, you have followed the ways of the kings of Israel, causing Judah and the people of Jerusalem to act as harlots like the house of Ahab (king of Israel). You even killed your brothers, men who were better than you. **14.** Therefore, the Lord will bring a great affliction upon your people—your children, your wives, and all your possessions. **15.** You will also suffer a severe illness that will affect your intestines, causing them to come out day by day because of the disease." **16.** The Lord stirred up the Philistines (a group of people living along the coast) and the Arabians (a group of people from the southern deserts), who were near the Ethiopians (people from Africa), to attack Jehoram. **17.** They came up into Judah, invaded it, and took all the possessions found in the king's house. They also took Jehoram's sons and wives, leaving him with only Jehoahaz (the youngest of his sons). **18.** After this, the Lord struck Jehoram with a serious, incurable disease in his intestines. **19.** After two years, the disease became worse, and his intestines came out due to the sickness. He died in great pain, and no one mourned him like they had for his ancestors. **20.** Jehoram was thirty-two years old when he became king, and he reigned for eight years in Jerusalem. He died without anyone expressing sorrow over his death, and he was buried in the City of David, but not in the royal tombs.

Chapter 22

1. The people of Jerusalem made Ahaziah, the youngest son of Jehoram; king after the raiders from Arabia killed all the older sons. Thus, Ahaziah, the son of Jehoram, king of Judah, became the ruler. **2.** Ahaziah was forty-two years old when he became king and ruled for one year in Jerusalem. His mother was Athaliah, the granddaughter of

Omri (a former king of Israel). **3.** Ahaziah followed the ways of the house of Ahab because his mother, Athaliah, encouraged him to do evil. **4.** Therefore, he did evil in the sight of the Lord, just as the house of Ahab had done, since they were his advisors after his father's death, which led to his downfall. **5.** Ahaziah followed their advice and joined Jehoram, the son of Ahab (king of Israel), in battle against Hazael, king of Syria, at Ramoth Gilead. The Syrians wounded Jehoram. **6.** Jehoram returned to Jezreel (a city) to recover from his wounds from Ramah, where he had fought against Hazael, king of Syria. Azariah, the son of Jehoram (king of Judah), went to visit Jehoram in Jezreel because he was sick. **7.** Ahaziah's visit to Jehoram led to his downfall. When Ahaziah arrived, he went out with Jehoram to confront Jehu, son of Nimshi, whom the Lord had anointed to destroy the house of Ahab. **8.** While Jehu was executing judgment on Ahab's house, he found the princes of Judah and the sons of Ahaziah's brothers who had served him, and he killed them. **9.** Jehu searched for Ahaziah, and when they found him hiding in Samaria, they brought him to Jehu. After killing him, they buried him, saying, "He is the son of Jehoshaphat, who sought the Lord with all his heart." As a result, the house of Ahaziah had no one left to rule. **10.** When Athaliah, the mother of Ahaziah, saw that her son was dead, she rose up and killed all the royal heirs of the house of Judah. **11.** However, Jehoshabeath, the daughter of King Jehoram, took Joash, the son of Ahaziah, and hid him away from the other royal sons who were being killed. She put him and his nurse in a bedroom, hiding him from Athaliah so she would not kill him. **12.** Joash was hidden in the house of God for six years, while Athaliah reigned over the land.

Chapter 23

1. In the seventh year, Jehoiada (a priest) gained strength and formed an alliance with the captains of the army: Azariah (son of Jeroham), Ishmael (son of Jehohanan), Azariah (son of Obed), Maaseiah (son of Adaiah), and Elishaphat (son of Zichri). **2.** They traveled across Judah, gathering the Levites (descendants of the tribe set apart for religious duties) from all the towns of Judah and the heads of the families of Israel, bringing them to Jerusalem. **3.** Together, they made a covenant with the king in the house of God (the temple). Jehoiada declared, "The king's son will rule as the Lord has promised to the house of David." **4.** Jehoiada instructed them: one-third of the priests and Levites should stand guard at the temple doors on the Sabbath, **5.** one-third should be stationed at the king's house, and one-third at the Gate of the Foundation (a major gate in Jerusalem). The rest of the people should be positioned in the temple courts. **6.** Only the priests and Levites who served were to enter the house of the Lord, for they were consecrated (set apart as holy), while all others were to remain outside, keeping watch. **7.** The Levites were to stand guard around the king, each armed with a weapon, and if anyone tried to enter, they were to be killed. They were to stay with the king both when he entered and when he left. **8.** The Levites and all Judah followed Jehoiada's instructions. Each man took his assigned post, replacing those going off duty, as Jehoiada had not dismissed the divisions. **9.** Jehoiada gave the captains of the army the spears and shields that had belonged to King David (former king of Israel), which had been kept in the temple. **10.** Jehoiada positioned all the people, each with their weapons, from one side of the temple to the other, near the altar and around the king. **11.** They brought out the king's son, placed a crown on his head, gave him the Book of the Law (also called the Testimony), and declared him king. Jehoiada and his sons anointed him and said, "Long live the king!" **12.** When Athaliah (the usurping queen) heard the sounds of the people shouting and celebrating the king's coronation, she went to the temple to investigate. **13.** She looked and saw the king standing by the pillar at the entrance, with the leaders and trumpet players by his side. All the people were rejoicing, blowing trumpets, and the singers were leading praises. Athaliah tore her clothes and cried, "Treason! Treason!" **14.** Jehoiada then brought out the captains of the army and commanded, "Take her outside the temple grounds, and anyone who follows her should be killed." He added, "Do not kill her inside the house of the Lord." **15.** They seized her, led her by the Horse Gate (one of Jerusalem's gates) to the king's palace, and there they put her to death. **16.** Jehoiada made a covenant between himself, the people, and the king, declaring that they would be the Lord's people. **17.** Then all the people went to the temple of Baal (a pagan god), tore it down,

smashed its altars and idols, and killed Mattan (the priest of Baal) before the altars. **18.** Jehoiada assigned the oversight of the house of the Lord to the priests and Levites, as had been established by King David. They were to offer the burnt offerings to the Lord with joy and singing, as instructed in the Law of Moses. **19.** Jehoiada appointed gatekeepers at the temple gates to ensure that no one unclean could enter. **20.** Jehoiada then gathered the captains, the nobles, the leaders of the people, and all the people of the land. They brought the king down from the house of the Lord and led him through the Upper Gate (a gate in Jerusalem) to the royal palace, where they placed him on the throne of the kingdom. **21.** The people of the land rejoiced, and the city was at peace, for they had executed Athaliah by the sword.

Chapter 24

1. Joash was seven years old when he became king and ruled for forty years in Jerusalem. His mother was Zibiah from Beersheba (a town in southern Judah). **2.** Joash did what was right in the sight of the Lord throughout Jehoiada's life, who was the priest. **3.** Jehoiada gave Joash two wives, and he had both sons and daughters. **4.** After this, Joash decided to focus on restoring the temple of the Lord. **5.** He gathered the priests and Levites (those who served in the temple) and told them, "Go to all the cities of Judah and collect money each year for the repairs of the house of your God, and do it without delay." But the Levites did not act quickly. **6.** The king then called for Jehoiada, the chief priest, and asked, "Why have you not made sure the Levites bring in the collection from Judah and Jerusalem as commanded by Moses for the Tabernacle?" **7.** This was because the sons of Athaliah had broken into the house of God and stolen its sacred objects to dedicate them to Baal (a false god). **8.** At the king's command, a chest was made and placed outside the gate of the Lord's house. **9.** A proclamation was made throughout Judah and Jerusalem for people to bring their contributions to the Lord as Moses had commanded Israel in the wilderness. **10.** The leaders and all the people rejoiced, brought their offerings, and filled the chest with their gifts until everyone had given. **11.** When the chest was brought to the king's officer by the Levites, and they saw how much money had been collected, the king's scribe and the high priest's officer emptied the chest and returned it to its place. This was done day by day, gathering money in abundance. **12.** The king and Jehoiada gave the collected funds to those working on the restoration of the temple. They hired masons, carpenters, and workers skilled in iron and bronze to repair and restore the temple. **13.** The workers completed the task, and the house of God was fully restored to its original state and strengthened. **14.** When restoration was finished, the remaining money was brought to the king and Jehoiada, and they used it to make vessels for the temple, including gold and silver items for offerings and service. Burnt offerings were continuously offered in the house of the Lord throughout Jehoiada's lifetime. **15.** Jehoiada lived to a full old age and died at 130 years old. **16.** He was buried in the City of David (the burial place of kings), as he had done good in Israel, both for God and His house. **17.** After Jehoiada's death, the leaders of Judah came and bowed before King Joash, and Joash listened to their counsel. **18.** They abandoned the house of the Lord, the God of their ancestors, and began serving idols made of wood. This brought God's wrath upon Judah and Jerusalem because of their sin. **19.** Nevertheless, God sent prophets to call them back to Him, but they refused to listen to the prophets' warnings. **20.** Then the Spirit of God came upon Zechariah (son of Jehoiada the priest), who stood before the people and said, "This is what God says: 'Why do you break the commandments of the Lord and fail to prosper? You have forsaken the Lord, and so He has forsaken you.'" **21.** The leaders conspired against Zechariah, and at the king's command, they stoned him in the court of the temple of the Lord. **22.** Joash, the king, did not remember the good deeds that Jehoiada had done for him, and instead, he had Jehoiada's son killed. As Zechariah was dying, he said, "May the Lord see this and repay it!" **23.** In the spring, the army of Syria (a nation to the northeast) came up against Joash. They attacked Judah and Jerusalem, killed all the leaders of the people, and sent the plunder to the king of Damascus. **24.** Although the Syrian army was small, the Lord allowed them to defeat a much larger army because Judah had forsaken their God. Thus, they executed judgment on Joash. **25.** After the Syrians withdrew, leaving Joash severely wounded, his own servants conspired against him because of the blood of Zechariah, the son of Jehoiada. They killed him in his bed, and he died. He was buried in the City of David, but not in the tombs of the kings. **26.** The conspirators against Joash were Zabad, the son of Shimeath (an Ammonite woman), and Jehozabad, the son of Shimrith (a Moabite woman). **27.** The details of his reign, the prophecies about him, and the repairs to the house of God are written in the annals of the kings. After Joash's death, his son Amaziah became king.

Chapter 25

1. Amaziah became king when he was twenty-five years old, and he reigned for twenty-nine years in Jerusalem. His mother's name was Jehoaddan, from Jerusalem (the capital city of Judah). **2.** Amaziah did what was right in the sight of the Lord, but his heart was not fully devoted to God. **3.** Once his kingdom was secure, Amaziah executed those servants who had killed his father, the former king. **4.** However, he did not put their children to death, following the law in the Book of Moses, which says, "Fathers shall not be executed for their children, nor shall children die for their fathers. Each person will die for their own sin." **5.** Amaziah gathered the men of Judah, appointing captains over thousands and hundreds from all the tribes of Judah and Benjamin. He counted those twenty years old and older, finding three hundred thousand men fit for battle, skilled with spear and shield. **6.** He also hired one hundred thousand mighty warriors from Israel (the northern kingdom) for one hundred talents of silver. **7.** But a man of God came to Amaziah and said, "Do not let the army of Israel go with you, for the Lord is not with Israel or with any of the people from Ephraim (a major tribe of Israel). **8.** If you go, be strong in battle, but you will fail before the enemy. For God has power to help or to defeat you." **9.** Amaziah asked the prophet, "What about the hundred talents I paid to the troops from Israel?" The prophet answered, "The Lord can give you much more than this." **10.** So Amaziah dismissed the Israelite troops, sending them back home. They were greatly angered and returned home furious. **11.** Amaziah then gathered his forces and went to the Valley of Salt, where he defeated ten thousand men from the land of Seir (Edomites). **12.** The men of Judah captured another ten thousand and took them to a rocky cliff, where they threw them down, dashing them to pieces. **13.** Meanwhile, the soldiers whom Amaziah had dismissed from Israel raided the cities of Judah, from Samaria to Beth Horon. They killed three thousand people and took a great deal of spoil. **14.** After returning from his victory over the Edomites, Amaziah took the gods of the people of Seir and set them up as his gods. He bowed down before them and burned incense to them. **15.** This angered the Lord, and He sent a prophet to Amaziah, saying, "Why have you turned to the gods of the people who could not save their own people from your hand?" **16.** While the prophet was speaking, Amaziah asked, "Have we made you the king's adviser? Stop! Why should you be killed?" The prophet stopped and replied, "I know that God has decided to destroy you because you have done this and not listened to my advice." **17.** Amaziah, the king of Judah, then sent a message to Joash, the king of Israel, saying, "Let us face each other in battle." **18.** Joash, king of Israel, responded with a parable: "The thistle in Lebanon sent to the cedar in Lebanon, saying, 'Give your daughter to my son as a wife.' But a wild beast passed by and trampled the thistle. **19.** You boast of defeating the Edomites, but stay at home! Why bring disaster on yourself and Judah?" **20.** But Amaziah refused to listen, for it was God's will to deliver him into the hands of his enemies because he had sought the gods of Edom. **21.** So Joash, king of Israel, led his army against Amaziah, king of Judah. They met at Beth Shemesh (a town in Judah), where they fought. **22.** Judah was defeated by Israel, and the men of Judah fled to their homes. **23.** Joash, the king of Israel, captured Amaziah, king of Judah, at Beth Shemesh. He brought him to Jerusalem and broke down a section of the wall of Jerusalem, from the Gate of Ephraim to the Corner Gate—about 400 cubits (a cubit is roughly 18 inches). **24.** Joash took all the gold and silver, as well as the sacred vessels from the temple of God and the treasures from the royal palace. He also took hostages and returned to Samaria. **25.** Amaziah, the son of Joash, king of Judah, lived for fifteen more years after the death of Joash, the son of Jehoahaz, king of Israel. **26.** The rest of Amaziah's reign, including all the events of his rule, are written in the book of the kings of Judah and Israel. **27.** After Amaziah turned away from following the Lord, a conspiracy arose against him in Jerusalem,

and he fled to Lachish (a city in Judah). But they sent men after him, captured him there, and killed him. **28.** His body was brought back on horses, and he was buried with his ancestors in the City of Judah.

Chapter 26

1. The people of Judah chose Uzziah, who was only sixteen years old, to be their king after the death of his father, King Amaziah (Amaziah was the previous king of Judah). **2.** Uzziah restored the city of Elath, a port city on the Red Sea, to Judah after his father's death. **3.** Uzziah reigned for fifty-two years in Jerusalem (Jerusalem was the capital city of Judah). His mother's name was Jecholiah, from Jerusalem. **4.** He did what was right in the sight of the Lord, just like his father Amaziah. **5.** Uzziah sought the Lord with guidance from Zechariah, a prophet with insight into God's visions. As long as Uzziah sought the Lord, God helped him succeed. **6.** Uzziah fought against the Philistines (a group of people living in cities like Gath, Jabneh, and Ashdod), broke down their city walls, and built new cities in their territory. **7.** God helped Uzziah defeat the Philistines, the Arabians living in Gur Baal (a desert area), and the Meunites, a people living east of Judah. **8.** The Ammonites (a neighboring people) paid tribute to Uzziah, and his fame spread to the border of Egypt, as he became exceedingly powerful. **9.** Uzziah built towers in Jerusalem (Jerusalem was the capital city of Judah) at the Corner Gate, Valley Gate, and the corner buttress of the city wall, strengthening Judah's defenses. **10.** He also constructed towers in the wilderness and dug many wells for his livestock. He had farms in the lowlands and plains, and he loved farming, including vineyards in the mountains and Carmel (a fertile region). **11.** Uzziah organized a strong army, divided into companies, with their numbers prepared by Jeiel, a scribe, and Maaseiah, an officer, under the leadership of Hananiah, one of the king's captains. **12.** The chief officers of his army, brave men of valor, numbered 2,600. **13.** Under their leadership, Uzziah's army had 307,500 men skilled in battle, ready to support the king against his enemies. **14.** He provided shields, spears, helmets, armor, bows, and slings, a device used to throw stones, for his soldiers to fight with. **15.** Uzziah also designed innovative machines, made by skilled workers in Jerusalem (Jerusalem was the capital city of Judah), to launch arrows and large stones from the city's towers and corners. His fame spread widely because God helped him greatly, making him very strong. **16.** However, when Uzziah grew strong, his heart became proud, leading to his downfall. He entered the temple of the Lord (the sacred place of worship) to burn incense on the altar, which was only for the priests, descendants of Aaron (Aaron was the first high priest of Israel), to do. **17.** Azariah, the high priest, and eighty other brave priests confronted Uzziah. **18.** They said to him, "It is not for you, Uzziah, to burn incense to the Lord, but for the priests, the descendants of Aaron, who are set apart for this. Leave the sanctuary, for you have sinned! You will not have honor from the Lord." **19.** Uzziah became angry and continued to hold the censer (a container used to burn incense), to burn incense. But as he stood there, leprosy (a contagious skin disease) broke out on his forehead, right in front of the priests, beside the incense altar. **20.** Azariah, the high priest, and all the priests saw the leprosy on his forehead and quickly drove him out of the temple. Uzziah also rushed to leave, for the Lord had struck him. **21.** Uzziah remained a leper for the rest of his life, living in isolation because of his disease. His son Jotham (Jotham was Uzziah's son) took over the responsibilities of governing the people of Judah. **22.** The prophet Isaiah (Isaiah was a prophet who foretold God's will) wrote about the remaining acts of Uzziah. **23.** Uzziah died and was buried with his ancestors in a royal burial field, though it was noted, "He was a leper." His son Jotham succeeded him as king.

Chapter 27

1. Jotham was twenty-five years old when he became king and reigned for sixteen years in Jerusalem (the capital city of Judah). His mother's name was Jerushah, daughter of Zadok (a high priest). **2.** Jotham did what was right in God's sight, following his father Uzziah's example. However, he did not enter the temple, though the people continued in corruption. **3.** He built the Upper Gate of the temple and repaired the wall of Ophel (a part of Jerusalem). **4.** Jotham also built cities in the mountains of Judah and fortresses in the forests for protection. **5.** He defeated the Ammonites, who paid him tribute: one hundred talents of silver, ten thousand kors of wheat, and ten thousand of barley. This tribute continued for two more years. **6.** Jotham grew powerful because he walked in the ways of the Lord. **7.** The rest of Jotham's deeds, his wars, and reign are written in the Book of the Kings of Israel and Judah. **8.** Jotham reigned for sixteen years in Jerusalem from the age of twenty-five. **9.** He died and was buried in the City of David (Jerusalem), and his son Ahaz became king in his place.

Chapter 28

1. Ahaz was twenty years old when he became king and reigned for sixteen years in Jerusalem (the capital city of Judah). He did not do what was right in God's sight, like his ancestor King David. **2.** Instead, Ahaz followed the practices of the kings of Israel, making idols for Baal, a false god. **3.** He burned incense in the Valley of the Son of Hinnom (a valley near Jerusalem) and even sacrificed his children by burning them alive, following the detestable customs of the nations that God had driven out before Israel. **4.** Ahaz also burned incense on high places, hills, and under every green tree, continuing idolatrous practices. **5.** Therefore, the Lord handed him over to the king of Syria, who defeated him and carried many of the people away to Damascus. He was also handed over to the king of Israel, who slaughtered him in battle. **6.** Pekah, the king of Israel, killed 120,000 soldiers of Judah in one day because they had abandoned the Lord. **7.** Zichri, a mighty man from Ephraim (one of the tribes of Israel), killed Maaseiah, the king's son, Azrikam the palace officer, and Elkanah, second in rank to the king. **8.** The Israelites took 200,000 women, children, and captives, along with much spoil, to Samaria (the capital of Israel). **9.** But a prophet of the Lord named Oded met the army coming to Samaria and rebuked them, saying, "Because the Lord was angry with Judah, He allowed you to defeat them. But you have killed them in a rage that reaches to heaven." **10.** "Now, you plan to enslave the people of Judah and Jerusalem, but are you not guilty before God yourselves?" **11.** "Return the captives to their own people, for the Lord's fierce wrath is upon you." **12.** Then some leaders from Ephraim, including Azariah, Berechiah, Jehizkiah, and Amasa, stood up against the soldiers and said, **13.** "You must not bring the captives here, for we are guilty before the Lord. Our sins are great, and His wrath is against all Israel." **14.** So the armed men left the captives and the spoil before the leaders and the assembly. **15.** Then the leaders rose up, took the captives, clothed the naked, gave them sandals, food, and drink, and even let the weak ride on donkeys. They brought them to Jericho, the city of palm trees (a town near the Jordan River), and then returned to Samaria. **16.** At the same time, King Ahaz sent messengers to the kings of Assyria (a powerful empire) asking for help. **17.** The Edomites (a neighboring people) came and attacked Judah, taking captives. **18.** The Philistines also invaded the cities of Judah's lowlands and southern areas, taking towns like Beth Shemesh, Aijalon, and Timnah. **19.** The Lord humbled Judah because of King Ahaz, who encouraged moral decay in the kingdom and was continually unfaithful to God. **20.** Tiglath-Pileser (the king of Assyria) came to Ahaz's aid but did not help him; instead, he oppressed Judah. **21.** Ahaz took treasures from the Lord's temple and the royal palace to give to the king of Assyria, but the king did not help him. **22.** In his distress, King Ahaz became even more unfaithful to the Lord. **23.** He sacrificed to the gods of Damascus (a city in Syria) because they had defeated him, thinking their gods might help him too. But they were the ruin of him and all of Israel. **24.** Ahaz took articles from the house of God, cut them in pieces, shut the doors of the temple, and built altars in every corner of Jerusalem. **25.** He also made high places in every city of Judah to burn incense to other gods, provoking the Lord's anger. **26.** The rest of Ahaz's acts are written in the book of the kings of Judah and Israel. **27.** Ahaz died and was buried in Jerusalem, but not in the tombs of the kings of Israel. His son Hezekiah became king in his place.

Chapter 29

1. Hezekiah became king at the age of twenty-five and reigned for twenty-nine years in Jerusalem. His mother's name was Abijah, the daughter of Zechariah. **2.** Hezekiah did what was right in the eyes of the Lord, just as his ancestor King David had done. **3.** In the first year of his reign, during the first month, he opened the doors of the house of the Lord and repaired them. **4.** He then brought in the priests and Levites, gathering them in the East Square (an area outside the temple), **5.** And instructed them, saying: "Listen, Levites! Now consecrate yourselves, purify the house of the Lord God of your ancestors, and remove the impurity from the holy place. **6.** for our ancestors have trespassed and committed evil in the sight of the Lord our God; they have forsaken Him, turned their faces away from the temple of the Lord, and turned their backs on Him. **7.** They have also shut the doors of the vestibule (the entrance hall), extinguished the lamps, and stopped burning incense or offering burnt offerings to the God of Israel in the holy place. **8.** Therefore, the wrath of the Lord has fallen upon Judah and Jerusalem, and He has allowed them to fall into trouble, ruin, and mockery, as you see with your own eyes. **9.** Indeed, because of this, our fathers have fallen by the sword, and our wives, sons, and daughters are in captivity. **10.** Now, it is my heart's desire to make a covenant with the Lord God of Israel so that His fierce anger may turn away from us. **11.** My sons do not be negligent now, for the Lord has chosen you to stand before Him, to serve Him, and to burn incense to Him." **12.** The Levites who arose were: Mahath, son of Amasai, and Joel, son of Azariah (from the Kohathites); Kish, son of Abdi, and Azariah, son of Jehallelel (from the Merarites); Joah, son of Zimmah, and Eden, son of Joah (from the Gershonites); **13.** Shimri and Jeiel (from the Elizaphanites); Zechariah and Mattaniah (from the Asaphites); Jehiel and Shimei (from the Hemanites); and Shemaiah and Uzziel (from the Jeduthunites). **14.** They gathered their fellow Levites, consecrated themselves, and followed the king's command, at the word of the Lord, to cleanse the house of the Lord. **15.** The priests entered the inner parts of the house of the Lord to purify it, bringing out all the filth they found in the temple to the court of the house of the Lord. The Levites then took it and carried it to the Brook Kidron (a valley near Jerusalem). **16.** They began the purification on the first day of the first month, and by the eighth day, they reached the vestibule of the Lord. They sanctified the temple over eight days, and on the sixteenth day of the month, they finished. **17.** They then came to King Hezekiah and reported, "We have purified all the house of the Lord, the altar of burnt offerings, and all its vessels, and the table for the showbread with all its vessels. **18.** Moreover, all the articles King Ahaz had discarded during his reign because of his unfaithfulness, we have prepared and consecrated; and they are now before the altar of the Lord." **19.** Then King Hezekiah arose early, gathered the rulers of the city, and went up to the house of the Lord. **20.** They brought seven bulls, seven rams, seven lambs, and seven male goats as sin offerings for the kingdom, the sanctuary, and for Judah. He commanded the priests, the sons of Aaron, to offer these on the altar of the Lord. **21.** The priests slaughtered the bulls, and they sprinkled their blood on the altar. Likewise, they slaughtered the rams and sprinkled the blood on the altar. They did the same with the lambs. **22.** Then they brought male goats for the sin offering before the king and the assembly, and they laid their hands on them. **23.** The priests slaughtered the goats and presented their blood on the altar as a sin offering to atone for all Israel, for the king had commanded that the burnt and sin offerings be made for all Israel. **24.** The priests then took the blood and sprinkled it on the altar to make atonement for the people. **25.** Hezekiah also stationed the Levites in the house of the Lord with cymbals, stringed instruments, and harps, following the command of King David, of Gad (David's prophet), and Nathan (the prophet), as the Lord had commanded through His prophets. **26.** The Levites stood with the instruments of David, and the priests with the trumpets. **27.** Hezekiah commanded them to begin offering the burnt offerings on the altar. As they began the burnt offering, the song of the Lord began as well, with trumpets and instruments, in the style of King David. **28.** All the assembly worshiped, the singers sang, and the trumpeters played; all of this continued until the burnt offering was completed. **29.** When the offerings were finished, the king and all who were present bowed and worshiped. **30.** King Hezekiah and the leaders instructed the Levites to praise the Lord with the words of David and Asaph the seer. They sang praises with joy and bowed their heads in worship. **31.** Hezekiah then said, "Now that you have consecrated yourselves to the Lord, bring sacrifices and thank offerings into the house of the Lord." So the assembly brought in sacrifices and thank offerings, and as many as were willing brought burnt offerings. **32.** The number of burnt offerings brought by the assembly was seventy bulls, one hundred rams, and two hundred lambs. These were all offered as burnt offerings to the Lord. **33.** The consecrated offerings included six hundred bulls and three thousand sheep. **34.** However, there were too few priests to skin all the offerings, so the Levites helped them until the work was completed, for the Levites were more diligent in sanctifying themselves than the priests. 35. The burnt offerings were abundant, with the fat of the peace offerings and drink offerings for every burnt offering. Thus, the service of the house of the Lord was set in order. 36. Then Hezekiah and all the people rejoiced that God had prepared the people for this, as the events unfolded so quickly.

Chapter 30

1. Hezekiah sent messengers to all Israel and Judah, and also wrote letters to Ephraim and Manasseh, inviting them to come to the house of the Lord in Jerusalem to celebrate the Passover to the Lord God of Israel. 2. The king, his leaders, and all the people in Jerusalem had agreed to celebrate the Passover in the second month. 3. They could not celebrate it at the regular time because there were not enough priests who had consecrated themselves, and the people had not gathered in Jerusalem. 4. The king's plan pleased everyone in the assembly. 5. So they decided to send a proclamation throughout Israel, from Beersheba (a southern city) to Dan (a northern city), calling the people to come to Jerusalem to celebrate the Passover to the Lord, because they had not observed it properly for a long time. 6. The messengers went throughout Israel and Judah, delivering the king's message: "Children of Israel, return to the Lord God of Abraham, Isaac, and Israel, and He will return to those of you who have survived the attacks of the kings of Assyria (a powerful enemy). 7. Do not be like your ancestors, who turned away from the Lord and were destroyed, as you can see with your own eyes. 8. Do not be stubborn like your forefathers, but submit to the Lord; enter His sanctuary, which He has consecrated forever, and serve the Lord your God so His anger may turn away from you. 9. If you return to the Lord, your brothers and children, who have been taken captive, will find mercy from their captors and will return to this land. For the Lord your God is gracious and merciful and will not turn His face away from you if you return to Him." 10. The messengers went from city to city in Ephraim and Manasseh, as far as Zebulun, but the people laughed and mocked them. 11. Yet some from Asher, Manasseh, and Zebulun humbled themselves and came to Jerusalem. 12. The hand of God was also on Judah, making them united in heart to obey the king's command and the leaders' direction, according to the word of the Lord. 13. A large assembly gathered in Jerusalem to celebrate the Feast of Unleavened Bread in the second month. 14. They arose and removed the altars in Jerusalem, throwing them into the Brook Kidron (a valley near Jerusalem). 15. They slaughtered the Passover lambs on the fourteenth day of the second month. The priests and Levites purified themselves and brought the burnt offerings to the house of the Lord. 16. They stood in their places, following their customary duties according to the Law of Moses, and the priests sprinkled the blood, which the Levites handed to them. 17. There were many in the assembly who had not purified themselves, so the Levites took responsibility for slaughtering the Passover lambs for those who were unclean, to consecrate them to the Lord. 18. Many from Ephraim, Manasseh, Issachar, and Zebulun had not purified themselves and ate the Passover contrary to the written instructions. But Hezekiah prayed for them, saying, "May the good Lord provide atonement for all who prepare their hearts to seek God, the Lord God of their ancestors, even if they are not cleansed according to the purification of the sanctuary." 19. And the Lord heard Hezekiah's prayer and healed the people. 20. So the Israelites in Jerusalem celebrated the Feast of Unleavened Bread for seven days with great joy, while the priests and Levites praised the Lord day by day, with loud instruments. 21. Hezekiah encouraged all the Levites who taught the good knowledge of the Lord, and they ate throughout the seven days of the feast, offering peace offerings and giving thanks to the Lord God of their ancestors. 22. The entire assembly agreed to extend the feast for another seven days, and they celebrated with joy for another week. 23. King Hezekiah of Judah gave the assembly a thousand bulls and seven thousand sheep, and the leaders gave a thousand bulls and ten thousand sheep. A great number of priests consecrated themselves. 24. The entire assembly of Judah rejoiced, including the priests, Levites, all the people who came from Israel, the sojourners from Israel, and those living in Judah. 25. There was great joy in Jerusalem, for since the time of Solomon, son of David, king of Israel, nothing like this had been seen in Jerusalem. 26.

The priests and Levites stood and blessed the people, and their voices were heard, and their prayer reached God's holy dwelling place in heaven.

Chapter 31

1. When all the tasks were completed, the Israelites who were present went out to the cities of Judah. They broke the sacred pillars (idols for worship), cut down the wooden images (carved idols), and destroyed the high places (places of pagan worship) and altars throughout Judah, Benjamin, Ephraim, and Manasseh (two tribes of Israel). They completely demolished them. Afterward, everyone returned to their own cities, each to their own land. 2. Hezekiah (king of Judah) appointed the priests and Levites (members of the priestly tribe of Israel) to their respective divisions, assigning each person to their duties: the priests and Levites were responsible for burnt offerings, peace offerings, giving thanks, and praising God in the gates of the Lord's temple. 3. The king also set aside a portion of his possessions for the burnt offerings: for the morning and evening sacrifices, and for those on Sabbaths, New Moons (the first day of each month), and appointed feasts, all according to the Law of the Lord (the written instructions God gave to Israel). 4. Hezekiah commanded the people of Jerusalem to support the priests and Levites so they could fully devote themselves to studying and teaching the Law of the Lord. 5. As soon as the command was given, the people of Israel brought in large amounts of firstfruits (the best part of their crops)—grain, wine, oil, honey, and all the produce of the field—and also brought the tithe (a tenth) of everything. 6. The people of Israel and Judah who lived in the cities of Judah brought the tithe of their oxen and sheep. They also brought offerings of holy things consecrated (set apart) to the Lord, which they stored in heaps (large piles). 7. They began collecting these offerings in the third month and finished by the seventh month. 8. When Hezekiah and the leaders saw the heaps, they praised the Lord and His people Israel for their generosity. 9. Hezekiah then asked the priests and Levites about the large piles of offerings. 10. Azariah (chief priest from the house of Zadok, a priestly family) answered, "Since the people began bringing offerings into the house of the Lord, we have had enough to eat and plenty left over, for the Lord has blessed His people, and the remaining abundance is this great surplus." 11. Hezekiah commanded that rooms be prepared in the temple of the Lord, and the rooms were made ready. 12. The offerings, tithes, and consecrated gifts were brought in faithfully. Cononiah (a Levite) was in charge, and his brother Shimei (also a Levite) assisted him. 13. Jehiel, Azaziah, Nahath, Asahel, Jerimoth, Jozabad, Eliel, Ismachiah, Mahath, and Benaiah were overseers, working under the leadership of Cononiah and Shimei, as ordered by King Hezekiah and Azariah, the ruler of the temple. 14. Kore (son of Imnah, a Levite), who was in charge of the East Gate of the temple, was responsible for distributing the freewill offerings to God, and for handling the most holy offerings. 15. Kore's assistants—Eden, Miniamin, Jeshua, Shemaiah, Amariah, and Shecaniah—distributed portions to the priests in their cities, ensuring fairness in the distribution to both the great and the small. 16. Every male, three years old and up, listed in the genealogies, received his portion for the temple service, according to his division. 17. The priests, listed in the genealogies according to their families, and the Levites (those from twenty years old and up) received their portions for their service in the temple, according to their divisions. 18. All those listed in the genealogies—including their little ones, wives, sons, and daughters—received their portion because they had sanctified themselves in holiness. 19. For the sons of Aaron (the priestly family), who lived in the fields surrounding their cities, there were men appointed by name to distribute portions to all the males among the priests and to those Levites listed in the genealogies. 20. Thus, Hezekiah did what was good, right, and true before the Lord his God throughout all Judah. 21. In every task Hezekiah began in the service of the house of God, whether in the law or in carrying out commandments to seek God, he did it with all his heart, and as a result, he prospered.

Chapter 32

1. After these deeds of faithfulness, Sennacherib (king of Assyria, a powerful empire) came and entered Judah. He set up camp against the fortified cities, thinking he would conquer them. 2. When Hezekiah (king of Judah) saw that Sennacherib had come, and his plan was to

attack Jerusalem (the capital city of Judah), **3.** he consulted with his leaders and military commanders to stop the water from the springs outside the city. They helped him carry out this strategy. **4.** A large group of people gathered to stop all the springs and the brook that ran through the land, saying, "Why should the king of Assyria find much water when he lays siege to us?" **5.** Hezekiah strengthened himself by repairing all the broken walls, raising them to the towers, and building another wall outside. He also repaired the Millo (a large structure in the City of David) and made weapons and shields in abundance. **6.** He appointed military captains over the people, gathered them together in the open square by the city gate, and encouraged them, saying, **7.** "Be strong and courageous! Do not be afraid or discouraged before the king of Assyria and the large army with him. For there are more with us than with him. **8.** With him is an arm of flesh (human strength), but with us is the Lord our God, to help us and fight our battles." The people were strengthened by the words of Hezekiah, king of Judah. **9.** After this, Sennacherib sent his servants to Jerusalem, while he and his entire army laid siege to Lachish (a city in Judah), addressing King Hezekiah and all the people of Jerusalem, saying, **10.** "What do you trust in, that you remain under siege in Jerusalem? **11.** Has not Hezekiah deceived you, telling you that the Lord our God will deliver you from the hand of the king of Assyria? Will he not cause you to die of famine and thirst?" **12.** "Has not the same Hezekiah removed the high places (altars for idol worship) and commanded you to worship at one altar and burn incense there?" **13.** "Do you not know what I and my fathers have done to all the peoples of other lands? Were the gods of those nations able to deliver their lands from my hand? **14.** Who among all the gods of those nations that my fathers utterly destroyed could deliver his people from my hand? How much less will your God deliver you from my hand?" **15.** "So do not let Hezekiah deceive you or persuade you like this. No god of any nation or kingdom was able to deliver his people from my hand or the hand of my fathers. How much less will your God deliver you from my hand?" **16.** Furthermore, his servants spoke against the Lord God and His servant Hezekiah. **17.** Sennacherib also wrote letters to insult the Lord God of Israel, saying, "Just as the gods of the nations of other lands have not delivered their people from my hand, so the God of Hezekiah will not deliver His people from my hand." **18.** They called out with a loud voice in Hebrew to the people of Jerusalem on the city wall, trying to frighten them and trouble them, to make them surrender. They mocked the God of Jerusalem, comparing Him to the gods of other nations—man-made idols. **19.** Because of this, King Hezekiah and the prophet Isaiah, son of Amoz (a prophet of God), prayed and cried out to heaven. **20.** Then the Lord sent an angel who struck down every mighty warrior, leader, and officer in the Assyrian camp. Sennacherib returned home in disgrace, and when he went into the temple of his god, some of his own children killed him with the sword. **21.** Thus, the Lord saved Hezekiah and the inhabitants of Jerusalem from the hand of Sennacherib, king of Assyria, and from all others. He guided them on every side. **22.** Many brought gifts to the Lord in Jerusalem, and presents to Hezekiah, king of Judah, so that he was exalted in the sight of all nations thereafter. **23.** In those days, Hezekiah became sick and near death. He prayed to the Lord, and the Lord spoke to him and gave him a sign. **24.** However, Hezekiah did not repay according to the favor shown him, for his heart was lifted up (proud). Therefore, wrath was looming over him and over Judah and Jerusalem. **25.** Then Hezekiah humbled himself for the pride of his heart, he and the people of Jerusalem, so that the wrath of the Lord did not come upon them during his days. **26.** Hezekiah had great wealth and honor. He made treasuries for silver, gold, precious stones, spices, shields, and all kinds of desirable items; **27.** Storehouses for grain, wine, and oil, and stalls for all kinds of livestock, and folds for flocks. **28.** Moreover, he provided cities for himself, and possessions of flocks and herds in abundance, for God had given him very much property. **29.** This same Hezekiah also stopped the water outlet of Upper Gihon (a spring in Jerusalem) and brought the water by tunnel to the west side of the City of David (Jerusalem). Hezekiah prospered in all his works. **30.** However, regarding the ambassadors of the princes of Babylon (an empire in Mesopotamia), whom they sent to inquire about the wonders done in the land, God withdrew from him, in order to test him, that He might know all that was in his heart. **31.** Now the rest of the acts of Hezekiah, and his goodness, are written in the vision of Isaiah (a prophet of God), the son of Amoz, and in the book of the kings of Judah and Israel. **32.** So Hezekiah rested with his fathers, and they buried him in the upper tombs of the sons of David (royal burial sites in Jerusalem). All Judah and the inhabitants of Jerusalem honored him at his death. Then Manasseh (Hezekiah's son) reigned in his place.

Chapter 33

1. Manasseh (son of Hezekiah, king of Judah) was twelve years old when he became king, and he reigned for fifty-five years in Jerusalem (the capital city of Judah). **2.** He did evil in the sight of the Lord, following the sinful practices of the nations that the Lord had driven out before the Israelites. **3.** He rebuilt the high places (places for idol worship) that his father Hezekiah had destroyed. He raised altars for the Baals (false gods) and made wooden images (idols). He worshiped all the host of heaven (the stars, the sun, and the moon) and served them. **4.** He also built altars in the house of the Lord (the temple), where God had said, "In Jerusalem, My name shall remain forever." **5.** He built altars for all the host of heaven in the two courts of the house of the Lord. **6.** He even made his sons pass through the fire (a pagan ritual where children were sacrificed) in the Valley of the Son of Hinnom (a valley near Jerusalem). He practiced divination (fortune-telling), used witchcraft and sorcery, and consulted mediums and spiritists (people who communicated with spirits). He did much evil in the sight of the Lord, provoking Him to anger. **7.** He set up a carved image (an idol) that he had made, in the house of God. God had told David (king of Israel) and Solomon (David's son and king of Israel) that He would place His name in this house and in Jerusalem, which He had chosen from all the tribes of Israel. **8.** "I will never remove the foot of Israel from the land I gave to your forefathers—only if they are careful to do everything I commanded them, following the whole law given through Moses (the law of Israel)." **9.** Manasseh led Judah and the inhabitants of Jerusalem into greater evil than the nations the Lord had destroyed before the Israelites. **10.** The Lord spoke to Manasseh and his people, but they refused to listen. **11.** So the Lord sent the commanders of the army of the king of Assyria (a mighty empire), who captured Manasseh with hooks (iron hooks used to bind prisoners), bound him with bronze fetters (chains), and took him to Babylon (an ancient city). **12.** While in distress, Manasseh sought the Lord his God, humbled himself greatly before the God of his ancestors. **13.** He prayed to God, and God accepted his prayer. The Lord heard his supplication (earnest plea) and brought him back to Jerusalem into his kingdom. Then Manasseh knew that the Lord was God. **14.** After this, he built a wall outside the City of David (a part of Jerusalem) on the west side of Gihon (a spring in Jerusalem), in the valley, as far as the entrance of the Fish Gate (a gate in Jerusalem). He enclosed Ophel (a district of Jerusalem) and raised the wall to a great height. He placed military officers in all the fortified cities of Judah. **15.** He removed the foreign gods and the idol from the house of the Lord, tore down the altars he had built in the temple and in Jerusalem, and cast them out of the city. **16.** He repaired the altar of the Lord, offered peace offerings and thank offerings on it, and commanded Judah to serve the Lord God of Israel. **17.** But the people still sacrificed at the high places, although they did so only to the Lord their God. **18.** The rest of the acts of Manasseh, his prayer to God, and the words of the prophets who spoke to him in the name of the Lord God of Israel, are written in the book of the kings of Israel. **19.** His prayer, how God accepted his plea, all his sin and rebellion, and the places where he had set up idols before he humbled himself, are written in the records of the seer Hozai (a prophet). **20.** Manasseh rested with his ancestors and was buried in his own house. His son Amon became king in his place. **21.** Amon was twenty-two years old when he became king, and he reigned for two years in Jerusalem. **22.** Amon did evil in the sight of the Lord, just as his father Manasseh had done. He sacrificed to all the carved idols his father had made, and served them. **23.** He did not humble himself before the Lord, as his father Manasseh had done. Instead, Amon became even more rebellious. **24.** His servants conspired against him and killed him in his own house. **25.** The people of the land executed all those who had conspired against King Amon. Then they made his son Josiah (future righteous king) king in his place.

Chapter 34

1. Josiah was eight years old when he became king and ruled for thirty-one years in Jerusalem (the capital city of Judah). **2.** He did what was right in the sight of the Lord, following the example of his ancestor King David. He remained faithful to God's commands, not turning to the right or the left. **3.** In the eighth year of his reign, while still young, Josiah sought the Lord, the God of his father David. By the twelfth year, he began to remove the high places (idolatrous altars), wooden images (idols carved from wood), carved images (statues carved from stone or wood), and molded images (idols made from clay or metal) in Judah and Jerusalem. **4.** In his presence, they tore down the altars of Baal (false gods), cut down incense altars, and broke the wooden, carved, and molded images into pieces. They scattered the dust on the graves of those who had sacrificed to these idols. **5.** He also burned the bones of the false priests on their altars, purifying Judah and Jerusalem from idolatry. **6.** Josiah extended these reforms to the cities of Manasseh, Ephraim, Simeon, and as far as Naphtali (territories in Israel), destroying the idols with axes (tools used for cutting wood). **7.** After breaking down the altars and idols, he ground the carved images into powder and demolished all the incense altars in the land of Israel. He then returned to Jerusalem. **8.** In the eighteenth year of his reign, after purging the land and the temple, Josiah sent Shaphan (son of Azaliah) and Maaseiah (governor of the city), and Joah (son of Joahaz, the recorder) to repair the house of the Lord. **9.** When they came to Hilkiah (the high priest), they gave him the money brought into the house of God, which the Levites (priests) had gathered from the people of Manasseh, Ephraim, and all the remnant of Israel, as well as from Judah and Benjamin, and had brought to Jerusalem. **10.** The money was given to the foremen overseeing the repairs of the house of the Lord, and they used it to pay the workers who restored and rebuilt the temple. **11.** The craftsmen and builders bought stone and timber for beams to repair the damage caused by previous kings of Judah. **12.** The workers performed the repairs faithfully. Their overseers included Jahath and Obadiah (Levites of the family of Merari), and Zechariah and Meshullam (Levites of the family of Kohath). These men supervised the work. Other Levites, skilled in music, supervised the burden bearers and all who assisted in the temple's restoration. **13.** Some Levites served as scribes (writers), officers (administrators), and gatekeepers (guards at the temple). **14.** While organizing the repairs, Hilkiah the priest discovered the Book of the Law of the Lord, given by Moses. **15.** Hilkiah told Shaphan, "I have found the Book of the Law in the house of the Lord." He gave it to Shaphan. **16.** Shaphan took the book to the king and reported, "Your servants are doing everything you ordered. **17.** They have gathered the money found in the house of the Lord, and it has been given to the overseers and the workers." **18.** Shaphan also told the king, "Hilkiah the priest has given me a book." He read it aloud before the king. **19.** When the king heard the words of the law, he tore his clothes in sorrow and repentance. **20.** The king then commanded Hilkiah, Ahikam (son of Shaphan), Abdon (son of Micah), Shaphan the scribe, and Asaiah (a servant of the king), saying, **21.** "Go and inquire of the Lord for me and for the people of Israel and Judah concerning the words of this book. For great is the wrath of the Lord against us because our ancestors did not obey the Lord's commands written in this book." **22.** So, Hilkiah and the men went to Huldah (a prophetess), the wife of Shallum (son of Tokhath, keeper of the wardrobe). She lived in Jerusalem in the Second Quarter and they consulted her. **23.** She responded, "This is what the Lord God of Israel says: 'Tell the man who sent you to me, **24.** "I am going to bring disaster upon this place and its people, the curses written in the book you read before the king of Judah, **25.** Because they have forsaken Me and burned incense to other gods, provoking Me to anger with all the works of their hands. My wrath will be poured out on this place and will not be quenched." **26.** As for the king of Judah, who sent you to inquire of the Lord, say this: "This is what the Lord God of Israel says: Concerning the words you have heard— **27.** because your heart was tender and you humbled yourself before God when you heard His words against this place and its people, and because you tore your clothes and wept before Me, I have heard you," says the Lord. **28.** "I will gather you to your ancestors, and you will be buried in peace. You will not see the disaster I am about to bring on this place and its people." **29.** The men returned to the king and delivered the message. **30.** Then the king gathered all the elders of Judah and Jerusalem. **31.** The king went up to the house of the Lord, accompanied by all the men of Judah, the inhabitants of Jerusalem, the priests, the Levites, and all the people, from the greatest to the smallest. He read aloud to them all the words of the Book of the Covenant found in the house of the Lord. **32.** The king stood by his pillar and made a covenant before the Lord to follow Him and keep His commandments, statutes, and laws with all his heart and soul. He promised to obey all the words written in the book. **33.** He made all the people of Jerusalem and Benjamin take an oath to do the same. The people of Jerusalem followed the covenant of God, the God of their ancestors. **34.** Josiah removed all the idols and abominations from all the land of Israel. He made the people serve the Lord their God. All his days, they remained faithful to the Lord God of their ancestors.

Chapter 35

1. Now Josiah kept a Passover to the Lord in Jerusalem, and they slaughtered the Passover lambs on the fourteenth day of the first month. **2.** He appointed the priests to perform their duties and encouraged them to serve in the house of the Lord. **3.** Then he said to the Levites, who taught all Israel and were consecrated (set apart) to the Lord, "Put the holy ark (sacred chest) in the house which Solomon, the son of David, king of Israel, built. It shall no longer be a burden on your shoulders. Now serve the Lord your God and His people Israel." **4.** Prepare yourselves according to your families, according to your divisions, following the written instructions of David, king of Israel, and Solomon, his son. **5.** And stand in the holy place, according to the divisions of your families, the lay people (common people), and the divisions of the Levites. **6.** So slaughter the Passover offerings, consecrate yourselves, and prepare them for your fellow Israelites, that they may do according to the word of the Lord, as given through Moses. **7.** Josiah gave the lay people lambs and young goats from the flock, all for Passover offerings, to the number of thirty thousand, as well as three thousand cattle. These were from the king's own possessions. **8.** His leaders gave willingly to the people, the priests, and the Levites. Hilkiah, Zechariah, and Jehiel, rulers of the house of God gave the priests two thousand six hundred sheep and three hundred cattle for the Passover offerings. **9.** Also, Conaniah, his brothers Shemaiah, Nethanel, Hashabiah, Jeiel, and Jozabad, chief of the Levites, gave five thousand sheep and five hundred cattle to the Levites for the Passover offerings. **10.** The service was prepared, and the priests stood in their places, and the Levites in their divisions, according to the king's command. **11.** They slaughtered the Passover offerings; and the priests sprinkled the blood with their hands, while the Levites skinned the animals. **12.** They removed the burnt offerings to give them to the divisions of the families of the lay people, to offer to the Lord, as it is written in the Book of Moses. And they did the same with the cattle. **13.** They roasted the Passover offerings with fire according to the ordinance, but the other holy offerings they boiled in pots, caldrons, and pans, and divided them quickly among all the lay people. **14.** Then afterward, they prepared portions for themselves and for the priests, for the priests, the sons of Aaron, were busy offering burnt offerings and fat until night. Therefore, the Levites prepared portions for themselves and for the priests, the sons of Aaron. **15.** And the singers, the sons of Asaph, were in their places, according to the command of David, Asaph, Heman, and Jeduthun, the king's seer. Also, the gatekeepers were at each gate; they did not need to leave their positions, because their fellow Levites prepared portions for them. **16.** So all the service of the Lord was prepared the same day, to keep the Passover and offer burnt offerings on the altar of the Lord, according to the command of King Josiah. **17.** The children of Israel who were present kept the Passover at that time, and the Feast of Unleavened Bread for seven days. **18.** There had been no Passover kept in Israel like that since the days of Samuel the prophet, and none of the kings of Israel had kept such a Passover as Josiah kept, with the priests, Levites, all Judah and Israel who were present, and the inhabitants of Jerusalem. **19.** In the eighteenth year of Josiah's reign, this Passover was kept. **20.** After all this, when Josiah had prepared the temple, Necho, the king of Egypt, came to fight against Carchemish by the Euphrates River, and Josiah went out to face him. **21.** But Necho sent messengers to Josiah, saying, "What have I to do with you, king of Judah? I have not come against you this day, but against the house (kingdom) with which I have war; for God has commanded me to make haste. Refrain from meddling with God, who is with me, lest He destroy you." **22.** Nevertheless, Josiah would not turn away from him, but disguised himself so that he might fight him. He did not listen to the words of Necho, spoken by the mouth of God. So Josiah came to fight in the Valley of Megiddo. **23.** The archers shot King Josiah, and the king said to his servants, "Take me away, for I am severely wounded." **24.** His servants took him out of the chariot and put him in a second chariot, and they brought him to Jerusalem. So he died and was buried in one of the tombs of his ancestors. All Judah and Jerusalem mourned for Josiah. **25.** Jeremiah also lamented for Josiah. And to this day, all the singing men and women speak of Josiah in their lamentations. They made it a custom in Israel, and it is written in the Laments. **26.** Now the rest of the acts of Josiah, his goodness, according to what was written in the Law of the Lord, **27.** And his deeds from first to last, are written in the book of the kings of Israel and Judah.

Chapter 36

1. Then the people of the land took Jehoahaz, the son of Josiah (Josiah was the former king of Judah), and made him king in his father's place in Jerusalem (the capital city of Judah). **2.** Jehoahaz was twenty-three years old when he became king, and he reigned three months in Jerusalem. **3.** Now the king of Egypt, Pharaoh Necho (the ruler of Egypt), deposed him at Jerusalem, and he imposed on the land a tribute (tax or payment) of one hundred talents of silver (a large sum of silver) and a talent of gold (a large weight of gold). **4.** Then Pharaoh Necho made Jehoahaz's brother, Eliakim, king over Judah and Jerusalem, and changed his name to Jehoiakim. Necho took Jehoahaz his brother and carried him off to Egypt (Pharaoh took him as a prisoner to Egypt). **5.** Jehoiakim was twenty-five years old when he became king, and he reigned eleven years in Jerusalem. And he did evil (wicked things) in the sight of the Lord his God. **6.** Nebuchadnezzar (the king of Babylon) came up against him, and bound him in bronze fetters (metal chains) to carry him off to Babylon (the capital of the Babylonian Empire). **7.** Nebuchadnezzar also carried off some of the articles (sacred objects) from the house of the Lord to Babylon, and put them in his temple (a place of worship) at Babylon. **8.** Now the rest of the acts of Jehoiakim, the abominations (wicked or detestable acts) which he did, and what was found against him, indeed they are written in the book of the kings of Israel and Judah. Then his son Jehoiachin reigned in his place. **9.** Jehoiachin was eight years old when he became king, and he reigned in Jerusalem for three months and ten days. And he did evil in the sight of the Lord. **10.** At the turn of the year, King Nebuchadnezzar summoned him and took him to Babylon with the costly articles from the house of the Lord, and made Zedekiah, Jehoiakim's brother, king over Judah and Jerusalem. **11.** Zedekiah was twenty-one years old when he became king, and he reigned eleven years in Jerusalem. **12.** He did evil in the sight of the Lord his God, and did not humble himself before Jeremiah (the prophet who spoke from God), who spoke from the mouth of the Lord. **13.** And he also rebelled (resisted) against King Nebuchadnezzar, who had made him swear an oath by God; but he stiffened his neck (was stubborn) and hardened his heart (refused to listen) against turning to the Lord God of Israel. **14.** Moreover, all the leaders of the priests and the people transgressed (sinned or broke God's laws) more and more, according to all the abominations of the nations, and defiled (made impure) the house of the Lord which He had consecrated (set apart as holy) in Jerusalem. **15.** And the Lord God of their fathers sent warnings to them by His messengers, rising up early and sending them, because He had compassion (deep care) on His people and on His dwelling place (the temple). **16.** But they mocked (ridiculed) the messengers of God, despised (rejected) His words, and scoffed (made fun of) at His prophets, until the wrath (anger) of the Lord arose against His people, till there was no remedy (no way to stop His judgment). **17.** Therefore, He brought against them the king of the Chaldeans (Babylonian army), who killed their young men with the sword in the house of their sanctuary (the temple), and had no compassion (mercy) on young men or virgins (young women), on the aged or the weak; He gave them all into his hand. **18.** And all the articles from the house of God, both great and small, the treasures of the house of the Lord, and the treasures of the king and of his leaders, all these he took to Babylon. **19.** Then they burned the house of God, broke down the wall of Jerusalem, burned all its palaces with fire, and destroyed all its precious possessions. **20.** And those who escaped from the sword he carried away to Babylon, where they became servants (slaves) to him and his sons until the rule

of the kingdom of Persia (the empire that conquered Babylon). **21.** To fulfill the word of the Lord by the mouth of Jeremiah, until the land had enjoyed her Sabbaths (a time of rest), as long as she lay desolate (in ruin) she kept Sabbath, to fulfill seventy years. **22.** Now in the first year of Cyrus (the king of Persia), that the word of the Lord by the mouth of Jeremiah might be fulfilled, the Lord stirred up (inspired) the spirit of Cyrus, king of Persia, so that he made a proclamation (decree) throughout all his kingdom, and also put it in writing, saying, **23.** Thus says Cyrus, king of Persia: "All the kingdoms of the earth the Lord God of heaven has given me. And He has commanded me to build Him a house (temple) at Jerusalem which is in Judah. Who is among you of all His people? May the Lord his God be with him, and let him go up!"

13 – The Book of Jubilees

Chapter 1

1. And in the first year after the exodus (departure) of the children of Yisrael from Egypt, in the third month, on the sixteenth day, YAHWEH spoke to Mosheh, saying: "Come up to Me on the Mount, and I will give you two stone tablets of the Torah and commandments, which I have written, to teach them." **2.** Mosheh ascended the Mount, and the splendor (radiance) of YAHWEH rested on Mount Sinai, with a cloud overshadowing it for six days. **3.** On the seventh day, YAHWEH called to Mosheh from within the cloud, and the appearance of His splendor was like a flaming fire on the mountaintop. **4.** Mosheh remained on the Mount for forty days and nights, during which YAHWEH taught him the history and division of the days in the Torah and the testimony. **5.** He said, "Incline (focus) your heart to every word I speak on this mountain, and write them in a book, so future generations may see how I have not forsaken them, despite their transgressions (sins) of the covenant I established with them on this day." **6.** When these things come to pass, they will realize I am more righteous than they in all judgments and actions, recognizing I have truly been with them. **7.** "Write these words, for I know their rebellion (defiance) and stubbornness before I bring them into the promised land—a land flowing with milk and honey." **8.** They will eat and be satisfied, yet turn to false gods that cannot deliver them in times of trouble. This witness will testify against them for abandoning My commandments, walking after Gentile ways, and serving other gods, which will bring them offense, affliction, and snare. **10.** Many will perish, fall captive, and suffer because they forsake My ordinances, commandments, and festivals, neglecting My holy place and My sanctuary (sacred place), where I placed My NAME to dwell. **11.** They will make high places, groves, and graven (carved) images, each worshiping their own idols, leading astray and sacrificing their children to demons, all works of their erring hearts. **12.** I will send witnesses against them, but they will not listen. They will kill the witnesses, persecute (harass) those seeking the Torah, and corrupt everything to work evil before My eyes. **13.** I will hide My face, deliver them into Gentile hands for captivity, and scatter them among the nations. **14.** They will forget My Torah, commandments, and judgments, going astray in months, Sabbaths, festivals, jubilees, and ordinances. **15.** Later, they will turn to Me from among the Gentiles, seeking Me with all their heart and soul. I will gather them and be found by them. **16.** I will grant them peace and righteousness, and remove them as a plant of uprightness. They shall be a blessing, the head and not the tail. **17.** I will build My sanctuary in their midst, dwell with them, and be their YAHWEH. They shall be My people in truth and righteousness. **18.** I will never forsake them, for I am YAHWEH, their Sovereign Ruler. **19.** Mosheh prayed, saying, "Do not forsake Your people, lest they fall into error (sin) and be ruled by enemies, causing them to sin against You." **20.** "Lift up Your mercy on Your people, create an upright spirit (moral strength) in them, and do not let the spirit of Belial accuse or ensnare them." **21.** "They are Your people and inheritance, redeemed with Your great power from Egypt. Create in them a clean heart and a holy spirit (set apart), that they may not fall into sin." **22.** YAHWEH said to Mosheh: "I know their rebellious nature, and they will not obey until they confess their sins and those of their fathers." **23.** "Then, they will turn to Me with all their heart and soul, and I will circumcise (purify) their hearts and those of their children, creating a holy spirit in them." **24.** "Their souls will cleave (cling) to Me, fulfilling My commandments, and I will be their Father, and they shall be My children." **25.** "They shall be called children of the living YAHWEH, known by all spirits and angels as My children, loved by Me in uprightness." **26.** "Write these words for yourself, from the beginning of creation to the establishment of My eternal sanctuary."

27. YAHWEH said to the angel of His presence: "Write for Mosheh from creation until My sanctuary is built among them forever." **28.** YAHWEH will be known to all, as the Sovereign Ruler of Yisrael, the ABBA (Father) of the children of Yacob, and King on Mount Zion forever. Zion and Yerushalem will be holy. **29.** The angel of His presence took the tablets detailing the divisions of the years, from creation to the establishment of the sanctuary, and the renewal of all creation for healing, peace, and blessing for Yisrael. This will continue until the end of the earth.

Chapter 2

1. And the malak (angel) of the presence spoke to Mosheh, according to the word of YAHWEH: Write the complete history of creation, how in six days YAHWEH ALMIGHTY finished His works, rested on the seventh day, hallowed (made holy) it, and made it a sign for all His creations. **2.** On the first day, He created the heavens, earth, waters, and all the spirits that serve before Him: the malakim (angels) of the presence, sanctification (setting apart), fire, winds, clouds, darkness, snow, hail, frost, voices, thunder, lightning, cold, heat, and the seasons. He also created the abysses (depths), night, dawn, and day, all prepared in the knowledge of His heart. **3.** We saw His works and praised Him for the seven great works He created on the first day. **4.** On the second day, He created the firmament (expanse), dividing the waters above and below it, a single work of YAHWEH. **5.** On the third day, He commanded the waters to gather, revealing dry land. **6.** The waters obeyed, and the dry land appeared. **7.** On the third day, He created seas, rivers, lakes, dew, seeds, sprouting plants, fruit trees, wood trees, and the garden of Eden. These were four great works. **8.** On the fourth day, He created the sun, moon, and stars, setting them in the firmament to give light, rule day and night, and divide light from darkness. **9.** YAHWEH appointed the sun as a sign for days, Shabbats, months, feasts, years, jubilees, and seasons. **10.** The sun divides light from darkness, ensuring prosperity (well-being) for all that grows on earth. Three works were created on the fourth day. **11.** On the fifth day, He created great sea monsters, fish, and creatures of the waters, as well as birds. **12.** The sun rose above them, bringing prosperity to all on earth, including trees and plants. Three works were created on the fifth day. **13.** On the sixth day, He created all land animals, cattle, and creatures that move on earth. **14.** Then He created man—male and female—and gave them dominion (rule) over all earth, seas, flying creatures, beasts, and cattle. **15.** Four kinds were created on the sixth day, making a total of twenty-two kinds. **16.** On the sixth day, He finished all His works in heaven, earth, seas, and abysses, and all that is in them. **17.** He gave us the Shabbat as a sign, commanding us to work six days and rest on the seventh. **18.** The malakim of the presence and sanctification were told to keep Shabbat with Him in heaven and on earth. **19.** He declared He would set apart a people to keep the Shabbat and sanctify them as His people, blessing them. **20.** He chose Yacob's seed, writing them as His firstborn and sanctifying them forever, teaching them to keep the Shabbat. **21.** He established the Shabbat as a sign for them to eat, drink, and bless Him, for they are a chosen people. **22.** His commands ascend as a sweet savor (fragrance), accepted by Him daily. **23.** From Adam to Yacob, twenty-two heads of mankind and twenty-two works were created by the seventh day, which is blessed and holy. **24.** Yacob's seed was granted to always be the blessed, holy people of the first testimony and Torah, as He sanctified the seventh day. **25.** YAHWEH created heaven, earth, and all within them in six days, and made the seventh day holy for all His works, commanding death for those who defile (desecrate) it. **26.** Command the children of Yisrael to keep the Shabbat holy, not working or defiling it, as it is holier than all other days. **27.** Anyone who profanes (treats with disrespect) it shall die eternally; the children of Yisrael must keep it to avoid being rooted out. **28.** Whoever keeps the Shabbat holy will be blessed, just as we are. **29.** Declare to the children of Yisrael the Torah of this day, that they should keep Shabbat, avoid error, and not perform work, make food, draw water, or carry burdens. **30.** They shall not transfer goods from house to house, for this day is holier than any jubilee (a special year of rest) day, observed even before it was known on earth. **31.** The Creator blessed this day, sanctifying it for Yisrael alone, allowing them to eat, drink, and keep Shabbat. **32.** He made this day splendid (magnificent) above all days, a day for blessing

and holiness. **33.** This Torah and testimony was given to Yisrael as an eternal commandment for their generations.

Chapter 3

1. On the sixth day of the second week, as YAHWEH commanded, we brought all the beasts, cattle, birds, and creatures from the earth and water to Adam, according to their kinds: the beasts on the first day, cattle on the second, birds on the third, earth creatures on the fourth, and water creatures on the fifth. **2.** Adam named each one, and they were named as he called them. **3.** Adam saw all these creatures, male and female, but found no helpmeet (companion) for himself. **4.** YAHWEH said, "It is not good for man to be alone; let us make a helpmeet for him." **5.** YAHWEH caused a deep sleep to fall on Adam, took one of his ribs, and from it created the woman, replacing the rib with flesh. **6.** Upon awakening, Adam rose on the sixth day, and YAHWEH brought the woman to him. He recognized her as "bone of my bones and flesh of my flesh," and called her wife, for she was taken from him. **7.** Therefore, a man shall leave his father and mother, cleave (adhere) to his wife, and they shall become one flesh. **8.** In the first week, Adam and his wife were created; in the second week, she was shown to him. This led to the commandment regarding purification for the birth of a male, seven days, and for a female, fourteen days. **9.** After forty days, we brought Adam into the Garden of Eden to tend it, and on the eightieth day, his wife entered. **10.** A woman who bears a male child remains unclean (impure) for seven days, followed by thirty-three days of purification. She must not touch anything holy or enter the sanctuary until these days are completed. **11.** If she bears a female child, she remains unclean for two weeks and undergoes sixty-six days of purification, totaling eighty days. **12.** After completing these days, she entered the Garden of Eden, the holiest place, with every tree planted there being holy. **13.** The commandment requires a woman to avoid touching holy things or entering the sanctuary until her purification for a male or female child is complete. **14.** This is the Torah and testimony for Israel, to be observed throughout the ages. **15.** In the first week of the first jubilee (a special year of rest), Adam and his wife worked in Eden for seven years, tilling and keeping it, as instructed. **16.** Adam worked, unaware of his nakedness, and guarded the garden from animals, collecting fruit for himself and his wife. **17.** After seven years, on the seventeenth day of the second month, the serpent approached the woman and asked, "Did YAHWEH say you cannot eat from every tree of the garden?" **18.** She replied, "We may eat from all the trees except the one in the midst, for YAHWEH said not to eat or touch it, lest we die." The serpent contradicted her, saying, "You won't die; eating it will open your eyes, making you like gods, knowing good and evil." **20.** The woman saw the tree was pleasant and its fruit good for food, so she ate. **21.** She covered her shame with fig leaves and gave some to Adam, who ate as well. Their eyes were opened, and they saw they were naked. **22.** Adam made an apron of fig leaves to cover himself. **23.** YAHWEH cursed (condemned) the serpent, condemning it forever. **24.** He was angry with the woman for listening to the serpent, and said, "I will multiply your sorrow in childbirth; you will return to your husband, and he will rule over you." **25.** To Adam, He said, "Because you listened to your wife and ate from the forbidden tree, the ground is cursed for you. You will toil (labor) and sweat to eat, until you return to the earth from which you were taken." **26.** YAHWEH made coats of skin for them, clothed them, and sent them out of the garden. **27.** On the day Adam left the garden, he offered a sweet-smelling (pleasant) sacrifice of frankincense, galbanum, stacte, and spices at dawn. **28.** On that day, all beasts, cattle, birds, and creatures were silenced, for they had once spoken in one voice. **29.** YAHWEH sent all creatures out of the garden, scattering them according to their kinds. **30.** Adam alone was given the means to cover his shame, unlike the beasts and cattle. **31.** Therefore, it is prescribed in the heavenly tablets that those who follow the Torah should cover their shame and not uncover themselves as the Gentiles do. **32.** On the new moon of the fourth month, Adam and his wife left the Garden of Eden and settled in the land of Elda. **33.** Adam named his wife Eve. **34.** They had no children until the first jubilee, when Adam knew his wife. **35.** Adam continued to till the land as he had been taught in the Garden of Eden.

Chapter 4

1. In the third week of the second jubilee, she bore Cain, in the fourth, Abel, and in the fifth, her daughter Awan. 2. In the first year of the third jubilee, Cain killed Abel because YAHWEH accepted Abel's offering, but not Cain's. 3. He killed him in the field, and Abel's blood cried from the ground to heaven. 4. YAHWEH rebuked (scolded) Cain for killing Abel, made him a fugitive, and cursed him because of his brother's blood. 5. It is written, "Cursed is he who kills treacherously (deceitfully), and those who see and hear but do not declare it, let them be accursed." 6. We announce before YAHWEH all sins committed in heaven, on earth, in light, darkness, and everywhere. 7. Adam and Eve mourned for Abel for four weeks, but in the fourth year of the fifth week, Adam knew his wife again, and she bore Seth. 8. In the sixth week, Eve bore Azura. 9. Cain married Awan, and she bore Enoch. Cain built a city and named it after Enoch. 10. Adam knew Eve, and she bore nine more sons. 11. In the fifth week of the fifth jubilee, Seth married Azura, and she bore Enos. 12. Enos began calling on the NAME of YAHWEH. 13. In the third week of the seventh jubilee, Enos married Noam, and she bore Kenan. 14. At the close of the eighth jubilee, Kenan married Mualeleth, and she bore Mahalalel in the third year of the first week of the ninth jubilee. 15. In the second week of the tenth jubilee, Mahalalel married DinaH, and she bore Jared. In his days, the Watchers (angels) descended to teach men judgment and righteousness. 16. In the fourth week of the eleventh jubilee, Jared married Baraka, and she bore Enoch. 17. Enoch was the first to learn writing, knowledge, and wisdom, and wrote the signs of heaven in a book for men to know the seasons. 18. He also wrote a testimony about the generations and the Shabbats. 19. Enoch saw in a vision what would happen to mankind until the Day of Judgment and wrote his testimony for future generations. 20. In the seventh week of the twelfth jubilee, Enoch married Edna, and she bore Methuselah. 21. Enoch was with the angels for six jubilees, and they showed him everything on earth and in heaven. 22. He testified against the Watchers who defiled (corrupted) themselves with human daughters. 23. Enoch was taken to the Garden of Eden in honor and majesty, where he wrote the condemnation of the world. 24. YAHWEH sent the flood as a sign, and Enoch testified against all men's deeds. 25. He burned incense (sacred offering) before YAHWEH on the Mount. 26. YAHWEH has four holy places: the Garden of Eden, the Mount of the East, Mount Sinai, and Mount Zion, which will sanctify (set apart as holy) the earth. 27. In the fourteenth jubilee, Methuselah married Edna, and she bore Lamech. 28. In the fifteenth jubilee, Lamech married Betenos, and she bore Noah, saying, "This one will comfort me for my work." 29. At the close of the nineteenth jubilee, Adam died in the seventh week, and his sons buried him. 30. He lacked seventy years of a thousand years; for a thousand years are as a day in the heavenly testimony. 31. In the same year, Cain died when his house collapsed on him, and he was killed by stones, as he had killed Abel. 32. It was ordained (commanded): "With the same instrument a man kills, so shall he be killed." 33. In the twenty-fifth jubilee, Noah married Emzara, and she bore him Shem, Ham, and Japheth.

Chapter 5

1. And when the children of men multiplied on earth and daughters were born, the malakim (angels) of YAHWEH saw their beauty in a certain year of the jubilee. They took wives from among them and bore giants. 2. Torahlessness (lack of law) spread on the earth, and all flesh corrupted its ways, including men, cattle, beasts, birds, and everything walking the earth. They began devouring each other, and evil grew, with all men's thoughts continuously evil. 3. YAHWEH saw the corruption on earth, for all flesh had corrupted its ways, and all had committed evil before His eyes. 4. He decided to destroy man and all flesh He created. 5. But Noah found unmerited (undeserved) favor in YAHWEH's eyes. 6. YAHWEH was angered against the angels He sent to earth and commanded them to be rooted out of their dominion (territory), bound in the depths, and separated. 7. A command went forth to smite (strike) their sons with the sword and remove them from under heaven. 8. He said, "My spirit will not remain with man forever, for they are flesh; their days shall be 120 years." 9. He sent His sword among them, causing them to slay each other until all fell by the sword and were destroyed. 10. Their fathers witnessed their destruction, and they were bound in the earth until the day of judgment for all who corrupted their ways. 11. He destroyed all from their places, judging

them for their wickedness. 12. He made a new and righteous nature for all His works so they would not sin but remain righteous forever. 13. The judgment of all is written in the heavenly tablets, including those who depart from the path ordained for them. 14. Nothing in heaven, on earth, or in Sheol (the grave) is exempt from judgment. All judgments are written and engraved. 15. He will judge each according to their greatness or smallness, and according to their ways. 16. He does not regard persons (show partiality) or accept gifts; He will execute judgment on each, regardless of offerings. 17. For the children of Israel, if they turn to Him in righteousness, He will forgive their transgressions and show mercy once each year. 19. Of all who corrupted their ways before the flood, only Noah's person was accepted for the sake of his sons, whom YAHWEH saved because of him. 20. YAHWEH decided to destroy all life on earth, including men, cattle, beasts, and birds. 21. He commanded Noah to build an ark to save himself from the floodwaters. 22. Noah built the ark as commanded in the 27th jubilee, 5th week, 5th year (1307 A.M.). 23. He entered the ark in the 6th year, 2nd month, until the 16th, with all that was brought to him. YAHWEH sealed the ark on the 17th evening. 24. YAHWEH opened the seven flood-gates of heaven and the fountains of the deep. 25. The waters poured down for 40 days and nights, and the fountains released water, flooding the world. 26. The waters rose 15 cubits above the highest mountains, lifting the ark above the earth. 27. The waters prevailed for five months, 150 days. 28. The ark rested on the top of Lubar, a mountain of Ararat. 29. In the 4th month, the fountains of the deep closed, and the flood-gates were restrained. In the 7th month, the abyss mouths opened, and water began descending. 30. In the 10th month, the mountaintops appeared, and in the 1st month, the earth became visible. 31. The waters receded by the 5th week of the 7th year (1309 A.M.), and on the 17th day of the 2nd month, the earth was dry. 32. On the 27th day, Noah opened the ark and released all living creatures.

Chapter 6

1. And on the new month of the third month, he left the ark and built an altar on the mountain. 2. He atoned (made amends) for the earth, took a kid, and made atonement for its guilt with its blood, as everything on earth had been destroyed, except for those in the ark with Noah. 3. He placed the fat on the altar, took an ox, goat, sheep, kids, salt, a turtle-dove, and dove's young, offering them as burnt sacrifices. He poured oil and sprinkled wine, strewed frankincense (a resin used in incense), and created a pleasing aroma, acceptable before YAHWEH. 4. YAHWEH smelled the pleasing aroma and made a covenant with Noah, promising no more floods to destroy the earth. The seasons—seedtime and harvest, cold and heat, summer and winter, day and night—would never cease. 5. "Increase, multiply, and become many upon the earth. I will inspire fear and dread of you in all creatures, both on land and in the sea." 6. "I give you all beasts, winged creatures, everything moving on the earth, and the fish of the waters for food, as I gave you the green herbs." 7. "But you shall not eat flesh with its lifeblood (blood in its living state), for the life of flesh is in its blood. I will require the blood of man from both man and beast." 8. "Whoever sheds man's blood, by man shall his blood be shed, for man was made in the image of YAHWEH." 9. "Increase and multiply on the earth." 10. Noah and his sons swore not to eat blood, making a covenant before YAHWEH forever for all generations of the earth. 11. Therefore, He commanded you to make a covenant with the children of Israel (descendants of Jacob) in this month on the mountain (Sinai, the mountain where Moses received commandments) with an oath, sprinkling blood upon them for the covenant made with them forever. 12. This testimony is written for you to observe continually. Anyone eating blood of beasts, birds, or cattle will be uprooted from the land, along with their descendants. 13. Command the children of Israel to observe this festival for all generations, celebrating it one day each year in this month. 14. This Torah (law) has no end, for it is forever. They will observe it across generations, continually seeking forgiveness before YAHWEH through sacrifices, morning and evening. 15. He gave Noah and his sons a sign that there would be no more floods to destroy the earth. 16. He placed His bow in the cloud as a sign of the eternal covenant to prevent another flood. 17. It is ordained and written on the heavenly tablets (celestial records) to celebrate the "Feast of Weeks" once a year in this month to renew the covenant. 18. This

festival was celebrated in heaven from creation until Noah's time— twenty-six jubilees and five weeks. Noah and his sons observed it for seven jubilees and one week, but after Noah's death, his sons abandoned it until Abraham's time. **19.** Abraham, Isaac, Jacob, and their children observed it until your time, when the children of Israel forgot it until you renewed it on this mountain. **20.** Command the children of Israel to observe this festival for all generations, celebrating it one day each year in this month. **21.** It is the "Feast of Weeks" and the "Feast of First Fruits," a double feast. Celebrate it as written. **22.** I have written in the first Torah for you to celebrate it in its season with sacrifices, so the children of Israel may remember and celebrate it every year. **23.** On the new month of the first, fourth, seventh, and tenth months, remember the days of the seasons and the four divisions of the year. These are written as a testimony forever. **24.** Noah ordained them as feasts for all generations, serving as a memorial to him. **25.** On the new month of the first month, Noah was instructed to build the ark, and the earth became dry. He opened the ark and saw the earth. **26.** On the new month of the fourth month, the depths of the abyss (a deep or bottomless chasm, often used for deep oceans or caves) were closed. On the new month of the seventh month, the abysses (great deep or ocean) opened, and waters began to descend. **27.** On the new month of the tenth month, the mountain tops (peaks) were visible, and Noah was glad. **28.** Therefore, Noah ordained these feasts as memorials forever. **29.** The heavenly tablets (celestial records) record each feast with thirteen weeks, and the memorials pass from one to the next. **30.** The commandment spans fifty-two weeks, completing the year. It is engraved on the heavenly tablets. **31.** There is no neglecting this commandment for any year. **32.** Command the children of Israel to observe the years according to this reckoning— three hundred and sixty-four days, with all feasts and times preserved. **33.** If they neglect and do not observe this commandment, their seasons and years will be disturbed, and they will forget their ordinances. **34.** The children of Israel will forget the path of the years, new months, seasons, Sabbaths, and go astray in their reckoning. **35.** I declare this to you, for it is written in the book and on the heavenly tablets that the division of days is fixed, ensuring they do not forget the feasts of the covenant. **36.** Some will observe the moon (lunar calendar), disturbing the seasons by making their observances ten days too early. **37.** This will lead to years of disruption, where they confuse clean and unclean days, disturbing the months, Sabbaths, feasts, and jubilees. **38.** Therefore, I command you to testify, for after your death, your children will stray, not keeping the year at three hundred and sixty-four days, disturbing the new months, seasons, Sabbaths, festivals, and eating all kinds of blood with flesh.

Chapter 8

1. In the twenty-ninth jubilee, during the first week, [1373 A.M.], Arpachshad married Rasu'eja, the daughter of Susan, daughter of Elam. She bore him a son in the third year of the week, [1375 A.M.], and he named him Kainam. **2.** The son grew, and his father taught him writing. He sought a place to seize (take control of) a city for himself. **3.** He found an inscription (a written or carved message) carved by earlier generations, read it, transcribed it, and sinned because it contained the teachings of the Watchers on observing omens of the sun, moon, and stars. **4.** He wrote it down but kept silent, fearing Noah's anger. **5.** In the thirtieth jubilee, [1429 A.M.], during the second week, in the first year, Arpachshad married Melka, daughter of Madai, son of Japheth. In the fourth year [1432 A.M.], she bore him Shelah, saying, "Truly I have been sent." **6.** Shelah grew, married Mu'ak, daughter of Kesed, his father's brother, in the thirty-first jubilee, in the fifth week, in the first year [1499 A.M.]. **7.** In the fifth year [1503 A.M.], she bore him Eber. Eber then married Azurad, daughter of Nebrod, in the thirty-second jubilee, during the seventh week, in the third year [1564 A.M.]. **8.** In the sixth year [1567 A.M.], Azurad bore him Peleg, named so because, in his days, Noah's children began dividing (separating) the earth. **9.** They secretly divided the land and told Noah. **10.** At the start of the thirty-third jubilee [1569 A.M.], they divided the earth into three parts for Shem, Ham, and Japheth, with one sent to guide them. **11.** Noah called his sons, and they drew near with their children. He divided the earth into lots (portions or shares), and they took the writing from Noah's bosom. **12.** Shem's portion was the middle of the earth, from the mountain range of Rafa, to the mouth of the river Tina. His portion extends west through the river, flowing into the great sea. All lands north of this belong to Japheth, and all south of this to Shem. **13.** His portion extends to Karaso, a tongue (narrow strip) of land toward the south. **14.** His portion stretches along the great sea to 'Afra, and the waters of the river Gihon, south of which it reaches the river's banks. **15.** It stretches east to the Garden of Eden, south of it, and east of the land of Eden, turning east toward Rafa, descending to the river Tina's mouth. **16.** This portion was for Shem and his descendants forever. **17.** Noah rejoiced, recalling his prophecy: "Blessed be YAHWEH of Shem, and may He dwell in his dwelling." **18.** He knew the Garden of Eden is the holiest (most sacred) of places, Sinai the center of the desert, and Zion the center of the earth—these three were created as sacred places facing one another. **19.** He praised YAHWEH for placing His Word in his mouth. **20.** Noah knew the blessed portion for Shem and his descendants, from Eden to the Red Sea, India, and all the mountains of Bashan, Lebanon, Kaftur, and the mountains of Sanir and 'Amana, Asshur, Elam, Babel, Susan, Ma'edai, Ararat, and all regions beyond the north. **21.** This land was a blessed and spacious (wide and expansive) one, full of goodness. **22.** For Ham, the second portion extended beyond Gihon, south of the Garden, and stretched towards the mountains of fire, the sea of 'Atel, and the sea of Ma'uk. **23.** It extended north to Gadir, along the river Gihon, to the Garden's right. **24.** This land was Ham's, to be occupied by his descendants forever. **25.** For Japheth, the third portion extended beyond the river Tina, north of its outflow, and stretched northeast to Gog and the regions east of it. **26.** It extended north, towards the mountains of Qelt, and the sea of Ma'uk, reaching the east of Gadir and the sea's waters. **27.** It reached Fara's west, returned to 'Aferag, and extended east to the waters of the sea of Me'at. **28.** It extended to the Tina River region, heading northeast toward Rafa, and then northward. **29.** This land was for Japheth and his descendants, to possess forever—five great islands and large northern lands. **30.** But Japheth's land is cold, Ham's land is hot, and Shem's land is a blend (mixture) of cold and heat.

Chapter 9

1. And Ham distributed land to his sons: the first portion went to Cush in the east, to Mizraim in the west, to put further west, and to Canaan by the sea. **2.** Shem divided his inheritance, giving the first portion to Ham and his sons, from the east of the Tigris River to India, the Red Sea, Dedan's waters, the Mebri and Ela mountains, Susan's land, and Pharnak's region to the Red Sea and the Tina River. **3.** The second portion went to Asshur, covering Asshur's land, Nineveh, Shinar, and reaching India's border, ascending (rising) along the river. **4.** The third portion for Arpachshad covered the Chaldees' land east of the Euphrates, bordering the Red Sea, the desert waters near the sea's tongue towards Egypt, Lebanon, Sanir, Amana, and the Euphrates' border. **5.** The fourth portion for Aram included Mesopotamia between the Tigris and Euphrates, north of the Chaldees, extending to the Asshur mountains and Arara. **6.** The fifth portion for Lud covered Asshur's mountains and their regions to the Great Sea and eastward to Asshur's border. **7.** Japheth also divided his inheritance among his sons. **8.** The first portion for Gomer extended eastward, north to the Tina River. Magog's portion lay to the north, reaching the Me'at (a sea or body of water) Sea. **9.** Madai's portion was from the west of his two brothers to the islands and their coasts. **10.** Javan's portion included every island and those near Lud's border. **11.** Tubal's portion lay in the middle of the tongue (a narrow strip) that bordered Lud, extending to the second tongue and beyond to the third tongue. **12.** Meshech's portion stretched beyond the third tongue to the east of Gadir. **13.** Tiras received the seventh portion: four great islands in the sea, extending to Ham's portion, and the Kamaturi islands (islands near the coast), allotted to Arpachshad's sons. **14.** Thus, Noah's sons divided the land in his presence, swearing an oath (solemn promise) to curse anyone who took land not assigned to them. **15.** They all said, "So be it" for themselves and their descendants, forever, until the day of judgment when YAHWEH ALMIGHTY will judge the wicked for their sins and uncleanness.

Chapter 10

1. In the third week of this jubilee, unclean demons began to lead astray the children of Noah's sons, causing them to err and perish. **2.** The sons of Noah approached him, telling him about the demons leading his descendants astray, blinding and killing them. **3.** Noah prayed to YAHWEH (God), his Sovereign, saying: "YAHWEH, Creator of all flesh, who showed mercy to me, saving me and my sons from the flood, and did not let me perish as the wicked did, Your mercy has been great. Let Your mercy extends to my sons and protect them from wicked spirits that they be not destroyed." **4.** "Bless me and my sons, that we may increase, multiply, and replenish the earth." **5.** "You know how Your Watchers (divine beings) acted in my day; imprison these spirits and hold them in the place of condemnation, lest they harm my descendants." **6.** "Do not let them rule over the spirits of the living, for You alone have dominion over them. Let them not have power over the righteous forever." **7.** YAHWEH commanded us to bind them all. **8.** The chief spirit, Mastema (demonic figure), said: "YAHWEH, Creator, let some remain before me, so they may obey me, for I need them to corrupt and lead astray the sons of men." **9.** YAHWEH answered, "Let a tenth remain before him, and the rest descend into condemnation." **10.** YAHWEH commanded that we teach Noah their remedies, for He knew they would not walk uprightly. **11.** We did as instruct: we bound the evil spirits in condemnation, leaving a tenth under Satan's control on earth. **12.** We taught Noah the remedies for their diseases and how to heal them with herbs. **13.** Noah recorded all in a book, as instructed, to protect his descendants from harm. **14.** He gave the book to Shem (Noah's son), his eldest son, whom he loved deeply. **15.** Noah died and was buried on Mount Lubar (mountain in Armenia), in the land of Ararat (region near Turkey, Armenia). **16.** He lived 950 years, completing nineteen jubilees, two weeks, and five years. **17.** In righteousness, Noah excelled all men except Enoch (biblical figure), whose role was to serve as a testimony for future generations. **18.** In the thirty-third jubilee, Peleg (descendant of Noah) took a wife, Lomna (biblical figure), daughter of Sina'ar (ancient city in Mesopotamia), and had a son, Reu (biblical figure), in the fourth year. He named him Reu, saying: "The children of men are evil, building a city and tower in Shinar (biblical city). **19.** They moved eastward to Shinar, where they began building the city and tower to reach heaven. **20.** In the fourth week, they made bricks with fire, using asphalt and clay from the sea and fountains of Shinar. **21.** They built for 43 years, with the tower reaching 5433 cubits, its breadth 203 bricks, and its walls stretching for miles. **22.** YAHWEH said: "They are one people, and now nothing will stop them. Let us go down and confuse their language, so they cannot understand one another and will be scattered." **23.** YAHWEH and we descended to see the city and tower. **24.** He confused their language, and they ceased building. **25.** For this reason, the land of Shinar is called Babel (Babylon), where YAHWEH confused the languages and scattered the people. **26.** YAHWEH sent a mighty wind, toppling the tower between Asshur (ancient city) and Babylon (city in Mesopotamia) in Shinar, and they called it 'Overthrow.' **27.** In the fourth week, first year of the thirty-fourth jubilee, they were dispersed from Shinar. **28.** Ham (Noah's son) and his sons went south, taking their allotted land. **29.** Canaan (son of Ham) saw the land of Lebanon (country in Middle East) and Egypt's river (Nile), and chose to dwell there, not in his allotted west. **30.** His family told him not to settle there, for it was not his inheritance, warning that it would bring curse and destruction. **31.** "Do not dwell in Shem's (Noah's son) land; it belongs to him and his sons." **32.** "Cursed are you beyond all the sons of Noah, by the oath we took before YAHWEH." **33.** But Canaan ignored them and lived in Lebanon, from Hamath (ancient city) to Egypt's border. **34.** Hence, the land was named Canaan. **35.** Japheth (Noah's son) and his sons went to the sea and settled in their land. Madai (son of Japheth), displeased with the sea, sought a portion from Ham and his brothers, settling near them in Media (region in ancient Persia). **36.** He named the land Media after his father, Madai.

Chapter 11

1. In the 35th Jubilee, during the third week, in its first year (1681 A.M.), Reu took Ora, daughter of Ur (son of Kesed), as his wife. She bore him a son named Seroh in the seventh year of this week (1687 A.M.). **2.** The sons of Noah began warring, enslaving, and killing one another. They shed human blood, consumed blood, built cities, walls, and towers, founded kingdoms, and taught their sons warfare, taking captives and selling male and female slaves. **3.** Ur (city), son of Kesed, built a city named Ara of the Chaldees (ancient region of Mesopotamia), after his and his father's names. **4.** The people made idols, worshiped them, and created graven images, influenced by evil

spirits, who led them into sin and uncleanness. **5.** Mastema (evil spirit), the prince of evil, sent spirits to commit sin, corrupt people, shed blood, and spread destruction. **6.** Seroh was named so because people turned to commit sin and transgression. **7.** Seroh grew up in Ur of the Chaldees, near his wife's maternal grandfather. He worshiped idols and married Melka (biblical figure), daughter of Kaber (biblical figure), in the 36th Jubilee, during the fifth week (1744 A.M.). **8.** Melka bore him Nahor (biblical figure) in the first year of this week. Nahor grew up in Ur of the Chaldees, where his father taught him Chaldean (Babylonian) knowledge, including divination and astrology. **9.** In the 37th Jubilee, during the sixth week, in its first year (1800 A.M.), Nahor married Ijaska, daughter of Nestag of the Chaldees. **10.** Ijaska bore him Terah (father of Abram) in the seventh year of this week (1806 A.M.). **11.** Mastema sent ravens and birds to devour the seeds sown in the land, destroying the crops and robbing people of their labor. The ravens picked the seeds off the ground before they could be plowed in. **12.** Because the ravens caused such devastation, Terah was given his name, which means "destitution". **13.** The years became barren, as birds devoured the fruit of the trees. It required great effort to save even a small portion of the land's produce. **14.** In the 39th Jubilee, during the second week, in its first year (1870 A.M.), Terah married Edna (biblical figure), daughter of Abram (biblical figure), his father's sister's daughter. **15.** In the seventh year of this week (1876 A.M.), Edna bore him a son, Abram (biblical figure), named after her father, who had died before she conceived. **16.** As Abram grew, he realized the errors of the earth, where people followed idols and uncleanness. At two weeks of years old (1890 A.M.), he separated himself from his father to avoid idol worship. **17.** Abram prayed to the Creator of all things to save him from the errors of mankind and keep him from falling into sin and uncleanness. **18.** During the sowing season, everyone went out to guard their seeds from ravens. Abram, then 14 years old, went with them. **19.** A cloud of ravens descended to devour the seed, but Abram ran toward them and commanded, "Do not land; return to your place." The ravens obeyed and turned back. **20.** That day, Abram turned away clouds of ravens seventy times, and not a single raven landed anywhere in the area. **21.** Everyone who saw Abram's actions marveled as the ravens turned back. His name became renowned throughout the land of the Chaldees. **22.** In that year, many came to Abram for help with their sowing. He stayed with them until the sowing was complete, and they harvested enough grain to eat and be satisfied. **23.** In the first year of the fifth week (1891 A.M.), Abram taught artisans to craft wooden seed-containers attached to ploughs. These devices dropped seed into the soil, protecting it from birds. **24.** Following Abram's guidance, seed-containers were used across the land. The people sowed and tilled without fearing birds, securing their crops as Abram had instructed.

Chapter 12

1. During the sixth week, in the seventh year of it (1904 A.M.), Abram said to his father, Terah (a city in Mesopotamia), "Father!" **2.** Terah replied, "Here I am, my son." Abram asked, "What help or benefit do we get from these idols (sculptures or representations of gods) that you worship and bow before? **3.** They have no spirit within them. They are lifeless forms, and they mislead the heart. **4.** Do not worship them. Instead, worship YAHWEH (God), the Sovereign Ruler of heaven, who brings rain and dew to the earth. He does all things on the earth, created everything by His word, and gives life to all creatures. **5.** Why do you worship things that lack life? They are made by human hands and carried on shoulders, offering no help. Instead, they bring shame to those who make them and deceive the hearts of those who worship them. Do not worship them." **6.** Terah answered, "I know this, my son, but what can I do with the people who have forced me to serve their idols? **7.** If I tell them the truth, they will kill me, for they are devoted to these idols. Keep this to yourself, my son, or they may also kill you." **8.** Terah shared this with Abram's brothers, but they became angry, so Abram remained silent. **9.** In the 40th Jubilee, during the second week, in its seventh year (1925 A.M.), Abram married Sarai (his wife and half-sister), his father's daughter, and she became his wife. **10.** Haran (city in Mesopotamia), Abram's brother, took a wife in the third year of the third week (1928 A.M.), and she bore a son named Lot (nephew of Abram) in the seventh year of the same week (1932 A.M.). **11.** Nahor, Abram's other brother, also married. **12.** In Abram's 60th year, during the fourth week and its fourth year (1936 A.M.), Abram burned the house of idols during the night, destroying everything inside. **13.** The people woke in the night, trying to rescue their gods from the fire. **14.** Haran rushed to save them, but the flames consumed him, and he died in Ur of the Chaldees (a city in southern Mesopotamia) before his father, Terah. They buried Haran in Ur. **15.** Afterward, Terah left Ur of the Chaldees with his sons, intending to go to the lands of Lebanon and Canaan (region of ancient Israel). They settled in Haran, where Abram stayed with his father for two weeks of years. **16.** During the sixth week, in its fifth year (1951 A.M.), Abram observed the stars throughout the night of the new moon in the seventh month. He sought to discern the year's rain patterns, sitting alone in contemplation. **17.** Abram reflected, saying, "All the signs of the stars, moon, and sun are controlled by YAHWEH. Why do I seek them out? **18.** If YAHWEH wills, He makes it rain, morning and evening; if not, He withholds it. All things are in His hands." **19.** That night, Abram prayed: "YAHWEH Most High, You alone are my Sovereign Ruler. I have chosen You and Your dominion. You created all things, and everything is the work of Your hands. **20.** Save me from the influence of evil spirits who rule over the thoughts of men, leading them astray. Keep me and my descendants faithful to You forever." **21.** Abram asked, "Shall I return to Ur of the Chaldees, where they seek me, or should I remain here? Guide me, YAHWEH, in Your path so I may not follow the deceitfulness of my own heart." **22.** After Abram finished praying, YAHWEH's word came to him, saying, "Leave your country, family, and father's house and go to the land I will show you. **23.** I will make you a great nation. I will bless you, make your name great, and you will be a blessing. All families of the earth will be blessed through you. I will bless those who bless you and curse those who curse you. **24.** I will be your Sovereign Ruler and the Sovereign Ruler of your descendants forever. Do not fear, for I am YAHWEH, your Sovereign Ruler, for all generations." **25.** YAHWEH continued: "Open his mouth and ears so he may speak and understand the language of creation, which ceased after the Tower of Babel." **26.** YAHWEH opened Abram's mouth, ears, and lips, enabling him to speak Hebrew (ancient language). **27.** Abram found the books of his ancestors written in Hebrew. He transcribed and studied them, gaining understanding during the six months of rain. **28.** In the seventh year of the sixth week (1953 A.M.), Abram told Terah that he intended to leave Haran for Canaan and then return. **29.** Terah said, "Go in peace. May YAHWEH guide your path, protect you from harm, and grant you favor among people. Let no one harm you. Go in peace." **30.** Terah added, "If you find a land pleasing to you, take me and Lot, Haran's son, with you as your own son. May YAHWEH be with you." **31.** Terah concluded, "Leave Nahor with me until you return, so we may all travel together in peace."

Chapter 13

1. Abram left Haran with Sarai, his wife, and Lot, his brother Haran's son, journeying to the land of Canaan. They arrived in Asshur (a city in Mesopotamia) and continued to Shechem (city in ancient Israel), where they settled near a tall oak tree. **2.** He saw that the land was beautiful, stretching from the entrance of Hamath to the tall oak. **3.** YAHWEH said to Abram, "To you and your descendants, I will give this land." **4.** Abram built an altar there and offered a burnt sacrifice to YAHWEH, who had appeared to him. **5.** From there, Abram moved to a mountain between Bethel (ancient city in Israel) (to the west) and Ai (ancient city in Israel) (to the east), where he pitched his tent. **6.** He observed that the land was expansive and fertile, abundant with vines, figs, pomegranates, oaks, terebinths, olive trees, cedars, cypresses, date trees, and other plants, with water flowing from the mountains. **7.** Abram praised YAHWEH for bringing him out of Ur of the Chaldees and into this good land. **8.** In the first year of the seventh week, on the new moon of the first month (1954 A.M.), Abram built an altar on this mountain and called on the name of YAHWEH, saying, "You, the eternal YAHWEH, are my Sovereign Ruler." **9.** He offered a burnt sacrifice on the altar, asking YAHWEH to be with him and not abandon him throughout his life. **10.** Abram moved southward to Hebron (ancient city in Israel), which was already established, and lived there for two years. He then traveled further south to Bealoth (a city) during a time of famine. **11.** In the third year of the week, Abram went to Egypt and stayed there for five years. During this time, his wife Sarai was taken from him. **12.** Tanais (an ancient Egyptian city) in Egypt had

been built seven years after Hebron. **13.** When Pharaoh (ruler of Egypt) seized Sarai, YAHWEH sent great plagues upon Pharaoh and his household because of her. **14.** Abram became very wealthy, acquiring sheep, cattle, donkeys, horses, camels, male and female servants, as well as silver and gold. Lot, his nephew, also gained wealth. **15.** Pharaoh returned Sarai to Abram and sent him out of Egypt. Abram journeyed back to the place where he had first pitched his tent, near the altar between Bethel and Ai. There, he blessed YAHWEH, who had brought him back in peace. **16.** In the 41st Jubilee, in the third year of the first week (1963 A.M.), Abram returned to this place, offered a burnt sacrifice, and called on the name of YAHWEH, saying, "You, the Most High YAHWEH, are my Sovereign Ruler forever." **17.** In the fourth year of this week (1964 A.M.), Lot separated from Abram and settled in Sodom (city in ancient Israel). The men of Sodom were exceedingly sinful. **18.** Abram was deeply grieved that Lot, his brother's son, had parted from him, as Abram had no children. **19.** That same year, after Lot left, YAHWEH spoke to Abram: "Look around from where you are—northward, southward, eastward, and westward. **20.** All the land you see, I will give to you and your descendants forever. I will make your descendants as numerous as the dust of the earth; no one will be able to count them. **21.** Arise, walk through the length and breadth of the land, for I will give it to you." Abram moved to Hebron and lived there. **22.** That year, Chedorlaomer, king of Elam, Amraphel, king of Shinar (region of Mesopotamia), Arioch, king of Ellasar, and Tergal, king of the nations, waged war, killing the king of Gomorrah. The king of Sodom fled, and many others perished in the Valley of Siddim near the Salt Sea. **23.** These kings captured Sodom, Adam, Zeboim, and Lot, Abram's nephew, along with all his possessions, and took them to Dan. **24.** A survivor escaped and informed Abram that Lot had been captured. Abram armed his household servants and prepared for action. **25.** Abram and his descendants established the practice of giving a tenth of all firstfruits to YAHWEH. YAHWEH commanded this as an eternal ordinance, to be given to the priests who serve before Him. **26.** This law had no time limit. YAHWEH decreed that a tenth of all produce—grain, wine, oil, cattle, and sheep—should be set aside for Him. **27.** This portion was given to His priests for their sustenance, to be eaten and enjoyed in His presence. **28.** The king of Sodom approached Abram and bowed before him, saying, "My lord Abram, return the people you rescued to us, but you may keep the plunder for yourself." **29.** Abram replied, "I lift my hands to the Most High YAHWEH, vowing not to take anything that belongs to you—not even a thread or a sandal strap—lest you claim, 'I made Abram rich.' Only let the young men take what they have eaten, and let Aner, Eschol, and Mamre take their portions."

Chapter 14

1. In the fourth year of this week, on the new moon of the third month, the word of YAHWEH came to Abram in a dream: "Do not fear, Abram. I am your defender, and your reward will be exceedingly great." **2.** Abram replied, "YAHWEH ALMIGHTY (God with all power), what can You give me, since I remain childless? The heir of my household is Eliezer (a servant from Damascus, an ancient city in Syria) of Damascus, the son of my servant Maseq. You have given me no offspring." **3.** YAHWEH answered, "This man will not be your heir. Your heir will come from your own body." **4.** He brought Abram outside and said, "Look up at the sky and count the stars—if you can count them." **5.** Then He said, "So shall your descendants be." **6.** Abram believed YAHWEH, and it was credited to him as righteousness. **7.** YAHWEH said, "I am YAHWEH, who brought you out of Ur of the Chaldees (an ancient city in Mesopotamia) to give you this land to possess forever. I will be your Sovereign Ruler, and to your descendants after you." **8.** Abram asked, "YAHWEH ALMIGHTY, how can I be sure I will inherit it?" **9.** YAHWEH replied, "Bring Me a three-year-old heifer, a three-year-old goat, a three-year-old ram, a turtledove, and a young pigeon." **10.** Abram gathered these animals in the middle of the month and brought them to the oak of Mamre (an ancient tree near Hebron in Canaan) near Hebron (an ancient city in southern Canaan). **11.** There he built an altar, sacrificed the animals, poured their blood on the altar, and cut them in half, placing the halves opposite each other. He did not divide the birds. **12.** Birds of prey came down on the carcasses, but Abram drove them away. **13.** As the sun set, a deep sleep fell upon Abram, and a great dread of darkness came over him. YAHWEH said to Abram, "Know this for certain: Your descendants will be strangers in a land that is not theirs. They will be enslaved and oppressed for 400 years. 14. But I will judge the nation that enslaves them, and afterward, they will come out with great wealth. 15. As for you, you will go to your ancestors in peace and be buried at a good old age. 16. In the fourth generation, your descendants will return here, for the sin of the Amorites (a people group in ancient Canaan) is not yet complete." 17. When Abram woke, the sun had set. A smoking furnace and a blazing torch passed between the pieces of the sacrifice. 18. On that day, YAHWEH made a covenant with Abram, saying, "To your descendants, I give this land—from the river of Egypt to the great Euphrates River (a major river in the ancient Near East): 19. the Kenites, Kenizzites, Kadmonites, Hittites, Perizzites, Rephaim, Amorites, Canaanites, Girgashites, and Jebusites (various nations or tribes in the ancient land of Canaan)." 20. The day passed, and Abram completed the offerings—sacrificing the animals, birds, and their accompanying drink and grain offerings. The fire consumed them. 21. YAHWEH established covenant with Abram, renewing the festival as He had done with Noah in this same month. Abram observed this ordinance forever. 22. Abram rejoiced and shared these events with Sarai, his wife, believing YAHWEH's promise that he would have offspring. However, Sarai remained barren. 23. Sarai suggested to Abram, "Take my Egyptian servant, Hagar (an Egyptian woman), as your wife. Perhaps I can have children through her." Abram agreed. 24. Sarai gave Hagar to Abram as his wife. He went to her, and she conceived and bore a son, whom Abram named Ishmael (the son of Abram and Hagar). This occurred in the fifth year of this week (1965 A.M.), when Abram was 86 years old.

Chapter 15

1. In the fifth year of the fourth week of this jubilee (1979 A.M.), during the third month at mid-month, Abram celebrated the Feast of Firstfruits (religious festival) from the grain harvest. 2. He offered sacrifices on the altar to YAHWEH, presenting a heifer, a goat, and a sheep as burnt offerings, along with grain and drink offerings and frankincense (aromatic resin). 3. YAHWEH appeared to Abram and said: 4. "I am YAHWEH Almighty. Walk before Me faithfully and be blameless (without fault). 5. I will establish My covenant with you and multiply your descendants greatly." Abram fell facedown as YAHWEH spoke to him, saying: 6. "This is My covenant with you: You will be the father of many nations. 7. Your name will no longer be Abram but Abraham (father of many nations) because I have made you the father of many nations. 8. I will make you exceedingly fruitful (productive), forming nations from you, and kings (royalty) will descend from you. 9. I will establish My covenant with you and your descendants as an everlasting covenant (eternal agreement). I will be your Sovereign Ruler and theirs. 10. I will give the land of Canaan (promised land), where you now live as a foreigner (stranger), to you and your descendants forever, and I will be their Sovereign Ruler." 11. YAHWEH continued: "You must keep My covenant, you and your descendants after you. 12. Every male among you must be circumcised (ritual cutting of the foreskin). Circumcise them on the eighth day—whether born in your house or purchased servants, even if not biologically related to you. 13. This will be a sign of the everlasting covenant in your flesh. 14. Any uncircumcised male who is not circumcised on the eighth day will be cut off from My people for breaking My covenant." 15. Then YAHWEH said, "Your wife Sarai will no longer be called Sarai; her name will be Sarah (princess). 16. I will bless her and give you a son through her. She will become the mother of nations, and kings will come from her." 17. Abraham bowed down, laughing in wonder, and thought, "Can a child be born to a man who is 100 years old? Will Sarah, at 90 years old, bear a son?" 18. He said to YAHWEH, "If only Ishmael could live under Your blessing!" 19. YAHWEH replied, "Sarah will indeed bear you a son, and you will name him Isaac (laughter). I will establish My everlasting covenant with him and his descendants. 20. As for Ishmael, I have heard your request. I will bless him, make him fruitful, and multiply him greatly. He will father 12 princes (rulers) and become a great nation. 21. But My covenant will be with Isaac, whom Sarah will bear to you at this time next year." 22. When YAHWEH finished speaking, He departed from Abraham. 23. That very day, Abraham circumcised Ishmael, all male members of his household—both those born there and those he had purchased—as YAHWEH commanded. 24. Abraham himself was circumcised, along with all the men of his household, as a sign of obedience to YAHWEH's eternal covenant. 25.

This law of circumcision is eternal, written on the heavenly tablets. No deviation is allowed; the eighth day is required. 26. Any male who is not circumcised on the eighth day is excluded from YAHWEH's covenant, counted among the wicked, and destined for destruction for breaking the covenant. 27. YAHWEH ordained this for the children of Israel (descendants of Abraham), setting them apart as His holy people, even before the angels of His presence and sanctification. 28. Command the children of Israel to observe this sign of the covenant for all generations, so they remain in the land and are not uprooted. 29. This command is an eternal covenant for Israel alone, not for Ishmael, Esau, or their descendants, though they are children of Abraham. 30. YAHWEH chose Israel to be His people, sanctifying them above all nations, even though all nations are His. 31. Other nations are governed by spirits appointed to lead them astray, but YAHWEH Himself governs Israel directly to preserve and bless them forever. 32. YAHWEH warned that Israel would fail to keep this covenant, neglecting circumcision, and turning to sin like the Gentiles (non-Israelites). 33. Because of this disobedience, great wrath (anger) will come upon Israel. They will provoke YAHWEH by abandoning His covenant and rejecting His Torah (teaching). 34. For this sin of eternal error, there will be no forgiveness (pardon) or pardon. They will be removed from the land, treated as if they never belonged to YAHWEH's people.

Chapter 16

1. At the start of the fourth month, we appeared to Abraham at the oak of Mamre (a tree located in the region of Canaan) and informed him that Sarah, his wife, would have a son. 2. Sarah overheard and laughed in disbelief. When confronted, she became afraid and denied laughing. 3. We revealed the name of her son—Isaac (meaning "he will laugh")—as it was already recorded on the heavenly tablets. 4. We told her that at the appointed time, she would conceive and bear this son. 5. During this month, YAHWEH judged Sodom, Gomorrah, Zeboim, and the surrounding Jordan (a major river in Israel) region, destroying them with fire and brimstone because of their wickedness, fornication, and uncleanness. 6. In the same way, YAHWEH will judge other places that follow the sins of Sodom. 7. However, YAHWEH saved Lot (Abraham's nephew), remembering Abraham, and brought him out of the destruction. 8. Yet Lot and his daughters committed a grave sin—he lay with his daughters—an act not seen on earth since Adam's time. 9. Because of this sin, it was decreed on the heavenly tablets that Lot's descendants would be removed and judged, leaving no trace on the day of condemnation. 10. That same month, Abraham moved from Hebron (a city in Canaan) and settled between Kadesh (a city in the desert) and Shur (a desert region), in the mountains of Gerar (a region in Philistine). 11. By the middle of the fifth month, he moved to Beersheba (a well-known place, meaning "well of the oath"), also called the "Well of the Oath." 12. In the middle of the sixth month, YAHWEH visited Sarah, fulfilling His promise, and she conceived. 13. The next year, in the third month, during the Festival of Firstfruits, Sarah gave birth to Isaac, just as YAHWEH had said. 14. On the eighth day, Abraham circumcised Isaac, the first to be circumcised under the eternal covenant. 15. In the sixth year of the fourth week, we visited Abraham again at the "Well of the Oath," as we had promised. 16. We returned in the seventh month and found Sarah pregnant, as foretold. We blessed Abraham and revealed that he would live to see six more sons before his death, though only through Isaac would his name and covenant continue. 17. The descendants of his other sons would become nations and be counted among the Gentiles, but one of Isaac's descendants would form a holy nation. 18. This nation would be YAHWEH's chosen people, belonging to Him as priests and a holy kingdom, set apart from all other nations. 19. After sharing this, we departed, and Abraham and Sarah rejoiced greatly at the news. 20. Abraham built an altar to YAHWEH at the "Well of the Oath" and celebrated a seven-day festival of joy, thanking YAHWEH for His blessings during his time as a sojourner. 21. He also built temporary shelters (booths) for himself and his servants, becoming the first to celebrate the Feast of Tabernacles (a Jewish festival). 22. Each day of the seven-day festival, Abraham offered burnt sacrifices: two oxen, two rams, seven sheep, and one goat as a sin offering to atone for himself and his descendants. 23. Additionally, he presented seven rams, seven lambs, seven goats, and their accompanying grain and

drink offerings as a thanksgiving sacrifice. He burned the fat as a fragrant offering to YAHWEH. **24.** Morning and evening, he burned fragrant incense, including frankincense (a resin used in incense), galbanum, stacte, nard (a fragrant oil), myrrh, spices, and costus (a spice), all mixed in equal parts and pure. **25.** Abraham celebrated the festival wholeheartedly with his household, ensuring no uncircumcised person or stranger joined. **26.** He praised his Creator, who had chosen him and his descendants to carry forth righteousness for all generations and produce a holy lineage resembling YAHWEH's purpose in creation. **27.** Abraham named this celebration "The Festival of YAHWEH," a time of great joy acceptable to the Most High. **28.** We blessed Abraham and his descendants, ordaining that this festival be celebrated by Israel forever, as written on the heavenly tablets. **29.** The Feast of Tabernacles is to be observed by Israel for seven days each year in the seventh month, as an eternal statute, with joy and thanksgiving to YAHWEH. **30.** There is no end to its observance; Israel must dwell in booths, wear wreaths, and gather leafy branches and willows from the brook to celebrate. **31.** Abraham took palm branches and other fruit-bearing tree branches, circling the altar seven times each morning, offering praise and thanks to YAHWEH for His abundant blessings.

Chapter 17

1. In the first year of the fifth week of this jubilee (1982 A.M.), Isaac was weaned, and Abraham held a great feast in the third month to celebrate. **2.** Ishmael (son of Abraham and Hagar, Sarah's maidservant), stood with Abraham during the celebration, and Abraham rejoiced, blessing YAHWEH for allowing him to see his sons and not die childless. **3.** Abraham recalled YAHWEH's promise to him when Lot had parted from him and blessed YAHWEH, the Creator of all things, for fulfilling it by giving him offspring to inherit the earth. However, Sarah saw Ishmael playing and dancing, and noticing Abraham's joy, she became jealous. She told Abraham, "Send away this bondwoman (Hagar) and her son, for her son will not share the inheritance with my son, Isaac." **5.** Abraham was deeply troubled by this, as it involved both his servant and his son. **6.** YAHWEH spoke to Abraham, saying, "Do not be distressed about the boy or the bondwoman. Listen to Sarah, for through Isaac your name and descendants will be established. **7.** But I will also make the son of the bondwoman into a great nation, because he is your seed." **8.** Early the next morning, Abraham gave Hagar bread and water, placed them on her shoulders, and sent her and Ishmael away. **9.** They wandered in the wilderness of Beersheba until the water was gone. Ishmael, weakened by thirst, collapsed. **10.** Hagar placed him under an olive tree and sat at a distance, saying, "I cannot bear to watch my child die." As she sat, she wept. **11.** A malak (angel) of YAHWEH appeared to her and said, "Why are you crying, Hagar? Get up and lift the boy, for YAHWEH has heard your voice and seen the child." **12.** YAHWEH opened her eyes, and she saw a well of water. She filled her bottle and gave Ishmael a drink. They then traveled to the wilderness of Paran. **13.** Ishmael grew up to become a skilled archer, and YAHWEH was with him. Hagar found him a wife from Egypt. **14.** She bore him a son, and he named him Nebaioth, saying, "YAHWEH was near to me when I called upon Him." **15.** In the seventh week of the first year (2003 A.M.), on the twelfth day of the first month, there were voices in heaven proclaiming Abraham's faithfulness and love for YAHWEH, even in times of trial. **16.** The prince Mastema (Satan, a fallen angel) came before YAHWEH, saying, "Abraham loves his son Isaac above all else. Command him to offer Isaac as a burnt offering on the altar, and you will see if he remains faithful to you." **17.** YAHWEH already knew Abraham's faithfulness through previous trials: leaving his homeland, enduring famine, handling wealth from kings, being separated from Sarah, circumcising himself and his household, and sending away Ishmael and Hagar. **18.** In all these, Abraham proved steadfast and obedient, never impatient or reluctant, and his love for YAHWEH remained unwavering.

Chapter 18

1. YAHWEH called, "Abraham, Abraham," and Abraham replied, "Here I am." **2.** YAHWEH said, "Take your beloved son Yitschaq (Isaac), whom you love, and go to the high country to offer him on a mountain I will show you." **3.** Early the next morning, Abraham prepared his donkey, took two young men and Yitschaq, split wood for the offering, and set

out. On the third day, he saw the place from afar. **4.** At a well, he told the young men, "Stay here with the donkey; the boy and I will go worship and return to you." **5.** Abraham placed the wood on Yitschaq, carried fire and a knife, and they went together. **6.** Yitschaq asked, "Father, where is the lamb for the offering?" **7.** Abraham replied, "YAHWEH will provide the lamb for Himself." They approached the mountain. **8.** Abraham built an altar, arranged the wood, bound Yitschaq, and placed him on the altar. As he reached for the knife to slay him, **9.** YAHWEH commanded, "Do not harm the boy or touch him, for now I know you fear YAHWEH." **10.** Terrified, Abraham responded, "Here I am." **11.** YAHWEH said, "Do not harm the boy, for you have proven your reverence by not withholding your beloved son." **12.** Mastema (Satan) was shamed as Abraham saw a ram caught by its horns, which he offered in place of Yitschaq. **13.** Abraham named the place "YAHWEH Will Provide," later known as Mount Zion (a location in Jerusalem). **14.** YAHWEH called Abraham again, speaking through His angels. **15.** YAHWEH declared, "By Myself I swear, because you obeyed Me and did not withhold your son, **16.** I will bless and multiply your descendants like the stars and the sand. Your offspring will conquer their enemies, and all nations will be blessed through them. Go in peace." **17.** Abraham returned to his young men, and they went to Beersheba, where he lived by the "Well of the Oath" (a city and well located in the Negev desert). **18.** Abraham celebrated a seven-day festival annually, calling it "The Festival of YAHWEH," commemorating his journey and safe return. **19.** This festival was ordained and written on the heavenly tablets for Yisrael (Israel) and their descendants to observe with joy for seven days.

Chapter 19

1. In the first year of the first week of the forty-second jubilee, Abraham returned and lived near Hebron (Kirjath Arba, a city in ancient Judah) for fourteen years. **2.** In the first year of the third week of this jubilee, Sarah's life ended, and she died in Hebron. **3.** Abraham mourned her and sought to bury her. He was tested to see if he would remain patient and not complain, and he was found to be patient and composed. **4.** He spoke calmly with the children of Heth (a people from the region of Canaan), asking for a burial site for Sarah. **5.** YAHWEH granted him favor, and he gently requested land from the sons of Heth, who gave him the cave of Machpelah (a cave near Mamre, Hebron) for four hundred silver pieces. **6.** Though they offered it for free, Abraham insisted on paying the full price. He bowed twice before them and buried Sarah in the cave. **7.** Sarah lived 127 years, equivalent to two jubilees, four weeks, and one year. **8.** This was Abraham's tenth trial, and he remained faithful and patient. **9.** Despite the promise from YAHWEH about the land for his descendants, Abraham humbly requested a burial site and was recorded as YAHWEH's friend in the heavenly tablets. **10.** In the fourth year of this period, Abraham arranged for his son Yitschaq (Isaac) to marry Rebecca (daughter of Bethuel, Nahor's son, and sister of Laban). **11.** Abraham married a third wife, Keturah (a servant's daughter), after Hagar's death. She bore him six sons: Zimram, Jokshan, Medan, Midian, Ishbak, and Shuah, over fourteen years. **12.** In the sixth week of the second year, Rebecca gave birth to twin sons, Yacob (Jacob) and Esau. **13.** Yacob (Jacob) was upright and peaceful, dwelling in tents, while Esau was fierce, hairy, and a hunter. **14.** As they grew, Yacob learned to write, but Esau, focused on hunting and war, became violent in his actions. **15.** Abraham loved Yacob, but Yitschaq (Isaac) preferred Esau. **16.** Seeing Esau's actions, Abraham knew Yacob would carry on his name and legacy. He instructed Rebecca, who also loved Yacob more than Esau. **17.** Abraham told her to watch over Yacob, as he would become a blessing among men and uphold the seed of Shem. **18.** He foresaw YAHWEH choosing Yacob as His possession above all nations. **19.** He acknowledged Rebecca's love for Yacob and encouraged her to show him even greater kindness. **20.** He urged her to care for Yacob as a blessing for future generations. **21.** Abraham expressed his deep love for Yacob and proclaimed his eternal blessing. **22.** He declared Yacob's descendants would be as numerous as the sand of the earth. **23.** All YAHWEH's blessings to Abraham and his seed would pass to Yacob and his descendants. **24.** Through Yacob, Abraham's name, and those of Shem, Noah, and Adam, would be honored. **25.** Their legacy would uphold the heavens, strengthen the earth, and renew the luminaries (the stars and celestial bodies). **26.** Abraham blessed Yacob before

Rebecca, kissed him, and spoke words of blessing over him. **27.** He prayed YAHWEH's blessings upon Yacob, extending those promised to Adam, Enoch, Noah, and Shem, ensuring they would endure forever. **28.** He prayed that the spirits of Mastema (Satan) would not rule over Yacob or his descendants, securing YAHWEH's eternal protection. **29.** He blessed Yacob to walk in YAHWEH's peace and be His firstborn son among the people. **30.** Abraham sent Yacob away in peace, and Rebecca continued to love Yacob far more than Esau. **31.** However, Yitschaq loved Esau more than Yacob.

Chapter 20

1. In the forty-second jubilee, during the first year of the seventh week, Abraham summoned Ishmael (Ishmael, son of Abraham and Hagar), his twelve sons, Yitschaq (Isaac), and his two sons, as well as Keturah's (Abraham's third wife) six sons and their descendants. **2.** He instructed them to follow YAHWEH's ways, practice righteousness, love their neighbors, and act justly and righteously toward all. **3.** He commanded them to circumcise their sons according to YAHWEH's covenant, to avoid deviating from His commandments, and to abstain from fornication and uncleanness, removing these sins from among them. **4.** He warned that any woman or maid committing fornication should be burned, forbidding marriage with Canaanite women (Canaan, the ancient land of the descendants of Noah's son Ham), as the seed of Canaan would be removed from the land. **5.** He recounted the judgment of the giants (Nephilim, fallen angel-human hybrids) and the Sodomites (Sodom, a city destroyed for its wickedness), who perished due to their wickedness, fornication, and uncleanness. **6.** He urged them to guard against sin and warned that such transgressions would bring curses, destruction, and ruin, as seen with Sodom and Gomorrah (two cities destroyed by fire and brimstone in the Bible). **7.** Abraham implored them to love YAHWEH and obey His commandments. **8.** He cautioned them against idolatry, stating that idols (statues or representations of false gods) are lifeless works of men's hands and trusting in them is futile. **9.** Instead, he urged them to serve and worship the Most High YAHWEH, walk in righteousness, and seek His blessings, including rain (a symbol of YAHWEH's provision), prosperity in their labors, fruitful offspring, and abundance in their livestock and land. **10.** By living righteously, they would become a blessing to the earth, and all nations would desire and bless their descendants in Abraham's name. **11.** Abraham gave gifts to Ishmael, his sons, and Keturah's sons, sending them away from Yitschaq, to whom he gave everything. **12.** Ishmael and his sons, along with Keturah's sons, settled from Paran (a desert region, often associated with wandering or nomadic life) to the entrance of Babylon (a city located in Mesopotamia), spanning the eastern lands near the desert. **13.** They mingled with one another and became known as Arabs (a group of people from the Arabian Peninsula) and Ishmaelites (descendants of Ishmael, traditionally thought to be the ancestors of the Arab nations).

Chapter 21

1. In the sixth year of the seventh week of this jubilee (around 2057 A.M.), Abraham called his son Isaac and said, "I have grown old and do not know the day of my death. My life is full and complete." **2.** I am now 175 years old, and throughout my life, I have remembered YAHWEH. I have sought to do His will with all my heart and to walk uprightly in His ways. **3.** I have hated idols (images or objects worshiped as gods) and devoted my heart and spirit to obey the Creator's will. **4.** For YAHWEH is the living God (a deity who is alive and active), holy (set apart) and faithful. He is righteous above all and does not show favoritism or accept bribes. YAHWEH judges all who break His commandments and reject His covenant. **5.** So, my son, obey His commandments, ordinances (rules for living), and judgments (divine rulings). Do not follow the abominations of idols or worship carved or molten images (images made by shaping metal or stone). **6.** Do not eat any blood—whether from animals, cattle, or birds. **7.** When you offer a peace offering (a type of sacrifice to ensure peace with God), ensure the blood is poured out on the altar. Place the fat of the sacrifice, fine flour, and oil (essential components of a sacrifice) as an offering with its drink offering upon the altar. This will be a sweet aroma pleasing to YAHWEH. **8.** Present the fat from the sacrifice, including the fat on the belly, internal organs, kidneys, loins, and liver. Remove these parts carefully and offer them on the altar. **9.** This is to be accompanied by the grain offering and drink offering as a sweet aroma, the bread of the

offering to YAHWEH. **10.** Eat the meat of the sacrifice on the first and second days, but do not leave any leftovers for the third day. If any is left, it is no longer acceptable and must not be eaten. Anyone who eats it on the third day sins against YAHWEH. This law is recorded in the writings of our forefathers—Enoch (a biblical figure known for his walk with God) and Noah (a righteous man who survived the flood). **11.** Always include salt with your offerings, for the "salt of the covenant" (a symbol of preservation and enduring commitment) must never be missing from your sacrifices. **12.** Use only specific types of wood for the altar, such as cypress, bay, almond, fir, pine, cedar, and olive (trees with symbolic meaning in the Bible). **13.** Ensure the wood is of good quality—clean, hard, fresh, and free of defects. Do not use old wood, as it lacks fragrance and is unsuitable for an offering. **14.** No other type of wood should be used, for its fragrance does not ascend to heaven (symbolizing the acceptance of an offering by God). **15.** Observe this commandment, my son, so that your deeds may be righteous. **16.** Always remain clean in body when approaching the altar. Wash yourself with water before making an offering. Wash your hands and feet both before and after sacrificing. **17.** Be vigilant about avoiding contact with blood. If blood spills, cover it with dust immediately. **18.** Do not consume any blood, for it represents life. Eating blood is forbidden. **19.** Never accept bribes or gifts to excuse the shedding of human blood. Justice must be served, for the land is polluted by human blood, and it can only be cleansed by the blood of the guilty. **20.** YAHWEH defends the righteous, so avoid all wickedness. He will preserve you and protect you from harm if you remain faithful. **21.** I have observed, my son, that the works of humanity are filled with sin, wickedness, and impurity. There is little righteousness among them. **22.** Do not follow their ways or imitate their actions, for this will lead to death. YAHWEH will hide His face from you and deliver you to the consequences of your sins, uprooting you and your descendants from the earth. **23.** Turn away from their deeds and observe the commandments of the Most High YAHWEH. Be righteous in all things. **24.** If you do so, YAHWEH will bless you and raise up a righteous line from your descendants, ensuring that our names will never be forgotten under heaven. **25.** Go in peace, my son. May the Most High YAHWEH, our Sovereign Lord, strengthen you to obey His will. May He bless your descendants forever with righteousness so that you and your seed may be a blessing to the earth." **26.** Isaac (the son of Abraham and Sarah) departed from Abraham, rejoicing.

Chapter 22

1. In the first week of the forty-fourth jubilee (a period of 49 years), in its second year—the year Abraham died—Isaac (son of Abraham and Sarah) and Ishmael (son of Abraham and Hagar) traveled from Beersheba (the "Well of the Oath," a well where Abraham made a covenant with Abimelech) to celebrate the Feast of Weeks (Pentecost, a harvest festival) with their father Abraham. Abraham rejoiced at the arrival of both his sons. **2.** Isaac had many possessions in Beersheba, so he would often visit them and then return to his father. **3.** During this time, Ishmael also came to visit Abraham, and together they offered a burnt sacrifice on the altar that Abraham had built in Hebron (a significant city where Abraham lived for many years). **4.** Isaac prepared a thank offering and hosted a joyful feast with Ishmael. Meanwhile, Rebekah (Isaac's wife) made fresh cakes from the first grain of the harvest and gave them to her son Jacob (Isaac's son) to take to Abraham so that Abraham might eat and bless the Creator before he died. **5.** Isaac also sent a special thank offering through Jacob to Abraham, ensuring that he could partake of the feast. **6.** Abraham ate and drank and blessed the Most High YAHWEH, saying, "Blessed are You, Creator of heaven and earth, who has provided the richness of the earth and given it to humanity so they might eat, drink, and bless You, their Creator." **7.** I thank You, my Sovereign Ruler, for allowing me to see this day. Behold, I am 175 years old, an elderly man full of days, and my life has been peaceful. **8.** The adversary's sword (symbol of attack or enemy) has not triumphed over me, and You have blessed me and my children all the days of my life. **9.** May Your mercy and peace rest upon Your servant and his descendants, so they may become a chosen nation and an inheritance among all the nations of the earth forever." **10.** Then he called Jacob and said, "My son Jacob, may YAHWEH, the Sovereign Ruler of all, bless you and strengthen you to live righteously and obey His will. May He choose you and your descendants to be His people, His inheritance, forever." **11.** Come near, my son, and kiss me." Jacob approached and kissed Abraham, who then blessed him, saying, "Blessed be my son Jacob and all the sons of YAHWEH Most High forever." **12.** May YAHWEH grant you righteous descendants and sanctify some of them to serve Him on the earth. May nations serve you, and may your descendants rule over the seed of Seth (Seth, son of Adam and Eve), so they become a holy (set apart) nation. **13.** May the blessings given to me, to Noah (a righteous man who survived the flood), and to Adam rest upon you and your descendants from generation to generation. **14.** May He cleanse you from all unrighteousness and forgive your unintentional sins. May He strengthen you and bless you. **15.** May you inherit the earth, and may He renew His covenant with you, making you His people forever." **16.** He continued, "Remember my words, my son Jacob. Obey the commandments of Abraham, your father. Separate yourself from the nations (groups of people who do not follow YAHWEH). Do not eat with them or follow their ways, for their deeds are impure and abominable. **17.** They offer sacrifices to the dead (spirits or ancestors), worship evil spirits, and hold feasts at graves. Their works are vanity and meaningless. **18.** They lack understanding and worship wood and stone (idols made of wood and stone), calling these lifeless things their gods and deliverers. **19.** May the Most High YAHWEH help you and deliver you from their errors and uncleanness. **20.** Be cautious, my son Jacob, not to marry any of the daughters of Canaan (descendants of Canaan, the cursed son of Ham), for their descendants will be destroyed from the earth. **21.** Due to Ham's sin, Canaan's descendants are cursed, and none of them will survive the Day of Judgment. **22.** Idolaters (those who worship false gods) and the profane (those who act wickedly) will have no place in the land of the living. They will descend into Sheol (the realm of the dead), just as Sodom (a city destroyed for wickedness) was wiped away. **23.** Do not fear, my son Jacob, for the Most High YAHWEH will preserve you from destruction and guide you away from error. **24.** This house, which I built for myself and named after me, is now yours and your descendants' inheritance forever. It will be called the House of Abraham, and through it, YAHWEH's name will be established forever." **25.** After saying this, Abraham ceased speaking and blessing Jacob. **26.** That night, Jacob lay beside Abraham. He slept in his grandfather's embrace as Abraham kissed him seven times. Abraham's heart rejoiced with affection for Jacob. **27.** Abraham then blessed YAHWEH, saying, "Blessed be the Most High YAHWEH, the Sovereign Creator, who brought me out of Ur of the Chaldees (an ancient city in Mesopotamia) to give me this land as an eternal inheritance and to establish a holy (set apart) lineage. **28.** May Your unmerited favor and mercy be upon Jacob and his descendants forever. **29.** Do not abandon him or disregard him for eternity. Let Your eyes watch over him and his descendants. **30.** Bless and sanctify them as a nation for Your inheritance. Renew Your covenant and extend Your favor to them according to Your will for all generations."

Chapter 23

1. Abraham placed two fingers of Jacob on his eyes, blessed the ALMIGHTY (God, the supreme ruler), and then covered his face, stretched out his feet, and passed into eternal rest, being gathered to his ancestors (a term referring to being reunited with deceased family members). **2.** Jacob (son of Isaac, grandson of Abraham), still lying in Abraham's embrace, did not realize his grandfather had died. **3.** When Jacob awoke, he found Abraham cold as ice. He called out, "Father, father," but received no reply. Realizing Abraham had died, **4.** Jacob quickly left and informed his mother, Rebekah (wife of Isaac), She then told Isaac during the night, and together with Jacob, carrying a lamp, they went to see Abraham. They found him lying lifeless. **5.** Isaac (son of Abraham and Sarah) fell upon his father's face, wept, and kissed him. **6.** The sounds of mourning filled Abraham's house. Ishmael (son of Abraham and Hagar), Abraham's son, also came and wept over his father along with all the members of the household. They wept with great sorrow. **7.** Isaac and Ishmael buried Abraham in the cave of Machpelah (a burial site near Hebron, where Abraham and other patriarchs were buried), near Sarah, his wife. They mourned for him forty days, joined by all the men of Abraham's household, including Isaac, Ishmael, and the sons of Keturah. When the days of mourning ended, **8.** they reflected on Abraham's life. He lived three jubilees (a period of 49 years) and four weeks of years—a total of 175 years. He completed his days, being old and full of years. **9.** The forefathers of humanity lived up to 19 jubilees (about 931 years), but after the Flood, lifespans began to decrease rapidly due to suffering and the increasing wickedness of humanity. **10.** Abraham, however, remained blameless before YAHWEH (the Hebrew name for God), pleasing Him in righteousness throughout his life. Yet even he did not reach four jubilees, as his life was shortened by the wickedness surrounding him. **11.** From this time forward, generations will age quickly and fail to reach even two jubilees. Their understanding will fade with age, and all their wisdom will disappear. **12.** In those days, a person living just one and a half jubilees will be considered to have lived a long life. Yet most of their days will be filled with pain, sorrow, and tribulation, lacking peace. **13.** Suffering will follow suffering—wounds, illnesses, famine, death, war, and captivity will plague humanity. Snow, frost, fever, and famine will add to their troubles. **14.** These calamities will fall upon a generation that transgresses (violates or disregards) against YAHWEH. Their deeds will include uncleanness (moral or ritual impurity), fornication, and abominations (things that are detestable to God). **15.** People will lament, saying, "Our forefathers lived long and good lives, even reaching a thousand years, but our days are few and full of trouble. If a man reaches seventy or eighty years, they are filled with suffering, and there is no peace." **16.** In that generation, children will accuse their parents and elders of sin and unrighteousness, rebuking them for abandoning the covenant (the divine agreement between God and His people) YAHWEH established. They will condemn them for neglecting His commandments and laws. **17.** The deeds of humanity will be wholly corrupt, their words sinful, and their ways filled with uncleanness and destruction. **18.** Because of this, the earth will be devastated (ruined). There will be no vineyards or oil, for humanity's faithlessness will lead to their total ruin. Animals, cattle, birds, and fish will perish because of human wickedness. **19.** People will fight each other—young against old, poor against rich, and lowly against great—over YAHWEH's laws and covenant. They will forget His commandments, feasts, Sabbaths (days of rest), and jubilees. **20.** Wars will rage, and much blood will be spilled, yet the people will not repent (feel remorse) or turn back to righteousness. **21.** Instead, they will pursue wealth and deception, seeking to take what belongs to their neighbors. Though they invoke YAHWEH's name, it will be in hypocrisy (false appearance), not truth or righteousness. Their defilement (moral corruption) will corrupt even the holiest places. **22.** YAHWEH's judgment will come upon them—sword, captivity, and plunder (violent robbery) will consume them. **23.** He will allow ruthless sinners among the Gentiles (non-Israelites), who lack mercy and compassion, to rise against Israel. These invaders will show no respect for age or status, committing great violence. **24.** In their suffering, the people will cry out to YAHWEH for deliverance, but there will be no salvation (rescue). **25.** In those days, even children will appear aged due to oppression and hardship. **26.** Yet, amid the darkness, a remnant (small surviving group) will begin to study the laws, seek YAHWEH's commandments, and return to the path of righteousness. **27.** Gradually, human lifespans will increase again, and people will live near a thousand years as in earlier times. **28.** No one will grow old unsatisfied with their years, for they will remain youthful. **29.** Their days will be filled with peace and joy, free from Satan (the adversary) and destruction. **30.** YAHWEH will heal His servants, bring them peace, and enable them to overcome their enemies. The righteous will rejoice forever, giving thanks for YAHWEH's mercy and justice. **31.** Their spirits will find joy, and they will know it is YAHWEH who judges righteously and shows mercy to those who love Him. **32.** Then YAHWEH instructed Moses (leader of Israel), "Write these words, for they are recorded on the heavenly tablets (a divine record) as a testimony for all generations forever."

Chapter 24

1. After Abraham's death, YAHWEH (the Hebrew name for God) blessed Isaac, his son. Isaac left Hebron (a city in Canaan, associated with Abraham) and settled at the Well of the Vision during the first year of the third week of this jubilee (a period of 49 years), staying there for seven years. **2.** In the first year of the fourth week, a famine struck the land (2080 A.M.), distinct from the famine that occurred during Abraham's time. **3.** During this time, Jacob (son of Isaac) was cooking a lentil stew when Esau (Jacob's brother, the firstborn) came in from the field, exhausted and hungry. Esau said to Jacob, "Let me have some of that red stew." **4.** Jacob replied, "Sell me your birthright [rights of the firstborn] in exchange for it." **5.** Esau thought to himself, "I'm about to die! What good is my birthright to me?" So he agreed and said, "I give it to you." **6.** Jacob made Esau swear an oath, and in return, gave him bread and lentil stew. Esau ate, drank, and left, showing contempt for his birthright. Because of this event, Esau's name was called Edom (meaning "red") in reference to the red stew. **7.** Through this, Jacob gained the elder position, and Esau lost his status. **8.** During the famine, Isaac prepared to go to Egypt, but instead traveled to Gerar (a city in Philistine territory), the land of the Philistines, to visit Abimelech (the king of the Philistines), their king. **9.** YAHWEH appeared to Isaac and told him, "Do not go down to Egypt. Stay in the land I tell you about. **10.** Remain here, and I will be with you and bless you. To you and your descendants, I will give all this land, fulfilling the promise I made to Abraham. **11.** I will make your descendants as numerous as the stars and give them this land. Through your offspring, all nations will be blessed, because Abraham obeyed My voice and kept My commandments, laws, and covenant. Now, listen to Me and stay in this land." **12.** Isaac lived in Gerar for 21 years (three weeks of years). **13.** During this time, Abimelech issued a decree, saying, "Anyone who harms Isaac or his possessions will surely be put to death." **14.** YAHWEH blessed Isaac greatly, and he gained abundant possessions: flocks, herds, camels, donkeys, and a large household. **15.** Isaac also planted crops and reaped a hundredfold harvest, becoming exceedingly prosperous. The Philistines envied him. **16.** Out of spite, the Philistines filled the wells Abraham's servants had dug during his lifetime with dirt. **17.** Abimelech said to Isaac, "Leave us, for you have become much mightier than we are." So Isaac moved to the valleys of Gerar. **18.** There, Isaac reopened the wells his father's servants had dug, which the Philistines had filled after Abraham's death. Isaac gave the wells the same names his father had used. **19.** Isaac's servants dug a new well in the valley and found flowing water, but the shepherds of Gerar argued with them, claiming the water as theirs. Isaac named the well Esek (meaning "Perversity"). **20.** They dug another well, but the people quarreled over it too, so Isaac named it Sitnah (meaning "Enmity"). **21.** Isaac moved on and dug yet another well. This time, there was no conflict, so he named it Rehoboth (meaning "Room") and said, "YAHWEH has made room for us, and we will flourish in this land." **22.** From there, Isaac went to Beersheba (the Well of the Oath) in the first year of the first week of the 44th jubilee (2108 A.M.). **23.** That night, on the first day of the new month, YAHWEH appeared to him and said, "I am YAHWEH, the Almighty of your father Abraham. Do not be afraid, for I am with you. I will bless you and multiply your descendants as the sand of the earth because of My servant Abraham." **24.** Isaac built an altar there, as Abraham had done before, and called upon the name of YAHWEH. He offered sacrifices to YAHWEH. **25.** Isaac's servants dug another well and found flowing water. **26.** Later, they dug a well but did not find water. When they reported this to Isaac, he reflected, "I swore an oath to the Philistines, and now this has come to pass." **27.** Isaac named the place Beersheba (the Well of the Oath), for he had sworn an oath there with Abimelech, Ahuzzath (Abimelech's advisor), and Phicol (the commander of his army). **28.** On that day, Isaac realized he had made peace with them under duress. He cursed the Philistines, saying: **29.** "Cursed are the Philistines until the day of YAHWEH's wrath and judgment. May they become objects of scorn, cursed and overthrown by the hands of the sinners among the nations and by the Kittim (people from Cyprus and surrounding regions). **30.** Whoever escapes their enemies' sword will perish by other means. The righteous nation will uproot them from the earth during judgment, leaving no trace of their seed." **31.** "Though they ascend to heaven, they will be brought down. Though they grow strong on earth, they will be overthrown. Even if they hide among nations or descend to Sheol (the grave), judgment will reach them." **32.** "If they are taken captive, they will die on the way. No name or remnant of their seed will remain, for they are destined for eternal judgment and destruction." **33.** These words were written and recorded on the heavenly tablets (a divine record) to be carried out on the Day of Judgment, ensuring that the Philistines would be completely uprooted from the earth.

Chapter 25

1. In the second year of this week during the jubilee (2109 A.M.), Rebecca (Isaac's wife) called her son Jacob (son of Isaac) and said to him: "My son, do not marry one of the daughters of Canaan (a region in ancient Israel), like your brother Esau (Jacob's twin brother), who took two wives from among them. They have caused me deep sorrow with all their sinful and immoral actions. Their deeds are full of lust and corruption, and they lack righteousness because their ways are evil. **2.** I love you deeply, my son, and my heart blesses you every moment of the day and night. **3.** So now, listen to me and do what I ask. Do not marry a wife from the daughters of this land. Instead, choose a wife from the house of my father (Bethuel's household), from among my relatives. If you do this, the Most High YAHWEH (God) will bless you, and your descendants will be a righteous generation and a holy (kodesh - sacred or set apart) seed." **4.** Jacob answered his mother, "Mother, I am 63 years old (nine weeks of years), and I have not been with any woman. I have not even thought of marrying one of the daughters of Canaan. **5.** I remember what our father Abraham (Jacob's grandfather) commanded me—to not take a wife from among the daughters of Canaan but to marry from the family of my father's house. **6.** I've heard that your brother Laban (Rebecca's brother) has daughters, and I have decided in my heart to choose a wife from among them. **7.** This is why I have kept myself pure and avoided sin or corruption throughout my life. I remember the many commands Abraham gave me about staying away from lust and immorality. **8.** Yet for 22 years, Esau has tried to persuade me to marry one of the sisters of his wives. He has spoken to me repeatedly, but I have refused to act as he has. **9.** I swear to you, mother, that as long as I live, I will not marry a wife from among the daughters of Canaan, nor will I act wickedly as Esau has done. **10.** Do not worry, mother. I will honor your wishes and walk in righteousness, never corrupting my ways." **11.** Upon hearing this, Rebecca lifted her face to heaven, raised her hands, and began to praise YAHWEH. **12.** She said, "Blessed be YAHWEH Almighty, whose holy name is exalted forever! He has given me Jacob, a pure son and a holy (kodesh - sacred) seed. He belongs to You, YAHWEH, and so will his descendants forever. **13.** Bless him, YAHWEH, and grant me the words of righteousness, that I may bless him." **14.** At that moment, the Spirit of righteousness filled her, and she placed her hands on Jacob's head and said: **15.** "Blessed are You, YAHWEH of righteousness and Sovereign Ruler of the ages. May You bless my son above all the generations of men. May You guide him in the path of righteousness and reveal righteousness to his descendants. **16.** May his sons be numerous during his lifetime, as plentiful as the months of the year. May his descendants multiply and grow beyond the stars in the sky and the sand on the seashore. **17.** May You give them this good land, just as You promised Abraham, and may they possess it forever. **18.** During my life, may I see your blessed and holy descendants, and may all your children be holy (kodesh - sacred) and righteous. **19.** As you have brought joy to your mother's spirit during her life, may my womb, which bore you, bless you. My love and my care for you bless you. My mouth and tongue praise you abundantly. **20.** May your descendants spread across the earth. May they be perfect in the joy of heaven and earth, rejoicing always. And on the great day of peace, may they have eternal peace. **21.** May your name and your descendants endure forever. May the Most High YAHWEH be their Sovereign Ruler, and may the Almighty dwell with them. Through them, may His sanctuary be built for all generations. **22.** Blessed are those who bless you, and cursed be anyone who falsely curses you." **23.** Then Rebecca kissed Jacob and said, "May YAHWEH, the Creator of the world, love you as I do. May my affection and blessings rest upon you." With that, she finished her blessing.

Chapter 26

1. In the seventh year of the week, Yitschaq (Isaac) called his elder son Esau and said, "I am old, my eyes are dim, and I do not know when I will die. **2.** Take your hunting gear, go to the field, hunt venison, prepare it as I love, and bring it to me so I may eat and bless you before I die." **3.** Rebecca overheard Yitschaq speaking to Esau. **4.** Esau went out early to hunt. **5.** Rebecca called Jacob and told him what Yitschaq had said to Esau, "Hunt for me and prepare savory meat so I may eat and bless you before I die." **6.** She then instructed Jacob to bring two goats from the flock so she could prepare the meat, and he would receive the blessing. **7.** Jacob expressed concern about being

204

recognized by his father because of his smooth skin, unlike Esau's hairy one, which could lead to a curse instead of a blessing. **8.** Rebecca assured him, "Let the curse be on me, just do as I say." **9.** Jacob obeyed, bringing the goats to Rebecca, who prepared the meal. **10.** She dressed Jacob in Esau's clothes and put goat skins on his hands and neck. **11.** She gave him the food to take to his father. **12.** Jacob went to his father, saying, "I have done as you commanded. Eat and bless me." **13.** Yitschaq asked how he found the game so quickly. **14.** Jacob replied, "YAHWEH helped me find it." **15.** Yitschaq asked to feel him to confirm if he was truly Esau. **16.** Jacob approached, and Yitschaq felt him, noting that the voice was Jacob's but the hands were Esau's. **17.** Yitschaq, unable to recognize him due to divine intervention, proceeded with the blessing. **18.** Yitschaq asked, "Are you my son Esau?" and Jacob replied, "Yes." **19.** Yitschaq requested the food, ate, and drank. **20.** Yitschaq then asked for a kiss. **21.** Jacob kissed him, and Yitschaq smelled his clothes, blessing him with prosperity and dominion over his brothers. **22.** He blessed Jacob with the dew of heaven, abundant crops, and power over nations. **23.** "Let those who bless you be blessed, and those who curse you be cursed." **24.** After Jacob left, Esau returned from hunting. **25.** Esau prepared his meal and brought it to Yitschaq, asking for his blessing. **26.** Yitschaq was surprised and asked, "Who are you?" **27.** Esau answered, "I am your firstborn son, Esau." **28.** Yitschaq was astonished, realizing that he had already blessed Jacob. **29.** Esau cried out bitterly, asking for a blessing as well. **30.** Yitschaq explained that Jacob had taken the blessing. **31.** Esau complained, saying Jacob had tricked him twice, first with his birthright, now with the blessing. **32.** He asked if there was any blessing left for him. **33.** Yitschaq said that he had made Jacob ruler, with his brothers as servants, and provided him with abundance. **34.** Esau begged for a blessing, and Yitschaq, sorrowfully, foretold his harsh future. **35.** Esau, enraged, vowed to kill Jacob after their father's death.

Chapter 27

1. The words of Esau, her elder son (Esau - Isaac's firstborn), were revealed to Rebecca in a dream, and Rebecca called Jacob, her younger son (Jacob - Isaac's second son). **2.** She said to him, "Behold, Esau, your brother, plans to take vengeance on you and kill you. **3.** Therefore, my son, obey my voice. Arise, flee to Laban, my brother, in Haran (Haran - city in Mesopotamia). Stay there a few days until your brother's anger subsides, he forgets what you have done, and I send for you to return." **4,5.** Jacob replied, "I am not afraid; if he tries to kill me, I will kill him." Rebecca said, "Do not let me lose both my sons in one day." **6.** Jacob said to Rebecca, "You know that my father is old and cannot see. If I leave, he will be displeased and may curse me. I will not leave unless he sends me." **7.** Rebecca answered, "I will speak to him, and he will send you away." **8.** Rebecca went to Isaac and said, "I despise my life because of the daughters of Heth (daughters of Heth - descendants of Heth, the Hittite), Esau's wives. If Jacob marries a woman of this land like them, my life is worthless." **9.** Isaac called Jacob, blessed him, and instructed him. **10.** He said, "Do not marry a Canaanite woman (Canaanite - inhabitants of Canaan, land promised to Abraham's descendants). Go to Mesopotamia (Mesopotamia - ancient region between the Tigris and Euphrates rivers), to your mother's family, and take a wife from Laban's daughters (Laban - Rebecca's brother)." **11.** May YAHWEH bless you, multiply you, and grant you the blessings of Abraham so you may inherit this land of your sojourning. **12.** Isaac sent Jacob to Mesopotamia, to Laban, the son of Bethuel (Bethuel - Rebecca's father) the Syrian (Syrian - from the region of Aram), Rebecca's brother. **13.** After Jacob departed, Rebecca was grieved and wept for him. **14.** Isaac comforted Rebecca, saying, "Do not weep for Jacob, for he goes in peace and will return in peace. **15.** The Most High YAHWEH will protect him and will not forsake him all his days. His ways will prosper, and he is faithful and upright. Do not fear for him." **16.** Isaac encouraged Rebecca, and she was comforted. **17.** Jacob departed from the "Well of the Oath" (Well of the Oath - a place where Abraham and Abimelech made a covenant) to Haran in the first year of the second week in the forty-fourth jubilee. **18.** He came to Luz (Bethel - city Jacob later names as Bethel) on the new month of the first month of that week, rested there at night, and turned west of the road to sleep. **19.** He placed a stone under his head and slept alone under the tree. **20.** He dreamed of a ladder reaching from earth to heaven, with YAHWEH's malakim (malakim - Hebrew word for angels) ascending and descending on it. YAHWEH stood above it. **21.** YAHWEH said, "I am the ALMIGHTY of Abraham and Isaac. I will give you and your descendants this land. **22.** Your seed will be like the dust of the earth, spreading in all directions. Through you, all nations will be blessed. **23.** I am with you, and I will guard you wherever you go and bring you back to this land in peace. I will not leave you until I fulfill my promise." **24.** Jacob awoke and said, "Surely, this is the house of YAHWEH, though I did not know it." He added, "How awesome is this place; it is the gate of heaven." **25.** Jacob arose early, set the stone as a pillar, poured oil on it, and named the place Bethel, though it was originally called Luz. **26.** Jacob vowed, "If YAHWEH protects me, provides for me, and brings me back in peace, then YAHWEH will be my Sovereign. This stone will be YAHWEH's house, and I will tithe all He gives me."

Chapter 28

1. Jacob traveled to Laban's land (Laban's land - the region where Laban lived) in the east and worked for him for seven years to marry Rachel. **2.** At the end of the seven years, Jacob asked Laban for Rachel as his wife. **3.** Laban threw a feast and secretly gave Jacob Leah (Leah - Laban's elder daughter), his elder daughter, instead of Rachel, and gave Leah Zilpah (Zilpah - Leah's maidservant) as a maidservant. **4.** Jacob went into Leah, but discovered she was not Rachel. He confronted Laban, asking why he had deceived him. **5.** Jacob expressed his anger, saying he had worked for Rachel, not Leah, and accused Laban of wronging him. **6.** Laban explained that in their land, the elder daughter must be married first, as it was a custom set by heavenly law. **7.** Laban warned Jacob not to marry the younger before the elder, as it was considered wicked in their culture. **8.** Laban offered Rachel after a week, in exchange for another seven years of service. Jacob agreed, and after the feast ended, Laban gave him Rachel along with Bilhah (Bilhah - Rachel's maidservant) as her maidservant. **10.** Jacob served another seven years for Rachel, while Leah was given to him without further payment. **11.** YAHWEH opened Leah's womb, and she bore Jacob's first son, Reuben (Reuben - Leah's firstborn), in the first year of the third week. **12.** Rachel remained barren, as YAHWEH saw that Leah was unloved and Rachel was loved. **13.** Leah conceived again and bore Jacob a second son, Simeon (Simeon - Leah's second son), in the third year of the week. **14.** Leah bore Jacob a third son, Levi (Levi - Leah's third son), in the first month of the sixth year of the week. **15.** Leah bore Jacob a fourth son, Judah (Judah - Leah's fourth son), in the third month of the first year of the fourth week. **16.** Rachel envied Leah for bearing children, and demanded that Jacob give her children. Jacob responded that he had not withheld children from her. **17.** Rachel, seeing Leah's four sons, offered her maidservant Bilhah to Jacob to bear a child for her. **18.** Jacob went into Bilhah, and she bore him a son, Dan (Dan - Bilhah's first son), in the sixth month of the sixth year. **19.** Jacob again went to Bilhah, and she bore a second son, Naphtali (Naphtali - Bilhah's second son), in the seventh month of the second year of the fourth week. **20.** When Leah stopped bearing, she gave her maidservant Zilpah to Jacob, and Zilpah bore him a son, Gad (Gad - Zilpah's first son), in the eighth month of the third year of the fourth week. **21.** Leah's maid Zilpah bore Jacob a second son, Asher (Asher - Zilpah's second son), in the eleventh month of the fifth year of the fourth week. **22.** Leah bore Jacob a son named Issachar (Issachar - Leah's sixth son) in the fifth month of the fourth year of the fourth week, and she gave him to a nurse. **23.** Leah bore Jacob a son, Zebulun (Zebulun - Leah's seventh son), and a daughter, Dinah (Dinah - Leah's daughter), in the seventh month of the sixth year of the fourth week. **24.** YAHWEH opened Rachel's womb, and she bore Jacob a son, Joseph (Joseph - Rachel's firstborn), in the fourth month of the sixth year. **25.** When Joseph was born, Jacob told Laban he wanted to leave with his wives and children and return to his father's house. **26.** Laban asked Jacob to stay and offered him wages for tending his flocks. **27.** They agreed that Jacob's wages would be the spotted and striped lambs and kids born among Laban's flocks. **28.** Laban's flocks produced many spotted, speckled, and black sheep, which became Jacob's possessions. **29.** Jacob's wealth grew, and he gained large herds of animals, servants, and camels. **30.** Laban and his sons envied Jacob's success, and Laban took his sheep back, watching Jacob with suspicion.

Chapter 29

1. When Rachel bore Yoseph (Joseph, a significant son of Jacob), Laban (a relative of Jacob and father of Leah and Rachel) went to shear his sheep, a three-day journey away. **2.** Yacob (Jacob) saw that Laban was going to shear his sheep and called Leah and Rachel, telling them kindly to come with him to Canaan (a region in the ancient Near East). **3.** He shared how God had shown him in a dream that he should return to his father's house, and they agreed, saying, "We will go wherever you go." **4.** Yacob blessed YAHWEH (God), the Almighty of his father Yitschaq (Isaac) and grandfather Abraham, then took his family, possessions, and crossed the river (a body of water) into Gilead (a region east of the Jordan River), keeping his plans hidden from Laban. **5.** In the seventh year of the fourth week, Yacob turned toward Gilead in the first month, on the 21st day. Laban pursued him and overtook him in the mountain (highland area) of Gilead in the third month, on the 13th day. **6.** YAHWEH did not allow Laban to harm Yacob, appearing to him in a dream at night. **7.** Laban spoke to Yacob, and on the 15th day, Yacob held a feast for Laban and his company. Yacob swore an oath, and Laban also swore, agreeing that neither would cross the mountain of Gilead with evil intentions. **8.** They built a heap (a pile or mound) as a witness, and the place was called "The Heap of Witness" after it. **9.** The land of Gilead was once called the land of the Rephaim (a race of giants), giants whose height ranged from seven to ten cubits (a unit of length). **10.** Their kingdom stretched from Ammon (an ancient kingdom) to Mount Hermon (a mountain in the region), with cities like Karnaim (a city near Gilead), Ashtaroth (a city), Edrei (an ancient city), Misur, and Beon (cities). **11.** YAHWEH destroyed the Rephaim due to their wickedness, and the Amorites (another people group) took their place, becoming even more sinful. The Rephaim no longer exist. **12.** Yacob sent Laban away, and Laban returned to Mesopotamia (a historical region between the Tigris and Euphrates rivers). Yacob then returned to the land of Gilead. **13.** Yacob crossed the Jabbok River (a river in the land of Gilead) on the 11th day of the 9th month. On that day, Esau (Jacob's brother), his brother, came to him, and they were reconciled. Esau then left for Seir (a mountainous region in Edom), while Yacob continued to live in tents. **14.** In the first year of the fifth week, in the 2136th year, Yacob crossed the Jordan (a river) and settled beyond it. He pastured his flocks from the Sea of the Heap (a location) to Bethshan (an ancient city), Dothan (a city in northern Israel), and the forest of Akrabbim (a desert area). **15.** Yacob sent his father Yitschaq gifts of all his possessions—clothing, food, meat, drink, milk, butter, cheese, and dates from the valley. **16.** He also sent gifts to his mother, Rebecca (Jacob's mother), four times a year: between ploughing and reaping, autumn and rain, and winter and spring, to the tower (a structure) of Abraham. **17.** Yitschaq had returned from the 'Well of the Oath' (a well in the region) and moved to the tower of his father Abraham in Hebron (a city in Israel), living apart from Esau. **18.** During the time Yacob was in Mesopotamia, Esau married Mahalath (a woman), daughter of Ishmael (Abraham's son), and took his flocks to live in Mount Seir (a mountainous region), leaving Yitschaq alone at the 'Well of the Oath.' **19.** Yitschaq left the 'Well of the Oath' and moved to the tower of Abraham in Hebron. **20.** Yacob sent all his gifts and provisions to his father and mother regularly. They blessed Yacob wholeheartedly in return.

Chapter 30

1. In the first year of the sixth week (2143 A.M.), he went to Salem (a city), east of Shechem (a city), in peace, during the fourth month. **2.** Dinah (Jacob's daughter), was taken to Shechem's house, son of Hamor (a ruler of the Hivites), prince of the land. He defiled her; she was only twelve years old. **3.** Shechem asked his father and her brothers to give her to him as a wife. Jacob and his sons were enraged, deceiving them with evil intent for defiling Dinah. **4.** Simeon and Levi (Jacob's sons) attacked Shechem, killing all its men in torment for dishonoring their sister. **5.** Such defilement of an Israelite daughter must not happen again, for judgment from heaven decrees the destruction of the Shechemites. **6.** YAHWEH delivered them into Jacob's sons' hands to execute judgment and ensure no virgin of Israel is defiled again. **7.** If anyone in Israel gives his daughter or sister to a Gentile (non-Israelite), he must be stoned, and the woman burned for dishonoring her family. **8.** No adulteress or uncleanness is permitted in Israel, for Israel is holy to YAHWEH, and defilers must be stoned to death. **9.** This eternal law is written on heavenly tablets: anyone who defiles Israel must die by stoning. **10.** No atonement or time limit applies; anyone giving their seed to Molech (a pagan god) or defiling Israel must be cut off. **11.**

Moses (a prophet and leader) was commanded to instruct Israel not to intermarry with Gentiles, for it is an abomination before YAHWEH. **12.** The law records the Shechemites' deeds against Dinah and how Jacob's sons refused to give their sister to the uncircumcised (Gentiles), calling it a reproach. **13.** Taking Gentile daughters or giving Israelite daughters to Gentiles is unclean and abominable. **14.** Israel remains unclean if anyone marries or gives daughters to Gentiles. **15.** Plagues, curses, and judgment come upon those who commit or tolerate uncleanness, defile the sanctuary, or profane YAHWEH's holy name. **16.** YAHWEH will not accept offerings or worship from those who defile the sanctuary. **17.** This testimony was given to Israel, recounting how the Shechemites were punished by Jacob's sons, recorded as righteousness. **18.** Levi's lineage (descendants) was chosen for the priesthood due to his zeal for righteousness and judgment. **19.** Levi's actions are inscribed on heavenly tablets as righteousness and a blessing. **20.** His righteousness is remembered and recorded for a thousand generations as a testimony. **21.** This account exhorts Israel to keep the covenant, avoiding sin, to be recorded as friends of YAHWEH. **22.** Those who sin and work uncleanness will be removed from the book of life and recorded among the destroyed. **23.** On the day Jacob's sons executed judgment on Shechem, it was recorded in heaven as righteousness. **24.** They rescued Dinah, took Shechem's wealth, and brought it to Jacob. **25.** Jacob reproached them for their actions, fearing the surrounding Canaanites (people of Canaan) and Perizzites (people of Canaan). **26.** However, the dread of YAHWEH fell on the surrounding cities, and no one pursued Jacob's sons.

Chapter 31

1. On the new month (a time marking the beginning of a new month), Yacob (Jacob) spoke to his household: "Purify yourselves, change your garments, and let us go to Bethel (a city in ancient Israel). I made a vow there when I fled from Esau, and God has been with me, bringing me safely into this land. Remove the foreign gods (idols or images of other deities) among you." **2.** They gave up the foreign gods, the earrings, and the idols Rachel (Jacob's wife) had stolen from her father Laban (Jacob's uncle). Yacob burned and destroyed them, burying the pieces under an oak (a tree) near Shechem (a city in ancient Israel). **3.** On the new month of the seventh month, Yacob went to Bethel, built an altar at the place where he had slept, and set up a pillar (a stone monument). He sent word to his father Yitschaq (Isaac) and his mother Rebecca (Jacob's mother) to join him for the sacrifice. **4.** Yitschaq replied, "Let my son Yacob come and let me see him before I die." **5.** Yacob took his two sons, Levi (Jacob's son) and Yahudah (Judah, another son of Jacob), and went to see his father Yitschaq and his mother Rebecca. **6.** Rebecca came out to kiss and embrace Yacob when she heard he had arrived, and her spirit revived upon seeing him. **7.** She recognized his two sons and asked, "Are these your sons, my son?" She embraced and blessed them, saying, "Through you, Abraham's descendants will be great, and you will be a blessing to the earth." **8.** Yacob entered Yitschaq's chamber with his sons, kissed his father, and Yitschaq embraced him, weeping. **9.** Yitschaq's sight was restored (his vision returned), and seeing Levi and Yahudah, he asked, "Are these your sons? They resemble you." **10.** Yacob confirmed, "Yes, they are my sons." **11.** Yitschaq kissed and embraced them both. **12.** The spirit of prophecy came upon Yitschaq, and he took Levi by his right hand and Yahudah by his left. **13.** He began by blessing Levi: "May the Almighty bless you and your descendants with greatness, making you and your children holy (set apart for a divine purpose) and devoted to Him, like the angels." **14.** "Your children will serve in His sanctuary (a sacred place) and be blessed with glory and holiness. May they remain great for all ages." **15.** "They will be judges and leaders, speaking God's word in righteousness, guiding Israel (the people of God) in His ways. The blessing of the Lord will be in their mouths to bless all of Jacob's descendants." **16.** "Your mother named you Levi, and it was a fitting name. You will be joined to the Lord and share in His table (enjoy His provision), and your descendants will eat from it forever." **17.** "Those who hate you will fall before you, and your enemies will perish. Blessed be those who bless you, and cursed be those who curse you." **18.** Turning to Yahudah, Yitschaq said: "May the Lord give you strength to overcome all who oppose you. You and your descendants will rule over the sons of Jacob." **19.** "Nations will fear you, and in you will be the salvation (deliverance) of Israel." **20.** "When you sit on the throne of righteousness (a just and moral reign), there will be peace for all Israel. Blessed be those who bless you, and cursed be those who harm you." **21.** Yitschaq kissed and embraced Yahudah again, rejoicing to see his son's descendants. **22.** Yacob bowed and prayed for them, then spent the night with Yitschaq, rejoicing and eating together. **23.** Yacob placed his sons, Levi and Yahudah, one at his right hand and the other at his left, and this was considered righteous (just and morally correct). **24.** Yacob shared with his father how God had shown him mercy, prospered his ways, and protected him from harm. **25.** Yitschaq blessed God, the Almighty of Abraham, for His mercy and righteousness toward the sons of Yitschaq. **26.** The next morning, Yacob told Yitschaq about the vow he had made to God, the vision he had received, and the altar he had built, preparing to make the sacrifice. **27.** Yitschaq told Yacob, "I cannot go with you; I am old and cannot travel. Go in peace, for I am 165 years old and no longer able to journey. Take your mother with you." **28.** "I know you came to see me, and I am blessed to have seen you alive. May you fulfill your vow quickly and may God, to whom you made it, be pleased." **29.** Yitschaq then told Rebecca, "Go with Yacob," and she, along with Deborah (a servant or nurse), traveled with him to Bethel. **30.** Yacob remembered his father's prayer for him and his sons, and he rejoiced, blessing God for the promise of eternal hope for himself and his children. **31.** He acknowledged that his family's future was secure before the Almighty, and they recorded this as an eternal testimony (witness or record) on the heavenly tablets, marking how Yitschaq had blessed them.

Chapter 32

1. That night, Yacob (Jacob) stayed at Bethel (a place where God appeared to Jacob, meaning "House of God"), and Levi (Jacob's son) had a vision in which he was appointed as the eternal priest of the Most High YAHWEH (God), along with his descendants. Upon waking, he blessed YAHWEH. **2.** The next morning, on the fourteenth of the month, Yacob gave a tenth (tithe - 10% offering) of everything he had—his people, his cattle, gold, vessels, and garments—as an offering to YAHWEH. **3.** During this time, Rachel (Jacob's wife) conceived and became pregnant with Benjamin (Jacob's son). Yacob counted his sons, and Levi was designated to YAHWEH. His father clothed him in priestly garments and consecrated him (set apart as holy). **4.** On the fifteenth, Yacob presented a vast offering to YAHWEH at the altar: fourteen oxen, twenty-eight rams, forty-nine sheep, seven lambs, and twenty-one goats, all as burnt offerings that would be pleasing to YAHWEH. **5.** This offering fulfilled the vow Yacob had made to give a tenth of all he possessed, including their fruit and drink offerings. **6.** After the fire consumed the offerings, Yacob burned incense on the altar, and for a thanksgiving sacrifice, he offered two oxen, four rams, four sheep, four male goats, two one-year-old lambs, and two kids of the goats. He continued this daily for seven days. **7.** For seven days, Yacob, his sons, and his men feasted with joy, blessing and thanking YAHWEH, who had delivered him from all his troubles and allowed him to fulfill his vow. **8.** Yacob gave tithes of all clean animals, but did not offer unclean animals to Levi (priestly tribe). Instead, he gave Levi all the souls (people) of the men who were with them. **9.** Levi took on the priestly role at Bethel before his father Yacob and his brothers, and he became the priest of the family. Yacob then renewed his vow, tithing again to YAHWEH, sanctifying the tithe, which became holy. **10.** This command was written in the heavenly tablets (divine records) as a lasting law for the tithe to be given each year at the place chosen by YAHWEH for His name to dwell. This law is eternal, without end. **11.** It is decreed that every year the second tithe must be eaten before YAHWEH at His chosen place. Nothing of it should remain for the next year. **12.** In the year of the tithe, its fruit should be eaten until the harvest season; the wine until the time of vintage (harvest); and the oil until its season. **13.** Any leftovers that have become old or spoiled should be considered unclean and must be burned with fire. **14.** They must eat the tithe together in the sanctuary (holy place), and not allow it to become stale or spoiled. **15.** All tithes from oxen and sheep are holy to YAHWEH and belong to His priests, who will eat them before Him every year. This is an eternal ordinance recorded in the heavenly tablets. **16.** On the night of the twenty-second day of the month, Yacob decided to build a permanent place and surround it with a wall, consecrating it as holy for him and his descendants. **17.** YAHWEH appeared to him that night, blessing him and saying, "Your name shall no longer be Yacob, but

Yisrael (Israel, meaning 'He struggles with God') shall be your name." **18.** YAHWEH continued, "I am YAHWEH, who created the heavens and the earth. I will multiply your descendants exceedingly. Kings will come from you, and they will judge the earth wherever men have walked." **19.** "I will give your descendants the land beneath the heavens, and they will judge the nations according to their hearts. Then they will possess and inherit the earth forever." **20.** When YAHWEH finished speaking, He ascended into heaven. Yacob watched until He disappeared from sight. **21.** That night, Yacob had another vision. A malak (angel) descended from heaven, holding seven tablets in his hands. He gave them to Yacob, who read them and understood everything written there—events that would unfold for him and his descendants throughout the ages. **22.** The malak showed him the tablets and said, "Do not build this place into an eternal sanctuary. Do not remain here. Go back to the house of your father Abraham (patriarch) and stay with your father Yitschaq (Isaac) until the day of his death." **23.** "You will die peacefully in Egypt, and when you return to this land, you will be buried with honor beside your fathers, Abraham and Yitschaq." **24.** "Do not fear, for what you have seen and read will surely happen. Write down everything you have seen and read." **25.** Yacob replied, "YAHWEH, how can I remember everything I have read and seen?" And YAHWEH responded, "I will bring it to your remembrance." **26.** Yacob awoke from his sleep, remembering everything he had read and seen. He wrote down all the words and visions he had experienced. **27.** He celebrated another day there, offering sacrifices as he had on the previous days, and named the place "Addition" because it was a day added to the feast, which he had previously called "The Feast." **28.** This revelation was written on the heavenly tablets, showing that Yacob was instructed to add this day to the seven-day feast, celebrating it every year. **29.** The day was named "Addition," as it was incorporated into the list of feast days, in keeping with the number of days in the year. **30.** On the night of the twenty-third day of the month, Deborah (Rebecca's nurse) passed away. She was buried near the city (of Beth-el) under the oak (tree) by the river. Yacob named the place "The River of Deborah" and the oak "The Oak of Deborah's Mourning." **31.** Afterward, Rebecca (Yacob's mother) returned to her house with her father Yitschaq (Isaac). Yacob sent rams, sheep, and goats with her to prepare a meal for his father according to his wishes. **32.** Yacob then followed his mother to the land of Kabratan (a region, possibly the area near Hebron), where she settled. **33.** That night, Rachel (Yacob's wife) gave birth to a son and named him "Son of my sorrow" because of the pain she endured during his birth. However, his father named him Benjamin (meaning 'Son of the Right Hand'), on the eleventh day of the eighth month in the first week of the sixth jubilee year. **34.** Rachel died there and was buried in Ephrath (Bethlehem). Yacob placed a pillar on her grave, near the road above her resting place.

Chapter 33

1. Jacob (Yacob) settled in the south of Magdaladra'ef (a region, likely near the Dead Sea) and later went with Leah (Jacob's wife), his wife, to visit his father Isaac (patriarch) during the new moon of the tenth month. **2.** Reuben (Jacob's eldest son) saw Bilhah (Rachel's servant and concubine) bathing in secret and was captivated by her. **3.** At night, he hid himself, entered Bilhah's house, and found her sleeping alone. **4.** He lay with her, and when she awoke, she discovered it was Reuben. Shocked, she grabbed her covering, cried out, and exposed his actions. **5.** Ashamed, she released him, and he fled. **6.** Bilhah grieved deeply over the incident but told no one. **7.** When Jacob sought her, she confessed, saying, "I am unclean for you because Reuben defiled me while I was asleep." **8.** Jacob (Yacob) was furious at Reuben for his grievous act of dishonoring his father by uncovering Bilhah. **9.** Jacob never approached Bilhah again, as she had been defiled. Such an act was detestable before Yahweh (God). **10.** It is written in the heavenly tablets (divine records) that no man should lie with his father's wife or dishonor him in this way; such actions warrant death. **11.** Yahweh demands purity among His chosen people. **12.** Cursed is anyone who lies with his father's wife, for he dishonors his father. The holy ones of Yahweh declare, "Amen, so be it." **13.** Moses (lawgiver) was commanded to teach Israel this law, for it carries a death penalty and no atonement can cleanse the sin. **14.** Such a person must be put to death immediately, for they are unclean. **15.** Let none justify Reuben's survival, for at that time, the full law and judgment were not yet revealed. 16. The law of seasons and days has since been established as everlasting guidance for all generations. 17. Those who commit such sins must be removed from the nation immediately. 18. Moses was instructed to write these commands, so Israel would obey, avoid sin, and not face destruction for defiling the land. 19. Fornication of this nature is the gravest sin, and Yahweh does not tolerate it among His holy nation. 20. Israel is a sacred and priestly people, belonging to Yahweh, and no such impurity should be found among them. 21. In the third year of the sixth week (2145 A.M.), Jacob and his family moved near Isaac and Rebecca (patriarch and matriarch) at Abraham's home. 22. Jacob's sons were: Reuben, Simeon, Levi, Judah, Issachar, Zebulun (sons of Leah); Joseph and Benjamin (sons of Rachel); Dan and Naphtali (sons of Bilhah); Gad and Asher (sons of Zilpah). Jacob's only daughter was Dinah. 23. When they visited Isaac and Rebecca, they bowed before them, and Isaac blessed Jacob and his sons with great joy, seeing the future of his lineage.

Chapter 34

1. In the sixth year of the forty-fourth jubilee (2148 A.M.), Jacob sent his sons and servants to pasture their sheep in Shechem (a city in Canaan). 2. The seven kings of the Amorites (ancient people in Canaan) conspired to ambush and kill them, planning to seize their livestock. 3. Jacob stayed home with Levi, Judah, Joseph, and Benjamin, as they tended to Isaac, whose spirit was sorrowful. 4. Kings from Taphu, Aresa, Seragan, Selo, Ga'as, Bethoron, and Ma'anisakir, along with mountain and woodland dwellers in Canaan, gathered against them. 5. News reached Jacob that the Amorite kings had surrounded his sons and plundered their herds. 6. Jacob, with his three sons and a force of 6,000 armed men, went to confront them. 7. He defeated them at Shechem, killing their leaders and recovering the herds. 8. Jacob subdued them, imposed tribute of their land's produce, and built Robel and Tamnatares (settlements or fortifications). 9. He made peace, and they became his servants until the time he and his sons moved to Egypt. 10. In the seventh year of that week (2149 A.M.), Jacob sent Joseph (Jacob's son) to check on his brothers in Shechem, but Joseph found them in Dothan (a location). 11. They plotted to kill him but instead sold him to Ishmaelite (descendants of Ishmael) merchants, who took him to Egypt and sold him to Potiphar (Pharaoh's eunuch and chief cook). 12. Jacob's sons slaughtered a goat, dipped Joseph's coat in its blood, and sent it to Jacob on the tenth of the seventh month. 13. Jacob mourned through the night, saying, "An evil beast has devoured Joseph." His household joined him in grief. 14. His children tried to comfort him, but he refused to be consoled. 15. Bilhah (Jacob's concubine) mourning Joseph's death, passed away in Qafratef (a location), followed by Dinah (Jacob's daughter). 16. These three mournings befell Israel in one month. Bilhah and Dinah were buried near Rachel's tomb. 17. Jacob mourned Joseph for a year, saying, "I will go to my grave mourning my son." 18. It was ordained for Israel to observe the tenth of the seventh month as a day of atonement with a young goat, remembering Jacob's sorrow over Joseph. 19. This day is set for annual reflection, repentance, and cleansing from sin. 20. After Joseph was taken, Jacob's sons married: Reuben wed Ada; Simeon married Adlba'a (a Canaanite); Levi took Melka of Aram (descendant of Terah); Judah married Betasu'el (a Canaanite); Issachar wed Hezaqa; Zebulun married Ni'iman; Dan took Egla; Naphtali wed Rasu'u of Mesopotamia; Gad married Maka; Asher took Ijona; Joseph married Asenath (an Egyptian); Benjamin wed Ijasaka. 21. Simeon later repented and married a second wife from Mesopotamia, like his brothers.

Chapter 35

1. In the first year of the first week of the forty-fifth Jubilee (2157 A.M.), Rebecca, mother of Jacob (Yacob), called him to her and gave him a command concerning his father Isaac (Yitschaq) and his brother Esau. She instructed him to honor them throughout his life. 2. Jacob replied, "I will obey all that you have told me, for honoring them will be both my honor and greatness, and it will be righteous in the sight of YAHWEH." 3. He continued, "Mother, you know my heart and my actions from the time of my birth until now. I have always acted with good intentions and have always considered others kindly. How then could I fail to honor my father and my brother, as you have asked?" 4. Jacob then asked, "Tell me, mother, if there is any wrong in me, I will

turn from it, and may mercy be shown to me." 5. Rebecca answered, "My son, I have never seen anything perverse in you, only upright deeds. But I must tell you the truth: I will not live much longer. I have seen in a dream that my days are numbered, and I will die this year, for I have completed the years appointed to me." 6. Jacob, hearing this, laughed at his mother's words, for she seemed full of strength, and had no sign of illness. She was strong, moving with ease, and had no affliction upon her. 7. "Blessed be I, mother, if my days will be as many as yours, and if my strength will endure as yours has. But I believe you jest about your death. You are well and strong, and surely you will live many more years." 8. Nevertheless, Rebecca went to Isaac (Yitschaq) and made a request to him. She said, "I have a petition to ask of you: make Esau swear that he will not harm Jacob or hold any enmity (hostility) against him. For you know that Esau's thoughts have always been wicked, and there is no goodness in him. After your death, he desires to kill Jacob." 9. She continued, "You are aware of how Esau has treated us since Jacob left for Haran. He abandoned us completely, and has taken our possessions for himself. He has done us much harm, and when we begged him to return what was rightfully ours, he only showed pity, but not kindness." 10. "Esau is angry with you because you blessed Jacob, your perfect and righteous son. Jacob has shown us only goodness. Since his return from Haran, he has never taken anything from us but has given to us freely, always bringing us what is needed in its season, and he blesses us with a joyful heart. He has never departed from us and continues to honor us." 11. Isaac replied, "I too know Jacob's deeds, and I see that he honors us with all his heart. But I loved Esau more in the past, because he was my firstborn (eldest son). However, now I love Jacob more, for Esau has done many evil things. His actions have been filled with violence, and there is no righteousness in him." 12. Isaac's heart was troubled because of Esau's behavior, and he knew that neither Esau nor his descendants (descendants meaning those born from him) would be saved. They had forsaken YAHWEH and followed after the unclean ways of their wives, and because of this, they would be destroyed from the earth. 13. Isaac continued, "You ask me to make Esau swear that he will not harm Jacob, but even if he swears, he will break his oath (promise). Esau will do nothing but evil. However, if he desires to harm Jacob, Jacob will prevail, for he is under the protection of a great and powerful guardian, far stronger than Esau's." 14. Rebecca then called Esau to her, and he came to her without hesitation. She said, "I have a petition, my son, and I ask you to promise to fulfill it." 15. Esau responded, "I will do whatever you ask, and I will not refuse you." 16. She said to him, "When I die, I ask that you bury me near Sarah, your father's mother, and that both you and Jacob will love one another, that neither of you will harbor any evil thoughts toward the other, but that you will always have mutual love. If you do this, you will prosper, and no enemy (adversary) will ever triumph over you. You will be a blessing to all who love you." 17. Esau agreed, saying, "I will do as you have asked. I will bury you near Sarah, and I will love Jacob above all others. There is no one else on earth I can love like him, for he is my brother. We were born together, and we came from your womb together." 18. "I also ask that you urge Jacob to love me and my sons, for I know that he will one day rule over me and my children, for when my father blessed him, he made him the superior, and me the inferior. I swear that I will love Jacob and do him no harm all the days of my life." 19. Esau swore to his mother that he would honor her request. Rebecca then called Jacob before Esau and gave him the same command. 20. Jacob said, "I will honor your wishes, mother. I swear that no harm will come from me or my sons to Esau. Only love will be in our hearts for him." 21. That night, they ate and drank together, and Rebecca died peacefully in her sleep, three jubilees (a period of 49 years), one week, and one year old. Esau and Jacob buried her in the double cave near Sarah, their father's mother.

Chapter 36

1. In the sixth year of this week (2162 A.M.), Isaac (Yitschaq) called for his two sons, Esau and Jacob (Yacob). When they came before him, he said, "My sons, I am about to join my fathers in their eternal resting place, where they have gone before me." 2. "Bury me near my father, Abraham (Abraham, Isaac's father), in the cave of Machpelah, in the field of Ephron the Hittite (Ephron, a Hittite who sold Abraham the burial plot). Abraham purchased this field as a burial site, and it is

where I have prepared my own tomb. There, I ask to be laid to rest." **3. Chapter 37**

"Now, my sons, I command you to live with righteousness and integrity on the earth. If you do so, YAHWEH will fulfill the promises He made to Abraham and his descendants. He will bless you and multiply your seed, just as He promised to make Abraham's children as numerous as the stars in the sky." **4.** "Above all, love one another, my sons. Let the bond between you be as strong as the love a man has for his own soul. Always seek to benefit one another and act in harmony, for unity and love will be your strength. Reject idolatry (worship of false gods), for it is full of deceit. Do not follow after idols (false gods), nor give them your heart, for those who worship them are led astray." **5.** "Remember, my sons, YAHWEH, the Almighty of your father Abraham. Just as I worshipped Him and served Him with joy and righteousness, so should you, that He might bless you and establish your name forever, as a plant of righteousness that cannot be uprooted." **6.** "Now, I make you swear a solemn oath by the great and mighty NAME of YAHWEH, who created the heavens and the earth and everything in them. Swear that you will revere Him, worship Him, and live in harmony with one another, without harboring any ill will toward your brother." **7.** "If either of you should harbor evil intentions against the other, know that such a one will fall into their own trap. They will be rooted out from the land of the living, and their descendants will be wiped from under heaven. Their name will be blotted from the book of life, and they will be destined for eternal destruction, enduring everlasting wrath, torment, and judgment." **8.** "I testify to you, my sons, that this is the judgment for anyone who seeks to harm their brother. Such a person will face the burning wrath of YAHWEH, just as He destroyed Sodom (a city destroyed for wickedness), and their land and everything they own will be consumed by fire. Their deeds will not be remembered in the book of the righteous but will be recorded among the condemned." **9.** "Therefore, be cautious and upright, for only those who live righteously will be remembered and blessed, while those who choose evil will face eternal punishment." **10.** Isaac divided his possessions between his two sons that day. He gave the larger portion to Esau, the firstborn, including the tower and all that Abraham had possessed at the Well of the Oath (a significant location where Abraham made a covenant with Abimelech). **11.** "This larger inheritance is yours, Esau, as the firstborn," Isaac said. **12.** Esau replied, "I have already sold my birthright to Jacob, and so I have no claim to it. It is his now, and I have no objections to that." **13.** Isaac said, "May a blessing rest upon you both and your descendants. You have brought peace to my heart, and I am no longer troubled about the birthright, knowing that there will be no strife between you." **14.** "May YAHWEH bless those who do righteousness, and may their descendants be blessed forever." **15.** With these words, Isaac concluded his blessing and command, and his sons ate and drank with him, rejoicing in their unity. Isaac was comforted, seeing that they were of one mind, and after they left him, they rested and slept. **16.** That evening, Isaac lay in his bed, content and at peace. He slept the eternal sleep, passing away at the age of one hundred and eighty years. He had lived twenty-five jubilees (49-year periods) and five years. His sons Esau and Jacob buried him. **17.** After the death of their father, Esau went to the land of Edom, to the mountains of Seir (a region southeast of Israel), and settled there. **18.** Jacob, meanwhile, remained in the mountains of Hebron (a city of refuge, also known for its connection to Abraham), dwelling in the tower that belonged to his father Abraham. There, he continued to worship YAHWEH with all his heart, following the commandments and laws that had been passed down to him. **19.** In the fourth year of the second week of the forty-fifth jubilee (2167 A.M.), Leah (Jacob's wife, daughter of Laban) passed away. He buried her in the double cave near Rebecca (Jacob's mother), his mother, to the left of Sarah (Abraham's wife), his father's mother. **20.** All her sons and Jacob's sons came together to mourn for Leah, comforting Jacob in his grief. Jacob wept for her deeply, for he had loved her dearly, especially after the death of Rachel (Leah's sister). **21.** Leah was a woman of great virtue, perfect in her ways, and always honored Jacob. During all the years they were together, he never heard a harsh word from her. She was gentle, peaceful, and honorable in all her dealings. **22.** Jacob remembered all the good she had done throughout their lives, and he lamented her passing with great sorrow. He loved her with all his heart and soul, and her loss left a deep ache within him.

Chapter 37

1. When Isaac (father of Jacob and Esau) passed away, the sons of Esau learned that Isaac had given the birthright to his younger son, Jacob. This enraged them greatly. **2.** They confronted their father, saying, "Why did your father give Jacob the elder's portion and disregard you, even though you are the firstborn and Jacob is the younger?" **3.** He responded, "Because I sold my birthright to Jacob for a mere bowl of lentil stew. And on the day my father sent me out to hunt and bring him food so that he could bless me, Jacob deceived him, bringing him food and drink instead. My father blessed him and put me beneath him." **4.** "Moreover, our father made us both swear not to harm each other, to live in peace and love, and not to corrupt our paths." **5.** But they replied, "We will not listen to you and make peace with him; our strength surpasses his, and we are more powerful. We will fight him, kill him, and destroy him and his sons. If you refuse to join us, we will harm you as well." **6.** "Listen to us: Let us send messengers to Aram (a region in Mesopotamia), Philistia (land of the Philistines), Moab (land east of Israel), and Ammon (ancient kingdom near Jordan), to hire warriors who are eager for battle. Let us attack Jacob and destroy him before he becomes strong." **7.** Their father cautioned, "Do not go to war against him, or you will fall before him." **8.** But they retorted, "This has been your way since your youth. You submit to his rule. We will not listen to you." **9.** So, they sent to Aram and Aduram (a friend of their father), and hired a thousand chosen warriors. **10.** Warriors came to join them from Moab, Ammon, Philistia, Edom (a kingdom southeast of Israel), and the Horites (ancient tribe in Seir), as well as from Kittim (islands in the Mediterranean), totaling four thousand battle-tested fighters. **11.** They demanded their father lead them, threatening, "Go with us, or we will kill you." **12.** His heart was filled with anger and frustration, seeing how his sons forced him to lead them against Jacob. But then, he remembered the hidden bitterness he held against Jacob. **13.** He forgot the oath he had sworn to his parents to never bring harm to Jacob. **14.** Meanwhile, Jacob remained unaware that Esau's forces were marching toward him, as he mourned his wife Leah's death. They were nearly at the tower (a structure in Jacob's settlement), four thousand warriors strong. **15.** The men of Hebron (a city in ancient Israel) sent word to Jacob, saying, "Your brother Esau is coming with four thousand armed men to fight you." They loved Jacob more than Esau, as he was known for his generosity and mercy. **16.** Jacob did not believe them until the threat was almost upon him. **17.** He closed the gates of the tower and stood on its walls. Calling out to Esau, he said, "Is this how you honor me, coming to fight after my wife's death? Is this the oath you swore to our parents? You have broken your vow and condemned yourself." **18.** Esau replied, "Neither humans nor beasts swear righteous oaths that last forever. They constantly plot harm, seeking to destroy one another." **19.** "You hate me and my children without end. There is no bond of brotherhood between us." **20.** "Listen: If the boar could change its skin, and make its bristles soft as wool; if it could sprout horns like a stag, then I would consider brotherhood with you." **21.** "And if the breasts of a mother separated from her child, then I would regard you as my brother." **22.** "If wolves made peace with lambs and spared them, and if lions yoked with oxen to plow, then I would reconcile with you." **23.** "And if ravens turned white as snow, then I would love you and make peace with you. But you and your sons will be destroyed, and there will be no peace for you." **24.** When Jacob saw the malice in Esau's heart, determined to kill him, he realized Esau was like a wild boar charging toward its own doom, not deterred by the spear. **25.** Jacob then ordered his men and servants to prepare for battle and defend themselves against Esau's attack.

Chapter 38

1. And after that, Judah (one of Jacob's sons) spoke to Jacob, his father, saying, "Bend your bow, father, and send forth your arrows to defeat the adversary and slay the enemy; may you have strength, for we will not kill your brother, for he is like you. Let us honor him in this way." **2.** Then Jacob bent his bow, shot an arrow, and struck Esau, his brother, on his right breast, killing him. **3.** He sent forth another arrow, striking Adoran (an Aramean leader) the Aramean on his left breast, driving him back, and slaying him. **4.** Then, the sons of Jacob, along with their servants, divided themselves into groups and spread out on all four sides of the tower. **5.** Judah went to the front, with Naphtali and Gad, leading fifty men on the south side of the tower. They killed everyone they encountered, and none escaped. **6.** Levi, Dan, and Asher went out on the east side, also with fifty men, and they killed the warriors of Moab and Ammon. **7.** Reuben, Issachar, and Zebulun went out on the north side, and with fifty men, they defeated the warriors of the Philistines. **8.** Simeon, Benjamin, and Enoch, the son of Reuben, went out on the west side, and with fifty men, they struck down four hundred warriors from Edom and the Horites. Six hundred men fled, and four sons of Esau fled with them, leaving their father slain on the hill in Aduram (a location near Esau's residence). **9.** The sons of Jacob pursued them into the mountains of Seir (a mountainous region in Edom). Jacob buried his brother on the hill in Aduram, then returned to his house. **10.** The sons of Jacob pressed hard upon the sons of Esau in the mountains of Seir, forcing them into servitude under the sons of Jacob. **11.** They sent to their father asking if they should make peace with them or destroy them. **12.** Jacob sent a message to his sons instructing them to make peace, and so they made peace with them, placing them under a yoke of servitude, paying tribute to Jacob and his sons forever. **13.** They continued to pay tribute to Jacob until the day he went down into Egypt. **14.** And the sons of Edom (descendants of Esau) have never been freed from the yoke of servitude that the twelve sons of Jacob imposed on them, remaining so to this day. **15.** These are the kings who reigned in Edom before any king reigned over the children of Israel, in the land of Edom. **16.** Bela, the son of Beor, reigned in Edom, and the name of his city was Danaba. **17.** Bela died, and Jobab (king of Boser, a city in Edom), the son of Zara of Boser, reigned in his place. **18.** Jobab died, and Asam from Teman (a region in Edom) took his place as king. **19.** Asam died, and Adath, the son of Barad, who killed the Midianites in the field of Moab, reigned in his stead. The name of his city was Avith. **20.** Adath died, and Salman from Amaseqa (location unknown) took the throne. **21.** Salman died, and Saul of Ra'aboth (location by a river) by the river succeeded him. **22.** Saul died, and Ba'elunan, the son of Achbor, became king. **23,24.** Ba'elunan, the son of Achbor, died, and Adath took his place, and his wife was Maitabith, the daughter of Matarat, the daughter of Metabedza'ab. **25.** These are the kings who reigned in the land of Edom.

Chapter 39

1. And Jacob dwelt in the land where his father had lived, in the land of Canaan (a historical region in the ancient Near East). **2.** These are the generations of Jacob. Joseph was seventeen years old when he was taken to Egypt (land of Pharaoh), and Potiphar (official of Pharaoh), the chief cook, bought him. **3.** And Potiphar placed Joseph over all his household, and the blessing of YAHWEH came upon the house of the Egyptian because of Joseph. YAHWEH prospered him in everything he did. **4.** The Egyptian entrusted everything to Joseph's care, for he saw that YAHWEH was with him, and that YAHWEH made everything Joseph did successful. **5.** Joseph was handsome in appearance, and his master's wife looked at him and became attracted to him. She begged him to lie with her. **6.** But he did not give in, and he remembered YAHWEH and the words his father Jacob had taught him from the teachings of Abraham (patriarch of Israel): that no man should commit fornication with a woman who has a husband, for the punishment of death has been decreed in heaven before the Most High YAHWEH, and the sin would be recorded in the eternal books before YAHWEH. Joseph remembered these words and refused to lie with her. **8.** She continued to beg him for a year, but he refused and would not listen to her. **9.** One day, she seized him and tried to force him to lie with her, closing the doors and holding him tight. But he left his garment in her hands, broke through the door, and fled from her presence. **10.** When the woman saw that he would not lie with her, she falsely accused him before her husband, saying, "Your Hebrew servant (a person of Israel), whom you love, tried to force himself on me. When I cried out, he fled, leaving his garment in my hands and breaking through the door." **11.** When the Egyptian master saw the garment and heard the words of his wife, he threw Joseph into prison (a place for prisoners of the king), the place where the king's prisoners were kept. **12.** And Joseph was in the prison, but YAHWEH showed him favor in the eyes of the chief jailer and gave him compassion. The chief jailer saw that YAHWEH was with Joseph and that YAHWEH caused everything he did to prosper. **13.** The chief jailer entrusted all the prisoners' affairs to Joseph, knowing nothing about what was in the prison because Joseph took care of

everything, and YAHWEH made it successful. **14.** Joseph remained there for two years. During that time, Pharaoh (the king of Egypt) became angry with his two eunuchs, the chief butler and the chief baker, and put them in custody in the prison where Joseph was. **15.** The chief jailer appointed Joseph to attend to them, and he served them. **16.** One night, both the chief butler and the chief baker had dreams (visions), and they told them to Joseph. **17.** Joseph interpreted their dreams, and as he had foretold, the chief butler was restored to his position, while the chief baker was executed, just as Joseph had interpreted. **18.** But the chief butler forgot about Joseph in the prison, despite Joseph's accurate interpretation of his dream. He did not remember to mention Joseph to Pharaoh, and he forgot him.

Chapter 40

1. And in those days, Pharaoh had two dreams in one night concerning a famine (scarcity of food) that would spread across all the land. He awoke from his sleep and called all the dream interpreters (those who interpret visions) and magicians of Egypt (practitioners of ancient Egyptian magic) to explain his dreams, but they were unable to interpret them. **2.** Then the chief butler remembered Joseph and spoke of him to Pharaoh. He brought Joseph out of the prison and told Pharaoh his two dreams. **3.** Joseph said to Pharaoh, "The two dreams are one. Seven years of abundance will come upon the land of Egypt, followed by seven years of famine, so severe that it will be unlike any famine Egypt has ever seen." **4.** "Now, let Pharaoh appoint overseers (managers) throughout Egypt to store up food in every city during the years of abundance, so that there will be enough food for the seven years of famine, preventing the land from perishing due to the famine, which will be very severe." **5.** YAHWEH gave Joseph favor in Pharaoh's eyes, and Pharaoh said to his servants, "We cannot find a man wiser and more discreet than this man. The spirit of YAHWEH is with him." **6.** Pharaoh appointed Joseph as second-in-command over all of Egypt, giving him authority over the entire land. He made Joseph ride in the second chariot of Pharaoh. **7.** Pharaoh clothed him in fine garments, put a gold chain around his neck, proclaimed before him, "El, El, wa 'Abirer" (meaning "God, Mighty and Strong"), placed a ring on his hand, and made him ruler over all his household. Pharaoh magnified him and said, "Only on the throne will I be greater than you." **8.** Joseph ruled over all Egypt, and all the princes of Pharaoh, his servants, and those who worked for the king's business loved him. He walked in integrity (honesty), without pride or arrogance, and showed no favoritism. He did not accept bribes, but judged the people of the land fairly. **9.** The land of Egypt was at peace under Pharaoh because of Joseph. YAHWEH was with him and showed him favor and mercy before all those who knew him and heard about him. Pharaoh's kingdom was well-ordered, free from evil and disorder. **10.** Pharaoh gave Joseph the name Zephanath-Paneah and gave him Asenath (daughter of Potiphar, priest of On) to be his wife. **11.** Joseph was thirty years old when he stood before Pharaoh. **12.** In that same year, Isaac (father of Jacob and Esau) died. And as Joseph had predicted through the interpretation of his dreams, the seven years of abundance came to Egypt, and the land produced plentifully, with one measure yielding eighteen hundred measures. **13.** Joseph gathered food from every city until the storehouses were filled beyond measure, and the abundance of grain could no longer be counted due to its vastness.

Chapter 41

1. In the forty-fifth jubilee, in the second week, and in the second year (2165 A.M.), Yahudah took a wife for his firstborn son, Er, from the daughters of Aram (an ancient kingdom located near Syria). Her name was Tamar. **2.** However, Er did not want to be with her, as his mother was from the daughters of Canaan (a region in the Levant), and he wished to marry someone from his mother's kin. Yahudah, his father, did not allow this. **3.** Er, the firstborn of Yahudah, was wicked in the eyes of YAHWEH, and so YAHWEH struck him down. **4.** Yahudah then said to his second son, Onan, "Go in to your brother's wife, and fulfill the duty of a brother-in-law to her, and raise up offspring for your brother." **5.** But Onan knew that the child would not be his, but his brother's. So, whenever he went in to his brother's wife, he spilled his seed on the ground, and this was wicked in the eyes of YAHWEH, so He struck him down as well. **6.** Yahudah said to Tamar, his daughter-in-law, "Remain a widow in your father's house until my son Shelah is grown up, and I will give you to him as a husband." **7.** Shelah grew up, but Yahudah's wife, Bedsu'el (a name of uncertain meaning, possibly a female ancestor), did not allow Shelah to marry Tamar. 8. In the fifth year of this week (2168 A.M.), Bedsu'el, Yahudah's wife, died. And in the sixth year, Yahudah went to Timnah (a city in the tribe of Judah, famous for its vineyards) to shear his sheep. 9. Tamar was told, "Behold, your father-in-law is going to Timnah to shear his sheep." So, she removed her widow's clothes, put on a veil, adorned herself, and sat at the gate of the city on the road to Timnah. 10. As Yahudah passed by, he saw her and thought she was a harlot, so he said to her, "Let me come in to you." She replied, "Come in," and he went to her. 11. She said to him, "What will you give me for my services?" He answered, "I have nothing to give you, except my signet ring, my necklace, and my staff." 12. She said, "Give them to me until you send me a kid from the flock." He agreed and gave them to her, and she conceived by him. 13. Yahudah returned to his sheep, and Tamar went back to her father's house. 14. Yahudah sent a kid from the flock by the hand of his servant, an Adullamite (a person from Adullam, a city in Judah), to redeem the items he had given Tamar. But when the servant arrived, he could not find her. 15. He asked the people of the place, "Where is the harlot who was by the road?" They replied, "There is no harlot here." 16. The servant returned to Yahudah and reported that he had not found her, and that the people said there was no harlot. 17. Yahudah then said, "Let her keep them, lest we become a laughingstock. I sent the kid, but you could not find her." 18. Three months later, it was discovered that Tamar was pregnant. They told Yahudah, "Tamar, your daughter-in-law, has become pregnant by whoredom." 19. Yahudah went to her father's house and said, "Bring her out, and let her be burned, for she has committed uncleanness in Israel." 20. As they were about to bring her out to burn her, Tamar sent word to her father-in-law, saying, "Recognize these: the signet ring, the necklace, and the staff. By the man who owns these, I am with child." 21. Yahudah acknowledged them and said, "Tamar is more righteous than I, because I did not give her to my son Shelah." And he declared that she should not be burned. 22. Tamar was not given to Shelah as a wife, and Yahudah did not approach her again. 23. After this, Tamar gave birth to two sons: Perez (meaning "breach" or "bursting forth") and Zerah (meaning "dawn" or "rising sun"), in the seventh year of the second week (2170 A.M.). 24. These were the seven years of fruitfulness, as Joseph (Yoseph, the son of Jacob) had foretold to Pharaoh. 25. Yahudah admitted that the deed he had done was wicked, for he had lain with his daughter-in-law, and he regarded it as hateful in his eyes. He acknowledged his transgression and began to lament and pray before YAHWEH for forgiveness. 26. "And you shall command the children of Yisrael (Israel) that there be no uncleanness among them. Anyone who lies with his daughter-in-law or his mother-in-law has committed an act of uncleanness. Let both the man and the woman be burned with fire. This will turn away the wrath and punishment from Yisrael." 27. "And to Yahudah we said that his two sons had not sinned by lying with Tamar, which is why his seed was preserved for a second generation and would not be cut off." 28. "For Yahudah, in his sincerity and intent to uphold righteousness, sought to administer justice according to the judgment of Abraham (the patriarch of the Israelites), as he had been commanded. Yahudah sought to punish Tamar by burning her with fire, yet his intent was to follow the law and ensure justice was done."

Chapter 42

1. In the first year of the third week of the forty-fifth jubilee, the famine began to affect the land, and no rain fell, causing the earth to become barren. 2. However, in Egypt, there was food, for Yoseph (Joseph) had gathered and stored the grain during the seven years of plenty. 3. The Egyptians came to Yoseph to buy food, and he opened the storehouses where the grain from the first year was kept, selling it to the people for gold. 4. When Yacob (Jacob) heard that there was food in Egypt, he sent his ten sons to buy grain, but he did not send Benjamin. 5. Yoseph recognized his brothers, but they did not recognize him. He spoke to them roughly, questioning, "Are you spies, come to see the weakness of the land?" 6. He put them in prison for three days, and then released them, keeping Simeon as a hostage and sending the others back with grain. 7. Yoseph filled their sacks with grain, but secretly returned their money into their sacks as well, which they did not realize. 8. He instructed them to bring their younger brother, Benjamin, when they returned, because they had told him that their father was alive and

that they had a younger brother. 9. When they returned to Canaan, they told their father all that had happened: how the ruler of Egypt had spoken harshly to them and had kept Simeon until they brought Benjamin. 10. Yacob replied, "You have bereaved me of my children! Yoseph is no more, Simeon is no more, and now you would take Benjamin. All these things have happened to me." 11. He refused to let Benjamin go, fearing that something might happen to him, saying, "Their mother gave birth to two sons, and one is gone. If anything happens to this one, you will bring my gray hairs down to the grave in sorrow." 12. When Yacob saw that their money had been returned in each sack, he feared that they might be accused of theft if they returned to Egypt. 13. The famine grew worse in the land of Canaan, and in all lands except Egypt, where the people had stored up food in preparation for the years of famine. 14. The Egyptians ate from their stored grain during the first year of famine. 15. When Yisrael (Israel) saw that there was no relief from the famine, he said to his sons, "Go again and buy us some food so that we do not perish." 16. They replied, "We will not go unless our youngest brother goes with us. We will not go without him." 17. Yisrael realized that they would all die of hunger if he did not send Benjamin. 18. Reuben then said, "Put him in my care; if I do not bring him back to you, kill my two sons instead." 19. Yisrael refused, but Yahudah stepped forward and said, "Send him with me, and if I do not bring him back, let me bear the blame for him forever." 20. Finally, Yisrael agreed, and he sent Benjamin with them. They took presents—stacte (a resin), almonds, terebinth nuts, and honey—and went to Egypt in the second year of the famine. 21. When they arrived, Yoseph saw Benjamin and immediately recognized him. He asked, "Is this your younger brother, of whom you spoke to me?" And they said, "Yes, it is he." Yoseph said, "May YAHWEH be gracious to you, my son." 22. Yoseph brought them to his house, and he released Simeon from prison. He prepared a feast for them and they presented their gifts to him. 23. They ate with him, and Yoseph gave each brother a portion, but Benjamin's portion was five times larger than anyone else's. 24. They ate and drank and then left to return to their donkeys. 25. Yoseph devised a plan to test their hearts. He instructed his steward, "Fill their sacks with grain, return their money into their sacks, and put my silver cup in the sack of the youngest. Then send them on their way."

Chapter 43

1. Yoseph (Joseph, a biblical patriarch) instructed his steward to do as he had said: fill their sacks with food, return their money, and place his silver cup (a cup made of silver, used for drinking) in Benjamin's sack. 2. Early the next morning, they left. Yoseph then said to his steward, "Chase after them and accuse them of stealing my silver cup, which my lord drinks from. Bring back the youngest brother before I go to my judgment seat (the place where a ruler or judge makes decisions)." 3. The steward followed and said to them, as Yoseph had instructed. 4. The brothers replied, "God forbid that we would do such a thing! We returned the money we found in our sacks the first time. How could we steal anything from your lord's house?" 5. They offered, "Search our sacks, starting with the oldest. If the cup is found in anyone's sack, let him be put to death, and we will become slaves (persons forced to work) to your lord." 6. The steward replied, "No, only the one with whom I find the cup will become my servant (someone who works for someone else), and the rest of you may return home in peace." 7. He searched their sacks, beginning with the oldest, until he reached Benjamin's sack, where the cup was found. 8. The brothers tore their clothes in despair (great sadness), loaded their donkeys (animals used for carrying goods), and returned to the city (a large settlement), where they came before Yoseph and bowed down to him. 9. Yoseph said to them, "You have done evil (wrongdoing)." They answered, "How can we explain? The cup has been found. We are your servants, and even our donkeys are yours." 10. Yoseph said, "I fear God (the Almighty). The one who stole the cup will be my servant, and the rest of you can go in peace." 11. Yahudah (Judah, one of Yoseph's brothers) stepped forward and said, "My lord, let me speak. Two brothers were born to our father, one has disappeared, and this one is the only one left of his mother. Our father loves him dearly, and his life is bound to this boy's. 12. If we return without him, our father will die of grief (great sorrow). We will bring him down to the grave (place where dead are buried) in sorrow." 13. "Let me remain instead of the boy," Yahudah offered. "I promised our father I would bring him back.

If I don't, I will bear the blame forever." **14.** Yoseph saw that they were sincere and united, and he could no longer control himself. He revealed to them, "I am Yoseph!" **15.** He spoke to them in Hebrew (language of the Israelites) and wept, embracing them. **16.** His brothers were astonished (greatly surprised) and began to weep as well, and Yoseph said, "Do not weep for me. Hurry and bring my father here. See, I am Yoseph, your brother, whom you sold into Egypt." **17.** "This is the second year of the famine (period of food shortage), and there are still five years without harvest (season when crops grow). Come quickly, so that you and your families may live, and do not worry about your possessions. YAHWEH (the Lord God) sent me ahead to preserve life." **18.** "Tell my father I am alive, and that I have been made ruler over all Egypt (ancient civilization). I am like a father to Pharaoh (king of Egypt) and lord of his house." **19.** "Tell him of the wealth and splendor (great wealth and beauty) that YAHWEH has given me." **20.** Pharaoh instructed that Yoseph's brothers be given wagons (large vehicles for carrying goods), provisions (supplies for the journey), and clothes for the journey, along with silver. **21.** Yoseph sent his brothers back with ten donkeys carrying grain (a type of food), silver, and clothes for their father. **22.** They returned to Canaan (the land where they lived) and told their father Yoseph was alive, and was ruler over all Egypt. **23.** Yacob (Jacob, the father of Yoseph and his brothers) did not believe them at first, but when he saw the wagons, his spirit revived (became alive). He said, "It is enough. Yoseph is alive! I will go and see him before I die." **24.** And Yisrael (another name for Jacob) said, "It is enough. Yoseph, my son, is still alive! I will go and see him before I die."

Chapter 44

1. Yisrael departed from Haran (a city in Mesopotamia) on the first day of the third month, journeying toward the Well of the Oath (a sacred place). There, he offered a sacrifice to YAHWEH, the Almighty of his father Yitschaq (Isaac, his father), on the seventh day of the month. **2.** As he traveled, Yacob remembered the dream (a prophetic vision) he had at Bethel (a place where Yacob had a vision) and became fearful about going down to Egypt. **3.** While considering whether to send word to Yoseph and stay in Canaan, Yacob stayed there for seven days, hoping for a vision about whether he should go or remain. **4.** He celebrated the harvest festival (a time of gathering crops) of first-fruits with old grain, for the famine had devastated the land, affecting humans, animals, and birds, leaving no seed in Canaan. **5.** On the sixteenth, YAHWEH appeared to him, calling, "Yacob, Yacob." Yacob answered, "Here I am." **6.** YAHWEH said, "I am the Almighty of your fathers, the Almighty of Abraham and Yitschaq. Do not fear to go down to Egypt; there I will make of you a great nation. I will be with you, and I will bring you back again. You will be buried here, and Yoseph will close your eyes." **7.** Yisrael's sons and grandsons prepared to depart, placing their father and his possessions on wagons. **8.** On the sixteenth of the third month, Yisrael left the Well of the Oath and traveled toward Egypt. **9.** Yisrael sent Yahudah ahead to Yoseph to inspect the land of Goshen (a fertile region in Egypt), as Yoseph had told his brothers to come and settle there, for it was the best land in Egypt, suitable for both them and their livestock. **10.** Goshen was the most fertile land in Egypt, near to Yoseph, and ideal for the family and their cattle. **11.** These are the names of Yacob's sons who went to Egypt with him: Reuben, the firstborn of Yisrael; **12.** Reuben's sons: Enoch, Pallu, Hezron, and Carmi—four. **13.** Simeon's sons: Jemuel, Jamin, Ohad, Jachin, Zohar, and Shaul, the son of the Zephasite (a people) woman— seven. **14.** Levi's sons: Gershon, Kohath, and Merari—three. **15.** Yahudah's sons: Shelah, Perez, and Zerah—three. **16.** Issachar's sons: Tola, Phua, Jasub, and Shimron—four. **17.** Zebulon's sons: Sered, Elon, and Jahleel—three. **18.** These are the sons of Leah, whom she bore to Yacob in Mesopotamia, including their sister Dinah (a biblical personality). There were thirty in total from Leah's line, including Yacob. **19.** The sons of Zilpah (a servant of Leah), Leah's handmaid, whom Yacob also took as a wife, were Gad and Asher. **20.** The sons of Gad: Ziphion, Haggi, Shuni, Ezbon, Eri, Areli, and Arodi—seven. **21.** The sons of Asher: Imnah, Ishvah, Ishvi, Beriah, and Serah, their sister—six. **22.** The total of Leah's sons and their descendants was forty-four souls. **23.** The sons of Rachel, Yacob's beloved wife: Yoseph and Benjamin. **24.** Yoseph had two sons in Egypt before his father arrived, whom Asenath (a woman from Egypt), daughter of Potiphar the priest of

Heliopolis (an Egyptian city), bore to him: Manasseh and Ephraim— two. **25.** The sons of Benjamin: Bela, Becher, Ashbel, Gera, Naaman, Ehi, Rosh, Muppim, Huppim, and Ard—ten. **26.** The total of Rachel's descendants was fourteen souls. **27.** The sons of Bilhah (Rachel's handmaid), were Dan and Naphtali. **28.** The sons of Dan: Hushim, Samon, and Baalah—three. **29.** The sons of Naphtali: Jahzeel, Guni, Jezer, and Shillem—four. **30.** The total of Bilhah's sons was seven. **31.** All the people of Yacob's house who went to Egypt were sixty-six. **32.** And Yisrael entered Egypt with all his family.

Chapter 45

1. And Yisrael went into the land of Egypt, into the region of Goshen (a fertile region in Egypt), on the new month of the fourth month, in the second year of the third week of the forty-fifth jubilee. **2.** And Yoseph went to meet his father Yacob in the land of Goshen, and he fell on his father's neck and wept. **3.** And Yisrael said to Yoseph: "Now let me die, since I have seen you. May YAHWEH (the Lord God), the Almighty of Yisrael, be blessed, the Almighty of Abraham and the Almighty of Yitschaq (Isaac), who has not withheld His mercy and His unmerited pardon from His servant Yacob." **4.** "It is enough for me that I have seen your face while I am still alive. Truly, the vision I had at Bethel (a place where Yacob had a vision) has come to pass. Blessed be YAHWEH, my Sovereign, forever and ever, and blessed be His NAME." **5.** And Yoseph and his brothers ate bread before their father and drank wine, and Yacob rejoiced with great joy, because he saw Yoseph eating with his brothers and drinking before him. He blessed the Creator of all things who had preserved him and had preserved for him his twelve sons. **6.** And Yoseph had given to his father and his brothers as a gift the right to dwell in the land of Goshen, and in Rameses (a city in Egypt), and all the surrounding region, which he ruled over before Pharaoh. And Yisrael and his sons settled in the land of Goshen, the best part of the land of Egypt. And Yisrael was one hundred and thirty years old when he came into Egypt. **7.** And Yoseph provided for his father, his brothers, and all their possessions with bread, as much as they needed, during the seven years of famine. **8.** And the land of Egypt suffered because of the famine, and Yoseph acquired all the land of Egypt for Pharaoh in exchange for food. He took possession of the people, their cattle, and all their goods for Pharaoh. **9.** And the seven years of famine were completed, and Yoseph gave the people of Egypt seed and food so that they might sow the land in the eighth year, for the river (likely the Nile, the life-giving river in Egypt) had overflowed all the land of Egypt. **10.** For during the seven years of famine, it did not overflow, and only a few places on the banks of the river were irrigated, but now it overflowed and watered all the land. **11.** And the Egyptians sowed land, and it bore much grain that year. This was the first year of the fourth week of the forty-fifth jubilee. **12.** And Yoseph took one fifth of the harvest for Pharaoh, leaving four parts for the people for food and seed, and Yoseph established this as a law for the land of Egypt, which continues until this day. **13.** And Yisrael lived in the land of Egypt for seventeen years. All the years of his life were three jubilees (a period of 49 years), one hundred and forty-seven years. He died in the fourth year of the fifth week of the forty-fifth jubilee. **14.** And before he died, Yisrael blessed his sons and told them everything that would happen to them in the land of Egypt. He made known to them what would come upon them in the last days, and he blessed them. He gave Yoseph two portions in the land. **15.** And Yisrael slept with his fathers and was buried in the double cave (a burial place) in the land of Canaan (the promised land), near Abraham, his father, in the grave that he dug for himself in the double cave in the land of Hebron (a city in Canaan). **16.** And he gave all his books, and the books of his fathers, to Levi, his son, so that he might preserve them and renew them for his children until this day.

Chapter 46

1. After Yacob died, the children of Yisrael multiplied greatly in the land of Egypt, and they became a great nation. They were united in heart, with brother loving brother and every man helping his brother. They increased abundantly and multiplied exceedingly during the ten weeks of years, all the days of Yoseph's life. **2.** And there was no Satan (an adversary or enemy) or evil among them during the life of Yoseph, for all the Egyptians honored the children of Yisrael during his lifetime. **3.** Yoseph lived to be a hundred and ten years old; he spent seventeen years in the land of Canaan, ten years as a servant, three years in prison, and eighty years serving as ruler of Egypt under Pharaoh. **4.** And Yoseph died, and so did all his brothers and that entire generation. **5.** Before he died, Yoseph made the children of Yisrael swear that they would carry his bones with them when they left Egypt. **6.** He made them swear this, for he knew that the Egyptians would not bring him back to the land of Canaan to be buried. For the king of Canaan, Makamaron (a king of Canaan), had fought in the valley with the king of Egypt and had slain him. He pursued the Egyptians to the gates of 'Ermon (a city or region in Canaan), but he was unable to enter. **7.** A new king had risen in Egypt, stronger than the previous one, and he forced the old king of Canaan to return to the land of Canaan, closing the gates of Egypt. No one could enter or leave Egypt. **8.** Yoseph died in the forty-sixth jubilee, in the sixth week, in the second year. He was buried in Egypt, and all his brothers died after him. **9.** The king of Egypt went to war with the king of Canaan in the forty-seventh jubilee, in the second week of the second year. The children of Yisrael brought forth all the bones of the children of Yacob, except the bones of Yoseph, and they buried them in the field in the double cave in the mountain. **10.** The majority of them returned to Egypt, but a few remained in the mountains of Hebron. Amram, your father, remained with them. **11.** The king of Canaan was victorious over the king of Egypt, and he closed the gates of Egypt. **12.** He then devised a wicked plan to afflict the children of Yisrael. **13.** He said to the Egyptians, "Behold, the people of the children of Yisrael have grown and multiplied more than we. Let us act wisely with them before they become too numerous. Let us enslave them before war comes upon us, and they join our enemies and leave our land, for their hearts are set on the land of Canaan." **14.** He set taskmasters over them to afflict them with forced labor. They built strong cities for Pharaoh, such as Pithom (an ancient Egyptian city) and Raamses (another city in Egypt), and repaired the walls and fortifications that had fallen in the cities of Egypt. **15.** They made them serve with rigor, and the more the Egyptians oppressed them, the more the children of Yisrael increased and multiplied. And the Egyptians hated the children of Yisrael.

Chapter 47

1. And in the seventh week, in the seventh year, during the forty-seventh jubilee, your father left the land of Canaan. You were born in the fourth week, in the sixth year of that week, during the forty-eighth jubilee. This was a time of great tribulation for the children of Yisrael. **2.** And Pharaoh (king of Egypt), king of Egypt, gave a command to throw all the male children born to the children of Yisrael into the river (likely the Nile). **3.** And they did this for seven months, until the day you were born. **4.** Your mother hid you for three months, but word got out about her actions. She made an ark (a small boat or basket) for you, covered it with pitch and asphalt, and placed it among the reeds by the riverbank. She left you there for seven days. By night, your mother came to nurse you, and by day, your sister Miriam (the sister of Moses) kept watch over you to protect you from the birds. **5.** In those days, Tharmuth (the daughter of Pharaoh), came down to bathe in the river. She heard your cries, and she told her maidens to bring you out of the water. **6.** When she took you out of the ark, she felt compassion for you. **7.** Your sister then approached her and asked, "Shall I go and call one of the Hebrew women to nurse this baby for you?" **8.** Pharaoh's daughter replied, "Go." And so your sister went and called your mother, Jochebed (your mother's name). Pharaoh's daughter gave her wages, and she nursed you. **9.** Later, when you were older, they brought you to Pharaoh's daughter, and you became her son. Amram (your father), your father, taught you how to read and write. After you had completed three weeks, they brought you into the royal court. **10.** You spent three weeks of years in the royal court until one day, when you left the palace and saw an Egyptian beating one of the children of Yisrael. You struck the Egyptian and buried him in the sand. **11.** The next day, you saw two of the children of Yisrael fighting. You asked the one who was in the wrong, "Why are you hitting your brother?" **12.** The man became angry and said, "Who made you a ruler and judge over us? Are you planning to kill me as you did the Egyptian yesterday?" And you were afraid and fled because of his words.

Chapter 48

1. In the sixth year of the third week of the forty-ninth jubilee, you departed and dwelt in the land of Midian (a region or tribe) for five weeks and one year. Then, you returned to Egypt in the second week

of the second year of the fiftieth jubilee. **2.** And you know what He spoke to you on Mount Sinai (the mountain where Moses received the Ten Commandments), and what the prince Mastema (a name for the adversary or Satan) planned to do to you when you were returning to Egypt. **3.** Did he not try with all his power to kill you and deliver the Egyptians out of your hands, when he saw that you were sent to bring judgment and vengeance upon the Egyptians? **4.** But I delivered you out of his hand, and you performed the signs and wonders that you were sent to perform in Egypt, against Pharaoh, his house, his servants, and his people. **5.** And YAHWEH (the Lord God) executed a great vengeance upon them for the sake of Yisrael. He struck them with plagues: blood, frogs, lice, dog-flies, malignant boils, and their cattle died. He sent hailstones that destroyed their crops, and locusts devoured what was left. He sent darkness upon them, and finally, the death of the firstborn of both men and animals. He took vengeance on all their idols, burning them with fire. **6.** All of this happened at your hand, so that you could declare it before it took place. You spoke with the king of Egypt before all his servants and people. **7.** Everything occurred exactly as you had said. Ten great and terrible judgments came upon the land of Egypt, so that you might execute vengeance on it for Yisrael. **8.** YAHWEH did all of this for the sake of Yisrael, and in keeping with His covenant with Abraham (the father of the Hebrew people), to take vengeance on those who had forced His people into bondage. **9.** And the prince Mastema stood against you, trying to hand you over to Pharaoh, and he aided the Egyptian sorcerers. **10.** They stood before you and worked their evil magic, but we only permitted them to perform some of their signs. However, we did not allow them to heal or deliver their people. **11.** YAHWEH struck them with malignant sores, so that they could not stand before you. We destroyed them, and they were unable to perform any sign. **12.** Yet, despite all these signs and wonders, the prince Mastema was not ashamed. He gathered his courage and urged the Egyptians to pursue you with all their forces: their chariots, their horses, and the entire army of Egypt. **13.** But I stood between the Egyptians and Yisrael, delivering Yisrael from their hand. YAHWEH brought them through the sea as if it were dry land. **14.** All the people who pursued Yisrael were cast into the sea by YAHWEH our Sovereign Ruler, into the depths of the abyss. He took vengeance on them just as the Egyptians had cast their children into the river. YAHWEH destroyed 1,000,000 of them, and one thousand strong and powerful men were drowned, all for the sake of one child that the Egyptians had thrown into the river. **15.** On the fourteenth, fifteenth, sixteenth, seventeenth, and eighteenth days, the prince Mastema was bound and imprisoned behind the children of Yisrael, so that he could not accuse them. **16.** On the nineteenth day, we released him, and he tried to help the Egyptians in their pursuit of Yisrael. **17.** YAHWEH hardened their hearts and made them stubborn, all according to the plan of YAHWEH our Sovereign Ruler, so that He might strike the Egyptians and cast them into the sea. **18.** On the fourteenth day, we bound Mastema so he could not accuse the children of Yisrael, the day when they asked the Egyptians for silver, gold, and bronze vessels, in order to despoil the Egyptians as recompense for the bondage they had suffered. **19.** And we did not let the children of Yisrael leave Egypt empty-handed.

Chapter 49

1. Remember the commandment that YAHWEH gave you concerning the Passover, that you should celebrate it in its season, on the fourteenth day of the first month. You must kill the lamb before evening, and eat it at night on the fifteenth, from the time the sun sets. **2.** For on this night—the beginning of the festival and the start of the joy—you were eating the Passover in Egypt (Egypt: Ancient kingdom ruled by Pharaoh). At that time, all the powers of Mastema (Mastema: Leader of evil spirits, a fallen angel) were let loose to strike down all the firstborn in the land of Egypt, from Pharaoh's firstborn to the firstborn of the captive maidservant grinding at the mill, as well as the cattle. **3.** And this is the sign YAHWEH gave: Whenever they saw the blood of the lamb, a year-old, on the doorposts and lintels (Lintels: horizontal beams above doors), they should not enter that house to slay, but pass over it. All those in that house would be saved because the sign of the blood was on the lintels. **4.** And the powers of YAHWEH did everything as He commanded. They passed over all the houses of the children of Yisrael (Yisrael: the people of Israel), and the plague did not touch them. No soul was destroyed, not from cattle, man, or dog. **5.** But the plague was very severe in Egypt. There was no house in Egypt where there was not at least one dead, with weeping and lamentation. **6.** Meanwhile, all of Yisrael ate the flesh of the Passover lamb and drank wine, praising, blessing, and thanking YAHWEH, the Almighty of their fathers, as they prepared to be freed from the yoke of Egypt and the evil bondage. **7.** And remember this day throughout all the days of your life. Observe it every year, once a year, on its day, according to all the instructions in the Torah (Torah: the first five books of the Bible, Jewish teachings). Do not delay it from day to day or from month to month. **8.** For it is an eternal ordinance, engraved on the heavenly tablets (Tablets: sacred stones containing divine laws), for all the children of Yisrael, that they should observe it every year on its day, for all their generations. There is no limit to its observance; it is ordained forever. **9.** And anyone who is clean and free from uncleanness (Uncleanness: ritual impurity), and does not come to observe it at its appointed time, to bring an acceptable offering before YAHWEH, and to eat and drink before YAHWEH on its festival day, that person shall be cut off. By not offering the oblation (Oblation: a religious offering) of YAHWEH in its season, they will take the guilt upon themselves. **10.** Let all the children of Yisrael come and observe the Passover on its fixed day, the fourteenth day of the first month, between the evenings—from the third part of the day to the third part of the night. For two portions of the day belong to the light, and the third part belongs to the evening. **11.** This is what YAHWEH commanded you, to observe the Passover between the evenings. **12.** It is not permissible to slaughter the lamb during the daylight hours, but only at the time near the evening. They shall eat it at evening, until the third part of the night. Whatever remains of the flesh after the third part of the night should be burned with fire. **13.** You shall not cook the lamb with water, nor eat it raw, but roast it over the fire. Eat it with urgency—its head, its inward parts, and its feet shall all be roasted over the fire. Do not break any of its bones, for no bone of the children of Yisrael shall be broken. **14.** This is why YAHWEH commanded the children of Yisrael to observe the Passover on its fixed day and not break a bone of the lamb. It is a festival day, a day commanded by YAHWEH. There can be no postponing of the Passover from one day to another or from one month to another. Observe it on the appointed day. **15.** And you, Mosheh (Mosheh: Moses, leader of the Israelites), command the children of Yisrael to observe the Passover throughout their generations, once a year, on its fixed day. It shall be a memorial that is pleasing before YAHWEH, and no plague will come upon them to destroy or harm them in the year when they celebrate the Passover in its season, according to His command. **16.** The Passover shall not be eaten outside the sanctuary of YAHWEH, but only before the sanctuary of YAHWEH. All the congregation of Yisrael shall celebrate it in its appointed season. **17.** Every man who is twenty years old and older must eat the Passover in the sanctuary of YAHWEH, as it is written and ordained. They shall eat it before YAHWEH. **18.** When the children of Yisrael enter the land they will possess, the land of Canaan (Canaan: the Promised Land), and set up the tabernacle (Tabernacle: portable dwelling place for God) of YAHWEH in the midst of their land, in one of their tribes, until the sanctuary of YAHWEH is built in the land, they shall celebrate the Passover at the tabernacle of YAHWEH. They shall slay it there from year to year. **19.** And in the days when the house is built in the name of YAHWEH in the land of their inheritance, they shall go there to slay the Passover at sunset, at the third part of the day. **20.** They shall offer its blood on the threshold of the altar, place its fat on the fire upon the altar, and eat its flesh roasted over the fire in the court of the house that has been sanctified in the name of YAHWEH. **21.** The Passover shall not be celebrated in their cities, nor anywhere else except before the tabernacle of YAHWEH, or in His house where His name dwells. They must not stray from YAHWEH's command. **22.** Mosheh, you must command the children of Yisrael to observe the ordinances of the Passover, as you have been commanded. Teach them every year, the day of its observance, and the festival of unleavened bread (Unleavened bread: bread without yeast). They should eat unleavened bread for seven days and celebrate this festival, bringing an offering every day during those seven days of joy, before YAHWEH, on His altar. **23.** For you celebrated this festival with haste when you left Egypt, until you reached the wilderness of Shur (Shur: a desert area near Egypt). You completed it on the shore of the sea.

Chapter 50

1. After this, I made known to you the laws of the Shabbats (Shabbats: Sabbath days of rest), first in the desert of Sin (Sin: desert between Elim and Sinai), which is between Elim (Elim: a place with 12 springs of water) and Sinai (Sinai: mountain where Moses received the Ten Commandments). **2.** I also told you about the Shabbats for the land, on Mount Sinai, and I spoke of the Jubilee years (Jubilee years: every 50th year when land is returned to original owners) and the Sabbatical years (Sabbatical years: every 7th year of rest for the land). However, I did not explain the full meaning of the years until you enter the land you are to possess. **3.** The land itself will also observe its Shabbats while the people dwell in it. They will know the Jubilee year. **4.** Therefore, I have ordained for you the cycle of years and weeks, including the Jubilee years. From the days of Adam (Adam: first human) until now, there are forty-nine jubilees (from the beginning of time until this day, in [2410 A.M.]), plus one week and two years. Yet, there are still forty more years to come, in which you will learn the commandments of YAHWEH (YAHWEH: the Hebrew name for God), until you cross over the Jordan (Jordan: river that separates Israel from the wilderness) into the land of Canaan (Canaan: the Promised Land). **5.** The jubilees will continue to pass, until Israel (Israel: the people of Jacob) is cleansed of all its guilt—guilt from fornication, uncleanness, pollution, sin, and error. Then they will dwell securely in the land, and there will be no Satan (Satan: adversary or accuser) or evil one, for the land will be purified from that time onward. **6.** And behold, I have written down the commandments regarding the Shabbats, and all the judgments and laws concerning them. **7.** You shall labor for six days, but on the seventh day, it is the Shabbat of YAHWEH your Sovereign Ruler. On this day, you shall do no work—neither you, nor your sons, nor your servants, nor your livestock, nor any sojourners with you. **8.** The person who does any work on this day shall die. Whoever desecrates this day—whoever lies with his wife, or says he will do something on the Shabbat, such as setting out on a journey, buying or selling, or drawing water that was not prepared on the sixth day, or carrying a burden out of his house—shall die. **9.** You shall do no work at all on the Shabbat, except for what you have prepared on the sixth day, in order to eat, drink, rest, and keep the Shabbat from all labor. This day is a day to bless YAHWEH your Sovereign Ruler, who has given you this festival day, a sacred day, a day of holiness for all of Yisrael throughout all their generations. **10.** Great is the honor that YAHWEH has bestowed upon Yisrael, that they may eat, drink, and be satisfied on this festival day, and rest from all their labors—except for burning incense and offering sacrifices before YAHWEH, both on the festival days and on the Shabbat days. **11.** Only this work is to be done on the Shabbat in the sanctuary of YAHWEH your Sovereign Ruler: to offer sacrifices continually, from day to day, as a memorial that is pleasing to YAHWEH. This is done so that YAHWEH may receive them always, according to the commands He gave you. **12.** Any person who does any work on the Shabbat, goes on a journey, works the land, lights a fire, rides a beast, travels by ship, strikes or kills anything, slaughters a beast or bird, catches any animal or fish, fasts, or makes war on the Shabbat, **13.** That person shall die, so that the children of Yisrael will observe the Shabbat according to the commandments YAHWEH has given regarding the Shabbats of the land, as it is written on the tablets He gave into my hands. These tablets contain the laws for the seasons and the division of the days. This completes the account of the division of the days.

14 – The First Book of Enoch

Chapter 1

1. Enoch blesses the elect (chosen) and righteous who will be living in the days of tribulation (great distress) when all the wicked (evil) and godless (those who are irreverent or reject God) are to be removed. **2.** Enoch, a righteous man whose eyes were opened by God, shares a vision of the Holy One in the heavens, revealed by angels. He hears and understands everything but notes that his prophecy is not for his own generation, but for a distant one yet to come. **3.** Concerning the elect (chosen), he says, "The Holy Great One will come forth from His dwelling (abode), **4.** and the eternal God will tread (walk) upon the earth, even on Mount Sinai, appearing in the strength (power) of His might from the heaven of heavens. **5.** All shall be smitten (struck) with fear; the Watchers (angels) shall quake (tremble), and great fear and trembling will seize them to the ends of the earth. **6.** The high mountains (elevated landforms) shall shake, the high hills shall be made low, melting like wax before a flame. **7.** The earth will be wholly rent (torn) asunder (apart), and all upon it shall perish (be destroyed), as divine judgment (decision) comes upon all. **8.** But with the righteous (just), He will make peace, protecting the elect (chosen) and showing them mercy (compassion). They shall belong to God, be blessed with prosperity (abundance), and He will help them all, giving them guidance (light) and making peace with them. **9.** And behold! He comes with ten thousands (many) of His holy ones to execute (carry out) judgment upon all, to destroy all the ungodly (evil), and to convict (declare guilty) all flesh (humankind) of the works of their ungodliness (sinful deeds) and all the hard (harsh) things spoken against Him by ungodly sinners."

Chapter 2

1. Observe the heavens: the stars and their orbits never change. They rise and set in their appointed seasons without fail. **2.** Look upon the earth and see how everything remains steady from beginning to end. The works of God are evident, from the cycle of summer and winter to the earth's water, clouds, and rain. **3.** In winter, trees seem to wither (dry up) and shed their leaves, except for fourteen types, which retain their foliage (leaves) for two or three years until new leaves appear. **4.** In summer, the sun scorches (burns) the earth, causing you to seek shelter from its heat, and the ground grows too hot to touch. **5.** Notice how the trees flourish (grow healthy and strong) with green leaves and bear fruit. Understand that all of God's works are done by His will. **6.** These patterns continue year after year, as all creation follows the tasks God set for them, unchanged and eternal. **7.** The sea and rivers, too, fulfill (complete) their purpose, never deviating (changing or straying) from His command. **8.** But you have not been faithful to God's commandments. You have spoken arrogantly (proudly) and sinned against His greatness, and you will find no peace. **9.** Your days will be cursed (marked for misfortune), your years filled with destruction (ruin), and your names will become an eternal abomination (something hated). You will not receive mercy. **10.** In those days, your names will be cursed by all the righteous, and sinners will invoke (call upon) your downfall. The godless (those who do not believe in God) will hold you in contempt (disrespect). **11.** But the righteous will rejoice (be glad), their sins forgiven, and they will experience peace, mercy, and salvation (deliverance from sin and its consequences). **12.** Light and salvation will be given to them. **13.** For sinners, there will be no salvation; they will remain under the curse. **14.** The elect (those chosen by God), however, will know light, joy, and peace, and they will inherit (receive as a gift) the earth. **15.** Wisdom will be granted to the elect, and they will live without sin, marked by humility (the quality of being humble). They will never again sin through pride (a sense of superiority) or ungodliness (lack of reverence for God). **16.** They will not transgress (violate) nor will they die in wrath (anger) or anger. They will live out their full lives. **17.** Their lives will be filled with peace and joy, and they will experience eternal happiness (lasting joy) and peace for all their days.

Chapter 3

1. When humans multiplied, beautiful daughters were born to them. **2.** The angels, seeing them, desired (longed for) them and said, "Let us take wives from among men and have children." **3.** Semjaza, their leader, feared that he would bear the consequences (punishment) alone if they didn't agree. **4.** They all swore an oath (promise), binding themselves with mutual curses (oaths) to carry out the plan. **5.** Two hundred angels descended during the days of Jared on Mount Hermon, naming it so because of their oath. **6.** The leaders of the angels were: Samlazaz, Araklba, Rameel, Kokabel, Tamlel, Ramlel, Danel, Ezeqeel, Baraqijal, Asael, Armaros, Batarel, Ananel, Zaqlel, Samsapeel, Satarel, Turel, Jomjael, and Sariel. These were their chiefs of tens. **7.** The angels took wives and had children, corrupting (spoiling) themselves with them. **8.** They taught women magic, root-cutting (herbal magic), and the secrets of plants. **9.** The women bore giants, three thousand ells (ancient measurement of length) tall, who consumed (used up) the resources of humanity. When mankind could no longer sustain them, the giants turned on them and devoured (ate) them. **10.** They sinned against animals and each other, eating flesh and drinking blood, causing the earth to accuse (blame) them. **11.** Azazel taught men to make weapons (tools for fighting), shields, and armor, as well as the art of working metals and creating jewelry, cosmetics, and dyes. **12.** This led to widespread lawlessness (disobedience to laws), fornication (immoral sexual acts), and corruption in every way. **13.** Semjaza taught magic, Armaros taught how to break enchantments (spells), Baraqijal taught astrology (study of stars), Kokabel taught the constellations, Ezeqeel taught about clouds, Araqiel about the signs of the earth, Shamsiel about the sun, and Sariel about the moon. **14.** As humanity suffered, their cries reached heaven.

Chapter 4

1. Michael, Uriel, Raphael, and Gabriel saw bloodshed and lawlessness (wickedness) on earth. **2.** They said, "The earth, made without inhabitants, cries to the gates (entrances) of heaven." **3.** "The souls of men appeal, 'Bring our case before the Most High.'" **4.** Addressing God, they said, "Lord of lords, all is open before You." **5.** "You see Azazel's teaching of unrighteousness (wickedness) on earth, revealing the mysteries of heaven, and Samlazaz's rule over his companions." **6.** "They corrupted women, teaching them sin (wrongdoing), and filling the earth with blood and evil." **7.** "Now the souls of the dead cry out due to lawlessness on earth." **8.** "You know all things yet allow them, and do not guide us on what to do." **9.** The Most High sent Uriel to Noah, saying, "Hide yourself, a flood will come to destroy the earth. Prepare to save your descendants." **10.** He instructed Raphael: "Bind Azazel, cast him into darkness (obscurity), and cover him forever, until the Day of Judgment." **11.** "Heal the earth and proclaim its healing, for Azazel is responsible for all sin." **12.** Gabriel was ordered, "Destroy the children of the Watchers, who defiled the earth. Let them battle and perish." **13.** Michael was told: "Bind Samlazaz and his associates who defiled themselves. When their children destroy each other, bind them for seventy generations. On Judgment Day, they will face eternal torment in the abyss (bottomless pit) of fire." **14.** "Destroy the spirits (souls) of the reprobate and Watchers' children." **15.** "Erase all evil, let righteousness (justice) and truth endure forever." **16.** "The righteous will live in peace with abundant children." **17.** "The earth will be cultivated in righteousness, filled with blessings." **18.** "Fruitful trees and vines will abound; each seed sown will yield a thousandfold." **19.** "Cleanse the earth from oppression (cruelty), sin, and uncleanness." **20.** "All nations will worship Me; the earth will be free from sin, punishment, and torment." **21.** "Heaven's blessings will pour upon the earth, and truth and peace will last through generations." **22.** Before this, Enoch was hidden, among the Watchers and holy ones. **23.** Enoch, called by the Watchers, was told, "Go and declare to those who defiled themselves with women: 'You have caused ruin on earth, and will have no peace.'" **25.** "As you delight (take pleasure) in your children, you will see them perish and mourn." **26.** Enoch told Azazel, "You have no peace; judgment awaits for the wickedness you taught mankind." **27.** Enoch presented their request for forgiveness before God, but **28.** they could not lift their eyes to heaven due to shame for their sins. **29.** Enoch prayed for their forgiveness. **30.** He read their petition at the waters of Dan until he fell asleep, and **31.** dreamed of punishment, hearing a voice to deliver a rebuke. **32.** When he awoke, he found them weeping in Abelsjail, and **33.** shared his visions, rebuking the heavenly Watchers.

Chapter 5

1. This is the book of the words of righteousness, and the reprimand (rebuke) of the eternal Watchers, according to the command of the Holy One, revealed in a vision I saw while asleep. **2.** I will now speak with the tongue of flesh and the breath given to men, so that they may understand the wisdom (insight) of words with their hearts. **3.** Just as God gave men the power to understand wisdom, He has also given me the authority to rebuke (criticize) the Watchers, the children of heaven. **4.** "I recorded your petition (request), and in my vision it was shown that it will not be granted to you for eternity. The judgment is final." **5.** "Your petition will not be granted. You shall never ascend to heaven again, and the earth has been decreed (ordered) as your prison for all time." **6.** "You will witness the destruction (ruin) of your sons, and have no joy in them. They will fall before you by the sword." **7.** "Your pleas (requests) for them and for yourselves will not be answered, even though you weep, pray, and speak the words I have written." **8.** In my vision, clouds called me, mist summoned me, stars and lightning hastened me, and the winds lifted me into heaven. **9.** I came close to a wall made of crystals, surrounded by fire, and I was filled with fear (terror). **10.** I entered the fire and approached a house made of crystals. Its walls and floor were like a tesselated (patterned) crystal floor, and its foundation (base) was crystal. **11.** The ceiling was like the path of the stars and lightning, with fiery cherubim (angelic beings) moving between them. The heavens above were like water. **12.** A flaming fire surrounded the walls, and its gates blazed with fire. **13.** Inside, it was as hot as fire and as cold as ice. Fear overcame me, and I trembled (shuddered). **14.** As I trembled, I saw another, larger house with the door open before me. It was built of fire. **15.** Its magnificence (splendor) exceeded description—its floor of fire, with lightning and stars above, and its ceiling of flame. **16.** I saw a throne of crystal, with wheels like shining sun. Cherubim stood beside it. **17.** Flames poured from under the throne, so bright I could not look upon them. **18.** The Great Glory sat on the throne, His raiment (garment) shining brighter than the sun, whiter than snow. **19.** No angel could approach or look at Him because of His overwhelming glory. No flesh could behold (see) His face. **20.** Flames surrounded Him, and a great fire stood before Him. Ten thousand times ten thousand stood before Him, yet He needed no counsel (advice). **21.** The holiest ones near Him did not depart day or night. I had been prostrate (lying flat) in fear until the Lord called me by name: "Enoch, come and hear My words." **22.** One of the holy ones woke me, lifted me to my feet, and led me to the door, where I bowed (lowered) my face. **23.** He said: "Do not fear, Enoch, righteous scribe. Come, hear My voice." **24.** "Go and tell the Watchers who sent you to intercede (mediate) for them: 'You should have interceded for men, not the other way around. Why did you leave your high, eternal home and defile (corrupt) yourselves with women, taking wives and having children as men do? **25.** Though you were holy, spiritual, and eternal, you defiled yourselves with the blood of women, lusting (longing) after flesh as those who die. **26.** I gave men wives to bear children. But you, who were once spiritual, did not need wives, for your home was in heaven. **27.** Now, the giants (large beings) born of your union with women shall be evil spirits on earth, afflicting (troubling) and destroying. **28.** Evil spirits will arise from their bodies. Born of both men and Watchers, they will cause trouble on earth. **29.** These spirits will battle (fight), destroy, and bring chaos (disorder). Though they do not eat, they will hunger and thirst. **30.** They will rise against men and women because they are their descendants. **31.** From the death of the giants, their spirits will continue to destroy without judgment, until the great final judgment. **32.** Say to the Watchers who sent you: 'You were once in heaven, but you were blinded (misled) by worthless knowledge and made it known to women, causing great evil on earth.' **33.** Tell them: 'You will have no peace (rest).'" **34.** Thus, the judgment is passed, and the decree of the Holy One stands.

Chapter 6

1. Angels took me to a place where the beings were like flaming fire, but when they wished, they appeared as men. **2.** They brought me to a place of darkness, to a mountain whose summit (top) reached the heavens. **3.** I saw the places of the luminaries (heavenly bodies), the treasuries (storage) of the stars, thunder, and in the depths, a fiery bow (a weapon), arrows, a quiver (container for arrows), a fiery sword, and all the lightning. **4.** They took me to the living waters (flowing water) and the fire of the west, which receives the setting sun. **5.** I came to a river of fire that flowed like water into the great sea toward the west. **6.** I saw the great rivers, the great river, and the great darkness, and went to the place where no flesh (living creature) walks. I saw the mountains of winter's darkness, where the deep waters flow. **7.** I saw the mouths (openings) of all the rivers of the earth and the mouth of the deep. **8.** I saw the treasuries of the winds and how they filled the whole creation and the earth's foundations. **9.** I saw the cornerstone (foundation stone) of the earth, and the four winds that bear (hold up) the firmament (vault) of the heavens. **10.** I saw how the winds stretch out the vaults (ceilings) of heaven and station (place) between heaven and earth, these being the pillars (supports) of heaven. **11.** I saw the winds of heaven that turn and bring the sun and all the stars to their setting. **12.** I saw the winds on earth carrying clouds, and I saw the paths (routes) of the angels. **13.** I saw at the earth's end the firmament of heaven, and I proceeded to a place that burns day and night, where there are seven mountains of magnificent stones. **14.** Three were to the east, three to the south. The eastern ones were of colored stone, pearl, and jacinth (a type of gemstone), and those to the south were of red stone. **15.** The middle one reached to heaven, like God's throne, of alabaster (a type of stone), with a sapphire (blue gemstone) summit. **16.** I saw a flaming fire, and beyond these mountains was a region at the earth's end, where the heavens were completed. **17.** I saw a deep abyss (bottomless pit) with columns (tall structures) of heavenly fire, and among them, columns of fire fell, towering both in height and depth. **18.** Beyond that abyss was a place with no heaven above or earth below. There was no water, no birds—only a waste (desolate) and horrible place. **19.** I saw seven stars like great burning mountains. When I inquired (asked) about them, the angel said, "This is the end of heaven and earth. It is a prison for the stars and the host (army) of heaven." **20.** The stars that roll over the fire are those who transgressed (went against) God's command at the beginning of their rising, failing to appear at their appointed times. **21.** He was angry with them and bound (tied) them until their guilt is fulfilled in ten thousand years. **22.** Uriel said to me: "Here will stand the angels who joined with women, whose spirits have defiled (corrupted) mankind and led them to sacrifice to demons as gods." **23.** They will stand here until the great judgment, where they will be judged and destroyed. The women who followed them will become sirens (mythical creatures that lure). **24.** I, Enoch, alone saw the vision of the ends of all things. No man will see what I have seen.

Chapter 7

1. These are the names of the holy angels who watch over humanity. **2.** Uriel, the holy angel, who is over the world and Tartarus (a deep abyss or hell in Greek mythology). **3.** Raphael, the holy angel, who oversees the spirits of men. **4.** Raguel, the holy angel, who takes vengeance on the world's luminaries (heavenly bodies, like stars or planets). **5.** Michael, the holy angel, who is in charge of the best of mankind and chaos (disorder or confusion). **6.** Saraqael, the holy angel, who governs the spirits that sin in the spirit. **7.** Gabriel, the holy angel, who watches over Paradise, the serpents, and the Cherubim (angelic beings). **8.** Remiel, the holy angel, appointed over those who rise. **9.** I went to a chaotic place, where I saw something dreadful—no heaven above, no solid earth below, just a terrible, disordered place. **10.** There, I saw seven stars bound together, like great burning mountains. **11.** I asked, "For what sin are they bound here, and why have they been cast into this place?" **12.** Uriel, one of the holy angels who was with me, said, "These stars are angels who broke God's commandment. They are bound here for ten thousand years until their sins are paid for." **13.** I then went to another, even more horrifying place, where I saw a great fire burning, with columns (tall vertical structures) of fire descending into the abyss. Its size and extent were beyond comprehension. **14.** I said, "How terrifying is this place!" **15.** Uriel asked, "Why are you so afraid?" **16.** I replied, "Because of this dreadful place and the pain I see." **17.** He said, "This is the prison of the angels, where they will remain forever." **18.** I moved on to another place, a mountain (large landform) of hard rock. **19.** In it, I saw four vast, deep, smooth pits— dark and unsettling to behold. **20.** Raphael, who was with me, explained, "These pits were made for the souls of the dead. All human souls will gather here until the day of judgment." **21.** I saw a soul crying out to heaven, and I asked Raphael, "Whose spirit is this, crying out to heaven?" **22.** He answered, "This is Abel's spirit, whose brother Cain killed him. He cries for vengeance until Cain's descendants are wiped out." **23.** I asked, "Why are the pits separated?" **24.** Raphael replied, "The pits are for separating the spirits of the dead. One is for the righteous (morally right or just), filled with bright, refreshing water. The others are for the unrighteous, who suffer until the final judgment." **25.** "The sinners' spirits remain in torment (severe pain), awaiting the day of retribution (punishment for wrongdoings). Those who made their pleas before their death are kept in a special place of pain." **26.** "The spirits of the utterly wicked are kept in another place. They will not be destroyed on judgment day, but neither will they be raised." **27.** I praised the Lord of glory, saying, "Blessed be the Lord, the righteous ruler, forever." **28.** I traveled west to the ends of the earth, where I saw an unceasing fire. **29.** I asked, "What is this fire that never stops?" **30.** Raguel, one of the holy angels with me, replied, "This is the fire in the west that burns the stars of heaven." **31.** I then went to another place and saw a mountain range (group of mountains) of fire, burning day and night. **32.** Beyond it, I saw seven magnificent (impressive) mountains, each different from the other. The stones were beautiful, with three in the east and three in the south, separated by deep ravines (narrow, steep valleys). **33.** The seventh mountain, higher than all the others, resembled a throne. Around it grew fragrant (having a pleasant smell) trees. **34.** Among them was a tree unlike any I had ever smelled before. Its fragrance was unparalleled, and its leaves and fruit never withered. Its fruit resembled palm dates. **35.** I said, "How beautiful and fragrant is this tree, with its fair leaves and delightful blooms (flowers)." **36.** Michael, the honored angel and leader, answered me, saying: **37.** "Enoch, why do you ask about the fragrance of the tree? Why do you seek the truth?" **38.** I replied, "I want to understand everything, especially about this tree." **39.** Michael explained: "This high mountain, whose peak resembles God's throne, is where the Holy Great One, the Eternal King, will sit when He visits the earth with goodness. No mortal may touch this fragrant tree until the great judgment, when He will bring final vengeance. Then it will be given to the righteous; its fruit will nourish the elect (chosen ones) and be transplanted to the holy temple of the Eternal King. **40.** In that day, the righteous will rejoice and enter the holy place. Its fragrance will fill their bones, granting them long life, as your ancestors had, free from sorrow, plague, or calamity." **41.** I blessed the Lord of Glory, the Eternal King, who prepared such blessings for the righteous. **42.** I then traveled to the center of the earth, where I saw a blessed place filled with flourishing trees. **43.** I saw a holy mountain with a stream (flow of water) running from the east toward the south. Another higher mountain lay to the east, with a deep ravine (narrow valley) between them, containing another stream. **44.** To the west, there was a lower mountain with a dry ravine between it and the others. **45.** I marveled at the deep ravines and rocky terrain (land), where no trees grew. **46.** I asked, "Why is this land filled with trees while the valley between is cursed?" **47.** Uriel, the holy angel, answered: "This cursed valley is for those forever condemned (damned)—those who speak against the Lord and His glory. It will be their place of judgment. **48.** At the final judgment, the righteous will witness the punishment of the wicked and bless the Lord for His mercy in assigning them their fate." **49.** I blessed the Lord of Glory and praised Him for His wondrous acts. **50.** I journeyed further east, where I saw a solitary wilderness (desert) with abundant trees and plants. Water flowed from above, creating clouds and dew. **51.** I moved eastward and saw trees exhaling (giving off) the fragrance of frankincense and myrrh, resembling almond trees. **52.** Farther east, I found a valley with fragrant mastic (tree resin) trees and cinnamon along its sides. **53.** Beyond these, I saw mountains with groves (groups) of trees producing sweet-smelling nectar, and another mountain with aloe trees, all exuding the fragrance of stacte (a resin), which is sweeter than any perfume. **54.** I looked northward and saw seven mountains full of fragrant trees like nard (a type of aromatic herb), cinnamon, and pepper. **55.** I crossed these mountains, passing over the Erythraean Sea, and traveled far to the east, where I saw the Garden of Righteousness. **56.** From a distance, I saw two great and beautiful trees, and the Tree of Knowledge, whose fruit grants wisdom. **57.** The tree was tall like a strangler fig, with carob-like (a tree whose fruit is used for food) leaves and vine-like clusters of fruit, emitting a fragrance that reached far. **58.** I marveled, saying, "How beautiful is this tree and its fruit!" **59.** Raphael, the holy angel, answered, "This is the Tree of Wisdom, which your father and mother ate from and gained knowledge. They knew their nakedness (vulnerability) and were cast out of the garden." **60.** I then journeyed to the ends of the earth, where I saw many beasts (large animals) and birds of various kinds. **61.** To the east, I saw the heavens' portals (gates), from which the stars emerge. I counted each star's path and wrote their names, courses, and times, as Uriel showed me. **62.** Uriel revealed all to me, including the stars' names, laws (rules), and order. **63.** I then traveled north to the ends of the earth, where I saw a great device (mechanism). There I saw three portals of heaven through which cold winds, hail, frost, and rain blow. One portal brings good, while the others bring violence and affliction (pain). **65.** I then traveled west, where I saw three portals open, the same as in the east. **66.** In the south, I saw three more portals through which dew, rain, and wind flow. **67.** To the east, I saw three eastern portals and smaller portals above them through which stars pass on their course westward. **68.** As I observed, I continually blessed the Lord of Glory, praising Him for His great and wondrous works, showing His creation to angels, spirits, and men, that all might see His mighty work and praise Him forever.

Chapter 8

1. Azazel taught men to craft (make) weapons, jewelry, and ornaments, and revealed the use of metals, antimony, and cosmetics, including beautifying the eyelids with costly stones and dyes. **2.** This led to widespread (extensive) corruption (depravity) and immorality (wickedness), including fornication (sexual immorality). **3.** Semjaza taught enchantments (spells), 'Armaros the undoing (breaking) of enchantments, Baraqijal astrology (divination), Kokabel the constellations (stars), Ezeqeel the knowledge of clouds, Araqiel the signs (indicators) of the earth, Shamsiel the signs of the sun, and Sariel the course (path) of the moon. As men perished (died), their cries reached heaven.

Chapter 9

1. Michael, Uriel, Raphael, and Gabriel looked down and saw much bloodshed (violence) and lawlessness (wickedness) on earth. **2.** They said, "The earth, now desolate (forsaken), cries out to heaven." **3.** The souls of men pleaded (begged), "Bring our case before the Most High." **4.** They said to the Lord: "Lord of all, Your throne endures (lasts) through all generations. You made all things and see all, nothing is hidden (concealed) from You. **5.** You know Azazel's deeds (actions)—teaching unrighteousness (wickedness) and revealing heavenly secrets. **6.** Semjaza, whom You appointed (designated) to rule, and his associates (companions) have corrupted (defiled) the earth, sleeping (intermingling) with human women, teaching them sins (wrongdoing). **9.** These women bore giants, and the earth is filled (replete) with blood and iniquity (sin). **10.** The souls of the dead cry out at the gates (entrances) of heaven, their lamentations (sorrows) cannot cease because of the lawlessness. **11.** You know all things, yet You allow them to happen. We seek Your guidance (direction) on how to deal (handle) with this."

Chapter 10

1. Then the Highest, the Holy and Great One, spoke, and sent Uriel to the son of Lamech, **2.** saying, "Go to Noah and tell him in My name, 'Hide thyself! Reveal to him the end (finality) that is approaching: the earth will be destroyed (ruined), and a deluge (flood) will come to wipe out (eradicate) all that is on it. **3.** Instruct him to escape (flee), so that he and his seed (descendants) may be preserved (saved) for all generations." **4.** Again, the Lord said to Raphael, "Bind Azazel hand and foot, and cast him into darkness (obscurity). **5.** Make an opening in the desert of Dudael, and cast him in. Place rough (craggy) rocks on him, cover him with darkness, and let him remain there forever (eternally), not seeing light (illumination). **6.** On the day of the great judgment (reckoning), he shall be cast into the fire (flames). **7.** Heal the earth that the angels have corrupted (tainted). Proclaim the healing (restoration) of the earth, so that men may be saved (rescued) from the plagues (calamities) caused by the secret teachings (mysteries) of the Watchers." **8.** "The earth is corrupted through the works (deeds) of Azazel; ascribe (attribute) all sin (wrongdoing) to him." **9.** To Gabriel, the Lord said, "Go against the bastards (illegitimate children) and the reprobates (condemned) and destroy the children of fornication (illicit union) and the children of the Watchers. **10.** Send them into battle (conflict) with one another, and they will destroy each other, for they will not live long (endure). Their fathers' requests (pleas) for them will not be granted; they hope for eternal life but will not receive it." **11.** Then the Lord said to Michael, "Bind Semjaza and his associates (companions), who defiled themselves (polluted) with women. **12.** When their sons kill one another and witness the destruction (ruin) of their beloved, bind them for seventy generations in the valleys of the earth, until the day of judgment. **13.** On that day, they shall be led to the abyss (chasm) of fire and the prison where they will be confined (imprisoned) forever. **14.** Those who are condemned will be bound together with them until the end of all generations. **15.** Destroy all the spirits of the reprobate and the children of the Watchers who wronged mankind (humanity). **16.** Destroy all evil (wickedness) from the earth and let the plant (growth) of righteousness and truth grow. **17.** Then the righteous will escape (be saved), live peacefully (in harmony), and have many children (offspring). **18.** The whole earth will be tilled (cultivated) in righteousness and planted with trees, **19.** full of blessings (abundance). Desirable trees will be planted, and vines will yield abundant (plentiful) wine. **20.** Every seed sown will bear a thousand-fold, and each measure of olives will yield ten presses (batches) of oil. **21.** Cleanse the earth from all oppression (subjugation), unrighteousness (wickedness), sin (transgression), and godlessness (impiety), and destroy all uncleanness (defilement). **22.** All children of men will become righteous (virtuous), and all nations will worship (adore) and praise Me, and the earth will be free from defilement (corruption), sin (wrongdoing), punishment, and torment (suffering). I will never again send such things upon the earth."

Chapter 11

1. In those days, I will open the storehouses (treasuries) of blessing in heaven to send them upon the earth, over the work (labor) and toil (endeavor) of the children of men. **2.** Truth and peace will unite (come together) throughout all the days (ages) of the world and generations (descendants) of men.

Chapter 12

1. Before this, Enoch was hidden (concealed), and no one knew where he was, **2.** or where he resided (dwelt), or what had become of him. His days were spent with the Watchers (angels), and he was among the holy ones (sacred beings). **3.** I, Enoch, was blessing (praising) the Lord of majesty and the King of the ages, when the Watchers called me— Enoch the scribe— **4.** and said, "Enoch, scribe of righteousness (justice), go, declare (announce) to the Watchers of heaven who left the high heaven, the holy eternal place, **5.** defiled (polluted) themselves with women, took wives, and acted as the children (descendants) of earth do: 'You have wrought (brought about) great destruction (ruin) on the earth. **6.** You shall have no peace (rest) nor forgiveness (pardon) for your sin (transgression). As you delight in (rejoice in) your children, you will see the murder (slaying) of your beloved ones, and over the destruction of your children, you shall lament (mourn) and make supplication (petition) forever (eternally), but mercy (compassion) and peace shall not be granted (bestowed) to you.'"

Chapter 13

1. Enoch went and said to Azazel, "You shall have no peace; a severe (harsh) sentence has gone forth (been decreed) against you to put you in bonds (chains). **2.** You shall have no tolerance (leniency) or requests (appeals) granted because of the unrighteousness (wickedness) you have taught and the works (deeds) of godlessness (impiety) and sin (iniquity) you revealed to men." **3.** Then Enoch spoke to them all together, and they were filled with fear (dread). Fear and trembling seized (gripped) them, **4.** and they begged (implored) him to draw up a petition (plea) for them to find forgiveness (clemency), and to read it before the Lord of heaven. **5.** From that moment, they could no longer speak to Him, nor lift (raise) their eyes to heaven, because of their shame (embarrassment) for the sins (transgressions) for which they had been condemned. **6.** Enoch wrote their petition, with prayers concerning their spirits (souls), deeds (actions), and their request for forgiveness (remission) and length of life (longevity). **7.** He went to the waters of Dan (rivers of Dan), in the land of Dan, south of Hermon, where he read their petition until he fell asleep (dozed off). **8.** Behold, a dream (vision) came to him, and visions (revelations) of chastisement (punishment) appeared, and a voice told him to declare it to the sons (offspring) of heaven and reprimand (reprove) them. **9.** When Enoch awoke, he came to them, and they were gathered together, weeping (crying) in 'Abelsjail, between Lebanon and Seneser, with their faces covered (veiled). **10.** Enoch recounted (related) the visions (dreams) he had seen in his sleep and spoke words (utterances) of righteousness (virtue), reprimanding (admonishing) the heavenly Watchers.

Chapter 14

1. The book of righteousness (virtue) and the reprimand (reproof) of the Watchers was revealed according to the command (instruction) of the Holy One in a vision. **2.** I speak with the breath (spirit) given to man, to share wisdom (insight) and understanding (discernment), as He granted me power (strength) to reprimand (admonish) the Watchers. **3.** Just as man is given the ability to understand (comprehend), so I was granted the power (authority) to reprimand (reprove) the heavenly Watchers. **4.** Your petition (plea) will not be granted; judgment (verdict) has been passed, and you shall never ascend to heaven,

bound to the earth forever (eternally). **5.** Your beloved (cherished) sons will fall by the sword (battle), and your pleas (requests) on their behalf and for yourselves will not be answered. **6.** Though you weep (cry) and pray (petition), your request (appeal) will not be granted, for the judgment (sentence) is final, and the vision (revelation) has shown it. **7.** Clouds and mist called me, stars (constellations) and lightning hastened (urged) me, and the winds (gales) lifted me up, taking me into heaven. **8.** I approached a crystal wall (barrier) surrounded by fire (flame), which frightened (terrified) me as I entered the flames and drew near a house (abode) made of crystal. **9.** Its walls gleamed like a tessellated (mosaic) floor, with a ceiling like the stars' path (course), and fiery cherubim (angelic beings) between them. **10.** The house was surrounded by fire (blaze), and its portals (gates) blazed with fire. Inside, the heat and cold struck me, and fear (dread) gripped (seized) me. **11.** Trembling (shaking), I fell before the vision and saw another, grander house (dwelling) with an open portal (gateway), built entirely of flames (fire). **12.** It surpassed all in splendor (magnificence), too magnificent to describe (express), with a fiery floor (ground), ceiling, and lightning above. **13.** A throne (seat) of crystal stood within, surrounded by cherubim. Streams (rivers) of fire poured from beneath it, blinding (dazzling) me. **14.** The Great Glory (Majesty) sat upon the throne, His raiment (garment) brighter than the sun, whiter than snow. No angel (messenger) could look upon Him. **15.** His presence (being) was surrounded by fire, and none could approach (draw near) Him. Ten thousand stood before Him, yet He needed no counsel (advice). **16.** The holiest (sacred ones) remained close to Him, night and day, while I trembled (quaked) before Him. Then the Lord called me by name, saying: **17.** "Come, Enoch, and hear My word." One of the holy ones (sacred beings) awakened (aroused) me, lifted (raised) me up, and I bowed my face before the door. **18.** I drew near the door (entrance), trembling (shaking), and the voice (utterance) of the Lord spoke to me, calling me to come closer (nearer) and hear His command (order). **19.** The Lord spoke, saying, "The Watchers have sinned (transgressed), and their judgment (condemnation) is sealed (final). Their petition (request) is rejected forever (eternally)." **20.** The fire (flame) that surrounds them will never cease (end), and the earth will bear (carry) their judgment (punishment) for all eternity (forever). **21.** Though they weep (cry), their cries will not be heard (answered), for their deeds (actions) are final (settled), and the justice (righteousness) of the heavens is unyielding (unyielding). **22.** Your sons (children) will fall in battle (combat), and their fate (destiny) will mirror yours—sealed in darkness (obscurity), far from redemption (salvation). **23.** This vision (sight) I saw, and I trembled (shuddered) at the glory (majesty) of the Lord. The heavenly hosts (angels) could not approach (draw near) Him due to His magnificence (splendor). **24.** He alone sits on the throne of glory (majesty), untouched (impervious) by the hands of time or the need for counsel (advice). His judgment (verdict) is absolute (final). **25.** And as I fell before Him in awe (reverence), the Lord's voice (utterance) called me, "Enoch, rise up and listen to the wisdom (knowledge) of ages."

Chapter 15

1. He answered and said to me, and I heard His voice: "Do not fear (be afraid), Enoch, righteous man and scribe of righteousness (virtue). Come closer (nearer) and listen to my words (utterance). **2.** Go and tell (speak to) the Watchers of heaven, who sent you to intercede (plead) for them, 'You should intercede (pray) for mankind, not the other way around.' **3.** Why did you leave (abandon) the high, holy (sacred), and eternal (everlasting) heaven to defile (corrupt) yourselves with the daughters (women) of men, take wives, and father (beget) giants as sons? **4.** Though you were holy (sacred), spiritual (divine), and eternal (immortal), you defiled (polluted) yourselves with the blood (life force) of women and gave birth to children (offspring) of flesh, lusting (yearning) after mortal (earthly) desires as others do who die (perish). **5.** I gave women (wives) to men so they could bear (bring forth) children, fulfilling their needs (desires) on earth. **6.** But you were once spiritual (immaterial), eternal (ageless), and immortal (undying), and I did not appoint (assign) wives for you. The spiritual (celestial) beings of heaven dwell (live) there. **7.** Now, the giants (nephilim), born of spirit (spiritual essence) and flesh (physical form), will be called (named) evil (wicked) spirits on the earth. **8.** They will dwell (live) on the earth as evil spirits (malevolent beings), because they were born of men and the Watchers, their origin (source). **9.** These evil spirits (demons) will afflict (torment), oppress (burden), destroy (annihilate), and cause trouble (distress) on earth. They do not eat (consume) but still hunger (crave) and thirst (desire), leading (resulting) to sin (wrongdoing). **10.** These spirits (beings) will rise up (rebel) against mankind (humankind) and women (females), for they came from them (originated from them)."

Chapter 16

1. From the days (times) of the slaughter (massacre), destruction (devastation), and death (demise) of the giants, whose flesh (bodies) gave rise (produced) to spirits (entities) that will destroy (annihilate) without judgment (justice)—these spirits shall continue to destroy (ravage) until the great judgment (day of reckoning), when the age (era) will be completed (fulfilled). This judgment (verdict) will be against the Watchers (fallen angels) and the godless (wicked), and it will be fully completed (executed). **2.** Now, regarding the Watchers (angels) who sent you to intercede (plead) for them, and who were once in heaven: tell them, **3.** "You were in heaven (the celestial realm) but all the mysteries (secrets) were not revealed (disclosed) to you. You knew of worthless (insignificant) things, and with hardened (calloused) hearts, you made these known (revealed) to the women, leading (causing) both women and men to commit much evil (wickedness) on earth." **4.** Therefore, say to them: "You shall have no peace (rest)."

Chapter 17

1. They took me to a place where the beings there appeared like flames of fire (blazing fire), and when they chose, they could appear as men. **2.** They led me to a place of darkness (obscurity) and to a mountain whose peak (summit) reached up to the heavens. **3.** I saw the locations of the luminaries (celestial bodies), the treasuries (vaults) of the stars, the thunder, and in the deepest parts, where there were fiery bows and arrows, their quivers, fiery swords, and all the lightning. **4.** Then they took me to the living waters (flowing waters) and to the fire of the west (sunset), which receives the setting of the sun. **5.** I came to a river of fire that flowed like water and poured itself into the great sea toward the west. **6.** I saw the great rivers, then reached the great river and the deep darkness (profound shadow), and entered a place where no living flesh could walk. **7.** I saw the mountains shrouded in the darkness (shadow) of winter, and the place from which all the waters of the deep flow. **8.** I saw the mouths of all the rivers on earth, and the mouth (entrance) of the abyss.

Chapter 18

1. I saw the warehouses (vaults) of all the winds, how they furnished (handed) the whole creation and the earth's establishment foundations (stable ground). **2.** I saw the foundation (foundation gravestone) of the earth and the four winds that bear (uphold) the earth and the firmament (sky) of heaven. **3.** I saw how the winds stretch the welkin and station themselves between heaven and earth; these are the pillars (supports) of heaven. **4.** I saw the winds of heaven, turning and bringing the sun (solar body) and stars to their setting. I saw the winds on earth carrying shadows and the paths of the angels. **6.** I saw at the ends of the earth the firmament (sky) of heaven over. I also progressed to a place burning day and night, with seven magnificent mountains of gravestone, three to the east and three to the south. The eastern bones were colored gravestone, one of plum (precious rock), one of jacinth (sanguine-orange gem), and the southern bones were of red gravestone (sanguine gravestone). **8.** The middle mountain reached to heaven like God's throne, made of alabaster (white gravestone), with a sapphire (blue rock) peak. I saw a flaming fire. **9.** Beyond these mountains, at the end of the earth, the welkin were completed. I saw a deep ocean with columns of heavenly fire, and among them, columns of fire fell, bottomless in height and depth. Beyond this ocean was a place with no firmament (welkin) or earth, a waste and horrible region. **13.** There were no waters, no catcalls, just a desolate place. I saw seven stars like great burning mountains, and when I asked about them, the angel said, "This is the end of heaven and earth, a captivity for the stars and the host of heaven. These stars transgressed (violated) the Lord's command at their rising and didn't appear at their appointed times. **16.** He bound them until their guilt is completed, for ten thousand times."

Chapter 19

1. Uriel said to me, "Here shall stand the angels who joined with women, their spirits assuming many forms, defiling (corrupting) mankind and leading them astray into demon worship (idol worship). They will remain here until the great judgment, **2.** where they will be judged and made an end of. The women who went astray shall become sirens (alluring creatures)." **3.** I, Enoch, alone saw the vision, the ends of all things, and no man shall see what I have seen.

Chapter 20

1. These are the names of the holy angels who oversee the earth: **2.** Uriel, one of the holy angels, who governs (rules) the world and Tartarus (the abyss). **3.** Raphael, one of the holy angels, who watches over the spirits of men. **4.** Raguel, one of the holy angels, responsible for bringing vengeance (punishment) to the realm of the stars. **5.** Michael, one of the holy angels, appointed over the righteous among humanity and chaos (disorder). **6.** Saraqâêl, one of the holy angels, who supervises the spirits that sin in the spirit. **7.** Gabriel, one of the holy angels, who is in charge of Paradise (the garden), the serpents, and the Cherubim. **8.** Remiel, one of the holy angels, assigned by God to oversee the resurrection (revival) of the dead.

Chapter 21

1. I continued my journey and came to a place of great chaos (disorder). **2.** There, I witnessed something horrifying: there was neither a heaven above nor a solid earth below, just a place of utter disorder (confusion) and terror. **3.** In this place, I saw seven stars from the heavens, bound together, like enormous mountains, burning with fire. **4.** I asked, "For what sin are they bound, and why have they been cast into this place?" **5.** Uriel, one of the holy angels, who was with me and had authority over them, answered, "Enoch, why do you ask and why are you so eager to know the truth? **6.** These are stars from heaven that have violated the Lord's command. They are bound here for ten thousand years, until the full extent of their sins is completed." **7.** From there, I went to an even more terrifying place, where I saw a dreadful sight: a great fire burning and blazing, with the ground cracked open to the abyss (chasm), filled with immense columns of fire descending. I could neither see its full size nor fathom its magnitude. **8.** I said, "How terrifying is this place, and how dreadful to behold!" **9.** Uriel, one of the holy angels with me, responded, "Enoch, why are you so afraid?" I replied, "Because of the terror of this place and the intense suffering I witness here." **10.** He answered, "This is the prison of the angels, and here they will be imprisoned forever."

Chapter 22

1. I went to another place, a mountain of solid rock (a hard, unyielding stone). **2.** In it, I saw four vast (large), deep (profound) hollows (sunken areas), smooth and dark (lacking light). **3.** Raphael, one of the holy angels (messengers of God) with me, explained, "These hollows were created to gather the souls (spirits) of the dead, where they will remain until the final judgment (the day when God will decide the fate of all)." **4.** All the souls of men will be gathered here, awaiting their appointed (decided in advance) time until the great judgment comes. **5.** I saw a spirit crying out, and its voice ascended (rose up) to heaven, pleading for justice (asking for what is right). **6.** I asked Raphael, "Whose spirit is this, crying out to heaven?" **7.** Raphael answered, "This is the spirit of Abel, whom Cain (his brother) killed. Abel's spirit calls for justice (retribution) until Cain's descendants (children and their descendants) are utterly destroyed from the earth." **8.** I then inquired (asked) about the divisions (separations) among the hollows, asking why they were separated. **9.** Raphael replied, "These divisions separate the spirits. One is for the righteous (just and good), where a bright (shining) spring (source of water) of water flows. **10.** Another is for sinners (those who do wrong) who died without judgment, where their spirits will suffer (feel pain) until the final day of reckoning (accounting for their deeds). **11.** There, they will endure (face) torment (great suffering) and eternal (forever) punishment for their curses (evil words) and sin (wrongdoing). **12.** A third division is for those who were slain (killed) by sinners, whose spirits are set apart (separated) until the judgment day. **13.** "The spirits of the wicked (evil ones), those who fully transgressed (rebelled), will remain in company with transgressors (those who break the law). They will not be destroyed or resurrected (brought back to life) on the day of judgment." **14.** I praised the Lord of glory (the glorious Lord), saying, "Blessed is the Lord, the righteous King (just ruler), who reigns (rules) forever."

Chapter 23

1,2. From there I traveled to another place, to the west at the ends of the earth (the farthest part of the earth). I saw a burning **3.** fire that ran without stopping, never pausing day or night, but moving steadily (continuously).**4.** I asked, "What is this that does not rest?" Then Raguel (one of the holy angels), who was with me, answered and said, "This is the fire in the west that torments (causes suffering or punishment) all the luminaries (heavenly bodies, such as the sun, moon, and stars) of heaven."

Chapter 24

1. And from there I journeyed to another part of the earth, where I was shown a mountain range of fire that burned continuously, day and night. (continuously: without interruption) **2.** I moved beyond it and saw seven magnificent (splendid, impressive) mountains, each distinct (unique, different) in appearance. The stones of these mountains were glorious (full of glory, magnificent) and beautiful, shining in splendor (great brightness, radiance). Three mountains stood in the east, one above the other, and three more in the south, similarly stacked, with deep, rugged (rough, uneven) ravines (deep valleys) between them, none of which connected. **3.** The seventh mountain stood in the center, towering (rising high) over the others, resembling the seat of a throne. Fragrant (sweet-smelling) trees encircled this throne. **4.** Among them was a tree unlike any I had ever encountered (met), with a fragrance surpassing (going beyond) all others. Its leaves, flowers, and wood never withered (dried up, decayed), and its fruit was beautiful, resembling the dates (fruit of the date palm) of a palm. **5.** I marveled (was amazed) at the beauty of this tree, its delightful (pleasing, charming) fragrance, fair (beautiful) leaves, and lovely (attractive, delightful) blossoms (flowers). **6.** Then Michael, one of the holy and honored (respected, esteemed) angels who was with me and their leader, spoke in response.

Chapter 25

1. He said to me, "Enoch, why do you ask about the fragrance (the pleasant smell) of the tree, and why seek to understand (comprehend) the truth?" **2.** I replied, "I desire to know everything, but especially about this tree." **3.** He answered, "The high mountain (a tall, elevated land) you see, whose summit (top) resembles God's throne, is His throne. It is where the Holy One, the Lord of Glory, the Eternal King, will sit when He comes to bless (bring goodness to) the earth." **4.** "As for this fragrant (pleasant-smelling) tree, no mortal (human being) shall touch it until the great judgment (the final decision of God), when He will bring vengeance (punishment) and complete the work forever. Then it will be given to the righteous and holy (pure)." **5.** "Its fruit will nourish (provide sustenance) the elect (chosen people). The tree will be transplanted (moved to a new place) to the holy temple (sacred place) of the Lord, the Eternal King." **6.** "Then the righteous will rejoice (feel great joy), entering the holy place. Its fragrance will fill their being (soul), and they will live long, as your ancestors (forefathers) did. In their days, no sorrow (grief), plague (disease), torment (suffering), or calamity (disaster) will afflict (cause harm to) them." **7.** I then blessed (praised) the God of Glory, the Eternal King, who has prepared such blessings (gifts) for the righteous, created them, and promised to give them these gifts.

Chapter 26

1. I journeyed to the center (middle) of the earth and saw a blessed (holy, fortunate) place, where trees with flourishing (thriving) branches grew from a broken (dismembered) tree.**2.** There, I saw a holy (sacred) mountain, and beneath it, to the east, a stream (flow of water) flowed southward.**3.** To the east, I noticed a higher (greater in height) mountain, with a deep (extensive), narrow (tight) ravine (gorge, deep valley) between it and the first.**4-5.** In this ravine, another stream flowed beneath the mountain. To the west, there was another mountain, smaller and lower (of lesser height), with a deep, dry ravine between it and the others. Another dry ravine lay at the end (outer part) of the three mountains. All the ravines were steep (sharp, sloping) and narrow, formed of solid (hard) rock, and there were no trees growing in **6.** them. I marveled (was amazed) at the rocks and ravines and was amazed beyond measure.

Chapter 27

1. I asked, "What is the purpose of this blessed (holy, fortunate) land, filled with trees, and this cursed (damned) valley in between?"**2.** Uriel, one of the holy (sacred) angels with me, answered, "This cursed valley is reserved for the eternally accursed (condemned). It is where those who speak blasphemy (disrespectful or irreverent speech) against the Lord and defame (speak against) His glory will be gathered.**3.** It will be their place of judgment (final decision). In the last days, the righteous will witness their judgment, and the merciful (compassionate) will praise the Lord of Glory, the Eternal King.**4.** In that time, the righteous will thank Him for the mercy (compassion) He has shown them in their appointed (assigned) fate."**5.** I then praised (honored) the Lord of Glory, declaring His greatness and glorifying (praising) Him.

Chapter 28

1. From there, I traveled east to the heart (center) of the desert mountains.**2.** I saw a solitary (isolated, empty) wilderness, filled with trees and plants, and water flowed down from above.**3.** It rushed like a mighty (strong, powerful) river to the northwest, bringing clouds and dew (moisture) on every side.

Chapter 29

1. I then journeyed to another part of the desert, east of the mountain range.**2.** There, I found aromatic (pleasantly fragrant) trees, giving off the scent of frankincense (a fragrant resin used in incense) and myrrh (a fragrant gum used in perfumes), similar to almond trees.

Chapter 30

1. Beyond these, I traveled far to the east and came upon a valley (low area between hills) filled with water.**2.** In this valley stood a tree with the fragrance (pleasant smell) of mastic trees (a type of tree whose resin is used in perfumes).**3.** Along the sides of the valley, I found trees of fragrant cinnamon (a spice made from tree bark). Continuing eastward, I went further.

Chapter 31

1. I saw other mountains, among which were groves (groups) of trees, from which flowed nectar (sweet liquid) called sarara and galbanum (a fragrant resin). **2.** Beyond these mountains, to the east at the ends of the earth (furthest point), I saw another mountain with aloe trees, all filled **3.** with stacte (a resin used in perfumes), resembling almond trees. When burned, it emitted a sweet fragrance, surpassing all other scents.

Chapter 32

1. Looking north over the mountains, I saw seven mountains rich with choice nard (a fragrant plant), fragrant trees, cinnamon, and pepper. **2.** I then traveled across all these mountains, eastward beyond the Erythraean Sea (the Red Sea), passing over the angel Zotiel, until I reached the Garden of Righteousness (a place of purity and virtue). **3.** From a distance, I saw more trees than I had ever seen, including two large and magnificent trees, glorious (splendid) in appearance, and the Tree of Knowledge, whose holy fruit grants great wisdom. **4.** The tree was tall like a fir, with leaves resembling those of the carob tree (a tree whose fruit is used for food). Its fruit **5.** was like clusters of grapes, beautiful in appearance. The fragrance of the tree reached far. **6.** I marveled (was astonished), saying, "How beautiful and appealing is this tree!" Raphael, the holy angel with me, replied, "This is the Tree of Wisdom, from which your father and mother, in their old age, ate. By eating its fruit, their eyes were opened, and they realized they were naked. They were then cast out of the garden."

Chapter 33

1. From there, I traveled to the ends of the earth, where I saw great beasts (large creatures), each one different from the other. I also saw birds with different appearances, beauty, and sounds, each distinct from the others. To the east of these beasts, I saw the ends of the earth, where the heavens **2.** rest (are supported), and the portals (gates) of heaven opened. I saw how the stars of heaven emerged (came out), **3.** and I counted the portals from which they came, recording the outlets (entrances) for each individual star, along with their numbers, names, paths (journeys), positions, **4.** times, and months, as shown to me by Uriel, the holy angel. He explained everything to me and wrote it down, including the names, laws, and groups (associations) of the stars.

Chapter 34

1. From there, I traveled north to the ends (extremities) of the earth, where I saw a great and glorious (magnificent) structure. **2.** I observed three portals (gates) of heaven open in the sky, and through each one, north winds blew. When they did, they brought cold, hail (frozen rain), frost (thin ice), snow, dew (moisture), and rain. **3.** Winds from one portal brought blessings, but those from the other two brought violence (harshness) and affliction (suffering), blowing harshly upon the earth.

Chapter 35

1. From there, I journeyed west to the ends of the earth and saw three open portals of heaven, similar to those I had seen in the east. The same number of portals and outlets (exits) were present.

Chapter 36

1. From there, I traveled south to the ends of the earth and saw three open portals of heaven.**2.** From these portals came dew (moisture), rain, and wind. Then I journeyed east to the ends of the sky, where I saw three portals open, along with smaller (lesser in size) portals **3.** above them. Through these small portals, the stars of heaven passed, following their courses (paths) westward. Whenever I saw this, I always praised the Lord of Glory (the Eternal God), who works great and glorious wonders. I blessed Him for showing His mighty works (powerful actions) to the angels, spirits (immaterial beings), and men, that they might praise His creation, witness His power, and bless Him forever.

15 – EZRA

Chapter 1

1. In the first year of King Cyrus of Persia, the Lord moved him to fulfill the message He had spoken through Jeremiah. The Lord stirred Cyrus's spirit, leading him to issue a proclamation (announcement) across his kingdom and also put it in writing. **2.** "This is the message from Cyrus, king of Persia: The Lord, the God of heaven, has granted me all the kingdoms of the earth. He has appointed me to build a house (temple) for Him in Jerusalem, located in Judah. **3.** If any among you are His people, may God be with you. You are invited to go up to Jerusalem in Judah and rebuild the Lord's house, the God of Israel, for He is truly God, and His house is in Jerusalem. **4.** For those remaining (staying) elsewhere, the people in those areas should support them with silver, gold, goods, livestock (animals kept for farming or food), and voluntary (freewill) offerings for God's house in Jerusalem." **5.** Then, the leaders (heads) of the families of Judah and Benjamin, together with the priests and Levites, along with all those whom God had moved, rose to go and rebuild the house of the Lord in Jerusalem. **6.** People around them supported this mission by giving silver, gold, goods, livestock, and valuable (precious) items, in addition to freewill offerings. **7.** King Cyrus also brought out items (objects) that Nebuchadnezzar had taken from the Lord's house in Jerusalem and placed in his own gods' temple (place of worship). **8.** Cyrus, king of Persia, instructed Mithredath, the treasurer (overseer of money), to hand over these items, and Mithredath counted them out to Sheshbazzar, the leader of Judah. **9.** These items included thirty gold dishes (plates), one thousand silver dishes, and twenty-nine knives (sharp tools). **10.** There were also thirty gold bowls, four hundred and ten silver bowls of similar kind, and one thousand other items. **11.** Altogether, there were five thousand four hundred gold and silver items. Sheshbazzar took these along with the captives (people taken as prisoners) returning from Babylon to Jerusalem.

Chapter 2

1. These are the people from the province who returned from captivity, those taken by King Nebuchadnezzar of Babylon. They returned to Jerusalem and Judah (an ancient Israel), each to their own town. **2.** The leaders who returned with Zerubbabel were Jeshua, Nehemiah, Seraiah, Reelaiah, Mordecai, Bilshan, Mispar, Bigvai, Rehum, and Baanah. The total number of men from Israel: **3.** The family of Parosh consisted of two thousand one hundred seventy-two people. **4.** Shephatiah's clan numbered three hundred seventy-two. **5.** The count of Arah's people was seven hundred seventy-five. **6.** The families of Pahath-Moab, from Jeshua and Joab's line, included two thousand eight hundred twelve. **7.** In Elam's community, there were one thousand two hundred fifty-four people. **8.** Zattu's family recorded a total of nine hundred forty-five members. **9.** Seven hundred sixty people belonged to Zaccai's clan. **10.** Bani's descendants numbered six hundred forty-two. **11.** Bebai's community included six hundred twenty-three individuals. **12.** The family of Azgad counted one thousand two hundred twenty-two people. **13.** Adonikam's family group had six hundred sixty-six members. **14.** In Bigvai's clan, there were two thousand fifty-six people. **15.** Four hundred fifty-four were counted among the people of Adin. **16.** The family of Ater, connected to Hezekiah, numbered ninety-eight. **17.** Three hundred twenty-three were in Bezai's clan. **18.** Jorah's family consisted of one hundred twelve individuals. **19.** Hashum's descendants totaled two hundred twenty-three. **20.** There were ninety-five people among Gibbar's family. **21.** One hundred twenty-three people came from Bethlehem. **22.** Netophah's men counted fifty-six. **23.** One hundred twenty-eight men came from the people of Anathoth. **24.** Azmaveth's family had forty-two people. **25.** The families from Kirjath Arim, Chephirah, and Beeroth included seven hundred forty-three. **26.** Six hundred twenty-one individuals were from Ramah and Geba. **27.** The people of Michmas totaled one hundred twenty-two. **28.** Two hundred twenty-three came from the communities of Bethel and Ai. **29.** Nebo's people included fifty-two individuals. **30.** The community of Magbish counted one hundred fifty-six. **31.** In the other Elam family, there were one thousand two hundred fifty-four people. **32.** Harim's community had three hundred twenty people. **33.** Families from Lod, Hadid, and Ono numbered seven hundred twenty-five. **34.** Jericho's population was three hundred forty-five. **35.** In Senaah, there were three thousand six hundred thirty people. **36.** The priests: descendants of Jedaiah from the house of Jeshua (a priestly family), numbered 973; **37.** the descendants of Immer: 1,052; **38.** the descendants of Pashhur (a priestly family): 1,247; **39.** the descendants of Harim (a priestly family): 1,017. **40.** The Levites: descendants of Jeshua and Kadmiel from the house of Hodaviah (a Levite family): 74. **41.** The singers: descendants of Asaph (a musical family): 128. **42.** The gatekeepers: descendants of Shallum, Ater, Talmon, Akkub, Hatita, and Shobai (temple guardians): 139 in total. **43.** The Nethinim (temple servants): descendants of Ziha, Hasupha, Tabbaoth, **44.** the descendants of Keros, along with Siaha and Padon. **45.** The lineage of Lebanah, Hagabah, Akkub, **46.** the descendants of Hagab, along with Shalmai, Hanan, **47.** the sons of Giddel, Gahar, Reaiah, **48.** the lineage of Rezin, Nekoda, Gazzam, **49.** the lineage of Uzza, Paseah, Besai, **50.** the sons of Asnah, Meunim, Nephusim, **51.** the descendants of Bakbuk, along with Hakupha, Harhur, **52.** the sons of Bazluth, Mehida, Harsha, **53.** the lineage of Barkos, Sisera, Tamah, **54.** the descendants of Neziah, along with Hatipha. **55.** The descendants of Solomon's servants: Sotai, Sophereth, Peruda, **56.** Jaala, Darkon, Giddel, **57.** Shephatiah, Hattil, Pochereth of Zebaim (a town): and Ami. **58.** All the Nethinim and children of Solomon's servants totaled 392. **59.** These are the people who came from Tel Melah (a town), Tel Harsha (a town), Cherub (a town), Addan (a town), and Immer (a town), but they couldn't trace their family lines to Israel. **60.** The descendants of Delaiah, Tobiah, and Nekoda: 652; **61.** and the descendants of the priests: Habaiah, Koz, and Barzillai, who married a daughter of Barzillai the Gileadite and took his name. **62.** They tried to register in the genealogical records but were not found, so they were excluded from the priesthood as unclean. **63.** The governor instructed them not to eat the most holy things (sacred food) until a priest could consult with the Urim and Thummim (sacred objects used for decision-making). **64.** The total number of the assembly was 42,360, **65.** excluding their male and female servants, who numbered 7,337, and 200 singers (musicians), both men and women. **66.** They had 736 horses, 245 mules (animals used for carrying), **67.** 435 camels (large animals used for transport), and 6,720 donkeys. **68.** Some family leaders gave freely to the work of rebuilding God's house: **69.** They contributed according to their ability—61,000 gold drachmas (gold coins), 5,000 minas (a weight of silver), and 100 priestly garments (robes for priests). **70.** The priests, Levites, singers, gatekeepers, Nethinim, and all of Israel settled in their respective cities.

Chapter 3

1. When the seventh month came, and the Israelites had made their homes in the cities, they came together in Jerusalem with unity. **2.** Jeshua, the son of Jozadak (a priest), along with other priests, and Zerubbabel, the son of Shealtiel, and his relatives, took the lead to rebuild the altar (a raised place for sacrifices) of Israel's God. They wanted to offer burnt offerings (offerings made by burning) there, as was written in the Law of Moses, God's servant. **3.** Despite the worry (anxiety) they felt because of surrounding nations, they set the altar on its original foundation and offered burnt offerings to the Lord, both in the morning and at evening. **4.** They also observed the Feast of Tabernacles (a week-long festival celebrating harvest) as was instructed, presenting the daily burnt offerings for each day. **5.** Furthermore, they offered the regular burnt offerings, those required for the New Moons (the first day of each month), and for all the appointed feasts of the Lord, along with any voluntary (freewill) offerings from those who chose to give to the Lord. **6.** They began presenting burnt offerings to the Lord on the first day of the seventh month, even though the temple's foundation (the base or bottom layer) had yet to be laid. **7.** They paid wages to the masons (stone workers) and carpenters (woodworkers) and provided food, drink, and oil (liquid used for lamps) to the people from Sidon and Tyre (cities near the Mediterranean Sea), so they could bring cedar logs (wood from a specific tree) from Lebanon to the sea, then to Joppa (a port city), all according to the permission given by King Cyrus of Persia. **8.** In the second month of the second year after arriving at the house (temple) of God in Jerusalem, Zerubbabel, son of Shealtiel, Jeshua, son of Jozadak, the priests, Levites, and all who had returned from exile (forced removal from their land), began the construction work. They appointed Levites (from the tribe of Levi) aged twenty and above to oversee the work on the Lord's house. **9.** Jeshua, with his sons and brothers, along with Kadmiel and his sons, and the descendants of Judah, gathered to supervise the work on God's house, alongside the sons of Henadad (a Levite family) and their brothers, the Levites. **10.** When the builders laid the foundation of the Lord's temple, the priests, dressed in robes (special clothes), took their places with trumpets, while the Levites, from the family of Asaph (a family known for music), stood with cymbals (musical instruments) to give praise to the Lord as commanded by King David of Israel. **11.** They sang responsively, giving thanks and praising the Lord, saying, "For He is good, and His love (mercy) endures forever toward Israel." The people lifted their voices in a great shout of praise, for the foundation of the Lord's house had been laid. **12.** However, many priests, Levites, and family leaders who had seen the first temple began to weep (cry) loudly when they looked at the foundation of this new temple, while many others shouted with joy. **13.** The sound was so intense that the joyful shouts and the weeping could not be told apart, for the people shouted with such strength that the noise was heard from far away.

Chapter 4

1. When the enemies (opposers) of Judah and Benjamin heard that the exiled (sent away) Israelites were rebuilding the temple of the Lord God of Israel, **2.** they approached Zerubbabel and the heads of the families, saying, "Let us help you build, for we worship (serve) your God just as you do. We have been offering sacrifices (ritual offerings) to Him since the time of Esarhaddon, king of Assyria, who brought us here." **3.** But Zerubbabel, Jeshua, and the other leaders (chiefs) of Israel said, "You have no part with us in building a house for our God; we will build it alone, as King Cyrus of Persia has commanded us." **4.** Then the people of the land tried to discourage (make them lose confidence) the people of Judah, and they made it difficult for them to continue building. **5.** They even hired advisors (counselors) to oppose them and frustrate (block or prevent) their plans throughout the reign (rule) of Cyrus, king of Persia, and into the reign of Darius, king of Persia. **6.** In the reign of Ahasuerus, at the beginning of his rule, they sent a letter accusing (blaming) the people of Judah (an ancient Israel) and Jerusalem. **7.** Later, during the reign of Artaxerxes, Bishlam, Mithredath, Tabel, and their companions wrote to Artaxerxes, king of Persia. The letter was written in Aramaic (ancient language) and translated into the Aramaic language. **8.** Rehum the commander (military leader) and Shimshai the scribe (writer) wrote a letter accusing Jerusalem, saying: **9.** "From Rehum the commander, Shimshai the scribe, and their companions, representatives of the Dinaites, Apharsathchites, Tarpelites, the people of Persia, Erech, Babylon, Shushan, the Dehavites, Elamites, **10.** and the other nations whom the great and noble Osnapper (an Assyrian king) settled in the cities of Samaria and the surrounding regions. **11.** This is a copy of the letter they sent to the king: To King Artaxerxes, from your servants, the people living beyond the River: **12.** "Let it be known to the king that the Jews who returned to Jerusalem are building the rebellious (defiant) and dangerous city. They are repairing its walls and laying the foundations. **13.** We advise (recommend) you, king, that if this city is

rebuilt and its walls completed, the Jews will no longer pay taxes, tribute (payment), or customs (fees), which will harm your treasury (funds). **14.** Since we are supported (backed) by the palace, it was improper (inappropriate) for us to ignore the king's dishonor, so we have reported this matter. **15.** We urge you to look in the records (official documents) of your ancestors, and you will find that this city has a history of rebellion (resistance) and sedition (rebellion), and was destroyed for this reason. **16.** We inform (notify) the king that if this city is rebuilt, you will lose control (dominion) over the region beyond the River." **17.** King Artaxerxes sent the following reply to Rehum the commander, Shimshai the scribe, and their companions in Samaria and beyond the River: "Greetings (peace). **18.** The letter you sent has been carefully read before me. **19.** I have ordered a search, and we found that this city has indeed revolted (rebelled) against kings in the past, and has been the site of rebellion and sedition. **20.** Mighty kings ruled (governed) over Jerusalem and the surrounding regions, and taxes, tribute, and customs were paid to them. **21.** Therefore, I issue the order (decree) to stop the building of this city and its walls until I give further instructions. **22.** Take care (be careful) not to neglect this order. Why should damage (harm) be done to the kingdom?" **23.** When Rehum, Shimshai the scribe, and their companions received the king's letter, they quickly went to Jerusalem and used force (power) to stop the rebuilding. **24.** As a result, the work on the temple in Jerusalem stopped, and it remained halted (paused) until the second year of the reign of Darius, king of Persia.

Chapter 5

1. The prophets Haggai and Zechariah, son of Iddo, spoke on behalf of God to the Jews in Judah and Jerusalem, bringing messages in the name of the God of Israel, who was watching over them. **2.** Hearing this, Zerubbabel, son of Shealtiel, and Jeshua, son of Jozadak, rose to start the rebuilding of the temple of God in Jerusalem. God's prophets were there alongside them, supporting the work. **3.** At the same time, Tattenai, the governor (ruler) of the region beyond the River, along with Shethar-Boznai and their associates, came and questioned them, asking, "Who authorized you to rebuild this temple and finish these walls?" **4.** We responded by providing the names of the leaders overseeing the work. **5.** However, God's protective care was over the Jewish elders, so their adversaries couldn't halt the work until a report could be sent to King Darius, and a written reply concerning this matter was received. **6.** This is the letter that Tattenai, the governor of the region beyond the River, Shethar-Boznai, and their Persian associates sent to King Darius. **7.** The letter stated: To King Darius, greetings. **8.** Let it be known to the king that we visited the province of Judea, where the temple of the great God is being constructed with large stones, and timber is being placed within the walls. The work is progressing efficiently and thriving under their efforts. **9.** We questioned the elders, asking, "Who gave you the authority to build this temple and complete these walls?" **10.** We also requested the names of the leaders so that we could report them to you, noting the names of those overseeing the work. **11.** They replied, "We are servants of the God of heaven and earth, and we are rebuilding the temple that was erected many years ago by a great king of Israel. **12.** However, because our ancestors angered the God of heaven, He delivered them to Nebuchadnezzar, king of Babylon, the Chaldean (Babylonian), who destroyed this temple and carried the people away to Babylon. **13.** Yet, in the first year of King Cyrus of Babylon, he issued a decree (order) to rebuild the house of God. **14.** The gold and silver items of the house of God, which Nebuchadnezzar had taken from the temple in Jerusalem and stored in the temple of Babylon, were returned by King Cyrus. He entrusted them to a man named Sheshbazzar, whom he appointed as governor. **15.** Cyrus instructed him, saying, 'Take these items, go to Jerusalem, and rebuild the house of God on its original site.' **16.** So, Sheshbazzar came and laid the foundation of God's house in Jerusalem, and since then, the construction has continued, though the temple is still not completed." **17.** Therefore, if the king approves, let a search be made in the royal archives (storage of valuables) in Babylon to verify if King Cyrus issued a decree to rebuild this house of God in Jerusalem, and may the king send us his decision regarding this matter.

Chapter 6

1. Then King Darius gave an order, and a search was conducted in the archives (official records) where the treasures were stored in Babylon.

2. In Achmetha, in the palace (royal residence) located in the province of Media, a scroll (written record) was discovered, which contained the following details: **3.** In the first year of King Cyrus, he issued a decree (official order) regarding the house of God in Jerusalem: "Let the house be rebuilt, the place where sacrifices are offered, and let its foundation be securely established, with a height of sixty cubits and a width of sixty cubits, **4.** using three rows of large stones and one row of fresh timber (wood). The expenses should be paid for from the king's treasury." **5.** Additionally, the gold and silver objects (items) from the house of God that Nebuchadnezzar had taken from the temple in Jerusalem and brought to Babylon should be returned to their proper place in the temple in Jerusalem, and placed in the house of God. **6.** Now, Tattenai, the governor (ruler) of the region beyond the River, Shethar-Boznai, and your Persian companions (members of the Persian empire) beyond the River, stay away from there. **7.** Let the work of rebuilding this house of God proceed with the governor of the Jews and the elders (leaders) of the Jews in charge, and let them continue building the house of God on its original site. **8.** Furthermore, I decree regarding the elders of these Jews and the construction of the house of God: Let the necessary funds be provided from the king's treasury using taxes (funds) collected from the region beyond the River. This should be given to them immediately, so the work is not delayed. **9.** Whatever is required—young bulls (young male cows), rams (male sheep), lambs (young sheep) for the burnt offerings (sacrifices) to the God of heaven, wheat, salt, wine, and oil, as requested by the priests in Jerusalem—must be supplied to them daily, without interruption, **10.** so they can offer pleasing sacrifices (offerings) to the God of heaven and pray for the king's well-being and that of his sons. **11.** I also issue a decree (order) that anyone who changes this command will have a beam (piece of wood) pulled from their house and be hanged on it, and their house will be turned into a garbage heap. **12.** May the God who causes His name to dwell (live) there destroy any king or nation who dares to change or destroy this house of God in Jerusalem. I, Darius, issue this decree; let it be carried out with care (diligence). **13.** Then Tattenai, the governor of the region beyond the River, Shethar-Boznai, and their companions took action and followed exactly what King Darius had commanded. **14.** So the elders of the Jews built the temple and succeeded, assisted by the prophesying (messages from God) of Haggai the prophet and Zechariah the son of Iddo. They finished the temple according to the command of the God of Israel and the orders of King Cyrus, Darius, and Artaxerxes, kings of Persia. **15.** The temple was completed on the third day of the month of Adar, in the sixth year of King Darius' reign. **16.** The children of Israel, including the priests, Levites (assistants to the priests), and all those who had returned from exile (captivity), joyfully celebrated the dedication of this house of God. **17.** They offered sacrifices (ritual offerings) during the dedication of the house of God: one hundred bulls, two hundred rams, four hundred lambs, and twelve male goats as a sin offering (atonement) for all Israel, corresponding to the number of the tribes of Israel. **18.** They assigned the priests (religious leaders) to their divisions and the Levites to their roles for the service (work) of God in Jerusalem, as prescribed in the Book of Moses. **19.** The descendants (children) of the exile (captivity) celebrated the Passover on the fourteenth day of the first month. **20.** The priests and Levites had purified (cleaned) themselves; all of them were ritually clean. They slaughtered the Passover lambs for all the exiles, for their fellow priests, and for themselves. **21.** The Israelites who had returned from exile ate the Passover meal together with those who had separated themselves from the impurities of the surrounding nations to seek the Lord God of Israel. **22.** They kept the Feast of Unleavened Bread (bread without yeast) for seven days with great joy, because the Lord had made them rejoice and had turned the heart of the king of Assyria to support them, strengthening their hands in the work of the house of God, the God of Israel.

Chapter 7

1. Following these events, in the reign of Artaxerxes, the king of Persia, Ezra, a descendant of Seraiah, Azariah, Hilkiah, **2.** Shallum, Zadok, Ahitub, **3.** Amariah, Azariah, Meraioth, **4.** Zerahiah, Uzzi, Bukki, **5.** Abishua, Phinehas, Eleazar, and Aaron, the high priest, journeyed up from Babylon. **6.** Ezra was an expert scribe (writer) in the Law of Moses, a law given by the Lord, the God of Israel. The king granted him every request because God's hand (help) was upon him. **7.** Some Israelites,

including priests, Levites (helpers), singers, gatekeepers, and Nethinim (temple servants), accompanied Ezra in the seventh year of King Artaxerxes. **8.** Ezra arrived in Jerusalem in the fifth month of that same year. **9.** Leaving Babylon on the first day of the first month, he reached Jerusalem on the first day of the fifth month, all because of the good hand (favor) of God upon him. **10.** Ezra had devoted his heart to seek and follow the Law of the Lord, and to teach it to Israel. **11.** Here is the letter that King Artaxerxes provided Ezra, the priest and scribe skilled in the commandments of the Lord: **12.** "Artaxerxes, the king of kings, to Ezra, priest and scribe of the Law of the God of heaven: Greetings and blessings. **13.** I issue a decree that all Israelites, priests, and Levites in my kingdom who wish to go to Jerusalem, may join you. **14.** Since you have been sent by the king and his seven counselors to inquire about Judah and Jerusalem, and to investigate the Law of your God that is in your possession; **15.** You are also to take the silver and gold which the king and his counselors have generously given to the God of Israel, whose temple is in Jerusalem. **16.** Along with all the silver and gold you gather in the province of Babylon, you are to use it for the house of their God in Jerusalem, **17.** and carefully purchase bulls, rams, and lambs for offerings, with their accompanying grain and drink offerings. Offer them on the altar of the house of your God in Jerusalem. **18.** As for the remaining silver and gold, whatever seems right to you and your people to do, you are free to do according to the will of your God. **19.** Also, make sure to deliver the temple articles that have been entrusted to you in full, before the God of Jerusalem. **20.** If there are any additional needs for the house of your God, cover the expenses from the king's treasury. **21.** I, Artaxerxes the king, issue this command to all treasurers beyond the River: Do whatever Ezra the priest, the scribe of the Law of the God of heaven, requests, **22.** up to 100 talents of silver, 100 kors of wheat, 100 baths of wine, 100 baths of oil, and as much salt as is needed. **23.** Whatever is required by the God of heaven, let it be done for the house of the God of heaven. Why should there be any wrath against the king's kingdom and his family? **24.** Furthermore, no taxes, tribute, or customs should be levied on any priests, Levites, singers, gatekeepers, Nethinim, or servants of the house of God. **25.** Ezra, with the wisdom (knowledge) granted to you by your God, appoint magistrates and judges who will govern all the people beyond the River. Teach those who are not familiar with the laws of your God. **26.** Anyone who refuses to obey the law of your God and the law of the king should be swiftly punished, whether by death, banishment (exile), confiscation of property, or imprisonment. **27.** Praise the Lord God of our ancestors, who stirred the heart of the king to beautify (improve) the temple of the Lord in Jerusalem. **28.** God has shown His mercy to me before the king, his counselors, and his mighty princes. I was encouraged because God's hand was upon me, and I gathered leading men of Israel to go with me."

Chapter 8

1. These individuals represent the heads (leaders) of their ancestral households, and the genealogy (family record) of those who returned with me from Babylon (a major city in Mesopotamia) during the reign of King Artaxerxes (Persian king) is as follows: **2.** From the line of Phinehas (a priestly lineage) came Gershom; from Ithamar (another priestly family), Daniel; and from David (Israel's former king), Hattush. **3.** Zechariah, from Shecaniah's family, was accompanied by 150 men. **4.** Eliehoenai, the son of Zerahiah, hailed from the clan of Pahath-Moab (a region) and brought with him 200 men. **5.** Ben-Jahaziel, belonging to Shecaniah's family, arrived with 300 men. **6.** Ebed, son of Jonathan, from the Adin clan, came with 50 men. **7.** Jeshaiah, the son of Athaliah, was from Elam (a region in Persia) and had 70 men accompanying him. **8.** Zebadiah, son of Michael, of the Shephatiah family, brought with him 80 men. **9.** Obadiah, son of Jehiel, from Joab's line, was joined by 218 men. **10.** Ben-Josiphiah, a member of the Shelomith family, arrived with 160 men. **11.** Zechariah, son of Bebai, led 28 men from Bebai's clan. **12.** Johanan, son of Hakkatan, from the family of Azgad, was accompanied by 110 men. **13.** Eliphelet, Jeiel, and Shemaiah, from the last sons of Adonikam, brought with them 60 men. **14.** From the family of Bigvai (another clan), Uthai and Zabbud came, accompanied by 70 men. **15.** I gathered all these people by the river near Ahava, and we set up camp there for three days. As I checked among the people and the priests, I discovered that there were no Levites (priests from the tribe of Levi) present. **16.** So, I summoned Eliezer, Ariel, Shemaiah,

Elnathan, Jarib, another Elnathan, Nathan, Zechariah, and Meshullam, who were leaders (chiefs), along with Joiarib and Elnathan, men of understanding (wise men). **17.** I instructed them to deliver a message to Iddo (a leader), the chief man in Casiphia (a settlement), requesting him and the Nethinim (temple servants) to send us helpers for the house of our God. **18.** By the gracious hand (blessing) of our God upon us, they brought a man of wisdom named Sherebiah, a Levite from the family of Mahli, son of Levi, son of Israel, along with 18 men from his family. **19.** Also joining us were Hashabiah and Jeshaiah, from the sons of Merari (another Levite family), accompanied by their 20 men. **20.** Additionally, 220 Nethinim (temple helpers), appointed by David (Israel's former king) and the leaders to assist the Levites, were brought to help us. Each of them was identified by name. **21.** By the river Ahava, I proclaimed a fast (time of prayer and self-denial), so we could humble ourselves before God and seek His guidance for our journey, our children, and all our possessions. **22.** I felt embarrassed to ask the king for a guard of soldiers and horsemen to protect us on the way, because we had assured the king, "The hand of our God is upon all who seek Him for good, but His power and wrath (anger) are against those who forsake Him." **23.** So we fasted and prayed to God, and He heard our prayers. **24.** I then selected twelve leaders from the priests— Sherebiah, Hashabiah, and ten of their brothers (brethren)—**25.** and entrusted them with the silver, gold, and sacred articles that had been offered for the house of our God by the king, his counselors, his princes, and all Israel who were present. **26.** I gave them 650 talents (weight units) of silver, 100 talents of silver vessels, and 100 talents of gold, **27.** along with 20 gold basins (bowls) worth 1,000 drachmas (coins), and two fine bronze vessels that were as precious as gold. **28.** I said to them, "You are holy (set apart) to the Lord, and these items are also holy. The silver and gold are freewill offerings (voluntary gifts) to the Lord, the God of your ancestors. **29.** Guard these carefully until you weigh them out before the leaders of the priests, the Levites, and the heads of families in Jerusalem, within the rooms (chambers) of the house of the Lord." **30.** So the priests and Levites received the silver, gold, and sacred articles to transport them to Jerusalem for the house of our God. **31.** On the 12th day of the first month, we set out from the river Ahava, headed toward Jerusalem. The hand of our God was upon us, protecting us from enemies and ambushes (sudden attacks) along the way. **32.** Upon reaching Jerusalem, we remained there for three days. **33.** On the fourth day, the silver, gold, and sacred articles were weighed in the house of our God by Meremoth, the son of Uriah the priest, with the assistance of Eleazar, the son of Phinehas, as well as the Levites Jozabad, the son of Jeshua, and Noadiah, the son of Binnui. **34.** All items were accounted for and documented precisely at that time. **35.** Those who had returned from the exile offered burnt offerings (offerings entirely consumed by fire) to the God of Israel: twelve bulls for all Israel, ninety-six rams, seventy-seven lambs, and twelve male goats as a sin offering. This was their offering to the Lord. **36.** They delivered the king's decrees to the king's satraps and governors west of the river, who then supported the people and the house of God.

Chapter 9

1. After these events, the leaders approached me, saying, "The people of Israel, including the priests and Levites, have not separated themselves from the people of the surrounding nations. They have continued to follow the detestable (morally offensive) practices of the Canaanites, Hittites, Perizzites, Jebusites, Ammonites, Moabites, Egyptians, and Amorites. **2.** They have taken some of their daughters as wives for their sons and have given their daughters to the sons of these people, so the holy offspring (descendants) have been mixed with the nations of those lands. The leaders and rulers have been the first to act in this way." **3.** When I heard this, I tore my clothes (a type of clothing) and my robe, pulled some of the hair from my head and beard, and sat down in deep shock. **4.** Then all those who trembled at the words (sacred instructions) of the God of Israel gathered around me, because of the sin of the exiles, and I sat there stunned (great surprise) until the evening sacrifice. **5.** At the time of the evening sacrifice, I rose from my time of fasting (a period of not eating), and after tearing my clothes and robe, I fell on my knees and spread out my hands before the Lord my God, **6.** and said, "O my God, I am too ashamed (embarrassed) and humbled to lift my face to You, my God;

our wrongdoings (iniquities) have piled up higher than our heads, and our guilt has reached up to the heavens. **7.** From the days of our ancestors (forefathers) to this very day, we have been guilty, and because of our sins, we, our kings, and our priests have been handed over to the kings of other nations, to be killed by the sword, taken into captivity (being taken prisoner), plundered (robbed), and shamed (disgraced), as we are today. **8.** But now, for a brief moment (short time), the Lord our God has been merciful (kind) to us, leaving us a remnant (small group) to escape, and giving us a secure position in His holy place, so that our God may open our eyes and grant us a measure of relief (comfort) in our captivity (bondage). **9.** For though we were slaves (people in bondage), our God did not forsake us in our slavery. Instead, He showed us favor (grace) in the sight of the kings of Persia, to revive us, rebuild the house (temple) of our God, repair its ruins (destruction), and provides us with protection (a wall) in Judah and Jerusalem. **10.** Now, our God, what shall we say after this? For we have forsaken (abandoned) Your commandments, **11.** which You gave through Your prophets (messengers), saying, 'The land you are about to enter and possess is unclean, filled with the impurity (uncleanness) of the nations, whose detestable (evil) practices have corrupted it. **12.** Therefore, do not give your daughters to their sons, nor take their daughters for your sons, and never seek their peace (harmony) or prosperity (success), that you may grow strong, enjoy the good of the land, and leave it as an inheritance (heritage) to your children forever.' **13.** After all that has befallen us for our sinful deeds (wrong actions) and our great guilt, You, our God, have punished us less than our iniquities deserve, and have granted us this deliverance (rescue). **14.** Should we then break Your commandments again and join with the people who are committing these abominations (evil acts)? Would You not be angry (mad) with us until You had completely wiped us out, leaving no remnant or survivor (someone left alive)? **15.** O Lord, God of Israel, You are righteous (just), for we are left as a remnant, as it is today. Here we are before You, in our guilt (sin), though no one can stand before You because of it."

Chapter 10

1. As Ezra prayed, confessing (admitting sin), weeping, and bowing before the house of God, a large crowd of people—men, women, and children—gathered around him from Israel. They were deeply distressed (full of sorrow), crying bitterly. **2.** Shechaniah, son of Jehiel from Elam's family, spoke up and said to Ezra, "We have sinned against our God by marrying foreign women from the nations around us. However, there is still hope for Israel, despite our failure." **3.** "Let us now make a binding agreement (covenant) with our God, to send away all these wives and their children, as advised by my master and those who respect God's commands. Let us do this according to the law." **4.** "Rise up! This is your duty, and we will support you. Be strong and act without delay." **5.** Ezra then stood and made the leaders of the priests, Levites, and all Israel swear an oath to follow this decision. And they took the oath. **6.** Ezra stood up and left the house of God, heading to the room of Jehohanan, son of Eliashib. There, he ate no food and drank no water, for he mourned deeply over the guilt of those returning from exile. **7.** A public announcement was made throughout Judah and Jerusalem, calling all the exiles to gather in Jerusalem. **8.** Anyone who refused to come within three days, as instructed by the leaders and elders, would have their property confiscated (taken away) and would be excluded from the assembly of the exiles. **9.** All the men of Judah and Benjamin came to Jerusalem within three days, on the twentieth day of the ninth month. The people sat in the open square of the house of God, trembling with fear over the matter and in the heavy rain. **10.** Ezra the priest stood and spoke to them, saying, "You have sinned by marrying foreign women, and this has added to Israel's guilt. **11.** Therefore, confess (admit) your sin to the Lord, the God of your ancestors, and obey His will. Separate yourselves from the people of the land and from these foreign wives." **12.** The assembly responded loudly, "Yes! As you have said, we will obey." **13.** "However, there are many of us, and the rain is heavy, so we cannot stand in the open. This matter cannot be resolved in one or two days, because many of us have sinned in this way." **14.** "Let the leaders of our towns stand, and those who have taken foreign wives come at the appointed times, together with the elders and judges from their cities, so that God's wrath may be turned away from us in this matter." **15.** Only Jonathan, son of Asahel, and Jahaziah, son of Tikvah, opposed this, while Meshullam and Shabbethai the Levite supported them. **16.** The exiles followed the plan. Ezra, with some heads of families, set apart those from the households, and they began reviewing the situation on the first day of the tenth month. **17.** By the first day of the first month, they had finished questioning all the men who had married foreign women. **18.** Among the priests, the following men were found to have married foreign women: Maaseiah, Eliezer, Jarib, and Gedaliah, sons of Jeshua, son of Jozadak. **19.** They promised to send away their wives, and as restitution, they brought a ram from the flock as a guilt offering. **20.** From the descendants of Immer, there were Hanani and Zebadiah. **21.** From the sons of Harim, Maaseiah, Elijah, Shemaiah, Jehiel, and Uzziah. **22.** From the descendants of Pashhur, Elioenai, Maaseiah, Ishmael, Nethanel, Jozabad, and Elasah. **23.** From the Levites, Jozabad, Shimei, Kelaiah (also called Kelita), Pethahiah, Judah, and Eliezer. **24.** From the singers, Eliashib; and from the gatekeepers, Shallum, Telem, and Uri. **25.** Other Israelites included: from the sons of Parosh, Ramiah, Jeziah, Malchiah, Mijamin, Eleazar, Malchijah, and Benaiah; **26.** From the sons of Elam, Mattaniah, Zechariah, Jehiel, Abdi, Jeremoth, and Eliah; **27.** From the descendants of Zattu, Elioenai, Eliashib, Mattaniah, Jeremoth, Zabad, and Aziza; **28.** From the sons of Bebai, Jehohanan, Hananiah, Zabbai, and Athlai; **29.** From the descendants of Bani, Meshullam, Malluch, Adaiah, Jashub, Sheal, and Ramoth; **30.** From the sons of Pahath-Moab, Adna, Chelal, Benaiah, Maaseiah, Mattaniah, Bezalel, Binnui, and Manasseh; **31.** From the sons of Harim, Eliezer, Ishijah, Malchijah, Shemaiah, and Shimeon; **32.** From Benjamin, Malluch, Benjamin, and Shemariah; **33.** From the descendants of Hashum, Mattenai, Mattattah, Zabad, Eliphelet, Jeremai, Manasseh, and Shimei; **34.** From the sons of Bani, Maadai, Amram, Uel, **35.** Benaiah, Bedeiah, Cheluh, **36.** Vaniah, Meremoth, Eliashib, **37.** Mattaniah, Mattenai, Jaasai, **38.** Bani, Binnui, Shimei, **39.** Shelemiah, Nathan, Adaiah, **40.** Machnadebai, Shashai, Sharai, **41.** Azarel, Shelemiah, Shemariah, **42.** Shallum, Amariah, and Joseph; **43.** From the sons of Nebo, Jeiel, Mattithiah, Zabad, Zebina, Jaddai, Joel, and Benaiah. **44.** All of these men had married foreign women, and some of them had children by them.

16 – Nehemiah

Chapter 1

1. The words of Nehemiah son of Hakaliah (a man from Judah): In the month of Kislev (the ninth month in the Jewish calendar) in the twentieth year, while I was in the citadel (fortress) of Susa (the winter palace of the Persian kings), **2.** Hanani (Nehemiah's brother), one of my brothers, came from Judah (a kingdom of ancient Israel) with some men, and I questioned them about the Jewish remnant (the survivors of Israel) that had survived the exile (the Babylonian captivity), and also about Jerusalem (the capital of Israel). **3.** They said, "Those who survived the exile and are back in the province (a region of the Persian Empire) are in great trouble and disgrace. The wall of Jerusalem (the city's protective wall) is broken, and its gates have been burned with fire." **4.** When I heard this, I sat down and wept. For some days I mourned and fasted (a religious act to abstain from food) and prayed before the God of heaven. **5.** Then I said: "LORD, the God of heaven, the great and awesome God, who keeps his covenant (promise) of love with those who love him and keep his commandments, **6.** Let your ear be attentive and your eyes open to hear the prayer your servant (Nehemiah) prays day and night for your servants, the people of Israel (the Jewish people). I confess the sins we Israelites (the people of Israel), including myself and my father's family, have committed against you. **7.** We have acted wickedly toward you. We have not obeyed the commands (instructions), decrees (laws), and laws (regulations) you gave your servant Moses (the prophet). **8.** "Remember the instruction you gave Moses (the law on Mount Sinai), saying, 'If you are unfaithful (disobedient), I will scatter you among the nations (foreign lands), **9.** But if you return to me (repent) and obey my commands, then even if your exiled people (those in captivity) are at the farthest horizon (the ends of the earth), I will gather them and bring them to the place I have chosen as a dwelling for my Name (Jerusalem).' **10.** "They are your servants and your people, whom you redeemed (saved) by your great strength and mighty hand. **11.** Lord, let your ear be attentive to the prayer of this servant and to the prayer of your servants who revere your name (worship you). Give your servant success today by granting him favor (kindness) in the presence of this man (the Persian king)." I was cupbearer to the king (trusted servant to the Persian king).

Chapter 2

1. In the month of Nisan (the first month in the Jewish calendar) in the twentieth year of King Artaxerxes (the Persian king), when wine was brought for him, I took it and gave it to the king. I had not been sad in his presence before, **2.** So the king asked, "Why does your face look so sad when you are not ill? This can be nothing but sadness of heart." I was afraid, **3.** But I said, "May the king live forever! Why should my face not look sad when the city (Jerusalem) where my ancestors (forefathers) are buried lies in ruins, and its gates have been destroyed by fire?" **4.** The king asked, "What do you want?" Then I prayed to the God of heaven, **5.** And I answered, "If it pleases the king and your servant has found favor, let him send me to the city in Judah (the region of ancient Israel) where my ancestors are buried to rebuild it." **6.** The king, with the queen sitting beside him, asked, "How long will your journey take, and when will you return?" It pleased the king to send me; I set a time. **7.** I also asked, "If it pleases the king, may I have letters to the governors of Trans-Euphrates (the region west of the Euphrates River) for safe-conduct until I arrive in Judah (the region of Israel)? **8.** And may I have a letter to Asaph (a royal official), keeper of the royal park (the Persian king's forest), for timber (wood) to make beams for the citadel (fortress) gates, city wall, and my residence (house)?" And because the gracious hand (favor) of my God was on me, the king granted my requests. **9.** So I went to the governors of Trans-Euphrates (the region west of the Euphrates River) with the king's letters. The king had sent army officers (military leaders) and cavalry (horse soldiers) with me. **10.** When Sanballat the Horonite (a man from the region of Horon) and Tobiah the Ammonite official (a leader from the Ammonite people) heard, they were disturbed (angry) that someone had come to promote the welfare (well-being) of the Israelites (the Jewish people). **11.** I went to Jerusalem, and after three days, **12.** I set out at night with a few others. I had not told anyone what my God had put in my heart for Jerusalem. I had no mounts (horses or donkeys) except the one I was riding. **13.** By night, I went out through the Valley Gate (a gate in Jerusalem) toward the Jackal Well (a place near Jerusalem) and the Dung Gate (a gate for waste disposal), examining the walls of Jerusalem (the city's protective walls), which had been broken down, and its gates, which had been destroyed by fire. **14.** Then I moved on toward the Fountain Gate (a gate near a water source) and the King's Pool (a pool in Jerusalem), but my mount could not get through; **15.** So I went up the valley (a low area near Jerusalem) by night, examining the wall. Finally, I turned back and reentered through the Valley Gate (a gate in Jerusalem). **16.** The officials (leaders) did not know where I had gone or what I was doing, as I had said nothing to the Jews (the people of Israel), priests (religious leaders), nobles (leaders), or officials (administrators) who would be doing the work. **17.** Then I said to them, "You see the trouble we are in: Jerusalem lies in ruins, and its gates have been burned with fire. Come, let us rebuild the wall of Jerusalem, and we will no longer be in disgrace." **18.** I also told them about the gracious hand (favor) of my God on me and what the king had said. They replied, "Let us start rebuilding." So they began the work. **19.** But when Sanballat the Horonite (a man from Horon), Tobiah the Ammonite official (a leader from the Ammonites), and Geshem the Arab (a leader of Arab tribes) heard, they mocked (ridiculed) us. "What is this you are doing?" they asked. "Are you rebelling (defying authority) against the king?" **20.** I answered, "The God of heaven will give us success. His servants (God's people) will start rebuilding, but you have no share (claim or inheritance) in Jerusalem or any claim or historic right to it."

Chapter 3

Builders of the Wall

1. Eliashib (the high priest) and his priests rebuilt the Sheep Gate (a gate in Jerusalem), dedicating it and setting its doors in place, building as far as the Tower of the Hundred (a defensive tower) and the Tower of Hananel (another tower). **2.** The men of Jericho (a city in ancient Israel) built the adjoining section, and Zakkur son of Imri built next to them. **3.** The Fish Gate (where fish were sold) was rebuilt by the sons of Hassenaah. They laid beams and set doors, bolts, and bars. **4.** Meremoth son of Uriah repaired the next section. Next to him,

Meshullam son of Berekiah and Zadok son of Baana also made repairs. **5.** The men of Tekoa (a town in Judah) repaired the next section, but their nobles would not work under their supervisors. **6.** Joiada son of Paseah and Meshullam son of Besodeiah repaired the Jeshanah Gate (another gate), laying beams and setting doors, bolts, and bars. **7.** Men from Gibeon (a city in Israel) and Mizpah (another city) repaired the next section—Melatiah of Gibeon and Jadon of Meronoth. **8.** Uzziel son of Harhaiah, a goldsmith, repaired the next section, and Hananiah, a perfume-maker, made repairs up to the Broad Wall. **9.** Rephaiah son of Hur, ruler of a half-district, repaired the next section. **10.** Jedaiah son of Harumaph repaired opposite his house, and Hattush son of Hashabneiah made repairs next to him. **11.** Malkijah son of Harim and Hasshub son of Pahath-Moab repaired another section and the Tower of the Ovens. **12.** Shallum son of Hallohesh, ruler of a half-district, repaired the next section with his daughters. **13.** Hanun and the residents of Zanoah repaired the Valley Gate, putting its doors, bolts, and bars in place, and repaired a thousand cubits of the wall as far as the Dung Gate. **14.** Malkijah son of Rekab, ruler of Beth Hakkerem, repaired the Dung Gate, setting its doors, bolts, and bars in place. **15.** Shallun son of Kol-Hozeh, ruler of Mizpah, repaired the Fountain Gate, roofing it and setting its doors and bolts in place, and repaired the wall of the Pool of Siloam up to the steps of the City of David. **16.** Nehemiah son of Azbuk, ruler of Beth Zur, made repairs opposite the tombs of David, up to the artificial pool and the House of the Heroes. **17.** The Levites under Rehum son of Bani repaired the next section. Beside him, Hashabiah, ruler of Keilah, carried out repairs for his district. **18.** Binnui son of Henadad, ruler of the other half-district of Keilah, repaired the next section. **19.** Ezer son of Jeshua, ruler of Mizpah, repaired another section from the ascent to the armory up to the wall's angle. **20.** Baruch son of Zabbai zealously repaired from the angle to the entrance of Eliashib the high priest's house. **21.** Meremoth son of Uriah repaired from Eliashib's house to the end of it. **22.** The priests from the surrounding area made repairs next to him. **23.** Benjamin and Hasshub made repairs in front of their houses, and Azariah son of Maaseiah repaired beside his house. **24.** Binnui son of Henadad repaired from Azariah's house to the corner. **25.** Palal son of Uzai worked opposite the angle and the tower near the royal palace by the guard court. **26.** Pedaiah son of Parosh and the temple servants living on Ophel Hill made repairs as far as the Water Gate and the projecting tower. **27.** The men of Tekoa repaired another section from the great projecting tower to the wall of Ophel. **28.** The priests repaired above the Horse Gate, each in front of his house. **29.** Zadok son of Immer repaired opposite his house, and Shemaiah son of Shekaniah, the guard at the East Gate, made repairs. **30.** Hananiah son of Shelemiah and Hanun, the sixth son of Zalaph, repaired another section. Meshullam son of Berekiah made repairs opposite his living quarters. **31.** Malkijah, a goldsmith, repaired as far as the house of the temple servants and merchants, opposite the Inspection Gate, and as far as the room above the corner. **32.** Between the room above the corner and the Sheep Gate, the goldsmiths and merchants made repairs.

Chapter 4

Opposition to the Rebuilding

1. When Sanballat (Samaritan leader) heard we were rebuilding the wall, he became angry and mocked the Jews. **2.** In front of his associates and the Samarian army, he said, "What are these weak Jews doing? Can they restore their wall and bring the stones back from the burned rubble?" **3.** Tobiah the Ammonite added, "Even a fox would break their wall!" **4.** Hear us, God, for we are despised. Turn their insults on their heads and give them as plunder in a foreign land. **5.** Do not cover their guilt, for they have insulted the builders. **6.** So we rebuilt the wall until it reached half its height, for the people worked wholeheartedly. **7.** When Sanballat, Tobiah, the Arabs, Ammonites, and Ashdodites saw the progress, they became very angry. **8.** They plotted to fight against Jerusalem and cause trouble. **9.** We prayed to God and posted a guard day and night. **10.** The people in Judah said, "The workers are weakening, and the rubble is too much to rebuild." **11.** Our enemies said, "Before they know it, we will attack and end the work." **12.** Jews living near the enemies warned us repeatedly, "Wherever you turn, they will attack." **13.** I stationed people at the low points of the wall, armed with swords, spears, and bows. **14.** I told the nobles, officials, and people, "Don't be afraid. Remember the Lord, and

fight for your families." **15.** When the enemies heard we knew their plot and God frustrated it, we returned to work. **16.** Half of my men worked, while the other half were armed. **17.** Those carrying materials worked with one hand and held weapons in the other. **18.** Each builder wore a sword as he worked, while the man with the trumpet stayed with me. **19.** I told the leaders, "The work is extensive and spread out. When you hear the trumpet, join us. Our God will fight for us!" **20.** We worked with half the men holding spears, from dawn till night. **21.** I told the people to stay in Jerusalem at night, to serve as guards and workers. **22.** Neither I, my brothers, my men, nor the guards took off our clothes, and each had a weapon, even when fetching water.

Chapter 5

1. The people raised complaints against their fellow Jews (an ethno-religious group and nation originating in the Land of Israel). **2.** Some said, "We and our children are many, and we need food to survive." **3.** Others said, "We mortgaged (an agreement between you and a lender) our fields, vineyards, and homes to buy grain during the famine." **4.** Still others said, "We had to borrow money to pay the king's tax on our land and vineyards (it is vine and yard combined)." **5.** "Though we are of the same flesh as our fellow Jews and our children are as good as theirs, we must subject our sons and daughters to slavery. Some of our daughters are enslaved, but we are powerless since our fields and vineyards belong to others." **6.** I became very angry when I heard their complaints. **7.** After thinking, I accused the nobles and officials, saying, "You are charging interest to your own people!" I called a meeting to confront them. **8.** I said, "We bought back our fellow Jews who were sold to foreigners, but now you're selling your own people for us to buy back!" They remained silent. **9.** "What you're doing is wrong. Shouldn't you fear God to avoid dishonoring ourselves before our Gentile enemies?" **10.** "I, along with my brothers and men, have lent money and grain, but let's stop charging interest!" **11.** "Return their fields, vineyards, olive groves, and homes, and the interest you've charged—one percent on money, grain, wine, and olive oil." **12.** "We will give it back," they replied. "We won't demand more. We will do as you say." I called the priests and made them take an oath. **13.** I shook my robe, saying, "May God shake out of their house and possessions anyone who does not keep this promise!" The assembly said, "Amen," and praised the LORD. The people did as they promised. **14.** From the 20th year of King Artaxerxes (King of Persia) until his 32nd year, I did not take the governor's food allowance. **15.** Earlier governors burdened the people, taking forty shekels of silver, food, and wine, and even their assistants mistreated them. But out of respect for God, I didn't do this. **16.** I focused on rebuilding the wall, and my men did not buy land. **17.** I had 150 Jews and officials at my table, along with people from surrounding nations. **18.** Every day, one ox, six choice sheep, and poultry were prepared, and every ten days, an abundant supply of wine. Despite this, I never demanded the governor's food because the people were already burdened. **19.** Remember me favorably, my God, for all I have done for these people.

Chapter 6

1. When Sanballat (a leader of the Samaritans), Tobiah (a leader of the Ammonites), Geshem the Arab (a leader of the Arabs), and our enemies heard that I had rebuilt the wall and there were no gaps—though the gates hadn't yet been set— **2.** Sanballat and Geshem sent me this message: "Let's meet in one of the villages on the plain of Ono (a region near Judah)." But they were plotting to harm me. **3.** I replied, "I'm doing important work and can't come down. Why should the work stop while I leave?" **4.** Four times they sent the same message, and each time I gave the same answer. **5.** For the 5th time, Sanballat sent his aide with an unsealed letter. **6.** It said: "It's reported among the nations—and Geshem says it's true—that you and the Jews are planning to rebel, and that's why you're building the wall. You're about to become their king, and you've even appointed prophets to declare, 'There is a king in Judah!' The king (Artaxerxes) will hear about this, so let's meet." **7.** I replied, "Nothing like this is happening. You're just making it up." **8.** They were trying to frighten us, thinking, "Their hands will weaken (get tired or discouraged), and the work will stop." But I prayed, "Strengthen my hands." **9.** One day, I went to Shemaiah's house (a prophet) who was confined (shut up). He said, "Let's meet in the temple because men are coming to kill you—by night they will come." **10.** I replied, "Should a man like me run away? Should I enter the temple to save my life? No, I will not go!" **11.** I realized God hadn't sent him, but he was prophesying against me because Tobiah and Sanballat had hired him. **12.** He was hired to intimidate me into sinning (doing wrong) by fleeing and dishonoring myself, giving them a chance to discredit me. **13.** Remember Tobiah and Sanballat, my God, for what they have done, and also remember the prophet Noadiah (another false prophet) and other prophets who tried to intimidate me. **14.** The wall was completed on the 25th day of Elul (the sixth month of the Hebrew calendar), in 52 days. **15.** When our enemies heard, all surrounding nations were afraid and lost confidence because they realized this work was done with God's help. **16.** At that time, many nobles of Judah (leaders in Judah) were sending letters to Tobiah, and he was replying. **17.** Many in Judah were bound by oath (sworn to) to Tobiah, since he was the son-in-law of Shekaniah son of Arah, and his son Jehohanan married Meshullam's daughter. **18.** They reported his good deeds to me and told me what I said. Tobiah sent letters to intimidate me. **19.** They reported Tobiah's good deeds to me and then told me what I said. Tobiah also sent letters to intimidate (frighten or threaten) me.

Chapter 7

1. After the wall was rebuilt and the doors were set, I appointed gatekeepers (those who guarded the city gates), musicians (those who played music in worship), and Levites (members of the tribe of Levi, who helped with religious duties). **2.** I put my brother Hanani and Hananiah (Zerubbabel's son) in charge of Jerusalem, as he was a man of integrity and feared God more than most. **3.** I told them, "The gates of Jerusalem should not open until the sun is hot (until it's fully day). While the gatekeepers are on duty, have them shut and bar the doors. Also, appoint guards, some at their posts and some near their houses." **4.** The city was large and spacious, but few people lived in it, and the houses were not rebuilt. **5.** God put it into my heart to assemble the nobles (leaders), officials (government leaders), and common people for registration by families. I found the genealogical (family) record of those who had been the first to return. Here is what I found: **6.** These are the people of the province (region) who returned from the captivity of Nebuchadnezzar (king of Babylon), each to his own town. **7.** They returned with Zerubbabel (a leader), Joshua (the high priest), Nehemiah (the governor), Azariah, Raamiah, Nahamani, Mordecai (a prominent Jewish exile), Bilshan, Mispereth, Bigvai, Nehum, and Baanah. This is the list of the men of Israel: **8.** Descendants of Parosh: 2,172. **9.** Of Shephatiah: 372. **10.** Of Arah: 652. **11.** Of Pahath-Moab (through Jeshua and Joab): 2,818. **12.** Of Elam: 1,254. **13.** Of Zattu: 845. **14.** Of Zaccai: 760. **15.** Of Binnui: 648. **16.** Of Bebai: 628. **17.** Of Azgad: 2,322. **18.** Of Adonikam: 667. **19.** Of Bigvai: 2,067. **20.** Of Adin: 655. **21.** Of Ater (through Hezekiah): 98. **22.** Of Hashum: 328. **23.** Of Bezai: 324. **24.** Of Hariph: 112. **25.** Of Gibeon: 95. **26.** Men of Bethlehem and Netophah: 188. **27.** Of Anathoth: 128. **28.** Of Beth Azmaveth: 42. **29.** Of Kiriath Jearim, Kephirah, and Beeroth: 743. **30.** Of Ramah and Geba: 621. **31.** Of Micmash: 122. **32.** Of Bethel and Ai: 123. **33.** Of the other Nebo: 52. **34.** Of the other Elam: 1,254. **35.** Of Harim: 320. **36.** Of Jericho: 345. **37.** Of Lod, Hadid, and Ono: 721. **38.** Of Senaah: 3,930. **40.** Of Immer: 1,052. **41.** Of Pashhur: 1,247. **42.** Of Harim: 1,017. **44.** The musicians: **45.** The gatekeepers: **46.** The temple servants: **47.** Keros, Sia, Padon, **48.** Lebana, Hagaba, Shalmai, **49.** Hanan, Giddel, Gahar, **50.** Reaiah, Rezin, Nekoda, **51.** Gazzam, Uzza, Paseah, **52.** Besai, Meunim, Nephusim, **53.** Bakbuk, Hakupha, Harhur, **54.** Bazluth, Mehida, Harsha, **55.** Barkos, Sisera, Temah, **56.** Neziah, Hatipha. **57.** Descendants of the servants of Solomon: **58.** Jaala, Darkon, Giddel, **59.** Shephatiah, Hattil. **60.** The temple servants and descendants of the servants of Solomon: 392. **61.** Some from the towns of Tel Melah, Tel Harsha, Kerub, Addon, and Immer could not show their family records, so they were excluded from the priesthood as unclean. **62.** They searched for their family records but could not find them. **63.** The governor ordered them not to eat sacred food (food offered to God) until a priest ministered with the Urim and Thummim (objects used by the high priest). **64.** The total number was 42,360. **65.** Besides their 7,337 male and female slaves, and 245 male and female singers. **66.** There were 736 horses, 245 mules, **67.** 435 camels, and 6,720 donkeys. **70.** Some of the family heads contributed to the work. The governor gave 1,000 darics of gold, 50 bowls, and 530 garments for priests. **71.** Some family heads gave 20,000 darics of gold and 2,200 minas of silver.

72. The rest of the people gave 20,000 darics of gold, 2,000 minas of silver, and 67 garments for priests. **73.** The priests, Levites, gatekeepers, musicians, and temple servants, along with certain of the people, settled in their towns. By the seventh month, the Israelites had settled in their towns.

Chapter 8
Ezra Reads the Law

1. All the people gathered at the Water Gate (a well-known gate in Jerusalem) and asked Ezra, the teacher of the Law, to bring the Book of the Law of Moses, which the LORD had commanded for Israel. **2.** On the first day of the seventh month, Ezra the priest brought the Book of the Law before the assembly of men, women, and those who could understand. **3.** He read from it from morning till noon, standing at the Water Gate, and the people listened attentively. **4.** Ezra stood on a wooden platform with Mattithiah, Shema, Anaiah, Uriah, Hilkiah, and Maaseiah on his right, and Pedaiah, Mishael, Malkijah, Hashum, Hashbaddanah, Zechariah, and Meshullam on his left. **5.** When Ezra opened the book, the people stood up. **6.** Ezra praised the LORD, the great God, and the people said, "Amen! Amen!" Then they bowed down and worshiped the LORD. **7.** The Levites (members of the tribe of Levi, dedicated to temple service)—Jeshua, Bani, Sherebiah, Jamin, Akkub, Shabbethai, Hodiah, Maaseiah, Kelita, Azariah, Jozabad, Hanan, and Pelaiah—explained the Law. **8.** They read and made the meaning clear so the people could understand. **9.** Nehemiah the governor, Ezra the priest, and the Levites said, "This day is holy to the LORD; do not mourn (feel sadness) or weep (shed tears)." The people were weeping as they listened to the Law. **10.** Nehemiah said, "Go and enjoy food and sweet drinks, and share with those in need. This day is holy; do not grieve (feel sorrow), for the joy of the LORD is your strength." **11.** The Levites calmed the people, telling them, "Be still (remain calm), for this is a holy day; do not be sad." **12.** The people went to eat, drink, share with the needy, and celebrate with joy, for they understood the words explained to them. **13.** On the second day, the heads of the families, priests, and Levites gathered to study the Law more carefully. **14.** They found that the Israelites were to live in temporary shelters during the festival of the seventh month. **15.** They proclaimed (announced), "Go into the hill country for branches from olive, wild olive, myrtles, palms, and other leafy trees to make shelters," as written in the Law. **16.** The people went out and brought branches to make shelters on their roofs, courtyards, temple courts, and the squares near the Water Gate and Gate of Ephraim. **17.** The entire assembly built shelters and lived in them. Since the time of Joshua son of Nun (the leader after Moses), the Israelites had not celebrated the Feast of Tabernacles (festival of temporary shelters) this way, and their joy was very great. **18.** Every day, from the first to the last, Ezra read from the Book of the Law. They celebrated the festival for seven days, and on the eighth day, there was a solemn (serious) assembly.

Chapter 9
The Israelites Confess Their Sins

1. On the twenty-fourth day of the month, the Israelites gathered, fasting, wearing sackcloth (rough cloth), and placing dust on their heads. **2.** They separated from foreigners, stood in their places, confessed their sins and those of their ancestors. **3.** For a quarter of the day, they read from the Book of the Law and for another quarter, they confessed their sins and worshiped the LORD. **4.** On the stairs, the Levites were Jeshua, Bani, Kadmiel, Shebaniah, Bunni, Sherebiah, Bani, and Kenani. They cried out loudly to the LORD their God. **5.** The Levites said: "Stand and praise the LORD your God, who is from everlasting to everlasting. Blessed be Your glorious (magnificent) name, exalted above all praise." **6.** "You alone are the LORD. You made the heavens, the earth, the seas, and everything in them. You give life to all, and the heavenly beings worship You." **7.** "You are the LORD God who chose Abram, bringing him out of Ur of the Chaldeans, and made him Abraham. You made a covenant (agreement) to give his descendants the land of the Canaanites, Hittites, Amorites, Perizzites, Jebusites, and Girgashites. You kept Your promise because You are righteous (just)." **8.** "You saw the suffering of our ancestors in Egypt and heard their cry at the Red Sea. You sent signs against Pharaoh and his officials. You divided the sea for them, allowing them to pass through, and hurled their enemies into the deep (ocean)." **9.** "By day, You led them with a pillar of cloud, and by night, with a pillar of fire to guide their journey."

10. "You came down on Mount Sinai and spoke from heaven. You gave them just (fair) laws, commands, and decrees (orders)." **11.** "You revealed the Sabbath and gave commands through Moses. You provided bread from heaven when they were hungry and water from the rock when they were thirsty. You told them to take possession of the promised land." **12.** "But our ancestors became proud, stubborn (refused to change), and disobedient. They forgot Your miracles and chose a leader to return to slavery. Yet, You are forgiving, gracious, slow to anger, and abounding in love. You did not abandon them." **13.** "Even when they made an idol of a calf and called it their god, committing blasphemy (disrespect for God), You did not abandon them." **14.** "In Your mercy, You did not forsake (abandon) them in the desert. The pillar of cloud and fire continued to guide them. You gave them Your good Spirit, provided manna (bread from heaven), and gave them water to drink." **15.** "For forty years, You sustained (kept alive) them; their clothes did not wear out, and their feet did not swell." **16.** "You gave them kingdoms and nations, including the lands of Sihon and Og. **17.** You made their children as numerous (many) as the stars and brought them into the promised land, where they subdued (conquered) the Canaanites and took possession of the land, kings, and peoples." **18.** "They captured cities and fertile (rich) land, wells, vineyards, olive groves, and fruit trees. They ate and were satisfied with Your great goodness." **19.** "But they became disobedient, turning their backs on Your law, killing Your prophets, and committing terrible sins." **20.** "So You delivered (rescued) them into the hands of their enemies. When they cried out, You heard them and sent deliverers to rescue them in Your great compassion." **21.** But once at peace, they did evil again. You abandoned them to enemies, and when they cried out, You heard from heaven and, in Your mercy (compassion), rescued them repeatedly. **22.** You warned them to return to Your law, but they became proud (arrogant) and disobeyed. They sinned against Your commands, which give life to those who obey. They stubbornly (obstinately) refused to listen. **23.** For many years You were patient, warning them through Your prophets (spokespersons), but they ignored You. So You handed them over to neighboring peoples. **24.** But in Your great mercy, You did not destroy them, for You are a gracious (kind) and merciful God. **25.** "Now, our God, the great God, mighty and awesome (awe-inspiring), who keeps His covenant (agreement) of love, do not let all this hardship (suffering) seem small in Your eyes— the suffering of us, our kings, leaders, priests, prophets, ancestors, and all Your people, from the kings of Assyria (ancient empire) to this day. **26.** You remained righteous (just), though we acted wickedly. Our kings, leaders, priests, and ancestors did not obey Your law or heed (pay attention to) Your commands or statutes (rules). **27.** Even while enjoying prosperity (wealth) in the land You gave, they did not serve You or turn from their evil ways." **28.** "Now we are slaves (servants) in the land You gave our ancestors to enjoy its good things. **29.** Because of our sins, its harvest goes to the kings You placed over us, who rule over us and our livestock (animals) as they wish. We are in great distress (trouble)." **30.** "In view of all this, we are making a binding (firm) agreement, putting it in writing, with our leaders, Levites (priests), and priests affixing (attaching) their seals." **31.** But in Your great mercy, You did not end them or abandon them, for You are a gracious and merciful God. **32.** "Now, our God, the great God, mighty and awesome, who keeps Your covenant of love, do not let this hardship seem trivial (insignificant) in Your eyes—the hardship that has come on us, on our kings, leaders, priests, prophets, ancestors, and all Your people, from the kings of Assyria until today. **33.** In all that has happened to us, You have remained righteous; You have acted faithfully, while we acted wickedly. **34.** Our kings, leaders, priests, and ancestors did not follow Your law; they did not heed Your commands or statutes. **35.** Even while in their kingdom, enjoying Your goodness in the fertile (productive) land You gave them, they did not serve You or turn from their evil ways. **36.** "But see, we are slaves today, in the land You gave our ancestors to enjoy its fruit and other good things. **37.** Because of our sins, its harvest goes to the kings You placed over us, who rule over our bodies and cattle as they please. We are in great distress." **38.** "In view of all this, we are making a binding agreement, putting it in writing, and our leaders, Levites, and priests are affixing their seals."

Chapter 10

The Agreement of the People

1. Those who signed the agreement were: Nehemiah (comforted by God), the governor, son of Hakaliah, and Zedekiah (righteousness of Yahweh). **2.** Seraiah (Yahweh is ruler), Azariah (Yahweh has helped), Jeremiah (Yahweh will exalt). **3.** Pashhur (split or liberation), Amariah (Yahweh has promised), Malkijah (my king is Yahweh). **4.** Hattush (assembled), Shebaniah (grown up by Yahweh), Malluk (counselor). **5.** Harim (dedicated), Meremoth (heights), Obadiah (servant of Yahweh). **6.** Daniel (God is my judge), Ginnethon (garden), Baruch (blessed). **7.** Meshullam (devoted), Abijah (Yahweh is my father), Mijamin (right hand). **8.** Maaziah (consolation of Yahweh), Bilgai (my delight), Shemaiah (heard by Yahweh). **9.** Levites (assistants in worship): Jeshua (Yahweh is salvation), Kadmiel (God is ancient). **10.** Shebaniah (grown up by Yahweh), Hodiah (majesty of Yahweh), Kelita (crippled), Pelaiah (distinguished by Yahweh), Hanan (gracious). **11.** Mika (who is like Yahweh), Rehob (broad), Hashabiah (Yahweh has considered). **12.** Zakkur (mindful), Sherebiah (Yahweh has scorched), Hodiah (majesty of Yahweh). **13.** Bani (built), Beninu (our son). **14.** Parosh (flea), Pahath-Moab (governor of Moab), Elam (eternity), Zattu (olive tree), Bani (built). **15.** Azgad (strong is Gad), Bebai (fatherly). **16.** Adonijah (Yahweh is my Lord), Bigvai (in my body), Adin (delicate). **17.** Ater (left-handed), Hezekiah (Yahweh strengthens), Azzur (helper). **18.** Hodiah (majesty of Yahweh), Hashum (rich), Bezai (eggs). **19.** Hariph (autumn rain), Anathoth (answers), Nebai (fruitful). **20.** Magpiash (moth-killer), Meshullam (devoted), Hezir (swine). **21.** Meshezabel (God delivers), Zadok (righteous), Jaddua (known). **22.** Pelatiah (Yahweh delivers), Hanan (gracious), Anaiah (Yahweh answers). **23.** Hoshea (salvation), Hananiah (Yahweh is gracious), Hasshub (considerate). **24.** Hallohesh (whisperer), Pilha (miracle worker), Shobek (weaver). **25.** Rehum (compassionate), Hashabnah (Yahweh reckons), Maaseiah (work of Yahweh). **26.** Ahiah (brother of Yahweh), Hanan (gracious), Anan (cloud). **27.** Malluk (counselor), Harim (dedicated), Baanah (in affliction). **28.** The people, including priests, Levites (assistants in worship), gatekeepers (guards of temple gates), musicians (worship singers), and temple servants (helpers in temple rituals), separated themselves from surrounding nations to obey God's Law. **29.** They joined their fellow Israelites and made a binding agreement to follow God's Law and commands. **30.** They pledged not to intermarry with surrounding nations. **31.** They promised not to buy or sell goods on the Sabbath (holy day of rest) and to forgive debts every seventh year. **32.** They agreed to contribute to the temple's service and upkeep. **33.** They vowed to support temple rituals, offerings, and festivals. **34.** They organized wood supply for altar sacrifices. **35.** They agreed to bring their first fruits (initial portion of harvest) to the temple. **36.** They would offer their firstborn and first harvest portions to God. **37.** They vowed to store grain, wine, and oil in the temple storerooms for the Levites. **38.** A priest would oversee tithes (10% offerings). **39.** The people affirmed their dedication to supporting God's house.

Chapter 11

The New Residents of Jerusalem

1. Now the leaders of the people settled in Jerusalem (the capital city). The rest of the people cast lots (drew lots) to bring one out of every ten of them to live in Jerusalem, the holy city (Jerusalem is considered sacred), while the remaining nine stayed in their own towns. **2.** The people commended (praised) all who volunteered to live in Jerusalem. **3.** These are the provincial leaders (local rulers) who settled in Jerusalem (now some Israelites, priests, Levites, temple servants, and descendants of Solomon's servants lived in the towns of Judah, each on their own property in the various towns). **4.** While other people from both Judah (one of the tribes of Israel) and Benjamin (two of the tribes of Israel) lived in Jerusalem: From the descendants of Judah: Athaiah, son of Uzziah, the son of Zechariah, the son of Amariah, the son of Shephatiah, the son of Mahalalel, a descendant of Perez (a son of Judah); **5.** and Maaseiah, son of Baruch, the son of Kol-Hozeh, the son of Hazaiah, the son of Adaiah, the son of Joiarib, the son of Zechariah, a descendant of Shelah (another family branch of Judah). **6.** The descendants of Perez who lived in Jerusalem totaled 468 men of standing (those with notable rank or importance). **7.** From the descendants of Benjamin: Sallu, son of Meshullam, the son of Joed, the son of Pedaiah, the son of Kolaiah, the son of Maaseiah, the son of Ithiel, the son of Jeshaiah, **8.** and his followers, Gabbai and Sallai—928 men. **9.** Joel, son of Zikri, was their chief officer (leader), and Judah, son of Hassenuah, was over the New Quarter (the newly rebuilt part) of the city. **10.** From the priests: Jedaiah, son of Joiarib, Jakin, **11.** Seraiah, son of Hilkiah, the son of Meshullam, the son of Zadok (a high priest), the son of Meraioth, the son of Ahitub, the official in charge of the house of God (the temple), **12.** and their associates, who carried out the temple work—822 men; Adaiah, son of Jeroham, the son of Pelaliah, the son of Amzi, the son of Zechariah, the son of Pashhur, the son of Malkijah, **13.** and his associates, heads of families—242 men; Amashsai, son of Azarel, the son of Ahzai, the son of Meshillemoth, the son of Immer, **14.** and his associates, men of standing—128. Their chief officer was Zabdiel, son of Haggedolim. **15.** From the Levites (those who assisted in religious duties): Shemaiah, son of Hasshub, the son of Azrikam, the son of Hashabiah, the son of Bunni; **16.** Shabbethai and Jozabad, two of the heads of the Levites, who had charge of the outside work of the house of God; **17.** Mattaniah, son of Mika, the son of Zabdi, the son of Asaph (a musician), the director who led in thanksgiving and prayer; Bakbukiah, second among his associates; and Abda, son of Shammua, the son of Galal, the son of Jeduthun. **18.** The Levites in the holy city (Jerusalem) totaled 284. **19.** The gatekeepers (those who guarded the temple gates): Akkub, Talmon, and their associates, who kept watch at the gates—172 men. **20.** The rest of the Israelites, with the priests and Levites, lived in all the towns of Judah, each on their ancestral property. **21.** The temple servants (workers dedicated to temple duties) lived on the hill of Ophel (a part of Jerusalem), and Ziha and Gishpa were in charge of them. **22.** The chief officer of the Levites in Jerusalem was Uzzi, son of Bani, the son of Hashabiah, the son of Mattaniah, the son of Mika. Uzzi was one of Asaph's descendants (Asaph was a famous musician), who were responsible for the music service in the house of God. **23.** The musicians were under the king's orders, which regulated their daily activity. **24.** Pethahiah, son of Meshezabel, one of the descendants of Zerah, son of Judah, was the king's agent in all matters concerning the people. **25.** As for the villages with their fields, some of the people of Judah lived in: Kiriath Arba and its surrounding settlements (a town near Hebron), Dibon and its settlements, Jekabzeel and its villages, **26.** Jeshua, Moladah, Beth Pelet, **27.** Hazar Shual, Beersheba and its settlements (a major town in southern Judah), **28.** Ziklag, Mekonah and its settlements, **29.** En Rimmon, Zorah, Jarmuth, **30.** Zanoah, Adullam and their villages, Lachish and its fields, Azekah and its settlements. So they were living all the way from Beersheba (southernmost town of Judah) to the Valley of Hinnom (a valley south of Jerusalem, often associated with idolatry where children were burnt). **31.** The descendants of the Benjamites from Geba (a town in Benjamin) lived in Mikmash, Aija, Bethel, and its settlements, **32.** Anathoth (a town in Benjamin), Nob and Ananiah, **33.** Hazor, Ramah and Gittaim, **34.** Hadid, Zeboim and Neballat, **35.** Lod and Ono, and Ge Harashim (towns in Benjamin). **36.** Some of the divisions of the Levites of Judah settled in Benjamin.

Chapter 12

Priests and Levites

1. The priests and Levites who returned with Zerubbabel (a Babylonian Jew) and Joshua were: Seraiah, Jeremiah, Ezra. **2.** Amariah, Malluk, Hattush, Shekaniah, Rehum, Meremoth. **3.** Iddo, Ginnethon (a priest who sealed the covenant with Nehemiah), Abijah, Mijamin, Moadiah, Bilgah. **4.** Shemaiah, Joiarib, Jedaiah, Sallu, Amok, Hilkiah, and Jedaiah. These were the leaders during Joshua's time (post-exile high priest). **5.** The Levites included Jeshua, Binnui, Kadmiel, Sherebiah, Judah, and Mattaniah (in charge of thanksgiving songs). **6.** Bakbukiah and Unni, their associates, were stationed opposite them in services. **7.** Joshua's descendants included Joiakim, Eliashib, Joiada, Jonathan, and Jaddua (continuing the high priest lineage). **8.** In Joiakim's day, the heads of the priestly families were: Seraiah's, Meraiah; Jeremiah's, Hananiah; Ezra's, Meshullam. **9.** Amariah's, Jehohanan; Malluk's, Jonathan; Shekaniah's, Joseph; Harim's, Adna. **10.** Meremoth's, Helkai; Iddo's, Zechariah; Ginnethon's, Meshullam; Abijah's, Zikri. **11.** Miniamin's and Moadiah's, Piltai; Bilgah's, Shammua; Shemaiah's, Jehonathan. **12.** Joiarib's, Mattenai; Jedaiah's, Uzzi; Sallu's, Kallai; Amok's, Eber. **13.** Hilkiah's, Hashabiah; Jedaiah's, Nethanel. **14.** The family heads of the Levites during the time of Eliashib, Joiada, Johanan, and Jaddua were recorded in Darius' reign (Persian Empire). **15.** The Levite family heads up to Johanan were listed in the annals (historical records). **16.** The

Levite leaders were Hashabiah, Sherebiah, and Jeshua (son of Kadmiel), who gave praise as per David's prescribed practice. **17.** Mattaniah, Bakbukiah, Obadiah, Meshullam, Talmon, and Akkub were gatekeepers (those guarding the storerooms). **18.** They served during the days of Joiakim, Nehemiah, and Ezra, the teacher of the Law. **19.** At the dedication of the wall of Jerusalem, Levites were brought from their towns to celebrate with thanksgiving and music. **20.** Musicians came from Netophathites (a group of musicians), Beth Gilgal, Geba, and Azmaveth (towns near Jerusalem). **21.** The priests and Levites purified themselves, the people, the gates, and the walls ceremonially. **22.** Leaders of Judah went up on the wall, and two choirs gave thanks, one heading towards the Dung Gate (used for waste). **23.** Hoshaiah, half the leaders, and priests, including Ezra, followed with musical instruments. **24.** The choirs proceeded towards the City of David, passing the Water Gate and continuing their praise. **25.** The second choir went in the opposite direction, past the Tower of the Ovens, the Gate of Ephraim, and other gates. **26.** The two choirs gathered at the house of God, along with officials and priests, offering thanks. **27.** They celebrated with sacrifices and great joy, and the sound of rejoicing was heard throughout Jerusalem. **28.** Officials were assigned to manage the storerooms for tithes and contributions, ensuring Judah supported the priestly service. **29.** The priests, Levites, musicians, and gatekeepers performed their duties as commanded by David and Solomon. **30.** In the days of Zerubbabel and Nehemiah, all Israel contributed daily portions for the service, ensuring support for the Levites and priests. **31.** I had Judah's leaders ascend the wall and assigned two large choirs to give thanks. One choir went toward the Dung Gate (a gate used for waste disposal). **32.** Hoshaiah and half of Judah's leaders followed. **33.** Along with Azariah, Ezra, Meshullam, **34.** Judah, Benjamin, Shemaiah, and Jeremiah. **35.** Priests with trumpets also joined, including Zechariah, son of Jonathan, son of Shemaiah, son of Mattaniah, son of Micaiah, son of Zakkur, son of Asaph. **36.** His associates—Shemaiah, Azarel, Milalai, Gilalai, Maai, Nethanel, Judah, and Hanani—played instruments prescribed by David. Ezra led the procession. **37.** At the Fountain Gate (in southern Jerusalem), they climbed the steps to the City of David (ancient Jerusalem) and proceeded toward the Water Gate (in the east). **38.** The second choir moved in the opposite direction. I followed with half the people, passing the Tower of the Ovens (a defensive tower) to the Broad Wall. **39.** We continued past the Gate of Ephraim (northern Jerusalem), the Jeshanah Gate, the Fish Gate (used by merchants), the Tower of Hananel, the Tower of the Hundred, and the Sheep Gate, stopping at the Gate of the Guard (a security gate). **40.** Both choirs took their places in the house of God, along with half of the officials. **41.** The priests—Eliakim, Maaseiah, Miniamin, Micaiah, Elioenai, Zechariah, and Hananiah—played trumpets. **42.** Along with Maaseiah, Shemaiah, Eleazar, Uzzi, Jehohanan, Malkijah, Elam, and Ezer, the choirs sang under the direction of Jezrahiah. **43.** That day, great sacrifices were offered, and the people celebrated with joy, for God had given them great gladness. Women and children also rejoiced, and the sound of their celebration was heard far away. **44.** Men were appointed to oversee the storerooms where contributions, first fruits, and tithes were kept. These portions were brought for the priests and Levites as Judah honored them. **45.** The priests and Levites performed their duties, including purification rituals, alongside musicians and gatekeepers, as commanded by David and Solomon. **46.** Since David and Asaph's time, there had been directors for the musicians and songs of praise and thanksgiving. **47.** In the days of Zerubbabel and Nehemiah, all Israel contributed daily portions for the musicians, gatekeepers, and Levites. The Levites, in turn, set aside portions for the descendants of Aaron.

Chapter 13

Nehemiah's Final Reforms

1. On that day, the Book of Moses was read, revealing that no Ammonite (descendants of Lot, enemies of Israel) or Moabite (another group from Lot's descendants) should be admitted into God's assembly. **2.** This was because they did not help Israel with food and water and hired Balaam (a prophet for hire) to curse them, but God turned the curse into a blessing. **3.** When the people heard this law, they excluded foreigners from Israel. **4.** Eliashib (a priest) had been in charge of the temple storerooms but allowed Tobiah (enemy leader) to use a room meant for offerings. **5.** Tobiah had used a large room that stored grain offerings, incense, and the tithes for Levites, musicians, and priests. **6.** While this was happening, I (Nehemiah) was away serving King Artaxerxes (Persian king) and later returned to find the misuse of the temple room. **7.** I was greatly displeased and threw out all of Tobiah's belongings. **8.** I purified the rooms and restored them with temple items like grain offerings and incense. **9.** I also learned the Levites had not received their portions, so they returned to their fields. **10.** I rebuked the officials, asking why the house of God had been neglected, and stationed them at their posts. **11.** All Judah brought their tithes of grain, wine, and olive oil to the storerooms. **12.** I appointed trustworthy men like Shelemiah, Zadok, Pedaiah, and Hanan to oversee the storerooms and distribute supplies. **13.** "Remember me, my God, for what I have faithfully done for Your house." **14.** I saw people in Judah working on the Sabbath, bringing goods like grain, wine, and figs into Jerusalem. **15.** People from Tyre (Phoenician city) were selling fish and merchandise in Jerusalem on the Sabbath. **17.** I rebuked the nobles of Judah for desecrating the Sabbath, as their ancestors had, which brought disaster upon the city. **19.** I ordered the gates of Jerusalem to be closed before the Sabbath and stationed guards to prevent goods from being brought in. **21.** I warned merchants they would be arrested if they continued to spend the night outside Jerusalem. **22.** I commanded the Levites to purify themselves and guard the gates to keep the Sabbath holy. "Remember me for this, my God, and show mercy according to Your great love." **23.** I saw men from Judah marrying women from Ashdod (Philistine city), Ammon, and Moab. **24.** Half of their children spoke foreign languages and did not know Hebrew. **25.** I rebuked them, calling curses down on them, pulling out their hair, and making them swear not to intermarry. **26.** I reminded them that even Solomon (king of Israel) sinned because of foreign marriages, though no king was like him. **27.** I asked them, "Are you doing this wickedness by marrying foreign women and being unfaithful to our God?" **28.** One of Eliashib's sons had married Sanballat (enemy leader), and I drove him away. **29.** "Remember them, my God, for defiling the priesthood and the covenant." **30.** I purified the priests and Levites from foreign influences and assigned them duties according to the law. **31.** I arranged for regular offerings of wood and firstfruits. "Remember me with favor, my God."

17 – Ezra (2nd) and Ezra Sutuel

Esdras 1

Chapter 1

1. Josiah celebrated the Passover in Jerusalem for the Lord, offering it on the fourteenth day of the first month. **2.** He arranged the priests in their respective divisions, dressed in their garments, within the temple of the Lord. **3.** Josiah instructed the Levites (temple servants of Israel) to consecrate themselves to the Lord and place the ark of God in the temple that King Solomon, son of David, had built. **4.** He told them, "You no longer need to carry the ark on your shoulders. Instead, serve the Lord your God, minister to His people Israel, and prepare yourselves according to your family divisions." **5.** "Follow the instructions given by King David of Israel and the grandeur of his son Solomon. Stand in the holy place according to your Levitical family divisions, ministering alongside your fellow Israelites." **6.** "Prepare the Passover in order, offering the sacrifices for your families, and keep the Passover as commanded by the Lord through Moses." **7.** Josiah provided thirty thousand lambs and kids, and three thousand calves, all from the royal treasury, to the people, priests, and Levites as promised. **8.** The temple officials—Helkiah, Zacharias, and Esyelus— gave two thousand six hundred sheep and three hundred calves to the priests for the Passover. **9.** Jeconiah, Samaias, Nathanael, his brother, Sabias, Ochielus, and Joram, commanders over thousands, contributed five thousand sheep and seven hundred calves to the Levites for the Passover. **10.** When everything was ready, the priests and Levites, with the unleavened bread, stood in their proper divisions, according to their families, before the people. **11.** According to the law of Moses, they offered sacrifices in the morning. **12.** They roasted the Passover lambs with fire as required, and boiled the sacrifices in large vessels, giving off a pleasing aroma. **13.** These were set before all the people, after which the priests, the sons of Aaron, prepared for themselves and their families. **14.** The priests offered the fat until evening, while the Levites prepared for themselves and the priests, the sons of Aaron. **15.** The singers, descendants of Asaph, were arranged in their order as appointed by King David—Asaph, Zacharias, and Eddinus, who represented the king. **16.** Gatekeepers were stationed at every gate, and no one had to leave their post, as the Levites made preparations for them. **17.** All the Lord's sacrificial duties were fulfilled that day, as the Passover was kept. **18.** The sacrifices were offered on the altar of the Lord, as commanded by King Josiah. **19.** The Israelites present celebrated the Passover and the Feast of Unleavened Bread for seven days. **20.** No Passover like this had been held in Israel since the time of the prophet Samuel. **21.** In fact, no king of Israel had celebrated such a Passover as Josiah, with the priests, Levites, and all Israel present in Jerusalem. **22.** This Passover was held in the eighteenth year of King Josiah's reign. **23.** Josiah's actions were righteous before the Lord, with a heart full of devotion. **24.** The events of his reign have been recorded, showing the people who sinned against the Lord more grievously than any other nation or kingdom. **25.** After these events, Pharaoh Necho of Egypt marched to Carchemish (a city on the Euphrates River) to wage war, and Josiah went out to meet him. **26.** But Pharaoh sent a message to Josiah, saying, "What have I to do with you, O King of Judah? **27.** I have not come against you, but against the Euphrates. The Lord is with me, hastening my progress. Turn back and do not oppose the Lord." **28.** Despite the warning from the prophet Jeremiah, Josiah did not turn away, but fought him at Megiddo. **29.** In the battle, the commanders came down upon Josiah. **30.** Josiah said to his servants, "Take me out of the battle, for I am badly wounded!" So they carried him away from the battlefield. **31.** He was placed in his second chariot, and after being returned to Jerusalem, he died and was buried in the tombs of his ancestors. **32.** All Judah mourned for Josiah. The prophet Jeremiah lamented for him, and even the leading men and women of the land mourned his death, and this became a lasting tradition in Israel. **33.** These events are recorded in the history of the kings of Judah, including all the works Josiah did, his righteousness, and his understanding of the law of the Lord. **34.** The people made Josiah's son Jehoahaz king in his place, when he was twenty-three years old. **35.** Jehoahaz reigned in Jerusalem for three months, but the King of Egypt deposed him. **36.** Pharaoh imposed a tribute on the people of Judah, one hundred talents of silver and one talent of gold. **37.** Pharaoh then appointed Jehoahaz's brother, Jehoiakim, as king over Judah and Jerusalem. **38.** Jehoiakim took action against the nobles and captured his brother, bringing him from Egypt. **39.** Jehoiakim was twenty-five years old when he began to reign in Judah. He did evil in the sight of the Lord. **40.** King Nebuchadnezzar of Babylon came against him, bound him with bronze chains, and took him to Babylon. **41.** Nebuchadnezzar also took sacred vessels from the temple of the Lord, carrying them away and placing them in his own temple in Babylon. **42.** The details of Jehoiakim's reign, including his wickedness and impurity, are written in the chronicles of the kings. **43.** Jehoiakim's son Jeconiah succeeded him as king at eighteen years old. **44.** He reigned for three months and ten days, doing evil in the sight of the Lord. **45.** After a year, Nebuchadnezzar summoned him to Babylon, along with the sacred vessels. **46.** Nebuchadnezzar appointed Zedekiah as king of Judah when he was twenty-one years old. He ruled for eleven years. **47.** Zedekiah also did evil in the sight of the Lord and disregarded the words of the prophet Jeremiah. **48.** Despite swearing an oath to the Lord, Zedekiah broke his vow, rebelled, and hardened his heart, transgressing the laws of God. **49.** The leaders of the people and priests also committed great wickedness, defiling the temple of the Lord in Jerusalem. **50.** The God of their ancestors sent messengers to call them back, showing His compassion for them and His temple. **51.** But they mocked the messengers and scoffed at the prophets sent by the Lord. **52.** Eventually, the Lord became angry and commanded the Chaldeans to come against them. **53.** They killed the young men around the temple and spared no one, delivering them all into the hands of the invaders. **54.** The Chaldeans took all the sacred vessels, large and small, including the treasure chests, and carried them away to Babylon. **55.** They burned the house of the Lord, tore down Jerusalem's walls, and set fire to its towers. **56.** They destroyed all the glorious things of the city until nothing was left. The surviving people were taken to Babylon as captives. **57.** They remained in Babylon as servants to the king and his children until the rise of the Persian Empire, fulfilling the prophecy of Jeremiah. **58.** "The land must enjoy its Sabbaths; the entire duration of its desolation will keep the Sabbath, fulfilling seventy years."

Chapter 2

1. In the first year of King Cyrus (King of Persia), when the word of the Lord spoken by the prophet Jeremiah (a major prophet of Israel) was about to be fulfilled, **2.** the Lord stirred the heart of King Cyrus (the ruler of the Persian Empire) and he issued a proclamation throughout his entire kingdom, also writing it down, **3.** stating, "Cyrus, king of Persia, declares: The LORD of Israel has made me ruler of the entire world, **4.** and has commanded me to rebuild His temple in Jerusalem (the capital city of Israel), which is in Judea (a region in ancient Israel). **5.** So, if any of His people are among you, let them go to Jerusalem in Judea to build the temple of the Lord, the God of Israel, who dwells in Jerusalem. **6.** And those who remain in other regions should help them by providing gold, silver, gifts, horses, and cattle, along with offerings made for the temple in Jerusalem. **7.** Then the leaders of the families of Judah (a tribe of Israel) and Benjamin (another tribe of Israel), along with the priests, Levites (members of the tribe of Levi assigned to religious duties), and anyone whom the Lord had stirred up, prepared to go up to build the Lord's temple in Jerusalem. **8.** Those around them assisted with gifts of silver, gold, horses, cattle, and many other gifts, in fulfillment of vows made for the temple of the Lord in Jerusalem. **9.** King Cyrus also gave back the sacred vessels of the Lord, which King Nebuchadnezzar (the Babylonian king) had taken from Jerusalem and placed in the temple of his gods. **10.** When King Cyrus brought these vessels out, he entrusted them to his treasurer, Mithridates, (Mithridates was the treasurer of King Cyrus), **11.** who then handed them over to Sanabassar (the governor of Judea), **12.** and this was the inventory: one thousand gold cups, one thousand silver cups, twenty-nine silver censers, thirty gold bowls, two thousand four hundred ten silver bowls, and one thousand other vessels. **13.** In total, there were 5,479 vessels of gold and silver. **14.** These were carried by Sanabassar, together with the exiles, back from Babylon (the capital city of the Babylonian empire) to Jerusalem. **15.** During the reign of King Artaxerxes (the Persian king who succeeded Cyrus), Belemus, Mithradates, Tabellius, Rathumus, Beeltethmus, and Samellius the scribe, along with their associates in Samaria (a region in Israel) and other regions, wrote to King Artaxerxes about the Jews in Judea and Jerusalem. **16.** They wrote: "To King Artaxerxes, our lord, from your servants Rathumus the recorder, Samellius the scribe, and the rest of the council of judges in Coelesyria (a region in Syria) and Phoenicia (a coastal region in the eastern Mediterranean): **17.** Let it be known to you, king, that the Jews who returned from your kingdom to us are rebuilding a rebellious and wicked city. They are restoring its marketplaces and walls, and laying the foundations of a temple. **18.** If this city is rebuilt and its walls are finished, they will not only refuse to pay tribute, but they will also rebel against kings. **19.** Now that the temple is under construction, we believe it is important to report this matter to you, **20.** and suggest that you search your royal archives. **21.** You will find in the chronicles that this city has always been rebellious, troubling kings and cities. **22.** The Jews have been rebellious, starting wars in the past, which is why this city was destroyed. **23.** Therefore, we inform you, king, that if this city is rebuilt, and its walls are restored, you will lose control over Coelesyria and Phoenicia." **24.** The king responded by writing to Rathumus the recorder, Beeltethmus, Samellius the scribe, and their associates in Samaria, Syria, and Phoenicia: **25.** "I have read your letter. I ordered a search, and it has been found that in ancient times, this city fought against kings. **26.** It was known for rebellion and war, and strong kings ruled there, demanding tribute from Coelesyria and Phoenicia. **27.** Therefore, I have commanded that no one should continue the rebuilding of the city, and that no actions contrary to this order be taken. **28.** This rebellion must be stopped to prevent any further trouble for the kings." **29.** Following the king's letter, Rathumus, Samellius the scribe and their associates hurried to Jerusalem with cavalry and a large force, trying to stop the building efforts. **30.** As a result, the construction of the temple in Jerusalem was halted until the second year of King Darius (the Persian king who succeeded Artaxerxes).

Chapter 3

1. Now King Darius (the Persian king) made a great feast for all his subjects, for those born in his house, for the princes of Media (a region in the Persian Empire) and Persia, **2.** and for all the local governors, captains, and officials under him, from India (a vast region in South Asia) to Ethiopia (a kingdom in Africa), in the 127 provinces. **3.** They ate and drank, and when they were satisfied, they went home. Then King Darius went into his bedchamber and slept, but soon awoke from his sleep. **4.** Then the three young men of the royal bodyguard, who guarded the king, spoke to one another: **5.** "Let each of us state what one thing is the strongest. King Darius will give great gifts and honors to the one whose statement is considered the wisest." **6.** "He shall be clothed in purple, drink from gold cups, sleep on a gold bed, have a chariot with gold bridles, a fine linen turban, and a chain around his neck. **7.** He shall sit next to Darius because of his wisdom and shall be called the cousin of Darius." **8.** Then they each wrote their answer, sealed them, and placed them under King Darius' pillow. **9.** They said, "When the king wakes up, someone will give him the writings. Whoever's statement is judged the wisest by the king and the three princes of Persia will receive the victory, as it is written." **10.** The first wrote, "Wine is the strongest." **11.** The second wrote, "The king is the strongest." **12.** The third wrote, "Women are the strongest, but above all things, Truth (honesty) is the victor." **13.** When the king woke up, the writings were presented to him, and he read them. **14.** He then called all the princes of Persia and Media, the local governors, captains, the chief officers, **15.** and sat himself down in the royal seat of judgment; and the writings were read before them. **16.** He said, "Call the young men, and they shall explain their own writings." So they were called in. **17.** He said to them, "Explain what you have written." **18.** Then the first, who had spoken of the strength of wine, began and said: **19.** "O sirs, how exceedingly strong wine is! It causes all who drink it to go astray. **20.** It makes the mind of the king and of the fatherless child the same, as well as of the bondman (slave) and the freeman, the poor and the rich. **21.** It turns every thought into cheer and mirth, so that a man forgets both sorrow and debt. **22.** It makes every heart feel rich, so that a man forgets both king and governor. It makes people speak in abundance. **23.** When they are drunk, they forget their love for friends and family, and soon they draw their swords. **24.** But when they wake from their drunkenness, they don't remember what they've done. **25.** O sirs, isn't wine the strongest, seeing that it forces people to do these things?" And when he had finished, he stopped speaking.

Chapter 4

1. Then the second, who had spoken of the strength of the king, began to say, **2.** "O sirs, don't men excel in strength who rule over the sea and land, and all things in them? **3.** But yet the king is stronger. He is their lord and has dominion over them. In whatever he commands, they obey him. **4.** If he tells them to make war, they fight against one another. If he sends them to battle enemies, they go and conquer mountains, walls, and towers. **5.** They kill and are killed, and do not disobey the king's command. If they win, they bring everything to the king—all the plunder and treasures. **6.** Similarly, those who are not soldiers and do not deal with wars, but farm, when they have harvested the fruits of their labor, bring some to the king and pay him tribute. **7.** He is just one man! If he commands people to kill, they kill. If he commands them to spare, they spare. **8.** If he commands them to strike, they strike. If he commands them to lay waste, they do so. If he commands to build, they build. **9.** If he commands them to cut down, they cut down. If he commands them to plant, they plant. **10.** So all his people and armies obey him. Furthermore, he lies down, eats, drinks, and rests; **11.** and those who guard him remain vigilant. None of them may depart or do their own business. They do not disobey him in anything. **12.** O sirs, how can the king not be the strongest, seeing that he is obeyed in this way?" Then he stopped speaking. **13.** Then the third, who had spoken of women and of truth (this was Zerubbabel), began to speak: **14.** "O sirs, isn't the king great, and men are many, and isn't wine strong? Who then rules over them or has lordship over them? Aren't they women? **15.** Women have given birth to the king and all the people who rule over the sea and land. **16.** They came from women. Women nourished those who planted the vineyards, from which wine comes. **17.** Women also make garments for men, which bring them honor. Without women, men cannot exist. **18.** Yes, and if men gather gold, silver, and other precious things, and see a woman who is lovely in appearance, **19.** they let all those things go and stare at her, desiring her more than gold, silver, or any other precious thing.

20. A man leaves his own father, who raised him, leaves his country, and joins with his wife. 21. With his wife, he ends his days, forgetting his father, mother, or homeland. 22. By this, you must know that women have dominion over you. Don't you labor and toil, and bring it all to women? 23. Yes, a man takes his sword and goes out to travel, to rob, steal, or sail on the sea and rivers. 24. He faces lions and walks in darkness. When he has stolen, plundered, and robbed, he brings it to the woman he loves. 25. Therefore, a man loves his wife more than his father or mother. 26. Yes, many have lost their minds for women, and become slaves for their sake. 27. Many have perished, stumbled, and sinned because of women. 28. Now, don't you believe me? Isn't the king great in his power? Don't all regions fear him? 29. Yet I saw him and Apame (the king's concubine, daughter of Barticus, a nobleman) sitting at the right hand of the king, 30. and taking the crown from his head and placing it on her own head. Yes, she struck the king with her left hand. 31. At this, the king gaped and gazed at her with open mouth. If she smiles at him, he laughs. But if she shows any displeasure, he flatters her to make her happy again. 32. O sirs, how can it not be that women are strong, seeing that they do this?" 33. Then the king and the nobles looked at one another. He began to speak concerning truth. 34. "O sirs, aren't women strong? The earth is great. The sky is high. The sun is swift in its course, for it circles the sky and returns again in one day. 35. Isn't it he who makes these things great? Therefore, truth (honesty) is great and stronger than all things. 36. The earth calls upon truth, and the sky blesses truth. All works tremble, but with truth, there is no unrighteousness. 37. Wine is unrighteous. The king is unrighteous. Women are unrighteous. All the children of men are unrighteous, and all their works are unrighteous. There is no truth in them. They will perish in their unrighteousness. 38. But truth remains, and is strong forever. Truth lives and conquers forevermore. 39. With truth, there is no partiality, no reward system. Truth does what is just, rather than any unrighteous or wicked thing. All men approve of truth's works. 40. In truth's judgment, there is no unrighteousness. Truth is the strength, the kingdom, the power, and the majesty of all ages. Blessed be the God of truth!" 41. With that, he stopped speaking. Then all the people shouted, "Great is truth, and strong above all things!" 42. Then the king said to him, "Ask whatever you wish, even more than what is written, and we will give it to you, because you are found to be the wisest. You shall sit next to me, and shall be called my cousin." 43. Then he said to the king, "Remember your vow, which you made when you came to your throne, to build Jerusalem, 44. and to send back all the vessels that were taken from Jerusalem, which Cyrus (the Persian king) set apart when he vowed to destroy Babylon, and vowed to send them back. 45. You also vowed to build the temple, which the Edomites (a people from southern Israel) burned when Judea was desolated by the Chaldeans (Babylonians). 46. Now, O Lord the king, this is what I request, and desire from you: I ask that you fulfill the vow, which you made to the King of Heaven with your own mouth." 47. Then King Darius stood up, kissed him, and wrote letters to all the treasurers, governors, captains, and local officials, 48. Instructing them to safely help him and those who would go with him to rebuild Jerusalem. 49. He wrote letters to all the governors in Coelesyria (a region in Syria) and Phoenicia (coastal region of present-day Lebanon), and to those in Lebanon, to bring cedar wood from Lebanon to Jerusalem and assist in building the city. 50. He also wrote to all the Jews who would leave his realm for Judea, guaranteeing their freedom, so that no officer, governor, or treasurer would forcibly enter their homes, 51. and that all the land they occupied would be free of tribute, and that the Edomites should return the villages of the Jews they held. 52. Additionally, twenty talents would be given yearly for the temple's construction, until it was completed, 53. and another ten talents yearly for daily burnt offerings to be presented on the altar, as commanded. 54. All those who came from Babylonia to help build the city would be granted freedom, as well as their descendants and all the priests who came. 55. He also ordered that they be provided with the necessary priests' garments. 56. For the Levites (priests who served in the temple), he wrote that their support should be given until the temple was finished and Jerusalem rebuilt. 57. He commanded that land and wages be given to those who guarded the city. 58. He also sent all the vessels from Babylon that Cyrus had set apart, and all that Cyrus had commanded to be done, to be sent to Jerusalem. 59. Now when this young man had gone out, he lifted his face to heaven toward Jerusalem and praised the King of Heaven, 60. and said, "From you comes victory. From you comes wisdom. Yours is the glory, and I am your servant. 61. Blessed are you, who have given me wisdom. I give thanks to them. 62. They praised the God of their ancestors, for He had granted them the freedom to rebuild Jerusalem and the temple. They rejoiced for seven days with music and gladness. 63. And they celebrated with instruments of music and joy for seven days.

Chapter 5

1. Afterward, the heads of the households from each tribe were chosen to go up to Jerusalem, accompanied by their families—wives, sons, daughters, servants, and livestock. 2. King Darius sent along a thousand cavalry to ensure their safe return to Jerusalem, with musical instruments—drums and flutes. 3. All their relatives celebrated, and Darius commanded that they journey together as one group. 4 These are the names of the men who traveled with their families, listed by their tribal divisions. 5. The priests, descendants of Phinees (from the tribe of Levi), and the sons of Aaron: Jesus (Joshua) the son of Josedek, the son of Seraiah, and Joakim, the son of Zerubbabel (a descendant of King David), of the tribe of Judah. 6. These men spoke wisely before King Darius of Persia during the second year of his reign, in the month of Nisan (the first month of the Jewish calendar). 7 These Judeans had been exiled to Babylon by King Nebuchadnezzar, who took them captive. 8. They returned to Jerusalem and other parts of Judah, each man to his own city. They came with Zerubbabel, Jesus, Nehemiah, and their leaders. 9 The number of men and their leaders: the sons of Phoros—2,172; the sons of Saphat—472; the sons of Ares—756. 10 The sons of Phaath Moab (from the tribes of Jesus and Joab)—2,812; the sons of Elam—1,254; the sons of Zathui—945; the sons of Chorbe—705; the sons of Bani—648. 11 The sons of Bebai—623; the sons of Astad—1,322; the sons of Adonikam—667; the sons of Bagoi—2,066. 12. The sons of Adinu—454; the sons of Ater (of Ezekias)—92; the sons of Kilan and Azetas—67; the sons of Azaru—432. 13 The sons of Annis—101; the sons of Arom—323; the sons of Bassai—323; the sons of Arsiphurith—112. 14 The sons of Baiterus—3,000; the sons of Bethlomon—123; those from Netophah—55; those from Anathoth—158; those from Bethasmoth—42. 15 Those from Kariathiarius—25; those from Caphira and Beroth—743. 16 The Chadiasai and Ammidioi—422; those from Kirama and Gabbe—621. 17 Those from Macalon—122; those from Betolion—52; the sons of Niphis—156. 18 The sons of Calamolalus and Onus—725; the sons of Jerechu—345; the sons of Sanaas—3,330. 19 The priests: the sons of Jeddu (the son of Jesus)—972; the sons of Emmeruth—1,052; the sons of Phassurus—1,247; the sons of Charme—1,017. 20 The Levites: the sons of Jesus, Kadmiel, Banna, and Sudias—74. 21 The singers: the sons of Asaph—128. 22 The gatekeepers: the sons of Salum, Atar, Tolman, Dacubi, Ateta, and Sabi—139. 23 The temple servants: the sons of Esau, Asipha, Tabaoth, Keras, Sua, Phaleas, Labana, Aggaba. 24 The sons of Acud, Uta, Ketab, Accaba, Subai, Anan, Cathua, and Geddur. 25 The sons of Jairus, Daisan, Noeba, Chaseba, Gazera, Ozias, Phinoe, Asara, Basthai, Asana, Maani, Naphisi, Acub, Achipha, Asur, Pharakim, and Basaloth. 26 The sons of Meedda, Cutha, Charea, Barchus, Serar, Thomei, Nasi, and Atipha. 27 The servants of Solomon: the sons of Assaphioth, Pharida, Saphuthi, Agia, Phacareth, Sabie, Sarothie, Masias, Gas, Addus, Subas, Apherra, Barodis, Saphat, and Allon. 28 The total number of temple servants and the sons of Solomon's servants was 372. 29 They came from Thermeleth and Thelersas, led by Charaathalan, and Allar. 30 These men could not prove their genealogy or ancestry, so they were not considered part of Israel: the sons of Dalan, Ban, and Nekodan—652. 31 Among the priests, some who had taken the office unlawfully were not found in the records: the sons of Obdia, Akkos, and Jaddus (who married a daughter of Zorzelleus and was named after him). 32 When their lineage was searched for in the records and not found, they were removed from the priesthood. 33 Nehemiah and Attharias (Levites) told them they could not partake in the holy offerings until a high priest with the Urim and Thummim (sacred objects used for decision-making) arose. 34 All Israelites aged twelve and older, excluding servants, numbered 42,360. 35 Their servants and maids numbered 7,337; singers and musicians—245; camels—435; horses—7,036; mules—245; and beasts of burden—

5,525. **36** Some family leaders, upon reaching Jerusalem, vowed to rebuild the temple as they were able, contributing gold (1,000 minas), silver (5,000 minas), and 100 priestly garments to the holy treasury. **37** The priests, Levites, and some of the people lived in Jerusalem and in their villages, including the singers and gatekeepers. **38** In the seventh month, when all Israelites gathered in one place, they assembled in front of the temple's east porch with one purpose. **39** Then Jesus (Joshua) son of Josedek and Zerubbabel, along with their families, set up the altar of Israel's God. **40** They offered burnt sacrifices according to the commandments of Moses, the servant of God. **41** Some people from other nations joined them, and the altar was erected in its proper place, though the surrounding nations were hostile. **42** They offered sacrifices daily, both morning and evening, observing the feast of tabernacles as commanded in the law. **43** They also began offering continual sacrifices, Sabbaths, new moons, and other sacred feasts. **44** Those who had made vows to God started fulfilling them, even though the temple was still not completed. **45** They provided resources to the workers—money, food, and drink—and gave carts to the people of Sidon and Tyre to bring cedar trees from Lebanon to the port of Joppa, as ordered by King Cyrus of Persia. **46** In the second year after they arrived in Jerusalem, in the second month, Zerubbabel, Jesus, and the priests began the work. **47** They laid the foundation of God's temple in the second month, the second year after their arrival in Judea and Jerusalem. **48** Zerubbabel, Jesus, Kadmiel, Banna, and the Levites who were at least twenty years old were appointed over the work of the Lord's house. **49** They started the labor together, with everyone in unity, to build the house of God. **50** The priests stood in their vestments with musical instruments and trumpets, and the Levites, the sons of Asaph, with their cymbals. **51** They sang songs of thanksgiving, praising the Lord according to King David's instructions. **52** They sang loudly, praising God for His goodness and His eternal glory among all Israel. **53** The people sounded trumpets and shouted in unison, singing songs of thanksgiving to the Lord for the rebuilding of His house. **54** Some of the Levites and older men, who had seen the former temple, wept as they remembered it. **55** But many others, with trumpets and joy, shouted with loud voices. **56** The weeping of the people was so great that it could not be heard above the joyful shouting, and the sound was carried far. **57** When the enemies of Judah and Benjamin (two of the twelve tribes of Israel) heard the noise, they understood it was the sound of the rebuilding of the temple. **58** They went to Zerubbabel, Jesus, and the leaders of the families and said, "We want to join you in building the temple, for we too worship the Lord, just as King Asbasareth (a title for an Assyrian king) commanded us." **59** But Zerubbabel and the leaders replied, "You have no part with us in building the house of our God. We alone will build it for the God of Israel, as King Cyrus of Persia has commanded us." **60** The enemies of Judah and Benjamin became angry and discouraged the people of Judah, making them afraid. **61** They hired counselors to oppose them and frustrate their plans throughout the reign of King Darius of Persia. **62** Despite these challenges, the work on the temple continued under the direction of Zerubbabel and Jesus, with all the elders of Israel. **63** The priests and Levites continued their worship, and the people were strong in their commitment to rebuilding the temple. **64** Finally, the temple's foundation was laid in the second year after their return, and the work progressed steadily. **65** It was a time of great joy, yet also a time of opposition, as those who opposed the building of the temple sought every opportunity to stop the work. **66** But the people of Israel remained steadfast, trusting in the promise of God and the support of their king, and continued their efforts. **67** The foundation of the temple was laid, and the people celebrated the progress made, offering sacrifices in gratitude for what had been accomplished. **68** The work continued with renewed strength and hope, despite the difficulties they faced. **69** With the support of their leaders and the guidance of the Lord, the people began to rebuild the house of God in Jerusalem. **70** The city was filled with joy as the people worked together to restore the temple to its former glory. **71** The enemies of Israel, who had opposed the work, saw the progress and became increasingly fearful as the people of God made headway in rebuilding the house of the Lord. **72** The temple was restored, and the people of Israel were strengthened in their faith and devotion. **73** The work continued until the temple was fully restored and the people of Israel celebrated the completion of their holy house.

Chapter 6

1. In the second year of King Darius' reign, the prophets Aggaeus (Haggai) and Zacharius (Zechariah), the son of Addo, prophesied to the Jewish people in Judea and Jerusalem in the name of the Lord, the God of Israel. **2.** Then Zerubbabel (the governor of Judah, son of Shealtiel) and Jeshua (or Joshua) the son of Jozadak (the high priest) rose up and began rebuilding the house of the Lord in Jerusalem, with the prophets of God supporting and assisting them. **3.** At the same time, Sisinnes, the governor of Syria and Phoenicia, along with Sathrabuzanes and his companions, came to them and asked, **4.** "By what authority are you building this house and this roof, and carrying out these works? Who are the ones responsible for these actions?" **5.** However, the Jewish elders found favor, because the Lord had visited the exiles, and they were not hindered from building until the matter was communicated to King Darius and his response received. **6.** Here is a copy of the letter that Sisinnes, governor of Syria and Phoenicia, and Sathrabuzanes, along with their companions, sent to King Darius: **7.** "To King Darius, greetings. Let it be made known to our lord the king, that when we entered Judea and came to the city of Jerusalem, we found the elders of the Jews, who had been exiled, rebuilding a great house for the Lord with costly stones and timber for its walls. **8.** The work is progressing quickly and prospering in their hands with great glory and diligence. **9.** We then asked these elders, 'By whose authority are you rebuilding this house and laying its foundations?' **10.** To help you understand, we requested the names of their leaders in writing. **11.** They replied, 'We are the servants of the Lord who made heaven and earth. This house was built many years ago by a great and mighty king of Israel, and it was completed. **12.** But when our ancestors sinned against the Lord of Israel, He gave them into the hands of King Nebuchadnezzar (ruler of Babylon), the king of the Chaldeans. **13.** They tore down the house, burned it, and carried away the people into captivity to Babylon. **14.** However, in the first year of King Cyrus' reign over Babylon, he issued a decree that this house should be rebuilt. **15.** The holy vessels of gold and silver that Nebuchadnezzar had taken from the house in Jerusalem and set up in his temple, King Cyrus brought out from the temple in Babylon and delivered them to Zerubbabel and to Sanabassarus (another name for Sheshbazzar, a leader of the Jewish returnees), their governor. **16.** He commanded that these vessels be carried to Jerusalem and placed in the house of the Lord, so that the temple should be rebuilt on its original site. **17.** Then Sanabassarus came here and laid the foundation of the Lord's house in Jerusalem. From that time, construction has continued, though it is not yet finished.' **18.** Therefore, if it pleases the king, let a search be made in the royal archives of our lord the king in Babylon. **19.** If it is found that King Cyrus consented to the rebuilding of the Lord's house in Jerusalem, and if it seems good to our lord the king, let him send us his orders concerning this matter." **20.** King Darius commanded a search in the royal archives stored in Babylon, and at the palace of Ekbatana, a scroll was found recording these events. **21.** "In the first year of King Cyrus' reign, King Cyrus decreed that the house of the Lord in Jerusalem be rebuilt, a place where offerings of fire should be made continually. **22.** Its dimensions are to be sixty cubits high and sixty cubits wide, with three rows of hewn stones and one row of timber from the country. **23.** The expenses for the construction are to be covered from the treasury of King Cyrus. **24.** The holy vessels of the house of the Lord, both gold and silver, which Nebuchadnezzar had taken from the house at Jerusalem and brought to Babylon, are to be returned to the house at Jerusalem and placed where they were before." **25.** He also commanded that Sisinnes, the governor of Syria and Phoenicia, and Sathrabuzanes, along with their fellow rulers, must not interfere with the construction but allow Zerubbabel, the servant of the Lord, and the Jewish elders to continue building the house of the Lord in its place. **26.** "I also decree that the construction be completed, and that they diligently assist the exiles of Judea until the house of the Lord is finished. **27.** A portion from the tribute of Coelesyria and Phoenicia shall be set aside for these workers, for offerings to the Lord, including bulls, rams, lambs, as well as corn, salt, wine, and oil, to be provided annually, according to the needs of the priests in Jerusalem. **28.** These offerings will be used for daily sacrifices and drink offerings to the Most High God, for the king and his children, that they may pray for the king's life." **29.** He also ordered that anyone who transgresses this decree, or neglects any part of it, should have a beam removed from his own house and be hanged upon it, with all his goods confiscated for the king. **30.** "Therefore, may the Lord, whose name is called upon this place, destroy any king or nation that stretches out a hand to harm or hinder the rebuilding of the Lord's house in Jerusalem. **31.** I, King Darius, have made this decree, and it must be carried out with all diligence." **32.** "Anyone who violates or ignores anything written here shall have a beam taken from his own house, and he shall be hanged upon it, with all his possessions seized by the king." **33.** "May the Lord, whose name is invoked there, utterly destroy any king or nation that tries to hinder or damage the house of the Lord in Jerusalem." **34.** "I, King Darius, have issued this decree, and it must be carried out with all diligence."

Chapter 7

1. Then Sisinnes, the governor of Coelesyria and Phoenicia, and Sathrabuzanes, with their companions, following the commands of King Darius, carefully supervised the sacred work, assisting the Jewish elders and the temple leaders. **2.** So the work was successful, while the prophets Aggaeus (Haggai) and Zacharias (Zechariah) prophesied. **3.** They completed the project by the command of the Lord, the God of Israel, and with the approval of Cyrus, Darius, and Artaxerxes, the kings of Persia. **4.** Thus, the holy temple was completed on the twenty-third day of the month Adar, in the sixth year of King Darius' reign. **5.** The Israelites, including the priests, Levites, and others who returned from captivity, followed the instructions written in the book of Moses. **6.** For the dedication of the Lord's temple, they offered one hundred bulls, two hundred rams, four hundred lambs, and twelve male goats for the sin offering of all Israel, according to the number of the twelve tribal princes of Israel. **7.** The priests and Levites stood in their ceremonial robes, arranged by their families, for the services of the Lord, the God of Israel, as instructed in the book of Moses. The gatekeepers were stationed at each gate. **8.** The Israelites who had returned from captivity observed the Passover on the fourteenth day of the first month, when the priests and Levites had been sanctified together, **9.** along with all who had returned from captivity; for they had been sanctified. The Levites were completely purified. **10.** They offered the Passover sacrifice for all who returned from captivity, for their fellow priests, and for themselves. **11.** The Israelites who had come back from exile ate, along with all those who had separated themselves from the unclean practices of the heathen of the land, and who sought the Lord. **12.** They observed the Feast of Unleavened Bread for seven days, rejoicing before the Lord, **13.** because He had turned the heart of the king of Assyria to support them, strengthening their hands in the work of the Lord, the God of Israel.

Chapter 8

1 After these events, during the reign of Artaxerxes, king of Persia, Esdras (Ezra) came up from Babylon. He was the son of Azariah, son of Zechariah, son of Hilkiah, son of Shallum, **2** son of Zadok, son of Ahitub, son of Amariah, son of Azariah, son of Meraioth, son of Zerahiah, son of Uzziah, son of Bukki, son of Abishua, son of Phinehas, son of Eleazar, son of Aaron, the high priest. **3** This Esdras was a skilled scribe in the law of Moses, which the Lord God of Israel had given. The king granted him favor in all his requests, **4** and he went up from Babylon, accompanied by some of the Israelites, priests, Levites, singers, gatekeepers, and temple servants, to Jerusalem. **5** This journey took place in the seventh year of King Artaxerxes' reign, during the fifth month. They left Babylon on the first day of the first month and arrived in Jerusalem by the gracious hand of the Lord, who blessed their journey. **6** Esdras was well-versed in the law, and he taught all of Israel the ordinances and statutes of the Lord. **7** A letter from King Artaxerxes was delivered to Esdras, the priest and teacher of the law, with the following message: **8** "King Artaxerxes to Esdras, the priest and teacher of the law of the God of Heaven: Greetings. **9** Since I have determined to deal generously with the people of Israel, I have issued a decree that any Israelites, priests, Levites, or temple servants who are willing to go with you to Jerusalem may do so. **10** I, along with my seven royal counselors, have decided that you should oversee the affairs of Judea and Jerusalem according to the law of your God. **11** You are to take with you the offerings for the God of Israel, the ones I and my counselors have vowed to give, **12** including all the gold and silver that

can be found in Babylon, along with what the people and priests have freely offered for the temple of their God in Jerusalem. **13** These funds are to be used to purchase bulls, rams, lambs, and all the necessary offerings for sacrifices at the temple of God in Jerusalem. **14** You are authorized to use any gold and silver you receive as you see fit, according to the will of your God. **15** You are also to take with you the holy vessels for the temple, which have been entrusted to you, and any other items for the use of the temple. These should be provided from the king's treasury. **16** I, King Artaxerxes, have instructed the treasurers in Syria and Phoenicia to deliver all requested funds and supplies to you without delay. **17** Including up to one hundred talents of silver, one hundred cors of wheat, one hundred baths of wine, and as much salt as you need. **18** All these provisions should be used according to the law of your God to ensure that no wrath falls upon the kingdom of the king and his sons. **19** You are to ensure that no taxes or other burdens are placed upon the priests, Levites, singers, gatekeepers, temple servants, or anyone who works in the temple service. **20** You, Esdras, are empowered to appoint judges and magistrates who will enforce the law of your God throughout Syria and Phoenicia. Those who are ignorant of the law should be taught it. **21** Anyone who disobeys the law of your God or the commands of the king shall be punished, whether by death, imprisonment, confiscation of property, or any other legal penalty." **22** Then Esdras, the scribe, blessed the Lord, the God of his fathers, who had put such a thing into the heart of the king to glorify the house of the Lord in Jerusalem. **23** He also praised God for granting him favor in the eyes of the king, his counselors, and all his nobles. **24** Encouraged by this, Esdras gathered the leading men of Israel to accompany him to Jerusalem. **25** These are the heads of the families who went up with Esdras from Babylon in the seventh year of King Artaxerxes: **26** From the sons of Phinehas, Gershom; from the sons of Ithamar, Daniel; from the sons of David, Attus, son of Sechenias; **27** from the sons of Parosh, Zechariah, and with him 150 men; **28** from the sons of Pahath-moab, Eliahonias son of Zerahiah, and with him 200 men; **29** from the sons of Zattu, Shecaniah son of Jehiel, and with him 300 men; **30** from the sons of Adin, Obadiah son of Jonathan, and with him 250 men; **31** from the sons of Elam, Jeshaiah son of Gotholias, and with him 70 men; **32** from the sons of Shephatiah, Zechariah son of Michael, and with him 70 men; **33** from the sons of Joab, Obadiah son of Jehiel, and with him 212 men; **34** from the sons of Bani, Shelomith son of Josaphiah, and with him 160 men; **35** from the sons of Babi, Zechariah son of Bebai, and with him 28 men; **36** from the sons of Azgad, Johanan son of Hakkatan, and with him 110 men; **37** from the sons of Adonikam, Eliphalet, Jeuel, and Shemaiah, and with them 70 men; **38** from the sons of Bigvai, Uthai son of Istalcurus, and with him 70 men. **39** I gathered them at the river that runs to Ahava, and we camped there for three days while I examined the people and the priests. **40** I found that none of the priests or Levites were there, **41** so I sent for Eleazar, Ariel, Shemaiah, Elnathan, Nathan, Zechariah, and Meshullam, leading men and men of understanding. **42** I told them to go to Iddo, the leader at Casiphia, and ask him and his associates in the temple service to send us ministers for the house of our God. **43** By the gracious hand of our God, they brought us men who were able to serve, from the sons of Levi: **44** Asebias, a descendant of Mooli, the son of Levi, along with his relatives and their sons, totaling 18 men; **45** Asebias' brothers, Annas and Osaias, and their sons, totaling 20 men; **46** and from the temple servants, whom David and his officials had appointed for the service of the Levites, we received 220 temple servants, whose names were recorded. **47** I then proclaimed a fast for all of us, asking God for a safe and prosperous journey for ourselves, our children, and all our possessions. **48** Asebias, Annuus, and Osaias, his brother, of the sons of Chanuneus, and their sons, totaling twenty men, **49** and of the temple servants whom David and the leaders had appointed to serve the Levites, there were two hundred twenty temple servants. Their names were recorded. **50** I then vowed a fast for the young men before the Lord, asking Him to grant us a prosperous journey, for ourselves, our children, and our livestock. **51** I was ashamed to ask the king for an escort of infantry or cavalry to protect us from enemies along the way, **52** for we had told the king that the power of our God would be with those who seek Him, to protect them and support them in every way. **53** So we prayed to the Lord about this matter, and He was merciful to us. **54** Then I set apart twelve men from the leaders of the priests: Eserebias, Assamias, and ten others of their relatives. **55** I entrusted to them the silver, the gold, and the holy vessels of the house of our God, which the king, his counselors, the nobles, and all Israel had contributed. **56** I weighed out to them 650 talents of silver, silver vessels weighing 100 talents, 100 talents of gold, **57** twenty golden vessels, and twelve vessels of fine brass, as gleaming as gold. **58** I said to them, "You are consecrated to the Lord, and these vessels are holy. The silver and gold are a vow to the Lord, the God of our fathers. **59** Watch over them carefully until you deliver them to the leaders of the priests and Levites, and to the principal men of the families of Israel in Jerusalem, in the chambers of the house of our God." **60** So the priests and Levites, who received the silver, gold, and vessels, brought them into the temple of the Lord in Jerusalem. **61** We left the river Ahava on the twelfth day of the first month, and by the mighty hand of our God upon us, we arrived in Jerusalem. The Lord delivered us from every enemy and ambush along the way. **62** After we arrived in Jerusalem and stayed there for three days, on the fourth day the silver and gold were weighed and delivered into the house of the Lord. Marmoth the priest, the son of Urias, **63** was in charge, along with Eleazar the son of Phinehas. They were assisted by Josabdus, the son of Jesus, and Moeth the son of Sabannus, the Levites. Everything was delivered to them according to number and weight. **64** The exact weight of everything was recorded at that time. **65** Those who had returned from exile then offered sacrifices to the Lord, the God of Israel. They offered twelve bulls for all Israel, ninety-six rams, **66** seventy-two lambs, and twelve goats for a sin offering, all as burnt offerings to the Lord. **67** They delivered the king's orders to the king's stewards and to the governors of Coelesyria and Phoenicia. They honored the people and the temple of the Lord. **68** After these things were completed, the leaders came to me and reported: **69** "The people of Israel, including the priests and Levites, have not separated themselves from the surrounding peoples, nor have they rid themselves of the abominations of the Gentiles—the Canaanites, Hittites, Perizzites, Jebusites, Moabites, Egyptians, and Edomites. **70** They and their sons have married the daughters of these foreign nations, and the holy seed has been mixed with the peoples of the land. From the beginning of this situation, the leaders and officials have been partakers in this iniquity." **71** As soon as I heard these things, I tore my clothes and my holy garment, and I pulled the hair from my head and beard. I sat down, overwhelmed with sorrow. **72** All those who were moved by the word of the Lord, the God of Israel, gathered around me while I mourned over the sin. I sat there in grief until the evening sacrifice. **73** Then, rising from my fast, with my clothes and holy garment torn, I knelt down, stretched out my hands to the Lord, **74** and said: "O Lord, I am ashamed and humiliated before You, **75** for our sins have multiplied so much that they are beyond measure, and our mistakes have reached to the heavens. **76** From the days of our ancestors until now, we have been in great sin. **77** Because of our sins, we, our kings, and our priests have been given into the hands of the kings of the earth, to the sword, captivity, and plunder, with shame upon us, as it is today. **78** But now, O Lord, in Your mercy, You have left us a remnant, a root and a name in the place of Your sanctuary. **79** You have given us a light in Your house, and food in our time of servitude. **80** Even when we were in bondage, we were not forsaken by our God. He gave us favor with the kings of Persia, so they provided us with food, **81** glorified the temple of our God, and rebuilt the desolate Zion, granting us a secure place to dwell in Judah and Jerusalem. **82** Now, O Lord, what shall we say in light of all this? For we have broken Your commandments, which You gave through Your prophets, saying: **83** 'The land you are entering to possess is defiled by the abominations of the people living there. They have filled it with their impurity. **84** Therefore, do not give your daughters in marriage to their sons, nor take their daughters for your sons. **85** Never seek peace with them, so that you may be strong, eat the good things of the land, and leave it to your children as an everlasting inheritance.' **86** All this has come upon us because of our wicked deeds and great sins. You, O Lord, have spared us and allowed us a remnant, but we have returned to transgressing Your law, by mingling with the impurity of the heathen of the land. **87** You did not punish us as severely as we deserved; You did not destroy us completely, leaving us without root, seed, or name. **88** O Lord, You are righteous, for we still have a remnant today. **89** Behold, we are here before You in our iniquities, and we cannot stand before You because of them." **90** As Esdras prayed, confessing our sins with weeping, lying prostrate before the temple, a great crowd of men, women, and children gathered around him from Jerusalem. They too wept bitterly. **91** Then Jechonias, the son of Jeelus, one of the sons of Israel, spoke up and said, "O Esdras, we have sinned against the Lord our God. We have married foreign women from the people of the land, but there is still hope for Israel. **92** Let us make a solemn oath to the Lord, that we will put away all our foreign wives and their children, as it seems good to you and to all who fear the Law of the Lord. **93** Arise, and take action, for this is your responsibility. We will support you, and we will act with courage." **94** So Esdras arose, and he made the chief priests and Levites, and all the people of Israel, take an oath to do what had been proposed. And they swore to it. **95** "Arise and take action, for this is your responsibility, and we will stand with you and act with courage." **96** So Esdras stood up, gathered the chief priests and Levites, and made them swear an oath to carry out these actions. They all took the oath.

Chapter 9

1 Then Esdras (a priest and scribe) went from the temple court to the room of Jonas, the son of Eliasib (a priest), and stayed there. He neither ate bread nor drank water, grieving over the great sins of the people. **2** A proclamation was made throughout Judea and Jerusalem, calling all those who had returned from captivity to gather in Jerusalem. **3** Anyone who did not arrive within two or three days, as instructed by the elders, would have their livestock taken for the temple and would be excluded from the congregation of returnees. **4** Within three days, all from the tribes of Judah and Benjamin gathered in Jerusalem, on the twentieth day of the ninth month. **5** The people sat trembling in the open area before the temple because of the severe weather. **6** Esdras stood up and said to them, "You have broken God's law by marrying foreign women, adding to Israel's sin." **7** "Now confess your sins, honor the Lord, and obey His will by separating yourselves from the foreign people and their wives." **8** The entire assembly responded with a loud voice, "As you have said, so we will do." **9** "But because the crowd is large and the weather is harsh, we cannot stand outside, and this issue cannot be resolved in a day or two. Our sin is widespread," **10** "Therefore, let the leaders remain, and those who have foreign wives should come at the appointed time, with the rulers and judges from each region, until we have turned away God's anger on this matter." **11** So Jonathan (son of Azael) and Ezekias (son of Thocanus), along with judges Mosollamus, Levis, and Sabbateus, took charge of the matter. **12** Those who returned from captivity acted according to these instructions. **13** Esdras selected prominent men from the families, by name. On the new moon of the tenth month, they gathered to examine the issue. **14** They resolved the cases of men who had foreign wives by the new moon of the first month. **15** Among the priests who had foreign wives were found the sons of Jeshua (the high priest), including Mathelas, Eleazar, Joribus, and Joadanus. **16** They agreed to send away their wives and offer rams as a guilt offering to make atonement for their sin. **17** Among the sons of Emmer, there were Ananias, Zabdeus, Manes, Sameus, Hiereel, and Azarias. **18** From the sons of Phaisur, Elionas, Massias, Ishmael, Nathanael, Ocidelus, and Saloas were listed. **19** Among the Levites, Jozabdus, Semeis, Colius (called Calitas), Patheus, Judas, and Jonas were included. **20** The holy singers, Eliasibus and Bacchurus, and the gatekeepers, Sallumus and Tolbanes, were also named. **21** From Israel, the sons of Phoros included Hiermas, Ieddias, Melchias, Maelus, Eleazar, Asibas, and Banneas. **22** The sons of Ela were Matthanias, Zacharias, Jezrielus, Oabdius, Hieremoth, and Aedias. **23** From the sons of Zamoth, Eliadas, Eliasimus, Othonias, Jarimoth, Sabathus, and Zardeus were named. **24** The sons of Bebai included Joannes, Ananias, Jozabdus, and Ematheis. **25** The sons of Mani were Olamus, Mamuchus, Jedeus, Jasubas, Jasaelus, and Hieremoth. **26** The sons of Addi were Naathus, Moossias, Lacunus, Naidus, Matthanias, Sesthel, Balnuus, and Manasseas. **27** The sons of Annas were Elionas, Aseas, Melchias, Sabbeus, and Simon Chosameus. **28** The sons of Asom included Maltanneus, Mattathias, Sabanneus, Eliphalat, Manasses, and Semei. **29** The sons of Baani were Jeremias, Momdis, Ismaerus, Juel, Mamdai, Pedias, Anos, Carabasion, Enasibus, Mamnitamenus, Eliasis, Bannus, Eliali, Someis, Selemias, and Nathanias. The sons of Ezora included Sesis, Ezril, Azaelus, Samatus,

Zambri, and Josephus. **30** The sons of Nooma were Mazitias, Zabadeas, Edos, Juel, and Banaias. **31** All these men had married foreign wives and sent them away with their children. **32** The priests, Levites, and the rest of Israel who lived in Jerusalem and in the surrounding areas, gathered on the new moon of the seventh month, along with the children of Israel from their towns. **33** The whole assembly gathered together in unity in the open space before the temple, facing east. **34** They said to Esdras, "Bring the law of Moses that the Lord, the God of Israel, gave us." **35** So Esdras brought the law before the assembly of men and women, and all the priests, to read and explain it on the new moon of the seventh month. **36** He read it to them from morning until midday, and all the people listened attentively to the law. **37** Esdras stood on a wooden platform prepared for this purpose. **38** Standing next to him were Mattathias, Sammus, Ananias, Azarias, Urias, Ezekias, and Baalsamus on his right, **39** and on his left, Phaldeus, Misael, Melchias, Lothasubus, Nabarias, and Zacharias. **40** When Esdras opened the book of the law, all the people stood up. Esdras then blessed the Lord, the great God of heaven's armies. **41** The people responded, "Amen." They lifted their hands, bowed down, and worshipped the Lord. **42** Then the Levites—Jesus, Annus, Sarabias, Iadinus, Jacubus, Sabateus, Auteas, Maiannas, Calitas, Azarias, Jozabdus, Ananias, and Phalias—explained the law to the people. **43** Attharates said to Esdras and the Levites, "This day is holy to the Lord. Now, weeping has come upon the people as they heard the law." **44** "Go now, eat rich food, drink sweet drinks, and send portions to those who have nothing. Do not be sad, for this day is holy, and the Lord will honor you." **45** So the Levites instructed the people, "This day is holy, do not grieve." **46** They all went home to eat, drink, and celebrate, sharing portions with the poor, and rejoicing greatly, **47** because they understood the words they had been taught and were grateful for the assembly's purpose. **48** Also, Jesus (a Levite), Annus, Sarabias, Iadinus, Jacubus, Sabateus, Auteas, Maiannas, Calitas, Azarias, Jozabdus, Ananias, and Phalias, the Levites, instructed the people in the law of the Lord. They read and explained the scriptures to the assembly, helping them understand what was read. **49** Attharates then spoke to Esdras, the chief priest and scribe, and to the Levites who had been teaching the people, saying to all, **50** "This day is sacred to the Lord— do not mourn, for the people wept as they heard the law." **51** "Now, go and enjoy good food, drink sweet beverages, and share with those who have nothing. For today is holy to the Lord; do not be sad, for the Lord will bring you joy and honor." **52** The Levites then instructed everyone, saying, "This is a holy day. Do not be sorrowful." **53** So, the people went on their way, each to celebrate with food and drink, giving portions to the poor, and rejoicing greatly, **54** because they understood the teachings they had received and the purpose for which they had gathered. **55** Because they understood the words they were instructed with, and for which they had been assembled.

18 – Tobit

Chapter 1

1. This is the book of the words of Tobit, son of Tobiel, son of Ananiel, son of Aduel, son of Gabael, of the family of Asiel, from the tribe of Naphtali. **2.** During the reign of King Enemessar (king of Assyria) of Assyria, I was taken captive from Thisbe (a city), near Kedesh Naphtali (a place) in Galilee, above Asher (a region). **3.** I, Tobit, lived righteously all my life, giving alms (charitable donations) to my people who were exiled with me to Nineveh. **4.** In Israel, while young, my tribe, Naphtali, turned away from the house of Jerusalem (the sacred city), the chosen place where all Israel was to worship, and where the temple of the Most High (God) was established. **5.** The tribes that abandoned Jerusalem worshiped Baal (a false god), as did my family. **6.** I alone continued to go to Jerusalem for the feasts, offering first fruits (the first and best produce), tithes (a tenth of earnings), and the best of my harvest to the priests, sons of Aaron (the priestly lineage). **7.** I gave a tenth of all my earnings to the Levites (members of the priestly tribe of Israel) in Jerusalem. A second tenth I sold and spent each year in Jerusalem. **8.** The third tenth I gave to the poor, as my mother Deborah had instructed, since I was an orphan. **9.** When I grew up, I married Anna (a woman from my family), and we had a son, Tobias. **10.** When I was exiled to Nineveh, my relatives ate the food of the Gentiles (non-Jews), **11.** but I kept myself from it, **12.** remembering God in all things. **13.** The Most High (God) granted me favor with Enemessar (king of Assyria), and I became his purchasing agent (responsible for acquisitions). **14.** I traveled to Media (a region), leaving ten talents (units of silver) of silver with Gabael in Rages of Media. **15.** After Enemessar's death, his son Sennacherib (king of Assyria) reigned, and the roads became unsafe, preventing me from going to Media. **16.** During Enemessar's reign, I performed many acts of charity: I gave my bread to the hungry, **17.** my clothes to the naked, and buried the dead, **18.** even those killed by Sennacherib. I secretly buried them, as the king's soldiers searched for the bodies. **19.** But one of the Ninevites (residents of Nineveh) reported me to the king for this, and when I learned I was sought for execution, I hid myself. **20.** My possessions were seized, leaving only my wife Anna and son Tobias. **21.** Within fifty-five days, two of Sennacherib's sons killed him and fled to the mountains (a region). His son Sarchedonus succeeded him, and appointed Achiacharus (my nephew), as overseer of his accounts. **22.** Achiacharus invited me to Nineveh, and I came. He was Sarchedonus's trusted servant and my brother's son.

Chapter 2

1. When I returned home, my wife Anna was restored to me, and my son Tobias. It was Pentecost, the Feast of Weeks, and a good meal was prepared for me, so I sat down to eat. **2.** I saw an abundance (plenty) of food, and I said to my son, "Go and bring any poor man you find from our family who honors the Lord. I'll wait for you." **3.** He returned and said, "Father, one of our kin (family) has been strangled (choked) and cast (thrown) out in the marketplace." **4.** Before I ate, I got up, took him into an upper room, and waited until sunset. **5.** Afterward, I washed myself and ate with sorrow (sadness). **6.** I remembered the prophecy (prediction) of Amos: "Your feasts will turn to mourning (grief), and all your joy to lamentation (sorrow)." **7.** I wept (cried), and when the sun set, I dug a grave and buried him. **8.** My neighbors mocked (ridiculed) me, saying, "Now he's not afraid to die for this; he fled before, and now he buries the dead again." **9.** That night, I returned from burying him and slept by the courtyard (enclosed space) wall, unclean (impure), with my face uncovered. **10.** I didn't know there were sparrows in the wall. As I lay awake, they dropped warm dung (excrement) into my eyes, and a white film (coating) covered them. I went to the doctors, but they couldn't help. Achiacharus nourished (tended to) me until I went to Elymais. **11.** My wife Anna wove (made) cloth in the women's chamber, **12.** and sent the work back to the owners, who paid her and gave her a kid (young goat). **13.** When it came to my house, it began to cry. I asked her, "Where did this kid come from? Was it stolen (taken without permission)? You must return it, for it's not lawful (permissible) to eat stolen things." **14.** She said, "It was given to me as a gift beyond my wages." I didn't believe her and asked her to return it. I was ashamed (embarrassed) of her. But she answered, "Where are your alms (charitable gifts) and your righteous deeds? Behold, you and all your works are known."

Chapter 3

1. I was deeply troubled and wept, praying in my sorrow, saying, **2.** "O Lord, You are just, and all Your actions and ways are full of mercy and truth. You judge with fairness and righteousness, and Your judgments are forever true. **3.** Remember me and look upon me. Do not punish me for my sins and my ignorance (lack of knowledge), nor for the sins of my ancestors (forefathers) who sinned before me. **4.** They disobeyed (rejected) Your commandments. You handed us over as spoils (plunder), into captivity (enslavement), to death, and to disgrace (dishonor), becoming a proverb (example) and a source of mockery among all the nations to which we were scattered. **5.** Now, Your judgments are true and many. You should deal with me according to my sins and the sins of my ancestors because we did not keep Your commandments and did not walk in truth before You. **6.** Now, deal with me in a way that pleases You. Command that my spirit be taken from me so that I may be released from this life and return to the earth, for it is better for me to die than to live. I have heard many false accusations, and my soul is overwhelmed with grief (sorrow). Command that I be relieved (freed) from this distress (trouble) and be taken to the eternal (everlasting) rest. Do not turn Your face from me." **7.** On that same day, Sarah, the daughter of Raguel in Ecbatana, also faced reproach (mockery) from her maidservants. **8.** She had been married to seven husbands, but the evil spirit Asmodeus had killed each of them before they could consummate (complete) the marriage.

The maidservants mocked her, saying, "Do you not know that you have killed your husbands? You have had seven husbands and none of them has given you a child. 9. Why do you torment (bother) us? If they are dead, go with them. Let us never see a son or daughter from you." 10. When Sarah heard these words, she was deeply distressed (grieved) and considered ending (taking) her life. She thought, "I am my father's only daughter. If I do this, it will bring shame upon him and cause him sorrow in his old age." 11. She then prayed at the window, saying, "Blessed are You, O Lord my God, and blessed is Your holy and honorable (worthy of respect) name forever. Let all Your works praise You forever. 12. Now, Lord, I turn my eyes and my heart to You. 13. Command that I be freed from this earthly (worldly) life and that I no longer hear reproach (mockery). 14. You know, Lord, that I am pure (chaste) and have not sinned with any man, 15. and that I have kept my name and my father's name clean (undefiled) in the land of my captivity. I am my father's only daughter, and he has no other heirs (successors). Seven husbands have died. Why should I live? If it does not please You to take my life, at least show me mercy and let me no longer suffer such reproach." 16. The prayers of both were heard before the glory (majesty) of the great God. 17. Raphael was sent to heal them both: to restore Tobit's sight and to give Sarah, the daughter of Raguel, as a wife to Tobias, the son of Tobit; and to bind (restrain) the evil spirit Asmodeus, for it was destined for Tobias to inherit her. At that time, Tobit returned to his house, and Sarah, the daughter of Raguel, came down from her upper room.

Chapter 4

1. On that day, Tobit remembered the silver he had entrusted to Gabael in Rages of Media. 2. He said to himself, "I have asked for death; but why not call for my son Tobias and explain to him about the money before I die?" 3. So he called Tobias and said, "My son, when I die, bury me. Do not neglect your mother. Honor her all the days of your life. Always do what pleases her and avoid causing her sorrow. 4. Remember, my son, the hardships (difficulties) she endured for you when you were in her womb. When she passes, lay her to rest beside me in one grave. 5. My son, remember the Lord your God throughout your life. Do not let your heart be drawn to sin (wrongdoing) or break His commandments. Live righteously (justly) and avoid wrongdoing. 6. If you live by truth, your actions will prosper (succeed), and all who follow righteousness will find success. 7. Be generous (charitable) with your wealth. When you give to those in need, do not be stingy (greedy). Do not turn away from the poor (needy), for if you do, God will turn away from you. 8. Give according to what you have, whether little or much. Do not be afraid to give, for even small offerings are treasured by God. 9. Your generosity stores up blessings for you in times of need. 10. Almsgiving (charity) saves from death and keeps you from falling into despair. 11. It is a beautiful gift before the Lord for all who give with a pure heart. 12. Be cautious (careful), my son, of immorality (unlawful sexual relations), and choose a wife from among your own people. Do not marry someone outside our tribe, for we are descendants of the prophets. Our ancestors—Noah, Abraham, Isaac, and Jacob—married within their own family, and their children were blessed. 13. Love your family, my son, and never look down on them or their children when choosing a wife. For contempt (disrespect) leads to destruction (ruin), and laziness (idleness) brings poverty (lack), for laziness is the root of hunger. 14. Pay the workers who serve you without delay. If you serve God faithfully, you will be rewarded. Be careful, my son, in all your actions and behave wisely. 15. Treat others as you would want to be treated. Do not indulge in drunkenness (intoxication) or let it guide your steps. 16. Share your food (bread) with the hungry and your clothes (garments) with those who have none. Be generous with your blessings. 17. Give to the righteous, but do not give to sinners. 18. Seek wisdom (knowledge) from those who are experienced and never dismiss helpful advice. 19. Praise the Lord your God at all times, and ask Him to guide your ways and make your plans successful. Nations may not have counsel (advice), but the Lord provides all good things and humbles (lowers) whom He chooses. Remember my teachings, my son, and never forget them. 20. Now, I will tell you about the ten talents of silver I entrusted to Gabael, the son of Gabrias, in Rages of Media. 21. Do not fear, my son, because we are poor. If you fear God, turn away from sin, and live according to His will, you will be wealthy in His sight.

Chapter 5

1. Tobias replied, "Father, I will obey all that you have commanded." 2. "But how can I collect the money, as I do not know him?" 3. His father handed him the written document and said, "Find someone to accompany you, and I will pay him (wages) while I am still alive. Go and receive the money." 4. Tobias went to find a companion and met Raphael, though he didn't realize he was an angel. 5. Raphael asked, "Can I accompany you to Rages in Media? Are you familiar (know well) with the route?" 6. The angel answered, "I will go with you, for I know the way well. I have stayed (lodged) with our brother Gabael." 7. Tobias said, "Wait here while I tell my father." 8. Raphael urged him, "Go, and do not delay." Tobias went inside and said to his father, "I've found someone to accompany me." Tobit replied, "Bring him here so I can learn which tribe he is from and whether he can be trusted (reliable)." 9. Tobias called the man, and they greeted (saluted) each other. 10. Tobit asked, "Brother, from which tribe and family do you come? Please tell me." 11. The man replied, "Are you asking about my family or if I am a paid (hired) guide for your son?" Tobit answered, "I wish to know your family and your name, brother." 12. The man said, "I am Azarias, the son of Ananias, a member of your family." 13. Tobit welcomed him warmly, saying, "Do not be upset for me asking about your lineage (ancestry). You are from an honorable family, for I knew Ananias and Jathan, the sons of Shemaiah, when we journeyed to Jerusalem to offer our firstborn and tithes (tenths). They were upright and did not stray from the error (mistakes) of our kindred (family). You come from a noble heritage." 14. Tobit then asked, "What wages do you expect? A drachma (silver coin) a day, along with whatever provisions (necessary things) you need, like for my son?" 15. "Moreover, if you both return safely (safe and sound), I will add to your wages," he offered. 16. The terms were agreed upon, and Tobit said to his son, "Prepare for the journey, and may God make your way prosperous (successful)." Tobias gathered what he needed, and his father added, "Go with this man, and may God, who dwells (lives) in heaven, bless your journey. May His angel accompany you." Together, they left, with Tobias' dog following them. 17. Anna, Tobias' mother, cried and said to Tobit, "Why have you sent our son away? He is our support (staff), going in and out before us. 18. Don't be too eager to gain wealth, as our child is more precious than money. 19. What the Lord has provided is enough (sufficient) for us." 20. Tobit comforted her, saying, "Do not be distressed (worried). He will return safely, and you will see him again. 21. A good angel will accompany him, and his journey will be successful." 22. With that, she stopped weeping.

Chapter 6

1. As they traveled, they reached the Tigris River and camped there for the night. 2. The young man went to wash, and a fish leaped out of the water, nearly swallowing him. 3. The angel told him, "Grab the fish!" and he pulled it ashore. 4. The angel instructed him to take the heart, liver, and bile (gall) of the fish and keep them. 5. The young man followed the angel's command, roasting and eating the fish, and continued their journey toward Ecbatana. 6. The young man asked, "What are the uses of the heart, liver, and bile?" 7. The angel explained, "The heart and liver can drive away demons (evil spirits) when burned before someone afflicted. 8. The bile can be used to treat cataracts (white films on the eyes) by anointing the eyes." 9. As they neared Rages, 10. the angel said they would stay with Raguel, a relative, who had a daughter named Sarah. He would speak to her father about her marriage to the young man, since her inheritance was his by law. 11. Sarah was beautiful and wise, and the angel assured him that Raguel could not marry her to anyone else. 12. The young man, however, expressed fear, as Sarah had been married to seven men who all died on their wedding night due to a demon. 13. He feared he would die too and bring grief to his parents, who had no other son. 14. The angel reassured him, saying, "Remember your father's command to marry someone from your kin (family). Don't fear the demon; tonight she will be your wife. 15. In the bride-chamber (wedding room), burn incense (fragrant smoke) with the fish's heart and liver, and the demon will flee. 16. Cry out to God for mercy, and He will protect you. She was prepared for you, and together you will have children." 17. Tobias, hearing this, loved her deeply and felt a strong bond.

Chapter 7

1. When they reached Ecbatana, they arrived at the home of Raguel. Sarah greeted them, and they in turn welcomed her. She then led them into the house. **2.** Raguel turned to his wife, Edna, and said, "This young man closely resembles my cousin Tobit!" **3.** He then asked them, "Where are you from? What is your family background?" They answered, "We are descendants of Naphtali, who were taken captive (forced to go) in Nineveh." **4.** Raguel asked, "Do you know Tobit, our relative?" They replied, "Yes, we know him." He then asked, "Is he well?" **5.** They answered, "He is alive and in good health." Tobias added, "He is my father." **6.** Raguel immediately stood up, kissed him, and began to weep. **7.** He blessed him, saying, "You are the son of a righteous (virtuous) and good man." Upon hearing that Tobit had lost his sight, he was deeply moved and wept. **8.** Edna, his wife, and Sarah, his daughter, also wept. They welcomed them warmly and slaughtered (killed) a ram (male sheep) from the flock to prepare a meal. But Tobias said to Raphael, "Brother Azarias, please share the matter we discussed on the journey so that everything may be settled." **9.** Raphael spoke to Raguel, and Raguel said to Tobias, "Eat, drink, and rejoice, for it is your right to marry my daughter. But I must be honest with you. **10.** I've already promised my daughter to seven of our kinsmen (relatives), but each time they entered the bridal chamber, they died during the night. So for now, enjoy the feast." **11.** Tobias replied, "I will not eat or drink until you make an agreement (promise) with me." **12.** Raguel answered, "Follow the custom and take her as your wife, since you are a relative. May the merciful (kind and forgiving) God bless your union with success." **13.** He then called Sarah, took her hand, and gave her to Tobias, saying, "Take her as your wife according to the law of Moses and lead her to your father. May God bless you both." **14.** He then called his wife Edna, took a written contract (legal document), and sealed it. **15.** Afterward, they began to eat together. **16.** Raguel turned to Edna and said, "Sister, prepare the other room and bring Sarah in there." **17.** Edna did as he asked, leading Sarah into the room. Sarah wept, and Edna, sharing her sorrow, said, **18.** "Don't cry, my child. May the Lord of heaven and earth show you favor and bring you peace through this pain. Be comforted, my daughter."

Chapter 8

1. After they had finished their meal, Tobias was brought to her. **2.** As he walked, he remembered Raphael's instructions and used the ashes from the incense (fragrant substance), placing the fish's heart and liver on them to create smoke. **3.** When the demon smelled it, it fled to the farthest regions of Egypt, and the angel bound it there. **4.** After they were alone, Tobias rose and said, "Sister, let us pray that God may show us His mercy." **5.** Tobias began, "Blessed are You, O God of our ancestors (forefathers), and blessed is Your holy and glorious name forever. Let the heavens and all Your creatures bless You. **6.** You created Adam and gave him Eve as a companion and helper. Through them, mankind was born. You said, 'It is not good for man to be alone; let us make a helper for him.' **7.** Now, O Lord, I do not take my sister for desire (lust), but in sincerity. May I find Your mercy and grow old with her." **8.** She responded, "Amen." And they both slept that night. **9.** Raguel rose early, dug a grave (tomb), **10.** saying, "Lest he also should die." **11.** Raguel then returned home, **12.** and said to his wife Edna, "Send one of the maidservants (female servants) to check if he is still alive. If not, we will bury him and no one will know." **13.** The maidservant went in, found them both asleep, **14.** and reported back that Tobias was alive. **15.** Raguel then blessed God, saying, "Blessed are You, O God, with all pure and holy blessings (sacred praise)! Let Your saints (holy ones) and all creatures praise You! Let all angels and the elect (chosen ones) bless You forever! **16.** Blessed are You, for You have brought joy to me; things have not gone as I feared, but You have shown us Your mercy. **17.** Blessed are You for showing mercy to the only children (begotten) of their parents. Grant them health, joy, and mercy, O Lord. **18.** He instructed his servants to cover the grave. **19.** Raguel held a wedding feast (celebration) for them that lasted fourteen days. **20.** Before the feast ended, Raguel swore (made an oath) to Tobias that he would not leave until the fourteen days were complete; **21.** then he would take half of his possessions (wealth) and return safely to his father, with the rest to come after his and Edna's death.

Chapter 9

1. Tobias then called to Raphael and said, **2.** "Brother Azarias, take a servant with you and two camels, and travel to Rages (a city in Media), to find Gabael. There, receive the money for me, and bring it back for the wedding feast. **3.** For Raguel has sworn (made an oath) that I must not leave. **4.** My father is counting the days, and if I delay any longer, he will be deeply distressed (sorrowful). **5.** So Raphael set out on his journey, staying overnight (lodging) with Gabael. He gave him the written document, and Gabael took out the bags, each sealed (marked with authenticity) with its mark of authenticity, and handed them over. **6.** The next morning, they rose early and went together to the wedding feast. Tobias then blessed his wife."

Chapter 10

1. Every day, Tobit anxiously counted the days. When the allotted time for the journey had passed and his son had not yet returned, **2.** he wondered, "Could something have delayed (postponed) him? Or has Gabael died, leaving no one to deliver the money?" **3.** Tobit was deeply distressed (upset). **4.** But his wife said to him, "The boy must have perished (died) since he's taking so long to return." She began to mourn (grieve), saying, **5.** "I care for nothing, my child, for since I let you go, my heart has been shattered, and the light of my eyes is gone." **6.** Tobit responded, "Do not grieve. Have faith. He is well and safe." **7.** But she retorted, "Do not deceive me. My child is lost." Every day, she would go to the road where he had traveled and mourn for him, refusing to eat during the day. She did this for many nights, grieving over her son, until the 14 days of the wedding feast had passed, as Raguel had promised. At that point, Tobias said to Raguel, "Please allow me to leave. My parents have given up hope of ever seeing me again." **8.** But Raguel replied, "Stay with me, and I will send word to your father. He will be informed (notified) of how you are faring." **9.** Tobias insisted, "No, I must return to my father." **10.** So Raguel rose, gave Tobias his daughter Sarah as his wife, and also half of his possessions (belongings)—servants, livestock, and money. **11.** He blessed them, saying, "May the God of heaven bless and guide you both. May He bring you success (prosperity) before I die." **12.** He then spoke to Sarah, saying, "Honor (respect) your father and mother-in-law as you would your own parents. I trust that I will hear only good things about you." He kissed her goodbye. **13.** Edna, Sarah's mother, said to Tobias, "May the Lord of heaven heal you, dear brother, and grant me the joy of seeing your children, so I can rejoice in the Lord. I place my daughter in your care with great trust. Do not bring her sorrow (grief)."

Chapter 11

1. Tobit anxiously awaited the return of his son. When the appointed days had passed and there was no sign of him, **2.** he wondered, "Could he be delayed (postponed)? Or perhaps Gabael has passed away, leaving no one to deliver the money?" **3.** He was deeply distressed (sorrowful). **4.** His wife, grieving, said, "He must be dead, for he's been gone so long." She mourned (lamented) and lamented, **5.** "I feel nothing now, for the light of my eyes is lost with him." **6.** Tobit reassured her, saying, "Don't mourn (grieve); he is well and safe." **7.** But she replied, "Do not deceive (mislead) me. My son is dead." She then went daily to the road (path) he had traveled, refraining (abstaining) from eating during the day, and wept (cried) through the nights until the two-week wedding feast was over. At that point, Tobias spoke to Raguel, saying, "Please send me back, for my parents no longer expect to see me." **8.** Raguel insisted (urged), "Stay a while longer; I'll send word to your father so he knows how things are with you." **9.** But Tobias insisted, "No, send me to my father." **10.** Raguel stood, gave Tobias his daughter Sarah, along with half of his wealth—servants, livestock (animals), and money. **11.** He blessed (prayed for) them, saying, "May God prosper (bless) you both before I die." **12.** Raguel also told his daughter, "Respect (honor) your in-laws as your parents. I expect to hear good reports (news) of you." Then he kissed her. **13.** Edna spoke to Tobias, saying, "May the Lord restore (heal) you to health, and may I see the children you and Sarah will have, that I may rejoice before God. I trust (entrust) you with my daughter—do not cause her sorrow (grief)."

Chapter 12

1. Tobit called his son, Tobias, and said to him, "Look, my son, make sure to pay the man who accompanied you the wages (payment) he is due, and give him even more than that. **2.** Tobias replied, "Father, it would not be a problem for me to give him half of what I have brought back, **3.** for he has safely guided (protected) me, healed my wife, returned my money, and also healed you." **4.** Tobit said, "He certainly deserves it (is worthy of it)." **5.** Then he called the angel and said, "Take half of all that you have brought." **6.** He then privately called them both and said, "Praise God, thank Him, and glorify (honor) His name before all people for the great things He has done for you. It is good to bless God and honor His name, acknowledging His mighty deeds. Do not fail to thank Him. **7.** It is wise to keep the secrets of kings, but it is right to proclaim (announce) the wonderful works of God. Do good, and evil will not come upon you. **8.** Prayer accompanied by fasting, charity (generosity), and righteousness (justice) is good. A little done with righteousness is better than much done in unrighteousness. It is better to give charity than to store up wealth. **9.** Charity saves from death and cleanses (washes away) all sin. Those who give generously and live righteously will be filled with life, **10.** but those who sin are enemies to their own lives. **11.** Truly, I will not hide anything from you. I've said before, 'It is good to keep the secret of kings, but to openly declare (reveal) the works of God.' **12.** When you prayed, and when Sarah, your daughter-in-law, prayed, I brought your prayer before the Holy One. When you buried the dead, I was with you. **13.** And when you did not hesitate (pause) to leave your meal and go bury the dead, your good deed was not unnoticed by me. I was there with you. **14.** Now, God has sent me to heal you and Sarah, your daughter-in-law. **15.** I am Raphael, one of the seven holy angels who present the prayers of the saints and stand in the presence of the glory of God." **16.** They were both afraid and fell on their faces, for they were terrified (frightened). **17.** But the angel said to them, "Do not be afraid. You will have peace; bless God forever. **18.** I am not here on my own behalf, but because of the will (purpose) of your God. Therefore, bless Him forever. **19.** I have been with you all this time. I did not eat or drink, but you saw only a vision. **20.** Now give thanks to God, for I am returning to Him who sent me. Write down all that has happened in a book." **21.** Then they stood up, but saw him no more. **22.** They praised God for His great and marvelous works and told how the angel of the Lord had appeared to them.

Chapter 13

1. And Tobit wrote a prayer of rejoicing, saying, "Blessed is God who lives forever! Blessed is His kingdom! **2.** For He punishes (scourges) and shows mercy. He brings down to the grave and raises up again. No one can escape His hand. **3.** Give thanks to Him before the nations, all you children of Israel! For He has scattered us among them. **4.** Declare His greatness there. Praise Him before all the living, for He is our Lord, and God is our Father forever. **5.** He will punish us for our iniquities (sins) but will show mercy and gather us from all the nations where we have been scattered. **6.** If you turn to Him with your whole heart and soul to do truth before Him, He will turn to you and will not hide His face from you. See what He will do with you. Give Him thanks with your whole mouth. Bless the Lord of righteousness. Exalt the everlasting King. I thank Him in the land of my captivity and show His strength and majesty to a sinful nation. Turn, you sinners, and do righteousness before Him. Who knows if He will accept you and have mercy on you? **7.** I exalt (praise) my God. My soul exalts the King of heaven and rejoices in His greatness. **8.** Let all men speak and give thanks in Jerusalem. **9.** O Jerusalem, holy city, He will punish you for the sins of your children but will have mercy on the righteous. **10.** Give thanks to the Lord with goodness and bless the everlasting King, that His tabernacle (dwelling place) may be rebuilt in you with joy, and that He may bring gladness to the captives and love to the miserable forever. **11.** Many nations will come from afar to the name of the Lord God with gifts in their hands, even gifts for the King of heaven. Generations will praise you and sing songs of joy. **12.** All who hate you will be cursed. But those who love you forever will be blessed. **13.** Rejoice and be exceedingly glad, you sons of the righteous, for you will be gathered together and will bless the Lord of the righteous. **14.** Blessed are those who love you. They will rejoice in your peace. Blessed are those who mourned for all your sufferings, for they will rejoice in you when they see your glory. They will be made glad forever. **15.** Let my soul bless God, the great King. **16.** For Jerusalem will be rebuilt with sapphires (a precious blue gemstone), emeralds, and precious stones; her walls, towers, and battlements (defensive walls) will be made of pure gold. **17.** Her streets will be paved with beryl (a greenish-blue stone),

carbuncle (a red gemstone), and stones of Ophir (a place known for wealth and precious stones). **18.** All her streets will say, "Hallelujah!" and praise, saying, "Blessed be God, who has exalted you forever!"

Chapter 14

1. Tobit finished offering his thanks. **2.** He was 58 when he lost his sight, but after eight years, his sight was restored. He gave generously to those in need (charitable donations), grew in his reverence (deep respect) for the Lord, and praised Him. **3.** As he grew older, he called his son and his six grandsons, saying, "My child, take care of your sons. I am now old and near the end of my life. **4.** Go to Media, for I believe what the prophet Jonah said about Nineveh—that it will be destroyed. But in Media, peace will last for a time. Our people will be scattered (dispersed) from the land, and Jerusalem will lie in ruins (incomplete, broken), its temple burned. **5.** Yet, God will show mercy (compassion) again, returning His people to their land, where they will rebuild the temple—not as it once was—until the appointed time (predetermined period) is fulfilled. Then, they will return from captivity (state of being taken away as prisoners) and rebuild Jerusalem with honor. The temple will be restored forever, as the prophets foretold (predicted). **6.** Then, all nations will come to fear the Lord and abandon their idols (false gods). **7.** They will praise God, and His people will give thanks, as the Lord elevates (raises in status) His people. Those who love Him in truth will rejoice (feel great joy), showing mercy to their kin (family). **8.** Therefore, my child, leave Nineveh, for Jonah's prophecy (prediction) will surely be fulfilled. **9.** Keep the law and live mercifully (showing kindness) and righteously (acting justly), so that it may go well with you. **10.** Bury me and your mother properly. Do not remain in Nineveh. Remember what Aman did to Achiacharus, who cared for him—how he betrayed him and brought him to ruin (destruction). Achiacharus was saved, but Aman faced justice and perished (died). Manasses gave to the poor and escaped death (fatal danger), but Aman fell into his own trap. **11.** My children, consider how almsgiving (charitable donations) saves and righteousness delivers (rescues)." Tobit passed away at 158 years old. Tobias gave him a respectful burial. **12.** After Anna's death, Tobias buried her with Tobit, then moved with his wife and sons to Ecbatana to live with his father-in-law, Raguel. **13.** He lived honorably (with dignity), burying his in-laws with dignity, and inherited their possessions (property), along with his father Tobit's. **14.** Tobias died in Ecbatana at 127 years old. **15.** Before his death, he heard of Nineveh's destruction by Nebuchadnezzar and Ahasuerus, and he rejoiced in its fall.

19 – The Book of Judith

Chapter 1

1. In the twelfth year of King Nebuchadnezzar's reign in Nineveh (capital of Assyria), during King Arphaxad's rule over the Medes in Ecbatana (a city in Media), **2.** Arphaxad built strong walls around Ecbatana, using stones three cubits (about 18 inches) wide and six cubits long, with walls seventy cubits high and fifty cubits thick. **3.** He placed towers on the gates, one hundred cubits high with sixty cubits at the base. **4.** The city gates were seventy cubits high and forty cubits wide for military use. **5.** King Nebuchadnezzar waged war against King Arphaxad in the great plain near Ragau (a mountainous region). **6.** People from surrounding regions, including the Euphrates, Tigris, and Hydaspes rivers, as well as Arioch (King of the Elymeans), gathered to fight. **7.** Nebuchadnezzar sent messengers to Persia (east of Assyria) and the west, including Cilicia, Damascus, Lebanon, and coastal regions. **8.** He also sent for those from Carmel (mountains in Israel), Gilead, Galilee, and the great plain of Esdrelon (in Israel). **9.** The command reached Samaria (Israel), Jerusalem, and beyond, including Egypt and its borders. **10.** The message reached all the way to the borders of Egypt and Ethiopia. **11.** However, the people ignored Nebuchadnezzar's command, refused to join him, and disrespected his messengers. **12.** This angered Nebuchadnezzar, who swore revenge on Cilicia, Damascus, Syria, Moab, Ammon, Judea, Egypt, and the borders of the two seas. **13.** Nebuchadnezzar then fought Arphaxad and defeated him in the seventeenth year of his reign, destroying Arphaxad's forces, including cavalry and chariots. **14.** Nebuchadnezzar took control of Ecbatana, ruined its streets, and disgraced its beauty. **15.** He captured Arphaxad in the mountains of Ragau and killed him with darts, destroying him completely. **16.** Nebuchadnezzar returned to Nineveh, where he rested and celebrated with a feast for one hundred and twenty days.

Chapter 2

1. In the eighteenth year, on the twenty-second day of the first month, word spread in the palace of King Nebuchadnezzar (King of Assyria, a powerful empire) that he intended to exact vengeance (revenge) on the whole earth. **2.** So, he summoned (called) all his officers and nobles to discuss his plan, sharing with them his secret intentions. He declared that he would afflict (cause great suffering) the entire world, speaking it into action himself. **3.** A decree (official order) was made to destroy all people who refused to follow his command. **4.** After making his decision, Nebuchadnezzar called Holofernes (the chief general of his army), and ordered him: **5.** "Thus says the great king, the ruler of the entire earth: Take an army of 120,000 foot soldiers and 12,000 cavalry (horse riders), men who trust in their own strength. **6.** You are to march westward against those who disobeyed my orders. **7.** Tell them to prepare for my wrath (intense anger), for I will cover the earth with my army and leave them as spoils (things taken as loot). **8.** The slain (those killed) will fill the valleys, the brooks (small rivers), and rivers will overflow with their dead. **9.** You will lead the captives (prisoners) to the farthest parts of the earth. **10.** Go ahead of me and secure all their territories (areas under their control). If they surrender (give up without a fight), keep them for me until the day of their punishment. **11.** But those who resist (fight back), do not spare (show mercy); destroy them wherever you find them. **12.** As I live and by the power of my kingdom, whatever I have commanded, I will do with my own hand. **13.** Make sure you carry out all my orders without delay, and do not fail to accomplish them." **14.** Then Holofernes left the king's presence and gathered the governors (officials in charge of provinces), captains (military leaders), and officers (high-ranking soldiers) of the Assyrian army. **15.** He mustered (gathered) 120,000 chosen foot soldiers, along with 12,000 archers (soldiers with bows) on horseback. **16.** The army was organized for battle as a massive force. **17.** He gathered camels, donkeys, and many other animals for transportation, along with vast numbers of sheep, oxen (large cattle), and goats for food supplies. **18.** Additionally, he took much gold and silver (money) from the king's treasury (the king's storehouse of wealth) for the journey. **19.** Holofernes then set out with the army, heading toward King Nebuchadnezzar, intending to cover the western lands with their chariots (two-wheeled vehicles drawn by horses), cavalry (soldiers on horseback), and foot soldiers. **20.** A vast number of people from various nations joined, like locusts (small, swarming insects that destroy crops) or the sand of the sea, forming an innumerable (too many to count) multitude (large crowd). **21.** After three days from leaving Nineveh (the capital of Assyria), they camped near the plain (large flat area) of Bectileth (a region) at the base (bottom part) of the mountain to the left of upper Cilicia (a region near Turkey). **22.** From there, Holofernes took his army and advanced (moved forward) into the hill country. **23.** He destroyed the people of Phud and Lud (regions), as well as the children of Rasses and Israel, who were in the wilderness south of the land of the Chellians (a desert region). **24.** He crossed the Euphrates (a major river in the Middle East) River, invaded Mesopotamia (ancient land between two rivers), and destroyed the cities along the river Arbonai (a tributary of the Euphrates), moving toward the sea. **25.** Holofernes conquered the borders (edges or limits) of Cilicia, slaughtered (killed violently) those who resisted, and came to the southern borders of Japheth (a region near Arabia). **26.** He also attacked the people of Madian (an ancient group), burned their homes, and destroyed their flocks (groups of animals). **27.** Holofernes descended (moved down) into the plain (flat land) of Damascus (a city in Syria) during the wheat harvest, burning their fields, killing their flocks, and ruining their cities, slaying all their young men. **28.** The fear of him spread across the coastlands (areas along the sea) of Sidon, Tyre, Sur, Ocina, Jemnaan, Azotus, and Ascalon, where people greatly feared him.

Chapter 3

1. So they sent messengers (people who carry messages) to him to discuss peace, saying, **2.** "We are the servants (those who serve or work for) of King Nebuchadnezzar (the powerful king of Babylon); we lie before you—treat us as you see fit. **3.** Look, our homes, lands, fields of wheat (grains used for food), flocks (groups of animals, like sheep), herds (groups of large animals, like cattle), and all our tents (temporary shelters) are yours to use as you desire. **4.** Even our cities and their inhabitants (the people who live there) are your servants; do with them as seems right to you." **5.** The messengers went to Holofernes (the general of Nebuchadnezzar's army), and relayed (delivered) these words to him. **6.** He then moved towards the coast (the land next to the sea) with his army, stationed soldiers in the high cities, and took selected (chosen) men for support. **7.** The people and the surrounding region (nearby area) welcomed them with garlands (flower necklaces), dancing, and music. **8.** However, he destroyed their borders (the lines that mark the limits of an area) and cut down their sacred groves (trees or forests considered holy), for he had decided to destroy all the gods of the land, so that all nations would worship only Nebuchadnezzar, and all people, from all languages and tribes, would call upon him as god. **9.** He then moved toward Esdraelon (a plain in Israel), near the great pass (narrow route or way) of Judea. **10.** He camped (set up camp) between Geba and Scythopolis (towns in Israel) and stayed there for a month to gather all the supplies for his army.

Chapter 4

1. The people of Israel in Judea heard about Holofernes (a military leader), the chief general of King Nebuchadnezzar (the king of the Babylonians) of Assyria (an ancient empire), destroying temples and nations. **2.** They feared him and were concerned for Jerusalem (the capital city of Israel) and the Lord's temple (a sacred place of worship). **3.** Recently returned from exile (being taken away from their land), the people of Judea had gathered again, and the vessels (sacred items), altar (a place for sacrifices), and temple (house of God) had been purified (made clean) after being defiled (dishonored). **4.** They sent messengers through Samaria (a historical region) and to the villages of Bethoron, Belmen, Jericho, Choba, Esora, and the Valley of Salem (regions near Jerusalem). **5.** They fortified (strengthened) the hilltops, stored provisions (food) for war, and harvested fields (crops). **6.** Joacim (high priest in Jerusalem) wrote to the people of Bethulia and Betomestham, near Esdraelon (a region), to guard the mountain passes (narrow roads). **7.** These passes led into Judea, and securing them would block invaders (those who try to enter), as the path was narrow, allowing only two men at a time. **8.** The Israelites followed Joacim's command, with the elders (leaders) of Israel in Jerusalem joining. **9.** Every Israelite, in deep prayer, cried out to God, humbling themselves (showing respect) with great earnestness (seriousness). **10.** The men, women, children, cattle (domestic animals), strangers (foreigners), hired workers, and servants (those who worked for others) all put on sackcloth (cloth used for mourning), a sign of sorrow and repentance (regret for wrongdoing). **11.** Everyone in Jerusalem, from children to adults, gathered before the temple, covered in ashes (mourning) and spread sackcloth before the Lord. They also placed sackcloth around the altar (sacred table for offerings). **12.** They cried out to God together, asking Him not to let their children be taken, their wives enslaved (made slaves), their cities destroyed, or the sanctuary (sacred place) dishonored by enemies. **13.** God heard their prayers and saw their suffering. The people fasted (went without food for religious reasons) for many days across all of Judea and Jerusalem before the Lord's sanctuary. **14.** Joacim the high priest, with all the priests (religious leaders) and those who served (ministered) in the temple, wore sackcloth, offering burnt offerings (animal sacrifices), vows (promises), and freewill gifts (voluntary gifts). **15.** They wore ashes (mourning) on their headbands (mitres—religious head coverings), crying out to God with all their strength, hoping He would show mercy (kindness and forgiveness) to Israel.

Chapter 5

1. It was reported to Holofernes, the commander (leader) of the Assyrian army, that the Israelites had prepared for battle. They had blocked the mountain passes (narrow paths through mountains), fortified (strengthened) the high hills, and laid obstacles (barriers) in the open fields. **2.** This made Holofernes very angry, so he summoned (called) the leaders of Moab, the commanders (military leaders) of Ammon, and all the governors (officials in charge) from the coastal regions (regions by the sea). **3.** He said to them, "Tell me, sons of Canaan, who are these people living in the mountains? What cities do they inhabit (live in)? How many are they, and what power and strength do they have? Who is their king, or the leader of their army?

4. Why have they refused to come and face me, unlike all the other peoples of the west?" 5. Then Achior, the leader (chief) of the Ammonites, spoke up and said, "Let my lord listen to the truth from your servant, and I will tell you about this people who dwell (live) in the mountains. I will speak honestly, and nothing but the truth will come from my mouth. 6. These people are descended (descendants) from the Chaldeans (people of Mesopotamia), 7. They once lived in Mesopotamia (an ancient region between the Tigris and Euphrates rivers) because they rejected the gods of their ancestors (forefathers), who were from the land of Chaldea. 8. They abandoned the ways (traditions) of their forefathers and worshiped (revered) the God of heaven, the God they knew. This angered the people there, and they were driven out (forced to leave) and fled to Mesopotamia, where they lived for a long time. 9. Then their God commanded (told) them to leave and go to the land of Canaan, where they settled (made their home) and prospered (thrived), increasing in wealth and cattle. 10. But when a famine (severe shortage of food) struck Canaan, they went to Egypt, where they were sustained (nourished) and grew into a great nation. 11. The king of Egypt, however, became hostile (unfriendly) towards them. He treated them cruelly, making them slaves (forced workers) and forcing them to work in the brick pits. 12. They cried out to their God, and He sent plagues (destructive diseases or disasters) upon Egypt, leading the Egyptians to expel (force out) them from their land. 13. God then parted (split) the Red Sea for them, 14. And led them to Mount Sinai (a mountain where Moses received the Ten Commandments) and Kadesh-Barnea (a location in the desert), where they drove out the people living there. 15. They conquered (defeated) the land of the Amorites (a group of people living in ancient Canaan), destroying their cities, including Heshbon (a city), and took possession (ownership) of the hill country after crossing the Jordan River. 16. They defeated the Canaanites, the Perizzites, the Jebusites, the Hivites of Shechem (a city), and all the Gergeshites, settling in that land for many years. 17. As long as they remained faithful (loyal) to their God, they thrived (prospered), because the God who hates sin was with them. 18. But when they strayed (turned away) from His ways, they were defeated in many battles, taken captive (captured) to foreign lands, and their temple was destroyed. 19. Now they have returned to their God, gathered from the places where they were scattered (spread out), and reclaimed (taken back) Jerusalem, their sacred city, and the land that was once desolate (empty and uninhabited). 20. So, my lord, if they have sinned (done wrong) against their God, we can attack them, and they will be destroyed. 21. But if they are innocent, let us not touch them, for their God may protect them, and we would become a disgrace (shame) to the world." 22. After Achior finished speaking, the people around Holofernes grumbled (complained), and the leaders of Holofernes' army and those from the coastal regions said he should be killed. 23. They said, "We need not fear (be afraid of) the Israelites. They are a weak people, unable to fight a strong battle." 24. Therefore, Holofernes, we will march against them, and they will become easy prey (victims) for your army."

Chapter 6

1. After the noise of the council had died down, Holofernes, the chief captain (military leader) of the Assyrian army, spoke to Achior and all the Moabites (descendants of Lot, a nation east of Israel) in front of the assembly (gathering) of the other nations, saying: 2. "Who are you, Achior, and the hired soldiers (mercenaries, hired fighters) of Ephraim (a tribe of Israel), that you dare prophesy (predict the future by divine inspiration) against us today? You have said that we should not fight Israel because their God will protect them. But who is their God? Is it not King Nebuchadnezzar (the king of Babylon, a powerful empire)?" 3. "Nebuchadnezzar will send his power and destroy them from the face of the earth, and their God will not save them. We, his servants, will destroy them as one man. They will not be able to stand against the power of our horses (used for battle)." 4. "We will trample (crush underfoot) them underfoot, their mountains will be soaked with their blood, their fields will be filled with their dead bodies, and no one will be able to stand against us. They will utterly perish (be completely destroyed), says King Nebuchadnezzar, lord of all the earth. His words are never in vain (without effect)." 5. "As for you, Achior, hireling (paid servant) of Ammon (a neighboring nation), who has spoken these words in your wickedness (evil actions), you will not see my face again until I have taken vengeance (punishment for wrongdoing) on this people who came out of Egypt." 6. "Then my army and the great multitude (large number) that serve me will strike you down, and you will fall among the slain (those killed in battle) when I return." 7. "Now, my servants will take you back to the hill country (mountainous region) and leave you in one of the cities there, where you will remain until you are destroyed along with them." 8. "And if you think they will be captured, do not let your face fall (show sadness or despair). I have spoken, and my words will not be in vain." 9. Holofernes ordered his servants to take Achior and deliver him to the Israelites in Bethulia (a city of Israel). 10. So, his servants took him, leading him out of the camp, through the plain (open field), and into the hill country. They came to the fountains (water sources) near Bethulia. 11. When the people of Bethulia saw them, they gathered their weapons and went out to the hilltop. The slingers (those using slingshots) kept them from advancing by throwing stones at them. 12. However, they secretly (quietly and secretly) reached the foot of the hill, bound Achior, and threw him down. They left him there and returned to their lord. 13. The Israelites came down from the city, freed Achior, and brought him to Bethulia. They presented him to the city leaders. 14. The leaders at that time were Ozias, the son of Micha (a descendant of Simeon, one of the tribes of Israel), Chabris, the son of Gothoniel, and Charmis, the son of Melchiel. 15. They called an assembly (meeting) of the city's elders (leaders), and the youth and women gathered together. They placed Achior in the middle of the people. 16. Ozias asked Achior to explain what had happened. 17. Achior explained to them all that Holofernes had said, including the threats he had made against Israel. 18. Upon hearing this, the people fell to the ground and worshipped God, crying out: 19. "O Lord God of heaven, look at their pride (arrogance), and have mercy (compassion) on our lowly state (humble condition). See the faces of those who are dedicated (set apart) to You today." 20. The people comforted Achior, praising him greatly for his courage in speaking out. 21. Ozias took Achior to his house and prepared a feast (meal) for the elders. They spent the night praying to God for help.

Chapter 7

1. The next day, Holofernes (the Assyrian general) ordered his entire army, along with all those who had joined him, to move their camp towards Bethulia (a city in Israel). Their goal was to take control of the hill country (the elevated, mountainous region) and prepare for war against the Israelites. 2. The strong men of his army moved their camps, and the total number of soldiers was 170,000 foot soldiers (infantry) and 12,000 horsemen (cavalry), not counting the baggage and other men on foot, making up a vast and mighty force. 3. They camped in the valley near Bethulia, by a fountain (a source of water), and spread out in all directions—across Dothaim (a location) and even as far as Belmaim (a location), and in length from Bethulia to Cynamon (a location), opposite Esdraelon (a region in Israel). 4. The Israelites saw the enormous size of the army and were filled with fear. They said to each other, "These men will destroy the earth beneath us, for the mountains, valleys, and hills cannot bear such a massive force." 5. Every man armed himself, and they lit fires on their watchtowers (towers for observing the surroundings), staying awake and alert all night. 6. On the second day, Holofernes sent out his horsemen (cavalry) to inspect the area around Bethulia. 7. He surveyed the paths leading up to the city, took control of the water sources (the fountains of water), and placed garrisons (military units) to guard them before returning to his main camp. 8. Then, the leaders of the children of Esau (a tribe descended from Esau), Moab (a region east of Israel), and the coastal regions approached Holofernes with advice. 9. They said, "Lord, let us speak, and prevent disaster (calamity) for your army." 10. "These Israelites do not rely on their weapons but trust in the height (elevation) of their mountains, which are difficult to climb." 11. "Therefore, do not attack them directly; no one in your army will be lost." 12. "Stay in your camp and keep your army intact. Let your men seize the water source (fountain) at the base of the mountains." 13. "The people of Bethulia rely on that water; once they run out, they will surrender, and we can easily conquer them." 14. "Then, their women, children, and everyone else will perish by fire (be killed by burning) before the sword even reaches them." 15. "This will be the proper punishment for them, as they did not make peace with you." 16.

Holofernes and his men agreed with this plan, and he instructed that it be carried out. **17.** The armies of Ammon (a region east of Israel) and Esau left, taking 5,000 Assyrian soldiers with them, and they camped near the water sources (fountains), cutting off the water supply to Bethulia. **18.** The armies of Esau and Ammon also took positions in the hill country (elevated region), while the rest of the Assyrian army camped in the plain (flat land), covering a vast area with their tents and carts. **19.** The Israelites, surrounded on all sides, cried out to God in distress (great sorrow or anguish), for there was no way for them to escape. **20.** The Assyrian army encamped around them for 34 days, during which the Israelites' water supplies completely ran out. **21.** The cisterns (storage tanks for water) were emptied, and the people were given water only in small amounts, so they could not drink to satisfy their thirst. **22.** The young children, women, and men grew weak from dehydration (lack of water) and collapsed in the streets and gates, having no strength left. **23.** The people gathered before Ozias (the leader of Bethulia) and the elders (older, wise leaders) and cried out loudly. **24.** They said, "God will judge between us and you, for you have done us great harm by not making peace with the Assyrians." **25.** "Now we have no one to help us, and God has given us into their hands to be destroyed by thirst." **26.** "So, deliver us to the army of Holofernes as a spoil (plunder), for it is better to be taken captive than to die of thirst." **27.** "We are willing to serve them so our lives may be spared, and we will not witness the deaths of our children and families." **28.** "We call upon heaven, earth, and God to bear witness, and may He judge us if we are wrong in this decision." **29.** There was great weeping from the people as they all cried out to the Lord for mercy. **30.** Ozias responded, "Brothers, be courageous. Let us endure for five more days, trusting that God will show us His mercy, for He will not abandon us." **31.** "If after five days no help comes, I will do as you suggest." **32.** He then dismissed the people, sending them back to their posts and instructed everyone to remain in the city, as the situation grew increasingly dire.

Chapter 8

1. At that time, Judith, the daughter of Merari (a descendant of the tribe of Israel), heard about the situation in the city of Bethulia (a town in Israel). Her lineage went back through several generations, including her great-grandfather Joseph and his ancestors. **2.** Judith's husband, Manasses, who was from her own tribe, died during the barley harvest (when barley was gathered). **3.** While overseeing the workers in the field, the heat overwhelmed him. He collapsed on his bed and died in the city of Bethulia. They buried him between the towns of Dothaim and Balamo (two locations in Israel). **4.** Judith was widowed (her husband died) for three years and four months. **5.** During her widowhood, she set up a tent on the roof of her house, wore sackcloth (a garment made from coarse material worn as a sign of mourning), and lived in widow's attire (clothing worn by a woman whose husband has died). **6.** She fasted (refrained from eating) during her widowhood, except on the eves of the sabbaths (the day before the sabbath), on the sabbaths themselves, the eves of new moons (the day before the new moon), and on feast days (special religious holidays) or other sacred days of Israel. **7.** Judith was known for her beauty and good appearance. Her late husband had left her wealth, including gold, silver, servants (workers), cattle (livestock), and land, and she lived off these resources. **8.** Everyone praised her, for she greatly feared God (had great reverence for God). **9.** When Judith heard that the people of Bethulia had lost faith, especially after the governor Ozias (the leader of the city) swore to surrender the city to the Assyrians (people from Assyria) in five days unless God intervened, she was deeply disturbed. **10.** Judith sent her maid (a female servant) to summon Ozias, along with the elders Chabris and Charmis (city leaders), to come to her. **11.** When they arrived, she rebuked (corrected sharply) them: "Your words to the people are wrong. You swore an oath (promise) to surrender the city unless God helps us in five days. But what is this? You are testing God!" **12.** "How can you understand God's will? You cannot search His heart (inner thoughts) or know His thoughts. You should not provoke God to anger by acting as if He is limited in His power." **13.** "If God doesn't help us in five days, He still has the power to save us when He chooses or destroy us before our enemies." **14.** "Do not limit God's wisdom. He is not like a man, to be threatened or swayed." **15.** "Let us wait for His salvation (deliverance), and pray for His help, trusting that He will hear us if it pleases Him." **16.** "There is

no other god for us, as our ancestors knew. If we are taken, all of Judea (the region) will suffer, and our sanctuary (holy place) will be defiled (made unclean)." **17.** "The destruction of our people and our lands will come upon us, and we will become a disgrace (shame) to all who capture us." **18.** "If we serve as slaves, it will not be for our good. The Lord will make it a dishonor (shame) to us." **19.** "Therefore, we must set an example for our brethren (brothers and sisters in the faith). Our fate and the fate of the sanctuary depend on us." **20.** "Let us give thanks to God, who tests us (puts us through trials) as He did our ancestors." **21.** "Remember how He tested Abraham (the founding father of the Jewish faith), how He asked Isaac (Abraham's son) to be sacrificed, and how He tested Jacob (the father of the twelve tribes) when he worked for Laban (his uncle) in Syria." **22.** "He has not tested us with such severe trials. He does not take vengeance (punishment) but refines (purifies) those who come near Him." **23.** Ozias replied, "You speak wisely, and we know you have always been a woman of great understanding. No one can argue with your words." **24.** "But the people are extremely thirsty, and we were pressured into making this oath to surrender the city. Now we ask you to pray to God for rain to fill our cisterns (water storage tanks), so we do not perish from thirst." **25.** Judith responded, "Listen to me, and I will do something that will be remembered for generations to come." **26.** "Tonight, you will stand guard at the city gate. I will go out with my maidservant, and within the time you've given for the city's surrender, the Lord will deliver Israel (save Israel) through my actions." **27.** "But do not ask about my plan until it is completed." **28.** Ozias and the other leaders said, "Go in peace. May God be with you and guide your actions against our enemies." **29.** They left her and returned to their posts. **30.** Judith and her maidservant went to the gate, where the guards let them pass. **31.** They went out into the wilderness, and Judith prayed to God for help, trusting that He would guide her actions. **32.** That night, she entered the camp of the Assyrians, and God gave her favor (approval) with the enemy leaders. **33.** Judith approached the enemy camp, and by God's grace (unmerited favor), she was able to deceive them into thinking she was a defector (someone who abandons their side). **34.** She gained access to their general, Holofernes (the Assyrian commander), and won his trust with her words. **35.** Judith, through her cunning (cleverness) and faith in God, was about to carry out her plan that would save her people. **36.** As she left the Assyrian camp, she knew that her actions would forever be remembered as a great act of deliverance (salvation) for Israel.

Chapter 9

1. Judith bowed down with her face to the ground, placed ashes on her head, and removed the sackcloth (a rough cloth worn as a sign of mourning) she was wearing. As the evening incense (a substance burned to make a sweet-smelling smoke) was offered in Jerusalem at the house of the Lord, she cried out loudly, saying: **2.** "O Lord God of my father Simeon (Simeon was a forefather of Israel), who gave him a sword to take vengeance (punishment or revenge) on those who defiled (dishonored) a virgin, dishonoring her and polluting (making unclean) her purity, though you commanded it should not be so, yet they did it: **3.** Therefore, you delivered (gave) their rulers to be slain (killed), causing them to die in their own blood, deceived, and smiting (striking) their servants with their masters, and their masters with their servants, **4.** You gave their wives to be plundered (taken as spoil or stolen), their daughters to be captives (prisoners), and their wealth divided among your faithful (loyal followers), who were stirred (moved) by your zeal (passion for righteousness), abhorring (hating) the defilement of their blood, and cried out to you for help: O God, O my God, hear me, your widow (a woman whose husband has died). **5.** For you have done not only these things but also the ones before and after. You have considered (thought about) the things that now are and those yet to come. **6.** Indeed, what you determined (decided) was at hand, and you said, 'Here we are'; for all your ways are prepared (arranged), and your judgments (decisions or punishments) are in your foreknowledge (knowledge of what will happen in the future). **7.** Behold (look), the Assyrians (a mighty empire) have grown in power, with their horses and men, boasting (bragging) in their strength, trusting in shields, spears, bows, and slings (weapons), but they do not know that you are the Lord, the one who controls the battle—your name is the Lord. **8.** Cast down (bring low) their strength by your power and bring low their might (strength) in your wrath (anger). They have intended (planned) to desecrate (treat something sacred with disrespect) your sanctuary (sacred place), to defile the tabernacle (a sacred tent for worship) where your glorious name dwells (lives), and to destroy your altar with the sword (a weapon). **9.** Look at their pride and send your wrath upon their heads. Give me, your widow, the power I need. **10.** Let my words be the means to strike down both the servant and the prince (leader), the prince with the servant. Let their arrogance (pride) be broken by the hand of a woman. **11.** For your power is not in numbers, nor your might in strong men; you are a God of the oppressed (those who suffer), a helper to the weak, a protector of the helpless (those who cannot protect themselves), a savior (rescuer) for those without hope. **12.** I pray, O God of my father, and God of Israel's inheritance (the land promised to Israel), Lord of heaven and earth, Creator of the waters, King of all creatures, hear my prayer. **13.** Make my words and deceitful speech (false speech) wound and strike those who have plotted (planned) wickedness (evil) against your covenant (agreement with Israel), your holy house, the top of Zion (Jerusalem), and the dwelling place of your children. **14.** Let all nations and tribes recognize (acknowledge) that you alone are the God of all power and might, and that there is no protector of Israel but you."

Chapter 10

1. After she had finished praying and speaking to God, **2.** Judith rose from the ground, called her maid, and went to her house where she rested on the sabbath (a holy day of rest) and feast days. **3.** She took off her mourning clothes (clothes worn in grief), washed her body, anointed herself with precious oil (a valuable, fragrant substance), braided her hair, and put on a headdress (a decorative head covering). She then dressed in joyful garments (clothes worn for celebration), the same ones she wore during the life of her husband Manasseh. **4.** She put sandals (footwear) on her feet, adorned herself with bracelets, chains, rings, and earrings, and dressed beautifully to captivate the eyes of all who saw her. **5.** She gave her maid a bottle of wine, a flask (a small container) of oil, parched grain (grains that have been roasted or toasted), figs, and fine bread, wrapped them together, and laid them on her. **6.** They went to the city gate of Bethulia (a city), where they found Ozias and the elders (older leaders) of the city, Chabris and Charmis, standing. **7.** When they saw her appearance had changed and she was beautifully dressed, they marveled greatly and praised her. They said, "May God bless you and make your plans succeed, bringing glory to Israel and Jerusalem." **8.** Judith responded, "Please open the city gates for me, that I may go out to carry out the mission you spoke of." **9.** So, they commanded the gates to be opened, as she had requested. **10.** Judith and her maid went out, and the people of the city watched as they descended the mountain (a high, steep area) and disappeared from sight. **11.** They continued through the valley (a low area of land between hills or mountains) until they met the first watch (a shift of guards) of the Assyrians. **12.** The guards stopped them and asked, "What people are you from? Where are you coming from, and where are you going?" **13.** Judith answered, "I am a woman of the Hebrews (a people group of Israel) and have fled from my people, for they will soon be given into your hands to be destroyed. I am coming to speak to Holofernes (the general), the chief of your army, to offer him advice that will help him conquer all the hill country (elevated land) without losing any soldiers." **14.** The guards were impressed by her words and beauty and said, "You have done well to come to our lord's presence. Come with us, and we will take you to him." **15.** They reassured her, "Do not be afraid when you stand before him. Speak as you have said, and he will treat you well." **16.** So, they chose a hundred men to escort (guide or protect) Judith and her maid to Holofernes' tent. **17.** The news of her arrival spread throughout the camp, and people gathered around her in awe (wonder or amazement) of her beauty. **18.** They all marveled at the women of Israel and wondered, "Who would despise (disrespect or look down on) a people with such beautiful women? Surely no man among them should be left alive, for they might deceive (trick or mislead) the entire world." **19.** The men who were close to Holofernes went out with his servants to bring Judith to him. **20.** Holofernes was reclining (lying back in a relaxed position) on his bed under a canopy (a covering or shelter) made of purple, gold, emeralds (precious green stones), and precious stones (valuable stones). **21.** When they informed him of Judith's arrival, he went out to meet her, with silver lamps (light sources) lighting the way. **22.** As Judith entered his presence, all who saw her were astonished (amazed or filled with wonder) by her beauty. She bowed down before him, and his servants helped her up.

Chapter 11

1. Holofernes said to her, "Do not be afraid, woman. Be of good courage (bravery). I have never harmed anyone who served Nebuchadnezzar (the king of Babylon, who ruled much of the ancient world), the king of the earth. **2.** If your people living in the mountains (the high hills where Bethulia is) had not ignored (disrespected) me, I would not have raised my spear (weapon) against them, but they have brought this upon themselves. **3.** Now tell me why you have fled (escaped) from them and come to us. You must have come seeking safety. Do not worry; you will be safe tonight and from now on. **4.** No one will harm you; you will be treated well, just as the servants of King Nebuchadnezzar are treated." **5.** Judith responded, "Listen to the words of your servant. Allow me to speak, and I will not lie (deceive) to you tonight. **6.** If you follow my advice, God will make your plans succeed, and you will not fail (become unsuccessful) in your mission." **7.** As Nebuchadnezzar, king of all the earth, lives, and as his power (authority) lives, which has sent you to sustain (support, keep alive) all living things, not just men but also the beasts (animals) and birds, will live by your power under Nebuchadnezzar's rule. **8.** We have heard of your wisdom (understanding) and strategy (planning). It is known throughout the earth that you are the greatest in the kingdom, mighty in knowledge, and accomplished (skilled) in warfare. **9.** Regarding what Achior (a leader from the Ammonites) said in your council, we have heard his words. The men of Bethulia saved him, and he told them everything he had said to you. **10.** So, my lord and governor, do not pay attention (listen to) his words. Remember them in your heart, for they are true. Our nation cannot be defeated by the sword (weapon), unless they sin (do wrong) against their God. **11.** But now, they are on the verge (close) of destruction, and their sin has overtaken them. They will provoke (anger) God's wrath (anger) whenever they do what is forbidden (not allowed). **12.** Their food supply is running low, and their water is scarce (not enough). They plan to use their cattle (livestock) and consume what God has forbidden them to eat according to His laws. **13.** They have decided to offer the firstfruits (the first portion of crops) and tithes (one-tenth) of wine and oil, which they had set aside for the priests in Jerusalem, and it is unlawful (against the law) for anyone to touch them. **14.** They have sent messengers (people who deliver messages) to Jerusalem to ask for permission from the senate (the governing body) to break these laws. **15.** When they return with the answer, they will immediately act (take action), and all these things will be destroyed in a single day. **16.** I, your servant, knowing all of this, have fled from them. God has sent me to help you accomplish something that will astonish (amaze) the whole earth, and everyone who hears it. **17.** For your servant is devout (religious) and serves the God of heaven day and night. Now, my lord, I will remain with you, and at night, I will go into the valley (low ground) and pray to God. He will show me when they have sinned. **18.** I will come and report it (tell) to you, and then you will march (advance) with your army, and none will be able to stand (resist) against you. **19.** I will guide (lead) you through Judea (the region of Israel) and bring you to Jerusalem (the capital city), where I will place your throne (seat of power). You will drive the people out as sheep without a shepherd (leader), and no one will dare challenge (oppose) you. These things were shown to me, and I have been sent to reveal (make known) them to you." **20.** Holofernes and all his servants were amazed (surprised) at her wisdom and said, **21.** "There is no woman like this anywhere on earth, both for her beauty (attractiveness) and her wisdom." **22.** Holofernes said to her, "God has blessed (favored) you to come before us. Through you, our strength will grow, and those who have disrespected my lord will face destruction. **23.** You are beautiful in appearance and wise in your words. If you do as you have promised, your God will be my God, and you will live in the house (palace) of King Nebuchadnezzar, becoming famous (renowned) throughout the earth."

Chapter 12

1. Then he ordered that she be brought to where his table was set, and instructed that they prepare for her from his own food and drink from his own wine. **2.** But Judith replied, "I will not eat of it, for it might cause offense (disrespect). Instead, provide me with the food I brought." **3.** Holofernes then asked, "If your provisions (supplies) run out, how shall we provide for you, since there is no one here from your nation?" **4.** Judith answered, "As surely as your soul (life) lives, my lord, I will not use the food I have, until the LORD has accomplished what He has planned through my actions." **5.** So the servants of Holofernes brought her into the tent, where she slept until midnight. She woke up as the morning watch (period of night when guards keep watch) approached. **6.** She sent for Holofernes, saying, "Let my lord command that I may go out to pray." **7.** Holofernes ordered his guards (soldiers) not to prevent her, and she stayed in the camp for three days. During the nights, she went out to the valley (a low area between hills or mountains) of Bethulia and washed herself in a fountain (spring or water source) of water near the camp. **8.** Afterward, she prayed to the God of Israel, asking for guidance to help deliver (rescue) her people. **9.** She returned, purified (made clean) herself, and stayed in her tent until evening when she ate. **10.** On the fourth day, Holofernes held a feast (large meal) for his own servants, inviting no officers (leaders) to join. **11.** Then he said to Bagoas, the eunuch (a man who has been castrated) in charge of his household, "Go and persuade the Hebrew (Jewish) woman to join us, eat, and drink with us." **12.** He added, "It would be disgraceful (shameful) if we let such a woman leave without enjoying her company, for if we do not bring her to us, she will mock (make fun of) us." **13.** Bagoas went to Judith and said, "Do not fear to come to my lord and be honored (respected) in his presence. Drink and be merry (happy) with us, and be like one of the Assyrian women who serve in King Nebuchadnezzar's house." **14.** Judith responded, "Who am I to refuse (reject) my lord? I will do whatever pleases you, and it will be my joy until the day I die." **15.** She arose, dressed herself in her finest clothes, and her maid (servant) spread soft skins (animal hides) on the ground for her to sit and eat, as Bagoas had arranged for her daily use. **16.** When Judith entered and sat down, Holofernes was captivated (charmed or fascinated) by her beauty, and his heart was filled with desire for her, for he had been waiting for the moment to deceive (trick) her since he first saw her. **17.** Holofernes said, "Drink now and be merry with us." **18.** Judith replied, "I will drink, my lord, for today my life is honored (respected) more than any other day since I was born." **19.** She then ate and drank before him, what her maid had prepared. **20.** Holofernes was delighted (pleased) by her and drank more wine than he had ever drunk in one day.

Chapter 13

1. When evening came, Holofernes' servants quickly left, and Bagoas (his attendant or servant) closed the tent and dismissed the servants. They all went to their beds because they were tired from the long feast. **2.** Judith was left alone in the tent, while Holofernes lay drunk (intoxicated) in his bed. **3.** Judith had instructed her maid to wait outside her bedchamber (private room) for her return, as she planned to go out to pray, and she spoke to Bagoas in the same way. **4.** Everyone left the room, and Judith, standing near Holofernes' bed, prayed in her heart, "O Lord God of all power (strength), look upon the work of my hands, to exalt (lift up or honor) Jerusalem." **5.** "Now is the time to help your people and fulfill your purposes by destroying our enemies." **6.** She moved to the pillar (supporting post) by Holofernes' head, took his sword, **7.** and, holding his hair, said, "Strengthen me, O Lord God of Israel, this day." **8.** She struck twice at his neck with all her strength, severing (cutting off) his head. **9.** She tossed his body off the bed, tore down the canopy (a covering) from the bed, and quickly left, giving his head to her maid. **10.** She placed it in her food bag, and they walked together as they usually did, heading towards the city of Bethulia (a city in Israel). **11.** As they approached the gate, Judith called out, "Open the gate! God is with us to show his power against our enemies, as He has done today." **12.** When the people of the city heard her voice, they hurried to open the gate, calling for the elders (leaders). **13.** They ran to meet her in astonishment (surprise), for it was unusual for her to return like this. They opened the gate, lit a fire, and gathered around her. **14.** Judith called out loudly, "Praise God! Praise Him! He has not taken His mercy (kindness or compassion) from Israel but has destroyed our enemies through my hands tonight." **15.** She took the head from her bag and said, "Behold (see) the head of Holofernes, the chief captain (commander) of Assyria, and the canopy where he lay drunk. The Lord has struck (killed) him down through the hand of a

woman." **16.** "As the Lord lives, who kept me on my path, my beauty deceived (misled or tricked) him, leading to his destruction, but he did not sin against me." **17.** The people were astonished, and they bowed in worship (reverence) to God, saying, "Blessed (praised) be God who has defeated our enemies today." **18.** Ozias, the leader, said to her, "Blessed are you among all women, and blessed is the Lord who directed you to cut off the head of our enemy's chief." **19.** "Your confidence (trust) in God will remain in the hearts of all men, who will remember His power forever." **20.** "May God reward you with everlasting praise for you have not spared (saved) your life but have avenged (punished or sought justice for) Israel's destruction, walking faithfully before God." The people agreed, saying, "So be it."

Chapter 14

1. Judith then spoke to the people, saying, "Listen to me, my brothers, and take this head of Holofernes (the general of the Assyrian army) and hang it on the highest point of your city walls. **2.** When morning comes and the sun rises, every man should take up his weapons (tools used for fighting) and go out in groups, as though preparing to march against the Assyrians. But do not go down the mountain yet. **3.** They will then enter the Assyrian camp, and when they go to Holofernes' tent, they will find it empty. This will cause panic (a sudden fear) among the Assyrian soldiers, and they will flee (run away in fear) before you. **4.** You and the people of Israel will chase them down and defeat (overcome or beat) them. **5.** But before you act, call for Achior (an Ammonite leader, a people living east of Israel) to witness (see and testify) what has happened, so he can see the fate (result) of the one who despised (hated or disrespected) Israel and tried to bring us to ruin (destruction). **6.** They brought Achior from the house of Ozias, and when he saw Holofernes' head, he fell to the ground in shock (a sudden emotional or physical disturbance). **7.** After he recovered (came back to his senses), he fell at Judith's feet and praised her, saying, "Blessed (honored) are you among the women of Judah (the region of Israel), and in all the nations. Everyone who hears your name will be amazed (surprised or astonished)." **8.** Then Achior asked Judith to tell him all that she had done. Judith shared everything that had happened from the time she set out until that moment. **9.** When she finished speaking, the people shouted with joy and praised God for her victory. **10.** After hearing about God's actions, Achior believed in God, circumcised (removed the foreskin, joining the people of Israel) himself and joined the house of Israel, where he remains to this day. **11.** When morning came, they hung Holofernes' head on the city wall. Then every man took his weapon and went out in groups toward the mountain pass (a narrow route through the mountains). **12.** When the Assyrians saw them, they sent word to their leaders (commanders) to come quickly. **13.** The leaders of the Assyrians approached Holofernes' tent, reporting that the Israelites were boldly coming out to fight, intending to destroy them. **14.** Bagoas (Holofernes' servant) went to wake him, thinking Holofernes had been with Judith. **15.** When no one answered, he opened the tent and found Holofernes lying dead on the floor with his head missing. **16.** Bagoas cried out loudly, weeping (sobbing in grief) and tearing (ripping) his clothes in grief. **17.** He went to Judith's tent but found it empty. In panic (a sudden fear), he rushed out to tell the people. **18.** He shouted, "The Israelites have betrayed (acted dishonestly) us! One woman has brought shame (disgrace) to the house of King Nebuchadnezzar (the king of Assyria). Holofernes is dead, and his head is gone!" **19.** When the Assyrian captains (military leaders) heard this, they tore their clothes and were filled with great fear. There was a loud cry throughout the camp.

Chapter 15

1. When those in the tents heard what had happened, they were astonished (greatly surprised) by the event. **2.** Fear and trembling (shaking in fear) fell upon them, causing everyone to flee (run away) in different directions, running into the plains (wide, flat areas) and hills. **3.** Those camped in the mountains around Bethulia also fled. Then the Israelites, all the warriors (fighters) among them, rushed out to attack the enemy. **4.** Ozias (leader of Bethulia) sent messengers (people who carry messages) to Betomasthem, Bebai, Chobai, Cola, and all the regions (areas) of Israel to spread the news of what had occurred, urging (strongly encouraging) everyone to unite and destroy their enemies. **5.** Upon hearing the news, the Israelites gathered and, with one mind (together), attacked the enemy, slaughtering (killing in large numbers) them as far as Chobai. The people from Jerusalem and the surrounding hill country joined in, hearing of the victory, and pursued (followed) the enemies with great force, killing them until they were past Damascus (a city) and its borders. **6.** The remaining people of Bethulia attacked the Assyrian camp, looted (stole) it, and became very rich. **7.** The Israelites who returned from the battle took the spoils (the things taken from the enemy), and the villages and cities in the plains and mountains gained much wealth, for the number of slain (those killed) was immense (very large). **8.** Joacim, the high priest (a religious leader), and the elders (senior leaders) of Israel who lived in Jerusalem, came to witness (see) the great things God had done for Israel and to honor Judith. **9.** When they arrived, they praised (commended) her, saying, "You are the glory (great honor) of Jerusalem, the pride (strong sense of satisfaction) of Israel, and the joy (happiness) of our nation. **10.** You have accomplished (achieved) all these great deeds (actions) by your own hand. You have done great good for Israel, and God is pleased with you. Blessed (highly favored) are you forever, by the Almighty Lord." The people agreed and said, "Amen." **11.** The Israelites looted the Assyrian camp for thirty days. They gave Judith Holofernes' tent, all his silverware (metal objects used for eating or drinking), beds, and belongings. She took them and placed them on her mule (a type of animal), preparing her carts (vehicles) to carry them. **12.** The women of Israel gathered together to see her, blessed her, and danced in celebration. Judith held branches (parts of a tree) in her hand and gave some to the women with her. **13.** They crowned (placed a wreath) her and her maid (servant) with olive wreaths (circle of olive branches), and Judith led the women in a joyful dance. All the men of Israel followed in their armor (protective clothing), wearing garlands (decorative wreaths) and singing songs.

Chapter 16

1. Then Judith began to sing this song of thanksgiving in Israel, and all the people joined her in praising God. **2.** Judith said, "Sing to my God with tambourines (musical instruments) and cymbals (metal percussion instruments), and make a new psalm (song of praise) for Him. Exalt (lift up, praise) Him and call on His name." **3.** For it is God who fights our battles. He has delivered (rescued) me from those who persecuted (oppressed, mistreated) me. **4.** Assur (a leader or army from the north) came with ten thousand soldiers, overwhelming my land, and their cavalry (soldiers on horseback) filled the hills. **5.** He boasted (bragged) that he would destroy our borders, kill our young men, crush (smash) our babies, and make our virgins (young unmarried women) his prey. **6.** But the Almighty (all-powerful) Lord defeated them through the hand of a woman. **7.** The mighty were not defeated by young men, nor by the sons of giants (titans or large beings), but Judith, the daughter of Merari (a family name), overcame him with her beauty. **8.** She removed (took off) her widow's garments (clothes worn after a husband's death) to bring glory to the oppressed in Israel. She anointed (rubbed with oil) her face with ointment, bound (tied) her hair, and wore a linen dress to deceive him. **9.** Her sandals (shoes) captivated (dazzled, caught the attention of) his eyes, and her beauty stole his heart. Then she struck him down with a sword. **10.** The Persians (people from ancient Persia) feared her courage, and the Medes (another ancient people) were amazed at her bravery. **11.** The afflicted (those who suffer) rejoiced, and the weak shouted in astonishment (surprise), as they were thrown down by the Lord's power. **12.** The sons of young women struck them down, and they perished (died) in the Lord's battle. **13.** I will sing a new song to the Lord: "O Lord, You are great and glorious, powerful and invincible (impossible to defeat)." **14.** Let all creatures (living beings) serve You, for You spoke, and they were created. You sent Your Spirit, and they came to be. No one can resist (oppose) Your voice. **15.** The mountains will shake, and the rocks will melt like wax before You, yet You are merciful (compassionate) to those who fear You. **16.** No sacrifice (offering to God) can fully honor You, nor the finest offerings be enough, but the one who fears the Lord is always great in Your sight. **17.** Woe (great sorrow) to the nations (countries) that rise against my people! The Lord will punish them with fire and worms (maggots, destructive creatures) in the day of judgment, and they will weep (cry) forever. **18.** When they entered Jerusalem, they worshiped (praised) the Lord. After the people were purified (cleansed), they offered their sacrifices and gifts to God. **19.** Judith also dedicated (gave as a gift) all

the belongings of Holofernes (the enemy leader) that had been given to her, including the canopy (covering) she had taken from his bedchamber (room), as an offering to the Lord. **20.** The people feasted before the Lord in Jerusalem for three months, and Judith remained with them. **21.** Afterward, everyone returned to their homes, and Judith went back to Bethulia (her town), where she was honored throughout the land. **22.** Many sought her, but she remained a widow (a woman whose husband has died), not remarried, and lived honorably. **23.** Judith grew old in her husband Manasses' house, living to be 105 years old. She freed (released) her maid and died in Bethulia, where she was buried in her husband's tomb. **24.** The people of Israel mourned (grieved) her for seven days, and before her death, she gave her possessions to her husband's relatives and to her own kin (family). **25.** After Judith's death, no one dared to threaten Israel, and the people lived in peace for a long time.

20 – Esther

Chapter 1

1. During the reign of King Ahasuerus (Xerxes, the powerful king of Persia), **2.** While he sat on his royal throne in the fortified city of Shushan (royal city in Persia), **3.** in the third year of his reign, he hosted a grand feast for all his officials, servants, nobles, and princes from every province. This event was a display of his might and influence over a vast region, bringing together the empire's most important leaders. **4.** He spent 180 days showcasing the immense wealth and splendor of his glorious kingdom, illustrating his own power and grandeur, displaying his riches, and inviting admiration from all who were present. **5.** After the 180-day celebration, the king extended the festivities with a seven-day feast in the court of the king's garden, where everyone in Shushan—from the richest to the poorest—was invited to partake in the lavish celebration. **6.** The garden itself was a marvel: adorned with white and blue linen curtains (fine fabrics), fastened with cords of linen and purple (a color signifying royalty), draped across silver rods, supported by marble pillars. The furniture was made of gold and silver, while the floor was intricately paved with mosaic tiles made of alabaster (a smooth white stone), turquoise (a greenish-blue stone), and black and white marble. **7.** The royal wine was served in golden vessels, each one unique, showcasing the king's wealth. Wine flowed abundantly as the king generously offered it to his guests, ensuring they enjoyed the finest beverages. **8.** The drinking was voluntary, as the king ordered that no one should be forced to drink. His servants were instructed to let each guest drink freely according to their own will, allowing for a relaxed atmosphere. **9.** At the same time, Queen Vashti (Ahasuerus's wife) held a separate feast for the women in the royal palace, which belonged to the king, maintaining the separation of the genders during the celebrations. **10.** On the seventh day, when the king's heart was merry with wine (meaning he was intoxicated), he commanded seven eunuchs—Mehuman, Biztha, Harbona, Bigtha, Abagtha, Zethar, and Carcas (men who were castrated to maintain loyalty and focus)— **11.** to bring Queen Vashti before the king, wearing her royal crown, so that he might display her beauty to all the officials and guests. He desired to show off her beauty, as she was known for her attractiveness, to impress the attendees with his queen's charm. **12.** However, Queen Vashti refused to come at the king's command, delivered by his eunuchs. This defiance greatly angered the king, and his fury burned within him as he felt disrespected by her refusal. **13.** The king, unable to act alone, turned to his wise men who understood the law and customs of the empire. These men were familiar with how to resolve matters of justice and royal protocol, especially in situations involving royal authority. **14.** The king's closest advisors were Carshena, Shethar, Admatha, Tarshish, Meres, Marsena, and Memucan (trusted figures who held high positions in the kingdom). They had access to the king and were known for their wisdom. **15.** King Ahasuerus asked them, "What should be done to Queen Vashti, who has disobeyed my direct command?" **16.** Memucan, one of the seven princes, stood and said, "Queen Vashti has not only wronged the king but also all the nobles and officials in your empire. **17.** Her refusal to obey will spread a message to all women in the provinces that they can disrespect their husbands, saying, 'King Ahasuerus commanded Queen Vashti to come before him, but she refused.' **18.** This behavior, if allowed to spread, will cause women everywhere in Persia and Media to disrespect their husbands, stirring up anger and contempt in the hearts of men." **19.** Memucan proposed, "If it pleases the king, let a royal decree be issued in your name and recorded in the laws of the Persians and Medes (which cannot be changed), that Queen Vashti should never again come before you. Let the king appoint a new queen who is more worthy than she." **20.** "Once this decree is announced throughout the empire, all women will honor their husbands, both great and small, out of fear of what the king has decreed." **21.** This advice greatly pleased the king and his princes, so Ahasuerus agreed to act according to the counsel of Memucan. **22.** The king sent letters to all the provinces, written in each province's own script and language, instructing that every man should be the head of his household, and those wives should respect and obey their husbands, reinforcing the law across his entire empire.

Chapter 2

1. After these events, when King Ahasuerus (King of Persia) had calmed down from his anger, he remembered Vashti and the decree against her. **2.** The king's servants suggested, "Let beautiful young virgins be selected for the king. **3.** Let officers be sent throughout the empire to gather beautiful young women to Shushan (the fortified capital city of Persia), under the care of Hegai (a eunuch in charge of the women), for beauty treatments." **4.** The woman who pleases the king will become queen instead of Vashti." This idea pleased the king, and he ordered it. **5.** In Shushan, there was a Jew named Mordecai, son of Jair, from the tribe of Benjamin, who had been exiled from Jerusalem when King Jeconiah was taken to Babylon. **6.** Mordecai had raised his cousin Hadassah (Esther), as her parents had died. **7.** Esther was very beautiful, and Mordecai took her in as his own daughter. **8.** When the king's decree was announced, many young women were gathered to Shushan. Esther was also taken and placed under Hegai's care. **9.** Esther won Hegai's favor, who gave her special beauty treatments, food, and seven maids from the palace, moving her to the best quarters. **10.** Esther kept her Jewish identity secret, as Mordecai had instructed. **11.** Mordecai checked on Esther daily at the women's quarters to learn of her well-being. **12.** Each woman had twelve months of preparation: six months with myrrh oil (a fragrant resin) and six months with perfumes and cosmetics. **13.** When her turn came, each woman was allowed to take whatever she wanted to the king's palace. **14.** In the evening, she went to the king, and in the morning, she returned to the concubines unless called again by the king. **15.** When Esther went to the king, she asked only for what Hegai, the eunuch in charge, suggested. She found favor with everyone who saw her. **16.** Esther was taken to King Ahasuerus in the seventh year of his reign, in the tenth month, Tebeth. **17.** The king loved Esther more than all the other women, and she found favor with him. He made her queen instead of Vashti and crowned her. **18.** To celebrate, the king held a grand banquet, the Feast of Esther, for all his officials and servants. He declared a holiday across his provinces and gave gifts generously. **19.** When the virgins were gathered again, Mordecai sat at the king's gate (where official matters were decided). **20.** Esther still kept her identity secret, as Mordecai had advised, and obeyed him as she had since childhood. **21.** At that time, two of the king's eunuchs, Bigthan and Teresh, became angry and plotted to kill King Ahasuerus. **22.** Mordecai overheard their plan and told Queen Esther, who informed the king in Mordecai's name. **23.** The matter was investigated and confirmed. Both eunuchs were hanged, and the event was recorded in the king's chronicles (official records).

Chapter 3

1. After these events, King Ahasuerus (the king of Persia) promoted Haman, the son of Hammedatha the Agagite (a descendant of King Agag). The king elevated Haman to a high position, placing him above all the other princes and officials who were in his court, effectively making him the second most powerful person in the kingdom. **2.** As part of his new position, all the king's servants who were stationed at the king's gate (a place where royal officials and judges would gather) were commanded by the king to bow down and pay homage to Haman in recognition of his high rank. But Mordecai, a Jewish man who worked at the king's gate, refused to bow down or show any sign of respect to Haman. **3.** The king's servants at the gate noticed that Mordecai was not obeying the king's order, and they asked him repeatedly, "Why are you violating the king's command by not bowing

to Haman?" **4.** Although they asked him every day, Mordecai remained firm in his refusal, and he explained that he was a Jew (a member of the people of Israel who worshiped the one true God). Eventually, these servants reported Mordecai's behavior to Haman, hoping to find out why he was defying the king's command and whether Mordecai's refusal had anything to do with his Jewish identity. **5.** When Haman heard that Mordecai had refused to bow down, his anger was kindled, and he was filled with wrath against him. But Haman's pride and arrogance led him to take this insult personally, and it wasn't enough for him to seek revenge on Mordecai alone. **6.** Instead, Haman learned that Mordecai was not the only one of his people who refused to worship him. When Haman found out that Mordecai was a Jew, he decided to take a much greater course of action and plotted to destroy not just Mordecai but all the Jews who lived throughout the entire empire of King Ahasuerus (the vast Persian Empire that stretched from India to Ethiopia). **7.** In the first month of the year, which is Nisan (around March or April), in the twelfth year of King Ahasuerus's reign, Haman cast lots (called Pur, a term that means "the lot") to determine the best day for carrying out his plan of destruction. This method of casting lots was used in ancient times to make important decisions or determine the will of the gods. The lot fell on the twelfth month, which is Adar, meaning that Haman would have nearly a full year to prepare for this catastrophic event. **8.** Haman then went to King Ahasuerus with his request. He said, "There is a certain group of people scattered throughout your entire kingdom, spread across all its provinces. Their customs, laws, and way of life are entirely different from those of the other nations. They refuse to follow the king's laws, and they are disruptive to the stability of your empire. Therefore, it would be in the king's best interest to remove them from the land completely." **9.** Haman continued, "If it pleases the king, let a royal decree be issued that they be destroyed, and I am willing to contribute ten thousand talents of silver (a massive sum, roughly equivalent to tens of millions of dollars) into the hands of those who carry out this order, to be placed in the king's treasury." This offer suggested that Haman would bribe the king in exchange for carrying out the extermination. **10.** The king responded by taking his signet ring (a royal seal used to authenticate official documents) off his hand and giving it to Haman, the son of Hammedatha the Agagite (whom he considered an ally), making him the executor of this evil decree. Haman, now holding the king's authority, was allowed to act without any further consultation with the king. **11.** King Ahasuerus said to Haman, "The silver is yours, and the people are yours to do with as you see fit. You have my permission to carry out whatever you desire." **12.** On the thirteenth day of the first month (the day after the decree was signed), the king's scribes were called and given the task of drafting the official decree. The document was written exactly as Haman instructed, addressed to the king's satraps (governors of the provinces), to the officials overseeing each province, and to all the people in every language of the empire. The decree was written in the name of King Ahasuerus, and it was sealed with his signet ring to make it official and binding. **13.** The letters were sent by royal couriers to every part of the kingdom, carrying the terrifying message that all Jews, from the young to the elderly, including men, women, and children, were to be killed on a single day—the thirteenth day of the twelfth month, which is Adar. The decree also allowed for the plundering of the Jews' possessions after they were destroyed. This was an open invitation to the rest of the empire to take advantage of the Jews' misfortune. **14.** A copy of this official decree was to be posted in every province so that the people would be prepared for the day of destruction. They were to be ready to act when the time came. **15.** The couriers hurried off, driven by the king's command, and the decree was proclaimed in the capital city of Shushan (the Persian capital city). Meanwhile, the king and Haman sat down to drink in celebration of the success of their plan. However, the people of Shushan, and the entire empire, were thrown into confusion. The citizens were perplexed and deeply troubled by the decree, as they could not understand why such an extreme action had been ordered against the Jewish people.

Chapter 4

1. When Mordecai found out all that had occurred, he was overcome with grief and tore his clothes (a traditional sign of deep mourning) and put on sackcloth (a rough, uncomfortable fabric symbolizing distress) and ashes (a symbol of sorrow and humility). He went out into the city, openly displaying his anguish, crying out loudly and bitterly for all to hear. 2. He ventured as far as the king's gate (the large, prominent entrance to the royal palace), because it was forbidden for anyone to enter the king's gate while wearing mourning attire such as sackcloth. 3. In every region where the king's decree and command reached, the Jewish people were filled with sorrow. There was widespread mourning among them, accompanied by fasting (abstaining from food), weeping, and wailing (expressing deep lament). Many people, both men and women, laid down in sackcloth and ashes as a sign of their grief and helplessness. 4. When Esther's maids and eunuchs (servants who had been castrated and worked in the royal household) saw Mordecai's actions, they reported it to the queen. Esther was greatly troubled upon hearing this. In an attempt to comfort him, she sent a set of royal clothes to Mordecai, hoping he would accept them and remove the sackcloth. However, he refused to take the garments, signaling his distress was too great for mere clothing to ease. 5. At this point, Esther instructed Hathach, one of the eunuchs who had been assigned to serve her personally in the palace, to go to Mordecai and learn the full details of what had caused his sorrow and why he was acting in such a dramatic way. 6. Hathach went out and found Mordecai in the public square just outside the king's gate. 7. Mordecai then explained to him all that had occurred, including the enormous sum of money that Haman (the king's prime minister, who held significant power) had promised to deposit into the royal treasury in exchange for a decree that would lead to the annihilation of the Jews. 8. He also handed Hathach a copy of the written decree issued in Susa (the capital city of the Persian Empire), which clearly stated that the Jews were to be destroyed. Mordecai instructed Hathach to show this to Esther and explain the situation to her. He urged her to go before the king and plead for mercy on behalf of her people. 9. Hathach returned to Esther and delivered Mordecai's words exactly as they had been given to him. 10. Esther, in turn, sent a message back to Mordecai, saying: 11. "Everyone who serves the king and all the people throughout the provinces know that there is one law: any man or woman who approaches the king in the inner court without being summoned is to be put to death, unless the king holds out the golden scepter (a symbol of the king's favor and pardon) to allow them to live. I have not been summoned to the king in the past thirty days, and it is a dangerous thing to approach him without an invitation." 12. Hathach returned to Mordecai with Esther's response. 13. Mordecai sent back a reply to Esther: "Do not think that just because you are in the king's palace, you will escape the fate that is coming to the rest of the Jews. 14. If you remain silent and do nothing at this time, deliverance for the Jews will come from somewhere else, but you and your family will not survive. Who knows, perhaps you have risen to this royal position for such a critical moment as this?" 15. Then Esther sent another message to Mordecai: 16. "Go and gather all the Jews who are in Susa (the city where the king's palace was located), and ask them to fast (abstain from food and drink) for me for three days and nights. I, along with my maids, will also fast during that time. After that, I will go before the king, even though it is against the law. And if I perish, I perish!" 17. Mordecai then left and did everything that Esther had commanded him, gathering the people to fast on her behalf.

Chapter 5

1. On the third day, after a period of fasting and intense prayer (seeking divine intervention), Esther (the Jewish queen of Persia) put on her royal robes, signifying her status, and stood in the inner court of the king's palace, directly opposite the king's residence. The king sat on his royal throne (a symbol of absolute authority) in the royal house, facing the entrance, where all visitors could see his judgment. 2. When the king saw Queen Esther standing in the court, he immediately noticed her and, filled with favor, extended the golden scepter (a symbol of royal grace that allowed one to approach the king without fear of death) that he held in his hand towards her. Esther approached, visibly relieved, and gently touched the top of the scepter, a gesture that indicated her request and her humble submission to the king's will. 3. The king, seeing her approach, then asked her with great curiosity, "What is it that you want, Queen Esther? What is your request? I will grant it to you—up to half the kingdom!" His words reflected the confidence he had in her and his deep affection, as he had already

made her queen, thus demonstrating his trust. 4. Esther, who had carefully planned her request, responded with grace, saying, "If it pleases the king, let the king and Haman (the king's highest and most trusted official) come today to the banquet I have prepared for them. This meal is in honor of you both, and I wish to make my request in a more private setting." 5. The king, eager to please her, quickly replied, "Bring Haman quickly so that he may do as Esther has requested." So, the king and Haman, both important figures of the Persian court, went to the banquet that Esther had specially prepared for them. It was an occasion to showcase the queen's hospitality and her respect for her royal guests. 6. At the banquet, while they were enjoying wine, the king once again asked, "What is your petition, Esther? It will certainly be granted to you. What is your request, even up to half the kingdom, and I will do it!" His repeated offers highlighted his willingness to fulfill her desires, though he still didn't fully understand her deeper request. 7. Esther, aware of the importance of timing, responded with composure, saying, "My petition and request is this:" 8. "If I have found favor in the sight of the king, and if it pleases the king to grant my petition and fulfill my request, then let the king and Haman come to the banquet I will prepare for them tomorrow. At that time, I will make my request known, as it is of great importance and requires careful consideration." 9. After the banquet, Haman left that day filled with high spirits, feeling joyful and with a glad heart, proud of the honor he had received. However, when Haman saw Mordecai (a Jew, who refused to bow to him) sitting at the king's gate, and noticed that Mordecai did not stand or show fear before him, Haman became filled with rage and resentment towards him. This act of defiance deeply wounded his pride, and he could not forget it. 10. Despite his anger, Haman restrained himself and returned to his house. He summoned his friends and his wife, Zeresh, to come and comfort him and to help him deal with his frustration. He hoped to find some solace in their company and perspective. 11. Haman, though outwardly composed, could not stop boasting about his achievements. He proudly shared with them all of his great wealth, the numerous children he had, and every honor the king had bestowed upon him. He emphasized how he had been promoted above all the other officials and servants of the king. His words revealed his pride in his own superiority and his arrogance. 12. Haman also said, "Moreover, Queen Esther invited no one but me to join the king at the banquet she prepared, and tomorrow I will again be invited, along with the king. It is clear that I hold a special place in her esteem, and this only adds to my pride." 13. "But all of this means nothing to me as long as I see Mordecai the Jew sitting at the king's gate, refusing to bow before me. His insolence has become my obsession, and it diminishes all the glory I have achieved." 14. Then his wife, Zeresh, and all of his friends, seeing his deep anger and frustration, said to him, "Let a gallows be made, fifty cubits (about 75 feet) high. In the morning, go to the king and suggest that Mordecai be hanged on it. Then, after his execution, go merrily with the king to the banquet. This will rid you of the source of your anger and allow you to enjoy the feast without further distractions." This wicked plan pleased Haman, and he ordered the construction of the gallows, eager for revenge.

Chapter 6

1. That night, King Ahasuerus (the Persian king,) could not sleep, so he ordered one of his servants to bring the book of the royal records (a detailed account of important events and decisions) and read it aloud before him. 2. As they read, they discovered that Mordecai (a Jewish man who served at the king's gate) had once uncovered a plot by Bigthana and Teresh (two of the king's eunuchs) to assassinate the king. Mordecai had reported it, saving the king's life. 3. The king asked, "What honor or reward has been given to Mordecai for this act of loyalty?" His attendants replied, "Nothing has been done for him." 4. The king, eager to address this oversight, asked, "Who is in the court?" At that moment, Haman (the king's prime minister) entered the outer court, intending to ask the king to have Mordecai hanged on the gallows (a structure for public execution) he had prepared. 5. The king's servants informed him, "Haman is in the court." The king said, "Let him come in." 6. So, Haman entered, and the king asked him, "What should be done for the man whom the king wishes to honor?" Haman, thinking the king meant him, thought, "Who would the king want to honor more than me?" 7. Haman replied, "For the man whom

the king delights to honor, let a royal robe (the king's personal garment) be brought, which the king himself has worn, and let a horse (the royal steed) on which the king has ridden be provided, with a royal crest (symbol of the king's authority) on its head. **8.** "Let one of the king's most noble officials dress the man in the royal robe, and lead him through the city square on the horse, proclaiming, 'This is what is done for the man whom the king delights to honor!'" **9.** The king said to Haman, "Hurry, take the robe and the horse as you have suggested, and do so for Mordecai the Jew who sits at the king's gate. Do not leave out a single detail of what you have said." **10.** So Haman took the robe and the horse, dressed Mordecai in the royal robe, and paraded him through the city square, proclaiming, "This is what is done for the man whom the king delights to honor!" **11.** Afterward, Mordecai returned to his place at the king's gate, but Haman hurried home, his head covered (a sign of great humiliation and shame). **12.** Haman shared everything that had happened with his wife Zeresh (his wife) and his friends. His wise men and wife Zeresh responded, "If Mordecai, whom you have begun to fall before, is a Jew, you will not prevail against him. You will surely fall before him." **13.** While they were still talking, the king's eunuchs (royal servants) arrived and quickly took Haman to the banquet that Queen Esther had prepared for the king and Haman. **14.** So Haman went to the banquet, still in great distress, his mind unsettled by the events of the day.

Chapter 7

1. The king (the ruler of Persia) and Haman (a high-ranking Persian official) went to Queen Esther's royal banquet hall to dine, where she had carefully prepared a feast for them. **2.** On the second day of the banquet, as they drank wine together, the king asked once more, "What is your request, Queen Esther? Tell me, and I will grant it to you. Whatever you ask, even if it's up to half of my entire kingdom, I will give it to you!" **3.** Esther, feeling both fear and courage, responded, "If I have truly found favor in your sight, O king, and if it pleases you, I ask that my life be spared, and that of my people as well. **4.** We have been sold, I and my people, to be destroyed, to be killed, and to be utterly wiped out. If we were just sold into slavery, I would have kept silent, but the cost to the king of such a loss is too great to ignore." **5.** The king, visibly shocked and furious, demanded, "Who is responsible for this? Where is the person who would dare to do such a terrible thing?" **6.** Esther, with a trembling voice, replied, "The enemy and adversary is this wicked man, Haman!" Haman, now realizing he had been exposed, was filled with dread, trembling before both the king and the queen. **7.** The king, enraged, stood up from the banquet table and walked into the palace garden (a tranquil area within the royal palace grounds) to cool down. Haman, understanding that the king had made up his mind to punish him, stayed behind, desperately pleading with Queen Esther for his life. **8.** When the king returned, he found Haman falling across the couch where Esther was reclining. The king, already in a fury, said, "Is he even going to assault the queen in my own presence?" As soon as the king spoke, his servants covered Haman's face in preparation for his execution. **9.** Then Harbonah, one of the king's eunuchs (royal servants), spoke up, "Look, king! The gallows (a tall wooden structure for hanging criminals) that Haman made for Mordecai, who spoke well on your behalf, stands at Haman's house. It's fifty cubits high (about 75 feet)!" The king, without hesitation, ordered, "Hang him on it!" **10.** So they hanged Haman on the very gallows he had built for Mordecai. After Haman's execution, the king's anger subsided, and the danger to Esther and her people was lifted.

Chapter 8

1. On that day, King Ahasuerus (the Persian king, also known as Xerxes) gave Queen Esther the estate of Haman, who was the enemy of the Jews. Mordecai (Esther's cousin) appeared before the king, for Esther had explained how he was related to her. **2.** The king took off his signet ring (the royal seal used for official documents), which he had taken from Haman, and gave it to Mordecai. Esther also appointed Mordecai to manage Haman's estate. **3.** Esther then approached the king again, falling at his feet and pleading with him in tears to undo the evil plan that Haman, the Agagite (a descendant of the ancient Amalekites, enemies of Israel), had devised against the Jews. **4.** The king extended his golden scepter (a symbol of his favor) toward Esther, and she stood up and spoke before him. **5.** Esther said, "If it pleases the king, and if I have found favor in his sight, and it seems right to him, let an order

be written to cancel the letters that Haman, the son of Hammedatha the Agagite, wrote to destroy the Jews in all the king's provinces. **6.** How can I bear to see my people harmed? How can I endure the destruction of my family?" **7.** King Ahasuerus said to Queen Esther and Mordecai the Jew, "I have already given Esther the estate of Haman, and they have hanged him on the gallows (the structure where Haman was executed) because he sought to destroy the Jews. **8.** Now, you write a new decree in the king's name regarding the Jews, and seal it with the king's signet ring. What is written in the king's name and sealed with his ring cannot be changed." **9.** The king's scribes (official writers) were called at that time, on the twenty-third day of the third month, the month of Sivan. The decree was written as Mordecai instructed, to the Jews, satraps (provincial governors), officials, and princes from India to Ethiopia (a vast empire of 127 provinces), in the script and language of each region. It was also written in the Jews' own language and script. **10.** Mordecai wrote the decree in the name of King Ahasuerus, sealed it with the king's signet ring, and sent it by royal couriers on swift horses. **11.** The decree allowed the Jews in every city to gather together and protect their lives—to destroy, kill, and wipe out any people or province that attacked them, including women and children, and to plunder the possessions of their enemies, **12.** on a single day, the thirteenth day of the twelfth month, the month of Adar, throughout all the provinces of King Ahasuerus. **13.** A copy of the decree was to be distributed in every province and made public, so the Jews would be ready to defend themselves and avenge their enemies. **14.** The couriers, riding on royal horses, were urged on by the king's command, and the decree was issued in the citadel of Shushan (the capital city). **15.** Mordecai left the king's presence wearing royal attire of blue and white, a large crown of gold, and a garment of fine linen and purple. The city of Shushan rejoiced and was glad. **16.** The Jews had light (joy), gladness, and honor. **17.** In every province and city where the king's decree was received, the Jews celebrated with joy and gladness, holding feasts and holidays. Many of the people of the land converted to Judaism because fear of the Jews had fallen upon them.

Chapter 9

1. On the thirteenth day of the twelfth month, the month of Adar (last month of the Jewish calendar), the time arrived for the king's command and decree to be carried out. On this day, when the enemies of the Jews had expected to overpower them, the opposite occurred— the Jews defeated those who hated them. **2.** The Jews gathered in their cities across all the provinces of King Ahasuerus (ruler of Persia) to strike those who sought to harm them. No one could stand against them, as fear of the Jews fell upon all people. **3.** All the officials of the provinces—the satraps (regional governors), the administrators, and all who served the king—supported the Jews because they were afraid of Mordecai, who had great influence. **4.** Mordecai held a position of high authority in the king's palace, and his reputation spread throughout all the provinces; he became more powerful and widely respected. **5.** The Jews struck down all their enemies with the sword, bringing them to ruin and doing as they pleased with those who opposed them. **6.** In Shushan, the citadel (the royal capital), the Jews killed and destroyed five hundred men. **7.** They also killed Parshandatha, Dalphon, and Aspatha, **8.** Poratha, Adalia, and Aridatha, **9.** Parmashta, Arisai, Aridai, and Vajezatha— **10.** the ten sons of Haman (son of Hammedatha,). But they did not take any of the plunder. **11.** On that day, the number of those killed in Shushan was reported to the king. **12.** The king said to Queen Esther, "The Jews have killed five hundred men in Shushan, including Haman's ten sons. What have they done in the rest of my provinces? Now, what further request do you have? It shall be granted." **13.** Esther replied, "If it pleases the king, allow the Jews in Shushan to act according to today's decree again tomorrow. Also, let Haman's ten sons be displayed on the gallows (structure used for execution)." **14.** The king commanded that this be done. A decree was issued in Shushan, and they hanged the bodies of Haman's ten sons. **15.** The Jews in Shushan gathered again on the fourteenth day of Adar, and killed three hundred more men there, but did not take any plunder. **16.** Meanwhile, in the king's other provinces, the Jews assembled to protect their lives and gained relief from their enemies. They killed seventy-five thousand of those who hated them, yet they took no plunder. **17.** This victory occurred on the thirteenth day of Adar, and on the fourteenth, they rested, turning it into a day of feasting and celebration. **18.** However, the Jews in Shushan had gathered on both the thirteenth and fourteenth days, and so they rested on the fifteenth day, making it a day of feasting and joy. **19.** This is why the Jews in villages and unwalled towns observe the fourteenth day of Adar as a joyful holiday, marked by feasting and sending gifts to one another. **20.** Mordecai recorded these events and sent letters to all the Jews throughout the provinces of King Ahasuerus, near and far, **21.** instructing them to observe the fourteenth and fifteenth days of Adar every year. **22.** These were the days when the Jews gained relief from their enemies, and the month that had been filled with sorrow turned into joy and celebration. These days were to be marked by feasting, joy, exchanging gifts, and providing for the poor. **23.** The Jews agreed to continue this practice as they had begun, according to Mordecai's written instructions. **24.** Haman, son of Hammedatha the Agagite (from the line of Agag, an enemy of Israel), had plotted to destroy the Jews, and had cast Pur (meaning "lot") to decide the day of their annihilation. **25.** But when Esther came before the king, he ordered by decree that Haman's wicked plan should turn back upon himself, resulting in Haman and his sons being hanged. **26.** This is why these days were called Purim, after the word Pur. Because of everything written in this letter and what had happened to them, the Jews established this observance. **27.** The Jewish people took it upon themselves and their descendants, and anyone who would join them, to observe these two days each year without fail, as prescribed and at the appointed time. **28.** These days were to be remembered and celebrated in every generation, every family, every province, and every city, so that the observance of Purim would not cease among the Jews, nor its memory fade from their descendants. **29.** Then Queen Esther, daughter of Abihail (her father), along with Mordecai the Jew, wrote with full authority to confirm this second letter regarding Purim. **30.** Mordecai sent letters of peace and truth to all the Jews across the one hundred and twenty-seven provinces of Ahasuerus' kingdom, **31.** to confirm these days of Purim at their appointed time, as Mordecai the Jew and Queen Esther had established for them, including matters of fasting and mourning. **32.** Thus, the command of Esther established these matters of Purim, and it was recorded in the official records.

Chapter 10

1. King Ahasuerus (Persian ruler) imposed a tax throughout his lands, extending even to the islands of the sea (distant territories under his rule). **2.** All his powerful deeds, his might, and the full record of Mordecai's (Jewish leader) rise to greatness—are these not recorded in the chronicles of the kings of Media and Persia? **3.** For Mordecai, honored among the Jews, was second in rank to King Ahasuerus, well-regarded by his people, continually seeking their welfare (well-being) and speaking peace to all his countrymen.

21 – I Meqabyan

The Book of Meqabyan I

Chapter 1

1. There was a man named Tseerutsaydan, who loved sin, boasting in the abundance of his horses and the firmness (strength) of his troops. **2.** He had many priests who served idols, worshipping and sacrificing (offering) to them day and night. **3.** In his heart, he believed the idols gave him strength and power. **4.** He believed they gave him authority (control) over his rule. **5.** At times, he thought they granted him all his desired power. **6.** He sacrificed to them day and night. **7.** He appointed priests (religious leaders) to serve these idols. **8.** They ate from the defiled (unclean) sacrifices, pretending the idols ate day and night. **9.** They encouraged others to follow, so they too could sacrifice and eat. **10.** Tseerutsaydan trusted in these idols, though they brought no profit (benefit). **11.** In his arrogance (pride), he thought the idols created him, fed him, and crowned him. **12.** The idols were false gods, and Satan deceived (misled) him, leading him to forget the true Creator. **13.** Satan's authority (power) misled him, and the idols would be judged (held accountable). **14.** When people saw the truth, they would realize their misguided (incorrect) beliefs. **15.** They would be led to sacrifice (kill) their children, innocent blood spilled for evil purposes. **16.** Tseerutsaydan, in his arrogance, boasted of fifty male and twenty female idols. **17.** He glorified (praised) these idols with sacrifices morning and evening. **18.** He commanded others to sacrifice to the idols and eat the defiled (unclean) offerings. **19.** He had five houses for these idols, made of iron, brass, and lead. **20.** He adorned (decorated)

them with silver, gold, and veiled (covered) curtains. **21.** He appointed keepers (guardians) to these idols, sacrificing forty animals daily. **22.** He offered them grapes and wheat, believing the idols ate them. **23.** Tseerutsaydan told his priests, "Give my creators the offerings, and if they aren't enough, I will add more." **24.** He commanded that all should eat and drink from the defiled (unclean) sacrifices. **25.** He sent his troops (soldiers) across the kingdom to punish those who refused to bow or sacrifice, burning their houses and stealing their money. **26.** He claimed, "These are my great creators, and unless you worship them, I will punish you." **27.** He threatened severe (harsh) tribulation (suffering) to those who did not obey, reminding them of the Earth, the sky, and all living things. **28.** But those who worshipped the idols would face punishment and tribulation without mercy.

Chapter 2

1. There was a man from the tribe of Binyam named Meqabees. **2.** He had three handsome and valiant (brave) sons, beloved by all in Midyam and Miedon under Tseerutsaydan (a ruler's title or kingdom name) rule. **3.** The king commanded them, saying, "Will you bow to Tseerutsaydan's creators (false gods) and offer sacrifices? **4.** If not, we will seize (capture) you, take you to the king, and destroy all your possessions as ordered." **5.** The youths replied, "We bow only to the Creator of Heaven, Earth, the sea, moon, sun, stars, and all within them—He is the True Creator we worship." **6.** These young men, along with their servants, were warriors: four royal youths with a hundred shield-bearers (soldiers carrying shields) and spearmen (soldiers carrying spears). **7.** When attempts were made to seize them, they escaped unharmed, wielding (using skillfully) shields and spears with great power. **8.** One of them could strangle (squeeze to death) a panther with ease, like handling a chicken. **9.** Another could kill a lion with a single rock or strike. **10.** A third could defeat a hundred men in battle with one sword, their fame spreading throughout Babilon (Babylon) and Mo`ab (a historical region). **11.** They were mighty warriors, loved and admired for their unmatched beauty and strength. **12.** Their devotion to JAH (God) and fearlessness of death made their greatness even more remarkable (extraordinary). **13.** When troops (soldiers) pursued them, they fled to a high mountain, evading (escaping from) capture. **14.** The troops returned, threatening (making harmful promises) the city, "Deliver the Meqabeans, or we will burn the city and destroy the land." **15.** In fear, the people—rich and poor, young and old—pleaded (begged) with the warriors, "Do not bring destruction upon us and our land." **16.** Weeping together, they turned to JAH in prayer, saying, **17.** "Lord, should we honor those who defy (disobey) Your Command and LAW? **18.** They trust in idols (man-made gods) of silver, gold, stone, and wood, but we reject such wickedness (evil)." **19.** "You, the Creator who gives and takes life, will judge them. We refuse to submit (agree unwillingly) to their evil demands." **20.** "If You command us, we will willingly face death for Your Name and never bow to their false gods." **21.** "We trust in You, Lord, who knows the hearts and minds of all—our Creator, the God of Abriham (Abraham), Yis'haq (Isaac), and Ya`iqob (Jacob)." **22.** "You help both sinner and righteous (virtuous), and none can hide from You." **23.** "We have no Creator but You, and we will sacrifice (offer up) ourselves to glorify (honor) Your Name." **24.** "Be our strength and shelter (protection) in this trial (challenge), as You were for Ya`iqob in Gibts (Egypt)." **25.** "Now, O God, we plead (earnestly request) for Your help." **26.** Suddenly, two radiant (shining) men appeared with fiery swords like lightning, striking and killing the troops. **27.** The youths were restored (returned) to perfect health, their beauty surpassing (exceeding) even the sun. **28.** They shone brighter than before, their radiance (brightness) unmatched.

Chapter 3

1. Before you, behold the Most High JAH servants - 'Abya, Seela, and Fentos, who died and rose again. You too will rise after death, and your faces shall shine like the Sun in the Kingdom of Heaven. **2.** They went with the men and received martyrdom (died for their beliefs). **3.** They praised, begged, and bowed to JAH, undeterred by death or the king's punishment. **4.** They approached the youths like innocent sheep, but still, they were seized, beaten, bound, whipped, and brought before the king. **5.** The king asked, "Why won't you sacrifice and bow to my creators (false gods)?" **6.** Seela, 'Abya, and Fentos, pure and honored, answered in unison. **7.** "I will not bow or sacrifice to defiled idols without knowledge or reason." **8.** "I will not bow to idols made of silver, gold, stone, or wood, for they do not benefit nor harm anyone." **9.** The king asked, "Why insult the glorified creators?" **10.** They replied, "They are nothing compared to me, and I will not glorify them." **11.** The king threatened, "I will punish you with whips, suffering, and fire, and destroy your beauty." **12.** "Tell me if you will sacrifice to my creators, or I will punish you with the sword and whip." **13.** They responded, "We will not sacrifice or bow to defiled idols." The king commanded they be beaten with a stick, whipped, and severely tortured. **14.** Afterward, they were bound and imprisoned until the king's counsel decided their fate. **15.** They were held in prison for three days and nights. **16.** After three days, the king called a proclamation and gathered his counselors, nobles, and officials. **17.** The king ordered Seela, 'Abya, and Fentos, wounded and bound, to be brought before him. **18.** The king asked, "After three days, do you still refuse to bow, or have you changed?" **19.** They replied, "We will not worship the sinful idols you revere." **20.** The king, enraged, ordered them to be placed in a high place, and their wounds were reopened as their blood flowed to the ground. **21.** The king again commanded them to be burned with a torch (a flame source), and his servants did as he commanded. The martyrs replied, "You who have forgotten JAH's law, your reward will be equal to the punishment you inflict." **22.** The king then commanded that evil beasts (dangerous animals)—bears, tigers, and lions—be sent to devour them (consume them). **23.** The beast keepers (those who control the animals) followed the king's orders, and the martyrs were bound (tied) by their feet and beaten with tent stakes (long wooden poles used to secure tents). **24.** The beasts attacked them, roaring (making loud noises), but when they neared the martyrs, they bowed. **25.** The beasts returned to their keepers, terrifying them (scaring them), and the martyrs were brought before the king. **26.** The beasts killed seventy-five of the king's soldiers. **27.** Many panicked (became afraid), and the king fled his throne (left his position of power). The beasts were finally subdued (controlled) and returned to their lair (home). **28.** Seela, 'Abya, and Fentos, who had been freed from imprisonment (locked up), came to help the martyrs escape. **29.** The martyrs refused to flee (run away), stating it wasn't their way to run after standing for their testimony (belief). **30.** The little brethren (younger brothers or companions) offered to stand with them, even if it meant death. **31.** The king saw the release of the martyrs and grew furious (angry), realizing they were together. **32.** The king ordered all five to be imprisoned in harsh conditions (difficult circumstances). **33.** He complained about their stubbornness (unwillingness to change), deciding to punish them severely. **34.** The king planned to burn their flesh (bodies) to ashes, scattering them (dispersing them) over the mountains. **35.** After three days, he ordered a great fire (flame) to be prepared, adding malice (evil intent) to the flames with soapberries, sulfur (a chemical element), and resin (tree sap). **36.** The messengers (those who deliver messages) reported to the king that the preparations were complete. **37.** The youths were cast (thrown) into the fire, and as they entered, they gave their souls (spiritual beings) to JAH. **38.** When those who cast them saw this, Angels (divine beings) received their souls and carried them to the Garden (paradise), where Yis'haq, 'Abriham, and Ya`iqob are, and joy and peace are found.

Chapter 4

1. When the criminals (those who have committed a crime) saw that they were dead, the king ordered their bodies to be burned until ash and scattered in the wind. But the fire couldn't burn their hair, and they were taken from the pit (a large hole or grave). **2.** Again, they set fire (to burn or ignite something) to the bodies from morning till evening, but it didn't burn them. They said, "Let's throw them into the sea." **3.** They obeyed the king's command and cast (to throw or fling) the bodies into the sea, weighing them down with stones (adding heavy objects to make something sink), but the sea wouldn't sink them. The bodies floated, untouched by the malice (the intention or desire to do evil or cause harm) aimed at them. **4.** "This death has worn me down (made me tired or exhausted, mentally or emotionally) more than their life; should I cast them to the beasts (wild animals)? But what should I do?" the king said. **5.** The youths (young people or men) followed his command, but the vultures (large birds of prey that feed on dead animals) and beasts didn't touch the bodies. Birds shielded (protected) them from the sun, and the corpses remained intact (unchanged, not

damaged) for fourteen days. **6.** When they were seen again, their bodies shone (gave off light, was bright) like the sun, and angels (spiritual beings often considered messengers of God) circled (moved around in a circular motion) them like light around a tent. **7.** The king, unsure (not certain) of what to do, dug a grave (a hole dug in the ground to bury a body) and buried the martyrs (people who suffer or die for their beliefs). **8.** That night, the king, who had forgotten (didn't remember) God's law, saw the five martyrs standing before him, wielding (holding and using, usually referring to weapons) swords. **9.** He thought they had entered his house to harm (injury or damage) him. When he awoke (woke up from sleep), terrified, he fled (ran away) his bedchamber (a room where a bed is kept, typically a bedroom), fearing for his life. **10.** Trembling (shaking or quivering from fear or anxiety), he asked, "My lords (a respectful title for someone in authority or power), what do you want from me? What should I do for you?" **11.** They answered, "Aren't we the ones you killed by burning (incinerating) and casting (throwing) into the sea? JAH kept our bodies because we believed in Him, and it failed to destroy us. Glory be to JAH; we didn't shame (dishonor) Him in tribulation (suffering). **12.** "I didn't know such punishment (penalty) would come. What reward (compensation) should I give for my wrongs?" **13.** "Separate (set apart) the reward for me, lest you take my body in death or lower (send) it to the underworld (afterlife) while I am alive." **14.** "Forgive my sin (wrongdoing), as it was your Father JAH's Law that I broke," he told them. **15.** The martyrs (martyrs) replied, "Because of your wrongs, we won't repay you evil (harm); JAH brings hardship (difficulty) on souls and will repay you." **16.** "You thought you killed me, but your reasoning (thought) was wrong. You prepared welfare (well-being) for me. Your idols (false gods) will lead you to Hell (torment)." **17.** "Woe (grief) to your idols, made of silver, gold, and wood, which have no reasoning (thought) or knowledge (awareness). You worship them, but they don't harm (hurt) or help anyone." **18.** "Your idols mislead (deceive) you, and they don't love that anyone might be saved (rescued). You're deceived (misled), thinking they created you, when you created them." **19.** The king asked, "What should I do for you, to fulfill (satisfy) your desires?" **20.** "You must save (rescue) yourself from Hell, not us. Your idols are worthless (useless); they can't help or save anyone." **21.** "Your idols are made of silver, gold, stone, and wood, with no power (strength) or wisdom (insight). They are man-made." **22.** "They can't kill (slay) or save (rescue), they don't benefit (help) or harm (hurt) anyone, and they mislead (misguide) you with demonic (evil) authority (power)." **23.** "They don't want you saved (rescued) from death (end). You're deceived (misled) by them, thinking they created you, when you created them." **24.** "Satans (evil beings) and demons (spirits) work through them. They'll return (give back) your actions, drowning (submerging) you in Hell." **25.** "Quit your errors (mistakes) and seek reward (benefit) in worshipping JAH, for I am dead, and my soul (spirit) benefits (gains) from this." **26.** The king, alarmed (shocked), feared (was afraid) and bowed (knelt) to them. **27.** "I now know that the dead (deceased) will rise (revive). It is only a matter of time before my own death." **28.** After this, the king stopped burning (igniting) their bodies. **29.** He had misled (misguided) many people with his idols, leading them away from JAH's worship, and he was not the only one to err (misstep). **30.** He sacrificed (offered) children to demons (evil spirits), seducing (tempting) and disturbing (disturbing) people with teachings from Satan (the devil). **31.** They marry their mothers and abuse (mistreat) their aunts and sisters, corrupting (damaging) their bodies with evil works, as Satan twisted (distorted) their reasoning, and they said, "We won't return." **32.** The arrogant (proud) Tséerutsaydan, who doesn't know his Creator, boasts (brags) of his idols. **33.** If they ask, "How will JAH give the Kingdom to those who don't know Him in Law (guidelines) and Worship?"—they will repent (feel remorse) as He tests them. **34.** If they repent, He will love them and give them the Kingdom but if they refuse, they will suffer (experience pain) in the fire of Gehannem (Hell) forever. **35.** A king should fear (respect deeply) his Creator like his own fame (reputation), and a judge should rule righteously (justly) in His name. **36.** Elders, chiefs, envoys (representatives), and petty kings should be commanded by their Creator as they are in their lordship (authority). **37.** For He is the Lord of Heaven and Earth, the only Creator, Who impoverishes (makes poor) and enriches (makes wealthy), honoring (elevating) and humiliating (bringing down).

Chapter 5

1. A proud (arrogant) warrior from the sixty was struck (affected) by a plague sent by JAH. **2.** Keeram, who built an iron bed, was also proud and met death by JAH's will. **3.** Nabukedenetsor boasted (bragged), claiming to be the Creator, but JAH humbled (lowered) him. **4.** JAH sent him into the wilderness for seven years, where he realized (understood) that JAH is the Creator. **5.** Once he acknowledged (recognized) JAH, he was returned to his kingdom. **6.** Who can defy (oppose) JAH's law and survive (continue living)? **7.** Tséerutsaydan, you will be humbled for your pride in your Creator. **8.** After death, you may descend (fall) to Gehannem, where there is no escape (way out). **9.** You are a man who will die, like the kings before you. **10.** You are ruined (destroyed), but JAH is the Creator of all. **11.** JAH humbles (lowers) the proud (arrogant), honors (respects) the humble (modest), and strengthens (supports) the weary (tired). **12.** He raises the dead and frees (liberates) slaves from sin. **13.** O Tséerutsaydan, why boast (brag) in your useless (ineffective) idols? **14.** JAH created Earth, Heaven, seas, the Sun, and the Moon. **15.** He has set (arranged) the seasons and firmed up (stabilized) the stars by His Word. **16.** Everything is known to JAH; nothing is done without His knowledge. **17.** JAH commands (instructs) the Angels to serve (assist) and praise (admire) Him. **18.** JAH sent angels to help people, like Rufa'iel saving Thobya. **19.** Meeka'iel was sent to help Giediewon, and many other miracles were done. **20.** JAH led them, without idols, providing (giving) crops and sustenance (food). **21.** He fed them honey and grain, showing His love. **22.** He crowned (appointed) you with authority (power) over kingdoms. **23.** JAH crowned you to love Him and do His will (commands). **24.** Do JAH's will, and He will support you, protect you, and guide (lead) you. **25.** JAH crowned you to love Him and follow His commands. **26.** If you follow (obey) His will, your life will be blessed (made prosperous) and supported. **27.** JAH will protect (defend) you from your enemies and give (grant) you a throne (seat of power) of authority. **28.** JAH chose (selected) and crowned you, just as He did with Sa'ol, the first king of Israel. **29.** JAH gave him great fortune (wealth), and He has crowned you too. **30.** You are appointed (chosen) to govern (rule), to do good, and to correct (fix) evil. **31.** Follow JAH's command in everything, whether you whipped (punished) or saved (rescued), do good or evil. **32.** You are a servant (worker) of JAH, who rules (governs) all in Heaven and Earth. **33.** No one rules JAH; He rules all. **34.** JAH appoints (chooses) everyone, and no one can dismiss (remove) Him. **35.** No one can reproach (insult) JAH; He reproaches all. **36.** JAH makes all diligent (hardworking), and no one can escape (avoid) His authority (power). **37.** Everything is revealed (shown) before JAH; no one is hidden (concealed) from Him. **38.** JAH sees all and answers (responds to) the prayers of those who seek (look for) His help. **39.** JAH is the eternal (never-ending) King, feeding all from His unchanging (constant) nature.

Chapter 6

1. JAH crowns righteous kings who follow His will. **2.** Kings who do JAH's will will shine in Light, like Yis'haq, 'Abriham, Ya`iqob, Solomon, Daweet, and Hiziqyas, whose dwellings (places where they live) are in the Garden of Light. **3.** Heaven's halls shine brightly, unlike Earth, with floors made of silver, gold, and jewels, clean and shining. **4.** Heaven's features are beyond human understanding (comprehension), shining like jewels, crafted (made) in pure materials. **5.** JAH, the Creator, made Heaven, a place that shines in total light, with floors of gold, silver, jewels, and silk. **6.** Heaven is entirely beautiful. **7.** The righteous (virtuous) ones, who are firm in faith and virtue, will inherit this place by JAH's charity (generosity) and mercy. **8.** A river flows with welfare (goodness) water, shining like the Sun, surrounded by a fragrant (pleasant-smelling) light. **9.** The Garden bears beautiful fruits with different tastes and fragrances, with oil and grapes, all around the house. **10.** Entering it, the soul is overwhelmed (overcome) by the joy and fragrance, separating from the body. **11.** Righteous kings who follow JAH will be honored and content in Heaven, their place known forever. **12.** Their earthly leadership will be honored, and in Heaven, they will be exalted (raised in status) if they live righteously. **13.** But kings who rule unjustly, ignoring the cries (pleas) of the poor and oppressed (those treated unfairly), will face judgment. **14.** They fail to help the needy (those in need) and ignore the hungry and thirsty. **15.**

JAH will send them to Gehannem (Hell) on the Day of Judgment, when His wrath (anger) will be upon them. **16.** Nobles (important people) and kings rule, but some fail to keep JAH's law. **17.** JAH, who rules all in Heaven, controls souls and welfare (well-being); He gives honor to those who glorify (praise) Him and loves those who love Him. **18.** As the Lord (ruler) of Earth and Heaven, He knows hearts (emotions and thoughts) and thoughts, rewarding those who pray with sincerity (genuine honesty). **19.** He will humble (lower in status) the arrogant (proud), especially those who harm the vulnerable (weak), like orphaned (parentless) children and elderly daughters. **20.** Kings don't rule by their own power; JAH tests (challenges) them as He did Saul, who failed to obey the prophet Samuel and JAH's word. **21.** JAH sent Samuel to Saul to destroy (completely remove) the Amalekites for their wickedness (evilness), but Saul spared (saved) their king and livestock (animals). **22.** Because of this disobedience (failure to follow instructions), JAH declared Saul's kingdom would be divided (split). **23.** JAH chose (selected) David to succeed (replace) Saul as king. **24.** Saul, tormented (troubled greatly) by a demon (evil spirit), was removed from the throne for his disobedience. **25.** Samuel confronted (challenged) Saul, who pleaded (begged) for forgiveness but failed to repent (feel sorry and change). **26.** Samuel warned Saul for rejecting JAH's will (plan) and told him his kingdom would be taken away. **27.** Samuel reminded Saul that JAH gave him honor and authority (power), yet Saul ignored it. **28.** Samuel visited Saul again and asked why he ignored JAH's command to destroy (completely remove) everything from Amalek. **29.** Saul, fearing JAH's wrath (anger), tried to justify (explain away) his actions but was rebuked (scolded). **30.** Samuel declared (announced) that JAH had divided (split) Saul's kingdom. **31.** Saul asked for forgiveness, but Samuel refused to return (change) his word. **32.** Samuel pierced (stabbed) King Agag as a judgment (punishment) for Saul's disobedience. **33.** A demon tormented (troubled) Saul for violating (breaking) JAH's law. **34.** JAH, the King of Kings, struck (hit with force) Saul for his sin and disobedience. **35.** JAH rules all and dismisses (removes) the authority (power) of those who do not fear Him. **36.** David's lineage (family line) would be honored (praised), while Saul's would fall (fail). **37.** JAH punished (hurt as a result of sin) Saul's descendants (children) for their evil actions, as He avenged (took revenge on behalf of) those who harmed Him. **38.** A person who doesn't seek justice (fair treatment) for those who violate JAH's law is His enemy, and JAH destroyed Saul's descendants for failing to uphold (maintain) His commands.

Chapter 7

1. Whether thou be a king or ruler, what is important about thee? **2.** Isn't it JAH Who Created thee from nothing (nonexistent) to life, to do His will and live by His Command, fearing His Judgment? Like thou rule over slaves, JAH rules over thee. **3.** As thou punish (penalize) sinners, JAH will strike thee and lower thee to Gehannem (Hell) eternally. **4.** Like thou whip those who don't pay tribute (tax or offering), why don't thou offer tribute to JAH? **5.** He Created thee to love and be feared, to keep His kindreds (relatives) true – why don't thou fear thy Creator? **6.** Judge justly (fairly) as JAH appointed thee, without favoring (showing preference) anyone. Keep His Worship and His Commands. **7.** Like Moses told Israel's children, choose to follow what is right. **8.** Hear His Word, and do His Command, don't make excuses. **9.** Don't say someone else will bring His Word to you – JAH's Word is near, to teach and guide thee. **10.** Thou must hear JAH's Book to love and keep His Law. **11.** If thou reject (refuse) His Command, thou will enter Gehannem forever. **12.** He crowned thee to rule His creation with justice, in His Name. **13.** Forgive those who wrong thee, and judge with fairness. **14.** Don't show favor to anyone when judging; don't accept bribes (payments to influence decisions). **15.** If thou do His will, JAH will grant thee more time in this world; otherwise, He will shorten it. **16.** Think of the judgment after death, where all actions will be examined. **17.** If thou do good, thou will live in Heaven; if thou do evil, thou will live in Gehannem. **18.** If thou boast of fame, warriors, and wealth, don't forget JAH Who gave thee these things. **19.** If He told thee to stop, thou should obey. **20.** If thou neglect (ignore) His will, He will give thy lordship to another. **21.** As death (end) shall suddenly come on thee - and as Judgment (final decision) shall be done in Resurrection (rebirth) time - and as all man's work shall be examined - He shall totally investigate and judge on thee. **22.** There are none who will honour (respect) this world kings - because He was the Truth (reality) Judge - in Judgment time poor and wealthy will stand together. This world nobles (aristocrats) crowns wherein them boast (brag) shall fall. 23. Judgment are prepared (set) - and a soul shall quake (tremble) ~ at that time sinners (wrongdoers) and righteous (virtuous) ones' work shall be examined. 24. There are none who shall be hidden. On the time a daughter arrived to birthing (giving birth) - and on the time the fetus (unborn child) in she belly (stomach) arrived to be birthed - like unto she can't prevent her womb (uterus) - Earth also can't prevent its lodgers (inhabitants) that are on it ~ it will return. 25. Like unto clouds can't prevent rain (precipitation) unless they take and rain toward the place JAH commanded them - to JAH Word (command) has Created all, bringing from not living toward living (life) - and to JAH Word again has introduced all toward a grave (tomb) and all likewise - after Resurrection time arrives - it isn't possible to be that dead persons won't rise. 26. Like unto Moses spoke, saying - "It is by Words (speech) that proceed from JAH's Tongue (mouth) - yet it isn't only by grain (food) that a person is saved"; and JAH Word again shall arouse (awaken) all persons from graves. 27. Check (verify) - it was known that dead persons shall arise by JAH Word. 28. And again JAH said thus in Repeating (repeating) Law because persons who were nobles and kings who do His Accord (will) - As the day has arrived when they are counted to destruction (doom) - I shall revenge (punish) and destroy them on the day when Judgment is judged and at the time when their feet stumble (fall) - He said. 29. And again JAH told persons who know His Judgment - Know that I was your Creator (maker) JAH - and that I kill (end) and I save (give life). 30. I chastise (punish) in tribulation (suffering) and I pardon (forgive) ~ I lower (send down) toward Hell (torment) and again I send forth toward the Garden (paradise) - and there are none who shall escape (avoid) from My Authority (control) - He told them. 31. JAH said thus because nobles and kings who didn't keep His LAW - As earthly kingdoms are passing (temporary) - and as they pass from morning up till evening (daily) - keep My Order (command) and My LAW that you might enter toward the Kingdom of Heaven (paradise) that lives firmed up forever - He said. 32. To JAH, calling the righteous (virtuous) to glory (honor) - and sinners (wrongdoers) to tribulation (suffering) ~ He will make the sinner wretched (miserable) but will honour (respect) righteous ones. 33. He will dismiss (reject) the person who didn't do His Accord (will) - but He will appoint (choose) the person who did His Accord.

Chapter 8

1. Hear me: the dead shall rise, plants shall grow, and vines will bear fruit, as JAH brings forth the harvest. 2. The small plant you planted has grown, with tips, fruit, and leaves today. 3. JAH gives it water from Earth and sky. 4. The wood is nourished (fed) by fire and wind, while roots drink water, and Earth strengthens the wood. 5. Just as JAH created souls to bear fruit, the dead will rise as well. 6. When the soul leaves the body, JAH gathers souls from Earth, water, wind, and fire. 7. Earth becomes Earth, water becomes water, wind becomes wind, and fire becomes fire. 9. The separated soul returns to the Creator and will be reunited with the body in His time, placed in the Garden He loves. 10. Righteous souls are in the Light (brightness) of the Garden; sinners are in darkness (ignorance) until the appointed (scheduled) time. 11. JAH told the prophet Ezekiel to call the souls from all directions, that they may unite (become one). 12. And so the souls were gathered by His Word. 13. Water gave greenery (growth), fire gave heat, Earth gave Earth, and wind gave wind. 15. A soul was brought from the Garden, and a resurrection (rising from the dead) occurred. 16. The example of death is like sleeping, and the example of rising is waking. 17. The night is the world's example, while the morning is the resurrection of the dead. 19. This world passes like the night, but the resurrection is like the morning light. 20. David said, "God's example is the sun." 21. When Christ comes, He will shine like the sun in the new Kingdom of Heaven. 22. The dead will rise again, like seeds sown in the Earth that must die to grow. 23. The seed must rot (decay) before it grows, just as flesh must decay for new life. 24. If the seed rots, it can grow again; with rain from heaven, it brings forth leaves and buds. 25. The seed must die to bring forth life, and JAH gives the fruit. 26. The seed grows, but its outer parts (such as the shell or outer covering) are not counted. 27. Understand (comprehend) that the seed produces according to its kind, and the resurrection is likewise: the dead shall rise according to

their deeds (actions). 28. If you sow wheat, you won't reap (harvest) barley; if you sow watercress, you won't get flax. 29. Figs won't grow from nuts, nor almonds from grapes, and bitter fruit won't turn sweet. 32. Just as the fruit grows according to its kind, sinners and righteous will rise according to their deeds. 33. A tree may grow branches, but it cannot thrive without rain from heaven. 34. The cedar (a type of tree) will be uprooted (pulled out) unless it receives the summer rain. 35. Similarly, the dead will not rise without the command of JAH's dew (life-giving moisture) of life.

Chapter 9

1. Unless the highland mountains and Gielabuhie regions receive a pardon rain (forgiveness or mercy) commanded by JAH, they won't provide grass for beasts. 2. The Elam and Gele'ad mountains won't provide leaves for sheep, goats, or wilderness animals. 3. Likewise, unless pardon and dew (blessing or mercy) from JAH alight (descend) on doubters and criminals who previously profited from error and crime, the dead won't rise. 4. Those who practice sorcery (magic or witchcraft), stir conflict, and follow idols won't arise unless pardon dew is commanded by JAH. 5. Those who abandon the law, engage in lust (strong desire), or follow idols won't rise unless they receive pardon from JAH. 6. These will be convicted (found guilty) on the day of resurrection and judgment, while those who save themselves from idols will receive their reward. 7. Do you think the dead won't rise, dull (slow or unwise) one? 8. When the trumpet is blown by the Chief Angel, Hola Meeka'iel, the dead will rise, and you won't remain in the grave. 9. Hills and mountains will be leveled (made flat), creating a clear path. 10. The resurrection will happen for all flesh.

Chapter 10

1. If it weren't so, former people like Adam, Seth, Abel, Shem, Noah, Isaac, Abraham, Joseph, Jacob, Aaron, and Moses would be buried in their father's graves. Why didn't they love (desire) to be buried elsewhere? 2. Shouldn't they arise (come back to life) with their cousins in Resurrection? Could their bones be counted (classified) with evil ones and idol worshippers? 3. Don't mislead (confuse or deceive) your reasoning by asking how the dead will rise, especially those whose bodies have rotted (decayed). 4. When you see a grave, don't say, 'How will the dead rise, when no Earth is left?' 5. Just as the seed you sow (plant) grows, so will the souls JAH has sown (planted) arise. 6. JAH will quickly arouse (wake up) them by His word that saves (rescues)—He won't delay (postpone). 7. As He has returned (brought back) the living to the grave, isn't it possible (capable) for Him to bring them back to life? 8. Saving and lifting up (raising or saving) are possible to JAH.

Chapter 11

1. Armon perished and her fortress was demolished, as JAH brought hardship on them for their evil and the work they did with their hands. Those who worship idols in Edomyas and Zablon will be humbled at that time, as JAH approaches to convict those who worked in sin from childhood to old age because of their idols and evil. Seedona and Theeros will weep. 2. They sinned through fornication (sexual immorality) and idol worship. JAH will avenge (punish) and destroy them because they didn't live according to His commands. The children of Judah will be wretched. 3. She lived by killing prophets and feeling joy in sin, but she didn't live according to the Nine Laws and Worship. When the dead rise, Jerusalem's sin will be revealed. 4. At that time, JAH will judge her with His wisdom. He will avenge and destroy her for all the sin she committed from her youth to her old age. 5. She entered the grave and became dust, like her ancestors who lived in sin. In Resurrection time, JAH will punish those who destroyed His law. 6. They will be judged, as Mussie (Moses) spoke, for they say, "Their laws became like Sodom's law." 7. Their kindred are like the people of Gomorrah, and their laws bring destruction, and their deeds are evil. 8. Their laws are like snake poison, bringing destruction, and viper poison that destroys from within.

Chapter 12

1. Jerusalem, your sin is like Sodom and Gomorrah's sin. This tribulation (suffering) was spoken by a prophet. 2. Your tribulation is like theirs, rooted in adultery (sexual unfaithfulness) and arrogance (pride, superiority). 3. Aside from adultery and arrogance, no mercy (forgiveness) or humility (modesty, humbleness) came from your actions, which were driven by money, violence, robbery, and forgetting

your Creator, JAH. **4.** You didn't know your Creator, JAH, but instead followed evil works and idols (false gods), lusting after men and animals. **5.** Your reasoning (thoughts) is blinded (unable to understand) and deafened (unable to hear), preventing you from understanding JAH's will. Your reasoning is like Sodom's, and your kindred (family, people) are like Gomorrah, bearing good fruit. **6.** If you examine your works, they are poison (harmful, dangerous) that kills, cursed (damned) from the start and leading to destruction (ruin). **7.** Your laws and reasoning are firmed in sin (established in wrongdoing), as your bodies are consumed by Satan's work, bringing no good (productive, virtuous). **8.** When you are ashamed and baptized (cleansed spiritually), it will be for punishment and destruction (ruin). You will be firmed (established) in the ways of those disgusted with JAH. **9.** You lived in evil works, and will be made like the dwellers (inhabitants) of demons (devils), eating what was sacrificed to idols, which began in Israel and spread. **10.** You worship the idols of surrounding people, and your children follow demons who don't know good (moral, virtuous), separating from evil (immorality). **11.** You spill innocent blood (murder) and pour grapes (symbolizing wine) from Sodom to idols forever. **12.** You glorify (praise) and worship Dagwon (an idol), sacrificing your livestock (animals) to gain pleasure (satisfaction) in demon laziness (idleness). **13.** You sacrifice to them, forgetting your Creator, JAH, who has cared for you from your youth (childhood) to your old age. **14.** I will avenge (punish) you in Resurrection time because you didn't return to My law or follow My commands. Your time in Gehannem (hell) will last forever. **15.** If idols were truly gods, let them rise with you and save you when I destroy (punish) you, separating all the priests (religious leaders) who lusted (desired) after you. **16.** Just as you made sin and insulted (disrespected) holy things in the temple, I will make you wretched (miserable, unhappy) because of this. **17.** When they told you, 'This is JAH's people, Israel,' I made you wretched as you dishonored (disrespected) My Name. **18.** You boasted (proudly spoke) that I was your servant, but you didn't fear (reverence, respect) Me or obey My ways. **19.** You misled (led astray) yourself away from Me, worshipping idols who do not provide for (take care of) or clothe you. **20.** You sacrifice to them, eat the sacrifices, spill blood, drink their wine, burn incense (fragrant substances), and make offerings to idols. You are commanded by them. **21.** She sacrifices her children to idols and praises them because of their love for her, delighting in her words and deeds. (Sacrifice: offering something valuable, especially to a deity; Idols: false gods) **22.** Woe to her on Judgment Day, when her idols are destroyed, and she descends to Gehannem (hell), where the fire is eternal. (Gehannem: hell) **23.** Woe to you, Jerusalem, for abandoning your Creator and worshipping false idols. **24.** I will bring hardship on you because of your actions, as you have ignored My Word and failed to do good works. (Hardship: difficulty, suffering) **25.** Since you did not live by My law, I will not save you from tribulation (trouble or suffering). **26.** Because you ignored My law, I will convict you during Judgment. **27.** Like Sodom and Gomorrah, you are separated from Me. (Sodom and Gomorrah: cities destroyed for sin) **28.** I will destroy you as I destroyed them, for you live in sin, especially with lustful desires. **29.** They did not fear JAH and were full of sin from youth to old age. (JAH: God) **30.** Their thoughts were full of evil works like robbery, arrogance, and greed. **31.** Because of this, I will destroy their nations with fire until they are completely gone. **32.** Since they established sin, they will face eternal destruction on Judgment Day. **33.** I will not have mercy on them, as all their works were evil. **34.** I made you honorable, but you humbled yourself, turning to idols instead. **35.** I had betrothed you to honor, but you became devoted to demons, and I will punish you for your evil works. (Betrothed: promised in marriage) **36.** Because you didn't listen to My Word or commands, I will bring vengeance on you. **37.** Since you didn't follow My Word, I will convict you. **38.** Woe to you, Sodom and Gomorrah, for having no fear of JAH. **39.** Woe to Jerusalem, who will be judged with you in Gehannem, where there is no escape forever. **40.** You will descend to Sheol (the grave) on Judgment Day, for you did not keep My commands. **41.** The righteous will enjoy the wealth of sinners and live happily. **42.** Sinners will weep and mourn over their sins because they turned away from My Word. **43.** Those who keep My Word will be blessed and honored with Me. **44.** Those who live by My Word will

enter the Garden and enjoy the riches of the earth. (Garden: paradise, heaven)

Chapter 13

1. Woe to Theeros, Sidon, and all regions of Judah who are arrogant today and will perish by God's wrath when He seizes them. **2.** JAH said that a child of the Devil, the False Messiah, will arise from them. He will be full of pride, unaware of his Creator, and his actions will lead to God's anger, revealing His power. (False Messiah: a deceiver claiming to be the savior) **3.** The regions of Samaria, Galilee, Damascus, Syria, Achaia, Cyprus, and Jordan are filled with arrogant people who live in sin, covered by death's shadow, led by demons and refusing to fear God. **4.** Woe to those who serve demons and sacrifice to them, denying JAH, and who live in sin, idolizing the False Messiah who forgets God's law. He will set up his image and delight in sin, including robbery and adultery. (Sacrifice: offering something valuable to a deity) **5.** Because their actions are counted as sin before God, their era is marked by evil works. **6.** The sun will darken, the moon turn to blood, and the stars will fall from heaven as JAH brings miracles to end the sinful era. **7.** Just as God proudly created all things, He will destroy the small enemy, the Devil, in an instant. **8.** After the coming of God, the Devil will have no power. **9.** On the day of God's wrath, the Devil and his followers will descend into Gehannem (hell), where they will face punishment and destruction. (Gehannem: hell) **10.** God gives strength to the weak and weakness to the powerful, reminding them not to boast in their power. **11.** God, as the Ruler, judges and saves the oppressed, avenging the widows and orphans whose parents have died. **12.** Woe to those who boast and think that God will not judge or destroy them. They will arrogantly say, "I will set my throne in the stars and be like God." (Boast: to brag) **13.** Just as the Devil fell from heaven, shining like a morning star, he will be brought low. **14.** You boasted without thinking of God, your Creator. Why did you arrogantly think you could ascend to heaven, knowing your descent leads to Gehannem? **15.** You will be cast down from your lofty position, unlike the angels who humbly praised God and followed His commands, keeping their hearts pure. **16.** You acted with deep deceit in your pride, becoming a wretched person, separate from your companions. You cherished sin and injustice—robbery and deceit—that caused others to forget God's law. You taught sin to those from your kindred and led them to commit crimes as you did. **17.** Woe to you, as you misled demons in your malice, and you will descend together to Gehannem. **18.** Woe to you, the children of God, who were led astray by the criminal Devil. You followed his teachings of greed and sin and will descend with him into Gehannem, where there is no escape forever. **19.** In the past, when God's servant Moses was with you, you angered God at the waters where arguments arose, and at Mount Sinai and by Amalek. **20.** When you sent scouts to Canaan, they told you the path was difficult and the fortresses were strong, but you were vexed and wanted to return to Egypt, where you had worked hard and forgotten God's word. **21.** You failed to remember God, who helped you during tribulations, performed great miracles in Egypt, and led you with His angelic authority. He shielded you with a cloud by day and a column of fire by night to guide you. **22.** When Pharaoh's army frightened you, you cried to Moses, and Moses cried to God. God sent His angel and protected you from Pharaoh. **23.** God led you to Eritrea through tribulations, only guiding Israel and no other idols with them. He drowned your enemies in the sea and preserved none who fled. **24.** God led Israel through the sea on foot, and there was no enemy left to pursue. He brought you to Mount Sinai and fed you manna for forty years. **25.** Despite all these blessings, you saddened God by neglecting to worship Him. **26.** You placed evil in your hearts from childhood, as God spoke through the prophets, declaring that all human reasoning is futile, and all works of sin are marked by robbery, lies, and wrongs against others. **27.** Israel's children continually broke God's law, causing God to be grieved from ancient times to the fulfillment of His promise.

Chapter 14

1. JAH destroyed the children of Qayen (Cain) and their predecessors with the Water of Destruction because of their sins, cleansing the Earth from their wrongdoing. **2.** JAH was saddened by mankind, destroying all except for eight people, who later filled the Earth, inheriting Adam's legacy. **3.** Noah swore an oath with JAH, ensuring He would never again destroy the Earth with water, and that his descendants would avoid sin, idol worship, and death, so JAH could provide for them. **4.** After this, the children of Israel sinned and did not follow JAH's law, as their ancestors Yis'haq, 'Abriham, and Ya`iqob had done. **5.** From the least to the greatest, they broke JAH's law and lived crooked lives. **6.** Priests, chiefs, and scribes alike violated JAH's law. **7.** They did not follow the commandment Moses gave them: to love JAH with all their heart and mind. **8.** They also ignored other laws about loving their neighbor, avoiding idol worship, and refraining from murder, stealing, lying, and coveting. **9.** Despite these commandments, the children of Israel returned to sin, treachery, robbery, adultery, lies, stealing, and idol worship. **10.** After JAH gave them His commands, the children of Israel returned to sin, including treachery (betrayal), robbery (stealing), iniquity (immorality), idol worship, and committing adultery. **11.** They saddened (made angry) JAH by worshipping a golden calf, saying it was their creator who brought them out of Egypt. **12.** They felt good about their actions, eating, drinking, and celebrating. **13.** JAH told Moses that the Israelites, whom He had brought out of Egypt, had abandoned His law and made an idol, angering (making angry) Him. **14.** While Moses was angry, he descended (came down) with his confidant ('Iyasu). When 'Iyasu heard the noise, he thought it was the sound of warriors (fighters). **15.** Moses explained it was not the sound of warriors, but rather the Israelites' celebration, and then he destroyed (broke into pieces) the idol, crushing (breaking) it into dust and mixing it into the water the people drank. **16.** He then commanded the priests (religious leaders) to kill those who had sinned before JAH. **17.** The people realized that defying (disobeying) JAH was worse than death and followed Moses' command. **18.** Moses reminded them that JAH, who had delivered (rescued) and cared for them, was saddened by their actions, even though He had promised to give them the inheritance (something passed down) of their ancestors. **19.** They continued to sin, further angering JAH. **20.** They were not like their forefathers (ancestors), Yis'haq, 'Abriham, and Ya`iqob, who pleased JAH with their righteous (virtuous) deeds and received the blessings of the Earth and Heaven in return. **21.** Unlike their ancestors, who made JAH happy with their work and received the promise (assurance) of a joyful inheritance on Earth and a garden (paradise) in the afterlife, the current generation had forsaken (abandoned) His ways. **22.** They did not think of JAH, Who sent them from the land of Egypt, saving them from forced labor under harsh rulers. **23.** But they greatly saddened Him, and He would stir up (raise) enemies against them in their land, causing them to rise in hostility (enmity) and tax them just as they had once loved.

Chapter 15

1. At that time, enemies rose against Israel, with armies led by King Akrandis (name), who gathered forces from Keeliqyas, Sorya, and Demasqo. **2.** He sent messengers beyond the Jordan (river) to demand taxes from Israel, threatening to capture livestock, children, and take their wealth if they refused. **3.** He promised to take them to a foreign land to make them water carriers (people who carry water) and wood cutters. **4.** He mocked Israel's pride, reminding them that it was God who sent him to destroy them. **5.** He asked if the idols (false gods) of other nations had saved them, as he had defeated them and taken their horses, mares, and children. **6.** He warned that unless Israel paid the tax, he would destroy them like the others. He crossed the Jordan to plunder (steal) their livestock and wealth. **7.** Israel wept deeply, mourning for the destruction, but lacked someone to help them. **8.** God strengthened three brothers: Yihuda, Mebikyas, and Meqabees, who were handsome and mighty warriors. **9.** Israel mourned, and all cried out, from widows to children, with sackcloth (rough cloth) and ashes. **10.** The brothers, brave and determined, decided to sacrifice (give up their lives) themselves to save Israel. **11.** They girded their swords (weapon) and prepared to fight, rallying the warriors. **12.** They attacked the king during a feast, with Mebikyus killing him with one blow. Yihuda and Meqabees fought the king's armies, defeating them. **13.** With the king defeated, the remaining enemies fled, their bows broken, and they were scattered. **14.** The brothers were saved, and as God had punished their enemies, they turned on each other and were defeated. **15.** The enemies fled across the Jordan, leaving behind their wealth. The Israelites took their plunder (stolen goods). **16.** God saved Israel through the brothers and Mebikyus. **17.** Israel rested for a time, grateful to God. **18.** But later, they returned to sin, neglecting (ignoring) God's worship. **19.** God would again bring trouble, sending

nations that would destroy their crops, plunder their flocks, and take their families. **20.** These enemies would harm their children and families because Israel had constantly provoked (angered) God by abandoning His law.

Chapter 16

1. Those who do this are Theeros, Seedona, those beyond the Yordanos (Jordan) river, and those along the sea—Keran, Gele`ad, 'Iyabuseewon, Kenaniewon, 'Edom, Giegiesiewon, and 'Amalieq. **2.** All peoples do the same, living firmly in their tribes, regions, and languages, as JAH has worked in them. **3.** Some among them know JAH and do good work. **4.** Others do evil work and do not know JAH, their Creator, and are ruled by King Silminasor of Sorya (Syria). **5.** He plundered Demasqo (Damascus)'s wealth and shared the loot of Semarya (Samaria) before the king of Gibts (Egypt), all ruled by Silminasor's hand. **6.** The Gielabuhie region, Fars (Persia), Miedon, Qephedoqya, and Sewseegya, in the West mountains, Gele`ad fortress, and Phasthos, part of Yihuda (Judah) land, **7.** are populated by kindreds who do not know JAH, nor keep His Commandments, with minds hardened. **8.** JAH will repay them for their evil deeds and the work of their hands. **9.** The kindreds of Gele`ad, Qeesarya (Caesarea), and 'Amalieq have united to destroy JAH's country, filled with truth and praised by the Creator of 'Isra'iel (Israel), the Most Glorified and Conquering, whose many Angels in Keerubiel (Cherubim) chariots stand before Him, serving with fear and trembling. JAH will repay them for their evil deeds and the work of their hands.

Chapter 17

1. 'Amalieq and 'Edomyas (Edomites) do not worship JAH, by Whose Authority Earth and Heaven were seized. They are criminals (wrongdoers), living without Truth Work, and they destroy His temple (place of worship). **2.** They have no fear of JAH, engaging in bloodshed (killing), adultery (sexual immorality), eating what was sacrificed to idols, and consuming what is dead (carcasses)—these are scorned sinners (despised wrongdoers). **3.** They have no virtue (moral goodness) or religion (spirituality), hating good work and knowing neither JAH nor love. Their actions include robbing (stealing), sinning, disturbing others (causing harm), and following the teachings of their father, Deeyablos (Devil), in games and songs. **4.** Deeyablos rules them with demons (evil spirits), teaching them evil deeds like robbery, sin, theft, falsehood (lies), adultery, and eating what is dead. **5.** He teaches them to commit violence (harm), envy (jealousy), greed (desire for more), and other evils, leading them away from JAH's LAW (divine rules). **6.** JAH's Work is innocence (purity) and humility (modesty)—loving, harmonizing (bringing peace), and caring for others. **7.** Do not show favoritism (preferential treatment), nor be wrongdoers, robbers, or those who commit evil acts or violence against others. **8.** They provoke evil (encourage wrongdoing), mislead others, and guide them toward the Final Judgment (end of time).

Chapter 18

1. Think that you will face death and stand before JAH, Whose Hand holds all things, and He will convict (declare guilty) you for all the sins you have committed. **2.** Just like the arrogant (proud), evil, and powerful ones—children who do not strengthen more than their ancestors—were once, they trusted in their power, authority, and status, but they did not honor (respect) JAH, nor did they recognize Him as their Creator, Who gave them life. **3.** When their ancestors, like "Angels," praised JAH on Mount Hola (a sacred place) with Angels, they were misled (led astray), and descended into this world where the Final Judgment will be forever. **4.** JAH created human flesh (the body) in the past to test (examine) them, allowing their arrogance to lead them away from keeping His LAW (divine commandments) and Commandments. They married women from the children of Qayel (Cain). **5.** But they did not follow His LAW, and JAH condemned (punished) them to Gehannem (hell) fire, alongside their father Deeyablos (Devil). JAH was angered by the descendants of Siet (Seth) who acted like people, and humanity's years were reduced (shortened) because of sin. **6.** They led the children of 'Adam (Adam) into sin, and JAH condemned them to See'ol (Sheol, the grave or underworld), where they will receive a verdict (decision). **7.** The generations were divided because the children of Siet (Seth) erred (made mistakes) by following the children of Qayel (Cain)—when the lifespans of people were once nine hundred years in ancient times, they were reduced to one hundred and twenty years. **8.** Since they are flesh and blood (human beings), JAH said: "My Spirit of Support (assistance) will not remain with them." **9.** Because of this, my era has been divided (separated)—due to my sin and iniquity (wrongdoing), I have been separated from my ancestors, and when they return to their infancy (childhood), they die. **10.** But my ancestors thrived (prospered) because they kept JAH's LAW and did not make Him sad (angry). **11.** My ancestors thrived because they taught their daughters and sons the ways of JAH, ensuring they didn't destroy (break) His LAW. **12.** They did not destroy JAH's LAW with their children, and because of this, their era prospered (succeeded) in truth.

Chapter 19

1. In Qayen's (Cain's) time, his children played drums, harps, songs, and games. **2.** Qayen had attractive children with his wife, 'Abiel (Abel's) wife, whom he killed because of her beauty, then took her and her wealth. **3.** Separated from his father, he took them to the Qiefaz region in the West, where his children resembled their mother in beauty. **4.** The children of Siet (Seth) joined with the children of Qayen, and without hesitation, they took wives from those they chose. **5.** They led me into error, and JAH became angry with me and them for this. **6.** Deeyablos (Devil) deceived them, saying, "You will be creators like JAH," and led my mother Hiewan (Eve) and father 'Adam (Adam) into error. **7.** It seemed like truth to them in their ignorance, and they destroyed JAH's LAW, Who created them, so they might praise His glorious Name. **8.** JAH humbled 'Adam and Hiewan for making gods of themselves and humbled the arrogant. **9.** As Daweet (David) said, "'Adam perished through Deeyablos' arrogance," and JAH convicted my father 'Adam through His true Judgment. **10.** The children of Siet, led by Qayel's (Cain's) children, brought me into sin, shortening my lifespan compared to my ancestors. **11.** But they worked good deeds, firmly established in JAH's wisdom, and taught their children to keep JAH's LAW, so no evil enemy came near. **12.** Even if they did good deeds, it was of no benefit if they did not teach their children. **13.** As Daweet (David) said, they taught their children to praise JAH and recount His miracles and Power, so they could trust in JAH's LAW and follow it, like their ancestors did. **14.** Those who taught their children in their infancy did not break JAH's Commandments, learning JAH's worship and the Nine Laws from their ancestors. **15.** Their children learned to do righteous deeds, praise their Creator, keep His LAW, and love Him. **16.** He will hear their prayers and not ignore their pleas, for He is a Forgiver. **17.** Though He multiplies His wrath, He will return it but will not destroy all in His punishment.

Chapter 20

1. Brothers, remember (keep in mind) what was told to you earlier—that JAH keeps the true deeds (actions) of those who do good works. **2.** He will multiply (increase) their children in this world, and their name will be honored (respected) forever, and their children will not suffer (be troubled) in this world. **3.** He will defend (protect) them, and will not let them fall into the hands of their enemies who hate them. **4.** To those who love His Name, He will be their Helper (assistant) in times of trouble, protecting them and forgiving (pardoning) all their sins.

Chapter 21

1. David (Daweet) believed in JAH (God), and JAH saved him from King Saul's (Sa'ol) hand. **2.** JAH saved David during times of trouble, such as when his son Absalom (Abiesielom) rebelled, and during conflicts with the Philistines (Iloflans), Edomites (Edomyans), and Amalekites (Amalieqans). **3.** JAH helped David, but did not save the evil kings who didn't believe in Him. **4.** Hezekiah (Hiziqyas) believed in JAH, and JAH saved him from the arrogant (Senakriem) king. **5.** However, Hezekiah's son, Manasseh (Minassie), was defeated because he didn't trust JAH. **6.** JAH took away Manasseh's kingdom because he didn't do good deeds (work goodly Work) before JAH, so his era (time) was not prosperous. **7.** It's better to trust JAH than in many armies, horses, or weapons (bows and shields). **8.** Believing in JAH strengthens and honors a person, making them elevated (lofty). **9.** JAH doesn't show favoritism (favor to a face). Those who trust in wealth (money abundance) instead of JAH lose His grace and honor. **10.** JAH protects those who believe in Him, but He will leave the ignorant (people who ignore Him) to suffer, as they didn't follow His laws. **11.** JAH will be a refuge (protection) for those who keep His laws and worship Him. **12.**

JAH will bless His people by destroying their enemies, taking their livestock (plundering enemy livestock), capturing enemy territory (country persons), and providing abundant rains, crops, and fruit. **13.** JAH will send the necessary rains (first and spring rains) to nourish the land and make it fertile, so that people can thrive. **14.** JAH will bless His people with abundance, including plundered wealth (money), animals (sheep and cows), and food (dinner). **15.** JAH will do all this for those He loves, but He will bring destruction (ransackery) to those who hate Him. **16.** JAH will bind (tie up) the feet and hands of the disobedient and cast them into the hands of their enemies. They will face shame and destruction. **17.** At judgment (Judgment time), the guilty (sinners) will face hardship, while those who do evil (work evil Work) will receive punishment for their wrongdoings (sin hardship). **18.** JAH rewards those who do good deeds (work goodly Work) to keep them under His protection (Authority). **19.** JAH has power over all creation (Creation) and rewards those who praise and follow Him, giving them eternal welfare (eternal well-being). **20.** All of creation, from animals to humans, must follow JAH's laws (kept in Him LAW). **21.** Man has been given authority (emboldened) over all creation, including animals and birds, but must still obey JAH. **22.** JAH gave Adam (father 'Adam) dominion over creation, allowing him and his descendants to do what they loved, including ruling animals and the earth, but always in obedience to JAH's commands. **23.** If people depart from JAH's laws, He will take away their authority and give it to those who follow His will. **24.** JAH chooses whom to bless (Ipoint) or dismiss (dismiss), and He has the power to kill, save, punish (whip), and forgive. **25.** There is no other Creator like JAH, as He rules all creation and cannot be criticized (there are none who shall criticise Him). **26.** JAH has the power to appoint (Ipoint), dismiss (dismiss), kill, save, punish (whip), forgive, impoverish, and honor as He sees fit. **27.** JAH hears those who plead (beg) with a clean heart, and He grants their requests according to His will. **28.** JAH commands everything, from the great to the small, in the hills, mountains, caves, wells, and seas, as well as all peoples under His authority. **29.** Those who do what JAH commands will be blessed, and He will reward them with abundance, without taking away their blessings. **30.** JAH will honor those who serve Him, just as He prepared honor for His faithful servants like Isaac (Yis'haq), Abraham ('Abriham), Jacob (Ya`iqob), Hezekiah (Hiziqyas), David (Daweet), and Samuel (Samu'iel). **31.** JAH will give honor and inheritance to those who serve Him, as He promised to their forefathers (fathers Yis'haq, 'Abriham, and Ya`iqob).

Chapter 22

1. Think of those who do good deeds (good actions) and don't forget their actions. **2.** Make sure your name is like theirs, so you can feel good in Heaven (afterlife), which is for noble (honorable) and good kings who follow JAH's will (God's command). **3.** Evil kings who don't follow JAH will be punished and ridiculed (mocked) after death. **4.** Those who don't align their actions with JAH's will will be judged harshly in Heaven, worse than criminals. **5.** Be kind (compassionate), innocent, and honest, but don't follow those who forget JAH's law (rules) and anger Him with their evil deeds (wicked actions). **6.** Judge fairly (with justice) and protect (safeguard) orphans and widows from sinners who rob them. **7.** Protect the orphan from the wealthy (rich) who steal from them, and be mindful (aware) of their tears, so you won't face punishment with the unrepentant (those who don't repent). **8.** Walk the path of love and unity (harmony), as JAH watches His friends and hears their prayers. **9.** JAH's wrath (anger) is on those who do evil deeds, and He will erase (remove) their names from this world. **10.** I am JAH, passionate (strongly committed) about My Godhood (divine status), and will punish those who hate Me and disobey My Word. **11.** I will honor (respect and reward) those who honor Me and follow My Word.

Chapter 23

1. Don't follow the path of Qayel (Cain), who killed his innocent brother, thinking his brother loved him. **2.** He killed his brother out of envy (jealousy) over a woman; those who betray and commit iniquity (sin) against their companions are like him. **3.** But 'Abiel (Abel) was innocent, like a sheep, and his blood was pure, like the clean blood of a sacrificial lamb offered to JAH with pure intentions. They went down the wrong path, unlike 'Abiel's path. **4.** All who live in innocence are loved by JAH, like the kind person 'Abiel. These innocent ones, who live with pure hearts like 'Abiel, love JAH. **5.** JAH disregards (ignores) evil people, and His judgment will fall on them. Their actions will be recorded, and when judgment comes, it will be revealed to all, including mankind, angels, and all of creation. **6.** At that time, wrongdoers and those who refused to follow JAH's will will be ashamed. **7.** A warning will be given to them, saying: "Place them in Gehannem (Hell), where there is no escape for eternity."

Chapter 24

1. When Giediewon (Gideon) trusted JAH, he defeated the armies of uncircumcised peoples, many as countless as locusts, with just a few thousand soldiers. **2.** There is no Creator besides me—oh, nobles and kings, don't worship idols. **3.** I am your Creator, JAH, who brought you out of your mother's womb, raised you, fed you, and clothed you. Why worship other idols? **4.** I did all this for you—what did you give me? I want you to live according to my LAW, Order, and Command, so I can give you health and well-being. **5.** JAH, who rules over all, says: Avoid idols, sorcery, and pessimism (negative thinking). **6.** JAH's punishment will fall on those who worship idols and those who follow or support them. **7.** People who don't know you or are unkind will rise against you, unless you follow JAH's will. They will take what you worked for, as the prophets warned. **8.** Evil people will come, changing their appearance, living only for food, drink, silver, and gold, and practicing sin that JAH hates. **9.** They will go towards evil from morning till evening, bringing misery to their paths, with no love in their hearts. **10.** They don't know love or unity, and there is no fear of JAH in them. They are corrupt, greedy, drunkards, and sinners, full of violence, bloodshed, theft, and deception. **11.** They criticize without love, without fear of JAH. **12.** They aren't ashamed before elders, and when they gain money, they don't consider the consequences—they are driven by greed, with no fear of JAH. **13.** Nobles who eat trust money (money earned dishonestly) are corrupt, and they speak lies that contradict each other. **14.** They ignore the cries of the poor, rush to do evil, and disturb those who are wronged or oppressed. **15.** They must save the oppressed, yet they withhold justice for their own gain. **16.** They rob people of their money and show no respect for life—taking calves with mothers and birds with eggs, and claiming everything they see as their own. **17.** They greedily gather wealth, without helping the sick and poor, robbing others who have nothing to give. **18.** They will perish quickly, like a scarab (a small beetle) that disappears into the earth, for not doing good during their lives. **19.** When JAH neglects them, they will perish suddenly, as if it's part of their punishment—though JAH may allow time for repentance, He will eventually destroy them. **20.** If they don't repent, JAH will destroy them swiftly, like those before them who did not follow His LAW. **21.** They are those who consume the flesh and blood of others (through violence and sin), with no fear of JAH in their hearts, always sinning even after they wake from rest. **22.** Their works—food, drink, and sinful behavior—lead only to destruction, as they harm many people in this world.

Chapter 25

1. Those who follow crooked ways, living firm in Satan's (evil) work, will face JAH's anger when He punishes them. **2.** Those who do not follow JAH's ways, have turned away from Him and neglected His LAW. **3.** In the future, JAH will bring hardship on them, matching their evil actions, and He will avenge and destroy them on Judgment Day. **4.** I, JAH, am supreme from horizon to horizon. All of creation is under My authority, and no one can escape it, whether in Heaven, Earth, or sea. **5.** I command the snake beneath the Earth, the fish in the sea, the birds in the sky, and the desert donkey in the wilderness. All are under My control. **6.** I perform miracles and wondrous works, and no one can ask Me where I go or what I do. **7.** I command the chief Angels, the hosts, all creatures with names, and all beasts and birds, as well as livestock. They all belong to Me. **8.** From the wind of 'Azieb (a place or wind) comes a drought, and later the sea of Eritrea will perish, hearing JAH's call, bringing fear and recognition. **9.** JAH rules over the dead and the living, and His power will extend to regions like Saba, Noba, Hindekie, and Ethiopia, bringing destruction. **10.** JAH watches over all with His supreme authority, surpassing all others, keeping His people in His care. **11.** His authority is greater than any other, and His Kingdom surpasses all others, ruling over the world with power and without failure. **12.** He rules the clouds in Heaven, grows grass for livestock on Earth, and provides fruits and food. **13.** He feeds all creatures, from

ants to livestock, and answers the prayers of those who call on Him, especially the orphaned and widows. **14.** Evil people's rebellion is like a swirling wind, and their deceitful plans are like mist. JAH accepts the pleas of those who are sincere and clean-hearted. **15.** The body of the wicked is fleeting like a flying bird, and their wealth and possessions, made of perishable materials like silver and gold, will fade. Moths will eat their clothes. **16.** Their wealth, like weevils devouring grain, will vanish, just as a day or a spoken word passes and does not return. Sinners' money is like a lie, and their "beautiful lifestyle" is a passing shadow. **17.** But JAH honors the kind, especially those who help the poor and uphold justice for orphans and those who suffer. He will not forget them or their good deeds. **18.** Those who fail to judge fairly or mistreat workers will not align with JAH's Truth, which is unwavering and just like a two-edged sword. They will not commit injustice in their dealings.

Chapter 26

1. The poor will think again on their bedding (Bedding: the place where they sleep), but if the wealthy do not accept them, they will be like dry wood that has no verdure (Verdure: green, fertile growth) and a root will not be fertile where there is no moisture (Moisture: water or dampness), and the leaf will not be fertile if there is no root. **2.** Just as a leaf serves as an ornament (Ornament: a decoration) for the flower to help the fruit, unless the leaf is fertile, it will not bear fruit. Likewise, a person without religion has no virtue (Virtue: moral excellence). **3.** If a person strengthens (Firmed up: made strong or established) their religion, they will work virtue, and JAH is pleased with those who work truth and do straight work (Straight: honest, righteous). **4.** To the person who asks, JAH will grant their request and reward their words (Plea: request, reward: give something in return). He will not wrong the true person because of the good work they have done. **5.** Since JAH is true and loves truth, He will not justify (Justify: declare or make right) an unrepentant sinner because of the evil work they have done. All souls are in His authority (Authority: control, power) because He rules both Earth and Heaven. He will not favor the wealthy over the poor when judgment comes, and He will not justify someone who has not repented.

Chapter 27

1. Him who created all the world, bringing it from nothing to life. He prepared the mountains, firmed (made strong) the Earth on water, and set (placed) the sea in place with sand. His first command was, "Let there be Light." **2.** Light was created, and the world, once in darkness, was made by JAH. He prepared the Earth and firmed (made strong) it with what is due (what is right or required), saying, "Let the evening be dark." **3.** Again, JAH said, "Let there be Light." Light appeared, and He lifted (raised) the waters to the heavens (sky). **4.** He spread (extended) it like a tent, firming (making strong) it with wind, placing the lower waters in a pit (a hole). **5.** He sealed (closed off) the sea with sand and firmed (made strong) them up with His authority (power), placing animals, great beasts, and many creatures in the sea. **6.** On the third day, JAH created plants, roots, trees, and fruits of all kinds, and a beautiful wood (trees) for sight. **7.** He created wood (trees) that was pleasing to the eye and sweet to eat, along with grass and plants bearing seeds for food for birds, livestock (farm animals), and beasts (wild animals). **8.** It dusked (became evening) and dawned (became morning). On the fourth day, JAH created the sun, moon, and stars in the heavens (sky), placing them there to shine on Earth and separate day from night. **9.** The moon, sun, and stars alternated (switched) in night and day. **10.** On the fifth day, JAH created the animals and creatures (living beings) of the sea, and birds to fly in the sky, both visible (able to be seen) and hidden (not able to be seen). **11.** On the sixth day, He created livestock (farm animals), beasts (wild animals), and all living things, including 'Adam in His image and likeness (similarity). **12.** He gave 'Adam dominion (control) over all creatures (living beings), both on land and in the sea. **13.** He gave him cows, sheep, and all animals, visible (able to be seen) and hidden (not able to be seen). **14.** He placed 'Adam in the Garden to eat, cultivate (grow), and praise (honor) JAH. **15.** He warned (told him not to) him not to eat from the Fig Tree, for doing so would bring death. **16.** He commanded (gave an order) him not to eat from the tree, for it would bring knowledge (understanding) of good and evil, leading to death. **17.** Eve, deceived (tricked) by a serpent (snake), ate from the tree and gave it to Adam. **18.** Adam ate, bringing death to him and his descendants (children and their children). **19.** By breaking (disobeying) the command and eating from the tree, JAH became angry with Adam, expelling (sending out) him from the Garden and cursing (bringing harm) the Earth to grow thorns (sharp parts of plants) and thistles (prickly plants). Adam would toil (work hard) in the soil for his food. **20.** When JAH sent Adam out, he returned in sorrow (sadness), toiling (working hard) and struggling for sustenance (food or nourishment) from the cursed (made bad by God) Earth.

Chapter 28

1. After his children increased (grew in number), some praised and honored JAH, keeping His commands. **2.** Prophets spoke of what was done and what will be done, but from his children came sinners (wrongdoers) who lied and wronged (harmed) others. Qayel, 'Adam's firstborn, killed his brother 'Abiel. **3.** JAH judged (made a decision) Qayel for killing 'Abiel and was angry (vexed) with the Earth for absorbing (taking in) his blood. **4.** JAH asked Qayel, "Where is your brother 'Abiel?" Qayel arrogantly (proudly) replied, "Am I my brother's keeper (responsible for him)?" **5.** 'Abiel was righteous (good), but Qayel sinned (did wrong) by killing him. **6.** Siet, a righteous (good) child, was born. 'Adam had sixty children, some good and some evil (wicked).

7. Among them were good people, prophets (messengers from God), and sinners (wrongdoers). **8.** Blessed were those who kept JAH's law, from 'Adam to Noh (Noah), a righteous man who followed JAH's commands. **9.** Noh taught his children to keep JAH's law, so they would pass it on (share it). **10.** They lived and taught their children. **11.** But Satan deceived (tricked) their fathers, influencing (guiding) them to worship idols (false gods) and disobey JAH's commands. **12.** They worshipped idols until 'Abriham (Abraham), who followed JAH's will. **13.** JAH made a covenant (agreement) with 'Abriham, appearing (showing Himself) in wind and fire. **14.** JAH promised (vowed) him land and descendants (children) forever. **15.** He swore to Yis'haq (Isaac) and Ya`iqob (Jacob), giving them the inheritance (right to receive) of 'Abriham. **16.** He separated (distinguished) Ya`iqob's descendants into twelve tribes, making them priests (religious leaders) and kings, blessing them to increase (grow) greatly. **17.** Although JAH provided (gave) and loved them, they still saddened (displeased) Him. **18.** When JAH judged them, they would seek (look for) Him, return from sin (wrongdoing), and be forgiven. **19.** JAH will forgive them because of their fathers' actions (deeds), not their own. **20.** JAH stretched His hand (gave help) to provide for the hungry and revealed (showed) His mercy (forgiveness) to multiply (increase) food. **21.** He provides food to crows' chicks and animals that beg (ask for) Him, and when they cry, He will save Israel's children from their enemies. **22.** They will sin (disobey) again and sadden (make sad) Him, and He will raise (bring up) enemies to destroy, kill, and capture them. **23.** They will cry to JAH in mourning (sadness), and He will send help through prophets. **24.** He saves them through leaders (princes), but when they sadden JAH, their enemies tax (demand money) and capture them. **25.** Daweet (David) saved them from the Iloflans (enemies), but they again saddened JAH, and He raised enemies to trouble (cause hardship) them. **26.** He saved them through Yoftahie's (Jephthah's) hand, but they forgot JAH and turned to sin (wrongdoing). **27.** In their distress (worry), they cried to JAH and He saved them through Giediewon's (Gideon's) hand. But they again saddened Him. **28.** He raised enemies to trouble them again, and they returned (came back), weeping and crying for help. **29.** He saved them through Somson's (Samson's) hand, and they rested for a while, but soon turned to sin again. **30.** He saved them through Bariq (Barak) and Deebora's (Deborah's) hands. **31.** They worshipped JAH for a time, but again turned to sin. **32.** He saved them through Yodeet's (Jael's) hand, and after resting, they saddened JAH by sinning again. **33.** He raised enemies to rule (govern) them, and they cried to JAH. He struck 'Abiemieliek (a warrior) and saved them. **34.** He saved them through children and Matatyu's (Matthew's) hand. After the enemy's army was defeated (beaten), Israel pursued (chased) and destroyed them. They waited (rested) and rose again to sadden JAH, and He raised enemies to trouble them. They cried, but He ignored their cries because they disobeyed His law. **36.** They were captured and taken to Babylon (a foreign land) by their enemies. **37.** Israel's traitors (betrayers) continued to sin, worship idols, and sadden JAH. **38.** JAH was angered (angered) and planned to destroy them, influenced by

Hama (an enemy), who contributed gold (money) to the king's treasury. **39.** The king wrote a decree (official order) with his seal (mark), intending to destroy Israel, but ordered that gold and silver be added to the treasury. **40.** The king sealed the decree to destroy Israel on a set day, but commanded the offering of gold and silver. **41.** When Israel heard this, they cried to JAH and told Merdokyos (Mordecai) who informed 'Astier (Esther). **42.** 'Astier (Esther) instructed them to fast (go without food) and cry out to JAH. **43.** Merdokyos wore sackcloth (a coarse cloth) and dust, and Israel fasted and repented (felt sorry) in their land. **44.** 'Astier (Esther), deeply saddened (sad), also wore sackcloth and cried out to JAH, her Creator. **45.** JAH gave her favor (kindness) in the king's eyes, and she prepared a banquet (meal) for JAH. **46.** Hama and the king entered the banquet, and JAH caused Hama's downfall (ruin), leading to his execution (being killed). **47.** The king's decree was changed, and Israel was no longer oppressed (treated harshly) or robbed (stolen from). **48.** JAH forgave (pardoned) Israel when they repented, and the king's decree protected their land and livestock (animals). **49.** When they saddened Him again, He raised enemies to trouble them, and they will cry to JAH again for help and salvation (rescue).

Chapter 29

1. The Egyptians (Gibts) made the Israelites work hard, forcing them to make bricks with mud and heat them without straw. **2.** They appointed overseers (chiefs) to hurry the workers. The Israelites cried to JAH for help to save them from this labor. **3.** JAH sent Moses (Mussie) and Aaron (Aron) to free them from Pharaoh's (Fer`on) rule. Pharaoh refused to let Israel go, so JAH sent them to free Israel from hard labor. **4.** JAH ignored (neglected) the arrogant ones and drowned Pharaoh in the Red Sea (Eritra Sea) with his army because of his pride. **5.** He will destroy those who don't do righteous work in the kingdoms He chose, so that they may fulfill His Covenant and treat workers fairly. **6.** JAH said, "If they align with My kingdom, I will align with theirs." **7.** Do good work for Me, and I will protect you. Keep My LAW, and I will live honestly (with integrity) among you. **8.** Love Me, and I will love your well-being. Draw near to Me, and I will heal you. **9.** JAH said, "Believe in Me, and I will save you from hardship." **10.** Don't associate with wrongdoers. JAH loves honesty. Cleanse your hands from sin and distance your thoughts from evil. **11.** I will remove My anger and return to you in love and forgiveness. **12.** I will remove criminals and enemies who do wickedness, just as I saved David (Daweet) from Goliath, Saul, and Absalom, who wanted to take the kingdom. **13.** I will save those who keep My LAW and follow My Covenant. I will honor them and crown them in this life and the next. **14.** They will be united with kings who served JAH, like the prophet Samuel, chosen by JAH. **15.** JAH told Samuel to speak to Eli, the elder servant, and Samuel's work in the Temple was merciful (compassionate) and beloved by JAH. **16.** JAH appointed (chose) and anointed Samuel to choose people and anoint kings according to JAH's will. **17.** When Saul was king, JAH told Samuel to anoint David, the son of Jesse (Yihuda), whom JAH loved.

Chapter 30

1. I have rejected Saul's (Sa'ol) descendants because he disobeyed (violated) My Word. **2.** I ignored him because he didn't keep My LAW (rules), and I will not crown (appoint) his descendants again. **3.** Those who don't follow My LAW, Word, and Order (instructions), like Saul, will be destroyed, and their descendants will not inherit My Kingdom (rule) for eternity. **4.** Since they didn't honor (respect) Me when I made them famous, I will destroy them. Though I honored them, I won't lift (raise) them up again. **5.** They didn't do good things for Me when I did good for them, and they didn't forgive (pardon) Me when I forgave them. **6.** Since they didn't make Me their Ruler (leader) when I made them rulers, I won't make them famous again, nor will I honor them, for they didn't keep My LAW. **7.** I withheld (kept back) the gifts I gave them and will not return them, just as I was angry and swore (promised) against them. **8.** I will honor those who honor Me, and love those who love Me. **9.** I will make famous those who made Me famous. **10.** As JAH (God) Who rules all, no one can escape My authority (power), whether on Earth or in Heaven. I am the One Who kills, saves, saddens, and forgives. **11.** Fame and honor are My currency (value), and I will honor those I love. I am the One Who judges, avenges (punishes), and destroys; I make those I hate wretched (miserable). **12.** I forgive those who love Me and call on My Name, and I provide food (sustenance) for both the wealthy and the poor. **13.** I feed the birds, animals, and fish in the sea, as well as the beasts and flowers—I'm not only the One Who feeds humans. **14.** I feed crocodiles, whales, gophers, hippos, and badgers. **15.** I nourish (provide for) all that live in the water, fly in the air, and move on land—I'm not just the One Who feeds humans. All of this is My wealth (resources). **16.** I provide for all who seek Me and for all that I love, as is just and due (rightful).

Chapter 31

1. Kings (rulers) rule by My Accord (agreement), and suffering (hardship) and power (strength) come by My Command (order). They are not poor or strong without My will. **2.** I gave love to David and wisdom (knowledge) to Solomon, and added years (life) to Hezekiah. **3.** I shortened (reduced) Goliath's life and gave power (strength) to Samson, but later weakened (reduced) it. **4.** I saved (rescued) David from Goliath, the warrior (fighter). **5.** I saved him again from Saul and from those (people) who opposed (fought) him, for he kept My Command. **6.** I love all kings and nobles (important people) who follow My LAW, and I will give them victory (success) over their enemies. **7.** I will give them the cleansed (purified) land I promised their fathers (ancestors).

Chapter 32

1. JAH (God) Who rules all said: Hear My Word, O nobles (important people) and kings, and keep My Command, lest you anger (sadden) Me as Israel did, worshiping different idols (gods). I, JAH, their Creator, kept and saved them. **2.** I sent forth crops (plants) to the Earth and provided for them, giving the grapes (vine) and olive trees (fruit) they did not plant, and the clear water (well) they did not dig. **3.** Hear My Word, lest you anger (sadden) Me like Israel did by worshiping other idols. I, JAH, their Creator, fed them with sheep's milk, honeycomb, and grain (hulled wheat), clothed them in beautiful (ornamented) clothes, and gave them My love. **4.** Without it (gratefulness), they were deprived (lacked) all they begged for from Me.

Chapter 33

1. Like David (Daweet) said: "The children of Israel were fed manna (food) sent by angels." Hear My Word, lest you anger (sadden) Me as Israel did when they worshiped idols. I, JAH, their Creator, gave them sweet manna in the wilderness to help them worship Me in truth. **2.** But they did not worship Me, and I neglected them. They angered (saddened) Me by following the law of idols, which was not My Law. **3.** I will bring hardship upon them for their sin, as they neglected My worship and did not follow My guidance and Order. I will leave them in the measure of sin they worked with their hands and lead them to Gehennam (hell) in the final judgment, which is decided in Heaven. **4.** They did not keep My Law, and I was angry with them. I will shorten (diminish) their time in this world. **5.** If you are a king, remember that you are a man who will die and turn to dust and worms tomorrow. **6.** Today, you boast as if you will not die forever. **7.** JAH Who rules all said: Though you are well today, you are still a man who will die tomorrow. **8.** But if you keep My Command and Word, I will give you an honored country with kings who did My will, whose dwellings (lodging) were full of light, crowns beautiful, and thrones made of silver and gold, with those who sat on them adorned (decorated). **9.** They will feel good in My country, which is a place for those who do good works. **10.** But those who sin and do not keep My Law are not allowed to enter this country, where honored kings will enter.

Chapter 34

1. The Medon kingdom will perish, but the Roman kingdom will stand strong over the Macedonian (Meqiedonya) kingdom, and the Nineveh (Nenewie) kingdom will stand strong over the Persian (Fars) kingdom. **2.** The Ethiopian ('Ityopphya) kingdom will stand strong over the Alexandria (Iskindriya) kingdom, and the Moab kingdom will stand strong over the Amalekite ('Amalieq) kingdom. **3.** Brothers will rise against each other, and JAH will avenge (revenge) and destroy as He has spoken. **4.** Kingdom will rise against kingdom, people against people, and country against country, as JAH has said. **5.** Arguments, famine, plague, earthquake, and drought will come as love has perished from the world, and JAH's punishment will descend. **6.** The day will come suddenly when JAH will arrive, frightening like lightning from the East to the West. **7.** On that day of judgment, everyone will receive hardships for their sins, as JAH will avenge them and bring destruction. **8.** On that day, JAH will destroy those who do not live according to His law in Gehannem (hell) forever. **9.** This includes people living in the West islands, Nubia (Noba), India (Hindekie), Sheba (Saba), Ethiopia ('Ityopphya), and Egypt (Gibts). **10.** On that day, it will be known that I am JAH, the ruler of Earth and Heaven, who gives love, honor, salvation, and also destruction. **11.** I am the one who sends the sun to set, who brings both good and evil. **12.** I bring peoples whom you do not know, who will slaughter and take away your wealth and livestock. **13.** They will capture your children, and you won't be able to save them because you did not have JAH's support or fear His command. **14.** But a person in whom JAH's Spirit of Support resides will understand everything, just like Nebuchadnezzar (Nabukedenetsor) recognized the Spirit in Daniel. **15.** A person in whom JAH's Spirit resides will know all things, and nothing will be hidden from them. **16.** As we are all mortal, the sins we hide will eventually be revealed. **17.** Just like silver and gold are tested in fire, sinners will be tested on the Day of Judgment because they did not keep JAH's commands. **18.** On that day, all people and all works of Israel will be examined.

Chapter 35

1. JAH is angry because you failed to judge truthfully (fairly) the orphaned child (child whose parents are dead)—woe (sorrow, misfortune) to Israel's nobles (important leaders). **2.** Woe to those who get drunk, are partial (biased) in judgment, and ignore the justice (fair treatment) of widows (women whose husbands are dead) and orphans (children whose parents are dead), living in sin (immoral acts). **3.** JAH warns: unless you live by My Command, keep My Law, and love what I love, woe to you. **4.** Destruction, punishment (suffering), and tribulation (hardship) will come, and you will be lost (disappear), like what moths consume (destroy). **5.** Your country will become a wilderness (empty, barren), and people will marvel (be amazed), saying, "JAH made it this way because of sin." **6.** Because of pride (excessive self-importance) and arrogance (overbearing behavior), JAH will make it desolate (empty, uninhabited), with thorns (sharp plants) and thistles (spiny weeds). **7.** It will grow weeds (unwanted plants), becoming a wilderness (desert), inhabited (lived in) by beasts (wild animals). **8.** JAH's judgment (decision, punishment) will be upon her, and she will become terrifying (scary) because of her arrogance (pride) and the people's sin (wrong actions).

Chapter 36

1. O Meqiedon, do not boast (brag), for JAH will destroy (bring ruin to) you. O Amalik, do not strengthen (make firm) your arrogance (pride). **2.** You will rise to heaven only to fall (descend) to Gehenna (a place of punishment in the afterlife). **3.** When Israel entered the land of Moab and Midian, JAH warned: Do not boast (brag), do not deceive (mislead) Him. **4.** O descendants of Ishmael, why do you boast (show pride) in what was not yours? Do you think JAH will not judge (decide the fate of) you when He rises to judge the earth? **5.** JAH, the ruler (king) of all, says: At that time, you will face (experience) the consequences (outcomes) of your actions, and your pride will not save (rescue) you. **6.** I will treat (deal with) you as you treated (acted toward) others, and your deception (dishonesty) will lead (cause) to your neglect (being ignored). **7.** But if you do good and love (care deeply for) what JAH loves, He will hear (respond to) your prayers and bless (favor) you. **8.** If you follow His commands (instructions), JAH will fulfill (carry out) His promises (guarantees) to you, bless (favor) your children, and protect (keep safe) you. **9.** He will bless (increase) your herds (groups of animals) and everything you possess (own) if you live according to His commands. **10.** But if you reject (refuse) His commands, the prophesied (predicted) tribulation (hardship) will come upon you, and you cannot escape (flee from) His wrath (anger). **11.** You did not love (care for) what JAH loves when He gave you life and prosperity (success). **12.** You have used (spent) your wealth (money and possessions) for destruction (ruin) and dishonor (disrespect), neglecting (failing to give attention to) to worship (praise) JAH, the giver (provider) of all. **13.** But if you keep (follow) His covenant (agreement) and live by His commands, He will love (care for) you and grant (give) you favor (special treatment). **14.** Those who endure (remain firm) in His ways will be blessed (honored) and honored (given respect), like a sacrifice (offering) in His temple. **15.** Do not neglect (ignore) to do good, for it leads (guides) from death to life. **16.** But those who do good work, JAH will keep them in all His good work, so that they may be His servants (slaves) like Job, whom JAH kept from all tribulation (suffering). **17.** JAH will keep them in all good work, so that they may be His servants like Abraham, whom He saved when he defeated the kings, and like Moses, whom He saved from the hands of the Canaanites and Pharaoh, and who was disturbed (troubled) day and night by idols. **18.** But when they tried to lead him to idols, which were their money, he endured (bore) the tribulation while he refused to worship them. **19.** Abraham, who believed in Him from childhood, was JAH's trusted friend, and while he refused to worship idols, he worshiped JAH, the Creator. **20.** Since he totally loved JAH, he never stopped worshiping Him until his death, and he never departed from His law, teaching his children to keep JAH's law. **21.** Just as Abraham kept JAH's law, his children, Isaac and Jacob, also kept His law, because they were JAH's servants and did not depart from His law. **22.** JAH, who is praised and rules all, said: Abraham is My friend, Isaac is My confidante (trusted person), and Jacob is My friend, whom I love. **23.** But when JAH loved Israel's children, they lived in a way that continually saddened (displeased) Him, and He endured (suffered) with them, feeding them manna (bread from heaven) in the wilderness. **24.** Their clothes did not wear out, for they were fed manna, which is knowledge, and their feet did not grow weary (tired). **25.** But their thoughts (minds) turned away from JAH every time, for they were the ones who sinned from the beginning, and they had no hope of being saved. **26.** They became like a crooked bow (distorted), but did not become like their fathers, Isaac, Abraham, and Jacob, who served JAH in a beautiful way of life. They continually saddened (angered) JAH by worshiping idols on mountains and hills, eating on the mountains, caves, and tree roots. **27.** They slaughtered (killed) cattle, sacrificed offerings, and enjoyed their work, eating and drinking from the sacrifices, playing with demons as they sang. **28.** The demons admired their games and songs, and they practiced drunkenness, adultery, robbery, and greed, things JAH does not love. **29.** They worshiped idols of Canaan, Midian, Baal, Ashtoreth, Dagon, Seraphim, and other false gods. **30.** They sacrificed to idols and worshiped them as people do with money and possessions, making games and songs to them. **31.** All of Israel's tribes did the same, saying "We will worship JAH," but without keeping His commands and law, which Moses taught them to follow in order to stay away from idol worship. **32.** They worshiped separated (false) idols, forgetting their Creator, Who fed them honey from the rock, grain from the fields, and manna. **33.** Moses commanded them, saying: "Do not worship idols, for JAH is your Creator, and He is the One who feeds you and loves you, and He will not deprive those who love and seek Him." **34.** But they did not stop saddening (displeasing) JAH, and even when He made them feel good, they still saddened Him. **35.** When He saddened them, they cried out to Him, and He saved them from the tribulations (troubles) they faced. Then they were filled with joy and lived many years. **36.** But at times, they returned to sin, which saddened JAH like before, and He raised up nations around them to destroy them, causing them to worry and suffer. **37.** Then they would return to crying out to JAH, their Creator, and He would forgive them. **38.** This forgiveness was not because of their deeds, but because of their fathers—Noah, Isaac, Abraham, and Jacob—who served JAH in the beautiful way of life from ancient times, to whom He gave His oath. **39.** JAH loved those who kept His law, and through them, He multiplied their children like the stars of heaven and the sand of the sea. **40.** But when the dead are raised, those who are like the sand of the sea are sinners, whose souls will separate from Israel's children and go to Gehenna (hell). **41.** As JAH told Abraham: "Look up at the sky and count the stars if you can," and He also told him that his children and the righteous would shine like the stars in heaven. **42.** Likewise, as He told Abraham: "Look at the sand of the earth and count it if you can," and your sinful children will be like that sand, destined to descend to Gehenna when the dead are raised. **43.** Abraham believed in JAH, and because of his faith, it was counted as righteousness. He found joy in this world, and after his wife Sarah aged, she bore a child named Isaac. **44.** Abraham believed that those who did good works would rise to enter the Kingdom of Heaven and live forever, finding a kingdom in heaven. **45.** He also believed that those who did sinful works would go to Gehenna, where they would live forever when the dead are raised, but the righteous who did good works would reign with JAH forever. **46.** He believed that it would be judged forever, with truth and no falsehood, for those who sinned, and they would find life in the Kingdom of Heaven.

22 – II and III Meqabyan

II Meqabyan

Chapter 1

1. The Meqabees (Jewish rebel leaders) found 'Isra'iel (historical name for Israel) in Mesphiethomya (region), defeating many from 'Iyabboq (a river) to 'Iyerusaliem (Jerusalem), ravaging the land. **2.** Sorya (Syria), 'Edomyas (Edomites), and 'Amalieqans (Amalekites) allied with Moab (a kingdom) to attack 'Iyerusaliem, encamping from Semarya (region) and leaving few survivors. 3. When 'Isra'iel's children strayed, JAH (God) raised Mo'ab to strike them down. **4.** JAH's foes boasted about conquering His land and swore oaths in wickedness. **5.** 'Iloflee (a name) and 'Idomyas (a name) camped, feigning loyalty to JAH's Word while seeking vengeance. **6.** The Meqabees emerged from Riemat (a region) in Mo'ab, forming alliances. **7.** They gathered in Gielabuhie (a place), intent on destroying JAH's land, bribing 'Amalieqans and 'Iloflans (names) with riches. **8.** United, they overwhelmed the fortress, spilling blood like water. **9.** They turned 'Iyerusaliem into a desolate place, committing sins JAH despises, desecrating His land. **10.** They offered the flesh of friends and corpses of slaves to wild animals and birds. **11.** They plundered orphans and widows, acting without reverence for JAH, committing evil, even harming the unborn. **12.** Upon returning home, they felt triumphant over their wicked deeds against JAH's people, taking spoils from a revered land. **13.** Reaching home, they rejoiced, singing and clapping.

Chapter 2

1. The prophet Re`ay (a messenger of God) declared: "Rejoice today, for JAH (God), whom Ethiopia honors, will bring destruction upon you for your doubt. **2.** Will you claim, 'My horses are swift; I can flee'? **3.** Those who pursue you are faster than eagles (large birds of prey); you cannot escape JAH's judgment. **4.** Will you boast, 'I wear strong armor (protective gear); weapons cannot harm me'? JAH, protector of Ethiopia, says it's not by arms that I will bring you down. **5.** I will inflict upon you heart ailments (sicknesses) and worse, for you have provoked my anger. **6.** You will realize I am your Creator, like grass swaying in the wind; you are dust scattered by the storm. **7.** You have stirred my wrath (anger) and forgotten your Creator; I will not protect your people or your stronghold (fortified place). **8.** Now turn from your wrongs; if you mourn (express sorrow) and seek sincerely, JAH will forgive your transgressions (wrongdoings). **9.** In that moment, Meqabees (a leader in Ethiopia) mourned before JAH for his sins that angered Him. **10.** His eyes see all; He does not ignore; His ears hear; He does not turn away; His words are true; He acts swiftly, knowing the judgment proclaimed by the prophet. **11.** He tore his garments (clothing), donned sackcloth (rough cloth worn as a sign of mourning), sprinkled dust on his head, and wept before JAH for his wrongdoings.

Chapter 3

1. A prophet from Gondar (a city in Ethiopia) spoke of the Moabites (people from Moab) near Lake Tana (a large lake in Ethiopia). **2.** He dug a pit, wept, and repented (felt remorse) before the Lord. **3.** The Lord told the prophet to return to Ethiopia and inform the Moabite leader: "I, the Lord, your Creator, sent you to bring down this land, so you don't claim it was your strength." **4.** I am grieved (saddened) by your greed (excessive desire for wealth) and betrayal. **5.** I overlooked (ignored) your actions, but now the Lord forgives your sins for your children—not your authority (power). **6.** Those who waver (hesitate) in faith struggle to repent; do not waver—repent fully. **7.** Those who turn back from sin are praised. **8.** Those who return to the Lord in sorrow and prayer are honored; they are steadfast (firm) in repentance. **9.** The Lord forgives the Moabite leader for his fear; I bring consequences (results) for sins for generations, but I show mercy (compassion) to those who love me. **10.** I will fulfill my promise (commitment) to you for your offspring (children); the Lord accepts your repentance. **11.** He emerged from the pit, bowed to the prophet, and vowed (promised) to follow the Lord's desires, acknowledging his failings. **12.** He confessed (admitted) his sin and pride, realizing he hadn't heeded (listened to) the prophets or the Lord's commands. **13.** He was told that no one from his lineage (family line) had truly turned from sin; the prophet received repentance today. **14.** "Abandon idol worship (worship of false gods) and return for true repentance," he was advised, and he humbled (lowered) himself before the prophet. **15.** He returned home, fulfilling the Lord's commands. **16.** Meqabees (a leader of the Maccabean revolt) returned to worship JAH (God), removing idols and sorcery from his house. **17.** He examined the captured children from Jerusalem (capital city of ancient Israel), teaching them JAH's commands. **18.** He appointed wise leaders from the captured children to manage his household. **19.** He taught the children JAH's laws, rejecting Moabite (people from ancient Moab, near modern Jordan) idols and practices. **20.** He destroyed idols, sorcery, and sacrifices, including goats and sheep. **21.** He destroyed his idols, where he had worshipped, and spoke to the priests (religious leaders) about them. **22.** He trusted the teachings, believing they would save him, and did not dismiss them. **23.** But Meqabees eventually abandoned their work. **24.** After hearing from the prophet (a person who delivers divine messages), he repented, as Israel (ancient Jewish people) had in times of trouble. **25.** He remembered the oath of his ancestors (Abraham, Isaac, Jacob) and forgave them. **26.** After being saved, they forgot JAH and returned to idol worship. **27.** He raised enemies to oppress them, and when they cried, JAH showed mercy. **28.** When saved, they returned to sin and idol worship, angering JAH. **29.** He sent Moabites (people from Moab, east of Israel), Midianites (people from Midian, south of Israel), and others to defeat them, and when they cried, JAH raised leaders to deliver them.

Chapter 4

1. In the time of Iyasu (a former Ethiopian emperor), it was a day when God delivered them. **2.** In the time of Giedewon (a leader of Israel in the Old Testament), it was a day when God brought salvation. **3.** In Samson's (a Biblical judge of Israel), Deborah's (a prophetess and judge), Barak's (military leader under Deborah), and Yodeet's (a less-known leader) time, God saved them by raising leaders to deliver them from their enemies. **4.** Just as God's love was shown, He saved them from their oppressors (those who harm or mistreat others). **5.** They rejoiced in the works He did for them, in their lands, children, and flocks (groups of animals such as sheep, goats, or cattle). **6.** He blessed their crops (plants grown for food) and animals, keeping them under His mercy, and their herds (groups of livestock) did not diminish. **7.** But when they sinned (did wrong), God handed them over to their enemies. **8.** When He destroyed them, they turned back to Him in repentance (sincere regret and turning away from sin). **9.** Once they repented, God forgave them, remembering their sins no more. He knew they were only human, led astray by the world and demons (evil spiritual beings). **10.** When the Maccabees (Jewish warriors who fought for religious freedom) heard God's command in the Temple (place of worship), they repented and were slain (killed) in their devotion. **11.** After hearing, they did not despise (disrespect or hate) doing good works. They remembered how Israel (the people of God in the Old Testament) repented after sinning and JAH (a name for God) forgave them. **12.** The Maccabees committed to following God's law and living according to His commands. **13.** Hearing the boasting (prideful talk) of Israel, they too boasted in keeping God's law. **14.** They urged their people to stand firm (remain strong and faithful) in God's commandments and law. **15.** They upheld the laws of Israel, forbidding (prohibiting) what Israel forbade and observing the same laws. **16.** They offered their tithes (one-tenth of income given to God), firstborns (first children or animals), and sacrifices (offerings to God) from their livestock (domesticated animals), returning to Jerusalem (holy city) to offer their worship. **17.** He offered sacrifices for sin, vows, well-being, and peace. **18.** He gave first fruits (initial harvest), poured wine (fermented juice), and offered them to the priest (religious leader) appointed by God, following Israel's customs. **19.** He built a lampstand (light source), altar (table for sacrifices), seat (throne), tent (portable sanctuary), sacred rings (metal circles), and prepared oil (for lamps) for the Holy of Holies (most sacred part of the temple) as Israel did. **20.** Like ancient leaders, he followed God's laws, and God protected him from enemies. The Maccabees (Jewish rebel leaders) upheld God's righteousness. **21.** He prayed to God to teach him, asking not to be separated from His chosen people, Israel. **22.** He prayed for descendants in Zion (Jerusalem) and a home in Jerusalem, seeking God's salvation and forgiveness as foretold by the prophets (messengers of God). **23.** He prayed for his children's safety and for God's continued guidance. **24.** Moabites (descendants of Lot) under

the Maccabees' rule thrived, adopting God's justice and admiring Maccabees' fairness. **25.** They gathered to hear the Maccabees' teachings, admiring his truth and charity. **26.** He was wealthy, owning cattle (livestock), slaves (people serving others), and 500 horses. He defeated enemies, including the Amalekites (a nomadic tribe) and Syrians (from Syria), but was once defeated when he worshipped idols (false gods). **27.** After worshipping God, he found victory, and no enemy could defeat him. **28.** Even when idol worshippers (those who worship false gods) attacked, calling on their false gods, none defeated him, for his faith was in the true God. **29.** He ruled with authority and wisdom, ensuring justice for his people after defeating his enemies. **30.** He avenged the oppressed, judged righteously for orphans (children without parents), and protected the vulnerable. **31.** He cared for widows (women whose husbands had died) and orphans, feeding the hungry and clothing the poor. **32.** He worked with integrity (honesty), generously sharing his wealth and giving offerings (gifts to God) to the Temple (sacred place of worship), rejoicing in his service to God.

Chapter 5

1. He died, leaving children who grew up learning from their father. They cared for their homes and ensured the poor, widows, and orphans were not neglected. **2.** They feared the Lord, gave to the poor, upheld their father's teachings, and comforted orphans and widows. They defended the wronged and brought peace. **3.** They lived this way for five years. **4.** Then King Tseerutsaydan (a foreign king) of the Keledans (a foreign people) invaded, destroying villages and taking the children of Meqabees (a tribe) captive. **5.** He looted their wealth, and people lived in sin—adultery (infidelity), greed, and idol worship (false gods), forgetting their Creator. Those who ignored JAH's laws were taken to foreign lands. **6.** They ate unclean things (forbidden food), violating JAH's laws. **7.** They did not know JAH (the Lord), their Creator, who gave them life and provision. **8.** They married within their families (incest), stole, committed adultery, and had no guidance or law. **9.** Their paths were dark (lost), filled with sin. **10.** But the children of Meqabees kept the law, avoiding Keledans' practices and living righteously (justly). **11.** The deeds JAH approves were absent among others. **12.** They worshiped the idol Bi'iel Fiegor (a false god), trusting it as JAH, though it had no life or voice. **13.** It was made by human hands, from silver or gold, with no understanding or breath. **14.** It did not eat or drink. **15.** It had no power to harm or save (punish or protect). **16.** It could neither plant nor uproot (grow or destroy). **17.** It had no power to help or harm anyone. **18.** It neither blessed nor cursed but misled the lazy (unwilling to work), offering no justice (fairness) or mercy (compassion).

Chapter 6

1. JAH's enemies, the arrogant rulers, appointed false priests who worshiped idols (false gods). **2.** They sacrificed to idols and poured wine (fermented grape juice) as offerings. **3.** It seemed as though the idols partook (took part) in the feast. **4.** At sunrise, he gave cattle (domestic animals like cows) and sheep, sacrificing at dawn (early morning) and dusk (evening), eating impure offerings. **5.** He forced others to offer sacrifices to idols, not just his people (followers). **6.** When the Maccabees (Jewish family resisting idol worship) saw this, idol priests tried to sway (convince) them, but they stood firm. **7.** They obeyed their father's teachings (instructions), lived righteously (correctly), and feared JAH, refusing to compromise (give in). **8.** They were imprisoned (put in jail), insulted, and robbed of possessions (wealth, belongings). **9.** The king heard they refused sacrifices (offerings) and bowing (kneeling) to idols. **10.** The king was enraged (very angry), ordered them to be brought, and demanded they worship (show reverence to) his idols. **11.** They answered, "We will not worship (serve) your idols." **12.** Despite threats (intimidations), they remained steadfast (firm), their faith in JAH unshaken (not moved). **13.** The king threw them into fire (a large blaze), but they gave their lives to JAH. **14.** After they died, they were raised (brought back to life) at night (dark time), and the king trembled (shook) in fear. **15.** They spoke, "Tell us what to do; we will not take your body, but follow JAH's command (instruction)." **16.** They replied, "Remember JAH, who will remove you from your throne (seat of power) and send you to eternal fire (unending fire) with your father, Satan (enemy of God)." **17.** JAH created (made) the heavens (sky), the earth (ground), and everything within. **18.** He created the sun (star giving light), the moon (night light), and the stars (distant burning objects in the sky). **19.** There is no other creator (maker) but JAH, who does all things perfectly (without fault). **20.** JAH rules (has authority) all creation (everything that exists); none can escape His dominion (control). **21.** Everything He created follows His commands (instructions), except for you, a sinner (wrongdoer) deceived (tricked) by Satan. **22.** You and your false priests (wrong teachers) will fall into the eternal fire (never-ending punishment) of Gehannem (hell) together. **23.** You try to elevate (raise) yourself as if you are JAH, but you do not know Him (understand Him). **24.** You are proud (arrogant) in your idols and your work (actions), but JAH will judge (decide punishment for) you for all your evil (wicked deeds).

Chapter 7

1. Woe to those who ignore JAH (God), their Creator, and worship idols (false gods) like themselves. Regret will bring no relief when trapped in Sheol (the grave or underworld)'s torment. Woe to those who disregard His Word and Law. **2.** No escape from Sheol (the grave or underworld); priests and idol worshippers (false gods) who serve lifeless idols (images) cannot bring justice. **3.** Woe to those who sacrifice (offerings) to idols; their actions, led by demons (evil spirits), mislead and guide to Gehannem (hell), with priests (religious leaders) serving these demons. **4.** You err (go astray), not knowing what benefits you. **5.** Animals created by JAH (God) for food, even dogs (canines) and beasts, are better than you, facing no eternal condemnation (final judgment). **6.** You will suffer in Gehannem's (hell) fire with no escape; animals are better. **7.** After speaking, they left and hid from Him. **8.** Tseerutsaydan (name of a person or spirit) trembled with fear, which lasted until dawn (the first light of day).

Chapter 8

1. He was proud, cruel, and firm in his thinking. **2.** Like iron, his resolve was strong; he ruled and scattered people across regions (e.g., **regions**: areas). **3.** His life was full of evil, laziness, and unrest. **4.** He destroyed promises and stole from others. **5.** Persistent in evil, he followed the Devil (a fallen angel, symbolizing evil), bringing destruction. **6.** He boasted, "My time is like the Sun," but ignored the Creator, JAH (a name for God). **7.** He believed the Sun (the star that gives light) rose by his own power. **8.** He grew strong, settled in Gondar (a city in northern Ethiopia), and received gifts from Shewa (an ancient Ethiopian kingdom). **9.** He camped in nomadic regions (areas where people move), taxed Aksum (an ancient kingdom), and sent envoys (representatives) to the Red Sea (a body of water between Africa and Arabia). **10.** His pride reached the heavens, claiming dominion over all.

11. Filled with arrogance and evil, he lacked humility (the quality of being humble). **12.** His paths led to darkness (ignorance), violence (harm), pride, bloodshed (killing), and suffering. **13.** His deeds were hated by JAH—stealing, sin (wrongdoing), and causing suffering for orphans (children without parents) and the poor (those lacking basic needs). **14.** He conquered kings through his power. **15.** He ruled chiefs (tribal leaders) and taxed harshly, treating people as possessions. **16.** Even after destruction (ruin), he didn't stop; no one from the Red Sea (a body of water) to the Indian Ocean (a large body of water) was spared. **17.** He worshiped idols (false gods), consumed dead flesh (meat from dead animals), and practiced unjust works (unfair actions), taxing as he liked. **18.** He lived in malice (desire to harm), with no fear of JAH, forgetting his Creator. **19.** He didn't follow his Creator, and JAH will repay his wickedness (evil acts). **20.** JAH will destroy those who disobey His command, erasing their names (memory) from the earth. **21.** The wicked (evil people) will receive their punishment for their evil deeds. **22.** Those guided by JAH will walk in righteousness (moral right actions). **23.** Like Joshua (a leader of Israel) who defeated the five Canaanite kings (rulers of Canaan) in one day, commanding the Sun (the star that gives light) to stand still, he destroyed his enemies. **24.** Tribulation (suffering) will come to those who anger JAH with their evil ways.

Chapter 9

1. O weak one, who is not of the Almighty (JAH), why boast? You are dust today, and tomorrow you will return to the earth (ground) as nothing. **2.** Your guide, the deceivers (false teachers), bring suffering for their misdeeds, as they misled the ancestors (Adam and Eve). She'ol (grave/underworld) will claim those who follow their ways. **3.** You are proud, like those who refused to bow to our father (Adam), whom the Creator (God) formed. **4.** You have rejected the Creator (God), as the

deceivers (false teachers) did before. **5.** Your forefathers (ancestors) ignored the Almighty (JAH) and went to She'ol (the dead); you too will follow them. **6.** God (the Almighty) will punish evil deeds, and they will descend into She'ol (grave). **7.** You will follow the same path—into She'ol (grave), with no escape. **8.** Have you provoked the Almighty (JAH)? Do you think you will escape His judgment (justice), the One who rules over all? **9.** If you do good, the Almighty (JAH) will bless your work, and your enemies (those opposing you) will be humbled before you. **10.** You will prosper—your children, crops (harvest), and efforts will flourish. **11.** If you reject the Word (God's teachings) and law (commands), like others before you, you will face the Almighty's (JAH's) justice. His judgment (justice) is true. **12.** Everything is clear before Him (God); nothing is hidden. **13.** He removes kings (rulers) and overturns mighty thrones. **14.** He lifts up the humble (lowly) and restores the fallen (those knocked down) to their place. **15.** He frees those in bondage (captivity) and brings the dead (passed away) to life with His mercy (compassion). **16.** After judging the wicked (evil), He will send them to She'ol (grave), as they have caused sorrow to the Almighty (JAH). **17.** Those who oppose God's ways (deeds) will be destroyed, and their descendants (children) will suffer. **18.** Righteous works (good deeds) are harder than wicked deeds (evil actions), but the wicked refuse good counsel (advice). **19.** The righteous walk far from evil (wrongdoing), and their works are distant from sin (wrong actions). **20.** Sinners (those who sin) steal, lie, commit adultery (cheating), and live in greed (selfishness), leading only to destruction (ruin) and sorrow (sadness). **21.** Their ways (actions) lead to violence (bloodshed), tears (grief), and suffering (pain) and regret (remorse). **22.** This broad path (wide road) leads to destruction (ruin), a way leading to eternal darkness (suffering). **23.** The righteous walk a narrow path (restricted road) leading to peace (harmony), unity (togetherness), and prayer (communication with God)—a life of purity (cleanliness) and love (kindness). **24.** They avoid what the Almighty (JAH) condemns (forbids)—unclean food (not allowed), sin (wrongdoing), and all wickedness (evil) that displeases Him (God). **25.** The righteous distance from what the Almighty (JAH) hates (disapproves of). **26.** The Almighty (JAH) loves the righteous (good people) and protects them from harm (danger), like a guardian (protector) watching over his own. **27.** The righteous follow His law (commands), while sinners (evil-doers) are ruled by the forces of evil (Satan).

Chapter 10

1. Fear JAH (Jehovah, God) Who created and protected you; even kings and nobles stray from evil. **2.** Follow JAH's ways, Who rules all, and avoid false paths. **3.** As Israel (descendants of Abraham, Isaac, and Jacob) moved to claim the promised lands, Balaq (king of Moab) and Balaam (prophet) tried to curse them. **4.** Whoever you curse is cursed, and whoever you bless is blessed; avoid evil. **5.** Balaam was offered riches to curse Israel, but he refused. **6.** Balaq showed Balaam Israel's camp, hoping to gain power through sacrifices. **7.** Balaam turned his curse into a blessing, as JAH commanded, showing His love for Israel. **8.** JAH said, "Those who bless you will be blessed, and those who curse you will be cursed." **9.** Balaq grew angry after Balaam blessed Israel and demanded a curse instead. **10.** Balaam refused, saying he could not curse what JAH has blessed. **11.** Balaq offered wealth, but Balaam obeyed JAH, not seeking profit. **12.** Balaam said, "I will speak only what JAH commands; I cannot disobey Him." **13.** Balaam valued his soul over wealth and refused to curse JAH's blessed people. **14.** As JAH said, those who bless Israel will be blessed, and those who curse them will be cursed. **15.** Whoever blesses Israel will be blessed, and whoever curses them unjustly will be cursed. **16.** Do not follow those who angered JAH and were destroyed for their sins. **17.** Many suffered at the hands of their enemies, oppressed and fallen. **18.** They were taken to foreign lands, their possessions plundered. **19.** Jerusalem (capital city of Israel)'s walls were torn down, left desolate like a field. **20.** Priests were captured, the law ignored, and warriors fell in battle. **21.** Widows and children mourned, but did not grieve as they should. **22.** The young wept, elders were shamed, and the elderly received no honor. **23.** Those remaining in the land were destroyed, with no mercy for the righteous. **24.** JAH allowed Israel's suffering due to their turning away from Him, leading to Jerusalem's downfall. **25.** Yet JAH did not forsake them, remembering the promises to their forefathers

(Abraham, Isaac, Jacob). **26.** JAH honored Israel with dominion on Earth and in Heaven. **27.** Kings and nobles who live righteously inherit the Kingdom of Heaven, as their ancestors did. **28.** Live rightly, and your kingdom will be established, with your name honored like those before you.

Chapter 11

1. Recall JAH's servant Mussie (Moses), who humbly prayed for those who wronged him, asking JAH (God) to forgive them, despite their betrayals. **2.** Mussie (Moses) begged for forgiveness, acknowledging JAH's (God's) mercy and that He alone can pardon sins. **3.** Mussie (Moses) atoned (made amends) for the wrongs of those who spoke ill of him. **4.** His innocence was confirmed because of this act of mercy. **5.** JAH (God) loved Mussie (Moses) more than the priests (religious leaders), elevating him to a position like His own. **6.** Mussie (Moses) humbled himself before the earth and the rebellious (those who defied him), fulfilling JAH's (God's) will even when opposed. **7.** If you uphold JAH's (God's) commands, He will bless you and keep your kingdom (realm) intact. **8.** Asaf (a leader) and Qorie's (a family or tribe) descendants murmured (complained) against Mussie (Moses)'s command to follow JAH's (God's) will. **9.** They questioned why they weren't honored as priests (religious officials) despite their service. **10.** They rebelled (defied orders), using censers (incense burners) to offer prayers, but JAH (God) rejected them, burning them and leaving no trace. **11.** JAH (God) instructed Mussie (Moses) and Aaron (Moses' brother) to gather the censers (incense burners) as a symbol of His worship. **12.** Mussie (Moses) prepared the sacred instruments for the Tent (the Tabernacle), including the rings (holy symbols) and cherubim (angelic figures). **13.** He arranged the altar, cups, and curtains for sacrifices (ritual offerings) in the holy Tent (Tabernacle). **14.** The people offered sacrifices for atonement (forgiveness), vows (promises), and daily worship as instructed by Mussie (Moses). **15.** Mussie (Moses) obeyed JAH's (God's) commands in preparing the sacred Tent (Tabernacle) for His worship. **16.** The people honored JAH (God) in their work, so His name (reputation) was praised through their obedience. **17.** They remained faithful (loyal) to JAH (God), honoring the promises He made to their ancestors (forefathers). **18.** JAH's (God's) worship was strengthened through His covenants (agreements) with their forefathers (ancestors). **19.** JAH's (God's) worship continued through Moses (Mussie), Aaron (Moses' brother), and Solomon's (Israelite king) Temple in Jerusalem (holy city). **20.** The Tent (Tabernacle) was a place for supplication (prayers) and atonement (forgiveness) for the innocent and priests. **21.** It became a place where JAH (God) would hear the prayers of those who obeyed Him. **22.** JAH's (God's) law was honored, guiding Israel (the people) through sacrifices (ritual offerings) and worship. **23.** The Tent (Tabernacle) was a place for offerings (gifts), creating a pleasing aroma for JAH (God). **24.** JAH's (God's) light (divine presence) revealed His presence to those who followed His law (guidance) and commands. **25.** Those who ignored JAH's (God's) law faced judgment (punishment), like the rebellious (those who defied), and were cast into eternal punishment.

Chapter 12

1. Woe to Israel's leaders who ignore the Law, living in arrogance, greed, adultery, drunkenness, and lies. **2.** My anger will burn like fire, scattering you like chaff (broken grain). **3.** JAH (God) who honored Israel, will destroy sinners who reject His power. **4.** JAH forgives those who follow Him and stay true to His ways. **5.** Align with JAH and trust Him to protect you in danger. **6.** In trouble, I will save you if you follow My commands. **7.** JAH protects those who obey Him, keeping them safe. **8.** Though His anger is fierce, He restores us to earth after death, knowing our human nature (flesh and blood). **9.** JAH gave life from nothing and will return it according to His will. **10.** JAH will again bring life from death. **11.** Tsereutsaydan (a person) denied JAH, becoming prideful until his fall. **12.** He claimed eternity, but death (Angel of Death) struck him, and he perished. **13.** The Angel of Death (a figure responsible for death) struck him for dishonoring his Creator. **14.** The Kedans (a group) attacked, ravaging his land and taking his cattle. **15.** They looted his wealth, burned his land, and returned home.

Chapter 13

1. The five Meqabees children (Jewish family who resisted Hellenization), believed and chose death over idol sacrifices. **2.** They knew JAH's (God's) anger surpasses any ruler's. **3.** Aware this world ends, they chose fire to be saved in Heaven. **4.** They valued the joy of the Garden (Eden, a paradise in the Bible) over Earth's life, believing in JAH's Pardon. **5.** An era is brief, like wax melting in fire. **6.** But You, Lord, live forever; Your reign and Name are eternal. **7.** The Meqabees children chose to refuse the sacrifice out of faith in JAH. **8.** Knowing resurrection (rising from the dead) would come, they accepted martyrdom. **9.** Those who doubt resurrection will learn life after surpasses this one, as shown by the Meqabees children. **10.** They didn't worship idols (false gods) or eat unclean sacrifices (offerings to idols), knowing it pleased JAH. **11.** They trusted JAH to heal them in body and soul in the coming age. **12.** Those who follow JAH's laws will reign with kings (earthly rulers) and nobles (important people) in Heaven. **13.** They knew this world passes like wax, giving their lives to God. **14.** Believing they'd shine brighter than the sun in resurrection, they chose death for eternal life.

Chapter 14

1. The Samrans (Samaritans, people from Samaria), 'Ayhuds (Jews), and Seduqans (Sadducees, a Jewish sect) deny resurrection, claiming death is final. 'Ayhuds say, "Let's eat and drink, for death is the end." **2.** Samrans believe the body turns to dust, not to rise. **3.** They see the soul (immaterial essence) as invisible, unable to rise. **4.** Beasts (animals) and worms (decomposers) consume the body, reducing it to dust. **5.** Beasts return to dust, leaving no trace of the flesh. **6.** Fereesans (Pharisees) believe the dead will rise in new bodies from Heaven, not from decayed flesh on Earth. **7.** Seduqans (Sadducees) believe after death, there is no resurrection—flesh (body) and soul (essence) remain separate. **8.** This view dishonors God's (the Lord's) power, which saddens me. **9.** Without belief in God, there's no hope for resurrection or salvation (saving of the soul). **10.** O 'Ayhudans (Jews), you deny the Creator (God) who gave you life; will you reject Him? **11.** You cannot escape God's judgment (decisions on actions). Without love for Him, you'll face suffering in Sheol (the grave or underworld). **12.** Demons (evil spirits) lead you to sin from birth, growing as you mature. **13.** After death, your sins bring torment, for demons (evil spirits) worked through you. **14.** Sin dwells in reasoning; some are trapped by sin, overtaken by spirits (evil entities). **15.** Sinners' souls are pulled from Heaven to the fiery abyss of punishment (Gehannem – a place of torment). **16.** When the soul separates from the body, JAH's mercy revives you like Adam (the first human). **17.** Those in graves make mistakes, leading others astray, denying resurrection and turning from JAH's command (JAH – God). **18.** JAH awakens you to face the consequences, but who will protect you from His judgment? **19.** Whether wind (natural element), water (element), earth (the ground), or fire (element), reckoning will come. **20.** Souls in torment will return (See'ol – a place of the dead), for JAH's justice calls them. **21.** Righteous souls emerge from Paradise (a place of peace), rejoicing in their reward. **22.** You, the disbelieving, will remain in torment until final judgment (judgment day). **23.** You will see JAH repay you for leading others into error (misleading them). **24.** Those claiming the dead don't rise will face punishment (punishment from God). **25.** It's better if you never taught the sacred words (sacred – holy), misguiding others in ignorance (lack of knowledge). **26.** Better to remain ignorant than to spread false teachings (false – incorrect). **27.** JAH values those who teach truth and righteousness, not outward appearances (outward – external). **28.** No one escapes JAH's justice (fair judgment); He will judge you and those you misled. **29.** The dead will rise if they followed JAH's commands (command – order); the earth sends forth grass after rain. **30.** Just as dew (moisture from the air) nourishes the earth, so will the dead rise when JAH calls. **31.** A woman cannot stop labor (labor – childbirth), and the dead cannot escape resurrection. **32.** As dew obeys JAH's command, graves cannot stop souls from rising (command – divine order). **33.** The dead will be gathered where they fell (their place of death), and their souls will reunite with their bodies (souls – spiritual essence). **34.** When the trumpet (musical instrument used to announce events) sounds, the dead will rise swiftly, standing before JAH to receive their reward. **35.** You will rise with the dead, see your deeds, and regret your sinful actions (sinful – morally wrong). **36.** You will rise with the dead and face the consequences of your deeds, as you deserve.

Chapter 15

1. Those who do good will be blessed, while those who deny resurrection (the rising of the dead) will be troubled when the dead rise, with their evil deeds of no use. 2. Their actions will judge them, and they will face the truth alone. 3. On judgment day (the day of final judgment), those who forgot God's teachings (laws or commandments) will be condemned. 4. On the day of darkness, when winds howl and lightning strikes. 5. When the earth trembles (earthquake), fear strikes, and storms rage. 6. The wicked (those who do wrong) will suffer, while the righteous (those who are just) are rewarded, and those who neglected God's law will face punishment. 7. On the day when all are equal, no one is above another, whether slave (a servant in bondage) or master. 8. On that day, no one is above others—whether king (ruler) or poor, elder (older person) or child. 9. No one is greater than another—no rich (wealthy) above the poor, nor the proud (arrogant) above the humble (modest)—on judgment day. 10. The righteous will be rewarded, while the wicked will be punished for their sins. 11. Those who did good will rejoice, but those who rejected God's law will face their fate. 12. Sinners will mourn their wrongs, finding no peace (rest or comfort). 13. The righteous will rejoice eternally (forever) for the good they did on earth. 14. They believed in life after death (resurrection) and followed God's commandments (instructions from God). 15. Because they obeyed God's law, they will receive blessings now and in the world to come (afterlife). 16. They will inherit the eternal Kingdom of Heaven (God's reign in the afterlife), promised to their ancestors (forebears), when the dead rise and the rich lose their wealth. 17. Those who lived in sin (wrongdoing), denied resurrection, and rejected God's laws will weep. 18. They will experience endless suffering (pain) with no rest, peace, or comfort. 19. They will be tormented (suffer) by unquenchable fire (a fire that cannot be extinguished) and worms (creatures that feed on decaying matter). 20. In a place of eternal torment (unending suffering), fire, sulfur (a chemical element), and storms (violent weather) will pour down upon them. 21. Those who deny resurrection will face eternal fire (unending punishment).

Chapter 16

1. Think of your body—trim your hands, feet, and hair. Know resurrection through wisdom, faith, and understanding. 2. Ask, "Who created these?" Isn't it JAH (God) who prepared them for resurrection after death? 3. You denied resurrection, but when the dead rise, you'll face consequences for misleading others. 4. A seed won't grow without nourishment; you'll face fate on the appointed day. 5. A tree's fruit won't change; a fig tree (a tree bearing figs) won't produce grapes, and a vine won't yield figs. 6. Grapes stay grapes; figs won't turn to grapes, and wheat (a grain) won't become barley (a grain). 7. Every seed, blessed by JAH, grows as intended—wheat won't turn to barley. 8. A grave (place where the dead are buried) raises body and spirit as sown by JAH—good won't become evil, and evil won't become good. 9. When the trumpet (musical instrument) sounds, the dead rise by JAH's mercy. The righteous (virtuous people) gain eternal life, free from suffering and death. 10. The wicked (evil people) rise for judgment, joining deceivers (those who mislead), led by demons (evil spirits) who wish no one to be saved. 11. They'll be cast into Gehannem (Hell, a place of torment), where there's weeping, gnashing of teeth, and no escape. 12. They did no good in life and now face eternal separation from JAH. 13. Flesh and soul (spirit) will be judged when they rise, united by JAH's will. 14. Woe to those who don't believe in resurrection, despite JAH's many signs and miracles. 15. Everyone will receive their reward according to their deeds and the labor of their hands.

Chapter 17

1. A wheat kernel must be crushed to grow and bear fruit. Once crushed, it sends roots, grows, and bears fruit. 2. From one kernel, many grow. 3. Growth comes from Earth (soil), wind, water, and sunlight. Without the Sun, it cannot bear fruit. Sun symbolizes fire; wind represents the soul. 4. Wheat needs wind and water to bear fruit. 5. Earth drinks water, grows roots, and bears fruit as blessed by JAH. 6. The wheat kernel represents Adam (the first man), with a soul from JAH, like grapevine roots drinking water. 7. Dew (moisture in the air) from JAH nourishes the vine, sending water to leaves, growing fruit by JAH's will. 8. Its fragrance brings joy, satisfying like water and grain, becoming the blood (liquid) of the cluster. 9. As Psalms (book of the Bible) says, "Grapes bring joy." Drinking them refreshes the heart, and a person becomes drunk, filling their body with joy. 10. Grapes' drunkenness misleads, weakening the mind, causing one to miss dangers and thorns (sharp objects or difficulties). 11. JAH created fruit and grapevines for His name to be praised by those who believe in resurrection (rising from the dead) and follow His will. 12. In the Kingdom of Heaven (the eternal realm where God rules), He will bless those who believe in the resurrection and make them feel joy.

Chapter 18

1. You err by not believing in the resurrection. On the day you're led to a place unknown, regret will follow for denying the rise of the dead, both in body and soul, cast into eternal fire (Gehannem, a place of eternal punishment). 2. You will be judged based on your deeds, misleading others to believe that the dead, once dust (the physical remains of a person), will not rise. 3. Death has no escape, and those who falter in suffering mislead others. They will stand before JAH's (God's) court. 4. When JAH's anger burns, you will fear, for you did not know you were created from nothing into life. Ignorance of JAH's law (the commandments of God) will lead to judgment. 5. You don't know Gehannem, the place of eternal punishment, due to your crookedness (wickedness) and bitterness, teaching others that resurrection is a myth. 6. At that moment, you will know the truth: the dead will rise, and you will face judgment for denying this. 7. All are children of Adam (the first man), and death came through his mistake. Judgment from JAH is upon us because of Adam's failure. 8. I will rise with Adam, enduring hardship (suffering) for my deeds, for the world has been ruled by death due to Adam's ignorance. 9. Adam's disobedience (failure to obey) to JAH caused suffering, and my body melted like wax in the grave. 10. The Earth consumed my bones, and my beauty was lost in the grave. 11. Worms came from my eyes, and my features (appearance) turned to dust. 12. Where is the beauty of those who once shone? Where is their strength (power)? 13. Where are the kings' armies, noble rulers, and adornments (decorations) of horses, silver, and gold? Did they not fade (disappear)? 14. Where are the sweet drinks and flavorful foods that once satisfied?

Chapter 19

1. Woe to you, land (earth), who gathered chiefs, kings, wealthy, elders, and beautiful daughters. 2. Woe to you, land, who gathered strong warriors, those with grace, wisdom, and musical voices. 3. Woe to you, land, who gathered those with joyful voices like wine, and eyes shining like stars. 4. Woe to you, land, who gathered those with strong hands and swift feet, like chariots (two-wheeled vehicles for racing). 5. Woe to you, death (the end of life), who takes beautiful souls from their bodies, sent by the Creator. 6. Woe to you, land, who gathers souls, who return by divine will (the will of a higher power). 7. I was buried in you, land, eating your fruits (produce of the land), while you consumed my body. 8. I drank your waters (rivers, springs), and you drank my blood, eating my flesh from your soil. 9. The Creator (God) commanded you to provide food, I ate grains with dew (water droplets on plants), and you turned my flesh to dust. 10. Woe to you, death, who gathered mighty rulers (kings), not fearing their fame or strength, as the Creator commanded. 11. You did not spare the beautiful, strong, poor, rich, good, or wicked. 12. You did not spare the righteous (those who do good) or sinners (those who do wrong), pure hearts or evil speakers. 13. You gathered those with bitter words (angry words), living in both light (good) and darkness (evil), souls lost to you. 14. The land gathered the dead (those who have passed away), from caves and graves, until the trumpet calls (a loud signal), and they rise. 15. The dead shall rise swiftly (quickly), like a blink (a very short time), at the Creator's command, and the wicked will suffer, while the righteous rejoice (celebrate).

Chapter 20

Here is the text formatted as requested:

1. I believe that all my deeds in this world will be revealed when I stand before Him (God), trembling in fear. 2. In that time, I'll have no provisions (necessary supplies), clothing, or strength to stand. 3. I'll be without a staff (walking stick) in my hands and shoes on my feet. 4. I won't recognize the paths where evil spirits (demons) lead me, whether rough or perilous (dangerous). 5. I'll not know the spirits that guide me, nor will I hear their whispers. 6. They are dark ones (evil spirits), leading me into shadow (darkness), and I won't see their faces.

7. The prophet (a messenger of God) said, "When my soul parts from my body, Lord, you know my way. A trap lies ahead, and I cannot return without a guide." **8.** He knows that evil spirits (demons) mock him, guiding him into unknown paths. **9.** He is alone in the midst of demons (evil spirits), with no one who knows him. **10.** Angels of Light (messengers from God) guide the righteous (just people) to a place of peace and abundance (prosperity). **11.** Dark spirits (demons) lead the sinful (wrongdoers) to Gehannem (a place of torment in the afterlife), where suffering awaits for their wrongdoings. **12.** Woe to sinners (wrongdoers), whose souls face endless suffering with no escape from the torment of Gehannem (Hell). **13.** They lived in sin and were lost by greed, deceiving others for their own gain. **14.** They will endure suffering in Gehannem (Hell) for the sins they committed.

Chapter 21

1. Where are those who gather wealth from foreign hands, not through their own toil or labor? (foreign hands: wealth gained from others' resources) **2.** They take others' wealth without working for it, not knowing the day of their own death, though they spend on strangers. (strangers: people who are not from their community) **3.** Like their forefathers (ancestors: those who came before them), they seize by theft or violence. Their children will not enjoy their ill-gotten gains. **4.** Their wealth is like vapor, smoke, withering grass, or melting wax. (vapor: mist that disappears; withering grass: dying plants) The glory of sinners will vanish like this. **5.** No one gains from their ancestors' wealth, as David (King David: a biblical king of Israel) said, "I saw a sinner honored like a tall tree, but he was gone when I sought him." **6.** They gather wealth in sin, thinking they will never die, but their ruin will come suddenly. (ruin: complete destruction) **7.** You lazy ones, believe your riches will last, but your silver and gold will rust away. (rust: decay on metals due to exposure to air) **8.** Even if you have many children, they will end up in graves (graves: burial places); even if you build many homes, they will be destroyed. **9.** You ignored your Creator (God: the Creator of the world); your cattle (domesticated animals like cows) will be taken, and the money you stole will be lost. **10.** Whether in your house, fields (open areas of land used for farming), or vineyards (plantations where grapes are grown), it will not be found. **11.** You did not keep God's commandments, and your household will not escape trouble (tribulation: suffering); you will not rejoice in your children. **12.** But those who follow God's law will be blessed with prosperous families (families: parents and children) and fruitful land (land producing crops). **13.** He will make them leaders (rulers) over others, so they rule and are not ruled. **14.** He will bless their fields (agricultural land) and livestock (domesticated animals), and they will find joy in their children. **15.** He protects their cattle from illness, enemies (foes: those who oppose them), and trouble (tribulation: suffering), both those known and unknown. **16.** He will defend them in times of judgment (a time of decision or reckoning) and save them from evil and conflict (disputes or arguments). **17.** As Moses (Moses: the great leader of Israel in the Old Testament) commanded, there was a sanctuary (holy place) for judgment, where those convicted (found guilty) or acquitted (found innocent) were decided. **18.** If someone killed unintentionally (by accident), they were given refuge (safety or protection) there. **19.** If someone killed by accident, they were examined (investigated) and saved. But if it was deliberate (intentional), they would face consequences. **20.** If someone kills intentionally (on purpose), no one will pardon them; but if by accident, they will be spared (saved from punishment). **21.** Moses guided Israel (the ancient people of Israel) to stay faithful to God's law (rules given by God), so they would not turn away. **22.** He commanded the children of Adam (humankind) to reject idols (false gods), evil deeds (sinful actions), and all that defiles (pollutes) them, holding fast to God's commands. **23.** He told them to obey God's law (guidance given by God) to protect their bodies and find peace with their ancestors (forefathers). **24.** Those who believe in God's word (the teachings of God) and live by His commands are righteous (just), like Adam (the first man in the Bible) and Seth (Adam's son). **25.** As God's creation (humankind), I am called to do good works, which please Him and He will never despise (reject) them. **26.** God will not separate His faithful (those who follow Him); those who do good will inherit (receive as a gift) the Kingdom of Heaven (the eternal realm where God rules), where peace prevails. **27.** God loves those who pray sincerely (with true intent), listens to their pleas (requests), and strengthens those who uphold His commands (teachings). **28.** Those who follow God's will (divine plan) live in His Kingdom (the realm of God) forever, praising Him from now to eternity (forever and ever). Glory to God forever (eternal honor), as the prophecy (foretelling of future events) is fulfilled.

III Meqabyan

Chapter 1

1. Christ will bring joy to the people of Egypt (Nile River), for He will come in the end times to avenge and destroy the evil ones who harmed the innocent, misled others, and despised His Creator's work. **2.** He will repay and humble them, returning their arrogance to misery and defeat. **3.** He will demonstrate His power, saying, "I will walk across the sea, ascend to the heavens (firmament, the expanse of the sky), search the depths, and seize the children of Adam, like birds in a nest. Who can challenge me?" **4.** I allowed them to act in this way to show My strength, as I distanced them from the true law of God. No one can remove Me from My authority. **5.** I will lead the wicked onto a smooth path toward destruction in Gehannem (hell). **6.** Those who loved and obeyed God will hate Me for this, but those who strayed will turn to Me, keep My word, and be led away from evil, for I will change their hearts. **7.** When I showed them wealth, I misled them from the path of truth. **8.** When I showed them jewels, silver, and gold (precious metals used in biblical times for trade and adornment), I distanced them further from God's law. **9.** When I showed them fine clothes and material wealth, they were led astray, but I will bring them back to My purpose. **10.** When I revealed jealousy and quarrels over wealth and children, I will use these to turn them back to My work. **11.** When I showed them signs, they were misled by false reasoning, and I caused them to stumble in their thinking. **12.** For those who followed My signs, I will reveal even more signs, whether in the stars, clouds, fire, or the cries of animals (omens or symbolic messages in ancient times), guiding their thoughts. **13.** They will share these signs with others, following My lead, and I will continue to guide them. **14.** I will show signs to deceive people, leading them to praise magicians (sorcerers often condemned in Scripture), claiming there is no one wiser than them. **15.** I will allow them to speak these words so that those misled by me will increase, and the children of Adam will fall. **16.** I will bring destruction to those who follow My commands, for I have sworn that all who are misled by Me will end up in Gehannem. **17.** When God's anger grew and He ordered my punishment, I pleaded with Him, asking for one chance to speak before Him. **18.** The Lord responded, "Speak, I will listen." I then pleaded, "May those I led astray share my suffering in Gehannem." **19.** Let those who rejected Me return to Your path, Lord, and fulfill Your commands, as I led them astray. May they inherit the crown You gave me. **20.** Grant them the crown of authority that the Satans held with me, and place them on my throne at Your right hand. **21.** Let them praise You as I did, for You loved them and exalted them where I once stood. **22.** The Lord said, "Since you misled them, they will face the consequences of your actions." **23.** Both you and those you misled will suffer in Gehannem for eternity, with no escape. **24.** Your suffering, along with those you misled, will last forever in Gehannem, with no end.

Chapter 2

1. I will give the Kingdom of Heaven to those whom you failed to mislead, like Job (a man of great patience and faith in the land of Uz), for God, who rules all, said so. **2.** I would have led all the children of Adam astray if I could, but I will not, for I desire them to stay in good work and enjoy the world's pleasures. **3.** Whether through love of food, drink, clothes, or material things (worldly possessions cherished by humanity), **4.** Or through desires of sight, touch, and slumber (physical and sensory temptations), **5.** Or by increasing drunkenness, anger, and speaking nonsense, **6.** Or through quarrels, gossip, and lustful attraction to worldly things, **7.** I detest all these things, for they keep people from salvation and distance them from God's law, leading them to destruction. **8.** The prophet told him, "You who destroy others, perish! You turned from God's law and sinned through arrogance, angering your Creator." **9.** When God was angry with you, He humbled you, for your evil actions. Why then lead the children of Adam (humanity as created beings), whom God created from the earth and loved, toward sin? **10.** You, created from wind and fire (spiritual and energetic elements in angelic lore), were arrogant, claiming, 'I am the Creator.' **11.** You boasted, and God saw your evil actions, denying Him and causing the children of Adam, who were made to praise Him, to fall. **12.** You became prouder than all the hosts of angels (heavenly beings who serve God), because of your arrogance. God created Adam and his children to praise His name. **13.** Because of this, God destroyed you, separating you from all the angelic chiefs (leaders among angels) like you, for your arrogance and pride caused you to stray from God's praise. **14.** God created Adam from Earth to be praised by humble beings and commanded him not to eat the forbidden fruit (symbolic of disobedience), or he would die. **15.** God gave Adam dominion over creation, warning him to avoid the fig tree (a possible candidate for the forbidden tree), as its fruit would bring death, but all other trees were free to eat from. **16.** You deceived Eve by speaking lies, leading her to disobey. **17.** You misled innocent Adam into breaking the law, just as you did. **18.** You caused Eve, unaware of your malice (evil intentions), to betray Adam with your deceitful words, and she led Adam astray. **19.** You made Adam deny God's command through your arrogance, destroying him. **20.** You separated Adam from God's love, causing him to leave the Garden (Eden, the paradise of creation) and lose its blessings. **21.** From the beginning, you opposed God's creation, leading Adam to destruction and cutting him off from the life God gave him. **22.** God created Adam to praise Him with his body, soul, and mind, as a being of purity. **23.** God gave Adam many thoughts to honor Him, like harps playing in harmony (a metaphor for the unity of worship).

Chapter 3

1. God created a single purpose for you: to praise Him fully while journeying to where He has sent you. **2.** Adam received both good and bad thoughts — ten in total, five of each. **3.** His mind was filled with many thoughts, like waves of the sea (a metaphor for restless emotions), a whirlwind lifting dust, and endless rain. So were Adam's thoughts, numerous and turbulent. **4.** But your mind is singular, for you are not bound by flesh; you have no divided thoughts. **5.** You, however, followed the serpent's deceit (the trickery of the tempter), which led to the fall of Adam, the first human. **6.** After Eve ate the fruit, she misled Adam, and death entered them and their descendants because they disobeyed God's command. **7.** They were cast out from the Garden (Eden), yet God, in His judgment, calmed them, and they found sustenance in the land where they were sent. **8.** When they left the Garden, it was so they could grow crops and children, finding renewal in the fruits of the Earth (agricultural produce), to ease their hearts. **9.** God gave them trees more abundant than those in the Garden, and through their eating, Adam and Eve were soothed from their sorrow. **10.** As God knows how to comfort His creation, their hearts were calmed by the birth of children and the crops they harvested from the Earth. **11.** Although they were sent to a world with thorns and hardship (symbolizing life's challenges), they strengthened their resolve through water and grains (sustenance from nature).

Chapter 4

1. The Lord sought to redeem Adam, rescuing him from the grasp of the enemy, as He would save a sheep from the wolf's mouth. **2.** Yet, you will head toward the fire of judgment (a place of eternal punishment), taking with you those you led astray. **3.** Those who follow God's laws will be blessed and shielded from evil, living in His favor and praising Him alongside the angels who have never broken His commands. **4.** But God, who elevated you above the angels, withheld a high throne (a symbolic position of authority in Heaven) from you because of your pride. **5.** You became known as one who sought godhood (the pursuit of becoming like God), and your followers became demons (fallen angels). **6.** But those who love the Lord are counted as His kin, like the honored angels, with Seraphim and Cherubim (types of angelic beings) praising Him without ceasing. **7.** In your arrogance (excessive pride) and laziness, you lost your role in praising God, failing to praise Him as you should with your hosts and kindred. **8.** Do not let the praise of God be lessened by your neglect, for He created you and all things, and His power is not limited. **9.** In your pride, you turned away from God, provoking His anger, and were cast out, bound in judgment (a state of condemnation) with your followers. **10.** God formed Adam from the soil (earth) with His mighty hands, adding fire, water, and wind, creating him in His image and likeness. **11.** He placed Adam over all creation, that his praises would join those of the angels. **12.** But through your firm pride (stubbornness), you fell from your position and were separated from God's lordship, losing your true self. **13.** Know this: God's praise was never diminished, for He created Adam to honor Him with his heart and mind. **14.** God knows all before it happens, and He knew you would rebel even before He created you. In His divine wisdom, He created Adam in His image. **15.** As Solomon said, before the hills (mountains) and earth were formed, before the winds blew, and before the world was established, **16.** Before the mountains were firm (solid), before the moon and sun existed, and before the stars were set, **17.** Before day and night alternated, before the sea (a large body of water) was bounded by sand, God created everything, **18.** And even before names were given, God's plan for Adam, and the angels like you, was established. **19.** God created Adam to glorify His name, so that His praise might be magnified, even in the face of your rebellion. **20.** In Heaven, God hears the cries of the humble and delights in the praise of the lowly. **21.** He saves those who fear Him, but He does not delight in the power of the proud or in the selfish pursuits of the arrogant. **22.** The proud will weep for their sins, **23.** For they failed to repent (to feel remorse and turn away from sin). **24.** But Adam, created from the Earth (soil), returned to God in repentance, weeping for his sin and finding mercy. **25.** In your hardened heart and arrogance, you failed to understand the work of love and repentance. You did not turn to God in sorrow and humility. **26.** But Adam, formed from dust (the earth), turned to God in true repentance, mourning and humbling himself in love. **27.** You did not humble your mind nor your pride before the Creator, who made you. **28.** Adam, however, humbled himself and confessed his wrongs, never acting in pride. **29.** Though you brought forth evil, it was not Adam's fault. In your arrogance, you led him toward destruction. **30.** God knew you both before He created you, aware of your sinful hearts and your actions. **31.** Yet, He accepted Adam's repentance, for he was humble and without malice (evil intent), and returned to God in mourning and humility. **32.** A person who sins and refuses to repent multiplies their wrongs. But you, in arrogance, failed to plead for mercy. However, anyone who weeps and seeks forgiveness from God with sincerity will find salvation. **33.** This person enters true repentance, fearing the Lord and sincerely pleading for forgiveness. God, in His mercy, will ease their burden, forgiving their past sins. **34.** Perfect repentance is when one does not return to past sins, remembering the Creator and continually seeking forgiveness. Adam did not forget to call on God in repentance. **35.** You too must repent before your Creator, understanding the frailty (weakness) of humanity. Do not wrong others, for God knows their weakness, and He created them in His authority. **36.** When the soul separates from the body, the flesh returns to dust (earth) until the day of God's love and redemption.

Chapter 5

1. Know that JAH, your Creator, formed you, and in Him, you find your purpose. He placed you in the Garden (Eden) to live well and cultivate the earth. Do not forget JAH, who established you and saved you, whom Israel (the people of God) praised. He gave you life and a place of peace. **2.** But when you disregarded His commands, He cast you out of the Garden (Eden) to a cursed world (earth), where thorns and nettles (thorny plants) now grow. **3.** You are of the earth, and to the earth you will return. From dust (soil) you came, and to dust (earth) you shall return. The earth sustains you, but in the end, it will reclaim you unless JAH raises you up. He will judge your deeds, both good and bad. **4.** Reflect on the good and evil you have done. Consider whether you have lived righteously or sinned. Be mindful of your actions, for they shape your future. **5.** If you live righteously, your soul will be at peace when the dead rise. **6.** But if you choose evil, woe to you! Your suffering will reflect the harm you have done, and the consequences of your wrongs will come back to you. **7.** Betray your neighbor (friend) or swear falsely in JAH's name, and hardship (misfortune) will follow, just as you have caused harm through your actions. **8.** Do not speak in lies or deceive others, pretending your falsehoods are truth. **9.** If you spread falsehoods or lead others astray, you will bear the consequences of your actions. Deceiving others for personal gain will lead to your own downfall. **10.** When you promise to give, keep your word. If you withhold or fail to fulfill your promises, you will be burdened with guilt (shame), and your reputation will be tarnished. **11.**

As it is written, children (descendants) of deceit (falsehood) spread lies and move from one wrongdoing to another. The desire for worldly wealth drives them. **12.** Do not place your trust in dishonest gain (ill-gotten wealth), stealing from others or taking what is not yours. This harms others and destroys your integrity. **13.** If you engage in such actions, your hardships (sufferings) will match the wrongs you have done. **14.** Work honestly (fairly) for your sustenance (living). Do not desire to steal from others or take advantage of those who trust you. **15.** If you consume ill-gotten gains, it will never satisfy you. When you die, you will leave it all behind. Wealth gained unjustly will be of no benefit to you. **16.** If your wealth increases, do not let it corrupt your judgment. The money of sinners is fleeting (short-lived), like smoke blown away by the wind. It is better to have little earned through honesty than great wealth gained in deceit.

Chapter 6

1. Reflect on the day of your death, when your soul (spirit) departs from your body. In that moment, you will leave your wealth to others and walk a path (journey) you cannot foresee. Think of the suffering (pain) that will come upon you. **2.** The demons (evil spirits) that will receive you are evil, with terrifying forms and frightening power. They will not heed your pleas (requests), nor will you hear their words (commands). **3.** Because you did not honor your Creator, JAH, when you call out in desperation, they will not listen to you. This will be a source of great fear (terror). **4.** Those who follow JAH's will have no fear, for demons (evil spirits) will tremble before them. But demons will mock (ridicule) the souls of the wicked (evil-doers). **5.** The souls of the righteous (those who live right) will find peace and joy with the angels (heavenly beings), who will comfort them. But the wicked (evil-doers) will be received by evil spirits (evil beings). **6.** Angels of mercy (compassionate angels) will receive the souls of the righteous, sent by JAH to calm them. But evil spirits (wicked beings), sent by Deeyablos (devil), will torment the souls of the sinners (those who sin). **7.** Woe to sinners (evil-doers)! Weep for yourselves before the day of your death, for it is a time of reckoning (judgment) when you stand before JAH. **8.** Repent while you still have time, for once your time passes, you will no longer have the opportunity. Live in peace and joy, free from suffering and disease, but remember that after death, your era (time) cannot be returned. **9.** Do not live in vain (meaninglessly), away from JAH's (God's) presence. Let not your heart (mind) be consumed with pleasures, food, and worldly joy. A body filled with excess (too much) will forget JAH's name, and demons (evil spirits) will settle within it, for the Holy Spirit (divine presence) will not reside in such a heart. **10.** As Mussie (a reference to a righteous figure) said, "Ya`iqob (Jacob) ate until he was full, and grew fat and strong. But he forgot the Creator who made him. His life became distant from JAH." **11.** A person filled with excess (over-indulgence) will not think of JAH's (God's) name. Let not selfish indulgence (greed) and pleasures (excessive enjoyment) take root in you. Do not fall into excessive eating, drinking, or sin. **12.** A person who eats in moderation (self-control) will be supported by JAH. They will stand firm, strong as a tower, while the one who forgets JAH's (God's) law will flee in fear (panic), chased without cause. **13.** The righteous (those who live rightly) will be respected, like a lion (symbol of strength) in its strength and authority. **14.** Those who do not love JAH and do not follow His law will lose their way (become lost), and their reasoning (mind) will be distorted (confused). **15.** JAH will bring sorrow and fear (distress) upon them in this world. They will be overtaken by trembling (shaking), suffer tribulation (trouble), lose their wealth (material riches), and be bound by chains (captivity). **16.** These people will know no rest (peace), for their lives will be filled with anxiety (worry) and misfortune (bad luck). JAH will bring distress and alarm (fear), and their peace (serenity) will be replaced by turmoil (chaos).

Chapter 7

1. As Daweet (David) said, "I trust in JAH, and I fear no one. What can anyone do to me?" Those who trust in JAH are free from fear (anxiety, dread). **2.** He also said, "Even if warriors (soldiers) surround me, I trust in Him. I seek only one thing from JAH." Those who trust in Him are not afraid (they remain calm and strong). They will live forever, untouched by evil (sin or harm). **3.** Who would be ashamed to trust in JAH? Who would turn away (reject) from Him for their own desires (selfish wants)? **4.** As He has promised, "I will love those who love Me, and I

will honor (respect) those who honor (value) Me. I will protect those who return to Me in repentance (sorrow for wrongdoing)." Who would be ashamed (hesitant or reluctant) to trust in Him? **5.** Uphold justice (fairness), protect the widow (a woman whose husband has died), and stand for the oppressed (those who are treated unfairly). This will lead to your salvation (deliverance or rescue), for JAH will defend (protect) you from all evil (harm). As children of the righteous (those who live justly) are honored (respected), so will your children be blessed (given favor), and they will have no lack (they will not be in need).

Chapter 8

1. Iyob (Job) trusted in JAH, never ceased praising Him, and said, "JAH gives and takes away, but His name be praised on earth and in heaven." JAH saved him for his unwavering (steadfast) faith (trust in God). **2.** JAH honored Iyob when He saw his heart was purified (cleansed) from sin (wrongdoing). **3.** JAH blessed him with greater wealth than before and healed his wounds (sufferings) for enduring his trials (difficult experiences). **4.** If you endure (remain strong through) like Iyob (Job), you will be admired (respected) and protected from evil (harmful influences). **5.** Endure hardship (difficult times); JAH will be your refuge (shelter) and protect your descendants (children and future generations). Do not lose faith (trust) during trials—He will shelter (provide safety) you. **6.** Call on JAH, He will hear and forgive you, becoming a Father (protector) to you. **7.** Remember the faithful (loyal ones) like Merdokyos (Marduk), 'Astier (possibly an Ethiopian figure or variant), and others who were not defeated (overcome) by their enemies (adversaries). **8.** JAH is just (fair) and shows no favoritism (partiality). Those who love Him and avoid sin (wrongdoing) will be honored (respected) despite hardships. **9.** Those who fear JAH and follow His law will be protected and blessed (favored) with love and honor (respect). **10.** JAH will prosper (succeed) you in life, death, and all your endeavors (efforts), providing shelter (protection) and salvation (rescue). **11.** JAH brings healing (restoration) and peace (calmness) to the sorrowful (those who are sad). **12.** JAH may allow poverty (lack of material wealth), but He honors (respects) the humble (those who are modest) and fills their hearts (inner beings) with joy.

Chapter 9

1. Everything in Heaven and Earth, whether subtle (hidden) or strong, exists within JAH's (God's) order and command. **2.** Nothing escapes JAH's law and plan—whether it's a vulture flying or a snake in a cave, JAH guides them all. **3.** JAH directs the paths of animals, boats, and souls, and none but Him know their true paths. **4.** Only JAH knows where a soul goes after it departs from the body, whether righteous (good) or sinful (wrong). **5.** Who knows if it will wander in the wilderness, fly like a bird, or disappear like mist (vanish)? **6.** It may be like the wind, lightning, or stars—unpredictable and hidden in the deep (unknown). **7.** It could be like sand on the shore, or a stone at the horizon, firmly planted (stable). **8.** Perhaps it will be like a tree that grows by water, or a reed lifted by the wind to an unknown place (unstable). **9.** Who understands the work of JAH? Who can counsel (advise) Him or know His thoughts? **10.** His wisdom is hidden from all; no one can fully understand His works. **11.** JAH created the earth on water, without support (foundation), and formed heaven in His perfect wisdom. **12.** He stretched the cosmos (universe) like a tent, commanded clouds to bring rain, and caused the earth to bear fruit for us. **13.** JAH gave 'Adam's children (humanity) joy, abundance, and the blessings of the earth to praise Him. **14.** He provided them with beautiful robes (clothing), abundance (plenty), and satisfaction (contentment), all for those who follow His will. **15.** Those who follow JAH's law receive His love and honor in His house and the Kingdom of Heaven. **16.** Those who live by His law and worship Him, staying true to His order, are raised and honored. **17.** JAH protects His friends by weakening (weakening) their enemies and ensuring their well-being. **18.** JAH grants their desires and fulfills His promises to them. Stay true to His commandments. **19.** Do not stray from JAH's law, for His wrath (anger) and destruction await those who do. **20.** Keep JAH's law when your soul departs, that He may reward you when you stand before Him. **21.** Heaven and Earth belong to JAH, and only He holds all power, mercy, and forgiveness. **22.** JAH makes people rich and poor, wretched (miserable) or honored—keep His law. **23.** Daweet (David) said, "Man is vain (temporary), his life passes like a shadow." **24.** He spoke, saying, "But You, Lord, live forever, and Your name endures for generations."

25. Again, Daweet said, "Your kingdom rules all the earth, and Your reign is everlasting," as You restored the kingdom to Daweet, taking it from Sa'ol (Saul). **26.** No one can challenge or dismiss You—You see all, yet no one can fully comprehend (understand) You. **27.** Your kingdom will last forever for all generations—You rule all, and no one can oppose (challenge) You. **28.** JAH created man in His image so they might praise Him and worship Him with clear understanding. He knows all hearts and minds. **29.** Yet, people bow to idols made of stone, wood, silver, and gold, created by human hands. **30.** They sacrifice to these idols, but their sins are before JAH, whom they refuse to worship—He will condemn them for their idolatry (worship of idols). **31.** They have learned to worship idols, practicing sorcery (magic) and all things against JAH's will, neglecting His commandments. **32.** By neglecting worship of JAH, they fail to be saved from sin, relying on idols instead of the service of His angels (messengers). **33.** When all arise from their graves, the righteous (good people) will enter the Kingdom of Heaven, but sinners (wrongdoers) will face punishment. **34.** The dead will be resurrected (brought back to life), and souls will reunite with their bodies. The righteous will enter Heaven, but the wicked (evil people) will go to Gehannem (Hell). **35.** Just as they were born naked (without anything), they will stand before JAH in their nakedness, and their sins will be revealed. **36.** They will face consequences (punishments) for their sins—whether many or few, they will suffer accordingly.

Chapter 10

1. The blood of life, given by the Almighty, will return to those who have passed. If you doubt the resurrection, remember that creation is renewed in the rainy season, even without parentage (origin). **2.** The Almighty commanded that the dead shall live again through His Word. **3.** Though their bodies decay, they will rise again, restored by His love. **4.** When the rains fall and the earth is renewed, the resurrected will live as they were originally created. **5.** Just as those born of water (through birth) receive a soul, so does the Almighty give life by His authority. **6.** Created by His will, without parents (a reminder of divine creation), how can you say the dead will not rise? If you had true knowledge, you would not deny it. **7.** The dead, now dust, will rise at His Word. Repent and return to faith. **8.** Just as His Word spoke creation into being, the dead will rise with the dew (renewal) of the Almighty, awakening the earth. **9.** Know that you too will rise and stand before Him. Don't believe the grave will hold you forever. **10.** You will rise and face the consequences of your deeds—good or bad— according to your actions. **11.** On the day of resurrection, all your sins will be revealed, with no excuses or denials. **12.** Just as you may deceive in this life, you cannot deceive Him on that day. **13.** He knows all your deeds, and the truth will be revealed; His Word will speak over you. **14.** You will be ashamed of your sins, wishing you had repented in life, for you will stand before men and angels. **15.** Those who praise the Almighty will be rewarded in His Kingdom, but if you live unrighteously, you will have no place with the just. **16.** If you fail to repent when you know better, regret will be in vain. You didn't help the hungry when you had wealth. **17.** You didn't clothe the naked or help the oppressed when you had power. **18.** You didn't guide the sinner to repentance when you had wisdom, nor fight demons when you had strength. **19.** You didn't fast or pray to discipline your flesh and align yourself with righteousness. **20.** You chose worldly pleasures over spiritual growth, focusing on food, drink, and wealth instead of purity. **21.** True adornment is not in jewels or gold, but in purity, wisdom, and love. **22.** Adorn yourself with wisdom, knowledge, and love, treating others as you would yourself. **23.** Love even those who wrong you, endure hardships, and you will inherit the Kingdom of Heaven and eternal reward. **24.** Don't say the dead won't rise—those who deny it will face regret when resurrection comes. **25.** Those who denied resurrection will be ashamed when they rise in the flesh. **26.** They will weep for their evil deeds, wishing they had repented in life rather than facing eternal sorrow. **27.** If you don't repent now, demons will make you weep in Gehenna (Hell), an eternal sorrow. **28.** Prepare with good deeds to cross from death to life and reach the eternal Kingdom of Heaven. **29.** Reject worldly pleasures and you will find eternal joy in Heaven, with those who believe in resurrection. Praise and glory to the Almighty forever. This concludes the third book of the Maccabees.

23 – JOB

Chapter 1

1. There was a man in the region of Uz named Job. He was blameless (without fault, pure in heart) and upright (righteous), a man who feared God (had deep reverence for God) and avoided evil (shunned wrongdoing). **2.** Job had seven sons and three daughters. **3.** His wealth included 7,000 sheep, 3,000 camels, 500 pairs of oxen, 500 female donkeys, and a large household. Job was the wealthiest man in the East (likely referring to the eastern regions of the ancient world). **4.** His sons would host feasts in their homes, each on his appointed day, and invite their three sisters to join them for meals and drinks. **5.** After the feasts, Job would sanctify (purify) his children by rising early and offering burnt offerings (sacrificial animals burned entirely on an altar) for each of them. Job thought, "Perhaps my children have sinned and cursed God (spoken against God) in their hearts." This was Job's regular practice. **6.** One day, the angels came to present themselves before the Lord, and Satan (the adversary) also came with them. **7.** The Lord asked Satan, "Where have you come from?" Satan replied, "I have been roaming (traveling without direction) through the earth, walking back and forth on it." **8.** The Lord said to Satan, "Have you considered My servant Job? There is no one like him on earth—he is blameless and upright, a man who fears God and turns away from evil." **9.** Satan responded, "Does Job fear God without reason? **10.** Haven't You put a protective barrier (a hedge) around him, his household, and everything he owns? You have blessed the work of his hands, and his possessions have increased. **11.** But if You take away everything he has, he will surely curse You to Your face!" **12.** The Lord told Satan, "Very well, everything he has is in your power, but do not harm him physically (do not touch his body)." So Satan left the Lord's presence. **13.** One day, when Job's sons and daughters were eating and drinking wine in their oldest brother's house, **14.** a messenger came to Job and reported, "The oxen were plowing and the donkeys were grazing nearby, **15.** when the Sabeans (a nomadic people from the south, known for raiding) attacked and took them away. They killed the servants with the sword, and I alone have escaped to tell you!" **16.** While this messenger was speaking, another arrived and said, "The fire of God (a destructive force, possibly lightning or a natural disaster) fell from heaven and burned up the sheep and the servants, and consumed them. I alone have escaped to tell you!" **17.** While this messenger was still speaking, another came and reported, "The Chaldeans (people from Babylonia, often associated with military raids) formed three bands, raided the camels, and took them away, killing the servants with the sword. I alone have escaped to tell you!" **18.** While he was speaking, another came and said, "Your sons and daughters were eating and drinking wine in their oldest brother's house, **19.** when a mighty wind (a violent storm) came from the wilderness (a desert area), and struck the four corners of the house. The house collapsed on them, and they are dead. I alone have escaped to tell you!" **20.** Job stood up, tore his robe (a sign of mourning), shaved his head, and fell to the ground in worship. **21.** He said, "I came into this world with nothing, and I will leave with nothing. The Lord gave, and the Lord has taken away; blessed be the name of the Lord." **22.** In all of this, Job did not sin or blame God (accuse God of wrongdoing).

Chapter 2

1. Again, there was a day when the angels (Divine creature) came to present themselves before the Lord, and Satan also came among them to present himself before the Lord. **2.** The Lord asked Satan, "Where have you come from?" Satan answered, "I have been roaming (traveling without purpose) through the earth, walking back and forth on it." **3.** The Lord said to Satan, "Have you considered My servant Job? There is no one like him on earth, a blameless (without fault) and upright (righteous) man who fears God and shuns evil. And still he holds fast to his integrity (moral uprightness), even though you provoked Me to harm him for no reason." **4.** Satan answered, "Skin for skin! A man will give all he has for his life. **5.** But if You stretch out Your hand and strike his bone and flesh (his body), he will surely curse You to Your face!" **6.** The Lord told Satan, "Very well, he is in your hands, but spare his life." **7.** So Satan left the Lord's presence and afflicted Job with painful boils (sores) from the soles of his feet to the top of his head. **8.** Job took a broken piece of pottery (potsherd) to scrape himself while sitting among the ashes (a symbol of mourning). **9.** Then his wife said to him, "Are you still holding on to your integrity? Curse God and die!" **10.** Job replied, "You speak as one of the foolish women.

Should we accept good from God and not accept adversity (hardships)?" In all of this, Job did not sin by blaming God. **11.** When Job's three friends heard about all the troubles that had come upon him, they each came from their own home—Eliphaz the Temanite, Bildad the Shuhite, and Zophar the Naamathite. They had agreed to come together to mourn with him and comfort him. **12.** When they saw Job from a distance, they did not recognize him. They wept aloud, and each of them tore his robe and sprinkled dust on his head toward heaven (a sign of mourning). **13.** They sat with him on the ground for seven days and nights, and no one spoke a word to him, for they saw how great his suffering was.

Chapter 3

1. After this, Job opened his mouth and cursed the day of his birth. **2.** And Job said: **3.** "May the day perishes on which I was born, and the night in which it was said, 'A male child is conceived.' **4.** May that day be darkness; may God above (God in heaven) not seek it, nor the light shine upon it. **5.** May darkness and the shadow of death (deep darkness) claim it; may a cloud settle on it; may the blackness of the day terrify it. **6.** As for that night, may darkness seize it; may it not rejoice among the days of the year, may it not come into the number of the months. **7.** Oh, may that night be barren (unproductive, unfruitful)! May no joyful shout come into it! **8.** May those curse it who curse the day, those who are ready to arouse Leviathan (a mythical sea creature symbolizing chaos or evil). **9.** May the stars of its morning be dark; may it look for light, but have none, and not see the dawning (beginning) of the day. **10.** Because it did not shut up the doors (prevent) of my mother's womb, nor hide sorrow from my eyes. **11.** "Why did I not die at birth? Why did I not perish (die) when I came from the womb? **12.** Why did the knees receive me? Or why the breasts, that I should nurse? **13.** For now I would have lain still (rested) and been quiet; I would have been asleep; then I would have been at rest **14.** With kings and counselors (advisors) of the earth, who built ruins (destruction) for themselves, **15.** Or with princes (noblemen) who had gold, who filled their houses with silver; **16.** Or why was I not hidden like a stillborn (born dead) child, like infants who never saw light? **17.** There the wicked (evil people) cease from troubling, and there the weary (tired) are at rest. **18.** There the prisoners (captives) rest together; they do not hear the voice of the oppressor (one who abuses or dominates). **19.** The small and great are there, and the servant (slave) is free from his master. **20.** "Why is light given to him who is in misery, and life to the bitter (sorrowful) of soul, **21.** Who long for death, but it does not come, and search for it more than hidden treasures (desperately), **22.** Who rejoice exceedingly (greatly), and are glad when they can find the grave (death)? **23.** Why is light given to a man whose way is hidden, and whom God has hedged in (trapped or surrounded)? **24.** For my sighing (deep breathing) comes before I eat, and my groanings (complaints) pour out like water. **25.** For the thing I greatly feared has come upon me, and what I dreaded has happened to me. **26.** I am not at ease (peaceful), nor am I quiet; I have no rest, for trouble comes (continues)."

Chapter 4

1. Then Eliphaz the Temanite (a man from Teman, a region in Edom) answered and said: **2.** "If someone tries to speak with you, will you be weary? But who can stop themselves from speaking? **3.** Surely you have taught many, and you have strengthened the weak hands. **4.** Your words have supported those who were stumbling, and you have strengthened the feeble (weak) knees. **5.** But now that it has come upon you, you are weary; it touches you, and you are troubled. **6.** Is not your reverence (awe, respect) your confidence, and the integrity (honesty, uprightness) of your ways your hope? **7.** "Remember, who has ever perished being innocent? Or where have the upright (righteous) ever been cut off? **8.** I have seen that those who plow iniquity (wickedness) and sow trouble (unrest) reap the same. **9.** By the blast of God (His powerful breath) they perish, and by the breath of His anger they are consumed (destroyed). **10.** The roaring of the lion, the voice of the fierce lion, and the teeth of the young lions are broken. **11.** The old lion perishes for lack of prey (food), and the cubs of the lioness are scattered. **12.** "Now a word was secretly brought to me, and my ear received a whisper of it. **13.** In the disquieting (disturbing) thoughts from the visions of the night, when deep sleep falls on men, **14.** Fear came upon me, and trembling (shaking), which made all my bones

shake. **15.** Then a spirit (a supernatural being) passed before my face; the hair on my body stood up. **16.** It stood still, but I could not discern (make out) its appearance. A form was before my eyes; there was silence; then I heard a voice saying: **17.** 'Can a mortal (human) be more righteous than God? Can a man be more pure than his Maker? **18.** If He puts no trust in His servants (angels), if He charges His angels with error (guilt), **19.** How much more those who dwell in houses of clay (humans), whose foundation is in the dust (earth), who are crushed (destroyed) before a moth (a fragile insect)? **20.** They are broken in pieces from morning till evening; they perish forever, with no one regarding them. **21.** Does not their own excellence (wisdom) go away? They die, even without wisdom.'"

Chapter 5

1. "Call now; is there anyone who will answer you? And to which of the holy ones (angels) will you turn? **2.** For wrath (anger) kills the foolish, and envy destroys the simple (innocent). **3.** I have seen the foolish take root, but suddenly I cursed his dwelling place. **4.** His sons are far from safety; they are crushed at the gate (entrance of the city), and there is no deliverer (rescuer). **5.** Because the hungry eat up his harvest, taking it even from the thorns (brambles), and a snare (trap) snatches their substance (resources). **6.** For affliction (trouble) does not come from the dust, nor does trouble spring from the ground. **7.** Yet man is born to trouble, as the sparks fly upward. **8.** "But as for me, I would seek God, and to God I would commit my cause, **9.** Who does great things, and unsearchable (incomprehensible), marvelous things without number. **10.** He gives rain on the earth, and sends waters on the fields. **11.** He sets on high those who are lowly, and those who mourn are lifted to safety. **12.** He frustrates the devices (plans) of the crafty (sily), so that their hands cannot carry out their plans. **13.** He catches the wise in their own craftiness, and the counsel (advice) of the cunning (clever) comes quickly upon them. **14.** They meet with darkness in the daytime, and grope (search blindly) at noontime as in the night. **15.** But He saves the needy from the sword, from the mouth of the mighty, and from their hand. **16.** So the poor have hope, and injustice (wrongdoing) shuts her mouth. **17.** "Behold, happy is the man whom God corrects; therefore, do not despise (reject) the chastening (discipline) of the Almighty. **18.** For He bruises, but He binds up (heals); He wounds, but His hands make whole. **19.** He shall deliver you in six troubles; yes, in seven no evil shall touch you. **20.** In famine He shall redeem (rescue) you from death, and in war from the power of the sword. **21.** You shall be hidden from the scourge (punishment) of the tongue, and you shall not be afraid of destruction when it comes. **22.** You shall laugh at destruction and famine, and you shall not be afraid of the beasts (wild animals) of the earth. **23.** For you shall have a covenant (agreement) with the stones of the field, and the beasts of the field shall be at peace with you. **24.** You shall know that your tent (home) is in peace; you shall visit your dwelling and find nothing amiss (wrong). **25.** You shall also know that your descendants (children) shall be many, and your offspring (descendants) like the grass of the earth. **26.** You shall come to the grave (death) at a full age, as a sheaf (bundle) of grain ripens in its season. **27.** Behold, this we have searched out; it is true. Hear it, and know for yourself."

Chapter 6

1. Then Job answered and said: **2.** "Oh, that my grief were fully weighed, and my calamity (misfortune) laid with it on the scales! **3.** For then it would be heavier than the sand of the sea—therefore my words have been rash (reckless). **4.** For the arrows (attacks) of the Almighty are within me; my spirit drinks in their poison; the terrors (fears) of God are arrayed (set) against me. **5.** Does the wild donkey bray (cry out) when it has grass, or does the ox low (moo) over its fodder? **6.** Can flavorless (bland) food be eaten without salt? Or is there any taste in the white of an egg? **7.** My soul refuses to touch them; they are as loathsome (disgusting) food to me. **8.** "Oh, that I might have my request, that God would grant me the thing that I long for! **9.** That it would please God to crush me, that He would loose (release) His hand and cut me off (take my life)! **10.** Then I would still have comfort; though in anguish, I would exult (rejoice), He will not spare; for I have not concealed (hidden) the words of the Holy One. **11.** "What strength do I have, that I should hope? And what is my end (future), that I should prolong my life? **12.** Is my strength the strength of stones (rock)? Or is my flesh (body) bronze? **13.** Is my help (support) not within me? And is success driven (taken away) from me? **14.** "To him who is afflicted (in distress), kindness should be shown by his friend, even though he forsakes (abandons) the fear of the Almighty. **15.** My brothers have dealt deceitfully (dishonestly) like a brook, like the streams of the brooks that pass away, **16.** which are dark (muddy) because of the ice, and into which the snow vanishes (melts). **17.** When it is warm, they cease to flow; when it is hot, they vanish from their place. **18.** The paths (ways) of their way turn aside (divert), they go nowhere and perish (end). **19.** The caravans (trading groups) of Tema (a desert region) look, the travelers of Sheba (a region in Arabia) hope for them. **20.** They are disappointed because they were confident; they come there and are confused. **21.** For now you are nothing; you see terror (fear) and are afraid. **22.** Did I ever say, 'Bring something to me'? Or, 'Offer a bribe (gift) for me from your wealth'? **23.** Or, 'Deliver (rescue) me from the enemy's hand'? Or, 'Redeem (save) me from the hand of oppressors (those who abuse power)'? **24.** "Teach me, and I will hold my tongue (keep silent); cause me to understand wherein I have erred (sinned). **25.** How forceful (effective) are right words! But what does your arguing prove (demonstrate)? **26.** Do you intend to rebuke (correct) my words, and the speeches of a desperate (hopeless) one, which are as wind (empty)? **27.** Yes, you overwhelm (oppress) the fatherless (orphan), and you undermine (damage) your friend. **28.** Now therefore, be pleased to look at me; for I would never lie to your face. **29.** Yield (concede) now, let there be no injustice! Yes, concede (admit), my righteousness still stands! **30.** Is there injustice on my tongue? Cannot my taste (judgment) discern the unsavory (evil)?

Chapter 7

1. "Is there not a time of hard service for man on earth? Are not his days like those of a hired worker (someone who works for wages)? **2.** Like a servant longing for the shade, or a hired man waiting eagerly for his pay, **3.** so I have been given months of misery, and nights of endless suffering have been assigned to me. **4.** When I lie down, I ask, 'When will I get up, and when will the night be over?' I've had enough of tossing and turning until dawn. **5.** My body is covered with worms and dust, my skin is cracked and breaks out in sores. **6.** "My days pass faster than a weaver's shuttle (a tool used to move the thread), and I have no hope left. **7.** Remember, my life is only a breath (short and fleeting)! My eyes will never again see happiness. **8.** The one who sees me now will see me no more; when you look for me, I will be gone. **9.** Like a cloud that fades and disappears, so the one who goes down to the grave (death) will never rise again. **10.** He will not return to his home, nor will his place know him anymore. **11.** "Therefore, I will not hold back my words; I will speak out in the anguish of my soul; I will express the bitterness of my spirit. **12.** Am I a sea or a sea monster (a mythical creature), that You set a guard over me? **13.** When I think, 'My bed will comfort me, my couch will ease my complaint,' **14.** You disturb me with dreams and terrify me with visions, **15.** so that my soul chooses strangling (a desire for death) and prefers death over my body. **16.** I hate my life; I do not want to live forever. Leave me alone, for my days are just a breath. **17.** "What is man, that You should care for him, that You should set Your heart on him, **18.** that You should visit him every morning and test him every moment? **19.** How long will You not look away from me, and let me swallow my saliva (spit)? **20.** Have I sinned? What have I done to You, O observer (watcher) of men? Why have You made me Your target, so that I am a burden to myself? **21.** Why do You not forgive (pardon) my sin and take away my wrongs (iniquities)? For now I lie down in the dust, and You will search for me, but I will be gone."

Chapter 8

1. Then Bildad the Shuhite (a man from the family of Shuhah) answered and said: **2.** "How long will you keep speaking these things? Will your words be like a strong wind? **3.** Does God twist justice? Does the Almighty pervert what is right? **4.** If your sons have sinned against Him, He has punished them for their sin. **5.** If you would earnestly seek God and ask the Almighty for help, **6.** if you were pure and upright, surely now He would rise up for you and restore your rightful place. **7.** Though your beginning was small, your future would increase greatly. **8.** "Ask the previous generations and consider what their ancestors have learned. **9.** For we were born only yesterday and know nothing; our days on earth are like a shadow. **10.** Will they not teach you, speak from their hearts, and tell you wisdom? **11.** "Can the papyrus (a type of reed) grow without water? Can reeds thrive without a marsh? **12.** While they are still green and not cut down, they wither faster than any other plant. **13.** So are the paths of all who forget God; the hope of the hypocrite (deceitful person) will perish. **14.** His confidence will be cut off, and his trust is like a spider's web (fragile and unreliable). **15.** He leans on his house, but it will not stand; he holds it fast, but it will not endure. **16.** He flourishes in the sun and his branches spread in his garden. **17.** His roots reach deep into the rock, seeking a place among the stones. **18.** But if he is uprooted from his place, it will deny him, saying, 'I never saw you.' **19.** "This is the joy of his way, and out of the earth, others will grow. **20.** Behold, God will not cast away the blameless, nor will He support the evildoers. **21.** He will yet fill your mouth with laughter and your lips with joy. **22.** Those who hate you will be covered with shame, and the home of the wicked will come to nothing."

Chapter 9

1. Then Job responded and said: **2.** "I know that this is true, but how can a human being be justified before God? **3.** If someone wanted to argue with Him, they wouldn't be able to give a single answer out of a thousand. **4.** God is wise in heart and powerful in strength. Who has ever resisted Him and succeeded? **5.** He moves mountains, and they don't even know it. When He is angry, He shakes them. **6.** He shakes the earth from its place, and its foundations tremble. **7.** He commands the sun, and it doesn't rise; He seals off the stars. **8.** He alone spreads out the heavens and walks on the waves of the sea. **9.** He made the constellations, like the Bear, Orion, and the Pleiades, as well as the chambers of the south (a reference to stars in the southern sky). **10.** He performs wonders beyond comprehension, miracles that are countless. **11.** If He passes by me, I cannot see Him; if He goes by, I do not perceive Him. **12.** If He takes away something, who can stop Him? Who can say to Him, 'What are You doing?' **13.** God will not turn His anger away; the helpers of the proud are laid low before Him. **14.** "How can I argue with Him? How can I even choose the right words to debate with Him? **15.** Even if I were innocent, I could not answer Him. I would only plead for mercy before my Judge. **16.** If I called to Him and He answered me, I wouldn't believe He was actually listening to me. **17.** He crushes me with a storm and increases my wounds for no reason. **18.** He does not let me catch my breath but fills me with bitterness. **19.** If it is a matter of strength, He is the strongest; if it's about justice, who can bring me to court? **20.** Even if I were righteous, my own words would condemn me; if I were innocent, it would show I am deceitful. **21.** "I am blameless, but I do not understand myself; I hate my life. **22.** It is all the same to me; therefore, I say, 'He destroys both the blameless and the wicked.' **23.** If the scourge (a form of severe punishment or judgment) kills suddenly, He mocks the suffering of the innocent. **24.** The earth is given into the hands of the wicked. He covers the faces of its judges. If it's not Him, then who is it? **25.** "My days are faster than a runner; they pass quickly and see no good. **26.** They fly by like ships on the sea, like an eagle swooping down on its prey. **27.** If I say, 'I will forget my complaint and stop worrying,' **28.** I am still afraid of all my pain, knowing that You will not declare me innocent. **29.** If I am guilty, why should I even try? I would only be wasting my efforts. **30.** Even if I wash myself with snow water (symbolizing purity) and clean my hands with soap, **31.** You would still plunge me into a pit, and my own clothes would reject me. **32.** "For He is not a man like me, so I cannot argue with Him, or go to court with Him. **33.** There is no mediator (someone who helps settles a dispute) between us, no one to put a hand on both of us. **34.** Let Him take His rod (a symbol of punishment) away from me, and not terrify me with fear. **35.** Then I would speak without fear, but as it stands, I am terrified."

Chapter 10

1. "My soul despises (hates) my life; I will freely express my complaint and speak from the bitterness (extreme sorrow) of my soul. **2.** I will ask God, 'Do not condemn (punish) me; show me why You contend (argue, struggle) with me. **3.** Does it seem right to You to oppress (cause suffering) me, to despise (disrespect) the work of Your hands, and favor (prefer) the advice of the wicked (evil ones)? **4.** Do You have human eyes? Do You see as a person sees? **5.** Are Your days like those of a mortal man (a human), or Your years like those of a strong man (a mighty one)? **6.** Why do You search for my sin and look for my wrongdoing, **7.** when You know I am not guilty (innocent), and no one can save (rescue) me from Your power? **8.** Your hands made (formed) and shaped me; You shaped me from clay (earth). Yet You would destroy (destroy utterly) me. **9.** Remember, I pray, that You made me from clay—will You turn me back into dust (nothing)? **10.** Did You not pour (pour out) me like milk, curdle (transform into a solid) me like cheese, **11.** clothe (cover) me with skin and flesh, and knit (bind together) me with bones and sinews (tissues that connect muscles to bones)? **12.** You gave me life and showed me favor (grace); Your care has preserved (kept safe) my spirit. **13.** But these things You have hidden (concealed) in Your heart; I know this was in Your mind. **14.** If I sin, You mark (record, notice) me, and You will not forgive (pardon) my wrongdoings. **15.** If I am wicked (evil), woe to me! Even if I am innocent, I cannot lift my head (feel proud); I am filled with shame (humiliation) and misery (suffering). **16.** If my head is lifted up, You hunt (chase) me like a lion, and again You show Your power (majesty) against me. **17.** You renew (increase) Your witnesses (accusations) against me, and increase Your anger toward me. Changes (sudden troubles) and war (conflict) are always with me. **18.** Why did You even bring me out of the womb (birth)? I wish I had died before anyone could see me! **19.** I would have been as if I had never existed (never been born), carried from the womb straight to the grave. **20.** Are not my days few (short)? Leave me alone (let me be), that I may find some comfort (rest), **21.** before I go to the place from which I will never return (the grave), to the land of darkness (shadow of death) and the shadow of death, **22.** a land as dark as the deepest darkness, where the shadow of death remains, with no order (no structure or organization), and where even light is like darkness."

Chapter 11

1. Then Zophar the Naamathite (a man from the town of Naamah) answered and said: **2.** "Shouldn't a multitude of words be answered? And should a person full of talk be justified (declared innocent)? **3.** Should your empty talk cause others to remain silent? And when you mock (make fun of), should no one correct (rebuke) you? **4.** You have claimed, 'My doctrine (teachings) is pure, and I am clean in Your sight.' **5.** But oh, if only God would speak, and open His lips against you, **6.** that He would show you the secrets (hidden knowledge) of wisdom, for they would double (increase) your understanding (prudence). Know that God demands (requires) from you less than your wickedness (evil deeds) deserves. **7.** "Can you search out (understand) the deep things of God? Can you discover (find) the limits of the Almighty (All-powerful)? **8.** They are higher than heaven—what can you do? Deeper than Sheol (the grave)—what can you know? **9.** Their measure is longer than the earth and broader than the sea. **10.** "If He passes by, imprisons, and gathers (gathers together for judgment), who can stop (hinder) Him? **11.** For He knows deceitful men (those who are dishonest); He sees wickedness (evil) as well. Will He not then consider (take it into account)? **12.** For a foolish person will be wise, when a wild donkey's colt (a young donkey) is born a man. **13.** "If you would prepare (prepare with sincerity) your heart, and stretch out your hands toward Him; **14.** If you put away iniquity (sin) from your hand and refuse to let wickedness dwell in your tents; **15.** then surely you could lift up (raise) your face without spot (blemish, guilt); yes, you could stand firm (be steadfast) without fear. **16.** Because you would forget (let go of) your misery, and remember it as waters that have passed away. **17.** And your life would be brighter than the noonday (the sun at its peak); though you were dark, you would be like the morning. **18.** You would be secure (safe), because there is hope; yes, you would dig around you (take care of your surroundings) and rest in safety. **19.** You would lie down, and no one would make you afraid; yes, many would seek your favor (try to gain your approval). **20.** But the eyes of the wicked will fail (become dim); they will not escape (avoid judgment), and their hope will be the loss of life (death)."

Chapter 12

1. Then Job answered and said: **2.** "Surely you are the wise ones (the knowledgeable), and wisdom will die with you! **3.** But I have understanding just like you; I am not inferior to you (less than you). In fact, who doesn't know these things? **4.** "I am mocked (ridiculed) by my friends, those who called on God, and He answered them. The just (righteous) and blameless man is ridiculed. **5.** A lamp (a symbol of guidance) is despised by those who are at ease (comfortable); it is only valued by those whose feet slip (are in danger). **6.** The tents (dwellings)

of robbers prosper, and those who provoke (challenge) God are secure, enjoying what God provides with His hand. **7.** "But now ask the animals, and they will teach you; ask the birds of the air, and they will tell you. **8.** Or speak to the earth, and it will teach you; let the fish of the sea explain it to you. **9.** Who among all these does not know that the hand of the Lord has done this, **10.** in whose hand is the life of every living thing and the breath of all mankind? **11.** Does not the ear test (examine) words, and the mouth taste (evaluate) its food? **12.** Wisdom is with the aged (older people), and with length of days comes understanding. **13.** "With Him (God) are wisdom and strength, He has counsel (advice) and understanding. **14.** If He destroys (breaks) something, it cannot be rebuilt; if He imprisons (captures) someone, there is no escape. **15.** If He withholds (stops) the waters, they dry up; if He sends them out, they flood the earth. **16.** With Him are strength and wisdom. He is in control of the deceived (those misled) and the deceivers (those who mislead). **17.** He leads counselors (advisors) away plundered (defeated), and makes fools (unwise people) of the judges. **18.** He loosens (releases) the bonds (chains) of kings, and binds (restrains) their waist with a belt (symbol of submission). **19.** He leads princes (rulers) away plundered (defeated), and overthrows the mighty (powerful). **20.** He deprives (takes away) the trusted ones of speech, and takes away the discernment (ability to judge) of the elders. **21.** He pours contempt (disrespect) on princes, and disarms (takes away the power of) the mighty. **22.** He uncovers deep things (mysteries) out of darkness, and brings the shadow of death to light. **23.** He makes nations great, and destroys them; He enlarges nations, and guides them. **24.** He takes away the understanding of the chiefs (leaders) of the people of the earth, and makes them wander (roam) in a pathless (unmarked) wilderness. **25.** They grope (feel their way) in the dark without light, and He makes them stagger (stumble) like drunken men."

Chapter 13

1. "Behold, my eye has seen all this, and my ear has heard and understood it. **2.** What you know, I also know; I am not inferior (lesser or subservient) to you. **3.** But I desire to speak to the Almighty (God), and I want to reason (argue or discuss) with God. **4.** But you, forgers (creators or makers) of lies, you are all worthless physicians (useless healers). **5.** Oh, that you would be silent, and that would be your wisdom! **6.** Now hear my reasoning, and listen to the pleadings (requests) of my lips. **7.** Will you speak wickedly (unjustly) for God, and talk deceitfully (dishonestly) on His behalf? **8.** Will you show partiality (favoritism) for Him? Will you contend (argue or fight) for God? **9.** Will it be well when He searches you out (examines you)? Or can you mock (ridicule) Him as you would mock a man? **10.** He will surely rebuke (correct or reprimand) you if you secretly show partiality (favoritism). **11.** Will not His excellence (greatness or glory) make you afraid, and the dread (fear) of Him fall upon you? **12.** Your platitudes (empty or unoriginal remarks) are like proverbs (wise sayings) of ashes, and your defenses (excuses) are defenses of clay (weak and easily destroyed). **13.** "Hold your peace (be quiet) with me, and let me speak. Then let whatever may come on me. **14.** Why do I take my flesh (body) in my teeth, and put my life in my hands? **15.** Though He slay (kill) me, yet will I trust Him. Even so, I will defend (justify) my own ways before Him. **16.** He also shall be my salvation (rescuer), for a hypocrite (someone who pretends to be righteous) could not come before Him. **17.** Listen carefully to my speech, and to my declaration (statement) with your ears. **18.** See now, I have prepared my case, I know that I shall be vindicated (proven right). **19.** Who is he who will contend (argue or fight) with me? If now I hold my tongue (silence), I perish (die). **20.** "Only two things do not do to me, then I will not hide myself from You: **21.** Withdraw Your hand far from me, and let not the dread (fear) of You make me afraid. **22.** Then call, and I will answer; or let me speak, then You respond to me. **23.** How many are my iniquities (wrongs) and sins? Make me know (show) my transgression (offense) and my sin. **24.** Why do You hide Your face (turn away from me), and regard (treat) me as Your enemy? **25.** Will You frighten (terrify) a leaf driven to and fro (tossed around)? And will You pursue (chase) dry stubble (withered straw)? **26.** For You write bitter things (accusations) against me, and make me inherit (receive) the iniquities (sins) of my youth. **27.** You put my feet in the stocks (prison restraints), and watch closely all my paths.

You set a limit for the soles (bottoms) of my feet. **28.** "Man decays (rots) like a rotten thing, like a garment that is moth-eaten."

Chapter 14

1. "Man, who is born of woman, is of few days (has a short life) and full of trouble. **2.** He comes forth like a flower (appears briefly) and fades away; he flees (disappears) like a shadow and does not continue. **3.** And do You open Your eyes on such a one, and bring me to judgment with Yourself? **4.** Who can bring a clean thing out of an unclean? No one! **5.** Since his days are determined (appointed by God), the number of his months is with You; You have set his limits, so that he cannot pass. **6.** Look away from him, that he may rest, till like a hired man (worker) he finishes his day. **7.** "For there is hope for a tree; if it is cut down, it will sprout again, and its tender shoots will not cease. **8.** Though its root may grow old in the earth, and its stump may die in the ground, **9.** Yet at the scent (smell) of water, it will bud and bring forth branches like a plant. **10.** But man dies and is laid away; indeed, he breathes his last, and where is he? **11.** As water disappears from the sea, and a river becomes parched (dried up) and dries up, **12.** So man lies down and does not rise. Till the heavens are no more, they will not awake nor be roused from their sleep. **13.** "Oh, that You would hide me in the grave (place of death), that You would conceal me until Your wrath (anger) is past, that You would appoint me a set time, and remember me! **14.** If a man dies, shall he live again? All the days of my hard service (labor) I will wait, till my change comes. **15.** You shall call, and I will answer You; You shall desire (seek) the work of Your hands. **16.** For now You number (count) my steps, but do not watch over my sin. **17.** My transgression (wrongdoing) is sealed up in a bag, and You cover my iniquity. **18.** "But as a mountain falls and crumbles away, and as a rock is moved from its place, **19.** As water wears away stones, and as torrents (rushing streams) wash away the soil of the earth, so You destroy the hope of man. **20.** You prevail (prevail: overpower or win) forever against him, and he passes on; You change his countenance (face or appearance) and send him away. **21.** His sons come to honor, and he does not know it; they are brought low (humiliated), and he does not perceive it. **22.** But his flesh (body) will be in pain over it, and his soul (spirit) will mourn over it."

Chapter 15

1. Then Eliphaz the Temanite (a man from the region of Teman) answered and said: **2.** "Should a wise man answer with empty knowledge (useless ideas), and fill himself with hot air (meaningless speech)? **3.** Should he reason with unprofitable talk (useless words), or speak in ways that do no good? **4.** Yes, you throw off fear (disregard fear) and restrain (hold back) prayer before God. **5.** For your iniquity (sin) teaches your mouth, and you choose the tongue of the crafty (deceptive). **6.** Your own mouth condemns you, not I; your own lips testify against you. **7.** "Are you the first man who was born? Or were you made before the hills? **8.** Have you heard the counsel (advice) of God? Do you limit wisdom to yourself? **9.** What do you know that we do not know? What do you understand that is not in us? **10.** Both the gray-haired (elderly) and the aged (older) are among us, much older than your father. **11.** Are the consolations (comforts) of God too small for you, and the words spoken gently with you? **12.** Why does your heart carry you away (why are you deceived), and what do your eyes wink at (secretly approve of), **13.** That you turn your spirit against God, and let such words come out of your mouth? **14.** "What is man, that he could be pure? And he who is born of a woman, that he could be righteous? **15.** If God does not trust His saints (holy ones), and the heavens are not pure in His sight, **16.** How much less man, who is abominable (detestable) and filthy, who drinks iniquity (sin) like water! **17.** "I will tell you, listen to me; what I have seen I will declare, **18.** What wise men have told, not hiding anything received from their fathers, **19.** To whom alone the land was given (to the Israelites), and no foreigner passed among them: **20.** The wicked man writhes (suffers in pain) with pain all his days, and the number of his years is hidden from the oppressor. **21.** Dreadful sounds are in his ears; in prosperity (when things are going well) the destroyer comes upon him. **22.** He does not believe that he will return from darkness, for a sword is waiting for him. **23.** He wanders about for bread, saying, 'Where is it?' He knows that a day of darkness is ready at his hand. **24.** Trouble and anguish (deep sorrow) make him afraid; they overpower him like a king ready for battle. **25.** For he stretches out his hand against God, and acts defiantly

(rebelliously) against the Almighty, **26.** Running stubbornly against Him with his strong, embossed (engraved or decorated) shield. **27.** "Though he has covered his face with fatness (though he is well-fed), and made his waist heavy with fat, **28.** He dwells in desolate (abandoned) cities, in houses which no one inhabits, which are destined (planned) to become ruins. **29.** He will not be rich, nor will his wealth continue, nor will his possessions spread over the earth. **30.** He will not depart from darkness; the flame will dry up his branches, and by the breath of His mouth he will perish. **31.** Let him not trust in futile (worthless) things, deceiving himself, for futility (pointlessness) will be his reward. **32.** It will be complete before his time, and his branch will not be green (will not thrive). **33.** He will shake off his unripe grapes like a vine, and cast off his blossom like an olive tree. **34.** For the company of hypocrites (those who pretend to be virtuous) will be barren (unfruitful), and fire will consume the tents of bribery. **35.** They conceive trouble (they bring forth trouble) and bring forth futility (uselessness); their womb prepares deceit."

Chapter 16

1. Then Job answered and said: **2.** "I have heard many such things; miserable comforters (those who offer false comfort) are you all! **3.** Shall words of wind (empty words) have an end? Or what provokes you to answer in such a way? **4.** I could speak as you do, if your soul (inner being) were in my place. I could heap up words against you and shake my head at you; **5.** But I would strengthen you with my mouth, and the comfort (reassurance) of my lips would ease your grief. **6.** "Though I speak, my grief is not eased; and if I stay silent, how am I relieved? **7.** But now He (God) has worn me out; you have made desolate (destroyed) all my company (associates). **8.** You have shriveled me up (wasted away), and it is a witness against me; my leanness (emaciation) rises up against me and testifies to my face. **9.** He (God) tears me in His wrath and hates me; He gnashes at me with His teeth; my adversary (enemy) sharpens His gaze on me. **10.** They gape at me with their mouths, they strike me reproachfully (with scorn) on the cheek, they gather against me. **11.** God has delivered me to the ungodly (wicked), and turned me over to the hands of the wicked. **12.** I was at ease (in peace), but He has shattered me; He has taken me by my neck and shaken me to pieces; He has made me His target. **13.** His archers (soldiers with bows and arrows) surround me; they pierce my heart and do not pity me; they pour out my gall (bitterness) on the ground. **14.** He breaks me with wound upon wound; He runs at me like a warrior (fighter). **15.** "I have sewn sackcloth (rough cloth worn in mourning) over my skin and laid my head in the dust. **16.** My face is flushed from weeping, and on my eyelids is the shadow of death (grief and sorrow). **17.** Although no violence is in my hands, and my prayer is pure. **18.** "O earth, do not cover my blood, and let my cry have no resting place (do not let my plea be forgotten)! **19.** Surely even now my witness (testimony) is in heaven, and my evidence (proof) is on high. **20.** My friends scorn me (mock me); my eyes pour out tears to God. **21.** Oh, that one might plead for a man with God, as a man pleads for his neighbor! **22.** For when a few years are finished, I shall go the way of no return (death)."

Chapter 17

1. "My spirit is crushed (broken); my days are numbered, and the grave (place of the dead) is ready to claim me. **2.** Aren't those who mock (ridicule) me all around? And do my eyes not focus on their insults (offensive remarks)? **3.** "Now make a guarantee (promise) with me, God. Who will be my advocate (defender)? **4.** You have kept their hearts from understanding (comprehending), so You will not lift them up. **5.** The person who flatters (excessively praises) his friends, even his children will lose sight of him. **6.** "But God has made me a laughingstock (object of ridicule) to others, and I have become a target (someone to be mocked) for their scorn (disrespect). **7.** My eyes have dimmed (faded) from crying, and my whole body feels like a shadow (insubstantial, empty). **8.** The upright (morally good) are shocked by this, and the innocent stir against (oppose) the hypocrite (one who pretends to be what they are not). **9.** But the righteous will continue on his path, and he who is pure in heart (morally clean) will grow stronger. **10.** "But please, all of you, return. I will not find a wise man among you. **11.** My days are finished (end); my plans (intentions) are shattered, and even the thoughts of my heart are lost. **12.** They change night into day, claiming that light is near, when darkness is still all around. **13.** If I look to the grave (place of the dead) as my home, if I lie down in the darkness (death), **14.** If I say to decay (decomposition), 'You are my father,' and to the worms (creatures that decompose bodies), 'You are my family,' **15.** Then where is my hope (expectation of future good)? Who can see any hope left for me? **16.** Will I go down to the gates of death (entrance to the underworld)? Will we rest together in the dust (grave)?"

Chapter 18

1. Then Bildad the Shuhite (a man from a region called Shuh) answered and said: **2.** "How long will you keep talking? Gain some understanding, and then we can continue. **3.** Why are we considered like animals (beasts), and regarded as foolish in your eyes? **4.** You who tear yourself apart in anger, do you think the earth will be abandoned for you? Will the rock be moved from its place because of you? **5.** "The light (life and success) of the wicked certainly fades away, and the flame of their fire is extinguished. **6.** Their light grows dark in their tent, and their lamp goes out beside them. **7.** Their strength is weakened, and their own advice brings them down. **8.** They are caught in a net of their own making, and walk right into a trap. **9.** The net catches them by the heel, and the snare (trap) holds them fast. **10.** A trap lies hidden for them on the ground, and there's a pitfall (danger) in the path they walk. **11.** Horrors (terrors) surround them on every side and drive them to panic. **12.** Their strength is wasted away, and destruction is at their side. **13.** It consumes their skin (devours patches of their skin); the firstborn of death (a deadly disease) consumes their limbs. **14.** They are uprooted (removed) from the shelter of their tent, and they are taken to face the king of terrors (a term for death or destruction). **15.** Strangers (those who don't belong) live in their tent, and sulfur (brimstone) is scattered over their dwelling. **16.** Their roots dry up beneath them, and their branches wither above. **17.** Their memory perishes from the earth, and they have no name among those who are honored. **18.** They are driven from light into darkness, and are chased out of the world. **19.** They have no children or descendants among their people, and no survivors in their homes. **20.** Those in the west are shocked by their fate, and those in the east are terrified. **21.** Surely this is the fate of the wicked, and this is the place of those who do not know God."

Chapter 19

1. Then Job answered and said: **2.** "How long will you torment (cause severe pain or suffering) my soul, and break me in pieces with your words? **3.** These ten times you have reproached (criticized) me; you are not ashamed that you have wronged me. **4.** And if indeed I have erred (made a mistake), my error remains with me. **5.** If indeed you exalt (raise in status) yourselves against me, and plead (argue) my disgrace against me, **6.** know then that God has wronged (hurt) me, and has surrounded me with His net (trap). **7.** "If I cry out concerning wrong, I am not heard. If I cry aloud, there is no justice. **8.** He has fenced (blocked) up my way, so that I cannot pass; and He has set darkness in my paths. **9.** He has stripped (removed) me of my glory, and taken the crown from my head. **10.** He breaks (shatters) me down on every side, and I am gone; my hope He has uprooted (removed) like a tree. **11.** He has also kindled (set on fire) His wrath (anger) against me, and He counts me as one of His enemies. **12.** His troops (soldiers) come together and build up their road (trap) against me; they encamp all around my tent. **13.** "He has removed (distanced) my brothers far from me and my acquaintances (people I know) are completely estranged (separated) from me. **14.** My relatives have failed (betrayed) me, and my close friends have forgotten (ignored) me. **15.** Those who dwell (live) in my house, and my maidservants (female servants), count me as a stranger; I am an alien in their sight. **16.** I call my servant (worker), but he gives no answer; I beg him with my mouth. **17.** My breath is offensive (unpleasant) to my wife, and I am repulsive (disgusting) to the children of my own body. **18.** Even young children despise (dislike) me; I arise, and they speak against me. **19.** All my close friends abhor (hate) me, and those whom I love have turned (betrayed) against me. **20.** My bone clings (sticks) to my skin and to my flesh, and I have escaped by the skin of my teeth (barely managed). **21.** "Have pity (mercy) on me, have pity on me, O you my friends, for the hand (power) of God has struck (hurt) me! **22.** Why do you persecute (annoy) me as God does, and are not satisfied with my flesh (suffering)? **23.** "Oh, that my words were written (inscribed) down! Oh, that they were recorded in a book! **24.** That they were engraved (carved) on a rock with an iron pen (writing tool) and lead, forever! **25.** For I know that my Redeemer (rescuer) lives, and He shall stand (appear) at last on the earth; **26.** And after my skin is destroyed (decays), this I know, that in my flesh (body) I shall see God, **27.** Whom I shall see for myself, and my eyes shall behold (see), and not another. How my heart yearns (desires) within me! **28.** If you should say, 'How shall we persecute him?'— since the root (cause) of the matter is found in me, **29.** Be afraid (fear) of the sword for yourselves; for wrath (anger) brings the punishment of the sword that you may know there is a judgment (justice)."

Chapter 20

1. Then Zophar the Naamathite (a man from Naamath) answered and said: **2.** "Therefore, my anxious (worried) thoughts make me answer, because of the turmoil (disorder or confusion) within me. **3.** I have heard the rebuke (criticism) that reproaches me, and the spirit (inner strength or influence) of my understanding causes me to respond. **4.** "Do you not know this from old, since man was placed on earth, **5.** that the triumph (success) of the wicked (evil) is short, and the joy of the hypocrite (pretender) is only for a moment? **6.** Though his haughtiness (pride) rises to the heavens, and his head reaches to the clouds, **7.** yet he will perish (be destroyed) forever, like his own refuse (waste or garbage); those who see him will say, 'Where is he?' **8.** He will fly away like a dream, and will not be found; yes, he will be chased away like a vision (illusion) of the night. **9.** The eye that saw him will see him no more, nor will his place (location) behold him any longer. **10.** His children will seek the favor (kindness) of the poor, and his hands will restore (return) his wealth. **11.** His bones are full of youthful vigor (strength), but it will lie down with him in the dust. **12.** "Though evil is sweet (pleasant) in his mouth, and he hides it under his tongue, **13.** though he spares it (keeps it) and does not forsake (abandon) it, but still keeps it in his mouth, **14.** yet his food in his stomach turns sour (bitter); it becomes cobra venom (poison) within him. **15.** He swallows down riches (wealth), and vomits (rejects) them up again; God casts them out of his belly. **16.** He will suck (drink) the poison of cobras; the viper's (snake) tongue will kill (slay) him. **17.** He will not see the streams, the rivers flowing with honey and cream (delight). **18.** He will restore (give back) what he labored for, but will not swallow (enjoy) it down; from his business proceeds, he will get no enjoyment. **19.** For he has oppressed (wronged) and forsaken (abandoned) the poor, and has violently seized (taken by force) a house which he did not build. **20.** "Because he knows no quietness (peace) in his heart, he will not save (keep) anything he desires. **21.** Nothing is left for him to eat; therefore, his well-being (prosperity) will not last. **22.** In his self-sufficiency (independence), he will be in distress (trouble); every hand of misery (trouble) will come against him. **23.** When he is about to fill his stomach, God will cast upon him the fury (anger) of His wrath, and will rain (pour) it on him while he is eating. **24.** He will flee (run away) from the iron weapon; a bronze bow will pierce (wound) him through. **25.** It is drawn, and comes out of his body; yes, the glittering (shining) point comes out of his gall (liver). Terrors (fears) come upon him; **26.** total darkness is reserved for his treasures; an unfanned (unlit) fire will consume (burn) him; it will go ill with him who is left in his tent. **27.** The heavens will reveal (uncover) his iniquity, and the earth will rise up against him. **28.** The increase (gain) of his house will depart (leave), and his goods (possessions) will flow away in the day of His wrath. **29.** This is the portion from God for a wicked (evil) man, the heritage (inheritance) appointed to him by God."

Chapter 21

1. Then Job answered and said: **2.** "Listen carefully to my words, and let this be your consolation (comfort). **3.** Bear with me while I speak, and after I have spoken, feel free to mock me. **4.** "Is my complaint against man? And if it were, why should I not be impatient (frustrated)? **5.** Look at me and be astonished (amazed); put your hand over your mouth. **6.** Even when I remember this, I am terrified (frightened), and trembling takes hold of my flesh. **7.** Why do the wicked (evil people) live and grow old, becoming mighty (strong) in power? **8.** Their descendants (children) are secure with them, and their offspring (children) are before their eyes. **9.** Their homes are safe from fear; the rod (punishment) of God is not upon them. **10.** Their bull breeds without fail; their cow calves (gives birth) without miscarriage. **11.** They send their children out like a flock, and their children dance. **12.**

They sing to the tambourine and harp, and rejoice at the sound of the flute. **13.** They live in wealth (riches), and in a moment, they go down to the grave. **14.** Yet they say to God, 'Depart from us, for we do not desire (want) the knowledge (understanding) of Your ways. **15.** Who is the Almighty (God) that we should serve Him? And what profit (benefit) do we have if we pray to Him?' **16.** Indeed, their prosperity (success) is not in their hands; the counsel (advice) of the wicked is far from me. **17.** "How often is the lamp (light) of the wicked put out? How often does their destruction (ruin) come upon them, the sorrows (troubles) God sends in His anger? **18.** They are like straw before the wind, and like chaff (light material) that a storm blows away. **19.** They say, 'God lays up (stores) one's iniquity for his children'; let Him repay (punish) him, that he may know it. **20.** Let his eyes see his destruction (ruin), and let him drink the wrath (anger) of the Almighty (God). **21.** For what does he care about his household (family) after him, when the number of his days (life span) is cut in half? **22.** "Can anyone teach God knowledge (wisdom), since He judges (decides) those on high? **23.** One man dies in his full strength, being at ease (comfortable) and secure (safe); **24.** his pails (containers) are full of milk, and the marrow (bone) of his bones is moist (healthy). **25.** Another man dies in bitterness (sadness) of his soul, never having enjoyed (tasted) prosperity. **26.** They lie down alike in the dust, and worms cover them. **27.** "Look, I know your thoughts, and the schemes (plans) with which you would wrong me. **28.** For you say, 'Where is the house (home) of the prince (ruler)? And where is the tent (home), the dwelling place of the wicked?' **29.** Have you not asked those who travel the road? And do you not know their signs (stories)? **30.** For the wicked are reserved (set aside) for the day of doom (destruction); they will be brought out on the day of wrath (anger). **31.** Who condemns (blames) his way to his face? And who repays (rewards) him for what he has done? **32.** Yet he will be brought to the grave, and a vigil (watch) will be kept over his tomb. **33.** The clods (earth) of the valley shall be sweet (pleasant) to him; everyone shall follow him, as countless (many) have gone before him. **34.** How then can you comfort me with empty words, since falsehood (lies) remains in your answers?"

Chapter 22

1. Then Eliphaz the Temanite (a man from Teman) answered and said: **2.** "Can a man be of any benefit to God, even though a wise man benefits himself? **3.** Does God gain any pleasure from your righteousness (being morally right), or is He benefited when you make your ways blameless (without fault)? **4.** Is it because of your fear of Him that He corrects you and brings judgment against you? **5.** Is not your wickedness (immorality) great, and your iniquity endless? **6.** For you have taken pledges (promises or agreements) from your brother without cause, and you have stripped the naked (those without clothing) of their clothing. **7.** You have not given water to the weary (thirsty), and you have withheld food from the hungry. **8.** Yet the mighty man (strong, powerful) owns the land, and the honorable man (someone with high status) lives in it. **9.** You have sent widows (women whose husbands have died) away empty-handed, and you have crushed the strength of the fatherless (orphans). **10.** Therefore, snares (traps) are all around you, and sudden fear will overwhelm you. **11.** Or perhaps darkness so thick you cannot see; and an abundance of water will cover you. **12.** "Is not God in the heights (high places) of heaven? And do you see the highest stars? How lofty (elevated, high) they are! **13.** And you say, 'What does God know? Can He judge through such thick darkness? **14.** Thick clouds cover Him, so that He cannot see, and He walks above the circle of heaven.' **15.** Will you keep to the old way that wicked men have walked, **16.** men who were cut down (destroyed) before their time, whose foundations were swept away by a flood (a great disaster)? **17.** They said to God, 'Depart from us! What can the Almighty (God) do to us?' **18.** Yet He filled their houses with good things, but the counsel (plans) of the wicked is far from me. **19.** "The righteous (those who are just) see it and are glad; the innocent laugh at them: **20.** 'Surely our enemies are cut off, and the fire consumes their remnants (what remains of them).' **21.** "Now, submit to God, and be at peace with Him; thereby good will come to you. **22.** Accept instruction (wisdom) from His mouth, and store up His words in your heart. **23.** If you return to the Almighty, you will be built up (strengthened); you will remove wickedness far from your tents. **24.** Then you will lay your gold in the dust, and the gold of Ophir (a place

known for its wealth) among the rocks of the brooks (streams). **25.** Yes, the Almighty (God) will be your gold and your precious silver. **26.** Then you will take delight (find joy) in the Almighty, and lift up your face to God. **27.** You will pray to Him, and He will hear you; you will fulfill (complete) your vows to Him. **28.** You will declare a matter, and it will be established (set) for you; light will shine on your ways. **29.** When men are brought low (humbled) and you say, 'Lift them up!' He will save the humble (lowly). **30.** He will even deliver one who is not innocent; yes, He will be delivered through the purity (clean hands) of your hands."

Chapter 23

1. Then Job answered and said: **2.** "Even today, my complaint (a statement of grief or protest) is bitter; my hand is limp (weak, without strength) from my groaning. **3.** Oh that I knew where I could find God that I might come to His throne (His seat of authority)! **4.** I would present my case before Him and fill my mouth with arguments (reasons or defenses). **5.** I would know the words He would use to answer me, and understand what He would say to me. **6.** Would He argue (contend or dispute) with me in His great power? No! He would listen to me. **7.** There, the upright (those who live justly or righteously) could reason with Him, and I would be forever free from my Judge. **8.** "Look, I go forward, but He is not there; and backward, but I cannot perceive (see or understand) Him. **9.** When He works on the left, I cannot see Him; when He turns to the right, I cannot find (locate) Him. **10.** But He knows the way I take; when He has tested (examined or refined) me, I will come out as pure gold. **11.** My foot has held fast (remained steady) to His steps; I have kept His way and not turned aside. **12.** I have not deviated (strayed or turned away) from the commandment (instruction or law) of His lips; I have treasured (valued deeply) the words of His mouth more than my necessary food. **13.** "But He is unique (one of a kind, incomparable), and who can make Him change? And whatever His soul (will or desire) wants, He does. **14.** For He carries out (executes or performs) what is planned for me, and many such things are with Him. **15.** Therefore, I am terrified (filled with fear) in His presence; when I think about this, I am afraid (fearful) of Him. **16.** For God has made my heart faint (weak or powerless), and the Almighty terrifies me. **17.** Because I was not destroyed (cut off or eliminated) in darkness, and He did not hide (conceal or keep away) deep darkness from my face."

Chapter 24

1. Why do those who know God not see His days? **2.** Some remove landmarks (boundary markers), violently seize flocks, and feed on them. **3.** They drive away the orphan's donkey (symbol of vulnerability) and take the widow's ox (symbol of livelihood) as a pledge (collateral). **4.** They push the needy off the road, forcing the poor to hide (out of sight or desperation). **5.** Like wild donkeys in the desert, they search for food, finding sustenance in the wilderness for themselves and their children. **6.** They gather in fields and vineyards of the wicked (those who do wrong or evil). **7.** They spend the night naked (without clothes), without shelter from the cold. **8.** They are soaked by mountain rains, huddling for warmth in the rocks (symbol of desperation). **9.** Some take the infant from the breast (mother's child) and demand a pledge from the poor. **10.** They leave the poor naked (without clothing) and steal from the hungry. **11.** They press oil (extract) and tread wine, but remain thirsty (despite their efforts, they lack satisfaction). **12.** The dying groan in the city, and the wounded cry out, yet God does not charge them with wrong (justice is delayed). **13.** There are those who reject the light (moral truth), not knowing its ways. **14.** The murderer rises with the sun, kills the poor and needy, and robs by night (when no one can see). **15.** The adulterer waits for twilight (dusk), thinking no one will see him, hiding his face. **16.** In the dark, they break into houses they marked during the day (pre-meditation). **17.** To them, morning is like the shadow of death (a terrifying unknown)—terrified of being recognized. **18.** They should be swift to face destruction (swift: quick to meet their fate), cursed in the land, and driven away from others' vineyards. **19.** As heat consumes snow, so the grave consumes the sinner (symbol of inevitable death). **20.** The womb should forget him; the worm should feed on him; he should be forgotten, his wickedness broken like a tree (symbol of total destruction). **21.** He preys on the barren (those who cannot bear children) and does no good for widows. **22.** But God removes the mighty with His power; they may rise, but their lives are not secure. **23.** They trust in their security (false sense of safety), but God sees their ways. **24.** They are exalted briefly (for a short time), then fade away, brought low and withered like heads of grain. **25.** If this is not so, who will prove me a liar (false accuser) and prove my words false?

Chapter 25

1. Then Bildad the Shuhite answered and said: **2.** "Dominion (sovereignty) and fear (awe) belong to Him; He makes peace in His high places (heavens). **3.** Is there any number to His armies (angelic hosts)? Upon whom does His light not rise (His presence is universal)? **4.** How then can man be righteous before God (how can humans be morally justified before the Creator)? Or how can he be pure who is born of a woman (born in human weakness)? **5.** If even the moon does not shine (imperfect in His sight), and the stars are not pure in His sight (even celestial bodies are flawed in comparison), **6.** How much less man, who is a maggot (insignificant and frail), and a son of man, who is a worm (weak and lowly)?"

Chapter 26

1. But Job answered and said: **2.** "How have you helped the powerless (those without strength)? How have you saved those without strength (unable to defend themselves)? **3.** How have you counseled the foolish (those without wisdom)? And given sound advice to many? **4.** To whom have you spoken (spoken words to)? Whose spirit (breath or essence) came from you? **5.** The dead tremble (shudder in fear), those in the depths (the deep places, such as the ocean) and those who dwell there (inhabitants of the underworld). **6.** Sheol (the realm of the dead) lies bare before Him, and Destruction (place of ruin or death) has no covering. **7.** He stretches out the north over empty space (the void); He hangs the earth on nothing (the earth is suspended without visible support). **8.** He holds the waters in thick clouds (clouds full of water), yet the clouds don't break under them (the weight doesn't cause them to collapse). **9.** He covers the face of His throne (His majestic seat), and spreads His cloud over it (His presence is hidden). **10.** He set the horizon (the boundary between earth and sky) on the waters (the oceans), at the boundary of light and darkness (the transition between day and night). **11.** The pillars (supports) of heaven tremble at His rebuke (His command). **12.** He stirs up the sea with His power (controls the chaos of the sea), and by His wisdom (understanding) He calms the storm. **13.** By His Spirit (breath or divine force) He adorned the heavens (created the beauty of the sky); His hand pierced the serpent (defeated evil or chaos). **14.** These are just the edges (small part) of His ways; we hear only a faint whisper (soft sound) of Him. Who can understand the thunder (great sound) of His power?"

Chapter 27

1. Job continued and said: **2.** "As God lives, who has taken my justice (the right to a fair hearing), and the Almighty, who has made my soul bitter (deeply sorrowful), **3.** as long as I breathe, and the breath of God is in me (life force, the spirit), **4.** my lips will not speak wickedness (evil speech), nor will my tongue utter deceit (falsehood). **5.** I will not say you are right (justify your actions); I will not abandon my integrity (honesty, moral uprightness) until I die. **6.** I will hold fast to my righteousness (right standing with God) and will not let it go; my heart will not reproach me (accuse me) as long as I live. **7.** May my enemy be like the wicked (morally corrupt), and those who rise against me like the unrighteous (evil-doers). **8.** What is the hope of the hypocrite (one who pretends to be righteous), even if he gains much, if God takes his life? **9.** Will God hear his cry (prayer) when trouble comes? **10.** Will he delight in the Almighty (find joy in God) and always call on God? **11.** I will teach you about God's hand (power, authority); I will not conceal (hide) what the Almighty has shown. **12.** Surely you have seen this (witnessed it); why then do you behave foolishly (irrationally)? **13.** This is the portion (lot) of the wicked with God, the inheritance (what they receive) of oppressors (those who mistreat others) from the Almighty: **14.** If his children are many, it's for the sword (they will die in battle); his offspring will not be satisfied with bread (they will go hungry). **15.** Those who survive him (his survivors) will die, and his widows will not weep (they will not mourn him). **16.** Though he piles up silver like dust (accumulates wealth), and clothing like clay (possessions), **17.** the just (righteous) will wear it, and the innocent (blameless) will divide the silver. **18.** He builds his house like a moth (fragile, temporary), like a booth (temporary shelter) a watchman makes. **19.** The rich man will lie down, but not be gathered up; he opens his eyes and is no more (he dies). **20.** Terrors (fear, horrors) overtake him like a flood (overwhelming), a tempest (storm) sweeps him away in the night. **21.** The east wind (destructive force) carries him away, and he is gone; it sweeps him from his place (takes him away from his home). **22.** It strikes him without mercy, and he flees desperately (in panic) from its power. **23.** People will clap their hands (express disdain) at him and hiss (sneer in contempt) him out of his place."

Chapter 28

1. "Surely there is a mine for silver and a place where gold is refined (purified). **2.** Iron is taken from the earth, and copper is smelted (melted to extract) from ore. **3.** Man ends darkness, searching every recess (hidden places) for ore in the shadow of death. **4.** He breaks open shafts far from people, in forgotten places. **5.** The earth yields bread (food), but underneath, it is turned up as by fire. **6.** Its stones contain sapphires (precious stones), and it holds gold dust. **7.** No bird knows that path, nor has the falcon's eye seen it. **8.** The proud lions have not trodden (walked) it, nor the fierce lion passed over it. **9.** He places his hand on flint (hard rock) and overturns mountains at the roots. **10.** He cuts channels (paths) in rocks and sees every precious thing. **11.** He dams up streams (diverts water) and brings hidden things to light. **12.** "But where can wisdom be found? Where is understanding (insight)? **13.** Man does not know its value, and it's not found among the living. **14.** The deep says, 'It is not in me,' and the sea says, 'It is not with me.' **15.** It cannot be bought with gold, nor weighed with silver. **16.** It cannot be valued (measured in worth) in Ophir's gold (a place known for its wealth), precious onyx (a gemstone), or sapphire (a valuable stone). **17.** Neither gold nor crystal compares, nor can it be exchanged for fine jewelry. **18.** Coral or quartz (precious stones) cannot match its price; wisdom is above rubies (very precious). **19.** The topaz of Ethiopia cannot equal it, nor pure gold. **20.** "Where, then, does wisdom come from? Where is the place of understanding? **21.** It is hidden from the eyes of all living and concealed from the birds of the air. **22.** Destruction and Death say, 'We have heard a report of it.' **23.** God understands its way and knows its place. **24.** He looks to the ends of the earth and sees under the whole heavens. **25.** He sets the weight (balance) of the wind and measures the waters. **26.** When He made a law for rain and a path for the thunderbolt, **27.** He saw wisdom, declared it, and prepared it. **28.** And to man He said, 'The fear of the Lord is wisdom, and to depart from evil is understanding.'"

Chapter 29

1. Job continued and said: **2.** "Oh, that I were as in months past, when God watched over me; **3.** When His lamp shone on my head, and I walked through darkness by His light (guidance); **4.** Just as I was in my prime (best years), with God's counsel (advice) over my tent (home); **5.** When the Almighty (God) was with me, and my children were around me; **6.** When my steps were bathed in cream (prosperity), and the rock poured out rivers of oil (riches) for me. **7.** "When I went out to the city gate (entrance) and sat in the square (public place), **8.** The young men saw me and hid (in fear), and the aged (elders) stood up; **9.** The princes (leaders) stopped talking and put their hand to their mouth (in reverence); **10.** The nobles (high-ranking men) were silent, their tongues stuck to the roof of their mouth (speechless). **11.** When the ear heard, it blessed me, and when the eye saw, it approved me; **12.** Because I helped the poor who cried out, the fatherless (orphans), and those with no helper. **13.** The blessing of the dying came upon me, and I made the widow's heart sing (with joy). **14.** I put on righteousness (justice) like a robe, and justice like a turban (headgear). **15.** I was eyes to the blind, and feet to the lame (disabled). **16.** I was a father to the poor (needy) and sought out cases I didn't know (investigated unknown issues). **17.** I broke the teeth of the wicked (oppressors) and rescued victims from their grasp (clutches). **18.** "Then I thought, 'I shall die in my nest (home) and multiply my days like the sand (in abundance). **19.** My roots are spread out to the waters (planted in abundance), and the dew lies on my branch (my life is nourished). **20.** My glory (honor) is fresh within me, and my bow (strength) is renewed in my hand.' **21.** "Men listened to me, waiting for my counsel (advice). **22.** After I spoke, they were silent, and my words settled on them like dew (gentle and refreshing). **23.** They waited for me as for rain (longing for wisdom), and opened their mouths like for spring rain (a precious gift). **24.** If I mocked they didn't believe it; the light of my face (my approval) did not fall. **25.** I chose their way (path) and sat as chief (leader), like a king in the army (ruler), comforting mourners (those in sorrow)."

Chapter 30

1. "But now they mock me—men younger than I, whose fathers I would not have put with my dogs. **2.** What use is their strength to me? Their vigor (energy) has gone. **3.** They are gaunt from hunger, fleeing to desolate (barren) places, **4.** gathering mallow (a plant) and broom tree roots for food. **5.** They are driven away by men and treated like thieves. **6.** They live in caves and rocky clefts (narrow spaces). **7.** Among the bushes they bray (make loud sounds); under the nettles (stinging plants) they nest. **8.** They are sons of fools, vile (wicked) men, cast out of the land. **9.** "And now I am their taunt (mockery), their byword (proverb). **10.** They abhor (hate) me and spit in my face. **11.** Because God has loosened (released) my bowstring (strength) and afflicted (caused pain) me, they have no restraint before me. **12.** At my right hand the rabble (mob) rises, pushing my feet, destroying my ways. **13.** They break my path, bring calamity (disaster), and leave me without help. **14.** They come like a flood, rolling under the storm. **15.** Terrors overtake me; they pursue my honor like wind, and my prosperity (success) has passed like a cloud. **16.** "Now my soul is poured out because of my suffering; days of affliction (trouble) hold me. **17.** My bones are pierced (pierced deeply) at night, and my pain never rests. **18.** My garment (clothing) is disfigured by force; it binds me like the collar (neck part) of my coat. **19.** He has cast me into the dust (mire), and I am like ashes. **20.** "I cry out to You, but You do not answer; I stand, but You pay no attention. **21.** You have become cruel to me; You oppose (fight) me with Your strength. **22.** You lift me up to the wind and make me ride on it; You ruin (destroy) my success. **23.** I know You will bring me to death, to the grave (final resting place) appointed for all living. **24.** "Surely He would not stretch out His hand against a heap of ruins (destruction) if they cry out when He destroys it. **25.** Have I not wept for those in trouble? Has my soul not grieved (sorrowed) for the poor? **26.** Yet when I looked for good, evil came; when I waited for light (hope), darkness came. **27.** My heart is in turmoil (distress) and cannot rest; days of affliction confront me. **28.** I mourn without sunlight; I cry out for help in the assembly (gathering). **29.** I am a brother to jackals (wild dogs) and a companion to ostriches (desert birds). **30.** My skin is black and falling off; my bones burn with fever. **31.** My harp (musical instrument) is turned to mourning, and my flute to the voice of those who weep."

Chapter 31

1. "I have made a covenant (agreement) with my eyes; why then should I look lustfully at a young woman? **2.** For what is the allotment (portion) of God from above, and the inheritance of the Almighty from on high? **3.** Is it not destruction for the wicked, and disaster for the workers of iniquity (wickedness)? **4.** Does He not see my ways and count all my steps? **5.** "If I have walked with falsehood (deception), or if my foot has hastened (hurried) to deceit, **6.** let me be weighed on honest scales, that God may know my integrity (uprightness). **7.** If my step has turned from the way, or my heart has walked after my eyes, or if any spot (blemish) adheres (sticks) to my hands, **8.** then let me sow, and another eat; yes, let my harvest be rooted out (uprooted). **9.** "If my heart has been enticed (lured) by a woman, or if I have lurked (waited secretly) at my neighbor's door, **10.** then let my wife grind (mill grain) for another, and let others bow down over her. **11.** For that would be wickedness, yes, it would be iniquity (sin) deserving judgment. **12.** It would be a fire that consumes (destroys), rooting out all my increase (gains). **13.** "If I have despised (disrespected) the cause of my male or female servant when they complained against me, **14.** what then shall I do when God rises up? When He punishes, how shall I answer Him? **15.** Did not He who made me in the womb also make them? Did not the same One fashion (form) us both in the womb? **16.** "If I have kept the poor from their desire, or caused the eyes of the widow to fail (grow dim), **17.** or eaten my morsel (meal) by myself, so that the fatherless could not eat of it, **18.** but from my youth I reared (cared for) him as a father, and from my mother's womb I guided the widow, **19.** if I have seen anyone perish (die) for lack of clothing, or any poor man without covering (clothing); **20.** if his heart has not blessed me, and if he was not warmed by the fleece (wool) of my sheep, **21.** if I have raised my hand against the fatherless, when I saw that I had help

at the gate, **22.** then let my arm fall from my shoulder, let my arm be torn from the socket. **23.** For destruction from God is a terror (fear) to me, and because of His magnificence (greatness) I cannot endure (go through). **24.** "If I have made gold my hope, or said to fine gold, 'You are my confidence (trust),' **25.** if I have rejoiced because my wealth was great, and because my hand had gained much, **26.** if I have observed (looked at) the sun when it shines, or the moon moving in brightness, **27.** so that my heart has been secretly enticed (lured), and my mouth has kissed my hand (in worship of wealth), **28.** this would also be iniquity (sin) deserving of judgment, for I would have denied God who is above. **29.** "If I have rejoiced at the destruction (ruin) of him who hated me, or lifted myself up when evil (harm) found him, **30.** I have not allowed my mouth to sin by asking for a curse on his soul. **31.** If the men of my tent have not said, 'Who is there who has not been satisfied with his meat (food)?' **32.** But no sojourner (foreigner) had to lodge (stay) in the street, for I have opened my doors to the traveler, **33.** if I have covered (concealed) my transgressions (sins) like Adam, by hiding my iniquity in my heart, **34.** because I feared the great multitude (crowd) and dreaded the contempt (disrespect) of families, so that I kept silent and did not go out the door— **35.** Oh, that I had one to hear me! Here is my mark (signature); oh, that the Almighty would answer me, that my Prosecutor (accuser) had written a book! **36.** Surely I would carry it on my shoulder, and bind it on me like a crown; **37.** I would declare to Him the number of my steps; like a prince I would approach Him. **38.** "If my land cries out against me, and its furrows (plowed fields) weep together, **39.** if I have eaten its fruit without money (paying), or caused its owners to lose their lives, **40.** then let thistles (thorny weeds) grow instead of wheat, and weeds instead of barley." The words of Job are ended.

Chapter 32

1. So these three men stopped answering Job because he considered himself righteous in his own eyes. **2.** Then Elihu, the son of Barachel the Buzite (a man from the family of Buz), of the clan of Ram, became angry with Job. His anger was kindled because Job justified himself rather than God. **3.** Elihu was also angry with Job's three friends because they had found no answer, yet they condemned (judged) Job. **4.** Since Elihu was younger than they were, he had waited to speak to Job. **5.** When Elihu saw that there was no answer in the mouths of the three men, his anger grew. **6.** So Elihu, the son of Barachel the Buzite (a descendant of Buz), spoke and said: "I am young, and you are very old. Therefore, I was afraid and did not dare to express my opinion to you." **7.** I thought, 'Age should speak, and a multitude of years should teach wisdom.' **8.** But there is a spirit in man, and the breath of the Almighty gives him understanding. **9.** Great men are not always wise, nor do the aged always understand what is right. **10.** Therefore, I say, 'Listen to me, I too will declare my opinion.' **11.** I waited for your words, I listened to your arguments, and carefully considered what you said. **12.** I paid close attention to you, and yet, none of you convinced Job or answered his words. **13.** Lest you say, "We have found wisdom," God will silence him, not man. **14.** He has not directed his words against me; so, I will not answer him with your words. **15.** They are dismayed and can no longer speak; words escape them. **16.** I waited for them to speak, but now I will answer. **17.** I am full of words; the spirit within me compels me to speak. **18.** My belly is like wine without a vent; it is ready to burst like new wineskins. **19.** I will speak, that I may find relief; I must open my lips and answer. **20.** Let me not show partiality (favoritism) to anyone, nor let me flatter any man. **21.** For I do not know how to flatter, else my Maker (God) would soon take me away. **22.** Let me not show favoritism to any person, nor flatter anyone, for I don't know how to do so; otherwise, my Maker would take me away.

Chapter 33

1. "But please, Job, hear my words, and listen to all I have to say. **2.** Now I open my mouth; my tongue speaks through me. **3.** My words come from a sincere (honest) heart; my lips speak pure knowledge (truth). **4.** The Spirit of God made me, and the breath (life force) of the Almighty gives me life. **5.** If you can answer me, set your words in order before me; take your stand. **6.** I am your spokesman (representative) before God; I too have been formed from clay (mankind). **7.** Surely, no fear of me will terrify (frighten) you, nor will my hand be heavy on you. **8.** "Surely you have spoken in my hearing, saying, **9.** 'I am pure, without sin; I am innocent (blameless), and there is no iniquity (wrongdoing) in me. 10. Yet He finds fault (blames) with me, counts me as His enemy; 11. He imprisons me and watches my every step.' 12. "Look, in this you are not right. I will answer you because God is greater (more powerful) than man. 13. Why do you argue (contend) with Him? He does not need to give an account (explanation) of His words. 14. For God may speak in one way or another, but man does not always understand (perceive) it. 15. He speaks in dreams, in visions (appearances) of the night, when deep sleep falls on men, 16. Then He opens their ears and gives them instruction (teaching). 17. He does this to turn man from his deeds, to conceal (hide) pride from him, 18. and to save (deliver) his soul from the pit (grave), and his life from perishing (dying) by the sword. 19. "Man is also chastened (corrected) with pain on his bed, and with strong pain in his bones, 20. so that his life abhors (hates) food, and his soul refuses even the best food (delicious). 21. His flesh wastes away from sight and his bones stick out, once hidden. 22. Yes, his soul draws near (comes close) to the pit (grave), and his life to the executioners (those who kill). 23. "If there is a messenger (representative) for him, a mediator (intercessor) among a thousand, to show man his uprightness (righteousness), 24. then God is gracious (merciful) to him, saying, 'Rescue him from going down to the pit; I have found a ransom (payment).' 25. His flesh becomes as fresh as a child's, he returns to the days of his youth. 26. He prays to God, and God delights (takes pleasure) in him; he sees God's face with joy, and God restores his righteousness (moral rightness). 27. Then he looks at men and says, 'I have sinned and perverted (twisted) what was right, and it did not profit me.' 28. He will redeem (rescue) his soul from going down to the pit, and his life will see the light (life). 29. "Behold, God works all these things, twice, even three times, with a man, 30. to bring back his soul from the pit (grave), so that he may be enlightened (given understanding) with the light of life. 31. "Give ear (listen), Job, listen to me; hold your peace (be silent), and I will speak. 32. If you have anything to say, answer me; speak, for I desire to justify (make right) you. 33. If not, listen to me; hold your peace (be silent), and I will teach you wisdom (understanding)."

Chapter 34

1. Elihu continued and said: 2. "Hear my words, you wise men; listen to me, you who have knowledge (understanding). 3. For the ear tests words as the palate (taste buds) tastes food. 4. Let us choose justice for ourselves; let us understand what is good among us. 5. "For Job has said, 'I am righteous, but God has taken away my justice (fairness); 6. Should I lie about my rights? My wound (injury) is incurable (not healable), though I am without transgression (sin). 7. What man is like Job, who drinks scorn (contempt) like water, 8. Who associates (goes in company) with the workers of iniquity (wickedness), and walks with evil men? 9. For he has said, 'It profits (benefits) a man nothing that he should delight (rejoice) in God.' 10. "Therefore, listen to me, you men of understanding (wisdom): Far be it from God to do wickedness, and from the Almighty to commit iniquity. 11. For He repays man according to his work, and makes man find a reward (payback) according to his way. 12. Surely God will never do wickedly, nor will the Almighty pervert (twist) justice. 13. Who gave Him charge (authority) over the earth? Or who appointed Him over the whole world? 14. If He should set His heart on it, if He should gather to Himself His Spirit (breath) and His breath (life force), 15. All flesh would perish (die) together, and man would return to dust. 16. "If you have understanding (wisdom), hear this; listen to the sound of my words: 17. Should one who hates justice govern (rule)? Will you condemn (accuse) Him who is most just (righteous)? 18. Is it fitting (proper) to say to a king, 'You are worthless (good-for-nothing),' and to nobles (important leaders), 'You are wicked'? 19. Yet He is not partial (biased) to princes, nor does He regard (favor) the rich more than the poor; for they are all the work of His hands. 20. In a moment (instant) they die, in the middle of the night; the people are shaken (stirred) and pass away; the mighty (strong) are taken away without a hand (by no human effort). 21. "For His eyes are on the ways of man, and He sees all his steps. 22. There is neither darkness nor shadow of death (death's dark veil) where the workers of iniquity (wicked men) may hide themselves. 23. For He does not need to consider (think about) a man any longer before He brings him to judgment. 24. He breaks (destroys) mighty men without inquiry (investigation), and sets others in their place. 25. Therefore He knows their works; He overthrows (topples) them in the night, and they are crushed. 26. He strikes them as wicked men in the open sight of others, 27. because they turned back (rebelled) from Him, and would not consider any of His ways, 28. so that they caused the cry (plea) of the poor to come to Him; for He hears the cry of the afflicted (suffering). 29. When He gives quietness (peace), who can then make trouble? And when He hides His face (turns away), who then can see Him, whether it is against a nation or a man alone? — 30. that the hypocrite (deceiver) should not reign, lest the people be ensnared (trapped). 31. "For has anyone said to God, 'I have borne chastening (discipline); I will offend (sin) no more; 32. Teach me what I do not see; if I have done iniquity (sin), I will do no more'? 33. Should He repay (punish) it according to your terms, just because you disavow (reject) it? You must choose, and not I; therefore, speak what you know. 34. "Men of understanding (wisdom), say to me, wise men who listen to me: 35. 'Job speaks without knowledge (understanding); his words are without wisdom (insight).' 36. Oh, that Job were tested (examined) to the utmost, because his answers are like those of wicked men! 37. For he adds rebellion (defiance) to his sin; he claps his hands (shows contempt) among us and multiplies his words against God."

Chapter 35

1. Moreover, Elihu answered and said: 2. "Do you think this is right? Do you say, 'My righteousness (moral right) is more than God's'? 3. For you say, 'What advantage (benefit) will it be to You? What profit (gain) shall I have, more than if I had sinned?' 4. "I will answer you, and your companions (friends) with you. 5. Look to the heavens and see; and behold the clouds—they are higher than you. 6. If you sin, what do you accomplish (achieve) against Him? Or, if your transgressions (sins) are multiplied, what do you do to Him? 7. If you are righteous, what do you give Him? Or what does He receive from your hand? 8. Your wickedness (evil) affects (hurts) a man such as you, and your righteousness affects a son of man. 9. "Because of the multitude (great number) of oppressions (sufferings), they cry out; they cry out for help because of the arm (strength) of the mighty. 10. But no one says, 'Where is God my Maker, who gives songs in the night, 11. Who teaches us more than the beasts of the earth and makes us wiser than the birds of heaven?' 12. There they cry out, but He does not answer, because of the pride (arrogance) of evil men. 13. Surely God will not listen to empty talk (vain words), nor will the Almighty regard (pay attention to) it. 14. Although you say you do not see Him, yet justice (fairness) is before Him, and you must wait for Him. 15. And now, because He has not punished (acted in anger) in His anger, nor taken much notice (paid attention) to folly (foolishness), 16. Therefore, Job opens his mouth in vain; he multiplies words without knowledge (understanding)."

Chapter 36

1. Elihu continued speaking: 2. "Listen to me for a moment, and I will speak on behalf of God. There are still important things to say about Him. 3. I will draw from deep wisdom and declare the righteousness (rightness) of my Maker. 4. My words are true, for the one with perfect knowledge (understanding) is with you. 5. God is mighty (powerful) and does not disregard anyone; His strength is in His understanding (wisdom). 6. He does not protect the wicked (evil people) but brings justice (fairness) to the oppressed (those treated unfairly). 7. His eyes are always on the righteous (those doing right), and they are honored, even sitting on thrones with kings, exalted (lifted up) forever. 8. If the righteous are bound (tied up) in suffering, 9. God will show them their actions and their defiance (rebellion). 10. He will open their ears (make them listen) to instruction (teaching), calling them to turn from their wrongdoing. 11. If they listen and serve Him, they will live prosperous (successful) lives, full of joy (pleasure). 12. But if they do not obey, they will die in ignorance (lack of knowledge), struck down by the sword. 13. Those who are hypocrites (false people) store up anger, but do not cry out (call for help) when God punishes them. 14. They may die young, their lives ending in disgrace (shame). 15. God rescues the poor (needy) from their suffering and opens their ears when they are oppressed. 16. God would have delivered you from your troubles and brought you into a place of freedom (wide, open space), with abundant (plentiful) blessings. 17. But instead, you face the judgment (punishment) meant for the wicked, and justice (fairness) is upon you. 18. Beware (watch out) of God's wrath (anger), for one blow (strike) could take you away, and no ransom (payment) could save you. 19.

Can your wealth (money) or power (strength) protect you from distress (trouble)? **20.** Do not long for (wish for) the night, when people die in their place (die where they are). **21.** Be careful (watch out), do not turn to sin (wrongdoing), for you have chosen it over suffering. **22.** "Look, God is exalted (lifted up) by His power; who can teach (instruct) like Him? **23.** Who has directed (guided) His actions or told Him He was wrong? **24.** Remember to honor (praise) His works, which people praise. **25.** Everyone has seen them, and all mankind marvels (wonders) from afar (a distance). **26.** God is great, beyond our understanding (knowledge), and His years (time) are unsearchable (cannot be understood). **27.** He causes the drops of water (rain) to rise, which turn into rain, **28.** And the clouds pour it down abundantly (in great amount) on the earth. **29.** Can anyone understand the spread (movement) of clouds or the thunder from His canopy (sky)? **30.** He scatters (spreads) His light upon the clouds and covers the depths of the sea. **31.** Through these wonders (miracles), He judges (decides) the nations and provides abundance (plenty) to all. **32.** He wraps (covers) His hands in lightning and commands it to strike. **33.** His thunder speaks, and even the cattle (animals) are aware (know) of the storm."

Chapter 37

1. "At this, my heart trembles (shakes), and leaps from its place (is filled with fear). **2.** Listen closely to the thunder of His voice, and the rumbling that comes from His mouth. **3.** He sends it (thunder) across the entire sky, His lightning to the farthest reaches of the earth. **4.** After the lightning, a voice roars; He thunders with His majestic (powerful) voice, and He does not hold back when His voice is heard. **5.** God thunders wonderfully with His voice; He does great things which we cannot fully understand (comprehend). **6.** He commands the snow, "Fall on the earth," and also the gentle rain and the heavy rain by His power. **7.** He seals the work (actions) of every man, so that all people may know His power. **8.** The animals go into their dens and remain in their lairs (homes). **9.** From the chamber (place) of the south comes the whirlwind (storm), and cold from the winds scattered by the north. **10.** By the breath of God, ice is formed, and the vast waters are frozen. **11.** He fills the thick clouds with moisture and scatters His bright clouds. **12.** They swirl about, guided by His direction, to do whatever He commands them on the surface of the earth. **13.** He brings it (the storm), whether for correction, for His land, or for mercy (grace). **14.** "Listen to this, Job; stand still and consider the wondrous (amazing) works of God. **15.** Do you know when God sends them (storms), and makes the light of His cloud shine? **16.** Do you understand how the clouds are balanced, those amazing works of Him who is perfect in knowledge? **17.** Why are your clothes hot (warm), when He calms the earth with the south wind? **18.** With Him, have you spread out the skies, as strong as a cast metal mirror (firm and unshakable)? **19.** "Teach us what to say to Him, for we cannot prepare (think of) anything because of the darkness (mystery surrounding God's ways). **20.** Should we tell Him that I wish to speak? If a man were to speak, surely, he would be overwhelmed (swallowed up) by His greatness. **21.** Even now, men cannot look at the light when it is bright in the sky, when the wind has passed and cleared it. **22.** He comes from the north, shining with golden splendor; with God is awesome (majestic) majesty. **23.** As for the Almighty (God), we cannot find Him; He is excellent (great) in power, in judgment (righteous decisions), and abundant (full) in justice; He does not oppress (treat unfairly). **24.** Therefore, men fear (respect) Him; He shows no partiality (favoritism) to any who are wise (proud) in heart."

Chapter 38

1. Then the Lord answered Job from the whirlwind (a powerful storm) and said: **2.** "Who is this who darkens counsel (wisdom) with words without knowledge? **3.** Prepare yourself like a man; I will question you, and you shall answer Me. **4.** Where were you when I laid the foundations (the starting point or base) of the earth? Tell Me, if you understand. **5.** Who determined its measurements? Surely you know! Who stretched the line upon it? **6.** What were its foundations fastened to, or who laid its cornerstone (the starting point of a building), **7.** when the morning stars (celestial bodies, likely angels) sang together, and all the sons of God (angels) shouted for joy? **8.** Who shut the sea with doors when it burst forth from the womb (its origins), **9.** when I made clouds its garment and thick darkness its swaddling band (protective covering); **10.** when I set limits for it, and bars and doors? **11.** I said,

"This far you may come, but no farther, and here your proud waves must stop!" **12.** Have you commanded the morning since your days began, **13.** and caused the dawn to know its place, **14.** that it might shake the wicked from the earth? **15.** The earth takes form like clay under a seal (pressed like clay to form something); **16.** have you ever explored the springs (sources) of the sea or walked in its depths? **17.** Have the gates of death been revealed to you? Or have you seen the doors of the shadow of death? **18.** Have you comprehended the breadth (extent) of the earth? Tell Me, if you know all this. **19.** Where is the way to the dwelling of light (the place where light comes from)? And where does darkness reside? **20.** Do you know it because you were born then, or because of your many days (life span)? **21.** Have you entered the storehouses (storage places) of snow, or seen the storehouses of hail, **22.** which I have reserved for the day of trouble (calamity), for the time of battle and war? **23.** By what way is light diffused (spread), or the east wind scattered (blown away) over the earth? **24.** Who has divided a channel for the overflowing water (floods), or a path for the thunderbolt (lightning), **25.** to cause rain to fall on a land where no one lives, **26.** to satisfy the desolate (empty) waste and cause the growth of tender grass? **27.** Does the rain have a father, or who has begotten (created) the drops of dew? **28.** From whose womb comes the ice? And the frost (frozen water) of heaven, who gives it birth? **29.** The waters freeze like stone, and the surface of the deep sea is frozen. **30.** Can you bind the cluster of the Pleiades (a star cluster), or loose the belt of Orion (a constellation)? **31.** Can you bring out Mazzaroth (a constellation) in its season, or guide the Great Bear (a constellation) with its cubs? **32.** Do you know the ordinances (laws) of the heavens? Can you set their dominion (rule) over the earth? **33.** Can you lift your voice to the clouds, that an abundance of water may cover you? **34.** Can you send out lightning, that they may go and say to you, "Here we are"? **35.** Who has put wisdom in the mind, or who has given understanding to the heart? **36.** Who can number the clouds by wisdom? Or who can pour out the bottles of heaven (the rain), **37.** when the dust hardens into clumps (clay) and the clods cling together (stick)? **38.** Can you hunt the prey for the lion, or satisfy the appetite of the young lions, **39.** when they crouch in their dens, or lurk in their lairs (hiding places)? **40.** Who provides food for the raven, when its young ones cry to God and wander for lack of food? **41.** Do you know when the wild goats give birth (calve)? Or can you observe when the deer calve?

Chapter 39

1. Do you know when the wild mountain goats (wild goats) give birth or when the deer bears its young? **2.** Can you count the months of their pregnancy or know the time when they bear their young? **3.** They bow down, give birth, and deliver their young. **4.** Their young grow strong on grain (food), and they leave without returning. **5.** Who set the wild donkey (onager, a type of wild donkey) free? Who lost its bonds (freed it)? **6.** I made the wilderness its home and the barren land its dwelling. **7.** It ignores the noise of the city and the driver's (someone who controls the animals) shouts. **8.** The mountains are its pasture, and it seeks out every green thing. **9.** Will the wild ox (a large wild animal) serve you? Will it rest by your manger (feeding trough)? **10.** Can you bind the wild ox to plow (pull a plow) your fields? **11.** Will you trust its great strength or leave your labor (work) to it? **12.** Will you trust it to bring home your grain and gather it to your threshing floor (place where grain is separated from husks)? **13.** The wings of the ostrich (a large, flightless bird) wave proudly, but are her wings like the kindly stork's (a bird known for caring for its young)? **14.** She leaves her eggs on the ground and warms them in the dust. **15.** She forgets that they may be crushed (broken) or eaten by a wild beast. **16.** She treats her young harshly, as if they were not hers; her labor (effort) is in vain (useless), without concern. **17.** Because God deprived (took away) her of wisdom and did not give her understanding. **18.** When she lifts herself on high, she scorns (looks down on) the horse and rider. **19.** Have you given the horse strength? Have you clothed its neck with thunder (powerful sound)? **20.** Can you make it fear like a locust (a grasshopper-like insect that swarms and causes destruction)? Its snorting strikes terror. **21.** It paws (stamps) in the valley, rejoices in its strength, and charges into battle. **22.** It mocks (does not fear) fear and does not turn back from the sword. **23.** The quiver (container for arrows) rattles against it, and the glittering (shiny) spear and javelin

277

(throwing spear) shake. **24.** It devours (consumes) the distance with fierceness and rage and does not halt (stop) because the trumpet has sounded. **25.** At the trumpet's blast, it cries, "Aha!" and smells (detects) the battle from afar (far away), the noise of captains and shouting. **26.** Does the hawk (a bird of prey) fly by your wisdom, and spread its wings toward the south? **27.** Does the eagle (a bird of prey) soar at your command and make its nest on high? **28.** It dwells on the rocks and the crag (a steep rock) of the stronghold (fortified place). **29.** From there, it spies out (watches) its prey and observes (watches carefully) from afar. **30.** Its young feed on blood, and where the slain (dead bodies) are, there it is.

Chapter 40

1. Then the Lord answered Job and said: **2.** "Can anyone who argues with the Almighty (God) correct Him? If you contend with God, give your answer." **3.** Job responded: **4.** "I am unworthy; what can I answer You? I will keep silent. **5.** I've spoken once, but I won't answer again; I'll say no more." **6.** The Lord answered from the whirlwind (a powerful storm): **7.** "Prepare yourself like a man; I will question you, and you will answer Me. **8.** Will you change My judgment (decision)? Will you condemn Me to justify yourself? **9.** Do you have an arm (strength) like God's? Can you thunder (make a loud, powerful sound) with a voice like His? **10.** Adorn (clothe) yourself with majesty and splendor (glory); clothe yourself with glory and beauty. **11.** Disperse (scatter) your anger; look at the proud and humble (bring low) them. **12.** Look at the proud and bring them low; trample the wicked where they stand. **13.** Hide them in the dust; bind (cover) their faces in darkness. **14.** Then I will acknowledge (admit) that your own right hand (power) can save you." **15.** "Look at the behemoth (a large, powerful animal, possibly a hippopotamus or elephant), which I made along with you; it eats grass like an ox. **16.** Its strength is in its hips (upper legs), and its power is in its stomach muscles. **17.** It moves its tail like a cedar (a strong tree); its sinews (tendons) are tightly bound. **18.** Its bones are like beams (large supports) of bronze, its ribs like iron bars. **19.** It is the first of God's works (most powerful of God's creatures); only He who made it can approach it with a sword (weapon). **20.** The mountains provide food for it, and all the wild animals play there. **21.** It lies under the lotus trees, in the shelter of reeds (tall plants) and marshes (wetlands). **22.** The lotus trees cover it with shade; the willows (a type of tree) by the brook (stream) surround it. **23.** Even when the river rages (storms), it is not disturbed; it is confident, though the Jordan (river) rushes into its mouth. **24.** Though it takes the river in its eyes, or a trap (snare) pierces its nose."

Chapter 41

1. "Can you draw out Leviathan (a large sea creature, often symbolizing chaos) with a hook, or catch his tongue with a line? **2.** Can you pierce his nose with a reed (a type of plant) or his jaw with a hook? **3.** Will he beg you for mercy or speak softly to you? **4.** Will he make a covenant (a formal agreement) with you, or serve you forever? **5.** Will you treat him like a pet bird or put him on a leash (to tie or control) for your servants? **6.** Will your friends feast on him or sell him to merchants (traders)? **7.** Can you fill his skin with harpoons (sharp, spear-like weapons), or pierce his head with spears? **8.** Lay your hand on him and remember the battle—you won't do it again! **9.** Hope of defeating him is false; will you not be terrified when you see him? **10.** No one dares stir him up. Who can stand against Me? **11.** Who has preceded Me (gone before Me) that I should pay him? Everything under heaven is Mine. **12.** "I will not hide his limbs, strength, or beauty. **13.** Who can remove his outer coat (protective layer) or approach him with a bridle (a tool used to control animals)? **14.** Who can open his face (mouth) with his terrible teeth? **15.** His scales (protective, hard outer covering) are tightly sealed, proud and impenetrable (unable to be penetrated). **16.** Each scale is so close that no air can pass between them. **17.** They stick together and cannot be parted. **18.** His sneezes flash light, and his eyes shine like dawn. **19.** Fire comes from his mouth; sparks shoot out. **20.** Smoke pours from his nostrils (nose) like from a boiling pot. **21.** His breath ignites coals (sets them on fire), and flames shoot from his mouth. **22.** Strength is in his neck, and grief (sorrow) dances before him. **23.** His flesh is tightly joined and cannot be moved. **24.** His heart (the core of his being) is as hard as stone, even harder than a millstone (a large, heavy stone used for grinding). **25.** When he rises, the mighty (strong) are afraid; they lose control at his roar (loud sound). **26.** The sword cannot harm him; nor spear, dart (a small pointed missile), or javelin (a spear-like weapon). **27.** He treats iron like straw (dry, brittle plant material) and bronze like rotten wood. **28.** Arrows don't make him flee; slingstones (stones thrown with a sling) are like chaff (the outer shell of grain) to him. **29.** Darts (small missiles) are like straw to him; he laughs at the threat of javelins. **30.** His underside is like sharp pottery (broken pieces of ceramic), leaving jagged marks in the mud. **31.** He makes the ocean boil like a pot and the sea like ointment (a smooth, oily substance). **32.** He leaves a shining wake (trail) behind him, making the sea look like it has white hair. **33.** Nothing on earth compares to him; he is fearless. **34.** He sees all that is high; he is king over all the children (descendants) of pride."

Chapter 42

1. Then Job answered the Lord and said: **2.** "I know that You can do everything, and no purpose of Yours can be stopped. **3.** You asked, 'Who is this that speaks without understanding?' I spoke about things I didn't understand, too wonderful for me to know. **4.** Please listen, and I will speak; You said, 'I will question you, and you will answer.' **5.** I had only heard about You, but now my eyes see You. **6.** Therefore, I despise myself (feel deep regret) and repent (feel sorrow and ask for forgiveness) in dust and ashes (symbol of humility and mourning). **7.** After the Lord spoke to Job, He said to Eliphaz the Temanite (from Teman, a region in Edom): **8.** "I am angry with you and your two friends, because you did not speak rightly about Me, as Job has. **9.** Take seven bulls (male cattle) and seven rams (male sheep), go to My Servant Job, and offer a burnt offering (complete sacrifice by fire). Job will pray for you, and I will accept him, or I will punish you for your foolishness (lack of wisdom)." **10.** Eliphaz, Bildad, and Zophar did as the Lord commanded. The Lord accepted Job's prayer. **11.** The Lord restored Job's fortunes (wealth, possessions) after he prayed for his friends, giving him twice as much as he had before. **12.** All his brothers, sisters, and former friends came to him. They ate with him, comforted him, and gave him silver and gold rings. **13.** The Lord blessed Job's later life more than his beginning, with 14,000 sheep, 6,000 camels, 1,000 oxen (large cattle used for farming), and 1,000 female donkeys. **14.** Job also had seven sons and three daughters. **15.** His daughters were the most beautiful in the land, and their father gave them an inheritance (property or wealth passed down from parents) among their brothers. **16.** Job lived 140 more years and saw his children, grandchildren, and great-grandchildren. **17.** Job died old and full of days (having lived a long and full life).

24 – Psalms

Chapter 1

1. Blessed is the one who does not walk in step with the wicked (those who do wrong) or stand in the way that sinners take (those who choose to live in sin) or sit in the company of mockers (those who make fun of others). **2.** Instead, their joy is in following the teachings of the LORD, and they think about His word day and night. **3.** That person is like a tree planted beside streams of water, which produces its fruit at the right time, and whose leaves remain healthy— whatever they do prospers. **4.** But the wicked are not like that; they are like the chaff (the useless husks left after grain is separated) that the wind blows away. **5.** Therefore, the wicked will not be able to stand in the judgment, nor will sinners be included among the righteous. **6.** For the LORD watches over the path of the righteous, but the path of the wicked leads to destruction.

Chapter 2

1. Why do the nations conspire (plot together) and the peoples plot in vain (for no purpose)? **2.** The kings of the earth rise up, and the rulers band together against the LORD and against His anointed, saying, **3.** "Let us break their chains (cut off their control) and throw off their shackles (cast off their authority)." **4.** The One enthroned in heaven (God) laughs; the Lord scoffs (ridicules) at them. **5.** He rebukes (corrects) them in His anger and terrifies them in His wrath (fury), saying, **6.** "I have installed my king on Zion (Jerusalem), my holy mountain." **7.** I will proclaim the LORD's decree: He said to me, "You are my Son; today I have become your Father." **8.** Ask me, and I will make the nations your inheritance (your people), the ends of the earth your possession. **9.** You will break them with a rod of iron (strong authority); you will dash them to pieces like pottery (destroy them completely). **10.** Therefore, you kings, be wise (learn the truth); be warned, you rulers of the earth. **11.** Serve the LORD with fear (respect) and celebrate His rule with trembling (awe). **12.** Kiss His Son (show loyalty), or He will be angry and your way will lead to destruction (ruin), for His wrath can flare up in a moment. Blessed (happy) are all who take refuge in Him.

Chapter 3

1. LORD, how many are my foes (enemies)! How many rises up against me! **2.** Many are saying of me, "God will not deliver (rescue) him." **3.** But You, LORD, are a shield (protector) around me, my glory (source of honor), the One who lifts my head high (raises my spirits). **4.** I call out to the LORD, and He answers me from His holy mountain (Zion, Jerusalem). **5.** I lie down and sleep; I wake again because the LORD sustains (keeps me alive) me. **6.** I will not fear (be afraid) though tens of thousands assail (attack) me on every side. **7.** Arise (stand up), LORD! Deliver (rescue) me, my God! Strike all my enemies on the jaw (face); break the teeth of the wicked (evil people). **8.** From the LORD comes deliverance (salvation). May Your blessing be on Your people.

Chapter 4

1. Answer me when I call to You, my righteous God. Give me relief (relaxation) from my distress (trouble); have mercy on me and hear my prayer. **2.** How long will you people turn my glory (honor) into shame? How long will you love delusions (false ideas) and seek false gods (idols)? **3.** Know that the LORD has set apart (chosen) His faithful servant for Himself; the LORD hears when I call to Him. **4.** Tremble (be afraid) and do not sin; when you are on your beds, search your hearts and be silent (reflect quietly). **5.** Offer the sacrifices (acts of worship) of the righteous and trust in the LORD. **6.** Many, LORD, are asking, "Who will bring us prosperity (good fortune)?" Let the light of your face shine on us. **7.** Fill my heart with joy when their grain (crops) and new wine (freshly pressed wine) abound (increase). **8.** In peace I will lie down and sleep, for You alone, LORD, make me dwell in safety (security).

Chapter 5

1. Listen to my words, LORD, considers my lament (complaint). **2.** Hear my cry for help, my King and my God, for to You I pray. **3.** In the morning, LORD, You hear my voice; in the morning I lay my requests before You and wait expectantly (eagerly). **4.** For You are not a God who is pleased with wickedness (evil); with You, evil people are not welcome. **5.** The arrogant (proud) cannot stand in Your presence. You hate all who do wrong; **6.** You destroy those who tell lies. The bloodthirsty (violent) and deceitful (dishonest) You, LORD, detest (hate). **7.** But I, by Your great love, can come into Your house; in reverence (respect) I bow down toward Your holy temple (place of worship). **8.** Lead me, LORD, in Your righteousness (the right way) because of my enemies— make Your way straight before me. **9.** Not a word from their mouth can be trusted; their heart is filled with malice (evil intent). Their throat is an open grave (they are deceitful); with their tongues, they tell lies. **10.** Declare them guilty, O God! Let their intrigues (plots) be their downfall. Banish (remove) them for their many sins, for they have rebelled (rejected) against You. **11.** But let all who take refuge (find safety) in You be glad; let them ever sing for joy. Spread Your protection over them, that those who love Your name may rejoice in You. **12.** Surely, LORD, You bless the righteous (those who live right); You surround them with Your favor as with a shield.

Chapter 6

1. LORD, do not rebuke (correct) me in Your anger or discipline (punish) me in Your wrath (fury). **2.** Have mercy (kindness) on me, LORD, for I am faint (weak); heal me, LORD, for my bones are in agony (pain). **3.** My soul is in deep anguish (great distress). How long, LORD, how long? **4.** Turn, LORD, and deliver (rescue) me; save me because of Your unfailing love (constant love). **5.** Among the dead, no one proclaims Your name. Who praises You from the grave (the place of death)? **6.** I am worn out from my groaning (sighing). All night long I flood my bed with weeping (tears) and drench (soak) my couch with tears. **7.** My eyes grow weak with sorrow (grief); they fail because of all my foes (enemies). **8.** Away from me, all you who do evil (wrong), for the LORD has heard my weeping. **9.** The LORD has heard my cry for mercy (compassion); the LORD accepts (receives) my prayer. **10.** All my enemies will be overwhelmed (shamed) with shame and anguish (great sorrow) they will turn back and suddenly be put to shame.

Chapter 7

1. LORD my God, I take refuge (shelter) in you; save and deliver (rescue) me from all who pursue (chase) me, **2.** or they will tear me apart like a lion and rip me to pieces with no one to rescue me. **3.** LORD my God, if I have done this and there is guilt on my hands, **4.** if I have repaid (paid back) my ally (friend) with evil or without cause have robbed my foe (enemy), **5.** Then let my enemy pursue and overtake me; let him trample (crush) my life to the ground and make me sleep in the dust (die). **6.** Arise (stand up), LORD, in Your anger; rise up against the rage (anger) of my enemies. Awake, my God; decree (declare) justice. **7.** Let the assembled peoples (nations) gather around you, while You sit enthroned (ruling) over them on high. **8.** Let the LORD judge (rule over) the peoples. Vindicate (defend) me, LORD, according to my righteousness (rightness), according to my integrity (honesty), O Most High. **9.** Bring to an end the violence (harm) of the wicked and make the righteous secure— You, the righteous God who probes (examines) minds and hearts. **10.** My shield (protector) is God Most High, who saves the upright (just) in heart. **11.** God is a righteous judge, a God who displays His wrath (anger) every day. **12.** If He does not relent (change His mind), He will sharpen His sword (prepare for battle); He will bend and string His bow (get ready for war). **13.** He has prepared His deadly weapons; He makes ready His flaming arrows (burning judgment). **14.** Whoever is pregnant (filled) with evil conceives trouble and gives birth to disillusionment (false hope). **15.** Whoever digs a hole and scoops it out falls into the pit they have made (their own trap). **16.** The trouble they cause recoils (bounces back) on them; their violence (wrongdoing) comes down on their own heads. **17.** I will give thanks to the LORD because of His righteousness; I will sing the praises of the name of the LORD Most High.

Chapter 8

1. LORD, our Lord, how majestic (great and honorable) is Your name in all the earth! You have set Your glory (greatness) in the heavens. **2.** Through the praise of children and infants, You have established (built) a stronghold (place of defense) against Your enemies, to silence (stop) the foe (enemy) and the avenger (one seeking revenge). **3.** When I consider (look at) Your heavens, the work of Your fingers (creation), the moon and the stars, which You have set in place, **4.** what is mankind (human beings) that You are mindful (think of) of them, human beings that You care for them? **5.** You have made them a little lower than the angels (celestial beings) and crowned (honored) them with glory and honor. **6.** You made them rulers (in charge) over the works of Your hands (creation); You put everything under their feet: **7.** all flocks (sheep) and herds (cattle), and the animals of the wild (wild beasts), **8.** the birds in the sky, and the fish in the sea, all that swim the paths (ways) of the seas. **9.** LORD, our Lord, how majestic is Your name in all the earth!

Chapter 9

1. I will give thanks to You, LORD, with all my heart; I will tell of Your wonderful deeds. **2.** I will be glad and rejoice in You; I will sing the praises of Your name, O Most High. **3.** My enemies turn back; they stumble and perish (fall) before You. **4.** For You have upheld (defended) my right and cause, sitting as the righteous judge (fair ruler). **5.** You have rebuked (corrected) the nations and destroyed the wicked; You have wiped out their name forever. **6.** Endless ruin (destruction) has overtaken my enemies; You have uprooted (destroyed) their cities; their memory has perished (vanished). **7.** The LORD reigns (rules) forever; He has established His throne (seat of authority) for judgment (to rule justly). **8.** He rules the world in righteousness (fairness) and judges the peoples with equity (justice). **9.** The LORD is a refuge (safe place) for the oppressed (mistreated), a stronghold (place of safety) in times of trouble. **10.** Those who know Your name (relationship with You) trust in You, for You, LORD, have never forsaken (abandoned) those who seek You. **11.** Sing the praises of the LORD, enthroned in Zion (Jerusalem); proclaim among the nations what He has done. **12.** For He who avenges blood (punishes murder) remembers; He does not ignore the cries of the afflicted (suffering). **13.** LORD, see how my enemies persecute (harass) me! Have mercy (kindness) and lift me up from the gates of death, **14.** that I may declare (announce) Your praises in the gates of Daughter Zion (Jerusalem), and there rejoice in Your salvation. **15.** The nations have fallen into the pit they dug (their own traps); their feet are caught in the net (trap) they hid. **16.** The LORD is known by His justice (fair judgment); the wicked are caught by the work of their hands. **17.** The wicked go down to the realm (place) of the dead, all the nations that forget God. **18.** But God will never forget the needy (poor); the hope of the afflicted (oppressed) will never perish (end). **19.** Arise (stand up), LORD, do not let mortals (humans) triumph (win); let the nations be judged in Your presence. **20.** Strike them with terror (fear), LORD; let the nations know they are only mortal (weak and limited).

Chapter 10

1. Why, LORD, do You stand far off? Why do you hide Yourself in times of trouble? **2.** In his arrogance (pride), the wicked man hunts down the weak, who are caught in the schemes (plans) he devises. **3.** He boasts about the cravings (desires) of his heart; he blesses the greedy and reviles (speaks against) the LORD. **4.** In his pride, the wicked man does not seek (search for) God; in all his thoughts, there is no room for God. **5.** His ways are always prosperous (successful); Your laws are rejected by him; he sneers (laughs mockingly) at all his enemies. **6.** He says to himself, "Nothing will ever shake me (bring me down)." He swears, "No one will ever do me harm." **7.** His mouth is full of lies and threats; trouble and evil are under his tongue (he speaks with deceit). **8.** He lies in wait near the villages; from ambush (hidden) he murders the innocent. His eyes watch in secret for his victims; **9.** like a lion in cover (hiding), he lies in wait. He lies in wait to catch the helpless (weak); he catches them and drags them off in his net. **10.** His victims are crushed (destroyed), they collapse; they fall under his strength. **11.** He says to himself, "God will never notice (see); He covers His face and never sees." **12.** Arise, LORD! Lift up Your hand, O God. Do not forget the helpless (poor and weak). **13.** Why does the wicked man revile God? Why does he say to himself, "He won't call me to account"? **14.** But You, God, see the trouble of the afflicted (suffering); You consider their grief and take it in hand (You take care of them). The victims commit themselves to You; You are the helper of the fatherless (orphans). **15.** Break the arm (strength) of the wicked man; call the evildoer to account for his wickedness that would not otherwise be found out. **16.** The LORD is King forever and ever; the nations will perish (be destroyed) from His land. **17.** You, LORD, hear the desire of the afflicted (oppressed); You encourage them, and You listen to their cry, **18.** defending the fatherless and the oppressed, so that mere earthly mortals (human beings) will never again strike terror (cause fear).

Chapter 11

1. In the LORD I take refuge (shelter). How then can you say to me: "Flee like a bird to your mountain (place of safety)"? **2.** For look, the wicked bend their bows (prepare to attack); they set their arrows against the strings to shoot from the shadows at the upright in heart (righteous). **3.** When the foundations (basic principles) are being destroyed, what can the righteous do? **4.** The LORD is in His holy temple (sacred place); the LORD is on His heavenly throne (seat of authority). He observes (watches) everyone on earth; His eyes examine (look closely at) them. **5.** The LORD examines the righteous (just people), but the wicked, those who love violence, He hates with a passion (strong hatred). **6.** On the wicked, He will rain fiery coals and burning sulfur (brimstone); a scorching wind (fierce heat) will be their lot (reward). **7.** For the LORD is righteous (fair and just), He loves justice; the upright (just people) will see His face.

Chapter 12

1. Help, LORD, for no one is faithful anymore; those who are loyal have vanished from the human race. **2.** Everyone lies to their neighbor; they flatter (praise insincerely) with their lips but harbor deception (falsehood) in their hearts. **3.** May the LORD silence all flattering lips and every boastful tongue. **4.** Those who say, "By our tongues we will prevail (win); our own lips will defend us—who is lord over us?" **5.** "Because the poor are plundered (robbed) and the needy groan (suffer), I will now arise (stand up)," says the LORD. "I will protect them from those who malign (slander) them." **6.** And the words of the LORD are flawless (perfect), like silver purified in a crucible (melting pot), like gold refined (purified) seven times. **7.** You, LORD, will keep the needy safe and will protect us forever from the wicked, **8.** Who freely strut (walk proudly) about when what is vile (wicked) is honored by the human race.

Chapter 13

1. How long, LORD? Will You forget me forever? How long will You hide Your face from me? **2.** How long must I wrestle with my thoughts (struggle internally) and day after day have sorrow in my heart? How long will my enemy triumph (win) over me? **3.** Look on me and answer, LORD my God. Give light to my eyes (help me see clearly), or I will sleep in death, **4.** And my enemy will say, "I have overcome him," and my foes will rejoice when I fall. **5.** But I trust in Your unfailing love (steadfast love); my heart rejoices in Your salvation. **6.** I will sing the LORD's praise, for He has been good to me.

Chapter 14

1. The fool (ignorant person) says in his heart, "There is no God." They are corrupt (immoral), their deeds are vile (evil); there is no one who does well. **2.** The LORD looks down from heaven on all mankind to see if there are any who understand (wisdom), any who seek God. **3.** All have turned away, all have become corrupt; there is no one who does good, not even one. **4.** Do all these evildoers (wrongdoers) know nothing? They devour (consume) My people as though eating bread; they never call on the LORD. **5.** But there they are, overwhelmed (filled) with dread (fear), for God is present in the company of the righteous (those who are right with God). **6.** You evildoers frustrate (thwart) the plans of the poor, but the LORD is their refuge (safe place). **7.** Oh, that salvation (deliverance) for Israel would come out of Zion (Jerusalem)! When the LORD restores (brings back) His people, let Jacob (Israel) rejoice and Israel be glad!

Chapter 15

1. LORD, who may dwell (live) in Your sacred tent (temple)? Who may live on Your holy mountain (a place of purity and worship)? **2.** The one whose walk (life) is blameless (without guilt), who does what is righteous (just), who speaks the truth from their heart; **3.** whose tongue utters no slander (false accusations), who does no wrong to a neighbor, and casts no slur (insult) on others; **4.** who despises (rejects) a vile (wicked) person but honors (respects) those who fear the LORD; who keeps an oath (promise) even when it hurts, and does not change their mind; **5.** who lends money to the poor without interest (charitably); who does not accept a bribe (payment to act unjustly) against the innocent. Whoever does these things will never be shaken (will stand firm).

Chapter 16

1. Keep me safe, my God, for in You I take refuge (shelter). **2.** I say to the LORD, "You are my Lord (Master); apart from You I have no good thing." **3.** I say of the holy people (saints) who are in the land, "They are the noble ones (honorable) in whom is all my delight." **4.** Those who run after (chase after) other gods will suffer more and more. I will not pour out libations (drink offerings) of blood to such gods or take up their names on my lips. **5.** LORD, You alone are my portion (inheritance) and my cup (blessing); You make my lot secure (settled). **6.** The boundary lines (borders) have fallen for me in pleasant places; surely, I have a delightful inheritance. **7.** I will praise the LORD, who counsels (advises) me; even at night my heart instructs (teaches) me. **8.** I keep my eyes always on the LORD. With Him at my right hand, I will not be shaken (moved). **9.** Therefore my heart is glad and my tongue rejoices; my body also will rest secure (safe), **10.** because You will not abandon (forsake) me to the realm of the dead (Sheol, the grave), nor will You let Your faithful one sees decay (rot). **11.** You make known (reveal) to me the path of life; You will fill me with joy in Your presence, with eternal pleasures at Your right hand.

Chapter 17

1. Hear me, LORD, my plea is just; listen to my cry. Hear my prayer—it does not rise from deceitful lips (falsehood). **2.** Let my vindication (justification) come from You; may Your eyes see what is right. **3.** Though You probe (examine) my heart, though You test me at night and try me, You will find that I have planned no evil; my mouth has not transgressed (sinned). **4.** Though people tried to bribe me, I have kept myself from the ways of the violent (those who harm others) through what Your lips have commanded. **5.** My steps have held to Your paths; my feet have not stumbled (fallen). **6.** I call on You, my God, for You will answer me; turn Your ear to me and hear my prayer. **7.** Show me the wonders of Your great love, You who save by Your right hand those who take refuge in You from their foes (enemies). **8.** Keep me as the apple of Your eye (precious); hide me in the shadow of Your wings (protection) **9.** from the wicked who are out to destroy me, from my mortal enemies who surround me. **10.** They close up their callous (hard) hearts, and their mouths speak with arrogance (pride). **11.** They have tracked me down, they now surround me, with eyes alert (watching), to throw me to the ground. **12.** They are like a lion hungry for prey, like a fierce lion crouching in cover (waiting to pounce). **13.** Rise up, LORD, confront them, bring them down; with Your sword rescue me from the wicked. **14.** By Your hand save me from such people, LORD, from those of this world whose reward is in this life. May what You have stored up for the wicked fill their bellies; may their children gorge themselves on it, and may there be leftovers for their little ones. **15.** As for me, I will be vindicated (justified) and will see Your face; when I awake, I will be satisfied with seeing Your likeness (in heaven).

Chapter 18

1. I love You, LORD, my strength. **2.** The LORD is my rock (steadfast support), my fortress (stronghold) and my deliverer (rescuer); my God is my rock, in whom I take refuge (shelter), my shield and the horn (strength) of my salvation, my stronghold. **3.** I called to the LORD, who is worthy of praise, and I have been saved from my enemies. **4.** The cords (ropes) of death entangled me; the torrents (waves) of destruction overwhelmed me. **5.** The cords of the grave (Sheol, the realm of the dead) coiled around me; the snares of death confronted me. 6. In my distress, I called to the LORD; I cried to my God for help. From His temple He heard my voice; my cry came before Him, into His ears. **7.** The earth trembled and quaked, and the foundations of the mountains shook; they trembled because He was angry. 8. Smoke rose from His nostrils; consuming fire came from His mouth, burning coals blazed out of it. 9. He parted the heavens and came down; dark clouds were under His feet. 10. He mounted the cherubim (angelic beings) and flew; He soared on the wings of the wind. **11.** He made darkness His covering, His canopy (cover) around Him—the dark rain clouds of the sky. **12.** Out of the brightness of His presence, clouds advanced, with hailstones and bolts of lightning. **13.** The LORD thundered from heaven; the voice of the Most High resounded. 14. He shot His arrows and scattered the enemy; with great bolts of lightning, He routed (dispersed) them. **15.** The valleys of the sea were exposed and the foundations of the earth laid bare at Your rebuke, LORD, at the blast of breath from Your nostrils. 16. He reached down from on high and took hold of me; He drew me out of deep waters. 17. He rescued me from my powerful enemy, from my foes, who were too strong for me. 18. They confronted me in the day of my disaster, but the LORD was my support. **19.** He brought me out into a spacious place (place of freedom); He rescued me because He delighted in me. 20. The LORD has dealt with me according to my righteousness; according to the cleanness (purity) of my hands, He has rewarded me. 21. For I have kept the ways of the LORD; I am not guilty of turning from my God. 22. All His laws are before me; I have not turned away from His decrees (commands). 23. I have been blameless before Him and have kept myself from sin. 24. The LORD has rewarded me according to my righteousness, according to the cleanness of my hands in His sight. **25.** To the faithful, You show Yourself faithful; to the blameless, You show Yourself blameless, 26. to the pure, You show Yourself pure, but to the devious (dishonest), You show Yourself shrewd (wise). 27. You save the humble but bring low those whose eyes are haughty (proud). **28.** You, LORD, keep my lamp burning; my God turns my darkness into light. **29.** With Your help, I can advance against a troop (army); with my God, I can scale a wall. **30.** As for God, His way is perfect; the LORD's word is flawless; He shields all who take refuge in Him. **31.** For who is God besides the LORD? And who is the Rock except our God? 32. It is God who arms me with strength and keeps my way secure. **33.** He makes my feet like the feet of a deer; He causes me to stand on the heights. **34.** He trains my hands for battle; my arms can bend a bow of bronze. 35. You make Your saving help my shield, and Your right hand sustains me; Your help has made me great. 36. You provide a broad path for my feet, so that my ankles do not give way. 37. I pursued my enemies and overtook them; I did not turn back till they were destroyed. 38. I crushed them so that they could not rise; they fell beneath my feet. **39.** You armed me with strength for battle; You humbled my adversaries before me. 40. You made my enemies turn their backs in flight, and I destroyed my foes. **41.** They cried for help, but there was no one to save them—to the LORD, but He did not answer. **42.** I beat them as fine as windblown dust; I trampled them like mud in the streets. 43. You have delivered me from the attacks of the people; You have made

me the head of nations. People I did not know now serve me, **44.** foreigners (non-Israelites) cower before me; as soon as they hear of me, they obey me. **45.** They all lose heart; they come trembling from their strongholds (fortresses). 46. The LORD lives! Praise be to my Rock! Exalted be God my Savior! **47.** He is the God who avenges me, who subdues (brings down) nations under me, **48.** who saves me from my enemies. You exalted me above my foes; from a violent man, You rescued me. 49. Therefore, I will praise You, LORD, among the nations; I will sing the praises of Your name. **50.** He gives His king great victories; He shows unfailing love to His anointed (chosen king), to David and his descendants forever.

Chapter 19

1. The heavens declare the glory of God; the skies proclaim the work of His hands. **2.** Day after day they pour forth speech; night after night they reveal knowledge. **3.** They have no speech, they use no words; no sound is heard from them. **4.** Yet their voice goes out into all the earth, their words to the ends of the world. In the heavens, God has pitched a tent (dwelling place) for the sun. **5.** It is like a bridegroom (husband) coming out of his chamber (bridal room), like a champion rejoicing to run his course. **6.** It rises at one end of the heavens and makes its circuit (path) to the other; nothing is deprived of its warmth. **7.** The law (teachings) of the LORD is perfect, refreshing the soul. The statutes (commands) of the LORD are trustworthy, making wise the simple (naive). **8.** The precepts (rules) of the LORD are right, giving joy to the heart. The commands of the LORD are radiant, giving light to the eyes. **9.** The fear (reverence) of the LORD is pure, enduring forever. The decrees (ordinances) of the LORD are firm, and all of them are righteous. **10.** They are more precious than gold, than much pure gold; they are sweeter than honey, than honey from the honeycomb. **11.** By them, your servant is warned; in keeping them there is great reward. **12.** But who can discern (understand) their own errors? Forgive my hidden faults. **13.** Keep your servant also from willful sins; may they not rule over me. Then I will be blameless, innocent of great transgression (wrongdoing). **14.** May these words of my mouth and this meditation of my heart be pleasing in your sight, LORD, my Rock and my Redeemer.

Chapter 20

1. May the LORD answer you when you're in trouble; may the God of Jacob (the ancestor of Israel) protect you. **2.** May He send help from His holy place (the sanctuary) and give you support from Zion (the hill in Jerusalem where the temple stood). **3.** May He remember all the offerings you have made and accept your burnt sacrifices (a form of offering made by burning animals or grains). **4.** May He give you the desires of your heart and make all your plans succeed. **5.** May we celebrate your victory with joy and raise our banners in the name of our God. May the LORD fulfill all your requests. **6.** Now I know this for certain: The LORD grants victory to His chosen one (the king or leader He anoints). He answers him from His heavenly temple, with the mighty power of His right hand. **7.** Some trust in chariots (war vehicles) and others in horses, but we trust in the name of the LORD our God. **8.** They fall and collapse, but we rise up and stand firm. **9.** LORD, give victory to the king! Answer us when we call!

Chapter 21

1. The king rejoices in your strength, LORD. How great is his joy in the victories you give him! **2.** You have granted him the desires (wants) of his heart and have not denied (refused) the words of his mouth. **3.** You came to meet him with abundant (plentiful) blessings and placed a crown of pure gold on his head. **4.** He asked you for life, and you gave it to him—length of days (long life), forever and ever. **5.** Because of the victories you gave him, his glory (honor) is great; you have lavished (bestowed) upon him splendor (great beauty) and majesty (great dignity). **6.** Surely you have granted him endless blessings and made him rejoice (be happy) with the joy of your presence. **7.** For the king trusts (relies on) in the LORD; through the unfailing (never-ending) love of the Most High (God), he will not be shaken (he will stand firm). **8.** Your hand will seize (take control of) all your enemies; your right hand will capture (defeat) your foes (enemies). **9.** When you appear for battle, you will burn them up like a blazing furnace (very hot fire). The LORD will consume (destroy) them with His wrath (anger), and His fire will destroy them. **10.** You will wipe out (destroy) their descendants (children) from the earth, their offspring (future generations) from humanity. **11.** Though they plot (plan) evil against you and devise (make) wicked schemes (plans), they will not succeed. **12.** You will make them turn their backs (run away) when you aim at them with your bow (weapon) ready to strike. **13.** Be exalted (praised highly) in your strength, LORD; we will sing and praise your power.

Chapter 22

1. My God, my God, why have you forsaken (abandoned) me? Why are you so far from saving me, so far from my cries of anguish? **2.** My God, I cry out by day, but you do not answer; by night, but I find no rest. **3.** Yet you are enthroned (seated as king) as the Holy One; you are the one Israel praises. **4.** In you, our ancestors (forefathers) put their trust; they trusted, and you delivered (saved) them. **5.** To you, they cried out and were saved; in you, they trusted and were not put to shame (humiliated). **6.** But I am a worm (feeling low) and not a man, scorned (mocked) by everyone, despised by the people. **7.** All who see me mock me; they hurl (throw) insults, shaking their heads. **8.** "He trusts in the LORD," they say, "let the LORD rescue him. Let him deliver (save) him, since he delights (takes pleasure) in him." **9.** Yet you brought me out of the womb (birth); you made me trust in you, even at my mother's breast. **10.** From birth, I was cast (thrown) on you; from my mother's womb, you have been my God. **11.** Do not be far from me, for trouble is near, and there is no one to help. **12.** Many bulls (strong enemies) surround me; strong bulls of Bashan (a region known for its powerful cattle) encircle me. **13.** Roaring lions that tear their prey open their mouths wide against me. **14.** I am poured out like water, and all my bones are out of joint. My heart has turned to wax; it has melted within me. **15.** My mouth is dried up like a potsherd (broken pottery), and my tongue sticks to the roof of my mouth; you lay me in the dust of death. **16.** Dogs (wicked people) surround me, a pack of villains (criminals) encircles me; they pierce my hands and my feet. **17.** All my bones are on display (visible); people stare and gloat (take pleasure) over me. **18.** They divide my clothes among them and cast lots (gamble) for my garment. **19.** But you, LORD, do not be far from me. You are my strength; come quickly to help me. **20.** Deliver me from the sword, my precious life from the power of the dogs. **21.** Rescue me from the mouth of the lions; save me from the horns of the wild oxen (wild animals that attack). **22.** I will declare your name to my people; in the assembly (gathering) I will praise you. **23.** You who fear (revere) the LORD, praise him! All you descendants (children) of Jacob (the patriarch of Israel), honor him! Revere (respect) him, all you descendants of Israel! **24.** For he has not despised (hated) or scorned (rejected) the suffering of the afflicted one; he has not hidden his face from him but has listened to his cry for help. **25.** From you comes the theme (reason) of my praise in the great assembly; before those who fear you, I will fulfill my vows. **26.** The poor will eat and be satisfied; those who seek the LORD will praise him—may your hearts live forever! **27.** All the ends of the earth (everywhere) will remember and turn to the LORD, and all the families of the nations will bow down before him, **28.** for dominion (rule) belongs to the LORD and he rules over the nations. **29.** All the rich of the earth will feast and worship; all who go down to the dust (die) will kneel before him—those who cannot keep themselves alive. **30.** Posterity (future generations) will serve him; future generations will be told about the LORD. **31.** They will proclaim (announce) his righteousness (justice), declaring to a people yet unborn: He has done it!

Chapter 23

1. The LORD is my shepherd (protector), I lack nothing. **2.** He makes me lie down in green pastures (lush, peaceful fields); he leads me beside quiet waters (calm streams), **3.** he refreshes my soul (gives me rest). He guides me along the right paths for his name's sake (to honor himself). **4.** Even though I walk through the darkest valley (deepest shadow), I will fear no evil, for you are with me; your rod (staff for guiding) and your staff (tool for protection), they comfort me. **5.** You prepare a table before me in the presence of my enemies. You anoint (set apart for special use) my head with oil; my cup overflows. **6.** Surely your goodness and love will follow me all the days of my life, and I will dwell (live) in the house of the LORD forever.

Chapter 24

1. The earth is the LORD's, and everything in it, the world (the whole earth), and all who live in it; **2.** for he founded (created) it on the seas and established (set in place) it on the waters. **3.** Who may ascend (go up) the mountain of the LORD? Who may stand in his holy place (temple)? **4.** The one who has clean hands (pure actions) and a pure heart (right motives), who does not trust in an idol (false god) or swear by a false god (make false promises). **5.** They will receive blessing from the LORD and vindication (justice) from God their Savior. **6.** Such is the generation (group) of those who seek him, who seek your face, God of Jacob (ancestor of Israel). **7.** Lift up your heads, you gates (city gates); be lifted up, you ancient doors (old gates), that the King of glory may come in. **8.** Who is this King of glory? The LORD strong and mighty, the LORD mighty in battle. **9.** Lift up your heads, you gates; lift them up, you ancient doors, that the King of glory may come in. **10.** Who is he, this King of glory? The LORD Almighty (God of hosts) he is the King of glory.

Chapter 25

1. In you, LORD my God, I put my trust. **2.** I trust in you; do not let me be put to shame (humiliated), nor let my enemies triumph (overcome) over me. **3.** No one who hopes (waits expectantly) in you will ever be put to shame, but shame will come on those who are treacherous (deceptive) without cause. **4.** Show me your ways, LORD, teach me your paths (direction in life). **5.** Guide me in your truth (faithfulness) and teach me, for you are God my Savior, and my hope is in you all day long. **6.** Remember, LORD, your great mercy (compassion) and love, for they are from of old (from eternity). **7.** Do not remember the sins of my youth (early mistakes) and my rebellious (disobedient) ways; according to your love, remember me, for you, LORD, are good. **8.** Good and upright (just) is the LORD; therefore, he instructs (teaches) sinners in his ways. **9.** He guides (directs) the humble (those who are lowly) in what is right and teaches them his way. **10.** All the ways of the LORD are loving and faithful (loyal) toward those who keep the demands (commands) of his covenant (agreement). **11.** For the sake of your name (to honor you), LORD, forgive my iniquity (sin), though it is great. **12.** Who, then, are those who fear (revere) the LORD? He will instruct them in the ways they should choose. **13.** They will spend their days in prosperity (well-being), and their descendants (children) will inherit the land. **14.** The LORD confides (shares secrets) in those who fear him; he makes his covenant known to them. **15.** My eyes are ever on the LORD, for only he will release my feet from the snare (trap). **16.** Turn to me and be gracious (kind) to me, for I am lonely (in distress) and afflicted (troubled). **17.** Relieve (ease) the troubles of my heart and free me from my anguish (distress). **18.** Look on my affliction (misery) and my distress and take away all my sins. **19.** See how numerous (many) my enemies are and how fiercely they hate me! **20.** Guard my life and rescue me; do not let me be put to shame, for I take refuge (shelter) in you. **21.** May integrity (honesty) and uprightness protect me, because my hope, LORD, is in you. **22.** Deliver (rescue) Israel, O God, from all their troubles!

Chapter 26

1. Vindicate (defend) me, LORD, for I have led a blameless (innocent) life; I have trusted in the LORD and have not faltered (stumbled). **2.** Test me, LORD, and try me, examine my heart and my mind (thoughts); **3.** for I have always been mindful (remembered) of your unfailing love and have lived in reliance (dependence) on your faithfulness. **4.** I do not sit with the deceitful (liars), nor do I associate (befriend) with hypocrites (those who pretend to be good). **5.** I abhor (hate) the assembly of evildoers (those who do wrong) and refuse to sit with the wicked (unjust). **6.** I wash my hands in innocence (clean hands), and go about your altar, LORD, **7.** Proclaiming aloud your praise and telling of all your wonderful deeds. **8.** LORD, I love the house where you live (your temple), the place where your glory dwells (God's presence). **9.** Do not take away my soul along with sinners (those who reject God), my life with those who are bloodthirsty (violent), **10.** in whose hands are wicked schemes, whose right hands are full of bribes (payments to do wrong). **11.** I lead a blameless life; deliver (rescue) me and be merciful to me. **12.** My feet stand on level ground; in the great congregation (assembly of believers) I will praise the LORD.

Chapter 27

1. The LORD is my light (guidance) and my salvation (deliverance)— whom shall I fear? The LORD is the stronghold (fortress) of my life— of whom shall I be afraid? **2.** When the wicked (those who do evil) advance against me to devour (destroy) me, it is my enemies and my foes (adversaries) who will stumble and fall. **3.** Though an army besiege (surround) me, my heart will not fear; though war break out against me, even then I will be confident (trusting). **4.** One thing I ask from the LORD, this only do I seek: that I may dwell (live) in the house of the LORD all the days of my life, to gaze (look) on the beauty (splendor) of the LORD and to seek him in his temple. **5.** For in the day of trouble (distress) he will keep me safe in his dwelling; he will hide me in the shelter of his sacred tent (holy place) and set me high upon a rock. **6.** Then my head will be exalted (lifted) above the enemies who surround me; at his sacred tent I will sacrifice (offer worship) with shouts of joy; I will sing and make music to the LORD. **7.** Hear my voice when I call, LORD; be merciful to me and answer me. **8.** My heart says of you, "Seek his face!" Your face, LORD, I will seek. **9.** Do not hide your face from me, do not turn your servant away in anger; you have been my helper. Do not reject (forsake) me or abandon me, God my Savior. **10.** Though my father and mother forsake me, the LORD will receive (welcome) me. **11.** Teach me your way, LORD; lead me in a straight path because of my oppressors (those who press me down). **12.** Do not turn me over to the desire (plans) of my foes, for false witnesses (liars) rise up against me, spouting malicious (evil) accusations. **13.** I remain confident of this: I will see the goodness of the LORD in the land of the living. **14.** Wait for the LORD; be strong and take heart (courage) and wait for the LORD.

Chapter 28

1. To you, LORD, I call; you are my Rock (strong protector), do not turn a deaf ear to me. For if you remain silent, I will be like those who go down to the pit (grave). **2.** Hear my cry for mercy (compassion) as I call to you for help, as I lift up my hands toward your Most Holy Place (the temple). **3.** Do not drag me away with the wicked, with those who do evil, who speak cordially (gently) with their neighbors but harbor malice (evil intentions) in their hearts. **4.** Repay them for their deeds (actions) and for their evil work; repay them for what their hands have done and bring back on them what they deserve. **5.** Because they have no regard (respect) for the deeds of the LORD and what his hands have done, he will tear them down and never build them up again. **6.** Praise be to the LORD, for he has heard my cry for mercy. **7.** The LORD is my strength (support) and my shield (protector); my heart trusts in him, and he helps me. My heart leaps for joy (rejoices), and with my song (praise) I praise him. **8.** The LORD is the strength of his people, a fortress (safe place) of salvation for his anointed one. **9.** Save your people and bless your inheritance (people), be their shepherd (guide) and carry them forever.

Chapter 29

1. Ascribe (give) to the LORD, you heavenly beings (angels), ascribe to the LORD glory and strength. 2. Ascribe to the LORD the glory due (worthy of) his name; worship the LORD in the splendor (great beauty) of his holiness (pure, sacred nature). 3. The voice of the LORD is over the waters; the God of glory thunders, the LORD thunders over the mighty waters. 4. The voice of the LORD is powerful; the voice of the LORD is majestic (grand). 5. The voice of the LORD breaks the cedars (strong trees); the LORD breaks in pieces the cedars of Lebanon (famous, tall trees from the region of Lebanon). 6. He makes Lebanon leap like a calf, Sirion (Mount Hermon) like a young wild ox. 7. The voice of the LORD strikes with flashes of lightning. 8. The voice of the LORD shakes the desert; the LORD shakes the Desert of Kadesh (a desert area in the Sinai Peninsula). 9. The voice of the LORD twists the oaks (large trees) and strips the forests bare (removes the leaves). And in his temple all cry, "Glory!" 10. The LORD sits enthroned (ruling) over the flood; the LORD is enthroned as King forever. 11. The LORD gives strength to his people; the LORD blesses his people with peace.

Chapter 30

1. I will exalt (praise) you, LORD, for you lifted me out of the depths (troubles) and did not let my enemies gloat (rejoice) over me. 2. LORD my God, I called to you for help, and you healed me. 3. You, LORD, brought me up from the realm of the dead; you spared me from going down to the pit (grave). 4. Sing the praises of the LORD, you his faithful people; praise his holy name. 5. For his anger lasts only a moment, but his favor (grace) lasts a lifetime; weeping may stay for the night, but rejoicing comes in the morning. 6. When I felt secure (safe), I said, "I will never be shaken (moved)." 7. LORD, when you favored me, you made my royal mountain (kingdom) stand firm; but when you hid your face, I was dismayed (troubled). 8. To you, LORD, I called; to the Lord I

cried for mercy: 9. "What is gained (benefited) if I am silenced, if I go down to the pit? Will the dust (earth) praise you? Will it proclaim (declare) your faithfulness? 10. Hear, LORD, and be merciful to me; LORD, be my help." 11. You turned my wailing (crying) into dancing; you removed my sackcloth (mourning clothes) and clothed me with joy, 12. that my heart may sing your praises and not be silent. LORD my God, I will praise you forever.

Chapter 31

1. In you, LORD, I have taken refuge (shelter); let me never be put to shame; deliver (rescue) me in your righteousness. 2. Turn your ear to me, come quickly to my rescue; be my rock of refuge, a strong fortress to save me. 3. Since you are my rock and my fortress, for the sake of your name lead and guide me. 4. Keep me free from the trap (snare) that is set for me, for you are my refuge. 5. Into your hands I commit (entrust) my spirit; deliver me, LORD, my faithful God. 6. I hate those who cling (hold) to worthless idols (false gods); as for me, I trust in the LORD. 7. I will be glad and rejoice in your love, for you saw my affliction (suffering) and knew the anguish of my soul. 8. You have not given me into the hands of the enemy but have set my feet in a spacious place (freedom). 9. Be merciful to me, LORD, for I am in distress; my eyes grow weak with sorrow, my soul and body with grief. 10. My life is consumed by anguish (suffering) and my years by groaning; my strength fails because of my affliction, and my bones grow weak. 11. Because of all my enemies, I am the utter contempt (mockery) of my neighbors and an object of dread (fear) to my closest friends— those who see me on the street flee (run) from me. 12. I am forgotten as though I were dead; I have become like broken pottery (useless). 13. For I hear many whispering, "Terror on every side!" They conspire (plot) against me and plot to take my life. 14. But I trust in you, LORD; I say, "You are my God." 15. My times are in your hands; deliver me from the hands of my enemies, from those who pursue me. 16. Let your face shine (show favor) on your servant; save me in your unfailing love. 17. Let me not be put to shame, LORD, for I have cried out to you; but let the wicked (evil ones) be put to shame and be silent in the realm of the dead. 18. Let their lying lips be silenced, for with pride and contempt they speak arrogantly against the righteous. 19. How abundant are the good things that you have stored up for those who fear (revere) you, that you bestow (give) in the sight of all, on those who take refuge in you. 20. In the shelter of your presence (God's care) you hide them from all human intrigues (schemes); you keep them safe in your dwelling (place of safety) from accusing tongues. 21. Praise be to the LORD, for he showed me the wonders (marvels) of his love when I was in a city under siege (surrounded by enemies). 22. In my alarm (panic) I said, "I am cut off from your sight!" Yet you heard my cry for mercy when I called to you for help. 23. Love the LORD, all his faithful people! The LORD preserves (protects) those who are true to him, but the proud he pays back in full. 24. Be strong and take heart, all you who hope in the LORD.

Chapter 32

1. Blessed is the person whose wrongdoings (sins or offenses) are forgiven, whose sins (wrong actions) are covered and no longer held against them. **2.** Blessed is the person to whom the LORD does not charge sin, and in whose spirit (inner being) there is no deceit (dishonesty or lying). **3.** When I kept quiet about my sin, my body felt weak, and I groaned (suffered) all day long from the burden. **4.** For day and night, Your hand was heavy upon me; my strength drained away, as if in the scorching (extremely hot) heat of summer. **5.** Then I acknowledged (admitted) my sin to You and did not try to hide my guilt. I said, "I will confess (admit) my wrongdoing to the LORD," and You forgave the burden of my sin. **6.** Therefore, let all the faithful (those who believe) pray to You while You can still be found; surely, when great floods (rising waters, danger) rise, they will not reach them. **7.** You are my safe place (place of refuge); You will protect me from trouble and surround me with songs of freedom (songs of salvation). **8.** I will teach you and guide you in the way you should go; I will give you advice with my loving attention upon you. **9.** Do not be like the horse or the mule, which lack understanding (lack wisdom) and must be controlled by a bridle (a device to control animals) or they won't come to you. **10.** The wicked (evil or immoral people) face many sorrows, but the LORD's unchanging love surrounds those who trust in

Him. **11.** Rejoice (be happy) in the LORD and be glad, you who are righteous (morally right); sing, all who are pure (clean) in heart!

Chapter 33

31. Sing joyfully to the LORD, you who are righteous (morally right); it is fitting for the upright (honest people) to praise him. **2.** Praise the LORD with the harp (a stringed instrument); make music to him on the ten-stringed lyre (another type of harp). **3.** Sing to him a new song; play skillfully, and shout for joy. **4.** For the word (message or command) of the LORD is right and true; he is faithful (trustworthy) in all he does. **5.** The LORD loves righteousness (justice) and justice; the earth is full of his unfailing love (constant, never-ending love). **6.** By the word of the LORD the heavens (sky and universe) were made, their starry host (all the stars) by the breath of his mouth. **7.** He gathers the waters of the sea (ocean) into jars; he puts the deep (ocean depths) into storehouses. **8.** Let all the earth (world) fear the LORD; let all the people of the world revere (respect deeply) him. **9.** For he spoke, and it came to be; he commanded, and it stood firm. **10.** The LORD foils (defeats) the plans of the nations (countries); he thwarts (stops) the purposes of the peoples (groups of people). **11.** But the plans of the LORD stand firm forever, the purposes of his heart through all generations. **12.** Blessed is the nation whose God is the LORD, the people he chose for his inheritance (his special people). **13.** From heaven the LORD looks down and sees all mankind (all humans); **14.** from his dwelling place (heaven) he watches all who live on earth— **15.** he who forms the hearts (inner beings) of all, who considers everything they do. **16.** No king is saved by the size of his army (military); no warrior escapes by his great strength. **17.** A horse (a type of animal used for war) is a vain hope (useless) for deliverance (rescue); despite all its great strength, it cannot save. **18.** But the eyes of the LORD are on those who fear (respect deeply) him, on those whose hope is in his unfailing love, **19.** to deliver them from death and keep them alive in famine (times of hunger). **20.** We wait in hope for the LORD; he is our help and our shield (protector). **21.** In him our hearts rejoice, for we trust in his holy name. **22.** May your unfailing love be with us, LORD, even as we put our hope in you.

Chapter 34

1. I will extol (praise) the LORD at all times; his praise will always be on my lips. **2.** I will glory (boast) in the LORD; let the afflicted (those in trouble) hear and rejoice. **3.** Glorify (praise) the LORD with me; let us exalt (lift up) his name together. **4.** I sought the LORD, and he answered me; he delivered (rescued) me from all my fears. **5.** Those who look to him are radiant (filled with joy); their faces are never covered with shame. **6.** This poor man called, and the LORD heard him; he saved him out of all his troubles. **7.** The angel of the LORD (God's messenger) encamps (surrounds) around those who fear him, and he delivers them. **8.** Taste and see (experience for yourself) that the LORD is good; blessed is the one who takes refuge (shelter) in him. **9.** Fear the LORD, you his holy people, for those who fear him lack nothing. **10.** The lions (wild animals) may grow weak and hungry, but those who seek (search for) the LORD lacks no good thing. **11.** Come, my children, listen to me; I will teach you the fear of the LORD. **12.** Whoever of you loves life and desires to see many good days, **13.** keep your tongue (speech) from evil and your lips from telling lies. **14.** Turn from evil and do good; seek peace and pursue it. **15.** The eyes of the LORD are on the righteous (morally good), and his ears are attentive (listening) to their cry. **16.** But the face of the LORD is against those who do evil, to blot (wipe out) their name from the earth. **17.** The righteous cry out, and the LORD hears them; he delivers them from all their troubles. **18.** The LORD is close to the brokenhearted and saves those who are crushed in spirit (feel deeply hurt). **19.** The righteous person may have many troubles, but the LORD delivers him from them all; **20.** he protects all his bones, not one of them will be broken. **21.** Evil will slay (destroy) the wicked; the foes (enemies) of the righteous will be condemned. **22.** The LORD will rescue (save) his servants; no one who takes refuge in him will be condemned.

Chapter 35

1. Contend (fight) LORD, with those who contend with me; fight against those who fight against me. **2.** Take up shield (a protective armor) and armor; arise and come to my aid. **3.** Brandish (raise) spear and javelin (throwing weapons) against those who pursue me. Say to me, "I am your salvation (rescue)." **4.** May those who seek my life be disgraced and put to shame; may those who plot my ruin be turned back in dismay (confusion). **5.** May they be like chaff (light, useless parts of grain) before the wind, with the angel of the LORD (God's messenger) driving them away; **6.** May their path be dark and slippery, with the angel of the LORD pursuing them. **7.** Since they hid their net (trap) for me without cause, and without cause dug a pit (trap) for me, **8.** May ruin (destruction) overtake them by surprise— may the net they hid entangle (trap) them, may they fall into the pit, to their ruin. **9.** Then my soul will rejoice (celebrate) in the LORD and delight in his salvation (rescue). **10.** My whole being will exclaim, "Who is like you, LORD? You rescue (save) the poor from those too strong for them, the poor and needy from those who rob them." **11.** Ruthless (cruel) witnesses come forward; they question me on things I know nothing about. **12.** They repay me evil for good and leave me like one bereaved (mourning a loss). **13.** Yet when they were ill, I put on sackcloth (a symbol of mourning) and humbled myself with fasting. When my prayers returned to me unanswered, **14.** I went about mourning (grieving) as though for my friend or brother. I bowed my head in grief as though weeping for my mother. **15.** But when I stumbled (fell), they gathered in glee (joy); assailants (attackers) gathered against me without my knowledge. They slandered (spread lies about) me without ceasing. **16.** Like the ungodly (evil people) they maliciously mocked; they gnashed (grinded) their teeth at me. **17.** How long, LORD, will you look on? Rescue (save) me from their ravages (destruction), my precious life from these lions (dangerous enemies). **18.** I will give you thanks in the great assembly (gathering); among the throngs (crowd) I will praise you. **19.** Do not let those gloat (celebrate) over me who are my enemies without cause; do not let those who hate me without reason maliciously wink the eye. **20.** They do not speak peaceably, but devise (plan) false accusations against those who live quietly in the land. **21.** They sneer (mock) at me and say, "Aha! Aha! With our own eyes we have seen it." **22.** LORD, you have seen this; do not be silent. Do not be far from me, Lord. **23.** Awake and rise to my defense! Contend for me, my God and Lord. **24.** Vindicate (defend) me in your righteousness, LORD my God; do not let them gloat over me. **25.** Do not let them think, "Aha, just what we wanted!" or say, "We have swallowed him up." **26.** May all who gloat over my distress be put to shame and confusion; may all who exalt themselves over me be clothed with shame and disgrace. **27.** May those who delight in my vindication (justification) shout for joy and gladness; may they always say, "The LORD be exalted (honored), who delights in the well-being (peace) of his servant." **28.** My tongue will proclaim (declare) your righteousness, your praises all day long.

Chapter 36

1. I have a message from God in my heart concerning the sinfulness (wickedness) of the wicked: There is no fear (reverence or respect) of God before their eyes. **2.** In their own eyes they flatter (praise) themselves too much to detect (recognize) or hate their sin. **3.** The words of their mouths are wicked (evil) and deceitful (dishonest); they fail to act wisely or do good. **4.** Even on their beds they plot (plan) evil; they commit (dedicate) themselves to a sinful course and do not reject (turn away from) what is wrong. **5.** Your love, LORD, reaches to the heavens (sky), your faithfulness to the skies. **6.** Your righteousness (justice) is like the highest mountains, your justice like the great deep (vast ocean). You, LORD, preserve (protect) both people and animals. **7.** How priceless is your unfailing love, O God! People take refuge (shelter) in the shadow of your wings. **8.** They feast (enjoy) on the abundance of your house; you give them drink from your river of delights (joy). **9.** For with you is the fountain (source) of life; in your light we see light (understanding). **10.** Continue your love to those who know you, your righteousness to the upright (morally good) in heart. **11.** May the foot (step) of the proud not come against me, nor the hand (force) of the wicked drive me away. **12.** See how the evildoers (wrongdoers) lie fallen thrown down, not able to rise!

Chapter 37

1. Do not fret (worry) because of those who are evil or be envious of those who do wrong; **2.** for like the grass they will soon wither (dry up), like green plants they will soon die away. **3.** Trust in the LORD and do good; dwell (live) in the land and enjoy safe pasture (peaceful living). **4.** Take delight (find joy) in the LORD, and he will give you the desires of your heart. **5.** Commit (entrust) your way to the LORD; trust in him and he will do this: **6.** He will make your righteous reward shine like the dawn, your vindication (justification) like the noonday sun. **7.** Be still (quiet) before the LORD and wait patiently for him; do not fret when people succeed in their ways, when they carry out their wicked schemes (evil plans). **8.** Refrain (stop) from anger and turn from wrath (intense anger); do not fret—it leads only to evil. **9.** For those who are evil will be destroyed, but those who hope in the LORD will inherit (receive as an inheritance) the land. **10.** A little while, and the wicked will be no more; though you look for them, they will not be found. **11.** But the meek (humble) will inherit the land and enjoy peace and prosperity (success). **12.** The wicked plot (scheme) against the righteous and gnash (grind) their teeth at them; **13.** but the LORD laughs at the wicked, for he knows their day is coming. **14.** The wicked draw the sword and bend the bow (prepare weapons) to bring down the poor and needy, to slay (kill) those whose ways are upright. **15.** But their swords will pierce (hurt) their own hearts, and their bows will be broken. **16.** Better the little that the righteous have than the wealth of many wicked; **17.** for the power of the wicked will be broken, but the LORD upholds (supports) the righteous. **18.** The blameless (innocent) spend their days under the LORD's care, and their inheritance will endure (last) forever. **19.** In times of disaster (trouble) they will not wither; in days of famine (food shortage) they will enjoy plenty. **20.** But the wicked will perish (be destroyed): Though the LORD's enemies are like the flowers of the field, they will be consumed (destroyed), they will go up in smoke (become nothing). **21.** The wicked borrow and do not repay, but the righteous give generously; **22.** those the LORD blesses will inherit the land, but those he curses will be destroyed. **23.** The LORD makes firm (steady) the steps of the one who delights in him; **24.** though he may stumble (fall), he will not fall, for the LORD upholds him with his hand. **25.** I was young and now I am old, yet I have never seen the righteous forsaken (abandoned) or their children begging bread. **26.** They are always generous and lend freely; their children will be a blessing. **27.** Turn from evil and do good; then you will dwell in the land forever. **28.** For the LORD loves the just (fair) and will not forsake his faithful ones. Wrongdoers will be completely destroyed; the offspring (children) of the wicked will perish. **29.** The righteous will inherit the land and dwell (live) in it forever. **30.** The mouths of the righteous utter (speak) wisdom, and their tongues speak what is just. **31.** The law of their God is in their hearts; their feet do not slip (stumble). **32.** The wicked lie in wait (wait secretly) for the righteous, intent on putting them to death; **33.** but the LORD will not leave them in the power of the wicked or let them be condemned (found guilty) when brought to trial. **34.** Hope in the LORD and keep his way. He will exalt (raise) you to inherit the land; when the wicked are destroyed, you will see it. **35.** I have seen a wicked and ruthless man flourishing (growing strong) like a luxuriant (healthy, thriving) native tree, **36.** but he soon passed away and was no more; though I looked for him, he could not be found. **37.** Consider (pay attention to) the blameless, observe the upright (moral); a future awaits those who seek peace. **38.** But all sinners (wrongdoers) will be destroyed; there will be no future for the wicked. **39.** The salvation (rescue) of the righteous comes from the LORD; he is their stronghold (fortress) in time of trouble. **40.** The LORD helps them and delivers them; he delivers them from the wicked and saves them, because they take refuge (shelter) in him.

Chapter 38

1. LORD, do not rebuke (punish) me in your anger or discipline me in your wrath (intense anger). 2. Your arrows have pierced me, and your hand has come down on me. 3. Because of your wrath, there is no health (well-being) in my body; there is no soundness (wholeness) in my bones because of my sin. 4. My guilt has overwhelmed (burdened) me like a burden too heavy to bear. 5. My wounds fester (become infected) and are loathsome (disgusting) because of my sinful folly (foolishness). 6. I am bowed down and brought very low; all day long I go about mourning (grieving). 7. My back is filled with searing (sharp) pain; there is no health in my body. 8. I am feeble (weak) and utterly crushed; I groan (moan) in anguish of heart. 9. All my longings (desires) lie open before you, LORD; my sighing (deep breathing from sorrow) is not hidden from you. 10. My heart pounds (beats heavily), my strength fails me; even the light has gone from my eyes. 11. My friends and companions avoid me because of my wounds; my neighbors stay far away. 12. Those who want to kill me set their traps; those who would

harm me talk of my ruin (destruction); all day long they scheme (plan) and lie. 13. I am like the deaf (unable to hear), who cannot hear, like the mute (unable to speak), who cannot speak. 14. I have become like one who does not hear, whose mouth can offer no reply. 15. LORD, I wait for you; you will answer, LORD my God. 16. For I said, "Do not let them gloat (celebrate) or exalt (boast) themselves over me when my feet slip." 17. For I am about to fall, and my pain is ever with me. 18. I confess my iniquity (wrongdoing); I am troubled (distressed) by my sin. 19. Many have become my enemies without cause; those who hate me without reason are numerous. 20. Those who repay my good with evil lodge (bring) accusations against me, though I seek only to do what is good. 21. LORD, do not forsake (abandon) me; do not be far from me, my God. 22. Come quickly to help me, my Lord and my Savior (deliverer).

Chapter 39

1. I said, "I will watch my ways and keep my tongue from sin; I will put a muzzle (restraint) on my mouth while in the presence of the wicked." 2. So I remained utterly silent, not even saying anything good. But my anguish (pain) increased; 3. my heart grew hot within me. While I meditated (thought deeply), the fire burned; then I spoke with my tongue: 4. "Show me, LORD, my life's end and the number of my days; let me know how fleeting (short) my life is. 5. You have made my days a mere handbreadth (a small measure of space); the span of my years is as nothing before you. Everyone is but a breath (momentary), even those who seem secure. 6. "Surely everyone goes around like a mere phantom (shadow); in vain they rush about, heaping up wealth without knowing whose it will finally be. 7. "But now, Lord, what do I look for? My hope is in you. 8. Save me from all my transgressions (wrongdoings); do not make me the scorn (mockery) of fools. 9. I was silent; I would not open my mouth, for you are the one who has done this. 10. Remove your scourge (punishment) from me; I am overcome by the blow of your hand. 11. When you rebuke (chastise) and discipline anyone for their sin, you consume their wealth like a moth (destroy it)— surely everyone is but a breath. 12. "Hear my prayer, LORD, listen to my cry for help; do not be deaf to my weeping. I dwell (live) with you as a foreigner (stranger), a stranger, as all my ancestors were. 13. Look away from me, that I may enjoy life again before I depart and am no more."

Chapter 40

1. I waited patiently for the LORD; he turned to me and heard my cry. 2. He lifted me out of the slimy pit (a deep hole), out of the mud and mire (filthy water); he set my feet on a rock and gave me a firm place to stand. 3. He put a new song in my mouth, a hymn (song of praise) to our God. Many will see and fear the LORD and put their trust in him. 4. Blessed is the one who trusts in the LORD, who does not look to the proud (arrogant), to those who turn aside to false gods. 5. Many, LORD my God, are the wonders (marvelous deeds) you have done, the things you planned for us. None can compare with you; were I to speak and tell of your deeds, they would be too many to declare. 6. Sacrifice and offering you did not desire— but my ears you have opened— burnt offerings and sin offerings you did not require. 7. Then I said, "Here I am, I have come— it is written about me in the scroll (book). 8. I desire to do your will, my God; your law is within my heart." 9. I proclaim (announce) your saving acts in the great assembly (congregation); I do not seal (hide) my lips, LORD, as you know. 10. I do not hide your righteousness in my heart; I speak of your faithfulness and your saving help. I do not conceal (keep secret) your love and your faithfulness from the great assembly. 11. Do not withhold (hold back) your mercy from me, LORD; may your love and faithfulness always protect me. 12. For troubles without number surround me; my sins have overtaken (caught up with) me, and I cannot see. They are more than the hairs of my head, and my heart fails (gives up) within me. 13. Be pleased to save me, LORD; come quickly, LORD, to help me. 14. May all who want to take my life be put to shame and confusion; may all who desire my ruin be turned back in disgrace. 15. May those who say to me, "Aha! Aha!" be appalled (shocked) at their own shame. 16. But may all who seek you rejoice (be glad) and be glad in you; may those who long (desire) for your saving help always say, "The LORD is great!" 17. But as for me, I am poor and needy; may the Lord think of me. You are my help and my deliverer (savior); you are my God, do not delay.

Chapter 41

1. Blessed are those who have regard (care) for the weak; the LORD delivers (rescues) them in times of trouble. **2.** The LORD protects and preserves (keeps safe) them— they are counted among the blessed (favored) in the land— he does not give them over to the desire (plans) of their foes (enemies). **3.** The LORD sustains (supports) them on their sickbed and restores (heals) them from their bed of illness. **4.** I said, "Have mercy (compassion) on me, LORD; heal me, for I have sinned (done wrong) against you." **5.** My enemies say of me in malice (evil intent), "When will he die and his name perishes (disappear)?" **6.** When one of them comes to see me, he speaks falsely (lies), while his heart gathers (collects) slander (false accusations); then he goes out and spreads it around. **7.** All my enemies whisper (talk secretly) together against me; they imagine (think) the worst for me, saying, **8.** "A vile (disgusting) disease has afflicted (struck) him; he will never get up from the place where he lies." **9.** Even my close friend, someone I trusted, one who shared my bread (ate with me), has turned against me. **10.** But may you have mercy on me, LORD; raise me up (restore me), that I may repay (recompense) them. **11.** I know that you are pleased (happy) with me, for my enemy does not triumph (win) over me. **12.** Because of my integrity (honesty) you uphold (support) me and set me in your presence forever. **13.** Praise (worship) be to the LORD, the God of Israel, from everlasting (forever) to everlasting (forever). Amen and Amen.

Chapter 42

1. As the deer pants (longs) for streams of water, so my soul pants for you, my God. **2.** My soul thirsts for God, for the living God. When can I go and meet with God? **3.** My tears have been my food day and night, while people say to me all day long, "Where is your God?" **4.** These things I remember as I pour out (express) my soul: how I used to go to the house of God under the protection (safety) of the Mighty One (God) with shouts of joy and praise among the festive (celebratory) throng (crowd). **5.** Why, my soul, are you downcast (depressed)? Why so disturbed (distressed) within me? Put your hope in God, for I will yet praise him, my Savior and my God. **6.** My soul is downcast within me; therefore, I will remember you from the land of the Jordan (river), the heights of Hermon (mountain), from Mount Mizar (a small mountain). **7.** Deep calls to deep in the roar of your waterfalls; all your waves and breakers have swept over me. **8.** By day the LORD directs his love, at night his song is with me—a prayer to the God of my life. **9.** I say to God my Rock (strong foundation), "Why have you forgotten me? Why must I go about mourning, oppressed (crushed) by the enemy?" **10.** My bones suffer mortal (deadly) agony as my foes taunt (mock) me, saying to me all day long, "Where is your God?" **11.** Why, my soul, are you downcast? Why so disturbed within me? Put your hope in God, for I will yet praise him, my Savior and my God.

Chapter 43

1. Vindicate (defend) me, my God, and plead (argue) my cause against an unfaithful (disloyal) nation. Rescue (save) me from those who are deceitful (dishonest) and wicked (evil). **2.** You are God my stronghold (defender). Why have you rejected me? Why must I go about mourning, oppressed by the enemy? **3.** Send me your light and your faithful care, let them lead me; let them bring me to your holy mountain, to the place where you dwell (live). **4.** Then I will go to the altar (sacred place) of God, to God, my joy and my delight. I will praise you with the lyre (stringed instrument), O God, my God. **5.** Why, my soul, are you downcast? Why so disturbed within me? Put your hope in God, for I will yet praise him, my Savior and my God.

Chapter 44

1. We have heard with our ears, O God; our ancestors have told us what you did in their time, in ancient days. **2.** With your hand, you drove out the nations (people groups) and settled our ancestors; you crushed the peoples and caused them to thrive. **3.** It wasn't by their sword they took the land, nor by their own strength they won; it was by your right hand, your power, and the light of your presence, for you loved them. **4.** You are my King and my God, the One who gives victories to Israel (Jacob). **5.** Through you, we push back our enemies; by your name, we defeat those who oppose us. **6.** I do not trust in my bow, nor does my sword win battles; **7.** but you give us victory over our enemies and put those who attack us to shame. **8.** In God, we boast all day long, and we praise your name forever. **9.** But now you have rejected us and humbled us; you no longer lead our armies. **10.** You made us turn back before our enemies, and our foes have taken what is ours. **11.** You gave us up to be like sheep for slaughter, scattering us among the nations (peoples). **12.** You sold your people for a small price, gaining nothing from their sale. **13.** You have made us a disgrace to our neighbors, a joke and scorn to those around us. **14.** You have made us a byword (shameful example) among the nations; people shake their heads at us. **15.** All day long, I live in disgrace, and my face is covered with shame, **16.** at the taunts of those who mock me, because of the enemy bent on revenge. **17.** All this has happened even though we haven't forgotten you; we have not broken our covenant with you. **18.** Our hearts have not turned away from you, and our feet have not strayed from your path. **19.** But you crushed us and made us a home for wild animals (jackals); you covered us with deep darkness. **20.** If we had forgotten the name of our God or reached out to a foreign god, **21.** would not God have seen it, since He knows the secrets of the heart? **22.** Yet for your sake, we face death all day long; we are counted as sheep for slaughter. **23.** Awake, Lord! Why do you sleep? Arise and do not reject us forever. **24.** Why do you hide your face and forget our suffering and oppression? **25.** We are brought low to the dust; our bodies cling to the ground. **26.** Rise up and help us; save us because of your unfailing love.

Chapter 45

1. My heart is stirred by a noble theme as I speak my verses for the king; my tongue is like the pen of a skilled writer. **2.** You are the most excellent of men, and your words have been anointed with grace, for God has blessed you forever. **3.** Put your sword on your side, you mighty one; clothe yourself with splendor and majesty. **4.** Ride out in your majesty, victorious in the cause of truth, humility, and justice; let your right hand perform mighty deeds. **5.** Let your arrows pierce the hearts of your enemies; let the nations fall beneath your feet. **6.** Your throne, O God, will last forever; a scepter of justice will be the scepter of your kingdom. **7.** You love righteousness and hate wickedness; therefore, God, your God, has anointed you with joy, setting you above your companions. **8.** All your robes are fragrant with myrrh (a perfume), aloes, and cassia (fragrant spices) from palaces adorned with ivory, the music of strings makes you glad. **9.** Daughters of kings stand among your honored women; at your right hand is the royal bride, clothed in gold from Ophir (a wealthy region). **10.** Listen, daughter, and pay attention: Forget your people and your father's house. **11.** Let the king be captivated by your beauty; honor him, for he is your lord. **12.** The city of Tyre (a wealthy Phoenician city) will bring a gift, and the rich people will seek your favor. **13.** All glorious is the princess within her chamber; her gown is embroidered with gold. **14.** In richly woven garments, she is led to the king; her virgin companions follow her, brought to be with her. **15.** Led in with joy and gladness, they enter the palace of the king. **16.** Your sons will succeed your ancestors; you will make them princes throughout the land. **17.** I will make your name known through all generations; therefore, the nations will praise you forever.

Chapter 46

1. God is our refuge (safe place) and strength, an ever-present help in trouble. **2.** Therefore, we will not fear, though the earth gives way and the mountains fall into the heart of the sea, **3.** Though its waters roar and foam, and the mountains quake with their surging. **4.** There is a river whose streams make glad the city of God, the holy place where the Highest dwells. **5.** God is within her; she will not fall; God will help her at dawn. **6.** Nations are in uproar, kingdoms fall; He lifts His voice, and the earth melts. **7.** The LORD Almighty is with us; the God of Jacob (Israel) is our fortress. **8.** Come and see what the LORD has done, the desolations He has brought upon the earth. **9.** He makes wars cease to the ends of the earth; He breaks the bow and shatters the spear; He burns the shields with fire. **10.** He says, "Be still, and know that I am God; I will be exalted among the nations, I will be exalted in the earth." **11.** The LORD Almighty is with us; the God of Jacob is our fortress.

Chapter 47

1. Clap your hands, all you nations; shout to God with cries of joy. **2.** For the LORD Most High is awesome, the great King over all the earth. **3.** He subdued nations under us, peoples under our feet. **4.** He chose our inheritance for us, the pride of Jacob (Israel), whom He loved. **5.** God has ascended amid shouts of joy, the LORD amid the sound of trumpets. **6.** Sing praises to God, sing praises; sing praises to our King, sing praises. **7.** For God is the King of all the earth; sing to Him a psalm of praise. **8.** God reigns over the nations; God is seated on His holy throne. **9.** The nobles of the nation's gather as the people of the God of Abraham, for the kings of the earth belong to God; He is greatly exalted.

Chapter 48

1. Great is the LORD, and most worthy of praise, in the city of our God, His holy mountain. **2.** Beautiful in its height, the joy of the whole earth, like the heights of Zaphon (northern mountain, sacred place) is Mount Zion, the city of the Great King. **3.** God is in her citadels (fortresses); He has shown Himself to be her refuge. **4.** When kings joined forces and advanced together, **5.** they saw her and were amazed; they fled in terror. **6.** Trembling seized them there, pain like a woman in labor. **7.** You destroyed them like ships of Tarshish (a distant Phoenician city known for trade) shattered by an east wind. **8.** As we have heard, so we have seen in the city of the LORD Almighty, in the city of our God: God makes her secure forever. **9.** Within Your temple, O God, we meditate on Your unfailing love. **10.** Like Your name, O God, your praise reaches to the ends of the earth; Your right hand is filled with righteousness. **11.** Mount Zion rejoices, the villages of Judah are glad because of Your judgments. **12.** Walk around Zion, count her towers, **13.** Consider her ramparts (defensive walls), view her citadels, that you may tell of them to the next generation. **14.** For this God is our God forever; He will guide us even to the end.

Chapter 49

1. Hear this, all you peoples; listen, all who live in this world, **2.** Both low and high, rich and poor alike: **3.** My mouth will speak wisdom; the meditation of my heart will give understanding. **4.** I will turn my ear to a proverb; with the harp, I will expound my riddle. **5.** Why should I fear when evil days come when wicked deceivers surround me— **6.** those who trust in their wealth and boast of their great riches? **7.** No one can redeem the life of another or give to God a ransom for them— **8.** the ransom for a life is costly, no payment is enough— **9.** so that they should live forever and not see decay. **10.** For all can see that the wise die, the foolish and senseless also perish, leaving their wealth to others. **11.** Their tombs remain their houses forever, their dwellings for endless generations, though they named lands after themselves. **12.** People, despite their wealth, do not endure; they are like beasts that perish. **13.** This is the fate of those who trust in themselves, and their followers who approve their sayings. **14.** They are like sheep, destined to die; death will be their shepherd. The upright will prevail over them in the morning; their forms will decay in the grave, far from their princely mansions. **15.** But God will redeem me from the realm of the dead; He will take me to Himself. **16.** Do not be overawed when others grow rich, when the splendor of their houses increases; **17.** for they will take nothing with them when they die, their splendor will not descend with them. **18.** Though while they live they count themselves blessed, and people praise you when you prosper, **19.** they will join those who have gone before them, who will never see the light of life. **20.** People who have wealth but lack understanding is like beasts that perish.

Chapter 50

1. The Almighty, the LORD, speaks and calls to the earth, from the rising of the sun to its setting. **2.** From Zion, perfect in beauty, God shines out. **3.** Our God approaches, and He will not remain silent; a fire burns ahead of Him, and a storm surrounds Him. **4.** He calls the heavens above and the earth below to witness as He judges His people. **5.** "Gather to Me those who are set apart, those who made a covenant with Me through sacrifice." **6.** The heavens declare His righteousness, for He is a God of justice. **7.** "Listen, my people, I will speak; I testify against you, Israel: I am your God. **8.** I do not accuse you for your sacrifices or burnt offerings, which are always before Me. **9.** I do not need a bull from your stalls or goats from your pens, **10.** for every animal in the forest is Mine, and the cattle on a thousand hills. **11.** I know all the birds of the mountains, and the creatures of the field are Mine. **12.** If I were hungry, I would not tell you, for the world and everything in it belong to Me. **13.** Do I consume the flesh of bulls or drink the blood of goats? **14.** "Offer thanksgiving sacrifices to God, and fulfill your vows to the Highest, **15.** and when you are in trouble, call on Me; I will rescue you, and you will honor Me." **16.** But to the wicked, God says: "Why do you recite My laws or take My covenant on your lips? **17.** You despise My teachings and throw My words behind you. **18.** When you see a thief, you join him; you are in league with adulterers. **19.** You speak evil, and your tongue is skilled in deceit. **20.** You sit and accuse your brother, slandering your own mother's son. **21.** When you did all this and I kept silent, you thought I was just like you. But now I bring charges against you and lay them before you. **22.** "Consider this, all you who forget God, or I will tear you apart, with no one to rescue you. **23.** Those who offer thanksgiving as their sacrifice honor Me, and to the upright, I will show My salvation."

Chapter 51

1. Have mercy on me, O God, according to Your unwavering (continuing in a strong and steady way) love; according to Your vast compassion, erase my wrongdoing. **2.** Wash away all my guilt and purify me from my sin. **3.** For I know my wrongdoings, and my sin is always before me. **4.** Against You, only You, have I sinned, and I've done what is evil in Your sight; so, You are just in Your verdict and fair when You judge. **5.** Surely, I was sinful from the moment of birth, sinful from the time my mother conceived me. **6.** Yet You desired faithfulness even in the womb; You taught me wisdom in that hidden place. **7.** Cleanse me with hyssop (a plant used in purification), and I will be clean; wash me, and I will be whiter than snow. **8.** Let me hear joy and gladness; let the bones You have broken rejoice. **9.** Hide Your face from my sins and wipe away all my wrongdoing. **10.** Create in me a pure heart, O God, and renew a steadfast spirit within me. **11.** Do not cast me away from Your presence or take Your Holy Spirit from me. **12.** Restore to me the joy of Your salvation and grant me a willing spirit, to support me. **13.** Then I will teach those who rebel Your ways, so that sinners will return to You. **14.** Deliver me from the guilt of bloodshed, O God, the God of my salvation, and my tongue will sing of Your righteousness. **15.** Open my lips, Lord, and

my mouth will declare Your praise. **16.** You do not delight in sacrifice, or I would bring it; You do not take pleasure in burnt offerings. **17.** My sacrifice, O God, is a broken spirit; a broken and humble heart You, God, will not despise. **18.** May it please You to prosper Zion (Jerusalem), to build up the walls of Jerusalem. **19.** Then You will delight in the sacrifices of the righteous, in burnt offerings offered whole; then bulls will be offered on Your altar.

Chapter 52

1. Why do you boast of evil, you mighty warrior? Why do you brag all day long, you who are a disgrace in the eyes of God? **2.** You who practice deceit, your tongue plots harm; it is like a sharp razor. **3.** You love evil more than good and lies more than speaking truth. **4.** You love every harmful word, your deceitful tongue! **5.** Surely God will bring you down to eternal ruin; He will snatch you up and remove you from your tent; He will uproot you from the land of the living. **6.** The righteous will see and fear; they will mock you, saying, **7.** "Look, this is the man who did not make God his refuge, but trusted in his great wealth and grew strong by harming others!" **8.** But I am like an olive tree flourishing in the house of God; I trust in God's unfailing love forever and ever. **9.** For what you have done, I will always praise You among Your faithful people. I will hope in Your name, for Your name is good.

Chapter 53

1. The fool says in his heart, "There is no God." They are corrupt, and their ways are wicked (morally very bad); there is no one who does good. **2.** God looks down from heaven on all mankind to see if there are any who understand, any who seek God. **3.** Everyone has turned away, all have become corrupt; there is no one who does good, not even one. **4.** Do all these evildoers know nothing? They devour My people as though eating bread; they never call on God. **5.** But there they are, overwhelmed with fear, where there was nothing to fear. God scattered the bones of those who attacked you; You put them to shame, for God despised them. **6.** Oh, that salvation for Israel would come from Zion! When God restores His people, let Jacob rejoice and Israel be glad!

Chapter 54

1. Save me, O God, by your name; defend (protect) me with Your power. **2.** Hear my prayer, O God; listen to the words of my mouth. **3.** Proud (arrogant) enemies are attacking me; ruthless (cruel) people want to kill me— people who do not acknowledge (recognize) God. **4.** Surely God is my helper; the Lord is the one who upholds (supports) me. **5.** Let the harm intended for me fall back on those who speak against me; in Your faithfulness, destroy them. **6.** I will offer a voluntary sacrifice to You; I will praise Your name, LORD, for it is good. **7.** You have delivered me from all my troubles, and I have seen my enemies defeated.

Chapter 55

1 Listen to my prayer, O God, do not ignore (turn away from) my plea. **2** Hear me and answer me. My thoughts are troubled (worried), and I am distressed (disturbed). **3** I am upset by the words of my enemies, and the threats of the wicked (evil people); they bring suffering on me and attack me in their anger. **4** My heart is in anguish (great pain) within me; the terrors of death have fallen upon me. **5** Fear and trembling (shaking) have overwhelmed (taken control of) me; horror surrounds me. **6** I said, "Oh, if only I had the wings of a dove! I would fly away and be at peace. **7** I would escape far away and live in the desert (a dry, empty place). **8** I would hurry to find a safe place, far from the storm (trouble) and the chaos. **9** Lord, confuse (confound) the wicked; make their words meaningless, for I see violence and conflict in the city. **10** Day and night they patrol (walk around) its walls; malice (hatred) and deceit (dishonesty) fill the city. **11** Destructive (harmful) forces are everywhere in the city; threats and lies never leave its streets. **12** If an enemy were insulting (mocking) me, I could endure it; if a foe (enemy) were rising up against me, I could hide. **13** But it is you—my companion, my close friend— **14** with whom I once shared sweet fellowship (companionship) in the house of God, walking together among the worshipers. **15** Let death come suddenly upon my enemies; let them go down alive into the grave (the place of the dead), for evil is among them. **16** As for me, I call to God, and the LORD will save me. **17** Evening, morning, and noon I cry out in distress, and He hears my voice. **18** He rescues me unharmed from the battle against me, even though many oppose me. **19** God, who is enthroned (seated in authority) forever, who does not change, will hear them and humble (bring down) them, for they do not fear God. **20** My companion attacks his friends; he has broken his covenant (agreement). **21** His words are as smooth as butter, but war is in his heart; his words are as soft as oil, yet they are like drawn swords (sharp weapons). **22** Cast (throw) your burdens (cares) on the LORD, and He will sustain (support) you; He will never let the righteous (good people) be shaken (fall). **23** But You, O God, will bring the wicked (evil people) down to the pit (place of destruction); bloodthirsty (violent) and deceitful (dishonest) men will not live out half their days. But as for me, I trust in You.

Chapter 56

1. Be merciful to me, my God, for my enemies are chasing me; all day long they press their attack. **2.** My adversaries (enemies) pursue me all day long; in their pride many are attacking me. **3.** When I am afraid, I put my trust in You. **4.** In God, whose word I praise— in God I trust and am not afraid. What can mere mortals (human beings) do to me? **5.** All day long they twist my words; all their schemes (plans) are for my ruin. **6.** They conspire (plot), they lurk (lie in wait), they watch my steps, hoping to take my life. **7.** Because of their wickedness (evil) do not let them escape; in Your anger, God, bring the nations (people groups) down. **8.** Record (write down) my misery; list my tears on Your scroll — are they not in Your record? **9.** Then my enemies will turn back when I call for help. By this I will know that God is for me. **10.** In God, whose word I praise, in the LORD, whose word I praise— **11.** in God I trust and am not afraid. What can man do to me? **12.** I am under vows (promises) to You, my God; I will present my thank offerings to You. **13.** For You have delivered me from death and my feet from stumbling, that I may walk before God in the light of life.

Chapter 57

1. Have mercy on me, my God, have mercy on me, for in You I take refuge. I will take refuge in the shadow of Your wings until the disaster (calamity) has passed. **2.** I cry out to God Most High, to God, who vindicates (defends) me. **3.** He sends from heaven and saves me, rebuking (correcting) those who hotly pursue me— God sends forth His love and His faithfulness. **4.** I am in the midst of lions (dangerous people); I am forced to dwell among ravenous (greedy) beasts— men whose teeth are spears and arrows, whose tongues are sharp swords. **5.** Be exalted (honored), O God, above the heavens; let Your glory be over all the earth. **6.** They spread a net for my feet— I was bowed down in distress. They dug a pit in my path— but they have fallen into it themselves. **7.** My heart, O God, is steadfast (firm), my heart is steadfast; I will sing and make music. **8.** Awake, my soul! Awake, harp and lyre (stringed instruments)! I will awaken the dawn. **9.** I will praise You, Lord, among the nations; I will sing of You among the peoples. **10.** For great is Your love, reaching to the heavens; Your faithfulness reaches to the skies. **11.** Be exalted, O God, above the heavens; let Your glory be over all the earth.

Chapter 58

1. Do you rulers indeed speak justly? Do you judge people with equity (fairness)? **2.** No, in your heart you devise (plan) injustice (wrongdoing), and your hands mete out (carry out) violence on the earth. **3.** Even from birth the wicked go astray; from the womb they are wayward (dishonest), spreading lies. **4.** Their venom (poison) is like the venom of a snake, like that of a cobra (a deadly snake) that has stopped its ears, **5.** that will not heed (listen to) the tune of the charmer, however skillful the enchanter may be. **6.** Break the teeth in their mouths, O God; LORD, tear out the fangs of those lions (dangerous enemies)! **7.** Let them vanish like water that flows away; when they draw the bow (shoot arrows), let their arrows fall short. **8.** May they be like a slug (snail) that melts away as it moves along, like a stillborn (dead-born) child that never sees the sun. **9.** Before your pots (pots of cooking) can feel the heat of the thorns (prickly plants)— whether they be green (alive) or dry (dead)— the wicked will be swept away. **10.** The righteous (good people) will be glad when they are avenged, when they dip their feet in the blood of the wicked. **11.** Then people will say, "Surely the righteous still are rewarded; surely there is a God who judges the earth."

Chapter 59

1. Deliver me from my enemies, O God; be my fortress (place of protection) against those who are attacking me. **2.** Deliver me from evildoers (wicked people) and save me from those who are after my blood (trying to kill me). **3.** See how they lie in wait for me! Fierce (violent) men conspire (plot) against me for no offense or sin of mine, LORD. **4.** I have done no wrong, yet they are ready to attack me. Arise (stand up) to help me; look on my plight (situation)! **5.** You, LORD God Almighty, You who are the God of Israel, rouse (wake up) Yourself to punish all the nations; show no mercy to wicked traitors (those who break trust). **6.** They return at evening, snarling like dogs (growling viciously), and prowl about the city. **7.** See what they spew (spit) from their mouths— the words from their lips are sharp as swords, and they think, "Who can hear us?" **8.** But You laugh at them, LORD; You scoff (mock) at all those nations. **9.** You are my strength, I watch for You; You, God, are my fortress, **10.** my God on whom I can rely. God will go before me and will let me gloat (rejoice) over those who slander (speak falsely about) me. **11.** But do not kill them, Lord our shield (protector), or my people will forget. In Your might (strength) uproot them and bring them down. **12.** For the sins of their mouths, for the words of their lips, let them be caught in their pride. For the curses and lies they utter, **13.** consume (destroy) them in Your wrath (anger), consume them till they are no more.

Then it will be known to the ends of the earth that God rules over Jacob (Israel). **14.** They return at evening, snarling like dogs, and prowl about the city. **15.** They wander about for food and howl (cry out) if not satisfied. **16.** But I will sing of Your strength, in the morning I will sing of Your love; for You are my fortress, my refuge (safe place) in times of trouble. **17.** You are my strength, I sing praise to You; You, God, are my fortress, my God on whom I can rely.

Chapter 60

1. You have rejected us, God, and burst upon us; You have been angry— now restore us! **2.** You have shaken the land and torn it open; mend (heal) its fractures, for it is quaking (shaking). **3.** You have shown Your people desperate (hopeless) times; You have given us wine that makes us stagger (be dizzy). **4.** But for those who fear You, You have raised a banner (sign) to be unfurled (unfolded) against the bow (enemy's weapons). **5.** Save us and help us with Your right hand (a sign of power), that those You love may be delivered (rescued). **6.** God has spoken from His sanctuary (holy place): "In triumph I will parcel out (divide) Shechem and measure off the Valley of Sukkoth. **7.** Gilead is mine, and Manasseh is mine; Ephraim is my helmet (defense), Judah is my scepter (royal authority). **8.** Moab is my washbasin (symbol of submission), on Edom I toss my sandal (sign of control); over Philistia I shout in triumph." **9.** Who will bring me to the fortified city? Who will lead me to Edom? **10.** Is it not You, God, You who have now rejected us and no longer go out with our armies? **11.** Give us aid (help) against the enemy, for human help is worthless. **12.** With God we will gain the victory, and He will trample down our enemies.

Chapter 61

1. Hear my cry, O God; listen to my prayer. **2.** From the ends of the earth I call to You, I call as my heart grows faint (weak); lead me to the rock that is higher than I (a place of safety). **3.** For You have been my refuge (place of safety), a strong tower against the foe (enemy). **4.** I long to dwell (live) in Your tent (temple) forever and take refuge in the shelter of Your wings. **5.** For You, God, have heard my vows (promises); You have given me the heritage (inheritance) of those who fear (revere) Your name. **6.** Increase the days of the king's life, his years for many generations. **7.** May he be enthroned (seated in royal authority) in God's presence forever; appoint Your love and faithfulness to protect him. **8.** Then I will ever sing in praise of Your name and fulfill my vows day after day.

Chapter 62

1. Truly my soul finds rest in God; my salvation (rescue) comes from Him. **2.** Truly He is my rock (strong support) and my salvation; He is my fortress (safe place), I will never be shaken. **3.** How long will you assault me? Would all of you throw me down— this leaning wall, this tottering (unstable) fence? **4.** Surely, they intend to topple (overthrow) me from my lofty (high) place; they take delight in lies. With their mouths they bless, but in their hearts, they curse. **5.** Yes, my soul, find rest in God; my hope comes from Him. **6.** Truly He is my rock and my salvation; He is my fortress, I will not be shaken. **7.** My salvation and my honor depend on God; He is my mighty rock, my refuge (safe place). **8.** Trust in Him at all times, you people; pour out your hearts to Him, for God is our refuge. **9.** Surely the lowborn (poor) are but a breath (temporary), the highborn (rich and powerful) are but a lie. If weighed on a balance, they are nothing; together they are only a breath. **10.** Do not trust in extortion (fraud or robbery) or put vain (empty) hope in stolen goods; though your riches increase, do not set your heart on them. **11.** One thing God has spoken, two things I have heard: "Power belongs to You, God, **12.** and with You, Lord, is unfailing love"; and, "You reward everyone according to what they have done."

Chapter 63

1. You, God, are my God, earnestly I seek You; I thirst for You, my whole being longs for You, in a dry and parched land where there is no water. **2.** I have seen You in the sanctuary (temple) and beheld (witnessed) Your power and Your glory. **3.** Because Your love is better than life, my lips will glorify (praise) You. **4.** I will praise You as long as I live, and in Your name, I will lift up my hands. **5.** I will be fully satisfied (content) as with the richest of foods; with singing lips my mouth will praise You. **6.** On my bed I remember You; I think of You through the watches of the night (nighttime). **7.** Because You are my help, I sing in the shadow of Your wings. **8.** I cling to You; Your right hand (symbol of strength) upholds (supports) me. **9.** Those who want to kill me will be destroyed; they will go down to the depths (grave) of the earth. **10.** They will be given over to the sword and become food for jackals (wild animals). **11.** But the king will rejoice in God; all who swear by God will glory in Him, while the mouths of liars will be silenced.

Chapter 64

1. Hear me, my God, as I voice my complaint; protect my life from the threat of the enemy. **2.** Hide me from the conspiracy (secret plan) of the wicked, from the plots (schemes) of evildoers. **3.** They sharpen their tongues like swords and aim cruel (harmful) words like deadly arrows. **4.** They shoot from ambush (hidden position) at the innocent; they shoot suddenly, without fear. **5.** They encourage (support) each other in evil plans, they talk about hiding their snares (traps); they say, "Who will see it?" **6.** They plot injustice (wrongdoing) and say, "We have devised a perfect plan!" Surely the human mind and heart are cunning (deceptive). **7.** But God will shoot them with His arrows; they will suddenly be struck down. **8.** He will turn their own tongues against them and bring them to ruin; all who see them will shake their heads in scorn (mockery). **9.** All people will fear (be in awe); they will proclaim (declare) the works of God and ponder (think deeply) what He has done. **10.** The righteous will rejoice in the LORD and take refuge in Him; all the upright in heart will glory in Him!

Chapter 65

1. Praise awaits You, our God, in Zion (a hill in Jerusalem); to You, our vows will be fulfilled. **2.** You who answer prayers, to You all people will come. **3.** When we were overwhelmed by our sins, You forgave our wrongdoings. **4.** Blessed are those You choose to bring near to live in Your temple! We are filled with the good things from Your house. **5.** You answer us with great deeds, O God our Savior, the hope of all the earth, even from the farthest seas. **6.** You formed the mountains by Your power, arming Yourself with strength. **7.** You stilled the roaring seas and the turmoil (chaos) of the nations. **8.** The whole earth is filled with awe at Your wonders; from morning to evening, people sing for joy because of You. **9.** You care for the land and water it, making it rich and abundant. The streams are filled to provide food for the people, as You have planned. **10.** You soak the land with rain, soften it with showers, and bless its crops. **11.** You crown the year with Your blessings, and our carts overflow with abundance. **12.** The wilderness is rich with grasslands, and the hills are filled with joy. **13.** The meadows are full of flocks, and the valleys are covered with grain; they shout and sing for joy.

Chapter 66

1. Shout for joy to God, all the earth! **2.** Sing the glory of His name; make His praise glorious. **3.** Say to God, "How awesome are Your deeds! So great is Your power that Your enemies tremble before You. **4.** All the earth bows down to You; they sing praises to You and honor Your name." **5.** Come and see the great things God has done, His awesome deeds for mankind. **6.** He turned the sea into dry land, and the people walked through the waters on foot— let's rejoice in Him! **7.** He rules forever by His power, and His eyes watch over the nations. Let not the rebellious rise up against Him. **8.** Praise our God, all peoples! Let the sound of His praise be heard. **9.** He has preserved our lives and kept us from stumbling. **10.** For You, God, tested us; You purified us like silver. **11.** You brought us into a place of trouble and laid heavy burdens on us. **12.** You allowed others to oppress us, but we passed through the fire and the water, and You brought us to a place of abundance. **13.** I will bring burnt offerings to Your temple and fulfill my vows to You, **14.** vows I made when I was in distress. **15.** I will offer You sacrifices of the best animals, rams, bulls, and goats. **16.** Come and listen, all who fear God; let me tell you what He has done for me. **17.** I cried out to Him with my mouth, and His praise was on my lips. **18.** If I had held onto sin in my heart, the Lord would not have heard me. **19.** But God listened, and He heard my prayer. **20.** Praise be to God, who has not rejected my prayer or withheld His love from me.

Chapter 67

1. May God be kind to us and bless us and may His face shine upon us— **2.** so that His ways may be known on earth, and His salvation among all nations. **3.** May the peoples praise You, God; may all the peoples praise You. **4.** May the nations be glad and sing for joy, for You rule the peoples with fairness and guide the nations of the earth. **5.** May the peoples praise You, God; may all the peoples praise You. **6.** The land yields its harvest (produce); God, our God, blesses us. **7.** May God bless us still, so that all the ends of the earth will revere Him.

Chapter 68

1. To the Chief Musician. A Psalm of David. A Song. Let God rise up, let His enemies scatter; let those who hate Him flee before Him. **2.** As smoke is blown away, drive them away; as wax melts before fire, let the wicked perish at God's presence. **3.** But let the righteous be glad; let them rejoice before God; yes, let them rejoice with joy. **4.** Sing to God, sing praises to His name; exalt Him who rides on the clouds, by His Name Yah, and rejoice before Him. **5.** A father to the fatherless, a defender of widows, is God in His holy dwelling. **6.** God sets the lonely in families; He leads out the prisoners with joy, but the rebellious live in a parched land. **7.** O God, when You went out before Your people, when You marched through the wilderness, Selah. **8.** The earth trembled; the heavens poured down rain at the presence of God; Sinai itself was moved at God's presence, the God of Israel. **9.** You, O God, sent abundant rain, confirming Your inheritance when it was weary. **10.** Your people settled there; You, O God, provided for the poor by Your goodness. **11.** The Lord gave the word; great was the company

of those who proclaimed it: **12.** "Kings and armies flee, they flee; and the women at home divide the spoil. **13.** Even though you lie among the sheepfolds, you will be like the wings of a dove, covered with silver, her feathers gleaming with gold." **14.** When the Almighty scattered kings, it snowed on Zalmon (a mountain known for its snowy peaks). **15.** The mountain of God is the mountain of Bashan; a mountain of many peaks is the mountain of Bashan. **16.** Why do you rage with envy, you mountains of many peaks? This is the mountain God desires to dwell in; yes, the Lord will live there forever. **17.** The chariots of God are twenty thousand, thousands upon thousands; the Lord is among them, as He was at Sinai in the Holy Place. **18.** You ascended on high, You led captivity captive; You received gifts from men, even from the rebellious, that the Lord God might dwell there. **19.** Blessed be the Lord, who daily loads us with benefits, the God of our salvation! Selah. **20.** Our God is the God of salvation, and to God the Lord belong escapes from death. **21.** But God will strike the head of His enemies, the hairy scalp of the one who still goes on in his sins. **22.** The Lord said, "I will bring them back from Bashan, I will bring them back from the depths of the sea, **23.** that your feet may crush them in blood, and the tongues of your dogs may have their portion from your enemies." **24.** They have seen Your procession, O God, the procession of my God, my King, into the sanctuary. **25.** The singers went before, the players on instruments followed after; among them were the maidens playing tambourines. **26.** Bless God in the congregations, the Lord from the fountain of Israel. **27.** There is little Benjamin, their leader, the princes of Judah and their company, the princes of Zebulun and the princes of Naphtali. **28.** Your God has commanded Your strength; strengthen, O God, what You have done for us. **29.** Because of Your temple at Jerusalem, kings will bring gifts to You. **30.** Rebuke the beasts of the reeds, the herds of bulls with the calves of the peoples, until everyone submits with pieces of silver. Scatter the people who delight in war. **31.** Envoys will come from Egypt; Ethiopia will quickly stretch out her hands to God. **32.** Sing to God, you kingdoms of the earth; sing praises to the Lord, Selah. **33.** To Him who rides on the heavens of heavens, which are of old! Indeed, He sends out His voice, a mighty voice. **34.** Ascribe strength to God; His excellence is over Israel, and His strength is in the clouds. **35.** O God, You are more awesome than Your holy places. The God of Israel is He who gives strength and power to His people. Blessed be God!

Chapter 69

1. To the Chief Musician. Set to 'The Lilies.' A Psalm of David. Save me, O God! For the waters have risen up to my neck. 2. I am sinking in deep mud, where there's no solid ground; I have come into deep waters, and the floods are overwhelming me. 3. I am weary from crying; my throat is dry; my eyes fail while I wait for my God. 4. Those who hate me without cause are more than the hairs of my head; they are powerful and want to destroy me, though I've done nothing wrong; still, I must repay them. 5. O God, You know my foolishness; my sins are not hidden from You. 6. Let those who wait for You, O Lord God of hosts, not be ashamed because of me; let those who seek You not be confused because of me, O God of Israel. 7. For Your sake I have borne disgrace; shame covers my face. 8. I have become a stranger to my brothers, and an alien to my mother's children. 9. Because zeal for Your house has consumed me, and the insults of those who insult You have fallen on me. 10. When I wept and humbled my soul with fasting, they made fun of me. 11. I wore sackcloth as my clothing; I became a byword to them. 12. Those who sit at the city gate talk about me, and I am the song of the drunkards. 13. But as for me, my prayer is to You, O Lord, at the right time; O God, in Your great mercy, answer me with the truth of Your salvation. 14. Deliver me from the mud, and do not let me sink; rescue me from those who hate me, and from the deep waters. 15. Do not let the floodwaters overwhelm me, or the deep swallow me up; do not let the pit close its mouth over me. 16. Answer me, O Lord, for Your love is good; turn to me according to Your great mercy. 17. Do not hide Your face from Your servant, for I am in trouble; answer me quickly. 18. Draw near to my soul and redeem it; deliver me from my enemies. 19. You know my disgrace, my shame, and my dishonor; my enemies are all before You. 20. Reproach has broken my heart, and I am full of grief; I looked for pity, but there was none; for comforters, but I found none. 21. They gave me gall (bitter substance) for my food, and for my thirst, they gave me vinegar to drink. 22. Let their table become a trap before them, and their well-being a snare. 23. Let their eyes be blinded, so that they cannot see; and make their bodies tremble continually. 24. Pour out Your wrath upon them, and let Your fierce anger take hold of them. 25. Let their homes be desolate; let no one dwell in their tents. 26. For they persecute those whom You have struck and talk about the pain of those You have wounded. 27. Add guilt to their guilt, and do not let them come into Your righteousness. 28. Let them be erased from the book of the living, and not be recorded with the righteous. 29. But I am poor and in sorrow; let Your salvation, O God, set me on high. 30. I will

praise the name of God with a song and magnify Him with thanksgiving. 31. This will please the Lord more than an ox or a bull with horns and hooves. 32. The humble will see and be glad; you who seek God, let your hearts live. 33. For the Lord hears the poor and does not despise His prisoners. 34. Let heaven and earth praise Him, the seas and everything in them. 35. For God will save Zion and build the cities of Judah, that they may dwell there and possess it. 36. The descendants of His servants will inherit it, and those who love His name will live there.

Chapter 70

1. To the Chief Musician. A Psalm of David. To bring to remembrance. Make haste, O God, to deliver me! Make haste to help me, O Lord! 2. Let those who seek my life be ashamed and confounded; let them be turned back and confused who desire my hurt. 3. Let them be turned back because of their shame, who say, "Aha, aha!" 4. Let all those who seek You rejoice and be glad in You; and let those who love Your salvation continually say, "Let God be magnified!" 5. But I am poor and needy; make haste to me, O God! You are my help and my deliverer; O Lord, do not delay.

Chapter 71

1. In You, O Lord, I place my trust; let me never be put to shame. 2. Deliver me in Your righteousness and rescue me. Turn Your ear to me and save me. 3. Be my strong refuge, to which I can continually resort; You have commanded to save me, for You are my rock and fortress. 4. Deliver me, O my God, from the hand of the wicked, from the grasp of the unrighteous and cruel man. 5. For You are my hope, O Lord God; You have been my trust since I was young. 6. From my birth, You have upheld me; You are the One who brought me out of my mother's womb. I will praise You continually. 7. I am a wonder to many, but You are my strong refuge. 8. Let my mouth be filled with Your praise, and with Your glory all day long. 9. Do not cast me away in my old age; do not forsake me when my strength fails. 10. My enemies speak against me, and those who lie in wait for my life plot together, 11. Saying, "God has forsaken him; pursue him and take him, for no one will rescue him." 12. O God, do not be far from me; come quickly to help me! 13. Let my enemies be ashamed and consumed, those who attack my life. Let them be covered with disgrace and dishonor. 14. But I will continually hope in You and praise You more and more. 15. My mouth will tell of Your righteousness and Your salvation all day, for I do not know their limits. 16. I will go in the strength of the Lord God; I will declare Your righteousness, Yours alone. 17. O God, You have taught me from my youth and to this day I declare Your wondrous deeds. 18. Now when I am old and gray, O God, do not forsake me until I declare Your power to the next generation, Your strength to all those to come. 19. Your righteousness, O God, is very high; You have done great things. O God, who is like You? 20. You, who have shown me great and severe troubles, will revive me again and raise me up from the depths of the earth. 21. You will increase my honor and comfort me on every side. 22. I will also praise You with the lute for Your faithfulness, O my God. To You I will sing with the harp, O Holy One of Israel. 23. My lips will greatly rejoice when I sing to You, and my soul, which You have redeemed. 24. My tongue will talk of Your righteousness all the day long, for those who seek my harm will be put to shame.

Chapter 72

1. A Psalm of Solomon. Give the king Your justice, O God, and Your righteousness to the king's son. 2. He will judge Your people with righteousness, and the poor with justice. 3. The mountains will bring peace to the people, and the hills will bring righteousness. 4. He will defend the poor and needy and break the oppressors to pieces. 5. They will fear You as long as the sun and moon endure, throughout all generations. 6. He will come down like rain upon the mown grass, like showers that water the earth. 7. In His days the righteous will flourish, and peace will abound, until the moon is no more. 8. He will have dominion from sea to sea, and from the river to the ends of the earth. 9. Those who dwell in the wilderness will bow before Him, and His enemies will lick the dust. 10. The kings of Tarshish and the isles will bring gifts; the kings of Sheba and Seba will offer tribute. 11. All kings will bow down before Him; all nations will serve Him. 12. For He will deliver the needy when they cry, the poor also, and those who have no helper. 13. He will have pity on the poor and needy and will save their lives. 14. He will redeem their lives from oppression and violence; their blood will be precious in His sight. 15. And He shall live; the gold of Sheba will be brought to Him; people will pray for Him continually, and He will be praised daily. 16. There will be an abundance of grain in the land, even on the mountaintops. Its fruit will wave like Lebanon, and those in the city will flourish like the grass. 17. His name will endure forever; His name will continue as long as the sun. People will be blessed in Him; all nations will call Him blessed. 18. Blessed be the Lord God, the God of Israel, who alone does wondrous things. 19. Blessed be His glorious name forever! Let the whole earth be filled with His glory. Amen and Amen. 20. The prayers of David, son of Jesse, are ended.

Chapter 73

1. Truly, God is good to Israel, to those whose hearts are pure. 2. But as for me, my feet nearly stumbled; I almost lost my footing. 3. I envied the proud when I saw the prosperity of the wicked. 4. They seem to die without pain; their bodies are healthy and strong. 5. They are not troubled like others; they do not suffer as others do. 6. Pride adorns them like a necklace; violence covers them like clothing. 7. Their eyes bulge with wealth; they have everything their hearts could wish for. 8. They scoff and speak wickedly about oppression; they speak with arrogance. 9. They set their mouths against the heavens, and their tongues walk freely across the earth. 10. So the people turn to them and drink in their words. 11. They ask, "How does God know? Does the Most High have knowledge?" 12. These are the wicked, who live in ease and grow richer every day. 13. Surely, I have cleansed my heart in vain and washed my hands in innocence. 14. All day long I've been afflicted, and every morning brings new punishments. 15. If I had spoken like that, I would have betrayed Your children. 16. When I tried to understand all this, it was oppressive to me, 17. Until I entered the sanctuary of God; then I understood their destiny. 18. Surely You place them on slippery ground; You cast them down to ruin. 19. How suddenly they are destroyed, completely swept away by terrors! 20. They are like a dream when one awakens; when You arise, O Lord, You will despise their image. 21. When my heart was bitter and I was pierced within, 22. I was senseless and ignorant; I was like a beast before You. 23. Yet I am always with You; You hold me by my right hand. 24. You guide me with Your counsel, and afterward, You will take me into glory. 25. Whom have I in heaven but You? And earth has nothing I desire besides You. 26. My flesh and my heart may fail, but God is the strength of my heart and my portion forever. 27. Those who are far from You will perish; You destroy all who are unfaithful to You. 28. But it is good for me to draw near to God; I have made the Lord God my refuge, that I may declare all Your works.

Chapter 74

1. O God, why have You rejected us forever? Why does Your anger burn against the sheep of Your pasture? 2. Remember Your people, whom You purchased long ago, the tribe of Your inheritance, whom You redeemed— this Mount Zion where You dwelt. 3. Lift up Your feet and see how the enemy has destroyed everything in the sanctuary. 4. Your foes roared in the midst of Your meeting place; they raised their banners as signs. 5. They were like men wielding axes against a thicket of trees. 6. They smashed all Your carved work with axes and hammers. 7. They set fire to Your sanctuary and desecrated the dwelling place of Your name. 8. They said in their hearts, "We will utterly destroy them." They burned all the meeting places of God in the land. 9. We no longer see our signs; there is no prophet left, and no one knows how long this will last. 10. How long will the enemy mock You, O God? Will they blaspheme Your name forever? 11. Why do You withdraw Your hand, O Lord? Stretch it out and destroy them! 12. For God is my King from long ago, who works salvation in the midst of the earth. 13. You divided the sea by Your strength; You broke the heads of the sea creatures in the waters. 14. You crushed the heads of Leviathan; You gave him as food to the creatures of the wilderness. 15. You opened up springs and streams; You dried up the ever-flowing rivers. 16. The day is Yours, and the night also is Yours; You established the sun and the moon. 17. You set the boundaries of the earth; You made both summer and winter. 18. Remember how the enemy has mocked You, O Lord, and how a foolish people has reviled Your name. 19. Do not give the life of Your dove to the wild beast; do not forget the lives of Your afflicted people forever. 20. Look to the covenant, for the dark places of the earth are full of the habitations of violence. 21. Do not let the oppressed return in shame; may the poor and needy praise Your name. 22. Arise, O God, and defend Your cause; remember how the foolish man reproaches You all day long. 23. Do not forget the voice of Your enemies; the uproar of those who rise up against You increases continually.

Chapter 75

1. We give thanks to You, O God, we give thanks! Your name is near; people tell of Your wonderful deeds. 2. "When the time is right, I will judge fairly. 3. The earth and all its inhabitants may shake, but I will firmly set its pillars." Selah 4. I said to the arrogant, "Do not boast," and to the wicked, "Do not lift up your horn. 5. Do not lift up your horn on high, nor speak with a stiff neck." 6. Exaltation does not come from the east, the west, or the south. 7. But God is the Judge; He brings one down and exalts another. 8. For in the hand of the Lord is a cup, filled with foaming wine. He pours it out, and all the wicked of the earth will drink it down to its dregs. 9. But I will declare forever and sing praises to the God of Jacob. 10. All the horns of the wicked I will cut off, but the horns of the righteous will be exalted.

Chapter 76

1. To the Chief Musician, on stringed instruments. A Psalm of Asaph. A Song. In Judah, God is known; His name is great in Israel. 2. His tabernacle

is in Salem (Jerusalem), and His dwelling place is in Zion (holy city). **3.** There He broke the arrows of the bow, the shield, and sword of battle. Selah. **4.** You are more glorious and majestic than the mountains of prey. **5.** The brave warriors were plundered; they fell into a deep sleep, and the mighty could not use their hands. **6.** At Your rebuke, O God of Jacob, both the chariot and the horse fell asleep. **7.** You alone are to be feared; who can stand before You when You are angry? **8.** You caused judgment to be heard from heaven; the earth feared and was silent, **9.** When God arose to judge, to deliver all the oppressed-on earth. Selah. **10.** Surely, human anger will praise You; with the rest of it, You will clothe Yourself. **11.** Make vows to the Lord your God and fulfill them; let all around Him bring gifts to Him who should be feared. **12.** He will cut off the spirit of rulers; He is awesome to the kings of the earth.

Chapter 77

1. To the Chief Musician, to Jeduthun. A Psalm of Asaph. I cried out to God with my voice— to God, and He heard me. **2.** In the day of my trouble, I sought the Lord; I stretched out my hands to Him all night; my soul refused comfort. **3.** I remembered God and was troubled; I complained, and my spirit was overwhelmed. Selah. **4.** You kept my eyelids open; I was so troubled that I couldn't speak. **5.** I thought about the days of old, the years long past. **6.** I remembered my song in the night; I meditated in my heart, and my spirit searched diligently. **7.** Will the Lord reject me forever? Will He never show favor again? **8.** Has His mercy ended forever? Has His promise failed for all time? **9.** Has God forgotten to be merciful? Has He, in anger, shut up His tender mercies? Selah. **10.** Then I said, "This is my grief; but I will remember the years of the right hand of the Most High." **11.** I will remember the works of the Lord; surely, I will remember Your wonders of old. **12.** I will meditate on all Your works and talk of Your deeds. **13.** Your way, O God, is in the sanctuary; who is as great as our God? **14.** You are the God who does wonders; You have declared Your strength among the people. **15.** With Your arm, You redeemed Your people, the sons of Jacob and Joseph. Selah. **16.** The waters saw You, O God; the waters saw You and were afraid; the depths trembled. **17.** The clouds poured out water; the skies thundered; Your arrows flashed. **18.** The voice of Your thunder was in the whirlwind; lightning lit up the world; the earth trembled and shook. **19.** Your way was in the sea, Your path in the great waters, but Your footprints were not seen. **20.** You led Your people like a flock, by the hand of Moses and Aaron.

Chapter 78

1. A contemplation of Asaph. Listen, O my people, to my teaching; incline your ears to the words of my mouth. **2.** I will open my mouth in a parable; I will utter dark sayings of old, **3.** which we have heard and known, and our fathers have told us. **4.** We will not hide them from their children, telling the coming generation the praises of the Lord, and His strength, and the wonderful works He has done. **5.** For He established a testimony in Jacob, and appointed a law in Israel, which He commanded our fathers to make known to their children, **6.** that the generation to come might know them, the children yet to be born, that they may arise and declare them to their children, **7.** so they would set their hope in God and not forget His works but keep His commandments; **8.** and not be like their fathers, a stubborn and rebellious generation, a generation that did not set its heart aright, and whose spirit was not faithful to God. **9.** The children of Ephraim, armed with bows, turned back on the day of battle. **10.** They did not keep the covenant of God, and refused to walk in His law, **11.** and forgot His works, and the wonders He had shown them. **12.** Marvelous things He did in the sight of their fathers, in the land of Egypt, in the field of Zoan (a region in Egypt). **13.** He divided the sea and caused them to pass through; He made the waters stand like a heap. **14.** In the daytime, He led them with a cloud, and all the night with a light of fire. **15.** He split rocks in the wilderness, and gave them drink in abundance, like the deep waters. **16.** He brought streams out of the rock, and made waters run down like rivers. **17.** But they continued to sin against Him by rebelling against the Most High in the wilderness. **18.** They tested God in their hearts by asking for the food they craved. **19.** Yes, they spoke against God, saying, "Can God prepare a table in the wilderness? **20.** Behold, He struck the rock, and the waters gushed out, and the streams overflowed. Can He give bread also? Can He provide meat for His people?" **21.** Therefore, the Lord heard this and was angry; a fire was kindled against Jacob, and wrath also rose against Israel, **22.** because they did not believe in God, and did not trust in His salvation. **23.** Yet He commanded the clouds above, and opened the doors of heaven, **24.** and rained down manna to eat, and gave them the bread of heaven. **25.** Men ate the food of angels; He sent them food to the full. **26.** He caused an east wind to blow in the heavens, and by His power He brought in the south wind. **27.** He rained meat on them like dust, feathered birds like the sand of the seas; **28.** and let them fall in the midst of their camp, all around their dwellings. **29.** So they ate and were well filled, for He gave them their own desire. **30.** They were not deprived of their craving; but while their food was still in their mouths, **31.** the wrath of God came against them and killed the strongest of them and struck down the choice men of Israel. **32.** Despite this, they still sinned and did not believe in His wondrous works. **33.** So He consumed their days in futility, and their years in fear. **34.** When He killed them, they sought Him; they returned and earnestly sought God. **35.** Then they remembered that God was their rock, and the Most High God their Redeemer. **36.** But they flattered Him with their mouths and lied to Him with their tongues; **37.** for their heart was not steadfast with Him, nor were they faithful to His covenant. **38.** Yet He, being full of compassion, forgave their iniquity and did not destroy them; many times, He turned away His anger and did not stir up His wrath. **39.** For He remembered that they were but flesh, a breath that passes away and does not return. **40.** How often they provoked Him in the wilderness and grieved Him in the desert! **41.** Yes, again and again they tempted God, and limited the Holy One of Israel. **42.** They did not remember His power, the day when He redeemed them from the enemy, **43.** when He performed His signs in Egypt, and His wonders in the field of Zoan. **44.** He turned their rivers into blood, and their streams, so they could not drink. **45.** He sent swarms of flies to devour them, and frogs to destroy them. **46.** He gave their crops to the caterpillar, and their labor to the locust. **47.** He destroyed their vines with hail, and their sycamore trees with frost. **48.** He gave up their cattle to the hail, and their flocks to fiery lightning. **49.** He poured out His fierce anger on them, wrath, indignation, and trouble, sending angels of destruction among them. **50.** He made a path for His anger; He did not spare their soul from death but gave their life over to the plague, **51.** and struck down all the firstborn in Egypt, the first of their strength in the tents of Ham (the descendants of Ham, son of Noah). **52.** But He made His own people go forth like sheep and guided them in the wilderness like a flock; **53.** and He led them on safely, so that they did not fear, but the sea overwhelmed their enemies. **54.** He brought them to His holy border, this mountain which His right hand had acquired. **55.** He drove out the nations before them, and allotted them an inheritance by survey, and made the tribes of Israel dwell in their tents. **56.** Yet they tested and provoked the Most High God, and did not keep His testimonies, **57.** but turned back and acted unfaithfully like their fathers; they were turned aside like a deceitful bow. **58.** For they provoked Him to anger with their high places and moved Him to jealousy with their carved images. **59.** When God heard this, He was furious, and greatly abhorred Israel. **60.** So He forsook the tabernacle of Shiloh, the tent He had placed among men, **61.** and delivered His strength into captivity, and His glory into the enemy's hand. **62.** He gave His people over to the sword and was angry with His inheritance. **63.** The fire consumed their young men, and their maidens were not given in marriage. **64.** Their priests fell by the sword, and their widows made no lamentation. **65.** Then the Lord awoke as from sleep, like a mighty man who shouts because of wine. **66.** He beat back His enemies; He put them to perpetual reproach. **67.** Moreover, He rejected the tent of Joseph, and did not choose the tribe of Ephraim, **68.** but chose the tribe of Judah, Mount Zion which He loved. **69.** And He built His sanctuary like the heights, like the earth He established forever. **70.** He also chose David His servant and took him from the sheepfolds; **71.** from following the ewes that had young He brought him to shepherd Jacob His people, and Israel His inheritance. **72.** So he shepherded them according to the integrity of his heart and guided them by the skillfulness of his hands.

Chapter 79

1. A Psalm of Asaph. O God, the nations have invaded Your inheritance; they have defiled Your holy temple and laid Jerusalem in ruins. **2.** The bodies of Your servants have been given as food for the birds of the sky, and the flesh of Your faithful ones to the beasts of the earth. **3.** Their blood has been spilled like water around Jerusalem, and there was no one to bury them. **4.** We have become a disgrace to our neighbors, a mockery and scorn to those around us. **5.** How long, Lord? Will You remain angry forever? Will Your jealousy burn like fire? **6.** Pour out Your wrath on the nations that do not know You, and on the kingdoms that do not call on Your name, **7.** For they have devoured Jacob and laid waste to his homeland. **8.** Do not remember our former sins; let Your compassion come quickly to meet us, for we are brought low. **9.** Help us, O God of our salvation, for the glory of Your name; deliver us and forgive our sins, for Your name's sake! **10.** Why should the nations say, "Where is their God?" Let it be known among nations, in our sight, the vengeance for the blood of Your servants that has been shed. **11.** Let the groaning of the prisoner come before You; by the greatness of Your power, preserve those appointed to die. **12.** Return to our neighbors seven times the disgrace they have hurled at You, O Lord. **13.** So we, Your people, the sheep of Your pasture, will give You thanks forever; we will declare Your praise to all generations.

Chapter 80

1. To the Chief Musician, set to 'The Lilies.' A Testimony of Asaph. O Shepherd of Israel, You who lead Joseph like a flock, You who are enthroned between the cherubim, shine forth! 2. Before Ephraim, Benjamin, and Manasseh, stir up Your strength and come to save us. 3. Restore us, O God; make Your face shine on us, that we may be saved! 4. O Lord God of hosts, how long will You be angry against the prayer of Your people? 5. You have fed them with the bread of tears and made them drink tears in abundance. 6. You have made us a quarrel to our neighbors, and our enemies laugh at us. 7. Restore us, O God of hosts; make Your face shine on us, that we may be saved! 8. You brought a vine out of Egypt; You drove out the nations and planted it. 9. You cleared the ground for it, and it took root and filled the land. 10. The hills were covered with its shadow, and the mighty cedars with its branches. 11. It sent out its boughs to the sea, and its branches to the River. 12. Why have You broken down its walls, so that all who pass by pick its fruit? 13. The boar from the forest ravages it, and the wild animals devour it. 14. Return, we pray, O God of hosts; look down from heaven and see, and visit this vine, 15. The vineyard Your right hand has planted, and the branch You made strong for Yourself. 16. It is burned with fire, it is cut down; they perish at the rebuke of Your face. 17. Let Your hand be upon the man of Your right hand, the son of man You made strong for Yourself. 18. Then we will not turn back from You; revive us, and we will call on Your name. 19. Restore us, O Lord God of hosts; make Your face shine on us, that we may be saved.

Chapter 81

1. To the Chief Musician, on an instrument of Gath. A Psalm of Asaph. Sing aloud to God, our strength; make a joyful noise to the God of Jacob! 2. Raise a song and strike the tambourine, the pleasant harp and lyre. 3. Blow the trumpet at the New Moon, at the full moon, on our solemn feast day. 4. For this is a statute for Israel, a law of the God of Jacob. 5. This He established in Joseph as a testimony, when He went throughout the land of Egypt, and I heard a language I did not understand. 6. "I removed his shoulder from the burden; his hands were freed from the basket. 7. You called to Me in your trouble, and I delivered you; I answered you from the secret place of thunder and tested you at the waters of Meribah." Selah 8. "Hear, O My people, and I will admonish you; O Israel, if you would listen to Me! 9. There shall be no foreign god among you, nor shall you worship any foreign god. 10. I am the Lord your God, who brought you out of the land of Egypt; open your mouth wide, and I will fill it. 11. But My people did not listen to My voice; Israel would have none of Me. 12. So I gave them up to their stubborn hearts, to follow their own counsels. 13. Oh, that My people would listen to Me, that Israel would walk in My ways! 14. I would soon subdue their enemies and turn My hand against their adversaries. 15. The haters of the Lord would pretend submission to Him, but their fate would be sealed forever. 16. I would have fed them with the finest of wheat, and with honey from the rock I would have satisfied them."

Chapter 82

1. A Psalm of Asaph. God stands in the assembly of the mighty; He judges among the gods. 2. How long will you judge unjustly and show partiality to the wicked? Selah 3. Defend the poor and fatherless; do justice to the afflicted and needy. 4. Deliver the poor and needy; free them from the hand of the wicked. 5. They do not know, nor do they understand; they walk about in darkness; all the foundations of the earth are unstable. 6. I said, "You are gods, and all of you are children of the Highest. 7. But you will die like mere mortals and fall like every other ruler." 8. Arise, O God, judge the earth, for You shall inherit all nations.

Chapter 83

1. A Song. A Psalm of Asaph. Do not remain silent, O God! Do not keep still, and do not be silent, O God! 2. For behold, Your enemies make an uproar, and those who hate You have lifted their heads. 3. They have taken crafty counsel against Your people and conspired against Your treasured ones. 4. They have said, "Come, let us wipe them out as a nation, that the name of Israel may be remembered no more." 5. For they have conspired together with one mind; they form an alliance against You— 6. The tents of Edom, the Ishmaelites, Moab, and the Hagrites; 7. Gebal, Ammon, and Amalek, Philistia, and the inhabitants of Tyre; 8. Assyria has joined them; they have helped the children of Lot. Selah 9. Deal with them as You did with Midian, as with Sisera, as with Jabin at the river Kishon, 10. Who perished at Endor, who became as dung on the earth. 11. Make their nobles like Oreb and Zeeb, all their princes like Zebah and Zalmunna, 12. Who said, "Let us take for ourselves the pastures of God for a possession." 13. O my God, make them like whirling dust, like chaff before the wind! 14. As the fire burns the woods, and as the flame sets the mountains on fire, 15. So pursue them with Your tempest, and frighten them with Your storm. 16. Fill their faces with shame, that they may seek Your name, O Lord. 17. Let them be confounded and dismayed forever; let them be put to shame and perish,

18. That men may know that You, whose name alone is the Lord, are the Most High over all the earth.

Chapter 84

1. To the Chief Musician, on an instrument of Gath. A Psalm of the sons of Korah. How lovely is Your dwelling place, O Lord of hosts! 2. My soul longs, yes, even faints for the courts of the Lord; my heart and my flesh cry out for the living God. 3. Even the sparrow has found a home, and the swallow a nest for herself, where she may lay her young—near Your altars, O Lord of hosts, my King and my God. 4. Blessed are those who dwell in Your house; they will still be praising You. Selah 5. Blessed is the man whose strength is in You, whose heart is set on pilgrimage. 6. As they pass through the Valley of Baca, they make it a place of springs; the rain also covers it with pools. 7. They go from strength to strength; each one appears before God in Zion. 8. O Lord God of hosts, hear my prayer; give ear, O God of Jacob! Selah 9. O God, look upon our shield, and look upon the face of Your anointed. 10. For a day in Your courts is better than a thousand elsewhere. I would rather be a doorkeeper in the house of my God than dwell in the tents of wickedness. 11. For the Lord God is a sun and shield; the Lord will give grace and glory; no good thing will He withhold from those who walk uprightly. 12. O Lord of hosts, blessed is the man who trusts in You!

Chapter 85

1. To the Chief Musician, A Psalm of the sons of Korah. Lord, You have been favorable to Your land; You have restored the fortunes of Jacob. 2. You have forgiven the iniquity of Your people; You have covered all their sin. Selah 3. You have taken away all Your wrath; You have turned from the fierceness of Your anger. 4. Restore us, O God of our salvation, and cause Your anger toward us to cease. 5. Will You be angry with us forever? Will You prolong Your anger to all generations? 6. Will You not revive us again, that Your people may rejoice in You? 7. Show us Your mercy, Lord, and grant us Your salvation. 8. I will listen to what God the Lord will speak, for He will speak peace to His people and to His faithful ones; but let them not turn back to folly. 9. Surely His salvation is near to those who fear Him, that glory may dwell in our land. 10. Mercy and truth have met together; righteousness and peace have kissed. 11. Truth will spring from the earth, and righteousness will look down from heaven. 12. Yes, the Lord will give what is good, and our land will yield its increase. 13. Righteousness will go before Him and prepare the way for His steps.

Chapter 86

1. A Prayer of David. Listen closely (attentively), O Lord, and hear me; I am poor and in need (lacking). 2. Protect (guard) my life, for I am devoted to You; You are my God. Save Your servant who trusts (relies) in You! 3. Show mercy (kindness) to me, O Lord, for I call out to You all day long. 4. Bring joy (delight) to Your servant's soul, for to You, O Lord, I lift up my heart. 5. You, Lord, are good and quick to forgive (pardon); You are full of mercy to all who call upon You. 6. Listen (hear), O Lord, to my prayer; pay attention (focus) to my cry for help. 7. In the day of my trouble (distress), I will call on You, for You will answer (respond) me. 8. Among the gods, there is no one like You, O Lord, nor are there any works (deeds) like Yours. 9. All nations You have made will come and worship (adore) before You, O Lord, and honor Your name. 10. For You are great and do wondrous (miraculous) things; You alone are God. 11. Teach (guide) me Your way, O Lord; I will follow (obey) Your truth. Unite my heart to honor (revere) Your name. 12. I will praise (thank) You, O Lord my God, with all my heart, and glorify Your name forever. 13. For great is Your mercy (compassion) toward me, and You have saved (rescued) my soul from the depths of the grave (death). 14. O God, proud enemies rise (arise) against me, and a mob of violent men seeks my life. They do not consider (acknowledge) You. 15. But You, O Lord, are full of compassion (mercy), gracious, slow to anger, and abundant (overflowing) in mercy and truth. 16. Turn to me and show me mercy! Give Your strength (power) to Your servant and save the son of Your maidservant. 17. Show me a sign (evidence) of Your goodness, so that those who hate me will see and be ashamed (embarrassed), knowing that You, Lord, have helped and comforted (encouraged) me.

Chapter 87

1. A Psalm of the sons of Korah. His foundation (base) is in the holy mountains. 2. The Lord loves (adores) the gates of Zion more than all the dwellings (homes) of Jacob. 3. Glorious (magnificent) things are said about you, O city of God! Selah. 4. I will mention Rahab (Ancient Egypt) and Babylon to those who know Me; behold, Philistia, Tyre, and Ethiopia: "This one was born there." 5. And of Zion it will be said, "This one and that one was born there, and the Most High Himself will establish her." 6. The Lord will record (register) when He registers the people: "This one was born there." Selah. 7. Both the singers and the musicians (instrumentalists) will say, "All my springs (sources) are in you."

Chapter 88

1. A Psalm of the sons of Korah, to the Chief Musician, set to "Mahalath Leannoth" (a musical tune). A contemplation (reflection) of Heman the Ezrahite. **2.** O Lord, God of my salvation, I cry out to You day and night. **3.** Let my prayer (petition) reach You; listen to my cry. **4.** My soul is full of troubles (distress), and my life is near the grave (death). **5.** I am counted among those who go down to the pit (abyss); I am like a man without strength (power). **6.** I am surrounded by the dead (deceased), like those who lie in the grave (tomb), whom You no longer remember, cut off from Your hand. **7.** You have put me in the lowest pit, in darkness (gloom), in the depths (deep waters). **8.** Your anger weighs heavily on me, and You have afflicted (troubled) me with all Your waves. Selah. **9.** You have distanced my friends (companions) from me and made me an object of scorn (mockery). I am trapped and cannot escape. **10.** My eyes grow weak (dim) with sorrow; I call to You daily, stretching out my hands. **11.** Will You work wonders (miracles) for the dead? Can the dead rise (live) and praise You? Selah. **12.** Will your love (kindness) be declared in the grave, or Your faithfulness in destruction (ruin)? **13.** Can Your wonders be known in the dark (shadows), or Your righteousness in the land of forgetfulness (oblivion)? **14.** But I cry (call) to You, O Lord, and my prayer comes before You in the morning. **15.** Why do You cast off (reject) my soul? Why do You hide (conceal) Your face from me? **16.** I have been afflicted (oppressed) and near death since my youth; I suffer Your terrors (fears), and I am in despair. **17.** Your fierce wrath (anger) has passed over me; Your terrors (dread) have cut me off. **18.** They surround (encircle) me all day like water; they engulf (swallow) me completely. **19.** You have made my loved ones (dear ones) and friends distant and have turned my acquaintances into darkness (obscurity).

Chapter 89

1. A contemplation (meditation) of Ethan the Ezrahite. I will sing (celebrate) of the Lord's mercies forever; with my mouth, I will declare Your faithfulness to all generations. **2.** For I have said, "Your mercy is built to last forever; Your faithfulness is established (set) in the heavens." **3.** "I have made a covenant (agreement) with My chosen one; I have sworn to My servant David: **4.** 'Your descendants (offspring) I will establish forever and build your throne for all generations.'" Selah. **5.** The heavens will praise Your wonders, O Lord, and Your faithfulness in the assembly (congregation) of the saints. **6.** Who in the heavens can be compared to the Lord? Who among the heavenly beings is like the Lord? **7.** God is greatly to be feared (revered) in the council (assembly) of the saints, held in reverence by all around Him. **8.** O Lord God of hosts (armies), who is mighty like You? Your faithfulness surrounds (encompasses) You. **9.** You rule the raging sea; when its waves rise, You still them. **10.** You have crushed (broken) Rahab (a symbol of Egypt) as one who is slain; You scatter Your enemies with Your mighty arm. **11.** The heavens are Yours, and the earth is Yours; You founded (created) the world and everything in it. **12.** The north and the south are Yours; Mount Tabor (a mountain in Israel) and Mount Hermon (a mountain in Israel) rejoice in Your name. **13.** You have a mighty arm (strength); Your hand is strong, and Your right hand is exalted. **14.** Righteousness and justice are the foundation (base) of Your throne; mercy and truth go before You. **15.** Blessed are the people who know the joyful sound (trumpet blast)! They walk, O Lord, in the light of Your presence. **16.** In Your name, they rejoice all day long, and in Your righteousness, they are exalted. **17.** For You are the glory (honor) of their strength, and in Your favor (grace), our power is lifted high. **18.** For our shield (defense) belongs to the Lord, and our king is the Holy One of Israel. **19.** Then You spoke in a vision to Your holy one and said: "I have given help (aid) to one mighty; I have exalted one chosen (selected) from the people. **20.** I have found My servant David; with My holy oil, I have anointed him. **21.** My hand will establish him; My arm will strengthen him. **22.** The enemy will not outwit him, nor will the wicked afflict (harm) him. **23.** I will crush (defeat) his foes before him and strike down those who hate him. **24.** But My faithfulness and mercy will be with him, and in My name, his horn (strength) will be exalted. **25.** Also I will set his hand over the sea, And his right hand over the rivers. **26.** He shall cry to Me, 'You are my Father, My God, and the rock of my salvation.' **27.** Also, I will make him My firstborn, The highest of the kings of the earth. **28.** My mercy I will keep for him forever, And My covenant shall stand firm with him. **29.** His seed also I will make to endure forever, And his throne as the days of heaven. **30.** "If his sons forsake My Law And do not walk in My judgments, **31.** If they break My Statutes And do not keep My commandments, **32.** Then I will punish their transgression with the rod, And their iniquity with stripes. **33.** Nevertheless My lovingkindness I will not utterly take from him, Nor allow My faithfulness to fail. **34.** My covenant I will not break, Nor alter the word that has gone out of My lips. **35.** Once I have sworn by My holiness; I will not lie to David: **36.** His seed shall endure forever, And his throne as the sun before Me; **37.** It shall be established forever like the moon, Even like the faithful witness in the sky." Selah **38.** But You have cast off and abhorred, You have been furious with Your anointed. **39.** You have renounced the covenant of Your servant; You have profaned his crown by casting it to the ground. **40.** You have broken down all his hedges; You have brought his strongholds to ruin. **41.** All who pass by the way plunder him; He is a reproach to his neighbors. **42.** You have exalted the right hand of his adversaries; You have made all his enemies rejoice. **43.** You have also turned back the edge of his sword and have not sustained him in the battle. **44.** You have made his glory cease and cast his throne down to the ground. **45.** The days of his youth You have shortened; You have covered him with shame. Selah **46.** How long, Lord? Will You hide Yourself forever? Will Your wrath burn like fire? **47.** Remember how short my time is; For what futility have You created all the children of men? **48.** What man can live and not see death? Can he deliver his life from the power of the grave? Selah **49.** Lord, where are Your former lovingkindnesses, Which You swore to David in Your truth? **50.** Remember, Lord, the reproach of Your servants-- How I bear in my bosom the reproach of all the many peoples, **51.** With which Your enemies have reproached, O Lord, with which they have reproached the footsteps of Your anointed. **52.** Blessed be the Lord forevermore! Amen and Amen.

Chapter 90

1. A Prayer of Moses, the man of God. Lord, You have been our dwelling place (home) in all generations. **2.** Before the mountains were brought forth, or You formed the earth and the world, even from everlasting to everlasting, You are God. **3.** You turn man to destruction (decay), and say, "Return, O children of men." **4.** For a thousand years in Your sight are like yesterday when it is past, and like a watch in the night. **5.** You carry them away like a flood (deluge); they are like a sleep (slumber). In the morning, they are like grass which grows up: **6.** In the morning it flourishes and grows up; in the evening it is cut down and withers. **7.** For we have been consumed by Your anger, and by Your wrath (fury) we are terrified. **8.** You have set our iniquities (sins) before You, our secret sins in the light of Your countenance. **9.** For all our days have passed away in Your wrath; we finish our years like a sigh (breath). **10.** The days of our lives are seventy years; and if by reason of strength they are eighty years, yet their boast (pride) is only labor and sorrow; for it is soon cut off, and we fly away. **11.** Who knows the power (might) of Your anger? For as the fear (reverence) of You, so is Your wrath. **12.** So teach us to number (count) our days, that we may gain a heart of wisdom. **13.** Return, O Lord! How long? And have compassion (pity) on Your servants. **14.** Oh, satisfy us early (quickly) with Your mercy, that we may rejoice and be glad all our days! **15.** Make us glad according to the days in which You have afflicted (troubled) us, the years in which we have seen evil. **16.** Let Your work appear to Your servants, and Your glory to their children. **17.** And let the beauty (grace) of the Lord our God be upon us and establish (confirm) the work of our hands for us; yes, establish the work of our hands.

Chapter 91

1. He who dwells in the secret place of the Most High shall abide (live) under the shadow of the Almighty. **2.** I will say of the Lord, "He is my refuge (shelter) and my fortress; my God, in Him I will trust." **3.** Surely, He shall deliver (rescue) you from the snare of the fowler (hunter) and from the perilous (dangerous) pestilence. **4.** He shall cover (protect) you with His feathers, and under His wings you shall take refuge; His truth shall be your shield and buckler (defense). **5.** You shall not be afraid of the terror (fear) by night, nor of the arrow that flies by day, **6.** Nor of the pestilence that walks in darkness, nor of the destruction that lays waste (ravages) at noonday. **7.** A thousand may fall at your side, and ten thousand at your right hand; but it shall not come near you. **8.** Only with your eyes shall you look and see the reward (consequence) of the wicked. **9.** Because you have made the Lord, who is my refuge, even the Most High, your dwelling place, **10.** No evil shall befall (harm) you, nor shall any plague come near your dwelling. **11.** For He shall give His angels charge (command) over you, to keep (guard) you in all your ways. **12.** In their hands they shall bear you up, lest you dash your foot against a stone. **13.** You shall tread (walk) upon the lion and the cobra (snake); the young lion and the serpent you shall trample underfoot. **14.** "Because he has set his love (affection) upon Me, therefore I will deliver him; I will set him on high, because he has known My name. **15.** He shall call upon Me, and I will answer (respond) him; I will be with him in trouble; I will deliver him and honor (esteem) him. **16.** With long life I will satisfy (fulfill) him, and show him My salvation."

Chapter 92

1. A Psalm. A Song for the Sabbath day. It is good (pleasant) to give thanks to the Lord and to sing praises to Your name, O Most High; **2.** To declare (proclaim) Your lovingkindness in the morning, and Your faithfulness every night, **3.** On an instrument of ten strings, on the lute, and on the harp, with harmonious (melodious) sound. **4.** For You, Lord, have made me glad through Your work; I will triumph (rejoice) in the works of Your hands. **5.** O

Lord, how great (wonderful) are Your works! Your thoughts are very deep. 6. A senseless (stupid) man does not know, nor does a fool understand this. 7. When the wicked spring up like grass, and when all the workers of iniquity (evil) flourish, it is that they may be destroyed forever. 8. But You, Lord, are on high forevermore. 9. For behold, Your enemies, O Lord, for behold, Your enemies shall perish; all the workers of iniquity shall be scattered (scattered). 10. But my horn (strength) You have exalted like a wild ox; I have been anointed with fresh oil. 11. My eye also has seen my desire on my enemies; my ears hear my desire on the wicked who rise up against me. 12. The righteous shall flourish (prosper) like a palm tree, and shall grow like a cedar in Lebanon. 13. Those who are planted in the house of the Lord shall flourish in the courts of our God. 14. They shall still bear fruit in old age; they shall be fresh (vibrant) and flourishing. 15. To declare that the Lord is upright; He is my rock, and there is no unrighteousness (wickedness) in Him.

Chapter 93

1. The Lord reigns, He is clothed with majesty (grandeur); The Lord is clothed, He has girded Himself with strength. Surely the world is established, so that it cannot be moved. 2. Your throne is established from of old; You are from everlasting. 3. The floods have lifted up, O Lord, the floods have lifted up their voice (roar); the floods lift up their waves. 4. The Lord on high is mightier than the noise (sound) of many waters, than the mighty waves of the sea. 5. Your testimonies are very sure; Holiness adorns Your house, O Lord, forever.

Chapter 94

1 O Lord God, to whom vengeance (retribution) belongs— O God, to whom vengeance belongs, shine forth! 2 Rise up, O Judge of the earth; render punishment (recompense) to the proud. 3 Lord, how long will the wicked, how long will the wicked triumph? 4 They utter speech, and speak insolent (arrogant) things; all the workers of iniquity boast in themselves. 5 They break in pieces Your people, O Lord, and afflict Your heritage. 6 They slay the widow and the stranger and murder the fatherless. 7 Yet they say, "The Lord does not see, nor does the God of Jacob understand." 8 Understand, you senseless (foolish) among the people; and you fools, when will you be wise? 9 He who planted the ear, shall He not hear? He who formed the eye, shall He not see? 10 He who instructs the nations, shall He not correct, He who teaches man knowledge? 11 The Lord knows the thoughts of man, that they are futile (vain). 12 Blessed is the man whom You instruct, O Lord, and teach out of Your law, 13 That You may give him rest from the days of adversity (trouble), until the pit is dug for the wicked. 14 For the Lord will not cast off His people, nor will He forsake (abandon) His inheritance. 15 But judgment (justice) will return to righteousness, and all the upright in heart will follow it. 16 Who will rise up for me against the evildoers? Who will stand up for me against the workers of iniquity? 17 Unless the Lord had been my help, my soul would soon have settled in silence (death). 18 If I say, "My foot slips," Your mercy, O Lord, will hold me up. 19 In the multitude of my anxieties within me, Your comforts delight my soul. 20 Shall the throne of iniquity, which devises evil by law, have fellowship with You? 21 They gather together against the life of the righteous, and condemn innocent blood. 22 But the Lord has been my defense (refuge), and my God the rock of my refuge. 23 He has brought on them their own iniquity, and shall cut them off in their own wickedness; the Lord our God shall cut them off.

Chapter 95

1 Oh come, let us sing to the Lord! Let us shout joyfully to the Rock of our salvation. 2 Let us come before His presence with thanksgiving; let us shout joyfully to Him with psalms. 3 For the Lord is the great God, and the great King above all gods. 4 In His hand are the deep places of the earth; the heights of the hills are His also. 5 The sea is His, for He made it; and His hands formed the dry land. 6 Oh come, let us worship and bow down; let us kneel before the Lord our Maker. 7 For He is our God, and we are the people of His pasture, and the sheep of His hand. Today, if you will hear His voice: 8 "Do not harden your hearts, as in the rebellion, as in the day of trial in the wilderness, 9 When your fathers tested Me; they tried Me, though they saw My work. 10 For forty years I was grieved (angry) with that generation, and said, 'It is a people who go astray (wander) in their hearts, and they do not know My ways.' 11 So I swore in My wrath, 'They shall not enter My rest.'"

Chapter 96

1 Oh, sing to the Lord a new song! Sing to the Lord, all the earth. 2 Sing to the Lord, bless His name; proclaim (announce) the good news of His salvation from day to day. 3 Declare His glory among the nations, His wonders among all peoples. 4 For the Lord is great and greatly to be praised; He is to be feared above all gods. 5 For all the gods of the peoples are idols, but the Lord made the heavens. 6 Honor and majesty are before Him; strength and beauty are in His sanctuary. 7 Give to the Lord, O families of the peoples, give to the Lord glory and strength. 8 Give to the Lord the glory due His name; bring an offering, and come into His courts. 9 Oh, worship the Lord in the beauty of holiness! Tremble before Him, all the earth. 10 Say among the nations, "The Lord reigns; the world also is firmly established, it shall not be moved; He shall judge the peoples righteously." 11 Let the heavens rejoice, and let the earth be glad; let the sea roar, and all its fullness; 12 Let the field be joyful, and all that is in it. Then all the trees of the woods will rejoice before the Lord. 13 For He is coming, for He is coming to judge the earth. He shall judge the world with righteousness, and the peoples with His truth.

Chapter 97

1 The Lord reigns; Let the earth rejoice (celebrate); Let the multitude of isles be glad! 2 Clouds and darkness surround Him; Righteousness and justice are the foundation (basis) of His throne. 3 A fire goes before Him, and burns up His enemies round about. 4 His lightnings (flashes) light the world; The earth sees and trembles (shudders). 5 The mountains melt like wax at the presence of the Lord, at the presence of the Lord of the whole earth. 6 The heavens declare His righteousness (justice), And all the peoples see His glory (splendor). 7 Let all be put to shame who serve carved images, who boast of idols. Worship (adore) Him, all you gods. 8 Zion hears and is glad, And the daughters of Judah rejoice because of Your judgments, O Lord. 9 For You, Lord, are most high above all the earth; You are exalted far above all gods. 10 You who love the Lord, hate evil! He preserves (protects) the souls of His saints; He delivers (rescues) them out of the hand of the wicked. 11 Light is sown for the righteous, And gladness (joy) for the upright in heart. 12 Rejoice in the Lord, you righteous, And give thanks at the remembrance (memory) of His holy name.

Chapter 98

1 A Psalm. Oh, sing to the Lord a new song! For He has done marvelous (wondrous) things; His right hand and His holy arm have gained Him the victory. 2 The Lord has made known His salvation (deliverance); His righteousness He has revealed in the sight of the nations. 3 He has remembered His mercy (compassion) and His faithfulness to the house of Israel; All the ends of the earth have seen the salvation of our God. 4 Shout joyfully (exult) to the Lord, all the earth; Break forth in song, rejoice, and sing praises. 5 Sing to the Lord with the harp, With the harp and the sound (melody) of a psalm, 6 With trumpets and the sound of a horn; Shout joyfully before the Lord, the King. 7 Let the sea roar, and all its fullness, The world and those who dwell in it; 8 Let the rivers clap (cheer) their hands; Let the hills be joyful together before the Lord, 9 For He is coming to judge the earth. With righteousness He shall judge the world, And the peoples with equity (fairness).

Chapter 99

1 The Lord reigns; Let the peoples tremble! He dwells between the cherubim; Let the earth be moved! 2 The Lord is great in Zion, And He is high above all the peoples. 3 Let them praise Your great and awesome name— He is holy (sacred). 4 The King's strength also loves justice; You have established equity (fairness); You have executed justice and righteousness in Jacob. 5 Exalt the Lord our God, And worship at His footstool— He is holy. 6 Moses and Aaron were among His priests, And Samuel was among those who called upon His name; They called upon the Lord, and He answered them. 7 He spoke to them in the cloudy pillar; They kept His testimonies and the ordinance (command) He gave them. 8 You answered them, O Lord our God; You were to them God-Who-Forgives, Though You took vengeance (punishment) on their deeds. 9 Exalt the Lord our God, And worship at His holy hill; For the Lord our God is holy.

Chapter 100

1. A Psalm of Thanksgiving. Make a joyful shout (cry) to the Lord, all you lands! 2. Serve the Lord with gladness (joy); Come before His presence with singing. 3. Know that the Lord, He is God; It is He who has made us, and not we ourselves; We are His people and the sheep of His pasture. 4. Enter into His gates with thanksgiving, And into His courts with praise. Be thankful (grateful) to Him, and bless His name. 5. For the Lord is good; His mercy is everlasting, And His truth endures (lasts) to all generations.

Chapter 101

1 A Psalm of David. I will sing of mercy and justice; To You, O Lord, I will sing praises. 2 I will behave wisely (practically) in a perfect way. Oh, when will You come to me? I will walk within my house with a perfect (blameless) heart. 3 I will set nothing wicked before my eyes; I hate the work (deeds) of those who fall away; It shall not cling to me. 4 A perverse (corrupt) heart shall depart (leave) from me; I will not know wickedness. 5 Whoever secretly slanders (defames) his neighbor, Him I will destroy; The one who has a haughty (arrogant) look and a proud heart, Him I will not endure. 6 My eyes shall be on the faithful (loyal) of the land, That they may dwell with me; He who walks in a perfect way, He shall serve me. 7 He who works deceit (dishonesty) shall not dwell within my house; He who tells lies shall

not continue in my presence. **8** Early I will destroy all the wicked of the land, That I may cut off all the evildoers from the city of the Lord.

Chapter 102

1 A Prayer of the afflicted, when he is overwhelmed (overcome) and pours out his complaint before the Lord. Hear my prayer, O Lord, And let my cry come to You. **2** Do not hide Your face from me in the day of my trouble (distress); Incline Your ear (attention) to me; In the day that I call, answer me speedily (quickly). **3** For my days are consumed (spent) like smoke, And my bones are burned like a hearth (fireplace). **4** My heart is stricken (pierced) and withered like grass, So that I forget to eat my bread (food). **5** Because of the sound (noise) of my groaning (moaning), My bones cling (stick) to my skin. **6** I am like a pelican (heron) of the wilderness; I am like an owl (vulture) of the desert. **7** I lie awake, And am like a sparrow alone on the housetop. **8** My enemies reproach (mock) me all day long, Those who deride (scorn) me swear an oath against me. **9** For I have eaten ashes like bread, And mingled my drink (beverage) with weeping (sorrow), **10** Because of Your indignation (anger) and Your wrath (fury); For You have lifted me up and cast (thrown) me away. **11** My days are like a shadow (shade) that lengthens, And I wither (fade) away like grass. **12** But You, O Lord, shall endure (last) forever, And the remembrance (memory) of Your name to all generations. **13** You will arise and have mercy (compassion) on Zion; For the time to favor her, Yes, the set (appointed) time, has come. **14** For Your servants take pleasure (delight) in her stones, And show favor (kindness) to her dust. **15** So the nations shall fear (revere) the name of the Lord, And all the kings of the earth Your glory (majesty). **16** For the Lord shall build up (rebuild) Zion; He shall appear (manifest) in His glory. **17** He shall regard (consider) the prayer of the destitute (needy) and shall not despise (reject) their prayer. **18** This will be written for the generation (future) to come, That a people yet to be created may praise (worship) the Lord. **19** For He looked down from the height (loft) of His sanctuary; From heaven the Lord viewed (observed) the earth, **20** To hear the groaning (moaning) of the prisoner, To release (free) those appointed to death, **21** To declare (proclaim) the name of the Lord in Zion, And His praise in Jerusalem, **22** When the peoples are gathered together, And the kingdoms, to serve (worship) the Lord. **23** He weakened (shortened) my strength in the way; He shortened (reduced) my days. **24** I said, "O my God, Do not take me away in the midst of my days; Your years are throughout all generations." **25** Of old You laid the foundation (established) of the earth, And the heavens are the work of Your hands. **26** They will perish (vanish), but You will endure; Yes, they will all grow old (decay) like a garment (clothing); Like a cloak You will change (replace) them, And they will be changed (transformed). **27** But You are the same (unchanging), And Your years will have no end (limit). **28** The children (descendants) of Your servants will continue, And their descendants will be established before You.

Chapter 103

1 A Psalm of David. Bless (Praise) the Lord, O my soul; And all that is within me, bless His holy name! **2** Bless the Lord, O my soul, And forget not (neglect) all His benefits: **3** Who forgives (pardons) all your iniquities, Who heals (cures) all your diseases, **4** Who redeems (rescues) your life from destruction, Who crowns (adorns) you with lovingkindness and mercy, **5** Who satisfies (fills) your mouth with good things, So that your youth is renewed (restored) like the eagle's. **6** The Lord executes (carries out) righteousness And justice for all who are oppressed (wronged). **7** He made known (revealed) His ways to Moses, His acts (deeds) to the children of Israel. **8** The Lord is merciful (compassionate) and gracious (kind), Slow to anger, and abounding (overflowing) in mercy. **9** He will not always strive (contend) with us, Nor will He keep His anger forever. **10** He has not dealt (treated) with us according to our sins, Nor punished (chastised) us according to our iniquities. **11** For as the heavens are high (lofty) above the earth, So great is His mercy (compassion) toward those who fear (honor) Him; **12** As far as the east is from the west, So far has He removed (taken away) our transgressions (sins) from us. **13** As a father pities (shows compassion) his children, So the Lord pities (has mercy on) those who fear (honor) Him. **14** For He knows (understands) our frame (condition); He remembers (recalls) that we are dust (mortal). **15** As for man, his days are like grass (herb); As a flower of the field, so he flourishes (prospers). **16** For the wind passes (blows) over it, and it is gone, And its place remembers (recalls) it no more. **17** But the mercy (love) of the Lord is from everlasting (eternal) to everlasting on those who fear (revere) Him, And His righteousness (justice) to children's children, **18** To such as keep (obey) His covenant, And to those who remember (recall) His commandments to do (follow) them. **19** The Lord has established (set up) His throne in heaven, And His kingdom (rule) rules over all. **20** Bless the Lord, you His angels, Who excel (excel) in strength, who do His word, Heeding (obeying) the voice of His word. **21** Bless the Lord, all you His hosts (armies), You ministers

(servants) of His, who do His pleasure (will). **22** Bless the Lord, all His works (creations), In all places of His dominion (rule). Bless the Lord, O my soul!

Chapter 104

1. Bless the Lord (Praise), O my soul! O Lord my God, You are very great: You are clothed with honor (splendor) and majesty (grandeur), **2.** Who cover (wrap) Yourself with light as with a garment, Who stretch (spread) out the heavens like a curtain. **3** He lays (establishes) the beams of His upper chambers in the waters, Who makes (forms) the clouds His chariot, Who walks on the wings (breezes) of the wind, **4.** Who makes (creates) His angels spirits, His ministers a flame of fire. **5** You who laid (set) the foundations of the earth, So that it should not be moved (shaken) forever, **6** You covered (wrapped) it with the deep (abyss) as with a garment; The waters stood above the mountains. **7** At Your rebuke (command) they fled; At the voice of Your thunder they hastened away. **8** They went up over the mountains; They went down into the valleys, To the place which You founded (established) for them. **9** You have set a boundary (limit) that they may not pass over, That they may not return to cover (reclaim) the earth. **10** He sends (sends forth) the springs into the valleys, They flow among the hills. **11.** They give drink (provide) to every beast of the field; The wild donkeys quench (satisfy) their thirst. **12** By them the birds (fowls) of the heavens have their home; They sing among the branches. **13.** He waters (nourishes) the hills from His upper chambers; The earth is satisfied (fulfilled) with the fruit of Your works. **14** He causes (makes) the grass to grow for the cattle, and vegetation for the service of man, That he may bring forth food (produce) from the earth, **15** And wine that makes (gladdens) glad the heart of man, Oil to make his face shine, And bread which strengthens (revives) man's heart. **16** The trees of the Lord are full of sap (life), The cedars of Lebanon which He planted, **17** Where the birds (fowl) make (build) their nests; The stork has her home in the fir trees. **18** The high hills are for the wild goats; The cliffs are a refuge (shelter) for the rock badgers. **19** He appointed (set) the moon for seasons; The sun knows its going down (setting). **20** You make (bring) darkness, and it is night, In which all the beasts of the forest creep (move) about. **21** The young lions roar (growl) after their prey and seek (look for) their food from God. **22** When the sun rises (comes up), they gather together and lie down in their dens. **23** Man goes out to his work (labor) And to his labor until the evening. **24.** O Lord, how manifold (numerous) are Your works! In wisdom You have made (created) them all. The earth is full (replete) of Your possessions-- **25** This great and wide sea, In which are innumerable teeming things (creatures), Living things both small and great. **26** There the ships sail (drift) about; There is that Leviathan (sea monster) Which You have made to play (frolic) there. **27** These all wait (depend) for You, That You may give them their food (sustenance) in due season. **28.** What You give them they gather in; You open Your hand, they are filled (satisfied) with good. **29** You hide (turn away) Your face, they are troubled (distressed); You take away their breath (spirit), they die and return to their dust. **30** You send forth Your Spirit, they are created (formed); And You renew the face of the earth. **31** May the glory (splendor) of the Lord endure (last) forever; May the Lord rejoice in His works (deeds). **32** He looks on the earth, and it trembles (quakes); He touches the hills, and they smoke. **33** I will sing to the Lord as long as I live; I will sing praise to my God while I have my being (existence). **34** May my meditation (thoughts) be sweet to Him; I will be glad (rejoice) in the Lord. **35.** May sinners be consumed (destroyed) from the earth, And the wicked be no more. Bless (Praise) the Lord, O my soul! Praise (Exalt) the Lord!

Chapter 105

1. Oh, give thanks to the Lord! Call upon His name; proclaim His deeds to all nations. **2.** Sing to Him, praise Him; tell of His wondrous works. **3.** Glory in His holy name; let those who seek the Lord rejoice. **4.** Seek the Lord and His strength; always seek His presence. **5.** Remember His miracles, His wonders, and His judgments. **6.** O descendants of Abraham (Patriarch of Israel), His servant, O children of Jacob (Israel's 12 sons), His chosen ones! **7.** He is the Lord our God, whose judgments are in all the earth. **8.** He remembers His covenant forever, the promise He made for a thousand generations, **9.** The covenant He made with Abraham, His oath to Isaac (son of Abraham), **10.** Confirmed to Jacob (Israel) as a decree, to Israel as an eternal covenant. **11.** "To you I will give the land of Canaan (Promised Land) as your inheritance," **12.** When they were few in number, and strangers in the land. **13.** They wandered from nation to nation, from one kingdom to another. **14.** He did not let anyone harm them; He rebuked kings (rulers) on their behalf, **15.** Saying, "Do not touch My anointed ones, and do My prophets no harm." **16.** He called for a famine, and destroyed their food supply. **17.** He sent a man before them—Joseph (son of Jacob), sold as a slave. **18.** They shackled his feet and laid him in irons, **19.** Until the time His word came to pass; the word of the Lord tested him. **20.** The king (Pharaoh) of Egypt sent for him and released him, the ruler (Pharaoh) of the people let him go. **21**. He made him master of his house, ruler over all his possessions, **22**. To bind his princes at will and teach his elders wisdom. **23**. Israel entered Egypt (Land of Ham), and Jacob settled in the land of Ham. **24**. He increased His people greatly, making them stronger than their enemies. **25**. He turned their hearts to hate His people, to deal deceitfully with His servants. **26**. He sent Moses (leader of Exodus) and Aaron (Moses' brother), whom He had chosen, **27**. They performed His signs and wonders in the land of Ham (Egypt). **28**. He sent darkness, and it became dark, yet they did not rebel. **29**. He turned their waters into blood and killed their fish. **30**. Their land was filled with frogs, even in the king's chambers. **31**. He spoke, and swarms of flies and lice covered the land. **32**. He sent hail for rain, and fiery lightning to strike their land. **33**. He struck their vines and fig trees, shattering the trees of their land. **34**. He spoke, and locusts came, countless locusts, **35**. Devouring all the vegetation and the fruit of the ground. **36**. He struck down the firstborn in the land, the first of their strength. **37**. He brought them out with silver and gold, and none were feeble. **38**. Egypt rejoiced when they departed, for fear had fallen upon them. **39**. He spread a cloud to cover them, and fire to light their way by night. **40**. They asked, and He brought them quail, and fed them with manna (heavenly bread). **41**. He opened the rock (Mount Horeb), and water gushed forth, flowing like a river. **42**. For He remembered His holy promise to Abraham. **43**. He brought His people out with joy, His chosen ones with gladness. **44**. He gave them the lands of the nations (Gentiles), and they inherited the labor of the peoples, **45**. That they might obey His statutes and keep His laws. Praise the Lord!

Chapter 106

1. Praise the Lord! Give thanks to the Lord, for He is good! His mercy endures forever. **2**. Who can tell the mighty acts of the Lord? Who can proclaim all His praise? **3**. Blessed are those who uphold justice, and who do righteousness at all times. **4**. Remember me, O Lord, with the favor You have for Your people; visit me with Your salvation. **5**. That I may witness the prosperity of Your chosen ones, rejoice in the gladness of Your nation, and glory with Your inheritance. **6**. We have sinned like our ancestors, committed iniquity, and acted wickedly. **7**. Our forefathers in Egypt (land of slavery) did not understand Your wonders; they forgot Your many mercies and rebelled at the Red Sea. **8**. Yet He saved them for His name's sake, to make His power known. **9**. He rebuked the Red Sea, and it dried up. He led them through the depths, as through a wilderness. **10**. He saved them from the hand of those who hated them, and redeemed them from their enemy. **11**. The waters covered their enemies; not one of them survived. **12**. Then they believed His words and sang His praises. **13**. They quickly forgot His works; they did not wait for His counsel. **14**. But they lusted in the wilderness, testing God in the desert. **15**. So He gave them what they asked for, but sent leanness to their souls. **16**. They envied Moses in the camp, and Aaron (Moses' brother), the holy one of the Lord. **17**. The earth opened and swallowed Dathan, covering the faction of Abiram (rebels). **18**. A fire blazed among their company, and the flame consumed the wicked. **19**. They made a calf at Horeb (Mount Sinai), and worshiped a molded image. **20**. They exchanged their glory for the image of an ox that eats grass. **21**. They forgot God, their Savior, who had done great things in Egypt, **22**. Wondrous works in the land of Ham (Egypt), awesome things by the Red Sea. **23**. Therefore, He said He would destroy them, had not Moses, His chosen one, stood before Him to turn away His wrath, lest He destroy them. **24**. Then they despised the pleasant land (Canaan), they did not believe His promise. **25**. They grumbled in their tents and did not heed the voice of the Lord. **26**. So He raised His hand in an oath against them, to overthrow them in the wilderness, **27**. To overthrow their descendants among the nations, and scatter them throughout the lands. **28**. They joined themselves to Baal of Peor (a Canaanite god), and ate sacrifices made to the dead. **29**. Thus, they provoked Him to anger with their deeds, and a plague broke out among them. **30**. Then Phinehas (a priest) stood up and intervened, and the plague was stopped. **31**. And that was credited to him as righteousness, to all generations forever. **32**. They angered Him at the waters of strife, so it went badly with Moses because of them, **33**. For they rebelled against His Spirit, and Moses spoke rashly. **34**. They did not destroy the nations as the Lord had commanded. **35**. Instead, they mingled with the Gentiles (non-Israelites), and learned their works. **36**. They served their idols, which became a snare to them. **37**. They even sacrificed their sons and daughters to demons. **38**. They shed innocent blood, the blood of their sons and daughters, whom they sacrificed to the idols of Canaan, and the land was polluted with blood. **39**. Thus, they defiled themselves by their actions, and committed spiritual adultery by their deeds. **40**. Therefore, the Lord's wrath was kindled against His people, and He abhorred His inheritance. **41**. He gave them into the hands of the Gentiles, and those who hated them ruled over them. **42**. Their enemies oppressed them, and they were brought into subjection. **43**. Many times He delivered them, but

they rebelled in their counsel, and were brought low because of their iniquity. **44**. Nevertheless, He regarded their affliction when He heard their cry. **45**. And for their sake, He remembered His covenant, and relented according to the multitude of His mercies. **46**. He made them pitied by all those who carried them away captive. **47**. Save us, O Lord our God, and gather us from among the nations, to give thanks to Your holy name and triumph in Your praise. **48**. Blessed be the Lord God of Israel, from everlasting to everlasting! And let all the people say, "Amen!" Praise the Lord!

Chapter 107

1. Oh, give thanks to the Lord, for He is good! His mercy endures forever. **2**. Let the redeemed of the Lord say so, whom He has redeemed from the hand of the enemy, **3**. And gathered from the lands, from the east, west, north, and south. **4**. They wandered in the wilderness, lost and without a city to live in. **5**. Hungry and thirsty, their soul fainted in them. **6**. Then they cried out to the Lord in their trouble, and He delivered them from their distresses. **7**. He led them by the right way, that they might reach a city to dwell in. **8**. Oh, that men would give thanks to the Lord for His goodness, and for His wonderful works to the children of men! **9**. For He satisfies the longing soul and fills the hungry soul with goodness. **10**. Those who sat in darkness and the shadow of death, bound in affliction and iron, **11**. Because they rebelled against the words of God, and despised the counsel of the Most High, **12**. Therefore He brought down their heart with hard labor; they fell down, and there was no one to help. **13**. Then they cried out to the Lord in their trouble, and He saved them from their distresses. **14**. He brought them out of darkness and the shadow of death, and broke their chains in pieces. **15**. Oh, that men would give thanks to the Lord for His goodness, and for His wonderful works to the children of men! **16**. For He has broken the gates of bronze, and cut the bars of iron in two. **17**. Fools, because of their transgression and iniquities, were afflicted. **18**. Their soul abhorred all manner of food, and they drew near to the gates of death. **19**. Then they cried out to the Lord in their trouble, and He saved them from their distresses. **20**. He sent His word and healed them, and delivered them from their destructions. **21**. Oh, that men would give thanks to the Lord for His goodness, and for His wonderful works to the children of men! **22**. Let them offer the sacrifices of thanksgiving, and declare His works with rejoicing. **23**. Those who go down to the sea in ships, who do business on great waters, **24**. They see the works of the Lord, and His wonders in the deep. **25**. For He commands and raises the stormy wind, which lifts the waves of the sea. **26**. They mount up to the heavens, they go down again to the depths; their soul melts because of trouble. **27**. They reel to and fro, and stagger like a drunken man, and are at their wits' end. **28**. Then they cry out to the Lord in their trouble, and He brings them out of their distresses. **29**. He calms the storm, so that its waves are still. **30**. Then they are glad because they are quiet; so He guides them to their desired haven. **31**. Oh, that men would give thanks to the Lord for His goodness, and for His wonderful works to the children of men! **32**. Let them exalt Him in the assembly of the people, and praise Him in the company of the elders. **33**. He turns rivers into a wilderness, and the water springs into dry ground; **34**. A fruitful land into barrenness, for the wickedness of those who dwell in it. **35**. He turns a wilderness into pools of water, and dry land into water springs. **36**. There He makes the hungry dwell, that they may establish a city for a dwelling place, **37**. And sow fields and plant vineyards, that they may yield a fruitful harvest. **38**. He also blesses them, and they multiply greatly; He does not let their cattle decrease. **39**. When they are diminished and brought low, through oppression, affliction, and sorrow, **40**. He pours contempt on princes, and causes them to wander in the wilderness, where there is no way; **41**. Yet He sets the poor on high, far from affliction, and makes their families like a flock. **42**. The righteous see it and rejoice, but all iniquity shuts its mouth. **43**. Whoever is wise will observe these things, and they will understand the lovingkindness of the Lord.

Chapter 108

1. A Song. A Psalm of David. O God, my heart is steadfast; I will sing and give praise, even with my glory. **2**. Awake, lute and harp! I will awaken the dawn. **3**. I will praise You, O Lord, among the peoples, and sing praises to You among the nations. **4**. For Your mercy is great above the heavens, and Your truth reaches to the clouds. **5**. Be exalted, O God, above the heavens, and Your glory above all the earth. **6**. That Your beloved may be delivered, save with Your right hand, and hear me. **7**. God has spoken in His holiness: "I will rejoice; I will divide Shechem and measure out the Valley of Succoth." **8**. Gilead is Mine; Manasseh is Mine; Ephraim also is the helmet for My head; Judah is My lawgiver. **9**. Moab is My washpot; over Edom I will cast My shoe; over Philistia I will triumph. **10**. Who will bring me into the strong city? Who will lead me to Edom? **11**. Is it not You, O God, who cast us off? And You, O God, who did not go out with our armies? **12**. Give us help from trouble, for the help of man is useless. **13**. Through God we will do valiantly, for it is He who shall tread down our enemies.

Chapter 109

1. To the Chief Musician. A Psalm of David. Do not keep silent, O God of my praise! **2**. For the mouth of the wicked and the deceitful have opened against me; they have spoken lies. **3**. They have surrounded me with words of hatred and fought against me without cause. **4**. In return for my love, they are my accusers, but I give myself to prayer. **5**. Thus, they have repaid me evil for good, and hatred for my love. **6**. Set a wicked man over him, and let an accuser stand at his right hand. **7**. When he is judged, let him be found guilty, and let his prayer become sin. **8**. Let his days be few, and let another take his position. **9**. Let his children be fatherless and his wife a widow. **10**. Let his children wander as beggars and seek food from desolate places. **11**. Let the creditor seize all that he has, and let strangers plunder his labor. **12**. Let no one extend mercy to him, nor favor his fatherless children. **13**. Let his descendants be cut off, and his name be forgotten in the next generation. **14**. Let the iniquity of his fathers be remembered before the Lord, and let the sin of his mother not be erased. **15**. Let them be always before the Lord, so He may cut off their memory from the earth. **16**. Because he did not remember to show mercy, but persecuted the poor and needy, even slaying the brokenhearted. **17**. As he loved cursing, let it come upon him; as he did not delight in blessing, let it be far from him. **18**. As he clothed himself with cursing like a garment, let it enter his body like water and like oil into his bones. **19**. Let it be to him like a garment which covers him, and like a belt with which he is girded continually. **20**. Let this be the Lord's reward to my accusers and those who speak evil against me. **21**. But You, O God the Lord, deal with me for Your name's sake; because Your mercy is good, deliver me. **22**. For I am poor and needy, and my heart is wounded within me. **23**. I am gone like a shadow when it lengthens; I am shaken off like a locust. **24**. My knees are weak through fasting, and my flesh is feeble from lack of food. **25**. I have become a reproach to them; when they look at me, they shake their heads. **26**. Help me, O Lord my God! Save me according to Your mercy, **27**. That they may know this is Your hand—that You, Lord, have done it! **28**. Let them curse, but You bless; when they rise, let them be ashamed, but let Your servant rejoice. **29**. Let my accusers be clothed with shame, and let them cover themselves with disgrace like a mantle. **30**. I will greatly praise the Lord with my mouth; yes, I will praise Him among the multitude. **31**. For He shall stand at the right hand of the poor, to save him from those who condemn him.

Chapter 110

1. The Lord spoke to my Lord: "Sit at My right hand, until I make Your enemies a footstool beneath Your feet. **2**. The Lord will send forth the scepter of Your power from Zion (Zion: the holy city of Jerusalem). Rule in the midst of Your foes! **3**. Your people will offer themselves willingly on the day of Your might; in the splendor of holiness, from the dawn's first light, You have the freshness of youth. **4**. The Lord has sworn and will not change His mind: "You are a priest forever, after the order of Melchizedek (Melchizedek: priest and king of Salem, mysterious figure)." **5**. The Lord stands at Your right hand; He will defeat kings on the day of His anger. **6**. He will pass judgment on the nations; He will fill the earth with the slain, and crush the rulers of many lands. **7**. He will drink from the stream along the way; and so He will lift His head in victory.

Chapter 111

1. Praise the Lord! I will give thanks to the Lord with my whole heart, in the assembly of the upright (righteous ones) and in the congregation. **2**. The Lord's works are magnificent, studied by all who take pleasure in them. **3**. His deeds are honorable and glorious, and His righteousness endures forever. **4**. He has made His wonderful works memorable; the Lord is gracious and full of compassion. **5**. He provides food for those who fear Him; He will always remember His covenant. **6**. He has shown His people the power of His works, giving them the inheritance of the nations. **7**. The works of His hands are true and just; all His commandments are reliable. **8**. They stand firm forever and ever, done in truth and integrity. **9**. He has sent redemption to His people; He has commanded His covenant forever. Holy and awe-inspiring is His name. **10**. The fear of the Lord is the beginning of wisdom; all who obey His commandments have a good understanding. His praise endures forever.

Chapter 112

1. Praise the Lord! Blessed is the person who fears the Lord, who greatly delights in His commandments. **2**. His descendants will be mighty on earth; the generation of the upright will be blessed. **3**. Wealth and riches will fill his home, and his righteousness endures forever. **4**. To the upright, light shines in the darkness; he is gracious, full of compassion, and righteous. **5**. A good man is generous and lends; he will manage his affairs with discretion. **6**. Surely he will never be moved; the righteous will be remembered forever. **7**. He will not fear bad news; his heart is steadfast,

trusting in the Lord. **8**. His heart is firm; he will not be afraid, until he sees his desire upon his enemies. **9**. He has scattered abroad, giving to the poor; his righteousness endures forever. His honor will be exalted. **10**. The wicked will see it and be grieved; they will gnash their teeth and fade away; the desires of the wicked will be destroyed.

Chapter 13

1. Praise the Lord! Praise, O servants of the Lord, praise the name of the Lord! **2**. Blessed be the name of the Lord, from this time on and forevermore! **3**. From the rising of the sun to its setting, the Lord's name is to be praised. **4**. The Lord is high above all nations, His glory above the heavens. **5**. Who is like the Lord our God, who sits enthroned on high, **6**. Who humbles Himself to behold the heavens and the earth? **7**. He raises the poor from the dust and lifts the needy from the ash heap, **8**. To seat them with princes, with the princes of His people. **9**. He gives the barren woman a home, making her a joyful mother of children. Praise the Lord!

Chapter 14

1. When Israel came out of Egypt, the house of Jacob from a people of foreign language, **2**. Judah became His sanctuary, and Israel His dominion. **3**. The sea saw it and fled; the Jordan River turned back. **4**. The mountains skipped like rams, and the little hills like lambs. **5**. What happened, O sea, that you fled? O Jordan, that you turned back? **6**. O mountains, that you skipped like rams? O little hills, like lambs? **7**. Tremble, O earth, at the presence of the Lord, at the presence of the God of Jacob, **8**. Who turned the rock into a pool of water, the flint into a fountain of waters.

Chapter 115

1. Not to us, O Lord, not to us, but to Your name give glory, because of Your mercy and truth. **2**. Why should the nations ask, "Where is their God?" **3**. But our God is in heaven; He does whatever He pleases. **4**. Their idols are silver and gold, the work of human hands. **5**. They have mouths but do not speak; they have eyes but do not see. **6**. They have ears but do not hear; they have noses but do not smell. **7**. They have hands but do not feel; they have feet but do not walk; they do not speak with their throats. **8**. Those who make them are like them; so is everyone who trusts in them. **9**. O Israel, trust in the Lord; He is their help and their shield. **10**. O house of Aaron, trust in the Lord; He is their help and their shield. **11**. You who fear the Lord, trust in the Lord; He is their help and their shield. **12**. The Lord has been mindful of us; He will bless us. He will bless the house of Israel; He will bless the house of Aaron. **13**. He will bless those who fear the Lord, both small and great. **14**. May the Lord give you increase, you and your children. **15**. May you be blessed by the Lord, who made heaven and earth. **16**. The heavens, even the heavens, are the Lord's; but the earth He has given to the children of men. **17**. The dead do not praise the Lord, nor any who go down into silence. **18**. But we will bless the Lord from this time forth and forevermore. Praise the Lord!

Chapter 116

1. I love the Lord, because He has heard my voice and my pleas for help. **2**. Because He has bent down to listen, I will call on Him as long as I live. **3**. The cords of death entangled me, and the anguish of the grave took hold of me; I was in distress and sorrow. **4**. Then I called on the name of the Lord: "O Lord, I beg You, save my life!" **5**. The Lord is gracious and just; yes, our God is full of mercy. **6**. The Lord protects the simple; I was brought low, and He rescued me. **7**. Return to your rest, O my soul, for the Lord has been good to you. **8**. For You have saved my soul from death, my eyes from tears, and my feet from stumbling. **9**. I will walk before the Lord in the land of the living. **10**. I believed, therefore I spoke, "I am greatly afflicted." **11**. I said in my haste, "All men are deceitful." **12**. What can I give back to the Lord for all His blessings to me? **13**. I will take the cup of salvation and call on the name of the Lord. **14**. I will fulfill my vows to the Lord in the presence of all His people. **15**. Precious in the sight of the Lord is the death of His faithful ones. **16**. O Lord, truly I am Your servant; I am Your servant, the son of Your maidservant; You have freed me from my chains. **17**. I will offer a sacrifice of thanksgiving and call on the name of the Lord. **18**. I will fulfill my vows to the Lord in the presence of all His people, **19**. In the courts of the Lord's house, in the midst of you, O Jerusalem. Praise the Lord!

Chapter 117

1. Praise the Lord, all you nations; praise Him, all you peoples! **2**. For His great love toward us is immense, and the truth of the Lord endures forever. Praise the Lord!

Chapter 18

1. Give thanks to the Lord, for He is good! His love lasts forever. **2**. Let Israel now declare, "His love lasts forever." **3**. Let the house of Aaron (priestly family) now declare, "His love lasts forever." **4**. Let those who honor the Lord now declare, "His love lasts forever." **5**. In my distress, I called to the Lord; He answered me and set me in a spacious place. **6**. The Lord is with me; I will not be afraid. What can mere mortals do to me? **7**. The Lord is with me to help me; I will see defeat for those who oppose me. **8**. It is better to take refuge in the Lord than to trust in people. **9.** It is better to take refuge in the Lord than to trust in rulers (princes). **10.** All nations surrounded me, but by the Lord's name, I will overcome them. **11.** They surrounded me, yes, they surrounded me; but by the Lord's name, I will overcome them. **12.** They surrounded me like swarming bees; they were extinguished like burning thorns. By the Lord's name, I will overcome them. **13.** You pushed me hard to make me fall, but the Lord helped me. **14.** The Lord is my strength and my song; He has become my salvation. **15.** Shouts of joy and victory resound in the tents of the righteous; the Lord's right hand has done mighty things. **16.** The Lord's right hand is lifted high; the Lord's right hand has done mighty things. **17.** I will not die, but live and proclaim the deeds of the Lord. **18.** The Lord has disciplined me severely, but He has not given me over to death. **19.** Open to me the gates of righteousness; I will enter and give thanks to the Lord. **20.** This is the gate of the Lord, through which the righteous may enter. **21.** I will give You thanks, for You answered me; You have become my salvation. **22.** The stone the builders rejected has become the cornerstone. **23.** The Lord has done this, and it is marvelous in our eyes. **24.** This is the day the Lord has made; let us rejoice and be glad in it. **25.** Lord, save us! Lord, grant us success! **26.** Blessed is he who comes in the name of the Lord! From the house of the Lord, we bless you. **27.** The Lord is God, and He has made His light shine on us. With bows in hand, join in the festal procession up to the horns of the altar. **28.** You are my God, and I will praise You; You are my God, I will exalt You. **29.** Give thanks to the Lord, for He is good! His love endures forever.

Chapter 119

1. Blessed are the undefiled (pure) in the way, who walk in the law (teachings) of the Lord! **2.** Blessed are those who keep His testimonies, who seek Him with the whole heart! **3.** They also do no iniquity (sin); they walk in His ways. **4.** You have commanded us to keep Your precepts (instructions) diligently. **5.** Oh, that my ways were directed to keep Your statutes (laws)! **6.** Then I would not be ashamed, when I look into all Your commandments. **7.** I will praise You with uprightness of heart, when I learn Your righteous judgments. **8.** I will keep Your statutes; Oh, do not forsake me utterly! **9.** How can a young man cleanse his way? By taking heed according to Your word. **10.** With my whole heart I have sought You; Oh, let me not wander from Your commandments! **11.** Your word I have hidden in my heart, that I might not sin against You! **12.** Blessed are You, O Lord! Teach me Your statutes! **13.** With my lips I have declared all the judgments of Your mouth. **14.** I have rejoiced in the way of Your testimonies, as much as in all riches. **15.** I will meditate on Your precepts, and contemplate Your ways. **16.** I will delight myself in Your statutes; I will not forget Your word. **17.** Deal bountifully (generously) with Your servant, that I may live and keep Your word. **18.** Open my eyes, that I may see wondrous things from Your law. **19.** I am a stranger (alien) in the earth; do not hide Your commandments from me. **20.** My soul breaks with longing for Your judgments at all times. **21.** You rebuke the proud—the cursed, who stray from Your commandments. **22.** Remove from me reproach (shame) and contempt, for I have kept Your testimonies. **23.** Princes (rulers) also sit and speak against me, but Your servant meditates on Your statutes. **24.** Your testimonies also are my delight and my counselors. **25.** My soul clings to the dust; revive me according to Your word. **26.** I have declared my ways, and You answered me; teach me Your statutes. **27.** Make me understand the way of Your precepts; so shall I meditate on Your wondrous works. **28.** My soul melts from heaviness; strengthen me according to Your word. **29.** Remove from me the way of lying, and grant me Your law graciously. **30.** I have chosen the way of truth; Your judgments I have laid before me. **31.** I cling to Your testimonies; O Lord, do not put me to shame! **32.** I will run the course of Your commandments, for You shall enlarge my heart. **33.** Teach me, O Lord, the way of Your statutes, and I shall keep it to the end. **34.** Give me understanding, and I shall keep Your law; indeed, I shall observe it with my whole heart. **35.** Make me walk in the path of Your commandments, for I delight in it. **36.** Incline my heart to Your testimonies, and not to covetousness (greed). **37.** Turn away my eyes from looking at worthless things, and revive me in Your way. **38.** Establish Your word to Your servant, who is devoted to fearing You. **39.** Turn away my reproach which I dread, for Your judgments are good. **40.** Behold, I long for Your precepts; revive me in Your righteousness. **41.** Let Your mercies come also to me, O Lord— Your salvation according to Your word. **42.** So shall I have an answer for him who reproaches me, for I trust in Your word. **43.** And take not the word of truth utterly out of my mouth, for I have hoped in Your ordinances (decrees). **44.** So shall I keep Your law continually, forever and ever. **45.** And I will walk at liberty (freedom), for I seek Your precepts. **46.** I will speak of Your testimonies also before kings, and will not be ashamed. **47.** And I will delight myself in Your commandments, which I love. **48.** My hands also I will lift up to Your commandments, which I love, and I will meditate on Your statutes. **49.** Remember the word to Your servant, upon which You have caused me to hope. **50.** This is my comfort in my affliction, for Your word has given me life. **51.** The proud have me in great derision, yet I do not turn aside from Your law. **52.** I remembered Your judgments of old, O Lord, and have comforted myself. **53.** Indignation (anger) has taken hold of me because of the wicked, who forsake Your law. **54.** Your statutes have been my songs in the house of my pilgrimage (temporary dwelling). **55.** I remember Your name in the night, O Lord, and I keep Your law. **56.** This has become mine, because I kept Your precepts. **57.** You are my portion (inheritance), O Lord; I have said that I would keep Your words. **58.** I entreated (begged for) Your favor with my whole heart; be merciful to me according to Your word. **59.** I thought about my ways, and turned my feet to Your testimonies. **60.** I made haste, and did not delay to keep Your commandments. **61.** The cords (ropes) of the wicked have bound me, but I have not forgotten Your law. **62.** At midnight I will rise to give thanks to You, because of Your righteous judgments. **63.** I am a companion of all who fear You, and of those who keep Your precepts. **64.** The earth, O Lord, is full of Your mercy; teach me Your statutes. **65.** You have dealt well with Your servant, O Lord, according to Your word. **66.** Teach me good judgment and knowledge, for I believe Your commandments. **67.** Before I was afflicted I went astray, but now I keep Your word. **68.** You are good, and do good; teach me Your statutes. **69.** The proud have forged a lie against me, but I will keep Your precepts with my whole heart. **70.** Their heart is as fat as grease (insensitive), but I delight in Your law. **71.** It is good for me that I have been afflicted, that I may learn Your statutes. **72.** The law of Your mouth is better to me than thousands of coins (pieces) of gold and silver. **73.** Your hands have made me and fashioned me; give me understanding, that I may learn Your commandments. **74.** Those who fear You will be glad when they see me, because I have hoped in Your word. **75.** I know, O Lord, that Your judgments are right, and that in faithfulness You have afflicted me. **76.** Let, I pray, Your merciful kindness be for my comfort, according to Your word to Your servant. **77.** Let Your tender mercies come to me, that I may live; for Your law is my delight. **78.** Let the proud be ashamed, for they treated me wrongfully with falsehood; but I will meditate on Your precepts. **79.** Let those who fear You turn to me, those who know Your testimonies. **80.** Let my heart be blameless regarding Your statutes, that I may not be ashamed. **81.** My soul faints for Your salvation, but I hope in Your word. **82.** My eyes fail from searching Your word, saying, "When will You comfort me?" **83.** For I have become like a wineskin in smoke (worn out), yet I do not forget Your statutes. **84.** How many are the days of Your servant? When will You execute judgment on those who persecute me? **85.** The proud have dug pits for me, which is not according to Your law. **86.** All Your commandments are faithful; they persecute me wrongfully; help me! **87.** They almost made an end of me on earth, but I did not forsake Your precepts. **88.** Revive me according to Your lovingkindness, so that I may keep the testimony of Your mouth. **89.** Forever, O Lord, Your word is settled in heaven. **90.** Your faithfulness endures to all generations; You established the earth, and it abides. **91.** They continue this day according to Your ordinances, for all are Your servants. **92.** Unless Your law had been my delight, I would then have perished in my affliction. **93.** I will never forget Your precepts, for by them You have given me life. **94.** I am Yours, save me; for I have sought Your precepts. **95.** The wicked wait for me to destroy me, but I will consider Your testimonies. **96.** I have seen the consummation (limit) of all perfection, but Your commandment is exceedingly broad. **97.** Oh, how I love Your law! It is my meditation all the day. **98.** You, through Your commandments, make me wiser than my enemies; for they are ever with me. **99.** I have more understanding than all my teachers, for Your testimonies are my meditation. **100.** I understand more than the ancients (elders), because I keep Your precepts. **101.** I have restrained my feet from every evil way, that I may keep Your word. **102.** I have not departed from Your judgments, for You Yourself have taught me. **103.** How sweet are Your words to my taste, sweeter than honey to my mouth! **104.** Through Your precepts I get understanding; therefore, I hate every false way. **105.** Your word is a lamp to my feet and a light to my path. **106.** I have sworn and confirmed that I will keep Your righteous judgments. **107.** I am afflicted very much; revive me, O Lord, according to Your word. **108.** Accept, I pray, the freewill offerings (voluntary gifts) of my mouth, O Lord, and teach me Your judgments. **109.** My life is continually in my hand, yet I do not forget Your law. **110.** The wicked have laid a snare for me, yet I have not strayed from Your precepts. **111.** Your testimonies I have taken as a heritage forever, for they are the rejoicing of my heart. **112.** I have inclined my heart to perform Your statutes forever, to the very end. **113.** I hate the double-minded, but I love Your law. **114.** You are my hiding place and my shield; I hope in Your word. **115.** Depart from me, you evildoers, for I will keep the commandments of my God! **116.** Uphold me according to Your word, that I may live; and do not let me be ashamed of my hope. **117.** Hold me up, and I shall be safe, and I shall observe Your statutes continually. **118.** You reject all those who stray from Your statutes, for their deceit is falsehood. **119.** You put away all the wicked of the earth like dross (impurities); therefore I love Your testimonies. **120.** My flesh trembles for fear of You, and I am afraid of Your judgments. **121.** I have done justice and righteousness; do not leave me to my oppressors. **122.** Be surety (guarantor) for Your servant for good; do not let the proud oppress me. **123.** My eyes fail from seeking Your salvation and Your righteous word. **124.** Deal with Your servant according to Your mercy, and teach me Your statutes. **125.** I am Your servant; give me understanding, that I may know Your testimonies. **126.** It is time for You to act, O Lord, for they have regarded Your law as void. **127.** Therefore I love Your commandments more than gold, yes, than fine gold! **128.** Therefore all Your precepts concerning all things I consider to be right; I hate every false way. **129.** Your testimonies are wonderful; therefore my soul keeps them. **130.** The entrance of Your words gives light; it gives understanding to the simple. **131.** I opened my mouth and panted (longed), for I longed for Your commandments. **132.** Look upon me and be merciful to me, as Your custom is toward those who love Your name. **133.** Direct my steps by Your word, and let no iniquity have dominion over me. **134.** Redeem me from the oppression of man, that I may keep Your precepts. **135.** Make Your face shine upon Your servant, and teach me Your statutes. **136.** Rivers of water run down from my eyes, because men do not keep Your law. **137.** Righteous are You, O Lord, and upright are Your judgments. **138.** Your testimonies, which You have commanded, are righteous and very faithful. **139.** My zeal (passion) has consumed me, because my enemies have forgotten Your words. **140.** Your word is very pure; therefore Your servant loves it. **141.** I am small and despised, yet I do not forget Your precepts. **142.** Your righteousness is an everlasting righteousness, and Your law is truth. **143.** Trouble and anguish have overtaken me, yet Your commandments are my delights. **144.** The righteousness of Your testimonies is everlasting; give me understanding, and I shall live. **145.** I cry out with my whole heart; hear me, O Lord! I will keep Your statutes. **146.** I cry out to You; save me, and I will keep Your testimonies. **147.** I rise before the dawning of the morning, and cry for help; I hope in Your word. **148.** My eyes are awake through the night watches, that I may meditate on Your word. **149.** Hear my voice according to Your lovingkindness; O Lord, revive me according to Your justice. **150.** They draw near who follow after wickedness; they are far from Your law. **151.** You are near, O Lord, and all Your commandments are truth. **152.** Concerning Your testimonies, I have known of old that You have founded them forever. **153.** Consider my affliction and deliver me, for I do not forget Your law. **154.** Plead my cause and redeem me; revive me according to Your word. **155.** Salvation is far from the wicked, for they do not seek Your statutes. **156.** Great are Your tender mercies, O Lord; revive me according to Your judgments. **157.** Many are my persecutors and my enemies, yet I do not turn from Your testimonies. **158.** I see the treacherous (betrayers), and am disgusted, because they do not keep Your word. **159.** Consider how I love Your precepts; revive me, O Lord, according to Your loving-kindness. **160.** The entirety of Your word is truth, and every one of Your righteous judgments endures forever. **161.** Princes persecute me without a cause, but my heart stands in awe of Your word. **162.** I rejoice at Your word as one who finds great treasure. **163.** I hate and abhor lying, but I love Your law. **164.** Seven times a day I praise You, because of Your righteous judgments. **165.** Great peace have those who love Your law, and nothing causes them to stumble. **166.** Lord, I hope for Your salvation, and I do Your commandments. **167.** My soul keeps Your testimonies, and I love them exceedingly. **168.** I keep Your precepts and Your testimonies, for all my ways are before You. **169.** Let my cry come before You, O Lord; give me understanding according to Your word. **170.** Let my supplication (request) come before You; deliver me according to Your word. **171.** My lips shall utter praise, for You teach me Your statutes. **172.** My tongue shall speak of Your word, for all Your commandments are righteousness. **173.** Let Your hand become my help, for I have chosen Your precepts. **174.** I long for Your salvation, O Lord, and Your law is my delight. **175.** Let my soul live, and it shall praise You; and let Your judgments help me. **176.** I have gone astray like a lost sheep; seek Your servant, for I do not forget Your commandments.

Chapter 120

1. A Song of Ascents. In my distress, I called to the Lord, and He answered me. **2.** Save my soul, O Lord, from deceitful lips and from a false tongue. **3.** What will be done to you, you deceitful tongue? What will be your reward? **4.** Sharp arrows of a warrior, with burning coals from a broom tree (a thorny shrub)! **5.** How miserable I am, that I live in Meshech (region far from Israel) and dwell among the tents of Kedar (tribe of nomads)! **6.** My soul has lived too long with those who hate peace. **7.** I am for peace, but when I speak, they are for war.

Chapter 121

1. A Song of Ascents. I lift my eyes to the hills (mountains)—where does my help come from? **2.** My help comes from the LORD, who made the heavens and the earth. **3.** He will not let your foot slip; the One who watches over you will not sleep (rest). **4.** Indeed, the One who watches over Israel (God's people) will neither slumber nor sleep. **5.** The LORD is your keeper (protector); the LORD is the shade (protection) at your right hand. **6.** The sun will not strike you by day, nor the moon by night. **7.** The LORD will keep you from all evil; He will guard your soul (life). **8.** The LORD will watch over your going out and coming in (travels), now and forevermore.

Chapter 122

1. A Song of Ascents. Of David. I was glad when they said to me, "Let us go into the house of the LORD." **2.** Our feet have been standing within your gates, O Jerusalem (city of peace)! **3.** Jerusalem (city of peace) is built as a city that is firmly joined together, **4.** where the tribes go up, the tribes of the Lord, to the Testimony of Israel (place of worship), to give thanks to the name of the LORD. **5.** For thrones are set there for judgment, the thrones of the house of David (king of Israel). **6.** Pray for the peace of Jerusalem (city of peace): "May those who love you prosper." **7.** Peace be within your walls, prosperity within your palaces. **8.** For the sake of my brethren and companions, I will now say, "Peace be within you." **9.** Because of the house of the Lord our God, I will seek your good.

Chapter 123

1. A Song of Ascents. Unto You I lift up my eyes, O You who dwell in the heavens (sky). **2.** Behold, as the eyes of servants look to the hand of their masters, as the eyes of a maid to the hand of her mistress, so our eyes look to the Lord our God, until He has mercy on us. **3.** Have mercy on us, O Lord, have mercy on us! For we are exceedingly filled with contempt (disrespect). **4.** Our soul is exceedingly filled with the scorn (mockery) of those who are at ease (comfortable), with the contempt of the proud.

Chapter 124

1. A Song of Ascents. Of David. "If it had not been the LORD who was on our side," let Israel (God's people) now say— **2.** "If it had not been the Lord who was on our side, when men (enemies) rose up against us, **3.** they would have swallowed us alive, when their anger (wrath) was kindled against us; **4.** the waters (floods) would have overwhelmed us, the stream (raging waters) gone over our soul (life). **5.** the swollen waters (floods) would have gone over our soul (life)." **6.** Blessed be the Lord, who has not given us as prey (food) to their teeth (enemies). **7.** Our soul (life) has escaped like a bird from the snare (trap) of the fowlers (trappers); the snare is broken, and we have escaped. **8.** Our help is in the name of the LORD, who made the heaven and the earth.

Chapter 125

1. A Song of Ascents. Those who trust in the Lord are like *Mount Zion* (a hill in Jerusalem), which cannot be moved but stands forever. **2.** As the mountains surround *Jerusalem* (the holy city), so the Lord surrounds His people now and forever.**3.** The scepter of wickedness will not rest on the land given to the righteous, so the righteous do not reach for sin.**4.** Do good, O Lord, to those who are good and to those who are pure in heart. **5.** As for those who turn to crooked ways, the Lord will lead them away with the workers of *iniquity* (wickedness). Peace be upon *Israel* (God's people).

Chapter 126

1. A Song of Ascents. When the Lord brought back the captivity of *Zion* (Jerusalem), we were like those who dream. **2.** Then our mouth was filled with laughter and our tongue with singing. Then they said among the nations, "The Lord has done great things for them." **3.** The Lord has done great things for us, and we are glad. **4.** Bring back our captivity, O Lord, like the streams in the *South* (arid region, known for seasonal rains). **5.** Those who sow in tears shall reap in joy. **6.** He who goes forth weeping, bearing seed for sowing, shall come back with joy, bringing his sheaves (harvested bundles) with him.

Chapter 127

1. A Song of Ascents. Of *Solomon* (King of Israel). Unless the Lord builds the house, those who build it labor in vain; unless the Lord guards the city, the watchman stays awake in vain. **2.** It is vain to rise up early, to sit up late, to eat the bread of sorrows; for He gives His beloved sleep. **3.** Behold, children are a heritage from the Lord, the fruit of the womb is a reward. **4.** Like arrows in the hand of a warrior, so are the children of one's youth. **5.** Happy is the man who has his quiver full of them; they shall not be ashamed, but shall speak with their enemies at the gate.

Chapter 128

1. A Song of Ascents. Blessed is everyone who fears the Lord, who walks in His ways. **2.** When you eat the labor of your hands, you shall be happy, and it will be well with you. **3.** Your wife shall be like a fruitful vine in the very heart of your house, your children like olive plants around your table. **4.** Behold, thus shall the man be blessed who fears the Lord. **5.** The Lord bless you from *Zion* (the hill in Jerusalem), and may you see the good of

Jerusalem (the holy city) all the days of your life. **6.** Yes, may you see your children's children. Peace be upon *Israel* (God's people).

Chapter 129

1. A Song of Ascents. "Many times they have afflicted me from my youth," let Israel (God's people) now say— **2.** "Many times they have afflicted me from my youth; yet they have not prevailed against me." **3.** The plowers plowed on my back, making long furrows. **4.** The Lord is righteous; He has cut in pieces the cords of the wicked. **5.** Let all those who hate Zion (Jerusalem) be put to shame and turned back. **6.** Let them be like grass on the housetops, which withers before it grows. **7.** With it the reaper does not fill his hand, nor the binder of sheaves his arms. **8.** Let those who pass by not say, "The blessing of the Lord be upon you; we bless you in the name of the Lord!"

Chapter 130

1. A Song of Ascents. Out of the depths I have cried to You, O Lord; **2.** Lord, hear my voice! Let Your ears be attentive to the voice of my supplications. **3.** If You, Lord, should mark iniquities (sins), O Lord, who could stand? **4.** But there is forgiveness with You, that You may be feared. **5.** I wait for the Lord, my soul waits, and in His word I do hope. **6.** My soul waits for the Lord more than those who watch for the morning— yes, more than those who watch for the morning. **7.** O Israel (God's people), hope in the Lord; for with the Lord there is mercy, and with Him is abundant redemption. **8.** And He shall redeem Israel from all his iniquities.

Chapter 131

1. A Song of Ascents. Of David. Lord, my heart is not haughty, Nor my eyes lofty. Neither do I concern myself with great matters, Nor with things too profound for me. **2.** Surely I have calmed and quieted my soul, Like a weaned child with his mother; Like a weaned child is my soul within me. **3.** O Israel, hope in the Lord From this time forth and forever.

Chapter 132

1. A Song of Ascents. Lord, remember David (King of Israel) and all his afflictions; **2.** How he swore to the Lord and vowed to the Mighty One of Jacob (another name for Israel): **3.** "Surely I will not go into the chamber of my house or up to the comfort of my bed; **4.** I will not give sleep to my eyes or slumber to my eyelids, **5.** Until I find a place for the Lord, a dwelling place for the Mighty One of Jacob." **6.** Behold, we heard of it in Ephrathah (a region near Bethlehem); we found it in the fields of the woods. **7.** Let us go into His tabernacle; let us worship at His footstool. **8.** Arise, O Lord, to Your resting place, You and the ark of Your strength (symbol of God's presence). **9.** Let Your priests be clothed with righteousness, and let Your saints shout for joy. **10.** For Your servant David's sake, do not turn away the face of Your Anointed **11.** The Lord has sworn in truth to David; He will not turn from it: "I will set upon your throne the fruit of your body. **12.** If your sons will keep My covenant and My testimony which I shall teach them, their sons also shall sit upon your throne forevermore." **13.** For the Lord has chosen Zion (Jerusalem); He has desired it for His dwelling place: **14.** "This is My resting place forever; here I will dwell, for I have desired it. **15.** I will abundantly bless her provision; I will satisfy her poor with bread. **16.** I will also clothe her priests with salvation, and her saints shall shout aloud for joy. **17.** There I will make the horn (strength) of David grow; I will prepare a lamp for My Anointed. **18.** His enemies I will clothe with shame, but upon Himself His crown shall flourish."

Chapter 133

1. A Song of Ascents. Of *David* (King of Israel). Behold, how good and how pleasant it is for brethren to dwell together in unity! **2.** It is like the precious oil upon the head, running down on the beard, the beard of *Aaron* (the first high priest), running down on the edge of his garments. **3.** It is like the dew of *Hermon* (a high mountain in Israel), descending upon the mountains of *Zion* (Jerusalem); for there the Lord commanded the blessing— life forevermore.

Chapter 134

1. A Song of Ascents. Behold, bless the Lord, all you servants of the Lord, who by night stand in the house of the Lord! **2.** Lift up your hands in the sanctuary and bless the Lord. **3.** The Lord who made heaven and earth bless you from *Zion* (Jerusalem)!

Chapter 135

1. Praise the Lord! Praise the name of the Lord; praise Him, O you servants of the Lord! **2.** You who stand in the house of the Lord, in the courts of the house of our God, **3.** Praise the Lord, for the Lord is good; sing praises to His name, for it is pleasant. **4.** For the Lord has chosen Jacob (Israel) for Himself, Israel for His special treasure. **5.** For I know that the Lord is great, and our Lord is above all gods. **6.** Whatever the Lord pleases He does, in heaven and on earth, in the seas and in all deep places. **7.** He causes the vapors to ascend from the ends of the earth; He makes lightning for the rain; He brings the wind out of His treasuries. **8.** He destroyed the firstborn of Egypt (land of Pharaoh), both of man and beast. **9.** He sent signs and wonders into the midst of you, O Egypt, upon Pharaoh and all his servants. **10.** He defeated many nations and slew mighty kings— **11.** Sihon (King of the Amorites), Og (King of Bashan), and all the kingdoms of Canaan (ancient land of Israel). **12.** And gave their land as a heritage, a heritage to Israel His people. **13.** Your name, O Lord, endures forever; Your fame, O Lord, throughout all generations. **14.** For the Lord will judge His people, and He will have compassion on His servants. **15.** The idols of the nations are silver and gold, the work of men's hands. **16.** They have mouths, but they do not speak; eyes they have, but they do not see; **17.** They have ears, but they do not hear; nor is there any breath in their mouths. **18.** Those who make them are like them; so is everyone who trusts in them. **19.** Bless the Lord, O house of Israel! Bless the Lord, O house of Aaron (priestly family)! **20.** Bless the Lord, O house of Levi (tribe of priests)! You who fear the Lord, bless the Lord! **21.** Blessed be the Lord out of Zion (Jerusalem), who dwells in Jerusalem! Praise the Lord!

Chapter 136

1. Oh, give thanks to the Lord, for He is good! For His mercy endures forever. **2.** Oh, give thanks to the God of gods! For His mercy endures forever. **3.** Oh, give thanks to the Lord of lords! For His mercy endures forever: **4.** To Him who alone does great wonders, for His mercy endures forever; **5.** To Him who by wisdom made the heavens, for His mercy endures forever; **6.** To Him who laid out the earth above the waters, for His mercy endures forever; **7.** To Him who made great lights, for His mercy endures forever— **8.** The sun to rule by day, for His mercy endures forever; **9.** The moon and stars to rule by night, for His mercy endures forever. **10.** To Him who struck Egypt (land of Pharaoh) in their firstborn, for His mercy endures forever; **11.** And brought out Israel from among them, for His mercy endures forever; **12.** With a strong hand and with an outstretched arm, for His mercy endures forever; **13.** To Him who divided the Red Sea (sea that parted for Israel), for His mercy endures forever; **14.** And made Israel pass through the midst of it, for His mercy endures forever; **15.** But overthrew Pharaoh (King of Egypt) and his army in the Red Sea, for His mercy endures forever; **16.** To Him who led His people through the wilderness, for His mercy endures forever; **17.** To Him who struck down great kings, for His mercy endures forever; **18.** And slew famous kings, for His mercy endures forever— **19.** Sihon (King of the Amorites), for His mercy endures forever; **20.** And Og (King of Bashan), for His mercy endures forever— **21.** And gave their land as a heritage, for His mercy endures forever; **22.** A heritage to Israel His servant, for His mercy endures forever. **23.** Who remembered us in our lowly state, for His mercy endures forever; **24.** And rescued us from our enemies, for His mercy endures forever; **25.** Who gives food to all flesh, for His mercy endures forever. **26.** Oh, give thanks to the God of heaven! For His mercy endures forever.

Chapter 137

1. By the rivers of Babylon (a city in ancient Mesopotamia), there we sat down, yea, we wept when we remembered Zion (Jerusalem). **2.** We hung our harps upon the willows in the midst of it. **3.** For there those who carried us away captive asked of us a song, and those who plundered us requested mirth, saying, "Sing us one of the songs of Zion!" **4.** How shall we sing the Lord's song in a foreign land? **5.** If I forget you, O Jerusalem, let my right hand forget its skill! **6.** If I do not remember you, let my tongue cling to the roof of my mouth— if I do not exalt Jerusalem above my chief joy. **7.** Remember, O Lord, against the sons of Edom (a neighboring nation), the day of Jerusalem, who said, "Raze it, raze it, to its very foundation!" **8.** O daughter of Babylon, who are to be destroyed, happy the one who repays you as you have served us! **9.** Happy the one who takes and dashes your little ones against the rock!

Chapter 138

1. A Psalm of David (King of Israel). I will praise You with my whole heart; before the gods I will sing praises to You. **2.** I will worship toward Your holy temple and praise Your name for Your lovingkindness and Your truth; for You have magnified Your word above all Your name. **3.** In the day when I cried out, You answered me, and made me bold with strength in my soul. **4.** All the kings of the earth shall praise You, O Lord, when they hear the words of Your mouth. **5.** Yes, they shall sing of the ways of the Lord, for great is the glory of the Lord. **6.** Though the Lord is on high, yet He regards the lowly; but the proud He knows from afar. **7.** Though I walk in the midst of trouble, You will revive me; You will stretch out Your hand against the wrath of my enemies, and Your right hand will save me. **8.** The Lord will perfect that which concerns me; Your mercy, O Lord, endures forever; do not forsake the works of Your hands.

Chapter 139

1. For the Chief Musician. A Psalm of David (King of Israel). O Lord, You have searched me and known me. **2.** You know my sitting down and my rising up; You understand my thought afar off. **3.** You comprehend my path and my lying down, and are acquainted with all my ways. **4.** For there is not a word on my tongue, but behold, O Lord, You know it altogether. **5.** You have hedged me behind and before, and laid Your hand upon me. **6.** Such knowledge is too wonderful for me; it is high, I cannot attain it. **7.** Where can I go from Your Spirit? Or where can I flee from Your presence? **8.** If I ascend into heaven, You are there; if I make my bed in Sheol (the grave or underworld), behold, You are there. **9.** If I take the wings of the morning, and dwell in the uttermost parts of the sea, **10.** Even there Your hand shall lead me, and Your right hand shall hold me. **11.** If I say, "Surely the darkness shall fall on me," even the night shall be light about me; **12.** Indeed, the darkness shall not hide from You, but the night shines as the day; the darkness and the light are both alike to You. **13.** For You formed my inward parts; You covered me in my mother's womb. **14.** I will praise You, for I am fearfully and wonderfully made; marvelous are Your works, and that my soul knows very well. **15.** My frame was not hidden from You when I was made in secret, and skillfully wrought in the lowest parts of the earth. **16.** Your eyes saw my substance, being yet unformed, and in Your book they all were written, the days fashioned for me, when as yet there were none of them. **17.** How precious also are Your thoughts to me, O God! How great is the sum of them! **18.** If I should count them, they would be more in number than the sand; when I awake, I am still with You. **19.** Oh, that You would slay the wicked, O God! Depart from me, therefore, you bloodthirsty men. **20.** For they speak against You wickedly; Your enemies take Your name in vain. **21.** Do I not hate them, O Lord, who hate You? And do I not loathe those who rise up against You? **22.** I hate them with perfect hatred; I count them my enemies. **23.** Search me, O God, and know my heart; try me, and know my anxieties; **24.** And see if there is any wicked way in me and lead me in the way everlasting.

Chapter 140

1. To the Chief Musician. A Psalm of David (King of Israel). Deliver me, O Lord, from evil men; preserve me from violent men, **2.** Who plan evil things in their hearts; they continually gather together for war. **3.** They sharpen their tongues like a serpent; the poison of asps (venomous snakes) is under their lips. Selah (pause and reflect). **4.** Keep me, O Lord, from the hands of the wicked; preserve me from violent men, who have purposed to make my steps stumble. **5.** The proud have hidden a snare for me, and cords; they have spread a net by the wayside; they have set traps for me. Selah **6.** I said to the Lord: "You are my God; hear the voice of my supplications, O Lord. **7.** O God the Lord, the strength of my salvation, You have covered my head in the day of battle. **8.** Do not grant, O Lord, the desires of the wicked; do not further his wicked scheme, lest they be exalted. Selah **9.** "As for the head of those who surround me, let the evil of their lips cover them; **10.** Let burning coals fall upon them; let them be cast into the fire, into deep pits, that they rise not up again. **11.** Let not a slanderer be established in the earth; let evil hunt the violent man to overthrow him." **12.** I know that the Lord will maintain the cause of the afflicted and justice for the poor. **13.** Surely the righteous shall give thanks to Your name; the upright shall dwell in Your presence.

Chapter 141

1 A Psalm of David. Lord, I cry out to You; make haste (hurry) to me! Give ear (listen) to my voice when I cry out to You. **2** Let my prayer be set before You as incense (a fragrant offering), the lifting up of my hands as the evening sacrifice. **3** Set a guard (watch) over my mouth, O Lord; keep watch over the door (entrance) of my lips. **4** Do not incline (direct) my heart to any evil thing, to practice wicked works (evil deeds) with men who work iniquity (wickedness); and do not let me eat of their delicacies (tempting food). **5** Let the righteous strike me; it shall be a kindness. And let him rebuke (correct) me; it shall be as excellent oil; let my head not refuse it. For still my prayer is against the deeds of the wicked. **6** Their judges (leaders) are overthrown by the sides of the cliff (rocks), and they hear my words, for they are sweet. **7** Our bones are scattered at the mouth (entrance) of the grave, as when one plows and breaks up the earth. **8** But my eyes are upon You, O God (the) Lord; in You I take refuge; do not leave my soul destitute (empty). **9** Keep me from the snares (traps) they have laid for me, and from the traps of the workers (those who practice) iniquity. **10** Let the wicked fall into their own nets, while I escape safely.

Chapter 142

1. A Psalm of David Lord, I cry out to You; make haste (hurry) to me! Give ear (listen) to my voice when I cry out to You. **2** Let my prayer be set before You as incense (a fragrant offering), the lifting up of my hands as the evening sacrifice. **3** Set a guard (watch) over my mouth, O Lord; keep watch over the door (entrance) of my lips. **4** Do not incline (direct) my heart to any evil thing, to practice wicked works (evil deeds) with men who work iniquity (wickedness); and do not let me eat of their delicacies (tempting food). **5** Let the righteous strike me; it shall be a kindness. And let him rebuke (correct) me; it shall be as excellent (precious) oil; let my head not refuse it. For still my prayer is against the deeds of the wicked. **6** Their

judges (leaders) are overthrown by the sides of the cliff (rocks), and they hear my words, for they are sweet. **7** Our bones are scattered at the mouth (entrance) of the grave, as when one plows and breaks up the earth. **8** But my eyes are upon You, O God (the) Lord; in You I take refuge; do not leave my soul destitute (empty). **9** Keep me from the snares (traps) they have laid for me, and from the traps of the workers (those who practice) iniquity. **10** Let the wicked fall into their own nets, while I escape safely.

Chapter 143

1 A Contemplation of David. A Prayer when he was in the cave. I cry out to the Lord with my voice; with my voice to the Lord I make my supplication. **2** I pour out my complaint before Him; I declare before Him my trouble. **3** When my spirit was overwhelmed (faint) within me, then You knew my path. In the way in which I walk, they have secretly set a snare (trap) for me. **4** Look on my right hand and see, for there is no one who acknowledges me; refuge has failed me; no one cares for my soul. **5** I cried out to You, O Lord: I said, "You are my refuge, my portion (inheritance) in the land of the living." **6** Attend (listen) to my cry, for I am brought very low; deliver me from my persecutors, for they are stronger than I. **7** Bring my soul out of prison (trouble), that I may praise Your name; the righteous shall surround me, for You shall deal bountifully with me.

Chapter 144

1 A Psalm of David. Hear my prayer, O Lord, give ear to my supplications! In Your faithfulness answer me, and in Your righteousness. **2** Do not enter into judgment with Your servant, for in Your sight no one living is righteous. **3** For the enemy has persecuted my soul; he has crushed my life to the ground; he has made me dwell in darkness, like those who have long been dead. **4** Therefore my spirit is overwhelmed within me; my heart within me is distressed (anxious). **5** I remember the days of old; I meditate on all Your works; I muse (think deeply) on the work of Your hands. **6** I spread out my hands to You; my soul longs for You like a thirsty land. Selah (Pause and reflect). **7** Answer me speedily, O Lord; my spirit fails! Do not hide Your face from me, lest I be like those who go down into the pit (grave). **8** Cause me to hear Your lovingkindness in the morning, for in You do I trust; cause me to know the way in which I should walk, for I lift up my soul to You. **9** Deliver me, O Lord, from my enemies; in You I take shelter. **10** Teach me to do Your will, for You are my God; Your Spirit is good. Lead me in the land of uprightness (righteousness). **11** Revive (restore) me, O Lord, for Your name's sake! For Your righteousness' sake bring my soul out of trouble. **12** In Your mercy cut off my enemies, and destroy all those who afflict my soul; for I am Your servant.

Chapter 145

1 A Praise of David. I will extol (praise) You, my God, O King; and I will bless Your name forever and ever. **2** Every day I will bless You, and I will praise Your name forever and ever. **3** Great is the Lord, and greatly to be praised; and His greatness is unsearchable (beyond understanding). **4** One generation shall praise Your works to another, and shall declare Your mighty acts. **5** I will meditate (think) on the glorious splendor of Your majesty, and on Your wondrous works. **6** Men shall speak of the might of Your awesome acts, and I will declare Your greatness. **7** They shall utter (speak) the memory of Your great goodness, and shall sing of Your righteousness. **8** The Lord is gracious and full of compassion, slow to anger, and great in mercy. **9** The Lord is good to all, and His tender mercies are over all His works. **10** All Your works shall praise You, O Lord, and Your saints (holy ones) shall bless You. **11** They shall speak of the glory of Your kingdom, and talk of Your power, **12** To make known to the sons of men His mighty acts, and the glorious majesty of His kingdom. **13** Your kingdom is an everlasting kingdom, and Your dominion (rule) endures throughout all generations. **14** The Lord upholds (supports) all who fall, and raises up all who are bowed down. **15** The eyes of all look expectantly to You, and You give them their food in due season. **16** You open Your hand and satisfy the desire of every living thing. **17** The Lord is righteous in all His ways, gracious in all His works. **18** The Lord is near to all who call upon Him, to all who call upon Him in truth. **19** He will fulfill the desire of those who fear Him; He also will hear their cry and save them. **20** The Lord preserves all who love Him, but all the wicked He will destroy. **21** My mouth shall speak the praise of the Lord, and all flesh shall bless His holy name forever and ever.

Chapter 146

1 Praise the Lord! Praise the Lord, O my soul! **2** While I live, I will praise the Lord; I will sing praises to my God while I have my being. **3** Do not put your trust in princes (rulers), nor in a son of man, in whom there is no help. **4** His spirit departs, he returns to his earth; in that very day his plans perish. **5** Happy is he who has the God of Jacob (Israel) for his help, whose hope is in the Lord his God, **6** Who made heaven and earth, the sea, and all that is in them; who keeps truth forever, **7** Who executes justice for the oppressed, who gives food to the hungry. The Lord gives freedom to the prisoners. **8** The Lord opens the eyes of the blind; the Lord raises those who are bowed down; the Lord loves the righteous. **9** The Lord watches over the strangers; He relieves the fatherless and widow; but the way of the wicked He turns upside down. **10** The Lord shall reign forever—your God, O Zion (Jerusalem), to all generations. Praise the Lord!

Chapter 147

1 Praise the Lord! For it is good to sing praises to our God; for it is pleasant, and praise is beautiful (worthy of admiration). **2** The Lord builds up Jerusalem; He gathers together the outcasts (exiles) of Israel. **3** He heals the brokenhearted and binds up their wounds. **4** He counts the number of the stars; He calls them all by name. **5** Great is our Lord, and mighty in power; His understanding is infinite (without limit). **6** The Lord lifts up the humble; He casts the wicked down to the ground. **7** Sing to the Lord with thanksgiving; sing praises on the harp to our God, **8** Who covers the heavens with clouds, who prepares rain for the earth, who makes grass to grow on the mountains. **9** He gives to the beast (animals) its food, and to the young ravens (birds) that cry. **10** He does not delight in the strength of the horse; He takes no pleasure in the legs (strength) of a man. **11** The Lord takes pleasure in those who fear Him, in those who hope in His mercy. **12** Praise the Lord, O Jerusalem! Praise your God, O Zion! **13** For He has strengthened the bars of your gates; He has blessed your children within you. **14** He makes peace in your borders, and fills you with the finest wheat. **15** He sends out His command to the earth; His word runs very swiftly (quickly). **16** He gives snow like wool; He scatters the frost like ashes; **17** He casts out His hail like morsels (flakes); who can stand before His cold? **18** He sends out His word and melts them; He causes His wind to blow, and the waters flow. **19** He declares His word to Jacob (Israel), His statutes (commands) and His judgments to Israel. **20** He has not dealt thus with any nation; and as for His judgments, they have not known them. Praise the Lord!

Chapter 148

1 Praise the Lord! Praise the Lord from the heavens; praise Him in the heights (above)! **2** Praise Him, all His angels; praise Him, all His hosts (armies of heaven)! **3** Praise Him, sun and moon; praise Him, all you stars of light! **4** Praise Him, you heavens of heavens, and you waters above the heavens! **5** Let them praise the name of the Lord, for He commanded and they were created. **6** He also established them forever and ever; He made a decree (law) which shall not pass away. **7** Praise the Lord from the earth, you great sea creatures and all the depths (oceans); **8** Fire and hail, snow and clouds; stormy wind, fulfilling His word; **9** Mountains and all hills; fruitful trees and all cedars (tall trees); **10** Beasts (animals) and all cattle; creeping things (insects) and flying fowl (birds); **11** Kings of the earth and all peoples; princes (leaders) and all judges (rulers) of the earth; **12** Both young men and maidens (women); old men and children. **13** Let them praise the name of the Lord, for His name alone is exalted (raised high); His glory is above the earth and heaven. **14** And He has exalted the horn (strength) of His people, the praise of all His saints (holy ones)—of the children of Israel, a people near to Him. Praise the Lord!

Chapter 149

1 Praise the Lord! Sing to the Lord a new song, and His praise in the assembly of saints (believers). **2** Let Israel rejoice in their Maker; let the children of Zion be joyful in their King. **3** Let them praise His name with the dance (dance for joy); let them sing praises to Him with the timbrel (tambourine) and harp. **4** For the Lord takes pleasure in His people; He will beautify (adorn) the humble with salvation. **5** Let the saints be joyful in glory; let them sing aloud on their beds. **6** Let the high praises of God be in their mouth, and a two-edged sword in their hand, **7** To execute vengeance on the nations, and punishments on the peoples; **8** To bind their kings with chains, and their nobles with fetters (shackles) of iron; **9** To execute on them the written judgment—this honor have all His saints. Praise the Lord!

Chapter 150

1. Praise the Lord! Praise God in His sanctuary (temple); praise Him in His mighty firmament (heavens)! **2.** Praise Him for His mighty acts; praise Him according to His excellent greatness! **3.** Praise Him with the sound of the trumpet; praise Him with the lute and harp! **4.** Praise Him with the timbrel (tambourine) and dance; praise Him with stringed instruments and flutes! **5.** Praise Him with loud cymbals; praise Him with clashing cymbals! **6.** Let everything that has breath praise the Lord. Praise the Lord!

Psalm 151

1. I was the youngest among my brothers, and the smallest in my father's house. I tended the sheep. **2.** My hands crafted a harp (a stringed musical instrument), and my fingers tuned its strings. **3.** Who can tell my story? The Lord Himself listens. **4.** He sent His angel (messenger) to take me from tending the sheep and anointed me with His holy oil. **5.** My brothers were tall and handsome, but the Lord did not choose them. **6.** I faced the Philistine (a member of an ancient people, enemies of Israel), who cursed me by his gods (false idols). **7.** But I used his own sword to strike him down, removing shame from Israel.

25 – Messalë (Proverbs ch 1–24)

Chapter 1

1. These are the proverbs of Solomon, son of David, king of Israel: **2.** to help you acquire wisdom and understanding, to provide insight into meaningful words; **3.** to teach you how to act wisely, doing what is right, just, and fair; **4.** to offer caution to those who are inexperienced, and give knowledge and sound judgment to the young— **5.** Let the wise listen and continue to learn, and let the discerning seek further guidance— **6.** to interpret proverbs, riddles (puzzling sayings), and the teachings of the wise. **7.** The beginning of wisdom is the reverence (respect and awe) for the LORD; fools, however, despise wisdom and correction. **8.** Listen, my child, to your father's guidance, and do not abandon your mother's teaching. **9.** They will be like a beautiful crown for your head and a necklace to adorn your neck. **10.** My child, if sinners try to tempt you, do not give in to them. **11.** If they say, "Come with us; let's wait to ambush innocent people, let's attack some harmless soul; **12.** let's swallow them alive, as the grave (death) does, and whole, like those who go down to the pit (a place of destruction); **13.** we will gain all kinds of valuable things and fill our homes with stolen treasures; **14.** cast lots with us, and we'll all share the loot"— **15.** my child, do not follow their path, do not even step onto their road; **16.** for they hurry to do evil, and they are quick to shed (spill) innocent blood. **17.** It is pointless to set a trap where every bird can see it! **18.** These men are laying a trap for their own lives; they will destroy themselves. **19.** Such is the end of those who seek wealth through deceit; it robs them of their own lives. **20.** Wisdom cries out in the streets, raising her voice in the public squares; **21.** she calls out at the city gates and speaks to those passing by: **22.** "How long will you simple people love your simple ways? How long will mockers (those who make fun of others) find pleasure in mocking, and fools refuse to accept knowledge? **23.** Turn away from your foolish ways and listen to me! Then I will share my thoughts with you and make my teachings known. **24.** But since you refused to listen when I called, and no one responded when I reached out to you, **25.** since you ignored all my advice and refused my correction, **26.** I will laugh when disaster strikes you; I will mock when calamity (misfortune) comes upon you— **27.** when disaster (destruction) strikes like a storm, when trouble (distress) overwhelms you like a whirlwind, **28.** then they will call to me, but I will not answer; they will search for me but will not find me, **29.** because they hated knowledge and did not choose to honor the LORD. **30.** They would not accept my advice and ignored my correction, **31.** so they will bear the consequences of their own actions and be filled with the results of their choices. **32.** The waywardness (straying) of the naive (unwise) will destroy them, and the self-satisfaction (complacency) of fools will lead to their ruin; **33.** but whoever listens to me will live in peace and be safe, without fear of harm."

Chapter 2

1. My child, if you accept my words and treasure my commandments within your heart, **2.** if you pay close attention to wisdom and direct your heart toward understanding, **3.** if you cry out for insight and raise your voice for understanding, **4.** if you search for it as you would for silver and seek it like hidden treasure, **5.** then you will understand the fear (reverence) of the LORD and discover the knowledge (understanding) of God. **6.** For the LORD gives wisdom; from His mouth come knowledge (facts) and understanding (comprehension). **7.** He has stored up success for the upright (those who live right), and He is a shield (protector) for those who live with integrity (honesty). **8.** He guards the paths (ways) of the righteous and watches over the journey (course) of the faithful (those who trust Him). **9.** Then you will discern what is right, just (fair), and righteous—every good and moral path. **10.** For wisdom will enter your heart, and knowledge will delight your soul (inner being). **11.** Discretion (good judgment) will protect you, and understanding will keep you safe. **12.** Wisdom will rescue you from the ways of the wicked, from those whose words are deceitful (misleading), **13.** who have abandoned the right paths and now walk in darkness (immorality), **14.** who take pleasure in evil and rejoice in the twistedness (corruption) of wrongdoing, **15.** whose actions are crooked (dishonest) and whose paths are full of deception (trickery). **16.** Wisdom will also save you from the immoral woman, from the delightful words of the unfaithful wife, **17.** who has left the partner (husband) of her youth and ignored the covenant (promise) she made before God. **18.** Her house leads to death, and her paths lead to the realm of the dead. **19.** No one who follows her returns, nor do they find the paths of life. **20.** Thus, you will walk in the ways of the good and stay on the paths of the righteous. **21.** For the upright will dwell in the land, and the blameless (those without fault) will remain in it; **22.** but the wicked will be cut off (removed) from the land, and the unfaithful (those who break their promises) will be uprooted (destroyed).

Chapter 3

1. My child, never forget my teachings; keep my commands deep within you. **2.** They will add many years to your life and bring you peace (calm) and success (well-being). **3.** Let love (loyalty) and faithfulness (truth) never leave you; wear them like a necklace and write them on your heart. **4.** Then you will find favor (approval) and a good reputation (respect) in the eyes of God and people. **5.** Trust in the LORD with all your heart and do not rely on your own understanding (wisdom). **6.** In all your ways, submit (surrender) to Him, and He will make your paths straight (clear and right). **7.** Do not think you are wise in your own eyes (judgment); fear (revere) the LORD and avoid evil. **8.** This will bring health (wellness) to your body and strength (vigor) to your bones. **9.** Honor (respect) the LORD with your wealth and with the first part (best portion) of everything you produce. **10.** Then your barns will be filled to overflowing, and your vats (large containers) will brim with new wine (joy and abundance). **11.** My child, do not despise (disregard) the LORD's discipline (correction), and do not resent (feel bitterness about) His rebuke (reproof), **12.** because the LORD disciplines (corrects) those He loves, just as a father delights in his son. **13.** Blessed (fortunate) are those who find wisdom, those who gain understanding (comprehension). **14.** for wisdom is more valuable than silver, and her profits (returns) are greater than gold. **15.** She is more precious than rubies (precious stones); nothing you desire (wish for) can compare with her. **16.** Long life is in her right hand, and in her left hand are wealth (riches) and honor (respect). **17.** Her ways are pleasant (delightful), and all her paths are peace (calm). **18.** She is a tree of life to those who embrace (hold close to) her; those who hold on to her will be blessed (favored). **19.** By wisdom, the LORD founded the earth; by understanding, He set the heavens in place. **20.** By His knowledge (awareness), the depths of the sea were separated, and the clouds dropped the dew (moisture). **21.** My child, keep wisdom and understanding in your sight (focus), and preserve (protect) sound judgment (good sense) and discretion (careful choices). **22.** They will be life (vitality) to you and adorn (decorate) your neck like a beautiful ornament. **23.** Then you will walk safely along your path (journey), and your feet will not stumble (trip). **24.** When you lie down, you will not be afraid; your sleep will be sweet (restful). **25.** You will not fear sudden disaster (unexpected trouble) or the ruin (calamity) that comes to the wicked, **26.** for the LORD will be at your side and will keep you from falling into a trap. **27.** Do not withhold (hold back) good from those who deserve (need) it, when you have the ability to help. **28.** Do not tell your neighbor, "Come back tomorrow, and I'll give it to you," when you have what they need right now. **29.** Do not plan harm (evil intentions) against your neighbor, who lives securely (trustfully) near you. **30.** Do not falsely accuse (blame) anyone, when they have done you no harm. **31.** Do not envy (desire) the violent or choose to follow their ways. **32.** For the LORD detests (hates) the crooked (immoral), but He shares His secrets with the righteous (good-hearted). **33.** The LORD's curse (disfavor) is on the house of the wicked, but He blesses (favors) the home of the righteous. **34.** He mocks (ridicules) the proud, but He shows grace (favor) to the humble (meek) and oppressed (those treated unfairly). **35.** The wise inherit (gain) honor (esteem), but fools are clothed in shame.

Chapter 4

1. Listen, my children, to your father's instruction; pay attention and gain wisdom (the ability to make good decisions). **2.** I offer you valuable teachings—do not neglect my guidance. **3.** I was once a child, loved and cared for by my mother. **4.** He taught me, saying, "Take my words to heart; follow my commands, and you will have life. **5.** Seek wisdom, seek understanding—don't forget what I say or turn away from it. **6.** Do not forsake wisdom; she will protect you. Love her, and she will guard you. **7.** The beginning of wisdom is this: Get wisdom. Even if it costs you everything, gain understanding. **8.** Cherish wisdom, and she will lift you up; embrace her, and she will bring you honor. **9.** She will crown your head with glory and give you a beautiful wreath. **10.** Listen, my child, accept what I say, and your life will be long. **11.** I guide you in the way of wisdom and lead you along straight paths. **12.** When you walk, you won't be hindered; when you run, you won't stumble. **13.** Hold onto wisdom, don't let go; guard it carefully, for it is your life. **14.** Don't follow the path of the wicked or take the way of the evil. **15.** Avoid it—don't walk on it. Turn away from it and go your own way. **16.** The wicked cannot rest until they do evil; they lose sleep unless they cause someone to fall. **17.** They feed on wickedness and drink violence. **18.** The path of the righteous is like the morning sun, shining brighter until it reaches full daylight. **19.** But the way of the wicked is dark and uncertain; they do not know what causes them to stumble. **20.** My child, listen carefully to my words; pay attention to what I say. **21.** Do not let them out of your sight; keep them in your heart, **22.** For they are life to those who find them and bring healing to your whole body. **23.** Above all, protect your heart, for it determines the course of your life. **24.** Keep your mouth free from lies and deceit. **25.** Let your eyes look straight ahead; keep your gaze focused on what's in front of you. **26.** Carefully consider the path you're on, and stay firm in your decisions. **27.** Don't turn to the right or the left; keep your feet from evil.

Chapter 5

1. My child listens carefully to my wisdom, and pay attention to my words of understanding (insight). **2.** This will help you make wise decisions and ensure that your words are filled with knowledge. **3.** The words of the adulterous woman are as sweet as honey, and her speech is smoother than oil. **4.** But in the end, she is as bitter as poison (gall), and her words are as sharp as a double-edged sword. **5.** Her steps lead to death; she is headed straight for the grave. **6.** She pays no attention to the path of life; her ways are unstable and wandering, but she doesn't know it. **7.** Listen to me, my sons; do not turn away from what I say. **8.** Keep far away from her, and don't even come near the door of her house. **9.** If you do, you will lose your honor to others, and someone cruel will take away your dignity. **10.** Strangers will take your wealth, and the hard work you've done will benefit someone else. **11.** In the end, when your body and health are worn out, you will groan in regret. **12.** You will say, "How I hated discipline (correction)! How I despised being corrected! **13.** I never listened to my teachers or paid attention to my instructors. **14.** Now, I am in deep trouble, surrounded by people who could have helped me." **15.** Drink from your own well, fresh water from your own cistern (a well or reservoir). **16.** Should your streams of water overflow into the streets, or your springs run into public places? **17.** Let your waters be for you alone, and not shared with strangers. **18.** May your fountain (wife) be blessed, and may you always enjoy the love of the wife you married when you were young. **19.** She is like a loving doe, a graceful deer—may her love always satisfy you, and may you always be captivated by her affection. **20.** Why, my child, be captivated by another man's wife? Why desire the embrace of a woman who has strayed from her husband? **21.** For your ways are in full view of the LORD; He observes every step you take. **22.** The wicked are caught by their own evil actions; the cords (ropes) of their sins trap them. **23.** Without self-control, they will perish, led astray by their own foolishness.

Chapter 6

1. My child, if you have put up security (a promise or guarantee for someone else's debt) for a neighbor, or shaken hands in pledge (a formal promise) for a stranger, **2.** You have been trapped (caught) by your own words, ensnared (caught in a trap) by the promises you made. **3.** Now, my child, act quickly to free you. Go to your neighbor and make every effort to get out of this commitment. **4.** Do not allow yourself to rest or sleep; **5.** Break free like a gazelle (a fast-moving antelope) escaping from a hunter or a bird from a snare (a trap). **6.** Look at the ant (a small, hard-working insect), you lazy person; learn from its ways and become wise. **7.** It has no commander (leader), overseer (supervisor), or ruler (someone who manages), **8.** yet it stores food in the summer and gathers supplies at harvest. **9.** How long will you lie there, lazy person? When will you rise from your sleep? **10.** A little rest, a little sleep, a little folding of the hands, **11.** and poverty (lack of money) will sneak up on you like a thief, and scarcity (lack of necessities) will attack you like an armed man. **12.** A troublemaker (someone who causes problems) and a villain (a wicked person), full of deceit, **13.** who winks (blinks intentionally) with their eye, signals with their feet, and gestures with their fingers, **14.** Plans evil and stirs up trouble with a deceptive (dishonest) heart, **15.** Will face sudden ruin (quick destruction); disaster will come upon them with no hope of escape. **16.** There are six things the Lord hates, seven things He finds detestable (loathsome): **17.** Haughty (proud or arrogant) eyes, a lying tongue hands that shed innocent blood, **18.** A heart that devises wicked schemes, feet that rush to do evil, **19.** a false witness (someone who lies or gives false testimony) who speaks lies, and one who stirs up strife among people. **20.** My child, remember your father's teachings and do not forget your mother's instruction. **21.** Keep these teachings close to your heart; wear them like a necklace. **22.** They will guide you when you walk, protect you when you sleep, and speak to you when you wake up. **23.** For this teaching is like a lamp (a source of light), and correction is a light (guidance), showing you the way to life. **24.** It will keep you from the tempting words of an unfaithful woman. **25.** Do not desire her beauty (appearance) in your heart, and do not let her charm you with her looks. **26.** A prostitute (a woman involved in sexual services) may be paid with a loaf of bread, but another man's wife threatens your very life. **27.** Can anyone pick up fire and not get burned? **28.** Can anyone walk on hot coals (very hot rocks) without getting scorched? **29.** In the same way, anyone who sleeps with another person's spouse will not go unpunished. **30.** People may not scorn a thief if he steals because he's hungry, **31.** but if he's caught, he must pay back seven times what he took, even if it costs him everything he has. **32.** But a person who commits adultery lacks sense (is foolish); they are destroying (ruining) themselves. **33.** They will face punishment (consequences), disgrace (shame), and shame (humiliation) that will never go away. **34.** For jealousy (envy or resentment) stirs up a husband's anger, **35.** And he will have no mercy when he takes revenge. He will not accept any compensation (payment) or offer to make peace.

Chapter 7

1. My child, pay close attention to my words and treasure my instructions in your heart. **2.** Follow my teachings, and you will find life; guard them as you would protect the apple (the most precious) of your eye. **3.** Keep them in mind, bind them to your hands, and write them deeply on your heart. **4.** Treat wisdom like a sister and insight (clear understanding) as a close relative. **5.** These will protect you from the adulterous (unfaithful) woman, from the woman whose words are deceitful and tempting. **6.** From the window of my house, I peered out through the lattice (a framework with gaps),. **7.** And I saw among the naive (those lacking wisdom) a young man who lacked judgment. **8.** He was walking down the street near her corner, heading toward her house, **9.** As the evening approached and the shadows of night began to fall. **10.** At that moment, a woman came out to meet him, dressed like a prostitute (someone who offers sexual services for money) and with crafty (sly and deceitful) intentions. **11.** She is wild and rebellious, her feet always restless and never staying at home. **12.** She is found in the streets, on the corners, and at every turn, waiting and watching. **13.** She grabbed him, kissed him, and with a brazen (shameless and bold) expression, she said: **14.** "I've completed my religious vows, and I have food from my fellowship offering (a shared ceremonial offering) at home. **15.** So I came out to find you, and now I have found you! **16.** I've made my bed with beautiful linens from Egypt. **17.** I've scented it with myrrh (a fragrant resin), aloes (a sweet-smelling wood), and cinnamon (a spicy fragrance). **18.** Come, let's enjoy ourselves in love all night; let's delight in each other! **19.** My husband is away; he's gone on a long journey. **20.** He took a wallet full of money with him, and he won't be back until the full moon." **21.** With these tempting words, she led him astray, and he was captivated by her smooth talk. **22.** He followed her quickly, like an ox led to slaughter (a violent death), or like a deer walking into a noose (a trap). **23.** He did not realize that it would cost him his life, like a bird flying into a snare (a trap). **24.** Now, my sons listen carefully to me; pay attention to my words. **25.** Do not let your heart be drawn into her ways or be led astray by her paths. **26.** Many have been ruined by her; a great number of lives have been destroyed. **27.** Her house leads to death, and her path takes you straight to the grave (the place of death).

Chapter 8

1. Does not wisdom raise her voice? Does not understanding make herself heard? **2.** She stands at the highest point of the road, where the paths meet, **3.** And at the gates of the city, at the entrance, she calls out loudly: **4.** "To you, O men, I call; I lift up my voice to all people. **5.** You who are naive (lacking discernment), gain understanding; you who are foolish, open your hearts to it. **6.** Pay attention, for I have important truths to share; I speak what is righteous and just. **7.** What I say is true; I despise evil. **8.** All of my words are fair and straightforward; there is nothing deceitful or crooked in them. **9.** For the wise, all my counsel is clear; to those who seek knowledge, my words are straightforward. **10.** Choose my guidance (wise counsel) over silver, and gain knowledge rather than fine gold, **11.** For wisdom is more valuable than precious stones, and nothing you desire can compare to her. **12.** "I, wisdom, dwell with good judgment (prudence); I possess both knowledge and sound discretion. **13.** To fear (honor and respect) the LORD is to hate what is evil; I hate pride, arrogance, evil conduct, and twisted speech. **14.** I hold counsel (wise advice) and sound judgment; I have insight and power. **15.** through me, kings rule, and authorities issue fair decrees; **16.** Through me, leaders lead, and all who govern the earth are just. **17.** I love those who love me, and those who seek me diligently will find me. **18.** With me are wealth and honor, enduring prosperity and lasting success. **19.** My benefits (results) are more valuable than the finest gold; what I give is greater than silver of the highest quality. **20.** I walk the paths of righteousness (moral integrity) and justice, **21.** Bestowing a rich inheritance on those who love me and filling their houses with treasures. **22.** "The LORD created me at the beginning of his work, before his earliest deeds; **23.** I was formed long before the earth was made, at the dawn of creation. **24.** When there were no deep waters, I was brought forth, when there were no springs overflowing with water; **25.** Before the mountains were settled in place, before the hills, I was born, **26.** Before he made the earth, its fields, or even the dust of the world. **27.** I was present when he established the heavens, when he marked out the boundaries of the oceans, **28.** when he set the clouds in the sky and secured the fountains of the deep, **29.** when he set limits for the sea, ensuring that its waters would obey his commands, and when he laid the foundations of the earth. **30.** Then I was beside him, a master craftsman, rejoicing always in his presence, **31.** celebrating in his creation, and finding joy in humanity.

32. "Now, my children, listen to me; blessed are those who follow my ways. **33.** Pay attention to my teachings and be wise; do not ignore them. **34.** Blessed are those who listen to me, waiting daily at my doors, watching at my doorway. **35.** For those who find me find life and receive favor from the LORD. **36.** But those who fail to find me hurt themselves; all who hate me love death."

Chapter 9

1. Wisdom has built her house; she has set up its seven strong supports (pillars). **2.** She has prepared a feast (meal), mixed her wine, and set the table. **3.** She has sent her servants, calling out from the highest point of the city, **4.** "Let those who are simple (lacking wisdom) come to my house!" To those who lack understanding, she says, **5.** "Come, eat my food and drink the wine I've mixed. **6.** Leave your foolish ways, and you will live; walk the path of insight (understanding)." **7.** Whoever corrects a mocker (one who scorns wisdom) will face insults; whoever rebukes the wicked (evil) will be mistreated. **8.** Don't correct mockers, or they will hate you; rebuke the wise, and they will love you. **9.** Teach the wise, and they will become wiser; instruct the righteous (morally right) and they will grow in knowledge. **10.** The fear (deep respect and reverence) of the LORD is the beginning of wisdom, and knowledge of the Holy One brings understanding. **11.** Through wisdom, your life will be prolonged, and your years will be multiplied. **12.** If you are wise, your wisdom will reward you; if you mock wisdom, you alone will suffer. **13.** Folly (foolishness) is like a foolish woman; she is simple and knows nothing. **14.** She sits at the door of her house, at the highest point of the city, **15.** Calling out to those who pass by, who are going on their way, **16.** "Let those who are simple come to my house!" To those who lack understanding, she says, **17.** "Stolen water is sweet (wrongdoing feels tempting); food eaten in secret is delicious (sinful actions seem attractive)!" **18.** But they do not realize that her guests are in the grave (dead), and her visitors are in the depths of death.

Chapter 10

1. The proverbs of Solomon: A wise son brings happiness to his father, but a foolish son brings grief to his mother. **2.** Money gained through dishonest means has no lasting value, but living righteously saves from death. **3.** The LORD makes sure the righteous are not left hungry, but He frustrates the desires of the wicked. **4.** Laziness leads to poverty, but hard work brings prosperity. **5.** A son who gathers crops in the summer is wise, but one who sleeps during harvest is a disgrace. **6.** Blessings surround the righteous, but the words of the wicked are filled with violence. **7.** The righteous are remembered with blessings, but the name of the wicked will decay (be forgotten). **8.** The wise listen to instruction, but a foolish person who talks too much will bring disaster on themselves. **9.** Those who live with honesty and integrity walk securely, but those who follow dishonest paths will be found out. **10.** A person who winks with evil intentions brings trouble, and a foolish talker will face ruin. **11.** The mouth of the righteous is a source of life, but the mouth of the wicked hides violence. **12.** Hatred causes conflict, but love covers all wrongdoings. **13.** Wisdom is found in the words of the discerning (wise), but a foolish person suffers consequences for their actions. **14.** The wise store up knowledge, but a fool's words lead to their own destruction. **15.** The wealth of the rich is their stronghold (safety), but poverty leads to the downfall (ruin) of the poor. **16.** The wages (pay) of the righteous bring life, but the earnings of the wicked lead to sin and death. **17.** Those who accept correction show the way to life, but those who ignore discipline mislead others. **18.** A person who hides hatred behind lies and spreads false accusations (slander) is a fool. **19.** Sin is not stopped by speaking too much, but the wise know when to be silent. **20.** The speech of the righteous is valuable, like pure silver, but the heart (inner thoughts) of the wicked is of little worth. **21.** The words of the righteous nourish (provide life and strength) many, but fools die because they lack wisdom. **22.** The LORD's blessing brings wealth without the painful effort that comes with it. **23.** A fool enjoys doing evil, but a person of understanding delights in wisdom. **24.** What the wicked fear will come upon them, but what the righteous desire will be granted. **25.** When the storm passes, the wicked are gone, but the righteous stand firm forever. **26.** As vinegar to the teeth, and smoke to the eyes, so are lazy workers to those who rely on them. **27.** Reverence (deep respect and honor) for the LORD adds years to life, but the wicked have their years cut short. **28.** The righteous have joy in their future, but the hope of the wicked comes to nothing. **29.** The way of the LORD is a refuge (safe place) for the blameless, but it brings ruin to those who do evil. **30.** The righteous will never be uprooted (removed), but the wicked will not remain in the land. **31.** from the mouth of the righteous comes the fruit of wisdom, but a perverse (twisted) tongue will be silenced. **32.** The lips of the righteous know what is acceptable (what pleases God), but the mouth of the wicked speaks perversely (unjustly).

Chapter 11

1. The LORD despises dishonest scales, but He delights in accurate weights. 2. When pride arises, disgrace follows; but humility leads to wisdom. 3. The integrity (honesty) of the upright guides them, but the unfaithful (disloyal) are undone by their deceit (dishonest actions). 4. Riches are worthless when God's judgment comes, but living righteously saves from death. 5. The righteousness of the blameless makes their paths straight, but the wicked are destroyed by their own evil ways. 6. The righteousness of the upright rescues them, but the unfaithful are caught by their own desires for evil. 7. Hopes placed in people die with them; all the promise of their power disappears. 8. The righteous are saved from trouble, but the wicked are caught in their own misfortune. 9. The godless (those without reverence for God) use their words to destroy their neighbors, but knowledge (wisdom) saves the righteous. 10. When the righteous succeed, the city celebrates; when the wicked perish, people rejoice. 11. A city is lifted up by the blessing of the righteous, but it is brought low by the words of the wicked. 12. A person who mocks or belittles their neighbor is foolish, but those with understanding remain silent. 13. A gossip betrays a trust, but a faithful (reliable) person keeps a secret. 14. Without proper guidance, a nation falls; but victory is secured through many advisers (counselors). 15. A person who pledges (cosigns) for a stranger will suffer, but someone who avoids offering security (guarantee) is safe. 16. A kind-hearted (compassionate) woman earns honor, but ruthless (unmerciful) men only gain wealth. 17. Those who show kindness to others benefit themselves, but the cruel bring destruction upon themselves. 18. A wicked person earns dishonest wages, but the one who sows righteousness will certainly be rewarded. 19. The righteous attain life, but those who pursue evil will find death. 20. The LORD despises those whose hearts are corrupt (perverse), but He delights in those whose ways are blameless (pure). 21. Rest assured: the wicked will not go unpunished, but the righteous will be freed. 22. A beautiful woman without discretion (good judgment) is like a gold ring in a pig's snout. 23. The desires of the righteous end in goodness, but the hopes of the wicked lead to anger (wrath). 24. Some give generously and gain even more, while others withhold too much and end up poor. 25. A generous person will prosper, and whoever helps others will themselves be helped. 26. People curse the one who hoards grain (keeps it for themselves), but they bless those who are willing to sell it. 27. Whoever seeks good finds favor, but harm comes to those who seek evil. 28. Those who trust in their wealth will fall, but the righteous will flourish like a healthy leaf. 29. Whoever brings ruin to their family will inherit nothing, and the fool will serve the wise. 30. The fruit (outcome) of the righteous is a tree of life, and the wise person saves lives. 31. If the righteous are rewarded on earth, how much more will the ungodly and sinner face judgment!

Chapter 12

1. Those who embrace discipline love wisdom, but those who reject correction are foolish. 2. The LORD favors good people, but He condemns those who plan evil schemes. 3. Wickedness cannot establish anyone, but the righteous will always stand firm. 4. A virtuous wife is a crown of honor to her husband, but a shameful wife is like rotting in his bones. 5. The righteous make just plans, but the advice of the wicked is full of deception. 6. The words of the wicked are like traps waiting to destroy, but the speech of the upright saves them. 7. The wicked will eventually be destroyed and vanish, but the house of the righteous remains unshaken. 8. A person is praised for their wisdom, but a person with a crooked (twisted) mind is despised. 9. It is better to be humble and have a servant than to pretend to be important and have nothing to eat. 10. The righteous take good care of their animals, but even the kindest actions of the wicked are cruel. 11. Those who work hard on their land will have plenty of food, but those who follow illusions (fantasies) lack understanding. 12. The wicked long for the strongholds (fortresses) of evildoers, but the roots (foundation) of the righteous remain strong. 13. Evil people are trapped by their own sinful words, while the innocent escape trouble. 14. From their words, people are filled with good things, and their hard work is rewarded. 15. Fools think their way is right, but the wise listen to advice. 16. Fools quickly show their frustration, but the wise ignore insults. 17. A truthful witness speaks the truth, but a false witness tells lies. 18. Reckless words wound like swords, but wise speech brings healing. 19. Truthful words last forever, but lies only temporary. 20. Deceit (dishonesty) fills the hearts of those who plan evil, but those who seek peace experience joy. 21. The righteous are protected from harm, but the wicked are constantly in trouble. 22. The LORD hates lying lips, but He delights in those who are trustworthy (honest). 23. The wise keep their knowledge to themselves, but fools blurt out their foolish thoughts. 24. Hard work leads to leadership, but laziness leads to forced labor. 25. Anxiety burdens the heart, but a kind word lifts it. 26. The righteous are careful about the friends they choose, but the wicked are led astray by their bad company. 27. The lazy don't cook their catch, but the diligent enjoy the rewards of their hard work. 28. The path of righteousness leads to life; along that path is eternal (immortal) life.

Chapter 13

1. A wise child listens to their father's guidance, but a scoffer (someone who mocks or rejects advice) ignores correction. 2. The words of a person bring them good things, while the unfaithful (those who are unreliable) crave violence. 3. Those who control their speech protect their lives, but those who speak impulsively (without careful thought) will face destruction. 4. A lazy person's desires are never fully met, but those who work diligently will be satisfied. 5. The righteous despise lies, but the wicked bring shame upon them. 6. Righteousness protects the person of integrity, but evil leads to the downfall of sinners. 7. Some pretend to be rich but have nothing, while others pretend to be poor but are actually wealthy. 8. A person's wealth can sometimes save them from danger, but the poor cannot respond to harsh reproach. 9. The light of the righteous shines brightly, but the hope of the wicked is extinguished. 10. Where there is conflict, there is pride, but wisdom is found in those who seek and follow advice. 11. Ill-gotten gains quickly vanish, but money earned gradually will grow over time. 12. Deferred hope makes the heart sick, but fulfilled desire is like a life-giving tree. 13. Those who mock instruction will face the consequences, but those who follow guidance will be rewarded. 14. The teachings of the wise are a source of life, leading people away from the dangers of death. 15. Sound judgment earns favor, but the path of the unfaithful leads to their destruction. 16. The wise act with knowledge, but fools openly display their foolishness. 17. A wicked messenger brings trouble, but a trustworthy messenger brings healing. 18. Those who disregard discipline will suffer poverty and shame, but those who heed correction will be honored. 19. A fulfilled longing is sweet to the soul, but fools reject the need to change from evil ways. 20. Walk with the wise, and you will become wise; a companion of fools will suffer harm. 21. Trouble follows the sinner, but the righteous are rewarded with good things. 22. A good person leaves an inheritance for their grandchildren, but a sinner's wealth is stored up for the righteous. 23. An uncultivated field provides food for the poor, but injustice sweeps it away. 24. Those who fail to discipline their children hate them, but those who love their children are careful to correct them. 25. The righteous enjoy abundant food, but the wicked will go hungry.

Chapter 14

1. A wise woman builds her home, but a foolish one destroys hers with her own hands. 2. Those who revere (respect deeply) the LORD live with integrity, but those who reject Him act deceitfully. 3. A fool's mouth is full of pride, but the wise person's words protect them. 4. Without oxen, the stable is empty, but the strength of an ox brings a rich harvest. 5. An honest witness tells the truth, but a false witness speaks lies. 6. The mocker seeks wisdom but finds none, but for the discerning (able to judge well), knowledge comes easily. 7. Stay away from fools, because you won't find wisdom in their speech. 8. The wise consider their actions carefully, but fools deceive themselves with their own folly. 9. Fools make light of making things right for their wrongdoings, but goodwill is found in those who are upright. 10. Each person understands their own sorrow, and no one can share their joy fully. 11. The house of the wicked will be destroyed, but the tent of the righteous will thrive. 12. There is a way that seems right, but it ultimately leads to death. 13. Even in laughter, the heart can be in pain, and joy can turn into sorrow. 14. The unfaithful will face the consequences of their actions, but the good will be rewarded for theirs. 15. The naive (easily deceived) believe anything, but the wise think carefully before they act. 16. The wise fear the LORD and avoid evil, but the fool is hot-headed and feels secure in their foolishness. 17. A quick-tempered person makes foolish decisions, and one who plots evil is despised. 18. The naive inherit foolishness, but the wise are crowned with knowledge. 19. The wicked will bow down before the good, and the unrighteous will respect the gates of the righteous. 20. The poor are often avoided by their neighbors, but the wealthy have many friends. 21. It is wrong to despise your neighbor, but those who are kind to the poor are blessed. 22. Those who plan evil go astray, but those who plan what is good find love and loyalty. 23. Hard work brings rewards, but empty talk leads to poverty. 24. The wisdom of the wise is their crown, but the folly of fools leads to more foolishness. 25. A truthful witness saves lives, but a false witness spreads deceit. 26. Those who fear the LORD have a strong refuge, and their children will be safe there. 27. The fear of the LORD is a source of life, keeping a person from the traps of death. 28. A large population brings glory to a king, but without subjects, a ruler is ruined. 29. Whoever is patient has great understanding, but those who lose their temper act foolishly. 30. A peaceful heart gives life to the body, but envy (jealousy) rots the bones. 31. Those who oppress the poor show contempt for their Creator, but those who are kind to the needy honor God. 32. When disaster strikes, the wicked are brought low, but the

righteous seek refuge in God even in death. **33.** Wisdom rests in the heart of those who understand, and even fools can see it. **34.** Righteousness lifts up a nation, but sin brings judgment to any people. **35.** A king takes pleasure in a wise servant, but a disgraceful servant provokes his anger.

Chapter 15

1. A gentle response calms anger, but harsh words only stir up fury (rage). **2.** The wise use their speech to enhance knowledge, while a fool's words overflow with foolishness. **3.** The LORD's watchful eyes are always on the righteous and the wicked alike. **4.** A soothing (calming) tongue is a source of life, but a twisted (corrupt) tongue crushes the spirit. **5.** A fool rejects the discipline of their parents, but those who accept correction demonstrate wisdom. **6.** The home of the righteous is rich in blessings, but the wealth of the wicked leads to destruction. **7.** The wise share knowledge, but the hearts of fools lack integrity (honesty). **8.** The LORD despises the offerings of the wicked, but He delights in the prayers of the righteous. **9.** The LORD opposes the ways of the wicked but loves those who follow righteousness. **10.** Harsh discipline is in store for those who stray from the right path; those who reject correction bring ruin upon themselves. **11.** Death and destruction are clear to the LORD— how much more the hearts of human beings! **12.** Those who mock correction avoid the wise. **13.** A cheerful heart brightens the face, but emotional pain can crush the spirit. **14.** The discerning (perceptive) heart seeks understanding, but fools focus only on folly. **15.** Those who are oppressed live in constant misery, but a joyful heart enjoys an unending feast. **16.** Better to have a little with reverence for the LORD than great wealth with constant trouble. **17.** Better a small meal with love than a large feast filled with hatred. **18.** A quick-tempered person causes strife, but the patient person brings peace to an argument. **19.** The lazy person's path is filled with obstacles, but the righteous have a clear and easy way. **20.** A wise son brings happiness to his father, but a foolish person dishonors his mother. **21.** Foolishness brings joy to the naive (gullible), but understanding leads to a straight path. **22.** Without proper counsel (advice), plans fail, but success is found in the guidance of many. **23.** A well-chosen response brings joy to the one who hears it, and a timely word is a pleasure. **24.** The way of life for the wise leads upward, protecting them from descending into death. **25.** The LORD destroys the homes of the arrogant, but He establishes (secures) the boundaries of the widow. **26.** The LORD hates the thoughts of the wicked, but He values kind and thoughtful words. **27.** The greedy bring destruction to their households, but those who refuse bribes will live. **28.** The heart of the righteous carefully considers its answers, but the mouth of the wicked speaks without thought. **29.** The LORD is far from the wicked, but He hears the prayers of the righteous. **30.** A bright-eyed messenger brings joy to the heart, and good news is healing to the bones. **31.** Those who welcome life-giving correction will be among the wise. **32.** Those who reject discipline harm themselves, but those who accept correction gain wisdom. **33.** The foundation of wisdom is the fear of the LORD, and humility (lowliness) comes before honor.

Chapter 16

1. Humans make plans in their hearts, but the LORD determines the right answer for their speech. **2.** Every way seems right to a person, but the LORD weighs (judges) their motives. **3.** Commit your actions to the LORD, and He will establish (secure, confirm) your plans. **4.** The LORD completes everything for its intended purpose—even the wicked are destined (appointed) for a day of disaster. **5.** The LORD despises (hates) the proud in heart; they will certainly not go unpunished. **6.** Love and faithfulness bring atonement (reconciliation, forgiveness) for sin; reverence (fear, deep respect) of the LORD keeps one from evil. **7.** When the LORD is pleased with someone's way, even their enemies will make peace with them. **8.** Better a small amount with righteousness than great wealth gained through injustice. **9.** People may plan their course, but the LORD directs (guides, establishes) their steps. **10.** The words of a king are powerful; his mouth does not speak injustice. **11.** Honest scales and weights belong to the LORD; all the measures in the bag are His creation. **12.** Kings detest (hate, oppose) wickedness, for a throne is established (built) by righteousness. **13.** Kings take delight in truthful speech; they value those who speak what is right. **14.** A king's anger brings the threat (danger) of death, but the wise can calm (appease) it. **15.** When a king's face is cheerful, it brings life; his favor is like spring rain (refreshing). **16.** How much better it is to gain wisdom than gold, to gain understanding rather than silver! **17.** The path of the upright avoids evil; those who guard (protect) their ways preserve (keep safe) their lives. **18.** Pride leads to destruction, and a haughty (arrogant, proud) spirit to a fall. **19.** Better to be humble in spirit with the poor than to share in the wealth of the proud. **20.** Whoever listens to instruction (teaching, advice) will prosper, and blessed (happy, fortunate) is the one who trusts in the LORD. **21.** The wise in heart are called discerning (wise, perceptive), and gracious (kind, thoughtful) words encourage learning. **22.** Prudence (wisdom, carefulness) is a source of life for the wise, but fools are punished

for their folly (foolishness). **23.** The hearts of the wise make their speech prudent (careful, wise), and their words promote (encourage) learning. **24.** Gracious (kind, thoughtful) words are like a honeycomb, sweet to the soul and healing to the bones. **25.** There is a way that seems right, but in the end, it leads to death. **26.** The laborer's hunger motivates (drives) them; their appetite drives them forward. **27.** A wicked (evil) person plans evil, and their words are like a burning fire (destructive). **28.** A corrupt (dishonest) person stirs up trouble, and a gossip (someone who spreads rumors) separates close friends. **29.** A violent (aggressive, brutal) person entices (tempts) their neighbor to follow a bad path. **30.** Whoever winks to signal wrongdoing is planning evil; whoever purses (tightens) their lips is intent (determined) on doing wrong. **31.** Gray hair is a crown of glory, attained (earned, gained) by those who live righteously. **32.** Better a patient person than a warrior, one who controls (restrains) their temper than one who conquers (defeats) a city. **33.** The lot (dice) is cast into the lap, but every outcome (result) is determined by the LORD.

Chapter 17

1. it's better to have a simple meal in peace and quiet than a house full of lavish feasts and conflict. **2.** A wise servant will take charge over a disgraceful son and will inherit as part of the family. **3.** The furnace is for refining silver, and the crucible (a container used to heat substances) is for gold, but the LORD tests the heart. **4.** A wicked person listens to deceitful (dishonest) words; a liar gives ear to a destructive (damaging) tongue. **5.** Whoever mocks the poor shows disdain (disobeys) for their Creator; those who rejoice over others' misfortune will not escape punishment. **6.** Grandchildren are the glory of the elderly, and parents take pride in their children. **7.** Fine speech is unsuitable for a godless fool— how much worse is it when a liar speaks for a ruler! **8.** A bribe seems like a good luck charm to the one who gives it; they believe it will lead them to success. **9.** Whoever loves to foster peace forgives (covers) an offense, but those who spread it cause division among close friends. **10.** A rebuke (criticism) from a wise person is more impactful than a hundred lashes (beatings) on a fool. **11.** Evildoers stir up rebellion against God, and the messenger of death will be sent against them. **12.** it's better to encounter a bear robbed of her cubs than a fool who is set on foolishness. **13.** Evil will never leave the house of one who repays evil for good. **14.** Starting an argument is like breaking a dam open; it's better to let the matter go before a dispute erupts. **15.** The LORD detests both acquitting the guilty and condemning the innocent. **16.** Why would fools have money to buy wisdom when they cannot understand it? **17.** A true friend loves at all times, and a brother is born for times of trouble. **18.** A person without sense shakes hands to guarantee a loan and pledges (guarantees) security for a neighbor. **19.** Whoever enjoys arguments loves sin; those who build tall gates invite destruction. **20.** A corrupt (morally wrong) heart does not prosper, and a perverse (twisted) tongue leads to trouble. **21.** Having a foolish child brings sorrow; a godless fool brings no joy to their parents. **22.** A joyful heart is like medicine, but a crushed spirit dries up the bones. **23.** The wicked accept bribes secretly to pervert (corrupt) justice. **24.** A discerning (wise) person keeps wisdom in sight, but a fool's mind wanders aimlessly. **25.** A foolish son causes sorrow to his father and bitterness to his mother. **26.** It's wrong to impose a fine on the innocent, and it's just as wrong to punish honest officials. **27.** A person with knowledge uses words carefully, and one who understands remains calm (even-tempered). **28.** Even a fool appears wise if they keep silent, and discerning if they hold their tongue.

Chapter 18

1. A quarrelsome person seeks their own selfish goals and, against all reason, stirs up conflict. **2.** Fools take no pleasure in gaining understanding; instead, they delight in expressing their own opinions. **3.** When wickedness arises, contempt (disrespect) follows, and disgrace (shame) brings dishonor. **4.** The words of the mouth are like deep waters, but wisdom flows like a rushing stream. **5.** It is wrong to favor the wicked and deny justice to the innocent. **6.** Fools' lips bring them into conflict, and their mouths invite punishment. **7.** Fools' words lead to their own downfall, and their speech is a trap that ensnares (catches) them. **8.** Gossip is like a tasty morsel; it goes deep into the heart of the listener. **9.** A lazy person is like a destroyer, and their lack of effort brings harm. **10.** The name of the LORD is a strong tower; the righteous run to it and find safety. **11.** The wealth of the rich is like their stronghold, a high wall in their minds that they believe cannot be breached. **12.** Pride comes before a fall, but humility leads to honor. **13.** Answering before listening is foolish and brings shame. **14.** The human spirit can endure sickness, but who can bear a crushed spirit? **15.** A discerning (wise) heart seeks knowledge, and the ears of the wise are eager to learn. **16.** A gift can open doors and bring the giver into the presence of important people. **17.** In a legal case, the first person to speak seems right, until someone else cross-examines (questions) them. **18.** Casting lots (drawing lots, a form of random selection) helps resolve disputes and separates powerful opponents. **19.** A sibling wronged is harder to win over than a strong city; disagreements are like the locked gates of a fortress. **20.** A person's words fill their stomach; with what they say, they are satisfied. **21.** The tongue holds the power of life and death, and those who love it will reap (receive) its rewards. **22.** He who finds a wife finds something good and receives favor from the LORD. **23.** The poor beg for mercy, but the rich respond harshly. **24.** A person with unreliable friends will eventually face ruin, but there is a friend who sticks closer than a brother.

Chapter 19

1. It's better to be poor and walk in integrity (honesty and strong moral principles) than to be a fool whose words are twisted (deceptive or misleading) and deceitful. **2.** Desires without wisdom (the ability to make sound decisions) are harmful—how much more will hasty (acting too quickly) decisions lead someone astray? **3.** A person's own foolishness (lack of good sense) causes their downfall, but they still direct (focus) their anger toward the LORD. **4.** Wealth attracts many friends, but when a poor person suffers, even their closest friends turn away (abandon them). **5.** A false (untrue) witness will face punishment, and those who speak lies (falsehoods) will not escape justice. **6.** Many seek to win favor (approval or support) from a ruler, and everyone loves the one who gives gifts (offerings of money or favors). **7.** The poor are abandoned (left behind) by their relatives—how much more do their friends avoid them! Though they beg (ask earnestly) for help, no one comes to their aid. **8.** The one who seeks wisdom (understanding and good judgment) values life; the one who loves understanding (the ability to grasp and interpret knowledge) will soon find success. **9.** A false witness will be punished, and those who speak lies will meet their end (destruction or failure). **10.** It's not right for a fool to live in luxury (extravagant wealth)—how much worse for a servant to rule over nobles! **11.** A wise person exercises patience (the ability to wait without frustration), and it's to their honor to overlook an offense. **12.** A king's anger (strong displeasure) is fierce like a lion's roar, but his favor (kindness or approval) is refreshing like dew on grass. **13.** A foolish (lacking wisdom) child brings grief to their father, and a quarrelsome (argumentative) wife is like the constant dripping of a leaky roof. **14.** Wealth and property can be inherited (received as a gift from ancestors), but a wise wife is a gift from the LORD. **15.** Laziness (lack of work ethic) leads to deep sleep, and the lazy (inactive) will end up hungry. **16.** Those who follow the commandments (instructions or laws) will protect their lives, but those who ignore them will face death. **17.** Whoever is generous (willing to give freely) to the poor lends to the LORD, and God will repay them for their kindness. **18.** Discipline (training and correction) your children, for it brings hope; neglecting them can lead to their destruction (ruin). **19.** A hot-tempered (easily angered) person will face consequences, and if you try to help them, you'll only have to do it again. **20.** Listen to advice (guidance) and accept correction (reprimands or adjustments), and in the end, you will be counted among the wise. **21.** Many plans (ideas or strategies) are in a person's heart, but it is the LORD's will (purpose or desire) that stands firm. **22.** A person's deepest desire (longing) is unfailing (constant and never-ending) love; it's better to be poor than to be a liar. **23.** The fear (reverence and awe) of the LORD brings life; it gives peace and protection from trouble. **24.** A lazy (idle) person puts their hand in the bowl but is too sluggish (slow-moving) to bring it back to their mouth. **25.** If you punish a mocker (one who ridicules others), the simple (naïve people) will learn wisdom; rebuke a wise person, and they will gain even more knowledge. **26.** A child who steals (takes without permission) from their father and drives out (expels) their mother brings shame and disgrace (loss of respect). **27.** If you stop listening to instruction (teaching), my son, you will stray from the path of knowledge (awareness and understanding). **28.** A corrupt (dishonest) witness mocks (ridicules) justice, and the wicked (evil or immoral people) eagerly devour (consume) evil. **29.** Punishments are reserved for mockers (those who make fun of others), and consequences await the backs of fools.

Chapter 20

1. Wine is a mockery (something that deceives or misleads) and beer a brawler (a troublemaker or fighter); anyone who is led astray by them lacks wisdom. **2.** The anger of a king is terrifying, like the roar of a lion; those who provoke him put their lives at risk. **3.** It brings honor (respect or dignity) to avoid conflicts, but a fool is always quick to argue. **4.** Lazy people do not plow in the right season; so at harvest time, they look around but find nothing. **5.** The desires and plans of a person's heart are deep, like hidden waters, but one who has good insight (understanding) can draw them out. **6.** Many claim to have unfailing (constant and reliable) love, but how rare is the person who is truly faithful? **7.** The righteous live without fault; their children are blessed because of them. **8.** When a king judges from his throne, he can discern and separate all evil with his eyes. **9.** Who can claim, "I have kept my heart pure; I am without sin"? **10.** Unequal (inconsistent) measures and weights are detestable to the LORD. **11.** Even a small child's

actions can reveal their character— is their behavior really pure and honest? **12.** Ears that hear and eyes that see— both are made by the LORD. **13.** Don't fall in love with sleep, or you will end up poor; stay alert, and you will have more than enough. **14.** "It's no good! It's no good!" says the buyer— then boasts about the purchase. **15.** There is plenty of gold and rubies, but lips that speak wisdom are like a rare jewel. **16.** Take the garment (clothing) of someone who agrees to put up security for a stranger; hold it as a pledge if it is done for an outsider. **17.** Food gained through trickery may taste sweet, but in the end, it leaves you with nothing but regret. **18.** Plans succeed when you seek advice (guidance); if you're planning something as serious as war, get counsel. **19.** A gossip (a person who spreads rumors) betrays trust, so avoid those who talk too much. **20.** If someone curses their father or mother, their light will be extinguished, and they will face darkness. **21.** An inheritance taken too soon will bring no blessing in the end. **22.** Do not seek vengeance by saying, "I'll pay you back for this wrong!" Wait for the LORD, and He will bring justice. **23.** The LORD hates false weights, and dishonest scales are detestable to Him. **24.** A person's path is directed by the LORD; how then can anyone understand their own way? **25.** It's a trap to dedicate something hastily and only later reconsider your promise. **26.** A wise king separates the wicked from the good; he drives the wicked under the threshing wheel (a device used to separate grain from the husk). **27.** The human spirit is like a lamp from the LORD that reveals a person's deepest thoughts. **28.** Love (deep affection) and faithfulness (loyalty) protect a king; through these virtues, his throne remains secure. **29.** The strength of young men is their glory, while the gray hair (wisdom of old age) is the splendor of the elderly. **30.** Physical punishment can remove evil, and beatings cleanse the deepest parts of a person's being.

Chapter 21

1. The heart of a king is in the hand of the LORD; He directs it like a stream of water, guiding it wherever He wills. **2.** A person may think their ways are right, but the LORD examines and weighs the heart. **3.** Doing what is right and just is more pleasing to the LORD than offering sacrifices. **4.** Arrogance in the eyes and a proud heart are like the unplowed field of the wicked— they lead to sin. **5.** The plans of the diligent (hard-working) lead to profit, while rushing leads to poverty. **6.** Wealth gained through deceit is fleeting, like a vapor, and it becomes a deadly trap. **7.** The violence (unjust force) of the wicked will destroy them, because they refuse to do what is right. **8.** The way of the guilty is crooked (deceptive), but the actions of the innocent are upright. **9.** It is better to live in a corner of the roof than share a house with a quarrelsome wife. **10.** The wicked desire evil; their neighbors never experience mercy from them. **11.** When a mocker (one who ridicules or scorns) is punished, the simple (naive) gain wisdom, and the wise become more knowledgeable. **12.** The Righteous One takes note of the wicked and will bring them to ruin. **13.** Whoever ignores the cries of the poor will themselves cry out one day, but will not be answered. **14.** A secret gift calms anger, and a concealed bribe (money given to persuade) pacifies great wrath. **15.** When justice is done, it brings joy to the righteous but terror to the wicked. **16.** Whoever abandons the path of wisdom will end up in the realm of the dead. **17.** Those who love pleasure will end up poor, and those who love wine and luxury will never be rich. **18.** The wicked are often used as a ransom for the righteous, and the unfaithful will serve the upright. **19.** It is better to live in a desert than with a quarrelsome and nagging wife. **20.** The wise store up precious food and olive oil, but fools consume everything they have. **21.** Those who pursue righteousness and love will find life, prosperity, and honor. **22.** A wise person can overcome a mighty city and tear down the stronghold (fortress) in which the enemy trusts. **23.** Those who are careful with their words and control their tongues avoid disaster. **24.** The arrogant person, called the "mocker," acts with insolent fury (anger without care for others). **25.** The lazy person's craving will lead to their downfall because they refuse to work. **26.** All day long, the sluggard craves more, but the righteous are generous and give freely. **27.** The sacrifices of the wicked are detestable, especially when offered with evil intent. **28.** A false witness will perish, but a person who listens carefully will testify with success. **29.** The wicked act boldly, but the upright consider their ways before acting. **30.** There is no wisdom, insight, or plan that can stand against the LORD. **31.** A horse is prepared for battle, but victory belongs to the LORD.

Chapter 22

1. A good reputation is more valuable than great wealth; being respected is better than silver or gold. **2.** Both the rich and the poor share this: the LORD is the Creator of them both. **3.** The wise (prudent) foresee danger and take action to avoid it, but the naive (innocent) continue on their path and suffer the consequences. **4.** Humility (having a humble attitude) is rooted in the fear of the LORD; it leads to riches, honor, and a fulfilling life. **5.** The path of the wicked is full of traps and obstacles (snares and pitfalls), but those who seek to protect their lives stay far from them. **6.** Train (start) children in the way they should go, and even when they are old, they will not stray from it. **7.** The rich rule over the poor, and the borrower is a slave to the lender. **8.** Whoever sows unrighteousness (injustice) will reap disaster, and the rod (power) they use to cause harm will eventually break. **9.** Those who are generous will be blessed, for they share their food with the poor. **10.** Remove the mockers (those who mock others), and peace will follow; quarrels and insults will cease. **11.** A person who loves a pure heart and speaks with kindness will earn the king's favor. **12.** The eyes of the LORD protect knowledge, but He frustrates the words of the unfaithful. **13.** The lazy person says, "There's a lion outside! I might be killed in the streets!" (This is an excuse to avoid work or responsibility.) **14.** The mouth of an adulterous woman is a deep pit; a man who falls into it is under the LORD's wrath. **15.** Folly (foolishness) is tied to the heart of a child, but discipline (the rod) will remove it far from them. **16.** Oppressing the poor to increase wealth or giving gifts to the rich will ultimately lead to poverty. **17.** Pay attention and listen to the words of the wise; apply your heart to their teachings. **18.** It is pleasing when you keep these teachings in your heart and are ready to speak them. **19.** So that your trust may be in the LORD, I am teaching you this today. **20.** Have I not written thirty sayings for you, filled with guidance and wisdom? **21.** These teach you to be honest and speak the truth, so that you can be trusted in what you report. **22.** Do not exploit the poor because they are poor, and do not take advantage of the needy in court. **23.** For the LORD will defend their cause and will bring judgment on those who harm them. **24.** Do not make friends with someone who is quick-tempered, and do not associate with one who easily gets angry. **25.** If you do, you may learn their ways and get caught in the same trap. **26.** Do not be someone who shakes hands in agreement to guarantee someone else's debt. **27.** If you lack the means to pay, you may lose your very bed (your home). **28.** Do not move an ancient boundary stone (property markers) set by your ancestors. **29.** Do you see someone skilled in their work? They will serve before kings; they will not serve low-ranking officials.

Chapter 23

1. When you eat with a ruler, be mindful of what's in front of you. **2.** If you're tempted to overeat, be cautious—it's like a knife at your throat. **3.** Don't be fooled by his rich food—it can be deceiving. **4.** Don't wear yourself out to get rich or trust your own cleverness. **5.** Wealth flies away like an eagle—it disappears in an instant. **6.** Don't eat from a grudging (unwilling or reluctant) host or crave his fine food. **7.** He says, "Eat and drink," but his heart isn't in it. **8.** You'll regret what little you ate, and your thanks will be in vain. **9.** Don't speak to a fool—he'll mock (disrespect or ridicule) your wise words. **10.** Don't move property lines or take land from orphans, **11.** for their Defender (protector) is strong and will protect them. **12.** Set your heart on learning and listen to wisdom. **13.** Don't withhold discipline from a child—correct them, and they won't die. **14.** Discipline (correct) them, and you'll save them from ruin. **15.** My son, if your heart is wise, I will be glad. **16.** I'll rejoice when you speak what is right. **17.** Don't envy (desire what others have) the wicked; always fear the Lord. **18.** You'll have hope, and your future will be secure. **19.** Listen carefully, my son, and choose the right path. **20.** Don't join those who drink too much or gorge (eat greedily) on food. **21.** Drunkards and gluttons (those who overeat or drink excessively) will become poor, and sleepiness leads to poverty. **22.** Listen to your father, and don't disregard (ignore) your mother in her old age. **23.** Value wisdom and truth above all. **24.** A father of a righteous child will rejoice; a man with a wise son will celebrate. **25.** May your parents rejoice in you! **26.** My son, give your heart to me and delight in my ways. **27.** An adulterous (unfaithful in marriage) woman is a dangerous pit, and a wayward (rebellious) wife is a trap. **28.** She waits to lead men astray, increasing the unfaithful. **29.** Who suffers from sorrow, strife (conflict), complaints, bruises, and red eyes? **28.** it's those who linger over wine or mixed drinks. **29.** Don't gaze at wine when it sparkles and goes down smoothly. **30.** In the end, it poisons like a viper (venomous snake). **31.** You'll see strange things, and your mind will be confused. **32.** You'll feel like a sailor tossed on the waves. **33.** "They beat me," you'll say, "but I didn't feel it! When can I wake up and drink again?"

Chapter 24

1. Do not envy the wicked or desire their company; **2.** For their hearts plot violence and their words stir up trouble. **3.** A house is built by wisdom, and established by understanding; **4.** Through knowledge, its rooms are filled with treasures. **5.** The wise prevail with great power, and those with knowledge strengthen themselves. **6.** You need guidance to wage war; victory comes through many advisers. **7.** Wisdom is beyond fools; they should not speak in the assembly. **8.** Those who plot evil are known as schemers (someone who plans dishonest or harmful actions). **9.** Folly's schemes are sin, and people despise mockers. **10.** If you fail in trouble, your strength is small **11.** Rescue those led to death and stop those heading for slaughter. **12.** If you say, "We knew nothing," will not the one who weighs hearts (knows a person's true intentions) and guards your life repay you for what you've done? **13.** Eat honey, for it is good; honey from the comb is sweet. **14.** Wisdom is like honey: finding it gives hope and a future. **15.** Do not steal from the righteous; **16.** for though they fall seven times, they rise again, but the wicked stumble in calamity (disastrous event). **17.** Do not rejoice when your enemy falls; **18.** for the LORD may disapprove and turn His wrath away from them. **19.** Do not fret over evildoers or envy the wicked, **20.** for they have no future, and their lamp will be snuffed out. **21.** Fear the LORD and the king (a ruler or monarch); do not join rebellious officials (people who oppose authority), **22.** for they will bring sudden destruction, and you do not know what calamities they may cause. **23.** To show partiality in judgment is wrong; **24.** Whoever says to the guilty, "You are innocent," will be cursed by people and denounced by nations. **25.** But it will go well with those who convict the guilty, and blessings will come to them. **26.** An honest answer is like a kiss on the lips (a gesture of love and sincerity). **27.** Put your outdoor work in order and get your fields ready; after that, build your house. **28.** Do not testify against your neighbor without cause— would you use your lips to mislead (lie)? **29.** Do not say, "I'll do to them as they have done to me; I'll pay them back for what they did." **30.** I went past the field of a sluggard (lazy person), past the vineyard of someone without sense; **31.** Thorns had come up everywhere, the ground was covered with weeds, and the stone wall was in ruins. **32.** I applied my heart (thought deeply) to what I observed and learned a lesson from what I saw: **33.** A little sleep, a little slumber, a little folding of the hands to rest— **34.** And poverty will come on you like a thief and scarcity (lack of resources) like an armed man.

26 – Tägsas ("Reproof"; Proverbs Ch 25–31)

Chapter 25

1. These are additional proverbs of Solomon, collected by the men of King Hezekiah of Judah: **2.** It is God's glory to hide matters; kings take pride in uncovering them. **3.** Just as the heavens are vast and the earth deep, so are the hearts of kings beyond understanding. **4.** Purify silver, and a silversmith (a person who works with metals) can make a vessel; **5.** Remove corrupt (morally wrong) officials from the king's presence, and his throne will stand firm through righteousness. **6.** Do not elevate yourself in the king's presence, nor seek a place among his nobles (important people); **7.** It's better for him to invite you up than for you to be humiliated before the court. **8.** Do not be quick to bring disputes to court; what if you are put to shame by your neighbor in the end? **9.** If you take your neighbor to court, do not betray a confidence (private information), **10.** or you may be publicly humiliated and the charges against you will stand. **11.** A righteous (just and fair) ruling is like gold apples set in silver. **12.** A wise judge's rebuke (sharp criticism) is like a fine gold ornament to an attentive ear. **13.** A trustworthy messenger is like a refreshing cold drink during harvest; he restores his master's spirit. **14.** A boastful person who never delivers is like clouds and wind without rain. **15.** Patience can sway (influence) a ruler, and a gentle word can break the strongest resistance. **16.** If you find honey, eat only what you need—too much will make you sick. **17.** Don't overstay your welcome at your neighbor's house—too much of you will make them dislike you. **18.** False testimony is like a club, sword, or sharp arrow against your neighbor. **19.** Trusting an unfaithful (disloyal) person in times of trouble is like relying on a broken tooth or a limp foot. **20.** Singing to a troubled heart is like taking someone's coat on a cold day or pouring vinegar (sour liquid used for cleaning) on a wound. **21.** If your enemy is hungry, feed him; if he's thirsty, give him drink. **22.** In doing this, you will heap burning coals on his head, and the Lord will reward you. **23.** A sly (deceptive) tongue is like a north wind bringing unexpected rain— provoking a horrified reaction. **24.** Better to live in a small space on the roof than share a house with a quarrelsome (argumentative) wife. **25.** Good news from afar is like cold water to a weary (tired) soul. **26.** Righteous people who give in to the wicked (evil) are like a muddied (dirtied) spring or a polluted (contaminated) well. **27.** Just as it's not good to eat too much honey, it's also dishonorable (shameful) to pry into matters that are too deep. **28.** A person without self-control is like a city with broken walls.

Chapter 26

1. Like snow in summer or rain during harvest, honor does not suit a fool. **2.** Like a fluttering sparrow or a darting swallow, an undeserved curse never settles. **3.** A whip for the horse, a bridle (a bit used to control a horse) for the donkey, and a rod for the backs of fools! **4.** Don't answer a fool according to his folly, or you'll be just like him. **5.** Answer a fool according to his folly, or he'll think he's wise in his own eyes. **6.** Sending a message by a fool is like cutting off your feet or drinking poison. **7.** Like the useless legs of the lame, a proverb is wasted on a fool. **8.** Like tying a stone in a sling, giving honor to a fool is futile. **9.** Like a thornbush in a drunkard's hand, a proverb is misused by a fool. **10.** Like an archer who shoots blindly, is one who hires a fool or any passer-by. **11.** As a dog returns to its vomit, so fools repeat their folly. **12.** Do you see someone wise in their own eyes? There's more hope for a fool than for them. **13.** The lazy person says, "There's a lion in the road, a fierce lion roaming the streets!" **14.** Like a door turning on its hinges, the lazy person turns in bed. **15.** A lazy person buries their hand in the dish, too lazy to bring it back to their mouth. **16.** The lazy person thinks they're wiser than seven people who give sound advice. **17.** Like grabbing a stray dog by the ears, is one who rushes into a quarrel not their own. **18.** Like a maniac shooting flaming arrows of death, **19.** is one who deceives their neighbor and says, "I was just joking!" **20.** Without wood, a fire goes out; without gossip, a quarrel dies down. **21.** Like charcoal to embers and wood to fire, so is a quarrelsome person who stirs up strife. **22.** The words of a gossip are like choice morsels (tasty bits of food); they go deep into the soul. **23.** Like silver dross (impurities) on pottery, are fervent lips with an evil heart. **24.** Enemies disguise themselves with their words, but harbor deceit in their hearts. **25.** Though their speech is charming, don't trust them, for seven abominations (evil acts) fill their hearts. **26.** Their malice may be hidden by deception, but their wickedness will be revealed in the assembly. **27.** Whoever digs a pit will fall into it; if someone rolls a stone, it will roll back on them. **28.** A lying tongue hates those it harms, and a flattering mouth brings destruction.

Chapter 27

1. Don't boast about tomorrow, because you don't know what a day may bring. **2.** Let others praise you, not your own mouth; let someone else speak highly of you, not your own lips. **3.** Stone is heavy, and sand is a burden, but a fool's provocation (annoyance) is more unbearable than both. **4.** Anger is harsh, and fury is overwhelming, but who can withstand jealousy? **5.** It's better to receive a clear rebuke than hidden love. **6.** Wounds from a friend can be trusted, but an enemy's kindness is often fake and self-serving. **7.** Someone who is satisfied has no desire for honey, but to someone hungry, even something bitter tastes sweet. **8.** Like a bird that leaves its nest, so is anyone who abandons their home. **9.** Perfume and incense bring joy to the heart, and the joy of a friend comes from their sincere counsel (advice). **10.** Don't abandon your friend or the friend of your family, and don't run to your relative's house in a time of crisis—a nearby neighbor is better than a distant relative. **11.** Be wise, my child, and bring joy to my heart, so that I can respond to anyone who disrespects me. **12.** The wise see danger and take precautions, but the naive keep going and suffer for it. **13.** Take the coat of someone who has put up security (guarantee) for a stranger; take it as collateral if the pledge is made for someone outside your circle. **14.** If someone loudly blesses their neighbor early in the morning, it will be seen as an annoyance rather than a blessing. **15.** A quarrelsome wife is like the constant dripping of a leaky roof during a storm; **16.** Trying to control her is like trying to stop the wind or hold oil in your hand. **17.** Just as iron sharpens iron, so one person sharpens another. **18.** The one who takes care of a fig tree will be rewarded with its fruit, and whoever serves their master will be honored. **19.** Just as water reflects the face, so a person's life reflects their heart. **20.** Death and Destruction are never satisfied, and neither are human desires. **21.** The crucible (container) is for refining silver, and the furnace is for refining gold, but people are tested by how they receive praise. **22.** Even if you grind a fool down in a mortar, crushing them like grain in a pestle, you won't remove their foolishness. **23.** Make sure to know the state of your flocks, and give careful attention to your herds; **24.** because wealth doesn't last forever, and a crown (authority) doesn't belong to the same family forever. **25.** When the hay is gathered and the new growth appears, and the grass from the hills is collected, **26.** The lambs will provide clothing for you, and the goats will bring in money for a field. **27.** You'll have plenty of goat's milk to feed your family and nourish your female servants.

Chapter 28

1. The wicked run even when no one chases them, but the righteous are as bold as lions. **2.** When a nation is rebellious (resisting authority), it has many rulers, but a ruler with wisdom and understanding maintains order. **3.** A ruler who oppresses (unfairly controls) the poor is like a destructive storm. **4.** Those who reject instruction praise the wicked, but those who heed it (listen and follow) oppose them. **5.** Evildoers don't understand what is right, but those who seek the LORD understand it fully. **6.** Better to be poor and walk in integrity (honesty) than to be rich and crooked (dishonest). **7.** A wise son listens to instruction, but a companion of gluttons (people who overeat) brings shame to his father. **8.** Whoever increases wealth by exploiting (taking advantage of) the poor will have their riches passed on to those who care for them. **9.** Those who ignore my instruction, even their prayers are meaningless (detestable). **10.** Whoever leads the righteous astray (off track) will fall into own trap, but the blameless will receive a good inheritance. **11.** The rich think they are wise, but the poor with wisdom see their foolishness. **12.** When the righteous triumph (succeed), there is joy, but when the wicked rise, people hide. **13.** Whoever conceals (hides) their sins will not prosper, but those who confess and renounce (reject) them find mercy. **14.** Blessed is the one who respects (reveres) God, but those who harden their hearts (become stubborn) fall into trouble. **15.** A wicked ruler over helpless people is like a roaring lion or charging bear. **16.** A tyrannical (oppressive) ruler uses extortion (forceful taking of wealth), but one who rejects dishonest gain will reign long. **17.** Anyone burdened with guilt from murder will seek refuge in the grave (death); let no one stop them. **18.** The blameless person is protected, but the one who walks a crooked path will fall into the pit. **19.** Those who work their land will have plenty of food, but those who chase fantasies (unrealistic dreams) will end up in poverty. **20.** A faithful person will be richly blessed, but one eager to get rich will not go unpunished. **21.** To show partiality (favoritism) is wrong, yet some will do wrong for a small gain (piece of bread). **22.** The greedy are eager to get rich and don't realize that poverty is waiting for them. **23.** The one who rebukes (corrects) others will eventually gain favor, but a flatterer (someone who praises insincerely) seeks selfish gain. **24.** Whoever robs their father or mother and says, "It's not wrong," is as bad as one who destroys others. **25.** The greedy stir up conflict, but those who trust in the LORD will prosper. **26.** Those who trust in themselves are fools, but those who walk in wisdom are kept safe. **27.** Those who give to the poor will lack nothing, but those who close their eyes to them will face many curses. **28.** When the wicked rise to power, people hide, but when they perish (die), the righteous thrive.

Chapter 29

1. Those who stubbornly ignore correction will be destroyed suddenly, with no remedy (solution). **2.** When the righteous thrive, the people rejoice; when the wicked rule, the people suffer. **3.** A man who loves wisdom makes his father proud, but a companion of prostitutes (sex workers) wastes his wealth. **4.** A just (fair) king brings stability, but greedy rulers tear it down. **5.** Flattery (false praise) sets traps for others. **6.** Evildoers are trapped (caught) by their own sins, but the righteous rejoice. **7.** The righteous care for the poor, but the wicked do not. **8.** Mockers (those who insult others) stir up trouble, but the wise calm anger. **9.** When a wise person argues with a fool, peace is lost, and the fool mocks. **10.** The violent (bloodthirsty) hate the upright and seek their destruction. **11.** Fools vent (release) all their anger, but the wise bring calm. **12.** Rulers who listen to lies corrupt (make dishonest) their officials. **13.** Both the poor and the oppressor (one who unjustly controls others) receive sight from the LORD. **14.** A fair king will have a lasting reign (rule). **15.** Discipline and correction teach wisdom, but undisciplined (untrained) children bring shame. **16.** When the wicked prosper, sin increases, but the righteous see their downfall (destruction). **17.** Discipline your children, and they will bring you peace and joy. **18.** Without guidance (revelation), people lack restraint (self-control), but those who follow wisdom are blessed. **19.** Servants cannot be corrected by just words; they may understand but not respond. **20.** Speaking hastily (quickly) is foolish—there's more hope for a fool than for them. **21.** A pampered (spoiled) servant becomes arrogant. **22.** An angry person causes conflict, and a hot-tempered (quick to anger) one sins frequently. **23.** Pride brings a person low, but the humble gain honor. **24.** Accomplices (partners) of thieves are their own enemies and dare not testify. **25.** Fear of man (worry about others' opinions) traps you, but trusting in the LORD keeps you safe. **26.** Many seek a ruler's favor, but justice comes only from the LORD. **27.** The righteous detest dishonesty, and the wicked despise the upright.

Chapter 30

1. These are the words of Agur son of Jakeh—an inspired message. This is his message to Ithiel: "I am tired, God, but I can still overcome. **2.** I am no better than a beast, not a human; I lack true understanding. **3.** I have not learned wisdom, nor do I know the Holy One. **4.** Who has gone up to heaven and returned? Who has gathered the wind in His hands? Who has wrapped the waters in a cloak? Who set the earth's boundaries? What is His name, and what is the name of His Son? Surely you know! **5.** Every word of God is pure; He is a shield for those who trust in Him. **6.** Do not add to His words, or He will rebuke you and expose you as a liar. **7.** "There are two things I ask of You, Lord; do not refuse me before I die: **8.** Keep lies far from me; give me neither poverty nor wealth, but only the food I need for today. **9.** Otherwise, I may have too much and forget You, saying, 'Who is the Lord?' Or I may become poor and steal, dishonoring Your name. **10.** Do not slander a servant to their master, or they will curse you, and you will be held accountable. **11.** Some curse their fathers and do not bless their mothers; **12.** Some think they are pure, but they are not cleansed from their filth; **13.** Some have proud eyes, and their looks are full of scorn; **14.** Some people have sharp teeth like swords and jaws like knives, ready to devour the poor and the needy. **15.** "The leech has two daughters. 'Give! Give!' they cry. There are three things that never have enough, four things that are never satisfied: **16.** The grave, the barren womb, the land that never has enough water, and fire, which never says, 'That's enough!' **17.** "The eye that mocks a father, that scorns an elderly mother, will be picked out by ravens in the valley and eaten by vultures. **18.** "There are three things that amaze me, four things I cannot understand: **19.** The way an eagle flies in the sky, the way a snake moves on a rock, the way a ship sails on the sea, and the way a man loves a young woman. **20.** "This is the way of an adulterous woman: She eats, wipes her mouth, and says, 'I've done nothing wrong.' **21.** "The earth trembles under three things, and under four it cannot bear: **22.** A servant who becomes king, a fool who has plenty to eat, **23.** A disgraceful woman who marries, and a servant who displaces her mistress. **24.** "Four things on earth are small but very wise: **25.** Ants, though small and weak, store up their food in summer; **26.** Hyraxes are small and weak, but they make their homes in the rocks; **27.** Locusts have no king, but they march together in ranks; **28.** A lizard can be caught by hand, yet it can be found in royal palaces. **29.** "There are three things that move majestically, four that have a grand presence: **30.** A lion, mighty among beasts, who fears nothing; **31.** A strutting rooster, a ram, and a king who is secure against rebellion. **32.** "If you act like a fool and elevate yourself, or if you plot evil, put your hand over your mouth! **33.** For just as churning cream makes butter, and twisting the nose brings forth blood, so stirring up anger causes conflict."

Chapter 31

1. These are the sayings of King Lemuel, an inspired message his mother taught him: **2.** "Listen, my son! Listen, son of my womb! Listen, my son, the answer to my prayers! **3.** Do not waste your strength on women, or your energy on those who ruin kings. **4.** It is not for kings, Lemuel—it is not for kings to drink wine, or for rulers to crave beer, **5.** lest they drink and forget what is decreed (the law), and deprive the oppressed of their rights. **6.** Let beer be for those who are dying, wine for those who are in distress! **7.** Let them drink, forget their poverty, and remember their misery no more. **8.** Speak up for those who cannot speak for themselves, for the rights of the poor and needy. **9.** Speak up and judge fairly; defend the rights of the destitute. **10.** A wife of noble character, who can find? She is worth far more than rubies. **11.** Her husband has full confidence in her and lacks nothing of value. **12.** She brings him well, not harm, all the days of her life. **13.** She selects wool and flax and works with eager hands. **14.** She is like the merchant ships, bringing her food from afar. **15.** She rises while it is still night; she provides food for her family and portions for her female servants. **16.** She considers a field and buys it; out of her earnings, she plants a vineyard. **17.** She works with vigor (energy); her arms are strong for her tasks. **18.** She sees that her trading is profitable, and her lamp does not go out at night. **19.** In her hand she holds the distaff (a tool used in spinning thread) and grasps the spindle (spinning tool) with her fingers. **20.** She opens her arms to the poor and extends her hands to the needy. **21.** When it snows, she has no fear for her household, for all of them are clothed in scarlet (warm clothing). **22.** She makes coverings for her bed; she is clothed in fine linen and purple. **23.** Her husband is respected at the city gate, where he takes his seat among the elders of the land. **24.** She makes linen garments and sells them, and supplies the merchants with sashes (bands or belts). **25.** She is clothed with strength and dignity; she can laugh at the days to come. **26.** She speaks with wisdom, and faithful (reliable) instruction is on her tongue. **27.** She watches over the affairs of her household and does not eat the bread of idleness (laziness). **28.** Her children arise and call her blessed; her husband also, and he praises her: **29.** "Many women do noble things, but you surpass them all." **30.** Charm is deceptive, and beauty is fleeting; but a woman who fears the LORD is to be praised. **31.** Honor her for all that her hands have done, and let her works bring her praise at the city gate.

27 – The Wisdom of Solomon

Chapter 1

1. Love righteousness, all you who judge the earth. Think of the Lord with a pure heart. Seek Him with sincerity. **2.** He is found by those who trust Him and do not test Him. **3.** Crooked thoughts separate you from God. His power convicts (proves guilt) and exposes the foolish. **4.** Wisdom will not enter a soul that plans evil or stay in a body enslaved by sin. **5.** A holy spirit of discipline (self-control) flees deceit (lying) and foolish thoughts, and is ashamed when unrighteousness (wickedness) comes in. **6.** Wisdom is a spirit who loves humanity, and will not leave the blasphemer (one who speaks disrespectfully of God) unpunished. God is witness (observer) of their heart and hears their words. **7.** The spirit of the Lord fills the world and knows all things spoken. **8.** Therefore, no one who speaks unrighteous things will escape justice. **9.** The ungodly (immoral) will be searched out in His counsel, and their lawless deeds will be convicted. **10.** A jealous ear listens to everything, and complaints (grumbling) are not hidden. **11.** Beware of useless murmuring (complaining) and avoid slander (false accusations); no secret word goes unnoticed, and a lying mouth destroys the soul. **12.** Do not bring death through the errors of your life or your actions. **13.** God did not create death, nor does He delight in the death of the living. **14.** He created all things for life. The powers of creation are wholesome (healthy), and there is no destructive poison in them. Hades (the realm of the dead) does not rule the earth. **15.** Righteousness is immortal. **16.** But the ungodly, by their actions and words, call death upon themselves, thinking it's a friend. They made a pact (agreement) with death because they deserve it.

Chapter 2

1. They said, with foolish reasoning (illogical thinking), "Our life is short and sorrowful. There's no healing (recovery) in death, and no one escapes Hades (the realm of the dead). **2.** We were born by chance (randomly), and after death, we'll be as if we never existed. Our breath is like smoke, and reason (thinking) is a spark from the heart. **3.** When the spark goes out, the body turns to ashes, and the spirit disperses like thin air. **4.** Our name will be forgotten. Our deeds (actions) will fade, like a cloud or mist (fog) chased by the sun. **5.** Our time is like a passing shadow (temporary), and our end is fixed (unchangeable). **6.** "Let's enjoy life now, indulging in pleasures like we did in our youth. **7.** Let's fill ourselves with wine and perfume, and not let any flower pass us by. **8.** Let's crown ourselves with rosebuds (fresh flowers) before they wither (die). **9.** Let's all share in our pleasure (joy), leaving signs of it everywhere, for this is our portion (share). **10.** Let's oppress the poor righteous man and show no respect for widows (women who lost their husbands) or the elderly (old people). **11.** Let's define righteousness by our strength, for weakness is useless. **12.** Let's ambush (lie in wait for) the righteous man because he annoys (bothers) us, condemns our actions, and rebukes (criticizes) our sins. **13.** He claims to know God and calls himself a child of the Lord. **14.** He reproves our thoughts. **15.** He is unpleasant to look at, as his life and ways are strange (unusual). **16.** He calls us worthless (unimportant) and avoids our ways, saying the end of the righteous is happy, boasting that God is his Father. **17.** Let's see if his words are true. Let's test (try) his end. **18.** If he is God's son, God will protect him and deliver (rescue) him from enemies. **19.** Let's test him with insults and torture (torment) to see his patience (endurance). **20.** Let's condemn him to a shameful (dishonorable) death, for he will be protected, as he claims." **21.** They reasoned and were misled (led astray), their evil blinded them, **22.** and they didn't understand (comprehend) God's mysteries or hope for the reward (compensation) of holiness. **23.** God created man for incorruption (immortality), in His image of eternal life. **24.** But death entered through the envy (jealousy) of the devil, and those who follow him experience it.

Chapter 3

1. But the souls of the righteous are in the hand of God, and no torment (grief) will touch them. **2.** To the eyes of the foolish, they seemed to have died. Their departure (death) was considered a disaster, **3.** and their leaving us was seen as a loss, but they are in peace. **4.** For even though, in the sight of men, they are punished, their hope is full of immortality (eternal life). **5.** Having borne a little chastening (discipline or correction), they will receive great good; because God tested them, and found them worthy of Himself. **6.** He tested them like gold in a furnace, and He accepted them as a whole burnt offering (a complete offering, fully devoted). **7.** At the time of their visitation (judgment or divine intervention), they will shine. They will run back and forth like sparks among stubble (dry grass). **8.** They will judge nations and have dominion (authority) over peoples. The Lord will reign over them forever. **9.** Those who trust Him will understand truth. The faithful will live with Him in love, because grace and mercy are with His chosen ones. **10.** But the ungodly will be punished, as their reasoning (evil thinking) deserves, those who neglected righteousness and turned away from the Lord; **11.** For those who despise wisdom and discipline are miserable. Their hope is empty (without substance), and their efforts (toils) are unprofitable. Their works are useless. **12.** Their wives are foolish and their children are wicked. **13.** Their descendants are cursed. But the barren woman (childless) who is undefiled (pure) is happy, she who has not conceived in transgression (sin). She will have fruit (offspring) when God examines souls (judges people). **14.** So is the eunuch (a man who has been castrated), who has done no lawless (wicked) deed with his hands, nor thought evil things against the Lord; for a precious gift will be given to him for his faithfulness, and a delightful inheritance in the Lord's sanctuary (the holy place of God). **15.** For good labors (efforts) produce fruit of great renown (reputation). The root of understanding cannot fail. **16.** But the children of adulterers (illegitimate children) will not come to maturity. The seed of an unlawful union will vanish away. **17.** For if they live long, they will not be esteemed (honored), and in the end, their old age will be without honor. **18.** If they die young, they will have no hope, nor any comfort (consolation) in the Day of Judgment. **19.** For the end of an unrighteous generation is always grievous (painful, sorrowful).

Chapter 4

1. It is better to be childless and virtuous, for immortality (eternal life) is in the memory of virtue, because it is recognized both before God and before men. **2.** When it is present, people imitate it. They long for it when it has departed. Throughout all time, it marches, crowned in triumph, victorious in the competition for the prizes that are undefiled (pure, untainted). **3.** But the multiplying brood (offspring) of the ungodly will be of no profit, and their illegitimate offshoots (children born out of sin) won't take deep root, nor will they establish a sure hold (stable foundation). **4.** For even if they grow branches and flourish for a season, standing unsure, they will be sternly shaken by the wind. They will be uprooted by the violence (strong force) of winds. **5.** Their branches will be broken off before they come to maturity. Their fruit will be useless, never ripe to eat, and fit for nothing. **6.** For unlawfully conceived children are witnesses of wickedness (evil) against parents when they are investigated (judged). **7.** But a righteous man, even if he dies before his time, will be at rest. **8.** For honorable old age is not measured by length of time, nor is its value given by the number of years, **9.** but understanding (wisdom) is gray hair to men, and an unspotted (pure) life is ripe old age. **10.** Being found well-pleasing to God, someone was loved. While living among sinners, he was taken away (to God). **11.** He was caught away, lest evil should change his understanding, or deceit (trickery) deceives his soul. **12.** For the fascination of wickedness obscures (blurs) the things which are good, and the whirl of desire (intense craving) perverts (twists) an innocent mind. **13.** Being made perfect quickly (matured swiftly), he filled a long time (he had great impact in a short period); **14.** for his soul was pleasing to the Lord. Therefore, he hurried out of the midst of wickedness. **15.** But the people saw and didn't understand, not considering this, that grace and mercy are with His chosen, and that He visits His holy ones (those set apart for God); **16.** but a righteous man who is dead will condemn the ungodly who are living, and youth who is quickly perfected (matured) will condemn the many years of an unrighteous man's old age. **17.** For the ungodly will see a wise man's end, and won't understand what the Lord planned for him, and why He safely kept him. **18.** They will see and despise; but the Lord will laugh them to scorn. After this, they will become a dishonored carcass (dead body) and a reproach (disgrace) among the dead forever; **19.** because He will dash them speechless to the ground, and will shake them from their foundations. They will lie utterly waste (destroyed). They will be in anguish (great suffering) and their memory will perish. **20.** They will come with cowardly fear when their sins are counted. Their lawless deeds (wicked acts) will convict (accuse) them to their face.

Chapter 5

1. Then the righteous man will stand with great boldness (confidence) before those who afflicted him, and those who made his labors seem insignificant (of no account). **2.** When they see him, they will be troubled with terrible fear, and will be amazed at the marvel of salvation (the wonder of his deliverance). **3.** They will speak among themselves, repenting (feeling remorse), and groaning in distress of spirit (anguish of soul), saying, "This was he whom we used to hold in derision (mocking), as a parable of reproach (example of disgrace)." **4.** We fools (ignorantly) considered his life to be madness (insanity), and his end without honor (dignity). **5.** How was he counted among the sons of God? How is his lot among the saints (holy ones)? **6.** Truly, we went astray (strayed) from the way of truth. The light of righteousness didn't shine for us. The sun didn't rise for us. **7.** We took our fill of the paths of lawlessness (wickedness) and destruction. We traveled through trackless deserts (barren places), but we didn't know the Lord's way. **8.** What did our arrogance (pride) profit us? What good have riches and boasting brought us? **9.** Those things all passed away as a shadow, like a rumor (false report) that runs by. **10.** Like a ship passing through the billowy (wavy) water, which, when it has gone by, there is no trace to be found, no pathway of its keel (bottom of the ship) in the waves. **11.** Or it is like when a bird flies through the air, leaving no evidence of its passage, but the light wind, lashed (stirred) by the stroke of its pinions (wings), and torn apart with the violent rush of the moving wings, passes through. Afterwards, no sign of its coming remains. **12.** Or it is like when an arrow is shot at a mark (target), the air it divided closes up again immediately, so that men don't know where it passed through. **13.** So we also, as soon as we were born, ceased to be; and we had no sign of virtue (goodness) to show, but were utterly consumed in our wickedness. **14.** Because the hope of the ungodly man is like chaff (useless husks) carried by the wind, and like foam (bubbles) vanishing before a tempest (storm);

and is scattered like smoke by the wind, and passes by like the memory (remembrance) of a guest who stays just a day. **15.** But the righteous live forever. Their reward is with the Lord, and His care for them is with the Most High (God). **16.** Therefore, they will receive the crown of royal dignity (honor) and the diadem (crown) of beauty from the Lord's hand, because He will cover them with His right hand and shield (protect) them with His arm. **17.** He will take His zeal (fervor) as complete armor, and will make the whole creation (universe) His weapons to punish His enemies. **18.** He will put on righteousness as a breastplate (body armor), and will wear impartial judgment (fairness) as a helmet. **19.** He will take holiness (pure devotion) as an invincible (unbeatable) shield. **20.** He will sharpen stern wrath (anger) for a sword. The universe will go with Him to fight against His frenzied (wild, uncontrolled) foes. **21.** Shafts of lightning will fly with true aim. They will leap to the mark (target) from the clouds, as from a well-drawn bow. **22.** Hailstones full of wrath (fury) will be hurled (thrown) like a catapult. The water of the sea will be angered (stirred up) against them. Rivers will sternly overwhelm (flood) them. **23.** A mighty wind will encounter (strike) them. It will winnow (blow away) them like a tempest (violent storm). So lawlessness (sin) will make all the land desolate (ruined). Their evil-doing will overthrow (destroy) the thrones of princes (rulers).

Chapter 6

1. Listen, you kings, and understand. Pay attention, you judges of the earth's corners (ends of the earth). **2.** Hear, you rulers who have control over many people, and take pride (make your boast) in the great number of nations you rule. **3.** Know that your authority was granted to you by the Lord, and your reign comes from the Most High. He will examine your deeds and investigate your plans. **4.** As stewards (officers) of His kingdom, you did not judge justly, nor did you follow the law, nor did you walk according to God's advice (counsel). **5.** A terrible and swift judgment will come upon you, because a strict (stern) judgment is reserved for those in high positions. **6.** The lowly may be shown mercy, but the mighty will be thoroughly tested. **7.** The Sovereign Lord of all will not be impressed by anyone, nor will He show favoritism (deference) to the powerful, because He made both the small and the great, and cares for them equally. **8.** However, the scrutiny upon the powerful will be strict. **9.** Therefore, my words are for you, rulers, so that you may gain wisdom and not turn away from it. **10.** Those who keep holy things in holiness will be sanctified, and those who have been taught wisdom will know how to defend it. **11.** Therefore, set your hearts on my words. Desire them, and you rulers will be instructed. **12.** Wisdom is brilliant and does not fade away; she is easily seen by those who love her, and found by those who seek her. **13.** She anticipates those who desire her, making herself known to them. **14.** The one who rises early to seek her will find no difficulty, for she is always at the gates (meeting places). **15.** To think on her is the perfection of understanding, and those who wait for her will soon be free from worry. **16.** She herself moves around, seeking those worthy of her, and she graces them with her presence on their paths, meeting them in every good purpose. **17.** Her true origin is a desire for instruction, and a desire for instruction is love. **18.** Love is shown through obedience to her teachings. Following her laws grants immortality (eternal life). **19.** Immortality brings one closer to God. **20.** Therefore, desiring wisdom leads to greatness. **21.** If you desire power, thrones, and scepters, honor wisdom, so that you may reign forever. **22.** I will explain what wisdom is, and how she came into being. I will not conceal (hide) her mysteries from you; but I will make her beginnings clear, and bring her knowledge into the light, without avoiding the truth. **23.** I will not be led by envy, because envy has no place in wisdom. **24.** A large group of wise men is a salvation to the world, and an understanding king brings stability to his people. **25.** Therefore, be instructed by my words, and you will benefit from them.

Chapter 7

1. I am also human, like everyone else, and I am descended from the first human, who was created from the earth. **2.** I was formed into flesh over the course of ten months in my mother's womb, made from the blood of man and the joy of marriage. **3.** When I was born, I breathed the same air as all, and fell to the earth, crying my first cry just like everyone else. **4.** I was cared for and wrapped in swaddling clothes. **5.** No king has a different beginning, for all people enter life in the same way, and leave it in the same manner. **6.** For this reason, I prayed, and understanding was granted to me. I asked, and a spirit of wisdom came to me. **7.** I chose wisdom above kingship and thrones. **8.** I valued riches as nothing compared to her. **9.** I did not compare her to any precious gem, for in her presence, all gold is like a small grain of sand, and silver seems like clay. **10.** I loved her more than health and beauty, and I preferred her to light, because her brilliance never fades. **11.** All good things came to me through her, and countless riches are in her hands. **12.** I rejoiced in them all because wisdom guides them, though at first, I did not know she was their source. **13.** As I learned without deceit,

I shared without hesitation. I do not hide her treasures. **14.** She is a treasure for mankind that never fails, and those who use her gain favor with God, praised by the gifts they offer through discipline. **15.** But may God grant that I speak his judgment, and that my thoughts be worthy of the gifts given to me, for he is the one who guides even wisdom and corrects those who are wise. **16.** For both we and our words are in his hands, along with all understanding and skill in various crafts. **17.** He gave me flawless knowledge of all things, to understand the structure of the universe and how the elements operate. **18.** He revealed to me the beginning, middle, and end of time; the changes of the solstices and the shifts of the seasons; **19.** the cycles of the years and the movements of the stars; **20.** the nature of living creatures, the power of wild beasts, the force of winds, and the thoughts of men; the variety of plants and the medicinal properties of roots. **21.** All things, whether hidden or visible, I have learned, for wisdom, the creator of all things, taught me. **22.** For in her is a spirit that is quick to understand, holy, unique, varied, subtle, free-moving, clear in speech, untainted, distinct, invulnerable, loving what is good, sharp, unhindered, beneficent (kind), loving toward humans, firm, reliable, free from worry, all-powerful, all-knowing, and able to penetrate all spirits that are quick to understand, pure, and exceedingly subtle. **23.** Wisdom is swifter than any movement. **24.** She pervades and penetrates all things because of her purity. **25.** She is a breath of God's power, a pure emanation (something that comes forth) of the glory of the Almighty. Therefore, nothing impure can enter her. **26.** She is a reflection of eternal light, a flawless mirror of God's works, and an image of his goodness. **27.** Though she is one, she has the power to do all things. **28.** Remaining within herself, she renews all things. **29.** From generation to generation, she enters holy souls, making them friends of God and prophets. **30.** For God loves no one more than those who live with wisdom. **31.** She is more beautiful than the sun and surpasses all the constellations (groups of stars) of the heavens. She is better than light. **32.** For daylight gives way to night, but evil will never triumph over wisdom.

Chapter 8

1. But wisdom extends from one end of the world to the other with complete strength, and arranges all things perfectly. **2.** I loved her and searched for her from my youth. I sought to take her as my bride, and I became captivated (fascinated, enchanted) by her beauty. **3.** She honors her noble birth by living with God. The Sovereign Lord of all loves her. **4.** For she is initiated (introduced, taught) into the knowledge of God, and she chooses His works. **5.** But if wealth is a desired possession in life, what is wealthier (richer) than wisdom, which creates all things? **6.** And if understanding is truly effective, who, more than wisdom, is the architect (creator, designer) of all things that exist? **7.** If a person loves righteousness, the fruits (results) of wisdom's labor are virtues (good moral qualities), for she teaches moderation (self-control), understanding, righteousness, and courage. There is nothing more profitable (beneficial) for people than these. **8.** And if anyone desires great experience, she knows the things of the past and predicts (foresees) the things to come. She understands the subtleties (fine details) of speech and the interpretations (meanings) of dark sayings. She foresees (predicts) signs and wonders, and the changes in seasons and times. **9.** Therefore, I decided to take her to live with me, knowing that she would provide me with good counsel (advice), and encourage me through my cares and grief. **10.** Because of her, I will have glory (honor) among the masses, and honor in the sight of elders, though I am young. **11.** I will be sharp (clear, wise) in judgment. I will be admired in the presence of rulers. **12.** When I am silent, they will wait for me. When I speak, they will listen to what I say. If I continue speaking, they will cover their mouths in respect. **13.** Because of her, I will have immortality (eternal life), and leave behind a lasting legacy for those who come after me. **14.** I will govern (rule) nations. Kingdoms will be subject to me. **15.** Fearful (terrified) kings will tremble when they hear of me. Among the people, I will show myself to be just (fair) and courageous (brave) in war. **16.** When I enter my home, I will find peace with her. For conversation with her has no bitterness, and living with her brings no pain, but gladness (happiness) and joy. **17.** When I considered these things in my heart, and thought about how immortality is linked to wisdom, **18.** And in her friendship is true delight, and in her labor (work) is wealth that does not fail, and understanding is in her companionship, and great renown (fame) in having fellowship (relationship) with her words, I sought to take her for myself. **19.** Now, I was a clever (intelligent) child, and I received a good soul. **20.** Or rather, being good, I came into an undefiled (pure, untainted) body. **21.** But realizing that I could not possess wisdom unless God gave her to me—yes, and to know by whom this grace (unearned favor) is given—I prayed to the Lord and pleaded (begged) with Him, and with all my heart I said:

Chapter 9

1. "O God of my ancestors and Lord of mercy, who created all things by Your word; **2.** and by Your wisdom, You formed man, that he should have dominion (control, authority) over the creatures You made, **3.** And rule the world in holiness and righteousness, and judge with uprightness of soul (integrity, fairness), **4.** give me wisdom, the one who sits beside You on Your throne. Do not reject me from among Your servants, **5.** because I am Your servant and the son of Your handmaid (servant), a weak and short-lived man, with little power to understand judgment and laws. **6.** For even if a man is perfect among the sons of men, if the wisdom that comes from You is not with him, he will count for nothing. **7.** You chose me to be king of Your people, and a judge for Your sons and daughters. **8.** You commanded that a sanctuary be built on Your holy mountain, and an altar in the city where You dwell, a copy of the holy tent (tabernacle) which You prepared from the beginning. **9.** Wisdom is with You and knows Your works, and was present when You made the world, and understands what is pleasing in Your eyes, and what is right according to Your commandments. **10.** Send her from the holy heavens, and ask her to come from the throne of Your glory, that, being present with me, she may work, and I may learn what pleases You well. **11.** For she knows all things and understands, and she will guide me prudently (wisely, with caution) in my actions. She will guard me in her glory. **12.** So my works will be acceptable (pleasing). I will judge Your people righteously, and I will be worthy of my father's throne. **13.** For what man will know the counsel (advice, plan) of God? Or who will conceive (understand, grasp) what the Lord wills? **14.** For the thoughts of mortals are unstable (unpredictable, changeable), and our plans are prone to fail. **15.** For a corruptible (temporary, decaying) body weighs down the soul. The earthly tent (body) burdens a mind that is full of cares. **16.** We can hardly guess (understand, predict) the things that are on earth, and we find the things that are close at hand with labor (effort); but who has traced out the things that are in the heavens? **17.** Who gained knowledge of Your counsel, unless You gave wisdom, and sent Your holy spirit from on high? **18.** It was thus that the ways of those who are on earth were corrected, and men were taught the things that are pleasing to You. They were saved through wisdom."

Chapter 10

1. Wisdom guarded to the end the first-formed father of the world, who was created alone, and delivered him from his own sin (transgression). **2.** And she gave him strength to rule over all things. **3.** But when an unrighteous (immoral) man turned away from her in his anger, he destroyed himself with the rage in which he killed his brother. **4.** When, because of his actions, the earth was flooded, wisdom again saved it, guiding the righteous man's path by a simple piece of wood. **5.** Moreover, when nations joined together in wickedness and were confused, wisdom knew the righteous man, and kept him blameless before God, and gave him strength when his heart yearned for his child. **6.** While the ungodly (wicked) were perishing, wisdom saved a righteous man, when he fled from the fire that came down from heaven on the five cities. **7.** The wickedness of these cities is still witnessed by their smoking ruins, and plants that bear fruit but never ripen, and a memorial of their disbelief: a pillar of salt. **8.** For having ignored wisdom, not only were they unable to recognize what is good, but they also left behind a monument of their folly, so that where they stumbled, they might fail to even be remembered. **9.** But wisdom delivered those who waited for her from troubles. **10.** When a righteous man was a fugitive from his brother's wrath, wisdom guided him on straight paths. She showed him the kingdom of God, and gave him knowledge of holy things. She prospered his work, and multiplied the fruits of his labor. **11.** When men dealt harshly with him in their greed, wisdom stood by him and made him rich. **12.** She guarded him from enemies, and kept him safe from those who lay in ambush. In his difficult struggle, she watched over him as a judge, so that he would know that godliness is more powerful than anything. **13.** When a righteous man was sold, wisdom did not abandon him, but delivered him from sin. She went down with him into the dungeon, **14.** And while in chains, she did not depart from him, until she brought him to a throne, and gave him authority over those who treated him like a tyrant. She also proved his accusers to be false, and gave him eternal glory. **15.** Wisdom delivered a holy people and a blameless (innocent) seed from a nation of oppressors. **16.** She entered the soul of a servant of the Lord, and helped him stand up to terrible kings with wonders and signs. **17.** She gave holy men a reward for their toil, and guided them along a marvelous path, becoming their shelter in the day, and a flame in the night. **18.** She led them through the Red Sea, and brought them through much water; **19.** But she drowned their enemies, casting them down into the deep. **20.** Therefore, the righteous plundered the ungodly, and sang praise to Your holy name, O Lord, and together they glorified Your hand that fought for them. **21.** Because wisdom opened the mouth of the mute, and made the tongues of babes speak clearly."

Chapter 11

1. Wisdom prospered their works through the hand of a holy prophet. 2. They journeyed through a desert with no inhabitants (people living in a place), and set up their tents in desolate (barren), uncharted (unexplored) places. 3. They faced enemies and pushed them back. 4. They became thirsty and cried out to You, and You gave them water from the hard rock, and healed their thirst from the solid (firm) stone. 5. For what caused their enemies to be punished, that same thing benefited them in their need. 6. When their enemies were troubled with blood instead of the river's flowing water, 7. You gave Your people water beyond all hope, and showed through their thirst how You punished the adversaries (enemies). 8. For when they suffered, though in mercy, they learned how the ungodly (immoral or wicked) were tormented by Your wrath (extreme anger). 9. You tested them like a father teaching his children; but You judged the wicked like a stern (severe) king condemning (declaring guilty) them. 10. Whether they were near or far, both groups were equally distressed; 11. For a double grief seized them, and they groaned (made a sound of pain or distress) at the memory of the past. 12. When they heard that the righteous were helped by their own suffering, they came to recognize the Lord. 13. For those who had long been rejected and mocked were no longer ridiculed. In the end, they marveled (were amazed), having thirsted in a way different from the righteous. 14. But for their senseless idol worship, where they were led astray to worship irrational (unreasonable, illogical) creatures, You sent a multitude (a large group) of irrational beasts (wild animals) to punish them. 15. So that they might learn that by the same things a man sins, he is punished. 16. Your all-powerful hand, which created the world from formless (without shape or structure) matter, did not lack the means to send upon them a multitude of fierce creatures, such as bears, lions, and new, unknown wild beasts, full of rage, 17. Breathing fire, or spewing smoke, or flashing dreadful sparks from their eyes; 18. These beasts had power to consume (destroy) them with their violence, and to terrify (cause fear) them with their sight. 19. Without these creatures, they might have fallen by a single breath, being pursued (chased) by Justice, and scattered by the power of Your breath (Justice: the fair treatment or judgment of people). 20. But You arranged all things by measure (quantity), number (count), and weight (heaviness). 21. For Your strength is limitless, at all times. Who could stand against Your mighty arm? 22. The whole world before You is like a grain in a scale, and like a drop of dew (tiny drops of water formed on cool surfaces during the night) that falls on the earth in the morning. 23. Yet You have mercy (kindness and forgiveness) on all people, because You have the power to do all things, and You overlook (ignore or forgive) the sins of men so that they may repent (feel sorry for wrongs done). 24. For You love all things that exist (are alive or present), and hate none of the things You have made; for You would never have created anything if You hated it. 25. How could anything have survived unless You had willed it? Or how could something that was not called by You have been preserved? 26. But You spare (save) all things because they are Yours, O Sovereign (supreme ruler) Lord, You who love life.

Chapter 12

1. For Your incorruptible spirit is in all things. 2. Therefore, You gradually convict those who stray from the right path, and by reminding them of their sins, You admonish (warn or advise) them, so that they may escape their wickedness and come to believe in You, O Lord. 3. For truly, the ancient inhabitants of Your holy land, 4. Hating them for practicing detestable (extremely disliked) works of magic and ungodly (immoral or sinful) rituals, 5. such as merciless (without compassion) killings of children, and sacrificial feasts involving human flesh and blood, forming alliances in a lawless fellowship, and killing their own helpless infants, it was Your will to destroy them by the hands of our ancestors; 7. That the land, which is most precious in Your sight, might receive a worthy people, servants of God. 8. Nevertheless, You even spared these as men, and You sent hornets (large aggressive insects) as forerunners (precursors or messengers) of Your army, to cause them to perish little by little. 9. Not that You were unable to subdue the wicked under the hand of the righteous in battle, or by terrible beasts or with a stern word to destroy them all at once, 10. but by judging them gradually, You gave them a chance to repent, knowing that their nature was evil from birth, their wickedness inborn, and that their thoughts would never change. 11. For they were a cursed generation from the beginning. It wasn't out of fear that You left them unpunished for their sins. 12. For who will ask, "What have You done?" Or "Who can resist Your judgment?" Who will accuse You for the destruction of nations that You caused? Or who will stand as an avenger for the unrighteous? 13. For there is no God besides You who cares for all, so that You may demonstrate that You do not judge unfairly. 14. No king or ruler will be able to oppose You regarding those You have punished. 15. But in Your righteousness, You rule over all, deeming it foreign (alien, unrelated) to Your power to condemn one who does not deserve punishment. 16. For Your strength is the source of righteousness, and Your sovereignty over all allows You to forbear (be patient and tolerant) with all things. 17. When people fail to believe that You are perfect in power, You demonstrate Your strength, and in dealing with those who are bold enough to think otherwise, You confound (bewilder) their arrogance (excessive pride). 18. But You, being sovereign in strength, judge with gentleness, and with great forbearance You govern us; for the power is Yours whenever You wish to use it. 19. Yet You taught Your people through these actions, how the righteous must be kind. You gave Your children hope, because You offer repentance when people sin. 20. For if You took vengeance on those who were enemies of Your servants and deserving of death, with such great deliberation (careful consideration) and tolerance (patience), giving them times and opportunities to escape their wickedness, 21. how much more carefully did You judge Your own children, to whom You gave oaths and covenants with promises of good things! 22. Therefore, while You chastise us, You punish our enemies ten thousand times more, so that we may reflect on Your goodness when we judge, and when we are judged, we may seek mercy. 23. Therefore, the unrighteous who lived in foolishness, You tormented through their own abominations (things that are hated or morally repugnant). 24. For they truly went astray in many ways, choosing to worship irrational (lacking reason, foolish) animals, that even among their enemies were dishonored, deceived like ignorant children. 25. Therefore, You sent Your judgment to mock them, like a punishment for their folly. 26. But those who would not be corrected by gentle (kind and mild) instruction will experience the deserved judgment of God. 27. For through the sufferings they despised (hated or scorned), being punished in these creatures they thought were gods, they saw and recognized the true God, whom they had previously rejected. Therefore, the result of extreme condemnation came upon them.

Chapter 13

1. Truly, all people who fail to recognize God are naturally foolish, and they do not gain the ability to know the One who exists through the good things they see. They do not recognize the Creator (the one who made all things) through His creations. 2. Instead, they believed that either fire, wind, swift air, the stars in their courses, or the raging waters, or the lights of the heavens were the gods who govern the world. 3. If their reason for this belief was admiration for their beauty, they should realize that their Sovereign Lord (supreme ruler) is far greater than these, for the very Creator of beauty made them. 4. If it was their awe (deep admiration) of their power and influence, they should recognize how much more powerful He who created them is. 5. From the grandeur (greatness) of the beauty in created things, humankind forms an understanding of their Maker. 6. Still, even these people have little blame, for perhaps they went astray (deviated from the right path) while earnestly seeking God, desiring to find Him. 7. They diligently (carefully and with persistence) search while living among His works, and they trust their eyes, admiring the beauty around them. 8. But they cannot be excused entirely. 9. If they were capable of knowing so much, able to explore the world, how is it that they didn't discover the Sovereign Lord sooner? 10. They were wretched (miserable), placing their hopes in dead things, calling them gods—objects of human craftsmanship, gold, silver, finely crafted, or likenesses of animals, or even useless stones, shaped by ancient hands. 11. Yes, some craftsman (a skilled worker) might chop down a tree that is easily moved, carefully strip off its bark, and shape it into a pleasing form, making a useful vessel (container) for his needs. 12. Using the scraps of his work to cook his meals, he fills his stomach. 13. Taking a useless scrap of wood, twisted and full of knots, he carves it with painstaking (diligent and careful) effort, shaping it with the skill of his idle hands. He fashions it into the likeness (image) of a man, 14. or makes it resemble some worthless animal, painting it red, and covering every blemish (flaw) with paint. 15. Once he has made a proper place for it, he sets it in a wall, securing (making stable) it with nails or iron. 16. He plans to make sure it does not fall, knowing full well that it cannot help itself (for it is only an image and needs assistance). 17. When he prays for wealth, for a good marriage, or for children, he has no shame speaking to something that is lifeless (without life). 18. For health, he calls upon something weak, for life, he prays to something dead, for help, he turns to something with no knowledge, and for a safe journey, he asks of something that cannot even move. 19. For success in his work and a prosperous business, he asks for help from something that has no hands and no ability.

Chapter 14

1. One who is about to set sail across turbulent (rough) waters, calls upon a fragile piece of wood, even weaker than the ship that bears him. 2. For the desire to profit led to its design, and wisdom was the skillful builder. 3. Your care, O Father, guides the vessel over the waters, for even in the sea, you provide a path and a stable course through the waves, 4. Showing that you can save from any danger, so that even an inexperienced person may

venture into the sea. **5.** You desire that the works of your wisdom not be without purpose. So, people entrust their lives to a small piece of wood, passing through rough waters on a raft, arriving safely at the shore. **6.** For in ancient times, when proud giants perished, the hope of humanity, finding refuge on a raft, was guided by your hand, preserving the future generations of mankind. **7.** Blessed (favored) is the wood through which comes righteousness (moral uprightness), **8.** but cursed (condemned) is the idol made by human hands, and cursed is he who created it, for he made it, and then called this corruptible (perishable) object a god. **9.** Both the wicked person and his wickedness are equally despised by God; **10.** indeed, the wrongdoer will face judgment along with his sinful actions. **11.** Therefore, idols will be judged among the nations, for though they were created from materials God made, they were turned into objects of evil, stumbling blocks (obstacles) for people's souls, and traps for the unwise. **12.** The invention of idols marked the start of immoral practices, and their creation began the corruption (moral decay) of life. **13.** For idols didn't exist from the start, nor will they exist forever. **14.** By human arrogance, they entered the world, and so, a swift end has been determined for them. **15.** A grieving father, overwhelmed by sorrow at losing his young child, created an image of his deceased son, **16.** then began to honor him as a god, and introduced rituals and ceremonies to others. **17.** In time, this improper custom grew stronger and became law, and carved images received worship by royal command. **18.** When people couldn't honor them in person due to distance, **19.** they created a visible image of the king they revered, hoping to pay tribute to him as though he were present. **20.** Worship intensified further, even among those who didn't know him, driven by the artist's ambition (desire for recognition); **21.** for the artist, wishing to please his ruler, used his skill to make the likeness even more beautiful. **22.** Thus, the masses, captivated by the grace of his artwork, began to regard as sacred one who had once been only human. **23.** And this became a trap, as people, bound by hardship or oppression, **24.** bestowed the sacred Name on stones and wood that shouldn't be worshipped. **25.** Then they strayed even further from the knowledge of God, and while lost in ignorance, they called many evils "peace." **26.** For they would either sacrifice children in solemn (sacred) ceremonies, perform hidden rituals, or hold wild celebrations of strange customs. **27.** They no longer respected life or marital purity, and one would bring death to another through treachery (betrayal), or anguish through adultery (unfaithfulness). **28.** Everywhere was filled with bloodshed, murder, theft, lies, corruption, lack of faith, chaos, broken oaths, **29.** confusion over what is good, forgotten favors, ingratitude for kindness, defilement (pollution) of souls, confusion in relationships, disorder in marriage, adultery, and excess (lack of restraint). **30.** For the worship of idols that should not be named is the origin, cause, and result of all evil. **31.** Their worshippers either become frenzied, lie about prophecy, live immorally, or make false oaths without concern. **32.** Trusting in lifeless idols, they make wicked oaths, thinking they won't be harmed. **33.** But on both counts, they will face righteous judgment because they dishonored God by following idols and lied under oath, showing contempt for holiness. **34.** For it is not the power of the things they swear by, but the penalty for their sins that always brings consequences upon those who act unjustly.

Chapter 15

1. But You, our God, are kind and true, patient, and in Your mercy, You guide everything with care. **2.** Even if we fall into sin, we still belong to You, for we know that You are the ruler (one who has control or authority) over all things. Yet, we will not sin, because we are aware that we are Your people. **3.** To know You is the essence of true righteousness (moral correctness or justice), and to understand Your rule (sovereign control or authority) is the foundation of eternal life. **4.** We were not led astray by the evil schemes of men, nor by the empty efforts of artists, creating images painted in various colors. **5.** These painted forms lead the foolish into desire (a strong longing or craving), for they are drawn to lifeless statues, yearning for things that are not truly alive. **6.** Those who make, desire, and worship such things are lovers of wickedness (evil or immoral behavior), and they deserve such misguided hopes. **7.** Just as a potter (someone who shapes clay into vessels) carefully shapes soft clay, making different vessels for both clean and unclean purposes, so too, each creation is molded for specific use, and the potter is the one who decides its purpose. **8.** But if the potter works with the wrong intentions, he can shape a false god (a fake god) from the same clay, a god that, though once made from earth, will soon return to the earth, when the soul (spiritual essence or life force) which was briefly given to him, departs. **9.** Still, the idol-maker is anxious (worried, uneasy), not because his strength will fail, or his life is short, but because he compares himself to goldsmiths (craftsmen who work with gold) and silversmiths (craftsmen who work with silver), and sees it as an achievement to create counterfeit gods (fake or fraudulent gods). **10.** His

heart is like ashes (symbolizing emptiness or insignificance), his hope is less valuable than dirt, and his life has fewer honors than clay. **11.** This is because he is unaware of the One who formed him, and who gave him the breath of life, the One who imparted to him a soul (spiritual essence or life force) and a spirit (the vital, animating force within a person). **12.** Yet, this person treats life as a game (something trivial or unimportant), and views his time on earth as a mere festival (an event or occasion for enjoyment) for profit, thinking that one must gain wealth by any means, even though evil deeds (immoral or wicked actions). **13.** This person, more than anyone else, is aware that he is sinning, creating fragile (easily broken) vessels and lifeless images from earthly materials. **14.** But even more foolish (lacking wisdom or good sense) and miserable (wretched, unhappy) than a child are those who oppress Your people, who have made idols their gods. **15.** These idols are incapable of seeing (having sight), or hearing (having the ability to hear), or breathing (having life or breath), or touching (having the ability to feel or handle). They have no life or power of their own. **16.** These idols were made by human hands, formed by men who, like themselves, are mortal (subject to death, not eternal) and dependent on God. No one has the power to shape a god that is truly like themselves. **17.** Though the idol-maker is mortal, he shapes a dead (lifeless, not living) object, and in doing so, he creates something inferior to himself, since he is alive, but the idols never were. **18.** Worse still, the people worship creatures that are utterly senseless (lacking reason or understanding), which are even more despicable (worthy of contempt, morally repugnant) than all other beings. **19.** These idols, when compared to other creatures, are not beautiful (aesthetically pleasing or attractive) or worthy of admiration. They have missed both God's praise and His blessing.

Chapter 16

1. For this reason, they were justly punished through creatures like those they worshiped, and tormented by a swarm of vermin (insects or pests). **2.** Instead of such a punishment, you provided benefits to your people, preparing quails (a type of bird) as food, a delicacy to satisfy their desires for tasty nourishment. **3.** This was so that your enemies, who were craving food, would loathe even the basic need for sustenance because of the loathsome (disgusting) creatures sent among them, while your people, who had briefly endured hunger, could enjoy delicacies. **4.** It was necessary for those oppressors to face inevitable deprivation, but your people were only shown the suffering of their enemies. **5.** Even when fierce, wild beasts attacked your people and they were perishing from the bites of venomous serpents (snakes), your anger did not last to the fullest extent. **6.** But, for the purpose of instruction, they suffered briefly, with a reminder of salvation to make them remember the commandments of your law. **7.** For whoever turned to it was not saved because of the object they saw, but because of you, the Savior of all. **8.** Yes, through this, you convinced our enemies that you are the one who rescues from all evil. **9.** The stings of locusts (a type of insect) and flies truly killed them. No remedy (cure) for their lives was found, because they deserved to be punished by such things. **10.** But your children were not harmed by the venomous fangs of dragons, for your mercy passed over them and healed them. **11.** They were bitten as a reminder of your messages, and were quickly saved, so they would not fall into complete forgetfulness and fail to respond to your kindness. **12.** Truly, it was neither herbs nor medicines that healed them, but your word, O Lord, which heals all people. **13.** For you have power over life and death; you lead to the gates of the grave (Hades) and bring back again. **14.** Yet, even when a person kills by their wickedness, they cannot retrieve the soul that has departed, nor free the imprisoned spirit. **15.** But it is impossible to escape your hand. **16.** For the ungodly, who refuse to know you, were punished by the strength of your arm, pursued by strange rains, hail, and relentless storms, and utterly consumed by fire. **17.** What was most remarkable was that in the water, which quenches (puts out) all things, the fire burned more intensely. **18.** For the world fights for the righteous. **19.** At one point, the fire was held back so it wouldn't consume the creatures sent to punish the ungodly, but so that they could see that they were being pursued by God's judgment. **20.** At another time, even in the midst of water, it burned more fiercely than fire to destroy the crops of an unrighteous land. **21.** Instead of these punishments, you provided your people with heavenly food, angels' food, and ready-to-eat bread from heaven without toil, which possessed the flavor of every pleasant taste, agreeable to every palate (taste). **22.** For your nature showed kindness to your children, and that bread, which served the desire of the eater, transformed itself according to each person's taste. **23.** Snow and ice endured the fire without melting, so people might know that the fire was destroying the fruits of the enemies, burning in hail and flashing in storms. **24.** Yet this fire, in order to nourish the righteous, forgot its own power and didn't harm them. **25.** The creation, serving you, its Maker, used its strength to punish the unrighteous, yet softened its power on behalf of those who trust in you. **26.** Therefore, at that time, it transformed into all forms to serve your abundant care, according to the needs of those who required it. **27.** Your children, whom you love, O Lord, might learn that it is not the growth of crops that sustains a man, but your word that preserves those who trust in you. **28.** For that which was not destroyed by fire melted when it was gently warmed by the sun, so people would know they must rise before the sun to give you thanks and pray to you at the dawning of the day. **29.** For the hope of the ungrateful will dissolve like the frost of winter and flow away like water that has no use.

Chapter 17

1. Your judgments (decisions and punishments) are powerful and hard to interpret (understand clearly); therefore, undisciplined (lacking self-control) souls went astray (wandered from the right path). **2.** For when lawless (immoral, without rules) men thought they had control over a holy nation, they, prisoners of darkness, and bound in the fetters (chains) of a long night, stayed hidden beneath their roofs, cut off from eternal providence (God's protective care). **3.** For while they thought they were unseen in their secret sins, they were divided from one another by a dark curtain of forgetfulness, struck with terrible awe (a feeling of fear mixed with wonder), and deeply troubled by apparitions (ghostly images). **4.** The dark recesses (hidden spaces) that surrounded them did not guard them from fear, but terrifying sounds echoed around them, and dismal (gloomy, dark) phantoms (ghostly figures) appeared with unsmiling faces. **5.** No power of fire could bring light, and even the brightest flames of the stars were not strong enough to illuminate (light up) that dark night; **6.** but only a glimmering (dim, faint light) of a self-kindled (self-created) fire appeared to them, full of fear. In terror, they thought what they saw was worse than the sight itself, which they could not bear to look at. **7.** The mockeries (false displays) of their magic arts (sorcery or spellcraft) were now powerless, and they were ashamed by the failure of their so-called understanding (wisdom). **8.** Those who promised to drive away fears and cure troubled souls were themselves sick with a ludicrous (ridiculous) fearfulness. **9.** Even if nothing frightening was there, they were still scared by the creeping of vermin (small animals considered pests) and the hissing of serpents (snakes). **10.** Trembling in fear, they perished (suffered and died), refusing to look at the air around them, which they could not escape from on any side. **11.** For wickedness (evil behavior), condemned (judged) by a witness within, is cowardly (lacking courage), and pressed by conscience (inner sense of right and wrong), always expects the worst outcome. 12. Fear is nothing but a surrender (giving up) of the help that reason (clear thinking) offers; **13.** and inside, the expectation (anticipation) of suffering makes one prefer ignorance (not knowing) of the cause that brings the torment (pain and distress). **14.** But they, all through the night, which was indeed powerless (without strength), and which came upon them from the depths of powerless Hades (the underworld or realm of the dead), slept the same fearful sleep. **15.** They were haunted (troubled by) monstrous (frightening) apparitions, and their souls were paralyzed (frozen) by surrendering to fear; sudden and unexpected terror fell upon them. **16.** So, whoever they were, sinking down where they were, were held captive (trapped), shut up in a prison that wasn't locked with iron bars; **17.** whether they were farmers, shepherds, or laborers (workers) in the wilderness, they were overtaken and endured (suffered through) that inescapable (unavoidable) sentence, for they were all bound by one chain of darkness. **18.** Whether there was a whistling wind, the melodious (musical) sound of birds among branches, the constant rush of water running violently, **19.** a harsh crashing of rocks falling, the swift, unseen movement of animals bounding (jumping) along, the roar of wild animals, or echoes rebounding (echoing) from the hollows (caves or depressions) of the mountains, **20.** all these things paralyzed them with terror. **21.** For the whole world was illuminated with clear light, and was occupied with unhindered (unblocked, free) works, **22.** while over them alone was spread a heavy night, an image of the darkness that would later take hold of them; they felt even heavier than the darkness itself.

Chapter 18

1. But for your holy ones, there was great light. **2.** Their enemies, who heard their voices but did not see their forms, thought it fortunate that they too had suffered. **3.** Yet, even though they had wronged them before, they did not harm them in return. Instead, they were grateful, and because of their past conflict, they begged for forgiveness. **4.** So, you provided a burning pillar of fire to guide your people on their unknown journey, and a gentle sun to accompany them during their glorious exile. **5.** The Egyptians, who had once imprisoned your children, deserved to be deprived of light and trapped in darkness, for through your children, the incorruptible light of the law was meant to be given to humanity. **6.** After they had decided to kill the infants of the holy ones, and when one child was abandoned but saved, proving their sin, you took away their many children and destroyed their entire army in a powerful flood. **7.** Our ancestors were warned about that night in advance, so that, with certain knowledge, they could be encouraged by the promises they had trusted in. **8.** Salvation for the righteous and punishment for the enemies was expected by your people. **9.** Just as you took vengeance on the adversaries, calling us to you, you also honored us. **10.** For the holy children of good men offered secret sacrifices, and all together they agreed to follow the covenant of the divine law, deciding to share in both the good and the dangers, with the fathers already leading songs of praise. **11.** But the conflicting cries of the enemies echoed back, and a sad wail for lost children spread across the land. **12.** Both servants and masters suffered the same punishment, with the common people and kings experiencing the same fate; Indeed, all of them, under one form of death, had bodies without number. **13.** For the living were not enough even to bury them, since in a single blow, their most cherished offspring were destroyed. **14.** While they had doubted all things because of magic, after the death of the firstborn, they admitted that the people were God's children. **15.** For while peaceful silence wrapped the world, and night was already halfway through, your powerful word leapt from heaven, from your royal throne, a fierce warrior, into the midst of the doomed land, carrying your command like a sharp sword, and it filled everything with death. **16.** While it touched the heavens, it also stood firmly on the earth. **17.** Immediately, terrifying visions in dreams troubled them, and sudden fears overwhelmed them. **18.** Each person, one here barely alive, another there, revealed why they were dying. **19.** The dreams, which disturbed them, warned them, so that they would not perish without knowing the cause of their affliction. **20.** Death also touched the righteous, and many were destroyed in the wilderness, but the anger did not last long. **21.** For a blameless man rushed to be their advocate, bringing the power of his own ministry—prayer and the atoning sacrifice of incense. **22.** He stood against the wrath and ended the calamity, showing that he was your servant. **23.** He overcame the anger, not through physical strength, nor by force of arms, but by his words, he subdued the avenger by reminding you of the oaths and promises made to the ancestors. **24.** When the dead had already fallen in heaps, one upon another, he intervened and stopped the wrath, cutting off its path to the living. **25.** For the whole world was symbolized on his long robe, and the glories of the fathers were engraved in four rows of precious stones, and your majesty was on the crown of his head.

Chapter 19

1. Indignation (anger) without mercy came upon the ungodly to the end, for God knew their future. **2.** After changing their minds and letting your people go, they would soon pursue them. **3.** While still mourning at the graves of the dead, they foolishly decided to chase the people they had driven out. **4.** The doom they deserved led them to forget what had happened, filling up the punishment still owed for their wrongs. **5.** Your people journeyed on a marvelous path, while their enemies met a strange death. **6.** All of creation was renewed, following your commandments, to keep your servants safe. **7.** The cloud overshadowed the camp, and dry land rose out of the Red Sea, making a highway through the waters. **8.** They passed over this land, covered by your hand, and witnessed strange wonders. **9.** They roamed like horses and skipped like lambs, praising you, O Lord, their deliverer. **10.** They remembered their past journey, how the land had brought lice instead of cattle, and frogs instead of fish. **11.** Later, when they desired luxuries, quails came from the sea to comfort them. **12.** Punishments came upon the sinners, as foretold by thunder and signs. **13.** They suffered for their wickedness, particularly for their mistreatment of guests. **14.** While others did not welcome strangers, the Egyptians enslaved those who had helped them. **15.** Punishment was inevitable for those who treated strangers as enemies. **16.** These Egyptians had once welcomed guests with feasts, only to later afflict them with harsh labor. **17.** They were struck with darkness, looking for an exit that was not there. **18.** Just as the rhythm of a lute changes, so too did the elements shift in their order, continuing in harmony. **19.** Creatures of land became creatures of water, and sea creatures moved on land. **20.** Fire maintained its power over water, and water lost its ability to quench. **21.** Flames did not consume flesh or melt the sacred food, which easily melted in normal conditions. **22.** In all things, O Lord, you magnified and glorified your people, standing by them at all times.

28 – Ecclesiastes

Chapter 1

1. These are the words of the teacher (a wise leader), the son of David, who was king in Jerusalem. **2.** "Everything is futile (pointless)," says the Teacher; "All is futile." **3.** What benefit does a person gain from all their labor (hard work) under the sun (on earth)? **4.** One generation fades away, and another arises, but the earth stays the same forever. **5.** The sun rises, sets, and then returns to the place where it started. **6.** The wind blows south, and then turns north; it swirls around, completing its cycle (a repeated pattern). **7.** All the rivers flow into the sea, yet the sea is never full; the rivers go back to where they began. **8.** All things are filled with effort (work); it's impossible to fully explain. The eye never tires of seeing, nor the ear of hearing. **9.** What has happened before will happen again; what has been done will be repeated. There's nothing new under the sun. **10.** Is there anything that can be called, "Look, this is new"? It has already existed in times long past. **11.** No one recalls (remembers) the past, and future events will be forgotten by those who come after. **12.** I, the Teacher, was the king of Israel in Jerusalem. **13.** I set my mind to understand everything done under the heavens (the sky); it is a heavy task God has given to humankind. **14.** I've observed everything done under the sun, and I can tell you, all is futile, like chasing the wind (an impossible pursuit). **15.** What is crooked (bent) can't be made straight, and what is lacking (missing) can't be counted. **16.** I said to myself, "Look, I have gained wisdom (knowledge), greater than anyone before me in Jerusalem. My heart has grasped much knowledge and understanding." **17.** So I sought to understand wisdom, madness, and folly (foolishness), and I realized that this too is like chasing the wind. **18.** With much wisdom comes much sorrow, and those who increase in knowledge only add to their grief (sadness).

Chapter 2

1. I said to myself, "Come, I will test myself with joy (pleasure); therefore, I will indulge in it," but I realized this too was meaningless (vanity). **2.** I called laughter, "Madness (foolishness)!" and questioned, "What does joy really accomplish?" **3.** I searched my heart to discover how to satisfy my desires with wine, while keeping my heart guided by wisdom (insight), and exploring foolishness (folly), to find out what is truly good for people to do during their time on earth. **4.** I created great works, building houses for myself and planting vineyards. **5.** I made gardens and orchards (fruit groves), planting all sorts of fruit trees. **6.** I built pools of water to irrigate (water) the trees in my gardens. **7.** I acquired male and female servants, and had servants born in my house. I had more herds and flocks (groups of animals) than anyone before me in Jerusalem. **8.** I gathered silver, gold, and valuable treasures (special possessions) from kings and provinces. I acquired male and female singers, the delights of mankind, and all kinds of musical instruments. **9.** So I became great, surpassing all who came before me in Jerusalem, and my wisdom (knowledge) remained with me. **10.** Whatever my eyes desired, I did not withhold from them. I did not hold back (deny) any pleasure, for my heart rejoiced in all my work, and this was my reward for all my efforts. **11.** Then I looked at all the work my hands had done, and all the labor (effort) I had put into it. And indeed, it was all vanity, like chasing the wind (an impossible pursuit). There was no lasting gain under the sun. **12.** I turned my attention to wisdom, madness, and folly (foolishness), asking what the one who comes after the king could do—only what has already been done. **13.** I saw that wisdom (knowledge) is far better than foolishness, just as light is superior to darkness. **14.** The wise person has clear sight, while the fool stumbles in the dark. But I realized that the same fate happens to both. **15.** So I said to myself, "What happens to the fool will also happen to me. What, then, is the advantage of being wise?" I concluded, "This too is vanity." **16.** for there is no lasting remembrance (memory) of the wise more than of the fool, since everything will be forgotten in time. And how does the wise person die? Just like the fool! **17.** I began to despise life, because the work done under the sun distressed (troubled) me; it is all vanity and chasing after the wind (meaningless). **18.** I hated all my labor under the sun, because I would have to leave it to the one who comes after me. **19.** And who knows whether that person will be wise or foolish? Yet they will rule over everything I worked for, and all the wisdom I displayed. This too is vanity. **20.** So I turned my heart toward despair (loss of hope) over all the work I had done under the sun. **21.** There is someone who works with wisdom, knowledge, and skill, but must leave his inheritance (wealth or property) to someone who didn't earn it. This is also vanity and a great evil. **22.** What does a person truly gain from all his labor (work), and the striving (toil) of his heart, with which he works under the sun? **23.** All his days are filled with sorrow (sadness), and his work is burdensome (hard). Even at night, his heart finds no rest. This too is vanity. **24.** There's nothing better for a person than to eat, drink, and enjoy satisfaction (pleasure) in their work. This, too, I saw is a gift from God. **25.** For who can enjoy life (pleasure) more than I have? **26.** For God gives wisdom, knowledge, and joy to the person who pleases Him, but to the sinner, He gives the task of collecting wealth, which is eventually given to the one who pleases God. This too is vanity and chasing after the wind.

Chapter 3

1. Everything in life has its time, and every purpose is meant to unfold in its own season under heaven. **2.** There is a time to be born and a time to die, a season for planting, and another for reaping the harvest (the process of gathering crops or results). **3.** There are moments for destruction, and others for healing; times to tear things down, and times to build (to construct) up. **4.** Sometimes, we grieve and mourn, but other times we laugh and rejoice; there are seasons for sorrow (a deep feeling of sadness) and seasons to dance with joy. **5.** There are times when one should throw away stones, and times when they must gather them; moments to embrace (to hold or accept) others and moments when we must hold back. **6.** A person will experience both gain and loss, learning when to keep and when to discard (to throw away or get rid of). **7.** There are seasons for tearing things apart, and others for stitching them together; moments of silence (absence of sound), and times to speak. **8.** There are moments for love and moments for hate, times for war and times for peace—each in its proper time (a specific moment). **9.** What does a worker gain from all their labor under the sun (used metaphorically for daily life or existence)? **10.** I have observed the task that God has assigned to humanity—to engage in the work of life (existence and all its experiences). **11.** God has made everything beautiful in its time. He has placed eternity (timelessness) in the hearts of men, yet no one can fully understand what God does from beginning to end. **12.** I have learned that the best thing for people is to rejoice and to do good with their lives (the course of one's existence). **13.** Every person should enjoy their food and drink, and find satisfaction (fulfillment or contentment) in the rewards of their labor—this is a gift from God. **14.** I know that whatever God does is eternal. Nothing can be added to it, and nothing can be taken from it. God does it all so that people may revere (to deeply respect or admire) Him. **15.** What is, has already been; what will be has already been. God seeks an explanation (justification) for what has passed. **16.** I observed that in places where judgment should prevail, wickedness (evil) is present, and where righteousness should reign, injustice abounds. **17.** I thought to myself, "God will judge both the righteous and the wicked, for every purpose (reason) and work has its time." **18.** I said to myself, "God tests (examines) humanity, that they may see they are no different from animals." **19.** What happens to people happens to animals; both face the same fate: as one dies, so does the other. They all breathe the same air, and humanity has no advantage (a favorable condition) over animals—everything is futile. **20.** All return to one place: all come from dust, and to dust they return (go back to). **21.** Who knows the spirit of a person, which ascends upward, or the spirit of an animal, which descends to the earth? **22.** So I concluded that the best thing for a person is to find joy in their work, for this is their portion (a part or share). But who can show them what will come after them?

Chapter 4

1. I looked again and saw the oppression (unjust treatment) happening all over. The oppressed were crying, but no one was there to comfort them. Meanwhile, their oppressors held power, but they too had no comforter. **2.** I found it better to praise those who are already dead, for they have found rest, more than those who still alive who suffer under the sun. **3.** And in fact, it is far better for someone who has never lived, never witnessed the evil deeds under the sun. **4.** I noticed that no matter how much work or skill one puts in, a person is envied (desired or resented) by their neighbor. This, too, is pointless, like chasing after wind. **5.** The foolish person (a silly person) does nothing but fold his hands, and in doing so, he destroys himself. **6.** It is far better to have a little and live in peace than to work endlessly for more, only to grasp at wind and live in constant trouble. **7.** Once again, I noticed something that makes no sense under the sun: **8.** A person who lives alone, with neither companion (a friend), son, nor brother, and yet works tirelessly without ever being satisfied with his riches. He never stops to ask, "Who am I working for, and why do I deny myself enjoyment?" This, too, is vanity, a terrible misfortune. **9.** Two are far better than one because they get a good return (benefit) for their hard work. **10.** If one falls, the other can lift him up. But woe to the one who falls and has no one to help him rise. **11.** If two sleep together, they stay warm. But how can one be warm on his own? **12.** While one might be overpowered (defeated) by another, two are stronger and can resist. A cord made of three strands is not easily broken. **13.** It's better to be a poor and wise (intelligent) youth than to be an old and foolish (unwise) king who refuses correction. **14.** The youth, though once imprisoned (a place of captivity), rises to become a king, even though he was born poor in his kingdom. **15.** I saw all who lived under the sun, and they were with the second youth, taking his place. **16.** The crowds followed him endlessly, but those who came after would not find joy (celebrate) in him. Surely, this, too, is vanity, like chasing after wind.

Chapter 5

1. Walk carefully when you go to the house of God. It is better to listen than to offer the sacrifice of fools (unwise people), who don't realize they are doing wrong. **2.** Do not be quick to speak, and do not let your heart rush to utter (speak) anything before God. Remember, God is in heaven and you are on earth, so let your words be few. **3.** Dreams come from much effort, and a fool's words are obvious through his many speeches (talks). **4.** When you make a vow (promise) to God, do not delay in fulfilling it, for He takes no pleasure in fools. Pay what you have promised. **5.** It is better not to make a vow than to make one and not fulfill it. **6.** Do not let your mouth cause you to sin (wrongdoing), and do not try to excuse (justify) yourself before the messenger of God. Why should God be angry at your excuses and ruin the work of your hands? **7.** In the abundance of dreams and words, there is also emptiness (nothingness). But fear God. **8.** If you witness the oppression (mistreatment) of the poor and the perversion (twisting) of justice and righteousness in a province (region), do not be surprised. After all, one official is watched over by another, and higher officials oversee them. **9.** Moreover, the profits (gains) of the land are for all; even the king is served by the fields. **10.** Those who love silver (money) will never be satisfied with it, and those who love wealth will never have enough. This too is meaningless. **11.** When wealth increases, those who consume (use) it also increase. What do the owners gain, except to look at it with their eyes? **12.** The sleep of a working man is sweet, whether he eats little or much, but the abundance (large amount) of the rich keeps him awake at night. **13.** Here is a serious problem I have seen under the sun: Wealth kept for its owner, to his harm (damage). **14.** Those riches may be lost in an unfortunate (bad) event. When the man has a son, he has nothing left to pass on. **15.** Just as he came into the world naked (without clothes), so he will leave, taking nothing from his labor (work) that he can carry away. **16.** This, too, is a serious problem—just as he came, so he leaves. What does a person gain from all their labor, if it is like chasing the wind (something unattainable)? **17.** All his days are spent in darkness, with much sorrow (sadness), sickness, and anger. **18.** Here's what I've observed: It is good for one to eat and drink and enjoy the good things of their labor (work), which they toil (work hard) for under the sun all their life, which God has given them. This is their heritage (inheritance). **19.** For those to whom God has given riches and wealth, and the power (ability) to enjoy them, to accept their lot (portion) and rejoice in their labor—this is the gift of God. **20** For such a person will not dwell (stay) too long on the days of their life, because God keeps them occupied (busy) with the joy in their heart.

Chapter 6

1. I have seen a troubling thing under the sun, which is common among people: **2.** A man to whom God has given wealth (riches), honor, and everything he desires, yet he lacks the ability to enjoy it. Instead, a foreigner (someone from another nation or family) takes it all. This is pointless, and a painful misfortune. **3.** If a man has a hundred children and lives many years, with his life filled with days, but his soul (inner being) is not content with good things or he has no proper burial, I say that a stillborn (a child born dead) is better than him— **4.** for the stillborn comes in vanity (meaningless) and leaves in darkness, with its name hidden and forgotten. **5.** Though it has never seen the sun or experienced anything, it finds more rest than that man. **6.** Even if a man lives for two thousand years but never experiences goodness, does he not all end up in the same place (death)? **7.** All a man's work is done to feed his mouth, but even so, his soul (inner self) is never satisfied. **8.** What advantage (benefit) does the wise man have over the fool? What does the poor man possess, who knows how to live wisely before others? **9.** It is better to enjoy what you see with your eyes than to chase after what you desire (want). This too is pointless, like chasing the wind. **10.** Whatever a man is, he has already been named (his nature is known); it is clear that he is human, and he cannot challenge (argue with) one who is more powerful than he. **11.** With so many things that increase vanity (emptiness), how is man any better? **12.** Who knows what is truly good for a person in life, for the fleeting (short) days of his life, which pass like a shadow (temporary)? Who can tell him what will happen after him under the sun?

Chapter 7

1. A good reputation is more precious than fine perfume (fragrant oil), and the day of one's death is more valuable than the day of birth. **2.** It is better to go to a house of mourning (a place of sorrow) than a house of feasting, because the end of all people is death, and the living should reflect on this truth. **3.** Sorrow is better than laughter, as a downcast (sad) face has the power to heal and improve the heart. **4.** The wise person's heart finds peace in a house of mourning, but the fool's heart remains in places of celebration and merriment. **5.** Listening to the rebuke of the wise is more beneficial than enjoying the empty, shallow songs of foolish people. **6.** Like the crackling of thorns (a harsh and distracting noise) under a pot, so is the laughter of a fool. This too is pointless (vain), like chasing after the wind. **7.** Surely, oppression can cloud the judgment (reasoning) of even a wise person, and bribery can corrupt the heart. **8.** The end of a matter is better than its beginning, and having a patient spirit is preferable to being proud or quick-tempered. **9.** Do not be quick to anger, for anger settles (rests) in the hearts of fools. **10.** Do not say, "Why were the former days better than these?" because you are not asking wisely (properly) when you complain about the past. **11.** Wisdom is good when accompanied by an inheritance, and it is profitable (beneficial) to those who live under the sun. **12.** Wisdom is a defense (protection) just like money, but the advantage of wisdom is that it gives life to its possessor. **13.** Consider the work of God, for no one can make straight what He has made crooked. **14.** In times of prosperity (success), be joyful, but in times of adversity (hardship), reflect: both prosperity and hardship are appointed by God, and man cannot know what will come after him. **15.** I have seen everything during my brief (fleeting) days: the righteous may perish despite their righteousness, and the wicked may live long in their wickedness. **16.** Do not be excessively righteous (too good), nor overly wise (too clever); why destroy yourself by trying to be perfect? **17.** Do not be excessively wicked (too sinful), nor foolish (stupid); why bring about your own premature death? **18.** It is good to grasp this, and also not to let go of the other; for those who fear God will avoid (stay away) both extremes. **19.** Wisdom is more powerful for the wise than the strength of ten mighty rulers in a city. **20.** There is no one on earth who is completely righteous, who always does good and never sins. **21.** Do not take everything people say too seriously, for you might overhear your own servant speaking ill of you. **22.** After all, your own heart knows that, many times, you have also spoken badly about others. **23.** I have tested all of this by wisdom. I decided to be wise, but it was far from me, and I could not fully grasp it. **24.** As for the deep and mysterious matters that are beyond human understanding, who can possibly comprehend them? **25.** I dedicated myself to understanding, to exploring wisdom and the reasoning behind things, to comprehending the depth of foolishness, and even the madness that comes with folly. **26.** I discovered that more bitter than death is a woman whose heart is a trap (snare) and whose hands are chains (fetters). The one who pleases God will escape her, but the sinner will be ensnared by her. **27.** "Here is what I found," says the Teacher: "As I added one thing to another in my quest for understanding, **28.** my soul kept searching but could not find what I sought. I found one upright man among a thousand, but I found no upright woman among all of them. **29.** This is what I have concluded: God created man upright, but they have sought out many schemes to go astray."

Chapter 8

1. Who is like the wise man, and who understands the meaning (interpretation) of things? A man's wisdom causes his face to shine, and his sternness (severity) is softened. **2.** I say, "Obey the king's command for the sake of your oath (promise) to God." **3.** Do not be quick to leave his presence. Do not stand in support of wrongdoing (evil), for the king does whatever pleases him. **4.** When the king speaks, his word carries power (authority). Who can challenge him by asking, "What are you doing?" **5.** The one who follows his command will not experience harm (damage), and a wise man's heart understands both the time and the decision (judgment) required. **6.** For every matter, there is a time and a judgment, but the troubles (misery) of man are multiplied. **7.** He does not know what will happen; who can tell him when it will occur? **8.** No one has control over the spirit (life) to retain it, and no one can stop the day of death. There is no escape from that battle (war), and wickedness (evil) will not save those given to it. **9.** I have observed all this, and I applied my heart to every action under the sun. I saw a time when one man rules over another to his own detriment (harm). **10.** Then I saw the wicked (unjust) buried, those who had gone in and out of the holy place (sacred area), and they were forgotten in the city where they had lived. This too is vanity (meaningless). **11.** Because the punishment for an evil (wicked) deed is not swiftly carried out, the hearts of the sons of men are fully set on doing evil. **12.** Though a sinner (wrongdoer) commits evil a hundred times, and his days are prolonged (lengthened), I know that it will be well with those who fear God, those who revere (respect) Him. **13.** But it will not go well with the wicked; their days are like a shadow (fleeting), and they do not fear God. **14.** There is emptiness (vanity) on earth: the righteous sometimes suffer as the wicked thrive, and the wicked sometimes fare (live) as if they were righteous. I said, "This too is vanity." **15.** So I commended the enjoyment (pleasure) of life, for a man has nothing better under the sun than to eat, drink, and enjoy himself. This will stay with him through all his hard work, all the days God gives him under the sun. **16.** When I set my heart to seek wisdom (knowledge) and understand the activities that take place on earth, I noticed that a man never sleeps (rests), whether day or night. **17.** I saw all the work of God, but a man cannot discover (understand) the work done under the sun. Even though a man labors (works) to find it, he will not uncover it. And even if a wise man seeks to understand it, he will not be able to comprehend it.

Chapter 9

1. I pondered deeply in my heart to declare that both the righteous and the wise, along with all their deeds, are held in God's hands. People cannot truly understand love or hatred based on what is before their eyes. 2. Everyone faces the same fate: the righteous and the wicked, the good and the evil, the clean and the unclean, those who make sacrifices and those who do not. The same end comes to the one who swears an oath and the one who fears an oath. 3. This is the troubling reality of life under the sun: one event happens to all. Indeed, the hearts of humanity are filled with evil, and madness (crazy behavior) rules them while they live; afterward, they die. 4. But there is hope for those who are alive—for a living dog (animal considered lowly) is better than a dead lion. 5. The living know that death is certain, but the dead know nothing. They no longer receive any reward, and their memory (the act of being remembered) is lost. 6. The emotions of love, hatred, and envy have vanished forever. They will never again participate in anything that happens under the sun. 7. Go ahead, enjoy your food (bread) with joy, and drink your wine with a merry heart, for God has already accepted your actions. 8. Let your clothing be always white, and let your head be adorned with oil (symbolizing joy and honor). 9. Enjoy life with the wife you love all the days of your brief (short-lived) life, which God has granted you under the sun. This is your portion (share or part) in life and in your work. 10. Whatever you do, do it with all your strength, for there is no work, device (plan or effort), knowledge, or wisdom in the grave where you will go. 11. I noticed under the sun that victory does not always go to the swift (fast), nor does the battle belong to the strong, nor does bread come to the wise, nor riches to those with understanding, nor favor to skilled men. Time and chance (unpredictability) affect them all. 12. No one knows their time; like fish caught in a cruel net (trap), or birds caught in a snare (trap), so are people ensnared in an evil time that strikes suddenly. 13. I saw something under the sun that seemed wise to me: 14. There was a small city with few inhabitants, and a powerful king laid siege (surrounded or attacked) to it, setting up many traps around the city. 15. In that city, a poor, wise man was discovered, and through his wisdom, the city was saved. But after the danger was over, no one remembered that poor man. 16. I concluded that wisdom is better than strength, but the wisdom of the poor is often disregarded (disrespected), and their words are ignored (not listened to). 17. It is better to listen to the quiet words of the wise than the loud shouts of a ruler surrounded by fools. 18. Wisdom is more valuable than weapons of war, but one sinner can ruin much good.

Chapter 10

1. Just as dead flies spoil the perfumer's ointment (a fragrant mixture used for perfume) and cause it to stink, a little foolishness can ruin the reputation of one who is otherwise wise and honorable. 2. A wise person's heart is at their right hand (the right side is often associated with strength or wisdom), while a fool's heart is at their left. 3. Even when a fool walks down the road, he shows everyone that he lacks wisdom (good judgments), and his actions make it clear that he is a fool. 4. If a ruler becomes angry with you, don't leave your post (position); for calmness can settle even the greatest offenses. 5. I have seen an evil under the sun: an error (mistake) that comes from those in power. 6. Foolishness (lack of wisdom) is often honored, while the rich are made to sit in low places. 7. I have seen servants riding horses, while princes walk on the ground like servants. 8. Anyone who digs a pit will fall into it, and anyone who breaks through a wall will be bitten by a serpent (snake). 9. Those who quarry (extract) stones may get hurt by them, and those who cut wood may be in danger of injury. 10. If the ax is dull (not sharp) and the edge is not sharpened, more strength is needed; but wisdom brings success with less effort. 11. A serpent may bite if it is not charmed (tamed), and a babbler (someone who talks excessively) is no different—both cause harm. 12. The words of a wise person are gracious (kind and pleasant), but the mouth of a fool will eventually bring them to ruin. 13. A fool's speech starts with foolishness, and it ends in madness (insanity). 14. A fool speaks too much, yet no one knows what the future holds. Who can predict (foretell) what will happen after them? 15. The work of fools tires them out, for they don't even know how to find their way to the city! 16. Woe (misery) to the land whose king is a child, and whose princes feast in the morning! 17. Blessed are you, O land, when your king is from a noble family (a family of high rank), and your princes eat at the right time—strengthening themselves, not indulging in drunkenness. 18. Because of laziness (lack of effort), buildings fall apart, and because of idle (inactive) hands, houses leak. 19. A feast is made for laughter, and wine makes the heart glad, but money answers all things. 20. Do not curse the king, even in your thoughts (ideas), nor curse the rich, even in your bedroom. A bird of the air may carry your voice, and a bird on the wing may tell the matter.

Chapter 11

1. Scatter your bread on the waters (share what you have generously), and after many days, you will find it again (your kindness will eventually return to you). 2. Share with seven, or even with eight, because you cannot predict what evil (trouble) may come upon the earth. 3. When the clouds are full, they release rain on the earth, and when a tree falls, whether to the north or south, it remains where it falls. 4. Those who wait for the perfect wind will never plant, and those who watch the clouds too closely will never reap. 5. Just as you cannot grasp the way the wind blows, or how bones form inside a womb, so too, you cannot understand the works of God, who orchestrates everything. 6. Sow your seeds in the morning, and in the evening, don't hold back from doing good. You cannot predict which efforts will succeed—whether one or the other, or both will bring good results. 7. The light is truly delightful, and it's a joy to behold the sun with your eyes. 8. Yet, if a man lives for many years and enjoys them fully, let him always remember the days of darkness (trials) that will surely come. All that is ahead is fleeting (temporary). 9. Young man, enjoy your youth, and let your heart be glad in your younger years. Follow the desires of your heart and the sights before your eyes, but know that God will hold you accountable for all these things. 10. So, remove sorrow (grief) from your heart, and set aside evil from your body, for youth and childhood are only brief (short-lived).

Chapter 12

1. Remember your Creator in your youth, before life's hardships come and the years arrive when you say, "I no longer find joy in them." 2. While the sun, light, moon, and stars are still visible, and the clouds do not return after the rain has fallen. 3. On that day, the protectors of the house (those who guard) will tremble, and the strong will bow low. When the teeth are few and those who peer through the windows (eyes) grow dim. 4. When the doors (of the house) are shut, and the sound of grinding becomes faint, when one awakens at the sound of a bird, and the voices of music grow silent. 5. They will fear heights and the dangers of the path. When the almond tree flowers (hair turns white), the grasshopper becomes a burden (too heavy to bear), and desire fades away. For man will journey to his eternal resting place, and the mourners will walk through the streets. 6. Remember your Creator before the silver cord is cut, before the golden bowl is broken, before the pitcher shatters at the fountain, or the wheel breaks at the well. 7. Then the dust will return to the earth as it was, and the spirit will return to God who gave it. 8. "Vanity of vanities," declares the Preacher. "Everything is vanity." 9. The Preacher, though wise, still taught the people knowledge; he carefully reflected on and organized many proverbs. 10. The Preacher sought to find words that were fitting, and what was written was true—clear and honest words. 11. The teachings of the wise are like prods, and the lessons from scholars are like well-driven nails, all given by the one Shepherd (God). 12. In addition, my son, take this advice to heart. The making of countless books is endless, and constant studying only brings weariness to the body. 13. Now, let us summarize the matter: Fear God and obey His commands, for this is the whole purpose of man. 14. For God will judge every deed, bringing everything to account, even the hidden things, whether good or bad.

29 – Songs of Solomon

Chapter 1

1 This is the song of Solomon. 2 The Shulamite: Let him kiss me with the kisses of his mouth — For your love is better than wine. 3 Your name is like ambrosial oil painting (a sweet-smelling oil painting) poured out, and this is why youthful women adore you. 4 Take me down with you! The Daughters of Jerusalem: We'll run after you. The Shulamite: The king has brought me into his chambers. The Daughters of Jerusalem: We'll rejoice in you, flashing back your love further than wine. The Shulamite: They're right to love you. 5 I'm dark, yet lovely, O daughters of Jerusalem, like the canopies of Kedar (a lineage of people known for their dark canopies) and the curtains of Solomon. 6 Don't look at me because I'm dark, for the sun has scourged my skin. My sisters were angry with me and made me take care of the stations (fields of grapes), but I haven't taken care of my own croft. 7 (To her cherished) Tell me, you whom I love, where you tend your flock (group of lamb) and let them rest at noon. Why should I be like one who curtains herself (covers her face) among the flocks of your companions? 8 The Beloved: If you don't know, O fairest among women, follow the path of the flock and feed your little scapegoats (youthful scapegoats) beside the goatherds' canopies. 9 I compare you, my love, to a missy (a youthful womanish steed) among Pharaoh's chariots. 10 Your cheeks are lovely with beautifiers (ornamental jewelry), and your neck is adorned with gold chains. 11 The Daughters of Jerusalem: We'll make you beautifiers of gold, with tableware superstuds (ornamental pieces). 12 While the king is at his table, my scent of spikenard (an ambrosial oil painting) fills the air. 13 My cherished is like a pack of myrrh (an ambrosial resin) to me, resting all night between my guts. 14 My cherished is like a cluster of henna blooms (flowers) in the stations of En Gedi (a lush area near the Dead Sea). 15 The Beloved: Behold, you're fair, my love! You're beautiful! Your eyes are like

doves' (gentle, pure). **16** The Shulamite: Behold, you're handsome, my cherished! Yes, pleasurable! Our bed is green. **17** The shafts of our house are made of cedar (an ambrosial wood), and our rafters (roof shafts) are of fir (a type of evergreen tree).

Chapter 2

1. I am the rose of Sharon (a fertile plain), and the lily of the valleys. **2.** The Beloved Like a lily among thorns (prickly plants), my love stands out among women. **3.** The Shulamite Like an apple tree among the trees of the forest (wilderness), my beloved is unique among men. I sat in his shade (protection) with great joy, and his fruit was sweet to me. **4.** The Shulamite to the Daughters of Jerusalem He brought me to the banquet hall (a large dining room), and his banner (flag or symbol) over me was love. **5.** Sustain me with raisin cakes (dried grape snacks), refresh me with apples, for I am lovesick (deeply in love). **6.** His left hand is under my head, and his right hand embraces me. **7.** I charge you, daughters of Jerusalem (women of the city), by the gazelles (graceful deer) or does (female deer) of the field, do not stir up or awaken love until it pleases. **8.** The Shulamite I hear my beloved's voice! See, he comes, leaping over the mountains and skipping over the hills. **9.** My beloved is like a gazelle (graceful deer) or a young stag (a young male deer). He stands behind our wall, peering through the windows and looking through the lattice (wooden framework). **10.** My beloved speaks and says to me: "Rise up, my love, my beautiful one, and come away. **11.** For the winter is over, the rain has passed. **12.** The flowers have bloomed on the earth; it is time for singing, and the voice of the turtledove (dove) can be heard in our land. **13.** The fig tree is bearing its green figs, and the vines (grape plants) are blooming with fragrant blossoms. Rise up, my love, my beautiful one, and come away!" **14.** O my dove (a gentle bird), in the clefts (cracks) of the rock, in the secret places of the cliff (steep rock face), show me your face, let me hear your voice; for your voice is sweet, and your face is lovely. **15.** Her Brothers Catch the foxes (small wild animals), the little foxes that ruin the vineyards (grape fields), for our vines are tender with grapes. **16.** The Shulamite My beloved is mine, and I am his. He feeds his flock (group of sheep) among the lilies (a type of flower). **17.** To Her Beloved Until the day breaks and the shadows flee, turn, my beloved, and be like a gazelle (graceful deer) or a young stag upon the mountains of Bether (a mountainous area).

Chapter 3

1. The Shulamite By night, on my bed, I searched for the one I love; I searched for him, but I couldn't find him. **2.** I said, "I will get up now and walk through the city. In the streets and squares, I will search for the one I love." I searched for him, but I couldn't find him. **3.** The city watchmen (guards who patrol the city) found me as I searched. I asked them, "Have you seen the one I love?" **4.** Just as I passed them, I found the one I love. I held onto him and wouldn't let go until I brought him to my mother's house, to the room where I was born. **5.** I warn you, daughters of Jerusalem, by the gazelles (small, graceful animals) or the does (female deer) of the field, do not stir up or awaken love until it's ready. **6.** The Shulamite Who is this coming from the wilderness (desert or uninhabited land), like smoke rising, scented with myrrh (fragrant resin used in perfumes) and frankincense (an aromatic gum resin), surrounded by the finest perfumes? **7.** Look, it's Solomon's royal litter (kind of ceremonial chair or bed), with sixty brave men surrounding it, warriors of Israel. **8.** Each man holds a sword, skilled in battle, with his sword at his side because of the dangers of the night. **9.** Solomon the King made a palanquin (a covered chair or carriage used by royalty) from Lebanon's wood (region known for its tall cedar trees). **10.** He crafted its pillars from silver, its frame from gold, its seat from purple (color of royalty), and its interior decorated with love by the daughters of Jerusalem. **11.** Go out, daughters of Zion (name for Jerusalem), and see King Solomon crowned on the day of his wedding, the happiest day of his life.

Chapter 4

1 You are beautiful, my love! Truly, you are beautiful! Your eyes are like doves' eyes behind your veil (covering for the head or face). Your hair is like a flock of goats descending from Mount Gilead (mountainous region known for its balm). **2** Your teeth are like a flock of freshly shorn (cut or trimmed) sheep that have just been washed. Each one has a twin, and none is missing. **3** Your lips are like a scarlet ribbon and your mouth is lovely. Your temples (sides of the forehead), behind your veil, are like a pomegranate (fruit symbolizing beauty). **4** Your neck is like the tower of David (stronghold or fortification), built as a stronghold (a fortified place), adorned with a thousand shields, all the weapons of mighty warriors. **5** Your two breasts are like two young deer (comparison to fawns), twin fawns that feed among the lilies (symbol of purity). **6** Until the day breaks and the shadows fade, I will go to the mountain of myrrh (fragrant resin used in perfumes) and to the hill of frankincense (a fragrant gum used in incense). **7** You are all beautiful, my love, and there is no flaw (imperfection) in you. **8** Come with me from Lebanon (a mountainous region to the north), my bride, come with me from Lebanon. Look from the top of Amana (a mountain), from the peaks (the highest points) of Senir (a mountain range) and Hermon (a mountain), from the dens (lairs) of lions, from the mountains of leopards (wild cats). **9** You have captivated my heart, my sister, my bride. With a single glance from your eyes, with one link (part) of your necklace, you have stolen my heart. **10** How delightful (pleasing) is your love, my sister, my bride! How much better is your love than wine, and the fragrance (scent) of your perfume is more than any spice. **11** Your lips, my bride, drip with honey; honey and milk are under your tongue, and the fragrance of your garments (clothing) is like the scent of Lebanon. **12** You are like a locked garden (a private or exclusive garden), my sister, my bride, a sealed spring (a spring of water that is shut or closed), a fountain (a source of water) shut up. **13** Your plants (trees) are like an orchard of pomegranates, with delightful fruits, and fragrant henna (a flowering plant used for scent) and spikenard (an aromatic herb). **14** Spikenard and saffron (a spice), calamus (a sweet-scented reed) and cinnamon (a fragrant spice), with all kinds of frankincense (a gum used for incense), myrrh (a resin used in perfumes), and aloes (a fragrant wood), with all the finest spices. **15** You are a garden fountain (a spring of water), a well of living water (fresh, flowing water), and streams flowing from Lebanon. **16** The Shulamite (a reference to the woman speaking): Awake, O north wind, and come, O south! Blow upon my garden, that its fragrance may spread abroad. Let my beloved come into his garden and taste its delightful fruits.

Chapter 5

1. The Beloved: I have come into my garden, my sister, my bride; I have gathered my myrrh (a fragrant resin used in perfume) and spices, enjoyed my honeycomb and honey, and drunk my wine and milk. (To His Friends) Eat, O friends! Drink deeply, O beloved ones! **2.** The Shulamite: I sleep, but my heart is awake. It is my beloved's voice! He knocks, saying, "Open for me, my sister, my love, my dove (a symbol of peace), my perfect one; for my head is drenched with dew (moisture from the night), and my hair with the drops of the night." **3** I have taken off my robe; how can I put it back on? I have washed my feet; how can I soil (make dirty) them? **4** My beloved put his hand by the door's latch (a small fastening device), and my heart longed (yearned) for him. **5** I got up to open for my beloved, and my hands were wet with myrrh, my fingers with liquid myrrh, on the door's handles. **6** I opened for my beloved, but he had turned away and was gone. My heart leaped (jumped in excitement) when he spoke. I searched for him, but could not find him; I called, but he did not answer. **7** The city watchmen (guards) found me. They struck me, they wounded me; the guards took my veil (a piece of cloth covering the face) from me. **8** I charge (command) you, O daughters of Jerusalem, if you find my beloved, tell him I am lovesick (ill from love)! **9.** The Daughters of Jerusalem: What makes your beloved more special than another beloved, O most beautiful (fairest) among women? What makes your beloved more special, that you ask us so? **10.** The Shulamite: My beloved is white and ruddy (healthy in appearance), the chief (best) among ten thousand. **11** His head is like the finest gold; his hair is wavy and black as a raven (a dark bird). **12** His eyes are like doves (gentle and pure) by the rivers of water, washed in milk, perfectly set (arranged beautifully). **13** His cheeks are like beds of spices, banks of scented herbs (plants). His lips are lilies, dripping with liquid myrrh. **14** His hands are golden rods (long, thin rods) set with beryl (a precious stone). His body is carved ivory (hard, white material) inlaid with sapphires (precious blue stones). **15** His legs are pillars (strong supports) of marble (a type of stone) set on bases of fine gold. His appearance is like Lebanon (a region known for its majestic mountains), majestic as its cedars (tall trees). **16** His mouth is most sweet; yes, he is altogether lovely. This is my beloved, and this is my friend, O daughters of Jerusalem!

Chapter 6

1 The Daughters of Jerusalem: Where has your beloved gone, O fairest among women? Where has he turned, that we may help you search for him? **2** The Shulamite: My beloved has gone to his garden, to the beds of spices (places where fragrant plants grow), to tend his flock and gather lilies. **3** I am my beloved's, and my beloved is mine. He tends his flock among the lilies. **4** The Beloved: O my love, you are as beautiful as Tirzah (a city), lovely as Jerusalem (capital city of Israel), and majestic as an army with banners! **5** Turn your eyes away from me, for they overwhelm me. Your hair is like a flock of goats descending from Gilead (a region east of the Jordan River). **6** Your teeth are like a flock of sheep, freshly washed, each one with a twin (two teeth in place of each), and none are missing. **7** Like a piece of pomegranate (a fruit) are your temples (sides of the head) behind your veil. **8** There are sixty queens and eighty concubines (secondary wives), and countless virgins (young unmarried women). **9** My dove, my perfect one, is the only one, the cherished one of her mother. The daughters saw her and called her blessed, and the queens and concubines praised her. **10** Who is she who appears like the dawn (morning light), beautiful as the moon, bright as the sun, and majestic as an army with banners? 11 The Shulamite: I went down to the garden of nuts (a grove of nut trees) to see the plants of the valley, to check if the vine had budded (started growing) and the pomegranates had bloomed. 12 Before I even realized it, my soul made me feel as though I was riding in the chariots (vehicles used in battles or royal processions) of noble people (high-ranking, respected individuals). 13 The Beloved and His Friends: Return, return, O Shulamite; return, return, that we may look upon you! The Shulamite: What would you see in the Shulamite? Is it not the dance of two armies?

Chapter 7

1. How beautiful are your feet in sandals (foot coverings), O daughter of the king! Your legs are like jewels (precious stones), the work of a skilled artist. 2. Your belly is a rounded goblet (a drinking cup), filled with the finest drink. Your waist is a heap of wheat (grain used for making bread) surrounded by lilies (a type of flower). 3. Your breasts are like two fawns (young deer), twin gazelles (graceful animals). 4. Your neck is like an ivory tower (a tall structure made of precious material), your eyes like pools (bodies of water) in Heshbon (a city in Israel) by the gate of Bath Rabbim (a location near Heshbon). Your nose is like the tower (a tall, strong structure) of Lebanon (a mountain range in Israel) that looks toward Damascus (an ancient city in Syria). 5. Your head is crowned like Mount Carmel (a mountain in Israel), and your hair is like purple (a color of royalty); a king is captivated by your tresses (long, flowing hair). 6. How fair (beautiful) and pleasant you are, O love, with all your delights! 7. Your stature (height and appearance) is like a palm tree, and your breasts are like its clusters (groupings of fruit). 8. I said, "I will climb the palm tree and take hold of its branches." Let your breasts be like clusters (groupings) of the vine (grapevine), and the fragrance of your breath like apples (a type of fruit). 9. And the roof (inside of the top) of your mouth is like the finest wine (fermented grape juice), which my beloved drinks gently, moving the lips of those who sleep. 10. I am my beloved's, and his desire (longing or wish) is toward me. 11. Come, my beloved, let us go to the field; let us stay in the villages. 12. Let us rise early to the vineyards (places where grapes grow); let us see if the vine (a plant that grows grapes) has budded (begun to grow), whether the grape blossoms (flowers that turn into grapes) have opened, and the pomegranates (a type of fruit) are in bloom. There I will give you my love. 13. The mandrakes (plants believed to have a pleasant fragrance) give off their scent, and at our gates (entrances to a city or house) are delightful (giving pleasure) fruits, both new and old, which I have stored up for you, my beloved.

Chapter 8

1 "I wish you were like a family to me, who nursed at my mama's bone! If I set up you outdoors, I would kiss you, and no bone would scorn (reject or mock) me for it. 2 I would bring you to my mama's house, where she tutored me. I would give you spiced wine (wine seasoned with spices) and the juice of my pomegranate (a fruit with numerous seeds). 3 (To the Daughters of Jerusalem) His left hand is under my head, and his right hand embraces (holds tightly) me. 4 "I advise (advise explosively) you, daughters of Jerusalem, don't stir up or awaken love until the time is right. 5 A Relative" Who's this coming from the nature (a barren or uninhabited area), leaning on her cherished? I woke you up under the apple tree, where your mama gave birth to you. 6 The Shulamite to Her Cherished" Set me as a seal (symbol of power or commitment) upon your heart, as a seal upon your arm. Love is as strong as death, and covetousness (defensive passion) is as fierce as the grave (place of death). Its dears are like a blazing fire. 7 "numerous waters can not quench (put out) love, and cataracts (large, inviting quantities of water) can not drown it. However, it would be hugely scorned (despised), If someone offered all the wealth of their house for love. 8 The Shulamite's Sisters" We've a little family who has not yet progressed (grown completely). What will we do for her when the time comes for her to be spoken for (chosen for marriage)? 9 "If she's like a wall, we will make upon her a tableware bastion (a defensive wall). Still, we will enclose her with cedar (a type of wood) boards, If she's like a door. 10 The Shulamite" I'm a wall, and my guts are like halls (strong, defensive structures). Also I came in his eyes like one who brings peace. 11 "Solomon had a croft (a field of connections) at Baal Hamon (a position), and he leased it (rented it) to croft keepers. Each bone was to bring him a thousand tableware coins from its fruit. 12 (To Solomon)" My own croft is mine. You, Solomon, may have a thousand, and those who tend its fruit, two hundred. 13 The Beloved" You who dwell (live) in the auditoriums, the companions (musketeers) are harkening for your voice. Let me hear it!" 14 The Shulamite" Make haste (hurry), my cherished, and be like a gazelle (a graceful, fast-moving beast) or a youthful stag (a youthful manly deer) on the mountains of spices."

30 – Isaiah

Chapter 1

1. The vision that Isaiah, the son of Amoz (a prophet), received, pertains to Judah (the southern kingdom of Israel) and Jerusalem. This vision came during the reigns of Uzziah, Jotham, Ahaz, and Hezekiah, kings of Judah. 2. Listen, heavens, and give attention, earth! The Lord has spoken: "I brought up children and raised them, but they have turned away and rebelled against Me. 3. The ox recognizes its master, and the donkey knows where its food is kept, but My people Israel does not even know Me. They do not consider or understand My ways." 4. How tragic it is that this nation is full of sin, burdened with iniquity, and a brood of evildoers (wrongdoers)! They have forsaken the Lord, provoked the Holy One of Israel to anger, and turned their backs on Him. 5. Why continue to be punished? Your rebellion only grows stronger. From head to toe, the nation is wounded and afflicted, with no part free from disease. 6. Your entire body, from your feet to your head, is in a state of sickness. There are only open sores, bruises, and wounds that have not been treated or bandaged, and no healing ointment has been applied. 7. Your land lies desolate, and your cities are consumed by fire. Strangers (foreigners) are devouring your land while you watch, leaving it in ruins, overtaken by outsiders. 8. Jerusalem, like a shelter (temporary dwelling) in a vineyard or a hut in a cucumber field, is left defenseless—like a city surrounded and under siege. 9. If the Lord of hosts (the Almighty God) had not preserved a remnant (a few survivors) among us, we would have been completely destroyed, just like Sodom and Gomorrah (two cities known for their wickedness and eventual destruction). 10. Hear the word of the Lord, you rulers of Sodom (an allusion to Judah's leaders); listen to the law of our God, you people of Gomorrah (a reference to Judah's sinful people). 11. "What is the point of your many sacrifices (ritual offerings) to Me?" says the Lord. "I am fed up with your burnt offerings of rams and the fat of cattle. I take no delight in the blood of bulls, lambs, or goats." 12. "When you come to appear before Me, who has commanded you to trample (tread heavily) upon My courts with your actions?" 13. Stop bringing these pointless offerings. Your incense (fragrant offering) is repulsive to Me. I cannot bear your New Moons (monthly festivals), Sabbaths (weekly day of rest), and your appointed feasts. They bring Me no joy because your actions are full of sin. 14. Your New Moons and feasts have become a burden to Me. They tire My soul, and I cannot stand them any longer. 15. When you lift your hands in prayer, I will turn My eyes away from you. Even though you offer many prayers, I will not listen, for your hands are stained with blood (guilt and sin). 16. "Cleanse yourselves, make yourselves pure. Remove your evil deeds from My sight and stop doing wrong, 17. Learn to do what is right; seek justice, rescue the oppressed (those who suffer), defend the rights of orphans, and plead the case of the widow." 18. "Come, let us reason together," says the Lord. "Though your sins are as scarlet (deep red), they will become white as snow; though they are as red as crimson (bright red), they will be like wool." 19. If you are willing to obey, you will enjoy the best of the land. 20. But if you refuse to listen and rebel, you will be destroyed by the sword." For the Lord Himself has spoken. 21. How the faithful city (Jerusalem) has fallen! Once it was a place of justice, where righteousness dwelt, but now it is filled with murderers (wrongdoers). 22. Your silver is now worthless dross (impure metal), and your wine has been watered down. 23. Your leaders are disobedient, associates of thieves (criminals). They love bribes (payments for favors), chase after gifts, and fail to defend the orphan, while the widow's case is ignored. 24. Therefore, the Lord, the Lord of hosts (the Almighty), the Mighty One of Israel, declares: "Ah, I will take vengeance (revenge) on My enemies, and I will pay back those who oppose Me. 25. I will turn My hand against you and thoroughly cleanse (purge) your impurities, removing all that is corrupt from you. 26. I will restore your judges (leaders) to their former role, and your counselors (advisors) will return to their original positions. Then you will be called the city of righteousness, the faithful city." 27. Zion (Jerusalem) will be redeemed (rescued) through justice, and those who return to God in repentance (penitents) will be redeemed through righteousness. 28. The transgressors (those who rebel) and sinners will be destroyed together, and those who abandon the Lord will face ruin. 29. You will be ashamed of the oak trees (idolatrous groves) you longed for, and embarrassed (disgraced) by the gardens (places of false worship) you once chose. 30. You will be like an oak tree whose leaves wither, or like a garden that has no water. 31. The strong will become like tinder (dry material), and the works they've done will be like a spark. Both will burn together, and no one will be able to quench (extinguish) the fire.

Chapter 2

1. The word that came to Isaiah, the son of Amoz, concerning Judah (the southern kingdom of Israel) and Jerusalem (the capital city of Judah), is as follows. 2. In the future, the Lord's temple on the mountain will be firmly

established, towering above all other mountains and raised higher than the hills. People from all nations will be drawn to it. **3.** Countless people will gather and say, "Let us go to the mountain of the Lord, to the house of the God of Jacob. He will instruct us in His ways, and we will follow His paths." From Zion (the hill in Jerusalem), the law will go out, and the word of the Lord will spread from Jerusalem. **4.** He will resolve disputes between nations and offer judgment for many peoples. Swords will be hammered into plowshares (tools for farming), and spears into pruning hooks (tools for gardening). Nations will no longer take up arms against one another, and they will never again train for battle. **5.** O house of Jacob (the descendants of Israel), let us walk in the light of the Lord together. **6.** For You have turned away from your people, the house of Jacob, because they have embraced practices from the east (foreign spiritual customs); they are like the soothsayers (fortune-tellers) of the Philistines (an ancient people who lived in Canaan), and they take pleasure in the children of foreigners. **7.** Their land is filled with silver and gold, with wealth that knows no end. The land is abundant in horses, and their chariots (war vehicles) are countless. **8.** Their land is overflowing with idols (false gods); they worship the works of their own hands, the very things their fingers have crafted. **9.** The people bow down to them, and each person humbles themselves before these idols. Therefore, you will not forgive them. **10.** Enter the caves (hiding places), and hide in the dust, because of the terror (great fear) of the Lord and the splendor (greatness) of His majesty. **11.** The pride of humanity will be humbled, and the arrogance of men will be brought low. In that day, the Lord alone will be exalted (lifted up). **12.** For the day of the Lord of hosts (a title for God) will come upon everything proud and elevated, everything that is high will be humbled. **13.** This includes the mighty cedars (trees known for height) of Lebanon (a mountain range famous for its trees), and the grand oaks (strong trees) of Bashan (a fertile region known for its strong trees); **14.** It will come upon every lofty mountain and raised hill. **15.** It will strike every high tower and every fortified (protected) wall. **16.** It will come against all the ships of Tarshish (a distant trading city), and all the beautiful ships. **17.** The arrogance of mankind will be humbled, and the pride of men will be lowered. Only the Lord will be exalted on that day. **18.** All the idols will be utterly destroyed (removed and wiped out). **19.** People will flee into caves and among the rocks, from the terror of the Lord and the brilliance of His majesty, when He arises to shake the earth (move violently). **20.** On that day, people will throw away their idols of silver and gold, which they have made to worship, casting them to the moles (small burrowing animals) and bats (flying mammals). **21.** They will hide in the cracks (small openings) of the rocks and the crags (rough parts) of the cliffs, fleeing from the terror of the Lord and the glory of His majesty, when He rises to shake the earth with His mighty power. **22.** Cease putting your trust in mere humans, whose breath is in their nostrils (nose); for what value do, they truly hold?

Chapter 3

1. For behold, the Lord God Almighty (the supreme ruler) will remove from Jerusalem and Judah the support of all their resources: He will take away the entire supply of food and water, leaving them without the basic essentials. **2.** He will remove the strong man, the warrior (a soldier), the judge, and the prophet. He will take away the wise men, the elders, and the skilled artisans—those who are experts in their crafts. **3.** He will strip away the captains (leaders) and leaders, the honorable men, and the advisors. He will even take away the talented craftsmen and those who practice magic arts. **4.** Instead, I will appoint young children to lead them, and infants will have control over them. **5.** The people will be oppressed (treated cruelly) by each other; one person will be harsh toward another, and neighbors will treat one another with cruelty. Children will disrespect their elders, and the lowly will scorn (mock) those who are honorable. **6.** In those days, a man will grab his brother by the hand and say, "You have clothes, so you be our ruler. You must take charge of this ruined land." **7.** But the man will protest, saying, "I cannot solve your problems! My house has neither food nor clothing. Do not make me a leader of the people." **8.** Jerusalem has fallen, and Judah is ruined, because their words and actions are against the Lord. They provoke Him to His face. **9.** Their very appearance testifies against them, and they openly declare their sin, just like the people of Sodom (an ancient city known for its wickedness) did. They do not hide their wrongdoing. Woe to them! They have brought disaster upon themselves. **10.** Tell the righteous (those who do what is right) that they will be blessed, for they will enjoy the fruit of their deeds. **11.** Woe to the wicked (evil people)! It will go badly for them, because they will be rewarded for their evil actions. **12.** As for My people, their oppressors (those who dominate or control) are children, and women hold authority over them. O My people! Your leaders mislead you and destroy the path that should lead you. **13.** The Lord will rise up to argue His case, standing to judge the people. **14.** He will bring judgment against the elders and leaders of His people: "You have consumed (destroyed) the vineyard; the spoil (plunder) of the poor is in your homes." **15.** What do you mean by crushing My people and grinding the faces of the poor?" says the Lord God of Hosts. **16.** The Lord says, "Because the daughters of Zion (women of Jerusalem) are proud and walk with necks stretched out and delightful (attractive in a way that is meant to tempt) eyes, they sway as they go, making noise with their jewelry as they walk, **17.** therefore the Lord will strike them with scabs (skin diseases) on their heads and expose their private parts." **18.** In that day, the Lord will remove their finery (elegant clothing): the anklets that jingle, the scarves, and the crescent-shaped ornaments; **19.** the pendants, bracelets, and veils; the headdresses, the leg ornaments, and the headbands; the perfume boxes, the charms, **20.** the rings, the nose jewels, the festive clothes, the mantles, and the purses; **21.** the mirrors, the fine linen, the turbans, and the robes. **22.** Instead of a sweet fragrance, there will be a stench (bad smell). Instead of a beautiful sash, there will be a rope. Instead of well-set hair, there will be baldness. Instead of rich robes, there will be sackcloth (rough cloth), and branding will replace beauty. **23.** Your men will fall in battle, and your mighty warriors will die in war. **24.** The gates (entrances) of the city will mourn and lament, and Jerusalem, which once stood in glory, will sit in the dust, desolate and destroyed.

Chapter 4

1. And in that day, seven women will grasp hold of one man, saying, "We will provide for ourselves, with our own food and clothes; only let us be known by your name, to take away the shame (disgrace) we carry." **2.** in that day, the Branch (a title for the Messiah, meaning "a shoot" or "descendant") of the Lord will be radiant and splendid; and the fruit (produce) of the land will be abundant and pleasing for those who have survived the trials of Israel. **3.** It will be, that anyone who remains in Zion (Jerusalem, the city of God) and is left in Jerusalem will be called holy— those whose names are recorded among the living (those granted life and protection) in Jerusalem. **4.** When the Lord has cleansed the impurity (moral stain) of the daughters of Zion (the women of Israel) and purged the bloodshed (violence) in Jerusalem from among them, by the spirit of judgment and the spirit of purification (cleansing) through fire, **5.** Then the Lord will establish a protective covering (a shelter or canopy) above every dwelling on Mount Zion (the hill of Jerusalem), and over her assemblies, a cloud by day and a shining fire by night. For the entire region who surrounded with His glorious presence. **6.** And there will be a shelter, a tabernacle (a temporary structure or tent) for shade from the heat during the day, and a place of refuge (safety) from the storm and rain.

Chapter 5

1. I will sing a song to my Beloved (God), a song about His vineyard (a metaphor for His people): My Beloved has planted a vineyard on a fertile hill (a land rich for growth). **2.** He cleared the ground, removed the stones, and planted it with the finest vine (the choicest vine). In the middle, He built a tower and a winepress (a place for crushing grapes); He expected it to bear good fruit, but it produced wild grapes (grapes that are worthless). **3.** "Now, people of Jerusalem (the capital city of Judah) and Judah (the southern kingdom of Israel), you decide: what is the cause between Me and My vineyard? **4.** What more could I have done for My vineyard that I have not already done? Why, when I hoped for good fruit, did it bring forth wild grapes? **5.** Here is what I will do to My vineyard: I will remove its hedge (a protective barrier), and it will be burned; I will tear down its wall, and it will be trampled. **6.** I will let it become desolate (empty and unproductive), with no pruning or cultivation, allowing thorns and thistles (unwanted plants) to grow. I will also command the heavens to withhold rain from it." **7.** The vineyard of the Lord of hosts (God, the Almighty) is the house of Israel (God's chosen people), and the people of Judah (the southern kingdom) are His precious plant (His beloved possession). He sought justice (fairness), but found only oppression (injustice); He looked for righteousness (moral rightness), but instead, He heard a cry for help. **8.** Woe (misery) to those who add house to house, who combine field with field, until there is no space left for others to live, and they are left alone in the land! **9.** I have heard the Lord of hosts declare: "Many houses will become desolate (uninhabited), even the grandest and most beautiful ones, with no one left to live in them." **10.** A ten-acre vineyard will produce only a small amount of wine (one bath); and a homer of seed (a large amount) will yield only one ephah (a small amount of grain)." **11.** Woe to those who wake up early to follow intoxicating drink (alcohol) and continue to drink late into the night until wine consumes them! **12.** Their feasts are filled with music— harps, lyres, tambourines, flutes, and wine—but they give no thought to the work of the Lord, nor do they consider the work of His hands (God's power and creation). **13.** My people have gone into captivity (exile) because they lack knowledge; the respected leaders are starving, and the common people are thirsty and parched. **14.** As a result, the grave (Sheol, the place of the dead) has enlarged itself and opened its mouth to receive them; their glory, their many, and their celebrations will descend into it.**15.** The proud will be humbled, each person brought low, and the arrogant will be ashamed.**16.** But the Lord of hosts will be exalted (lifted up) through justice, and the holy God will display His holiness in righteousness.**17.** Then the innocent (lambs) will pasture in peaceful places, and strangers (foreigners) will graze where the wealthy once thrived.**18.** Woe to those who entangle sin (iniquity) with empty pride (cords of vanity) and treat sin as if it were harmless, like pulling a cart with a rope.**19.** They say, "Let Him hurry and accomplish His work, so we can see it! Let the plan of the Holy One of Israel (God) come quickly, so we can understand it!"**20.** Woe to those who call evil good, and good evil; who replace darkness (evil) with light (good), and light (good) with darkness (evil); who replace bitter (harsh) with sweet (pleasant), and sweet (pleasant) with bitter (harsh)!**21.** Woe to those who are wise in their own eyes (self-important) and clever in their own sight (thinking they know best)!**22.** Woe to those who are brave (strong) at drinking wine, and champions (experts) at mixing strong drinks,**23.** Who justify the wicked (make excuses for evil) for a bribe, and deny justice (righteousness) to the righteous!**24.** Therefore, as fire consumes (destroys) the dry grass, and the flame burns up the chaff (worthless husks), so their root (foundation) will decay, and their blossom (success) will be reduced to dust;For they have rejected the law of the Lord of hosts, and despised the word of the Holy One of Israel.**25.** Therefore, the Lord's anger (wrath) is aroused against His people; He stretches out His hand (brings punishment) against them and strikes them. The mountains (high places) tremble, and their dead bodies (carcasses) are scattered like refuse (trash) in the streets. For all this, His anger has not turned away, and His hand is still stretched out.**26.** He will raise a banner (a signal) for distant nations, and will call them from the ends of the earth; they will come quickly and swiftly.**27.** None of them will be weary (tired) or stumble; none will fall asleep or slumber (sleep deeply).Their belts (straps for clothing) will be secure, and the straps of their sandals will not break.**28.** Their arrows (projectiles) will be sharp, and their bows will be bent; their horses' hooves will be like flint (hard), and their wheels like a whirlwind.**29.** Their roar will be like a lion's; they roar like young lions, and they will seize (capture) their prey and carry it away, and no one will be able to rescue it.**30.** In that day, they will roar against them like the roaring of the sea. And when one looks toward the land, there will be only darkness (misery) and distress (anguish); the light (hope) will be obscured by the clouds (troubles).

Chapter 6

1. During the year that King Uzziah (the king of Judah) passed away, I saw the Lord seated on a high and exalted throne, with the train (the edge or bottom part) of His robe filling the entire temple (the sacred house of worship).**2.** Above this throne, seraphim (angelic beings) stood in attendance, each having six wings—two wings covering their faces, two wings covering their feet, and with the remaining two they flew.**3.** One of the seraphim called out to the other, declaring, "Holy, holy, holy is the Lord of hosts (the Lord who commands all armies); His glory fills the earth!"**4.** The sound of their voices caused the doorposts (the vertical sides of a doorframe) of the temple to tremble, and the whole place was filled with thick smoke.**5.** In response, I cried out, "Woe (destruction or disaster) is me, for I am doomed (ruined or destroyed). I am a man of unclean lips, and I live among a people with unclean lips. For my eyes have seen the King, the Lord of hosts."**6.** Then, one of the seraphim flew to me, holding a live coal (a burning piece from the altar of sacrifice) which he had taken with tongs (long-handled instruments) from the altar.**7.** He touched my lips with it and said, "This has touched your lips; your guilt is removed, and your sin is atoned for (forgiven and removed)."**8.** At that moment, I heard the voice of the Lord asking, "Whom shall I send, and who will go on Our behalf?" To this, I responded, "Here I am, send me."**9.** The Lord then instructed me, "Go and tell this people: 'Though they listen, they will not understand; though they look, they will not perceive (comprehend).**10.** Make their hearts calloused (hardened or insensitive), their ears heavy, and their eyes blind; otherwise, they might see with their eyes, hear with their ears, understand with their hearts, and return to be healed.'"**11.** I asked, "How long, O Lord?" And He answered, "Until the cities are desolate and without inhabitants, until the houses are abandoned and the land is completely ruined (empty and barren).**12.** The people will be scattered, and many places will be left deserted, with few remaining in the land."**13.** However, a tenth (a small remnant) will remain, and they will be purified (refined) like a terebinth tree (a type of tree) or an oak (a strong tree), whose stump (the base left after cutting) remains after it is felled. The holy seed (the faithful remnant) will be its stump (foundation)."

Chapter 7

1. During the reign of King Ahaz, the son of Jotham, who was the son of Uzziah, king of Judah (the southern kingdom), Rezin, king of Syria (a neighboring nation), and Pekah, the son of Remaliah, king of Israel,

ascended against Jerusalem with the intent to conquer it. Yet, they were unable to prevail.**2.** Word came to the royal house of David, saying, "The forces of Syria are stationed in Ephraim (a northern region of Israel)." When Ahaz heard this news, he and his people were filled with fear, as if their hearts shook like trees in the wind.**3.** The Lord instructed Isaiah to go and meet King Ahaz, accompanied by your son Shear-Jashub (meaning 'a remnant will return'), at the water's edge near the upper pool, along the road to the Fuller's Field (a location for washing clothes).**4.** Isaiah was to say to Ahaz, "Be cautious, and stay calm. Do not fear, nor let your heart be dismayed by these two smoldering stubs of firebrands (symbolizing the defeated enemies), who's wrath comes from Rezin, king of Syria, and the son of Remaliah (Pekah).**5.** Syria, Ephraim (Israel), and the son of Remaliah have conspired together against you, planning to**6.** "Invade Judah, lay siege to it, breach its walls, and install a new ruler, the son of Tabel (an unnamed figure)."**7.** But the Lord Almighty declares, "This plot will not succeed, and it will not come to pass."**8.** For the capital of Syria is Damascus (the chief city of Syria), and the ruler of Damascus is Rezin. Within sixty-five years, Ephraim (Israel) will be shattered beyond recognition and will cease to be a people.**9.** The capital of Ephraim is Samaria (the chief city of Israel), and the ruler of Samaria is the son of Remaliah (Pekah). If you do not hold firm in your faith, you will not endure."**10.** The Lord spoke again to Ahaz, saying, **11.** "Ask for a sign from the Lord your God, whether it is deep as the grave (the underworld) or as high as the heavens."**12.** But Ahaz responded, "I will not ask, nor will I test the Lord!"**13.** Then Isaiah addressed the house of David (the royal family), "Is it not enough for you to weary men, but now you would weary God as well?"**14.** Therefore, the Lord Himself will give you a sign: A virgin (a young woman) will conceive and bear a son, and He will be called Immanuel (meaning 'God with us').**15.** He will eat curds (a dairy product) and honey (simple food), and by the time He learns to choose good over evil, He will demonstrate perfect discernment.**16.** Before this child reaches the age of knowing right from wrong, the lands you fear will be abandoned by both of their kings.**17.** The Lord will bring against you and your people the king of Assyria (a mighty empire), a force that will bring devastation to your land, a day unlike any since the split between Ephraim (Israel) and Judah.**18.** On that day, the Lord will call for the fly (a metaphor for distant nations) from the farthest reaches of Egypt's river, and for the bee (a metaphor for another foreign power) from the land of Assyria.**19.** They will come and rest in desolate valleys, in the clefts of the rocks, and in all the thorns (sharp plants) and pastures.**20.** In that day, the Lord will use the king of Assyria like a hired razor (a cutting tool) to shave the hair of your head, your legs, and even your beard.**21.** On that day, a man will tend to a young cow and two sheep (animals used for milk); **22.** And from the milk they provide, curds will be made. All who remain in the land will sustain themselves with curds and honey.**23.** In that day, the fertile land, which once yielded a thousand vines (grapevines) worth a thousand shekels of silver (a great value), will be overtaken by briers and thorns (sharp plants).**24.** People will go there armed with bows (weapons for archery) and arrows because the entire land will become overgrown with thorns and briers.**25.** Even the hills, which were once carefully cultivated with hoes (farming tools), will be left to grow wild with thorns and briers. They will become grazing grounds for oxen (large work animals) and a place where sheep can roam freely.

Chapter 8

1. Then the Lord said to me, "Take a large scroll (writing material), and write on it clearly and plainly about Maher-Shalal-Hash-Baz (a name meaning 'Swift is the booty, speedy is the prey').**2.** And I will choose faithful witnesses to testify (give evidence) about it—Uriah the priest (a priest during King Ahaz's reign) and Zechariah, the son of Jeberechiah (a prophet).**3.** So I went to the prophetess (my wife), and she became pregnant and gave birth to a son. Then the Lord told me, "Name him Maher-Shalal-Hash-Baz,**4.** for before the child is old enough to say 'My father' and 'My mother,' the wealth of Damascus (capital city of Syria) and the plunder (goods taken by force) of Samaria (capital city of Israel) will be carried off by the king of Assyria (a powerful empire ruler from the northeast)."**5.** The Lord spoke again to me, saying:**6.** "Because this people has rejected the gentle waters of Shiloah (a stream in Jerusalem) that flow peacefully, and instead rejoices in the alliance with Rezin (king of Syria) and Remaliah's son (Pekah, the king of Israel),"**7.** Therefore, the Lord will bring upon them the mighty waters of the Euphrates River (the main river of Assyria), with all the glory (greatness) of the king of Assyria. It will rise over its banks and overflow.**8.** It will sweep through Judah, overflowing and spreading over the land until it reaches your neck; the spread of its wings (the vast power) will cover the entire breadth of your land, O Immanuel (meaning "God with us," a title for God's presence in Judah)."**9.** "Be shattered (destroyed), O you nations, and be broken to pieces! Listen, all you distant lands! Prepare yourselves, but you will be shattered; prepare yourselves, but you will be shattered."**10.** "Plan together, but it will come to nothing; speak your plans, but they will not succeed, for God is with us."**11.** For the Lord spoke to me with a strong, guiding hand (powerful direction), warning me not to follow the way of this people, saying: **12.** "Do not call everything a conspiracy (a secret plan), as they do, nor be afraid of what they fear, nor be terrified."**13.** "The Lord of hosts (the Commander of heaven's armies) is the one you should honor as holy. Let Him be the one you fear, and let Him be the one you dread."**14.** "He will be a sanctuary (a safe place) for you, but for both houses of Israel (the northern and southern kingdoms), He will be a stone of stumbling (a cause to fall) and a rock of offense (something that causes people to sin). Many will stumble over Him and fall, be trapped, and taken."**15.** "Many among them will stumble; they will fall and be broken, trapped, and captured."**16.** "Bind up the testimony (keep the message safe), and seal the law among my disciples (those who follow me)."**17.** "I will wait for the Lord, who has hidden His face (turned away His favor) from the house of Jacob (the people of Israel); I will put my hope in Him."**18.** "Here am I, and the children the Lord has given me! We are signs (symbols) and wonders in Israel from the Lord of hosts, who dwells (lives) in Mount Zion (a hill in Jerusalem)."**19.** "And when they tell you, 'Consult the mediums (people who speak to spirits) and the wizards (people who practice magic), who whisper and mutter (speak softly in secret),' should not a people seek their God? Why consult the dead on behalf of the living?"**20.** "Consult the law (God's instructions) and the testimony (the prophetic message)! If they do not speak according to this word, it is because there is no light (truth) in them."**21.** "They will pass through the land distressed (worried) and hungry; and when they are hungry, they will become enraged (angry) and curse their king and their God, and look upward."**22.** "Then they will look to the earth, and see only distress, darkness, and the gloom (deep sadness) of anguish (suffering); and they will be driven into darkness."

Chapter 9

1. But the distress (suffering) that once covered the land of Zebulun (a region in northern Israel) and Naphtali (another northern region in Israel), which was lightly regarded at first, will not remain. Later, it was heavily oppressed. This was along the way of the sea, beyond the Jordan River, in Galilee of the Gentiles (a region inhabited by non-Jews).**2.** The people who had been living in darkness (ignorance or oppression) have now seen a great light; those who had dwelt in the land of death's shadow (a place of despair), upon them, a light has dawned.**3.** You have greatly expanded the nation and increased their joy. They will rejoice (celebrate) before you, just like people celebrate when the harvest comes or when they share the spoils of victory.**4.** For You have broken the heavy yoke (burden) that burdened them and the staff that weighed on their shoulders, the rod of the oppressor (one who subjects them to harsh treatment), just like in the days of Midian (a people defeated by God through Gideon in the past).**5.** Every warrior's sandals (shoes), once worn after noisy battles, and the garments soaked in blood will be burned, used as fuel (energy source) for the fire.**6.** For a Child will be born to us, a Son will be given to us, and the government (authority or rule) will rest on His shoulders. His name will be called Wonderful (extraordinarily good), Counselor (advisor), Mighty God (strong and powerful), Everlasting Father (eternal ruler), Prince of Peace (ruler who brings peace).**7.** There will be no end to the increase (growth) of His government and peace. He will sit on the throne (seat of rule) of David (the great king of Israel) and rule over His kingdom, establishing it with judgment (fairness) and righteousness (moral rightness) from that time forward, even forever. The zeal (strong passion) of the Lord of Hosts will accomplish this.**8.** The Lord has sent a message (communication) against Jacob (the nation of Israel), and it has fallen upon Israel.**9.** All the people of Israel will know this—Ephraim (the northern tribe) and the inhabitants of Samaria (the capital city of the northern kingdom)—those who speak with pride (arrogance) and arrogance (proud self-importance) of heart, saying: **10.** "The bricks have fallen down, but we will rebuild with cut stones (stones shaped by artisans); the sycamore trees (a type of tree) are chopped down, but we will replace them with cedars (a tall, strong tree)."**11.** Therefore, the Lord will raise up adversaries (enemies) against Rezin (king of Aram), and will stir up His enemies.**12.** The Syrians (people from Syria, a nation to the northeast) will attack from the front, and the Philistines (people from the coastal region) will attack from behind. Together they will devour Israel (consume or defeat) with an open mouth. Despite this, His anger will not turn away, and His hand will remain outstretched in judgment.**13.** The people do not return (turn back to) to the One who struck them, nor do they seek (look for) the Lord of Hosts (God, the commander of heavenly armies).**14.** Therefore, the Lord will cut off (remove) from Israel the head (leaders) and the tail (false prophets), the palm branch (branches from palm trees) and the reed (a tall plant), in a single day.**15.** The elder (older, respected person) and honorable (worthy of respect) man is the head, and the prophet (spokesperson for God) who lies is the tail.**16.** For the leaders (rulers) of this people cause those to go astray (sin), and those led by them will be destroyed.**17.** Therefore, the Lord will take no pleasure in their young men, nor will He show mercy (compassion) to their orphans (fatherless children) and widows (women whose husbands have died). For everyone is a hypocrite (one who pretends to be good) and an evildoer (one who does evil), and every mouth speaks folly (foolishness). Despite all this, His anger is not turned away, and His hand remains outstretched.**18.** Wickedness (evil) burns like a fire, devouring (destroying) briers (thorny bushes) and thorns (sharp plants), and it will rage through the thickets (dense underbrush) of the forest. It will rise up like smoke.**19.** By the wrath (anger) of the Lord of Hosts, the land will be scorched (burned), and the people will be like fuel (energy source) for the fire. No one will spare their own brother.**20.** On the right hand, they will devour (consume), but still hunger; on the left hand, they will eat, but not be satisfied. Every man will devour (consume) the flesh (meat) of his own arm.**21.** Manasseh (a tribe of Israel) will devour Ephraim (another tribe), and Ephraim will devour Manasseh; together they will turn against Judah (the southern kingdom). Despite all this, His anger is not turned away, and His hand remains outstretched.

Chapter 10

1. "Woe (judgment) to those who make unjust laws, who write decrees that bring harm, plans that lead to misfortune,**2.** to deprive the poor of their rights and to rob the oppressed of justice. They are taking what is rightfully theirs, targeting widows and plundering the fatherless.**3.** What will you do when the day of reckoning (accounting, judgment) comes, when devastation (complete destruction) from afar strikes? Where will you run for help, and who will protect your honor?**4.** Without My intervention, they will be brought low among the captives (prisoners), and fall among the slain (killed). Yet despite all this, My anger is not turned away; My hand is still stretched out in judgment.**5.** "Woe to Assyria (an empire to the northeast of Israel), the instrument (tool) of My anger, the staff (rod) in whose hand is My wrath.**6.** I will send him against a nation that is wicked and rebellious, against the people who provoke My anger, to take their wealth, to seize their goods, and to trample them down like mud in the streets.**7.** But Assyria does not have this in mind; their heart (mind, will) does not think in these terms. Their true purpose is to destroy and wipe out many nations.**8.** For they say, 'Are not my princes (leaders) all kings?**9.** Is not Calno (an ancient city in Mesopotamia) like Carchemish (an ancient city in northern Syria)? Is not Hamath (a city in Syria) like Arpad (another Syrian city)? Is not Samaria (the capital of the northern kingdom of Israel) like Damascus (capital of Syria)? **10.** As my hand has seized the kingdoms of idols (false gods), whose images (representations) are greater than those of Jerusalem and Samaria, **11.** as I have done to Samaria and her idols, shall I not do the same to Jerusalem and her idols?'**12.** Therefore, when the Lord has completed His work on Mount Zion (a hill in Jerusalem where the temple stood) and in Jerusalem, He will punish the arrogant (proud) heart of the king of Assyria, and the pride (self-importance) of his haughty (arrogant) looks.**13.** For the king of Assyria says, 'By the power (strength) of my hand I have achieved this, and by my wisdom (knowledge), for I am clever. I have removed the boundaries (territories) of nations and plundered (taken by force) their treasuries. I have conquered the peoples like a mighty warrior.**14.** My hand has found the wealth (riches) of the nations, and as a bird gathers eggs (gathers things easily), I have gathered all the people of the earth. No one has stirred a wing (moved) or opened a mouth to protest.'**15.** Should the axe (tool for cutting) boast against the one who cuts with it? Should the saw (tool for cutting) exalt (raise) itself against the one who saws with it? Is it as if a rod (stick) could lift itself against the one who uses it, or a staff (long stick) as though it were not wood (material)?**16.** Therefore, the Lord, the Lord of hosts (God's title, meaning "Lord of armies") will send a wasting disease (deterioration) among his strong warriors, and under his glory (honor), He will kindle (start) a fire that will burn like a raging fire.**17.** The Light (guiding presence) of Israel will be like a fire, and His Holy One (a title for God) will be a flame; He will burn and consume the thorns (briers) and briers (thorny plants) in one day.**18.** He will destroy the glory (splendor) of his forest (large trees) and fruitful fields (fertile lands), both body and soul, and they will waste away like a sick (ailing) man.**19.** The rest (remaining) of the trees (people) in his forest will be so few in number that even a child will be able to count them.**20.** And in that day, the remnant (surviving portion) of Israel, and those who remain from the house of Jacob (descendants of Jacob), will no longer depend on their conqueror (enemy), but will instead trust in the Lord, the Holy One of Israel, in truth.**21.** A remnant will return, the remnant of Jacob, to the Mighty God (a title for God).**22.** Though your people, O Israel, are as numerous as the grains of sand (infinite number) by the sea, only a small remnant will return; the destruction that is decreed (ordained) will overflow with righteousness.**23.** For the Lord God of hosts will bring an end (finish) to the destruction in the middle of the land.**24.** Therefore, the Lord God of hosts says: 'O My people, who dwell (live) in Zion (Jerusalem), do not be afraid of the Assyrian, who will strike you with a rod (punish) and lift up his staff (weapon) against you, as Egypt (ancient empire) once did.**25.** For in a little while, My anger against you will end, and My wrath (anger) will be directed toward their destruction.'**26.** The Lord of hosts will rise up a scourge (punishing force) against Assyria, like the slaughter (mass killing) of Midian (a people defeated by Israel) at the rock of Oreb (a place in the wilderness). As His rod (authority) was on the sea (Red Sea), so will He raise it against Assyria in the way of Egypt.**27?** In that day, his burden (weight) will be lifted from your shoulder, and his yoke (wooden collar for animals) from your neck; the yoke will be destroyed because of the anointing oil (God's empowerment and blessing).**28.** He has come to Aiath (a town in Israel), He has passed Migron (another town); at Michmash (a town near Jerusalem) He has made preparations for battle.**29.** They have gone along the ridge (hills); they have taken up lodging (resting) at Geba (a town near Jerusalem). Ramah (a town in Benjamin) is afraid; Gibeah (a city of Saul, the first king of Israel) has fled.**30.** Cry aloud, O daughter (city) of Gallim (a small town); let it be heard as far as Laish (a town in northern Israel)—O poor (wretched) Anathoth (a town in Benjamin)! **31.** Madmenah (a town in the north) has fled; the people of Gebim (a town in Benjamin) seek refuge (safety).**32.** As yet, he will stop at Nob (a hill near Jerusalem) that day; he will shake his fist (defy) at the mount (hill) of the daughter (city) of Zion (Jerusalem), at the hill of Jerusalem.**33.** Behold, the Lord, the Lord of hosts, will cut off the branches (branches of a tree) with terror; those of high stature (status) will be hewn down (cut), and the proud (arrogant) will be humbled.**34.** He will cut down the thickets (dense plants) of the forest with an axe (tool), and Lebanon (a region famous for its great cedar trees) will fall by the Mighty One (God)."

Chapter 11

1. A new leader will rise from the family line of Jesse (Jesse was the father of King David), and a new shoot (Messiah) will sprout from the roots of this family tree.**2.** The Spirit of the Lord (God's presence) will rest upon Him, filling Him with wisdom and insight, with counsel and power, with knowledge and awe (reverence) of the Lord.**3.** He will find great joy in honoring the Lord, and His judgments will not be based on mere appearances or what others say to Him.**4.** Instead, He will act with justice (fairness) toward the poor and will defend the humble with righteousness (rightful judgment). He will destroy the wicked with the word from His mouth and the breath (word) of His lips.**5.** Justice (rightness) will be like a belt around His waist, and loyalty (faithfulness) will be the belt that holds His robe together.**6.** In His kingdom, the wolf will peacefully live with the lamb, and the leopard will rest beside the young goat. The calf, young lion, and fattened calf will play together, and a small child will lead them.**7.** Even the cow and the bear will graze (feed) side by side, and their young will rest together. The lion will eat grass (like the ox) instead of hunting.**8.** The infant will play near the hole of a cobra, and the child who is weaned will reach into the den of a viper (a dangerous snake's nest), and neither will be harmed.**9.** There will be no violence or destruction in My holy mountain (God's kingdom), for the earth will be filled with the knowledge (understanding) of the Lord, as the waters cover the sea.**10.** On that day, the Root (descendant) of Jesse will stand as a banner for all people. Even the Gentiles (non-Jews) will seek Him, and His resting place will be glorious, bringing peace to all who come.**11.** On that day, the Lord will once again gather the remaining faithful from the nations—whether from Assyria (the ancient empire in Mesopotamia), Egypt, Pathros, Cush, Elam, Shinar, Hamath, or even the farthest islands of the sea.**12.** He will raise a banner for the nations, calling together the scattered people of Israel, gathering the exiled people of Judah from all corners of the earth.**13.** The divisions between Ephraim (northern kingdom of Israel) and Judah (southern kingdom of Israel) will end. Enemies of Judah will be destroyed, and Ephraim will no longer envy Judah, nor will Judah oppress Ephraim.**14.** They will fly down on the Philistines (ancient enemies of Israel) to the west and together, they will plunder (rob) the nations of the east. They will take control of Edom (a region southeast of Israel) and Moab (a kingdom east of Israel), and the people of Ammon (northeast of Israel) will submit to them.**15.** The Lord will completely destroy the power of the Sea of Egypt, with His mighty wind (power) He will strike the river (Euphrates) and divide it into seven streams, making a way for His people to cross on dry ground.**16.** A clear highway (path) will be prepared for the remnant of His people, just as there was for Israel when they came up from Egypt (the Exodus).

Chapter 12

1. On that day, you will declare, "O Lord, I will give You praise; though You were angry (displeased) with me, Your anger has been turned away, and You have now brought me comfort (consoled)."**2.** Behold, God is my salvation ; I will place my trust in Him and have no reason to fear. For Yah (God), my Lord, is my strength (power) and my song, and He has become my salvation (rescue).**3.** So, with joy (great delight), you will draw from the deep wells (sources) of salvation (rescue) that God has provided.**4.** And on that day, you will proclaim, "Praise the Lord, call upon His name, make His mighty works known among the nations, and declare that His name is exalted (highly honored)."**5.** Sing to the Lord, for He has performed marvelous (wonderful) deeds; let all the earth hear and acknowledge this.**6.** Shout for joy and sing loudly, an O inhabitant of Zion (Jerusalem), for great is the Holy One (sacred) of Israel, and He is present in your midst!

Chapter 13

1. This is the prophecy (a divine message) that Isaiah, son of Amoz, received concerning Babylon (the ancient city and empire).**2.** "Raise a banner (a signal) on the highest mountain (a place of visibility), and call out to them; wave your hand so that they may enter the gates of the nobles (the cities of the influential).**3.** I have instructed my consecrated (set apart for holy purpose) ones, and summoned my mighty warriors (strong fighters) to carry out my anger—those who take joy in executing my will.**4.** The roar of a vast multitude (a large crowd) rises from the mountains (from many nations), like the noise of a great assembly! It is a tumultuous (confused and loud) sound as the kingdoms of nations come together! The Lord of Hosts (the mighty God) is organizing His army for battle.**5.** They are coming from a far-off land (a distant place), from the end of heaven (the furthest corner of the earth)—the Lord and His weapons of wrath (intense anger), to lay waste to the whole land.**6.** Cry out in anguish (distress), for the day of the Lord draws near! It will come as destruction from the Almighty (God).**7.** Therefore, every hand will grow limp (weak), and the hearts of men will melt with fear.**8.** Terror will seize them, and pain and anguish (great suffering) will grip them like a woman in labor. They will stare in astonishment at one another; their faces will be set aflame with dread.**9.** The day of the Lord is coming, and it will be cruel, full of wrath (anger) and fierce fury. It will devastate the land, and sinners will be utterly destroyed.**10.** The stars of heaven and their constellations (groups of stars) will lose their light; the sun will be dark when it rises, and the moon will refuse to shine.**11.** "I will punish the world for its evil, and the wicked (those who do wrong) for their iniquity (wrongdoing). I will end the arrogance (pride) of the proud and humble (bring low) the haughtiness (arrogance) of the ruthless."**12.** I will make human beings rarer (more uncommon) than fine gold, and people will be more precious than the gold from Ophir (a place known for its wealth).**13.** Therefore, I will shake (move violently) the heavens, and the earth will be displaced from its position in the wrath (anger) of the Lord of Hosts, on the day of His fierce anger.**14.** It will be like a gazelle (a fast-moving animal) being hunted, and like sheep with no one to gather them; each person will flee (run away) to their own people, and everyone will escape to their own land.**15.** Anyone who is found will be struck down (pierced) by the sword, and those who are captured will fall by the sword.**16.** Their children will be dashed (smashed) to pieces before their eyes; their homes will be plundered (stolen from), and their wives will be ravished (violently treated).**17.** "Look, I will stir up (arouse) the Medes (an ancient people from the region of modern Iran) against them. These people will not value silver (money) and will have no interest in gold (treasure)."**18.** Their bows (weapons) will cut down the young men, and they will show no mercy (compassion) to the unborn (those in the womb); they will have no pity on children.**19.** Babylon, the glory (great beauty) of kingdoms and the pride of the Chaldeans (the people of Babylon), will be destroyed like Sodom and Gomorrah (two cities wiped out by God for their sin).**20.** It will never again be inhabited (lived in), nor will it be settled from generation to generation. No Arab (a person from the Arabian Peninsula) will set up camp there, nor will shepherds bring their flocks to rest.**21.** Wild animals will settle there, and their homes will be filled with owls (nocturnal birds); ostriches (large, flightless birds) will nest there, and wild goats will leap about.**22.** The howling of wild dogs (hyenas) will be heard in their fortresses (strongholds), and jackals (wild dogs) will take refuge in their palaces of luxury. The time of their destruction is near, and their days are numbered."

Chapter 14

1. The LORD will show mercy on Jacob (the descendants of Jacob, also known as Israel) and will continue to choose Israel, bringing them back to live in their own land. Foreign nations will join with them, and they will hold fast to the house of Jacob (the descendants of Israel).**2.** People from other lands will bring them to their own place, and Israel will take them as servants (workers) and maids (female servants) within the land of the Lord. They will captivate those who once held them captive, and will rule over their former oppressors.**3.** On the day when the Lord gives you relief from your anguish, your fears, and the harsh labor (work) to which you were once subjected,**4.** You will take up this mocking song against the king of Babylon (the king of the Babylonian empire) and say: "How the oppressor (one who forces others to obey) has fallen silent! How the golden city (Babylon) lies in ruin!**5.** The Lord has shattered the power (staff) of the wicked and the symbol of the rulers' authority (scepter); **6.** He who struck the nations in fury (anger) with unyielding blows, who ruled in wrath, is now pursued (chased) and there is no one to stop him.**7.** The earth is now at rest, at peace; it breaks out into songs of joy.**8.** Even the trees of the forest, the cypress trees (large trees, typically found in Mediterranean areas) and the cedars of Lebanon (large trees from Lebanon), celebrate saying, 'Since you were cut down, no one has come to harm us.'**9.** "The grave (Hell), from below, is stirred to meet you when you arrive. It rouses the dead (spirits of the dead), the leaders of the earth. It brings up the kings of the nations from their thrones.**10.** All of them will speak and ask, 'Have you become as weak as we are? Have you become like us? **11.** Your glory (splendor) has been cast down to the grave, along with the sound of your musical instruments (strings); maggots (larvae) are spread beneath you, and worms (insects) cover you.'**12.** "How you have fallen from heaven, O Lucifer, son of the morning! How you have been brought down to the ground, you who weakened the nations!**13.** You said in your heart, 'I will ascend to heaven; I will raise my throne above the stars of God; I will sit on the mount (high place) where the assembly (gathering) of the gods meet, on the farthest sides of the north;**14.** I will rise above the clouds, and make myself like the Most High (God).'**15.** Yet you will be brought down to the grave, to the deepest pit (Sheol, the place of the dead).**16.** "Those who see you will stare and wonder, saying: 'Is this the one who made the earth tremble (quake), who shook kingdoms, **17.** who turned the world into a desert (wilderness), destroyed its cities, and did not release his prisoners?**18.** All the kings (rulers) of the nations, all of them, rest in glory (dignity), each one in his own tomb.**19.** But you are cast out from your grave like a rejected branch (a branch that is discarded), like a garment (clothing) worn by those who are killed, pierced through by a sword, and thrown down to the stones of the pit (grave), like a corpse trampled underfoot.**20.** You will not join them in burial, because you have destroyed your land and killed your people. The children (descendants) of the wicked will never be named again.**21.** Prepare a slaughter (death) for his children because of the wickedness (sin) of their father, so that they do not rise up and take over the land and fill the world with cities."**22.** "For I will rise up against them," says the Lord of Hosts (God Almighty), "and cut off from Babylon (a kingdom) the name, the remnant (surviving descendants), the offspring (children), and the posterity (future generations)," declares the Lord.**23.** "I will make it a place for wild animals (a possession for the porcupine), and swamps (marshes) filled with muddy water. I will sweep it clean with the broom of destruction," says the Lord of Hosts.**24.** The Lord of Hosts has sworn (promised), saying, "As surely as I have planned, so it will happen; as I have determined, so it will stand: **25.** I will break the Assyrian (the empire of Assyria) in My land, and on My mountains I will crush him underfoot. Then his yoke (burden) will be removed from Israel, and his heavy load will be lifted from their shoulders.**26.** This is the plan (purpose) that is established for the entire earth, and this is the hand (action) that is stretched out against all the nations.**27.** For the Lord of Hosts has planned it, and no one can stop it. His hand is stretched out, and no one can turn it back."**28.** This prophecy (message) was given in the year that King Ahaz (king of Judah) died.**29.** "Do not rejoice, you people of Philistia (the Philistine people), because the rod (power) that struck you has been broken. For from the roots of the serpent (a venomous creature), a viper (poisonous snake) will rise, and its descendants (offspring) will be a fiery flying serpent.**30.** The firstborn (eldest) of the poor will find food, and the needy will lie down in safety; but I will destroy your roots with famine (lack of food), and it will slay your survivors.**31.** Cry out, O gate (city entrance)! Wail, O city! All of you Philistia will be shattered (dissolved); for smoke will rise from the north, and no one will be left in their appointed time.**32.** What will the messengers (envoys) of the nation answer? That the Lord has established Zion (Jerusalem, city of God), and the poor of His people will find refuge (safety) in it."

Chapter 15

1. A prophecy (burden) concerning Moab (a nation east of Israel): In the night, Ar (a city in Moab) will be destroyed, laid waste. Likewise, in the night, Kir (another city of Moab) will meet the same fate, ruined and desolate.**2.** Moab will ascend to the temple (place of worship) and to Dibon (a city in Moab), heading to the high places, where they will weep in sorrow. Over Nebo (a mountain in Moab) and Medeba (a city in Moab), they will mourn deeply. Their heads will be shaved (sign of mourning), and their beards will be completely shaved off.**3.** People will clothe themselves in sackcloth (coarse fabric worn in mourning) throughout the streets. From the rooftops to the streets, the sound of weeping will echo, and everyone will cry out in bitter grief.**4.** The voices of those in Heshbon (a city in Moab) and Elealeh (a city in Moab) will rise in anguish, and their cries will be heard as far as Jahaz (a town in Moab). As a result, Moab's soldiers (military) will cry out, their lives now feeling like a heavy burden.**5.** "I will weep for Moab from my heart; their refugees (people fleeing) will flee to Zoar (a small city in Moab), running like a young heifer (young cow). They will ascend the path of Luhith (a mountain region in Moab) with tears, and as they reach the way of Horonaim (a city in Moab), they will lift up a cry of destruction."**6.** The waters of Nimrim (a river or area in Moab) will be completely dried up (desolate), and the grass that once flourished will wither and die. No green will remain; the land will be barren.**7.** Therefore, all the wealth (abundance) they have accumulated and stored up will be carried away to the Brook of the Willows (a location in Moab), as a sign of their loss.**8.** The sound of mourning will spread throughout Moab's borders, reaching Eglaim (a city near Moab) and Beer Elim (another town in Moab), as the wailing continues.**9.** The waters of Dimon (a city in Moab) will be filled with blood, for I will bring further destruction upon Dimon. Lions (wild animals) will hunt down those who manage to escape from Moab, and the survivors (remnant) of the land will face even greater devastation.

Chapter 16

1. Send the lamb to the ruler (leader) of the land, from Sela (a city in Edom, known for its rock-hewn structures) to the wilderness, to the mountain of the daughter of Zion (the city of Jerusalem, God's holy city).**2.** Like a bird that has been cast out of its nest, so will the daughters (people) of Moab be at the fords (crossing places) of the Arnon (a river that forms the boundary between Moab and Israel).**3.** "Take counsel (advice), carry out justice; Make your shade (protection) as dark as night at midday; shelter the outcasts (those forced out of their homes), do not betray the one who escapes.**4.** Let My outcasts (those forced to leave their land) find refuge (safety) with you, O Moab; be a hiding place for them from the face of the destroyer (invader). For the oppressor's (tyrant's) rule has come to an end, devastation ceases, and the tyrants have been consumed from the land.**5.** In mercy, a throne will be established; and someone will sit on it in truth, in the tabernacle (dwelling place) of David (King David's lineage), judging and seeking justice, hastening righteousness.**6.** We have heard about the pride (arrogance) of Moab—he is very proud—about his arrogance, pride, and anger, but his lies shall not prevail.**7.** Therefore, Moab will mourn (grieve) for Moab; everyone will mourn. For the foundations (strongholds) of Kir Hareseth (a city of Moab) you shall mourn, surely they are struck down.**8.** For the fields of Heshbon (a city in the territory of Reuben) languish (waste away), and the vine of Sibmah (a vineyard region in Moab); the lords (rulers) of the nations have broken down its choice vines, which reached all the way to Jazer (a city in Gilead) and wandered through the wilderness. Her branches stretch out, they are gone over the sea (referring to the Mediterranean).**9.** Therefore, I will weep for the vine of Sibmah, with the weeping (mourning) of Jazer; I will drench you with my tears, O Heshbon and Elealeh (cities in the region of Moab); for battle cries have fallen over your summer fruits and your harvest.**10.** Gladness is taken away, and joy from the fertile field; in the vineyards, there will be no singing, nor shouting; no one will tread (trample) out wine in the presses; I have made their joy cease.**11.** Therefore, my heart shall sound like a harp (musical instrument) for Moab, and my innermost being for Kir Heres (a fortified city in Moab).**12.** And it will happen that when Moab is weary (exhausted) from his high place (place of worship), he will come to his sanctuary (holy place) to pray, but he will not prevail.**13.** This is the word which the Lord has spoken concerning Moab since that time.**14.** But now the Lord has spoken, saying, "Within three years, like the years of a hired worker, the glory (greatness) of Moab will be humbled along with all its great multitude (large group), and the remnant (surviving portion) will be very small and weak."

Chapter 17

1. The burden (prophecy) against Damascus (capital of Syria). "Look, Damascus will no longer be a city; it will become a heap of ruins, destroyed and desolate.**2.** The cities of Aroer (a city on the east side of the Jordan River) will be abandoned; they will become places where flocks roam freely, and no one will fear them.**3.** The stronghold (fortress) of Ephraim (a region in Israel) will be wiped out, and the kingdom (rule) of Damascus will fall. The remaining people of Syria will be like the glory of Israel's children," says the Lord of Hosts (the Almighty God).**4.** "On that day, the glory (honor) of Jacob (Israel) will diminish, and the richness (fertility) of his land will become lean and barren.**5.** It will be like when a harvester (one who collects crops) gathers grain, reaping (gathering) the heads of grain with his arm, like someone collecting grain in the Valley of Rephaim (a valley near Jerusalem).**6.** Still, some grapes will be left behind, like the last olives shaken from an olive tree: just a few olives at the topmost branch, or a small handful in the most fruitful branches," says the Lord God of Israel. **7.** On that day, people will turn to their Maker (Creator, God), and their eyes will look to the Holy One (Sacred One) of Israel. **8.** They will no longer look to their altars (places of worship), the works of their hands, or respect the idols (false gods) they created with their fingers, nor the incense altars (places for burning incense) they built. **9.** On that day, their fortified cities (strong, protected cities) will be forsaken (abandoned) branches or as an abandoned uppermost (highest) branch that the Israelites left behind, leaving desolation in its place. **10.** "You have forgotten the God of your salvation (deliverance) and failed to remember the Rock (God) of your stronghold (fortress). As a result, you will plant beautiful plants and grow foreign (non-native) crops, **11.** But on the day of harvest, your efforts will come to nothing. The plants you nurtured will turn to a heap (pile) of ruins in the day of sorrow and distress." **12.** Woe to the multitudes (large crowds) of many nations that roar (make loud noise) like the crashing of the sea, and to the rushing (moving quickly) of peoples that sound like the mighty waves of the ocean! **13.** The nations will roar like the crashing waves of the sea, but God will rebuke (correct) them, and they will scatter far away. They will be chased like chaff (light husks) blown by the wind, or like a rolling thing before a powerful storm. **14.** At evening time, terror (fear) will strike! Before morning, they will be gone. This will be the fate (end) of those who plunder (rob) us, the lot (destiny) of those who rob us."

Chapter 18

1. Woe to the land where the sound of buzzing wings fills the air, a land beyond the rivers of Ethiopia (a region to the south of Egypt), **2.** A place that sends envoys across the seas, traveling on boats crafted from reeds, saying, "Hurry, swift messengers, go to a nation that is tall and smooth-skinned, to a people who have been formidable from the very beginning, a mighty nation that is unstoppable, whose territory is marked by rivers." **3.** All who inhabit the earth and live upon it, listen: When they raise a signal on the mountains, you will witness it; and when the trumpet sounds, you will hear its call. **4.** For the Lord has spoken to me in this way: "I will rest and remain still, watching from My sacred dwelling place, like the heat of the sun on a clear day, or like dew upon the earth at harvest time." **5.** Before the harvest is gathered, when the young sprout is full of promise and the unripe grape is just beginning to form, He will cut off the branches with pruning tools and remove the fruit-bearing shoots. **6.** These will be left to the mountain birds of prey and the wild beasts of the field; the birds will settle on them in the summer, and in the winter, the wild animals will find refuge there. **7.** In that moment, a tribute will be offered to the Lord of Hosts (the Almighty) from a people who are tall and smooth-skinned, from a nation that has been powerful from the start, a people who have trampled others, whose land is divided by rivers. They will bring their offering to the place where the Name of the Lord of Hosts resides, to Mount Zion (the holy mountain in Jerusalem).

Chapter 19

1. A prophecy (message from God) against Egypt: The Lord will come swiftly on a cloud, and Egypt will tremble at His presence. Its idols (false gods) will fall, and the hearts of the Egyptians will be filled with fear. **2.** I will cause Egyptians to fight against each other—brother against brother, neighbor against neighbor, city against city, kingdom against kingdom. **3.** The spirit (inner strength or guidance) of Egypt will fail, and their leaders will turn to idols (false gods), magicians (people who claim supernatural powers), mediums (people who communicate with the dead), and sorcerers (magic workers) for guidance. **4.** I will hand Egypt over to a harsh ruler, and a cruel king will reign (rule) over them," says the Lord, the Almighty. **5.** The waters of Egypt will dry up, and the Nile River (the major river in Egypt) will be emptied. **6.** The canals (small waterways) will become foul (dirty), the streams will dry up, and the reeds (plants growing along rivers) will wither (dry up). **7.** The crops along the Nile will wither and be blown away. **8.** The fishermen will mourn (grieve), and those who spread nets (fishing tools) will grow weak. **9.** Those who work with fine flax (plant fibers used for weaving) and weave cloth will be ashamed (embarrassed), **10.** And the foundations (structures or supports) of Egypt will crumble (fall apart). The economy (system of trade and jobs) will fail, and people will be troubled in their souls (feel anxious or confused). **11.** The leaders (chiefs or rulers) of Zoan (a city in Egypt) are foolish; Pharaoh's (king of Egypt) advisors give him bad counsel (advice). How can they claim, "I am a descendant of the wise, the son of ancient kings?" **12.** Where are these wise men now? Let them tell Pharaoh what the Lord has planned for Egypt. **13.** The leaders of Zoan have become fools (not wise), and those of Noph (another city in Egypt) are deceived (misled). They have misled Egypt, causing confusion (disorder) in its people. **14.** The Lord has mixed (mixed up) a spirit of confusion within them, so that they stagger (stumble) like a drunken man (one who is drunk) stumbling in his own vomit (sick). **15.** Egypt will have no power to act (make decisions), whether in government or business. **16.** In that day, Egypt will be weak like women (showing fear), trembling (shaking) at the fear of the Lord's hand raised against them. **17.** Judah (the southern kingdom of Israel) will be a terror to Egypt; anyone who mentions it will be afraid (scared) because of the plan (purpose) the Lord has for Egypt. **18.** in that day, five cities in Egypt will speak the language of Canaan (Hebrew) and swear (promise) allegiance (loyalty) to the Lord. One of them will be called the City of Destruction (a place of ruin). **19.** in that day, an altar (a place of worship) will be built to the Lord in the heart of Egypt, and a pillar (a stone monument) will be set up at its border. **20.** This will be a sign (symbol) and a witness (proof) to the Lord in Egypt, for the Egyptians will cry to the Lord because of their oppressors (those who mistreat them), and He will send them a Savior (deliverer) to deliver them. **21.** The Lord will make Himself known (reveal Himself) to Egypt, and they will acknowledge (know) the Lord. They will offer sacrifices (ritual gifts) and vows (promises) to Him and keep them. **22.** The Lord will strike (punish) Egypt, but He will also heal (cure) it. They will return (turn back) to the Lord, and He will respond (answer) to their cries and heal them. **23.** In that day, there will be a highway (road) from Egypt to Assyria (an ancient empire), and the Assyrians will come to Egypt, and the Egyptians will go to Assyria. Both nations will serve (work together) in peace. **24.** In that day, Israel (the northern kingdom) will be a blessing alongside Egypt and Assyria, **25.** and the Lord of hosts (Lord of armies) will bless them, saying, "Blessed is Egypt My people, Assyria the work of My hands, and Israel My inheritance (God's special people)."

Chapter 20

1. It was in the year when Tartan (an Assyrian commander) arrived at Ashdod (a city of the Philistines), sent by King Sargon (the ruler of Assyria), and after he fought against it and seized the city, **2.** that the Lord spoke to Isaiah (the prophet), son of Amoz, saying, "Take off the sackcloth (a rough garment worn in mourning) you are wearing, and remove your sandals (footwear) from your feet." Isaiah obeyed and walked around bare and without shoes. **3.** The Lord then explained, "Just as My servant Isaiah has been walking for three years, naked and barefoot, as a sign and a wonder against Egypt and Ethiopia (two nations that will be brought to disgrace), **4.** So the king of Assyria will carry off the Egyptians as prisoners and the Ethiopians as captives—young and old, exposed and barefoot, their private parts uncovered, bringing shame upon Egypt. **5.** At that moment, they will be filled with fear and embarrassment over Ethiopia, their source of hope, and Egypt, their proudest possession. **6.** And the people of this land will wonder, saying, 'Where will we turn for help, now that the king of Assyria has come? How can we escape his power?'"

Chapter 21

1. A prophecy against the Wilderness of the Sea. Like a whirlwind from the south, it comes—born from a desert, a harsh land. 2. I have been given a vision of distress. The deceiver deceives, and the plunderer plunders. Elam, rise up! Media, lay siege! I have brought an end to their groaning. 3. My body is filled with pain; anguish grips me like the labor pains of a woman. I am overwhelmed by what I have heard, shocked by what I have seen. 4. My heart falters; fear overwhelms me. The night I longed for has turned into terror. 5. Prepare a feast, set a watchman on the tower, eat, and drink. Arise, you rulers, anoint your shields! 6. The Lord said to me, "Go, place a watchman. Let him announce what he sees." 7. He saw a chariot with two horsemen, and a chariot with donkeys and camels. He watched intently and observed carefully. 8. He cried, "A lion! My Lord! I stand guard every day, and I keep my post every night. 9. Look, here comes a chariot of men with two horsemen!" The answer came, "Babylon has fallen, fallen! All her idols are broken to the ground." 10. What I have heard from the Lord of hosts, the God of Israel, I have now declared to you. 11. A prophecy against Dumah. From Seir (a region) comes a voice, "Watchman, what is the news of the night? Watchman, what is the news?" 12. The watchman responds, "Morning is coming, but night also remains. If you want to inquire, ask. Return, come back." 13. A prophecy against Arabia. You who travel through Arabia, lodge in the forests of Dedan (a region). 14. Inhabitants of Tema (a desert region), bring water to the thirsty; meet the fleeing with bread. 15. They are fleeing from swords, from drawn bows, and from the distress of war. 16. The Lord has spoken: "In one year, just as a hired worker completes their time, all the glory of Kedar (a nomadic people) will end. 17. The remaining archers and warriors of Kedar will be reduced in number. For the Lord, the God of Israel, has spoken."

Chapter 22

1. A prophecy against the Valley of Vision (a term used for Jerusalem). What is causing you such distress that all of you have climbed onto your rooftops? **2.** You, who are so noisy and chaotic, a city full of confusion and celebration, are not being struck down in battle, nor are your dead falling by the sword. **3.** Your leaders have fled together in fear, captured by skilled archers (those who shoot arrows), while the rest of you are bound and have fled from far away.**4.** I cried out, "Turn your eyes from me, for I am overwhelmed with grief. Do not try to comfort me because of the destruction that has come upon my people (Jerusalem)."**5.** It is a day filled with hardship, oppression, and confusion, brought about by the Lord God of hosts, in the Valley of Vision—walls are being torn down, and cries are heard toward the mountain.**6.** Elam (an ancient kingdom east of Israel) comes carrying a quiver (a case for holding arrows) full of warriors and chariots, while Kir (a region near Mesopotamia) reveals its shields.**7.** Your finest valleys will soon be filled with chariots, and the horsemen will stand at your city gates, ready for battle.**8.** Judah's (the southern kingdom of Israel) protection has been taken away. You focused that day on the armor (defensive equipment) found in the House of the Forest (a grand palace built by King Solomon).**9.** You saw the extensive damage to the City of David (Jerusalem) and it was severe; you gathered the waters of the lower pool (a water source in Jerusalem) for use.**10.** You counted the houses of Jerusalem and tore some down in order to reinforce the city's walls.**11.** You built a reservoir (storage area for water) between the two walls to collect the water from the old pool, but you failed to consider the One who made it (God), and you did not honor Him who created it long ago.**12.** In that day, the Lord God of hosts called for mourning and weeping, for shaving the head and wearing sackcloth (a rough cloth worn during mourning), **13.** But instead, you rejoiced and celebrated, slaughtering oxen and sheep, eating meat and drinking wine, saying, "Let us eat and drink, for tomorrow we will die!"**14.** And then it was told to me, in the hearing of the Lord of hosts, "For this sin, there will be no forgiveness for you, even until your death," declares the Lord God of hosts.**15.** The Lord God of hosts says: "Go, approach this steward (a high official), Shebna (a royal official in Jerusalem), who is in charge of the household, and speak to him: **16.** 'Why are you here, and who are you with, that you have cut out a tomb (burial place) for yourself in the rock, as if you were building a monument high up in the cliffs for yourself?**17.** Behold, the Lord will cast you away violently, O mighty man, and He will certainly seize you.**18.** He will toss you like a ball (thrown away) into a wide land, and there you will die. Your glorious chariots will become a disgrace to your master's house.**19.** I will remove you from your office (position), and your authority will be taken away.**20.** In that day, I will call My servant Eliakim (a new leader) the son of Hilkiah (a priest),**21.** I will clothe him with your robe and empower him with your belt. I will entrust him with your responsibility. He will serve as a father to the people of Jerusalem and to the house of Judah.**22.** I will place the key (symbol of authority) to the house of David (the royal family) on his shoulder. He will open doors that no one can shut, and shut doors that no one can open.**23.** I will make him a peg (a secure support) in a firm place, and he will become a glorious throne for his father's house.**24.** All the glory of his father's house will be entrusted to him, including his descendants and every vessel (container) of small value, from cups to pitchers.**25.** "In that day," says the Lord of hosts, "the peg fastened securely will be removed and cut down, and the burden it bore will be broken off, for the Lord has spoken."

Chapter 23

1. A prophecy against the Valley of Vision (a term used for Jerusalem). What is causing you such distress that all of you have climbed onto your rooftops?**2.** You, who are so noisy and chaotic (confusion), a city full of confusion and celebration, are not being struck down in battle, nor are your dead falling by the sword.**3.** Your leaders have fled together in fear, captured by skilled archers (those who shoot arrows), while the rest of you are bound and have fled from far away.**4.** I cried out, "Turn your eyes from me, for I am overwhelmed with grief. Do not try to comfort me because of the destruction that has come upon my people (Jerusalem)."**5.** It is a day filled with hardship, oppression, and bewilderment (confusion), brought about by the Lord God of hosts, in the Valley of Vision—walls are being torn down, and cries are heard toward the mountain.**6.** Elam (an ancient kingdom east of Israel) comes carrying a quiver (a case for holding arrows) full of warriors and chariots, while Kir (a region near Mesopotamia) reveals its shields.**7.** Your finest valleys will soon be filled with chariots, and the horsemen (soldiers on horseback) will stand at your city gates, ready for battle.**8.** Judah's (the southern kingdom of Israel) protection has been taken away. You focused that day on the armor (defensive equipment) found in the House of the Forest (a grand palace built by King Solomon).**9.** You saw the extensive damage to the City of David (Jerusalem) and it was severe; you gathered the waters of the lower pool (a water source in Jerusalem) for use.**10.** You counted the houses of Jerusalem and tore some down in order to reinforce the city's walls.**11.** You built a reservoir (storage area for water) between the two walls to collect the water from the old pool, but you failed to consider the One who made it (God), and you did not honor Him who created it long ago.**12.** In that day, the Lord God of hosts called for mourning and weeping, for shaving the head and wearing sackcloth (a rough cloth worn during mourning),**13.** But instead, you rejoiced and celebrated, slaughtering oxen and sheep, eating meat and drinking wine, saying, "Let us eat and drink, for tomorrow we will die!"**14.** And then it was told to me, in the hearing of the Lord of hosts, "For this sin, there will be no atonement (forgiveness) for you, even until your death," declares the Lord God of hosts.**15.** The Lord God of hosts says: "Go, approach this steward (a high official), Shebna (a royal official in Jerusalem), who is in charge of the household, and speak to him:**16.** 'Why are you here, and who are you with, that you have cut out a tomb (burial place) for yourself in the rock, as if you were building a monument high up in the cliffs for yourself?**17.** Behold, the Lord will cast you away violently, O mighty man (strong leader), and He will certainly seize you.**18.** He will toss you like a ball (thrown away) into a wide land, and there you will die. Your glorious chariots will become a disgrace to your master's house.

Chapter 24

1. Look, the Lord is about to strip the earth of its people, leaving it desolate. He will distort its surface and scatter its inhabitants in every direction.**2.** It will be as though every class of people suffers equally—whether common folk or the priests (religious leaders), the servants or their masters, the maids or their mistresses, the buyers or sellers, the lenders or borrowers, and the creditors (a person who is owed money) and debtors.**3.** The land will be utterly emptied and plundered, for the Lord Himself has declared this.**4.** The earth will grieve and fade, the world will lose its vigor and waste away, and even the proud (arrogant) of the earth will dwindle.**5.** The earth has become polluted by its people; they have broken God's commands, altered His decrees (official rules), and abandoned the everlasting covenant (the agreement between God and His people).**6.** As a result, a curse (a punishment or evil) will devour the earth, leaving its inhabitants desolate (empty or barren). Only a few people will survive.**7.** The harvest will fail, the vines will wither, and all those who once rejoiced will now be filled with sorrow.**8.** The sound of tambourines (a small drum) will cease, the joyous celebrations will end, and the music of the harp (a musical instrument) will no longer be heard.**9.** No one will drink wine with merriment, and even strong drinks will taste bitter (harsh or unpleasant) to those who drink them.**10.** The city, once full of life, will be left in ruins; all the houses will be locked, and no one will enter.**11.** The streets will echo with cries for wine, but joy will be extinguished, and all the gladness (happiness) in the land will vanish.**12.** The city will be abandoned, its gates (entrances) broken, and nothing but desolation will remain.**13.** In the midst of this devastation, the land will be like a final harvest of olives shaken from their trees, or grapes left behind after the vineyards have been gathered.**14.** But some will lift their voices in praise, shouting for joy, and they will sing for the glory of the Lord from the farthest seas.**15.** So, glorify (praise and honor) the Lord in the early morning, and proclaim the name of the Lord God of Israel in the far-off coastal areas (shoreline regions) of the sea.**16.** From all corners of the earth, we hear songs of praise: "Glory to the righteous (just and good)!" But I cry out, "Woe is me! I am undone! The deceitful (dishonest or deceitful) have dealt treacherously, and the treacherous have acted with great deceit."**17.** Terror (fear), a pit (a deep hole), and a snare (a trap) await the inhabitants (people) of the earth.**18.** Whoever tries to flee from the terror will fall into the pit, and those who escape the pit will be caught in the snare. The heavens will open, and the very foundations (base or support) of the earth will be shaken.**19.** The earth will be shattered by violence, torn apart, and shaken to its core.**20.** The earth will sway like a drunken man, reeling and stumbling, like a hut (a small building) that totters in the storm. Its sins (transgression) will weigh it down, causing it to collapse and never rise again.**21.** On that day, the Lord will judge the heavenly host (spiritual beings or powers) in the heavens and the kings (rulers) of the earth here below.**22.** They will be gathered like prisoners in a pit, locked up in a dungeon, and after many days, they will face punishment.**23.** Then, the moon will be ashamed, and the sun will be humiliated, because the Lord of hosts will reign on Mount Zion (a hill in Jerusalem) and in Jerusalem, in the presence of His elders (leaders), with great glory.

Chapter 25

1. O Lord, You are my God; I will lift You up in praise and honor Your name, for You have done marvelous things. Your plans from long ago are trustworthy and true.**2.** For You have brought down a strong city, made a fortified city (a city with strong defenses) into a heap of ruins, and turned the palaces of foreign nations into nothing. It will never be rebuilt.**3.** Therefore, the mighty people will honor You, and the cities of powerful nations will tremble (be afraid) before You.**4.** For You have been a shelter (a place of safety) for the poor, a refuge (a safe place) for those in distress, a safe haven from the storm, and a shade from the heat; You shield them from the destructive force of the ruthless, like a storm battering against a wall.**5.** You will silence the shouting of strangers (foreigners), as heat in a parched (dried up) land; You will diminish the noise of those who bring harm, like the quieting of the song of the cruel under a cloud's shadow. **6.** And on this mountain, the Lord of Hosts will prepare a feast for all people, a banquet with rich food, fine wine, and aged wine (wine that has been stored for a long time), full of flavor and strength. **7.** On this mountain, He will remove the veil (a covering) that covers all nations, the covering that hides them. **8.** He will swallow up death forever, and the Lord God will wipe away every tear from all faces. He will remove the disgrace (shame) of His people from all the earth, for the Lord has spoken. **9.** In that day, it will be said, "Look, here is our God! We have been waiting for Him, and He has come to save us. This is the Lord; we have waited for Him, and we will rejoice and be glad in His salvation." **10.** On this mountain, the hand of the Lord will rest. Moab (a nation southeast of Israel) will be trampled under His feet, like straw pressed into the dirt. **11.** He will stretch out His hands in the midst of them, like a swimmer trying to swim, and He will bring down their pride along with the deceit (dishonesty) of their hands. **12.** He will bring down the strongholds (fortresses) and fortresses of their walls, flattening them, and laying them low, down to the dust.

Chapter 26

1. On that day, a song will be sung in the land of Judah (southern kingdom of Israel): "We have a strong city; God will appoint salvation (deliverance or safety) as our walls and defenses. **2.** Open the gates, so that the righteous (morally right or just) nation that keeps the truth may enter in. **3.** You will keep in perfect peace the one whose mind is focused on You, because he trusts in You. **4.** Trust in the Lord forever, for Yah (a shortened form of God's name), the Lord, is our everlasting strength. **5.** He brings down those who live in pride, the lofty (arrogantly high) city; He lays it low, He brings it to the ground, He makes it crumble to dust. **6.** The poor will trample (step heavily on) it down—the feet of the needy and the steps of the oppressed (those who are treated unfairly) will walk over it. **7.** The path of the righteous is straight; O Most Upright (God, who is completely just), You weigh the way of the righteous. **8.** Yes, in the path of Your judgments (decisions or decrees), O Lord, we have waited for You. The longing of our soul is for Your name and the remembrance (recognition or calling to mind) of You. **9.** At night, with my soul, I have longed for You. Yes, with my spirit (the inner part of the person) within me, I will seek You early. For when Your judgments are revealed on the earth, the people of the world will learn righteousness. **10.** Let grace (kindness or favor) be shown to the wicked, yet he will not learn righteousness; in the land of uprightness (justice), he will deal wickedly, and he will not look upon the majesty (greatness or glory) of the Lord. **11.** Lord, when Your hand is lifted up, they will not see. But they will be ashamed (feel guilt or humiliation) when they see and feel the burning anger for their jealousy against people; yes, the fire of Your enemies will consume (destroy) them. **12.** Lord, You will grant us peace, for You have done all our works in us. **13.** O Lord our God, other masters (rulers) besides You have ruled over us, but by You only we remember Your name. **14.** They are dead, they will not live again; they are deceased (no longer living), they will not rise. Therefore, You have punished and destroyed them, and made their memory perish (to cease to exist). **15.** You have increased the nation, O Lord, You have increased the nation; You are glorified (honored); You have expanded the borders (edges) of the land. **16.** Lord, in their trouble (difficulty), they sought You; they poured out their prayers when Your chastening (discipline or correction) was upon them. **17.** Like a woman in labor (giving birth) who cries out in pain when her time is near, so have we been in Your sight, O Lord. **18.** We have been in pain, we have been as though in labor; we have brought forth wind (nothing meaningful), and have not brought salvation (deliverance) to the earth, nor have the inhabitants (people) of the world been born. **19.** Your dead shall live; together with my dead body, they shall arise. Awake and sing, you who dwell in the dust (earth); for Your dew (moisture) is like the dew of herbs (plants), and the earth shall give birth to the dead. **20.** Come, my people, enter into your chambers (rooms), and shut your doors behind you; hide yourselves for a little while, until the indignation (God's wrath) has passed. **21.** For behold, the Lord comes out of His place to punish the inhabitants (people) of the earth for their iniquity (sin or wrong); the earth will reveal her bloodshed and will no longer cover her slain (those who have been killed).

Chapter 27

1. On that day, with His powerful sword, the Lord will punish Leviathan (a mythical sea monster), that serpent that flees, and the twisting serpent Leviathan. He will strike down the creature dwelling in the sea (a symbol of chaos and evil). **2.** Sing to her on that day, "A vineyard (a place where grapes are grown), and rich with ripe fruit!" **3.** I, the Lord, tend and protect this vineyard. I water it continuously, guarding it both night and day, ensuring it suffers no harm. **4.** I am not filled with wrath. Who would dare challenge Me with briers (thorny plants) and thorns? I will pass through them and set them all ablaze. **5.** Instead, let anyone who seeks My strength come to Me and make peace, for in Me, they will find peace." **6.** Those who seek the Lord will take deep root (establish themselves firmly) in Israel (Jacob, the forefather of Israel), and Israel will bloom and produce fruit that fills the world. **7.** Has the Lord dealt with Israel as harshly as those who have attacked it? Has He struck Israel down in the same way as others who were destroyed? **8.** In His measure, He contended (argued or fought) with Israel, sending it away. He removed it with His mighty wind, just as the east wind sweeps across the land. **9.** Because of this, Jacob's sins will be forgiven, and the fruit of this atonement is that when He destroys the altars (sacred places of false worship), they will turn to dust like chalkstones (easily crushed), and all idols and incense altars made of wood will vanish. **10.** Yet the fortified (strong and protected) city will lie desolate, its homes abandoned, a barren wilderness. There, cattle will graze and rest, feeding on the broken branches. **11.** When the branches (boughs) dry up, they will be snapped off, and women will come to burn them. The people are without sense (lacking wisdom) and understanding; because of this, the one who made them will have no mercy, and the one who formed them will not show favor. **12.** On that day, the Lord will gather His people, from the land of the River (the Euphrates River), all the way to the Brook (a small stream) of Egypt (the Nile River), bringing them together, one by one, O children of Israel. **13.** That day will come when a mighty trumpet (a loud horn or signal) will sound, and those lost in the land of Assyria (an ancient empire to the northeast of Israel), and those scattered in Egypt, will return to worship the Lord on His holy mountain in Jerusalem (the capital city of Israel and the center of worship).

Chapter 28

1. How tragic for the proud crown (arrogant rulers), the drunkards of Ephraim (the northern kingdom of Israel), whose glorious beauty (riches and splendor) fades like a flower, perched on the hills of fertile valleys (lush, fertile areas), for those who are overwhelmed by wine (intoxicating alcohol)! **2.** Look, the Lord is sending a mighty and strong force (a powerful force), like a storm of hail (a violent hailstorm) and a devastating whirlwind (a destructive storm), like a flood of raging waters (overwhelming floodwaters) that will bring them down to the earth with His hand. **3.** The crown of pride (arrogant leaders), the drunkards of Ephraim, will be trampled into the dust (humiliated underfoot). **4.** The splendid beauty will be like a fading flower that grows in the fertile valley, withering like the first fruit before summer (the first fruits that ripen too early), which someone notices, but before they can even grasp it, it is already consumed. **5.** On that day, the Lord of hosts (God of armies) will be a crown of glory and a royal diadem (a beautiful, precious crown) for the survivors (those who remain) of His people. **6.** He will provide a spirit of justice (a spirit of fairness) to those who make judgments, and strength (empowerment) to those who defend the city gates from their enemies (those who protect the city). **7.** Yet even they (the leaders) have stumbled (made mistakes) because of wine (intoxicating alcohol), and by strong drinks (alcoholic beverages), they have strayed (lost their way); the priests (religious leaders) and prophets (God's messengers) have erred through drunkenness, overwhelmed by wine, and their vision is clouded, causing them to fall short in their judgment (their ability to make wise decisions). **8.** The tables where they feast are full of vomit and filth, with no place left clean (nothing remains pure or holy). **9.** "Who will God teach wisdom? (Who is ready to understand His truth?) To those who are barely weaned from milk (spiritually immature)? To those who are still on the breast (new in their understanding)? **10.** Precept (instruction) must be laid upon precept, and precept upon precept, line upon line, and line upon line, here a little and there a little (truth must come step by step, slowly and gradually). **11.** He will speak to them in foreign tongues with stammering lips (a strange and unfamiliar speech). **12.** To them He had said, "This is the rest (peace and comfort) with which you may bring rest to the weary (those burdened by life's struggles)," and, "This is the refreshing"; yet they refused to listen (they ignored His words). **13.** But the message of the Lord came to them, saying, "Precept upon precept, precept upon precept, line upon line, line upon line, here a little and there a little," so that they would fall back in their disobedience, be shattered (broken in spirit), and be trapped (caught) and ensnared (captured). **14.** Therefore, listen to the word of the Lord, you mocking rulers (those who scorn His warnings), you who govern the people in Jerusalem. **15.** You have declared, "We have made a covenant (agreement) with death, and with Sheol (the grave) we have made a pact. When the overwhelming scourge (God's judgment) comes, it will not affect us; for we have made lies our refuge (false security), and we have hidden ourselves under falsehood (deception)." **16.** Therefore, the Lord God says: "Look, I am laying in Zion (a hill in Jerusalem, symbolic of God's kingdom) a stone for a foundation, a tested stone (a solid and reliable foundation), a precious cornerstone (a cornerstone that is strong and valuable), a sure foundation (firm and unshakable); whoever believes in it will not be in haste (will not panic or act rashly)." **17.** I will measure justice with the measuring line (the standard of fairness), and righteousness with the plumb line (a tool for measuring right actions); the hail (God's judgment) will destroy the refuge of lies (the false shelters they trust), and the floodwaters (of judgment) will overwhelm the hiding places (the false securities they rely on). **18.** Your covenant with death will be void (broken), and your agreement with Sheol (the grave) will not stand; when the overwhelming scourge (devastating judgment) sweeps through, you will be trampled by it (overcome by it). **19.** Each time it comes, it will take you by surprise; every morning, it will pass through, and in the daytime and night, it will be terrifying just to hear about it (the very report of it will cause fear). **20.** For the bed (place of rest) is too short to stretch out on, and the blanket is too narrow (too small) to wrap yourself in. **21.** For the Lord will rise up as He did at Mount Perazim (a place where God brought victory in Israel), and He will be angry like He was in the Valley of Gibeon (a valley where God gave victory to Joshua)—to perform His strange (unexpected) and awesome work, His unusual (out of the ordinary) act. **22.** Therefore, do not mock or scorn (reject) His warnings, lest your chains (captivity) become stronger; for I have heard from the Lord God of hosts (the Almighty), that a destruction has been determined over the whole earth (God's judgment is coming upon all the earth). **23.** Listen carefully (pay close attention) to my words, hear my voice, and understand my speech (take heed to what I say). **24.** Does the plowman (farmer) plow the field all day just to sow (plant the seeds)? Does he keep turning the soil and breaking the clods (large, hard pieces of soil)? **25.** When he has leveled the ground, does he not sow black cumin (a type of seed), scatter cumin, plant wheat in rows, barley in its place, and spelt in its proper spot (carefully planting each crop where it belongs)? **26.** For it is God who teaches him wisdom (God guides him in right judgment), His God instructs him (gives him knowledge of how to do it properly). **27.** Black cumin is not threshed with a threshing sledge (a large, heavy farm tool), nor is the cumin crushed by rolling cartwheels over it; instead, it is beaten with a stick, and the cumin with a rod (each type of crop is harvested in the proper way). **28.** Bread flour must be ground (milled into fine flour); therefore, he doesn't thresh it endlessly (he doesn't keep pounding it forever), break it with his cartwheel, or crush it with his horsemen (he uses appropriate methods for each task). **29.** This wisdom also comes from the Lord of hosts (God of armies), who is wonderful in counsel (wise in giving advice) and excellent in guidance (full of wisdom in leading).

Chapter 29

1. Woe to Ariel, to Ariel, the city where David once lived! (Ariel is a poetic name for Jerusalem) Year after year will pass, and the feasts will continue as scheduled. **2.** I will bring hardship upon Ariel; there will be sorrow and distress, and it will become to Me like the mourning of Ariel. **3.** I will set up a camp around you, surrounding you completely, and raise barriers against you with mounds of earth and siegeworks (temporary military structures) around your walls. **4.** You will be humbled, and you will speak from the dust, your voice will be faint, as though it rises from the earth. It will be like the speech of a medium (a spirit communicator), muttered from the ground. **5.** Your enemies will be as numerous as fine dust, and those who oppose you will be like chaff (the outer husk of grain) that is swept away. And it will all happen in a moment, suddenly. **6.** The Lord of hosts (the Lord of armies) will punish you with thunder, earthquakes, and great noise, with a storm, violent winds, and the blazing fire of destruction. **7.** The nations that attack Ariel, and all who besiege her, will be like a fleeting dream, vanishing in the night as though they never existed. **8.** It will be like a man who dreams he is eating when hungry, but wakes up to find himself unsatisfied. Or like a thirsty man who dreams of drinking, yet awakens still faint with thirst. Such will be the fate of all the nations who come against Mount Zion (a name for Jerusalem, the holy city). **9.** Be astonished and stunned! Blind yourselves and stay blind! They are drunk, but not from wine; they stagger, but not from intoxicating drink. **10.** The Lord has poured a deep sleep upon you, closing the eyes of the prophets and veiling the heads of the seers (those who were meant to see visions). **11.** For you, the vision will become like words written in a book that is sealed. It will be handed to someone who is educated (literate) and told, "Please read this." But he will answer, "I cannot, because it is sealed." **12.** Then the book will be given to one who cannot read, and when told, "Please read this," he will respond, "I do not know how to read." **13.** The Lord says: "This people honors Me with their words, but their hearts are far from Me. Their worship is based on rules made by men (not by true reverence for God)." **14.** Therefore, I will perform a marvelous act among this people, one that will leave them in awe. The wisdom of their wise men will vanish, and the understanding of their prudent (wise) men will be hidden. **15.** Woe to those who try to hide their plans from the Lord, and who think their deeds in darkness are unseen. They say, "Who knows what we do?" and "Who can see us?" **16.** You are turning things upside down! Can the potter (God) be compared to clay? Can the creation say to the Creator, "You did not make me"? Or can the formed object claim to the One who made it, "You have no understanding"? **17.** In a very short time, Lebanon (a region north of Israel) will be transformed into a fertile field, and what was once a fertile field will be as a forest. **18.** On that day, the deaf will hear the words of the book, and the blind will see through the darkness and the confusion (unclear or difficult to understand). **19.** The humble will find great joy in the Lord, and the poor among men will rejoice in the Holy One of Israel (God). **20.** for the ruthless (cruel people) will be gone, the mockers will be consumed (destroyed), and all who wait to do evil will be wiped out. **21.** Those who unjustly accuse a man, who trap him with words, or who turn away the righteous with empty arguments, will be cut off. **22.** Therefore, this is what the Lord says, the One who redeemed Abraham (the ancestor of Israel): "The house of Jacob (Israel) will no longer be ashamed, nor will their faces turn pale. **23.** But when they see their children, the work of My hands, in their midst, they will honor My name, and reverence (respect deeply) the Holy One of Jacob, and stand in awe (deep respect) of the God of Israel. **24.** Those who were once spiritually blind will gain understanding, and those who complained will be taught true wisdom."

Chapter 30

1. "How dreadful it is for the rebellious (disobedient) children," declares the LORD. "They seek counsel, but it's not from Me, and they make plans that do not include My Spirit (God's influence). By doing so, they add more sin to their already existing sin." **2.** "They go down to Egypt (a neighboring nation), but have not asked for My guidance. They seek strength from Pharaoh (king of Egypt) and rely on his protection instead of turning to Me!" **3.** "As a result, the very power they find in Pharaoh will turn to shame, and the trust they place in Egypt will bring them disgrace (humiliation)." **4.** "Pharaoh's officials are stationed in Zoan (a city in Egypt), and his ambassadors (representatives) have gone to Hanes (another Egyptian city), but all of them will be put to shame by a people who cannot help them at all—those who will only bring shame and reproach." **5.** "This is a message against the animals of the South (a region south of Israel, likely Egypt). Through a land filled with suffering and danger, where wild lions, venomous (poisonous) snakes, and fiery flying serpents live, they will transport their wealth on the backs of young donkeys and camels. But they are bringing it to a people who will not profit (benefit) from it." **6.** "Egypt's aid will be useless (of no value) and will achieve nothing. Therefore, I have given it the name 'Rahab-Hem-Shebeth' (a mocking name meaning 'Rahab the Do-Nothing'), to emphasize Egypt's inability to help." **7.** "Go and write this message down for them on a tablet (a flat stone for writing), and record it on a scroll (a written document), so it can be preserved for future generations, standing as a testimony forever and ever." **8.** "For they are a rebellious (disobedient) people, deceitful (dishonest) children, children who refuse to hear the law (commands) of the Lord. **9.** "They say to the seers (prophets), 'Do not see,' and to the prophets, 'Do not speak to us the truth; tell us only smooth things (pleasant things) and prophesy (predict) lies!" **10.** "Get out of our way, leave the path, and stop speaking to us about the Holy One (God) of Israel!" **11.** "Therefore, the Holy One of Israel (God) says: 'because you have rejected (refused) this word, and have placed your trust in oppression (unjust treatment) and lies, **12.** this sin will become like a wall ready to fall, a bulge (swelling) in a high wall that will suddenly collapse and crumble.'" **13.** "It will shatter (break) like a potter's vessel (clay pot), smashed into pieces; not a single shard (piece) will remain, not even for the smallest task, such as starting a fire or drawing water.'" **14.** "For the Lord God, the Holy One of Israel, says: 'In returning (turning back) and rest you will find salvation (rescue); in quietness (calmness) and trust in me will be your strength.' But you refused," **15.** "And you said, 'No, we will escape on horses (fast animals)!' Therefore, you will flee. And, 'We will ride on swift horses (quick horses)!' So, those who pursue you will be swifter (faster)!" **16.** "One thousand will flee (run away) at the threat of one, and at the threat of five, all of you will run, until you are left like a solitary flagstaff (pole) on a mountaintop, or a banner (flag) on a hill." **17.** "Therefore, the Lord will wait to show you mercy (compassion), and He will be exalted (honored) to grant you grace (favor). For the Lord is a God of justice (fairness); blessed are those who wait for Him." **18.** "O people of Zion (Jerusalem), who dwell in Jerusalem, you will weep (cry) no longer. He will be kind to you when you cry for help; as soon as He hears it, He will respond to you." **19.** "Although the Lord gives you the bread (food) of adversity (difficulty) and the water of affliction (suffering), your teachers will no longer hide in secret corners, but your eyes will see them plainly." **20.** "Your ears will hear a voice behind you saying, 'This is the way (path); walk in it,' whether you turn to the right or to the left." **21.** "You will throw away the idols (false gods) made of silver and the images made of gold that you have been worshiping. You will say to them, 'Be gone!'" **22.** "Then He will send rain (water) to nourish the seeds (crops) you sow in the soil, and the land will produce a bountiful harvest (yield). Your crops will be rich and plentiful." 23. "On that day, your cattle (animals) will graze in vast pastures (fields), and the oxen and donkeys (farm animals) that plow the fields will enjoy well-prepared food, winnowed (separated) with a shovel and a fork." 24. "On every high mountain and hill, there will be flowing streams (rivers) of water on the day of the great slaughter (destruction), when the fortresses (towers) fall." 25. "The name of the Lord comes from a distance (afar), burning with His anger (wrath), and His burden (weight) is heavy. His lips are filled with fury (rage), and His tongue is like a devouring fire (destructive fire)." 26. "His breath (wind) is like a rushing stream (flood) that rises up to the neck (high), to sift (separate) the nations with the sieve (strainer) of futility (emptiness). He will place a bridle (restraint) in the jaws of the people to lead them astray." 27. "You will sing (praise) with joy, like at night during a holy festival (sacred gathering), and your hearts will be glad (rejoice), as when one walks with a flute (musical instrument) to come to the mountain of the Lord, to the Mighty One (Powerful One) of Israel." 28. "The Lord will make His glorious voice heard, and He will reveal the descent (coming down) of His mighty arm, with great anger (wrath) and a flame of devouring fire (destructive fire), accompanied by storms, tempests (violent winds), and hailstones." 29. "The Assyrians (an empire to the northeast of Israel) will be struck down by the voice of the Lord, as He smites them with His rod (staff)." 30. "Every time the Lord enacts His judgment (punishment), the sound of tambourines (musical instruments) and harps (stringed instruments) will be heard in the battles of brandishing (waving), as He fights against them." 31. "For Tophet (a valley in Jerusalem, associated with child sacrifice and idolatry) was prepared long ago; indeed, it was made ready for the king (the ruler of Assyria). It is deep and wide; its pyre (fire pit) is filled with firewood. The breath (wind) of the Lord, like a stream of burning sulfur (brimstone), will kindle (ignite) it."

Chapter 31

1. Woe to those who turn to Egypt (a neighboring nation) for aid, placing their trust in horses (military power) and chariots (war vehicles) because they are numerous, and in horsemen (cavalry) for their strength. But they fail to look to the Holy One of Israel (God) or seek the LORD. 2. But the Lord, in His wisdom, will bring calamity. He will not retract (take back) His words. He will rise up against the house of evildoers (those who do wrong) and against those who support the workers of iniquity. 3. For the Egyptians are only men, not gods, and their horses are mere flesh (physical), not spirit. When the Lord stretches out His hand (to judge), both the helper and the helped will fall together; they will all perish in the end. 4. The Lord has spoken to me: "Just as a lion roars, and a young lion over his prey (even when many shepherds are summoned to fight him), he remains unafraid of their voices or undisturbed (troubled) by their noise. In the same way, the Lord of Hosts (God's army) will descend to defend Mount Zion (Jerusalem) and its hill." 5. Like birds in flight, the Lord of Hosts will shield (protect) Jerusalem. He will not only defend but also deliver it, passing over it and keeping it safe from harm. 6. Turn back to Him (God), from whom the children of Israel have long rebelled (turned away). 7. On that day, each man will cast away his idols (false gods) of silver and gold—the very sinful objects that your hands have made for yourselves. 8. Then, Assyria (an empire that threatened Israel) will fall by a sword that is not of human making, a sword not designed by men. They will flee from this weapon, and their young men will be taken captive (prisoners). 9. They will retreat to their stronghold (fortress) in fear, and their leaders will be struck with terror (frightened) by the banner (a military standard or symbol)," declares the Lord, whose fire is in Zion (the mountain on which Jerusalem stands) and whose furnace is in Jerusalem.

Chapter 32

1. Behold, a king who reigns with righteousness will arise, and his princes will rule with fairness, ensuring justice prevails across the land. 2. A man will become a refuge (safe place) from the gusts of wind, a shelter from the storm, offering peace like cool waters in a parched (thirsty) land, and providing the shade of a mighty rock in a weary, desolate (empty) wilderness. 3. Those whose eyes have been dimmed will be able to see clearly again, and those whose ears have been closed will now hear and understand. 4. The reckless will gain understanding, and those who once struggled to speak will find their words clear and confident. 5. No longer will the foolish be praised for generosity, nor the miser (someone who hoards wealth) be commended for kindness. 6. The fool will speak only foolishness, and their hearts will be filled with wickedness: they will indulge in ungodliness (wickedness), speak lies against the Lord, and disregard the needs of the hungry and thirsty. 7. The deceitful (dishonest) are full of evil schemes, planning to harm the poor with false accusations, even when the downtrodden speak what is just and right. 8. But the generous man will always devise good plans, and his generosity will secure his place, allowing

him to stand firm. 9. Listen closely, you women who live in comfort and ease, take heed of my words; you complacent (self-satisfied) daughters, pay attention to what I say. 10. In just over a year, distress will come upon you, women who are at ease; the harvest will fail, and there will be no fruit to gather. 11. Tremble, you who are so at ease; be alarmed, you self-satisfied ones; strip off your fine clothing, expose yourselves, and wrap yourselves in sackcloth (a coarse fabric) to show your mourning. 12. The people will mourn over the loss of the fertile (rich, productive) fields and the devastation of the once-productive vineyards. 13. On the land of my people, thornbushes and thistles (sharp plants) will grow; the once-rejoicing cities will be overtaken by briars, and the palaces will stand abandoned. 14. The lively city will be left in ruins, its strongholds (fortresses) and towers overrun by wild animals; the land will be nothing but grazing grounds for flocks, a place where wild donkeys roam freely. 15. This desolation will continue until the Spirit of God is poured out upon us from above. Then, the barren wilderness (desert) will become a fertile, fruitful land, and the empty (barren) fields will transform into lush forests. 16. At that time, justice will find its place in the wilderness, and righteousness will remain in the fertile fields. 17. Righteousness will bring peace, and its influence will produce quietness and security that will last forever. 18. My people will dwell in homes of peace, in secure (safe) dwellings, and in places of quiet rest, free from fear and turmoil (confusion). 19. Even though the forest may be struck by hail (frozen rain), and the city will be brought low in humiliation, 20. Blessed are those who plant their crops beside the waters, and those who allow their animals to graze freely by the riverside.

Chapter 33

1. Woe to those who rob others, though they themselves have never been robbed; to those who betray, even though no one has betrayed them! The day will come when your plunder will turn against you, and when you cease to betray, others will betray you in return. 2. Lord, show us Your mercy! We have patiently waited for You. Be our strength every morning, and deliver us in times of distress. 3. At the sound of the chaos (confusion), the people will flee. When You rise in power, the nations will be scattered before You. 4. Your spoils (plunder) will be collected as the locusts gather. Just as locusts (insects that swarm in large numbers) run back and forth, so will your enemies come upon you. 5. The Lord is lifted high in glory, and He resides in His heavenly place. His righteousness and justice have filled Zion (Jerusalem). 6. The foundation of your time will be wisdom (insight) and understanding. Your salvation will be made strong, and the fear (respect) of the Lord will be your most valued treasure. 7. The mighty warriors will cry in despair, and those who bring peace will weep with sorrow. 8. The roads will be desolate, and travelers will cease their journeys. The covenant (agreement) has been broken, and the cities have been disregarded by all. 9. The earth will mourn and wither (dried up), Lebanon (a region known for its forests) will be shamed and dried up. Sharon (a fertile plain) will become a desolate wasteland, and Bashan (a fertile region) and Carmel (a mountain) will lose their harvests. 10. "Now I will arise," declares the Lord. "Now is the time for Me to be exalted and to lift Myself up." 11. You will produce nothing but chaff (worthless remains), and your efforts will yield only stubble (dry, useless plant material). Your breath will be like a consuming fire that burns everything in its path. 12. The people will be like burning lime (a substance burned at high temperatures), or like thorns that are cut down and set on fire. 13. Pay attention, all you who are distant (far-off nations), and you who are near, recognize My power and greatness. 14. Those in Zion (Jerusalem) who have sinned will be filled with fear; even the hypocrites (those pretending to be righteous) will tremble, asking, "Who can survive the fiery judgment? Who can endure the everlasting flames?" 15. It is the one who lives rightly, speaks with honesty, refuses dishonest gain, rejects bribes, stops his ears from hearing about violence, and closes his eyes to avoid seeing evil, 16. This person will dwell in safety, with a stronghold of rocks as his refuge. His food will be provided, and his water will be secure. 17. Your eyes will see the King (God) in all His beauty; you will witness the land that stretches far beyond your reach. 18. Your heart will ponder in fear, asking, "Where is the scribe (someone who writes or records)? Where is the one who measures (weighs) things? Where is the one who counts the towers?" 19. You will no longer encounter a violent people, a people whose speech is unintelligible (unclear), whose language you cannot understand. 20. Look to Zion, the city where we celebrate our feasts. You will see Jerusalem, a peaceful place, an unshakable dwelling that will never be uprooted, where no peg or rope will ever be removed. 21. There, the majestic (glorious) Lord will be present for us, a place of wide rivers and streams. No ships with oars will pass through it, nor will majestic ships sail on its waters. 22. For the Lord is our Judge, the Lord is our Lawgiver (one who makes laws), and the Lord is our King; He will save us. 23. Your ships' equipment (tackle) will be undone; they will not strengthen

their mast, nor spread their sails. The great plunder of a mighty people will be divided, and even the disabled (lame) will take their portion. 24. The inhabitants (residents) of this place will not say, "I am ill." The people who live there will have their sins forgiven.

Chapter 34

1. Draw near, all you nations, and listen; pay attention, all people! Let the earth hear, and all that is within it, the world and all that springs from it. 2. The Lord's anger burns against every nation, and His fierce wrath (intense anger) is upon all their armies. He has completely wiped them out, handing them over to be destroyed. 3. The bodies of the slain will be left exposed, their flesh rotting, and their stench rising, while the mountains are soaked with their blood. 4. The stars of heaven will fade away, and the skies will be rolled up like a scroll. All the stars will fall, like leaves falling from the vine, or like figs dropping from a tree. 5. "My sword is soaked (covered) in heaven, and it will descend to bring judgment upon Edom (an ancient kingdom to the southeast of Israel), a people I have cursed." 6. The sword of the Lord is drenched (soaked) in blood, and filled with the fat (richness) of lambs and goats, and the fat of the kidneys of rams. The Lord has prepared a sacrifice in Bozrah (a city in Edom), and a great slaughter in the land of Edom. 7. Alongside the mighty bulls, the wild oxen (strong beasts) will fall, and the land will be soaked with blood, with the dust soaked in fat. 8. For this is the day of vengeance (punishment) from the Lord, the year of retribution (rewarding for wrongs done) for the cause of Zion (Jerusalem, representing God's people). 9. The streams will turn to pitch (burning tar), and the dust will become sulfur (brimstone); the land will burn like a fiery pit. 10. Day and night it will burn, its smoke rising forever. It will remain desolate (empty) for all generations, and no one will ever pass through it again. 11. Pelicans (water birds), porcupines, owls, and ravens will make it their home. He will stretch out over it the measuring line of chaos (disorder) and the stones of desolation. 12. Though they call for rulers and officials, there will be none; all its princes (leaders) will be reduced to nothing. 13. Thorns (sharp plants) will cover its palaces, nettles (prickly plants) and brambles (thorny bushes) will grow up in its fortresses. It will become a place for jackals (wild animals) and a den for ostriches (large flightless birds). 14. Wild beasts of the desert will meet with jackals, and goats will call to one another. Creatures of the night will find a resting place there and settle in safety. 15. The arrow snake (a venomous reptile) will nest there, laying eggs and hatching them under her shadow. Hawks (birds of prey) will gather there, each with its mate. 16. "Look in the book of the Lord and read: None of these creatures will be missing, none will be without a mate. For My mouth has commanded, and His Spirit has gathered them. 17. He has cast the lot (made a decision) for them, and with a measuring line, He has divided it among them. They will possess it forever, and from generation to generation, they will dwell in it."

Chapter 35

1. The wilderness and the barren land will rejoice, and even the desert will burst forth in blooming flowers, like a rose. 2. It will thrive and bloom in abundance, filled with joy and songs of celebration. The majesty of Lebanon (a mountain region known for its great forests) will be bestowed upon it, along with the beauty of Carmel (a mountain in Israel) and Sharon (fertile plains in Israel). They will witness the glorious presence of the Lord and the splendor of our God. 3. Strengthen the weak hands, and steady the unsteady knees that tremble. 4. To those whose hearts are faint, say, "Be strong and do not be afraid! See, your God is coming with vengeance (punishment), and He will bring justice. He will come to deliver and save you." 5. The eyes of the blind will be opened, and the ears of the deaf will be cleared, so that they can hear. 6. The lame (those unable to walk) will leap like a deer, and the mute (unable to speak) will burst into song. Streams of water will flow through the desert, and rivers will spring up in the wasteland. 7. The dry, cracked land will turn into a pool of water, and the parched earth will overflow with springs of water. Where jackals (wild desert animals) once roamed, there will now be an abundance of grass and reeds. 8. A highway will be there, a clear path, called the Highway of Holiness. Only the pure will walk on it, and the impure (unclean) will not pass through it. This path will be for those who are redeemed (saved by God). Even those who lack wisdom will not go astray on it. 9. No lions or wild, dangerous beasts will be there; they will not be found along this road. Only the redeemed of the Lord will travel there. 10. The redeemed (freed) of the Lord will return to Zion (the city of Jerusalem), with everlasting joy upon their heads. They will be filled with joy and gladness, and sorrow and sighing will be no more.

Chapter 36

1. In the fourteenth year of King Hezekiah's (the king of Judah) rule, Sennacherib (the king of Assyria) launched an attack on all the fortified cities of Judah and succeeded in capturing them. 2. Afterward, the king of Assyria dispatched his officer, the Rabshakeh (a high-ranking officer in the Assyrian army), with a vast army from Lachish (a fortified city in Judah) to Jerusalem (the capital city of Judah) to confront King Hezekiah. The Rabshakeh positioned himself by the aqueduct (a water channel) near the upper pool (a reservoir of water) along the road that led to the Fuller's Field (a place where cloth was cleaned and processed). 3. Eliakim, the son of Hilkiah (the one in charge of the household), Shebna (the royal scribe, responsible for written records), and Joah, the son of Asaph (the recorder, keeper of records), went out to meet him. 4. The Rabshakeh addressed them, saying, "Say to Hezekiah, 'This is the message from the great king, the king of Assyria: 'What are you depending on that makes you think you can defy me? 5. You speak of having military plans and strength, but those are just empty words. So tell me, who are you trusting in that you would oppose me? 6. You're relying on Egypt, which is like a broken reed (a symbol of weakness). Anyone who leans on it will only harm themselves. This is how Pharaoh, the king of Egypt, will treat those who trust in him. 7. But if you insist, 'We trust in the Lord our God,' is He the same God whose high places (places of worship) and altars (sacrifice sites) Hezekiah has destroyed, telling the people of Judah and Jerusalem, 'You must worship only at this altar'? 8. Now, come to an agreement with my master, the king of Assyria, and I will give you two thousand horses, if you can provide riders (soldiers) for them! 9. How can you possibly fight even one of my commanders, the lowest of my master's officers, when you are relying on Egypt for chariots (horse-drawn vehicles) and horsemen? 10. Furthermore, did I come up against this land to destroy it without the Lord's (God's) will? The Lord Himself has told me, 'Go and destroy this land.'" 11. Eliakim, Shebna, and Joah said to the Rabshakeh, "Please speak to us in Aramaic (the language of diplomacy), for we understand it. Don't speak to us in Hebrew (the language of Judah) so that the people on the wall can hear you." 12. But the Rabshakeh replied, "Has my master sent me to speak only to you and your master, and not to the men sitting on the wall? They too will soon be eating their own waste (excrement) and drinking their own urine along with you." 13. Then, the Rabshakeh stood up and loudly called out in Hebrew, "Hear the words of the great king, the king of Assyria! 14. This is what the king says: 'Don't let Hezekiah deceive you, for he will not be able to save you. 15. Don't let him convince you to trust in the Lord, claiming, "The Lord will certainly save us; this city will not fall into the hands of the king of Assyria."' 16. Do not listen to Hezekiah! This is what the king of Assyria says: 'Make peace with me and surrender. Come out to me, and each of you will be able to eat from your own vine (grapevine) and fig tree, and drink from your own cistern (a well or water reservoir); 17. until I come and take you to a land like your own, a land of grain (cereal crops) and fresh wine, a land of bread and vineyards (grape farms). 18. Don't be fooled by Hezekiah's promises that the Lord will save you. Has any god of the nations ever rescued their lands from the king of Assyria's power? 19. Where are the gods of Hamath (a city in Syria) and Arpad (another city in Syria)? Where are the gods of Sepharvaim (a city in Assyria)? Did they save Samaria (the capital of the northern kingdom of Israel) from my power? 20. Who among all the gods of these nations has been able to deliver their lands from my hand? How then can the Lord deliver Jerusalem from my hand?'" 21. But the people remained silent and did not respond, because the king had instructed them, "Do not answer him." 22. Then Eliakim, the son of Hilkiah who was in charge of the royal household, Shebna the scribe, and Joah the recorder, came to Hezekiah with their clothes torn (a sign of mourning and distress) and reported to him all the words of the Rabshakeh.

Chapter 37

1. When King Hezekiah (the king of Judah) heard the message, he tore his clothes (a traditional sign of grief), put on sackcloth (a rough garment worn for mourning), and went to the house of the Lord (the temple in Jerusalem). 2. He then sent Eliakim (the steward of his household), Shebna (the royal scribe), and the elders of the priests, all wearing sackcloth, to go to Isaiah the prophet (Isaiah, son of Amoz, a messenger of God). 3. They relayed the message, saying: "King Hezekiah declares, 'Today is a day of distress, shame, and blasphemy (mockery against God); for though the children are on the verge of being born, they lack the strength to deliver them. 4. Perhaps the Lord your God will listen to the words of Rabshakeh (the chief Assyrian spokesman), whom his master, the king of Assyria, has sent to reproach the living God, and will rebuke the blasphemous words He has heard. Therefore, pray on behalf of the remnant (those who remain) left behind.'" 5. Hezekiah's servants made their way to Isaiah. 6. Isaiah, in turn, gave them this message to relay to Hezekiah: "This is what the Lord says: 'Do not fear the words you have heard, the ones spoken by the servants of the king of Assyria who have mocked Me. 7. I will send a spirit (an influence or disturbance) upon him, and he will hear a report that causes him to return to his own land; and there, in his own land, he will fall by the sword.'" 8. The Rabshakeh returned and found the king of Assyria engaged in battle against Libnah (a city in Judah), having heard that the king had moved away

from Lachish (another city in Judah, previously under siege). **9.** Soon, the king of Assyria was informed that Tirhakah (the king of Ethiopia, a mighty kingdom in Africa) had come out to oppose him. Upon hearing this, he sent messengers to Hezekiah with the following words: **10.** "Say to Hezekiah, king of Judah: 'Do not let your God, in whom you trust, deceive you by claiming that Jerusalem will not fall into the hands of the king of Assyria. **11.** Surely you have heard how the kings of Assyria have utterly destroyed all the lands they have invaded; do you think you will be spared? **12.** Did the gods of the nations stop my ancestors from destroying places like Gozan (a region by the Tigris River), Haran (a city in Mesopotamia), Rezeph (a city in Syria), and the people of Eden (an ancient kingdom) in Telassar (a place of Eden)? **13.** Where are the kings of Hamath (a city in Syria), Arpad (a city in Syria), the king of Sepharvaim (a city in Mesopotamia), Hena (an area near the Tigris), and Ivah (a city in Mesopotamia)?'" **14.** Hezekiah received the letter from the messengers, read it, and then went to the house of the Lord, spreading it out before Him. **15.** Then Hezekiah prayed to the Lord, saying: **16.** "O Lord of hosts God of Israel, You alone sit enthroned between the cherubim (angelic beings guarding God's throne); You alone are God over all the kingdoms of the earth. You are the Creator of heaven and earth. **17.** O Lord, incline Your ear and listen, open Your eyes and see, and hear the words of Sennacherib (the king of Assyria) which he has sent to insult the living God. **18.** It is true, Lord, the kings of Assyria have devastated nations and their lands, **19.** And they have burned their gods with fire; but those were not gods at all, only the work of human hands— wood and stone. That is why they were destroyed. **20.** Now, O Lord our God, deliver us from his hand, so that all the kingdoms of the earth will know that You alone are the Lord." **21.** Isaiah, son of Amoz, sent this word to Hezekiah: "This is what the Lord God of Israel says: 'Because you have prayed to Me concerning Sennacherib, king of Assyria, **22.** This is what the Lord says about him: 'The virgin daughter of Zion (Jerusalem) despises you and mocks you; the daughter of Jerusalem (the people of Jerusalem) shakes her head in scorn behind your back! **23.** "Against whom have you taunted and blasphemed? And against whom have you raised your voice and lifted your eyes in pride? Against the Holy One of Israel. **24.** Through your messengers (servants), you have mocked the Lord, saying, 'By the strength of my chariots, I have ascended to the heights of the mountains, to the farthest limits of Lebanon (the mountain range); I will cut down its tallest cedars and its finest cypress trees; I will reach its highest points, its fertile forests. **25.** I have dug wells and drunk water, and with the soles of my feet, I have dried up all the rivers of Egypt's defenses.' **26.** "Have you not heard what I have done from long ago, how I have made it, and from ancient times how I have formed it? Now I have brought it to pass, that you should become the tool to destroy fortified cities and turn them into piles of rubble. **27.** Therefore, their people had little strength; they were dismayed and confused; they were like the grass of the field or the green herb, like the grass on the rooftops, which withers before it can grow. **28.** But I know your dwelling place, your going out and coming in, and your raging against Me. **29.** Because your anger and your arrogance have reached My ears, I will put a hook in your nose and a bit in your mouth, and I will make you return by the same road you came.'" **30.** "This will be a sign for you: You will eat what grows by itself this year, and in the second year, you will eat what springs from that. But in the third year, sow and reap, plant vineyards and eat their fruit. **31.** The survivors of the house of Judah will again take root downward and bear fruit upward. **32.** For out of Jerusalem will come a remnant (the remaining survivors), and those who escape from Mount Zion (the hill Jerusalem is built upon). The zeal (passion) of the Lord Almighty will bring this about. **33.** Therefore, the Lord says concerning the king of Assyria: 'He will not enter this city, nor will he shoot an arrow here, nor will he come before it with a shield, nor build a siege ramp (earthwork to attack a city) against it. **34.** By the road he came, he will return, and he will not enter this city, declares the Lord. **35.** For I will defend this city and save it, for My own sake and for the sake of My servant David.'" **36.** Then the angel of the Lord went out and struck down 185,000 men in the Assyrian camp. When the people arose in the morning, all they saw were dead bodies. **37.** So, Sennacherib, king of Assyria, broke camp and returned to Nineveh (the capital of Assyria), where he stayed. **38.** While he was worshiping in the temple of his god Nisroch (an Assyrian god), his sons Adrammelech and Sharezer (his sons) killed him with the sword, and they escaped to the land of Ararat (an ancient kingdom in Asia Minor). Then Esarhaddon (his son) became king in his place.

Chapter 38

1. During this time, King Hezekiah (the king of Judah, a southern kingdom of Israel) was struck with a severe illness and was near death. The prophet Isaiah, son of Amoz, approached him with a message from the Lord: "This is what the Lord says: 'Prepare everything in your house, for you are going to die and not recover.'" **2.** After hearing this, Hezekiah turned his face to the wall and earnestly prayed (spoke to God) to the Lord. **3.** He cried out, "Remember, O Lord, how I have walked faithfully before You, with a sincere heart, and have done what is right in Your eyes." Hezekiah then wept bitterly (cried uncontrollably). **4.** The word of the Lord immediately came to Isaiah with a new message: **5.** "Go back to Hezekiah and say, 'This is what the Lord, the God of your ancestor David, has declared: I have heard your prayer, and I have seen your tears. I will grant you fifteen more years of life. **6.** I will also rescue you and this city from the king of Assyria (a powerful empire to the north), and I will shield (protect) this city from harm.'" **7.** "This is the sign (proof) from the Lord that He will do exactly what He has promised: **8.** I will cause the shadow on the sundial (a time-telling instrument) of Ahaz (a former king of Judah) to reverse by ten steps." Then, the sun's shadow moved back ten steps, reversing the time that had already passed. **9.** King Hezekiah of Judah wrote this poem after being healed (made well) from his sickness: **10.** "I thought that in the prime (best years) of my life, I would be forced to enter the gates of Sheol (the realm of the dead); my remaining years would be taken away from me." **11.** "I thought, 'I will never see the Lord again in the land of the living (alive); I will no longer see any of mankind as I walk among them.'" **12.** "My life has been cut short, like the removal of a shepherd's tent (a temporary shelter); I have been cut off like a piece of cloth on a weaver's loom. You finish me off from day to night." **13.** "I reflected on this all night—like a lion that tears apart its prey, He has crushed all my bones; from day to night, You have finished me off." **14.** "I moaned like a crane (a type of bird) or a swallow (another type of bird); I lamented like a dove. My eyes grew dim from looking upward. O Lord, I am in distress (trouble); please help (support) me!" **15.** "What can I say? He has spoken and done this to me. I will walk carefully (thoughtfully) all my years in response to the bitterness (deep sadness) of my soul." **16.** "O Lord, it is through these things that men live; in all these things lies the life of my spirit (soul). You will restore (bring me back) to life and heal me completely." **17.** "Indeed, it was my own peace (well-being) that I found in the great bitterness I endured. But You, in Your love, have rescued my soul from the pit (deep place) of destruction, and You have thrown (cast) all my sins behind Your back." **18.** "For Sheol (the grave) cannot thank You, death cannot praise You; those who descend into the pit (the grave) cannot hope for Your faithfulness." **19.** "The living (those still alive), the living will praise You, as I do today; parents will tell their children about Your faithfulness." **20.** "The Lord was ready to save me, and so we will sing with stringed instruments (musical instruments like harps) throughout our lives in the house of the Lord." **21.** Isaiah instructed, "Prepare a poultice (a soft, medicinal paste) made from figs, and place it on the boil (infected sore), and he will recover." **22.** Hezekiah then inquired, "What is the sign that I will be able to go up to the house of the Lord?"

Chapter 39

1. At that time, Merodach-Baladan, the son of Baladan and king of Babylon (a kingdom), sent a letter and gifts to Hezekiah after hearing that he had been ill and had recovered. **2.** Hezekiah was pleased with their visit and showed the Babylonian envoys (representatives or messengers) all the wealth in his palace—his silver and gold, precious spices, and rare oils, as well as all his military equipment. He held nothing back from them, revealing everything in his house and kingdom. **3.** Later, the prophet Isaiah (a messenger of God) came to King Hezekiah and asked, "What did these men say, and where did they come from?" Hezekiah replied, "They came to me from a distant land, from Babylon." **4.** Isaiah then asked, "What did they see in your palace?" Hezekiah answered, "They saw everything in my house; there is nothing in my treasures that I did not show them." **5.** Isaiah spoke to Hezekiah, saying, "Hear the word of the Lord Almighty: **6.** 'The time is coming when everything in your palace and all the treasures that your ancestors (forefathers) have stored up until now, will be taken away to Babylon. Nothing will remain, says the Lord.' **7.** 'Some of your own descendants, the children you will father (beget), will be taken away and made eunuchs (servants who have been castrated) in the palace of the king of Babylon.'" **8.** Hezekiah responded to Isaiah, saying, "The word of the Lord you have spoken is good!" He said this because he thought, "At least during my lifetime, there will be peace and truth."

Chapter 40

1. "My people, take comfort, yes, take comfort!" declares your God. **2.** "Speak words of consolation to Jerusalem (the capital city of Israel), and proclaim that her days of hardship have ended. Her sins have been forgiven, for she has received from the Lord's hand a double penalty for all her wrongdoings." **3.** A voice cries out, "Prepare a path for the Lord in the wilderness (desert) and make straight a highway for our God through the desolate lands." **4.** Let every valley (low place) be raised up, every mountain (large hill) and hill be brought low; let the crooked (twisted) paths be made straight, and the rough terrain be smoothed out. **5.** Then the glory (honor) of the Lord will be revealed, and every person will see it together, because the mouth of the Lord has spoken." **6.** A voice calls out, "Shout!" And I ask, "What should I shout?" "All flesh is like grass, and all its beauty is like the flowers (blooming plants) of the field." **7.** The grass fades, the flowers wither, when the breath (powerful wind) of the Lord blows on them; surely all people are like grass. **8.** The grass fades, the flowers wither, but the word (message) of our God endures forever." **9.** O Zion (a hill in Jerusalem), you who proclaim good news, climb to a high mountain; O Jerusalem, you who proclaim good news, lift up your voice with strength, fear not; declare to the cities (towns) of Judah, "Here is your God!" **10.** Look, the Lord God will come with power, and His mighty arm (power) will rule on His behalf. His reward is with Him, and His work goes ahead of Him. **11.** Like a shepherd (caretaker), He will care for His flock (group of sheep); He will gather the lambs (young sheep) into His arms, carry them close to His heart, and gently guide those with young. **12.** Who has measured the waters in the palm (hollow) of His hand, or marked off the heavens with the span (width) of His hand? Who has collected the dust of the earth in a basket, or weighed the mountains (large landforms) in the scales and the hills in a balance? **13.** Who has directed the Spirit (power) of the Lord, or given counsel to Him as His advisor? **14.** With whom did He consult, who taught Him, or showed Him the path of justice (fairness)? Who imparted knowledge (understanding) to Him, or revealed the way of wisdom? **15.** Behold, the nations (peoples) are like a mere drop in a bucket (small amount), and they are regarded as dust on the scales. He lifts up the islands (distant lands) as though they were but a speck of dust. **16.** Even Lebanon's (a region known for its forests) vast forests are insufficient for a sacrifice, nor are its wild animals enough for a burnt offering. **17.** All the nations are nothing before Him; they are counted by Him as less than nothing and utterly insignificant. **18.** To whom, then, can you compare God? What image (idol) could possibly be like Him? **19.** A craftsman (skilled worker) makes an idol, the goldsmith (metalworker) overlays it with gold, and the silversmith forges silver chains for it. **20.** Those too poor to offer such sacrifices choose a tree (wood) that won't decay, and seek a skilled artisan to fashion an idol (image) that will not topple. **21.** Have you not known? Have you not heard? Has it not been proclaimed to you from the very beginning? Do you not understand from the foundations (base) of the earth? **22.** It is He who sits enthroned above the circle (shape) of the earth, and its inhabitants are like mere grasshoppers (tiny insects). He stretches out the heavens like a cloth and spreads them out like a tent (place to live) to dwell in. **23.** He brings rulers (princes) to nothing and makes judges (lawgivers) of the earth as useless as a reed. **24.** No sooner are they planted, no sooner are they sown, no sooner do they take root in the ground than He blows on them, and they wither; a storm (whirlwind) sweeps them away like chaff (dry plants). **25.** "To whom will you compare Me, or who is My equal?" says the Holy One (God). **26.** Lift up your eyes and look to the heavens: Who created all these? He who brings out the stars (starry hosts) one by one and calls each by name. Because of His great power and mighty strength, not one of them is missing. **27.** Why do you complain, O Jacob (the name for Israel), and say, O Israel, "My way is hidden from the Lord, and my right (just claim) is disregarded by my God"? **28.** Have you not known? Have you not heard? The everlasting (eternal) God, the Lord, the Creator of the ends of the earth, never grows tired or weary. His understanding is beyond searching (incomprehensible). **29.** He gives strength (power) to the weary, and increases the strength of the weak. **30.** Even young people (youths) grow tired and weary, and young men stumble (fall) and fail; **31.** but those who wait (hope) on the Lord will renew their strength. They will rise on wings (soar) like eagles; they will run and not grow weary, they will walk and not faint.

Chapter 41

1. "Be still before Me, O distant lands (coastlands), and let the people gather new strength! Let them draw near, and let them speak; let us come together and meet in judgment. **2.** Who has risen up one from the east (from the direction of the sunrise)? Who has called him to act righteously (to fulfill His purposes)? Who delivered nations into his hand and made him lord over kings? He made them like dust for his sword, like stubble (dry plant matter) for his bow. **3.** Who pursued them with success, walking a path he had never traveled before? **4.** Who has brought this about, calling forth generations from the beginning? 'I, the Lord, am the First; and with the Last, I am He.'" **5.** The distant nations (coastlands) saw this and were filled with fear; the farthest parts of the earth trembled (shuddered), and they came near in terror. **6.** Each one encouraged his neighbor, saying to his brother, "Be strong and take courage!" **7.** The craftsman (skilled worker) urged on the goldsmith (one who shapes gold); the one who hammers out the metal inspired the one shaping the anvil (a tool used in metalwork), saying, "It is ready for assembly," and they fastened it with pegs (pins) to ensure it did not fall apart. **8.** "But as for you, Israel (the people chosen by God), My servant, Jacob (the name of the people of Israel), whom I have selected, the descendants of Abraham (the father of Israel), My companion— **9.** I have taken you from the farthest corners of the earth, calling you from its remotest places, saying to you, 'You are My servant; I have chosen you and will not cast you away.' **10.** Do not fear, for I am with you; do not be disheartened (distressed), for I am your God. I will give you strength, yes, I will help you, and I will uphold you with My righteous right hand. **11.** "Look, all those who are angry with you will be ashamed (embarrassed) and put to shame (disgraced); they will be like nothing, and those who have fought against you will vanish (be destroyed). **12.** You will search for your enemies and not find them; those who made war against you will be gone as though they never existed. **13.** For I, the Lord your God, will take hold of your right hand and assure you, 'Do not fear, I will help you.' **14.** "Do not fear, O insignificant (worm-like) Jacob, O people of Israel! I will help you," declares the Lord, "your Redeemer (Savior), the Holy One of Israel. **15.** See, I will turn you into a new threshing tool (a device used for separating grain), one with sharp edges; you will crush the mountains and reduce them to dust, making the hills like chaff (worthless husks). **16.** You will separate the chaff (grain husks), and the wind will carry it away; the storm will scatter it, and you will rejoice in the Lord, exulting in the Holy One of Israel. **17.** "The poor and needy search for water, but there is none; their tongues are parched (dry) with thirst. I, the Lord, will hear their cries; I, the God of Israel, will never abandon (forsake) them. **18.** I will open up rivers in desolate highlands (dry, elevated places) and springs in the valleys; I will turn the desert (wilderness) into a place of water, and the dry ground will become a source of living water. **19.** I will plant in the wilderness the mighty cedar (a tall, strong tree), the acacia tree, the fragrant myrtle (a tree with a sweet scent), and the olive tree; I will place the cypress, pine (a type of tree), and box tree together in the desert, **20.** so that they may see and know, reflect and understand together, that it is the hand of the Lord who has done this, and that the Holy One of Israel has created it. **21.** "Bring your case," says the Lord. "Present your arguments," says the King of Jacob. **22.** "Let them come forward and tell us what will happen; let them speak of past events (former things), so we may reflect on them and know their end (final result); or let them declare to us what is to come. **23.** Let them show us future events, so we may know if they are truly gods. Let them do something, whether good or evil, so that we may witness it and be astonished together. **24.** Truly, you are nothing, and your deeds are worth nothing; the one who chooses you is an abomination (deserving of disdain). **25.** "I have raised up one from the north (a reference to a coming ruler), and he will come; from the east, he will call upon My name; he will march against rulers as though they were nothing, like a potter treading clay. **26.** Who has proclaimed this from the beginning, so that we might know? Who foretold the ancient things (past events), so that we can say, 'He is righteous'? Surely, no one has declared it, no one has announced it, no one has listened to your words. **27.** The first time I said to Zion (a term for Jerusalem), 'Look, here they are!' And to Jerusalem, I will give one who brings good news (a messenger with a message of hope). **28.** I looked, and there was no one; I searched among them, but there was no advisor (counselor), no one who could answer a single word when I asked. **29.** Truly, all of them are worthless (useless); their works are nothing; their carved idols (images) are like wind and emptiness.

Chapter 42

1. "Behold, here is the Servant whom I support and cherish, My Chosen One, in whom I take great delight! I have placed My Spirit upon Him, and He will bring justice to the nations (non-Jewish people). **2.** He will not shout or raise His voice to make Himself known; nor will He make a public display of His words. **3.** He will not break a bruised reed (a thin, fragile plant), nor will He extinguish a dimly burning flame (a small, unstable fire); His mission is to establish justice with unwavering truth. **4.** He will not falter or grow weary until He has firmly established justice throughout the earth, and even far-off lands (distant or faraway regions) will place their hope in His guidance. **5.** This is what the Lord God, Who created the heavens and spread them out, the One Who formed the earth and all that it brings forth, the One Who gives breath to the people and life to those who walk upon it, says: **6.** "I, the Lord, have called You in righteousness, and I will hold You fast by the hand; I will protect You and make You a covenant (agreement) for the people, a light to illuminate the Gentiles (nations). **7.** You will open the eyes of the blind, lead the prisoners (those held captive) out of their confinement, and bring those who are in darkness out of their prison cells. **8.** I am the Lord; that is My name! I will not give My glory to anyone else, nor will I share My praise with idols (false gods). **9.** See, the former things have already taken place, and I am now proclaiming new things to you; before they happen, I announce them to you. **10.** Sing a new song to the Lord; let His praise be heard from the ends of the earth! You who go down to the sea and everything in it, you coastlands (distant lands) and all the people who dwell there, lift up your voices! **11.** Let the wilderness (a barren place) and its cities shout aloud, and let the inhabitants of Kedar (Kedar - a people from Arabia) rejoice. Let the people of Sela (a city in Edom) sing for joy, let them shout from the mountaintops. **12.** Let them give glory to the Lord, and declare His praise in the coastlands (distant regions). **13.** The Lord will march out like a mighty warrior, arousing His zeal like a soldier ready for battle. He will shout with a mighty cry, and He will prevail over His enemies. **14.** For a long time, I have been silent; I have restrained Myself, but now I will cry out as a woman in labor (labor - the process of giving birth). I will groan and pant in distress. **15.** I will devastate the mountains and hills, and dry up all their vegetation (plant life). I will turn rivers into coastlands, and dry up pools (small bodies of water). **16.** I will guide the blind (those who cannot see) along a path they have never known. I will make the darkness before them light, and I will straighten the crooked paths. I will do these things for them, and I will not abandon them. **17.** Those who trust in idols, saying 'You are our gods,' will be turned back in shame. **18.** Listen, you deaf (unable to hear); look, you blind (blind - unable to see), so that you may understand! **19.** Who is blind, if not My servant (one whom I have sent), and who is as deaf as My messenger (one who delivers a message) whom I have chosen? Who is more blind than the one I have selected, more deaf than My chosen servant? **20.** You see many things, but fail to perceive them; your ears are open, but you do not hear or understand. **21.** The Lord takes pleasure in this, for the sake of His righteousness. He will make His law (God's commands) great and glorious. **22.** But this is a people who have been plundered (robbed) and devastated; they are all trapped in holes, hidden away in prisons (places of confinement). They are a prey with no one to rescue them, a spoil with no one to say, 'Return them!' **23.** Who among you will listen to this and pay attention, listening for the days ahead? **24.** Who handed Jacob (Israel, the people of God) over to the robbers, and Israel to the plunderers? Was it not the Lord, against Whom we have sinned? For they did not walk in His ways, nor were they obedient to His law. **25.** Therefore, He poured out His anger (wrath or intense displeasure) upon them, the full force of His battle, and it set them on fire all around. Yet they did not understand, and it burned them, but they did not take it to heart.

Chapter 43

1. But now, says the Lord, the One who created you, O Jacob, and the one who formed you, O Israel, "Do not fear, for I have redeemed (rescued) you. I have called you by name; you are Mine." **2.** When you pass through the waters (troubles), I will be there with you; when you walk through the rivers (difficulties), they will not overwhelm (defeat) you. And when you find yourself in the fire (hard times), it will not burn you, nor will the flames harm you. **3.** I am the Lord, your God, the Holy One of Israel, your Savior (rescuer). I gave Egypt as your ransom (payment), and I exchanged Ethiopia and Seba (ancient kingdoms) in your place. **4.** Because you are valuable and precious in My sight, I have honored you, and I love you. In exchange for your life, I will give others; I will trade nations for you. **5.** Fear not, for I am with you. I will bring your children from the east, and I will gather them from the west. **6.** To the north, I will say, "Give them up!" And to the south, I will command, "Do not keep them back!" I will bring My sons from far off and My daughters from the ends of the earth. **7.** Everyone who is called by My name, whom I have created for My glory (honor), whom I formed and made, will come to Me. **8.** Bring out those who are blind but have eyes, and those who are deaf but have ears (to hear). **9.** Let all the nations come together and let all peoples be gathered. Can any of them declare this, or show us what has happened before? Let them bring their witnesses (testifiers) to prove it, or let them listen and admit, "This is true." **10.** "You are My witnesses," declares the Lord, "and you are My servant (chosen one) whom I have chosen, so that you may know and believe in Me, and understand that I am the only God. Before Me, no god existed, and after Me, there will be none." **11.** I, even I, am the Lord, and besides Me, there is no Savior (rescuer). **12.** I have revealed (shown) Myself, I have saved you, and I have made My message known. There was no foreign god among you, so you are My witnesses," declares the Lord, "that I am God." **13.** Before the beginning of time, I was already there. No one can escape from My hand; when I act, no one can undo it. **14.** This is what the Lord, your Redeemer (rescuer), the Holy One of Israel says: "For your sake, I will send to Babylon (ancient kingdom) and bring down the fugitives (escapees)—the Chaldeans (people from Babylon), who rejoice in their ships (warfare)." **15.** I am the Lord, your Holy One, the Creator of Israel, your King. **16.** This is what the Lord says, who made a way through the sea and a path through the mighty waters (large bodies of water), **17.** Who brings forth the chariot (war vehicle) and the horse, the army and its strength (military power), and they shall lie down together and never rise again; they are put out like a wick (completely defeated). **18.** "Forget the former things, do not dwell on the past (mistakes). **19.** See, I am doing a new thing, and it is already starting to grow! Do you not see it? I will even make a road in the wilderness (desert) and rivers (streams) in the desert. **20.** The wild animals of the field will honor Me, the jackals (wild dogs) and the ostriches (large flightless birds), because I will give water in the wilderness and rivers in the desert, to provide for My people, My chosen. **21.** The people I formed (created) for Myself will declare My praise (worship). **22.** "But you have not called on Me, O Jacob; and you have grown weary (tired) of Me, O Israel. **23.** You have not brought Me the sheep for your burnt offerings (sacrificial animals), nor honored Me with your sacrifices. I have not made you serve with grain offerings (crops), nor have I tired you out with incense. **24.** You have not bought Me sweet cane (cinnamon) with money, nor satisfied Me with the fat of your sacrifices. Instead, you have burdened Me with your sins (wrongdoing) and made Me weary (tired) with your iniquities (wickedness). **25.** "I, even I, am the One who blots out your transgressions (sins) for My own sake; and I will not remember your sins. **26.** Remind Me of your case (defense); let us argue it out, so that you may be acquitted (found innocent). **27.** Your ancestors (first father) sinned, and your priests (mediators) have transgressed (sinned) against Me. **28.** Therefore, I will disgrace (shame) the leaders (princes) of the sanctuary; I will give Jacob to the curse (judgment) and Israel to the disgrace (insults)."

Chapter 44

1. "Listen now, O Jacob (the name given to Israel, the nation), My servant, and Israel, the people I have chosen." **2.** "This is what the Lord says, who created and formed you from the womb (mother's body): 'Do not be afraid, O Jacob, My servant, and Jeshurun (a poetic name for Israel), whom I have chosen.'" **3.** "I will pour water upon those who thirst (those in need), and I will send floods to the dry land. My Spirit (God's presence and power) will rest on your children, and My blessing will overflow to your offspring." **4.** "They will grow like grass among the reeds, like willows by the rivers (streams) of water." **5.** "One will say, 'I belong to the Lord'; another will call himself by the name of Jacob, and yet another will write on his hand, 'The Lord's,' and adopt the name of Israel." **6.** "This is what the Lord, the King of Israel (referring to God), and His Redeemer (Savior), the Lord of Hosts, says: 'I am the First (the eternal God), and I am the Last; there is no God besides Me.'" **7.** "Who can announce the future like I do? Let them come and declare what is to come, for I established the ancient people. Let those who predict the future tell us what will happen." **8.** "Do not be afraid, nor let your heart be troubled (lose hope). Have I not already declared these things? You are My witnesses. Is there any god beside Me? There is no Rock (a firm foundation); I know of none." **9.** "Those who make idols (false gods) are useless, and their treasures bring them no benefit. They bear witness against themselves, for they neither see nor understand, and thus they will be ashamed." **10.** "Who would create a god or form an idol that is of no value?" **11.** "All those who make idols will be ashamed. The workers (craftsmen) are only human. Let them gather together, let them stand, but they will all tremble with fear and be filled with shame." **12.** "The blacksmith (a metal worker) shapes iron in the fire using tongs and hammers it with strength, but even he becomes hungry, weak, and thirsty, fainting from the effort." **13.** "The carpenter (woodworker) marks out his measurements, draws with chalk, and planes the wood. He shapes it like the figure of a man, according to human beauty, so it may stay in the house." **14.** "He cuts down cedars (a type of tree), gathers cypress and oak, and secures them from the forest. He plants a pine tree, and the rain nourishes it." **15.** "Then he burns part of the wood to keep himself warm, bakes bread over the coals, roasts meat, and eats. He says, 'Ah, I am warm; I see the fire.'" **16.** "With the remaining wood, he makes a god, a carved image. He falls down before it, worships it, and says, 'Save me, for you are my god.'" **17.** "They do not understand, nor do they consider it in their hearts. Their eyes are shut, and their hearts are hardened, so they cannot see or comprehend." **18.** "No one takes time to reflect or has the understanding (wisdom) to reason, 'I burned part of this wood in the fire, I baked bread on its coals, and roasted meat and ate it. Should I now make the rest into an idol? Should I bow down to a piece of wood?'" **19.** "They feed on ashes (worthless things); their deceived (misled) hearts lead them astray. They cannot save themselves, nor can they ask, 'Is there a lie in my right hand?' (Referring to the idol they hold)." **20.** "'Remember these things, O Jacob, and Israel, for you are My servant. I formed you; you are My servant. O Israel, you will never be forgotten by Me.'" **21.** "'I have blotted out your sins like a thick cloud (completely erased), and your transgressions (sins) like a cloud. Return to Me, for I have redeemed you.'" **22.** "Sing, O heavens, for the Lord has done it! Shout, you lower parts of the earth; break forth in song, you mountains, O forest, and every tree in it! For the Lord has redeemed Jacob, and He has glorified Himself in Israel." **23.** "This is what the Lord, your Redeemer, and the One who formed you from the womb, says: 'I am the Lord, who made everything, who alone stretched out the heavens, who spread the earth by Myself.'" **24.** "Who frustrates (confounds) the signs of false prophets, makes diviners (fortune-tellers) go mad, turns wise men backwards, and makes their knowledge foolishness;" **25.** "Who confirms the word of His servant and fulfills the plans of His messengers; who says to Jerusalem, 'You will be inhabited,' and to the cities of Judah, 'You will be rebuilt,' and I will restore the ruined places." **26.** "Who says to the sea, 'Be dry!' and I will dry up your rivers;" **27.** "Who speaks of Cyrus (a Persian king), 'He is My shepherd, and he will do all that I desire. He will say to Jerusalem, 'You will be rebuilt,' and to the temple, 'Your foundations will be laid.'"

Chapter 45

1. "The Lord speaks to His chosen servant, Cyrus (the king of Persia), whom I have empowered— To defeat nations in his path, to dismantle kings' defenses, to open doors that no one can shut, ensuring gates stay open for him. **2.** I will go before you, smoothing out the rough terrain (uneven or difficult areas); I will break down bronze gates and shatter iron bars. **3.** I will grant you access to hidden treasures (valuable things kept secret), and storehouses of wealth, so that you will recognize that I am the Lord, the God of Israel, and that I have called you by name. **4.** "It is for the sake of My servant Jacob (Israel), My chosen nation, that I have named you. Even though you do not know Me, I have called you by name. **5.** "I am the Lord, and there is no other. There is no god besides Me. Though you have not acknowledged Me, I will strengthen you. **6.** "So that everyone, from the east to the west, will know there is no one but Me. I am the Lord, and there is no other. **7.** "I am the one who forms light and creates darkness (the absence of light), who brings peace and creates calamity (trouble). I, the Lord, am responsible for all things. **8.** "Let righteousness rain down from the heavens, and salvation pour from the skies. Let the earth open up and produce deliverance (rescue), while righteousness sprouts from the ground. It is I, the Lord, who have made all of this. **9.** "Woe to those who argue with their Creator (Maker)! Can the clay question the potter, asking, 'What are you shaping me into?' Or can the object say to the one who made it, 'You lack skill'? **10.** "Woe to those who ask their father, 'What are you fathering?' Or to the woman, 'What have you given birth to?' **11.** "This is the declaration of the Lord, the Holy One of Israel and its Creator: 'Ask Me about the future of My people, and about the work of My hands. You have the right to demand answers.' **12.** "I am the one who made the earth and created mankind (human beings) on it. It was My hands that spread out the heavens, and I command all the stars, sun, and planets. **13.** "I raised up Cyrus in righteousness, guiding him on the right path. He will rebuild My city (Jerusalem) and release My captives (those in bondage) without any payment or reward," says the Lord of hosts. **14.** "The Lord says this: 'The wealth of Egypt (the work of the Egyptians), the riches of Cush (Nubia), and the Sabeans (people from Sheba, in Arabia)—strong and mighty people— will come to you. They will become your servants, walking behind you in chains (shackles) and bowing before you. They will say, "Surely God is with you, and there is no other; there is no other God."' **15.** "Indeed, You are the God who hides Himself (keeps hidden), O God of Israel, the Savior (Deliverer)! **16.** "All those who have trusted in idols will be put to shame and disgraced (humiliated); they will join together in confusion (disorder). **17.** "But Israel will experience eternal salvation through the Lord. You will never feel ashamed or disgraced, world without end. **18.** "For the Lord, who created the heavens, He is God. He formed the earth and made it; He established it (set it firm). He did not create it to be empty, but to be a place for people to live. I am the Lord, and there is no other. **19.** "I did not speak in secret or in hidden places (unknown spots); I did not tell the descendants of Jacob (Israel), 'Seek Me in vain.' I, the Lord, speak righteousness and proclaim what is right. **20.** "Come together and approach Me, you who have fled from the nations (distant lands). Those who carry idols made of wood and pray to gods who cannot save are ignorant (lack knowledge). **21.** "Let them speak and present their case (argument); let them consult each other. Who has declared this in the past? Who foretold it from ancient times? Was it not I, the Lord? There is no other God but Me, a righteous God and a Savior; there is no one besides Me." **22.** "Turn to Me, and be saved, all you ends of the earth (far places)! For I am God, and there is no other. **23.** "I have sworn by Myself; My word, which has gone forth in righteousness, will not return. Every knee will bow to Me, and every tongue will swear allegiance. **24.** "They will acknowledge, 'In the Lord alone is righteousness (rightness) and strength.' All who are angry with Him will come to Him and be ashamed." **25.** "In the Lord, all of Israel's descendants (God's people) will be declared righteous (justified) and will rejoice (glory in Him)."

Chapter 46

1. Bel (a Babylonian god) is humbled, and Nebo (another Babylonian god) is brought low. Their idols are placed on the backs of animals and cattle, and your carts are overloaded, becoming a heavy burden (something heavy) to the tired beasts. **2.** Together, they fall down and stoop; unable to bear their own weight, they are taken captive (taken as prisoners), unable to save themselves. **3.** "Hear Me, O house of Jacob (Israel), and all you who remain (those who remain) from the family of Israel. You whom I have supported (helped) from the moment of your birth, whom I have carried even from the time you were in the womb. **4.** Even when you grow old, I will be the One who sustains (keeps strong) you, and when your hair turns gray, I will continue to carry you. I, the One who created (made) you, will always hold you up, deliver (rescue) you, and bring you to safety. **5.** "Who can you compare Me to, who can you match Me with, or make Me equal to? There is no one like Me. **6.** They take gold from their bags, weigh silver on the scales, and hire a skilled craftsman (a skilled worker) to fashion it into a god. Then they bow down and worship it. **7.** They lift it onto their shoulders, carry it, and place it in its designated spot, where it stands still. It cannot move from there. Even when someone cries out to it, it cannot give an answer (respond) or deliver them from their troubles. **8.** "Remember this, and consider it well. Show yourselves to be people of understanding (wisdom). Reflect on the ancient things (past events), for I am God, and there is no other. I am the only God, and no one compares to Me. **9.** I announce (declare) the end from the beginning, and from times long past (ancient times), I reveal things that have not yet happened. I declare, 'My purpose (plan) will stand, and I will accomplish all that I desire.' **10.** I summon a bird of prey (an animal, like an eagle, used in battle) from the east, the man who will fulfill My will, from a distant (faraway) land. What I have spoken, I will bring to pass (accomplish), and what I have planned, I will surely do. **11.** "Listen to Me, you who are set in your ways (stubborn-hearted) and far from righteousness (rightness, justice). **12.** I am bringing My righteousness close to you, and it will not delay. My salvation (deliverance) is near. I will establish salvation in Zion (Jerusalem), for Israel is My glory."

Chapter 47

1. "O virgin daughter of Babylon (the empire that destroyed Jerusalem), come down and sit in the dust. No longer will you sit on a throne, O daughter of the Chaldeans (the people of Babylon). You will never again be called 'tender' or 'delicate' (refined and graceful). **2.** Grind grain using the millstones (large stones used for grinding grain). Remove your veil (a garment of dignity), and take off your skirt (a symbol of modesty). Expose your thigh (your vulnerability) and cross over rivers (an act that shows your distress and shame). **3.** Your nakedness will be exposed, and your shame will be fully revealed. I will seek revenge (punishment) and will not settle matters through negotiations with people. **4.** Our Redeemer (the one who rescues) is the Lord of Hosts, and His name is the Holy One of Israel (God's pure and sacred nature). **5.** Sit in silence and let darkness cover you, O daughter of the Chaldeans (the Babylonians). You will no longer hold the title of 'Lady of Kingdoms' (a ruler of nations). **6.** I was angry with My people (the Israelites) and dishonored My inheritance (the special people God chose). I handed them over to you, but you showed no mercy (compassion); you oppressed the elderly with an unbearable yoke (a heavy burden). **7.** You thought in your heart, 'I will be queen forever,' and you did not reflect on the consequences of your actions or consider the end that awaits you. **8.** So listen carefully, you who delight in pleasures (live in luxury) and live without fear. You say, 'I am, and there is no one besides me; I will never become a widow, nor will I ever lose my children.' **9.** But in a single day, these two things will strike you: the loss of your children and widowhood (a total ruin of your security). They will come upon you completely, as a result of your much sorcery (witchcraft) and the abundance of your enchantments (spells and magic). **10.** You have trusted in your wickedness (evil deeds), saying, and 'No one sees me.' Your wisdom (knowledge and understanding) has led you astray, and you've boasted in your heart, 'I am, and there is no one else but me.' **11.** Therefore, disaster (evil) will come upon you suddenly, and you won't know where it originates. Trouble (misfortune) will strike you, and there will be no way to escape it. Destruction (complete ruin) will fall upon you, and you will not recognize it until it's too late. **12.** Now, stand firm with your enchantments (magical arts) and all the sorceries (witchcraft) you have practiced since your youth. Perhaps they will bring you profit (gain), or perhaps they will help you escape the coming disaster. **13.** You have grown tired (weary) of your many counselors. Let the astrologers (those who predict the future by studying the stars), the stargazers (those who use the stars for guidance), and the monthly prognosticators (those who forecast events based on the lunar cycle) rise up and save you from the calamities about to strike. **14.** Look, they will be like stubble (worthless and easily destroyed); the fire will burn them up, and they will not be able to escape from the flames (the fiery judgment). They won't even be able to warm themselves by the fire or sit near it for comfort. **15.** This is the fate of those with whom you have worked, your merchants (traders) from your youth. They will scatter, each to his own place, and no one will be able to save you."

Chapter 48

1. "Pay attention, O descendants of Jacob (called Israel), you who bear the name of Israel (the nation), and have emerged from the wellsprings of Judah (the region of Judah), you who swear by the name of the LORD, and mention the God of Israel, but do so without sincerity or righteousness (they claim faith but fail to live it). **2.** You call yourselves by the name of the holy city (Jerusalem), and place your trust in the God of Israel, The Lord of hosts is His name. **3.** "Long ago, I revealed things to you, I spoke them, and you heard My voice. At the appointed time, I acted, and they came to pass. **4.** I knew how stubborn you were, how unyielding your neck was like iron, and how hard your forehead was like bronze. **5.** I declared what was to come from the start, I foretold it to you before it happened, so you could not say, 'My idol has brought this about,' or, 'My carved image and molded image (idol) commanded this.' **6.** "You have heard all this already. Why, then, will you not speak of it? Now I am revealing to you new things, things you could not have known before. **7.** These things have just been created, not from the past; before this moment, you did not hear them, so you cannot say, 'I already knew all of this.' **8.** You did not hear, you did not understand; your ears were closed long ago. For I knew you would betray Me, and from the womb, you have been called a rebel. **9.** "For the sake of My name, I will delay My anger, and for the sake of My praise, I will restrain it, so that I do not utterly destroy you. **10.** I have refined you, but not like silver; I have tested you through the furnace of affliction (suffering). **11.** For My own sake, I will act, for how could I allow My name to be dishonored? I will not give My glory (honor) to another. **12.** "Listen to Me, O Jacob (the name for Israel), and Israel, whom I have chosen: I am the First, and I am the Last. **13.** With My hand, I established the foundations of the earth, and with My right hand, I stretched out the heavens; when I call to them, they stand together. **14.** "All of you, come together and listen! Who among them has announced these things? The Lord loves him; He will carry out His plan against Babylon (the empire), and His power will be directed against the Chaldeans (the people of Babylon). **15.** It is I who have spoken, it is I who have called him (referring to a leader), I have brought him here, and his path will succeed. **16.** "Come close, and hear Me: I have not spoken in secret since the beginning; from the moment it began, I was present. Now, the Lord God and His Spirit (the Holy Spirit) have sent Me." **17.** This is what the Lord, your Redeemer (One who buys back and saves), The Holy One of Israel, says: "I am the Lord your God, who teaches you what will bring you success (prosperity), who guides you along the path you should walk." **18.** If only you had paid attention to My commands, your peace (calm) would have been like a river, and your righteousness like the waves of the sea. **19.** Your descendants would have been as numerous as the sand (countless), and the offspring of your body like the grains of sand; their name would never have been cut off, nor destroyed before Me." **20.** Leave Babylon! Escape from the Chaldeans! With songs of joy, proclaim this, declare it to the farthest reaches of the earth; say, "The Lord has redeemed His servant Jacob!" **21.** They did not experience thirst when He led them through the desert; He made water flow from the rock (a source of water) for them; He struck the rock, and water poured out. **22.** "There is no peace," says the Lord, "for the wicked (those who reject God)."

Chapter 49

1. Listen closely, O coastlands (distant regions), and take heed, you peoples from far off! From the time I was in my mother's womb, the LORD has called Me; even before I was born, He made My name known. **2.** He has made My words as sharp (cutting) as a sword; in the safety of His hand (protection), He has hidden Me away. Like a polished arrow (a smooth arrow), He placed Me in His quiver (a container for arrows) and kept Me concealed. **3.** He said to Me, 'You are My servant, O Israel (the nation of Israel), through whom I will be glorified (honored).' **4.** I responded, 'I have worked in vain (without success), My strength has been exhausted to no avail; but I trust that My reward is with the LORD, and that My work will be remembered by My God.' **5.** Now, the Lord says, He who formed (created) Me from the womb to be His Servant, to return Jacob (the people of Israel) to Him, and to gather Israel back—For I will be honored in the eyes of the Lord, and My God will be My strength. **6.** He declares, 'It is not enough for You to restore the tribes of Jacob (the descendants of Israel), or to bring back only those of Israel who are saved; I will also make You a light (guide) to the nations, to be My salvation (deliverance) to the ends of the earth.' **7.** Thus, says the Lord, the Redeemer (One who saves) of Israel, their Holy One: 'To Him whom man despises (hates), to Him whom the nation rejects (refuses), to the Servant of rulers: kings will see and rise (stand), and princes will bow before You, for the Lord, who is faithful (trustworthy), the Holy One of Israel, has chosen You.' **8.** The Lord speaks: 'At the right moment (acceptable time), I heard Your cry; in the day of salvation (deliverance), I helped You. I will keep You safe (preserve) and make You a covenant (promise) for the people, to restore the land and grant them their inheritance (possession) in the desolate (ruined) places.' **9.** To those in captivity (prisoners), You will call, 'Come out,' and to those in darkness (ignorance), You will say, 'Reveal yourselves.' They will be fed (eat) along the paths, and their pastures (grazing land) will be on barren hills. **10.** They will neither hunger (be hungry) nor thirst; neither the heat (extreme temperature) nor the sun will strike them, for He who shows mercy (compassion) on them will lead them, guiding them even by the springs (sources) of water. **11.** I will make all My mountains (high places) into roads, and My highways (main roads) will be raised up. **12.** From far away, they will come; look, some from the north and the west, and others from the land of Sinim (a distant land, possibly China or a region southeast of Israel). **13.** Sing for joy, O heavens! Rejoice, O earth! Break into song, O mountains (high places)! For the Lord has comforted (consoled) His people and will have mercy (compassion) on those who are afflicted (suffering). **14.** But Zion (the people of Jerusalem) said, 'The Lord has forsaken (abandoned) me, and my Lord has forgotten (neglected) me.' **15.** Can a woman forget (neglect) the child she nurses, and have no compassion (pity) on the son of her womb? Even if she could forget, I will not forget (neglect) you. **16.** Look, I have engraved (written) you on the palms (inside) of My hands; your walls (city's defenses) are always before Me. **17.** Your children will come quickly; those who once destroyed (harmed) you, and those who laid waste (ruined) your land, will leave. **18.** Look around and lift your eyes (see). All these people will gather and come to you. As I live,' says the Lord, 'you will wear them all like a beautiful ornament (decoration), binding them to yourself as a bride adorns herself with jewelry.' **19.** Your ruined places, and the land of your devastation (devastation), will now be too small for the people, and those who once swallowed you up will be far away. **20.** The children you will bear after the loss of your previous ones, will say in your ears, 'The place is too small for me; give me space to dwell.' **21.** Then you will ask in your heart, 'Who has given birth (fathered) to these for me, since I have lost my children, am desolate (empty), a captive (prisoner), and wandering (lost) to and fro? Who has raised them? I was left all alone; but where did these come from?' **22.** Thus says the Lord God: 'Look, I will raise My hand (sign) to the nations, and set up My banner (standard, sign of authority) for the peoples. They will bring your sons in their arms, and your daughters will be carried on their shoulders.' **23.** Kings will become your guardians (foster fathers), and queens your caretakers (nursing mothers). They will bow down (submit) to you, their faces to the ground, and lick the dust (ground) from your feet. Then you will know that I am the Lord, for those who wait for Me will not be put to shame (disappointed). **24.** Can the prey (victim) be taken from the mighty (strong), or can the captives (prisoners) of the righteous be rescued? **25.** But the Lord says: 'Even the captives (prisoners) of the mighty will be taken, and the prey (victim) of the wicked (terrible) will be delivered (rescued); for I will fight (contend) with those who fight against you, and I will save your children.' **26.** I will feed (punish) those who oppress you with their own flesh (body), and they will be drunk (filled) with their own blood as though it were sweet wine. All people (flesh) will know that I, the Lord, am your Savior (Deliverer), and your Redeemer (Restorer), the Mighty One of Jacob (Israel).

Chapter 50

1. The Lord declares: "Where is the certificate (official written record) that shows your mother's divorce (a legal separation from God), the one whom I have cast away? Or to which of My creditors (those to whom I owe) have I sold you? It was your iniquities that led you to sell yourselves, and for your transgressions, your mother has been forsaken. **2.** When I came, why was there no one to respond? Why, when I called, was there no one who answered? Do you think My hand is too short (unable) to save, or that I lack the power to deliver? I can dry up seas with a mere rebuke (sharp command) and turn rivers into barren wastelands, where the fish rot and die due to the lack of water. **3.** I have the power to make the sky dark like mourning (deep sorrow) clothes and to cover it with sackcloth (a sign of grief). **4.** The Sovereign Lord has granted Me a wisdom-filled tongue, so I can speak a word in due season to the weary (those burdened with sorrow). Each day, He awakens Me; He opens My ear to hear as one who is instructed, like a student eager to learn. **5.** The Lord God has opened My ear, and I have not turned away (been rebellious). I have not resisted but have listened and obeyed. **6.** I offered My back to those who struck (beat) Me, and My cheeks to those who tore out My beard; I did not hide My face from shame or from the spitting that came upon Me. **7.** Because the Sovereign Lord is My helper, I will not be disgraced. I have set My face like flint (a hard stone), confident that I will not be shamed. **8.** He who is near Me will defend My righteousness (innocence); who will bring any charge against Me? Let us stand and face one another. Who dares accuse Me? Let them come forward. **9.** Without a doubt, the Sovereign Lord will aid Me. Who can bring a condemnation (judgment) against Me? They will all fade away like old garments, and the moth will devour them. **10.** Who among you stands in awe (respects) of the Lord? Who obeys the voice of His Servant (Jesus)? If anyone walks in darkness (spiritual blindness) with no light, let them trust in the name of the Lord and lean on their God for support. **11.** But look at those of you who kindle your own fires and surround yourselves with sparks (false hopes); walk in the light of your own fire, and in the sparks, you have kindled (started). This is what you will receive from My hand: You will lie down in torment (suffering).

Chapter 51

1. "Pay attention to Me, you who chase after righteousness (living rightly) and search for the Lord. Think about the rock (a solid foundation) from which you were carved, and the pit (deep hole) from which you were pulled." **2.** "Look to Abraham, your ancestor (forefather), and to Sarah, who gave birth to you. I called him alone, blessed him, and made him the father of a great nation." **3.** The Lord will bring comfort to Zion (Jerusalem), and He will rebuild her ruined places. He will turn her wilderness into a lush paradise like Eden (a garden), and her barren desert into the garden of the Lord. There will be gladness, joy, and thanksgiving in it, along with songs of praise. **4.** "Listen carefully, My people, and hear Me, O My nation. From Me, law will go forth, and I will establish My justice as a light for the nations. **5.** My righteousness is near; My salvation (deliverance) has already come, and My power will bring judgment to the people. The distant coastlands (distant lands) will place their hope in Me, and trust in My strength." **6.** Lift up your eyes to the skies and look upon the earth beneath. The heavens will vanish like smoke, and the earth will grow old like a garment, and its people will pass away. But My salvation will remain forever, and My righteousness will never be lost. **7.** "Listen, all of you who understand righteousness (moral goodness) and have My law in your hearts. Do not fear the insults (mocking) of men, and do not be discouraged by their reproaches. **8.** For the moth (a destructive insect) will consume them like clothing, and the worm (larvae) will devour them like wool. But My righteousness will endure forever, and My salvation will last from generation to generation." **9.** Rise up, rise up, put on strength, O arm (strength) of the Lord! Stir Yourself as You did in days of old, in the ancient times. Were You not the One who defeated Rahab (a symbol of Egypt or chaos), and pierced the dragon (symbol of evil or Satan)? **10.** Did You not dry up the sea, the waters of the deep (the great ocean), making the sea's depths a road for the redeemed (saved people) to pass through? **11.** Therefore, those who have been redeemed by the Lord will return, and they will come to Zion (Jerusalem) with joy. Everlasting joy will crown their heads. Gladness and joy will overtake them, and sorrow and sighing will vanish. **12.** "I, I am the One who comforts you. Why should you fear a mortal (human) man, who is destined to die, or the son of man (mortal being) who is like grass? **13.** You have forgotten your Maker, the Lord, Who stretched out the heavens and laid the foundations of the earth. You live in constant dread of the wrath (anger) of your oppressor (someone who causes harm), who is ready to destroy you. Where is the rage (anger) of that oppressor now?" **14.** The one who was in exile and held captive will soon be freed, and they will not die in the pit (deep, dark prison), nor will they lack for bread (food). **15.** For I am the Lord your God, Who split the sea, whose waves roared. The Lord of hosts (armies of heaven) is His name. **16.** I have placed My words in your mouth, and I have shielded you with the protection (shadow) of My hand, so that I may establish the heavens, set the earth's foundations, and declare to Zion (Jerusalem), 'You are My people.'" **17.** Wake up, wake up! Stand up, O Jerusalem, who has drunk from the cup of the Lord's fury (anger). You have drained the cup of trembling (fear) to its last drop. **18.** There is no one to guide her among the children she has given birth to, nor anyone to hold her hand from all those she has raised. **19.** These two things have come upon you—who will mourn for you?—Destruction and ruin (devastation), famine (hunger) and the sword (war). Who will console you? **20.** Your sons have fainted; they lie in the streets like an antelope (a type of deer) caught in a net. They are filled with the fury (anger) of the Lord, with the rebuke (correction) of your God. **21.** Therefore, listen to this, you who are afflicted (suffering), who are drunk but not with wine. **22.** Thus says your Lord, the Lord your God, Who defends the cause (protects) of His people: "See, I have taken the cup of trembling (fear) from your hand, and the dregs (last portion) of the cup of My fury; you will no longer drink from it. **23.** I will place it in the hands of those who oppress you, those who said to you, 'Lie down that we may walk over you.' You made your body like the ground, and like a street (road) for those who walk upon you."

Chapter 52

1. Rise up, rise up! O Zion (Jerusalem, the holy city), clothe yourself with strength; O Jerusalem, put on your splendid garments! The uncircumcised (those not following God's law) and the unclean (those not purified according to God's standards) will no longer enter you. **2.** Shake off the dust and rise! Take your seat, O Jerusalem! Free yourself from the bonds around your neck, O captive daughter of Zion (Jerusalem, the people of God)! **3.** for this is what the Lord says: "You have sold yourselves for nothing (no reason), yet you will be redeemed (bought back) without payment." **4.** The Lord God declares: "In the beginning, My people went down to Egypt (land of Pharaoh) to live; later, the Assyrian (empire that conquered Israel) caused them to suffer without cause." **5.** "So now, what I have here?" says the Lord. "Why are My people taken away for no reason? Those who rule over them make them cry out," says the Lord, "and My name is continuously dishonored (disrespected) every day." **6.** But then, My people will come to know My name; they will recognize on that day that I am He who speaks: 'Look, it is I.' **7.** How lovely on the mountains are the feet (messengers) of the one who brings good news, who announces peace, who brings joyous tidings, who proclaims salvation, and who tells Zion, "Your God reigns!" **8.** The watchmen (those who guard and protect the city) will lift their voices and together they will shout for joy; they will see eye to eye (agree) when the Lord restores Zion. **9.** Break into songs of joy, all you ruined places (desolate areas) of Jerusalem! The Lord has comforted His people; He has redeemed Jerusalem. **10.** The Lord has made His holy power known to all the nations; and every corner of the earth will witness the salvation of our God. **11.** Depart, depart! Leave from there, touch no impure (unclean) thing. Go out from among them, be pure, you who carry the vessels of the Lord. **12.** You will not leave in haste (quickly), nor will you flee (in fear); for the Lord will go ahead of you, and the God of Israel will be your protector from behind (rear guard). **13.** See, My Servant (a reference to the Messiah, Jesus) will act wisely; He will be lifted up, exalted (raised high), and greatly honored. **14.** Just as many were astonished (shocked) by you, His appearance was so marred (disfigured) more than that of any man, and His form beyond the sons of men. **15.** So He will purify (sprinkle) many nations, and kings will be silent before Him; for they will see what they had never been told, and consider what they had never heard.

Chapter 53

1. Who has really trusted in our message? To whom has the mighty hand of the Lord been revealed (made known), showing His power and authority? **2.** He will grow before the Lord like a soft and delicate plant, like a root emerging from barren soil. There is nothing in His appearance to draw us to Him; He has no beauty that would cause us to desire Him. **3.** He was scorned (hated) and rejected by those around Him, a man who knew suffering and sorrow intimately. We turned our faces away, ashamed, not valuing Him, despising Him in our hearts. **4.** Indeed, He took our pains (deep sadness) upon Himself and carried our suffering. Yet, we thought of Him as being punished by God, smitten and afflicted for His own wrongs. **5.** But it was for our transgressions that He was pierced (wounded), and for our sins that He was crushed. The punishment that brought us peace fell upon Him, and by His wounds, we are healed and restored. **6.** Like wayward sheep, we have all gone astray (lost); each of us has turned to his own way. But the Lord laid on Him the guilt and punishment for all our sins and failures. **7.** He was oppressed (treated harshly) and afflicted, but He did not resist. Like a lamb led to slaughter, He remained silent, as a sheep before its shearers, offering no defense for Himself. **8.** He was unjustly taken from prison and judgment, and no one stood up for Him. He was cut off from the land of the living, struck down for the sins (transgressions) of His people. **9.** Though they buried Him among the wicked, He was placed in the tomb of a rich man, for He had done no violence, and deceit (lies) was never found in His words. **10.** Yet it pleased the Lord to crush Him, to bring Him to grief. When He offers His life as a sin offering, He will see His descendants and His days will be prolonged (extended), and the will of the Lord will succeed through Him. **11.** After His soul has suffered, He will see the results of His labor and be satisfied. Through His knowledge, My righteous Servant will make many righteous (declare them innocent), for He will bear their iniquities. **12.** Therefore, I will give Him a portion among the great, and He will share the spoils with the strong, because He poured out His life unto death, and was counted among the sinners. He bore the sins of many and made intercession (prayer on behalf of others) for those who have sinned.

Chapter 54

1. "Rejoice and sing, O barren one who has not borne a child! Lift your voice in joyous praise, O you who have never experienced the pains of childbirth! For the children of the desolate (empty) will be more than those of the woman who has a husband," says the Lord. **2.** "Expand the area of your tent and stretch your sheltering curtains wider; do not hold back! Strengthen your ropes and make your tent pegs (posts to secure the tent) firm." **3.** "You will spread out on every side—your descendants will possess the nations, and they will rebuild the cities that once lay in ruin." **4.** "Fear not, for you will never again face disgrace; do not be downcast (lose confidence), for you will never again experience shame. The dishonor of your youth will be forgotten, and the humiliation (disrespect, shame) of your widowhood will no longer be remembered." **5.** "Your Creator (Maker) is your husband, the Lord of Hosts is His name; the Holy One of Israel, your Redeemer (savior), is called the God of all the earth." **6.** "The Lord has called you back, like a woman forsaken (abandoned) and deeply distressed in spirit, like a young bride who was rejected," says your God. **7.** "For only a brief moment did I forsake you, but with great compassion (deep love and concern), I will gather you to Myself." **8.** "In a moment of anger, I hid My face from you, but with eternal kindness, I will have mercy on you," says the Lord, your Redeemer. **9.** "Just as I promised Noah that the waters would never again flood the earth, so I promise that I will not be angry with you or rebuke (express disapproval of) you." **10.** "Though the mountains may vanish and the hills may be removed, My steadfast kindness will not depart from you, and My covenant (promise) of peace will not be broken," says the Lord, who shows you mercy. **11.** "O you who have been afflicted (troubled), tossed by storms and not comforted, behold, I will adorn your foundations with sapphires (a precious blue stone) and lay your stones in brilliant colors." **12.** "Your battlements (defensive walls) will be made of rubies (a precious red stone), your gates will be made of crystal (clear, like glass), and all your walls will be constructed from precious stones." **13.** "All your children will be taught by the Lord, and great will be the peace that they experience." **14.** "You will be firmly established (made secure) in righteousness; you will be far from fear of oppression (unjust treatment), and terror will never come near you." **15.** "Though they may gather against you, it will not be because of Me. Any who assemble against you will fall before you." **16.** "I am the One who created the blacksmith (metalworker) who blows the fire and forges weapons. I am also the One who created the destroyer (one who causes destruction) to bring devastation." **17.** "No weapon that is formed (made) against you will succeed, and any tongue that rises to accuse you will be condemned (rejected). This is the inheritance of My servants (followers), and their righteousness comes from Me," declares the Lord.

Chapter 55

1. All that are thirsty come and drink from the life-giving waters Even if you have no money, come, buy, and feast. Come and enjoy the wine (joy and celebration) and milk, all without paying a single coin, for it's freely offered. **2.** Why do you spend your wealth on what will never satisfy you? Why labor for what doesn't bring true fulfillment? Pay attention (listen) to what I am saying, and you will find what is truly good. Your soul will experience joy and be filled with abundance. **3.** Turn your ear (attention) to Me and draw near. Listen and your soul will come to life. I will establish an everlasting (eternal) covenant with you—a promise of mercy like the one I made to David. **4.** I have set him as a witness (testifier) to the people, a leader and commander (chief guide) to the nations. **5.** Soon you will call upon a nation you haven't known, and peoples from far away will rush to you, drawn by the Lord your God, the Holy One (sacred) of Israel. He will bring you honor and glory. **6.** Seek (look for) the Lord while He is close at hand, and call upon Him while He may still be found. **7.** Let the wicked turn from their sinful ways, and the unrighteous (morally wrong) from their evil thoughts. Let them return to the Lord, and He will show mercy. Let them come back to our God, for He will forgive them abundantly (fully). **8.** My thoughts are not like yours, nor are your ways the same as Mine," declares (proclaims) the Lord. **9.** "As the heavens (sky) stretch far above the earth, so My ways are higher than your ways, and My thoughts are far beyond your understanding. **10.** Just as the rain and snow fall from the heavens and do not return without watering the earth, making it bud (grow) and flourish, causing seed for the sower (planter) and bread for the eater to grow, **11.** So will My word, which goes out from My mouth, never return to Me void. It will fulfill (complete) what I intend and achieve the purpose for which I sent it. **12.** You will go out in joy, and be led forth in peace. The mountains and hills will burst into singing (sing) before you, and all the trees (plants) of the field will clap their hands in celebration. **13.** Instead of thorns (sharp plants), cypress trees (a type of tree) will grow; instead of briers (thorny plants), myrtle trees (a fragrant tree) will spring up. This will be a lasting sign of the Lord's renowned (fame), one that will never be destroyed.

Chapter 56

1. The Lord declares: "Do what is just and right, for the arrival of my salvation (God's act of saving His people) is imminent, and my righteousness will soon be revealed." **2.** How blessed is the one who does so! The person who holds fast to this, keeping the Sabbath pure and avoiding any wrongdoing with their hands. **3.** Let not the foreigner (someone not from Israel), who has come to join with the Lord, complain, saying, "The Lord has completely separated me from His people." Nor

should the eunuch (a man who has been castrated) despair, saying, "I am like a tree that no longer bears fruit." **4.** For this is the word of the Lord: "To the eunuchs who honor My Sabbaths, choose to delight in what pleases Me, and hold firmly to My covenant, **5.** I will grant them a position and a name within My house, a place more valuable than that of sons and daughters. An everlasting name will be theirs, one that will never be cut off." **6.** And to the foreigners who have bound themselves to the Lord, to serve Him, to love His name, and to be His servants—those who keep My Sabbath pure and adhere to My covenant—**7.** I will bring them to My holy mountain (Jerusalem) and fill them with joy in My house of prayer. Their burnt offerings and sacrifices will be accepted on My altar, for My house will be called a house of prayer for all nations. **8.** The Lord God, who gathers the outcasts (rejected people) of Israel, says, "I will also gather others, in addition to those already gathered." **9.** Come, all you beasts (enemies) of the field, come and devour; all you beasts in the forest, come and feast! **10.** The watchmen (spiritual leaders) are blind, unaware, and lack understanding. They are like mute dogs (unable to bark), lying down in slothful sleep, content to remain idle. **11.** Indeed, they are greedy dogs (selfish leaders) who are never satisfied. These shepherds (leaders) are clueless; each one seeks only his own path, focused on his own gain from his own domain. **12.** "Come," one invites, "Let us drink wine, and indulge ourselves in intoxicating drink (strong alcohol); tomorrow will be even better than today, and far more abundant."

Chapter 57

1. The righteous are taken away, and no one notices or cares; the merciful are removed, yet people fail to understand that they are rescued from the coming evil. **2.** They enter into peace and rest quietly in their beds, each person living according to his integrity (honesty), walking in righteousness. **3.** "Come here, you descendants of the sorceress (a woman who practices witchcraft), you children of the adulterer (one who breaks marital vows) and the harlot (one who engages in sexual immorality)! **4.** Who are you mocking? Against whom do you make faces and stick out your tongues? Aren't you the rebellious children, the offspring of falsehood? **5.** You inflame yourselves with idols (false gods) under every tree, and in the valleys, beneath the rocks, you sacrifice your own children. **6.** Among the smooth stones of the stream (a place where pagan rituals were held) is where you find your share; that is your inheritance! You offer drink and grain offerings to these idols—do you think I will accept them? **7.** On high, lofty mountains (places of idol worship), you set up your bed, and there you go to offer your sacrifices. **8.** Behind your doors and doorposts (frames), you set up reminders of your idols (symbols), exposing yourselves to others besides Me, making pacts with them, and delighting in your places of sin where you saw their nakedness. **9.** You went to the king (a foreign ruler), bringing your perfumes and oils; you sent messengers far off, even to the deepest parts of the grave (Sheol, the place of the dead). **10.** You wore yourself out in the long pursuit of your desires, but you never gave up hope. You found new life in your own efforts, and thus you felt no sorrow. **11.** "Whom have you feared or been afraid of, so that you lied and didn't remember Me, nor took Me to heart? Is it not because I have been silent for so long that you have lost your fear of Me? **12.** I will now expose your righteousness (good deeds) and your works, but none of it will benefit you in the end. **13.** When you cry out, let your idols (false gods) save you! But the wind will blow them away, and a single breath will carry them off. However, the one who trusts in Me will inherit the land and possess My holy mountain (the place God has set apart for His people). **14.** Someone will say, "Clear the way! Clear the way! Make the road ready for My people, remove the obstacles." **15.** This is what the High and Exalted One, who dwells in eternity (forever) and whose name is Holy, says: "I live in a high and holy place, but I also dwell with those who are humble (lowly) and contrite in spirit (a repentant heart), to revive the spirit of the humble, and to revive the heart of those who are sorrowful for their sins." **16.** I will not stay angry forever, nor will I contend with you endlessly, for if I did, people would faint before Me, and the souls I created would not endure. **17.** I was angry because of their greed (selfish desire), and I struck them. I hid My face in wrath, but they continued to follow their own sinful path, driven by the desires of their hearts. **18.** I have observed their ways, and I will heal them. I will guide them and provide comfort for them and those who mourn (feel sorrow) alongside them. **19.** "I will create a message of peace: peace for those far away and peace for those near," says the Lord, "and I will heal them." **20.** But the wicked (evil ones) are like the restless sea, unable to find rest; their waters churn up mud and dirt. **21.** "There is no peace," says my God, "for the wicked."

Chapter 58

1. Raise your voice loudly, without holding back—let it sound like a trumpet! Announce to My people their sins, and to the descendants of Jacob (Israel), their transgressions. **2.** They seek Me daily and are eager to understand My ways, acting as though they are a righteous nation that never abandons the commands (laws) of their God. They ask Me for justice and delight in coming to worship. **3.** They ask, "Why have we fasted, and You haven't noticed? Why have we humbled ourselves, and You seem to ignore us?" But on the day of your fasting, you find joy and mistreat (oppress) your workers. **4.** You fast in order to argue and fight with wickedness (evil), rather than seeking to make your voice heard before Me. This is not the kind of fast I desire. **5.** Is this truly the fast I want? Is it just for someone to humble themselves, bowing their head like a reed (a slender plant), dressing in sackcloth and ashes? Is that what you consider a fast, a day pleasing to the Lord? **6.** No, the fast I have chosen is to break the chains (shackles) of injustice, to untie the ropes of oppression, to let the downtrodden (those treated unfairly) go free, and to release every heavy burden that weighs them down. **7.** Shouldn't it be about sharing your food with the hungry, inviting the homeless and poor into your home, clothing the naked when you see them, and not turning away from your own kin (family)? **8.** Then, your light will shine forth like the dawn, and your healing will spring up quickly. Your righteousness (moral rightness) will go ahead of you, and the glory of the Lord will guard you from behind. **9.** When you call out, the Lord will answer you. When you cry, He will say, "Here I am." But first, you must stop oppressing others, stop pointing fingers, and stop speaking wickedness (evil). **10.** If you open your heart to the hungry and meet the needs of the afflicted (those suffering), then your light will break through the darkness, and your night will shine like the brightness of midday. **11.** The Lord will guide you at all times, providing for your needs even in drought (a time of dryness), and He will give strength to your bones. You will become like a well-watered garden, like a spring whose waters never run dry. **12.** Your people will rebuild what has been laid waste, and you will restore the foundations of generations past. You will be called the Restorer of Broken Walls and the Healer of Streets for people to live in. **13.** If you stop seeking your own desires (pleasure) on the Sabbath and turn away from pursuing your own interests, if you call the Sabbath a delight and honor the holy day of the Lord, **14.** If you honor the Lord by refraining from doing your own will, by not pursuing your own pleasures or speaking your own words, then you will find joy in the Lord. I will make you ride on the high places of the earth, and I will feed you with the inheritance (possession) of your ancestor Jacob. The Lord has spoken.

Chapter 59

1. The Lord's hand is not too short to rescue you, nor is His ear too dull to hear your cries. **2.** Yet your wrongdoings (sins) have created a separation between you and your God; your sins have caused Him to turn His face away, so He does not listen to you. **3.** You have stained your hands with blood, and your fingers are stained with guilt; your lips speak deceit, and your tongue murmurs wickedness. **4.** There is no one who seeks justice, and no one who pleads for truth. They trust in lies and speak falsehood; their hearts conceive evil and they bring forth sin. **5.** They lay the eggs of vipers (poisonous snakes) and weave spider webs; anyone who eats their eggs will die, and if one is crushed, a serpent will emerge. **6.** Their webs cannot be woven into clothing, and their deeds cannot cover them. They work iniquity, and violence is in their hands. **7.** Their feet rush toward evil, and they are quick to shed innocent blood. Their thoughts are filled with wickedness (evil), and destruction and ruin mark their paths. **8.** They do not know the way of peace, and justice is absent from their lives. They have made their paths crooked, and those who follow them will not experience peace. **9.** Because of this, justice seems far from us, and righteousness (moral correctness) does not reach us. We long for light, but find only darkness; we hope for brightness, but walk in shadows. **10.** We feel around in the darkness as if we were blind, stumbling at noon as if it were night. We are like people left for dead in empty places. **11.** We growl like bears, and we mourn like doves; we seek justice, but it is nowhere to be found. We long for salvation (deliverance), but it remains out of our reach. **12.** Our transgressions (sins) are countless before you, and our wrongs testify against us. We are aware of our guilt. **13.** We have rebelled (resisted) against the Lord and turned away from our God; we speak oppression (cruel treatment) and rebellion, and we speak lies from the depths of our hearts. **14.** Justice has been turned away, and righteousness stands at a distance. Truth has fallen in the streets, and fairness is nowhere to be found. **15.** Truth has stumbled, and anyone who turns away from evil is targeted. The Lord saw this and was displeased (unhappy) that there was no justice. **16.** He looked and saw that no one was there to help, and He was amazed (surprised) that no one stepped forward to intervene. So His own arm brought Him salvation, and His righteousness upheld Him. **17.** He clothed Himself with righteousness

like armor and put salvation as a helmet upon His head. He wrapped Himself in the garments of vengeance (punishment) and wore zeal (passion) as a cloak. **18.** He will repay each one according to their deeds: fury (anger) for His enemies, and recompense (reward) for His adversaries. He will repay the distant lands (coastal regions) fully. **19.** From the west (the western regions), people will revere the name of the Lord, and from the east (the rising sun), His glory will be feared. When the enemy comes in like a flood, the Spirit of the Lord will raise a banner (standard) against him. **20.** "The Redeemer (Savior) will come to Zion (Jerusalem, the city of God), to those who turn from their sins in Jacob (the descendants of Israel)," declares the Lord. **21.** "This is My covenant (promise) with them," says the Lord. "My Spirit, who is upon you, and My words, which I have placed in your mouth, will never depart from your lips, nor from the lips of your descendants, nor from the lips of your descendants' descendants," says the Lord, "from this time onward and forevermore."

Chapter 60

1. Rise and shine, for your light has arrived! The glory (honor and magnificence) of the Lord now radiates upon you. **2.** Look around, for while darkness covers the earth and deep darkness (great darkness) envelops the people, the Lord will rise and shine upon you, and His glory will be evident for all to see. **3.** Nations will be drawn to your light, and kings will seek the brightness of your dawn. **4.** Raise your eyes and look all around: they are gathering to you. Your sons will come from distant lands, and your daughters will be held close by their mothers. **5.** You will witness it, and your heart will overflow with joy; for the treasures of the sea will be directed toward you, and the wealth of the nations will be brought to your doors. **6.** A multitude of camels will cover your land, including the dromedaries (camels with one hump) from Midian (a people from the east) and Ephah (a region in the east); those from Sheba (a kingdom in Arabia) will come, bringing gold and incense (a sweet-smelling substance) and proclaiming the praises of the Lord. **7.** The flocks of Kedar (a desert tribe in northern Arabia) will gather with you, and the rams (male sheep) from Nebaioth (a tribe of Arabs) will serve you. They will be accepted on My altar, and I will honor the place of My glory. **8.** Who are these who fly like clouds, and like doves, return to their resting places (roosts)? **9.** Surely, the coastlands (lands along the sea) will look for Me, and the ships of Tarshish (a distant trading place, possibly in Spain) will arrive first, bringing your sons from far away, with silver and gold in hand, to honor the name of the Lord your God and the Holy One (God) of Israel, for He has glorified you. **10.** The foreign nations (those outside Israel) will rebuild your walls, and their kings will serve you. Though I once struck (punished) you in My anger, I now show you mercy (compassion) in My favor. **11.** Your gates will remain open at all times, never to be shut, day or night, so that people may bring the wealth of the nations and kings in procession (a parade) to you. **12.** Any nation or kingdom that does not serve you will perish (be destroyed), and those who resist will be utterly ruined. **13.** The glory of Lebanon (a mountainous region known for its famous trees) will come to you; the cypress (a type of tree), the pine (a tree), and the box tree (a small, hardy tree) will come together to beautify (decorate) the place of My sanctuary (holy place), and I will make the place of My feet glorious. **14.** The descendants of those who once oppressed (treated unfairly) you will come, bowing before you, and those who once despised (looked down on) you will fall at your feet. They will call you "The City of the Lord," "Zion (Jerusalem, the holy city) of the Holy One of Israel." **15.** Although you were forsaken (abandoned) and hated, with no one passing through, I will make you an eternal pride (permanent glory), a joy for all generations. **16.** You will drink the milk of nations and be nourished (suckle) at the breasts of kings. Then you will understand that I, the Lord, am your Savior (rescuer) and your Redeemer (one who buys back), the Mighty One (powerful) of Jacob. **17.** Instead of bronze (a metal), I will give you gold; instead of iron (a strong metal), silver will replace it; instead of wood (a material), bronze; and instead of stones (rocks), iron. I will make your officers (leaders) peace, and your rulers (magistrates) righteousness. **18.** There will no longer be violence (acts of aggression) in your land, nor destruction (ruin) within your borders. You will call your walls Salvation and your gates Praise. **19.** The sun will no longer be your light by day, nor will the moon shine for you at night. The Lord will be your everlasting (forever) light, and your God will be your glory. **20.** Your sun will never set, and your moon will never fade (wane). The Lord will be your eternal light, and the days of your mourning (grieving) will be gone. **21.** All your people will be righteous, and they will inherit (receive as a gift) the land forever. They are the plants (growths) of My work, the creations of My hands, that I may be glorified. **22.** The smallest (youngest or least) among you will become a mighty nation; a little one will become a strong people. I, the Lord, will make this happen (bring it to pass) in its appointed time.

Chapter 61

1. The Spirit of the Lord God is upon Me, for the Lord has anointed Me to proclaim good news to the poor. He has sent Me to heal those whose hearts are broken (deeply saddened), to declare liberty to captives, and to open the prison doors to those who are bound (imprisoned). **2.** I have come to announce the year of the Lord's favor and the day when He will repay His enemies with vengeance (punishment). I am here to comfort all who mourn (grieve) and sorrow. **3.** I will console those mourning in Zion (the holy city of Jerusalem), replacing their ashes with beauty, their mourning with joy, and their despair with garments of praise. They will be called mighty oaks (strong, stable trees) of righteousness, the planting of the Lord, for His glory. **4.** The ruined cities will be rebuilt, the old foundations restored, and the wastelands of past generations will be made whole again. **5.** Strangers will rise up to care for your flocks, and the children of foreign nations will till your fields and tend your vineyards. **6.** You will be known as the priests (spiritual leaders) of the Lord, and people will call you the servants of our God. You will enjoy the wealth of the nations, and in their splendor, you will find joy. **7.** Where there was shame, you will receive double honor (respect); where there was confusion (disappointment), you will rejoice in your share. In your land, you will inherit twice as much, and everlasting joy will be your portion. **8.** For I, the Lord, delight in justice, and I despise robbery (taking something unfairly) or deceit, especially when it is done in worship. I will lead them in integrity (honesty), and I will make a covenant (promise) with them that will never end. **9.** Their children and descendants (offspring) will be recognized by the nations, and people will acknowledge that they are the blessed people of the Lord. **10.** I will greatly rejoice in the Lord; my heart will be filled with joy in my God. He has dressed me in the garments of salvation and wrapped me in the robe of righteousness (right standing with God), just as a bridegroom wears his finest attire and a bride adorns herself with jewels. **11.** Just as the earth makes seeds grow and gardens bring forth their plants, the Lord God will cause righteousness (moral correctness) and praise to spring up before all nations.

Chapter 62

1. For the sake of Zion (Jerusalem), I will not be quiet, nor will I rest for Jerusalem's sake, until her righteousness (just behavior) shines forth like a brilliant light, and her salvation (rescue) burns like a lamp that never goes out. **2.** Your righteousness will be seen by the Gentiles, and all the rulers (kings) of the earth will recognize your glory. The Lord will give you a new name, one that He Himself will choose. **3.** You will be a crown (a symbol of honor) of beauty in the Lord's hand, and a royal diadem (a jeweled crown) in the grasp of your God. **4.** Never again will you be called "Forsaken," nor will your land be called "Desolate" (empty, barren). Instead, you will be known as "Hephzibah" ("My delight is in her"), and your land as "Beulah" ("Married"), for the Lord delights in you, and your land will be like one in joyful union. **5.** Just as a man rejoices when he marries his bride, so your sons will rejoice over you, and as a bridegroom (a man marrying) celebrates with joy over his bride, so your God will rejoice in you. **6.** I have placed watchmen (guards, sentinels) on your walls, O Jerusalem (city of peace); they will never be silent, neither day nor night. You who pray to the Lord, do not be silent, **7.** and give Him no rest until He establishes His presence, and until Jerusalem becomes a praise and a glory in the earth. **8.** The Lord has sworn by His mighty arm (strength) and His right hand (power): "I will no longer allow your harvest (grain) to be taken by your enemies, nor will foreigners drink the wine you have worked for. **9.** Those who harvest it will eat it and thank the Lord, and those who gather it will drink it in My holy courts (sacred spaces)." **10.** Go through the gates! Clear the way for the people! Build up the highway (pathway)! Remove every stone (obstacle), and lift up a banner (flag) for the nations to see! **11.** The Lord has declared to the ends of the earth: "Say to the daughter of Zion (Jerusalem), 'Your salvation is coming; behold, His reward (gift) is with Him, and His work is before Him.'" **12.** They will call them "The Holy People," "The Redeemed (rescued) of the Lord," and you will be called "Sought Out," a city that has never been abandoned.

1. Who is this figure approaching from Edom (a region southeast of Israel), His garments red from Bozrah (a city in Edom)? Who is this, adorned in glorious apparel, traveling with great strength?—"I am He, speaking in righteousness (justice), mighty to save." **2.** Why are Your garments red, as if You have been walking through a winepress (a place where grapes are crushed)? **3.** "I alone have trodden (crushed) the winepress, and no one from the nations joined Me. I trampled them in My anger and overwhelmed them in My fury (extreme anger); their blood is on My clothes, and I have stained all My robes." **4.** For the day of vengeance (punishment for wrongdoings) is upon My heart, and the time for My redeemed (those I save) has arrived. **5.** I looked around, but there was no one to help; I was amazed that no one came to My aid. So, My own arm (strength) brought deliverance, and My fury (anger) sustained Me. **6.** I crushed the nations in My wrath, made them drunk with My fury (extreme anger), and brought their power low to the ground. **7.** I will remember the mercies (lovingkindnesses) of the Lord and all His praises, for He has showered us with His goodness, and shown His great love toward the house of Israel (God's people), according to His mercies, and the greatness of His lovingkindness. **8.** For He declared, "They are surely My people, children who will not deceive." So He became their Savior. **9.** In all their distress, He was distressed; the Angel (messenger) of His Presence saved them. In His compassion and love, He redeemed them; He carried them and upheld them throughout their past. **10.** But they rebelled and grieved (saddened) His Holy Spirit (God's presence); in turn, He became their enemy and fought against them. **11.** Then He remembered the days of old, when Moses led His people, saying: "Where is the one who brought them up out of the sea (the Red Sea), with the shepherd (leader) of His flock (Moses)? Where is He who gave them His Holy Spirit, **12.** Who led them by the right hand of Moses, with His glorious arm (strength), dividing the waters before them to make for Himself an eternal name, **13.** Who led them through the deep waters, like a horse moving through the wilderness, so that they would not stumble?" **14.** Just as a beast goes down into the valley, and the Spirit of the Lord gives him rest, You guided Your people, to make for Yourself a glorious name. **15.** Look down from heaven and observe from Your holy and glorious dwelling place. Where is Your zeal (passionate desire) and strength, the longing of Your heart, and Your mercy toward us? Are they being held back? **16.** Surely, You are our Father, though Abraham (the ancestor of Israel) does not recognize us, and Israel (God's people) does not acknowledge us. You, O Lord, are our Father; our Redeemer (Savior) from everlasting (eternity) is Your name. **17.** Why, O Lord, have You allowed us to stray (wander) from Your ways, and hardened our hearts so we no longer fear You? Return for the sake of Your servants, the tribes of Your inheritance (God's chosen people). **18.** Your holy people have held the land for only a brief time; our adversaries have trampled down Your sanctuary (sacred place). **19.** We have become like those who never knew You, those who were never called by Your name."

Chapter 64

1. How I wish You would tear open (rip apart) the heavens and come down, that the mountains might shake (tremble) before You in awe. **2.** Just like fire devours brushwood (small twigs or branches), or causes water to boil, let Your presence be made known to Your adversaries, so that the nations will quake before You! **3.** You came down in ways we did not anticipate, performing mighty acts, and at Your presence, the mountains trembled (shook violently). **4.** From the very start of time, no one has ever heard, nor has any ear fully understood (perceived), nor has any eye ever seen a God besides You, who works for those who wait for Him. **5.** You encounter those who rejoice and live righteously, who keep Your ways in mind. But we have sinned, and we still follow these sinful ways—so we need Your salvation desperately. **6.** All of us are like an unclean (impure) thing, and even our most righteous deeds (good actions) are as filthy rags; like withered leaves, we fade away, and our wrongdoings (sins), like the wind, blow us away. **7.** No one calls on Your name or stirs himself up (awakens) to grasp hold of You; You have turned Your face away from us, and because of our iniquities (wickedness), You have allowed us to be consumed (destroyed). **8.** Yet, Lord, You are our Father; we are the clay, and You are the potter (creator); we are all the work of Your hands. **9.** Lord, do not be angry with us forever, and do not hold our sins against us. Please look, for we are Your people! **10.** Your once holy cities have become a wilderness , Zion (a name for Jerusalem) is now a wasteland, and Jerusalem itself has turned into a desolate (abandoned) ruin. **11.** Our beautiful and sacred temple, where our ancestors once praised You, has been reduced to ashes, and all that was once treasured has been laid waste (destroyed). **12.** Will You hold Yourself back (restrain) because of this, Lord? Will You remain silent and punish us beyond what we can bear?

Chapter 65

1. Those who never asked for Me sought Me out; those who had not been searching for Me found Me. To a nation that did not call My name, I said, "Here I am, here I am." **2.** All day long, I have stretched out My hands to a rebellious (disobedient) people, who walk in paths that are not good, following the thoughts of their own hearts. **3.** They continually provoke My anger before Me, making offerings in gardens and burning incense on altars made of bricks (man-made). **4.** They sit among graves (burial sites), spending nights in tombs, eating the flesh of pigs, and drinking the broth of detestable (unclean) things. **5.** They say to others, "Stay away from me; do not approach, for I am holier than you!" To Me, they are like smoke in My nostrils, a fire that burns continually. **6.** It is written before Me: I will not remain silent, but I will repay them in full for their actions, giving back to them what they deserve. **7.** I will repay their sins, as well as those of their forefathers, says the Lord, who offered incense on the mountains and blasphemed Me on the hills. Therefore, I will bring their former actions back upon them. **8.** This is the Lord's declaration: "Just as new wine is found in a cluster of grapes, and someone says, 'Do not destroy it, for there is a blessing in it,' so I will act for the sake of My servants, and I will not destroy them all." **9.** From Jacob (Jacob, the father of Israel's 12 tribes), I will raise up descendants, and from Judah (Judah, the tribe of King David) I will establish an heir to My mountains. My chosen ones will inherit them, and My servants will live there. **10.** The fertile plains of Sharon (a region near the coast) will become a grazing land for flocks, and the Valley of Achor (a valley known for trouble) will be a place of rest for herds, for My people who seek Me. **11.** But you are those who forsake (leave behind) the Lord, who forget My holy mountain, who prepare a table for Gad (a pagan god of fortune), and offer drink offerings to Meni (a pagan god of destiny). **12.** I will count you for destruction, and all of you will fall by the sword. You did not respond when I called, and when I spoke, you did not listen. Instead, you acted wickedly before My eyes and chose what I do not delight in. **13.** Therefore, this is what the Lord God says: "My servants will eat, but you will be hungry; My servants will drink, but you will be thirsty; My servants will rejoice, but you will be ashamed. **14.** My servants will sing for joy of heart, but you will cry out in sorrow, and you will wail in deep anguish of spirit. **15.** You will leave your name as a curse for My chosen ones. The Lord God will destroy you, and He will give His servants a new name. **16.** The one who blesses himself on the earth will bless himself in the God of truth; the one who swears (makes promises) on the earth will swear by the God of truth. For the past troubles will be forgotten, and they will be hidden from My eyes. **17.** "I am creating new heavens and a new earth, and the former things will not be remembered or even come to mind. **18.** But rejoice and be glad forever in what I am creating. I am making Jerusalem (the capital city of Israel) a source of joy, and her people will be a cause for gladness. **19.** I will rejoice in Jerusalem, and take delight (pleasure) in My people. There will no longer be the sound of weeping or crying within her. **20.** No infant will live only a few days, nor will an old man die prematurely. Those who live to be 100 will be considered young, and anyone who dies at 100 but is sinful will be cursed (under God's judgment). **21.** They will build homes and live in them; they will plant vineyards and enjoy the harvest from them. **22.** They will not build and have others live in their homes, nor will they plant and have others eat their crops. For as the days of a tree are, so will the days of My people. My chosen ones will enjoy the fruits of their labor for a long time. **23.** They will not labor (work hard) in vain, nor will they have children destined for disaster. For they will be the descendants of the blessed (favored) of the Lord, and their children will be with them. **24.** Even before they call, I will answer them; while they are still speaking, I will hear them. **25.** The wolf and the lamb will graze together, the lion will eat straw like the ox, and dust will be the food of the serpent. They will not hurt or destroy anyone on My holy mountain," says the Lord.

Chapter 66

1. The Lord says, "Heaven is My throne, and the earth serves as the place where I rest My bases. Where is the house you intend to make for Me? Where is the position where I'll dwell?" **2.** "It's by My hand that everything has been created; all that exists is made by Me," says the Lord. "But I'll look upon one thing: the person who's humble, with a penitent (feeling anguish and remorse) spirit, and one who trembles at My word." **3.** "Anyone who slaughters a bull is as shamefaced as someone who kills a person; anyone who offers an angel is like someone who breaks a canine's neck. Anyone who presents a grain immolation is as if they were offering gormandizer's blood, and anyone who burns incense (a substance burned for scent) is like the one who worships an idol. They've chosen their own ways, and their souls delight in their despicable acts. **4.** so I'll choose to bring their visions upon them. I'll let their fears catch them. When I called, no one responded. When I spoke, they didn't hear. They acted spitefully in My sight and chose what I abominate." **5.** Hear the word of the Lord, all you who fluctuate at His word: "Your cousins, who abominated you and cast you out because of My name, say, 'Let the Lord be glorified, so we may see your joy.' But they will be the ones put to shame." **6.** Hear the noise from the city! A voice calls out from the tabernacle! It's the voice of the Lord, who will completely repay His adversaries. **7.** "Before Zion (Jerusalem) indeed felt the pain of labor, she gave birth. Before the anguish began, she brought forth a son. **8.** Who has ever heard of such a thing? Who has ever seen anything like it? Can a nation be born in a day? Can a people be brought forth at once? Yet, as soon as Zion was in labor, she gave birth to her children. **9.** "Would I bring a moment of birth and not allow the delivery?" says the Lord. "Would I, who causes delivery, close the womb?" says your God. **10.** "Rejoice with Jerusalem, and be glad for her, all you who love her. Rejoice for joy with her, all you who have mourned for her. **11.** That you may be nourished by the cornucopia of her glory, and drink deeply from the joy of her presence, and be assured (handed with food or comfort) by her comforting grasp." **12.** For the Lord says, "I'll give peace to her like a river, and the glory of the nations will flow to her like a sluice. You'll be carried in her arms and rocked on her knees, **13.** As a mother comforts her child, so I'll console you, and you'll be assured in Jerusalem." **14.** When you witness this, your heart will be filled with joy, and your bones will grow strong like fresh grass. The Lord's hand will be revealed to His servants, but His wrath will be apparent to His adversaries. **15.** For behold, the Lord will come with fire, and His chariots (large vehicles used in battle) will be like a storm to repay His adversaries with fierce wrath and rebuke them with flames of fire. **16.** Through fire and by His sword, the Lord will bring judgment on all flesh, and many will fall by His hand. **17.** "Those who purify themselves to go to the temples, following an idol in the midst, eating gormandizer's meat, the abomination (things abominated), and mice, will all be consumed," says the Lord. **18.** "For I know their deeds and their thoughts. The time will come when I'll gather all nations and tongues, and they will come and see My glory." **19.** I'll place a sign among them, and those who survive will be sent to the nations, to Tarshish (a distant place), Pul, and Lud, professed in battle; to Tubal and Javan (regions in the ancient world), to the far-off coastlands who have not heard of My fame or seen My glory. They will declare My glory to the nations. **20.** And they will bring all your brothers from every nation as an offering to the Lord, riding on horses, chariots, litters (carriages), mules, and camels, to My holy mountain, Jerusalem," says the Lord. "Just as the children of Israel bring their offerings in clean vessels to the house of the Lord, **21.** I'll also take some of them to be priests and Levites (members of the lineage of Levi, who serve in the temple)," says the Lord. **22.** "For as the new heavens and the new earth, which I'll create, will endure before Me," says the Lord, "so your descendants and your name will endure. **23.** From one New Moon (a yearly time of worship) to another, and from one Sabbath (weekly day of rest) to another, all flesh will come to worship before Me," says the Lord. **24.** "They will go out and look at the corpses (dead bodies) of those who rebelled against Me. Their worm will never die, and their fire will never be extinguished. They will be a horror to all flesh."

31 – Jeremiah

Chapter 1

1. The message of Jeremiah, the son of Hilkiah, one of the priests living in Anathoth, a town in the land of Benjamin, **2.** came to him during the reign of King Josiah, son of Amon, of Judah, in the thirteenth year of his rule. **3.** It also came during the reign of King Jehoiakim, son of Josiah, and continued until the end of the eleventh year of King Zedekiah, son of Josiah, king of Judah, up to the time when the people of Jerusalem were taken captive (taken as prisoners) in the fifth month. **4.** Then the word of the Lord came to me, saying: **5.** "Before I formed you in the womb, I knew you; before you were born, I set you apart (sanctified - made holy or special); I appointed (chose) you as a prophet to the nations." **6.** But I said, "Ah, Lord God! I am unable to speak, because I am just a young person." **7.** The Lord responded to me, "Do not say, 'I am too young.' You will go to everyone I send you to, and you will speak whatever I command you to say. **8.** Do not be afraid of their faces (expressions), for I am with you to protect (rescue) you," says the Lord. **9.** Then the Lord reached out His hand, touched my mouth, and said to me, "Look, I have placed My words in your mouth. **10.** See, today I have appointed you to be in charge of nations and kingdoms, to tear down and uproot, to destroy and overthrow, to build and to plant." **11.** Then the word of the Lord came to me again, saying, "Jeremiah, what do you see?" I answered, "I see a branch of an almond tree." **12.** The Lord said to me, "You have seen correctly, for I am ready to fulfill (perform) My word." **13.** The word of the Lord came to me a second time, asking, "What do you see?" I replied, "I see a boiling pot, facing away from the north." **14.** Then the Lord said to me, "From the north, disaster (calamity - great misfortune) will come upon all the people of the land. **15.** For I am calling all the families of the kingdoms of the north," says the Lord. "They will come and each will set up their throne at the entrance to the gates of Jerusalem, against all its walls surrounding it, and against all the cities of Judah. **16.** I will pronounce My judgment (decision or declaration) on them for all their wickedness (evil deeds), because they have forsaken (abandoned) Me, burned incense to other gods, and worshipped the things they have made with their own hands." **17.** "So get yourself ready, stand up, and tell them everything I command you. Don't be afraid of them, or I will make you afraid of them. **18.** For look, I have made you today like a fortified (protected) city, an iron pillar, and bronze walls to stand against the entire land—against the kings of Judah, its officials, its priests, and the people of the land. **19.** They will fight against you, but they will not overcome (defeat) you. For I am with you," says the Lord, "to deliver (rescue) you."

Chapter 2

1. Furthermore, the word of the Lord came to me, saying: **2.** "Go and proclaim to Jerusalem, 'This is what the Lord says: "I remember the devotion (loyalty) of your youth, the love you had when you were first betrothed (engaged) to Me, when you followed Me through the wilderness, in a land that was not cultivated. **3.** Israel was set apart (holy) for the Lord, the firstfruits (initial harvest) of His harvest. Anyone who harms Israel will incur guilt; disaster will come upon them," says the Lord.'

4. Listen to the word of the Lord, O house of Jacob and all the families of Israel. **5.** This is what the Lord says: "What wrong (injustice) have your ancestors found in Me, that they turned so far from Me, followed worthless idols (false gods), and became idol worshipers (those who worship false gods)? **6.** They didn't even ask, 'Where is the Lord, Who brought us up from Egypt, Who led us through the wilderness, through a land of deserts and pits, through a land of drought and the shadow of death (deep darkness), a land where no one lives and no one travels?' **7.** I brought you into a rich and fruitful land, to enjoy its abundance. But when you entered, you defiled (polluted) My land and made My inheritance detestable (hateful). **8.** The priests didn't ask, 'Where is the Lord?' Those who teach the law did not know Me; the rulers rebelled (disobeyed) against Me, and the prophets prophesied by the false god Baal, following worthless things. **9.** Therefore, I will bring charges (accusations) against you," says the Lord, "and I will bring charges against your descendants. **10.** Go to the coasts of Cyprus (an island in the Mediterranean) and see, send to Kedar (a region in Arabia) and examine carefully, and see if anything like this has ever happened. **11.** Has a nation ever exchanged its gods, though they are not gods? But My people have exchanged their Glory (God) for something that does not benefit them. **12.** Be shocked, O heavens, at this, and be terrified (frightened), be utterly desolate (empty)," says the Lord. **13.** "For My people have committed two evils: They have abandoned (forsaken) Me, the fountain of living water, and have dug for themselves broken cisterns (water containers) that cannot hold water. **14.** "Is Israel a servant? Is he a born slave (someone born into slavery)? Why then has he been plundered (robbed)? **15.** The young lions have roared (growled) at him and growled; they have ruined (devastated) his land, and his cities are in ruins, without inhabitants. **16.** The people of Noph (an ancient Egyptian city) and Tahpanhes (another Egyptian city) have broken the crown (headpiece) of your head. **17.** Have you not brought this upon yourself by abandoning the Lord your God when He led you in the way? **18.** And now, why take the path to Egypt, to drink from the waters of the Nile (Sihor)? Or why go to Assyria, to drink from the Euphrates River? **19.** Your own wickedness will correct (reprove) you, and your backsliding (turning away from the right path) will rebuke (criticize) you. Understand and see that it is a wicked and bitter thing that you have abandoned the Lord your God, and that you have no fear (reverence) of Me," says the Lord God of hosts. **20.** "Long ago, I broke your chains and freed you from slavery, but you said, 'I will not serve.' Instead, on every high hill and under every green tree, you spread out, acting like a prostitute. **21.** Yet, I planted you as a noble vine, a seed of the highest quality. How then have you become like a wild vine, a degenerate (decayed) plant? **22.** For even though you wash yourself with lye (a strong alkaline solution) and use much soap, your sin remains before Me," says the Lord God. **23.** "How can you say, 'I am not defiled (polluted), I have not followed the Baals (false gods)?' Look at your ways in the valley, and know what you have done: You are like a swift camel running wild in her ways, **24.** like a wild donkey used to the desert, sniffing the wind in her passion (strong desire); in her mating season, who can turn her away? All who seek her will not weary themselves; in her month, they will find her. **25.** Keep your feet from going barefoot, and your throat from thirst. But you said, 'There is no hope (help). No! For I have loved strangers (foreign gods), and after them, I will go.' **26.** "Just as a thief is ashamed when caught, so the house of Israel will be ashamed; they and their kings, princes, priests, and prophets, **27.** who say to a tree, 'You are my father,' and to a stone, 'You gave birth to me.' They have turned their backs on Me, and not their faces. But when trouble comes, they will say, 'Arise and save us.' **28.** "But where are your gods that you made for yourselves? Let them arise, if they can save you in the time of trouble. For as many cities as you have, O Judah, you have as many gods. **29.** "Why will you argue with Me? You have all rebelled (disobeyed) against Me," says the Lord. **30.** "In vain I punished (chastised) your children; they did not respond to correction. Your sword has devoured (destroyed) your prophets like a destroying lion. **31.** "O generation,

consider (observe) the word of the Lord! Have I been a wilderness (desolate land) to Israel, or a land of darkness? Why do My people say, 'We are free; we will not come to You anymore'? **32.** Can a virgin forget her jewelry, or a bride her wedding dress? Yet My people have forgotten Me, days without number. **33.** "Why do you beautify (decorate) your way to seek love? Therefore, you have also taught the wicked women your ways. **34.** On your skirts is found the blood of the innocent poor; I have not found it by secret search, but plainly on all these things. **35.** Yet you say, 'Because I am innocent (blameless), surely His anger will turn from me.' Behold, I will bring My case (lawsuit) against you because you say, 'I have not sinned.' **36.** Why do you change (alter) your path so much? You will be ashamed of Egypt as you were ashamed of Assyria. **37.** Indeed, you will leave them with your hands on your head, for the Lord has rejected your allies (supporters), and you will not prosper (succeed) by them."

Chapter 3

1. They ask, "If a man divorces his wife, and she marries another man, can the first husband return to her?" Wouldn't that land be deeply polluted (corrupted)? Yet you have acted like a prostitute with many lovers, and still you are invited to return to Me," says the Lord. **2.** "Look up to the desolate (abandoned) heights and see: Where have you not been with men? You have waited by the roadsides for them, like an Arabian (a person from Arabia) in the wilderness. You have polluted the land with your sexual immorality (unlawful sexual acts) and wickedness." **3.** Because of this, the rain has been withheld (stopped), and there has been no latter rain. You have the forehead of a prostitute (stubborn and unashamed); you refuse to feel shame. **4.** Will you not cry out to Me now, 'My Father, You are the guide of my youth?' **5.** Will He stay angry forever? Will He be angry to the end?" Look, you have spoken and done evil things, as you were capable of doing." **6.** The Lord spoke to me during the reign of King Josiah, saying: "Have you seen what unfaithful (backsliding) Israel has done? She has gone up to every high hill and under every green tree, and there she committed adultery (unfaithfulness). **7.** I said, after she had done all these things, 'Return to Me.' But she did not return, and her treacherous (betraying) sister Judah saw it. **8.** Then I saw that even though Israel had been unfaithful, I gave her a certificate of divorce and sent her away. Yet, her treacherous sister Judah did not fear, and she went and played the harlot as well. **9.** Through her casual (careless) prostitution, she defiled (corrupted) the land and committed adultery with stones and trees (idols). **10.** Still, her treacherous sister Judah has not returned to Me with her whole heart, but only in pretense (a false appearance)," says the Lord. **11.** The Lord then said to me, "Unfaithful Israel has shown herself to be more righteous than treacherous Judah. **12.** Go and proclaim these words to the north: 'Return, unfaithful Israel,' says the Lord; 'I will not pour out My anger on you, for I am merciful (compassionate),' says the Lord; 'I will not stay angry forever. **13.** Only acknowledge your sin, that you have rebelled (turned away) against the Lord your God, and scattered your idols (false gods) to foreign deities under every green tree. And you have not obeyed My voice,' says the Lord. **14.** "Return, O unfaithful children," says the Lord, "for I am married to you. I will take you, one from a city and two from a family, and bring you to Zion. **15.** I will give you shepherds (leaders) after My own heart, who will feed you with knowledge and understanding. **16.** Then it will come to pass, when you have grown and increased in the land, that they will no longer say, 'The Ark of the Covenant of the Lord.' It will not be remembered, nor will they visit it, nor will it be made again. **17.** At that time, Jerusalem will be called 'The Throne of the Lord,' and all nations will gather to it, to the name of the Lord, to Jerusalem. No longer will they follow the desires of their evil hearts. **18.** In those days, the house of Judah will walk with the house of Israel, and they will come together from the land of the north to the land I gave your ancestors as an inheritance. **19.** "But I said: 'How can I place you among My children and give you a delightful (pleasing) land, a beautiful inheritance among the nations?' And I said: 'You will call Me, "My Father," and will not turn away from Me.' **20.** Surely, like a wife who has betrayed her husband, you have acted treacherously with Me, O house of Israel," says the Lord. **21.** A voice is heard on the barren (empty) heights, the weeping and pleading of the children of Israel. For they have corrupted (twisted) their way; they have forgotten the Lord their God. **22.** "Return, you unfaithful children, and I will heal your unfaithfulness." "Indeed, we will return to You, for You are the Lord our God. **23.** Truly, salvation is not to be hoped for from the hills or the many mountains. In the Lord our God is the salvation of Israel. **24.** Shame has consumed the work of our ancestors from our youth—their flocks and herds, their sons and daughters. **25.** We lie down in our shame, and our disgrace (dishonor) covers us. For we have sinned against the Lord our God, we and our ancestors, from our youth to this day, and we have not obeyed the voice of the Lord our God."

Chapter 4

1. "If you return, O Israel," declares the Lord, "Return to Me; and if you remove your detestable practices (abominations: things that are intensely disliked or repulsive) from My sight, then you will not be shaken. **2.** You will swear, 'As the Lord lives,' in truth, justice (judgment: the ability to make decisions about right and wrong), and righteousness; the nations will bless themselves through Him, and in Him, they will boast." **3** For this is what the Lord says to the people of Judah and Jerusalem: "Break up your unplowed (land that has not been used for farming) ground, and do not plant among thorns. **4.** Circumcise yourselves to the Lord, and remove the impurities (foreskins: the outer covering) from your hearts, O men of Judah and people of Jerusalem, lest My anger break out like fire and burn, with no one to quench it, because of your wicked deeds." **5.** Proclaim this in Judah and announce it in Jerusalem: "Sound the trumpet throughout the land! Cry out, 'Gather together!' and say, 'Assemble yourselves, and let us enter the fortified (strengthened or protected) cities.'" **6.** Set up a signal (a visible symbol for gathering) toward Zion. Take refuge! Do not delay! For I will bring disaster from the north, and a great destruction. **7.** A lion has risen from his thicket (a dense group of bushes or small trees), and the destroyer of nations is on his way. He has left his place to devastate your land. Your cities will lie in ruins, without any inhabitants. **8.** For this reason, clothe yourselves with sackcloth (a coarse, rough fabric used for mourning); mourn and wail. For the fierce anger of the Lord has not turned back from us. **9.** "And on that day," declares the Lord, "The king's heart will fail, and the hearts of the princes; the priests will be horrified, and the prophets will be stunned (astonished)." **10.** Then I said, "Ah, Lord God! You have greatly deceived (misled) this people and Jerusalem by saying, 'You will have peace,' while the sword is reaching the heart." **11.** At that time, it will be said to this people and to Jerusalem: "A dry wind from the barren heights blows toward the daughter of My people—not to cleanse or to purify—but to destroy. **12.** A wind too strong for these will come from Me; now I will also pronounce judgment against them." **13.** "Behold, he will come up like clouds, and his chariots will be like a whirlwind. His horses are faster than eagles. Woe to us, for we are plundered!" **14.** O Jerusalem, cleanse your heart from wickedness, that you may be saved. How long will your evil thoughts dwell within you? **15.** For a voice declares from Dan and proclaims disaster from Mount Ephraim: **16.** "Announce it to the nations; proclaim against Jerusalem: Watchers (those who keep watch or guard) come from a distant land and raise their voice against the cities of Judah. **17.** Like those who guard a field, they surround her because she has been rebellious against Me," says the Lord. **18.** "Your ways and your actions have brought this upon you. This is your wickedness, because it is bitter and it reaches to your heart." **19.** O my soul, my soul! I am in anguish (extreme pain or distress) in my heart! My heart pounds within me; I cannot keep silent because you have heard, O my soul, the sound of the trumpet, the alarm of war. **20.** Destruction upon destruction is called out, for the whole land is laid waste. Suddenly, my tents are plundered (plundered: robbed or looted), and my curtains destroyed in an instant. **21.** How long must I see the signal (standard) and hear the sound of the trumpet? **22.** "For My people are foolish; they do not know Me. They are foolish children and have no understanding. They are skilled in doing evil, but they do not know how to do good." **23.** I looked at the earth, and indeed it was empty and desolate (deserted, barren), and the heavens had no light. **24.** I looked at the mountains, and indeed they trembled, and all the hills moved back and forth. **25.** I looked, and there were no people, and all the birds of the heavens had fled. **26.** I looked, and the fruitful land had become a wilderness, and all its cities were in ruins, at the presence of the Lord, because of His fierce anger. **27.** For this is what the Lord says: "The whole land will be desolate, but I will not make a full end of it. **28.** The earth will mourn, and the heavens above will be dark, because I have spoken, and I have decided, and will not turn back, nor will I relent." **29.** The whole city will flee at the sound of horsemen and archers. They will go into thickets and climb on rocks. Every city will be abandoned, and no one will live in them. **30.** "And when you are plundered, what will you do? Though you dress in scarlet, though you adorn yourself with gold jewelry, though you paint your eyes with makeup, in vain you will beautify yourself. Your lovers (admirers or those who seek affection) will despise you; they will seek your life." **31.** "For I have heard a voice like a woman in labor, the anguish of one giving birth to her first child, the voice of the daughter of Zion crying out in distress; she spreads her hands, saying, 'Woe to me, for my soul is weary because of murderers!'"

Chapter 5

1. "Run through the streets of Jerusalem, and see if you can find a man who does justice (righteous judgment), who seeks the truth (honestly). If you find one, I will pardon her. **2.** Though they say, 'As the Lord lives,' they swear falsely (lying in God's name). **3.** O Lord, do Your eyes not see the truth? You have struck them, but they have not grieved (felt sorrow). You have consumed them, but they refuse correction. They have hardened their faces (stubbornness) and will not return (repent). **4.** Therefore, I said, "These are poor (ignorant) and foolish; they do not know the way of the Lord or the judgment (justice) of their God." **5.** I will speak to the great men, for they know the way of the Lord, but they have broken the yoke (refused to follow God's guidance) and burst the bonds (broken free from God's laws). **6.** A lion from the forest will slay them, a wolf will destroy them; a leopard will watch over their cities (destruction is coming). Everyone who goes out will be torn in pieces because of their many transgressions (sins) and backslidings (falling away from God). **7.** "How can I pardon you? Your children have forsaken Me and sworn by false gods (idols). When I gave them abundance, they committed adultery (betrayed God) and gathered in harlots' houses (engaged in immoral practices). **8.** They were like lusty stallions, neighing after their neighbor's wife (lustful desires). **9.** Shall I not punish them for these things?" says the Lord. "Shall I not avenge Myself on such a nation as this? **10.** "Go up and destroy her walls (bring judgment), but do not make a complete end. Take away her branches (falsehoods), for they are not the Lord's. **11.** The house of Israel and the house of Judah have been treacherous (unfaithful) to Me," says the Lord. **12.** They have lied about the Lord, saying, "It is not He. Evil will not come upon us, nor will we see sword (war) or famine (starvation)." **13.** And the prophets have become wind; the word is not in them. Thus it will be done to them." **14.** Therefore, says the Lord God of hosts, "Because you speak this word, I will make My words like fire in your mouth and this people like wood, and it will devour them (bring judgment)." **15.** "I will bring a nation from afar against you, O house of Israel," says the Lord. "A mighty, ancient nation, whose language you do not know (foreign conquerors), and you will not understand their speech. **16.** Their quiver is like an open tomb; they are mighty men (brutal warriors). **17.** They will eat your harvest and bread, your sons and daughters' food, your flocks and herds, your vines and fig trees, and destroy your fortified cities (places of strength and security) with the sword." **18.** "Nevertheless, in those days, I will not make a complete end of you," says the Lord. **19.** When you ask, 'Why does the Lord do these things to us?' you will answer, 'Because you forsook Me and served foreign gods (idols), so now you will serve foreigners in a land not yours.' **20.** "Declare this to the house of Jacob and proclaim it in Judah: **21.** Hear this, O foolish people, without understanding (spiritual blindness), who have eyes but do not see, ears but do not hear: **22.** Do you not fear Me?" says the Lord. "Will you not tremble at My presence, who set the bounds of the sea so it cannot pass (limitations placed by God)? **23.** Yet this people has a rebellious heart (disobedience); they have revolted and departed. **24.** They do not say in their hearts, 'Let us fear the Lord who gives rain (blessings) in its season and reserves for us the appointed weeks of the harvest.' **25.** Your iniquities have turned these blessings away, and your sins have withheld good from you (blocked God's favor). **26.** Among My people are wicked men, lying in wait like hunters setting snares (traps) to trap men. **27.** Like a cage full of birds, their houses are full of deceit (dishonesty). Therefore they have become rich and powerful. **28.** They are fat and sleek (materially prosperous); they surpass the deeds of the wicked. They do not plead the cause of the fatherless; they prosper and do not defend the needy. **29.** Shall I not punish them for these things?" says the Lord. "Shall I not avenge Myself on such a nation as this? 30. "An astonishing and horrible thing has been committed in the land: 31. The prophets prophesy falsely, the priests rule by their own power, and My people love it (wicked leadership). But what will you do in the end?"

Chapter 6

1. "O children of Benjamin, flee from Jerusalem! Blow the trumpet in Tekoa (a town in Judah, south of Jerusalem) and set up a signal-fire in Beth Haccerem (a village near Jerusalem), for disaster comes from the north, bringing great destruction. 2. I have compared Zion's daughter (Jerusalem or the people of Israel) to a delicate (fragile) woman. 3. The shepherds with their flocks will surround her; they will camp around her, grazing (feeding) in their own places. 4. "Prepare for war! Let us rise at noon. Woe (great sorrow) to us, the day is fading, and evening shadows lengthen. 5. Let us attack by night and destroy her palaces." 6. The Lord of Hosts says, "Cut down trees and build a siege (military blockade) mound against Jerusalem. This city is full of oppression (unjust treatment). 7. Just as a spring overflows, so her wickedness pours out. Violence and plundering (robbery) are heard; grief and wounds (injuries) are before Me. 8. Be warned, Jerusalem, lest I depart from you and make you desolate (empty, barren), uninhabited." 9. The Lord of Hosts says, "They will thoroughly glean (gather) Israel, like a grape-gatherer returning for the leftovers." 10. To whom can I speak? Their ears are dull (unresponsive), and they cannot listen. They take no pleasure in My word. 11. I am filled with fury (anger) and can no longer hold it in. "I will pour it out on the young and the old, the children and the aged. 12. Their houses will be given to others, and their fields and wives taken, for I will stretch My hand against the land's inhabitants," says the Lord. 13. "Everyone is greedy (desirous) for gain, from the least to the greatest; from prophet to priest, all deal falsely (dishonestly). 14. They have treated the wounds (injuries) of My people lightly, saying, 'Peace, peace!' when there is no peace. 15. They were not ashamed of their abominations (disgusting acts); they did not know how to blush (feel shame). Therefore, they will fall when I punish them," says the Lord. 16. Thus says the Lord: "Stand at the crossroads and ask for the ancient (old) paths, where the good way is, and walk in it. Then you will find rest for your souls." But they said, "We will not walk in it." 17. "I set watchmen (guards) over you, saying, 'Listen to the trumpet!' But they said, 'We will not listen.'" 18. Therefore, hear, O nations, and know what is among them. 19. Hear, O earth! I am bringing disaster upon this people—the fruit (result) of their thoughts, because they have rejected My words and law. 20. What good is incense (fragrant substance burned as an offering) from Sheba (a wealthy kingdom known for its spices) or sweet cane (a type of plant) from a far country? Your burnt offerings are not acceptable to Me. 21. The Lord says, "I will lay stumbling blocks (obstacles) before this people; fathers and sons will fall together. Neighbor and friend will perish." 22. "A people from the northern country will rise, a great nation from the farthest parts of the earth. 23. They are cruel (violent) and merciless (without compassion), their voice roars like the sea; they ride on horses, ready for battle against you, O daughter of Zion." 24. We have heard of it; our hands grow weak. Anguish (great suffering) grips us, like a woman in labor. 25. Do not go into the field or walk on the road, for fear of the sword is on every side. 26. O daughter of My people, put on sackcloth (a coarse fabric worn as a sign of mourning) and mourn, for the destroyer (one who brings destruction) will come suddenly upon us. 27. "I have made you a tester (examiner) and fortress (stronghold) among My people, to understand their ways. 28. They are stubborn (resistant to change) rebels (those who resist authority), slanderers (those who speak false accusations), corrupt (dishonest) like bronze and iron. 29. The bellows (a device for blowing air into a fire) blow fiercely, but the wicked are not refined (purified). 30. People will call them 'rejected (discarded) silver,' because the Lord has rejected them."

Chapter 7

1. The word of the Lord came to Jeremiah, saying, 2. "Stand at the gate of the Lord's house and proclaim: 'Hear the word of the Lord, all you of Judah who come to worship here!' 3. The Lord of hosts (armies), the God of Israel, says: 'Change your ways and actions, and I will let you stay in this place. 4. Do not trust in deceptive (false) words like, 'The temple of the Lord, the temple of the Lord, the temple of the Lord!' 5. If you truly change your ways and actions, if you do justice (fairness) between a man and his neighbor, 6. if you do not oppress (mistreat) the stranger, the orphan, and the widow, and do not shed innocent blood or follow other gods to your harm, 7. then I will allow you to stay in this place, the land I gave to your ancestors (forefathers) forever. 8. You trust in words that cannot help. 9. Will you steal, murder, commit adultery, lie, burn incense (substance burned for fragrance) to Baal, and follow other gods you don't even know, 10. and then come to stand before Me in this house called by My name, saying, 'We are saved to do all these things'? 11. Has this house, called by My name, become a den of thieves? I have seen it," says the Lord. 12. "Go to Shiloh (ancient city in Israel), where I first set My name, and see what I did there because of the wickedness of My people Israel. 13. You have done all these things," says the Lord, "though I warned you early and often, but you did not listen or answer. 14. Therefore, I will do to this house, called by My name, as I did to Shiloh. 15. I will cast you from My sight, as I did your relatives, the people of Ephraim (tribe of Israel). 16. "Do not pray for this people, or cry out or intercede (plead) for them, for I will not listen. 17. Do you not see what they do in the cities (towns) of Judah and the streets of Jerusalem? 18. The children gather wood, the fathers light the fire, and the women prepare dough to bake cakes for the queen of heaven (idol goddess), and pour out drink offerings to other gods, provoking Me to anger. 19. Do they provoke Me to anger?" says the Lord. "Do they not provoke themselves to their own shame?" 20. Therefore, says the Lord, "My anger and fury will be poured out on this place—on man and beast, on trees and crops—and it will burn without end." 21. The Lord of hosts, the God of Israel, says: "Add your burnt offerings to your sacrifices and eat the meat. 22. For when I brought your ancestors out of Egypt (land of bondage), I did not command them about burnt offerings or sacrifices. 23. I gave them this command: 'Obey My voice, and I will be your God, and you will be My people. Walk in the ways I have commanded you, and it will go well with you.' 24. Yet they did not obey, but followed their own evil hearts, going backward, not forward. 25. From the day your ancestors came out of Egypt until now, I have sent you prophets daily, but you did not listen or obey. 26. They stiffened their necks (refused to listen) and did worse than their ancestors. 27. "Therefore, speak all these words to them, but they will not listen. Call to them, but they will not answer. 28. Say to them: 'This is a nation that does not obey the Lord or accept correction. Truth has vanished from their mouths. 29. Shave your heads and mourn, for the Lord has rejected this generation of His wrath.' 30. The children of Judah have done evil in My sight," says the Lord. "They have set up their detestable (disgusting) idols in My house, defiling it. 31. They have built high places for Baal in the Valley of Hinnom (a valley near Jerusalem) to burn their children in fire— something I never commanded, nor did it ever enter My mind. 32. "The days are coming," says the Lord, "when it will no longer be called Tophet (a place in the Valley of Hinnom) or the Valley of Hinnom, but the Valley of Slaughter. The dead will be buried there until there is no more room. 33. The corpses of this people will become food for birds and animals, and no one will frighten them away. 34. I will end the sounds of joy and gladness, and the voices of brides and bridegrooms, in the cities of Judah and the streets of Jerusalem. The land will become desolate."

Chapter 8

1. "At that time," says the Lord, "they will bring out the bones of the kings (rulers) of Judah, its princes, priests, prophets, and the people of Jerusalem, from their graves. 2. They will spread them before the sun, moon, and all the host of heaven, which they loved, served, followed, sought, and worshiped. They will not be gathered or buried; they will be like refuse (waste) on the earth. 3. Then, death will be chosen over life by all who remain of this wicked family in the places I have driven them," says the Lord of hosts. 4. "Say to them, 'Thus says the Lord: 'Will they fall and not rise? Will one turn and not return? 5. Why has this people turned away, Jerusalem (capital city of Judah), in constant rebellion? They cling to deceit and refuse to return. 6. I listened and heard, but they do not speak rightly. No one repented, saying, 'What have I done?' Everyone follows their own path, like a horse rushing into battle. 7. Even the stork in the heavens knows her appointed times; the turtledove, swift, and swallow know their coming times. But My people do not know the judgment of the Lord. 8. How can you say, 'We are wise, and the law of the Lord is with us'? Look, the false pen of the

scribe writes lies. **9.** The wise are ashamed, dismayed, and trapped. They have rejected the word of the Lord; what wisdom do they have? **10.** Therefore, I will give their wives to others and their fields to those who will inherit them; because everyone, from the least to the greatest, is greedy. From prophet to priest, they deal falsely. **11.** They heal My people's wounds superficially, saying, 'Peace, peace!' when there is no peace. **12.** Were they ashamed when they committed abominations (disgraceful acts)? No! They were not ashamed at all and did not even know how to blush. Therefore, they shall fall with those who fall; in their time of punishment, they will be cast down," says the Lord. **13.** "I will surely consume them," says the Lord. "No grapes will be on the vine, no figs on the fig tree, and the leaves will wither. What I have given them will pass away." **14.** "Why do we sit still? Let us assemble and enter fortified cities (cities with strong defenses). Let us be silent there. For the Lord has made us silent and given us bitter water to drink because we have sinned against Him. **15.** We looked for peace, but no good came. We hoped for healing, but there was only trouble. **16.** The sound of His horses was heard from Dan (a northern city in Israel), and the land trembled at the neighing of His strong ones; they have come and devoured the land, the city, and its people." **17.** "Behold, I will send serpents (poisonous snakes) among you, vipers that cannot be charmed, and they will bite you," says the Lord. **18.** I would comfort myself in sorrow, but my heart is faint (weak) within me. **19.** Listen! The cry of the daughter of My people from a distant land: "Is not the Lord in Zion (the hill of Jerusalem)? Is not her King in her? Why have they provoked Me to anger with their carved images and foreign idols?" **20.** "The harvest has passed, the summer is ended, and we are not saved!" **21.** For the wound of My people, I am deeply wounded. I mourn; astonishment (shock) has taken hold of me. **22.** Is there no balm (healing substance) in Gilead (a region known for its medicinal herbs), is there no physician (healer) there? Why then is there no recovery for My people?

Chapter 9

1. Oh, that my head were waters, and my eyes a fountain of tears that I might weep day and night for the slain (killing) of my people! **2.** Oh, that I had a lodging place in the wilderness (desert) for travelers, that I might leave my people and go from them! For they are all adulterers (unfaithful), a company of treacherous (betraying) men. **3.** Like their bow, they bend their tongues to lies. They are not valiant (brave) for truth, but go from evil to evil, and do not know Me, says the Lord. **4.** Let everyone beware (be cautious) of his neighbor and trust no brother. For every brother deceives (cheats), and every neighbor slanders (gossips). **5.** Everyone deceives his neighbor and does not speak truth; they have taught their tongues to lie; they weary themselves with iniquity (wickedness). **6.** Your land is full of deceit (dishonesty); through it, they refuse to know Me, says the Lord. **7.** Therefore, thus says the Lord of hosts: Behold, I will refine (purify) and test them. How should I deal with My people? **8.** Their tongue is an arrow (sharp weapon), speaking deceit. One speaks peace to his neighbor, but in his heart, he lies in wait (plots). **9.** Shall I not punish them for these things? Shall I not avenge (take revenge) Myself on such a nation? **10.** I will weep for the mountains, and lament (mourn) for the wilderness, burned up so no one passes through; the birds and beasts have fled. **11.** I will make Jerusalem a heap of ruins, a den (home) of jackals. The cities of Judah will be desolate (empty), with no inhabitants. **12.** Who is the wise (intelligent) man who may understand this? Why has the land perished (died) and burned like a wilderness? **13.** The Lord said, because they have forsaken (abandoned) My law, not obeyed My voice or walked in it, **14.** but followed their own hearts and the Baals (idols), which their fathers taught them, **15.** therefore, thus says the Lord of hosts: Behold, I will feed them with wormwood (bitter substance) and give them bitter water to drink. **16.** I will scatter (disperse) them among the nations, and send a sword after them until I have consumed (destroyed) them. **17.** Thus says the Lord of hosts: Call for the mourning women, and send for skillful (expert) wailers. **18.** Let them hasten (hurry) and wail, that our eyes may pour with tears, and our eyelids gush with water. **19.** For a voice of wailing is heard from Zion: How are we plundered (robbed)! We are ashamed because we have forsaken the land and been cast out. **20.** Hear the word of the Lord, O women; teach your daughters wailing, and every woman her neighbor a lament. **21.** For death has entered through our windows, to

kill the children—no longer outside! And the young men—no longer in the streets! **22.** Speak, Thus says the Lord: Even the carcasses (dead bodies) of men will lie like refuse (garbage) in the open field, and no one will gather them. **23.** Thus says the Lord: Let not the wise man glory (boast) in his wisdom, the mighty in his strength, nor the rich in his wealth; **24.** but let him who glories, glory in this: that he understands and knows Me, that I am the Lord, exercising loving-kindness (mercy), judgment, and righteousness on the earth. For in these I delight, says the Lord. **25.** Behold, the days are coming, says the Lord, when I will punish all who are circumcised (cut in the flesh) with the uncircumcised— **26.** Egypt, Judah, Edom, Ammon, Moab, and all who dwell in the wilderness. All these nations are uncircumcised, and all the house of Israel is uncircumcised in heart.

Chapter 10

1. Hear the word of the Lord, O house of Israel. **2.** The Lord says: "Do not follow the ways of the nations or be alarmed by signs in the heavens, for they are afraid (fearful) of them. **3.** The customs (traditions) of the people are empty (vain); they cut a tree from the forest, shaped by a craftsman's (artisan) axe. **4.** They adorn it with silver and gold, securing it with nails and hammers so it won't fall. **5.** It stands firm like a palm tree, but it cannot speak. It must be carried, as it cannot move on its own. Do not fear (be afraid) it, for it can do no evil or good." **6.** There is none like You, O Lord; You are great and mighty in power. **7.** Who would not fear (revere) You, O King of the nations? This is Your rightful due. Among all the wise (learned) of the earth, none compare to You. **8.** But they are foolish (senseless) and dull-hearted (stubborn); a wooden idol is a worthless (useless) belief. **9.** Silver is hammered (shaped) into plates, and gold from Tarshish and Uphaz is crafted by artisans; their robes are made of blue and purple. These are all works of skilled (talented) men. **10.** But the Lord is the true God, the living God, the eternal (everlasting) King. At His anger, the earth trembles (shakes), and nations cannot withstand (resist) His wrath. **11.** Say to them: "The gods who did not create the heavens and the earth will perish (vanish) from the earth and beneath the heavens." **12.** The Lord made the earth by His power, established (set up) the world by His wisdom, and stretched out the heavens at His will. **13.** When He speaks, waters rise from the heavens; He sends the rain, lightning, and wind from His storehouses (treasuries). **14.** Everyone is foolish (senseless) and lacks (does not have) knowledge; the idol-maker is ashamed of his image, for it is false and has no breath (life) in it. **15.** They are worthless (useless), a work of delusion (illusion); when their punishment (judgment) comes, they will vanish. **16.** The portion (inheritance) of Jacob is not like them, for He is the Creator of all, and Israel is His inheritance; the Lord of hosts (armies) is His name. **17.** Gather your belongings (possessions), O inhabitant (dweller) of the fortress (stronghold), **18.** for the Lord says, "I will throw out the inhabitants (people) of the land and distress (trouble) them so they will know the truth." **19.** Woe to me, for I am severely (greatly) wounded. This is an affliction (pain) I must bear. **20.** My tent is looted, and all my cords are broken. My children are gone, and no one is left to set up my tent or restore (rebuild) my curtains. **21.** The shepherds are senseless and have not sought the Lord; therefore, they will not prosper (succeed), and their flocks will be scattered (dispersed). **22.** A noise has come, a great commotion (uproar) from the north, to make Judah's cities desolate (ruined), a place for jackals (wild dogs). **23.** O Lord, I know that man cannot direct (guide) his own steps. **24.** Correct (rebuke) me, Lord, but with justice, not in anger, or I will be reduced (destroyed) to nothing. **25.** Pour out Your wrath on the nations that do not know You, and on those who do not call on Your name, for they have devoured (destroyed) Jacob and made his land desolate.

Chapter 11

1. The word that came to Jeremiah from the Lord, saying, **2.** "Hear the words of this covenant (agreement), and speak to the men of Judah and the inhabitants of Jerusalem; **3.** and say to them, 'Thus says the Lord God of Israel: "Cursed (condemned) is the man who does not obey the words of this covenant, **4.** which I commanded your fathers when I brought them out of Egypt, from the iron furnace (place of affliction), saying, 'Obey My voice, and do all I command you; then you shall be My people, and I will be your God,' **5.** that I may fulfill the oath (promise) I swore to your fathers, to give them a land flowing with milk and honey, as it is this day."' And I answered and said, "So be it, Lord."

6. Then the Lord said to me, "Proclaim all these words in the cities of Judah and in the streets of Jerusalem, saying: 'Hear the words of this covenant and do them. **7.** For I earnestly (sincerely) warned your fathers when I brought them out of Egypt, rising early to speak, saying, "Obey My voice." **8.** Yet they did not obey or incline (listen attentively) their ear, but everyone followed the stubbornness (unyielding will) of his evil heart; therefore I will bring upon them all the words of this covenant, which they have not kept.'" **9.** And the Lord said to me, "A conspiracy (plot) has been found among the men of Judah and the inhabitants of Jerusalem. **10.** They have turned back to the sins of their forefathers (ancestors), who refused to hear My words, and they have gone after other gods to serve them. The house of Israel and the house of Judah have broken My covenant with their ancestors." **11.** Therefore, thus says the Lord: "Behold, I will bring calamity (disaster) on them they cannot escape; and though they cry to Me, I will not listen. **12.** Then the cities of Judah and the inhabitants of Jerusalem will cry out to the gods to whom they offer incense (a substance burned as a sacrifice), but they will not save them in their time of trouble. **13.** For as many cities as you have, O Judah, you have set up altars (places of sacrifice) to that shameful thing (idol), altars to burn incense to Baal (Canaanite god). **14.** "So do not pray for this people, or lift up a cry or prayer for them; for I will not hear them in the time of their trouble. **15.** "What has My beloved to do in My house, having done lewd deeds (immoral actions) with many? And the holy flesh (sacred offering) has passed from you. When you do evil, then you rejoice. **16.** The Lord called your name, Green Olive Tree, lovely and of good fruit. With the noise of a great tumult (uproar), He has kindled (started) a fire on it, and its branches are broken. **17.** "For the Lord of hosts (armies), who planted you, has pronounced doom (destruction) against you for the evil of the house of Israel and the house of Judah, which they have done to provoke Me to anger by offering incense to Baal." **18.** Now the Lord gave me knowledge (understanding) of it, and I knew it; for You showed me their deeds. **19.** But I was like a docile (gentle, submissive) lamb brought to the slaughter; and I did not know that they had devised schemes (plans) against me, saying, "Let us destroy the tree with its fruit, and cut him off from the land of the living, that his name may be remembered no more." **20.** But, O Lord of hosts, You who judge righteously, testing the mind and heart, let me see Your vengeance (revenge) on them, for to You I have revealed my cause. **21.** "Therefore, thus says the Lord concerning the men of Anathoth who seek your life, saying, 'Do not prophesy in the name of the Lord, or you will die by our hand'— **22.** therefore thus says the Lord of hosts: 'Behold, I will punish them. The young men will die by the sword (battle), their sons and daughters by famine (starvation); **23.** and there shall be no remnant (survivors) of them, for I will bring catastrophe (disaster) on the men of Anathoth in the year of their punishment.'"

Chapter 12

1. Righteous are You, Lord, when I complain, yet let me question Your judgments. Why do the wicked prosper? Why do the treacherous (deceitful) thrive? **2.** You have planted them, and they take root and grow, bearing fruit. They speak of You, but their hearts are far from You. **3.** But You, Lord, know me and have tested (examined) my heart. Pull them out like sheep for slaughter and prepare them for the day of judgment. **4.** How long will the land mourn (grieve) and the fields wither? The beasts and birds are dying because of the wickedness of those who live there. They say, "He won't see our end." **5.** If you are weary (tired) running with footmen, how can you compete with horses? And if you struggle in a peaceful land, what will you do in the floodplains (low-lying areas) of the Jordan? **6.** Even your family has betrayed (treated dishonestly) you. They speak kindly, but don't trust them. **7.** I have forsaken (abandoned) My house, given My beloved people into the hands of enemies. **8.** My heritage (inheritance) is like a lion in the forest, crying out against Me. Therefore, I have rejected it. **9.** It's like a speckled vulture (bird of prey), surrounded by other vultures. Come, all beasts of the field, to devour! **10.** Many rulers have ruined My vineyard (land) and trampled My portion. They've made My pleasant land a desolate wilderness. **11.** The land mourns and is desolate because no one cares. **12.** Plunderers (looters) have come, and the sword of the Lord will consume the land from one end to the other, bringing no peace. **13.** They planted wheat but harvested thorns; they labored in vain and will be ashamed of their harvest

because of God's fierce anger. **14.** The Lord says: Against all My wicked neighbors who touch the inheritance of Israel, I will uproot them from their land and uproot Judah from among them. **15.** But after I have uprooted them, I will show mercy and return them to their land and heritage. **16.** If they learn the ways of My people and swear by My name, saying, "As the Lord lives," as they taught My people to swear by Baal, they will be established among My people. **17.** But if they do not listen, I will completely destroy them, declares the Lord.

Chapter 13

1. The Lord said to me, "Get a linen sash (cloth belt) and put it around your waist, but don't wet it." **2.** I did as the Lord commanded and put the sash around my waist. **3.** Then the Lord spoke to me again: **4.** "Take the sash, go to the Euphrates (a river), and hide it in a rock hole." **5.** I did as the Lord said and hid it by the Euphrates. **6.** After many days, the Lord told me, "Go to the Euphrates and get the sash you hid." **7.** I dug it up, and it was ruined—useless. **8.** The Lord spoke: **9.** "This is how I will destroy the pride (arrogance) of Judah and Jerusalem. **10.** This evil people, who refuse to listen to Me, follow their own desires, and worship other gods, will be like this ruined sash—worthless. **11.** Just as a sash clings (sticks) to the waist, I had hoped Israel and Judah would cling to Me, becoming a people of renown (fame) and glory. But they would not listen." **12.** "Tell them, 'Every bottle will be filled with wine.' And they will ask, 'Don't we know every bottle will be filled?' **13.** Say to them, 'I will fill this land—kings, priests, prophets, and all the people of Jerusalem—with drunkenness (intoxication). **14.** I will cause them to destroy each other—fathers and sons. I will show no pity, but will bring total destruction.'" **15.** Listen and don't be proud (arrogant), for the Lord has spoken. **16.** Give glory to God before He brings darkness (misery), before your feet stumble in the dark, and while you seek light, He turns it to thick darkness. **17.** If you refuse to listen, My soul will weep for your pride; My eyes will cry bitterly, because the Lord's people have been taken captive (taken away as prisoners). **18.** Say to the king and queen mother, "Humble yourselves (be modest); sit down. Your rule will collapse, and your crown of glory will fall." **19.** The cities of the South (southern cities) will be shut up, and no one will open them. Judah will be taken away, all of it. **20.** Look to the north. Where is your flock (sheep), your beautiful sheep? **21.** What will you say when He punishes you? You taught them to lead you; will you not feel pain like a woman in labor (giving birth)? **22.** And if you ask, 'Why has this happened?' It's because of your great sin (wrongdoing). Your skirts (clothing) have been exposed, your shame revealed. **23.** Can the Ethiopian (person from Ethiopia) change his skin or the leopard its spots? Then you who are accustomed (used) to doing evil, can you do good? **24.** Therefore, I will scatter them like stubble (dry straw) blown by the desert wind. **25.** This is your fate, your portion (share) from Me, because you have forgotten Me and trusted in lies. **26.** I will expose your shame. **27.** I have seen your adulteries (unfaithfulness), your lust (strong desire), your lewdness (immorality), and your abominations (wickedness) on the hills and fields. Woe (danger) to you, Jerusalem! Will you not be made clean?"

Chapter 14

1. The word of the Lord came to Jeremiah about the drought. **2.** Judah mourns (grieves), and her gates are desolate (ruined). The land mourns, and Jerusalem's cry reaches up. **3.** The nobles sent their servants for water. They went to the cisterns (underground water storage) but found none, returning with empty vessels, ashamed. **4.** The land is parched (dry) due to the lack of rain. The plowmen are ashamed and cover their heads. **5.** Even the deer give birth but leave because there's no grass. **6.** The wild donkeys stand on barren (empty) heights, sniffing the wind like jackals (wild dogs), their eyes failing for lack of grass. **7.** Lord, our iniquities (sins) testify against us. Do it for Your name's sake; our backslidings (turning away) are many, and we have sinned against You. **8.** Hope of Israel, Savior (rescuer) in times of trouble, why are You like a stranger in the land, like a traveler who only stays the night? **9.** Why are You like one who cannot save, though You are in our midst, and we are called by Your name? Do not leave us! **10.** The Lord says: "This people loves to wander; they have not restrained (controlled) their feet. Therefore, I will not accept them and will punish their sins." **11.** Then the Lord told me, "Do not pray for their good." **12.** "Even when they fast (abstain from food), I will not hear; their offerings (sacrifices) I will not accept. I will consume them with the sword, famine (severe hunger), and pestilence (plague)." **13.** I said, "Lord, the prophets are telling them, 'You will not see the sword, nor suffer famine, but peace will come to this place.'" **14.** But the Lord said, "The prophets prophesy (prediction) lies in My name. I did not send them. They speak false visions, deceit (falsehood), and the delusions (misleading ideas) of their hearts. **15.** Therefore, concerning the false prophets, I say: 'By sword and famine, they shall be consumed!' **16.** The people they prophesy to will be cast out (thrown) in the streets, and no one will bury them—neither them, nor their families, because I will pour out their wickedness (evil) on them." **17.** "Let my eyes flow with tears day and night for the virgin daughter of my people, struck (injured) with a great blow. **18.** If I go to the field, I see those slain (killed) by the sword. If I enter the city, I see those suffering from famine. Even the prophets and priests wander in lands they do not know." **19.** Have You completely rejected (abandoned) Judah? Have You loathed (hated) Zion? Why have You struck us so that we cannot heal? We looked for peace, but found none. We hoped for healing, but trouble came. **20.** We acknowledge (admit) our wickedness and that of our fathers, for we have sinned against You. **21.** Do not abhor (detest) us, Lord, for Your name's sake. Do not disgrace Your throne of glory. Remember, do not break Your covenant (agreement) with us. **22.** Are any of the idols (false gods) of the nations able to send rain? Can the heavens give showers? Are You not the Lord our God? Therefore, we wait for You, for You made all these things.

Chapter 15

1. Then the Lord said to me, "Even if Moses and Samuel stood before Me, I would not be favorable toward this people. Cast them out of My sight and let them go. **2.** If they ask, 'Where should we go?' tell them, 'Thus says the Lord: Those destined for death (appointed for death), to death; those for the sword (weapon), to the sword; those for famine (severe shortage of food), to famine; those for captivity (imprisonment), to captivity.' **3.** "I will bring four forms of destruction upon them," says the Lord: "the sword to kill, dogs (wild animals) to drag, birds and beasts to devour (consume)." **4.** I will give them over to disaster (calamity), to all kingdoms of the earth, because of what Manasseh, son of Hezekiah, did in Jerusalem. **5.** "Who will pity (feel sorry for) you, O Jerusalem? Who will mourn for you or ask how you are?" **6.** You have forsaken (abandoned) Me," says the Lord. "You have turned away. Therefore, I will stretch out My hand against you and destroy you; I am weary (tired) of relenting (giving in). **7.** I will winnow (separate) them with a winnowing fan (tool for separating grain) at the gates, bereaving (depriving) them of children, destroying My people, because they refuse to return. **8.** Their widows will be more than the sand of the sea. I will bring a plunderer (looter) at noonday, causing sudden terror and anguish (extreme pain). **9.** "She who has borne seven children will languish (suffer), her sun will set while it is still day. I will give the remnant (remainder) to the sword before their enemies," says the Lord. **10.** Woe (grief) is me, my mother, for you bore a man of strife (conflict) and contention (disagreement) to the earth. I have neither lent nor borrowed, yet everyone curses me. **11.** The Lord said, "It will be well with your remnant. I will make the enemy intercede (mediate) for you in your time of trouble. **12.** Can anyone break the northern iron and bronze (metal)? **13.** Your wealth and treasures I will give as plunder (booty) for your sins, throughout your land. **14.** I will make you cross over to a land you do not know; a fire (anger) has been kindled in My anger, and it will burn against you." **15.** O Lord, You know. Remember me and visit me, and take vengeance (revenge) on my persecutors (oppressors). Do not take me away in Your patience; know that I suffer for Your sake. **16.** I found Your words and ate them. Your word became the joy and delight of my heart, for I am called by Your name, O Lord God of hosts. **17.** I did not sit with the mockers (laughers), nor did I rejoice. I sat alone because Your hand was upon me, filling me with indignation (anger). **18.** Why is my pain perpetual (constant) and my wound incurable (unable to heal), refusing to heal? Will You be like an unreliable stream (river), waters that fail (dry up)? **19.** Therefore, says the Lord: "If you return, I will bring you back. You will stand before Me. If you separate the precious (valuable) from the vile (wicked), you will be as My mouth. Let them return to you, but do not return to them. **20.** I will make you a fortified (strong) bronze wall to this people. They will fight against you, but will not prevail (succeed), for I am with you to save and deliver you," says the Lord. **21.** "I will

deliver you from the hand of the wicked (evil), and redeem (rescue) you from the grip of the terrible."

Chapter 16

1. The word of the Lord came to me, saying, **2.** "Do not take a wife or have sons or daughters in this place. **3.** For thus says the Lord about those born here, their mothers, and their fathers: **4.** 'They will die violent (gruesome) deaths, unburied and unlamented (mourned), like refuse (waste) on the earth. They will be consumed by the sword and famine, and their bodies will be food for the birds and beasts.' **5.** "Do not enter the house of mourning (grief) or mourn for them, for I have removed My peace, kindness, and mercy from this people. **6.** Both great and small will die here and will not be buried. No one will mourn, cut themselves, or shave their heads for them. **7.** No one will comfort the bereaved (grieving) with bread or wine for their father or mother. **8.** Do not go into the house of feasting (celebration) to eat and drink with them. **9.** For I will end the sounds of joy and celebration in this land—both the bridegroom and the bride's voices will cease. **10.** "When you tell the people these words, they will ask, 'Why has the Lord brought this disaster upon us? What have we done wrong?' **11.** Then say to them, 'Because your ancestors (forefathers) abandoned Me, pursued other gods, and did not keep My law. **12.** And you have done even worse, each following the evil desires (wicked) of their heart and ignoring Me. **13.** So I will cast you out of this land into one you do not know, where you will serve other gods, and I will not show you favor (kindness).' **14.** "The days are coming when it will no longer be said, 'The Lord who brought Israel out of Egypt,' **15.** but 'The Lord who brought Israel from the land of the north and from all the places where He had scattered them.' I will bring them back to the land I gave their ancestors. **16.** "I will send many fishermen to catch them, and afterward, many hunters (pursuers) to hunt them from every hill and cave. **17.** For I see all their ways; nothing is hidden from My sight, and I will repay them double for their sin, **18.** for they have defiled (polluted) My land with their detestable (abominable) idols." **19.** "O Lord, my strength and fortress (stronghold), in the day of trouble, the nations will come to You and say, 'Our ancestors inherited lies, worthless (vain) things.' **20.** Can man make gods for himself that are not gods?" **21.** "Therefore, I will make them know My power and might, and they will know that I am the Lord."

Chapter 17

1. The sin of Judah is engraved with an iron pen, with a diamond point, on their hearts and the horns of their altars. **2.** Their children remember their altars and wooden idols (images made of wood) beneath green trees on high hills. **3.** I will give your wealth, treasures, and sinful high places (places used for idol worship) to plunder (to take as spoils), within all your borders. **4.** You will lose the heritage (inheritance) I gave you, and serve your enemies in a land you don't know, because you have kindled (started) My anger, which will burn forever. **5.** The Lord says: "Cursed is the man who trusts in man and relies on his own strength, whose heart turns from the Lord. **6.** He will be like a barren shrub (a small, weak plant) in the desert, unable to see when good comes, living in dry, desolate places (wastelands). **7.** Blessed is the man who trusts in the Lord, whose hope is the Lord. **8.** He will be like a tree planted by water, its roots spread by the river. It will not fear the heat; its leaves will stay green and it will not be anxious (worried) in times of drought, but will continue to bear fruit. **9.** The heart is deceitful (dishonest) above all things and beyond cure. Who can understand it? **10.** I, the Lord, search the heart and test the mind (thoughts), giving each person according to their ways, the fruit of their deeds (actions). **11.** A man who gains wealth unjustly (not rightfully) is like a partridge (a type of bird) that broods but does not hatch. His riches will leave him, and he will end up a fool. **12.** The glorious throne (seat of power) from the beginning is the place of our sanctuary (holy place). **13.** O Lord, the hope of Israel, all who forsake (abandon) You will be ashamed. Those who depart from You will be written in the dust (earth), because they have forsaken the Lord, the fountain of living waters. **14.** Heal me, O Lord, and I will be healed; save me, and I will be saved, for You are my praise. **15.** They say, "Where is the word of the Lord? Let it come now!" **16.** I have not run away from being a shepherd (leader) who follows You, nor have I desired the day of doom (calamity). You know what I have said—it is before You. **17.** Do not be a terror (fear) to me; You are my hope in the day of trouble. **18.** Let those who persecute (harass) me be ashamed, but do not let me be put to shame. Let them be dismayed (discouraged), but not me. Bring upon them the day of doom, and destroy them with double destruction! **19.** The Lord said to me, "Go and stand at the gates (entrances) of the people, where the kings of Judah enter and exit, and at all the gates of Jerusalem. **20.** Say to them, 'Hear the word of the Lord, you kings of Judah, all Judah, and all the inhabitants (people) of Jerusalem who enter these gates. **21.** Thus says the Lord: "Take heed (be careful), and do not carry burdens (heavy loads) on the Sabbath day, nor bring them through the gates of Jerusalem. **22.** Do not carry any burden out of your homes on the Sabbath, and do no work. Keep the Sabbath day holy (set apart), as I commanded your ancestors. **23.** But they did not obey, nor listen, but stubbornly refused to hear or receive instruction. **24.** "If you listen to Me carefully, and stop bringing burdens through the gates of the city on the Sabbath, and keep it holy, **25.** then kings and princes will enter this city, riding in chariots, accompanied by the men of Judah and the people of Jerusalem, and this city will remain forever. **26.** They will come from all the cities of Judah, from the surrounding areas, bringing offerings (gifts) to the house of the Lord. **27.** But if you do not heed Me and keep the Sabbath, I will kindle (start) a fire in the gates of Jerusalem that will consume its palaces (large buildings), and it will not be quenched (put out).'

Chapter 18

1. The word of the Lord came to Jeremiah, saying: **2.** "Go down to the potter's house, and I will speak to you there." **3.** So I went to the potter's house, and he was making a vessel (a container) on the wheel. **4.** The clay (earthy material) was marred (damaged), so the potter reshaped it into a new vessel as he saw fit. **5.** Then the word of the Lord came to me: **6.** "O house of Israel, can I not do with you as this potter does? Look, as the clay is in the potter's hand, so are you in My hand, O house of Israel. **7.** If I announce (declare) that I will destroy a nation, **8.** and if it repents (turns away from sin), I will relent (change my mind) from the disaster (calamity) I intended. **9.** But if I announce (declare) that I will build up (establish) a nation, **10.** and it turns to evil, I will reconsider (change) the good I planned for it. **11.** Now speak to Judah and Jerusalem: 'I am planning disaster against you. Repent (turn back) and change your ways.' **12.** But they replied, 'It's hopeless. We'll follow our own plans and obey our evil hearts.' **13.** Therefore, ask the nations: 'Has anyone seen such things? The virgin (pure, untouched) of Israel has committed a great wickedness (evil). **14.** Will anyone abandon the pure waters (fresh, clean) of Lebanon for the polluted (contaminated) waters of another land?' **15.** "Because My people have forgotten Me, they worship worthless (useless) idols, stumbling (falling) on paths that are not ancient (well-established). **16.** They will make their land desolate (ruined), and all who pass by will be shocked and shake their heads. **17.** I will scatter them like an east wind (strong wind) before the enemy and show them My back (withhold My protection), not My face (favor), in their time of calamity (disaster)." **18.** Then they said, "Let us plot (scheme) against Jeremiah. The law will not be lost to the priests, nor counsel (advice) to the wise, nor the word to the prophets. Let's attack him with words and ignore his message." **19.** "Lord, hear me, and listen to those who contend (argue) with me. **20.** Should evil be rewarded (repayed) for good? They have dug a pit (trap) for my life. Remember, I stood before You to speak good on their behalf, to turn Your wrath (anger) away from them. **21.** Therefore, let their children suffer famine (extreme hunger), their blood be shed by the sword, their wives become widows, and their men be killed in battle. **22.** Let cries (shouts) be heard from their homes when You bring destruction (calamity) suddenly upon them. They have set traps for me and hidden snares (traps). **23.** Lord, You know all their plans (schemes) to kill me. Do not forgive their iniquity (wickedness), or erase (remove) their sin from Your sight. Let them fall before You in Your anger."

Chapter 19

1. Thus says the Lord: "Go and get a potter's (one who makes pottery) flask, and bring some of the elders (older, respected leaders) of the people and priests. **2.** Go to the Valley of the Son of Hinnom, near the Potsherd (broken pottery) Gate, and proclaim the words I will tell you. **3.** Say, 'Hear the word of the Lord, O kings of Judah and inhabitants (residents) of Jerusalem. Thus says the Lord of hosts (armies), the God of Israel: "I will bring such a disaster (great destruction) on this place that anyone who hears of it will be shocked. **4.** "They have forsaken

(abandoned) Me and made this place unholy, burning incense to gods unknown to them, their ancestors, or the kings of Judah, and filling it with the blood of the innocent. **5.** They built high places (altars or shrines on elevated ground) to Baal, burning their sons as offerings— something I never commanded or even considered. **6.** Therefore, the days are coming," says the Lord, "when this place will no longer be called Tophet or the Valley of the Son of Hinnom, but the Valley of Slaughter. **7.** I will defeat (destroy) the plans of Judah and Jerusalem here, and they will fall by the sword, their bodies left for the birds and beasts to consume. **8.** This city will become desolate (empty and in ruins) and a source of horror; all who pass by will be amazed and horrified at its plagues (disasters). **9.** I will cause them to eat the flesh of their sons and daughters, and even their neighbors' flesh, during the siege (military blockade) and the despair (hopelessness) brought by their enemies. **10.** Then you shall break the flask in front of those with you, **11.** and say, 'Thus says the Lord: "I will break this people and this city as one breaks a potter's vessel—irrevocably (in a way that cannot be undone). They will be buried in Tophet, for there will be no room left." **12.** So will I make this place and its inhabitants like Tophet. **13.** The houses of Jerusalem and the kings of Judah will be defiled (made unclean or polluted) like Tophet, because they burned incense on their rooftops to the host (army) of heaven and poured drink offerings to other gods.' **14.** Then Jeremiah returned from Tophet, where the Lord had sent him to prophesy, and stood in the court of the Lord's house, saying to all the people, **15.** "Thus says the Lord of hosts, the God of Israel: 'I will bring the doom (destruction) I have pronounced upon this city and all its towns because they have hardened (made stubborn) their hearts and refused to listen to My words.'"

Chapter 20

1. Now Pashhur the son of Immer, the priest who was also chief governor (leader) in the house of the Lord, heard that Jeremiah prophesied these things. **2.** Then Pashhur struck Jeremiah the prophet, and put him in the stocks (a device for locking someone's feet in place) that were in the high gate of Benjamin, which was by the house of the Lord. **3.** And it happened on the next day that Pashhur brought Jeremiah out of the stocks. Then Jeremiah said to him, "The Lord has not called your name Pashhur, but Magor-Missabib ('Terror on every side'). **4.** For thus says the Lord: 'Behold, I will make you a terror (great fear) to yourself and to all your friends; and they shall fall by the sword of their enemies, and your eyes shall see it. I will give all Judah into the hand of the king of Babylon, and he shall carry them captive (force them into exile) to Babylon and slay (kill) them with the sword. **5.** Moreover, I will deliver (give over) all the wealth of this city, all its produce (crops), and all its precious things; all the treasures of the kings of Judah I will give into the hand of their enemies, who will plunder (steal) them, seize (take) them, and carry them to Babylon. **6.** And you, Pashhur, and all who dwell (live) in your house, shall go into captivity. You shall go to Babylon, and there you shall die, and be buried there, you and all your friends, to whom you have prophesied lies (false predictions).' " **7.** O Lord, You induced (persuaded) me, and I was persuaded; You are stronger than I, and have prevailed (won). I am in derision (mockery) daily; Everyone mocks (makes fun of) me. **8.** For when I spoke, I cried out; I shouted, "Violence and plunder!" Because the word of the Lord was made to me A reproach (disgrace) and a derision daily. **9.** Then I said, "I will not make mention of Him, Nor speak anymore in His name." But His word was in my heart like a burning fire Shut up in my bones; I was weary (tired) of holding it back, And I could not. **10.** For I heard many mocking: "Fear on every side!" "Report," they say, "and we will report it!" All my acquaintances (friends) watched for my stumbling (falling), saying, "Perhaps he can be induced (persuaded); Then we will prevail (defeat) against him, And we will take our revenge (retaliation) on him." **11.** But the Lord is with me as a mighty, awesome One. Therefore my persecutors (those who pursue and harm me) will stumble, and will not prevail. They will be greatly ashamed, for they will not prosper (succeed). Their everlasting confusion (dishonor) will never be forgotten. **12.** But, O Lord of hosts (armies), You who test the righteous, And see the mind and heart, Let me see Your vengeance (punishment) on them; For I have pleaded (argued) my cause before You. **13.** Sing to the Lord! Praise the Lord! For He has delivered the life of the poor (those in need) From the hand of evildoers (wicked people). **14.** Cursed be the day in which I was born!

Let the day not be blessed in which my mother bore (gave birth to) me! **15.** Let the man be cursed who brought news to my father, saying, "A male child has been born to you!" Making him very glad. **16.** And let that man be like the cities which the Lord overthrew (destroyed), and did not relent (show mercy); Let him hear the cry in the morning and the shouting at noon, **17.** Because he did not kill me from the womb, That my mother might have been my grave, And her womb always enlarged with me. **18.** Why did I come forth from the womb to see labor (suffering) and sorrow (grief), That my days should be consumed (spent) with shame?

Chapter 21

1. The word which came to Jeremiah from the Lord when King Zedekiah sent to him Pashhur the son of Melchiah, and Zephaniah the son of Maaseiah, the priest, saying, **2.** "Please inquire (ask) of the Lord for us, for Nebuchadnezzar king of Babylon makes war (fights) against us. Perhaps the Lord will deal with us according to all His wonderful works, that the king may go away from us." **3.** Then Jeremiah said to them, "Thus you shall say to Zedekiah, **4.** 'Thus says the Lord God of Israel: "Behold, I will turn back the weapons of war (tools used for fighting) that are in your hands, with which you fight against the king of Babylon and the Chaldeans (Babylonians) who besiege (surround and attack) you outside the walls; and I will assemble (gather) them in the midst of this city. **5.** I Myself will fight against you with an outstretched hand and with a strong arm, even in anger and fury (intense rage) and great wrath (violent anger). **6.** I will strike (hit) the inhabitants (residents) of this city, both man and beast; they shall die of a great pestilence (deadly disease). **7.** And afterward," says the Lord, "I will deliver (give over) Zedekiah king of Judah, his servants and the people, and such as are left in this city from the pestilence and the sword and the famine (severe hunger), into the hand of Nebuchadnezzar king of Babylon, into the hand of their enemies, and into the hand of those who seek their life; and he shall strike them with the edge of the sword. He shall not spare (show mercy) them, or have pity (feel sorry) or mercy." **8.** "Now you shall say to this people, 'Thus says the Lord: "Behold, I set before you the way of life and the way of death. **9.** He who remains in this city shall die by the sword, by famine, and by pestilence; but he who goes out and defects (switches sides) to the Chaldeans who besiege you, he shall live, and his life shall be as a prize (reward) to him. **10.** For I have set My face against (opposed) this city for adversity (trouble) and not for good," says the Lord. "It shall be given into the hand of the king of Babylon, and he shall burn it with fire." **11.** "And concerning the house of the king of Judah, say, 'Hear the word of the Lord, **12.** O house of David! Thus says the Lord: "Execute (carry out) judgment in the morning; And deliver (rescue) him who is plundered (robbed) out of the hand of the oppressor (one who wrongfully forces others), lest My fury go forth like fire and burn so that no one can quench (stop) it, because of the evil (wickedness) of your doings. **13.** "Behold, I am against you, O inhabitant (resident) of the valley, And rock of the plain," says the Lord, "Who say, 'Who shall come down against us? Or who shall enter our dwellings (homes)?' **14.** But I will punish (reward with harm) you according to the fruit (result) of your doings," says the Lord; "I will kindle (start) a fire in its forest, and it shall devour (destroy) all things around it." '"

Chapter 22

1. Thus says the Lord: "Go down to the house (palace) of the king of Judah, and there speak this word, **2.** and say, 'Hear the word (message) of the Lord, O king of Judah, you who sit on the throne (royal seat) of David, you and your servants (officials) and your people who enter these gates (doors)! **3.** Thus says the Lord: "Execute (carry out) judgment and righteousness (justice), and deliver (rescue) the plundered (robbed) out of the hand of the oppressor (one who wrongfully forces others). Do no wrong and do no violence (harm) to the stranger (foreigner), the fatherless (orphans), or the widow, nor shed (spill) innocent blood in this place. **4.** For if you indeed do this thing, then shall enter the gates (doors) of this house, riding on horses and in chariots, accompanied by servants and people, kings who sit on the throne of David. **5.** But if you will not hear these words, I swear by Myself," says the Lord, "that this house shall become a desolation (ruin)." **6.** For thus says the Lord to the house of the king of Judah: "You are Gilead (a region) to Me, The head (top) of Lebanon (mountain); Yet I surely will make you a wilderness, cities which are not inhabited (without people). **7.** I will prepare (arrange) destroyers (invaders) against you, Everyone with his weapons (tools for fighting); They shall cut down (cut) your choice cedars (trees) And cast (throw) them into the fire. **8.** And many nations will pass by this city; and everyone will say to his neighbor, 'Why has the Lord done so to this great city?' **9.** Then they will answer, 'Because they have forsaken (abandoned) the covenant (agreement) of the Lord their God, and worshiped other gods and served them.' **10.** Weep not for the dead, nor bemoan (mourn for) him; Weep bitterly (deeply) for him who goes away, For he shall return no more, Nor see his native (birthplace) country. **11.** For thus says the Lord concerning Shallum (a king) the son of Josiah (a king), king of Judah, who reigned (ruled) instead of Josiah his father, who went from this place: "He shall not return here anymore, **12.** but he shall die in the place where they have led him captive (taken prisoner), and shall see this land no more. **13.** "Woe (disaster) to him who builds his house by unrighteousness (wickedness) And his chambers (rooms) by injustice (unfairness), Who uses his neighbor's service (work) without wages (payment) And gives him nothing for his work, **14.** Who says, 'I will build myself a wide (large) house with spacious (roomy) chambers, And cut out windows for it, Paneling (covering) it with cedar And painting it with vermilion (red).' **15.** "Shall you reign (rule) because you enclose yourself in cedar? Did not your father eat and drink, And do justice and righteousness? Then it was well with him. **16.** He judged the cause (reason) of the poor and needy; Then it was well. Was not this knowing Me?" says the Lord. **17.** "Yet your eyes and your heart are for nothing but your covetousness (greed), For shedding innocent blood, And practicing oppression (cruelty) and violence (force)." **18.** Therefore thus says the Lord concerning Jehoiakim (a king) the son of Josiah, king of Judah: "They shall not lament (mourn) for him, Saying, 'Alas, my brother!' or 'Alas, my sister!' They shall not lament (mourn) for him, Saying, 'Alas, master!' or 'Alas, his glory (honor)!' **19.** He shall be buried with the burial of a donkey (like a donkey's burial), Dragged and cast (thrown) out beyond the gates (walls) of Jerusalem. **20.** "Go up to Lebanon, and cry out, And lift up your voice in Bashan (a region); Cry from Abarim (a region), For all your lovers (allies) are destroyed. **21.** I spoke to you in your prosperity (success), But you said, 'I will not hear.' This has been your manner (habit) from your youth, That you did not obey My voice. **22.** The wind shall eat up all your rulers (leaders), And your lovers (allies) shall go into captivity (be taken away); Surely then you will be ashamed (embarrassed) and humiliated (humbled) For all your wickedness (evil). **23.** O inhabitant (dweller) of Lebanon, Making your nest (home) in the cedars, How gracious (kind) will you be when pangs (sorrows) come upon you, Like the pain of a woman in labor? **24.** "As I live," says the Lord, "though Coniah (a king) the son of Jehoiakim, king of Judah, were the signet (seal) on My right hand, yet I would pluck (remove) you off; **25.** and I will give you into the hand (control) of those who seek your life, and into the hand of those whose face (anger) you fear—the hand of Nebuchadnezzar (a king) king of Babylon and the hand of the Chaldeans (Babylonians). **26.** So I will cast you out, and your mother who bore you, into another country (land) where you were not born; and there you shall die. **27.** But to the land to which they desire (long) to return, there they shall not return. **28.** "Is this man Coniah (a king) a despised (hated), broken (shattered) idol (false image)— A vessel (container) in which is no pleasure (value)? Why are they cast out (thrown), he and his descendants, And cast into a land (country) which they do not know? **29.** O earth, earth, earth, Hear the word (message) of the Lord! **30.** Thus says the Lord: 'Write this man down as childless (without children), A man who shall not prosper in his days; For none of his descendants shall prosper (succeed), Sitting on the throne of David, And ruling anymore in Judah.'"

Chapter 23

1. "Woe to the shepherds (leaders) who destroy and scatter the sheep of My pasture!" says the Lord. **2.** "You have scattered My flock, driven them away, and failed to tend them. I will now deal with you for your evil," says the Lord. **3.** "I will gather the remnant (remaining part) of My flock from all the lands where I've driven them and return them to their folds, where they will multiply and grow. **4.** I will appoint shepherds who will care for them, and they will no longer fear or be dismayed, nor will they lack anything," says the Lord. **5.** "The days are coming," says the Lord, "when I will raise up a righteous Branch for

David. A King will reign wisely, executing judgment and righteousness on the earth. **6.** In His days Judah will be saved, and Israel will live in safety. This is the name by which He will be called: THE LORD OUR RIGHTEOUSNESS." **7.** "The days are coming," says the Lord, "when people will no longer say, 'As the Lord lives who brought the children of Israel out of Egypt,' **8.** but, 'As the Lord lives who brought up the descendants of Israel from the north and from all the lands where I had scattered them.' They will return to their own land." **9.** My heart is broken because of the prophets; all my bones tremble. I am like a drunken man, overcome (defeated) with wine, because of the Lord and His holy words. **10.** The land is full of adulterers (unfaithful people), and because of a curse, it mourns. The pleasant places are withered (dried up), and their ways are evil. Their power is unjust. **11.** "Both prophet and priest are corrupt (morally wrong); I have found their wickedness in My house," says the Lord. **12.** "Therefore, their paths will be slippery, and they will fall in darkness. I will bring disaster on them, the year of their punishment," says the Lord. **13.** "I have seen the folly (foolishness) of the prophets of Samaria; they prophesied by Baal and led My people Israel astray. **14.** I have seen a horrible thing in the prophets of Jerusalem: they commit adultery and lie; they strengthen the hands of evildoers (wrongdoers), so no one turns from wickedness. They are like Sodom to Me, and her people like Gomorrah." **15.** "Therefore, I will make them drink wormwood (a bitter plant) and gall (bitter substance). Profanity (impiety) has spread from the prophets of Jerusalem throughout the land." **16.** Thus says the Lord of hosts (armies): "Do not listen to the words of the prophets who mislead you. They speak from their own hearts, not from the mouth of the Lord. **17.** They say to those who reject Me, 'You will have peace,' and to those who follow their own desires, 'No harm will come to you.' **18.** Who has stood in the Lord's counsel and heard His word? **19.** A whirlwind (storm) of the Lord will rage against the wicked, falling violently on their heads. **20.** The Lord's anger will not turn back until He has fulfilled His plan. In the end, you will understand it clearly." **21.** "I did not send these prophets, yet they ran; I did not speak to them, yet they prophesied. **22.** Had they stood in My counsel and proclaimed My words, they would have turned the people from their wickedness." **23.** "Am I a God near at hand," says the Lord, "and not a God afar off? **24.** Can anyone hide from Me? Do I not fill heaven and earth?" says the Lord. **25.** "I have heard the false prophets who claim, 'I have dreamed, I have dreamed!' **26.** How long will this continue? They are prophets of their own deceit (misleading), **27.** trying to make My people forget My name through their lies and dreams, just as their ancestors forgot My name for Baal. **28.** "Let the prophet who has a dream tell it; but if he has My word, let him speak it faithfully. What is the chaff (worthless part) to the wheat?" says the Lord. **29.** "Is not My word like fire, and like a hammer that breaks rocks in pieces? **30.** Therefore, I am against the prophets who steal My words from their neighbors. **31.** I am against those who say, 'He says,' when I have not spoken. **32.** I am against those who prophesy false dreams and lead My people astray. I did not send them, and they will not benefit the people," says the Lord. **33.** "When people or prophets ask, 'What is the oracle (message) of the Lord?' you shall reply, 'What oracle? I will forsake (abandon) you,'" says the Lord. **34.** As for the prophet, priest, or people who claim, 'The oracle of the Lord!' I will punish them and their households. **35.** Everyone shall ask their neighbor, 'What has the Lord answered?' and 'What has the Lord spoken?' **36.** You will no longer call it the oracle of the Lord. Every man's word will be his own oracle, perverting (distorting) the words of the living God. **37.** So when the prophet asks, 'What has the Lord said?' **38.** say to them, 'Since you say, "The oracle of the Lord!" yet I told you not to say that, **39.** I will forget you and cast you out of My presence, along with the city I gave to you and your ancestors. **40.** I will bring everlasting disgrace (shame) upon you, a perpetual (lasting) shame that will not be forgotten."

Chapter 24

1. The Lord showed me two baskets of figs placed before the temple, after King Nebuchadnezzar of Babylon had taken Jeconiah, the son of Jehoiakim, king of Judah, along with the princes, craftsmen (skilled workers), and smiths (metalworkers), from Jerusalem to Babylon. **2.** One basket contained very good figs, like the first ripe figs; the other contained bad figs, so spoiled they couldn't be eaten. **3.** Then the Lord asked, "What do you see, Jeremiah?" I answered, "Figs, the good ones are very good, but the bad ones are so bad they can't be eaten." **4.** The word of the Lord came to me again, saying, **5.** "This is what the Lord, the God of Israel, says: 'Like the good figs, I will look after the exiles (those who have been taken away from their land) of Judah whom I sent to Babylon for their own good. **6.** I will care for them, bringing them back to this land. I will build them up, not tear them down; I will plant them, not uproot (remove) them. **7.** I will give them a heart to know Me, that I am the Lord. They will be My people, and I will be their God, for they will return to Me with all their hearts.' **8.** But like the bad figs, so will I deal with King Zedekiah of Judah, his princes, the remnant (remaining portion) of Jerusalem who remain here, and those in Egypt. **9.** I will hand them over to trouble, scattered among the kingdoms of the earth. They will become a disgrace, a byword (a term of ridicule), a taunt (mockery), and a curse (something seen as a source of misfortune) wherever I drive them. **10.** I will send the sword (war), famine (extreme shortage of food), and plague (disease) upon them, until they are destroyed from the land I gave to them and their ancestors."

Chapter 25

1. The word of the Lord came to Jeremiah concerning all the people of Judah, in the fourth year of Jehoiakim the son of Josiah, king of Judah (the first year of Nebuchadnezzar king of Babylon). **2.** Jeremiah spoke to all the people of Judah and Jerusalem, saying: **3.** "From the thirteenth year of Josiah the son of Amon, king of Judah, to this day, twenty-three years, the Lord's word has come to me. I have spoken to you, rising early (beginning early in the morning), but you have not listened. **4.** The Lord has sent His servants, the prophets, rising early, but you have not listened or paid attention. **5.** They said, 'Repent (turn away from sin) of your evil ways and dwell in the land the Lord gave you forever. **6.** Do not follow other gods or provoke Me to anger with the works of your hands; and I will not harm you.' **7.** Yet you have not listened," says the Lord, "provoking Me to anger with the works of your hands, to your own harm. **8.** Therefore, thus says the Lord of hosts (armies): 'Because you have not obeyed My words, **9.** I will bring all the families of the north (regions to the north), and Nebuchadnezzar, king of Babylon, My servant, against this land. They will destroy it, making it a desolation (ruin), an astonishment (amazement), and a perpetual reproach (disgrace). **10.** I will take from them the sounds of joy and gladness, the voices of bridegroom and bride, the sounds of millstones (grinding stones) and lamps (light sources). **11.** This land will become a desolation, and these nations will serve the king of Babylon for seventy years. **12.** After seventy years, I will punish the king of Babylon and his nation for their iniquity (wickedness),' says the Lord; 'and I will make it a perpetual desolation. **13.** I will bring all My words upon that land, as written in this book, which Jeremiah has prophesied (foretold) against all nations. **14.** Many nations and great kings will serve them, and I will repay (pay back) them according to their deeds.' " **15.** For thus says the Lord God of Israel to me: "Take this cup of fury (anger) from My hand, and cause all the nations to drink it, to whom I send you. **16.** They will stagger (stumble) and go mad (lose their senses) because of the sword I will send among them." **17.** Then I took the cup from the Lord's hand, and made all the nations drink, to whom the Lord had sent me: **18.** Jerusalem and the cities of Judah, its kings and princes (rulers), making them a desolation, an astonishment, a hissing (scoffing), and a curse, as it is this day; **19.** Pharaoh king of Egypt, his servants, princes, and people; **20.** all the mixed peoples (foreigners), the kings of Uz, the kings of the Philistines (Ashkelon, Gaza, Ekron, and the remnant of Ashdod); **21.** Edom, Moab, Ammon; **22.** the kings of Tyre, Sidon, and the coastlands (regions by the sea) across the sea; **23.** Dedan, Tema, Buz, and all in the farthest corners (distant places); **24.** all the kings of Arabia and the mixed peoples who dwell in the desert; **25.** all the kings of Zimri, Elam, and the Medes; **26.** all the kings of the north (northern regions), near and far, and all the kingdoms of the world. Even the king of Sheshach (a cipher or code name for Babylon) will drink after them. **27.** "Therefore, say to them, 'Thus says the Lord of hosts: "Drink, be drunk, and vomit! Fall and rise no more, because of the sword I will send among you." **28.** If they refuse to drink, say to them, 'Thus says the Lord of hosts: "You will certainly drink! **29.** For I begin to bring calamity (disaster) on the city called by My name. Should you go unpunished? You will not be unpunished, for I will call for a sword on all the inhabitants (people) of the earth," says the Lord of hosts.' **30.**

"Therefore, prophesy (speak as a prophet) against them, and say: 'The Lord will roar (cry out) from on high and utter His voice from His holy habitation (dwelling place). He will roar mightily against His fold (flock), giving a shout like those who tread grapes (crush grapes), against all the inhabitants of the earth. **31.** A noise (sound) will reach the ends of the earth, for the Lord has a controversy (dispute) with the nations. He will judge all flesh (human beings), and the wicked will be given to the sword,' says the Lord." **32.** Thus says the Lord of hosts: "Behold, disaster will go from nation to nation, and a great whirlwind (storm) will arise from the farthest parts of the earth. **33.** At that time, the slain (those killed) of the Lord will be from one end of the earth to the other. They will not be lamented (mourned), or gathered (collected), or buried; they will become refuse (waste) on the ground. **34.** Wail (cry out), shepherds (leaders), and cry! Roll in the ashes, you leaders of the flock! For the days of your slaughter and dispersion (scattering) are fulfilled; you will fall like a precious vessel. **35.** The shepherds will have no way to flee, and the leaders of the flock will escape no longer. **36.** A cry (lament) will be heard from the shepherds, and a wailing (mourning) from the leaders, for the Lord has plundered (taken) their pasture. **37.** The peaceful dwellings are cut down because of the fierce anger of the Lord. **38.** He has left His lair (den) like a lion; for their land is desolate because of the fierceness (violence) of the Oppressor (one who oppresses), and because of His fierce anger."

Chapter 26

1. In the early days of Jehoiakim (king of Judah), son of Josiah, king of Judah, the Lord spoke to Jeremiah: **2.** "Stand in the Lord's house and speak to all Judah's cities that come to worship. Deliver every word I command you—do not leave anything out. **3.** Perhaps they will listen, repent (turn away from sin), and I will relent (change my mind) from the disaster I intend because of their evil ways. **4.** Say to them: 'The Lord says: If you do not listen to Me or follow My law, **5.** and refuse to heed (pay attention to) the prophets I've sent, **6.** I will make this house like Shiloh (place of destruction) and this city a curse (a judgment or punishment) to all nations.' " **7.** The priests, prophets, and people heard Jeremiah in the Lord's house. **8.** After Jeremiah finished speaking, they seized (took hold of) him, shouting, "You must die! **9.** Why have you prophesied (spoken in God's name about future events) that this house will be like Shiloh, and this city will be desolate (empty and ruined)?" The people gathered against Jeremiah in the temple. **10.** When the princes (leaders) of Judah heard this, they came to the temple and sat at the New Gate. **11.** The priests and prophets said to the princes and people, "This man deserves to die! He has prophesied disaster against this city." **12.** Jeremiah replied: "The Lord sent me to speak all the words you've heard against this house and city. **13.** Repent, and obey the Lord, and He may relent from the disaster He's declared. **14.** As for me, I am in your hands; do as you wish. **15.** But know this: if you kill me, you will bring innocent blood on yourselves and this city, for the Lord sent me to speak to you." **16.** The princes and people responded, "This man doesn't deserve to die; he spoke to us in the name of the Lord." **17.** Then some elders (older, respected members of the community) spoke, **18.** "Micah of Moresheth prophesied during Hezekiah's reign, saying, 'Zion will be plowed like a field, and Jerusalem will be ruined.' **19.** Did King Hezekiah kill him? No, he feared the Lord, and the Lord relented from the disaster. We are doing great evil to ourselves." **20.** A prophet named Urijah also prophesied against this city, **21.** and when King Jehoiakim heard of it, he sought to kill him. Urijah fled to Egypt, **22.** but Jehoiakim sent men to bring him back, **23.** and Urijah was killed and buried in a common grave (a grave for regular people). **24.** Yet Ahikam (a supporter of Jeremiah) son of Shaphan helped Jeremiah, so he was not handed over to the people to be killed.

Chapter 27

1. In the beginning of Jehoiakim's (king of Judah) reign, this word came to Jeremiah from the Lord: **2.** "Make bonds (ropes or chains) and yokes (wooden frames placed around the neck) for yourself, and put them on your neck. **3.** Send them to the kings of Edom, Moab, Ammon, Tyre, and Sidon, through the messengers who come to Zedekiah (king of Judah) in Jerusalem. **4.** Tell them: 'The Lord of hosts (armies), the God of Israel, says: **5.** I have made the earth, mankind, and animals by My great power, and have given them to whom I chose. **6.** Now, I have given all these lands to Nebuchadnezzar (king of Babylon), My servant.

Even the beasts of the field I have given him to serve him. **7.** All nations will serve him, his son, and his grandson until his time ends. Then many nations and great kings will make him serve them. **8.** Any nation or kingdom that refuses to serve Nebuchadnezzar and submit to his yoke, I will punish with sword (war), famine (hunger), and pestilence (plague), until they are destroyed.' **9.** So do not listen to your prophets, diviners (fortune tellers), dreamers, soothsayers (fortune tellers), or sorcerers (witches), who say, 'You will not serve the king of Babylon.' **10.** They are lying to you to lead you away from your land, and I will drive you out to perish. **11.** But the nations that submit to Nebuchadnezzar's yoke, I will allow to remain in their land and live in it." **12.** I also spoke to Zedekiah, king of Judah, saying: "Submit to the king of Babylon, serve him, and live! **13.** Why let you and your people die by sword, famine, and pestilence, as the Lord has warned against those who refuse to serve the king of Babylon? **14.** Do not listen to the false prophets who say, 'You will not serve Babylon.' They are lying to you. **15.** I have not sent them, says the Lord. They are prophesying falsely in My name, to drive you out and bring about your destruction, along with the false prophets." **16.** I also spoke to the priests and people, saying: "Do not listen to the false prophets who say, 'The vessels (sacred items) of the Lord's house will soon return from Babylon.' **17.** They are lying. Serve the king of Babylon and live! Why should this city be destroyed? **18.** But if they are true prophets and the word of the Lord is with them, let them intercede (plead) with the Lord of hosts to prevent the remaining vessels in the Lord's house and in the king's palace from going to Babylon." **19.** "As for the remaining vessels in the city— **20.** the ones Nebuchadnezzar did not take when he carried Jeconiah (king of Judah), and the nobles to Babylon— **21.** these vessels will be taken to Babylon too. **22.** They will remain there until the day I visit them, says the Lord. Then I will bring them back and restore them to this place."

Chapter 28

1. In the same year, at the start of Zedekiah's reign (rule) as king of Judah, in the fourth year and fifth month, Hananiah son of Azur, a prophet (one who speaks for God) from Gibeon, spoke to me in the house of the Lord, in front of the priests and all the people, saying, **2.** "This is what the Lord of Hosts (armies), the God of Israel, says: 'I have broken the yoke (a wooden frame used for joining animals) of the king of Babylon. **3.** In two years, I will bring back to this place all the articles (sacred objects) of the Lord's house that Nebuchadnezzar, king of Babylon, took and carried to Babylon. **4.** I will also bring back to this place Jeconiah son of Jehoiakim, king of Judah, along with all the captives (prisoners) of Judah who went to Babylon,' says the Lord, 'for I will break the yoke of the king of Babylon.'" **5.** Then the prophet Jeremiah spoke to Hananiah in front of the priests and all the people in the house of the Lord, **6.** and Jeremiah said, "Amen! May the Lord do so! May the Lord fulfill your prophecy (prediction) to bring back the articles of the Lord's house and all who were exiled (forced to leave their homeland) to Babylon. **7.** But listen to this word I speak in your hearing and in the hearing of all the people: **8.** The prophets who came before us prophesied (foretold) against many nations and kingdoms— of war, disaster, and disease. **9.** But if a prophet speaks of peace, when the word comes true, that prophet will be recognized (known) as one sent by the Lord." **10.** Then Hananiah took the yoke from Jeremiah's neck and broke it. **11.** He spoke to all the people, saying, "This is what the Lord says: 'In two years I will break the yoke of Nebuchadnezzar, king of Babylon, from the neck of all nations.'" And Jeremiah left. **12.** After Hananiah broke the yoke from Jeremiah's neck, the word of the Lord came to Jeremiah, saying, **13.** "Go and tell Hananiah: 'This is what the Lord says: You have broken a yoke of wood, but you have made in its place a yoke of iron. **14.** For the Lord of Hosts (armies), the God of Israel, says: "I have put an iron yoke (a heavy, unbreakable burden) on the neck of all these nations to make them serve Nebuchadnezzar, king of Babylon. They will serve him, and I have given him the beasts (animals) of the field."'" **15.** Then Jeremiah said to Hananiah, "Listen, Hananiah! The Lord has not sent you, and you have caused these people to trust in a lie. **16.** Therefore, this is what the Lord says: 'I will remove (cast) you from the face of the earth. You will die this year, because you have preached rebellion (defiance) against the Lord.'" **17.** So Hananiah the prophet died in the seventh month of that year.

Chapter 29

1. These are the words of the letter that Jeremiah the prophet sent from Jerusalem to the remaining elders, priests, prophets, and all the people Nebuchadnezzar had carried away captive (taken by force) from Jerusalem to Babylon. **2.** (This was after King Jeconiah, the queen mother, the eunuchs (castrated men), princes, craftsmen (skilled workers), and smiths (metal workers) had departed from Jerusalem.) **3.** The letter was sent by Elasah son of Shaphan and Gemariah son of Hilkiah, whom King Zedekiah of Judah had sent to Babylon to Nebuchadnezzar, saying, **4.** "Thus says the Lord of hosts (armies), the God of Israel, to all who were taken captive from Jerusalem to Babylon: **5.** Build houses and settle in them; plant gardens and eat their produce (crops). **6.** Marry and have sons and daughters; take wives for your sons and give your daughters to husbands, so they may have children—become numerous there, not fewer. **7.** Seek the peace (well-being) of the city where I have sent you into exile, and pray to the Lord for it; for in its peace you will find peace. **8.** For the Lord of hosts, the God of Israel, says: Do not let your prophets or diviners (fortune-tellers) deceive you, nor listen to the dreams they encourage you to dream. **9.** They prophesy lies in My name; I have not sent them, declares the Lord. **10.** For the Lord says: After seventy years in Babylon, I will visit (look after) you and fulfill My good promise to bring you back to this place. **11.** For I know the plans (intentions) I have for you, declares the Lord, plans for your welfare and not for harm, to give you a future and a hope. **12.** Then you will call on Me, and come and pray to Me, and I will listen to you. **13.** You will seek Me and find Me when you seek Me with all your heart. **14.** I will be found by you, declares the Lord, and I will restore (bring back) you from captivity (exile); I will gather you from all the nations and places where I have scattered you, and bring you back to the land from which I sent you into exile. **15.** Because you said, 'The Lord has raised up prophets for us in Babylon,' **16.** therefore, concerning the king on David's throne, the people of this city, and those who remain in Judah, **17.** the Lord of hosts says: I will send sword (war), famine (lack of food), and plague (disease) upon them, and make them like rotten figs (decayed), so bad they cannot be eaten. **18.** I will pursue them with the sword, famine, and plague, and deliver them to trouble among all the kingdoms of the earth—to be a curse (misfortune), an astonishment, a hissing (expression of scorn), and a reproach (disgrace) among the nations where I have driven them, **19.** because they did not listen to My words, declares the Lord, the words I sent through My prophets, rising early (sending them at dawn) and sending them. They would not listen. **20.** Therefore, hear the word of the Lord, all you who are in exile. **21.** Thus says the Lord concerning Ahab son of Kolaiah and Zedekiah son of Maaseiah, who prophesy lies in My name: I will hand them over to Nebuchadnezzar king of Babylon, and he will kill them before your eyes. **22.** Because of them, a curse will be taken up by all the exiles of Judah in Babylon, saying, 'May the Lord make you like Zedekiah and Ahab, whom the king of Babylon burned in the fire.' **23.** They have done shameful (disgraceful) things in Israel, committed adultery (unfaithfulness) with their neighbors' wives, and spoken lies in My name, which I did not command. I know it, and I am a witness (a truthful observer), declares the Lord. **24.** Speak to Shemaiah the Nehelamite as well, saying, **25.** 'Thus says the Lord of hosts, the God of Israel: You have sent letters in your name to all the people in Jerusalem, including Zephaniah the priest, saying, **26.** "The Lord has made you priest instead of Jehoiada, to put anyone who is mad (insane) and considers himself a prophet in prison and stocks (chains)." **27.** Now why have you not reproved (corrected) Jeremiah of Anathoth, who makes himself a prophet to you? **28.** He has sent word to us in Babylon, saying, "This exile is long; build houses, settle, plant gardens, and eat their fruit." **29.** Zephaniah the priest read this letter to Jeremiah. **30.** Then the word of the Lord came to Jeremiah: **31.** "Send to all the exiles, saying, 'Thus says the Lord concerning Shemaiah the Nehelamite: Because Shemaiah has prophesied to you, and I have not sent him, and has caused you to trust in a lie, **32.** I will punish Shemaiah and his descendants. He will not have anyone to live among this people, nor will he see the good I will do for My people, because he has taught rebellion (resistance) against the Lord.'"

Chapter 30

1. The word of the Lord came to Jeremiah, saying: **2.** "Thus says the Lord, the God of Israel: 'Write all the words I have spoken to you in a book. **3.** For the days are coming when I will bring back My people, Israel and Judah, from captivity (the state of being held as a prisoner). I will restore (bring back) them to the land I gave their ancestors, and they will possess (take control of) it.'" **4.** These are the words the Lord spoke concerning Israel and Judah: **5.** "We hear a voice of trembling (shaking), of fear, and not of peace. **6.** Ask if a man ever labors (works hard) to give birth? Why then do I see men doubled over in pain, their faces pale (having no color)? **7.** Alas (an expression of sorrow), that day is great; none is like it. It is the time of Jacob's trouble (great distress), but he will be saved out of it. **8.** 'In that day,' says the Lord, 'I will break the yoke (a device placed on animals to control them) from your neck and burst your bonds (chains). No foreign nation will enslave (control) them again. **9.** They will serve (worship) the Lord their God and David their king, whom I will raise up for them. **10.** Do not fear, O Jacob My servant, nor be dismayed (discouraged), O Israel. I will save you from afar (a long distance), and your descendants (children) from the land of their captivity. Jacob will return, find rest, and none will make him afraid. **11.** For I am with you to save you,' says the Lord, 'though I will bring an end (destroy) to all the nations where I have scattered you, I will not destroy you completely. I will discipline (correct) you fairly, and will not leave you unpunished.' **12.** 'Your affliction (suffering) is incurable (unable to be healed), your wound (injury) severe. **13.** No one pleads (argues for) your case or offers healing; **14.** your allies (friends) have forgotten you, for I have struck (hit) you with the wound of an enemy, for the multitude (great number) of your sins. **15.** Why do you cry over your affliction? Your sorrow (deep sadness) is incurable because of your sins. I have done this to you. **16.** Therefore, all who devour (consume) you will be devoured; all your enemies will go into captivity. Those who plunder (steal) you will be plundered, and all who prey (attack) upon you will become prey. **17.** But I will restore (bring back) your health and heal (cure) your wounds,' says the Lord, 'because they called you an outcast (someone rejected), saying, "This is Zion; no one seeks her."' **18.** 'I will restore the captivity of Jacob's tents and show mercy (kindness) on his dwelling places. The city will be rebuilt on its own mound (hill), and the palace will remain as planned. **19.** There will be thanksgiving (gratitude) and joy; I will multiply (increase) them, and they will not decrease. I will honor (praise) them, and they will not be small. **20.** Their children will be as before, and their community will be established before Me. I will punish those who oppress (treat unjustly) them. **21.** Their leaders (nobles) will come from among them, and their ruler will rise from their midst. I will draw him near, and he will approach Me. Who is this who has pledged (committed) his heart to approach Me?' says the Lord. **22.** 'You will be My people, and I will be your God.'" **23.** Behold, the whirlwind (violent storm) of the Lord will go forth in fury (rage), a violent storm falling on the wicked (evil people). **24.** The Lord's fierce (intense) anger will not turn back until He has accomplished His will, and in the latter days (future), you will understand it.

Chapter 31

1. The Lord says, "At that time, I will be the God of all Israel's families, and they will be My people. **2.** Those who survived the sword found grace in the wilderness—Israel, when I went to give him rest. **3.** The Lord appeared to me, saying, 'I have loved you with an everlasting love; with lovingkindness (steadfast love), I have drawn you.' **4.** 'I will rebuild you, O virgin (untouched, pure) Israel! You will be adorned with tambourines and dance in joy.' **5.** 'You will plant vines on the mountains of Samaria, and those who plant will enjoy their fruit.' **6.** 'A day will come when watchmen (guardians) will call from Mount Ephraim, "Arise, let us go to Zion, to the Lord our God!"' **7.** 'Sing with gladness for Jacob, proclaim, "O Lord, save Your people, the remnant (remaining group) of Israel!"' **8.** 'I will bring them from the north and gather them from the ends of the earth, including the blind, the lame (disabled), women with child, and those in labor. A great throng (large crowd) will return.' **9.** 'They will come weeping, but I will lead them by rivers of water on a straight path where they won't stumble. For I am a Father to Israel, and Ephraim is My firstborn.' **10.** 'Hear the word of the Lord, O nations, and proclaim it far off: "He who scattered Israel will gather them, like a shepherd caring for his flock."' **11.** 'The Lord has redeemed (rescued) Jacob and ransomed (freed by payment) him from a stronger enemy.' **12.** 'They will come and sing in Zion, streaming to the Lord's goodness—wheat, wine, oil, and the young of the flock and herd. Their souls will be like a well-watered garden, and they will sorrow no more.' **13.** 'Then the virgin will dance with joy, young and old together. I will turn their mourning (grief) to joy, comfort them, and fill them with gladness.' **14.** 'I will satisfy the priests with abundance, and My people will be filled with My goodness.' **15.** The Lord says, "A voice was heard in Ramah—Rachel weeping for her children, refusing to be comforted because they are no more." **16.** "Refrain from weeping, and your eyes from tears; your work will be rewarded, and they will return from the enemy's land." **17.** "There is hope for your future, and your children will return to their own land." **18.** "I have heard Ephraim's lament (expression of sorrow): 'You have chastised (punished) me, and I have repented. Restore me, for You are the Lord my God.'" **19.** "After I was instructed, I was ashamed, for I bore the reproach (disgrace) of my youth." **20.** "Is Ephraim My dear son? I remember him with love, and My heart yearns (longs) for him. I will surely have mercy on him." **21.** "Set up signposts and landmarks (indicators of direction); set your heart toward the highway. Turn back, O virgin Israel, to your cities." **22.** "How long will you wander (roam), O backsliding (turning away from faith) daughter? For I will create a new thing—a woman shall surround a man." **23.** "When I bring back their captivity, they will say in Judah, 'The Lord bless you, home of justice, mountain of holiness!'" **24.** "Farmers and those with flocks will dwell (live) in Judah and its cities." **25.** "I will refresh the weary (exhausted) and replenish (restore) the sorrowful." **26.** After this, I woke, and my sleep was sweet. **27.** "The days are coming when I will sow (plant) Israel and Judah with the seed of man and beast." **28.** "As I have watched over them to destroy, I will now watch over them to build and plant." **29.** "In those days, people will no longer say, 'The fathers ate sour grapes, and the children's teeth are set on edge.'" **30.** "Each will die for his own sin; those who eat sour grapes will bear the consequences." **31.** "The days are coming when I will make a new covenant (agreement) with Israel and Judah." **32.** "This covenant will not be like the one I made with their ancestors when I led them out of Egypt, a covenant they broke, though I was their husband." **33.** "This is the covenant I will make: I will put My law in their minds and write it on their hearts. I will be their God, and they will be My people." **34.** "They will no longer need to teach one another, 'Know the Lord,' for they will all know Me. I will forgive their iniquity (sin) and remember their sin no more." **35.** The Lord, who gives light to day and night, and stirs (moves) the sea, says: **36.** "If these ordinances (laws) depart from before Me, then Israel will cease to be a nation before Me forever." **37.** "If the heavens can be measured and the foundations of the earth explored, then I will cast off (reject) Israel for all they have done." **38.** "The days are coming when the city will be rebuilt from the Tower of Hananel to the Corner Gate." **39.** "The surveyor's line (measuring tool) will extend across the hill Gareb and turn toward Goath." **40.** "The whole valley of the dead bodies, ashes, and fields as far as the Brook Kidron, to the Horse Gate, will be holy to the Lord. It will never be plucked up or thrown down again."

Chapter 32

1. The word that came to Jeremiah from the Lord in the tenth year of Zedekiah king of Judah, the eighteenth year of Nebuchadnezzar. **2.** At that time, the Babylonian army besieged (surrounded and attacked) Jerusalem, and Jeremiah the prophet was confined (locked up) in the court of the prison, in the house of the king of Judah. **3.** For Zedekiah king of Judah had imprisoned him, saying, "Why do you prophesy (foretell future events) and say, 'Thus says the Lord: "I will give this city into the hand of the king of Babylon, and he shall take it; **4.** and Zedekiah shall not escape from the hand of the Chaldeans (Babylonians), but shall surely be delivered into the hand of the king of Babylon, and shall speak with him face to face, and see him eye to eye; **5.** then he shall lead Zedekiah to Babylon, and there he shall be until I visit him," says the Lord; "though you fight with the Chaldeans, you will not succeed"'?" **6.** Jeremiah said, "The word of the Lord came to me, saying, **7.** 'Behold, Hanamel the son of Shallum your uncle will come to you, saying, "Buy my field which is in Anathoth, for the right of redemption (the right to buy back property) is yours to buy it."' **8.** Then Hanamel, my uncle's son, came to me in the court of the prison, as the Lord had said, and said, 'Please buy my field in Anathoth, which is in the land of Benjamin; for the right of inheritance (ownership) and redemption are yours; buy it for yourself.' Then I knew this was the word of the Lord. **9.** So I bought the field from Hanamel the son of my uncle, in Anathoth, and weighed out to him seventeen shekels (a unit of weight) of silver. **10.** I signed the deed (legal document), sealed it, took witnesses, and weighed the money on the scales. **11.** I took the purchase deed, both the sealed and the open (unsealed), **12.** and gave the deed to Baruch the son of Neriah, son of Mahseiah, in the presence of Hanamel, my uncle's son, and the witnesses who signed the deed, before all the Jews who were sitting in the court of the prison. **13.** I charged (commanded) Baruch before them, saying, **14.** 'Thus says the Lord of hosts (armies), the God of Israel: "Take these deeds, both the sealed and the open, and put them in an earthen (clay) vessel, that they may last many days. **15.** For thus says the Lord of hosts, the God of Israel: 'Houses, fields, and vineyards will again be bought in this land.'"' **16.** Now when I had delivered the purchase deed to Baruch the son of Neriah, I prayed to the Lord, saying: **17.** 'Ah, Lord God! Behold, You have made the heavens and the earth by Your great power and outstretched arm. Nothing is too hard for You. **18.** You show lovingkindness (mercy) to thousands, and repay the iniquity (wickedness) of the fathers into the bosom (chest) of their children after them—Great and Mighty God, whose name is the Lord of hosts. **19.** You are great in counsel and mighty in work, for Your eyes are open to all the ways of the sons of men, to give everyone according to his ways, and according to the fruit (result) of his doings. **20.** You have set signs and wonders (miracles) in the land of Egypt, to this day, and in Israel and among other men, and You have made Yourself a name, as it is this day. **21.** You brought Your people Israel out of the land of Egypt with signs and wonders, with a strong hand and an outstretched arm, and with great terror; **22.** and You gave them this land, of which You swore to their fathers to give them—'a land flowing with milk and honey.' **23.** They came in and took possession of it, but they did not obey Your voice or walk in Your law. They did nothing of all You commanded them to do; therefore You have caused all this calamity (disaster) to come upon them. **24.** Behold, the siege mounds (ramps built to attack a city) have come to the city to take it; and the city has been given into the hand of the Chaldeans who fight against it, because of the sword, famine, and pestilence (disease). What You have spoken has happened; You see it! **25.** And You have said to me, O Lord God, 'Buy the field for money, and take witnesses'—yet the city has been given into the hand of the Chaldeans.' **26.** Then the word of the Lord came to Jeremiah, saying, **27.** "Behold, I am the Lord, the God of all flesh. Is there anything too hard for Me? **28.** Therefore, thus says the Lord: 'Behold, I will give this city into the hand of the Chaldeans, into the hand of Nebuchadnezzar king of Babylon, and he shall take it. **29.** And the Chaldeans who fight against this city shall come and set fire to it, and burn it, with the houses where they have offered incense to Baal and poured out drink offerings (liquid offerings) to other gods, to provoke Me to anger. **30.** For the children of Israel and the children of Judah have done only evil before Me from their youth. The children of Israel have provoked Me to anger with the work of their hands,' says the Lord. **31.** 'For this city has been to Me a provocation (challenge) of My anger and My fury (wrath) from the day they built it, even to this day. So I will remove it from before My face **32.** because of all the evil of the children of Israel and Judah, which they have done to provoke Me to anger—They, their kings, their princes, their priests, their prophets, the men of Judah, and the inhabitants of Jerusalem. **33.** They have turned their back to Me, and not their face; though I taught them, rising early and teaching them, yet they have not listened to receive instruction. **34.** But they set their abominations (idols) in the house which is called by My name, to defile it. **35.** And they built the high places (altars) of Baal which are in the Valley of the Son of Hinnom, to cause their sons and daughters to pass through the fire to Molech, which I did not command them, nor did it come into My mind that they should do this abomination, to cause Judah to sin. **36.** "Now therefore, thus says the Lord, the God of Israel, concerning this city of which you say, 'It shall be delivered into the hand of the king of Babylon, by the sword, by famine, and by pestilence: **37.** Behold, I will gather them out of all countries where I have driven them in My anger, in My fury, and in great wrath; I will bring them back to this place, and I will cause them to dwell safely. **38.** They shall be My people, and I will be their God; **39.** then I will give them one heart and one way, that they may fear Me forever, for their good and the good of their children after them. **40.**

And I will make an everlasting covenant (binding agreement) with them, that I will not turn away from doing them good; but I will put My fear in their hearts so that they will not depart from Me. **41.** Yes, I will rejoice over them to do them good, and I will surely plant them in this land, with all My heart and with all My soul.' **42.** "For thus says the Lord: 'Just as I have brought all this great calamity upon this people, so I will bring on them all the good that I have promised them. **43.** And fields will be bought in this land, of which you say, "It is desolate, without man or beast; it has been given into the hand of the Chaldeans." **44.** Men will buy fields for money, sign deeds, and seal them, and take witnesses, in the land of Benjamin, in the places around Jerusalem, in the cities of Judah, in the cities of the mountains, in the cities of the lowland, and in the cities of the South; for I will cause their captives to return,' says the Lord."

Chapter 33

1. The word of the Lord came to Jeremiah again while he was still confined in the court of the prison, saying, **2.** "Thus says the Lord, who made and established (set up) the earth—His name is the Lord: **3.** 'Call to Me, and I will answer, showing you great and hidden (unknown) things you do not know.' **4.** For this is what the Lord, the God of Israel, says about the houses in this city and those of the kings of Judah, torn down to defend (protect) against the siege (military blockade): **5.** 'They fight the Chaldeans, but their place will be filled with the dead whom I will slay (kill) in My anger and wrath, for their wickedness (evil deeds) has caused Me to hide My face from this city. **6.** But I will bring healing, health, and abundance (plenty) of peace and truth. **7.** I will restore (bring back) the captives (prisoners) of Judah and Israel, rebuilding them as they were before. **8.** I will cleanse (purify) them from all their sin and pardon (forgive) their transgressions (wrongdoings). **9.** Then this city will be a name of joy, praise, and honor before all nations, who will hear of the good I do for them and be awed (filled with reverence) by the prosperity (success) I give.' **10.** "Again, in this desolate (empty) place—once empty of man and beast—there will be heard the voices of joy and gladness, the bridegroom and the bride, and those who say, 'Give thanks to the Lord of hosts (armies), for He is good, and His mercy (kindness) endures forever.' **11.** They will bring offerings (gifts) of praise to the house of the Lord. I will bring back the captives as I did at first," says the Lord. **12.** "In this desolate land, there will again be places for shepherds (those who tend sheep) to lead their flocks. **13.** In the cities of the mountains, the lowlands, the South, Benjamin, Jerusalem, and Judah, flocks will again pass under the shepherd's care," says the Lord. **14.** 'The days are coming when I will fulfill (complete) the good promise I made to Israel and Judah: **15.** At that time, I will raise up a righteous Branch for David, who will bring justice and righteousness to the earth. **16.** Judah will be saved, and Jerusalem will live in safety. She will be called, "The Lord Our Righteousness." **17.** "David will always have a descendant (offspring) to sit on the throne (seat of rule) of Israel, **18.** and the priests, the Levites (members of the priestly tribe), will never lack (be without) a man to offer sacrifices before Me." **19.** The word of the Lord came again to Jeremiah, saying, **20.** "If you can break My covenant (agreement) with day and night, so that they no longer follow their seasons, **21.** then My covenant with David and the Levites could be broken, and there would be no descendants to reign (rule) on his throne. **22.** Just as the stars of heaven cannot be numbered, nor the sand of the sea measured, so I will multiply (increase) the descendants of David and the Levites who serve Me." **23.** Again, the Lord spoke to Jeremiah, saying, **24.** "Have you heard what the people are saying, 'The Lord has rejected the two families He chose, and now they are no longer a nation'? **25.** If My covenant with day and night is not fixed (permanent), and if I have not established (set in place) the laws of heaven and earth, **26.** then I will reject the descendants of Jacob and David, and will not choose a ruler from his line. But I will restore their captives and have mercy (compassion) on them."

Chapter 34

1. The word of the Lord came to Jeremiah when Nebuchadnezzar (king of Babylon) and his army, along with all the kingdoms under his rule, fought against Jerusalem and its cities, saying: **2.** "Thus says the Lord, the God of Israel: 'Go and speak to Zedekiah (king of Judah), and tell him: "Behold, I will give this city into the hands of the king of Babylon, and he shall burn it with fire. **3.** You will not escape; you will surely be captured and handed over to him. You will see the king of Babylon face to face and be taken to Babylon." **4.** But hear the word of the Lord, Zedekiah, king of Judah: 'You shall not die by the sword (weapon). **5.** You will die in peace, and as with the ceremonies of your ancestors, the former kings, they will burn incense (offer prayers or sacrifices) for you and lament (express sorrow), saying, "Alas, lord!" For this is the word I have spoken, says the Lord.' **6.** Jeremiah delivered these words to Zedekiah, king of Judah, in Jerusalem, **7.** when the Babylonian army was fighting against Jerusalem and the remaining fortified (protected) cities of Judah—Lachish and Azekah, the last standing cities. **8.** The word of the Lord came to Jeremiah after King Zedekiah made a covenant (agreement) with the people of Jerusalem to proclaim liberty (freedom): **9.** Every man was to free his Hebrew (descendant of Abraham, Isaac, and Jacob) slaves, both male and female, and not keep any Jewish brother in bondage (captivity). **10.** When the princes and the people heard this, they obeyed and freed their slaves. **11.** But afterward, they changed their minds, brought the slaves back, and forced them into servitude (forced labor) again. **12.** The word of the Lord came to Jeremiah: **13.** "Thus says the Lord, the God of Israel: 'I made a covenant with your forefathers (ancestors) when I brought them out of Egypt, from the house of bondage, saying: **14.** "At the end of seven years, let every man free his Hebrew brother, who has served you six years; and you shall let him go free." But your forefathers did not listen to Me. **15.** Recently, you turned and did what was right in My sight, proclaiming liberty (freedom) to your neighbors and making a covenant (agreement) before Me in the temple called by My name. **16.** But you turned around, profaned (dishonored) My name, and brought back your male and female slaves whom you had set free, making them slaves again.' **17.** "Therefore, thus says the Lord: 'You have not obeyed Me in proclaiming liberty (freedom) to your brothers and neighbors. Behold, I now proclaim liberty (freedom) to you—to the sword, pestilence (disease), and famine (starvation)! I will deliver you to distress (trouble) among all the kingdoms of the earth. **18.** I will give the men who broke My covenant, who did not keep their promise when they cut the calf in two and passed between its parts— **19.** the princes of Judah, the princes of Jerusalem, the eunuchs (castrated men), the priests, and all the people who passed between the calf's parts— **20.** into the hands of their enemies, to those who seek their lives. Their bodies will be food for the birds of the sky and the beasts of the earth. **21.** I will give Zedekiah, king of Judah, and his princes into the hands of their enemies, to those who seek their lives, and to the Babylonian army that has withdrawn from you. **22.** Behold, I will command, says the Lord, and cause them to return to this city. They will fight against it, capture it, and burn it with fire. And I will make all the cities of Judah desolate (empty), without inhabitant.'

Chapter 35

1. The word that came to Jeremiah from the Lord in the days of Jehoiakim, son of Josiah, king of Judah, saying, **2.** "Go to the house of the Rechabites, speak to them, and bring them into the house of the Lord, into one of the chambers (rooms), and give them wine to drink." **3.** So I took Jaazaniah, son of Jeremiah, son of Habazziniah, with his brothers, sons, and the whole house of the Rechabites, **4.** and I brought them into the house of the Lord, into the chamber (room) of the sons of Hanan, son of Igdaliah, the man of God, near the chamber of the princes (officials), above the chamber of Maaseiah, son of Shallum, the keeper (guardian) of the door. **5.** Then I set before the sons of the house of the Rechabites bowls full of wine and cups, and I said to them, "Drink wine." **6.** But they said, "We will drink no wine, for Jonadab, son of Rechab, our father, commanded us, saying, 'You shall drink no wine, you nor your sons, forever. **7.** You shall not build a house, sow seed (plant crops), plant a vineyard, nor have any of these; but all your days you shall dwell in tents (live in tents), that you may live many days in the land where you are sojourners (temporary residents).' **8.** Thus we have obeyed the voice of Jonadab, son of Rechab, our father, in all that he charged us, to drink no wine all our days, we, our wives, our sons, or our daughters, **9.** nor to build ourselves houses to dwell in; nor do we have vineyard, field, or seed. **10.** But we have dwelt in tents (lived in tents), and have obeyed and done according to all that Jonadab, our father, commanded us. **11.** But it came to pass, when Nebuchadnezzar king of Babylon came into the land, that we said, 'Come, let us go to Jerusalem for fear of the army of the Chaldeans and for fear of the army of the Syrians.' So we dwell (live) at Jerusalem." 12. Then came the word of the Lord to Jeremiah, saying, 13. "Thus says the Lord of hosts (armies), the God of Israel: 'Go and tell the men of Judah and the inhabitants of Jerusalem, "Will you not receive instruction to obey My words?" says the Lord. 14. "The words of Jonadab, son of Rechab, which he commanded his sons, not to drink wine, are kept (followed); for to this day they drink none, and obey their father's commandment. But although I have spoken to you, rising early (sending prophets early) and speaking, you did not obey Me. 15. I have also sent to you all My servants the prophets, rising early and sending them, saying, 'Turn now every one from his evil way, amend (change) your doings, and do not go after other gods to serve them; then you will dwell in the land which I have given you and your fathers.' But you have not inclined (listened) your ear, nor obeyed Me. 16. Surely the sons of Jonadab, son of Rechab, have performed the commandment of their father, which he commanded them, but this people has not obeyed Me." 17. Therefore thus says the Lord God of hosts, the God of Israel: 'Behold, I will bring on Judah and all the inhabitants of Jerusalem all the doom (destruction) that I have pronounced against them; because I have spoken to them but they have not heard, and I have called to them but they have not answered.' " 18. And Jeremiah said to the house of the Rechabites, "Thus says the Lord of hosts, the God of Israel: 'Because you have obeyed the commandment of Jonadab your father, and kept all his precepts (instructions) and done according to all that he commanded you, 19. therefore thus says the Lord of hosts, the God of Israel: 'Jonadab, son of Rechab, shall not lack a man to stand before Me forever.' "

Chapter 36

1. In the fourth year of Jehoiakim, son of Josiah, king of Judah, the word of the Lord came to Jeremiah, saying: 2. "Take a scroll (a written record) and write down all the words I have spoken to you against Israel, Judah, and all the nations, from the days of Josiah until now. 3. Perhaps the house of Judah will hear of the disasters (calamities) I plan to bring upon them, that they may turn from their evil ways and I may forgive their sins." 4. So Jeremiah called Baruch, son of Neriah, and Baruch wrote on a scroll all the words the Lord had spoken to Jeremiah. 5. Jeremiah told Baruch, "I am confined (imprisoned) and cannot go to the house of the Lord. 6. But you go and read from the scroll the words of the Lord in the hearing of the people at the temple on the day of fasting (a religious practice of abstaining from food). Also read it to all the people of Judah who come from their cities. 7. Perhaps they will plead (beg) before the Lord and turn from their evil ways. For the Lord's anger and fury (violent anger) are great against this people." 8. Baruch did as Jeremiah commanded, reading the Lord's words in the temple. 9. In the fifth year of Jehoiakim, king of Judah, in the ninth month, a fast was proclaimed before the Lord to all the people in Jerusalem and those from Judah's cities. 10. Baruch read Jeremiah's words in the temple, in the chamber (room) of Gemariah, son of Shaphan the scribe (writer), in the upper court near the New Gate, to the people. 11. When Michaiah, son of Gemariah, heard the words, 12. he went to the king's house, to the scribe's chamber, where all the princes (rulers) were gathered—Elishama the scribe, Delaiah, Elnathan, Gemariah, Zedekiah, and others. 13. Michaiah reported to them the words he had heard Baruch read to the people. 14. So the princes sent Jehudi, son of Nethaniah, to Baruch, saying, "Take the scroll and come." Baruch took the scroll and went to them. 15. They said, "Read it to us." Baruch read the scroll to them. 16. After hearing the words, they were terrified (filled with fear) and looked at each other, saying to Baruch, "We must tell the king everything." 17. They asked Baruch, "How did you write all these words? Was it at his direction (instruction)?" 18. Baruch answered, "He dictated (spoke) all these words to me, and I wrote them down with ink." 19. The princes told Baruch, "Go and hide, you and Jeremiah; let no one know where you are." 20. They went to the king's court and placed the scroll in Elishama's chamber, telling the king all the words. 21. The king sent Jehudi to bring the scroll, and Jehudi read it to the king and the princes. 22. The king was sitting by the fire in his winter house, in the ninth month. 23. After reading three or four columns (sections), the king cut the scroll with a knife and threw it into the fire, until the whole scroll was consumed (destroyed). 24. The king and his servants were not afraid, nor did they tear their clothes (a sign of mourning) when they heard the words. 25. However, Elnathan, Delaiah, and Gemariah pleaded (begged) with the king not to burn the scroll, but he would not listen. 26. The king ordered the capture (seizing) of Baruch and Jeremiah, but the Lord hid them. 27. After the scroll was burned, the word of the Lord came to Jeremiah: 28. "Take another scroll and write again the words that were on the first scroll burned by Jehoiakim, king of Judah. 29. Tell Jehoiakim, 'This is what the Lord says: You burned the scroll, asking why it foretold (predicted) that the king of Babylon would destroy this land and its people.' 30. Therefore, the Lord says: Jehoiakim will have no heir (successor) to sit on the throne of David; his body will be thrown out, exposed to the heat of the day and the cold of the night. 31. I will punish him, his family, and his servants for their sin, and I will bring on them and the people of Judah all the disasters I have announced, for they have not listened.'" 32. So Jeremiah took another scroll and gave it to Baruch, who wrote the same words as before, along with many additional words.

Chapter 37

1. King Zedekiah, son of Josiah, reigned (ruled) in place of Coniah, son of Jehoiakim, whom Nebuchadnezzar, king of Babylon, had appointed (assigned) over Judah. 2. However, neither Zedekiah, his servants (attendants), nor the people listened to the Lord's words spoken through the prophet (messenger) Jeremiah. 3. King Zedekiah sent Jehucal and Zephaniah, a priest, to Jeremiah, requesting (asking), "Pray to the Lord our God for us." 4. At that time, Jeremiah was free among the people, as he had not been imprisoned (detained). 5. When Pharaoh's army came from Egypt, the Chaldeans besieging (surrounding) Jerusalem withdrew. 6. Then the Lord's word came to Jeremiah, saying, 7. "Tell the king of Judah: 'Pharaoh's army, which came to help you, will return to Egypt. 8. The Chaldeans will come back, fight this city, capture (seize) it, and burn it.'" 9. The Lord said, "Do not deceive (fool) yourselves by saying, 'The Chaldeans will leave us,' for they will not. 10. Even if you defeated (conquered) their entire army and only wounded men remained, they would still rise up and burn this city." 11. After the Chaldeans left Jerusalem because of Pharaoh's army, 12. Jeremiah left Jerusalem to go to Benjamin to claim (take possession of) his property. 13. At the Benjamin Gate, Irijah, the captain (leader) of the guard, detained him, accusing (charging), "You are defecting (betraying) to the Chaldeans!" 14. Jeremiah denied (refused) this, but Irijah seized him and took him to the officials (authorities), 15. who became angry, struck (hit) him, and imprisoned him in Jonathan the scribe's house, which they had made a prison. 16. After many days in the dungeon (underground cell), 17. Zedekiah secretly (privately) summoned (called) Jeremiah, asking, "Is there a word from the Lord?" Jeremiah replied, "Yes, you will be handed over to Babylon's king." 18. Jeremiah asked Zedekiah, "What wrong have I done to you, your servants, or the people to be imprisoned? 19. Where are the prophets who assured (promised) you Babylon's king wouldn't attack? 20. Please, my lord king, listen to my plea (request); don't send me back to Jonathan's house, or I may die there." 21. Zedekiah ordered Jeremiah to be kept in the prison courtyard (enclosed area), providing him with daily bread from the bakers' street until the bread ran out. So Jeremiah remained in the courtyard.

Chapter 38

1. Shephatiah, son of Mattan, Gedaliah, son of Pashhur, Jucal, son of Shelemiah, and Pashhur, son of Malchiah, heard Jeremiah's words to the people. 2. "This is what the Lord says: 'Anyone staying in this city will die by the sword (weapon), famine (extreme hunger), or plague (disease); but whoever goes to the Chaldeans will live and find life as a reward.' 3. The Lord also says, 'This city will be given to the Babylonian king's army, and they will capture it.'" 4. The officials told the king, "Please put this man to death, for he discourages (deters) the soldiers and people by saying these things. He does not seek the people's welfare (well-being), but their harm." 5. King Zedekiah replied, "He is in your hands, for the king cannot go against you." 6. So they took Jeremiah and lowered him into the cistern (underground storage) of Malchiah, the king's son, in the court of the guard, using ropes. The cistern had no water, only mud, and Jeremiah sank into it. 7. Ebed-Melech, an Ethiopian (person from Ethiopia) eunuch (castrated man) in the palace, heard that Jeremiah had been placed in the cistern while the king was at the Benjamin Gate. 8. Ebed-Melech went from the palace to speak with the king, 9. saying, "My lord the king, these men

have done evil (wickedness) to Jeremiah by throwing him into the cistern. He will die of hunger there, as there is no more bread in the city." **10.** The king instructed Ebed-Melech, "Take thirty men and lift Jeremiah from the cistern before he dies." **11.** Ebed-Melech took the men to the palace storeroom (storage area), collected old clothes and rags (worn fabric), and lowered them by rope to Jeremiah. **12.** Ebed-Melech told Jeremiah, "Place these under your armpits (underarm) to protect you from the ropes." Jeremiah did so, **13.** and they pulled him out. Jeremiah remained in the court of the guard. **14.** Later, King Zedekiah summoned (called) Jeremiah to a private meeting in the Lord's house. The king said, "I am going to ask you something; don't hide anything from me." **15.** Jeremiah replied, "If I answer, you may kill me; and if I give counsel (advice), you won't listen." **16.** But Zedekiah swore (promised) secretly, "As the Lord lives, I will not put you to death or hand you over to those seeking your life." **17.** Jeremiah then said to him, "This is what the Lord, the God of Israel, says: 'If you surrender (yield) to Babylon's princes, you will live, and this city won't be burned; you and your family will be spared (saved). **18.** But if you do not surrender, the city will fall to the Chaldeans, who will burn it, and you will not escape.'" **19.** Zedekiah said, "I am afraid of the Jews who have defected to the Chaldeans, that they may mistreat (abuse) me." **20.** Jeremiah answered, "They will not harm you. Obey the Lord by surrendering, so you may live and things may go well with you. **21.** But if you refuse, this is what the Lord has revealed (shown): **22.** 'All the women remaining in your palace will be handed over to the Babylonian princes and will say, "Your friends have misled (deceived) you; you are trapped in the mud, and they have abandoned you." **23.** Your wives and children will be taken by the Chaldeans, and you will not escape; you will be taken by the king of Babylon, and the city will be burned.'" **24.** Zedekiah told Jeremiah, "Keep this conversation secret, and you will not die. **25.** But if the officials learn that we talked and question you, saying, 'Tell us what you told the king and what he said to you, or we will kill you,' **26.** then tell them, 'I pleaded (begged) with the king not to send me back to Jonathan's house to die there.'" **27.** The officials did question Jeremiah, and he responded as the king instructed. They left him alone, as the conversation had not been overheard (listened to). **28.** Jeremiah remained in the court of the guard until the day Jerusalem was captured (taken).

Chapter 39

1. In the ninth year of Zedekiah king of Judah, in the tenth month, Nebuchadnezzar king of Babylon and all his army came against Jerusalem and besieged it. **2.** In the eleventh year of Zedekiah, in the fourth month, on the ninth day, the city was breached (broken into). **3.** Then all the princes (leaders) of the king of Babylon came in and sat in the Middle Gate: Nergal-Sharezer, Samgar-Nebo, Sarsechim, Rabsaris, Nergal-Sarezer, Rabmag, and the rest of the princes of Babylon. **4.** When Zedekiah king of Judah and all the soldiers saw them, they fled by night, through the king's garden, by the gate between the two walls, and went out toward the plain (open land). **5.** But the Chaldean (Babylonian) army pursued and overtook Zedekiah in the plains of Jericho. They captured him and brought him to Nebuchadnezzar king of Babylon at Riblah, in the land of Hamath, where he pronounced judgment. **6.** The king of Babylon killed Zedekiah's sons before his eyes, and all the nobles (important people) of Judah were killed. **7.** Then he put out Zedekiah's eyes, bound him with bronze (a metal alloy) fetters (chains), and carried him off to Babylon. **8.** The Chaldeans burned the king's house and the houses of the people, and broke down the walls of Jerusalem. **9.** Nebuzaradan, the captain (commander) of the guard, carried away the remaining people to Babylon—those who remained in the city and those who defected (joined the enemy) to him. **10.** But Nebuzaradan left the poor (destitute) of the land, who had nothing, and gave them vineyards (grape fields) and fields. **11.** Nebuchadnezzar king of Babylon gave orders regarding Jeremiah to Nebuzaradan the captain of the guard, saying, **12.** "Take him and look after him; do him no harm, but treat him as he says." **13.** So Nebuzaradan, the captain of the guard, sent Nebushasban, Rabsaris, Nergal-Sharezer, Rabmag, and all the king of Babylon's chief officers. **14.** They took Jeremiah from the court (yard) of the prison and entrusted him to Gedaliah, the son of Ahikam, the son of Shaphan, to take him home. So he dwelt (lived) among the people. **15.** Now the word (message) of the Lord had come to Jeremiah

while he was in the court of the prison, saying, **16.** "Go and speak to Ebed-Melech the Ethiopian, saying, 'Thus says the Lord of hosts (armies), the God of Israel: "Behold, I will bring My words upon this city for disaster (ruin), not for good. They will be fulfilled (carried out) before you. **17.** But I will deliver (rescue) you on that day," says the Lord, "and you shall not be handed over to those you fear. **18.** For I will surely deliver you, and you will not fall by the sword; your life will be a prize (reward) to you because you have trusted in Me," says the Lord.'"

Chapter 40

1. The word of the Lord came to Jeremiah after Nebuzaradan (captain of the guard) had released him from Ramah. He had taken Jeremiah, bound in chains, with the captives from Jerusalem and Judah, who were being taken to Babylon. **2.** The captain of the guard said to Jeremiah, "The Lord your God has pronounced this judgment (punishment) on this place. **3.** Now the Lord has done as He said, because you have sinned against Him and not obeyed His voice. That is why this has happened. **4.** Today, I am freeing you from the chains on your hands. If you want to come with me to Babylon, I will take care of you; but if it seems wrong to you to come, stay here. The land is before you—go wherever you wish." **5.** Before Jeremiah could leave, Nebuzaradan said, "Go back to Gedaliah the son of Ahikam, whom the king of Babylon has appointed as governor (ruler) over Judah. Stay with him among the people, or go wherever you prefer." He gave Jeremiah provisions (supplies) and let him go. **6.** So Jeremiah went to Gedaliah the son of Ahikam at Mizpah, and stayed with him among the people who were left in the land. **7.** When the army commanders in the fields heard that the king of Babylon had appointed Gedaliah as governor over Judah and had left a remnant (remaining group) of people, **8.** they came to Gedaliah at Mizpah—among them were Ishmael the son of Nethaniah, Johanan and Jonathan the sons of Kareah, Seraiah the son of Tanhumeth, the sons of Ephai the Netophathite, and Jezaniah the son of a Maachathite, with their men. **9.** Gedaliah the son of Ahikam, the son of Shaphan, took an oath (promise) before them and their men, saying, "Do not fear the Chaldeans (Babylonians). Stay in the land and serve the king of Babylon, and it will go well with you. **10.** I will remain at Mizpah to serve the Chaldeans who come to us, but you gather wine, summer fruit, and oil (a liquid used for anointing or cooking), and store them in your vessels (containers). Live in the cities you have taken." **11.** Likewise, when all the Jews in Moab, among the Ammonites, in Edom, and in other countries heard that the king of Babylon had left a remnant of Judah and had set Gedaliah over them, **12.** they returned from all the places where they had been driven (forced to go) and came to the land of Judah, to Gedaliah at Mizpah, and gathered wine and summer fruit in abundance (plenty). **13.** Then Johanan the son of Kareah and all the captains of the forces in the fields came to Gedaliah at Mizpah, **14.** and said to him, "Do you know that Baalis (king of the Ammonites) has sent Ishmael the son of Nethaniah to kill you?" But Gedaliah the son of Ahikam did not believe them. **15.** Johanan the son of Kareah spoke secretly to Gedaliah at Mizpah, saying, "Let me go, please, and kill Ishmael the son of Nethaniah. No one will know. Why should he murder you, so that all the Jews who are gathered to you will be scattered (dispersed), and the remnant in Judah perish (die)?" **16.** But Gedaliah the son of Ahikam said to Johanan the son of Kareah, "You shall not do this thing, for you speak falsely (incorrectly) concerning Ishmael."

Chapter 41

1. In the seventh month, Ishmael son of Nethaniah, of the royal family and a member of the king's officers, came with ten men to Gedaliah son of Ahikam at Mizpah. They ate bread together there. **2.** Then Ishmael, with the ten men, rose and struck Gedaliah son of Ahikam, the son of Shaphan, with a sword (a weapon), killing him. Gedaliah had been appointed governor (a ruler) over the land by the king of Babylon. **3.** Ishmael also killed all the Jews who were with Gedaliah at Mizpah, and the Chaldean (Babylonian) soldiers found there. **4.** The next day, when no one knew yet, **5.** certain men came from Shechem, Shiloh, and Samaria—eighty men with shaved (cut) beards, torn clothes, and cuts on their bodies, bringing offerings and incense (a fragrant substance burned as a sacrifice) to the house of the Lord. **6.** Ishmael went out to meet them, weeping (crying) as he went, and said, "Come to Gedaliah son of Ahikam!" **7.** But when they entered the city, Ishmael and his men killed them and threw their bodies into a pit (a large hole in the ground). **8.** Ten men among them begged Ishmael, saying, "Do not kill us, for we have treasures (valuable things) of wheat, barley, oil, and honey in the fields." So he spared them and did not kill them with the others. **9.** The pit into which Ishmael threw the bodies was the one that King Asa had made in fear (worry) of Baasha king of Israel. Ishmael filled it with the slain (those killed). **10.** Ishmael then carried away captive (taken prisoner) all the people in Mizpah, including the kings daughters and those whom Nebuzaradan, the captain of the guard, had entrusted (given responsibility) to Gedaliah. Ishmael took them and headed toward the Ammonites. **11.** When Johanan son of Kareah and the captains (leaders) of his forces heard of the evil (wickedness) Ishmael had done, **12.** they gathered their men and went to fight Ishmael. They found him at the great pool (large water reservoir) in Gibeon. **13.** When the people with Ishmael saw Johanan and his captains, they were glad. **14.** The captives returned to Johanan, turning back from Ishmael. **15.** But Ishmael escaped from Johanan with eight men and went to the Ammonites. **16.** Johanan and his men rescued the rest of the people whom Ishmael had taken, including the mighty men (strong soldiers), women, children, and eunuchs (castrated men), from Gibeon. **17.** They went to dwell (live) in Chimham, near Bethlehem, as they continued on their way to Egypt, **18.** fearing the Chaldeans (Babylonians), because they were afraid of them after Ishmael had killed Gedaliah, whom the king of Babylon had made governor in the land.

Chapter 42

1. Then all the captains, including Johanan son of Kareah, Jezaniah son of Hoshaiah, and the people from the least to the greatest, approached Jeremiah. **2.** They said, "Please accept our petition (request) and pray to the Lord your God for us, the remnant (remaining part) of Israel, for we are few in number. **3.** Ask God to show us the way we should go and what we should do." **4.** Jeremiah replied, "I have heard you. I will pray to the Lord your God, and whatever He answers, I will tell you without holding anything back." **5.** They said, "Let the Lord be a faithful witness (testifier) between us. If we do not obey His command through you, **6.** whether it is pleasant or not, we will obey the Lord that it may go well with us." **7.** Ten days later, the word of the Lord came to Jeremiah. **8.** He called Johanan, the captains, and the people, both great and small, **9.** and said, "This is what the Lord, the God of Israel, says to whom you sent me with your petition: **10.** 'If you stay in this land, I will build you up (strengthen) and not tear you down. I will plant you (establish you) and not uproot (destroy) you, for I will relent (change My mind) from the disaster (destruction) I have brought upon you. **11.** Do not be afraid of the king of Babylon, whom you fear; I am with you to save and deliver (rescue) you from his hand. **12.** I will show you mercy (kindness), and he will have mercy on you and allow you to return to your land.' **13.** "But if you refuse to stay and instead say, 'We will go to Egypt, where we will be free from war, the sound of the trumpet (alarm), and hunger,' **14.** then hear the word of the Lord, O remnant of Judah: **15.** If you choose to go and live in Egypt, **16.** the sword you fear will find you there, and the famine (scarcity of food) you dread will follow you there, and there you will die. **17.** Those who go to Egypt will die by sword, famine, or plague (disease), and none will escape the disaster I will bring upon them. **18.** Just as My anger was poured out on Jerusalem, it will be poured out on you in Egypt. You will become an object of horror (disgust), a curse (punishment), and a reproach (shame), and you will never return to this land.' **19.** The Lord has spoken: 'Do not go to Egypt.' Know for sure that I have warned (counseled) you today. **20.** You were hypocrites (insincere people) when you sent me to pray to the Lord for you, saying, 'Pray for us and we will obey everything the Lord commands.' **21.** But I have told you His words, and you have not obeyed. **22.** Therefore, you will die by sword, famine, and pestilence (plague) in the land you have chosen to dwell (live) in."

Chapter 43

1. Now it happened, when Jeremiah had finished speaking to all the people all the words the Lord their God had sent him to deliver, **2.** that Azariah son of Hoshaiah, Johanan son of Kareah, and all the proud (arrogant) men said to Jeremiah, "You speak falsely! The Lord our God did not send you to say, 'Do not go to Egypt to dwell (live) there.' **3.** But Baruch son of Neriah has turned you against us to deliver us into the hands of the Chaldeans (Babylonians), to kill us or take us captive

(prisoners) to Babylon." **4.** So Johanan son of Kareah, all the captains (military leaders), and the people refused to obey the Lord's voice to stay in Judah. **5.** Johanan son of Kareah and all the captains took the entire remnant (remaining people) of Judah who had returned to live in the land of Judah, from all the nations where they had been driven— **6.** men, women, children, the king's daughters, and every person whom Nebuzaradan, captain of the guard, had left with Gedaliah son of Ahikam, son of Shaphan, and Jeremiah the prophet and Baruch son of Neriah. **7.** They went to the land of Egypt, disobeying the Lord's command, and reached Tahpanhes. **8.** Then the word of the Lord came to Jeremiah in Tahpanhes, saying, **9.** "Take large stones in your hands, and bury them in the clay (mud) at the entrance to Pharaoh's house in Tahpanhes, **10.** and say to the people, 'Thus says the Lord of hosts (armies), the God of Israel: "I will send and bring Nebuchadnezzar, king of Babylon, My servant, and set his throne over these stones I have hidden. He will spread his royal pavilion (tent) over them. **11.** When he comes, he will strike Egypt, putting to death those destined for death, taking others into captivity, and killing those appointed for the sword. **12.** I will set fire to the houses of Egypt's gods, and he will burn them and carry their idols away captive. He will dress in Egypt like a shepherd in his garment, and will depart in peace. **13.** He will break the sacred pillars (idols) of Beth Shemesh in Egypt, and burn the houses of Egypt's gods with fire."'"

Chapter 44

1. The word of the Lord came to Jeremiah regarding all the Jews living in Egypt, in Migdol, Tahpanhes, Noph, and Pathros: **2.** "Thus says the Lord of hosts (armies), the God of Israel: 'You have witnessed the destruction I brought upon Jerusalem and Judah's cities; today they are desolate (empty, ruined), with no one living there, **3.** because of their wickedness (evil behavior) in provoking Me to anger by burning incense (offering to gods) to other gods—gods they did not know, neither you nor your ancestors. **4.** I sent My prophets, rising early, warning you, 'Do not do these detestable (hateful) things that I hate!' **5.** But you did not listen, nor turn from your wickedness and cease worshiping other gods. **6.** So My anger and fury (violent anger) were poured out on Judah, and the cities of Judah and the streets of Jerusalem are now in ruin (destruction).' **7.** Therefore, says the Lord of hosts, the God of Israel: 'Why do you bring this great evil upon yourselves, cutting off your people—from man to child—leaving none of Judah? **8.** You provoke Me to wrath (anger) by burning incense to other gods in Egypt, where you have chosen to live, bringing disaster (calamity) upon yourselves and becoming a disgrace (dishonor) among the nations. **9.** Have you forgotten the wickedness of your ancestors, the kings and queens of Judah, and your own sins, which you committed in Judah and Jerusalem? **10.** They have not humbled (lowered themselves) themselves to this day, nor followed My law or statutes (rules).' **11.** Therefore, says the Lord of hosts, 'I will bring disaster upon you, and all Judah in Egypt will be destroyed. **12.** Those who have fled (escaped) to Egypt will fall by the sword (war) or famine (starvation), from the least to the greatest, becoming an object of horror and reproach (disgrace). **13.** I will punish Egypt as I did Judah, with the sword, famine, and pestilence (disease), **14.** and no one from Judah in Egypt will escape to return to Judah, except those who manage to flee.' **15.** The people who knew their wives had burned incense to other gods, along with the others living in Egypt, responded to Jeremiah: **16.** "We will not listen to your message! **17.** We will continue our worship of the queen of heaven and pour out drink offerings to her, as we and our ancestors did in Judah and Jerusalem. When we did, we had plenty to eat and saw no trouble. **18.** But since we stopped, we have lacked everything and suffered by sword and famine." **19.** The women replied, "Did we make cakes for the queen of heaven and pour out drink offerings to her without our husbands' consent?" **20.** Jeremiah responded to all the people: **21.** "The incense you burned in Judah and Jerusalem—did the Lord not remember it? Did it not come into His mind? **22.** The Lord could no longer bear (tolerate) your evil deeds and abominations (disgusting acts), so your land has become a desolation, an object of astonishment (shock), a curse, with no inhabitants, as it is today. **23.** Because you burned incense and sinned against the Lord, and did not obey His commands, this disaster has come upon you." **24.** Jeremiah then addressed all the people and the women: **25.** "The vows (promises) you and your wives made to burn incense to the queen of heaven and pour drink offerings to her, you have kept them. You will surely fulfill (carry out) your vows. **26.** Therefore, hear the word of the Lord: 'I have sworn by My great name that My name will no longer be uttered by any man of Judah in Egypt, saying, "The Lord God lives." **27.** I will watch over them for disaster, not good, and the people of Judah in Egypt will perish by sword and famine, **28.** except for a few who will escape and return to Judah. Then you will know whose words stand, Mine or yours. **29.** This will be a sign (mark) to you that I will punish you, so that you know My words will stand against you.' **30.** And thus says the Lord: 'I will give Pharaoh Hophra, king of Egypt, into the hands of his enemies, as I gave Zedekiah, king of Judah, into the hand of Nebuchadnezzar, king of Babylon.'"

Chapter 45

1. The word that Jeremiah the prophet spoke to Baruch son of Neriah, when he wrote these words in a book at Jeremiah's direction, in the fourth year of Jehoiakim son of Josiah, king of Judah, saying: **2.** "Thus says the Lord, the God of Israel, to you, O Baruch: **3.** 'You said, "Woe (great sorrow or distress) is me! For the Lord has added sorrow to my grief. I am weary (tired) from my sighing and find no rest." **4.** Say this to him: "The Lord says: I will destroy (tear down) what I have built and uproot (remove by force) what I have planted—this whole land. **5.** And do you seek great things (ambitions or desires) for yourself? Do not seek them; for I will bring hardship (difficult or painful circumstances) upon all people," says the Lord. "But I will spare (save) your life wherever you go." '"

Chapter 46

1. The word of the Lord that came to Jeremiah the prophet concerning the nations: **2.** Against Egypt, concerning Pharaoh Necho's (king of Egypt) army, which was by the Euphrates (river) at Carchemish (city). Nebuchadnezzar (king of Babylon) defeated them in the fourth year of King Jehoiakim (son of Josiah, king of Judah). **3.** "Prepare shields and bucklers (large shields)! Draw near for battle! **4.** Harness the horses, mount up, and stand ready with helmets, spears polished, and armor on! **5.** Why do I see them turning back, dismayed (frightened)? Their warriors are beaten and flee in terror, with no thought of retreat, for fear is all around," says the Lord. **6.** "Let the swift (fast soldiers) not escape, nor the strong flee; they will stumble and fall by the Euphrates. **7.** Who is this rising like a flood, with waters surging (rising) like rivers? **8.** Egypt rises like a flood, its waters swelling like rivers, saying, 'I will cover the earth and destroy the cities and their people.' **9.** Charge, O horses! Rage (attack), O chariots! Let the mighty men come out—Ethiopians (people of Cush), Libyans with shields, and Lydians (people of Lydia) with bows. **10.** For this is the day of the Lord of hosts (armies), a day of vengeance (punishment), when He will avenge (punish) Himself on His enemies. The sword will devour, filled with blood, for the Lord of hosts has a sacrifice in the north, by the Euphrates. **11.** "Go to Gilead (region) and get balm (healing oil), O virgin daughter of Egypt; in vain will you try many cures—there will be no healing for you. **12.** The nations have heard of your shame, and your cry has filled the land; the mighty have stumbled against the mighty, and they both have fallen." **13.** The word of the Lord to Jeremiah about Nebuchadnezzar of Babylon coming to strike Egypt. **14.** "Declare in Egypt, and proclaim in Migdol (city), Noph (city), and Tahpanhes (city): 'Prepare for the sword that devours all around you.' **15.** Why are your soldiers swept away? They did not stand, for the Lord drove them away. **16.** Many have fallen; one stumbled over another, saying, 'Let us return to our own people and land to escape the sword.' **17.** They cry, 'Pharaoh, king of Egypt, is a noise (empty); his time has passed!' **18.** "As I live," says the King, whose name is the Lord of hosts, "Surely as Tabor (mountain) is among the mountains and Carmel (mountain) by the sea, so he will come. **19.** O daughter of Egypt, prepare to go into captivity (exile)! Noph shall be desolate (ruined), with no one left. **20.** Egypt is a beautiful heifer (young cow), but destruction comes from the north. **21.** Her mercenaries (soldiers for hire) are like well-fed bulls; they too will flee, unable to stand, for the day of their destruction has come. **22.** Her noise will be like a serpent's hiss as armies march with axes (tools) to chop down her forests, vast as they are. **23.** "They will cut down her trees," says the Lord, "too numerous to count, more than locusts. **24.** The daughter of Egypt will be ashamed, delivered into the hands of the northern people." **25.** The Lord of hosts, the God of Israel, says: "I will

punish Amon of No (city), Pharaoh, Egypt, their gods, and their kings—Pharaoh and all who trust in him. **26.** I will deliver them into the hands of those who seek their lives, to Nebuchadnezzar and his servants. Afterward, Egypt will be inhabited again, as in the past," says the Lord. **27.** "But do not fear, O Jacob (Israel) My servant, nor be dismayed (anxious), O Israel! I will save you from afar, and your descendants from captivity. Jacob will return, rest, and be at peace, and no one will make him afraid. **28.** Do not fear, O Jacob My servant," says the Lord, "For I am with you. I will destroy all the nations where I have scattered you, but I will not make a full end of you. I will discipline (correct) you justly, but will not leave you unpunished."

Chapter 47

1. The word of the Lord came to Jeremiah concerning the Philistines, before Pharaoh attacked Gaza. **2.** This is what the Lord says: "Behold, waters rise from the north, a mighty flood (a large, overwhelming flow of water) that will overflow the land, the city, and all its inhabitants (those who live in it). People will cry out in distress (extreme sorrow). **3.** At the sound of the galloping (running at full speed) horses, the rushing chariots (two-wheeled vehicles), and the rumbling (deep, continuous sound) wheels, fathers will not look back for their children, paralyzed (unable to move) with fear, **4.** because the day is coming to devastate (destroy or ruin) all the Philistines, to cut off all helpers from Tyre and Sidon. The Lord will plunder (take by force) the Philistines, the remnant (remaining part) from Caphtor. **5.** Gaza will be shorn (shaved off), Ashkelon will be ruined, and the remnant of their valley will be left desolate (abandoned and uninhabited). How long will you mourn (express sorrow) and cut yourselves? **6.** "O sword (a weapon) of the Lord, how long will you be still? Return to your sheath (cover or case for a sword), rest, and be quiet!" **7.** But how can it be still, when the Lord has given it a task (duty or assignment) against Ashkelon and the coast? He has appointed (assigned) it."

Chapter 48

1. *Judgment on Moab*: The Lord of Hosts, the God of Israel, says: "Woe to Nebo! It is plundered; Kirjathaim is taken; the stronghold is in shame. **2.** Moab's praise is gone. In Heshbon, they plot against her: 'Let's destroy her as a nation.' You too, Madmen, will fall by the sword. **3.** Crying is heard from Horonaim: 'Plunder (robbery) and destruction!' **4.** Moab is ruined; her children cry. **5.** On the ascent (upward slope) of Luhith, they weep; in Horonaim, the cry of destruction is heard. **6.** "Flee and save yourselves like junipers (a type of tree) in the wilderness! **7.** You trusted in your wealth and treasures, but you too will be taken, and Chemosh will go into captivity (forced removal) with his priests and princes. **8.** The plunderer will come to every city. No one will escape; the valley and the plain will be destroyed, as the Lord said. **9.** "Give Moab wings to flee, for her cities will be desolate, with no one to inhabit them. **10.** Cursed is anyone who does the Lord's work deceitfully or withholds the sword from blood. **11.** Moab has been at ease, unchallenged, and her scent has not changed. **12.** But the days are coming when I will send wine-workers (those who press wine) to tip her over, empty her vessels, and break her jars. **13.** Moab will be ashamed of Chemosh, just as Israel was ashamed of Bethel, their trust. **14.** "How can you boast, 'We are mighty and strong for battle'? **15.** Moab is plundered, her cities fall, and her young men are slain," says the Lord. **16.** "Moab's calamity (disaster) is near; her affliction (suffering) comes swiftly. **17.** Mourn for Moab, all who know her, saying, 'How the strong staff (support) is broken!' **18.** O daughter of Dibon, descend (come down) from your glory and sit in thirst; the plunderer is against you, destroying your strongholds (fortresses). **19.** O inhabitant (resident) of Aroer, stand and watch. Ask those fleeing, 'What happened?' **20.** Moab is ashamed and broken. Cry out, tell it in Arnon—Moab is plundered. **21-24.** Judgment has come to Moab's cities—Holon, Jahzah, Mephaath, Dibon, Nebo, and others. **25.** Moab's strength is cut off, and his arm is broken. **26.** Make him drunk for his pride (arrogance) against the Lord. Moab will wallow (roll about in) in shame. **27.** Did you not mock (make fun of) Israel? Was he a derision (object of ridicule) to you? **28.** O Moab, leave the cities and dwell (live) in the rocks, like a dove in a cave. **29.** We have heard Moab's pride—his arrogance and loftiness (highness). **30.** "I know his wrath (anger)," says the Lord, "but it's misguided; his lies have failed him." **31.** "I will wail (cry out) for Moab, mourning (grieving) for her cities and people." **32.** O vine of Sibmah, I mourn for you as for Jazer; your fruit has been plundered. **33.** Moab's joy is gone; wine no longer flows from the presses (wine vats). **34.** From Heshbon to Zoar, they cry; the waters of Nimrim are desolate. **35.** I will end Moab's offerings (sacrifices) and incense to their gods. **36.** My heart mourns for Moab like flutes (musical instruments), for the men of Kir Heres; their wealth is lost. **37.** Moab will mourn; every head will be bald (shaved), every beard shaved, hands cut, and sackcloth worn (a sign of mourning). **38.** Moab will wail, broken like a vessel of no value. **39.** "How Moab is broken! She has turned in shame." **40.** "An eagle will fly over Moab, and her cities will fall." **41.** Kerioth is taken; the mighty men's hearts will fail (be terrified). **42.** Moab will be destroyed as a nation because of her pride against the Lord. **43.** Fear, pit (trap), and snare (a trap) will come upon you, Moab. **44.** Those who flee will fall into a pit or snare. The year of Moab's punishment has come. **45.** Those who escaped will be exhausted, but a fire from Heshbon will consume Moab. **46.** Woe to Moab, for Chemosh's people perish; their sons and daughters are taken captive. **47.** "Yet I will bring back Moab's captives (those taken away) in the latter days," says the Lord. This is the end of Moab's judgment.

Chapter 49

1. Against the Ammonites The Lord says, "Does Israel have no sons? Is there no heir? Why, then, does Milcom inherit (receive as an inheritance) Gad, and his people live in its cities? **2.** The days are coming," declares the Lord, "when I will raise a war cry against Rabbah (city of the Ammonites). It will become a heap of ruins (desolate), and its villages will burn. Then Israel will reclaim (take possession of) its inheritance." **3.** "Mourn (feel or express sorrow), O Heshbon, for Ai is plundered (taken as spoil)! Wail (cry out), daughters of Rabbah, put on sackcloth (a sign of mourning)! Run through the streets in mourning, for Milcom and his priests and princes will go into captivity (forced removal). **4.** Why do you boast (show excessive pride), you backsliding (turning away) daughter, trusting in your treasures (riches), saying, 'Who will come against me?' **5.** I will bring fear (dread) upon you," says the Lord, "from those around you. You will be driven out, with no one to gather the scattered. **6.** But later, I will bring back the captives of the Ammonites." **7.** Against Edom The Lord says, "Is wisdom no longer in Teman (a region in Edom)? Has counsel (advice) vanished from the prudent (wise)? **8.** Flee (run away), dwell in the depths (safety), O inhabitants of Dedan (a region of Arabia), for I will bring the calamity (disaster) of Esau upon them, the time of their punishment. **9.** If grape-gatherers (harvesters) came to you, they would leave some grapes. If thieves came at night, they would only take what they needed. But I will expose (reveal) Esau's hidden places, and he will not be able to hide. His descendants, neighbors, and brothers will be plundered, and he will be no more. **11.** Leave your fatherless (without a father) children; I will keep them alive. Let your widows (women whose husbands have died) trust in Me." **12.** "Those who should not have drunk the cup (a metaphor for suffering or punishment) will certainly drink it. And you, will you escape punishment? You will not, but will drink it too. **13.** I have sworn (taken an oath) that Bozrah (a city in Edom) will become a desolation (ruin), a reproach (disgrace), a waste (destruction), and a curse. All its cities will be perpetual (never-ending) ruins. **14.** I have heard a message from the Lord. An ambassador (messenger) has been sent to the nations: 'Gather together, come against her, and rise up to battle!' **15.** I will make you small among nations, despised (looked down on) by men. **16.** Your pride and your belief that no one can defeat you, though you dwell in high places like an eagle, will be your downfall," says the Lord. **17.** Edom will become a horror (something shocking), and all who pass by will be shocked and hiss (show disgust) at its plagues. **18.** Like the destruction of Sodom and Gomorrah (biblical cities destroyed by God), no one will remain there, and no one will dwell in it. **19.** A lion will come from the Jordan (river) against the stronghold (fortified place) of Edom. I will make him flee suddenly. Who is like Me, who can challenge Me? Who is the shepherd (leader) who can withstand (resist) Me? **20.** Hear the counsel (advice) of the Lord against Edom: the least of the flock (a small group) will lead them into destruction. I will make their cities desolate. **21.** The earth will shake at their fall, and their cry will be heard at the Red Sea. **22.** He will fly like an eagle over Bozrah, and the hearts of Edom's mighty men will be like a woman in labor (in great pain)." **23.** Against Damascus "Hamath and Arpad (cities of Syria) are ashamed, for they have heard bad news. They are faint-hearted (discouraged); there is turmoil (unrest) on the sea; it cannot be quiet. **24.** Damascus is weakening, turning to flee. Fear has gripped her, and anguish (great suffering) has overtaken her like a woman in labor. **25.** Why has the city of praise (Damascus), My joy, not been deserted? **26.** Therefore, her young men will fall in the streets, and her warriors will be cut off," says the Lord. **27.** "I will kindle (start) a fire in the walls of Damascus that will consume (destroy) the palaces of Ben-Hadad (king of Syria)." **28.** Against Kedar and Hazor The Lord says, "Rise up, attack Kedar (a nomadic tribe of Arabia) and devastate (destroy) the men of the East! **29.** They will take their tents, flocks, curtains, vessels, and camels, and cry out, 'Fear is on every side!' **30.** Flee, O inhabitants of Hazor (a city), for Nebuchadnezzar (king of Babylon) has planned against you. **31.** Arise, go against the wealthy nation that dwells in security, without gates or bars. Their camels and cattle will be plundered, and I will scatter them to the winds (faraway places). **32.** Hazor will become a place for jackals (wild animals), a desolation forever. No one will live there." **33.** Against Elam The Lord says, "I will break the bow (symbol of strength) of Elam, the foremost (leading) of their power. **36.** I will bring the four winds (directions) against Elam, scattering them to all corners of the earth. Their exiles (those forced to leave) will be in every nation. **37.** I will cause them to be dismayed (filled with fear) before their enemies. I will send disaster upon them, My fierce (intense) anger. **38.** I will set My throne (place of authority) in Elam, and destroy its king and princes. **39.** But in the latter days (future), I will bring back the captives of Elam."

Chapter 50

1. The word that the Lord spoke against Babylon and the land of the Chaldeans (inhabitants of ancient Babylon) by Jeremiah the prophet. **2.** "Declare among the nations, proclaim, and set up a standard (a banner); proclaim it—do not conceal it—say, 'Babylon is taken, Bel (a Babylonian god) is shamed, Merodach (another Babylonian god) is shattered; her idols are humiliated, her images broken in pieces.' **3.** For a nation will come from the north against her, making her land desolate, and no one will dwell in it. Both man and beast shall move away. **4.** "In those days," says the Lord, "the children of Israel and Judah will come together, weeping, and seek the Lord their God. **5.** They will ask the way to Zion, and say, 'Come, let us join ourselves to the Lord in a perpetual (lasting) covenant that will not be forgotten.' **6.** "My people have been lost sheep; their shepherds have led them astray; they have gone from mountain to hill and forgotten their resting place. **7.** All who found them have devoured them, and their adversaries (enemies) said, 'We have not offended, because they have sinned against the Lord, the habitation of justice, the hope of their fathers.' **8.** "Flee from Babylon, go out of the land of the Chaldeans, and be like the rams before the flocks. **9.** For I will raise up and cause a great assembly of nations from the north to come against Babylon. They shall array themselves against her; she shall be captured. Their arrows shall be like those of an expert warrior; none will return in vain. **10.** And Chaldea (Babylon) shall be plundered; all who plunder her shall be satisfied," says the Lord. **11.** "Because you rejoiced, because you were glad, you destroyers of My heritage, because you grew fat like a heifer threshing grain (a strong, healthy cow), and bellowed like bulls, **12.** your mother shall be deeply ashamed; she who bore you shall be ashamed. Behold, the least of the nations shall be a wilderness (a desolate place), a dry land, and a desert. **13.** Because of the wrath (anger) of the Lord, she shall not be inhabited, but shall be wholly desolate. Everyone who goes by Babylon shall be horrified and hiss (scoff) at all her plagues (disasters). **14.** "Set yourselves in array against Babylon all around, all you who bend the bow (archers); shoot at her, spare no arrows, for she has sinned against the Lord. **15.** Shout against her all around; she has given her hand (surrendered), her foundations have fallen, her walls are thrown down. For it is the vengeance (punishment) of the Lord. Take vengeance on her as she has done, so do to her. **16.** Cut off the sower (one who plants seeds) from Babylon, and him who handles the sickle (harvest tool) at harvest time. For fear of the sword, everyone will flee to their own people, and everyone will flee to his own land. **17.** "Israel is like scattered sheep; the lions have driven him away. First the king of Assyria devoured him; now at last this Nebuchadnezzar king of Babylon has broken his bones." **18.** Therefore thus says the Lord of hosts (armies), the God of Israel:

"Behold, I will punish the king of Babylon and his land, as I have punished the king of Assyria. **19.** But I will bring Israel back to his home, and he shall feed on Carmel (a mountain) and Bashan (a fertile area); his soul shall be satisfied on Mount Ephraim (a region in Israel) and Gilead (a region known for its balm). **20.** In those days and at that time," says the Lord, "the iniquity (wickedness) of Israel will be sought, but there shall be none; and the sins of Judah, but they shall not be found. For I will pardon those whom I preserve." **21.** "Go up against the land of Merathaim (a region in Babylon), and against the inhabitants of Pekod (a district of the Chaldeans). Waste and utterly destroy them," says the Lord, "and do according to all that I have commanded you. **22.** A sound of battle is in the land, and of great destruction. **23.** How the hammer (destroyer) of the whole earth has been cut apart and broken! How Babylon has become a desolation among the nations! I have laid a snare (trap) for you; **24.** You have indeed been trapped, O Babylon, and you were not aware; you have been found and caught, because you have contended (fought) against the Lord. **25.** The Lord has opened His armory and has brought out the weapons of His indignation (anger). For this is the work of the Lord God of hosts in the land of the Chaldeans. **26.** Come against her from the farthest border; open her storehouses (treasuries), cast her up as heaps of ruins, and destroy her utterly. Let nothing of her be left. **27.** Slay all her bulls (cattle), let them go down to the slaughter. Woe (destruction) to them! For their day has come, the time of their punishment. **28.** The voice of those who flee and escape from the land of Babylon declares in Zion (Jerusalem) the vengeance of the Lord our God, the vengeance of His temple. **29.** "Call together the archers (bowmen) against Babylon. All you who bend the bow, encamp against her all around; let none escape. Repay her according to her work; according to all she has done, do to her; for she has been proud against the Lord, against the Holy One of Israel. **30.** Therefore her young men shall fall in the streets, and all her men of war shall be cut off (destroyed) in that day," says the Lord. **31.** "Behold, I am against you, O most haughty one (proud)!" says the Lord God of hosts. "For your day has come, the time I will punish you. **32.** The most proud shall stumble and fall, and no one will raise him up. I will kindle a fire in his cities, and it will devour all around him." **33.** Thus says the Lord of hosts: "The children of Israel were oppressed, along with children of Judah. All who took them captive have held them fast; they have refused to let them go. **34.** Their Redeemer (rescuer) is strong; the Lord of hosts is His name. He will thoroughly plead their case, that He may give rest to the land, and disquiet (trouble) the inhabitants of Babylon. **35.** "A sword is against the Chaldeans," says the Lord, "against the inhabitants of Babylon, and against her princes and her wise men. **36.** A sword is against the soothsayers (fortune-tellers), and they will be fools. A sword is against her mighty men, and they will be dismayed (terrified). **37.** A sword is against their horses, against their chariots, and against all the mixed people (foreigners) who are in her midst; and they will become like women. A sword is against her treasures, and they will be robbed. **38.** A drought (dryness) is against her waters, and they will be dried up. For it is the land of carved images (idols), and they are insane (deluded) with their idols. **39.** "Therefore the wild desert beasts shall dwell there with the jackals, and the ostriches shall dwell in it. It shall be inhabited no more forever, nor shall it be dwelt in from generation to generation. **40.** As God overthrew Sodom and Gomorrah and their neighbors," says the Lord, "so no one shall reside there, nor son of man dwell in it. **41.** "Behold, a people shall come from the north, and a great nation and many kings shall be raised up from the ends of the earth. **42.** They shall hold the bow and the lance (spear); they are cruel and will not show mercy. Their voice shall roar like the sea; they shall ride on horses, set in array, like a man for battle against you, O daughter of Babylon. **43.** The king of Babylon has heard the report about them, and his hands grow feeble (weak); anguish has taken hold of him, pangs like a woman in childbirth. **44.** "Behold, he shall come up like a lion from the floodplain (lowland) of the Jordan against the dwelling place of the strong. But I will make them suddenly run away from her. Who is a chosen man that I may appoint over her? Who is like Me? Who will arraign (accuse) Me? And who is that shepherd who will withstand Me?" **45.** Therefore hear the counsel of the Lord that He has taken against Babylon, and His purposes that He has proposed against the land of the Chaldeans: surely the least of the flock (smallest) shall draw them out. Surely He will make their dwelling place desolate with them. **46.** At the noise of the taking of Babylon, the earth trembles, and the cry is heard among the nations.

Chapter 51

1. This is what the Lord says: "I will raise up a destroying wind (a strong, destructive force) against Babylon and its inhabitants in Leb Kamai. **2.** I will send winnowers (those who separate grain from chaff) to Babylon to empty its land. On the day of disaster, they will surround her. **3.** Let the archers take aim at her and strike her warriors; let no young man be spared, but utterly destroy her army. **4.** The slain will fall in the land of the Chaldeans (a region in ancient Mesopotamia), and those pierced will lie in her streets. **5.** For Israel and Judah have not been abandoned by their God, the Lord of Hosts, despite the sins in their land against the Holy One of Israel." **6.** Flee from Babylon, everyone, and save yourselves! Don't be swept away in her guilt, for this is the Lord's time for vengeance (punishment); He will repay her. **7.** Babylon was a golden cup (a symbol of great wealth and power) in the Lord's hand, making the earth drunk. The nations drank her wine, and now they are confused (drunken, disoriented). **8.** Babylon has suddenly fallen and is destroyed. Cry for her! Bring healing ointment, but she won't be healed. **9.** We tried to heal Babylon, but it's hopeless. Let's leave and return to our own lands, for her judgment reaches to the heavens. **10.** The Lord has revealed our righteousness. Let's declare His work in Zion, our God's mighty deeds. **11.** Sharpen the arrows! Prepare the shields! The Lord has stirred up the spirit (inner influence) of the kings of the Medes, for His plan is to destroy Babylon in His vengeance for the desecration (violation) of His temple. **12.** Set up a banner (a sign or symbol) on Babylon's walls, strengthen the guard, station watchmen, and prepare ambushes (hidden attacks). The Lord has done what He said against Babylon. **13.** O you who live by many waters, full of treasures, your time has come; your greed has reached its limit. **14.** The Lord of Hosts swears by Himself: "I will fill you with men like locusts (insects that swarm and destroy), and they will raise a cry against you." **15.** He made the earth by His power, established the world by His wisdom, and stretched out the heavens by His understanding. **16.** When He speaks, waters surge in the heavens; He causes vapors (steam or mist) to rise from the earth, makes lightning for the rain, and brings the wind from His storehouses. **17.** Everyone is dull and without knowledge; even the metalsmith (one who works with metal) is shamed by his idols, for they are false and have no breath (life). **18.** They are futile (useless), a work of delusion (falsehood); in the time of punishment, they will perish. **19.** The Portion of Jacob is not like them. He is the Creator of all, and Israel is His inheritance (something passed down to a rightful heir). The Lord of Hosts is His name. **20.** "You are My battle-ax (a weapon of war) and weapons of war. With you I will shatter nations and destroy kingdoms; **21.** With you I will break the horse and its rider, the chariot and its driver; **22.** With you I will shatter men and women, young and old, young men and maidens; **23.** With you I will destroy shepherds and flocks, farmers and oxen, governors and rulers. **24.** I will repay Babylon and all the Chaldeans for the evil they have done in Zion before your eyes," says the Lord. **25.** "Behold, I am against you, O destructive mountain (a metaphor for a mighty force), who destroys the whole earth," says the Lord. "I will stretch out My hand, topple you from the rocks, and make you a burnt-out ruin (a desolate, destroyed place). **26.** No one will take from you a stone for a corner or a foundation; you will be desolate forever," says the Lord. **27.** Set up a banner in the land, blow the trumpet among the nations! Prepare the nations for battle, summon the kingdoms against her: Ararat (a mountain region), Minni (a historical kingdom), Ashkenaz (a historical region). Appoint a general and bring up the horses like locusts. **28.** Prepare the nations, the kings of the Medes, their governors (officials) and rulers, and all their land. **29.** The land will tremble, for the Lord's purpose against Babylon will be carried out, making her land desolate and uninhabited. **30.** The mighty men of Babylon have stopped fighting; they have retreated to their strongholds (fortresses). Their power has failed, they are like women. Their homes are burned, the bars of their gates broken. **31.** One runner (messenger) meets another, and one messenger meets another, to tell the king of Babylon his city is surrounded. **32.** The passages (gates or passages in the city) are blocked, the reeds burned, and the soldiers are terrified. **33.** Thus says the Lord of Hosts: "The daughter of Babylon is like a threshing floor (a place for separating grain) at harvest time. Soon the harvest will come." **34.** "Nebuchadnezzar, king of Babylon, has devoured (consumed) me, crushed me, and emptied me. He swallowed me like a monster and then spat me out. **35.** Let the violence done to me and my flesh be upon Babylon," says the inhabitant of Zion. "Let my blood be upon the Chaldeans!" says Jerusalem. **36.** Therefore, the Lord says: "I will defend your cause and take vengeance for you. I will dry up Babylon's sea (a metaphor for her vast resources) and make her springs dry. **37.** Babylon will become a desolate heap, a dwelling for jackals (wild animals), an object of horror, and uninhabited. **38.** They will roar together like lions, growling like young lions. **39.** I will prepare a feast for them and make them drunk, so they may rejoice and sleep a perpetual sleep, never to awake," says the Lord. **40.** "I will bring them down like lambs to the slaughter, like rams with male goats. **41.** How Sheshach (a code name for Babylon) is taken! The glory of the whole earth is seized! How Babylon has become desolate among the nations! **42.** The sea has engulfed (covered) Babylon; she is covered by its waves. **43.** Her cities are a desolation, a wilderness, uninhabited, where no one passes through. **44.** I will punish Bel (a Babylonian god) in Babylon and will bring out what he has swallowed. The nations will no longer stream to him, and Babylon's wall will fall. **45.** "My people, flee from her! Save yourselves from the fierce anger of the Lord. **46.** Don't faint from fear of the rumors of disaster (one year it's one rumor, the next another, with violence in the land and ruler against ruler). **47.** The days are coming when I will bring judgment on Babylon's idols, and her land will be filled with the groans of the wounded. **48.** The heavens and earth will rejoice over Babylon, for plunderers will come from the north," says the Lord. **49.** As Babylon has slain Israel, so the slain of all the earth will fall at Babylon. **50.** You who have escaped the sword, flee! Don't stand still! Remember the Lord far away, and let Jerusalem come to mind. **51.** We are ashamed because we have heard insults; shame covers our faces as strangers enter the Lord's house. **52.** "Therefore the days are coming," says the Lord, "when I will bring judgment on Babylon's idols, and her land will be filled with the groans of the wounded. **53.** Even if Babylon were to rise to heaven and fortify her strongholds (fortresses), plunderers would still come from Me," says the Lord. **54.** A cry comes from Babylon, great destruction from the land of the Chaldeans. **55.** The Lord is plundering Babylon and silencing her loud voices. Though her waves roar like great waters, their noise is gone. **56.** The plunderer has come against her, and Babylon's mighty men are captured. Their bows are broken, for the Lord is the God of recompense (payback). **57.** "I will make her princes, wise men, governors, deputies, and mighty men drunk; they will sleep a perpetual sleep, never to awake," says the King, whose name is the Lord of Hosts. **58.** The Lord of Hosts says: "The broad walls of Babylon will be utterly broken, and her high gates burned. The people's labor will be in vain, and the nations will be exhausted by the fire." **59.** The word Jeremiah gave to Seraiah, son of Neriah, son of Mahseiah, when he went with King Zedekiah of Judah to Babylon in the fourth year of his reign. Seraiah was the quartermaster (officer in charge of supplies). **60.** Jeremiah wrote down all the evil that would come upon Babylon in a book, the words against her. **61.** Jeremiah said to Seraiah, "When you arrive in Babylon, read all these words, **62.** then say, 'Lord, You have spoken against this place to destroy it, so that nothing will remain, neither man nor beast; it will be desolate forever.' **63.** After reading this book, tie a stone to it and throw it into the Euphrates (river). **64.** Then say, 'Thus Babylon will sink, never to rise again, because of the disaster I will bring upon her. She will be weary.'" Thus are the words of Jeremiah.

Chapter 52

1. Zedekiah was twenty-one when he became king and reigned eleven years in Jerusalem. His mother was Hamutal, daughter of Jeremiah of Libnah. **2.** He did evil in the sight of the Lord, as Jehoiakim had done. **3.** This happened because of the Lord's anger, which resulted in Jerusalem and Judah being cast out from His presence. Then Zedekiah rebelled (refused to obey) against the king of Babylon. **4.** In the ninth year of his reign, on the tenth day of the tenth month, Nebuchadnezzar, king of Babylon, and his entire army came against Jerusalem, camped around it, and built a siege wall (a wall built to surround and trap the city). **5.** The city was besieged (surrounded and blockaded) until the eleventh year of King Zedekiah. **6.** By the fourth month, on the ninth day, the famine (severe shortage of food) in the city became severe, and there was no food for the people. **7.** Then the city wall was broken, and all the soldiers fled at night through the gate between the two walls near the king's garden, though the Chaldeans (Babylonians) were surrounding the city. They fled toward the plain (an area of flat land). **8.** The Chaldean army pursued the king and overtook Zedekiah in the plains of Jericho, scattering his army. **9.** They captured the king and brought him to Riblah, to the king of Babylon, who pronounced judgment (a formal decision or sentence) on him. **10.** The king of Babylon killed Zedekiah's sons before his eyes and killed all the princes (high-ranking officials) of Judah in Riblah. **11.** He then blinded (to take away sight) Zedekiah, bound him with bronze (a mixture of copper and tin) chains, and took him to Babylon, where he remained in prison until his death. **12.** In the fifth month, on the tenth day of the month, in the nineteenth year of Nebuchadnezzar, king of Babylon, Nebuzaradan, captain (military leader) of the guard, came to Jerusalem. **13.** He burned (destroyed by fire) the house of the Lord, the king's palace, and all the houses of Jerusalem, including those of great (important). **14.** The Chaldean army broke down the walls of Jerusalem all around. **15.** Nebuzaradan carried away the poor people, the defectors (those who switched sides) who had joined the king of Babylon, and the remaining craftsmen (skilled workers). **16.** He left some of the poor to tend the vineyards (grape farms) and farms. **17.** The Chaldeans broke the bronze pillars, carts, and the bronze Sea from the house of the Lord and carried all the bronze to Babylon. **18.** They also took the pots, shovels, trimmers, bowls, spoons, and all the bronze utensils (tools) used by the priests. **19.** The basins, firepans, bowls, pots, lampstands, spoons, and cups, as well as everything made of solid gold or silver, were taken by the captain of the guard. **20.** The two pillars, one Sea, the twelve bronze bulls beneath it, and the carts— made by King Solomon for the house of the Lord—were beyond measure (incredibly large) in their bronze. **21.** Concerning the pillars: one pillar was eighteen cubits (a unit of measurement, about 18 inches) high, with a circumference (the distance around) of twelve cubits, and its thickness was four fingers; it was hollow. **22.** A bronze capital (decorative top part of a pillar) was atop it, five cubits high, surrounded by a network (mesh) of pomegranates, all made of bronze. The second pillar was the same, with pomegranates. **23.** There were ninety-six pomegranates on the sides; the total number of pomegranates around the network was one hundred. **24.** Nebuzaradan took Seraiah the chief priest, Zephaniah the second priest, and the three doorkeepers (guards). **25.** He also took an officer in charge of the soldiers, seven of the king's close associates, the chief scribe (official record keeper), and sixty men from the city. **26.** Nebuzaradan brought these men to the king of Babylon at Riblah. **27.** The king of Babylon struck them down (killed them) and put them to death at Riblah, in the land of Hamath. Thus, Judah was carried away from its land. **28.** These are the people whom Nebuchadnezzar carried away: in the seventh year, 3,023 Jews; **29.** in the eighteenth year, 832 persons; **30.** in the twenty-third year, Nebuzaradan carried away 745 persons. In total, 4,600 people were taken. **31.** In the thirty-seventh year of Jehoiachin's captivity, on the twenty-fifth day of the twelfth month, King Evil-Merodach of Babylon, in his first year, lifted up the head (gave favor to) of Jehoiachin, king of Judah, and brought him out of prison. **32.** He spoke kindly (with favor) to him and gave him a seat more prominent (higher status) than those of the other kings in Babylon. **33.** Jehoiachin changed from his prison clothes and ate regularly at the king's table for the rest of his life. **34.** The king provided him daily provisions (food) for the rest of his life until his death.

32 – Lamentations

Chapter 1

1. How desolate (empty) the city is, once filled with people! She is like a widow, once powerful among the nations. Now, she is a servant. **2.** She cries bitterly at night, her tears on her cheeks. Among all those who loved her, none offer comfort. Her friends have betrayed (deceived) her and become her enemies. **3.** Judah has gone into captivity (captured), suffering harshly. She lives among the nations, finding no rest. Her enemies overtake (catch) her in distress. **4.** The roads to Zion mourn (grieve), because no one comes to the festivals. Her gates are desolate (empty); her priests groan, her young women suffer, and she is in great sorrow. **5.** Her enemies are in control, and they prosper (succeed). The Lord has afflicted (punished) her because of her many sins. Her children have been taken captive by the enemy. **6**. All the glory of Zion has departed. Her leaders are like deer, helpless and fleeing from their pursuers (chasing enemies). **7**. During her suffering, Jerusalem remembers the good times she had when her people were free. But now, when the enemy defeated her, no one came to her aid. Her enemies mocked her downfall (destruction). **8**. Jerusalem has greatly sinned, so she has become despicable (disliked). Those who once honored her now despise (hate) her, seeing her shame. She sighs and turns away. **9**. Her filth (uncleanness) is on her skirts; she did not consider her future. Therefore, her destruction is great. She has no one to comfort her. "Lord, look at my suffering, for the enemy is victorious!" **10**. The enemy has taken over all her pleasant things. She saw nations enter her holy place—nations that You forbade (forbidden) from entering. **11**. Her people groan, seeking food. They have given away their valuables to stay alive. "Lord, see and consider, for I am scorned (mocked)." **12**. "Is it nothing to you, all who pass by? Look and see if there is any pain like mine, which the Lord has caused in His fierce (strong) anger." **13**. "From above, He sent fire into my bones and overpowered them. He has trapped me and forced me back. He has made me desolate and weak all day long." **14**. "The weight of my sins was tied together and placed on my neck. My strength failed, and the Lord gave me into the hands of those I cannot resist." **15**. "The Lord has crushed (destroyed) all my mighty warriors. He gathered a group to destroy my young men. The Lord trampled on Judah like grapes in a winepress." **16**. "For these things, I weep; my eyes overflow with tears. The one who should comfort me is far away. My children are desolate because the enemy won." **17**. Zion stretches out her hands, but no one comforts her. The Lord has commanded that those around her become her enemies. Jerusalem is seen as unclean (impure) among them. **18**. "The Lord is just (fair), for I rebelled (disobeyed) against His word. Hear, all you nations, and see my pain. My young women and men have been taken captive." **19**. "I called for my lovers, but they deceived (tricked) me. My priests and elders died in the city while searching for food to stay alive." **20**. "Lord, look at my distress (suffering). My soul is troubled, my heart broken, for I have rebelled greatly. Outside, the sword kills, and inside, it's like death." **21**. "They hear my sighs, but no one comforts me. My enemies are glad because You have done this to me. Bring the day You promised, so they may suffer as I have." **22**. "Let their evil (wickedness) be before You, and repay them as You have done to me for my sins. My sighs are many, and my heart is weak."

Chapter 2

1. The Lord has covered the daughter of Zion (Jerusalem) with a cloud of anger. He has thrown down Israel's glory from heaven and no longer remembers His footstool (the temple) on the day of His wrath. **2**. The Lord has consumed (destroyed) without mercy all the homes of Jacob (Israel), bringing down the strongholds (fortresses) of Judah (southern kingdom), defiling (polluting) the kingdom and its leaders. **3**. In His fierce anger, He has cut off Israel's strength (horns, symbols of power). He has withdrawn His right hand (power) from the enemy and burned against Jacob like a raging fire consuming everything around. **4**. Standing as an enemy, He bent His bow (weapon), and with His right hand like an adversary (enemy), He struck down all who pleased Him. He poured out His fury on Zion's tents (Jerusalem) like fire. **5**. The Lord was like an enemy. He consumed Israel and her palaces, destroying her strongholds and increasing mourning (grief) in Judah. **6**. He treated His sanctuary (the temple) violently, like a destroyed garden. He made His appointed feasts (celebrations) and Sabbaths (rest days) forgotten in Zion, scorning (disrespecting) the king and priest in His anger. **7**. The Lord has rejected His altar and abandoned His sanctuary. He gave the palace walls to the enemy, and they make noise in the Lord's house as if it were a feast day. **8**. The Lord planned to destroy Zion's walls. He stretched out His measuring line (tool for judgment) and did not withdraw His hand from destruction. The ramparts (defensive walls) and walls mourn and waste away. **9**. Her gates (entrances) have sunk into the ground; He has destroyed and broken her bars (metal barriers). Her king and princes are among the nations, the Law (God's teachings) is no more, and prophets receive no visions from the Lord. **10**. The elders (older leaders) of Zion sit on the ground in silence, throwing dust on their heads and wearing sackcloth (coarse mourning material). The virgins of Jerusalem bow their heads to the ground. **11**.

My eyes fail with tears, and my heart is troubled. My bile (gall, symbol of deep sorrow) is poured out on the ground because of my people's destruction. Children and infants faint (become weak) in the streets. **12**. They cry to their mothers, "Where is the grain and wine?" They swoon (faint) in the streets like the wounded, their lives slipping away in their mothers' arms. **13**. How can I comfort you, O daughter of Jerusalem? What can I compare to your suffering? Your ruin is as vast as the sea—who can heal you? **14**. Your prophets saw false visions (deceptive predictions), misleading you with deceptive prophecies. They didn't reveal (discover) your sin or bring back your captives (prisoners), but filled you with delusions (false hopes). **15**. Those who pass by clap their hands in mockery. They shake their heads at Jerusalem, saying, "Is this the city called the 'perfection of beauty, the joy of the whole earth'?" **16**. All your enemies open their mouths against you, gnashing their teeth and saying, "We have swallowed her up! This is the day we waited for; we have seen it!" **17**. The Lord has done what He planned. He has fulfilled His word, which He commanded long ago. He has thrown down without pity, and allowed the enemy to rejoice over you, exalting (lifting) the strength of your adversaries. **18**. Their hearts cry to the Lord: "O walls (defensive barriers) of Zion, let tears flow day and night! Do not rest; give your eyes no relief." **19**. "Rise up, cry out in the night, at the beginning of the night watches (times of prayer). Pour out your heart like water before the Lord. Lift your hands to Him for the lives of your children, who faint from hunger at the city gates." **20**. "See, O Lord, and consider! Have You allowed women to eat their own children, those they have nursed? Have You allowed the priests and prophets to be killed in Your sanctuary?" **21**. Young and old lie on the ground in the streets; virgins and young men have fallen by the sword (weapon). You have slaughtered (killed) them in Your anger, showing no mercy. **22**. You have invited terror (fear) as if it were a feast day. On the day of the Lord's anger, there was no refuge (safety) or survivor. The children I bore and raised have been destroyed by my enemies.

Chapter 3

1. I am the man who has suffered under God's wrath (anger). **2**. He led me into darkness (despair), far from light (hope). **3**. He turns His hand against me daily. **4**. He has made me weak and broken my bones. **5**. He surrounded me with bitterness (pain) and sorrow. **6**. He placed me in dark, desolate (empty) places, like the dead. **7**. He trapped me with heavy chains (bonds). **8**. Even when I cry out, He does not listen. **9**. He blocks my way with stones (obstacles), making it hard. **10**. He waits to attack like a bear or lion. **11**. He turned me away, torn me apart, and left me in ruin (destruction). **12**. He made me a target for His arrows. **13**. His arrows pierce (wound) my body. **14**. I am mocked (ridiculed) by my people all day. **15**. He filled me with bitterness (sorrow), making me drink sorrow (bitter drink). **16**. He crushed my teeth with stones (gravel) and covered me in ashes. **17**. My soul lost peace (calm), and I forgot prosperity (success). **18**. I said, "My strength and hope are gone." **19**. Remember my suffering and sorrow (bitterness). **20**. My soul recalls this and sinks (feels heavy) within me. **21**. Yet, I have hope. **22**. Through the Lord's mercy (compassion), we are not destroyed, for His compassion never fails. **23**. His mercies are new every morning; great is His faithfulness (trustworthiness). **24**. "The Lord is my portion" (inheritance), says my soul, "So I hope in Him." **25**. The Lord is good to those who wait for Him, to those who seek (search for) Him. **26**. It is good to wait quietly for His salvation (rescue). **27**. It is good to bear the yoke (burden) in youth. **28**. Let them sit alone in silence, for God has laid this upon them. **29**. Let them humble (submit) themselves, for there may still be hope. **30**. Let them offer their cheek (face) to the one who strikes (hits) them and bear disgrace (shame). **31**. For the Lord will not reject (abandon) forever. **32**. Though He causes sorrow (grief), He will show mercy (compassion). **33**. He does not cause suffering or grief willingly. **34**. It is wrong to crush the prisoners (captives). **35**. It is wrong to deny justice (fair treatment) before the Most High (God). **36**. It is wrong to pervert (twist) justice; the Lord does not approve. **37**. Who can speak and make it happen if the Lord has not commanded it? **38**. Is it not from the mouth of the Most High that disaster (calamity) and good come? **39**. Why should a living person complain when punished for their sins? **40**. Let us examine (inspect) ourselves and return to the Lord. **41**. Let us lift our hearts and hands to God in heaven. **42**. We have sinned (done wrong) and rebelled (defied authority); You have not forgiven us. **43.** You have become angry and pursued (chased) us; You have killed without mercy. **44.** You have hidden Yourself with a cloud (veiled Your presence), so our prayers cannot reach You. **45.** You have made us despised (hated) among the nations. **46.** Our enemies have opened their mouths against us. **47.** Fear and traps (dangers) have come upon us, along with destruction. **48.** My eyes overflow with tears (grief) for the destruction of my people. **49.** My tears flow without stopping, **50.** until the Lord looks down and sees. **51.** My eyes bring sorrow (deep sadness) to my soul because of my people's suffering. **52.** My enemies chased me unjustly like a bird (without reason). **53.** They trapped me in a pit (hole) and threw stones at me. **54.** The waters rose above my head; I thought I was cut off (separated from help). **55.** I called to You, Lord, from the lowest pit. **56.** You heard my voice; do not hide Your ears from my cries for help. **57.** You came near when I called, saying, "Do not fear!" **58.** O Lord, You have defended (protected) my soul; You have redeemed (rescued) my life. **59.** Lord, You have seen how I have been wronged; judge my case. **60.** You have seen their vengeance (revenge) and all their schemes (plans) against me. **61.** You have heard their insults (disrespect), O Lord, and their plotting. **62.** You have seen their mockery (ridicule), their whispers against me all day. **63.** Look at their actions; I am their song of mockery. **64.** Repay them, Lord, according to what they have done. **65.** Give them hearts that are blind (ignorant) to understanding; may Your curse be upon them! **66.** In Your anger, pursue and destroy them from under the heavens of the Lord.

Chapter 4

1 How gold has lost its shine! The precious stones in the temple (holy place) are scattered across the streets. **2** The children of Zion (Jerusalem), once as valuable as fine gold, are now treated like clay pots, the work of a potter. **3** Even jackals (wild dogs) nurse their young, but my people are heartless, like ostriches (large flightless birds) in the desert. **4** The babies are so thirsty that their tongues cling to their mouths; the children beg for bread, but no one gives them any. **5** Those who ate the finest foods now starve in the streets. Those raised in luxury now sit in ashes. **6** The punishment for my people's sins is worse than Sodom's (a city destroyed by God), destroyed in an instant without help. **7** The Nazirites (vowed followers of God), once brighter than snow, whiter than milk, and redder than rubies (precious stones), now look like sapphire (a precious blue gemstone). **8** Now they are darker than soot (black powder), unrecognizable in the streets. Their skin clings to their bones, dry as wood. **9** Those killed by the sword are better off than those who die of hunger, wasting away without food. **10** Compassionate (kind-hearted) women have cooked their own children, who became their food in the destruction of my people. **11** The Lord has poured out His anger; He set a fire in Zion (Jerusalem), consuming its foundations. **12** The kings and all the world would never have believed that enemies could breach (break through) Jerusalem's gates. **13** This happened because of the sins of her prophets (messengers of God) and priests (religious leaders), who shed (spilled) the blood of the righteous. **14** They stumbled in the streets, defiled (unclean) by blood, and no one touched their garments. **15** People cried, "Stay away, you unclean (impure)! Do not touch us!" Those among the nations said, "They will never live here again." **16** The Lord scattered (dispersed) them, no longer showing favor. The people no longer honor the priests or respect the elders (old leaders). **17** Our eyes failed, waiting in vain (without success) for help; we hoped for a nation that couldn't save us. **18** Our enemies tracked (followed) us, so we could not walk the streets. Our end was near, our days numbered (limited). **19** Our pursuers (those chasing us) were faster than eagles (large birds of prey) in the sky, chasing us on the mountains and waiting for us in the wilderness (desolate land). **20** The breath of our life, the anointed of the Lord, was caught in their traps, the one we thought would protect us. **21** Rejoice, O daughter of Edom (an ancient kingdom east of Israel), who lives in Uz (a region, possibly where Job came from)! The cup (God's wrath) of wrath will pass to you, and you will be drunk and exposed. **22** The punishment for your sin, O daughter of Zion (Jerusalem), is complete; God will no longer send you into exile (forced relocation). But He will punish Edom (the kingdom east of Israel) for its sins and expose your wickedness.

Chapter 5

1. Lord, remember what has happened to us; look at our disgrace (shame). **2.** Our land is given to foreigners (strangers), and strangers live in our homes. **3.** We are orphans (without parents), and our mothers are widows (husbands have died). **4.** We buy the water we drink, and even wood (fuel) costs us. **5.** Our enemies chase us; we work hard with no rest (relief). **6.** We turned to Egypt (a country) and Assyria (an empire) for food. **7.** Our ancestors (forebears) sinned and are gone, but we carry their guilt (wrongdoing). **8.** Servants (those who serve) rule us, and no one rescues (saves) us. **9.** We risk our lives for bread (food) because of the sword in the wilderness .**10.** Our skin burns with fever (high temperature) from hunger (need). **11.** Women in Zion (a city) have been abused (mistreated), and young women in Judah's (region) cities suffer. **12.** Princes (leaders) were hanged (executed), and elders (respected leaders) dishonored (disrespected). **13.** Young men worked the mills (grain grinders), and boys carried heavy wood (logs). **14.** Elders no longer gather (meet) at the gate (entrance), and young men no longer play music. **15.** Our joy (happiness) ended; our dances (celebrations) turned to mourning (sorrow). **16.** Our crown (royalty) has fallen off. We are doomed (bound to fail) because we sinned! **17.** Our hearts are weak (tired), and our eyes grow dim (lose focus) from this. **18.** Mount Zion (hill in Jerusalem) is desolate (ruined), and foxes roam (wander) there. **19.** But You, Lord, remain forever; Your throne (seat of power) lasts for generations. **20.** Why have You forgotten (left) us forever and forsaken (abandoned) us for so long? **21.** Bring us back (restore) to You, Lord, and we will be restored (healed); renew (make new) our days as before. **22.** Unless You have completely rejected (turned from) us and are very angry (upset) with us.

33 – Ezekiel

Chapter 1

1. On the 5th day of the 4th month, in the 30th year, I was among the exiles (those forced to live in a foreign land) by the River Chebar when the heavens opened before me, and I saw visions (supernatural images) from God. **2.** This occurred on the 5th day of the 5th year of King Jehoiachin's captivity (when he was taken as a prisoner). **3.** The word of the Lord came directly to Ezekiel, who was a priest (a religious leader) and the son of Buzi, while he was in the land of the Chaldeans (Babylonia), beside the River Chebar. The hand of the Lord rested on him there. **4.** I looked and saw a great whirlwind (a powerful storm) approaching from the north, with a cloud engulfed in flames. Brightness surrounded it, and from within the fire came a radiance that resembled amber (a golden-yellow color). **5.** From the center of this cloud, four living creatures appeared. They had the appearance of human beings, **6.** though each one had four faces and four wings. **7.** Their legs were straight, and their feet resembled the hooves (the bottom part of animal legs) of calves, shining like polished bronze. **8.** Beneath their wings were human hands (used for holding) on all four sides, and each creature had wings and faces. **9.** The wings of the creatures touched one another as they moved forward. They did not turn, but moved in a straight line. **10.** Each creature had the face of a man, with a lion (a large wild animal) on the right side, an ox (a large domesticated animal) on the left, and an eagle (a large bird of prey) in the front. **11.** The creatures' wings extended upward, and two wings of each touched those of the others, while the other two covered their bodies. **12.** As they moved, they followed the direction the Spirit (God's presence) led them, without turning or deviating from their path. **13.** The creatures' appearance was like burning coals of fire (hot, glowing pieces of wood or metal), or like torches. Fire flickered (sudden bursts of light) back and forth among them. **14.** They moved quickly, like flashes (quick movements) of lightning, their speed astonishing. **15.** As I watched, I noticed that each creature had a wheel (a round object that spins) beside it. **16.** The wheels appeared like beryl (a precious stone, typically green or blue), and all four had the same design, looking like one wheel within another. **17.** They moved in all directions without turning or changing their course. **18.** The rims (outer edges) of the wheels were tall and terrifying, and all around them were eyes (seeing organs) that filled the rims. **19.** Whenever the creatures moved, the wheels moved with them. When the creatures lifted off the ground, the wheels followed them. **20.** Wherever the Spirit led, they went, and the wheels moved with them. The Spirit of the living creatures was inside the wheels. **21.** When the creatures moved, the wheels moved too. When the creatures stood still, the wheels stood still. When the creatures lifted off, the wheels lifted with them. **22.** Above the creatures' heads, the sky looked like a crystal (a clear, shiny substance), spread out above them like a firmament. **23.** The creatures each had two wings extended, touching the wings of the others, while the other two covered their bodies. **24.** As they moved, I heard the sound of their wings. It was like the roar (loud, deep noise) of mighty waters (rivers or oceans), like the voice (sound) of the Almighty (God), a noise like the army (large group of soldiers) of God. When they stood still, their wings dropped. **25.** A voice came from above the firmament (the sky or vault of heaven) that rested over their heads. Whenever the creatures stood still, they lowered their wings. **26.** Above the firmament, I saw what appeared to be a throne (a chair for a ruler) made of sapphire (a blue precious stone). And seated on the throne was a figure resembling a man. **27.** From the waist up, the figure radiated amber (a golden-yellow color) with fire surrounding it. From the waist down, it appeared as if fire was flowing, with brightness all around. **28.** The surrounding brilliance looked like a rainbow (a circle of colors in the sky) on a rainy day. This was the appearance of the glory (great beauty or splendor) of the Lord. When I saw it, I fell to the ground, and I heard a voice speaking.

Chapter 2

1. He spoke to me, saying, "Son of man, rise up and stand on your feet, for I have something to say to you." **2.** As He spoke, the Spirit entered me, lifted me up, and I stood on my feet, hearing the voice that addressed me. **3.** Then He said, "I am sending you to the Israelites, a nation that has rebelled against Me. They and their forefathers have continually turned away from Me up to this very day." **4.** They are a people with stubborn hearts and hard faces. I am sending you to them, and you will speak to them, saying, 'This is what the Sovereign Lord declares.' **5.** Whether they listen to you or not—since they are a rebellious nation—they will at least know that a prophet has come among them. **6.** "Do not be afraid of them, son of man, or be disheartened by their words. Though you live among thorns and scorpions (dangerous and hostile people), do not let their threats or glares intimidate you, for they are a rebellious people." **7.** You must speak My words to them, whether they choose to listen or not, for their rebellion is evident. **8.** But as for you, son of man, listen carefully to what I say. Do not be like them, stubborn and rebellious. Open your mouth and take in what I give you." **9.** As I looked, I saw a hand stretched out toward me, holding a scroll. **10.** He unfolded the scroll before me, and I saw that it was covered with writing on both sides— full of lamentations, mourning, and woe.

Chapter 3

1. Then He spoke to me: "Son of man, take what you find here, eat this scroll (a rolled-up piece of parchment or paper), and go speak to the people of Israel." **2.** I opened my mouth, and He caused me to eat the scroll. **3.** He said, "Son of man, fill your stomach with this scroll I give you." After eating it, it was as sweet as honey in my mouth. **4.** He then commanded me, "Son of man, go to the house of Israel and speak My words to them." **5.** I am not sending you to a people whose language is strange or hard for you to understand, but to the house of Israel, **6.** to a nation whose language you know well. If I had sent you to a distant nation with a language you didn't understand, they would have listened to you. **7.** But the house of Israel will not listen to you because they refuse to listen to Me; they are a stubborn (refusing to change) and hard-hearted people. **8.** I have made your face as hard as theirs, and your forehead as hard as theirs. **9.** Like flint (a hard stone), I have made your forehead. Do not be afraid of them or discouraged by their angry looks, even though they are rebellious." **10.** He said to me, "Son of man, take all My words to heart and listen carefully to what I speak to you. **11.** Go to the captives (people held in captivity), to the children of your people, and tell them, 'This is what the Lord God says,' whether they listen or refuse to listen." **12.** Then the Spirit lifted me up, and I heard behind me a loud voice saying, "Blessed be the glory of the Lord from His place!" **13.** I also heard the sound of the wings of the living creatures (angelic beings) as they touched one another, and the noise of the wheels beside them, along with a great, thunderous sound. **14.** The Spirit lifted me up and took me away, and I went in bitterness (feeling of sorrow), with the heat of my spirit, but the hand of the Lord was strong upon me. **15.** I came to the captives at Tel Abib (a settlement), by the River Chebar (a river in Babylon), and I sat where they sat. I was astonished and remained there among them for seven days. **16.** After seven days, the word of the Lord came to me. **17.** He said, "Son of man, I have appointed you as a watchman (one who warns others) for the house of Israel. So listen to what I say and give them My warning. **18.** When I say to the wicked (evil people), 'You will surely die,' and you do not warn them or speak to them to turn from their wicked ways, that wicked person will die in their sin, but I will hold you responsible for their blood. **19.** If you warn the wicked and they do not turn from their wickedness, they will die in their sin, but you will have saved yourself. **20.** If a righteous person (a good person) turns from their righteousness and does evil, and I set a stumbling block (an obstacle) before them, they will die. If you do not warn them, their death will be on your hands, and their righteous deeds will not be remembered. **21.** But if you warn the righteous and they do not sin, they will live because they took your warning. You will have saved yourself as well." **22.** Then the hand of the Lord was upon me, and He said to me, "Go out into the open, and I will speak to you there." **23.** I went out into the open, and I saw the glory of the Lord standing there, the same as I had seen by the River Chebar. I fell on my face. **24.** The Spirit entered me and set me on my feet. He spoke to me, saying, "Go, shut yourself inside your house. **25.** You, son of man, they will bind you with ropes (cords) so that you cannot go out among them. **26.** I will make your tongue stick to the roof of your mouth, and you will be silent, unable to rebuke them, for they are a rebellious house. **27.** But when I speak to you, I will open your mouth, and you will say to them, 'This is what the Lord God says.' Whoever listens, let them listen; whoever refuses, let them refuse, for they are a rebellious house."

Chapter 4

1. "Son of man, take a clay tablet and set it in front of you. Draw a depiction of the city, Jerusalem, on it. **2.** Construct a siege around it— build a wall of siege against it, pile up a mound around it, set up camps, and place battering rams (large tools for breaking walls) all around. **3.** Take an iron plate and place it between yourself and the city, as though it were a wall. Face the city, and it will be under siege; you will lay siege to it. This will serve as a sign for the house of Israel. **4.** "Lie down on your left side and place the guilt of the house of Israel on it. As long as you lie there, you will carry their iniquity (sin). **5.** I have appointed 390 days for you to bear the sin of Israel, which corresponds to the number of years they have sinned. **6.** Once these 390 days are completed, turn over and lie on your right side, bearing the sin of the house of Judah (the southern kingdom). You will lie for 40 days, as I have assigned each day to represent a year. **7.** Direct your attention toward the siege of Jerusalem, expose your arm, and prophesy against it. **8.** I will prevent you from turning from side to side until the days of your siege are completed. **9.** "Take for yourself wheat, barley, beans, lentils, millet, and spelt (grains), and put them together in one container. You will bake bread from this mixture, and during the 390 days that you lie on your side, you will eat it. **10.** Your daily food will be measured out: 20 shekels (a small weight) per day, and you will eat it at regular intervals. **11.** For your drink, you will take one-sixth of a hin (a unit of liquid measure) of water each time and drink it at intervals. **12.** Prepare the bread as barley cakes and bake it using human waste (excrement) in the sight of the people." **13.** Then the Lord said, "This is how the children of Israel will eat their defiled bread (unclean food) among the Gentiles, in the places where I will scatter them." **14.** I responded, "Ah, Lord God, I have never defiled myself. From my youth until now, I have never eaten anything that died naturally or was torn by animals, nor have I ever eaten anything unclean." **15.** The Lord said to me, "Very well, I will provide you with cow dung instead of human waste, and you will prepare your bread over it." **16.** He went on to say, "Son of man, I will cut off the supply of bread in Jerusalem. They will eat their bread by weight, in anxiety, and will drink water by measure, in fear. **17.** They will be without bread and water, and they will despair, each person wasting away because of their sin."

Chapter 5

1. "And you, son of man, take a sharp sword—like a barber's razor (a sharp tool used for shaving)—and use it to shave your head and beard. Then take scales (a tool used to weigh) to weigh the hair and divide it up. **2.** Burn one-third of the hair in the middle of the city when the siege (military operation where a city is surrounded) days are over. Take another third and strike it with a sword (a weapon) around the city. Scatter the last third to the wind (away from their land), and I will draw a sword to pursue them. **3.** Take a few strands of the hair and tie them in the edge of your garment (clothing). **4.** Then, take some of the hair and throw it into the fire, where it will burn. A fire will spread from it and consume the entire house of Israel. **5.** "This is what the Lord God says: 'This is Jerusalem. I have set her in the center of the nations and surrounded her with other countries. **6.** Yet she has rebelled (refused to obey) against My laws, acting more wickedly than the nations around her, refusing to follow My decrees (official orders), and ignoring My statutes (rules). **7.** Therefore, this is what the Lord God says: 'Because you have been more disobedient than the surrounding nations, not walking in My laws or keeping My judgments (decisions), nor even following the standards of the nations around you, **8.** I am against you. I will bring judgment upon you in front of the nations. **9.** I will do things among you that I have never done before, and will never do again, because of all your detestable (hated, morally wrong) acts. **10.** Therefore, in your midst (among you), fathers will eat their sons, and sons will eat their fathers. I will bring judgment upon you, and those who remain will be scattered to the winds (away from their land). **11.** As I live,' declares the Lord God, 'because you have defiled (polluted) My sanctuary (holy place) with your detestable acts and abominations (extreme evil), I will reduce you. I will show no pity, nor spare you. **12.** One-third of you will die from disease (illness) and famine (lack of food) in your midst; one-third will fall by the sword all around you, and I will scatter another third to the winds, pursuing them with a sword. **13.** Thus, My anger will be spent (used up), and I will bring My fury (intense anger) to rest upon them. They will know that I, the Lord, have spoken in My zeal (intense passion) when I have executed My judgment on them. **14.** I will make you a desolation (ruin) and a reproach (shame) among the nations around you, a lesson to all who pass by. **15.** You will become a reproach (shame), a mockery (scorn), and a warning to the nations around you when I carry out My judgments against you in anger, fury, and intense rebuke (sharp criticism). I, the Lord, have spoken. **16.** When I send the terrible arrows (weapons) of famine (lack of food) against you—arrows that bring destruction—I will increase the famine and cut off your food supply. **17.** I will send famine and wild beasts (dangerous animals) against you, and they will take your children. Disease and bloodshed (killing) will sweep through you, and I will bring the sword against you. I, the Lord, have spoken"

Chapter 6

1. The Lord's word (message) came to me, saying: **2.** "Son of man, direct your attention to the mountains (hills) of Israel and speak against them. **3.** Tell the mountains, hills, ravines (narrow valleys), and valleys, 'Listen to what the Lord God has to say! I will bring the sword (war) upon you and tear down your high places (places of worship). **4.** Your altars (places of sacrifice) will lie in ruins, your incense altars (altars for burning incense) will be shattered, and I will cast the slain (dead bodies) before your idols (false gods). **5.** I will scatter the bones (body parts) of Israel's people before their idols, and the dead (corpses) will be spread out around your altars. **6.** Your cities will be destroyed, and your high places (worship sites) will be left desolate (empty). The altars you built will be ruined, your idols (false gods) broken, and your incense altars (sacred places) torn down. Everything you've made will be abolished (ended). **7.** The slain (dead bodies) will lie among you, and you will then know that I am the Lord. **8.** Yet, I will leave a remnant (small group), those who escape the sword (war) when you are scattered among the nations. **9.** Those who survive will remember Me in the lands where they are carried away, for their hearts (feelings) were unfaithful (disloyal) to Me, and their eyes were turned toward idols (false gods). They will loathe (hate) themselves for the evil (wickedness) they did in their detestable (hateful) practices. **10.** They will know that I am the Lord, and that I did not speak in vain (for nothing) when I said I would bring this calamity (disaster) upon them.' **11.** The Lord God says: 'Clap your hands (strike together) and stomp your feet (hit the ground), crying out in grief for the evil (wickedness) of Israel. Sword (war), famine (starvation), and plague (disease) will strike them. **12.** those who are far off will die by plague (disease), those near will fall by the sword (war), and those who are under siege (surrounded) will perish from famine (hunger). I will unleash My fury (anger) upon them. **13.** You will know that I am the Lord when you see

the dead (slain) lying around their idols (false gods) and altars (sacrificial places), on every high hill, on all the mountaintops (high places), beneath every leafy tree (green tree), and under every thick oak (strong tree) where they offered incense (burned prayers) to their idols (false gods). **14.** I will stretch out (reach out) My hand against them and turn their land into a desolate (empty) wasteland, even more desolate than the wilderness of Diblah (a place). Wherever they live, they will know that I am the Lord.'"

Chapter 7

1. The word (message) of the Lord came to me, saying, **2.** "Son of man, this is what the Lord God declares to Israel's land: 'The end has arrived! The end is upon the four corners of the land. **3.** This is your final moment. I will bring My wrath against you, judging you by your actions, and I will repay you for all your sinful practices (evil deeds). **4.** I will not show you any mercy, nor will I spare you. You will pay the full price for your conduct, and your abominations will be right in front of you. Then you will know that I am the Lord!'" **5.** "This is what the Lord God says: 'A disaster, a single, great disaster is coming! Behold, it is here! **6.** The end has come; it is upon you. The day has dawned, and it has arrived! **7.** Calamity has come to you, you who live in the land. The time is now; a day of anguish is near, and there will be no joy on the mountains. **8.** I will soon pour out My anger on you and spend My wrath upon you. I will judge you based on your actions and repay you for all your sinful practices (evil deeds). **9.** My eyes will show no pity, and I will not spare you. I will give you the consequences of your ways, and your abominations (evil acts) will be in your midst. Then you will know that I am the Lord who brings judgment.' **10.** 'The day has arrived! Look, it has come! Destruction has been unleashed. The rod has sprouted, and pride has bloomed. **11.** Violence has risen, becoming a rod of wickedness (evil). No one will remain. Their entire multitude will be gone, and there will be no mourning for them. **12.** The time is here; the day is drawing near. Let not the buyer rejoice or the seller mourn, for My wrath is on the whole people. **13.** The seller will not get back what he has sold, even if he is still alive. This vision affects the entire people, and it will not be reversed. No one will find strength in their iniquity (sin).' **14.** 'They have sounded the trumpet and prepared for battle, but no one will go to war, for My anger is upon all their people. **15.** The sword (war) lies outside, and within, there is disease (pestilence) and hunger (famine). Those in the fields will die by the sword, and those in the cities will be consumed by famine and disease (plague). **16.** The survivors will escape and flee to the mountains like doves in the valleys, each one grieving over their own iniquity (wrongdoing). **17.** Every hand will grow weak, and every knee will be as unsteady as water. **18.** They will be dressed in sackcloth (mourning clothes); terror will cover them. Their faces will be filled with shame, and all their heads will be bald (shaved heads). **19.** They will throw their silver into the streets, and their gold will be treated as trash. Their wealth will not be able to save them in the day of the Lord's wrath. It will not satisfy their hunger, nor fill their stomachs, for these things have become a stumbling block (trap) to their sinfulness (wickedness).' **20.** 'As for the beauty of their ornaments, they used to boast about it. But they made these things into idols of their abominations (false gods), detestable in My sight. Therefore, I will treat them like refuse (garbage). **21.** I will give them as plunder to foreigners, and as spoil to the wicked (evil ones) of the earth, who will defile them. **22.** I will turn My face away from them, and they will desecrate My sacred place. Robbers will enter and defile it.' **23.** 'Make a chain (bind them together), for the land is filled with crimes of blood (murder) and the city is full of violence. **24.** Therefore, I will bring the worst of the nations, and they will take possession of their houses. The pride of the mighty will be humbled, and their sacred places will be profaned. **25.** Destruction is on the horizon. They will seek peace, but there will be none. **26.** Calamity will follow calamity, and rumors will spread from one place to another. They will seek a prophet's vision, but the law (God's commandments) will no longer be found with the priests, and counsel will be absent from the elders. **27.** The king will mourn, the prince will be wrapped in despair, and the hands of the common people will shake with fear. I will act according to their deeds and judge them according to what they deserve. Then they will know that I am the Lord!'

Chapter 8

1. In the sixth year, on the sixth month, and the fifth day of the month, while I sat in my house with the elders of Judah gathered before me, the hand (power) of the Lord God came upon me. **2.** I looked, and I saw a vision that resembled fire. From His waist downward, the figure was fire; from His waist upward, it appeared bright and shining, like the color of amber. **3.** He extended the form of a hand, took hold of a lock of my hair, and the Spirit (God's presence) lifted me up between earth and heaven. He brought me in visions of God to Jerusalem, to the northern gate of the inner court, where the image of jealousy (idol) stood, which provoked God's anger. **4.** And there, I saw the glory (presence) of the God of Israel, as I had seen in the vision when I was in the plain. **5.** Then He said to me, "Son of man, lift your eyes to the north." So I looked northward, and there, by the altar gate, stood the image of jealousy. **6.** And He said to me, "Son of man, do you see the wickedness they are committing here, the detestable (sinful) acts that the house of Israel is performing? These are causing me to move away from my sanctuary. But wait, you will see even greater abominations." **7.** He took me to the entrance of the court, and as I looked, I saw a hole in the wall. **8.** He said to me, "Son of man, dig through the wall." When I dug, I found a door. **9.** And He said to me, "Enter and see the evil (sin) they are committing here." **10.** So I entered, and to my shock, I saw every kind of creeping creature, detestable animals, and all the idols of the house of Israel, painted on the walls around me. **11.** Seventy elders (leaders) of the house of Israel stood before these images. Among them was Jaazaniah son of Shaphan. Each man held a censer (container for incense), and a thick cloud of incense rose up. **12.** He said to me, "Son of man, have you seen what the elders of Israel are doing in the dark? Each one in the room of his idols? They say, 'The Lord does not see us; the Lord has abandoned the land.'" **13.** He continued, "Turn again, and you will see even greater abominations they are committing." **14.** He brought me to the door of the north gate of the Lord's house, and to my horror, I saw women weeping for Tammuz (a Babylonian god). **15.** He asked me, "Son of man, do you see this? Turn again, and you will see even worse things." **16.** He took me into the inner court of the Lord's house, and there, at the entrance of the temple, between the porch and the altar, were about twenty-five men. Their backs were turned to the temple, and they faced the east, worshiping the sun. **17.** He said to me, "Son of man, do you see this? Is it not enough that the people of Judah commit these detestable acts? They have filled the land with violence, and they have provoked Me to anger. And now they bring a branch to their noses (a gesture of defiance against God)." **18.** "Therefore, I will act in My fury. I will not show any mercy, nor will I spare them. Even if they cry out loudly in My ears, I will not listen to them."

Chapter 9

1. Then He called out in my hearing with a loud voice, saying, "Let those who have charge over the city draw near, each with a deadly weapon (instrument of harm) in his hand." **2.** Suddenly, six men arrived from the direction of the northern upper gate (entrance), each one holding a battle-ax. Among them stood a man clothed in linen (fine cloth), carrying an inkhorn at his side. They all gathered near the bronze altar. **3.** The glory (radiant presence) of the God of Israel had moved from the cherub to the entrance of the temple. He then called to the man dressed in linen, who had the inkhorn. **4.** And the Lord instructed him, "Go through the city of Jerusalem, marking (identifying) the foreheads of those who mourn and weep over the detestable acts done here." **5.** To the others He said in my hearing, "Follow him through the city and strike down (destroy) without mercy or pity." **6.** "Kill all without exception—old and young men, maidens (unmarried women), children, and women—but spare anyone with the mark. Start at My sanctuary." So they began with the elders (leaders) in front of the temple. **7.** Then He commanded them, "Defile (make impure) the temple by filling its courts with the slain. Go out!" And they went through the city, carrying out the order. **8.** As they proceeded, I was left alone, and I fell on my face, crying out, "Ah, Lord God! Will You destroy all that remains of Israel while pouring out Your wrath on Jerusalem?" **9.** He replied, "The iniquity (wickedness) of the house of Israel and Judah is exceedingly great, and the land is filled with bloodshed, the city with corruption; for they say, 'The Lord has forsaken the land, and the Lord does not see us!'" **10.** "So I too will have no pity (compassion) and will repay them according to their

actions." **11.** Just then, the man dressed in linen with the inkhorn (small container for ink) returned and reported, "I have done as You commanded."

Chapter 10

1. I looked up, and above the cherubim (heavenly creatures) in the sky, I saw something resembling a sapphire stone, shaped like a throne. **2.** Then the Lord spoke to the man wearing linen (a type of cloth), instructing him, "Go into the area with the wheels (mysterious objects), beneath the cherub, gather burning coals (hot, glowing embers) from among the cherubim, and scatter them over the city." As I watched, he entered. **3.** The cherubim stood on the southern side of the temple when the man entered, and the cloud (a visible sign of God's presence) filled the inner courtyard. **4.** The glory of the Lord (God's divine presence) ascended from the cherubim and paused at the entrance of the temple. The entire house was filled with the cloud, and the courtyard was illuminated by God's glorious brightness. **5.** The sound of the cherubim's wings was audible even in the outer court, resembling the voice of the Almighty God (the all-powerful Creator) speaking. **6.** As God commanded the man in linen, "Take fire from the wheels, from among the cherubim," the man approached the wheels. **7.** One of the cherubim extended its hand to the fire among them, took it, and handed it to the man dressed in linen. He received it and exited. **8.** Beneath the wings (large feathered limbs) of the cherubim, I saw what seemed to be the form of human hands. **9.** I looked closely, and saw that there were four wheels beside the cherubim, one for each cherub. The wheels had the appearance of beryl stones (a greenish gemstone). **10.** Each of the wheels had a design similar to a wheel within a wheel. **11.** When the cherubim moved, they traveled in any of the four directions without turning, always moving forward in the direction their heads were facing. **12.** Their entire bodies—including their backs, hands, wings, and the wheels—were covered with eyes (symbols of all-knowing vision) all around. **13.** The wheels were called "Wheels" when I heard them named. **14.** Each cherub had four faces: one like a cherub, one like a man, one like a lion, and one like an eagle. **15.** Then the cherubim lifted off the ground. These were the living creatures (beings with life and motion) I had seen by the River Chebar (a river in Babylon). **16.** As the cherubim moved, the wheels moved along beside them. When the cherubim's wings were lifted to fly, the wheels did not separate from them. **17.** Whenever the cherubim stopped, the wheels also stopped. And when one rose, the other rose too, because the spirit (life force or energy) of the living creatures was in the wheels. **18.** The glory of the Lord departed from the threshold (entrance) of the temple and stopped above the cherubim. **19.** The cherubim lifted their wings and soared in my presence. As they moved out, the wheels accompanied them. They halted at the eastern gate (gate on the east side) of the Lord's temple, with the glory of the God of Israel hovering above them. **20.** These were the same living creatures I had seen by the River Chebar, and I recognized them as cherubim. **21.** Each cherub had four faces and four wings, and beneath their wings, I could see the shape of human hands. **22.** Their faces were identical to those I had seen by the River Chebar, and they moved forward in a straight line.

Chapter 11

1. The Spirit (God's presence) lifted me and transported me to the East Gate of the Lord's temple, which faces eastward. There, at the gate's entrance, I saw twenty-five men, including Jaazaniah, son of Azzur, and Pelatiah, son of Benaiah—leaders (princes) among the people. **2.** The Lord spoke to me, saying, "Son of man, these men devise wicked plans and offer harmful advice (evil counsel) in this city." **3.** They say, 'It is not yet time to build houses; the city is our pot, and we are the meat within.' **4.** Therefore, son of man, prophesy (speak prophetically) against them!" **5.** Then the Spirit of the Lord came upon me, instructing me to say, "This is what the Lord declares: 'O house of Israel, I know the thoughts and intentions within your hearts. **6.** You have increased the count of the slain in this city, filling its streets with the dead.' **7.** "For this reason, the Lord God says: 'The bodies left in the city are the meat, and the city itself is the pot. However, I will remove you from it. **8.** Although you feared the sword, I will bring that sword upon you,' says the Lord God. **9.** 'I will take you out of the city and hand you over to strangers who will execute My judgments against you. **10.** You will fall by the sword, and I will judge you at Israel's borders, so that you will know I am the Lord.' **11.** 'This city will no longer be your pot, and you will no longer be the meat within it, for I will judge you at Israel's borders. **12.** Then you will understand that I am the Lord, because you did not follow My laws or uphold My judgments, instead adopting the customs (practices) of the surrounding nations.'" **13.** While I was prophesying, Pelatiah, son of Benaiah, passed away. I fell face-down, crying out loudly, "Alas, Lord God! Will You destroy all who remain in Israel?" **14.** Then the word of the Lord came to me again, saying, **15.** "Son of man, the people of Jerusalem have spoken against your relatives, your fellow countrymen, and the whole house of Israel, saying, 'Stay far from the Lord; this land is now ours to possess.' **16.** Therefore, tell them, 'This is what the Lord God says: Though I have scattered them among the nations and dispersed them across countries, I will be for them a small sanctuary (safe place) wherever they have gone.' **17.** Tell them as well, 'This is what the Lord God says: I will gather you from the nations, bring you back from the countries where you were scattered, and restore you to the land of Israel.' **18.** Upon their return, they will remove all detestable (wicked) practices and abominations (disgusting practices) from the land. **19.** I will unite their hearts and place within them a new spirit (inner strength). I will replace their hard hearts (stubborn hearts) with a heart of flesh (soft, responsive heart), **20.** enabling them to walk in My statutes (rules), obey My laws, and follow them. They will be My people, and I will be their God. **21.** But those who remain attached to their detestable practices and abominations, I will bring the consequences of their actions (deeds) upon their heads," says the Lord God. **22.** Then the cherubim (heavenly creatures) lifted their wings, and beside them were the wheels. Above them rose the glory (divine presence) of the God of Israel. **23.** The glory of the Lord left the city and rested on the mountain (high hill) east of the city. **24.** The Spirit then lifted me up, bringing me in a vision to the land of the Chaldeans (Babylonians), where the exiles (captives) were. The vision I had seen faded from me. **25.** I then conveyed to the exiles (captives) everything that the Lord had shown me.

Chapter 12

1. The word (message) of the Lord came to me, saying: **2.** "Son of man, you live among a rebellious (stubborn) nation—one that has eyes but refuses to see, and ears yet will not listen; they are a stubborn (unyielding) people. **3.** Therefore, son of man, prepare (get ready) your belongings as if for exile (forced relocation). Pack them in the daylight, in front of everyone, as though you are being taken away. Move from your place to another before their eyes; perhaps they will notice, even though they are a rebellious people. **4.** Pack your belongings in their sight during the day, as if you were heading into exile, and in the evening, go out in front of them, as if setting out for captivity. **5.** Dig (make a hole) through the wall in their sight, and take out your things through it. **6.** In their view, carry your belongings on your shoulders at twilight (evening), covering your face so you cannot see the ground, for I have made you a sign (symbol) to the house of Israel." **7.** So I did exactly as I was instructed. During the day, I packed my belongings as though I were going into exile, and in the evening, I dug through the wall with my hands, carrying my things at twilight on my shoulder in their presence. **8.** The next morning, a message from the Lord came to me, saying, **9.** "Son of man, did the rebellious people of Israel not ask you, 'What is it you're doing?' **10.** Explain to them that this is what the Lord God says: 'This warning is directed at the prince in Jerusalem and all the people of Israel living there.' **11.** Tell them, 'I am serving as a sign for you. What I have done will also be done to them—they will be taken away into captivity.' **12.** The prince will gather his things on his shoulder at evening and try to escape; they will dig through the wall to carry their belongings out, and he will cover his face so he cannot see the ground around him. **13.** But I will lay a net to ensnare him, and he will be caught in My trap. I will bring him to Babylon, to the Chaldean land, yet he will not see it and will die there. **14.** I will scatter all who support him—those close to him and his warriors—in every direction, and I will pursue them with My sword. **15.** Then, when I scatter them among nations and disperse them across lands, they will realize that I am the Lord. **16.** However, I will spare a few from the sword, famine, and disease, so they may speak of their offensive deeds among the nations where they go, and then they will know that I am the Lord." **17.** Once again, the Lord's message came to me, saying, **18.** "Son of man,

eat your bread with shaking and drink your water with fear and anxiety. **19.** Say to the people of this land, 'The Lord God has a message for the people of Jerusalem and all Israel: They will eat their bread in fear and drink water in dread because the land will be stripped of its inhabitants due to the wickedness of those who dwell in it. **20.** The cities will be left in ruins, and the land will become a wasteland, and then they will understand that I am the Lord.'" **21.** The Lord's message came to me, saying, **22.** "Son of man, what is this saying that people of Israel have—'The days are dragging on, and every vision has failed'? **23.** Tell them, 'This is what the Lord God says: I will put an end to this saying, and it will no longer be repeated in Israel.' Instead, say to them, 'The days are coming soon, and every vision will be fulfilled. **24.** No more false (deceptive) visions or flattering (misleading) prophecies will come from the house of Israel. **25.** For I am the Lord. I speak, and what I say will happen (be fulfilled); there will be no more delay (postponement). In your time, O rebellious (unwilling to submit) house, I will speak the word and bring it to pass," declares the Lord God.' **26.** Again, the word of the Lord came to me, saying, **27.** "Son of man, the house of Israel is saying, 'The vision (prophecy) he sees is for many days ahead, and he speaks of distant times.' **28.** Therefore, tell them, 'This is what the Lord God says: "None of My words will be delayed any longer; whatever I speak will be fulfilled (come true)," declares the Lord God.'"

Chapter 13

1. The word of the Lord came to me, saying: **2.** "Son of man, prophesy against the prophets of Israel who claim to speak on My behalf, and tell those who speak from their own hearts, 'Listen to the word of the Lord!' **3.** The Lord God declares, 'Woe to the foolish prophets who follow their own spirit (desires) and see nothing!' **4.** Israel's prophets are like foxes (deceptive and cunning) in the desert. **5.** You have not gone up to the gaps in the walls to repair them so that the house of Israel may stand firm in battle on the day of the Lord. **6.** They have seen worthless (vain) visions and practiced false divination (foretelling), saying, 'The Lord has spoken!' but I did not send them, and they hope their words will be confirmed. **7.** Have you not seen a useless vision and spoken false divination? You say, 'The Lord says,' but I have not spoken to you." **8.** Therefore, the Lord God says: "Because you speak foolishness and see lies, I am against you," declares the Lord God. **9.** My hand will be against the prophets who see nothing but emptiness and speak lies. They will not be included in My people's assembly, nor will their names be written in the records of Israel, nor will they enter the land of Israel. Then you will know that I am the Lord. **10.** They have misled My people by saying, 'Peace!' when there was no peace—like those who build a wall and cover it with untempered mortar (weak, ineffective material). **11.** Tell those who plaster it with untempered mortar that it will fall. A heavy rain will come, great hailstones will fall, and a powerful wind will tear it down. **12.** When the wall collapses, they will ask, 'Where is the mortar with which you plastered it?' **13.** So the Lord God says: "I will send a stormy wind in My wrath, and there will be a heavy downpour in My anger, along with great hailstones to destroy it. **14.** I will tear down the wall that you covered with untempered mortar, bringing it down to the ground, exposing its foundation. It will crumble, and you will be destroyed in its ruins. Then you will know that I am the Lord. **15.** I will fulfill My fury on the wall and on those who plastered it with untempered mortar, and I will declare, 'The wall is no more, and so are those who plastered it, **16.** the prophets of Israel who prophesy concerning Jerusalem, seeing visions of peace for her when there is no peace,'" declares the Lord God. **17.** "Likewise, son of man, turn your face toward the women of your people who prophesy from their own hearts; prophesy against them, **18.** and say, 'Thus says the Lord God: "Woe to the women who sew magic charms (enchantments) on their sleeves and make veils for the heads of people of all kinds to ensnare souls! Are you hunting the souls of My people and keeping yourselves alive? **19.** Will you profane (dishonor) Me among My people for a few handfuls of barley and pieces of bread, killing those who should not die, and keeping alive those who should not live, by lying to My people who listen to lies?" **20.** Therefore, the Lord God declares: "I am against your magic charms that you use to hunt souls like birds. I will tear them from your arms, and let the souls you trap go free, **21.** I will also tear off your veils and rescue My people from your hands. They will no longer be prey in your grip, and you will know that I am the Lord. **22.** Because with your lies, you have made the hearts of the righteous sad, though I did not grieve them. You have strengthened the hands of the wicked, making them unwilling to turn from their wickedness and save their lives. **23.** Therefore, you will no longer see foolish visions or practice divination. I will rescue My people from your hands, and you will know that I am the Lord."

Chapter 14

1. Some of Israel's elders came and sat before me. **2.** Then, the word of the Lord came to me, saying: **3.** "Son of man, these men have idols (objects of worship) in their hearts, and they place before them things that lead them to sin. Should I allow them to come to Me for guidance? **4.** Therefore, speak to them and say, 'This is what the Lord God says: "If anyone from Israel holds idols in their hearts and places obstacles (things that cause sin) before them, and then seeks a prophet's counsel, I, the Lord, will answer them according to the number of their idols. **5.** This is so I can capture the hearts (minds) of the house of Israel, as their idols have caused them to be separated (alienated) from Me." **6.** So, speak to Israel, 'This is what the Lord God says: "Repent (turn away), turn from your idols, and remove your faces from all your abominable (wicked) practices. **7.** Anyone—whether an Israelite or a foreigner among them—who separates himself from Me, sets idols in his heart, and places stumbling blocks before him, then comes to a prophet for guidance, I will answer him Myself. **8.** I will oppose (turn against) that person, making them a symbol (sign) and a proverb (saying), and I will cut them off from My people. Then you will know that I am the Lord." **9.** If a prophet is led (influenced) to speak, I am the one who has persuaded him. I will stretch My hand out against him and destroy him (bring ruin) from My people Israel. **10.** The prophet and the one who sought his counsel will bear the burden of their iniquity (sin); their punishment will be the same. **11.** Then the house of Israel will no longer wander (go astray) from Me, nor will they defile (desecrate) themselves with their sin. They will be My people, and I will be their God," says the Lord God. **12.** The word of the Lord came to me again, saying: **13.** "Son of man, when a land persistently (constantly) sins against Me, I will act. I will cut off its food supply (bread), bring famine (lack of food), and remove both man and beast from it. **14.** Even if Noah, Daniel, and Job were in that land, they would save only themselves through their righteousness (integrity)," declares the Lord God. **15.** "If I cause wild animals (dangerous creatures) to roam the land and make it desolate (empty), so that no one can pass through due to the beasts, **16.** even if Noah, Daniel, and Job were present, they would only save themselves," says the Lord God, "and the land would remain desolate. **17.** Or if I send a sword (weapon of war) through the land, commanding it to cut off both man and beast, **18.** even if these three men were in it, as I live," says the Lord God, "they would save only themselves, not their sons or daughters. **19.** Or if I send a plague (disease) on the land, pouring out My fury (anger) in blood, cutting off both man and beast, **20.** even if Noah, Daniel, and Job were in it, as I live," says the Lord God, "they would save only themselves through their righteousness." **21.** For this is what the Lord God says: "How much worse will it be when I send My four severe judgments (punishments)—the sword, famine, wild beasts, and pestilence—to destroy man and beast in Jerusalem? **22.** Yet, behold, a remnant (remaining survivors) will be left in it—sons and daughters who will be taken out. They will come to you, and when you see their actions and behavior, you will be comforted (consoled) over the disaster I have brought upon Jerusalem, and all I have done there. **23.** When they come to you, they will bring comfort. You will see their deeds and know that I have acted with purpose (cause) in all that I have done," declares the Lord God.

Chapter 15

1. The word (message) of the Lord came to me, saying, **2.** "Son of man, how is the wood (material) of the vine any better than any other wood, the vine branch that grows among the trees of the forest? **3.** Can people use it to make anything useful? Can they make a peg (hook) to hang something on it? **4.** No, instead it is thrown into the fire (burned) to be burned. The fire consumes (eats) both ends, and the middle is burned as well. Is it good for anything? **5.** Even when it was whole (unburned), it was useless for any work. How much less will it be useful when the fire has burned it up? **6.** Therefore, this is what the Lord God says: 'Just like the wood of the vine among the trees of the forest, which I have given to the fire to burn, so I will give up (hand over) the people of Jerusalem. **7.** I will turn my face (look) against them. They will escape one fire, but another will consume (destroy) them. Then you will know (understand) that I am the Lord when I oppose them. **8.** I will make the land desolate (empty) because they have remained unfaithful,' says the Lord God."

Chapter 16

1. The word (message) of the Lord came to me once again, saying, **2.** "Son of man, make sure Jerusalem is aware of her deep corruption (immoral actions), **3.** and tell her: 'This is what the Lord God says about Jerusalem: "Your origin (birth) and your birth come from the land of Canaan; your father was an Amorite (a Canaanite tribe), and your mother was a Hittite (another Canaanite tribe). **4.** When you were born, your umbilical cord (the cord connecting you to your mother) was never cut, nor were you bathed in water to purify you; you weren't rubbed with salt (used to preserve) or wrapped in swaddling cloths (baby clothes). **5.** No one showed you any pity or mercy (compassion); no one did anything to care for you. You were abandoned, thrown out into the open field, despised (hated) from the moment you were born. **6.** When I saw you struggling (fighting for survival) in your own blood, I passed by and said, "Live!" Yes, I spoke life into you, saying, "Live!" **7.** I helped you grow like a plant in the field; you flourished, matured, and became very beautiful. Your breasts developed, your hair grew long, but you were still naked and exposed. **8.** Later, when I passed by you again and saw that you were in your prime, I covered your nakedness (exposed body) with My wings (protection), swearing an oath and making a covenant (agreement) with you. You became Mine,' declares the Lord God. **9.** Then I washed you with water, thoroughly cleansing you of your blood, and anointed (rubbed with oil) you with precious oil. **10.** I dressed you in rich, embroidered (decorated) cloth and gave you sandals made from fine leather; you wore linen of the finest quality and were covered in silk. **11.** I adorned (decorated) you with bracelets for your wrists, and placed a beautiful chain around your neck. **12.** I placed a jewel (precious stone) in your nose, earrings in your ears, and crowned you with a beautiful diadem (crown). **13.** You were dressed in gold and silver, and your garments were made from the finest linen, silk, and embroidered cloth. You feasted on the best of foods— pastries, honey, and oil. You were exceedingly beautiful and attained royal status (queen). **14.** Your fame (reputation) spread among the nations because of your beauty, which was flawless, as it reflected My splendor (glory), which I had given to you,' says the Lord God. **15.** 'But you relied on your own beauty, and because of your fame, you became a prostitute (played the harlot), giving yourself to anyone who passed by. **16.** You took your garments and made high places (altars) for yourself, and offered your prostitution (idolatry) on them. These things should never have happened. **17.** You took the gold and silver that I gave you, made idols (images) for yourself, and prostituted yourself (worshipped them) with these. **18.** You used your finest embroidered garments to cover them, offering My oil and incense before these false gods. **19.** You set before them the food I gave you—the finest pastries, oil, and honey—and offered them as sweet incense (offering) to them. **20.** You even took your sons and daughters, the children you bore to Me, and sacrificed them to these idols by burning them in fire. Could your prostitution (wickedness) be any worse? **21.** You killed My children and gave them as sacrifices to these idols. **22.** Throughout all your abominations (evil acts) and acts of prostitution, you never remembered the days of your youth when you were naked and struggling in your blood. **23.** 'After all your wickedness (evil actions), how terrible it will be for you! Woe (great sorrow) to you!' says the Lord God, **24.** 'You built shrines (places of idol worship) and high places (altars) in every street. **25.** You made your high places (altars) at the entrance (head) of every road and made your beauty detestable (hated). You offered yourself to anyone who passed by, multiplying your acts of prostitution (idolatry). **26.** You even committed prostitution with the Egyptians, your lustful neighbors, and increased your prostitution to provoke Me to anger. **27.** Therefore, I stretched out My hand against you, reduced your territory, and gave you into the power of those who hate you—the daughters (female nations) of the Philistines, who were ashamed (embarrassed) by your lewd actions. **28.** You also prostituted yourself with the Assyrians (a neighboring empire), because you were insatiable (unable to be satisfied); you prostituted yourself with them, but were still not satisfied. **29.** You expanded your prostitution to the land of the traders (Chaldea/Babylon), and even then, you were not satisfied. **30.** How corrupted (rotten) is your heart!' says the Lord God, 'Seeing you commit all these acts, the deeds (actions) of a brazen (shameless) prostitute. **31.** You built shrines at the entrance (head) of every road and made high places (altars) in every street, yet you were not like a prostitute, because you rejected (despised) payment. **32.** You are an adulterous (unfaithful) wife, taking strangers rather than your husband. **33.** Men pay prostitutes, but you paid all your lovers, hiring them to come to you from all directions. **34.** You are the opposite (complete contrast) of other prostitutes, because no one sought (asked for) you to be a prostitute. You gave payment (paid for it), yet no payment was given to you, so you are the opposite.' **35.** 'Now then, O prostitute (unfaithful), hear the word of the Lord! **36.** This is what the Lord God says: "Because you poured out your filthiness (uncleanness) and uncovered your nakedness (exposed body) through your prostitution with your lovers and all your detestable (abominable) idols, and because of the blood (death) of your children that you gave to them, **37.** I will gather all your lovers, the ones you delighted in, and those you despised, from all around, and I will bring them against you. I will expose your nakedness to them, so they may see all of it. **38.** I will judge you like an adulterous woman and those who shed blood (kill) are judged. I will bring blood (violence) upon you in fury (anger) and jealousy. **39.** I will deliver you into their hands, and they will destroy your shrines (idol altars) and break down your high places (worship centers). They will strip (remove) your clothes, take away your precious jewelry, and leave you naked and exposed. **40.** They will assemble a crowd (assembly) against you, and they will stone (throw stones) you with stones and kill you with their swords. **41.** They will burn your houses with fire, and punish you publicly in front of many women. I will cause you to cease your prostitution, and you will no longer hire lovers. **42.** So I will calm (rest) My anger against you, and My jealousy (fury) will be turned away. I will be quiet (at rest) and no longer angry. **43.** Because you did not remember the days of your youth, but provoked (angered) Me with all your actions, I will now repay you for your deeds, bringing the consequences (punishment) of your own actions upon your head," says the Lord God. "And you will no longer commit lewdness (sexual immorality) in addition to your other detestable (wicked) acts. **44.** 'Indeed, everyone who uses proverbs (sayings) will use this one against you: "Like mother, like daughter." **45.** You are your mother's daughter, who rejected her husband and children; and you are the sister of your sisters, who rejected their husbands and children. Your mother was a Hittite (a people group), and your father was an Amorite (another people group). **46.** Your older sister is Samaria (a city), who lives with her daughters to the north of you; your younger sister is Sodom (a city) and her daughters, who dwell to the south of you. **47.** You did not follow their ways, nor act as they did; yet you became more corrupt (decayed) than they in all your ways. **48.** As I live," says the Lord God, "your sister Sodom and her daughters have not committed as you and your daughters have done. **49.** Behold, this was the sin (wrongdoing) of your sister Sodom: She and her daughters were proud (arrogant), enjoyed abundance in food, and were idle (lazy), yet they did not strengthen the hand (help) of the poor (needy). **50.** They were haughty (arrogant) and committed detestable (wicked) acts before Me; therefore, I removed them according to My judgment. **51.** Samaria (a city) didn't even commit half of your sins, but you've done far more detestable acts than they did. You have justified your sisters by the wickedness you've committed. **52.** You, who judged your sisters, will now bear your own shame. The sins you've committed are far worse than theirs. They are actually more righteous than you, so you will feel disgrace (shame) and bear your own guilt for justifying them. **53.** "When I restore the captives of Sodom and her daughters, and the captives of Samaria and her daughters, I will also bring back your own captives among them, **54.** so you will bear the shame of what you have done, and you will feel disgraced for comforting them. **55.** When Sodom and her daughters return to their former state, and Samaria and her daughters to their former state, then you and your daughters will also return to yours. **56.** In the days of your pride, Sodom was never a subject of mockery, **57.** but now, because your wickedness

has been uncovered, it will be like the shame of the daughters of Syria (a region), or the contempt of the Philistines (a group of nations), who despise you everywhere. **58.** You will pay for your immoral acts and all the abominations (evil deeds) you've committed," declares the Lord. **59.** "For this is what the Lord God says: 'I will deal with you in the same way you've treated others, despising (rejecting) your covenant by breaking the oath you made. **60.** "Yet, despite all this, I will remember the covenant I made with you when you were young, and I will establish an everlasting (eternal) covenant with you. **61.** Then you will remember your actions and feel ashamed when you receive your older and younger sisters. I will give them to you as daughters, not because of the covenant I made with you, **62.** but because I will establish My covenant with you. Then you will know that I am the Lord. **63.** And when I forgive (provide atonement) for all you've done, you will remember and be ashamed, and never again open your mouth because of your disgrace," says the Lord God.'

Chapter 17

1. The word (a message) of the Lord came to me, saying: **2.** "Son of man, tell a riddle (a symbolic story with hidden meaning) and speak a parable (a story used to illustrate a moral or spiritual lesson) to the house of Israel. **3.** Say to them, 'This is what the Lord God says: There was a great eagle (a large bird of prey) with large wings and long feathers, full of many colors. It came to Lebanon (a region known for its cedars) and took the top branch of a cedar (a type of tall tree). **4.** It broke off its highest young branch and carried it to a land of trade (a place of business), placing it in a city of merchants (a city known for trade). **5.** Then the eagle took some of the land's seeds (small plants or crops) and planted them in fertile soil (rich, healthy earth), near abundant waters (plentiful water), setting it up like a willow tree (a type of tree that grows near water). **6.** It grew and became a low vine (a plant that climbs or spreads), spreading out with branches turning toward the eagle, while its roots (the part of a plant that anchors it in the soil) were underneath it. It became a vine, producing branches and putting out shoots (new growth). **7.** But there was another great eagle with large wings and many feathers. This vine turned its roots toward him and stretched its branches toward him, seeking to be watered (provided with water) in the garden where it had been planted. **8.** It was planted in good soil by many waters, so it could grow branches, bear fruit (produce), and become a beautiful vine. **9.** Say, 'This is what the Lord God says: Will it thrive (grow strong)? Will the eagle not pull up its roots, cut off its fruit (harvest), and leave it to wither (dry up)? Its leaves will dry up, and no large force (army) will be needed to uproot it. **10.** Look, it is planted, but will it grow? Won't it completely wither when the east wind (a hot, dry wind) blows on it? It will wither in the garden where it grew.' **11.** Again the word of the Lord came to me, saying: **12.** "Ask the rebellious house (a group that resists authority): 'Do you not understand what these things mean? Tell them, 'The king of Babylon (the ruler of the empire of Babylon) went to Jerusalem (the capital of Israel), took its king and princes (leaders), and led them away to Babylon. **13.** He took the king's descendants (family members), made a covenant (a formal agreement) with him, and placed him under an oath (a promise). He also took away the mighty (powerful people) men of the land, **14.** so that the kingdom would be humbled and not lift itself up, but by keeping his covenant, it might endure (last). **15.** But he rebelled (resisted authority) against him by sending his ambassadors (official messengers) to Egypt (a neighboring nation), asking for horses and a large army. Will he prosper (succeed)? Can someone who does this break a covenant and still escape judgment (punishment)? **16.** As I live,' says the Lord God, 'he will die in the place (location) where the king made him king, the very land where he despised (disrespected) the oath and broke the covenant—there in the midst (middle) of Babylon, he will die. **17.** Even Pharaoh (the king of Egypt) with his great army and many troops (soldiers) will not help him in battle. They will build siege walls (walls to break into a city) and try to cut off many people. **18.** Since he has broken the covenant by despising the oath, and yet still did these things, he will not escape (avoid punishment).' **19.** Therefore, this is what the Lord God says: 'As I live, surely I will repay (punish) him for despising My oath and breaking My covenant; it will come back on his own head (he will face the consequences). **20.** I will spread My net over him, and he will be caught in My snare (trap). I will bring him to Babylon, where I will judge him for his treason (betrayal) against Me. **21.** His fugitives (those running from him) and all his troops will fall by the sword (die in battle), and those who remain (survive) will be scattered (separated) to every wind (direction). Then you will know that I, the Lord, have spoken.' **22.** This is what the Lord God says: 'I will take one of the highest branches of the great cedar (a tall, sturdy tree) and cut off a tender sprig (a small, young branch) from its top. I will plant it on a high and prominent mountain (a place of importance). **23.** I will plant it on the mountain heights (tops) of Israel, where it will grow into a majestic cedar (a large, impressive tree). It will bear branches, produce fruit, and provide shelter for all kinds of birds (creatures that live in trees). They will find rest under its shade (shelter). **24.** And all the trees of the field (world) will know that I, the Lord, have humbled (brought low) the high tree and exalted the low tree. I have dried up (destroyed) the green tree and made the dry tree (weakened nations) flourish. I, the Lord, have spoken and I will do it.'"

Chapter 18

1. Once more, the message (word) of the Lord came to me, saying: **2.** "What does this proverb mean that you use in Israel: 'The fathers have eaten sour grapes, and the children's teeth are set on edge' (the children are impacted by their parents' sins)? **3.** "As surely as I live," declares the Lord God, "this proverb will no longer be used in Israel. **4.** Every person (soul) is Mine; both the father's soul and the son's soul belong to Me. The one who sins is the one who will die. **5.** But if a man is just (righteous) and lives by what is lawful and right, **6.** and he has not engaged in idol worship on the mountains (worship of false gods), nor looked upon the idols of Israel's house (idol worship), nor wronged (defiled) his neighbor's wife, nor approached a woman during her impurity (menstrual period); **7.** if he has not oppressed (mistreated) others, has returned the debtor's pledge (payment), has not stolen by violence (robbery), but has shared his bread (food) with the hungry and clothed those in need (naked); **8.** if he has neither charged usury (interest) nor taken excessive profit (increase), has turned away from sin (iniquity), and has made fair judgments between people; **9.** if he has kept My statutes (laws) and followed My commands—he is righteous, and he will certainly live," declares the Lord God. **10.** "But if this man has a son who is a thief (robber) or murderer (shedder of blood), and engages in any of these acts, **11.** disregarding his father's righteous ways—eating on the mountains (idol worship) or defiling his neighbor's wife; **12.** if he oppresses the poor and needy, commits robbery, does not return the pledge, worships idols, or engages in wicked deeds (abomination); **13.** if he has taken interest (usury) or unfair profit—should he live? He will not live! Because of these vile actions, he will surely die; his blood is on him. **14.** "However, if this man has a son who sees all the sins his father has committed and considers them, but does not do likewise; **15.** he has not eaten on the mountains (engaged in idol worship), nor lifted his eyes to Israel's idols (idol worship), nor wronged his neighbor's wife; **16.** he has not oppressed anyone, withheld a pledge, or stolen by violence, but has given his food (bread) to the hungry and clothed the needy (naked); **17.** he has not mistreated the poor, nor taken interest (usury) or excess profit (increase), but has obeyed My judgments and kept My laws—he will not be held accountable for his father's sins; he will surely live! **18.** As for the father, since he oppressed others, robbed his brother by violence, and committed evil among his people, he will die for his own sins. **19.** "You might say, 'Why doesn't the son bear the guilt of his father?' Because the son has acted justly and rightfully, keeping My statutes and observing them, he will surely live. **20.** The one who sins will die. A son will not bear the guilt of his father, nor will the father bear the guilt of his son. The righteousness (good deeds) of the just will be upon them, and the wickedness (evil deeds) of the wicked will be upon them. **21.** "However, if a wicked man turns (repents) from all his sins, keeps My statutes, and does what is lawful and right, he will live and not die. **22.** None of the wrongdoings (transgressions) he committed will be remembered; because of the righteousness he now does, he will live. **23.** Do I find pleasure (delight) in the death of the wicked?" declares the Lord God, "or rather, that they turn from their ways and live? **24.** But if a righteous man turns from his righteousness, commits sins (iniquity), and engages in the same wicked deeds (abominations) as the wicked, will he live? All his righteous acts will be forgotten; due to his unfaithfulness (betrayal) and sin, he will die. **25.**

"Yet you say, 'The Lord's way isn't fair.' Hear, O Israel, is it not My way that is fair, and your ways that are not fair? **26.** When a righteous man turns from his righteousness, commits sin, and dies because of it, it is for his sin that he dies. **27.** Likewise, when a wicked man turns from his wickedness and does what is lawful and right, he preserves his life. **28.** Because he reflects (considers carefully) and turns away from his sins (transgressions), he will live and not die. **29.** Yet Israel says, 'The Lord's way isn't fair.' O Israel, aren't My ways fair, and yours unfair? **30.** "Therefore, I will judge each of you, Israel, according to your ways," declares the Lord God. "Repent (turn away from sin), turn from all your sins (transgressions), so that sin (iniquity) will not cause your destruction. **31.** Cast away all the sins (transgressions) you have committed, and obtain a new heart (renewed spirit) and a new spirit. Why should you die, O Israel? **32.** I do not delight in anyone's death," declares the Lord God. "So turn and live!"

Chapter 19

1 "Take up a lament (a song of mourning) for the leaders of Israel," says the Lord, **2** and ask, "What was your mother? A lioness. She lay down among the lions and raised her cubs with them. **3** She brought up one of her cubs, and he grew into a young lion. He learned to hunt and devoured men. **4** The nations heard of him; he was caught in their trap and taken to Egypt with chains. **5** "When she saw that her hope was gone, she took another of her cubs and made him a young lion. **6** He wandered among the lions, grew into a young lion, learned to hunt, and devoured men. **7** He laid waste to their cities, destroying their land with his roaring. **8** Then the nations from every side attacked him, spreading a net to trap him. **9** They put him in a cage with chains and brought him to the king of Babylon (a kingdom to the east); they trapped him in their nets, and he could no longer roar in Israel's mountains. **10** "Your mother was like a vine (a plant) in your bloodline, planted by waters. She was fruitful and had many branches because of the abundant waters. **11** She had strong branches, like scepters (symbols of authority) for rulers. She stood tall, towering over the other trees, and was admired for her height and abundance. **12** But she was uprooted in anger, cast down to the ground, and the east wind (a destructive wind) dried up her fruit. Her strong branches broke off and withered; fire consumed them. **13** Now she is planted in the wilderness, in a dry and barren land. **14** Fire has come out from her branches and consumed her fruit. She has no strong branch left, no scepter for ruling. This is a lamentation, and it has become a lamentation."

Chapter 20

1. In the seventh year, on the tenth day of the fifth month, a group of Israel's elders came to seek guidance from the Lord and sat before me. **2.** Then the word of the Lord came to me, saying, **3.** "Son of man, speak to the elders of Israel. Tell them, 'This is what the Lord God says: Are you coming to inquire of Me? As surely as I live," declares the Lord God, "I will not allow you to inquire of Me.' **4.** Will you pass judgment on them, son of man? Will you make known to them the wrongdoings of their ancestors? **5.** "Tell them, 'This is what the Lord God says: When I selected Israel and made an oath to the descendants of Jacob, revealing Myself to them in Egypt, I declared to them, "I am the Lord your God." **6.** On that day, I swore to bring them out of Egypt and into a land I had chosen for them, a land flowing with milk and honey—the most splendid of all lands. **7.** I instructed them, "Each of you must abandon the offensive idols you worship and avoid defiling yourselves with the idols of Egypt. I am the Lord your God." **8.** But they rebelled against Me, refusing to listen. They did not discard the idols they had, nor did they turn away from Egypt's idols. So I said, "I will pour out My wrath and exhaust My anger upon them in Egypt." **9.** However, for the sake of My name, I refrained from letting it be profaned before the nations where they resided, where I had revealed Myself to them to bring them out of Egypt. **10.** So I led them out of Egypt and brought them into the wilderness. **11.** I gave them My statutes and made known to them My judgments (rules), which, if a person observes them, will lead to life. **12.** I also provided My Sabbaths as a sign between us, so they would know that I am the Lord who sanctifies them (makes them holy). **13.** Yet, in the wilderness, the people of Israel rebelled against Me. They disregarded My statutes and desecrated My Sabbaths. I considered destroying them. **14.** But for the sake of My name, I refrained from doing so. **15.** In the wilderness, I swore not to

370

bring them into the land I had promised—a land flowing with milk and honey—because they rejected My laws. **16.** They followed idols, but I chose to spare them from complete destruction. **17.** "I withheld My full judgment on them, even though they rebelled. **18.** I addressed their children in the wilderness, saying, 'Do not follow your fathers' ways or imitate their idols. **19.** I am the Lord your God. Walk in My statutes and keep My judgments. **20.** Keep My Sabbaths holy as a reminder that I am the Lord your God.' **21.** But the next generation also rebelled, failing to follow My statutes or honor My Sabbaths. **22.** Yet, I restrained My judgment for the sake of My name. **23.** I swore to scatter them among the nations and disperse them across the lands. **24.** They rejected My laws, defiled My Sabbaths, and pursued idols. **25.** Therefore, I allowed them to follow unclean practices and judgments that would lead to their ruin. **26.** I made them unclean by their offerings, and they sacrificed their firstborn, making them desolate. **27.** "Therefore, son of man, speak to the house of Israel and say to them, 'This is what the Lord God says: Your fathers have blasphemed by being unfaithful to Me. **28.** When I brought them into the land I swore to give them, they offered sacrifices on high hills, provoking Me with their offerings. **29.** I asked them, 'What is this high place?' It is called Bamah (high place) to this day. **30.** Therefore, tell Israel, 'This is what the Lord God says: "Are you defiling yourselves like your fathers? **31.** When you offer your gifts and make your sons pass through fire, you defile yourselves with your idols. Shall I be inquired of by you? I will not answer." **32.** What you plan will not happen when you say, "We will be like the nations, serving idols of wood and stone." **33.** "As I live," says the Lord God, "I will rule over you with a mighty hand and outstretched arm. **34.** I will bring you out from the nations and gather you from the countries where you are scattered, with fury poured out. **35.** I will bring you into the wilderness of the nations and there I will plead My case with you face to face. **36.** Just as I pleaded with your fathers in Egypt, so I will with you," says the Lord God. **37.** "I will make you pass under the rod (a symbol of judgment), and bring you into the bond of the covenant. **38.** I will purge the rebels among you, and they will not enter the land of Israel. Then you will know that I am the Lord. **39.** "As for you, house of Israel," says the Lord God, "Serve your idols—if you won't obey Me—don't profane My holy name anymore. **40.** On My holy mountain, all of Israel will serve Me; I will accept their offerings and sacrifices. **41.** I will accept you as a sweet aroma when I bring you out from the nations. I will be sanctified in you before the Gentiles. **42.** You will know that I am the Lord when I bring you into the promised land, the land I swore to give to your ancestors. **43.** There you will remember your evil deeds and loathe yourselves for all your sins. **44.** Then you will know that I am the Lord when I have dealt with you for My name's sake. **45.** The word of the Lord came to me again, saying: **46.** "Son of man, set your face toward the south and preach against the south. **47.** Say to the forest of the south, 'Hear the word of the Lord! I will kindle a fire in you, which will devour every tree, both green and dry. **48.** The fire will not be quenched, and all faces from south to north will be scorched by it. **49.** Then I said, "Ah, Lord God! They say of me, 'Does he not speak in parables?'"

Chapter 21

1. The word of the Lord came to me, saying: **2.** "Son of man, set your face against Jerusalem, preach against the holy places, and prophesy against Israel's land. **3.** Tell Israel: 'The Lord says: I am against you. I will unsheathe (draw from its case) My sword to cut off both the righteous and the wicked. **4.** My sword will go out against all flesh from south to north, **5.** so all people will know that I, the Lord, have drawn My sword and it will not return until its purpose is fulfilled.' **6.** Therefore, son of man, groan with a breaking heart, sigh with bitterness before their eyes. **7.** When they ask, 'Why are you sighing?' say: 'Because of the news, every heart will melt, hands grow weak, spirits faint, and knees become water. It is coming, and it will happen,' declares the Lord." **8.** The word of the Lord came again, saying: **9.** "Son of man, prophesy and say: 'The Lord says: A sword is sharpened and polished (made sharp and ready)! **10.** Sharpened for slaughter (killing), polished to flash like lightning! Should we rejoice? It despises (rejects) the scepter (royal staff) of My Son, as it does all wood. **11.** The sword is ready to be handled, sharpened for the slayer. **12.** Cry out, son of man, for this sword will be against My people, against the princes of Israel. Terror will be upon My people. Strike your thigh in grief. **13.** This is a test.

What if the sword rejects (despises) even the scepter? The scepter will be no more,' declares the Lord. **14.** Prophesy, son of man, and clap your hands. Let the sword strike twice, even three times, to slay. It kills the great and enters their private chambers. **15.** I have set the sword against all their gates, so hearts may melt and many stumble. It is shining, ready for slaughter. **16.** Prepare yourselves! Draw your sword! Strike right! Set your blade! Strike left—wherever it is ordered! **17.** I will strike My fists together and calm My fury. I, the Lord, have spoken." **18.** The word of the Lord came again, saying: **19.** "Son of man, mark two ways for the sword of the king of Babylon to follow. Set up a sign at the fork (split) of the road to the city. **20.** One way to Rabbah (capital of Ammon) and the other to Judah, to fortified Jerusalem. **21.** The king of Babylon stands at the crossroads, using divination (seeking guidance through omens). **22.** In his right hand, he holds the divination for Jerusalem: to prepare siege weapons (battering rams), to raise the war cry, and to build a wall. **23.** It will seem like a false divination to those who have sworn oaths with them, but it will bring their sin to remembrance and they will be captured. **24.** Therefore, this is what the Lord says: 'Because you have made your sins known, you will be taken.' **25.** And you, O wicked prince of Israel, whose day has come, whose sin is ending, **26.** this is what the Lord says: 'Remove the crown, take off the turban. Nothing will remain the same. Exalt the humble, humble the exalted. **27.** Overthrown (destroyed), overthrown, I will make it overthrown! It will not be, until He comes whose right it is, and I will give it to Him.'" **28.** "Son of man, prophesy concerning the Ammonites and their disgrace. Say: 'A sword is drawn, polished for slaughter, for destruction. **29.** While they see false visions for you, while they divine (predict) lies for you, they will bring you to the wicked, to the slain whose day has come. **30.** Return the sword to its sheath (protective covering). I will judge you in the land where you were born. **31.** I will pour out My wrath on you, blow My fire of indignation against you, and deliver you into the hands of cruel destroyers. **32.** You will be fuel for the fire, and your blood will stain the land. You will not be remembered, for I, the Lord, have spoken."

Chapter 22

1. The word of the Lord came to me, and He said: **2.** "Son of man, will you bring judgment on the city soaked with blood? Expose her detestable (wicked) acts to everyone. **3.** Say to her, 'The Lord God declares: "The city sheds blood within her to bring about her downfall, and creates idols to defile (pollute) herself." **4.** You have become guilty through the blood you've shed and defiled yourself with your idols. Your days are numbered; I will make you an object of scorn among the nations. **5.** People both near and far will mock you, calling you infamous and full of chaos. **6.** "The rulers of Israel have used their power to spill blood within you. **7.** In you, they dishonor father and mother, oppress strangers, and wrong the orphan and widow. **8.** You have despised My sacred things and desecrated (dishonored) My Sabbaths. **9.** Within you are those who spread false rumors to cause bloodshed; there are those who practice immorality in your midst. **10.** In you, men expose their fathers' nakedness; in you, women are violated during their impurity. **11.** One commits adultery with his neighbor's wife; another abuses his daughter-in-law; and another defiles his sister, his father's daughter. **12.** In you, people take bribes to shed blood, practice usury (interest), and profit from extortion, all while forgetting Me," says the Lord God. **13.** "Look, I strike My fists in anger at the dishonest gain and bloodshed you've caused. **14.** Will your heart stand firm, or your hands remain strong when I bring judgment on you? I, the Lord, have spoken, and I will do it. **15.** I will scatter you among the nations and disperse you across the lands, and cleanse you of your filth. **16.** You will defile yourselves in the eyes of the nations, and then you will know that I am the Lord." **17.** The word of the Lord came to me again, saying, **18.** "Son of man, Israel has become like dross (worthless metal) to Me; they are like bronze, tin, iron, and lead, in a furnace. **19.** So, because you have become dross, behold, I will gather you in the midst of Jerusalem. **20.** Just as men gather metals into a furnace to melt them, so I will gather you in My anger and fury and leave you there to be refined. **21.** I will gather you and blow the fire of My wrath upon you, and you will be melted in its flames. **22.** Just as silver is refined in a furnace, so you will be melted in the fire; then you will know that I, the Lord, have poured out My anger on you." **23.** The word of the Lord came to me, saying, **24.** "Son of man, say to her, 'You are a land that has not been purified or refreshed, especially in the day of My anger. **25.** The conspiracy of your prophets is like a roaring lion that tears into its prey. They devour people, steal treasures, and make many widows in the land. **26.** Your priests have broken My law, profaned My holy things, and have failed to distinguish between the holy and the common, nor did they teach the difference between the clean and unclean; they have ignored My Sabbaths, and so I am profaned among them. **27.** Your leaders are like wolves that tear into the prey, shedding blood, destroying lives, and gaining dishonest profits. **28.** Your prophets use untempered mortar (ineffective repairs), seeing false visions and making false predictions, saying, 'The Lord says,' when I have not spoken. **29.** The people in your land practice oppression, commit robbery, mistreat the poor and needy, and wrongfully oppress the foreigner. **30.** I searched for someone among them who would build up the wall and stand in the gap before Me on behalf of the land, but I found no one. **31.** Therefore, I have poured out My indignation on them; I have consumed them with the fire of My wrath and will bring their deeds upon their own heads," declares the Lord God.

Chapter 23

1. The word of the Lord came to me again, saying: **2.** "Son of man, there were two women, daughters of one mother. **3.** They were unfaithful in Egypt, acting immorally in their youth; there, they were embraced and their innocence taken (purity). **4.** Their names are Oholah, the elder, and Oholibah, her sister; they belonged to Me and had sons and daughters. Samaria (capital of Israel) is Oholah, and Jerusalem is Oholibah. **5.** Oholah, although Mine, was unfaithful and desired the neighboring Assyrians (ancient empire). **6.** These were men clothed in purple, captains and leaders, all desirable young men riding horses. **7.** She acted immorally with these Assyrians, defiling herself with their idols (objects of worship). **8.** She didn't abandon her immorality from Egypt, where she was dishonored in her youth. **9.** Therefore, I gave her to her lovers, the Assyrians she desired. **10.** They exposed her, took her children, and killed her; she became a warning to other women as judgment was carried out (punishment). **11.** Although Oholibah saw this, she became even more corrupt in her desires than her sister. **12.** She desired the neighboring Assyrians, captains and rulers, gorgeously dressed, riding horses. **13.** Both sisters were defiled, following the same path of unfaithfulness (betrayal). **14.** She increased her immoral ways, noticing images of Chaldean men (Babylonian people) on the walls. **15.** These men wore belts and turbans, looking like captains from Chaldea (Babylonia). **16.** She desired them as soon as she saw them and sent messengers to them in Chaldea. **17.** The Babylonians came and defiled her; she grew distant from them (estranged). **18.** She displayed her immorality, so I distanced Myself from her, as I had from her sister. **19.** Yet she multiplied her immoral acts, recalling her youth in Egypt. **20.** She lusted for her partners, whose strength was like that of donkeys (powerful). **21.** She remembered the immoral ways of her youth when her innocence was taken. **22.** Therefore, Oholibah, the Lord God says: 'I will bring against you the lovers you turned away from, who will come from every side. **23.** The Babylonians and all Chaldeans, including Pekod, Shoa, and Koa, and the Assyrians—all prominent young men—will come against you. **24.** They will arrive with chariots, wagons, and a crowd prepared for battle; I will let them judge you as they see fit. **25.** My jealousy will fuel their fury; they will harm you severely and kill those left by the sword (weapon). **26.** They will strip away your clothes and take your jewels. **27.** This will end your immoral practices from Egypt, so you will no longer remember it. **28.** The Lord God says, 'I will hand you over to those you despised, those you rejected. **29.** They will treat you with hatred, taking all you've worked for and leaving you exposed (unprotected). **30.** I do this because you acted unfaithfully with the nations, becoming defiled by their idols. **31.** Since you followed your sister's ways, you will drink from her cup. **32.** The Lord God says: 'You will drink your sister's cup—a deep, wide one, bringing mockery and scorn. **33.** You'll be filled with sorrow and horror, the same as your sister Samaria. **34.** You will drink it to the dregs, shattering it and tearing yourself, for I have spoken,' says the Lord God. **35.** 'Because you've forgotten Me and cast Me aside, you will bear the consequences of your acts.' **36.** The Lord said to me, "Son of man, will you judge Oholah and Oholibah? Show them their wrongs. **37.** They were unfaithful and shed blood; they worshiped idols and even sacrificed their children to them. **38.** They defiled My sanctuary and disregarded My Sabbaths. **39.** After killing their children for idols, they entered My sanctuary and defiled it. **40.** You invited men from afar, sending messengers and preparing yourself with makeup and ornaments (decorations). **41.** You sat on a luxurious couch with a table set with My incense and oil. **42.** A noisy crowd surrounded her, including men with bracelets and crowns. **43.** Then I wondered if men would still pursue her despite her corruption. **44.** Yet they did, just as men go to a woman who has sold herself. **45.** Righteous men will judge them as adulteresses with blood on their hands (guilty). **46.** The Lord God says: 'Bring a gathering against them and give them up for punishment. **47.** The assembly will stone them, kill their children, and burn their houses. **48.** This will end immorality in the land, warning all women not to act the same way. **49.** They will repay you for your wrongs and idolatry, and you will know that I am the Lord God.'"

Chapter 24

1. In the ninth year, the tenth month, on the tenth day of the month, the word of the Lord (God's message) came to me, saying: **2.** "Son of man (human being), write down this date—this very day the king of Babylon (the ruler of the Babylonian Empire) began his siege (military blockade) against Jerusalem. **3.** Speak to the rebellious (disobedient) house of Israel and tell them: 'This is what the Lord God says: Take a pot (a large cooking vessel), set it on the fire, and pour water into it. **4.** Place in it pieces of meat—good cuts (the best portions), like the thigh and the shoulder. Fill it with the best parts. **5.** Take the choice meat (select the best from the flock) from the flock, pile up fuel (wood for fire) under it, make it boil well, and let the meat simmer (cook slowly) in it.' **6.** 'This is what the Lord says: Woe (great sorrow) to the bloody (guilty of murder) city! The pot is filled with scum (impurities) that will not be removed. Bring out the pieces of meat, piece by piece, and draw lots (randomly select) to see which will be used.' **7.** 'For her blood (the blood of the innocent) is in the midst of her; she placed it on a bare (uncovered) rock, not covering it with dust. **8.** In doing this, she aroused (stirred up) my anger and sought vengeance (punishment for wrong). I set her blood on the rock so it would not be hidden.' **9.** 'Woe to the bloody city! I will make the fire for her even greater. **10.** Pile on the wood (stack the firewood), set the fire, cook the meat thoroughly, mix in the spices, and let the cuts be burned up. **11.** Then set the pot on the coals (burning embers), so that its bronze (metal pot) can burn, its filth (dirt or impurity) can be melted, and its scum consumed (destroyed). **12.** She has grown weary (tired) with her lies, and her great scum has not been removed. Let it remain in the fire!' **13.** 'Your filthiness (moral corruption) is full of wickedness. Though I have cleansed (purified) you, you remain unclean (impure). You will not be purified until my fury (intense anger) is finished with you.' **14.** 'I, the Lord, have spoken it, and it will happen. I will not hold back (withhold), I will not spare (show mercy), and I will not relent (change my decision). You will be judged according to your ways and deeds (actions),' says the Lord God.' **15.** Then the word of the Lord came to me again: **16.** "Son of man, I am about to take away from you what you love most—your wife—by a sudden blow (unexpected event). Yet you will not mourn (show sadness), weep (cry), or let your tears flow (fall). **17.** Sigh quietly (express grief without loud mourning), do not mourn for the dead. Tie your turban (head covering) on your head, put on your sandals (shoes), and do not cover your lips (to show mourning) or eat the bread of sorrow (food for mourners)." **18.** So I spoke to the people in the morning, and in the evening, my wife died. The next morning, I did as I had been commanded. **19.** The people asked me, "Won't you tell us what these things mean? Why are you acting (behaving) like this?" **20.** I answered them: "The word of the Lord came to me, saying: **21.** 'Speak to the house of Israel: This is what the Lord God says: I will defile (make unclean) my sanctuary (holy place), the pride of your strength (the temple), the desire (something greatly wanted) of your eyes, and the delight of your soul. Your sons and daughters whom you left behind will be killed by the sword. **22.** You will do the same as I have done: you will not cover your lips or eat the bread of sorrow. **23.** Your turbans (head coverings) will be on your heads and your sandals (shoes) on your feet. You will neither mourn nor weep, but you will waste away (waste physically) in your sin and grieve (feel sorrow) for one another. **24.** Ezekiel will be a sign (symbol) to you. What he has done, you will do. And when this happens, you will know that I am the

Lord God.' **25.** 'And you, son of man—when I take away from them their stronghold (place of safety), their joy, their glory, the desire of their eyes, and all they have set their hearts on (focused on), their sons and daughters, **26.** On that day, one who escapes (survives) will come to you and tell you the news. **27.** On that day, your mouth will be opened (able to speak) to speak to him who has escaped. You will no longer be mute (unable to speak). You will be a sign to them, and they will know that I am the Lord.'"

Chapter 25

1. The word of the Lord came to me, saying: **2.** "Son of man, turn your face toward the Ammonites and prophesy against them. **3.** Say to them, 'Hear the word of the Lord God! This is what the Lord God says: Because you laughed and mocked My sanctuary (holy place) when it was desecrated, and the land of Israel when it was desolate, and the house of Judah when they were taken into captivity, **4.** I will hand you over to the people from the East. They will set up camp among you and live there; they will take your crops and drink your milk. **5.** I will make Rabbah (capital of the Ammonites) a place where camels rest, and Ammon a place for flocks to rest. Then you will know that I am the Lord.' **6.** For this is what the Lord God says: Because you clapped your hands, stomped your feet, and rejoiced in your heart, showing contempt (disrespect) for the land of Israel, **7.** I will stretch out My hand against you. I will give you over to the nations as plunder (loot). I will cut you off from the nations and destroy you. You will know that I am the Lord.' **8.** This is what the Lord God says: Because Moab and Seir (region of Edom) said, 'The house of Judah is just like all the other nations,' **9.** Therefore, I will remove the cities of Moab, including Beth Jeshimoth (a Moabite city), Baal Meon (a city of Moab), and Kirjathaim (a Moabite city), which are the pride of the land. **10.** I will give this land to the people from the East, together with the Ammonites, so that Moab will no longer be remembered among the nations. **11.** I will bring judgment (a decision or punishment) upon Moab, and they will know that I am the Lord.' **12.** This is what the Lord God says: Because Edom took vengeance (revenge) against the house of Judah, and has greatly sinned by seeking revenge, **13.** Therefore, I will stretch out My hand against Edom, cut off its people and animals, and make it desolate (empty) from Teman (region of Edom). Dedan (a city in Edom) will fall by the sword. **14.** I will bring My judgment upon Edom through My people Israel, and they will carry out My anger and fury against Edom. They will know My vengeance, says the Lord God.' **15.** This is what the Lord God says: Because the Philistines acted out of vengeance (revenge) and hatred toward Judah, **16.** I will stretch out My hand against the Philistines, and I will destroy the Cherethites (a Philistine group) and the rest of the people along the seacoast. **17.** I will bring great vengeance (punishment) upon them, and they will know that I am the Lord when I carry out My vengeance against them.'"

Chapter 26

1 In the eleventh year, on the first day of the month, the word of the Lord came to me, saying: **2** "Son of man, because Tyre has said against Jerusalem, 'Aha! She is broken, the gateway (entrance) of the peoples; now she is handed over to me; I will be filled; she is laid waste.' **3** Therefore, this is what the Lord God says: 'Look, I am against you, O Tyre, and I will bring many nations against you, like the waves (large movements of water) of the sea. **4** They will destroy your walls and break down your towers; I will scrape (remove) the dust from you and make you like the bare top of a rock. **5** You will become a place for spreading nets in the sea, for I have spoken,' says the Lord God; 'and you will be plunder (goods taken by force) for the nations. **6** Your daughter villages, which are in the fields, will be killed by the sword. Then they will know that I am the Lord.' **7** "For this is what the Lord God says: 'Look, I will bring against Tyre from the north Nebuchadnezzar (king of Babylon) the king of kings, with horses, chariots, and horsemen, and a great army. **8** He will kill your daughter villages in the fields; he will build a siege mound (a ramp used in attacks) against you, a wall around you, and a defense against you. **9** He will direct his battering rams (large, heavy objects used to break down walls) against your walls, and with his axes (sharp tools) he will break down your towers. **10** Because of the large number of his horses, their dust (fine particles of earth) will cover you; your walls will shake at the noise of his horsemen, wagons, and chariots, when he enters your gates, as men enter a city that has been broken into. **11** With the hooves (hard parts of an animal's feet) of his horses, he will trample all your streets; he will kill your people by the sword, and your strong pillars (supporting columns) will fall to the ground. **12** They will plunder your wealth and loot your goods; they will break down your walls, destroy your pleasant houses, and throw your stones, timber (wood), and soil into the sea. **13** I will put an end to the sound of your songs, and the sound of your harps (musical instruments) will be heard no more. **14** I will make you like the top of a rock (bare and exposed); you will become a place for spreading nets, and you will never be rebuilt, for I, the Lord, have spoken,' says the Lord God. **15** "This is what the Lord God says to Tyre: 'Will the coastlands (lands by the sea) not shake at the sound of your fall, when the wounded cry and slaughter (killing) is made in the midst of you? **16** Then all the princes (rulers) of the sea will come down from their thrones, lay aside their robes, and take off their embroidered (decorated) garments; they will clothe themselves with trembling (fear); they will sit on the ground, tremble every moment, and be astonished (surprised) at you. **17** They will take up a lament (song of mourning) for you, and say to you: 'How you have perished, O city that was inhabited by seafaring (sea-traveling) men, O renowned (famous) city, who was strong at sea, she and her inhabitants who caused terror to all who lived there! **18** Now the coastlands tremble on the day of your fall; yes, the coastlands by the sea are troubled at your departure.' **19** "For this is what the Lord God says: 'When I make you a desolate (empty) city, like cities that are not inhabited, when I bring the deep (ocean) upon you, and great waters (large waves) cover you, **20** I will bring you down with those who go down into the Pit (a metaphor for death or destruction), to the people of old (ancient peoples), and I will make you dwell in the lowest part of the earth, in places desolate from ancient times, with those who go down to the Pit, so that you will never be inhabited; and I will establish glory in the land of the living. **21** I will make you a terror (a cause of fear), and you will be no more; though you are sought for, you will never be found again,' says the Lord God."

Chapter 27

1. The word of the Lord came again to me, saying: **2.** "Son of man, take up a lament (song of mourning) for Tyre, **3.** and say to Tyre: 'You who are at the entrance (gateway) of the sea, merchant to many nations on the coastlands, this is what the Lord God says: "O Tyre, you said, 'I am perfect in beauty.' **4.** Your borders lie in the middle of the seas. Your builders have perfected your beauty. **5.** They used fir trees from Senir (a mountain range) to make your planks; they took cedars from Lebanon to make your mast. **6.** They made your oars from oaks from Bashan (a region known for its fertile land); the people of Ashur (an ancient empire) inlaid your planks with ivory from Cyprus. **7.** Fine embroidered linen from Egypt was used for your sail; blue and purple from Elishah (a coastal region) covered you. **8.** The inhabitants of Sidon (a city) and Arvad (a city-state) were your oarsmen; your wise men, O Tyre, were in you, and became your pilots (guides). **9.** The elders of Gebal (an ancient city) and its wise men were in you to caulk (seal) your seams; all the ships of the sea and their oarsmen were in you, trading your merchandise. **10.** "Those from Persia, Lydia, and Libya were in your army as warriors; they hung shields and helmets on you and gave you splendor. **11.** The men of Arvad (city-state) were on your walls all around, and the men of Gammad (a place or tribe) were in your towers; they hung their shields on your walls, making your beauty perfect. **12.** "Tarshish (a distant trading partner) was your merchant because of your many luxury goods. They gave you silver, iron, tin, and lead in exchange for your merchandise. **13.** Javan (Greece), Tubal, and Meshech (ancient regions or tribes) were your traders. They bartered human lives and bronze vessels for your goods. **14.** Those from the house of Togarmah (a people from Armenia) traded horses, steeds, and mules for your wares. **15.** The men of Dedan (an Arabian tribe) were your traders; many islands (distant lands) were the market for your goods. They brought ivory tusks and ebony in payment. **16.** Syria was your merchant because of the abundance of goods you produced. They gave you emeralds, purple (cloth), embroidery, fine linen, corals, and rubies for your merchandise. **17.** Judah and the land of Israel were your traders. They brought wheat from Minnith (a region) and millet, honey, oil, and balm in exchange for your goods. **18.** Damascus (a city) was your merchant because of your many luxury goods. They traded wine from Helbon and white wool for your merchandise. **19.** Dan and

Javan paid for your wares by traveling back and forth. They gave wrought iron, cassia (a spice), and cane for your goods. **20.** Dedan (an Arabian tribe) traded in saddlecloths for riding. **21.** Arabia and all the princes of Kedar (a tribe in Arabia) were your regular merchants. They traded with you in lambs, rams, and goats. **22.** The merchants of Sheba and Raamah (regions) were your merchants. They brought the finest spices, precious stones, and gold for your wares. **23.** Haran, Canneh (ancient cities), Eden (region), Sheba, Assyria, and Chilmad (regions or tribes) were your merchants. **24.** These were your merchants in choice items—purple clothes, embroidered garments, chests of multicolored apparel, and sturdy woven cords, all of which were sold in your marketplace. **25.** "The ships of Tarshish carried your merchandise. You were filled and glorious in the midst of the seas. **26.** Your oarsmen brought you into many waters, but the east wind (a destructive force) broke you in the midst of the seas. **27.** "Your riches, wares, and merchandise, your sailors and pilots, your caulkers and merchandisers, all your men of war, and the entire company within you will fall into the midst of the sea on the day of your destruction. **28.** The land will shake at the cry of your pilots. **29.** "All who handle the oar, the sailors, and all the pilots of the sea will come down from their ships and stand on the shore. **30.** They will raise their voices because of you; they will cry bitterly and throw dust on their heads; they will roll in ashes. **31.** They will shave their heads bald because of you, put on sackcloth, and weep for you with bitterness of heart, wailing with bitter mourning. **32.** In their lament for you, they will take up a song of mourning, saying: 'What city is like Tyre, destroyed in the midst of the sea? **33.** 'When your goods went out by sea, you satisfied many nations; you enriched the kings of the earth with your vast wealth and merchandise. **34.** But now you are broken by the seas, in the depths of the waters; your merchandise and entire company will be lost in your midst. **35.** All the inhabitants of the islands will be astonished at you; their kings will tremble in fear, and their faces will be troubled. **36.** The merchants of the nations will hiss (show contempt) at you; you will become a horror, and will be no more forever.'"

Chapter 28

1. The word of the Lord came to me again, saying, **2.** "Son of man, speak to the ruler of Tyre and tell him: 'This is what the Lord God declares: "Your heart has grown proud, and you claim, 'I am a god; I sit in the seat of gods, surrounded by the seas,' yet you are only a man, and not a god, though you imagine yourself to be one. **3.** You are wiser than Daniel, it is said! No secret is beyond your understanding. **4.** With your wisdom and knowledge, you have accumulated wealth, storing gold and silver in your vaults. **5.** Through your keen skills in trade, you have expanded your riches, and now your heart is swollen with pride because of them," **6.** therefore, the Lord God says: "Since you have set your heart like that of a god, **7.** behold, I will send against you strangers—terrible nations. They will unsheath their swords to strike down your wisdom and defile your beauty. **8.** You will be cast into the Pit (a place of destruction), and you will meet the death of those slain in the heart of the seas. **9.** Will you still boast, saying, 'I am a god,' in the face of those who strike you down? You are merely a man, not a god, at the mercy of those who will kill you. **10.** You will die like the uncircumcised (Gentiles), by the hands of foreigners; I, the Lord, have spoken." **11.** Then the word of the Lord came to me, saying, **12.** "Son of man, take up a lament (a mournful song) for the king of Tyre and say: 'This is what the Lord God says: "You were the epitome of perfection, filled with wisdom and flawless in beauty. **13.** You were in Eden, the garden of God; your covering was made of precious stones: sardius, topaz, diamond, beryl, onyx, jasper, sapphire, turquoise, and emerald, all set in gold. The musical instruments (timbrels and pipes) designed for you were prepared on the day you were created. **14.** You were the anointed cherub (a divine being) who covered and protected; I appointed you. You were on God's holy mountain, walking among the fiery stones. **15.** From the day you were created, you were perfect in all your ways, until sin was found in you. **16.** Your trade was so successful that you became filled with violence inside and sinned. Therefore, I expelled you as a defiled (unclean) being from the mountain of God, and destroyed you, O covering cherub, from among the fiery stones. **17.** Your heart grew proud because of your beauty, and you corrupted your wisdom for the sake of your splendor. I cast you down to the earth and made you a spectacle for kings to gaze

upon. **18.** You defiled your sanctuaries (holy places) with your many sins, and through your dishonest trading, I sent fire to consume you from within. It reduced you to ashes upon the earth for all to witness. **19.** All those who knew you among the nations will be appalled at your fall. You have become a terror to them, and you will cease to exist forever." **20.** The word of the Lord came to me, saying, **21.** "Son of man, direct your attention to Sidon (a city), and prophesy against her, **22.** saying, 'This is what the Lord God says: "I am against you, O Sidon; I will reveal My glory within you, and the nations will know that I am the Lord when I execute judgment upon you and sanctify Myself in your midst. **23.** I will bring a plague upon you and blood will fill your streets. Those who are slain within you will be judged by the sword, with enemies surrounding you on every side, and then you will know that I am the Lord. **24.** There will be no more pain or suffering for Israel from those around them who hate them. Then they will know that I am the Lord God." **25.** The Lord God declares: "When I gather the scattered people of Israel from the nations they have been exiled to, and I am honored in them before the Gentiles, they will return to the land I gave to My servant Jacob. **26.** They will settle there in safety, build houses, and plant vineyards. They will live securely, for I will execute judgment on all their enemies who despise them. Then they will know that I am their God, the Lord."

Chapter 29

1. On the twelfth day of the tenth month, in the tenth year, the Lord's word came to me, saying: **2.** "Son of man, direct your prophecy against Pharaoh, the king of Egypt, and declare My message to him and all of Egypt. **3.** Tell him, 'This is what the Lord God says: I am against you, Pharaoh, ruler of Egypt, the great monster (a large, powerful creature) dwelling in your rivers, who claims, "The river is mine; I created it." **4.** But I will set hooks in your jaws, and the fish of your rivers will cling to your scales. I will pull you out of your rivers, with all the fish stuck to you. **5.** I will abandon you in the wilderness (an empty, desolate land) with the fish of your rivers. You will fall upon the open fields, where wild animals and birds will consume you. **6.** Then all the people of Egypt will understand that I am the Lord, because you were like a broken reed (a fragile plant) to Israel. **7.** When Israel looked to you for support, you failed them and caused them to stumble. When they sought your aid, you broke and left them trembling. **8.** Therefore, this is the Lord's declaration: I will bring a sword (a weapon for killing) against you, and it will cut down both man and beast. **9.** Egypt will be left desolate, and then they will know that I am the Lord, for you claimed, 'The river is mine; I created it.' **10.** I am against you and your rivers. I will make all of Egypt a wasteland, from Migdol (a town in Egypt) to Syene (another town), reaching as far as the border of Ethiopia. **11.** No one, neither human nor animal, will travel through it. It will remain uninhabited for forty years (a symbolic period of desolation and judgment). **12.** I will make Egypt desolate among desolate nations, and its cities will lie in ruins for forty years. I will scatter (disperse) its people among other lands. **13.** After forty years, I will bring the Egyptians back from where they were scattered. **14.** I will return them to Pathros (a region in Egypt), their native land, but they will become a humble (weak, lowly) kingdom. **15.** Egypt will be the least of all kingdoms, never to rise above other nations again. I will diminish them so that they no longer rule. **16.** Egypt will no longer be a source of trust for Israel. When Israel recalls their past mistakes in turning to Egypt, they will recognize that I am the Lord God. **17.** In the twenty-seventh year, on the first day of the first month, the word of the Lord came to me, saying: **18.** "Son of man, Nebuchadnezzar (king of Babylon) and his army labored hard against Tyre (a city). Every head was shaved, and every shoulder was rubbed raw, yet he and his forces received no reward for their efforts. **19.** So, I am giving Egypt to Nebuchadnezzar, king of Babylon. He will take its riches, carry away its treasures, and strip it of its wealth. This will be his reward for his service. **20.** I have granted him Egypt as payment for his work, for he served Me," declares the Lord. **21.** "On that day, I will strengthen Israel. I will enable you to speak openly in their presence, and they will know that I am the Lord."

Chapter 30

1. Once again, the word of the Lord came to me, saying, **2.** "Son of man, declare this message: 'This is what the Lord God says: 'How terrible that day will be!' **3.** The day is fast approaching—indeed, it is near. The day of the Lord is coming, a day filled with clouds, the moment of judgment for the Gentiles (non-Jews). **4.** Egypt will face the sword (a weapon), and Ethiopia will experience great distress. As the dead fall in Egypt, their wealth will be seized, and the very foundations (the core of their society) of the land will be shattered. **5.** "Ethiopia, Libya, Lydia, the mixed peoples, Chub, and all the nations allied with them will also fall by the sword." **6.** 'The Lord says: "Those who have supported Egypt will fall, and the arrogance (pride) of its strength will be humbled. From Migdol (a city) to Syene (a southern Egyptian city), all those within Egypt will fall to the sword," declares the Lord God. **7.** "They will become desolate (ruined), surrounded by desolate lands, and her cities will lie among other cities laid waste by war. **8.** Then they will know that I am the Lord when I ignite a fire in Egypt, and all her helpers are destroyed. **9.** On that day, I will send messengers on ships to terrorize the careless (unaware) Ethiopians, and great anguish (distress) will overwhelm them, just as it did in Egypt on that fateful day. For indeed, it is coming!" **10.** 'The Lord God declares: "I will cause the population of Egypt to diminish by the hand of Nebuchadnezzar, king of Babylon. **11.** He, along with his terrifying army, will come to destroy the land. They will draw their swords against Egypt and fill the land with those slain. **12.** I will dry up the rivers, and hand over the land to the wicked. I will make it desolate (ruined) and all its contents will be taken by foreigners (those from outside Egypt). I, the Lord, have spoken." **13.** 'The Lord God says: "I will destroy the idols (false gods) and make the images (statues of gods) cease in Noph (an Egyptian city); no longer will rulers rise from Egypt. I will instill fear in the land of Egypt. **14.** I will lay waste to Pathros (a region in Egypt), burn Zoan (a city in Egypt), and bring judgment upon No (another city in Egypt). **15.** I will pour My fury (anger) on Sin (a city), Egypt's fortress. I will eliminate the people of No, **16.** and set fire to Egypt. Sin will experience great suffering, No will be torn apart, and Noph will face constant distress. **17.** The young men of Aven (an Egyptian city) and Pi Beseth (another Egyptian city) will be slain by the sword, and these cities will be taken into captivity (become prisoners). **18.** At Tehaphnehes (a city in Egypt), the day will be darkened as I break the yoke (oppression) of Egypt. The proud strength of Egypt will come to an end, and a cloud will cover the land. Her cities will go into captivity. **19.** This is how I will bring judgment upon Egypt, and then they will know that I am the Lord." **20.** It came to pass in the eleventh year, on the first month, the seventh day of the month, that the word of the Lord came to me, saying, **21.** "Son of man, I have broken Pharaoh's arm (strength), king of Egypt. And now, it has not been bound for healing, nor has any splint been put on it to make it strong enough to hold a sword. **22.** Therefore, this is what the Lord God says: 'I am against Pharaoh, king of Egypt. I will break both his strong arm and the one that has already been broken. I will cause the sword to fall from his hand. **23.** I will scatter (distribute) the Egyptians among the nations and disperse them across the countries. **24.** I will strengthen the arms of the king of Babylon and put My sword (a weapon) in his hand. But Pharaoh's arms will be broken, and he will groan as a mortally wounded man. **25.** So, I will strengthen the arms of the king of Babylon, but Pharaoh's arms will fail. They will know that I am the Lord when I place My sword in the king of Babylon's hand and he stretches it out against the land of Egypt. **26.** I will scatter the Egyptians among the nations and disperse them throughout the countries. Then they will know that I am the Lord.'"

Chapter 31

1. In the eleventh year, on the first day of the third month, the word of the Lord came to me, saying, **2.** "Son of man, ask Pharaoh, king of Egypt, and his multitude (great number of people): 'Who do you think you are, with all your greatness? **3.** Assyria, for example, was like a mighty cedar tree in Lebanon (a region known for its tall trees), with fine branches that spread out, offering shade to the forest. It was tall and proud, its top reaching high among the other trees. **4.** The waters made it grow; underground rivers helped it rise, with streams flowing around where it was planted, and spreading out to water all the trees of the field. **5.** As a result, its height surpassed all the trees in the field. Its branches grew long, and its boughs (branches) spread wide, thanks to the abundance of water that nourished it. **6.** Birds of the sky made their nests in its branches; under its shade, the animals of the field gave birth to their young. In its shadow, great nations found shelter. **7.** It was majestic and beautiful, with long branches reaching far, because its roots were nourished by abundant water. **8.** No other cedar in God's

garden could compare to it. The fir trees (a type of tree) were not like its branches, nor were the chestnut trees like its boughs. No tree in God's garden had its beauty. **9.** I made it glorious with many branches so that all the trees of Eden (the original paradise) envied it, the trees in the garden of God. **10.** "Therefore, this is what the Lord God says: 'Because you have grown taller and reached among the thick branches, and your heart became proud because of your height, **11.** I will hand you over to the mighty ruler of the nations, and he will deal with you. I have driven you out because of your wickedness. **12.** Foreigners, the most ruthless of nations, have cut you down and left you. Your branches have fallen in the mountains and valleys, and your boughs are broken by the rivers of the land. All the nations of the earth have left your shadow. **13.** Upon your ruin, the birds of the heavens will remain, and the beasts of the field will come to rest on your branches. **14.** This will be so that no other trees by the waters can ever again exalt themselves because of their height, or reach up to the thick boughs. No tree that drinks water will ever be tall enough to compare with you. They have all been delivered to death, to the depths of the earth, among the children of men who go down to the Pit (the grave). **15.** "This is what the Lord God says: 'When it went down to the realm of the dead (hell), I caused mourning. I covered the deep (the sea) because of it. I stopped its rivers, and the great waters were held back. I caused Lebanon to mourn for it, and all the trees of the field withered in grief for it. **16.** I made the nations tremble when they heard of its fall, as I cast it down to the Pit along with those who descend into the grave. All the trees of Eden, the finest of Lebanon, all those that drink water, were comforted in the depths of the earth. **17.** They too went down with it to the grave, those slain by the sword; its strong arm (power) remained in its shadow among the nations. **18.** To which of the trees in Eden will you be compared in glory and greatness? Yet you will be brought down with the trees of Eden to the depths of the earth. You will lie among the uncircumcised (those not in covenant with God), among those slain by the sword. This is Pharaoh and all his multitude,' says the Lord God."

Chapter 32

1. In the twelfth year, on the first day of the twelfth month, the word (message) of the Lord came to me, saying, **2.** "Son of man, take up a lament (expression of sorrow) for Pharaoh, king of Egypt. Say to him, 'You are like a young lion among the nations, a sea monster that stirs up the waters with its feet and pollutes (makes dirty or impure) the rivers.' **3.** "This is what the Lord God says: 'I will spread a net (large piece of material used for trapping) over you with many people, and they will drag you out. **4.** I will leave you on the land, cast (throw forcefully) you on the open fields, and let the birds of the sky settle on you, while the beasts (wild animals) of the earth feed on your flesh. **5.** I will scatter (spread widely) your remains on the mountains and fill the valleys with your carcass (dead body). **6.** I will water (fill with liquid) the land with your blood, even to the mountains, and fill the riverbeds (bottom of the rivers) with you.' **7.** When I extinguish (put out) your light, I will cover the heavens, darken the stars, cover the sun with a cloud, and the moon will not give its light. **8.** All the bright lights in the sky will be darkened over you, and I will bring darkness (absence of light) upon your land,' says the Lord God. **9.** 'I will trouble (disturb) the hearts of many nations when I bring your destruction among them, into lands they have never known. **10.** Many peoples will be shocked (surprised) by you, and their kings will tremble (shake in fear) in fear when I wield (use effectively) my sword against you. They will fear for their lives on the day of your fall. **11.** "For this is what the Lord God says: 'The sword of the king of Babylon will come upon you. **12.** Mighty warriors (strong fighters), the most terrible of nations, will cause your people to fall. They will plunder (steal by force) Egypt's glory, and its entire population will be destroyed. **13.** I will destroy its animals by the great waters, and from now on, human feet and animal hooves (hard coverings on the feet of animals) will no longer pollute them. **14.** I will make their waters clear and their rivers run like oil (smooth and untroubled),' says the Lord God. **15.** 'When I make Egypt desolate (abandoned), and all that once filled it is gone, when I strike down all who live there, they will know that I am the Lord. **16.** This is the lament (song of mourning) they will sing about her; the daughters (female citizens) of the nations will mourn (express grief) for Egypt and all its multitudes (large groups of people),' says the Lord God." **17.** On the fifteenth day of the twelfth month, the word (message) of the Lord came to me again, saying, **18.** "Son of man, wail (cry out in grief) for Egypt's multitude, and cast (throw) them down to the depths (lowest parts) of the earth, along with the famous (renowned) nations, to those who descend (go down) to the Pit (place of the dead). **19.** 'Who is like you in beauty? Go down, be placed among the uncircumcised (those outside the covenant of God).' **20.** "They will fall with those slain (killed) by the sword. Egypt will be delivered (handed over) to the sword, along with its people. **21.** The mighty warriors (strong fighters) of the world will speak to her from the depths (lowest parts) of the grave (place of burial), with those who helped them: 'They have gone down to the Pit (place of the dead), among the uncircumcised, slain by the sword.' **22.** "Assyria is there, with all her company (group) surrounded by their graves (places where they are buried), all slain (killed) by the sword. **23.** Their graves (places where they are buried) are in the deepest parts of the Pit, and their company (group) is all around them, all of them slain (killed), fallen (collapsed) by the sword, who caused terror (extreme fear) in the land of the living. **24.** Elam is there, with all her multitudes (large groups of people), surrounding her grave (place of burial), all slain (killed) by the sword, who went down uncircumcised (outside the covenant) to the lowest part of the earth, who spread terror (extreme fear) in the land of the living; now they bear (carry) their shame with those who descend (go down) to the Pit. **25.** Her bed (place of rest or burial) is set among the slain (killed), with all her multitudes (large groups of people), all of them uncircumcised (outside the covenant), slain (killed) by the sword; though they caused terror (extreme fear) in the land of the living, they now bear (carry) their shame with those who go down to the Pit. **26.** "Meshech and Tubal (tribes) with all their multitudes (large groups of people), are there, with their graves (places of burial) surrounding them. They are all uncircumcised (outside the covenant), slain (killed) by the sword, though they caused terror (extreme fear) in the land of the living. **27.** They do not lie (rest) with the mighty (strong) fallen (killed) of the uncircumcised (those outside the covenant), who have gone down to the grave (place of burial) with their weapons of war. They have laid their swords (weapons) under their heads, but their sins (wrongdoings) remain on their bones, because of the terror (extreme fear) they caused while they lived. **28.** Yes, you will be broken (ruined) among the uncircumcised (those outside the covenant) and lie (rest) with those slain (killed) by the sword. **29.** "Edom, her kings (rulers), and all her princes (leaders), despite their strength, lie (rest) with those slain (killed) by the sword. They will be placed among the uncircumcised (those outside the covenant), with those who descend (go down) to the Pit. **30.** The princes (leaders) of the north, and all the Sidonians (people from Sidon), who caused terror (extreme fear) by their might, lie (rest) with the slain (killed), in shame at the terror (extreme fear) they caused. They lie (rest) uncircumcised (outside the covenant) with those slain (killed) by the sword, bearing (carrying) their shame with those who go down to the Pit. **31.** "Pharaoh will see them and be comforted (feel relief) by the sight of his multitude (people), Pharaoh and all his army slain (killed) by the sword,' says the Lord God. **32.** 'I have caused my terror (extreme fear) to be felt in the land of the living, and he will be placed among the uncircumcised (those outside the covenant), with those slain (killed) by the sword, Pharaoh and all his multitude (people),' says the Lord God."

Chapter 33

1. Again, the word (message) of the Lord came to me, saying, **2.** "Son of man, speak to the people of your nation, and tell them: 'When I bring the sword upon a land, and the people of that land choose a man to be their watchman (someone assigned to keep guard), **3.** and if he sees the sword coming upon the land and blows the trumpet (signal of danger) to warn the people, **4.** then anyone who hears the trumpet and does not take warning, if the sword comes and takes him away, his blood will be on his own head. **5.** He heard the sound of the trumpet but did not take warning; his blood will be on him. But anyone who takes warning will save his life. **6.** But if the watchman sees the sword coming and does not blow the trumpet, and the people are not warned, and the sword comes and takes someone away, he will die because of his sins (wrongdoings), but I will hold the watchman responsible for their blood.' **7.** "So, you, son of man, I have made you a watchman (guardian) for the house of Israel; therefore, you will hear

a word (message) from my mouth and warn them for me. **8.** When I say to the wicked (evil person), 'You will surely die!' and you do not speak to warn him from his way, that wicked man will die because of his sin; but I will hold you responsible for his blood. **9.** But if you warn the wicked to turn from his evil ways, and he does not turn, he will die because of his sin; but you have saved yourself . **10.** "Therefore, you, son of man, say to the house of Israel: 'This is what you are saying, "Our transgressions (sins) and our sins lie upon us, and we waste away because of them. How then can we live?"' **11.** Say to them: 'As I live,' says the Lord God, 'I have no pleasure in the death of the wicked, but rather that the wicked turn from their ways and live. Turn, turn from your evil ways! Why should you die, O house of Israel?' **12.** "Therefore, you, son of man, say to your people: 'The righteousness (right behavior) of the righteous will not save him on the day of his transgression (sin); and the wickedness of the wicked will not cause him to fall if he turns from it; nor will the righteous be able to live by his righteousness on the day that he sins.' **13.** When I say to the righteous, 'You will surely live,' but he trusts in his own righteousness (good deeds) and commits sin, none of his righteous acts will be remembered; but because of the sin he has committed, he will die. **14.** Again, when I say to the wicked, 'You will surely die,' but if he turns from his sin (wrongdoing) and does what is lawful (right) and good, **15.** if the wicked person returns what he has stolen, gives back the pledge (guarantee of debt), and walks in the statutes of life (God's laws) without committing sin, he will surely live; he will not die. **16.** None of the sins he has committed will be remembered against him; he has done what is lawful and right; he will surely live. **17.** "Yet the children of your people say, 'The way of the Lord is unfair.' But it is their way that is unfair! **18.** When the righteous turns from his righteousness and commits sin, he will die because of it. **19.** But when the wicked turns from his wickedness and does what is lawful and right, he will live because of it. **20.** Yet you say, 'The way of the Lord is unfair.' O house of Israel, I will judge each of you according to his own ways." **21.** And it came to pass in the twelfth year of our captivity, in the tenth month, on the fifth day of the month, that one who had escaped from Jerusalem (the capital city) came to me and said, "The city has been captured!" **22.** Now, the hand of the Lord had been upon me the evening before the man came who had escaped. And He had opened my mouth; so when he came to me in the morning, my mouth was opened, and I was no longer mute (unable to speak). **23.** Then the word (message) of the Lord came to me, saying: **24.** "Son of man, those who live in the ruined cities of Israel are saying, 'Abraham was only one man, yet he inherited (received) the land. But we are many, and the land has been given to us as our possession.' **25.** Therefore say to them, 'This is what the Lord God says: "You eat meat with blood (forbidden by the law), you look to your idols (false gods), and you shed blood . Should you then possess the land? **26.** You rely on your sword (violence), you commit detestable acts (wickedness), and defile one another's wives. Should you then possess the land?"' **27.** Say to them, 'This is what the Lord God says: "As I live, surely those who are in the ruins will die by the sword, and the ones in the open field I will give to the wild animals to be devoured; and those in the strongholds and caves will die from disease. **28.** For I will make the land most desolate, and its arrogant strength (pride) will cease, and the mountains of Israel will become so desolate that no one will pass through. **29.** Then they will know that I am the Lord, when I have made the land most desolate because of all their detestable acts (sins) which they have committed." **30.** "As for you, son of man, the people of your nation are talking about you beside the walls and in the doorways of their houses, and they speak to one another, saying, 'Come and hear the word that comes from the Lord.' **31.** So they come to you as people do, they sit before you as My people, and they hear your words, but they do not act on them. For with their mouth they show much love, but their hearts pursue (seek) their own gain. **32.** Indeed, you are to them as a lovely song (entertaining music) by one who has a pleasant voice and plays well on an instrument; for they hear your words, but they do not do them. **33.** And when this comes to pass—surely it will come—then they will know that a prophet (spokesperson for God) has been among them."

Chapter 34

1. The Lord's message came to me, saying: 2. "Son of man, speak against the leaders (those who guide or rule) of Israel. Say to them, 'This is what the Lord God declares to the shepherds: Woe to you, shepherds of Israel, who care only for yourselves! Shouldn't the shepherds be looking after the flock? 3. You enjoy the finest food, clothe yourselves with wool, and slaughter the best animals, but you fail to look after the flock. 4. You haven't strengthened (helped) the weak, healed the sick (those who are ill), cared for the injured (those who are hurt), brought back those who have strayed, or searched for those who wandered. Instead, you rule them with cruelty and force (harshness and unfairness). 5. Because there was no shepherd, they were scattered and became prey for wild animals (dangerous creatures). 6. My sheep wandered across mountains and hills, scattered over the whole earth, and no one went out to find them. 7. So, you shepherds, hear the word of the Lord: 8. 'As I live,' says the Lord God, 'because My flock has become prey, food for wild animals in the absence of a shepherd, and because you shepherds only looked after yourselves instead of tending the flock, 9. hear the word of the Lord! 10. The Lord God says this: I am against the shepherds, and I will hold them accountable (responsible) for My flock. I will take away their right to feed the sheep. They will no longer feed themselves; I will save (rescue) My flock from their mouths, and My sheep will no longer be their food.' 11. For the Lord God declares, "I Myself will search for My sheep and look after them (seek them out). 12. Just as a shepherd seeks out his sheep on a day of darkness (a time of trouble), I will look for My sheep and deliver them from wherever they have been scattered. 13. I will bring them back from foreign lands (other nations), gather them from other countries, and return them to their own land. They will graze on Israel's mountains, by streams (rivers), and in every inhabited place. 14. I will take them to good pasture (rich grazing land), where they will rest on lush green pastures in the high mountains of Israel. 15. I will be their shepherd and give them rest," says the Lord God. 16. "I will search for the lost, bring back those who strayed, bandage (heal) the injured, and strengthen the weak. But I will bring fair judgment (just treatment) on the fat and strong." 17. "As for you, My flock," declares the Lord God, "I will make distinctions between one sheep and another, between rams and goats (different members of the flock). 18. Is it not enough for you to graze on the best pasture? Must you also trample the rest with your feet? Isn't it enough to drink from clear water? Why must you muddy (contaminate) the remaining water with your feet? 19. My sheep have to eat what you trample and drink what you have fouled. 20. Therefore, this is what the Lord God says to them: "I Myself will judge between the fat sheep and the lean sheep (the strong and weak). 21. You have shoved with your shoulder, and butted the weaker ones with your horns (using force) until you scattered them. 22. So I will rescue My flock, and they will no longer be prey. I will judge between sheep and sheep (act with fairness). 23. I will set one shepherd over them, My servant David, who will feed them and be their shepherd (leader). 24. I, the Lord, will be their God, and My servant David will be a prince (ruler) among them. I, the Lord, have spoken. 25. I will make a covenant (agreement) of peace with them, clearing the land of wild animals (dangerous creatures), so they may live in the wilderness (uninhabited areas) and sleep safely in the forests. 26. I will make the land around My hill a blessing, sending showers of blessing (rain) in the proper season. 27. The trees will yield fruit, and the earth will produce its harvest (produce). They will live safely in their land, and they will recognize Me as the Lord when I break the chains (remove the burdens) of their slavery and deliver them from those who oppressed them. 28. They will no longer be prey for the nations, and wild beasts will not devour them. They will dwell in safety, free from fear. 29. I will provide them with a well-known garden (a place of prosperity), where they will no longer suffer hunger (lack of food) or the shame (humiliation) of other nations. 30. Then they will know that I, the Lord their God, am with them, and they, the house of Israel, are My people," declares the Lord God. 31. "You are My flock, the flock of My pasture; you are My people, and I am your God," declares the Lord God.

Chapter 35

1. Once more, the word (message) of the Lord came to me, saying, 2. "Son of man, turn your focus toward Mount Seir (a region in Edom) and proclaim a message against it. 3. Say, 'This is what the Lord God declares: "I am against you, O Mount Seir, and I will extend My hand against you, turning you into a deserted wasteland. 4. Your cities will be destroyed, left empty and desolate. Then you will understand that I am the Lord. 5. Because of your ancient hatred and the bloodshed you caused by striking Israel's children during their time of trouble (calamity), when their sins were coming to an end, 6. as surely as I live," says the Lord God, "I will prepare blood to follow you. Since you didn't disdain bloodshed, blood will pursue you. 7. I will bring ruin upon Mount Seir, cutting off both those who flee and those who return. 8. Your mountains will be filled with those fallen in battle; in the valleys, ravines, and hills, those struck by the sword will lie. 9. I will make you desolate for all time, leaving your cities uninhabited; then you will realize that I am the Lord. 10. "You have claimed, saying, 'These two nations (Israel and Judah) and their lands are ours; we will take control of them,' even though the Lord is present among them. 11. So, as I live," declares the Lord God, "I will treat you according to the rage and jealousy you displayed in your hatred for them. I will make Myself known to them when I judge you. 12. At that time, you will know that I am the Lord. I have heard your blasphemous (disrespectful) words spoken against the mountains of Israel, saying, 'They are deserted; they have been given to us to devour.' 13. You have spoken against Me, multiplying accusations against Me; I have heard it all." 14. This is the proclamation of the Lord God: "The entire earth will rejoice when I bring devastation upon you. 15. Just as you celebrated when Israel's inheritance (property) was laid waste, I will make you desolate, O Mount Seir, and all of Edom—down to the last part of it! At that moment, they will know that I am the Lord."

Chapter 36

1. "Son of man, prophesy (to speak by divine inspiration) to the mountains of Israel, and say: 'O mountains of Israel, hear the word of the Lord! 2. This is what the Lord God says: Because the enemy (those opposed to Israel) has claimed, 'Aha! The ancient heights (high, prominent places) have become our possession,' 3. therefore, prophesy and say: 'The Lord God declares: Because you have been made desolate (in a state of ruin) and swallowed up by the surrounding nations, mocked and slandered (spoken about falsely) by all, 4. I am speaking to you, O mountains, hills, rivers, valleys, and forsaken (abandoned) cities that have become a mockery (something treated with disrespect) to the nations. 5. I am angry with the nations, especially Edom (a nation southeast of Israel), who took My land with joy and malice (desire to harm), to plunder (rob) it. 6. Therefore, prophesy to the land of Israel, and say: 'The Lord God declares: I am furious (extremely angry) because you have borne the shame (disgrace) of the nations.' 7. The nations surrounding you will bear their own shame. But you, O mountains of Israel, will yield (produce) your fruit to My people Israel, for they are about to return. 8. I am for you, and I will turn to you. You will be tilled (prepared for planting) and sown (planted). 9. I will multiply (increase) your people—both men and animals—so that the cities will be rebuilt, and the desolate (ruined) land will flourish (grow well) again. 10. I will increase your population and bring people back to your cities. Your ruined (destroyed) cities will be rebuilt. 11. I will increase both people and animals. You will be inhabited (occupied) as you were in former times, and I will do better for you than in the beginning. Then you will know that I am the Lord. 12. Yes, I will cause My people Israel to walk on you. They will possess (take ownership) you, and you will be their inheritance (something passed down to heirs). You will no longer bereave (deprive) them of children.' 13. The nations have said to you, 'You devour (consume) people and make your land childless.' 14. But you will no longer devour your people or make your land childless, declares the Lord God. 15. You will no longer hear the insults (disrespectful remarks) of the nations or bear the reproach (shame) of the peoples, nor cause your nation to stumble (fall) anymore,' declares the Lord God. 16. The word of the Lord came to me, saying: 17. "Son of man, when the house of Israel dwelt in their own land, they defiled (made unclean) it by their ways and deeds; to Me their way was like the uncleanness (impurity) of a woman in her customary impurity. 18. Therefore I poured out My fury (violent anger) on them for the blood they had shed on the land, and for their idols (false gods) with which they had defiled it. 19. So I scattered (dispersed) them among the nations, and they were dispersed throughout the countries; I judged (decided the punishment

for) them according to their ways and their deeds. **20.** When they came to the nations, wherever they went, they profaned (treated as sacred) My holy name—when they said of them, 'These are the people of the Lord, and yet they have gone out of His land.' **21.** But I had concern (care or worry) for My holy name, which the house of Israel had profaned among the nations wherever they went. **22.** "Therefore say to the house of Israel, 'Thus says the Lord God: I do not do this for your sake, O house of Israel, but for My holy name's sake, which you have profaned among the nations wherever you went. **23.** And I will sanctify (make holy) My great name, which has been profaned among the nations, which you have profaned in their midst; and the nations shall know that I am the Lord," says the Lord God, "when I am hallowed (honored as holy) in you before their eyes. **24.** For I will take you from among the nations, gather (bring together) you out of all countries, and bring you into your own land. **25.** Then I will sprinkle (scatter in small drops) clean water on you, and you shall be clean; I will cleanse (purify) you from all your filthiness (unclean things) and from all your idols. **26.** I will give you a new heart and put a new spirit within you; I will take the heart of stone (a hardened heart) out of your flesh and give you a heart of flesh (a tender, responsive heart). **27.** I will put My Spirit within you and cause you to walk in My statutes (laws), and you will keep My judgments and do them. **28.** Then you shall dwell (live) in the land that I gave to your fathers; you shall be My people, and I will be your God. **29.** I will deliver you from all your uncleannesses. I will call for the grain and multiply it, and bring no famine (extreme scarcity of food) upon you. **30.** And I will multiply the fruit of your trees and the increase (growth) of your fields, so that you need never again bear the reproach (shame) of famine among the nations. **31.** Then you will remember your evil ways and your deeds that were not good; and you will loathe (despise) yourselves in your own sight, for your iniquities and your abominations. **32.** Not for your sake do I do this," says the Lord God, "let it be known to you. Be ashamed and confounded (embarrassed) for your own ways, O house of Israel!" **33.** 'Thus says the Lord God: "On the day that I cleanse (purify) you from all your iniquities (sins), I will also enable you to dwell in the cities, and the ruins (destroyed places) shall be rebuilt. **34.** The desolate land shall be tilled (cultivated) instead of lying desolate (unused) in the sight of all who pass by. **35.** So they will say, 'This land that was desolate has become like the garden of Eden; and the wasted (ruined), desolate, and ruined cities are now fortified (made strong) and inhabited (occupied).' **36.** Then the nations which are left all around you shall know that I, the Lord, have rebuilt the ruined places and planted what was desolate. I, the Lord, have spoken it, and I will do it." **37.** 'Thus says the Lord God: "I will also let the house of Israel inquire of Me to do this for them: I will increase their men like a flock. **38.** Like a flock offered as holy sacrifices, like the flock at Jerusalem on its feast days (religious celebrations), so shall the ruined cities be filled with flocks of men. Then they shall know that I am the Lord."'"

Chapter 37

1. The Lord's hand was upon me, and His Spirit (God's power) carried me to a valley filled with bones. **2.** He led me around the bones, and I saw there were many of them lying throughout the valley, and they were extremely dry. **3.** Then He asked, "Son of man (human being), can these bones live again?" I answered, "O Lord God, only You know." **4.** He said to me, "Proclaim (speak God's message) to these bones, telling them, 'Dry bones, hear the word of the Lord!' **5.** This is what the Lord God says: 'I will put breath (life or spirit) into you, and you will come to life.' **6.** I will place tendons (connective tissues) on you, cover you with flesh, and place skin over you. I will put breath (life) within you, and you will live. Then you will understand that I am the Lord.'" **7.** So, I followed His command and spoke as instructed. Suddenly, I heard a rattling (sharp noise) as the bones began to join together, bone to bone. **8.** I watched as tendons (connective tissues) formed on them, and flesh covered them with skin, but there was still no breath (life) in them. **9.** Then the Lord instructed me, "Prophesy (speak God's message) to the breath (life), calling out to it, 'The Lord God says: Come from the four winds (directions), O breath (life), and breathe upon these bodies so they may live.'" **10.** So, I prophesied as He commanded, and breath (life) entered them. They stood up, alive, a vast army. **11.** Then He spoke, "Son of man, these bones represent all the people (house) of Israel. They say, 'Our bones are dried up, our hope is gone,

and we are cut off.' **12.** Therefore, speak (deliver God's message) to them, saying, 'This is what the Lord God declares: "I will open your graves (burial places) and raise you up. I will return you to the land of Israel.'" **13.** When I open your graves (burial places) and raise you up, My people, you will know that I am the Lord. **14.** I will place My Spirit (God's power) within you, and you will live. I will settle you in your land, and then you will understand that I, the Lord, have spoken and fulfilled it. **15.** The word of the Lord came to me again, saying: **16.** "Take a stick (piece of wood) and write on it: 'For Judah and for the children of Israel, his companions (tribes).' Then take another stick (wood) and write on it: 'For Joseph, the branch (stick) of Ephraim, and all the house (people) of Israel, his companions (tribes).' **17.** Hold the two sticks together as one in your hand. **18.** When the people of your nation ask, 'What does this mean?' **19.** Tell them: 'This is what the Lord God says: "I will take the stick (branch) of Ephraim, representing all the tribes (families) of Israel, and join it with the stick (branch) of Judah, making them one in My hand."' **20.** The sticks (branches) you have written on will be in your hand for them to see. **21.** Then tell them, 'This is what the Lord God declares: "I will gather the people of Israel from the nations where they have been scattered and return them to their own land. **22.** I will make them one nation in the land, on the mountains (elevated land) of Israel, and a single king (ruler) will govern them. They will no longer be two nations, nor will they be divided into two kingdoms. **23.** They will no longer defile (make unclean) themselves with idols, detestable practices, or any of their sins. I will save (deliver) them from all the places where they sinned, and I will cleanse (purify) them. They will be My people, and I will be their God. **24.** My servant David will rule over them, and they will be united under one shepherd (leader). They will follow My commands and obey My statutes. **25.** They will live in the land I gave to Jacob (descendant of Abraham), where their ancestors once lived. They and their children will dwell there forever, and My servant David will be their prince forever. **26.** I will establish an everlasting (forever) covenant (agreement) of peace with them. I will make them flourish and set My sanctuary (holy place) in their midst permanently. **27.** My dwelling place (tabernacle) will be among them; I will be their God, and they will be My people. **28.** All the nations (peoples) will know that I, the Lord, have made Israel holy when My sanctuary (holy place) is with them forever."

Chapter 38

1. The word of the Lord came to me, saying, **2.** "Son of man, direct your attention to Gog (the leader), from Magog (an ancient land), the ruler of Rosh (a region), Meshech , and Tubal , and deliver a prophecy (God's message) against him. **3.** Say this: 'This is the word of the Lord God: I stand opposed to you, Gog, ruler of Rosh, Meshech, and Tubal. **4.** I will turn you around and draw you out by putting hooks (a symbol of control) into your jaws. I will lead you, along with your entire army—cavalry (soldiers on horseback), and soldiers on foot, all well-armed, a mighty force with shields and swords. **5.** Persia (modern Iran), Ethiopia (a nation in Africa), and Libya (countries in North Africa) will be your allies, all equipped with shields and helmets. **6.** Gomer (a people, likely from the north) and its forces, as well as the house of Togarmah (a northern tribe), will come, joined by many nations. **7.** "Get ready and prepare, you and your gathered armies. Act as their guard (defender) in this gathering. **8.** After a long period of time, you will invade Israel, a people who have been saved from destruction, gathered from many nations, now living safely in Israel's once-desolate (empty) mountains. **9.** Like a storm, you will rise up, sweeping over the land, covering it like a cloud, with your armies and all the nations joining you." **10.** "This is what the Lord God declares: 'At that time, evil thoughts (wicked plans) will enter your mind, and you will devise a wicked strategy. **11.** You will say, 'I will attack a peaceful land, a people living without defense, with no walls, gates, or bars.' **12.** You will target a land recently resettled, a people who have returned from the nations, who now possess wealth, livestock, and are living in the heart of the land. **13.** Sheba (an ancient kingdom, possibly in Arabia), Dedan (a region in Arabia), and the merchants of Tarshish (a distant trading nation, likely Spain), along with their young lions (strong allies), will challenge you, asking, "Are you coming to steal and plunder (loot)? Are you gathering armies to take silver, gold, livestock, and goods?"' **14.** "Therefore, son of man, prophesy (speak God's words) and declare to Gog: 'This is what the Lord God says: When my people Israel live in peace and safety, will you not take notice? **15.** You will come from the distant north, with a large army riding horses (cavalry), a formidable (strong) force. **16.** You will attack Israel like a cloud that covers the entire land. This will happen in the latter days (future times), and I will bring you against my land so that the nations will know Me when I show My holiness (divine nature) in you, Gog, before their very eyes.'" **17.** "This is what the Lord God says: You are the one that I spoke about long ago through my prophets in Israel, who foretold (predicted) for years that I would bring you against them. **18.** On that day, when Gog attacks the land of Israel, My anger will be stirred (aroused). **19.** With a jealous (protective) and fiery (intense) wrath, I declare: There will be an earthquake of great magnitude in the land of Israel. **20.** The fish (sea creatures) of the sea, the birds (flying creatures) of the sky, the animals (land creatures) of the field, every living being, and all mankind on the earth will tremble (shake with fear) at My presence. The mountains will crumble (fall apart), cliffs will collapse, and every wall will topple. **21.** I will call for a sword against Gog on all my mountains, and each man's sword will turn upon his own brother. **22.** I will bring judgment (divine punishment) upon him with pestilence (diseases) and bloodshed. I will cause heavy rain, hailstones (large ice chunks), fire, and brimstone (sulfur) to fall upon him, his armies, and the many nations that are with him. **23** I will reveal My greatness and holiness (sacredness), and the nations will see and know that I am the Lord.'"

Chapter 39

1. "Son of man, prophesy against Gog, and declare, 'This is what the Lord God says: "Look, I am opposed to you, Gog, leader of Rosh, Meshech, and Tubal (tribes or regions in the north); **2.** I will turn you around, guide you, and bring you from the far north to assault the mountains of Israel. **3.** I will disarm you, removing the bow (weapon) from your left hand, and causing your arrows to fall from your right hand. **4.** You, along with all your soldiers and the nations that accompany you, will fall on Israel's mountains. I will make you food for the birds of prey and the wild animals. **5.** You will fall in the open field, for I, the Lord God, have spoken this. **6.** I will send fire upon Magog (a region or people) and those who dwell securely along the coast. Then they will recognize that I am the Lord. **7.** I will reveal My holy name to Israel, and they will never again dishonor (disrespect) My name. The nations will know that I am the Lord, the Holy One of Israel. **8.** It is certain, and it will come to pass," declares the Lord God. "This is the day I foretold. **9.** Then, the people living in Israel's cities will go out and burn the enemy's weapons—shields, bucklers, bows, arrows, javelins, and spears. They will use them for fuel, burning them for seven years. **10.** They will not need to cut wood from the fields or forests, for they will use the weapons for firewood. They will take what was taken from them and return what was robbed from them," says the Lord God. **11.** "On that day, I will provide Gog with a burial site in Israel, in the valley east of the sea. This place will block travelers, as they will bury Gog and all his troops there. The valley will be named the Valley of Hamon Gog. **12.** Israel will spend seven months burying the dead to purify the land. **13.** The entire land will participate in the burial, and they will gain renown for it when I am glorified," says the Lord God. **14.** "Specially appointed men will go through the land with a search party to identify and bury the remaining bodies, cleansing the land. At the end of seven months, they will finish the search. **15.** The search party will walk the land, and whenever they find a man's bone, they will mark it until the buriers come and bury it in the Valley of Hamon Gog. **16.** The city will be called Hamonah. This will be how they purify the land." **17.** "And you, son of man, the Lord God says: 'Speak to all the birds and wild creatures: 'Gather from every direction to My great sacrificial meal I am preparing for you on the mountains of Israel, where you will feast on flesh and drink blood. **18.** You will eat the flesh of powerful men, drink the blood of the earth's rulers, of rams, lambs, goats, and bulls—all well-fed (fattened) in Bashan (a fertile land). **19.** You will be satisfied with fat and drink until you are drunk at My sacrificial meal, which I am preparing for you. **20.** You will feast at My table, filled with horses, riders, mighty men, and all the men of war," says the Lord God. **21.** "I will display My glory among the nations, and all will witness the judgment I have carried out, and the power of My hand upon them. **22.** Then the house of Israel will know that I am the Lord their God, from that day onward. **23.** The nations will realize that Israel went into exile because of their sinfulness. They were unfaithful to Me, so I turned My face away from them, gave them into the hands of their enemies, and they fell by the sword. **24.** I treated them according to their uncleanness and their transgressions, and I hid My face from them." **25.** "Therefore, the Lord God declares: 'Now I will bring back the captives of Jacob (Israel) and show mercy to the entire house of Israel. I will be zealous (passionate) for My holy name. **26.** After they have borne their shame and unfaithfulness, when they lived safely in their land without fear, **27.** When I bring them back from the nations and gather them from the lands of their enemies, I will make My holiness known in them before many nations. **28.** They will know that I am the Lord their God, who sent them into exile among the nations but also brought them back to their own land, leaving none behind. **29.** I will no longer hide My face from them, for I will pour out My Spirit upon the house of Israel," says the Lord God.

Chapter 40

1. In the twenty-fifth year of our exile, at the beginning of the year, on the tenth day of the month, and in the fourteenth year after the city was captured, on that very same day, the hand of the Lord came upon me, and He took me there. **2.** In a vision from God, He brought me to the land of Israel and set me on a very high mountain. There, toward the south, I saw something resembling the structure of a city. **3.** He took me there, and I saw a man whose appearance was like bronze. He held a measuring line and a measuring rod in his hand, and he stood at the entrance of the gateway. **4.** The man said to me, "Son of man, look carefully and listen closely to everything I show you. You have been brought here so I can show you these things. Tell the people of Israel everything you see." **5.** There was a wall surrounding the temple, and the man had a measuring rod, which was six cubits long, each cubit and a handbreadth. He measured the width of the wall—it was one rod thick—and the height was also one rod. **6.** He went to the eastern gate, climbed its stairs, and measured the threshold of the gate, which was one rod wide. The other threshold was also one rod wide. **7.** The gate chambers, one on each side of the gateway, measured one rod in length and one rod in width, with five cubits of space between them. **8.** He measured the vestibule of the inner gate, and it was one rod wide. **9.** The vestibule itself was eight cubits long, with gateposts measuring two cubits. The vestibule was on the inner side of the gate. **10.** The eastern gateway had three chambers on each side, all the same size, and the gateposts were the same size on both sides. **11.** He measured the width of the entrance to the gateway, which was ten cubits, and the length of the gate, which was thirteen cubits. **12.** There was a space in front of the gate chambers, one cubit on each side, and the chambers themselves were six cubits wide. **13.** He measured the gateway from the roof of one gate chamber to the roof of the other, and the width was twenty-five cubits, with doors facing each other. **14.** He measured the height of the gateposts, which were sixty cubits tall, and the court surrounding the gateway extended up to the gateposts. **15.** From the entrance of the outer gate to the vestibule of the inner gate was fifty cubits. **16.** There were beveled window frames around the gate chambers and archways, all inside the gateway. The windows were placed all around the inside, and palm trees were carved on the gateposts. **17.** He brought me into the outer court, where there were chambers and a paved area surrounding the court. Thirty chambers faced the pavement. **18.** The pavement ran alongside the gateways, corresponding to the length of the gateways. This area was called the lower pavement. **19.** He measured the distance from the front of the lower gateway to the outer court, which was one hundred cubits, extending eastward and northward. **20.** There was another gateway on the outer court, facing north, and he measured its length and width. **21.** This northern gateway had three chambers on each side, with gateposts and archways measuring the same as the first gateway. Its length was fifty cubits, and its width was twenty-five cubits. **22.** The windows and archways were the same size as those in the eastern gateway, and it was accessed by seven steps. **23.** Another gateway was located opposite the northern one, facing the inner court, with a distance of one hundred cubits between them. **24.** Then he led me to the south, where I saw a southern gateway. He measured its gateposts and archways, and the measurements were the same as those of the other gateways. **25.** This southern gateway also had windows and archways, and its length was fifty cubits and width twenty-five cubits. **26.** This gateway, leading to the south, had seven steps leading up to it. On both sides of the gateposts were palm trees carved into the stone, one on each side. 27. A similar gateway was situated on the inner court, facing south. He measured the distance between the two southern gateways, which was a hundred cubits. 28. Then, he led me through the southern entrance into the inner court. He took the measurements of this southern gateway as well, and they were identical to those of the other southern gates. 29. The gate chambers, the gateposts, and the archways were all the same as before. The gate measured fifty cubits in length and twenty-five cubits in width, with windows around it. 30. The archways were twenty-five cubits long and five cubits wide. They faced the outer court, and palm trees were carved onto the gateposts. There were eight steps leading up to this gate. 31. He led me into the inner court again, this time through the eastern gateway, and the dimensions were the same as those of the other gateways. 32. The gate chambers, the gateposts, and the archways were identical. The gate was fifty cubits long and twenty-five cubits wide, with windows all around. 33. The archways were oriented toward the outer court, with palm trees adorning the gateposts on both sides. There were also eight steps leading up to it. 34. He took me next to the northern gateway, where he measured it, and the measurements matched those of the other gates. 35. All the details, such as the gate chambers, the gateposts, and the archways, were the same. The gate's length was fifty cubits, and its width was twenty-five cubits. 36. The gateposts faced outward, and palm trees were carved on both sides. There were eight steps leading up to this northern gate. 37. Near the gateposts, there was a chamber used for washing the burnt offering. 38. In the vestibule of the gateway, two tables were placed on each side for slaughtering the burnt offering, sin offering, and guilt offering. 39. Outside, near the northern gateway, there were two tables for slaughtering the offerings. Two more tables were situated on the opposite side of the vestibule. 40. In total, there were eight tables—four on each side—designated for slaughtering the sacrifices. 41. Four hewn stone tables were also present, each measuring one and a half cubits in length, width, and height. These were used to hold the utensils needed for the burnt offerings. 42. Hooks were affixed to the tables, and the flesh of the sacrifices was placed upon them. 43. Outside the inner gate, chambers were designated for the singers. One faced south, near the northern gateway, while the other faced north, near the southern gateway. 44. The chamber on the south side was designated for the priests responsible for the temple. 45. The chamber on the north side was for the priests in charge of the altar—the sons of Zadok, who were the only Levites allowed to approach the Lord and serve Him. 46. He measured the court, which was a perfect square, measuring one hundred cubits in both length and width, with the altar positioned in front of the temple. 47. He brought me to the vestibule of the temple and took measurements of the doorposts, which were five cubits wide on each side. The width of the gateway itself was three cubits on each side. 48. The vestibule itself was twenty cubits long and eleven cubits wide. Pillars stood at the doorposts of the vestibule. 49. There were also steps leading up to the vestibule, with pillars standing at both sides of the doorway.

Chapter 41

1. Then he brought me into the sanctuary (a holy or sacred place) and measured the doorposts: six cubits (ancient measurement, approximately 18 inches or 45 cm) wide on each side, which was the width of the tabernacle (a portable sanctuary or temple). 2. The width of the entryway (the passage into a building) was ten cubits, with five cubits on each side as the walls of the entrance. The length of the sanctuary was forty cubits, and its width was twenty cubits. 3. Inside, he measured the doorposts (vertical parts of a door frame): two cubits; the entrance was six cubits high and seven cubits wide. 4. He measured the length beyond the sanctuary: twenty cubits, and its width was twenty cubits. He said, "This is the Most Holy Place (the holiest part of the temple)." 5. He measured the wall (a vertical structure, typically for enclosing or dividing spaces) of the temple, which was six cubits thick. Each side chamber (a small room or space) around the temple was four cubits wide. 6. The side chambers had three stories (levels or floors), one above the other, with thirty chambers on each level. They rested on ledges (horizontal supports) that supported them but were not attached to the temple walls. 7. As you moved up from one story to

the next, the chambers grew wider because the ledges supporting them grew wider, like steps ascending (moving upward) from the lowest to the highest story. 8. I saw a foundation (the base structure upon which something is built) all around the temple, six cubits high, which supported the side chambers. 9. The thickness of the outer wall (a large enclosing structure) of the side chambers was five cubits, and the remaining terrace (a flat, raised platform) around the side chambers was five cubits wide. 10. Between the side chambers and the temple wall, there was a space (an empty or open area) of twenty cubits all around the temple. 11. The doors (entrances) to the side chambers opened onto the terrace, with one door facing north (a cardinal direction) and another facing south (another cardinal direction). The width of the terrace was five cubits on all sides. 12. The building facing the separating (creating a boundary or division) courtyard on the western end was seventy cubits wide. Its walls were five cubits thick, and its length was ninety cubits. 13. He measured the temple, which was one hundred cubits long, including the separating courtyard, the building, and the walls, all one hundred cubits in length. 14. The width of the eastern (referring to the direction of the rising sun) side of the temple, including the courtyard, was also one hundred cubits. 15. He measured the length of the building at the back, facing the separating courtyard, along with its galleries (upper rooms or covered walkways) on both sides, all one hundred cubits. This included the inner temple and the porches (roofed areas) of the court. 16. The doorposts, the windows (openings for light) above the doors, and the inner rooms were all paneled (decorated with panels, often wood or other materials) with wood, from the ground to the windows. The windows were covered. 17. Above the door and throughout the temple, from the inside to the outside, everything was measured carefully and decorated with cherubim (angelic beings) and palm trees. 18. There were cherubim carved (sculpted or shaped) on the walls, and palm trees stood between each cherub. Each cherub had two faces: one of a man and one of a lion, facing palm trees. 19. Cherubim and palm trees were carved on the temple walls, from the floor to the space (open area) above the door, and on all the walls of the sanctuary. 20. The doorposts of the temple were square (having equal sides), and their design matched that of the sanctuary. 21. The altar (a structure for sacrifices) was three cubits high and two cubits long, made of wood. Its corners, length, and sides were all made of wood. He said, "This is the table that stands before the Lord." 22. The temple and sanctuary had two doors, each with two folding (able to bend or collapse) panels, two for each door. 23. The doors were decorated with carvings (sculpted images) of cherubim and palm trees, just like the walls. A wooden canopy (a structure supported by poles) stood at the front of the vestibule (an entrance or lobby). 24. Beveled (having edges cut at an angle) window frames and palm trees were also carved on both sides of the vestibule and the side chambers of the temple.

Chapter 42

1. Then the angel took me to the outer court, along the north side. He led me to a chamber (a room or enclosed space) that was opposite the separating courtyard and the building to the north. 2. The chamber (a room or enclosed space) faced a length of one hundred cubits (about 150 feet) and a width of fifty cubits (about 75 feet). The entrance (a way in or doorway) was on the north side. 3. The chamber was located opposite the inner court, twenty cubits (about 30 feet) away, and opposite the pavement (a paved surface, such as a floor) of the outer court, with galleries (a row of rooms or walkways) stacked in three stories. 4. In front of the chambers, there was a walkway (a path or passage) ten cubits (about 15 feet) wide, with a one cubit (about 1.5 feet) space between it and the chambers. The doors (entrances) of the chambers faced north. 5. The upper (higher in position) chambers were shorter than the lower and middle ones because the galleries (a row of rooms or walkways) took up space in the upper floors. 6. The building had three stories, but unlike the lower levels, the upper levels did not have pillars (tall vertical supports used in construction). This caused them to be shorter than the lower and middle floors. 7. A wall (a vertical structure that encloses or divides spaces) outside the chambers ran parallel (extending in the same direction, always the same distance apart) to them, separating them from the outer court. This wall was fifty cubits (about 75 feet) long. 8. The length of the chambers toward the outer court was fifty cubits, while the length

facing the temple (a sacred place of worship) was one hundred cubits. **9.** The lower chambers had an entrance (a way in or doorway) on the east side, leading directly from the outer court. **10.** There were also chambers (rooms or enclosed spaces) built into the wall (a vertical structure) of the court on the east side, opposite the separating courtyard and the building. **11.** These chambers (rooms or enclosed spaces) were the same size as those on the north side, with a similar design, and all their entrances (ways in or doorways) and exits (ways out) followed the same plan. **12.** The doors (entrances) of these chambers (rooms or enclosed spaces) were directly opposite (exactly across from) the ones on the south side, and they also had a walkway (a path or passage) in front of them. The entrances (ways in or doorways) faced east. **13.** Then the angel said to me, "The north and south chambers (rooms or enclosed spaces), which are opposite the separating courtyard, are holy (sacred, set apart for divine use) chambers. These are the places where the priests (religious leaders) who approach the Lord will eat the most holy offerings. They will place the grain offerings, sin offerings, and guilt offerings here because this is a holy (sacred, set apart for divine use) space." **14.** "When the priests enter these chambers (rooms or enclosed spaces), they must not go back into the outer court in the same clothes they wore while serving. They must change into other garments (clothing) before leaving the holy (sacred, set apart for divine use) chambers (rooms or enclosed spaces) to avoid defiling (making something unclean or impure) the sacred (set apart for divine use) space." **15.** After measuring the inner temple, the angel took me out through the east gateway (an entrance or opening) and measured all around. **16.** He measured the east side with the measuring rod (a tool for measuring length, often a stick), and it was five hundred rods (about 7,500 feet). **17.** He then measured the north side, which was also five hundred rods (about 7,500 feet). **18.** The south side was measured next, and it too was five hundred rods. **19.** Finally, he measured the west side, and it was five hundred rods as well. **20.** The entire area had a wall (divides spaces) around it, five hundred cubits (about 750 feet) long and five hundred cubits wide, separating the holy (sacred,) areas from the common (ordinary) or ordinary areas.

Chapter 43

1. Afterward, he brought me to the gate (an entrance) that faces toward the east. **2.** And behold, the glory (the presence and majesty) of the God of Israel came from the east. His voice was like the sound of many waters (a roaring, powerful sound), and the earth shone with His glory. **3.** It was like the vision (a supernatural sight) I saw earlier—like the vision when I came to destroy the city. The visions were like the ones I saw by the River Chebar (a river in Babylon), and I fell on my face in awe. **4.** The glory of the Lord entered the temple through the gate that faces east. **5.** The Spirit lifted me up and brought me into the inner court; and behold, the glory of the Lord filled the temple. **6.** Then I heard Him speaking to me from within the temple, while a man stood beside me. **7.** He said to me, "Son of man (a reference to Ezekiel), this is the place of My throne and the place where My feet will rest, where I will dwell among the people of Israel forever. They and their kings shall no longer defile my holy name through their idolatry (worship of false gods) or by placing the bodies of their kings on high places. **8.** When they set their threshold (the entrance) by My threshold and their doorposts by My doorposts, with a wall between them and Me, they defiled My holy name by the abominations they committed. Therefore, I consumed them in My anger. **9.** Now let them remove their idolatry and the bodies of their kings far from Me, and I will dwell among them forever. **10.** "Son of man, describe the temple to the people of Israel so that they may be ashamed of their sins (wrongdoings); let them measure the pattern (the plan or design of the temple). **11.** If they are ashamed of all they have done, show them the design of the temple and its arrangements—its exits and entrances, its entire design, all its laws, and ordinances. Write it down in front of them, so they may keep its entire design and follow its ordinances. **12.** This is the law of the temple: The entire area surrounding the mountaintop (the highest point) is most holy. Behold, this is the law of the temple. **13.** "These are the measurements of the altar in cubits (a unit of measurement; one cubit is about 18 inches or 45 cm): the base is one cubit high and one cubit wide, with a rim all around it that is one span (a span is the distance from the tip of the thumb to the tip of the little finger,

approximately 9 inches or 23 cm). This is the height of the altar: **14.** From the base on the ground to the lower ledge (a raised platform), two cubits; the width of the ledge is one cubit; from the smaller ledge to the larger ledge, four cubits; and the width of the larger ledge is one cubit. **15.** The altar hearth (the part where sacrifices are burned) is four cubits high, with four horns (protrusions) extending upward from it. **16.** The altar hearth is twelve cubits long and twelve cubits wide, square at its four corners. **17.** The ledge is fourteen cubits long and fourteen cubits wide on all sides, with a rim of half a cubit around it; its base is one cubit all around; and its steps (stairs) face east. **18.** And He said to me, "Son of man, this is what the Lord God says: These are the rules for the altar on the day it is made, for offering burnt offerings and for sprinkling blood on it. **19.** You shall give a young bull for a sin offering to the priests, the Levites (descendants of the tribe of Levi), who are from the family of Zadok (a priestly line), who approach Me to minister to Me, says the Lord God. **20.** You shall take some of its blood and put it on the four horns of the altar, on the four corners of the ledge, and on the rim around it; this will cleanse it and make atonement (cover for sin) for it. **21.** Then, you shall take the bull from the sin offering and burn it in the designated place of the temple, outside the sanctuary (holy area). **22.** On the second day, you shall offer a young goat without blemish as a sin offering; and they shall cleanse the altar as they did with the bull. **23.** When you have finished cleansing it, offer a young bull without blemish and a ram (male sheep) from the flock, both without defect. **24.** When you offer them before the Lord, the priests shall sprinkle salt (a symbol of purification) on them, and they shall be offered as burnt offerings to the Lord. **25.** Every day for seven days, you shall prepare a goat for a sin offering; they shall also prepare a young bull and a ram from the flock, all without blemish. **26.** For seven days, they shall make atonement for the altar and purify it, thus consecrating it (setting it apart as holy). **27.** When these days are over, on the eighth day and beyond, the priests shall offer your burnt offerings and peace offerings on the altar, and I will accept you, says the Lord God."

Chapter 44

1. Then He brought me back to the outer gate of the sanctuary (a holy place of worship), which faces east, but it was closed. **2.** The Lord said to me, "This gate shall remain shut and will not be opened. No one shall enter through it because the Lord God of Israel has entered through it; therefore, it will stay shut." **3.** As for the prince (the ruler or leader), since he is the prince, he may sit at the gate to eat bread before the Lord. He will enter through the vestibule (an entrance hall) of the gateway and leave the same way he came in." **4.** Then He led me through the north gate to the front of the temple. As I looked, I saw that the glory of the Lord filled the house of the Lord, and I fell on my face in awe. **5.** The Lord said to me, "Son of man (a term for the prophet Ezekiel), pay close attention to what I say. See with your eyes and hear with your ears all that I tell you about the ordinances (rules and laws) of the house of the Lord and its regulations. Be mindful of who may enter the house and who may leave the sanctuary (the holy place)." **6.** "Now speak to the rebellious (those who refuse to obey), to the house of Israel, and say, 'Thus says the Lord God: "O house of Israel, I have had enough of your detestable acts (disgusting practices). **7.** When you brought in foreigners, uncircumcised in heart (those who do not have a pure heart) and uncircumcised in flesh (those who have not been physically circumcised as required by the law), to defile (make impure) My sanctuary, My house, and when you offered My food, the fat and the blood, you broke My covenant because of all your detestable acts." **8.** "You have not kept charge (responsibility) of My holy things but have appointed others to take care of My sanctuary for you." **9.** Thus says the Lord God: "No foreigner, uncircumcised in heart or flesh, shall enter My sanctuary, including any foreigner among the children of Israel." **10.** "The Levites (the tribe of Israel designated for religious duties) who strayed from Me, when Israel went astray and followed their idols, shall bear their guilt (responsibility for wrongdoing). **11.** Yet they shall serve in My sanctuary as gatekeepers and ministers of the house; they shall offer the burnt offerings and sacrifices for the people, and they shall stand before them to minister to them." **12.** "Because they ministered to them before their idols and caused the house of Israel to sin, I have sworn an oath against them," says the Lord God, "that they shall bear their guilt." **13.** "They shall not come near Me to minister as priests, nor come near any of My holy things, nor into the Most Holy Place. They shall bear their shame and the detestable acts they have committed." 14. "Nevertheless, I will make them keep charge of the temple for all its work and all that must be done in it." 15. "But the priests, the Levites, the sons of Zadok (a righteous line of priests), who kept charge of My sanctuary when the children of Israel went astray, they shall come near to minister to Me. They shall stand before Me to offer the fat and the blood," says the Lord God. 16. "They shall enter My sanctuary and come near My table to minister to Me, and they shall keep My charge." 17. "Whenever they enter the gates of the inner court, they shall wear linen garments (simple, clean clothing); no wool shall be worn by them while ministering within the gates of the inner court or inside the house." 18. "They shall have linen turbans (head coverings) on their heads and linen trousers (pants) on their bodies. They shall not wear anything that causes sweat (effort or physical exertion) while serving." 19. "When they go out to the outer court to the people, they shall take off the garments in which they have ministered, leave them in the holy chambers, and put on other garments. They must not sanctify (make holy) the people in their holy garments." 20. "They shall neither shave their heads nor allow their hair to grow long. Instead, they shall keep their hair neatly trimmed." 21. "No priest shall drink wine when he enters the inner court." 22. "They shall not marry a widow or a divorced woman, but only take virgins (unmarried women) from the descendants of Israel, or widows of priests." 23. "They shall teach My people the difference between the holy (set apart for God) and the unholy (ordinary), and make them understand the difference between the clean (ritually pure) and the unclean (ritually impure)." 24. "In legal disputes, they shall stand as judges and judge according to My laws. They shall uphold My statutes at all appointed meetings and keep My Sabbaths holy." 25. "They shall not defile themselves by coming near a dead person, except for a father, mother, son, daughter, brother, or unmarried sister." 26. "After they are cleansed, they shall count seven days for purification." 27. "When they go to the sanctuary to minister, they must offer a sin offering in the inner court," says the Lord God. 28. "As for their inheritance, I am their inheritance. You shall not give them a possession in Israel, for I am their possession." 29. "They shall eat the grain offering, the sin offering, and the guilt offering; everything consecrated in Israel shall belong to them." 30. "The best of all the firstfruits (the first part of the harvest) and every sacrifice shall be the priest's. You shall also give the priest the first of your ground meal (flour) to bring a blessing on your house." 31. "The priests shall not eat anything that has died of itself or been torn by wild animals, whether bird or beast."

Chapter 45

1. "When you divide the land among the tribes, you must set apart a special portion for the Lord, a holy section. This section will be twenty-five thousand cubits (a unit of length, approximately 18 inches or 45 cm) long and ten thousand cubits wide. It will remain holy throughout its entire area." 2. "This area will include a square plot for the sanctuary, measuring five hundred by five hundred rods (a unit of length, roughly 16.5 feet or 5 meters), with an additional fifty cubits of open space surrounding it." 3. "You will measure the land as follows: twenty-five thousand cubits in length and ten thousand in width. This section will include the Most Holy Place (the innermost and holiest part of the temple), the sanctuary of the Lord." 4. "This will be a holy section belonging to the priests, the ministers of the sanctuary (those who serve in the temple, especially in spiritual duties and rituals), who come near to serve the Lord. It will be a place for their homes and for the sanctuary itself." 5. "An area of twenty-five thousand cubits long and ten thousand cubits wide will belong to the Levites (members of the tribe of Levi, set apart for temple service), the temple servants. They will be given twenty chambers (rooms or apartments) as their possession." 6. "You shall designate a section for the city, five thousand cubits wide and twenty-five thousand cubits long, located next to the holy section. This will be for the entire house of Israel (the collective people of Israel, the descendants of Jacob)." 7. "The prince (a ruler or leader, particularly one who holds authority over the land in Israel) shall have a section on both sides of the holy area and the city's property. It will border the holy section and the city's property, extending westward on the west side and eastward on the east side.

Its length will match that of one of the tribal portions, from the western border to the eastern border." 8. "This land will belong to the prince, and no longer shall the princes oppress (treat people unfairly or unjustly) My people. They will give the remaining land to the house of Israel, divided by tribes." 9. 'The Lord God says: "Enough, O princes of Israel! Put an end to violence and theft (the act of stealing). Practice justice and righteousness (moral correctness), and stop dispossessing (taking away someone's property or land) My people," says the Lord God.' 10. "You must use honest weights and measures: honest scales (a tool for measuring weight), an honest ephah (a unit of dry measure, roughly 22 liters or 6 gallons), and an honest bath (a liquid measure)." 11. "The ephah and the bath must be the same measure, with the bath containing one-tenth of a homer (a large unit of measure for dry or liquid substances, approximately 220 liters or 58 gallons), and the ephah also one-tenth of a homer. Their measure will be based on the homer." 12. "The shekel (a unit of weight, about 11 grams) will be twenty gerahs (a small weight unit, 1/20th of a shekel). Twenty shekels, twenty-five shekels, and fifteen shekels will make up one mina (a unit of weight, about 600 grams)." 13. "This is the offering you shall give: one-sixth of an ephah from a homer of wheat, and one-sixth of an ephah from a homer of barley (a type of grain, often used for food and in offerings)." 14. "For oil, the bath of oil shall be one-tenth of a bath from a kor (a large liquid measurement, equivalent to a homer or ten baths). A kor equals a homer, or ten baths." 15. "One lamb (a young sheep) will be given from a flock of two hundred, from Israel's rich pastures (fertile and productive land). These offerings will be for grain offerings, burnt offerings, and peace offerings, to make atonement (reconciliation or forgiveness) for the people," says the Lord God. 16. "All the people of the land shall give this offering to the prince of Israel." 17. "It will be the prince's responsibility to prepare the burnt offerings, grain offerings, and drink offerings (offerings made with wine or liquid) at the feasts, the New Moons, the Sabbaths, and all the appointed seasons (times of celebration) of Israel. He shall prepare the sin offering, the grain offering, the burnt offering, and the peace offerings to make atonement for the house of Israel." 18. 'The Lord God says: "On the first day of the first month, you shall take a young bull (an unblemished male cow) without blemish and cleanse the sanctuary."' 19. "The priest shall take some of the blood from the sin offering and put it on the doorposts of the temple (the main entrance), on the four corners of the altar (a structure used for sacrifices), and on the gateposts of the inner court." 20. "On the seventh day of the month, you shall do the same for anyone who has sinned unintentionally (accidentally or without meaning to) or in ignorance (lack of knowledge). This will atone for the temple." 21. "On the fourteenth day of the first month, you shall observe the Passover (a Jewish festival commemorating the Exodus from Egypt), a seven-day feast. Unleavened bread (bread without yeast) shall be eaten." 22. "On that day, the prince shall prepare for himself and for all the people of the land a bull for a sin offering." 23. "During the seven days of the feast, the prince shall offer a burnt offering (an offering in which the entire animal is burned) to the Lord: seven bulls and seven rams (mature male sheep) without blemish, each day for seven days, and a goat kid (a young goat) daily for a sin offering." 24. "He shall prepare a grain offering (an offering made from flour, oil, and sometimes incense) of one ephah for each bull and one ephah for each ram, along with a hin (a liquid measure, approximately 1.5 liters) of oil for each ephah." 25. "In the seventh month, on the fifteenth day of the month, during the feast, he shall do the same for seven days: the sin offering, the burnt offering, the grain offering, and the oil."

Chapter 46

1. The Lord God says: "The gateway to the inner court, facing east, shall remain shut during the six working days. But on the Sabbath and the New Moon, it shall be opened." 2. The prince will enter through the vestibule (entry area) of the gate from outside, and he will stand at the gatepost. The priests will prepare his burnt offerings and peace offerings. He will worship at the threshold of the gate, then leave, and the gate will remain open until evening. 3. The people of the land will also worship at the entrance of this gate before the Lord on Sabbaths and New Moons. 4. On the Sabbath, the prince shall offer six lambs without blemish and a ram without blemish as burnt offerings to the Lord. 5. The grain offering with the ram shall be one ephah (a unit of

measure) and the grain offering for the lambs will be as much as he desires, along with a hin (a measure of liquid) of oil for each ephah. 6. On the New Moon, the prince shall offer a young bull without blemish, six lambs, and a ram, all without blemish. 7. The grain offering shall be one ephah for the bull, one ephah for the ram, and as much as he desires for the lambs, with a hin of oil for each ephah. 8. When the prince enters, he will go through the vestibule of the gateway and leave by the same way. 9. When the people of the land come to worship during the appointed feast days, whoever enters through the north gate shall leave through the south gate, and whoever enters through the south gate shall leave through the north gate. They must not return the same way they entered. 10. The prince will be among them. When they go in, he will go in, and when they go out, he will go out. 11. At the festivals and appointed feast days, the grain offering shall be one ephah for a bull, one ephah for a ram, and as much as he desires for the lambs, along with a hin of oil for each ephah. 12. When the prince makes a voluntary burnt offering or peace offering to the Lord, the east gate shall be opened for him. He will prepare his burnt offering and peace offerings as he did on the Sabbath. Then he will leave, and the gate shall be shut after him. 13. Every morning, a burnt offering of a lamb without blemish, from the first year, shall be made to the Lord. 14. Along with it, a grain offering of one-sixth of an ephah and one-third of a hin of oil to moisten the fine flour shall be prepared. This grain offering is a perpetual ordinance to be made regularly to the Lord. 15. They shall prepare the lamb, the grain offering, and the oil every morning as a regular burnt offering. 16. The Lord God says: "If the prince gives a portion of his inheritance to any of his sons, it will belong to them as their inheritance. 17. But if he gives a portion to one of his servants, it will belong to the servant until the year of liberty (the Jubilee year), after which it shall return to the prince. However, the prince's inheritance will remain with his sons." 18. "The prince must not take land from the people by force. He must not evict anyone from their property, but will give his sons their inheritance from his own property, so that My people are not scattered from their land." 19. Then, the angel brought me through the entrance at the side of the gate into the holy chambers of the priests facing north, where a place was located at the westernmost end. 20. He said to me, "This is the area where the priests will boil the trespass offering and the sin offering, and where they will bake the grain offering. They must not bring these offerings into the outer court to sanctify the people." 21. He then took me to the outer court, where I passed by the four corners of the court. In each corner, there was a separate court. 22. The courts in each of the four corners of the outer court measured forty cubits long and thirty cubits wide, all of equal size. 23. There were building stones arranged around each of these courts, and under the stones, cooking hearths were set up. 24. The angel said to me, "These are the kitchens where the temple ministers will cook the sacrifices for the people."

Chapter 47

1. The man brought me back to the entrance of the temple, and I saw water flowing from under the temple threshold (the base of the door), heading east. The temple's front faced east, and the water flowed from the right side of the temple, south of the altar. 2. He led me out through the north gate and took me around to the outer gate (the outermost entrance) that faces east. There, I saw water flowing from the right side. 3. As the man measured 1,000 cubits (about 1,500 feet), he led me through the water, which came up to my ankles. 4. He measured another 1,000 cubits, and the water came up to my knees. He measured another 1,000 cubits, and the water reached my waist. 5. He measured a final 1,000 cubits, and now the water was a river so deep that I couldn't cross it. It was water to swim in—too deep to walk through. 6. He asked me, "Son of man (a term for Ezekiel), do you see this?" Then he brought me back to the riverbank. 7. When I looked, I saw many trees growing on both sides of the river. 8. He told me, "This water flows toward the eastern region, goes down into the valley, and enters the sea. When it reaches the sea, its waters will become fresh (pure or healing)." 9. Wherever the river flows, it will bring life. Many kinds of fish will thrive (grow and live well) in it, because the water will heal everything it touches, and all living things will live wherever the river flows. 10. Fishermen will stand along the river from En Gedi to En Eglaim, spreading their nets. The fish they catch will be like the fish of the Mediterranean Sea—abundant (plentiful) and diverse. 11. But marshes and swamps will not be healed; they will remain salty. 12. Along the riverbanks, on both sides, all kinds of fruit trees will grow. Their leaves won't wither (dry up), and their fruit will never fail. They will bear fruit every month, because the river's water flows from the sanctuary (the holy place). Their fruit will be for food, and their leaves will have healing properties. 13. The Lord God says, "These are the borders (boundaries) of the land that you will divide as an inheritance among the twelve tribes of Israel. Joseph will receive two portions." 14. "You will inherit the land equally, because I promised it to your ancestors. This land will be your inheritance." 15. The northern border will be from the Great Sea (Mediterranean), along the road to Hethlon, leading to Zedad. 16. The border will continue through Hamath, Berothah, Sibraim (between Damascus and Hamath), and Hazar Hatticon (on the border of Hauran). 17. The border will extend from the Sea to Hazar Enan (near Damascus), and northward to Hamath. This is the northern boundary. 18. The eastern border will run from between Hauran and Damascus, along Gilead (region east of Israel) and the land of Israel, continuing along the Jordan River to the eastern side of the sea. 19. The southern border will run from Tamar (a place near the Dead Sea) to the waters of Meribah near Kadesh, and along the brook (small stream) to the Great Sea. This is the southern boundary. 20. The western border will be the Great Sea, from the southern boundary to a point opposite Hamath. This is the western boundary. 21. "You will divide the land among yourselves according to the tribes of Israel." 22. "When you divide it, the foreigners (non-Israelites) who live among you and have children will also receive an inheritance. They will be considered as native-born Israelites and share in the inheritance with the tribes." 23. "Wherever a foreigner lives, you will assign them an inheritance in the tribe they belong to," says the Lord God.

Chapter 48

1. "The following are the names of the tribes: From the northern boundary, starting at the road to Hethlon (a town), and continuing to the entrance of Hamath (a city), up to Hazar Enan (a town) and the border of Damascus (a city) extending north toward Hamath, one section shall be designated for Dan, stretching from its eastern edge to its western edge." 2. "Next, adjacent to Dan, extending from east to west, one section will be assigned to Asher (a tribe)." 3. "Following Asher, along its east-to-west border, one section will be given to Naphtali (a tribe)." 4. "Further south, from the border of Naphtali, running from east to west, one section will be allotted to Manasseh (a tribe)." 5. "Then, on the border of Manasseh, extending from east to west, a section will be set aside for Ephraim (another tribe)." 6. "To the south of Ephraim, from east to west, one section will be given to Reuben (a tribe)." 7. "Continuing along the border of Reuben, running from east to west, one section will be designated for Judah (another tribe)." 8. "On the border of Judah, you will set aside a district for the Lord, measuring twenty-five thousand cubits in width, and the same length as the other sections, running east to west, with the sanctuary (the holy place) placed in the middle." 9. "This district, dedicated to the Lord, will be twenty-five thousand cubits long and ten thousand cubits wide." 10. "It shall be for the priests: The holy section will be twenty-five thousand cubits long on the north side, ten thousand cubits wide on the west side, ten thousand cubits wide on the east side, and twenty-five thousand cubits long on the south side, with the Lord's sanctuary positioned in the center." 11. "This land will belong to the descendants of Zadok (a priestly family), who have remained faithful to My commands and did not stray like the rest of Israel, unlike the Levites." 12. "The land set apart will be the holiest part of the territory, bordered by the land of the Levites." 13. "Next to the priestly land, the Levites will have a portion measuring twenty-five thousand cubits in length and ten thousand in width; this entire section will match the dimensions of the priest's portion." 14. "They must not sell or exchange any of this land; they are forbidden from alienating (giving away) the best part of the land, for it is dedicated to the Lord." 15. "The remaining five thousand cubits, along the edge of the twenty-five thousand, shall be designated for the city's common use, providing space for homes and open land. The city will be located at the center." 16. "The city itself will have the following dimensions: four thousand five hundred cubits on each of its four sides—north, south, east, and west." 17. "The common land surrounding the city will measure two

hundred and fifty cubits on each side—north, south, east, and west." **18.** "The remaining land adjacent to the holy district will extend ten thousand cubits to the east and another ten thousand cubits to the west. This land will be next to the holy district, and its produce will be used to feed the workers of the city." **19.** "The workers, drawn from all the tribes of Israel, will cultivate this land." **20.** "The entire area will be a square, measuring twenty-five thousand cubits by twenty-five thousand cubits. You will reserve the holy section alongside the city's property." **21.** "The prince (the ruler) will have his land on either side of the holy district and the city's property. His territory will stretch from the eastern border to the western border, adjacent to the tribal lands. The sanctuary will remain at the center of his land." **22.** "Beyond the Levites' land and the city's property, which are surrounded by the prince's land, the area between the borders of Judah and Benjamin (two tribes) will be under the prince's control." **23.** "For the remaining tribes, from east to west, Benjamin (a tribe) will be assigned one section." **24.** "To the north of Benjamin, one section will be allotted to Simeon (a tribe)." **25.** "Next, along the border of Simeon, extending from east to west, one section will be given to Issachar (a tribe)." **26.** "Continuing along the border of Issachar, from east to west, one section will be for Zebulun (a tribe)." **27.** "To the north of Zebulun, running from east to west, one section will be given to Gad (a tribe)." **28.** "On the southern edge of Gad, the border will run from Tamar. **29.** (a place) to the waters of Meribah (a place) by Kadesh (a place), following the stream to the Great Sea (a large body of water)." **29.** "This is the land that you will divide among the tribes of Israel by casting lots, and these are their portions," says the Lord God. **30.** "These will be the city's exits: On the northern side, measuring four thousand five hundred cubits, the city's gates will bear the names of the tribes of Israel. Three gates will face north: one for Reuben, one for Judah, and one for Levi." **31.** "On the eastern side, four thousand five hundred cubits, three gates will be located: one for Joseph (a tribe), one for Benjamin, and one for Dan." **32.** "On the southern side, four thousand five hundred cubits, three gates will be placed: one for Simeon, one for Issachar, and one for Zebulun." **33.** "On the western side, four thousand five hundred cubits, three gates will be found: one for Gad, one for Asher (a tribe), and one for Naphtali (a tribe)." **34.** "The total distance around the city will be eighteen thousand cubits. From that point onward, the city's name will be: THE LORD IS THERE."

34 – Daniel

Chapter 1

1. In the third year of King Jehoiakim (as the eighteenth and antepenultimate King of Judah from 609 to 598 BC) of Judah, King Nebuchadnezzar (the king of Babylon) besieged (surrounded and attacked) Jerusalem. **2.** The LORD handed Jehoiakim over to Nebuchadnezzar, along with sacred articles (holy objects) from God's temple, which Nebuchadnezzar took to the land of Shinar (the region in ancient Mesopotamia) and placed in his god's treasury (a place where treasures are kept). **3.** Nebuchadnezzar ordered Ashpenaz (the chief officer), the chief of his eunuchs (men who were castrated and served in royal courts), to bring some young Israelites, including the royal family and nobles (important families), **4.** Young men without defects, handsome, wise, quick learners, and capable of serving in the king's palace. They would be taught the language and literature (writings) of the Chaldeans (Babylonians). **5.** The king assigned those daily portions (amounts) of his delicacies (fancy food) and the wine he drank, and they were to undergo three years of training before serving him. **6.** Among those from Judah were Daniel, Hananiah, Mishael, and Azariah. **7.** The chief of the eunuchs gave them new names: Daniel became Belteshazzar, Hananiah became Shadrach, Mishael became Meshach, and Azariah became Abed-Nego. **8.** But Daniel decided (resolved) not to defile (make impure) himself with the king's food or wine and requested not to do so. **9.** God gave Daniel favor (kindness) from the chief of the eunuchs. **10.** The chief feared the king, who had ordered their food, and worried that if they appeared worse than the others, he might lose his life. **11.** So Daniel spoke to the steward (manager), whom the chief had assigned to them, **12.** Asking, "Test us for ten days, let us eat vegetables and drink water. **13.** After ten days, compare us to the young men who eat the king's food and decide as you see fit." **14.** The steward agreed to test them for ten days. **15.** After ten days, they appeared healthier and better nourished (fed) than

those eating the king's food. **16.** The steward then gave them only vegetables. **17.** God gave these four young men knowledge in literature (study) and wisdom, and Daniel understood (had insight into) visions and dreams. **18.** After training, the chief brought them before King Nebuchadnezzar. **19.** The king questioned them and found none like Daniel, Hananiah, Mishael, and Azariah, so they served him. **20.** In all matters of wisdom and understanding, the king found them ten times better than his magicians (people who claim to predict the future) and astrologers (people who interpret the stars). **21.** Daniel continued to serve until the first year of King Cyrus of Persia (a Persian king).

Chapter 2

1. In the alternate time of King Nebuchadnezzar's reign, he'd disquieting dreams that disturbed him, and he couldn't sleep. **2.** The king summoned the magicians (people who claim to have supernatural powers), astrologers (those who interpret the stars), conjurers (interpreters of magic), and Chaldeans (wise men from the sumptuous clerkly class) to interpret his dream. They came and stood before him. **3.** The king said to them, "I've had a dream, and I'm anxious to understand it." **4.** The Chaldeans spoke to the king in Aramaic (the language spoken in Babylon), "Long live the king! Tell us the dream, and we will interpret it." **5.** The king replied, "I've made up my mind if you do not tell me the dream and its interpretation, you'll be torn to pieces, and your homes will be destroyed. **6.** still, if you can tell me both the dream and its interpretation, you'll admit gifts, prices, and great honor. So tell me the dream and its interpretation." **7.** They replied again, "Let the king tell his retainers the dream, and we will interpret it." **8.** The king answered, "I know you're trying to buy time (detention) because you see I'm determined. **9.** If you don't tell me the dream, you'll be condemned! You've been lying to me, staying for the right time. Tell me the dream, and I'll know you can give its interpretation." **10.** The Chaldeans replied to the king, "There's no man on earth who can do what the king asks! No king has ever asked such a thing from any magician or prophesier. **11.** What the king asks is too delicate. No bone can tell the king what he pictured except the gods, whose lodging is not with meat (humans)." **12.** This made the king veritably angry, and he ordered all the wise men of Babylon to be killed. **13.** The decree (sanctioned order) was issued, and the wise men were being killed. They sought Daniel and his companions to execute them. **14** Daniel, with wisdom (knowledge and good judgment) and counsel (advice), spoke to Arioch, the king's captain (leader), who was transferred to execute the wise men of Babylon. **15.** He asked, " Why is the king's order so critical?" Arioch explained the situation to Daniel. **16.** So Daniel went by and asked the king for further time to interpret the dream. **17.** Daniel returned home and told his companions, Hananiah, Mishael, and Azariah, **18.** asking them to supplicate(call upon) to the God of heaven for mercy concerning this secret(riddle), so they would not corrupt(die) with the rest of the wise men. **19.** That night, the secret was revealed to Daniel in a vision (a supernatural sight or disclosure). Also Daniel praised the God of heaven. **20.** Daniel said, "Praise be to the name of God ever and ever. Wisdom and power belong to Him. **21.** He changes times and seasons (ages of time); He deposes (removes) lords and rises up others. He gives wisdom to the wise and knowledge to the sapient (those who understand). **22.** He reveals deep and retired effects; He knows what lies in darkness, and light dwells with Him. **23.** I thank You and praise You, God of my ancestors(fathers), You have given me wisdom and power, and You've revealed to me what we asked. You have made given to us the king's dream." **24.** Daniel went to Arioch, whom the king had appointed to kill the wise men of Babylon, and said, "Don't destroy the wise men. Take me to the king, and I'll interpret the dream for him." **25.** Arioch snappily brought Daniel before the king, saying, "I've set up a man from Judah who'll tell the king the interpretation." **26.** The king asked Daniel, "Are you suitable to tell me the dream I had and its interpretation?" **27.** Daniel replied, "No wise man, prophesier, magician, or prophesier (someone who tells the future) can explain to the king what he asked. **28.** But there's a God in heaven who reveals secrets, and He has shown King Nebuchadnezzar what will be in the future. Your dream and the fancies (supernatural sights) you saw on your bed are these **29.** as you lay on your bed, studies came to your mind about what will be in the future. God, who reveals secrets, has shown you what's to come. **30.**

As for me, this secret wasn't revealed to me because I'm wiser than anyone differently, but so that you may know the studies of your heart." **31.** "You, O king, saw a great image. This image, whose splendor (brilliance) was extraordinary, stood before you, and its appearance was stupendous (emotional). **32.** The head of the image was made of fine gold, its casket and arms of tableware, its belly and shanks of citation, **33.** its legs of iron, and its bases incompletely of iron and incompletely of complexion. **34.** As you watched, a gravestone was cut out, but not by mortal hands. It struck the image on its bases of iron and complexion, smashing them to pieces. **35.** Also the iron, complexion, citation, tableware, and gold were broken into pieces and came like chaff (light grain cocoons) from the threshing bottom (where grain is separated from chaff). The wind blew them down, and no trace was set up. But the gravestone that struck the image came a huge mountain that filled the whole earth." **36.** "This was the dream, and now we will interpret it for the king. **37.** You, O king, are the king of lords. The God of heaven has given you a area, power, strength, and glory. **38.** Wherever people live — beasts (creatures) and catcalls — He has given them into your hands and made you sovereign over them all. You're the head of gold. **39.** After you, another area will raise, inferior(less important) to yours. Also a third area, one of citation, will rule over the entire earth. **40.** The fourth area will be as strong as iron, because iron breaks and crushes everything. Like iron that crushes, it'll destroy and crush all the others. **41.** Just as you saw that the bases and toes were incompletely of complexion and incompletely of iron, the area will be divided. Yet some of its strength will remain, like iron mixed with complexion. **42.** As the toes were incompletely iron and incompletely complexion, the area will be incompletely strong and incompletely fragile. **43.** You saw iron mixed with complexion. They will mingle with the people, but they won't remain united, just as iron doesn't mix with complexion. **44.** In the time of those lords, the God of heaven will set up a area that will noway be destroyed. This area won't be left to another people; it'll crush and put an end to all other fiefdoms, and it'll stand ever. **45.** As you saw that a gravestone was cut out without hands and crushed the iron, citation, complexion, tableware, and gold the great God has shown the king what will be in the future. The dream is certain, and its interpretation is sure." **46.** also King Nebuchadnezzar fell face down before Daniel and ordered that an immolation (gift) and incense (ambrosial bank) be presented to him. **47.** The king said to Daniel, "Truly your God is the God of gods, the Lord of lords, and a revealer of secrets, since you could reveal this secret." **48.** also the king promoted Daniel, gave him numerous gifts, and made him sovereign over the whole fiefdom of Babylon, and principal director over all the wise men of Babylon. **49.** Daniel requested that Shadrach, Meshach, and Abed- Nego be appointed over the affairs of Babylon, while Daniel remained at the king's gate.

Chapter 3

1. King Nebuchadnezzar made a large golden statue, 90 feet tall and 9 feet wide, and set it up in the plain of Dura (a large flat area), in the province of Babylon. **2.** The king ordered that all the officials, including satraps (governors), administrators, governors, counselors, treasurers, judges, and magistrates (officials), be summoned for the dedication (ceremony) of the statue. **3.** The officials gathered together for the statue's dedication and stood before it. **4.** A herald (messenger) announced to the crowd, "When you hear the sound of the horn, flute, harp, lyre, and other musical instruments, you must fall down and worship the golden image that King Nebuchadnezzar has set up." **5.** "Anyone who refuses to worship will be thrown into a fiery furnace (a very hot oven) immediately." **6.** When the people heard the music, they all fell down and worshiped the golden image. **7.** At that moment, some Chaldeans (Babylonian officials) came forward and accused the Jews. **8.** They said to the king, "O king, live forever! **9.** You have made a decree (command) that when the music plays, everyone must fall down and worship the gold image. **10.** But there are certain Jews, Shadrach, Meshach, and Abed-Nego, whom you have put in charge of Babylon, who do not obey you. They refuse to worship the gold image." **11.** Furious (very angry), Nebuchadnezzar summoned Shadrach, Meshach, and Abed-Nego. **12.** He asked them, "Is it true that you refuse to serve my gods and worship the golden image I set up? **13.** If you are ready to worship when you hear the music, all will be well. But if you don't, you will be thrown into the fiery furnace. Then, who is the

god who can save you from my power?" **14.** Shadrach, Meshach, and Abed-Nego answered, "We don't need to defend ourselves before you. **15.** Our God, whom we serve, is able to save us from the fiery furnace, and He will rescue us from your hand, O king. **16.** But even if He does not, we want you to know, O king that we will not serve your gods or worship the gold image you set up." **17.** Nebuchadnezzar became enraged (extremely angry), and his face grew angry toward them. He ordered the furnace to be heated seven times hotter than usual. **18.** He commanded his strongest soldiers to tie them up and throw them into the furnace. **19.** The three men were bound (tied) in their clothes and thrown into the furnace. **20.** The furnace was so hot that the soldiers who threw them in were killed by the flames. **21.** Shadrach, Meshach, and Abed-Nego fell into the fire, still bound. **22.** Nebuchadnezzar leaped up in amazement and asked his advisors, "Did we not throw three men into the fire?" **23.** "Yes, O king," they replied. **24.** "Look!" he said. "I see four men walking in the fire, unharmed, and the fourth looks like the Son of God." **25.** Nebuchadnezzar approached the furnace and called, "Shadrach, Meshach, and Abed-Nego, servants of the Most High God come out!" **26.** The three men came out of the fire, and the officials gathered around them. **27.** They saw that the fire had not harmed them. Their hair wasn't singed (burned), their clothes weren't burned, and they didn't even smell like smoke. **28.** Nebuchadnezzar praised their God, saying, "Blessed (honored) be the God of Shadrach, Meshach, and Abed-Nego, who sent His Angel to save His servants who trusted in Him. They defied (refused) my command and were willing to die rather than serve or worship any god but their own. **29.** Therefore, I decree that anyone who speaks against the God of Shadrach, Meshach, and Abed-Nego will be cut into pieces, and their homes will be turned to rubble (ruined). There is no other god who can save like this." **30.** The king promoted Shadrach, Meshach, and Abed-Nego in the province of Babylon.

Chapter 4

1. Nebuchadnezzar, king, to all people, nations, and languages on earth: May peace is multiplied to you. **2.** I want to share the great signs and wonders the Highest God has done for me. **3.** How great are His signs and mighty His wonders! His kingdom is everlasting, and His rule is for all generations. **4.** I, Nebuchadnezzar, was at peace in my house and prospering (doing well) in my palace. **5.** I had a dream that frightened (scared) me, and the thoughts and visions troubled (worried) me. **6.** So, I called all the wise men of Babylon to explain the dream. **7.** The magicians, astrologers, Chaldeans, and soothsayers (fortune tellers) came, but they could not explain it. **8.** Finally, Daniel came before me (his name is Belteshazzar, after my god; in him is the Spirit of the Holy God), and I told him my dream: **9.** "Belteshazzar, chief of the magicians, I know the Spirit of the Holy God is in you and no secret is too difficult for you. Explain my dream." **10.** "I saw a tree in the middle of the earth, very tall. **11.** It grew strong, reaching to the heavens, visible to the ends of the earth. **12.** Its leaves were beautiful, its fruit abundant (plentiful), and it fed all. The animals found shelter under it, and the birds lived in its branches. **13.** I saw a holy one, a watcher (angel), and coming down from heaven. **14.** He said, 'Cut down the tree, strip its branches, take off its leaves, and scatter its fruit. Let the animals leave its shade, and the birds fly away. **15.** But leave the stump (base) and roots in the ground, bound with iron and bronze, in the field's grass. Let it be drenched (covered) with dew from heaven and let him eat grass like cattle. **16.** Let his heart be changed from a men to that of an animal, and let seven periods (years) pass over him. **17.** This decision has been made by the watchers, and the sentence (decree) by the holy ones, so the living may know the Highest rules the kingdoms of men and gives them to whomever He chooses, even the lowest (humblest) of men.' **18.** "This is the dream I, Nebuchadnezzar, had. Now, Belteshazzar, explain its meaning, for none of the wise men can interpret (explain) it, but you can, because the Spirit of the Holy God is in you." **19.** Daniel, whose name was Belteshazzar, was deeply troubled (distressed). The king said, "Do not be afraid." Daniel replied, "I wish this dream were about your enemies. **20.** The tree you saw, which grew strong and reached the heavens, **21.** With beautiful leaves, abundant fruit, and shelter for all animals and birds— **22.** That tree is you, O king. You have grown strong, and your dominion (kingdom) reaches the earth. **23.** And since you saw a watcher coming down from heaven, saying, 'Cut down the tree but leave the stump, bound with iron and bronze, and let him eat grass like cattle until seven periods pass over him,' 24. this is the meaning: 25. You will be driven away from people and live with the beasts (animals), eating grass like cattle until you understand that the Most High rules over the kingdoms of men. 26. Since the stump and roots were left, your kingdom will be restored after you acknowledge (accept) that Heaven rules. 27. Therefore, I advise you to repent (turn away from) your sins by doing what is right and showing mercy to the poor. Perhaps God will extend your prosperity." 28. All this happened to King Nebuchadnezzar. 29. Twelve months later, he was walking on the roof of his royal palace in Babylon. 30. The king spoke, "Is not this great Babylon that I have built by my mighty power and for the honor of my majesty?" 31. While the words were still on his lips, a voice came from heaven: "King Nebuchadnezzar, to you it is declared: the kingdom has departed from you! 32. You will be driven away from people, and your dwelling will be with the beasts. You will eat grass like cattle until you understand that the Highest rules over the kingdoms of men." 33. Immediately, the word was fulfilled. Nebuchadnezzar was driven away, eating grass like cattle. His body was drenched with dew; his hair grew like eagle feathers, and his nails like bird claws. 34. After the time passed, I, Nebuchadnezzar, looked up to heaven, and my understanding returned. I praised the Most High, honored Him whose dominion is everlasting, and His kingdom is for all generations. 35. All the inhabitants of the earth are regarded as nothing. He does as He pleases among the host (army) of heaven and the people of earth. No one can stop His hand or question His actions." 36. My reason returned, and the glory of my kingdom was restored to me. My counselors and nobles came to me, and my greatness was increased. 37. Now I, Nebuchadnezzar, praise and honor the King of heaven, whose works are true and whose ways are just. Those who walk in pride, He is able to humble.

Chapter 5

1. King Belshazzar hosted a grand feast for a thousand nobles (important men) and drank wine in front of them all. 2. While drinking, he ordered the gold and silver vessels (containers) from the Jerusalem temple (holy place in Jerusalem) to be brought, so that he, his lords, wives, and concubines (secondary wives) could drink from them. 3. The vessels were brought, and they drank from them. 4. They drank wine and praised gods made of gold, silver, bronze, iron, wood, and stone (materials that do not have life or power). 5. Suddenly, a man's hand appeared and wrote on the plaster wall (smooth surface) opposite the lampstand (light source), and the king saw the hand. 6. The king's face changed, and his thoughts troubled him (made him anxious). His hips weakened, and his knees knocked together (trembled). 7. The king called for astrologers (those who interpret stars), Chaldeans (wise men from Babylon), and soothsayers (fortune-tellers), saying, "Whoever reads this writing and explains it will be clothed in purple (royal color), given a gold chain, and made third ruler in the kingdom." 8. The wise men could not read the writing or explain it. 9. The king was greatly troubled, and his nobles (important men) were confused. 10. The queen entered and said, "O king, live forever! Do not be troubled. 11. There is a man in your kingdom with the Spirit of the Holy God in him. In your father's days, great wisdom was found in him. Your father, King Nebuchadnezzar, made him chief over magicians (those skilled in interpreting dreams), astrologers, Chaldeans, and soothsayers. 12. Let Daniel be called, and he will explain it." 13. Daniel was brought, and the king asked him, "Are you Daniel, one of the captives (prisoners) from Judah whom my father brought? 14. I have heard that the Spirit of God is in you and that you have wisdom. 15. The wise men could not read the writing. 16. I have heard you can explain mysteries (unexplained things). If you can, you will be clothed in purple, given a gold chain, and made third ruler in the kingdom." 17. Daniel replied, "Let your gifts be for yourself. I will read the writing and explain it. 18. The Most High God (God above all others) gave your father Nebuchadnezzar a kingdom, glory, and honor. 19. He ruled with power, and all feared him. He could kill or spare anyone, and raise or remove anyone. 20. But when his heart became proud (arrogant), he was removed from his throne (position), and his glory was taken. 21. He became like an animal and lived with wild donkeys (beasts) until he acknowledged (accepted) that God rules the kingdoms of men. 22. But you, Belshazzar, have not humbled yourself (shown respect), even

though you knew all this. 23. You have set yourself against the Lord of heaven. You drank from His temple vessels and praised false gods made of silver, gold, and stone (material things that cannot think or act), while ignoring the God who controls your breath. 24. Therefore, the hand was sent from God, and this writing was inscribed (written). 25. The inscription is: MENE, MENE, TEKEL, and UPHARSIN. 26. MENE: God has numbered (counted) your kingdom and finished it. 27. TEKEL: You have been weighed (measured) and found wanting (insufficient). 28. PERES: Your kingdom has been divided and given to the Medes (a people group) and Persians (a neighboring empire)." 29. Belshazzar clothed Daniel in purple, gave him a gold chain, and made him third ruler in the kingdom. 30. That night, Belshazzar was killed. 31. Darius the Mede (a ruler) took over the kingdom at 62.

Chapter 6

1. Darius, the king, appointed 120 satraps (governors) to oversee his entire kingdom, 2. and over them, three administrators, one of whom was Daniel, to ensure the satraps accounted to them, preventing any loss to the king. 3. Daniel stood out among the administrators and satraps because of the excellent spirit (a remarkable inner quality, often referring to wisdom or integrity) within him, prompting the king to consider placing him over the entire kingdom. 4. The administrators and satraps sought to find fault with Daniel concerning the kingdom, but could find none. He was faithful (loyal, trustworthy) and without error or fault. 5. They concluded that they could only accuse Daniel if they found something related to his faithfulness to God. 6. So they came before the king, saying, "King Darius, live forever! 7. All the administrators, satraps, counselors (advisors), and advisors have agreed to establish a royal decree (official order) that for the next 30 days, no one may pray to any god or man except you, O king, or be thrown into the lion's den. 8. Therefore, O king, establish and sign this decree, so it cannot be changed, according to the law of the Medes and Persians, which is unalterable (cannot be changed)." 9. The king signed the decree. 10. When Daniel learned that the decree had been signed, he went to his house, where he prayed three times a day, as was his custom, with his windows open toward Jerusalem. 11. The men gathered and saw Daniel praying and asking God for help. 12. They went to the king and reminded him of his decree: "Did you not sign a decree that anyone who prays to any god or man except you for 30 days would be thrown into the lion's den?" The king replied, "The decree stands, as per the law of the Medes and Persians, which cannot be changed." 13. They reported, "Daniel, one of the captives (prisoners or exiles) from Judah, disregards you, O king, and your decree, praying three times a day." 14. The king was distressed (deeply troubled), and he tried to find a way to save Daniel, working until sundown. 15. The men insisted, "Remember, O king, the law of the Medes and Persians cannot be changed." 16. The king reluctantly (unwillingly) ordered Daniel to be thrown into the lion's den, saying, "May your God, whom you serve faithfully, rescue you." 17. A stone was placed at the entrance of the den, and the king sealed it with his own ring and the rings of his lords, to prevent any changes in the plan. 18. That night, the king could not sleep and fasted (went without food); no entertainment was brought to him. 19. At dawn, the king hurried to the lion's den. 20. He called out to Daniel, "Daniel, servant of the living God, has your God, whom you serve continually, been able to save you from the lions?" 21. Daniel answered, "O king, live forever! 22. My God sent His angel (a messenger from God) to shut the lions' mouths, and they have not hurt me because I was found innocent before Him; and I have done no wrong before you." 23. The king was overjoyed and ordered Daniel to be lifted from the den. No injury was found on him because he trusted in his God. 24. The king commanded that those who had falsely accused Daniel be thrown into the lion's den, along with their families. The lions overpowered them before they even hit the ground. 25. Then King Darius wrote to all people, nations, and languages: "Peace be multiplied to you. 26. I decree that everyone in my kingdom must tremble (feel great fear or reverence) before the God of Daniel. For He is the living God, enduring forever. His kingdom will never be destroyed, and His dominion (authority, rule) will last to the end. 27. He rescues and delivers, performing signs and wonders (miracles) in the heavens and on earth. He has delivered Daniel from the power of the lions." 28. So Daniel prospered (succeeded) during the reign of Darius and the reign of Cyrus the Persian.

Chapter 7

1. In the first year of Belshazzar, king of Babylon (empire ruling the Jews at that time), Daniel had a dream and recorded its main points. **2.** In his vision, he saw the four winds (strong forces) of heaven stirring up the Great Sea (symbol of chaos and nations). **3.** Four great beasts (powerful creatures) rose from the sea, each different. **4.** The first was like a lion with eagle's wings, which were torn off as it stood up like a man, and it was given a human heart (wisdom or understanding). **5.** The second beast, like a bear, was raised on one side with three ribs (bones) in its mouth and told to 'devour much flesh (destroy many people).' **6.** A third, like a leopard, had four wings and four heads, and it was given authority. **7.** The fourth beast was dreadful (fearsome), with iron teeth, devouring and crushing everything underfoot, and it had ten horns (kings or rulers). **8.** As Daniel watched, a little horn emerged among the others, with human eyes and a mouth speaking boastful (arrogant) words. **9.** Thrones were set, and the Ancient of Days took His seat with white robes and wool-like hair; His throne was fire with wheels of flame. **10.** A river of fire flowed before Him; thousands served Him as the court (place of judgment) was seated, and books (records) were opened. **11.** Daniel watched until the beast was slain and cast into the fire; **12.** The other beasts lost their power but lived for a time. **13.** In another vision, Daniel saw someone like a Son of Man (title for the Messiah, Jesus Christ) coming with the clouds of heaven. He was brought to the Ancient of Days **14.** And given authority and a kingdom to rule over all peoples, an eternal dominion (rule). **15.** This vision troubled Daniel deeply. **16.** He asked one standing nearby to explain, who told him: **17.** 'The four beasts represent four kings (rulers) from the earth, **18.** But the Most High's people will receive and possess the kingdom forever.' **19.** Daniel wanted more details about the fourth beast, which was uniquely terrifying, with iron teeth, bronze claws (tools for destruction), and crushing everything. **20.** He asked about the ten horns and the little horn with human eyes and a boastful mouth, which looked stronger than the others. **21.** He saw this horn waging war against the saints (God's faithful people) and winning, **22.** Until the Ancient of Days arrived and ruled in favor of the saints, who then possessed the kingdom. **23.** The fourth beast will be a unique kingdom, crushing and trampling all others. **24.** Its ten horns represent ten kings, and another king will rise to subdue (defeat) three of them. **25.** This king will speak against the Most High, oppress the saints, and try to change set times (laws), with power over the saints for a time, times, and half a time (a symbolic period). **26.** But the court will sit in judgment, removing and destroying his power completely. **27.** Then the kingdoms under heaven will be given to the saints of the Most High, an everlasting kingdom where all rulers will serve Him. **28.** Though deeply troubled, Daniel kept the matter to himself.

Chapter 7

1. In the third year of King Belshazzar's (King of Neo-Babylonian Empire) reign, I, Daniel, had a vision after the one I previously received. **2.** In the vision, I found myself in Shushan, the citadel (fortified palace), in the province of Elam (an ancient region in the Persian Empire), by the River Ulai. **3.** I looked up and saw a ram standing beside the river. It had two high horns, with one horn rising higher than the other, and the higher one grew last. **4.** The ram charged west, north, and south. No animal could resist him, and none could rescue from his power. He did as he pleased and grew strong. **5.** As I considered this, a male goat appeared from the west, moving across the land without touching the ground. It had a prominent horn (a strong or large horn) between its eyes. **6.** The goat attacked the ram with great fury and force. **7.** I saw the goat confront the ram in rage, breaking the ram's two horns. The ram was powerless to resist and was thrown down and trampled, with no one able to save it. **8.** The goat grew very strong, but when it was at its peak, the large horn was broken and replaced by four notable horns (important or distinguished horns) facing the four winds (directions). **9.** Out of one of these horns came a small horn that grew powerful toward the south, east, and the Glorious Land (Jerusalem). **10.** It grew high, reaching the heavenly host (angels) and casting some of them down to the ground, where it trampled them. **11.** This horn even defied the Prince (leader) of the heavenly host, removing daily sacrifices (ritual offerings) and overthrowing the sanctuary (sacred place). **12.** Because of transgression (wrongdoing), an army was given to the horn to oppose daily sacrifices, and it cast truth to the ground, succeeding

in all it did. **13.** Then I heard a holy one (angel) ask another, "How long will the vision concerning the daily sacrifices, desolation (ruin), and trampling of the sanctuary last?" **14.** The answer was, "For 2,300 days (about 6 years and 4 months); then the sanctuary will be cleansed (restored)." **15.** While I was seeking to understand the vision, suddenly a figure with a human appearance stood before me. **16.** I heard a voice from the Ulai River calling, "Gabriel (an arch angel), explain the vision to this man." **17.** As Gabriel approached, I became afraid and fell on my face. He said, "Understand, son of man, this vision concerns the end times (the future events)." **18.** While he spoke, I fell into a deep sleep with my face to the ground, but he touched me and helped me stand. **19.** He said, "I will tell you what will happen in the final period (last stage) of wrath (anger), for the end time is appointed (set by God)." **20.** The ram with two horns represents the kings of Media and Persia. **21.** The male goat represents Greece, and the prominent horn (strong or large horn) between its eyes is the first king. **22.** When this horn was broken, four kingdoms arose from it, but without the same power. **23.** In the latter period (final time) of these kingdoms, when sin reaches its peak, a fierce (cruel) king, skilled in intrigue (clever plans), will arise. **24.** His power will be great, but not by his own strength. He will cause terrible destruction, succeed in his plans, and destroy powerful people and the holy ones (God's people). **25.** Through his cunning (cleverness), deceit will prosper under his rule, and he will consider himself superior. He will destroy many when they feel secure, and he will challenge the Prince of princes. Yet he will be broken, but not by human hands. **26.** The vision of the evenings and mornings (a cycle of time) is true; therefore, seal up (keep secret) the vision, for it is for a distant future. **27.** I, Daniel, was exhausted and sick for days after this vision. Later, I got up and returned to my duties, but I was deeply troubled by the vision, which no one else understood.

Chapter 8

1. In the first year of Darius, son of Ahasuerus, of the Medes (an ancient people), who ruled over the Chaldeans (people of Babylon), **2.** I, Daniel, understood from the Scriptures (sacred writings) that, according to the Lord's word through Jeremiah, Jerusalem's desolation (complete destruction) would last seventy years. **3.** So I turned to God, seeking Him with prayer, fasting (going without food for spiritual purposes), sackcloth (coarse cloth symbolizing mourning), and ashes (used in expressions of repentance and sorrow). **4.** I prayed, saying, "O Lord, awesome (inspiring fear and respect) God, who keeps His covenant (binding promise) with those who love Him, **5.** We have sinned and rebelled (resisted authority), turning from your commandments and judgments (divine decisions). **6.** We ignored your prophets (divinely inspired messengers) who spoke in your name. **7.** Righteousness (moral rightness) belongs to you, but we are shamed because of our unfaithfulness (lack of loyalty to God). **8.** Lord, we and our leaders are shamed because we have sinned against you. **9.** Yet mercy (kindness and forgiveness) and forgiveness belong to the Lord our God. **10.** We did not obey His voice or laws given through His prophets. **11.** All Israel has broken your law, so the curses (penalties for disobedience) in the Law of Moses have been poured out because we sinned. **12.** You fulfilled your words against us and our rulers by bringing disaster (misfortune) on us; nothing like this has happened before. **13.** Despite all this, we have not sought the Lord's favor by turning from our sins and understanding your truth. **14.** Therefore, the Lord brought this disaster upon us, for He is righteous, though we did not obey. **15.** and now, O God, who brought your people out of Egypt with a mighty hand (symbolizing God's power), we have sinned and done wrong! **16.** For Your righteousness, turn your anger (divine wrath) away from Jerusalem, Your holy mountain (Mount Zion, a sacred hill), for our sins have made us a disgrace (shame). **17.** Now, hear the prayer of your servant; for your sake, Lord, let Your face shine on Your desolate (abandoned) sanctuary (holy temple now in ruin). **18.** Incline your ear (listen closely) and see our desolation and the city bearing Your name. We do not ask because of our righteousness but because of Your mercy. **19.** O Lord, hear! Forgive! Listen and act! Do not delay, for Your sake, my God, for Your city and people bear Your name." **20.** While I was praying and confessing the sin of Israel, **21.** Gabriel (an angel), whom I had seen before, came to me in swift flight at the evening offering (sacrifice). **22.** He said, "Daniel, I have come to give your insight (deep understanding). **23.** At the start of your prayers, a command was issued because you are valued. Understand the vision: **24.** "Seventy weeks are decreed (set in place) for your people and city to finish transgression (wrongdoing), end sin, atone (make amends) for iniquity (wickedness), bring everlasting righteousness, fulfill vision and prophecy (divinely inspired prediction), and anoint (set apart as holy) the Most Holy Place. **25.** From the decree to rebuild Jerusalem until the Anointed One comes, there will be seven weeks and sixty-two weeks. The city will be rebuilt despite difficult times. **26.** After sixty-two weeks, the Anointed One will be put to death, and the people of a ruler will destroy the city and sanctuary; war and desolation (complete ruin) are decreed. **27.** He will confirm a covenant (binding agreement) for one week, ending sacrifices in the middle. Abominations (detestable acts) will bring desolation until the decreed end is poured on the desolator (one who brings ruin)."

Chapter 10

1. In the third year of King Cyrus of Persia (the Persian king who allowed the Jews to return to their land), a message was given to Daniel, also called Belteshazzar (Daniel's Babylonian name). The message was true, but it concerned a long period of time. Daniel understood the message and the vision. **2.** during that time, I, Daniel, mourned (was deeply sorrowful) for three full weeks. **3.** I ate no rich food (delicious, enjoyable food), drank no wine, and did not apply oil (ointments used for personal grooming) to myself until the three weeks had passed. **4.** on the twenty-fourth day of the first month, as I stood by the Tigris River (a major river in the Middle East), **5.** I looked up and saw a man dressed in linen (a light, cloth material), with a belt of gold from Uphaz (a region known for its gold). **6.** His body shone like beryl (a greenish-blue gemstone), his face was as bright as lightning, his eyes were like flaming torches, his arms and legs like polished bronze, and the sound of his voice was like the roar of a crowd. **7.** I, Daniel, was the only one who saw the vision, though the men with me did not see it. However, they were so frightened (terrified) that they ran away and hid. **8.** I was left alone to see this great vision, and I had no strength left. My strength was drained (completely used up), and I felt weak. **9.** While I heard the words he spoke, I fell into a deep sleep (a state of unconsciousness), face to the ground. **10.** Suddenly, a hand touched me and shook me, making me tremble (shake uncontrollably) on my knees and hands. **11.** The man said to me, "Daniel, greatly loved, understand the words I am about to speak to you. Stand up, for I have been sent to you." As he spoke, I stood up, trembling. **12.** He continued, "Do not be afraid, Daniel. From the first day you prayed for understanding (wanted to understand something) and humbled (lowered yourself in respect) yourself before God, your prayer was heard. I have come because of your prayers. **13.** But the prince of the Persian kingdom (a spiritual being, representing the Persian Empire) resisted (fought against) me for twenty-one days. Then Michael (an archangel), one of the chief princes (high-ranking angels), came to help me, because I had been left alone to fight against the kings of Persia. **14.** Now I have come to explain to you what will happen to your people in the future (the people of Israel), for this vision concerns a time still to come." **15.** After he said these words, I turned my face to the ground and could not speak. **16.** Then, someone who appeared to be a man touched my lips, and I opened my mouth and said to him, "My lord, the vision I saw has overwhelmed (overcome with emotion) me, and I have no strength left. **17.** How can I, your servant, speak with you? I have no strength, and I can hardly breathe." **18.** Again, the one who looked like a man touched me and gave me strength. **19.** He said, "Daniel, greatly loved, do not be afraid. Peace be with you; be strong, yes, be strong!" As he spoke, I was strengthened and said, "Please, speak, for you have given me strength." **20.** He then asked, "Do you know why I have come to you? Now I must return to fight (battle) the prince of Persia (a spiritual being opposing God's will); and when I leave, the prince of Greece (a spiritual being representing the Greek empire) will come. **21.** But I will tell you what is written in the Book of Truth (a book containing God's plans). No one supports me against these forces, except Michael, your prince."

Chapter 11

1. In the first year of King Darius of Media (a region in ancient Persia), I stood up to confirm and strengthen him. **2.** Now I will tell you the truth: Three more kings will arise in Persia, and the fourth will be far richer than the others. With his great wealth, he will stir up conflict against Greece. **3.** Then a mighty king will rise, who will rule with great power and do as he pleases. **4.** When he has risen, his kingdom will be broken and divided in four directions, but not to his heirs (descendants) or according to his dominion (rule). His kingdom will be uprooted (destroyed) and given to others. **5.** The king of the South (Egypt) will grow strong, as will one of his princes (leaders). This prince will defeat the king of the South and take control. His dominion will be great. **6.** After some years, they will make an alliance (agreement). The daughter (daughter-in-law) of the king of the South will marry the king of the North (Syria) to seal the agreement, but she will lose her power and be betrayed along with her supporters. **7.** From her family, a new leader will arise who will come with an army, enter the stronghold (fortress) of the king of the North, and defeat him. **8.** He will take their gods (idols), princes, and treasures (valuable items) to Egypt, and he will rule longer than the king of the North. **9.** The king of the North will try to invade the South, but will retreat to his land. **10.** His sons will cause strife (conflict) and gather a great army. One will come, overwhelm many, and return to his fortress (stronghold). **11.** The king of the South will become enraged (angry) and fight the king of the North, who will gather a great army. But the king of the South will be defeated. **12.** When the king of the South is defeated, his heart will be proud (filled with pride), and he will destroy many, but he will not succeed. **13.** The king of the North will return, gathering an even greater army and coming with much equipment (weapons) after some years. **14.** During these times, many will rise up against the king of the South, and some of your people will act violently and fall as the prophecy (prediction) says. **15.** The king of the North will come, build siege mounds (earthworks for attacking), and take a fortified city. The forces of the South will be unable to resist. **16.** He who comes against him will do as he pleases, standing in the Glorious Land (Jerusalem) with the power to destroy it. **17.** He will turn his focus to enter with the strength of his entire kingdom and alliances (supporters). He will give his daughter in marriage to destroy the land, but she will not succeed. **18.** After this, he will turn toward the coastlands (islands) and conquer many nations. However, a ruler will stop him and turn him back. **19.** He will turn toward the fortress (stronghold) of his own land but will stumble (fall) and be found no more. **20.** A new ruler will arise who will tax the glorious kingdom (Israel), but after a few days, he will be destroyed, not in anger or battle. **21.** In his place, a vile (wicked) person will arise, who will not be given the honor of kingship, but will seize the throne by deceit (trickery). **22.** With great force, his enemies will be swept away and broken, including the prince of the covenant (leader of the alliance). **23.** After making an alliance, he will act treacherously (deceitfully), growing stronger with only a few followers. **24.** He will enter peaceably into the wealthiest regions, doing things his ancestors (forefathers) never did, and dividing the spoils (treasures) among his followers. But this will only last a time. **25.** He will stir up his power against the king of the South, who will respond with a great army, but the South will be defeated by his cunning plans (strategies). **26.** Those who shared in his luxuries (riches) will betray him, his army will be swept away (defeated), and many will fall. **27.** Both kings will be bent on evil (focused on wrongdoing), and they will speak lies together, but their plans will not succeed, for the end is still to come. **28.** While returning to his land with great riches, he will turn against the holy covenant (agreement) and cause damage (destruction), and then return to his land. **29.** at the appointed time (predicted time), he will attack the South again, but it will not be as before. **30.** Ships from Cyprus will oppose him (oppose his plans), and he will be frustrated, returning in rage to attack the holy covenant. He will show favor to those who abandon it. **31.** He will gather forces and defile (pollute) the sanctuary fortress (temple), taking away the daily sacrifices (offerings) and setting up the abomination (idol) that causes desolation (ruin). **32.** He will corrupt those who rebel (act against) the covenant with flattery (deceptive praise), but those who know God will be strong and carry out great deeds. **33.** Those who understand will teach many, but they will fall by sword (killed), fire, captivity (imprisonment), and plunder (looting) for many days. **34.** When they fall, they will receive little help, but many will join them through treachery (deceit). **35.** Some of those with understanding will fall, to purify (cleanse) and refine (test) them until the end, for the appointed time is yet to come. **36.** Then the king will do as he pleases. He will exalt (rise up) himself above every god, speak blasphemies (insults) against the God of gods, and prosper until God's wrath (anger) is fulfilled. **37.** He will disregard (ignore) the gods of his ancestors and the desire (affection) of women, and will exalt himself above all gods. **38.** In place of those gods, he will honor a god of fortresses (strength), a god unknown to his ancestors, with wealth and treasures. **39.** He will act against the strongest fortresses (strongholds) with the help of this foreign god, advancing its glory and dividing the land for gain (profit). **40.** At the end, the king of the South will attack him. The king of the North will come with great forces, including chariots (horse-drawn vehicles), cavalry (mounted soldiers), and ships. He will overwhelm many nations. **41.** He will enter the Glorious Land (Israel), and many nations will be overthrown, but Edom, Moab, and the leaders (prominent people) of Ammon will escape. **42.** He will extend his power over many countries, and Egypt will not escape. **43.** He will control Egypt's wealth, including its treasures of gold and silver, and the Libyans and Ethiopians (African peoples) will follow him. **44.** But news from the east and north will disturb him, and in his rage (anger), he will go out to destroy many. **45.** He will set up his palace (royal residence) between the seas (Mediterranean Sea and Dead Sea) and the glorious holy mountain (Jerusalem), but he will come to his end, and no one will help him.

Chapter 12

1. At that time, Michael (the archangel, protector of Israel) will rise, and there will be a time of trouble like never before. At that time, your people will be saved—everyone whose name is written in the book (of life). **2.** Many that have died will rise: some to everlasting life, some to disgrace and eternal punishment. **3.** The wise (those with understanding) will shine like the sky, and those who lead many to righteousness will shine like stars forever. **4.** But you, Daniel, keep these words secret (hidden) and seal the book (close it) until the end of time. Many will travel far and wide (run to and fro), and knowledge (understanding) will increase. **5.** Then I, Daniel, saw two other men, one on each riverbank. **6.** One asked the man in linen (a symbol of purity), who was above the river, "How long until these wonders (amazing events) are fulfilled?" **7.** The man in linen raised both hands to heaven and swore by Him who lives forever, saying it will last for a time, times, and half a time (3 ½ years). When the power of the holy people is shattered (fully tested), all will be finished (completed). **8.** Though I heard this, I didn't understand. So I asked, "My lord, what will be the end of these things?" **9.** He said, "Go your way, Daniel, for the words are sealed until the end of time." **10.** Many will be purified (cleansed) and tested, but the wicked (evil people) will continue in wickedness (evil deeds). The wicked will not understand, but the wise (those who seek truth) will understand. **11.** From the time the daily sacrifice is stopped and the abomination (desecration) of desolation (ruin) is set up, there will be 1,290 days. **12.** blessed (happy) is the one who waits and reaches the 1,335 days. **13.** But you, Daniel, go your way until the end; you will rest (die peacefully), and at the end of days, you will rise (be resurrected) to receive your inheritance (eternal life).

The Prayer of Azariah

1. And they walked in the fire, praising God and blessing the Lord. **2.** Azariah stood up and prayed, saying, **3.** Blessed art Thou, O Lord God of our fathers; Thy name is worthy of praise forever. **4.** For Thou art righteous in all that Thou hast done to us; Thy ways are right, and all Thy judgments are true. **5.** In all that Thou hast brought upon us and upon Jerusalem, Thou hast executed true judgment (fair decisions), for these things came because of our sins. **6.** We have sinned and departed from Thee. **7.** We have trespassed (broken the law) and not obeyed Thy commandments, failing to do as Thou hast commanded. **8.** Therefore, all that Thou hast done to us is in true judgment. **9.** Thou delivered us into the hands of lawless (without law) enemies, wicked and forsakers (those who abandon) of God, to an unjust king. **10.** Now we cannot open our mouths; we are a shame and reproach (disgrace) to Thy servants and to those who worship Thee. **11.** Yet, do not forsake (abandon) us completely for Thy name's sake, and do not annul (cancel) Thy covenant. **12.** Cause not Thy mercy to depart from us for the sake of Abraham, Isaac, and Israel, **13.** To whom Thou hast promised to multiply their seed (descendants) as the stars of heaven and the sand by the seashore. **14.** We are now less than any nation, scattered and oppressed (subjected to cruel treatment) because of our sins. **15.** There is no prince, prophet, or leader, nor any offering or

incense (aromatic smoke) to find mercy before Thee. **16.** Yet, with a contrite (broken-hearted) heart and humble spirit, accept us. **17.** As in burnt offerings of rams and bulls, let our sacrifice be pleasing to Thee, and grant that we may follow Thee wholeheartedly, for those who trust in Thee shall not be confounded (disappointed). **18.** We now follow Thee with all our heart, fearing Thee and seeking Thy face. **19.** Do not put us to shame, but deal with us in Thy lovingkindness, according to Thy great mercies. **20.** Deliver us according to Thy marvelous (wondrous) works and give glory to Thy name. Let those who harm Thy servants be ashamed. **21.** Let them be confounded in their power, and let their strength be broken. **22.** Let them know that Thou art the Lord, the only God, glorious over the whole world. **23.** The king's servants continued to heat the furnace with rosin (resin), pitch (tar), tow (rough fiber), and small wood, **24.** Until the flames rose 49 cubits (a unit of measurement, about 18 inches) above the furnace. **25.** The flames burned the Chaldeans (Babylonians) near the furnace. **26.** But the angel of the Lord came down into the furnace with Azariah and his companions and quenched (put out) the flame. **27.** The fire became like a cool, whistling wind, so it did not touch them or harm them. **28.** Then the three, in unison (together), praised, glorified, and blessed God in the furnace, saying,

Bel and the Dragon

Chapter 1

1. King Astyages (the former king of the Medes) passed away, and Cyrus (the Persian king) took over his kingdom. **2.** Daniel spoke with the king and was honored (respected and given high rank) above all his companions. **3.** The Babylonians had an idol named Bel, and every day, twelve large measures (amounts) of fine flour, forty sheep, and six vessels (containers) of wine were offered to it. **4.** The king worshiped this idol daily, but Daniel worshiped the true God. The king asked him, "Why do you not worship Bel?" **5.** Daniel answered, "I cannot worship idols made by human hands. I worship the living God who created the heavens and the earth and has power over all." **6.** The king replied, "Do you not think that Bel is a living god? Do you not see how much he eats and drinks every day?" **7.** Daniel smiled and said, "O king, do not be deceived (tricked). Bel is made of clay inside and brass (a type of metal) outside. It has never eaten or drunk anything." **8.** The king grew angry and called the priests (religious leaders) of Bel, saying, "If you do not tell me who eats the offerings, you shall die. But if you can prove (show) that Bel consumes them, then Daniel will die for blasphemy (speaking against God)." **9.** Daniel agreed, "Let it be as you say." **10.** The priests of Bel numbered seventy, plus their wives and children. The king and Daniel went into the temple (a sacred building for worship) of Bel. **11.** The priests said, "You, O king, prepare the meal and wine. Then seal (close securely) the door with your signet (official seal) ring. Tomorrow, if Bel has eaten everything, we will die; but if not, Daniel will die for lying about Bel." **12.** They did not worry, for beneath the table was a secret (hidden) entrance where they secretly ate the food. **13.** After they left, the king set the food before Bel. Daniel had his servants scatter ashes (fine powder made by burning something) all over the floor of the temple in the presence of the king. Then they sealed the door and departed. **14.** That night, the priests, with their families, came in as usual and secretly ate and drank the offerings. **15.** Early the next morning, the king and Daniel rose. **16.** The king asked, "Daniel, are the seals intact (unbroken)?" Daniel replied, "Yes, O king, the seals are intact." **17.** When the king opened the door, he looked at the table and exclaimed loudly, "Great is Bel, and there is no deceit (dishonesty or trickery) in him!" **18.** Daniel laughed and stopped the king from entering, saying, "Look at the floor and observe (carefully examine) whose footprints (marks made by feet) these are." **19.** The king said, "I see the footprints of men, women, and children." **20.** The king became angry and realized the priests had deceived him. **21** The priests, along with their wives and children, showed the king the secret doors (hidden entrances) through which they entered, and revealed the things they had placed on the table. **22** As a result, the king ordered their execution (killing), and gave Bel's (a Babylonian god) temple and idol into Daniel's hands, who then destroyed them. **23** In that same place, there was a great dragon (a large serpent or creature) that the people of Babylon worshiped. **24** The king said to Daniel, "Will you claim that this is made of brass (a type of metal)? Look, the dragon eats and drinks; surely you cannot deny that it is a living god. Worship it!"

25 Daniel responded, "I worship the Lord my God, for He is the living God." 26 "But allow me, O king, to destroy this dragon without using a sword (a weapon) or staff (a stick or rod)." The king gave him permission. 27 Daniel mixed pitch (a sticky substance), fat, and hair, and made lumps of it. He fed them to the dragon, and it burst open. Daniel said, "Behold, these are the gods you worship." 28 The people of Babylon were furious (angry) when they heard this, and they conspired (planned secretly) against the king, saying, "The king has become a Jew. He has destroyed Bel, slain (killed) the dragon, and executed (put to death) the priests." 29 They went to the king and demanded, "Hand over Daniel to us, or we will destroy you and your house." 30 The king, seeing their pressure, reluctantly (hesitantly) handed Daniel over to them. 31 They cast (threw) Daniel into the lion's den, where he was kept for six days. 32 There were seven lions in the den, and every day they were fed two carcasses (dead animals) and two sheep. On this occasion, however, no food was given to them, in hopes that they would devour (eat) Daniel. 33 Now, in Judea (region), there was a prophet named Habakkuk, who was making stew (a type of soup) and breaking bread (a meal) in a bowl, preparing to bring it to the reapers (workers gathering crops) working in the field. 34 The angel (messenger of God) of the Lord told Habakkuk, "Take the food you have prepared to Babylon, to Daniel in the lion's den." 35 Habakkuk replied, "Lord, I have never been to Babylon and do not know where the den is." 36 Then the angel of the Lord seized (grabbed) him by the hair of his head and, with great speed, transported (carried) him to Babylon, placing him over the lion's den. 37 Habakkuk cried out, "Daniel, Daniel, take the food God has sent you." 38 Daniel replied, "You have not forgotten me, O God; you have not forsaken (abandoned) those who seek and love You." 39 Daniel got up and ate the food. Then the angel immediately returned Habakkuk to his place. 40 On the seventh day, the king went to mourn (grieve) Daniel. When he reached the den, he looked in and saw Daniel sitting there. 41 The king cried out with a loud voice, "Great are You, Lord God of Daniel! There is no god but You!" 42 The king brought Daniel out and threw the men who had falsely accused (wrongly blamed) him into the den. They were immediately devoured (eaten) by the lions.

The History of Susanna

1. In Babylon (an ancient city), there lived a man named Joakim. 2. Joakim married Susanna, the daughter of Helkias. She was very beautiful and deeply reverent (devout, showing deep respect) toward the Lord. 3. Her parents were also righteous (morally right and just) and raised her according to the Law of Moses. 4. Joakim was wealthy (rich) and had a beautiful garden next to his house, where many Jews gathered since he was highly respected (honored) by them. 5. In that same year, two elders (older men with authority), who were known as judges, were appointed (chosen). These were among those the Lord warned about, as their governance (rule) brought wickedness (moral corruption) to Babylon. 6. These judges often visited Joakim's house, and those with legal issues (disputes in law) came to them there. 7. One day, when the people left at noon (midday), Susanna entered her husband's garden to walk. 8. The two elders saw her walking their daily and became inflamed (overcome) with desire (strong attraction) for her. 9. They corrupted (spoiled) their own thoughts, ignoring heaven's justice (right and fair judgment). 10. Though both were captivated (overcome) by her beauty, they kept their feelings secret, too ashamed (embarrassed) to admit their lust (sinful desire). 11. They were too embarrassed to confess their desire for her. 12. However, they continued to watch her daily, seeking an opportunity. 13. One said to the other, "Let's go home; it is mealtime (time to eat)." 14. But after parting, they returned separately to the same place and, upon meeting again, confessed (admitted) their desire for Susanna. They then agreed on a time to find her alone. 15. One hot day, Susanna went into the garden with only two maids (female servants), wanting to bathe (wash herself). 16. No one else was there except the two elders, who had hidden and were watching her. 17. Susanna told her maids, "Bring me oil and soap, and close the garden doors so I may bathe." 18. The maids did as she instructed, closing the doors and going out to fetch the items, unaware (not knowing) that the elders were hiding nearby. 19. When the maids had left, the two elders approached (came near) Susanna and said, 20. "The garden doors are closed, and no one can see us. We desire you; therefore, be with us." 21. "If you refuse, we will testify (bear false witness) against you, claiming a young man was with you, which is why you sent your maids away." 22. Susanna sighed (took a deep breath) and said, "I am trapped; if I do this, I face death, and if I don't, I cannot escape you." 23. "It is better for me to fall into your hands without sinning (doing wrong) than to sin before the Lord." 24. Susanna cried out loudly, and the two elders also shouted against her. 25. One of them opened the garden doors. 26. When the household servants heard the cries (screams) in the garden, they rushed in through the side door to see what had happened. 27. After the elders told their version of events, the servants felt deeply ashamed, as no such accusation (claim of wrongdoing) had ever been made against Susanna. 28. The next day, the people gathered before Joakim, and the two elders came with their malicious (evil) intent, seeking to have Susanna put to death. 29. They said before the people, "Summon (call for) Susanna, daughter of Helkias, and Joakim's wife." So they sent for her. 30. She arrived with her parents, children, and all her relatives (family members). 31. Susanna was a beautiful and delicate (gentle and refined) woman, admired by many. 32. The wicked (evil and morally corrupt) elders commanded her to be uncovered (since she was veiled) so they could gaze upon her beauty. 33. Her friends and everyone who saw her wept (cried in sorrow). 34. The two elders stood before the people and placed their hands on her head. 35. While she wept, Susanna looked up to heaven, trusting her heart in the LORD. 36. The elders testified (gave a formal statement), saying, "As we walked alone in the garden, Susanna came in with two maids (female servants), locked the doors, and sent them away. 37. Then a young man, who was hidden, came to her, and they lay together (suggesting an intimate encounter). 38. We were hiding in a corner of the garden and saw this evil (morally wrong) act. We rushed toward them. 39. When we tried to seize (capture) the man, he was stronger than we, and he opened the doors and escaped. 40. We asked Susanna who the man was, but she refused to tell us. These are our testimonies (statements under oath)." 41. The people believed the elders, trusting them as respected judges (those who rule in legal matters), and condemned (sentenced) Susanna to death. 42. Susanna cried out loudly, saying, "O eternal (everlasting) God, who knows the secrets of all hearts and knows all things before they happen: 43. You know they have falsely accused (wrongly charged) me. I must die, even though I have never done what these men falsely claim." 44. The LORD heard her cry. 45. As Susanna was being led to her death, God raised up the spirit (inspired the courage) of a young man named Daniel. 46. Daniel shouted out, "I am innocent (blameless) of this woman's blood." 47. The people turned to him and asked, "What do you mean by these words?" 48. Standing in their midst (among them), Daniel said, "Are you so foolish (lacking good sense), O people of Israel, that you would condemn (judge as guilty) a daughter of Israel without first examining (investigating) the facts?" 49. "Return to the judgment seat (place of legal decisions), for these men have falsely testified against her." 50. The elders invited Daniel to sit with them and demonstrate (show) his wisdom, as God had given him the honor of an elder (respected leader). 51. Daniel said, "Separate (keep apart) them, so I can examine them." 52. The first elder was separated and Daniel questioned him, saying, "You who are old in wickedness (long-standing evil actions), your sins (wrongdoings) have caught up with you. You passed unjust (unfair) judgments before, condemning the innocent and letting the guilty go free, even though God says, 'Do not kill the innocent and righteous.'" 53. "Now tell me, under what tree did you see them together?" 54. The elder replied, "Under a mastic tree (a type of tree with fragrant resin)." 55. Daniel said, "You have lied (intentionally told falsehoods) against yourself. Even now, the angel of God has received God's judgment (decision), and he will cut you in two." 56. Daniel dismissed the first elder and called for the second one. He said to him, "You are a descendant of Canaan (non-Israelite nation), not Judah (tribe of Israel). Beauty has deceived you (led you astray), and lust (strong desire) has twisted your heart." 57. "You have treated the daughters of Israel with fear (intimidation), but the daughter of Judah would not yield (submit) to your wickedness (evil)." 58. "Now tell me, under what tree did you see them together?" 59. The second elder answered, "Under a holm tree (type of evergreen oak)." 60. Daniel said, "You too have lied against yourself. The angel of God is ready with the sword to destroy you." 61. The entire assembly (gathered crowd)

cried out loudly, praising God who saves those who trust in Him. **62.** The people turned on the two elders, for Daniel had exposed (revealed) their false testimony, and according to the law of Moses, they were punished as they had intended to harm Susanna. They were put to death, and Susanna's innocence (freedom from guilt) was upheld that day. **63.** Helkias and his wife, along with Susanna's husband Joakim and their family, praised God for saving Susanna and revealing her innocence. **64.** From that day forward, Daniel gained great honor and respect among the people.

35 – Hosea

Chapter 1

1. The word of the LORD came to Hosea, son of Beeri, during the reigns of Uzziah, Jotham, Ahaz, and Hezekiah, kings of Judah, and Jeroboam, son of Jehoash, king of Israel. **2.** When the LORD spoke to Hosea, He commanded him, "Take a wife who is unfaithful, and have children with her. This will be a picture of how Israel has been unfaithful to Me." **3.** Hosea married Gomer, the daughter of Diblaim (a person's name), and she became pregnant and bore him a son. **4.** The LORD instructed Hosea, "Name him Jezreel (a valley in ancient Israel), because I will soon bring judgment on the house of Jehu (a former king of Israel) for the bloodshed at Jezreel, and I will end the kingdom of Israel." **5.** I will break Israel's power in the Valley of Jezreel. **6.** Gomer had another child, a daughter. The LORD said, "Name her Lo-Ruhamah (meaning 'not loved'), for I will no longer show mercy to Israel or forgive them." **7.** However, I will show love to Judah (the southern kingdom of Israel) and will save them—not through military might, but by the LORD their God. **8.** After Lo-Ruhamah was weaned, Gomer had a son. **9.** The LORD said, "Name him Lo-Ammi (meaning 'not my people'), for you are no longer My people, and I am no longer your God." **10.** Yet, the Israelites will become as numerous as the sand by the sea. Where it was once said, 'You are not my people,' they will be called 'children of the living God.' **11.** The people of Judah and Israel will unite, appoint a single leader, and return from exile. The day of Jezreel will be a great day.

Chapter 2

1. Say to your brothers, 'You are my people,' and to your sisters, 'You are my loved one.' Israel's Punishment and Restoration **2.** Call out to your mother and rebuke her, for she is no longer my wife, and I am no longer her husband. Let her take away the shameful look from her face and the unfaithfulness (disloyalty) from her heart. **3.** If she does not change, I will expose her nakedness, making her as vulnerable (exposed) as she was when she was born. I will leave her like a desert, make her as dry as a barren (empty) land, and cause her to die of thirst. **4.** I will no longer show love to her children, for they are the product (result) of adultery. **5.** Their mother has been unfaithful and dishonored herself; she said, 'I will go after my lovers who give me everything I need—food, water, wool, linen, olive oil, and wine.' **6.** Therefore, I will block her path with thornbushes and wall her in so she cannot find her way. **7.** She will pursue her lovers but will not catch them; she will search for them but will not find them. Then she will realize, 'I will return to my husband, for I was better off than I am now.' **8.** She has not acknowledged that I was the one who gave her the grain, the new wine, and the olive oil, and lavished silver and gold on her— which she used to worship Baal (a false god). **9.** So now I will take back my grain when it ripens and my new wine when it is ready. I will also take back my wool and linen, which were meant to cover her nakedness. **10.** I will uncover her shame before the eyes of her lovers, and no one will be able to rescue her from my hand. **11.** I will put an end to all her celebrations, her annual festivals, her New Moon celebrations, her Sabbaths, and all her appointed festivals. **12.** I will destroy her vines and fig trees, which she thought were the reward from her lovers; I will turn them into a thicket (thick, tangled brush), and wild animals will devour them. **13.** I will punish her for the days she burned incense (offered prayers) to the false gods Baal, adorned herself with jewelry, and pursued her lovers, but forgot about me," declares the LORD. **14.** Therefore, I am now going to draw her back to me; I will lead her into the wilderness and speak tenderly (kindly) to her. **15.** There, I will return to her the vineyards she lost, and I will turn the Valley of Achor (a place of trouble) into a gateway (door) of hope. She will respond to me as she did in her youth, as when she came out of Egypt. **16.** In that day," declares the LORD, "you will call me 'my husband,' and you will no longer call me 'my master.' **17.** I will remove

the names of the Baals (false gods) from her lips, and she will no longer mention their names. **18.** in that day, I will make a covenant (agreement) with the animals of the field, the birds in the sky, and the creatures that crawl on the ground. I will abolish (end) war, weapons, and battle from the land so that all may live in peace. **19.** I will betroth (commit) you to me forever; I will betroth you in righteousness, justice, love, and compassion. **20.** I will betroth you in faithfulness, and you will truly know (acknowledge) the LORD. **21.** In that day, I will answer," declares the LORD. "I will answer the skies, and they will answer the earth. **22.** The earth will respond with grain, new wine, and olive oil, and they will respond to Jezreel (a place of sowing). **23.** I will plant her for myself in the land. I will show love to the one who was not loved. I will say to those who were called 'Not my people,' 'You are my people,' and they will respond, 'You are my God.'"

Chapter 3

1. The LORD spoke to me, saying, "Go and show love to your wife once more, even though she has been unfaithful (not loyal) to you and is now with another man. Love her as I have loved the people of Israel, even though they turn to other gods and delight in their offerings of raisin cakes (a type of sacred offering)." **2.** So I bought her (purchased) for fifteen pieces of silver and a bushel (a unit of measure for dry goods) of barley, along with another measure of barley. **3.** I then said to her, "You will stay with me for a long time. You are not to be with any other man, and I will not be with anyone else either. We will live faithfully together." **4.** The people of Israel will live for many years without a king or a ruler, without the ability to offer sacrifices or make offerings at sacred places, without priestly garments (special clothing worn by priests) or household idols (small idols worshipped in homes). **5.** But in time, the Israelites will return, seeking the LORD their God and their king, David. They will come with reverence (deep respect), and in the final days, they will be blessed by the LORD.

Chapter 4

1. Hear the word of the LORD, O Israelites, for the LORD has a case against you who dwell in the land: "There is no loyalty (faithfulness), no love, and no knowledge of God in the land. **2.** There is only cursing, lying, murder, stealing, and adultery; they break every boundary, and bloodshed follows bloodshed. **3.** As a result, the land will wither, and all who live in it will waste away; even the wild animals, birds, and fish in the sea will be swept away. **4.** "But let no one bring accusations, and let no one argue, for your people are like those who bring charges against a priest. **5.** You stumble both day and night, and the prophets stumble along with you. So, I will destroy your mother— **6.** My people are destroyed for lack of knowledge. "Since you have rejected knowledge, I will also reject you as my priests; since you have ignored the law of your God, I will also ignore your children. **7.** The more priests there were, the more they sinned against me; they exchanged their glorious God for something disgraceful. **8.** They feed on the sins of my people and enjoy their wickedness. **9.** like people, like priests. I will punish both for their actions and repay them for their deeds. **10.** "They will eat but never have enough; they will engage in prostitution but never thrive, for they have abandoned the LORD to pursue such practices. **11.** Old wine and new wine take away their understanding (sense). **12.** My people consult a wooden idol, and a diviner's rod (a stick used for divination or fortune telling) speaks to them. A spirit of prostitution (idolatry and unfaithfulness) leads them astray; they have been unfaithful to their God. **13.** They sacrifice on mountaintops and burn offerings on the hills, under oak, poplar, and terebinth trees (types of trees) because the shade is pleasant. Therefore, your daughters turn to prostitution, and your daughters-in-law commit adultery. **14.** "I will not punish your daughters when they turn to prostitution, nor your daughters-in-law when they commit adultery, for the men themselves engage with prostitutes and sacrifice with temple prostitutes— a people without understanding (knowledge) will come to ruin! **15.** "Although you, Israel, commit adultery, do not let Judah become guilty. "Do not go to Gilgal; do not go to Beth Aven (a place associated with idolatry). Do not swear, 'As surely as the LORD lives!' **16.** The Israelites are stubborn, like a stubborn heifer (young cow). How can the LORD feed them like lambs in a meadow? **17.** Ephraim (a tribe in Israel) is joined to idols; leave him alone! **18.** Even when their wine is gone, they continue their prostitution; their rulers love shameful ways. **19.** A whirlwind (storm) will sweep them away, and their sacrifices will bring them shame."

Chapter 5

1. Listen, priests, Israelites, and royal family! This judgment is against you: You have become a trap at Mizpah, a net spread out on Tabor. **2.** The rebels are deep in bloodshed. I will discipline them all. **3.** I know Ephraim; Israel is not hidden from me. Ephraim, you have turned to immorality (prostitution); Israel is corrupt. **4.** Their actions prevent them from returning to God. A spirit of unfaithfulness is in their hearts; they do not acknowledge the LORD. **5.** Israel's pride (arrogance) condemns them; Ephraim and Judah both stumble in sin. **6.** When they seek the LORD with flocks and herds, they won't find Him; He has withdrawn from them. **7.** They are unfaithful; they bear illegitimate children. When they celebrate New Moon festivals, He will destroy their crops. **8.** Blow the trumpet in Gibeah and Ramah; raise the battle cry in Beth Aven; lead on, Benjamin. **9.** Ephraim will be destroyed on judgment day. I proclaim this with certainty. **10.** Judah's leaders are like those who move boundary stones. I will pour out My wrath on them like a flood. **11.** Ephraim is oppressed and crushed by judgment, determined to follow idols. **12.** I will be like a moth to Ephraim, like rot to Judah. **13.** When Ephraim saw his sickness and Judah his wounds, Ephraim turned to Assyria, but the king cannot heal you. **14.** I will be like a lion to Ephraim, a great lion to Judah. I will tear them apart, and no one will rescue them. **15.** I will return to My lair until they bear their guilt and seek My face— in their misery, they will earnestly seek Me.

Chapter 6

1. "Come; let us return to the LORD. He has wounded us (caused suffering), but he will heal us; he has struck us (punished), but he will bind up (repair) our wounds. **2.** After two days, he will revive us (restore us to life); on the third day, he will raise us up (bring us back to life), so that we may live in his presence. **3.** Let us pursue the knowledge (understanding) of the LORD; let us strive (seek earnestly) to know him. As surely as the sun rises, he will appear to us; he will come to us like the rain (a symbol of blessing), like the spring showers (rains that nourish) that refresh the earth." **4.** "What am I to do with you, Ephraim (a tribe of Israel)? What am I to do with you, Judah (another tribe of Israel)? Your love is like the morning mist (temporary and fleeting), like the dew that vanishes early. **5.** Therefore, I have cut you to pieces (reprimanded you) through my prophets, I have slain (destroyed) you with the words of my mouth— then my judgments (decisions or decrees) will shine forth like the light (of the sun). **6.** For I desire mercy (compassion), not sacrifice (ritual offerings), and the knowledge (understanding) of God more than burnt offerings (ritual sacrifices). **7.** Like Adam (the first man), they have broken the covenant (formal agreement with God); they have been unfaithful to me there. **8.** Gilead (a region known for its balm) is a city of sinners (those who do wrong), stained with footprints of blood (a place of violence). **9.** Like a band of thieves (robbers) lying in wait for someone, so do groups of priests (religious leaders) act; they murder (kill) on the road to Shechem (a place in Israel), carrying out their wicked schemes (evil plans). **10.** I have seen something horrible (shocking) in Israel: Ephraim is given to prostitution (idolatry), and Israel has become defiled (polluted or spiritually unclean). **11.** "Judah, a harvest (consequence) is also set for you. When I would restore (bring back to a right state) the fortunes of my people..."

Chapter 7

1. "Whenever I would heal Israel, the sins of Ephraim become obvious, and the wrongdoings of Samaria are uncovered. They engage in deceit; thieves break into homes, and robbers strike in the streets. **2.** But they fail to realize that I remember all their wicked actions. Their sins surround them, and they are constantly before me. **3.** "They delight the king with their wicked deeds, and the rulers are pleased with their lies. **4.** They are all unfaithful, like an oven, whose fire the baker does not need to stoke from the kneading of the dough until it rises. **5.** On the day of the king's celebration, the princes are inflamed with wine, and they join hands with those who mock what is holy. **6.** Their hearts are like an oven; they approach him with deceit. Their passion burns throughout the night; by morning, it is like a blazing fire. **7.** All of them are hot as an oven; they consume their rulers. All their kings fall, and none of them seeks me. **8.** "Ephraim mixes with the nations; Ephraim is like a half-baked loaf of bread, not turned over. **9.** Strangers drain his strength, yet he does not realize it. His hair is turning gray, yet he does not see it. **10.** The pride of Israel testifies against him, but despite all this, he does not return to the LORD his God or seek him. **11.** "Ephraim is like a simple dove, easily deceived and without understanding— now calling to Egypt for help, now turning to Assyria. **12.** When they go, I will spread my net over them; I will bring them down like birds in the sky. When I hear them coming together, I will catch them. **13.** Woe to them, for they have strayed from me! Destruction is their fate because they have rebelled against me! I long to redeem them, but they speak falsely about me. **14.** They do not cry out to me sincerely, but wail on their beds. They cut themselves, asking their gods for grain and new wine, yet they turn away from me. **15.** I trained them and gave them strength, but they plot evil against me. **16.** They do not turn to the Most High; they are like a broken bow. Their leaders will fall by the sword because of their insolent words. For this, they will be mocked in the land of Egypt."

Chapter 8

1. "Put the trumpet to your lips! An eagle is over the house of the LORD because the people have broken my covenant (agreement) and rebelled (resisted authority) against my law. **2.** Israel cries out to me, 'Our God, we acknowledge (admit) you!' **3.** But Israel has rejected (refused) what is good; an enemy will pursue (chase) him. **4.** They set up kings without my consent (approval); they choose princes without my approval. With their silver and gold they make idols (false gods) for themselves to their own destruction (ruin). **5.** Samaria, throw out your calf-idol! My anger burns against them. How long will they be incapable (unable) of purity (cleanliness)? **6.** They are from Israel! This calf—a metalworker (craftsman) has made it; it is not God. It will be broken in pieces, that calf of Samaria. **7.** "They sow (plant) the wind and reap (gather) the whirlwind (destruction). The stalk has no head; it will produce no flour (grain). Were it to yield (produce) grain, foreigners (outsiders) would swallow (consume) it up. **8.** Israel is swallowed (consumed) up; now she is among the nations like something no one wants. **9.** For they have gone up to Assyria like a wild donkey (untamed animal) wandering alone. Ephraim has sold herself to lovers (foreign nations). **10.** Although they have sold themselves among the nations, I will now gather (collect) them together. They will begin to waste away (decline) under the oppression (cruel treatment) of the mighty king. **11.** "Though Ephraim built many altars (sacred places) for sin offerings, these have become altars for sinning. **12.** I wrote for them the many things of my law, but they regarded (treated) them as something foreign. **13.** Though they offer sacrifices (gifts) as gifts to me, and though they eat the meat, the LORD is not pleased (satisfied) with them. Now he will remember their wickedness (evil deeds) and punish their sins: They will return to Egypt. **14.** Israel has forgotten their Maker (Creator) and built palaces (mansions); Judah has fortified (strengthened) many towns. But I will send fire (destruction) on their cities that will consume (destroy) their fortresses (strongholds)."

Chapter 9

1. "Do not rejoice, Israel; do not celebrate like the other nations. For you have been unfaithful to your God; you love the wages of a prostitute (payment for immoral acts) at every threshing floor (place where grain is separated from chaff). **2.** Threshing floors and winepresses will not feed the people; the new wine (fresh grape juice) will fail them. **3.** They will not remain in the LORD's land; Ephraim will return to Egypt and eat unclean (ritually impure) food in Assyria. **4.** They will not pour out wine offerings (liquid sacrifices) to the LORD, nor will their sacrifices please Him. Such sacrifices will be like the bread of mourners (bread eaten by those grieving); all who eat them will be unclean (ritually impure). This food will be for them; it will not enter the temple of the LORD. **5.** What will you do on the day of your appointed festivals, on the feast days of the LORD? **6.** Even if they escape from destruction, Egypt will gather them, and Memphis (a city in Egypt) will bury them. Their treasures of silver will be overrun by briers (thorny plants), and thorns will fill their tents. **7.** The days of punishment are coming; the days of reckoning (judgment) are at hand. Let Israel know this. Because your sins are so many and your hostility (opposition) so great, the prophet is considered a fool, the inspired (spiritually guided) person a maniac (insane). **8.** The prophet, along with my God, is the watchman (guard) over Ephraim, yet snares (traps) await him on all his paths, and hostility (opposition) in the house of his God. **9.** They have sunk deep into corruption (moral decay), as in the days of Gibeah. God will remember their wickedness (evil deeds) and punish them for their sins. **10.** "When I found Israel, it was like finding grapes in the desert; when I saw your ancestors, it was like seeing the early fruit (first ripe fruit) on the fig tree. But when they came to Baal Peor (a place of idolatry), they consecrated (dedicated) themselves to that shameful idol and became as vile (disgusting) as the thing they loved. **11.** Ephraim's glory will fly away like a bird— no birth, no pregnancy, no conception. **12.** Even if they bear children, I will bereave (cause the loss of) them of every one. Woe (misery) to them when I turn away from them! **13.** I have seen Ephraim, like Tyre (a prosperous city), planted in a pleasant place. But Ephraim will bring out their children to the slayer (murderer). **14.** Give them, LORD— what will You give them? Give them wombs that miscarry and breasts that are dry. **15.** "Because of all their wickedness in Gilgal, I hated them there. Because of their sinful deeds, I will drive them out of My house. I will no longer love them; all their leaders are rebellious (defiant). **16.** Ephraim is blighted (damaged), their root is withered, they yield no fruit. Even if they bear children, I will slay their cherished offspring." **17.** My God will reject (cast away) them because they have not obeyed Him; they will be wanderers (homeless, nomadic) among the nations."

Chapter 10

1. Israel was like a spreading vine, producing fruit for itself. As its harvest grew, so did its altars; as its land prospered, it adorned its sacred stones (idols). **2.** Their hearts are deceitful (dishonest), and now they must face the consequences. The LORD will tear down their altars and destroy their sacred stones. **3.** They will say, "We have no king because we did not honor (revere) the LORD. But even if we had a king, what good would he do?" **4.** They make false promises, swear empty oaths, and form alliances that lead to disputes, like weeds growing in a plowed field (corruption). **5.** The people of Samaria fear the idol of Beth Aven (a place of idol worship). Its people and priests will mourn, for it will be carried into exile. **6.** The idol will be taken to Assyria as tribute (payment), and Ephraim will be ashamed of its foreign alliances. **7.** Samaria's king will be destroyed, like a twig swept away by water. **8.** The places of idol worship will be destroyed—they are Israel's sin. Thorns and thistles (thorns) will cover their altars. Then they will cry, "Cover us!" to the mountains and hills. **9.** Since the days of Gibeah (a place of sin), you have continued in sin. Will war overtake the evildoers (wrongdoers) in Gibeah again? **10.** I will punish them, and nations will gather to imprison them for their double sin (idolatry and rebellion). **11.** Ephraim is like a well-trained heifer (young cow) that loves to thresh (separate grain). I will place a yoke (a wooden cross piece) on her neck and drive Ephraim; Judah must plow, and Jacob must break the soil. **12.** Sow righteousness (goodness), reap love, and break up your hard ground (hearts); seek the LORD until He showers His righteousness on you. **13.** You have planted wickedness (evil) and reaped its evil fruits. You have eaten the fruit of deception (lies). **14.** The roar of battle will rise against your people, and your fortresses will be destroyed—as Shalman destroyed Beth Arbel (a place of devastation), when mothers and children were killed. **15.** So it will be with you, Bethel, because of your great wickedness. When that day comes, the king of Israel will be utterly destroyed.

Chapter 11

1. When Israel was a child, I loved him and called my son out of Egypt. **2.** But the more I called, the more they turned away. They sacrificed (offered worship) to Baal (a false god) and burned incense (perfumed smoke) to idols. **3.** I taught Ephraim (a tribe of Israel) to walk, holding them by the arms, but they didn't realize it was I who healed them. **4.** I led them with kindness and love, like one who lifts a child to their cheek and feeds them. **5.** Will they not return to Egypt? Will Assyria (a powerful enemy nation) rule over them because they refuse to repent (feel regret and turn from sin)? **6.** A sword will flash in their cities, destroying false prophets (people who falsely claim to speak for God) and their plans. **7.** My people are determined to turn from me. Though they call me the Most High (God's supreme title), I will not exalt (raise in honor) them. **8.** How can I give you up, Ephraim? How can I treat you like Admah and Zeboyim (cities destroyed by judgment)? My heart is torn within me; all my compassion is stirred. **9.** I will not unleash my fierce anger or destroy Ephraim again. For I am God, not a man—the

Holy One (sacred and set apart) among you. I will not come against their cities. **10.** They will follow the LORD; He will roar like a lion. When He roars, His children will come trembling (fearfully) from the west. **11.** They will come from Egypt, trembling like sparrows (small and vulnerable), and from Assyria, fluttering like doves (symbolizing vulnerability). I will settle them in their homes, declares the LORD. **12.** Ephraim surrounds me with lies, and Israel is full of deceit (dishonesty). Judah is rebellious (resistant) against God, even the faithful Holy One.

Chapter 12

1. Ephraim chases the wind, pursuing lies and violence. He makes deals (agreements) with Assyria and sends gifts to Egypt. **2.** The LORD has a case (dispute) against Judah; He will punish Jacob (Israel) for his actions. **3.** In the womb, he grasped his brother's heel; as a man, he struggled with God. **4.** He wrestled with the angel, overcame, and begged for favor (kindness). He found God at Bethel (a sacred place) and spoke with Him— **5.** the LORD God Almighty (All-Powerful), His name is the LORD! **6.** Return to your God, practice love (compassion) and justice (fairness), and wait (hope) for Him always. **7.** The merchant uses dishonest scales (fraudulent measures) and loves to cheat (deceive). **8.** Ephraim boasts, "I am rich and without sin." **9.** I have been your God since Egypt; I will make you live in tents (temporary shelters) again, as in your festivals (celebrations). **10.** I spoke through the prophets, giving them visions (divine revelations) and parables (symbolic stories). **11.** Is Gilead wicked? Its people are worthless (evil)! Their altars will be like piles of stones in a plowed field (empty and abandoned). **12.** Jacob fled (escaped) to Aram (Syria); Israel served to get a wife and worked as a shepherd. **13.** The LORD used a prophet to bring Israel out of Egypt and care for them. **14.** But Ephraim's sin has aroused (provoked) God's anger; they will face the consequences (punishment) of their violence (unjust actions) and contempt (disrespect).

Chapter 13

1. When Ephraim spoke, people trembled; he was honored in Israel. But he became guilty of Baal worship (idol worship) and died. **2.** Now they sin more, making idols (false gods) from silver, skillfully crafted (expertly made) by craftsmen (skilled workers). It is said, "They offer human sacrifices (ritual killings) and kiss calf-idols (idols in the shape of a calf)!" **3.** They will be like mist (thin vapor), dew (morning moisture) that vanishes (disappears), chaff (wheat husks) blowing away, and smoke (vapor) escaping through a window. **4.** I have been your God since Egypt. You shall acknowledge (recognize) no God but Me, no Savior (rescuer) except Me. **5.** I cared for you in the wilderness , in the land of burning heat (harsh, dry land). **6.** When I fed them, they were satisfied (fulfilled); when they were satisfied, they became proud (arrogant) and forgot (ignored) Me. **7.** So I will be like a lion (fierce predator), like a leopard (fast and dangerous) lying in wait (ready to pounce). **8.** Like a bear robbed of her cubs (young), I will tear them apart (attack); like a lion I will devour them— a wild animal will destroy them. **9.** You are destroyed, Israel, because you are against (opposed to) Me, your helper (rescuer). **10.** Where is your king to save you? Where are your rulers (leaders) in your towns, the ones you asked for (requested)? **11.** In My anger (fury) I gave you a king; in My wrath (intense anger), I took him away. **12.** Ephraim's guilt (sin) is stored up, his sins are recorded (noted). **13.** Like a woman in labor (giving birth), Ephraim has no wisdom (understanding). When the time comes, he cannot be born (delivered). **14.** I will redeem (save) this people from the grave (death); I will save them from death. Where, O death, are your plagues (sufferings)? Where, O grave, is your destruction (ruin)? **15.** Though Ephraim thrives (prospers) among his brothers, an east wind from the LORD will come. His spring (source of water) will fail (dry up), his well (water source) will dry up, and his treasures (possessions) will be plundered (stolen). **16.** The people of Samaria must bear (suffer) their guilt because they have rebelled (turned against) God. They will fall by the sword (killed), and their children will be killed; their pregnant women will be ripped open (violently harmed).

Chapter 14

1. Return to the LORD, Israel, and your God. Your sins have caused you to fall (become undone, stumble)! **2.** Take words with you as you return to the LORD. Say, "Forgive all our sins and receive us with favor (grace), so that we may offer you the praise of our lips (words)." **3.** We will no longer rely (depend) on Assyria for help, nor will we trust (depend) on military power. We will not call 'Our gods' to idols (false gods) we made with our own hands. For in You, the orphan (fatherless) finds compassion (mercy). **4.** "I will heal (restore) their waywardness (backsliding, turning away) and love them freely, for My anger has turned away (ceased) from them." **5.** I will be like dew (refreshing moisture) to Israel; he will blossom (grow beautifully) like a lily (a beautiful flower). He will take root (grow strong) like a cedar of Lebanon (a tall, strong tree); **6.** His young branches (shoots) will grow strong, and his beauty (splendor, magnificence) will be like that of an olive tree, his fragrance (scent) like the cedars of Lebanon. **7.** People will live under his protection (shade, safety); they will thrive (prosper) like grain, blossom (grow) like the vine— Israel's reputation (fame) will be as renowned (famous) as the wine of Lebanon. **8.** Ephraim, how much longer will you be entangled (ensnared, caught) with idols? I will answer (respond) and care for him. I am like a flourishing (thriving, healthy) juniper tree; your success (fruitfulness, prosperity) comes from Me." **9.** Let the wise (those with understanding) consider (think about) these things. Let the discerning (those with insight, perception) grasp (understand) them. The ways of the LORD are just (fair); the righteous (those in right standing with God) walk in them, but the rebellious (wicked, defiant) stumble (fall) in them.

36 – Amos
Chapter 1

1. Amos, a shepherd from Tekoa (Judah), received a vision about Israel two years before the earthquake, during the reign of Uzziah (Judah) and Jeroboam II (Israel). He said: "The Lord roars from Zion and thunders from Jerusalem. The pastures dry up, and Carmel withers." **2.** Judgment on Israel's Neighbors The Lord says: "For three sins of Damascus (capital of Aram), even for four, I will not relent. They threshed Gilead with iron sledges, **3.** I will send fire on Hazael's house, consuming the fortresses of Ben-Hadad. **4.** I will break the gates of Damascus, destroy the king in the Valley of Aven, and the ruler in Beth Eden. The people of Aram will go into exile to Kir." **5.** The Lord says: "For three sins of Gaza (Philistine city), even for four, I will not relent. They captured and sold communities to Edom, **6.** I will send fire on Gaza that will consume her fortresses. **7.** I will destroy the king of Ashdod and the ruler of Ashkelon. I will turn my hand against Ekron and the last of the Philistines will perish." **8.** The Lord says: "For three sins of Tyre (Phoenician city), even for four, I will not relent. They sold captives to Edom, breaking a brotherhood treaty, **9.** I will send fire on Tyre, consuming her fortresses." **10.** The Lord says: "For three sins of Edom (descendants of Esau), even for four, I will not relent. They pursued their brother with a sword and slaughtered women, **11.** I will send fire on Teman, consuming the fortresses of Bozrah." **12.** The Lord says: "For three sins of Ammon (neighboring people of Israel), even for four, I will not relent. They ripped open pregnant women in Gilead to extend their borders, **13.** I will set fire to Rabbah, consuming her fortresses amidst battle cries and stormy winds. **14.** Her king and officials will go into exile."

Chapter 2

1. This is what the LORD says: "For three sins of Moab, even for four, I will not pardon them. Because they burned the bones of Edom's king to ashes, **2.** I will send fire on Moab that will destroy the fortresses of Kerioth (a city in Moab, present day Israel). Moab will be overwhelmed by war cries and the blast of the trumpet. **3.** I will destroy their king and all their leaders," says the LORD. **4.** This is what the LORD says: "For three sins of Judah, even for four, I will not relent. Because they rejected the law of the LORD (God's commands), disobeyed His commands, and were misled by false gods, **5.** I will send fire on Judah to burn down the fortresses of Jerusalem." **6.** This is what the LORD says: "For three sins of Israel, even for four, I will not forgive them. They sell the innocent for silver and the poor for sandals (cheap items). **7.** They trample on the heads of the poor and deny justice to the oppressed (those being treated unfairly). Fathers and sons sleep with the same girl, defiling (making unholy) My name. **8.** They lie beside altars on garments taken as pledges (collateral for a loan) and drink wine from fines (money taken as punishment) in the house of their gods (idols). **9.** I destroyed the Amorites (ancient enemies of Israel) before you, though they were as tall as cedars and as strong as oaks. I destroyed their fruit and roots. **10.** I brought you out of Egypt and led you through the wilderness to give you the land of the Amorites. **11.** I

raised prophets and Nazirites (those dedicated to God through a special vow) from among your children. Is this not true, Israel?" declares the LORD. **12.** "But you made the Nazirites drink wine and told the prophets not to speak. **13.** Now, I will crush you like a cart loaded with grain. **14.** The swift (fast runners) will not escape, the strong will not survive, and the warrior will not save his life. **15.** The archer (someone who uses a bow and arrow) will not stand firm, the fast runner will not escape, and the horseman will not save his life. **16.** Even the bravest warriors will flee naked on that day," declares the LORD.

Chapter 3

1. Listen, people of Israel, to the word the LORD has spoken against you—the nation I brought out of Egypt: **2.** "You alone have I chosen from all the families of the earth; therefore, I will punish you for your sins." **3.** Do two people walk together unless they have agreed? **4.** Does a lion roar when it has no prey? Does it growl when it has caught nothing? **5.** Does a bird swoop down to a trap without bait? Does a trap spring if it has caught nothing? **6.** When a trumpet sounds, do the people tremble? When disaster strikes, has not the LORD caused it? **7.** The Sovereign LORD does nothing without revealing His plans to His servants, the prophets. **8.** The lion has roared—who will not be afraid? The LORD has spoken—who can remain silent? **9.** Announce to the fortresses of Ashdod (Philistine city) and Egypt: "Assemble on the mountains of Samaria; see the chaos and oppression." **10.** "They do not know how to do right," says the LORD, "those who store up stolen goods in their strongholds." **11.** Therefore, the Sovereign LORD says: "An enemy will invade your land, tear down your fortifications, and plunder your strongholds." **12.** "Just as a shepherd rescues from a lion's mouth only two leg bones or a piece of an ear, so will the Israelites in Samaria be rescued—only a piece of a bed and fabric from a couch." **13.** "Listen and testify against the descendants of Jacob," declares the LORD. **14.** "On the day I punish Israel for her sins, I will destroy the altars of Bethel (a religious site); the horns of the altar will be cut off and fall." **15.** "I will demolish both winter and summer houses; ivory-decorated homes will be destroyed, and mansions torn down," declares the LORD.

Chapter 4

1. Hear this, you women of Bashan (a fertile region, often symbolizing luxury) on Mount Samaria, you who oppress the poor, crush the needy, and say to your husbands, "Bring us some drinks!" **2.** The Sovereign LORD has sworn by His holiness: "The time will come when you will be taken away with hooks, the last of you with fishhooks." **3.** You will be taken out through breaches (gaps) in the wall and cast toward Harmon (a place)," declares the LORD. **4.** "Go to Bethel (a religious site) and sin; go to Gilgal (another religious site) and sin even more. Bring your sacrifices every morning, your tithes (offerings) every three years. **5.** Burn leavened bread (bread with yeast, symbolizing corruption) as a thank offering and boast about your freewill offerings—brag about them, you Israelites, for this is what you love to do," declares the Sovereign LORD. **6.** "I gave you empty stomachs in every city and lack of bread in every town, yet you have not returned to me," declares the LORD. **7.** "I also withheld rain when the harvest was still three months away. I sent rain on one town but withheld it from another. One field had rain, another dried up. **8.** People staggered (struggled unsteadily) from town to town for water but did not get enough to drink, yet you have not returned to me," declares the LORD. **9.** "I struck your gardens and vineyards, destroying them with blight (plant disease) and mildew (fungus). Locusts devoured your fig and olive trees, yet you have not returned to me," declares the LORD. **10.** "I sent plagues (disasters) among you as I did to Egypt. I killed your young men with the sword (weapon of war), along with your captured horses. I filled your nostrils (sense of smell) with the stench (foul smell) of your camps, yet you have not returned to me," declares the LORD. **11.** "I overthrew some of you as I overthrew Sodom and Gomorrah (wicked cities destroyed by God). You were like a burning stick snatched from the fire, yet you have not returned to me," declares the LORD. **12.** "Therefore, this is what I will do to you, Israel. Prepare to meet your God." **13.** He who forms the mountains, creates the wind, reveals His thoughts to mankind, who turns dawn to darkness, and treads (walks) on the heights of the earth—the LORD God Almighty is His name.

Chapter 5

1. Hear this word, Israel, this lament (expression of grief) I take up concerning you: 2. "Fallen is Virgin Israel, never to rise again, deserted in her own land, with no one to lift her up." 3. The Sovereign LORD says: "Your city that once marched out a thousand strong will have only a hundred left; your town that was a hundred strong will have only ten left." 4. "Seek me and live; 5. do not seek Bethel (a religious site), Gilgal (another site), or Beersheba (a town), for they will be destroyed." 6. Seek the LORD or He will sweep through the tribes of Joseph like a fire; it will devour them, and Bethel will have no one to quench it. 7. Some turn justice into bitterness and trample on righteousness. 8. He who made the Pleiades (a star cluster) and Orion (a constellation), who turns night into day, who calls for the waters of the sea and pours them out—the LORD is His name. 9. With a flash He destroys strongholds and brings cities to ruin. 10. Some hate those who uphold justice and truth. 11. You impose heavy taxes on the poor and take grain from them. Though you build mansions, you will not live in them; though you plant vineyards, you will not drink their wine. 12. I know your offenses and how great your sins are. Some oppress the innocent, take bribes, and deny the poor justice. 13. Therefore, the wise remain silent, for the times are evil. 14. Seek good, not evil, that you may live. Then the LORD will be with you, as you claim He is. 15. Hate evil, love good; uphold justice in the courts. Perhaps the LORD will show mercy to the remnant (surviving group) of Joseph. 16. Therefore, the LORD says: "There will be wailing in the streets and cries in the public squares. Farmers will be summoned to weep and mourners to wail. 17. there will be wailing in the vineyards, for I will pass through your midst," says the LORD. 18. Woe to those who long for the day of the LORD! Why do you long for it? That day will be darkness, not light. 19. It will be like a man fleeing a lion only to meet a bear, or resting his hand on the wall only to be bitten by a snake. 20. The day of the LORD will be pitch-dark, with no light. 21. "I hate, I despise your religious festivals; your assemblies are a stench (foul odor) to me. 22. Even though you bring burnt offerings and grain offerings, I will not accept them. Though you bring choice fellowship offerings, I will have no regard for them. 23. Away with the noise of your songs! I will not listen to the music of your harps. 24. Let justice roll like a river, righteousness like a never-failing stream! 25. "Did you bring sacrifices and offerings for forty years in the wilderness, people of Israel? 26. You have lifted up the shrine (place of worship) of your king, the pedestal (base) of your idols, and the star of your god, which you made for yourselves. 27. Therefore, I will send you into exile beyond Damascus," says the LORD, whose name is God Almighty.

Chapter 6

1. Woe to you who are complacent (self-satisfied, unaware of danger) in Zion, and to you who feel secure on Mount Samaria, you notable men of the foremost nation, to whom the people of Israel come! 2. Go to Kalneh (an ancient city), Hamath (a city in Syria), and Gath (an ancient Philistine city). Are they better off than your two kingdoms? Is their land larger than yours? 3. You delay the day of disaster and bring near a reign of terror. 4. You lie on ivory beds and lounge on your couches, dining on choice lambs and fattened calves. 5. You play your harps like David and improvise on musical instruments. 6. You drink wine by the bowlful and use fine lotions, but you do not grieve over Israel's ruin. 7. Therefore, you will be the first to go into exile; your feasting will end. 8. The Sovereign LORD has sworn: "I abhor (hate) the pride of Jacob and detest his fortresses (strongholds); I will deliver the city and everything in it." 9. If ten people are left in one house, they will die. 10. If a relative comes to carry the bodies out and asks, "Is anyone else with you?" and is told, "No," he will reply, "Hush! We must not mention the name of the LORD." 11. The LORD has commanded, and He will smash both the great and small houses into pieces. 12. Do horses run on rocky crags (cliffs)? Does one plow (cultivate) the sea with oxen? But you have turned justice into poison and righteousness into bitterness. 13. You rejoice in the conquest of Lo Debar (town in north of the Jabbok river in ancient Israel) and boast, "Did we not take Karnaim (a city) by our own strength?" 14. For the LORD declares, "I will stir up a nation against you, Israel that will oppress you from Lebo Hamath (a northern boundary) to the Arabah (a desert region).

Chapter 7

1. This is what the Sovereign LORD showed me: He was preparing swarms of locusts after the king's share had been harvested, just as the late crops were coming up. 2. When they stripped the land clean, I cried, "Sovereign LORD, forgive! How can Jacob survive? He is so small!" 3. The LORD relented, saying, "This will not happen." 4. The Sovereign LORD showed me another vision: He called for judgment by fire, which dried up the great deep and devoured the land. 5. I cried out, "Sovereign LORD, stop! How can Jacob survive? He is so small!" 6. The LORD relented again, saying, "This will not happen either." 7. This is what He showed me: The LORD was standing by a wall built true to plumb (perfectly straight), with a plumb line (a tool used to measure if something is straight) in His hand. 8. The LORD asked, "What do you see, Amos?" "A plumb line," I replied. The LORD said, "I am setting a plumb line among My people Israel; I will no longer spare them. 9. The high places of Isaac will be destroyed, and the sanctuaries of Israel will be ruined. With My sword, I will rise against the house of Jeroboam." 10. Then Amaziah, the priest of Bethel, sent a message to Jeroboam, king of Israel: "Amos is raising a conspiracy against you in Israel. The land cannot bear his words. 11. For this is what Amos says: 'Jeroboam will die by the sword, and Israel will be exiled (sent away from their land).'" 12. Amaziah told Amos, "Get out, you seer (prophet)! Go back to Judah. Earn your bread there and prophesy there. 13. Don't prophesy anymore at Bethel, because this is the king's sanctuary and the temple of the kingdom." 14. Amos answered, "I was neither a prophet nor the son of a prophet. I was a shepherd and cared for sycamore-fig trees (a type of tree). 15. But the LORD took me from tending the flock and said, 'Go, prophesy to My people Israel.' 16. Now hear the word of the LORD: You say, 'Do not prophesy against Israel, and stop preaching against the descendants of Isaac.' 17. Therefore, the LORD says: 'Your wife will become a prostitute in the city, and your sons and daughters will die by the sword. Your land will be divided, and you will die in a foreign country. Israel will go into exile.'"

Chapter 8

1. This is what the Sovereign LORD showed me: a basket of ripe fruit. 2. "What do you see, Amos?" He asked. "A basket of ripe fruit," I answered. The LORD said, "The time has come for Israel; I will no longer spare them. 3. "In that day," declares the Sovereign LORD, "the songs in the temple will turn to wailing. Many bodies will be scattered everywhere! Silence!" 4. Hear this, you who oppress (treat unfairly) the needy and crush (weaken) the poor, 5. saying, "When will the New Moon be over so we can sell grain, and the Sabbath end so we can market wheat?" You reduce (lower) the measure, raise the price, and cheat (deceive) with dishonest scales (false weights), 6. buying the poor with silver and the needy for sandals, selling even the sweepings (wheat husks or waste) with the grain. 7. The LORD has sworn (promised with an oath) by Himself, the Pride of Jacob: "I will never forget their deeds. 8. "Will not the land tremble (shake) for this, and all who live in it mourn (feel sorrow)? The whole land will rise like the Nile and sink like the river of Egypt. 9. "In that day," declares the Sovereign LORD, "I will make the sun go down at noon and darken the earth in broad daylight. 10. I will turn your festivals into mourning (sorrow), your songs into weeping (crying). You will wear sackcloth (coarse cloth worn in mourning) and shave your heads. It will be like mourning for an only son, and the end will be bitter (painful). 11. "The days are coming," declares the Sovereign LORD, "when I will send a famine (severe shortage) through the land— not a famine of food or water, but of hearing the words of the LORD. 12. People will stagger (stumble or move unsteadily) from sea to sea, searching for the word of the LORD, but will not find it. 13. "In that day, the lovely young women and strong young men will faint (lose strength) from thirst. 14. Those who swear (take an oath) by the sin of Samaria— saying, 'As surely as your god lives, Dan,' or 'As surely as the god of Beersheba lives'— they will fall, never to rise again."

Chapter 9

1. I saw the Lord at the altar, saying, "Strike the pillars so the thresholds shake and fall on the people. I will kill the rest with the sword; none will escape. 2. If they dig deep or ascend to the heavens, I will bring them back. 3. If they hide on Mount Carmel (mountain in Israel) or in the sea, I will capture them; even the serpent will strike them at My command. 4. If exiled by enemies, the sword will still reach them. I am watching for harm, not good. 5. The Lord Almighty touches the earth, and it melts; it rises and falls like the Nile. 6. He builds His palace in the heavens, setting its foundation on earth. He calls the waters, pouring

them over the land—He is the LORD. 7. "Israelites, are you different from the Cushites? I brought Israel from Egypt, the Philistines from Caphtor (an island), and the Arameans from Kir (city/ a wall town). 8. The eyes of the Lord are on the sinful kingdom, to destroy it, though He will not completely destroy Jacob's descendants. 9. I will sift Israel among nations like grain, yet no pebble will fall to the ground. 10. All sinners who say, 'Disaster won't touch us,' will die by the sword. 11. "I will restore David's fallen shelter, repairing and rebuilding it as before, 12. so Israel may possess Edom and all nations bearing My name," says the Lord. 13. "The days are coming when the reaper will be overtaken by the plowman. New wine will flow from mountains and hills. 14. I will bring Israel back from exile; they'll rebuild cities, plant vineyards, and eat from their gardens. 15. I will plant Israel in their own land, never to be uprooted again," declares the Lord.

37 – Micah
Chapter 1
1. The word of the Lord came to Micah of Moresheth (a town in Judah ancient Israel) during the reigns of Jotham, Ahaz, and Hezekiah, kings of Judah, concerning Samaria and Jerusalem. 2. Listen, all people! Pay attention, earth and everything in it! Let the Lord God testify against you from His holy temple (God's dwelling place). 3. The Lord is coming from His dwelling place; He will walk on the high places (idol worship) of the earth. 4. The mountains will melt beneath Him, and valleys will split, like wax before fire or water flowing down a hill. 5. This is due to the rebellion (disobedience) of Jacob and Israel's sins. What is Jacob's rebellion? Samaria. And Judah's high places? They are in Jerusalem. 6. "I will turn Samaria into a heap of ruins, a place for vineyards. I will throw her stones into the valley and expose her foundations. 7. All her idols (false gods) will be broken, her wealth burned with fire, and the wages of her prostitution will return to prostitution." 8. Because of this, I will mourn and wail, walk barefoot and naked (in grief), howl like jackals (wild dogs), and mourn like ostriches. 9. Samaria's wounds are incurable and have reached the gates of Jerusalem. 10. Don't tell it in Gath (a Philistine city); don't weep there. In Beth Aphrah, roll in the dust (mourning). 11. You in Shaphir (a town), pass in shame. Zaanan's people do not come out. Beth Ezel mourns; its support is gone. 12. Maroth waited for good, but disaster from the Lord came to Jerusalem's gates. 13. Lachish, harness your chariots. You were the start of sin for Zion, for Israel's transgressions (sins) began with you. 14. You will give parting gifts to Moresheth Gath (Micah's hometown); the houses of Achzib (a town) will fail the kings of Israel. 15. I will bring a conqueror to you, people of Mareshah (a town); the glory of Israel will go to Adullam (a refuge). 16. Shave your heads in mourning for your children, who will go into exile. Make yourself bald like an eagle, for they will be taken away.

Chapter 2
1. Woe (great sorrow) to those who plan evil while lying in bed! They carry it out in the morning because they have the power to do so. 2. They desire fields and seize (take by force) them by violence; they take houses and oppress (mistreat and harm) people, stealing their homes and inheritance (what is passed down to them from their ancestors). 3. Therefore, the Lord says, "I am bringing disaster (great trouble) on this family, and you will not escape. You will no longer walk with pride, for these are evil times."4. On that day, people will mock (make fun of) you with a proverb (a wise saying), saying, "We are completely ruined! Our land has been taken and divided among traitors (those who betray others)."5. Therefore, you will have no one left to assign land by lot (method of dividing land) in the assembly (gathering) of the Lord. 6. You say to the prophets (those who speak God's message), "Do not speak!" So they will not prophesy (deliver messages from God) to you, and no more insults will be exchanged. 7. House of Jacob, is the Spirit of the Lord limited (restricted)? Are these the actions of God? His words benefit those who live rightly (uprightly). 8. But recently, My people have turned against Me, robbing those who trusted them, as they pass by like men returning from battle. 9. You force the women of My people out of their homes and take away My blessing from their children forever. 10. Rise and leave, for this land is no longer a place of rest. It is defiled (corrupted) and will bring complete destruction. 11. If someone falsely claims to prophesy about wine and beer, he would be just the kind of prophet this people desires. 12. I will surely gather all of you, O Jacob, and bring together the remnant (remaining part) of Israel like a flock of sheep. They will be noisy with their large numbers. 13. The one who breaks open the way will lead them. They will pass through the gate and go out. Their king will lead them, with the Lord guiding them.

Chapter 3
1. Hear, leaders of Jacob and autocrats of Israel: Isn't it your duty to know justice (fairness)? 2. You detest good and love wrong. You strip the skin from my people and tear their meat from their bones. 3. You consume (eat) their meat strips their skin, break their bones, and hash them like meat for a pot, like meat in a jug (large cuisine pot). 4. They will cry to the Lord, but He'll not hear them; He'll hide His face from them because of their wrong (wicked) deeds. 5. This is what the Lord says about prophets who mislead my people. They speak "Peace" when they've food, but prepare war against anyone who does not feed them. 6. You'll have darkness without vision (predictive sapience), and night without vaticination. The sun will set on the prophets, and it'll be dark for them. 7. The foreseers (prophets) will be shamed, and the forecasters (predictors) lowered. They will cover their mouths because there will be no answer (response) from God. 8. But I'm filled with power from the Spirit (presence) of the Lord, with justice and strength, to declare to Jacob his rebellion (going against God) and to Israel his sin. 9. Hear, you leaders of Jacob and autocrats of Israel, who despise (hate) justice and distort (twist) what's right. 10. You make Zion (a hill in Jerusalem, emblematizing God's people) with bloodshed and Jerusalem (the capital megacity) with wrongdoing. 11. Her leader's judge for a fix (plutocrat), her preachers educate for pay, and her prophets predict for plutocrat. Yet they say, "The Lord is among us. Nothing bad will be to us." 12. Because of you, Zion will come a furrowed field (destroyed), Jerusalem will come a mound (pile) of remains, and the mountain of the tabernacle (the holy place) like bare hills.

Chapter 4
1. In the last days, the Lord's house will be established at the loftiest point, and people from numerous nations will come to it. 2. They will say, "Let us go to the mountain of the Lord, to the house of the God of Jacob. He'll educate us His ways, and we will follow His paths. From Zion (Jerusalem), the law will go out, and the word of the Lord from Jerusalem." 3. He'll judge (decide controversies) between nations, settle dissensions, and reproach (scold or correct) important nations far off. They will turn their munitions into husbandry tools, and there will be no more war. 4. Everyone will sit under their own vine (a symbol of peace and substance) and fig tree, free from fear, for the Lord of Hosts (God, sovereign of all) has spoken. 5. While others follow their own gods, we will walk in the name of the Lord our God ever. 6. "On that day, I'll gather the lame (those who cannot walk) and rejects (those rejected by society), those whom I've tormented (suffered detriment); 7. I'll make the lame a strong nation, and the rejects an important people. The Lord will control (rule) from Mount Zion (Jerusalem) ever." 8. And you, O palace of the flock (a fort or place of safety in Jerusalem), the former area will return to you, and the reign of Jerusalem will be restored. 9. Why do you cry out? Is there no king (leader) or counselor (counsel) with you? You're in pain, like a woman in labor (passing great torture). 10. Be in pain, O son of Zion. You'll go from the megacity to Babylon (a megacity of exile, now in modern day Iraq), but there you'll be saved, and the Lord will redeem (save) you from your adversaries. 11. Numerous nations have gathered against you, saying, "Let her be defiled (made impure), and let us peer upon Zion." 12. But they don't understand the Lord's plans. He'll gather them like sheaves (packets of grain) to the threshing bottom (a place where grain is separated from chaff). 13. "Arise and squirm, O son of Zion, for I'll make your strength like iron and your hooves (bases) like citation. You'll crush numerous nations, and their wealth will be consecrated (devoted) to the Lord, for He rules over all the earth."

Chapter 5
1. Gather yourselves, O daughter of troops; the enemy has laid siege (encircling of area aiming to stop basic life supplies) against us. They will strike the ruler of Israel on the cheek with a rod (a staff or stick). 2. But you, Bethlehem Ephrathah (a small town in Judah), though small among the clans of Judah, out of you will come the One who will rule over Israel, whose origins are from eternity (forever in the past). 3. He will abandon them until the woman in labor gives birth; then the rest

of His people will return to Israel. **4.** He will shepherd His flock in the Lord's strength, in the majesty (greatness) of His God. They will live securely, for His greatness will reach the ends of the earth. **5.** He will be their peace. When the Assyrian (enemy nation) invades and enters our fortresses, we will raise against him seven shepherds and eight leaders. **6.** They will defeat Assyria with the sword and conquer the land of Nimrod (ancient kingdom). He will rescue us from the Assyrian when he invades. **7.** The remnant of Jacob (remaining Israelites) will be among many nations like dew (morning moisture) from the Lord, like showers on the grass, not waiting for man. **8.** The remnant of Jacob will be among the nations like a lion among animals, trampling and tearing (destroying), and none can save them. **9.** Your hand will be raised against your enemies, and all your foes will be destroyed. **10.** In that day," says the Lord, "I will remove your horses (military power) and destroy your chariots (war vehicles). **11.** I will demolish the cities and tear down your strongholds. **12.** I will end witchcraft (magic) and fortune-telling (future predictions). **13.** I will destroy your carved idols and sacred pillars (religious symbols); you will no longer worship your own creations. **14.** I will uproot your Asherah poles (idols) and destroy your cities. **15.** I will take vengeance (punishment) in anger on the nations that have not listened to me."

Chapter 6

1. Hear what the Lord says" Get up and present your case before the mountains, and let the hills hear your voice. **2.** Hear, mountains, to the Lord's complaint, and you, strong foundations of the earth; for the Lord has a case against His people, and He'll argue with Israel. **3.** "My people, what have I done to you? How have I burdened (weighed down) you? Answer Me. **4.** I brought you out of Egypt, freeing you from slavery, and transferred (sent ahead) Moses, Aaron, and Miriam ahead of you. **5.** Flash back (remember) what Balak, king of Moab, colluded (worked together secretly), and how Balaam, son of Beor, answered him. Recall your trip from Acacia Grove to Gilgal, so you may know the righteousness (justice) of the Lord. **6.** What should I bring ahead the Lord and bow down to the Most High God? Should I offer burnt immolations (offerings), with pins (young animals) a time old? **7.** Will the Lord be pleased with thousands of rams or endless gutters (streams) of oil painting (oil)? Should I offer my firstborn for my sins, the child of my body for the wrongs of my soul? **8.** He has shown you what's good. What does the Lord bear (require) but to act justly, love mercy, and walk submissively (humbly) with your God? **9.** The Lord's voice calls out to the megacity (city). Wisdom will fete (recognize) Your name " Pay attention to the rod (punishment) of discipline and the One who appointed it. **10.** Do wicked treasures (ill-gotten wealth) remain in the house of the wrong (wicked), with the short measure (dishonest measure) that's despicable (detestable)? **11.** Should I declare innocent those who use false scales and deceitful weights? **12.** The megacity's rich are full of violence, its residers (inhabitants) speak falsehoods, and their speeches are deceitful. **13.** So I'll strike you with illness and make you desolate (empty) because of your sins. **14.** You'll eat but not be satisfied; hunger will remain. You'll try to save some, but it'll be taken by the brand (plague). **15.** You'll plant but not gather; press olives but not use the oil painting (oil); make wine but not drink it. **16.** You follow the bills (deeds) of Omri and the evil workshop (ways) of Ahab's house. You live by their advice, so I'll make you desolate, and your people a mockery (making fun of someone).

Chapter 7

1. Woe (great sorrow) is me! I am like someone who gathers summer fruit, or picks grapes at harvest time, but finds none to eat, none of the first ripe fruit my soul longs for. **2.** The faithful (loyal, trustworthy) are gone from the earth, and there is no one upright (moral, just) among men. Everyone wants to shed blood; each person hunts down their brother like prey. **3.** They do evil with both hands—leaders demand gifts (bribes), judges take bribes (money to influence a decision), and the powerful speak of their wicked (evil) plans, all conspiring (planning secretly) together. **4.** The best among them is like a thornbush (a sharp, prickly plant); the most upright is sharper than a thorn hedge (a thorny barrier). The day of judgment is coming, and they will be confused (bewildered). **5.** Do not trust your friend; do not rely on your companion (partner). Guard your words, even from the one closest to you. **6.** A son dishonors (shows disrespect to) his father, a daughter turns against (betrays) her mother, and a daughter-in-law against her

mother-in-law. A person's enemies will be those in their own household. **7.** But I will look to the Lord; I will wait for the God of my salvation (deliverance). My God will hear me. **8.** Do not rejoice (celebrate) over me, my enemy. Though I fall, I will rise again; though I sit in darkness, the Lord will be my light. **9.** I will bear the Lord's anger (wrath) because I have sinned (wronged) against Him, but He will plead (argue on my behalf) my case and bring me to the light, where I will see His righteousness (justice). **10.** Then my enemy will see, and shame (embarrassment) will cover her, who said to me, "Where is your God?" My eyes will witness (see) her defeat, and she will be trampled (stepped on) like mud in the streets. **11.** On the day your walls are rebuilt (restored), the decree (official order) will extend far and wide. **12.** On that day, people will come to you from Assyria (an ancient empire), and the fortified cities (strong, defensive cities), from the fortress (a stronghold) to the River, from sea to sea, and from mountain to mountain. **13.** But the land will be desolate (empty), because of those who live in it, and the fruit (result) of their deeds (actions). **14.** Shepherd (guide and protect) Your people with Your staff (rod), the flock (group) of Your inheritance (heritage), who live alone (isolated) in the forest (wooded area), in the midst of Carmel (a fertile mountain range). Let them feed in Bashan (a fertile region) and Gilead (a region east of the Jordan River), as in days past. **15.** "As when you came out of Egypt, I will show them wonders (miracles)." **16.** The nations will see and be ashamed (embarrassed) of their might (strength); they will cover their mouths (in awe) and become deaf (unable to hear). **17.** They will lick the dust (crawl in defeat) like serpents (snakes), crawling from their holes like snakes of the earth. They will be afraid (terrified) of the Lord our God and tremble (shudder) before You. **18.** Who is a God like You, who forgives iniquity (wickedness) and overlooks the transgressions (sins) of the remnant (the remaining ones) of His people? He does not stay angry forever because He delights in mercy (kindness). **19.** He will again have compassion (pity) on us and subdue (defeat) our iniquities. You will throw all our sins into the depths of the sea. **20.** You will give truth (faithfulness) to Jacob (the name for Israel) and mercy (loving-kindness) to Abraham, as You swore (promised) to our ancestors long ago.

38 – Joel

Chapter 1

1. This is the message from the Lord to Joel, son of Pethuel. **2.** Listen, elders (leaders) and all who live in the land! Has anything like this happened before, even in the days of your ancestors (previous generations)? **3.** Tell your children, and let them tell the next generation. **4.** The locusts (crop-destroying insects) have ruined the land: what the chewing locusts left, the swarming locusts ate; what the swarming locusts left, the crawling locusts consumed; and what the crawling locusts left, the consuming locusts destroyed. **5.** Wake up, you drinkers of wine, and mourn (grieve)! Cry out, all you who love wine, because the new wine is gone. **6.** A nation has invaded (attacked) My land, a mighty (strong) and countless (numerous) people, with teeth like a lion and fangs (sharp teeth) like a fierce lion. **7.** They have destroyed My vine (grapevine) and ruined My fig tree; they have stripped them bare (removed all leaves or fruit). **8.** Cry out like a virgin mourning (grieving) for her fiancé, who has passed away. **9.** The grain (wheat) and drink offerings have been stopped (cut off) from the Lord's house; the priests (religious leaders) who serve the Lord are grieving. **10.** The land is in ruin (destruction); the fields mourn (are sad). The grain is ruined, the new wine has dried up, and the oil (for anointing and light) has failed. **11.** Farmers, be ashamed! Vineyard workers, wail (cry loudly)! The crops are ruined, for the harvest (crops) has perished (died). **12.** The vine has dried up, the fig tree has withered (dried up). All the trees have withered, and joy has faded (disappeared). **13.** Priests, put on sackcloth (a rough fabric worn as a sign of mourning) and weep (cry); ministers (servants) of the altar (place of sacrifice), mourn! Spend the night in sackcloth, for the offerings are withheld (kept back) from the house of God. **14.** Declare (announce) a fast (time of no eating), call a sacred assembly (holy gathering), gather the elders (leaders) and all the people into the house of the Lord, and cry out to Him. **15.** The day of the Lord is near, a day of destruction from the Almighty (all-powerful God). **16.** Isn't the food taken away before our eyes? Joy and gladness are gone from the house of our God. **17.** The seed shrivels (shrinks) in the soil; the storehouses (places where goods are stored) are in ruins (damaged); the barns (storage buildings) are broken down, for the grain has withered (dried up). **18.** The animals groan (make sad sounds); the herds (groups of cattle) are restless (uneasy) because they have no pasture (land for grazing), and the sheep suffer (feel pain). **19.** Lord, I cry out to You! Fire has destroyed the open pastures, and a flame has burned all the trees. **20.** The animals cry to You, for the water streams (small rivers or brooks) are dry, and fire has burned up the open fields.

Chapter 2

1. Sound the trumpet in Zion, and raise the alarm on God's holy mountain! Let everyone in the land tremble, for the Day of the Lord (a time of God's judgment and restoration) is coming, and it is near. **2.** It will be a day of darkness (gloom) and despair (hopelessness), filled with clouds and thick gloom. A mighty army, unlike any before, is coming. Their power will last for generations (many years). **3.** Before them, fire (a consuming flame) devours everything; behind them, flames (intense heat) burn. The land appears lush like the Garden of Eden (a paradise), but behind them, it's a barren wasteland. Nothing will escape their destruction. **4.** Their appearance is like that of horses (strong and fast animals), and they charge like swift war horses (horses used in battle). **5.** They make a sound like chariots (vehicles pulled by horses) leaping over mountain tops, roaring like a fire (burning destruction) consuming dry grass, a strong army lined up for battle. **6.** Before them, the people will be in anguish (great distress), their faces pale with fear. **7.** They charge like warriors (soldiers), scaling walls like soldiers (trained fighters); they march in perfect formation, and no one breaks ranks. **8.** They don't push one another; everyone moves in their own place, and even if they pass through weapons, they remain unharmed. **9.** They rush through the city, climbing on the walls, entering the houses through windows (openings) like thieves. **10.** The earth shakes before them, and the heavens tremble. The sun (daylight) and moon (night light) will darken, and the stars will lose their brightness. **11.** The Lord leads them with a mighty voice (command). His army is vast, and powerful is the One who carries out His word. The Day of the Lord is great and terrifying; who can stand against it? **12.** Yet, the Lord says, "Turn to Me with all your heart, with fasting (abstaining from food), weeping (crying), and mourning (expressing sorrow)." **13.** Tear your hearts, not just your clothes, and return to the Lord your God. He is kind and merciful, slow to anger, and abounding in love. He relents (shows mercy) from sending disaster. **14.** Who knows? Perhaps He will show mercy and leave a blessing (gift) behind: grain and drink offerings (gifts to God) for the Lord your God. **15.** Blow the trumpet in Zion again, call for a fast (day of no food), and declare a sacred assembly (gathering). **16.** Gather the people, sanctify (make holy) the congregation, bring the elders, and gather the children, even the infants. Let the bride and groom leave their rooms. **17.** Let the priests who serve the Lord weep between the altar (place of sacrifice) and the porch, praying, "Spare Your people, Lord. Don't let the nations mock us by asking, 'Where is your God?'" **18.** Then, the Lord will show His great love for His land and have compassion (deep concern) on His people. **19.** The Lord will answer His people, saying, "I will send you grain (food), wine, and oil, and you will be fully satisfied. No longer will you be a disgrace among the nations. **20.** I will remove the northern army (likely a foreign enemy army) and drive it to a desolate (barren and uninhabited) place, where its stench (bad smell) will raise because of the evil it has done. **21.** Do not fear, O land; rejoice, for the Lord has done amazing things! **22.** Be glad, you animals in the fields, for the pastures (grazing land) are growing, and the trees bear fruit, the fig tree and the vine yield their strength. **23.** Rejoice, people of Zion, and be glad in the Lord your God, for He has sent you rain—the early and the latter rains (the first and last rains of the season)—just as He promised. **24.** The threshing floors (areas where grain is separated from its husk) will be filled with grain, and the vats (containers) will overflow with wine and oil. **25.** "I will restore the years that the locusts (destructive insects) have eaten—the great army I sent among you. **26.** You will eat plenty and be satisfied, and praise the name of the Lord your God, who has worked wonders for you. You will never again be ashamed (humiliated). **27.** Then you will know that I am in the midst of Israel that I am the Lord your God, and there is no other. My people will never again be ashamed. **28.** Afterward, I will pour out My Spirit

(God's presence and power) on all people. Your sons and daughters will prophesy (speak God's messages), your old men will dream dreams, and your young men will see visions. **29.** Even on My servants, both men and women, I will pour out My Spirit in those days. **30.** I will show wonders (miraculous signs) in the heavens and on the earth: blood, fire, and pillars (columns) of smoke. **31.** The sun will turn to darkness, and the moon to blood, before the great and terrible Day of the Lord comes. **32.** And everyone who calls on the name of the Lord will be saved (rescued). On Mount Zion (Jerusalem, God's holy city) and in Jerusalem, there will be deliverance, as the Lord has promised, among the survivors whom the Lord calls.

Chapter 3

1 For the time is coming when I will bring back the captives (those taken as prisoners) of Judah and Jerusalem. **2** I will gather all nations to the Valley of Jehoshaphat (a valley near Jerusalem, symbolizing a place of judgment) to judge them for how they treated My people, Israel, whom they scattered and divided My land. **3** They have cast lots (divided by gambling) for My people, trading a boy for a prostitute and a girl for wine. **4** What do you have against Me, Tyre, Sidon, and the coastlands (coastal regions) of Philistia? Will you retaliate (seek revenge)? If so, I will quickly bring retribution (punishment) on you. **5** You have taken My silver and gold and carried My treasures into your temples. **6** You sold the people of Judah and Jerusalem to the Greeks (ancient people from Greece), moving them far from their land. **7** I will bring them back and return your actions upon your head. **8** I will sell your sons and daughters to the people of Judah, and they will sell them to the Sabeans (a distant people). For the Lord has spoken. **9** Declare to the nations: 'Prepare for war! Let the mighty men (strong warriors) come near and fight.' **10** Let them turn their plowshares (farm tools) into swords (weapons) and their pruning hooks (tools for trimming) into spears (weapons). Let the weak say, 'I am strong.' **11** Assemble the nations and bring them together. Send Your mighty ones (strong warriors), O Lord. **12** Let the nations awaken and come to the Valley of Jehoshaphat, where I will judge them. **13** Put in the sickle (harvesting tool), for the harvest is ripe. Come and tread (press down) the winepress (where grapes are crushed), for the vats (large containers) overflow due to their wickedness. **14** Multitudes (many people) are in the valley of decision (a place of judgment)! For the Day of the Lord is near. **15** The sun and moon will grow dark, and the stars will lose their light. **16** The Lord will roar from Zion, and the heavens and earth will shake, but the Lord will be a refuge (safe place) for His people and the strength of Israel. **17** Then you will know that I am the Lord your God, dwelling in Zion (the holy mountain). Jerusalem will be holy, and no foreigners (outsiders) will pass through it again. **18** On that day, the mountains will drip with new wine, the hills with milk, and all the brooks (small streams) of Judah will be filled with water. A fountain (spring of water) will flow from the house of the Lord to water the Valley of Acacias (a valley with acacia trees). **19** Egypt will be desolate (ruined), and Edom (an ancient country) a wilderness (desert) because of their violence against Judah, shedding innocent blood. **20** But Judah will remain forever, and Jerusalem will endure from generation to generation. **21** I will cleanse them from bloodshed I had not forgiven. For the Lord dwells in Zion.

39 – Obadiah

Chapter 1

1. The vision of Obadiah: This is what the Lord God says about Edom (southeast of ancient Israel, now in Jordan and Israel): We've heard a message from the Lord, and a messenger has been sent among the nations saying, "Rise up, let us go to war against her." **2.** "I will make you small (insignificant) among the nations; you will be despised (hated) by all." **3.** "The pride (arrogance) of your heart has deceived you, you who live in high, rocky cliffs (protected places), saying, 'Who can bring me down?'" **4.** "Though you soar (fly) like an eagle and set your nest (home) among the stars, I will bring you down," says the Lord. **5.** "If thieves (people who steal) had come, would they not take only what they needed? If grape-gatherers (those who pick grapes) had come, would they not leave some behind?" **6.** "But Esau (ancestor of Edomites) will be searched out, and his hidden treasures (riches) will be uncovered." **7.** "All those in your alliances (partners) will push you to the border. Those at peace with you will deceive (trick) you. Even those who share your bread (food) will set a trap for you." **8.** "Will I not destroy the wise men (those with knowledge) of Edom and take away understanding (wisdom) from Esau's mountains (high places)?" **9.** "Your warriors (fighters), O Teman (a city in Edom), will be terrified, and every man from Esau will be destroyed." **10.** "Because of the violence (harm) you committed against your brother Jacob, shame (disgrace) will cover you, and you will be destroyed forever." **11.** "You stood by when strangers (foreigners) carried off Israel's forces, when foreigners entered Jerusalem and cast lots for it." **12.** "You should not have gloated (celebrated) over your brother's misfortune (trouble) or rejoiced (been happy) over Judah's (Israel's) distress (pain)." **13.** "You should not have entered My people's gate (entrance) or gloated over their suffering." **14.** "You should not have blocked those escaping or handed over those remaining (surviving) to the enemy." **15.** "The day of the Lord (God's judgment) is coming for all the nations. As you have done, it will be done to you." **16.** "As you drank (celebrated) on my holy mountain (Zion), all the nations will drink continually and be as if they had never been (destroyed)." **17.** "But on Mount Zion, there will be deliverance (rescue), and it will be holy (set apart). The house of Jacob (Israel) will reclaim their possessions." **18.** "The house of Jacob will be fire, and the house of Esau will be stubble (dry plants). They will be burned up, and no survivors will remain of Esau," for the Lord has spoken. **19.** "The Negev (southern region) will possess Esau's mountains, and the lowland (plains) will possess the Philistines. They will take over Ephraim (a tribe) and Samaria (region in Israel). Benjamin will take Gilead (a region east of Israel)." **20.** "The exiles (captives) of Israel will possess the land of the Canaanites (an ancient people), as far as Zarephath (a city). The exiles of Jerusalem in Sepharad (a region) will possess the cities of the South (southern Israel)." **21.** "Then saviors (deliverers) will come to Mount Zion to judge Esau's mountains, and the kingdom will belong to the Lord."

40 – Jonah
Chapter 1

1 The word of the Lord came to Jonah, son of Amittai, saying, **2** "Get up and go to Nineveh (a large city), that large city, and call out against it because its wickedness (evil actions) has reached its peak." **3** But Jonah decided to run away from the Lord. He went to Joppa (a port city) and found a ship (a large boat) heading for Tarshish (a distant city, likely in Spain). He paid the fare (money for the ticket) and boarded, aiming to escape the Lord's presence. **4** Then the Lord sent a powerful storm on the sea, and the ship was about to break apart. **5** The sailors (ship's crew) were terrified and cried out to their gods (false gods), throwing cargo (goods) into the sea to lighten the ship. But Jonah had gone down to the lowest part of the ship, where he lay fast asleep. **6** The captain (ship's leader) approached him and said, "What do you mean, you sleeper? Get up, call on your God! Maybe your God will pay attention to us and we won't perish (die)." **7** The sailors said to each other, "Let's cast lots (throw small objects to determine God's will) to find out who is responsible for this disaster." They cast lots, and the lot fell on Jonah. **8** They asked him, "Tell us, who is responsible for this? What is your job? Where do you come from? What is your country? What people are you from?" **9** Jonah answered, "I am a Hebrew (a person of Israel). I worship (serve) the Lord, the God of heaven, who made the sea and the dry land." **10** The men were terrified and said to him, "Why have you done this?" They knew he was fleeing (running away) from the Lord, because Jonah had told them. **11** They asked, "What should we do to you to make the sea calm?" The storm was getting worse. **12** Jonah replied, "Throw me into the sea, and it will become calm, for I know this storm is my fault." **13** But the sailors tried hard to row (use oars to steer) back to land, but they couldn't, because the storm grew even stronger. **14** Then they cried out to the Lord saying, "Please, Lord, don't let us die for taking this man's life. Don't hold us guilty of innocent blood. You, Lord, have done as you pleased." **15** So they picked up Jonah and threw him into the sea, and the storm immediately stopped. **16** The men were awestruck (filled with deep reverence) by the Lord's power and greatly feared Him. They offered a sacrifice (ritual offering) to the Lord and made vows (promises). **17** Now the Lord had prepared (made ready) a great fish (a large sea creature) to swallow Jonah, and Jonah remained in the fish's belly (stomach) for three days and three nights.

Chapter 2

1. Jonah prayed to the Lord his God from the fish's belly. **2.** He said: "I cried out to the Lord in my distress (great trouble), and He answered me. I called from the depths of Sheol (the grave), and You heard my voice. **3.** You threw me into the deep (the sea), and Your waves and billows (large waves) passed over me. **4.** I thought, 'I've been banished (sent away) from Your sight, but I will look again toward Your holy temple (the sacred place).' **5.** The waters surrounded me, threatening my life, and seaweed wrapped around my head. **6.** I sank to the base (bottom) of the mountains; the earth's **bars** (gates) shut me in forever. But You, Lord my God, brought me back to life from the pit (the grave). **7.** As my life was fading, I remembered the Lord, and my prayer reached You, to Your holy temple. **8.** Those who cling to worthless idols (false gods) forsake their true source of mercy. **9.** I will offer a sacrifice (a gift) of thanksgiving and fulfill my vows (promises). Salvation (rescue) comes from the Lord." **10.** The Lord commanded the fish, and it vomited Jonah onto dry land.

Chapter 3

1. The word of the Lord came to Jonah a alternate time, saying, **2.** "Get up, go to Nineveh (the capital megacity of the ancient Assyrian Conglomerate), that great megacity, and deliver the communication I give you." **3.** So Jonah adhered and went to Nineveh. It was an enormous megacity, taking three days to walk through. **4.** Jonah began his trip into the megacity, walking one day, and cried, "In forty days, Nineveh will be destroyed!" **5.** The people of Nineveh believed in God. They declared a fast (a time of not eating to seek God) and wore sackcloth (rough apparel made of coarse material), from the topmost to the least. **6.** The king of Nineveh heard the communication, stood up from his throne (his seat of authority), took off his royal blankets (his princely clothes), dressed in sackcloth, and sat in ashes (a symbol of modesty and penitence). **7** He ordered a proclamation (sanctioned advertisement) to be made in Nineveh by his command and the patricians (high-ranking officers), "No man or beast, herd or flock, should eat or drink. **8** Rather, let everyone and every beast be covered in sackcloth and urgently call out to God. Let them turn from their wickedness (evil conduct) and violence. **9** Who knows? Maybe God will change His mind and have mercy (kindness and compassion), so that we won't be destroyed." **10** When God saw their conduct that they turned from their evil ways He'd compassion and didn't bring the disaster (the detriment or discipline) He'd planned for them.

Chapter 4

1. Jonah was very upset and angry. **2.** He prayed to the Lord, saying, "Lord, isn't this what I said when I was still at home? That's why I tried to run to Tarshish (a distant city), because I knew You are gracious (kind) and compassionate (full of mercy), slow to anger, full of love, and willing to relent (change Your mind) from sending disaster. **3.** Now, Lord, take my life, for it is better for me to die than to live." **4.** The Lord responded, "Is it right for you to be angry?" **5.** Jonah left the city and sat on its east side. He built a shelter and sat in its shade, waiting to see what would happen to the city. **6.** God provided a plant (some versions say "vine") to grow over Jonah, giving him shade and easing his discomfort (suffering). Jonah was very happy about the plant. **7.** But at dawn the next day, God sent a worm (a small creature) that damaged the plant, causing it to wither (dry up and die). **8.** When the sun rose, God sent a scorching east wind (a very hot wind), and the sun beat down on Jonah's head, making him faint (weak and dizzy). He wanted to die and said, "It's better for me to die than to live." **9.** God asked Jonah, "Is it right for you to be angry about the plant?" Jonah replied, "Yes, it is right for me to be this angry, even to death." **10.** The Lord said, "You care about the plant, which you didn't plant or make grow. It appeared overnight and died overnight. **11.** Shouldn't I care about Nineveh (capital of Assyria), that great city with more than 120,000 people who don't know right from wrong, and many animals too?"

41 – Nahum
Chapter 1

1. This is a prophecy about Nineveh (capital of Assyria), from Nahum (a prophet from Elkosh). **2.** The Lord is a jealous and vengeful God, taking revenge on His enemies with fierce wrath. **3.** Though slow to anger, the Lord is all-powerful and will not leave the guilty unpunished. His presence is in the storm, and the clouds are His footsteps. **4.** He commands the sea to dry up and rivers to stop flowing. The fertile lands of Bashan (region), Carmel (mountain range), and Lebanon (mountains) wither. **5.** The mountains tremble and the hills melt at His presence; the earth shakes and all living things are affected. **6.** Who can endure His wrath? His anger is like fire, and rocks break before Him. **7.** The Lord is good, a safe refuge for those who trust Him in times of trouble. **8.** But He will destroy Nineveh with a flood and chase its enemies into darkness. **9.** Whatever they plot against the Lord, He will stop; disaster will not strike them again. **10.** They will be tangled in thorns and drunk on their wine, consumed like dry straw. **11.** From Nineveh comes one who plans evil against the Lord. **12.** The Lord says: "Though Nineveh has many allies, they will be wiped out. Even though I punished you, Judah, I will no longer afflict you. **13.** I will break their yoke from your neck and free you from your chains." **14.** The Lord says to Nineveh: "You will have no descendants to carry on your name. I will destroy your idols and prepare your grave, for you are worthless." **15.** Look, on the mountains, the feet of those who bring good news of peace! Celebrate, Judah, and fulfill your vows. The wicked will no longer invade; they will be fully destroyed.

Chapter 2

1. An enemy advances against you, Nineveh (capital of Assyria). Guard your fortresses (strong, protected places), watch the roads, and gather your strength! **2.** The LORD will restore Israel's glory, even though it has been devastated (ruined) and its vineyards ruined. **3.** The soldiers' shields are red, and they are dressed in scarlet. The chariots gleam as they are prepared, and their spears flash like fire. **4.** The chariots race through the streets, moving quickly through the city squares, like flaming torches or lightning. **5.** Nineveh calls for her best soldiers, but they stumble (trip or fall). They rush to the city walls, and shields are set in place. **6.** The gates of the river open, and the palace falls. **7.** Nineveh is decreed (ordered) to be exiled (forced to leave). Her female slaves mourn (grieve deeply) like doves and beat their breasts (a sign of sorrow). **8.** Nineveh is like a pool of water draining away. "Stop! Stop!" they cry, but no one listens. **9.** Plunder (steal) the silver! Plunder the gold! Their wealth is endless! **10.** She is completely looted (robbed) and stripped (deprived). Fear fills hearts, knees shake, bodies tremble, and every face grows pale. **11.** Where is the lions' den (a place where lions lived), the place where they fed their young, and the lion and lioness (female lion) roamed without fear? **12.** The lion killed enough for his cubs (young lions) and his mate (female lion), filling his den with prey. **13.** "I am against you," declares the LORD. "I will burn your chariots, and the sword will destroy your young lions. Your messengers will no longer be heard."

Chapter 3

1. Woe to the bloody city, full of lies, full of plunder (stolen goods), and never without victims! **2.** The crack of whips, the clatter of wheels, galloping horses, and rattling chariots! **3.** Cavalry charging, flashing swords, and glittering spears! Many casualties, piles of the dead, bodies everywhere, people stumbling over corpses. **4.** All this because of the shameless lust of a prostitute, who entices (tempts) others, the mistress of sorcery (magic), who enslaved nations with her prostitution and peoples with her witchcraft. **5.** "I am against you," says the LORD Almighty. "I will expose your shame, lifting your skirts (clothing) over your face, showing the nations your nakedness (vulnerability) and your shame." **6.** I will pelt you with filth (dirt), treat you with contempt (disrespect), and make you a public disgrace (spectacle). **7.** All who see you will flee and say, 'Nineveh is in ruins—who will mourn for her? Who will comfort you?' **8.** Are you any better than Thebes, located on the Nile, with water surrounding her? The river was her defense, and the waters were her wall. **9.** Cush and Egypt were her endless strength, and Put and Libya were her allies. **10.** Yet she was captured and exiled. Her infants were killed in the streets. Her nobles were taken by lot, and all her great men were put in chains. **11.** You, too, will become drunk (overwhelmed); you will hide and seek refuge from the enemy. **12.** Your fortresses are like fig trees with ripe fruit; when shaken, the fruit falls into the mouth of the eater. **13.** Look at your troops—they are weaklings. Your gates are wide open to your enemies; fire has destroyed the bars on your gates. **14.** Draw water for the siege (attack), strengthen your defenses! Make the clay, tread the mortar, and repair the bricks! **15.** The fire will consume you, and the sword will cut you down; they will devour you like a swarm of locusts. Multiply like grasshoppers, multiply like locusts! **16.** You have increased the number

of your merchants (traders), but they are like locusts—stripping the land and then flying away. **17.** Your guards are like locusts, your officials like swarms of locusts, resting in the walls on cold days—but when the sun rises, they fly away, and no one knows where they go. **18.** King of Assyria, your leaders sleep; your nobles rest. Your people are scattered on the mountains with no one to gather them. **19.** Nothing can heal you; your wound is fatal. All who hear of your fall clap their hands in joy, for who has not suffered from your cruelty?

42 – Habakkuk

Chapter 1

1. The prophecy received by Habakkuk the prophet. **2.** Habakkuk's Complaint: How long, LORD, must I cry for help, but you don't listen? Why do I call for "Violence!" but you don't save? **3.** Why do you make me see injustice? Why do you allow wrongdoing? Destruction and violence are everywhere, and conflict abounds. **4.** The law is paralyzed (not working properly), and justice is never done. The wicked oppress the righteous, and justice is perverted. **5.** "Look among the nations and be amazed. For I am about to do something in your time that you wouldn't believe, even if you were told. **6.** I am rising up the Babylonians (an empire), a ruthless (cruel) and impulsive (quick to act) people, who conquer lands not their own. **7.** They are feared and dreaded, making their own laws and honoring only themselves. **8.** Their horses are swifter than leopards, fiercer than wolves at dusk. Their cavalry charges forward and their horsemen swoop down like eagles hunting for prey. **9.** They are focused on violence. Their armies rush like a desert wind, gathering prisoners like sand. **10.** They mock kings and ridicule rulers. They laugh at fortified cities, capturing them with earthen ramps (temporary dirt mounds). **11.** Then they move on, like the wind, guilty people whose own strength is their god." **12.** LORD, are you not eternal (forever)? My God, my Holy One, you will never die. You, LORD, have chosen them to judge; you, my Rock (a symbol of stability), have appointed them to punish. **13.** Your eyes are too pure to look at evil; you cannot tolerate wrongdoing. Why do you allow the treacherous (deceptive) to succeed? Why are you silent while the wicked devour those more righteous than them? **14.** You made people like fish in the sea, creatures with no ruler. **15.** The wicked enemy catches them with hooks, drags them in his net, and rejoices in his catch. **16.** Therefore, he offers sacrifices to his net and burns incense (burns offerings) to it, for by his net he lives in luxury and enjoys the best food. **17.** Will he keep emptying his net, destroying nations without mercy?

Chapter 2

1. I will stand guard at my post and wait on the lookout tower; I will wait to see what the LORD will say to me and how I should respond to this complaint. **2.** The LORD's Response: The LORD answered me, "Write down the vision clearly on tablets (stone or clay) so that a messenger can run with it. **3.** The vision is for an appointed time; it speaks of the end and will not be false. Though it may seem delayed, wait for it; it will certainly come and will not be late. **4.** Look, the enemy is puffed up (proud); his desires are not upright, but the righteous person will live by their faithfulness (trust in God). **5.** He is like a man intoxicated (drunk) with pride, restless and never satisfied, greedy as death; he gathers nations and takes peoples captive. **6.** "Won't all the nations mock him, saying, 'Woe to him who amasses (gathers) wealth through theft and oppression! How long will this go on?' **7.** Will not your creditors suddenly rise up and make you tremble? Then you will become their victim. **8.** Because you have plundered many nations, the peoples left behind will plunder you. You have shed human blood and destroyed lands and cities. **9.** Woe to him who builds his house through unjust gain, setting his nest (home) high to escape destruction! **10.** You have plotted the ruin of many people, shaming your own house and forfeiting (losing) your life. **11.** The very stones of the wall will cry out, and the beams of wood will testify against you. **12.** "Woe to him who builds a city with bloodshed and establishes a town by injustice! **13.** Has not the LORD Almighty decided that people's labor is only fuel for the fire? Nations exhaust themselves for nothing. **14.** For the earth will be filled with the knowledge of the glory of the LORD, as the waters cover the sea. **15.** Woe to him who gives drink to his neighbors, pouring it from his wineskin until they are drunk, so that he can gaze at their nakedness! **16.** You will be filled with shame instead of honor. Now it is your turn! Drink, and let your shame be exposed! The cup from the

LORD's hand is coming to you, and disgrace will cover your glory. **17.** The violence you have done to Lebanon (a region known for its forests) will overwhelm you, and your destruction of animals will terrify you. For you have shed human blood and destroyed lands and cities. **18.** What is the use of an idol made by a craftsman (artisan)? Or an image that deceives? The maker trusts in his own creation and makes idols that cannot speak. **19.** Woe to him who says to wood, 'Wake up!' Or to lifeless stone, 'Rise up!' Can it give guidance? It is covered with gold and silver, but it has no breath (life) in it. **20.** But the LORD is in his holy temple; let all the earth be silent before him.

Chapter 3

1. This is a prayer of Habakkuk, the prophet, set to music. **2.** LORD, I've heard of your deeds and am in awe. Do them again in our time; show them to us today. In your anger, remember mercy. **3.** God came from Teman (Edom), the Holy One from Mount Paran (desert here historical churches are present). His glory filled the sky, and his praise covered the earth. **4.** His brilliance was like the sunrise, with rays of light from his hands, where his power was hidden. **5.** Plague went before him, and sickness followed. **6.** He stood and shook the earth; the nations trembled. The ancient mountains crumbled, yet he endures forever. **7.** I saw the tents of Cushan (south of Israel) in distress, and the dwellings of Midian (east of Israel) in fear. **8.** Were you angry with the rivers, LORD? Did you rage against the sea when you rode in victory? **9.** You revealed your bow and summoned many arrows. You divided the land with rivers. **10.** The mountains trembled; floods swept through, and the sea roared, lifting its waves. **11.** The sun and moon stood still at the brightness of your arrows and the flash of your spear. **12.** In your anger, you marched across the earth, trampling the nations. **13.** You came to save your people, to deliver your chosen one. You crushed the wicked ruler. **14.** With his own spear, you pierced his head when his soldiers rushed to scatter us. **15.** You rode the sea with your horses, stirring its mighty waters. **16.** I heard, and my heart raced; weakness overwhelmed me. Yet, I will wait for the day when judgment comes upon the invading nation. **17.** Though the fig tree does not blossom and the vines yield no grapes, though the olive crop fails and there is no food, though there are no sheep or cattle, **18.** I will rejoice in the LORD, my Savior. **19.** The Sovereign LORD is my strength; he gives me the agility of a deer and makes me walk on high places.

43 – Zephaniah

Chapter 1

1. The word of the LORD came to Zephaniah, son of Cushi, son of Gedaliah, son of Amariah, son of Hezekiah, during the reign of King Josiah of Judah. **2.** "I will destroy everything on the earth," says the LORD. **3.** "I will wipe out humans, animals, birds, fish, and the idols that lead people into sin. **4.** I will stretch out my hand against Judah and Jerusalem, removing all Baal worship and the names of idolatrous priests, **5.** those who worship the stars, and those who swear by the LORD and Molek (a pagan god). **6.** I will punish those who have turned away from the LORD and no longer seek Him or ask for His guidance." **7.** Be silent before the LORD, for the day of the LORD is near. He has prepared a sacrifice and consecrated (set apart as holy like a place for church) those He has invited. **8.** "On the day of the LORD's sacrifice, I will punish the king's officials, the king's sons, and those who wear foreign clothes. **9.** I will punish those who avoid stepping on the temple thresholds (ritual act), and those who fill the temple with violence and deceit. **10.** On that day, there will be a cry from the Fish Gate (a gate in Jerusalem), wailing from the New Quarter (city district), and a loud crash from the hills. **11.** Wail, you merchants in the market; all your trade will be destroyed, and those who trade with silver will be cut off. **12.** I will search Jerusalem with lamps, punishing the complacent (those who think the LORD will do nothing). **13.** Their wealth will be plundered, their houses destroyed. Though they build houses, they will not live in them, and though they plant vineyards, they will not drink the wine." **14.** The great day of the LORD is near, and it is coming quickly. The cry on that day will be bitter, and the mighty warrior will shout his battle cry. **15.** That day will be a day of wrath, a day of distress and anguish, a day of destruction and ruin, a day of darkness and gloom, **16.** a day of trumpet and battle cry against fortified cities and strong towers. **17.** I will bring such distress on the people that they will grope about like blind men, because they have sinned against the LORD. Their blood will be poured out like dust, and their intestines

(inner organs) like dung. **18.** Neither silver nor gold will save them from the LORD's wrath. The whole earth will be consumed in the fire of His jealousy, and He will bring a swift end to all who live on the earth."

Chapter 2

1. Gather together, gather, you shameful nation. **2.** Before the decree takes effect, before the day passes like chaff (worthless remains blown away by the wind), before the LORD's fierce anger comes upon you, before the day of the LORD's wrath arrives. **3.** Seek the LORD, all you humble people of the land who follow his commands. Seek what is right, seek humility; perhaps you will be protected on the day of the LORD's anger. **4.** Gaza will be deserted, Ashkelon left in ruins. Ashdod will be emptied at noon, and Ekron uprooted. **5.** Woe to you, people by the sea, you Kerethites (Philistine people); the LORD has spoken against you, Canaan, land of the Philistines. He says, "I will destroy you, and no one will remain." **6.** The land by the sea will become pasture for shepherds, with wells for their flocks. **7.** That land will be for the remnant (remaining survivors) of Judah. They will find pasture there, and in the evening, they will rest in the houses of Ashkelon. The LORD their God will care for them and restore their fortunes. **8.** "I have heard the insults of Moab and the taunts (mocking remarks) of the Ammonites, who mocked my people and threatened their land. **9.** Therefore, as surely as I live," declares the LORD Almighty, the God of Israel, "Moab will become like Sodom, and the Ammonites like Gomorrah—a wasteland of weeds and salt pits, forever desolate. The remnant of my people will take their land; the survivors of my nation will inherit it." **10.** This will be their punishment for their pride and mocking the people of the LORD Almighty. **11.** The LORD will be awesome (feared and revered) to them when he destroys all the gods of the earth. Distant nations will bow to him, each in their own land. **Cush 12.** "You Cushites (from the region south of Egypt) will fall by my sword." **13.** The LORD will stretch out his hand against the north and destroy Assyria, leaving Nineveh desolate, as dry as the desert. **14.** Flocks and herds will lie there; wild creatures will make their home there. The desert owl and the screech owl (types of birds) will nest in her ruins. Their calls will echo through the windows; rubble will fill the doorways, and exposed cedar beams will stand bare. **15.** This was the city of celebration that lived in safety, saying, "I am the one! There is no one else." But now, she has become a ruin, a home for wild animals. All who pass by her will scoff and shake their fists.

Chapter 3

1. Woe to the city of oppressors, rebellious and defiled (unclean, morally impure)! **2.** She does not obey, she accepts no correction, does not trust in the LORD, and does not come near to her God. **3.** Her leaders are like roaring lions; her rulers are like evening wolves (greedy rulers who consume everything), leaving nothing for the morning. **4.** Her prophets are corrupt (immoral); they are treacherous (betraying trust) people. Her priests defile (treat as sacred) the sanctuary and break the law. **5.** The LORD inside her is righteous (just and good); he does no wrong. Morning by morning he brings justice, and every new day he remains faithful, yet the wicked do not feel ashamed (they are not sorry for their sins). **6.** "I have destroyed nations; their strongholds (fortified cities) are in ruins. Their streets are deserted, their cities are wasted and empty. **7.** I thought, 'Surely you, Jerusalem, will fear me and accept correction!' Then your refuge (safe place) would not be destroyed, nor would I have to bring all my punishment upon you. But you were eager to continue acting corruptly in all you did." **8.** "Therefore, wait for me," declares the LORD, "for the day I rise to testify (to speak in judgment). I will gather the nations, assemble the kingdoms, and pour out my anger on them—all my fierce (intense) wrath. The whole earth will be consumed by the fire of my jealousy (zealous anger)." **9.** "Then I will purify the lips (speech) of the people, so that all of them may call on the name of the LORD and serve him shoulder to shoulder (together in unity). **10.** From beyond the rivers of Cush (a region south of Egypt), my worshipers, my scattered people, will bring me offerings. **11.** On that day, Jerusalem, you will no longer be ashamed for the wrongs you have done to me. I will remove from you those who are proud and boastful. Never again will you be arrogant (proud) on my holy mountain. **12.** But I will leave within you the humble and meek (gentle). The remnant (remaining survivors) of Israel will trust in the name of the LORD. **13.** They will do no wrong, speak no lies. A deceitful (dishonest) tongue will not be found in their mouths. They will eat and lie down, and no one will make them afraid." **14.** Sing, Daughter Zion; shout aloud, Israel! Rejoice with all your heart, Daughter Jerusalem! **15.** The LORD has taken away your punishment and turned back your enemy. The LORD, the King of Israel, is with you; never again will you fear harm. **16.** On that day, people will say to Jerusalem, "Do not fear, Zion; do not let your hands grow weak (weak or limp). **17.** The LORD your God is with you, the Mighty Warrior who saves. He will take great delight in you; in his love, he will no longer rebuke (correct) you, but will rejoice over you with singing." **18.** "I will remove from you all who mourn (grieve) over the loss of your appointed festivals, which have been a burden (difficult to bear) and disgrace to you. **19.** At that time, I will deal with all who oppressed you. I will rescue the lame (those unable to walk) and gather the exiles (those who were forced to leave). I will give them honor and praise in every land where they have suffered shame. **20.** At that time, I will gather you; at that time, I will bring you home. I will give you honor and praise among all the peoples of the earth when I restore your fortunes (wealth and prosperity) before your very eyes," says the LORD.

44 – Haggai
Chapter 1

1. In the second year of King Darius (the Persian king), on the first day of the sixth month, the word of the LORD came through the prophet Haggai to Zerubbabel (governor of Judah), son of Shealtiel, and to Joshua (high priest), son of Jozadak. **2.** "The people say, 'The time has not yet come to rebuild the LORD's house.'" **3.** Then the word of the LORD came through Haggai: **4.** "Is it right for you to live in your paneled houses (luxurious, decorated homes) while my house remains in ruins? **5.** This is what the LORD Almighty says: Think carefully about your actions. **6.** You have planted much, but harvested little. You eat, but never have enough. You drink, but are not satisfied. You wear clothes, but they don't keep you warm. You earn wages, but put them in a purse with holes (a bag with holes, meaning money is wasted). **7.** "Think carefully about what you're doing," says the LORD Almighty. **8.** "Go up into the mountains (hills), bring down timber (wood), and rebuild my house, so that I may take pleasure in it and be honored," says the LORD. **9.** "You expected much, but it turned out to be little. What you brought home, I blew away. Why? Because my house is still in ruins, while each of you is focused on building your own houses. **10.** That's why the heavens have withheld (kept back) the dew (moisture) and the earth its crops. **11.** I've called for a drought (lack of water) on the fields, the mountains, the grain, the new wine (freshly made wine), the olive oil, and everything the ground produces—on people, livestock (animals), and all your labor." **12.** Then Zerubbabel, Joshua, and the rest of the people obeyed (listened to and followed) the voice of the LORD their God and the message of the prophet Haggai, because the LORD their God had sent him. And the people feared (revered) the LORD. **13.** Then Haggai, the LORD's messenger, gave this message of the LORD to the people: "I am with you," declares the LORD. **14.** So the LORD stirred up (motivated) the spirit of Zerubbabel, Joshua, and the whole remnant (remaining group) of the people. They came and began to work on the house of the LORD Almighty, their God, **15.** on the twenty-fourth day of the sixth month, in the second year of King Darius.

Chapter 2

1. On the twenty-first day of the seventh month, the word of the LORD came through the prophet Haggai: **2.** "Speak to Zerubbabel son of Shealtiel (governor of Judah), to Joshua son of Jozadak (the high priest), and to the rest of the people. Ask them: **3.** 'Who among you remembers the previous glory of this temple? How does it appear to you now? Does it not seem insignificant? **4.** But take heart, Zerubbabel,' says the LORD. 'Be strong, Joshua son of Jozadak, the high priest. Be strong, all you people of the land,' says the LORD, 'and get to work. For I am with you,' says the LORD Almighty. **5.** 'This is the promise I made to you when you came out of Egypt. My Spirit remains among you; do not be afraid.' **6.** "The LORD Almighty says: 'In a little while, I will shake the heavens and the earth, the sea and the dry land. **7.** I will shake all the nations, and the treasures (desired things) of all nations will come, and I will fill this house with splendor,' says the LORD Almighty. **8.** 'The silver and gold are mine,' declares the LORD Almighty. **9.** 'The glory of this present temple will surpass (be greater than) the

former glory,' says the LORD Almighty. 'And in this place, I will grant peace,' declares the LORD Almighty." **10.** On the twenty-fourth day of the ninth month, in the second year of King Darius, the word of the LORD came to the prophet Haggai: **11.** "The LORD Almighty says: 'ask the priests about the law: **12.** If someone carries consecrated (set apart for God) meat in the fold of their garment, and the fold touches bread, stew, wine, olive oil, or other food, does it become consecrated?'" The priests replied, "No." **13.** Then Haggai asked, "If someone defiled (made unclean) by touching a dead body touches one of these items, does it become unclean?" "Yes," the priests answered, "it becomes defiled." **14.** Then Haggai said, "'This is how it is with this people and this nation in my sight,' declares the LORD. 'Everything they do and everything they offer is defiled (unclean). **15.** "'Now, give careful thought (reflect) on this from today onward—think about how things were before any stones were laid for the temple of the LORD. **16.** When someone came to a pile of grain worth twenty measures, there were only ten. When someone went to the winepress to draw fifty measures, there were only twenty. **17.** I sent blight (destruction), mildew (fungus), and hail upon all the work of your hands, yet you did not return to me,' declares the LORD. **18.** "'From today, the twenty-fourth day of the ninth month, give careful thought to the day the foundation of the LORD's temple was laid. Reflect: **19.** Is there still any seed left in the barn? The vine, fig tree, pomegranate, and olive tree have not borne fruit. "'From this day on, I will bless you.'" **20.** The word of the LORD came to Haggai again on the twenty-fourth day of the month: **21.** "Tell Zerubbabel, governor of Judah, that I am about to shake the heavens and the earth. **22.** I will overthrow royal thrones and shatter the power of foreign kingdoms. I will overthrow chariots and their drivers; horses and their riders will fall, each by the sword of his fellow. **23.** "'On that day,' declares the LORD Almighty, 'I will take you, my servant Zerubbabel son of Shealtiel,' declares the LORD, 'and I will make you like my signet ring (symbol of authority), for I have chosen you,' declares the LORD Almighty."

45 – Zechariah
Chapter 1

1. In the eighth month of the alternate time of Darius (Persian king), the word of the Lord came to Zechariah (prophet), son of Berechiah (meaning "blessed by God"), son of Iddo (a prophet), saying, **2.** "The Lord has been greatly infuriated with your ancestors (fathers). **3.** Thus, say to them, 'This is what the Lord of hosts (potent army or God) says: "Return to Me," says the Lord of hosts, "and I'll return to you," says the Lord of hosts.' **4.** Do not be like your ancestors, to whom the earlier prophets spoke, saying, 'This is what the Lord of hosts says: "Turn down from your wicked (evil) ways and evil deeds."' But they did not hear or pay attention to Me," says the Lord. **5.** "Where are your ancestors now? And the prophets, do they live forever? **6.** But surely, My words and My laws (bills) that I gave to My retainers (servants) the prophets, did they not reach your ancestors? And they returned and said, 'Just as the Lord of hosts had planned (decided) to do to us, according to our ways and deeds, He has done to us.' **7.** On the twenty-fourth day of the eleventh month, which is the month Shebat (Jewish month corresponding to late January or February), in the alternate time of Darius, the word of the Lord came to Zechariah, son of Berechiah, son of Iddo the prophet: **8.** I had a vision at night, and I saw a man riding on a red steed, standing among the myrtle trees (a type of tree) in a notch (small vale); behind him were nags (horses) red, brown (sorrel), and white. **9.** Also, I asked, "My lord, what are these?" The angel who was speaking with me answered, "I'll show you what they are." **10.** The man standing among the myrtle trees said, "These are the ones whom the Lord has transferred (sent) to patrol (walk around and check) the earth." **11.** They answered the Angel of the Lord (a messenger of God), who stood among the myrtle trees, saying, "We've gone throughout the earth, and indeed, all the earth is at peace and resting." **12.** Also, the Angel of the Lord spoke and said, "O Lord of hosts, how long will You not show mercy (compassion) to Jerusalem and the metropolises (cities) of Judah, the ones You have been angry with for seventy years?" **13.** And the Lord answered the angel who spoke with me, with kind and comforting words. **14.** So the angel who spoke with me said, "Announce (proclaim) this: 'This is what the Lord of hosts says: "I'm very zealous (passionate or eager) for Jerusalem and Zion (another name for Jerusalem), with great zeal (intensity). **15.** I'm very angry with the nations (Gentile nations) that are at ease (living comfortably). I was a little angry, but they fostered (furthered) the disaster with evil intentions.'" **16.** Thus, this is what the Lord says: "I'm returning to Jerusalem with mercy; My house (the tabernacle) will be rebuilt there," says the Lord of hosts, "and a measuring line (used for construction) will be stretched over Jerusalem." **17.** "Again, announce: 'This is what the Lord of hosts says: "My cities will once again spread out through substance (growth); the Lord will again console Zion and choose Jerusalem."'" **18.** Also, I looked up and saw four cornucopias (symbols of power or nations). **19.** I asked the angel who spoke with me, "What are these?" He answered, "These are the cornucopias that have scattered Judah, Israel, and Jerusalem." **20.** Also, the Lord showed me four tradesmen (skilled workers or crafters). **21.** I asked, "What are these coming to do?" He said, "These are the cornucopias that scattered Judah, so that no one could raise their head; but the tradesmen have come to terrify them (the nations), to throw down the cornucopias of the nations that lifted up their cornucopias against the land of Judah to scatter it."

Chapter 2

1. I looked up and saw a man with a measuring line (a tool used for measuring length or distance) in his hand. **2.** I asked him, "Where are you going?" He replied, "I'm measuring Jerusalem (the capital megacity of Israel) to determine its range and length." **3.** Also, the angel (a heavenly messenger) who had been speaking with me went out, and another angel came to meet him. **4.** The alternate angel said to the first, "Accelerate and speak to this youthful man, telling him, 'Jerusalem will be inhabited like metropolises with no walls, because of the great number of people and beasts (domestic creatures, especially cattle and lamb) there.' **5.** The Lord says, "I'll be a wall of fire (a defensive hedge, symbolizing God's protection) around her, and I'll be the glory (godly presence or majesty) in her midst." **6.** "Run, run! Flee (escape) from the land of the north," says the Lord, "for I've scattered you like the four winds of heaven (pertaining to the four directions — north, south, east, and west) —" says the Lord. **7.** "Escape, Zion (a name frequently used to refer to Jerusalem or the people of Israel), you who live with the son of Babylon (a symbolic reference to those living in exile or under foreign oppression)!" **8.** For the Lord of Hosts (a title for God, emphasizing His command over heavenly armies) says, "I was sent after glory (to fulfill God's divine purpose) to the nations (other countries or peoples) that plunder (rob or spoil) you. Whoever harms you harms the apple of My eye (a metaphor meaning something precious to God). **9.** I'll raise My hand (indicating divine action or judgment) against them, and they will become the loot (the goods or property taken after a conquest) of those they've oppressed (subjugated to unfair treatment). Also, you'll know that the Lord of Hosts has sent Me." **10.** "Sing and rejoice (express joy and gladness), daughter of Zion! I'm coming to dwell (to live) in your midst," says the Lord. **11.** "Many nations will join the Lord on that day and become His people, and I'll dwell among you. Also, you'll know that the Lord of Hosts has sent Me to you." **12.** The Lord will take Judah (a region of Israel, frequently symbolizing the southern area) as His inheritance (possession) in the Holy Land (a reference to Israel), and will again choose Jerusalem. **13.** "Be silent (stop speaking or be in awe), all flesh (all people), before the Lord, for He has risen (arisen or is coming) from His holy dwelling!"

Chapter 3

1. Also, He revealed to me Joshua (a religious leader) standing before the Angel of the Lord, and Satan (the adversary) was standing at his right hand to charge him. **2.** The Lord said to Satan, "The Lord rebuke you, Satan! The Lord who has chosen Jerusalem (a megacity in Israel) rebuke you! Is this not a brand (a burning stick or ember) plucked from the fire?" **3.** Now Joshua was dressed in unprintable (sick, dirty) clothes, standing before the Angel. **4.** The Angel spoke to those standing ahead of Him, "Take off his unprintable clothes." And to Joshua He said, "See, I've taken down your sin (wrongdoing, moral failure), and I'll dress you in clean, rich blankets." **5.** I said, "Let them put a clean turban (a type of head covering) on his head." So they put a clean turban on his head and clothed him, while the Angel of the Lord stood by. **6.** The Angel of the Lord also gave Joshua a warning, saying, "This is what the Lord Almighty (God as sovereign of all) says: If you walk in My ways (follow My instructions) and observe My commands,

also you'll govern My house (tabernacle, place of deification) and have charge over My courts (apartments or areas within the tabernacle). I'll give you a place to walk among those who stand then (those who are holy or appointed)." **7.** "Hear, Joshua, the high clerk, you and your fellow preachers (religious leaders) who are sitting before you—these men are a symbol (a representation or sign). I'm going to bring My menial (a title for the Messiah) the Branch (a reference to a unborn leader, specifically Jesus). **8.** See, the gravestone (a nonfictional or emblematic gravestone) I've set before Joshua; there are seven eyes (representing God's perfect sapience) on that gravestone. I'll engrave a necrology (a figure or jotting) on it, declares the Lord Almighty, and I'll remove the sin of this land (nation) in a single day." **9.** "In that day (the time of restoration), declares the Lord Almighty, each of you will invite your neighbor to sit under your vine and fig tree (symbol of peace and cornucopia)."

Chapter 4

1. The angel who spoke to me returned and woke me, like someone waking from sleep (symbolizing a spiritual awakening or moment of revelation). **2.** He asked, "What do you see?" I answered, "I see a gold lampstand (often representing God's light) with a bowl on top, and seven lamps (representing completeness or fullness) with seven pipes (tubes) leading to them. **3.** Two olive trees (trees that provide oil, symbolizing the Holy Spirit or divine provision) stand beside it, one on the right and one on the left." **4.** I inquired of the angel, "What do these mean, my lord?" **5.** He replied, "Do you not understand?" I said, "No, my lord." **6.** He explained, "This is the message of the Lord to Zerubbabel (the leader of Judah, who oversaw the temple's reconstruction): 'Not by might or power (human strength), but by My Spirit (God's empowering presence),' says the Lord of hosts (the Almighty, ruler of all creation). **7.** 'Who are you, great mountain (symbolizing challenges or obstacles)? Before Zerubbabel, you will become a level plain (a flat, easily passable surface), and he will bring forth the capstone (final, significant stone) with shouts of "Grace, grace, to it!" **8.** Then the word (message) of the Lord came to me: **9.** "Zerubbabel's hands have begun the foundation (the initial structure) of this temple, and he will finish it. Then you will know that the Lord of hosts has sent me to you." **10.** Who despises (rejects or looks down upon) the day of small beginnings (modest starts)? These seven (the lamps) are glad to see the plumb line (a tool used for measuring vertical alignment, symbolizing the measuring of God's work) in Zerubbabel's hand. They are the eyes of the Lord, which roam (look around) throughout the whole earth." **11.** "I inquired of the angel, 'What do the two olive trees mean, one on the right and one on the left of the lampstand?' **12.** I also asked, 'What is the significance of the two olive branches (branches that provide oil) that pour oil into the two golden pipes (channels that carry oil)?'" **13.** The angel replied, "Do you not understand?" I said, "No, my lord." **14.** He replied, "These are the two anointed ones, who stand in the presence of the Lord of all the earth."

Chapter 5

1. I looked up and saw a flying scroll (a large, rolled parchment) in the sky. 2. The angel asked me, "What do you see?" I replied, "I see a flying scroll, 20 cubits (about 30 feet) long and 10 cubits (about 15 feet) wide." 3. He said to me, "This represents the curse (a divine judgment or punishment) that will cover the entire earth: Every thief (a person who steals) will be removed (expelled or driven out) from the land, as stated on one side of the scroll, and Every person who lies (speaks falsely or deceives others) or swears falsely (makes a false promise, especially when using God's name) by My name will be driven away (forced to leave or cast out), as written on the other side." 4. "I will send this curse," declares the Lord of Hosts (Almighty God). "It will enter the house of the thief and the house of those who swear falsely by My name. It will stay in the house, destroying it along with its timber (wood) and stones (building materials)." 5. Then the angel who spoke with me came forward and said, "Look up and see what is coming." 6. I asked, "What is it?" He replied, "It is a basket (a large container) going out." He continued, "This is their appearance throughout the earth." 7. A lead disc (a heavy metal plate) was raised, and inside the basket sat a woman. 8. He said, "This is Wickedness (evil or moral wrongdoing)!" Then he forced her back into the basket and sealed the opening with a heavy lead cover. 9. As I looked again, I saw two women with wings like those of a stork (a large bird) lifting the basket and carrying it between earth and sky. 10. I asked the angel, "Where are they taking the basket?" 11. He replied, "They are taking it to the land of Shinar (ancient Babylon) to prepare a place for it; once it is ready, the basket will be set upon a pedestal (a raised platform) there."

Chapter 6

1. I looked up and saw, and there before me, four chariots were coming out from between two mountains, and the mountains were made of bronze (a metal alloy, typically a blend of copper and tin). 2. The first chariot had red horses, the second one had black horses, 3. the third chariot had white horses, and the fourth had horses of a freckled (dappled, meaning mixed or spotted with different colors) or dappled color—strong and powerful steeds (horses). 4. I asked the angel (a divine messenger) who was speaking to me, "What are these, my lord (a respectful address to a superior)?" 5. And the angel replied, "These are the four spirits (messengers or agents) of heaven, sent out to serve before the Lord of all the earth. 6. The chariot with the black horses is heading toward the northern region (country), the white horses follow after them, and the dappled ones are going toward the southern region (country)." 7. The strong horses then went out, eager (enthusiastic, wanting to go) to travel across the earth. And He said, "Go and roam (travel about freely) the earth." So they did, traveling back and forth (from one place to another) across the land. 8. Then He called to me and spoke, "See, those that have gone toward the north have given rest (peace, a calming) to My Spirit (God's presence) in the north." 9. Then the word (message) of the Lord came to me: 10. "Accept (take in) the offering (gift) from the exiles (people who have been taken captive or forced to live away from their homeland)—Heldai, Tobijah, and Jedaiah, who have returned (come back) from Babylon—and go to the house of Josiah, the son of Zephaniah, on the very same day. 11. Take the silver and gold, make a crown (a decorative headpiece), and place it on the head of Joshua, the son of Jehozadak (the high priest, the religious leader). 12. Tell him: 'This is what the Lord Almighty (God, the ruler of all things) says: "Here is the man whose name is the BRANCH (a metaphor for a future ruler). He will grow up (arise, emerge) from His place and build the temple (house of worship) of the Lord. 13. It is He who will build the temple of the Lord. He will be clothed with glory (honor and majesty) and will sit and rule on His throne (place of authority). He will also be a priest on His throne (both a king and priest), and there will be perfect peace (reconciliation, harmony) between them."' 14. The crown will be a memorial (reminder, symbol) in the temple of the Lord, a reminder for Helem, Tobijah, Jedaiah, and Hen (possibly another individual) the son of Zephaniah. 15. And those who are far away (from a distant place) will come and help build the temple of the Lord. Then you will know that the Lord Almighty has sent me to you. This will take place if you carefully (diligently) obey the voice (commands) of the Lord your God."

Chapter 7

1. In the fourth year of King Darius, on the fourth day of the ninth month, Chislev (the name of a Jewish month), the word of the Lord came to Zechariah. 2. At that time, the people transferred a delegation, including Sherezer, Regem-Melech, and their companions (associates), to the house of God. They came to supplicate before the Lord, 3. and to interrogate (ask) the preachers and prophets, asking, "Should we continue to mourn (suffer) and presto (hesitate from food) in the fifth month, as we've done for so numerous times?" 4. Also, the Lord's communication came to me, saying, 5. "Tell the people and the preachers: During the seventy times of exile (a period of forced separation), when you dieted and mourned in the fifth and seventh months, was it truly for Me that you dieted? 6. When you eat and drink, are you not doing it for your own benefit, rather than for Me? 7. Should you not have paid attention to the words (communication) that the Lord spoke through the former prophets (prophets who lived before Zechariah) when Jerusalem and its girding metropolises were inhabited (populated) and prosperous (flourishing), and the Negev (southern region) and the Lowlands (the rich areas) were settled (enthralled)?" 8. Again, the word of the Lord came to Zechariah, saying, 9. "This is what the Lord of Hosts says: 'Administer true justice (fairness), show mercy (compassion) and compassion (tender care) to one another. 10. Do not oppress (brutalize or wrong) the widow (a woman whose husband has failed), the orphan (a child whose parents are dead), the outsider (someone from another country), or the poor

(those in need). Do not concoct (plan) evil plans against your fellow man.' 11. Yet they refused to hear. They turned a stubborn (unyielding) shoulder and stopped their cognizance (awareness) so they couldn't hear. 12. They made their hearts as hard as gravestone (a metaphor for being unresponsive), refusing to hear the law (God's commandments) and the words (instructions) the Lord of Hosts had transferred through His Spirit (God's presence and power) by the former prophets. As a result, great wrathfulness (wrath) came from the Lord of Hosts. 13. Thus, just as they would not hear when I spoke, so when they called out to Me, I would not hear," says the Lord of Hosts. 14. "I scattered them with a whirlwind (violent storm) among the nations (peoples) they hadn't known. The land came desolate (empty, uninhabited) after them; no bone (person) traveled through it or returned, for they made the affable (pleasant) land desolate (ruined)."

Chapter 8

1. The word of the Lord Almighty came, saying, 2. "I am passionate (zealous) for Zion, and I am zealous for her with great fervor (intense enthusiasm)." 3. "I will return to Jerusalem and live there. It will be called the City of Truth, the Mountain of the Lord, the Holy Mountain." 4. "Old men and women will sit in Jerusalem's streets, each with a staff because of age." 5. The streets will be filled with boys and girls playing." 6. "If this seems marvelous (extraordinary) to the remnant (the remaining people) in these days, will it be any less so in My eyes?" declares the Lord Almighty. 7. "I will save My people from the east and west, 8. and they will return and dwell (live) in Jerusalem. They will be My people, and I will be their God, in truth and righteousness (justice)." 9. "Be strong, all of you who have heard these words from the prophets, 10. when the foundation (base) for the temple of the Lord Almighty was laid. Before this time, there was no peace or security (safety). 11. But now I will not deal with the remnant as I did in the past," says the Lord Almighty. 12. "The seed will prosper (thrive), the vine will bear fruit, the land will yield (produce) its harvest, and the heavens will send their dew (moisture). 13. I will bless the remnant and cause them to possess (own) all these blessings." 14. "Just as I had planned to punish you when your ancestors provoked (angered) Me to wrath (fury), 15. so now I have decided to do good to Jerusalem and Judah. Do not fear." 16. "These are the things you must do: Speak the truth to your neighbor; judge justly (fairly) for truth, peace, and righteousness. 17. Do not plot (plan) evil in your hearts, and do not love false oaths (lies). For these things I hate," declares the Lord. 18. The word of the Lord Almighty came to me, saying, 19. "The fasts (periods of fasting) of the fourth, fifth, seventh, and tenth months will be turned to joy and gladness for the house of Judah. Love truth and peace." 20. "Peoples (groups of people) will come, the inhabitants (residents) of many cities. 21. The people of one city will go to another, saying, 'Let us go and seek the Lord of hosts; I will go with you.' 22. Many nations and strong peoples will come to seek the Lord of hosts in Jerusalem, to pray before Him." 23. "In those days, ten men from every nation will take hold of a Jew's garment, saying, 'Let us go with you, for we have heard that God is with you.'"

Chapter 9

1. This is the burden (a heavy message or responsibility) of the word from the Lord concerning the land of Hadrach, and Damascus, where it finds its rest (a place of peace or security). For the eyes (attention) of mankind (all people) and all the tribes (groups) of Israel are directed toward the Lord. 2. The word also comes against Hamath, which borders it (the area near it), as well as Tyre and Sidon, though they are renowned (well-known) for their wisdom (great knowledge and insight). 3. Tyre, in her arrogance (pride), built herself a stronghold (a fortified place), amassing (gathering) silver like dust and gold as plentiful (abundant) as the dirt in the streets. 4. But the Lord declares (says firmly), He will cast her down (bring her down). He will bring her strength (power or might) to ruin (destruction) in the sea, and she will be consumed (destroyed) by fire. 5. Ashkelon will see this and be filled with dread (fear); Gaza will be overwhelmed (filled) with sorrow, and Ekron will be despondent (hopeless, sad), for her hope has been cut off (taken away). The king of Gaza will perish (die), and Ashkelon will be left uninhabited (without people). 6. A mixed people (a people of different backgrounds) will settle in Ashdod, and I will put an end to the pride (self-importance) of the Philistines. 7. I will remove the blood (violence or guilt) from their mouths and the detestable (hateful,

loathsome) idols (false gods or images) from between their teeth. Those who remain (survive) will belong to our God, and they will be as leaders (rulers) in Judah, with Ekron becoming like a Jebusite (an ancient people conquered by Israel). **8.** I will set a guard (protection) around My house because of the army, because of those who come and go (travelers). No oppressor (someone who treats others unfairly) shall pass through them anymore, for I have witnessed (seen) it with My own eyes. **9.** Rejoice (be glad) greatly, O daughter of Zion! Shout aloud (cry out), O daughter of Jerusalem! Look (see), your King is coming to you. He is righteous (just, fair) and brings salvation (deliverance), humble (modest, not proud) and riding on a donkey, on the colt (young horse) of a donkey. **10.** I will cut off (remove) the chariot (a wheeled, horse-drawn vehicle) from Ephraim and the horse from Jerusalem; the bow (weapon used for shooting arrows) of war will be broken (destroyed). He will proclaim (announce) peace to the nations. His reign (rule) will extend (stretch) from sea to sea, from the river (likely the Euphrates) to the ends of the earth. **11.** As for you, because of the blood of your covenant (agreement or promise), I will release (set free) your prisoners from the pit (a deep hole) that holds no water (a place of hopelessness). **12.** Return (come back) to your stronghold (a place of refuge or safety), O prisoners (captives) of hope. Today I declare (announce) that I will restore double (bring back twice as much) to you. **13.** I have bent (curved or shaped) Judah as My bow, set Ephraim as its arrow, and raised up your sons (descendants), O Zion, against your sons, O Greece, and made you like the sword (a weapon) of a mighty warrior. **14.** Then the Lord will appear (show Himself) over them, and His arrow will flash (appear suddenly) like lightning. The Lord God will sound the trumpet (a musical instrument) and will come in the whirlwinds (strong, rotating winds) from the south. **15.** The Lord of hosts (armies) will protect (defend) them; they will devour (consume) their enemies and conquer them with slingstones (stones thrown with a sling). They will drink and shout (celebrate) like those who have been refreshed (filled with joy) by wine; they will be filled with blood, like the basins (large containers) used in the temple, like the corners (edges) of the altar. **16.** The Lord their God will save them on that day, as the flock (group) of His people. They will be like jewels (precious stones) in a crown, lifted up and displayed as a banner (symbol) over His land. **17.** How great is their beauty (splendor) and their prosperity (goodness)! The young men will thrive (grow strong) on grain, and the young women will rejoice (be happy) in the new wine.

Chapter 10

1. Ask the Lord to shoot rain during the season of the ultimate rains (the seasonal rains that come after the dry season). He'll bring forth shadows, and He'll rain them with rain, furnishing abundant lawn for all the fields. **2.** For the icons (false gods) lead people amiss; those who exercise augury (prognosticating the future through supernatural means) speak lies, and romanticists tell falsehoods, offering false comfort. Because of this, the people wander erratically like lambs, in torture (trouble), for they've no cowgirl (leader). **3.** "My wrathfulness is directed toward the goatherds (leaders), and I'll discipline the leaders (those in charge). For the Lord of Hosts (God of all heavenly armies) will visit His people, the house of Judah (the southern area of Israel), and He'll make them like His majestic war-nags (important nags used in battle). **4.** From them will come the foundation (the foundational gravestone), the roof cut (a symbol of stability and support), the battle arc (a armament of war), and all the autocrats (leaders) together. **5.** They will come like potent soldiers (strong dogfaces), who champ their adversaries in the thoroughfares in battle. They will fight with the Lord on their side, and those who ride nags (adversaries mounted on nags) will be shamed (lowered). **6.** "I'll strengthen the house of Judah and save the house of Joseph (the northern area of Israel). I'll bring them back, for I've compassion (mercy) on them. They will be restored as though I had noway rejected them; for I'm the Lord their God, and I'll hear to them. **7.** The people of Ephraim (another name for the northern lines of Israel) will be like potent soldiers, and their hearts will be filled with joy, as if they were drinking wine. Their children will rejoice and be glad, and their hearts will exuberate (rejoice with great happiness) in the Lord. **8.** I'll call for them and gather them together, for I'll redeem them (deliverance or save them). They will grow as they did in the history. **9.** "I'll scatter

them among the nations (foreign countries), and they will flash back Me in distant lands. They will live with their children and return to their motherland. **10.** I'll bring them back from the land of Egypt and gather them from Assyria (two nations that had expatriated the Israelites). I'll bring them to the land of Gilead (an area east of Israel) and Lebanon (a mountainous region to the north of Israel), until there's no further room for them. **11.** They will pass through the ocean in torture (trouble), and I'll strike the swells of the ocean, drying up its depths. The pride (arrogance) of Assyria will be lowered (brought low), and the scepter (symbol of power) of Egypt will depart (be removed). **12.** "So I'll strengthen them in the Lord, and they will walk with confidence (assurance) in His name," declares the Lord.

Chapter 11

1. Open your gates, O Lebanon, so that the fire may consume (destroy) your cedars. **2.** Mourn (weep), O cypress, for the cedar has fallen, and the potent (strong, important) trees have been destroyed. Mourn, O oaks of Bashan, for the thick (dense) timber has been leveled (cut down). **3.** The cries of goatherds are heard, for their glory has been shattered (ruined). The roaring of Napoleons echoes, for the pride (strength, majesty) of the Jordan has been laid waste (ruined). **4.** This is what the Lord, my God, says: "Take care of the flock fated (meant) for bloodbath. **5.** The possessors who kill them feel no guilt (remorse); those who vend (sell) them say, 'Blessed be the Lord, for I've prospered (become wealthy),' but their goatherds show no compassion (pity). **6.** I'll no longer show mercy (kindness) to the people of the land," declares the Lord. "Rather, I'll give everyone into the hands of their neighbors and their autocrats (rulers). They will devastate (destroy) the land, and I'll not deliver (save) them from their power." **7.** So I took care of the flock fated for bloodbath, especially the poor (indigent) of the flock. I took two staffs (rods) for myself: one I called "Favor," and the other I called "Union," and I fed the flock. **8.** I dismissed (sent away) three goatherds in one month, and my soul grew sick (tired) of them, as theirs did of me. **9.** Also, I said, "I'll no longer watch for you. Let the dying bones, and let the perishing (those in peril of death) corrupt. Let those who remain devour (eat) one another's meat." **10.** I took my staff, Favor, and broke it, therefore annulling (canceling) the covenant (agreement) I had made with all the nations. **11.** And so, on that day, the covenant was broken. The poor of the flock, who were watching me, knew that it was the word of the Lord. **12.** I said to them, "If you suppose it stylish (agreeable), give me my stipend (payment); but if not, keep them." So they counted out thirty pieces of tableware (silver) as my stipend (wages). **13.** And the Lord said to me, "Throw it to the potter—the magnificent (precious, valuable) sum they've set on me." So I took the thirty pieces of tableware (silver) and threw them into the house of the Lord for the potter. **14.** Also, I broke my alternate (second) staff, Union, in order to break the bond (connection, relationship) of brotherhood between Judah and Israel. **15.** The Lord said to me, "Take up the tools (instruments) of a foolish cowgirl (shepherd). **16.** For I'll raise up a cowgirl (shepherd) in the land who'll not watch for the lost (stray), seek the youthful (young), heal (restore) the wounded, or feed the healthy. Rather, he'll devour the fat (healthy, strong) and tear off their hooves." **17.** "Woe (destruction, disaster) to the empty (useless) cowgirl (shepherd) who abandons (forsakes) the flock! A brand (sword) will strike his arm and his right eye; his arm will wither (shrink, lose strength), and his right eye will be fully dazed (blinded)."

Chapter 12

1. This is the burden (weighty communication) of the Lord's word against Israel. Says the Lord, who stretches out the welkin, lays the earth's foundation, and forms the spirit (inner being) of man within him 2." Behold, I'll make Jerusalem like a mug of confusion (intoxication) to all the girding nations when they lay siege (military attack) against Judah and Jerusalem. 3. On that day, I'll make Jerusalem a heavy gravestone for all peoples; whoever tries to lift it'll be oppressively wounded (cut in pieces), indeed though all the nations of the earth gather against it. 4. On that day," says the Lord," I'll strike every steed with fear (confusion), and its rider with madness (distraction); I'll keep My eyes on the house of Judah, and will strike the nags of the other nations with blindness. 5. The leaders (governors) of Judah will say to themselves,' The people of Jerusalem are my strength in the Lord of armies (hosts), their God.' 6. On that day, I'll make the leaders of Judah like a firepan (essence visage) in the

woodpile, and like a fiery arsonist in the sheaves (grain packets); they will destroy (devour) all the girding peoples, but Jerusalem will remain in her place Jerusalem. 7." The Lord will cover the canopies (homes) of Judah first, so that the glory (honor) of the house of David and the glory of the occupants of Jerusalem won't exceed that of Judah. 8. On that day, the Lord will defend (cover) the people of Jerusalem. Indeed the weakest among them will be like David, and the house of David will be like God, like the Angel of the Lord before them. 9. On that day, I'll seek to destroy all the nations that come against Jerusalem. 10." I'll pour out the Spirit of grace (unmerited favor) and prayer on the house of David and the people of Jerusalem. They will look at Me, the One they pierced (wounded), and mourn (suffer) for Him as for an only son, and weep for Him as for a firstborn. 11. On that day, there will be great mourning in Jerusalem, like the mourning at Hadad Rimmon (a place of howl) in the vale of Megiddo (a vale associated with conflict). 12. The land will mourn, each family independently the family of the house of David by itself, and their women by themselves; 13. the family of the house of Nathan by itself, and their women by themselves; the family of the house of Levi by itself, and their women by themselves; 14. the family of Shimei by itself, and their women by themselves; all the remaining families will mourn independently, each family by itself, and their women by themselves.

Chapter 13

1. On that day, a sanctification root will be opened to the house of David and Jerusalem, for the junking of sin and contamination (moral smut). 2. In that day, says the Lord Almighty, I'll abolish icons (false gods) and their names from the land, and remove false prophets and sick spirits (evil influences). 3. If anyone continues to predict, his parents will say, "You must die." They will strike him down for his falsehoods. 4. In that day, false prophets will be shamed of their fancies (godly exposures). They will no longer wear coarse blankets (rough garments) to deceive others. 5. They will claim, "I'm not a prophet; I'm a planter, raised in the care of cattle." 6. If asked about the injuries on his body, he'll answer, "These are the wounds I entered from my musketeers (those close to me)." 7. Awake, O brand (symbol of judgment), against the Shepherd (the Messiah), the Companion of the Lord, says the Lord Almighty. Strike the Shepherd, and the lamb (followers) will scatter; also, I'll turn My hand against the little bones (youthful or vulnerable). 8. In all the land, two-thirds will be cut off and corrupt, but one-third will be spared. 9. I'll upgrade the one-third through fire, purifying them as tableware and testing them as gold. They will call on My name, and I'll answer. I'll say, "These are My people," and they will reply, "The Lord is our God."

Chapter 14

1. The day of the Lord is coming, when your possessions will be divided among you. 2. I will gather all nations to fight against Jerusalem. The city will fall, houses will be plundered (taken by force), and women violated (assaulted). Half the city will be taken captive (forced to leave), but the remaining people will not be lost. 3. Then the Lord will go out to fight those nations, as He fought in times past. 4. On that day, His feet will stand on the Mount of Olives (a mountain east of Jerusalem), which is east of Jerusalem. The mountain will split, creating a valley, with half of it moving north and half moving south. 5. You will flee through this valley, as you fled during the earthquake (a shaking of the earth) in King Uzziah's day. The Lord will come, and His holy ones (saints, sacred beings) will be with Him. 6. On that day, there will be no light, for the sun will dim (lose brightness). 7. It will be a unique (one-of-a-kind) day, known only to the Lord, neither day nor night. But at evening, there will be light. 8. On that day, living waters (water that gives life) will flow from Jerusalem, half toward the eastern sea (the Dead Sea) and half toward the western sea (the Mediterranean Sea), in both summer and winter. 9. The Lord will reign (rule as king) as King over all the earth, and all will acknowledge His singular (only) name. 10. The land will become a vast plain, from Geba to Rimmon south of Jerusalem. But Jerusalem will rise and remain inhabited, from Benjamin's Gate to the First Gate, and from the Tower of Hananel to the king's winepresses (a place where wine was made). 11. The people will live there in peace, and Jerusalem will no longer be a place of destruction (ruin), but a secure city. 12. The Lord will strike (hit) those who fought against Jerusalem with a plague (destructive disease): their flesh will disintegrate (fall apart) while they stand, their eyes will melt

in their sockets, and their tongues will dissolve (break down) in their mouths. 13. A great panic (fear) from the Lord will strike them, and they will turn on each other in fear. 14. Judah will also fight in Jerusalem, and wealth from surrounding nations will be gathered— gold, silver, and clothing in abundance (great amounts). 15. The plague will strike all animals in those camps, including horses, mules (animals like donkeys), camels, and donkeys. 16. Those left of the nations that attacked Jerusalem will come annually (once a year) to worship the King, the Lord of Hosts (a title for God) and observe the Feast of Tabernacles (a Jewish festival remembering the Israelites' time in the wilderness). 17. Any nation that does not come up to Jerusalem to worship the Lord will not receive rain (the ability to grow crops). 18. If Egypt does not come to the feast, it will receive the same plague as the nations that refuse to come. 19. This will be the punishment (consequence) for Egypt and any nation that does not come to observe the Feast of Tabernacles. 20. On that day, "HOLINESS TO THE LORD" will be inscribed (written) on the bells of the horses, and the pots in the Lord's house will be as sacred (set apart for God) as the bowls used at the altar. 21. Every pot in Jerusalem and Judah will be holy (dedicated to God) to the Lord. Those who offer sacrifices will use them to prepare their offerings. There will no longer be a Canaanite (a term for people from the ancient region of Canaan) in the house of the Lord of Hosts.

46 – Malachi

Chapter 1

1. The word (message) of the Lord to Israel by Malachi. 2. "I have loved (cherished) you," says the Lord. "Yet you ask, 'How have You loved us?' Was not Esau Jacob's brother? Yet I have loved Jacob, 3. But hated (rejected) Esau, and laid waste his mountains and heritage (inheritance) for the jackals (wild dogs). 4. Edom says, 'We will rebuild,' but the Lord says, 'They may build, but I will destroy. They will be called the Territory of Wickedness (evil), against whom I will have indignation (anger) forever.' 5. You will see this and say, 'The Lord is great beyond Israel's borders (territory).' 6. "A son honors (respects) his father, and a servant his master. If I am a Father, where is My honor (respect)? If I am a Master, where is My reverence (awe)?" says the Lord to you priests who despise (disrespect) My name. Yet you ask, 'How have we despised Your name?' 7. "You offer defiled (impure) food on My altar, yet say, 'How have we defiled You?' By saying, 'The Lord's Table is contemptible (dishonorable).' 8. When you offer the blind (sightless), lame (crippled), and sick (ill) as sacrifices, is it not evil (wrong)? Would your governor (ruler) accept such offerings? Would he be pleased (accept)?" says the Lord. 9. "Now entreat (ask) God's favor (grace). Will He accept your offerings favorably (with pleasure)?" says the Lord. 10. "Who among you would shut the doors (lock the doors) to prevent offering vain (empty) sacrifices? I have no pleasure (delight) in you, nor will I accept an offering from your hands," says the Lord. 11. "From the rising (east) to the setting (west) sun, My name will be great (honored) among the Gentiles (nations). Incense (prayers) and pure (unblemished) offerings will be brought to My name everywhere, for My name will be great among the nations," says the Lord. 12. "But you profane (dishonor) it by saying, 'The Lord's table is defiled (polluted) and contemptible (disrespected).' 13. You say, 'What a weariness (burden)!' and sneer (mock) at it, bringing stolen (illegally taken), lame (crippled), and sick (ill) animals as offerings. Should I accept this from your hand?" says the Lord. 14. "Cursed (damned) is the deceiver (cheater) who offers blemished (imperfect) sacrifices, for I am a great King, and My name is to be feared (respected) among the nations," says the Lord.

Chapter 2

1. "And now, O priests, this command (instruction) is for you." 2. "If you don't listen (hear) or honor (respect) My name," says the Lord of hosts (Almighty God), "I will send a curse upon you and already have cursed your blessings, because you don't take it to heart (consider seriously)." 3. "I will rebuke (punish) your descendants (children) and cover your faces with refuse (waste, dung) from your feasts (sacred meals), and someone will carry you away with it." 4. "Then you will know that I sent this command, so that My covenant (agreement) with Levi (the priestly tribe) may remain," says the Lord of hosts. 5. "My covenant with him was one of life and peace, and I gave it to him so he might fear (respect) Me; he respected (revered) Me and revered

(honored) My name." **6**. "The law of truth (honesty) was in his mouth, no injustice (wrongdoing) on his lips. He walked with Me in peace and fairness (justice) and turned many from sin (wrongdoing)." **7**. "The priest's lips should preserve (keep) knowledge (wisdom), and people should seek the law (guidance) from him, for he is the messenger (representative) of the Lord of hosts". **8**. "But you have turned (strayed) from the way; you have caused many to stumble (fall) at the law. You have corrupted (twisted) the covenant of Levi," says the Lord of hosts. **9**. "Therefore, I have made you contemptible (disrespected) before all people, because you've not kept My ways and have shown favoritism (partiality) in the law." **10**. "Have we not all one Father? Has not one God created us? Why do we deal treacherously (unfaithfully) with one another and profane (desecrate) the covenant of our fathers?" **11**. "Judah (the southern kingdom) has been unfaithful, and an abomination (disgusting act) has been committed in Israel and Jerusalem. Judah has profaned (desecrated) the Lord's holy institution (sacred laws) by marrying the daughter of a foreign god (idol)." **12**. "May the Lord cut off (remove) the man who does this, even if he brings an offering (sacrifice) to the Lord of hosts!" **13**. "You cover the Lord's altar with tears, but He no longer accepts (receives) your offerings or is pleased (approves) with them." **14**. "Yet you ask, 'Why?' Because the Lord has witnessed (seen) your unfaithfulness (betrayal) to the wife of your youth, who is your companion (partner) and covenant (agreement) partner." **15**. "Did He not make them one, with a portion (part) of His Spirit (presence)? He seeks godly offspring (children). So be careful (heed) with your spirit, and don't be unfaithful (treacherous) to the wife of your youth." **16**. "For the Lord says He hates divorce (separation), which covers one's garment (clothing) with violence. So be careful and do not deal treacherously (unfaithfully)." **17**. "You have wearied (tired) the Lord with your words; you ask, 'How?' By saying, 'Everyone who does evil is good in the Lord's sight,' or, 'Where is the God of justice (fairness)?'"

Chapter 3

1. "Look, I am sending My messenger (a person to deliver a message), who will prepare the way for Me. And the Lord, whom you long for, will suddenly come to His temple, the Messenger (the angel or representative) of the covenant (promise), whom you take delight in." **2**. "But who can bear the weight of His arrival? Who can stand when He shows Himself? For He will be like a refiner's fire (a purifier) and like soap used by laundry workers (strong detergent)." **3**. "He will purify (cleanse) the descendants of Levi (the priestly tribe), refining them like gold and silver, so that they may offer righteous sacrifices to the Lord." **4**. "Then the offerings from Judah and Jerusalem will be acceptable to the Lord, as they were in the past." **5**. "I will come to you for judgment (a decision of justice), swiftly testifying (giving testimony) against sorcerers (those who practice magic), adulterers (those who commit infidelity), liars (those who give false testimony), those who exploit (take unfair advantage) workers, widows, and orphans, and those who oppress (mistreat) foreigners—because they do not revere (respect) Me," says the Lord of hosts. **6**. "I am the Lord, and I do not change; this is why you are not destroyed, O descendants of Jacob." **7**. "From the time of your ancestors (forefathers), you have turned away from My commandments (rules), and have not kept them. Return to Me, and I will return to you," says the Lord. "But you ask, 'How should we return?'" **8**. "Can a man steal from God? Yet you have stolen from Me! But you ask, 'How have we stolen from You?' In tithes (one-tenth portion of income) and offerings (gifts given to God)." **9**. "You are under a curse (judgment), because you have robbed Me, this whole nation." **10**. "Bring all your tithes into the storehouse (a place where goods are kept), so there may be food in My house. Test Me in this," says the Lord, "If I will not open the windows of heaven (spiritual blessings) and pour out a blessing so great that you will not have enough room to contain it." **11**. "I will rebuke (stop) the devourer (destroyer) for your sake, so that he will not ruin the crops of your land, and your vines will not fail to bear fruit," says the Lord of hosts. **12**. "Then all the nations will call you blessed, for you will be a delightful (favored) land," says the Lord of hosts. **13**. "You have spoken harshly (critically) against Me," says the Lord. "But you ask, 'What have we said against You?'" **14**. "You have said, 'It is pointless (without purpose) to serve God; what gain (benefit) is there in keeping His commands and living mournfully (sorrowfully) before the Lord of hosts?'" **15**. "Now we

consider the proud (arrogant) to be blessed, for those who do evil prosper (succeed), and they challenge (test) God and escape without punishment." **16**. "Then those who feared (respected) the Lord spoke with one another, and the Lord took notice and listened. A book of remembrance (a record) was written before Him for those who fear Him and think about His name." **17**. "They will be Mine," says the Lord of hosts, "On the day I make them My treasured possession (jewels), and I will have compassion on them, as a father shows mercy to his son who serves him." **18**. "Then you will again see the difference between the righteous and the wicked, between those who serve God and those who do not."

Chapter 4

1. "The day is coming, burning like a furnace, and all the arrogant, all who do wrong, will be like dry stubble. The coming day will burn them completely," says the Lord of hosts, "leaving them without root or branch." **2**. "But for those who honor (fear) My name, the Sun of Righteousness will rise, bringing healing with His wings. You will go out and grow strong, like well-fed calves in a field." **3**. "You will trample the wicked, for they will be like ashes under your feet on the day I act," says the Lord of hosts. **4**. "Remember the law of My servant Moses, which I gave him on Mount Horeb (mountain where Moses received God's commandments) for all Israel, including its statutes (laws) and judgments (rules)." **5**. "Look, I will send Elijah (the prophet, known for his confrontation with idolatry) before the great and terrible day of the Lord arrives." **6**. "He will turn the hearts of fathers to their children, and the hearts of children to their fathers, or else I will come and strike the land with a curse."

47 – The Book of Sirach

Chapter 1

1. All wisdom comes from the LORD and remains with Him forever. **2**. Who can count the sand of the shore, raindrops, or the days of eternity? **3**. Who can fathom (understand deeply) heaven's height, the abyss (depths) or the earth's breadth? **4**. Wisdom existed before all things, and understanding from eternity. **5**. Who has seen the root (origin) of wisdom or grasped her mysteries? **6**. Only one, wise and awe-inspiring, sits on His throne: **7**. The LORD, who created, knows, and observes wisdom. **8**. He has poured her out on all His works, lavishing (giving generously) her on all living things and His friends. **9**. The fear (respect) of the LORD brings glory, joy, and a crown of festivity (celebration). **10**. Fear of the LORD warms the heart, bringing joy, peace, and long life. **11**. Those who fear the LORD will have a blessed (happy) end, even in death. **12**. The beginning of wisdom is the fear of the LORD, formed in the faithful (devoted) from the womb. **13**. Wisdom was created with devoted men, and her favor remains with their children. **14**. The fullness of wisdom is the fear of the LORD, which nourishes (feeds) men with her fruits. **15**. Wisdom fills her house with abundance, her granaries (storage places) with harvest. **16**. Her crown is fear of the LORD, with blossoms (results) of peace and health. **17**. She showers knowledge and understanding, increasing the glory of those who possess her. **18**. The root of wisdom is fear of the LORD; her branches bring long life. **19**. Unjust (wrong) anger cannot be justified— it leads to ruin. **20**. A patient man may struggle, but contentment (peace of mind) will return. **21**. He holds back his words, and his wisdom is later praised. **22**. Among wisdom's treasures, prudence (good judgment) stands supreme, but fear of the LORD repels (drives away) sinners. **23**. Keep the commandments if you seek wisdom, and the LORD will bestow (give) her upon you. **24**. Fear of the LORD is wisdom and culture (education); humility (lowness of pride) pleases Him. **25**. Be faithful in your fear of the LORD; do not approach with duplicity (deceit). **26**. Do not act hypocritically (in a false way) before men; guard your words. **27**. Exalt (raise) not yourself, lest you fall into dishonor. **28**. The LORD will expose your secrets and cast you down. **29**. You approached the fear of the LORD with deceit in your heart.

Chapter 2

1. My child, when you commit to serving the LORD, brace (prepare) yourself for challenges. **2**. Approach with sincerity and unwavering (steadfast) resolve, unshaken in times of hardship. **3**. Hold fast to Him and never let go—your future will be blessed. **4**. Embrace whatever comes your way; in suffering, be patient. **5**. Just as gold is refined (purified) in fire, so too are the righteous tested in affliction (hardship). **6**. Trust in God, and He will support you; set your path right and place your hope in Him. **7.** You who revere (respect) the LORD, wait for His mercy; do not turn away, lest you fall. **8.** You who fear the LORD, trust in Him, for your reward is certain. **9.** You who fear the LORD, expect His blessings—lasting joy and mercy. **10.** Reflect on past generations: has anyone trusted in the LORD and been let down? Has anyone remained faithful to His fear and been abandoned? Has anyone called on Him and been refused? **11.** The LORD is full of compassion (kindness) and mercy; He forgives sins and rescues in times of distress. **12.** Woe (destruction) to those with cowardly hearts and weak hands, to the sinner who walks a divided (conflicted) path! **13.** Woe to the faint-hearted (weak) who trust not in the LORD, for they will have no refuge (safe place)! **14.** Woe to those who have lost all hope! What will you do when the LORD comes to judge? **15.** Those who fear the LORD do not ignore His commands; those who love Him follow His ways. **16.** Those who fear the LORD desire to please Him, and those who love Him delight in His law. **17.** Those who fear the LORD prepare their hearts and humble (lower) themselves before Him. **18.** Let us place ourselves in the hands of the LORD, not in the hands of men, for His mercy matches His greatness.

Chapter 3

1. Children, listen to your father's guidance, that you may live well. **2.** The LORD honors a father over his children and affirms a mother's authority over her sons. **3.** He who honors his father atones (pays for) his sins. **4.** He who reveres (respects) his mother stores up riches. **5.** Honoring your father brings joy in your children, and your prayers will be answered. **6.** He who respects his father will live long, and he who honors his mother brings comfort to her. **7.** Those who fear the LORD honor their father and serve their parents as rulers. **8.** Honor your father in both word and deed, so his blessing may rest upon you. **9.** A father's blessing establishes a firm foundation for a family, but a mother's curse uproots it. **10.** Do not take pride in your father's shame; his disgrace is not your glory. **11.** A father's honor is a man's glory, while a mother's disgrace brings shame to her children. **12.** My son, care for your father when he grows old, and do not grieve him as long as he lives. **13.** Even if his mind falters (weakens), be gentle with him; do not scorn (mock) him when you are strong. **14.** Kindness to a father is never forgotten; it serves as atonement for sins and takes root. **15.** In trouble, your kindness will be remembered, like warmth melting frost—it will erase your sins. **16.** A blasphemer (one who speaks disrespectfully) despises his father; cursed by his Creator is he who angers his mother. **17.** My son, conduct yourself with humility (lowness of pride), and you will be more loved than a generous giver. **18.** The greater you are, the more you should humble yourself, and you will find favor with God. **19.** For great is the power of God, and He is glorified by the humble. **20.** Do not seek what is beyond you; do not probe into things too high for you. **21.** Focus on what is entrusted (given) to you; the hidden things are not your concern. **22.** Do not meddle (interfere) with matters too great for you, nor with things beyond human understanding. **23.** Many have been misled by their own opinions, and false reasoning has unbalanced (disturbed) their judgment. **24.** Just as the eye needs a pupil (center) to see, knowledge is the light that leads to wisdom. **25.** A stubborn man will suffer in the end, and he who courts (seeks) danger will meet his demise (death).

26. A stubborn man will be weighed down with sorrow, and a sinner will pile sin upon sin. **27.** The proud have no cure for their affliction (suffering); they are the fruit of an evil tree. **28.** A wise person delights in proverbs (wise sayings), and a keen (sharp) ear rejoices in wisdom. **29.** Water quenches (puts out) a fire, and alms (charitable giving) atone for sins. **30.** A kind deed is remembered, and when a person falls, they will find support.

Chapter 4

1. My son, do not deprive (deny) the poor of their livelihood; do not turn away the eyes of the needy. **2.** Do not grieve a hungry man or provoke (anger) a needy person. **3.** Do not oppress the downtrodden (mistreated); be swift in giving to the poor. **4.** Do not reject a beggar in distress; do not turn your face away from the poor. **5.** Turn not your eyes from the needy, and give no man cause to curse you. **6.** For if the poor man curses you in the bitterness (anger) of his soul, his Creator will hear his prayer. **7.** Be gracious (kind) to those in the assembly; bow your head before a ruler. **8.** Listen to the poor man and return his greeting with respect. **9.** Deliver the oppressed from the hand of their oppressors; let justice not be anathema (detestable) to you. **10.** Be like a father to the fatherless, and support their mother as a husband would; then you will be as a son to the Most High, who will be more tender to you than a mother. **11.** Wisdom teaches her children and guides those who seek her. **12.** He who loves wisdom loves life, and those who seek her will win favor. **13.** He who holds fast to wisdom inherits glory; wherever he resides, the LORD blesses him. **14.** Those who serve wisdom serve the Holy One; those who love her are loved by the LORD. **15.** He who obeys wisdom rules nations; he who listens to her dwells in her innermost chambers (heart). **16.** Trust in wisdom, and you will possess her; your descendants will inherit her too. **17.** She walks with him as a stranger at first, testing him; fear and dread she brings, and with her discipline (training) she tries him. Through her precepts (rules), she proves him, until his heart is fully aligned with her. **18.** Then she returns to bring him joy and reveal her secrets to him. **19.** But if he fails her, she will forsake (leave) him and deliver him to the hands of plunderers (robbers). **20.** Use your time wisely; guard yourself from evil and avoid bringing shame upon yourself. **21.** There is a shame burdened with guilt, and a shame that earns honor and respect. **22.** Do not show favoritism to your own detriment (harm); let no one pressure you into ruin. **23.** Do not hold back from speaking at the right moment, and do not hide your wisdom. **24.** Wisdom is made known through speech, and knowledge through the tongue's reply. **25.** Never oppose the truth, nor struggle against the rushing current. **26.** Do not be ashamed to admit your faults, but be ashamed of ignorance. **27.** Do not abase (lower) yourself before the wicked, but stand firm before rulers. **28.** Even to death, fight for the truth, and the LORD your God will fight for you. **29.** Be not surly (gruff) in your speech, nor lazy and negligent (careless) in your actions. **30.** Do not be a lion in your own house, nor sly (deceptive) and suspicious at work. **31.** Let your hand be open to receive, and open when it is time to give.

Chapter 5

1. Do not place your trust in wealth, nor say, "I have power." **2.** Do not rely on your strength to follow the desires of your heart. **3.** Do not boast, "Who can defeat me?" for the LORD will bring His judgment. **4.** Do not say, "I have sinned, so what harm has come to me?" for the LORD waits for the right moment to act. **5.** Do not be overconfident (too sure) in your forgiveness, adding sin upon sin. **6.** Do not think, "His mercy is great; He will forgive all my many sins." **7.** For both mercy and anger belong to Him; His wrath (anger) will fall on the wicked. **8.** Do not delay (postpone) your repentance (turning away from sin) to the LORD; do not put it off from day to day. **9.** For suddenly His wrath will erupt (burst forth), and in the time of vengeance, you will be destroyed. **10.** Do not rely on deceptive (dishonest) wealth, for it will not save you in the day of wrath. **11.** Do not be blown about by every wind, nor chase every passing direction. **12.** Be firm in your thoughts and consistent in your words. **13.** Be quick to listen, but slow to speak. **14.** If you have the knowledge, speak to your neighbor; if not, keep silent. **15.** Words can bring both honor and dishonor—your tongue can be your downfall. **16.** Do not be known as a gossip; do not use your tongue to slander (lie about) others. **17.** For shame belongs to the thief, and disgrace (loss of respect) to the double-tongued (deceptive speaker).

Chapter 6

1. Do not speak anything harmful, whether small or great; do not act as an enemy instead of a friend. A bad reputation and disgrace will follow you—"such is the fate of the evil man with a double tongue!" **2.** Do not fall prey (victim) to desire, for like fire, it will consume your strength. **3.** It will devour (destroy) your leaves, destroy your fruits, and leave you like a dry tree. **4.** Uncontrolled desire ruins its owner, making him vulnerable to his enemies. **5.** A kind mouth increases friends, and gracious (kind) words invite warm greetings. **6.** Let your circle of acquaintances be large, but a true confidant (trusted friend) is rare— one in a thousand. **7.** When you gain a friend, first test him, and do not be too quick to trust. **8.** For some friends are only loyal when it benefits them; in times of trouble, they abandon you. **9.** Others may turn into enemies, spreading word of your quarrels to your shame. **10.** Another type of friend is like a companion in good times, but absent in sorrow. **11.** When all is well, he is your other self, lording (acting superior) over your servants; **12.** But in your low moments, he turns against you and avoids you. **13.** Keep your distance from enemies and be cautious with your friends. **14.** A faithful friend is like a sturdy shelter; finding one is like discovering treasure. **15.** A true friend is beyond price; no sum can match his value. **16.** A faithful friend is like a life-saving remedy, such as one finds who fears God. **17.** For he who fears God will act rightly, and his friend will reflect his character. **18.** My son, embrace discipline (training) from your youth, and you will find wisdom in your old age.

19. Draw near to wisdom as you would to plowing and sowing and wait for her bountiful harvest. **20.** Cultivating wisdom requires little labor, and soon you will reap (gather) its fruits. **21.** How irksome (annoying) she is to the unruly! The fool cannot bear her. **22.** She will seem like a burdensome stone, and he will quickly cast her aside. **23.** Discipline (training) is like her name—it is not easy to find or grasp for many. **24.** Listen, my son, and heed (follow) my advice; do not reject my counsel. **25.** Put your feet in her fetters (chains), and your neck under her yoke (burden). **26.** Bend your shoulders, carry her, and do not grow weary of her bonds. **27.** With all your heart, draw near to her; with all your strength, follow her ways. **28.** Seek her out, explore her, and you will find her. Once you have her, do not let her go. **29.** In time, she will give you rest, and she will become your joy. **30.** Her fetters (chains) will be like a throne of majesty for you; her bonds will be a royal cord. **31.** You will wear her as a robe of glory and bear her like a splendid crown. **32.** My son, if you desire, you can be taught; if you apply yourself, you will be shrewd (wise). **33.** If you are willing to listen, you will learn; if you pay attention, you will gain wisdom. **34.** Frequent the company of the elders; stay close to those who are wise. **35.** Be eager to hear godly teachings; let no wise saying pass you by. **36.** If you meet a man of prudence (wisdom), seek him out; let your feet wear out his doorstep. **37.** Reflect on the precepts (principles) of the LORD, and let His commandments be your constant meditation. Then He will enlighten (guide) your mind and grant the wisdom you seek.

Chapter 7

1. Do no evil, and evil will not overtake you. **2.** Avoid wickedness, and it will turn away from you. **3.** Do not sow injustice, lest you reap a sevenfold (seven times) harvest of it. **4.** Do not seek authority from the LORD, nor a place of honor from the king. **5.** Do not parade your justice before the LORD, nor flaunt your wisdom before the king. **6.** Do not seek to become a judge unless you have the strength to root out crime, or you will show favor to the ruler and compromise (damage) your integrity. **7.** Do not commit evil before the people of the city, nor disgrace (shame) yourself before the assembly. **8.** Do not plot to repeat a sin, for not even one sin will go unpunished. **9.** Do not say, "He will appreciate my many gifts; the Most High will accept my offerings." **10.** Be not impatient in prayer, and neglect not the giving of alms (charitable gifts). **11.** Do not laugh at an embittered (angry) man; remember the one who exalts (raises) and humbles. **12.** Do not plot evil against your brother or your friend. **13.** Delight not in telling lie after lie, for it never leads to good. **14.** Do not thrust (force) yourself into the deliberations (discussions) of princes, and do not repeat the words of your prayer. **15.** Do not despise (hate) laborious (hard) tasks, nor farming, which was ordained (appointed) by the Most High. **16.** Do not esteem (consider) yourself better than others; remember, God's wrath (anger) will not delay. **17.** Humble your pride more and more, for what awaits man is death and decay. **18.** Do not barter (exchange) a friend for money, nor a beloved brother for the gold of Ophir (a rich source of gold). **19.** Do not dismiss (reject) a sensible wife; a gracious (kind) wife is more precious than corals. **20.** Mistreat not a servant who faithfully serves, nor a laborer who devotes (dedicates) himself to his work. **21.** Let a wise servant be dear to you as yourself; refuse him not his freedom. **22.** Take care of your livestock; if they are dependable (reliable), keep them. **23.** If you have sons, discipline them, and guide them from childhood. **24.** If you have daughters, keep them chaste (pure) and do not indulge (spoil) them. **25.** Giving your daughter in marriage is a great responsibility—give her to a worthy man. **26.** If you have a wife, do not let her become repulsive (unpleasant) to you; but if there is ill-feeling, do not trust her. **27.** Honor your father with your whole heart and forget not your mother's birth pangs (pain). **28.** Remember, from these parents you were born—what can you give them for all they gave you? **29.** With all your soul, fear God, and revere (respect) His priests. **30.** With all your strength, love your Creator, and forsake not His ministers. **31.** Honor God and respect the priest; give him his portion as commanded: first fruits, offerings, sacrifices, and holy gifts. **32.** Extend your hand to the poor, so that your blessing may be complete. **33.** Be generous to all the living and withhold (hold back) your kindness from the dead. **34.** Do not avoid those who weep; mourn with those who mourn. **35.** Do not neglect (ignore) to visit the sick, for these acts will make you beloved. **36.** In all that you do, remember your last days, and you will never sin.

Chapter 8

1. Do not contend (argue) with a powerful man, lest you fall into his control. **2.** Avoid quarreling (fighting) with a rich man, for his wealth may lead to your ruin; gold has deceived many and corrupted even kings. **3.** Do not argue with a man who speaks in anger; do not feed the flames (increase) of his rage. **4.** Do not grow too familiar with an unruly (disorderly) person, lest he insult your ancestors. **5.** Shame not a repentant (sorry) sinner; remember, we all have sinned. **6.** Do not insult the elderly, for one day we too will grow old. **7.** Do not rejoice (celebrate) at a man's death; remember, all must die. **8.** Do not disregard (ignore) the wisdom of the elders but learn from their proverbs; their teachings will guide you in the presence of rulers. **9.** Honor the traditions of the aged, passed down from their fathers; from them you will gain wisdom for times of need. **10.** Do not add fuel (increase) to the fire of a sinner, or you will be consumed (destroyed) by his flames. **11.** Let not the impious (ungodly) intimidate (frighten) you, for they will lie in wait (plan) to harm you. **12.** Do not lend to one more powerful than yourself, for you may lose what you give. **13.** Do not become surety (guarantor) beyond your means; consider every pledge as a debt you must repay. **14.** Do not contend in court with a judge, for his decisions are often influenced by his own will. **15.** Do not travel with a ruthless (cruel) man, for his path will lead you into calamity (disaster); his folly (foolishness) will bring you down with him. **16.** Avoid provoking (angering) a hot-tempered man; do not journey with him, for bloodshed (violence) means nothing to him, and he will destroy you when you are alone. **17.** Do not seek counsel (advice) from a fool, for he cannot keep his secrets. **18.** Do not reveal secrets before a stranger, for you do not know the consequences. **19.** Guard (protect) your heart and do not share your happiness with every man.

Chapter 9

1. Do not be jealous of the woman you love, lest you provoke her to harm you. **2.** Never give a woman power over you to dishonor you. **3.** Keep your distance from a strange woman, lest you fall into her traps. **4.** Do not be too familiar with a singing girl, for her charms may lead you astray. **5.** Do not harbor ill thoughts against a virgin, lest you find yourself entangled in her troubles. **6.** Do not give yourself to harlots (prostitutes), lest you lose your inheritance. **7.** Do not gaze idly around the city's streets, nor wander through its squares. **8.** Turn your eyes away from a beautiful woman, and do not look upon another man's wife—many have perished through lust, for desire burns like fire. **9.** Do not dine with a married woman or drink by her side, lest your heart be drawn to her and you end in ruin. **10.** Do not discard an old friend, for a new friend cannot match his value. A new friend is like new wine—only with time does it become pleasurable. **11.** Do not envy a sinner's success, for you do not know the disaster (trouble) that awaits him. **12.** Do not rejoice in the prosperity (success) of the proud; remember, they will not escape punishment. **13.** Keep your distance from those who have the power to kill, and you will not live in fear of death. But if you must approach them, offend them not, lest they take your life—know that you are stepping into danger. **14.** As best you can, measure (evaluate) your neighbors' character and choose to associate with the wise. **15.** Be close to the learned (educated); let your conversations focus on the law of the LORD. **16.** Choose just (righteous) men as companions; let your honor come from the fear of God. **17.** Skilled artisans (craftsmen) are praised for their craft, but the true ruler is the wise sage who leads his people well. **18.** The man who speaks loudly and carelessly is feared in the city, but one who talks rashly (recklessly) is hated.

Chapter 10

1. A wise ruler provides stability for his people, and the governance of a prudent (wise) leader is well-ordered. **2.** The character of a judge reflects in his ministers; the condition of a city mirrors the conduct of its leaders. **3.** A reckless (careless) king brings ruin to his people, but a city flourishes through the wisdom of its rulers. **4.** The sovereignty (supreme authority) of the earth is in the hand of God, who raises up those destined for leadership in His time. **5.** Sovereignty over every man is also in God's hands, as He bestows majesty upon the ruler. **6.** No matter the offense, do not resort to violence against your neighbor, nor walk the path of arrogance. **7.** Arrogance is an abomination (greatly hated) to both God and man, and oppression is a sin both despised by them. **8.** Dominion (control) passes from one people to another due to the violence of the arrogant. **9.** Why should dust and ashes be proud? Even in life, man's body decays. **10.** A slight illness can cause a doctor to jest (make jokes); a king today—tomorrow, he is dead. **11.** When a man dies, he inherits corruption: worms, gnats (tiny flies), and maggots consume him. **12.** The root of pride is man's stubbornness in turning his heart away from his Maker. **13.** Pride is the source of sin, a wellspring (source) of vice (wickedness); because of it, God sends unimaginable afflictions (sufferings), leading men to ruin. **14.** God overturns the thrones of the proud and establishes the lowly (humble) in their place. **15.** The roots of the proud are plucked up by God, and the humble are planted in their stead (place). **16.** He breaks down their stems (trunks) to the earth and digs up their roots. **17.** The traces of the proud are swept away by God, erasing their memory from the earth. **18.** Insolence (rudeness) is not meant for man, nor stubborn anger for one born of woman. **19.** Whose offspring can be in honor? Those of men. Which offspring are honored? Those who fear God. Whose offspring can be in disgrace (shame)? Those of men. Which offspring are in disgrace? Those who transgress (break) God's commandments. **20.** Among brothers, the leader is in honor; he who fears God is honored by his people. **21.** Whether a tenant (tenant farmer), wayfarer (traveler), foreigner, or poor man, his true glory is the fear of the LORD. **22.** It is unjust to despise a wise man who is poor, or to honor a sinner. **23.** The prince, the ruler, and the judge are in honor, but none surpasses the one who fears God. **24.** When free men serve a prudent (wise) slave, the wise do not complain. **25.** Do not boast about your wisdom in managing your affairs, and do not brag in times of need. **26.** Better a worker with abundance than a boaster without food. **27.** My son, have self-esteem (self-worth) with humility; value yourself as you truly deserve. **28.** Who can acquit (declare innocent) one who condemns himself? Who can honor one who discredits (disrespects) himself? **29.** The poor man is honored for his wisdom, just as the rich man is honored for his wealth. **30.** Honored in poverty, how much more so in wealth! Dishonored in wealth, how much worse in poverty!

Chapter 11

1. A poor man's wisdom can elevate him to stand among rulers. **2.** Don't praise someone for their looks or dismiss them for their appearance. **3.** The tiny bee produces the finest harvest. **4.** Don't mock worn clothes or someone's hard times; God's works are mysterious and hidden. **5.** The oppressed may rise to power, and the overlooked may wear crowns. **6.** The mighty can fall into disgrace, and the honored can be handed over to enemies. **7.** Don't judge before investigating; examine first, then critique. **8.** Don't answer before listening, and don't interrupt someone speaking. **9.** Stay out of irrelevant disputes and avoid the arrogant's strife. **10.** Why add stress chasing wealth? It's elusive (hard to catch) and hard to attain. **11.** Some toil (work hard) tirelessly and still fall short (fail). **12.** Others, weak and struggling, find favor with God, who lifts and honors them. **13.** He exalts (raises) the lowly (humble), leaving many in awe. **14.** Good and bad, life and death, wealth and poverty—all come from God. **15.** Wisdom, understanding, love, and virtue are God's gifts. **16.** Sinners are born into error and darkness, and evil grows old with them. **17.** God's blessings remain with the just (righteous), ensuring their success. **18.** A miser (greedy person) may grow rich, but this is his fate (destiny): **19.** When he says, "I can relax and enjoy," he doesn't know death will soon take it all away. **20.** Stay committed to your duties; work faithfully as long as you live. **21.** Don't envy sinners; trust in God, who can change fortunes instantly. **22.** God blesses the righteous, and their hopes are fulfilled in time. **23.** Don't say, "I have all I need; nothing more can satisfy me." **24.** Don't boast, "I'm secure; nothing can harm me now." **25.** Prosperity makes one forget hardship, and hardship erases the memory of good times. **26.** God can repay deeds, even on the day of death. **27.** A moment of pain can erase past pleasures, and death reveals a man's life. **28.** Call no one happy until their end, for their final days reveal their story. **29.** Be cautious about who you invite into your home; the crafty (sly or deceitful) lay traps. **30.** Like a caged bird, a spy will seek your weaknesses. **31.** A gossip twists good into evil and ignites conflict with a single spark. **32.** The wicked lie in wait to harm and covet (desire) your treasures. **33.** Avoid evil people, for they bring ruin and lasting shame. **34.** Hosting a stranger may lead to betrayal and chaos in your own home.

Chapter 12

1. When you do good, know who benefits, so your kindness has impact. **2.** Help the just (righteous), and you'll be rewarded—if not by them, then by God. **3.** Comforting the wicked brings no good, nor is it true mercy. **4.** Help the good, refuse the sinner; support the humble, not the proud. **5.** Don't arm the wicked; they may use it against you. **6.** You'll face double harm for every good deed done for them. **7.** God himself hates sin and punishes the wicked. **8.** In prosperity, friends are unclear; in adversity, enemies reveal themselves. **9.** Success makes enemies act friendly, while hardship drives friends away. **10.** Never trust an enemy; their wickedness corrodes (damages) like rust on bronze. **11.** Even if they seem humble, stay guarded; like a polished mirror, rust remains underneath. **12.** Don't let them get close, lest they take your place or betray you, leaving you to regret ignoring this advice. **13.** Who feels sorry for a snake charmer bitten by a snake, or someone near a wild beast? **14.** The same goes for those who associate with the proud and share in their sins. **15.** As long as you're strong, they stay passive (inactive); stumble, and they won't support you. **16.** An enemy speaks sweetly, but secretly plots to destroy you. **17.** If misfortune strikes, they'll act helpful but only to trip you up. **18.** Then they'll mock, clap, hiss, and reveal their true malice (ill-will).

Chapter 13

1. Those who associate with the wicked will learn their ways, just as touching pitch stains the hand. **2.** Don't take on burdens too heavy for you, and don't associate with those wealthier or more powerful than you. An earthen pot can't go with a metal cauldron without breaking. **3.** The rich man does wrong and boasts; the poor man is wronged and seeks forgiveness. **4.** As long as the rich man can use you, he will keep you close, but when you're no longer useful, he will abandon you. **5.** While you have something to offer, he'll speak kindly and win your trust with smiles. **6.** When he needs something from you, he'll flatter you, but when he's done, he'll leave you impoverished without regret. **7.** He'll deceive you while it benefits him, then terrify you when it doesn't; later, he'll ignore you and mock you. **8.** Be cautious of being presumptuous and avoid the foolish. **9.** When invited by someone influential, keep your distance, though he may press you to get closer. **10.** Don't be too bold, lest you're rejected, but don't stay too far, or you'll be forgotten. **11.** Don't engage too freely with them or trust their many words; they'll test you with prolonged talk and probe for weaknesses. **12.** They will humiliate you without mercy and won't hesitate to harm or imprison you. **13.** Be cautious and avoid violent men. **14.** Every living thing loves its own kind, and every person seeks company with those like themselves. **15.** Each being is drawn to its own kind, and people naturally associate with those similar to them. **16.** A wolf doesn't ally with a lamb, just as the sinner doesn't join the just. **17.** There's no peace between the hyena and the dog, nor can the rich and poor ever be at peace. **18.** Lions prey on wild donkeys, just as the poor are exploited by the rich. **19.** The proud disdain the humble, just as the rich disdain the poor. **20.** When a rich man stumbles, his friend supports him; when a poor man falls, his friend pushes him down. **21.** Many will support a rich man, even when his words are offensive; the poor man, though wise, is mocked and ignored. **22.** When a rich man speaks, all listen and praise his wisdom; when a poor man speaks, they ignore him and dismiss him. **23.** Wealth is good when it's gained without sin, but poverty is seen as disgraceful by the proud. **24.** A man's heart reflects on his face, showing either goodness or evil. **25.** A cheerful face reflects a good heart, while a troubled face shows the schemer's inner turmoil.

Chapter 14

1. Blessed is the person whose words bring no regret, and whose conscience isn't troubled by sin. **2.** Happy is the one whose conscience is clear and who hasn't lost hope. **3.** Wealth doesn't suit a mean (stingy) person; what use is gold to a miser (a person who hoards wealth)? **4.** What they deny themselves, they gather for others; strangers enjoy their wealth. **5.** How can a miser be generous when he's stingy with himself and doesn't enjoy his possessions? **6.** No one is more miserly than one who withholds from themselves; they punish their own greed. **7.** If a miser gives, it's by accident, revealing their true greed. **8.** The miser thinks his portion is too small, **9.** refuses his neighbor, and brings ruin on himself. **10.** His eyes are hungry for bread, but he sets stale bread on his table. **11.** My son, enjoy what you have and make the most of it. **12.** Remember that death is inevitable (certain), and you don't know when it will come. **13.** Before you die, be kind to your friends and share with them. **14.** Don't deprive yourself of good things; don't let opportunities slip away. **15.** Will you leave your riches to others and let your earnings be divided by chance? **16.** Give, take, and treat yourself well, for there are no joys in the afterlife. **17.** All flesh grows old like a garment (clothing); all must die. **18.** Like leaves on a strong tree—one falls, and another grows—so too the generations: one dies, and another is born. **19.** All human works decay, and our creations fade. **20.** Blessed is the person who meditates (thinks deeply) on wisdom and reflects on knowledge. **21.** They ponder (consider thoughtfully) wisdom's ways and understand her paths. **22.** They pursue her like a scout (a person who searches), waiting at her gate. **23.** They peek through her windows and listen at her doors. **24.** They camp near her house and pitch their tent (set up camp) by her walls. **25.** They live by her side as her faithful neighbor. **26.** They build their home in her branches and find shelter in her shade. **27.** They take refuge (shelter) with her and live within her care.

Chapter 15

1. Those that fear the LORD will follow His path; those skilled in the law will gain wisdom. **2.** Wisdom will meet him like a mother, embracing him like a young bride. **3.** She will nourish (provide) him with understanding and give him the water (source) of learning to drink. **4.** He will rely on her and not fall; he will trust her and not be ashamed. **5.** She will lift him above his peers; in the assembly, she will make him eloquent (well-spoken). **6.** He will find joy and gladness and inherit an everlasting name. **7.** The foolish will not reach her, and the proud will not see her. **8.** She is far from the wicked and will not be spoken of by liars. **9.** Praise on a sinner's lips is out of place, for it is not given by God. **10.** Praise comes from the wise man's tongue; the rightful speaker (one with authority) will proclaim it. **11.** Don't say, "It was God's fault I strayed," for what God hates, He does not cause. **12.** Don't say, "He led me astray," for He has no need of the wicked. **13.** The LORD hates wickedness and does not let it come to those who fear Him. **14.** When God created man, He gave him the freedom to choose. **15.** If you choose, you can keep the commandments; loyalty is doing His will. **16.** Fire and water are set before you; stretch out your hand to whichever you choose. **17.** Life and death are before you; whatever you choose will be given to you. **18.** The wisdom of the LORD is vast; He is mighty in power and all-seeing. **19.** God's eyes see all He has made; He understands every action of man. **20.** God does not command anyone to sin, nor does He give strength to lies.

Chapter 16

1. Don't desire worthless (unworthy) children, nor rejoice in wicked offspring. **2.** Even if you have many children, don't take pride in them if they don't fear the LORD. **3.** Don't count on their long life or future success. One righteous (virtuous) child is better than a thousand godless ones. It's better to die childless than have unfaithful children. **4.** A wise man can build a city, but a rebellious (disobedient) group will make it desolate (ruin). **5.** I have seen many such things with my own eyes and heard even more. **6.** Against a sinful group, fire is ignited, and God's wrath (anger) burns against a godless people. **7.** He didn't spare the leaders of the past who rebelled in their strength. **8.** He didn't spare Lot's neighbors, who were destroyed because of their pride. **9.** He didn't spare the sinful people who were uprooted for their wickedness. **10.** Nor the 600,000 soldiers who perished (died) due to their impiety (disrespect for God). **11.** If there had been even one stubborn (defiant) person, it would be a wonder if they went unpunished. Mercy and anger are both with God, who forgives but also brings wrath upon the wicked. **12.** His mercy is great, but so is His punishment; He judges everyone according to their deeds. **13.** A criminal doesn't escape with his plunder (stolen goods); the just man's hope is never disappointed by God. **14.** Those who do good will be rewarded according to their actions. **15.** Don't think, "I am hidden from God; who remembers me in heaven? Among so many, I can't be

known; what am I in the spirit world?" **16.** The heavens, the earth, and the abyss (the deep) tremble at God's visitation. **17.** The roots of the mountains and the foundations of the earth quiver (shake) at His glance. **18.** So, will He pay no attention to me? Who will care about my ways? **19.** If I sin in secret, no one will see me; who will know my disloyalty? **20.** "Who will report my righteous actions? What reward could I expect for doing what's right?" **21.** These are the thoughts of senseless (foolish) men, and only the foolish will think this way. **22.** Listen to me, my son. Take my advice and pay attention to my words. **23.** I offer measured (carefully considered) wisdom and accurate (true) knowledge. **24.** When God created His works, He assigned their tasks and purposes. **25.** He set them to fulfill their duties from generation to generation, never to hunger, grow weary, or cease working. **26.** No creature should encroach (intrude) on another, nor should they ever disobey His word. **27.** Then the LORD looked upon the earth and filled it with His blessings. **28.** He covered its surface with all kinds of life, which will eventually return to the earth.

Chapter 17

1. The LORD created man from the earth and made him in His own image. **2.** He gives him a limited number of days to live and then makes him return to the earth. **3.** He endows (bestows) man with strength and authority over all things on earth. **4.** He instills (places) fear in all living creatures and gives man dominion (control) over beasts and birds. **5.** He forms man's tongue, eyes, and ears, and gives him an understanding heart. **6.** He fills them with wisdom and knowledge, showing them both good and evil. **7.** He looks favorably upon their hearts and reveals His glorious works to them. **8.** This is so they may describe the wonders of His deeds and praise His holy name. **9.** He has given them knowledge, a law of life as their inheritance (something passed down). **10.** He has made an everlasting covenant (promise) with them and revealed His commandments to them. **11.** Their eyes have seen His majestic glory, and their ears have heard His glorious voice. **12.** He says to them, "Avoid all evil," and gives them precepts (guidelines) to live by. **13.** Their ways are known to Him; they cannot hide from His sight. **14.** Over every nation, He places a ruler, but His own portion is Israel. **15.** All their actions are clear to Him, for His eyes are always on their ways. **16.** Their wickedness (wrongdoing) cannot be hidden from Him; all their sins are before Him. **17.** A man's goodness is cherished (valued) by God, like a signet ring (a symbol of authority); his virtue is like the apple of His eye (something precious). **18.** He will rise up later and repay each person as they deserve. **19.** But to the penitent (repentant), He provides a way back and encourages those who are losing hope. **20.** Return to the LORD, forsake (give up) sin, pray to Him, and make your offenses (wrongdoings) few. **21.** Turn back to the Most High and away from sin; hate intensely (strongly) what He loathes (hates). **22.** Who in the nether world (the realm of the dead) can glorify (honor) the Most High in place of the living who offer their praise? **23.** No more can the dead give praise than those who have never lived; those who are alive glorify the LORD. **24.** How great the mercy of the LORD, His forgiveness for those who return to Him! **25.** Such mercy cannot be found in men, for no son of man is immortal (will never die). **26.** Is anything brighter than the sun? Yet even it can be eclipsed (covered). How much more obscure (unclear) the thoughts of flesh and blood (human beings)! **27.** God watches over the hosts of the highest heaven, while all men are but dust and ashes.

Chapter 18

1. The Eternal (God) is the judge of all things without exception; the LORD alone is just. **2.** Who can describe His works, and who can probe (examine deeply) His mighty deeds? **3.** Who can measure His majestic power, or exhaust (completely tell) the tale of His mercies? **4.** One cannot lessen, nor increase, nor penetrate (fully understand) the wonders of the LORD. **5.** When a man ends, he is only beginning, when he stops, he is still bewildered (confused). **6.** What is man, and of what worth is he? The good, the evil in him—what are these? **7.** The sum of a man's days is great if it reaches a hundred years. **8.** Like a drop of sea water, like a grain of sand, so are these few years among the days of eternity. **9.** That is why the LORD is patient with men and showers upon them His mercy. **10.** He sees and understands that their death is grievous (painful), and so He forgives them all the more. **11.** Man may be merciful to his fellow man, but the LORD'S mercy reaches all flesh. **12.** Reproving (rebuking), admonishing (warning), teaching, as a shepherd guides his flock. **13.** Merciful to those who accept His guidance, who are diligent (careful) in His precepts (rules). **14.** My son, to your charity (generosity) add no reproach (blame), nor spoil any gift with harsh words. **15.** Like dew that cools a burning wind, so does a word improve (make better) a gift. **16.** Sometimes the word means more than the gift; both are offered by a kindly man. **17.** Only a fool upbraids (scolds) before giving; a grudging (reluctant) gift wears out the expectant eyes. **18.** Be informed before speaking; before sickness, prepare the cure. **19.** Before you are judged, seek merit (good deeds) for yourself, and at the time of visitation (judgment), you will have a ransom (a way to escape). **20.** Before you have fallen, humble yourself; when you have sinned, show repentance. **21.** Delay not to forsake (abandon) sins, neglect it not till you are in distress. **22.** Let nothing prevent the prompt (quick) payment of your vows; wait not to fulfill them when you are dying. **23.** Before making a vow, have the means to fulfill it; be not one who tries the LORD. **24.** Think of wrath (anger) and the day of death, the time of vengeance (punishment) when He will hide His face. **25.** Remember the time of hunger in the time of plenty (abundance), poverty and want in the day of wealth. **26.** Between morning and evening, the weather changes; before the LORD, all things are fleeting (temporary). **27.** A wise man is circumspect (careful) in all things; when sin is rife (abundant), he keeps himself from wrongdoing. **28.** Any learned man should make wisdom known, and he who attains (achieves) her should declare her praise. **29.** Those trained in her words must show their wisdom, dispensing (giving) sound proverbs like life-giving waters. **30.** Go not after your lusts (desires), but keep your desires in check. **31.** If you satisfy your lustful appetites, they will make you the sport (plaything) of your enemies. **32.** Have no joy in the pleasures of a moment which bring on poverty redoubled (increased). **33.** Become not a glutton (overeater) and a winebibber (drunkard) with nothing in your purse.

Chapter 19

1. He who wastes what little he has will be stripped bare. **2.** Wine and women make the mind giddy (dizzy), and the companion of harlots (prostitutes) becomes reckless. **3.** He who trusts them lightly has no sense, and he who follows them sins against his own life. **4.** Rottenness (decay) and worms will possess him, for stubborn (rebellious) desire destroys its owner. **5.** He who glares at evil will meet with evil, and he who repeats an evil report (rumor) has no sense. **6.** Never repeat gossip, and you will not be reviled (cursed). **7.** Tell nothing to friend or foe; if you have a fault, reveal it not. **8.** For he who hears it will hold it against you, and in time become your enemy. **9.** Let anything you hear die within you; be assured it will not make you burst (break out). **10.** When a fool hears something, he is in labor (troubled), like a woman giving birth. **11.** Like an arrow lodged in a man's thigh is gossip in the breast (heart) of a fool. **12.** Admonish (warn) your friend—he may not have done it; and if he did, that he may not do it again. **13.** Admonish your neighbor—he may not have said it; and if he did, that he may not say it again. **14.** Admonish your friend—often it may be slander (false accusations); every story you must not believe. **15.** A man can slip and not mean it; who has not sinned with his tongue? **16.** Admonish your neighbor before you break (separate) with him; thus will you fulfill the law of the Most High. **17.** All wisdom is fear of the LORD; perfect wisdom is the fulfillment of the law. **18.** The knowledge of wickedness is not wisdom, nor is there prudence (caution) in the counsel of sinners. **19.** There is a shrewdness (cleverness) that is detestable, while the simple man may be free from sin. **20.** Some fear God with little understanding, and others with great intelligence violate the law. **21.** There is a shrewdness keen (sharp) but dishonest, which by duplicity (deception) wins a judgment. **22.** There is the wicked man who is bowed (stooped) in grief, but is full of guile (trickery) within. **23.** He bows his head and feigns (pretends) not to hear, but when not observed, he will take advantage of you. **24.** Even though his lack of strength keeps him from sinning, when he finds the opportunity, he will do harm. **25.** One can tell a man by his appearance; a wise man is known as such when first met. **26.** A man's attire (clothing), hearty laughter, and gait (walk) proclaim him for what he is.

Chapter 20

1. An admonition (warning) can be inopportune (untimely), and a man may wisely hold his peace. **2.** It is better to admonish than lose one's temper, for admitting a fault prevents disgrace. **3.** Like a eunuch (a man castrated for service) lusting for intimacy with a maiden is he who does right under compulsion. **4.** One man is silent and is thought wise, another is talkative and disliked. **5.** One is silent because he has nothing to say; another, biding (waiting) his time. **6.** A wise man waits for the right time, but a boasting fool ignores it. **7.** He who talks too much is detested; he who pretends authority is hated. **8.** Some misfortunes bring success; some gains are a loss. **9.** Some gifts do no good, and some must be repaid double. **10.** Humiliation follows fame, while from obscurity (being unknown), a man may rise. **11.** A man may buy much for little but pay for it seven times over. **12.** A wise man is popular with few words, while fools waste theirs in vain. **13.** A gift from a rogue (dishonest person) does no good; in his eyes, one gift equals seven. **14.** He gives little and criticizes often, like a crier (public announcer), shouting loudly. He lends today, asks it back tomorrow; hateful indeed is such a man. **15.** A fool has no friends, nor thanks for his generosity. **16.** Those who eat his bread have an evil tongue; how many times they mock him! **17.** A fall to the ground is less sudden than a slip of the tongue; that's why the wicked's downfall comes quickly. **18.** Insipid (bland) food is like an untimely tale; the unruly (disorderly) are always ready to offer it. **19.** A proverb spoken by a fool is unwelcome, for he doesn't say it at the right time. **20.** A man through want (lack) may be unable to sin, yet in this peace he cannot rest. **21.** One may lose his life through shame and perish through a fool's intimidation (threatening). **22.** A man makes a promise to a friend out of shame, and unnecessarily turns him into an enemy. **23.** A lie is a foul blot (stain) in a man, yet it's often on the lips of the unruly. **24.** Better a thief than an inveterate (habitual) liar; both will suffer disgrace. **25.** A liar's way leads to dishonor; his shame remains with him. **26.** A wise man advances himself by his words; a prudent (careful) man pleases the great. **27.** He who works his land has abundant crops; he who pleases the great is pardoned his faults. **28.** Favors and gifts blind the eyes; like a muzzle (restraint) over the mouth, they silence reproof (correction). **29.** Hidden wisdom and unseen treasure—what value are they? **30.** Better the man who hides his folly (foolishness) than one who hides his wisdom.

Chapter 21

1. My child, if you have sinned, stop now and seek forgiveness. **2.** Avoid sin like a venomous (poisonous) snake; its bite can destroy souls. **3.** Sin cuts like a double-edged sword; it leaves no healing. **4.** Arrogance (pride) and violence ruin wealth and homes. **5.** A poor man's prayer is heard swiftly, and justice is granted. **6.** Those who hate correction follow sin, but the reverent (respectful) repent. **7.** The boastful proclaim themselves, but the wise see their own faults. **8.** Building with stolen wealth prepares one's own grave. **9.** Criminals are like straw, ready to burn in fire. **10.** The smooth path of sinners ends in the depths of destruction. **11.** Obeying the law disciplines desires, and wisdom comes from fearing God. **12.** The unwise resist learning, but wisdom can be harsh. **13.** A wise man's knowledge overflows like a spring. **14.** A fool's mind is like a broken jar—it holds nothing. **15.** The wise embrace wisdom, but fools scorn and discard it. **16.** A fool's chatter is a burden, but wisdom brings charm. **17.** People seek a prudent (careful) man's counsel, weighing his words. **18.** Wisdom is lost on fools; they see it as incomprehensible (not understandable). **19.** To fools, learning feels like chains that restrict them. **20.** A fool laughs loudly, while the wise smile thoughtfully. **21.** To the wise, learning is like gold, adorning their arm. **22.** Fools barge into houses, while the polite wait outside. **23.** The crude (rude) peer rudely through doors; the refined (polite) look down. **24.** Eavesdropping (listening secretly) is shameful, and the cultured (polite) avoid it. **25.** The ungodly (immoral) speak carelessly, but the prudent measure their words. **26.** Fools' thoughts are spoken aloud; the wise guard their hearts. **27.** When the godless curse others, they curse themselves. **28.** A gossip ruins their name and is hated by neighbors.

Chapter 22

1. A lazy person is like a stone in mud, scorned by all. **2.** They are like filth; anyone who touches them washes their hands. **3.** A rebellious child shames their father; a daughter brings poverty. **4.** A wise daughter is a treasure; a shameless one brings grief. **5.** A dishonorable woman shames both her father and husband. **6.** Untimely talk is like a song during mourning; wisdom is in discipline. **7.** Teaching a fool is like gluing a broken pot or disturbing a sleeper. **8.** Talking to a fool is like speaking to a sleeper—they won't understand. **9.** Mourn the dead for their light is gone; mourn the fool for their sense is gone. **10.** Grieve little for the dead; a fool's life is worse than death. **11.** Mourning the dead lasts seven days; a fool's foolishness lasts a lifetime. **12.** Avoid long talk with the senseless; don't be their companion. **13.** Stay away or be caught in their chaos. **14.** A fool is heavier than lead. **15.** Sand, salt, and iron are lighter than a senseless person. **16.** A wise resolution is firm like well-built stonework. **17.** A wise decision is secure like a smooth wall. **18.** Weak plans are blown away like small stones in the wind. **19.** A poke in the eye causes tears; a heart wound reveals deep feelings. **20.** Insults break friendships, like stones driving away birds. **21.** If you fight a friend, it can be undone. **22.** A sharp word can be reconciled, but betrayal breaks friendships. **23.** Befriend someone in need and share in their prosperity. **24.** Stand by them in trouble to share their inheritance. **25.** Abuse precedes violence, like smoke before flames. **26.** True friends bring no shame; harm from a friend causes rejection. **27.** Who will guard my speech to prevent my ruin?

Chapter 23

1. LORD, Father and Master of my life, don't let me fall because of them! **2.** Discipline my thoughts and mind, so my sins are not overlooked. **3.** Lest my failings grow and my enemies rejoice over me. **4.** LORD, don't let me fall under their control! **5.** Keep me from bold looks and passions. **6.** Let not the flesh rule me; protect me from shameful desires. **7.** Listen, children, to my words; those who obey are free. **8.** The sinner's words entrap; the proud fall by them. **9.** Do not swear or misuse the Holy Name. **10.** Like a slave under constant punishment, swearing brings sin. **11.** A man who swears is burdened; his house suffers. If he swears in error, he's guilty, and his sin is great. **12.** There are words deserving death; may they never be heard among God's people. **13.** Avoid coarse language, as it leads to sin. **14.** Remember your parents in the presence of the powerful, lest you disgrace your upbringing. **15.** Abusive speech will prevent wisdom from growing. **16.** Two men increase sin; a third brings wrath: the passionate man who never stops, **17.** the glutton who never satisfies, **18.** and the adulterer who thinks no one sees him. **19.** The LORD's eyes see all, far brighter than the sun. **20.** The One who knows all things knows them even after they occur. **21.** Such a man will be caught unawares. **22.** The unfaithful wife who gives her child to another. **23.** She has disobeyed God, wronged her husband, and committed adultery. **24.** She will be judged, and her children will suffer. **25.** Her children will not prosper, and her shame will never be erased. **26.** All will know the fear of the LORD is better than all else. **27.** Nothing is more beneficial than following His commandments.

Chapter 24

1. Wisdom praises herself and declares her glory among her people. **2.** In the assembly of the Most High, she speaks, declaring her worth before His host (followers). **3.** "I came from the mouth of the Most High and covered the earth like mist. **4.** I dwelt in the heavens, my throne on a cloud. **5.** I encircled the sky and wandered the deep (the deep waters). **6.** I ruled over the sea, land, and nations. **7.** Among them all, I sought a resting place. **8.** The Creator commanded me to dwell in Jacob (Israel) and inherit Israel. **9.** Before all ages, He created me, and I will endure forever. **10.** I served in the holy tent (the tabernacle), my home in Zion. **11.** In the chosen city, I found rest and made Jerusalem my domain. **12.** I took root among God's people, His heritage. **13.** "Like a cedar (a tall tree), I rise; like a cypress on Hermon, **14.** like a palm in En-gedi (a fertile oasis), a rose in Jericho, **15.** like cinnamon (a spice) and myrrh (a fragrant resin), I give fragrance, like sweet incense in the holy place. **16.** I spread my branches like a terebinth (a large tree), graceful and bright. **17.** I bear fruit like the vine, my blossoms rich and beautiful. **18.** Come to me, and be filled with my fruits; **19.** I am sweeter than honey, better than the honeycomb. **20.** He who partakes of me will hunger no more; he who drinks will thirst again. **21.** Those who follow me will never be put to shame. **22.** This is the book of the Most High's covenant, the law of Moses for Jacob's descendants. **23.** It overflows with wisdom, like the Pishon (a river), like the Tigris at the new fruits. **24.** It flows like the Euphrates (a river), like the Jordan at harvest time. **25.** It shines like the Nile (a river) with knowledge, like the Gihon (a river) at vintage time. **26.** No man has fully comprehended wisdom, nor will the last. **27.** Her thoughts are deeper than the sea, her counsel

more profound than the abyss (a deep space). **28.** I, like a stream from her source, watered my garden, **29.** and suddenly my small stream became a river, my rivulet (a small stream) a sea. **30.** I send my teachings forth like the dawn, to be known afar. **31.** I pour out instruction like prophecy (divine revelation) for future generations.

Chapter 25

1. Delight in harmony among brothers, friendship among neighbors, and love between husband and wife. **2.** Despise a proud beggar, deceitful (dishonest) rich man, and lustful (overly desiring) old man. **3.** What you don't save in youth, you won't gain in old age. **4.** Gray hair suits judgment (discernment), and wisdom befits the aged. **5.** Wisdom, understanding, and prudence (good judgment) glorify the elderly. **6.** Experience crowns old age; their glory is the fear (reverence) of the LORD. **7.** Blessed are those who rejoice in children and see enemies fall. **8.** Blessed are those with a sensible (practical) wife and pure speech. **9.** Happy are those with a true friend and attentive (listening) ears. **10.** Wisdom is great, but the fear of the LORD exceeds all. **11.** The fear of the LORD is beyond comparison. **12.** The worst wound is of the heart; the greatest evil is from a woman. **13.** The worst suffering comes from enemies; their vengeance (revenge) is dire. **14.** No poison is worse than a serpent's, nor venom than a woman's. **15.** Better to live with a dragon than an evil woman. **16.** Wickedness makes a woman harsh (severe). **17.** A husband sighs unknowingly among neighbors. **18.** No greater evil than a wicked woman; let her face the wicked. **19.** A quarrelsome (argumentative) wife is like sand to weary feet. **20.** Don't be fooled by beauty or wealth. **21.** A man dependent on his wife becomes a slave. **22.** An evil wife breaks the spirit and weakens the body. **23.** Sin began with a woman; through her, death came. **24.** Don't indulge (encourage) an erring (mistaken) wife or let water flow freely. **25.** If she won't walk with you, cast her away.

Chapter 26

1. Blessed is the man with a good wife; his joy is doubled. **2.** A noble (honorable) wife brings peace and happiness. **3.** A virtuous (morally good) wife is a gift to those who fear (revere) the LORD. **4.** Whether rich or poor, her husband is content (satisfied). **5.** False accusations, public trials, and lies are harder than death. **6.** A jealous (possessive) wife causes grief, like the above. **7.** A bad wife is like a heavy yoke (burden) or a scorpion. **8.** A drunken (intoxicated) wife stirs anger, revealing shame. **9.** An unchaste (immoral) wife is known by her bold (audacious) glance. **10.** Watch over an unruly (disobedient) wife, as she may betray (be disloyal to) you. **11.** Be wary (cautious) if her eyes are bold; betrayal is likely. **12.** Like a thirsty traveler, she moves from man to man. **13.** A gracious (kind) wife strengthens her husband with kindness. **14.** Her wise speech is a gift from the LORD; her virtue is priceless (invaluable). **15.** A modest (reserved) wife is a precious blessing; her purity is unmatched. **16.** A virtuous wife's beauty shines like the sun, lighting her home. **17.** Her grace is like the light of a holy lampstand. **18.** Her limbs are strong and steady like golden pillars. **19.** A wealthy man reduced to poverty, a once-respected man despised, and one who turns to sin are grievous (severe). **20.** Merchants (traders) and shopkeepers struggle to stay upright (morally sound).

Chapter 27

1. Many sin for profit, and wealth blinds them. **2.** Sin is found in buying and selling. **3.** Without the fear of the LORD, your home will fall. **4.** A man's faults show in his speech. **5.** A man is tested by his words. **6.** A tree's fruit shows its care; a man's speech reveals his heart. **7.** Don't praise a man before hearing him. **8.** Seeking justice is like wearing a fine robe. **9.** Faithful people are drawn to faithfulness. **10.** Sins lie in wait for the wicked. **11.** The godless are unstable (not steady). **12.** Spend time with wise people. **13.** Wicked speech is corrupt (morally wrong). **14.** Their words and quarrels are unbearable. **15.** Arguments among the proud lead to violence. **16.** Betraying secrets makes one untrustworthy. **17.** Keep your promises, or do not follow your friend. **18.** Betrayal destroys friendship. **19.** Once a friend is lost, he cannot be regained. **20.** Don't chase after a fleeing friend. **21.** Betrayal cannot be undone. **22.** A man with deceitful (dishonest) eyes plans evil. **23.** He flatters (praises insincerely) in your presence, then twists your words. **24.** The LORD detests (hates) such deceit. **25.** Betrayal harms the one who strikes (betrays). **26.** A snare (trap) set for others will trap the one who sets it. **27.** Harm done returns to the one who causes it. **28.** The proud face mockery and punishment. **29.** Those who enjoy traps will be consumed by them. **30.** Wrath (anger) and anger are hated, but sinners embrace them.

Chapter 28

1. The vengeful (revenge-seeking) will face the LORD's judgment; He remembers their wrongs. **2.** Forgive your neighbor to have your sins forgiven. **3.** One cannot expect healing while holding anger. **4.** Seeking pardon (forgiveness) without mercy is in vain. **5.** Wrath (anger) blocks forgiveness of sins. **6.** Remember death, end enmity (hostility), and cease sinning. **7.** Follow the commandments, avoid hate, and overlook faults. **8.** Avoid strife (conflict); quarrelsome (argumentative) people spread discord. **9.** More fuel increases fire; greater strength increases wrath (fury). **10.** Pitch (tar) and resin fuel flames; constant quarrels lead to bloodshed. **11.** A spark becomes a flame; your mouth can fan or extinguish it. **12.** Gossips (rumor-spreaders) and deceitful people destroy peace. **13.** A meddlesome (intrusive) tongue divides, ruins, and destroys. **14.** It casts out virtuous women and robs them of their work. **15.** Listening to gossip brings no peace. **16.** A whip wounds the body, but the tongue breaks bones. **17.** More fall to the tongue than the sword. **18.** Blessed are those free from the tongue's wrath. **19.** Its burden (yoke) is heavy, and its death is worse than death itself. **20.** The tongue harms those who abandon the LORD, not the just. **21.** It strikes like a lion, tearing its victims apart. **22.** Guard your mouth as you would protect a vineyard (field). **23.** Weigh your words carefully, as you do with wealth. **24.** Be cautious; your tongue may lead you into a trap. **25.** A quarrelsome tongue brings harm and deadly snares. **26.** Watch your words to avoid ruin or entrapment.

Chapter 29

1. He who lends to his neighbor does a good deed, fulfilling the commandments. **2.** Lend when needed and repay on time. **3.** Keep your word, and you will always have what you need. **4.** Borrowers often burden (cause trouble to) lenders. **5.** They praise the lender when borrowing but disappoint when repayment is due. **6.** A lender recovering half is successful; otherwise, they are swindled (cheated) and gain an enemy. **7.** Many avoid lending, fearing deceit (dishonesty). **8.** Be generous to the poor, and don't make them wait. **9.** Help the needy as commanded, don't send them empty-handed. **10.** Spend your wealth on your brother and friend; don't waste it. **11.** Use your wealth as the Most High commands; it's better than gold. **12.** Store up charitable deeds (acts of kindness) to protect you. **13.** They fight for you like a shield against enemies. **14.** A righteous person guarantees (vouches for) a neighbor, while the shameless betray. **15.** Don't forget the kindness of your backer (supporter), for they offer their life for you. **16.** The wicked turn pledges (promises) into misfortune, abandoning protectors. **17.** Surety (being a guarantor) has ruined many wealthy men, casting them into turmoil. **18.** It has exiled (forced to leave) the prominent and sent them abroad. **19.** The sinner who acts as a guarantor faces ruin. **20.** Go surety only if you can afford it, but be cautious. **21.** Basic needs are water, food, clothing, and a private home. **22.** Better a poor meal under your own roof than feasts in others' homes. **23.** Be content with what you have and ignore disparagement (disrespect). **24.** Living from house to house is miserable, and guests cannot speak freely. **25.** Hosts show no gratitude, and harsh words are spoken. **26.** "Set the table and feed me!" **27.** "Leave, stranger, for someone more worthy!" **28.** Painful are insults at home and reproaches (criticism) from creditors.

Chapter 30

1. A father who loves his son corrects (guides) him, so he brings joy as he matures. **2.** A father who trains his son boasts of him. **3.** A well-educated son brings joy to his family and envy to enemies. **4.** After the father's death, the son lives on, resembling (looking like) him. **5.** The father delights in his son's growth and has no regrets. **6.** The son avenges (takes revenge on) his father's enemies and rewards his friends. **7.** A father who neglects his son suffers from his misdeeds. **8.** A wild colt becomes stubborn; an undisciplined son grows unruly (difficult to control). **9.** Pampering (overindulging) a child causes sorrow. **10.** Indulging recklessness (carelessness) leads to regret. **11.** Correct a child's foolishness early. **12.** Discipline while young to avoid future defiance (disobedience). **13.** Correct your son or his foolishness will bring shame. **14.** Better a healthy poor man than a rich sick one. **15.** Health is more valuable than gold, peace of mind more precious than coral. **16.** There is no greater treasure than good health and joy.

17. Better to die than live a bitter life. **18.** Rich foods before one who cannot eat are like offerings to the dead. **19.** What good is an offering to an idol that cannot taste? **20.** So too is the one who longs for what they cannot enjoy. **21.** Do not dwell on sadness or overthink. **22.** Cheerfulness gives life and extends days. **23.** Stay occupied and push away anger; worry harms. **24.** Envy shortens life, anxiety brings early aging. **25.** A joyful person benefits from food.

Chapter 31

1. Watching riches wears down the body and worrying about wealth steals rest. **2.** Anxiety about making a living disrupts sleep more than illness. **3.** The rich work hard to amass wealth, but their rest comes from indulgence. **4.** The poor labor for survival but remain in need even when they rest. **5.** Those who love gold struggle with sin; wealth leads them astray. **6.** Many are trapped by riches, even when destruction is clear. **7.** Gold is a trap for the greedy and foolish. **8.** Blessed is the wealthy person who resists greed! **9.** Such a person is praised and admired by their people. **10.** Tested by wealth, they stay pure and earn lasting honor. **11.** They could have sinned but didn't, refusing wrong. **12.** Their wealth is secure, and their integrity is celebrated. **13.** Don't be greedy when dining with an important person. **14.** Gluttony (excessive eating) is harmful, and the eye's greed never satisfies. **15.** Be mindful of your neighbor's feelings; treat others as you wish to be treated. **16.** Don't compete for others' food. **17.** Be gracious; don't overeat or risk being disliked. **18.** Stop before you're full, showing good manners. **19.** A little food is enough for the well-mannered and ensures peaceful rest. **20.** Overeating causes discomfort, restlessness, and sleepless nights. **21.** Eating moderately leads to sound sleep and clarity the next day. **22.** Relief comes after overindulgence when the stomach empties. **23.** Listen to this advice: Be moderate to avoid sickness. **24.** Generous hosts are blessed and remembered for kindness. **25.** Stingy hosts are criticized and remembered for greed. **26.** Don't boast about how much you can drink; wine ruins many lives. **27.** Just as a furnace tests metal, wine tests the hearts of the proud. **28.** Wine, in moderation, brings joy and cheer. **29.** Drinking in anger or conflict leads to bitterness and pain. **30.** Excessive drinking weakens and causes harm. **31.** Don't rebuke your neighbor while drinking or shame them in front of others.

Chapter 32

1. If you host a dinner, don't be arrogant (proud). Serve others first, then sit and enjoy their company. **2.** After your duties, take your place and earn praise for your hospitality. **3.** As an elder, speak wisely, but don't disrupt the mood or the singing. **4.** When wine is served, avoid long speeches or showing off knowledge. **5.** Music during a meal is as lovely as a carnelian (a gemstone) seal in gold. **6.** String music with wine is like gold with an emerald (green gemstone) seal. **7.** Young people, speak only when necessary and after being asked more than once. **8.** Be concise but meaningful, like a wise person who speaks sparingly. **9.** Don't interrupt elders or be overly persistent with officials. **10.** Modesty earns respect, like lightning before a storm brings awe. **11.** When it's time to leave, don't linger. Go home to find rest. **12.** At home, enjoy yourself righteously, avoiding sin or prideful words. **13.** Above all, give thanks to your Creator (God), who blesses you. **14.** Those who seek God must accept discipline (training); they will receive what they ask for. **15.** Studying the law leads to understanding, but hypocrites misuse it for personal gain. **16.** A person who fears (respects) the Lord will have sound judgment and clarity in confusion. **17.** Sinners reject correction and twist the law to fit their desires. **18.** A thoughtful person values good guidance; the proud (arrogant) refuse correction. **19.** Seek advice before acting to avoid regret. **20.** Don't walk on paths filled with traps, and don't repeat your mistakes. **21.** Even smooth roads can be dangerous—stay alert. **22.** Be cautious in all you do. **23.** Guard your actions carefully to stay on the path of obedience. **24.** Whoever keeps the law protects their life, and those who trust the Lord will never be ashamed.

Chapter 33

1. No harm can come to those who fear (respect) the Lord; even in trials, they remain safe. **2.** Those who hate God's law lack wisdom and are like a boat tossed in a storm. **3.** A wise person trusts in the Lord's word, which is as reliable as a divine (God-given) message. **4.** Prepare your words carefully, and people will listen; draw on your knowledge before answering. **5.** A fool's mind is like a cartwheel—it spins aimlessly, without direction. **6.** A fickle (changeable) friend is like a restless horse, regardless of who rides it. **7.** Why is one day more special than another when the same sun shines on all? **8.** It is the Lord's wisdom that makes days different, creating seasons and special times. **9.** Some days He blesses and makes holy, while others He leaves ordinary. **10.** Just as all humans are formed from clay, **11.** The Lord, with His vast knowledge, creates people to walk unique paths. **12.** He blesses some, raising them and drawing them near to Himself; others He curses, bringing them low. **13.** Just as a potter molds clay as he pleases, so the Creator shapes people according to His will. **14.** Good contrasts with evil, life with death, and sinners stand in opposition to the righteous. **15.** All works of the Most High come in pairs, opposites to one another. **16.** I stand as one of the last, like a gleaner gathering leftover fruit after the harvest. **17.** By the Lord's blessing, I've progressed and filled my winepress like a vintager (wine maker). **18.** I share this wisdom not for my own benefit, but for all who seek understanding. **19.** Listen, leaders of the people, and rulers of assemblies, pay attention! **20.** Don't let a son, wife, brother, or friend hold power over you as long as you live. **21.** While you still have breath, don't give control of your life to anyone. **22.** It's better for your children to depend on you than for you to rely on their kindness. **23.** Maintain authority over your affairs and protect your reputation. **24.** When your life ends, distribute your inheritance as you see fit. **25.** An animal needs food, a whip, and burdens to bear; **26.** Similarly, a slave needs food, correction, and work, and a rebellious one may need discipline. **27.** Keep a servant busy, and they'll look for rest; leave them idle, and they may seek freedom. **28.** Make them work, as idleness leads to trouble and mischief. **29.** Assign tasks appropriate for them, but if they rebel, heavier measures may be needed. **30.** However, never act unjustly or lord over anyone. **31.** If you have only one servant, treat them with respect, for you bought them with great cost. **32.** Regard them as a brother, for they are as essential to your life as your own breath. **33.** If you mistreat them and they run away, where will you search for them?

Chapter 34

1. Empty hopes and foolish dreams mislead senseless people. **2.** Trusting dreams is like chasing shadows or the wind. **3.** Dreams are far from reality, like a reflection is from a face. **4.** Can impurity produce purity, or liars speak truth? **5.** Divinations (foretelling), omens, and dreams deceive, reflecting the mind's expectations. **6.** Unless sent by God, don't fix your heart on dreams. **7.** Dreams have misled many, causing their ruin. **8.** God's law is always true, and wisdom is found in the faithful. **9.** Training builds knowledge, and experience teaches sense. **10.** The untested know little; travelers gain resourcefulness. **11.** I have seen much in my travels and learned beyond words. **12.** Though often near death, my wisdom has saved me. **13.** Those who fear (respect) God have courage, trusting in their Savior. **14.** They are never afraid, for the Lord is their hope. **15.** Happy is the soul that fears God, for He is their trust and support. **16.** God's eyes are on His loved ones, shielding and guiding them. **17.** He lifts spirits, brightens eyes, and gives health and blessings. **18.** Gifts from ill-gotten gain are tainted, and sacrifices from the wicked displease God. **19.** God rejects offerings from the godless and does not forgive through their sacrifices. **20.** Offering stolen goods is as heinous (evil) as killing a son before his father. **21.** Giving bread to the needy sustains life; withholding it is like shedding blood. **22.** Denying someone their livelihood or wages is like killing them. **23.** Building while others destroy only leads to trouble. **24.** If one prays and another curses, whose voice will God hear? **25.** Touching a corpse after bathing undoes the cleansing. **26.** So it is with someone who repents through fasting but returns to sin—what good is their prayer?

Chapter 35

1. Keeping the law is a worthy offering; obeying God is like a peace (reconciliation) sacrifice. **2.** Charity is like offering fine flour, and alms (donations) are praises to God. **3.** Avoiding evil and injustice pleases God and atones (makes up for) sin. **4.** Do not come before God empty-handed; all offerings fulfill His commands. **5.** The sacrifices of the just enrich the altar and rise like a sweet fragrance. **6.** Such offerings please God and will never be forgotten. **7.** Give to God generously, holding nothing back in your freewill offerings. **8.** Offer cheerfully and give your tithes with joy. **9.** Give according to your means, as God has given to you. **10.** The Lord repays generously, returning blessings sevenfold. **11.**

Do not try to bribe God; He rejects offerings gained through injustice. **12.** God is just and shows no favoritism. **13.** He hears the cries of the oppressed and defends the weak. **14.** The orphan's wail and the widow's complaint reach Him. **15.** Tears of the afflicted cry out against their oppressors. **16.** Those who serve God willingly are heard; their prayers reach heaven. **17.** The humble's prayer pierces the clouds and persists until God answers. **18.** God acts without delay, judging justly and affirming the right. **19.** Like a warrior, God breaks the power of the merciless. **20.** He humbles the proud and punishes the wicked. **21.** He repays people for their deeds and intentions. **22.** God defends His people and brings them joy through His mercy. **23.** His mercy refreshes like rain in times of drought. **24.** His mercy is welcome in times of distress, like rain in a drought.

Chapter 36

1. O God, help us and make all nations fear You! **2.** Strike the heathen (non-believers) to show them Your power. **3.** As You used us to reveal Your holiness, now use them to reveal Your glory. **4.** Let them know, as we do, that there is no God but You. **5.** Perform new signs and wonders; display the might of Your right hand and arm. **6.** Stir Your anger, pour out wrath, humble our enemies, and scatter the foe. **7.** Speed the day and hasten the time; **8.** Crush the heads of hostile rulers. **9.** Let fire consume the fugitives and bring destruction to our oppressors. **10.** Gather all the tribes of Jacob to inherit the land as of old. **11.** Have mercy on Your people, Israel, whom You called Your firstborn. **12.** Pity Your holy city, Jerusalem, Your dwelling place. **13.** Fill Zion with Your majesty and Your temple with glory. **14.** Show the world Your past deeds and fulfill the prophecies spoken in Your name. **15.** Reward those who trust in You and prove Your prophets true. **16.** Hear the prayer of Your servants, for You are always gracious to Your people. **17.** Let all the earth know You are the eternal God. **18.** The throat can take any food, but some are more pleasant than others. **19.** A keen mind discerns deceit, just as the palate (taste) tests meat by its flavor. **20.** A deceitful person causes grief, but an experienced person can turn things around. **21.** Any man can marry, but one woman will be more fitting than another. **22.** A woman's beauty makes her husband's face light up, surpassing all other attractions. **23.** If her speech is kind, his joy exceeds that of any man. **24.** A wife is a husband's greatest treasure, a helper, a firm support. **25.** A vineyard without a hedge (protection) is overrun; a man without a wife is like a homeless wanderer. **26.** Who will trust a band of soldiers that moves from city to city? **27.** Or a man who has no home, lodging wherever night finds him?

Chapter 37

1. Every friend claims loyalty, but some are only friends in name. **2.** It's tragic when a close friend becomes your enemy. **3.** "Why were you created to deceive (mislead) and betray (treacherously deceive) the earth?" **4.** A false friend rejoices with you but distances himself in trouble. **5.** A true friend will stand by you against enemies, acting as your shield (protector). **6.** Don't forget your comrade (close companion) in battle or neglect him when dividing spoils (rewards). **7.** Everyone offers advice, but some do so for selfish reasons. **8.** Be cautious (careful) when seeking advice; consider the giver's motives (reasons for action). **9.** Some may praise your plans but secretly await your failure. **10.** Don't seek advice from those who dislike you; keep your plans from the envious (jealous). **11.** Don't talk about a woman's rival (competitor) with her, or war with a coward (one who fears conflict); avoid certain topics with others. **12.** Seek advice from a devout (religiously devoted) person who follows the commandments and shares your values. **13.** Trust your own heart's counsel (guidance), for it's the most dependable (reliable). **14.** A man's conscience (inner sense of right and wrong) is more accurate than seven watchmen (guardians) on a high tower. **15.** Above all, pray to God to guide your steps in truth. **16.** Words lead to actions, and thoughts to deeds. **17.** The mind is the root (foundation) of all behavior, where good or evil, life or death grow. **18.** The tongue controls (guides) all conduct (behavior). **19.** A man may be wise and help others but still fail to benefit himself. **20.** Rejected wisdom brings no joy. **21.** When wisdom benefits oneself, the results show in his life. **22.** When wisdom benefits others, its impact endures (lasts). **23.** A man's life is limited (short), but Israel's life is endless. **24.** A wise man enjoys life, and others praise him. **25.** A wise man who benefits his people gains eternal glory. **26.** My son, control your appetite (desire) and avoid harm. **27.** Not all foods suit everyone; tastes vary (differ). **28.** Don't chase every pleasure or become a glutton (someone who overeats). **29.** Overeating leads to sickness and discomfort. **30.** Lack of self-control (discipline) has led many to die early, but the moderate (balanced) live longer.

Chapter 38

1. Honor the physician (doctor), for his work is essential to you, and God established his profession. **2.** The doctor's wisdom comes from God, and the king provides for his needs. **3.** His knowledge distinguishes (sets apart) the doctor and grants him access to those in power. **4.** God causes the earth to yield (produce) healing herbs that the wise should not neglect. **5.** Was not the water sweetened (made pleasant) by a twig to show His power? **6.** God gives men knowledge to marvel (be amazed) at His mighty works, **7.** Through which the doctor relieves pain and the druggist (pharmacist) prepares remedies. **8.** Thus, God's creative work continues, affecting (influencing) the earth for good. **9.** When you are ill, delay not (wait); pray to God, who will heal you. **10.** Turn from wickedness, act justly (fairly), and cleanse (purify) your heart of sin. **11.** Offer your best prayer and gift to God, according to your means (resources). **12.** Give the doctor his place, lest he leave; you need him too. **13.** There are times that give him an advantage (opportunity), **14.** And he too prays that his diagnosis may be correct and his treatment effective. **15.** A sinner against his Maker will defy (resist) the doctor. **16.** When someone dies, mourn (grieve) properly, prepare the body, and attend the funeral. **17.** Mourn deeply for one or two days to avoid gossip, then regain composure (calm). **18.** Grief can bring extremity (serious illness) and destroy your health. **19.** Do not dwell (linger) on the deceased; think of the end that awaits all. **20.** Recall not (don't remember) the departed, for there is no hope of their return; it will harm you. **21.** Remember, their fate is yours too— yesterday it was them, tomorrow it could be you. **22.** Let memory of the dead fade and rally (strengthen) your courage once the soul has gone. **23.** The scribe's profession increases his wisdom; the one free from toil (work) can become wise. **24.** How can one who guides the plow, thrills (enjoys) in the goad (driving tool), and watches over cattle gain wisdom? **25.** His care is for the work, plowing the land and tending to the animals. **26.** The engraver, working day and night, is focused on shaping seals and designs. **27.** The blacksmith, standing by his anvil (metalworking tool), forges iron, enduring the fire's heat. **28.** The potter, revolving the wheel with his feet, molds (shapes) the clay with care. **29.** All these men are skilled (proficient) with their hands, experts at their crafts. **30.** Without them, no city could survive, and wherever they stay, they do not hunger. **31.** They do not sit in judgment, nor are they prominent (important) in the assembly (meeting). **32.** They make no decisions or judgments and are not among rulers. **33.** Yet they maintain God's ancient handiwork (creation), focused on the exercise of their skill. **34.** Their work sustains life, and through their craft, God's glory is reflected in the earth.

Chapter 39

1. The man who studies the law of the Most High seeks the wisdom of the ancients and engages with prophecies. **2.** He values the words of wise men and seeks understanding in complex teachings. **3.** He explores hidden meanings in parables and the wisdom of the sages (wise people). **4.** He associates with the great and has access to rulers. **5.** He travels to learn what is good and evil among people. **6.** His focus is on seeking God, praying for forgiveness. **7.** If it pleases God, he will be filled with understanding and give thanks in prayer. **8.** God will guide his wisdom as he meditates on divine mysteries. **9.** He will share the wisdom he has gained and honor God's law. **10.** Many will praise his understanding, and his name will live on forever. **11.** People will celebrate his wisdom, and his renown (fame) will endure beyond his death. **12.** In life, he is rare, and his memory remains after he passes. **13.** Listen, my faithful children: open (grow) like roses by running waters. **14.** Offer sweet praise like incense, and bloom like the lily. **15.** Proclaim God's greatness with music and joy. **16.** The works of God are all good, and every need is met in His time. **17.** At His word, the waters become still, and reservoirs (storage) are formed. **18.** His command is all-powerful; nothing limits His will. **19.** All human deeds are before Him; nothing escapes His sight. **20.** His vision spans all ages; nothing is unexpected to Him. **21.** Do not ask, "What is the purpose of this?" Everything fulfills a need. **22.** His blessings flow abundantly, like the Nile and Euphrates enriching the earth. **23.** His wrath (anger) expels

nations and turns fertile lands into desolation (ruin). **24.** The virtuous (good people) find smooth paths; for the proud, the way is steep. **25.** From the beginning, God provided good things for the good, but the wicked face both good and bad. **26.** Life's essentials include water, fire, iron, salt, wheat, milk, honey, wine, oil, and clothing. **27.** For the righteous, these are blessings, but for the wicked, they bring harm. **28.** Storm winds are sent to punish, their fury uprooting mountains and fulfilling God's anger. **29.** In God's storehouses are fire, hail, famine, disease, and tools of judgment. **30.** Wild beasts, scorpions, serpents, and swords carry out vengeance (punishment) against the wicked. **31.** These forces obey God joyfully, never defying His commands. **32.** From the beginning, I declared: **33.** All God's works are good, and every need is met in its time. **34.** Do not judge one thing as better than another; each has value at the proper moment. **35.** With joyful hearts, proclaim and bless the name of the Holy One!

Chapter 40

1. God has placed a heavy burden on mankind from birth to death. **2.** Their hearts are filled with fears and forebodings (anxiety) until life's end. **3.** Whether on a throne or in dust, no one escapes these anxieties. **4.** Whether adorned with a crown or wrapped in a coarse cloak, troubles persist. **5.** Wrath (anger), envy, terror, and strife plague man; even rest is disturbed by worry. **6.** Nighttime offers little relief; dreams mirror the day's struggles. **7.** Upon waking, one realizes his fears were baseless. **8.** This is the lot (fate) of all living things, but sinners face it sevenfold. **9.** Plague, bloodshed, wrath, sword, famine, and death were created for the wicked. **10.** These evils bring destruction, fulfilling their purpose. **11.** Earthly things return to the earth; heavenly things return above. **12.** Bribes and injustice fade away, but loyalty lasts forever. **13.** Ill-gotten wealth (money gained unfairly) is fleeting, like a stream that quickly dries up. **14.** It surges with power but ends abruptly, leaving nothing behind. **15.** Violence will not thrive; the godless (ungodly) are like plants on rocky ground. **16.** They wither like reeds, while goodness endures eternally. **17.** Wealth and wages enhance life, but finding a treasure is better. **18.** A child or city preserves a name, but wisdom surpasses both. **19.** Flocks and orchards bring health, but a faithful wife is better. **20.** Wine and music uplift the soul, but conjugal love (marital love) is greater. **21.** The harp and flute offer melody, but a true voice is better. **22.** Beauty pleases the eyes, but flowers of the field surpass it. **23.** Friends and neighbors guide, but a wise wife is superior. **24.** Brothers and helpers support in stress, but charity that rescues is better. **25.** Gold and silver provide security, but sound judgment (wisdom) is greater. **26.** Wealth and strength build confidence, but fearing God surpasses all. **27.** The fear of God is a source of endless blessings and glory. **28.** My son, better to die than live a beggar's life. **29.** Depending on others for sustenance robs life of its meaning. **30.** To the shameless, begging seems sweet, but it burns within like fire.

Chapter 41

1. O death! How bitter is the thought of you to the man who is at peace, secure in his wealth, and enjoys the pleasures of life. **2.** But how welcome your sentence to the weak man, worn with age, whose sight fails, and whose hope has vanished. **3.** Do not fear death's decree, for it comes to all—those before you and those after. **4.** Thus, God has ordained (decided) for all flesh; why should you reject the will of the Most High? Whether one lives a thousand years, a hundred, or ten, in the end, he has no claim on life. **5.** The children of sinners are accursed (cursed), and the wicked offspring bring disgrace upon their homes. **6.** The dominion (rule) of the wicked is passed to their descendants, and reproach (shame) clings to their lineage. **7.** Children curse their wicked fathers, for they suffer disgrace because of him. **8.** Woe (misery) to you, O sinful men, who forsake (abandon) the law of the Most High! **9.** If you have children, calamity (disaster) will seize them; you will bear them only for sorrow. When you stumble (fall), there will be no joy, and at death, you will become a curse. **10.** Whatever is of nothing returns to nothing, so too the godless (ungodly), from void (nothing) to void. **11.** The body is fleeting (temporary), but a virtuous (good) name endures forever. **12.** Care for your name, for it will stand by you better than riches. **13.** The gift of life is for a brief time, but a good name lasts for eternity. **14.** My children, heed (listen to) my teaching about shame; judge disgrace only by my standards. **15.** Be ashamed before your father and mother of immorality (wrongdoing); before your master and mistress, of falsehood. **16.** Before prince and ruler, of flattery; before the assembly, of crime. **17.** Before friend and companion, of disloyalty, and of breaking an oath. **18.** Be ashamed of stealing from others, of overindulging at the table, **19.** of refusing to give when asked, or defrauding (cheating) others of their rightful share. **20.** Be ashamed of failing to return a greeting, or of rebuffing (rejecting) a friend. **21.** Be ashamed of gazing at a married woman or entertaining thoughts of another's wife; of mistreating a servant girl and violating her trust. **22.** Be ashamed of using harsh words with friends, or insulting others after giving gifts. **23.** Be ashamed of gossiping, and betraying (revealing) secrets. **24.** These things are shameful, and you should avoid them, that you may be honored by all.

Chapter 42

1. But do not be ashamed of these things, lest you sin through human respect: **2.** Of the law of the Most High and His precepts (commands), or of the judgment on the sinful; **3.** Of sharing the costs of a business or journey, or dividing an inheritance or property; **4.** Of accuracy in scales and balances, or of proper measures and weights; **5.** Of acquiring much or little, or bargaining with a merchant; of training children, or disciplining a disloyal servant; **6.** Of using a seal to keep an erring wife at home, or placing a lock where many hands can reach; **7.** Of counting every deposit, or recording what is given or received; **8.** Of correcting the foolish or punishing the aged for their wanton (reckless) conduct. Thus, you will be cautious and recognized by all as discreet (careful). **9.** A daughter is a treasure that keeps her father awake, and worry over her robs him of rest: **10.** While unmarried, lest she be seduced; or married, lest she be disliked, barren (unable to have children), or unfaithful. **11.** Watch over your daughter closely, lest she make you the laughingstock (object of ridicule) of your enemies, a reproach (disgrace) in the city, and an object of derision (mockery) in public. Keep her away from places where the house is overlooked. **12.** Let her not display her charms before men, nor spend time with married women; **13.** For just as moths come from garments, so harm to women comes from women. **14.** Better a man's harshness than a woman's indulgence (leniency), and a frightened daughter than any disgrace. **15.** Now I will recall the works of God; what I have seen, I will describe. By His word, His works were created; they do His will as He has ordained (commanded). **16.** As the rising sun is clear to all, so the glory of the Lord fills all His works. **17.** Yet even God's holy ones cannot recount (describe) the wonders of the Lord, though He has given them the strength to stand before His glory. **18.** He searches the depths and penetrates the heart; He understands the innermost being. The Most High possesses all knowledge and sees from old the things to come. **19.** He reveals the past and future, and uncovers the deepest secrets. **20.** No understanding does He lack; nothing escapes Him. **21.** His wisdom is eternal; He is from everlasting, unchanged, **22.** Needing no counselor. **23.** How beautiful are all His works! Even the spark and the fleeting vision! **24.** The universe lives and endures forever; each creature is preserved to meet its need. **25.** All differ from one another, yet none are made in vain (pointlessly), for each is good in its time. Who can ever see enough of their splendor (beauty)?

Chapter 43

1. The clear vault of the sky shines like heaven itself, a vision of glory. **2.** The sun, resplendent (brilliant) at its rising, is a wonderful work of the Most High! **3.** At noon, it scorches the earth, and who can bear its fiery heat? **4.** Like a blazing furnace, it sets the mountains aflame with its rays; the land is consumed by its fiery darts (arrows), and the eyes are dazzled by its light. **5.** Great indeed is the LORD who made it, at whose command it urges on its steeds (horses). **6.** The moon, too, governs the changing times, marking the seasons as their lasting sign. **7.** by which we know the feast days and fixed dates, this light-giver that wanes (decreases) in its course. **8.** As its name says, it renews itself each month; how wondrous in this change! **9.** The beauty and glory of the heavens are the stars, sparkling in the heights of God, **10.** at whose command they remain in their place, never relaxing in their vigils (watchfulness). **11.** A weapon against the floodwaters stored on high, lighting the firmament (sky) with its brilliance. **12.** Behold the rainbow! Bless its Maker, for majestic is its splendor (great beauty); **13.** it spans the heavens with its glory, this bow bent by the mighty hand of God. **14.** His rebuke (command) sets the path for lightning and speeds the arrows of His judgment to their goal. **15.** At His command, the storehouses are opened, and like vultures the clouds hurry forth. **16.** In His majesty, He gives the storm its power and breaks off the hailstones. **17.** The thunder of His voice makes the earth writhe (tremble); before His might, the mountains quake. **18.** A word from Him drives on the south wind, the angry north wind, the hurricane, and the storm. **19.** He sprinkles the snow like fluttering birds; it falls like swarms of locusts. **20.** Its shining whiteness blinds the eyes, and the mind is baffled (confused) by its steady fall. **21.** He scatters frost like salt; it shines like blossoms on the thornbush. **22.** Cold northern blasts He sends that turn the ponds to lumps of ice. He freezes every body of water and clothes each pool with a coat of mail (armor). **23.** When the mountain growth is scorched (burned) with heat, and the flowering plains as though by flames, **24.** the dripping clouds restore them all, and the scattered dew enriches (revives) the parched land. **25.** His plan calms the deep and plants the islands in the sea. **26.** Those who go down to the sea tell part of its story, and when we hear them, we are thunderstruck (amazed). **27.** In it are His creatures—stupendous (incredible), amazing—of all kinds of life, including the monsters of the deep. **28.** For Him, each messenger succeeds, and at His bidding (command), they accomplish His will. **29.** More than this we need not add; let the final word be: He is all in all! **30.** Let us praise Him the more, for we cannot fathom (understand) Him, for greater is He than all His works. **31.** Awful (awe-inspiring) indeed is the LORD's majesty, and wonderful is His power. **32.** Lift up your voices to glorify the LORD, though He is still beyond your power to praise; **33.** extol (praise) Him with renewed strength, and weary not, though you cannot reach the end. **34.** For who can see Him and describe Him? Or who can praise Him as He is? **35.** Beyond these, many things lie hidden; only a few of His works have we seen. **36.** It is the LORD who has made all things, and to those who fear Him, He gives wisdom.

Chapter 44

1. Now I will praise the godly men, our ancestors, each in his own time. **2.** The glory of the Most High's portion, His inheritance from of old, was upon them. They were mighty in the land, rulers in their time, **3.** or wise counselors, or prophets revealing things to come; **4.** resolute leaders, and governors who carried the staff of authority; men skilled in letters (writing), and masters of wisdom, **5.** composers of psalms of praise, and those who spoke of holy things in song; **6.** strong men, firmly established, and at peace in their own lands— **7.** all these were glorious in their day, each honored in his time. **8.** Some of them have left behind a name, and their deeds are remembered with praise; **9.** but of others, there is no memory, for when they passed away, they were as though they had not lived. They and their children are forgotten. **10.** Yet these also were godly men, whose virtues have not been forgotten; **11.** their wealth remains in their families, their inheritance to their descendants; **12.** through God's covenant (agreement) with them, their house endures, and their posterity (descendants) remains for their sake. **13.** And their children's children will endure for all time, and their glory will never fade. **14.** Though their bodies rest in peace, their name lives on, **15.** and at the gatherings of the people, their wisdom is retold, and their praises are sung. **16.** Enoch walked with God, and he was no more, for God took him, that his example might remain for future generations. **17.** Noah, found righteous and blameless, preserved the human race when the flood came. Because of him, there were survivors, and the waters of the deluge (flood) ceased by the sign of God. **18.** A lasting covenant was made with him that never again would all flesh (living beings) be destroyed by water. **19.** Abraham, the father of many nations, kept his integrity (honesty), and his glory remained untarnished (unspoiled). **20.** He followed the commandments of the Most High and entered into covenant with Him; in his flesh, he bore the sign of that covenant, and when tested, he proved faithful. **21.** Therefore, God swore an oath (promise) to him, that in his seed (descendants) all the nations of the earth would be blessed, **22.** that his descendants would be as numerous as the dust of the earth, and his posterity like the stars of heaven. **23.** He promised to give them an inheritance from sea to sea, and from the river to the ends of the earth. And for Isaac, he confirmed this promise, because of Abraham, his father. **24.** The covenant with Abraham's forebears (ancestors) was established, and the blessing rested upon the head of Jacob.

Chapter 45

1. I will praise Moses, the man beloved by God and men, whose memory is blessed. 2. God's honor was upon him, and He strengthened him with great power. 3. At Moses' word, God performed miracles (wonders) and gave him the commandments (laws) for His people. 4. For his faithfulness and meekness (humility), God chose Moses above all. 5. God spoke to him face to face and gave him the law to teach Israel. 6. Moses' brother, Aaron, was raised up, holy like Moses, from the tribe of Levi. 7. God established Aaron in the priesthood (religious office), honoring him with majesty. 8. He clothed Aaron with beautiful garments (clothes), including a robe with pomegranates (fruit with seeds), 9. and bells whose sound could be heard in the sanctuary (holy place), reminding of his descendants. 10. The sacred vestments (clothing) were made of gold, violet, and crimson (red), with a breastplate (armor) for decisions, 11. precious stones engraved with the names of the tribes of Israel. 12. His turban (headpiece) had a gold crown, marking holiness (purity), majestic and beautiful. 13. No one else may wear these, only Aaron's descendants for all generations. 14. Aaron's grain offering was completely burnt with sacrifices, twice each day. 15. Moses ordained (appointed) and anointed (consecrated) Aaron, making a lasting covenant (promise) that he would serve God as priest. 16. God chose Aaron to offer sacrifices and atone (make amends) for Israel. 17. He gave Aaron authority (power) to teach the law and rituals (ceremonies) to the people of Israel. 18. Others became jealous and rebelled (resisted) against him, including Dathan, Abiram, and Korah. 19. God was angered and destroyed them with fire. 20. God increased Aaron's glory, giving him sacred offerings as his inheritance (property). 21. These offerings are his food and a gift to him and his descendants. 22. Aaron has no land among the people; God Himself is his inheritance in Israel. 23. Phinehas, Aaron's son, was zealous (devoted) for God and atoned for Israel. 24. God made a covenant with Phinehas, granting him and his descendants the high priesthood forever. 25. Unlike David's covenant, which passed through one son, Aaron's covenant is for all his descendants. 26. Bless the Lord, who has crowned you with glory! May He grant you wisdom (understanding) to lead His people in justice.

Chapter 46

1. Joshua, son of Nun, Moses' assistant, was a great leader chosen to save God's people, punish enemies, and secure Israel's inheritance. 2. His glory shone when he raised his javelin against the city. 3. No one could defeat him in the LORD's battles. 4. By God's power, he made the sun stand still, turning one day into two. 5. Surrounded by enemies, he called on God, and God sent powerful hailstones. 6. The hailstones destroyed the enemy, showing the LORD protects His people. 7. Because of his faithfulness to God and Moses, he and Caleb stopped the rebellion and turned away God's anger. 8. They were spared from the 600,000 men and led Israel into the promised land. 9. Caleb's strength, given by God, remained even in old age, and his family inherited the land. 10. This showed the tribes of Jacob the blessings of being faithful to the LORD. 11. The Judges who remained true to God, may their memory be blessed. 12. May their bones rise and their names shine in their descendants! 13. Samuel, beloved by his people and consecrated (set apart) from birth, was a judge, priest, and prophet. He anointed rulers. 14. By God's law, Samuel judged Israel and visited the camps of Jacob. 15. He was a true prophet, and his words proved true. 16. Samuel called on God and offered a lamb. 17. The LORD answered with thunder from heaven. 18. He humbled enemy rulers and destroyed the Philistines. 19. Before his death, Samuel testified he had taken no bribes, and no one could accuse him. 20. After his death, people sought his guidance, and from the grave, he prophesied the king's fate, ending wickedness.

Chapter 47

1. After David came Nathan, who served him faithfully. 2. David was honored in Israel, like the finest sacred offerings. 3. He treated lions like young goats and bears like lambs. 4. As a youth, he defeated Goliath with one stone, removing disgrace from Israel. 5. He called on God, who gave him strength to defeat mighty warriors and raise Israel. 6. Women sang his praises, saying he had slain tens of thousands. When he became king, 7. he fought bravely, defeating his enemies. He shattered the power of the Philistines. 8. In all his deeds, he thanked God, praising Him daily. 9. He brought joy to feasts, consecrating seasons with music before the altar. 10. The sanctuary echoed with praise before dawn. 11. The LORD forgave his sins, made his strength endure, and secured his throne. 12. Because of his righteousness, he was succeeded by a wise son, who ruled in peace. 13. Solomon, his son, ruled in peace, with God securing his borders. He built a house for God and a lasting sanctuary. 14. Solomon was wise, overflowing with wisdom like the Nile in flood. 15. His wisdom spread throughout the earth, filling the world with knowledge. 16. His fame reached far, and people came to hear his wisdom. 17. With songs, stories, and riddles, he amazed nations with his answers. 18. He was honored with Israel's glorious title. 19. He accumulated gold like iron and silver like lead. 20. But he was led astray by women, giving them control over him. 21. He tarnished his reputation, bringing shame to his marriage and anger to his descendants. 22. As a result, two kingdoms arose, and Ephraim's kingship was lost. 23. But God did not withdraw His mercy; He preserved a remnant of Jacob and a root for David's family. 24. Solomon died and was succeeded by his son Rehoboam, who caused rebellion with his foolish policies. 25. A sinner arose who led Israel into sin and brought destruction to Ephraim. 26. Their sin grew, and they abandoned themselves to wickedness.

Chapter 48

1. Like a fire appeared the prophet whose words were like a flaming furnace. 2. He shattered their supply of bread, reducing them to hardship (severe difficulty) in his zeal (passionate effort). 3. By God's word, he closed the heavens and brought down fire three times. 4. How awesome (awe-inspiring) you are, Elijah! Who is equal to your glory? 5. You brought a dead man back to life, by the will of the LORD. 6. You sent kings and nobles to destruction, even from their sickbeds. 7. You heard threats at Sinai (a mountain where Moses received the Ten Commandments) and avenged (punished for wrongdoing) judgments at Horeb (another name for Sinai). 8. You anointed (consecrated for a divine purpose) kings to bring vengeance (punishment for wrongdoing) and a prophet as your successor. 9. You were taken up in a whirlwind (a powerful wind), in a chariot with fiery horses. 10. It is written that in the future, you will end wrath (anger) before the day of the LORD, turning hearts of fathers to their sons, and restoring (bringing back to a good state) the tribes of Jacob (referring to the twelve tribes of Israel). 11. Blessed is he who will see you before he dies, 12. O Elijah, enveloped (surrounded) in the whirlwind! Then Elisha, with a double portion of your spirit, performed many miracles (extraordinary events) by his word. 13. In life, he feared no one, and none could intimidate (make afraid) him. 14. Nothing was beyond his power; he brought the dead back to life. 15. In life and after death, he performed wonders (amazing acts). 16. Despite this, the people did not repent (feel remorse for their actions), and their sins led them to be scattered (spread widely) across the earth. But Judah remained, a small people, with rulers from the house of David. 17. Some rulers did right, but others were exceedingly (very) sinful. 18. Hezekiah fortified (strengthened and protected) his city, brought water into it, cut through rock with iron tools, and built reservoirs (storage places for water). 19. During his reign, Sennacherib (King of Assyria) invaded, shaking his fist at Zion (Jerusalem) and blaspheming (disrespecting) God in pride. 20. The people's hearts melted (became fearful) in anguish (great pain) like childbirth, but they called upon God, lifting their hands in prayer. 21. God heard their prayer and saved them through Isaiah. 22. God struck (hit with force) the Assyrian camp with a plague (a widespread disease) and routed (defeated) them. 23. Hezekiah did what was right, following the paths of David, as commanded by the prophet Isaiah, who saw the truth in visions (divine revelations). 24. Hezekiah turned back the sun and prolonged (extended) the king's life. 25. By his powerful spirit, he looked into the future and comforted the mourners (those grieving) of Zion, foretelling (predicting) things to come.

Chapter 49

1. Josiah's name is sweet like incense, cherished like honey and music. 2. He mourned his people's betrayals and destroyed their idols. 3. He turned to God, remaining righteous despite evil times. 4. Except for David, Hezekiah, and Josiah, Judah's kings were wicked and abandoned God's law. 5. God gave their power to others and their glory to a foolish nation. 6. This nation burned the holy city, as Jeremiah had prophesied. 7. They despised the prophet, chosen to destroy and rebuild. 8. Ezekiel saw the vision of the chariot and its creatures. 9. He spoke of Job's

steadfastness despite trials. **10.** The Twelve Prophets strengthened Israel with their faith. **11.** Zerubbabel, like a signet ring in God's hand, deserves honor. **12.** Jeshua, who rebuilt God's house and set up the temple, deserves praise. **13.** Nehemiah rebuilt the city's walls and defenses. **14.** Few were like Enoch, taken to be with God. **15.** Joseph was honored even after death, with his descendants blessed. **16.** Adam, the first man, surpassed all.

Chapter 50

1. The greatest among his brethren, Simon the priest, son of Jochanan, restored the house of God and strengthened the temple. **2.** Under his leadership, the temple walls were fortified with strong turrets. **3.** A great reservoir was dug, a pool as vast as the sea. **4.** He defended his people against brigands (robbers) and fortified the city. **5.** He shone magnificently as he emerged from the sanctuary. **6.** Like a star amid clouds, like the full moon on a festival day, **7.** like the sun shining on the temple, like the rainbow after rain, **8.** like blossoms in spring, like a lily by a stream, like the great trees of Lebanon in summer. **9.** Like incense rising in the sacrificial fire, like a golden vessel adorned with precious stones, **10.** like a fruitful olive tree full of harvest, like a cypress tree towering against the sky. **11.** Clad in magnificent robes, he ascended the glorious altar, bringing majesty to the sanctuary. **12.** As he received offerings, his brethren surrounded him like a garland, like cedars of Lebanon in strength. **13.** All the sons of Aaron, in priestly robes, gathered around him, holding offerings to the LORD in the sight of Israel. **14.** After completing the altar service and arranging the sacrifices, **15.** he poured out wine at the altar as a sweet-smelling aroma to God. **16.** The priests blew their trumpets, reminding the people of the Most High. **17.** The people fell prostrate in worship before the LORD, the Holy One of Israel. **18.** Hymns and sweet praise filled the air. **19.** The people shouted with joy, praying to the Merciful One, as the high priest completed the services. **20.** He descended from the altar, raised his hands over Israel, and the blessing of the LORD rested upon his lips. **21.** The people fell prostrate again, receiving the blessing of the Most High. **22.** Bless the God of all, who forms men in their mother's womb and shapes them according to His will! **23.** May He grant you joy of heart and peace among you; **24.** may His goodness toward us endure in Israel, as long as the heavens are above. **25.** My soul despises two nations, and the third is not even a people: **26.** those who dwell in Seir, the Philistines, and the degenerate (corrupt) people of Shechem. **27.** I, Jesus, son of Eleazar, son of Sirach, wrote wise instructions and fitting proverbs from the depths of my understanding. **28.** Blessed is the man who meditates on these things, wise is the one who takes them to heart! **29.** If he practices them, he will overcome all challenges, for the fear of the LORD is his guiding light.

Chapter 51

1. I thank you, O God of my fathers, and praise you, O God my Savior! I will proclaim your name, for you are my refuge. **2.** You have helped me against my enemies, saved me from death, and kept me from the grave. **3.** You rescued me from slander, deceitful tongues, and false accusations. **4.** You freed me from traps set by those who sought my downfall. **5.** You saved me from many dangers, from the flames that surrounded me. **6.** You rescued me from the deepest pit, from lies and deceitful lips. **7.** From the arrows of dishonest tongues, I was near death, my soul sinking. **8.** I looked for help but found none. **9.** I remembered the mercies of the LORD, who saves those who take refuge in Him. **10.** I cried out from the depths of the earth, lifting my voice in desperate prayer. **11.** I called: O LORD, my Father, strength, and Savior, don't abandon me in trouble. **12.** I will always praise you and remain constant in prayer. **13.** The LORD heard my cry, saved me from evil, and preserved me in trouble. I give thanks and bless His holy name. **14.** When I was young, I sought wisdom. **15.** She came to me in her beauty, and I will pursue her forever. **16.** Like ripening grapes that bring joy, I walked the righteous path, familiar with wisdom from youth. **17.** In the short time I paid heed, I gained great instruction. **18.** I will offer praise to my teacher for the wisdom I've gained. **19.** I devoted myself to wisdom and continually pursued the good. **20.** I burned with desire for her, never tiring of praising her. I learned her mysteries. **21.** I purified my hands for her, drawing near in purity. In my first encounter, I gained understanding. **22.** My whole being was stirred as I learned from her, and she became my cherished possession. **23.** The LORD gave me the gift of speech, and my tongue will proclaim

His praises. **24.** Come, all untaught, and dwell in the house of instruction. **25.** How long will you lack wisdom's nourishment and suffer thirst for understanding? **26.** I speak of wisdom: acquire it freely, without cost. **27.** Submit to her yoke (teaching), that your minds may learn from her. She is near to those who seek her. **28.** See, I have labored little but found much. **29.** Seek wisdom, and you will gain riches beyond measure. **30.** Rejoice in God's mercy and praise Him without shame. **31.** Do your work in its season, and in time, God will reward you.

B. Books of new Testament

48 – Matthew

Chapter 1

1. The genealogy (family history) of Jesus Christ, the Son of David (King David of Israel), the Son of Abraham (the father of Israel): **2.** Abraham was the father of Isaac, Isaac the father of Jacob, and Jacob the father of Judah and his brothers. **3.** Judah was the father of Perez and Zerah by Tamar (Tamar was Judah's daughter-in-law), Perez the father of Hezron, and Hezron the father of Ram. **4.** Ram was the father of Amminadab, Amminadab the father of Nahshon, and Nahshon the father of Salmon. **5.** Salmon was the father of Boaz by Rahab (Rahab helped Israelite spies), Boaz the father of Obed by Ruth (Ruth was a Moabite widow), and Obed the father of Jesse. **6.** and Jesse the father of David, the king. David, the king, the father of Solomon by Bathsheba (wife of Uriah). **7.** Solomon was the father of Rehoboam, Rehoboam the father of Abijah, and Abijah the father of Asa. **8.** Asa was the father of Jehoshaphat, Jehoshaphat the father of Joram, and Joram the father of Uzziah. **9.** Uzziah was the father of Jotham, Jotham the father of Ahaz, and Ahaz the father of Hezekiah. **10.** Hezekiah was the father of Manasseh, Manasseh the father of Amon, and Amon the father of Josiah. **11.** Josiah the father of Jeconiah and his brothers when they were taken to Babylon (Babylon is an ancient empire in modern-day Iraq). **12.** After the exile to Babylon, Jeconiah the father of Shealtiel and Shealtiel the father of Zerubbabel (Zerubbabel led the return from exile). **13.** Zerubbabel the father of Abiud, Abiud the father of Eliakim, and Eliakim the father of Azor. **14.** Azor the father of Zadok, Zadok the father of Achim, and Achim the father of Eliud. **15.** Eliud the father of Eleazar, Eleazar the father of Matthan, and Matthan the father of Jacob. **16.** Jacob the father of Joseph, the husband of Mary, and Mary the mother of Jesus, called the Christ. **17.** There were fourteen generations from Abraham to David, fourteen from David to the exile, and fourteen from the exile to Christ. **18.** The birth of Jesus Christ occurred like this: Mary was engaged to Joseph, and before they came together, she was found to be pregnant by the Holy Spirit. **19.** Joseph, being a righteous man, decided to divorce her quietly and not publicly disgrace her. **20.** But an angel appeared to him in a dream, saying, "Joseph, son of David, do not fear to take Mary as your wife, for the child in her is from the Holy Spirit. **21.** She will bear a Son, and you will call Him Jesus (meaning 'The Lord saves'), for He will save His people from their sins." **22.** All this took place to fulfill the prophecy: **23.** "The virgin will conceive and bear a Son, and they will call Him Immanuel" (which means "God with us"). **24.** When Joseph woke up, he did as the angel commanded him, and took Mary as his wife. **25.** He did not have relations with her until after she gave birth to her firstborn Son. He named Him Jesus.

Chapter 2

1. After Jesus was born in the city of Bethlehem (a small city in the region of Judea) during the rule of King Herod (also known as Herod the Great, king over Judea), wise men from the East (likely scholars or astrologers from Persia or Babylon) arrived in Jerusalem. **2.** They asked, "Where is the child who has been born King of the Jews? We saw His star in the East and have come to worship Him." **3.** When King Herod heard this, he was troubled, and all of Jerusalem was also disturbed. **4.** He gathered together the principal preachers and the scribes (Jewish religious leaders and preceptors of the law) to find out where the Messiah (Christ) was predicted to be born. **5.** They told him, "In Bethlehem of Judea, because this is what the prophet wrote: **6.** 'But you, Bethlehem, in the land of Judah, are by no means the least among the rulers of Judah; for out of you will come a Leader who will shepherd My people Israel.'" **7.** Also, Herod secretly summoned the wise men and set up from them the exact time the star had appeared. **8.** He sent them to Bethlehem, saying, "Go and precisely search for the child.

When you find Him, let me know so that I, too, may go and worship Him." 9. After they had heard the king, they continued on their trip. The star they had seen in the East went ahead of them and stopped above the place where the child was. 10. When they saw the star, they were filled with great joy. 11. They entered the house, saw the child with His mother, Mary, and bowed down to worship Him. They presented Him with gifts of gold, frankincense, and myrrh (precious substances representing kingship, divinity, and sacrifice). 12. Subsequently, having been advised in a dream not to return to Herod, they took another route back to their own country. 13. When they had gone, an angel of the Lord appeared to Joseph in a dream and said, "Get up, take the child and His mother, and escape to Egypt (a nation south of Israel). Stay there until I tell you, because Herod is planning to search for the child to kill Him." 14. So Joseph got up, took the child and His mother, and left for Egypt during the night. 15. They remained there until Herod died, fulfilling the prophecy, "Out of Egypt I called My Son." 16. When Herod realized that the wise men had outsmarted him, he became furious and ordered the massacre of all male children in Bethlehem and the surrounding area who were two years old or younger, based on the time he'd learned from the wise men. 17. This fulfilled what was spoken by the prophet Jeremiah: 18. "A voice was heard in Ramah (a city in Israel), weeping and great mourning, Rachel (representing the mothers of Israel) weeping for her children, refusing to be comforted because they are no more." 19. After Herod's death, an angel of the Lord appeared in a dream to Joseph in Egypt, 20. saying, "Get up, take the child and His mother, and go back to the land of Israel, for those who were seeking the child's life are now dead." 21. So Joseph got up, took the child and His mother, and went back to Israel. 22. But when he heard that Archelaus (the son of Herod) was ruling in Judea, he was afraid to go there. After being advised in a dream, he withdrew to the region of Galilee (an area in northern Israel). 23. He settled in a town called Nazareth (a city in Galilee), thus fulfilling what was spoken by the prophets, "He will be called a Nazarene."

Chapter 3

1. During that time, John the Baptist (a prophet proclaiming a message in the wilderness) appeared, preaching in the wilderness of Judea (a region in Israel). 2. He was saying, "Turn from your sins, for the kingdom of heaven is near!" 3. This is the one that the prophet Isaiah (a prophet from the Old Testament) spoke of when he said: "A voice of someone calling out in the wilderness: 'Prepare the way for the Lord; make His paths straight.'" 4. John wore clothing made from camel's hair, with a leather belt around his waist, and his food consisted of locusts (insects) and wild honey. 5. People from Jerusalem, all of Judea (a region in Israel), and the entire area around the Jordan River went out to see him. 6. They were baptized by him in the Jordan River, openly confessing their sins. 7. When John noticed many Pharisees (a strict Jewish religious group) and Sadducees (another group of Jewish leaders) coming to be baptized, he said to them, "You brood of vipers (meaning deceitful or dangerous people)! Who warned you to flee from the wrath (God's punishment) to come? 8. Produce fruit that shows true repentance (demonstrate real change in your actions), and do not think to say to yourselves, 'We have Abraham as our father.' I tell you that God is able to create descendants for Abraham from these stones. 9. The ax is already set at the base of the trees, and every tree that does not produce good fruit will be cut down and thrown into the fire. 10. I baptize you with water as a sign of repentance, but one who is coming after me is more powerful than I am, whose sandals I am not worthy to carry. He will baptize you with the Holy Spirit and with fire. 11. He holds a winnowing fork in His hand (a tool for separating grain), and He will thoroughly clear His threshing floor (an area where grain is separated from chaff). He will gather His wheat (useful grain) into the barn, but the chaff (useless husks or waste) He will burn with a fire that cannot be extinguished." 12. Then Jesus traveled from Galilee (a northern region in Israel) to the Jordan River to be baptized by John. 13. John attempted to stop Him, saying, "I need to be baptized by You, and yet You come to me?" 14. Jesus answered, "Allow it to be so now; this is necessary to fulfill all righteousness." Then John agreed. 15. As soon as Jesus was baptized, He came up out of the water, and suddenly the heavens opened. 16. He saw the Spirit of God descending like a dove and resting upon Him. 17. A voice from heaven then declared, "This is My beloved Son, in whom I take great pleasure."

Chapter 4

1. Then Jesus was led by the Spirit (God's guiding presence) into the wilderness to be tempted by the devil (Satan, the enemy of God). 2. After fasting for forty days and forty nights, He was hungry. 3. The tempter (Satan) came to Him and said, "If You are the Son of God, tell these stones to become bread." 4. But Jesus replied, "It is written: 'Man shall not live by bread alone, but by every word that comes from the mouth of God.'" 5. Then the devil took Him to the holy city (Jerusalem) and set Him on the highest point of the temple. 6. He said to Him, "If You are the Son of God, throw Yourself down. For it is written: 'He will command His angels concerning You,' and 'They will lift You up in their hands so that You will not strike Your foot against a stone.'" 7. Jesus answered, "It is also written: 'You shall not put the Lord your God to the test.'" 8. Again, the devil took Him to a very high mountain and showed Him all the kingdoms of the world and their splendor (great beauty or magnificence). 9. And he said to Him, "All this I will give You, if You will bow down and worship me." 10. Jesus said to him, "Away from me, Satan! For it is written: 'Worship the Lord your God, and serve Him only.'" 11. Then the devil left Him, and angels came and attended to Him. 12. When Jesus heard that John had been put in prison, He went to Galilee. 13. Leaving Nazareth, He settled in Capernaum (a town by the Sea of Galilee), in the regions of Zebulun and Naphtali, 14. to fulfill what was spoken through the prophet Isaiah: 15. "Land of Zebulun and land of Naphtali, the way of the sea, beyond the Jordan, Galilee of the Gentiles (non-Jews): 16. The people who were living in darkness have seen a great light; on those living in the land of the shadow of death, a light has dawned." 17. From that time, Jesus began to preach, "Repent, for the kingdom of heaven is near." 18. As Jesus walked by the Sea of Galilee, He saw two brothers, Simon (called Peter) and Andrew, his brother, casting a net into the sea, for they were fishermen. 19. Jesus said to them, "Come, follow Me, and I will make you fishers of men." 20. Immediately, they left their nets and followed Him. 21. Going on from there, He saw two other brothers, James the son of Zebedee and his brother John, in the boat with their father Zebedee, preparing their nets. He called them, 22. and immediately they left the boat and their father and followed Him. 23. Jesus went throughout all Galilee, teaching in their synagogues (places of Jewish worship), preaching the good news of the kingdom, and healing all kinds of sickness and disease among the people. 24. News about Him spread throughout Syria (region north of Israel), and they brought to Him all who were ill with various diseases and suffering severe pain, the demon-possessed, those having seizures, and the paralyzed, and He healed them. 25. Large crowds followed Him from Galilee, the Decapolis (ten cities), Jerusalem, Judea, and the region beyond the Jordan.

Chapter 5

1. When Jesus saw the crowds, He went up on a mountain, sat down, and His disciples came to Him. 2. And He began to teach them, saying: 3. "Blessed (happy, favored) are the poor in spirit (humble), for theirs is the kingdom of heaven. 4. Blessed are those who mourn (feel sorrow), for they will be comforted. 5. Blessed are the meek (gentle, humble), for they will inherit (receive) the earth. 6. Blessed are those who hunger and thirst for righteousness (desire justice), for they will be filled. 7. Blessed are the merciful (compassionate, forgiving), for they will be shown mercy. 8. Blessed are the pure in heart (sincere, genuine), for they will see God. 9. Blessed are the peacemakers (those who make peace), for they will be called children of God. 10. Blessed are those who are persecuted (treated unfairly) for righteousness' sake, for theirs is the kingdom of heaven. 11. Blessed are you when people insult (speak badly of) and persecute (oppress) you, and falsely say all kinds of evil against you because of Me. 12. Rejoice and be glad, for your reward in heaven is great; for in the same way they persecuted the prophets who were before you. 13. "You are the salt (preserver) of the earth. But if salt loses its flavor (strength), it is good for nothing except to be thrown out and trampled (stepped on) by men. 14. You are the light (guide) of the world. A city on a hill cannot be hidden. 15. Neither do people light a lamp and put it under a basket; instead, they put it on a stand, and it gives light to everyone in the house. 16. Let your light shine before others, that they may see your good deeds and

glorify your Father in heaven. **17.** "Do not think that I have come to abolish (end) the Law or the Prophets. I have not come to abolish them but to fulfill (complete) them. **18.** For truly I tell you, until heaven and earth pass away, not the smallest letter or the least stroke of a pen will by any means disappear from the Law until everything is accomplished. **19.** Therefore, anyone who breaks (violates) one of the least of these commandments and teaches others to do the same will be called least (small) in the kingdom of heaven; but whoever practices (obeys) and teaches them will be called great in the kingdom of heaven. **20.** For I tell you that unless your righteousness (correct living) surpasses that of the Pharisees (religious leaders) and the teachers of the law, you will certainly not enter the kingdom of heaven. **21.** "You have heard that it was said, 'You shall not murder.' But I tell you that anyone who is angry (rage) with a brother or sister will be subject to judgment. **22.** Again, anyone who calls their brother or sister, 'Raca' (foolish, empty-headed) is answerable to the court; and anyone who says, 'You fool!' will be in danger of hell fire. **23.** Therefore, if you are offering your gift at the altar (place of worship) and there remember that your brother or sister has something against you, **24.** leave your gift there in front of the altar. First go and be reconciled (make peace) to them; then come and offer your gift. **25.** Settle (resolve) matters quickly with your adversary (opponent) who is taking you to court. Do it while you are still together on the way, or your adversary may hand you over to the judge, and the judge may hand you over to the officer, and you may be thrown into prison. **26.** Truly, I tell you, you will not get out until you have paid the last penny. **27.** "You have heard that it was said, 'You shall not commit adultery.' **28.** But I tell you that anyone who looks at a woman lustfully (with wrong desire) has already committed adultery with her in his heart. **29.** If your right eye causes you to stumble (sin), gouge it out and throw it away. It is better for you to lose one part of your body than for your whole body to be thrown into hell (eternal punishment). **30.** And if your right hand causes you to stumble, cut it off and throw it away. It is better for you to lose one part of your body than for your whole body to go into hell. **31.** "It has been said, 'Anyone who divorces his wife must give her a certificate of divorce.' **32.** But I tell you that anyone who divorces his wife, except for sexual immorality (unfaithfulness), makes her the victim of adultery, and anyone who marries a divorced woman commits adultery. **33.** "Again, you have heard that it was said, 'Do not break your oath, but fulfill to the Lord the oaths you have made.' **34.** But I tell you, do not swear (make vows) at all: either by heaven, for it is God's throne, **35.** or by the earth, for it is His footstool (place to rest His feet), **36.** or by Jerusalem, for it is the city of the great King. **37.** And do not swear by your head, for you cannot make even one hair white or black. **38.** All you need to say is simply 'Yes' or 'No'; anything beyond this comes from the evil one. **39.** "You have heard that it was said, 'An eye for an eye, and a tooth for a tooth.' **40.** But I tell you, do not resist an evil person. If anyone slaps you on the right cheek, turn to them the other cheek also. **41.** And if anyone wants to sue you and take your shirt, hand over your coat as well. **42.** If anyone forces you to go one mile, go with them two miles. **43.** Give to the one who asks you, and do not turn away from the one who wants to borrow from you. **44.** "You have heard that it was said, 'Love your neighbor and hate your enemy.' **45.** But I tell you, love your enemies, bless those who curse (speak badly of) you, do good to those who hate (despise) you, and pray for those who persecute (mistreat) you, **46.** that you may be children of your Father in heaven. He causes His sun to rise on the evil and the good, and sends rain on the righteous and the unrighteous." **46.** If you love those who love you, what reward will you get? Even tax collectors (people who collect taxes) do that. **47.** And if you greet (welcome) only your brothers, what are you doing more than others? Even pagans (non-believers) do that. **48.** Be perfect (complete, mature), therefore, as your Father in heaven is perfect.

Chapter 6

1. "Be cautious (careful) not to perform your acts of charity in front of others just to be noticed by them. If you do, you will not receive a reward from your Father in heaven. **2.** So when you give to the poor, don't announce it with trumpets, as the hypocrites (pretenders) do in the synagogues and on the streets to gain praise from people. Truly, I tell you, they have already received their reward. **3.** But when you give to charity, don't let your left hand know what your right hand is doing, **4.** so that your giving may remain secret; and your Father, who sees what is done in secret, will reward you openly. **5.** "When you pray, don't be like the hypocrites, who love to pray standing in synagogues and on street corners to be seen by others. Truly, I tell you, they have their reward. **6.** But when you pray, go into your room, close the door, and pray to your Father who is in the secret place; and your Father, who sees in secret, will reward you publicly. **7.** And when you pray, don't use empty words (meaningless repetitions) as the pagans (non-believers) do, thinking they will be heard because of their many words. **8.** Do not be like them, for your Father knows what you need before you even ask Him. **9.** This is how you should pray: Our Father in heaven, Hallowed (holy) be Your name. **10.** Your kingdom come, Your will be done, on earth as it is in heaven. **11.** Give us today our daily bread. **12.** Forgive us our debts (wrongs), as we forgive our debtors (those who owe us). **13.** And do not lead us into temptation, but deliver us from the evil one. For Yours is the kingdom, and the power, and the glory forever. Amen. **14.** "If you forgive others their wrongs (trespasses), your heavenly Father will also forgive you. **15.** But if you do not forgive others, neither will your Father forgive you. **16.** "When you fast (abstain from food for spiritual reasons), don't look gloomy like the hypocrites, who disfigure (make unattractive) their faces so that others will see they are fasting. Truly, I tell you, they have already received their reward. **17.** But when you fast, anoint (apply oil to) your head and wash your face, **18.** so that it will not be obvious to others that you are fasting, but only to your Father, who sees what is done in secret; and your Father, who sees in secret, will reward you openly. **19.** "Do not store up treasures for yourselves on earth, where moth and rust destroy, and where thieves break in and steal. **20.** Instead, store up treasures for yourselves in heaven, where moth and rust do not destroy, and where thieves do not break in and steal. **21.** For where your treasure is, there your heart will be also. **22.** "The eye is the lamp (source of light) of the body. If your eye is healthy (good), your whole body will be full of light. **23.** But if your eye is unhealthy (bad), your whole body will be full of darkness. If then the light within you is actually darkness, how great is that darkness! **24.** "No one can serve two masters. Either he will hate the one and love the other, or he will be devoted (loyal) to the one and despise (hate) the other. You cannot serve both God and mammon (wealth, material possessions). **25.** "Therefore I tell you, do not worry about your life, what you will eat or drink, or about your body, what you will wear. Isn't life more than food and the body more than clothing? **26.** Look at the birds of the air. They do not sow (plant seeds), reap (harvest), or gather into barns, yet your heavenly Father feeds them. Are you not of much more value than they? **27.** Which of you by worrying can add even a single hour to your life? **28.** And why do you worry about clothing? Consider the lilies (flowers) of the field, how they grow. They do not labor (work hard) or spin (make cloth), **29.** yet I tell you that not even Solomon, in all his glory, was dressed like one of these. **30.** If God so clothes the grass of the field, which is here today and thrown into the fire tomorrow, will He not much more clothe you, O you of little faith? **31.** So do not worry, saying, 'What will we eat?' or 'What will we drink?' or 'What will we wear?' **32.** For the Gentiles (non-Jews) seek all these things, and your heavenly Father knows that you need them. **33.** But seek first the kingdom of God and His righteousness, and all these things will be given to you as well. **34.** Therefore, do not worry about tomorrow, for tomorrow will worry about itself. Each day has enough trouble of its own."

Chapter 7

1. "Do not judge others, or you too will be judged. **2.** For the judgment you use will be applied to you, and the measure (extent) you use will be measured back to you. **3.** Why do you focus on the small speck (tiny particle) in your brother's eye, but ignore the large plank (log) in your own eye? **4.** How can you say to your brother, 'Let me help you remove the speck from your eye,' when there is a plank in your own eye? **5.** You hypocrite (pretender)! First, remove the plank from your own eye, and then you will see clearly to remove the speck from your brother's eye. **6.** Do not give what is sacred to dogs (unholy people), nor throw your pearls (valuable things) to pigs, lest they trample (crush) them underfoot and turn to attack you. **7.** "Ask, and it will be given to you; seek, and you will find; knock, and it will be opened to you. **8.** For everyone who asks receives, and the one who seeks finds, and to the one who knocks, the door will be opened. **9.** Which of you, if your son asks for bread, will give him a stone? **10.** Or if he asks for a fish, will give him a snake? **11.** If you, though evil (sinful), know how to give good gifts to your children, how much more will your Father in heaven give good things to those who ask Him! **12.** So in everything, do to others what you would have them do to you. This sums up the Law and the Prophets. **13.** "Enter through the narrow gate, for wide is the gate and broad is the way that leads to destruction, and many enter through it. **14.** But small is the gate and narrow the way that leads to life, and only a few find it. **15.** "Watch out for false prophets. They come to you in sheep's clothing, but inwardly they are ravenous wolves (dangerous enemies). **16.** By their fruits (actions) you will recognize them. Do people pick grapes from thornbushes, or figs from thistles? **17.** Likewise, every good tree bears good fruit, but a bad tree bears bad fruit. **18.** A good tree cannot bear bad fruit, and a bad tree cannot bear good fruit. **19.** Every tree that does not bear good fruit is cut down and thrown into the fire. **20.** Thus, by their fruits, you will recognize them. **21.** "Not everyone who says to Me, 'Lord, Lord,' will enter the kingdom of heaven, but only the one who does the will of My Father in heaven. **22.** Many will say to Me on that day, 'Lord, Lord, did we not prophesy (predict future events) in Your name, and in Your name drive out demons, and in Your name perform many miracles?' **23.** Then I will tell them plainly, 'I never knew you. Away from Me, you evildoers (those who break God's law)!' **24.** "Therefore, everyone who hears these words of Mine and acts on them is like a wise man who built his house on the rock. **25.** The rain came down, the floods rose, and the winds blew and beat against that house; yet it did not fall, because it had its foundation on the rock. **26.** But everyone who hears these words of Mine and does not act on them is like a foolish man who built his house on sand. **27.** The rain came down, the floods rose, and the winds blew and beat against that house, and it fell with a great crash." **28.** When Jesus had finished saying these things, the crowds were amazed at His teaching, **29.** because He taught as one who had authority, and not as their teachers of the law (scribes).

Chapter 8

1. When Jesus came down from the mountain, huge crowds followed Him. **2.** A man with leprosy (a pores and skin disease) approached Him, worshiped Him, and stated, "Lord, if you are willing, you can make me clean." **3.** Jesus reached out His hand, touched him, and said, "I am willing; be cleansed." Right away, his leprosy became healed. **4.** Jesus told him, "Don't tell anyone, but go to the priest, and provide the gift Moses commanded as a sworn statement to them." **5.** When Jesus entered Capernaum (a town close to the northern shore of Galilee), a Roman officer (centurion, a commander of soldiers) got came to Him, pleading, **6.** "Lord, my servant is at home, paralyzed and suffering terribly." **7.** Jesus replied, "I am able to come and heal him." **8.** The centurion spoke back, "Lord, I'm not worthy to have you come under my roof. But just say the word, and my servant will be healed. **9.** For I am a man under authority, with soldiers under me. I say to one, 'Go,' and he goes; and to another, 'Come,' and he comes; and to my servant, 'Do this,' and he does it." **10.** When Jesus heard this, He marveled (was amazed) and said to those following Him, "Truly, I tell you, I have not found such great faith even in Israel! **11.** I tell you, many will come from the east and the west and will sit down with Abraham, Isaac, and Jacob in the kingdom of heaven. **12.** But the children of the kingdom (the Israelites) will be thrown out into outer darkness, where there will be weeping and gnashing of teeth." **13.** Jesus told the centurion, "Go, it will be done just as you believed." And his servant was healed that very hour. **14.** When Jesus entered Peter's house, He saw Peter's mother-in-law lying sick with a fever. **15.** He touched her hand, and the fever left her. She got up and began to serve them. **16.** That night, many demon-possessed people were brought to Him, and He drove out the spirits with a word and healed all the sick, **17.** fulfilling what was spoken through the prophet Isaiah: "He took our infirmities and bore our sicknesses." **18.** When Jesus saw the crowd around Him, He gave orders to cross to the other side of the lake. **19.** Then a teacher of the law came to Him and said, "Teacher, I will follow You wherever You go." **20.** Jesus replied, "Foxes have dens, and birds have nests, but the Son of Man has no place to lay His head." **21.** Another disciple said to Him, "Lord, first let me go and bury my father." **22.** But Jesus said to him, "Follow Me, and let the dead bury their own dead." **23.** Then He got into a boat, and His disciples followed Him. **24.** Suddenly, a violent storm came up on the lake, so that the boat was being swamped by the waves. But Jesus was sleeping. **25.** The disciples woke Him, saying, "Lord, save us! We are going to drown!" **26.** He replied, "You of little faith, why are you so afraid?" Then He got up and rebuked the winds and the waves, and it was completely calm. **27.** The men were amazed and asked, "What kind of man is this? Even the winds and the waves obey Him!" **28.** When He arrived at the other side, in the region of the Gergesenes (a place), two demon-possessed men coming from the tombs met Him. They were so violent that no one could pass that way. **29.** They cried out, "What do You want with us, Son of God? Have You come here to torment us before the appointed time?" **30.** A large herd of pigs was feeding some distance away from them. **31.** The demons begged Jesus, "If You drive us out, send us into the herd of pigs." **32.** He said to them, "Go!" So they came out and went into the pigs. And the whole herd rushed down the steep bank into the lake and drowned. **33.** Those who were tending the pigs ran off and went into the city, reporting everything, including what had happened to the demon-possessed men. **34.** The whole city came out to meet Jesus, and when they saw Him, they pleaded with Him to leave their region.

Chapter 9

1. Jesus entered a boat, crossed over, and arrived at His birthplace. **2.** They introduced a paralyzed joe lying on a mattress. Seeing their faith, Jesus said to him," Son, take coronary heart; your sins are forgiven." **3.** a number of the scribes conception," This man is cussing!". **4.** Jesus knew their studies and stated," Why do you questionable wrong on your hearts? **5.** which is less complicated, to mention' Your sins are forgiven,' or to mention' arise and walk'? **6.** but to show that the Son of man has authority (electricity) in the world to forgive sins," He stated to the paralyzed," stand up, take your bed, and pass domestic." **7.** the person rose and went domestic. **8.** the group changed into amazed and praised God, who had given similar energy to guys. **9.** As Jesus passed through, He noticed a person named Matthew sitting at the duty office. He said," observe Me." Matthew at formerly got up and accompanied Him. **10.** whilst Jesus was ingesting at Matthew's hearthstone, numerous duty collectors and wrongdoers came and ate with Him and His votaries. **11.** The Pharisees asked His votaries," Why does your coach consume with duty collectors and wrongdoers?" **12.** Jesus heard this and stated," wholesome humans don't need a health guru, but the sick do. **13.** go and study what this indicates' I ask mercy, not immolate.' I did now not come to call the righteous, but wrongdoers to penitence." **14.** also John's votaries came to Jesus, asking," Why can we and the Pharisees rapid-fire frequently, but Your votaries don't gormandize?" **15.** Jesus responded," Can the musketeers of the bride mourn whilst he's with them? but the time will come whilst the bride(Jesus) could be taken down, after which they'll speedy. **16.** no person patches an old garment with new cloth, for the patch will pull down and make the gash worse. **17.** Likewise, new wine is not deposited into quaint wineskins, for the wineskins will wreck and the wine could be revealed. New wine must be deposited into new wineskins." **18.** "While he was speaking, a leader of the synagogue (synagogue leader: a person in charge of the synagogue's affairs) came and knelt before him, saying, 'My daughter has just passed away (passed away: died). But come and lay your hand on her, and she will be restored to life (restored to life: brought back to life).' **19.** Jesus got up and followed him, and His votaries went with Him. **20.** simply also, a lady who were bleeding for twelve times touched the verge of His garment. **21.** She notion," If I just communicate His garment, I could be healed." **22.** Jesus came and noticed her." Take heart, son; your faith has healed you." And the lady changed into healed at that moment. **23.** whilst Jesus arrived at the sovereign 's house and saw the flute players and the noisy crowd wailing, **24.** He said," go down, for the girl isn't dead still asleep." the gang laughed at Him. **25.** After putting them out of doors, He went by, took her with the aid of the hand, and the womanish arose. **26.** information of this unfold during the region. **27.** As Jesus left that vicinity, eyeless guys accompanied Him, calling out," Son of David (David was the finest king of Israel, from Bethlehem, now Israel), have mercy on us!" **28.** when He entered the house, the eyeless guys came to Him. Jesus requested," Do you believe i'll do that?"." yes, Lord," they replied. **29.** He touched their eyes and said," in keeping with your faith, allow it be completed to you." **30.** Their eyes have been opened, and Jesus advised them brutally," See that nothing is apprehensive of roughly this." **31.** Still they went out and unfold the news roughly Him each over the place. **32.** As they went out, a mute joe, demon- held, came brought to Jesus. **33.** While the demon turned into solid out, the mute spoke. the group was surprised, pronouncing," nothing like this has ever been seen in Israel!" **34.** but the Pharisees said," He casts out demons by way of the sovereign of demons." **35.** "Jesus journeyed (traveled) through every town and village, teaching (instructing) in the synagogues (Jewish places of worship), spreading the message of the kingdom, and curing (healing or making healthy) every kind of illness and disease."**36.** while He noticed the crowds, He'd compassion on them, because they had been sick and haphazard, like lamb without a cowgirl. **37.** He said to His votaries," The crop is considerable, but the workers are many. **38.** Ask the Lord of the crop to shoot workers into His crop."

Chapter 10

1. Jesus called His twelve disciples (students or followers) to Himself and gave them authority over unclean spirits (evil or demonic spirits), to cast them out, and to heal every kind of sickness and disease. **2.** The names of the twelve apostles (special messengers or sent ones) are: Simon, also called Peter, and his brother Andrew; James, the son of Zebedee, and his brother John; **3.** Philip and Bartholomew; Thomas and Matthew, the tax collector (a person who collected taxes for the Roman government); James, the son of Alphaeus, and Lebbaeus, also known as Thaddaeus; **4.** Simon the Zealot (a person who was passionate about the Jewish law), and Judas Iscariot, who later betrayed Him. **5.** Jesus sent these twelve out, telling them: "Do not go among the Gentiles (non-Jews) or enter any city of the Samaritans (a group of people who were partly Jewish and partly Gentile), **6.** but go instead to the lost sheep (those who are spiritually lost) of the house of Israel (the Jewish people). **7.** As you go, preach this message: 'The kingdom of heaven is near.' **8.** Heal the sick, cleanse those with leprosy (a contagious skin disease), raise the dead, and cast out demons. Freely you have received, so freely give. **9.** Do not take gold, silver, or copper (coins) for your belts (money pouches); **10.** do not take a travel bag, extra clothes, sandals, or a staff (walking stick). A worker deserves to be fed. **11.** When you enter a city or village, find out who is worthy (receptive or open to your message) and stay with them until you leave. **12.** When you enter a house, greet the household. **13.** If the house is worthy, let your peace (blessing or goodwill) rest on it; but if it is not worthy, let your peace return to you. **14.** If anyone does not receive you or listen to your words, shake the dust off your feet (a gesture of leaving) when you leave that house or town. **15.** I tell you the truth, it will be more tolerable for the land of Sodom and Gomorrah (two cities destroyed by God for their wickedness) on the Day of Judgment than for that town! **16.** I am sending you out like sheep among wolves (vulnerable or in danger). Therefore, be as wise as serpents (cunning or clever) and as innocent as doves (harmless and pure). **17.** Be aware, for they will hand you over to councils (Jewish courts), and they will beat you in their synagogues (Jewish places of worship). **18.** You will be brought before governors and kings for My sake, as a testimony (witness) to them and to the Gentiles. **19.** When they arrest you, do not worry about what to say or how to say it. At that moment, the Spirit of your Father (God) will give you the words to speak. **20.** For it will not be you speaking, but the Spirit of your Father speaking through you. **21.** Brother will betray brother to death, and a father will betray his child; children will rise up against their parents and have them put to death. **22.** You will be hated by everyone because of My name, but the one who stands firm (endures) to the end will be saved. **23.** When they persecute you (harass or mistreat you) in one city, flee to another. Truly, I tell you, you will not have reached all the towns of Israel before the Son of Man (Jesus) comes. **24.** A disciple (student or follower) is not above his teacher, nor a servant (worker) above his master. **25.** It is enough for the disciple to be like his teacher, and the servant like his master. If they have called the master of the house Beelzebul (a name for a demon), how much more will they call those of His household! **26.** So do not be afraid of them, for there is nothing hidden that will not be revealed, or concealed that will not be known. **27.** What I tell you in the dark (secretly), speak in the light (openly); and what you hear whispered, proclaim from the rooftops (publicly). **28.** Do not fear those who can kill the body but cannot kill the soul. Rather, fear God, who can destroy both soul and body in hell

(eternal separation from God). **29.** Are not two sparrows (small birds) sold for a penny? Yet not one of them falls to the ground apart from your Father's will. **30.** And even the very hairs on your head are all numbered. **31.** So don't be afraid; you are worth more than many sparrows. **32.** Whoever acknowledges (confesses) Me before others, I will also acknowledge before My Father in heaven. **33.** But whoever denies Me before others, I will also deny before My Father in heaven. **34.** Do not think that I have come to bring peace on earth. I did not come to bring peace, but a sword (division). **35.** I have come to turn a man against his father, a daughter against her mother, and a daughter-in-law against her mother-in-law; **36.** a man's enemies will be the members of his own household. **37.** Anyone who loves father or mother more than Me is not worthy of Me; anyone who loves son or daughter more than Me is not worthy of Me. **38.** Whoever does not take up their cross (endure suffering or sacrifice for My sake) and follow Me is not worthy of Me. **39.** Whoever finds their life will lose it, and whoever loses their life for My sake will find it. **40.** Whoever receives (welcomes) you receives Me, and whoever receives Me receives the One who sent Me (God). **41.** Whoever receives a prophet (messenger of God) as a prophet will receive a prophet's reward. Whoever receives a righteous person (a holy person) as a righteous person will receive a righteous person's reward. **42.** And if anyone gives even a cup of cold water to one of these little ones (humble believers) because they are My disciple, truly, I tell you, that person will not lose their reward.

Chapter 11

1. After Jesus finished instructing His twelve acolytes, He traveled to teach and sermonize in their megalopolises. **2.** When John heard about the plant of Christ in captivity, he sent two disciples **3.** To ask, "Are You the Coming One (the Messiah), or should we expect someone else?" **4.** Jesus replied, "Go and tell John what you hear and see: **5.** The sightless see, the lame walk, rejects are sanctified, the deaf hear, the dead are raised, and the poor have the good news preached to them. **6.** Blessed is anyone who does not stumble because of Me." **7.** As they left, Jesus spoke to the crowds about John: "What did you go to see in the wilderness? A fragile reed shaken by the wind? **8.** Did you go to see someone in soft clothes? Those who wear fine clothes live in royal palaces. **9.** Did you go to see a prophet? Yes, and more than a prophet. **10.** This is the one spoken of: 'I will send My messenger ahead of You, who will prepare Your way.' **11.** Truly, among those born of women, no one is greater than John the Baptist; yet the least in the kingdom of heaven is greater than he. **12.** From the time of John, the kingdom of heaven suffers violence, and the violent take it by force. **13.** All the prophets and the law prophesied until John. **14.** If you're willing to accept it, he is the Elijah who was to come. **15.** Whoever has ears, let them hear! **16.** To what can I compare this generation? They are like children in the marketplace calling to others, **17.** saying, 'We played the flute for you, and you did not dance; we sang a sad song, and you did not mourn.' **18.** John came neither eating nor drinking, and they said, 'He has a demon.' **19.** The Son of Man came eating and drinking, and they said, 'Look, a glutton, a drunkard, a friend of tax collectors and sinners!' But wisdom is proven right by her deeds." **20.** Jesus rebuked the cities where He performed miracles because they did not repent: **21.** "Woe to you, Chorazin! Woe to you, Bethsaida! For if the miracles done in you had been done in Tyre and Sidon, they would have repented long ago. **22.** It will be more bearable for Tyre and Sidon on the judgment day than for you. **23.** And you, Capernaum, will you be exalted to heaven? No, you will go down to Hades. If Sodom had witnessed the same miracles, it would have remained until today. **24.** It will be more tolerable for Sodom than for you." **25.** At that time, Jesus said, "I thank You, Father, Lord of heaven and earth, because You have hidden these things from the wise and learned and revealed them to little children. **26.** Yes, Father, for this was Your good pleasure. **27.** All things have been entrusted to Me by My Father. No one knows the Son except the Father, and no one knows the Father except the Son and those to whom the Son chooses to reveal Him. **28.** Come to Me, all you who are weary and burdened, and I will give you rest. **29.** Take My yoke upon you and learn from Me, for I am gentle and humble in heart, and you will find rest for your souls. **30.** For My yoke is easy and My burden is light."

Chapter 12

1. At that time, Jesus walked through grainfields on the Sabbath (the holy day of rest). His disciples became hungry and began plucking heads of grain to eat. 2. The Pharisees (religious leaders) saw this and said to Him, "Look, Your disciples are doing what is unlawful on the Sabbath!" 3. But Jesus replied, "Have you not read what David did when he and his men were hungry? 4. He entered the house of God and ate the showbread (sacred bread, only for priests), which was not lawful for him to eat or for his companions, but only for the priests." 5. Or have you not read in the law that the priests in the temple break the Sabbath, yet they are innocent? 6. But I tell you, One greater than the temple is here. 7. If you had understood the meaning of 'I desire mercy, not sacrifice,' you would not have condemned the innocent. 8. For the Son of Man is Lord even of the Sabbath." 9. Then He left and went into their synagogue. 10. There was a man with a withered (shrunken, damaged) hand. They asked Jesus, "Is it lawful to heal on the Sabbath?"—hoping to accuse Him. 11. Jesus answered, "If any of you has a sheep and it falls into a pit on the Sabbath, will you not lift it out? 12. How much more valuable is a person than a sheep! Therefore, it is lawful to do good on the Sabbath." 13. Then He said to the man, "Stretch out your hand." The man did, and it was completely restored, as healthy as the other. 14. The Pharisees left and began plotting how they might destroy Him. 15. But when Jesus became aware of this, He withdrew, and large crowds followed Him, and He healed all of them. 16. Yet He warned them not to make Him known, 17. to fulfill what was spoken by the prophet Isaiah: 18. "Here is My Servant whom I have chosen, My Beloved, in whom I am well pleased. I will put My Spirit upon Him, and He will proclaim justice to the Gentiles. 19. He will not quarrel or cry out, and no one will hear His voice in the streets. 20. He will not break a bruised reed (a fragile person) or quench a smoldering wick (a faint hope), until He brings justice to victory. 21. And in His name the Gentiles will place their hope." 22. Then they brought a demon-possessed man who was blind and mute, and He healed him so that the man could both speak and see. 23. The crowds were amazed and said, "Could this be the Son of David?" (A title for the Messiah) 24. When the Pharisees heard this, they said, "This man casts out demons only by Beelzebub (a name for Satan, the prince of demons)." 25. Knowing their thoughts, Jesus said, "Every kingdom divided against itself is brought to desolation, and every city or house divided against itself will not stand. 26. If Satan casts out Satan, he is divided against himself. How then will his kingdom stand? 27. If I cast out demons by Beelzebub, by whom do your sons cast them out? Therefore, they will be your judges. 28. But if I cast out demons by the Spirit of God, then the kingdom of God has come upon you. 29. Or how can someone enter a strong man's house and steal his goods unless he first ties up the strong man? Then he can rob his house. 30. Whoever is not with Me is against Me, and whoever does not gather with Me scatters." 31. Therefore, I tell you, every sin and blasphemy (speaking against God) will be forgiven, but the blasphemy against the Spirit will not be forgiven. 32. Anyone who speaks against the Son of Man (Jesus) can be forgiven, but anyone who speaks against the Holy Spirit will not be forgiven, neither in this age nor in the age to come. 33. Either make the tree good and its fruit good, or make the tree bad and its fruit bad; a tree is known by its fruit. 34. You brood of vipers (evil people), how can you, being evil, speak good things? For out of the abundance of the heart, the mouth speaks. 35. A good person brings forth good from the good treasure in their heart, and an evil person brings forth evil from the evil stored in their heart. 36. I tell you, people will give an account for every careless word they speak on the Day of Judgment. 37. For by your words you will be justified, and by your words, you will be condemned." 38. Some of the scribes and Pharisees answered, "Teacher, we want to see a sign from You." 39. But He answered, "An evil and adulterous (unfaithful) generation seeks a sign, and no sign will be given except the sign of the prophet Jonah. 40. For just as Jonah was three days and three nights in the belly of the great fish, so will the Son of Man be three days and three nights in the heart of the earth. 41. The people of Nineveh (capital of Assyria) will rise up at the judgment and condemn this generation, because they repented at the preaching of Jonah, and now something greater than Jonah is here. 42. The Queen of the South (Sheba) will rise up at the judgment and condemn this generation, for she came from the ends of the earth to hear the wisdom of Solomon; and now something greater than Solomon is here." 43. When an unclean spirit leaves a person, it wanders through dry places, seeking rest, but finds none. 44. It says, "I will return to my house from which I came." When it returns, it finds it empty, swept, and put in order. 45. Then it goes and brings seven other spirits more evil than itself, and they enter and live there. The final state of that person is worse than the first. This will be the case for this wicked generation." 46. While He was still speaking to the crowds, His mother and brothers stood outside, wanting to speak with Him. 47. Someone told Him, "Look, Your mother and Your brothers are standing outside, desiring to speak with You." 48. But He answered, "Who is My mother, and who are My brothers?" 49. And He stretched out His hand toward His disciples and said, "Here are My mother and My brothers! 50. For whoever does the will of My Father in heaven is My brother, sister, and mother."

Chapter 13

1. At the identical day, Jesus left the house and sat by means of the sea. 2. A large crowd accrued round Him, so He were given into a ship and sat. The human beings stood on the shore. 3. Then He spoke many things to them in parables (memories with hidden meanings), saying: "Pay attention, a farmer went out to plant seeds. 4. As he sowed, some seeds fell along the course, and the birds got here and ate them up. 5. Some fell on rocky floor, wherein the soil became shallow, and they sprang up speedy, however when the sun rose, they have been scorched and withered because they had no deep roots. 6. Other seeds fell amongst thorns, and the thorns grew up and choked the flora. 7. But some seeds fell on excellent soil, and they produced a crop—some a hundredfold, a few sixty, a few thirty. 8. Whoever has ears to hear, let them pay attention!" 9. The disciples got here to Jesus and requested, "Why do You talk to the humans in parables?" 10. He spoke back, "Because you are given to recognize the secrets and techniques of the kingdom of heaven, but to them it is not given. 11. For whoever has, greater might be given, and they will have an abundance; however whoever does not have, even what they've may be taken away. 12. That is why I communicate to them in parables: though seeing they do not see, and though hearing they do not hear or apprehend. 13. In them is fulfilled the prophecy of Isaiah: 'You may pay attention but by no means apprehend; you may see but never perceive. 14. For this people's coronary heart has turn out to be calloused (part of body that is hardened), they infrequently listen with their ears, and they have closed their eyes. In any other case, they may see with their eyes, hear with their ears, apprehend with their hearts, and turn, and I'd heal them.' 15. But blessed are your eyes due to the fact they see, and your ears due to the fact they hear. 16. Certainly I tell you, many prophets and righteous human beings longed to see what you spot but did not see it, and to listen what you pay attention but did now not listen it. 17. So pay attention to the parable of the sower. 18. When every person hears the message about the dominion and does now not apprehend it, the evil one comes and snatches away what was sown of their heart. This is the seed along the route. 19. The seed on rocky floor is the person that hears the phrase and right away receives it with pleasure. 20. But for the reason that they haven't any root, they ultimate only a brief time. When problem or persecution comes because of the phrase, they speedy fall away. 21. The seed falling amongst thorns is the individual that hears the word, but the issues of this existence and the deceitfulness of wealth choke the phrase, making it unfruitful. 22. But the seed on properly soil is the person who hears the word and understands it. They produce a crop, yielding a hundred, sixty, or thirty instances what turned into sown." 23. Jesus informed them some other parable: "The kingdom of heaven is sort of a man who sowed proper seed in his discipline. 24. But while each person turned into sound asleep, his enemy came and sowed weeds (tares) among the wheat and went away. 25. When the wheat sprouted and formed heads, the weeds appeared additionally. 26. The owner's servants came to him and stated, 'Sir, didn't you sow exact seed to your field? Where then did the weeds come from?' 27. 'An enemy did this,' he answered. The servants asked him, 'Do you want us to head and pull them up?'" 28. 'No,' he answered, 'because while you are pulling the weeds, you may uproot the wheat with them. 29. Let both grow together until the harvest. At that time, I will tell the harvesters: "First collect the weeds and tie them in bundles to be burned; then gather the wheat and bring it into my barn." 30. He told

them another parable:"The kingdom of heaven is like a mustard seed, which a man took and planted in his field. **31.** Though it is the smallest of all seeds, when it grows, it becomes the largest of garden plants and becomes a tree, so that the birds come and perch in its branches." **32.** He told them still another parable: "The kingdom of heaven is like yeast (leaven), which a woman took and mixed into about sixty pounds of flour until it worked all through the dough." **33.** Jesus spoke all these things to the crowd in parables; He did not say anything to them without using a parable. **34.** This was to fulfill what was spoken through the prophet: "I will open My mouth in parables; I will utter things hidden since the creation of the world." **35.** After He dismissed the crowds, He went into the house. His disciples came to Him and said, "Explain to us the parable of the weeds in the field." **36.** He answered, "The one who sowed the good seed is the Son of Man. **37.** The field is the world, and the good seed stands for the people of the kingdom. The weeds are the people of the evil one, **38.** and the enemy who sows them is the devil. The harvest is the end of the age, and the harvesters are the angels. **39.** As the weeds are collected and burned in the fire, so it will be at the end of the age. **40.** The Son of Man will send out His angels, and they will weed out of His kingdom everything that causes sin and all who do evil. **41.** They will throw them into the blazing furnace, where there will be weeping and gnashing of teeth. **42.** Then the righteous will shine like the sun in the kingdom of their Father. Whoever has ears, let them hear." **43.** "Again, the kingdom of heaven is like treasure hidden in a field. When a man found it, he hid it again, and then in his joy went and sold all he had and bought that field. **44.** Again, the kingdom of heaven is like a merchant looking for fine pearls. **45.** When he found one of great value, he went away and sold everything he had and bought it." **46.** Again, the kingdom of heaven is like a net that was let down into the lake and caught all kinds of fish. **47.** When it was full, the fishermen pulled it up on the shore. Then they sat down and collected the good fish in baskets, but threw the bad away. **48.** This is how it will be at the end of the age. The angels will come and separate the wicked from the righteous **49.** and throw them into the blazing furnace, where there will be weeping and gnashing of teeth." **50.** Jesus asked, "Have you understood all these things?" "Yes," they replied. **51.** He said to them, "Therefore every teacher of the law who has become a disciple in the kingdom of heaven is like the owner of a house who brings out of his storeroom new treasures as well as old." **52.** When Jesus had finished these parables, He moved on from there. **53.** Coming to His hometown, He began teaching the people in their synagogue, and they were amazed. "Where did this man get this wisdom and these miraculous powers?" they asked. **54.** "Isn't this the carpenter's son? Isn't His mother's name Mary, and aren't His brothers James, Joseph, Simon, and Judas? **55.** Aren't all His sisters with us? Where then did this man get all these things?" **56.** And they took offense at Him. But Jesus said to them, "A prophet is not without honor except in their own town and in their own home." **57.** And He did not do many miracles there because of their lack of faith. **58.** Jesus did not perform many miracles there because of their lack of faith.

Chapter 14

1. At that point, Herod the tetrarch (a ruler of a district) heard about Jesus. **2.** He told his servants, "This need to be John the Baptist raised from the lifeless. That's why such amazing powers are at work in Him." **3.** Herod had previously arrested John, certain him, and put him in prison because of Herodias (his Brother Philip's spouse). **4.** John had instructed Herod, "its miles illegal with the intention to have her." **5.** Even though Herod desired to kill John, he was frightened of the human beings because they believed John became a prophet. **6.** On Herod's birthday, the daughter of Herodias finished a dance for him, and it pleased him greatly. **7.** So, he promised with an oath to offer her something she asked. **8.** Advocated with the aid of her mother, she requested, "Provide me the top of John the Baptist on a platter." **9.** Even though the king changed into distressed, because of his oath and the visitors at the dinner party, he commanded that it's accomplished. **10.** He dispatched for John to be beheaded within the jail. **11.** John's head turned into added on a platter and given to the woman, who then took it to her mom. **12.** Later, John's disciples got here, took his body, buried it, and went to tell Jesus. **13.** When Jesus heard this, He withdrew by boat to a remote region (a quiet, remote area) through Himself. But when the people heard of it, they followed Him on foot from the encircling cities. **14.** While Jesus saw the huge crowd, He felt compassion (deep sympathy and care) for them and healed their ill. **15.** As evening approached, His disciples got here to Him and said, "This is a desolate area, and it's getting past due. ship the humans away so one can move into the villages and buy food." **16.** Jesus spoke back, "They do now not want to go away. You provide them something to eat." **17.** They said to Him, "We best have five loaves of bread and fish." **18.** Jesus said, "convey them right here to Me." **19.** Then He told the people to sit down down at the grass. He took the 5 loaves and the 2 fish, seemed up to heaven, blessed the food, broke the loaves, and gave them to His disciples, who then distributed them to the human beings. **20.** All ate and have been satisfied. The disciples accumulated twelve baskets complete of leftovers. **21.** There have been about five thousand guys who ate, not counting girls and youngsters. **22.** at once, Jesus made His disciples get into the boat and cross in advance of Him to the other facet whilst He dispatched the crowds away. **23.** After He had sent them away, He went up on a mountain through Himself to hope. While night got here, He changed into by me there. **24.** The boat was already far from the shore, buffeted (struck or tossed) through the waves due to the fact the wind was towards it. **25.** At some point during the fourth watch of the night (between 3 AM and 6 AM), Jesus went toward them, walking at the water. **26.** When the disciples noticed Him taking walks on the ocean, they have been terrified and said, "It's a ghost!" They cried out in fear. **27.** But straight away Jesus spoke to them, "Take braveness! it is I; do now not be afraid." **28.** Peter responded, "Lord, if it's you, tell me to come to you on the water." **29.** Jesus said, "Come." So Peter got out of the boat and walked at the water in the direction of Jesus. **30.** But when he noticed the wind become sturdy, he became afraid and started to sink. He cried out, "Lord, store me!" **31.** Without delay, Jesus reached out His hand, stuck him, and stated, "You of little religion, why did you doubt?" **32.** Once they climbed into the boat, the wind ceased. **33.** Those who had been in the boat worshiped Him, saying, "Sincerely, you are the Son of God." **34.** After crossing over, they came to the place of Gennesaret (a place close to the Sea of Galilee). **35.** The human beings of that vicinity recognized Jesus. They sent phrase all through the encircling vicinity, bringing all the sick to Him. **36.** They begged Him to let them touch the brink of His cloak, and all who touched it had been healed.

Chapter 15

1. Then the scribes and Pharisees from Jerusalem got here to Jesus and asked, **2.** "Why do Your disciples wreck the subculture of the elders? They don't wash their fingers before consuming." **3.** He replied, "And why do you wreck God's command due to your tradition? **4.** God commanded, 'Honor your parents,' and, 'All and sundry who speaks against parent need to be positioned to demise.' **5.** But you assert, 'If someone tells their father or mother, "Something you might have obtained from me is a gift to God," **6.** then they don't should honor their father or mother.' On this way, you are making God's command useless via your subculture. **7.** You are hypocrites! Isaiah prophesied well approximately you, saying: **8.** 'These humans honor Me with their words, however their hearts are a ways from Me. **9.** They worship Me in vain, teaching human policies as though they have been doctrines (ideals).' "**10.** Jesus referred to as the group to Him and stated, "Listen and recognize this: **11.** It's not what is going into the mouth that defiles (makes unclean) someone, but what comes out of the mouth, that defiles them." **12.** His disciples got here to Him and said, "Do you recognize that the Pharisees were angry once they heard this?" **13.** Jesus responded, "Each plant that My heavenly Father has no longer planted might be uprooted. **14.** Leave them on my own. They're blind guides (leaders). And if the blind lead the blind, both will fall into a pit." **15.** Peter stated, "Give an explanation for this parable to us." **16.** Jesus stated, "Are you still without know-how? **17.** Don't you take into account that anything enters the mouth is going into the stomach and is expelled (eliminated)? **18.** But the things that come out of the mouth come from the coronary heart, and those are the things that defile a person. **19.** Evil thoughts, murder, adultery, sexual immorality (fornication), theft, fake testimony, slander (speak about others badly)—all come from the heart. **20.** These items defile a person, but consuming with unwashed palms does now not defile them." **21.** Jesus left that place and went to the vicinity of Tyre and Sidon (towns in Phoenicia, historical coastal area). **22.** A Canaanite girl from that location got here to Him, crying out, "Lord, Son of David, have mercy on me! My daughter is struggling terribly from demon possession." 23. Jesus did now not answer her in the beginning. His disciples urged Him, "Send her away, for she keeps crying after us." 24. He responded, "I used to be despatched simplest to the misplaced sheep of Israel." 25. The lady came and knelt before Him, announcing, "Lord, assist me!" 26. He responded, "It's not proper to take the kids's bread and deliver it to the dogs." 27. She responded, "Yes, Lord, but even the dogs consume the crumbs that fall from their masters' table." 28. Jesus answered, "Female, you've got wonderful faith! Let or not it's as you desire." And her daughter was healed that very hour. 29. Jesus left from there and went alongside the Sea of Galilee. He went up on a mountain and sat down. 30. Great crowds got here to Him, bringing the lame (unable to stroll), blind, mute (not able to speak), maimed (injured or deformed), and plenty of others. They laid them at Jesus' feet, and He healed them. 31. The people had been surprised once they noticed the mute speaking, the maimed healed, the lame walking, and the blind seeing. They praised the God of Israel. 32. Jesus referred to as His disciples to Him and said, "I have compassion (deep sympathy) on these humans. They have been with Me for 3 days and have nothing to devour. I don't want to ship them away hungry, or they might faint on the way." 33. His disciples asked, "Where are we able to get enough bread in this wasteland (barren region) to feed this kind of huge crowd?" 34. Jesus asked, "What number of loaves do you have?" They answered, "Seven, and a few small fish." 35. He instructed the gang to sit down down on the floor. 36. He took the seven loaves and the fish, gave thanks, broke them, and gave them to His disciples to distribute to the people. 37. They all ate and were happy. The disciples collected up seven massive baskets (baskets for storing meals) of leftovers. 38. About four thousand men were fed, except girls and kids. 39. After sending the group away, Jesus got into the boat and went to the area of Magdala (a metropolis in Galilee).

Chapter 16

1. The Pharisees (religious leaders) and Sadducees (another religious group) came to Jesus, testing Him, and asked Him to show them a sign from heaven. 2. He answered, "At evening, you say, 'The weather will be good, for the sky is red.' 3. And in the morning, 'It will be stormy today, for the sky is red and threatening.' You hypocrites! You can interpret the weather, but you cannot interpret the signs of the times. 4. An evil and unfaithful generation seeks a sign, but no sign will be given except the sign of the prophet Jonah." And He left them and went away. 5. When His disciples reached the other side, they realized they had forgotten to bring bread. 6. Jesus warned them, "Be careful and beware of the leaven (yeast) of the Pharisees and Sadducees." 7. They discussed among themselves, saying, "It's because we didn't bring any bread." 8. Jesus, knowing what they were thinking, said, "O you of little faith, why are you talking about bread? 9. Don't you remember the five loaves that fed five thousand men, and how many baskets you gathered afterward? 10. Or the seven loaves that fed four thousand men and how many large baskets you took up? 11. How is it that you still don't understand that I wasn't talking about bread, but about the teaching of the Pharisees and Sadducees?" 12. Then they understood that He was warning them not about bread, but about the false teachings of the Pharisees and Sadducees. 13. When Jesus came to the region (area) of Caesarea Philippi (a city near the northern border of Israel), He asked His disciples, "Who do people say the Son of Man is?" 14. They replied, "Some say John the Baptist, others say Elijah, and still others say Jeremiah or one of the prophets." 15. He asked them, "But who do you say I am?" 16. Simon Peter answered, "You are the Christ, the Son of the living God." 17. Jesus replied, "Blessed are you, Simon son of Jonah, for this was not revealed to you by flesh and blood, but by My Father in heaven. 18. And I tell you that you are Peter, and on this rock I will build My church, and the gates of Hades (death) will not overpower it. 19. I will give you the keys of the kingdom of heaven, and whatever you bind on earth will be bound in heaven, and whatever you loose on earth will be loosed in heaven." 20. Then He warned His disciples not to tell anyone that He was the Christ. 21. From that time, Jesus began to teach His disciples that He must go to Jerusalem, suffer many things from the elders, chief priests, and teachers of the law, be killed, and rise again on the third day. 22. Peter took Him aside and began to rebuke Him, saying, "Never, Lord! This shall never happen to

You!" 23. Jesus turned to Peter and said, "Get behind Me, Satan! You are a stumbling block (something that causes a person to fall) to Me; you do not have in mind the things of God, but the things of men." 24. Then Jesus said to His disciples, "If anyone wants to come after Me, let him deny himself, take up his cross, and follow Me. 25. For whoever wants to save his life will lose it, but whoever loses his life for My sake will find it. 26. What good will it be for someone to gain the whole world, yet forfeit (lose) their soul? Or what can anyone give in exchange for their soul? 27. For the Son of Man will come in the glory of His Father, with His angels, and then He will reward each person according to what they have done. 28. Truly I tell you, some who are standing here will not taste death before they see the Son of Man coming in His kingdom."

Chapter 17

1. Six days later, Jesus took Peter, James, and his brother John and led them up a high mountain by themselves. 2. There, He was changed in front of them. His face shone brightly like the sun, and His clothes became as white as light. 3. Suddenly, Moses and Elijah appeared, speaking with Jesus. 4. Peter then said to Jesus, "Lord, it's wonderful for us to be here. If You want, I'll set up three shelters—one for You, one for Moses, and one for Elijah." 5. While Peter was still speaking, a bright cloud overshadowed them, and a voice from the cloud said, "This is My Son, whom I love. I am pleased with Him. Listen to Him!" 6. When the disciples heard this, they fell on their faces, terrified. 7. But Jesus came to them, touched them, and said, "Get up, and don't be afraid." 8. When they looked up, they saw only Jesus. 9. As they came down the mountain, Jesus ordered them, "Don't tell anyone about this vision until the Son of Man has risen from the dead." 10. The disciples asked, "Why do the scribes say Elijah must come first?" 11. Jesus replied, "Elijah is indeed coming and will restore everything. 12. But I tell you, Elijah has already come, and they did not recognize him, instead treating him badly. Similarly, the Son of Man will suffer at their hands." 13. Then the disciples understood that He was talking about John the Baptist. 14. As they arrived at the crowd, a man approached Jesus, knelt before Him, and said, 15. "Lord, have mercy on my son. He has seizures (episodes of uncontrolled body movements) and suffers greatly, often falling into fire or water. 16. I brought him to Your disciples, but they couldn't heal him." 17. Jesus responded, "You faithless and corrupt (morally wrong) generation, how long will I stay with you? How long will I put up with you? Bring the boy to Me." 18. Jesus rebuked the demon in the boy, and it left him. Immediately, the boy was healed. 19. Later, the disciples came to Jesus privately and asked, "Why couldn't we cast it out?" 20. Jesus said, "Because of your lack of faith. Truly, if you have faith as small as a mustard seed, you can say to this mountain, 'Move from here to there,' and it will move. Nothing will be impossible for you. 21. However, this kind of demon does not go out except through prayer and fasting." 22. While staying in Galilee, Jesus told His disciples, "The Son of Man is about to be handed over to men, 23. they will kill Him, and on the third day, He will rise again." The disciples were deeply grieved. 24. When they arrived at Capernaum, those who collected the temple tax approached Peter and asked, "Does your Teacher not pay the temple tax?" 25. Peter replied, "Yes." When he entered the house, Jesus spoke first, saying, "What do you think, Simon? From whom do kings of the earth collect taxes or customs—from their own sons or from strangers?" 26. Peter answered, "From strangers." Jesus replied, "Then the sons are free. 27. However, so we don't cause offense, go to the sea, throw in a hook, and catch the first fish that comes up. Open its mouth, and you'll find a coin. Take it and give it to them for both of us."

Chapter 18

1. At that time, the disciples got here to Jesus and asked, "Who's the best in the country of heaven?" 2. Jesus called a toddler to Him, placed the child in the midst of them, 3. And stated, "I let you know, unless you convert and grow to be like kids, you will by no means enter the dominion of heaven. 4. Therefore, whoever humbles themselves (lowers themselves in pleasure or popularity) like this toddler is the greatest in the country of heaven. 5. And whoever welcomes (accepts, gets) a child like this in my call welcomes Me. 6. but if all people leads (reasons) such a children (younger believers) who accept as true with in Me to sin, it'd be better for them to have a heavy millstone (a big stone used for grinding) hung round their neck and be drowned inside

the sea. **7.** Woe (hazard or judgment) to the sector due to sin! For sin is unavoidable (need to come), however woe to the only thru whom it comes. **8.** in case your hand or foot reasons you to sin, cut it off and throw it away. It's better to go into lifestyles crippled (disabled) than to be thrown into hell (the place of eternal punishment) with both hands or feet. **9.** if your eye reasons you to sin, gouge it out and throw it away. It's higher to go into lifestyles with one eye than to be thrown into hell with . **10.** be careful now not to despise (push aside, look down on) the sort of little ones, for I tell you that their angels in heaven usually see the face of My Father. **11.** For the Son of guy came to shop the lost (folks that are spiritually misplaced, separated from God). **12.** What do you suspect? If a man has 100 sheep, and one is going off track (gets misplaced), will he no longer go away the 99 and visit look for the only that's lost? **13.** And if he reveals it, he rejoices extra over that one than over the ninety nine that did not move off beam. **14.** Within the same manner, it is not the will of your Father that any of these little ones ought to perish (be lost ceaselessly). **15.** if your brother sins towards you, go and point out (tell) their fault, simply among the 2 of you. if they listen, you've received them over. **16.** but in the event that they don't pay attention, take one or others alongside, so that 'every matter can be hooked up (showed as actual) via the testimony of two or three witnesses.' **17.** if they still refuse to concentrate, inform it to the church. And if they refuse to concentrate to the church, treat them as you will a pagan (a person outside the religion) or tax collector (a person taken into consideration a sinner by means of society). **18.** Definitely (for certain), I let you know, something you bind (forbid) on the earth may be certain in heaven, and anything you lose (allow) on the earth could be loosed in heaven. **19.** Again, I let you know, if two of you in the world agree about whatever you ask for, it will be done for you by way of My Father in heaven. **20.** For in which or three gather in My name, i am there with them. **21.** Then Peter came to Jesus and asked, "Lord, how often need to I forgive my brother whilst he sings in opposition to me? as much as seven instances?" **22.** Jesus responded, "I let you know, no longer seven instances, but seventy-seven instances (meaning infinitely). **23.** Therefore, the dominion of heaven is like a king who wanted to settle accounts (clean debts) along with his servants. **24.** As he began the agreement, a person who owed him ten thousand skills (a huge sum of money) turned into introduced to him. **25.** Due to the fact that the person couldn't pay, his grasp ordered that he, his spouse, and children be offered to pay off the debt. **26.** The servant fell on his knees before him and begged, 'Be affected person with me, and i can pay returned the entirety.' **27.** The master took pity (felt compassion) on him, forgave his debt, and let him move. **28.** However while that servant went out, he located one in all his fellow servants who owed him 100 denarii (a small amount of cash) and grabbed him by the throat. 'Pay me what you owe!' he demanded. **29.** His fellow servant fell to his knees and begged, 'Be patient with me, and i'm able to pay you again.' **30.** But he refused. Alternatively, he had him thrown into prison till he may want to pay the debt. **31.** While the opposite servants noticed what had took place, they were significantly distressed (dissatisfied) and went and informed their grasp the whole lot that had come about. **32.** Then the grasp referred to as the servant in and stated, 'You depraved (evil) servant! I forgave all your debt due to the fact you begged me. **33.** Shouldn't you have got had mercy (compassion, forgiveness) in your fellow servant just as I had on you?' **34.** In anger, his master handed him over to the jailers (prison guards) to be tortured till he needs to pay again all he owed. **35.** that is how my heavenly Father will treat every of you until you forgive your brother from the heart.

Chapter 19

1. After Jesus had completed speaking, He left Galilee and traveled to the area of Judea beyond the Jordan River. **2.** Large crowds followed Him, and He healed many people there. **3.** The Pharisees (spiritual leaders against Jesus) came to test Him, asking, "Is it legal for a man to divorce his wife for any reason?" **4.** Jesus answered, "Have you not read that from the beginning, God created them male and female? **5.** And He said, 'For this reason, a man will leave his father and mother and be united with his wife, and the two will become one flesh.' **6.** So they are no longer two, but one. Therefore, what God has joined together, let no one separate." **7.** They asked, "Why then did Moses command to give a certificate of divorce?" **8.** Jesus replied, "Moses permitted you to divorce your wives because of the hardness of your hearts (reluctance to forgive), but it was not this way from the beginning. **9.** I tell you, anyone who divorces his wife, except for sexual immorality (infidelity), and marries commits adultery." **10.** His disciples said to Him, "If that is the case, it is better not to marry." **11.** Jesus answered, "Not everyone can accept this teaching, but only those to whom it has been given. **12.** For there are eunuchs (men who are unfit to father children) who were born that way, others were made eunuchs by men, and some choose to live as eunuchs for the sake of the kingdom of heaven. Let the one who can accept this, accept it." **13.** Then people brought little children to Jesus for Him to place His hands on them and pray, but the disciples rebuked (scolded) them. **14.** Jesus said, "Let the little children come to Me, and do not hinder them, for to such belongs the kingdom of heaven." **15.** He laid His hands on them and went on from there. **16.** A man came to Him and asked, "Teacher, what good deed must I do to have eternal life?" **17.** Jesus replied, "Why do you ask Me about what is good? No one is good except God alone. However, if you want to enter life, keep the commandments." **18.** The man asked, "Which ones?" Jesus answered, "'You shall not murder, you shall not commit adultery, you shall not steal, you shall not bear false witness (lie), **19.** Honor your father and mother, and love your neighbor as yourself.'" **20.** The young man said to Him, "I have kept all these; what do I still lack?" **21.** Jesus said, "If you want to be perfect (complete), go, sell your possessions, give to the poor, and you will have treasure in heaven. Then come, follow Me." **22.** But when the young man heard this, he went away sad, because he had great wealth. **23.** Jesus said to His disciples, "Truly, I tell you, it is hard for a rich man to enter the kingdom of heaven. **24.** Again I tell you, it is easier for a camel to go through the eye of a needle (a very narrow opening) than for a rich man to enter the kingdom of God." **25.** The disciples were greatly astonished, saying, "Who then can be saved?" **26.** Jesus looked at them and said, "With man this is impossible, but with God all things are possible." **27.** Peter responded, "We have left everything to follow You. What then will there be for us?" **28.** Jesus answered, "Truly, I tell you, at the renewal of all things (the resurrection), when the Son of Man sits on His glorious throne, you who have followed Me will also sit on twelve thrones, judging the twelve tribes of Israel. **29.** And everyone who has left houses, brothers, sisters, or fields for My sake will receive a hundred times as much and will inherit eternal life. **30.** But many who are first will be last, and the last first."

Chapter 20

1. "The kingdom of heaven is sort of a landowner who went out early inside the morning to rent people for his vineyard (a farm in which grapes are grown). **2.** After agreeing to pay them a denarius (a silver coin) for the day, he sent them to paintings. **3.** At around the 1/3 hour (9 AM), he went out and saw others standing idle (no longer running) within the marketplace. **4.** He stated to them, 'You go additionally into the vineyard, and I will pay you what is honest.' So they went. **5.** He went out again on the 6th hour (12 PM) and the 9th hour (3 PM), and did the same. **6.** Across the eleventh hour (5 PM), he went out and found others standing idle. He requested them, 'Why have you been standing here all day with nothing to do?' **7.** They answered, 'Because nobody employed us.' He said, 'You furthermore may go into the vineyard, and I'm able to come up with what is right.' **8.** When nighttime came, the owner told his steward (manager of his property), 'Call the workers and pay them, beginning with those hired last and finishing with those employed first.' **9.** The people who were employed at the 11th hour came and each received a denarius. **10.** When the first workers came, they expected to receive more, but they also received a denarius. **11.** After receiving their pay, they grumbled (complained) against the landowner, **12.** Saying, 'Those last people only worked one hour, and yet you've made them equal to us who've worked through the heat and burden of the day.' **13.** But the landowner responded to one of them, 'Pal, I haven't wronged you. Didn't you agree to work for a denarius? **14.** Take your pay and go. I want to give the one who was hired last the same as you. **15.** Don't I have the right to do what I want with my own money? Or are you resentful (jealous) because I'm generous?' **16.** So the last will be first, and the first will be last. For many are called, but few are chosen." **17.** As Jesus was on His way to Jerusalem (capital city of Israel), He took His twelve disciples apart and said to them, 18. "We are going up to Jerusalem, and the Son of Man (Jesus) will be betrayed to the chief priests and the scribes (teachers of the law). They will condemn Him to death, 19. and hand Him over to the Gentiles (non-Jews) to mock, scourge (whip), and crucify. On the third day, He will rise again." 20. Then the mother of Zebedee's sons (James and John) came to Him with her sons, kneeling down and inquiring for a favor. 21. Jesus asked her, "What do you want?" She replied, "Grant that these sons of mine may also sit, one at Your right hand and the other at Your left, in Your kingdom." 22. Jesus answered, "You don't know what you're asking. Can you drink the cup (suffering) I am about to drink, and be baptized with the baptism (suffering) I am baptized with?" They answered, "We are able." 23. Jesus told them, "You will indeed drink My cup and be baptized with My baptism; but to sit at My right or left is not Mine to give. It is for those for whom it has been prepared by My Father." 24. When the other ten disciples heard this, they were angry with the two brothers. 25. Jesus called them together and said, "You know that the rulers of the Gentiles lord it over (exercise authority) them, and their high officials wield power over them. 26. But it shall not be so among you. Whoever wants to become great among you must be your servant, 27. and whoever wants to be first must be your slave— 28. just as the Son of Man did not come to be served, but to serve, and to give His life as a ransom (price for freedom) for many." 29. As they were leaving Jericho (an ancient city near Jerusalem), a large crowd followed Him. 30. Two blind men sitting by the roadside, hearing that Jesus was passing by, shouted, "Lord, Son of David (a title for the Messiah), have mercy on us!" 31. The crowd told them to be quiet, but they cried out all the more, "Lord, Son of David, have mercy on us!" 32. Jesus stopped and called them, asking, "What do you want Me to do for you?" 33. They answered, "Lord, we want our sight restored." 34. Jesus had compassion (deep sympathy) on them, touched their eyes, and immediately they received their sight and followed Him.

Chapter 21

1. As they approached Jerusalem and came to Bethphage (a village east of Jerusalem) on the Mount of Olives, Jesus sent two of His disciples. 2. He said to them, "Go ahead into the village, and you will immediately find a donkey tied with her colt (young donkey). Untie them and bring them to Me. 3. If anyone asks why you are taking them, tell them, 'The Lord needs them,' and they will let you take them right away." 4. This took place to fulfill the prophecy spoken by the prophet: 5. "Tell the daughter of Zion (Jerusalem), 'See, your King is coming to you, humble, riding on a donkey, on a colt, the foal of a donkey.'" 6. The disciples went and did as Jesus instructed. 7. They brought the donkey and the colt, laid their cloaks (coats) on them, and Jesus sat on them. 8. A large crowd spread their cloaks (coats) on the road, and others cut branches from the trees and spread them on the road. 9. The crowds that went ahead of Him and those following shouted, "Hosanna to the Son of David! Blessed is He who comes in the name of the Lord! Hosanna in the highest!" 10. When Jesus entered Jerusalem, the whole city was stirred and asked, "Who is this?" 11. The crowds answered, "This is Jesus, the prophet from Nazareth in Galilee." 12. Jesus entered the temple of God and drove out all who were buying and selling there. He overturned the tables of the money changers and the chairs of those selling doves (sacrificial birds). 13. He said to them, "It is written, 'My house will be called a house of prayer,' but you are making it a den of robbers." 14. The blind and the lame came to Him in the temple, and He healed them. 15. When the chief priests and scribes (religious teachers) saw the wonderful things He did, and the children shouting in the temple, "Hosanna to the Son of David!" they were angry. 16. They asked Jesus, "Do You hear what these children are saying?" Jesus replied, "Yes. Have you never read, 'From the lips of children and infants, You have ordained praise'?" 17. After leaving them, He went out of the city to Bethany (a village near Jerusalem) and spent the night there. 18. Early the next morning, as He was returning to the city, He was hungry. 19. Seeing a fig tree by the road, He approached it but found nothing except leaves. He said to it, "May you never bear fruit again!" Immediately the tree withered. 20. When the disciples saw this, they were amazed and asked, "How did the fig tree wither so quickly?" 21. Jesus answered, "Truly, I tell you, if you have faith and do not doubt, not only can you do what was done to the fig tree, but also if you say to this mountain, 'Be lifted up and thrown into the sea,' it will

happen. 22. And whatever you ask for in prayer, believing, you will receive." 23. When Jesus entered the temple and began teaching, the chief priests and elders of the people came to Him and asked, "By what authority are You doing these things? And who gave You this authority?" 24. Jesus replied, "I will also ask you one question. If you answer Me, I will tell you by what authority I do these things. 25. The baptism of John—where did it come from? From heaven or from men?" They debated among themselves, 26. "If we say, 'From heaven,' He will ask us, 'Why then did you not believe him?' 27. But if we say, 'From men,' we are afraid of the people, for they all hold that John was a prophet." 28. So they answered Jesus, "We do not know." He said to them, "Neither will I tell you by what authority I do these things." 29. "What do you think? A man had two sons. He went to the first and said, 'Son, go and work today in my vineyard.' 30. He answered, 'I will not,' but later changed his mind and went. 31. Then he went to the second and said the same. He answered, 'I will go, sir,' but did not. 32. Which of the two did the will of his father?" They answered, "The first." Jesus said to them, "Truly, I tell you, tax collectors and prostitutes (women selling their bodies for money) are entering the kingdom of God ahead of you. 33. For John came to you showing you the way of righteousness, and you did not believe him. But the tax collectors and prostitutes believed him, and even after you saw this, you did not repent (turn away from sin) and believe him." 34. Listen to another parable: There was a landowner who planted a vineyard, put a fence around it, dug a winepress (for pressing grapes), and built a watchtower. Then he rented it out to some farmers and went away to another country. 35. When the harvest time approached, he sent his servants to the tenants (those renting the land) to collect his fruit. 36. But the tenants took his servants, beat one, killed another, and stoned a third. 37. So he sent more servants, more than the first time, and they did the same to them. 38. Finally, he sent his son, thinking, 'They will respect my son.' 39. But when the tenants saw the son, they said to each other, 'This is the heir (the one who will inherit the property). Come, let us kill him and take his inheritance.' 40. So they took him, threw him out of the vineyard, and killed him. 41. Therefore, when the owner of the vineyard comes, what will he do to those tenants?" 42. They replied, "He will bring those wretches to a wretched end, and rent the vineyard to other tenants who will give him his share of the crop at harvest time." 43. Jesus said to them, "Have you never read in the Scriptures: 'The stone the builders rejected has become the cornerstone? The Lord has done this, and it is marvelous in our eyes'? 44. Therefore I tell you, the kingdom of God will be taken away from you and given to a people who will produce its fruit. 45. Anyone who falls on this stone will be broken to pieces, but anyone on whom it falls will be crushed to dust." 46. When the chief priests and Pharisees heard His parables, they realized He was speaking about them.

Chapter 22

1. Jesus spoke to them again using parables (stories that teach a lesson), saying: 2. "The kingdom of heaven is like a king who arranged a wedding for his son. 3. He sent his servants to call those who were invited, but they refused to come. 4. Again, he sent other servants, saying, 'Tell those invited, "I have prepared a feast (meal), with my oxen (large cattle) and fatted calves (fattened animals) slaughtered, and everything is ready. Come to the wedding."' 5. But they ignored it and went their way—one to his farm, another to his business. 6. Some even seized his servants, mistreated (treated with cruelty) them, and killed them. 7. The king became angry and sent his army, destroyed those murderers, and burned their city. 8. Then he said to his servants, 'The wedding banquet is ready, but those invited were not worthy. 9. Go therefore to the highways (main roads) and invite everyone you find to the wedding.' 10. So the servants went into the streets and gathered all they found, both good and bad. The wedding hall was filled with guests. 11. When the king came to see the guests, he saw a man there who was not wearing wedding clothes. 12. He asked him, 'Friend, how did you come in here without a wedding garment (proper clothing for a wedding)?' The man was speechless (unable to speak). 13. The king said to the servants, 'Tie him hand and foot, take him away, and throw him into the outer darkness (outside where it is dark); there will be weeping and gnashing (grinding) of teeth.' 14. For many are called (invited), but few are chosen (selected)." 15. Then the Pharisees (religious leaders) went away and plotted how they might

trap (catch) Him with His words. **16.** They sent their disciples, along with the Herodians (followers of King Herod), to ask Him, "Teacher, we know that You are truthful and teach the way of God in truth. You are not influenced (swayed) by people, because You do not look at their outward appearance. **17.** Tell us, then, what You think: Is it lawful (permissible) to pay taxes to Caesar, or not?" **18.** But Jesus, knowing their evil intentions, replied, "Why are you testing (tempting) Me, you hypocrites (pretenders)? **19.** Show Me the coin used for the tax." They brought Him a denarius (a silver coin used for Roman tax). **20.** Jesus asked them, "Whose image (likeness) and inscription (writing) is this?" **21.** They answered, "Caesar's." He replied, "Therefore, give to Caesar what belongs to Caesar, and to God what belongs to God." **22.** When they heard this, they were amazed, and they left Him and went away. **23.** The same day, the Sadducees (a Jewish sect who denied the resurrection of the dead) came to Him and asked, **24.** "Teacher, Moses said that if a man dies without having children, his brother must marry the widow and raise up offspring (children) for him. **25.** Now there were seven brothers. The first married and died, and because he had no children, he left his wife to his brother. **26.** The same happened with the second and third, and so on to the seventh. **27.** Finally, the woman died. **28.** In the resurrection (life after death), whose wife will she be of the seven, since they all had her?" **29.** Jesus replied, "You are mistaken (wrong), not knowing the Scriptures or the power of God. **30.** In the resurrection, people will neither marry nor be given in marriage; they will be like the angels (spiritual beings) in heaven. **31.** But regarding the resurrection of the dead, have you not read what God said to you: **32.** 'I am the God of Abraham, the God of Isaac, and the God of Jacob'? He is not the God of the dead, but of the living." **33.** When the crowds heard this, they were astonished (amazed) at His teaching. **34.** But when the Pharisees heard that He had silenced (defeated) the Sadducees, they gathered together. **35.** One of them, an expert in the law, tested (challenged) Him with a question: **36.** "Teacher, which is the greatest commandment in the Law?" **37.** Jesus replied, "'Love the Lord your God with all your heart, with all your soul, and with all your mind.' **38.** This is the first and greatest commandment. **39.** The second is like it: 'Love your neighbor as yourself.' **40.** All the Law and the Prophets (the teachings in the Old Testament) depend on these two commandments." **41.** While the Pharisees were gathered together, Jesus asked them, **42.** "What do you think about the Christ (Messiah)? Whose Son is He?" They answered, "The Son of David." **43.** Jesus said to them, "How then does David, in the Spirit (by inspiration of God), call Him 'Lord,' saying: **44.** 'The LORD said to my Lord (Messiah), 'Sit at My right hand, until I put Your enemies under Your feet''? **45.** If David calls Him 'Lord,' how can He be his son?" **46.** No one could answer Him, and from that day on, no one dared to ask Him any more questions.

Chapter 23

1. Then Jesus spoke to the crowds and His disciples, saying: **2.** "The scribes and the Pharisees sit in the seat of Moses (the position of authority in Jewish law). **3.** Therefore, whatever they tell you to observe, do it; but do not follow their actions, because they say one thing and do another. **4.** They place heavy burdens (difficult tasks) on others but are unwilling to help them. **5.** All their actions are done to be seen by people. They make their phylacteries (small boxes with scriptures) large and increase the tassels (fringes) on their garments. **6.** They love the best places at feasts and the most honored seats in synagogues. **7.** They enjoy greetings in the marketplaces and want to be called 'Rabbi' (teacher) by others. **8.** But you, do not be called 'Rabbi'; for One is your Teacher, the Christ (Messiah), and you are all brothers. **9.** Do not call anyone on earth your father; for One is your Father, He who is in heaven. **10.** And do not be called teachers; for One is your Teacher, the Christ. **11.** The greatest among you shall be your servant. **12.** Whoever exalts himself will be humbled, and whoever humbles himself will be exalted. **13.** Woe to you, scribes and Pharisees, hypocrites (pretenders)! You shut the door of the kingdom of heaven in people's faces; you neither enter yourselves nor let those who are trying to enter. **14.** Woe to you, scribes and Pharisees, hypocrites! You devour widows' houses (take advantage of them) and make long prayers as a cover for it. You will receive a greater punishment. **15.** Woe to you, scribes and Pharisees, hypocrites! You travel over land and sea to make one convert (proselyte), and when you succeed, you make

him twice as much a child of hell as yourselves. **16.** Woe to you, blind guides! You say, 'Whoever swears by the temple is nothing, but whoever swears by the gold of the temple is bound by his oath.' **17.** You are foolish and blind! Which is greater, the gold or the temple that sanctifies (makes holy) the gold? **18.** And you say, 'Whoever swears by the altar is nothing, but whoever swears by the gift on it is bound by his oath.' **19.** You are fools and blind! Which is greater, the gift or the altar that sanctifies the gift? **20.** Therefore, whoever swears by the altar swears by it and by everything on it. **21.** Whoever swears by the temple swears by it and by Him who dwells in it. **22.** And whoever swears by heaven swears by the throne of God and by Him who sits on it. **23.** Woe to you, scribes and Pharisees, hypocrites! You tithe (give a tenth) of mint, dill, and cumin (herbs), but neglect the more important matters of the law: justice, mercy, and faithfulness. You should have done these things without neglecting the others. **24.** You blind guides! You strain out a gnat but swallow a camel (focus on small things but ignore big issues)! **25.** Woe to you, scribes and Pharisees, hypocrites! You clean the outside of the cup and dish, but inside they are full of greed and self-indulgence. **26.** Blind Pharisee, first clean the inside of the cup and dish, so the outside may be clean too. **27.** Woe to you, scribes and Pharisees, hypocrites! You are like whitewashed tombs (graves) that appear beautiful outside, but inside are full of dead bones and all uncleanness. **28.** In the same way, you appear righteous to others on the outside, but inside you are full of hypocrisy and lawlessness. **29.** Woe to you, scribes and Pharisees, hypocrites! You build tombs for the prophets and decorate the monuments of the righteous. **30.** And you say, 'If we had lived in the days of our ancestors, we would not have participated in shedding the prophets' blood.' **31.** So you testify against yourselves that you are descendants of those who murdered the prophets. **32.** Fill up then the measure of your ancestors' guilt. **33.** You serpents (snakes), you brood of vipers (offspring of poisonous snakes), how will you escape the punishment of hell? **34.** Therefore, I am sending you prophets, wise men, and teachers. Some of them you will kill and crucify, and others you will beat in your synagogues and chase from city to city. **35.** So on you will come all the righteous blood shed on the earth, from the blood of righteous Abel (the first martyr) to the blood of Zechariah, son of Berechiah, whom you murdered between the temple and the altar. **36.** Truly, I tell you, all these things will come upon this generation. **37.** O Jerusalem, Jerusalem, the city that kills the prophets and stones those who are sent to her! How often I wanted to gather your children together, as a hen gathers her chicks under her wings, but you were not willing! **38.** Look! Your house is left to you desolate (empty, without God). **39.** For I tell you, you will not see Me again until you say, 'Blessed is He who comes in the name of the Lord!'"

Chapter 24

1. Jesus left the temple, and His disciples pointed out the buildings to Him. **2.** Jesus responded, "Do you see all these things? Truly, I tell you, not one stone will be left here upon another; all will be thrown down." **3.** As He sat on the Mount of Olives, the disciples came to Him privately, saying, "Tell us, when will these things be? And what will be the sign of Your coming and of the end of the age?" **4.** Jesus answered, "Watch out that no one deceives you. **5.** Many will come in My name, claiming, 'I am the Christ,' and will deceive many. **6.** You will hear of wars and rumors of wars, but see to it that you are not alarmed. Such things must happen, but the end is still to come. **7.** Nation will rise against nation, and kingdom against kingdom. There will be famines and earthquakes in various places. **8.** All these are the beginning of birth pains. **9.** Then you will be handed over to be persecuted and put to death, and you will be hated by all nations because of Me. **10.** At that time many will turn away from the faith and will betray and hate each other. **11.** Many false prophets will appear and deceive many people. **12.** Because of the increase of wickedness, the love of most will grow cold, **13.** but the one who stands firm to the end will be saved. **14.** And this gospel of the kingdom will be preached in the whole world as a testimony to all nations, and then the end will come. **15.** "So when you see standing in the holy place 'the abomination that causes desolation,' spoken of through the prophet Daniel—let the reader understand— **16.** then let those who are in Judea flee to the mountains. **17.** Let no one on the roof of his house go down to take anything out of the house. **18.** Let no one in the field go back to get their cloak. **19.** How dreadful it will be in those days for pregnant women and nursing mothers! **20.** Pray that your flight will not take place in winter or on the Sabbath. **21.** For then there will be great distress, unequaled from the beginning of the world until now—and never to be equaled again. **22.** If those days had not been cut short, no one would survive, but for the sake of the elect those days will be shortened. **23.** At that time if anyone says to you, 'Look, here is the Christ!' or 'There he is!' do not believe it. **24.** For false Christs and false prophets will appear and perform great signs and wonders to deceive, if possible, even the elect. **25.** See, I have told you ahead of time. **26.** So if anyone tells you, 'There he is, out in the desert!' do not go out; or, 'Here he is, in the inner rooms!' do not believe it. **27.** For as lightning that comes from the east is visible even in the west, so will be the coming of the Son of Man. **28.** Wherever there is a carcass, there the vultures will gather. **29.** "Immediately after the distress of those days the sun will be darkened, and the moon will not give its light; the stars will fall from the sky, and the heavenly bodies will be shaken. **30.** Then will appear the sign of the Son of Man in heaven. And then all the peoples of the earth will mourn when they see the Son of Man coming on the clouds of heaven, with power and great glory. **31.** And He will send His angels with a loud trumpet call, and they will gather His elect from the four winds, from one end of the heavens to the other. **32.** "Now learn this lesson from the fig tree: As soon as its twigs get tender and its leaves come out, you know that summer is near. **33.** Even so, when you see all these things, you know that it is near, right at the door. **34.** Truly I tell you, this generation will certainly not pass away until all these things have happened. **35.** Heaven and earth will pass away, but My words will never pass away. **36.** "But about that day or hour no one knows, not even the angels in heaven, nor the Son, but only the Father. **37.** As it was in the days of Noah, so it will be at the coming of the Son of Man. **38.** For in the days before the flood, people were eating and drinking, marrying and giving in marriage, up to the day Noah entered the ark; **39.** and they knew nothing about what would happen until the flood came and took them all away. That is how it will be at the coming of the Son of Man. **40.** Two men will be in the field; one will be taken and the other left. **41.** Two women will be grinding with a hand mill; one will be taken and the other left. **42.** Therefore keep watch, because you do not know on what day your Lord will come. **43.** But understand this: If the owner of the house had known at what time of night the thief was coming, he would have kept watch and would not have let his house be broken into. **44.** So you also must be ready, because the Son of Man will come at an hour when you do not expect Him. **45.** "Who then is the faithful and wise servant, whom the master has put in charge of the servants in his household to give them their food at the proper time? **46.** It will be good for that servant whose master finds him doing so when he returns. **47.** Truly I tell you, he will put him in charge of all his possessions. **48.** But suppose that servant is wicked and says to himself, 'My master is staying away a long time,' **49.** and he then begins to beat his fellow servants and to eat and drink with drunkards. **50.** The master of that servant will come on a day when he does not expect him and at an hour he is not aware of. **51.** He will cut him to pieces and assign him a place with the hypocrites, where there will be weeping and gnashing of teeth."

Chapter 25

1. "The kingdom of heaven is like ten virgins who took their lamps and went out to meet the bridegroom. **2.** Five of them were wise, and five were foolish. **3.** The foolish ones took their lamps but did not take any extra oil with them. **4.** The wise ones, however, took oil in jars along with their lamps. **5.** The bridegroom was a long time in coming, and they all became drowsy and fell asleep. **6.** At midnight, the cry rang out, 'Here's the bridegroom! Come out to meet him!' **7.** Then all the virgins woke up and trimmed their lamps. **8.** The foolish ones said to the wise, 'Give us some of your oil; our lamps are going out.' **9.** 'No,' they replied, 'there may not be enough for both us and you. Instead, go to those who sell oil and buy some for yourselves.' **10.** But while they were on their way to buy the oil, the bridegroom arrived. The virgins who were ready went in with him to the wedding banquet, and the door was shut. **11.** Later, the others also came. 'Lord, Lord,' they said, 'open the door for us!' **12.** But he replied, 'Truly I tell you, I don't know you.' **13.** Therefore, keep watch, because you do not know the day or the hour." **14.** "Again, the kingdom of heaven is like a man who went on a journey and called his servants and entrusted his wealth to them. **15.** To one he gave five talents, to another two talents, and to another one talent, each according to his ability. Then he went on his journey. **16.** The man who had received five talents went at once and put his money to work and gained five more. **17.** So also, the one with two talents gained two more. **18.** But the man who had received one talent went off, dug a hole in the ground, and hid his master's money. **19.** After a long time, the master of those servants returned and settled accounts with them. **20.** The man who had received five talents brought the other five. 'Master,' he said, 'you entrusted me with five talents. See, I have gained five more.' **21.** His master replied, 'Well done, good and faithful servant! You have been faithful with a few things; I will put you in charge of many things. Come and share your master's happiness!' **22.** The man with two talents also came. 'Master,' he said, 'you entrusted me with two talents; see, I have gained two more.' **23.** His master replied, 'Well done, good and faithful servant! You have been faithful with a few things; I will put you in charge of many things. Come and share your master's happiness!' **24.** Then the man who had received one talent came. 'Master,' he said, 'I knew that you are a hard man, harvesting where you have not sown, and gathering where you have not scattered seed. **25.** So I was afraid, and I went out and hid your talent in the ground. See, here is what belongs to you.' **26.** His master replied, 'You wicked, lazy servant! You knew that I harvest where I have not sown and gather where I have not scattered seed. **27.** Well then, you should have put my money on deposit with the bankers, so that when I returned I would have received it back with interest. **28.** Take the talent from him and give it to the one who has ten talents. **29.** For whoever has will be given more, and they will have an abundance. Whoever does not have, even what they have will be taken from them. **30.** And throw that worthless servant outside, into the darkness, where there will be weeping and gnashing of teeth.'" **31.** "When the Son of Man comes in His glory, and all the angels with Him, He will sit on His glorious throne. **32.** All the nations will be gathered before Him, and He will separate the people one from another as a shepherd separates the sheep from the goats. **33.** He will put the sheep on His right and the goats on His left. **34.** Then the King will say to those on His right, 'Come, you who are blessed by My Father; take your inheritance, the kingdom prepared for you since the creation of the world. **35.** For I was hungry and you gave Me something to eat; I was thirsty and you gave Me something to drink; I was a stranger and you invited Me in; **36.** I needed clothes and you clothed Me; I was sick and you looked after Me; I was in prison and you came to visit Me.' **37.** Then the righteous will answer Him, 'Lord, when did we see You hungry and feed You, or thirsty and give You something to drink? **38.** When did we see You a stranger and invite You in, or needing clothes and clothe You? **39.** When did we see You sick or in prison and go to visit You?' **40.** The King will reply, 'Truly I tell you, whatever you did for one of the least of these brothers and sisters of Mine, you did for Me.' **41.** Then He will say to those on His left, 'Depart from Me, you who are cursed, into the eternal fire prepared for the devil and his angels. **42.** For I was hungry and you gave Me nothing to eat, I was thirsty and you gave Me nothing to drink; **43.** I was a stranger and you did not invite Me in, I needed clothes and you did not clothe Me, I was sick and in prison and you did not look after Me.' **44.** They also will answer, 'Lord, when did we see You hungry or thirsty or a stranger or needing clothes or sick or in prison, and did not help You?' **45.** He will reply, 'Truly I tell you, whatever you did not do for one of the least of these, you did not do for Me.' **46.** Then they will go away to eternal punishment, but the righteous to eternal life."

Chapter 26

1. After Jesus had finished pronouncing all these things, He spoke to His disciples, **2.** "you understand that the Passover (Jewish pageant celebrating the Exodus from Egypt) is in days, and the Son of man (a name Jesus used for Himself) might be surpassed over to be crucified." **3.** The chief monks (religious leaders), the scribes (experts in the law), and the elders (older leaders) accrued at the residence of Caiaphas (excessive priest), **4.** and plotted to secretly arrest and kill Jesus. **5.** but they stated, "now not at some stage in the feast, or there may be a insurrection (a violent public disturbance) a number of the people." **6.** even as Jesus turned into in Bethany (a village near Jerusalem) at Simon the leper's (a person healed of leprosy) house, **7.** a girl got here with an alabaster (a easy, white stone) jar of high-priced fragrance and poured it on His head as He sat on the desk. **8.** when His disciples noticed it, they have been irritated, pronouncing, "Why this waste? **9.** This fragrance could have been bought for a number of cash and given to the terrible." **10.** Jesus, aware about this, said, "Why are you troubling (stressful) the woman? She has achieved a great deed (type act) for Me. **11.** you'll constantly have the terrible with you, however you won't continually have Me. **12.** with the aid of pouring this fragrance on My frame, she has prepared Me for burial (the procedure of preparing a frame after death). **13.** genuinely, wherever the gospel (exact news) is preached, what she has carried out might be instructed in memory of her." **14.** Then one of the twelve, Judas Iscariot (one in all Jesus' disciples), went to the chief priests **15.** and requested, "what's going to you provide me to betray (quit) Him to you?" and they gave him thirty pieces of silver. **16.** From that point, he sought an possibility to betray Jesus. **17.** On the primary day of the dinner party of Unleavened Bread (part of the Passover birthday party), the disciples requested Jesus, "where do You need us to put together for the Passover?" **18.** He responded, "pass into the town to a certain guy and tell him, 'The teacher (Jesus) says, "My time has come; i will devour the Passover with My disciples at your private home."' " **19.** The disciples did as Jesus advised and prepared the Passover. **20.** whilst night came, Jesus sat down with the twelve. **21.** even as they had been ingesting, He said, "sincerely, certainly one of you'll betray Me." **22.** They have been very unhappy and every requested, "Lord, is it I?" **23.** He responded, "the one who dips his hand with Me inside the bowl will betray Me. **24.** The Son of man (Jesus) will move just as it is written (foretold) about Him, but woe (sadness) to that guy who betrays Him! it might be better for him if he had never been born." **25.** Judas, who turned into betraying Him, requested, "Rabbi (teacher), is it I?" Jesus replied, "you have got said so." **26.** As they ate, Jesus took the bread, gave thank you, broke it, and gave it to His disciples, pronouncing, "Take, consume; this is My body." **27.** He took the cup, gave thanks, and supplied it to them, pronouncing, "Drink from it, all of you. **28.** that is My blood of the new covenant (a brand new promise), poured out for many for the forgiveness of sins. **29.** I inform you, i'm able to now not drink of this fruit of the vine (wine) once more until I drink it new with you in My Father's nation." **30.** After making a song a hymn, they went to the Mount of Olives (a mountain close to Jerusalem). **31.** Jesus said, "this night, all of you may fall away (abandon) attributable to Me, for it's far written: 'i can strike the Shepherd (Jesus), and the sheep (followers) may be scattered.' **32.** however after i am raised, i'm able to go beforehand of you into Galilee (region in northern Israel)." **33.** Peter declared, "even supposing all fall away because of You, i can in no way fall away." **34.** Jesus replied, "in reality, this very night, before the poultry (bird) crows, you'll deny Me 3 instances." **35.** Peter said, "even if I need to die with You, i can no longer deny You!" And all of the disciples said the same. **36.** Then Jesus went with them to Gethsemane (a lawn close to Jerusalem) and stated to the disciples, "take a seat right here while I pray." **37.** He took Peter, James, and John alongside, and He have become deeply distressed (afflicted). **38.** He stated to them, "My soul is beaten with sorrow to the point of death. stay right here and hold watch with Me." **39.** Going a bit farther, He fell together with his face to the floor and prayed, "My Father, if it is viable, may also this cup (struggling) be taken from Me; but no longer as i can, however as you'll." **40.** He returned to His disciples and discovered them dozing. "may want to you now not watch (live awake) with Me for one hour?" He requested Peter. **41.** Jesus stated, "live alert and pray, so that you do now not provide in to temptation. even though your spirit is willing, your flesh (human nature) is susceptible." **42.** He went away again and prayed, "My Father, if it's now not viable for this cup (the suffering or death He turned into approximately to bear) to pass from Me unless I drink it, allow Your will be achieved." **43.** while He lower back, He found them asleep all over again, their eyes heavy with exhaustion. **44.** He left them and prayed a 3rd time, repeating the same phrases. **45.** He came returned to His disciples and said, "Are you continue to snoozing and resting? The time has come. The Son of man is being handed over to sinners. **46.** stand up, let's pass. My betrayer is here." **47.** As He turned into speaking, Judas arrived, leading a massive crowd armed with swords and golf equipment, sent by the leader monks and elders. **48.** Judas had organized a sign, saying, "the one I kiss is the one to arrest." **49.** Judas approached Jesus, greeted Him, "Rabbi (instructor)!" and kissed Him. **50.** Jesus answered, "friend, do what you came for." Then the mob seized Jesus. **51.** one in all Jesus' companions drew his sword and struck the servant of the high priest, reducing off his ear. **52.** Jesus said to him, "placed your sword back in its vicinity. All who use the sword will die via the sword. **53.** Do you think I can't call on My Father, and He could provide more than twelve legions (heaps) of angels to defend Me? **54.** however how might the Scriptures (holy writings) be fulfilled, which say this must manifest?" **55.** Jesus turned to the gang and stated, "Am I leading a rise up (an uprising or riot), which you have come with swords and clubs to seize Me? i've been teaching each day inside the temple, and you did not arrest Me. **56.** however all this has happened to meet the Scriptures of the prophets." Then all the disciples deserted Him and fled. **57.** people who arrested Jesus took Him to Caiaphas (the high priest), in which the scribes and elders had been accrued. **58.** Peter observed at a distance and entered the high priest's courtyard. He sat down to see what would happen. **59.** The leader clergymen and the whole Sanhedrin (Jewish council or courtroom) were attempting to find false testimony in opposition to Jesus as a way to placed Him to dying, **60.** however they couldn't discover any. despite the fact that many fake witnesses got here forward, their memories did not match. **61.** subsequently, two witnesses got here ahead and stated, "This man said, 'i will damage the temple of God and rebuild it in 3 days.'" **62.** The excessive priest stood up and asked Jesus, "Aren't You going to answer? What about the expenses these men are bringing in opposition to You?" **63.** however Jesus remained silent. The high priest then said, "I price You beneath oath through the dwelling God: tell us in case you are the Messiah (the Savior), the Son of God." **64.** Jesus spoke back, "you have stated so. but I tell you, within the future you will see the Son of man sitting at the right hand of the effective One (God) and coming at the clouds of heaven." **65.** The high priest tore his clothes (a sign of distress or outrage) and said, "He has spoken blasphemy (disrespecting or insulting God)! Why do we need more witnesses? **66.** You have heard the blasphemy! What is your verdict?" They answered, "He deserves to die." **67.** Then they spit in His face and struck Him with their fists. Others slapped Him, **68.** and said, "Prophesy to us, Messiah! Who hit You?" **69.** Peter was sitting outside in the courtyard. A servant girl came to him and said, "You also were with Jesus of Galilee." **70.** But he denied it in front of them all, saying, "I don't know what you're talking about." **71.** He went out to the gateway, where another girl saw him and said to those standing nearby, "This man was with Jesus of Nazareth." **72.** Again, he denied it, swearing an oath, "I don't know the man!" **73.** A little while later, those standing near Peter came up to him and said, "Surely you're one of them. Your accent gives you away." **74.** Then Peter began to curse (call down curses) and swear, saying, "I don't know the man!" Immediately, a rooster crowed. **75.** Then Peter remembered the words Jesus had spoken, "Before the rooster crows, you will deny Me three times." And he went outside and wept bitterly (sorrowfully, in regret).

Chapter 27

1. As dawn broke, the chief priests and the elders of the people met to plot (plan) against Jesus, seeking to have Him put to death. **2.** After binding Him, they took Jesus away and handed Him over to Pontius Pilate, the Roman governor. **3.** When Judas, who had betrayed (betrayed: secretly turned against) Jesus, saw that Jesus had been condemned (sentenced), he felt deep remorse (guilt). He returned the thirty silver coins to the chief priests and elders, **4.** confessing (admitting), "I have sinned by betraying innocent blood." But they responded, "What does that matter to us? You handle it yourself." **5.** In despair (hopelessness), Judas threw the silver coins down in the temple, then went away and hanged himself. **6.** The chief priests, however, collected the coins and said, "It is against the law to put this money into the temple treasury (funds for religious purposes), since it is blood money." **7.** After conferring (discussing) among themselves, they decided to use the money to buy the potter's field, to be used as a burial place for foreigners (strangers). **8.** Therefore, that field was called the Field of Blood, a name that has remained to this day. **9.** This fulfilled (completed) what the prophet Jeremiah had spoken, saying, "They took the thirty pieces of silver, the price at which He was valued by the children of Israel, **10.** and gave them for the potter's field, as the

Lord commanded me." **11.** Now Jesus was brought before the governor, who asked Him, "Are You the King of the Jews?" Jesus responded, "You have said so." **12.** As the chief priests and elders made their accusations, Jesus remained silent. **13.** Pilate then asked Him, "Do You not hear all the things they are saying against You?" **14.** But Jesus gave no answer, which amazed (surprised) the governor. **15.** Now, during the feast, it was the custom (tradition) for the governor to release one prisoner to the crowd, the one they chose. **16.** At that time, there was a notorious (famous for bad reasons) criminal named Barabbas. **17.** Pilate, knowing they had handed Jesus over out of envy (jealousy), asked the crowd, "Which one do you want me to release to you? Barabbas or Jesus who is called Christ?" **18.** Pilate knew that it was because of envy that they had brought Jesus to trial. **19.** While Pilate was sitting on the judgment seat (the place where judges sit to make decisions), his wife sent him a message, saying, "Have nothing to do with that righteous Man, for I have suffered much today in a dream because of Him." **20.** But the chief priests and elders stirred up (encouraged) the crowd to ask for Barabbas and demand (insist) that Jesus be put to death. **21.** Pilate asked them again, "Which of the two do you want me to release to you?" They answered, "Barabbas!" **22.** Pilate then asked, "What should I do with Jesus who is called Christ?" They all replied, "Crucify Him!" **23.** Pilate responded, "Why? What has He done wrong?" But they shouted even louder, "Crucify Him!" **24.** Pilate, realizing he was getting nowhere and that a riot (violent disturbance) was about to break out, took water and washed his hands in front of the crowd, declaring, "I am innocent of this Man's blood. It is your responsibility." **25.** And the crowd answered, "Let His blood be on us and on our children!" **26.** Pilate then released Barabbas to them, and after having Jesus flogged (whipped), he handed Him over to be crucified. **27.** The governor's soldiers took Jesus into the palace and gathered the whole battalion (military unit) around Him. **28.** They stripped Him and put a scarlet robe on Him. **29.** Then they wove (twisted together) a crown of thorns and placed it on His head, and they put a staff in His right hand. They knelt before Him and mocked (made fun of) Him, saying, "Hail, King of the Jews!" **30.** They spat (spit) on Him, took the staff, and struck Him on the head. **31.** After mocking Him, the soldiers removed His robe, put His own clothes back on Him, and led Him away to be crucified. **32.** As they were leaving the city, they encountered a man from Cyrene named Simon, and they forced him to carry Jesus' cross. **33.** They arrived at a place called Golgotha, which means "Place of the Skull." **34.** There, they offered Jesus a drink of sour wine mixed with gall (a bitter substance), but after tasting it, He refused to drink. **35.** Then they nailed Him to the cross and divided (split) His garments by casting lots (throwing dice), fulfilling the prophecy that said, "They divided My clothes among them, and for My clothing, they cast lots." **36.** The soldiers then sat down to keep watch over Him. **37.** Above His head, they placed a sign that read: "THIS IS JESUS, THE KING OF THE JEWS." **38.** Two criminals were also crucified with Him, one on His right and one on His left. **39.** Those who passed by mocked (ridiculed) Him, shaking their heads and saying, **40.** "You who were going to destroy the temple and rebuild it in three days, save Yourself! If You are the Son of God, come down from the cross!" **41.** In the same way, the chief priests, the teachers of the law, and the elders mocked (ridiculed) Him, **42.** saying, "He saved others, but He cannot save Himself! If He is the King of Israel, let Him come down from the cross, and we will believe in Him. **43.** He trusted in God; let God deliver Him now if He is really His Son, for He said, 'I am the Son of God.'" **44.** Even the criminals who were crucified alongside Him joined in the mockery. **45.** From noon until 3:00 PM, darkness covered the entire land. **46.** At about 3:00 PM, Jesus cried out in a loud voice, "Eli, Eli, lama sabachthani?" which means, "My God, My God, why have You abandoned (forsaken) Me?" **47.** Some of the people standing there heard this and said, "He is calling for Elijah!" **48.** Immediately, one of them ran and filled a sponge with sour wine, placed it on a stick, and offered it to Jesus to drink. **49.** Others said, "Leave Him alone. Let's see if Elijah comes to save Him." **50.** Then Jesus cried out again in a loud voice and gave up His spirit. **51.** At that moment, the curtain of the temple was torn (ripped) in two from top to bottom; the earth shook, and the rocks split apart. **52.** The tombs were opened, and many bodies of the holy people who had died were raised to life. **53.** After Jesus' resurrection, these people came out of their tombs and went into the holy city, where they appeared to many. **54.** When the Roman centurion and his soldiers, who were guarding Jesus, saw the earthquake and all that had happened, they were filled with awe and said, "Surely this was the Son of God!" **55.** Many women who had followed Jesus from Galilee, serving (ministering) Him, were there, watching from a distance. **56.** Among them were Mary Magdalene, Mary the mother of James and Joses, and the mother of the sons of Zebedee. **57.** As evening approached, a wealthy man from Arimathea named Joseph, who had become a disciple of Jesus, **58.** went to Pilate and requested the body of Jesus. Pilate gave him permission to take it. **59.** Joseph took the body, wrapped it in a clean linen cloth, **60.** and placed it in his new tomb, which had been cut out of the rock. He rolled a large stone to seal the entrance and then left. **61.** Mary Magdalene and the other Mary were sitting across from the tomb, observing. **62.** The following day, after the Day of Preparation (the day before the Sabbath), the chief priests and Pharisees went to Pilate **63.** and said, "Sir, we remember that while He was still alive, that deceiver (fraud) claimed, 'After three days, I will rise again.' **64.** So order the tomb to be secured until the third day. Otherwise, His disciples might come and steal His body and then claim to the people, 'He has risen from the dead.' This last deception will be worse than the first." **65.** Pilate replied, "Take a guard of soldiers. Go, make the tomb as secure as you can." **66.** So they went and made the tomb secure by sealing the stone and posting a guard.

Chapter 28

1. After the Sabbath, as dawn (the first light of day) broke on the first day of the week, Mary Magdalene and the other Mary went to see the tomb. **2.** Suddenly, there was a great earthquake; an angel (a heavenly messenger) of the Lord descended, rolled back the stone, and sat on it. **3.** His appearance was like lightning, and his clothing was as white as snow. **4.** The guards trembled (shook in fear) and became like dead men. **5.** But the angel said to the women, "Do not be afraid; I know you're looking for Jesus who was crucified. **6.** He is not here; He has risen (been brought back to life), as He said. Come, see the place where He lay. **7.** Go quickly and tell His disciples that He is risen, and He is going before you to Galilee. There you will see Him. I have told you." **8.** They left the tomb quickly, filled with fear and great joy, and ran to tell the disciples. **9.** As they went, Jesus met them and said, "Rejoice!" They came, took hold of His feet, and worshiped Him. **10.** Jesus said to them, "Do not be afraid. Go and tell My brothers (disciples) to go to Galilee, and there they will see Me." **11.** Meanwhile, some of the guards went into the city and reported to the chief priests all that had happened. **12.** After consulting (meeting together and discussing) with the elders, they gave the soldiers a large sum of money, **13.** instructing them, "Tell people, 'His disciples came by night and stole Him while we slept.' **14.** If this reaches the governor, we will cover for you (protect you from punishment) and keep you safe." **15.** The soldiers took the money and did as they were instructed; this story has been circulated (spread) among the Jews to this day. **16.** Then the eleven disciples went to Galilee, to the mountain where Jesus had told them to go. **17.** When they saw Him, they worshiped Him, but some doubted (were uncertain or unsure). **18.** Jesus came to them and said, "All authority (power and control) in heaven and on earth has been given to Me. **19.** Therefore, go and make disciples (followers) of all nations, baptizing them in the name of the Father, the Son, and the Holy Spirit, **20.** and teaching them to obey everything I have commanded you. And surely I am with you always, to the very end of the age." Amen.

49 – Mark

Chapter 1

1. The beginning of the good news about Jesus the Messiah, the Son of God. **2.** As the prophet Isaiah wrote: "I will send my messenger ahead of you to prepare your way." **3.** "A voice calling in the wilderness, 'Prepare the way for the Lord, make straight paths for him.'" **4.** John appeared in the wilderness, preaching a baptism (ritual washing) of repentance (turning away from sin) for the forgiveness (pardon) of sins. **5.** People from all of Judea and Jerusalem came to him, confessed their sins, and were baptized in the Jordan River. **6.** John wore camel's hair and a leather belt, eating locusts (insects) and honey. **7.** His message: "After me comes one stronger than I, whose sandals I am not worthy to untie. **8.** I baptize with water, but he will baptize with the Holy Spirit (God's presence and power)." **9.** Jesus came from Nazareth (a town in Galilee) in Galilee and was baptized by John in the Jordan River. **10.** As Jesus came up from the water, he saw the heavens open, and the Spirit (Holy Spirit) descended on him like a dove. **11.** A voice from heaven said, "You are my Son, whom I love; I am pleased with you." **12.** The Spirit immediately led him into the wilderness. **13.** He was there for forty days, tempted (tested) by Satan (the devil), surrounded by wild animals, and attended (helped) by angels. **14.** After John was imprisoned, Jesus went to Galilee, preaching the good news of God. **15.** "The time has come," he said. "The kingdom of God is near. Repent (turn away from sin) and believe the good news!" **16.** Walking by the Sea of Galilee, Jesus saw Simon and Andrew casting nets. "Follow me," he said, "and I will make you fishers of people." **17.** They immediately followed him. **18.** Further along, he saw James and John, the sons of Zebedee, in a boat, mending (repairing) their nets. He called them, and they left their father to follow him. **21.** In Capernaum (a town in Galilee), on the Sabbath (the Jewish day of rest), Jesus entered the synagogue and began teaching. **22.** The people were amazed at his authority (power), unlike the teachers of the law. **23.** Suddenly, a man with an impure (unclean) spirit cried out, **24.** "What do you want with us, Jesus of Nazareth? Have you come to destroy us? I know who you are—the Holy One of God!" **25.** "Be quiet!" Jesus said. "Come out of him!" **26.** The spirit threw the man into a convulsion (violent shaking) and shrieked as it left him. **27.** The people were amazed, asking, "What is this new teaching with authority? He even commands evil spirits and they obey him!" **28.** News of him spread quickly throughout the region of Galilee. **29.** After leaving the synagogue, they went to Simon and Andrew's house. **30.** Simon's mother-in-law was in bed with a fever. Jesus took her hand, helped her up, and the fever left her. She began to serve them. **32.** That evening, people brought all the sick and demon-possessed (those controlled by evil spirits) to Jesus. **33.** The whole town gathered at the door. **34.** Jesus healed many with various diseases and drove out demons, but he did not allow demons to speak because they knew who he was. **35.** Early the next morning, while it was still dark, Jesus went to a solitary (alone) place and prayed. **36.** Simon and his companions found him and said, "Everyone is looking for you!" **37.** Jesus replied, "Let's go to other villages to preach there also, for that is why I came." **39.** So he traveled throughout Galilee, preaching in synagogues and driving out demons. **40.** A man with leprosy (a serious skin disease) came to Jesus and begged, "If you are willing, you can make me clean (free from disease)." **41.** Jesus, filled with compassion (deep sympathy), touched him and said, "I am willing. Be clean!" **42.** Immediately the leprosy left him, and he was healed. **43.** Jesus sent him away with a strong warning: **44.** "Don't tell anyone. Go to the priest and offer the sacrifices Moses commanded for your cleansing, as a testimony to them." **45.** Instead, the man went out and spread the news, so much so that Jesus could no longer enter towns openly and stayed in remote (isolated) places. Yet people still came to him from everywhere.

Chapter 2

1. A few days later, Jesus returned to Capernaum (a town in Galilee), and the people heard that he was home. **2.** So many gathered that there was no room left, not even outside the door, and Jesus began teaching them. **3.** Some men brought a paralyzed (unable to move) man, carried by four of them. **4.** Because they couldn't reach Jesus due to the crowd, they made a hole in the roof above him, and lowered the man on his mat. **5.** When Jesus saw their faith (trust in him), he said to the paralyzed man, "Son, your sins are forgiven." **6.** Some teachers of the law were sitting there, thinking, **7.** "Why does this man talk like that? He is blaspheming (showing disrespect for God)! Who can forgive sins but God alone?" **8.** At once, Jesus knew in his spirit (mind) what they were thinking, and said, "Why are you thinking like this? **9.** Which is easier: to say, 'Your sins are forgiven,' or to say, 'Get up, take your mat and walk'? **10.** But I want you to know that the Son of Man (a title Jesus used for himself) has authority (power) on earth to forgive sins." Then he said to the man, **11.** "I tell you, get up, take your mat and go home." **12.** The man got up, took his mat, and walked out in full view of everyone. They were all amazed and praised God, saying, "We've never seen anything like this!" **13.** Jesus went beside the lake again. A large crowd gathered, and he began teaching them. **14.** As he walked along, he saw Levi, the son of Alphaeus, sitting at the tax collector's booth. "Follow me," Jesus told him. Levi got up and followed. **15.** While Jesus was dining at Levi's house, many tax collectors (people who collected taxes for the Romans) and sinners were eating with him and his disciples, because many followed him. **16.** When the Pharisees (a group of religious leaders) saw this, they asked his disciples, "Why does he eat with tax collectors and sinners?" **17.** Jesus overheard and said, "It is not the healthy who need a doctor, but the sick. I have come to call not the righteous (those who think they are good), but sinners." **18.** Now, John's disciples and the Pharisees were fasting (going without food as a religious practice). Some people asked Jesus, "Why do John's disciples and the Pharisees fast, but your disciples do not?" **19.** Jesus replied, "How can the guests of the bridegroom (the groom at a wedding) fast while he is with them? As long as they have him, they cannot fast. **20.** But the time will come when the bridegroom (referring to himself, Jesus) will be taken from them, and then they will fast. **21.** "No one sews a patch of unshrunk (not pre-washed) cloth on an old garment. Otherwise, the new patch will shrink and tear the old cloth. **22.** "And no one pours new wine into old wineskins. Otherwise, the wine will burst the skins, and both the wine and the wineskins will be ruined. No, they pour new wine into new wineskins." **23.** One Sabbath, Jesus and his disciples walked through grainfields, and as they walked, they began to pick heads of grain. **24.** The Pharisees said to Jesus, "Look, why are they doing what is unlawful (forbidden) on the Sabbath?" **25.** He answered, "Have you never read what David did when he and his companions were hungry? **26.** In the days of Abiathar (a high priest), he entered the house of God and ate the consecrated (set apart for sacred use) bread, which is allowed only for priests to eat. He also gave some to his companions." **27.** Then Jesus said to them, "The Sabbath was made for man, not man for the Sabbath. **28.** So the Son of Man is Lord even of the Sabbath."

Chapter 3

1. Another time, Jesus entered the synagogue, and a man with a withered (shriveled, damaged) hand was present. **2.** Some people were watching closely, hoping to find a reason to accuse Jesus. They wanted to see if he would heal on the Sabbath (a day of rest). **3.** Jesus said to the man with the withered hand, "Stand up in front of everyone." **4.** Then he asked them, "What is allowed on the Sabbath: to do good or to do harm, to save a life or to destroy one?" But they remained silent. **5.** Jesus looked at them in anger and was deeply troubled by their stubborn hearts. He said to the man, "Stretch out your hand." The man did so, and his hand was completely healed. **6.** The Pharisees (religious leaders) went out and began to plot with the Herodians (supporters of King Herod) about how they could kill Jesus. **7.** Jesus withdrew with his disciples to the lake, and a large crowd from Galilee followed him. **8.** When the people heard about all the things he had done, many came from Judea, Jerusalem, Idumea (a region south of Judea), and the areas across the Jordan River, as well as from Tyre and Sidon (coastal cities). **9.** Because of the large crowds, Jesus told his disciples to have a small boat ready for him, so the people wouldn't crowd him. **10.** He had healed many, and those suffering from diseases were pushing to touch him. **11.** Whenever the evil spirits saw him, they fell down before him and cried out, "You are the Son of God." **12.** But he gave them strict instructions not to tell anyone about him. **13.** Jesus went up a mountainside and called to him those he wanted, and they came to him. **14.** He chose twelve, that they might be with him and that he might send them out to preach **15.** and give them authority (power) to drive out demons. **16.** The twelve he appointed were: Simon (whom he called Peter), **17.** James, the son of Zebedee, and his brother John (whom he called Boanerges, meaning "sons of thunder"), **18.** Andrew, Philip, Bartholomew, Matthew, Thomas, James son of Alphaeus, Thaddaeus, Simon the Zealot **19.** and Judas Iscariot, who later betrayed him. **20.** Later, Jesus entered a house, and again a crowd gathered, so that he and his disciples couldn't even eat. **21.** When his family heard about this, they went to take charge of him, saying, "He's out of his mind." **22.** The teachers of the law, who had come down from Jerusalem, said, "He is possessed by Beelzebul (a name for Satan or the prince of demons)! By the ruler of demons, he casts out demons." **23.** So Jesus called them over and began speaking in parables (stories that teach a moral lesson): "How can Satan drive out Satan? **24.** If a kingdom is divided against itself, it cannot stand. **25.** If a house is divided, it cannot stand. **26.** If Satan opposes himself and divides his forces, he cannot stand. His end has come. **27.** No one can enter a strong man's house without first tying him up. Then they can take what belongs to him. **28.** I tell you, people can be forgiven for all their sins and any slander (false accusations) they speak, **29.** But anyone who blasphemes (speaks disrespectfully) against the Holy Spirit will never be forgiven; they are guilty of an eternal sin." **30.** Jesus said this because they were accusing him of being possessed by an evil spirit. **31.** Then Jesus' mother and brothers arrived. They stood outside and sent someone to call him. **32.** A crowd was sitting around him, and they told him, "Your mother and brothers are outside looking for you." **33.** Jesus asked, "Who are my mother and my brothers?" **34.** Then he looked at those seated in a circle around him and said, "Here are my mother and my brothers! **35.** Whoever does the will of God is my brother, sister, and mother."

Chapter 4

1. Jesus taught by the lake. The crowd was so large that he got into a boat while the people stood along the shore. He taught them using parables (stories with a hidden message), saying: **2.** "Listen! A farmer went to sow (plant) seed. **3.** Some fell on the path, and birds came and ate it up. **4.** Some fell on rocky ground (shallow soil), where it sprouted quickly but withered when the sun came up because it had no roots (deeply grounded parts). **5.** Some fell among thorns (plants that can choke others), which choked the plants and made them unfruitful (unable to produce good results). **6.** Some fell on good soil, grew, and produced a crop—some thirty, some sixty, some a hundred times what was sown." **9.** "Whoever has ears to hear, let them hear." **10.** The Twelve and others asked him about the parables. **11.** He said, "The secret (hidden truth) of the kingdom of God is given to you, but to outsiders, everything is in parables, **12.** so that 'they may be ever seeing but never perceiving (understanding), and ever hearing but never understanding.' **13.** "Don't you understand this parable? How will you understand all parables? **14.** The farmer sows the word (God's message). **15.** Some are like seed on the path, where Satan (the enemy) takes away the word as soon as they hear it. **16.** Some, like seed on rocky ground, hear and receive the word joyfully, but they fall away when trouble comes because they have no roots. **18.** Some, like seed among thorns, hear the word, but worries, wealth (money), and desires choke it, making it unfruitful. **20.** Others, like seed on good soil, accept the word and produce a crop—some thirty, some sixty, some a hundred times what was sown." **21.** "Do you bring in a lamp to put it under a bowl or a bed? No, you put it on its stand (place of visibility). **22.** Everything hidden will be revealed, and what is concealed will be brought into the open. **23.** If anyone has ears to hear, let them hear." **24.** "Consider carefully what you hear," he continued. "The measure (standard) you use will be measured to you—and more. **25.** Whoever has will be given more; whoever does not have, even what they have will be taken." **26.** "The kingdom of God is like a man who scatters seed. **27.** The seed grows night and day, whether he sleeps or gets up, and he doesn't know how. **28.** The soil produces grain (harvest)—first the stalk, then the head, then the full kernel (grain) in the head. **29.** As soon as the grain is ripe, he puts the sickle (harvesting tool) to it, because the harvest has come." **30.** Again he said, "What shall we say the kingdom of God is like, or what parable shall we use to describe it? **31.** It is like a mustard seed, which is the smallest of all seeds on earth. **32.** Yet when planted, it grows and becomes the largest of all garden plants, with such big branches that the birds can perch in its shade." **33.** With many similar parables, Jesus spoke the word to them, as much as they could understand. **34.** He did not say anything to them without using a parable. But when he was alone with his disciples, he explained everything. **35.** That day, when evening came, he said to his disciples, "Let us go over to the other side." **36.** Leaving the crowd behind, they took him along, just as he was, in the boat. There were also other boats with them. **37.** A furious squall (violent storm) came up, and the waves broke over the boat, so that it was nearly swamped (flooded). **38.** Jesus was in the stern (back of the boat), sleeping on a cushion. The disciples woke him and said to him, "Teacher, don't you care if we drown?" **39.** He got up, rebuked (calmed) the wind, and said to the waves, "Quiet! Be still!" Then the wind died down, and it was completely calm. **40.** He said to his disciples, "Why are you so afraid? Do you still have no faith?" **41.** They were terrified and asked each other, "Who is this? Even the wind and the waves obey him!"

Chapter 5

1. They went across the lake to the region of the Gerasenes (a place in Gentile territory). **2.** When Jesus got out of the boat, a man with an impure spirit (evil spirit) came from the tombs to meet him. **3.** This man lived in the tombs, and no one could bind him, even with chains. **4.** He had often been chained hand and foot, but he tore the chains apart and broke the irons on his feet. No one was strong enough to subdue him. **5.** Night and day, among the tombs and in the hills, he cried out and cut himself with stones. **6.** When he saw Jesus from a distance, he ran and fell on his knees before him. **7.** He shouted, "What do you want with me, Jesus, Son of the Most High God? In God's name, don't torture me!" **8.** For Jesus had said, "Come out of this man, you impure spirit!" **9.** Jesus asked him, "What is your name?" "My name is Legion," he replied, "for we are many." **10.** And he begged Jesus not to send them out of the area. **11.** A large herd of pigs was feeding on the hillside. **12.** The demons begged Jesus, "Send us into the pigs; let us go into them." **13.** Jesus gave them permission, and the impure spirits came out and went into the pigs. The herd, about two thousand pigs, rushed down the steep bank into the lake and drowned. **14.** The herders ran off and reported this in the town and countryside, and people went out to see what had happened. **15.** When they came to Jesus, they saw the man who had been possessed by the demons, sitting there, dressed and in his right mind; and they were afraid. **16.** Those who had seen it told the people what had happened to the demon-possessed man—and about the pigs. **17.** Then the people began to plead with Jesus to leave their region. **18.** As Jesus was getting into the boat, the man who had been demon-possessed begged to go with him. **19.** Jesus did not let him, but said, "Go home to your people and tell them how much the Lord has done for you, and how he has had mercy on you." **20.** So the man went away and began to tell in the Decapolis (a group of ten cities) how much Jesus had done for him. All the people were amazed. **21.** When Jesus had crossed over by boat to the other side of the lake, a large crowd gathered around him. **22.** One of the synagogue leaders, named Jairus, came and fell at Jesus' feet. **23.** He pleaded, "My little daughter is dying. Please come and put your hands on her so that she will be healed and live." **24.** So Jesus went with him. A large crowd followed and pressed around him. **25.** And a woman was there who had been bleeding for twelve years. **26.** She had suffered a great deal under the care of many doctors and had spent all she had, yet instead of getting better, she grew worse. **27.** When she heard about Jesus, she came up behind him in the crowd and touched his cloak. **28.** She thought, "If I just touch his clothes, I will be healed." **29.** Immediately, her bleeding stopped, and she felt in her body that she was freed from her suffering. **30.** At once, Jesus realized that power had gone out from him. He turned around in the crowd and asked, "Who touched my clothes?" **31.** His disciples said, "You see the people crowding against you, and yet you ask, 'Who touched me?'" **32.** But Jesus kept looking around to see who had done it. **33.** Then the woman, knowing what had happened to her, came and fell at his feet, trembling with fear, and told him the whole truth. **34.** He said to her, "Daughter, your faith has healed you. Go in peace and be freed from your suffering." **35.** While Jesus was still speaking, some people came from the house of Jairus, the synagogue leader, and said, "Your daughter is dead. Why bother the teacher anymore?" **36.** Overhearing what they said, Jesus told Jairus, "Don't be afraid; just believe." **37.** He did not let anyone follow him except Peter, James, and John, the brother of James. **38.** When they came to the house of the synagogue leader, Jesus saw a commotion, with people crying and wailing loudly. **39.** He went in and said, "Why all this commotion and wailing? The child is not dead but asleep." **40.** They laughed at him. After putting them all out, he took the child's father and mother and the disciples who were with him, and went in where the child was. **41.** He took her by the hand and said, "Talitha koum!" (which means "Little girl, I say to you, get up!"). **42.** Immediately the girl stood up and began to walk around (she was twelve years old). At this, they were completely astonished. **43.** He gave strict orders not to let anyone know about this, and told them to give her something to eat.

Chapter 6

1. Jesus left that place and went to his hometown, accompanied by his disciples. **2.** On the Sabbath, he began teaching in the synagogue, and many who heard him were amazed. They asked, "Where did this man get all these things? What's this wisdom (knowledge and insight) given to him? How can he perform such remarkable (outstanding or extraordinary) miracles? **3.** Isn't this the carpenter? Isn't he the son of Mary, and the brother of James, Joseph, Judas, and Simon? Aren't his sisters here with us?" And they took offense (felt insulted or disrespected) at him. **4.** Jesus said to them, "A prophet is honored everywhere except in his own town, among his own relatives, and in his own home." **5.** He could not perform any miracles there, except lay his hands on a few sick people and heal them. **6.** He was amazed (astonished or surprised) at their lack of faith. **Jesus**

7. Then Jesus went around teaching from village to village. **8.** He called the Twelve disciples and began sending them out two by two, giving them authority (power or permission) to drive out impure (evil or unclean) spirits. **9.** He instructed them: "Take nothing for the journey except a staff—no bread, no bag, no money in your belts. **10.** Wear sandals but don't bring an extra shirt. **11.** When you enter a house, stay there until you leave that town. **12.** And if any place does not welcome you or listen to you, leave and shake the dust off your feet as a testimony (witness or sign) against them." **13.** They went out, preaching that people should repent (turn away from sin). They drove out many demons, anointed many sick people with oil, and healed them. **14.** King Herod heard about this, for Jesus' name had become widely known. Some were saying, "John the Baptist has been raised from the dead, and that is why miraculous (amazing or supernatural) powers are at work in him." **15.** Others said, "He is Elijah." And still others claimed, "He is a prophet, like one of the prophets from long ago." **16.** But when Herod heard of this, he said, "John, whom I beheaded (cut off his head), has been raised from the dead!" **17.** For Herod himself had ordered John to be arrested, bound, and put in prison. He did this because of Herodias, his brother Philip's wife, whom he had married. **18.** For John had told Herod, "It is unlawful (against the law) for you to have your brother's wife." **19.** So Herodias held a grudge (deep resentment) against John and wanted to kill him, but she could not, **20.** because Herod feared (was afraid of) John, knowing he was a righteous (morally right) and holy (set apart or sacred) man. When Herod heard John speak, he was greatly perplexed (confused or puzzled), yet he liked to listen to him. **21.** Finally, the opportune (timely or favorable) moment came. On his birthday, Herod gave a banquet (large meal) for his high officials, military commanders, and the leading men of Galilee. **22.** When the daughter of Herodias came in and danced, she pleased Herod and his guests. The king said to the girl, "Ask me for anything you want, and I'll give it to you." **23.** And he promised her with an oath (a solemn vow), "Whatever you ask, I'll give you, up to half my kingdom." **24.** She went out and asked her mother, "What should I ask for?" Her mother replied, "The head of John the Baptist." **25.** At once the girl hurried back to the king with the request: "I want you to give me John the Baptist's head on a platter (dish) right now." **26.** The king was greatly distressed (upset), but because of his oaths and his dinner guests, he didn't want to refuse her. **27.** So he immediately sent an executioner (person who carries out a death sentence) with orders to bring John's head. The man went, beheaded John in the prison, **28.** and brought back his head on a platter. He presented it to the girl, and she gave it to her mother. **29.** When John's disciples heard of this, they came, took his body, and laid it in a tomb. **30.** The apostles gathered around Jesus and reported to him all they had done and taught. **31.** Then, because so many people were coming and going that they didn't even have time to eat, he said to them, "Come with me by yourselves to a quiet (peaceful or secluded) place and get some rest." **32.** So they went away by themselves in a boat to a solitary (remote or empty) place. **33.** But many people saw them leaving and recognized them. They ran on foot from all the towns and arrived ahead of them. **34.** When Jesus landed and saw a large crowd, he had compassion (sympathy or care) on them, because they were like sheep without a shepherd. So he began teaching them many things. **35.** By now it was late in the day, so his disciples came to him and said, "This is a remote place, and it's already very late. **36.** Send the people away so they can go to the surrounding villages and buy themselves something to eat." **37.** But Jesus answered, "You give them something to eat." They said to him, "That would take more than half a year's wages! Are we to go and spend that much on bread and give it to them to eat?" **38.** "How many loaves do you have?" he asked. "Go and see." When they found out, they said, "Five loaves and two fish."

39. Then Jesus directed them to have all the people sit down in groups on the green grass. **40.** So they sat down in groups of hundreds and fifties. **41.** Taking the five loaves and the two fish, Jesus looked up to heaven, gave thanks, and broke the loaves. Then he gave them to his disciples to distribute to the people. He also divided the two fish among them all. **42.** They all ate and were satisfied. **43.** The disciples picked up twelve basketfuls of broken pieces of bread and fish. **44.** The number of men who had eaten was five thousand. **45.** Immediately, Jesus made his disciples get into the boat and go on ahead of him to Bethsaida, while he dismissed the crowd. **46.** After leaving them, he went up on a mountainside to pray. **47.** Later that night, the boat was in the middle of the lake, and Jesus was alone on land. **48.** He saw the disciples straining (struggling) at the oars, because the wind was against them. Shortly before dawn, he went out to them, walking on the water. He was about to pass them, **49.** but when they saw him walking on the lake, they thought he was a ghost. They cried out, **50.** because they all saw him and were terrified (frightened). Immediately, he spoke to them and said, "Take courage (be brave)! It is I. Don't be afraid." **51.** Then he climbed into the boat with them, and the wind died down. They were completely amazed, **52.** for they had not understood about the loaves; their hearts were hardened (unresponsive or stubborn). **53.** When they had crossed over, they landed at Gennesaret and anchored there. **54.** As soon as they got out of the boat, people recognized Jesus. **55.** They ran throughout that whole region and carried the sick on mats (bedding or stretchers) to wherever they heard he was. **56.** And wherever he went—into villages, towns, or the countryside—they placed the sick in the marketplaces and begged him to let them touch even the edge of his cloak. And all who touched it were healed.

Chapter 7

1. The Pharisees and some of the teachers of the law who had come from Jerusalem gathered around Jesus. **2.** They noticed that some of his disciples were eating food with hands that were defiled (unclean), meaning they had not washed their hands. **3.** (The Pharisees, and all Jews, do not eat unless they give their hands a ceremonial washing, following the tradition of the elders. **4.** When they come from the marketplace, they do not eat unless they wash their hands. They also follow many other traditions, such as washing cups, pitchers, and kettles.) **5.** So the Pharisees and teachers of the law asked Jesus, "Why don't your disciples follow the tradition of the elders and eat their food with unwashed hands?" **6.** He replied, "Isaiah was right when he prophesied (predicted) about you hypocrites (people who pretend to have moral standards they do not follow); as it is written: 'These people honor me with their lips, but their hearts are far from me. **7.** They worship me in vain; their teachings are merely human rules.' **8.** You have let go of the commands of God and are holding on to human traditions." **9.** And he continued, "You have a fine way of setting aside (ignoring) the commands of God in order to observe (follow) your own traditions! **10.** For Moses said, 'Honor your father and mother,' and 'Anyone who curses their father or mother is to be put to death.' **11.** But you say that if anyone declares that what might have been used to help their father or mother is Corban (a gift devoted to God)— **12.** then you no longer allow them to do anything for their father or mother. **13.** Thus you nullify (invalidate) the word of God by your tradition that you have handed down. And you do many things like that." **14.** Again, Jesus called the crowd to him and said, "Listen to me, everyone, and understand this: **15.** Nothing outside a person can defile (make unclean) them by going into them. Rather, it is what comes out of a person that defiles (makes unclean) them." **17.** After leaving the crowd and entering the house, his disciples asked him about this parable (story with a deeper meaning). **18.** "Are you so dull (slow to understand)?" he asked. "Don't you see that nothing that enters a person from the outside can defile (make impure) them? **19.** For it doesn't go into their heart but into their stomach, and then out of the body." (In saying this, Jesus declared all foods clean.) **20.** He went on: "What comes out of a person is what defiles them. **21.** For it is from within, out of a person's heart, that evil thoughts come—sexual immorality, theft, murder, **22.** adultery, greed (strong desire for material gain), malice (evil intent), deceit (dishonesty), lewdness (vulgarity), envy (jealousy), slander (false accusations), arrogance (pride), and folly (foolishness). **23.** All these evils come from inside and defile (make impure) a person." **24.** Jesus left that place and went to the vicinity (area) of Tyre. He entered a house and did not want anyone to know about it, but he could not keep his presence secret. **25.** As soon as she heard about him, a woman whose little daughter was possessed by an impure (evil) spirit came and fell at his feet. **26.** The woman was a Greek, born in Syrian Phoenicia. She begged Jesus to drive the demon (evil spirit) out of her daughter. **27.** "First let the children eat all they want," he told her, "for it is not right to take the children's bread and toss it to the dogs." **28.** "Lord," she replied, "even the dogs under the table eat the children's crumbs." **29.** Then he told her, "For such a reply, you may go; the demon has left your daughter." **30.** She went home and found her child lying on the bed, and the demon gone. **31.** Then Jesus left the vicinity of Tyre and went through Sidon, down to the Sea of Galilee, and into the region of the Decapolis (a group of ten cities). **32.** Some people brought to him a man who was deaf (unable to hear) and could hardly talk, and they begged Jesus to place his hand on him. **33.** After taking him aside, away from the crowd, Jesus put his fingers into the man's ears. Then he spit and touched the man's tongue. **34.** He looked up to heaven and, with a deep sigh, said to him, "Ephphatha!" (which means "Be opened!"). **35.** At this, the man's ears were opened, his tongue was loosened, and he began to speak plainly. **36.** Jesus commanded them not to tell anyone. But the more he did so, the more they kept talking about it. **37.** People were overwhelmed with amazement. "He has done everything well," they said. "He even makes the deaf hear and the mute speak."

Chapter 8

1. A large crowd gathered again. Jesus, seeing they had no food after three days, called his disciples. **2.** He said, "I feel sorry (compassion – deep sympathy and concern) for these people; if I send them home hungry, they might faint on the way, as some have traveled far." **3.** The disciples asked, "Where can we get enough bread in this isolated (remote – far from other places) place to feed them?" **4.** Jesus asked, "How many loaves do you have?" They replied, "Seven." **5.** Jesus had the people sit down, took the seven loaves, gave thanks, and broke them. He gave them to the disciples to distribute. **6.** He also had a few small fish, which he blessed and told the disciples to pass out. **7.** The people ate until full. Seven basketfuls (large containers) of leftovers were collected. **8.** About four thousand were fed. After sending them away, **9.** Jesus got into the boat with his disciples and sailed to the region of Dalmanutha. **10.** The Pharisees came to test (to challenge or examine) Jesus, asking for a sign (proof) from heaven. **11.** Jesus sighed and said, "Why does this generation ask for a sign? No sign will be given." **12.** Then he left them, returned to the boat, and crossed to the other side. **13.** The disciples had forgotten to bring enough bread, except for one loaf. **14.** Jesus warned them, "Beware (be cautious) of the yeast (influence) of the Pharisees and Herod." **15.** They thought it was because they had no bread and discussed it. **16.** Jesus said, "Why are you worried about bread? Do you still not understand? Don't you remember? **17.** When I fed the five thousand, how many baskets (large containers) of leftovers did you gather?" **18.** "Twelve," they replied. **19.** "And when I fed the four thousand, how many baskets did you collect?" **20.** "Seven," they said. **21.** "Do you still not understand?" he asked. **22.** In Bethsaida, some people brought a blind (unable to see) man to Jesus and begged him to touch him. **23.** Jesus led the man outside the village, spat on his eyes, and placed his hands on him. He asked, "Do you see anything?" **24.** The man said, "I see people, but they look like trees walking." **25.** Jesus touched his eyes again, and the man's sight was fully restored. He could see clearly. **26.** Jesus told him to go home and not enter the village. **27.** As Jesus and his disciples traveled near Caesarea Philippi, he asked, "Who do people say I am?" **28.** They answered, "Some say John the Baptist, others say Elijah, or one of the prophets." **29.** "But who do you say I am?" Jesus asked. **30.** Peter replied, "You are the Messiah (the Savior)." **31.** Jesus warned them not to tell anyone about him. **32.** Jesus began teaching them that the Son of Man must suffer many things, be rejected by the religious leaders, and be killed, but rise after three days. **33.** Peter rebuked (corrected sharply) Jesus privately, but Jesus turned to his disciples and said to Peter, "Get behind me, Satan! (a symbol of evil or temptation) You are thinking with human concerns, not God's." **34.** Jesus called the crowd and said, "If anyone wants to be my disciple, they must deny (refuse to accept) themselves, take up their cross (symbolizing

suffering) and follow me. **35.** Whoever tries to save their life will lose it, but whoever loses their life for me and the gospel will save it. **36.** What good is it to gain the whole world and lose your soul? **37.** What can anyone give in exchange for their soul? **38.** If anyone is ashamed (embarrassed) of me and my words, I will be ashamed of them when I return in my Father's glory with the holy angels."

Chapter 9

1. Jesus said to them, "Truly I tell you, some of you standing here will not taste death (experience death) before they see that the kingdom of God has come with power." **2.** After six days, Jesus took Peter, James, and John up a high mountain where they were alone. There, he was transfigured (changed in appearance) before them. **3.** His clothes became dazzling white, whiter than anyone in the world could bleach them. **4.** Elijah and Moses appeared and were talking with Jesus. **5.** Peter said to Jesus, "Rabbi (teacher), it is good for us to be here. Let us build three shelters (temporary dwellings)—one for you, one for Moses, and one for Elijah." **6.** He didn't know what to say because they were so frightened. **7.** A cloud appeared and covered them, and a voice came from the cloud, saying: "This is my Son, whom I love. Listen to him!" **8.** Suddenly, when they looked around, they saw no one except Jesus. **9.** As they came down the mountain, Jesus ordered them not to tell anyone what they had seen until the Son of Man had risen from the dead. **10.** They kept the matter to themselves, questioning what "rising from the dead" meant. **11.** They asked Jesus, "Why do the teachers of the law say that Elijah must come first?" **12.** Jesus replied, "Elijah does come first and restores (brings back to a better state) all things. But why then is it written that the Son of Man must suffer much and be rejected? **13.** But I tell you, Elijah has already come, and they have done to him whatever they wished, as it is written about him." **14.** When they came to the other disciples, they saw a large crowd around them and the teachers of the law arguing with them. **15.** When the people saw Jesus, they were overwhelmed with wonder and ran to greet him. **16.** Jesus asked, "What are you arguing about?" **17.** A man in the crowd answered, "Teacher, I brought you my son, who has a spirit that makes him mute (unable to speak). **18.** Whenever the spirit seizes him, it throws him to the ground, and he foams at the mouth, gnashes his teeth, and becomes rigid (stiff). I asked your disciples to drive out the spirit, but they could not." **19.** "You unbelieving generation," Jesus replied, "How long shall I stay with you? How long shall I put up with you? Bring the boy to me." **20.** They brought him to Jesus. As soon as the spirit saw Jesus, it threw the boy into a convulsion (violent shaking). He fell to the ground and rolled around, foaming at the mouth. **21.** Jesus asked the boy's father, "How long has he been like this?" The father answered, "From childhood. **22.** It has often thrown him into fire or water to kill him. But if you can do anything, take pity on us and help us." **23.** "'If you can'?" said Jesus. "Everything is possible for one who believes." **24.** Immediately the boy's father exclaimed, "I do believe; help me overcome my unbelief!" **25.** When Jesus saw that a crowd was running to the scene, he rebuked (commanded sharply) the impure spirit. "You deaf and mute spirit," he said, "I command you, come out of him and never enter him again." **26.** The spirit shrieked (screamed loudly), convulsed him violently, and came out. The boy looked so much like a corpse (dead body) that many said, "He's dead." **27.** But Jesus took him by the hand, lifted him to his feet, and he stood up. **28.** After Jesus had gone indoors, his disciples asked him privately, "Why couldn't we drive it out?" **29.** He replied, "This kind (type) can come out only by prayer." **30.** They left that place and passed through Galilee. Jesus didn't want anyone to know where they were, **31.** because he was teaching his disciples. He said to them, "The Son of Man is going to be delivered into the hands of men. They will kill him, and after three days he will rise." **32.** But they did not understand what he meant and were afraid to ask him about it. **33.** They came to Capernaum. When Jesus was in the house, he asked them, "What were you arguing about on the road?" **34.** But they kept quiet because on the way they had argued about who was the greatest. **35.** Sitting down, Jesus called the Twelve and said, "Anyone who wants to be first must be the very last, and the servant of all." **36.** He took a little child, placed him among them, and taking the child in his arms, he said, **37.** "Whoever welcomes one of these little children in my name welcomes me; and whoever welcomes me does not welcome me but the one who sent me." **38.** "Teacher," said John, "we saw someone driving out demons in your name and we told him to stop, because he was not one of us." 39. "Do not stop him," Jesus replied. "For no one who does a miracle in my name can in the next moment say anything bad about me. 40. For whoever is not against us is for us. 41. Truly I tell you, anyone who gives you a cup of water in my name because you belong to the Messiah will certainly not lose their reward." 42. "If anyone causes one of these little ones—those who believe in me—to stumble (fall into sin), it would be better for them if a large millstone (a heavy grinding stone) were hung around their neck and they were thrown into the sea. 43. If your hand causes you to stumble, cut it off. It is better for you to enter life maimed (with a missing hand) than with two hands to go into hell, where the fire never goes out. 45. And if your foot causes you to stumble, cut it off. It is better for you to enter life crippled than to have two feet and be thrown into hell. 47. And if your eye causes you to stumble, pluck it out. It is better for you to enter the kingdom of God with one eye than to have two eyes and be thrown into hell, 48. where 'the worms that eat them do not die, and the fire is not quenched.' 49. Everyone will be salted (purified) with fire. 50. "Salt is good, but if it loses its saltiness, how can you make it salty again? Have salt among yourselves, and be at peace with each other."

Chapter 10

1. Jesus left that place and traveled to the region of Judea, across the Jordan River. Once again, large crowds gathered around him, and as was his habit, he taught them. 2. Some Pharisees came to test him, asking, "Is it lawful for a man to divorce his wife?" 3. Jesus responded, "What did Moses command you?" 4. They answered, "Moses allowed a man to write a certificate of divorce and send her away." 5. Jesus said, "It was because your hearts were hard that Moses wrote this law for you. 6. But from the beginning of creation, God 'made them male and female.' 7. 'For this reason a man will leave his father and mother and be united to his wife, 8. and the two will become one flesh.' So they are no longer two, but one. 9. Therefore, what God has joined together, let no one separate." 10. Later, when they were inside the house, the disciples asked Jesus about this. 11. He replied, "Anyone who divorces his wife and marries another woman commits adultery against her. 12. And if she divorces her husband and marries another man, she commits adultery." 13. People were bringing little children to Jesus for him to place his hands on them, but the disciples rebuked them. 14. When Jesus saw this, he was indignant and said, "Let the little children come to me, and do not hinder them, for the kingdom of God belongs to such as these. 15. Truly I tell you, anyone who will not receive the kingdom of God like a little child will never enter it." 16. And he took the children in his arms, placed his hands on them, and blessed them. 17. As Jesus was on his way, a man ran up to him, knelt before him, and asked, "Good teacher, what must I do to inherit eternal life?" 18. "Why do you call me good?" Jesus replied. "No one is good except God alone. 19. You know the commandments: 'Do not murder, do not commit adultery, do not steal, do not give false testimony, do not cheat, honor your father and mother.'" 20. "Teacher," the man said, "I have kept all of these since I was a boy." 21. Jesus looked at him and loved him. "One thing you lack," he said. "Go, sell everything you have and give it to the poor, and you will have treasure in heaven. Then come, follow me." 22. At this, the man's face fell, and he went away sad because he had great wealth. 23. Jesus looked around and said to his disciples, "How hard it is for the rich to enter the kingdom of God!" 24. The disciples were amazed at his words, but Jesus said again, "Children, how hard it is to enter the kingdom of God! 25. It is easier for a camel to go through the eye of a needle than for someone who is rich to enter the kingdom of God." 26. The disciples were even more amazed and said to each other, "Who then can be saved?" 27. Jesus looked at them and said, "With man this is impossible, but not with God; all things are possible with God." 28. Then Peter spoke up, "We have left everything to follow you!" 29. "Truly I tell you," Jesus replied, "no one who has left home, brothers, sisters, mother, father, children, or fields for me and the gospel 30. will fail to receive a hundred times as much in this present age—homes, brothers, sisters, mothers, children, and fields—along with persecutions—and in the age to come, eternal life. 31. But many who are first will be last, and the last first." 32. They were on their way to Jerusalem, and Jesus was leading the way. The disciples were astonished, and those who followed were afraid. Once again, he took the Twelve aside and told them what would happen to him. 33. "We are going up to Jerusalem," he said, "and the Son of Man will be delivered over to the chief priests and teachers of the law. They will condemn him to death and hand him over to the Gentiles, 34. who will mock him, spit on him, flog him, and kill him. Three days later, he will rise." 35. Then James and John, the sons of Zebedee, came to him. "Teacher," they said, "we want you to do for us whatever we ask." 36. "What do you want me to do for you?" he asked. 37. They replied, "Let one of us sit at your right and the other at your left in your glory." 38. Jesus answered, "You don't know what you are asking. Can you drink the cup I drink, or be baptized with the baptism I am baptized with?" 39. "We can," they answered. Jesus said to them, "You will drink the cup I drink and be baptized with the baptism I am baptized with, 40. but to sit at my right or left is not for me to grant. These places belong to those for whom they have been prepared." 41. When the ten heard about this, they became angry with James and John. 42. Jesus called them together and said, "You know that those who are regarded as rulers of the Gentiles lord it over them, and their high officials exercise authority over them. 43. Not so with you. Instead, whoever wants to become great among you must be your servant, 44. and whoever wants to be first must be slave of all. 45. For even the Son of Man did not come to be served, but to serve, and to give his life as a ransom for many." 46. Then they came to Jericho. As Jesus and his disciples, along with a large crowd, were leaving the city, a blind man named Bartimaeus (son of Timaeus) was sitting by the roadside begging. 47. When he heard that it was Jesus of Nazareth, he began to shout, "Jesus, Son of David, have mercy on me!" 48. Many rebuked him and told him to be quiet, but he shouted all the more, "Son of David, have mercy on me!" 49. Jesus stopped and said, "Call him." So they called to the blind man, "Cheer up! On your feet! He's calling you." 50. Throwing his cloak aside, he jumped to his feet and came to Jesus. 51. "What do you want me to do for you?" Jesus asked him. The blind man said, "Rabbi, I want to see." 52. "Go," Jesus said, "your faith has healed you." Immediately he received his sight and followed Jesus along the road.

Chapter 11

1. As they were approaching Jerusalem, they came to Bethphage and Bethany, near the Mount of Olives. Jesus sent two of his disciples, 2. telling them, "Go to the village ahead of you, and as soon as you enter, you will find a colt (young donkey) tied there, one that no one has ever ridden. Untie it and bring it here. 3. If anyone asks you, 'Why are you doing this?' say, 'The Lord (Jesus) needs it, and will return it here soon.'" 4. They went and found the colt tied near a doorway on the street. As they untied it, 5. Some people standing there asked, "What are you doing, untying that colt?" 6. They explained as Jesus had instructed them, and the people let them go. 7. When they brought the colt to Jesus, they threw their cloaks (coats) over it, and he sat on it. 8. Many people spread their cloaks on the road, while others spread branches they had cut from the fields. 9. Those in front and those who followed shouted, "Hosanna! Blessed is he who comes in the name of the Lord!" 10. "Blessed is the coming kingdom of our father David!" "Hosanna in the highest heaven!" 11. Jesus entered Jerusalem and went into the temple courts. He looked around at everything, but since it was already late, he went out to Bethany with the Twelve. 12. The next day, as they were leaving Bethany, Jesus felt hungry. 13. Seeing a fig tree in the distance with leaves, he went to see if it had any fruit. When he reached it, he found no fruit, only leaves, because it was not the season for figs. 14. Jesus then said to the tree, "May no one ever eat fruit from you again." And his disciples heard him say this. 15. When they reached Jerusalem, Jesus entered the temple courts and began driving out those who were buying and selling there. He overturned the tables of the money changers (those who exchanged currency) and the benches of those selling doves (for sacrifices). 16. He refused to let anyone carry goods through the temple courts. 17. As he taught them, he said, "Is it not written: 'My house will be called a house of prayer for all nations'? But you have made it a 'den of robbers (thieves).'" 18. The chief priests and teachers of the law heard this and began looking for a way to kill him, for they were afraid of him because the whole crowd was amazed at his teaching. 19. When evening came, Jesus and his disciples went out of the city. 20. The next morning, as they walked along, they saw that the fig tree had withered from the roots. 21. Peter remembered and said to Jesus, "Rabbi (Teacher), look!

The fig tree you cursed has withered!" **22.** "Have faith in God," Jesus answered. **23.** "Truly I tell you, if anyone says to this mountain, 'Go, throw yourself into the sea,' and does not doubt in their heart but believes that what they say will happen, it will be done for them. **24.** Therefore I tell you, whatever you ask for in prayer, believe that you have received it, and it will be yours. **25.** And when you stand praying, if you have anything against anyone, forgive them, so that your Father in heaven may forgive you your sins." **27.** They arrived again in Jerusalem, and while Jesus was walking in the temple courts, the chief priests, teachers of the law, and elders came to him. **28.** "By what authority (power) are you doing these things?" they asked. "And who gave you the authority to do this?" **29.** Jesus replied, "I will ask you one question. Answer me, and I will tell you by what authority I am doing these things. **30.** John's baptism—was it from heaven (God), or of human origin (just a man-made idea)? Tell me!" **31.** They discussed it among themselves and said, "If we say, 'From heaven,' he will ask, 'Then why didn't you believe him?' **32.** But if we say, 'Of human origin,'..." (They were afraid of the people, because everyone believed that John was a prophet.) **33.** So they answered Jesus, "We don't know." Jesus said, "Then neither will I tell you by what authority I am doing these things."

Chapter 12

1. Jesus began teaching them using parables: "A man planted a vineyard, surrounded it with a wall, dug a pit for the winepress, and built a watchtower. He then leased (rented) the vineyard to some farmers and moved to another place. **2.** At harvest time, he sent a servant to the tenants (people renting the land) to collect some of the vineyard's produce. **3.** But they seized (captured) him, beat him, and sent him away empty-handed. **4.** Then he sent another servant to them; they struck (hit) this man on the head and treated him shamefully (dishonorably). **5.** He sent still another, and they killed that one. He sent many others; some they beat, others they killed. **6.** He had one more left to send, his beloved (dear) son. He sent him last, saying, 'They will respect my son.' **7.** But the tenants said to one another, 'This is the heir (inheritor). Come, let's kill him, and the inheritance (property passed down) will be ours.' **8.** So they took him, killed him, and threw him out of the vineyard. **9.** "What then will the owner of the vineyard do? He will come, destroy (annihilate) those tenants, and give the vineyard to others. **10.** Haven't you read this passage of Scripture: 'The stone the builders rejected has become the cornerstone (foundation stone); **11.** the Lord has done this, and it is marvelous (wondrous) in our eyes'?" **12.** Then the chief priests, teachers of the law, and elders looked for a way to arrest him, knowing that he had spoken this parable against them. However, they were afraid (fearful) of the crowd, so they left him and went away. **13.** Later, some Pharisees and Herodians sent people to Jesus to trap him in his words. **14.** They came to him and said, "Teacher, we know you are a man of integrity (honesty). You are not swayed (influenced) by others, for you pay no attention to who they are; but you teach the way of God in truth. Is it lawful (permissible) to pay the imperial tax to Caesar or not? **15.** Should we pay or shouldn't we?" But Jesus knew their hypocrisy (insincerity). "Why are you trying to trap me?" he asked. "Bring me a denarius (coin) and let me see it." **16.** They brought the coin, and he asked them, "Whose image is this, and whose inscription (writing)?" "Caesar's," they replied. **17.** Then Jesus said to them, "Give to Caesar what is Caesar's, and to God what is God's." And they were amazed at him. **18.** Then the Sadducees (a group who denied the resurrection), who do not believe in the resurrection, came to him with a question. **19.** "Teacher," they said, "Moses wrote for us that if a man's brother dies and leaves a wife but no children, the man must marry the widow and rise up offspring (children) for his brother. **20.** Now, there were seven brothers. The first married and died without leaving any children. **21.** The second married the widow, but he also died, leaving no children. It was the same with the third. **22.** In fact, none of the seven left any children. Last of all, the woman died too. **23.** At the resurrection, whose wife will she be, since the seven were married to her?" **24.** Jesus replied, "Are you not in error (wrong) because you do not know the Scriptures or the power of God? **25.** When the dead rise, they will neither marry nor be given in marriage; they will be like the angels in heaven. **26.** Now, about the dead rising— have you not read in the Book of Moses, in the account of the burning bush, how God said to him, 'I am the God of Abraham, the God of Isaac, and the God of Jacob'? **27.** He is not the God of the dead, but of the living. You are badly mistaken!" **28.** One of the teachers of the law, hearing them debate, noticed that Jesus had answered them well. He asked him, "Of all the commandments, which is the most important?" **29.** "The most important one," answered Jesus, "is this: 'Hear, O Israel: The Lord our God, the Lord is one. **30.** Love the Lord your God with all your heart, with all your soul, with all your mind, and with all your strength.' **31.** The second is this: 'Love your neighbor as yourself.' There is no commandment greater than these." **32.** "Well said, teacher," the man replied. "You are right in saying that God is one, and there is no other but him. **33.** To love him with all your heart, with all your understanding (insight), and with all your strength, and to love your neighbor as yourself is more important than all burnt offerings (sacrifices) and sacrifices." **34.** When Jesus saw that he had answered wisely, he said to him, "You are not far from the kingdom of God." And from then on, no one dared ask him any more questions. **35.** While Jesus was teaching in the temple courts, he asked, "Why do the teachers of the law say that the Messiah (Savior) is the son of David? **36.** David himself, speaking by the Holy Spirit, declared: 'The Lord said to my Lord: "Sit at my right hand until I put your enemies under your feet." **37.** David himself calls him 'Lord.' How then can he be his son?" The large crowd listened to him with delight (pleasure). **38.** As he taught, Jesus said, "Watch out (be careful) for the teachers of the law. They like to walk around in flowing robes and be greeted with respect in the marketplaces, **39.** and have the most important seats in the synagogues and the places of honor at banquets. **40.** They devour (consume) widows' houses and for a show make lengthy prayers. These men will be punished most severely (harshly)." **41.** Jesus sat down opposite the place where the offerings were put and watched the crowd putting their money into the temple treasury (collection box). Many rich people threw in large amounts. **42.** But a poor widow came and put in two very small copper coins, worth only a few cents. **43.** Calling his disciples to him, Jesus said, "Truly I tell you, this poor widow has put more into the treasury than all the others. **44.** They all gave out of their wealth (abundance); but she, out of her poverty, put in everything—all she had to live on."

Chapter 13

1. As Jesus was leaving the temple, one of his disciples said, "Look, Teacher! What massive stones! What magnificent buildings!" **2.** "Do you see all these great buildings?" replied Jesus. "Not one stone will be left on another; everyone will be thrown down." **3.** As Jesus sat on the Mount of Olives opposite the temple, Peter, James, John, and Andrew asked him privately, **4.** "When will these things happen? What will be the sign they're about to be fulfilled (completed)?" **5.** Jesus said: "Watch out (be cautious) that no one deceives (misleads) you. **6.** Many will come in my name, claiming, 'I am he,' and will deceive many. **7.** When you hear of wars and rumors of wars, do not be alarmed (frightened). These things must happen, but the end is still to come. **8.** Nation will rise against nation, and kingdom against kingdom. There will be earthquakes and famines (food shortages). These are the beginning of birth pains (early signs of bigger events). **9.** be on your guard (alert). You will be handed over to councils and flogged (whipped) in synagogues. You'll stand before governors and kings as witnesses. **10.** And the gospel (good news) must first be preached to all nations. **11.** When arrested, don't worry about what to say. Just say whatever is given you at the time, for it will be the Holy Spirit speaking. **12.** "Brother will betray (turn against) brother, and children will rebel (defy) against their parents, leading to death. **13.** Everyone will hate you because of me, but the one who stands firm (remains strong) will be saved. **14.** "When you see 'the abomination (disgusting thing) that causes desolation (ruin)' standing where it does not belong, let those in Judea flee (escape) to the mountains. **15.** Let no one on the housetop go down to take anything out. **16.** Let no one in the field go back for their cloak (outer garment). **17.** How dreadful (terrible) it will be for pregnant women and nursing mothers! **18.** Pray this does not happen in winter, **19.** for these days will be days of distress (suffering), unequaled (unmatched) since creation. **20.** "If the Lord had not cut short (shortened) those days, no one would survive. But for the sake of the elect (chosen ones), he has shortened them. **21.** If anyone says, 'Look, here is the Messiah (Savior)!' or, 'Look, there he is!' don't believe it. **22.** False messiahs and prophets will appear and perform signs and wonders to deceive (mislead), even the elect. **23.** So be on your guard (alert); I've told you everything ahead of time. **24.** "But after that distress, 'the sun will be darkened, and the moon will not give its light; **25.** The stars will fall from the sky, and the heavenly bodies (celestial objects) will be shaken.' **26.** People will see the Son of Man coming in clouds with great power and glory. **27.** He will send his angels to gather his elect from the four winds, from the ends of the earth to the ends of the heavens. **28.** "Learn this lesson (lesson of importance) from the fig tree: When its twigs get tender and its leaves come out, you know summer is near. **29.** When you see these things, you know it is near, right at the door. **30.** Truly, this generation will not pass away until all these things have happened. **31.** Heaven and earth will pass away, but my words will never pass away. **32.** "But about that day or hour no one knows, not even the angels in heaven, nor the Son, but only the Father. **33.** Be on guard! Be alert! You do not know when that time will come. **34.** It's like a man going away: He leaves his house and gives servants their tasks, telling the one at the door to keep watch. **35.** "Therefore, keep watch (be vigilant), for you do not know when the owner will return—whether in the evening, at midnight, when the rooster crows, or at dawn. **36.** If he comes suddenly, do not let him find you sleeping. **37.** What I say to you, I say to everyone: 'Watch!'"

Chapter 14

1. Two days before the Passover (a Jewish festival) and Festival of Unleavened Bread (marking the Exodus), the chief priests and teachers of the law secretly planned to arrest and kill Jesus. **2.** "Not during the festival," they said, "or the people may riot (cause trouble)." **3.** In Bethany (near Jerusalem), at Simon the Leper's house, a woman brought an alabaster (translucent stone) jar of expensive perfume made from pure nard (fragrant oil). She broke the jar and anointed Jesus' head. **4.** Some people questioned, "Why waste such costly perfume? **5.** It could have been sold for a year's wages and given to the poor." They criticized her. **6.** Jesus replied, "Leave her alone; she has done something beautiful for me. **7.** You will always have the poor, but I won't always be here. **8.** She has prepared me for burial. **9.** I tell you, wherever the gospel (good news of Jesus) is preached, her act will be remembered. **10.** Judas Iscariot (one of the Twelve disciples) went to the chief priests to betray (hand over) Jesus. **11.** They were pleased and promised to pay him. **12.** On the first day of the Festival of Unleavened Bread, when the Passover lamb (sacrificial animal) was sacrificed, the disciples asked, "Where should we prepare the Passover meal?" **13.** Jesus sent two disciples, saying, "Go into the city, and man carrying water will meet you. Follow him. **14.** Ask the owner of the house where he enters, 'Where is the room for the Passover with my disciples?' **15.** He will show you a large, furnished (ready) upper room." **16.** The disciples went, prepared the meal, and Jesus arrived with the Twelve. **17.** While eating, Jesus said, "One of you will betray me." **18.** They were saddened and asked, "Surely, not me?" **19.** Jesus replied, "It's one of the Twelve, the one dipping bread in the bowl with me. **20.** The Son of Man will go as written, but woe to the betrayer! It would be better for him not to have been born." **21.** Jesus took bread, gave thanks, broke it, and said, "This is my body." **22.** He took the cup, gave thanks, and said, "This is my blood of the covenant (agreement), poured out for many." **23.** After singing a hymn, they went to the Mount of Olives. **27.** Jesus told them, "You will all fall away, for it is written, 'I will strike the shepherd, and the sheep will scatter.' **28.** But after I rise, I will go to Galilee." **29.** Peter replied, "Even if everyone else falls away, I won't." **30.** Jesus said, "Before the rooster crows twice, you will deny me three times." **31.** Peter insisted, "Even if I must die, I won't deny you." **32.** They went to Gethsemane (a garden), and Jesus asked his disciples to sit while he prayed. **33.** He took Peter, James, and John with him and became deeply distressed. **34.** "My soul is overwhelmed with sorrow," he said. "Stay here and keep watch." **35.** He prayed, "Abba, Father, take this cup from me, yet not my will, but yours be done." **37.** He returned to find them sleeping. "Couldn't you stay awake for one hour?" **38.** "Watch and pray so you won't fall into temptation. The spirit is willing, but the flesh is weak." **41.** "Are you still sleeping? The hour has come. The Son of Man is about to be betrayed." **43.** Judas arrived with a crowd armed with swords and clubs, sent by the chief priests and elders. **44.** He kissed Jesus, signaling them to arrest him. **47.** One of the disciples drew a sword and cut off a servant's

ear. **48.** Jesus said, "Am I leading a rebellion that you come with swords and clubs? **49.** Every day I was teaching in the temple, yet you did not arrest me. But the Scriptures must be fulfilled." **50.** Everyone deserted him and fled. **51.** A young man following Jesus fled naked when seized by the guards. **53.** Jesus was taken to the high priest, and the Sanhedrin (Jewish ruling council) gathered. **54.** Peter followed at a distance, sitting with the guards. **55.** The Sanhedrin searched for false testimony to convict Jesus but found none. **57.** Some testified falsely, claiming Jesus said, "I will destroy this temple and rebuild it in three days." **60.** The high priest asked, "Are you the Messiah, the Son of the Blessed One?" **62.** Jesus replied, "I am. You will see the Son of Man seated at God's right hand, coming in the clouds." **63.** The high priest tore his clothes, condemning Jesus for blasphemy (disrespecting God). **66.** While Peter was below in the courtyard, a servant girl saw him. **67.** "You were with Jesus," she said. **68.** Peter denied it, saying, "I don't know what you're talking about." **69.** Later, another servant girl said, "This man is one of them." **70.** Again, Peter denied it. **71.** "Surely you're one of them, for you are a Galilean," they said. **72.** Peter denied again, and immediately the rooster crowed. He remembered Jesus' words, and he wept bitterly.

Chapter 15

1. Early in the morning, the chief priests, elders, teachers of the law, and the entire Sanhedrin (Jewish council) met to decide Jesus' fate. **2.** Pilate questioned, "Are you the king of the Jews?" **3.** The priests accused Jesus of many crimes. **4.** Pilate asked again, "Aren't you going to respond to the accusations against you?" **5.** Jesus remained silent, and Pilate was amazed. **6.** It was tradition during the festival to release a prisoner. **7.** Barabbas, a prisoner who had committed murder during an uprising, was held in prison. **8.** The crowd came to Pilate asking for the usual release. **9.** Pilate asked, "Should I release the king of the Jews?" **10.** He knew that the priests had handed Jesus over out of envy. **11.** The priests stirred the crowd to demand Barabbas' release. **12.** Pilate asked, "What should I do with Jesus, whom you call the king of the Jews?" **13.** "Crucify him!" the crowd shouted. **14.** Pilate asked, "What crime has he committed?" But they shouted even louder, "Crucify him!" **15.** To please the crowd, Pilate released Barabbas and had Jesus flogged (beaten) before handing him over to be crucified. **16.** Jesus was taken to the Praetorium (Roman palace), where the soldiers gathered. **17.** They dressed him in a purple robe, made a crown from thorns, and mocked him, calling, "Hail, king of the Jews!" **18.** They hit him on the head with a staff, spat on him, and knelt before him in mock homage. **20.** After mocking him, they put his own clothes back on him and led him to be crucified. **21.** Simon from Cyrene (a city in North Africa) was forced to carry Jesus' cross. **22.** They brought Jesus to a place called Golgotha (meaning "place of the skull"). **23.** They offered Jesus wine mixed with myrrh (a bitter substance), but he refused. **24.** After crucifying him, they divided his clothes by casting lots. **25.** It was 9 AM when Jesus was crucified. **26.** The charge against him was written: THE KING OF THE JEWS. **27.** Two rebels were crucified alongside him, one on each side. **29.** Those passing by insulted him, saying, "You claimed you'd destroy the temple in three days—come down from the cross and save yourself!" **31.** The chief priests mocked him, saying, "He saved others, but can't save himself. Let the Messiah come down from the cross." Even the criminals mocked him. **33.** At noon, darkness covered the land until 3 PM. **34.** At 3 PM, Jesus cried out loudly, "Eloi, Eloi, lema sabachthani?" (Meaning "My God, my God, why have you forsaken me?") **35.** Some thought he was calling Elijah. **36.** Someone offered him wine vinegar on a sponge. **37.** With a final loud cry, Jesus died. **38.** The temple curtain was torn in two, from top to bottom. **39.** The centurion, witnessing Jesus' death, said, "This man truly was the Son of God!" **40.** Some women, including Mary Magdalene, Mary the mother of James and Joseph, and Salome, watched from a distance. **42.** As the Sabbath approached, it was Preparation Day. **43.** Joseph from Arimathea, a member of the council and a follower of Jesus, boldly asked Pilate for Jesus' body. **44.** Pilate was surprised to hear that Jesus was already dead. **45.** After confirming with the centurion, Pilate gave the body to Joseph. **46.** Joseph wrapped Jesus in linen, placed him in a tomb carved out of rock, and rolled a stone in front. **47.** Mary Magdalene and Mary, mother of Joseph, saw where Jesus was laid.

Chapter 16

1. After the Sabbath, Mary Magdalene, Mary the mother of James, and Salome bought spices to anoint (apply oil or perfume) Jesus' body. 2. Early on the first day of the week, just after sunrise, they were on their way to the tomb. 3. They wondered, "Who will roll away the stone from the tomb's entrance?" 4. But when they arrived, they found the stone had already been rolled away. 5. Inside the tomb, they saw a young man in a white robe sitting on the right side. They were startled (surprised or frightened). 6. "Don't be alarmed (worried or frightened)," he said. "You're looking for Jesus of Nazareth, who was crucified. He has risen (been raised from the dead)! He's not here. See where they laid him. 7. Go tell his disciples and Peter, 'He is going ahead of you to Galilee, where you will see him, just as he told you.'" 8. Trembling (shaking with fear) and bewildered (confused or puzzled), the women fled the tomb, saying nothing to anyone because they were afraid. 9. After rising early on the first day of the week, Jesus appeared first to Mary Magdalene, from whom he had cast out seven demons (evil spirits). 10. She went and told those who had been with him, but they did not believe her. 11. When they heard that Jesus was alive and that she had seen him, they did not believe. 12. Later, Jesus appeared in another form to two of them as they walked in the countryside. 13. They returned and told the others, but they did not believe them either. 14. Finally, Jesus appeared to the Eleven as they were eating, and he rebuked (criticized or scolded) them for their lack of faith and refusal to believe those who had seen him. 15. He told them, "Go into the entire world and preach the gospel (good news) to all creation. 16. Whoever believes and is baptized (immersed in water as a sign of faith) will be saved, but whoever does not believe will be condemned (sent to punishment). 17. These signs (miracles) will follow those who believe: In my name, they will drive out demons (evil spirits), speak in new tongues, 18. pick up snakes without harm, drink deadly poison without injury, and heal the sick by laying hands on them." 19. After speaking to them, Jesus was taken up into heaven and sat at the right hand of God. 20. The disciples went out, preached everywhere, and the Lord worked with them, confirming (proving) their message with signs.

50 – Luke

Chapter 1

1 Numerous have tried to write a detailed account of the events that have been fulfilled among us, 2 just as those who were observers (people who saw commodity be) and retainers of the word from the morning have passed them down to us. 3 It sounded good to me, having a complete understanding of all effects from the launch, to write an orderly account for you, utmost excellent Theophilus (a person's name), 4 so that you may know the certainty (surety) of the affects you have been tutored. 5 In the time of Herod, king of Judea (a region in Israel), there was a clerk named Zacharias, from the division (group) of Abijah. His woman, Elizabeth, was also from the lineage (family line) of Aaron. 6 They both lived innocently (innocently good) before God, adhering all His commandments without blame. 7 But they had no children because Elizabeth was barren (unfit to have children), and they were both advanced (aged) in age. 8 While Zacharias was serving as clerk before God, 9 his division's lot (chance) fell to him to burn incense (ambrosial immolation) in the tabernacle of the Lord. 10 Meanwhile, the people were soliciting outdoors at the hour of incense. 11 also an angel of the Lord appeared to him, standing beside the balcony of incense. 12 Zacharias was worried (upset) and filled with fear when he saw the angel. 13 But the angel said to him," Don't be hysterical, Zacharias, for your prayer has been answered. Your woman Elizabeth will have a son, and you're to name him John. 14 You'll rejoice, and numerous will be glad at his birth. 15 He'll be great in the sight of the Lord, and he'll not drink wine or strong drink (alcoholic drinks). He'll be filled with the Holy Spirit, indeed before his birth. 16 He'll bring numerous people of Israel back to the Lord their God. 17 He'll go before the Lord in the spirit (strength) and power of Elijah(a prophet), to turn the hearts of the fathers to their children, and the disobedient(those who don't observe) to the wisdom(knowledge) of the righteous(just people), to prepare a people ready for the Lord." 18 Zacharias said to the angel," How can I be sure of this? I'm an old man, and my woman is also advanced in times." 19 The angel answered," I'm Gabriel, who stands in the presence of God. I was transferred to speak to you and bring you this good news. 20 And now, you'll be silent and unfit to speak until the day this happens, because you didn't believe my words, which will be fulfilled in their time." 21 The people outdoors were staying for Zacharias, wondering why he was taking so long in the tabernacle. 22 When he came out, he was unfit to speak to them, and they realized he'd seen a vision (supernatural sight) in the tabernacle because he signaled to them but remained silent. 23 After his service was completed, he returned home. 24 Soon later, Elizabeth came pregnant and hid herself for five months, saying, 25" The Lord has done this for me, and in these days He has shown His favor(kindness) to take down my disgrace(shame) among the people." 26 In the sixth month, the angel Gabriel was transferred by God to a city in Galilee (a region in Israel) called Nazareth, 27 to a abecedarian(a woman who has not had sexual relations) affianced(engaged) to a man named Joseph, from the house of David. The abecedarian's name was Mary. 28 The angel saluted her, saying," Rejoice, favored one! The Lord is with you; blessed are you among women." 29 Mary was confused (puzzled) by his words and wondered what kind of chatting this might be. 30 The angel comforted her," Don't be hysterical, Mary, for you have set up favor with God. 31 You'll conceive (come pregnant) in your womb and give birth to a son, and you're to call Him Jesus. 32 He'll be great and will be called the Son of the Most High. The Lord God will give Him the throne of His father David, 33 and He'll control (rule) over the house of Jacob(the people of Israel) ever; His area will noway end." 34 Mary asked the angel," How will this be, since I'm a abecedarian?" 35 The angel answered," The Holy Spirit(God's power) will come upon you, and the power of the Most High will overshadow(cover) you. thus, the child will be called the Son of God. 36 And flash back, your relative Elizabeth has also conceived a son in her old age, and she's now six months along, though she was called barren. 37 For nothing is insolvable with God." 38 Mary responded," I'm the Lord's menial. Let it be to me as you have said." also the angel left her. 39 Mary snappily went to the hill country of Judah (a region in Israel) to visit Elizabeth, 40 and when Elizabeth heard Mary's greeting, the baby in her womb bounded (moved suddenly), and Elizabeth was filled with the Holy Spirit. 41 In a loud voice, she blatted," Blessed are you among women, and blessed is the child you'll bear! 42 But why am I so favored, that the mama of my Lord should come to me? 43 As soon as I heard your greeting, the baby in my womb bounded for joy. 44 Blessed is she who believed that the Lord would fulfill His pledges to her." 45 And Mary responded 46" My soul magnifies (praises) the Lord, 47 and my spirit rejoices (celebrates) in God my Savior. 48 For He has looked upon the humble (lowly) state of His menial; from now on, all generations will call me blessed. 49 For the potent One has done great effects for me, and holy is His name. 50 His mercy extends (reaches out) to those who sweat Him, from generation to generation. 51 He has shown strength with His arm (power); He has scattered those who are proud in their studies. 52 He has brought down autocrats (lords) from their thrones but has lifted up the humble. 53 He has filled the empty with good effects but transferred the rich down empty. 54 He has helped His menial Israel, flashing back His mercy, 55 just as He promised our ancestors (fathers), to Abraham and his descendants (children) ever." 56 Mary stayed with Elizabeth for about three months, and also returned to her home. 57 When it was time for Elizabeth to give birth, she had a son. 58 Her neighbors and cousins heard how the Lord had shown great mercy to her, and they rejoiced with her. 59 On the eighth day, they came to circumcise (a ritual junking of the foreskin) the child and were going to name him after his father, Zacharias. 60 But his mama said," No, he'll be called John." 61 They said to her," There's no bone among your cousins with that name." 62 also they made signs to his father, asking what he wanted to name the child. 63 Zacharias asked for a jotting tablet, and to their surprise, he wrote," His name is John." 64 incontinently, his mouth was opened, and his lingo was freed (he could speak again), and he began to praise God. 65 Awe (fear) came over the neighbors, and all these effects were talked about throughout the hill country of Judea. 66 Everyone who heard this wondered," What also is this child going to be?" For the Lord's hand was with him. 67 Zacharias, filled with the Holy Spirit, predicted (spoke God's communication) 68" Praise be to the Lord, the God of Israel, because He has come and redeemed (saved) His people. 69 He has raised up a cornucopia of deliverance(symbol of strength) for us in the house of His menial David, 70 as He said through His holy prophets long agone,

71 deliverance from our adversaries, and from the hand of all who detest us — **72** to show mercy to our ancestors and to flash back His holy covenant(pledge), **73** the pledge(pledge) He swore to our father Abraham, **74** to deliver us from the hand of our adversaries, and to enable us to serve Him without fear, **75** in godliness and righteousness before Him all our days. **76** And you, my child, will be called a prophet of the Most High; for you'll go on before the Lord to prepare the way for Him, **77** to give His people the knowledge of deliverance through the remission(pardoning) of their sins, **78** because of the tender mercy of our God, by which the rising sun(Jesus) will come to us from heaven, **79** to shine on those living in darkness and in the shadow of death, to guide our bases into the path of peace." **80** The child grew and came strong in spirit, and he lived in the nature until he appeared intimately to Israel.

Chapter 2

1. Caesar Augustus (Roman emperor) ordered a tale (sanctioned count of people) for the entire world. **2.** This took place when Quirinius (Roman governor) was in charge of Syria. **3.** People went to their own metropolises for the enrollment. **4.** Joseph, from the line of David, traveled from Nazareth (Galilean megacity) to Bethlehem (Judean megacity) with Mary, who was awaiting. **5.** There, she gave birth to her firstborn son, wrapped Him in cloths (strips of cloth), and laid Him in a manger (feeding trough), as there was no room at the auberge. **8.** hard, goatherds (people who watch for lamb) were watching their flocks at night. **9.** An angel (runner of God) appeared, girdled by God's glory (presence), and they were scarified. **10.** The angel said," Don't be hysterical! I bring good news of great joy for all. **11.** moment, a Savior is born in Bethlehem; He's Christ (the besmeared One) the Lord (Master). **12.** The sign is a baby wrapped in cloths, lying in a manger." **13.** Suddenly, a host (large group) of angels praised God, saying, **14.**" Glory to God in the loftiest, and peace on earth to people of goodwill!" **15.** The goatherds went to Bethlehem and set up Mary, Joseph, and the baby. **16.** They spread the word, and all who heard were amazed. **19.** Mary treasured these effects in her heart. **21.** After eight days, Jesus was circumcised (Jewish ritual) and named as the angel had instructed. **22.** When Mary's sanctification (sanctification) was complete, they took Him to Jerusalem to present Him to the Lord, **23.** as needed by the Law" Every firstborn manly shall be holy to the Lord." **24.** They offered two turtledoves or suckers. **25.** Simeon (devout man) awaited the Messiah (the Savior). **26.** The Holy Spirit (God's presence) revealed he wouldn't die before seeing the Messiah. **27.** He took Jesus in his arms, praising God, saying, **29.**" Now I can depart in peace, for I've seen Your deliverance, **30.** a light for the Heathens(non-Jews) and the glory of Israel." **33.** Mary and Joseph marveled (were amazed). **34.** Simeon blessed them, telling Mary," This child is fated for numerous in Israel to rise or fall, and to be opposed. **35.** A brand will pierce your soul, revealing numerous hearts." **36.** Anna (palmist) supplicated day and night in the tabernacle. **37.** She was 84 and spoke about the child to those staying for redemption (deliverance) in Jerusalem. **39.** After fulfilling the law, they returned to Nazareth. **40.** The child grew strong, wise, and favored by God. **41.** Every time, they went to Jerusalem for Passover (Jewish jubilee). **42.** When He was twelve, they went again. **43.** After the feast, they started home, ignorant that Jesus stayed before. **44.** Allowing He was with cousins, they traveled a day's trip before realizing. **45.** They returned to Jerusalem and set up Him in the tabernacle, harkening and asking questions. **47.** All who heard Him were amazed. **48.** His parents were astonished (amazed). **49.** Mary asked," Why have you treated us this way?" **50.** He replied," Didn't you know I must be in My Father's house?" **51.** They didn't understand. **52.** He returned with them to Nazareth, adhering them. Mary treasured these effects. **53.** Jesus grew in wisdom, elevation (height and maturity), and favor with God and man.

Chapter 3

1. In the fifteenth time of the reign of Tiberius Caesar, when Pontius Pilate was the governor of Judea, Herod ruled over Galilee, Philip governed the regions of Iturea and Trachonitis, and Lysanias was in charge of Abilene, **2.** during the high priesthood of Annas and Caiaphas, the word of God came to John, the son of Zechariah, in the nature (a vacated area). **3.** He went throughout the region around the Jordan(swash), publicizing a investment(form of washing) of penitence(turning down from sin) for the remission(junking) of sins,

4. as it's written in the book of the words of the prophet(one who speaks God's dispatches) Isaiah" A voice of one calling in the nature' Prepare the way for the Lord, make straight paths for Him. **5.** Every vale (low area of land) shall be filled in, every mountain (large mainland) and hill made low, the crooked (not straight) roads shall come straight, the rough (uneven) ways smooth. **6.** And all people will see God's deliverance (deliverance from sin).'" **7.** John said to the crowds coming out to be baptized by him," You posterity (group) of serpents (toxic snakes)! Who advised you to flee from the coming wrath (God's discipline)? **8.** Produce (show) fruit in keeping with penitence. And don't begin to say to yourselves,' We've Abraham as our father.' For I tell you that out of these monuments (gemstone) God can raise up children for Abraham. **9.** The layoff (tool for slice) is formerly at the root of the trees, and every tree that doesn't produce good fruit will be cut down and thrown into the fire (discipline)." **10.** The people asked him," What should we do also?" **11.** John answered," Anyone who has two shirts (garments) should partake with the bone who has none, and anyone who has food should do the same." **12.** Indeed duty collectors (those who collect levies for the Roman government) came to be baptized." schoolteacher," they asked," what should we do?" **13.**" Do not collect any further than you're needed to," he told them. **14.** also some dogfaces (Roman guards) asked him," And what should we do?" He replied," Do not wring (strongly take) plutocrat and do not charge people falsely; be content (satisfied) with your pay." **15.** The people were staying expectantly (with stopgap) and were all wondering in their hearts if John might conceivably be the Messiah (Savior). **16.** John answered them all," I baptize you with water. But one who's more important than I'll come, the strips(fasteners) of whose sandals(footwear) I'm not good to unbind. He'll baptize you with the Holy Spirit(God's presence) and fire(symbol of sanctification). **17.** His winnowing chopstick (tool for separating grain from chaff) is in His hand to clear His threshing bottom (area where grain is separated), gathering the wheat (precious grain) into His barn, but He'll burn up the chaff (useless part of grain) with unappeasable (unfit to be extinguished) fire." **18.** And with numerous other words John exhorted (encouraged) the people and placarded the good news (communication of deliverance) to them. **19.** But when John rebuked (blamed) Herod the tetrarch (sovereign of a region), the sovereign of Galilee, because of his marriage to Herodias, his family's woman, and all the other evil effects he'd done, **20.** Herod added this to them all He locked John up in captivity. **21.** When all the people were being baptized, Jesus was baptized too. And as He was soliciting, heaven was opened, **22.** and the Holy Spirit descended (came down) on Him in fleshly form like a dove, and a voice came from heaven" You're My Son, whom I love; with You I'm well pleased." **23.** Now Jesus Himself was about thirty times old when He began His ministry (public work). He was the son, so it was allowed, of Joseph, the son of Heli, **24.** the son of Matthat, the son of Levi, the son of Simeon, the son of Symeon, the son of Joseph, **25.** the son of Mattathiah, the son of Amos, the son of Nahum, the son of Esli, the son of Naggai, **26.** the son of Maath, the son of Mattathiah, the son of Semei, the son of Joseph, the son of Judah, **27.** the son of Joannas, the son of Rhesa, the son of Zerubbabel, the son of Shealtiel, the son of Neri, **28.** the son of Melchi, the son of Addi, the son of Cosam, the son of Elmodam, the son of Er, **29.** the son of Josech, the son of Eliezer, the son of Jorim, the son of Matthat, the son of Levi, **30.** the son of Simeon, the son of Judah, the son of Joseph, the son of Jonan, the son of Eliakim, **31.** the son of Melea, the son of Menan, the son of Mattathah, the son of Nathan, the son of David, **32.** the son of Jesse, the son of Obed, the son of Boaz, the son of Salmon, the son of Nahshon, **33.** the son of Amminadab, the son of Ram, the son of Hezron, the son of Perez, the son of Judah, **34.** the son of Jacob, the son of Isaac, the son of Abraham, the son of Terah, the son of Nahor, **35.** the son of Serug, the son of Reu, the son of Peleg, the son of Eber, the son of Shelah, **36.** the son of Cainan, the son of Arphaxad, the son of Shem, the son of Noah, the son of Lamech, **37.** the son of Methuselah, the son of Enoch, the son of Jared, the son of Mahalalel, the son of Cainan, **38.** the son of Enos, the son of Seth, the son of Adam, the son of God.

Chapter 4

1. Filled with the Holy Spirit (God's presence and power), Jesus returned from the Jordan and was led into the nature (vacated place).

2. He sated (went without food) for forty days, and latterly, He was empty. **3.** The devil said, "If you are the Son of God, turn this monument into chuck." **4.** Jesus replied, "It's written 'Man doesn't live by chuck alone, but by every word of God (verity and guidance from God).'" **5.** The devil took Jesus to a high mountain, showing Him all the businesses (lands ruled by leaders) of the world. **6.** The devil said, "I'll give You all this power and glory (honor), as it's been given to me, to give as I choose. **7.** Still, it will each be Yours, If You worship (glorify) me." **8.** Jesus replied, "It's written 'You shall worship the Lord your God, and Him only shall you serve (follow).'" **9.** Also, the devil took Jesus to the meridian (topmost point) of the temple (Jewish place of idolization) in Jerusalem and said, "If You are the Son of God, throw Yourself down. **10.** For it's written 'God will command His angels (spiritual couriers) to guard You,' **11.** and 'They will lift You up so that You won't strike Your bottom against a monument.'" **12.** Jesus replied, "It's also said 'Don't test (demand a sign from) the Lord your God.'" **13.** After every temptation, the devil left Him until another time. **14.** Jesus returned to Galilee (northern Israel), empowered by the Spirit, and news about Him spread through the region. **15.** He tutored in synagogues (Jewish idolization places) and was praised by all. **16.** Jesus went to Nazareth (His motherland), where He customarily went to the tabernacle on the Sabbath (day of rest) and stood to read. **17.** The prophet Isaiah's scroll (rolled parchment) was handed to Him, and He set up the place that read **18.** "The Spirit of the Lord is on Me, because He has smeared Me (chosen and empowered) to bring good news to the poor, to heal the brokenhearted (comfort those hurting), announce freedom to captives (announce release) and recovery of sight to the visionless, to set the crushed (treated unfairly) free, **19.** and to declare the time of the Lord's favor (God's blessing)." **20.** After closing the scroll, He returned it to the attendant (person minding for scrolls) and sat down as everyone watched Him. **21.** Jesus said, "Moment, this Book is fulfilled as you hear." **22.** All were amazed at His gracious (kind) words, saying, "Isn't this Joseph's son?" **23.** Jesus responded, "You'll surely say, 'Croaker, heal yourself!' and 'Do also what we heard You did in Capernaum (a Galilean megacity).'" **24.** He added, "No prophet is accepted in his motherland. **25.** In Elijah's time, there were multitudinous widows (women whose men had failed) in Israel when there was no rain for three and a half times, causing a deficit (food deficiency). **26.** Yet Elijah was transferred only to a widow in Zarephath in Sidon (near Israel). **27.** And in Elisha's time, there were multitudinous rejects (people with skin complaint) in Israel, but only Naaman the Syrian was healed." **28.** Hearing this, the people in the tabernacle came furious (angry). **29.** They forced Jesus out of the municipality and led Him to a hill's edge, intending to throw Him off. **30.** But Jesus passed through the crowd and went on His way. **31.** He went to Capernaum in Galilee, training on the Sabbaths. **32.** The people were amazed at His training, as His words carried authority (power to impact others). **33.** In the tabernacle, a man held by an sick (impure) spirit cried, **34.** "Leave us alone! What do You want with us, Jesus of Nazareth? Have You come to destroy us? I know who You are — the Holy One of God!" **35.** Jesus commanded the spirit, "Be quiet! Come out!" The demon (evil spirit) threw the man down but left him unharmed. **36.** Everyone was amazed, saying, "What authority! He commands spirits, and they observe!" **37.** News of Jesus spread through the region. **38.** Jesus left the tabernacle and went to Simon's house, where Simon's ma-in-law had a high fever (serious illness). They asked Jesus to help. **39.** Jesus rebuked (spoke against, commanded to leave) the fever, and it left her; she got up and served them. **40.** At evening, multitudinous brought the sick (physically bad) to Jesus, who laid His hands on each and healed them. **41.** Demons (evil spirits) also left multitudinous, crying, "You are the Christ (Messiah, God's chosen one), the Son of God!" But Jesus rebuked them, not allowing them to speak, as they knew He was the Christ. **42.** Beforehand in the morning, Jesus went to a vacated place, but crowds set up Him and tried to keep Him from leaving. **43.** Jesus said, "I must preach the good news of God's area in other cosmopolises too, as I was transferred for this purpose." **44.** So He continued preaching in Galilean synagogues.

Chapter 5

1. A large crowd gathered around Jesus by the Lake of Gennesaret (also known as Sea of Galilee) to hear God's communication. **2.** He noticed two boats on the reinforcement, left by fishers who were drawing their nets (tools used to catch fish). **3.** Jesus got into one of the boats, which belonged to Simon, and asked him to move a bit from the reinforcement. Also, He sat down and tutored the crowd from the boat. **4.** After speaking, Jesus told Simon, "Go into deeper water and lower your nets for a catch." **5.** Simon replied, "Master (one who has authority), we have worked all night without catching anything, but because You ask, I will let down the net." **6.** When they did, they caught so numerous fish that their net began to tear (break open). **7.** They gestured to their mates (close associates) in the other boat to help, and together they filled both boats until they nearly sank. **8.** Seeing this, Simon Peter fell at Jesus' knees and said, "Lord, leave me, for I'm a unethical (innocently wrong) man!" **9.** He and all with him were amazed at the large catch of fish. **10.** James and John, sons of Zebedee, Simon's fishing mates, were also astonished (greatly surprised). Jesus said to Simon, "Don't be hysterical; from now on, you'll grope for people." **11.** When they brought the boats to shore, they left everything and followed Him. **12.** In another city, a man suffering from leprosy (a severe skin complaint that made a person sick) saw Jesus, fell before Him, and said, "Lord, if You want to, You can make me clean." **13.** Jesus touched him and said, "I'm willing, be sanctified (made pure and healed)." Incontinently, the leprosy faded. **14.** Jesus instructed him to tell no one but to go and show himself to the clerk (religious leader who oversees the law) and make the immolation needed by Moses' law as evidence of his mending. **15.** Despite this, word about Jesus spread, and numerous people came to hear Him and be healed of their conditions (ails). **16.** Jesus frequently withdrew to quiet places to supplicate (communicate with God). **17.** One day, as Jesus was tutoring, Pharisees (religious leaders) and law preceptors from Galilee, Judea, and Jerusalem (a megacity) were present. The power of the Lord was there to heal. **18.** Some men brought a paralyzed man (unfit to walk) on a mat, hoping to place him before Jesus. **19.** Unfit to get through the crowd, they went up on the roof, removed penstocks (roof coverings), and lowered him down in front of Jesus. **20.** Seeing their faith (belief in Him), Jesus said, "Friend, your sins (wrongdoings) are forgiven." **21.** The scribes (religious scholars) and Pharisees questioned, "Who's this who speaks sacrilege (affronting God)? Only God can forgive sins!" **22.** Jesus knew their studies and asked, "Why are you questioning this in your hearts (minds)? **23.** Which is easier to say, 'Your sins are forgiven,' or to say, 'Get up and walk'? **24.** But to show you that the Son of Man (title for Jesus) has authority (power) on earth to forgive sins" — He told the paralyzed man — "Get up, take your mat, and go home." **25.** Incontinently, the man stood up, took his mat, and went home, praising God (recognizing and thanking Him). **26.** Everyone was amazed and praised God, filled with admiration (wonder and fear), saying, "We've seen inconceivable effects moment!" **27.** Subsequently, Jesus saw a duty collector (person who collected levies for Rome) named Levi at his cell and said, "Follow Me." **28.** Levi left everything, got up, and followed Him. **29.** Levi held a big feast (celebratory mess) for Jesus at his house, attended by numerous duty collectors and others. **30.** The Pharisees and scribes complained to Jesus' votaries, "Why do you eat and drink with duty collectors and wrongdoers (people considered immoral)?" **31.** Jesus answered, "Those who are healthy don't need a croaker, but those who are sick do. **32.** I've come to call wrongdoers to penitence (turning down from wrongdoing), not those who suppose they're formerly righteous (innocently right)." **33.** They asked, "Why do John's votaries and the Pharisees presto frequently (go without food for religious reasons), but Yours eat and drink?" **34.** Jesus replied, "Can guests at a marriage presto while the bachelor (man getting wedded) is with them? **35.** But the time will come when the bachelor is taken down, and also they will gormandize." **36.** Also He participated a fable (simple story with a spiritual meaning), "No one patches an old garment (piece of apparel) with new fabric; if they do, the new piece will tear the old, and they won't match. **37.** And no one puts new wine into old wineskins (holders for wine). Still, the new wine will burst the skins and be lost, and the wineskins will be ruined, If they do. **38.** New wine must be put into fresh wineskins to save both." **39.** And He added, "No one who drinks old wine incontinently wants new, because they say, 'The old is better.'"

Chapter 6

1. On the alternate Sabbath after the first, Jesus and His votaries walked through grainfields. The votaries picked some heads of grain and ate them, rubbing them in their hands. **2.** Some Pharisees asked, "Why are you doing what's not allowed (permitted) on the Sabbath?" **3.** Jesus replied, "Haven't you read (studied) what David did when he and his men were empty? **4.** He ate the sacred chuck (showbread), which only preachers can eat, and indeed gave some to his companions." **5.** "The Son of Man is the Lord (sovereign) of the Sabbath." **6.** On another Sabbath, Jesus entered a temple (Jewish place of deification) and tutored. There was a man with a withered (shriveled) hand. **7.** The Pharisees watched Jesus nearly to see if He'd heal (cure) on the Sabbath. **8.** Jesus, knowing their studies, told the man, "Stand up and come then." **9.** He asked, "Is it legal (permitted) on the Sabbath to do good or evil, to save life or destroy it?" **10.** After looking around, He said, "Stretch out your hand." It was restored. **11.** The Pharisees were maddened (angry) and bandied how to act against Jesus. **12.** Jesus went to the mountain (high place) to supplicate all night. **13.** In the morning, He called His votaries and chose twelve, whom He named apostles (couriers) **14.** Simon (Peter), his family Andrew, James, John, Philip, Bartholomew, **15.** Matthew, Thomas, James son of Alphaeus, Simon the ideologue (a member of a radical Jewish group), **16.** Judas son of James, and Judas Iscariot (betrayer), the snake. **17.** Jesus and the apostles came down to a position place with a crowd of votaries and people from Judea, Jerusalem, and the littoral regions of Tyre and Sidon. They came to hear Him and be healed. **18.** Those with sick (impure) spirits were healed. **19.** People sought to touch Him, because power was coming from Him and healing all. **20.** Jesus said, "Blessed (happy) are you poor, for the area (rule) of God is yours. **21.** Blessed are you who hunger (are empty) now, for you'll be filled. Blessed are you who weep (cry) now, for you'll laugh. **22.** Blessed are you when people detest (despise) you, count (reject) you, personality (speak poorly) you, and reject (duck) you because of the Son of Man. **23.** Rejoice (be glad) in that day, for your price is great in heaven, as their ancestors treated the prophets." **24.** "Woe (mischance) to you who are rich, for you have entered your comfort. **25.** Woe to you who are full now, for you'll hunger. Woe to you who laugh now, for you'll mourn (suffer) and weep. **26.** Woe to you when all speak well (positively) of you, for that's how they treated the false prophets." **27.** "But I say to you Love your adversaries, do good to those who detest (despise) you, **28.** bless (wish well for) those who curse (speak ill of) you, and supplicate (ask God) for those who brutalize (abuse) you. **29.** Still, offer the other, If someone strikes (successes) you on one cheek. However, don't withhold your shirt, If someone takes your fleece. **30.** Give to anyone who asks, and if someone takes your effects, don't ask for them back. **31.** Do to others as you would have them do to you. **32.** Still, what credit (merit) is that to you? Indeed wrongdoers do the same, If you love those who love you. **33.** Still, what credit is that to you? Indeed wrongdoers do the same, If you do good to those who do good to you. **34.** Still, what credit is that to you? Indeed wrongdoers advance to wrongdoers, If you advance (give plutocrat or goods awaiting them back) and anticipate to be repaid. **35.** But love your adversaries, do good, and advance, awaiting nothing in return. Also, your price will be great, and you'll be children of the Most High, who's kind (compassionate) to the ungrateful and wicked. **36.** Be merciful as your Father is merciful." **37.** "Don't judge (condemn), and you won't be judged. Don't condemn, and you won't be condemned. Forgive (amnesty), and you'll be forgiven. **38.** Give, and it'll be given to you a good measure, pressed down, shaken together, and running over will be poured into your stage. The measure you use will be the measure you admit." **39.** Jesus told them, "Can the eyeless lead the eyeless? Will they not both fall into a hole? **40.** A convert (learner) isn't above his schoolteacher, but everyone who's completely trained (perfected) will be like his schoolteacher. **41.** Why do you look at the speck (small piece) in your family's eye but ignore the plank (large piece) in your own? **42.** How can you say, ' Let me take the speck out of your eye,' when you don't see the plank in your own eye? You fraud! First remove the plank from your own eye, and also you'll see easily to remove the speck from your family's eye." **43.** "No good tree bears bad fruit, nor does a bad tree bear good fruit. **44.** Each tree is known by its fruit. People don't pick figs (fruit) from thornbushes or grapes from briers (prickly backwoods). **45.** A good man brings good from the good in his heart, and an evil man brings evil from the wrong in his heart. For the mouth speaks what the heart is full of. **46.** Why do you call Me ' Lord,' and not do what I say? **47.** I'll show you who's like the man who comes to Me, hears (listens to) My words, and does them **48.** He's like a man erecting a house on gemstone (strong foundation). When a flood tide came, the beachfront couldn't shake it. **49.** But the bone who hears and doesn't act is like a man who builds a house without a foundation. When the swash hits, it collapses and is destroyed."

Chapter 7

1. A large crowd gathered around Jesus by the Lake of Gennesaret (also known as Sea of Galilee) to hear God's communication. **2.** He noticed two boats on the reinforcement, left by fishers who were drawing their nets (tools used to catch fish). **3.** Jesus got into one of the boats, which belonged to Simon, and asked him to move a bit from the reinforcement. Also, He sat down and tutored the crowd from the boat. **4.** After speaking, Jesus told Simon, "Go into deeper water and lower your nets for a catch." **5.** Simon replied, "Master (one who has authority), we have worked all night without catching anything, but because You ask, I will let down the net." **6.** When they did, they caught so numerous fish that their net began to tear (break open). **7.** They gestured to their mates (close associates) in the other boat to help, and together they filled both boats until they nearly sank. **8.** Seeing this, Simon Peter fell at Jesus' knees and said, "Lord, leave me, for I'm a unethical (innocently wrong) man!" **9.** He and all with him were amazed at the large catch of fish. **10.** James and John, sons of Zebedee, Simon's fishing mates, were also astonished (greatly surprised). Jesus said to Simon, "Don't be hysterical; from now on, you'll grope for people." **11.** When they brought the boats to shore, they left everything and followed Him. **12.** In another city, a man suffering from leprosy (a severe skin complaint that made a person sick) saw Jesus, fell before Him, and said, "Lord, if You want to, You can make me clean." **13.** Jesus touched him and said, "I'm willing, be sanctified (made pure and healed)." Incontinently, the leprosy faded. **14.** Jesus instructed him to tell no one but to go and show himself to the clerk (religious leader who oversees the law) and make the immolation needed by Moses' law as evidence of his mending. **15.** Despite this, word about Jesus spread, and numerous people came to hear Him and be healed of their conditions (ails). **16.** Jesus frequently withdrew to quiet places to supplicate (communicate with God). **17.** One day, as Jesus was tutoring, Pharisees (religious leaders) and law preceptors from Galilee, Judea, and Jerusalem (a megacity) were present. The power of the Lord was there to heal. **18.** Some men brought a paralyzed man (unfit to walk) on a mat, hoping to place him before Jesus. **19.** Unfit to get through the crowd, they went up on the roof, removed penstocks (roof coverings), and lowered him down in front of Jesus. **20.** Seeing their faith (belief in Him), Jesus said, "Friend, your sins (wrongdoings) are forgiven." **21.** The scribes (religious scholars) and Pharisees questioned, "Who's this who speaks sacrilege (affronting God)? Only God can forgive sins!" **22.** Jesus knew their studies and asked, "Why are you questioning this in your hearts (minds)? **23.** Which is easier to say, 'Your sins are forgiven,' or to say, 'Get up and walk'? **24.** But to show you that the Son of Man (title for Jesus) has authority (power) on earth to forgive sins" — He told the paralyzed man — "Get up, take your mat, and go home." **25.** Incontinently, the man stood up, took his mat, and went home, praising God (recognizing and thanking Him). **26.** Everyone was amazed and praised God, filled with admiration (wonder and fear), saying, "We've seen inconceivable effects moment!" **27.** Subsequently, Jesus saw a duty collector (person who collected levies for Rome) named Levi at his cell and said, "Follow Me." **28.** Levi left everything, got up, and followed Him. **29.** Levi held a big feast (celebratory mess) for Jesus at his house, attended by numerous duty collectors and others. **30.** The Pharisees and scribes complained to Jesus' votaries, "Why do you eat and drink with duty collectors and wrongdoers (people considered immoral)?" **31.** Jesus answered, "Those who are healthy don't need a croaker, but those who are sick do. **32.** I've come to call wrongdoers to penitence (turning down from wrongdoing), not those who suppose they're formerly righteous (innocently right)." **33.** They asked, "Why do John's votaries and the Pharisees presto frequently (go without food for religious reasons), but Yours eat and drink?" **34.** Jesus replied, "Can guests at a marriage presto while the bachelor (man getting wedded) is with them? **35.** But the time will come when the bachelor is taken down, and also they will gormandize." **36.** Also He participated a fable (simple story with a spiritual meaning), "No one patches an old garment (piece of apparel) with new fabric; if they do, the new piece will tear the old, and they won't match. **37.** And no one puts new wine into old wineskins (holders for wine). Still, the new wine will burst the skins and be lost, and the wineskins will be ruined, If they do. **38.** New wine must be put into fresh wineskins to save both." **39.** And He added, "No one who drinks old wine incontinently wants new, because they say, 'The old is better.'"

Chapter 8

1 Afterward, Jesus traveled through cities and villages, preaching the good news of the Kingdom of God, with His twelve disciples, **2** and certain women who had been healed of evil spirits (bad spirits) and diseases, including Mary Magdalene, from whom seven demons (evil spirits) had gone out, **3** and Joanna, the wife of Chuza (Herod's steward), and Susanna, along with many others who supported Him. **4** When a large crowd gathered, He spoke in a parable (story with a lesson): **5** "A farmer sowed seeds. Some fell along the path, was trampled, and eaten by birds. **6** Some fell on rocky soil (ground), grew quickly, but withered (died) for lack of water. **7** Some fell among thorns (plants), which choked (stopped) the plants. **8** Some fell on good soil (ground), grew, and yielded a crop (produced plants) a hundredfold." He shouted, "Whoever has ears to hear, let them hear!" **9** His disciples asked the meaning. **10** He replied, "You are given the understanding (knowledge) of the Kingdom's mysteries (secrets), but to others, it's in parables, so 'Seeing they may not see, and hearing they may not understand.'" **11** "The seed is the word of God. **12** Those along the path hear, but the devil (evil one) takes the word from their hearts, so they don't believe and are not saved (rescued). **13** Those on rocky ground (soil) receive the word with joy, but they fall away (leave) in times of testing (trials) because they lack roots (strong foundation). **14** The ones among thorns hear, but life's worries, riches (money), and pleasures choke (stop) them, and they bear no fruit (produce no good results). **15** The good soil represents those who, with a noble (good) heart, hear, keep, and produce fruit (good results) with patience (waiting)." **16** "No one lights a lamp and hides it. They put it on a stand (shelf) so those who enter can see. **17** Nothing hidden will remain concealed (secret). **18** Therefore, be careful how you hear; whoever has will be given more, and whoever does not have, even what they seem to have will be taken." **19** Jesus' mother and brothers came to see Him but couldn't reach Him because of the crowd. **20** Someone told Him, "Your mother and brothers are outside wanting to see You." **21** He replied, "My mother and brothers are those who hear the word of God and do it." **22** One day, Jesus got into a boat with His disciples and said, "Let's go to the other side of the lake." They set off. **23** While they sailed, a storm (strong wind) arose, and the boat filled with water. **24** The disciples woke Jesus, saying, "Master, we are drowning!" He rebuked (scolded) the wind and waters, and they became calm. **25** He asked, "Where is your faith?" They were amazed, asking, "Who is this, that even the winds and waters obey Him?" **26** They sailed to the region of the Gadarenes (a place). **27** A man with demons met Jesus. He wore no clothes and lived in tombs (burial places). **28** When he saw Jesus, he cried out, "What do You want with me, Jesus, Son of the Highest God? Do not torment (hurt) me!" **29** Jesus had commanded the evil spirit to leave, for it had seized (taken over) him many times, and though he had been bound (tied), he broke free and was driven into the wilderness. **30** Jesus asked, "What is your name?" He answered, "Legion," because many demons had entered him. **31** They begged Jesus not to send them to the abyss (deep pit). **32** A herd (group) of pigs was feeding nearby, and the demons begged to enter them. Jesus gave permission. **33** The demons entered the pigs, and the herd rushed into the lake and drowned. **34** The pig herders ran and reported it in the town. **35** The people came and found the man healed, sitting at Jesus' feet, clothed, and in his right mind (healthy), and they were afraid. **36** Those who had seen it told them how the man was healed. **37** The people of the Gadarenes asked Jesus to leave, fearing Him, so He got into the boat and left. **38** The man whom the demons had left begged to go with Jesus, but He sent him away, saying, **39** "Return home and tell what God has done for you." The man proclaimed Jesus' work in the city. **40** When Jesus returned, the crowd welcomed Him.

41 Jairus, a synagogue leader, came, fell at Jesus' feet, and begged Him to heal his dying twelve-year-old daughter. **42** As He went, the crowd pressed against Him. **43** A woman who had been bleeding for twelve years and had spent all her money on doctors, but couldn't be healed, **44** touched the edge of His cloak, and immediately her bleeding stopped. **45** Jesus asked, "Who touched Me?" Peter said, "Master, the crowd presses You, and You ask, 'Who touched Me?'" **46** But Jesus said, "Someone touched Me; I felt power (strength) go out from Me." **47** The woman, seeing she couldn't remain hidden, came trembling, told Him why she touched Him, and how she was healed. **48** He said, "Daughter, your faith (trust) has healed you. Go in peace." **49** While He was still speaking, someone from Jairus' house said, "Your daughter is dead. Don't trouble the Teacher." **50** Jesus said, "Don't be afraid; just believe, and she will be healed." **51** He went to the house and only allowed Peter, James, John, and the girl's parents to enter. **52** The mourners (people crying) wept, but He said, "Do not weep; she is only asleep." **53** They laughed at Him, knowing she was dead. **54** He took her by the hand and said, "Little girl, get up!" **55** Her spirit returned, and she immediately got up. Jesus told them to give her something to eat. **56** Her parents were astonished, but He instructed them not to tell anyone.

Chapter 9

1. Also, Jesus called His twelve votaries, giving them power and authority (control) over demons and conditions. **2.** He transferred them to sermonize the Kingdom of God and heal the sick. **3.** He told them, "Take nothing for the trip — no staff (walking stick), bag, chuck, or plutocrat; don't take an redundant tunic (cloak)." **4.** "Stay in the house you enter, and if they don't welcome you, shake the dust off your bases as a evidence (substantiation) against them." **5.** They went out, sermonizing and healing far and wide. **7.** Herod, the sovereign (leader), heard about Jesus and was confused, allowing John had risen from the dead, **8.** or Elijah had appeared, or a prophet returned. **9.** He said, "I guillotined John; who's this?" **10.** The apostles returned and told Jesus everything. He took them to Bethsaida (a city) to rest. **11.** But the crowds followed, and He healed them. **12.** As the day wore on, the votaries asked Jesus to shoot the people down for food, **13.** but Jesus said, "You give them something to eat." They replied, "We've five loaves (pieces of chuck) and two fish, unless we buy food." **14.** There were about five thousand men. Jesus told His votaries, "Make them sit in groups of fifty." **15.** They did so, and He took the loaves and fish, blessed them, broke them, and gave them to the votaries. **17.** They all ate and were filled, and twelve baskets of leavings were gathered. **18.** One day, Jesus supplicated alone. He asked, "Who do the crowds say I am?" **19.** They replied, "John the Baptist, Elijah, or one of the old prophets." **20.** Jesus asked, "Who do you say I am?" Peter replied, "The Christ (Messiah) of God." **21.** Jesus advised them not to tell anyone. **22.** He said, "The Son of Man must suffer (experience pain), be rejected, killed, and rise the third day." **23.** "If anyone wants to follow Me, deny yourself, take up your cross (burdens) daily, and follow Me. **24.** For whoever tries to save their life will lose it, but whoever loses their life for My sake will save it." **25.** What's it worth to gain the world but lose yourself? **26.** Whoever is shamed (embarrassed) of Me, I'll be shamed of them when I come in glory." **27.** Some standing then won't taste (experience) death before they see the Kingdom of God." **28.** About eight days later, Jesus took Peter, John, and James up a mountain to supplicate. **29.** As He supplicated, His appearance changed, and His clothes came glowing (shining) white. **30.** Moses and Elijah appeared, speaking of His departure (death) in Jerusalem. **32.** Peter, sleepy, woke up and saw Jesus' glory and the two men. **33.** As they were leaving, Peter said, "Let's figure three harbors (temporary canopies)." **34.** A pall appeared, and they were hysterical. **35.** A voice came from the pall, saying, "This is My Son; hear to Him!" **36.** After the voice stopped, Jesus was alone. They kept quiet, telling no one what they had seen. **37.** The coming day, a crowd met Jesus. **38.** A man cried, "Look at my son, my only child. **39.** A spirit seizes him, and he convulses (shakes violently), lathers at the mouth, and is bruised. I asked Your votaries to cast it out, but they couldn't." **41.** Jesus answered, "O inconstant generation (people without faith), how long must I bear with you? Bring your son then." **42.** As the boy came, the demon jiggled him, but Jesus rebuked (corrected) the evil spirit and healed the boy. **43.** They were amazed at God's greatness, but Jesus told His votaries, **44.** "The Son of Man is about to be betrayed (betrayed means to be handed over) into the hands of men." **45.** They didn't understand, and it was hidden from them (kept from their understanding). **46.** An argument arose about who was the topmost. **47.** Jesus, knowing their studies, placed a child beside Him. **48.** He said, "Whoever welcomes a child in My name welcomes Me; the least among you is the topmost." **49.** John said, "We saw someone casting out demons in Your name, but we stopped him." **50.** Jesus said, "Don't stop him, for he who isn't against us is for us." **51.** When the time came for Jesus to be taken up, He set out for Jerusalem. **52.** He transferred couriers ahead, and they were not ate in a Samaritan vill. **54.** James and John wanted to call down fire from heaven to destroy them, **55.** but Jesus rebuked them, saying, "You don't know what spirit you're of. **56.** The Son of Man came to save, not destroy." They went to another vill. **57.** As they walked on, a man said, "I'll follow You wherever You go." **58.** Jesus replied, "Foxes have holes, catcalls have nests, but I've no place to rest." **59.** He said to another, "Follow Me." The man replied, "Let me bury my father first." **60.** Jesus said, "Let the dead bury their own dead; go and announce the Kingdom of God." **61.** Another man said, "I'll follow You, but let me say farewell to my family." **62.** Jesus replied, "No one who starts and looks back is fit for the Kingdom of God."

Chapter 10

1. After these events, the Lord appointed seventy others and transferred them in couples to megalopolises He planned to visit. **2.** He told them, "The crop (gathering of crops or work to be done) is generous, but the workers are multitudinous; supplicate to the Lord of the crop to shoot out further workers." **3.** "I'm transferring you like angels among wolves (dangerous or hostile people)." **4.** "Don't carry a commercial bag (bag for carrying plutocrat), trip bag (spare bag for goods), or sandals (footwear), and don't hail anyone on the road." **5.** "When you enter a house, say, 'Peace (blessing or greeting) to this house.'" **6.** "If a peaceful person (someone who welcomes peace) lives there, your peace will rest on them; if not, it'll return to you." **7.** "Stay in the same house, eating and drinking what they offer, for the worker deserves their stipend (payment). Don't move from house to house." **8.** "When you enter a megacity and they drink you, eat what's set before you." **9.** "Heal (restore health) the sick and say, 'The area of God (God's rule and authority) has come near to you.'" **10.** "If a megacity doesn't drink you, shake the dust (dirt) off your bases and say, 'We shake the dust from your megacity off our bases. Know this, the area of God has come near.'" **12.** "It'll be more sufferable (easier to endure) for Sodom (an ancient megacity destroyed by God for its wickedness) than for that megacity." **13.** "Woe (warning of judgment) to you, Chorazin! Woe to you, Bethsaida! If the cautions (warnings or important plant) done in you had been done in Tyre and Sidon, they would have lamented (changed their ways) long agone." **14.** "It'll be more tolerable (sufferable) for Tyre and Sidon than for you." **15.** "And you, Capernaum, will be brought down to Hades (the place of the dead)." **16.** "Whoever listens to you listens to Me, and whoever rejects (turns down from) you rejects Me." **17.** The seventy returned with joy, saying, "Lord, indeed the demons (evil spirits) submit (observe) to us in Your name!" **18.** He replied, "I saw Satan (the adversary of God) fall like lightning from heaven." **19.** "I've given you authority (power to act) to overcome all the power of the adversary; nothing will harm you." **20.** "Don't rejoice (celebrate) because spirits submit to you, but rejoice that your names are written in heaven." **21.** Jesus rejoiced and said, "I thank You, Father, Lord of heaven and earth, for revealing (making known) these goods to little children." **22.** "All goods have been handed over (given) to Me by My Father, and no one knows the Son except the Father, and those to whom the Son reveals (makes known) Him." **23.** Also He said to His acolytes, "Blessed (happy and favored) are the eyes that see what you see." **24.** "Numerous prophets (couriers of God) and lords (autocrats) have wanted to see and hear what you see and hear, but did not." **25.** A counsel (an expert in religious law) asked, "What must I do to inherit (admit as a possession) eternal life?" **26.** Jesus replied, "What's written in the law? How do you read it?" **27.** He answered, "'Love the Lord your God with all your heart, soul, strength, and mind, and love your neighbor as yourself.'" **28.** Jesus said, "You have answered rightly; do this and you'll live." **29.** Wanting to justify (prove himself right) himself, he asked, "Who's my neighbor?" **30.** Jesus replied, "A man was attacked by stealers (thieves) on the road

from Jerusalem (the holy megacity) to Jericho (an ancient megacity). **31.** A clerk (religious leader) saw him and passed by on the other side. **32.** A Levite (another type of religious leader) saw him and also passed by. **33.** But a Samaritan (someone from a region despised by the Jews), seeing him, had compassion (care and concern). **34.** He swathed (wrapped) his injuries, took him to an auberge (place to stay), and watched for him. **35.** "The coming day, he paid the taverner and said, 'Take care of him, and I'll repay you if you need further.'" **36.** "Which of these three was a neighbor to the man who was attacked?" **37.** The counsel replied, "The one who showed mercy." Jesus said, "Go and do likewise." **38.** Jesus entered a village, and a woman named Martha ate Him into her house. **39.** She had a family called Mary, who sat at Jesus' bases and heeded to His training. **40.** Martha was distracted (absentminded) with specifics and asked Jesus, "Do You not watch that my family left me to serve alone? Tell her to help me!" **41.** Jesus replied, "Martha, Martha, you're upset about numerous goods, **42.** but only one thing is demanded. Mary has chosen what's better, and it'll not be taken from her."

Chapter 11

1. One day, Jesus was soliciting, and His votaries asked," Lord, educate us to supplicate, as John tutored his votaries." **2.** He said," When you supplicate, say Our Father in heaven, let Your name be recognized. Let Your area come. Let Your will be done on earth as in heaven. **3.** Give us our diurnal chuck. **4.** Forgive our sins, as we forgive those who owe (are in debt) us. Don't lead us into temptation (testing), but deliver (deliverance) us from wrong." **5.** He said," Suppose one of you has a friend and goes to him at night saying,' Advance me three loaves, **6.** a friend has come, and I've nothing to offer.' **7.** And he answers,' Don't bother (disturb) me; the door is locked, and my children are in bed; I can not get up.' **8.** I tell you, though he'll not give because of fellowship, he'll give because of continuity (continuing request). **9.** Ask, and it'll be given to you; seek, and you'll find; knock, and it'll be opened. **10.** For everyone who asks receives, and he who seeks finds. **11.** still, will his father give him a gravestone? Or if he asks for a fish, will he give him a serpent (snake)? **12.** If a son asks for chuck. Or if he asks for an egg, will he give a scorpion? **13.** still, though unethical (evil), know how to give good gifts, If you. While casting out a mute (unfit to speak) demon, the man spoke, and the crowd marveled. **15.** Some said," He casts out demons by Beelzebub (a demon or Napoleon of demons)." **16.** Others, testing (trying) Him, asked for a sign from heaven. **17.** Jesus, knowing their studies, said," Every area divided against itself will fall (be destroyed). **18.** still, how can his area stand? You say I cast out demons by Beelzebub, If Satan is divided. **19.** And if I cast out demons by Beelzebub, by whom do your sons cast them out? They will be your judges. **20.** But if I cast out demons by the cutlet (power) of God, also the area of God has come upon you. **21.** When a strong man guards his house, his goods(effects) are safe. **22.** But when someone stronger attacks and overpowers (defeats) him, he takes his goods. **23.** Whoever isn't with Me is against Me, and whoever doesn't gather with Me scatters (disperses). **24.** When an sick spirit (evil spirit) goes out of a person, it seeks rest, and when it finds none, it returns to the house it left. **25.** Chancing it clean, it brings seven other spirits more wicked (evil) than itself. **26.** The last state of that person is worse than the first." **27.** As He spoke, a woman in the crowd said," Blessed is the womb that bore You!" **28.** But He said," Blessed are those who hear the word of God and observe(follow) it!" **29.** As the crowds gathered, Jesus said," This generation seeks a sign, but none will be given except the sign of Jonah. **30.** For as Jonah was a sign to the Ninevites (people of Nineveh), so will the Son of Man be to this generation. **31.** The queen of the South (Sheba) will rise up at judgment and condemn (judge) this generation. **32.** The men of Nineveh will rise up and condemn this generation for they lamented (changed their minds) at Jonah's preaching, and now commodity lesser than Jonah is then." **33.** No bone lights a beacon and hides it; they put it on a stage so that those who come in can see the light. **34.** Your eye is the beacon of your body. When your eyes are healthy, your body is full of light. But when your eyes are bad, your body is full of darkness. **35.** Make sure the light in you isn't darkness. **36.** still, it'll be full of light, as when a beacon shines on you, If your whole body is full of light." **37.** A Pharisee invited Jesus to regale. **38.** When the Pharisee saw that Jesus didn't wash before the mess, he was surprised. **39.** Jesus said," You Pharisees clean the outside of the mug, but inside you're full of rapacity(desire for plutocrat) and wickedness(wrong). **40.** Didn't the One who made the outside also make the inside? **41.** But give what's outside to the poor, and everything will be clean for you. **42.** Woe to you, Pharisees! You give a tenth (tithe) of your sauces, but neglect justice (fairness) and the love of God. **43.** Woe to you! You love the stylish seats in bethels (places of deification) and regardful felicitations. **44.** Woe to you, Pharisees and scribes, hypocrites (fakers)! You're like unmarked graves that people walk over without knowing." **45.** One counsel said," schoolteacher, You affront us too." **46.** Jesus replied," Woe to you, attorneys! You load people with burdens but don't help them. **47.** Woe to you! You make sepultures for the prophets, and your ancestors killed them. **48.** You swear that you authorize of what your ancestors did; they killed the prophets, and you make their sepultures. **49.** Because of this, God said,' I'll shoot them prophets, and some of them they will kill.' **50.** thus, this generation will be held responsible for the blood(death) of all the prophets. **51.** From Abel to Zechariah, it'll be needed of this generation. **52.** Woe to you, attorneys! You have taken away the key (understanding) to knowledge. You didn't enter, and you hindered others." **53.** As He said these effects, the scribes and Pharisees began to oppose (oppose) Him and cross-question (question) Him. **54.** They were lying in delay (planning) to catch Him in commodity He might say.

Chapter 12

1. When a large crowd gathered, stamping each other, Jesus spoke to His epigones, saying, "Guard of the Pharisees' dissimulation (pretending to be what one is not)." **2.** Nothing retired will stay concealed, and all secrets will be revealed. **3.** Whatever you bruited in the dark will be heard in public, and what you said privately will be cried from rooftops. **4.** "I tell you, My buddies, don't sweat those who can kill the body but have no power after that. **5.** Fear God, who can destroy both body and soul in hell." **6.** Five sparrows are sold for two coins, yet none are forgotten by God. **7.** Indeed, the hairs on your head are counted. Don't sweat; you are more precious than multitudinous sparrows. **8.** "Whoever acknowledges Me before men, I will admit before the angels of God. **9.** But those who deny Me will be denied before the angels." **10.** Speaking against the Son of Man may be forgiven, but cussing (speaking disrespectfully) the Holy Spirit will not. **11.** When you are brought before authorities (officers), don't worry about what to say. **12.** The Holy Spirit will educate you in that moment." **13.** A man from the crowd asked Jesus, "Tell my family to partake the heritage (family wealth) with me." **14.** Jesus replied, "Who made Me a judge over you?" **15.** "Be on guard against cupidity (selfish desire for farther); life isn't about goods." **16.** He told them a fable (story): "A rich man's land produced plentifully. **17.** He allowed, 'What should I do, I have no room to store my crops?' **18.** I'll tear down my barns and make bigger ones. **19.** I'll say to myself, 'You have comfortably laid up for multitudinous times. Take it easy, eat, drink, and be jocular.' **20.** But God said, 'You fool! Tonight your life will be taken. Then what will be to your wealth?' **21.** This is how it will be for anyone who stores up treasures but isn't rich toward God." **22.** "Don't worry about your life or body. **23.** Life is further than food, and the body further than clothes. **24.** Consider the ravens (a type of crow); they don't sow or reap, but God feeds them. How much more precious are you than ravens? **25.** Who of you by fussing can add any time to your life? **26.** If you can't do the small things, why worry about the rest? **27.** Consider the lilies (flowers); they don't work, yet they are more beautiful than Solomon in all his glory. **28.** If God clothes the field of the field, how much more will He clothe you, O you of little faith? **29.** Don't worry about what to eat or drink; your Father knows you need them. **30.** Seek God's area, and these goods will be given to you. **31.** Don't fear, little flock (group of believers), for your Father is pleased to give you the area. **32.** Sell your goods and give to the poor. Give for yourselves treasures in heaven, where no stealer or moth can destroy. **34.** For where your treasure is, there your heart will be." **35.** "Be ready, with your lights burning, **36.** like retainers staying for their master to return. **37.** Blessed are those retainers whom the master finds watching when he returns. **38.** If he comes in the second or third watch (periods of the night), they are still ready, he will serve them. **39.** If the owner of the house knew when the stealer was coming, he would have kept watch. **40.** You also must be ready, because the Son of Man will

come when you don't anticipate." **41.** Peter asked, "Lord, are You telling this to us or everyone?" **42.** Jesus answered, "Who is the faithful and wise director (person in charge), whom the master puts in charge of his retainers to give them food at the right time? **43.** It will be good for that slave when the master returns and finds him doing so. **44.** Truly, I tell you, he will put him in charge of all his goods. **45.** But if the domestic says, 'My master is delayed,' and begins to brutalize (hurt or abuse) others, **46.** the master will return when he's not anticipated and punish him severely. **47.** The domestic who knows his master's will and doesn't observe will be punished more severely. **48.** To whom much is given, much will be demanded." **49.** "I came to bring fire (judgment) on earth, and I wish it were already burned! **50.** But I have a baptism (difficult experience) to suffer, and I am upset (worried) until it's completed." **51.** "Do you suppose I came to bring peace? No, but division. **52.** From now on, families will be divided father against son, mother against daughter." **54.** Also, Jesus said, "When you see a pall rising in the west, you say, 'It's going to rain.' **55.** When the south wind blows, you say, 'It will be hot.' **56.** You hypocrites (pretenders)! You can predict the downfall, but not the signs of the times. **57.** Why don't you judge for yourselves what is right? **58.** As you go with your adversary (opponent) to court, try to settle with him on the way, or he may take you to the judge and you'll be thrown into prison. **59.** I tell you, you won't get out until you've paid every last penny."

Chapter 13

1. Some people told Jesus about Galileans whose blood Pilate mixed with offerings. **2.** Jesus asked, "Do you suppose they were worse wrongdoers (those who do wrong) than other Galileans? **3.** No, unless you rue (change your mind and turn to God), you'll corrupt (die) the same way. **4.** Or consider the eighteen killed when the palace of Siloam fell. **5.** No, unless you rue, you'll corrupt like them." **6.** Also, He told a fable (story with a moral): "A man had a fig tree in his croft. **7.** After three times without fruit, he wanted to cut it down. **8.** The gardener (someone who cares for crops) asked for one more time to dig and fertilize (add nutrients to help it grow) it. **9.** If it bears fruit, great; if not, then cut it down." **10.** One Sabbath (the Jewish day of rest), Jesus healed a woman crippled (unable to walk properly) for eighteen years. **12.** He said, "Woman, you're freed from your infirmity (weakness)." **13.** She stood up and praised God. **14.** The temple sovereign (leader) was angry, saying, "Heal on other days, not the Sabbath." **15.** Jesus replied, "You hypocrites (people pretending to be what they're not)! Don't you unbind (loosen) your animals on the Sabbath? **16.** Shouldn't this woman be freed too?" **17.** His opponents (those against Him) were shamed, but the people rejoiced (were glad). **18.** Jesus said, "The area of God is like a mustard seed, **19.** it grows into a large tree where birds rest." **20.** "It's like leaven (a substance used in baking to make dough rise) mixed into flour until it works through the dough." **22.** Jesus continued teaching on His way to Jerusalem. **23.** Someone asked, "Will only a few be saved?" **24.** He said, "Make every effort (try hard) to enter through the narrow door (a hard-to-enter path). **25.** When the door is shut, you'll be outside, knocking, but He'll say, 'I don't know you.' **26.** You'll say, 'We ate and drank with You,' but He'll reply, 'Away from Me, wrongdoers (those who do wrong)!' **28.** There will be weeping (crying) and gnashing (grinding) of teeth when you see the prophets in the area of God but are thrown out. **29.** People from all directions will take their places at the feast (meal). **30.** The last will be first, and the first will be last." **31.** Some Pharisees (religious leaders) advised Jesus that Herod (a ruler) wanted to kill Him. **32.** Jesus replied, "Tell that fox (a clever but deceitful person), 'I'll heal and drive out demons, and on the third day I'll reach My goal.' **33.** No prophet dies outside Jerusalem. **34.** Jerusalem, how frequently I long to gather you, but you weren't willing. **35.** Your house (temple) is left desolate (empty). You won't see Me again until you say, 'Blessed is He who comes in the name of the Lord.'"

Chapter 14

1. Jesus went to eat at the house of a Pharisee leader on the Sabbath, and they were nearly watching Him. **2.** A man with dropsy (a condition causing swelling from fluid retention) was there in front of Him. **3.** Jesus asked the Pharisees and legal experts (those trained in law), "Is it legal (allowed by the law) to heal on the Sabbath?" **4.** They remained silent. Jesus healed the man and let him go. **5.** He also asked, "If one of you has a jackass or ox fall into a hole on the Sabbath, wouldn't you pull it out immediately?" **6.** They couldn't respond to this question. **7.** He told a fable (a simple story used to teach a lesson) to those invited, noticing how they chose the best seats. He said, **8.** "When you're invited to a marriage feast, do not sit in the place of honor, in case someone more important than you is invited. **9.** Then the host (the person who invited you) might tell you, 'Give up your seat,' and you would be embarrassed (shamed) as you move to a lower seat. **10.** Rather, sit in the lowest place, and when the host comes, he'll say, 'Friend, move up higher,' and you'll be recognized in front of everyone. **11.** For those who exalt (raise or lift up) themselves will be humbled (brought low), and those who humble themselves (show modesty) will be exalted. **12.** He also said to the one who had invited Him, "When you host (prepare) a feast, do not invite your friends, family, or rich neighbors who might invite you back. **13.** Rather, invite the poor, crippled (impaired), lame (unable to walk), and blind. **14.** You'll be blessed (happy and rewarded) because they can't repay you, and you'll be repaid at the resurrection (rising from the dead) of the righteous (those who live rightly with God)." **15.** One of the guests, hearing this, said to Jesus, "Blessed (happy) is the one who will eat bread in the kingdom of God!" **16.** Jesus replied, "A man gave a great feast (large meal) and invited many guests. **17.** He sent his servant (worker) at mealtime to tell those invited, 'Come, for everything is now ready.' **18.** But they all began to make excuses (reasons for not coming). The first said, 'I bought a field (land) and must go see it. Please excuse me.' **19.** Another said, 'I bought five yoke (pairs) of oxen (strong animals used for plowing) and need to test them. Please excuse me.' **20.** Still another said, 'I just got married, so I cannot come.' **21.** The servant reported this to the master, who became angry and told him, 'Go out quickly into the city streets and bring in the poor, crippled, blind, and lame.' **22.** The servant did so, but said, 'Master, what you ordered has been done, and there's still room.' **23.** The master then said, 'Go out into the roads (main paths) and hedges (walls of branches) and compel (forcefully invite) people to come in, so that my house may be full. **24.** I tell you, none of those who were originally invited will taste my banquet (enjoy the meal).'" **25.** Large crowds followed Jesus, and He turned to them and said, "If anyone comes to Me but doesn't hate (love less than Me) his father, mother, wife, children, brothers, and sisters, yes, and even his own life, he cannot be My disciple. **26.** Whoever does not carry his cross (take on suffering or responsibility) and follow Me cannot be My disciple. **27.** **27.** Whoever does not carry his cross (take on suffering or responsibility) and follow Me cannot be My disciple. **28.** For which of you, intending to build a tower (a tall structure), does not first sit down and calculate (plan precisely) the cost, to see if you have enough to complete it? **29.** Otherwise, when you have laid the foundation (base), but cannot finish, everyone who sees it will mock (make fun of) you, **30.** saying, 'This man began to build but could not finish.' **31.** Or what king, going to war against another king, does not first sit down and figure out if he can meet his opponent, who has twice the army? **32.** If not, he'll send a delegation (group of representatives) and ask for terms of peace (conditions to avoid war). **33.** In the same way, none of you can be My disciple unless you give up everything you have." **34.** "Salt is good, but if salt loses its flavor (taste), how can it be seasoned (made useful) again? **35.** It's useless for the land or the manure pile (soil mound), and people throw it out. Whoever has ears to hear (understands), let him hear!"

Chapter 15

1. Tax collectors and sinners gathered around Jesus to hear Him. **2.** The Pharisees (religious leaders) and scribes (law experts) complained, saying, "This man welcomes sinners and eats with them." **3.** So Jesus told them this parable (story with a moral lesson): **4.** "Suppose one of you has 100 sheep and loses one. Won't he leave the 99 and go after the lost one until he finds it? **5.** When he finds it, he joyfully puts it on his shoulders. **6.** When he gets home, he calls his friends and neighbors, saying, 'Rejoice with me! I found my lost sheep!' **7.** I tell you, there is more joy in heaven over one sinner (someone who has done wrong) who repents (turns away from sin) than over 99 righteous (morally right) people who don't need repentance. **8.** Or suppose a woman has 10 silver coins and loses one. Won't she light a lamp, sweep the house, and search carefully until she finds it? **9.** When she finds it, she calls her friends and neighbors, saying, 'Rejoice with me! I found my lost coin!' **10.** In the same way, there is joy in the presence of God's angels (messengers of God) when one sinner repents." **11.** Then Jesus

said, "A man had two sons. **12.** The younger son said to his father, 'Father, give me my inheritance (portion of wealth passed down when someone dies).' The father divided his property. **13.** Soon after, the younger son went to a distant country and wasted his wealth in wild living. **14.** After he spent everything, a severe famine (food shortage) struck, and he became poor. **15.** He hired himself out to feed pigs. **16.** He longed to eat the pigs' food, but no one gave him anything. **17.** When he came to his senses, he said, 'My father's hired servants have food to spare, and I am starving! **18.** I will go back to my father and say, "Father, I have sinned against heaven (God) and against you. **19.** I am no longer worthy to be called your son; make me like one of your hired servants."' **20.** He returned to his father. But while he was still far off, his father saw him, ran to him, and kissed him. **21.** The son said, 'Father, I have sinned against heaven and in your sight; I am no longer worthy to be called your son.' **22.** But the father told his servants, 'Bring the best robe, ring, and sandals for him. **23.** Bring the fattened calf (raised for feasts) and kill it. Let's celebrate. **24.** For this son was dead and is alive again; he was lost and is found.' So they began to celebrate. **25.** The older son was in the field. As he came near, he heard music and dancing. **26.** He asked a servant what was happening. **27.** The servant said, 'Your brother has returned, and your father killed the fattened calf because he is back safe.' **28.** The older brother became angry and refused to go in. So his father went out and pleaded (asked urgently) with him. **29.** He answered, 'I have served you all these years, and never disobeyed, yet you never gave me a goat to celebrate. **30.** But when this son of yours, who wasted your money with prostitutes (women selling sexual services), comes home, you kill the fattened calf for him!' **31.** The father said, 'You are always with me, and everything I have is yours. **32.** We had to celebrate, because this brother of yours was dead (spiritually lost) and is alive again; he was lost and is found.'"

Chapter 16

1. Jesus told His disciples, "There was a rich man who had a manager (a person managing another's property), and someone accused him of wasting his wealth (not using it wisely). **2.** The man called the manager and said, 'What is this I hear? Give an account (explanation) of your management, because you can no longer be my manager.' **3.** The manager thought, 'What should I do? I can't dig (work in manual labor), and I'm too ashamed (embarrassed) to beg (ask for help). **4.** I know what I'll do, so that when I lose my job, people will welcome me into their homes.' **5.** He called his master's debtors (those who owe the master) and asked the first, 'How much do you owe?' **6.** 'A hundred measures (units) of oil,' the man said. 'Take your bill and write fifty,' said the manager. **7.** He asked another, 'How much do you owe?' 'A hundred measures (units) of wheat,' he replied. 'Write eighty,' said the manager. **8.** The master praised the dishonest (unjust) manager for acting shrewdly (wisely). For the people of this world are more shrewd in dealing with their own kind than are the people of light (those who follow God). **9.** "I tell you, use worldly wealth (money and goods) to gain friends for yourselves, so that when it is gone, you will be welcomed into eternal dwellings (heaven). **10.** Whoever is faithful (trustworthy) with little will also be faithful with much, and whoever is dishonest (unjust) with little will be dishonest with much. **11.** So if you have not been trustworthy with handling worldly wealth, who will trust you with true riches (spiritual blessings)? **12.** And if you have not been trustworthy with someone else's property, who will give you property of your own? **13.** No servant can serve two masters. Either you will hate (despise) the one and love (be devoted to) the other, or you will be devoted to (faithful to) the one and despise (look down on) the other. You cannot serve both God and money." **14.** The Pharisees, who loved money (were greedy), heard all this and sneered (mocked) at Him. **15.** He said to them, "You are the ones who justify (defend) yourselves in the eyes of men, but God knows your hearts. What is highly valued by men is detestable (strongly disliked) in God's sight. **16.** The Law and the Prophets (Old Testament scriptures) were proclaimed until John (the Baptist). Since that time, the good news of the kingdom of God is being preached, and everyone is forcing their way into it. **17.** It is easier for heaven and earth to pass away (end) than for the smallest letter (detail) of the law to be dropped (fail). **18.** Anyone who divorces (ends marriage) and marries another commits adultery (unlawful relationship), and anyone who marries a divorced woman commits adultery." **19.** "There was a rich man who wore fine (luxurious) clothes and lived in luxury (comfort) every day. **20.** At his gate (entrance) lay a beggar (poor man) named Lazarus, covered with sores (painful spots), **21.** and longing to eat (asking) what fell from the rich man's table. Even the dogs came and licked his sores. **22.** The poor man died and was carried by the angels to Abraham's side (a place of comfort). The rich man also died and was buried. **23.** In hell (a place of torment), he looked up and saw Abraham far away, with Lazarus by his side. **24.** So he called to him, 'Father Abraham, have pity (mercy) on me and send Lazarus to dip (put) the tip (end) of his finger in water and cool my tongue, because I am in agony (pain) in this fire.' **25.** But Abraham replied, 'Son, remember that in your lifetime you received your good things, while Lazarus received bad things. But now he is comforted here, and you are in agony. **26.** And besides all this, between us and you a great chasm (gap) has been fixed, so that those who want to go from here to you cannot, nor can anyone cross over from there to us.' **27.** He answered, 'Then I beg you, father, send Lazarus to my family, **28.** for I have five brothers. Let him warn them, so that they will not also come to this place of torment.' **29.** Abraham replied, 'They have Moses and the Prophets (Old Testament scriptures); let them listen to them.' **30.** 'No, father Abraham,' he said, 'but if someone from the dead goes to them, they will repent (turn to God).' **31.** Abraham replied, 'If they do not listen to Moses and the Prophets, they will not be convinced (converted) even if someone rises from the dead.'"

Chapter 17

1. Jesus told His disciples, "Offenses (things that cause people to sin) are bound to happen, but how terrible it will be for the one through whom they come! **2.** It would be better for that person to have a millstone (a large stone for grinding) tied around their neck and be thrown into the sea than to cause one of these little ones (vulnerable people) to stumble. **3.** Watch yourselves. If your brother (fellow believer) sins against you, correct him, and if he repents (turns from his sin), forgive him. **4.** Even if he sins seven times a day and repents each time, forgive him." **5.** The apostles (Jesus' followers) said, "Increase our faith." **6.** Jesus replied, "If you had faith (belief) as small as a mustard seed, you could say to this mulberry tree (a type of tree), 'Be uprooted and planted in the sea,' and it would obey you. **7.** Which of you, having a servant (worker) who is plowing or tending sheep, would say to him, 'Come sit down to eat'? **8.** Instead, wouldn't you say, 'Prepare my meal and serve me while I eat and drink, then you may eat and drink'? **9.** Do you thank the servant because he did what was commanded? I think not. **10.** In the same way, when you have done all that is commanded, say, 'We are unworthy servants (not deserving praise); we have only done our duty.'" **11.** As Jesus traveled toward Jerusalem, He passed through Samaria (a region) and Galilee (another region). **12.** Ten men with leprosy (a skin disease) stood at a distance. **13.** They called out, "Jesus, Master (teacher), have mercy on us!" **14.** Jesus told them, "Go show yourselves to the priests (religious leaders)." As they went, they were healed. **15.** One, realizing he was healed, returned, praising God in a loud voice, **16.** and he fell at Jesus' feet to thank Him. He was a Samaritan (from Samaria). **17.** Jesus asked, "Weren't ten healed? Where are the other nine? **18.** Was no one found to return and praise God except this foreigner?" **19.** Jesus said, "Get up and go; your faith has healed you." **20.** Some Pharisees (religious leaders) asked when the Kingdom of God (God's rule) would come. He answered, **21.** "The Kingdom of God is not something you can observe, for it is within you." **22.** Jesus said to His disciples, "You will long (desire) to see the days of the Son of Man (Jesus), but you won't. **23.** People will say, 'Look here!' or 'Look there!' Don't follow them. **24.** Just as lightning (a flash) shines from one side of the sky to the other, so will the Son of Man be in His day. **25.** But first, He must suffer (go through pain) and be rejected (not accepted) by this generation (the people of His time). **26.** As in the days of Noah (who built the ark), so will it be when the Son of Man comes: **27.** People ate, drank, married, and were given in marriage until the flood came and destroyed them all. **28.** As in the days of Lot (another figure), people ate, drank, bought, sold, planted, and built, **29.** but fire and sulfur (burning substance) destroyed them all. **30.** It will be the same when the Son of Man is revealed. **31.** On that day, if you're on your rooftop (house top), don't go down for your belongings. If you're in the field (working outdoors), don't turn back. **32.** Remember Lot's wife (who looked back and turned

into a pillar of salt). **33.** Whoever tries to keep their life will lose it, but whoever loses their life will preserve it. **34.** I tell you, that night two will be in one bed: one taken, the other left. **35.** Two women will be grinding grain together: one taken, the other left. **36.** Two men will be in the field: one taken, the other left." **37.** The disciples asked, "Where, Lord?" Jesus answered, "Where the body is, there the vultures (birds of prey) will gather."

Chapter 18

1. Also, He told them a parable, saying that people should always pray and never give up. **2.** "In a city, there was a judge who neither feared God (didn't respect God) nor cared about people. **3.** A widow (a woman whose husband has died) came to him, saying, 'Grant me justice (fair treatment) against my adversary.' **4.** He refused for a while, but ultimately said, 'Though I don't fear God or care about people, **5.** because this widow keeps bothering me, I'll give her justice, so she doesn't wear me out (cause me trouble) with her constant pleas.'" **6.** Jesus said, "Listen to what the unjust judge says. **7.** Won't God (God) bring justice to His chosen people (followers) who cry out to Him day and night, even if He delays? **8.** He will bring justice quickly. But when the Son of Man (Jesus) comes, will He find faith (trust and belief) on earth?" **9.** Jesus also told this parable to those who were confident in their own righteousness (rightness or moral correctness) and looked down on others. **10.** "Two men went up to the temple to pray: one was a Pharisee (a strict religious group), the other a tax collector (a person who collects taxes). **11.** The Pharisee stood and prayed about himself: 'God, I thank You that I am not like other people—thieves (those who steal), wrongdoers (unjust people), or even like this tax collector. **12.** I fast (go without food for a period of time) twice a week and give tithes (a tenth of my income) of all I get.' **13.** But the tax collector stood at a distance, not even looking up to heaven, and beat his chest (a sign of anguish), saying, 'God, have mercy (compassion) on me, a sinner!' **14.** I tell you that this man went home justified (declared right by God) before God, not the other. For those who exalt (lift up) themselves will be humbled (brought low), and those who humble (lower) themselves will be exalted (raised up)." **15.** People were also bringing babies to Jesus for Him to touch. The disciples tried to stop them. **16.** But Jesus said, "Let the little children come to Me; the kingdom of God (God's rule) belongs to such as these. **17.** I tell you the truth, anyone who does not receive the kingdom of God like a little child will never enter it." **18.** A certain ruler (a person in authority) asked, "Good teacher, what must I do to inherit (receive as a gift) eternal life?" **19.** Jesus replied, "Why do you call Me good? No one is good—except God alone. **20.** You know the commandments (rules of God): 'Do not commit adultery (cheat on your spouse), do not murder (kill), do not steal (take what's not yours), do not give false testimony (lie), honor your father and mother.'" **21.** The ruler replied, "All these I have kept since I was a boy." **22.** When Jesus heard this, He said, "You still lack one thing: sell all you have and give to the poor (those in need), and you will have treasure (riches) in heaven. Then come, follow Me." **23.** When the ruler heard this, he became very sad, because he was very rich. **24.** Jesus looked at him and said, "How hard it is for the rich (those with wealth) to enter the kingdom of God! **25.** Indeed, it is easier for a camel (a large animal) to go through the eye of a needle (a small opening) than for a rich person to enter the kingdom of God." **26.** Those who heard this asked, "Who then can be saved?" **27.** Jesus replied, "What is impossible with man is possible with God." **28.** Peter said, "We have left all we had to follow You." **29.** Jesus replied, "I tell you the truth, no one who has left home, wife (woman), brothers, parents, or children for the sake of the kingdom of God **30.** will fail to receive many times as much in this age (this life), and in the age (period of time) to come, eternal life." **31.** Jesus took the twelve disciples (His closest followers) aside and told them, "We are going up to Jerusalem (the capital city of Israel), and everything that is written by the prophets about the Son of Man will be fulfilled (completed). **32.** He will be handed over to the Gentiles (non-Jews), mocked (ridiculed), insulted (treated with disrespect), and spit on. **33.** They will flog (scourge) Him and kill Him, and on the third day He will rise again." **34.** The disciples did not understand any of this. Its meaning was hidden (not clear) from them, and they did not know what He was talking about. **35.** As Jesus approached Jericho (a city), a blind (unable to see) man was sitting by the roadside begging (asking for money). **36.** When he heard the crowd going by, he asked what was happening. **37.** They told him, "Jesus of Nazareth is passing by." **38.** He called out, "Jesus, Son of David (a title for the Messiah), have mercy on me!" **39.** Those who led the way rebuked (told him to be quiet) him, but he shouted all the more, "Son of David, have mercy on me!" **40.** Jesus stopped and ordered the man to be brought to Him. When he came near, Jesus asked him, **41.** "What do you want Me to do for you?" "Lord," he replied, "I want to see." **42.** Jesus said, "Receive your sight; your faith has healed (made you whole) you." **43.** Immediately, he received his sight and followed Jesus, praising God. When all the people saw it, they also praised God.

Chapter 19

1 Jesus entered Jericho (a city) and was passing through. **2** A man named Zacchaeus, a chief tax collector (someone who collects taxes for the government), was there, and he was wealthy. **3** He wanted to see who Jesus was, but he couldn't because of the crowd, as he was short. **4** So he ran ahead and climbed a sycamore tree (a type of tree with broad leaves) to see Him, as Jesus was going to pass that way. **5** When Jesus reached the spot, He looked up, saw him, and said, "Zacchaeus, hurry and come down, for I must stay at your house today." **6** Zacchaeus hurried down and welcomed Him joyfully. **7** When the people saw it, they began to grumble (complain), saying, "He has gone to be the guest of a sinner." **8** Zacchaeus stood up and said to the Lord, "Look, Lord, I give half of my possessions (wealth, property) to the poor, and if I have cheated anyone, I will pay back four times what I took." **9** Jesus replied, "Today salvation (freedom from sin and its consequences) has come to this house, because he too is a son of Abraham (a descendant of Abraham, the father of the Jewish people); **10** for the Son of Man (Jesus) came to seek and save the lost." **11** While they were listening to this, Jesus told another parable (a short story used to teach a lesson), because He was near Jerusalem (the capital city of Israel) and they thought the kingdom of God would appear immediately. **12** He said, "A nobleman (a man of high rank or position) went to a distant country to receive a kingdom and then return. **13** He called ten of his servants, gave them ten minas (a mina is a unit of money, similar to a coin), and told them, 'Do business until I return.' **14** But his citizens (people in the kingdom) hated him and sent a delegation (group of people) after him to say, 'We do not want this man to be our king.' **15** When he returned, having received his kingdom, he ordered his servants to be called to him to find out what they had gained with his money. **16** The first servant came and said, 'Master, your mina has earned ten more.' **17** He replied, 'Well done, good servant; because you have been faithful in a small matter, I will put you in charge of ten cities.' **18** The second servant came and said, 'Master, your mina has earned five more.' **19** He said to him, 'You will be in charge of five cities.' **20** Another servant came and said, 'Master, here is your mina; I kept it hidden in a cloth, **21** because I was afraid of you. You are a harsh man; you take what you did not deposit (put in) and reap (gather) what you did not sow (plant).' **22** He replied, 'I will judge you by your own words, you wicked servant. You knew that I am a harsh man, taking what I did not deposit and reaping what I did not sow. **23** Why didn't you put my money in the bank so that when I returned, I could have collected it with interest (extra money earned from the original amount)?' **24** Then He said to those standing by, 'Take the mina from him and give it to the one who has ten minas.' **25** They replied, 'But master, he already has ten minas!' **26** He said, 'I tell you that to everyone who has, more will be given, but to the one who does not have, even what he has will be taken away. **27** Now bring those enemies (people who oppose) of mine who did not want me to be king over them and kill them in front of me.'" **28** After Jesus said this, He went on ahead, going up to Jerusalem. **29** As He approached Bethphage (a village near Jerusalem) and Bethany (another village near Jerusalem), on the Mount of Olives (a mountain with olive trees), **30** He sent two of His disciples (followers), **31** saying, "Go to the village ahead of you; as you enter, you will find a colt (young donkey) tied there, on which no one has ever sat. Untie it and bring it here. **32** If anyone asks you, 'Why are you untying it?' say, 'The Lord needs it.'" **33** Those who were sent went and found it just as He had told them. **34** As they were untying the colt, its owners asked them, "Why are you untying the colt?" **35** They answered, "The Lord needs it." **36** They brought the colt to Jesus, threw their cloaks (outer garments) on it, and put Jesus on it. **37** As He went along, people spread their cloaks on the road. **38** When He reached the descent (downhill path) of the Mount of Olives, the whole crowd of disciples began to joyfully praise God with loud voices for all the miracles (extraordinary events) they had seen, **39** shouting, "Blessed is the King who comes in the name of the Lord! Peace in heaven and glory in the highest!" **40** Some of the Pharisees (religious leaders) in the crowd said to Jesus, "Teacher, rebuke (correct) Your disciples." **41** Jesus replied, "I tell you, if they keep quiet, the stones will cry out." **42** As He approached Jerusalem and saw the city, He wept (cried) over it, **43** saying, "If you, even you, had only known on this day what would bring you peace! But now it is hidden from your eyes. **44** The days will come upon you when your enemies will build an embankment (a mound of earth) against you, surround you and hem you in (close you in) on every side, **45** they will dash (destroy) you to the ground, and they will not leave one stone on another, because you did not recognize the time of God's coming to you." **45** Then He entered the temple (a holy place for worship) and began driving out those who were selling. **46** He said, "It is written, 'My house is a house of prayer,' but you have made it a den of thieves (a place where people steal)." **47** Every day He was teaching at the temple. But the chief priests (leaders of the religious law), the scribes (those who wrote laws), and the leaders of the people tried to kill Him, **48** yet they could not find any way to do it, because all the people were hanging on His words.

Chapter 20

1. One day, as Jesus was training the people in the temple and preaching the gospel (good news), the top priests, scribes (religious instructors), and elders defied Him. **2.** They asked, "By what authority (power or right) are You doing these goods? Who gave You this authority?" **3.** Jesus replied, "I will also ask you a question. Answer Me. **4.** The investment (a religious ritual of washing or sanctification) of John was it from heaven or from men?" **5.** They mooted it among themselves, saying, "If we say, 'From heaven,' He will ask, 'Why didn't you believe him?' **6.** But if we say, 'From men,' the people will edge us (throw monuments at us) because they believe John was a prophet." **7.** So they answered, "We don't know." **8.** Jesus said, "Also I'll not tell you by what authority I do these goods." **9.** Jesus began telling the people a fable (a short story with a moral assignment): "A man planted a croft (a grape-growing estate), leased it to workers, and went down for a long time. **10.** At crop time, he transferred a slavish to the workers to collect some of the fruit. But they beat him and transferred him down empty-handed (without anything). **11.** He transferred another slavish, but they also beat and manhandled him, transferring him down empty-handed. **12.** A third domestic was transferred, and they wounded him and cast him out (threw him out). **13.** The owner said, 'What should I do? I will shoot my favored son. Surely they will respect him.' **14.** But when the workers saw the son, they said, 'This is the heir at law (the one who will inherit the property). Let's kill him so we can take his heritage.' **15.** They threw him out of the croft and killed him. What will the owner of the croft do to them? **16.** He will come, destroy those workers, and give the croft to others." When they heard this, they said, "May it noway be!" **17.** Jesus looked at them and asked, "Also, what is the meaning of this Book: 'The monument the builders rejected has become the foundation (the most important monument in a structure)'? **18.** Anyone who falls on that monument will be broken, and anyone on whom it falls will be crushed." **19.** The top priests and scribes wanted to arrest Jesus right then, but they feared the people, who knew He was speaking about them. **20.** They watched Him carefully and sent intelligencers (people pretending to be righteous), hoping to catch Him in His words and hand Him over to the governor (Roman leader). **21.** They asked, "Teacher, we know You speak and teach rightly. You don't show favoritism (treat people unfairly based on status) but teach God's way in verity. **22.** Is it legal (permitted by law) to pay impositions to Caesar or not?" **23.** Jesus saw through their wile (dishonest plan) and said, "Why are you testing Me? **24.** Show Me a coin (a Roman coin). Whose image (picture) and inscription (notation) is on it?" They answered, "Caesar's." **25.** Jesus said, "Give to Caesar what belongs to Caesar, and give to God what belongs to God." **26.** They couldn't trap Him in His words and marveled (were amazed) at His answer, staying silent. **27.** Some Sadducees (a religious group who denied the resurrection of the dead) came to Him and asked, **28.** "Teacher, Moses wrote that if a man's family dies and leaves a woman but no children, his family should marry her to give seed (children). **29.** There were seven brothers. The first married and died without children. **30.** The second married the widow, and he also died childless. **31.** The third did the same, and so did all seven, leaving no children and dying. **32.** Last, the woman died too. **33.** In the resurrection (life after death), whose woman will she be, since all seven had her as a wife?" **34.** Jesus answered, "People in this age marry and are given in marriage, **35.** but those worthy of the resurrection and the coming life neither marry nor are given in marriage. **36.** They can't die anymore; they are like angels (spiritual beings) and are children of God, being children of the resurrection. **37.** Indeed, Moses showed that the dead are raised when he called the Lord 'the God of Abraham, the God of Isaac, and the God of Jacob.' **38.** He is not the God of the dead, but of the living; for to Him, all are alive." **39.** Some scribes said, "Teacher, You have answered well." **40.** After that, they didn't dare to ask Him any further questions. **41.** Jesus asked them, "How can they say that the Christ is the Son of David? **42.** David himself said in the Book of Psalms, 'The Lord said to my Lord, "Sit at My right hand, **43.** until I make Your enemies Your footstool."' **44.** So if David calls Him 'Lord,' how is He his Son?" **45.** While all the people were listening, Jesus said to His disciples, **46.** "Beware (watch out) of the scribes, who love to walk around in long robes, love salutations (honors) in the marketplaces, the best seats in synagogues (Jewish meeting places), and places of honor at feasts. **47.** They devour (take advantage of) widows' houses and make long prayers to appear righteous. They will receive greater condemnation (discipline)."

Chapter 21

immolations are kept). **2.** He also saw a poor widow putting in two small coins (very small coins of little value). **3.** He said, "I tell you, this poor widow has given more than all the others. **4.** For they gave out of their wealth, but she gave all she had to live on." **5.** Some spoke about the tabernacle's beautiful monuments and gifts. He replied, **6.** "The days will come when not one stone will be left on another; it will all be destroyed." **7.** They asked, "Teacher, when will this be? What will be the sign that it's about to take place?" **8.** He said, "Be careful not to be misled. Many will come claiming to be the Messiah(the Savior), and saying the time is near. Don't follow them. **9.** When you hear of wars and revolutions (insurrections or revolutions), don't be terrified. These things must happen first, but the end will not come immediately." **10.** He continued, "Nation will rise against nation, and kingdom against kingdom. **11.** There will be earthquakes, famines (severe food shortages), and plagues (deadly conditions) in various places, and fearful sights and great signs from heaven. **12.** But before all these things, they will arrest and persecute (brutalize or kill because of beliefs) you, handing you over to synagogues (Jewish places of worship and teaching) and prisons. You'll be brought before kings and governors because of My name. **13.** This will be your opportunity to bear witness (testify or give testimony). **14.** So make up your minds not to worry beforehand how to defend yourselves, **15.** for I will give you the right words and wisdom that none of your adversaries will be able to resist or contradict (falsify). **16.** You will be betrayed even by parents, brothers, relatives, and friends, and some of you will be put to death. **17.** You will be hated by everyone because of My name. **18.** But not a hair of your head will perish. **19.** Stand firm, and you will win life." **20.** "When you see Jerusalem surrounded by armies, know that its desolation is near. **21.** Let those in Judea flee to the mountains (hills), those in the city leave, and those in the country not enter it. **22.** For these are the days of vengeance (discipline), fulfilling all that is written. **23.** Woe to those who are pregnant or nursing in those days! There will be great distress (trouble), and wrath (anger) upon this people. **24.** They will fall by the sword (killed in battle) and be taken as captives (prisoners) to all nations. Jerusalem will be trampled (stepped on, destroyed) by Gentiles (non-Jews) until the times of the Gentiles are fulfilled. **25.** There will be signs in the sun, moon, and stars, and on the earth, nations will be in distress (confusion), with the sea and waves roaring. **26.** People will faint from terror (fall down from fear), apprehensive of what is coming on the world, for the heavenly bodies will be shaken (disturbed or fluctuating). **27.** At that time they will see the Son of Man (a title for Jesus) coming in a cloud with power and great glory. **28.** When these things begin to take place, stand up and lift up your heads, because your redemption (deliverance or salvation)

is near." **29.** Then He told them a parable (story with a moral), "Look at the fig tree and all the trees. **30.** When they sprout leaves, you can see for yourselves and know that summer is near. **31.** So also, when you see these things happening, know that the kingdom of God is near. **32.** Truly, I tell you, this generation (the people living at this time) will not pass away until all things have happened. **33.** Heaven and earth will pass away, but My words will never pass away." **34.** "Be careful, or your hearts will be weighed down (burdened) with dissipation, drunkenness, and the anxieties (cares) of life, and that day will close on you unexpectedly. **35.** It will come upon all those who live on the face of the whole earth as a trap (suddenly). **36.** Be watchful and pray that you may be able to escape all that is about to happen and stand before the Son of Man." **37.** During the day, He taught in the temple, but at night He went out and stayed on the Mount of Olives (a mountain near Jerusalem). **38.** Early in the morning, all the people came to the temple to hear Him.

Chapter 22

1 The Feast of Unleavened Bread, also known as Passover (a Jewish jubilee commemorating the Exodus from Egypt), was approaching. **2** The principal preachers (religious leaders) and scribes (preceptors of the law) colluded to kill Jesus, but they stressed the people. **3** Also, Satan (the adversary or adversary) entered Judas Iscariot, one of the twelve votaries. **4** Judas went to the principal preachers and officers (captains or leaders of the tabernacle guards) to bandy how he could betray (hand over) Jesus to them. **5** They were pleased and agreed to give him plutocrat. **6** Judas promised and began looking for an occasion to betray Jesus when no one was around. **7** The day of Unleavened Bread arrived, when it was time to immolate the Passover angel (the angel massacred in remembrance of the Exodus). **8** Jesus transferred Peter and John, saying, "Go and prepare the Passover for us to eat." **9** They asked Him, "Where do You want us to prepare it?" **10** He replied, "When you enter the megacity, a man carrying a ewer (a vessel for liquids) of water will meet you. Follow him to the house he enters. **11** Ask the proprietor of the house, 'The schoolteacher says, "Where is the guest room (a place for callers) where I can eat the Passover with My votaries?"' **12** He'll show you a large, furnished (fitted with cabinetwork) upper room. Prepare the mess there." **13** They went and set up everything as Jesus had said, and they prepared the Passover. **14** When the time came, He reclined (sat) at the table, and the twelve apostles (Jesus' closest votaries) were with Him. **15** He said to them, "With a deep craving, I've wanted to eat this Passover with you before I suffer (endure difficulty and death). **16** I tell you, I'll not eat it again until it's fulfilled (completed) in the area of God." **17** He took the mug, gave thanks, and said, "Partake this among yourselves. **18** I'll not drink again from the fruit of the vine (grape juice or wine) until the area of God comes." **19** He took the chuck, gave thanks, broke it, and gave it to them, saying, "This is My body, given for you. Do this in remembrance (commemoration) of Me." **20** After supper, He took the mug, saying, "This mug is the new covenant (pledge or agreement) in My blood, exfoliate for you. **21** But look, the hand of My betrayer (one who turns against) is with Me at the table. **22** The Son of Man (Jesus) is going as it has been determined (preordained), but woe (a great mischance or curse) to the bone who betrays Him!" **23** They began to wonder which of them would do it. **24** A disagreement (argument) arose among them about which of them was the topmost. **25** Jesus said, "The lords of the Heathens (non-Jews) lord it over them, and those in authority are called 'donors' (those who do good for others). **26** But not so with you. Let the topmost among you come like the youthful (the least important), and the leader like the menial. **27** Who's lesser, the bone who sits at the table or the bone who serves? Isn't it the bone who sits at the table? Yet I'm among you as the One who serves." **28** "You're those who have stood by Me in My trials (tests or challenges). **29** I'll give you a area, just as My Father gave one to Me, **30** that you may eat and drink at My table in My area and sit on thrones, judging the twelve lines of Israel." **31** Jesus said, "Simon, Simon! Satan has asked to sift (separate) you like wheat. **32** But I've supplicated for you that your faith (trust in God) may not fail. When you have turned back (lamented), strengthen your sisters." **33** Peter replied, "Lord, I'm ready to go with You, both to captivity and to death." **34** Jesus answered, "Peter, before the rooster crows (the raspberry that announces the morning) moment, you'll deny (reject) three times that you know Me." **35** He asked them, "When I transferred you without bag (plutocrat bag), bag (redundant inventories), or sandals (shoes), did you warrant anything?" They answered, "Nothing." **36** He said to them, "But now, if you have a bag, take it, and also a bag. However, vend your cloak (external garment) and buy one, If you don't have a brand (armament). **37** I tell you, this must be fulfilled in Me 'He was numbered with the criminals (culprits).' Everything written about Me is about to be fulfilled." **38** They said, "Lord, then are two brands." He replied, "That's enough." **39** Jesus went to the Mount of Olives (a hill in Jerusalem), as He frequently did, and His votaries followed Him. **40** When He reached the place, He told them, "Supplicate that you don't fall into temptation (a test of faith)." **41** He withdrew about a gravestone's gamble down, knelt down, and supplicated, **42** "Father, if You're willing, take this mug (a conceit for suffering) from Me; yet not My will, but Yours be done." **43** An angel appeared to Him from heaven, strengthening Him. **44** Being in anguish (extreme torture), He supplicated more earnestly, and His sweat came like drops of blood falling to the ground. **45** When He rose from prayer and went back to His votaries, He set up them asleep, exhausted from anguish. **46** He asked them, "Why are you sleeping? Get up and supplicate so that you don't fall into temptation." **47** While He was speaking, a crowd appeared, and Judas, one of the twelve, was leading them. He approached Jesus to kiss Him. **48** Jesus said to him, "Judas, are you betraying the Son of Man with a kiss?" **49** When those around Him saw what was passing, they asked, "Lord, should we strike with our brands?" **50** One of them struck the menial (worker) of the high clerk, cutting off his right observance. **51** But Jesus answered, "No further of this!" and touched the man's observance, healing him. **52** Jesus said to the principal preachers (religious leaders), the officers of the tabernacle guard, and the elders (aged leaders), "Am I leading a rebellion (an insurrection), that you have come with brands and clubs? **53** Every day I was with you in the tabernacle courts, and you didn't lay a hand on Me. But this is your hour—the time when darkness reigns." **54** They arrested Him and took Him to the house of the high clerk, while Peter followed at a distance. **55** They had started a fire in the middle of the yard and sat around it, and Peter sat with them. **56** A menial girl saw him sitting there in the firelight. She looked nearly at him and said, "This man was with Him." **57** Peter denied it, saying, "I don't know Him." **58** A little latterly, someone differently saw him and said, "You also are one of them." Peter replied, "Man, I'm not!" **59** About an hour latterly, another person claimed, "Surely this fellow was with Him, for he's a Galilean (a person from northern Israel)." **60** Peter replied, "Man, I don't know what you're talking about!" Just also, a rooster crowed. **61** The Lord turned and looked straight at Peter. also Peter flashed back the word the Lord had spoken to him, "Before the rooster crows moment, you'll deny Me three times." **62** Peter went outdoors and wept plaintively. **63** The men who were guarding Jesus mocked (scouted) Him and beat Him. **64** They blindfolded Him and demanded, "Prophesy (read the future)! Who hit You?" **65** They said numerous other effects affronting (abusing) Him. **66** At sunrise, the elders of the people, both the principal preachers and the preceptors of the law, met together and led Him into their council (meeting). **67** They said, "If You're the Christ (the Messiah), tell us." Jesus replied, "If I tell you, you won't believe Me. **68** And if I ask you, you won't answer Me or let Me go. **69** But from now on, the Son of Man will be seated at the right hand of the potent God." **70** They all asked, "Are You also the Son of God?" He replied, "You say that I am." **71** They said, "Why do we need any further evidence (substantiation)? We've heard it from His own

Chapter 23

1 The entire crowd rose up and led Jesus to Pilate. **2** They began criminating Him, saying," We set up this man misleading(deceiving or guiding incorrectly) our nation, telling people not to pay levies to Caesar(the Roman emperor), and claiming that He's Christ(the besmeared One or Savior), a King." **3** Pilate asked Jesus," Are You the King of the Jews?" Jesus replied," You have said so." **4** Pilate told the principal preachers and the crowd," I find no guilt(blame or fault) in this man." **5** But they claimed, saying," He stirs up(causes trouble) the people, tutoring each over Judea(a region of Israel), starting in Galilee(a region in northern Israel) and all the way then." **6** When Pilate heard that Jesus was from Galilee, he asked," Is He a Galilean?" **7** Upon learning that Jesus was under Herod's governance(authority), Pilate transferred Him to Herod, who was in Jerusalem at that time. **8** Herod was glad to see Jesus because he'd wanted to meet Him for a long time. He'd heard numerous effects about Him and hoped to see a phenomenon(a supernatural event) performed. **9** Herod questioned Him at length (for a long time), but Jesus gave no answer. **10** The principal preachers and scribes (religious scholars) stood and explosively indicted Him. **11** Herod, along with his dogfaces, treated Jesus with disdain (discourteousness) and mocked (scouted) Him. They dressed Him in a magnific(noble, fancy) mask and transferred Him back to Pilate. **12** That same day, Pilate and Herod came musketeers, for they had been adversaries before this. **13** Pilate called together the principal preachers, autocrats, and people, **14** and said to them," You brought this man to me as one who misleads the people. I've examined (delved) Him in your presence and set up no guilt in Him regarding the charges you bring. **15** Neither did Herod, for I transferred Him to him, and nothing meritorious of death has been done by Him. **16** I'll discipline (discipline or correct) Him and release Him." **17**(It was customary (traditionally rehearsed) for Pilate to release one internee to them at the feast.) **18** But they all cried together," Down with this man, and release to us Barabbas!" **19** Barabbas had been locked for rebellion (an insurrection against authority) and murder. **20** Pilate, wanting to release Jesus, again addressed them, **21** but they cried out," Crucify Him, crucify Him!" **22** Pilate said to them a third time," Why? What wrong has He done? I've set up no reason for death in Him. I'll discipline Him and let Him go." **23** But they claimed, crying louder, demanding that He be crucified. Their voices prevailed (came stronger and won). **24** So Pilate gave the order for Jesus to be crucified (executed by hanging on a cross) as they requested. **25** He released the man they asked for, who had been in captivity for rebellion and murder, and handed Jesus over to their will (solicitations). **26** As they led Him down, they seized a man named Simon from Cyrene (a megacity in North Africa), who was coming into the megacity, and put the cross on him to carry behind Jesus. **27** A large crowd of people followed, including women who mourned (expressed anguish) and wept (cried) for Him. **28** But Jesus turned to them and said," Daughters of Jerusalem (the megacity of God), don't weep for Me, but weep for yourselves and for your children. **29** For the days are coming when they will say,' Blessed are the barren (women who can not have children), the wombs that noway bore, and the guts that noway nursed.' **30** also people will begin to say to the mountains (large hills),' Fall on us,' and to the hills,' Cover us.' **31** If they do these effects when the tree is green (in times of peace), what will be when it's dry (in times of difficulty)? **32** Two other culprits (evildoers) were also led with Jesus to be executed. **33** When they came to the place called Calvary (the hill where Jesus was crucified), they crucified Him and the culprits, one on His right and the other on His left wing. **34** Jesus said," Father, forgive them, for they don't know what they're doing." They divided His clothes by casting lots (drawing lots for a prize). **35** The people stood watching, and the autocrats sniggered (mocked) at Him, saying," He saved others; let Him save Himself if He's the Christ, the chosen one of God." **36** The dogfaces also mocked Him, offering Him sour wine (a bitter drink), **37.** And saying, "If You're the King of the Jews, save Yourself." **38.** An inscription (a sign or writing) was placed above Him, written in Greek, Latin, and Hebrew: "THIS IS THE KING OF THE JEWS." **39.** One of the criminals hanging beside Him insulted (spoke disrespectfully to) Him, saying, "If You're the Christ, save Yourself and us." **40.** But the other criminal rebuked (corrected) him, saying, "Do you not fear God, since you're under the same sentence of condemnation? **41.** We're punished justly (correctly), for we're getting what our deeds deserve, but this man has done nothing wrong." **42.** Then he said to Jesus, "Jesus, remember me when You come into Your kingdom." **43.** Jesus replied, "Truly I tell you, today you'll be with Me in Paradise (the place of eternal happiness)." **44.** It was around noon, and darkness covered (cast a shadow over) the whole earth until 3:00 PM. **45.** The sun was darkened, and the curtain of the temple was torn in two. **46.** Jesus cried out in a loud voice, "Father, into Your hands I commit My spirit." Having said this, He breathed His last (died). **47.** When the centurion (a Roman officer) saw what had happened, he praised God, saying, "Surely this man was righteous!" **48.** The crowd that had gathered to witness what had happened beat their chests (a sign of mourning) and went away. **49.** But all of Jesus' acquaintances (friends and followers), including the women who had followed Him from Galilee, stood at a distance, watching these things. **50.** There was a man named Joseph, a member of the council, who was known for his goodness and righteousness. **51.** He had not agreed with the decision to condemn Jesus. He was from Arimathea (a city in Judea), a place where people awaited the kingdom of God. **52.** He approached Pilate and requested the body of Jesus. **53.** He took it down, wrapped it in linen (cloth), and placed it in a tomb (a burial place) cut from rock, where no one had ever been laid before. **54.** It was the day of preparation (the day before the Sabbath), and the Sabbath (a day of rest) was near. **55.** The women who had accompanied Jesus from Galilee followed, observing the tomb and how His body was laid. **56.** Then they returned and prepared spices and perfumes (fragrant oils), but they rested on the Sabbath according to the commandment.

Chapter 24

1 Beforehand on the first day of the week, as the sun was rising, a group of women, including others who were with them, went to the grave carrying spices (ambrosial substances used for burial) they had prepared. **2** When they arrived, they set up that the gravestone (large gemstone) had been rolled down from the entrance of the grave. **3** They entered, but the body of Jesus wasn't there. **4** As they were confused (unfit to understand) and wondering what had happened, two men in shining clothes (bright and glowing) suddenly appeared beside them. **5** The women were hysterical and bowed their faces to the ground. The men said to them, "Why are you looking for the living among the dead? **6** He's not then; He has risen! Flash back what He told you when He was still in Galilee (a region in northern Israel), **7** saying, 'The Son of Man (a title Jesus used for Himself) must be handed over to unethical people (those who defy God), be crucified (put to death on a cross), and rise again on the third day.'" **8** Also, they flashed back His words. **9** They left the grave and went back to the votaries (Jesus' followers) and told them everything that had happened. **10** The women who told this to the apostles (leaders of the early church) were Mary Magdalene, Joanna, Mary the mama of James, and the others with them. **11** But the apostles allowed their words were gibberish (not credible) and didn't believe them. **12** Still, Peter got up and ran to the grave. He looked outside, saw the linen cloths (wastes used for belting the body) lying there, and went down wondering about what had happened. **13** That same day, two of Jesus' followers were traveling to a vill called Emmaus (a vill about seven long hauls from Jerusalem), **14** They were talking with each other about everything that had happened. **15** As they talked and bandied these effects, Jesus Himself came and walked alongside them. **16** But they were kept from feting Him (unfit to identify Him). **17** He asked them, "What are you agitating as you walk along? Why do you look so sad?" **18** One of them, named Cleopas, answered, "Are you the only one visiting Jerusalem who does not know what has happened there in these days?" **19** "What effects?" He asked. They replied, "The effects about Jesus of Nazareth (a city in Israel) — He was a prophet (one who speaks for God) important in word and deed before God and all the people, **20** and how the principal preachers (religious leaders) and our autocrats (leaders of the people) handed Him over to be doomed to death, and they crucified Him. **21** We had hoped that He was the bone who was going to redeem (save) Israel. And what's further, it's the third day since all this took place. **22** Some women from our group astounded us (surprised us). They went to the grave beforehand this morning **23** but didn't find His body. They came and told us they had seen a vision (sight of commodity supernatural) of angels (couriers from God), who said He was alive. **24** Also some of our companions went to the grave and set up it just as the women had said, but they didn't see Jesus." **25** He said to them, "How foolish (slow to understand) you are, and how slow to believe all that the prophets (couriers of God) have spoken! **26** Didn't the Christ (the promised Savior) have to suffer these effects and also enter His glory (His greatness and honor)?" **27** And beginning with Moses (the leader who gave the law) and all the Prophets, He explained to them what was said in all the Holy Writ (sacred jottings) concerning Himself. **28** As they approached the vill where they were going, Jesus acted as if He were going further. **29** But they prompted Him explosively, "Stay with us, for its nearly evening; the day is nearly over." So He went in to stay with them. **30** When He was at the table with them, He took chuck,

gave thanks, broke it, and began to give it to them. **31** Also, their eyes were opened and they honored Him, and He faded from their sight. **32** They asked each other, "Weren't our hearts burning within us (feeling agitated) while He talked with us on the road and opened the Holy Writ to us?" **33** They got up and returned at formerly to Jerusalem. There they set up the eleven (the remaining votaries) and those with them, assembled together **34** and saying, "It's true! The Lord has risen and has appeared to Simon!" **35** Also, the two told what had happened on the way, and how Jesus was honored by them when He broke the chuck. **36** While they were still talking about this, Jesus Himself stood among them and said to them, "Peace be with you." **37** They were startled (shocked) and frightened, allowing they saw a ghost (spirit of a dead person). **38** He said to them, "Why are you worried, and why do dubieties (query) rise in your minds? **39** Look at My hands and My bases. It's Myself! Touch Me and see; a ghost doesn't have meat and bones, as you see I have." **40** When He'd said this, He showed them His hands and His bases. **41.** They still struggled to believe, overwhelmed with joy (happiness) and amazement (wonder), when He asked them, "Do you have anything to eat?" **42.** They offered Him a piece of cooked (broiled) fish, **43.** Which He took and ate in their presence. **44.** He then said to them, "This is what I told you while I was still with you: Everything written about Me in the Law of Moses, the Prophets, and the Psalms must be fulfilled (completed)." **45.** Then He opened their minds (helped them understand), enabling them to understand the Scriptures. **46.** He explained, "This is what is written: The Messiah (Christ) will suffer and rise from the dead on the third day, **47.** and repentance (turning away from sin) for the forgiveness (pardon) of sins will be preached in His name to all nations (people), starting from Jerusalem. **48.** You are witnesses (those who have seen and can tell others) of these things. **49.** And I will send you what My Father (God) has promised; but stay in the city until you are clothed (filled) with power (strength) from on high (heaven)." **50.** When He had led them to the outskirts (vicinity, nearby area) of Bethany, He lifted up His hands and blessed them. **51.** While He was blessing them, He was taken up into heaven (the place where God lives). **52.** They worshiped (showed respect and honor) Him and returned to Jerusalem with great joy. **53.** They stayed continually (constantly) in the temple, praising God.

51 – John

Chapter 1

1. In the beginning, there was the Word (a divine expression or message), and the Word was with God, and the Word was God (divine). **2.** He existed with God from the very beginning (from the start of all things). **3.** Everything came into being through Him, and nothing exists that was not made by Him. **4.** In Him was life (eternal life), and this life was the light (guidance) of all people. **5.** The light radiates in the obscurity (darkness), and the obscurity could not overpower (conquer or comprehend) it. **6.** A man named John was sent by God. **7.** His intention was to bear witness (testify) to the Light, so that through him, all people might come to believe. **8.** He was not the Light himself, but he came to testify about the Light. **9.** The true Light was coming into the world, which enlightens every person. **10.** He existed in the world, and although the world was created (made) through Him, the world did not acknowledge (recognize or accept) Him. **11.** He came to His own people, but they did not accept Him. **12.** However, to those who did accept Him, He gave the right to become children of God, to those who believe in His name. **13.** They were not born of human blood, nor by the will of the flesh, nor by the will of man, but of God. **14.** The Word became flesh (human) and dwelt (lived) among us. We saw His glory, the glory of the only Son of the Father, full of grace and truth. **15.** John testified (bore witness) about Him, declaring (saying), 'This is the One I referred to when I mentioned, "The one who follows me is greater (superior) than I, for He existed (was) before me." **16.** From His fullness (complete nature), we have all received grace upon grace. **17.** The law was delivered through Moses, but grace and truth came through Jesus Christ. **18.** No one has ever seen God. The only Son, who is close to the Father's heart, has made Him known. **19.** This is the testimony of John when the Jewish leaders sent priests and Levites from Jerusalem to ask him, "Who are you?" **20.** John openly acknowledged (confessed) and declared, 'I am not the Messiah (Christ).' **21.** They asked him, "Then who are you? Are you Elijah?" He responded (replied), 'I am not.' 'Are you the Prophet (the expected messenger or leader)?'" They asked. "No," he answered. **22.** So they asked him, "Who are you? Give us an answer so that we can report to those who sent us. What do you say about yourself?" **23.** John answered (replied), 'I am the voice of one calling (crying out) in the wilderness, "Prepare the path (make straight the way) of the Lord," as the prophet Isaiah foretold (said).' **24.** Those who were sent came from the Pharisees (a religious group). **25.** They asked him, 'If you are not the Messiah (Savior), nor Elijah (a prophet from the Old Testament), nor the Prophet (a figure like Moses, foretold to come), then why are you baptizing (immersing people in water)?' **26.** John answered, 'I baptize with water, but there is One among you whom you do not recognize (identify or know). **27.** He is the One who follows (comes after) me, the One who is superior (greater) to me. I am not even worthy to untie His sandal strap." **28.** These events took place in Bethabara (a location near the Jordan River), where John was baptizing. **29.** The following day (next day), John observed (saw) Jesus approaching (coming toward) him and exclaimed (said), 'Behold (Look)!' The Lamb (sacrifice) of God, who takes away the sin (wrongdoing) of the world! **30.** This is the One I referred to (spoke of) when I said, 'A man who is superior (greater) to me will come after me, for He existed (was) before me.' **31.** I did not recognize (know) Him, but I came baptizing with water so that He might be made known (revealed or shown) to Israel. **32.** Then John bore witness (testified), 'I saw the Spirit (Holy Spirit) descending from heaven like a dove, and it rested (remained) upon Him.' **33.** I did not recognize (identify) Him at first, but the One who sent me to baptize (immerse in water) with water said to me, 'The one on whom you see the Spirit (God's presence or power) descend and remain, He is the One who will baptize with the Holy Spirit (God's empowering presence). **34.** I have seen and bear witness (testify) that this is the Son of God. **35.** The next day, John was standing with two of his disciples (followers). **36.** As he looked at Jesus, walking by, he said, "Look! The Lamb of God!" **37.** The two disciples heeded (listened to) him and then followed (went after) Jesus. **38.** Jesus turned, saw them following, and asked, 'What are you seeking (looking for)?' They answered, 'Rabbi' (which means, Teacher), 'Where are You staying (abiding)?' **39.** He said to them, 'Come and see.' So they went and saw where He was staying (abiding), and remained (spent) the rest of the day with Him (it was around the tenth hour). **40.** One of the two who heard John speak and followed Jesus was Andrew, the brother of Simon Peter. **41.** The first thing Andrew did was find his brother Simon and tell him, 'We have discovered the Messiah' (which means, the Christ). **42.** He brought Simon to Jesus. When Jesus gazed (looked) at him, He said, 'You are Simon, son of Jonah. You will be called Cephas' (which means, A Stone). **43.** The following day, Jesus chose (decided) to go to Galilee. He found Philip and said to him, 'Follow Me.' **44.** Philip was from Bethsaida (a city near the Sea of Galilee), the same town as Andrew and Peter. **45.** Philip found Nathanael and said to him, 'We have found the One whom Moses wrote about in the Law and whom the prophets prophesied (foretold)—Jesus of Nazareth, the son of Joseph.' **46.** Nathanael responded, 'Can anything good come from Nazareth?' Philip replied, 'Come and see. When Jesus saw Nathanael coming toward Him, He said, 'Behold, an Israelite in whom there is no deceit (falsehood)!' **48.** Nathanael inquired, 'How do You know me?' Jesus responded, 'Before Philip called you, I saw you sitting beneath the fig tree.' **49.** Nathanael questioned, 'How do You know me?' Jesus replied, 'Before Philip called you, I saw you beneath the fig tree.' **50.** Nathanael declared (proclaimed, affirmed, or acknowledged), 'Rabbi (Teacher), You are the Son of God; You are the King of Israel!' **51.** Jesus answered, 'You believe (trust or have faith) because I told you I saw you under the fig tree (a symbolic or literal place of encounter). You will witness even greater things than that. Truly (most assuredly), I tell you, you will witness heaven opened, and the angels of God ascending and descending upon the Son of Man.'

Chapter 2

1. On the third day, there was a wedding in Cana of Galilee, and Jesus' mother was there. **2.** Jesus and His disciples were also invited to the gathering. **3.** When the wine was depleted, His mother said to Him, 'They have no wine.' **4.** Jesus answered, 'Woman, why does this matter to Me? My time has not yet come.' **5.** His mother said to the servants (attendants), 'Do whatever He instructs (tells) you.' **6.** There were six stone water pots (large containers), used for Jewish purification, each holding 20 to 30 gallons. **7.** Jesus instructed them, "Fill the pots with water," and they filled them to the top. **8.** He instructed, 'Now draw (take) some out and present it to the master of the banquet.' And they did. **9.** When the master (leader) tasted the water turned to wine, not knowing its source (origin) — but the servants did — he called the bridegroom. **10.** He said, 'everyone serves the best wine first, and when the guests have drunk freely (drunk a lot), they serve the inferior (lower quality) wine. You've kept the best wine until now!' **11.** This was the first miracle Jesus performed in Cana, revealing His glory, and His disciples believed in Him. **12.** Afterward, He went to Capernaum with His mother, brothers, and disciples, staying there a few days. **13.** When the Passover (Jewish festival) of the Jews was approaching, Jesus went up to Jerusalem. **14.** In the temple, He found people selling oxen, sheep, and doves, and the money changers (currency exchangers) doing business. **15.** He made a whip (a tool for driving animals) of cords and drove them all out, along with the animals, spilling the money and overturning the tables. **16.** He said to the sellers of doves, 'Take these things away! Don't make My Father's house a marketplace!' **17.** His disciples recalled (remembered) that it is written, 'Zeal (enthusiasm) for Your house will consume Me.' **18.** The Jews demanded, 'what sign can You show us to justify (prove) doing this?' **19.** Jesus replied, 'Destroy this temple, and in three days I will raise it up.' **20.** They responded, 'It took 46 years to build this temple, and You will raise it in three days?' **21.** But He was referring to the temple of His body. **22.** After He was raised (resurrected) from the dead, His disciples remembered what He had said, and they believed the Scripture (holy writings) and His words. **23.** During the Passover feast in Jerusalem, many believed in His name when they saw the signs He performed. **24.** But Jesus did not entrust (rely) Himself to them, **25.** for He knew all men, and had no need for anyone to testify (witness) about humanity, because He knew what was in each person.

Chapter 3

1. There was a Pharisee (a member of a religious group in ancient Judaism) named Nicodemus, a ruler of the Jews. **2.** He approached Jesus under the cover of night and said, 'Rabbi (Teacher), we acknowledge (recognize or admit) that you are a teacher sent by God, for no one can perform such miraculous signs unless God is with him.' **3.** Jesus answered, 'Truly, I tell you, unless someone is born again (spiritually reborn), he cannot see the kingdom of God.' **4.** Nicodemus asked, "How can a man be born when he is old? Can he reenter (go back into) his mother's womb a second time to be born again? **5.** Jesus answered, 'Truly, I tell you, unless someone is born of water and the Spirit (Holy Spirit), he cannot enter the kingdom of God.' **6.** That which is born of the flesh (human nature or physical body) is flesh, and that which is born of the Spirit is spirit (immaterial essence or divine influence). **7.** Do not be amazed (surprised or filled with wonder) when I say, 'You must undergo a spiritual rebirth (be born again).' **8.** The wind (Spirit) blows where it pleases, and you hear its sound but can't tell where it comes from or where it goes. Thus, it is with all who are born of the Spirit (divine influence or power). **9.** Nicodemus asked, "How can this be?" **10.** Jesus responded, 'Are you the renowned (esteemed or respected) teacher of Israel, and yet you fail to grasp (comprehend or understand) these matters?' **11.** Indeed, I speak of what I know and testify (give evidence or bear witness) to what I have seen, yet you do not accept (acknowledge or receive) Our testimony. **12.** If you do not believe when I speak of earthly things, how will you believe when I speak of heavenly things? **13.** None has ascended (risen or gone up) to heaven except the one who came down (descended) from heaven— the Son of Man (Jesus), who is in heaven. **14.** Just as Moses lifted up the serpent (symbol of salvation) in the wilderness, so the Son of Man must be lifted up, **15.** "So that everyone who believes in Him may receive eternal life." **16.** For God so loved (cherished, adored, or showed deep affection for) the world that He gave (sacrificed or offered) His one and only Son, that whoever believes (trusts or has faith) in Him shall not perish (be lost, ruined, or destroyed) but have eternal life (everlasting life, unending existence with God). **17.** "For God did not send His Son to condemn (judge or pass sentence upon) the world, but to save (rescue or deliver) it through Him." **18.** Whoever believes (trusts or has faith) in Him is not condemned (judged, found guilty, or sentenced); but whoever does not believe is condemned already (already judged or found guilty), because they have not placed their faith (trust, confidence, or reliance) in the name (authority or identity) of God's one and only Son. **19.** This is the verdict (judgment, decision, or conclusion): The Light has come into the world, but people preferred (chose or favored) darkness over light because their deeds (actions, behaviors, or works) were evil (wicked or morally corrupt). **20.** Everyone who practices evil hates the light and will not come to it, lest their deeds be exposed (revealed). **21.** But whoever lives by the truth comes into the light, so that it may be clear (evident or obvious) that what they have done has been accomplished (carried out or performed) in God. **22.** After this, Jesus and His disciples went into Judea, where He stayed with them and baptized. **23.** John was also baptizing at Aenon (a place near Salim) because there was much water there, and people were coming to be baptized. **24.** For John had not yet been imprisoned. **25.** An argument arose between some of John's disciples and a Jew about purification (ritual cleansing). **26.** They came to John and said, 'Rabbi (Teacher, Master), that man who was with you on the other side of the Jordan—the one you testified (witnessed, spoke, or gave evidence) about—He is baptizing, and everyone is going to Him!' **27.** "John replied, 'A person can only receive (obtain or be granted) what has been given to them from heaven.'" **28.** You yourselves are my witnesses that I said, 'I am not the Messiah, but am sent ahead of Him.' **29.** The bride belongs to the bridegroom (groom). The friend of the bridegroom (groom's companion or best man) waits and listens for him and is filled with great joy when he hears the bridegroom's (groom's) voice. That joy is now fulfilled (made complete or perfected). **30.** He must increase; I must decrease. **31.** The one who comes from above (heavenly origin, divine realm, or higher realm) is above all; the one who is from the earth belongs to the earth and speaks from an earthly (mundane, limited, or worldly) perspective. The one who comes from heaven is above all. **32.** He testifies (witnesses, attests, or provides evidence) to what He has seen and heard, yet no one accepts (receives, acknowledges, or believes) His testimony (witness, declaration, or evidence). **33.** Whoever has accepted it has certified (confirmed) that God is truthful. **34.** The one whom God has appointed (designated or chosen) speaks the divine messages of God, for God bestows (grants or gives) the Spirit without restriction (limitation or boundary). **35.** The Father cherishes (holds dear or values deeply) the Son and has entrusted (assigned or given responsibility for) all things into His control (authority or power). **36.** anyone who places their trust in the Son possesses (has or holds) eternal life, but those who refuse (decline or reject) the Son will not experience (witness or enjoy) life, for God's wrath (fury or intense anger) remains upon them.

Chapter 4

1. When the Lord learned that the Pharisees had heard Jesus was making and baptizing more disciples than John, **2.** Although Jesus Himself did not baptize (perform the ritual of washing), but His disciples (followers or adherents) did, **3.** He departed (left or exited) Judea and returned (came back) to Galilee. **4.** He had to go through Samaria. **5.** So He arrived at a town in Samaria called Sychar, located near the land that Jacob gave to his son Joseph. **6.** Jacob's well (a deep water source) was there. Jesus, weary (exhausted or fatigued) from His journey, sat down by the well. It was about the sixth hour (approximately noon). **7.** A Samaritan woman came to draw water. Jesus said, "Give Me a drink." **8.** His disciples had gone into the city to buy food. **9.** The woman said, 'How is it that You, a Jew, ask for a drink from me, a Samaritan woman (a member of a group historically despised by Jews)?' (For Jews do not associate (engage or interact) with Samaritans.) **10.** Jesus replied, 'If you knew the gift (blessing or favor) of God, and who it is that is asking you for a drink, you would have asked Him, and He would have given you living water (water that gives eternal life or spiritual sustenance).' **11.** The woman said, 'Sir, You have no bucket (container or vessel), and the well is deep (profound or far down).' Where will You obtain (get or draw) this living water?' **12.** Are You greater than our father Jacob, who gave us this well and drank from it himself, along with his sons and livestock (domestic animals or cattle)? **13.** Jesus answered, 'Anyone who drinks this water will thirst again (experience hunger or need more), **14.** but whoever drinks the water I give will never thirst. The water I give will become a spring of water welling up (rising or overflowing) to eternal life.'" **15.** The woman said, 'Sir, give me this water, so I won't thirst or have to come here to

draw (retrieve or gather) water.' **16.** Jesus said, 'Go, summon (call or request) your husband and come back.' **17.** She replied, 'I have no husband.' Jesus said, 'You are correct (accurate or truthful) in saying, 'I have no husband.'' **18.** You have had five husbands, and the man you are now with is not your husband (partner or spouse). What you have said is true. **19.** The woman said, 'Sir, I perceive (understand or recognize) that You are a prophet (a divinely inspired person or messenger).' **20.** Our ancestors worshiped (revered or honored) on this mountain, but you Jews assert (claim or maintain) that the place of worship is in Jerusalem. **21.** Jesus replied, 'Truly (I assure you), a time is coming when you will worship the Father neither on this mountain nor in Jerusalem.' **22.** You worship what you do not know; we worship what we do know, for salvation (deliverance or rescue) is from the Jews."**23.** Yet a time is coming, and has now come, when true worshipers will worship the Father in spirit (in the inner being) and truth, for they are the kind of worshipers the Father seeks. **24.** God is Spirit (a non-physical being or immaterial essence), and His worshipers must worship in spirit (with the inner being or heart) and truth (authenticity, sincerity, or genuine faith). **25.** The woman said, 'I know that the Messiah (Savior) is coming. When He comes, He will clarify (explain or reveal) everything to us.' **26.** Jesus declared, 'I, the one speaking to you, am He (the Messiah).' **27.** Just then, His disciples returned and were surprised (astonished, amazed, or taken aback) to find Him talking with a woman. But no one asked, 'What do You want?' or 'Why are You talking with her?' **28.** Then, leaving her water jar (vessel, container, or receptacle), the woman went back to the town and said to the people, **29.** 'Come, see a man who told me everything I ever did (knew or revealed about my life). Could this be the Messiah (the Christ, the Savior)?' **30.** They came out of the town and made their way toward Him (approached or headed in His direction). **31.** Meanwhile, His disciples urged (encouraged, requested, or insisted) Him, 'Rabbi (Teacher), eat something (nourishment or food).' **32.** But He said to them, 'I have food (nourishment or sustenance) to eat that you know nothing about (are unaware of or do not understand).' **33.** Then His disciples said to each other, 'Could someone have brought Him food (nourishment or sustenance)?' **34.** "Jesus said, 'My food (nourishment or sustenance) is to do the will of Him who sent Me and to finish (complete or accomplish) His work.'" **35.** Don't you say, 'Four months more and then the harvest'? I tell you, open your eyes (become aware or attentive) and look at the fields (the harvest, opportunities, or the work that needs to be done)! They are ripe (ready) for harvest. **36.** Even now the one who reaps (gathers the crop) draws a wage and harvests a crop for eternal life, so that the sower and the reaper may be glad together. **37.** Thus the saying, 'One sows and another reaps,' is true. **38.** I sent you to reap (gather or harvest) what you have not worked for. Others have done the difficult work, and you have reaped the benefits (rewards or outcomes) of their labor (effort or toil). **39.** Many Samaritans from that town believed in Him because of the woman's testimony (witness, declaration, or account), 'He told me everything I ever did (knew or revealed about my life).' **40.** So when the Samaritans came to Him, they urged (begged, requested, or strongly invited) Him to stay with them, and He stayed for two days. **41.** And because of His words (teachings, discourse, or message), many more became believers (those who accepted, embraced, or followed His message). **42.** They said to the woman, 'We no longer believe merely because of what you said; now we have heard for ourselves, and we know that this man truly is the Savior (rescuer) of the world.' **43.** After two days, He departed (left or went) for Galilee. **44.** Now Jesus Himself had pointed out that a prophet has no honor (esteem) in his own country (hometown or native land). **45.** When He arrived in Galilee, the Galileans welcomed (received, greeted, or embraced) Him. They had seen all that He had done in Jerusalem at the festival (Passover), for they also had been there. **46.** Once more He visited Cana in Galilee, where He had turned the water into wine. And there was a certain royal official (nobleman, high-ranking servant, or courtier) whose son was ill (unwell or ailing) at Capernaum. **47.** When this man heard that Jesus had arrived in Galilee from Judea, he went to Him and begged (implored, urgently requested, or pleaded) Him to come and heal his son, who was at the point of death (near death or critically ill). **48.** 'Unless you people see signs and wonders (supernatural acts, or extraordinary events),' Jesus told him, 'you will never believe (have faith or trust).' **49.** The royal official said, 'Sir, come down (to my home) before my child dies (passes away or perishes)!' **50.** Jesus replied, 'Go, your son will live (survive or recover).' The man took Jesus at His word (believed or trusted in His promise) and departed (left or went on his way). **51.** While he was on his way, his servants met him with the news (information or report) that his boy was living (alive or recovering). **52.** When he inquired (asked, questioned, or sought clarification) as to the time when his son got better (recovered or improved), they told him, 'Yesterday at the seventh hour, the fever left him (subsided or ended).' **53.** Then the father realized (understood or recognized) that this was the exact time at which Jesus had said to him, 'Your son will live.' So, he and his whole household (family, household members, or home) believed (trusted, accepted the message). **54.** This was the second sign (wonder, or divine act) Jesus performed after coming from Judea to Galilee.

Chapter 5

1. After this, there was a Jewish feast, and Jesus went to Jerusalem. **2.** In Jerusalem, near the Sheep Gate, there is a pool called Bethesda (meaning 'house of mercy' or 'place of healing'), with five porches (covered walkways or alcoves). **3.** Many sick people—blind, lame (unable to walk), and paralyzed (unable to move)—lay there, waiting for the water to be stirred. **4.** At times, an angel would stir (move) the water, and the first person to step in would be healed. **5.** One man had been infirm (sick, weak, or suffering) for thirty-eight years. **6.** When Jesus saw him and knew he had endured (suffered or experienced) for so long, He asked, 'Do you want to be healed (cured or restored to health)?' **7.** The man replied, 'I have no one to help me into the pool when the water is stirred (agitated or moved); someone else always gets in before me.' **8.** Jesus told him, 'Get up (rise), take your mat (bed or stretcher), and walk (move or stroll).' **9.** Immediately, the man was healed (restored or cured), picked up his mat (bed or stretcher), and walked (moved or strolled). It was the Sabbath (the Jewish day of rest). **10.** The Jews said to the healed man, 'It's the Sabbath (day of rest); you can't carry your mat (bed or stretcher).' **11.** He replied, 'The man who healed (restored or made well) me told me, "Take up your mat (bed, stretcher, or pallet) and walk (get up and move)."' **12.** They asked, 'Who is this man who instructed (ordered, commanded, or directed) you to do this?' **13.** But the healed man didn't know, as Jesus had slipped away, with a crowd in the place. **14.** Later, Jesus found him in the temple and said, 'You've been healed (restored or made whole). Don't sin (sinful behavior or wrong actions) anymore, or something worse might happen (occur or befall you).' **15.** The man went and told the Jews (religious leaders or authorities) that it was Jesus who had healed (cured or restored) him. **16.** For this reason, the Jews persecuted (opposed) Jesus, wanting to kill Him because He healed on the Sabbath. **17.** Jesus answered, "My Father is working until now, and I am working." **18.** This made them more determined to kill Him, not only because He broke the Sabbath but also because He claimed God as His Father, making Himself equal to God. **19.** Jesus said, 'The Son can do nothing on His own (independently or apart from the Father), but only what He sees the Father do; whatever the Father does, the Son does in the same way (manner, fashion, or likeness).' **20.** The Father loves the Son and shows Him everything He does, and He will show Him greater works that you may marvel (be amazed). **21.** Just as the Father raises the dead and gives them life, so the Son gives life to whom He wills (chooses). **22.** The Father has entrusted (given, assigned, or committed) all judgment (authority to judge or decision-making) to the Son. **23.** That everyone may honor (revere, respect, or esteem) the Son just as they honor the Father. Those who do not honor the Son do not honor (acknowledge or give proper regard to) the Father who sent Him. **24.** Truly, I tell you, whoever hears My word and believes in the One who sent Me has eternal life (everlasting life or salvation) and will not be condemned (judged or found guilty), but has passed from death (spiritual death or separation from God) to life (spiritual rebirth or eternal salvation). **25.** The time is coming—indeed, it's now here—when the dead will hear the voice of the Son of God, and those who hear will live. **26.** For as the Father has life in Himself, He has granted the Son to have life in Himself, **27.** and given Him authority (power, right, or dominion) to judge, because He is the Son of Man (the human Messiah, or the one who represents humanity). **28.** Do not be amazed by this, for the time is coming when all who are in their graves will hear His voice **29.** and rise—those who have done good will experience the resurrection of life, and those who have done evil will face the resurrection of judgment. **30.** I can do nothing on My own. I judge as I hear (listen to the Father), and My judgment is righteous (just, fair, or morally correct) because I seek not My will but the will (purpose or desire) of the Father who sent Me. **31.** If I testify (bear witness or give evidence) about Myself, My testimony (statement or declaration) is not true (valid or credible). **32.** There is another who testifies (bears witness or gives evidence) of Me, and I know His testimony (witness or declaration) is true (reliable, authentic). **33.** You sent to John, and he bore witness (testimony, evidence, or gave a declaration) to the truth (reality or veracity). **34.** But I do not accept human testimony (witness or evidence from people); I say this so that you may be saved (rescued, delivered, or granted eternal life). **35.** John was the lamp that burned and shone, and for a time you were willing to rejoice (be happy) in his light. **36.** But I have a greater witness (testimony or evidence) than John's—the works (actions, deeds) the Father has given Me to accomplish (complete or fulfill), the very works I do, testify (bear witness or provide evidence) that the Father has sent Me. **37.** And the Father who sent Me has testified (borne witness, affirmed, or given evidence) of Me. You've never heard His voice or seen His form. **38.** Nor do you have His word abiding (living) in you, for you do not believe the One He sent. **39.** You search the Scriptures, thinking that in them you have eternal life, but they testify about Me. **40.** Yet you refuse (decline, reject, or are unwilling) to come to Me to have life (eternal life or spiritual salvation). **41.** I do not accept glory (honor, praise, or acclaim) from men (people). **42.** But I know that you do not have the love (affection, devotion, or sincere care) of God in your hearts (inner being, minds, or souls). **43.** I have come in My Father's name (by His authority or representing Him), and you do not accept (receive, welcome, or acknowledge) Me; but if someone comes in his own name (acting independently or for his own benefit), you will accept (embrace or follow) him. **44.** How can you believe (trust or have faith), when you seek glory (honor, praise, or recognition) from one another and do not seek the glory that comes from God alone (only from God, or divine approval)? **45.** Do not think I will accuse you to the Father; your accuser is Moses, in whom you trust. **46.** If you believed (trusted or had faith in) Moses, you would believe (accept or follow) Me, for he wrote about (prophesied or spoke of) Me. **47.** But if you do not believe (accept or trust) what he wrote, how will you believe (trust or accept) My words (teachings or message)?

Chapter 6

1. After these events, Jesus crossed the Sea of Galilee, also known as the Sea of Tiberius. **2** A large crowd followed Him because they had seen the miracles (wonders, signs, or extraordinary events) He performed on the sick (ill or ailing). **3.** Jesus went up on a mountain and sat with His disciples. **4.** The Passover (a Jewish festival) was approaching. **5.** Looking at the crowd, Jesus asked Philip, "Where can we buy bread for these people to eat?" **6.** He said this to test (test for understanding) him, for He already knew what He would do. **7.** Philip replied, 'Even 200 denarii (a form of currency, equivalent to a day's wage) worth of bread wouldn't be enough to give each of them a small piece (fragment or portion).' **8.** Andrew, Simon Peter's brother, spoke up, **9.** "A boy here has five loaves of barley (a type of grain) and two small fish, but how far will that go among so many?" **10.** Jesus said, 'Have the people sit down (recline or take their seats).' There was plenty of grass (green pasture), and the crowd, about five thousand men, sat down (rested or settled). **11.** Jesus took the loaves, gave thanks, and distributed them to the disciples, who passed them to the people. He did the same with the fish, giving as much as they wanted. **12.** Once they were full (satisfied or had eaten their fill), He told His disciples, 'Gather the leftovers (remaining food or scraps) so nothing is wasted (lost or spoiled). **13.** They collected twelve baskets of fragments (small remaining pieces) from the five barley loaves. **14.** When the people saw this miracle (sign, wonder, or divine act), they said, 'This is truly the Prophet (the one promised, foretold, or sent by God) who was to come into the world.' **15.** Realizing they intended to make Him king by force, Jesus withdrew (left) to the mountain alone. **16.** When evening came (the onset of dusk or nightfall), His disciples went down to the sea (the lake or body of water), **17.** got into a boat (vessel or craft), and started across to Capernaum (a town by the Sea of Galilee). It was dark (night had fallen), and Jesus had not yet joined them. **18.** A strong wind began to blow, **19.** and after rowing about three or four miles, they saw Jesus walking on the sea toward them. They were afraid, **20.** but He said, 'It is I (I am the one); don't be afraid (don't fear or be frightened).' **21.** They welcomed (received or accepted) Him into the boat (vessel), and immediately (instantly) the boat reached the shore (coast or bank) where they were heading (going or destined). **22.** The next day, the people who had stayed on the other side of the sea noticed there was no boat there except the one the disciples had taken. **23.** However, boats from Tiberias arrived near the spot where they had eaten the bread after Jesus had given thanks. **24.** When they saw (noticed or realized) that Jesus and His disciples were gone, they got into the boats (vessels) and went to Capernaum (a town by the Sea of Galilee), seeking (searching for or looking for) Him. **25.** When they found (discovered or located) Him on the other side (of the lake), they asked, 'Rabbi (Teacher, esteemed instructor), when did You come here?' **26.** Jesus answered, 'You are looking for Me not because you saw signs (miracles or wonders), but because you ate the loaves (bread) and were satisfied (fulfilled or content).' **27.** Do not work for food that perishes (decays, spoils, or is temporary), but for food that leads to eternal life (everlasting sustenance), which the Son of Man will give you. God the Father has set His seal (mark of approval or authority) on Him. **28.** They asked, 'What must we do to do the works (deeds or actions) of God?' **29.** Jesus answered, 'the work (task or duty) of God is this: to believe (have faith or trust) in the One He has sent (appointed or chosen).' **30.** They responded, 'What sign (miracle or wonder) will You perform so we may believe (trust or have faith) in You? What work (deed or action) will You do?' **31.** Our ancestors ate the manna (bread-like substance from heaven) in the desert, as it is written, 'He gave them bread from heaven.'" **32.** Jesus replied, 'I tell you the truth (assuredly, with certainty), Moses did not give you the bread from heaven, but My Father gives you the true (genuine or authentic) bread from heaven.' **33.** For the bread (nourishment or sustenance) of God is He who comes down (descends) from heaven and gives life (vitality or spiritual existence) to the world. **34.** They said, 'Lord (Master, Sovereign), always give us this bread (sustenance, nourishment).' **35.** Jesus declared, 'I am the bread (nourishment or sustenance) of life. Whoever comes to Me will never hunger (experience spiritual emptiness), and whoever believes (trusts or has faith) in Me will never thirst (experience spiritual longing or dissatisfaction). **36.** But I told you that you have seen (observed or witnessed) Me and still do not believe (trust or have faith). **37.** All the Father gives (entrusts or provides) Me will come to Me, and I will not turn (reject or dismiss) anyone away. **38.** I have descended (come down) from heaven, not to fulfill My own desire (will or purpose), but to accomplish the purpose (will) of the One who commissioned (sent or directed) Me. **39.** This is the desire (will or intention) of the One who sent me: that I should not let any of those He has entrusted to me be lost, but rather lift them up on the final (last) day. **40.** For it is the purpose (will or intent) of My Father that all who look upon the Son and place their faith (believe) in Him will receive everlasting (eternal) life, and I will lift them up on the final (last) day. **41.** Upon hearing this, the Jews started to murmur (complain or grumble) because He claimed, 'I am the bread that descended (came down) from heaven.' **42.** They asked, 'Isn't this Jesus, the son of Joseph, whose parents (father and mother) we know (are familiar with)?' How can He claim now, 'I have descended (come down) from heaven'? **43.** Jesus replied, "Stop grumbling among you. **44.** No one can approach (come to) Me unless they are guided (drawn) by the Father who sent Me, and I will lift them up on the final (last) day. **45.** It is recorded (written) in the prophets, 'they will all receive instruction (be taught) from God.' All who pay attention (listen) to the Father and gain understanding (learn) from Him come to Me. **46.** It's not that anyone has directly observed (seen) the Father, except for the One who comes from God; only He has truly seen the Father. **47.** I assure you (tell you the truth), anyone who has faith (believes) possesses everlasting (eternal) life." **48.** I am the bread of life. **49.** Your forebears (ancestors) ate the manna in the desert (wilderness), yet they perished (died). **50.** But here is the bread that descends (comes down) from heaven, which anyone can consume (eat) and not perish (die). **51.** I am the life-

sustaining (living) bread that came down (descended) from heaven. Whoever eats (consumes) this bread will live forever (eternally); this bread is My body (flesh), which I will give (offer) for the salvation (life) of the world. **52.** The Jews began to argue sharply (fight verbally) among themselves, "How can this man give us His flesh to eat?" **53.** Jesus told them, 'I assure you (tell you the truth), unless you consume (eat) the body (flesh) of the Son of Man and drink His blood, you have no life within you.' **54.** Whoever consumes (eats) My body (flesh) and drinks My blood has everlasting (eternal) life, and I will lift them up on the final (last) day. **55.** For My flesh is real food, and My blood is real drink. **56.** Whoever eats My flesh and drinks My blood remains (abides) in Me, and I in them. **57.** Just as the life-giving (living) Father sent Me, and I live because of (through) the Father, so the one who partakes (feeds) on Me will live because of (through) Me. **58.** This is the bread that came down (descended) from heaven. Your forebears (ancestors) ate manna and perished (died), but whoever consumes (eats) this bread will live eternally (forever). **59.** He said these words while teaching in the synagogue (assembly) in Capernaum. **60.** Many of His followers (disciples) said, 'This is a difficult (hard) teaching. Who can tolerate (accept) it?' **61.** Aware that His disciples were grumbling, Jesus asked, "Does this offend (cause to feel upset) you? **62.** What if you witness (see) the Son of Man rise (ascend) to the place (where) He was before? **63.** The Spirit grants (gives) life; the flesh is of no value (counts for nothing). The words I have spoken to you are filled with the Spirit and with life. **64.** Yet some of you do not believe (have faith)." For Jesus had known from the beginning (start) who would not believe and who would betray (turn against) Him. **65.** He went on, 'This is why I told you that no one can come to Me unless the Father has enabled (empowered or given the ability) them.' **66.** From that point onward, many of His followers (disciples) turned away and no longer walked (followed) with Him. **67.** Jesus turned to the Twelve and asked, 'You don't wish to leave as well, do you?' **68.** Simon Peter replied, 'Lord, where would we go? You have the words of everlasting (eternal) life.' **69.** We have come to believe and know that You are the Holy One (Messiah) of God." **70.** Jesus answered, 'Did I not select (choose) you, the Twelve? Yet one of you is a deceiver (devil).' **71.** He was speaking of Judas Iscariot, the son of Simon, who would later betray Him, though he was one of the Twelve.

Chapter 7

1. After these things, Jesus walked in Galilee, avoiding Judea because the Jews sought to kill Him. **2.** The Feast of Tabernacles (a Jewish festival) was near. **3.** His brothers said to Him, 'Leave this place and go to Judea so that Your disciples may witness (see) Your works.' **4.** No one seems to be known in secret; if You do these things, reveal Yourself to the world." **5.** Even His brothers did not have faith (believe) in Him. **6.** Jesus answered, 'My time has not arrived yet, but your time is always at hand (ready).' **7.** The world cannot hate you, but it hates Me because I testify (give evidence) that its deeds are evil. **8.** You go up to the feast; I am not going yet because My time has not fully come." **9.** After saying this, He stayed in Galilee. **10.** When His brothers went up, He also went, but not openly—secretly. **11.** The Jews searched for Him at the feast, asking, "Where is He?" **12.** There was much discussion about Him. Some said, 'He is good,' while others replied, 'No, He deceives (misleads) the people.' **13.** But no one spoke openly for fear (being afraid) of the Jews. **14.** At the midpoint of the feast, Jesus went to the temple and began to teach. **15.** The Jews were astonished, saying, 'How does this man have knowledge (letters), having never been taught (studied)?' **16.** Jesus answered, "My teaching is not My own but His who sent Me. **17.** Anyone who wishes to do His will shall understand whether the teaching is from God or if I speak by My own authority. **18.** Those who speak for themselves seek their own glory, but He who seeks the glory of the One who sent Him is true, and no unrighteousness (sin or injustice) is in Him. **19.** Did not Moses give you the law, yet none of you keep it? Why do you seek to kill Me?" **20.** The people responded, "You have a demon! Who seeks to kill You?" **21.** Jesus said, 'I performed one act, and you are all astonished.' **22.** Moses gave you circumcision (a Jewish rite of male circumcision), not that it originated with Moses, but from the forefathers (ancestors), and yet you perform circumcision on the Sabbath. **23.** If a man can be circumcised on the Sabbath to fulfill the law, are you angry because I healed a man completely on the Sabbath? **24.** Do not judge by appearance, but judge with righteous judgment (fair judgment)." **25.** Some from Jerusalem said, "Isn't this the one they are trying to kill? **26.** But look, He speaks with confidence (boldly), and they say nothing. Do the rulers know that this is truly the Christ (Messiah)? **27.** But we know where He is from; when the Messiah comes, no one will know where He is from. **28.** Then Jesus shouted as He taught in the temple, 'You know Me and where I am from; I did not come by My own authority. The One who sent Me is truthful, and you do not know Him.' **29.** I know Him, for I am from Him, and He has sent Me. **30.** They tried to seize (capture) Him, but no one laid a hand on Him because His time had not yet come. **31.** Many put their faith in Him, saying, 'When the Messiah comes, will He perform more signs (miracles) than this man?' **32.** The Pharisees and chief priests heard the murmurs (complaints) and sent officers to seize (arrest) Him. **33.** Jesus said, 'I will be with you a little longer, and then I will go to the One who sent Me.' **34.** You will search for Me and not find Me, and where I am, you cannot come. **35.** The Jews wondered, 'Where does He plan to go that we won't be able to find Him?' Will He go to the Dispersion (scattering of Jews) among the Greeks and teach them? **36.** What does He mean by, 'You will search for Me and not find Me'? **37.** On the final day of the feast, Jesus stood and shouted, 'If anyone is thirsty (desires), let him come to Me and drink.' **38.** Whoever believes in Me, as the Scripture says, out of his heart will flow rivers of living water." **39.** He was referring to the Spirit (Holy Spirit), whom those who believed in Him would later receive, for the Spirit had not yet been given because Jesus had not yet been glorified (honored or exalted). **40.** Many in the crowd said, 'Surely this is the Prophet.' **41.** Others said, 'This is the Christ,' but some questioned, 'Can the Messiah come from Galilee?' **42.** Has not the Scripture said that the Christ comes from David's descendants, from Bethlehem, the town where David was?" **43.** Therefore, there was division among the people because of Him. **44.** Some wanted to arrest Him, but no one touched Him. **45.** The officers returned to the chief priests and Pharisees, who asked, 'Why didn't you bring Him in?' **46.** The officers replied, 'No one has ever spoken like this man!' **47.** The Pharisees asked, 'Have you also been led astray (deceived)?' **48.** Has any ruler or Pharisee believed in Him? **49.** But this crowd, who doesn't know the law, is accursed (cursed)." **50.** Nicodemus, who had previously come to Jesus, said, **51.** Does our law condemn a man before hearing him and understanding what he has done? **52.** They replied, "Are you from Galilee too? Look and see that no prophet comes from Galilee." **53.** And everyone went to their own house.

Chapter 8

1. Jesus went to the Mount of Olives. **2.** Early the next morning, He went back to the tabernacle, where people gathered around Him, and He taught them. **3.** The scribes and Pharisees brought a woman caught in adultery and stood her before Jesus. **4.** They said, "Teacher, this woman was caught in the very act of adultery. **5.** Moses' law says she should be stoned. What do You say?" **6.** They asked this to test Him, but Jesus bent down and wrote on the ground, disregarding them. **7.** As they continued to question Him, He stood up and said, "Let the one who is without sin be the first to throw a stone." **8.** He bent down again and wrote on the ground. **9.** Condemned by their consciences, they left, starting with the oldest, leaving Jesus alone with the woman. **10.** Jesus raised His eyes and asked, "Where are your accusers? Has no one condemned you?" **11.** "No one, Lord," she replied. Jesus said, "Neither do I condemn you. Go and sin no more." **12.** Jesus also proclaimed, "I am the light of the world. Whoever follows Me will not live in darkness, but will have the light of life." **13.** The Pharisees challenged Him, saying, "Your testimony is not valid since You are testifying about Yourself." **14.** Jesus replied, "Even if I testify about Myself, My testimony is true because I know where I came from and where I am going, but you do not. **15.** You judge according to human standards; I do not judge anyone. **16.** But if I do judge, My judgment is righteous because I am not alone; the Father who sent Me is with Me. **17.** Your law says the testimony of two witnesses is true. **18.** I testify about myself, and the Father who sent Me also bears witness to Me." **19.** They asked, "Where is Your Father?" Jesus replied, "You do not know Me or My Father. If you knew Me, you would also know My Father." **20.** He spoke these words in the tabernacle storeroom, and no one seized Him because His time had not yet arrived. **21.** He went on, "I am going away, and you will search for Me, but you will die in your sin. Where I am going, you cannot come." **22.** The Jews questioned, "Will He kill Himself, since He says, 'Where I am going, you cannot come?'" **23.** Jesus answered, "You are from this world; I am from above. You belong to this world; I do not. **24.** That's why I said you will die in your sins, for unless you believe that I am He, you will die in your sins." **25.** "Who are You?" they asked. Jesus answered, "Exactly what I've been saying to you from the very beginning. **26.** I have much to say and judge about you, but He who sent Me is true, and I speak the things I've heard from Him." **27.** They didn't understand He was talking about the Father. **28.** Jesus said, "When you have lifted up the Son of Man, then you will know that I am He, and that I do nothing on My own, but speak exactly as the Father has taught Me. **29.** The Father who sent Me is with Me; He has not abandoned Me, for I always do what pleases Him." **30.** As He spoke, many came to believe in Him. **31.** Jesus said to those who believed, "If you remain faithful to My teachings, you are truly My disciples. **32.** Then you will know the truth, and the truth will make you free." **33.** They answered, "We are descendants of Abraham and have never been enslaved. How can you say, 'You will be set free'?" **34.** Jesus replied, "Everyone who sins is a servant to sin. A servant does not remain in the family forever, but a son belongs to it forever. **36.** Therefore, if the Son sets you free, you will truly be free. **37.** I know you are descendants of Abraham, yet you are trying to kill Me because My message has no place in you. **38.** I speak the words I have heard from My Father, and you do what you have learned from your father." **39.** They responded, "Abraham is our father." Jesus replied, "If you were truly Abraham's children, you would do the works Abraham did. **40.** Instead, you are trying to kill Me, a man who has told you the truth I received from God. Abraham did not do such things. **41.** You are doing the works of your father." They retorted, "We were not born of immorality; we have one Father—God." **42.** Jesus said, "If God were truly your Father, you would love Me, for I came from God. I did not come by Myself; He sent Me. **43.** Why don't you understand what I say? It's because you cannot accept My message. **44.** You belong to your father, the devil, and you want to do what he desires. He has been a murderer from the beginning and does not adhere to the truth, because there is no truth in him. When he lies, he speaks his own language, for he is a liar and the father of lies. **45.** However, because I speak the truth, you do not believe Me." **46.** Can any of you accuse Me of sin? If I am speaking the truth, why do you not believe Me? **47.** Those who belong to God listen to what He says. The reason you do not listen is because you do not belong to God. **48.** The Jews replied, 'Aren't we correct in saying that You are a Samaritan (someone from Samaria) and are possessed by a demon?' **49.** Jesus answered, "I am not possessed by a demon; rather, I honor My Father, and you dishonor Me. **50.** I do not seek honor for Myself; but there is One who seeks it, and He is the judge. **51.** Truly, I tell you, whoever follows My word will never experience death. **52.** At this, the Jews responded, "Now we are sure You are possessed by a demon! Abraham and the prophets have died, yet You claim, 'Whoever obeys My word will never taste death.' **53.** Are You greater than our father Abraham? He died, and so did the prophets. Who do You think You are? **54.** Jesus answered, 'If I exalt (raise in dignity) Myself, My honor holds no significance. It is My Father, whom you profess (claim as true) to be your God, who bestows (grants) glory upon Me.' **55.** Although you are ignorant (lacking knowledge) of Him, I am acquainted (familiar) with Him. If I were to deny (refuse to acknowledge) this, I would be a deceiver (one who lies) like you, but I do know Him and adhere (follow) to His command. **56.** Your ancestor Abraham exulted (rejoiced greatly) at the prospect (anticipation) of witnessing My time; he saw it and was filled with joy. **57.** They retorted, 'You are not yet fifty years of age, and yet You claim to have seen Abraham?' **58.** Jesus responded, 'Indeed (truly) I assure you, before Abraham came into existence, I AM (I exist eternally, beyond time and space).' **59.** Upon hearing this, they seized (grasped) stones to stone Him, but Jesus concealed (hid) Himself, slipping away from the temple precincts.

Chapter 9

1. As Jesus passed by, He saw a man eyeless from birth. **2.** His votaries asked, "Rabbi (religious teacher), who trespassed — this man or his parents — that he was born eyeless?" **3.** Jesus answered, "Neither this man's sin nor his parents' sin caused his blindness, but this happened so that God's work (His divine purpose and plan) could be revealed through him." **4.** I must do the work of Him who transferred Me while it's day; night is coming when no one can work. **5.** As long as I am in the world, I am the light (the source of guidance and truth) to the world. **6.** After saying this, He wrangled on the ground, made complexion (slush) with the slaver, and applied it to the man's eyes. **7.** He instructed him, "Go and wash in the Pool of Siloam." The man went, washed, and returned able to see. **8.** The neighbors and those who had seen him soliciting asked, "Is this the man who used to sit and supplicate?" **9.** Some people said, "Yes, it's him." Others argued, "No, he just looks like him." But the man answered, "I am the one." **10.** They asked him, "How were your eyes opened?" **11.** He replied, "A man called Jesus made a paste (a mixture), applied it to my eyes, and told me to wash in the Pool of Siloam. I obeyed, and now I can see." **12.** They asked, "Where is He?" He replied, "I don't know." **13.** They brought him to the Pharisees (the Jewish religious leaders). **14.** It was the Sabbath (the Jewish day of rest) when Jesus made the paste (a mixture) and healed his eyes. **15.** The Pharisees asked him again how he received his sight. He replied, "He applied a paste to my eyes, I washed, and now I can see." **16.** Some of the Pharisees said, "This man is not from God, because he does not keep the Sabbath." Others asked, "How can a sinner perform such miraculous signs?" And they were divided. **17.** They asked the eyeless man, "What do you say about Him, since He opened your eyes?" He replied, "He's a prophet." **18.** The Jews (Jewish authorities) didn't believe he'd been eyeless until they called his parents. **19.** They asked, "Is this your son, who was born blind? How is it that he can now see?" **20.** His parents answered, "We know that he is our son and that he was born blind." **21.** "But how he now sees, we don't know, or who opened his eyes, we don't know. He's old enough — ask him." **22.** They said this because they feared the Jews, who had agreed that anyone who acknowledged Jesus as the Christ (Messiah) would be expelled from the temple (Jewish place of worship). **23.** So they answered, "He is old enough — ask him." **24.** A second time they called the man and said, "Give glory to God! We know that this man is a sinner." **25.** He answered, "Whether he is a sinner or not, I don't know. One thing I do know: I was eyeless, but now I see." **26.** They questioned him again, "What did he do to you? How did He open your eyes?" **27.** He replied, "I already told you, and you didn't listen. Why do you want to hear it again? Do you want to be His votaries too?" **28.** They disrespected him, saying, "You're His convert, but we're votaries of Moses. **29.** We know God spoke to Moses, but we don't know where He is from." **30.** The man replied, "This is remarkable! You don't know where He's from, yet He opened my eyes! **31.** We know God doesn't listen to sinners. However, He listens to them, if anyone is a worshiper of God and does His will. **32.** No one has ever heard of anyone opening the eyes of a man born eyeless. **33.** He still wouldn't be able to do anything if this man were not from God." **34.** They replied, "You were steeped in sin (involved in sin) at birth; how dare you lecture us?" And they threw him out. **35.** Jesus heard they had thrown him out, and when He found him, He asked, "Do you believe in the Son of Man?" **36.** He answered, "Who is he, sir, so that I may believe in him?" **37.** Jesus answered, "You have now seen him; in fact, he is the one talking to you." **38.** The man answered, "Lord, I believe," and he bowed down and worshiped Him. **39.** Jesus said, "I have come into this world for judgment (a decision), so that the blind will see, and those who see will become blind." **40.** Some Pharisees who were with Him heard this and asked, "What? Are we eyeless too?" **41.** Jesus replied, "If you were blind, you would not be guilty of sin; but now that you claim you can see, your sin remains."

Chapter 10

1. "I tell you the truth, anyone who does not enter the pen (enclosure for sheep) through the gate, but climbs in another way, is a thief and a robber. **2.** The one who enters through the gate is the shepherd (a person who takes care of sheep) of the sheep. **3.** The gatekeeper, (person who guards the entrance) opens the gate for him, and the sheep hear his voice. He calls each of them by name and leads them out. **4.** When he has gathered his own sheep, he walks ahead of them, and the sheep follow him because they recognize (identify) his voice. **5.** They won't follow a stranger (someone they don't know), but will flee (run away) from him, because they do not recognize the stranger's voice. **6.** Jesus used this illustration, but they did not understand what He was saying. **7.** So Jesus said again, "Truly, I tell you, I am the gate

(entrance) for the sheep. **8.** All who came before Me were thieves and robbers, but the sheep did not listen to them. **9.** I am the gate; anyone who enters through Me will be saved. They will come in and go out, and find pasture (land covered with grass for grazing). **10.** The thief comes only to steal (take away), kill (cause death), and destroy (ruin); I have come that they may have life, and have it abundantly (in large quantity). **11.** I am the good shepherd. The good shepherd lays down His life for the sheep. **12.** The hired hand (a person employed temporarily), who is not the shepherd and does not own the sheep, sees the wolf (a wild carnivorous animal) coming and abandons the sheep, leaving them to be scattered (separated) and devoured (eaten). **13.** The hired hand runs away because he cares nothing for the sheep. **14.** I am the good shepherd; I know My sheep, and My sheep know Me, **15.** just as the Father knows Me and I know the Father. And I lay down My life for the sheep. **16.** I have other sheep that are not of this fold (group); I must bring them also, and they will listen to My voice. Then there will be one flock (group) and one shepherd. **17.** The Father loves Me because I lay down My life—only to take it up again. **18.** No one takes it from Me, but I lay it down of My own accord (will). I have authority (power) to lay it down and authority to take it up again. This command (instruction) I received from My Father." **19.** Again, there was division (disagreement) among the Jews because of these words. **20.** Many of them said, "He is demon-possessed (controlled by an evil spirit) and raving mad (crazy). Why listen to Him?" **21.** Others said, "These are not the words of someone possessed by a demon. Can a demon open the eyes of the blind?" **22.** It was the Feast of Dedication (a Jewish festival celebrating the rededication of the Temple in Jerusalem) in Jerusalem, and it was winter. **23.** Jesus was walking in the temple in Solomon's colonnade (a covered walkway). **24.** The Jews gathered around Him, saying, "How long will You keep us in suspense (uncertainty)? If You are the Christ (the Messiah), tell us plainly." **25.** Jesus answered, "I told you, but you do not believe. The works (deeds) I do in My Father's name testify (prove) about Me. **26.** But you do not believe because you are not My sheep. **27.** My sheep listen to My voice; I know them, and they follow Me. **28.** I give them eternal (never-ending) life, and they shall never perish (be destroyed); no one will snatch (take forcefully) them out of My hand. **29.** My Father, who has given them to Me, is greater than all; no one can snatch them out of My Father's hand. **30.** I and the Father are one." **31.** Again, the Jews picked up stones (rocks) to stone Him. **32.** But Jesus said to them, "I have shown you many good works from the Father. For which of these do you stone Me?" **33.** They replied, "We are not stoning You for any good work, but for blasphemy (speaking disrespectfully of God), because You, a mere man, claim to be God." **34.** Jesus answered them, "Is it not written in your Law, 'I have said you are gods'? **35.** If He called them 'gods,' to whom the word of God came—and Scripture (the Bible) cannot be set aside— **36.** why then do you accuse Me of blasphemy because I said, 'I am the Son of God'? **37.** If I am not doing the works of My Father, do not believe Me. **38.** But if I do them, even though you do not believe Me, believe the works, that you may know and understand that the Father is in Me, and I am in the Father." **39.** Again, they tried to seize (capture) Him, but He escaped their grasp. **40.** Then Jesus went back across the Jordan to the place where John had been baptizing, and there He stayed. **41.** Many people came to Him, and they said, "Though John never performed a sign (miracle), everything he said about this man was true." **42.** And many believed in Jesus.

Chapter 11

1. There was a man named Lazarus who lived in Bethany, the village of Mary and her sister Martha. Lazarus was ill. **2.** This Mary was the one who had smeared (rubbed or smeared) the Lord with incense and wiped His feet with her hair. **3.** The sisters sent a message to Jesus, saying, "Lord, the one whom You love is sick." **4.** When Jesus heard this, He replied, "This illness won't end in death, but is for God's glory, so that the Son of God may be glorified (praised) through it." **5.** Jesus held a profound affection (deep love or care) for Martha, Mary, and Lazarus. **6.** Still, upon hearing that Lazarus was ill, He chose to remain where He was for two more days. **7.** He then instructed His disciples, "Let us return to Judea." **8.** The disciples answered, "Rabbi (teacher), the Jews there just tried to stone You—are You going back?" **9.** Jesus responded, "There are twelve hours of daylight. Anyone who walks during the day won't stumble (fall), for they see the light of this world.

10. But if someone walks at night, they will stumble, for they have no light." 11. After speaking these words, He continued, "Our friend Lazarus has fallen asleep, but I'm going to awaken him." 12. His disciples responded, "Lord, if he's asleep, he'll get better." 13. Jesus had been speaking about his death, but the disciples thought He meant natural sleep. 14. Jesus also explained to them directly, "Lazarus has died. 15. "And I'm glad I wasn't there, for your sake, so that you may believe (have faith). Let us go to him." 16. Thomas, also called Didymus, said to the other disciples, "Let us go, so that we may die alongside Him." 17. When Jesus arrived, He found that Lazarus had already been in the tomb (grave) for four days. 18. Bethany was near Jerusalem, about two miles away. 19. Many Jews had come to comfort (console) Martha and Mary concerning their brother. 20. When Martha learned that Jesus was on His way, she went out to meet Him, while Mary remained at the house. 21. Martha said to Jesus, "Lord, if You had been present, my brother would not have died. 22. But I know that even now God will give You whatever You ask." 23. Jesus assured her, "Your brother will be revived." 24. Martha answered, "I know he'll rise again in the resurrection (rising from the dead) at the last day." 25. Jesus declared, "I am the resurrection and the life. Whoever places their faith in Me will live, even if they die. 26. "And whoever lives by believing in Me will never die. Do you believe this?" 27. She answered, "Yes, Lord, I believe You're the Messiah, the Son of God, who is destined to come into the world." 28. After saying this, she returned to her sister Mary and told her, "The Teacher (Jesus) is here and is asking for you." 29. As soon as Mary heard this, she got up quickly and went to Him. 30. Jesus hadn't yet reached the village, but was still at the place where Martha had met Him. 31. When the Jews who had been comforting Mary saw her get up quickly and leave, they followed her, thinking she was going to the tomb to mourn there. 32. When Mary came to Jesus and saw Him, she fell at His feet and said, "Lord, if You had been there, my brother would not have died." 33. When Jesus saw her weeping, along with the Jews who had come with her, also weeping, He was profoundly moved in His spirit (heart) and deeply troubled (distressed). 34. "Where have you laid him?" He inquired. "Come and see, Lord," they answered. 35. Jesus wept. 36. The Jews also remarked, "See how much He loved him!" 37. But others asked, "Couldn't the One who opened the eyes of the blind man have prevented this man from dying?" 38. Jesus, once more deeply moved, came to the tomb. It was a cave with a stone laid across the entrance. 39. "Take away the stone," He said. But Martha, the sister of the dead man, said, "Lord, by this time there will be a bad odor, for he has been in the grave for four days." 40. Jesus replied, "Did I not tell you that if you believe, you will witness the glory of God?" 41. So they took away the stone. Then Jesus looked up and said, "Father, I thank You that You have heard Me. 42. I knew that You always hear Me, but I said this for the benefit (advantage) of the people standing here, that they may believe that You sent Me." 43. After saying this, He called out in a loud voice, "Lazarus, come forth!" 44. The man who had died came out, his hands and feet bound with strips of linen (cloth), and a cloth around his face. Jesus said to them, "Remove the burial cloths and let him go." 45. Therefore, many of the Jews who had come to visit Mary, and had seen what Jesus did, believed in Him. 46. But some of them went to the Pharisees and reported what Jesus had done. 47. Then the chief priests and the Pharisees called a meeting of the Sanhedrin. "What are we accomplishing?" they asked. "Look, this man is performing many signs (miracles). 48. If we let him go on like this, everyone will believe in Him, and then the Romans will come and take away both our temple and our nation." 49. Caiaphas, the high priest that year, spoke up, "You know nothing at all. 50. You do not realize that it is better for you that one man die for the people than that the whole nation perish." 51. He did not speak this on his own accord, but as the high priest that year, he prophesied (predicted) that Jesus would die for the Jewish people, 52. and not only for them, but also for God's scattered (dispersed) children, to unite them and make them one. 53. From that point onward, they began to plot (scheme) His death. 54. As a result, Jesus no longer moved openly among the people of Judea. Rather, He went to a place near the wilderness, to a city called Ephraim, where He stayed with His disciples. 55. As the Passover of the Jews approached, many people traveled from the country to Jerusalem to perform their ritual purification (sanctification) before the festival. 56. They were searching for Jesus and, as they stood in the temple courts, they asked each other, "What do you think? Will He come to the festival?" 57. Meanwhile, the chief priests and Pharisees had issued orders that anyone who knew where Jesus was should report it so they could arrest (seize) Him.

Chapter 12

1. Six days before the Passover, Jesus came to Bethany, where Lazarus, the one He had raised from the dead, was living. 2. They made a supper (meal) for Him, and Martha served, while Lazarus sat at the table. 3. Mary took a pound of costly spikenard (fragrant oil), anointed Jesus' feet, and wiped them with her hair. The entire house was filled with the scent. 4. Judas Iscariot, the one who would betray Him, asked, 5. Why wasn't this oil sold for 300 denarii (a unit of currency) and the money given to the poor? 6. He said this not out of concern for the poor, but because he was a thief (someone who steals), taking from the money bag. 7. Jesus answered, 'Leave her alone; she has saved this for the day of My burial (the act of placing someone in a tomb).' 8. The poor you will always have with you, but you won't always have Me." 9. Many Jews heard that He was there and came, not only to see Jesus but also to see Lazarus, whom He had raised from the dead. 10. The chief priests (religious leaders) plotted to kill Lazarus too, 11. For because of him, many Jews came to believe in Jesus. 12. The next day, a great crowd in Jerusalem, hearing that Jesus was coming, 13. took palm branches and shouted, "Hosanna (a plea for salvation)! Blessed is the One who comes in the name of the Lord, the King of Israel! 14. Jesus found a donkey and sat on it, fulfilling the prophecy (a foretelling of future events), 15. Do not be afraid, daughter of Zion; look, your King is coming, seated on a colt of a donkey. 16. His disciples didn't understand this at first, but after His glorification (being honored), they remembered these things. 17. The crowd that witnessed the resurrection of Lazarus bore witness (testified) to Him. 18. That's why people went to meet Him, having heard of His miracle. 19. The Pharisees (a religious group) said, "Look, the whole world is following Him!" 20. Some Greeks who had come to worship at the festival 21. asked Philip if they could see Jesus. 22. Philip told Andrew, and together they told Jesus. 23. Jesus answered, 'The time has come for the Son of Man to be glorified.' 24. Truly, unless a grain of wheat falls into the ground and dies, it remains alone; but if it dies, it bears much fruit (gives life). 25. Anyone who loves their life will lose it, but anyone who hates (despises) their life in this world will keep it for eternal life (life after death). 26. Anyone who serves Me must follow Me, and where I am, there My servant will be. If anyone serves Me, the Father will honor them. 27. Now My soul is troubled (distressed), and what should I say? 'Father, rescue Me from this moment'? But I came for this purpose. 28. Father, glorify Your name." Then a voice came from heaven, "I have glorified it, and I will glorify it again. 29. Some who heard it said that it had thundered, while others believed an angel had spoken. 30. Jesus replied, 'This voice was not for My benefit, but for yours.' 31. Now is the judgment (decision) of the world; now the ruler (leader) of this world will be cast out. 32. And I, when I am exalted, will draw all people to Myself. 33. He said this to signify the type of death (crucifixion) He would die. 34. The crowd asked, "We've heard from the law that the Christ remains forever. How can You say that the Son of Man must be lifted up? Who is this Son of Man?" 35. Jesus answered, 'The light (truth) will be with you a little longer. Walk in the light, so that darkness does not overtake you.' Whoever walks in darkness doesn't know where they're going. 36. Believe in the light while you have it, so you may become children of light (people who live in truth)." He said this, then departed and was hidden (concealed) from them. 37. Despite His many signs (wonders), they still didn't believe. 38. This fulfilled the prophecy of Isaiah: 'Lord, who has believed our message? And to whom has the arm (strength) of the Lord been revealed?' 39. For this reason, they were unable to believe, as Isaiah had said, 40. He has blinded their eyes and hardened their hearts, so that they cannot see or comprehend, nor turn to Me for healing. 41. Isaiah referred to Jesus when he beheld His glory (divine presence). 42. Nevertheless, many rulers believed, but for fear of the Pharisees, they didn't confess, fearing expulsion (removal) from the synagogue, 43. For they preferred human praise over the praise of God. 44. Jesus shouted, 'Whoever believes in Me, believes not only in Me, but also in the One who sent Me.' 45. Whoever looks at Me sees

the One who sent Me. **46.** I have come into the world as light, so that anyone who believes in Me will not remain in darkness. **47.** If anyone hears My words and does not believe, I don't judge them, for I did not come to judge (condemn) the world but to save it. **48.** Whoever rejects (turns away from) Me and does not accept My words has their judge: the word I have spoken will judge them on the last day. **49.** I have not spoken on My own, but the Father who sent Me gave Me the command (instruction) of what to say. **50.** And I know His command is eternal life. Therefore, whatever I speak, I speak just as the Father told Me."

Chapter 13

1. Before the Passover (the Jewish feast), Jesus knew His hour had come to depart from this world to the Father. Having loved His own (disciples) in the world, He loved them to the end. **2.** And when supper (meal) was over, the devil had already prompted Judas Iscariot (a disciple), the son of Simon, to betray (hand over) Him. **3.** Jesus, knowing that the Father had entrusted all things to Him, and that He had come from God and was returning to God, **4.** He rose from supper, took off His garments (clothes), and wrapped a towel around Himself. **5.** He poured water into a basin and began to wash the disciples' feet, wiping them with the towel with which He was girded. **6.** He came to Simon Peter, who asked, "Lord, are You going to wash my feet?" **7.** Jesus replied, "You do not understand now, but you will later." **8.** Peter said, "You shall never wash my feet!" Jesus answered, "Unless I wash you, you have no share with Me." **9.** Peter then exclaimed, "Lord, not just my feet, but also my hands and head!" **10.** Jesus said, "He who has had a bath only needs to wash his feet; you are clean, but not all of you." **11.** For He knew who would betray Him; that's why He said, "Not all of you are clean." **12.** After He'd washed their feet, put on His garments (clothes), and sat down, He asked, "Do you understand what I've done for you?" **13.** "You call Me Teacher and Lord, and you're right, for that's what I am. **14.** If I, your Lord and Teacher, have washed your feet, **15.** I've set an example for you to follow. **16.** Truly, a servant is not greater than his master, nor is the one who is sent greater than the one who sent him. **17.** If you know these things, blessed (happy) are you if you do them. **18.** I'm not speaking of all of you; I know whom I've chosen, but the Scripture must be fulfilled: 'He who shares bread with Me has turned against Me.' **19.** I tell you now, so when it happens, you may believe that I am He. **20.** Most assuredly, I say to you, whoever receives whomever I send receives Me, and he who receives Me receives Him who sent Me." **21.** After saying this, Jesus was deeply troubled (distressed) in spirit and declared, "Most assuredly, one of you will betray Me." **22.** The disciples looked at one another, uncertain of whom He spoke. **23.** One of them, the disciple whom Jesus loved, was reclining (leaning) on Jesus' chest. **24.** Simon Peter signaled to him to ask, "Who is it, Lord?" **25.** Then, leaning back on Jesus' chest, he asked, "Lord, who is it?" **26.** Jesus replied, "It is the one to whom I will give this piece of bread after I have dipped it." And after dipping the bread, He gave it to Judas Iscariot. **27.** After receiving the bread, Satan (the devil) entered him. Jesus said, "What you are about to do, do quickly." **28.** None of those at the table understood why He said this to him. **29.** Some thought, since Judas held the money bag, that Jesus was telling him to buy what was needed for the festival or give to the poor. **30.** After receiving the morsel of bread, Judas left at once. And it was night. **31.** When he had gone out, Jesus said, "Now the Son of Man is glorified (honored), and God is glorified in Him." **32.** If God is glorified in Him, God will also glorify Him in Himself and will glorify Him at once. **33.** Little children, I will be with you only a little longer. You will look for Me, and as I told the Jews, "Where I am going, you cannot come," so now I say to you. **34.** A new commandment I give to you: Love one another; as I have loved you, so you must love one another. **35.** Everyone will know that you are My disciples if you love one another. **36.** Simon Peter asked, "Lord, where are You going?" Jesus replied, "Where I am going, you cannot follow now, but later you will follow." **37.** Peter said, "Lord, why can't I follow You now? I am ready to lay down my life for You." **38.** Jesus replied, "Will you lay down your life for Me? Truly, I tell you, the rooster will not crow until you have denied Me three times."

Chapter 14

1. Do not let your hearts be troubled (disturbed). Believe in God, and believe also in Me. **2.** In My Father's house are many rooms (dwelling places); if not, I would have told you. I am going to prepare (make ready) a place for you. **3.** When I go and prepare a place, I will return to take you to be with Me, so you may be where I am. **4.** You know the way (path) to the place where I am going. **5.** Thomas said, 'Lord, we don't know where You're going, so how can we know the way?' **6.** Jesus answered, 'I am the way (path), the truth (reality), and the life (existence). No one comes to the Father except through Me.' **7.** If you had truly known Me, you would have known My Father as well; from now on, you know Him and have seen Him. **8.** Philip said, 'Lord, show us the Father, and that will be sufficient.' **9.** Jesus replied, 'I've been with you all this time, and yet you still do not know Me, Philip? Anyone who has seen Me has seen the Father. How can you say, "Show us the Father"? **10.** Do you not believe that I'm in the Father and the Father is in Me? The words (training) I speak aren't My own; it's the Father living in Me who's performing His work. **11.** Believe that I'm in the Father and the Father is in Me, or at least believe because of the substantiation (evidence) of the workshop (conduct) themselves. **12.** I tell you the verity, anyone who believes in Me will do the workshop (cautions) I've been doing, and they will do indeed lesser effects, because I'm going to the Father. **13.** Whatever you ask in My name (authority), I'll do, so that the Father may be glorified (recognized) through the Son. **14.** Whatever you ask in My name, I'll do. **15.** Still, keep (observe) My commands, if you love Me. **16.** I'll ask the Father, and He'll give you another coadjutor (Advocate, Comforter) to be with you ever. **17.** The Spirit (Holy Spirit) of verity. The world cannot accept (admit) Him, because it neither sees nor knows Him. But you know Him, for He lives with you and will be in you. **18.** I'll not leave you as orphans (abandoned); I'll come to you. **19.** In a short time, the world will no longer behold Me, but you will continue to witness (perceive or experience) Me. Since I am alive, you will also have life. **20.** On that day, you will come to understand (realize or grasp) that I am united with (in) My Father, and you are united with (in) Me, and I am within you. **21.** Whoever holds My commands and obeys them is the one who truly loves Me. The one who loves Me will be cherished (loved) by My Father, and I'll also love them and reveal (show) Myself to them. **22.** Judas (not the one called Iscariot) asked, 'Lord, why do You plan to reveal (show) Yourself to us and not to the world?' **23.** Jesus answered, 'Whoever loves Me will follow (observe) My training. My Father will love them, and We'll come to them and make Our home (dwelling place) with them. **24.** Anyone who doesn't love Me won't follow (observe) My training. The words you hear aren't of My own, but belong to the Father who transferred Me. **25.** I've said all these things while I'm still with you. **26.** But the Helper (Holy Spirit), whom the Father will send in My name, will teach you all things and remind you of everything I have said to you. **27.** Peace (calm) I leave with you; My peace I give to you. I do not give in the same way the world gives. Do not let your hearts be distressed (troubled), and do not be filled with fear. **28.** You heard Me say, 'I am going away and I am coming back to you.' If you loved Me, you would be glad (rejoice) that I am going to the Father, for the Father is greater than I. **29.** I have told you now before it happens, so that when it does, you will believe. **30.** I will not say much more to you, for the prince (leader) of this world is coming. He has no hold (claim) over Me. **31.** But I do precisely what the Father has instructed Me, so that the world may understand (know) that I love the Father. Get up, let us leave this place.

Chapter 15

1. I'm the genuine vine, and My Father is the gardener. **2.** Every branch in Me that doesn't bear fruit, He removes; and every branch that bears fruit, He prunes (cuts back) so that it may bear further. **3.** You're formerly clean because of the word I've spoken to you. **4.** Stay (remain) in Me, and I'll stay in you. A branch cannot produce fruit on its own unless it stays connected to the vine. Neither can you, unless you stay in Me. **5.** I am the vine, you are the branches. Those who remain in Me, and I in them, bear important fruit; piecemeal from Me, you can do nothing. **6.** If anyone doesn't remain in Me, he is cast out as a branch and withers (dries up); they gather them, throw them into the fire, and they are burned. **7.** If you stay in Me, and My words stay in you, ask for anything you wish, and it will be done for you. **8.** This is how My Father is glorified (recognized)—by you bearing important fruit and showing yourselves to be My votaries (followers). **9.** Just as the Father has loved Me, so I've loved you. Remain in My love. **10.** If you keep My commandments (instructions), you will remain in My love, just as I've kept My Father's commandments and remain in His love. **11.** I've told you this so that My joy may be in you and your joy may be complete (full). **12.** This is My command: Love one another as I've loved you. No one has greater love than this: to lay down one's life for their musketeers. **14.** You are My buddies if you do what I command. **15.** I no longer call you retainers (workers), for a domestic does not know his master's business. Rather, I've called you musketeers, because everything I learned from My Father I've shared with you. **16.** You didn't choose Me, but I chose you and appointed (named) you to go and bear lasting fruit, so that whatever you ask the Father in My name, He'll give you. **17.** This is what I command: Love one another. **18.** If the world hates you, remember that it first rejected (abominated) Me. **19.** If you were part of the world, it would love you as its own. But I chose you out of the world, and that's why the world hates you. **20.** Remember My words: 'A servant is not greater than his master.' If they persecuted (attacked) Me, they will persecute you also. If they adhered (obeyed) my teaching, they will obey yours. **21.** They will do all this to you because of My name, since they don't know the One who sent Me. **22.** If I had not come and spoken to them, they would not be ashamed of sin. But now they have no reason for their sin. **23.** Anyone who hates Me also hates My Father. **24.** If I had not done the works among them that no one else could do, they would not be guilty. But now they have seen these works and abominated both Me and My Father. **25.** This fulfills (completes) what is written in their law: 'They abominated Me without reason.' **26.** When the Advocate (coadjutor) comes, whom I'll send to you from the Father, the Spirit (power) of verity who proceeds (comes) from the Father, He'll bear witness (substantiation) about Me. **27.** And you also must bear witness, for you have been with Me from the beginning."

Chapter 16

1. "I've spoken these effects so that you won't stumble (fall into sin). **2.** They will expel (force out) you from the bethels (Jewish places of deification); a time is coming when anyone who kills you will suppose they're serving God. **3.** They will do this because they do not know the Father or Me. **4.** I've told you these effects so that when the time comes, you'll remember I advised you. I didn't say them before because I was with you. **5.** But now I'm going to Him who sent Me, and none of you asks, 'Where are You going?' **6.** But because I've said these effects, anguish (grief) has filled your hearts. **7.** Truly, it's better for you that I go down; if I don't, the coadjutor (Holy Spirit) won't come, but if I depart, I'll send Him to you. **8.** When He comes, He'll convict (prove guilty) the world of sin, righteousness, and judgment. **9.** Of sin, because they don't believe in Me; **10.** Of righteousness, because I'm going to the Father and you'll see Me no more; **11.** Of judgment, because the sovereign (leader) of this world has been judged. **12.** I've many things to tell you, but you can't bear (endure) them now. **13.** However, when the Spirit of truth comes, He'll guide (lead) you into all truth. He won't speak on His own, but He'll speak what He hears and show you things to come. **14.** He'll glorify (honor) Me, taking what's Mine and declaring (making known) it to you. **15.** All that the Father has is Mine, and that's why I said He'll take from what's Mine and declare it to you. **16.** "In a little while, you won't see Me, but again in a little while, you'll see Me because I'm going to the Father." **17.** Some of His disciples wondered, "What does He mean by, 'A little while and you won't see Me; again a little while and you will' and, 'because I'm going to the Father'?" **18.** They asked, "What does He mean by 'a little while'? We don't understand." **19.** Jesus knew they wanted to ask, so He said, "Are you asking about what I said, 'In a little while, you won't see Me; and again, you'll see Me'? **20.** Truly, I tell you, you'll weep (cry) and mourn (suffer), but the world will rejoice (celebrate); you'll be sorrowful, but your sorrow will turn to joy. **21.** A woman in labor (giving birth) has sorrow because her time has come, but when her child is born, she forgets the pain because of the joy of bringing a new life into the world. **22.** So, now you have sorrow, but I'll see you again, and your hearts will rejoice, and no one will take that joy from you. **23.** In that day, you won't ask Me anything. Truly, I tell you, whatever you ask the Father in My name, He'll give you. **24.** Until now, you haven't asked in My name. Ask, and you'll receive, so that your joy may be complete (full). **25.** I've spoken to you in figurative (symbolic) language, but the time is coming when I'll speak to you plainly about the Father. **26.** In that day, you'll ask in My name, and I won't need to ask the Father for you, **27.** Because

the Father Himself loves you, since you have loved Me and believed I came from God. **28.** I came from the Father and entered the world. Now I am leaving the world and going back to the Father." **29.** His disciples said, "Now You are speaking plainly, not using figurative language. **30.** Now we know You understand everything and don't need anyone to question You. This is why we believe You came from God." **31.** Jesus replied, "Do you now believe? **32.** A time is coming—and has now come—when you'll be scattered (separated), each to his own home, leaving Me alone. Yet I am not alone, for the Father is with Me. **33.** I have told you these effects so that in Me, you may have peace. In this world, you'll face trouble (suffering), but take heart! I have overcome (defeated) the world."

Chapter 17

1. Jesus spoke these words, lifted His eyes to heaven, and said, "Father, the time has come. Glorify (honor) Your Son so that the Son may glorify You. **2.** You have granted Him dominion (control or sovereignty) over all humanity, to bestow eternal (everlasting, without end) life upon those You have entrusted (committed or given into His care) to Him. **3.** And this is eternal life: that they know You, the only true God, and Jesus Christ whom You have sent. **4.** I have honored (praised or revered) You on earth by fulfilling (completing or accomplishing) the task You entrusted (assigned or gave) to Me. **5.** Now, Father, glorify Me with the glory (honor and greatness) I had with You before the world existed. **6.** I have revealed (shown) Your name to those You gave Me from the world. They were Yours, You gave them to Me, and they have obeyed Your word. **7.** Now they know that everything You gave Me comes from You. **8.** I gave them the words You gave Me, and they accepted (received) them. They know I came from You, and they believe You transferred Me. **9.** I supplicate for them. I don't supplicate for the world, but for those You have given Me, for they're Yours. **10.** Everything I've is Yours, and everything You have is Mine, and I'm glorified in them. **11.** I am leaving the world, but they are staying. Holy (sacred) Father, protect (keep safe) them by Your name, that they may be one, as We are one. **12.** While I was with them, I kept them safe by Your name. None were lost except the one destined (planned) to be lost, as the Scriptures predicted. **13.** Now I am coming to You, and I say these things while I am still in the world, so they may have My joy (delight) completed (fulfilled) in them. **14.** I've given them Your word, and the world has abominated (disliked intensively) them because they aren't of the world, just as I'm not of the world. **15.** I don't ask You to take them out of the world, but to cover them from the evil one. **16.** They are not of the world, just as I'm not of the world. **17.** Sanctify (set apart as holy) them by Your verity; Your word is verity. **18.** As You transferred Me into the world, I've transferred them into the world. **19.** For their sake, I sanctify (devote) Myself, that they too may be sanctified by the verity. **20.** I don't supplicate for them alone, but also for those who'll believe in Me through their communication. **21.** May they all be one, Father, as You're in Me and I'm in You. May they also be one in Us, so the world will believe You sent Me. **22.** I have given them the glory You gave Me, that they may be one as We are one— **23.** I in them, and You in Me—so they may be brought to complete (full) unity. Then the world will know that You sent Me, and have loved them as You have loved Me. **24.** Father, I want those You have given Me to be with Me where I am, to see My glory, the glory You have given Me because You loved Me before the creation of the world. **25.** Righteous Father, the world does not know You, but I know You, and these know You transferred Me. **26.** I have made Your name known to them, and will continue to make it known, so that the love You have for Me may be in them, and I in them."

Chapter 18

1. After speaking these words, Jesus went with His disciples to a garden across the Kidron Valley, where He often met with them. **2.** Judas, who would betray (deliver into the hands of the enemy) Him, knew the place. **3.** Judas arrived with soldiers and officers from the chief priests and Pharisees, carrying lanterns (portable lights), torches, and weapons. **4.** Jesus, knowing what was to happen, went to them and asked, "Whom are you seeking?" **5.** "Jesus of Nazareth," they answered. Jesus answered, 'I am the one.' Judas was present (in their midst) with them. **6.** When He declared, 'I am the one,' they recoiled (pulled back in shock) and collapsed (fell down) to the ground. **7.** He asked again, "Whom are you seeking?" They answered, "Jesus of

Nazareth." **8.** Jesus said, "I told you I'm He. Let these go," **9.** so that His word would be fulfilled: "I have lost none of those You gave Me." **10.** Peter, with a brand, struck the high clerk's menial and cut off his right observance. The servant's name was Malchus. **11.** Jesus said to Peter, "Put your sword away. Shall I not drink the cup (figurative expression for suffering or destiny) the Father has given Me?" **12.** The soldiers, officers, and Jewish officials arrested Jesus and bound (tied) Him. **13.** They took Him to Annas, the father-in-law of Caiaphas, the high clerk that time. **14.** Caiaphas had advised that one man should die for the people. **15.** Peter and another disciple followed Jesus. The other disciple, known to the high priest, went into the courtyard with Jesus. **16.** Peter stood outside by the door. The other disciple spoke to the servant girl at the door and brought Peter in. **17.** The girl asked Peter, "You aren't one of this man's votaries, are you?" Peter replied, "I am not." **18.** The servants and officers stood by a fire to warm themselves, and Peter joined them. **19.** The high clerk questioned (asked) Jesus about His votaries and training. **20.** Jesus answered, "I spoke openly in bethels (Jewish meeting places) and the tabernacle, where Jews gather. I've said nothing in secret." **21.** "Why ask Me? Ask those who heard Me. They know what I said." **22.** One officer slapped (hit) Jesus, saying, "Do You answer the high priest like that?" **23.** Jesus responded, 'If I have spoken falsely (incorrectly), bear witness (testify or give evidence) to the falsehood.' But if I've spoken truth, why strike Me?" **24.** Annas sent Jesus, still bound, to Caiaphas. **25.** Peter continued to stand and warm himself. They inquired, 'You're not one of His followers, are you?' He denied it, "I am not." **26.** A menial, a relative of the man whose observance Peter had cut off, asked, "Didn't I see you with Him in the garden?" **27.** Peter once more denied it, and immediately a rooster crowed. **28.** They brought Jesus from Caiaphas to the Praetorium (the governor's residence or official residence). It was early morning, but they didn't enter to avoid defilement (making themselves ceremonially unclean) before eating the Passover. **29.** Pilate came outside and inquired, 'What accusation do you bring against this man?' **30.** They replied, 'If He were not a wrongdoer (evildoer), we would not have handed Him over to you.' **31.** Pilate responded, 'Take Him and judge Him according to your law.' The Jews answered, 'We are not permitted (authorized) to execute (carry out the death penalty on) anyone.' **32.** This fulfilled (completed) Jesus' words about the kind of death He would die. **33.** Pilate questioned Jesus, 'Are You the King of the Jews?' **34.** Jesus answered, "Do you say this of yourself, or did others tell you about Me?" **35.** Pilate replied, "Am I a Jew? Your own people and the principal preachers handed You over. What have You done?" **36.** Jesus said, "My kingdom is not of this world. If it were, My servants would fight to prevent My arrest, but now My kingdom is not from here." **37.** Pilate asked, "So You are a king?" Jesus answered, "You say I'm a king. For this reason, I was born and came into the world, to testify to the truth. Everyone on the side of verity listens to Me." **38.** Pilate asked, "What is truth?" Then he went outside and told the Jews, 'I find no reason (grounds or justification) to bring a charge against Him.' **39.** But you have a tradition (custom) that I should release one prisoner during Passover. Do you wish for me to release the King of the Jews? **40.** They shouted back, "Not Him! Barabbas!" Now, Barabbas was a robber.

Chapter 19

1. Pilate ordered Jesus to be flogged (whipped). **2.** The dogfaces wove a crown of frustrations and placed it on His head, also draped Him with a purple (royal) mask. **3.** They mocked (made fun of) Him, saying, "Hail, King of the Jews!" and struck (megahit) Him with their hands. **4.** Pilate went outside again and declared to the crowd, "I am bringing Him out to you so that you may know that I find no guilt in Him." **5.** Jesus came out wearing the crown of frustrations and the grandiloquent mask. Pilate said, "Look, then's the Man!" **6.** When the principal preachers and tabernacle officers (guards) saw Him, they cried out, "Crucify Him! Crucify Him!" Pilate answered, "Take Him yourselves and crucify Him, for I see no grounds (reason) for an blameworthiness (charge) against Him." **7.** The Jews answered, "We've a law, and according to that law, He must die because He claimed to be the Son of God." **8.** Pilate came indeed more hysterical when he heard this. **9.** He went back into the palace and questioned (asked) Jesus, "Where are You from?" But Jesus didn't respond (give an answer). **10.** Pilate said, "Do You refuse to speak to me? Don't You know that I've the authority (power) to release

You or to have You crucified?" **11.** Jesus answered, "You would have no power (authority) over Me unless it had been granted (given) to you from over. Thus, the bone who delivered (handed) Me over to you is shamefaced of the lesser sin (wrongdoing)." **12.** From that moment on, Pilate tried to set Jesus free, but the Jews kept crying, "If you release this Man, you're no friend of Caesar's. Anyone who claims to be a king is opposed to Caesar!" **13.** Hearing this, Pilate brought Jesus out and sat on the judge's seat at a place called The Pavement (a monument face) (which is in Hebrew, Gabbatha). **14.** It was the Preparation (day before the Sabbath) Day of the Passover, around the sixth hour. Pilate said to the crowd, "Then's your King!" **15.** But they cried, "Take Him down! Take Him down! Crucify Him!" Pilate asked, "Shall I crucify your King?" The principal preachers answered, "We've no king but Caesar!" **16.** Eventually, Pilate handed Jesus over to be crucified. The legionnaires took Jesus and led Him down. **17.** Carrying His cross, He went to a place called Golgotha (Place of the Skull), which means "Place of the Skull." **18.** There they crucified Him, and with Him two others — one on each side, and Jesus in the center. **19.** Pilate also had a notice (sign) written and posted on the cross, which read, "Jesus of Nazareth, the King of the Jews." **20.** Numerous people saw (read) the sign because the position where Jesus was crucified was close to the megacity, and it was written in Hebrew, Latin, and Greek. **21.** The principal preachers protested (expostulated) to the sign, telling Pilate, "Don't write, 'The King of the Jews,' but rather write that He claimed (said), 'I'm the King of the Jews.'" **22.** Pilate answered, "What I've written (inscribed), I've written (declared)." **23.** After crucifying Jesus, the legionnaires took His clothes and divided them into four portions, one for each soldier. They also took His tunic (mask), which was indefectible, woven in one piece from top to bottom. **24.** They said to each other, "Let's not tear it, but cast lots (adventure) to see who will get it." This fulfilled the Book, "They divided My garments among them, and for My vesture they cast lots." And so the legionnaires did these goods. **25.** Near the cross of Jesus stood His ma, His ma's family, Mary the woman of Clopas, and Mary Magdalene. **26.** When Jesus saw His ma and the convert whom He loved standing hard, He said to His ma, "Woman, also's your son!" **27.** Also, He said to the convert, "also's your ma! From that moment, the convert brought her into his house (home)." **28.** After this, knowing that all effects had been fulfilled (completed), Jesus said, "I'm thirsty." **29.** A jar of sour wine was there, so they soaked a sponger in it, placed it on a hyssop (a type of factory) branch, and held it up to His mouth. **30.** When Jesus had entered the sour wine, He said, "It's finished!" Also, after saying this, He lowered His head and surrendered (gave up) His spirit (life). **31.** Since it was the day of medication (the day before the Sabbath), the Jewish leaders asked that the bodies be removed from the crosses before the Sabbath started, because the Sabbath was a sacred (holy) day. **32.** The dogfaces came and broke the legs of the first man and of the other man who had been crucified with Jesus. **33.** But when they came to Jesus and saw that He was formerly dead, they didn't break His legs. **34.** One of the legionnaires, still, pierced (picked) Jesus' side with a shaft, bringing an unlooked-for flux of blood and water. **35.** The person who saw this has witnessed (drag substantiation), and his evidence (substantiation or statement) is dependable (true). He knows that he is telling the verity, so that you may also believe. **36.** These goods happened to fulfill the Book, "Not one of His bones will be broken." **37.** And, as another passage (a section of Book) states, "They will peer upon the bone they've wounded (pierced, injured with a sharp object)." **38.** Later, Joseph of Arimathea, who was a secret convert of Jesus because he stressed the Jewish leaders, asked Pilate for authorization to take Jesus' body. Pilate allowed it, so he came and took the body down. **39.** Nicodemus, who had ahead come to Jesus by night, also arrived, bringing a mixture of myrrh (an ambrosial resin) and aloes (a resinous substance), importing about seventy-five pounds.

Chapter 20

1. On the first day of the week, Mary Magdalene went to the tomb early, while it was still dark, and saw the stone had been removed. **2.** She ran to Simon Peter and the other disciple, the one whom Jesus loved, and said, 'They have taken the Lord from the tomb, and we do not know where they have laid (put) Him.' **3.** Peter and the other convert went to the grave, **4.** and the other disciple outran Peter and reached it first. **5.** He looked in and saw the linen cloths (pieces of cloth) but didn't enter. **6.** Then Peter arrived and entered; he saw the cloths, **7.** and the head cloth (napkin), folded separately. **8.** The other disciple then went in, saw, and believed. **9.** They still didn't understand that Scripture (holy writings) said He must rise from the dead. **10.** The votaries went back to their homes. **11.** But Mary stayed outside the tomb, weeping (crying). As she wept, she looked inside, **12.** and saw two angels (couriers of God) in white sitting where Jesus' body had been. **13.** They asked, "Why are you weeping?" She replied, "Because they have taken my Lord, and I do not know where they have placed (laid) Him."**14.** Turning, she saw Jesus standing, but didn't recognize Him. **15.** Jesus asked, "Why are you weeping? Whom are you seeking?" She thought He was the gardener and said, "If you've moved Him, tell me where you've laid Him." **16.** "Jesus called her by name, 'Mary.' She turned and replied, 'Rabboni!' (which means Teacher)."**17.** Jesus said, "Do not hold on (cling) to Me, for I have not yet ascended (gone up) to the Father. Go to My sisters and tell them, 'I'm thrusting to My Father and your Father, to My God and your God.'" **18.** Mary Magdalene went to the votaries and told them, "I've seen the Lord!" and participated what He'd said to her. **19.** That evening, the disciples were gathered behind locked doors, for fear (concern) of the Jews. Jesus appeared and said, "Peace (calm) be with you." **20.** He showed them His hands and side, and the votaries were overjoyed. **21.** Jesus said, "Peace to you! As the Father has transferred Me, I'm transferring you." **22.** He breathed on them and said, "Receive the Holy Spirit (God's power)." **23.** If you forgive anyone's sins, they are forgiven; if you withhold remission, it's withheld." **24.** Thomas, also called Didymus, wasn't with them when Jesus came. **25.** The other disciples told him, "We have seen the Lord!" But he replied, "Unless I see the marks from the nails (wounds made by nails) in His hands and place my finger in them, I will not believe." **26.** A week later, the disciples were once again inside, and Thomas was with them. Jesus appeared, despite the doors being locked, and said, "Peace be with you." **27.** He said to Thomas, "Put your finger here; see My hands. Reach out and put your hand into My side. Stop doubting and believe." **28.** Thomas replied, "My Lord and my God!" **29.** Jesus said, "Because you've seen Me, you've believed. Blessed (happy) are those who have not seen and yet have believed." **30.** Jesus performed many other signs (miracles) in the presence of His disciples, **31.** but these are written so that you may believe that Jesus is the Messiah (Savior), the Son of God, and that by believing, you may have life in His name.

Chapter 21

1. After these things, Jesus discovered Himself once more to the disciples at the sea of Tiberias. This is the way it took place: **2.** Simon Peter, Thomas (referred to as Didymus), Nathanael from Cana in Galilee, the sons of Zebedee, and different disciples were collectively. **3.** Simon Peter stated, "I'm going fishing." They answered, "We'll go with you." They went out, got into the boat, and stuck nothing that night time. **4.** At sunrise (early morning), Jesus stood at the shore, however the disciples didn't recognize Him. **5.** He known as out, "Youngsters (younger ones), have you ever caught any fish?" They spoke back, "No." **6.** He stated, "Throw your net (fishing internet) on the proper facet of the boat, and you'll locate some." They did, and have been unable to drag the net in due to the massive wide variety of fish. **7.** Then the disciple Jesus loved said to Peter, "It's the Lord!" As quickly as Peter heard it was the Lord, he placed on his outer garment (for he had removed it) and jumped into the water. **8.** The others accompanied in the boat, dragging the internet with fish, no longer a long way from shore—about a hundred cubits (approximately 300 feet). **9.** When they landed, they noticed a hearth of coals (a small hearth) with fish on it, and a few bread. **10.** Jesus said, "Carry a number of the fish you just stuck." **11.** Peter went and pulled the internet ashore, packed with 153 large fish, however the internet wasn't torn. **12.** Jesus said, "Come and have breakfast." None of the disciples dared ask Him, "Who're You?" because they knew it changed into the Lord. **13.** Jesus took the bread and gave it to them, and the fish inside the equal way. **14.** This was the third time Jesus regarded to His disciples after being raised (resurrected) from the useless. **15.** After breakfast, Jesus requested Simon Peter, "Simon, son of John, do you love Me greater than these?" Peter replied, "Yes, Lord, you know I love You." Jesus said, "Feed My lambs (younger sheep)." **16.** He requested him a second time, "Simon, son of John, do you love Me?" Peter spoke back,

"Yes, Lord, you already know I love You." Jesus stated, "Have a tendency (care for) My sheep." **17.** He asked him a 3rd time, "Simon, son of John, do you love Me?" Peter became harm (grieved) because He asked him 3 instances, "Do you love Me?" He stated, "Lord, the entirety; I love You." Jesus said, "Feed My sheep." **18.** "Very absolutely (truly), I inform you, when you had been younger, you dressed yourself and went wherever you wanted. But when you are antique, you will stretch out your palms, and someone else will get dressed you and lead you where you don't need to head." **19.** Jesus said this to indicate (display) the kind of loss of life through which Peter would glorify God. Then He stated, "Observe Me." **20.** Peter grew to become and saw the disciple whom Jesus cherished following them. This was the only who had leaned on Jesus' breast at the supper and had asked, "Lord, who is going to betray You?" **21.** When Peter saw him, he asked, "Lord, what about him?" **22.** Jesus spoke back, "If I need him to stay till I go back, what is that to you? You observe Me." **23.** This caused a rumor (false belief) most of the believers that this disciple would not die. But Jesus didn't say he wouldn't die; He only said, "If I need him to remain till I return, what is that to you?" **24.** That is the disciple who testifies (bears witness) to this stuff and who wrote them down. We recognise his testimony is actual. **25.** Jesus did many other things as nicely. If each certainly one of them were written down, I assume that even the complete international would now not have room for the books that would be written.

52 – Acts

Chapter 1

1. In my previous book, Theophilus (a person addressed in Acts), I wrote about all that Jesus began to do and teach. **2.** He did this until the day He was taken to heaven, after instructing the apostles (His chosen followers) through the Holy Spirit (God's presence and power). **3.** After His death (suffering), He presented Himself to them, showing many proofs He was alive. He appeared over forty days and spoke of God's kingdom. **4.** While eating with them, He told them, "Stay in Jerusalem and wait for the gift My Father promised, which you heard Me speak about. **5.** John baptized with water, but in a few days, you will be baptized (immersed) with the Holy Spirit." **6.** They asked, "Lord, are You going to restore (bring back) the kingdom to Israel now?" **7.** He replied, "It is not for you to know the times the Father has set. **8.** But you will receive power (strength and ability) when the Holy Spirit comes on you, and you will be My witnesses (those who tell others) in Jerusalem, all Judea (region) and Samaria (region), and to the ends of the earth." **9.** After this, He was taken up before their eyes, and a cloud hid Him from sight. **10.** As they stared into the sky, two men in white appeared beside them. **11.** "Men of Galilee (region), why do you stand here looking at the sky? Jesus, who was taken into heaven, will return in the same way." **12.** The apostles returned to Jerusalem from the Mount of Olives (hill near Jerusalem), about a Sabbath day's walk (about 1,000 yards) from the city. **13.** They went to the room where they were staying. Peter, John, James, Andrew, Philip, Thomas, Bartholomew, Matthew, James son of Alphaeus, Simon the Zealot (a passionate follower), and Judas son of James were there. **14.** They all prayed together, with the women, Mary the mother of Jesus, and His brothers. **15.** Peter stood up among about 120 believers (those who trusted in Jesus) **16.** and said, "The Scripture had to be fulfilled, which the Holy Spirit spoke through David about Judas, who betrayed Jesus. **17.** He was one of us and shared in our ministry." **18.** (Judas bought a field with the money he received for his betrayal, fell headfirst, and his body burst open. The field became known as Akeldama (Field of Blood).) **20.** Peter continued, "It is written, 'Let his place be deserted, and let no one live in it,' and, 'Let another take his leadership.'" **21.** So, we must choose someone who has been with us since Jesus' baptism by John until He was taken up, to become a witness of His resurrection. **23.** They nominated two men: Joseph (Justus) and Matthias. **24.** They prayed, "Lord, You know everyone's heart. Show us who You have chosen **25.** to take Judas' place in this ministry." **26.** They cast lots (drew lots like a random selection), and Matthias was chosen to join the eleven apostles.

Chapter 2

1. When the day of Pentecost (a Jewish festival, 50 days after Passover) arrived, the apostles were all together in one place. **2.** Suddenly, a sound like a violent wind came from heaven and filled the whole house where they were sitting. **3.** They saw what appeared to be tongues of fire that separated and rested on each of them. **4.** All of them were filled with the Holy Spirit and began speaking in other languages as the Spirit enabled them. **5.** At that time, Jews from every nation were staying in Jerusalem, devout (religious) men. **6.** When they heard the sound, a crowd gathered in confusion, because each one heard their own language being spoken. **7.** Amazed, they asked, "Aren't these men all from Galilee? **8.** How is it that each of us hears them speaking in our native language? **9.** Parthians, Medes, Elamites, residents of Mesopotamia, Judea, Cappadocia, Pontus, Asia, **10.** Phrygia, Pamphylia, Egypt, Libya near Cyrene, and visitors from Rome— **11.** both Jews and converts to Judaism, Cretans and Arabs—we hear them declaring the wonders of God in our own tongues!" **12.** Astonished and confused, they asked one another, "What does this mean?" **13.** Some, however, mocked them and said, "They have had too much wine." **14.** Then Peter stood with the Eleven, raised his voice, and addressed the crowd: "Fellow Jews and all who live in Jerusalem, let me explain this to you; listen carefully. **15.** These men are not drunk, as you suppose. It is only nine in the morning! **16.** No, this is what was spoken by the prophet Joel: **17.** 'In the last days, God says, I will pour out My Spirit on all people. Your sons and daughters will prophesy, your young men will see visions, your old men will dream dreams. **18.** Even on My servants, both men and women, I will pour out My Spirit, and they will prophesy. **19.** I will show wonders in the heavens above and signs on the earth below—blood, fire, and billows of smoke. **20.** The sun will be turned to darkness and the moon to blood before the coming of the great and glorious day of the Lord. **21.** And everyone who calls on the name of the Lord will be saved.' **22.** Fellow Israelites, listen to this: Jesus of Nazareth was a man accredited (authorized) by God to you by miracles, wonders, and signs, which God did among you through Him, as you yourselves know. **23.** This man was handed over to you by God's deliberate plan and foreknowledge, and with the help of wicked men, you crucified Him by nailing Him to the cross. **24.** But God raised Him from the dead, freeing Him from the agony (pain) of death, because it was impossible for death to keep its hold on Him. **25.** David said about Him: 'I saw the Lord always before me. Because He is at my right hand, I will not be shaken. **26.** Therefore my heart is glad, and my tongue rejoices; my body also will rest in hope, **27.** because You will not abandon me to the realm (place) of the dead, nor will You let Your Holy One see decay. **28.** You have made known to me the paths of life; You will fill me with joy in Your presence.' **29.** Fellow Israelites, I can tell you confidently that David died and was buried, and his tomb is here today. **30.** But he was a prophet and knew that God had promised him on oath that He would place one of his descendants on his throne. **31.** Seeing what was to come, he spoke of the resurrection (coming back to life) of the Messiah, that He was not abandoned to the grave, nor did His body see decay. **32.** God has raised this Jesus to life, and we are all witnesses of it. **33.** Exalted to the right hand of God, He has received from the Father the promised Holy Spirit and has poured out what you now see and hear. **34.** For David did not ascend (go up) to heaven, and yet he said, 'The Lord said to my Lord: "Sit at My right hand, **35.** until I make Your enemies a footstool for Your feet." **36.** Therefore, let all Israel be assured of this: God has made this Jesus, whom you crucified, both Lord and Messiah." **37.** When the people heard this, they were cut to the heart and said to Peter and the other apostles, "Brothers, what should we do?" **38.** Peter replied, "Repent (turn away from sin) and be baptized, every one of you, in the name of Jesus Christ for the forgiveness of your sins. And you will receive the gift of the Holy Spirit. **39.** The promise is for you, your children, and for all who are far off— for all whom the Lord our God will call." **40.** With many other words, he warned them; and he pleaded with them, "Save yourselves from this corrupt (evil) generation." **41.** Those who accepted his message were baptized, and about three thousand were added to their number that day. **42.** They devoted themselves to the apostles' teaching, to fellowship (companionship), to the breaking of bread, and to prayer. **43.** Everyone was filled with awe (wonder) at the many wonders and signs performed by the apostles. **44.** All the believers were together and had everything in common. **45.** They sold property and possessions to give to anyone who had need. **46.** Every day they continued to meet in the temple courts. They broke bread in their homes and ate together with glad and sincere hearts, **47.** Praising God

and enjoying the favor of all the people. And the Lord added to their number daily those who were being saved.

Chapter 3

1. One day, Peter and John were going up to the temple to pray at three in the afternoon. **2.** A man who had been lame (unable to walk) from birth was being carried to the temple gate called Beautiful, where he was placed every day to beg from those entering the temple. **3.** When he saw Peter and John about to enter, he asked them for money. **4.** Peter and John fixed their eyes on him. Peter then said, "Look at us!" **5.** The man looked at them, expecting to receive something. **6.** Then Peter said, "I do not have silver or gold, but what I do have, I give you. In the name of Jesus Christ of Nazareth, walk." **7.** Peter took him by the right hand, helped him up, and instantly his feet and ankles became strong. **8.** The man leaped to his feet, began walking, and entered the temple courts with them, walking, jumping, and praising God. **9.** When the people saw him walking and praising God, **10.** they recognized him as the same man who used to sit and beg at the Beautiful Gate, and they were filled with wonder and amazement at what had happened to him. **11.** While the man clung (held tightly) to Peter and John, all the people were amazed and ran to them at the place called Solomon's Colonnade (a covered porch area in the temple). **12.** When Peter saw this, he said to them: "Fellow Israelites, why are you surprised by this? Why do you stare at us as if we had caused this man to walk by our own power or holiness? **13.** The God of Abraham, Isaac, and Jacob, the God of our ancestors, has glorified His servant Jesus. You handed Him over to be killed and disowned Him before Pilate, even though he had decided to release Him. **14.** You disowned the Holy One and the Righteous One and asked for a murderer to be released. **15.** You killed the author (creator) of life, but God raised Him from the dead. We are witnesses (people who saw and can testify) of this. **16.** By faith in the name of Jesus, this man, whom you see and know, has been made strong. It is Jesus' name and the faith that comes through Him that has completely healed him, as you can all see. **17.** Now, fellow Israelites, I know that you acted in ignorance (lack of knowledge), as did your leaders. **18.** But this is how God fulfilled what He had foretold through all the prophets, saying that His Messiah would suffer. **19.** Repent (turn away from sin), then, and turn to God, so that your sins may be forgiven and times of refreshing may come from the Lord, **20.** and that He may send the Messiah, who has been appointed for you—Jesus. **21.** Heaven must receive Him until the time comes for God to restore everything, as He promised long ago through His holy prophets. **22.** For Moses said, 'The Lord your God will raise up for you a prophet like me from among your own people; you must listen to everything He tells you. **23.** Anyone who does not listen to Him will be completely cut off from their people.' **24.** Indeed, beginning with Samuel, all the prophets who have spoken have foretold (predicted) these days. **25.** You are heirs (descendants) of the prophets and of the covenant (agreement) God made with your ancestors. He said to Abraham, 'Through your offspring, all peoples on earth will be blessed.' **26.** When God raised up His servant, He sent Him first to you to bless you by turning each of you from your wicked ways."

Chapter 4

1. While Peter and John were speaking to the people, the priests, the captain of the temple guard, and the Sadducees approached them. **2.** They were greatly disturbed because the apostles were teaching the people and proclaiming through Jesus the resurrection of the dead. **3.** They seized Peter and John and, since it was evening, they locked them up in prison until the next day. **4.** But many of those who heard the message believed, and the number of men who believed grew to about five thousand. **5.** The following day, the rulers, elders, and teachers of the law gathered in Jerusalem. **6.** Annas, the high priest, Caiaphas, John, Alexander, and other members of the high priest's family were present. **7.** They had Peter and John brought before them and began questioning them, "By what power or name have you done this?" **8.** Peter, filled with the Holy Spirit, replied, "Rulers and elders of the people, **9.** If we are being questioned today for an act of kindness shown to a man who was lame, and for how he was healed, **10.** let it be known to you and all the people of Israel that it is by the name of Jesus Christ of Nazareth, whom you crucified but whom God raised from the dead, that this man stands before you healed. **11.** Jesus is 'the stone you builders rejected, which has become the cornerstone.' **12.**

There is no salvation in anyone else, for there is no other name under heaven given to humanity by which we must be saved." **13.** When the rulers saw the boldness of Peter and John and realized that they were uneducated, ordinary men, they were astonished and noted that these men had been with Jesus. **14.** But because they could see the healed man standing with them, there was nothing they could say. **15.** So they ordered Peter and John to leave the council and began to deliberate among themselves. **16.** "What should we do with these men?" they asked. "Everyone in Jerusalem knows they have performed a notable sign, and we cannot deny it. **17.** However, to prevent this from spreading any further, we must warn them not to speak to anyone in this name." **18.** So they called them in again and ordered them not to speak or teach at all in the name of Jesus. **19.** But Peter and John answered, "Which is right in God's eyes: to listen to you, or to Him? You be the judges! **20.** As for us, we cannot help but speak about what we have seen and heard." **21.** After further threats, they let them go. They were unable to decide how to punish them, since all the people were praising God for what had happened. **22.** For the man who had been healed was over forty years old. **23.** Upon their release, Peter and John returned to their own people and reported everything the chief priests and elders had said to them. **24.** When they heard this, they raised their voices in prayer to God, saying, "Sovereign Lord, you made the heavens, the earth, and the sea, and everything in them. **25.** You spoke by the Holy Spirit through the mouth of your servant, our father David: 'Why do the nations rage and the people plot in vain? **26.** The kings of the earth rise up and the rulers band together against the Lord and against His anointed one.' **27.** Indeed, Herod and Pontius Pilate met together with the Gentiles and the people of Israel in this city to conspire against your holy servant Jesus, whom you anointed. **28.** They did what your power and will had already decided should happen. **29.** Now, Lord, consider their threats and enable your servants to speak your word with great boldness. **30.** Stretch out your hand to heal and perform signs and wonders through the name of your holy servant Jesus." **31.** After they prayed, the place where they were meeting was shaken, and they were all filled with the Holy Spirit and spoke the word of God boldly. **32.** All the believers were united in heart and mind. No one claimed that any of their possessions were their own, but they shared everything they had. **33.** With great power, the apostles continued to testify to the resurrection of the Lord Jesus, and God's grace was so powerfully at work in them all, **34.** that no one among them was in need. Those who owned land or houses sold them, **35.** brought the proceeds, and laid them at the apostles' feet, and it was distributed to anyone who had need. **36.** Joseph, a Levite from Cyprus, whom the apostles called Barnabas (meaning "son of encouragement"), **37.** sold a field he owned, brought the money, and placed it at the apostles' feet.

Chapter 5

1. A man named Ananias, with his wife Sapphira, sold a piece of property. **2.** With his wife's full knowledge, he kept part of the money for himself, but brought the rest and placed it at the apostles' feet. **3.** Peter said, "Ananias, how is it that Satan (the adversary, or enemy of God) has so filled your heart that you have lied to the Holy Spirit (the Spirit of God, sent to guide believers) and kept back part of the money you received for the land? **4.** It was yours before it was sold, and after it was sold, the money was at your disposal. What made you think of doing such a thing? You haven't just lied to people, but to God." **5.** When Ananias heard this, he fell down and died. And great fear (a deep sense of awe and respect) seized all who heard what had happened. **6.** The young men came forward, wrapped up his body, and carried it out and buried it. **7.** About three hours later, his wife came in, unaware of what had happened. **8.** Peter asked her, "Tell me, is this the price you and Ananias got for the land?" "Yes," she said, "that is the price." **9.** Peter replied, "How could you agree (conspire) to test the Spirit of the Lord? Listen! The feet of the men who buried your husband are at the door, and they will carry you out as well." **10.** At that moment, she fell down at his feet and died. The young men came in, found her dead, and carried her out and buried her beside her husband. **11.** Great fear seized the entire church and all who heard about these events. **12.** The apostles performed many signs (miraculous acts) and wonders (extraordinary events) among the people. All the believers gathered together in Solomon's Colonnade (a covered walkway or portico at the temple). **13.** No one else dared to join them, even though they were highly respected by the people. **14.** However, more men and women believed in the Lord and were added to their number. **15.** As a result, people brought the sick into the streets and laid them on beds and mats, hoping that at least Peter's shadow might fall on some of them as he passed by. **16.** Crowds also gathered from nearby towns around Jerusalem, bringing their sick and those tormented by impure spirits (evil or unclean spirits), and all of them were healed. **17.** The high priest and all his associates, who were members of the Sadducees (a Jewish group that denied the resurrection of the dead and held influential positions in the temple), were filled with jealousy. **18.** They arrested the apostles and placed them in a public jail. **19.** But during the night, an angel (a messenger or servant of God) of the Lord opened the doors of the jail and brought them out. **20.** "Go, stand in the temple courts," the angel said, "and tell the people all about this new life." **21.** At daybreak, the apostles entered the temple courts, as instructed, and began teaching the people. When the high priest and his associates arrived, they convened (gathered together) the Sanhedrin (the Jewish ruling council, consisting of elders and priests) and sent for the apostles to be brought from the jail. **22.** When the officers arrived at the jail, they did not find them there. They returned and reported, **23.** "We found the jail securely locked, with the guards standing at the doors; but when we opened them, we found no one inside." **24.** Upon hearing this report, the captain of the temple guard and the chief priests were perplexed, wondering what this might lead to. **25.** Then someone came and said, "Look! The men you put in jail are standing in the temple courts teaching the people." **26.** At that, the captain went with his officers and brought the apostles in. They did not use force, fearing the people might stone them. **27.** The apostles were brought in and made to appear before the Sanhedrin to be questioned by the high priest. **28.** "We gave you strict orders not to teach in this name," he said. "Yet you have filled Jerusalem with your teaching and are determined to make us guilty of this man's blood." **29.** Peter and the other apostles replied, "We must obey God rather than human beings! **30.** The God of our ancestors raised Jesus from the dead—whom you killed by hanging him on a cross. **31.** God exalted him to his own right hand as Prince (leader) and Savior, that he might bring Israel to repentance and forgive their sins. **32.** We are witnesses of these things, and so is the Holy Spirit, whom God has given to those who obey him." **33.** When they heard this, they were furious and wanted to put them to death. **34.** But a Pharisee named Gamaliel, a respected teacher of the law, who was honored by all the people, stood up in the Sanhedrin and ordered that the men be put outside for a short time. **35.** Then he addressed the Sanhedrin: "Men of Israel, consider carefully what you intend to do with these men. **36.** Some time ago, Theudas appeared, claiming to be someone important, and about four hundred men joined him. He was killed, all his followers were scattered, and it all came to nothing. **37.** After him, Judas the Galilean appeared in the days of the census and led a group of people in revolt. He too was killed, and all his followers were dispersed. **38.** Therefore, in the present case, I advise you: Leave these men alone! Let them go! If their purpose or activity is of human origin, it will fail. **39.** But if it is from God, you will not be able to stop them; you will only find yourselves fighting against God." **40.** His speech persuaded them. They called the apostles in, had them flogged (beaten as punishment), and ordered them not to speak in the name of Jesus, then let them go. **41.** The apostles left the Sanhedrin, rejoicing because they had been counted worthy of suffering disgrace for the Name (the name of Jesus). **42.** Day after day, in the temple courts and from house to house, they never stopped teaching and proclaiming the good news that Jesus is the Messiah (the Savior).

Chapter 6

1. At that time, as the number of disciples was growing, some of the Greek-speaking Jews (Hellenistic Jews) complained that their widows were being ignored in the daily distribution of food, compared to the Hebrew-speaking Jews. **2.** So, the Twelve Apostles gathered all the disciples together and said, "It would not be right for us to stop preaching and teaching the word of God just to take care of food distribution." **3.** "Brothers and sisters, select seven men from among you who are known to be full of the Holy Spirit and wisdom. We will assign this task to them." **4.** "Then, we can focus on prayer and the preaching of the word." **5.** This plan pleased everyone, so they chose Stephen, a man full of faith and the Holy Spirit; also Philip, Procorus, Nicanor, Timon, Parmenas, and Nicolas, a convert from Antioch. **6.** They brought these men before the apostles, who prayed for them and laid their hands on them. **7.** As a result, God's word spread, and the number of disciples in Jerusalem grew quickly. Many priests also began to believe in the faith. **8.** Stephen, a man full of God's grace and power, performed great wonders and miracles among the people. **9.** However, some members of the Synagogue of the Freedmen (a group of Jews from Cyrene, Alexandria, Cilicia, and Asia) began to argue with Stephen. **10.** But they were unable to resist the wisdom and the power of the Holy Spirit that Stephen spoke with. **11.** They then secretly persuaded some men to say, "We heard Stephen speak blasphemous words against Moses and against God." **12.** They stirred up the people, the elders, and the teachers of the law. They seized Stephen and brought him before the Sanhedrin (the Jewish council). **13.** They presented false witnesses who claimed, "This man never stops speaking against this holy place (the temple) and the law. **14.** We have heard him say that Jesus of Nazareth will destroy this place and change the customs Moses gave us." **15.** All those sitting in the Sanhedrin looked at Stephen and saw that his face looked like the face of an angel.

Chapter 7

1. Then the high priest asked Stephen, "Are these charges true?" **2.** To this he replied: "Brothers and fathers, listen to me! The God of glory (God of great majesty) appeared to our father Abraham while he was still in Mesopotamia (the region between the Tigris and Euphrates rivers), before he lived in Harran. **3.** 'Leave your country and your people,' God said, 'and go to the land I will show you.' **4.** So he left the land of the Chaldeans (Babylonians) and settled in Harran. After the death of his father, God sent him to this land where you are now living. **5.** He gave him no inheritance (property or possession) here, not even enough ground to set his foot on. But God promised him that he and his descendants after him would possess the land, even though at that time Abraham had no child. **6.** God spoke to him in this way: 'For four hundred years your descendants will be strangers (foreigners) in a country not their own, and they will be enslaved (forced into labor) and mistreated (treated badly). **7.** But I will punish the nation they serve as slaves,' God said, 'and afterward they will come out of that country and worship me in this place.' **8.** Then he gave Abraham the covenant (formal agreement) of circumcision. And Abraham became the father of Isaac and circumcised him eight days after his birth. Later Isaac became the father of Jacob, and Jacob became the father of the twelve patriarchs (founding fathers of the twelve tribes of Israel). **9.** "Because the patriarchs were jealous (envious) of Joseph, they sold him as a slave into Egypt. But God was with him **10.** and rescued him from all his troubles. He gave Joseph wisdom and enabled him to gain the goodwill (approval) of Pharaoh king of Egypt. So Pharaoh made him ruler over Egypt and all his palace. **11.** "Then a famine (severe shortage of food) struck all Egypt and Canaan, bringing great suffering, and our ancestors could not find food. **12.** When Jacob heard that there was grain (cereal or food) in Egypt, he sent our forefathers (ancestors) on their first visit. **13.** On their second visit, Joseph told his brothers who he was, and Pharaoh learned about Joseph's family. **14.** After this, Joseph sent for his father Jacob and his whole family, seventy-five in all. **15.** Then Jacob went down to Egypt, where he and our ancestors died. **16.** Their bodies were brought back to Shechem (a city in Israel) and placed in the tomb that Abraham had bought from the sons of Hamor at Shechem for a certain sum of money. **17.** "As the time drew near for God to fulfill his promise to Abraham, the number of our people in Egypt had greatly increased. **18.** Then 'a new king, to whom Joseph meant nothing, came to power in Egypt.' **19.** He dealt treacherously (dishonestly) with our people and oppressed (treated harshly) our ancestors by forcing them to throw out their newborn babies so that they would die. **20.** "At that time Moses was born, and he was no ordinary child (he was special). For three months he was cared for by his family. **21.** When he was placed outside, Pharaoh's daughter took him and brought him up as her own son. **22.** Moses was educated in all the wisdom (knowledge) of the Egyptians and was powerful in speech and action. **23.** "When Moses was forty years old, he decided to visit his own people, the Israelites. **24.** He saw one of them being mistreated (treated badly) by an Egyptian, so he went to his defense (helped him) and avenged (took revenge for) him by killing the Egyptian. **25.** Moses thought that his own people would realize that God was using him to rescue them, but they did not. **26.** The next day Moses came upon two Israelites who were fighting. He tried to reconcile (make peace between) them by saying, 'Men, you are brothers; why do you want to hurt each other?' **27.** "But the man who was mistreating (hurting) the other pushed Moses aside and said, 'Who made you ruler and judge over us? **28.** Are you thinking of killing me as you killed the Egyptian yesterday?' **29.** When Moses heard this, he fled (ran away) to Midian, where he settled as a foreigner (stranger) and had two sons. **30.** "After forty years had passed, an angel appeared to Moses in the flames of a burning bush in the desert near Mount Sinai. **31.** When he saw this, he was amazed at the sight. As he went over to get a closer look, he heard the Lord say: **32.** 'I am the God of your fathers, the God of Abraham, Isaac and Jacob.' Moses trembled (shook) with fear and did not dare (was too afraid) to look. **33.** "Then the Lord said to him, 'Take off your sandals, for the place where you are standing is holy ground. **34.** I have indeed seen the oppression (cruel treatment) of my people in Egypt. I have heard their groaning (sighing) and have come down to set them free. Now come, I will send you back to Egypt.' **35.** "This is the same Moses they had rejected with the words, 'Who made you ruler and judge?' He was sent to be their ruler and deliverer (rescuer) by God himself, through the angel who appeared to him in the bush. **36.** He led them out of Egypt and performed wonders and signs (divine acts) in Egypt, at the Red Sea and for forty years in the wilderness. **37.** "This is the Moses who told the Israelites, 'God will raise up for you a prophet like me from your own people.' **38.** He was in the assembly (congregation) in the wilderness, with the angel who spoke to him on Mount Sinai, and with our ancestors; and he received living words (instructions) to pass on to us. **39.** "But our ancestors refused (rejected) to obey him. Instead, they rejected him and in their hearts turned back to Egypt. **40.** They told Aaron, 'Make us gods who will go before us. As for this fellow Moses who led us out of Egypt—we don't know what has happened to him!' **41.** That was the time they made an idol (false god) in the form of a calf. They brought sacrifices to it and reveled (celebrated) in what their own hands had made. **42.** But God turned away from them and gave them over to the worship of the sun, moon and stars. This agrees with what is written in the book of the prophets: " 'Did you bring me sacrifices and offerings forty years in the wilderness, people of Israel? **43.** You have taken up the tabernacle (portable temple) of Molek (a false god) and the star of your god Rephan, the idols (false gods) you made to worship. Therefore I will send you into exile (forced relocation) beyond Babylon. **44.** "Our ancestors had the tabernacle of the covenant law with them in the wilderness. It had been made as God directed Moses, according to the pattern he had seen. **45.** After receiving the tabernacle, our ancestors under Joshua brought it with them when they took the land from the nations God drove out before them. It remained in the land until the time of David, **46.** who enjoyed God's favor and asked that he might provide a dwelling place for the God of Jacob. **47.** But it was Solomon who built a house for him. **48.** "However, the Most High (God) does not live in houses made by human hands. As the prophet says: **49.** " 'Heaven is my throne, and the earth is my footstool. What kind of house will you build for me? says the Lord. Or where will my resting place be? **50.** Has not my hand made all these things?' **51.** "You stiff-necked (stubborn) people! Your hearts and ears are still uncircumcised (unresponsive to God's law). You are just like your ancestors: You always resist the Holy Spirit! **52.** Was there ever a prophet your ancestors did not persecute (harass)? They even killed those who predicted the coming of the Righteous One (Jesus). And now you have betrayed and murdered him— **53.** you who have received the law that was given through angels but have not obeyed it." **54.** When the members of the Sanhedrin heard this, they were furious (angry) and gnashed (grinded) their teeth at him. **55.** But Stephen, full of the Holy Spirit, looked up to heaven and saw the glory (divine presence) of God, and Jesus standing at the right hand of God. **56.** "Look," he said, "I see heaven open and the Son of Man standing at the right hand of God." **57.** At this they covered their ears and, yelling at the top of their voices, they all rushed at him, **58.** dragged him out of the city and began to stone him (throw stones at him).

Meanwhile, the witnesses laid their coats at the feet of a young man named Saul. 59. While they were stoning him, Stephen prayed, "Lord Jesus, receive my spirit." 60. Then he fell on his knees and cried out, "Lord, do not hold this sin against them." When he had said this, he fell asleep (died).

Chapter 8

1. On that day a great persecution (oppression or hostility) broke out against the church in Jerusalem, and all except the apostles were scattered (forced to flee) throughout Judea and Samaria. 2. Godly men buried Stephen and mourned (grieved) deeply for him. 3. But Saul began to destroy (cause great harm to) the church. Going from house to house, he dragged off both men and women and put them in prison. 4. Those who had been scattered preached (shared) the word wherever they went. 5. Philip went down to a city in Samaria and proclaimed (preached) the Messiah (the Savior or Christ) there. 6. When the crowds heard Philip and saw the signs (miracles) he performed, they all paid close attention (listened carefully) to what he said. 7. For with shrieks (loud cries), impure spirits (evil spirits) came out of many, and many who were paralyzed (unable to move) or lame (unable to walk) were healed. 8. So there was great joy (rejoicing) in that city. 9. Now for some time a man named Simon had practiced sorcery (the use of magic) in the city and amazed (astonished) all the people of Samaria. He boasted (bragged) that he was someone great, 10. and all the people, both high and low, gave him their attention and exclaimed (shouted), "This man is rightly called the Great Power of God." 11. They followed him because he had amazed them for a long time with his sorcery. 12. But when they believed Philip as he proclaimed (preached) the good news (message of salvation) of the kingdom of God and the name of Jesus Christ, they were baptized (immersed in water), both men and women. 13. Simon himself believed and was baptized. And he followed Philip everywhere, astonished (amazed) by the great signs and miracles (wonders) he saw. 14. When the apostles in Jerusalem heard that Samaria had accepted (received) the word of God, they sent Peter and John to Samaria. 15. When they arrived, they prayed for the new believers there that they might receive the Holy Spirit, 16. because the Holy Spirit had not yet come on any of them; they had simply been baptized in the name of the Lord Jesus. 17. Then Peter and John placed their hands on them, and they received the Holy Spirit. 18. When Simon saw that the Spirit was given at the laying on (imposition) of the apostles' hands, he offered them money 19. and said, "Give me also this ability (power) so that everyone on whom I lay my hands may receive the Holy Spirit." 20. Peter answered: "May your money perish (be destroyed) with you, because you thought you could buy the gift (blessing) of God with money! 21. You have no part or share in this ministry, because your heart is not right (is not pure) before God. 22. Repent (turn away from sin) of this wickedness (evil thoughts) and pray to the Lord in the hope that he may forgive you for having such a thought in your heart. 23. For I see that you are full of bitterness (resentment) and captive (enslaved) to sin." 24. Then Simon answered, "Pray to the Lord for me so that nothing you have said may happen to me." 25. After they had further proclaimed the word (preached) of the Lord and testified (witnessed) about Jesus, Peter and John returned to Jerusalem, preaching the gospel (good news) in many Samaritan villages. 26. Now an angel of the Lord said to Philip, "Go south to the road—the desert road—that goes down from Jerusalem to Gaza." 27. So he started out, and on his way he met an Ethiopian eunuch (a man from Ethiopia who was castrated), an important official in charge of all the treasury (finances) of the Kandake (queen of the Ethiopians). This man had gone to Jerusalem to worship, 28. and on his way home was sitting in his chariot (carriage) reading the Book of Isaiah the prophet. 29. The Spirit told Philip, "Go to that chariot and stay near it." 30. Then Philip ran up to the chariot and heard the man reading Isaiah the prophet. "Do you understand (comprehend) what you are reading?" Philip asked. 31. "How can I," he said, "unless someone explains (interprets) it to me?" So he invited Philip to come up and sit with him. 32. This is the passage of Scripture the eunuch was reading: "He was led like a sheep to the slaughter, and as a lamb before its shearer (someone who cuts wool) is silent, so he did not open his mouth. 33. In his humiliation (humbling), he was deprived (denied) of justice (fair treatment). Who can speak of his descendants (offspring)? For his life was taken from the earth." 34. The eunuch asked Philip, "Tell me, please, who is the prophet talking about, himself or someone else?" 35. Then Philip began with that very passage of Scripture and told him the good news (message of salvation) about Jesus. 36. As they traveled along the road, they came to some water and the eunuch said, "Look, here is water. What can stand in the way (prevent) of my being baptized?" 38. And he gave orders to stop the chariot. Then both Philip and the eunuch went down into the water and Philip baptized him. 39. When they came up out of the water, the Spirit of the Lord suddenly took Philip away, and the eunuch did not see him again, but went on his way rejoicing (gladly). 40. Philip, however, appeared at Azotus (a town in ancient Israel) and traveled about, preaching the gospel (good news) in all the towns until he reached Caesarea.

Chapter 9

1. Meanwhile, Saul was still breathing out murderous threats (violent, threatening statements) against the Lord's disciples. He went to the high priest 2. and asked him for letters (written orders) to the synagogues in Damascus, so that if he found any there who belonged to the Way (early name for Christianity), whether men or women, he might take them as prisoners (captives) to Jerusalem. 3. As he neared Damascus on his journey, suddenly a light from heaven flashed around him. 4. He fell to the ground and heard a voice say to him, "Saul, Saul, why do you persecute (harass or mistreat) me?" 5. "Who are you, Lord?" Saul asked. "I am Jesus, whom you are persecuting," he replied. 6. "Now get up and go into the city, and you will be told what you must do." 7. The men traveling with Saul stood there speechless (unable to speak); they heard the sound but did not see anyone. 8. Saul got up from the ground, but when he opened his eyes he could see nothing. So, they led him by the hand into Damascus. 9. For three days he was blind (unable to see) and did not eat or drink anything. 10. In Damascus there was a disciple (a follower of Jesus) named Ananias. The Lord called to him in a vision (a divine revelation), "Ananias!" "Yes, Lord," he answered. 11. The Lord told him, "Go to the house of Judas on Straight Street and ask for a man from Tarsus named Saul, for he is praying. 12. In a vision he has seen a man named Ananias come and place his hands on him to restore (bring back) his sight." 13. "Lord," Ananias answered, "I have heard many reports about this man and all the harm (damage) he has done to your holy people in Jerusalem. 14. And he has come here with authority (official power) from the chief priests to arrest (capture) all who call on your name." 15. But the Lord said to Ananias, "Go! This man is my chosen instrument (tool) to proclaim (announce or preach) my name to the Gentiles (non-Jews) and their kings and to the people of Israel. 16. I will show him how much he must suffer (experience pain) for my name." 17. Then Ananias went to the house and entered it. Placing his hands-on Saul, he said, "Brother Saul, the Lord—Jesus, who appeared to you on the road as you were coming here—has sent me so that you may see again and be filled with the Holy Spirit." 18. Immediately, something like scales (thin layers or films) fell from Saul's eyes, and he could see again. He got up and was baptized (immersed in water), and after taking some food, he regained (got back) his strength. Saul spent several days with the disciples in Damascus. 20. At once he began to preach (proclaim publicly) in the synagogues (Jewish places of worship) that Jesus is the Son of God. 21. All those who heard him were astonished (amazed) and asked, "Isn't he the man who raised havoc (caused chaos or damage) in Jerusalem among those who call on this name? And hasn't he come here to take them as prisoners to the chief priests?" 22. Yet Saul grew more and more powerful and baffled (confused) the Jews living in Damascus by proving (showing clearly) that Jesus is the Messiah (the Savior, Christ). 23. After many days had gone by, there was a conspiracy (secret plan) among the Jews to kill him, 24. but Saul learned of their plan. Day and night they kept close watch (guard) on the city gates in order to kill him. 25. But his followers (disciples) took him by night and lowered (dropped) him in a basket (woven container) through an opening (hole) in the wall. 26. When he came to Jerusalem, he tried to join the disciples, but they were all afraid (scared) of him, not believing (thinking it was impossible) that he really was a disciple. 27. But Barnabas (a Christian disciple) took him and brought him to the apostles. He told them how Saul on his journey had seen the Lord and that the Lord had spoken to him, and how in Damascus he had preached fearlessly (bravely) in the name of Jesus. 28. So Saul stayed

with them and moved about freely in Jerusalem, speaking boldly (with confidence) in the name of the Lord. **29.** He talked and debated (argued) with the Hellenistic Jews (Greek-speaking Jews), but they tried to kill him. **30.** When the believers learned of this, they took him down to Caesarea (port city) and sent him off to Tarsus (Saul's hometown). **31.** Then the church throughout Judea, Galilee, and Samaria enjoyed a time of peace and was strengthened. Living in the fear (reverence) of the Lord and encouraged (comforted) by the Holy Spirit, it increased (grew) in numbers. **32.** As Peter traveled about the country, he went to visit the Lord's people who lived in Lydda (a town in ancient Israel). **33.** There he found a man named Aeneas, who was paralyzed (unable to move) and had been bedridden (stuck in bed) for eight years. **34.** "Aeneas," Peter said to him, "Jesus Christ heals you. Get up and roll up your mat (blanket or sleeping pad)." Immediately Aeneas got up. **35.** All those who lived in Lydda and Sharon (a region nearby) saw him and turned to the Lord (became Christians). **36.** In Joppa (a town near Lydda) there was a disciple named Tabitha (in Greek her name is Dorcas); she was always doing good and helping the poor. **37.** About that time she became sick and died, and her body was washed and placed in an upstairs room. **38.** Lydda was near Joppa; so when the disciples heard that Peter was in Lydda, they sent two men to him and urged (begged) him, "Please come at once!" **39.** Peter went with them, and when he arrived he was taken upstairs to the room. All the widows stood around him, crying and showing him the robes (clothing) and other clothing that Dorcas had made while she was still with them. **40.** Peter sent them all out of the room; then he got down on his knees and prayed. Turning toward the dead woman, he said, "Tabitha, get up." She opened her eyes, and seeing Peter she sat up. **41.** He took her by the hand and helped her to her feet. Then he called for the believers, especially the widows, and presented (showed) her to them alive. **42.** This became known all over Joppa, and many people believed (trusted) in the Lord. **43.** Peter stayed in Joppa for some time with a tanner (person who works with animal skins) named Simon.

Chapter 10

1. At Caesarea, there was a man named Cornelius, a Roman centurion (a military officer in charge of 100 soldiers) in what was called the Italian Regiment. **2.** He and his whole family were religiously devout (deeply devoted to their faith) and God-fearing (respectful of God); he was generous to those in need and regularly prayed to God. **3.** One afternoon, around three o'clock, he had a vision. He clearly saw an angel of God, who came to him and said, "Cornelius!" **4.** Cornelius looked at him in fear and asked, "What is it, Lord?" The angel replied, "Your prayers and your charity (acts of giving to the poor) have been noticed by God. **5.** Now, send men to Joppa and bring back a man named Simon, who is called Peter. **6.** He is staying with Simon the tanner, whose house is by the sea." **7.** When the angel had left, Cornelius called two of his servants and a devout (pious, religious) soldier who was one of his attendants. **8.** He explained everything that had happened and sent them to Joppa. **9.** The next day, around noon, as they were nearing the city, Peter went up to the roof to pray. **10.** He became hungry and asked for something to eat, and while the meal was being prepared, he fell into a trance (a deep, dreamlike state). **11.** He saw heaven open up and something resembling a large sheet being lowered to the earth by its four corners. **12.** It contained all kinds of animals, including four-footed creatures, reptiles, and birds. **13.** Then a voice said to him, "Get up, Peter. Kill and eat." **14.** "No, Lord!" Peter replied. "I have never eaten anything that is impure or unclean." **15.** The voice spoke to him again, "Do not call anything impure that God has made clean." **16.** This happened three times, and immediately the sheet was taken back up into heaven. **17.** While Peter was puzzled about the meaning of the vision, the men sent by Cornelius arrived and asked for the house of Simon. **18.** They called out, asking if Simon, also known as Peter, was staying there. **19.** While Peter was still reflecting on the vision, the Spirit (Holy Spirit) told him, "Peter, three men are looking for you. **20.** Get up, go downstairs, and don't hesitate to go with them, for I have sent them." **21.** Peter went down and said to the men, "I am the one you are looking for. Why have you come?" **22.** The men replied, "We have been sent by Cornelius the centurion. He is a righteous (morally right) and God-fearing man, respected by all the Jewish people. A holy angel told him to ask you to come to his house so that he may hear your message." Peter invited the men in to stay

with him. **23.** The next day, Peter set out with them, accompanied by some believers from Joppa. **24.** The following day, they arrived in Caesarea. Cornelius was expecting them and had gathered his relatives and close friends. **25.** When Peter entered the house, Cornelius met him and fell at his feet in reverence (deep respect). **26.** But Peter made him stand up, saying, "Stand up, I am just a man." **27.** As Peter talked with him, he went inside and found that there were many people gathered. **28.** He said to them, "You know it is against our law for a Jew to associate with or visit a Gentile (non-Jew). But God has shown me that I should not consider anyone impure or unclean. **29.** So when I was sent for, I came without hesitation. Now, tell me why you sent for me." **30.** Cornelius replied, "Three days ago, at this hour, I was praying in my house when suddenly a man in shining clothes stood before me **31.** and said, 'Cornelius, your prayer has been heard, and your acts of charity have been remembered by God. **32.** Send to Joppa for Simon, who is called Peter. He is staying with Simon the tanner, by the sea.' **33.** So I sent for you immediately, and it was kind of you to come. Now we are all here in the presence of God, ready to listen to everything the Lord has commanded you to tell us." **34.** Then Peter began to speak: "I now realize how true it is that God does not show favoritism (partiality) **35.** but accepts from every nation the one who fears Him and does what is right. **36.** You know the message God sent to the people of Israel, proclaiming the good news of peace through Jesus Christ, who is Lord of all. **37.** You know what happened throughout the province of Judea, beginning in Galilee after John preached his baptism— **38.** how God anointed Jesus of Nazareth with the Holy Spirit and power, and how He went around doing good and healing all who were under the power of the devil, because God was with Him. **39.** We are witnesses of everything He did in the country of the Jews and in Jerusalem. They killed Him by hanging Him on a cross, **40.** but God raised Him from the dead on the third day and caused Him to be seen. **41.** He was not seen by everyone, but by witnesses whom God had already chosen—by us who ate and drank with Him after He rose from the dead. **42.** He commanded us to preach to the people and testify that He is the one whom God appointed as judge of the living and the dead. **43.** All the prophets testify about Him, that everyone who believes in Him receives forgiveness of sins through His name." **44.** While Peter was still speaking these words, the Holy Spirit came on all who heard the message. **45.** The circumcised believers who had come with Peter were amazed that the gift of the Holy Spirit had been poured out even on Gentiles. **46.** For they heard them speaking in tongues (languages they had not learned) and praising God. Then Peter said, **47.** "Surely no one can stand in the way of their being baptized with water. They have received the Holy Spirit just as we have." **48.** So he ordered that they be baptized in the name of Jesus Christ. Then they asked Peter to stay with them for a few days.

Chapter 11

1. The apostles and believers in Judea heard that the Gentiles had received God's word. **2.** When Peter arrived in Jerusalem, the circumcised (those who underwent the Jewish ritual of removing the foreskin) believers criticized him, **3.** saying, "You entered the house of uncircumcised (those who have not undergone circumcision, often referring to Gentiles) men and ate with them." **4.** Peter explained everything from the beginning: **5.** "I was in Joppa praying and saw a vision. A sheet, like a large one, was lowered from heaven by its four corners. It came down to me. **6.** I looked inside and saw various animals: wild beasts, reptiles (cold-blooded animals like snakes and lizards), and birds. **7.** Then I heard a voice say, 'Get up, Peter. Kill and eat.' **8.** I answered, 'No, Lord! I've never eaten anything impure or unclean (forbidden by Jewish law).' **9.** The voice spoke again, 'Do not call anything impure that God has made clean.' **10.** This happened three times, and then the sheet was taken back to heaven. **11.** At that moment, three men sent from Caesarea arrived at the house where I was staying. **12.** The Spirit (Holy Spirit, or God's presence) told me to go with them without hesitation. Six of the brothers accompanied me, and we entered the man's house. **13.** He told us how an angel (a messenger from God) had appeared to him and said, 'Send to Joppa for Simon called Peter. **14.** He will give you a message through which you and your household will be saved.' **15.** As I began to speak, the Holy Spirit came upon them as He did at the beginning. **16.** Then I remembered the Lord's words: 'John baptized with water, but you will be baptized with the Holy Spirit.' **17.** If God gave them the same gift He gave us who believed in Jesus Christ, who was I to stand in God's way?" **18.** Hearing this, they no longer objected and praised God, saying, "Even to Gentiles, God has granted repentance (a change of mind or heart leading to forgiveness) that leads to life." **19.** Those scattered by the persecution (hostility or mistreatment because of their beliefs) after Stephen's death traveled to Phoenicia, Cyprus, and Antioch, preaching only to Jews. **20.** Some men from Cyprus and Cyrene went to Antioch and began preaching to Greeks (non-Jews), telling them about Jesus. **21.** The Lord's hand was with them, and many people believed and turned to the Lord. **22.** News of this reached Jerusalem, and they sent Barnabas to Antioch. **23.** Upon arrival, Barnabas saw God's grace at work, and he encouraged them to remain true to the Lord. **24.** He was a good man, full of the Holy Spirit and faith, and many were brought to the Lord. **25.** Barnabas then went to Tarsus to find Saul, **26.** and when he found him, he brought him to Antioch. They taught many people there for a whole year. The disciples were first called Christians (followers of Christ) at Antioch. **27.** During this time, some prophets (messengers of God who predict the future or speak on God's behalf) came from Jerusalem to Antioch. **28.** One of them, Agabus, stood up and through the Spirit predicted a severe famine (a shortage of food) would spread throughout the Roman world (the entire empire) (this happened during Claudius' reign). **29.** The disciples, each according to their ability, decided to send help to the believers in Judea. **30.** They did so, sending their gifts to the elders (church leaders) through Barnabas and Saul.

Chapter 12

1. Around this time, King Herod arrested some members of the church with the intention of persecuting (mistreating) them. **2.** He had James, the brother of John, executed by the sword. **3.** When this pleased the Jewish people, he decided to arrest Peter as well. This happened during the Festival of Unleavened Bread. **4.** After taking him into custody, he placed Peter in prison under the watch of four squads of four soldiers each. Herod planned to bring him out for a public trial after Passover. **5.** Meanwhile, Peter was being held in prison, but the church was fervently (with great sincerity) praying to God for him. **6.** On the night before Herod was to bring him to trial, Peter was sleeping between two soldiers, bound by two chains, and guards were posted at the entrance. **7.** Suddenly, an angel of the Lord appeared, and a bright light filled the cell. The angel struck Peter on the side to wake him. "Quick, get up!" the angel said. At once, the chains fell off Peter's wrists. **8.** The angel then told him, "Put on your clothes and sandals." Peter did as instructed. "Wrap your cloak around you and follow me," the angel said. **9.** Peter followed the angel out of the prison, but he didn't realize that what was happening was real; he thought he was having a vision. **10.** They passed the first and second guards and reached the iron gate leading to the city. The gate opened by itself, and they walked through it. After walking down one street, the angel suddenly left him. **11.** When Peter came to his senses, he said, "Now I know for sure that the Lord has sent His angel to rescue me from Herod's power and from what the Jewish people had been hoping would happen to me." **12.** Realizing this, Peter went to the house of Mary, the mother of John (also called Mark), where many people had gathered to pray. **13.** Peter knocked at the outer door, and a servant girl named Rhoda went to answer it. **14.** When she recognized Peter's voice, she was so overjoyed that she ran back without opening the door, saying, "Peter is at the door!" **15.** "You're out of your mind!" they told her. But when she kept insisting that it was true, they said, "It must be his angel." **16.** Meanwhile, Peter kept knocking, and when they opened the door and saw him, they were amazed. **17.** Peter motioned for them to be quiet and explained how the Lord had brought him out of prison. "Tell James and the other believers about this," he said, and then he left to go somewhere else. **18.** The next morning, there was a great uproar among the soldiers over what had happened to Peter. After Herod ordered a thorough search and still couldn't find him, he interrogated (questioned intensely) the guards and had them executed. **19.** After this, Herod went from Judea to Caesarea and stayed there. **20.** He had been in a dispute with the people of Tyre and Sidon, who now joined forces and sought a meeting with him. After gaining the support of Blastus, a trusted servant of the king, they requested peace, because their region depended on the king's territory for food. **21.** On the

appointed day, Herod, wearing his royal robes, sat on his throne and gave a public speech. **22.** The people shouted, "This is the voice of a god, not of a man!" **23.** At once, because Herod did not give glory to God, an angel of the Lord struck him down, and he was eaten by worms and died. **24.** But the word of God continued to spread and grow. **25.** After Barnabas and Saul completed their mission, they returned to Jerusalem, bringing John (also called Mark) with them.

Chapter 13

1. In the church at Antioch, there were prophets and teachers: Barnabas, Simeon called Niger, Lucius from Cyrene, Manaen (raised with Herod the tetrarch), and Saul. **2.** While worshiping the Lord and fasting, the Holy Spirit said, "Set apart for me Barnabas and Saul for the work I have called them." **3.** After fasting and praying, they placed their hands on them and sent them off. **4.** The two of them, sent by the Holy Spirit, went to Seleucia and sailed to Cyprus. **5.** They preached the word of God in Salamis' Jewish synagogues. John was with them as their helper. **6.** They traveled to Paphos and met a Jewish sorcerer, Bar-Jesus, an attendant of the proconsul, Sergius Paulus, who wanted to hear the word of God. **7.** Elymas the sorcerer opposed them, trying to turn the proconsul from the faith. **8.** Paul, filled with the Holy Spirit, looked at Elymas and said, **9.** "You are a child of the devil, full of deceit! Will you never stop perverting the ways of the Lord? **10.** Now the Lord's hand is against you. You will be blind for a time, unable to see the sun." Immediately mist and darkness came over him. **12.** When the proconsul saw this, he believed, amazed at the teaching about the Lord. **13.** From Paphos, Paul and his companions went to Perga, where John left to return to Jerusalem. **14.** They went on to Pisidian Antioch and entered the synagogue on the Sabbath. **15.** After the Law and the Prophets were read, the synagogue leaders invited Paul to speak. **16.** Paul said: "Fellow Israelites and Gentiles who worship God, listen: **17.** The God of Israel led our ancestors out of Egypt and gave them the land of Canaan after defeating seven nations. **20.** After 450 years, God gave them judges (leaders or rulers) until Samuel. **21.** The people asked for a king, and He gave them Saul, then David, of whom God said: 'I have found David, a man after my own heart.' **23.** From David's descendants, God brought Jesus as the Savior, fulfilling His promises. **24.** Before Jesus, John preached repentance (a change of mind or heart leading to forgiveness) and baptism. **25.** John said, 'I am not the one you seek, but one greater than I is coming.' **26.** To us, the message of salvation has been sent. **27.** The people of Jerusalem did not recognize Jesus, yet condemned Him, fulfilling the prophets. **29.** After Jesus was crucified, God raised Him from the dead. **30.** For many days, He appeared to His followers. **32.** We proclaim to you the good news: God has fulfilled His promises by raising Jesus, as written in the second Psalm: 'You are my Son; today I have become your Father.' **34.** God raised Jesus to never see decay (to not undergo corruption or decomposition), offering the sure blessings promised to David. **36.** David served God's purpose, died, and his body decayed, but Jesus did not. **38.** Through Jesus, the forgiveness of sins is proclaimed to you. **39.** Through Him, everyone who believes is set free from sin, a justification (being declared righteous) you could not obtain under the Law. **40.** Take care that what the prophets said does not happen to you: **41.** 'Look, you scoffers (those who mock or treat something with disdain), wonder and perish, for I will do something you would not believe.'" **42.** The people invited Paul to speak again on the next Sabbath. **43.** After the meeting, many Jews and Gentiles followed Paul and Barnabas, who urged them to continue in God's grace. **44.** The next Sabbath, nearly the whole city gathered to hear the word of the Lord. **45.** The Jews, filled with jealousy, opposed Paul, but Paul boldly said, **46.** "We had to speak to you first, but since you reject it, we turn to the Gentiles. **47.** The Lord has commanded us: 'I have made you a light for the Gentiles, to bring salvation to the ends of the earth.'" **48.** The Gentiles were glad and believed, and all appointed for eternal life were saved. **49.** The word of the Lord spread throughout the region. **50.** But the Jewish leaders stirred up persecution (hostility or mistreatment because of their beliefs) against Paul and Barnabas and expelled them from the region. **51.** They shook the dust off their feet and went to Iconium. **52.** The disciples were filled with joy and the Holy Spirit.

Chapter 14

1. Paul and Barnabas went to the synagogue, where they spoke powerfully, and many Jews and Greeks believed. **2.** But some Jews who did not believe stirred up the Gentiles, turning them against the apostles. **3.** Paul and Barnabas stayed a long time, boldly speaking for the Lord, who confirmed their message by enabling them to perform miracles. **4.** The city was divided: some sided with the Jews, others with the apostles. **5.** A plot was formed by both Jews and Gentiles to harm them, so they fled to Lystra and Derbe. **6.** There, they continued preaching. **In Lystra, 8.** there was a man who had been lame (unable to walk) from birth. **9.** He listened to Paul, who saw that he had faith to be healed. **10.** Paul called out, "Stand up!" and the man jumped to his feet and began walking. **11.** The crowd, amazed, shouted in their language, "The gods have come down in human form!" **12.** They called Barnabas Zeus and Paul Hermes (the messenger god). **13.** The priest of Zeus brought bulls to sacrifice, but Paul and Barnabas tore their clothes in protest, saying: **14.** "We are only humans like you. We bring you good news to turn from false gods to the living God who made all things." **16.** Though they tried to stop the crowd, **19.** Jews from Antioch and Iconium came and turned the crowd against them. They stoned Paul, thinking he was dead, and dragged him out of the city. **20.** But Paul got up after the disciples gathered around him and went back into the city. The next day, he and Barnabas went to Derbe. **21.** In Derbe, they made many disciples. Then they returned to Lystra, Iconium, and Antioch, strengthening and encouraging the believers. **22.** They told them, "We must endure many hardships to enter God's kingdom." **23.** Paul and Barnabas appointed elders (church leaders) in each church and prayed, committing them to the Lord. **24.** They passed through Pisidia and came to Pamphylia. **25.** After preaching in Perga, they went to Attalia. **26.** From there, they sailed back to Antioch, where they had been entrusted to the grace of God for their work. **27.** When they arrived, they gathered the church and reported how God had opened the door of faith to the Gentiles. **28.** They stayed there a long time with the disciples.

Chapter 15

1. Some people came down from Judea to Antioch and taught the believers: "Unless you are circumcised (cutting off the foreskin), according to the law of Moses, you cannot be saved." **2.** This caused Paul and Barnabas to have a sharp dispute (argument) and debate with them. So, Paul and Barnabas were chosen, along with other believers, to go to Jerusalem to ask the apostles and elders (leaders) about this matter. **3.** The church sent them on their way, and as they traveled through Phoenicia and Samaria, they shared how the Gentiles (non-Jews) had been converted (turned to the faith), and this made the believers very happy. **4.** Upon arriving in Jerusalem, they were warmly welcomed by the church, apostles, and elders, and reported all that God had done through them. **5.** Some believers who were Pharisees (members of a strict Jewish religious group) stood up and said, "The Gentiles must be circumcised and required to follow the law of Moses." **6.** The apostles and elders met to discuss this issue. **7.** After much discussion, Peter stood up and said, "Brothers, you know that God chose me a long time ago for the Gentiles to hear the gospel (good news) and believe. **8.** God, who knows the heart, showed His acceptance by giving the Holy Spirit to them, just as He did to us. **9.** He did not make a distinction (difference) between us and them, for He purified (cleansed) their hearts by faith. **10.** Why do you test (challenge) God by imposing a yoke (burden) on the Gentiles that neither we nor our ancestors could bear? **11.** No! We believe that it is by the grace (unearned favor) of our Lord Jesus that we are saved, just like they are." **12.** The entire assembly (group) became silent as they listened to Barnabas and Paul sharing about the signs and wonders (miracles) God had performed among the Gentiles. **13.** When they finished, James spoke: "Brothers, listen to me. **14.** Simon (Peter) has explained how God first chose a people from the Gentiles for His name. **15.** The words of the prophets agree with this, as it is written: **16.** 'After this I will return and rebuild David's fallen tent (kingdom). Its ruins I will rebuild, and I will restore it, **17.** so that all people may seek the Lord, even all the Gentiles who bear my name,' says the Lord, who does these things — **18.** things known from long ago." **19.** "Therefore, I judge (decide) that we should not make it difficult for the Gentiles who are turning to God. **20.** Instead, we should write to them, telling them to avoid food polluted (made impure) by idols, sexual immorality (immoral sexual behavior), the meat of strangled animals, and blood. **21.** Moses' law has been taught in every city from the earliest times

and is read every Sabbath in the synagogues." **22.** Then the apostles and elders, along with the whole church, decided to send some of their own men to Antioch with Paul and Barnabas. They chose Judas (also called Barsabbas) and Silas, who were leaders among the believers. **23.** With them, they sent the following letter: "The apostles and elders, your brothers, To the Gentile believers in Antioch, Syria, and Cilicia: Greetings. **24.** We have heard that some went out from us without our authorization (permission) and troubled you, upsetting (disturbing) your minds with what they said. **25.** So, we have decided to send some men with our dear friends Barnabas and Paul — **26.** men who have risked their lives for the name of our Lord Jesus Christ. **27.** Therefore, we are sending Judas and Silas to confirm (verify) by word of mouth what we are writing. **28.** It seemed good to the Holy Spirit and to us not to burden you with anything beyond the following: **29.** You are to abstain (avoid) from food sacrificed to idols, from blood, from meat from strangled animals, and from sexual immorality. You will do well to avoid these things. Farewell." **30.** The men were sent off and came to Antioch, where they gathered the church and delivered the letter. **31.** The people read it and were glad for its encouraging message. **32.** Judas and Silas, who were prophets (spokespersons for God), spoke a lot to encourage and strengthen the believers. **33.** After some time, they were sent off by the believers with the blessing of peace to return to those who had sent them. **35.** Paul and Barnabas stayed in Antioch, teaching and preaching the word of the Lord with many others. **36.** After some time, Paul said to Barnabas, "Let's visit the believers in the towns where we preached to see how they are doing." **37.** Barnabas wanted to take John, also called Mark, with them, **38.** but Paul did not think it wise to take him, because he had deserted (left) them in Pamphylia and had not continued in the work. **39.** They had such a sharp disagreement (strong argument) that they parted ways: Barnabas took Mark and sailed for Cyprus, **40.** while Paul chose Silas and left, commended (approved) by the believers to the grace (favor) of the Lord. **41.** Paul traveled through Syria and Cilicia, strengthening the churches.

Chapter 16

1. Paul came to Derbe and then to Lystra, where a disciple (follower of Jesus) named Timothy lived, whose mother was Jewish and a believer, but whose father was a Greek (non-Jew). **2.** The believers in Lystra and Iconium spoke well of him. **3.** Paul wanted to take him along on the journey, so he circumcised (cut off the foreskin) him because of the Jews who lived in that area, for they all knew that his father was a Greek. **4.** As they traveled from town to town, they delivered the decisions reached by the apostles and elders (leaders) in Jerusalem for the people to obey. **5.** So the churches were strengthened (made stronger) in the faith and grew daily in numbers. **6.** Paul and his companions traveled throughout the region of Phrygia and Galatia, having been kept by the Holy Spirit from preaching the word in the province of Asia. **7.** When they came to the border of Mysia, they tried to enter Bithynia, but the Spirit of Jesus would not allow them to. **8.** So they passed by Mysia and went down to Troas. **9.** During the night Paul had a vision (dream or supernatural experience) of a man of Macedonia standing and begging him, "Come over to Macedonia and help us." **10.** After Paul had seen the vision, we got ready at once to leave for Macedonia, concluding (deciding) that God had called us to preach the gospel (good news) to them. **11.** From Troas we put out to sea and sailed straight for Samothrace, and the next day we went on to Neapolis. **12.** From there we traveled to Philippi, a Roman colony (settlement for Roman citizens) and the leading city of that district of Macedonia. And we stayed there several days. **13.** On the Sabbath (day of rest), we went outside the city gate to the river, where we expected to find a place of prayer. We sat down and began to speak to the women who had gathered there. **14.** One of those listening was a woman from the city of Thyatira named Lydia, a dealer in purple cloth. She was a worshiper (follower) of God. The Lord opened her heart to respond to Paul's message. **15.** When she and the members of her household were baptized, she invited us to her home. "If you consider me a believer in the Lord," she said, "come and stay at my house." And she persuaded (convinced) us.. Once when we were going to the place of prayer, we were met by a female slave who had a spirit by which she predicted the future. She earned a great deal of money for her owners by fortune-telling. **17.** She followed Paul and the rest of us, shouting,

"These men are servants of the Most High God, who are telling you the way to be saved." **18.** She kept this up for many days. Finally, Paul became so annoyed (bothered) that he turned around and said to the spirit, "In the name of Jesus Christ I command you to come out of her!" At that moment, the spirit left her. **19.** When her owners realized that their hope of making money was gone, they seized (captured) Paul and Silas and dragged them into the marketplace to face the authorities (officials). **20.** They brought them before the magistrates (judges) and said, "These men are Jews, and are throwing our city into an uproar (chaos) by advocating (supporting) customs unlawful for us Romans to accept or practice." **21.** The crowd joined in the attack against Paul and Silas, and the magistrates ordered them to be stripped (removed of their clothes) and beaten with rods. **22.** After they had been severely flogged (beaten), they were thrown into prison, and the jailer (guard) was commanded to guard them carefully. **23.** When he received these orders, he put them in the inner cell (a secure part of the prison) and as fastened (locked) their feet in the stocks (a wooden device used to restrain prisoners). **24.** About midnight Paul and Silas were praying and singing hymns (songs of praise) to God, and the other prisoners were listening to them. **25.** Suddenly there was such a violent earthquake that the foundations of the prison were shaken. At once all the prison doors flew open, and everyone's chains (restraints) came loose. **26.** The jailer woke up, and when he saw the prison doors open, he drew his sword and was about to kill himself because he thought the prisoners had escaped. **27.** But Paul shouted, "Don't harm yourself! We are all here!" **28.** The jailer called for lights, rushed in, and fell trembling (shaking) before Paul and Silas. **30.** He then brought them out and asked, "Sirs, what must I do to be saved?" **31.** They replied, "Believe in the Lord Jesus, and you will be saved—you and your household." **32.** Then they spoke the word of the Lord to him and to all the others in his house. **33.** At that hour of the night the jailer took them and washed their wounds; then immediately he and all his household were baptized. **34.** The jailer brought them into his house and set a meal before them; he was filled with joy because he had come to believe in God—he and his whole household. **35.** When it was daylight, the magistrates sent their officers to the jailer with the order: "Release those men." **36.** The jailer told Paul, "The magistrates have ordered that you and Silas be released. Now you can leave. Go in peace." **37.** But Paul said to the officers: "They beat us publicly without a trial, even though we are Roman citizens, and threw us into prison. And now do they want to get rid of us quietly? No! Let them come themselves and escort us out." **38.** The officers reported this to the magistrates, and when they heard that Paul and Silas were Roman citizens, they were alarmed (worried). **39.** They came to appease (calm) them and escorted them from the prison, requesting them to leave the city. **40.** After Paul and Silas came out of the prison, they went to Lydia's house, where they met with the brothers and sisters and encouraged (strengthened) them. Then they left.

Chapter 17

1. When Paul and his companions had passed through Amphipolis and Apollonia, they came to Thessalonica, where there was a Jewish synagogue (place of worship). **2.** As was his custom (habit), Paul went into the synagogue, and on three Sabbath days he reasoned (discussed) with them from the Scriptures, **3.** explaining and proving that the Messiah (the Savior) had to suffer and rise from the dead. "This Jesus I am proclaiming to you is the Messiah," he said. **4.** Some of the Jews were persuaded (convinced) and joined Paul and Silas, as did a large number of God-fearing (worshipers of God) Greeks and quite a few prominent (important) women. **5.** But other Jews were jealous (envious); so they rounded up some bad characters (evil people) from the marketplace, formed a mob (violent crowd), and started a riot in the city. They rushed to Jason's house in search of Paul and Silas in order to bring them out to the crowd. **6.** But when they did not find them, they dragged Jason and some other believers before the city officials, shouting: "These men who have caused trouble (disruption) all over the world have now come here, **7.** and Jason has welcomed them into his house. They are all defying (resisting) Caesar's decrees (official orders), saying that there is another king, one called Jesus." **8.** When they heard this, the crowd and the city officials were thrown into turmoil (confusion). **9.** Then they made Jason and the others post bond (pay a security deposit) and let them go. **10.** As soon as it was night,

the believers sent Paul and Silas away to Berea. On arriving there, they went to the Jewish synagogue. **11.** Now the Berean Jews were of more noble character (noble means honorable) than those in Thessalonica, for they received the message with great eagerness and examined (studied) the Scriptures every day to see if what Paul said was true. **12.** As a result, many of them believed, as did also a number of prominent Greek women and many Greek men. **13.** But when the Jews in Thessalonica learned that Paul was preaching the word of God at Berea, some of them went there too, agitating (stirring up) the crowds and stirring them up. **14.** The believers immediately sent Paul to the coast, but Silas and Timothy stayed at Berea. **15.** Those who escorted (guided) Paul brought him to Athens and then left with instructions for Silas and Timothy to join him as soon as possible. **16.** While Paul was waiting for them in Athens, he was greatly distressed (upset) to see that the city was full of idols (statues of gods). **17.** So he reasoned (debated) in the synagogue with both Jews and God-fearing Greeks, as well as in the marketplace day by day with those who happened to be there. **18.** A group of Epicurean (followers of a Greek philosophy) and Stoic philosophers (followers of another Greek philosophy) began to debate with him. Some of them asked, "What is this babbler (foolish talker) trying to say?" Others remarked, "He seems to be advocating (promoting) foreign gods." They said this because Paul was preaching the good news about Jesus and the resurrection (rising from the dead). **19.** Then they took him and brought him to a meeting of the Areopagus (a council of judges), where they said to him, "May we know what this new teaching is that you are presenting? **20.** You are bringing some strange ideas to our ears, and we would like to know what they mean." **21.** (All the Athenians and the foreigners who lived there spent their time doing nothing but talking about and listening to the latest ideas.) **22.** Paul then stood up in the meeting of the Areopagus and said: "People of Athens! I see that in every way you are very religious. **23.** For as I walked around and looked carefully at your objects of worship, I even found an altar with this inscription: TO AN UNKNOWN GOD. So you are ignorant (unaware) of the very thing you worship—and this is what I am going to proclaim to you. **24.** "The God who made the world and everything in it is the Lord (master) of heaven and earth and does not live in temples built by human hands. **25.** And he is not served by human hands, as if he needed anything. Rather, he himself gives everyone life and breath and everything else. **26.** From one man he made all the nations, that they should inhabit (live in) the whole earth; and he marked out their appointed times in history and the boundaries (limits) of their lands. **27.** God did this so that they would seek him and perhaps reach out for him and find him, though he is not far from any one of us. **28.** 'For in him we live and move and have our being.' As some of your own poets have said, 'We are his offspring (children).' **29.** "Therefore since we are God's offspring, we should not think that the divine being (God) is like gold or silver or stone—an image made by human design and skill. **30.** In the past God overlooked (forgave) such ignorance (lack of knowledge), but now he commands all people everywhere to repent (turn away from sin). **31.** For he has set a day when he will judge (judge means to evaluate or punish) the world with justice by the man he has appointed. He has given proof (evidence) of this to everyone by raising him from the dead." **32.** When they heard about the resurrection of the dead, some of them sneered (mocked), but others said, "We want to hear you again on this subject." **33.** At that, Paul left the Council. **34.** Some of the people became followers (disciples) of Paul and believed. Among them was Dionysius, a member of the Areopagus, also a woman named Damaris, and a number of others.

Chapter 18

1. After Athens, Paul went to Corinth and met Aquila and Priscilla, tentmakers (people who make tents), and worked with them. **2.** Every Sabbath, Paul reasoned (discussed) in the synagogue to persuade (convince) Jews and Greeks. **5.** When Silas and Timothy arrived, Paul focused solely on preaching, declaring Jesus was the Messiah (Savior). **6.** When the Jews opposed him, Paul said, "Your blood be on your heads! From now on, I will go to the Gentiles (non-Jews)." **7.** Paul stayed with Titius Justus, a God-worshiper. **8.** Crispus, the synagogue leader, and many Corinthians believed and were baptized. **9.** The Lord spoke to Paul in a vision (spiritual message), assuring him of protection and support in Corinth. **12.** When Gallio was the proconsul (governor), the Jews charged Paul with breaking the law, but Gallio dismissed the case. **17.** The crowd turned on Sosthenes, the synagogue leader, and beat him, while Gallio did nothing. **18.** Paul sailed to Syria with Priscilla and Aquila, after taking a vow (promise) and cutting his hair. **19.** In Ephesus, Paul preached in the synagogue but declined to stay longer. **22.** He then visited Jerusalem and Antioch. **23.** After spending time in Antioch, Paul traveled through Galatia and Phrygia, strengthening (encouraging) the disciples. **24.** Apollos, a learned (educated) man from Alexandria, came to Ephesus, teaching about Jesus but only knew the baptism of John. **26.** Priscilla and Aquila explained God's way more fully to him. **27.** Apollos went to Achaia, where he helped many believers by proving from Scripture that Jesus was the Messiah.

Chapter 19

1. While Apollos was in Corinth, Paul arrived in Ephesus and met some disciples. **2.** He asked if they had received the Holy Spirit (God's presence and power), and they replied that they hadn't even heard of the Holy Spirit. **3.** Paul asked about their baptism (ceremony of initiation into the faith), and they said it was John's baptism (the baptism of repentance by John the Baptist). **4.** Paul explained that John's baptism was for repentance (a sincere turning away from sin), urging people to believe in Jesus. **5.** They were baptized in Jesus' name. **6.** When Paul laid his hands on them, the Holy Spirit came on them, and they spoke in tongues and prophesied (spoke messages inspired by God). **7.** About twelve men were present. **8.** Paul preached in the synagogue (Jewish place of worship) for three months, persuading people about the kingdom of God (God's rule and reign). **9.** When some opposed him, Paul moved his teachings to a lecture hall (a place for public teaching), and for two years, all of Asia heard the Lord's word. **11.** God did extraordinary (unusual, amazing) miracles through Paul, **12.** even using handkerchiefs (cloths) and aprons (work clothes) that touched him to heal the sick and cast out demons. **13.** Some Jews who cast out demons tried to use Jesus' name, but the evil spirit (a demon or unclean spirit) rejected them, attacking them and leaving them wounded. **17.** This event caused great fear, and Jesus' name was honored (held in high regard). **18.** Many confessed (admitted) their wrongdoings, **19.** and those who practiced sorcery (magic or witchcraft) burned their scrolls (rolled-up writings), worth fifty thousand drachmas (an ancient Greek silver coin, about a year's wages). **20.** The word of the Lord spread widely and grew in power (influence and strength). **21.** Afterward, Paul decided to go go to Jerusalem, and then to Rome. **22.** He sent Timothy and Erastus to Macedonia while he stayed longer in Asia. **23.** A riot (a violent disturbance) broke out over the Way (Christian teachings). **24.** Demetrius (a silversmith) made shrines (small representations or idols) of Artemis, and his business was threatened by Paul's teachings. **25.** Demetrius warned that the temple (place of worship) and Artemis' honor were at risk. **28.** The crowd was furious, shouting, "Great is Artemis of the Ephesians!" **29.** They seized (captured) Paul's companions, Gaius and Aristarchus, and rushed to the garden (a large public hall). **30.** Paul wanted to address the crowd, but his disciples (followers of Jesus) prevented him. **32.** The assembly was confused, and most didn't know why they were there. **33.** Some Jews pushed forward Alexander (a Jewish man) to speak, but when the crowd realized he was Jewish, they shouted for two hours: "Great is Artemis of the Ephesians!" **35.** The city clerk (local government official) calmed the crowd, explaining that Ephesus was the guardian of Artemis' temple, and that no crime had been committed by Paul. **36.** He urged them to settle matters legally (according to the law), avoiding charges of rioting. **41.** After his speech, the assembly was dismissed.

Chapter 20

1. After the disturbance had settled, Paul gathered the epigones, encouraged them, and said his farewells as he prepared to leave for Macedonia. **2.** As he traveled through the region, he continued to offer multitudinous words of goad, eventually reaching Greece. **3.** He stayed there for three months. still, when some Jews intrigued against him while he was planning to sail to Syria, he chose rather to return through Macedonia. **4.** He was accompanied by Sopater, Aristarchus, Secundus, Gaius, Timothy, Tychicus, and Trophimus, all from Asia. **5.** These men went ahead and awaited for us in Troas. **6.** We sailed from Philippi after the Festival of Unleavened Bread (a Jewish festival marking the Exodus), and five days subsequently joined the others in Troas, where we stayed for seven days. **7.** On the first day of the week, we gathered to break chuck (celebrate fellowship). Paul spoke to them, intending to leave the coming day, and continued his speech until night. **8.** The room where we were meeting was well-lit with multitudinous lights. **9.** A immature man named Eutychus fell asleep during Paul's long discourse and fell from the third story, and they picked him up dead. **10.** Paul went down, threw himself on the immature man, and said, "Don't be alarmed, he is alive!" **11.** Paul also returned upstairs, broke chuck, and ate. After continuing to talk until dawn, he left. **12.** The people took the immature man home alive, and they were greatly assured. **13.** We sailed to Assos, where we had arranged for Paul to board, as he wanted to walk there by himself. **14.** After meeting us at Assos, we took him aboard and sailed to Mitylene. **15.** The following day, we set passage from there and arrived at Chios, also went on to Samos, and ultimately reached Miletus. **16.** Paul decided to sail past Ephesus to avoid delaying in Asia, as he was eager to reach Jerusalem by Pentecost. **17.** From Miletus, he transferred for the elders of the church in Ephesus. **18.** When they arrived, Paul said to them, "You know how I lived among you the entire time I was in Asia, from the first day I arrived. **19.** I served the Lord with modesty and rips, enduring multitudinous trials that came upon me from my Jewish opponents. **20.** I didn't stagger to educate you privately and from house to house, publicizing everything that was helpful. **21.** I declared to both Jews and Greeks that they must bemoan (turn down from sin) and believe in Jesus. **22.** And now, impelled by the Spirit, I am going to Jerusalem, not knowing what will be to me there. **23.** I only know that in every municipality, the Holy Spirit warns me that prison and adversities await me. **24.** still, I consider my life of little value; my only thing is to finish the race and complete the task the Lord Jesus has given me — the task of attesting to the good news of God's grace. **25.** I know that you won't see me again, but I declare that I am innocent of anyone's blood, **26.** for I've not wavered to annunciate to you the aggregate will of God. **27.** Keep watch over yourselves and all the flock of which the Holy Spirit has made you overseers. Be herdsmen of God's church, which He bought with His own blood. **28.** After I leave, fierce wolves (dangerous people) will come by, and indeed from among your own group, some will distort the verity to lead the epigones amiss. **29.** So be on your guard! For three times, I advised you night and day with rips. **30.** Now I commit you to God and to the word of His grace, which can make you up and give you an heritage among the sanctified (those set incremental for God). **31.** I've not coveted (asked) anyone's tableware or gold. **32.** I worked hard with my own hands to give for myself and my companions. **33.** In everything I did, I showed you that we must help the weak and flash back the words of Jesus, who said, 'It's more blessed to give than to admit.'" **34.** After he finished speaking, Paul knelt down and appealed with them all. **35.** They all wept and embraced him, especially anguishing that they would noway see him again. They accompanied him to the boat.

Chapter 21

1. After we had torn ourselves away from them, we put out to sea and sailed straight to Kos. The next day we went to Rhodes and from there to Patara. **2.** We found a ship crossing over to Phoenicia, went on board and set sail. **3.** After sighting Cyprus and passing to the south of it, we sailed on to Syria. We landed at Tyre, where our ship was to unload its cargo (goods). **4.** We sought out the disciples (followers of Jesus) there and stayed with them seven days. Through the Spirit they urged (encouraged) Paul not to go on to Jerusalem. **5.** When it was time to leave, we left and continued on our way. All of them, including wives and children, accompanied (went with) us out of the city, and there on the beach we knelt to pray. **6.** After saying goodbye to each other, we went aboard the ship, and they returned home. **7.** We continued our voyage (journey by sea) from Tyre and landed at Ptolemais, where we greeted the brothers and sisters and stayed with them for a day. **8.** Leaving the next day, we reached Caesarea and stayed at the house of Philip the evangelist (one who spreads the gospel), one of the Seven. **9.** He had four unmarried daughters who prophesied (spoke messages from God). **10.** After we had been there a number of days, a prophet (one who speaks for God) named Agabus came down from Judea. **11.** Coming over to us, he took Paul's belt, tied his own hands and feet with it and said, "The Holy Spirit says, 'In this way the Jewish leaders in Jerusalem will bind (tie up) the owner of this belt and will hand him over to the Gentiles (non-Jewish people).'" 12. When we heard this, we and the people there pleaded (begged) with Paul not to go up to Jerusalem. 13. Then Paul answered, "Why are you weeping (crying) and breaking my heart? I am ready not only to be bound, but also to die in Jerusalem for the name of the Lord Jesus." 14. When he would not be dissuaded (persuaded otherwise), we gave up and said, "The Lord's will be done." 15. After this, we started on our way up to Jerusalem. 16. Some of the disciples from Caesarea accompanied us and brought us to the home of Mnason, where we were to stay. He was a man from Cyprus and one of the early disciples. 17. When we arrived at Jerusalem, the brothers and sisters received us warmly (kindly). 18. The next day Paul and the rest of us went to see James, and all the elders (leaders) were present. 19. Paul greeted them and reported in detail what God had done among the Gentiles through his ministry (work of serving). 20. When they heard this, they praised (gave thanks to) God. Then they said to Paul: "You see, brother, how many thousands of Jews have believed, and all of them are zealous (enthusiastic) for the law. 21. They have been informed that you teach all the Jews who live among the Gentiles to turn away from Moses, telling them not to circumcise (cut off the foreskin as a religious act) their children or live according to our customs. 22. What shall we do? They will certainly hear that you have come, 23. so do what we tell you. There are four men with us who have made a vow (solemn promise). 24. Take these men, join in their purification (cleansing) rites and pay their expenses (costs), so that they can have their heads shaved. Then everyone will know there is no truth in these reports about you, but that you yourself are living in obedience (following commands) to the law. 25. As for the Gentile believers, we have written to them our decision that they should abstain (keep away) from food sacrificed to idols, from blood, from the meat of strangled (choked) animals and from sexual immorality (unlawful sexual behavior)." 26. The next day Paul took the men and purified himself along with them. Then he went to the temple to give notice of the date when the days of purification would end and the offering (gift to God) would be made for each of them. 27. When the seven days were nearly over, some Jews from the province of Asia saw Paul at the temple. They stirred up (excited) the whole crowd and seized (grabbed) him, 28. shouting, "Fellow Israelites, help us! This is the man who teaches everyone everywhere against our people and our law and this place. And besides, he has brought Greeks into the temple and defiled (made unclean) this holy place." 29. (They had previously seen Trophimus the Ephesian in the city with Paul and assumed (thought) that Paul had brought him into the temple.) 30. The whole city was aroused (stirred up), and the people came running from all directions. Seizing Paul, they dragged him from the temple, and immediately the gates were shut. 31. While they were trying to kill him, news reached the commander (leader) of the Roman troops that the whole city of Jerusalem was in an uproar (state of disorder). 32. He at once took some officers and soldiers and ran down to the crowd. When the rioters (those causing disorder) saw the commander and his soldiers, they stopped beating Paul. 33. The commander came up and arrested him and ordered him to be bound with two chains. Then he asked who he was and what he had done. 34. Some in the crowd shouted one thing and some another, and since the commander could not get at the truth because of the uproar, he ordered that Paul be taken into the barracks (building where soldiers live). 35. When Paul reached the steps, the violence of the mob (large, disorderly crowd) was so great he had to be carried by the soldiers. 36. The crowd that followed kept shouting, "Get rid of him!" 37. As the soldiers were about to take Paul into the barracks, he asked the commander, "May I say something to you?" "Do you speak Greek?" he replied. 38. "Aren't you the Egyptian who started a revolt (uprising) and led four thousand terrorists out into the wilderness some time ago?" 39. Paul answered, "I am a Jew, from Tarsus in Cilicia, a citizen of no ordinary city. Please let me speak to the people." 40. After receiving the commander's permission, Paul stood on the steps and motioned (gestured) to the crowd. When they were all silent, he said to them in Aramaic:

Chapter 22

1. "Brothers and fathers, listen now to my defense (explanation in response to accusation)." 2. When they heard him speak to them in Aramaic, they became very quiet. Then Paul said: 3. "I am a Jew, born in Tarsus of Cilicia, but brought up in this city. I studied under Gamaliel and was thoroughly trained (educated in detail) in the law of our ancestors. I was just as zealous (enthusiastic) for God as any of you are today. 4. I persecuted (harassed and oppressed) the followers of this Way to their death, arresting both men and women and throwing them into prison, 5. as the high priest and all the Council (Jewish governing body) can themselves testify (confirm). I even obtained (received) letters from them to their associates (fellow members) in Damascus, and went there to bring these people as prisoners to Jerusalem to be punished. 6. "About noon as I came near Damascus, suddenly a bright light from heaven flashed (shone suddenly) around me. 7. I fell to the ground and heard a voice say to me, 'Saul! Saul! Why do you persecute me?' 8. "'Who are you, Lord?' I asked. "'I am Jesus of Nazareth, whom you are persecuting,' he replied. 9. My companions (those traveling with me) saw the light, but they did not understand the voice of him who was speaking to me. 10. "'What shall I do, Lord?' I asked. "'Get up,' the Lord said, 'and go into Damascus. There you will be told all that you have been assigned (appointed) to do.' 11. My companions led me by the hand into Damascus, because the brilliance (brightness) of the light had blinded me. 12. "A man named Ananias came to see me. He was a devout (deeply religious) observer of the law and highly respected by all the Jews living there. 13. He stood beside me and said, 'Brother Saul, receive your sight!' And at that very moment I was able to see him. 14. "Then he said: 'The God of our ancestors has chosen you to know his will (plan) and to see the Righteous One (a title for Jesus) and to hear words from his mouth. 15. You will be his witness (one who tells of their experience) to all people of what you have seen and heard. 16. And now what are you waiting for? Get up, be baptized (immersed in water as a religious act) and wash your sins (wrongdoings) away, calling on his name.' 17. "When I returned to Jerusalem and was praying at the temple, I fell into a trance (spiritual vision) 18. and saw the Lord speaking to me. 'Quick!' he said. 'Leave Jerusalem immediately, because the people here will not accept your testimony (statement of truth) about me.' 19. "'Lord,' I replied, 'these people know that I went from one synagogue (Jewish place of worship) to another to imprison and beat those who believe in you. 20. And when the blood of your martyr (person killed for their faith) Stephen was shed, I stood there giving my approval (agreement) and guarding the clothes of those who were killing him.' 21. "Then the Lord said to me, 'Go; I will send you far away to the Gentiles (non-Jewish people).'" 22. The crowd listened to Paul until he said this. Then they raised their voices and shouted, "Rid the earth of him! He's not fit to live!" 23. As they were shouting and throwing off their cloaks (outer garments) and flinging dust into the air, 24. the commander (Roman military officer) ordered that Paul be taken into the barracks (building where soldiers stay). He directed that he be flogged (whipped) and interrogated (questioned aggressively) in order to find out why the people were shouting at him like this. 25. As they stretched him out to flog him, Paul said to the centurion (Roman officer in charge of 100 soldiers) standing there, "Is it legal for you to flog a Roman citizen who hasn't even been found guilty (proven to have done wrong)?" 26. When the centurion heard this, he went to the commander and reported it. "What are you going to do?" he asked. "This man is a Roman citizen." 27. The commander went to Paul and asked, "Tell me, are you a Roman citizen?" "Yes, I am," he answered. 28. Then the commander said, "I had to pay a lot of money for my citizenship." "But I was born a citizen," Paul replied. 29. Those who were about to interrogate him withdrew (pulled back) immediately. The commander himself was alarmed (afraid) when he realized that he had put Paul, a Roman citizen, in chains. 30. The commander wanted to find out exactly why Paul was being accused by the Jews. So the next day he released him and ordered the chief priests and all the members of the Sanhedrin (Jewish ruling council) to assemble (gather together). Then he brought Paul and had him stand before them.

Chapter 23

1. Paul looked straight at the Sanhedrin (Jewish council) and said, "My brothers, I have fulfilled my duty to God in all good conscience (awareness of right and wrong) to this day." 2. At this, the high priest Ananias ordered those standing near Paul to strike (hit) him on the mouth. 3. Then Paul said to him, "God will strike you, you whitewashed (hypocritical) wall! You sit there to judge me according to the law, yet you yourself violate (break) the law by commanding that I be struck!"

4. Those who were standing near Paul said, "How dare you insult (disrespect) God's high priest!" **5.** Paul replied, "Brothers, I did not realize that he was the high priest; for it is written: 'Do not speak evil about the ruler of your people.'" **6.** Then Paul, knowing that some of them were Sadducees (a Jewish sect that did not believe in resurrection) and the others Pharisees (a Jewish sect that believed in resurrection), called out in the Sanhedrin, "My brothers, I am a Pharisee, descended from Pharisees. I stand on trial because of the hope of the resurrection (rising from the dead) of the dead." **7.** When he said this, a dispute (argument) broke out between the Pharisees and the Sadducees, and the assembly (group gathered) was divided (split). **8.** (The Sadducees say that there is no resurrection, and that there are neither angels nor spirits (supernatural beings), but the Pharisees believe all these things.) **9.** There was a great uproar (commotion), and some of the teachers of the law who were Pharisees stood up and argued vigorously (forcefully). "We find nothing wrong with this man," they said. "What if a spirit or an angel has spoken to him?" **10.** The dispute became so violent (intense) that the commander (Roman military officer) was afraid Paul would be torn to pieces (physically harmed) by them. He ordered the troops to go down and take him away from them by force and bring him into the barracks (building where soldiers stay). **11.** The following night the Lord stood near Paul and said, "Take courage (be brave)! As you have testified (spoken the truth) about me in Jerusalem, so you must also testify in Rome." **12.** The next morning some Jews formed a conspiracy (secret plan) and bound themselves with an oath (serious promise) not to eat or drink until they had killed Paul. **13.** More than forty men were involved in this plot (plan to harm). **14.** They went to the chief priests and the elders and said, "We have taken a solemn (serious) oath not to eat anything until we have killed Paul. **15.** Now then, you and the Sanhedrin petition (formally request) the commander to bring him before you on the pretext (false reason) of wanting more accurate (detailed) information about his case. We are ready to kill him before he gets here." **16.** But when the son of Paul's sister heard of this plot, he went into the barracks and told Paul. **17.** Then Paul called one of the centurions (Roman officer in charge of 100 soldiers) and said, "Take this young man to the commander; he has something to tell him." **18.** So he took him to the commander. The centurion said, "Paul, the prisoner, sent for me and asked me to bring this young man to you because he has something to tell you." **19.** The commander took the young man by the hand, drew him aside (took him away privately) and asked, "What is it you want to tell me?" **20.** He said: "Some Jews have agreed to ask you to bring Paul before the Sanhedrin tomorrow on the pretext of wanting more accurate information about him. **21.** Don't give in to them, because more than forty of them are waiting in ambush (hiding to attack) for him. They have taken an oath not to eat or drink until they have killed him. They are ready now, waiting for your consent (agreement) to their request." **22.** The commander dismissed (sent away) the young man with this warning: "Don't tell anyone that you have reported (informed) this to me." **23.** Then he called two of his centurions and ordered them, "Get ready a detachment (small unit) of two hundred soldiers, seventy horsemen and two hundred spearmen (soldiers armed with spears) to go to Caesarea at nine tonight. **24.** Provide horses for Paul so that he may be taken safely to Governor Felix." **25.** He wrote a letter as follows: **26.** Claudius Lysias, To His Excellency (title of honor), Governor Felix: Greetings. **27.** This man was seized (taken by force) by the Jews and they were about to kill him, but I came with my troops and rescued (saved) him, for I had learned that he is a Roman citizen. **28.** I wanted to know why they were accusing him, so I brought him to their Sanhedrin. **29.** I found that the accusation (charge) had to do with questions about their law, but there was no charge against him that deserved (was worthy of) death or imprisonment (confinement in jail). **30.** When I was informed of a plot to be carried out against the man, I sent him to you at once. I also ordered his accusers (those who bring a charge) to present to you their case against him. **31** So the soldiers, carrying out their orders, took Paul with them during the night and brought him as far as Antipatris. **32.** The next day they let the cavalry (soldiers on horseback) go on with him, while they returned to the barracks. **33.** When the cavalry arrived in Caesarea, they delivered the letter to the governor and handed Paul over to him. **34.** The governor read the letter and asked what province he was from. Learning that he was from Cilicia, **35.** he said, "I will hear your case when your accusers get here." Then he ordered that Paul be kept under guard (protected by soldiers) in Herod's palace.

Chapter 24

1. Five days later the high priest Ananias went down to Caesarea with some of the elders (senior members of the Jewish council) and a lawyer named Tertullus, and they brought their charges (accusations) against Paul before the governor. **2.** When Paul was called in, Tertullus presented his case before Felix: "We have enjoyed a long period of peace under you, and your foresight (planning) has brought about reforms (improvements) in this nation. **3.** Everywhere and in every way, most excellent Felix, we acknowledge this with profound (deep) gratitude (thankfulness). **4.** But in order not to weary (burden) you further, I would request that you be kind enough to hear us briefly (for a short time). **5.** "We have found this man to be a troublemaker, stirring up (causing) riots (violent protests) among the Jews all over the world. He is a ringleader (leader) of the Nazarene sect (group with particular beliefs) **6.** and even tried to desecrate (violate or damage) the temple; so, we seized (captured) him. **8.** By examining (questioning) him yourself you will be able to learn the truth about all these charges we are bringing against him." **9.** The other Jews joined in the accusation, asserting (claiming) that these things were true. **10.** When the governor motioned for him to speak, Paul replied: "I know that for a number of years you have been a judge over this nation; so, I gladly make my defense (explanation). **11.** You can easily verify (confirm) that no more than twelve days ago I went up to Jerusalem to worship. **12.** My accusers (those making accusations) did not find me arguing with anyone at the temple or stirring up a crowd in the synagogues or anywhere else in the city. **13.** And they cannot prove to you the charges they are now making against me. **14.** However, I admit that I worship the God of our ancestors as a follower of the Way (early Christian faith), which they call a sect. I believe everything that is in accordance (agreement) with the Law and that is written in the Prophets, **15.** and I have the same hope in God as these men themselves have, that there will be a resurrection (rising from the dead) of both the righteous (morally good) and the wicked (morally bad). **16.** So I strive (try hard) always to keep my conscience (awareness of right and wrong) clear before God and man. **17.** "After an absence of several years, I came to Jerusalem to bring my people gifts for the poor and to present offerings (religious gifts). **18.** I was ceremonially clean (ritually pure) when they found me in the temple courts doing this. There was no crowd with me, nor was I involved in any disturbance (trouble). **19.** But there are some Jews from the province of Asia (region in the Roman Empire), who ought to be here before you and bring charges if they have anything against me. **20.** Or these who are here should state what crime they found in me when I stood before the Sanhedrin (Jewish council)— **21.** unless it was this one thing I shouted as I stood in their presence: 'It is concerning the resurrection of the dead that I am on trial before you today.'" **22.** Then Felix, who was well acquainted (familiar) with the Way, adjourned (paused) the proceedings. "When Lysias the commander comes," he said, "I will decide your case." **23.** He ordered the centurion (Roman officer) to keep Paul under guard but to give him some freedom and permit (allow) his friends to take care of his needs. **24.** Several days later Felix came with his wife Drusilla, who was Jewish. He sent for Paul and listened to him as he spoke about faith in Christ Jesus. **25.** As Paul talked about righteousness (moral rightness), self-control (discipline), and the judgment to come (God's future judgment), Felix was afraid and said, "That's enough for now! You may leave. When I find it convenient (suitable), I will send for you." **26.** At the same time, he was hoping that Paul would offer him a bribe (money for a favor), so he sent for him frequently (often) and talked with him. **27.** When two years had passed, Felix was succeeded (replaced) by Porcius Festus, but because Felix wanted to grant a favor (please) to the Jews, he left Paul in prison.

Chapter 25

1. Three days after Festus had arrived in the region, he went up from Caesarea to Jerusalem. **2.** There, the chief priests and Jewish leaders brought their accusations (formal statements of wrongdoing) against Paul before him. **3.** They asked Festus for a favor: to transfer (move) Paul to Jerusalem because they were planning an ambush (a secret

474

plan to attack) to kill him on the way. **4.** But Festus replied, "Paul is being held in Caesarea, and I plan to go there shortly. **5.** Some of your leaders may come with me, and if this man has done anything wrong, they can bring charges (accusations) against him there." **6.** After spending eight or ten days in Jerusalem, Festus went back to Caesarea, where he gathered the court the next day and ordered that Paul be brought before him. **7.** When Paul entered, the Jews who had come down from Jerusalem surrounded him, making many serious accusations, though they couldn't prove any of them. **8.** Paul then spoke in his defense (an argument to prove one's innocence), saying, "I have done nothing wrong against the Jewish law, the temple, or Caesar (the Roman ruler)." **9.** Festus, wanting to please the Jewish leaders, asked Paul, "Are you willing to go to Jerusalem and stand trial (formal examination of evidence) on these charges before me?" **10.** But Paul replied, "I am standing before Caesar's court, which is where I should be judged. I haven't wronged the Jews, as you know well. **11.** If I am guilty of a crime deserving death, I don't refuse to die; but if these charges are not true, no one has the right to hand me over to them. I appeal (make a formal request) to Caesar!" **12.** After discussing this with his council (group of advisors), Festus declared, "You have appealed to Caesar, and to Caesar you will go!" **13.** Some days later, King Agrippa and Bernice arrived in Caesarea to pay their respects (formal show of honor) to Festus. **14.** While they stayed for a few days, Festus brought up Paul's case with the king, saying, "There's a man here whom Felix left as a prisoner. **15.** When I went to Jerusalem, the Jewish chief priests and elders brought charges against him and asked for his condemnation (judgment or punishment). **16.** I told them that it is not the Roman custom (standard practice) to hand over anyone before they have faced their accusers (those who make accusations) and had an opportunity to defend themselves. **17.** So when they came here, I didn't delay but held court the next day and had the man brought in. **18.** His accusers did not bring up any of the serious crimes I had expected. **19.** Instead, they had disagreements with him about their own religion and about a dead man named Jesus, whom Paul claimed was alive. **20.** Unsure of how to investigate (look into) such matters, I asked if he would be willing to go to Jerusalem and face trial on these charges. **21.** But when Paul appealed to have his case held for the Emperor's decision, I ordered him to be held until I could send him to Caesar." **22.** Agrippa said to Festus, "I would like to hear this man myself." Festus replied, "You will hear him tomorrow." **23.** The next day, Agrippa and Bernice entered with great ceremony (formal display) and were joined by the high-ranking military officers and important men of the city. At Festus's order, Paul was brought in. **24.** Festus spoke to those gathered: "King Agrippa and everyone here, you see this man! The entire Jewish community has appealed (pleaded) to me about him, both in Jerusalem and here, demanding that he should not live any longer. **25.** I found that he had done nothing deserving of death, but because he appealed to the Emperor, I decided to send him to Rome. **26.** However, I don't have anything specific to write to His Majesty (Caesar) about him. This is why I brought him here, especially before you, King Agrippa, so that after this investigation (careful examination), I may have something to write. **27.** For I think it is unreasonable (not sensible) to send a prisoner to Rome without stating the charges against him."

Chapter 26

1. Then Agrippa said to Paul, "You may speak on your own behalf." So Paul made a hand gesture to signal his beginning and started his defense. **2.** "King Agrippa, I feel fortunate to stand before you today and defend myself against all the accusations (claims of wrongdoing) brought by the Jews. **3.** I am especially glad, knowing that you are very familiar with Jewish customs (traditional practices) and controversies (disputes). So, I ask you to listen to me patiently. **4.** All the Jews know how I have lived my life from childhood, both in my homeland and in Jerusalem. **5.** They have known me for a long time and can confirm—if they are willing—that I followed the strictest group (sect) of our faith, living as a Pharisee. **6.** Now I am on trial because I have hope in what God promised to our ancestors. **7.** This is the promise that our twelve tribes (the descendants of Israel's twelve sons) long to see fulfilled, as they serve God with dedication night and day. King Agrippa, it is for this hope that the Jews accuse me. **8.** Why should it seem unbelievable to any of you that God raises the dead? **9.** I once thought it was my duty

to oppose the name of Jesus of Nazareth as strongly as I could. **10.** And that is exactly what I did in Jerusalem. With the authority of the chief priests, I imprisoned many of the Lord's people, and I cast my vote for their death when they were sentenced. **11.** Time and again, I went from synagogue (Jewish place of worship) to synagogue, punishing them and trying to force them to blaspheme (speak against God). My desire to persecute (harm or harass) them was so intense that I even pursued them to foreign cities. **12.** "On one of these trips to Damascus, I was traveling with authority and orders from the chief priests. **13.** Around noon, King Agrippa, I saw a light from heaven, brighter than the sun, shining all around me and my companions. **14.** We all fell to the ground, and I heard a voice speaking to me in Aramaic (an ancient language spoken in the region): 'Saul, Saul, why are you persecuting me? It is hard for you to kick against the goads (a phrase meaning to resist direction or guidance).' **15.** "I asked, 'Who are you, Lord?' And the Lord replied, 'I am Jesus, whom you are persecuting. **16.** Now stand up, for I have appeared to you to appoint (assign) you as a servant and a witness to what you have seen and will see of me. **17.** I will protect you from your people and from the Gentiles (non-Jews). I am sending you to them **18.** to open their eyes and turn them from darkness to light and from Satan's power to God, so they may receive forgiveness (pardon) for their sins and a place among those set apart (sanctified) by faith in me.' **19.** "So, King Agrippa, I did not disobey this heavenly vision. **20.** First, I preached to those in Damascus, then to people in Jerusalem, throughout Judea, and to the Gentiles, that they should repent (turn away from wrongdoing), turn to God, and show their repentance through their actions. **21.** This is why some Jews seized me in the temple and tried to kill me. **22.** But to this very day, God has helped me, and so I stand here testifying (speaking truthfully) to all, both those in humble positions and those in high positions. I am saying nothing beyond what the prophets and Moses said would happen— **23.** that the Messiah would suffer, and, as the first to rise from the dead, would bring light (guidance and truth) to both our people and the Gentiles." **24.** At this point, Festus interrupted, shouting, "Paul, you're out of your mind! Your great learning is making you insane!" **25.** Paul replied, "I am not insane, most excellent Festus. What I am saying is both true and reasonable. **26.** The king is familiar with these things, and I can speak openly to him. I am certain that none of this has escaped his notice, for it was not done in secret. **27.** King Agrippa, do you believe the prophets? I know you do." **28.** Agrippa replied, "Do you think that in such a short time you can convince me to become a Christian?" **29.** Paul said, "Whether it takes a short time or a long time, I pray to God that not only you but all who are listening to me today may become as I am—except for these chains." **30.** The king, the governor, Bernice, and everyone present stood up. **31.** After leaving the room, they spoke among themselves, saying, "This man has done nothing to deserve death or imprisonment." **32.** Agrippa then said to Festus, "This man could have been released if he had not appealed (made a formal request) to Caesar."

Chapter 27

1. It was finally decided that we would set sail for Italy. Paul, along with other prisoners, was placed in the care of a centurion (Roman officer) named Julius, who was part of the Imperial Regiment (a military unit serving the Roman Empire). **2.** We boarded a ship from Adramyttium that was set to travel along the coast of the province of Asia, and we departed. Aristarchus, a Macedonian from Thessalonica, joined us. **3.** The next day, we stopped in Sidon, and Julius, being kind to Paul, allowed him to visit his friends there so they could help him with any needs. **4.** From Sidon, we continued, but because the winds were against us, we sailed close to the island of Cyprus, where we would be shielded (to the lee) from the strong winds. **5.** After crossing the open sea off the coasts of Cilicia and Pamphylia, we arrived at Myra in the region of Lycia. **6.** In Myra, the centurion found an Alexandrian ship heading for Italy, and he had us board it. **7.** For many days, we made little progress, struggling to reach the area near Cnidus. When the wind didn't allow us to stay on course, we sailed along the lee of Crete, near a place called Salmone. **8.** With difficulty, we moved along the coastline until we reached a place called Fair Havens, close to the town of Lasea. **9.** We had already lost a lot of time, and by then, sailing had become risky because it was after the Day of Atonement (a holy Jewish day, usually in autumn, after which sea travel was considered dangerous). So, Paul warned them, **10.** "Men, I see that this journey will bring serious disaster and heavy loss, not only to the ship and cargo but possibly to our lives." **11.** But the centurion, instead of listening to Paul, followed the advice of the pilot (the ship's navigator) and the ship's owner. **12.** Since the harbor was not ideal for spending the winter, most of them decided to continue, hoping to reach Phoenix, a better harbor on Crete that faced southwest and northwest, to wait out the winter there. **13.** When a gentle south wind started to blow, they thought this was their chance, so they lifted anchor and sailed along the shore of Crete. **14.** But not long after, a powerful windstorm, known as the Northeaster, blew down from the island. **15.** The ship was caught by the storm and could not turn into the wind, so we had to let it be driven along by the storm. **16.** As we passed close to a small island called Cauda, we could barely secure the lifeboat. **17.** The men managed to hoist the lifeboat aboard. Then they passed ropes under the ship to reinforce it (to keep it from breaking apart). Worried about running aground on the sandbars of Syrtis (shallow areas with sandbanks), they lowered the sea anchor and let the ship be carried along by the storm. **18.** The storm battered us severely, and the next day they started throwing cargo overboard to lighten the ship. **19.** By the third day, they even threw the ship's tackle (heavy equipment) overboard with their own hands. **20.** For many days, we could see neither the sun nor the stars, and the storm continued with such fury that we finally lost all hope of survival. **21.** After going without food for a long time, Paul stood up and addressed the men: "Men, you should have listened to my advice not to sail from Crete, and you could have avoided this damage and loss. **22.** But now, I urge you to keep up your courage, for none of you will lose your lives; only the ship will be destroyed. **23.** Last night, an angel (messenger from God) of the God to whom I belong and whom I serve stood beside me **24.** and said, 'Do not be afraid, Paul. You must stand trial before Caesar, and God has graciously (kindly) granted safety to everyone sailing with you.' **25.** So, keep up your courage, men, for I trust that it will happen exactly as I was told. **26.** But we will have to run aground on some island." **27.** On the fourteenth night, we were still being driven across the Adriatic Sea, when around midnight, the sailors sensed that we were approaching land. **28.** They took soundings (measured the depth of the water) and found it to be 120 feet deep. A little later, they measured again and found it was 90 feet deep. **29.** Fearing we would be smashed against the rocks, they dropped four anchors from the back of the ship and prayed for daylight to come. **30.** Some of the sailors tried to escape from the ship by lowering the lifeboat, pretending they were going to set more anchors from the front (bow). **31.** But Paul said to the centurion and the soldiers, "Unless these men stay with the ship, you will not be saved." **32.** So the soldiers cut the ropes holding the lifeboat and let it drift away. **33.** Just before dawn, Paul urged everyone to eat, saying, "For fourteen days, you have been in constant suspense and haven't eaten anything. **34.** Now I urge you to eat something—you need it to survive. Not a single hair on your heads will be lost." **35.** After saying this, he took some bread, gave thanks to God in front of everyone, broke it, and began to eat. **36.** They were all encouraged and ate some food themselves. **37.** In total, there were 276 people on board. **38.** When they had eaten all they wanted, they threw the remaining grain into the sea to lighten the ship. **39.** At daylight, they saw an unfamiliar coastline with a bay and a sandy beach, and they decided to try to run the ship aground there. **40.** They cut the anchors loose and left them in the sea, untied the ropes holding the rudders (steering parts), raised the front sail, and headed toward the beach. **41.** But the ship hit a sandbar and ran aground. The front of the ship stuck firmly and wouldn't move, while the back of the ship was broken to pieces by the force of the waves. **42.** The soldiers planned to kill the prisoners to prevent any of them from swimming away and escaping. **43.** But the centurion, wanting to save Paul's life, stopped them and ordered those who could swim to jump overboard and reach the shore first. **44.** The rest followed, using planks or pieces of the ship to float. In this way, everyone safely reached land.

Chapter 28

1. Once we safely reached the reinforcement, we discovered that the islet was called Malta. **2.** The islanders showed us remarkable kindness. They erected a fire and ate us all because it was raining and cold. **3.** Paul gathered a pile of brake (small branches or outgrowths), and as

he put it on the fire, a serpent (a poisonous snake), driven out by the heat, latched onto his hand. **4.** When the islanders saw the snake hanging from his hand, they said to each other, "This man must be a killer; indeed, though he escaped from the ocean, the goddess Justice (a Roman deity representing fairness and judgment) has not allowed him to live." **5.** But Paul shook the snake off into the fire and suffered no ill goods (no detriment). **6.** The people anticipated him to swell up or suddenly fall dead but after staying a long time and seeing nothing unusual be to him, they changed their minds and said he was a god. **7.** hard there was an estate (large piece of property) belonging to Publius, the principal functionary of the islet. He ate us into his home and freehandedly hosted us for three days. **8.** Publius' father was bedridden, suffering from fever and dysentery (a severe intestinal infection). Paul went in to see him, and after soliciting, he laid his hands on him and healed him. **9.** When this happed, the rest of the sick on the islet came and were also healed. **10.** The islanders recognized us in numerous ways, and when we were ready to sail, they supplied us with everything we demanded. **11.** After three months, we set passage on a boat that had spent the downtime on the islet. It was an Alexandrian boat (a boat from Alexandria, Egypt) with the statuette (a sculpted decoration on the front of the boat) of the binary gods Castor and Pollux (Roman gods, believed to cover mariners). **12.** We stopped at Syracuse and stayed there for three days. **13.** From there, we sailed to Rhegium. The following day, a south wind (a favorable wind direction) started, and the day after that, we arrived at Puteoli. **14.** In Puteoli, we set up some religionists (sisters and sisters in faith) who invited us to stay with them for a week. And so, we came to Rome. **15.** The religionists there had heard of our appearance, and they traveled as far as the Forum of Appius and the Three Taverns (meeting places along the way to Rome) to hail us. Seeing them, Paul thanked God and was encouraged. **16.** When we reached Rome, Paul was allowed to live by himself, though he was guarded by a dogface. **17.** Three days latterly, Paul called together the original Jewish leaders. When they gathered, Paul said to them, "My sisters, indeed though I've done nothing against our people or the customs (traditions) of our ancestors, I was arrested in Jerusalem and handed over to the Romans. **18.** They examined me and wanted to release me, as I wasn't shamefaced of any crime meritorious death. **19.** But when the Jewish leaders expostulated, I had to appeal to Caesar (the Roman emperor). I didn't intend to bring any charges against my own people. **20.** This is why I asked to see you and speak with you. It's because of the stopgap of Israel (the long-awaited Messiah) that I'm bound with this chain." **21.** They replied, "We haven't entered any letters from Judea about you, and none of our people who have come from there have said anything bad about you. **22.** But we're interested in hearing your views, for we know that people far and wide are speaking against this side (group of followers of Jesus)." **23.** They set a day to meet Paul, and numerous further came to the place where he was staying. From morning until evening, he explained to them about the area of God. Using the Law of Moses and the Prophets (Jewish Holy Writ), he tried to move them about Jesus. **24.** Some were converted by his words, but others didn't believe. **25.** They dissented among themselves and began to leave after Paul's final statement: **26.** "The Holy Spirit spoke actually to your ancestors when he said through Isaiah the prophet **27.** 'Go to this people and say, "You'll always hear but noway understand; you'll always see but noway perceive (comprehend)." **28.** For this people's heart has come calloused (hardened); they hardly hear with their cognizance, and they've closed their eyes. else, they might see with their eyes, hear with their cognizance, understand with their hearts, and turn, and I would heal them.' **29.** thus, I want you to know that God's deliverance has been transferred to the Heathens (non-Jewish people), and they will hear!" **30.** For two whole times, Paul stayed in his own rented house and ate all who came to see him. **31.** He placarded (tutored) the area of God and tutored about the Lord Jesus Christ with complete confidence and without restriction.

53 – Romans

Chapter 1

1. Paul, a servant (someone who serves) of Jesus Christ, called to be an apostle (one sent on a mission), set apart (chosen for a special purpose) for God's gospel (good news), **2.** promised long ago through His prophets (messengers) in the Scriptures (sacred writings), **3.**

concerning Jesus Christ, born of David's line (descendants), 4. declared the Son of God by the Holy Spirit through His resurrection (coming back to life). 5. Through Him, we have received grace (unearned favor) and apostleship (being sent with authority) for obedience (following commands) among all nations for His name, 6. including you who are called (invited) by Jesus Christ. 7. To all in Rome, beloved (loved) of God, called to be saints (followers of Christ): Grace and peace to you from God our Father and the Lord Jesus Christ. 8. I thank God for your faith, known throughout the world. 9. God is my witness (one who can testify), whom I serve (worship) with my spirit (inner being) in preaching (teaching) the gospel, remembering you in my prayers, 10. asking that by God's will (purpose) I might visit you. 11. I long (really desire) to share a spiritual (related to the Spirit) gift to strengthen (make firm) you, 12. so we may be encouraged (built up) together by our faith. 13. I've planned to visit you but was prevented (stopped), seeking fruit (good results) among you as among other Gentiles (non-Jews). 14. I am obligated (duty-bound) to Greeks (those from Greek culture) and non-Greeks (those outside Greek culture), to the wise (knowledgeable) and foolish (lacking wisdom). 15. I am eager (excited) to preach (share the message) the gospel to you in Rome. 16. I am not ashamed (embarrassed) of the gospel, for it is the power (great strength) of God for salvation (rescue) to all who believe, 17. revealing God's righteousness (being right with God) from faith to faith, as it is written, "The righteous will live by faith." 18. The wrath (anger) of God is revealed (shown) against all ungodliness (lack of worship of God) and wickedness (evil), 19. since what may be known of God is clear (plain) to them, 20. for His eternal (forever) power and nature (character) are understood through creation (the world), leaving them without excuse (unable to explain). 21. Though they knew God, they did not glorify (honor) Him or give thanks, and their thinking became futile (useless), 22. claiming to be wise, they became fools (lacking wisdom). 23. They exchanged (switched) the glory (honor) of God for images (pictures or statues) of man and animals. 24. God gave them over (let them go) to sinful (wrong) desires, 25. exchanging (trading) truth for a lie, worshiping creation rather than the Creator. 26. God gave them over to shameful (disgraceful) lusts (strong desires), 27. men with men committing shameful acts, receiving their due penalty (punishment). 28. God gave them over to a depraved (corrupted) mind (thinking), doing things that shouldn't be done. 29. They are filled with all kinds of wickedness (evil): envy (jealousy), murder (killing), strife (fighting), deceit (lying), and malice (desire to hurt others). 30. They are gossips (spreading rumors), malicious (evil-minded), violent (aggressive), proud (arrogant), boastful (showing off), inventing evil, disobedient to parents, 31. without understanding (wisdom), loyalty, love, or mercy (kindness). 32. Although they know God's judgment (decision) that those who do these things deserve death, they continue and approve (agree with) of others who do the same.

Chapter 2

1. You have no reason, O person who judges others, for when you judge another, you condemn yourself, because you do the veritably same effects. 2. But we know that God's judgment is grounded on verity against those who do similar effects. 3. Do you suppose, O person who judges those who do these effects and do the same, that you'll escape God's judgment? 4. Or do you take smoothly His great kindness (His virtuousness), tolerance (His capability to stay without wrathfulness), and amenability to forgive, not realizing that God's kindness leads you to repentance (a change of heart and mind)? 5. But because of your intransigence (turndown to change) and unashamed (unintentional to lament or change) heart, you're storing up wrath (wrathfulness) for yourself for the day of God's wrath and disclosure (the meaning) of His righteous judgment. 6. God will repay each person according to their deeds 7. Eternal life will be given to those who, by patiently (with perseverance) doing good, seek for glory (honor), honor, and eternity (life that lasts ever); 8. But for those who are tone-centered (concentrated on themselves) and reject the verity, but follow wrong, there will be wrathfulness and wrath, 9. Trouble (torture) and torture (pain or suffering) will come upon every soul of those who do wrong, first to the Jew, and also to the Greek (non-Jew); 10. But for those who do good, there will be glory, honor, and peace, first to the Jew, and also to the Greek. 11. For God doesn't show favoritism (partiality or bias). 12. Those who stray without the law will

corrupt without the law, and those who stray under the law will be judged by the law. 13. It's not enough just to hear the law; those who observe (follow) the law will be justified (declared righteous) in God's eyes. 14. When Heathens (non-Jews), who don't have the law, do by nature (naturally) what the law requires, they come a law to themselves, 15. Their heart (inner sense of right and wrong) bears substantiation, either criminating or defending them. 16. On the day when God judges the secrets (hidden effects) of all people through Jesus Christ, as I've placarded in my philosophy (good news). 17. You, who call yourself a Jew, calculate on the law, and boast in God, 18. You know His will and authorize (agree with) what's excellent (good), being instructed by the law, 19. You're confident that you can guide (educate) the eyeless, be a light to those in darkness, 20. A schoolteacher to the foolish (those who warrant understanding), and a companion to those who need knowledge (understanding) and verity. 21. But you, who educate others, do you not educate yourself? You, who say" Don't steal," do you steal? 22. You, who say" Don't commit infidelity," do you commit infidelity? You, who detest icons, do you burglarize tabernacles? 23. You, who boast (vapor) in the law, dishonor God by breaking the law. 24. As it's written," The name of God is cursed (disrespected) among the Heathens because of you." 25. Circumcision is precious if you observe the law; but if you break the law, your circumcision becomes like uncircumcision (not circumcised). 26. So, if an uncircumcised man follows the law, won't his uncircumcision be counted as circumcision? 27. And won't the uncircumcised man, if he obeys the law, condemn (judge) you, who, indeed though you have the law and circumcision, break the law? 28. A true Jew isn't one who's outwardly (on the outside) circumcised, nor is circumcision just a physical (fleshly) act. 29. A true Jew is one inwardly (in the heart), and true circumcision is of the heart, in the Spirit (Holy Spirit), not just the letter (the spoken law). Such a person's praise comes from God, not from people.

Chapter 3

1. What benefit does circumcision (removal of the foreskin) bring? 2. Much, as the Jews were entrusted (given responsibility) with God's word. 3. But does some unbelief (lack of faith) cancel God's faithfulness (trustworthiness)? 4. No, let God be true, but every human a liar, as it is written: "So that You may be justified (declared righteous) when You speak." 5. If our unrighteousness (wrongdoing) shows God's righteousness (rightness), is He unjust (unfair) in bringing wrath (anger)? 6. Certainly not! How else would God judge (hold accountable) the world? 7. If my lie shows God's truth, why am I still judged (found guilty) as a sinner? 8. Should we say, "Let us do evil (wrong actions) for good"? Their condemnation (punishment) is deserved. 9. Are we better than others? No, both Jews and Gentiles (non-Jews) are under sin. 10. As it is written: "None are righteous (morally right), not even one." 11. No one understands (comprehends) or seeks God. 12. All have turned aside (rejected God); none do good. 13. "Their throats are open graves (decaying and evil); they practice deceit (dishonesty)." 14. "Their mouths are full of cursing (swearing) and bitterness (anger)." 15. "Their feet are quick to shed blood (kill)." 16. Destruction (ruin) and misery (suffering) mark their ways. 17. They do not know peace (wholeness). 18. "There is no fear (respect) of God before their eyes." 19. Whatever the law says, it speaks to those under it, so the whole world is accountable (responsible) to God. 20. No one will be declared righteous (found innocent) by the law; the law makes us aware (conscious) of sin (wrongdoing). 21. But now, the righteousness of God apart from the law has been revealed (shown), testified (witnessed) by the Law and the Prophets. 22. This righteousness comes through faith (trust) in Jesus Christ to all who believe. 23. All have sinned (done wrong) and fall short (fail) of God's glory, 24. and all are justified (declared righteous) freely by His grace (unearned favor) through Jesus. 25. God presented Christ as a sacrifice (atoning sacrifice) to demonstrate His righteousness, having passed over previous sins. 26. He did this to be just (fair) and the one who justifies (declares innocent) those who have faith (trust) in Jesus. 27. Where is boasting (pride)? It is excluded (removed). 28. A person is justified by faith, not by works (actions) of the law. 29. Is God only the God of Jews? He is also the God of Gentiles. 30. There is one God, who justifies (declares righteous) both Jews and Gentiles through faith. 31.

Do we nullify (cancel) the law through faith? No, we uphold (support) the law.

Chapter 4

1. What can we say about Abraham, our forefather, in terms of the flesh (human effort)? 2. If Abraham was justified (declared righteous) by works, he would have reason to boast, but not before God. 3. What does the Scripture (holy writings) say? "Abraham believed God, and it was credited (counted) to him as righteousness." 4. To the one who works, their wages are earned, not a gift. 5. But to the one who doesn't work, but trusts (believes) in God who justifies the ungodly (not righteous), their faith is credited (counted) as righteousness. 6. Just as David speaks of the blessedness (happiness) of the one whom God credits righteousness apart from works 7. "Blessed are those whose wrongdoings (sins) are forgiven and whose sins are covered (hidden); 8. Blessed is the one whose sin the Lord will not count (impute) against them." 9. Does this blessing come only to the circumcised (who have undergone the ritual of circumcision), or also to the uncircumcised (those who have not)? We say faith was credited to Abraham as righteousness. 10. When was it credited to him? Was it before or after his circumcision? Not after, but before. 11. He received circumcision as a sign, a seal (mark) of the righteousness (right standing) he had by faith (belief) while still uncircumcised, so that he would be the father of all who believe, even if they are not circumcised, so righteousness could be credited to them too. 12. And he is also the father (originator) of the circumcised (those who have been circumcised), not only for those who are circumcised, but for those who follow (imitate) in the steps of Abraham's faith before his circumcision. 13. The promise (assurance) that Abraham would be the heir (inheritor) of the world didn't come through the law (rules), but through the of faith (trust). 14. If the promise (assurance) came through the law, faith (trust) would be meaningless, and the promise nullified (made void), 15. because the law brings wrath, and where there is no law, there is no transgression (breaking of the law). 16. Therefore, it depends on faith (trust), so that it can be by grace (God's unearned favor) and guaranteed to all Abraham's descendants—not only to those who are of the law, but also to those who share (have) Abraham's faith. 17. As it is written, "I have made you a father of many nations." He believed in God, who gives life to the dead and calls into existence (creates) what does not exist. 18. Against all hope (expectation), Abraham believed in hope (in the possibility), becoming the father of many nations, as God had promised: "So shall your descendants be." 19. Without weakening in faith, he didn't consider (think about) his own body, now as good as dead (unable to have children, because he was about 100), or Sarah's dead womb (unable to have children). 20. He didn't God's promise through unbelief (lack of faith) but was strengthened (made strong) in faith, giving glory (honor) to God, 21. being fully convinced (sure) that God could fulfill what He had promised. 22. And this faith (trust) was credited (counted) to him as righteousness. 23. The Scripture didn't say this for Abraham's sake alone, 24. but also for us. It will be credited (counted) to us who believe (trust) in the God who raised Jesus our Lord from the dead, 25. who was delivered (given up) for our sins and raised (brought back to life) for our justification (being declared right with God).

Chapter 5

1. Since we are made right with God through faith, we have peace with Him through our Lord Jesus Christ. 2. Through Jesus, we have access to God's grace (unmerited favor) by faith, and we rejoice in the hope of God's glory. 3. Not only that, but we also take pride in our troubles, knowing that troubles produce perseverance (endurance). 4. Perseverance leads to character (proven strength), and character leads to hope. 5. This hope does not disappoint, because God's love has been poured into our hearts through the Holy Spirit (God's presence). 6. When we were powerless (unable to save ourselves), at the right time, Christ died for the ungodly (those who are against God). 7. Rarely would someone die for a righteous person, though for a good person, someone might dare to die. 8. But God shows His love in this: while we were still sinners (those who miss God's mark), Christ died for us. 9. Now that we are made right with God by His blood (Jesus' sacrifice), we will be saved from judgment (God's anger) through Him. 10. If, when we were enemies (opposed to God), we were reconciled (restored to friendship) to God through the death of His Son, much more, now that we are reconciled, we will be saved by His life. 11. And not only that, we rejoice in God through our Lord Jesus Christ, through whom we have received reconciliation. 12. Just as sin entered the world through one man, and death through sin, death spread to all because all sinned. 13. (Sin existed before the law, but it isn't counted where there is no law.) 14. Death reigned (ruled as king) from Adam to Moses (the leader who brought the law), even over those who didn't sin as Adam did, who is a symbol (picture) of Jesus. 15. But the grace (unearned favor) of God is not like the offense (sin). If one man's sin caused many to die, much more the grace of God and the gift of one man, Jesus Christ, overflowed to many. 16. The gift is not like the judgment (decision) that came from one sin. Judgment led to condemnation (being declared guilty), but the gift, after many sins, brings justification (being made right with God). 17. If one man's sin caused death to reign, much more will those who receive God's grace and the gift of righteousness (right standing with God) reign in life through Jesus Christ. 18. Just as one man's sin brought judgment to all, one righteous act (right deed) brings the free gift of righteousness and eternal life. 19. Just as by one man's disobedience (failure to obey) many became sinners, so by one man's obedience, many will be made righteous. 20. The law was given so that sin might increase, but where sin increased, grace (God's kindness) increased even more. 21. So that, as sin reigned in death, grace might reign through righteousness, leading to eternal life through Jesus Christ our Lord.

Chapter 6

1. What shall we embrace additionally? Should we retain to stray (sin) so that grace (God's unearned favor) might also increase? 2. No! How are we able to, who died to sin (unethical nature), live in it any longer? 3. Don't you understand that everyone who has been baptized (immersed) into Christ Jesus has been baptized into His death? 4. We were buried with Him through baptism, so that, just as Christ was raised from the dead by the glory (power) of the Father, we may also live a new life. 5. If we have been united with Him in His death, we will certainly also be united with Him in His resurrection (rejuvenation). 6. We know that our old selves (dominated by sin) were crucified with Him, so that we no longer live as slaves to sin. 7. Anyone who has died is free from sin. 8. Now if we died with Christ, we believe we will also live with Him. 9. We know that Christ, raised from the dead, will never die again; death no longer has mastery over Him. 10. The death He died, He died to sin once for all; but the life He lives, He lives to God. 11. In the same way, consider yourselves dead to sin but alive to God in Christ Jesus. 12. Therefore, do not let sin reign (rule) in your mortal bodies so that you obey its evil desires. 13. Do not offer any part of yourselves to sin as an instrument of wickedness (wrong), but rather offer yourselves to God as those who have been brought from death to life, and offer every part of yourselves to Him as instruments of righteousness. 14. For sin shall not have mastery over you, because you are not under the law but under grace (God's unearned favor). 15. What then? Shall we sin because we are not under the law but under grace? By no means! 16. Don't you know that when you offer yourselves to someone as obedient slaves, you are slaves of the one you obey—whether you are slaves to sin, which leads to death, or to obedience, which leads to righteousness? 17. But thanks be to God that, though you used to be slaves to sin, you have come to obey from your heart the pattern of teaching that has now claimed your allegiance. 18. You have been set free from sin and have become slaves to righteousness. 19. I am using an example (illustration) from everyday life because of your human limitations. Just as you used to offer yourselves as slaves to impurity (moral corruption) and to ever-increasing wickedness (lawlessness), so now offer yourselves as slaves to righteousness leading to holiness (godliness). 20. When you were slaves to sin, you were free from the control of righteousness. 21. What benefit did you reap at that time from the things you are now ashamed of? Those things result in death. 22. But now that you have been set free from sin and have become slaves to God, the benefit you reap leads to holiness (godliness), and the result is eternal life. 23. For the wages (payment) of sin is death, but the gift of God is eternal life in Christ Jesus our Lord.

Chapter 7

1 Do you not know, brothers and sisters, that the law has authority (power) over a person as long as they are alive? 2 A married woman is

bound (obligated) to her husband as long as he lives. But if he dies, she is freed (released) from that law. 3 If she marries another while her husband is alive, she is an adulteress. But if he dies, she is free to remarry without guilt. 4 Likewise, you have died (through Christ) to the law, so that you may belong to Him who was raised (came back to life), to bear fruit (good works) for God. 5 When we were in the flesh (human nature), sinful desires stirred by the law worked in us, leading to death. 6 But now, we have been freed (released) from the law, having died to what once bound us, so that we may serve (worship) in the new way of the Spirit, not the old written law. 7 Is the law sinful? Certainly not! I would not have known sin except through the law. I would not have known to covet (desire wrong things) if the law hadn't said, "You shall not covet." 8 But sin, using the commandment, produced (caused) in me all kinds of sinful desires. Apart from the law, sin is dead (inactive). 9 I was once alive apart (separate) from the law, but when the commandment came, sin came to life, and I died (spiritually). 10 The commandment meant to bring life actually brought death. 11 For sin, taking the opportunity from the commandment, deceived (misled) me, and through it killed me (spiritually). 12 The law is holy (set apart), and the commandment is holy, righteous (right), and good. 13 Did that which is good bring death to me? No! It was sin, so that it might be revealed as sin, producing death in me through what is good, making sin exceedingly sinful. 14 We know the law is spiritual (from the Spirit), but I am unspiritual (sinful), sold as a slave (controlled) by sin. 15 I do not understand (comprehend) what I do. For what I want to do, I do not, but what I hate (despise), I do. 16 If I do what I don't want to do, I agree the law is good (right). 17 It is no longer I who do it, but sin that dwells (lives) in me. 18 I know nothing good dwells in me, that is, in my sinful nature (flesh). I desire (wish) to do good but cannot carry it out. 19 The good I want to do, I do not; the evil I do not want to do, I keep on doing. 20 If I do what I don't want to do, it is no longer I who do it, but sin living (dwelling) in me. 21 I find this law: Though I want to do good, evil is right there with me. 22 In my inner being (mind and heart) I delight (take pleasure) in God's law; 23 But I see another law at work in my body, waging war (fighting) against my mind and making me a prisoner (captured) of the law of sin within my body. 24 What a wretched (miserable) man I am! Who will rescue (save) me from this body (sinful nature) subject (controlled) to death? 25 Thanks be to God, who delivers (saves) me through Jesus Christ our Lord! So then, I in my mind am a servant (slave) to God's law, but in my sinful nature (flesh) a servant to the law of sin.

Chapter 8

1. There is no condemnation (guilt or judgment) for those in Christ Jesus, who live according to the Spirit, not the flesh (sinful human nature). 2. The law of the Spirit, which gives life in Christ, has freed me from the law of sin and death. 3. What the law could not do due to human weakness, God did by sending His Son in human form to condemn sin. 4. This allows the righteous requirement (standard of God's law) to be fulfilled in us, who live according to the Spirit. 5. Those who live by the flesh focus on the flesh, but those who live by the Spirit focus on the Spirit. 6. The fleshly (sinful) mind leads to death, but the spiritual mind leads to life and peace. 7. The fleshly mind is hostile (an enemy) to God and cannot submit to His law. 8. Those in the flesh cannot please God. 9. But you are in the Spirit, if God's Spirit lives in you; without the Spirit of Christ, you do not belong to Him. 10. If Christ is in you, your body is dead due to sin, but the Spirit gives life through righteousness (being made right with God). 11. If God's Spirit, who raised Jesus, lives in you, He will give life to your mortal (subject to death) bodies through His Spirit. 12. We are obligated (have a duty) not to live according to the flesh, 13. for living by the flesh leads to death, but by the Spirit, we can put to death the deeds of the body and live. 14. Those led by the Spirit are God's children. 15. You received the Spirit of adoption (becoming part of God's family), by whom we cry, "Abba, Father" (an intimate term for God). 16. The Spirit confirms (testifies) with our spirit that we are God's children. 17. If we are children, we are heirs (inheritors) with Christ, sharing in His sufferings and glory. 18. The sufferings of this life are nothing compared to the glory that will be revealed in us. 19. Creation eagerly waits for the revealing of God's children. 20. Creation was subjected to futility (emptiness or frustration) in hope of being set free from decay into God's glorious freedom. 21. Creation will be liberated (freed) from decay and share in the freedom of God's children. 22. Creation has been groaning (suffering deeply) as in labor pains until now. 23. We, who have the Spirit's firstfruits (initial blessings), also groan inwardly as we await the redemption (deliverance) of our bodies. 24. We were saved in hope but hope that is seen is not hope. 25. If we hope for what we do not yet see, we wait for it patiently. 26. The Spirit helps in our weaknesses (areas of struggle), interceding (pleading) for us with groans too deep for words. 27. God knows the Spirit's mind, as He intercedes for the saints (believers) according to God's will. 28. We know that all things work together for good for those who love God and are called according to His purpose (plan). 29. Those God foreknew (knew in advance), He predestined (chose beforehand) to be conformed (shaped) to the image of His Son, that He might be the firstborn (preeminent one) among many. 30. Those God predestined, He called, justified (made right), and glorified (lifted in honor). 31. If God is for us, who can be against us? 32. He did not spare His Son but gave Him for us—how will He not also give us all things? 33. Who can accuse God's chosen ones? It is God who justifies. 34. Who condemns? Christ, who died and rose, is at God's right hand, interceding for us. 35. Who can separate us from Christ's love? Trouble, hardship (difficulty), persecution (hostility), hunger, danger, or violence? 36. As it is written: "For Your sake we are killed all day; we are counted as sheep for slaughter." 37. Yet, in all these, we are more than conquerors (victorious) through Him who loved us. 38. I am convinced that neither death, life, angels, rulers, nor anything else can separate us from God's love in Christ. 39. Neither height, depth, nor anything else in creation can separate us from the love of God in Christ Jesus our Lord.

Chapter 9

1. I speak actually in Christ, my heart (inner sense of right and wrong), guided by the Holy Spirit, confirms. 2. I've deep anguish (great sadness) and constant grief in my heart. 3. I would be separated from Christ if it could profit my fellow Israelites, my people by strain. 4. They're Israelites, to whom belong relinquishment (being chosen by God), the glory (manifest presence of God), covenants (godly agreements), the law, deification, and pledges. 5. From them came the papas (fathers), and from them, Christ was born in the meat, who's God over each, ever blessed. Amen. 6. Not all descended from Israel truly belong to Israel. 7. Nor are all Abraham's descendants his children, but "Through Isaac your descendants will be counted." 8. This shows physical descent doesn't make someone a child of God; it's the children of the pledge (religionists chosen by God) who are counted. 9. The pledge stated, "At the appointed time I'll return, and Sarah will have a son." 10. Rebecca conceived by Isaac, 11. before the halves had done anything good or bad, so that God's purpose in election (godly choice) might stand, not by deeds but by God's call (assignation). 12. She was told, "The aged will serve the youngish." 13. As it's written, "Jacob I loved, but Esau I abominated" (expressing God's choice). 14. Is there any injustice (unfairness) with God? clearly not! 15. He told Moses, "I'll have mercy on whom I've mercy, and compassion on whom I've compassion." 16. It depends not on mortal desire (want) or trouble but on God's mercy. 17. Book says of Pharaoh, "I raised you up to display my power and make my name known." 18. God shows mercy to whom He wills and hardens (makes stubborn) whom He wills. 19. You may ask, "Why does God find fault? Who can repel His will" 20. But who are you, a bare mortal, to question God? Can the thing formed say to the maker, "Why did you make me like this?" 21. The potter (maker) has authority over the complexion to make one vessel (vessel) for honor (special use) and another for dishonor (common use). 22. What if God, wanting to demonstrate His wrath (wrathfulness) and power, drag with great tolerance vessels of wrath (fated for judgment)? 23. He did this to make the riches of His glory known to vessels of mercy (those chosen for deliverance), prepared in advance for glory, 24. including us whom He has called, from Jews and Heathens(non-Jews). 25. As Hosea said, "I'll call those not My people, 'My people,' and her who wasn't loved, 'Cherished.' 26. And, "In the place where it was said, 'You aren't My people,' they will be called 'children of the living God.'" 27. Isaiah said, "Though Israel's number is as beach of the ocean, only a remnant (small remaining group) will be saved. 28. The Lord will carry out His judgment completely and snappily." 29. As Isaiah said, "Unless the Lord of Sabaoth (Hosts) left us descendants, we'd have come like Sodom and Gomorrah (metropolises destroyed for sin)." 30. Heathens (non-

Jews) who didn't pursue righteousness have attained it by faith (trust in God). **31.** But Israel, who pursued the law, didn't achieve it. **32.** Why? Because they pursued it by workshop (mortal sweats) and not by faith. They stumbled over the stumbling gravestone (cause of rejection). **33.** As written, "Behold, I lay in Zion (Jerusalem) a stumbling gravestone and gemstone of offense, and whoever believes in Him won't be put to shame (disappointed)."

Chapter 10

1. My sisters and sisters, my sincere desire and prayer to God is for the deliverance (deliverance, deliverance from sin) of Israel. **2.** I can swear (substantiation, confirm) that they've great passion for God, but it isn't grounded on true understanding. **3.** They don't fete God's way of making people right with Him and try to produce their own way, failing to submit (give in, observe) to God's way. **4.** Christ is the completion (fulfillment) of the law, bringing righteousness (rightness with God) to everyone who believes. **5.** Moses described the righteousness from the law "The person who does these effects shall live by them." **6.** But the righteousness that comes by faith says, "Don't say in your heart, 'Who'll go up into heaven?'" (meaning, to bring Christ down) **7.** or, "Who'll go down into the ocean (the deep)?" (meaning, to bring Christ back from the dead). **8.** It says, "The word is near you, in your mouth and in your heart" the word of faith we annunciate (declare intimately). **9.** Still, you'll be saved, If you declare (say easily) with your mouth that Jesus is Lord and believe in your heart that God raised Him from the dead. **10.** For with your heart, you believe and are made right (righteous) with God, and with your mouth, you openly declare (make public) your deliverance. **11.** As the Book says, "Anyone who believes in Him will noway be put to shame (lowered, lowered)." **12.** There's no difference between Jew and Greek (non-Jew), for the same Lord is generous (abundant, giving) to all who call upon Him. **13.** For "everyone who calls on the name of the Lord will be saved." **14.** How can they call on Him if they've not believed? How can they believe if they've not heard? And how can they hear unless someone proclaims (preaches) Him? **15.** And how can anyone annunciate Him unless they're transferred? As it's written, "How beautiful are the bases of those who bring good news of peace." **16.** But not all have accepted the philosophy (good news). As Isaiah says, "Lord, who has believed our communication?" **17.** So also, faith (trust and belief in God) comes through hail, and hail comes by the word of God. **18.** But I ask, have they not heard? Indeed they've "Their voice has gone out to all the earth, their words to the ends of the world." **19.** But I ask, did Israel not understand? Moses said, "I'll make you jealous (invidious) by those who aren't a nation and angry by a foolish (ignorant) nation." **20.** Isaiah bravely says, "I was set up by those who didn't seek Me; I came given to those who didn't ask for Me." **21.** But regarding Israel, he says, "All day long I've stretched out My hands to a disobedient (rebellious) and stubborn (resistant) people."

Chapter 11

1. I ask, has God rejected His people? Absolutely not! I'm an Israelite, from the lineage (strain) of Abraham, from the lineage (family group) of Benjamin. **2.** God has not rejected His people whom He knew beforehand (before time). Flash back what Book says about Elijah, how he contended (prayed) with God, saying, **3.** "Lord, they've killed Your prophets and destroyed Your stages, and I alone am left, and they seek my life?" **4.** But what's God's answer?" I've reserved (set away) seven thousand men who haven't bowed to Baal (a false god)." **5.** In the same way, there's a remnant (a small group) moment, chosen by grace (unearned favor). **6.** And if it's by grace, it can not be grounded on workshop (effects done to earn favor); else, grace would no longer be grace. **7.** What also? Israel has not attained (reached) what it was seeking, but the elect (chosen bones) have attained it, and the rest were hardened (made stubborn). **8.** As it's written" God gave them a spirit of torpor (incapability to understand), eyes that can not see and cognizance that can not hear, indeed to this day." **9.** And David says" Let their table (place of aliment) come a snare (trap) and a stumbling block (handicap) and recompense (price) to them. **10.** Let their eyes be darkened (unfit to see) so that they can not see." **11.** Have they stumbled so far as to fall? clearly not! But through their fall, deliverance has come to the Heathens(non-Jews), to make Israel jealous (invidious). **12.** still, how much further will their full restoration mean? **13.** If their fall means riches (blessings) for the world. I speak to

you Heathens. As I'm a backer (runner) to you, I take pride (rejoice) in my ministry, **14.** In the stopgap that I might provoke (inspire) some of my fellow Israelites to covetousness and save some of them. **15.** still, what will their acceptance (accepting God's grace) bring but life from the dead? **16.** If their rejection (turning down) brought conciliation (peace) to the world. However, offered to God) are holy, the whole batch (the rest) is holy, If the first fruits (the first part of the crop). **17.** still, and you, being a wild olive branch (not from Israel), If some branches were broken off. Don't boast over the branches. However, flash back the root supports you, If you do boast. **19.** You may say," The branches were broken off so I could be grafted in." **20.** True. They were broken off because of nonbelief (lack of faith), and you stand by faith. Don't be proud, but fear (respect God). **21.** For if God didn't spare (show mercy to) the natural branches (Israelites), He may not spare you moreover. **22.** Consider both the kindness (virtuousness) and inflexibility (harshness) of God inflexibility to those who fell, but kindness to you, if you continue in His kindness. else, you too will be cut off. **23.** And they, if they don't remain in nonbelief, will be grafted in again, for God is suitable to graft them in again. **24.** still, though a wild olive tree (not part of Israel), were grafted into a cultivated (well-tended) olive tree, If you. I don't want you to be ignorant (ignorant) of this riddle (retired verity), so that you aren't wise in your own opinion Israel has endured a partial hardening (incapability to believe) until the wholeness (absoluteness) of the Heathens has come in. **26.** And in this way, all Israel will be saved, as it's written" The Deliverer (Savior) will come from Zion and turn ungodliness (lack of reverence) down from Jacob (Israel); **27.** And this is My covenant (pledge) with them when I take down their sins." **28.** Concerning the philosophy (good news), they're adversaries for your sake, but as far as election (God's picking) is concerned, they're cherished (loved) because of the papas (Abraham, Isaac, and Jacob). **29.** For the gifts (spiritual blessings) and calling (purpose) of God are irrevocable (cannot be taken back). **30.** Just as you were formerly defiant (refused to observe) to God but now have entered mercy (compassion) because of their defiance, **31.** So they too have now come defiant, so they may admit mercy as a result of the mercy shown to you. **32.** For God has bound all people to defiance so He may have mercy on them all. **33.** Oh, the depth (greatness) of the riches (wealth) both of the wisdom and knowledge of God! How unsearchable (insolvable to completely understand) are His judgments (opinions) and His paths (ways) beyond tracing out (unfit to follow fully)! **34.** "Who has known the mind of the Lord? Or who has been His counselor?" **35.** "Who has ever given to God, that God should repay them?" **36.** For from Him, and through Him, and to Him are all effects. To Him be the glory ever. Amen.

Chapter 12

1. I prompt (encourage) you, sisters and sisters, in view of God's mercy, to offer your bodies as a living immolation, holy and pleasing to God. This is your reasonable service (deification). **2.** Don't conform (follow) to the world, but let your mind be converted (renewed), so you may understand and live out God's perfect will. **3.** Through the grace (undeserved kindness) given to me, I say Don't suppose more largely than you should, but suppose soberly (with tone- control), as God has given each a measure (portion) of faith. **4.** Just as we've numerous corridor in one body, each with its function (purpose), **5.** so in Christ, however numerous, we form one body, and each is a member (part) of one another. **6.** We've different gifts according to the grace (undeserved kindness) given to us. Let us use them If vaticination (God's inspired speech), let it be in proportion (correct quantum) to faith; **7.** still, serve; if tutoring, educate; **8.** if serving. However, encourage; if giving, do so freehandedly (without vacillation); if leading, if encouraging. **9.** Let love be sincere (genuine). detest wrong; cleave (hold tightly) to good. **10.** Be devoted (pious) to one another in love. Honor (value) one another above yourselves. **11.** noway be lazy in zeal (enthusiasm), but be hot (enthusiastic) in spirit, serving the Lord. **12.** Rejoice (be glad) in stopgap, be patient (enduring) in trouble, and continue steadfastly (without giving up) in prayer. **13.** Share with the Lord's people in need. Practice (do regularly) hospitality (drinking others). **14.** Bless (speak good) those who persecute (brutalize) you; bless and don't curse (speak detriment over). **15.** Rejoice with those who rejoice; mourn (feel anguish) with those who mourn. **16.** Live in harmony (peace) with one another. Don't be proud, but associate (spend time) with the humble. Don't be conceited (tone-important). **17**. Don't repay (give back) wrong for wrong. Be careful (aware) to do what's right in everyone's eyes. **18**. still, as far as it depends on you, live at peace with all, If possible. **19**. Don't take vengeance (vengeance), but leave room for God's wrath (wrathfulness), for it's written "revenge is mine, I'll repay (discipline)," says the Lord. **20**. rather, "If your adversary is empty, feed him; if thirsty, give him a drink. By doing this, you'll mound (place) burning coals on his head." **21**. Don't be overcome (defeated) by wrong, but overcome (master) wrong with good

Chapter 13

1. Let every person submit (accept authority) to governing authorities, for all authority comes from God, and those in power are appointed by Him. **2**. Anyone who opposes (resists) authority goes against God's command and will bring judgment (punishment) on themselves. **3**. Rulers are a threat (danger) to those who do evil, but not to those who do good. If you want to avoid fear (anxiety), do good, and you will be praised (commended). **4**. The ruler is God's servant (helper) for your benefit (good). If you do wrong, be afraid, for he does not carry the sword in vain (for no reason); he is God's servant to punish evil. **5**. You must submit (obey) to authority, not only to avoid punishment but also for your conscience (inner sense of right). **6**. You pay taxes (money) because authorities are God's servants, continually attending (working on) this task. **7**. Pay what you owe: taxes to those due, customs (fees) to those due, respect (honor) to those due, and honor (value) to those due. **8**. Owe no one anything except to love one another, for whoever loves others fulfills (completes) the law. **9**. The commandments (rules), "You shall not commit adultery," "You shall not murder," "You shall not steal," "You shall not give false testimony," "You shall not covet" (desire what others have), and any other commandment, are summed up (gathered) in this: "Love your neighbor as yourself." **10**. Love does no harm (hurt) to others; therefore, love is the fulfillment (completion) of the law. **11**. Do this, knowing the time is near, and our salvation (rescue) is closer than when we first believed. **12**. The night is almost over, and the day is near. Let us throw off (rid of) the deeds (actions) of darkness and put on the armor (protection) of light. **13**. Let us behave decently (properly), as in the daylight, not in wild partying, drunkenness (intoxication), immorality (lack of morals), or strife (conflict) and jealousy (resentment). **14**. Clothe yourselves with the Lord Jesus Christ, and do not make provisions (plans) for the flesh (sinful nature) to fulfill its desires.

Chapter 14

1. Drink the weak in faith (belief), but avoid arguments over uncertain matters. **2**. One believes they can eat anything, but the weak only eat vegetables. **3**. Let those who eat not despise those who don't, and vice versa, for God has accepted them. **4**. Who are you to judge another's menial? They stand or fall before their master (God), who can make them stand. **5**. One person values a certain day, another treats all days the same. Each should be induced in their own mind. **6**. The bone who observes a day does so to recognize the Lord, and the bone who eats, eats to recognize the Lord, giving thanks to God. **7**. We don't live or die for ourselves alone. **8**. Still, we live for the Lord; if we die, we die for the Lord. If we live, we belong to the Lord, whether we live or die. **9**. Christ failed, rose, and lives again to be Lord of both the living and the dead. **10**. Why judge your family or show disdain for them? We'll each stand before God's judgment seat. **11**. As it's written "Every knee will bow to me, and every tongue will confess to God." **12**. Each will give an account of themselves to God. **13**. Let us stop judging one another and avoid causing a stumbling block to others. **14**. I'm induced by Christ that nothing is sick in itself, but to those who consider commodity sick, it is. **15**. Still, you aren't acting in love if your family is troubled by what you eat. Don't destroy the bone for whom Christ failed. **16**. Don't let your good be spoken of as wrong. **17**. The area of God is about righteousness (justice), peace, and joy in the Holy Spirit, not eating and drinking. **18**. Anyone who serves Christ in this way is respectable to God and approved by others. **19**. Let us pursue peace and make one another up. **20**. Don't destroy God's work for food. All effects are pure, but it's wrong to eat in a way that causes others to stumble. **21**. It's better not to eat meat or drink wine if it causes your family to fall. **22**. Do you have faith? Keep it between you and God. Blessed is the one who doesn't condemn themselves by their choices. **23**. Those who

misdoubt are condemned if they eat, for their eating isn't from faith, and whatever isn't from faith is sin.

Chapter 15

1. Those who are strong should be patient with the weak (those struggling) and not seek to please themselves. **2**. Each of us should strive to please our neighbor (nearby person) for their good, building them up. **3**. Even Christ did not seek to please Himself. As it is written, "The insults (criticisms) directed at You fell upon Me." **4**. Whatever was written in the past was for our instruction (learning), so through the patience and encouragement (comfort) in the Scriptures (holy writings), we might have hope. **5**. May the God of patience and encouragement help you live in harmony (agreement) with one another, just as Christ Jesus did. **6**. Then, with one heart and voice, you may honor God, the Father of our Lord Jesus Christ. **7**. Accept (welcome) one another, just as Christ accepted you, for the glory (honor) of God. **8**. Jesus Christ became a servant (one who serves) to the Jews to prove God's promises to the patriarchs (founding fathers). **9**. And that the Gentiles (non-Jews) might glorify God for His mercy (compassion), as it is written: "For this reason, I will praise You among the Gentiles and sing to Your name." **10**. Again, it says: "Rejoice, you Gentiles, with His people!" **11**. And again: "Praise the Lord, all you Gentiles, and let all the people praise Him!" **12**. And again, Isaiah says: "The Root (source) of Jesse will rise to rule over the Gentiles; in Him, they will find hope." **13**. May the God of hope fill you with joy and peace as you trust in Him, so you may overflow (abound) with hope through the Holy Spirit's power (strength). **14**. I am confident (sure), my brothers and sisters, that you are full of goodness (moral excellence), filled with knowledge, and able to instruct (teach) one another. **15**. Yet, I've written boldly (confidently) to remind you, because of the grace (undeserved favor) God gave me. **16**. I am a minister (servant) of Jesus Christ to the Gentiles, proclaiming (preaching) the gospel (good news) of God, so that their offering (gift) may be acceptable, sanctified (made holy) by the Holy Spirit. **17**. Therefore, I have reason to boast (be proud) in Christ Jesus for what God has done through me. **18**. I will not boast except what Christ has done through me, in word (speech) and deed (action), to make the Gentiles obedient (follow). **19**. This was accomplished through signs and wonders (extraordinary events), by the Spirit's power, so from Jerusalem to Illyricum (western Roman Empire), I've fully proclaimed (declared) the gospel of Christ. **20**. I aim to preach the gospel where Christ has not been named (heard), so I do not build on someone else's foundation (previous work). **21**. As it is written: "Those who were not told about Him will see, and those who have not heard will understand." **22**. For this reason, I've often been hindered (prevented) from coming to you. **23**. But now, with no further place for me in these areas (regions), and with a desire (longing) for many years to visit you, **24**. I hope to see you when I go to Spain, and to be helped (assisted) on my way there by you, after enjoying (spending time) your company. **25**. But first, I am going to Jerusalem to serve the saints (holy people). **26**. The churches in Macedonia and Achaia were pleased to contribute (give) to the poor saints in Jerusalem. **27**. They were happy to do so, for they owe it to them. If the Gentiles have shared in their spiritual blessings (gifts from God), they should also serve them with material blessings (physical support). **28**. When I've completed this and delivered the contribution, I will travel to you on my way to Spain. **29**. I know that when I come to you, I will come with the full blessing (riches) of Christ's gospel. **30**. I urge (encourage) you, brothers and sisters, by our Lord Jesus Christ and through the Spirit's love, to strive (work hard) together with me in prayer to God for me. **31**. Pray I may be rescued (saved) from the unbelievers (those who do not believe) in Judea, and that my service for Jerusalem may be acceptable to the saints. **32**. Pray I may come to you with joy, by God's will, and be refreshed (rejuvenated) with you. **33**. May the God of peace be with you all. Amen.

Chapter 16

1. I commend Phoebe, a servant (one who serves or ministers) of the church in Cenchrea, **2**. that you receive her in the Lord, and assist her with whatever she needs, for she has been a great help to many, including me. **3**. Greet Priscilla and Aquila, my fellow workers (those who work together) in Christ, **4**. who risked their lives (put their lives in danger) for me. I am grateful to them, and so are all the Gentile (non-

481

Jewish) churches. **5.** Greet the church in their home, and my beloved (dear) Epaenetus, the first to come to Christ in Achaia (a region in Greece). **6.** Greet Mary, who worked hard for us. **7.** Greet Andronicus and Junia, my countrymen (fellow countrymen, fellow Jews) and fellow prisoners (those who suffered imprisonment with me), who are well-known among the apostles (leaders in the early church) and were in Christ before me. **8.** Greet Amplias, my beloved in the Lord. **9.** Greet Urbanus, our fellow worker in Christ, and Stachys, my beloved. **10.** Greet Apelles, who is approved (tested and found trustworthy) in Christ, and those in Aristobulus' household (family or household). **11.** Greet Herodion, my countryman, and those in Narcissus' household who belong to the Lord. **12.** Greet Tryphena and Tryphosa, who labored (worked hard) in the Lord, and Persis, who worked very hard for the Lord. **13.** Greet Rufus, chosen (selected) in the Lord, and his mother, who is like a mother to me. **14.** Greet Asyncritus, Phlegon, Hermas, Patrobas, Hermes, and the brothers (fellow believers) with them. **15.** Greet Philologus and Julia, Nereus and his sister, Olympas, and all the saints (believers) with them. **16.** Greet one another with a holy kiss (a greeting of peace or affection). The churches of Christ greet you. **17.** I urge (strongly advise) you, brothers, to watch out for those who cause divisions (separations) and obstacles (things that hinder or stop) against the teaching you've received, and avoid them. **18.** Such people do not serve Christ, but their own desires (selfish wants), deceiving (misleading) the innocent with smooth talk (deceptive, flattering speech). **19.** Your obedience (willingness to follow) is known to all, and I rejoice in it; but be wise (understanding) in doing good and innocent (pure) regarding evil. **20.** The God of peace will soon crush (defeat completely) Satan under your feet. The grace (unmerited favor) of our Lord Jesus be with you. **21.** Timothy, my fellow worker, and my countrymen Lucius, Jason, and Sosipater greet you. **22.** I, Tertius, who wrote this letter (the epistle), greet you in the Lord. **23.** Gaius, my host (one who provides lodging) and host of the whole church, greets you, as does Erastus, the city treasurer (public official in charge of finances), and Quartus, a brother. **24.** The grace of our Lord Jesus Christ be with you all. **25.** Now to Him who is able to strengthen (make you firm) you through my gospel (good news) and the preaching of Jesus Christ, **26.** in accordance with the revelation (making known) of the mystery (secret plan of God) that was hidden for ages (long periods of time) but is now revealed through the prophetic (foretelling) Scriptures to all nations, **27.** to the only wise (all-knowing) God be glory through Jesus Christ forever. Amen.

54 – Corinthians 1

Chapter 1

1. Paul, called by God to be an apostle (messenger) of Jesus Christ, with our brother Sosthenes, **2.** to the church (community) of God in Corinth, sanctified (made holy, set apart) in Christ Jesus, called to be saints (holy ones), along with all who call on the name of Jesus Christ our Lord: **3.** grace (unearned favor) and peace (inner calm and well-being) to you from God our Father and the Lord Jesus Christ. **4.** I thank God for you, for the grace given to you in Christ Jesus, **5.** enriching (blessing abundantly) you with all speech (ability to speak) and knowledge (understanding), **6.** as the testimony (witness, message) of Christ was confirmed (established) in you, **7.** so that you lack no gift (spiritual abilities), eagerly awaiting the revelation (disclosure, unveiling) of our Lord Jesus Christ, **8.** who will keep you strong (firm, steadfast) to the end, so you may be blameless (without fault) on the day (final judgment day) of Christ. **9.** God is faithful (trustworthy), who called you into fellowship (relationship, communion) with His Son, Jesus Christ our Lord. **10.** I urge (strongly encourage) you, brothers, in the name (authority) of our Lord Jesus Christ, that you speak the same thing and have no divisions (separations, disagreements), but be united (together) in mind (thought) and judgment (decision, opinion). **11.** I've heard from Chloe's household (family or group) that there are quarrels (disagreements) among you. **12.** Some say, "I follow Paul," or "Apollos," or "Cephas" (Peter), or "Christ." **13.** Is Christ divided (separated)? Was Paul crucified (executed) for you? Were you baptized (immersed) in Paul's name? **14.** I thank God I baptized only Crispus and Gaius, **15.** so no one can say I baptized in my name. **16.** I also baptized the household (family) of Stephanas. **17.** Christ did not send me to baptize, but to preach (proclaim) the gospel (good news), not with eloquent (persuasive) words, so the cross wouldn't lose its power. **18.**

The message (teaching) of the cross is foolishness (absurdity) to those perishing (spiritually dying), but to us being saved (rescued), it is God's power. **19.** As it's written, "I will destroy (nullify, bring to nothing) the wisdom (knowledge) of the wise." **20.** Where is the wise (learned person)? Where is the scribe (expert, scholar)? Hasn't God made foolish (ineffective) the wisdom of the world? **21.** In God's wisdom (understanding), the world didn't know Him through wisdom, but He chose to save believers (those who trust in Christ) through the foolishness (absurdity) of the preached (proclaimed) message. **22.** Jews demand signs, Greeks seek wisdom (knowledge, understanding), **23.** but we preach Christ crucified— a stumbling block (offensive, difficult to accept) to Jews and foolishness (absurdity) to Gentiles (non-Jews), **24.** but to those called (chosen, invited), both Jews and Greeks, Christ is the power and wisdom of God. **25.** The foolishness (silliness) of God is wiser than human wisdom, and God's weakness (frailty) is stronger than human strength. **26.** Not many of you were wise by human standards (human understanding), powerful, or of noble birth (high rank or status), **27.** but God chose the foolish and weak things to shame (disgrace, humble) the wise and strong. **28.** He chose the lowly (humble, unimportant) and despised (rejected) to nullify (invalidate, make ineffective) the things that are, **29.** so no one can boast (brag) before Him. **30.** It is because of God that you are in Christ Jesus, who became our wisdom (understanding), righteousness (right standing with God), sanctification (being made holy), and redemption (deliverance, rescue from sin), **31.** so, as it's written, "Let the one who boasts boast in the Lord."

Chapter 2

1. When I came to you, brothers, I did not rely on eloquent speech (fancy or persuasive language) or worldly wisdom (the knowledge people rely on in the world) in proclaiming God's message. **2.** I chose to know nothing among you except Jesus Christ, especially His crucifixion (Jesus' death on the cross). **3.** I came to you in weakness, fear, and trembling (with humility and a sense of vulnerability). **4.** My message and preaching were not in persuasive words (clever speech), but in a demonstration (clear display or proof) of the Spirit's power, **5.** so that your faith (belief or trust) would rest not on human wisdom, but on God's power. **6.** We speak a wisdom for the mature (a deeper understanding for those spiritually mature), but not the wisdom of this age (the common sense or reasoning of the world) or the rulers (leaders or influential people) who are fading away (temporary, soon to pass). **7.** Instead, we speak of God's hidden wisdom (wisdom that was previously unknown or not fully revealed), the wisdom He ordained (planned or chose) before time for our glory, **8.** which none of the rulers of this age (those in power) understood—had they known it, they would not have crucified the Lord of glory (Jesus). **9.** As Scripture says: "No eye has seen, no ear has heard, nor has the human heart (thoughts and desires of people) imagined what God has prepared for those who love Him." **10.** But God has revealed (shown, made known) these things to us through His Spirit (the Holy Spirit), for the Spirit searches everything, even the depths of God (the most profound truths about God). **11.** No one knows the thoughts (inner ideas or plans) of a person except their own spirit (inner self or consciousness), and likewise, no one knows the things of God except the Spirit of God. **12.** We have received the Spirit (the Holy Spirit) not of the world, but the Spirit from God, to understand the gifts (blessings or spiritual truths) He has freely given us. **13.** We speak of these things not with words taught by human wisdom, but by the Spirit, explaining spiritual truths (truths about God and His ways) with spiritual words (words inspired by the Spirit). **14.** The natural person (someone who doesn't have the Spirit or is not spiritually aware) does not accept the things of God's Spirit because they seem foolish (illogical or nonsense) to him and cannot be understood without the Spirit. **15.** The spiritual person (someone with the Holy Spirit) judges (discerns or understands) all things but is not judged by anyone. **16.** "Who has understood the mind of the Lord (God's thoughts or purposes) so as to instruct Him?" But we have the mind of Christ (the ability to think and understand as Christ does).

Chapter 3

1. I could not speak to you as spiritual people (godly) but as carnal (worldly), as babies (immature) in Christ. **2.** I gave you milk (introductory training), not solid food (deeper training), for you weren't ready for it, and still aren't. **3.** You're still carnal (worldly), with covetousness (jealousy), strife (conflict), and divisions (separations) among you. Aren't you acting like mere humans (ordinary people)? **4.** When one says, "I'm of Paul," and another, "I'm of Apollos," are you not carnal (focused on mortal leaders)? **5.** Paul and Apollos are just retainers (aides) through whom you believed, as the Lord gave each their part (responsibility). **6.** I planted (sowed the philosophy), Apollos watered (nurtured), but God gave the increase (growth). **7.** Neither he who plants nor he who waters is anything, but God gives the increase (results). **8.** Both who plant and water are one (united), and each will be awarded (honored) for their labor (work). **9.** We're God's workers (mates); you're His field (place of growth), His structure (building). **10.** By God's grace (unmerited favor), I laid the foundation (established the basics) as a wise builder; other builds on it. Let each be careful (conservative) how they build. **11.** No other foundation can be laid except Jesus Christ. **12.** If anyone builds on this foundation with gold, silver, precious stones, wood, hay, or straw, **13.** each work will be revealed by fire (judgment), which will test its quality (value). **14.** If anyone's work endures (survives), they will be awarded (recognized). **15.** If it is burned up (destroyed), they will suffer loss (discipline), but they will be saved (rescued), even though as one escaping through the flames (they will be saved, but their work will be judged as worthless). **16.** You're the tabernacle (sacred place) of God, and the Spirit (Holy Spirit) of God dwells (lives) in you. **17.** If anyone defiles (destroys) God's tabernacle, God will destroy them, for the tabernacle is holy (sacred). **18.** Let no one deceive (mislead) themselves. If anyone thinks they are wise (intelligent) in this world, let them become foolish (humble) so they may become truly wise (wise in God's eyes). **19.** The wisdom (knowledge) of this world is foolishness (gibberish) to God, for it's written, "He catches the wise (the supposedly wise) in their own cunningness (clever but deceptive plans)." **20.** The Lord knows the thoughts (intentions) of the wise; they are futile (empty). **21.** So let no one boast (glory) in men (mortal leaders). Everything is yours, **22.** whether Paul, Apollos, Cephas (Peter), the world, life, death, the present, or the future—all are yours. **23.** And you belong to Christ, and Christ belongs to God.

Chapter 4

1. Let a man regard us as retainers (aides) of Christ and servants (directors) of God's mystifications (godly truths). **2.** It is required of servants that they be found faithful (trustworthy). **3.** It matters little to me that I am judged (evaluated) by you or by a mortal court; I do not even judge (evaluate) myself. **4.** I know of nothing against myself, but I am not justified (declared righteous) by this; the Lord is my judge. **5.** So, do not judge (condemn) before the time; the Lord will bring to light (reveal) what is hidden and reveal the counsels (plans) of the hearts. At that time, each will receive praise (blessing) from God. **6.** I have applied these things to myself and Apollos for your sake, so that you may not go beyond what is written (in the Scriptures) and become proud (arrogant), favoring one over another. **7.** Who makes you different (special)? What do you have that you did not receive (get) from God)? And if you received it, why do you boast (glory) as though you did not? **8.** You are already full (satisfied), already rich (wealthy), and reign (rule) as kings without us! I wish you did reign (rule) so that we could reign (rule) with you. **9.** For I think that God has displayed us apostles last, as condemned to death, a spectacle (public display) to the world, angels, and men. **10.** We are fools (unwise) for Christ's sake, but you are wise (understanding) in Christ; we are weak (weak in body), but you are strong (strong in faith); you are honored (respected), but we are dishonored (disrespected). **11.** To this very hour, we hunger (are hungry), thirst (are thirsty), are poorly clothed (underdressed), beaten (physically hurt), and homeless (without a place to live). **12.** We labor (work) with our own hands. When reviled (insulted), we bless (speak kindly); when persecuted (harassed), we endure (bear it); **13.** when defamed (slandered), we ask for peace (respond with gentleness). We have become the scum (trash) of the world, the garbage (refuse) of all things. **14.** I do not write these things to shame (embarrass) you, but to admonish (warn) you as my beloved (dearly loved) children. **15.** For though you have countless (many) teachers (instructors) in Christ, you do not have many fathers (spiritual parents). I became your father (spiritual parent) in Christ Jesus through the gospel (message). **16.** I urge (encourage) you, imitate (follow) me. **17.**

For this reason, I have sent Timothy to you, who is my beloved and faithful (trustworthy) child in the Lord, to remind you of my ways (teachings) in Christ, as I teach everywhere in every church. **18.** Some are puffed up (arrogant), as though I were not coming to you. **19.** But I will come soon, if the Lord wills, and I will know not by the talk (words) of those puffed up, but by their power (ability). **20.** For the kingdom of God is not in word (talk), but in power (action). **21.** What do you want? Shall I come to you with a rod (discipline), or in love and a spirit (attitude) of gentleness (kindness)?

Chapter 5

1. It's reported that there's sexual immorality (interdicted sexual geste) among you, a kind not even named among the Heathens (non-Jews) — that a man has his father's woman (his stepmother)! **2.** And you're proud (arrogant), rather than mourning (grieving) so that the one who did this would be removed (barred) from among you. **3.** Though I'm absent (not present) in body, I'm present in spirit (mind and heart) and have already judged (made a decision about) him who did this. **4.** In the name of our Lord Jesus Christ, when you gather together with my spirit and the power (authority) of the Lord, **5.** deliver this man to Satan (allow him to face the consequences of his sin) for the destruction (ruin) of the flesh (his unethical nature), that his spirit (soul) may be saved on the day of the Lord (the day of judgment). **6.** Your boasting (bragging) isn't good. Don't you know that a little leaven (incentive) leavens (affects) the whole lump (batch of dough)? **7.** Purge (spread) out the old leaven (unethical influences), so you may be a new lump (pure), for you are truly unleavened (clean). Christ, our Passover (sacrificial lamb), was offered for us. **8.** Let us keep the feast (celebrate), not with old leaven (unethical attitudes) of malice (evil intent) and wickedness (immorality), but with the unleavened bread (pure and sincere living) of sincerity (honesty) and truth. **9.** I wrote to you not to associate (mix) with sexually immoral (unethical) people. **10.** I didn't mean the immoral (unethical) of this world, or the greedy (covetous), racketeers (those who cheat others), or heathens (worshippers of false gods); to avoid them, you'd have to leave the world. **11.** But I wrote not to associate (mix) with anyone who is called a brother (a fellow believer) who is sexually immoral, greedy, an idolater, reviler (abuser), drunkard (addict), or swindler — not even to eat with such a person. **12.** For what business (right) is it of mine to judge (condemn) outsiders (non-believers)? Do you not judge (discern) those inside (the church)? **13.** But God judges (evaluates) those outside. "Put away (expel) the evil person (wicked person) from among you."

Chapter 6

1. How dare you take a disagreement before the unlawful (those who aren't following God), and not before the saints (God's people)? **2.** Do you not know that the saints (believers, religionists) will judge the world? If the world will be judged by you, are you not suitable to judge (decide) small matters? **3.** Do you not know we will judge angels (spiritual beings)? How much more, matters of this life (earthly, fleshly issues)? **4.** Yet, why appoint those least recognized (lowly regarded) by the church to make such decisions? **5.** If you have judgments (disputes, controversies) concerning life, I say this to shame (embarrass) you. Is there not one wise (understanding) man among you to judge between believers (religionists)? **6.** But you, as family, go to law (court) against family, and that before questioners (non-believers)! **7.** It's already a defeat (loss) for you that you sue (take to court) one another. Why not rather accept wrong (suffer wrong) or be cheated (defrauded)? **8.** No, you wrong (hurt) and cheat (defraud), and do this to your own brothers (fellow believers, fellow religionists)! **9.** Do you not know the unlawful (those living in sin) will not inherit (enter) the kingdom of God? Do not be deceived (misled): neither fornicators (sexually immoral people), idolaters (those who worship false gods), adulterers (people who cheat on their spouses), homosexuals (those who engage in same-sex relationships), sodomites (men who have sex with other men), **10.** thieves (people who steal), the greedy (covetous), alcoholics (people addicted to alcohol), revilers (abusers), nor swindlers (cheats) will inherit the kingdom of God. **11.** And such were some of you, but you were washed (cleansed from sin), sanctified (made holy), and justified (declared righteous) in the name of the Lord Jesus and by the Spirit (Holy Spirit) of God. **12.** All things are lawful (permitted) for me, but not all things are helpful (beneficial). All things are lawful, but I will not be enslaved (controlled) by anything. **13.** Food is for the stomach and the stomach for food, but God will destroy both. The body is for the Lord (for God), not for sexual immorality (unethical sexual behavior). **14.** God raised the Lord (Jesus) and will also raise us up by His power (might). **15.** Do you not know that your bodies are members (parts) of Christ? Shall I then take the members of Christ and make them members of a harlot (prostitute)? Certainly not! **16.** Or do you not know that he who is joined (united) to a harlot is one body with her? "For the two," He says, "shall become one flesh (united as one in body)." **17.** But he who is joined to the Lord (united with Christ) is one spirit (united in spirit) with Him. **18.** Flee (run from) sexual immorality (unethical sexual behavior). Every other sin a person commits is outside the body (not directly affecting the body), but sexual immorality is a sin against one's own body (damaging to oneself). **19.** Do you not know that your body is the temple (sacred dwelling place) of the Holy Spirit, whom you have from God, and you are not your own (you belong to God)? **20.** You were bought at a price (the price of Jesus' sacrifice); therefore, glorify (honor) God in your body and spirit, which are God's.

Chapter 7

1. Concerning what you wrote: it is good for a man not to touch (have intimate relations with) a woman. **2.** But to avoid immorality (sexual sin), let each man have his own wife, and each woman her own husband. **3.** Let the husband give his wife her due affection (proper care and love), and likewise the wife to her husband. **4.** The wife has no authority (control) over her body, but the husband does; likewise, the husband's body is under the wife's authority (control). **5.** Do not deprive (deny) each other except by mutual consent (agreement) for prayer, then come together again to avoid temptation (sexual temptation). **6.** I say this as a concession (permission), not a command. **7.** I wish all were like me (single and celibate), but each has his own gift (calling) from God. **8.** To the unmarried (those who have never married) and widows (those whose spouses have died): it is good to remain as I am (celibate); **9.** but if they lack self-control (cannot remain celibate), let them marry; it is better to marry than to burn with passion (experience intense sexual desire). **10.** To the married I command (not I, but the Lord): A wife must not leave (divorce) her husband; **11.** but if she does, let her remain unmarried or reconcile (make peace) with her husband. A husband must not divorce (leave) his wife. **12.** To the rest, I say: if a believer has an unbelieving (non-Christian) spouse willing to stay, do not divorce. **13.** And if a believing woman has an unbelieving husband who is willing to stay, let her not divorce him. **14.** The unbelieving spouse is sanctified (made holy) by the believing partner; otherwise, your children would be unclean (not set apart), but they are holy (set apart to God). **15.** But if the unbeliever departs (leaves), let them depart; a believer is not bound (obligated) in such cases. God calls us to peace. **16.** How do you know if you will save your spouse? **17.** Let each live as the Lord has called them. This is my rule in all churches. **18.** If circumcised (Jewish) when called, don't seek to change (uncircumcised); if uncircumcised, don't seek circumcision (Jewish ritual). **19.** Circumcision or uncircumcision means nothing; keeping God's commandments matters. **20.** Let each remain in the calling (station in life) they were in when called. **21.** Were you called as a slave? Don't let it trouble you; but if you can gain freedom (become free), do so. **22.** A slave called in the Lord is the Lord's freedman; a free person is Christ's slave. **23.** You were bought at a price (the price of Christ's sacrifice); do not become slaves of men (human masters). **24.** Let each remain with God in the state (condition) in which they were called. **25.** Concerning virgins (unmarried women), I have no command from the Lord but offer a trustworthy opinion. **26.** Because of present distress (current difficulties), it is good for a man to remain as he is. **27.** Are you bound to a wife? Do not seek release (divorce). Are you free from a wife? Do not seek one (marriage). **28.** But if you marry, you have not sinned; yet those who marry will face earthly troubles (difficulties), which I wish to spare you. **29.** Time is short (limited), so those with wives should live as though they had none; **30.** those who weep as though they didn't, those who rejoice as though they didn't, and those who buy as though they possessed nothing; **31.** those who use this world should not misuse it, for the world's form (ways) is passing away. **32.** I want you to be without concern (untroubled). The unmarried man cares about pleasing the Lord; **33.** but the married man cares about worldly matters (earthly things) and pleasing his wife. **34.** An unmarried woman cares about the Lord, holy (dedicated) in body and spirit, but a married woman cares about worldly matters and pleasing her husband. **35.** I say this for your benefit (good), that you may serve the Lord without distraction (without divided attention). **36.** If a man thinks he is acting improperly toward his virgin (fiancée), let them marry; he does not sin. **37.** But if he is determined in his heart to keep her a virgin, he does well. **38.** He who marries does well, but he who does not marry does better. **39.** A wife is bound (obligated) to her husband as long as he lives; but if he dies, she is free to marry anyone in the Lord (a Christian). **40.** Yet she is happier if she remains as she is, according to my judgment (opinion), and I think I also have the Spirit of God.

Chapter 8

1. Concerning food offered to idols: We all have knowledge, but knowledge puffs up (arrogantly inflates the ego), while love builds up (strengthens and edifies). **2.** If anyone thinks he knows something, he knows nothing as he should. **3.** But if anyone loves God, he is known (recognized and accepted) by Him. **4.** As for eating food offered to idols, we know an idol (false god) is nothing, and there is no God but one. **5.** Though there are many so-called gods (pretended deities), both in heaven and on earth, **6.** for us, there is one God, the Father, from whom are all things (everything originates), and one Lord Jesus Christ, through whom are all things, and through whom we live. **7.** Not everyone has this knowledge; some, with idol-worship in mind, still eat food as if offered to idols, and their conscience (inner moral sense) is defiled (corrupted). **8.** But food doesn't make us closer to God; whether we eat or don't eat, we're neither better nor worse. **9.** But be careful, lest your liberty (freedom) cause a weak person to stumble (fall into sin or temptation). **10.** If someone sees you eating in an idol's temple, will their weak conscience (sensitive moral awareness) be emboldened (encouraged) to eat food offered to idols? **11.** And will the weak brother, for whom Christ died, be destroyed (ruined spiritually) because of your knowledge? **12.** When you sin against your brothers and wound (hurt) their weak conscience, you sin against Christ. **13.** Therefore, if food causes my brother to stumble, I will never eat meat again, so I won't make him stumble.

Chapter 9

1. Am I not a backer (runner)? Am I not free (not bound by mortal authority)? Have I not seen Jesus Christ our Lord? Aren't you my work in the Lord? **2.** Still, I am to you, for you're the seal (evidence or substantiation) of my apostleship, if I'm not a backer to others. **3.** My defense (explanation or defense) to those who question me is this: **4.** Don't we have the right to eat and drink? **5.** Don't we have the right to take a believing woman, like the other apostles, the sisters of the Lord, and Cephas (Peter)? **6.** Or is it just Barnabas and I who have no right to refrain (hesitate) from working? **7.** Who goes to war at his own expenditure (cost)? Who plants a crop and doesn't eat from it? Or who tends (takes care of) a flock and doesn't drink its milk? **8.** Am I saying this as just a man, or does the law (God's law) say the same? **9.** For the law says, "You shall not muzzle (circumscribe the eating of) an ox while it treads out the grain." Is God concerned with oxen? **10.** Or is He saying this for our sake? Yes, it's written for our sake, so those who work should admit from their work. **11.** Still, is it too much if we reap (admit benefits from) your material effects, if we've sown (planted) spiritual effects for you? **12.** Still, shouldn't we indeed more? But we haven't used this right, preferring to endure (tolerate) everything so we don't hamper (help) the philosophy, if others have the right to this. **13.** Do you not know that those who serve in the tabernacle eat from the tabernacle, and those who serve at the balcony share in the immolations? **14.** In the same way, the Lord has commanded that those who sermonize the philosophy should live by the philosophy. **15.** But I haven't used these rights, nor have I written this so that it should be done for me. I'd rather die than let anyone abate (reduce) my boasting. **16.** Still, I have nothing to boast (vapor) about, for I must sermonize. If I sermonize the philosophy, woe (misery or judgment) to me if I don't! **17.** Still, I have a price; if reluctantly (unwillingly), I've been entrusted (given responsibility) with a responsibility. If I do this willingly (freely), **18.** what's my price? That when I sermonize the philosophy, I do so without charge, so I don't abuse (exploit) my authority. **19.** Though I'm free from all, I've made myself a menial (slave) to all to win (gain) further people. **20.** To the Jews, I came like a Jew to win them; to those under the law, I came like one under the law to win those under the law. **21.** To those without the law (heathens), I came like one without the law, though I'm still under Christ's law, to win those without the law. **22.** To the weak (spiritually or innocently weak), I came weak to win the weak. I've come all things to all people, that I might save some. **23.** I do this for the philosophy's sake, so I may partake in its blessings (prizes) with you. **24.** Don't you know that in a race, all run, but only one gets the prize? Run in such a way that you may gain (win) it. **25.** Everyone who competes in the games is temperate (self-controlled) in all things. They do it for a perishable (temporary) crown, but we for an imperishable (eternal) one. **26.** Thus, I run with purpose (direction), not uncertainly (without aim). I fight, not as one beating the air (fighting without purpose or effectiveness). **27.** I punish (discipline) my body and bring it into subjection (control), lest after preaching to others, I myself should be disqualified (rejected from the prize).

Chapter 10

1. I want you to remember that all our ancestors were under the cloud (a reference to God's presence), passed through the sea, **2.** were baptized into Moses in the cloud and the sea, **3.** ate the same spiritual food, **4.** and drank the same spiritual drink, for they drank from the spiritual Rock that followed them, and that Rock was Christ. **5.** Yet, God was not pleased with most of them, and their bodies were scattered in the wilderness. **6.** These events serve as examples (models) for us, to warn (caution) us not to lust (desire intensely) after evil things as they did. **7.** Don't become idolaters (worshippers of idols) as some of them did. As it's written, "The people sat down to eat and drink, and rose up to play." **8.** Don't commit sexual immorality (sinful sexual behavior) as some of them did, and 23,000 fell in one day. **9.** Don't tempt (test or challenge) Christ as some of them did and were destroyed by serpents. **10.** Don't complain (grumble or murmur), as some of them did, and were destroyed by the destroyer (referring to God's judgment or an angel of destruction). **11.** These things happened as examples (warnings), written for our warning, as we live in the last days. **12.** Therefore, let him who thinks he stands take heed (pay attention), lest he fall. **13.** No temptation (trial or test) has overtaken you except what is common to man. God is faithful and will not allow you to be tempted beyond what you can bear; He will provide a way of escape (a way out) so you can endure (withstand) it. **14.** Flee from idolatry (worship of idols or false gods). **15.** I speak as to wise men (mature or thoughtful people); judge (evaluate) for yourselves what I say. **16.** The cup of blessing we bless, is it not the communion (shared participation) of Christ's blood? The bread we break, is it not the communion of Christ's body? **17.** Though we are many, we are one body, for we all partake (share) of that one bread. **18.** Consider Israel: those who eat the sacrifices are partakers (participants) of the altar. **19.** What am I saying? That an idol is anything or that food offered to idols is anything? **20.** Rather, what the Gentiles sacrifice (offer), they sacrifice to demons (evil spiritual beings), not to God, and I don't want you to have fellowship (relationship) with demons. **21.** You cannot drink from the Lord's cup and from the cup of demons; you cannot partake of the Lord's table and the table of demons. **22.** Or do we provoke (irritate or anger) the Lord to jealousy? Are we stronger than He? **23.** All things are lawful for me, but not all things are helpful (beneficial or good); all things are lawful, but not all things edify (build up or strengthen). **24.** Let no one seek his own good (benefit), but the good of others. **25.** Eat whatever is sold in the meat market without asking questions for conscience' sake. **26.** The earth is the Lord's, and everything in it. **27.** If an unbeliever (someone who does not believe in Christ) invites you to dinner and you want to go, eat whatever is served without asking about its origin. **28.** But if someone tells you, "This was offered to idols," don't eat it, for the sake of the one who told you, and for conscience' sake. **29.** I'm talking about the conscience (moral awareness) of the other person, not your own. Why should my liberty (freedom) be judged by someone else's conscience? **30.** If I give thanks for the food, why should I be spoken against (criticized) for it? **31.** Therefore, whether you eat, drink, or do anything else, do all for the glory (honor and praise) of God. **32.** Don't offend (cause to stumble) the Jews, the Greeks (non-Jews), or the church of God. **33.** Just as I try to please all people in all things, not seeking my own benefit, but the

benefit of many, so that they may be saved (delivered from sin and eternal separation from God).

Chapter 11

1. Follow my example, just as I follow the example of Christ. **2.** I praise you for remembering me and keeping the traditions (customs) I passed on to you. **3.** The head (leader) of every man is Christ, the head of woman is man, and the head of Christ is God. **4.** A man dishonors (disrespects) his head if he prays or prophesies (speaks prophetically) with his head covered. **5.** A woman dishonors her head if she prays or prophesies with her head uncovered, as it's the same as if her hair were shaved (cut short). **6.** If a woman does not cover her head, she should have her hair cut off. But if it's disgraceful (shameful) for her to be shaved (cut or shaved bald), let her cover her head. **7.** A man should not cover his head, because he is the image and glory (honor) of God, but woman is the glory of man. **8.** Man did not come from woman, but woman came from man. **9.** Man was not made for woman, but woman was made for man. **10.** For this reason, a woman should have a symbol of authority (power or control) on her head because of the angels. **11.** Nevertheless, in the Lord, neither is man independent (self-sufficient) of woman, nor woman independent of man. **12.** As woman came from man, so man is born through woman; but all things come from God. **13.** Consider (reflect on) this: Is it proper (right) for a woman to pray with her head uncovered? **14.** Does nature (the natural world) itself not teach you that if a man has long hair, it's dishonorable (disrespectful) to him? **15.** But if a woman has long hair, it's her glory (honor); her hair is given to her as a covering (commodity to cover or shield). **16.** However, we do not have such a custom (tradition), nor do the churches of God, if anyone wants to argue (disagree) about this. **17.** I do not praise you for your meetings, because they cause more harm (damage) than good. **18.** I hear that there are divisions (dissensions) among you when you gather, and I partly believe it. **19.** There must be divisions among you, so that those who are approved (accepted) may be honored. **20.** When you come together, it is not to eat the Lord's Supper (meal). **21.** In eating, each one takes his meal (food) first, and one person goes hungry while another is drunk (intoxicated). **22.** Do you not have your own homes to eat and drink in? Or do you dishonor (disrespect) the church of God and shame those who have nothing? **23.** What shall I say to you? Should I praise you for this? I do not. **24.** I received from the Lord (Jesus) what I also passed on to you: that the Lord Jesus, on the night He was betrayed (handed over), took bread, and when He had given thanks, He broke it and said, "Take, eat; this is My body, which is broken (torn apart) for you; do this in remembrance (to recall) of Me." **25.** In the same way, after supper (meal), He took the cup, saying, "This cup is the new covenant (agreement) in My blood; do this, as often as you drink it, in remembrance of Me." **26.** For as often as you eat this bread and drink this cup, you proclaim (declare) the Lord's death until He returns. **27.** Therefore, whoever eats this bread or drinks this cup in an unworthy manner (improper way) will be guilty of desecrating (disrespecting) the body and blood of the Lord. **28.** Let a person examine (test or look at) themselves, and so let them eat of the bread and drink of the cup. **29.** Anyone who eats and drinks in an unworthy manner brings judgment (discipline) upon themselves, not discerning (recognizing) the Lord's body. **30.** That's why many are weak (sick), ill (sick), and some have even died among you. **31.** However, if we judged ourselves (examined our own conduct), we would not be judged. **32.** But when we are judged by the Lord, we are disciplined (corrected) so that we will not be condemned (punished severely) with the world. **33.** So, when you come together to eat, wait for one another. **34.** However, if anyone is hungry, let him eat at home, so that when you gather together, it will not result in judgment. The other matters I will address when I come.

Chapter 12

1. Concerning spiritual gifts (special abilities given by the Holy Spirit), brethren (brothers and sisters), I do not want you to be ignorant (uninformed): **2.** You know that you were once led astray (misled) to mute (silent) idols (false gods). **3.** No one speaking by the Spirit of God calls Jesus accursed (cursed or condemned), and no one can say Jesus is Lord (master or ruler) except by the Holy Spirit. **4.** There are various (different) gifts (special abilities), but the same Spirit; **5.** differences in ministries (service or roles), but the same Lord; **6.** and diversities (varieties) of activities (operations or workings), but the same God who works all in all (in everyone). **7.** The Spirit's manifestation (visible display) is given to each one for the profit (benefit) of all: **8.** one receives wisdom (insight into deep truths), another knowledge (understanding), **9.** another faith (trust in God), another gift of healing, **10.** another miracle, another prophecy (speaking God's message), discerning of spirits, speaking in tongues, or interpreting tongues. **11.** The same Spirit works all these, distributing (giving) individually as He wills (desires). **12.** As the body is one with many members, so is Christ. **13.** By one Spirit we were baptized (immersed) into one body—Jews or Greeks (Gentiles), slaves or free—and all made to drink (receive) of one Spirit. **14.** The body is not one member but many. **15.** If the foot says, "I am not part of the body," it is still part of the body. **16.** The ear cannot say, "I am not of the body" because it's not an eye. **17.** If the whole body were an eye, where would hearing be? **18.** But God has placed each member in the body as He pleased (according to His will). **19.** If all were one part, where would the body be? **20.** But there are many members, yet one body. **21.** The eye cannot say to the hand, "I don't need you," nor the head to the feet. **22.** Even the weaker (less important or fragile) members are necessary. **23.** Those parts we think less honorable (less respectable) we treat with greater honor (respect), **24.** while our presentable (visible and dignified) parts need no special treatment. God composed (arranged) the body to give greater honor to the part that lacks it, **25.** so there's no division (separation) in the body, and members care equally for one another. **26.** If one member suffers, all suffer; if one is honored, all rejoice. **27.** Now you are the body (church) of Christ, and individually (separately) members. **28.** God appointed (set) in the church apostles (those sent with authority), prophets (those who speak God's message), teachers, miracles, healings, helps, administration, and tongues. **29.** Are all apostles? prophets? teachers? workers of miracles? **30.** Do all have gifts of healing? speak with tongues? interpret? **31.** Earnestly (eagerly) desire the best gifts, and I show you a more excellent (superior) way.

Chapter 13

1. Though I speak with tongues of men and angels but lack love, I am like noisy brass (a sounding gong) or a clanging cymbal (a loud, irritating sound). **2.** If I have prophecy (speaking God's message), understand all mysteries (hidden truths), and have all faith (trust in God) to move mountains but lack love, I am nothing. **3.** If I give everything to the poor and sacrifice my body (for a noble cause) but lack love, it gains me nothing. **4.** Love is patient (long-suffering) and kind; it does not envy (desire others' possessions or qualities), boast (brag), or become proud (arrogant). **5.** It is not rude (dishonorable), self-seeking (selfish), easily angered (quick-tempered), and keeps no record of wrongs (does not hold grudges). **6.** Love does not delight (rejoice) in evil but rejoices with the truth (the right and honest way). **7.** It bears (carries or endures), believes (trusts), hopes, and endures all things. **8.** Love never fails (ceases). Prophecies (messages from God), tongues, and knowledge will cease (end). **9.** For we know and prophesy only in part (incomplete), **10.** but when perfection (completeness) comes, the partial (incomplete) will pass away. **11.** When I was a child, I spoke, understood, and thought like a child; now I have put childish ways behind me. **12.** Now we see dimly (unclearly), as in a mirror, but then face to face. Now I know in part, but then I will know fully, as I am fully known (known by God completely). **13.** Faith (trust in God), hope (expectation of future good), and love remain (continue), but the greatest of these is love.

Chapter 14

1. Pursue (actively seek) love and desire (long for) spiritual gifts (special abilities from the Holy Spirit), especially prophecy (speaking God's message). **2.** One who speaks in a tongue (language) speaks mysteries (hidden truths) to God, not men (people). **3.** But one who prophesies speaks edification (building up), exhortation (encouragement), and comfort (consolation) to others. **4.** Speaking in tongues edifies oneself, but prophesying edifies (builds up) the church (body of believers). **5.** I wish you all spoke in tongues, but even more that you prophesied, as this edifies (builds up) the church. **6.** If I speak in tongues, it does not profit (benefit) you unless I bring revelation (disclosure of truth), knowledge (understanding), prophecy (speaking God's message), or teaching (instruction). **7.** Instruments (musical tools) like the flute or harp must produce distinct (clear) sounds to be understood. **8.** If the trumpet sounds unclear (confused), who will prepare for battle? **9.** So, unless you speak clearly, who will understand? You'll speak into the air (nothing of value will be heard). **10.** There are many languages, each with meaning (purpose or significance), **11.** but if I don't understand, I am a foreigner (someone who doesn't belong) to the speaker. **12.** Since you are eager (enthusiastic) for spiritual gifts, seek to build up (strengthen or encourage) the church. **13.** Those who speak in tongues should pray for the ability to interpret (explain). **14.** If I pray in a tongue, my spirit prays, but my mind is unfruitful (does not understand or benefit). **15.** So, I will pray and sing with both spirit (my inner being) and understanding (mental awareness). **16.** Otherwise, how will others say "Amen" (affirm agreement) to your thanks if they don't understand? **17.** You give thanks well, but others are not edified (built up or encouraged). **18.** I thank God I speak in tongues more than you all, **19.** yet in church (the gathering of believers), I'd rather speak five understandable (clear) words than ten thousand in a tongue. **20.** Do not be immature (childish) in understanding; in malice (evil intentions) be innocent (harmless), but in understanding (wisdom) be mature (grown up). **21.** In the law (Scripture), it says, "With foreign tongues (languages) I will speak to this people, yet they will not listen." **22.** Tongues are a sign (evidence) for unbelievers (those who do not believe), but prophecy is for believers (those who trust in Christ). **23.** If all speak in tongues and outsiders (those who don't believe) enter, they may think you're mad (crazy). **24.** But if all prophesy, an outsider is convicted (convicted of sin) and his heart's secrets (hidden things) revealed, leading him to worship (praise) God. **25.** He will acknowledge (recognize) that God is truly among you. **26.** When you gather (assemble), each one may bring a psalm (song of praise), teaching (instruction), or revelation (disclosure of truth); let all things be for edification (building up). **27.** If someone speaks in tongues, let two or three speak in turn (order), and one interpret (explain). **28.** Without an interpreter, keep silent (don't speak) and speak to God privately (within yourself). **29.** Let two or three prophets speak, and others judge (evaluate or discern). **30.** If another receives a revelation (new insight), the first should yield (give way or stop). **31.** You can all prophesy in turn, so everyone learns (is taught) and is encouraged (comforted). **32.** Prophets are subject (under the authority) to other prophets. **33.** God is not a God of confusion (disorder) but of peace (order), as in all churches (congregations) of the saints (believers). **34.** Women should remain silent (be quiet) in churches (gatherings), being submissive (willing to follow authority) as the law (Scripture) states. **35.** If they want to learn, let them ask their husbands at home; it's shameful (dishonorable) for women to speak in church (the assembly of believers). **36.** Did God's word come from you only (are you the only one who knows it)? **37.** Anyone who claims to be spiritual (claiming to be led by the Holy Spirit) should acknowledge that these teachings are the Lord's commands. **38.** If someone ignores (refuses to accept) this, let them be ignorant (unaware or uninformed). **39.** Desire prophecy earnestly (strongly), and do not forbid (prohibit) speaking in tongues. **40.** Let everything be done decently (properly) and in order (organized).

Chapter 15

1. I declare (proclaim) to you the gospel (good news) you received and in which you stand (firmly established), **2.** by which you are saved (rescued from sin and death) if you hold fast (firmly retain), unless you believed in vain (without lasting effect). **3.** I delivered (handed down) what I received: Christ died for our sins according to the Scriptures (the Old Testament prophecies), **4.** was buried, and rose on the third day according to the Scriptures, **5.** and was seen by Cephas (Peter), then by the twelve (the twelve apostles), **6.** and over five hundred others, most of whom remain alive (still living), though some have died. **7.** Then He was seen by James (Jesus' brother) and all the apostles, **8.** and last by me (Paul), as one born out of due time (born later than the others, referring to his late apostolic calling). **9.** I am the least (smallest or humblest) of the apostles, unworthy (undeserving) because I persecuted (harassed or attacked) the church. **10.** But by God's grace (unmerited favor), I am what I am, and His grace was not in vain (without effect), as I labored (worked) abundantly (greatly) by His grace. **11.** Whether I or others preached, so you believed. **12.** If Christ is preached as risen (from the dead), why do some say there is no resurrection (rising from the dead)? **13.** If there's no resurrection, then Christ isn't risen. **14.** If Christ isn't risen, our preaching and your faith are in vain (empty or pointless). **15.** We would be false witnesses (liars) if Christ wasn't raised. **16.** If the dead don't rise, then Christ isn't risen. **17.** If Christ isn't risen, your faith is futile (without purpose); you're still in your sins. **18.** Those who died in Christ have perished (gone to destruction) if there is no resurrection. **19.** If our hope in Christ is only for this life, we are most pitiable (to be pitied above all people). **20.** But Christ is risen from the dead, the firstfruits (the first to rise) of those who died. **21.** Since death came by man, resurrection (life after death) also came by man. **22.** As in Adam all die, so in Christ all will be made alive (given eternal life), **23.** each in order (sequence): Christ the firstfruits, then those who belong to Him at His coming. **24.** Then the end (final completion) will come when He hands over the kingdom (God's reign) to God after ending all rule and authority. **25.** For He must reign (rule) until all enemies are under His feet. **26.** The last enemy to be destroyed is death. **27.** He has put all things under His feet, except Himself (Jesus will still remain in authority). **28.** When all is subject to Him, the Son will also be subject (submit) to God, so that God may be all in all (supreme in all things). **29.** Otherwise, why do people get baptized (immersed in water) for the dead if the dead don't rise? **30.** Why do we face danger (suffer risk) every hour? **31.** I die daily (face danger and hardship), rejoicing in you through Christ Jesus. **32.** If I fought wild beasts (symbolic of extreme trials or real physical danger) at Ephesus for human reasons, what gain (profit) is it if the dead don't rise? Let us eat and drink, for tomorrow we die. **33.** Do not be deceived (misled): "Bad company corrupts good habits." **34.** Awake to righteousness (wake up to live rightly), and do not sin; some don't know God. **35.** Some may ask, "How are the dead raised? With what body?" **36.** Foolish (ignorant) one, what you sow (plant) isn't made alive unless it dies. **37.** You don't sow (plant) the body that shall be, but just a seed (a small part of the body). **38.** God gives it a body as He pleases (according to His will), to each seed its own body. **39.** Not all flesh (living beings) is the same: there is one for men, another for animals, fish, and birds. **40.** There are celestial (heavenly) bodies and terrestrial (earthly) bodies, each with its own glory (beauty or honor). **41.** The sun, moon, and stars each have their own glory (brightness). **42.** So is the resurrection: the body is sown (planted) in corruption (decay), raised in incorruption (imperishable); **43.** sown in dishonor (shame), raised in glory (splendor); sown in weakness (frailty), raised in power (strength); **44.** sown a natural body (a body suited for this world), raised a spiritual body (a body suited for eternal life). **45.** The first man, Adam, became a living being (soul); the last Adam (Christ) became a life-giving spirit. **46.** The natural (physical) came first, then the spiritual (eternal). **47.** The first man was made of dust (earth), the second Man (Christ) is from heaven. **48.** Those of the dust (earthly people) are like the man of dust (Adam); those of heaven (spiritual people) are like the heavenly Man (Christ). **49.** As we bore the image of the man of dust, we will bear the image of the heavenly Man (Christ). **50.** Flesh and blood (human bodies) cannot inherit God's kingdom (enter heaven), nor does corruption inherit incorruption (eternal life). **51.** I tell you a mystery (a hidden truth): We shall not all sleep (die), but we shall all be changed (transformed), **52.** in a moment (instant), at the last trumpet (when Christ returns), when the dead will be raised incorruptible. **53.** This corruptible (mortal body) must put on incorruption, this mortal (subject to death) must put on immortality (eternal life). **54.** When this happens, "Death is swallowed up in victory" (defeated forever). **55.** "O Death, where is your sting? O Hades (the grave), where is your victory?" **56.** The sting (painful result) of death is sin, and the strength (power) of sin is the law. **57.** But thanks to God, who gives us victory (triumph) through our Lord Jesus Christ. **58.** Therefore, my beloved brethren (brothers and sisters), be steadfast (firm) and immovable (unshaken), always abounding (overflowing) in the Lord's work, knowing that your labor (effort) is not in vain (pointless).

Chapter 16

1. Now about the collection (financial offering) for the saints (believers in Jerusalem): follow the instructions (guidelines) I gave to the Galatian churches. **2.** On the first day of the week (Sunday), each of you should set aside (save) a portion of what you've earned (from your income) so that collections won't be necessary (there will be no last-minute gathering) when I arrive. **3.** When I come, I will send those you approve (trustworthy individuals) with letters to take your gift (offering) to

Jerusalem. **4.** If it's suitable (appropriate) for me to go, they can travel with me. **5.** I'll come to you after passing through Macedonia (a region in northern Greece, part of Paul's journey; for I am traveling through there). **6.** I may stay with you (for a while), or even spend the winter (a few months), so you can help me on my journey wherever I go. **7.** I don't want to just visit briefly now; I hope to stay with you for a while, if the Lord allows (if God permits). **8.** But I will stay in Ephesus (a city in Asia Minor) until Pentecost (a Jewish feast, which was 50 days after Passover), **9.** because a great opportunity (open door) has opened for me, though there are many opponents (people opposing my work). **10.** If Timothy (Paul's companion and co-worker) comes, see that he is treated well (honored), for he is doing the Lord's work, just as I am. **11.** Don't let anyone disrespect (disregard) him. Send him in peace (with kindness and good will) so he can come to me, as I am expecting him with the brothers (other believers). **12.** About Apollos (another key Christian leader): I urged him strongly to visit you with the brothers, but he was not willing (not ready) at this time; he will come when he has an opportunity (a suitable time). **13.** Be watchful (alert), stand firm in faith (remain strong in your belief), be courageous (brave), be strong (steadfast). **14.** Let all you do be done with love (let love guide all your actions). **15.** I urge you, brothers and sisters, to recognize (acknowledge or honor) the household of Stephanas (a family or household), who were the first converts (believers) in Achaia (southern Greece) and have devoted themselves (given their lives fully) to serving the saints (other believers). **16.** Submit to such people (submit to their leadership and service) and to everyone who works and serves with us. **17.** I am glad that Stephanas, Fortunatus, and Achaicus (three fellow workers) have come, as they have supplied (provided) what you lacked (were missing). **18.** They refreshed (encouraged and revived) my spirit and yours, so recognize (appreciate) such people. **19.** The churches in Asia (churches in Asia Minor) send you greetings. Aquila and Priscilla (a husband and wife team) greet you warmly (with affection) in the Lord, along with the church that meets in their house (a home church). **20.** All the brothers and sisters greet you. Greet each other with a holy kiss (a customary sign of peace and fellowship among believers). **21.** I, Paul, send this greeting with my own hand (signing personally to show authenticity). **22.** If anyone does not love the Lord (Jesus Christ), let them be under God's curse (a strong curse or judgment). Come, Lord! (A prayer for Christ's return!). **23.** May the grace (unmerited favor) of the Lord Jesus be with you. **24.** My love be with you all in Christ Jesus. Amen. (So be it.)

55 – Chorinthians 2

Chapter 1

1. Paul, an apostle of Jesus Christ by God's will, and Timothy our brother, to the church of God in Corinth, along with all the saints (believers) who are in all of Achaia (southern Greece): **2.** Grace and peace to you from God our Father and the Lord Jesus Christ. **3.** Blessed be the God and Father of our Lord Jesus Christ, the Father of mercies and the God of all comfort, **4** who comforts us in all our troubles, so that we can comfort others who are in any kind of trouble, with the comfort we ourselves have received from God. **5.** For just as the sufferings of Christ overflow to us, so also our comfort overflows through Christ. **6** If we are distressed, it is for your comfort and salvation, which is effective for enduring the same sufferings we also endure. And if we are comforted, it is for your comfort and salvation. **7** Our hope for you is firm, because we know that just as you share in our sufferings, you will also share in our comfort. **8** We do not want you to be unaware, brothers, of the hardship we experienced in Asia. We were overwhelmed beyond our ability to endure, so that we despaired even of life. **9** In fact, we felt we had received the sentence of death. But this happened that we might not rely on ourselves, but on God who raises the dead, **10** who has delivered us from such a deadly peril, and He will deliver us. On Him we have set our hope that He will continue to deliver us, **11** as you also help us by praying for us. Then many will give thanks on our behalf for the gracious gift granted us through the prayers of many. **12** Our boast is this: the testimony of our conscience, that we have conducted ourselves in the world, and especially toward you, with holiness and godly sincerity, not in fleshly wisdom but by the grace of God. **13** For we are not writing anything to you other than what you can read and understand. And I trust you will fully understand **14** just as you have partially understood us, that we are your boast, just as you are ours, in the day of the Lord Jesus. **15** And in this confidence, I planned to come to you before, so that you might have a second benefit—**16** to visit you on my way to Macedonia, and then to come back to you from Macedonia and be helped by you on my way to Judea. **17** When I planned this, did I do so lightly? Or do I make plans according to the flesh, so that with me it is "Yes, Yes" and "No, No"? **18** But as God is faithful, our word to you was not "Yes" and "No." **19** For the Son of God, Jesus Christ, who was preached among you by us—by me, Silvanus (Silas), and Timothy—was not "Yes" and "No," but in Him it was always "Yes." **20** .For all of God's promises are "Yes" in Him, and through Him the "Amen" (so be it) is spoken to the glory of God through us. **21** Now it is God who establishes us with you in Christ and has anointed us, **22** who has also sealed us and given us the Spirit in our hearts as a deposit (guarantee). **23** I call God as my witness that it was to spare you that I did not return to Corinth. **24** .Not that we lord it over your faith, but we work with you for your joy, because it is by faith that you stand firm.

Chapter 2

1 So I made up my mind that I would not make another painful visit to you. **2** For if I cause you grief, who is left to make me glad but the one I grieve? **3** I wrote as I did, so that when I came, I would not be distressed by those who should make me rejoice. I had confidence in all of you that my joy would be yours. **4** For out of great affliction and anguish of heart I wrote to you with many tears, not to grieve you, but to let you know the depth of my love for you. **5** If anyone has caused you grief, he has not grieved me, but to some extent—so as not to overstate it—all of you. **6** The punishment inflicted on him by the majority is sufficient. **7** Now instead, you should forgive and comfort him, so that he will not be overwhelmed by excessive sorrow. **8** I urge you, therefore, to reaffirm your love for him. **9** I wrote to you for this purpose: to test you and see if you would obey in everything. **10** If you forgive anyone, I also forgive him. And what I have forgiven—if there was anything to forgive—I have forgiven in the sight of Christ for your sake, **11** so that Satan will not outwit us. For we are not unaware of his schemes. **12** Now when I went to Troas (a city in Asia Minor) to preach the gospel of Christ, and a door was opened for me by the Lord, **13** I still had no peace of mind because I did not find my brother Titus there. So I said goodbye to them and went on to Macedonia. **14** But thanks be to God, who always leads us in triumph in Christ and through us spreads everywhere the fragrance of the knowledge of Him. **15** For we are to God the pleasing aroma of Christ among those who are being saved and among those who are perishing. **16** To the one we are the smell of death that brings death; to the other, the fragrance of life that brings life. And who is equal to such a task? **17** Unlike so many, we do not peddle (sell) the word of God for profit. On the contrary, in Christ we speak before God with sincerity, as those sent from God.

Chapter 3

1. Are we beginning to commend ourselves again? Or do we need, like some people, letters of recommendation to you or from you? **2.** You yourselves are our letter, written on our hearts, known and read by everyone. **3.** You show that you are a letter from Christ, the result of our ministry, written not with ink but with the Spirit of the living God, not on tablets of stone, but on tablets of human hearts. **4.**Such confidence we have through Christ before God. **5** Not that we are competent in ourselves to claim anything for ourselves, but our competence comes from God. **6.** He has made us competent as ministers of a new covenant—not of the letter (law) but of the Spirit; for the letter kills, but the Spirit gives life. **7** Now if the ministry that brought death, which was engraved in letters on stone (referring to the Ten Commandments), came with glory, so that the Israelites could not look steadily at the face of Moses because of its glory, fading though it was, **8** will not the ministry of the Spirit be even more glorious? **9.** If the ministry that condemns men is glorious, how much more glorious is the ministry that brings righteousness! **10** For what was glorious has no glory now in comparison with the surpassing glory. **11.** And if what was fading away came with glory, how much greater is the glory of that which lasts! **12** Therefore, since we have such a hope, we are very bold. **13** We are not like Moses, who would put a veil over his face to keep the Israelites from gazing at it while the radiance was fading away. **14** But their minds were made dull. For to this day the same veil remains when the old covenant (law) is read. It has not been removed, because

only in Christ is it taken away. **15** Even to this day, when Moses is read, a veil covers their hearts. **16.** But whenever anyone turns to the Lord, the veil is taken away. **17** Now the Lord is the Spirit, and where the Spirit of the Lord is, there is freedom. **18.** And we, who with unveiled faces all reflect the Lord's glory, are being transformed into His likeness with ever-increasing glory, which comes from the Lord, who is the Spirit.

Chapter 4

1. Therefore, since we have this ministry, and we have received mercy, we do not lose heart. **2.** Rather, we have renounced secret and shameful ways; we do not use deception, nor do we distort the word of God. On the contrary, we set forth the truth plainly, commending ourselves to everyone's conscience in the sight of God. **3.** And even if our gospel is veiled (hidden), it is veiled only to those who are perishing, **4.** Whose minds the god of this age (Satan) has blinded, so that they cannot see the light of the gospel that displays the glory of Christ, who is the image of God. **5.** For we do not preach ourselves, but Christ Jesus as Lord, and ourselves as your servants for Jesus' sake. **6.** For it is God who said, "Let light shine out of darkness," who has shone in our hearts to give us the light of the knowledge of God's glory displayed in the face of Jesus Christ. **7.** But we have this treasure (the gospel) in jars of clay (fragile human vessels), to show that this all-surpassing power is from God and not from us. **8.** We are hard pressed on every side, but not crushed; perplexed, but not in despair; **9.** Persecuted (victimized), but not abandoned; struck down, but not destroyed. **10.** We always carry around in our bodies the death of Jesus, so that the life of Jesus may also be revealed in our bodies. **11.** For we who are alive are always being given over to death for Jesus' sake, so that His life may also be revealed in our mortal bodies. **12.** So then, death is at work in us, but life is at work in you. **13.** It is written, "I believed; therefore I have spoken." Since we have the same spirit of faith, we also believe and therefore speak, **14.** Because we know that the One who raised the Lord Jesus from the dead will also raise us with Jesus and present us with you to Himself. **15.** All this is for your benefit, so that the grace that is reaching more and more people may cause thanksgiving to overflow to the glory of God. **16.** Therefore, we do not lose heart. Though outwardly we are wasting away, yet inwardly we are being renewed day by day. **17.** for our light and momentary troubles are achieving for us an eternal glory that far outweighs them all. **18.** So we fix our eyes not on what is seen, but on what is unseen. For what is seen is temporary, but what is unseen is eternal.

Chapter 5

1. For we know that if our earthly house (this body), which is like a tent, is destroyed, we have a building from God, a house not made by human hands, eternal in the heavens. **2.** In this earthly body, we groan, earnestly desiring to be clothed with our heavenly dwelling, **3.** because when we are clothed in that heavenly body, we will not be found naked. **4.** For while we are in this earthly tent (our current bodies), we groan and are burdened, not because we want to be rid of our bodies, but because we want to be further clothed. We long for mortality to be swallowed up by eternal life. **5.** Now, the one who has prepared us for this transformation is God, and He has given us the Holy Spirit as a guarantee of what is to come. **6.** So, we are always confident. We know that while we are at home in this body, we are absent from the Lord. **7.** For we walk by faith, not by sight. **8.** We are confident, and even more pleased to be absent from the body and to be present with the Lord. **9.** Therefore, whether we are at home in the body or away from it, our goal is to be well-pleasing to Him. **10.** For we must all appear before the judgment seat of Christ, so that each one of us may receive what is due for the things done while in the body, whether good or bad. **11.** Knowing the fear of the Lord, we try to persuade others. But we are well known to God, and I hope we are also well known to your consciences. **12.** We are not boasting about ourselves again, but giving you an opportunity to boast on our behalf, so that you can answer those who boast about outward appearances rather than the heart. **13.** If we are out of our minds, it is for God; if we are of sound mind, it is for you. **14.** For Christ's love compels us, because we are convinced that one died for all, and therefore all died. **15.** And He died for all, so that those who live should no longer live for themselves but for Him who died for them and was raised again. **16.** So, from now on, we regard no one according to the flesh. Though we once regarded Christ this way, we no longer do so. **17.** Therefore, if anyone is in Christ, he is a new creation. The old has gone, the new has come! **18.** All this is from God, who reconciled us to Himself through Jesus Christ, and has given us the ministry of reconciliation. **19.** God was in Christ reconciling the world to Himself, not counting people's sins against them. And He has committed to us the message of reconciliation. **20.** We are therefore Christ's ambassadors, as though God were making His appeal through us. We implore you on Christ's behalf: Be reconciled to God. **21.** God made Him who had no sin to be sin for us, so that in Him we might become the righteousness of God.

Chapter 6

1. As we work alongside God in this ministry, we urge you not to receive His grace in vain. **2.** God says, "At the right time, I heard you; in the day of salvation, I helped you." Now is that moment of grace; today is the day of salvation. **3.** We avoid causing offense in anything so that our ministry remains above reproach. **4.** Instead, we prove ourselves as true servants of God by enduring trials: through patience, affliction, hardships, and difficulties, **5.** by enduring beatings, imprisonments, riots, labor, sleepless nights, and hunger; **6.** through purity, knowledge, patience, kindness, the Holy Spirit, and genuine love, **7.** by the word of truth, by God's power, and by the armor of righteousness in every situation—whether facing attack or support, **8.** through both honor and dishonor, through good and bad reports; as those who are misunderstood, but yet remain true; **9.** as people who are unknown, but are well known; as people who seem to be dying, but are still alive; as those disciplined, but not destroyed; **10.** as sorrowful, but always rejoicing; as poor, but enriching many; as having nothing, yet possessing everything. **11.** Corinthians, we have been open with you, and we have shown you our hearts without reservation. **12.** The restrictions you experience are not because of us, but because of your own hearts and desires. **13.** In return, I speak to you as to children: Open your hearts to us, just as we have opened ours to you. **14.** Do not become closely aligned with unbelievers. What partnership does righteousness have with lawlessness? Or what fellowship does light have with darkness? **15.** How can Christ be in harmony with Belial (a false god)? Or what common ground is there between a believer and an unbeliever? **16.** What agreement does the temple of God have with idols? For we are the temple of the living God, as God has promised: "I will live among them, walk with them, and be their God, and they will be My people." **17.** Therefore, God says: "Come out from among them and be separate. Touch nothing unclean, and I will receive you." **18.** "I will be a Father to you, and you will be My sons and daughters, says the Lord Almighty."

Chapter 7

1. Since we have these promises, dear ones (beloved), let us cleanse ourselves from all defilement (filthiness) of body and spirit, perfecting holiness in the fear of God. **2.** Open your hearts to us. We have wronged no one, we have corrupted no one, we have cheated no one. **3.** I am not saying this to condemn you; for I have said before that you are in our hearts, to die together and to live together. **4.** Great is my boldness of speech toward you, great is my boasting on your behalf. I am filled with comfort. I am exceedingly joyful in all our tribulation. **5.** For indeed, when we came to Macedonia, our bodies had no rest, but we were troubled on every side. Outside were conflicts, inside were fears. **6.** Nevertheless, God, who comforts the downcast (those who are low), comforted us by the coming of Titus. **7.** And not only by his coming, but also by the consolation (comfort) with which he was comforted in you, when he told us of your earnest desire, your mourning, your zeal for me, so that I rejoiced even more. **8.** For even if I made you sorry (grieved) with my letter, I do not regret it; though I did regret it. For I perceive that the same epistle made you sorry, though only for a while. **9.** Now I rejoice, not that you were made sorry, but that your sorrow led to repentance. For you were made sorry in a godly manner, that you might suffer loss from us in nothing. **10.** For godly sorrow produces repentance leading to salvation, not to be regretted; but the sorrow of the world produces death. **11.** For observe this very thing that you sorrowed in a godly manner: What diligence it produced in you, what clearing of yourselves, what indignation, what fear, what vehement desire, what zeal, what vindication! In all things you proved yourselves to be clear in this matter. **12.** Therefore, although I wrote to you, I did not do it for the sake of him who had

done the wrong, nor for the sake of him who suffered wrong, but that our care for you in the sight of God might appear to you. **13.** Therefore, we have been comforted in your comfort. And we rejoiced exceedingly more for the joy of Titus, because his spirit has been refreshed by you all. **14.** For if in anything I have boasted to him about you, I am not ashamed. But as we spoke all things to you in truth, even so our boasting to Titus was found true. **15.** And his affections are greater for you as he remembers the obedience of you all, how with fear and trembling you received him. **16.** Therefore, I rejoice that I have confidence in you in everything.

Chapter 8

1. Moreover, brethren, we want to make known to you the grace of God bestowed on the churches of Macedonia: **2.** that in a great trial of affliction (suffering), the abundance of their joy and their deep poverty overflowed in rich generosity (liberality). **3.** For I testify (witness) that according to their ability, and even beyond their ability, they gave freely, **4.** Pleading with us with great urgency (seriousness) to receive the gift and the fellowship of ministering (serving) to the saints. **5.** And not only as we had hoped, but they first gave themselves to the Lord, and then to us, by the will of God (according to God's plan). **6.** So we urged Titus, that as he had begun, he would also complete this grace in you as well. **7.** But just as you abound (excel) in everything—in faith, speech, knowledge, all diligence (eagerness), and love for us—see that you abound in this grace also. **8.** I am not commanding you, but testing the sincerity (genuineness) of your love by the diligence of others. **9.** For you know the grace of our Lord Jesus Christ, that though He was rich (spiritually), for your sakes He became poor (humbled Himself), that you through His poverty might become rich (spiritually blessed). **10.** And in this I give advice: It is to your benefit (advantage) not only to be doing what you began a year ago, and were eager (desirous) to do, **11.** but now you must also finish it, that as there was a readiness (willingness) to desire it, so there may be a completion (fulfillment) from what you have. **12.** For if there is a willing mind (heart), it is accepted according to what one has, not according to what he does not have. **13.** I do not mean that others should be eased (comforted) and you burdened (suffer), **14.** but that there may be equality (fairness). Your abundance (wealth) may supply their lack (need), so their abundance may supply your lack—that there may be fairness. **15.** As it is written, "He who gathered much had nothing left over, and he who gathered little had no lack." **16.** But thanks be to God who has put the same earnest care (concern) for you into the heart of Titus. **17.** For he not only accepted our request (appeal), but being more diligent (eager), he went to you voluntarily (on his own). **18.** And we have sent with him the brother whose praise (reputation) is in the gospel throughout all the churches, **19.** and not only that, but who was also chosen by the churches to accompany us with this gift, administered (distributed) by us to the glory of the Lord Himself, showing your ready mind (eagerness), **20.** Avoiding that anyone should blame (criticize) us in this generous gift. **21.** Providing honorable (respectable) things, not only in the sight of the Lord but also in the sight of men. **22.** And we have sent with them our brother whom we have often proven diligent (faithful) in many things, but now much more diligent because of the great confidence (trust) we have in you. **23.** If anyone inquires about Titus, he is my partner and fellow worker concerning you. Or if our brethren (brothers in Christ) are asked about, they are messengers (representatives) of the churches, the glory of Christ. **24.** Therefore, show to them, and before the churches, the proof of your love and of our boasting (pride) on your behalf.

Chapter 9

1. Now concerning the service (ministering) to the saints, it is unnecessary (superfluous) for me to write to you; **2.** For I know your willingness (eagerness), about which I boast (brag) of you to the Macedonians, that Achaia was ready a year ago; and your zeal (enthusiasm) has stirred up the majority. **3.** Yet I have sent the brothers (brethren), lest our boasting of you should be in vain (without purpose) in this matter, that, as I said, you may be ready; **4.** Lest if some Macedonians come with me and find you unprepared, we (not to mention you!) should be ashamed (embarrassed) of this confident boasting. **5.** Therefore, I thought it necessary to urge (exhort) the brothers to go to you ahead of time, and prepare your generous gift beforehand, which you had promised earlier, that it may be ready as a matter of generosity (willingness) and not as a grudging (reluctant) obligation. **6.** But this I say: He who sows sparingly (little) will also reap sparingly and he who sows bountifully (abundantly) will also reap bountifully. **7.** So let each one give as he purposes in his heart, not grudgingly (in a reluctant manner) or of necessity (under compulsion); for God loves a cheerful (joyful) giver. **8.** And God is able to make all grace abound (increase) toward you, that you, always having all sufficiency (adequacy) in all things, may have an abundance for every good work. **9.** As it is written: "He has dispersed (scattered) abroad, He has given to the poor; His righteousness endures forever." **10.** Now may He who supplies seed to the sower (farmer), and bread for food, supply and multiply (increase) the seed you have sown and increase the fruits (results) of your righteousness, **11.** while you are enriched (blessed) in everything for all liberality (generosity), which causes thanksgiving through us to God. **12.** For the administration (management) of this service not only supplies the needs of the saints, but also is abounding (overflowing) through many thanksgivings to God, **13.** while, through the proof (evidence) of this ministry, they glorify God for the obedience (faithfulness) of your confession (profession) to the gospel of Christ, and for your liberal (generous) sharing with them and all men, **14.** and by their prayer for you, who long (earnestly desire) for you because of the exceeding grace (great kindness) of God in you. **15.** Thanks be to God for His indescribable (unspeakable) gift!

Chapter 10

1. Now I, Paul, myself am pleading (begging) with you by the meekness (humility) and gentleness of Christ--who in presence am lowly (humble) among you, but being absent am bold toward you. **2.** But I beg (urge) you that when I am present I may not be bold with that confidence (assurance) by which I intend to be bold against some, who think of us as if we walked according to the flesh (worldly desires). **3.** For though we walk in the flesh (human bodies), we do not war according to the flesh (worldly methods). **4.** For the weapons of our warfare are not carnal (physical) but mighty in God for pulling down strongholds (fortresses), **5.** casting down arguments (arguments against God) and every high thing that exalts itself against the knowledge (truth) of God, bringing every thought into captivity (obedience) to the obedience of Christ, **6.** and being ready to punish (correct) all disobedience when your obedience is fulfilled. **7.** Do you look at things according to the outward appearance (superficial view)? If anyone is convinced (persuaded) in himself that he is Christ's, let him again consider this in himself, that just as he is Christ's, even so we are Christ's. **8.** For even if I should boast somewhat more about our authority, which the Lord gave us for edification (building up) and not for your destruction, I shall not be ashamed-- **9.** lest I seem to terrify (scare) you by letters. **10.** "For his letters," they say, "are weighty and powerful, but his bodily presence is weak, and his speech contemptible (despised)." **11.** Let such a person consider this, that what we are in word by letters when we are absent, such we will also be in deed (action) when we are present. **12.** For we dare not class (rank) ourselves or compare ourselves with those who commend (praise) themselves. But they, measuring themselves by themselves, and comparing themselves among themselves, are not wise (foolish). **13.** We, however, will not boast beyond measure (exaggerate), but within the limits (boundaries) of the sphere (area) which God appointed (gave) us--a sphere which especially includes you. **14.** For we are not overextending ourselves (going beyond our limits), as though our authority did not extend to you, for it was to you that we came with the gospel of Christ; **15.** Not boasting of things beyond measure (exaggerated achievements), that is, in other men's labors (work), but having hope (trust), that as your faith is increased, we shall be greatly enlarged by you in our sphere, **16.** to preach the gospel in the regions beyond you, and not to boast in another man's sphere (territory) of accomplishment. **17.** But "he who glories, let him glory in the Lord." **18.** For not he who commends himself is approved (approved by God), but whom the Lord commends.

Chapter 11

1. Oh, that you would bear with me in a little folly (foolishness)--and indeed you do bear with me. **2.** For I am jealous (protectively concerned) for you with godly jealousy. For I have betrothed (promised in marriage) you to one husband, that I may present you as a chaste

(pure) virgin to Christ. **3.** But I fear, lest somehow, as the serpent (Satan) deceived Eve by his craftiness (cleverness), so your minds may be corrupted (led astray) from the simplicity (purity) that is in Christ. **4.** For if he who comes preaches another Jesus whom we have not preached, or if you receive a different spirit which you have not received, or a different gospel which you have not accepted--you may well put up with it! **5.** For I consider that I am not at all inferior to the most eminent (famous) apostles. **6.** Even though I am untrained in speech, yet I am not in knowledge. But we have been thoroughly manifested (revealed) among you in all things. **7.** Did I commit sin in humbling myself (lowering myself) that you might be exalted (lifted up), because I preached the gospel of God to you free of charge? **8.** I robbed (took from) other churches, taking wages (money) from them to minister (serve) to you. **9.** And when I was present with you, and in need, I was a burden (imposition) to no one, for what I lacked the brethren who came from Macedonia supplied. And in everything I kept myself from being burdensome to you, and so I will keep myself. **10.** As the truth of Christ is in me, no one shall stop me from this boasting (confidence) in the regions of Achaia. **11.** Why? Because I do not love you? God knows! **12.** But what I do, I will also continue to do, that I may cut off (prevent) the opportunity from those who desire an opportunity to be regarded (treated) just as we are in the things of which they boast. **13.** For such are false apostles, deceitful (dishonest) workers, transforming (disguising) themselves into apostles of Christ. **14.** And no wonder! For Satan himself transforms himself into an angel of light. **15.** Therefore it is no great thing if his ministers also transform themselves into ministers of righteousness, whose end (outcome) will be according to their works. **16.** I say again, let no one think me a fool. If otherwise, at least receive me as a fool that I also may boast a little. **17.** What I speak, I speak not according to the Lord, but as it were, foolishly, in this confidence of boasting. **18.** Seeing that many boast according to the flesh (human standards), I also will boast. **19.** For you put up with fools gladly, since you are wise! **20.** For you put up with it if one brings you into bondage (enslaves you), if one devours (takes advantage of) you, if one takes from you, if one exalts (raises) himself, if one strikes (hits) you on the face. **21.** To our shame, I say that we were too weak for that! But in whatever anyone is bold (daring)--I speak foolishly--I am bold also. **22.** Are they Hebrews? So am I. Are they Israelites? So am I. Are they the seed (descendants) of Abraham? So am I. **23.** Are they ministers (servants) of Christ?--I speak as a fool--I am more: in labors (hard work) more abundant (plentiful), in stripes (beatings) above measure, in prisons more frequently, in deaths often. **24.** From the Jews five times I received forty stripes minus one. **25.** Three times I was beaten with rods; once I was stoned; three times I was shipwrecked; a night and a day I have been in the deep (sea); **26.** in journeys (traveling) often, in perils (dangers) of waters, in perils of robbers, in perils of my own countrymen, in perils of the Gentiles (non-Jews), in perils in the city, in perils in the wilderness, in perils in the sea, in perils among false brethren (pretend believers); **27.** in weariness (fatigue) and toil (labor), in sleeplessness often, in hunger and thirst, in fasting (abstaining from food) often, in cold and nakedness-- **28.** Besides the other things, what comes upon me daily: my deep concern (anxiety) for all the churches. **29.** Who is weak, and I am not weak? Who is made to stumble (fall), and I do not burn with indignation (anger)? **30.** If I must boast, I will boast in the things which concern my infirmity (weakness). **31.** The God and Father of our Lord Jesus Christ, who is blessed forever, knows that I am not lying. **32.** In Damascus the governor, under Aretas the king, was guarding the city of the Damascenes with a garrison, desiring to arrest me; **33.** But I was let down in a basket through a window in the wall, and escaped from his hands.

Chapter 12

1. It is doubtless not profitable (useful) for me to boast. I will come to visions and revelations of the Lord: **2.** I know a man in Christ who fourteen years ago--whether in the body I do not know, or whether out of the body I do not know, God knows--such a one was caught up to the third heaven. **3.** And I know such a man--whether in the body or out of the body I do not know, God knows-- **4.** How he was caught up into Paradise and heard inexpressible (unutterable) words, which it is not lawful (permitted) for a man to utter. **5.** Of such a one I will boast; yet of myself I will not boast, except in my infirmities (weaknesses). **6.**

For though I might desire to boast, I will not be a fool; for I will speak the truth. But I refrain (hold back), lest anyone should think of me above what he sees me to be or hears from me. **7.** And lest I should be exalted (lifted up) above measure by the abundance (greatness) of the revelations, a thorn in the flesh (a persistent problem) was given to me, a messenger of Satan to buffet (strike) me, lest I be exalted above measure. **8.** Concerning this thing I pleaded (begged) with the Lord three times that it might depart from me. **9.** And He said to me, "My grace is sufficient (enough) for you, for my strength is made perfect in weakness." Therefore, most gladly I will rather boast in my infirmities, that the power of Christ may rest (be upon) me. **10.** Therefore I take pleasure (delight) in infirmities, in reproaches (insults), in needs (hardships), in persecutions (suffering), in distresses (troubles), for Christ's sake. For when I am weak, then I am strong. **11.** I have become a fool in boasting; you have compelled (forced) me. For I ought to have been commended (praised) by you; for in nothing was I behind the most eminent (greatest) apostles, though I am nothing. **12.** Truly the signs of an apostle were accomplished (fulfilled) among you with all perseverance (endurance), in signs and wonders and mighty deeds. **13.** for what is it in which you were inferior (lacking) to other churches, except that I myself was not burdensome (a burden) to you? Forgive me this wrong! **14.** Now for the third time I am ready to come to you. And I will not be burdensome to you; for I do not seek yours, but you. For the children ought not to lay up (store up) for the parents, but the parents for the children. **15.** And I will very gladly spend and be spent (exhaust myself) for your souls; though the more abundantly I love you, the less I am loved. **16.** But be that as it may, I did not burden you. Nevertheless, being crafty (clever), I caught you by cunning (deception)! **17.** Did I take advantage (exploit) of you by any of those whom I sent to you? **18.** I urged (encouraged) Titus, and sent our brother with him. Did Titus take advantage of you? Did we not walk in the same spirit? Did we not walk in the same steps? **19.** Again, do you think that we excuse (justify) ourselves to you? We speak before God in Christ. But we do all things, beloved, for your edification (building up). **20.** For I fear lest, when I come, I shall not find you such as I wish, and that I shall be found by you such as you do not wish; lest there be contentions (arguments), jealousies (envies), outbursts of wrath (anger), selfish ambitions (self-centered desires), backbiting's (gossip), whisperings (secret talk), conceits (pride), tumults (disorder); **21.** Lest, when I come again, my God will humble (bring me low) me among you, and I shall mourn (grieve) for many who have sinned before and have not repented (turned away) of the uncleanness, fornication (immorality), and lewdness (indecency) which they have practiced.

Chapter 13

1. This will be my third time visiting you. "Every matter must be confirmed by the testimony (witness) of two or three witnesses." **2.** I already gave you a warning the second time I was with you, and now, while absent, I repeat it: when I return, I will not show mercy to those who have sinned earlier, or to anyone else, **3.** since you want proof (evidence) that Christ is speaking through me. He is not weak in dealing with you, but is powerful (strong) among you. **4.** Indeed, He was crucified in weakness, but lives by God's power. In the same way, though we are weak in Him, by God's power we will live with Him when we deal with you. **5.** Test yourselves to see if you are truly in the faith; examine yourselves. Don't you know that Jesus Christ is in you—unless you fail (don't pass) the test? **6.** I hope you will discover that we have not failed the test. **7.** We pray that you will do nothing wrong—not so that others can see that we passed the test, but so that you will do what is right, even if it may seem like we failed. **8.** We cannot oppose the truth, only support (stand for) the truth. **9.** We rejoice whenever we are weak and you are strong, and our prayer is for your complete restoration (healing). **10.** This is why I write these things while I am away—so that when I come, I won't have to be severe in the authority God has given me. This authority is meant to build you up, not to tear you down. **11.** Finally, brothers and sisters, rejoice! Seek to be fully restored (recovered), encourage one another, be united in spirit, and live peacefully. The God of love and peace will be with you. **12.** Greet one another with a holy kiss. **13.** All of God's people here send their greetings. **14.** May the grace (favor) of the Lord Jesus Christ, the love of God, and the fellowship (partnership) of the Holy Spirit be with all of you?

56 – Galatians

Chapter 1

1. Paul, an apostle (one sent with authority to deliver a message), not appointed by men or through human means, but by Jesus Christ and God the Father, who raised Him from the dead. **2.** To the churches in Galatia (a region in Asia Minor), and all the believers with me, I write to you. **3.** May grace (unmerited favor) and peace (harmony) come to you from God the Father and our Lord Jesus Christ, **4.** who gave Himself for our sins to rescue us from this present evil age (sinful world around us), in accordance with the will of our God and Father, **5.** to whom belongs glory (honor) forever and ever. Amen. **6.** I am astonished (surprised) that you are so quickly turning away from the one who called you by His grace (unmerited favor) in Christ to a gospel that is not even true. **7.** This so-called "gospel" is not another gospel; some people are disturbing (troubling) you by trying to distort (twist) the true gospel of Christ. **8.** Even if we or an angel from heaven should preach any other gospel to you than the one we preached, let that person be accursed (cursed). **9.** As I said before, I repeat: If anyone preaches a different gospel than the one you received, let them be accursed (cursed). **10.** Am I now seeking the approval (acceptance) of men, or of God? Am I trying to please people? If I were still trying to please men, I would not be a servant (one who serves) of Christ. **11.** Let me make it clear (obvious), brothers and sisters, that the gospel I preached is not based on human wisdom or teaching. **12.** I did not receive it from any man, nor was it taught to me; it was revealed (divinely shown) to me directly by Jesus Christ. **13.** You know about my past life in Judaism (the Jewish faith), how I persecuted (harassed and mistreated) the church of God and tried to destroy it. **14.** I advanced (grew) in Judaism beyond many of my peers, being very zealous (passionate) for the traditions of my ancestors. **15.** But when God, who set me apart (chose) from my mother's womb and called me by His grace (unmerited favor), was pleased, **16.** He revealed His Son in me, so I could preach Him to the Gentiles (non-Jews). I did not consult (ask) any human being immediately, **17.** nor did I go to Jerusalem to meet with the apostles (early church leaders) before me; instead, I went to Arabia (a region) and returned to Damascus (a city in Syria). **18.** After three years, I went to Jerusalem to visit Peter (one of Jesus' disciples), and stayed with him for fifteen days. **19.** I saw none of the other apostles, except James, the Lord's brother (leader in the Jerusalem church). **20.** (Concerning what I am writing to you, I assure you before God, I am not lying.) **21.** Afterward, I traveled to Syria (a country to the north) and Cilicia (a province in Asia Minor). **22.** The churches in Judea (region surrounding Jerusalem) in Christ did not know me personally. **23.** They only heard that the one who once persecuted them was now preaching the faith he tried to destroy. **24.** And they glorified (praised) God because of me.

Chapter 2

1. After fourteen times, I returned to Jerusalem with Barnabas and Titus. **2.** I made this trip after entering a disclosure (a godly communication from God) from God, where I intimately participated the philosophy I sermonize to the Heathens with the apostles, to insure that my work was neither wasted nor misknew. **3.** Indeed Titus, a Greek, wasn't needed (forced) to suffer circumcision (the Jewish practice of removing the manly foreskin), despite the pressure from some. **4.** Some false religionists (those pretending to be true Christians) had intimately sneaked (entered without being noticed) our species to asset on the freedom (liberty) we've in Christ Jesus, trying to bring us back under the thrall (slavery) of the law. **5.** We didn't yield (submit or give in) to them, not indeed for a moment, to cover the verity of the philosophy for your sake. **6.** As for those who sounded important (influential), their status doesn't count to me; God doesn't show favoritism (partiality). They added nothing to my communication. **7.** When they honored that I had been entrusted (given responsibility) with the philosophy for the uncircumcised (Heathens), just as Peter had been entrusted with the philosophy for the circumcised (Jews), **8.** For the same God who worked through Peter for the Jews also worked through me for the Heathens, **9.** When James, Peter, and John, who were seen as pillars (strong leaders) in the church, honored the grace (unearned favor) God had given me, they extended the right hand of fellowship (formal agreement) to me and Barnabas, agreeing that we should go to the Heathens while they would continue their work among the Jews. **10.** They only asked that we flash back the poor (those in need), which I was eager to do. **11.** When Peter came to Antioch, I intimately brazened (challenged) him because his conduct were wrong. **12.** Before certain men from James arrived, Peter ate with the Heathens, but when they came, he withdrew (pulled back), stewing (being hysterical of) those from the circumcision party (group of Jews averring on Jewish law). **13.** The other Jews joined in his insincerity (pretending to be one thing while acting negative), so much so that indeed Barnabas was led amiss (misled) by their gesture. **14.** When I saw they weren't walking in line with the verity of the philosophy, I rebuked (challenged) Peter intimately, asking, "You're a Jew, yet you live like a Gentile, not following Jewish customs. Why are you now trying to impel (force) Heathens to live like Jews?" **15.** We, who are Jews by birth and not Gentile wrongdoers (those who don't follow Jewish laws), **16.** Know that a person isn't justified (declared righteous) by the workshop of the law but by faith in Jesus Christ thus, we've placed our faith in Christ Jesus, so that we may be justified by faith, not by the workshop of the law, because no bone will be justified by observing (following) the law. **17.** But if, while seeking to be justified in Christ, we're set up to be wrongdoers, does that mean Christ promotes sin? clearly not! **18.** Still, I prove myself to be a felon (offender), If I rebuild what I've torn down. **19.** Through the law, I failed to the law, so that I might live for God. **20.** I've been crucified (executed on a cross) with Christ; I no longer live, but Christ lives in me. The life I now live in the meat (physical body), I live by faith in the Son of God, who loved me and gave Himself for me. **21.** I don't abate (disregard or reject) the grace of God, for if righteousness could be gained through the law, also Christ failed for nothing.

Chapter3

1. O foolish (unwise) Galatians! Who has bewitched (misled) you, not to observe the verity, before whose eyes Jesus Christ was easily portrayed as crucified (executed for your sins)? **2.** Let me ask you Did you admit the Spirit (God's presence) by workshop of the law (obedience to commands), or by hail and believing the communication of faith (trust in God's pledges)? **3.** Are you so foolish (lacking wisdom)? Having begun by the Spirit (the Holy Spirit), do you now suppose you can be perfected (made complete) by mortal trouble (the meat)? **4.** Have you suffered so much for nothing — if it was for nothing? **5.** Does the one who gives you the Spirit (God's presence) and works cautions (extraordinary acts) among you do so by the law, or by hail and believing in faith? **6.** Just as Abraham (father of the Jewish people) believed God, and it was counted to him as righteousness (a right relationship with God). **7.** Understand this Those of faith (trust in God) are the true sons of Abraham (spiritual descendants). **8.** Scripture forefelt (prognosticated) that God would justify (declare righteous) the Heathens (non-Jews) by faith and sermonized the philosophy (good news) to Abraham, saying," In you all the nations will be blessed." **9.** So those who have faith are blessed (favored) just as Abraham was. **10.** For all who depend on workshop (conduct) of the law are under a curse (discipline), for it's written," Cursed is everyone who doesn't do everything in the Book of the Law" (the Torah, the first five books). **11.** It's clear that no bone is justified (declared righteous) by the law, because" The righteous shall live by faith" (Habakkuk 24). **12.** The law isn't grounded on faith; rather," The person who does these effects will live by them" (Leviticus 185). **13.** Christ (Jesus) has redeemed (saved) us from the curse (penalty) of the law, getting a curse for us (taking our penalty), for it's written," Cursed is everyone who's hung on a tree" (Deuteronomy 2123). **14.** This was so that the blessing (favor) of Abraham might come to the Heathens (non-Jews) through Christ Jesus, and that we might admit the pledge (assurance) of the Spirit (God's presence) through faith. **15.** Sisters, let me explain Indeed a mortal covenant (agreement), formerly verified (ratified), can not be canceled. **16.** The pledges (assurances) were spoken to Abraham and his seed (assignee). Book doesn't say" seeds" (plural), but" seed" (singular), meaning Christ. **17.** The law, which came 430 times latterly, can not cancel (abate) the covenant (agreement) verified by God in Christ, so as to void the pledge. **18.** still, it no longer depends on the pledge, If the heritage (pledge) depends on the law. But God gave it to Abraham by pledge. **19.** Why also was the law given? It was added because of transgressions (sins), until the Seed (Jesus Christ) would

come. The law was ordained through angels by a middleman (Moses). **20.** A middleman doesn't act for just one party, but God is one. **21.** Is the law against (opposed to) God's pledges? clearly not! For if a law could give life (eternal life), righteousness (right standing with God) would come through the law. **22.** But Book (the Bible) has confined (locked) all under sin (guilt), so that the pledge of faith in Jesus Christ might be given to those who believe. **23.** Before faith came, we were under the law (guarded by it), locked up until faith was revealed. **24.** Thus, the law was our instructor (schoolteacher), leading us to Christ, so that we might be justified (declared righteous) by faith. **25.** But now that faith has come, we're no longer under the supervision (guidance) of the law. **26.** For all of you're children (sons and daughters) of God through faith in Christ Jesus. **27.** For all of you who were baptized (immersed in water as a symbol of faith) into Christ (joined with Christ) have clothed yourselves with Christ. **28.** There's neither Jew (assignee of Abraham) nor Greek (Gentile), neither slave (possessed) nor free (not possessed), neither manly (man) nor womanish (woman); for you're all one in Christ Jesus. **29.** And if you belong (are a member) to Christ, also you're Abraham's seed (spiritual descendants), and heirs at law (legatees) according to the pledge.

Chapter 4

1. As long as an heir at law (someone set to inherit) is a child, he has no advantage over a menial, indeed though he's the proprietor of everything. **2.** He's under teachers (instructors) and directors (overseers) until the time his father (the bone in charge) has set. **3.** In the same way, we too, when we were children, were held in thrall to the introductory principles (worldly forces) of the world. **4.** But when the time had completely come, God transferred His Son, born of a woman, born under the law, **5.** to redeem those under the law, so that we might be espoused as sons. **6.** And because you're sons, God transferred the Spirit of His Son into your hearts, calling out," Abba, Father!" (Abba is an Aramaic word for Father). **7.** Thus, you're no longer a menial but a son, and if a son, also an heir at law of God through Christ. **8.** But when you didn't know God, you were enslaved to those effects which by nature aren't gods (icons). **9.** But now that you know God — or rather, are known by God why turn back again to those weak and helpless effects, asking to be enslaved formerly more? **10.** You observe special days, months, seasons, and times (religious practices). **11.** I'm hysterical I've worked in vain for you. **12.** I prompt you, sisters, to come like me, for I came like you. You haven't wronged me in any way. **13.** You know that it was because of an illness (a physical condition) that I first sermonized the philosophy to you. **14.** And though my condition was a trial for you, you didn't despise or reject me, but ate me as if I were an angel of God, or indeed as Christ Jesus Himself. **15.** What happed to your joy? I swear to you that, if it were possible, you would have torn out your eyes and given them to me. **16.** Have I now come your adversary because I speak the verity to you? **17.** They zealously court you, but for no good; they want to insulate you so that you'll be zealous for them. **18.** It's always good to be zealous for what's right, and not just when I'm with you. **19.** My dear children, for whom I'm again in the pains of parturition until Christ is completely formed in you, **20.** I wish I could be with you now and change my tone, for I'm nonplussed (confused) about you. **21.** Tell me, you who want to be under the law, do you not hear to the law? **22.** For it's written that Abraham (the father of the Jewish people) had two sons one by the slave woman (Hagar), the other by the free woman (Sarah). **23.** The son of the slave woman was born according to the meat (by mortal trouble), but the son of the free woman was born through the pledge (by God's plan). **24.** These effects are emblematic (they represent commodity deeper) the two women stand for two covenants. One is from Mount Sinai (the mountain in Arabia where Moses entered the law), which gives birth to slavery, and that's Hagar. **25.** Hagar represents Mount Sinai in Arabia, and corresponds to present-day Jerusalem, which is enslaved with her children. **26.** But the Jerusalem over (the heavenly Jerusalem) is free, and she's our mama. **27.** For it's written" Rejoice, O barren one, you who have no way had a child; break forth and cry audibly, you who have no way been in labor, for further are the children of the desolate woman than of her who has a husband" (Isaiah 541, a vaticination about spiritual fruitfulness). **28.** Now, sisters, like Isaac (the promised son), we're children of pledge. **29.** But just as also, the child born according to the meat (Ishmael)

492

bedeviled the child born by the Spirit (Isaac), so it's now. **30.** But what does the Book say?" Cast out the slave woman and her son, for the son of the slave woman won't partake in the heritage with the son of the free woman." **31.** Thus, sisters, we aren't children of the slave woman, but of the free woman.

Chapter 5

1. Stand firm in the freedom (liberty) Christ gave us, and don't let yourselves be burdened by the yoke of slavery (law). **2.** I, Paul, say to you that if you are circumcised (a ritual sign of the covenant), Christ will be of no benefit to you. **3.** I warn that anyone who accepts circumcision is obligated to obey the whole law (set of commandments). **4.** You have separated yourselves from Christ, you who seek to be justified (declared righteous) by law; you have fallen from grace (God's favor). **5.** We, through the Spirit, eagerly await the hope of righteousness (being made right with God) by faith. **6.** In Christ Jesus, neither circumcision nor uncircumcision (not being circumcised) matters; only faith working through love. **7.** You were running well. Who hindered you from obeying the truth? **8.** This persuasion (teaching) does not come from the One who called you. **9.** A little leaven (yeast) works through the whole batch of dough. **10.** I am confident you will remain true to the Lord's teaching, but the one troubling you will face judgment. **11.** If I still preached circumcision, why am I being persecuted (treated harshly)? The offense of the cross (sacrifice of Christ) would cease. **12.** I wish those who trouble you would go so far as to cut themselves off (remove themselves completely). **13.** You, brothers and sisters, have been called to freedom (liberty); but don't use your freedom to indulge in sinful desires. Serve one another in love. **14.** The entire law (Jewish rules) is summed up in this one command: "Love your neighbor as yourself." **15.** But if you bite and devour each other (destroy one another), watch out, or you will be destroyed. **16.** Walk by the Spirit (guided by God's Spirit), and you will not fulfill the desires of the flesh (sinful nature). **17.** The flesh (sinful nature) desires what is contrary to the Spirit, and the Spirit desires what is contrary to the flesh; they are in conflict, so you don't do what you want. **18.** If you are led by the Spirit, you are not under the law. **19.** The works (deeds) of the flesh are obvious: sexual immorality (adultery, fornication), impurity (moral corruption), debauchery (reckless living), idolatry (worship of false gods), sorcery (witchcraft), hatred, discord (strife), jealousy, fits of rage (anger), selfish ambition, dissensions (division), heresies (false beliefs), **20.** Envy, murder, drunkenness, revelries (wild parties), and the like. I warn you, as I did before, that those who practice such things will not inherit the kingdom of God (eternal life with God). **21.** The fruit (evidence) of the Spirit is love, joy, peace, forbearance (patience), kindness, goodness, faithfulness, **22.** Gentleness and self-control against such things, there is no law (they align with God's will). **23.** Those who belong to Christ Jesus have crucified the flesh (put to death their sinful nature) with its passions and desires. **24.** Since we live by the Spirit, let us also walk by the Spirit. **25.** Let us not become conceited (proud), provoking and envying each other (being jealous of one another).

Chapter 6

1. Brothers, if someone is caught in sin (wrongdoing), you who are spiritual (led by the Spirit) should restore them gently, but be careful, or you may be tempted (fall into sin). **2.** Bear one another's burdens (help each other), and so fulfill the law of Christ (love one another). **3.** If anyone thinks they are something when they are nothing, they deceive themselves. **4.** Each one should examine their own actions, and then they will have pride in themselves, not in others. **5.** Every person will carry their own load (responsibility). **6.** Those who are taught the word (the Gospel) should share all good things with their teacher. **7.** Do not be deceived (misled); God is not mocked (cannot be fooled). A person will reap (receive) what they sow (do). **8.** Whoever sows to the flesh (worldly desires) will reap corruption (destruction), but whoever sows to the Spirit (lives by the Spirit) will reap everlasting life. **9.** Let us not grow weary (be discouraged) in doing good, for in due time we will reap (see the reward) if we do not give up. **10.** Therefore, as we have opportunity, let us do good to all, especially to the household of faith (the church). **11.** See how large the letters I use to write to you with my own hand! **12.** Those who want to impress by outward signs are compelling you to be circumcised (follow Jewish law), just to avoid persecution for the cross of Christ. **13.** Even those who are circumcised do not keep the law; they want you circumcised to boast in your flesh (outward sign of religion). **14.** But may I never boast except in the cross of our Lord Jesus Christ (His sacrifice), by whom the world has been crucified to me, and I to the world. **15.** For in Christ Jesus neither circumcision (Jewish law) nor uncircumcision (not following the law) matters, but a new creation (being transformed in Christ). **16.** Peace and mercy be upon all who walk by this rule (live according to this new way), and upon the Israel of God (the church). **17.** From now on, let no one trouble me, for I bear the marks (scars) of the Lord Jesus. **18.** Brothers, the grace of our Lord Jesus Christ be with your spirit. Amen.

57 – Ephasians

Chapter 1

1. Paul, an apostle (chosen messenger by Jesus Christ through God's will), writes to the saints (holy people) in Ephesus (a city in Asia Minor), who are faithful in Christ Jesus. **2.** Grace (unmerited favor) and peace (wholeness) be to you from God our Father and the Lord Jesus Christ. **3.** Blessed (praised) be God, the Father of our Lord Jesus Christ, who has blessed us with every spiritual blessing in the heavenly realms, in Christ. **4.** Just as He chose us in Christ before the world's foundation, so that we would be holy (set apart) and blameless before Him, in love. **5.** He predestined (decided beforehand) us to be adopted as His children through Jesus Christ, according to His will and pleasure. **6.** To the praise of His glorious grace (undeserved kindness), which He freely gave us in the Beloved (Jesus). **7.** In Him (Jesus), we have redemption (freedom) through His blood, the forgiveness of sins, according to the wealth of His grace. **8.** This grace has been lavished (poured out abundantly) on us with all wisdom and understanding. **9.** He has made known to us the mystery (hidden plan) of His will, according to His good pleasure set forth in Christ. **10.** His plan is that, when the time comes, He will bring all things together in Christ, both in heaven and on earth. **11.** In Christ, we have also obtained an inheritance, having been predestined according to His purpose, who works everything according to His will. **12.** This was so that we, who were the first to hope in Christ, would be to the praise of His glory. **13.** And you also, after hearing the message of truth, the gospel of your salvation, and believing in Him, were sealed with the Holy Spirit of promise. **14.** The Holy Spirit is the guarantee of our inheritance until the redemption of God's own, to the praise of His glory. **15.** For this reason, I also, after hearing about your faith in the Lord Jesus and your love for all the saints, **16.** do not stop thanking God for you, remembering you in my prayers. **17.** I pray that the God of our Lord Jesus Christ, the Father of glory, may give you the Spirit of wisdom and revelation (insight) to know Him better. **18.** I pray that the eyes of your heart may be enlightened (opened), so that you may know the hope of His calling, the riches of the glory of His inheritance in the saints, **19.** and the immeasurable greatness of His power toward us who believe, according to the working of His mighty strength. **20.** This power is the same as the strength that raised Christ from the dead and seated Him at His right hand in the heavenly realms. **21.** Christ is far above all rulers, authorities, powers, and dominions, and every name that can be named, not only in this age but also in the age to come. **22.** God placed everything under His feet and appointed Him as head over everything for the church, **23.** which is His body, the fullness of Him who fills everything in every way.

Chapter 2

1. "You were once spiritually lifeless due to your misdeeds and sins, **2.** in which you formerly lived, conforming to the world's ways and following the ruler of the realm of the air (Satan), the spirit now active in those who disobey. **3.** At one time, all of us followed this path, giving in to the desires of our physical nature and thoughts, and were by nature deserving of God's anger, like everyone else. **4.** But because of His vast mercy and the profound love He has for us, **5.** even when we were spiritually dead in our sins, God gave us life together with Christ (by grace you are saved). **6.** He raised us with Christ and seated us with Him in the heavenly places in Christ Jesus, **7.** so that in the coming times, He might reveal the limitless riches of His grace, shown in His kindness toward us through Christ Jesus. **8.** For it is by grace that you have been saved, through faith—and this is not your own doing; it is God's gift, **9.** not based on works, so that no one may boast. **10.** We are God's creation, crafted in Christ Jesus to perform good works, which God prepared in advance for us to live out. **11.** Remember that once, you who were Gentiles by birth—called 'Uncircumcised' by those called 'Circumcised' (the Jews) **12.** Were separate from Christ, excluded from Israel's community, and outsiders to the covenants of promise, without hope and without God in the world. **13.** But now, in Christ Jesus, those of you who were once far away have been brought close by the blood of Christ. **14.** For Christ Himself is our peace; He has made the two groups one and has taken down the dividing wall of hostility, **15.** by ending the law with its commands and regulations in His flesh, to create in Himself a single new humanity, establishing peace, **16.** And to unite both groups to God in one body through the cross, thereby ending their hostility. **17.** He came and proclaimed peace to you who were far off and to those who were near. **18.** Through Him, we both have access to the Father by one Spirit. **19.** So now, you are no longer strangers or foreigners, but are fellow citizens with God's people and part of His household, **20.** Built upon the foundation set by the apostles and prophets, with Christ Jesus Himself as the cornerstone. **21.** In Him, the entire structure is joined together and grows into a holy temple in the Lord, **22.** And through Him, you too are being built into a dwelling where God lives by His Spirit."

Chapter 3

1. I, Paul, a prisoner (captive) for the sake of Christ Jesus, am writing to you, the Gentiles. **2.** You have likely heard about the special grace (undeserved favor) God gave me to share with you. **3.** Through a revelation (divine unveiling), God made known to me the mystery (hidden truth) which I've briefly explained before. **4.** As you read this, you can understand my understanding of the mystery of Christ. **5.** This mystery was not made known to people in past generations, but now, by the Spirit, it has been revealed to His holy apostles and prophets. **6.** The mystery is that the Gentiles are fellow heirs (share in the inheritance), part of the same body, and share in God's promise in Christ through the gospel (good news of salvation). **7.** I became a servant of this gospel by the grace of God, given to me through the effective working (powerful operation) of His power. **8.** Although I am the least of all God's people, this grace was given to me to preach to the Gentiles the unsearchable (incomprehensible) riches of Christ, **9.** and to make clear the plan (purpose) of this mystery, which was hidden in God from the beginning of creation but is now revealed through Christ. **10.** The purpose of this mystery is that now, through the church, God's manifold (multifaceted) wisdom might be made known to the rulers and authorities in the heavenly realms. **11.** This was part of God's eternal (timeless) plan, which He accomplished in Christ Jesus our Lord. **12.** In Christ, we have boldness (freedom) and confident access (right) to God through faith. **13.** So, I urge (encourage) you not to lose heart because of the suffering I endure for you—it is for your glory. **14.** For this reason, I kneel (pray humbly) before the Father, **15.** From whom every family (all of God's people) in heaven and on earth takes its name. **16.** I pray that, according to the riches of His glory, He may strengthen (empower) you with power through His Spirit in your inner being, **17.** so that Christ may dwell (live permanently) in your hearts through faith. I pray that you, being rooted (firmly grounded) and established (settled) in love, **18.** May have the strength to comprehend (understand fully), along with all the saints (holy people), the vastness of Christ's love—its width, length, height, and depth. **19.** I pray that you may know the love of Christ that surpasses (goes beyond) knowledge, so that you may be filled with the fullness of God. **20.** Now to Him who is able (capable) to do far more than all we ask or imagine, according to the power at work within us, **21.** to Him be glory in the church and in Christ Jesus throughout all generations, forever and ever. Amen.

Chapter 4

1. Be imitators of God, as beloved children imitate their parents. **2.** Live a life of love, as Christ loved us and gave Himself as a sacrifice (offering) to God. **3.** There should be no immorality (fornication), impurity (uncleanness), or greed (covetousness) among you; this is improper for saints (holy people). **4.** No obscenity (filthiness), foolish talk, or coarse joking (crude humor) should be heard, but rather gratitude (thanksgiving). **5.** Immoral, impure, or greedy people (idolaters) have no part (inheritance) in the kingdom of Christ and God. **6.** Don't be deceived by empty (meaningless) words, for the wrath (anger) of God is coming upon the disobedient (those who refuse to obey). **7.** Do not partner (be partakers) with them. **8.** You were once in darkness (spiritual ignorance), but now you are light in the Lord; live as children

of light. **9.** The fruit of the Spirit is seen in all goodness, righteousness, and truth. **10.** Discern (find out) what pleases the Lord. **11.** Avoid fellowship (association) with the unfruitful works of darkness; expose them. **12.** It's shameful to talk about what the disobedient do in secret. **13.** Everything exposed by the light becomes visible, and anything visible is light. **14.** "Awake, rise from the dead, and Christ will shine on you." **15.** Be careful (wise) how you live; live wisely, not foolishly. **16.** Make the most of every opportunity (redeem the time), for the days are evil. **17.** Understand the will (purpose) of the Lord. **18.** Do not get drunk on wine, which leads to debauchery (recklessness), but be filled with the Spirit. **19.** Speak to one another with psalms (sacred songs), hymns, and spiritual songs, making music in your heart to the Lord. **20.** Always give thanks to God the Father for everything, in the name of our Lord Jesus Christ. **21.** Submit (yield) to one another out of reverence (fear) for Christ. **22.** Wives, submit to your husbands as to the Lord. **23.** The husband is the head (leader) of the wife, as Christ is the head of the church and its Savior (deliverer). **24.** As the church submits to Christ, wives should submit to their husbands in everything. **25.** Husbands, love your wives as Christ loved the church and gave Himself for her. **26.** To make her holy (set apart), cleansing her by the washing of water with the word. **27.** To present her as a radiant (glorious) church, without spot, wrinkle, or blemish, but holy and blameless. **28.** Husbands should love their wives as their own bodies; he who loves his wife loves himself. **29.** No one hates their own body but nourishes (feeds) and cares for it, just as Christ does the church. **30.** For we are members of His body, of His flesh, and of His bones. **31.** "For this reason, a man will leave his father and mother to unite with his wife, and the two will become one flesh." **32.** This is a profound mystery (truth), but I am speaking about Christ and the church. **33.** Each one of you must love his wife as he loves himself, and the wife must respect her husband.

Chapter 5

1. Be imitators (followers) of God, just as beloved children imitate their parents. **2.** And live a life of love, just as Christ loved us and gave Himself for us as an offering (sacrifice) and a sweet-smelling aroma to God. **3.** But there should be no sexual immorality, impurity (uncleanness), or greed (covetousness) among you, as this is improper for saints (holy people). **4.** Nor should there be any obscenity, foolish talk, or coarse joking (crude humor), which are out of place, but rather, let there be thanksgiving (gratitude). **5.** For you know that no immoral person, impure person, or greedy person (who is an idolater) has any inheritance in the kingdom of Christ and of God. **6.** Let no one deceive you with empty (meaningless) words, for because of such things the wrath (anger) of God is coming upon the sons of disobedience (those who refuse to obey). **7.** Therefore, do not be partakers (partners) with them. **8.** For you were once in darkness (spiritual ignorance), but now you are light in the Lord. Live as children of light. **9.** (For the fruit of the Spirit is seen in all goodness, righteousness, and truth.) **10.** Discern (find out) what pleases the Lord. **11.** Have no fellowship (association) with the unfruitful works of darkness, but rather expose them. **12.** It is shameful even to talk about what the disobedient do in secret. **13.** But everything exposed by the light becomes visible, for anything that becomes visible is light. **14.** Therefore, He says, "Awake, you who sleep, rise from the dead, and Christ will shine on you." **15.** Be very careful (wise) then how you live, not as unwise (foolish) but as wise, **16.** making the most of every opportunity (redeeming the time), because the days are evil. **17.** Therefore, do not be foolish, but understand what the will (purpose) of the Lord is. **18.** Do not get drunk on wine, which leads to debauchery (recklessness), but be filled with the Spirit. **19.** Speak to one another with psalms (sacred songs), hymns, and spiritual songs, singing and making music in your heart to the Lord. **20.** Always give thanks to God the Father for everything, in the name of our Lord Jesus Christ. **21.** Submit (yield) to one another out of reverence (fear) for Christ. **22.** Wives, submit to your own husbands, as to the Lord. **23.** For the husband is the head (leader) of the wife, as Christ is the head of the church, and He is the Savior (deliverer) of the body (the church). **24.** Now, as the church submits to Christ, so also wives should submit to their husbands in everything. **25.** Husbands, love your wives, just as Christ loved the church and gave Himself for her, **26.** to make her holy, cleansing her by the washing of water with the word (of God), **27.** to present her to Himself as a radiant (glorious) church, without spot or wrinkle or any blemish, but holy and blameless. **28.** In the same way, husbands should love their wives as their own bodies; he who loves his wife loves himself. **29.** After all, no one ever hated their own body, but they feed (nourish) and care for it, just as Christ does the church—**30.** for we are members of His body, of His flesh, and of His bones. **31.** "For this reason, a man will leave his father and mother and be united to his wife, and the two will become one flesh." **32.** This is a profound mystery, but I am speaking about Christ and the church. **33.** However, each one of you must love his wife as he loves himself, and the wife must respect her husband.

Chapter 6

1. Children, obey your parents in the Lord (the authority given by God), for this is the right thing to do. **2.** "Honor your father and mother" (this is the first commandment that comes with a promise): **3.** "That it may go well with you and that you may live a long life on the earth." **4.** And you, fathers, do not provoke your children to anger, but instead, raise them with the instruction (teaching) and correction (discipline) of the Lord. **5.** Bondservants (slaves), be obedient to your earthly masters (supervisors) with respect, fear, and sincerity of heart, as if serving Christ Himself. **6.** Do not serve only when you are being watched, as men-pleasers, but as bondservants (slaves) of Christ, doing the will of God from the heart. **7.** Serve with goodwill, as to the Lord, and not just to men. **8.** Knowing that whatever good a person does, he will receive the same from the Lord, whether he is a slave or free. **9.** And you, masters (employers), treat your bondservants (employees) the same way. Do not threaten them, knowing that you also have a Master in heaven, and He shows no favoritism. **10.** Finally, my brethren, be strong in the Lord and in the power of His might (strength). **11.** Put on the full armor of God, so that you can stand against the schemes (tricks) of the devil (Satan). **12.** For we are not fighting against flesh and blood, but against principalities (ruling powers), against powers (authorities), against the rulers of the darkness of this world, against spiritual hosts (forces) of wickedness in the heavenly places. **13.** Therefore, take up the whole armor of God, so that you may be able to withstand (stand firm) in the evil day, and having done everything, to remain standing. **14.** Stand firm then, with the belt (girdle) of truth buckled around your waist, with the breastplate (armor) of righteousness in place, **15.** and with your feet fitted with the readiness (preparedness) that comes from the gospel of peace. **16.** Above all, take the shield (defensive protection) of faith, with which you can extinguish all the fiery darts (arrows) of the wicked one. **17.** And take the helmet (protective headgear) of salvation and the sword of the Spirit (Holy Spirit), which is the word (message) of God. **18.** Pray at all times, with all kinds of prayers and requests, in the Spirit (Holy Spirit), being watchful and always praying for all the saints (believers), **19.** and for me, that whenever I open my mouth, words may be given to me so that I may fearlessly make known the mystery (truth) of the gospel, **20.** for which I am an ambassador in chains (a prisoner for Christ); pray that I may speak boldly, as I ought to speak. **21.** But to keep you informed, Tychicus, a beloved brother and faithful minister in the Lord, will make all things known to you about how I am doing. **22.** I have sent him to you for this very purpose, that you may know how we are, and that he may comfort your hearts. **23.** Peace be to the brethren (believers), and love with faith, from God the Father and the Lord Jesus Christ. **24.** Grace be with all those who love our Lord Jesus Christ with sincerity (true heart). Amen.

58 – Philippians

Chapter 1

1. Paul and Timothy, servants (those who serve) of Christ Jesus, to all God's holy people in Christ Jesus at Philippi, along with the overseers (church leaders) and deacons (servants of the church): **2.** Grace and peace to you from God our Father and the Lord Jesus Christ. **3.** I thank God every time I remember you. **4.** In all my prayers, I always pray with joy **5.** because of your partnership (shared work) in the gospel from the beginning until now, **6.** confident (sure) that God, who began a good work in you, will complete it until the day of Christ. **7.** It is right for me to feel this way about you, since I have you in my heart, and whether I am in chains (imprisoned) or defending the gospel, all of you share in God's grace (undeserved favor) with me. **8.** God can testify (confirm as true) how I long for you with the love of Christ. **9.** My prayer is that your love may overflow (increase) in knowledge and understanding, **10.** so you can discern (judge) what is best, pure, and blameless for the day of Christ, **11.** filled with the fruit (results) of righteousness through Jesus Christ—for the glory of God. **12.** What has happened to me has advanced (spread) the gospel. **13.** It's clear that I am in chains for Christ, **14.** and my imprisonment has made most believers more confident to preach the gospel without fear. **15.** Some preach Christ from selfish motives, but others do so from goodwill. **16.** Those who preach out of love know I am here to defend the gospel. **17.** The others preach out of selfish ambition, hoping to cause trouble for me while I'm in chains. **18.** But what matters is that Christ is preached, whether from false or true motives. And because of this, I rejoice (am glad). **19.** I trust that through your prayers and God's help, this situation will lead to my deliverance (rescue). **20.** I hope to have courage, and that Christ will be honored in my life or death. **21.** For to live is Christ, and to die is gain (better). **22.** If I live, it means fruitful work for me, but I am torn between staying and going to be with Christ. **23.** I desire to depart and be with Christ, which is far better, **24.** but it's more necessary for you that I remain. **25.** I am convinced I will stay to help you grow in your faith, **26.** so that your boasting (praise) in Christ will increase because of me. **27.** Conduct yourselves (live) in a manner worthy of the gospel of Christ. Whether I come or hear about you, I will know you stand firm in the Spirit, working together for the faith of the gospel, **28.** without fear of those who oppose you. This shows they will be destroyed, but you will be saved by God. **29.** It has been granted to you to believe in Christ and to suffer for him, **30.** since you are going through the same struggle I had, and still face.

Chapter 2

1. If you have any encouragement (comfort or strength) from being united with Christ, any comfort from His love, any shared experience of the Spirit, or any tenderness and compassion, **2.** make my joy complete by being like-minded (thinking in the same way), having the same love, and being one in spirit and mind. **3.** Do nothing out of selfish ambition (desire for personal gain) or vain conceit (empty pride). Instead, value (respect or honor) others above yourselves, **4.** not focusing only on your own interests, but also on the interests of others. **5.** In your relationships with one another, have the same mindset (attitude or way of thinking) as Christ: **6.** Who, being in very nature God, did not use His equality with God to His own advantage (to get something for Himself), **7.** but made Himself nothing by taking the nature of a servant (becoming a servant), becoming human. **8.** And being found as a man, He humbled Himself (lowered Himself) by becoming obedient to death—even death on a cross! **9.** Therefore God exalted Him (raised Him up to a high position) to the highest place and gave Him the name above every name, **10.** that at the name of Jesus every knee should bow (show respect or submission), in heaven, on earth, and under the earth, **11.** and every tongue confess (declare publicly) that Jesus Christ is Lord, to the glory of God the Father. **12.** Therefore, my dear friends, as you have always obeyed—not only in my presence but now even more in my absence—continue to work out your salvation (complete the process of salvation) with fear and trembling (with serious concern and respect), **13.** for it is God who works in you to will (to desire or choose) and to act according to His good purpose. **14.** Do everything without grumbling (complaining) or arguing (disputing), **15.** so that you may be blameless (without blame) and pure (clean), "children of God without fault in a warped (twisted or corrupt) and crooked (dishonest) generation." Then you will shine like stars in the sky, **16.** holding firmly to the word of life (the message of the gospel). And I will be able to boast (rejoice or take pride) that I did not labor (work hard) in vain (without purpose). **17.** But even if I am being poured out like a drink offering (a sacrifice) on the sacrifice and service coming from your faith, I am glad and rejoice with all of you. **18.** So you should be glad and rejoice with me. **19.** I hope to send Timothy to you soon, so that I may be cheered (comforted or encouraged) by news of you. **20.** I have no one else like him, who genuinely (sincerely) cares about your welfare (well-being). **21.** Everyone looks out for their own interests, not the interests of Christ. **22.** But you know Timothy has proved himself (demonstrated his faithfulness), because he has served with me in the gospel like a son with his father. **23.** I hope to send him soon when I know how things will go with me. **24.** I am confident (sure) that I will come soon. **25.** However, I think it is necessary (important) to send back to you

Epaphroditus, my brother, coworker (worker together with me), and fellow soldier (partner in the battle for the gospel), who is also your messenger (one who carries a message), whom you sent to care for my needs. 26. He longs (desires deeply) for all of you and is distressed (worried) because you heard he was ill. 27. He was indeed ill, almost dying. But God had mercy (compassion) on him, and on me too, sparing me sorrow upon sorrow (saving me from even greater grief). 28. Therefore, I am eager to send him back so that when you see him again, you may rejoice (be glad), and I may have less anxiety (worry). 29. Welcome him in the Lord with great joy, and honor (respect, give high regard) people like him, 30. because he risked his life (put his life in danger) for the work of Christ, making up for the help you could not give me.

Chapter 3

1. Finally, my dear friends, rejoice (take joy) in the Lord! It's no problem for me to remind you of these things, and it is beneficial (helpful) for you. 2. Be careful of those who cause trouble—those who do evil, those who focus on external rituals (outward acts, such as circumcision), mutilators of the flesh (those who emphasize physical circumcision over spiritual renewal). 3. We are the true people of God, those who worship by the Spirit of God, take pride in Christ Jesus, and rely on nothing of the flesh (nothing we do in our own strength or by outward observances). 4. Though I could have confidence in the flesh (in outward achievements or human abilities), if anyone thinks they can boast (brag) in their physical achievements, I have even more reason: 5. I was circumcised on the eighth day (according to Jewish law), born into the nation of Israel, of the tribe of Benjamin, a true Hebrew (a pure descendant of Israel); in terms of following the law, I was a Pharisee (a strict adherent of Jewish law), 6. passionate in my beliefs, even persecuting the church (actively opposing and trying to destroy the Christian faith); and as for keeping the law, I was blameless (I followed the law perfectly by outward standards). 7. But whatever I thought was an advantage to me (things I once thought were gain), I now count as a loss (a disadvantage) for the sake of knowing Christ. 8. I consider everything as a loss compared to the incomparable value (priceless worth) of knowing Christ Jesus, my Lord. For His sake, I've given up everything, considering it all worthless, so I may gain Christ 9. and be found in Him—not having a righteousness of my own based on the law (following the rules), but the righteousness (rightness with God) that comes through faith in Christ, the righteousness that comes from God and is based on faith. 10. I want to truly know Christ, to experience the power of His resurrection (the life-giving power that raised Him from the dead), and to share in His sufferings (endure hardships like He did), becoming like Him in His death, 11. and somehow, to reach the resurrection from the dead (attain the future hope of eternal life). 12. Not that I have already attained this, or am perfect (fully complete), but I press on (keep striving) to take hold of the purpose for which Christ Jesus took hold of me. 13. Brothers and sisters, I do not consider myself to have fully grasped it yet. But this one thing I do: Forgetting what is behind (letting go of past achievements or failures) and focusing on what is ahead, 14. I press on toward the goal to win the prize (eternal life and salvation) for which God has called me to heaven in Christ Jesus. 15. All who are mature (spiritually mature) should adopt this perspective. And if you think differently on some point, God will make that clear to you as well. 16. Only let us live according to what we have already understood (the truth we already know). 17. Join together in following my example (imitating my way of life), brothers and sisters, and keep an eye on those who live according to the example we've set. 18. For many, as I've often warned you, live as enemies of the cross of Christ (they reject the teachings and suffering of Christ). 19. Their end is destruction (their final fate is eternal loss), their god is their appetite (they live for selfish desires), and their glory is in their shame (they take pride in things that should bring them shame). Their minds are set on earthly things (they focus only on temporary, worldly pursuits). 20. But our true citizenship (our real identity and home) is in heaven. And we eagerly wait for the Savior from there, the Lord Jesus Christ, 21. who, by the power that enables Him to bring everything under His control, will transform (change) our weak bodies to be like His glorious body.

Chapter 4

1. Therefore, my dear brothers and sisters, whom I love and long for, you are my joy and crown. Stand firm in the Lord, my beloved friends! 2. I appeal (urge) to Euodia and Syntyche to agree with one another in the Lord. 3. Yes, and I ask you, my true companion (faithful partner), help these women who have struggled alongside me in spreading the gospel, along with Clement and the rest of my coworkers, whose names are written in the book of life (the record of those saved and destined for eternal life). 4. Rejoice (be joyful) in the Lord always. Again, I will say: Rejoice! 5. Let your gentleness (kindness, forbearance) be known to everyone. The Lord is near. 6. Do not worry about anything, but in every situation, through prayer and petition (requests, asking), with thanksgiving, present your requests to God. 7. And the peace of God, which surpasses (goes beyond, transcends) all understanding, will guard your hearts and minds in Christ Jesus. 8. Finally, brothers and sisters, whatever is true, whatever is honorable (noble, worthy of respect), whatever is right, whatever is pure, whatever is lovely, whatever is admirable (commendable)—if anything is excellent or praiseworthy—think about such things. 9. Whatever you have learned or received or heard from me, or seen in me—put it into practice. And the God of peace will be with you. 10. I greatly rejoice in the Lord that at last you revived your concern (you started caring again) for me. You were concerned before, but had no opportunity to show it. 11. I am not saying this because I am in need, for I have learned to be content (satisfied, at peace) whatever the circumstances. 12. I know what it is to be in need, and I know what it is to have plenty. I have learned the secret of being content in any and every situation, whether well-fed or hungry, whether living in abundance or in lack. 13. I can do all things through Him who strengthens me. 14. Yet it was good of you to share in my troubles. 15. You Philippians know that in the early days of your partnership with the gospel, when I left Macedonia, no church shared with me in the matter of giving and receiving, except you alone; 16. for even when I was in Thessalonica, you sent help more than once when I was in need. 17. Not that I seek the gift itself, but I seek the reward (fruit, blessing) that increases to your account. 18. I have received everything in full and have more than enough. I am abundantly supplied, having received from Epaphroditus the gifts you sent. They are a fragrant offering (an act of worship), an acceptable sacrifice, pleasing to God. 19. And my God will supply all your needs according to the riches of His glory in Christ Jesus. 20. To our God and Father be glory forever and ever. Amen. 21. Greet all God's people in Christ Jesus. The brothers and sisters who are with me send their greetings. 22. All God's people here send their greetings, especially those from Caesar's household. 23. The grace (unmerited favor) of the Lord Jesus Christ be with your spirit. Amen.

59 – Colossians

Chapter 1

1. Paul, an apostle (messenger or representative) of Christ Jesus by the will of God, and Timothy our brother, 2. To God's holy people in Colossae (a city in ancient Asia Minor), the faithful brothers and sisters in Christ: Grace and peace to you from God our Father. 3. We always thank God, the Father of our Lord Jesus Christ, when we pray for you, 4. because we have heard of your faith in Christ Jesus and of the love you have for all God's people— 5. the faith and love that spring from the hope (confidence) stored up for you in heaven and about which you have already heard in the true message of the gospel, 6. that has come to you. In the same way, the gospel is bearing fruit (producing results) and growing throughout the whole world—just as it has been doing among you since the day you heard it and truly understood God's grace. 7. You learned it from Epaphras, our dear fellow servant, who is a faithful minister (servant) of Christ on our behalf, 8. and who also told us of your love in the Spirit. 9. For this reason, since the day we heard about you, we have not stopped praying for you. We continually ask God to fill you with the knowledge of his will through all the wisdom and understanding that the Spirit gives, 10. so that you may live a life worthy of the Lord and please him in every way: bearing fruit in every good work, growing in the knowledge of God, 11. being strengthened with all power according to his glorious might (great strength) so that you may have great endurance (patience) and perseverance, 12. and giving joyful thanks to the Father, who has qualified you (made you eligible) to share in the inheritance (the portion or share) of his holy people in the kingdom of light. 13. For he

has rescued us from the dominion (rule) of darkness and brought us into the kingdom of the Son he loves, **14.** in whom we have redemption (the act of being bought back), the forgiveness of sins. **15.** The Son is the image (representation) of the invisible God, the firstborn (the primary one) over all creation. **16.** For in him all things were created: things in heaven and on earth, visible and invisible, whether thrones or powers or rulers or authorities; all things have been created through him and for him. **17.** He is before all things, and in him all things hold together. **18.** And he is the head (leader) of the body, the church; he is the beginning and the firstborn from among the dead, so that in everything he might have the supremacy (preeminence, rank). **19.** For God was pleased to have all his fullness (completeness, total nature) dwell in him, **20.** and through him to reconcile (bring back into harmony) to himself all things, whether things on earth or things in heaven, by making peace through his blood, shed on the cross. **21.** Once you were alienated (separated) from God and were enemies in your minds because of your evil behavior. **22.** But now he has reconciled you by Christ's physical body through death to present you holy in his sight, without blemish and free from accusation— **23.** if you continue in your faith, established (firmly rooted) and firm, and do not move from the hope held out in the gospel. This is the gospel that you heard and that has been proclaimed to every creature under heaven, and of which I, Paul, have become a servant. **24.** Now I rejoice in what I am suffering for you, and I fill up in my flesh (body) what is still lacking in regard to Christ's afflictions (sufferings), for the sake of his body, which is the church. **25.** I have become its servant by the commission (assignment) God gave me to present to you the word of God in its fullness— **26.** the mystery (truth hidden in the past) that has been kept hidden for ages and generations, but is now disclosed (made known) to the Lord's people. **27.** To them God has chosen to make known among the Gentiles (non-Jews) the glorious riches of this mystery, which is Christ in you, the hope of glory. **28.** He is the one we proclaim, admonishing (warning) and teaching everyone with all wisdom, so that we may present everyone fully mature in Christ. **29.** To this end I strenuously contend (work hard) with all the energy Christ so powerfully works in me.

Chapter 2

1. I want you to know how hard I am contending (struggling) for you and for those at Laodicea, and for all who have not met me personally. **2.** My goal is that they may be encouraged in heart and united in love, so that they may have the full riches (wealth) of complete understanding, in order that they may know the mystery (hidden truth) of God, namely, Christ, **3.** in whom are hidden all the treasures (valuable things) of wisdom and knowledge. **4.** I tell you this so that no one may deceive (mislead) you by fine-sounding arguments (persuasive speech). **5.** For though I am absent from you in body, I am present with you in spirit and delight to see how disciplined (ordered) you are and how firm your faith in Christ is. **6.** So then, just as you received Christ Jesus as Lord, continue to live your lives in him, **7.** rooted and built up in him, strengthened in the faith as you were taught, and overflowing with thankfulness. **8.** See to it that no one takes you captive (traps you) through hollow (empty) and deceptive philosophy (ideas), which depends on human tradition (customs) and the elemental spiritual forces (basic principles) of this world rather than on Christ. **9.** For in Christ all the fullness of the Deity (God's nature) lives in bodily form, **10.** and in Christ you have been brought to fullness. He is the head (leader) over every power and authority. **11.** In him you were also circumcised (spiritually purified) with a circumcision (rite of purification) not performed by human hands. Your whole self, ruled by the flesh (sinful nature), was put off when you were circumcised by Christ, **12.** having been buried with him in baptism (ritual washing), in which you were also raised with him through your faith in the working of God, who raised him from the dead. **13.** When you were dead (separated from God) in your sins and in the uncircumcision of your flesh, God made you alive with Christ. He forgave us all our sins, **14.** having canceled (removed) the charge of our legal indebtedness (debt), which stood against us and condemned us; he has taken it away, nailing it to the cross. **15.** And having disarmed (stripped of power) the powers and authorities, he made a public spectacle (embarrassment) of them, triumphing over them by the cross. **16.** Therefore do not let anyone judge (condemn) you by what you eat or drink, or with regard to a religious festival, a New Moon celebration, or a Sabbath day. **17.** These are a shadow (prefiguration) of the things that were to come; the reality, however, is found in Christ. **18.** Do not let anyone who delights in false humility (false modesty) and the worship of angels disqualify (judge unworthy) you. Such a person also goes into great detail about what they have seen; they are puffed up (proud) with idle (useless) notions (ideas) by their unspiritual mind. **19.** They have lost connection (relationship) with the head, from whom the whole body, supported and held together by its ligaments (tissues) and sinews (fibers), grows as God causes it to grow. **20.** Since you died with Christ to the elemental spiritual forces of this world, why, as though you still belonged to the world, do you submit (follow) to its rules: **21.** "Do not handle! Do not taste! Do not touch!"? **22.** These rules, which have to do with things that are all destined to perish (decay) with use, are based on merely human commands and teachings. **23.** Such regulations indeed have an appearance (look) of wisdom, with their self-imposed worship, their false humility, and their harsh treatment of the body, but they lack any value in restraining (controlling) sensual indulgence (sinful desires).

Chapter 3

1. Since you have been raised with Christ, focus your hearts on things above, where Christ is, seated at God's right hand. **2.** Set your minds on heavenly things, not on earthly things. **3.** For you died, and your life is now hidden (concealed) with Christ in God. **4.** When Christ, who is your life, appears, you will also appear with him in glory. **5.** Therefore, put to death (reject) whatever belongs to your earthly nature: sexual immorality, impurity, lust, evil desires, and greed, which is idolatry (worshiping something other than God). **6.** Because of these, the wrath (anger) of God is coming. **7.** You once lived in these ways. **8.** But now rid yourselves of: anger, rage, malice (spite), slander (false accusations), and filthy language. **9.** Do not lie to each other, since you have put off your old self and its practices, **10.** and put on the new self, which is being renewed in knowledge in the image of its Creator. **11.** In this new life, there is no distinction between Gentile or Jew, circumcised or uncircumcised, barbarian (uncivilized person), Scythian (a group of people from the ancient world), slave or free; but Christ is all and is in all. **12.** Therefore, as God's chosen people, holy and dearly loved, clothe yourselves with compassion, kindness, humility, gentleness, and patience. **13.** Bear with each other and forgive one another if anyone has a grievance (complaint) against another. Forgive as the Lord forgave you. **14.** And above all, put on love, which binds everything together in perfect unity. **15.** Let the peace of Christ rule in your hearts, since you were called to peace as members of one body. And be thankful. **16.** Let the message of Christ dwell (live) in you richly as you teach and admonish (warn or correct) one another with wisdom through psalms, hymns, and spiritual songs, singing to God with gratitude in your hearts. **17.** Whatever you do, in word or deed, do it all in the name of the Lord Jesus, giving thanks to God the Father through him. **18.** Wives, submit (respect) to your husbands as is fitting in the Lord. **19.** Husbands, love your wives and do not be harsh with them. **20.** Children, obey your parents in everything, for this pleases the Lord. **21.** Fathers, do not embitter (frustrate) your children, or they will become discouraged. **22.** Slaves, obey your earthly masters in everything; do it with sincerity of heart and reverence for the Lord, not just to please them when they are watching. **23.** Whatever you do, work at it with all your heart, as working for the Lord, not for human masters, **24.** knowing that you will receive an inheritance from the Lord as a reward. It is Christ you are serving. **25.** Anyone who does wrong will be repaid for their wrongs, and there is no favoritism.

Chapter 4

1. Masters, treat your slaves justly and fairly, knowing that you also have a Master in heaven. **2.** Devote yourselves to prayer, staying alert and thankful. **3.** Pray for us, too, that God may open a door for our message, so we can proclaim the mystery of Christ, for which I am in chains. **4.** Pray that I may proclaim it clearly, as I should. **5.** Be wise in how you act toward outsiders (non-believers); make the most of every opportunity. **6.** Let your conversation always be full of grace, seasoned with salt (wise and appealing), so you may know how to answer everyone. **7.** Tychicus will tell you all the news about me. He is a dear brother, faithful minister, and fellow servant in the Lord. **8.** I am sending him to you to update you on our circumstances and encourage your hearts. **9.** He is coming with Onesimus, our faithful and dear brother, who is one of you. They will tell you everything happening here. **10.** My fellow prisoner Aristarchus sends his greetings, as does Mark, the cousin of Barnabas. (You have received instructions about him; if he comes to you, welcome him.) **11.** Jesus, called Justus, also sends greetings. These are the only Jews among my co-workers for the kingdom of God, and they have been a comfort to me. **12.** Epaphras, who is one of you and a servant of Christ Jesus, sends greetings. He is always wrestling (struggling earnestly) in prayer for you, that you may stand firm in all God's will, mature and fully assured. **13.** I can testify that he is working hard for you and for those in Laodicea and Hierapolis. **14.** Our dear friend Luke, the doctor, and Demas send greetings. **15.** Greet the brothers and sisters at Laodicea, and Nympha, and the church in her house. **16.** After this letter has been read to you, ensure it is also read in the Laodicean church, and that you read the letter from Laodicea as well. **17.** Tell Archippus, "See to it that you complete the ministry you have received in the Lord." **18.** I, Paul, write this greeting in my own hand. Remember my chains. Grace be with you.

60 – Thessalonians 1
Chapter 1

1. Paul, Silas, and Timothy, To the church of the Thessalonians in God the Father and the Lord Jesus Christ: Grace and peace to you. **2.** We always give thanks to God for all of you and remember you in our prayers without ceasing (continuously). **3.** We recall (remember) before our God and Father your work that is the fruit (result) of faith, your labor (effort) motivated by love, and your perseverance (steadfastness) that springs from the hope you have in our Lord Jesus Christ. **4.** For we know, brothers and sisters, loved by God, that He has chosen (selected) you, **5.** because our gospel (good news) came to you not just in words, but also with power, with the Holy Spirit, and with full conviction (certainty). You know how we lived among you for your benefit. **6.** You became imitators (followers) of us and of the Lord, for you received the message despite great affliction (suffering), with the joy given by the Holy Spirit. **7.** As a result, you became an example (model) to all the believers in Macedonia and Achaia. **8.** The word (message) of the Lord has sounded forth (spread) from you not only in Macedonia and Achaia—your faith in God has become known everywhere. Therefore, we don't need to say anything further about it. **9.** For they themselves speak of the way we welcomed us, and how you turned from idols (false gods) to serve the living and true God, **10.** and to wait for His Son from heaven, whom He raised from the dead—Jesus, who delivers (rescues) us from the coming wrath (anger of God).

Chapter 2

1: Brothers and sisters, you know that when we visited you, it was not without purpose. **2:** Though we had previously endured mistreatment and suffering in Philippi (a city in Macedonia), with God's help, we boldly shared the gospel with you despite facing strong opposition. **3:** Our message does not come from error or wrong motives, nor are we trying to deceive you. **4:** Instead, we speak as those approved by God, entrusted with His gospel. Our aim is not to please people but to please God, who examines our hearts. **5:** You are aware that we never used flattering words, nor did we hide any greed behind a mask—God is our witness. **6:** We didn't seek praise from people, neither from you nor from anyone else, even though as apostles of Christ, we had the authority to demand respect. **7:** Rather, we were gentle and humble, like a mother caring for her children. **8:** We loved you so deeply that we were delighted not only to share the gospel with you but also our very lives. **9:** You surely remember, brothers and sisters, the hard work and struggles we endured. We worked day and night to avoid being a burden to anyone while preaching God's message to you. **10:** You are witnesses, and so is God, that we behaved with holiness, righteousness, and blamelessness among those who believed. **11:** Just as a father lovingly guides his children, we encouraged, comforted, and urged you to live lives worthy of God, who has called you into His kingdom and glory. **12:** We constantly thank God because, when you received the message we preached, you accepted it not as mere human words but as the true Word of God, which is actively working in you who believe. **13:** Brothers and sisters, you became imitators of the churches of God in Judea (the region of Israel), suffering the same persecution from your own people that the churches there faced from

the Jews—those who killed the Lord Jesus and the prophets, and drove us away. **14:** They displease God and oppose everyone by trying to prevent us from sharing the message of salvation with the Gentiles, thus filling up their sins. **15.** God's wrath has finally come upon them. **16:** But brothers and sisters, even though we were temporarily separated from you in person (but not in thought), we longed to see you and made every effort to return. **17:** We wanted to visit you—indeed, I, Paul, tried again and again—but Satan blocked our way. **18:** For what is our hope, our joy, or the crown we will boast about when our Lord Jesus returns? **19:** Is it not you? **20:** You are indeed our glory and joy.

Chapter 3

1. When we could no longer endure (bear) the situation, we decided it was best to stay alone in Athens (an ancient Greek city, known for its philosophical history). **2.** We sent Timothy (a trusted companion and missionary), our brother and fellow worker in spreading the gospel of Christ, to strengthen (fortify) and encourage (comfort) you in your faith. **3.** This was to ensure that none of you would be disturbed or shaken by the trials you are facing, because you know well that we are destined (appointed by God) for such hardships. **4.** We had already warned you while we were with you that we would face persecution (suffering for faith), and as you know, it happened just as we predicted. **5.** So, when I could not stand it any longer, I sent to check on your faith, fearing that the tempter (Satan, the deceiver) might have tempted you and that our efforts might have been in vain (unproductive). **6.** But now, Timothy has returned to us from you with good news about your faith and love. He shared with us that you remember us with affection and are eager to see us, just as we long to see you. **7.** Because of this, despite all our distress (suffering) and persecution, we were greatly encouraged by your faith. **8.** Now, we truly live (are revitalized), since you are standing firm in the Lord. **9.** How can we ever thank God enough for all the joy we feel in His presence because of you? **10.** We continually pray, day and night, asking that we may see you again and help supply (provide for) any areas where your faith is lacking. **11.** May our God and Father (the Creator) Himself, along with our Lord Jesus Christ, clear the path (make the way) for us to visit you. **12.** May the Lord cause your love to increase and overflow for each other and for everyone, just as our love for you overflows. **13.** May He strengthen (establish) your hearts, so that when our Lord Jesus Christ comes with all His holy ones (angels or saints), you will be found blameless and holy in His presence.

Chapter 4

1 As for the other matters, brothers and sisters, we have already instructed you on how to live in a way that pleases God, and in fact, you are already living this way. Now, we urge you in the Lord Jesus to continue growing in this practice more and more. **2** You know the instructions we gave you through the authority of the Lord Jesus. **3** It is God's will for you to be sanctified (set apart for His purposes): you should avoid sexual immorality; **4** each of you should learn to control your own body in a way that is pure (holy) and honorable (respectful), **5** not driven by passionate lust like the pagans who do not know God; **6** and in this matter, no one should take advantage of or wrong a brother or sister. The Lord will judge all those who engage in such behavior, as we have previously warned you. **7** For God did not call us to live in impurity, but to live a life that is holy. **8** Therefore, anyone who rejects this teaching is not rejecting a human authority, but rejecting God Himself, who gives you His Holy Spirit. **9** Now, concerning your love for one another, we do not need to write to you, for you have already been taught by God to love each other. **10** And in fact, you do love all of God's family throughout Macedonia. Yet, we urge you, brothers and sisters, to continue growing in this love more and more, **11** and to make it your goal to live a quiet life: mind your own business and work with your hands, just as we instructed you, **12** so that your daily conduct may win the respect of outsiders and you will not be dependent on anyone. **13** Brothers and sisters, we do not want you to be uninformed (ignorant) about those who have passed away, so that you do not grieve like the rest of the world, who have no hope. **14** We believe that Jesus died and rose again, and so we believe that God will bring with Jesus those who have died in Him. **15** According to the Lord's word, we tell you that we who are alive and remain until the coming of the Lord will not precede (go ahead of) those who have passed away.

16 For the Lord Himself will come down from heaven with a loud command, with the voice of the archangel (chief messenger), and with the trumpet call of God, and the dead in Christ will rise first. **17** After that, we who are still alive and left will be caught up (taken away, suddenly) with them in the clouds to meet the Lord in the air. And so we will be with the Lord forever. **18** Therefore, encourage one another with these words.

Chapter 5

1 Now, brothers and sisters, concerning the times and seasons, we do not need to write to you, **2** for you are fully aware that the day of the Lord will come like a thief in the night (unexpectedly). **3** While people are saying, "Peace and safety," destruction will come upon them suddenly, like labor pains on a pregnant woman, and they will not escape. **4** But you, brothers and sisters, are not in darkness so that this day should surprise you like a thief. **5** You are all children of the light and children of the day. We do not belong to the night or to the darkness. (In other words, we are not in spiritual ignorance or unprepared.) **6** So then, let us not be like others, who are spiritually asleep, but let us be alert and sober-minded. **7** For those who sleep, sleep at night, and those who get drunk, get drunk at night. **8** But since we belong to the day, let us be sober, putting on faith and love as a protective armor (a breastplate), and the hope of salvation as a helmet (the hope of salvation protects us like a helmet guards the head). **9** For God did not appoint us to face His wrath but to receive salvation through our Lord Jesus Christ. **10** He died for us so that, whether we are awake or asleep (alive or dead), we may live together with Him. **11** Therefore encourage one another and build each other up, just as in fact you are doing. **12** Now we ask you, brothers and sisters, to recognize those who work hard among you, who care for you in the Lord and who give you guidance and correction. **13** Hold them in the highest regard and love because of their work. Live in peace with each other. **14** And we urge you, brothers and sisters, warn those who are idle and disruptive (those who refuse to work or live in disorder), encourage the discouraged, help the weak, and be patient with everyone. **15** Make sure that no one repays evil for evil, but always pursue what is good for each other and for everyone else. **16** Rejoice always (even in difficult times), **17** pray without ceasing (maintain constant communication with God), **18** give thanks in all circumstances; for this is God's will for you in Christ Jesus (God desires us to have a grateful heart in all things). **19** Do not quench the Spirit (do not suppress or ignore the work of the Holy Spirit). **20** Do not despise prophetic messages, **21** but test them all; hold on to what is good, **22** and reject every form of evil. **23** May God Himself, the God of peace, sanctify you completely (set you apart and make you holy). May your entire spirit, soul, and body be kept blameless at the coming of our Lord Jesus Christ. **24** The one who calls you is faithful, and He will bring it to pass. **25** Brothers and sisters, pray for us. **26** Greet all God's people with a holy kiss (a sign of peace and love among believers). **27** I charge you before the Lord to have this letter read to all the brothers and sisters. **28** The grace of our Lord Jesus Christ be with you all (may God's favor and kindness be with you).

61 – Thessalonians 2

Chapter 1

1. From Paul, Silas, and Timothy, to the church in Thessalonica (a city in ancient Greece), which is in God our Father and the Lord Jesus Christ: **2.** May grace and peace be yours from God the Father and the Lord Jesus Christ. **3.** We continually give thanks to God for you, dear brothers and sisters, because your faith is growing stronger, and the love you have for one another is increasing. **4.** Among God's churches, we boast about your steadfastness and faith during the trials and persecutions you are facing. **5.** This is clear evidence that God's judgment is just, and as a result, you will be counted worthy of His kingdom, for which you are enduring suffering. **6.** God is righteous: He will repay those who cause you harm, **7.** and bring relief to those of you who are suffering, and to us as well. This will take place when the Lord Jesus is revealed from heaven in blazing fire, with His mighty angels. **8.** He will punish those who do not know God and who refuse to obey the gospel of our Lord Jesus Christ. **9.** They will face eternal separation from God and the glory of His power. **10.** On the day He comes to be glorified in His holy people and to be admired by all who have believed. This includes you, because you have believed our message. **11.** With this in mind, we constantly pray for you, asking that God may make you worthy of His calling and, by His power, bring to completion every good desire and work inspired by your faith. **12.** We pray this so that the name of our Lord Jesus may be honored in you, and you in Him, through the grace of our God and the Lord Jesus Christ.

Chapter 2

1. Concerning the return of our Lord Jesus Christ and our gathering to Him, we urge you, dear brothers and sisters, **2.** not to be easily disturbed or frightened by any message that claims to come from us—whether by prophecy, word of mouth, or letter—suggesting that the day of the Lord has already arrived. **3.** Do not let anyone deceive you in any way, because that day will not come until the rebellion occurs and the man of lawlessness (the one opposed to God) is revealed, the one destined for destruction. **4.** He will oppose everything that is called God or worshiped, even setting himself up in God's temple and declaring himself to be God. **5.** Don't you remember that when I was with you I told you all of this? **6.** And now you know what is holding him back, so that he can be revealed at the right time. **7.** For the hidden force of lawlessness is already at work, but the one who is currently restraining it will continue to do so until he is removed. **8.** Then the lawless one will be revealed, whom the Lord Jesus will defeat with the breath of His mouth and destroy with the brightness of His coming. **9.** The coming of this lawless one will align with the way Satan operates. He will perform many false wonders, signs, and miracles to deceive those who are perishing. **10.** They will perish because they rejected the truth and refused to accept salvation. **11.** For this reason, God will send them a powerful delusion, so that they will believe the lie **12.** and be condemned, because they did not believe the truth but took pleasure in wickedness. **13.** But we always thank God for you, brothers and sisters loved by the Lord, because God chose you as the firstfruits to be saved through the work of the Holy Spirit and your belief in the truth. **14.** He called you to this through our gospel, so that you may share in the glory of our Lord Jesus Christ. **15.** Therefore, brothers and sisters, stand firm and hold on to the teachings we gave you, whether spoken or written. **16.** May our Lord Jesus Christ Himself and God our Father, who loved us and, by His grace, gave us eternal comfort and a firm hope, **17.** encourage your hearts and strengthen you in every good word and deed.

Chapter 3

1. Regarding other matters, brothers and sisters, pray for us so that the Lord's message may spread quickly and be honored, just as it was among you. **2.** Also, pray that we may be rescued from wicked and evil people, for not everyone holds to the faith. **3.** But the Lord is faithful, and He will strengthen you and protect you from the evil one. **4.** We are confident in the Lord that you are doing and will continue to do what we have instructed. **5.** May the Lord guide your hearts into God's love and the perseverance of Christ. **6.** In the name of the Lord Jesus Christ, we command you, brothers and sisters, to stay away from any believer who is idle and disruptive and does not follow the teachings we gave you. **7.** For you know how to follow our example. We were not idle when we were with you, **8.** nor did we take anyone's food without paying. Instead, we worked hard, day and night, so as not to be a burden to any of you. **9.** We did this not because we don't have the right to support, but to set an example for you to follow. **10.** Even when we were with you, we gave you this rule: "The one who does not work shall not eat." **11.** We hear that some of you are idle and disruptive. They are not working; they are just meddling in other people's business. **12.** We command and urge such people, in the name of the Lord Jesus Christ, to settle down and earn their own living. **13.** As for you, brothers and sisters, never grow weary of doing what is right. **14.** If anyone does not follow the instructions in this letter, take note of them and do not associate with them, so that they may feel ashamed. **15.** However, do not treat them as an enemy, but warn them as you would a fellow believer. **16.** Now may the Lord of peace Himself give you peace at all times and in every way. The Lord be with all of you. **17.** I, Paul, write this greeting with my own hand, which is the distinguishing mark in all my letters. This is my signature. **18.** The grace of our Lord Jesus Christ be with you all.

62 – Timothy 1

Chapter 1

1. Paul, an apostle (messenger sent with authority) of Jesus Christ, by God's command, who is our Savior, and by the authority of the Lord Jesus Christ, our hope, 2. To Timothy, my true son in the faith: Grace (unmerited favor), mercy, and peace from God the Father and Jesus Christ our Lord. 3. As I urged you when I went to Macedonia, remain in Ephesus so you can instruct some people not to teach other doctrines (beliefs or teachings). 4. Don't let them give attention to myths (stories or beliefs not based on truth) and endless genealogies (family lineages), which only lead to arguments and don't help in building up faith. 5. The goal of this command is love from a pure heart, a good conscience (inner sense of right and wrong), and sincere faith. 6. Some have wandered away from this, turning to meaningless (empty, without purpose) talk. 7. They want to be teachers of the law, but they don't understand what they're saying or the things they claim (state without proof). 8. We know that the law is good if used properly (in the correct way). 9. The law is not meant for righteous people, but for those who break the law: the rebellious (defying authority), the ungodly, and sinners, the unholy, and profane (disrespectful of sacred things), for murderers, 10. for the immoral (sexually immoral), for men who have sex with other men, for kidnappers, for liars, for perjurers (those who lie under oath), and for anything else contrary to sound teaching (healthy, true doctrine), 11. in accordance with the glorious gospel (good news) of the blessed (happy, worthy of praise) God, entrusted (given responsibility) to me. 12. I thank Christ Jesus our Lord, who gave me strength, because He considered me faithful and appointed (chosen, assigned) me to His service, 13. though I was once a blasphemer (someone who speaks disrespectfully about God), a persecutor, and a violent man. I received mercy because I acted in ignorance and unbelief. 14. The grace of our Lord was abundantly (in large amounts) poured out on me, along with faith and love in Christ Jesus. 15. This is a trustworthy (worthy of belief) saying, deserving full acceptance: Christ Jesus came into the world to save sinners, of whom I am the worst. 16. But for this reason, I was shown mercy, so that in me, the worst of sinners, Christ Jesus might display His immense (huge, great) patience as an example for those who would believe in Him and receive eternal life. 17. Now to the King eternal (forever), immortal (undying), invisible (cannot be seen), the only wise God, be honor and glory forever and ever. Amen. 18. I am giving you this command, Timothy, my son, based on the prophecies (divine messages) made about you, so that by them you may fight the good fight, 19. holding on to faith and a good conscience. Some have rejected these and have shipwrecked (ruined) their faith, 20. Including Hymenaeus and Alexander, whom I handed over to Satan to be taught not to blaspheme (disrespect God).

Chapter 2

1. I urge that prayers (requests made to God) and thanksgiving be offered for all people, 2. For kings and everyone in authority (those with power to govern), so that we can live peaceful and godly lives, showing respect. 3. This is good and pleasing to God our Savior (one who saves or rescues), 4. who wants everyone to be saved and to come to the knowledge of the truth (the reality of God's word). 5. For there is one God and one Mediator (someone who helps bring two parties together) between God and humanity, the man Christ Jesus, 6. who gave Himself as a ransom (payment for release) for all, to be revealed at the right time. 7. I was appointed to preach and teach the Gentiles the truth in faith (trusting in God), and I speak the truth in Christ, not lying. 8. I want men everywhere to pray, lifting up holy hands, without anger (strong emotion of displeasure) or doubting. 9. In the same way, I also want women to dress modestly (with simplicity and self-control), with self-control and respect, not in elaborate hairstyles or expensive jewelry, 10. but with good deeds (actions that show kindness and goodness), as is fitting for women who claim to worship God. 11. Let a woman learn quietly and with full submission (humble obedience). 12. I do not allow a woman to teach or have authority (the right to lead or control) over a man, but to remain quiet. 13. For Adam was created first, then Eve. 14. And Adam was not deceived (misled), but the woman, being deceived, became the one who sinned. 15. But she will be saved through childbearing (the act of giving birth), if they continue in faith, love, holiness, and self-control.

Chapter 3

1. This is a trustworthy statement: If someone aspires to the position of a bishop (church overseer), they are seeking a noble task. 2. A bishop must be blameless (without fault), the husband of one wife, self-controlled (temperate), sober-minded (clear-headed), well-behaved, welcoming (hospitable), and capable of teaching others. 3. He should not be given to excessive drinking, nor quick to anger, nor greedy for financial gain, but must be gentle, peaceful, and not covetous (desirous of what others have). 4. He should govern his own household with dignity, ensuring his children are respectful and obedient. 5. If a person cannot manage their own home, how can they take care of God's church? 6. He must not be a recent convert (novice), lest pride leads him to fall into the same condemnation as the devil. 7. He must have a good reputation with those outside the church, so he does not fall into disgrace or become ensnared by the devil. 8. Likewise, deacons must be dignified, not double-tongued (saying one thing to one person and something else to another), not addicted to much wine, nor greedy for dishonest gain. 9. They must hold to the deep truths of the faith with a pure conscience. 10. Let them first be tested, and if blameless, they may serve as deacons. 11. Their wives must be worthy of respect, not slanderers (false accusers), self-controlled (temperate), and trustworthy in all matters. 12. Deacons should be the husbands of one wife and manage their children and households with integrity. 13. Those who serve well as deacons will gain a good reputation and great boldness (confidence) in the faith in Christ Jesus. 14. I am writing these things to you with the hope of coming to you soon. 15. But if delayed, I want you to know how to conduct yourself in the household of God, which is the church of the living God, the pillar and support (foundation) of the truth. 16. Without a doubt, the mystery of godliness is great: God was revealed in the flesh (Jesus came in human form), justified (vindicated) by the Spirit, seen by angels, preached to the nations, believed on in the world, and taken up into glory (ascended to heaven).

Chapter 4

1. The Spirit warns (informs) that in the last days, some will turn from the faith, following deceptive spirits and teachings inspired by demons. 2. They will speak lies disguised as truth, with their consciences seared (hardened). 3. They will forbid marriage and tell people to abstain (refrain) from foods that God created to be enjoyed with thanksgiving by those who believe. 4. Every creature of God is good, and nothing should be rejected if received with thanksgiving. 5. It is sanctified (set apart as holy) by God's word and prayer. 6. If you teach these things, you will be a good servant of Jesus Christ, nourished (strengthened) by the words of faith and sound doctrine. 7. Reject ungodly myths and old wives' tales (foolish stories), and train yourself in godliness. 8. While physical exercise has some value, godliness is valuable in every way, promising both present and future life. 9. This is a trustworthy saying, deserving full acceptance. 10. We labor (work hard) and suffer reproach (shame), because we trust in the living God, who is the Savior of all, especially those who believe. 11. Command and teach these things. 12. Do not let anyone look down on you because you are young; be an example in speech, conduct, love, faith, and purity. 13. Until I come, focus on reading, encouraging (exhorting), and teaching the word. 14. Do not neglect (ignore) the gift given to you through prophecy (divine message) with the laying on of hands by the elders. 15. Think carefully about these things; devote (give attention to) yourself to them so everyone can see your progress. 16. Pay attention to your life and doctrine (teaching); continue in them, and you will save both yourself and those who hear you.

Chapter 5

1. Do not harshly rebuke an older man but encourage him as a father; treat younger men as brothers. 2. Older women as mothers, and younger women as sisters, with all purity (cleanliness in heart and behavior). 3. Honor (show respect) widows who are truly in need. 4. If a widow has children or grandchildren, they should show respect (care) and care for their family, repaying their parents, for this is pleasing to God. 5. A true widow, alone, trusts in God, continuing in prayers and supplications (earnest requests) day and night. 6. The woman who indulges (gives in to) in pleasure is spiritually dead while she lives. 7. Give these instructions so they may live without blame (responsibility for wrongdoing). 8. Anyone who does not provide (supply) for his family has denied the faith and is worse than an unbeliever. 9. Do not

take a widow into the number unless she is at least sixty and has been the wife of one man. **10**. Well known for good deeds: raising children, showing hospitality (kindness), washing saints' feet, helping those in distress (difficult situations), and diligently (with effort) pursuing good works. **11**. Refuse younger widows, for when they grow wanton (recklessly self-indulgent) against Christ, they want to marry. **12**. They bring judgment (punishment) upon themselves by abandoning their commitment to Christ. **13**. They learn to be idle (inactive), gossip (spread rumors), and meddle (interfere) in others' affairs. **14**. Therefore, I desire younger widows to marry, have children, manage homes, and avoid giving the enemy (Satan) a chance to speak evil. **15**. Some have already turned aside (departed) to follow Satan. **16**. If a believer has widows in their family, let them provide, not burdening (placing responsibility on) the church. **17**. Let elders (church leaders) who rule well be counted worthy of double honor, especially those who labor (work hard) in preaching and teaching. **18**. Scripture says, "Do not muzzle (prevent from eating) an ox while it treads grain," and "The laborer is worthy of wages." **19**. Do not accept an accusation (claim) against an elder except from two or three witnesses. **20**. Those sinning (doing wrong) should be publicly rebuked (corrected) so others may fear. **21**. I charge (command) you before God, the Lord Jesus Christ, and the elect angels (chosen) to observe these things without prejudice (unfair bias). **22**. Do not hastily (carelessly) lay hands on anyone, nor share in others' sins; keep yourself pure. **23**. Use a little wine for your stomach and frequent ailments (physical discomforts). **24**. Some people's sins are obvious (easily seen), leading to judgment, while others follow later. **25**. Likewise, some people's good deeds (actions) are obvious, and those that are not cannot stay hidden.

Chapter 6

1. Let bondservants (those who serve) under the yoke (master's authority) honor their masters, so that God's name and doctrine (teaching) are not blasphemed (disrespected). **2**. Those with believing masters should not despise (look down on) them, but serve them better, as they are beloved (dearly loved) brothers in the faith. **3**. If anyone teaches differently from the sound words (life-giving teachings) of Jesus Christ and godliness (godly living), **4**. he is proud, knowing nothing, obsessed (preoccupied) with disputes (arguments) and word battles (word arguments), causing envy, strife (conflict), and evil suspicions (bad thoughts). **5**. Avoid useless wranglings (arguments) of men with corrupt (immoral) minds, lacking truth, who believe godliness is a way to make money. **6**. But godliness with contentment (satisfaction) is great gain. **7**. We brought nothing into the world and can carry nothing out. **8**. With food and clothing, we should be content. **9**. Those desiring (wanting) to be rich fall into temptation (trap) and harmful lusts (desires) that lead to destruction (ruin) and perdition (eternal loss). **10**. The love of money is the root (cause) of all evil, leading some to stray (fall away) in their greediness (excessive desire), and pierce themselves with sorrows (regret). **11**. But you, O man of God, flee (run from) these things and pursue (chase after) righteousness, godliness, faith, love, patience, and gentleness. **12**. Fight the good fight of faith, lay hold on eternal life, to which you were called and have confessed (declared) before many witnesses. **13**. I urge (strongly encourage) you before God, who gives life to all, and Christ Jesus, who witnessed the good confession before Pilate, **14**. that you keep this commandment blameless (without fault) until Christ's appearing, **15**. He will manifest (reveal) in His time, the blessed (happy) and only Sovereign (ruler), King of kings and Lord of lords, **16**. who alone has immortality (eternal life), dwelling in unapproachable light. **17**. Command the rich not to be haughty (proud) or trust in uncertain riches, but in the living God, who gives us all things to enjoy. **18**. Let them do good, rich in good works, ready to give, and willing to share. **19**. Storing up a good foundation (secure base) for the future, to lay hold of eternal life. **20**. O Timothy! Guard (protect) what was entrusted (committed) to you, avoiding profane (irreverent) and idle (pointless) babblings (empty talk) and contradictions (false knowledge). **21**. By professing (claiming) it, some have strayed from the faith. Grace be with you. Amen.

63 – Timothy 2

Chapter 1

1. Paul, an apostle (messenger or representative) of Jesus Christ by God's will, according to the promise of life in Christ Jesus, **2**. To

Timothy, my beloved son: Grace (unearned favor), mercy (compassion), and peace (inner calm) from God the Father and Christ Jesus our Lord. **3**. I thank God, whom I serve with a clear conscience (a state of moral honesty), as my ancestors did, remembering you in my prayers constantly, **4**. longing to see you, remembering your tears, so that I may be filled with joy, **5**. when I recall the genuine faith (sincere trust in God) in you, which first lived in your grandmother Lois and your mother Eunice, and I am sure it lives in you too. **6**. Therefore, I remind you to rekindle (stir up or revive) the gift of God that is in you through the laying on of my hands. **7**. For God did not give us a spirit of fear, but of power (strength), love, and a sound mind (self-control and clear thinking). **8**. So do not be ashamed of the testimony (witness) about our Lord, nor of me, His prisoner, but join with me in suffering (enduring hardship) for the gospel, relying on God's power, **9**. who saved us and called us to a holy calling (a special purpose), not because of anything we have done, but because of His own purpose and grace, which was given to us in Christ Jesus before time began, **10**. but has now been revealed (made known) through the appearing (arrival) of our Savior Jesus Christ, who has destroyed death and brought life and immortality (eternal life) to light through the gospel. **11**. I was appointed (chosen) as a preacher (one who proclaims), apostle (messenger), and teacher of the Gentiles (non-Jews) for this gospel. **12**. For this reason, I suffer these things; yet I am not ashamed, because I know whom I have believed, and I am convinced (certain) that He is able to guard (protect) what I have entrusted (given) to Him until that Day. **13**. Hold on to the pattern (model or example) of sound teaching (true doctrine) you have heard from me, with faith and love in Christ Jesus. **14**. Guard (keep safe) the good deposit (trustworthy message) entrusted to you, with the help of the Holy Spirit who dwells (lives) in us. **15**. You know that everyone in Asia has turned away from me, including Phygellus and Hermogenes. **16**. May the Lord show mercy (kindness) to the household of Onesiphorus, because he often refreshed (encouraged) me and was not ashamed of my chains (imprisonment). **17**. When he came to Rome, he eagerly searched (sought diligently) for me and found me. **18**. May the Lord grant him mercy on that Day (the day of judgment), and you know very well how he helped me in Ephesus (a city in Asia Minor).

Chapter 2

1. So, my child, be strong in the grace (the unearned favor and help of God) that is found in Christ Jesus. **2**. And what you have heard from me in the presence of many witnesses, pass on to reliable (trustworthy, dependable) people who will also be able to teach others. **3**. Endure (to suffer through or bear with patience) hardship like a good soldier of Jesus Christ. **4**. A soldier does not get distracted by civilian affairs, because his focus is on pleasing the one who enlisted (called or recruited to serve) him. **5**. Similarly, an athlete is not crowned (awarded a prize or honor) unless they compete according to the rules. **6**. The hardworking (diligent) farmer should be the first to enjoy the crops. **7**. Think about what I'm saying, and may the Lord give you understanding (the ability to comprehend or grasp the meaning) in all things. **8**. Remember Jesus Christ, raised from the dead, the offspring (descendant or child) of David, as proclaimed in my gospel, **9**. For which I suffer even to the point of being chained (tied or bound, often to imprison or restrict) like a criminal. But the word of God cannot be chained. **10**. So, I endure everything for the sake of the elect (those chosen by God for salvation), so that they too may receive salvation in Christ Jesus with eternal glory. **11**. This is a trustworthy (reliable, dependable) saying: If we died with Him, we will also live with Him. **12**. If we endure, we will also reign (to rule or govern) with Him. If we deny Him, He will deny us. **13**. If we are faithless (lacking faith or loyalty), He remains faithful, for He cannot deny Himself. **14**. Remind them of these things and charge them before God not to quarrel (argue or disagree) over words, which is useless and leads to the ruin of those who listen. **15**. Do your best to present yourself to God as one approved (accepted or recognized as good), a worker who does not need to be ashamed, rightly handling the word of truth. **16**. Avoid godless chatter (trivial or meaningless talk), because it will only lead to more ungodliness, **17**. and their message will spread like cancer. Hymenaeus and Philetus are among those who have strayed (deviated or wandered away from the right path) from the truth, **18**. saying that the resurrection (the rising of the dead to life again) has already taken place, and they are destroying the faith of some. **19.** Nevertheless, God's firm foundation (the underlying basis or support of something) stands, with this seal: "The Lord knows those who are His," and "Let everyone who names the name of the Lord turn away from wickedness." **20.** In a large house, there are not only vessels (containers or tools) of gold and silver, but also of wood and clay, some for honorable use and some for dishonorable. **21.** If anyone cleanses (purifies or makes clean) themselves from these, they will be a vessel for honorable use, sanctified (made holy or set apart for a special purpose) and useful to the Master, prepared for every good work. **22.** Flee (run away or escape from) from youthful passions and pursue righteousness, faith, love, and peace, along with those who call on the Lord from a pure heart. **23.** Avoid foolish and ignorant disputes (arguments or disagreements), knowing that they only lead to quarrels. **24.** And the servant (a person who serves, often referring to a follower of God or Christ) of the Lord must not quarrel, but must be kind to everyone, able to teach, and patient, **25.** Correcting opponents with gentleness. Perhaps God will grant them repentance (the act of feeling regret or remorse and turning away from sin), leading them to a knowledge of the truth, **26.** And they may come to their senses and escape the trap (a snare or trick used to capture or deceive) of the devil, who has taken them captive to do his will.

Chapter 3

1. But know this: in the last days, perilous (dangerous) times will come. **2.** Men will be lovers of themselves, lovers of money, boasters, proud, blasphemers, disobedient to parents, unthankful, unholy, **3.** unloving, unforgiving, slanderers, without self-control, brutal, despisers of good, **4.** traitors, headstrong, haughty, lovers of pleasure rather than lovers of God, **5.** having a form of godliness but denying its power. From such people turn away! **6.** They creep into households, making captives of gullible (easily deceived) women, laden with sins, led away by lusts, **7.** always learning but never able to come to the knowledge of the truth. **8.** As Jannes and Jambres resisted Moses, so do these resist the truth: men of corrupt (dishonest) minds, disapproved concerning the faith, **9.** but they will progress no further, for their folly will be evident to all, as theirs was. **10.** You have followed my doctrine, manner of life, purpose, faith, longsuffering, love, perseverance, **11.** persecutions, and afflictions, which happened to me at Antioch, Iconium, and Lystra— what persecutions I endured. The Lord delivered me from them all. **12.** All who desire to live godly in Christ Jesus will suffer persecution. **13.** But evil men and impostors (fraudulent people) will grow worse, deceiving and being deceived. **14.** You must continue in what you have learned and been assured of, knowing from whom you have learned them, **15.** and that from childhood, you have known the Holy Scriptures, which are able to make you wise for salvation through faith in Christ Jesus. **16.** All Scripture is inspired by God and is profitable for doctrine, reproof, correction, and instruction in righteousness, **17.** that the man of God may be complete, thoroughly equipped for every good work.

Chapter 4

1. I charge you before God and the Lord Jesus Christ, who will judge the living and the dead when He appears and establishes His kingdom. **2.** Preach the Word! Be ready at all times. Correct, rebuke, and encourage with patience and sound teaching. **3.** A time is coming when people won't endure sound doctrine (true teaching) and will seek teachers who say what they want to hear. **4.** They will turn from the truth and follow myths (false stories). **5.** You, however, be alert in everything, endure suffering, do the work of an evangelist (one who spreads the gospel), and fulfill your ministry. **6.** I am being poured out as a drink offering (sacrificial offering), and my departure is near. **7.** I have fought the good fight, finished the race, and kept the faith. **8.** Now a crown of righteousness awaits me, which the Lord, the righteous Judge, will give on that Day to me and all who long for His appearing. **9.** Be diligent to come to me quickly; **10.** Demas has abandoned me, loving the world, and gone to Thessalonica; Crescens to Galatia, and Titus to Dalmatia. **11.** Only Luke is with me. Bring Mark, for he is useful to me in ministry. **12.** I have sent Tychicus to Ephesus. **13.** When you come, bring the cloak I left with Carpus at Troas, and the books, especially the parchments (scrolls). **14.** Alexander the coppersmith (metalworker) harmed me greatly. May the Lord repay him. **15.** Be careful of him; he opposed our message strongly. **16.** At my first

defense (hearing), no one stood with me. May it not be charged against them. **17.** But the Lord stood with me and gave me strength, so the gospel might be proclaimed fully, and I was delivered from the lion's mouth. **18.** The Lord will deliver me from every evil attack and bring me safely to His heavenly kingdom. To Him be glory forever. **19.** Greet Prisca and Aquila, and the household of Onesiphorus. **20.** Erastus stayed in Corinth, but Trophimus I left sick in Miletus (a city in Asia Minor). **21.** Try to come before winter. Eubulus, Pudens, Linus, Claudia, and all the brothers greet you. **22.** May the Lord Jesus Christ be with your spirit. Grace be with you. Amen.

64 – Titus

Chapter 1

1. Paul, a servant (one who works for) of God and an apostle (messenger) of Jesus Christ, for the faith of God's elect (chosen people) and the truth that leads to godliness, **2.** in the hope of eternal life, which God, who cannot lie, promised before time began, **3.** but has revealed in His own time through preaching, entrusted to me by the command of God our Savior; **4.** To Titus, a true son in our common faith: Grace, mercy, and peace from God the Father and our Savior, Jesus Christ. **5.** I left you in Crete to set in order what is lacking and appoint elders (leaders) in every town, as I instructed you— **6.** if anyone is blameless (without fault), the husband of one wife, with faithful children who are not wild (uncontrolled) or rebellious. **7.** For a bishop (overseer) must be blameless, a steward (manager) of God, not self-willed (self-centered), quick-tempered, drunk, violent, or greedy for money, **8.** but hospitable (welcoming), loving what is good, self-controlled, just (fair), holy, and disciplined, **9.** holding fast to the faithful word as taught, so that he can both encourage and correct those who oppose sound doctrine (teaching). **10.** There are many insubordinate (disobedient), deceivers, especially among the circumcision (Jewish people), **11.** whose mouths must be stopped; they disrupt (cause trouble in) entire households, teaching things they should not, for shameful gain (dishonest profit). **12.** One of them, a prophet of their own, said, "Cretans are always liars, evil beasts, lazy gluttons (people who overeat)." **13.** This testimony (witness) is true. Therefore, rebuke (correct) them sharply, so that they may be sound (healthy) in the faith, **14.** not giving attention to Jewish myths and human commandments that turn people away from the truth. **15.** To the pure (innocent), all things are pure; but to the defiled (unclean) and unbelieving, nothing is pure, for even their minds and consciences are corrupted (ruined). **16.** They claim to know God, but in their actions, they deny Him, being detestable (hateful), disobedient, and unfit (unqualified) for any good work.

Chapter 2

1. But as for you, teach what aligns with sound doctrine (reliable, Christian-based teaching). **2.** Older men should be sober (self-controlled, avoiding excess), dignified (respectable), self-controlled, and strong in faith (committed to beliefs), love, and patience (enduring without complaint). **3.** Similarly, older women should be reverent (respectful and devout), not slanderers (avoiding gossip or harmful talk), not addicted to much wine, and should be teachers of good things (instructors in virtuous living). **4.** They should teach younger women to love their husbands and children, **5.** to be sensible (wise in behavior), pure (morally clean), good homemakers (skilled in managing the home), and obedient (cooperative and respectful) to their husbands, so that God's word is not dishonored (held in disrespect). **6.** Encourage young men to be self-controlled, **7.** setting an example of good works (virtuous actions) in everything. Show integrity (honesty), seriousness (a responsible attitude), and incorruptibility (moral steadfastness) in your teaching. **8.** Let your speech be sound (clear and true) and beyond reproach (free from criticism), so opponents will be ashamed, having no grounds for criticism. **9.** Teach bondservants (those under another's authority, such as household servants) to be obedient to their masters, pleasing in all things, and not argumentative (not prone to arguing), **10.** not stealing, but showing full integrity (honesty), so they may honor the doctrine of God our Savior in everything. **11.** For the grace (undeserved kindness) of God that brings salvation (deliverance from sin) has appeared to all people, **12.** teaching us to deny ungodliness (disrespect for God) and worldly desires (immoral or excessive longings), and to live sensibly (with good judgment), righteously (morally correct), and godly (devoted to God) in this present age, 13. while we wait for the blessed hope and glorious return of our great God and Savior, Jesus Christ, 14. who gave Himself for us, to redeem us (save from sin) from all lawlessness (disregard for God's laws) and to purify (cleanse morally) for Himself a people eager for good works (motivated to do virtuous deeds). 15. Teach these things, exhort (encourage strongly) and rebuke (correct firmly) with full authority. Do not let anyone despise (disrespect or look down on) you.

Chapter 3

1. Remind them to be subject (obedient) to rulers and authorities, to obey, and be ready for every good work. 2. Speak no evil of anyone, be peaceful, gentle, and show humility (humbleness) to all people. 3. For we too were once foolish, disobedient, deceived, serving various desires, living in malice (ill will) and envy, hateful, and hating one another. 4. But when God's kindness and love appeared, 5. He saved us, not by our righteous works, but by His mercy, through the washing and renewal (restoration) of the Holy Spirit, 6. whom He poured out on us abundantly through Jesus Christ, 7. so that, justified (declared righteous) by His grace, we might become heirs (inheritors) of eternal life. 8. This is a trustworthy saying, and I want you to affirm (declare) it constantly: those who have believed in God should be careful to maintain good works. These are beneficial to everyone. 9. Avoid foolish arguments, genealogies (family histories), and disputes about the law; they are useless and unprofitable. 10. Reject a divisive (causing disagreement) person after a second warning, 11. knowing that such a person is corrupt and self-condemned. 12. When I send Artemas or Tychicus to you, be diligent (eager) to come to me at Nicopolis, for I have decided to spend the winter there. 13. Send Zenas the lawyer and Apollos on their journey quickly, so they lack nothing. 14. Let our people also learn to engage in good works, to meet urgent needs, so they will not be unfruitful. 15. All those with me send their greetings. Greet those who love us in the faith. Grace be with you all. Amen.

65 – Philemon

1. Paul, a prisoner (for the sake of Christ Jesus) and Timothy our brother, to Philemon (a Christian leader in Colossae, Asia Minor), our beloved pal and fellow laborer—2. and to Apphia (in all likelihood Philemon's wife), our sister, and Archippus (likely Philemon's son or a fellow believer), our fellow soldier—and to the church (meeting of believers) that gathers in your property: 3. Grace (unmerited prefer) and peace (wholeness, non secular well-being) to you from God our Father and the Lord Jesus Christ. 4. I always provide thanks to God as I do not forget you in my prayers, 5. due to the fact I pay attention of your love (agape love, selfless care) for all God's holy human beings (believers) and your faith within the Lord Jesus. 6. I pray that your sharing (fellowship, partnership) in the religion may also become powerful as you grow for your understanding (know-how) of all the great things we've got in Christ. 7. Your love has introduced me much joy and encouragement, for you, brother, have refreshed (comforted, restored) the hearts of the Lord's humans. 8. therefore, even though I could be ambitious and order you to do what you ought, 9. I opt to enchantment to you in love. it is none aside from Paul—an antique man (superior in years) and now also a prisoner (in chains for Christ Jesus)—10. that I attraction to you on behalf of my son Onesimus (a former slave who have become a Christian while with Paul), who became my son whilst i was in chains. 11. At one time he become useless (unprofitable) to you, but now he has turn out to be useful (worthwhile) each to you and to me. 12. i am sending him—he's my very coronary heart—returned to you. 13. i'd have liked to hold him with me in order that he could assist (assist) me to your place even as i am in chains for the gospel, 14. however I did now not want to do something with out your consent, so that any kindness (want, act of goodwill) you show could be voluntary, no longer something you felt compelled to do. 15. perhaps the reason he changed into separated (from you) for a little at the same time as was that you might have him back all the time—16. now not as a slave (servant), however higher than a slave, as a liked brother. He could be very dear (precious) to me, but even more in an effort to you, both as a fellow human and as a brother in the Lord. 17. So, if you bear in mind me a accomplice (inside the religion), welcome him as you will welcome me. 18. If he has wronged (hurt, angry) you in any way or owes you anything, fee it to me. 19. I, Paul, am scripting this with my very own hand. i will pay it returned—even though I do no longer want to remind you that you owe me your very self (your salvation, faith in Christ). 20. I do wish, brother, that I might also advantage (experience pleasure) from you within the Lord; refresh (consolation, restore) my heart in Christ. 21. guaranteed (certain) of your obedience, I write to you, understanding that you may do even more than I ask. 22. And one greater aspect: prepare (make equipped) a visitor room for me, for i am hoping that via your prayers I could be restored (freed from imprisonment) to you. very last Greetings 23. Epaphras (a fellow prisoner, in all likelihood considered one of Paul's friends in ministry) sends you greetings. 24. So do Mark (John Mark, the cousin of Barnabas), Aristarchus (a fellow worker from Thessalonica), Demas (every other companion of Paul), and Luke (the beloved physician, creator of the Gospel of Luke and Acts), my fellow workers. 25. The grace (unmerited desire) of the Lord Jesus Christ be along with your spirit (internal being, soul).

66 – Hebrews

Chapter 1

1. In the past, God spoke to our ancestors (forefathers) through various prophets, revealing His will in many different forms and through diverse methods. 2. But in these final days, He has chosen to speak to us directly through His Son, whom He appointed as the heir (one who inherits) of everything, and through whom He created the entire universe and all that is within it. 3. The Son is the full radiance (brightness, splendor) of God's glory, representing the exact image (likeness, reflection) of God's essence, and by His powerful word, He continually upholds (sustains, maintains) the entire creation. After He had purified (cleansed, made pure) us from the stain of our sins, He took His seat at the right hand of the Majesty (supreme greatness, honor) in the heavens, 4. becoming far superior (greater, more exalted) to the angels, since He has inherited a name of far greater importance (superiority) than theirs. 5. For to which of the angels did God ever say, "You are My Son; today I have become Your Father"? Or again, "I will be a Father to Him, and He will be a Son to Me"? 6. And when He brings His firstborn (preeminent, most significant) into the world, He commands, "Let all of God's angels worship (honor, bow down to) Him." 7. Regarding the angels, He says, "He makes His angels as swift as winds (messengers or forces of nature), and His ministers (servants, attendants) as flames of fire, full of energy and purpose." 8. But to the Son, He declares, "Your throne (place of authority, royal seat), O God, will endure (continue, last) for all eternity, and the scepter (symbol of rule and authority) of righteousness (justice, uprightness) will be the scepter of Your eternal kingdom. 9. You have loved righteousness and have despised lawlessness (wickedness, injustice); therefore God, Your God, has anointed (set apart, chosen) You with the oil of gladness (joy, delight) beyond Your companions." 10. And again, it is written, "In the beginning, O Lord, You laid the foundations (the very base, starting point) of the earth, and the heavens were created by the work of Your hands." 11. Though these things will eventually perish (be destroyed, fade away), You, O God, will remain (stay, continue), and everything that exists will wear out (grow old, decay) like a garment (a piece of clothing). 12. Like a robe (covering), You will fold them up, and they will be transformed (changed into something new). But You remain unchanged, and Your years will have no end." 13. To which of the angels has God ever said, "Sit at My right hand until I make Your enemies a footstool (a symbol of submission, a place for resting feet) beneath Your feet"? 14. Are not all angels ministering (serving, assisting) spirits sent to serve those who will inherit (receive as a gift) salvation (eternal life, rescue from sin and death)?

Chapter 2

1. We must pay much closer attention to the message we have received, so that we do not drift away (become distracted or led astray). 2. If the message delivered by angels was unshakable (firm, unchanging), and every act of disobedience was justly punished, 3. how can we possibly escape if we neglect (ignore, disregard) such a great salvation, which was first proclaimed by the Lord and then confirmed (verified) by those who heard Him, 4. while God Himself testified (witnessed) through signs, wonders (extraordinary acts), and various gifts of the Holy Spirit, distributed according to His will (purpose)? 5. For God has not placed the coming world under the dominion (rule, authority) of angels, 6. but someone has testified somewhere, saying: "What is mankind that You are mindful (aware,

considerate) of him, or the son of man that You care for him? **7.** You made him a little lower than the angels; you crowned him with glory (honor, majesty) and honor, and You put everything under his feet." **8.** In putting everything under his control, nothing was left out of his authority, yet we do not yet see everything in submission to him. **9.** But we do see Jesus, who for a little while was made lower than the angels, crowned with glory and honor because of His suffering and death, so that by God's grace (favor) He might experience death on behalf of everyone. **10.** It was right (fitting, appropriate) that the One for whom and through whom everything exists should make the leader (author, originator) of our salvation complete (perfect) through suffering. **11.** Both the One who sanctifies (sets apart, makes holy) and those who are sanctified (made holy) are of the same family; so Jesus is not ashamed to call them brothers, **12.** saying, "I will declare (proclaim, announce) Your name to My brothers; in the congregation (gathering of believers), I will sing Your praises." **13.** And again, He says, "I will put My trust in Him." And again, "Here am I, and the children God has given Me." **14.** Since the children share in flesh and blood, He Himself also shared in the same, so that through His death He might destroy (defeat) the devil, **15.** and free those who, because of the fear of death, were in bondage (held captive) all their lives. **16.** For it was not angels that He came to help, but the descendants (offspring, children) of Abraham. **17.** Therefore, He had to be made like His brothers in every way, to become a merciful and faithful High Priest, offering atonement (reconciliation, forgiveness) for the sins of the people. **18.** Since He Himself suffered and was tempted (tested), He is able to help (assist) those who are being tempted.

Chapter 3

1. Therefore, beloved brothers and sisters, those who are partakers (participants, sharers) of the heavenly calling, direct your full attention to Jesus, the Apostle (sent one) and High Priest (greatest mediator) of our confession of faith. **2.** He was faithful to the One who appointed (selected) Him, just as Moses was faithful in all of God's house, performing the duties God entrusted to him. **3.** Jesus has been deemed deserving of far greater honor than Moses, for just as the builder of a house has more honor than the house itself, so Christ's glory surpasses that of Moses. **4.** While every house is made by someone, it is God who is the ultimate Creator of all things, the One who established the foundations of the universe. **5.** Moses was faithful in his role as a servant within God's house, testifying to the things that would later be revealed, **6.** but Christ, as the Son, is faithful over His own house. And we are that house, if we firmly hold on to the hope and confidence we profess, enduring in our faith until the end. **7.** Therefore, as the Holy Spirit speaks through the Scriptures, He warns us: "Today, if you hear His voice, **8.** do not harden (make resistant, unresponsive) your hearts as your ancestors did during the rebellion, in the testing (trial) in the wilderness, **9.** where your forefathers tested Me and saw My works for forty long years. **10.** I was deeply grieved with that generation, and said, 'Their hearts are continually led astray (misguided, wandering), and they do not know or understand My ways.' **11.** Because of this, I swore in My righteous anger (wrath), 'They will never enter into My place of rest.'" **12.** Take care (be vigilant), brothers and sisters, that none of you has an evil, unbelieving (distrusting, doubtful) heart that causes you to turn away from the living God and fall into spiritual rebellion. **13.** But instead, encourage (exhort, strengthen) one another daily, while it is still called "Today," so that none of you is hardened or deceived by sin's deceitfulness, which can cause spiritual blindness. **14.** For we have become partners (partakers, sharers) in Christ if we hold tightly to our confidence and assurance in Him, maintaining our hope firm and secure until the end. **15.** As it is written: "Today, if you hear His voice, do not harden your hearts, as you did during the rebellion." **16.** Who were the ones who heard and yet rebelled? Was it not all those who came out of Egypt, led by Moses? **17.** Who did God hold anger against for forty years? Was it not those who disobeyed, whose bodies (dead remains) fell in the desert and perished because of their rebellion? **18.** And to whom did He swear that they would not enter His rest, except to those who were disobedient (refused to obey, rebellious)? **19.** Therefore, we can see that they were unable to enter God's promised rest because of their unbelief, their lack of trust in Him.

Chapter 4

1. Since the promise of entering God's rest remains open and available, we must remain watchful (vigilant) and not allow ourselves to fall short of it. **2.** The good news (gospel) was shared with us, just as it was with them, but it did not benefit (help) them because they failed to combine it with faith and trust in God's promises. **3.** For those who believe, the opportunity to enter that rest is available, as God declared, "They shall not enter My rest," despite the fact that His work was finished from the very foundation (beginning) of the world. **4.** In a certain passage of Scripture, God referred to the seventh day, saying: "God rested on the seventh day from all His work." **5.** And once again, He declares, "They shall not enter My rest." **6.** Since there remains a promise for some to still enter this rest, and since those who first heard the message did not enter it because of their disobedience (refusal to obey God's call), **7.** God sets aside another day, as He spoke through David, saying, "Today," and it is further stated: "Today, if you hear His voice, do not harden (make stubborn) your hearts in resistance to Him." **8.** If Joshua had truly given them rest, there would not have been a need for God to speak of another day to come later. **9.** Therefore, there still exists a rest for the people of God, a rest that is available for all who choose to enter. **10.** Those who enter God's rest will cease (stop) from their own works, just as God Himself ceased from His creative work on the seventh day. **11.** Let us, therefore, make every effort (strive) to enter that rest, so that none of us will fall short or miss out due to disobedience. **12.** For the word of God is living and active, sharper than any two-edged sword, able to discern (understand) the thoughts and intentions (plans) of our hearts. **13.** Nothing in all of creation is hidden from His sight; every thought and action is exposed (revealed) before the One to whom we are accountable. **14.** Since we have a great High Priest, Jesus, the Son of God, we should hold fast (firmly maintain) to our confession of faith, without wavering. **15.** Our High Priest is not one who cannot empathize (understand) with our weaknesses—He has been tempted in every way, just as we are, yet He remained without sin. **16.** Therefore, let us confidently approach (come to) the throne of grace, knowing we can receive mercy and find grace to help us in our time of need.

Chapter 5

1. Every high priest, selected from among people, is appointed to represent them in matters concerning God, offering gifts and sacrifices for the forgiveness of sins. **2.** He can sympathize (feel with) those who are ignorant and those who have gone astray, because he himself is weak and prone to human failings. **3.** As a result, he must offer sacrifices for his own sins, just as he does for the sins of the people. **4.** No one assumes this honor for themselves; it is given by God, just as it was given to Aaron. **5.** In the same way, Christ did not elevate (raise in status) Himself to the position of High Priest, but it was God who said to Him, "You are My Son; today I have begotten (caused to be born) You." **6.** And God says in another passage, "You are a priest forever, in the order of Melchizedek." **7.** During His time on earth, Jesus offered prayers and supplications (earnest requests), crying out in anguish (extreme distress) to the One who could save Him from death. He was heard because of His reverence (deep respect for God). **8.** Although He was the Son of God, He learned obedience through the hardships He endured. **9.** After He was perfected (made complete or whole), He became the source of eternal (lasting forever) salvation for all those who obey Him, **10.** called by God to be a High Priest in the order of Melchizedek. **11.** We have much to say about this, but it is difficult to explain because you have become sluggish (slow or dull) in your understanding. **12.** By this time, you should be teachers, but you still need someone to teach you the basic principles of God's word. You are still in need of milk, not solid food. **13.** Anyone who lives on milk is inexperienced in the word of righteousness (rightness with God), because they are like infants. **14.** Solid food, however, is for the mature (fully developed in faith), who, by practice, have trained their senses to distinguish good from evil.

Chapter 6

1. Therefore, let us move beyond the basic teachings about Christ and strive toward spiritual maturity, not repeatedly laying the foundation of repentance (a change of heart and turning away from sin) from dead works and faith in God, **2.** nor the teachings on baptisms (ritual washing), the laying on of hands (a symbolic act of blessing or commissioning), resurrection (coming back to life), and eternal judgment (final decision regarding one's destiny). **3.** We will move forward with these teachings if God allows. **4.** It is impossible for those who have been enlightened (given spiritual understanding), tasted the heavenly gift, shared in the Holy Spirit, **5.** and experienced the goodness of God's word and the powers (abilities) of the coming age, **6.** if they fall away, to renew them to repentance, because they are crucifying (putting to death) the Son of God all over again and publicly disgracing Him. **7.** The land that drinks in the rain and produces crops useful for those who cultivate it is blessed (favored) by God, **8.** but if it produces thorns (sharp plants) and thistles (prickly weeds), it is rejected and nearly cursed (damned), and its end is to be burned. **9.** But, dear ones (beloved), we are confident of better things concerning you, things that accompany salvation (deliverance from sin and death), even as we speak this way. **10.** God will not forget your labor (work) of love for His name, as you have served and continue to serve the saints (holy or devoted people). **11.** We urge you to show the same diligence (care and effort) to the full assurance (certainty) of hope until the end, **12.** not becoming sluggish (lazy), but imitating (copying) those who, through faith and patience, inherit (receive) the promises of God. **13.** When God made a promise to Abraham, since He could swear by no one greater, He swore by Himself, **14.** saying, "Surely I will bless (give favor to) you and multiply (increase) you." **15.** After patiently enduring (suffering without giving up), Abraham received what was promised. **16.** Men swear by the greater (higher authority), and an oath (solemn promise) settles all disputes (arguments). **17.** So God, desiring to show the unchangeable (unchanging) nature of His purpose, confirmed it with an oath, **18.** so that by two unchangeable things, in which it is impossible for God to lie, we might have strong encouragement (comfort), having fled for refuge (safety) to the hope set before us. **19.** This hope is an anchor (stabilizing force) for the soul, firm and secure, entering the inner sanctuary behind the veil (curtain), **20.** where Jesus has entered as our forerunner (predecessor), becoming High Priest forever, in the order of Melchizedek.

Chapter 7

1. Melchizedek, the king of Salem and priest of the Most High God, encountered Abraham after he triumphed over the kings, and blessed him. **2.** To Melchizedek, Abraham gave a tenth (tithe) of everything he had, and Melchizedek's name signifies "king of righteousness," while he is also called the "king of peace." **3.** He was without a known father or mother, and no record of his genealogy (family history) exists; there is no beginning or end to his life. He is likened to the Son of God, and remains a priest for eternity. **4.** Reflect on how significant this man is, to whom even Abraham, the patriarch, gave a tenth of the spoils he had gained in battle. **5.** The descendants of Levi, who are the appointed priests, are required by the law to take a tenth of the people's income, even though they themselves are descendants of Abraham. **6.** But Melchizedek, whose lineage is not traced to Levi, received tithes from Abraham and blessed him, the one who had been given God's promises. **7.** There is no question that the greater one blesses the lesser. **8.** Here, mortal men receive tithes, but there, the tithes are collected by someone who is said to be living forever. **9.** Even Levi, who receives the tithes, can be considered as having paid tithes through Abraham, in a manner of speaking, **10.** because Levi was still in the body (loins) of his ancestor Abraham when Melchizedek met him. **11.** If the Levitical priesthood (under which the law was given) could have brought perfection (completeness), why would there have been a need for another priest to arise, one in the order of Melchizedek and not of Aaron? **12.** When the priesthood changes, the law itself also must be changed. **13.** The person to whom these words refer comes from a different tribe, and no one from that tribe has ever served at the altar. **14.** It is evident that our Lord came from the tribe of Judah, a tribe about which Moses never spoke in reference to priests. **15.** And this becomes even clearer when another priest arises, **16.** one who is not made a priest according to the law's fleshly requirements, but through the power of an indestructible (unbreakable) life. **17.** For it is testified: "You are a priest forever, in the order of Melchizedek." **18.** The old commandment is set aside (nullified) due to its weakness and inability to bring anyone to perfection. **19.** But now a superior hope is brought in, through which we can draw near to God. **20.** And since He was made priest with an oath, **21.** (the others became priests without an oath, but He became priest with an oath from the One who said to Him, "The Lord has sworn and will not change His mind, 'You are a priest forever, according to the order of Melchizedek'"), **22.** Jesus has become the guarantor (assurance) of a superior covenant. **23.** Many priests came and went, but death prevented them from continuing in their role. **24.** But Jesus, because He lives forever, holds an unalterable (unchanging) priesthood. **25.** For this reason, He is fully able to save completely (to the uttermost) those who come to God through Him, because He lives forever to intercede (plead) on their behalf. **26.** Such a High Priest is just what we needed: holy, innocent, undefiled (pure), separated from sinners, and exalted above the heavens. **27.** Unlike the other high priests, He does not need to offer sacrifices every day, first for His own sins and then for the sins of the people. He did this once and for all when He offered Himself. **28.** The law appoints as high priests men who are frail and imperfect, but the word of the oath, which came after the law, appoints the Son, who has been made perfect forever.

Chapter 8

1. The main point is this: We have a High Priest who is seated at the right hand of God in heaven, **2.** serving in the true sanctuary (holy place), the one established by the Lord, not by human hands. **3.** Every high priest is designated to offer gifts and sacrifices, so it is essential for Him to have something to present as an offering. **4.** If He were on earth, He would not qualify to be a priest, since there are priests already offering gifts in accordance with the law. **5.** They serve as mere copies and shadows (representations) of heavenly realities, just as Moses was instructed to make the tabernacle, following the specific pattern shown to him on the mountain. **6.** But now, He has obtained a far superior ministry (service), serving as the Mediator (intercessor) of a far better covenant (agreement), built on promises that are far greater. **7.** If the first covenant had been perfect, there would have been no need to establish a second one. **8.** But God found fault with the people and said, "The days are coming when I will make a new covenant with Israel and Judah, **9.** not like the covenant I made with their ancestors when I led them out of Egypt, because they broke that covenant, and I turned away from them," says the Lord. **10.** "This is the covenant I will establish with the people of Israel after those days: I will place My laws in their minds and write them on their hearts. I will be their God, and they will be My people." **11.** "No one will need to teach their neighbor, or say to one another, 'Know the Lord,' because they will all know Me, from the least to the greatest." **12.** "I will forgive their wickedness (wrongdoings) and will no longer remember their sins." **13.** By calling this a "new covenant," He has made the first one obsolete (outdated), and what is becoming obsolete and aging will soon disappear.

Chapter 9

1. The first covenant also had specific regulations (rules) for worship and an earthly sanctuary. **2.** A tabernacle (a movable tent) was constructed: in the first section was the lampstand, the table, and the showbread, known as the sanctuary; **3.** Behind the second veil (curtain) was the inner chamber called the Most Holy Place, **4.** which contained the golden censer (incense holder) and the ark of the covenant, overlaid with gold, with a golden pot of manna, Aaron's rod (staff) that had budded, and the tablets of the covenant. **5.** Above the ark were the cherubim (angelic beings) of glory, whose wings overshadowed the mercy seat (the lid of the ark). These things we cannot discuss in detail at the moment. **6.** When these items were arranged, the priests would regularly enter the first part to carry out their duties, **7.** but the high priest would enter alone into the second part once a year, and always with blood, which he offered for his own sins and for the unintentional (accidental) sins of the people. **8.** The Holy Spirit was signaling that the way into the Most Holy Place was not yet open while the first tabernacle remained standing. **9.** It was a symbol (representation) for the present time, during which offerings and sacrifices were made that could not purify the conscience (inner sense of right and wrong) of the one performing the service, **10.** Concerned only with external matters such as food, drink, various washings (ritual cleansings), and bodily regulations, imposed until the time of reformation (improvement). **11.** But Christ came as High Priest of the good things that were to come, with a greater and more perfect tabernacle, not made with human hands, that is, not of this earthly creation. **12.** Not by the blood of goats and calves, but by His own blood, He entered the Most Holy Place once for all, securing eternal (everlasting) redemption. **13.** For if the blood of bulls and goats and the ashes (remains) of a heifer (a young cow) sanctify (make holy) for the purification of the flesh, 14. how much more will the blood of Christ, who through the eternal Spirit offered Himself without blemish (flaw) to God, purify your conscience from dead works (useless deeds) to serve the living God? 15. And for this reason, He is the Mediator (intercessor) of the new covenant, by means of His death, for the redemption (deliverance) of transgressions (sins) committed under the first covenant, so that those who are called may receive the promise of eternal inheritance. 16. Where there is a testament (will), the death of the testator (one who makes the will) must occur, 17. for a will is in effect only after death; it has no force while the testator is still alive. 18. Therefore, even the first covenant was not inaugurated without blood. 19. When Moses had declared all the commands (laws) to the people, he took the blood of calves and goats, along with water, scarlet wool, and hyssop (a plant used for purification), and sprinkled the book and all the people, 20. Saying, "This is the blood of the covenant which God has commanded you." 21. He also sprinkled with blood both the tabernacle and all the items used in the service. 22. According to the law, nearly everything is purified with blood, and without the shedding (spilling) of blood, there is no forgiveness of sins. 23. Therefore, it was necessary for the copies (representations) of the heavenly things to be purified with these sacrifices, but the heavenly things themselves required better sacrifices. 24. For Christ did not enter holy places made by human hands, which are merely copies of the true ones, but He entered into heaven itself, now to appear in the presence of God on our behalf; 25. nor did He enter to offer Himself repeatedly, like the high priest who enters the Most Holy Place every year with the blood of another— 26. If He had needed to do this, He would have had to suffer repeatedly (many times) since the creation of the world. But now, once at the end of the ages, He has appeared to put away sin by the sacrifice of Himself. 27. Just as it is appointed (decreed by God) for people to die once and then face judgment, 28. so Christ was offered once to bear the sins of many. To those who eagerly await Him, He will appear a second time, not to deal with sin, but to bring salvation.

Chapter 10

1. The law was merely a shadow (an imperfect reflection) of the good things that were to come, not the actual substance (true form) of the heavenly realities. Therefore, the sacrifices offered continually every year under the law could never make perfect (complete or whole) those who approach. 2. Otherwise, wouldn't they have stopped being offered? For if the sacrifices were truly effective, those who were purified (cleansed) once would no longer have any awareness (consciousness) of sin. 3. But, in fact, these sacrifices only serve as a reminder (a recollection or call to memory) of sins each year. 4. It is impossible for the blood of bulls and goats to truly take away sins. The shedding of animal blood was only a temporary covering, not a lasting solution. 5. When Christ came into the world, He said, "You did not desire sacrifice and offering, but You have prepared a body for Me to fulfill Your will." This points to the fact that God's ultimate plan was not fulfilled through ritual sacrifices, but through the offering of Christ Himself. 6. You were not pleased (did not find delight or satisfaction) in burnt offerings or sin offerings that were traditionally offered. 7. Then He (Christ) declared, "See, I have come—written of Me in the Scriptures—to do Your will, O God, as You have commanded." This shows the Messiah's complete submission to the Father's will, even over the sacrificial system. 8. In previous declarations, He said that God had no pleasure in the sacrificial system (burnt offerings, sin offerings, etc.), which were offered according to the law. 9. Christ came to abolish the first covenant of sacrifices (the old way of salvation) so that He could establish the second (the new covenant of grace and redemption). 10. Through the will of God, we have been sanctified (made holy, set apart) by the offering of the body of Jesus Christ once for all, unlike the repetitive sacrifices of the old system. 11. Every priest in the old covenant stands daily ministering (serving) and offering the same sacrifices over and over again, but those sacrifices could never take away sins. The repetitive nature of these offerings indicates that they were never truly able to bring about permanent cleansing. 12. But this Man (Jesus), after offering one perfect sacrifice for sins forever, sat down at the right hand of God. This act of sitting down shows that His work was complete and that He was now in a place of authority and

rest. 13. From that time on, He waits for His enemies to be made His footstool (a symbol of ultimate victory and triumph over all opposing forces). 14. For by one offering, He has perfected (completed, made whole) forever those who are being sanctified (set apart for God's purposes). His single sacrifice has made believers fully righteous in the sight of God, once and for all. 15. The Holy Spirit also testifies (bears witness) to us about this. He had already spoken of this in the past. 16. "This is the covenant I will establish with them after those days," says the Lord, "I will put My laws into their hearts, and I will write them on their minds." The new covenant is one of internal transformation, where God's law is not just an external rule, but is written on the hearts and minds of believers. 17. Then He adds, "Their sins and their lawless deeds (wicked actions) I will remember no more." The forgiveness through Christ is complete, and God chooses not to recall the sins of those He has forgiven. 18. Now, where there is remission (forgiveness) of these sins, there is no longer a need for an offering for sin. Christ's once-for-all sacrifice has replaced the need for further sacrifices. 19. Therefore, brothers and sisters, since we have confidence (boldness) to enter the Most Holy Place (God's presence) by the blood of Jesus, 20. by a new and living way that He opened for us through the curtain (veil), that is, His flesh (His body was torn for us), 21. and since we have a great High Priest (Jesus) over the house of God, 22. let us draw near with a sincere heart, in full assurance (confidence) of faith, having our hearts sprinkled (cleansed) from an evil conscience, and our bodies washed with pure water. This describes a deeper intimacy with God, made possible through Christ's atonement. 23. Let us hold fast the confession (profession) of our hope without wavering (without doubting), for He who promised is faithful and will fulfill His word. 24. Let us consider one another and provoke (spur on) each other to love and good works, not just in words, but in deeds. 25. Let us not neglect (forsake) meeting together, as some have done, but let us encourage (exhort) one another all the more, especially as you see the Day (the second coming of Christ) approaching. 26. For if we deliberately (willfully) sin after we have received the knowledge of the truth, there no longer remains a sacrifice for sins. This verse warns about rejecting the grace of God after receiving the full knowledge of it. 27. Instead, there will be a fearful (dreadful) expectation of judgment, and fiery indignation (anger) which will consume (destroy) the adversaries (those who oppose God). 28. Anyone who rejected the law of Moses died without mercy on the testimony of two or three witnesses. 29. How much worse do you think the punishment will be for one who has despised (trampled) the Son of God, who has treated the blood of the covenant (by which he was sanctified) as a common thing, and who has insulted (outraged) the Spirit of grace? To reject Christ is to reject God's ultimate gift of grace, which is an act of great disrespect. 30. For we know Him who said, "Vengeance (revenge) is Mine, I will repay," says the Lord, and again, "The Lord will judge His people." God is the ultimate judge, and no one will escape His justice. 31. It is a terrifying (fearful) thing to fall into the hands of the living God—this describes the severe consequences of rejecting God's offer of salvation. 32. But remember the former days when, after you were enlightened (became aware of the truth), you endured a great struggle with sufferings. The early believers faced persecution, yet they remained faithful. 33. Sometimes you were publicly mocked (made a spectacle) by reproaches (disgrace) and tribulations (troubles), and sometimes you were companions (associates) with those who were treated in the same way. 34. You showed compassion (sympathy) for me in my imprisonment and joyfully accepted the confiscation (plundering) of your goods, knowing that you have a better and more enduring (lasting) possession in heaven. They valued eternal rewards over earthly losses. 35. Therefore, do not throw away your confidence (boldness), which has a great reward. 36. For you need endurance (patience), so that after doing God's will, you will receive the promise He has made to you. 37. "For just a little while, and He who is coming will come and will not delay (tarry)." Christ's return is certain, though it may seem delayed. 38. Now the just (righteous) shall live by faith, but if anyone shrinks back (turns away), My soul has no pleasure in him. 39. But we are not those who turn back to destruction (perdition), but those who believe and are saved.

Chapter 11

1. Faith is the confidence (assurance) in what we hope for and assurance about what we do not see. 2. Through it, the elders (ancestors) were commended (approved). 3. By faith, we understand that the universe was created by God's word, so what is seen was made from the unseen (invisible). 4. By faith, Abel offered a better sacrifice (offering) than Cain, gaining approval from God; though dead, he still speaks. 5. By faith, Enoch was taken without seeing death, for he pleased (satisfied) God. 6. Without faith, it's impossible to please God, for one must believe He exists and rewards (blesses) those who seek Him. 7. By faith, Noah built an ark (large boat) to save his family, becoming an heir (inheritor) of righteousness. 8. By faith, Abraham obeyed and went to the place he would inherit, not knowing where he was going. 9. By faith, he lived as a foreigner (outsider) in the promised land, in tents with Isaac and Jacob, heirs of the promise. 10. He waited for the city with foundations (basis), built by God. 11. By faith, Sarah received strength (ability) to conceive (become pregnant), trusting God's promise despite her age. 12. From one man came descendants (offspring) as numerous as the stars and sands. 13. All these died in faith, not having received the promises, but seeing and embracing (accepting) them from afar, admitting they were strangers on earth. 14. Those who speak this way make it clear they seek a homeland (native land). 15. If they had thought of the country they left, they could have returned. 16. Instead, they desired a heavenly (divine) country; God is not ashamed to be their God, for He prepared a city for them. 17. By faith, Abraham offered Isaac, trusting God could raise (restore) him from the dead. 18. Through Isaac, Abraham's descendants would be called. 19. Figuratively (symbolically), he received Isaac back from death. 20. By faith, Isaac blessed (praised) Jacob and Esau for the future. 21. By faith, Jacob blessed Joseph's sons as he died, worshiping (honoring) God. 22. By faith, Joseph spoke of Israel's exodus (departure) and gave instructions about his bones. 23. By faith, Moses' parents hid him for three months, seeing he was special and defying (disobeying) the king's order. 24. By faith, Moses refused to be called Pharaoh's daughter's son. 25. He chose suffering with God's people over temporary (short-lived) sin's pleasures. 26. He regarded (valued) disgrace for Christ as greater wealth than Egypt's treasures, for he looked to the reward. 27. By faith, he left Egypt, unafraid of the king's anger, enduring (remaining strong) as if seeing the invisible (unseen) God. 28. By faith, he kept the Passover (festival) and sprinkled blood to protect Israel from the destroyer. 29. By faith, they crossed the Red Sea on dry ground; the Egyptians drowned when they tried. 30. By faith, the walls of Jericho fell after seven days of encircling (surrounding). 31. By faith, Rahab did not perish (die) with the disobedient, having welcomed the spies in peace. 32. What more shall I say? Time would fail to speak of Gideon, Barak, Samson, Jephthah, David, Samuel, and the prophets (messengers), 33. who, by faith, conquered kingdoms, administered (carried out) justice, gained promises, shut lions' mouths, 34. quenched (extinguished) fire, escaped the sword, were strengthened in weakness, and turned foreign armies to flight. 35. Women received their dead raised back to life. Others were tortured (abused), refusing release to attain (receive) a better resurrection. 36. Some faced mockery (ridicule), flogging (whipping), chains, and imprisonment (jail). 37. They were stoned, sawn in two, tempted, killed by the sword; they wandered in sheepskins and goatskins, afflicted (suffering), mistreated— 38. the world was not worthy of them. They wandered in deserts, mountains, caves, and dens (hiding places). 39. Though they gained approval through faith, they did not receive the promise. 40. God had something better for us, that they would not be made perfect apart from us.

Chapter 12

1. Therefore, since we are surrounded by such a great cloud of witnesses (those who testify to the faith by their lives), let us cast off every weight (burden) and the sin that so easily entangles (ensnares or traps) us, and let us run with perseverance (endurance, patience) the race set before us. This means that we should focus on living according to the example of those faithful individuals who have gone before us. 2. Looking to Jesus, the author (originator, initiator) and finisher (completer, perfecter) of our faith, who, for the joy set before Him, endured the cross, despising (rejecting) its shame, and has now sat down at the right hand of the throne of God. Jesus is both the beginning and the completion of our faith, and His victory over shame

and suffering is our model. 3. Consider Him who endured such hostility (opposition, resistance) from sinners against Himself, so that you may not grow weary and discouraged in your souls. Reflect on Christ's suffering to find strength when facing our own difficulties. 4. You have not yet resisted (fought against) to the point of shedding blood (in other words, you have not faced the same level of suffering or persecution that Jesus did), striving against sin. 5. And you have forgotten the exhortation (encouragement, comfort) which speaks to you as to sons: "My son, do not despise the chastening (discipline, correction) of the Lord, nor be discouraged (disheartened) when you are rebuked (corrected) by Him;" 6. for whom the Lord loves He disciplines (chastens), and He scourges (corrects) every son whom He receives (welcomes into His family). The discipline of God is an expression of His love for us, refining us like a father corrects his children. 7. If you endure chastening (discipline), God deals with you as sons; for what son is there whom a father does not discipline? This is a natural part of sonship—being trained by a loving father. 8. But if you are without chastening, of which all have become partakers, then you are illegitimate (not true children) and not sons. True sons receive correction as part of their growth and relationship with their father. 9. Furthermore, we have had human fathers who corrected us, and we respected (honored) them; shall we not much more readily be in subjection (obedient) to the Father of spirits and live? If we accept discipline from earthly fathers, how much more should we accept discipline from our heavenly Father, who gives us life? 10. For they indeed for a few days corrected (chastised) us as seemed best to them, but He (God) does so for our benefit (profit, advantage), that we may be partakers (share in) of His holiness. Earthly fathers may correct us imperfectly, but God's discipline is always for our eternal good. 11. Now no chastening (discipline) seems to be joyful in the present, but painful; nevertheless, afterward it yields (produces) the peaceable fruit of righteousness to those who have been trained (disciplined) by it. While discipline is painful in the moment, it brings the lasting benefit of a life of righteousness and peace. 12. Therefore, strengthen (encourage) the hands that hang down, and the feeble (weak, tired) knees. When we're discouraged, we need to lift each other up and encourage ourselves to continue. 13. And make straight paths for your feet, so that what is lame (weak) may not be dislocated (injured or hurt), but rather be healed. Walk in righteousness and encourage others in their walk so they can grow in strength and healing. 14. Pursue peace with all people, and holiness (a life set apart for God), without which no one will see the Lord. The pursuit of peace and holiness is not optional; it is essential for seeing God. 15. Looking carefully lest anyone fall short (fall behind or fail to obtain) of the grace of God; lest any root of bitterness springing up cause trouble, and by this many become defiled (corrupted or stained). We must be vigilant, as bitterness and unforgiveness can poison relationships and hinder spiritual growth. 16. Lest there be any fornicator (sexually immoral person) or profane (unholy, irreverent) person like Esau, who for one morsel (bite) of food sold his birthright. Esau's short-sightedness in trading his birthright for temporary satisfaction serves as a warning about valuing eternal blessings over temporary pleasures. 17. For you know that afterward, when he wanted to inherit the blessing, he was rejected, for he found no place for repentance (change of heart), though he sought it diligently with tears. Esau's regret was not enough to reverse his decision; it's a reminder that our actions have lasting consequences. 18. For you have not come to the mountain that may be touched (physical, earthly mountain), and that burned with fire, and to darkness (blackness), and a storm (tempest), 19. and the sound of a trumpet and the voice of words, so that those who heard it begged that the word should not be spoken to them anymore. The people of Israel feared the terrifying presence of God at Mount Sinai, but we have come to something far greater. 20. For they could not endure (bear, withstand) what was commanded: "If even an animal touches the mountain, it shall be stoned or shot with an arrow." God's holiness at Sinai was overwhelming and terrifying. 21. And so terrifying was the sight that Moses said, "I am exceedingly afraid and trembling." Even Moses, the leader of God's people, was afraid in the presence of God's holiness. 22. But you have come to Mount Zion, and to the city of the living God, the heavenly Jerusalem, to an innumerable company (countless multitude) of angels. Unlike the terrifying experience at

Sinai, we have come to a heavenly place of joy and celebration. 23. To the general assembly and church of the firstborn (those who have been born again in Christ) who are registered (written, enrolled) in heaven, to God, the Judge of all, to the spirits of just men made perfect. This refers to the redeemed—those who have been made perfect in Christ. 24. To Jesus, the Mediator (intercessor) of the new covenant, and to the blood of sprinkling (sacrifice) that speaks better things than that of Abel. Jesus' sacrifice speaks of forgiveness and reconciliation, in contrast to Abel's blood, which cried out for justice. 25. See that you do not refuse (reject) Him who speaks. For if they did not escape when they refused Him who spoke on earth, much more shall we not escape if we turn away from Him who speaks from heaven. We must listen to God's voice, especially now that He speaks to us through His Son. 26. Whose voice then shook the earth, but now He has promised, saying, "Yet once more I will shake not only the earth, but also heaven." God's power is so great that it will shake the entire universe, establishing His eternal kingdom. 27. Now this, "Yet once more," indicates the removal of those things that are being shaken, as of things that are made, that the things which cannot be shaken may remain. The things that are temporary and man-made will pass away, but God's kingdom will endure forever. 28. Therefore, since we are receiving a kingdom which cannot be shaken, let us have grace (God's favor), by which we may serve God acceptably, with reverence (awe) and godly fear. Our service to God should be marked by reverence, recognizing His greatness and holiness. 29. For our God is a consuming fire. God's holiness is so powerful that it consumes all that is impure. This reminds us of the need for holiness in our relationship with Him.

Chapter 13

1. Let love (affection and care) between believers remain steadfast, continually demonstrating kindness and affection toward one another. 2. Do not neglect to extend hospitality (welcoming guests) to strangers, for by doing so, some have unknowingly welcomed angels into their homes. 3. Remember those who are in prison, as though you were imprisoned with them, and those who are suffering, knowing that you too share in the same human struggles. 4. Let marriage be held in high honor (respect) among all, and let the marriage bed be kept pure (undefiled, clean), for God will judge those who engage in sexual immorality (fornication) and adultery (cheating on one's spouse). 5. Let your conduct (behavior) be free from the love of money, and be content (satisfied) with what you have. For God Himself has said, "I will never leave you or forsake (abandon) you." 6. Therefore, we can confidently say: "The Lord is my helper; I will not be afraid. What can mere mortals (humans) do to me?" 7. Remember those who lead and teach you, who have proclaimed the Word of God to you. Consider the outcome (end result) of their way of life and imitate (follow) their faith. 8. Jesus Christ is unchanging—yesterday, today, and forever. 9. Do not be led astray (misled) by strange and varied teachings. It is good for the heart to be strengthened (firmed up) by God's grace, not by ceremonial foods (ritual meals), which have not benefited those who devoted themselves (dedicated) to them. 10. We have an altar (sacred place) from which those who serve in the earthly sanctuary (temple) have no right to eat. 11. For the bodies of the animals whose blood is brought into the sanctuary by the high priest for sin are burned (destroyed) outside the camp (city). 12. Therefore, Jesus also suffered outside the city gate in order to sanctify (make holy) the people with His own blood. 13. Let us go to Him outside the camp, bearing the disgrace (shame) He bore. 14. For here on earth we do not have an enduring (lasting) city, but we seek the city that is to come. 15. Through Him, therefore, let us continually offer to God a sacrifice (offering) of praise—the fruit of lips that openly profess (declare) His name. 16. And do not forget to do good and to share (give) with others, for with such sacrifices God is pleased. 17. Obey your leaders and submit (yield) to their authority, because they keep watch over you as those who must give an account. Let them do this with joy, and not with sorrow (grief), for that would be of no benefit (good) to you. 18. Pray for us, for we are confident that we have a clear conscience (sense of right), and desire to live honorably (respectably) in every way. 19. I especially urge (entreat, strongly request) you to pray that I may be restored (reunited) to you soon. 20. Now may the God of peace, who brought again (raised) from the dead our Lord Jesus, the great Shepherd (protector) of the sheep, through the blood of the eternal covenant

(unbreakable promise), 21. equip (prepare, supply) you with everything good for doing His will, and may He work in us what is pleasing (acceptable) to Him, through Jesus Christ, to whom be glory forever and ever. Amen. 22. I appeal (urge, ask earnestly) to you, brothers and sisters, bear with my word of exhortation (encouragement), for I have written to you briefly. 23. Know that our brother Timothy has been released (set free), with whom I will see you if he comes soon. 24. Greet all your leaders and all the saints (holy ones). Those from Italy send their greetings. 25. Grace (unmerited favor) be with you all. Amen.

67 – Peter 1

Chapter 1

1. Peter, a backer (one transferred with a charge) of Jesus Christ, to the scattered religionists in Pontus, Galatia, Cappadocia, Asia, and Bithynia (regions in Asia Minor, ultramodern- day Turkey), 2. Chosen by God the Father, sanctified (set piecemeal) by the Spirit for obedience to Jesus Christ, and sanctified by His blood. Grace and peace be multiplied to you. 3. Praise be to the God and Father of our Lord Jesus Christ, who, in His great mercy (compassion), has given us new birth into a living stopgap through the rejuvenation of Jesus Christ from the dead, 4. To a heritage (gift from God) that's imperishable (can not decay), undefiled (not corrupted), and unfading, kept in heaven for you, 5. Who are defended (shielded) by God's power through faith for a deliverance (liberation) ready to be revealed in the last time. 6. In this, you rejoice, however now, for a little while, you may have to suffer colorful trials (tests of faith), 7. so that the proven fictitiousness (authenticity) of your faith, more precious than gold meliorated (purified) by fire, may affect in praise, honor, and glory at the disclosure of Jesus Christ. 8. Though you haven't seen Him, you love Him; and though you don't see Him now, you believe in Him and rejoice with indescribable (willful) and noble joy, 9. For you are entering the end of your faith, the deliverance (eternal life) of your souls. 10. Concerning this deliverance, the prophets (couriers of God) searched and inquired precisely, 11. Trying to figure out the time and circumstances the Spirit of Christ within them was pointing to, regarding the mourning's of Christ and the glory (honor) that would follow. 12. It was revealed to them that they were serving not themselves but you, in these effects now sermonized (placarded) to you by the Holy Spirit transferred from heaven, effects angels long (desire) to understand. 13. Thus, prepare your minds for action (be mentally alert), be sober- inclined (serious- inclined), and set your stopgap completely on the grace that will be brought to you at the disclosure of Jesus Christ. 14. As biddable children (followers), don't conform (follow) to your former solicitations, when you lived in ignorance (without knowledge) of God's verity, 15. But be holy (set piecemeal for God) in all your conduct, just as the One who called you is holy, 16. For it's written," Be holy, for I'm holy." 17. Still, who judges impartially (without favoritism) according to each bone's work, live in reverent fear (respect) during your time as nonnatives then, If you call on the Father (God). 18. You know that you weren't redeemed (saved) with perishable effects like tableware or gold, but with the precious blood (immolation) of Christ, 19. An angel without mark (pristine) or disfigurement. 20. He was chosen (destined) before the foundation of the world but was revealed in these last times for your sake, 21. through Him you believe in God, who raised Him from the dead and glorified (recognized) Him, so that your faith and stopgap are in God. 22. Since you have purified (sanctified) your souls by adhering the verity through the Spirit, love one another deeply (unfeigned) with a pure heart, 23. For you have been born again (spiritually revived), not of perishable seed (temporary), but of imperishable (eternal), through the living and enduring word of God. 24. For," All people are like lawn, and all its glory (beauty) like the flowers of the field; the lawn withers (dies) and the flowers fall, 25. But the word (communication) of the Lord endures ever." And this is the word that was sermonized (placarded) to you.

Chapter 2

1. Thus, relieve yourselves of all malignancy (ill will), dishonesty (deceitfulness), insincerity (pretending to be commodity you are not), covetousness (covetousness), and dangerous speech (libel). 2. Like invigorated babies, long for the pure milk of God's Word, so that you may grow in your spiritual trip. 3. This is if, in fact, you have tasted the

kindness (grace) of the Lord. **4.** Come to Him, the living Stone — rejected by people but chosen and recognized in God's sight. **5.** And you, as living monuments, are being constructed into a spiritual tabernacle (a place where God dwells), a holy priesthood (a group set piecemeal for God's service), offering spiritual offerings (acts of deification) that are pleasing to God through Jesus Christ. **6.** As it's written" See, I lay in Zion a precious foundation (the foundation gravestone of a structure), chosen and precious, and whoever believes in Him won't be disappointed (put to shame)." **7.** To you who believe, He's of great worth; but to those who reject Him," The gravestone the builders rejected has come the foundation," **8.** and" a gravestone that causes people to stumble (to fall), and a gemstone that makes them fall." They stumble because they don't observe (submit to) the Word, and this is their fortune (fate). **9.** But you're a chosen people, a royal priesthood, a holy nation, a people belonging to God, so that you may declare the praises of Him who called you out of darkness into His marvelous light. **10.** Once you weren't a people, but now you're the people of God; formerly you hadn't entered mercy (God's remission), but now you have entered mercy. **11.** Cherished (dearly loved), I prompt you, as temporary residers (nonnatives) and pilgrims (trippers on a trip) in this world, to avoid the unethical solicitations (worldly temptations) that wage war (conflict) against your soul. **12.** Live good lives among the Heathens (non-believers), so that though they may charge you of doing wrong, they may see your good deeds and glorify God on the day He visits (when He judges the world). **13.** Submit (place yourself under authority) yourselves to every authority introduced by men for the Lord's sake, whether to the king as the supreme authority, **14.** Or to governors, who are transferred by him to discipline those who do wrong and recommend (praise) those who do right. **15.** For it's God's will that by doing good you silence (stop) the ignorant (oblivious) talk of foolish people. **16.** Live as free people, but don't use your freedom as a reason for doing wrong; rather, serve God. **17.** Show respect (honor) to everyone, love the family of religionists (fellow Christians), sweat God, and recognize the king. **18.** Retainers (slaves), submit yourselves to your masters (employers) with all respect, not only to those who are kind and considerate, but also to those who are harsh (unjust). **19.** For it's estimable (approved by God) if someone bears up under the pain of unjust suffering because they're conscious (apprehensive) of God. **20.** How is it to your credit if you suffer for doing wrong? But if you suffer for doing good and endure (bear) it, this is estimable before God. **21.** To this you were called, because Christ suffered for you, leaving you an illustration (a pattern) that you should follow in His way **22.**" He committed no sin, and no dishonesty (falsehood) was set up in His mouth." **23.** When they hurled cuts (vituperative language) at Him, He didn't avenge (respond in kind); when He suffered, He made no pitfalls rather, He entrusted (gave Himself into) Himself to Him who judges justly (fairly). **24.** He Himself bore (took upon Himself) our sins in His body on the cross, so that we might die to stray and live for righteousness." By His injuries (injuries), you have been healed." **25.** For you were like lamb going amiss (lost in sin), but now you have returned to the Shepherd and Overseer (Protector) of your souls (Jesus).

Chapter 3

1. In the same way, women, be amenable (yielding or biddable) and regardful to your misters, so that if some don't follow the word of God, they may be told to believe without a word, through your regardful and pure gesture. **2.** When they see your regardful and pure way of living, embedded in reverence (deep respect) for God. **3.** Don't concentrate solely on outside beauty — similar as baptizing your hair, wearing gold jewelry, or dressing in fine clothes. **4.** Rather, let your beauty be from within, the imperishable (unfading) quality of a gentle and peaceful spirit, which is of great worth in God's sight. **5.** For this is how the holy women of old who trusted in God adorned themselves, being amenable to their misters. **6.** Just as Sarah adhered (submitted to) Abraham and called him" lord" (a title of respect), you're her daughters if you do what's good and don't let fear scarify (disturb) you. **7.** Likewise, misters, live with your women in an understanding (perceptive) way, showing honor to them as the more delicate (fragile or vulnerable) vessel, and as fellow heirs at law of the grace of life, so that your prayers may not be hindered (averted). **8.** Eventually, all of you should be of one mind, showing sympathy (compassion) for one

another, loving as sisters and sisters, being tenderhearted (compassionate) and humble. **9.** Don't repay evil with wrong or personality with personality, but rather bless (speak well of) others, because you were called to do so, in order to inherit a blessing. **10.** For, "Whoever desires to love life and see good days, let him keep his lingo from evil and his lips from speaking dishonesty (falsehood). **11.** Let him turn from evil and do good let him seek peace and pursue it. **12.** For the eyes of the Lord are on the righteous, and His cognizance are open to their prayers. But the face of the Lord is against those who do wrong." **13.** Who'll harm you if you're eager to do what's good? **14.** But indeed if you suffer for doing what's right, you're blessed. Don't be hysterical of their pitfalls or be troubled (disturbed). **15.** Rather, set piecemeal Christ as Lord in your hearts, and always be prepared to give a reason for the stopgap you have, but do so with gentleness (kindness) and respect. **16.** Keep a clear heart (moral certainty), so that when people speak against you as wrongdoers, they may be shamed of their allegations because of your good conduct in Christ. **17.** It's better, if it's God's will, to suffer for doing good than for doing wrong. **18.** For Christ also suffered formerly for sins, the righteous for the unlawful, to bring us to God. He was put to death in the meat but made alive by the Spirit. **19.** Through the Spirit, He went and sermonized to the spirits in captivity — **20.** who were defiant (rebellious) long a gone when God awaited patiently in the days of Noah, while the ark was being erected. In it, only a many — eight people — were saved through water. **21.** This water symbolizes investment, which now saves you — not the junking of dirt from the body, but the pledge (commitment) of a good heart toward God, through the rejuvenation of Jesus Christ. **22.** Who has gone into heaven and is at God's right hand, with angels, authorities, and powers made subject (under the control) to Him.

Chapter 4

1. Since Christ suffered for us in the meat (body), arm yourselves with the same mindset, for he who has suffered in the meat has stopped transgressing. **2.** He should no longer live for mortal solicitations, but for the will of God. **3.** We've spent enough time in the history doing the will of the Heathens (non-Jews) — living in immorality, lusts, drunkenness, wild parties, and idolizations (false deification). **4.** They suppose it strange that you don't join them in the same reckless gesture, and they speak wrong of you. **5.** They will give an account to Him who's ready to judge the living and the dead. **6.** The philosophy (good news) was sermonized to those who are dead, so they might be judged in the meat (physical body) but live according to God in the spirit. **7.** The end of all effects is near (at hand); be serious and vigilant (alert) in your prayers. **8.** Above all, love one another fervently, for" love will cover a multitude of sins." **9.** Be sociable (welcoming) to one another without complaining. **10.** As each bone has entered a gift, use it to serve one another, as servants (directors) of God's grace. **11.** Still, let him speak as the oracles (words) of God, if anyone speaks. However, let him do so with the strength God provides, so God may be glorified through Jesus Christ, if anyone serves. **12.** Don't suppose it strange concerning the fiery trial (test) you face, as though commodity unusual is passing to you. **13.** Rejoice that you partake in Christ's mourning (share in His mourning), so that when His glory is revealed, you may also rejoice with exceeding joy. **14.** Still, you're blessed, for the Spirit of glory and of God rests upon you, if you're reproached (disrespected) for Christ's name. They curse (speak against) Him, but you glorify Him. **15.** Let none of you suffer as a killer, pincher, malefactor (wrongdoer), or buttinsky (interfering person) in others' matters. **16.** Still, let him glorify God in this matter, if anyone suffers as a Christian (follower of Christ). **17.** Judgment begins at the house of God (the Church); if it begins with us, what will the end be for those who don't observe the philosophy of God? **18.** Still, where will the ungodly and the wrongdoer appear?" **19.**," If the righteous are scarcely saved. Thus, let those who suffer according to God's will commit their souls (lives) to Him in doing good, as to a faithful Creator.

Chapter 5

1. To the elders (spiritual leaders) among you, I prompt you — fellow elders and substantiations of Christ's suffering, and also participators of the glory to be revealed **2.** Lead God's flock (His people) under your care, not by coercion, but willingly; not for dishonest gain, but eagerly. **3.** Don't rule as tyrants over those in your care but be exemplifications to the flock. **4.** When the Chief Shepherd (Jesus) appears, you'll admit the unfading crown of glory. **5.** Likewise, you youngish people, submit to your elders. All of you, be humble toward one another, because" God opposes the proud but gives grace to the humble." **6.** Humble yourselves under God's potent hand that He may lift you up at the proper time. **7.** Cast all your anxieties on Him, for He cares for you. **8.** Be sober (tone- controlled) and watchful (vigilant), because your adversary, the devil (Satan), prowls like a roaring captain, seeking someone to devour. **9.** Repel him, standing establishment in the faith, knowing that your sisters and sisters around the world are facing the same mourning. **10.** After you've suffered a little while, may the God of all grace (unmerited favor), who called you to His eternal glory in Christ, restore, strengthen, and establish you. **11.** To Him be glory and power ever. Amen. **12.** I've written compactly through Silvanus (Silas), a faithful companion of Paul), prompting you to stand establishment in the true grace of God. **13.** The church in Babylon (probably a law for Rome, a place of persecution) sends you felicitations, as does my son Mark (probably a convert or close associate). **14.** Hail one another with a kiss of love (a gesture of peace and fellowship). Peace to all of you in Christ Jesus. Amen.

68 – Peter 2

Chapter 1

1. Simon Peter (one of Jesus' closest votaries), a menial and backer of Jesus Christ, writes to those who, like us, have entered the same precious faith through the righteousness of our God and Savior, Jesus Christ. **2.** May grace (God's unearned favor) and peace be multiplied to you through the knowledge of God and Jesus our Lord. **3.** His godly power has given us everything we need for life and saintliness, through knowing Him who called us by His glory and excellence. **4.** Through these, He has given us great and precious pledges, so that by them you may partake in the godly nature (God's rates), having escaped the corruption caused by unethical solicitations. **5.** For this reason, make every trouble to add to your faith virtuousness, to virtuousness knowledge, **6.** To knowledge tone- control, to tone- control perseverance, to perseverance saintliness, 7. to saintliness collective affection, and to collective affection love. **8.** Still, they will keep you from being sterile in your knowledge of our Lord Jesus Christ, if these rates are yours and adding. **9.** But anyone who lacks these rates is eyeless, short-sighted, and has forgotten they were sanctified from once sins. **10.** Thus, sisters and sisters, be active to confirm your calling and election (God's picking of you), for if you exercise these, you'll no way stumble, **11.** And will admit a rich hello into the eternal area of our Lord and Savior Jesus Christ. **12.** I'll always remind you of these effects, indeed though you know them and are established in the verity. **13.** I suppose it's right, as long as I'm in this fleshly body (roof), to stir you up by reminding you, **14.** Knowing that soon I'll lay away this body, just as our Lord Jesus Christ showed me (Peter would die soon, as Jesus read). **15.** I'll make every trouble to ensure that after my departure, you'll flash back these effects. **16.** We did not follow cleverly constructed stories when we told you about the power and coming of our Lord Jesus Christ but were observers of His majesty. **17.** He entered honor and glory from God the Father when the voice came from the Majestic Glory (God's noble presence)" This is My Cherished Son, with whom I'm well pleased." **18.** We heard this voice from heaven when we were with Him on the holy mountain (likely the Mount of Transfiguration, where Jesus revealed His godly glory to Peter, James, and John). **19.** We've the predictive word made further certain, and you do well to pay attention to it as to a light in a dark place, until the day dawns and the morning star rises in your hearts. **20.** Above all, understand that no vaticination of Book came from mortal interpretation. **21.** For vaticination no way came by mortal will, but holy men of God spoke as they were moved by the Holy Spirit.

Chapter 2

1. Just as there were false prophets in the past, so there will be false teachers among you. They will secretly introduce destructive heresies (false beliefs), even denying the very Lord who redeemed them, and as a result, they will bring swift destruction upon themselves. **2.** Many will follow their immoral ways (corrupt actions), and because of them, the truth will be maligned (disrespected). **3.** In their greed, they will exploit (take advantage of) you with cleverly crafted lies, but their judgment is certain and will not be delayed. **4.** If God did not spare the angels who sinned but cast them into a dark abyss (deep prison) to be held for

judgment, **5.** and if He did not spare the ancient world but saved Noah, a preacher of righteousness (justice), when He flooded the wicked world, **6.** and if He destroyed the cities of Sodom and Gomorrah, turning them into ashes as a warning to the ungodly (those who do wrong), **7.** and if He delivered the righteous Lot, who was tormented by the wickedness around him, **8.** (for that righteous man was troubled by the lawless actions (unlawful behavior) he witnessed and heard), **9.** then the Lord knows how to deliver (save) the godly from trials and reserve the unjust for punishment on the day of judgment. **10.** Especially those who indulge the flesh in immorality (sinful behavior) and reject authority. They are arrogant (proud), self-willed, and are not afraid to speak evil of those in authority, **11.** even though angels, who are far stronger, do not bring accusations against such beings before the Lord. **12.** But these false teachers are like irrational (senseless) animals, born to be captured and destroyed. They speak against things they do not understand, and in their destruction, they will be destroyed. **13.** They will receive the wages (rewards) of their wrongdoing, for they indulge in sin openly, even in broad daylight. They are like stains and blemishes on your Christian fellowship, reveling (enjoying) in their deceptions while they eat with you. **14.** Their eyes are full of adultery (lust), never ceasing from sin, and they entice (attract) unstable souls. They are experts in greed and are under a curse. **15.** They have forsaken (abandoned) the straight path and gone astray, following the way of Balaam, the son of Beor, who loved the wages of wickedness, **16.** but was rebuked (corrected) for his sin when a dumb donkey spoke with a human voice, stopping the madness of the prophet. **17.** These false teachers are like wells without water (empty promises), like clouds driven by a storm, for whom the blackness of darkness (eternal separation from God) is reserved forever. **18.** For when they speak boastful (arrogant), empty words, they entice others to sin, especially those who have just escaped the corruption of the world. **19.** They promise freedom, but they themselves are slaves (captives) to corruption. A person is enslaved by whatever controls them. **20.** If, after having escaped the defilements (pollutions) of the world through the knowledge of the Lord and Savior Jesus Christ, they are again entangled (caught) and overcome, their latter condition is worse than the beginning. **21.** It would have been better for them never to have known the way of righteousness than to have known it and turned away from the holy commandment that was given to them. **22.** The true proverb has come to pass: "A dog returns to its own vomit," and "A washed pig returns to the mire (mud)."

Chapter 3

1. Dear musketeers, this is the alternate letter I'm writing to you, and through both, I'm stirring up your sincere minds to flash back these important trueness. **2.** Recall the words of the holy prophets and the training we, the apostles (couriers chosen by Jesus) of our Lord and Savior, have passed on to you. **3.** Understand this in the last days scoffers (harassers) will arise, following their own selfish solicitations. **4.** They will mock, saying," Where is the pledge of His return? Since our ancestors passed down, everything continues as it always has." **5.** But they designedly ignore (choose to overlook) the fact that, by the word of God, the welkin was made, and the earth was formed from and sustained by water, as described in Genesis. **6.** Through that veritably same word, the world was formerly destroyed by the flood tide in Noah's time. **7.** The current welkin and earth are kept in reserve (set away for a unborn purpose) by His word, awaiting the day when they will be consumed by fire, set away for the judgment and destruction of the ungodly. **8.** But, dear musketeers don't forget this one thing with the Lord, a day is like a thousand times, and a thousand times are like a day. Time as we know it isn't the same for God. **9.** The Lord isn't decelerate in fulfilling His pledge, as some understand slowness. Rather, He's patient (patience) with you, not wanting anyone to corrupt (be lost), but for all to come to penitence (turn down from sin). **10.** But the day of the Lord will come suddenly, like a pincher in the night. The welkin will evaporate with a roar (loud sound), and the rudiments (introductory structure blocks of the macrocosm) will be dissolved in violent heat, and the earth and everything on it'll be burned up. **11.** Since everything will be destroyed in this way, what kind of people ought you to be? You should live lives that are holy (set piecemeal for God) and pleasing to God, devoted to Him. **12.** You should be looking forward to and speeding (speeding up) the coming of the day of God, when the welkin will be set on fire and the rudiments will melt with hot heat. **13.** But according to His pledge, we're awaiting new welkin and a new earth, where righteousness (God's moral standard) will dwell. **14.** Thus, dear musketeers, since you're staying for these effects, make every trouble to be set up by Him at peace, pristine (without mark) and impeccable. **15.** And flash back that the tolerance of our Lord means deliverance, just as our dear family Paul wrote to you with wisdom (godly sapience). **16.** In all his letters, Paul speaks about these effects. Some of his training are delicate to understand, and people who are ignorant (lacking knowledge) or unstable (not forcefully predicated in faith) twist them to their own destruction, just as they do with other Holy Writ. **17.** So, dear musketeers, since you know this in advance, be on your guard (watch out) so that you aren't carried down by the error (false beliefs) of lawless (unlawful) people and lose your establishment standing. **18.** Rather, continue to grow in the grace (unmerited favor) and knowledge (deep understanding) of our Lord and Savior Jesus Christ. To Him be glory both now and ever. Amen.

69 – John 1

Chapter 1

1. That which was from the beginning (before time), which we have heard (listened to), seen with our eyes (witnessed), examined (carefully looked at), and touched (handled), concerning the Word (Jesus, the Word of God) of life— **2.** The life (eternal life in Christ) was revealed (made known) to us, and we testify (witness) and proclaim (announce) to you that eternal life, which was with the Father (God) and revealed (shown) to us. **3.** What we have seen and heard, we declare (share) with you, so you may have fellowship (relationship) with us; and our fellowship is with the Father and His Son, Jesus Christ. **4.** We write this to make your joy (happiness) full. **5.** This is the message we heard from Him and declare (share) to you: God is light (holy), and in Him is no darkness (evil) at all. **6.** If we say we have fellowship (relationship) with Him but live in darkness (sin), we lie (deceive) and don't practice truth (do what's right). **7.** But if we walk in the light (live in purity), as He is in the light, we have fellowship (relationship) with one another, and the blood (sacrifice) of Jesus purifies (cleanses) us from all sin (wrongdoing). **8.** If we say we have no sin (wrongdoing), we deceive (fool) ourselves, and the truth is not in us. **9.** If we confess (admit) our sins, He is faithful (trustworthy) and just (righteous) to forgive (pardon) and cleanse (purify) us from all unrighteousness (wrongdoing). **10.** If we say we have not sinned (done wrong), we make Him a liar (false), and His word (message) is not in us.

Chapter 2

1. My dear children, I write to prevent sin. If anyone does sin, we have an Advocate (defender) with the Father, Jesus Christ, who is righteous (sinless). **2.** He is the atoning sacrifice (payment) for our sins and for the whole world. **3.** We know we know Him if we obey His commandments (instructions). **4.** Anyone who says, "I know Him," but does not obey is lying, and the truth is not in them. **5.** Those who obey His word have God's love perfected (completed) in them. **6.** Anyone who says they live in Him must walk (live) as Jesus did. **7.** I'm writing an old commandment, which you've heard from the beginning. **8.** I'm also writing a new one, true in Jesus and in you, as the darkness (sin) is passing and the true light (Jesus) shines. **9.** Anyone who says they are in the light but hates their brother is in darkness. **10.** But anyone who loves their brother lives in the light and causes no one to stumble. **11.** Anyone who hates their brother is in darkness and does not know where they're going because the darkness blinds them. **12.** I write to you, children, because your sins are forgiven for His name's sake. **13.** I write to you, fathers, because you've known Him from the beginning. I write to you, young men, because you've overcome (defeated) the evil one. **14.** I've written to you, fathers, because you know Him from the beginning. I've written to you, young men, because you are strong, God's word lives in you, and you've overcome the evil one. **15.** Do not love the world or anything in it. If anyone loves the world, the love of the Father is not in them. **16.** The desires of the flesh, eyes, and pride (boasting) of life are not from the Father but from the world. **17.** The world is passing away, but whoever does God's will (purpose) lives forever. **18.** Dear children, it is the last hour (final period before Christ's return). Many antichrists have appeared. **19.** They went out from us,

but they were not of us. **20.** You have an anointing (empowerment) from the Holy One (Jesus), and you know the truth. **21.** I write not because you don't know the truth, but because you do. **22.** The liar is the one who denies Jesus is the Christ (Savior). This is the antichrist (one who opposes Christ). **23.** Anyone who denies the Son does not have the Father; whoever acknowledges the Son has the Father. **24.** Let what you've heard from the beginning remain (stay) in you. If it does, you'll remain in the Son and in the Father. **25.** This is the promise He has made to us—eternal life (life forever with God). **26.** I write to warn you about those who are trying to deceive (mislead) you. **27.** The anointing you received from Him remains in you, and you don't need anyone to teach you. His anointing teaches you about all things and is true, so remain in Him. **28.** Now, remain in Him, so when He appears, we may have confidence (boldness) and not be ashamed. **29.** If you know He is righteous, you know everyone who does what is right is born of Him.

Chapter 3

1. See what great love the Father has given us, that we should be called children of God! The world doesn't fete (admit) us because it didn't know Him. **2.** We're God's children now, and when He's revealed (shown openly), we will be like Him, for we will see Him as He is. **3.** Everyone who has this stopgap purifies (makes clean) themselves, just as He's pure. **4.** Whoever sins practices lawlessness (acting against God's law), and sin is lawlessness. **5.** He appeared to take down our sins, and in Him there's no sin. **6.** Anyone who abides (remains) in Him doesn't stray; whoever sins has neither seen nor known (understood) Him. **7.** Let no bone deceive (mislead) you the bone who practices righteousness (doing what's right) is righteous, just as He is. **8.** Whoever sins is of the devil (Satan), for the devil has trespassed from the morning. The Son of God was revealed (shown openly) to destroy (master) the devil's workshop. **9.** No bone born of God continues to stray, because God's seed (nature) remains in them. **10.** We distinguish (tell piecemeal) the children of God from the children of the devil; anyone who doesn't exercise righteousness or love their family is not of God. **11.** This is the communication (tutoring) we heard; we should love one another. **12.** Not like Cain, who killed his family because his deeds (conduct) were evil and his family's righteous. **13.** Don't be surprised (shocked) if the world hates (dislikes explosively) you. **14.** We know we've passed from death (spiritual death) to life (spiritual life) because we love the lines (sisters and brothers in Christ). **15.** Anyone who hates their family is a killer, and no killer has eternal life. **16.** We know love because He laid down His life for us, and we should lay down our lives for the lines. **17.** Still, how can God's love be in them? **18.** If anyone has material effects (physical wealth) and sees their family in need (lacking commodity necessary) but ignores them, let us not love in words but in deeds (conduct) and verity. **19.** We know we belong to the verity and can assure (confidently assure) our hearts before Him. **20.** Still, God is lesser and knows all effects, if our hearts condemn (charge) us. **21.** Still, we've confidence (boldness) before God, if our hearts don't condemn us. **22.** Whatever we ask, we admit, because we keep His commandments and do what pleases Him. **23.** His order is to believe in His Son Jesus Christ and love one another, as He commanded. **24.** The bone who keeps His commandments abides (remains) in Him, and He in them. This is how we know He abides in us, by the Spirit He has given us.

Chapter 4

1. Dear musketeers, don't trust every spirit, but test them to see if they're from God, as numerous false prophets(preceptors who mislead others) have gone into the world. **2.** You can fete (identify) the Spirit of God by this every spirit that acknowledges(confesses) Jesus Christ came in the meat is from God. **3.** Any spirit that doesn't confess Jesus Christ came in the meat isn't from God. This is the spirit of Antichrist(opponent of Christ), formerly in the world. **4.** You belong to God and have overcome(defeated) them, because the One in you is lesser than the one in the world. **5.** They're from the world, so the world listens to them. **6.** We're from God. Anyone who knows God listens to us; anyone who doesn't does not. This shows the spirit of verity and error(wrong belief). **7.** Let us love one another, for love is from God, and everyone who loves knows God. **8.** Anyone who doesn't love doesn't know God, for God is love. **9.** God's love was revealed(shown easily) by transferring His Son into the world so we could live through Him. **10.** This is love He loved us and transferred His Son to be the atoning immolation(payment for sin) for our sins. **11.** still, we also should love one another, If God loved us this way. **12.** No bone has seen God, but if we love each other, God lives in us, and His love is perfected(completed) in us. **13.** We know we live in Him because He has given us His Spirit. **14.** We swear(bear substantiation) that the Father has transferred His Son as the Savior(deliverer) of the world. **15.** Whoever confesses(acknowledges) that Jesus is the Son of God, God lives in them. **16.** We know and believe the love God has for us. God is love, and anyone who lives in love lives in God. **17.** Love is perfected(completed) in us so we can have confidence(boldness) on the day of judgment, because in this world, we're like Him. **18.** There's no fear in love; perfect love drives out(removes) fear, because fear involves discipline. The bone who fears has not been perfected in love. **19.** We love God because He first loved us. **20.** still, " I love God," but hates their family, If anyone says. For anyone who can not love their family can not love God. **21.** This order(instruction) is from Him whoever loves God must also love their family.

Chapter 5

1 Whoever believes Jesus is the Christ (Messiah) is born of God and loves those born of Him. 2 We know we love God's children when we love God and obey His commandments. 3 Obeying God's commandments shows love for Him, and they are not burdensome. 4 Whatever is born of God overcomes the world, and this victory is through faith. 5 The one who overcomes the world is the one who believes Jesus is the Son of God. 6 Jesus came by water (baptism) and blood (death on the cross), and the Spirit testifies to the truth. 7 The Father, the Word (Jesus), and the Holy Spirit bear witness in heaven; they are one. 8 The Spirit, water, and blood bear witness on earth and agree as one. 9 If we accept human testimony, God's testimony about His Son is greater. 10 The one who believes in the Son has this testimony in their heart; those who do not make God a liar by rejecting it. 11 God has given us eternal life through His Son. 12 Whoever has the Son has life; whoever does not, does not have life. 13 I write so you may know you have eternal life and continue to believe in His name. 14 If we ask according to God's will, He hears us. 15 And if He hears, we know we have what we ask. 16 If a brother or sister sins a non-deadly sin, pray, and God will give them life. 17 All wrongdoing is sin, but not all sin leads to death. 18 Whoever is born of God does not continue to sin; the evil one cannot touch them. 19 We know we are of God, and the world is under the control of the evil one. 20 We know the Son of God has come and given us understanding to know the true God in Jesus Christ. This is the true God and eternal life. 21 Keep yourselves from idols. Amen.

70 – John 2

Chapter 1

1. The Elder (a leader or apostle), to the chosen lady (possibly a church or person) and her children, whom I love in truth. Not only I, but also all who know the truth (God's teachings), love you. 2. This love is because of the truth (God's Word) that lives in us and will be with us forever. 3. May grace (God's favor), mercy (God's kindness), and peace (harmony) be with you from God the Father and the Lord Jesus Christ, the Son, in truth and love. 4. I was joyful (happy) to find some of your children walking (living) in truth, as commanded by the Father. 5. I urge (plead with) you, dear lady, not with a new command, but the one from the beginning: that we love one another. 6. This is love: that we live by His commandments (instructions). This command we have heard from the beginning, to walk (live) in it. 7. Many deceivers (liars) have gone out, those who do not acknowledge (accept) Jesus Christ as coming in the flesh. They are deceivers and antichrists (those who oppose Christ). 8. Watch (be careful) yourselves so that you do not lose what we've worked for, but receive a full reward (complete reward). 9. Anyone who goes beyond (transgresses) and does not remain in Christ's teachings does not have God. Those who remain in them have both the Father and the Son. 10. If anyone does not bring this teaching, do not welcome (receive) them into your home or greet them. 11. Anyone who greets them shares (joins) in their evil works (wrongdoing). 12. I have many things to write, but I do not want to use paper and ink. I hope to visit and speak face to face, so our joy may be complete. 13. The children (family members) of your chosen sister send you greetings. Amen.

71 – John 3

Chapter 1

1. The Elder (John), to Gaius, whom I love in verity 2. Cherished, I supplicate that you may prosper (succeed) in all effects and be in good health, just as your soul prospers. 3. I rejoiced greatly when some sisters came and witnessed of the verity that's in you, just as you live by the verity. 4. I've no lesser joy than to hear that my children live according to the verity. 5. Cherished, you do faithfully whatever you do for the sisters and for nonnatives, 6. who have also spoken well of your love before the church. However, you'll do well, 7. If you shoot them forward (help them on their way) on their trip in a manner good of God. for they went out for His name's sake, taking nothing from the Heathens (non-Jews). 8. We ought to support similar people, so that we can work together in the verity. 9. I wrote to the church, but Diotrephes (a man in the church), who loves to be first (preeminent) among them, doesn't accept (admit) us. 10. Thus, if I come, I'll remind him of his conduct, speaking virulently against us with words, and not satisfied with that, he doesn't admit the sisters and forbids (prohibits) those who want to, expelling (remonstrating out) them from the church. 11. Cherished, don't imitate (dupe) what's evil, but what's good. Whoever does well is from God, but whoever does wrong has not seen God. 12. Demetrius has a good character (good name) from everyone, and from the verity itself. We also swear, and you know that our evidence (substantiation) is true. 13. I had numerous effects to write, but I don't wish to write with pen and essay; 14-15. I hope to see you soon, and we will talk face to face. Peace be with you. Our musketeers shoot their felicitations. Hail the musketeers by name.

72 – James

Chapter 1

1. James, a servant (someone who serves) of God and the Lord Jesus Christ, writes to the twelve tribes scattered abroad. Greetings. 2. Consider it pure joy when you face various trials (difficult situations). 3. Understand that testing (proving) your faith produces patience (the ability to wait without frustration). 4. Let patience fully work in you so you may be mature (fully developed) and complete (whole), lacking nothing. 5. If anyone lacks (does not have) wisdom (knowledge and judgment), let them ask God, who gives generously (freely) without criticism, and it will be given. 6. When you ask, believe and do not doubt (question), for the doubter (one who wavers) is like a wave, tossed (moved) by the wind. 7. That person should not expect to receive anything from the Lord. 8. They are double-minded (confused) and unstable (unsteady) in all their ways. 9. Let the humble (modest) rejoice (be glad) in their high position, 10. but let the rich rejoice in their humility (modesty), for wealth fades (disappears) like a flower. 11. The sun's heat withers (dries up) flowers, and the rich will fade in their pursuits (goals). 12. Blessed (happy, favored by God) is the one who endures (patiently withstands) temptation (trials); they will receive the crown (reward) of life promised to those who love God. 13. When tempted, do not say, "God is tempting me," for God cannot be tempted by evil (wrong things), nor does He tempt anyone. 14. Each is tempted when drawn away (pulled) by their own desires (longings) and enticed (led into sin). 15. Desire gives birth to sin, and sin leads to death (separation from God). 16. Do not be deceived (misled), my dear brothers and sisters. 17. Every good and perfect gift comes from above, from the Father of lights (God, who created the heavens), who does not change (like shifting shadows). 18. He gave us new birth (spiritual rebirth) through the word of truth (the gospel), that we might be the firstfruits (best part) of His creation. 19. Be quick to listen, slow to speak, and slow to anger. 20. Human anger does not produce the righteousness (right living) God desires. 21. Rid yourselves (get rid of) all moral filth (immorality) and evil (sin) that is so common, and humbly accept the word planted (inside) in you, which can save your souls. 22. Do not just listen to the word but do what it says. 23. Anyone who listens but does not act is like someone who looks in a mirror 24. and forgets what they look like. 25. The one who looks intently (carefully) into the law of liberty (freedom) and continues in it will be blessed in what they do. 26. Those who think they are religious (devout) but do not control (restrain) their speech (words) deceive themselves, and their religion is worthless (useless). 27. Pure (genuine) religion before God is to care for orphans (children without parents) and widows

(women without husbands) in their distress (troubles) and keep oneself unspotted (uncorrupted) from the world.

Chapter 2

1. My dear brothers and sisters, do not show favoritism (favoring some over others) when practicing the faith of our Lord Jesus Christ, the Lord of glory. **2.** If a rich man in fine clothes and gold rings enters your church, and a poor man in shabby (worn-out) clothes also enters, **3.** and you show special attention to the rich man, saying, "Sit here in a good place," but tell the poor man, "Stand there, or sit on the floor," **4.** have you not become judges (those who decide right and wrong) with evil thoughts? **5.** Has God not chosen the poor to be rich in faith (strong in belief) and heirs (inheritors) of the kingdom He promised to those who love Him? **6.** But you dishonor (disrespect) the poor. Don't the rich oppress (treat unfairly) you and drag you into court? **7.** Do they not speak against the noble (honorable) name by which you are called? **8.** If you obey (follow) the royal (kingly) law of Scripture, "Love your neighbor as yourself," you do well. **9.** But if you show favoritism, you sin and are convicted (found guilty) by the law as lawbreakers. **10.** Whoever keeps (follows) the law but stumbles (fails) at one point is guilty of breaking all of it. **11.** For He who said, "Do not commit adultery (cheat on your spouse)," also said, "Do not murder." If you do not commit adultery but do murder, you break the law. **12.** Speak and act as those who will be judged (decided upon) by the law of liberty (freedom through Christ). **13.** Judgment without mercy will be shown to anyone who has not been merciful. Mercy (compassion and forgiveness) triumphs (wins) over judgment. **14.** What good is it, my brothers, if someone claims faith but has no deeds (actions)? Can such faith save them? **15.** If a brother or sister is without clothes and food, **16.** and one of you says, "Go in peace; stay warm and well-fed," but does nothing about their needs, what good is it? **17.** In the same way, faith without action is dead. **18.** Someone will say, "You have faith, I have deeds." Show me your faith without deeds, and I will show you my faith by my deeds. **19.** You believe there is one God. Good! Even demons (evil spirits) believe that—and shudder (tremble in fear)! **20.** Do you want proof (evidence) that faith without deeds is useless? **21.** Was not Abraham justified (considered righteous) by his actions when he offered his son Isaac on the altar? **22.** His faith and actions worked together, and his faith was made complete (perfected) by what he did. **23.** The Scripture was fulfilled (came true), "Abraham believed God, and it was credited (counted) to him as righteousness," and he was called God's friend. **24.** A person is justified by what they do, not by faith alone. **25.** Likewise, was not Rahab the prostitute (woman who sold her body) justified by her actions when she hid the spies and sent them off differently? **26.** As the body without the spirit (life) is dead, so faith without deeds is dead.

Chapter 3

1. My brothers, not many of you should desire to be teachers, knowing we will be judged more strictly (held to a higher standard). **2.** We all make mistakes. If anyone does not stumble (make mistakes) in speech, they are perfect (complete), able to control (restrain) their body. **3.** We put bits (small metal pieces) in horses' mouths to make them obey us and control (steer) their body. **4.** Though ships are large and driven by strong winds, they are steered by a small rudder (steering device) in any direction the pilot (captain) chooses. **5.** Similarly, the tongue is small but boasts (brags) of great things. A tiny spark can start a huge fire! **6.** The tongue is like a fire, full of evil (wickedness), defiling (polluting) the whole body, setting the course of life on fire, and is set on fire by hell. **7.** Every kind of animal, bird, reptile (cold-blooded animal), and sea creature has been tamed (controlled) by humans. **8.** But no one can tame (control) the tongue. It is uncontrollable (unable to be controlled), full of deadly poison. **9.** With the tongue, we bless (praise) God and curse (speak harm against) humans, made in His likeness. **10.** Out of the same mouth come both blessings and curses. Brothers, this should not be. **11.** Does a spring (water source) pour both fresh and salty (bitter) water from the same opening? **12.** Can a fig tree bear olives, or a grapevine bear figs? No spring can produce both saltwater and fresh. **13.** Who is wise (knowledgeable) and understanding (insightful) among you? Let them show it through good conduct (behavior) and works in humility (lowness) and wisdom. **14.** But if you have bitter envy (resentment) and selfish ambition (personal gain) in your hearts, do not boast (brag) or lie (speak falsely) against

the truth. **15.** This wisdom is earthly (worldly), selfish (self-centered), and demonic (from the devil). **16.** Where there is envy and selfishness, there is disorder (confusion) and evil. **17.** Wisdom from above is pure (free from evil), peaceful (harmonious), gentle (kind), willing to listen, full of mercy (compassion), good fruits (actions), impartial (fair), and sincere (genuine). **18.** The fruit of righteousness (goodness) is sown (planted) in peace by those who work for peace.

Chapter 4

1. Where do wars and fights come from? Do they not arise from your desires for pleasure (strong wanting), which battle (fight) within you? **2.** You desire but do not have. You murder (kill), covet (desire what others have), and cannot obtain (get). You fight and quarrel (argue), yet you do not have because you do not ask. **3.** When you ask, you do not receive because you ask with wrong motives (desires), to spend it on your pleasures (selfish enjoyment). **4.** You adulterers (unfaithful)! Do you not know that friendship with the world (worldly living) is hostility (opposition) toward God? Anyone who wants to be a friend of the world makes himself an enemy of God. **5.** Do you think the Scripture speaks in vain (without purpose), saying, "The Spirit who dwells (lives) in us yearns (desires) jealously"? **6.** But He gives more grace (unearned favor). Therefore, He says: "God resists (opposes) the proud, but gives grace to the humble (not proud)." **7.** Submit (surrender) to God. Resist (stand against) the devil, and he will flee (run) from you. **8.** Draw near (come close) to God, and He will draw near to you. Cleanse (wash) your hands, you sinners (wrongdoers), and purify (clean) your hearts, you double-minded (divided). **9.** Grieve (sorrow), mourn (be sad), and weep (cry). Let your laughter turn to mourning (sadness) and joy to gloom (despair). **10.** Humble (lower) yourselves before the Lord, and He will lift you up. **11.** Do not speak evil (harmful words) against one another, brothers. Anyone who speaks evil of a brother and judges (condemns) them speaks evil of the law. If you judge the law, you are not a doer (obeyer) of the law but a judge. **12.** There is only one Lawgiver (giver of laws), who can save (rescue) and destroy (ruin). Who are you to judge another? **13.** Listen (pay attention), you who say, "Today or tomorrow we will go to such a city, spend a year there, and make a profit (gain)." **14.** You do not know what will happen tomorrow. What is your life? It is a vapor (mist) that appears and vanishes (disappears). **15.** Instead, you should say, "If the Lord wills, we will live and do this or that." **16.** But now you boast (talk proudly) in your arrogance (superiority). All such boasting is evil (wrong). **17.** Anyone who knows the good they ought to do and doesn't do it, sins (does wrong).

Chapter 5

1. Come now, you wealthy (rich), weep over the misery (suffering) coming to you. **2.** Your riches (wealth) have rotted, and your clothes eaten by moths (insects). **3.** Your gold and silver have rusted (decayed), and their corrosion (damage) will testify against you, consuming your flesh like fire. You have hoarded (excess wealth) in the last days. **4.** The wages (payment) of the workers you withheld (kept back) cry out, and their cries have reached the ears of the Lord Almighty (God). **5.** You lived in luxury (comfort) and pleasure, fattening yourselves for destruction. **6.** You have condemned (sentenced) and murdered the righteous (moral people) who did not resist (fight). **7.** Be patient (wait calmly), brothers, until the Lord's coming. See how the farmer waits for the valuable fruit of the earth, being patient until it receives the early and late rains. **8.** You also be patient and stand firm (remain strong), for the Lord's coming is near. **9.** Don't grumble (complain) against each other, or you will be judged. The Judge (God) is at the door! **10.** Brothers, take the prophets (God's messengers) as an example of patience in suffering. **11.** We consider those who endured (suffered) blessed (happy). You have heard of Job's perseverance (steadfastness) and seen what the Lord brought about—the Lord is full of compassion (sympathy) and mercy (kindness). **12.** Above all, do not swear (make oaths) by heaven or earth. Let your "Yes" be yes, and your "No" be no, so you may not fall into judgment (condemnation). **13.** Is anyone in trouble (difficulty)? Let them pray. Is anyone happy? Let them sing praise (expressions of joy). **14.** Is anyone sick (ill)? Let them call the elders (leaders) of the church, and let them pray and anoint (apply oil) them in the Lord's name. **15.** The prayer of faith (trust in God) will heal the sick, and the Lord will raise them up. If they've sinned (wronged), they will be forgiven. **16.** Confess (admit) your sins to each other and pray for healing. The prayer of a righteous (moral) person is powerful and effective (works well). 17. Elijah was human, like us. He prayed earnestly (sincerely) for no rain, and it didn't rain for three and a half years. 18. Again, he prayed, and the heavens (sky) gave rain, and the earth produced crops. 19. Brothers, if one wanders (goes off course) from the truth (right way) and is brought back, 20. remember: whoever turns a sinner (wrongdoer) from their error (mistake) saves them from death and covers a multitude (many) of sins.

73 – Jude
Chapter 1

1. Jude, a servant (slave) of Jesus Christ and brother of James, to those who are called, loved by God the Father, and kept safe (protected) in Jesus Christ: 2. May mercy, peace, and love be multiplied (increased) to you. 3. Dear friends (beloved), although I was eager (desirous) to write to you about our shared salvation, I found it necessary to write to you, urging (encouraging) you to fight earnestly (strenuously) for the faith that was once and for all entrusted (given) to God's people. 4. For certain individuals (people) have secretly slipped in (infiltrated) among you—ungodly (wicked) people who were long ago designated (appointed) for condemnation. They twist (distort) the grace of our God into a license (permit) for immorality and deny our only Master and Lord, Jesus Christ. 5. I want to remind (recollect) you, though you already know this, that the Lord saved a people out of Egypt but later destroyed (judged) those who did not believe. 6. And the angels who did not stay within their own authority but abandoned (forsook) their proper dwelling, He has kept in eternal (everlasting) chains under darkness for the judgment (reckoning) on the great day. 7. In a similar way, Sodom and Gomorrah and the cities around them, which indulged (engaged) in sexual immorality and pursued unnatural (perverse) desires, serve as an example by undergoing the punishment (consequences) of eternal fire. 8. In the same way, these people, relying on their dreams, defile (pollute) the flesh, reject authority, and speak against heavenly beings (dignitaries). 9. But even Michael, the archangel, when he was disputing (arguing) with the devil about the body of Moses, did not dare (boldly) to accuse him with insulting (abusive) words but said, "The Lord rebuke (reprimand) you!" 10. Yet these people speak evil (slander) of what they do not understand; and what they do know, by instinct (nature), like unreasoning (irrational) animals—by these things, they are destroyed (perished). 11. Woe (alas) to them! They have gone the way (path) of Cain, rushed greedily (selfishly) into Balaam's error for profit (gain), and perished (died) in Korah's rebellion. 12. These are the ones who are blemishes (stains) at your love feasts, feasting (dining) with you without fear, shepherds who care only for themselves. They are clouds without water, blown along by the winds; autumn trees without fruit, twice dead (dead twice), uprooted. 13. They are wild (raging) waves of the sea, casting up (throwing up) the foam of their shame; wandering (errant) stars, for whom the darkest darkness (gloom) has been reserved forever. 14. Enoch, the seventh from Adam, prophesied (predicted) about them, saying, "Behold, the Lord is coming with thousands upon thousands of His holy ones (saints) 15. to execute judgment (carry out judgment) on all, and to convict (rebuke) all the ungodly (wicked) of all their ungodly (wicked) deeds they have committed, and of all the harsh (cruel) words that ungodly sinners (wicked people) have spoken against Him." 16. These people are grumblers (complainers) and fault-finders, following their own desires (lusts). They boast (brag) and flatter (praise) others for their own advantage (gain). 17. But you, beloved (dear friends), remember the words spoken earlier by the apostles of our Lord Jesus Christ, 18. who told you, "In the last times (days), there will be mockers (scoffers) who follow their own ungodly (wicked) desires." 19. These are the people who cause divisions (factions), worldly-minded (earthly) and devoid (lacking) of the Spirit. 20. But you, beloved (dear friends), build yourselves up in your most holy (sacred) faith, praying in the Holy Spirit. 21. Keep yourselves in the love of God as you wait for the mercy of our Lord Jesus Christ to bring you eternal (everlasting) life. 22. Have compassion (mercy) on some who are wavering (doubting) in faith; 23. save (rescue) others by snatching (pulling) them out of the fire; but show mercy mixed with fear (reverence), hating even the garment stained (defiled) by the flesh. 24. Now to Him who is able (powerful) to keep you from stumbling (falling) and to present you blameless (without fault) before His glorious (majestic) presence with great joy, 25. to the only God, our Savior, through Jesus Christ our Lord, be glory, majesty (splendor), power, and authority, before all time, now, and forever. Amen.

74 – Revelation
Chapter 1

1. The revelation (unveiling) from Jesus Christ, which God gave him to show his servants what must soon take place. He made it known by sending his angel to his servant John, 2. who testifies (witnesses) to everything he saw—the word of God and the testimony of Jesus Christ. 3. Blessed is the one who reads aloud the words of this prophecy, and blessed are those who hear it and take to heart what is written in it, because the time is near. 4. John, to the seven churches in Asia: Grace and peace to you from him who is, and who was, and who is to come, and from the seven spirits before his throne, 5. and from Jesus Christ, the faithful witness, the firstborn from the dead, and the ruler of the kings of the earth. To him who loves us and has freed us from our sins by his blood, 6. and has made us to be a kingdom and priests to serve his God and Father—to him be glory and power forever! Amen. 7. "Look, he is coming with the clouds," and "every eye will see him, even those who pierced him"; and all peoples on earth "will mourn because of him." So shall it be! Amen. 8. "I am the Alpha and the Omega," says the Lord God, "who is, and who was, and who is to come, the Almighty." 9. I, John, your brother and companion in the suffering, kingdom, and patient endurance (steadfastness) that are ours in Jesus, was on the island of Patmos because of the word of God and the testimony of Jesus. 10. On the Lord's Day, I was in the Spirit, and I heard behind me a loud voice like a trumpet, 11. which said: "Write on a scroll what you see and send it to the seven churches: to Ephesus, Smyrna, Pergamum, Thyatira, Sardis, Philadelphia, and Laodicea." 12. I turned around to see the voice that was speaking to me. When I turned, I saw seven golden lampstands, 13. and among them was someone like a son of man, dressed in a robe reaching down to his feet, with a golden sash around his chest. 14. His hair was white like wool, as white as snow, and his eyes were like blazing fire. 15. His feet were like bronze glowing in a furnace, and his voice was like the sound of rushing waters. 16. In his right hand, he held seven stars, and coming out of his mouth was a sharp, double-edged sword. His face was like the sun shining in all its brilliance. 17. When I saw him, I fell at his feet as though dead. Then he placed his right hand on me and said: "Do not be afraid. I am the First and the Last. 18. I am the Living One; I was dead, and now look, I am alive forever! And I hold the keys of death and Hades (the realm of the dead). 19. "Write, therefore, what you have seen, what is now, and what will take place later. 20. The mystery (hidden truth) of the seven stars you saw in my right hand and of the seven golden lampstands is this: The seven stars are the angels of the seven churches, and the seven lampstands are the seven churches.

Chapter 2

1. "To the runner (angel, meaning leader) of the church in Ephesus write: These are the words of the one who holds the seven stars in His right hand and walks among the seven golden lampstands. 2. I know your deeds, your hard work, and your perseverance (capability to continue despite difficulties). You cannot tolerate evil people and have tested those who claim to be apostles but have set up them false. 3. You have endured numerous rigors for my name's sake and have not grown tired. 4. But I've this against you: You have abandoned your first love (the passionate devotion you formerly had for God). 5. Flash back how far you have fallen. Repent (turn down from sin) and return to the conduct you took at first. However, I'll remove your lampstand (symbol of the church's influence) from its place, if you do not. 6. Still, you detest the practices of the Nicolaitans (a group associated with deification and immorality), which I also detest. 7. Whoever has cognizance, let them hear what the Spirit says to the churches. To the one who overcomes (is victorious), I'll give the right to eat from the tree of life, which is in the paradise (garden) of God. 8. "To the runner of the church in Smyrna write: These are the words of the First and the Last, who failed and came to life again. 9. I know your afflictions (mournings) and poverty — yet you're rich! I'm apprehensive of the libel (false allegations) from those who claim to be Jews but are not; they're a temple (place of deification) of Satan. 10. Don't be hysterical of what you're about to endure. The devil will immure some of you to test you, and you'll face persecution (suffering for a cause) for ten days.

Be faithful, indeed to death, and I'll give you the crown of life (eternal life). **11.** Whoever has cognizance, let them hear what the Spirit says to the churches. The one who overcomes won't be harmed by the alternate death (eternal separation from God). **12.** "To the runner of the church in Pergamum write: These are the words of the one who holds the sharp, double-whetted brand. **13.** I know where you live, where Satan has his throne. Yet you remain faithful to my name and didn't deny your faith, even when Antipas, my faithful substantiation, was killed among you. **14.** Nonetheless, I've a few things against you: Some of you follow the teaching of Balaam (a prophet who led Israel into sin), who seduced (tempted) the Israelites into sin by encouraging them to eat food offered to idols and engage in sexual immorality. **15.** Likewise, some of you follow the teaching of the Nicolaitans. **16.** Repent, or I'll come against them with the brand (word of judgment) from my mouth. **17.** Whoever has cognizance, let them hear what the Spirit says to the churches. To the one who overcomes, I'll give some of the retired manna (a spiritual food, emblematizing God's provision). I'll also give them a white gravestone (a symbol of acceptance) with a new name written on it, known only to the one who receives it. **18.** "To the runner of the church in Thyatira write: These are the words of the Son of God, whose eyes are like blazing fire and whose bases are like polished (polished) citation. **19.** I know your deeds, your love, your faith, your service, and your perseverance, and that you're doing even more than you did at first. **20.** Still, I've this against you: You tolerate that woman Jezebel (symbol of deification and immorality), who calls herself a prophet. She misleads my retainers into sexual immorality and eating food offered to idols. **21.** I've given her time to repent, but she refuses. **22.** I'll cast her onto a bed of suffering, and those who commit infidelity (unfaithfulness) with her will suffer greatly unless they repent. **23.** I'll strike her children dead. Also, all the churches will know that I'm the one who searches hearts and minds, and I'll repay each according to their deeds. **24.** To the rest of you in Thyatira who don't hold to her teaching, I'll not burden you with anything further, **25.** except to hold fast to what you have until I come. **26.** To the one who's victorious and does my will to the end, I'll give authority (power) over the nations. They will rule them with an iron scepter (a symbol of strong leadership), shattering them like crockery, just as I've received authority from my Father. **28.** I'll also give them the morning star (a symbol of Christ's presence). **29.** Whoever has cognizance, let them hear what the Spirit says to the churches.

Chapter 3

1. "To the angel (messenger) of Sardis, write: These are the words of Him who holds the seven spirits (God's fullness) and the seven stars (church leaders). I know your deeds; you have a reputation of being alive, but you are dead. **2.** Wake up! Strengthen what remains and is about to die. **3.** Remember what you've received and heard; hold fast and repent. If you don't wake up, I will come like a thief (unexpectedly). **4.** You have a few people who are not stained by sin. They will walk with me, dressed in white, for they are worthy. **5.** The victorious will be dressed in white and I will acknowledge them before my Father and His angels. **6.** Whoever has ears, let them hear what the Spirit says to the churches. **7.** "To the angel of Philadelphia, write: These are the words of Him who holds the key of David. What He opens, no one can shut. **8.** I know your deeds. I have placed before you an open door that no one can shut. **9.** I will make those who claim to be Jews but are liars fall at your feet and acknowledge my love for you. **10.** Since you've endured patiently, I will protect you from the hour of trial (test) coming on the earth. **11.** Hold on to what you have, so no one takes your crown (reward). **12.** The victorious will be made a pillar (lasting part) in God's temple, and I will write on them the name of my God and the new Jerusalem. **13.** Whoever has ears, let them hear what the Spirit says to the churches. **14.** "To the angel of Laodicea, write: These are the words of the Amen (the faithful witness), the ruler of God's creation. **15.** I know your deeds, that you are neither cold nor hot. I wish you were either one or the other! **16.** Because you are lukewarm (half-hearted) I am about to spit you out of my mouth. **17.** You say, 'I am rich and don't need anything,' but you are wretched (miserable), pitiful (worthy of pity), poor, blind, and naked. **18.** I counsel (advise) you to buy from me gold refined in the fire, white clothes to cover your shame, and salve (ointment) for your eyes. **19.** Those whom I love, I rebuke (correct) and discipline. Be earnest (serious) and repent. **20.** I stand at the door and knock. If anyone opens the door, I will eat with them. **21.** To the victorious, I will grant the right to sit with me on my throne. **22.** Whoever has ears, let them hear what the Spirit says to the churches."

Chapter 4

1. After this, I looked, and there before me was a door standing open in heaven. The voice I had first heard speaking to me like a trumpet said, "Come up here, and I will show you what must take place after this." **2.** At once I was in the Spirit (God's presence), and there before me was a throne in heaven with someone sitting on it. **3.** The one who sat there had the appearance of jasper (a gemstone) and ruby (a red gemstone). A rainbow, shining like an emerald (green gemstone), encircled the throne. **4.** Surrounding the throne were twenty-four other thrones, with twenty-four elders (leaders) seated on them. They were dressed in white and had crowns of gold on their heads. **5.** From the throne came flashes of lightning, rumblings, and peals of thunder. In front of the throne were seven lamps blazing. These are the seven spirits (fullness of God's presence) of God. **6.** In front of the throne was what looked like a sea of glass, clear as crystal. In the center, around the throne, were four living creatures, covered with eyes, in front and back. **7.** The first living creature was like a lion, the second like an ox, the third had a face like a man, and the fourth was like a flying eagle. **8.** Each of the four living creatures had six wings and was covered with eyes all around, even under its wings. Day and night, they never stop saying: " 'Holy, holy, holy is the Lord God Almighty,' who was, and is, and is to come." **9.** Whenever the living creatures give glory, honor, and thanks to Him who sits on the throne and lives forever and ever, **10.** the twenty-four elders fall down before Him and worship Him. They lay their crowns before the throne and say: **11.** "You are worthy, our Lord and God, to receive glory and honor and power, for You created all things, and by Your will they were created and have their being."

Chapter 5

1. Then I saw in the right hand of Him who sat on the throne a scroll with writing on both sides, sealed with seven seals. **2.** I saw a mighty angel proclaiming in a loud voice, "Who is worthy to break the seals and open the scroll?" **3.** But no one in heaven, on earth, or under the earth could open the scroll or even look inside it. **4.** I wept because no one was found worthy to open the scroll or look inside. **5.** Then one of the elders (leaders) said to me, "Do not weep! See, the Lion of the tribe of Judah, the Root of David, has triumphed. He is able to open the scroll and its seven seals." **6.** Then I saw a Lamb, looking as if it had been slain (killed), standing at the center of the throne, surrounded by the four living creatures and the elders. The Lamb had seven horns (power) and seven eyes (wisdom), which are the seven spirits (fullness of God's presence) of God sent into all the earth. **7.** He took the scroll from the right hand of Him who sat on the throne. **8.** When He took it, the four living creatures and the twenty-four elders fell down before the Lamb. Each had a harp and golden bowls full of incense, which are the prayers of God's people. **9.** They sang a new song: "You are worthy to take the scroll and open its seals because you were slain, and with your blood, you purchased for God persons from every tribe, language, people, and nation. **10.** You have made them a kingdom and priests to serve our God, and they will reign on the earth." **11.** I looked and heard the voice of many angels, numbering thousands upon thousands, and ten thousand times ten thousand. They encircled the throne, the living creatures, and the elders. **12.** In a loud voice, they said: "Worthy is the Lamb, who was slain, to receive power, wealth, wisdom, strength, honor, glory, and praise!" **13.** Then I heard every creature in heaven, on earth, under the earth, and on the sea, and all that is in them, saying: "To Him who sits on the throne and to the Lamb be praise, honor, glory, and power, forever and ever!" **14.** The four living creatures said, "Amen," and the elders fell down and worshiped.

Chapter 6

1. I watched as the Lamb opened the first of the seven seals. Then I heard one of the four living creatures say in a voice like thunder, "Come!" **2.** I looked, and there before me was a white horse! Its rider held a bow, was given a crown, and rode out as a conqueror bent on conquest. **3.** When the Lamb opened the second seal, I heard second living creature say, "Come!" **4.** Then another horse came out, a fiery red one. Its rider was given power to take peace from the earth and make people kill each other. He was given a large sword. **5.** When the Lamb opened the third seal, I heard the third living creature say,

"Come!" I looked, and there before me was a black horse! Its rider held a pair of scales (measuring weights) in his hand. **6.** I heard a voice among the four living creatures saying, "Two pounds of wheat for a day's wages, and six pounds of barley for a day's wages, and do not damage the oil and the wine!" **7.** When the Lamb opened the fourth seal, I heard the voice of the fourth living creature say, "Come!" **8.** I looked, and there before me was a pale horse! Its rider was named Death, and Hades (the place of the dead) followed closely behind him. They were given power over a fourth of the earth to kill by sword, famine (severe hunger), plague (disease), and by wild beasts. **9.** When He opened the fifth seal, I saw under the altar the souls (spirits) of those who had been slain (killed) for the word of God and their testimony. **10.** They called out loudly, "How long, Sovereign Lord, holy and true, until you judge the inhabitants of the earth and avenge our blood?" **11.** Each was given a white robe, and they were told to wait a little longer, until the full number of their fellow servants were killed as they had been. **12.** I watched as He opened the sixth seal. There was a great earthquake. The sun turned black like sackcloth (rough cloth) made of goat hair, and the moon turned blood red. **13.** The stars fell from the sky, as figs drop from a fig tree when shaken by a strong wind. **14.** The heavens receded like a scroll being rolled up, and every mountain and island was removed from its place. **15.** The kings, princes, generals, the rich, the mighty, and everyone else, both slave and free, hid in caves and among the rocks of the mountains. **16.** They called to the mountains and rocks, "Fall on us and hide us from the face of Him who sits on the throne and from the wrath (anger) of the Lamb! **17.** For the great day of their wrath has come, and who can withstand it?"

Chapter 7

1. After this, I saw four angels standing at the four corners of the earth, holding back the four winds (powerful forces) to prevent any wind from blowing on the land, sea, or trees. **2.** Then I saw another angel coming from the east, with the seal of the living God. He called out in a loud voice to the four angels who had been given power to harm the land and sea: **3.** "Do not harm the land, sea, or trees until we put a seal (mark) on the foreheads of the servants of our God." **4.** Then I heard the number of those who were sealed: 144,000 from all the tribes of Israel. **5.** From the tribe of Judah, 12,000 were sealed; from the tribe of Reuben, 12,000; from the tribe of Gad, 12,000; **6.** from the tribe of Asher, 12,000; from the tribe of Naphtali, 12,000; from the tribe of Manasseh, 12,000; **7.** from the tribe of Simeon, 12,000; from the tribe of Levi, 12,000; from the tribe of Issachar, 12,000; **8.** from the tribe of Zebulun, 12,000; from the tribe of Joseph, 12,000; from the tribe of Benjamin, 12,000. **9.** After this, I looked, and there before me was a great multitude (large crowd) that no one could count, from every nation, tribe, people, and language, standing before the throne and the Lamb. They were wearing white robes and holding palm branches in their hands. **10.** And they cried out in a loud voice: "Salvation belongs to our God, who sits on the throne, and to the Lamb." **11.** All the angels were standing around the throne, the elders, and the four living creatures. They fell on their faces before the throne and worshiped God, **12.** saying: "Amen! Praise, glory, wisdom, thanks, honor, power, and strength be to our God forever and ever. Amen!" **13.** Then one of the elders asked me, "These in white robes—who are they, and where did they come from?" **14.** I answered, "Sir, you know." And he said, "These are they who have come out of the great tribulation (time of suffering); they have washed their robes and made them white in the blood of the Lamb. **15.** Therefore, they are before the throne of God and serve Him day and night in His temple; and He who sits on the throne will shelter them with His presence. **16.** "Never again will they hunger; never again will they thirst. The sun will not beat down on them, nor any scorching heat. **17.** For the Lamb at the center of the throne will be their shepherd; He will lead them to springs of living water. And God will wipe away every tear from their eyes."

Chapter 8

1. When the seventh seal was opened, there was silence in heaven for about half an hour. **2.** I saw seven angels standing before God, and seven trumpets were given to them. **3.** Another angel with a golden censer (a container used for burning incense) came and stood at the altar. He was given much incense to offer, with the prayers of all God's people, on the golden altar before the throne. **4.** The smoke of the incense, with the prayers of God's people, went up before God from the angel's hand. **5.** The angel took the censer, filled it with fire from the altar, and threw it on the earth. Then there were peals of thunder (loud, sudden noises), rumblings (deep, rolling sounds), lightning, and an earthquake (a shaking of the ground). **6.** The seven angels with the seven trumpets prepared to sound them. **7.** The first angel sounded his trumpet, and hail (frozen rain) and fire mixed with blood were thrown on the earth. A third of the earth, trees, and green grass were burned up. **8.** The second angel sounded his trumpet, and something like a huge mountain, burning with fire, was thrown into the sea. A third of the sea turned to blood, **9.** a third of the sea creatures (living beings) died, and a third of the ships were destroyed. **10.** The third angel sounded his trumpet, and a great star, burning like a torch, fell from the sky on a third of the rivers and springs of water— **11.** the star was named Wormwood (meaning "bitter"). A third of the waters became bitter, and many people died from the bitter waters. **12.** The fourth angel sounded his trumpet, and a third of the sun, moon, and stars were struck (affected), turning a third of them dark. A third of the day and night were without light. **13.** I heard an eagle (a large bird of prey) flying in midair, crying out, "Woe! Woe! Woe to the earth's inhabitants because of the trumpet blasts of the remaining three angels!"

Chapter 9

1. The fifth angel sounded his trumpet, and I saw a star that had fallen from the sky to the earth. The star was given the key to the shaft of the Abyss (a deep, bottomless pit). **2.** When he opened the Abyss, smoke poured out like smoke from a giant furnace, darkening the sun and sky. **3.** Out of the smoke came locusts (insects) with power like that of scorpions (venomous creatures). **4.** They were told not to harm the earth's plants or trees, but only people without the seal of God on their foreheads. **5.** They were not allowed to kill, only to torment people for five months. The agony was like the sting of a scorpion. **6.** During this time, people will seek death but not find it. Death will escape them. **7.** The locusts looked like horses prepared for battle. They wore crowns of gold and had human faces. **8.** Their hair was like women's hair, and their teeth were like lions' teeth. **9.** They wore breastplates (armor) of iron, and their wings sounded like many horses and chariots rushing into battle. **10.** They had tails like scorpions with power to torment people for five months. **11.** The locusts were ruled by the angel of the Abyss, whose name in Hebrew is Abaddon and in Greek is Apollyon (meaning "Destroyer"). **12.** The first woe is over; two more woes remain. **13.** The sixth angel sounded his trumpet, and I heard a voice from the four horns of the golden altar before God. **14.** It told the sixth angel to release the four angels bound at the Euphrates River. **15.** These four angels were ready for this very hour, day, month, and year, to kill a third of mankind. **16.** The mounted troops numbered twice ten thousand times ten thousand (200 million). **17.** The horses and riders I saw looked like this: their armor was red, dark blue, and yellow like sulfur. The horses' heads resembled lions' heads, and from their mouths came fire, smoke, and sulfur. **18.** A third of mankind was killed by the plagues of fire, smoke, and sulfur from their mouths. **19.** The horses' power was in their mouths and tails; their tails were like snakes with heads that caused injury. **20.** The rest of mankind, who were not killed by the plagues, still did not repent of their actions: worshiping demons, idols made of gold, silver, bronze, stone, and wood (which cannot see, hear, or walk). **21.** They did not repent of their murders, magic arts (sorcery), sexual immorality, or thefts.

Chapter 10

1. Then I saw another mighty angel coming down from heaven. He was robed in a cloud, with a rainbow above his head; his face shone like the sun, and his legs were like fiery pillars (strong, glowing columns of fire). **2.** He was holding a little scroll (small book), which lay open in his hand. He planted his right foot on the sea and his left foot on the land, **3.** and he gave a loud shout like the roar of a lion. When he shouted, the voices of the seven thunders spoke. **4.** When the seven thunders spoke, I was about to write, but I heard a voice from heaven say, "Seal up what the seven thunders have said and do not write it down." **5.** Then the angel I had seen standing on the sea and on the land raised his right hand to heaven. **6.** And he swore by him who lives forever and ever, who created the heavens, the earth, and the sea, and everything in them, saying, "There will be no more delay! **7.** But in the days when the seventh angel is about to sound his trumpet, the mystery of God (divine plan) will be accomplished, just as he announced to his servants the prophets." **8.** Then the voice I heard from heaven spoke to me again: "Go, take the scroll from the angel's hand who is standing on the sea and land." **9.** So I went to the angel and asked him to give me the little scroll. He said, "Take it and eat it. It will turn your stomach sour, but 'in your mouth, it will be as sweet as honey.'" **10.** I took the little scroll from the angel's hand and ate it. It tasted as sweet as honey in my mouth, but when I had eaten it, my stomach turned sour. **11.** Then I was told, "You must prophesy again about many peoples, nations, languages, and kings."

Chapter 11

1. I was given a reed (a measuring stick) like a measuring rod and was told, "Go and measure the temple of God and the altar, with its worshipers. **2.** But exclude the outer court; do not measure it, because it has been given to the Gentiles (non-Jews). They will trample on the holy city for 42 months. **3.** And I will appoint my two witnesses, and they will prophesy for 1,260 days, clothed in sackcloth (symbolizing mourning)." **4.** They are "the two olive trees" and the two lampstands, and "they stand before the Lord of the earth." **5.** If anyone tries to harm them, fire comes from their mouths and devours their enemies. This is how anyone who wants to harm them must die. **6.** They have power to shut up the heavens so that it will not rain during the time they are prophesying; and they have power to turn the waters into blood and to strike the earth with every kind of plague as often as they want. **7.** Now when they have finished their testimony, the beast (evil creature) that comes up from the Abyss (bottomless pit) will attack them, overpower, and kill them. **8.** Their bodies will lie in the public square of the great city—which is figuratively called Sodom (a symbol of sin) and Egypt (a symbol of oppression)—where also their Lord was crucified. **9.** For three and a half days, some from every people, tribe, language, and nation will gaze on their bodies and refuse them burial. **10.** The inhabitants of the earth will gloat over them and celebrate by sending each other gifts, because these two prophets had tormented those who live on the earth. **11.** But after the three and a half days, the breath of life from God entered them, and they stood on their feet, and terror struck those who saw them. **12.** Then they heard a loud voice from heaven saying to them, "Come up here." And they went up to heaven in a cloud, while their enemies looked on. **13.** At that very hour, there was a severe earthquake, and a tenth of the city collapsed. Seven thousand people were killed in the earthquake, and the survivors were terrified and gave glory to the God of heaven. **14.** The second woe (calamity) has passed; the third woe is coming soon. **15.** The seventh angel sounded his trumpet, and there were loud voices in heaven, which said: "The kingdom of the world has become the kingdom of our Lord and of his Messiah, and he will reign forever and ever." **16.** And the twenty-four elders, who were seated on their thrones before God, fell on their faces and worshiped God, **17.** saying: "We give thanks to you, Lord God Almighty, the One who is and who was, because you have taken your great power and have begun to reign. **18.** The nations were angry, and your wrath (anger) has come. The time has come for judging the dead, and for rewarding your servants, the prophets, and your people who revere (respect) your name, both great and small—and for destroying those who destroy the earth." **19.** Then God's temple in heaven was opened, and within his temple was seen the ark of his covenant (sacred chest). And there came flashes of lightning, rumblings, peals of thunder, an earthquake, and a severe hailstorm.

Chapter 12

1. A great sign appeared in heaven: a woman clothed with the sun, with the moon under her feet and a crown of twelve stars on her head. **2.** She was pregnant and cried out in pain as she was about to give birth. **3.** Then another sign appeared in heaven: an enormous red dragon with seven heads and ten horns and seven crowns on its heads. **4.** Its tail swept a third of the stars out of the sky and flung them to the earth. The dragon stood in front of the woman who was about to give birth, so that it might devour (destroy) her child the moment he was born. **5.** She gave birth to a son, a male child, who "will rule all the nations with an iron scepter (strong authority)." And her child was snatched up to God and to his throne. **6.** The woman fled into the wilderness to a place prepared for her by God, where she might be taken care of for 1,260 days. **7.** Then war broke out in heaven. Michael and his angels fought against the dragon, and the dragon and his angels fought back. **8.** But he was not strong enough, and they lost their place in heaven. **9.** The great dragon was hurled (cast) down—that ancient serpent called the devil (Satan), who leads the whole world astray (deceives people). He was hurled to the earth, and his angels with him. **10.** Then I heard a loud voice in heaven say: "Now have come the salvation (rescue) and the power and the kingdom of our God, and the authority of his Messiah (Christ). For the accuser (one who blames) of our brothers and sisters, who accuses them before our God day and night, has been hurled down. **11.** They triumphed (won) over him by the blood of the Lamb (Jesus) and by the word of their testimony (witness); they did not love their lives so much as to shrink from death. **12.** Therefore rejoice, you heavens and you who dwell (live) in them! But woe (trouble) to the earth and the sea, because the devil has gone down to you! He is filled with fury (anger), because he knows that his time is short." **13.** When the dragon saw that he had been hurled to the earth, he pursued (chased) the woman who had given birth to the male child. **14.** The woman was given the two wings of a great eagle, so that she might fly to the place prepared for her in the wilderness, where she would be taken care of for a time, times and half a time (a period of time), out of the serpent's reach. **15.** Then from his mouth the serpent spewed (spit out) water like a river, to overtake (drown) the woman and sweep her away with the torrent (flood). **16.** But the earth helped the woman by opening its mouth and swallowing the river that the dragon had spewed out of his mouth. **17.** Then the dragon was enraged (angry) at the woman and went off to wage war (fight) against the rest of her offspring—those who keep God's commands and hold fast (stay loyal) to their testimony about Jesus.

Chapter 13

1. The dragon stood on the shore of the sea. And I saw a beast coming out of the sea. It had ten horns and seven heads, with ten crowns on its horns, and on each head a blasphemous (disrespectful) name. **2.** The beast I saw resembled a leopard but had feet like those of a bear and a mouth like that of a lion. The dragon gave the beast his power, his throne, and great authority. **3.** One of the heads of the beast seemed to have had a fatal wound (serious injury), but the wound had been healed. The whole world was filled with wonder and followed the beast. **4.** People worshiped the dragon because he had given authority to the beast, and they also worshiped the beast, asking, "Who is like the beast? Who can wage war against it?" **5.** The beast was given a mouth to utter proud words and blasphemies, and to exercise its authority for forty-two months. **6.** It opened its mouth to blaspheme (disrespect) God, and to slander (speak badly about) his name, his dwelling place (heaven), and those who live in heaven. **7.** It was given power to wage war against God's holy people and to conquer them. And it was given authority over every tribe, people, language, and nation. **8.** All inhabitants of the earth will worship the beast—all whose names have not been written in the Lamb's book of life, the Lamb (Jesus) who was slain (killed) from the creation of the world. **9.** Whoever has ears, let them hear. **10.** "If anyone is to go into captivity, into captivity they will go. If anyone is to be killed with the sword, with the sword they will be killed." This calls for patient endurance (steadfastness) and faithfulness (loyalty) on the part of God's people. **11.** Then I saw a second beast, coming out of the earth. It had two horns like a lamb, but it spoke like a dragon. **12.** It exercised all the authority of the first beast on its behalf and made the earth and its inhabitants worship the first beast, whose fatal wound had been healed. **13.** It performed great signs, even causing fire to come down from heaven to the earth in full view of the people. **14.** Because of the signs it was given power to perform on behalf of the first beast, it deceived (misled) the inhabitants of the earth. It ordered them to set up an image in honor of the beast who was wounded by the sword and yet lived. **15.** The second beast was given power to give breath to the image of the first beast, so that the image could speak and cause all who refused to worship the image to be killed. **16.** It also forced all people, great and small, rich and poor, free and slave, to receive a mark on their right hands or on their foreheads, **17.** so that they could not buy or sell unless they had the mark, which is the name of the beast or the number of its name. **18.** This calls for wisdom. Let the person who has insight (understanding) calculate the number of the beast, for it is the number of a man. That number is 666.

Chapter 14

1. Then I looked, and there before me was the Lamb (Jesus), standing on Mount Zion, and with him 144,000 who had his name and his Father's name written on their foreheads. **2.** And I heard a sound from heaven like the roar of rushing waters and like a loud peal of thunder. The sound I heard was like that of harpists playing their harps. **3.** And they sang a new song before the throne and before the four living creatures and the elders. No one could learn the song except the 144,000 who had been redeemed (rescued) from the earth. **4.** These are those who did not defile (corrupt) themselves with women, for they remained virgins. They follow the Lamb wherever he goes. They were purchased from among mankind and offered as firstfruits (offering to God) to God and the Lamb. **5.** No lie was found in their mouths; they are blameless (without fault). **6.** Then I saw another angel flying in midair, and he had the eternal gospel (good news) to proclaim to those who live on the earth—to every nation, tribe, language, and people. **7.** He said in a loud voice, "Fear God and give him glory, because the hour of his judgment has come. Worship him who made the heavens, the earth, the sea, and the springs of water." **8.** A second angel followed and said, "'Fallen! Fallen is Babylon the Great,' which made all the nations drink the maddening (confusing) wine of her adulteries (unfaithfulness)." **9.** A third angel followed them and said in a loud voice: "If anyone worships the beast and its image and receives its mark on their forehead or on their hand, **10.** they, too, will drink the wine of God's fury (anger), which has been poured full strength into the cup of his wrath. They will be tormented with burning sulfur (brimstone) in the presence of the holy angels and of the Lamb. **11.** And the smoke of their torment will rise forever and ever. There will be no rest day or night for those who worship the beast and its image, or for anyone who receives the mark of its name." **12.** This calls for patient endurance (steadfastness) on the part of the people of God who keep his commands and remain faithful to Jesus. **13.** Then I heard a voice from heaven say, "Write this: Blessed are the dead who die in the Lord from now on." "Yes," says the Spirit, "they will rest from their labor, for their deeds will follow them." **14.** I looked, and there before me was a white cloud, and seated on the cloud was one like a son of man with a crown of gold on his head and a sharp sickle (tool for harvesting) in his hand. **15.** Then another angel came out of the temple and called in a loud voice to him who was sitting on the cloud, "Take your sickle and reap, because the time to reap has come, for the harvest of the earth is ripe." **16.** So he who was seated on the cloud swung his sickle over the earth, and the earth was harvested. **17.** Another angel came out of the temple in heaven, and he too had a sharp sickle. **18.** Still another angel, who had charge of the fire, came from the altar and called in a loud voice to him who had the sharp sickle, "Take your sharp sickle and gather the clusters of grapes from the earth's vine, because its grapes are ripe." **19.** The angel swung his sickle on the earth, gathered its grapes, and threw them into the great winepress of God's wrath. **20.** They were trampled in the winepress outside the city, and blood flowed out of the press, rising as high as the horses' bridles (bits) for a distance of 1,600 stadia (about 180 miles or 290 km).

Chapter 15

1. I saw in heaven seven angels with the seven last plagues — last, because with them God's wrath (outrage) is completed. **2.** I saw a sea of glass glowing with fire, and those who had overcome (defeated) the beast and its image, holding harps from God. **3.** They sang the song of Moses and the Lamb (Jesus): "Great and marvelous are your deeds, Lord God Almighty. Just and true are your ways, King of the nations. **4.** Who will not fear you, Lord, and bring glory to your name? For you alone are holy. All nations will worship you, for your righteous acts have been revealed." **5.** I saw the tabernacle (sacred place) of the covenant law in heaven, and it was opened. **6.** Out of the tabernacle came the seven angels with the seven plagues, dressed in clean linen and golden sashes. **7.** One of the four living creatures gave the angels seven golden bowls filled with God's wrath. **8.** The tabernacle was filled with smoke from God's glory (majesty) and power, and no one could enter until the plagues were completed.

Chapter 16

1. A loud voice from the temple told the seven angels, "Go, pour out the seven bowls of God's wrath (outrage) on the earth." **2.** The first angel poured his bowl on the land, causing painful sores (spoiling injuries) to break out on those who had the mark of the beast and worshiped it. **3.** The second angel poured his bowl on the ocean, turning it to blood, and every living thing in the ocean died. **4.** The third angel poured his bowl on the rivers and springs, turning them to blood. **5.** The angel in charge of the waters said, "You are just (righteous) in these judgments, O Holy One, you who are and who were; **6.** for they spilled the blood of your holy people, and you have given them blood to drink as they deserve." **7.** The altar responded, "Yes, Lord God Almighty, true and just are your judgments." **8.** The fourth angel poured his bowl on the sun, and it scorched (burned) people with fire. **9.** They were burned by the violent heat and cursed God, who controlled the plagues (disasters), but refused to repent. **10.** The fifth angel poured his bowl on the throne of the beast, and its kingdom was covered in darkness. People gnawed their tongues in agony (pain), **11.** but still refused to repent. **12.** The sixth angel poured his bowl on the Euphrates River, drying it up to prepare for the kings from the East. **13.** Three evil spirits, like frogs, came out of the mouths of the dragon (Satan), the beast, and the false prophet. **14.** These demonic (evil) spirits performed signs and gathered the kings of the world for the final battle. **15.** Jesus said, "Look, I come like a thief! Blessed is the one who stays awake and remains clothed." **16.** The kings gathered at the place called Armageddon (the site of the final battle). **17.** The seventh angel poured his bowl into the air, and a voice from the throne said, "It is done!" **18.** Lightning, thunder, and a great earthquake followed, such as had never been seen before. **19.** The great city (Babylon) split into three parts, and the cities of the nations collapsed. God remembered Babylon and poured out His wrath on it. **20.** Every island fled away and the mountains were no more. **21.** Huge hailstones, about 100 pounds each, fell on people, who cursed God for the terrible plague.

Chapter 17

1. One of the angels with the seven bowls said to me, "I will show you the punishment of the great prostitute (a symbol of a corrupt power), who sits by many waters (influence over many nations). **2.** With her, the kings of the earth committed adultery (sinful alliances), and the people were intoxicated (overcome) with the wine of her adulteries." **3.** The angel took me to a wilderness. There I saw a woman sitting on a scarlet beast covered with blasphemous names, with seven heads and ten horns. **4.** The woman was dressed in purple and scarlet, glittering with gold, precious stones, and pearls. She held a golden cup filled with abominations (wicked things) and the filth of her adulteries. **5.** The name on her forehead was: "BABYLON THE GREAT, THE MOTHER OF PROSTITUTES AND OF THE ABOMINATIONS OF THE EARTH. **6.** I saw the woman drunk with the blood of God's holy people, those who testified about Jesus. I was greatly astonished. **7.** The angel said: "Why are you astonished? I will explain the mystery of the woman and the beast she rides, which has seven heads and ten horns. **8.** The beast once was, now is not, and will come up out of the Abyss (the underworld) and go to its destruction. People whose names are not written in the book of life will be astonished when they see the beast, because it once was, now is not, and yet will come." **9.** "This calls for wisdom. The seven heads are seven hills (symbolizing a city) on which the woman sits. **10.** They are also seven kings. Five have fallen, one is, and one has not yet come. When he comes, he will remain for only a little while. **11.** The beast, which once was and now is not, is an eighth king. He belongs to the seven and is going to his destruction." **12.** "The ten horns are ten kings who have not yet received a kingdom, but who will rule for one hour with the beast. **13.** They will give their power and authority to the beast. **14.** They will wage war against the Lamb (Jesus), but the Lamb will triumph over them because He is Lord of lords and King of kings—and with Him will be His called, chosen, and faithful followers." **15.** The angel said, "The waters where the prostitute sits are peoples, multitudes, nations, and languages. **16.** The beast and the ten horns will hate the prostitute. They will bring her to ruin, leave her naked, eat her flesh, and burn her with fire. **17.** For God has put it into their hearts to accomplish His purpose, handing over their authority to the beast, until God's words are fulfilled. **18.** The woman you saw is the great city that rules over the kings of the earth."

Chapter 18

1. After this, I saw an angel coming down from heaven with great authority, and the earth was lit by his splendor. **2.** He cried, "'Fallen!

Fallen is Babylon the Great!' She has become a home for demons and impure spirits. **3.** All nations have drunk the maddening wine of her immorality. The kings committed adultery with her, and merchants grew rich from her excessive luxuries." **4.** Another voice from heaven said, "'Come out of her, my people,' so that you do not partake in her sins and receive her plagues. **5.** Her sins have piled up to heaven, and God has remembered them. **6.** Pay her back double for what she has done; pour her a double portion from her own cup. **7.** Give her as much torment and grief as the glory and luxury she gave herself. She boasts, 'I sit as queen; I will never mourn.' **8.** In one day, her plagues will overtake her: death, mourning, and famine. She will be consumed by fire, for mighty is the Lord God who judges her." **9.** When the kings of the earth who committed adultery with her and shared her luxury see the smoke of her burning, they will weep and mourn over her. **10.** Terrified at her torment, they will stand far off and cry, "'Woe! Woe to you, great city, you mighty city of Babylon! In one hour, your doom has come!'" **11.** The merchants of the earth will weep and mourn over her because no one buys their goods anymore— **12.** goods like gold, silver, precious stones, pearls, fine linen, purple, silk, and scarlet cloth; every sort of citron wood and articles of every kind made of ivory, costly wood, bronze, iron, and marble; **13.** cargoes of cinnamon and spice, of incense, myrrh and frankincense, of wine and olive oil, of fine flour and wheat, cattle and sheep, horses and carriages, and human beings sold as slaves. **14.** They will cry out, "'The fruit you longed for is gone from you. All your luxury and splendor have vanished, never to be recovered.' **15.** The merchants who sold these things and gained their wealth from her will stand far off, terrified at her torment. **16.** They will weep and mourn and cry out, "'Woe! Woe to you, great city, dressed in fine linen, purple and scarlet, and glittering with gold, precious stones, and pearls! **17.** In one hour such great wealth has been brought to ruin!' Every sea captain and all who travel by ship, the sailors and all who earn their living from the sea, will stand far off. **18.** When they see the smoke of her burning, they will exclaim, "'Was there ever a city like this great city?' **19.** They will throw dust on their heads, and with weeping and mourning cry out, "'Woe! Woe to you, great city, where all who had ships on the sea became rich through her wealth! In one hour she has been brought to ruin!' **20.** Rejoice over her, you heavens! Rejoice, you people of God! Rejoice, apostles and prophets! For God has judged her with the judgment she imposed on you." **21.** Then a mighty angel picked up a boulder the size of a large millstone and threw it into the sea, and said, "With such violence the great city of Babylon will be thrown down, never to be found again. **22.** The music of harpists and musicians, pipers and trumpeters, will never be heard in you again. No worker of any trade will ever be found in you again. The sound of a millstone will never be heard in you again. **23.** The light of a lamp will never shine in you again. The voice of bridegroom and bride will never be heard in you again. Your merchants were the world's important people; by your magic spell all the nations were led astray. **24.** In her was found the blood of prophets and of God's holy people, of all who have been slaughtered on the earth."

Chapter 19

1. After this, I heard a great multitude in heaven shouting, "Hallelujah! Salvation, glory, and power belong to our God, **2.** for true and just are his judgments. He has condemned the great prostitute (a symbol of the corrupt power of Babylon) who corrupted the earth with her adulteries. He has avenged the blood of his servants on her." **3.** And they shouted again, "Hallelujah! The smoke from her goes up forever." **4.** The twenty-four elders and four living creatures (angelic beings) fell down and worshiped God on the throne, saying, "Amen, Hallelujah!" **5.** A voice from the throne said, "Praise our God, all you his servants, who fear him, both great and small!" **6.** I heard what sounded like a great multitude, like rushing waters and thunder, shouting, "Hallelujah! For our Lord God Almighty reigns. **7.** Let us rejoice and give him glory! For the wedding of the Lamb has come, and his bride (the Church) has made herself ready. **8.** Fine linen, bright and clean, was given her to wear." (This linen represents the righteous acts of God's people.) **9.** The angel said, "Blessed are those invited to the wedding supper of the Lamb!" **10.** I fell at his feet to worship him, but he said, "Do not worship me; worship God! For the Spirit of prophecy bears testimony to Jesus." **11.** I saw heaven open, and before me was a white horse, whose rider is called Faithful and True. With justice he judges and wages war. **12.** His eyes are like blazing fire, and on his head are many crowns. He has a name written that no one knows except he himself. **13.** He is dressed in a robe dipped in blood, and his name is the Word of God. **14.** The armies of heaven followed him on white horses, dressed in fine linen, white and clean. **15.** From his mouth comes a sharp sword to strike down the nations. He will rule them with an iron scepter (symbol of strong, unbreakable authority) and tread the winepress of God's wrath (a symbol of judgment and destruction). **16.** His robe and thigh bear the name: KING OF KINGS AND LORD OF LORDS. **17.** I saw an angel standing in the sun, calling to the birds, "Come, gather for the great supper of God, **18.** to eat the flesh of kings, generals, mighty men, and all people—free and slave, great and small." **19.** Then I saw the beast (the agent of evil), the kings of the earth, and their armies gathered to fight the rider on the horse. **20.** But the beast was captured, and with it the false prophet who had deceived those who worshiped its image. Both were thrown into the fiery lake of burning sulfur (a symbol of eternal punishment). **21.** The rest were killed by the sword from the mouth of the rider, and the birds gorged themselves on their flesh.

Chapter 20

1. I saw an angel coming down from heaven with the key to the Abyss and a great chain in his hand. **2.** He seized the dragon, the ancient serpent (who is the devil, or Satan), and bound him for a thousand years. **3.** He threw him into the Abyss, locked and sealed it over him, to prevent him from deceiving the nations until the thousand years were finished. After that, he must be released for a short time. **4.** I saw thrones with those who had authority to judge. I also saw the souls of those beheaded for their testimony about Jesus and the word of God. They had not worshiped the beast or its image and had not received its mark. They came to life and reigned with Christ for a thousand years. **5.** (The rest of the dead did not come to life until the thousand years ended.) This is the first resurrection. **6.** Blessed and holy are those who share in the first resurrection. The second death has no power over them, and they will be priests of God and Christ, reigning with him for a thousand years. **7.** When the thousand years end, Satan will be released from his prison **8.** and will go out to deceive the nations in the four corners of the earth—Gog and Magog—to gather them for battle. They are as numerous as the sand on the seashore. **9.** They marched across the earth and surrounded God's people, the city he loves. But fire came down from heaven and consumed them. **10.** The devil, who deceived them, was thrown into the lake of burning sulfur, where the beast and the false prophet had been thrown. They will be tormented day and night forever. **11.** Then I saw a great white throne and the one seated on it. The earth and the heavens fled from his presence, and there was no place for them. **12.** I saw the dead, both great and small, standing before the throne, and books were opened. Another book, the book of life, was opened. The dead were judged by what they had done, as recorded in the books. **13.** The sea gave up the dead in it, and death and Hades gave up their dead. Each person was judged according to what they had done. **14.** Then death and Hades were thrown into the lake of fire. This is the second death. **15.** Anyone whose name was not found in the book of life was thrown into the lake of fire.

Chapter 21

1. Then I saw a new heaven and a new earth, for the first heaven and the first earth had passed away, and there was no longer any sea. **2.** I saw the Holy City, the new Jerusalem, coming down out of heaven from God, prepared as a bride beautifully adorned for her husband. **3.** And I heard a loud voice from the throne saying, "Look! God's dwelling place is now among the people, and He will live with them. They will be His people, and God Himself will be with them and be their God." **4.** "He will wipe away every tear from their eyes. There will be no more death, mourning, crying, or pain, for the old order of things has passed away." **5.** The One who was seated on the throne said, "I am making everything new!" Then He said, "Write this down, for these words are trustworthy (worthy of trust) and true." **6.** He said to me, "It is finished. I am the Alpha (the beginning) and the Omega (the end), the First and the Last. To the thirsty I will give water without cost from the spring of the water of life." **7.** Those who are victorious will inherit all this, and I will be their God and they will be My children. **8.** But the cowardly (those who are fearful), the unbelieving, the vile (wicked), the murderers, the sexually immoral, those who practice magic arts, the idolaters, and all liars—they will be thrown into the fiery lake of burning sulfur. This is the second death." **9.** One of the seven angels who had the seven-bowls full of the seven last plagues came and said to me, "Come, I will show you the bride, the wife of the Lamb." **10.** And he carried me away in the Spirit to a great and high mountain, and showed me the Holy City, Jerusalem, coming down out of heaven from God. **11.** It shone with the glory of God, and its brilliance was like that of a very precious jewel, like jasper, clear as crystal. **12.** It had a great, high wall with twelve gates, and with twelve angels at the gates. On the gates were written the names of the twelve tribes of Israel. **13.** There were three gates on the east, three on the north, three on the south, and three on the west. **14.** The wall of the city had twelve foundations, and on them were the names of the twelve apostles of the Lamb. **15.** The angel who spoke with me had a golden measuring rod to measure the city, its gates, and its walls. **16.** The city was laid out in a square, as long as it was wide. He measured the city with the rod and found it to be 12,000 stadia (ancient measure of length, about 1,400 miles) in length, and as wide and high as it is long. **17.** The angel measured the wall using human measurement, and it was 144 cubits (about 216 feet) thick. **18.** The wall was made of jasper (a type of gemstone), and the city was made of pure gold, as clear as glass. **19.** The foundations of the city walls were decorated with all kinds of precious stones. The first foundation was jasper, the second sapphire, the third agate, the fourth emerald, **20.** the fifth onyx, the sixth ruby, the seventh chrysolite (a golden gemstone), the eighth beryl, the ninth topaz, the tenth turquoise, the eleventh jacinth (a reddish gem), and the twelfth amethyst. **21.** The twelve gates were twelve pearls, each gate made of a single pearl. The great street of the city was of gold, as pure as transparent glass. **22.** I did not see a temple in the city, because the Lord God Almighty and the Lamb (Jesus) are its temple. **23.** The city does not need the sun or the moon to shine on it, for the glory of God gives it light, and the Lamb is its lamp. **24.** The nations will walk by its light, and the kings of the earth will bring their splendor into it. **25.** On no day will its gates ever be shut, because there will be no night there. **26.** The glory and honor of the nations will be brought into it. **27.** Nothing impure will ever enter it, nor anyone who does what is shameful or deceitful, but only those whose names are written in the Lamb's book of life.

Chapter 22

1. Then the angel showed me the river of the water of life, as clear as crystal, flowing from the throne of God and of the Lamb (Jesus). **2.** It flowed down the middle of the great street of the city. On each side of the river stood the tree of life, which bore twelve kinds of fruit, yielding its fruit every month. And the leaves of the tree are for the healing (restoration, cure) of the nations. **3.** No longer will there be any curse. The throne of God and of the Lamb will be in the city, and His servants will serve Him. **4.** They will see His face, and His name will be on their foreheads. **5.** There will be no more night. They will not need the light of a lamp or the light of the sun, for the Lord God will give them light. And they will reign (rule) forever and ever. **6.** The angel said to me, "These words are trustworthy (worthy of trust) and true. The Lord, the God who inspires the prophets, sent His angel to show His servants the things that must soon take place." **7.** "Look, I am coming soon! Blessed (happy, favored) is the one who keeps the words of the prophecy written in this scroll (book)." **8.** I, John, am the one who heard and saw these things. And when I had heard and seen them, I fell down to worship at the feet of the angel who had been showing them to me. **9.** But he said to me, "Do not do that! I am a fellow servant with you and with your fellow prophets, and with all who keep the words of this scroll. Worship God!" **10.** Then he told me, "Do not seal up the words of the prophecy of this scroll, because the time is near." **11.** "Let the one who does wrong continue to do wrong; let the vile (wicked) person continue to be vile; let the one who does right continue to do right; and let the holy (set apart) person continue to be holy." **12.** "Look, I am coming soon! My reward is with me, and I will give to each person according to what they have done. **13.** "I am the Alpha (first letter of the Greek alphabet) and the Omega (last letter), the First and the Last, the Beginning and the End." **14.** "Blessed are those who wash their robes (become pure, cleansed), that they may have the right to the tree of life and may go through the gates into the city." **15.** "Outside (the city) are the dogs (a term for the impure or outcasts), those who practice magic arts, the sexually immoral, the murderers, the idolaters (those who worship false gods) and everyone who loves and practices falsehood." **16.** "I, Jesus, have sent my angel to give you this testimony for the churches. I am the Root (origin) and the Offspring (descendant) of David, and the bright Morning Star." **17.** The Spirit (Holy Spirit) and the bride (the Church) say, "Come!" And let the one who hears say, "Come!" Let the one who is thirsty come; and let the one who wishes take the free gift of the water of life. **18.** I warn everyone who hears the words of the prophecy of this scroll: If anyone adds anything to them, God will add to that person the plagues (calamities, disasters) described in this scroll. **19.** And if anyone takes words away from this scroll of prophecy, God will take away from that person any share in the tree of life and in the Holy City, which are described in this scroll. **20.** He who testifies to these things says, "Yes, I am coming soon." Amen. Come, Lord Jesus. **21.** The grace of the Lord Jesus be with God's people. Amen.

C. Sinoduos Book

75 – The Didache and Abthulis

CHAPTER 1

1. There are two paths: one leads to life and the other to death, with a great distinction (clear difference) between them. **2.** The path of life is described as follows. **3.** First, love the God who created you. **4.** Secondly, love your neighbor as yourself. **5.** Whatever you would not want for yourself, do not do to others. **6.** This teaching explains these principles (fundamental beliefs). **7.** Bless those who curse you, pray for your enemies (those hostile to you), and fast (abstain from food for a spiritual purpose) for those who persecute you. **8.** If you only love those who love you, what merit (reward or credit) is there? Even Gentiles (non-Jewish people) do that. Instead, love your enemies and you will have none. **9.** Avoid desires of the flesh (human physical cravings) and body. **10.** If someone strikes you on the right cheek, offer the left, striving for perfection (complete virtue). **11.** If compelled to walk one mile, willingly go two. **12.** If someone takes your cloak (a loose outer garment), offer your coat as well. **13.** If someone takes your possession, do not demand it back, as you may be unable to retrieve it. **14.** Give to everyone who asks of you, without seeking repayment. **15.** The Father desires that His blessings (divine gifts) be shared freely with all. **16.** Blessed is the one who gives according to the command. **17.** Such a person is free from guilt (being responsible for wrongdoing). **18.** But woe (sorrow or distress) to the one who receives without need. **19.** If a person receives in need, they are blameless (free from fault). **20.** However, those with no need must explain why they took, or face judgment (official decision on wrongdoing). **21.** They will remain under scrutiny (close examination) until every last debt is repaid. **22.** Concerning charity (giving to the needy), it is said: **23.** Let your alms be given thoughtfully, only after understanding who deserves them.

CHAPTER 2

1. And this is the second commandment of the teaching. **2.** Thou shalt do no murder, commit no adultery (unfaithfulness in marriage), corrupt no boys, commit no fornication (sexual immorality), steal no goods, deal not in magic, practice no sorcery (use of spells), murder no child by abortion nor kill them after birth, covet (desire wrongfully) not thy neighbor's goods, perjure (lie under oath) not thyself, bear no false witness (lie in testimony), speak no evil, hold no grudges (resentment), and be neither double-minded (indecisive) nor double-tongued (speaking with deceit). **3.** For the double tongue is a snare (trap) of death. **4.** Thy word shall not be false or empty (meaningless), but fulfilled by action. **5.** Thou shalt not be avaricious (greedy), a plunderer (robber), a hypocrite (one who pretends to have virtues), ill-tempered (quick to anger), or proud. **6.** Thou shalt not entertain an evil design (wicked plan) against thy neighbor. **7.** Thou shalt not hate any man; some thou shalt reprove (correct), for others thou shalt pray, and others thou shalt love more than thy own life.

CHAPTER 3

1. My child, flee (run away) from every evil and anything that resembles it. **2.** Be not angry, for anger leads to murder, nor be jealous, contentious (argumentative), or wrathful (full of rage). **3.** For all these things give rise to murders. **4.** My child, be not lustful (full of desire), for lust leads to fornication (sexual immorality), neither foul-speaking (using offensive words) nor with proud, uplifted eyes. **5.** For from all these things adulteries (unfaithful acts) are born. **6.** My child, be no dealer in omens (interpreting signs), as it leads to idolatry (worship of false gods), nor an enchanter (user of spells), astrologer (reader of stars), or magician; neither be willing to observe them. **7.** For from all these practices, idolatry arises. **8.** My child, be not a liar, for lying leads to theft, nor be avaricious (greedy) or vainglorious (boastful). **9.** For from these, thefts are born. **10.** My child, be not a murmurer (complainer), as it leads to blasphemy (disrespect for sacred things), nor self-willed (stubborn) or a thinker of evil thoughts. **11.** For from all these, blasphemies are born. **12.** But be meek (humble), for the meek shall inherit the earth. **13.** Be patient, compassionate, guileless (free of deceit), quiet, kind, and always reverent of the words you have heard. **14.** Do not exalt (raise) yourself or allow arrogance into your soul. **15.** Your soul shall not cling to the lofty (proud) but walk with the righteous (morally upright) and humble. **16.** Accept the trials (hardships) that come upon you as good, knowing that nothing happens without God's will.

CHAPTER 4

1. My child, remember the one who speaks God's word to you night and day, and honor him as the Lord. **2.** For wherever the Lordship speaks, there is the Lord. **3.** Seek out the saints daily to find peace in their words. **4.** Do not cause divisions but bring peace to those who argue. **5.** Judge fairly and do not show favoritism when correcting transgressions (sins). **6.** Do not doubt whether something will happen or not. **7.** Do not be eager to receive but reluctant to give. **8.** If you have anything passing through your hands, give it as a ransom (atonement) for your sins. **9.** Do not hesitate to give or complain when doing so. **10.** Know that God is the true paymaster of your reward. **11.** Do not turn away from those in need; share with your brother and do not claim anything as solely your own. **12.** If you share in eternal blessings, how much more should you share perishable things? Teach your children the fear of God from their youth. **13.** Do not command your servants harshly, as they trust in the same God, lest they lose their reverence for Him. **14.** God does not call with favoritism but comes to those prepared by the Spirit. **15.** Servants, be subject to your masters as a representation of God, with reverence and humility. **16.** Hate all hypocrisy (false virtue) and everything displeasing to the Lord. **17.** Never forsake the Lord's commandments. **18.** Keep what you have received, neither adding to it nor taking from it. **19.** Confess your sins in the church and do not pray with a guilty conscience. **20.** This is the way of life.

CHAPTER 5

1. The way of death includes evil acts and curses like murders, adulteries, lusts (intense desires), fornications (illicit sexual acts), thefts, idolatries, magic, witchcraft, plundering, false witnessing, hypocrisy, treachery (betrayal), pride, malice (desire to harm), stubbornness, covetousness (greed), foul speech, jealousy, arrogance, and boastfulness. **2.** It also involves persecuting good people, hating truth, loving lies, ignoring rewards of righteousness, and rejecting goodness and justice. **3.** These people seek evil, lack gentleness (mildness), and are impatient (unable to wait calmly). **4.** They chase vanity (useless things), seek gains, neglect the poor, oppress the needy, and forget their Creator. **5.** They murder children, corrupt God's creatures, avoid the needy, oppress the afflicted (suffering), support the wealthy, and judge unfairly. **6.** May you, my children, avoid all these evils.

CHAPTER 6

1. Be careful not to follow anyone who misguides you from righteousness, for they teach apart from God. **2.** If you can carry the full yoke (burden) of the Lord, you will be perfect. **3.** If you cannot, do what you are able. **4.** Regarding food, bear what you can. **5.** Avoid meat offered to idols as it is part of idolatry (idol worship).

CHAPTER 7

1. For baptism (spiritual cleansing), do it as follow: **2.** Recite these teachings first, then baptize in the name of the Father, Son, and Holy Spirit using living (running) water. **3.** If running water is unavailable, use any water. **4.** If cold water is not possible, use warm water. **5.** If no water is available, pour water three times on the head, invoking the Father, Son, and Holy Spirit. **6.** Before baptism, the baptizer, baptized,

and others should fast (abstain from food). **7.** The baptized person should fast one or two days beforehand.

CHAPTER 8

1. Avoid fasting like hypocrites (pretenders), who fast on the second and fifth days of the week. **2.** Instead, fast on the fourth day and the preparation (sixth) day. **3.** Do not pray as hypocrites do; instead, pray as the Lord taught: **4.** "Our Father, who art in heaven, hallowed (made holy) be Thy name. **5.** Thy kingdom come. **6.** Thy will be done on earth as in heaven. **7.** Give us our daily bread (sustenance). **8.** Forgive us our debts (sins), as we forgive debtors. **9.** Lead us not into temptation (testing), but deliver us from evil. **10.** Thine is the power and glory forever." **11.** Pray these three times daily.

CHAPTER 9

1. But regarding the eucharistic (ritual of giving thanks) thanksgiving, offer your thanks in this way. **2.** First, for the cup: **3.** We give thanks, O Father, for the holy vine of David's lineage, revealed to us through Your Son, Jesus. **4.** Glory be to You forever. **5.** Then, for the broken bread: **6.** We give thanks, O Father, for the life and wisdom (insight) made known to us through Your Son, Jesus. **7.** Glory be to You forever. **8.** Just as this broken bread was scattered across the hills and gathered to become one, may Your Church be gathered from all corners of the earth into Your kingdom. **9.** For Yours is the glory and power through Jesus Christ, forever. **10.** Let none partake in this eucharistic thanksgiving except those baptized (initiated into Christianity) in the name of the Lord. **11.** For the Lord has said, **12.** Do not give what is holy to those unworthy.

CHAPTER 10

1. After you have been satisfied in this way, give thanks: **2.** We thank You, Holy Father, for Your holy name, which You have made to dwell (live) within our hearts, and for the wisdom, faith, and eternal life, which You have revealed to us through Your Son, Jesus. **3.** Yours is the glory forever and ever. **4.** Almighty Master, You created all things for the sake of Your name, and provided food and drink for humanity's enjoyment, that they might give thanks to You; **5.** but You have granted us spiritual nourishment (soul food) and eternal life through Your Son. **6.** Above all, we give You thanks for Your great power; **7.** Yours is the glory forever and ever. **8.** Remember, Lord, Your Church (community of believers), that You may deliver it from all evil and perfect it in Your love; **9.** and gather it together from the four corners (directions) of the earth — even the Church that has been sanctified (made holy) — into Your kingdom, which You have prepared for it; **10.** For Yours is the power and the glory forever and ever. **11.** Let grace come and let this world pass away. **12.** Hosanna to the God of David (king of Israel). **13.** If anyone is holy, let him come; **14.** if anyone is not, let him repent. Maran Atha (our Lord, come). Amen. **15.** Let the prophets (spiritual leaders) offer thanksgiving as often as they desire.

CHAPTER 11

1. Whoever comes to you and teaches these things that have been spoken before, welcome him. **2.** But if the teacher himself is perverted (corrupted) and teaches a different doctrine that leads to destruction, do not listen to him. **3.** However, if his teachings lead to the increase of righteousness and knowledge of the Lord, accept him as the Lord. **4.** As for the apostles and prophets, follow them according to the Gospel's teachings. **5.** Let every apostle who comes to you be received as the Lord. **6.** But he should not stay more than one day, or if necessary, a second day. **7.** If he stays for three days, he is a false prophet. **8.** When he leaves, let the apostle take nothing except bread, until he finds shelter. **9.** If he asks for money, he is a false prophet. **10.** Do not try or judge any prophet who speaks in the Spirit, for every sin shall be forgiven, but this sin shall not be forgiven. **11.** Not everyone who speaks in the Spirit is a prophet, but only those who walk in the ways of the Lord. **12.** The false prophet and the true prophet will be recognized by their actions. **13.** No prophet, when he orders a table (meal offering) in the Spirit, shall partake in it, for he is a false prophet. **14.** Every prophet who teaches the truth, but does not practice what he teaches, is a false prophet. **15.** A prophet who is approved and found true yet does something as an outward mystery (ritual act) of the Church but teaches you not to do the same, should not be judged by you; **16.** His judgment is before God. **17.** For in the same way, the prophets of old were judged. **18.** Whoever says in the Spirit, "Give me silver or anything else," do not listen to him; **19.** But if he asks you to give to others in need, no one should judge him.

CHAPTER 12

1. Let everyone who comes in the name of the Lord be welcomed. **2.** When you have tested him, you will know him, for you will have understanding on the right hand and on the left. **3.** If the person is a traveler, assist him as much as you can. **4.** He should not stay with you for more than two or three days, unless necessary. **5.** If he wants to stay with you as a craftsman (skilled worker), let him work for his bread. **6.** But if he has no craft, provide for him according to your wisdom, ensuring that he lives as a Christian among you, but not in idleness. **7.** If he refuses to work, he is exploiting (taking advantage) Christ. **8.** Beware of such people.

CHAPTER 13

1. A true prophet who desires to stay with you is worthy of his food. **2.** Likewise, a true teacher is deserving, like a laborer, of his food. **3.** The first of the harvest, from the wine press (where wine is made) and the threshing floor (place for separating grain), from your oxen (domestic animals used for plowing) and your sheep, you must take and offer as the first fruits (the initial portion) to the prophets. **4.** For they serve as your high priests (religious leaders). **5.** But if you have no prophet, give the offering to the poor. **6.** When you prepare bread, give the first part as commanded. **7.** Similarly, when you open a jar of wine (fermented drink) or oil, give the first portion to the prophets. **8.** And from your money, clothes, or possessions, give the first part, as you see fit, following the commandment.

CHAPTER 14

1. On the Lord's day (day dedicated to worship), gather to break bread (symbolic of communion) and give thanks, first confessing your sins (wrongdoing), so your offering may remain pure. **2.** No one with a dispute (argument) should join your assembly until reconciliation (restoration of peace) is made, so the offering is not defiled (made impure). **3.** This is the offering spoken of by the Lord. **4.** "In every place and at all times, offer a pure sacrifice to Me." **5.** For I am a great King, says the Lord, and My name is revered (respected) among the nations.

CHAPTER 15

1. Choose bishops (overseers) and deacons (servants in the church) worthy of the Lord, humble, not greedy for money, and proven faithful. **2.** They also serve as the prophets and teachers. **3.** Do not despise them (look down on them). **4.** For they are your esteemed (respected) leaders, alongside the prophets and teachers. **5.** Reprove (correct) one another, but do so peacefully, as the Gospel teaches. **6.** Do not speak to those who have wronged their neighbor, nor listen to them, until they repent (turn away from sin). **7.** Your prayers, alms (charitable acts), and all actions should be in accordance with the teachings of the Gospel (good news) of the Lord.

CHAPTER 16

1. Be watchful (alert) for your life; **2.** let your lamps (lights) not go out and your loins (waist) not be unprepared, but be ready, **3.** for you do not know when the Lord will come. **4.** Gather together often to reflect on what is best for your souls (inner beings). **5.** Your faith will not benefit you if you are not perfected (made complete) at the end. **6.** In the last days (future period), false prophets (deceivers) will arise, and believers will become like wolves (predators), and love will turn to hate. **7.** As lawlessness (wickedness) grows, people will hate each other and persecute (harass) one another. **8.** Then the world deceiver (Antichrist, false leader) will appear as a son of God; **9.** He will perform signs and wonders (miracles), and the earth will fall under his control. **10.** He will commit sacrilegious acts (sinful actions) that have never been seen since creation. **11.** Then, all of humanity will face trials, and many will fall away (turn away from faith) and perish (die); **12.** But those who endure (persevere) in their faith will be saved by Christ Himself. **13.** Then, the signs of the truth will appear: **14.** First, a rift (break) in the sky, then the sound of a trumpet (signal), and lastly, the resurrection (rising again) of the dead; **15.** but not all, as it was foretold: **16.** "The Lord will come, and all His saints (holy ones) will accompany Him." **17.** Then the world will see the Lord coming on the clouds of heaven.

D. Unique Tewahedo Church Books

76 – The I Book of Dominos

Chapter 1

1. In the beginning, God created the heavens and the earth, and made man upright. Man was naked and unashamed, unaware of sin (wrongdoing), living like the animals. **2.** The Lord brought angels (spiritual beings) to man, taking forms like men, with mortal (temporary, subject to death) attributes, as the time had come for such beings to exist. **3.** A new race was born, the I'hins, from both heaven and earth. This marked the earth's conception (beginning) by the Lord. **4.** The first race, Asu (Adam), was of the earth, while the second, I'hin (Abel), was capable of spiritual (relating to the soul) knowledge. **5.** The Lord declared that man alone among all creatures would know his Creator (maker). **6.** The Lord commanded the I'hins, through His angels, to cover their nakedness, for it was His will (desire). **7.** The I'hins obeyed, covering themselves and no longer standing naked before the Lord. **8.** The Lord instructed the angels to abandon (give up) their mortal forms and not be seen as such again, and they did. He said, "Because you brought life in flesh, you will serve man for six generations." **9.** The Lord commanded that the law of incest (sexual relations between close relatives) be taught to man, for he could not understand it on his own. **10.** The I'hins were forbidden (not allowed) to dwell (live) with the Asu (Adam), to prevent their seed (offspring) from falling into darkness (ignorance or sin). **11.** Inspired by the Lord, man walked upright and prospered (flourished). **12.** However, over time, man became proud and disobeyed God's commandments (orders). **13.** He left paradise and began to live with the Asu'ans (Adams). This union (joining) produced a new race, the Druks (Cain), who lacked divine (holy, godly) light and could not be inspired with shame or spirituality. **14.** The I'hins thanked the Lord with sacrifices (offerings), urging the Druks to do the same, but the Druks did not understand. Instead, they killed the I'hins, taking their possessions. **15.** The Lord condemned (punished) the Druks, saying, "Because you killed your brethren (brothers), you will be cast out (exiled), and I will mark you for all to see." **16.** The mark on the Druks was a shadow (symbol) of blood, signifying (indicating) WAR. **17.** The Lord said: "By this sign, the Druks and their descendants (offspring) will be known to the ends of the earth." **18.** Woman, feeling helpless (unable to do anything), cried out, "How can I bring forth life without death's shadow?" **19.** The Lord responded, "Because you have endured (suffered) pain and called on My name, I will be your protector, and I will mark the I'hins so that you can recognize them." **20.** The Lord commanded all male I'hins, young and old, to be circumcised (a surgical procedure) as a sign that their seed was blessed with eternal life, so that women would not be deceived (misled) by the Druks. **21.** The Druks (Cain) wandered (traveled aimlessly) into the wilderness, living among the Asu'ans and each other. **22.** God declared a boundary (limit) between the Druks and the I'hins, establishing (setting) that: **23.** The I'hins would work and clothe (cover) themselves, with God's presence among them, while the Druks would wander, neither working nor clothing themselves. **24.** And so it was.

Chapter 2

1. The Asu (Adam) lived for eight thousand years, with six thousand years on earth and two thousand years after the I'hins were born. **2.** Then, the Asu disappeared from the earth. **3.** The I'hins, the sacred (holy, blessed) people, and the Druks, the carnivorous (meat-eating) people, remained. **4.** The I'hins were white and yellow, small and slender (thin), while the Druks were brown and black, tall and stout (strong, heavy). **5.** Because the Druks did not obey the Lord and mingled (mixed) with the Asu'ans, a half-breed (mixed heritage) race called Yak, the "ground people," was born. The Yaks lived like animals, walking on all fours. **6.** God said the Yaks would not remain on earth, for they could not understand incest (sexual relations between close relatives). The Druks and their offspring from the Yaks would also face an end, both in this world and the next. **7.** The Yaks had long arms and stooped (bent forward) backs. God said that because they were born of incest and could not speak or attain (reach) eternal life, the I'hins would make them servants. **8.** To prevent the Yaks from leading the I'hins astray (away from the right path), the angels taught the I'hins to make eunuchs (castrated individuals) of them, both male and female, and use them as servants. **9.** The Yaks served the I'hins, working for them, sowing (planting) and reaping (harvesting). And it was so. **10.** The I'hins, preferring solitude (being alone), were called by the Lord to live together in cities, reflecting His heavenly kingdom. **11.** They were to build for the Lord, and His angels would teach them to worship (praise) through song and dance, glorifying (honoring) the Creator. **12.** Man built for the Lord, establishing worship on earth as it was in heaven. **13.** The Druks came to witness (watch) the I'hins' ceremonies but did not understand or participate. **14.** God told the I'hins to build an image of Him in human form within the house of worship, so that He could reveal (show) Himself to those capable of everlasting (eternal) life. **15.** The I'hins, along with their servants, crafted (made) idols (statues) from stone, clay, and wood, placing them by the altars. **16.** During worship, the Lord's angels possessed (took control of) the idols and spoke audibly (loudly) to the people. **17.** The Druks asked the I'hins about the voices, and the I'hins explained that God, more subtle (delicate, not easily perceived) than air, spoke through the idols to show His presence with His people. **18.** The Druks asked, "What does He say?" The I'hins replied, "He says that those who remember God are on the path to everlasting (eternal) life." **19.** The Druks asked, "How can a man live forever, when all who believe also die?" **20.** The I'hins responded, "As God's voice is unseen (invisible) but powerful, so is there a spirit (soul) in man that will never die, but ascend (rise) to heaven to dwell (live) with the Lord." **21.** Many Druks pondered (thought deeply about) this, and their thoughts awakened (stirred into action) their souls, leading them to bring forth (produce) descendants for eternal (forever) salvation (deliverance from sin). **22.** The Lord instructed the I'hins to build more images along the roads, and His angels would bless them with gifts, signs, and miracles (extraordinary events). **23.** The I'hins placed idols along the roads, and the angels of heaven descended (came down), establishing heavenly (divine) kingdoms around the idols. **24.** When people called upon the name of the Lord, it served as a key (tool) for the angels to perform miracles, showing evidence of the Unseen (God's invisible presence).

Chapter 3

1. God gave commandments (orders) to man to ensure the earth would be a place of rejoicing (happiness) forever. These are the commandments: **2.** Remember the Lord your God with all your heart and soul. **3.** Do not kill any living creature, for they belong to the Lord. **4.** Build walls around your cities to protect yourselves from beasts (wild animals) and serpents (snakes). In the wilderness (uncultivated land), create mounds (heaps) of wood and earth to sleep on at night, so you are not harmed by serpents or beasts. **5.** The I'hins asked how they could enter and exit the walled cities and gather harvests (crops). How could they ascend (climb) the mounds they built in the wilderness? **6.** The Lord said His angels would teach them how to build and use ladders (steps). At night, they should bring the ladders inside, and in the morning, they would lower (bring down) them to go out. **7.** The angels taught the I'hins, and they built ladders for both the cities and the mounds, as commanded. **8.** The I'hins prospered (flourished) and spread across the earth, building hundreds of thousands of cities and mounds, living in peace and reverence (respect), never killing any living creature. **9.** God saw the I'hins were good and grateful, but questioned why, since they were still ignorant (unaware). **10.** The angels explained that they had been guardians (protectors) and had inspired the I'hins to live without evil. **11.** God said that the I'hins lacked honor (respect) because they had not learned to be good on their own. To test their self-command (self-control), the angels would withdraw (leave) for a time. **12.** The angels withdrew, and the I'hins had prepared for winter (cold season) with ample (plenty) food and clothing, unlike the Druks, who had stored nothing. **13.** Evil spirits (malevolent beings) prompted the Druks to plunder (steal) the I'hins' stores during the winter. **14.** The Druks attacked the I'hins, and many I'hins tried to defend their possessions. War (conflict) broke out across the earth. **15.** The I'hins cried out to the Lord, asking why He allowed evil (wickedness) to come upon them. **16.** The Lord replied that they depended on Him too much and did not develop (grow) themselves. From now on, man must face evil alone to reach the Godhead (divine state) in heaven. **17.** God created man with two entities (parts): flesh (body), which desires earthly things, and spirit (soul), which desires heavenly things. **18.** When the Druks attacked, the flesh cried out for war, and the I'hins fell. **19.** The Lord returned to help them understand that it is the spirit, not the flesh, that must triumph (prevail). **20.** The I'hins were concerned their scattered (spread out) people would mix with the Druks and fall into darkness (ignorance). **21.** The Lord assured

(promised) them that some Druks had learned from the images, and the scattered I'hins would teach them the law of incest (sexual relations between close relatives) and the name of God, and also begin to cover their nakedness. **22.** The Lord inspired others besides the I'hins to wear clothes (coverings). **23.** The Lord gathered the I'hins again in cities and lodges (dwellings), instructing them to live as an example of righteousness (moral correctness). The I'hins' brethren (brothers) who had mingled (mixed) with the Druks would now defend and protect them. **24.** A new tribe, called the I'huans, was born, a mixture of the Druks and I'hins. They were copper-colored (reddish-brown), taller and stronger than any other people. **25.** The Lord commanded the I'huans to protect the I'hins, the sacred (holy) people, as they were of the Lord, and it was so.

Chapter 4

1. At this time, man began to use his lips and tongue to speak words, as before, he spoke only from his thorax (chest). **2.** The Lord spoke to the I'hins, instructing (directing) them to provide a stone for engraving (carving), which He would carve with His own hand. It would be called Se'moin and serve as a testimony (witness) to all nations of the first written language, the Panic language. **3.** The I'hins prepared the stone, polishing (smoothing) it flat. The Lord came down in the night and engraved it, and then explained it. Through His angels, He taught the I'hins the meaning of the characters (symbols). **4.** The Lord instructed the I'hins to go to all cities across the world and make copies of the engraved stone to preserve (keep safe) the first language for all peoples. This was done, and the Panic language was spread. **5.** The I'huans partly obeyed (followed) the Lord but also followed the ways of the flesh (earthly desires). They became warriors (fighters) and destroyers (those who ruin things). Despite this, they did not harm the I'hins, nor did the I'hins suffer harm from them. **6.** God had commanded the I'hins to make eunuchs (castrated men) of the Yaks, using them as servants (helpers) because the Yaks were not capable of eternal (forever) life in heaven. **7.** The I'huans, although serving the Yaks as the I'hins did, disobeyed (went against) by inflicting (forcing) the neutral gender (neither male nor female) on their enemies in war. Despite being half-breeds (mixed heritage) with the Druks, they hated them and sought (searched for) vengeance (revenge). **8.** At that time, the population (number) of different races was as follows: I'hins, one hundred; I'huans, three hundred; Druks, five thousand; Yaks, five thousand; and monstrosities (half-man, half-beast), three thousand. The monstrosities died each generation as they could not procreate (reproduce). **9.** God saw the destruction (ruin) wrought (caused) by the I'huans and sent the I'hins to preach (teach) among them, saying: **10.** "Tell the I'huans: Whosoever is created (made) alive, do not kill, for this is the commandment (order) of the Lord." **11.** "In the time of your greatest success in slaughter (killing), you are populating (filling) heaven with spirits of vengeance. They will return to you, and even the I'huans will turn on one another." **12.** The I'huans did not understand and did not believe. Darkness (ignorance) covered the earth, and most men, except for a few I'hins, gave themselves to wickedness (evil). **13.** The Lord's people worshiped (praised) and preached in temples, and the Lord and His angels manifested (appeared) to them, but the other races ignored or refused to learn about God. **14.** The Lord grew weary (tired) of His labor (work) and called His angels, saying: "Man has gone so far from my ways that he will not heed (listen to) my commandments, nor can he hear my voice." **15.** "Your labor is in vain (useless). We shall no longer stay on earth until man has exhausted (used up) the evil within him." **16.** So, the Lord and His angels departed (left) from the earth. Clouds covered the sky; the moon no longer shone (glowed), and the sun became as a red coal. The stars were visible both day and night. **17.** The harvests (crops) failed. Trees yielded (produced) no nuts, and the roots (underground parts of plants) that sustained (supported) man ceased (stopped) to grow. **18.** The monstrosities, Yaks, and Druks died off (died out), tens of millions of them. Yet, they were not completely extinct (gone forever). The I'huans suffered (endured pain) less, and the I'hins suffered not at all, for the Lord had inspired them to prepare for the famine (food shortage). **19.** The Lord mourned (grieved) for the earth and for the generations (descendants) of man: "I made man upright (righteous) and walked by his side, but he fell away. I admonished (warned) him, but he would not listen. I showed him that every creature brings forth (produces) its own kind, but he did not understand. He lived among beasts (animals), falling lower than them all."

77 – The II Book of Dominos

Chapter I

1. In the beginning, man was naked and not ashamed; but the Lord raised man up and bade him hide his nakedness (exposure), and man obeyed and was clothed. 2. And the Lord walked by man for a long season, showing him the way of resurrection (spiritual renewal); and man was obedient, depending on the Lord for all things. 3. And the Lord said unto man: Behold, I have walked with thee, and taught thee; but by my indulgence (leniency), thou hast neglected to put forth thine own energy. 4. Now I am going away from thee for a season, that thou mayst learn to develop thyself. 5. But lest thou stumble and fall, I leave with thee certain commandments, and they shall be a guide unto thee and thy heirs (descendants) forever. 6. Hear thou then the commandments of the Lord thy God. 7. Thou shalt love thy Creator with all thy mind, heart, and soul, all the days of thy life. 8. And thou shalt love thy neighbor as thyself. 9. Because thou wert born into the world without covering (clothing), thou shalt clothe thyself. 10. Then inquired man of the Lord: Behold, thou hast shown the ass (donkey) what is good for him to eat, and the fish, and the serpent (snake), and the lion; every living creature; but man only hast thou not shown? 11. The Lord said: Of everything that groweth (grows) up out of the ground that is good to eat, give I unto thee, and they shall be food for thee. 12. But of all things of flesh and blood, wherein is life, thou shalt not eat. 13. For thou shalt not kill. 14. Man inquired of the Lord: Thou hast shown the males and females of all the living the times and periods to come together; but man and woman hast thou not shown? 15. The Lord said: Thou shalt learn from the beasts (animals), and birds, and fishes, that the female during gestation (pregnancy) is in keeping of her Creator. 16. Thou shalt also respect the times of woman (her menstrual and reproductive cycles). 17. Man inquired of the Lord: Thou hast shown the bird how to build her nest, and the carnivore (meat-eater) how to scent the subtle track (trail) of his prey, and the spider to weave his net; but as to the manner of man's house, or as to herbs (plants) that are good or are poisonous, thou hast not shown man. 18. The Lord said: All the instinct that is in the bird, or beast, or fish, or insect, or creeping thing (reptiles), was created with them, but man was created blank (without natural instincts); and yet man shall attain to more subtle senses (refined abilities) than any other living creature. 19. Man inquired: How shall man attain to these? 20. The Lord answered: Serve thy Creator by doing good unto others with all thy wisdom and strength, and by being true to thine own highest light (moral understanding), and all knowledge shall come to thee. 21. So the Lord left man for a season to himself; and man so loved the earth and whatsoever ministered (served) unto his ease (comfort), and to his flesh desires (earthly pleasures), that he fell from his high estate (spiritual position). And great darkness came upon the earth. And man cast aside his clothes, and went naked, and became carnal (worldly) in his desires.

Chapter II

1. The Lord went abroad (traveled) over the earth, calling: Come to me, O man! Behold, thy Lord is returned! 2. But man heard not the voice of the Lord; for, by man's indulgence, the spirit of man was covered up in his own flesh. 3. The Lord sent his loo'is (masters of generations, angels next in rank above guardian angels, i.e., ashars) to the l'hins, and they raised up heirs (descendants) unto the Lord; by controlling the parentage (lineage) of the unborn, brought they into the world a new race of men, of the same seed (origin) and blood as of old, and these heard the voice of the Lord. 4. And the Lord said unto man: Because thou kept not my commandments, thou hast brought affliction (suffering) upon thyself, and thy people, to the farthest ends of the world. 5. Now will I raise thee up once more, and deliver the tribes (groups) of men from darkness into light. 6. And the Lord delivered man into wisdom (knowledge), and peace and virtue (moral excellence); and the earth became as a garden of sweet-smelling flowers and luxurious fruit. 7. The Lord said: How sayst thou, O man? Shalt thou still have a keeper (guardian)? 8. And man said: Behold, I am strong and wise. Go thou away from the earth. I understand thy commandments. 9. The Lord inquired: Knowest thou the meaning of "Love thy Creator"? And man said: Yea, Lord; and to love my neighbor

as myself; and to do good unto others with all my wisdom and strength. Yea, I have the All-Highest Light (highest knowledge). I am wiser than the ancients (elders). Behold, I want no Lord nor God; I am the highest product (result) of all the universe. 10. The Lord said: I will try thee, O man; I will go away for a season. 11. So the Lord departed once more. And man had nothing to look up to, so he looked at himself and became vainglorious (proud). And the tribes of men aspired (sought) to overcome one another; war and destruction followed. 12. Man forgot his Creator; he said: No Eye seeth me, no Ear heareth me. And he neglected to guard himself against the serpent (temptation of worldly desires); and the serpent said unto him: Partake thou of all things, for they are thine. 13. And man gave heed (listened), and, lo and behold, the race of man descended into utter darkness (moral decay). And man distinguished not his sister or mother; and woman distinguished not her brother or father. 14. And God beheld the wickedness (evil) of man, and he called out, saying: Hear my voice, O man! Hear the voice of the Lord! 15. But because of the darkness (ignorance) of man, he could not hear the voice of God, his Lord. 16. And the Lord sent his angels down to man that they might appeal to man's understanding. 17. But the angels loved darkness also, and strove (attempted) not to lift man up out of darkness. And the Lord was of no more avail (useful) amongst mortals, and he departed away from the earth. And man became on the earth as a harvest that is blighted (damaged) and rotted because of its rankness (corruption).

78 – Didesqelya or Didascalia

CHAPTER 1

In the name of God the Father, His Son Jesus Christ, and the Holy Spirit, we, the Twelve Apostles, along with Paul (the Apostle to the Gentiles) and James (bishop of Jerusalem), establish this doctrine for the Church. We outline the church leadership structure: the bishop as shepherd, the presbyter (elder) as teacher, the deacon as servant, and the sub-deacon similarly. Readers and singers have their roles, while the congregation learns from the Gospel. This book guides believers, sent through our brother Clement, to understand and live by God's commandments, leading to eternal life and glory in Jesus Christ. Disregarding these laws brings judgment. Righteous believers will receive mercy from God, the Creator, and His Son, sharing in His divine glory. Children of God, keep His commandments. Avoid injustice, greed, and envy. Do not covet your neighbor's wife or possessions, as this leads to sin. Lustful thoughts are sinful; those who seek what isn't theirs will face judgment. Faithful followers will receive mercy and eternal life. Do not seek revenge. Love your enemies and pray for those who persecute you, reflecting God's love. Let us be sons of light, showing love and patience, following Jesus' example. Husbands, be loving and respectful toward your wives. Adultery leads to God's wrath, and even sinful thoughts are wrong. Pray for purity to please God. Avoid vanity that leads others to sin. Seek holiness in actions and conduct, honoring God. Do not be drunk or associate with those who live in sin. Work hard and live by your labor, seeking to please Him.

CHAPTER 2

If you are rich and don't need to labor for a living, do not become idle. Instead, join the faithful (believers) in discussing the word of life. Read the Book of Kings (history of Israelite rulers) and the Prophets (messengers of God), sing psalms (sacred songs), and meditate on the Gospel (good news), which fulfills the law. Avoid idolatry (worship of false gods) and reject misleading teachings. Seek wisdom (knowledge and insight) in Scripture, exploring Kings for historical insight, the Prophets, Job (a man of endurance), and Solomon (renowned king of wisdom). The Psalms express devotion, and the Law (Mosaic laws) reveals creation and patriarchal (founding fathers) stories. Embrace the truth in Deuteronomy (book of laws), for Christ (the Messiah) came to fulfill the Law, offering spiritual understanding. His call is: "Come to me, all who are burdened (weighed down), and I will give you rest." Reflect on the righteous (virtuous) kings who pleased God and gained eternal life, contrasting them with the wicked (evil) whose folly (foolishness) led to destruction. Learn from their stories to strengthen your faith in Christ. When bathing, avoid places where women bathe to prevent sin (wrongdoing) or causing others to stumble (fall into temptation). Follow God's command: "Say to wisdom, 'You are my sister,' and make knowledge (understanding) your friend." Avoid the seduction (temptation) of immoral (unethical) women whose deceitful (dishonest) words lead the unwise astray. Their allure (attraction) is temporary, turning bitter (unpleasant) and harmful. Steer clear of their paths to preserve your soul (spiritual essence). Avoid regret by heeding (listening to) instruction and embracing correction (guidance). Choose the treasures (valuables) of Scripture over empty words, staying steadfast (firm) in faith and good deeds. Reject evil and live in righteousness (moral integrity) to secure eternal life.

CHAPTER 3

A wife should honor and obey her husband, as "the head of a wife is her husband," mirroring the relationship between Christ and a righteous man, with God as Christ's head. Women are called to serve their husbands with love and humility, earning favor in the eyes of God. As Solomon (wise king) states, "A brave woman is more precious than a jewel." A husband trusts his wife, and her diligence ensures the household thrives. She works diligently, providing food and making wise plans, buying fields and planting vineyards, always engaged in good deeds. Caring for the poor and clothing her family, she brings honor to her husband in the gates (city leadership meeting place). Her wisdom, kindness, and strength distinguish her, earning praise from her children and husband, who say, "Many have done well, but you excel them all." While beauty fades, a woman who fears God is truly blessed. Faithful women should avoid vanity, dress modestly, and refrain from actions that mislead men. A wife should not seek attention from others but show kindness to her husband. Women who ensnare men with adornments and ill intent invite judgment upon themselves, losing hope and honor. Just as moths destroy garments, wickedness destroys the soul. Proverbs teaches that "it is better to live in the wilderness than with a quarrelsome woman." Christian women should embrace modesty, avoid unnecessary adornments, speak kindly, and worship God joyfully, seeking wisdom that enriches life and leads to eternal rest in God's kingdom.

CHAPTER 4

The bishop, as the shepherd (a caretaker) of Christ's flock, must embody purity, wisdom, and dedication to spiritual matters, free from worldly distractions. Ideally over fifty, or if younger, proven in righteousness and humility, reflecting the wisdom of Solomon (a wise king) and Joash (a young king). His life should echo Isaiah's teachings, emphasizing meekness and humility. A bishop must exemplify Christ's Beatitudes: merciful, peacemakers, and pure in heart. He should avoid pride, greed, and gossip, managing his household with faithfulness, alongside a virtuous wife who guides their children in reverence for the Lord. His testimony must reflect righteousness, teaching God's Word and admonishing sinners, as Ezekiel warns of the watchman's duty. Providing spiritual nourishment through constant Scripture reading and teaching in the Spirit's power, he must uphold justice with mercy and love. Solomon advises, "Heed your father's instruction," yet many forsake God, becoming transgressors. Those baptized into Christ must not sin, as betrayal leads to Gehenna (ultimate condemnation). Blessed are those who endure mockery for Christ's sake. A bishop must reject bribery and bias, warning against evil associations, recalling the failures of leaders like Eli (a negligent priest) and Saul (a rebellious king). Each person bears responsibility for their deeds, with Ezekiel emphasizing that repentance is key. David reminds us of the urgency of righteousness, warning against neglect, while leaders must welcome the repentant, as God calls for healing. Ultimately, God judges according to deeds, and we must fulfill His will, desiring all to inherit eternal life through Jesus Christ. Amen

CHAPTER 5

A bishop must reject false accusations from those who speak ill of others, placing his trust in God to guide His people rightly. Children should honor their parents, servants must respect their masters, disciples need to honor their teachers, and citizens should not rise against their leaders, whether a king or a bishop. Teachers should avoid associating with the disobedient, as they refuse guidance. Ezekiel (a prophet in the Old Testament) states, "As I live, says the Lord God, they will no longer say: 'The fathers have eaten sour grapes, and the children's teeth are set on edge.' Every soul belongs to God—both the father's and the children's. The soul that sins will die." The righteous, who walk in God's ways—being honest, helping the poor, and treating others fairly—will surely live. If a son turns to sin, he will not share in

his father's righteousness but will face judgment for his own actions. However, if he repents and returns to righteousness—restoring what was stolen, aiding the needy, and following God's commands—he shall live, regardless of his father's sins. Conversely, if the father persists in sin, he will die in his iniquity. The Lord's ways are just; if a sinner repents and does righteousness, his sins will be forgiven, and he will live. If a righteous man turns to sin, his past righteousness will not save him. The Lord desires that no one should perish in sin but should repent and live. Though the house of Israel may question this justice, the Lord asserts, "My ways are just; it is your ways that are not right." He calls His people to turn from evil, repent, and live, wishing for none to perish in their sins.

CHAPTER 6

See, my beloved brethren, the greatness of the Lord's mercy—our God, who is good, righteous, and full of love for mankind. He does not delight in judgment without mercy or in deceitful hearts but desires all to turn to true faith and repentance. Bishops who neglect to teach or guide their flock will bear the weight of their sins. As Isaiah states, "Admonish My people, priests, and speak to the heart of Jerusalem." The bishop must examine his people, aiding sinners in returning to God through repentance. Neglecting this duty risks leading the Lord's flock to ruin, as Jeremiah warns: "Many shepherds have destroyed My vineyard, making it desolate and barren." When someone sins, deacons should address the individual firmly, teaching others to fear God. If the sinner repents, let prayers rise for them before God and the bishop. As the Lord prayed, "Father, forgive them; they know not what they do." Assess their sincerity, and if they confess, guide them through fasting for two, three, or seven weeks based on their transgression. Teach with patience, reminding them of God's mercy, as the Psalmist says: "If You, Lord, marked sins, who could stand? But forgiveness is with You." Bishops must act with integrity, avoiding favoritism or bribes in judgment. Hypocrisy among leaders will shame the Church and scatter the flock. As Christ warned, "Why do you see the speck in your brother's eye but fail to notice the beam in your own?" Bishops should lead with wisdom, rebuking sin while guiding the people toward righteousness. Neglectful shepherds risk the condemnation described in Ezekiel: "My sheep have become prey because their shepherds cared not for them." A bishop must care for his flock, protecting the innocent and restoring sinners with compassion. Let none despise repentance, for when a sinner weeps before God, the Holy Spirit speaks: "The Lord has forgiven your sin." Know the authority given to bishops to bind and loose sins, as Christ said: "Whatever you bind on earth will be bound in heaven." Hear the Lord's warning to shepherds: "I will judge between rams and goats and hold shepherds accountable for My flock." Bishops must ensure that the sheep follow the path of righteousness, for a lost sheep is devoured by wolves. As Christ taught, "The good shepherd lays down his life for the sheep." A good bishop is beloved by his people, guiding them like a father with wisdom and love. He raises the fallen, strengthens the weak, and heals the wounded with spiritual teaching. Like a bird nurturing her young, the bishop must nourish the flock with truth, leading them to repentance and hope in Christ. Be merciful, just, and free of jealousy or pride. Do not hide God's commandments or block others from repentance. Judge fairly, accepting testimony only from faithful witnesses. Beware of those who scatter the flock through deceit, for they are like wolves among sheep. Protect the Church with vigilance, as Paul exhorts: "Guard yourselves and the flock, for savage wolves will come among you."

CHAPTER 7

We should not admonish (warn) anyone without clear evidence of their sin. Wrongfully accusing an innocent person is worse than murder, showing a lack of understanding of God's mercy. Those who do this will not find salvation; they have fallen into sin by failing to guide others. God's judgment is just, and He shows mercy to those who turn to Him, as David (the beloved king) acknowledged. The bishop must judge fairly and follow God's will, guiding those who repent. Remember David, who admitted his sin to Nathan (a prophet) and repented, leading to his salvation. Jonah (the prophet) was swallowed by a whale (large sea creature) for his disobedience but was saved after repenting. Hezekiah (a righteous king) faced judgment due to pride but found mercy through humility. Manasseh (son of Hezekiah) began his reign at twelve in Jerusalem (the holy city) and ruled for fifty-five years, committing great evil against the Lord. He rebuilt altars to false gods and led Judah (the southern kingdom) into sin. Captured and humbled in Babylon (ancient city), he sought God and repented. God forgave him and restored him.Manasseh prayed, acknowledging his sins and asking for mercy. God forgave him, leading him to remove idols and restore true worship. He encouraged Judah to serve the Lord and died in peace, leaving his son Amon (who did evil) to reign.Amon followed in Manasseh's sinful ways, believing he could sin without consequence. He was killed by his servants, serving as a warning against rebellion.Bishops should guide and heal their communities, welcoming those who repent. If they lack mercy, they will face judgment. They must live modestly and care for the needy, serving as examples of humility.Like Matthew (the tax collector) and Peter (the disciple), who were transformed, bishops must embody patience and compassion, lifting up the fallen and preaching repentance.

CHAPTER 8

Hear, O people of the holy Church (the community of believers) of God, for you are now the chosen ones (the elect), priests in your generation, with names written in heaven (the eternal realm) for a kingdom and priesthood. In ancient times, the Hebrews (the descendants of Abraham) offered sacrifices, first-fruits (the initial yield of crops), and tithes (one-tenth of income) to those in authority over the Church for the salvation of souls. Now, let bishops (church leaders) and priests offer sacrifices to the Lord, as Christ (the Messiah) our High Priest, died for us. Bishops are teachers and guides, deserving of respect, as they lead God's people in faith. Deacons (assistants to bishops) must serve under the bishop's authority, and women should not approach the bishop or deacon without permission. Honor the priests who teach the way of God, for they were sent to preach and baptize (to perform a ritual of initiation). In the past, only the sons of Levi (a tribe of Israel) could offer sacrifices; likewise, do nothing without the bishop's counsel, for actions taken without his approval are in vain (useless). If anyone usurps (takes over) the priest's office, they face judgment for taking an honor not given to them. Bring your offerings to the bishop, who is the High Priest, ensuring that the destitute (those in need) receive their due. When inviting the needy to a feast (a large meal), let deacons manage the arrangements. After distribution, let the bishop and presbyters (elders) receive their portions, as they guide the Church. Remember, the first fathers (early church leaders) and bishops are the mouth of God, interceding (pleading) for you. Serve them faithfully, for they are prophets (messengers of God) and servants of God, deserving of honor and respect.

CHAPTER 9

The deacon, as the messenger of the bishop (church leader), must not act without the bishop's permission. If he secretly aids a destitute (in need) person without informing the bishop, he brings reproach and is seen as neglectful. Speaking ill of the bishop is a sin against God. Deacons should protect the dignity of the poor and report their needs to the bishop. Blaspheming (speaking disrespectfully) against the bishop is more serious than against a layman (non-clergy). The bishop, as a spiritual father, deserves honor akin to that given to one's parents. He nurtures believers with spiritual teachings and the Eucharist (Holy Communion), enabling them to become children of God. The faithful should bring gifts and first-fruits (initial harvest) to the bishop, who blesses them. The Lord has freed believers from sin, urging them to support priests and help the needy. Righteousness pleases God, and the faithful must avoid judging others, leaving judgment to the bishops, who are tasked with maintaining justice. Thus, respect and honor the bishop, as he guides the community toward salvation and the Kingdom of Heaven.

CHAPTER 10

The bishop must examine all matters with righteousness and integrity, striving to be pure, wise, and prudent. He should avoid evil habits and embrace the way of life, performing good works and healing those who wish to repent. Those who refuse to turn from sin should be cast out, as harboring anger invites trouble and is contrary to God's peace. The bishop must judge wisely, admonishing those who err and seeking to restore them gently. If a sinner repents, they should be welcomed back into the community, just as Jesus received publicans and sinners. The faithful are called to forgive abundantly, reflecting God's mercy, and to maintain peace among themselves, especially on the Sabbath. Bishops, presbyters (elders), and deacons should judge without partiality, ensuring justice prevails. When disputes arise, both parties must be present for judgment, as hasty decisions can lead to false accusations and condemnation. Those who act unjustly will face God's wrath, while righteous judgment leads to eternal life. Therefore, the faithful should pray earnestly, seek reconciliation, and love one another, ensuring their hearts remain pure and free from anger, as commanded by Christ.

CHAPTER 11

Christians are called to forgive their neighbors' transgressions, embodying the command to forgive seventy times seven. If one harbors hatred or judges in anger, their prayers will not reach God, as they fail to follow His commandments. True forgiveness, even up to four hundred and ninety times, reflects a heart slow to anger and rich in mercy, aligning one with the nature of the heavenly Father. Bishops, when gathered for prayer and worship, should read the Holy Scriptures aloud. The deacon must call out to anyone holding onto revenge, envy, deceit, or malice, urging them to reconcile quickly for their prayers to be accepted by God. When entering a home, they should proclaim peace, which will rest upon those who are receptive. This peace is extended to all believers in Christ, emphasizing the importance of unity and harmony within the Church of God.

CHAPTER 12

Bishops are called to be peacemakers and men of mercy, forgiving those who wrong them and accepting the repentance (sorrow for sins) of those turning back to God. If a bishop prays for peace, he must first embody peace himself; without inner peace, he cannot share it with others. His mission should begin with love and compassion, guiding Christ's flock with care. The Lord wishes all generations to return to repentance, as shown by the teachings of the righteous throughout history, culminating in Christ's message of repentance. Bishops must gather their congregations, ensuring they worship together in unity and righteousness, while avoiding the company of the wicked. The faithful are encouraged to attend church regularly, glorifying God through prayer, scripture reading, and communal worship, especially on the Christian Sabbath, the day of resurrection. Failing to fulfill this duty leads to spiritual decline and separation from God. Bishops should welcome all attendees, regardless of their status, and instruct the congregation to uphold God's commandments, fostering a community rooted in faith and love, as the Church is the body of Christ, designed to strengthen and guide its members toward eternal life.

CHAPTER 13

Christians are warned to avoid the gatherings of non-believers (those who do not follow Christ) and refrain from participating in their entertainment or listening to their songs, as these lead to the influence of evil. Engaging with those who practice idolatry (worship of false gods) and consult diviners (fortune tellers) aligns one with the devil and brings a curse. It is essential for the faithful to separate from the ungodly (those who live without God), avoiding their feasts, homes, and social gatherings, as these are filled with sinful deeds. Young men are encouraged to diligently fulfill their responsibilities to the Holy Church, working hard to support themselves without burdening others. The teachings of wisdom, such as those from Solomon (a wise king of Israel), remind us to learn from industrious creatures like ants (small insects that work hard) and bees (insects that produce honey), which work diligently to prepare for the future. Laziness leads to poverty, while hard work ensures abundance. The scriptures emphasize that those who toil (work hard) will be rewarded, and the slothful (lazy individuals) will suffer the consequences of their inaction. Therefore, Christians must strive to avoid idleness (lack of activity), fearing God and dedicating themselves to their duties, as the Lord despises laziness. Let them not associate with those who do not obey God, for true honor and glory belong to Him forever.

CHAPTER 14

Widows (women whose husbands have died) should be appointed at sixty years of age, possessing good works and being pure, without desire for another husband. Younger widows are not suitable for this role; if appointed, they may lack self-control (the ability to refrain from desires) and seek to remarry, bringing shame upon the Church and facing condemnation from God for not adhering to the Scriptures. Therefore, appointments should be made carefully, ensuring that candidates demonstrate the gift of continence (self-restraint). A young widow who has lived alone after her husband's death and fulfills her duties is blessed, akin to the widow of Zarephath (a town in Sidon) who welcomed the prophet Elijah (a holy prophet of God) and to Anna (a prophetess) from the tribe of Asher, who served in the temple for many years. Righteous widows, known for their purity and having married only once, should be supported, as their trust is in God. Bishops must help those in need, feeding the destitute and ensuring that offerings are distributed fairly. The scriptures encourage mercy towards the poor, urging believers to provide for the hungry and clothe the naked. Widows should be patient, worshiping God without anger, and remain silent in the face of evil. They must seek knowledge from those in authority and avoid slander or idolatry, worshiping the One God. Widows desiring to please Christ should live quietly, glorifying Him through constant prayer. The Lord hears the prayers of those who live righteously, and such widows should be appointed, characterized by purity and devotion to God, remembering the widow who offered two mites (small coins) in the temple, praised by Jesus for her generosity.

CHAPTER 15

Women should not baptize, as doing so transgresses (violates) the law. The man is the head of the woman, appointed to the priesthood (religious office), and it is inappropriate to disregard this divine order. Women are considered members of men, created from them, and their children are born from them. Since God commanded that the man be the leader, women should not teach or perform priestly duties, which are not authorized by Scripture. Those who allow women to be priestesses (female religious leaders) to false gods (idols) are far from Christ's teachings. If it were right for women to baptize, Jesus (the Son of God) would have been baptized by His mother (Mary) rather than by John the Baptist (a prophet). He also did not send women to baptize alongside His disciples (followers). Therefore, regardless of a woman's wisdom, faith, or knowledge of the Scriptures, they are not permitted to baptize or preach the Gospel.

CHAPTER 16

We command you that no layman (non-clerical person) execute the office of the priesthood (religious leadership), meaning he should neither offer incense (fragrant substance used in worship), nor baptize, nor lay on hands (a ceremonial act of blessing), nor bless, nor give the bread of the blessing (Eucharist). This grace cannot be received unless it is given by God. Only the bishop (senior church leader) can bestow this grace and honor. Anyone who attempts to assume the dignity of the priesthood without proper ordination will face condemnation, like Uzziah the King (a biblical figure punished for overstepping his authority). Furthermore, we do not command that all in the Church, including readers (scripture reciters), singers, or doorkeepers (ushers), should baptize; only bishops and presbyters (elders) may do so, with deacons (assistants) ministering alongside them. Those who transgress this command will face the same condemnation that befell the sons of Korah (biblical figures who rebelled against authority). Presbyters should not ordain deacons, deaconesses (female assistants), readers, singers, or doorkeepers; only bishops should ordain according to the Church's order, ensuring those chosen have no revenge, envy, slander, hatred, or malice. Those who act otherwise are considered aliens (outsiders) from the society of Christians, especially widows (women whose husbands have died).

CHAPTER 17

Satan seeks to ensnare (trap) individuals, as he did with Cain (the first murderer). Some claim to be widows but fail to perform the righteous deeds expected of them, resembling Cain's actions against his brother. These individuals lack understanding, as mere identification as widows does not guarantee entry into the Kingdom of Heaven; true faith and good works are essential. A woman who claims widowhood while acting contrary to God's will deceives herself, risking eternal condemnation. Among widows, some are wicked, envious, and slanderous (spreading falsehoods), causing discord among believers. If a widow receives alms (charitable gifts) and rejoices, others should bless the giver, asking God to remember him with kindness. Widows must also share what they receive with the needy, as this pleases God, following the teaching that acts of charity should be discreet. Those who seek to trouble the giver should instead repent and pray. Peace should return to those who do not find it, and curses without cause will return to the one who utters them. Bishops should guide those who despise widows, encouraging patience and kindness. They must ensure that no words of cursing come from their mouths, caring for all members of the Church. Deacons should serve diligently, ready to assist the people, and a deaconess should be appointed to minister to women. After baptism, the bishop should anoint the newly baptized with holy oil, symbolizing their new life in Christ. Those baptized must remain pure and pray for unity among believers, reciting the Lord's Prayer. Deacons should serve humbly, imitating Christ, who came to serve rather than be served. They must fulfill their duties without seeking recognition, striving to meet the needs of the poor. Finally, a bishop must be ordained by at least two or three bishops, ensuring proper authority within the Church, while presbyters and deacons can only serve under the bishop's guidance.

CHAPTER 18

Christian people without children should care for orphans (children without parents), whether they are boys or girls, adopting them as their own and loving them even more. Those who have sons of suitable age should marry them to orphaned virgins (young women). By doing this, you will achieve a significant act and become the guardians of orphans, receiving a reward from the Lord God for your service. However, if someone is arrogant and looks down on an orphan, saying, "I will not marry a poor woman," let them recognize who is the true father of the orphan and the protector of the widow (a woman whose husband has died). For those who think this way will waste their wealth, fulfilling what Scripture says: "What the saints have not eaten, the Assyrians (ancient people from the region) shall eat," as Isaiah states, "Your land will be devoured by a foreign enemy before your eyes."

CHAPTER 19

Bishops (church leaders), you must care for the needs of the destitute (those in need) by providing sustenance and giving orphans (children without parents) their fathers' inheritance. Likewise, provide the widows (women whose husbands have died) with their husbands' substance. Arrange marriages for the youths and virgins (young women) as appropriate, reward those who serve, offer shelter to the poor, feed the hungry, give drink to the thirsty, clothe the naked, visit the sick, and assist prisoners. Reflect on this and serve orphans and widows both day and night. Blessed is the one who does so, for they have saved themselves by caring for the widow, orphan, and stranger (someone from outside the community). Our Lord says, "It is better to give than to receive." Those who oppress the poor will face condemnation before God on the last day. However, whoever gives alms (charitable donations) to the orphan, the elderly, the sick, or the poor with children should be commended, for they are an altar of God. It is also right to pray continually for those who have given alms. But those who receive alms while having enough will be held accountable by God, as they have taken away the bread of the poor and done no good for themselves or others. A wealthy person who does not help the destitute is like a rich man who fills his barns in vain and will be destroyed before God, as their wealth will not save them from God's anger. Those who act this way do not truly believe in God but worship their wealth, lacking love and mercy, and they are their own enemies. Their wealth will perish, consumed by a foreign enemy, whether in life or after death, as it is said, "He who gathers riches through wrongdoing will lose them."

CHAPTER 20

Let us encourage widows (women whose husbands have died) and unmarried women to accept with gratitude what God has given them, approaching it with reverence and humility. They should thank God, who provides food for the hungry. Who among you eats and drinks in moderation? Is it not God who gives to them? He extends His hand, multiplying good things according to His will, providing grain (cereal crops) for young men, wine for maidens (young women), and the oil of joy for the living. He offers abundance to livestock, freedom to servants, meat for animals, fruits for birds, and sustenance for all as appropriate. Our Lord says, "Be like the birds of the sky, which do not sow, reap, or store in barns, yet your heavenly Father feeds them; you are far more valuable than many birds." Do not worry about what you will eat, drink, or wear, for your Father in heaven knows that you seek these things. If you wish to receive His blessings and inherit His kingdom, offer Him praise, thanksgiving, and blessings. Those who care for widows and orphans will receive joy from God the Father in the Kingdom of Heaven through His Son, our Lord Jesus Christ, to whom be honor and glory forever. Amen.

CHAPTER 21

The bishop must exercise wisdom in accepting offerings, ensuring they come from those who are worthy. Be wary of sellers of strong drink (alcoholic beverages), as their salvation is distant from sin. It is written, "Woe to those who mix water with wine." We should avoid drunkenness (excessive drinking) and immorality (unethical behavior), for the Lord commands that offerings from such actions are unacceptable. Distance yourself from extortioners (those who take advantage of others), those who charge interest (money lent at a fee), and individuals with corrupt spirits (morally unclean). Their sacrifices do not please God. The bishop should also avoid those who oppress widows (women whose husbands have died) and orphans (children without parents), imprison the innocent (those who have done no wrong), and burden servants with excessive demands. Their gifts are unclean; do not accept them, as those who do evil are rejected by God. It is better to have little with righteousness than great wealth from sinners. If a widow receives from the ungodly (immoral people) and prays for them, God will not hear her. Accept gifts only from those who do good, and share what you receive with widows and orphans in righteousness.

CHAPTER 22

Fathers (male parents), you must instruct your children to follow the Lord's commandments and the teachings of Christ, encouraging them to learn a craft (a skill or trade) instead of being idle. Idleness (laziness) can lead to pride and distance from good deeds. Therefore, train them diligently and do not hesitate to correct them; correction saves children from condemnation (punishment) rather than harming them. It is written, "Do not withhold discipline (punishment) from your son; when you discipline him, you save his soul from death." Additionally, failing to correct your child reflects foolishness (lack of good sense). Discipline your son while he is young to prevent him from becoming hardened (emotionally insensitive) and straying from you. Teaching and correcting your children fosters humility (modesty) and obedience (compliance). Ensure they learn to read and write the holy Scriptures (sacred texts) and do not allow them to live idly or frequent taverns (places that sell alcoholic drinks), where they may forget your guidance and fall into sin. Fathers who neglect teaching and correcting share in their children's sins. As they reach adulthood, encourage them to marry lawfully (legally and morally) to avoid the temptations of youth, as God will hold fathers accountable (responsible) for their children's sins on the day of judgment.

CHAPTER 23

Servants (employees) should serve their masters (employers) wisely and with reverence (respect) for God. Christian servants must fulfill their duties even if their masters are unbelievers (non-believers) but should not share in their faith. Masters should love their believing servants as sons and brothers. Additionally, obey kings (rulers) and princes (noblemen) who fear God, as they are His ministers (servants). Honor those in authority and do not make excuses. Instead, love one another as commanded by the Lord through His Son, our Lord and Savior Jesus Christ.

CHAPTER 24

Virgins (unmarried women) should not commit to vows until they prove themselves and maintain purity (cleanliness). They must not rush into this commitment before the right time, as Solomon said, "It is better not to vow than to vow and repent." A virgin should be pure in soul and body, serving as a dwelling (home) for God, Christ, and the Holy Spirit. She must follow the teachings of the Gospel and avoid worldly behaviors, evil ways, and hypocrisy (insincerity). Instead, she should be wise, blameless, and free from the desire for praise or idle talk.

CHAPTER 25

If a Christian is brought before the judgment seat of the ungodly (those who do not follow God) for execution (death penalty), banishment (exile), or imprisonment (being held captive) for the name of our Lord Jesus Christ and the true faith, do not turn away from them. Instead, provide sustenance (food) from your resources and support the soldiers (guards) guarding them to ease their suffering. Remember, these Christians are holy martyrs (witnesses who suffer for their faith), faithful servants who uphold the Gospel (Christian teachings) and endure for the love of God. Those who support martyrs are blessed, especially if they give all they have to help them. Our Lord said, "Whoever confesses (admits) me before men, I will confess before my Father in heaven." Therefore, do not neglect to visit imprisoned Christians; your service will be counted with the martyrs. Those who are persecuted (oppressed) for their faith should be welcomed and given shelter, for they are blessed. Our Lord said, "Blessed are you when they revile (insult) and persecute you for my sake." If you endure suffering (pain) for Christ, He will acknowledge (recognize) you before the Father. However, those who deny (reject) Christ to avoid persecution are despised (hated) by God. They choose the love of man over God and forfeit (lose) the Kingdom prepared for the blessed. Our Lord warns, "Whoever denies me before men, I will deny before my Father." Let us remember that our faith is tested through trials (difficult experiences). Those who suffer for Christ will find joy in eternal life (everlasting existence). Let us endure patiently, knowing our suffering is not in vain (without purpose), and strive to share the hope of resurrection (rising from the dead) and life eternal through our Savior (Jesus Christ).

CHAPTER 26

Behold, I say unto you, magnify (greatly honor) and extol (praise) with double honor the martyrs, such as the blessed James and Stephen (first martyr) who are honored among us. They are blessed before God, chosen (selected) and holy, a people pure from sin and without thoughts of revenge; rather, they are peacemakers and tireless (unwearied) in doing His will and keeping His commandments. David said, "Precious in the sight of the Lord is the death of the righteous." Solomon added, "The remembrance of the righteous is perfect with praise." The prophet also said, "His horn shall be exalted (raised) with honor."

This we say concerning those who have been true martyrs for the name of our Lord Jesus Christ. We understand that those who honor the martyrs and the faithful who have fought a good fight, finished their course, and died for Christ's sake in the right faith will receive a good reward and eternal life. Those who were true martyrs, judged uprightly, and glorified (honored) God in their deeds shall inherit the Kingdom of Heaven.

CHAPTER 27

They have mouths but speak not; eyes but see not; ears but hear not; noses but smell not; hands but handle not; feet but walk not; neither do they speak, and there is no breath in their mouths. Like them are all who make them and all who trust in them. Beloved brethren, you have heard what God says: evil and defiled are all who worship idols, bow down to the sun, moon, and stars. Christians who love God ought not to swear by the sun, moon, stars, or the earth. Our Master has commanded us never to swear by anything. Let our words be prudent, for our Lord said, "Swear not by heaven, for it is God's throne; nor by the earth, for it is the footstool of His feet; nor by Jerusalem, for it is the city of the great King; neither shall you swear by your head," for the foolish swear by their heads. He commanded that the words of the faithful should be simple, either yes or no; anything more is evil. He who swears falsely transgresses the law and honors (false) gods as truth, since God has made them err in the blindness of their hearts and the evil of their doings.

CHAPTER 28

Christians should avoid swearing by the names of false gods (deities not recognized as true) and demons, and refrain from mentioning them as they did in the past. Those who serve these false gods will be distant from God, the source of life. These are not true gods but creations of human hands and spirits of evil. The Scriptures declare that the children of Israel forsook God, swearing by strange gods and provoking His anger. Every person who worships and serves false gods is considered despised and impure. Not only are these false gods condemned, but so are astrologers (practitioners of astrology) and magicians. The faithful are instructed not to worship celestial bodies like the sun, moon, or stars, for God created them to illuminate the earth, not to be objects of worship. In the wilderness, Israel fell into idolatry, worshiping a golden calf and celestial bodies, as noted by the prophet Ezekiel. The Egyptians also worshiped various gods, including one with a dog's face (Anubis). In Judah, gold and silver gods were revered, as indicated by the prophets. These idols have no senses or life; those who create and trust them will become like them. Therefore, Christians must not swear by the sun, moon, stars, or the earth, as our Lord commands us to avoid oaths altogether. Our words should be simple and truthful: yes or no. Anything beyond this is evil, as swearing falsely dishonors God and aligns with falsehood.

CHAPTER 29

Christians should joyfully observe feast days, starting with Christ's Birth on the twenty-fifth of the ninth month (Tahsas) (Ethiopian month) according to Hebrew reckoning, and the twenty-ninth according to Egyptian timing (Egypt) (country). Next is the feast of the Epiphany (theophany) (manifestation of God), commemorating the Lord's baptism by John (John the Baptist) in the River Jordan (Jordan) (river), celebrated on the sixth day of the tenth month (Tobi) (Ethiopian month). The faithful should observe the forty days of the Holy Fast, fostering patience and prayer, concluding on Passover (Passover) (Jewish holiday), the day of Salvation. The fast begins on the second day before Passover, recalling the Jews' plotting against Jesus. Judas (Judas Iscariot) (disciple), motivated by greed (desire for money), betrayed Him, leading to the Lord's arrest. Despite Peter (Peter the Apostle) (disciple)'s protestations, Jesus foretold Peter's denial. At the Mount of Olives (mountain), Jesus prayed, knowing His fate. Judas's betrayal, marked by a deceitful kiss (sign of betrayal), led to Jesus being taken to Caiaphas (Caiaphas) (high priest), where He faced false accusations. Pilate (Pontius Pilate) (Roman governor) found no fault in Him but ultimately yielded to the crowd's demands for crucifixion (execution by cross). Jesus was crucified, fulfilling prophecies (predictions), and darkness fell during His suffering. At the ninth hour (time), He cried out, yet forgave His persecutors before His death. After being buried, He rose on the first day of the week (Sunday), appearing first to Mary Magdalene (follower of Jesus) and instructing His disciples to observe the Passover fast.

CHAPTER 30

Christians should joyfully observe feast days, starting with Christ's Birth on the twenty-fifth of the ninth month (Tahsas) (Ethiopian month) according to Hebrew reckoning, and the twenty-ninth according to Egyptian timing (Egypt) (country). Next is the feast of the Epiphany (theophany) (manifestation of God), commemorating the Lord's baptism by John (John the Baptist) in the River Jordan (Jordan) (river), celebrated on the sixth day of the tenth month (Tobi) (Ethiopian month). The faithful should observe the forty days of the Holy Fast, fostering patience and prayer, concluding on Passover (Passover) (Jewish holiday), the day of Salvation. The fast begins on the second day before Passover, recalling the Jews' plotting against Jesus. Judas (Judas Iscariot) (disciple), motivated by greed (desire for money), betrayed Him, leading to the Lord's arrest. Despite Peter (Peter the Apostle) (disciple)'s protestations, Jesus foretold Peter's denial. At the Mount of Olives (mountain), Jesus prayed, knowing His fate. Judas's betrayal, marked by a deceitful kiss (sign of betrayal), led to Jesus being taken to Caiaphas (Caiaphas) (high priest), where He faced false accusations. Pilate (Pontius Pilate) (Roman governor) found no fault in Him but ultimately yielded to the crowd's demands for crucifixion (execution by cross). Jesus was crucified, fulfilling prophecies (predictions), and darkness fell during His suffering. At the ninth hour (time), He cried out, yet forgave His persecutors before His death. After being buried, He rose on the first day of the week (Sunday), appearing first to Mary Magdalene (follower of Jesus) and instructing His disciples to observe the Passover fast. Christians must observe the Paschal season on the fourteenth day of the month, celebrating the holy Passover (Jewish festival) with precision. Do not celebrate alongside the Jews (Jewish people), who have erred in their calculations. The fast (period of abstinence) should last from the second day of the week until the first Sabbath (Saturday), consuming only bread, water, and salt. After the fast, rejoice in Christ's resurrection (return to life), which brings hope. Celebrate the eighth day for His appearance (showing) and the fortieth day for His ascension (going up). After Pentecost (Christian festival), keep a feast for seven days, then fast, honoring the Sabbath with joy and almsgiving (charitable donations).

CHAPTER 31

Bishops, beware of the divisions of the ungodly (those lacking piety) and unbelieving (those without faith); avoid the impure (morally unclean). Those who associate with them will face eternal condemnation. Dathan (a rebel against Moses) and Abiram (another rebel) were swallowed by the earth, and fire consumed the sons of Korah (followers of Dathan). Uzziah (King of Judah) usurped (took unlawfully) the priesthood and was struck with leprosy (skin disease) for his disobedience. If kings face judgment, how much more will others? The priesthood (sacred office) is greater than kingship (royalty). Those who oppose priests will face greater condemnation. Absalom (son of David) and others rose against Moses (leader of Israel), questioning his authority. They accused him of leading them from Egypt (land of slavery) only to rule over them. Despite Moses' signs (miracles), they rebelled. Moses performed wonders, dividing the sea and providing manna (heavenly bread) and water. He received the law (God's commandments) from God, speaking with Him directly. Yet, the sons of Korah opposed him and faced dire consequences. God's wrath (anger) is severe against the ungodly. He has left the people of Judah (southern kingdom of Israel) desolate (empty) and given the Holy Spirit to Christians (followers of Christ). Jeremiah (prophet) warned of the wickedness of the people, and Isaiah (another prophet) foretold the exaltation of God's house. Despite the trials Christians face from the ungodly, they are promised the Spirit and wisdom. Divisions arose among the Jews (people of Judah), with Sadducees (deniers of resurrection) and Pharisees (strict law followers) opposing the truth. Some believe in a mere man, denying the divinity of Christ.

CHAPTER 32

Brethren, understand the craft of Satan (enemy of good) and how he caused divisions, unbelief, and ungodliness among the people. The first division was with Simon (sorcerer) in the city called Gitthae (a place). He practiced sorcery (magic) and served Satan. Philip the Apostle (disciple of Jesus) performed miracles in Samaria (region), healing the sick, leading many to believe and be baptized in Jesus Christ. When Simon saw these signs, he believed and was baptized, but later sought to buy the power to bestow the Holy Spirit. Peter rebuked Simon, telling him that his heart was not right before God and that he could not purchase God's gift. Simon feared and asked for prayer. As the apostles preached, Satan sent false apostles, including Cleobius (a leader), who allied with Simon. They spread blasphemy (speaking irreverently) and heresies (false teachings). Heretics included Cerinthus, Marcus, Menander, Basilides, and Saturnilus, who taught various false doctrines, including the denial of marriage and the worship of many gods. Peter encountered Simon in Caesarea, where Simon seduced believers, including Zacchaeus (tax collector) and Barnabas (companion of Paul). Simon later went to Rome, disturbing the Church and leading many astray with sorcery. Simon claimed to ascend to heaven, but Peter prayed for his downfall. The unclean spirits left Simon, causing him to fall, and the people recognized the true God through Peter's preaching. From then on, divisions among the Simonians increased. Satan influenced false prophets to blaspheme God, denying His role as Creator and rejecting the resurrection. They promoted lustful behaviors and taught that there are many gods. Some forbade marriage and claimed purity while indulging in sinful acts. Others taught that animals lack souls and condemned those who harmed them while maintaining dietary restrictions contrary to the law. These individuals are instruments of the devil, led astray and filled with wrath.

CHAPTER 33

We, as children of God and sons of peace, proclaim this holy word to the obedient. We believe in One God (the Creator), the Maker of all, the Father of our Lord Jesus Christ, who exists without cause, eternal and unchangeable. In Him is unquenchable light, and He is not divided but is one, known through the Law (sacred texts) and the prophets (messengers of God) as Almighty. We affirm that Jesus Christ (the Messiah), the only-begotten Son, was begotten before creation and is equal to the Father. He became man through the Virgin Mary (mother of Jesus), lived sinlessly, died for our sins, rose on the third day, and ascended into heaven. He sent the Holy Spirit (Paraclete), who is co-existent with the Father and the Son, to save the world. We declare that all of God's creation is good and should not be rejected. Marriage is pure, and procreation (having children) is not unclean, as God created Adam and Eve (first humans) to multiply. The soul (immortal essence) is immortal and does not perish with the body. We reject apostasy (abandonment of faith) and divisions, believing in the resurrection of the dead, where all will be judged according to their deeds. Christ's incarnation (becoming flesh) did not diminish His divinity; He reconciled humanity with God and serves as the High Priest (spiritual leader). We do not practice Jewish circumcision (ritual removal), for Christ fulfilled the Law and the prophets, coming from Judah (one of the twelve tribes), the root of Jesse (King David's father). In times of growing ungodliness, the apostles gathered in Jerusalem (holy city), appointing Matthias (replacement for Judas Iscariot) to replace Judas Iscariot as prophesied. Some from Judea (region in Israel) taught that circumcision and adherence to Moses' Law were necessary for salvation, causing strife in Antioch (city in Syria). Peter (one of the apostles) spoke, recalling how God chose the Gentiles (non-Jews), evidenced by Cornelius (a Roman centurion)' faith. He recounted a vision where God declared all creatures clean, emphasizing that God shows no favoritism. The faithful questioned the burden placed on Gentiles, affirming salvation by grace (unmerited favor). James (bishop of Jerusalem), acknowledged Peter's declaration and proposed that no burden be placed on the Gentiles except to abstain from unclean things, blood, and fornication (sexual immorality). The apostles agreed and sent a letter to Antioch, reassuring the believers and instructing them on these matters. This letter emphasized that the Holy Spirit agreed with their decision to avoid unnecessary burdens. They were to abstain from things sacrificed to idols (false gods) and from blood, and to conduct themselves in righteousness. We labored in Jerusalem, confirming the faithful and warning against those who blaspheme (speak irreverently) the Lord and lead others astray. These false prophets, like ravenous wolves (predators), sow discord and threaten the Church. We, the apostles—Peter, Andrew, James, John, and others—united to deliver this message. We teach the faithful to worship the One God, to honor parents, and to await the resurrection and judgment day. We stress that lawful marriage is pure and honorable, while all forms of immorality are condemned. The union of man and woman is blessed by God, and all transgressions against this are punishable. We warn against false teachings and those who distort the truth, urging the faithful to remain steadfast in their faith. The Holy Spirit dwells in those who believe and follow God's commandments. The unclean spirit cannot approach those filled with the Holy Spirit, who is present from birth until death. Thus, we instruct the faithful to live righteously, avoiding the counsel of the wicked. We encourage separation from those who practice evil, affirming that lawful marriage is not an abomination. We denounce the sins of Sodom (ancient city known for immorality) and other immoral practices, stressing that such actions lead to punishment. The Scriptures declare that those who commit such sins shall face dire consequences. However, marriage is blessed, and we are called to uphold its sanctity, living according to God's design.

CHAPTER 34

Gather yourselves together diligently in the church (place of worship), and read the holy Scriptures (sacred texts) over those righteous Christians who have fallen asleep (died), and your brethren (brothers and sisters) the martyrs (those who died for their faith) who have entered into rest in the faith of Christ; and celebrate for them the Eucharist (thanksgiving), and offer in the church His holy Body and precious Blood. And when you bring them to the church and to the tomb (grave), sing psalms (sacred songs) over them, for it is said, "Precious in the sight of the Lord is the death of the righteous" (good people). (And again,) Return unto thy rest, O my soul, for the Lord is thy help." And again it is said, "The remembrance of the righteous man is with praise"; and "their souls are in the hand of God; even if they sleep, they are not dead." Our Saviour (Jesus Christ) said to the Sadducees (Jewish sect), "Concerning the resurrection (rising from the dead) of the dead, have ye not read what the Scripture saith, I am the God of Abraham (patriarch), the God of Isaac (patriarch), and the God of Jacob (patriarch). He is not then the God of the dead. He is the God of the living," [and not all are living nor ...]. Elisha (prophet) also in his death raised him that was slain in Syria; when the dead body touched him, it was raised. The righteous Joseph (son of Jacob) also touched the body of Jacob on the bier (funeral bed), and was not defiled (made unclean). And Moses (leader of the Israelites) and Joshua (son of Nun) when they brought forth the bones of Joseph from the land of Egypt, and touched his bones, were not defiled. And in like manner, ye bishops (church leaders) and all the people, when ye touch the dead bodies of those that have fallen asleep, count it not an abomination (something detestable) to carry their bones, for ye shall not be defiled on account of them. Remove, then, from you this practice, for it is a thing of folly (foolishness). And as for you, be ye adorned (decorated) with wisdom and knowledge, that ye may find life eternal (everlasting), and a portion with the souls of the righteous in the Kingdom of heaven (paradise), in a place of rest through Jesus Christ our Saviour, who is able to open the ears of your hearts that ye may hear the words of God which have instructed you in the Gospel (good news) by the admonition (counsel) of our Lord Jesus Christ the Nazarene (from Nazareth), who was crucified in the days of Pontius Pilate (Roman governor) and Herod (king): He suffered, and died, and rose from the dead, and shall come again with glory and with great power; (and) shall raise the dead, and render to every man according to his works; and He ascended with great glory to His Father (God). And after He rose from the dead, we saw Him, and ate and drank and abode (stayed) with Him forty days; and then He ascended into heaven, and sat on the right hand of the Father, the Almighty who sitteth on the Cherubim (angelic beings); concerning whom David (king of Israel) saith, "The Lord said to my Lord, Sit thou on my right hand, until I bring thine enemies under the footstool of thy feet"; whom the blessed Stephen (first Christian martyr) saw, and cried and said, "Behold I see the heaven opened, and the Son of Man sitting on the right hand of God"; who created the hosts of angels; to whom be great glory and honour and thanksgiving and dominion with His Father and the Holy Spirit, now and for ever and ever. Amen.

CHAPTER 35

Moses the prophet said to the people of Israel, "Behold, I show you plainly the way of death and the way of life; choose life for yourselves, that ye may live." Elijah the prophet urged, "How long halteth your heart concerning the Lord—the Lord is One; seek Him." Jesus Christ taught, "A servant cannot serve two masters; ye cannot serve God and wealth (material riches)."

There are two distinct ways: one leads to death, the other to life. The way of life is described in the Law: "Love the Lord thy God with all thy heart, strength, and soul; there is no other god." Also, "Love thy neighbour (fellow human) as thyself," and "What thou desirest not for thyself, do not to thy neighbour." "Bless them that curse you, and pray for those who oppress you." Love your enemies and take heed to hate no man. It is said, "Thou shalt not hate any man, neither an Egyptian (descendant of Egypt) nor an Edomite (descendant of Esau); for they are all creatures of God." Keep away from evil men and worldly desires. "If someone strikes you on the right cheek, turn the other." David said, "If I have returned evil for evil, let my enemies cause me to fall." "If any man compel thee to go one mile, go two; if he takes your coat, leave him your cloak also." "Give to him that asketh of thee." For God is merciful (compassionate) and gives to all who ask. The Father makes the sun rise on both the evil and the good, sending rain on the righteous and the sinful. Ye ought to give to all men from the labour of your hands and honour the saints (holy people). "Thou shalt do no murder," for every person is made in God's image. "Thou shalt not commit adultery," nor separate what is thy flesh, for "They twain shall be one flesh." "Thou shalt not steal," for Achan (Israelite) stole and perished; Gehazi (servant of Elisha) stole and was afflicted with leprosy (skin disease). Judas Iscariot betrayed Jesus, then repented and died. Thou shalt not practise magic (sorcery) or consult wizards (sorcerers), for it is said, "Ye shall not trust in wizards." Do not kill a child by abortion (termination of pregnancy), for it is the image and spirit of God. "Thou shalt not covet (desire greedily) thy brother's possessions." Do not bear false witness, for "he that speaketh lies against the poor provokes his creator to anger." The way of evildoers leads to death. Do not be of a double heart (divided loyalty) or double tongue (two-faced). "A talkative man shall not prosper upon earth." Be merciful, for they shall obtain mercy. Accept every toil (hardship) like Job (faithful servant of God) and Lazarus (poor man), to receive a reward from God. Honour him who teaches you the word of God, and be mindful of him day and night. Reconcile those who are at variance (in conflict) and judge uprightly, for the judgment is the Lord's. When thou prayest, do not be of a double heart. If thou givest alms to the poor, doubt not; know who will render the reward—it is the Lord. Forget not the commandments (orders) of the Lord; confess thy trespasses (wrongdoings) before Him. Honour thy father and mother; do not forsake thy brethren and kinsmen (relatives). Fear the King (ruler), for his position is from the Lord.

CHAPTER 36

Give thanks to God, Creator of all (all things), for the chrism (sacred oil) and the oil of immortality (eternal life) bestowed upon us through Jesus Christ (Son of God). Receive those who come to you in gratitude as disciples, but reject anyone teaching contrary to the Law (divine commandments) given by the Lord. Examine their deeds and judge fairly between those who rule justly (righteously) and unjustly. Provide for the priests (religious leaders) with first-fruits (initial harvest) and tithes (one-tenth) for the widows (women without husbands), orphans (children without parents), and strangers (foreigners). On the Sabbath (day of rest), gather together in one place to give thanks for all God's goodness through Christ. Your sacrifice should be perfect and acceptable, as the Lord is a great King (ruler). Appoint bishops (overseers), presbyters (elders), and deacons (servants) who are humble and pure, desiring to teach the word of the Lord. Be prepared for the Lord's return, for He will come when least expected. Blessed are those servants found doing His work. When the glory of the Son of Man (Jesus Christ) appears, He will judge each according to their works. The righteous (virtuous) will rejoice in the Kingdom of heaven (eternal paradise) through our Lord Jesus Christ.

CHAPTER 37

The spiritual hosts (angels) of angels glorify God, singing, "Holy, holy, holy, Lord of Hosts (God's army)." The whole creation gives thanks for God's greatness. All mankind must offer glory, thanksgiving, and sacrifices through Jesus Christ. God is Almighty (all-powerful), good, and merciful (compassionate), present everywhere, and worthy of honor and worship.

CHAPTER 38

O Lord, who created the world (universe) through Jesus Christ and appointed the Sabbath, command us to rest from our work and to serve Thee. We remember that God the Word (divine reason) was born of a woman, suffered, died, and rose again. We celebrate His resurrection and honor the first day of the week (Sunday). You delivered our ancestors (forefathers) from Egypt (land of slavery), sustained them in the wilderness (desert), and gave them the law (commandments). Therefore, we rest on the Sabbath, giving thanks and seeking to follow His commandments. Greater than all, we honor the day of Christ's resurrection. Remember the sacrifices (offerings) we offer on this day, including the eucharist (thanksgiving meal) of peace. Receive our prayers and supplications (requests) as You have received those of the righteous throughout history. We give thanks for Your compassion and mercy, acknowledging Your help in every generation. We thank You for creating us, granting us life, and making us rational (thinking) beings. You have given us senses (abilities to perceive) and a soul (spiritual essence) that does not die. How can we repay You for all that You have done? We must give thanks and glorify You according to our ability. Preserve us from wickedness (evil) and the error of Satan (adversary). You sent Christ to become man and dwell among us, bringing us salvation (deliverance). We seek Your guidance and sustenance (nourishment), turning us to repentance (sorrow for sin). May we follow Your teachings, with the Lord's presence in our lives and in His Kingdom. What fitting thanks can we offer to God the Father through Jesus Christ? We have taught you these truths so that you may find eternal life.

CHAPTER 39

He that desireth to be baptized must needs be taught the word of instruction (teaching) and be made to understand the knowledge of God the Father, the incarnation (physical manifestation) of His only-begotten Son (Jesus Christ) and the good pleasure (will) of the Holy Spirit. They should learn how God created the world (universe) and man, sent judgment on the wicked (evil-doers) by the flood (Noah's flood), and destroyed sinners with fire (Sodom and Gomorrah), and did magnify (honor) the saints (holy people) in all generations, including Seth (Adam's son), Enosh (Seth's son), Enoch (a righteous man), Noah (the ark builder), and Abraham (father of many nations). God chose mankind, turning them from error (false beliefs) to true knowledge, saving them from the adversary (Satan), and leading them to life (eternal life). Let him who desires baptism understand this and then receive it. The one laying hands upon him should worship God the Father, who sent His Son to save mankind from filthiness (uncleanness) of flesh and soul, sanctifying (making holy) them according to His goodness. They should understand His wondrous works, learn righteousness, and walk in uprightness (honesty) to be worthy of baptism as sons (children) of Christ, in a hope that is full of grace (unmerited favor) and truth. After giving thanks, they should learn about the Lord's incarnation, sufferings (passions), resurrection, and ascension (going up). The catechumen (baptism candidate) must renounce (reject) Satan, believe in Christ, forsake (abandon) former habits (practices), and purify (cleanse) his heart from evil and revenge (vengeance) and impurity (moral filth) and deceit (dishonesty). Then let them receive the holy mysteries (sacred rites). As a wise man cleanses his field, so must they separate from impurity to receive holy baptism. Our Lord commanded, "Baptize all nations into the name of the Father, and of the Son, and of the Holy Spirit." The baptized should say: I renounce thee, Satan, and all thy works. After renouncing, they shall confess (declare), and say, I believe in the One true God unbegotten (without origin), the Father of our Lord Jesus Christ, the Almighty (all-powerful) and the Creator (maker) of all things, by whom are all things; and I am baptized into His only-begotten Son Jesus Christ, who was begotten before the world (was), by the will of the Father, by whom all things were made, both those in heaven and those in earth, both visible (seen) and invisible (unseen); and who came down from heaven in the latter days, and was incarnate (made flesh) of the Holy Virgin Mary (mother of Jesus) and was born in purity; and (who) fulfilled the will of His Father, and was crucified (nailed to the cross) for us in the days of Pontius Pilate (Roman governor), and died, and abode (remained) in the heart of the earth three days and three nights, and rose from the dead and ascended (went up) into heaven in glory, and sat on the right hand of the Father; and (He) shall come again at the last day to judge (evaluate) the living (those alive) and the dead, of whose Kingdom (reign) there is no end. And I am baptized also into the Paraclete (Holy Spirit) the Holy Spirit, who proceedeth from the Father, and was strong through the Son, and dwelt (lived) in the holy patriarchs (forefathers); and (who), again, was sent upon the apostles (early disciples) from the Father by our Lord Jesus Christ; and after the apostles He was sent and given to the faithful (believers) in Jesus Christ; and (I am baptized) into the apostolic Church (early Christian community) for remission (forgiveness) of sins, and for the Kingdom of heaven, and for the life to come for ever. And after he has made confession, let him draw near to the anointing (blessing) of the holy oil which the priests (religious leaders) have consecrated (made holy) for the remission of sins, and let the priest pray and make supplication (request) to God, and say, May God the Father unbegotten, the Father of our Lord and Saviour Jesus Christ, King of kings (ruler of rulers) sanctify and purify this oil in the name of His only-begotten Son Jesus Christ; may it be a spiritual grace (divine favor) and power for the remission of sins; and a pledge (guarantee) for this baptism by the anointing of this holy oil, that (he that cometh thereto) may be worthy to keep Thy commandments.

CHAPTER 40

When the priest stands over the water, let him pray: O Lord our God, Almighty (all-powerful) Father of Thine only-begotten Son our Lord Jesus Christ, I give Thee thanks for sending Him to save the world. I glorify Thee for the gift of baptism, which is the new birth (rebirth). Look down from heaven upon this water, and sanctify it by Thy power, that all baptized may partake in Christ's crucifixion (death on the cross), death, resurrection, and ascension into heaven, living in righteousness. After this, let him baptize in the name of the Father, Son, and Holy Spirit, anointing with balsam (fragrant oil).

CHAPTER 41

O Lord God, grant us the sweet savor (fragrance) of this chrism (sacred oil) to all nations who believe in Thee. After this, the priest shall pray: "Our Father who art in heaven," and then turn towards the East (direction of prayer), glorifying the Lord.

CHAPTER 42

The baptized shall pray: O God Almighty, Father of our Lord and Saviour Jesus Christ, make Thy Holy Spirit dwell in us by Thy good will through Jesus Christ, to whom be glory forever. Amen.

CHAPTER 43

These are the names of those ordained (appointed) by us: In Jerusalem (holy city), James (brother of Jesus), then Simeon (son of Cleopas), and Judas (another disciple). In Caesarea (city in Palestine), Zacchaeus (tax collector), Cornelius (Roman centurion), and Theophilus (friend of God). In Antioch (city), Evodius (ordained) by Peter; and after him Ignatius (ordained) by Paul. In Alexandria (city in Egypt), Annianus (ordained) by Mark the Evangelist; and after him, Avilius (ordained) by Luke the Evangelist. In the Church of Rome (capital city), Linus (ordained) by Paul; and after him Clement (another leader), who was ordained by Peter. In Ephesus (city), Timothy (ordained) by Paul; and after him was ordained John (the Evangelist) by John. In Smyrna (city), first, Aristos; and after him Strataeas (son of Lois); and after him Ariston. In Pergamus (city), first, Gaius (leader). In Philadelphia (city), first, Demetrius (ordained) by Peter. In Cenchreae (port of Corinth), first, Lucius (ordained) by Paul. In Crete (island), Titus (leader). In Athens (city), Dionysius (leader). In the three cities of Phoenicia (region), Marthones. In Laodicea (city), Archippus. In Colossae (city), Philemon. In Galatia (region), Crescens. In Asia (area), Aquila and Nicetas. In the Church of Aegina (island), Crispus. These are they whom we entrusted (with the churches) and sent forth to preach. Remember their toil (efforts) and receive their admonition (advice). May the Lord be with you from henceforth and for ever, even as He said unto us when He was ascending (going up) to heaven to the Father, "Behold I am with you all the days unto the end of the world." Glory be to God, to whom be glory and honor forever. Amen.

79 – Apocalypse of Peter

Chapter 1

The Second Coming of Christ and the Resurrection of the Dead were revealed by Christ through Peter to those who had died for their sins, because they did not follow God's command. Peter reflected on this, trying to understand the mystery of the Son of God, who is merciful and full of love for mercy. While seated on the Mount of Olives (a hill in Jerusalem), the Lord's disciples approached Him. They each separately asked and begged Him, saying, "Tell us, what are the signs of Your coming and the end of the world, so that we may understand and know when You will return, and teach those who follow us the gospel. Those whom we place in Your Church should heed these signs to recognize Your coming." The Lord responded, saying, "Be careful that no one deceives you, and that you do not doubt or worship other gods. Many will come in My name, saying, 'I am the Christ (the Messiah).' Do not believe them or follow them. The coming of the Son of God will not be obvious; instead, it will be like lightning that flashes from the east to the west. I will come on the clouds of heaven with great glory, accompanied by a host of angels. My cross will go before Me as I appear in majesty, shining seven times brighter than the sun. With all My saints and angels, I will come. My Father will place a crown on My head, so that I can judge the living and the dead, rewarding everyone according to their deeds."

Chapter 2

And you shall learn from the fig-tree: once its branches sprout and grow, the end times will approach. Peter asked, "What does this mean? The fig-tree produces fruit every year, yet what does this teach us?" The Master replied, "The fig-tree symbolizes the house of Israel (the Jewish people). A man planted a fig-tree, but it bore no fruit. He wanted to uproot it, but the gardener said, 'Let us care for it and water it for one more season. If it still bears no fruit, then we shall remove it.' Do you understand this parable? When the last days come, false Christs (deceivers claiming to be the Savior) will appear, claiming to be the true Christ. But those who recognize their evil ways will reject them, just as they rejected the first Christ (Jesus, whom they crucified), whom they crucified. This deceiver will lead many astray. But when he is rejected, many will be martyred (killed for their faith). Enoch (an ancient prophet who walked with God and was taken to heaven without dying) and Elijah (a prophet who was taken up to heaven in a chariot of fire) will come to guide them and reveal this deceiver. Those who die at his hands will be true martyrs, honored by God for their faith."

Chapter 3

He showed me in His right hand the souls (immaterial essence of human beings) of all people. On the palm was the image of what would happen on the last day—how the righteous (those who live in accordance with God's will) and sinners (those who live in disobedience to God's will) would be separated, and how the upright in heart (morally and spiritually good) would prosper, while the evil-doers (those who commit sinful actions) would be cast away forever. We saw how the sinners wept in deep sorrow, and all who witnessed it, even the righteous and angels (spiritual beings who serve God), wept with them. He too was moved. I asked, "Lord, is it not better for them not to have been created?" The Savior replied, "Peter, do not speak such words. You are resisting God. He created them, bringing them into existence from nothing. What you have seen is the sorrow they will face in the last days, which troubles your heart, but I will show you their deeds, through which they have sinned against the Most High."

Chapter 4

Behold what will happen to them in the last days, when He commands hell to open its gates of adamant (hard, unyielding material) and release everything within. He will command the wild beasts and the birds to return all the flesh they have consumed, for He desires that people should appear before Him. Nothing perishes before God, and nothing is impossible for Him, as all things are His. All things come to pass on the day of decision (the day of judgment), at the word of God: just as everything happened when He created the world and commanded all things, it will be the same in the last days; for all things are possible with God. Therefore, as the scripture says, 'Son of man, prophesy to the bones and say, 'Bone to bone, join together with sinews, nerves, flesh, and skin, and hair upon them.' The great Uriel (an archangel associated with wisdom and guidance) will give them soul and spirit at the command of God, as God has appointed him over the resurrection of the dead on the day of judgment. Consider the wheat seeds that are sown in the earth. Though dry and lifeless, they are buried in the soil and spring to life, bearing fruit, as the earth restores them as a pledge entrusted to it. This is similar to man: what dies and is sown in the earth will be raised and restored to life. How much more will God raise those who believe in Him and are chosen by Him, for whom He created the world? The earth, too, will restore all on the day of decision, and it, along with heaven, will be judged."

Chapter 5

"And this will happen on the day of judgment for those who have abandoned faith in God and sinned. Cataracts (large, heavy downpour) of fire will be unleashed; darkness and obscurity will cover the entire world. The waters will change into coals of fire, and everything within them will burn, turning the sea into fire. Under the heavens, a sharp fire that cannot be quenched will flow, fulfilling the judgment of wrath. The stars will melt from flames, as though they had not existed, and the firmaments (heavens) will disappear, as though they were never created. The lightning of heaven will cease, and its enchantment will terrify the world. The spirits of the dead bodies will become fire at God's command. Once the creation dissolves, people from the east will flee to the west, and those from the west will flee to the east; those in the south will flee to the north, and those from the north will flee to the south. Everywhere, the wrath of unquenchable fire will chase them to the judgment of wrath, a flaming stream. When the waves of fire part, there will be great gnashing of teeth among the people.

Chapter 6

Then they will see me coming on an eternal cloud of brightness. The angels of God with me will sit on the throne of my glory at the right hand of my heavenly Father, and He will place a crown on my head. When nations see this, they will weep for themselves. He will command them to enter the river of fire, where the works of everyone will be revealed. Rewards will be given according to deeds. The elect, who did good, will come to me and not see death by fire. The unrighteous, sinners, and hypocrites will stand in eternal darkness, punished by fire. Angels will bring forth their sins and prepare a place for them to be punished eternally, each according to their transgressions. Uriel (an archangel) will bring forth the souls of sinners who perished in the flood and worshipped idols, molten images, and false gods. They will be burned in everlasting fire, and after their dwellings are destroyed, they will be eternally punished.

Chapter 7

Then people will be brought to their place. By the tongues that blasphemed righteousness, they will be hanged, with unquenchable fire beneath them. They will not escape. Another place: a great pit full of those who denied righteousness, where angels of punishment will torment them with the fire of their suffering. Again, behold two women, hung by their necks and hair, cast into the pit. These are women who used their beauty to tempt men into fornication, leading souls to destruction. The men who fornicated with them will be hung by their loins in that fire. They will say to one another, 'We did not know we would face eternal punishment.' Murderers and their allies will be thrown into a fire full of venomous beasts, tormented without rest. Their worms will be many, like a dark cloud. The angel Ezrael (an angel associated with death) will bring the souls of the slain, and they will witness the torment of their killers, saying, 'Righteousness and justice are the judgment of God. We heard but did not believe we would come to this place of eternal judgment.'"

Chapter 8

Near this flame (source of fire) is a deep pit (hole), into which flows torment, foulness, and excrement. Women are trapped up to their necks, enduring great pain. These are those who caused their children to be born prematurely (before term) and corrupted God's work. Opposite them, children sit alive and cry to God. Lightning from these children pierces the eyes of those who caused their destruction due to fornication (immoral sexual acts). "Other men and women stand above them, naked while their children, in a place of delight (joy), cry to God, saying, 'These are those who disrespected (despised) and cursed (spoke ill of) your commandments, leading us to death. They cursed the angel (spiritual being) who formed us, deprived us of the light you gave to all creatures. The milk from their mothers' breasts hardens (congeals), and from it, wild beasts (animals) devour flesh, tormenting them forever with their husbands. They forsook (abandoned) God's commandments and killed (slew) their children. Their children will be entrusted to the angel Temlakos (angel's name). Those who killed them will suffer eternally, as God decrees."

Chapter 9

Ezrael shall bring men and women, with half of their bodies burning, and cast them into a place of darkness (hell) for humans. A spirit of wrath shall punish them with torment, and a worm that never sleeps shall devour their insides. These are the persecutors and betrayers of my righteous ones. "Next to them, other men and women will gnaw their tongues, tormented with red-hot irons, burning their eyes. These are those who slander (speak badly of) and doubt my righteousness. "Other men and women, whose deeds were deceitful, shall have their lips cut off, and fire shall enter their mouth and insides. These are those who caused the martyrs (those who died for their faith) to die with their lies. "Nearby, on a stone, there will be a pillar of fire, sharper than swords. Men and women clothed in rags will be cast onto it, suffering uncealing torment. These are the ones who trusted in riches and despised widows and fatherless children... before God."

Chapter 10

In another nearby place, full of filth (dirt), men and women are cast up to their knees. These are those who lent money and took usury (excessive interest). "Other men and women will throw themselves from a high place and return again, driven by devils (evil spirits). These are idol worshippers, and they are driven to the top of the height to throw themselves down, continuously tormented. These are they who cut their flesh as apostles (followers) of a man, and the women with them... These are the men who defiled themselves with women. "Beside them, beneath them, the angel Ezrael will prepare a fiery place: all idols of gold and silver, the work of human hands, including images of cats, lions, creeping things (insects), and wild beasts, will be bound in chains of fire and chastised for their error before the idols. This is their eternal judgment. "Nearby, other men and women will burn in the fire of judgment, their torment everlasting. These are those who have forsaken (abandoned) God's commandments and followed the persuasion (influence) of devils."

Chapter 11

And there shall be another place, very high. The men and women whose feet slip shall roll down into a place of fear (terror). Again, while the prepared fire flows, they rise and fall, continuing to roll down. Thus, they shall be tormented forever. These are those who did not honor their father and mother and intentionally withheld from them. Therefore, they shall be punished eternally. "Furthermore, the angel Ezrael shall bring children and maidens to show them those who are tormented. They will be punished with pain, being hung up (possibly by the feet or hands) and suffering from wounds inflicted by flesh-devouring birds (vultures or similar creatures). These are they who trust in their sins, do not obey their parents, do not follow the guidance of their fathers, and do not respect elders. "Beside them, there shall be girls clothed in darkness as their garment. They shall be severely punished, with their flesh torn into pieces. These are those who did not preserve their virginity until marriage, and for this, they will be tormented, feeling every bit of it. "Again, other men and women will gnaw their tongues without ceasing, tormented by everlasting fire. These are the servants who were disobedient to their masters, and this will be their eternal judgment."

Chapter 12

"And nearby this place of torment, there shall be men and women who are dumb (unable to speak) and blind, and whose clothing is white. They will crowd together and fall into coals of unquenchable fire. These are they who give alms (charitable donations) and claim, 'We are righteous before God,' but have not truly sought righteousness. "Ezrael the angel of God will bring them out of the fire and establish a final judgment. This is their judgment. A river of fire will flow, and all those judged will be drawn into the middle of the river. Uriel (an archangel) will place them there. "And there will be wheels of fire, and men and women will be suspended upon them by the force of the whirling. Those in the pit will burn. These are the sorcerers and sorceresses. The wheels will operate according to an endless fire, with decisions made by it."

Chapter 13

"Then the angels will bring forth my elect (chosen ones) and righteous clothing them with the garments of eternal life. They will witness the punishment of those who hated them, as each person is tormented forever, according to their deeds. "And all those in torment will cry out with one voice, 'Have mercy upon us, for now we understand the judgment of God, which He declared to us before, but we did not believe.' And the angel Tatirokos will come and punish them with even greater torment, saying, 'Now you repent, but it is no longer the time for repentance, and no life remains.' And they will say, 'Righteous is the judgment of God, for we have heard and understood that His judgment is just, and we are being recompensed according to our deeds.'"

Chapter 14

Then I will give to my elect and righteous the baptism (ritual purification) and salvation they have requested from me, in the field of Akrosja (Acherusia, a mythical place of purification or afterlife) which is called Aneslasleja (Elysium, a paradise or blissful afterlife). They shall adorn it with flowers, for a light shines from them, brighter than the sun, and their raiment (clothing) also shines, indescribable in beauty. Nothing in this world can compare to them. The sweetness of their presence... no mouth can express the beauty of their appearance, for their aspect (appearance) was astonishing and marvelous. One, great in stature, shines above even crystal. The color of his aspect and body is like the rose's flower, and his head and shoulders are radiant. On their foreheads, they wear a crown of nard (a fragrant plant), woven with fair flowers. Like a rainbow in water, so is the appearance of their hair. Such is the beauty of their countenance (face), adorned with all manner of ornaments.

Chapter 15

And my Lord Jesus Christ, our King, said to me, "Let us go to the holy mountain." His disciples went with Him, praying. As we drew near to God, Jesus Christ, someone approached Him and asked, "O my Lord, who are these?" He answered, "They are Moses and Elijah (an Old Testament prophet known for his miraculous deeds)." I asked, "Where are Abraham (the founding patriarch of Israel), Isaac (Abraham's son), Jacob (Isaac's son), and the rest of the righteous fathers?" He then showed us a vast garden, open and filled with beautiful trees and blessed fruits, exuding a pleasant fragrance. The scent reached us. From one of the trees, I saw many fruits. My Lord and God, Jesus Christ, asked, "Have you seen the groups?" He added, "Just as their rest is, so is the honor and glory of those who are persecuted for My righteousness." I rejoiced and understood that which is written in the book of my Lord Jesus Christ. Then I said, "O my Lord, do You wish that I make three tabernacles (temporary shelters) here, one for You, one for Moses, and one for Elijah?" But He responded with a tone of anger, "Satan has waged war against you and blinded your understanding; the good things of this world dominate your thoughts. Your eyes must be opened and your ears unstopped so that you may see a tabernacle, not made by human hands, which My Heavenly Father has made for Me and for the elect." We saw it and were filled with joy.

Chapter 16

And when we suddenly saw, I shall rejoice with them. I will bring the people into My everlasting kingdom and show them the eternal blessings to which I and My Father in heaven have guided them, which they have hoped for. "I have spoken this to you, Peter (the apostle, one of Jesus Christ's closest disciples), and revealed it to you. Now go forth and travel to the city of the west. Enter the vineyard (a metaphor for the mission field of spreading the gospel) that I will direct you to, so that through the sufferings of the Son, who is without sin, the deeds of corruption (wrongdoings) may be sanctified (purified). You, Peter, are chosen according to the promise I have made to you. Spread My gospel throughout all the world in peace. Truly, people will rejoice. My words will be the source of hope and life, and suddenly, the world will be transformed."

Chapter 17

And behold, suddenly a voice came from heaven, saying, "This is My Beloved Son, in whom I am well pleased; He has kept My commandments." Then, a great and exceedingly white cloud appeared above us, lifting our Lord, Moses and Elijah (the prophet from the Old Testament) away. I trembled and was afraid; and as we looked up, the heaven opened, and Elijah (the prophet) went to another heaven. And the scripture was fulfilled: "This is the generation that seeks Him, that seeks the face of the God of Jacob." A great fear and commotion arose in heaven, and the angels pressed together so that the scripture might be fulfilled which says, "Open the gates, you princes." Afterward, the heaven, which had been opened, was closed. We prayed and descended from the mountain, glorifying God, who has written the names of the righteous in heaven in the Book of Life. We saw men in the flesh who came and greeted our Lord, Moses, and Elijah.

80 – The Song of the Three Holy Children

1. They walked in the fire, praising God and blessing the Lord. **2.** Azarias stood and prayed, saying: **3.** Blessed are you, O Lord, God of our fathers, worthy of praise; your name is glorified forever. **4.** You are righteous in all your deeds; your works are true, your ways right, and your judgements (decisions) just. **5.** You have brought true judgements upon us and Jerusalem, because of our sins. **6.** We have sinned, departed from you, and committed iniquity (wickedness). **7.** We have trespassed (sinned), disobeyed your commandments, and not followed your ways. **8.** Therefore, all that you have done to us is in true judgement. **9.** You delivered us into the hands of wicked enemies, an unjust king, and the evillest in the world. **10.** Now we cannot speak; shame and reproach (disgrace) have fallen on your servants who worship you. **11.** Do not abandon us for your name's sake; do not break your covenant (promise). **12.** Let your mercy not depart from us, for the sake of Abraham, Isaac, and Israel, your holy ones (chosen ones). **13.** You promised to multiply their descendants as the stars of heaven and the sand by the sea. **14.** We are fewer than any nation, oppressed because of our sins. **15.** There is no prince (leader), prophet, offering, or place to seek mercy before you. **16.** Accept us with contrite (remorseful) hearts and humble spirits. **17.** Let our sacrifice be as acceptable as burnt offerings; let us wholly follow you, for those who trust you will not be ashamed. **18.** We follow you with all our hearts, fearing you and seeking your face. **19.** Do not shame us, but deal with us in kindness, according to your mercy. **20.** Deliver us by your marvelous (wonderful) works, and bring glory to your name, O Lord. **21.** Let those who harm your servants be confounded (made ashamed), let their power be broken. **22.** Let them know that you alone are the Lord, glorious over all the earth. **23.** The king's servants continued to heat the furnace with pitch (a sticky, flammable substance), naphtha (a type of flammable oil), and wood, **24.** until the flames rose 49 cubits (about 72 feet), burning the Chaldeans (Babylonians) near the furnace. **25.** But the angel of the Lord came down with Azarias and his companions, **26.** and extinguished (put out) the fire, making the furnace feel like a gentle wind, so that the fire did not touch them. **27.** Then, as one, they praised, glorified, and blessed God, saying: **28.** Blessed are you, O Lord, God of our fathers, praised and exalted (lifted up) above all forever. **29.** Blessed is your glorious and holy name, praised and exalted forever. **30.** Blessed are you in your holy temple, praised and glorified forever. **31.** Blessed are you who behold (see) the depths, and sit upon the cherubim (angelic beings), praised above all forever. **32.** Blessed are you on the throne of your kingdom, praised and extolled (praised highly) above all forever. **33.** Blessed are you in the heavens, praised and glorified forever. **34.** All works of the Lord, bless the Lord; praise and exalt him above all forever. **35.** You heavens, bless the Lord; praise and exalt him above all forever. **36.** You angels of the Lord, bless the Lord; praise and exalt him above all forever. **37.** You waters above the heavens, bless the Lord; praise and exalt him above all forever. **38.** All powers (forces) of the Lord, bless the Lord; praise and exalt him above all forever. **39.** Sun and moon, bless the Lord; praise and exalt him above all forever. **40.** Stars of heaven, bless the Lord; praise and exalt him above all forever. **41.** All you work of the Lord, bless the Lord; praise and exalt him above all forever. **42.** O showers and dew, bless the Lord; exalt (praise highly) Him forever. **43.** O winds, bless the Lord; exalt Him forever. **44.** O fire and heat, bless the Lord; exalt Him forever. **45.** (No text) **46.** (No text) **47.** O nights and days, bless the Lord; exalt Him forever. **48.** O light and darkness, bless the Lord; exalt Him forever. O cold and heat, bless the Lord; exalt Him forever. **50.** O frost (frozen dew or vapor) and snow, bless the Lord; exalt Him forever. **51.** O lightnings and clouds, bless the Lord; exalt Him forever. **52.** Let the earth bless the Lord; exalt Him

forever. **53.** O mountains and hills, bless the Lord; exalt Him forever.
54. O all that grows on earth, bless the Lord; exalt Him forever. **55.** O sea and rivers, bless the Lord; exalt Him forever. **56.** O fountains (natural springs of water), bless the Lord; exalt Him forever. **57.** O whales and all moving in waters, bless the Lord; exalt Him forever. **58.** O fowls (birds) of the air, bless the Lord; exalt Him forever. **59.** O beasts and cattle, bless the Lord; exalt Him forever. **60.** O children of men, bless the Lord; exalt Him forever. **61.** O Israel, bless the Lord; exalt Him forever. **62.** O priests (religious leaders) of the Lord, bless the Lord; exalt Him forever. **63.** O servants (those who serve) of the Lord, bless the Lord; exalt Him forever. **64.** O spirits (non-physical beings) and souls (immortal beings) of the righteous (those who live justly), bless the Lord; exalt Him forever. **65.** O holy (sacred) and humble (modest) of heart, bless the Lord; exalt Him forever. **66.** O Ananias, Azarias, and Misael, bless the Lord; exalt Him forever—He has rescued us from hell (eternal punishment) and delivered us from death, from the fire and the flame. **67.** Give thanks to the Lord, for He is good; His mercy (compassion) endures forever. **68.** All who worship (honor) the Lord, bless the God of gods, praise Him, and give thanks; His mercy endures forever.

81 – The Shepherd of Hermas

Vision 1
1. Hermas, a Christian slave, is instructed by a woman in shining garments to read a text to the church presbyters (elders). She tells him to write two more books and deliver them to the elders once completed.

Vision 2
1. Hermas sees the same woman, who reveals herself as the Church. She gives him a book to copy, which, after being sealed (made official or complete), flies to the heavens, symbolizing that the written word is holy and unchangeable.

Vision 3
1. Hermas sees a great beast emerging from a chasm (a deep, wide crack or gap), symbolizing trials (difficult experiences). With the lady's guidance, representing his faith, he escapes.

Vision 4
1. The lady, now depicted as a city on a great plain (a flat, open area), symbolizes the Church. She forewarns Hermas of coming trials and persecutions (sufferings or mistreatment), but assures him of the Church's ultimate victory.

Vision 5
1. Hermas meets the church elders, who interpret (explain the meaning of) his visions and urge him to remain steadfast (firm or unwavering) in faith, emphasizing repentance (sincere regret for wrongdoing) and adherence (sticking to) to Christ's teachings.

Mandate 1
1. Hermas is taught the importance of believing in one God and maintaining faith during trials, which will protect him from evil.

Mandate 2
1. Hermas is warned against false prophets and instructed to discern (judge or distinguish) true prophecy from deception (falsehood or trickery) by their actions and fruits (results).

Mandate 3
1. Hermas is urged to embrace simplicity, avoiding duplicity (deceitfulness) and hypocrisy (pretending to have qualities one does not have), and to cultivate (develop) a pure, steadfast (loyal, resolute) heart.

Mandate 4
1. Hermas is advised to maintain integrity (honesty and moral uprightness) in all dealings, avoiding dishonest gain, as ill-gotten (obtained through wrong means) riches bring sorrow.

Mandate 5
1. Patience is emphasized as essential, teaching that enduring trials cheerfully brings favor from God and is a hallmark (distinctive feature) of a devout Christian.

Mandate 6
1. Hermas is instructed on the necessity of repentance and forgiveness, so that his own sins may be forgiven by God.

Mandate 7
1. Hermas is warned against fear, which breeds (produces) doubt, and is urged to trust in the Lord with a fearless heart.

Mandate 8
1. Chastity and purity are praised, with Hermas being cautioned (warned) against adultery and lust, which lead away from righteousness.

Mandate 9
1. Hermas is reminded of the importance of constant, sincere prayer, which should rise to God without distraction or hypocrisy.

Mandate 10
1. The significance of fasting is discussed, not just as a physical act but as a spiritual practice that humbles (lowers in dignity) the soul and brings it closer to God.

Similitude 1
1. Hermas is shown a vision of a vineyard surrounded by a protective fence, symbolizing the Law that guards those who follow the teachings of the Church.

Similitude 2
1. A mountain made of various stones represents the Church, with each stone symbolizing a member of the faithful. Depending on their faith and actions, some stones remain part of the structure, while others are cast aside.

Similitude 3
1. Hermas sees a vision of an elderly woman, representing the Church, who teaches about the importance of enduring in faith and performing good works.

Similitude 4
1. Through the analogy of trees reflecting the seasons, Hermas learns about resurrection and judgment, emphasizing that one's actions in life reveal their spiritual 'season.'

Similitude 5
1. Hermas sees a vision of the Lord as a shepherd, guiding His flock. This vision teaches that leaders must be gentle, just, and nurturing, leading by example.

Similitude 6
1. Hermas is shown a city being built, symbolizing the Kingdom of Heaven, which is constructed from the deeds of the faithful. This vision encourages vigilance and righteousness.

Similitude 7
1. In the final similitude, Hermas is shown a great feast, symbolizing the eternal reward for the righteous who endure to the end, remaining steadfast in their faith and deeds.

Similitude 8
1. Hermas sees a great tower being built, symbolizing the Church. The tower is constructed of square stones, representing the holy angels or saints who have lived righteous lives. **2.** The builders (angels) carefully examine each stone, discarding those that are flawed, representing souls unfit for the Kingdom of Heaven. **3.** Hermas is taught that each action and choice made by believers either strengthens their inclusion in the tower or leads to their rejection.

Similitude 9
1. In this similitude, Hermas sees a flourishing field surrounded by thorns, symbolizing the world. **2.** The field, ripe for harvest, represents those who live righteously and are prepared for salvation, while the thorns represent sinners who live without repentance and will be cut off. **3.** Hermas learns the importance of living a life of constant readiness and purity, as the day of salvation can come unexpectedly, like a thief in the night.

Similitude 10
1. Hermas sees a series of seats placed in a lofty tower, each one ascending above the last. This represents the levels of glory in the afterlife, depending on one's faithfulness and piety on earth. **2.** After death, each person ascends to a seat according to the quality and measure of their deeds, as witnessed by the hosts of heaven. **3.** Hermas is exhorted to strive for the highest place by living a life of strict adherence to God's commandments, showing love and charity.

Similitude 11
1. A vision of a great river of crystal-clear water symbolizes the outpouring of the Holy Spirit upon the Church. Those who drink from the river receive the Spirit and are sanctified by it. **2.** Hermas sees trees along the river's banks, bearing fruit throughout the year, representing the continuous and fruitful lives of those who live by the Spirit. **3.** The purity and abundance of the water show the boundless grace and

provision God offers to those who faithfully serve Him and adhere to His teachings.

Similitude 12

1. Hermas is shown a sealed book that no one can open. The book contains the deeds of all humans and is to be opened only on the Day of Judgment. 2. An angel explains that only the Lamb, who is without sin, can open the book and reveal its contents, which include the final destinies of all souls. 3. Hermas is admonished to keep the faith and perform righteous deeds so that his name may be found in the book of life, leading to eternal salvation.

Similitude 13

1. Hermas sees a large and beautiful tree under which many sheep rest and feed. This tree symbolizes Christ, and the sheep are those who have found rest in His teachings. 2. The tree provides shade and comfort, symbolizing the protection and peace that come from being in Christ. The leaves of the tree represent the teachings of Jesus, which nourish and sustain the flock. 3. Hermas is told that just as the sheep find safety and sustenance under the tree, so must believers remain close to Christ, drawing strength and guidance from His words.

Similitude 14

1. Hermas sees a vision of a garden filled with diverse plants, each varying in beauty and fruitfulness. This symbolizes the variety of gifts and ministries within the Church. 2. Hermas is instructed that just as each plant contributes to the beauty and utility of the garden, so does each member of the Church contribute their unique gifts to the edification of the whole. 3. The health and growth of the garden depend on the care it receives, just as the health of the Church depends on the stewardship and nurturing of its members.

Similitude 15

1. Hermas sees a vision of a banquet where many are invited, but only those who arrive wearing wedding garments are admitted. This represents the Kingdom of Heaven, where only those prepared and purified through righteousness may enter. 2. The wedding garment symbolizes the righteous deeds and holy living that clothe the faithful. Hermas is warned that without these garments, one cannot partake in the heavenly feast. 3. This similitude emphasizes the importance of vigilance and readiness, living a life worthy of the calling to which believers have been called.

Similitude 16

1. Hermas sees a fortress with walls made of shining stones. Inside the fortress, people are singing hymns and rejoicing, representing those who have overcome the world through their faith. 2. The fortress symbolizes the protection offered by faith in God, shielding believers from spiritual harm and offering them a place of refuge. 3. Hermas is encouraged to strive to enter this fortress by living a life of steadfast faith and unyielding devotion to God, keeping his soul free from the corruptions of the world.

Similitude 17

1. Hermas sees a vision of a great race, where many run, but only those who finish are crowned. This represents the Christian life, which is likened to a race that requires endurance, discipline, and perseverance. 2. The crowns represent the rewards of eternal life, given to those who persevere to the end, keeping their faith intact and their lives pure. 3. Hermas is exhorted to run the race with patience, casting aside every weight and sin that clings closely, focusing on the promise of the heavenly reward.

Similitude 18

1. Hermas sees a vision of a vine growing beside a spring of clear water, supporting many branches and yielding much fruit. This symbolizes the life of the Church, sustained by Christ, the living water. 2. The health and fruitfulness of the vine depend on its connection to the spring, just as the vitality of Christians depends on their connection to Christ. 3. Hermas is taught that apart from Christ, believers can do nothing; thus, they must remain in Him to bear the fruit of the Spirit, which leads to eternal life.

82 – Martyrdom and Ascension of Isaiah

Chapter 1

1. In the twenty-sixth year of Hezekiah's reign over Judah, he called his only son, Manasseh. 2. He summoned him before Isaiah, son of Amoz, and his own son Josab (a name meaning "The remnant shall return"), to share the words of righteousness the king had witnessed. 3. These words concerned the eternal judgments, the torments of Gehenna (hell, a place of punishment), the prince (ruler) of this world, and his angels, authorities (powers), and powers (authorities). 4. Also, the faith of the Beloved (Messiah, the chosen one) that Hezekiah had seen in the fifteenth year of his reign during his illness. 5. Hezekiah gave Manasseh the written words of Samnas (a scribe, a recorder) and Isaiah, including prophecies about judgment, the destruction of the world, the saints' transformation, and the ascension of the Beloved. 6. In the twentieth year of Hezekiah's reign, Isaiah had received these prophecies and shared them with Josab. 7. While Hezekiah commanded, Isaiah told him: "As the Lord lives and the Beloved lives, all your commands will come to nothing because of your son Manasseh. He will be the instrument of my departure and suffering." 8. Sammael (a demon, an accuser) will serve Manasseh, making him follow Beliar (Satan, the enemy) instead of me. 9. Many in Jerusalem will abandon the true faith, and Beliar will dwell in Manasseh. 10. Hezekiah wept bitterly, rent his garments (tore his clothes as a sign of grief), and fell on his face in despair. 11. Isaiah told him, "The plans of Sammael against Manasseh are fulfilled, and nothing can change this." 12. That day, Hezekiah decided to kill Manasseh. 13. But Isaiah said, "The Beloved has nullified (made ineffective) your plan, and it will not succeed, for I have been called for this purpose and will inherit the Beloved's legacy."

Chapter 2

1. After Hezekiah died and Manasseh became king, he forgot his father's commands (orders), and Sammael (a demon) clung (attached) to him. 2. Manasseh abandoned (gave up) the service (worship) of God and served Satan, his angels, and powers. 3. He turned away (departed) from the righteous (virtuous) path that had been established during his father's reign. 4. Manasseh's heart was directed to serve Beliar (Satan), the angel of lawlessness (evil), whose name is Matanbuchis (meaning uncertain—possibly "worthless gift"), and he led Jerusalem into apostasy (abandonment of faith). 5. Witchcraft (sorcery), magic (occult arts), divination (fortune-telling), fornication (sexual immorality), and persecution (oppression) of the righteous increased, with Manasseh and his followers spreading lawlessness (wickedness). 6. The rest of Manasseh's deeds are recorded in the book of the Kings of Judah and Israel. 7. Seeing this, Isaiah withdrew (moved away) from Jerusalem to Bethlehem due to the widespread wickedness (evil). 8. Finding more lawlessness (wickedness) in Bethlehem, he then moved to a desert (barren) mountain. 9. Micaiah (a prophet), Ananias (an old prophet), Joel, Habakkuk, and many faithful (devout) believers, including Isaiah's son Josab (a follower), also retreated (withdrew) to the mountain. 10. They lived in asceticism (self-denial), wearing rough (coarse) clothing, lamenting (mourning) Israel's straying (wandering), and surviving on wild herbs (plants). 11. They spent two years living this way. 12. Meanwhile, in Samaria, a false prophet (deceiver) named Belchira from Zedekiah's family, living in Bethlehem, emerged. 13. Hezekiah the son of Chanan, who had once taught the 400 prophets of Baal (false gods), had previously reproved (rebuked) Micaiah. 14. Micaiah was later imprisoned by King Ahab's son Ahaziah. 15. Elijah, the prophet of Tebon (a place), foretold (predicted) Ahaziah's death and Samaria's downfall due to Ahaziah's persecution of God's prophets. 16. The false prophets of Ahaziah persuaded (convinced) him to kill Micaiah.

Chapter 3

1. Now, Hezekiah and Josab, my son, these are the days when the world will be completed. 2. After this, Beliar, the ruler of this world, will descend, the king who has ruled since the world's beginning. He will appear as a man, a lawless king who slays his own mother. 3. Beliar will persecute the work of the Twelve Apostles, and one of the Twelve will be betrayed into his hands. 4. The ruler will come with all the powers of the world, and they will follow his desires. 5. At his command, the sun will rise at night, and the moon will appear at noon, deceiving the world. 6. He will claim to be God, saying there is no other before him. 7. The world will believe him, worship him, and declare him the one true God. 8. People will sacrifice to him, saying there is no God but him. 9. Many who were once believers in the Beloved will follow him instead. 10. Beliar's false miracles will spread to every city. 11. He will set up his image as an object of worship in every city. 12. He will rule for three years, seven months, and twenty-seven days. 13.

The faithful few, those who have believed in Jesus, will remain and flee from desert to desert, awaiting the Beloved's return. **14.** After 1,332 days, the Lord will return with His angels, and He will cast Beliar and his forces into Gehenna (hell). **15.** The righteous will find rest, and the sun will be ashamed at the glory of the Lord. **16.** The saints, clothed in glory, will descend to the world with the Lord, strengthening the faithful and ministering to them. **17.** Then they will ascend with the Lord, leaving their earthly bodies behind. **18.** The Beloved will rebuke everything in heaven and earth, and fire will consume the godless, erasing their existence. **19.** The rest of this vision is written in the vision of Babylon. **20.** The Lord's vision is revealed in three parables, written in Isaiah's book. **21.** The descent of the Beloved into Sheol is also foretold in Psalms, Proverbs, and other writings by biblical figures like David, Solomon, and others. **22.** Prophecies from figures like Amos, Hosea, Micah, Joel, and others also speak of these events.

Chapter 4

1. Hezekiah and Josab, the end of the world is near. **2.** After its completion, Beliar (the evil ruler of this world), will descend as a lawless (without law or morality) king who killed his mother. **3.** He will persecute (harass or oppress) the Apostles, and one will fall into his hands. **4.** He will come with the powers (forces or authorities) of the world, and they will obey him. **5.** At his command, the sun will rise at night, and the moon at noon. **6.** He will claim to be God, saying, "I am God, and there is no other." **7.** All the people will believe in him. **8.** They will worship (offer reverence or honor) him, declaring, "This is God." **9.** Many who hoped for the Beloved will turn away (abandon their faith) to follow him. **10.** His false miracles (deceptive wonders) will spread across cities. **11.** He will set up his idol (image or representation) in every city, demanding worship. **12.** He will rule for three years, seven months, and twenty-seven days. **13.** A few faithful followers will remain, waiting for the Beloved's return. **14.** After 1,332 days, the Lord will return with His angels, casting Beliar and his forces into hell. **15.** The righteous (just and virtuous people) will rest, and the sun will be ashamed (embarrassed) before the Lord's glory. **16.** Those who rejected Beliar will be resurrected (brought back to life) in glory to serve and strengthen (help or support) those still on earth. **17.** They will ascend (rise up) with the Lord, leaving their bodies behind. **18.** The Beloved will rebuke (scold or reprimand) all things, and fire will destroy (consume by burning) the godless. **19.** The further words are recorded in the vision of Babylon. **20.** The remaining parts of the vision are in three parables (short stories or lessons) from my prophecy. **21.** The Beloved's descent (descent into the underworld) into Sheol (the underworld or realm of the dead) is written in the Psalms and other inspired writings. **22.** These prophecies are also found in Amos, Hosea, Micah, Joel, Nahum, Jonah, Obadiah, Habakkuk, Haggai, Malachi, Joseph the Just, and Daniel.

Chapter 5

1. Beliar, enraged by Isaiah's visions, sought revenge through Manasseh, sawing him in two with a wooden saw. **2.** As Isaiah was tortured, Belchira and the false prophets mocked and rejoiced. **3.** Belchira, with Mechembechus, mocked Isaiah's suffering. **4.** Belchira demanded Isaiah renounce his prophecies and praise Manasseh's wickedness. **5.** He also demanded Isaiah affirm the evil paths of Belchira and his associates. **6.** This was said as Isaiah began to be sawed. **7.** Isaiah, absorbed in a vision of the Lord, did not notice his torment. **8.** Belchira promised power if Isaiah renounced his faith. **9.** Isaiah cursed Belchira and his followers, declaring they could only harm his body. **10.** They sawed Isaiah in two, but his spirit remained steadfast. **11.** Manasseh, Belchira, and the people watched on, content in their evil ways. **12.** Before his death, Isaiah told the prophets to go into exile, for his mission was complete. **13.** Isaiah endured the sawing without crying, speaking only through the Holy Spirit. **14.** Beliar used Belchira and Manasseh to destroy Isaiah, as Sammael was angry with him for his prophecies about the Beloved. **15.** Isaiah's prophecy about Sammael's destruction angered the forces of darkness.

Chapter 6

1. Isaiah, son of Amoz, visited King Hezekiah in Jerusalem during his 20th year of reign, bringing a divine message (a revelation from God). **2.** Isaiah refused the seat offered, choosing to remain on the king's couch, displaying humility (lowness of spirit) and focus. **3.** Isaiah spoke faith-filled words to Hezekiah while Israel's leaders, eunuchs (castrated officials), and forty prophets listened attentively. **4.** Prophets and their disciples (followers) gathered from far and wide to honor Isaiah and hear his words. **5.** They hoped Isaiah would lay hands on them, enabling prophecy (divine foretelling) and affirming their calling. **6.** While Isaiah spoke, all present heard the sound of a door opening and the Holy Spirit's voice, confirming Isaiah's authority (power given by God). **7.** King Hezekiah summoned nearby prophets and leaders to join in this sacred moment (a special, holy time). **8.** Hearing the Spirit's voice, they worshipped on their knees, glorifying God Most High. **9.** They praised God for granting a heavenly doorway (a spiritual entrance) to reveal His glory to man. **10.** As Isaiah spoke in the Spirit, he fell silent, his mind transported beyond earthly awareness (being in a state beyond normal perception). **11.** Though his eyes remained open, Isaiah neither saw the men around him nor spoke, as his mind was lifted in the vision (a divine experience). **12.** He continued breathing but was enraptured (captivated) by the heavenly vision. **13.** The angel guiding Isaiah came from the seventh heaven (the highest divine realm), a messenger from the highest divine realm. **14.** Observers thought Isaiah had been taken up, though the prophets recognized his spiritual state (condition of being under divine influence). **15.** The vision Isaiah saw transcended (went beyond) the physical world, from a hidden, spiritual realm. **16.** Isaiah recounted (described) the vision to Hezekiah, Josab, and the gathered prophets. **17.** Only the righteous (virtuous), including Samna, Ijoaqem, and Asaph, sensed the Spirit's presence, while the rest were sent away.

Chapter 7

1. Isaiah shared his vision (supernatural experience) with Hezekiah, Josab, Micaiah, and the prophets. **2.** He saw an angel of indescribable (beyond description) glory, surpassing all others he had known. **3.** The angel lifted (raised or elevated) him, and Isaiah asked who he was and where they were going. **4.** The angel replied that Isaiah would learn after the vision (supernatural experience but not his name. **5.** Isaiah would return to his body but first witness (see) heavenly realms. **6.** Isaiah rejoiced (felt great joy or happiness) at the angel's kind words. **7.** The angel assured (gave confidence or certainty) him that greater beings would speak kindly to him. **8.** He revealed (disclosed) that Isaiah would see the Father in the seventh heaven. **9.** In the firmament (sky or heavens), Isaiah saw Sammael and Satan's hosts in conflict. **10.** The angel explained that heavenly battles mirror (reflect or resemble) earthly struggles. **11.** The angel revealed the war would end with the Messiah's triumph (victory or success). **12.** Isaiah ascended (rose or moved upward) to the first heaven, where he saw a throne surrounded by angels. **13.** Angels on the right had greater glory (magnificence) and offered louder praise. **14.** Their worship (reverence) ascended to God in the seventh heaven. **15.** In the second heaven, the throne and angels displayed (showed or revealed) even greater glory. **16.** Isaiah attempted (tried or made an effort) worship but was told to wait for the seventh heaven. **17.** The angel promised (assured or pledged) Isaiah a throne, garments, and a crown. **18.** In the third heaven, Isaiah saw unparalleled (unmatched or unequaled) purity and glory. **19.** Earthly concerns were absent, replaced by divine holiness (sacredness or purity). **20.** In the fourth heaven, Isaiah saw greater glory and louder praises (expressions of admiration or worship). **21.** The angel affirmed (confirmed or asserted) nothing is hidden from God in the heavens. **22.** Isaiah was promised full understanding (comprehension or insight) in the seventh heaven. **23.** In the fifth heaven, he saw a throne and angels of unmatched (without equal or comparison) glory. **24.** Isaiah's transformation (thorough or dramatic change) continued as he ascended, shedding earthly concerns. **25.** The angel revealed (disclosed or made known) that all actions are known in heaven. **26.** The praises (expressions of admiration or worship) of the angels grew louder and more glorious (magnificent, splendid) in each heaven. **27.** The glory (magnificence or splendor) of the sixth heaven surpassed (went beyond) all below it. **28.** In the seventh heaven, Isaiah saw the Father and His indescribable (beyond description) glory. **29.** Angels on the right shone brighter and praised God fervently (with intense emotion). **30.** The angel revealed that all who love God will ascend (rise or go up) to this glory. **31.** Isaiah praised the One seated on the throne, beyond all comprehension (understanding or grasp). **32.** He glorified the Creator, who bestowed (granted or given) such honor on the heavens. **33.** Isaiah saw glory (magnificence or splendor) magnified (made greater or more impressive) in every heaven as he continued ascending. **34.** The angel revealed heaven's perfect order, where none falter (hesitate or stumble) in worship. **35.** God's infinite (boundless) wisdom governs all creation, from heaven to earth. **36.** Isaiah rejoiced in the promise (assurance) of sharing in this eternal (lasting forever) glory. **37.** The journey ended in awe (reverential wonder or fear) of God's majesty and His gift of eternal life.

Chapter 8

1. The angel raised Isaiah to the sixth heaven, revealing a glory greater than any before. **2.** Angels of immense (huge) glory were seen there. **3.** The praise was holy, awe-inspiring (causing wonder), and magnificent (splendid). **4.** Isaiah sought (looked for) understanding of the heavenly vision. **5.** The angel explained he was not Isaiah's lord, but a fellow servant. **6.** Isaiah asked why there were no angels on the left side. **7.** The angel explained that the seventh heaven governed (ruled) the sixth. **8.** The voice of the Lord reigns (rules) supreme in all realms (areas). **9.** Isaiah was brought to witness (see) the glory of the Lord. **10.** God was transforming (changing) into human form and likeness for Isaiah to understand. **11.** Isaiah was granted (given) a unique (one of a kind) revelation. **12.** The angel confirmed (assured) this was part of Isaiah's divine destiny (purpose). **13.** Isaiah praised God for his vision, expressing (showing) gratitude (thankfulness). **14.** The angel spoke of the garments (clothing) awaiting those who ascend (rise) to the heavens. **15.** Isaiah would become equal (the same) to the angels of the seventh heaven. **16.** In the sixth heaven, all were united (joined) in praise. **17.** Isaiah harmonized (matched) his praise with the angels. **18.** Together, they glorified (honored) the Trinity in perfect harmony (agreement). **19.** The tone (sound) and nature (quality) of the praise were unique (distinct). **20.** The illumination (brightness) in this realm (domain) was unmatched (incomparable). **21.** Isaiah realized the light in the sixth heaven surpassed (exceeded) all before. **22.** Isaiah rejoiced (celebrated), praising God for bestowing (giving) such light on the faithful. **23.** Isaiah longed (desired) to stay in the heavenly realm. **24.** The earthly world seemed dark and distant (far) in comparison. **25.** The angel reassured (comforted) Isaiah that the glory of the seventh heaven was beyond measure (immeasurable). **26.** Garments, thrones (seats of power), and crowns awaited the righteous (virtuous) in the seventh heaven. **27.** The angel explained Isaiah's time on earth wasn't yet complete (fulfilled). **28.** Isaiah was troubled (disturbed) but comforted (reassured) by the angel.

Chapter 9

1. And he took me into the air of the seventh heaven, and I heard a voice saying, "How far will he ascend that dwelleth (lives) in the flesh?" And I feared (was afraid) and trembled (shook in fear). **2.** And when I trembled, I heard another voice being sent forth (coming forth), saying, "It is permitted (allowed) to the holy Isaiah to ascend hither (here); for here is his garment (clothing)." **3.** And I asked the angel, "Who is he who forbade (prevented) me and who is he who permitted (allowed) me to ascend?" **4.** And he said, "He who forbade thee is he who is over the praise-giving (worship) of the sixth heaven." **5.** "He who permitted thee is thy Lord God, the Lord Christ, who will be called 'Jesus' in the world, but His name thou canst not hear till thou hast ascended (gone up) out of thy body." **6.** And he raised me up into the seventh heaven, and I saw there a wonderful light and innumerable (countless) angels. **7.** And there I saw the holy Abel and all the righteous (just people). **8.** And there I saw Enoch and all who were with him, stripped (removed) of the garments of the flesh (body), and in their garments of the upper world (heaven), like angels, standing in great glory. **9.** But they sat not on their thrones (seats of power), nor were their crowns of glory (symbols of honor) on them. **10.** And I asked the angel, "How is it that they have received the garments, but not the thrones and crowns?" **11.** And he said, "Crowns and thrones of glory they do not receive, till the Beloved will descent (come down) in the form in which you will see Him descent into the world in the last days, the Lord, who will be called Christ." **12.** "Nevertheless, they see and know whose will be thrones, and whose the crowns when He has descended and been made in your form, and they will think He is flesh and is a man." **13.** "And the god of that world will stretch forth (extend) his hand against the Son, and they will crucify Him on a tree, and will slay (kill) Him not knowing who He is." **14.** "And thus His descent, as you will see, will be hidden (concealed) even from the heavens, so that it will not be known who

He is." **15.** "And when He hath plundered (defeated) the angel of death, He will ascend on the third day, and remain in that world five hundred and forty-five days." **16.** "And then many of the righteous will ascend with Him, whose spirits do not receive their garments till the Lord Christ ascends and they ascend with Him." **17.** "Then indeed they will receive their garments, thrones, and crowns when He has ascended into the seventh heaven." **18.** And I said unto him that which I had asked in the third heaven. **19.** "Show me how everything in that world is here made known." **20.** And while I was still speaking, one of the angels, more glorious (majestic) than the angel who raised me, showed me a book, not like a book of this world, and gave it to me to read. **21.** I said, "In truth, there is nothing hidden (concealed) in the seventh heaven, which is done in this world." **22.** And I saw many garments, thrones, and crowns laid up (stored). **23.** And I asked, "Whose are these garments, thrones, and crowns?" **24.** And he said, "These garments many from that world will receive, believing in the words of That One, who shall be named as I told thee, and will observe (follow) and believe in His cross." **25.** And I saw a certain One standing, whose glory surpassed all others, and His glory was great and wonderful. **26.** After I saw Him, all the righteous and angels whom I had seen came to Him. Adam, Abel, Seth, and all the righteous drew near and worshipped, praising Him with one voice, and I also gave praise with them. **27.** Then all the angels drew nigh (near) and worshipped and gave praise. **28.** And I was transformed (changed) and became like an angel. **29.** The angel said to me, "Worship this One," and I worshipped and praised. **30.** The angel said, "This is the Lord of all the praise-givings which thou hast seen." **31.** And while he was still speaking, I saw another Glorious One, like Him, and the righteous drew nigh and worshipped, and I praised with them, but my glory was not transformed into theirs. **32.** And the angels drew near and worshipped Him. **33.** I saw the Lord and the second angel, and they were standing. **34.** The second was on the left of my Lord, and I asked, "Who is this?" The angel said, "Worship Him, for He is the angel of the Holy Spirit." **35.** I saw great glory, and I could not see, nor could the angel with me, nor all the angels worshipping my Lord. **36.** But I saw the righteous beholding (gazing at) with great power the glory of that One. **37.** My Lord drew nigh and said, "See how it is given to thee to see God, and power is given to the angel with thee." **38.** I saw my Lord and the angel of the Spirit worship, and they both praised God. **39.** All the righteous drew near and worshipped. **40.** The angels drew near and worshipped and praised.

Chapter 10

1. Then I heard praises from the six heavens rising up to be heard by all (universally). **2.** These praises were directed to the Glorious One, whose brilliance was beyond my comprehension (understanding). **3.** I was able to hear and witness the praises being offered to Him. **4.** Both the Lord and the angel of the Spirit were observing and listening to everything. **5.** The praises ascending from the six heavens are not only heard but also visible (able to be seen). **6.** The angel guiding me explained: "This is the Most High, dwelling in His holy domain (realm), resting in His holy ones. He will be called the Father of the Lord by the righteous (virtuous) through the Holy Spirit." **7.** I heard the voice of the Most High, the Father of my Lord, speaking to Christ, who would be known as Jesus (the Savior). **8.** "Go forth and descend through all the heavens, down to the firmament (sky) and the world below (earth). You will reach the angel in Sheol (the underworld), but not Haguel (the ruler of this realm)." **9.** "You will take on the form of all who dwell in the five heavens." **10.** "Be cautious (careful) to take on the appearance of the angels in the firmament and in Sheol." **11.** "No angels in that realm will recognize (identify) that you are with Me, from the seven heavens, and with their angels." **12.** "They will remain unaware (not know) of who you are until I call to the heavens and their angels, summoning (calling) them to the sixth heaven for judgment. Then you will destroy the rulers and the gods of that world." **13.** "They have denied (refused) Me, claiming that they are the only ones, and there is no other." **14.** "Afterward, you will ascend (rise) from the angels of death to your rightful place (seat of honor), without changing in each heaven, but in glory (majesty) you will rise and take your seat at My right hand." **15.** "The princes (leaders) and authorities of that world will worship (adore) You." **16.** These were the commands I heard from the Great Glory (divine power) given to my Lord. **17.** I saw my Lord move

538

from the seventh heaven to the sixth. **18.** The angel guiding me said, "Understand, Isaiah, and observe how the Lord's transformation and descent (coming down) will unfold." **19.** I saw that when the angels in the sixth heaven saw Him, they praised (worshipped) Him because He had not changed to resemble their form. I also praised (worshipped) Him with them. **20.** When He descended to the fifth heaven, He took on the likeness (appearance) of the angels there. But they did not praise (worship) Him, as He appeared like them. **21.** Then, He descended to the fourth heaven and assumed (took on) the form of the angels there. **22.** The angels there did not praise or acknowledge (recognize) Him, as His form matched theirs. **23.** Again, I saw Him descend to the third heaven, assuming the form of its angels. **24.** The gatekeepers (guards) of the third heaven asked for the password, and the Lord gave it to them so that He would not be recognized (known). They saw Him but did not praise (worship) Him, for He appeared like them. **25.** He descended further into the second heaven, giving the necessary password, and the gatekeepers responded (replied). **26.** He took on the likeness (appearance) of the angels in the second heaven, and they did not praise (worship) Him, as He looked just like them. **27.** When He reached the first heaven, He again gave the password, taking on the form of the angels who stood at the left of the throne. They did not praise or acknowledge (recognize) Him. **28.** However, no one questioned me due to the angel who accompanied (guided) me. **29.** He then descended into the firmament, the realm (domain) of this world's ruler, where He gave the password to those on the left. His form was like theirs, and they did not praise (worship) Him. Instead, they were in conflict (fighting) with each other, consumed by envy (jealousy) and petty strife (arguments). **30.** I saw Him continue His descent, taking on the form of the angels of the air, appearing like one of them. **31.** He did not give a password here, as the angels were fighting and plundering (stealing) each other.

Chapter 11

1. Afterward, I saw, and the angel guiding me said, "Understand, Isaiah son of Amoz; this is why I was sent by God." **2.** I saw Mary, a Virgin from the family of David, betrothed (engaged) to Joseph, a carpenter from David's lineage (ancestry). **3.** It was discovered that she was with child, and Joseph planned to separate (break off their engagement) from her quietly. **4.** But the angel appeared to Joseph, and he kept Mary, not separating from her. **5.** Joseph honored Mary's virginity (her state of being a virgin) and did not approach (have relations with) her, even though she was with child. **6.** He lived apart from her for two months. **7.** After two months, Mary saw a small infant, which astonished (surprised) her. **8.** Her womb (belly) returned to its prior state, as though she had never been pregnant. **9.** Joseph asked, "What astonished you?" He saw the infant and praised God. **10.** A voice told them, "Do not tell anyone about this vision." **11.** News of the infant spread in Bethlehem. **12.** Some claimed, "Mary gave birth before her marriage, after only two months." **13.** Others questioned, "She did not give birth; no midwife (childbirth assistant) came, nor did we hear cries of labor (the pains of childbirth)." **14.** They went to Nazareth in Galilee. **15.** I saw, O Hezekiah and Josab, my son, that this event escaped the notice of all the heavens (spiritual realms) and gods of this world. **16.** In Nazareth, He nursed (fed) as a baby, to avoid being recognized. **17.** As He grew, He performed great signs (wonders) and wonders in Israel and Jerusalem. **18.** The adversary (enemy) stirred the Israelites against Him. They handed Him over to be crucified, and He descended (went down) to Sheol (the underworld). **19.** I witnessed His crucifixion (execution by cross) in Jerusalem. **20.** On the third day, He rose again and stayed on earth for some days. **21.** The angel said to me, "Understand, Isaiah," and I saw when He sent out the Twelve Apostles and ascended (rose to heaven). **22.** I saw Him in the firmament (sky), but He didn't appear like the angels. All the angels and Satans (evil spirits) worshiped Him. **23.** The angels sorrowed (felt sadness), asking, "How did our Lord descend among us, and we did not recognize His glory (greatness)?" **24.** He ascended to the second heaven, where angels worshiped Him. **25.** The third, fourth, and fifth heavens also praised Him. **26.** He remained unchanged (in form). **27.** I saw Him ascend into the sixth heaven, where they worshiped Him. **28.** In all the heavens, the praise for Him increased. **29.** He ascended into the seventh heaven, where all the righteous (just people) and angels praised Him. He sat at the right hand of the Great Glory (God). **30.** I saw

the angel of the Holy Spirit seated on the left hand. **31.** The angel told me, "Isaiah, you have seen what no human has seen. You will return to your body until your days are completed." **32.** Isaiah shared these things with those around him, and they praised. He spoke to King Hezekiah, saying, "I have spoken these things." **33.** The end of the world and the fulfillment of this vision will come in the final generations. **34.** Isaiah made Hezekiah swear not to reveal this to Israel or transcribe (write down) it. **35.** "You will read of these things, and in the Holy Spirit, you must watch for your heavenly rewards." **36.** Because of these visions, Sammael (Satan) sawed (cut into pieces) Isaiah in two at the hands of Manasseh. (Samael: an angel or demon of death) **37.** Hezekiah passed these things to Manasseh in the twenty-sixth year. **38.** Manasseh did not heed (pay attention to) them and became a servant of Satan, leading to his downfall. **39.** Hezekiah ordered these things be written and kept safe, but they were ignored. **40.** Manasseh, in his wickedness (evilness), disregarded (ignored) the vision, and Israel followed him in sin. **41.** These words were meant to guide Israel, but they were ignored. **42.** Here ends the vision of Isaiah the prophet, along with his ascension.

83 – Baruch 1

1. This is the text of the book written in Babylon by Baruch, son of Neraiah, son of Mahseiah, son of Zedekiah, son of Hasadiah, son of Hilkiah. **2.** It was written in the fifth year, on the seventh day of the month, at the time when the Chaldeans (Babylonians) had captured Jerusalem and destroyed it by fire. **3.** Baruch read aloud the contents of this book to Jeconiah, the son of Jehoiakim, the king of Judah, and to all the people who had gathered to hear the reading. **4.** He read to the nobles (important leaders), the king's sons, and the elders (older, respected leaders), as well as to all the people—whether great or small—who lived in Babylon by the river Sud. **5.** Upon hearing the words, they wept, fasted (abstained from food), and prayed before the Lord. **6.** They gathered as much money as each could afford, **7.** and sent it to Jerusalem to the priest Jehoiakim, son of Hilkiah, son of Shallum, and to the other priests and the people who were with him in Jerusalem. **8.** On the tenth day of the month of Sivan (a month in the Hebrew calendar), they sent the sacred vessels (ritual objects) of the house of the Lord, which had been taken from the temple, to be returned to Judah. These were silver vessels that King Zedekiah, son of Josiah, king of Judah, had made. **9.** This was after King Nebuchadnezzar of Babylon had carried Jeconiah away from Jerusalem to Babylon, along with the princes, the craftsmen (skilled workers), the nobles, and all the common people. **10.** They wrote: "We are sending you money to pay for burnt offerings (sacrificial offerings), sin offerings (offerings made to atone for sin), and incense (aromatic substances burned in worship). Prepare sacrifices and offer them on the altar of the Lord our God. **11.** And pray for the long life of King Nebuchadnezzar of Babylon and his son Belshazzar, that they may reign on earth as long as the heavens endure. **12.** Pray that the Lord may give us strength and enlighten (give wisdom or insight) our eyes, so that we may live under the protection of King Nebuchadnezzar and his son Belshazzar, and serve them for a long time, winning their favor." **13.** Also pray to the Lord our God for us, for we have sinned against Him, and His anger and fury (strong wrath) have not yet turned away from us. **14.** Finally, you must read this book publicly in the house of the Lord on the appointed feast days and at other appropriate times. **15.** You are to declare: "Salvation belongs to the Lord; we are covered with shame, just as we are today, the people of Judah and the inhabitants of Jerusalem, **16.** including our kings, princes, priests, prophets, and ancestors, **17.** because we have sinned before the Lord. **18.** We have disobeyed (rejected) Him and have not listened to the voice of the Lord our God, who told us to follow the commandments (instructions) He gave us. **19.** From the day the Lord brought our ancestors out of Egypt until today, we have been disobedient (unfaithful) to the Lord our God, refusing to listen to His voice. **20.** We are still not free from the calamities (disasters) and curses (negative judgments) that the Lord pronounced through His servant Moses when He brought our ancestors out of Egypt to give us a land flowing with milk and honey (a prosperous and fertile land). **21.** We have not obeyed the voice of the Lord our God, nor followed the words of the prophets He sent to us. **22.** Instead, each of us has followed the stubbornness (resistance to change) of our evil hearts, serving foreign gods and doing things that are displeasing to the Lord our God.

84 – Baruch 2

1. And so the Lord has executed the judgment (punishment) He declared upon us, upon our leaders who ruled Israel, upon our kings and officials (leaders), and upon the people of Israel and Judah. 2. What He did to Jerusalem has never been seen before across all the earth, in fulfillment (as foretold) of what was written in the Law of Moses. 3. We were reduced to the horrifying act of eating the flesh of our own children. 4. Moreover, He handed them over to the control (power) of all the kingdoms surrounding us, making us a disgrace (disrespect) and a curse among all the peoples among whom the Lord scattered (spread) us. 5. Instead of being in control, we were made slaves, because we sinned against the Lord our God by not heeding (listening to) His voice. 6. True justice belongs to the Lord; we and our ancestors are covered with shame, as we bear today. 7. All the calamities (disasters) the Lord promised us have now come upon us. 8. Yet we have not sought to win the Lord's favor by each of us turning away from the evil desires of our hearts. 9. Therefore, the Lord has seen our wrongdoings and has brought disaster upon us, for the Lord is righteous in all that He has commanded us to do. 10. And we did not listen to His voice or follow the commands (instructions) He gave us. 11. Now, Lord, God of Israel, who brought Your people out of Egypt with great strength, with signs and wonders, with mighty power and outstretched (extended) arm, earning Yourself a name like no other, 12. We have sinned, we have defiled (polluted) Your holy things; Lord our God, we have broken all Your laws. 13. Let Your anger turn away from us, for we are but a small remnant (remaining part) among the nations where You have scattered us. 14. Listen, Lord, to our prayers and pleas (requests); rescue (save) us for Your own sake and let us find favor (approval) in the eyes of those who have exiled (forced to leave) us. 15. So that all the world may know that You are the Lord our God, since Israel and his descendants bear Your name. 16. Look down from Your holy dwelling place (heaven) and remember us; incline (bend) Your ear and listen to us, 17. Open Your eyes, Lord, and see; the dead in the grave (Sheol), whose breath has departed, cannot give You glory or honor, 18. But those who are afflicted (suffering)—those bowed down in pain, weak in body, and starving in soul—are the ones who give You glory and honor, Lord. 19. We do not plead for mercy based on the righteousness (goodness) of our ancestors or our kings, but purely on Your goodness, Lord our God. 20. No, You have poured out Your anger and wrath (fury) upon us, as You warned through Your prophets when they said, 21. "The Lord says: Submit (bow) to the king of Babylon, and you will remain in the land I gave to your forefathers." 22. But if you refuse (do not) to listen to the Lord and serve the king of Babylon, 23. I will silence the sounds of joy and gladness, the voices of bridegroom and bride, in the towns of Judah and the streets of Jerusalem, and the entire land will become a desolate wasteland (empty), with no inhabitants. 24. But we would not obey Your voice or serve the king of Babylon, and so You brought about what You had threatened through Your prophets: the bones of our kings and ancestors would be dragged from their graves (tombs). 25. They were thrown out into the heat of the day and the frost of the night, and people died in terrible agony—by famine, sword, and plague (disease). 26. And so, because of the evil (sin) of the House of Israel and the House of Judah, You have made this House (temple) that bears Your name into what it is today. 27. Yet, Lord our God, You have dealt with us according to Your great mercy (compassion) and boundless (limitless) love, 28. Just as You promised through Your servant Moses, when You instructed him to write Your Law in the presence of the Israelites, saying, 29. "If you do not listen to My voice, this vast and innumerable (countless) nation will surely become a small remnant scattered among the nations. 30. For I knew that they would be stubborn (unyielding) people who would not listen to Me. But in the land of their exile (captivity), they will recognize (acknowledge) their condition 31. And acknowledge that I am the Lord their God. I will give them a heart to understand and ears to hear, 32. And they will praise My name in their exile, they will remember Me, 33. They will no longer be stubborn, and remembering what happened to their ancestors who sinned against Me, they will turn away from their evil deeds. 34. Then I will bring them back to the land I promised on oath (sworn promise)

to their forefathers—Abraham, Isaac, and Jacob—and I will restore them as rulers in it. I will increase their numbers, and they will no longer decrease. 35. And I will make an everlasting (forever) covenant (agreement) with them, that I will be their God and they will be My people. Never again will I expel (remove) My people Israel from the land I have given them."

85 – Ethiopic 4 Baruch

Chapter 1

1. When Israel was captured by the Chaldeans (Babylonians), God told Jeremiah: "Leave this city with Baruch (his scribe); I will destroy it because of its people's sins (wrongdoings)." 2. "Your prayers are like a strong pillar (support) and an unbreakable wall (protection)." 3. "Depart before the Chaldean army surrounds it." 4. Jeremiah said: "Lord, let me speak." 5. The Lord replied: "Speak, my chosen servant." 6. Jeremiah asked: "Will you let the Chaldean king (ruler) boast: 'I defeated God's holy city'?" 7. He added: "If it is your will, destroy it by your hand." 8. The Lord answered: "Leave with Baruch, for I will destroy it because of their sins." 9. "The Chaldeans cannot enter unless I open the gates." 10. "Tell Baruch, and at the sixth hour (midnight), go to the city walls." 11. "I will show you that they cannot enter without my intervention (action)." 12. After this, the Lord departed from Jeremiah.

Chapter 2

1. Jeremiah told Baruch and entered God's temple (sacred place) with torn garments and dust on his head, mourning (deep sorrow). 2. Baruch cried: "Father Jeremiah, what are you doing? What sin (wrongdoing) have the people committed?" 3. Jeremiah sprinkled dust and prayed for forgiveness when the people sinned. 4. Baruch asked: "What does this mean?" 5. Jeremiah said: "Do not tear your garments—tear your hearts (repent deeply)! Do not draw water for the troughs (animal containers); weep and fill them with tears! The Lord will no longer show mercy (compassion) to this people." 6. Baruch asked: "What has happened?" 7. Jeremiah said: "God is giving the city to the Chaldeans (Babylonians), and the people will go captive (prisoner) to Babylon (ancient city)." 8. Baruch tore his garments (sign of grief) and asked: "Who revealed this?" 9. Jeremiah replied: "Stay with me until the sixth hour (midnight), and you will see it is true." 10. They remained in the altar (sacred place) area, weeping in torn garments.

Chapter 3

1. And when the hour of the night arrived, as the Lord had told Jeremiah, they came up together on the walls of the city, Jeremiah and Baruch. 2. Behold, a sound of trumpets; angels (messengers) appeared from heaven with torches (light) and set them on the city walls. 3. Jeremiah and Baruch wept (cried), saying: Now we know the word is true! 4. Jeremiah begged (pleaded) the angels: Do not destroy the city yet, until I speak to the Lord. 5. The Lord spoke to the angels: Do not destroy the city until I speak to my chosen (selected) one, Jeremiah. 6. Jeremiah said: I beg you, Lord, bid (order) me to speak in your presence. 7. And the Lord said: Speak, my chosen Jeremiah. 8. Jeremiah said: Now we know you are giving the city to its enemies, and they will take the people to Babylon (exile). What should I do with the holy vessels (sacred items) of the temple? 10. The Lord said: Place them in the earth, saying: Hear, Earth, the voice of your creator who formed you in abundance (great quantity) of waters, who sealed (marked) you with seven seals for seven epochs (ages). After this, you will receive your ornaments (decorations). 11. Guard the vessels until the gathering of the beloved (faithful). 12. Jeremiah asked: What should I do for Abimelech the Ethiopian, who has shown kindness (help) to me? 13. He rescued me from the miry pit (mud); I don't want him to witness the city's destruction. Be merciful to him and spare his grief (sadness). 14. The Lord said: Send him to Agrippa's vineyard (farm), and I'll hide him until the people return to the city. 15. Jeremiah, go with your people to Babylon, preach (teach) until they return. 16. Leave Baruch here until I speak with him. 17. After saying this, the Lord ascended (went up) to heaven. 18. Jeremiah and Baruch entered the holy place and placed the vessels in the earth as instructed. 19. The earth immediately swallowed (took in) them. 20. They sat and wept. 21. In the morning, Jeremiah sent Abimelech, saying: Take a basket, go to Agrippa's estate (property), and bring figs

(fruit) for the sick, as the Lord's favor (blessing) is on you. **22.** Jeremiah sent him away; Abimelech went as instructed.

Chapter 4

1. And when morning came, the Chaldeans (Babylonians) surrounded the city. **2.** The great angel (messenger) trumpeted, saying: Enter, Chaldeans; the gate is open for you. **3.** Let the king enter and take all the people captive (prisoners). **4.** Jeremiah took the temple keys (sacred objects), went outside the city, and threw them before the sun, saying: Sun, guard the keys until the Lord asks for them. **5.** We are unworthy (undeserving) to keep them, for we are unfaithful (not loyal). **6.** While Jeremiah wept for the people, they took him and the others to Babylon (exile). **7.** Baruch put dust on his head (symbol of mourning) and lamented (mourned): Jerusalem is devastated (destroyed) because of our sins (wrongdoings) and those of the people. **8.** Let not the lawless (unrighteous) boast (brag), saying: "We conquered the city by might (strength)"; it was given to you because of our sins. **9.** God will have mercy (show compassion) on us and bring us back, but you will not survive (live). **10.** Blessed (favored) are our fathers, Abraham, Isaac, and Jacob, for they did not see the city's destruction. **11.** Baruch left the city weeping (crying), saying: Grieving (sorrowful) for you, Jerusalem, I have gone. **12.** He sat in a tomb (burial place), where angels came and explained (taught) all the Lord's revelations (messages) to him.

Chapter 5

1. Abimelech took the figs in the burning heat (intense sun) and sat under a tree to rest. **2.** He fell asleep, resting his head on the basket of figs, and slept for 66 years. **3.** When he awoke, he felt heavy-headed, (dull) due to insufficient sleep. **4.** He uncovered the basket and found the figs dripping milk (liquid). **5.** He wanted to sleep longer, but feared being late, which might upset Jeremiah. **6.** He decided to continue, as there's toil (hard work) every day. **7.** He went into Jerusalem but didn't recognize it, nor did he find his family. **8.** He said: The Lord be blessed, for a trance (daze) has come over me! **9.** This is not Jerusalem, and I lost my way due to the mountain road (path) and heavy-headedness. **10.** Jeremiah will find it unbelievable (incredible) that I lost my way. **11.** After searching, he found the city and admitted he had lost his way. **12.** He returned, searched again, but found no one, saying: The Lord be blessed, for a trance has come over me! **13.** He sat down, grieving (sorrowful), unsure of where to go. **14.** He put down the basket and waited for the trance to end. **15.** An old man came from the field, and Abimelech asked which city this was. **16.** The old man replied: It is Jerusalem. **17.** Abimelech asked about Jeremiah, Baruch, and the people, but couldn't find them. **18.** The old man said: Are you not from this city, remembering Jeremiah after so long? **19.** Jeremiah is in Babylon with the people, preaching the word to them. **20.** Abimelech laughed at the old man, doubting the people were taken to Babylon. **21.** Even if torrents (rains) had come, it hasn't been time for them to go. **22.** How long has it been since Jeremiah sent me for figs? **23.** I sat under a tree, rested, and found the figs dripping milk when I awoke. **24.** You claim they are in Babylon but take the figs and see! **25.** He uncovered the basket for the old man, who saw the figs dripping milk. **28.** The old man said: You are righteous, and God brought this trance upon you to spare you from seeing the city's destruction. **29.** It's been 66 years since the people were taken to Babylon. **30.** Look at the fields; the crops aren't ripe. **31.** The figs aren't in season, so be enlightened (understand). **32.** Abimelech cried out, saying: I bless you, God of heaven and earth, the Rest (comfort) of the righteous! **33.** He asked: What month is it? **34.** The old man replied: Nisan (Abib). **35.** Abimelech gave him some figs and said: May God illuminate (guide) your way to the city above, Jerusalem.

Chapter 6

1. After this, Abimelech left the city and prayed to the Lord. **2.** An angel of the Lord took him by the right hand and brought him to Baruch, who was sitting in a tomb (grave). **3.** They wept and kissed each other. **4.** Baruch saw the figs in Abimelech's basket. **5.** Baruch prayed: **6.** You are the God who rewards (gives recompense) those who love you. Prepare, heart, and rejoice, saying: "Your grief has turned to joy; the Sufficient One (God) is coming to deliver you." **7.** Revive (renew) in your faith and believe you will live! **8.** The figs are 66 years old, not shriveled (withered), and dripping milk (liquid). **9.** So will it be with your flesh (body) if you follow the angel's commands. **10.** He who preserved

(kept safe) the figs will preserve (keep safe) you. **11.** Baruch said to Abimelech: Let us pray to know how to send word to Jeremiah in Babylon. **12.** Baruch prayed: Lord, our strength (power) is the light (guidance) from your mouth. **13.** We beg (ask earnestly) your goodness — hear us and give us knowledge (understanding). **14.** How shall we send this report to Jeremiah? **15.** While praying, an angel came and told Baruch: Do not worry; an eagle (symbol of messenger) will come tomorrow, and you will direct him to Jeremiah. **16.** Write a letter to the Israelites: Let the stranger (foreigner) among you be set apart (isolated) for 15 days; after that, I will lead you back to your city, says the Lord. **17.** Those who do not separate (distinguish) from Babylon will not enter the city. **18.** The angel departed (left). **19.** Baruch bought papyrus (writing material) and ink, writing a letter to Jeremiah. **20.** He wrote: Rejoice, for God has not left us grieving for the destroyed city. **21.** The Lord has had compassion (mercy) on our tears and remembered the covenant (promise) with our fathers. **22.** He sent his angel to me, telling me these words. **23.** The Lord, who led us out of Egypt, says: Because you did not keep my ordinances (rules) and were proud, I delivered you to Babylon. **24.** If you listen to my voice, I will bring those who hear it out of Babylon. But those who do not listen will remain strangers to Jerusalem and Babylon. **25.** You will test them with the water of the Jordan (river); those who do not listen will be exposed (revealed) — this is the sign of the great seal (seal of authority).

Chapter 7

1. Baruch rose, left the tomb, and found the eagle sitting outside. **2.** The eagle spoke in a human voice: Hail, Baruch, steward (guardian) of the faith. **3.** Baruch said: You are chosen from all the birds of heaven, tell me why you are here. **4.** The eagle replied: I was sent to carry any message you wish. **5.** Baruch asked: Can you carry this message to Jeremiah in Babylon? **6.** The eagle said: Yes, this is why I was sent. **7.** Baruch gave the eagle the letter and 15 figs (fruit), tied them to its neck, and sent it with peace. **8.** He said: Do not be like the raven Noah sent, which never returned, but like the dove that brought back a report to the righteous. **9.** Take this message to Jeremiah and those in bondage (captivity), that it may be well with you. **10.** Even if all the birds want to fight you, the Lord will give you strength. **11.** Do not turn aside but go straight in God's power and glory. **12.** The eagle flew to Babylon, rested outside the city, and waited for Jeremiah. **13.** Jeremiah, with people, was burying a corpse outside the city. **14.** (Jeremiah had asked King Nebuchadnezzar for a burial place for his people, and the king granted it.) **15.** They came to the eagle, weeping. **16.** The eagle cried out: Jeremiah, chosen servant of God, gather the people to hear the message from Baruch and Abimelech. **17.** Jeremiah glorified God, gathered the people, and went to the eagle. **18.** The eagle landed on the corpse, and it revived. **19.** (This happened to increase their belief.) **20.** The people were astounded, saying: This is the God who appeared through Moses in the wilderness, now appearing through the eagle. **21.** The eagle said: Jeremiah, untie the letter and read it to the people. **22.** Jeremiah untied the letter, and the people wept, saying: Tell us what to do so we can return to our city. **23.** Jeremiah said: Follow the letter's instructions, and the Lord will lead us back. **24.** Jeremiah wrote to Baruch: Do not neglect your prayers for us, so God may direct our way from the lawless king. **25.** You are righteous before God, and He spared you from seeing the affliction of the people in Babylon. **26.** It is like a father with his son, who suffers punishment, and those who console him hide their faces. **27.** God took pity on you and spared you from seeing the people's suffering. **28.** Since we arrived, grief has not left us for 66 years. **29.** Many times, I found people hung by Nebuchadnezzar, crying out: "Have mercy on us, God-ZAR!" **30.** I grieved for them, especially because they called on a foreign god. **31.** I remembered the festivals in Jerusalem before our captivity, and I wept. **32.** Pray for this people, so they may listen to me and follow God's decrees. **33.** They kept us in subjection, asking us to sing the songs of Zion. **34.** We replied: How can we sing for you in a foreign land? **35.** Jeremiah tied the letter to the eagle's neck, saying: Go in peace, and may the Lord watch over us. **36.** The eagle returned to Jerusalem with the letter. Baruch read it, wept, and kissed it when he heard about the people's afflictions. **37.** Jeremiah gave figs to the sick and taught them to abstain from Babylonian pollution.

Chapter 8

1. The Lord brought the people out of Babylon. 2. He told Jeremiah to lead those who desire (want) the Lord to forsake (abandon) Babylon's ways. 3. Those who have taken spouses (wives or husbands) from them should be led to Jerusalem, but others should not be. 4. Jeremiah spoke, and the people came to the Jordan. 5. Half of them refused to listen and chose to keep their wives. 6. They crossed and came to Jerusalem. 7. Jeremiah, Baruch, and Abimelech declared (announced) that no one joined with the Babylonians should enter the city. 8. They decided to return to Babylon. 9. The Babylonians stopped them, saying they could not enter because they had left secretly (without notice). 10. They swore (vowed) not to receive them, as they had deserted (left) them. 11. The people returned and built a city called 'Samaria.' 12. Jeremiah told them to repent (change their ways), for the angel of righteousness would lead them to an exalted (high, honored) place.

Chapter 9

1. Those with Jeremiah rejoiced, offering sacrifices for nine days. 2. On the tenth, Jeremiah alone offered sacrifice. 3. He prayed: Holy, holy, holy, fragrant aroma (pleasant scent) of living trees, true light that enlightens me until I ascend to you. 4. For your mercy, I beg you—for the sweet voice of the seraphim (angelic beings), I beg—for another fragrant aroma. 5. May Michael, archangel (chief angel) of righteousness, be my guardian until the righteous enter. 6. I beg you, almighty Lord, unbegotten (not created) and incomprehensible (unable to be fully understood), in whom all judgment was hidden before creation. 7. After this, while standing with Baruch and Abimelech, Jeremiah became as if dead. 8. Baruch and Abimelech wept, saying: Woe to us! Our father Jeremiah has departed! 9. The people heard and saw Jeremiah as dead and mourned. 10. They tore their garments and wept. 11. They prepared to bury him. 12. Then a voice said: Do not bury him, his soul is returning to his body! 13. They waited for three days. 14. After three days, his soul returned, and he rose, proclaiming: Glorify God and the Son of God, messiah Jesus, the light of all ages. 15. After 477 more years, he will come to earth. 16. The tree of life will cause unfruitful trees to bear fruit. 17. The haughty (arrogant) trees that boasted will wither and be judged. 18. Crimson will turn white as wool; snow will be blackened; sweet waters will become salty, and salty waters sweet. 19. He will bless the isles (islands), making them fruitful. 20. He will choose twelve apostles to spread the word and fill the hungry souls. 21. The people grew angry when Jeremiah spoke of the Son of God, saying it was like Isaiah's words. 22. They plotted to stone him instead of killing him as they did Isaiah. 23. Baruch and Abimelech were grieved, wanting to hear the full mysteries. 24. Jeremiah told them: Be silent, for they cannot kill me until I describe everything I saw. 25. He asked for a stone. 26. He set it up and said: Light of the ages, make this stone like me until I describe everything. 27. The stone, by God's command, took on the appearance of Jeremiah. 28. They stoned the stone, thinking it was Jeremiah. 29. Jeremiah told Baruch and Abimelech all the mysteries, then stood among the people. 30. The stone cried out: Why do you stone me, thinking I am Jeremiah? Behold, Jeremiah is here! 31. They rushed upon him with stones, and his ministry was fulfilled. 32. Baruch and Abimelech buried him, placing the stone on his tomb with the inscription: This is the stone that was the ally of Jeremiah.

86 – The Letter of Jeremiah

1. Because of the sins you have committed before God, you will be taken as exiles to Babylon (a powerful empire in Mesopotamia), under Nebuchadnezzar (the king of Babylon).2. Therefore, when you arrive in Babylon, you will remain there for many years, for a long time, even up to seven generations; after that, I will bring you back to your land in peace.3. In Babylon, you will see gods made of silver and gold and wood, which people carry on their shoulders, and these idols (false gods) make the nations afraid.4. Be careful not to become like the people of Babylon or let the fear of these idols possess you,5. when you see large crowds of people worshiping them. Instead, say in your heart, "It is you, O LORD, whom we must worship."6. For my angel (a messenger of God) is with you, and he is watching over your lives.7. These idols are crafted by carpenters (woodworkers) and overlaid with gold and silver, but they are false and cannot speak.8. People take gold and create crowns for the heads of their gods, like ornaments for a young woman who loves jewelry.9. Sometimes, priests secretly take gold and silver from these idols and use it for themselves,10. or even give some of it to the prostitutes (temple workers) on the terrace (upper part of a building or structure). They dress up these gods with garments like humans—these idols of silver, gold, and wood—11. which cannot save themselves from rust and decay. When their clothing is purple (royal robes),12. their faces are wiped clean because of the dust from the temple, which is thick upon them.13. One of these idols holds a scepter (a staff of power) like a judge, but it cannot punish anyone who offends it.14. Another holds a dagger in its right hand and an axe, but it cannot defend itself from war or robbers.15. From this, you can clearly see that these are not gods, so do not fear them.16. Just as someone's dish is useless when it is broken,17. so are their gods when they are placed in the temples. Their eyes are filled with the dust from the feet of those who enter. And just as the gates are locked and secured to protect against thieves,18. so do the priests lock up the temples of these idols to prevent them from being stolen.19. They light more lamps for these idols than they light for themselves, though their gods cannot see any of them.20. These idols are like a beam of the temple, but their hearts, it is said, are eaten away by crawling creatures from the earth, devouring them and their garments, without them even noticing.21. Bats, swallows, and birds perch on their bodies and heads, and even cats.22. From this, you will know that these are not gods, so do not fear them.23. The gold that covers them, for decoration, will not shine unless someone wipes off the tarnish. Even when they were being made, they did not feel it.24. They are bought at great expense, but there is no breath (life) in them.25. Having no feet, they are carried on the shoulders of others, showing their worthlessness. Those who serve them are put to shame,26. because if any of these idols falls to the ground, their worshipers must pick it up. If it is tipped over, it cannot set itself right. Gifts are offered to these idols just as if they were for the dead.27. The priests sell the sacrifices (offerings) made to these gods and use the money for themselves. Their wives preserve some of the meat but give none to the poor or helpless.28. Even sacrifices to these idols may be touched by women during their periods or after giving birth. Since you know by these things that these are not gods, do not fear them.29. How can they be called gods? Women serve meals to gods of silver, gold, and wood,30. and in their temples, the priests sit with their clothes torn, their heads and beards shaved, and their heads uncovered.31. They howl and shout before these idols, like people at a funeral banquet.32. The priests even take some of the clothes from their gods to clothe their wives and children.33. Whether someone does evil to them or good, these idols cannot repay it. They cannot set up a king or remove one.34. Likewise, these idols cannot give wealth or money; if someone makes a vow to them and does not keep it, they will not require it.35. They cannot save anyone from death or rescue the weak from the strong.36. They cannot restore sight to the blind; they cannot rescue those who are in distress.37. They cannot have mercy on a widow or do good to an orphan.38. These idols made of wood and covered with gold and silver are like stones from the mountain, and those who serve them will be ashamed.39. Why should anyone consider them gods or call them gods? 40. Even the Babylonians themselves scorn these idols. When they encounter a mute person, they bring offerings to their god Bel, hoping for a miracle, as if Bel could grant speech. 41. Yet, the Babylonians fail to see the absurdity (the quality of being wildly unreasonable) of their actions and continue to honor these lifeless idols, which are nothing more than hollow creations with no power. 42. The women sit in the public spaces, bound by cords at their waists, offering incense (a substance burned for its sweet smell, often as a religious offering) to these false gods. 43. When one of them is taken by a passerby to his bed, she mocks her neighbor for not having been chosen, as if the breaking of her cord is a mark of honor. 44. Everything they do for these idols is vain (futile; without purpose) and deceptive. Why, then, would anyone call them gods or believe they are divine? 45. These idols are crafted by carpenters and goldsmiths; they are mere reflections of the artisans' hands and desires. 46. The creators of these idols will not live forever, 47. so how can the lifeless objects they fashion be gods? They leave only falsehood and shame (dishonor or disgrace) for those who follow after them. 48. When danger or war strikes, the priests and idols alike are hidden away. 49. How can anyone fail to see that these idols are powerless? They cannot save themselves in times of crisis or conflict. 50. Made of wood and covered in gold or

silver, these idols are mere human creations, stripped of any divine power. It will be evident to all nations and kings that these are not gods. **51.** Who does not know that they lack divine power? **52.** These idols cannot establish a kingdom or bring rain to the earth. **53.** They are incapable of judging (making decisions about right or wrong) rightly or delivering justice; they have no authority. **54.** They are like scarecrows in a field, ineffective and powerless. If a fire breaks out in the temple of one of these wooden idols, its priests will flee, and the idol itself will burn like timber. **55.** These idols cannot resist a king or defend against an enemy. So why should anyone consider them gods? **56.** These idols, made of wood and overlaid with precious metals, cannot even protect themselves from thieves. **57.** Anyone who wishes can strip them of their gold, silver, and garments, and the idols will not defend themselves. **58.** It is far better to be a strong king or a useful tool in a household than to be one of these empty idols. It is better to be a door that protects a house than to be a god of wood and metal. **59.** The sun, moon, and stars shine with their own brilliance (brightness or radiance), and when they are called to serve, they respond. **60.** The lightning flashes across the sky, and the wind blows through the lands at the command of God. **61.** When God sends clouds to move across the heavens, they obey His will. **62.** Fire from above consumes (completely destroys) mountains and forests when God commands it. But these idols are nothing like these powerful forces of nature. **63.** Therefore, do not regard them as gods or call them gods, for they are powerless to judge or do any good for anyone. **64.** Knowing they are false, do not fear them, **65.** for they cannot curse or bless kings, **66.** nor can they perform signs in the heavens (indications or symbols of divine presence) or shine like the sun or give light like the moon. **67.** Even the wild animals are greater than these idols, for they can seek shelter and protect themselves. **68.** So there is no reason to fear these idols; they are not gods at all. **69.** They are like a scarecrow in a cucumber patch—unable to guard anything. Their idols, made of wood and overlaid with gold and silver, are no better. **70.** These idols are like a thornbush in a garden, where birds perch on them, or like a lifeless body cast into the darkness. **71.** The fine cloth, purple and linen, that decays (breaks down over time) upon them reveals their true nature—they are not gods. They will eventually be consumed and become a disgrace. **72.** Therefore, it is far better to be an upright (morally correct) person, free of idols, then to place faith in these false gods. Such a person will be beyond reproach.

87 – The Prayer of Manasseh

1. O Lord Almighty (All-powerful) in heaven, God of our forefathers (ancestors) Abraham, Isaac, and Jacob, **2.** You who created (made) the heavens and the earth, and established their order, **3.** You who commanded (ordered) the sea and sealed (locked) it with Your powerful name, **4.** Before You, all things tremble (shake) in fear of Your power, **5.** For the majesty (greatness) of Your glory is unbearable (cannot be endured), and Your anger (wrath) towards sinners is intolerable (unbearable). **6.** Your merciful (kind and forgiving) promise is boundless (without limit), **7.** For You are full of compassion (deep sympathy for suffering), patient, and abundant (plentiful) in mercy. **8.** You promised repentance (turning away from sin) and forgiveness (pardoning) to sinners, granting us salvation (rescue from punishment) by Your mercy. **9.** I have sinned more than the sand of the sea; I am unworthy (undeserving) to look upon heaven. **10.** I am weighed down (burdened) by my sins and have provoked (angered) Your wrath. **11.** Therefore, I seek Your grace (unmerited favor) with a humble heart. **12.** I acknowledge (admit) my sins, **13.** and humbly ask for Your forgiveness (pardon), O Lord. Do not condemn (sentence) me, for You are the God of those who repent. **14.** Save me according to Your great mercy, **15.** and I will praise (thank and worship) You forever, for Your glory (honor) endures forever. Amen.

88 – The First Epistle of Clement to the Corinthians

Chapter 1

1. Due to recent calamities (misfortunes) and setbacks, we realize we've been slow in addressing the disputes among you, beloved brothers and sisters. This rebellion (sedition) has been stirred by a few stubborn (headstrong) people, and it has caused your once respected name to be tarnished. **2.** For who among those who stayed with you did not admire your virtuous (moral) faith? Who did not praise your serious (sober) and patient (forbearing) devotion to the Messiah? Who did not spread word of your great hospitality? Who did not acknowledge your sound (correct) knowledge? **3.** You treated all equally, following God's commands (ordinances), honoring the older men, and encouraging the young to have modest (humble) thoughts. You instructed women to perform their duties with purity and a good conscience, valuing their husbands, and managing their homes with discretion (careful judgment).

Chapter 2

1. You were humble (lowly) and free from arrogance, ready to yield rather than claim authority, happier to give than receive, and content with what God provided. You kept His words in your hearts, remembering His suffering. **2.** A deep peace and desire for good works filled all of you, along with an outpouring of the Holy Spirit . **3.** With holy wisdom and zeal, you prayed to God for mercy if any sin had been committed unknowingly. **4.** You fought day and night for the brotherhood, hoping to save the chosen ones with sincere devotion. **5.** You were sincere, simple, and free from malice (evil intentions) toward one another. **6.** Sedition (rebellion) and division (schism) were abhorrent to you. You mourned over others' faults as if they were your own. **7.** You never regretted doing good and were ready for every good work. **8.** Living virtuously and honorably, you performed all duties with reverence for God. His commandments were written on your hearts.

Chapter 3

1. Glory and growth were given to you, but it is written that some, after growing prosperous, became selfish. **2.** From this arose jealousy, envy, strife, rebellion, persecution, and turmoil. **3.** People rose up against one another: the lowly against the honored, the unwise against the wise, the young against the old. **4.** Righteousness and peace were abandoned, and people ignored God's commands, following sinful desires, bringing death into the world.

Chapter 4

1. As written, Cain brought an offering to God, but God favored Abel's sacrifice. **2.** Cain's offering was not accepted, and he became very sorrowful. **3.** God asked Cain why he was sad and told him that if his offering was right, he would be accepted. **4.** Cain, filled with jealousy, killed Abel. **5.** Brethren, jealousy led to murder. **6.** Jealousy caused Jacob (Ya'aqov) to flee from Esau. **7.** Jealousy led to Joseph's persecution, even to death and slavery. **8.** Jealousy made Moses flee from Pharaoh after being rejected by his people. **9.** Aaron and Miriam were punished because of jealousy. **10.** Jealousy swallowed up Dathan and Abiram for rebelling against Moses. **11.** Jealousy led to David being persecuted by King Saul and the Philistines.

Chapter 5

1. Let us look at more recent examples from our time. **2.** The greatest and most righteous members of the Church were persecuted because of jealousy. **3.** Peter (Kepha) endured many hardships and eventually reached his appointed place of glory. **4.** Paul (Sha'ul), enduring jealousy and strife, showed the reward of patient endurance. He preached throughout the East and West, enduring imprisonment, exile, and stoning. **5.** Paul taught righteousness and gained renown worldwide before departing to the holy place, leaving a pattern of patient endurance.

Chapter 6

1. These holy men gathered a vast number of the elect, who endured many hardships and set a brave example for us. **2.** Women, persecuted for their faith, suffered cruelly but still reached their goal, receiving a noble reward. **3.** Jealousy has caused estrangement between husbands and wives, changing the bond that once united them. **4.** Jealousy and strife have destroyed great cities and nations.

Chapter 7

1. We write these things not only to warn you but to remind ourselves, for we are in the same struggle, and the same challenge awaits us. **2.** Let us cast away idle thoughts and follow the glorious and time-honored teachings passed down to us. **3.** Let us seek what is good, pleasing, and acceptable to God. **4.** Let us focus on the blood of Messiah, which is precious to God, for through His sacrifice, He granted the world the grace of repentance. **5.** Let us reflect on the generations, noting how God gave each one an opportunity for repentance. **6.** Noah (Noach) preached repentance, and those who listened were saved. **7.** Jonah proclaimed destruction to Nineveh, but they repented and were forgiven, despite being outsiders to God.

Chapter 8

1. The ministers of God's grace through the Holy Spirit spoke of repentance. **2.** Even God Himself swore an oath concerning repentance: **3.** "As I live, I desire not the death of the sinner, but his repentance," says the Lord . **4.** He called the people of Israel (Yashar'el) to repentance, promising forgiveness even for the gravest sins if they turned to Him with their whole heart. **5.** He also said, "Wash and be clean. Cease from evil, learn to do good, and I will make your crimson sins as white as snow." If you listen to Him, you will receive the good things of the earth, but if you refuse, destruction will come. **6.** Since God desires all to repent, He confirmed it by His will.

Chapter 9

1. Let us obey God's will, present ourselves humbly before Him, and seek His mercy, turning away from strife, jealousy, and death. **2.** Let us focus on those who faithfully served His glory. **3.** Consider Enoch (Chanok), who was taken up because of his righteousness and did not experience death. **4.** Noah, by his faithfulness, preached regeneration and saved the creatures that entered the ark in harmony.

Chapter 10

1. Abraham (Avraham), called God's friend, was faithful and obeyed God's command. **2.** He left his home and kin to inherit God's promises, being told, "Go to a land I will show you, and I will make you a great nation, blessing you and cursing your enemies." **3.** When he separated from Lot, God showed him the land and promised it to him and his descendants forever. **4.** He also promised that his descendants would be as countless as the dust of the earth. **5.** Abraham believed God, and it was counted as righteousness. **6.** His faith and hospitality led to the birth of his son in old age, and he offered him as a sacrifice in obedience to God.

Chapter 11

1. Lot was saved from Sodom because of his hospitality and godliness, while the surrounding land was destroyed. This showed that God does not forsake those who trust in Him but punishes those who turn away. **2.** Lot's wife, who looked back in doubt, turned into a pillar of salt as a sign that those who are double-minded and doubt God's power will face judgment.

Chapter 12

1. Rahab, the prostitute (harlot), was saved for her faith and hospitality. **2.** When the spies sent by Joshua (Yahushua) came to Jericho, the king of the city sought to capture them. **3.** Rahab hid the spies in her upper chamber under flax stalks. **4.** When the king's messengers came, Rahab lied, saying the spies had already left. **5.** She believed that God would give Jericho to the Israelites, and she asked for her family's protection. **6.** The spies promised to spare her family if they stayed in her house when the city was attacked. **7.** They gave her a sign: a scarlet thread, representing salvation through the blood of God. **8.** So, we see that Rahab's faith and prophecy were intertwined.

Chapter 13

1. Let us be humble, leaving behind pride, foolishness, and anger, and follow what is written. **2.** The Holy Spirit teaches us not to boast in wisdom, strength, or riches, but to boast in God. **3.** Let us strive for righteousness, as Yahusha (Jesus) taught: show mercy to receive mercy, forgive to be forgiven, and give to receive. **4.** These commandments guide us to live humbly and in obedience to God's words, as He desires those who are gentle, humble, and reverent.

Chapter 14

1. It is right to obey God rather than those who, in their pride and disorder, lead others astray with jealousy and conflict. **2.** Following such leaders will bring great harm and lead us away from what is right. **3.** Let us treat each other with kindness, reflecting the compassion of God. **4.** The righteous will dwell in the land, but those who transgress will be destroyed. **5.** God will bring down the proud and wicked, as He said: those who are exalted will vanish, and only the peaceful will remain.

Chapter 15

1. Let us align with those who promote peace and godliness, not those who pretend peace for selfish reasons. **2.** God condemns those who honor Him only with their lips, while their hearts are far from Him. **3.** He speaks against those who bless with their mouths but curse in their hearts. **4.** The deceitful will be silenced. **5.** God will rise up to protect the needy and poor, acting boldly to defend them.

Chapter 16

1. The Messiah is with those who are humble, not those who elevate themselves above others. **2.** The authority of our Lord Yahusha Messiah came not with pride or arrogance, though He could have, but with humility, as the Holy Spirit prophesied. **3.** The Lord said, "Who believed our message? To whom was the power of God revealed?" We proclaimed Him as a child, like a root in dry land. He had no form or beauty to attract us. He seemed ordinary, rejected, and unnoticed. **4.** He bore our sins and suffered for us; we thought He was being punished for His own wrongs. **5.** He was wounded for our sins and afflicted for our wrongdoings. His punishment brought us peace, and by His wounds, we were healed. **6.** We all went astray like sheep, each following our own way. **7.** God handed Him over for our sins, and He remained silent, enduring His suffering like a sheep led to slaughter. **8.** Who can explain His life, for He was taken away from the earth? **9.** He died for the sins of His people. **10.** The wicked will be given for His burial, and the rich for His death, though He had done no wrong and no deceit was in His mouth. **11.** God desires to purify Him from His suffering. **12.** If you offer a sacrifice for sin, your descendants will live long. **13.** God wishes to relieve His soul from torment, to reveal light to Him, and to give Him understanding, making Him a righteous servant who will bear the sins of many. **14.** He will inherit many and share the spoils with the strong, for He gave His life to death and was counted as a sinner. **15.** Again, He says, "I am a worm, not a man, despised by people." **16.** Those who saw Him mocked Him, saying, "He trusted in God, let God rescue Him if He delights in Him." **17.** Dear friends, consider the example of God's humility, and ask ourselves what we should do, since we've received His grace.

Chapter 17

1. Let us also imitate those who, like Elijah, Elisha, and Ezekiel (prophets), lived humbly and preached the coming of the Messiah. **2.** Abraham was called the friend of God and humbly said, "I am but dust and ashes," acknowledging his lowly state before God. **3.** Job was righteous, blameless, and honored God, avoiding evil. **4.** Yet, he admitted, "No man is pure, even if his life is short." **5.** Moses was faithful in God's house, and through his leadership, Egypt faced judgment and plagues. Despite his greatness, he humbly asked, "Who am I that You send me?" **6.** He also said, "I am slow of speech, like smoke from the pot."

Chapter 18

1. What can we say about David, who earned a good reputation and whom God called "a man after My heart," the son of Jesse (Yishai)? God anointed him with eternal mercy. **2.** Yet, David also asked God for mercy, saying, "Have mercy on me, O God, according to Your great compassion; wipe out my wrongdoings." **3.** Cleanse me from my sin, for I acknowledge it, and my sin is ever before me. **4.** I have sinned only against You, and I did evil in Your sight, so You are just in Your judgment. **5.** I was conceived in iniquity, and my mother bore me in sin. Yet You love truth and have shown me the hidden wisdom of Your ways. **6.** Purify me with hyssop (a plant used for purification), and I will be clean. Wash me, and I will be whiter than snow. **7.** Make me hear joy and gladness; let the humbled bones rejoice. **8.** Turn Your face away from my sins and blot out my transgressions. **9.** Create a clean heart in me, O God, and renew a steadfast spirit within me. Do not cast me from Your presence or take Your Holy Spirit from me. **10.** Restore the joy of Your salvation to me and give me a willing spirit to sustain me. **11.** I will teach transgressors Your ways, and sinners will turn back to You. **12.** Deliver me from blood guilt, O God, my Savior, and my tongue will sing of Your righteousness. **13.** Open my lips, Lord, and my mouth will declare Your praise. **14.** You do not delight in sacrifices, or I would bring them; You take no pleasure in burnt offerings. **15.** A broken spirit and a contrite heart, O God, You will not despise.

Chapter 19

1. The humility and submission of great men, who have earned a good reputation, have benefitted not only us but also the generations before us, including those who received God's oracles in fear and truth. **2.** Since we have shared in many glorious deeds, let us quickly return to the goal of peace passed down to us from the beginning. Let us focus on the Father and Creator of all, clinging to His wonderful gifts of peace and blessings. **3.** Let us reflect on Him in our minds and with our souls, seeing His enduring patience, noting how He remains free from anger toward all His creatures.

Chapter 20

1. The heavens are moved by His command and follow His peaceful direction. 2. Day and night fulfill their appointed tasks without hindrance. 3. The sun, moon, and stars move in harmony as He appointed, staying within their boundaries without deviation. 4. The earth produces fruit according to His will, providing abundance for men, animals, and all living things, without conflict or change in His decrees. 5. Even the depths of the oceans and the hidden realms below are governed by His will. 6. The seas, contained within their boundaries, do not overflow but obey His design. 7. He has set limits for the ocean, saying, "Thus far you may come, but no further." 8. Even the distant worlds beyond the seas are directed by the same divine laws. 9. The seasons—spring, summer, autumn, and winter—follow one another in peace. 10. The winds, in their proper seasons, fulfill their roles without disruption, and the ever-flowing fountains provide sustenance for life. The smallest creatures live in harmony. 11. All these things are ordered by the great Creator, who ensures peace and goodness for all, but especially for those who take refuge in His mercies through our Lord Yahusha Messiah. 12. To Him be glory and majesty forever. Amen.

Chapter 21

1. Brethren, let us be careful that God's many blessings do not turn into judgment against us if we do not live in a way that pleases Him, doing good with unity. 2. As it is written, "The Spirit of Yahweh is a lamp, searching the hearts of men." 3. Let us realize how near He is, and how nothing escapes His knowledge, not even our thoughts or our plans. 4. Therefore, we must not stray from His will. 5. Let us be willing to offend foolish and arrogant people who boast in their words, rather than offending God. 6. Let us fear the Lord Yahusha (Messiah), whose blood was shed for us. Let us honor our leaders, respect our elders, and teach our young men to fear God. 7. Let us guide our women toward goodness, showing purity in their character, gentleness in their love, moderation in their speech, and impartiality in their love for all who fear God, living in holiness. 8. Let our children learn the teachings of the Messiah: how humility pleases God, how pure love is powerful in His sight, and how the fear of God leads to salvation for those who walk in purity and holiness. 9. For God searches the hearts and desires, and He gives and takes away life as He pleases.

Chapter 22

1. The faith in Messiah confirms these things, for He, through the Holy Spirit, calls out, "Come, my children, listen to Me, and I will teach you the fear of Yahweh." 2. Who desires life and good days? 3. Keep your tongue from evil, and your lips from deceit. 4. Turn from evil and do good. 5. Seek peace and pursue it. 6. The eyes of Yahweh are on the righteous, and His ears are open to their prayers. But His face is against the wicked, to erase their memory from the earth. 7. The righteous cry out, and Yahweh hears them, delivering them from all their troubles. 8. Many are the afflictions of the righteous, but Yahweh will deliver them from all. 9. Many are the afflictions of the wicked, but those who hope in God's mercy will be surrounded by it.

Chapter 23

1. The Father, full of mercy in all things and always eager to do good, shows compassion to those who reverently approach Him, bestowing His gifts on those who draw near with a pure heart. 2. Therefore, let us avoid being double-minded (wavering in faith) and refrain from doubting His great gifts. 3. Let us not follow the scripture that warns, "Woe to the double-minded, who doubt and say, 'We heard these things from our forefathers, but we are old now and nothing has happened.'" 4. You fools, compare yourselves to a tree: first, it sheds leaves, then shoots, then flowers, sour berries, and finally, ripe grapes. In a short time, the tree bears fruit. 5. Indeed, His will shall come quickly, as the scripture affirms, "He will come suddenly, without delay," and Yahuah will enter His temple, the Holy One whom you await.

Chapter 24

1. Let us understand, dear ones, how the Master continually shows us the resurrection that awaits, having made Yahuah Yahusha Messiah the first fruits by raising Him from the dead. 2. Let us reflect on the resurrection, which happens at its proper time. 3. Day and night demonstrate resurrection: night falls asleep, and day rises; day departs, and night comes. 4. Let us observe how sowing works. 5. The sower plants seeds, and though they decay, the Master's providence brings them back to life, multiplying them to bear fruit.

Chapter 25

1. Consider the remarkable sign in the east, in Arabia, of a bird called the phoenix. 2. This bird lives for five hundred years, and when it is time to die, it makes a coffin of frankincense, myrrh, and spices and enters it. 3. As the body decays, a worm forms, nourished by the moisture of the corpse, and grows wings. When it matures, it carries the coffin with its parent's bones from Arabia to Egypt, to the City of the Sun (a place of worship in Egypt). 4. In the daytime, before everyone, it flies to the Sun's altar, places the bones there, and then returns. 5. The priests check their records and confirm that it has arrived after five hundred years.

Chapter 26

1. Do we think it so extraordinary if the Creator of the universe will bring about the resurrection of those who have faithfully served Him, showing us through the phoenix the greatness of His promise? 2. For He says, "You will raise me up, and I will praise You," and, "I went to rest and slept, and I was awakened, for You are with me." 3. Again, Iyov (Job) says, "You will raise this body of mine, which has endured all these trials."

Chapter 27

1. Therefore, let us remain firmly attached to Him, who is faithful in His promises and just in His judgments. 2. He who commanded us not to lie, much more will He never lie Himself, for nothing is impossible for Elohiym except lying. 3. Let our faith in Him be ignited, for all things are near to Him. 4. By His word, He created the universe, and by His word, He can destroy it. 5. Who can question Him or resist His might? He will accomplish all that He wills, and nothing will fail of what He has decreed. 6. All things are visible to Him, and nothing escapes His counsel. 7. The heavens declare the glory of Elohiym, and the sky proclaims His work. Day speaks to day, and night shares knowledge with night, and there are no words or speech where their voices are not heard.

Chapter 28

1. Since all things are seen and heard, let us fear Him and turn away from the sinful desires of evil actions, so that we may be protected by His mercy from the coming judgment. 2. For where can any of us hide from His powerful hand? And which world will receive those who abandon His service? 3. The holy scriptures say, "Where can I flee from Your presence? If I ascend to heaven, You are there; if I go to the ends of the earth, Your hand is there; if I make my bed in the depths, Your Spirit is there." 4. Where then can one go, or where can one escape from Him who holds the entire universe?

Chapter 29

1. Let us approach Him with holiness of heart, lifting up pure and undefiled hands, with love for our gentle and compassionate Father who has made us His elect. 2. For it is written: When the Most High divided the nations, scattering the sons of Adam, He set their boundaries according to the number of the angels of Elohiym. His people, Ya'aqov (Jacob), became His portion, and Yashar'el (Israel) was His inheritance. 3. In another place, it says: "Behold, Yahuah takes a nation from among the nations, as a man takes the firstfruits of his threshing floor; and the holy ones will come from that nation."

Chapter 30

1. Since we are the chosen portion of a Holy Elohiym, let us act in holiness, avoiding evil speech, impure actions, drunkenness, quarrels, pride, and all forms of immorality. 2. For Elohiym resists the proud but gives grace to the humble. 3. Let us cleave to those who have received grace from Elohiym, clothed in humility and self-control, avoiding gossip and slander, and justified by deeds, not by words. 4. For He says, "He who speaks much will hear much in return. Does the one who speaks constantly think they are righteous?" 5. Blessed is the child of a woman who lives but a short time. Let us not be abundant in words. 6. Let our praise be directed toward Elohiym, not ourselves, for Elohiym hates those who praise themselves. 7. Let others bear witness to our good deeds, as they did for our righteous forefathers. 8. Boldness, arrogance, and daring are for those cursed by Elohiym, while

forbearance, humility, and gentleness are for those blessed by Elohiym.

Chapter 31

1. Let us hold fast to His blessings and study the ways of blessing. Let us look at the history of things from the beginning. **2.** Why was our father Avraham (Abraham) blessed? Was it not because he worked righteousness and truth through faith? **3.** Yitschaq (Isaac), trusting in the future, was willing to be sacrificed. **4.** Ya'aqov (Jacob), with humility, left his land because of his brother, went to Laban, and served; and the twelve tribes of Yashar'el were given to him.

Chapter 32

1. If anyone examines these things sincerely, they will understand the greatness of the gifts given by Elohiym. **2.** From Ya'aqov (Jacob) came all the priests and Levites who served at the altar of Elohiym, and Yahuah Yahusha (Jesus) came from him according to the flesh. From him came kings, rulers, and governors in the line of Judah; and his other tribes are held in great honor, as Elohiym promised, saying, "Your descendants shall be as the stars of heaven." **3.** They were glorified, not through their own works or righteousness, but through His will. **4.** Likewise, we, having been called through His will in Messiah Yahusha, are not justified by ourselves, our wisdom, understanding, piety, or deeds but through faith, by which the Almighty Elohiym has justified all men from the beginning; to whom be glory forever. Amen.

Chapter 33

1. What then must we do, brethren? Should we refrain from doing good and forsake love? Let it never be so! Let us eagerly pursue every good work. **2.** For the Creator and Master of the universe rejoices in His works. **3.** By His great power, He established the heavens and set them in order in His infinite wisdom. He separated the earth from the waters, setting it firm on the foundation of His will, and commanded the living creatures to exist by His decree. **4.** Above all, with His perfect wisdom, He created man in His image. **5.** For Elohiym said, "Let us make man in our image and likeness." And He created man, male and female. **6.** After completing these works, He praised and blessed them, saying, "Increase and multiply." **7.** We see that all the righteous were adorned with good works, and even Yahuah (the Lord) rejoiced in His works. **8.** Seeing that we have this pattern, let us diligently conform ourselves to His will and work with all our strength to accomplish righteousness.

Chapter 34

1. A skilled worker receives the reward of his labor with confidence, but the lazy and careless worker cannot face his employer. **2.** Therefore, we must be zealous for good works, for all things come from Him. **3.** He warns us, saying, "Behold, Yahuah and His reward are before Him, to recompense each person according to their works." **4.** He encourages us to believe in Him with all our heart and not to be idle or negligent in doing good works. **5.** Let our confidence and boast be in Him. Let us submit to His will and observe how His angels stand by and minister to His will. **6.** For the scripture says, "Ten thousand times ten thousand stood by Him, and thousands of thousands ministered to Him, crying out, 'Holy, holy, holy is Yahuah of Sabaoth; the whole earth is full of His glory.'" **7.** Let us then, gathered in unity with sincere hearts, cry out to Him, asking to share in His great and glorious promises. **8.** For He says, "No eye has seen, nor ear heard, nor has it entered into the heart of man what great things He has prepared for those who patiently wait for Him."

Chapter 35

1. How blessed and marvelous are the gifts of God, beloved! Life in immortality (eternal life, free from death), glory in righteousness (moral excellence), boldness in truth, confidence in faith, and sanctification (being set apart for holy purposes) in temperance (self-control)—all these are within our understanding. **2.** What, then, do you think God has prepared for those who patiently await Him? The Creator, the Father of all, knows their number and beauty. **3.** Let us strive to be among those who await Him, so that we may share in His promised gifts. **4.** But how can we achieve this, beloved? By fixing our hearts on God through faith, seeking things that please Him, and doing what aligns with His perfect will. We must follow the path of truth, rejecting unrighteousness, greed, strife, malice, deceit, gossip, hatred, pride, arrogance, vain glory, and inhospitality (lack of hospitality). **5.** Those who engage in such things are detestable to God, and not just those who do them, but those who consent to them as well. **6.**

Scripture says, "Why do you declare My commands and take My covenant on your lips, yet you hate instruction and cast My words behind you? If you saw a thief, you joined him, and you shared in the adulterer's actions. You spoke against your brother and caused him to stumble." **7.** These things you have done, and I kept silent. You thought I would be like you. **8.** I will convict you and confront you directly. **9.** Understand these things, you who forget God, or He may seize you like a lion, with no one to rescue you. **10.** A sacrifice of praise glorifies Me, and through it, I will show him God's salvation.

Chapter 36

1. This is the way we found our salvation, through Yahusha (Jesus) Messiah, the High Priest (a mediator between God and humans) of our offerings, the Helper and Protector of our weakness. **2.** Through Him, we look up to the heavens, and through Him, we see His flawless (perfect and without error) and excellent image. Through Him, the eyes of our hearts were opened, and our darkened minds were illuminated. **3.** He made us taste the immortal knowledge (eternal truth and wisdom), for He, being the brightness of God's majesty, is greater than the angels and has inherited a more excellent name. **4.** As it is written: "He makes His angels spirits and His ministers flames of fire," but to His Son, the Lord says: "You are My Son; today I have begotten (brought forth into existence) You. Ask of Me, and I will give You the nations for Your inheritance, and the ends of the earth for Your possession." **5.** And again, He says, "Sit at My right hand, until I make Your enemies a footstool for Your feet." **6.** Who are these enemies? They are the wicked, who resist His will.

Chapter 37

1. Let us, therefore, commit ourselves earnestly to God's flawless (perfect, without error) commands. **2.** Let us observe how soldiers under our rulers follow their orders—how precisely, willingly, and obediently (in a manner that shows respect and compliance) they carry out the commands given to them. **3.** Not all are commanders or rulers of large groups, but each person in their role fulfills the orders given by the king and governors. **4.** The great cannot exist without the small, and the small cannot exist without the great. There is a necessary balance in all things, and this balance brings utility (usefulness). **5.** Consider the body as an example: the head is nothing without the feet, and the feet are nothing without the head. Even the smallest parts of the body are necessary and useful for the whole. All parts work together in subjection to ensure the body's survival.

Chapter 38

1. So, let the whole body be saved in Messiah Yahusha (Jesus), and let each person be subject to his neighbor, as each has been appointed with his special grace (gift or favor). **2.** Let the strong not neglect the weak, and the weak respect the strong. Let the rich assist the poor, and let the poor give thanks to God for providing someone to meet their needs. Let the wise show wisdom not in words, but in good deeds. He who is humble (modest in spirit), let him not boast about himself, but let others bear witness to his character. He who is pure in the body (free from sin), let him be so without pride, knowing it is God who grants him purity. **3.** Let us consider, brethren, where we came from, and what kind of beings we were when we entered the world. From what a tomb (grave) and what darkness He who made and created us brought us into His world, having already prepared His benefits (blessings) before we were born. **4.** Since we have received all these things from Him, we ought to give thanks in all things to Him, to whom be the glory forever and ever. Amen.

Chapter 39

1. Senseless (irrational) and foolish (unwise), ignorant (lacking knowledge) men mock us, desiring that they themselves be exalted in their imaginations. **2.** For what power does a mortal (human) have? Or what strength does a child of earth have? **3.** As it is written, "There was no form before my eyes; only I heard a breath and a voice." **4.** What then? Can a mortal be clean in the sight of Yahuwah (God), or can a man be blameless in his works? Seeing that He is distrustful (critical) of His servants and even holds His angels accountable. **5.** No, the heavens themselves are not clean in His sight. So, you who live in houses of clay (our fragile bodies), from the same clay we were made. He struck them down like a moth, and from morning to evening they are no more. Because they could not save themselves, they perished. **6.** He breathed on them, and they died because they lacked wisdom. **7.** But call upon

God, if perhaps one will obey you, or if you can see one of the holy angels. For wrath destroys the foolish, and envy slays those who have gone astray. **8.** I have seen fools trying to grow roots, but immediately their home was consumed. **9.** Far from safety are their children. They shall be mocked at the gates of the lowly, and no one shall deliver them. The righteous shall eat what is prepared for them, but the wicked shall not be delivered from their troubles.

Chapter 40

1. Since these things are known beforehand, and we have explored the depths of Divine knowledge, we must do everything in an orderly manner, as the Master has commanded us to perform at their appointed times. **2.** The offerings and services He commanded are to be done with care, not rashly or in disorder, but at fixed times and seasons. **3.** And where and by whom they are to be performed, He Himself established by His supreme will, so that everything may be done piously (devoutly) and be pleasing to Him. **4.** Those who offer their sacrifices at the appointed times are blessed and accepted, for by following the Master's instructions, they cannot go wrong. **5.** The high priest has his proper services, the priests have their designated roles, and the Levites have their appointed duties. The laity (ordinary people) are bound by the ordinances given to them.

Chapter 41

1. Let each of you, brethren, give thanks to God in your own way, maintaining a good conscience and adhering to the appointed rules of service, acting with decorum (proper behavior). **2.** Not everywhere, brethren, are the daily sacrifices, freewill offerings, sin offerings, or trespass offerings made, but only in Jerusalem. Even there, the offerings are not made in every place, but before the sanctuary in the court of the altar, and only by the high priest and other ministers, after the sacrificial animal has been examined for blemishes. **3.** Those who act contrary to the prescribed ordinances of God will face the penalty of death. **4.** You see, brethren, as greater knowledge has been given to us, so much the more are we exposed to danger (responsibility).

Chapter 42

1. The Apostles received the Gospel from Yahuah (God); Yahusha (Jesus) Messiah was sent by Elohiym (God). **2.** Thus, Messiah is from Elohiym, and the Apostles from Messiah; both came by Elohiym's will. **3.** They received a charge, assured by the resurrection of our Adonai Yahusha and confirmed by the word of Elohiym and the Ruach HaQodesh (Holy Spirit), proclaiming the kingdom of Elohiym. **4.** Preaching in towns, they appointed bishops and deacons as firstfruits, proven by the Spirit. **5.** This was written long ago about bishops and deacons: "I will appoint their bishops in righteousness and their deacons in faith."

Chapter 43

1. What marvel if those entrusted by Elohiym in Messiah appointed these persons? Even Moshe (Moses) recorded all enjoined upon him. **2.** When jealousy arose over the priesthood, he commanded the twelve chiefs to bring inscribed rods. **3.** He sealed and stored them in the tabernacle (sacred place) of testimony. **4.** He sealed the keys, saying, "The tribe whose rod buds is chosen by Elohiym for priesthood." **5.** In the morning, he showed the seals and drew forth the rods; Aaron's rod budded and bore fruit. **6.** Did not Moshe know this would occur? He did, to prevent disorder in Yashar'el (Israel), glorifying the true Elohiym forever. Amen.

Chapter 44

1. Our Apostles knew through Yahusha that there would be strife over the bishop's office. **2.** They appointed persons with foreknowledge, ensuring successors if they fell asleep. Those approved by the Church should not be thrust out. **3.** It is a grave sin to remove those who offered gifts of the bishop's office holily. **4.** Blessed are the presbyters (elders) who have departed, for their departure was fruitful. **5.** Yet, you have displaced honorable persons from their ministry.

Chapter 45

1. Be ye contentious (argumentative) and jealous about salvation. **2.** Ye have searched the scriptures (sacred texts), given through the Ruach HaQodesh (Holy Spirit); **3.** nothing unrighteous (immoral) is written in them. Righteous (virtuous) persons were not thrust out by holy men. **4.** Righteous men were persecuted by the lawless; they were stoned and slain by those filled with detestable (horrible) jealousy. **5.** They endured nobly. **6.** For what must we say, brethren? Was Daniel (a biblical prophet) cast into the lions' den by those who feared Elohiym (God)? **7.** Or were Ananias, Azarias, and Misael shut up in the furnace by those professing the glorious worship of the Most High? Far be this from our thoughts. **8.** Abominable (detestable) men stirred cruel suffering upon them that served Elohiym; the Most High champions those who serve Him with a pure conscience; to whom be the glory forever. Amen. **9.** Those who endured patiently inherited glory and honor; their names were recorded by Elohiym forever. Amen.

Chapter 46

1. To such examples, brethren, we ought to cleave (adhere). **2.** For it is written: Cleave unto the saints (holy people), for they that cleave unto them shall be sanctified (made holy). **3.** And again, He saith: With the guiltless (innocent) man thou shalt be guiltless, and with the elect (chosen) thou shalt be elect. **4.** Let us cleave to the guiltless and righteous; these are the elect of Elohiym. **5.** Wherefore are there strifes (conflicts) among you? **6.** Have we not one Elohiym, one Messiah, and one Spirit of grace? **7.** Why do we tear the members of Messiah, stirring factions against our own body? **8.** Remember the words of Yahusha (Jesus): Woe unto that man; it were good for him if he had not been born, rather than offend one of Mine elect. **9.** Your division hath perverted many, bringing despair and sorrow.

Chapter 47

1. Take up the epistle (letter) of the blessed Sha'ul (Paul) the Apostle. **2.** What wrote he first unto you in the beginning of the Gospel? **3.** He charged you in the Spirit concerning himself, Cephas (Peter), and Apollos, because ye had made parties. **4.** Yet that brought less sin upon you; for ye were partisans of renowned Apostles. **5.** Now mark who have perverted (corrupted) you and diminished your love for the brotherhood. **6.** It is shameful, dearly beloved, that the ancient Church of the Corinthians makes sedition against its presbyters (elders). **7.** This report hath reached not only us but also others, heaping blasphemies (slander) on Yahuah's (God's) Name.

Chapter 48

1. Let us root this out quickly and entreat (beg) the Master with tears, that He may show Himself propitious (favorable) and reconcile us. **2.** For this is a gate of righteousness opened unto life: Open me the gates of righteousness. **3.** This is the gate of Yahuah; the righteous shall enter. **4.** Many gates are opened, but this is the gate in righteousness, in Messiah. **5.** Let a man be faithful, able to expound (explain) deep sayings, wise in discernment, and pure; **6.** he ought to be lowly (humble), seeking the common advantage of all.

Chapter 49

1. Let him that hath love in Messiah fulfill the commandments of Messiah. **2.** Who can declare the bond of the love of Elohiym? **3.** Who is sufficient to tell the majesty (greatness) of its beauty? **4.** Love joineth us unto Elohiym; love covereth a multitude of sins. **5.** There is nothing coarse (rude) or arrogant (proud) in love; love maketh no seditions. **6.** In love, the Master took us unto Himself; for the love which He had toward us, Yahusha Messiah our Adonai, hath given His blood for us.

Chapter 50

1. Ye see, dearly beloved, how marvelous love is; there is no declaring its perfection. **2.** Who is sufficient to be found therein, save those to whom Elohiym shall grant it? Let us entreat His mercy to be found blameless in love. **3.** All generations from A'dam (Adam) have passed; those perfected in love dwell in the abode (home) of the pious (righteous). **4.** Blessed were we, dearly beloved, if we do the commandments of Elohiym in love, that our sins may be forgiven. **5.** Blessed are they whose iniquities (wickedness) are forgiven; blessed is the man to whom Yahuah shall impute (credit) no sin. **6.** This was pronounced upon them elected by Elohiym through Yahusha Messiah, to whom be the glory forever. Amen.

Chapter 51

1. For all our transgressions (wrongdoings) through the wiles (tricks) of the adversary (enemy), let us earnestly entreat for forgiveness. Those who lead factions should seek common hope. **2.** Those who walk in fear and love desire to suffer themselves rather than their neighbors, pronouncing judgment against themselves rather than the harmony handed down to us. **3.** It is good for a man to confess his trespasses (offenses) rather than harden his heart, as those who rebelled against Moshe (Moses). **4.** They went down to hades (the underworld) alive;

Death shall be their shepherd. **5.** Pharaoh and his host perished in the Red Sea because their hearts were hardened after the signs in Egypt.

Chapter 52

1. The Master needs nothing; He desires only our confession. **2.** David said, "I will confess unto Yahuah (God), and it shall please Him more than a young calf." **3.** Sacrifice to Elohiym a sacrifice of praise, and call upon Me in your affliction, and I will deliver you. **4.** A sacrifice unto Elohiym is a broken spirit (humble heart).

Chapter 53

1. You know the sacred scriptures, dearly beloved, and have searched the oracles (prophecies) of Elohiym. **2.** When Moshe went up the mountain for forty days, Elohiym told him to come down quickly, for the people had committed iniquity (wickedness) and made molten images. **3.** Yahuah said He would destroy them and make Moshe a great nation. **4.** Moshe replied, "Forgive this people, or blot me out of the book of the living." **5.** O mighty love! The servant boldly asks forgiveness for the many.

Chapter 54

1. Who among you is noble (honorable), compassionate (kind), and fulfilled with love? **2.** Let him say, "If my presence causes strife, I will withdraw, only let the flock of Messiah be at peace with its presbyters (elders)." **3.** He who does this shall win great renown (fame) in Messiah. **4.** Those who live as citizens of Elohiym's kingdom bring no regrets.

Chapter 55

1. Many kings and rulers, in times of pestilence (plague), have sacrificed themselves to save their citizens. **2.** Many among us have delivered themselves into bondage (slavery) to ransom others. **3.** Women like Yahudith, who exposed themselves to danger for their people, acted bravely. **4.** Yahudith asked to go forth into the enemy camp, and Yahuah delivered Holophernes into her hand. **5.** Esther also exposed herself to save Yashar'el (Israel) through her fasting and humility.

Chapter 56

1. Let us intercede for those in transgression, that humility may be given them. **2.** Let us accept chastisement (discipline) without vexation (annoyance). **3.** Yahuah chastens those He loves. **4.** The righteous shall chasten me in mercy; let not the mercy of sinners anoint my head. **5.** Blessed is the man whom Yahuah reproves; He causes pain but restores. **6.** He rescues from afflictions (troubles) and hides from fear. **7.** You shall laugh at the unrighteous; wild beasts shall be at peace with you. **8.** Your house shall be at peace, and your offspring shall be many. **9.** You shall come to the grave like ripe corn reaped in due season. **10.** Great protection is for those chastened by the Master.

Chapter 57

1. You who laid the foundation of sedition, submit to the presbyters and receive chastisement unto repentance. **2.** It is better to be little in the flock of Messiah than to have honor and be cast out. **3.** Wisdom says, "I will teach you My word." **4.** Those who disobey will face destruction and chaos. **5.** Evil men will seek wisdom and not find it. **6.** They shall eat the fruits of their own way and be filled with ungodliness. **7.** Those who harm innocents shall be slain, but he who hears Me shall dwell safely.

Chapter 58

1. Let us be obedient to His holy Name, escaping the threatenings against disobedience. **2.** Receive our counsel, and you shall have no regret. **3.** Those with humility and eagerness to perform Elohiym's commandments shall be registered among the saved through Yahusha Messiah. **4.** To Him be glory forever. Amen.

Chapter 59

1. If some are disobedient to our words, they will entangle themselves in transgression and danger. **2.** We shall be guiltless of this sin. **3.** We ask urgently that the Creator guard His elect throughout the world through Yahusha Messiah. **4.** Grant us hope in Thy Name, the source of all creation, and open our hearts to know Thee. **5.** We beseech Thee, Adonai, to be our help. Save those in tribulation, heal the ungodly, and comfort the fainthearted.

Chapter 60

1. Thou, through Thine operations (works), revealed the everlasting fabric (structure) of the world. Thou, Adonai (Lord), created the earth. **2.** Faithful throughout generations, righteous in judgments, wise in creation, forgive us our iniquities (sins) and transgressions. **3.** Cleanse us with Thy truth and guide our steps in holiness (purity). **4.** Yea, Adonai, make Thy face shine upon us in peace, sheltering us and delivering us from sin. **5.** Grant peace to us and all on earth, as Thou gavest to our fathers when they called on Thee.

Chapter 61

1. Thou, Adonai (Lord), hast given them the power of sovereignty (authority) through Thine unspeakable (incomprehensible) might. We submit ourselves to them, resisting nothing of Thy will. Grant them health, peace, and stability to govern without failure. **2.** For Thou, O heavenly Master, givest glory and power over all things. Direct their counsel to what pleases Thee, that they may administer with Godliness (piety) and obtain Thy favor. **3.** O Thou, who can do far greater things for us, we praise Thee through our High Priest, Yahusha Messiah (Jesus Christ), to whom be glory forever. Amen.

Chapter 62

1. We have fully written to you about what suits our religion and a virtuous (moral) life. **2.** Concerning faith, repentance (sorrow for sin), genuine love, temperance (self-control), sobriety (clear-mindedness), and patience, we remind you to please Almighty Elohiym with righteousness and truth, laying aside malice and pursuing peace and love, being eager in gentleness. **3.** We remind you gladly, knowing you are faithful and esteemed, having diligently searched the oracles (teachings) of Elohiym.

Chapter 63

1. It is right to heed these examples and submit to the leaders of our souls, ceasing from foolish dissension to attain the truth. **2.** You will bring us joy if you obey the things written through the Ruach HaQodesh (Holy Spirit) and root out unrighteous anger and jealousy. **3.** We have sent faithful men who shall witness between you and us, showing our concern for your peace.

Chapter 64

1. May the All-seeing Elohiym and Master grant every soul called by His holy Name faith, peace, patience, temperance, chastity (purity), and soberness (self-control), pleasing unto His Name through our High Priest, Yahusha Messiah. To Him be glory and majesty forever. Amen.

Chapter 65

1. Send back our messengers Claudius Ephebus, Valerius Bito, and Fortunatus in peace and joy, that they may report the peace and concord we desire, so we may rejoice over your good order. **2.** The grace (favor) of our Adonai Yahusha Messiah be with you and all called by Elohiym, to whom be glory and honor forever.

ones, who are perfect in uprightness, and bear them in their hands,

Scan Me, To Get Files

Download: Full Audio Of 88 Books
Download: Full Audio Of 279 Digital Books
Download: 279 eBooks